THE OXFORD STUDY BIBLE

Revised English Bible with
the Apocrypha

CONTRIBUTORS

PAUL J. ACHTEMEIER   LLOYD R. BAILEY

ALBERT BAUMGARTEN   WILLIAM A. BEARDSLEE   DIANNE BERGANT

†RICHARD V. BERGREN, JR.   †SHELDON H. BLANK   MYLES M. BOURKE

D. PETER BURROWS   ELIZABETH A. CLARK   JAMES L. CRENSHAW

EDWARD J. CROWLEY   DEMETRIUS DUMM   LOREN R. FISHER

RICHARD ELLIOTT FRIEDMAN   VICTOR P. FURNISH

ROBERT GOLDENBERG   EDWIN M. GOOD   PAUL HAMMER

JOHN H. HAYES   RICHARD A. HENSHAW   MARTHA HIMMELFARB

W. LEE HUMPHREYS   JOHN C. HURD   LEANDER E. KECK

DENNIS R. MAC DONALD   NEIL J. MC ELENEY   JAMES L. MAYS

WAYNE A. MEEKS   CAROL MEYERS   PATRICK D. MILLER, JR.

JAMES R. MUELLER   CAROL A. NEWSOM   DAVID L. PETERSEN

KATHARINE DOOB SAKENFELD   JAMES A. SANDERS   CHOON-LEONG SEOW

BYRON E. SHAFER   DAVID M. STANLEY   CARROLL STUHLMUELLER

M. JACK SUGGS   ARNOLD J. TKACIK   MARY ANN TOLBERT

GENE M. TUCKER   DAVID B. WEISBERG   JAY A. WILCOXEN

CLYDE M. WOODS

The Oxford Study

BIBLE

REVISED ENGLISH BIBLE
WITH THE APOCRYPHA

EDITED BY

M. JACK SUGGS

KATHARINE DOOB SAKENFELD

JAMES R. MUELLER

New York
OXFORD UNIVERSITY PRESS

OXFORD UNIVERSITY PRESS

Oxford   New York   Toronto
Delhi   Bombay   Calcutta   Madras   Karachi
Petaling Jaya   Singapore   Hong Kong   Tokyo
Nairobi   Dar es Salaam   Cape Town
Melbourne   Auckland

and associated companies in
Berlin   Ibadan

1 3 5 7 9 8 6 4 2
Printed in the United States of America

Contents

UNDERSTANDING THE BIBLE AND ITS COMMUNITIES

THE BIBLICAL TEXT WITH ANNOTATIONS

Note: The page numbering distinguishes between the two sections of this volume: the *articles section* (which provides general scholarly information about the Bible and its times as a background for study) and the *biblical books with annotations and introductions.* The biblical text is numbered uninterruptedly in ordinary Arabic numerals from Genesis to the Revelation of John, including the Apocrypha. The page numbers of the articles are marked with an asterisk (*). Readers will thus be able to determine immediately where they are in the text.

The Editors' Preface

The Oxford Study Bible continues a project which at an earlier stage was called *The New English Bible: Oxford Study Edition.* The idea of such a project was conceived by the late Samuel Sandmel and encouraged by Wilbur Ruggles (then Vice President for Religious Publishing at Oxford University Press). Sandmel was especially taken with the translation—its accuracy, of course, but especially its "clarity and readability." Here was a committee translation which provided readers with a plain, unstilted rendering of the text. It was Sandmel's conviction that a volume which combined such a superior translation with basic study aids would meet the needs of interested students and other lay readers. A further consideration, which was noted in the preface to the *Study Edition,* made the project especially important to Sandmel: "In our times the scholarly study of the Bible cuts across sectarian lines; hence both the editors and the contributors represent a diversity of religious persuasions and traditions." This volume embraces the aim of providing useful, non-sectarian encouragement to intelligent reading of the Bible.

Committees responsible for modern versions provide, as needed, updated translations. The appearance of the *Revised English Bible* in 1989 signaled the need for a revision of the *Study Edition* as well. The annotations, composed as they were for the *New English Bible,* required accommodation to the new translation and occasional adjustments of other kinds. The need for revision also provided the opportunity to conform the language of the study helps to inclusive standards. Further, in the interim since the *Study Edition,* the technology of paper and book production has advanced so as to permit an expanded section of essays. The happy consequence is that a group of four "Special Articles" in the previous edition has become a section of nineteen articles in the new book.

Readers should be advised of a number of editorial decisions with respect to the included material. For example, biblical citations in the essays are from the *Revised English Bible,* except in rare instances where a linguistic point has required an author to supply a special translation. Calendar references are made by using B.C.E. (before the common era) and C.E.—temporal equivalents to B.C. and A.D. American, rather than British, spellings are used in the annotations and essays ("labor" instead of "labour," for example). The format of a volume like this is important and is explained in the article on "Reading This Bible."

The annotations constitute a large part of the aids to study. The editors wish to express their appreciation to the annotators, whose work for the 1976 edition proved remarkably durable.

Paul J. Achtemeier
Acts of the Apostles, 1 and
2 Timothy, Titus

Lloyd R. Bailey
Genesis, Exodus, Leviticus,
Numbers, Deuteronomy

Albert Baumgarten
Wisdom of Solomon

William A. Beardslee
Ecclesiasticus

Sheldon H. Blank
Jeremiah

Myles M. Bourke
*Ephesians, Philippians,
Colossians, 1 and 2
Thessalonians, Philemon*

James L. Crenshaw
Job, Proverbs, Ecclesiastes

Edward J. Crowley
*Joshua, Judges, Ruth,
Esther*

Demetrius Dumm, O.S.B.
*Tobit, Judith, Rest of
Esther*

Loren R. Fisher
The Psalms

Victor P. Furnish
*Hebrews, James, 1 and 2
Peter, Jude*

Edwin M. Good
The Twelve Prophets

Paul Hammer
Revelation

Richard A. Henshaw
*Song of Songs,
Lamentations, Daniel*

John C. Hurd
*Romans, 1 and 2
Corinthians, Galatians*

Neil J. McEleney, C.S.P.
1 and 2 Maccabees

David M. Stanley, S.J.
*The Gospel of John,
1, 2, and 3 John*

Carroll Stuhlmueller, C.P.
Letter of Jeremiah, Baruch

M. Jack Suggs
Matthew, Mark, Luke

Arnold J. Tkacik
Ezekiel

Gene M. Tucker
Isaiah

David B. Weisberg
Ezra, Nehemiah, 1 Esdras

Jay A. Wilcoxen
*1 and 2 Samuel, 1 and 2
Kings, 1 and 2 Chronicles*

Clyde M. Woods
*2 Esdras, The Prayer of
Azariah and the Song of
the Three, Daniel and Susanna,
Daniel, Bel, and the
Snake, The Prayer of Manasseh*

For the most part, the revising of the annotations required by the new translation was done by Katharine Doob Sakenfeld (Old Testament editor), James R. Mueller (Apocrypha editor), and M. Jack Suggs (New Testament editor). In a small number of instances involving a substantial volume of material, the editorial work was done by others: William A. Beardslee, *Ecclesiasticus;* James L. Crenshaw, *Job, Proverbs, Ecclesiastes;* Neil J. McEleney, *1 and 2 Maccabees;* Patrick D. Miller, Jr., *The Psalms;* and Gene M. Tucker, *Isaiah.* Also, James C. VanderKam reviewed the annotations for two books of the Apocrypha. Prof. Sakenfeld's graduate assistants, Nancy Bowen and Carolyn Pressler, did valuable, basic work, especially with the Pentateuch, *Jeremiah,* and *Ezekiel.* Prof. Mueller was aided in certain aspects of technical editing by his graduate assistant, Patricia Woods.

As the preceding paragraph suggests, there was a division of editorial labor with respect to annotations. However, the remaining editorial work—from the design of the essay section to the final approval of essays—was not divided. Though Suggs served as Senior Editor, the editors developed a way of working together which insured that even small tasks were shared and decisions were based largely on consensus.

The collection of essays provides basic information about issues and approaches which are important for informed study of the Bible. The writers of the essays are distinguished scholars who are authorities in the fields about which they have written.

Dianne Bergant, C.S.A.
"The Perspective of Wisdom"

Elizabeth A. Clark
"Biblical Interpretation in the Early Church"

Richard Elliott Friedman
"Torah and Covenant"

Robert Goldenberg
"Hebrew Scriptures in Early Post-Biblical Judaism, with Special Reference to the Rabbinic Tradition"

John H. Hayes
"Deity in the Biblical Communities and among Their Neighbors"

Martha Himmelfarb
"The Apocalyptic Vision"

W. Lee Humphreys
"Historical Contexts of the Biblical Communities"

Leander E. Keck
(with Gene M. Tucker)
"Literary Forms of the Bible"
(Revised by Keck)

Dennis R. MacDonald
"Early Christian Literature"

James L. Mays
"The Phenomenon of Prophecy"

Wayne A. Meeks
"The Social World of the New Testament"

Carol Meyers
"The Contributions of Archaeology"

Carol A. Newsom
"The Dead Sea Scrolls and Other Jewish Literature"

David L. Petersen
"The Social World of the Old Testament"

James A. Sanders
"Communities and Canon"

Choon-Leong Seow
"Literature of the Ancient Near East"

Byron E. Shafer
"Relationship to God: Public and Private Worship"

M. Jack Suggs
"Reading This Bible"

Mary Ann Tolbert
"Reading the Bible"

Gene M. Tucker
(with Leander E. Keck)
"Literary Forms of the Bible"

Three additional essays on special topics appear in the pages of the biblical text, each introduced at the beginning of the Old Testament, Apocrypha or New Testament. For these, the editors are responsible: Sakenfeld for the article on "The Pentateuch," Mueller for "The Place and Significance of the Apocrypha" and Suggs for "The Gospels."

Finally, a "Select Index to People, Places, and Themes in the Bible," originally prepared by Richard V. Bergren, Jr., and D. Peter Burrows, has been revised for this edition.

A project such as this is possible only because of people who share the vision of opening the Bible to lay readers. The editors are mindful of such colleagues. We are grateful for scholars willing to translate technical jargon into the language of common discourse to assist readers who are not specialists. Donald Kraus has been "Oxford University Press" for us, shielding us from the details of book production and encouraging us in myriad ways; we know that he, his colleague Herbert J. Addison, and their associates (artists, compositors, copy readers, marketing representatives) have undertaken work that has permitted us to do the "fun things." The editors also wish to thank the following people, whose contributions made this volume possible: Elizabeth M. Edman, Henry Engel, Doug Gunden, June Gunden, Piera F. Paine, Leslie Phillips, and Shelley Ruh. Special thanks are due to Mr. Gordon Clem, Headmaster, and the St. Thomas Choir School, New York City, for hosting several editorial planning meetings. The editors and all these collaborators in the task will feel rewarded if the book accomplishes for its readers what we intended—letting the Bible be intelligible and the reading of it a joy.

THE EDITORS

Preface
to the Revised English Bible

The second half of the twentieth century has produced many new versions of the Bible. One of the pioneers was The New English Bible, which was distinctive inasmuch as it was a new translation from the ancient texts and was officially commissioned by the majority of the British Churches.

The translators themselves were chosen for their ability as scholars, without regard to Church affiliation. Literary advisers read and criticized the translators' drafts.

The translation of the New Testament appeared in 1961. The Old Testament and the Apocrypha were published with a limited revision of the New Testament in 1970; The New English Bible was then complete. Two years later a new impression appeared with some very minor corrections, and The New English Bible has remained substantially as it was first produced until the present day. It has proved to be of great value throughout the English-speaking world and is very widely used.

The debt of the Churches to those who served on the various committees and panels is very considerable and has been gladly acknowledged on many occasions. One name that will always be associated with The New English Bible is that of Dr C. H. Dodd, who as Director from start to finish brought to the enterprise outstanding leadership, sensitivity, and scholarship. It is fitting also to recall with gratitude the roles of Professor Sir Godfrey Driver, Joint Director from 1965, and Professor W. D. McHardy, Deputy Director from 1968.

It was right that The New English Bible in its original form, like any other version, should be subject to critical examination and discussion, and especially the Old Testament, which had not had the advantage of even a limited general revision. From the beginning helpful suggestions and criticisms had come in from many quarters. Moreover the widespread enthusiasm for The New English Bible had resulted in its being frequently used for reading aloud in public worship, the implications of which had not been fully anticipated by the translators. As a result it became desirable to review the translation, and in 1974 the Joint Committee of the Churches decided to set in train what was to become a major revision of the text.

New translators' panels were constituted under the chairmanship of Professor W. D. McHardy, who was appointed Director of Revision. The result of their work is The Revised English Bible, a translation standing firmly in the tradition established by The New English Bible. This substantial revision expresses the mind and conviction of biblical scholars and translators of the 1980s, as The New English Bible expressed the mind of a previous generation of such specialists, and it is fortunate that some distinguished scholars have been able to give their services throughout the entire process. To them we owe a great deal, and to none more than to Professor McHardy, who has served with great devotion throughout and made this a large part of his life's work.

The original initiative for making the New English Bible translation had come from the Church of Scotland in 1946, and a number of other Churches later joined them and formed a committee which was to plan and direct a new translation in contemporary language. The Joint Committee comprised representatives of the Baptist Union of Great Britain and Ireland, the Church of England, the Church of Scotland, the Congregational Church of England and Wales, the Council of Churches for Wales, the Irish Council of Churches, the London Yearly Meeting of the Religious Society of Friends, the Methodist Church of Great Britain, and the Presbyterian Church of England, as well as of the British and Foreign Bible Society and the National Bible Society of Scotland. Roman Catholic representatives later attended as observers.

After publication of the complete translation, there were changes in the composition of the Joint Committee. The Roman Catholic Church entered into full membership, with representatives from the hierarchies of England and Wales, Scotland, and Ireland. Following the union of the Presbyterian Church of England with the Congregational Church as the United Reformed Church, the united church was represented on the Committee. After the review began, the Committee was joined by representatives of the Salvation Army and the Moravian Church.

The progress of the work of the revisers has been regularly reported to meetings of the Joint Committee, taking place once and sometimes twice a year in the Jerusalem Chamber, Westminster Abbey. The Committee has much appreciated the courtesy of the Dean and Chapter in making the Chamber available for these meetings.

Members of the Joint Committee have given guidance and support to the Director of Revision throughout, and have had the opportunity of inspecting drafts as the work on each book approached its final stage, in many cases making detailed comments and criticisms for the consideration of the Director and revisers.

Care has been taken to ensure that the style of English used is fluent and of appropriate dignity for liturgical use, while maintaining intelligibility for worshippers of a wide range of ages and backgrounds. The revisers have sought to avoid complex or technical terms where possible, and to provide sentence structure and word order, especially in the Psalms, which will facilitate congregational reading but will not misrepresent the meaning of the original texts. As the 'you'-form of address to God is now commonly used, the 'thou'-form which was preserved in the language of prayer in The New English Bible has been abandoned. The use of male-oriented language, in passages of traditional versions of the Bible which evidently apply to both genders, has become a sensitive issue in recent years; the revisers have preferred more inclusive gender reference where that has been possible without compromising scholarly integrity or English style.

The revision is characterized by a somewhat more extensive use than in The New English Bible of textual subheadings printed in italic type. These headings are used, for example, to mark broad structural divisions in the writing or substantial changes of direction or theme. They should not be regarded in any way as part of the biblical text. The headings in the Psalms are a special case; these have been translated from those prefixed in ancient times to the Hebrew Psalms.

The traditional verse numbering of the Authorized (King James) Version is retained in The Revised English Bible for ease of reference. Where the Authorized Version contains passages which are found in the manuscripts on which that version rests, but which are absent from those followed by The Revised English Bible, these passages are reproduced in footnotes, in order to explain gaps in the verse numbering.

A table of measures, weights, and values will be found on pages xxvii-xxviii. The ancient terms usually appear in the text, but modern equivalents have been used when it seemed appropriate to do so.

The Joint Committee commends The Revised English Bible to the Churches and to the English-speaking world with due humility, but with confidence that God has yet new light and truth to break forth from his word. The Committee prays that the new version will prove to be a means to that end.

DONALD COGGAN
Chairman of the Joint Committee

Churches Sponsoring
the Revised English Bible

*The Revised English Bible was planned
and directed by representatives of*

THE BAPTIST UNION OF GREAT BRITAIN

THE CHURCH OF ENGLAND

THE CHURCH OF SCOTLAND

THE COUNCIL OF CHURCHES FOR WALES

THE IRISH COUNCIL OF CHURCHES

**THE LONDON YEARLY MEETING OF THE RELIGIOUS
SOCIETY OF FRIENDS**

THE METHODIST CHURCH OF GREAT BRITAIN

THE MORAVIAN CHURCH IN GREAT BRITAIN AND IRELAND

THE ROMAN CATHOLIC CHURCH IN ENGLAND AND WALES

THE ROMAN CATHOLIC CHURCH IN IRELAND

THE ROMAN CATHOLIC CHURCH IN SCOTLAND

THE SALVATION ARMY

THE UNITED REFORMED CHURCH

THE BIBLE SOCIETY

THE NATIONAL BIBLE SOCIETY OF SCOTLAND

The Books of the Bible and the Apocrypha

THE OLD TESTAMENT

THE APOCRYPHA

THE NEW TESTAMENT

Alphabetical Listing of the
Books of the Bible and the Apocrypha

Abbreviations of the Books of the Bible and the Apocrypha in Alphabetical Order

ABBREVIATION, LOCATION, TITLE

Acts   NT   Acts of the Apostles

Amos   OT   Amos

Bar.   APOC.   Baruch

Bel & Snake   APOC.   Daniel, Bel, and the Snake

1 Chr.   OT   1 Chronicles

2 Chr.   OT   2 Chronicles

Col.   NT   Colossians

1 Cor.   NT   1 Corinthians

2 Cor.   NT   2 Corinthians

Dan.   OT   Daniel

Deut.   OT   Deuteronomy

Eccles.   OT   Ecclesiastes

Ecclus.   APOC.   Ecclesiasticus or the Wisdom of Jesus Son of Sirach

Eph.   NT   Ephesians

1 Esd.   APOC.   1 Esdras

2 Esd.   APOC.   2 Esdras

Esther   OT   Esther

Exod.   OT   Exodus

Ezek.   OT   Ezekiel

Ezra   OT   Ezra

Gal.   NT   Galatians

Gen.   OT   Genesis

Hab.   OT   Habakkuk

Hag.   OT   Haggai

Heb.   NT   Hebrews

Hos.   OT   Hosea

Isa.   OT   Isaiah

Jas.   NT   James

Jdt.   APOC.   Judith

Jer.   OT   Jeremiah

Jn.   NT   John

1 Jn.   NT   1 John

2 Jn.   NT   2 John

3 Jn.   NT   3 John

ABBREVIATION, LOCATION, TITLE

Job   OT   Job

Joel   OT   Joel

Jonah   OT   Jonah

Josh.   OT   Joshua

Jude   NT   Jude

Judg.   OT   Judges

1 Kgs.   OT   1 Kings

2 Kgs.   OT   2 Kings

Lam.   OT   Lamentations

Lev.   OT   Leviticus

Lk.   NT   Luke

L. of Jer.   APOC.   Letter of Jeremiah

1 Macc.   APOC.   1 Maccabees

2 Macc.   APOC.   2 Maccabees

Mal.   OT   Malachi

Matt.   NT   Matthew

Mic.   OT   Micah

Mk.   NT   Mark

Nahum   OT   Nahum

Neh.   OT   Nehemiah

Num.   OT   Numbers

Obad.   OT   Obadiah

1 Pet.   NT   1 Peter

2 Pet.   NT   2 Peter

Phil.   NT   Philippians

Philem.   NT   Philemon

Pr. of Az.   APOC.   Prayer of Azariah

Pr. of Man.   APOC.   Prayer of Manasseh

Prov.   OT   Proverbs

Ps(s).   OT   Psalms

Rest of Esth.   APOC.   Rest of Esther

Rev.   NT   Revelation of John

Rom.   NT   Romans

Ruth   OT   Ruth

1 Sam.   OT   1 Samuel

2 Sam.   OT   2 Samuel

ABBREVIATION, LOCATION, TITLE

S. of S.   OT   Song of Songs
S. of Three   APOC.   Song of the Three
Sus.   APOC.   Daniel and Susanna
1 Thess.   NT   1 Thessalonians
2 Thess.   NT   2 Thessalonians
Ti.   NT   Titus

ABBREVIATION, LOCATION, TITLE

1 Tim.   NT   1 Timothy
2 Tim.   NT   2 Timothy
Tob.   APOC.   Tobit
Wisd.   APOC.   Wisdom
Zech.   OT   Zechariah
Zeph.   OT   Zephaniah

Other Abbreviations and Notes

An explanation of terms, names of ancient versions, etc., as used in footnotes to the text, appears in the Introductions to the Old Testament, the Apocrypha, and the New Testament where appropriate.

Ant.	Flavius Josephus, *Antiquities of the Jews*
Apoc.	Apocrypha
Aq.	Aquila, Greek version of the Hebrew Scriptures
Aram.	Aramaic
B.C.E.	Before the Common Era (= B.C.)
B.J.	Flavius Josephus, *The Jewish War*
ca.	*circa,* approximately
C.E.	Common Era (= A.D.)
cf.	*confer,* compare
ch(s).	chapter(s)
cp.	compare
e.g.	*exempli gratia,* for example
Gk.	Greek (language or version)
Heb.	Hebrew
i.e.	*id est,* that is
Lat.	Latin version
lit.	literally
Lives	Diogenes Laertius, *Lives and Opinions of Eminent Philosophers*
Luc.	Lucian's edition of the Septuagint
mng.	meaning
MS(S).	manuscript(s)
MT	Masoretic Text
n(n).	note(s)
NT	New Testament
om.	omit(s)
or	indicates an alternative interpretation
OT	Old Testament
Pesh.	Peshitta, Syriac version of Hebrew Scriptures
poss.	possible
prob.	probable
rdg	reading
Samar.	Samaritan Pentateuch
Scroll	text drived from the Dead Sea Scrolls
Sept.	Septuagint, Greek version of Hebrew Scriptures (with additional books now included in Apocrypha)
Symm.	Symmachus, Greek version of Hebrew Scriptures
Syr.	Syriac
Targ.	Targum
Tfn.	translators' footnotes
Theod.	Theodotion, Greek version of Hebrew Scriptures
Vg.	Vulgate, Latin version of the Bible
v(v).	verse(s)
Vs(s).	Version(s)
[ ]	In keywords, square brackets enclose words that are included for clarity of reference, but are not themselves the subject of the note.

Measures, Weights, and Values

No precise modern equivalents can be given for the units of measurement, weight, and value used in the ancient world, which themselves varied at different times, in different places, and in different contexts of use. The approximate equivalents given below may be helpful as an indication of the order of magnitude implied by a particular term.

LENGTH

Unit	Approx. equivalent in metres	As read at
hand's breadth	0.075	Ezek. 40:5
span	0.225	1 Sam. 17:4Tfn.
cubit (short) = 6 hand's breadths	0.45	Judg. 3:16Tfn.
cubit (long) = 7 hand's breadths	0.525	2 Chr. 3:3

WEIGHTS AND VALUES

Unit	Approx. equivalent in grammes	As read at
gerah	0.6	Ezek. 45:12
shekel (sacred) = 20 gerahs	12	Lev. 27:25
mina = 50 shekels	600	1 Kgs. 10:17
mina = 60 shekels	720	Ezek. 45:12
talent = 3000 shekels	36000	Exod. 38:25

Mention is made (Gen. 23:16) of a shekel of 'the standard recognized by merchants'; its relationship to the sacred standard is uncertain.

The 'pound' of the New Testament (John 12:3) may be referred to the Roman standard of about 317 grammes.

Related to gold or silver, the weights tabulated above are frequently used as measures of value. In the Old Testament 'beka' (*lit.* half) is used to signify a half-shekel (Exod. 38:26). The 'talent' of the New Testament (Matt. 18:24) evidently signifies a large but not precise monetary value.

COINS

The 'daric' (1 Chr. 29:7) was a gold coin weighing just over 8 grammes, said to have been equivalent to a month's pay for a soldier in the Persian army. What is referred to as a 'drachma' (Neh. 7:70) may have been a silver coin of about 4.4 grammes.

The 'denarius' of the New Testament (Mark 14:5) is said to have been the equivalent of a day's wage for a labourer.

MEASURES OF CAPACITY: DRY MEASURES

Unit	Approx. equivalent in litres	As read at
kab	2.5	2 Kgs. 6:25
omer	4.5	Exod. 16:32
seah	15	1 Sam. 25:18Tfn.
ephah = 10 omers	45	Exod. 16:36
kor = 10 ephahs	450	1 Kgs. 4:22
homer = 10 ephahs	450	Ezek. 45:11

LIQUID MEASURES

Unit	Approx. equivalent in litres	As read at
log	1	Lev. 14:10
hin = 12 log	12	Num. 15:7
bath = 6 hin	72	Ezek. 45:14
kor = 10 bath	720	Ezek. 45:14

Understanding the Bible
and its Communities

Reading the Bible

MARY ANN TOLBERT

No person was ever born knowing how to read, for reading is neither instinctual nor hereditary. It is, instead, a *learned* skill. Throughout the centuries the people who could read were taught to do so by their societies in the course of public education or private family socialization, and the methods and content of that teaching often varied greatly from culture to culture and from generation to generation. Even in our contemporary world, people are taught to read in many different languages that display varying grammatical conventions, distinct alternatives of expression, and often non-translatable vocabulary. Moreover, learning to read a new language with real understanding always involves also acquiring a wide variety of cultural information about customs, social relationships, and history out of which each different language system grows and upon which it depends. The difficulty of this process is well known to anyone who has studied a "foreign" langauge and is amusingly, if xenophobicly, detailed by the American humorist Mark Twain in his essay, "The Awful German Language." After listing all of his frustrations in mastering German cases, grammatical gender, and word arrangement, the English-speaking Twain sardonically concludes by asserting, "My philological studies have satisfied me that a gifted person ought to learn English (barring spelling and pronouncing) in thirty hours, French in thirty days, and German in thirty years." Of course, a German faced with learning English might argue the reverse of Twain's listing as the more justifiable one! Becoming conversant with any new language is a formidable and time-consuming task, for it actually requires entering a new world of meaning.

The texts of the Bible were not written in English, nor, for that matter, in German or French, but in languages now "dead": biblical Hebrew, Aramaic, and koinē* Greek. To make these texts accessible to contemporary audiences who have neither thirty years nor a lifetime to give to language study, translators schooled in these languages have produced the *Revised English Bible* and other modern language translations. While the benefits of such translations are easy to perceive, however, they also

---

*Meaning "common." Koinē is the form of Greek commonly used in the Mediterranean world during the few centuries before and after the Common Era.

present certain important limitations. Since all languages are deeply embedded in the cultural systems out of which they come, to understand a text written in another language requires some understanding of that other culture as well, and simply reading an English translation does not provide that vital cultural information. Although people taught to read English can easily read this *Revised English Bible,* if they were to do so as though it were a modern English text coming out of contemporary social experience, they would be seriously *mis*-reading the ancient narratives, laws, letters, and poetry produced by the ancient authors and editors and understood by the first audiences of the Bible. To comprehend the Bible in ways similar to its original audiences, a modern reader must *learn* something of the alien and long-dead cultures standing behind these texts, and it is precisely to assist readers with such learning that the articles of this study edition are dedicated.

To speak of people *reading* the Bible in itself points to one of the most striking, yet often least recognized, differences between the modern reader and the ancient one. While literacy today is widespread and common, in the ancient world of the Hebrew people and even the later world of the Greeks very few people acquired the skills of reading and writing. Consequently, the authors of the biblical documents belonged to a tiny literate elite within largely illiterate societies. Since the majority of the Hebrew people and the early Christians could not read, most of the biblical texts were written primarily to be heard with the ear rather than read with the eye, allowing those few who could read to read aloud for the benefit of the larger group. Hearing a text, rather than seeing it, affected the way ancient material was fashioned; repetition, puns, prologues, and summaries are all prevalent stylistic devices in biblical material because of the requirements of the ear. While modern readers are taught to use chapter titles, tables of contents, paragraphing, and internal headings as ways of orienting themselves in books or articles, these "eye helps" did not exist in ancient writings (the verse numbers in the Bible, for instance, were not added until the sixteenth century C.E. by the famous Parisian printer Stephanus). Stops and starts, the organization of material, and the type (or genre) of writing had to be signaled in ways accessible to the ear for an ancient audience. Thus, repeated opening and closing patterns, sharply defined genres like proverbs, pronouncement stories (a brief narrative scene ending with a direct saying by the major character), hymns, oracles, laws, letters, and straightforward, reliable narration are all important aspects of biblical literature that appear quite differently and much less extensively in modern writing.

Not only were the writings of the Bible composed for the ear, but much of the material in those writings, especially in the Hebrew Bible (or the Christian Old Testament), existed for years, perhaps centuries, as *oral* tradition before ever being written down. The stories were passed orally from one generation to the next, adapted to new occasions and altered to fit changing social and political circumstances. After a time, collections of these oral stories were made and eventually committed to writing. Some of the materials in the four gospels of the New Testament may also have been part of an oral tradition, though for a much briefer period, before the gospel writers incorporated them into their narratives. Hence, the absence of widespread literacy in antiquity meant that *oral* communication was the medium of critical importance; in the ancient world, persuasive speech had to be ear-oriented. Therefore, in order to understand the Bible as its first audiences did, modern readers must learn to *hear* its texts as well as read them.

Even referring to *the* Bible may encourage contemporary readers to *mis*-read, for *the* Bible is not one book but a collection of many books coming from many different centuries and several quite distinct cultures. The Hebrew Bible contains books written from the tenth century B.C.E. to the second century B.C.E., almost a millennium of human history. The present shape of many of these books evolved over centuries of editing and reworking, from the early legends about the origins of the Hebrew people, most of which originally circulated as oral tradition, to the later apocalyptic visions of the end of the world in the Book of Daniel. Because of this complex process of composition, these documents often reflect not only the evolving religious ideas of the Hebrew people but also their changing social and political fortunes in the maelstrom of ancient Near Eastern diplomacy. Yet, since the first audiences were themselves living that political and social history, it generally stands behind the biblical stories as context rather than in them as subject matter; for contemporary readers to understand the stories fully, however, this essential historical information needs to be learned.

Although the New Testament books were written over the much shorter period of about 100 years, from perhaps 41 or 51 C.E. for Paul's earliest letter to as late as 150 C.E. for some of the catholic epistles (or general letters), the political history of that century, containing the war between Rome and the Jews, the subsequent fall of Jerusalem and Qumran, and the destruction of the Jerusalem temple, as well as—probably—the destruction of the Christian community in Jerusalem, plays a crucial role in the outward growth of the Christian movement. Actually, the twenty-seven separate letters and books that now compose the official New Testament canon (or authoritative list) are only a small selection from a much larger body of writings by Christians during the first several centuries of the Common Era. Thus, in order to appreciate the full variety and vitality of early Christian history, this larger fund of material— ranging from long-recognized writings like the letters of Clement or *The Shepherd of Hermas* to recently discovered works like the gnostic documents of Nag Hammadi—needs to be studied and assessed. Moreover, why some of these texts were determined to be authoritative (or canonical) by later third- and fourth-century Christians, while other texts were not, provides insight into the debates that came to shape medieval Christianity and indeed Christianity today.

The Hebrew Bible and the New Testament, the two major divisions of the Bible, clearly display certain similarities in form and content: they both draw upon oral traditions; they are both made up of various types of literature, written at diverse times, directed to separate groups of people for a variety of reasons; they both relate the continuing story of God's involvement with the Jewish people and the surrounding Gentile world; and they often present mutually complementary moral and theological positions. To view these similarities as establishing a uniformity of perspective for *the* Bible, however, would again be a serious *mis*-reading of the material, for the cultural matrix informing each set of writings is fundamentally different. The very fact that they were composed in two quite distinct languages, Hebrew (Aramaic, a semitic language similar to Hebrew, also occurs in small sections of Ezra-Nehemiah and Daniel) and Greek, points to their involvement in two divergent cultural systems. One good illustration of that dissimilarity can be seen in the general world-views, or conceptions of the universe and the place of humanity and divinity in it, that dominated the thinking of each cultural period.

In the ancient Near Eastern world of the Sumerians, Babylonians, and Hebrew people, the universe was an intimate and fairly compact affair, which might be visualized as three stories, separated by the solid firmament of the earth below and of the heavens above. The top story, formed by the heavens, was the abode of the gods and was surrounded at its outermost limits by water, which the gods could allow to fall upon the earth by opening windows in the heavens, a practice engendering considerable anxiety among the human population for fear that the gods might forget or decide not to close those windows and thus flood the earth. The second story, the space between the earth and the heavens, was the location of humanity, while the bottom story with its limits also defined by water, which could rise to the earth above through rivers and oceans, belonged to the spirits of the underworld. All three stories were closely connected to each other; for example, in the sixth century B.C.E. priests estimated the distance between the temple in Jerusalem and the heavenly dwelling of God to be about two miles. In such a small universe, encounters between the divine and human worlds were expected and regular. Only when one element or another was out of place or not performing its assigned tasks (e.g., the gods were asleep or on a journey when they were needed [see 1 Kgs. 18.27] or the king refused to rebuild the city walls or the farmer neglected the time of harvest) was the harmony of the entire system put at risk by an eruption of chaos. Order and a strong sense of place created a very secure world, and religion provided the map or contract or set of rules needed to maintain the established order.

By the beginnings of Christianity, that secure, compact universe had exploded. Only a few other periods in the history of Western civilizations can rival the extensive change in perspective that occurred during the Greco-Roman era. Galileo's discoveries in the sixteenth and seventeenth centuries or perhaps Einstein's theories in the contemporary world have initiated similar revolutions in thought and society, but such cataclysmic shifts are rare. The exact causes of that ancient transformation remain unclear, but it was surely influenced by the increasingly sophisticated developments in astronomy, science, and mathematics in Greek circles as well as the growth of large, multi-national urban centers around the Mediterranean basin, where cultural, economic, and religious exchange could flourish. These intellectual and social innovations coupled with the new mobility permitted by the widespread use of koinē Greek as a general language of commerce and the relative stability of Greek and then of Roman rule, extended the limits of the universe far beyond anything imaginable by earlier peoples.

The cosmology conceived during the Greco-Roman period, formally codified by Claudius Ptolemy in the second century C.E., might best be visualized as an expanding series of concentric spheres, all in eternal motion around a tiny, stationary earth. The first seven spheres contained the moon and the fixed stars or planets, each moving in its appointed round and in the process, rubbing against other spheres to produce musical notes (the "music of the spheres" found in hymnody). The planets were not the only inhabitants of each sphere, however, for Greco-Roman people also believed that each sphere housed an order of angels or demons, constantly watching the activities of the human world below, and the closer the sphere to the earth, the nastier were its tenants, with the demons responsible for illness, birth defects, and pains of all kinds lodging in the space between the moon and the earth. It is true that the earth was the stable center of this vast, moving universe, but its centrality was not an assertion of human pride, for like the stationary bull's-eye in a cosmic target the earth was now the focus of active, mobile evil. The intimate, secure universe of the earlier age had disappeared into the vast, threatening reaches of the cosmos, and God no longer dwelt a short distance away but instead resided out beyond the farthest sphere. Religion in such an age existed to help people escape the fears of daily life and to assure them of God's continued care in this world and the next across the outstretched spaces of the stars. Paul's ringing conviction in Rom. 8.38–39 speaks precisely to this situation: "For I am convinced that there is nothing in death or life, in the realm of spirits or superhuman powers, in the world as it is or the world as it shall be, in the forces of the universe, in heights or depths—nothing in all creation that can separate us from the love of God in Christ Jesus our Lord."

Today we live neither in the ancient three-story universe of the Hebrew people nor even in the Ptolemaic universe of the early Christians. In reading about worries over sleeping deities or threatening demonic powers, modern people probably think of metaphorical language or symbolic meanings, for in modern writings those images would surely function in that fashion. The Bible, however, is not a modern book or collection of modern books. The people who told, wrote, and heard these stories faced uncertain and dangerous worlds which they attempted to understand as God's creation in the ways their societies and theories pictured it. In order to read the Bible in a manner similar to the way they might have heard it, we must *learn* its old language anew and hear its words with ears more attuned to its ancient cadences.

Reading This Bible

M. JACK SUGGS

The preceding essay suggests that knowledge and skills other than those needed to read the morning newspaper are important for "Reading the Bible" intelligently. Originally written in languages with which most speakers of modern English are unfamiliar, the Bible's many documents were composed or compiled in the remote past and over an extended period, in social settings and for cultures different from the reader's own. Therefore, the Bible must be translated from ancient languages to contemporary English, to be sure. But information about its ancient historical and cultural environment also increases understanding. *The Oxford Study Bible* is meant to facilitate informed reading by bringing together a superior modern translation and a collection of basic study aids.

The Translation

The translation was carried out by a broadly ecumenical team of distinguished scholars. There is a "Preface" to the translation on pp. xv–xvii which briefly tells both the story and the history of the translation. The translation is, as one would expect, based on the best manuscript evidence and provides important alternative meanings in translators' footnotes. But it is especially notable for its English style. To a degree seldom achieved in committee translations, the language of this version is modern and fluid. Indeed, the readability of the *Revised English Bible* and its predecessor, the *New English Bible,* led to their becoming offerings of the Book-of-the-Month Club. The ancient-to-modern language translation does not make reading effortless, but certainly sense and meaning are more accessible in the smooth idiom of this superb translation.

Aids to Better Understanding

What many students want in addition to the translation is information that will help to bridge the gap between original historical settings and the reader's modern setting, between ancient and contemporary cultures. An array of annotations, introductions and articles serve this purpose by providing an orientation to current scholarly opinion about biblical literature and methods of study.

INTRODUCTIONS AND ANNOTATIONS. The reader will find that Introductions and annotations have been supplied for each biblical book. These are meant to furnish the modest but essential information which enables a student to begin reading the Bible with understanding. In contrast to the highly individual and distinctive judgments in technical books and commentaries which scholars address to each other, what the reader can expect here are common opinions, views generally shared by scholars. If one consults the list of contributors, it will also be seen that this kind of scholarly consensus represents a broad spectrum of confessional positions. The annotations and Introductions, written by contributors who come from Jewish, Roman Catholic and various Protestant traditions, exhibit a methodology which cuts across lines of religious affiliation.

An Introduction appears at the very beginning of each book and provides information about the history and character of the book. Such information is important for understanding the document, so consulting the Introduction when reading a book is always an advantage. For example, the Introduction will ordinarily indicate a book's historical context. Thus, the reader who turns to the Introduction to Deuteronomy (p. 181) learns that Deuteronomy is to be seen in relation to the events of the seventh and eighth centuries B.C.E. Similarly, the Introduction to the Gospel according to John (p. 1365) includes the information that it probably was written near the end of the first century C.E. in Asia Minor. Also, an Introduction will discuss special literary features of a book. Thus, Proverbs (one learns from the Introduction, p. 652) is made up of several collections of "wisdom" instruction; the Revelation of John is an apocalyptic document (Introduction, p. 1556). Clues of this nature enlighten the reading of a book in advance.

The annotations furnish information about matters in the text of the book and are located at the foot of the page on which the verse or passage is printed. Typically, annotations provide clarification of historical and geographical references, identification of characters, definitions of words with special meanings, and other basic information. A good example of how annotations illuminate a passage may be seen at Isa. 7.1–9, where notes supply such information as: description of the historical setting of the account, identification of *Ahaz*, explanation of *house of David*, elucidation of the name *Shear-jashub*. The notes are not a set of detailed comments, nor do they intend to supply a comprehensive interpretation of the passage. What is supplied is basic knowledge for informed reading.

The annotations also incorporate references to other biblical passages which are pertinent because they are being quoted, or offer a parallel account or otherwise shed light on the text. Where there is a literary relation between books (i.e., one uses the other as a source) these references receive special treatment. Because they were used as sources, for example, the books of Samuel and Kings are referenced frequently and pointedly in the annotations on Chronicles. The fact that the Synoptic Gospels (Matthew, Mark, Luke) have a literary relationship has led to a special way of citing parallel units: the parallels are cross-referenced in parentheses which immediately follow paragraph headings in the annotations. Thus, the annotation heading for Mark **9.2–8: The transfigu-**

ration is followed by reference in parenthesis to the parallels Matt. 17.1–8 and Lk. 9.28–36.

OTHER STUDY AIDS. In addition to the Introductions and annotations which accompany the text, another two dozen "aids to study" in the form of articles, charts and maps undergird informed reading in other ways. These additional aids address subjects that are broader than the issues of specific passages and furnish orientations to areas that are relevant to the Bible as a whole or to a sizable portion of it. The positions advanced in these articles are, by and large, consensus judgments. A student who uses these materials will gain an impression of the common understandings of issues in biblical studies developed by contemporary scholars.

The idea of turning to these aids may come as a result of the reader's experience with the biblical text that presses for their use. Thus the "Maps and Notes" may be consulted initially when it becomes apparent that an understanding of geographical setting will enhance a story's significance. Or, in the course of reading Hosea, the student may decide to turn to the article on "The Phenomenon of Prophecy." The articles are, in fact, sufficiently relevant to the process of reading that many of them may be encountered out of just such a practical motivation.

However, while a student's attention may be drawn to a particular study aid by an encountered "problem" or "issue," a better approach would be to read the assembled articles as a small book which furnishes a survey laying the foundation for good understanding. Although the realization that one is reading chapters of the Bible printed as poetry might suggest turning to the article on "Literary Forms of the Bible," the study of the entire Bible would be better served by having learned in advance to expect a variety of types of books (such as poetry, letters, or narrative) and diverse small units (such as parables, proverbs, or prayers). Again, the dramatic story of Moses, the burning bush, and the revelation of the God who is called "I am" (Exod. 3.1–15) might suggest looking at the article on "Deity in the Biblical Communities and among their Neighbors"; still, that article is important far beyond the specific Exodus account and should be allowed to inform general reading in the Bible. Other articles provide general overviews which supply relevant background information; "Historical Contexts of the Biblical Communities" and "The Social World of the New Testament" are only two of the more obvious examples. The reader should explore the articles and other aids with a view to finding how they facilitate the enjoyment of Bible study.

For millennia, the Bible's story has fascinated its readers and its message has inspired both courage and faith. *The Oxford Study Bible* is offered in the hope of encouraging the reader's discovery of the book and of enhancing the meaning of its story and message.

Literary Forms of the Bible

LEANDER E. KECK AND GENE M. TUCKER

The Bible can be read from many perspectives. From a historical view, one can read it to learn about the past; from the standpoint of religion, one can read it to clarify or strengthen faith; from a literary angle, one can appreciate its poetry, its narrative style, and its use of imagery. Another kind of concern is developed here—an attempt to acquaint the reader with the many literary forms which the Bible represents.

Awareness of literary form is fundamental to understanding. In reading poetry we do not look for the same thing that we look for in reading novels; legal contracts use language different from that which is used in short stories. Moreover, because in a typical biblical book various kinds of material stand side by side, the reader must know what the natural unit is. Furthermore, later use frequently obscured the original shape of the material; but awareness of the form can help the student distinguish earlier from later layers. The Bible is such a rich and diverse book that only a general sketch, with a few examples, can be undertaken here, with the hope that the reader will be encouraged to pursue the study of literary form independently.

In terms of literary form, the Bible as a whole ought not to be taken for granted. We shall therefore begin by noting its structure and history. From there we shall look at the kinds of books in the Bible, then at the kinds of literary forms within the individual books. Finally, we shall reflect on the value of pursuing this kind of analysis.

The Bible As a Whole

WHAT IS THE BIBLE? From a literary point of view the Bible is an anthology, or a collection of literature, containing narratives, poetry, prophetic books, letters, and apocalypses. It is not organized according to types of literature; rather, different kinds of literature (called "books") stand side by side. Furthermore, many individual books themselves juxtapose narratives, poetry, and legal codes. Understanding the Bible from a literary point of view requires us to see the character of the anthology as a whole, and how it came to be what it now is.

In the first place, the contents of the collection depend on whose Bible we are talking about. What Jews call "the Bible," Christians call "the Old Testament"; moreover, because of the Apocrypha, Christians have not always agreed among themselves, nor with the Jews, on what constitutes the Old Testament. Roman Catholics have always included the Apocrypha in the Old Testament, but Protestants sometimes printed the books between the Old and New Testaments, or omitted them entirely. (The

Revised English Bible places the Apocrypha between the two Testaments.) The reasons for this are complex, but the facts are simple enough: the Protestant Old Testament is the Bible of the Palestinian synagogue as determined by the rabbis after the fall of Jerusalem in 70 C.E. The Apocrypha, on the other hand, was part of the Bible of the Greek synagogues. This Bible in turn became the Scripture of the Greek-speaking church; later it was translated into Latin. However, in the sixteenth century, Reformation Protestants reverted to the Palestinian canon for their Old Testament, and relegated the Apocrypha to the status of books "good and useful to read," while denying them full authority as Scripture, but at the Council of Trent Catholics determined to continue to include them in the Old Testament.

Nor did Christians always agree about the content of the New Testament. The earliest list of books which agrees with our present New Testament comes from 367 C.E., yet it was not until many centuries later that all Christians agreed on what constituted the New Testament. From this rudimentary sketch, it is clear that what the word "Bible" refers to depends on the particular religious community one has in view, and on the history of these communities with their Scriptures.

In the second place, the way in which the anthology called the Bible is organized also depends on whether one has in mind the Jewish or the Christian Bible. The Hebrew Bible, quite apart from the placement of the Apocrypha, is structured differently from the Christian Old Testament. It has three divisions: the Torah ("the Law"), the Prophets (subdivided into "the former prophets" and "the latter prophets"), and the Writings. When Christians adopted the Greek Bible, they also accepted a different order. For example, in the Christian Old Testament, the literary prophets (called "latter prophets" in the Hebrew Bible) come at the very end.

In the third place, the content of the New Testament is the result of many historical factors, especially the rejection of Marcion, a second-century heretic. Marcion demanded that Christians discard the Synagogue Bible altogether and rely solely on a Christian Bible consisting of the Gospel of Luke and the Letters of Paul (from both of which he had deleted passages favorable to Judaism and the God of the Old Testament). In rejecting Marcion, the church retained the Old Testament; it also insisted that the New Testament should have four gospels and the letters of more than one apostle. Eventually the Book of Revelation was included as well. These factors, succinctly stated here, explain why "the Bible" refers to several anthologies, and why the tables of contents vary as they do.

It is difficult to classify a piece of literature precisely if it was edited subsequently, or if it is itself a compilation of several writings. But this is exactly what we have in most books of the Bible. On the one hand, some works came to be divided into several books. For example, what we now know as 1 and 2 Chronicles, Ezra, and Nehemiah were originally a single work. The long work became divided and the divided parts acquired individual names. On the other hand, books which are essentially compilations are common. In the Hebrew Bible the twelve (minor) prophets are a single "book" which compiled the individual works into one scroll. Second Corinthians probably combines parts of at least five letters.

Broadly speaking, nonetheless, we may classify the books of the Bible into five kinds of literature: 1. Narrative books (e.g., Genesis, Samuel, Kings, Maccabees, the Gospels, the Acts of the Apostles); 2. Poetry (e.g., Psalms, Song of Songs, Proverbs); 3. Prophetic books; 4. Epistles (e.g., the Letters of Paul); 5. Apocalypses (Daniel, 2 Esdras [4 Ezra], Revelation). Each of these will be discussed below. First, however, several considerations merit attention.

To begin with, the distribution is of interest. Narrative and apocalypse are found throughout the Old and New Testaments, and the Apocrypha. On the other hand, except for the Letter of Jeremiah in some manuscripts, epistles as separate writings are found only in the New Testament, while only the Old Testament has books of poetry and collections of proverbs. Second, many types of literature do not appear in the Bible at all: drama, satire, autobiography, myth (an extended narrative about the gods), commentaries. Third, none of the literary types found in the Bible is peculiarly biblical. Therefore, the study of types or genres of literature in general, and especially those of antiquity, illumines the particular biblical literature. Fourth, most of the books contain several literary forms. For example, Exodus contains narrative, laws, and poetry; Jeremiah contains narrative, poetry, and letters; some of the epistles contain poetic passages, such as 1 Corinthians, ch. 13.

Multiple literary forms may exist within a given book either because it is a compilation (e.g., Daniel begins with stories and then becomes reports of visions) or because its author used various kinds of materials in writing it. For example, the Deuteronomic history (Deuteronomy, Joshua, Judges, 1 and 2 Samuel, 1 and 2 Kings) used earlier documents, such as annals and previous histories.

AUTHORSHIP. The biblical writers were not self-conscious literary figures writing for a public, nor were they writing to express their personal views. They were writing for religious communities which they sought to address as effectively as possible. In doing so, some of them recorded and adapted fixed traditions. They were not professional authors who earned their livelihood by writing. Indeed, to what extent the writers were self-conscious "authors" is highly uncertain. We know few of their names. The vast majority of the books are anonymous; "authors" were assigned to them at a later date by the communities as acts of piety. Thus, the Pentateuch was attributed to Moses, the Psalms to David, Proverbs to Solomon, the Gospels to apostles or their associates. Furthermore, some of the literature was actually written in the name of well-known figures. All apocalypses, except the Revelation of John, claim to be written by persons long dead. Certain letters of Paul (Ephesians, Timothy, Titus), and probably the letters of James, Jude, Peter, and John were written in the name of these apostles. More important, the identity of none of the compilers is known, nor are the names of many of the writers whose works have been incorporated in books which we now have. In many instances it is not at all clear whether the compilation was done by an individual or by a group. For example, it is customary to speak of "the Yahwist" or "the Priestly writer" of certain strata of the Pentateuch, or of the "author" of the Fourth Gospel. But no one knows whether these works represent the efforts of a single mind or of a group. Similarly, the Gospels are end products of a process of development to which several persons or groups made their contribution. For example, the Gospel according to Matthew appropriates most of Mark, some of which was rewritten, and supplements it with a collection (itself restructured) of Jesus' teachings and with other material. Most of the individuals who wrote the literature of the Bible drew on materials already known. The creativity of the writer usually expressed itself in the use of existing material. Thus, biblical literature is much less the product of creative writing than the product of creative editing done within the context of communities of faith.

Types of Books

NARRATIVE WORKS. Many of the books are essentially narratives. As such, they include at least the rudiments of a plot, an indication of where the events transpired, and some greater or lesser portrayal of the characters. Ordinarily the larger narratives have a chronological order. The various narrative genres may be distinguished from one another on the basis of plot, setting, and characterization, and on the basis of specific purposes. Was a work composed in order to entertain, to edify, or to transmit factual information?

A great many different narrative genres appear in the Bible. A number of the books and literary works may be classified as histories, though not in the modern scholarly sense. A history is a written narrative of past events which is governed by facts, as far as the writer could ascertain and interpret them, and not by thematic or aesthetic organization. It will, then, in most cases be chronological in sequence. Most of the biblical histories are popular histories; that is, the writer's determination of the facts was not based on critically assessed and reliable sources (such as eye-witness testimony or accurate records), but on traditional material (such as stories and legends). Much of the popular history of the Bible could also be called salvation history, since it aims at showing how the sequence of events was directed by God. A major example of history in these senses is the Deuteronomic sequence (see above), which includes many diverse literary types, but viewed as a whole comprises a single interpretative account of the history of Israel from the Exodus to the Exile. The Tetrateuch ("four books": Genesis, Exodus, Leviticus, Numbers) likewise is such a history, though its sequence is not so neatly ordered because of its history of composition; furthermore, it includes within its historical framework a considerable amount of legal material. Critical analysis of the Tetrateuch has shown that it is composed of two or more originally separate but complete histories of salvation, the works of the Yahwist and the Priestly writer. Other major examples of salvation histories are the Chronicler's work (1 and 2 Chronicles, Ezra, and Nehemiah), 1 and 2 Maccabees, 1 Esdras, and Acts.

Some narrative books are essentially stories, that is, their structure is determined primarily by plot. Stories create interest by arousing tension (suspense) and releasing it. In addition to stories, such as the Joseph narrative, employed in larger works, a number of separate books belong to this category. Many of these owe their content or shape to popular tradition, and thus may be called tales. The Book of Ruth is a short story which probably rests on a folktale; Jonah is a didactic (teaching) story developed from legend. In terms of content, the Book of Esther could be called a historical novel, or in terms of purpose, a festival legend, since it seems to have been written to explain the meaning and significance of the Feast of Purim. In the Apocrypha the books of Tobit; Judith; Daniel and Susanna; and Daniel, Bel, and the Snake are imaginative didactic stories—works of fiction, novelistic in character, and written in order to convey lessons.

Generally speaking, gospels are narratives about Jesus. Their literary form is basically similar to ancient biographies of popular teachers. The title "gospel" was attached to a rather diverse body of narratives about Jesus, only four of which were included in the New Testament. The canonical Gospels generally narrate the public ministry of Jesus; each of them has its own structure, though they all culminate in the story of Jesus' death and resurrection. The apocryphal gospels (those never included in the canon), on the other hand, vary considerably in content. Some, such as the infancy *Gospel of Thomas* or the *Gospel of Peter*, fill in "gaps," that is, give information not provided by the canonical Gospels. Others claim to furnish secret traditions; one recently found gospel, that of Thomas, is a collection of sayings but without any real narrative at all.

The canonical Gospels are the results of the transmission and use of traditions about Jesus, including his teachings. The so-called "Synoptics" (the first three Gospels) are interdependent, since Matthew and Luke used Mark; John apparently did not use the Synoptics but did have access to some materials found also in the others. Essentially, however, John's traditions were independent of the Synoptics, and were developed in distinctive ways. The canonical Gospels were written forty to seventy years after the events which they report. All of the Gospels were probably developed for various uses in the Christian congregations, whose problems are reflected both in the selection of the individual traditions and in the emphases of the individual Gospels.

POETIC BOOKS. Many books of the Bible are poetic works, but this category is not adequate as a generic classification because there are several very distinct types. Moreover, though the prophetic books contain a considerable amount of poetry, they are sufficiently distinctive to merit a separate classification. Divided broadly, there are two kinds of poetic books: cultic poetry and Wisdom literature. The primary example of the former is the Book of Psalms, which is not simply a collection of poems but is the hymn and prayer book of the temple in late Old Testament times. For the most part the psalms and cultic poems are lyrical, that is, meant to be sung (see below). The only other book of cultic poetry in the Old Testament is Lamentations, a collection of dirges and mourning liturgies concerning national disaster. In the Apocrypha, books of liturgical poetry are represented by the Prayer of Manasseh, a short devotional piece, and the Prayer of Azariah and The Song of the Three, added to the Book of Daniel on its translation into Greek.

The other poetic books are more difficult to classify. They generally are considered Wisdom literature, itself a wide range of types. The Song of Songs, for example, is lyrical poetry. Though sometimes interpreted as the liturgy of a sacred marriage ceremony, it is in reality a collection of secular love poetry, perhaps assembled for use at weddings. Other Wisdom poetry ranges from the collection of sayings and poems in the Book of Proverbs (see below) through the lengthy instructions in the apocryphal Book of Ecclesiasticus, to the carefully constructed poem of Job. Still other examples of this literature are Ecclesiastes and the apocryphal Wisdom of Solomon. All of these works have in common a certain literary self-consciousness seldom found in other biblical literature. Behind these works often stand poets in the sense of creative individuals.

In the Revised English Bible, as in most modern translations, poetry can be recognized by its verse (metrical) form. The basic principle of Hebrew poetry is the parallelism of members, or the "thought rhyme" of two (or sometimes three) successive lines. For example, in Ps. 29.8 we have:

> The voice of the LORD makes the wilderness writhe in travail,
> the LORD makes the wilderness of Kadesh writhe.

The second line introduces no new thought, but parallels the first. Scholars have recognized different types of parallelism. In the example cited, the two lines are synonymous. Others are antithetical, that is, the second line verbalizes the opposite of the first, or states negatively what the first had presented positively. Thus Job 22.29:

> but God brings down the pride of the haughty
> and keeps safe those who are humble.

Still others have been called synthetic or formal parallelism, for the second line may develop the thought of the first. Other poetic features more familiar to us, such as meter, rhyme, alliteration, assonance, and the like

appear, but they are not as basic as parallelism. There is usually some
regularity of meter in the sense of balanced numbers of accented sylla-
bles, but this feature seems to be derived from the balancing of parallel
lines.

PROPHETIC BOOKS. While prophets were found elsewhere in antiquity, no
other culture, before or since, has developed prophetic literature as did
ancient Israel. Prophets were known in ancient Mesopotamia, but not
prophetic books. Books called prophecies were written in Egypt, but they
are quite different from the Old Testament prophetic books. Neither are
there prophetic books in the Apocrypha nor in the New Testament,
though the Book of Revelation has some affinities with prophetic literature.

The prophetic books receive their distinctive stamp from the prophets'
self-understanding as messengers for God. The prophets, on the basis of
a particular call and special revelations, announced God's word concerning Israel and other nations as well. They were preoccupied with declaring God's actions in the immediate future.

We must distinguish the prophetic words themselves from the prophetic books. Study of the prophets in recent generations has emphasized
that they were not authors who wrote books, but speakers. It was usually
their followers or other listeners who committed their words to writing.
Occasionally we catch a glimpse of the way the spoken words were written down, eventually to form books or parts of books, as in Jeremiah
ch. 36. Isaiah, when he was not heeded, decided to "tie up the message,
seal the instruction" (Isa. 8.16). It seems clear from such texts and other
indications that something new and significant had occurred when the
words were written down. At least two factors were involved. First, writing the speeches preserved the revelation and kept it from being stifled
when the prophet was either prevented from speaking, or ignored. Second, there arose a concern that future generations should know that
what they were experiencing had already been set into motion by God's
word once spoken through his prophets.

The first prophetic "books" doubtless were collections of the sayings of
individual prophets. As we shall see, those sayings were of many different
types, but for the most part they were short, poetic units. But the prophetic books contain other classes of literature as well, such as narratives.
Most of these are reports of prophetic activities, either in autobiographical or biographical style. They range from short accounts, setting the
occasions for particular speeches, to lengthy tales; from reports of the
prophet's call to accounts of symbolic actions performed as messages.
The third genre found in the prophetic books is prayer, such as the
so-called complaints of Jeremiah in the Book of Jeremiah, or the hymnic
fragments in the Book of Amos.

From the jotting down of the first prophetic utterance to the books we
read today was a long journey. The details of that journey elude us, but

some of the landmarks can be reconstructed from the evidence in the books themselves. In most cases, the first stage was the recording of individual speeches and small collections of sayings. Often we can recognize some of these earlier collections within the present books; Isa. 2.1, for instance, appears to be the heading for such a unit. Then other materials were added, sometimes organized loosely on the basis of similar content or type, or on the basis of chronology. Most of these emerging books continued to be expanded by later additions which claimed the authority of the original prophet of God. As a result, most of the books now reflect the experience and the thought of several generations. At least two centuries after the death of Isaiah, for example, prophetic writings still were being added to the book bearing that name.

The prophetic books were read and expounded in the Israelite communities which developed and preserved them long before they were canonized as sacred Scriptures. When the Babylonian exiles in the sixth century B.C.E. heard the voice of Amos of the eighth century announcing punishment, they understood their experience as arising from God's activity, and they could turn to the future which they believed lay in God's hands. Again, Jeremiah's pronouncements against Judah were used as texts for sermons exhorting obedience. And Deutero-Isaiah (Isaiah chs. 40–55) argued that Israel's Lord was the only God of history and human affairs, for this God had announced beforehand through the prophets what was to come.

LETTERS. The New Testament is dominated by letters. Of the twenty-seven books, twenty-one are called epistles (the Greek word for letters), most of which are linked to Paul. The letter form became the most important genre in early Christianity. This development is best appreciated when it is seen in light of the Hellenistic letter-writing conventions. Hebrew or Aramaic letters do not appear to have been as influential as the Greek.

Even before the emergence of Christianity, the Greek letter had already become a remarkably stable literary form, despite the diverse kinds of letters which were written. It is useful to distinguish private letters (correspondence between friends or business letters) from public letters. A considerable quantity of private correspondence, mostly on papyrus, has been preserved; much of it has been published since the late nineteenth century. The public letter could be an official correspondence between a public official and a city council, or a series of discussions of moral or political topics cast in letter form, a letter-essay, or a body of magical information made available as a letter. Almost any kind of material could be presented in the form of a public letter, for it was intended for publication and sale.

Both the private and the public letters followed established conventions, with considerable flexibility in detail. The Hellenistic letter had three main parts: the introduction, the body, and the conclusion. The introduction normally named the writer and the recipient, stated a greeting, and may have included the writer's thanksgiving for deliverance from illness and/or a wish for the reader's health. The body could be short and to the point in private correspondence, or lengthy in essays cast as letters. The conclusion expressed greetings and wishes for the persons known to both the writer and the reader, a final greeting, and sometimes the date. Christian letters followed these conventions and modified them at the same time.

A rigid distinction between public and private letters will not work for Paul's correspondence because of the nature of his writing. Paul responded to particular issues by means of letters only because he could not deal with the issues face to face. His letters stand somewhere between private correspondence and public letters; they were not designed to be published and sold in the book stalls, but rather to be read to his congregations and then exchanged (in some cases at least) with other congregations.

Paul follows the convention of naming the writer and the readers (X to Y): but he modifies this by frequently naming his associates, by characterizing the receiving congregation, and by changing the greeting from "Greetings" (Greek *charein*) to "Grace" (*charis*) and by adding "peace" (from the Hebrew *shalom*). In Romans, possibly the last letter genuinely from Paul, the opening becomes more complex, for in it Paul summarized the Gospel in six verses before proceeding to write "to all of you in Rome, who are loved by God and called to be his people." Generally, Paul also modified the thanksgiving; instead of expressing thanks for his own safety and health, he wrote his thanks for the life of the congregation, and did so in a way as to subtly indicate the theme of the body of the letter which followed. The body of the letter was developed according to the needs of the occasion, but regularly included exhortations and a section in which he spoke of his travel plans, expressing a desire to visit the congregation personally. The closing not only amplified the greeting pattern, but frequently included a personal word in his own hand (e.g., 1 Cor. 16.21 ff.; Gal. 6.11 ff.; Philem. 19 ff.) in accord with the practice of official letters in Hellenistic times.

The post-Pauline generation not only imitated Paul's letter writing but developed the catholic (general) epistle to the church at large (e.g., 1 John) or to the churches of a region (1 Peter). The post-Pauline letters tended to become letter-treatises, from which the personal touches are generally absent (e.g., Ephesians, Hebrews, 1 John, 2 Peter); 2 John and 3 John are exceptions. In the second century, the letter-writing tradition continued to flourish but did not enter the canon.

In the New Testament, the epistles stand in a clear order: first, those associated with Paul, with Hebrews standing at the end because it was once thought to be from Paul, and then the Catholic Epistles. Of the Pauline Epistles, those addressed to churches stand first, then come four letters addressed to individuals. The Catholic Epistles begin with James, traditionally thought to be Jesus' brother and head of the Jerusalem church, followed by letters attributed to Peter, John, and Jude. Thus the sequence of letters in the epistle section of the New Testament disregards chronological order.

APOCALYPSES. The only book in the Bible that calls itself an apocalypse is the Revelation of John ("apocalypse" means revelation). In the past two centuries, scholars have come to use this self-designation for a great variety of writings with which the Revelation of John shares important features. Although many such writings from the biblical era have come to light, the Bible contains but three books that are commonly deemed apocalypses: Daniel in the Old Testament, 2 Esdras (4 Ezra) in the Apocrypha, and the Revelation of John in the New Testament. The texts commonly regarded as apocalypses are so diverse that it has proven exceedingly difficult to identify a literary form that characterizes them all. On the one hand, many "apocalypses" juxtapose blocks of quite different types of material. For example, Daniel begins with stories about Daniel, the Book of Revelation begins with seven letters to as many churches, and of the sixteen chapters of 2 Esdras only chs. 3–14 constitute an apocalypse. On the other hand, many books not considered apocalypses also contain apocalypse-like sections (e.g., Isaiah, Ezekiel, Zechariah, *Jubilees, Testaments of the Twelve Patriarchs,* the *Life of Adam and Eve* [also called the *Apocalypse of Moses*], the Synoptic Gospels, 1 and 2 Thessalonians, and 2 Peter).

What, then, is an "apocalypse"? Essentially, it is a text that reports that an other-worldly being (angel or archangel) has given a revelation whose content, be it ever so important, cannot otherwise be known to humans. An apocalypse usually tells how and by whom the revelation was given, and frequently includes directions for preserving it in writing. The means of the revelation vary from dreams to visions to journeys through the heavenly world or to the underworld. The content also varies greatly: cosmological "information," descriptions of end-time catastrophes, portrayals of the Last Judgment and the ultimate fate of the righteous and the wicked, the destruction of Satan and Satan's minions, allegorical overviews of the history of the oppressed righteous, and predictions of what is about to happen. The Revelation of John is the only apocalypse which identifies its author as a contemporary of the readers. Otherwise, apocalypses are pseudonymous: they claim to record revelations given to ancient figures like Adam, Enoch, Moses, Ezra, Baruch (Jeremiah's associate)—though the *War of the Sons of Light and the Sons of Darkness* (one of the Dead Sea Scrolls) is anonymous. Christian apocalypses were often written in the name of an apostle: Peter, Paul, James, etc. Pseudonymity confers on the texts the authority of a hero; by presenting the revelation as something disclosed to an ancient figure, the author conveys an important point: history is neither unintelligible nor meaningless; rather, history has happened, is happening, and will happen exactly as God determined that it would and disclosed long ago. The "historically-oriented" apocalypses are thus pamphlets of encouragement.

The adjective "apocalyptic" is commonly used to refer to a particular view of eschatology (the doctrine of "last things"), one which emphasizes inevitable, imminent disaster. But just as not every eschatology is apocalyptic, so apocalypses are not simply visions of doom. "Apocalyptic" is also used frequently as a noun (instead of "apocalypticism") to refer to a mindset of a particular religious development in Judaism and Christianity at the turn of the eras. Basic to this outlook (not limited to apocalypses or to apocalyptic sections of other books) is the notion of discontinuity between "this age" (the whole of history) and "the age to come," the God-given alternative which will replace it. This too is portrayed in various ways, sometimes as the rejuvenated earth free of suffering and wickedness, sometimes as the Messiah's reign in Israel, or as the arrival of a "new heaven and new earth" as in the Revelation of John. An array of images and motifs portrays this discontinuity; e.g., the return of primeval chaos (stars fall and the moon turns to blood), unprecedented wars and calamities climax evil's rebellion (e.g., Armageddon). There are many scenarios of the end-time. The modern idea of progress, however, is almost the exact opposite of the apocalyptic view of history, according to which things will get worse, not better, until history itself is replaced by the "age to come."

Oppressed and persecuted communities repeatedly have been encouraged by the apocalyptic promise that this history will be replaced, that the Great Judgment will reward the good and punish the wicked, and that paradise will be restored if not surpassed. According to this outlook, such assurances cannot be inferred; they depend rather on revelation, on apocalypse. Thus literary form, language and imagery, and theological content are compatible. No part of the Bible has had a greater influence on the imagination in Western art and literature than its apocalyptic materials.

Genres Within Books

We have already noted that a given book may contain diverse types of materials either because it is a compilation or because the author used and reproduced diverse sources (documents); moreover, the utilized sources themselves contain various forms. Our task now is to suggest the range of diverse materials, and to account, in a sketchy way, for their inclusion in the biblical documents.

The diversity of genres is so rich and the problem of distinguishing one from the other sometimes so complex, that only a general sampling can be undertaken here. Nonetheless, it may show both the variety in the Bible's forms, and the importance of paying attention to them for understanding the text itself. One fundamental factor must be borne in mind—that much of the content of the Bible was handed down by word of mouth (technically called "oral tradition") before it was written.

NARRATIVES. It is important to recognize that there are different narrative genres within the biblical books, for they arose in different social settings and served different purposes. Histories, because they attempt to reconstruct the past on the basis of the best information available, are more reliable documents for the modern historian than, for example, fables. And impersonal records or reports are more reliable still.

The Old Testament document which most closely approximates history in the modern sense is not the longer popular or salvation histories mentioned above, but the court history of David (2 Sam. chs. 9–20; 1 Kgs. chs. 1–2). Its writer, having access to excellent sources of information, reconstructed a segment of the past into a meaningful account, and interpreted the events in terms of cause and effect. The sense of divine providence and activity is here implicit rather than explicit, as it is in the Book of Judges.

A great many of the individual narratives in the Bible are stories; as noted earlier, they generate interest by arousing tension and releasing it. Most stories in the Old Testament—such as ancestral narratives in Genesis—are folktales; that is, they use motifs, patterns, and techniques supplied by the oral tradition. Stories serve many different purposes: to amuse, to teach, to enlighten, or to present the most profound theological affirmations. If a story is primarily concerned with the wonderful and aimed at edification, it is a legend (though a legend need not take the form of a story; it may be a simple report). Legends ordinarily deal with holy people, holy places, or religious ceremonies. They speak of the miraculous and the awesome. But the legends of Elisha, for example, do not mean to boast of the prophet's power as such, but to bear witness to the power of Israel's God made visible through him. Very often legends or other stories of sacred places or religious ceremonies are etiological, that is, they explain the sacredness of the place or the importance of the ritual by an account of its origin. For example, the story of Jacob's dream at Bethel (Gen. 28.10 ff.) is told—in part—to explain how the place was known to be holy, and how it got its name.

In the New Testament, and especially in the Gospels, many different traditional narrative genres are employed. Often the shape and content of these types are clues to their use in the oral tradition handed down by the earliest Christian communities. One genre is the pronouncement story or paradigm, a short, concise narrative which focuses upon a memorable saying of Jesus. The story provides the occasion for the saying. Thus the story of the disciples eating grain on the sabbath (Mk. 2.23–28) is the framework for the saying, "The sabbath was made for man, and not man for the sabbath." Another kind is the miracle story, which concentrates on Jesus himself (instead of on his sayings) and secondarily on the other characters. Most of these stories tersely report the malady, the healing, and the onlookers' response of wonder. The Christian miracle stories are similar to those in Hellenistic culture generally, but unlike the latter, they seldom report the techniques of the miracle worker. The

New Testament also contains narratives which are classed as legends because they express the church's esteem for the hero, such as the story of Peter's release from prison (Acts ch. 12) or the accounts of Jesus' temptations.

PROPHETIC GENRES. In understanding prophetic literature, the reader's first step, as noted above, must be an effort to distinguish the individual units from one another. The meaning of individual lines depends in large measure on the context to which they belong, including the limits of the unit of which they are a part. (The chapter and verse divisions are misleading as often as they are helpful; anyway they date from medieval times.) In distinguishing one unit from another, the reader should be aware of the formulas and genres of prophetic literature, their typical structures, and intentions. Certain formulas, for example, indicate quite clearly the beginning of speeches. Among these are the call to attention, "Listen to these words . . . ," and the expression, "The word of the Lord came to me. . . ."

We have noted that generally speaking the prophetic books contain speeches, narratives, and a few prayers, but in order to recognize the units and interpret them we must be more specific. The range of types of speech found in prophetic utterance is wide; the prophets employed virtually every possible form of verbal communication known in their culture. While the freedom with which they borrowed and adapted from all spheres of life has led some to doubt that there is a distinctively prophetic form of speech, it is preferable to recognize that there are some genres which are particularly and intimately related to the prophetic role. The frequent recurrence of the messenger formula, "thus says the LORD," and the fact that the prophets speak for the Lord often quoting God directly, have led many scholars in recent years to characterize prophetic address as messenger speech. Whether "messenger speech" or simply "prophecy" is the most apt description of the prophetic addresses, it is clear that the prophets regarded themselves as persons speaking for the Lord both revealing and setting into motion God's future activities.

One of the genres most frequently encountered in the preexilic prophets is the prophecy of punishment (or prophetic "*judgment* speech"). This type has two main elements, a statement of reasons for punishment (or accusation) and the announcement of punishment (or *judgment*), bound together by a transition which emphasizes that the latter is the result of the former. Such speeches were addressed to individuals, to groups, or to the nation as a whole. On the other hand, in later prophets such as Deutero-Isaiah and in the additions to the preexilic books, prophecies of salvation predominate. In these addresses the prophets announce the Lord's intervention on behalf of Israel, usually without giving reasons.

Other genres closely related to the prophetic office itself are reports of visions, reports of God's call of the prophet, and reports of symbolic actions. Vision reports range from the brief accounts in Amos to the lengthy and detailed descriptions in Ezekiel which often approach the imagery of apocalyptic literature, but they ordinarily include an account of what was seen and an interpretation of its meaning. The "call reports" are not presented in order to give autobiographical information, but rather to authenticate the person and message of the prophet. So, too, the symbolic action stories are not biographical or autobiographical, but means of communicating the prophetic word.

The prophet's freedom to employ forms of speech from all spheres of Israelite life seems unlimited, but when such genres were used they usually were modified. When Amos sings a dirge, for example, it has become an announcement of punishment: "She has fallen, to rise no more, the virgin Israel, prostrate on her own soil, with no one to lift her up" (Amos 5.2). Proverbs, parables, and other forms of speech associated with Wisdom literature are employed freely. And though the prophets should not be viewed primarily as preachers of repentance, but as proclaimers of God's future, they often instruct, admonish, exhort, and warn their hearers. Further, the image of the prophets as consistent opponents of the cult is tempered when we recognize their frequent use of cultic genres. Second Isaiah (chs. 40–55), for example, often speaks in the words of the "salvation oracle," a genre similar to the Old Testament priestly absolutions. Often, of course, the prophets employ cultic expressions to criticize the cult, as when Amos (4.4) uses a call to worship ironically. And frequently we recognize that the prophets are speaking in juridical terms, either in allusions to Israel's laws or in using expressions and motifs from the legal procedure.

LEGAL GENRES. Since the time of the Apostle Paul, Christians often have thought of the Old Testament, in whole or in part, as "the law." This impression stems in large measure from the Greek title of the first part of the Jewish canon, the Torah, which Greek Jews translated "law." But to characterize the Torah (the Pentateuch) as "law" obscures as much as it reveals. We have already observed that the first five books of the Bible are narratives, not law books. But a considerable body of legal material is presented within that narrative framework, either as the report of what was revealed at Sinai or—in Deuteronomy—as part of the report of the last will and testament of Moses.

In fact, none of the books of the Bible can be accurately described as a law book. What we do find, however, are legal codes of different kinds. It seems clear that most of these codes had been organized and handed down in the context of juridical and cultic activity long before they were placed in their present literary contexts. Some of these codes are quite short; they are the collections of ten or twelve laws found in Exodus chs. 20 and 34, and Deuteronomy ch. 5. Other codes are "the book of the covenant" (Exodus chs. 21–23), containing laws mainly concerned with what we would call civil and criminal matters; the Holiness Code (Lev. chs. 17–26), which is not so much a code as sermons on law. (In view of its expansive literary character it is doubtful that we should call the large body of instructions in the Priestly document—Exodus ch. 25–Numbers ch. 10—a law code.) The Old Testament law codes are similar in many ways to their ancient Near Eastern predecessors: all are collections which tend to organize laws loosely on the basis of content and form; all are the results of many centuries of growth; and there are some distinct similarities of form and content.

In recent scholarship the individual laws in the Old Testament have been classified into two categories. The first is casuistic or case law. These laws closely parallel those in the ancient Near Eastern codes both in form and content. Each has two main parts, a conditional clause describing a case and a conclusion specifying the penalty: "When [or if] a man steals an ox or a sheep and slaughters or sells it, he must repay five beasts for the ox and four sheep for the sheep" (Exod. 22.1). Such laws must have been related to the everyday practice of law. The second genre has been called apodictic, absolute commands or prohibitions which require no accompanying argumentation or condition, since they are taken to be expressions of the will of God. As the Ten Commandments reveal, their content is not limited to specifically religious or cultic affairs, but include social relationships. Whatever the origin of these different genres may have been, eventually all of Israel's laws were associated with Moses and the covenant at Sinai.

In addition to laws, the Old Testament contains a considerable body of material from the judicial process itself. This material is in the form of reports of legal proceedings, allusions to the practice of law in court and cult, and judicial genres and formulas employed in different contexts, such as prophetic speeches. Viewing this data as a whole gives us a picture of the formalities of the trial, of the way contracts were formalized, of the way priests instructed the laity concerning the interpretation or application of cultic laws, and of how law was related to the life of Israel.

WISDOM AND INSTRUCTION. The proverb is one of the most widely known forms of expression and its original oral character is beyond dispute. Proverbs are found in many parts of the Bible apart from the book bearing the name. Proverbs are folk wisdom distilled into pithy, memorable sayings. In isolation, a proverb expresses a general insight (e.g., "haste makes waste"); inevitably one can think of exceptions or of other proverbs which express an apparently conflicting insight. Thus, proverbs must not be treated as first principles but rather as practical wisdom gained from experience. In contrast with divine oracles and apocalyptic visions, proverbs themselves do not claim to be revealed knowledge but distilled human insight. Their specific meaning depends almost entirely on the context in which they are used.

Biblical proverbs or wisdom sayings have many forms. Some are simple declarative statements, such as, "Where the carcass is, there will the vultures gather" (Lk. 17.37). More common is the doublet in which the second half contrasts with the first, as in, "A simpleton believes every word he hears; a clever person watches each step" (Prov. 14.15). Others are structured according to the principle of synonymous parallelism, as in, "Experience uses few words; discernment keeps a cool head" (Prov. 17.27). Sometimes a proverb is put in the form of a comparison, as, "Better live humbly with those in need than divide the spoil with the proud" (Prov. 16.19).

Because proverbs express wisdom, it is natural that in the Book of Proverbs wisdom itself is extolled, and even spoken of as if she (the word "wisdom" is feminine) were a person. Furthermore, the proverbs are then regarded as "wisdom's counsel": "My son, keep my words; store up my commands in your mind" (Prov. 7.1). Wisdom can also tell a story (in poetic form), as occurs in Proverbs ch. 7 and especially in Ecclesiasticus. In the Wisdom of Solomon wisdom guides the history of Israel. Wisdom materials were originally secular; however, there developed the view that human wisdom is derived from divine Wisdom. Indeed, divine Wisdom—especially when personified—came to be regarded as the self-manifestation of God; inevitably, the sages came to regard both the Wisdom tradition and the Torah as revealed.

Wisdom materials are found in various parts of the biblical literature, especially in the Synoptic Gospels. Often proverbs have been expanded to make the meaning explicit, as in the case of "No one can serve two masters," to which has been added, "for either he will hate the first and love the second, or he will be devoted to the first and despise the second. You cannot serve God and Money" (Matt. 6.24). On the other hand, proverbs have also been added to teachings to provide a broader application. Thus, some form of "Whoever gains his life will lose it; whoever loses his life for my sake will gain it" (Matt. 10.39), is added to various sayings of Jesus (Matt. 16.25; Lk. 17.33). Wisdom materials need to be read on two levels: the inherent meaning of the original material (usually discerned by noting the balanced structure of the phrases and ideas), and the specific meaning which the material receives from its present context.

The most famous genre associated with Jesus is the parable—the New Testament rendering of the Hebrew *mashal,* which refers to a variety of forms found in the Old Testament and in various post-biblical texts: the riddle, epigram, and story. Although Jesus did not invent the parable, so fully did he exploit its potential that it is widely assumed to be the hallmark of his teaching. Like the *mashal,* Jesus' parables range from epigrams (e.g., "nothing that goes into a person from the outside can defile him," Mk. 7.15) to terse comparisons (e.g., "the kingdom of Heaven is like yeast, which a woman took and mixed . . .", Matt. 13.33) to short stories like the Prodigal Son (Lk. 15.11–32). Students have found it useful, however, to distinguish the parable from closely related forms, especially the simile, the metaphor, and the allegory. The *simile* (A is *like* B) uses the typical to ask one to recognize the truth of a comparison already made; e.g., "Like a lightning-flash, that lights the sky from east to west, will be the coming of the Son of Man" (Matt. 24.27). The *metaphor*, on the other hand, unexpectedly transfers an image from one domain to another (A *as* B), thereby breaking the literal meaning. Thus: "[You] Vipers' brood!" (Matt. 3.7); it requires the hearer to share the speaker's assessment or reject the figure of speech. Thus in Matt. 16.11 Jesus warns against "the leaven of the Pharisees and Sadducees." To this the evangelist adds, "then they understood: they were to be on their guard, not against baker's leaven, but against the teaching of the Pharisees and Sadducees." The *parable* is a brief narrative whose plot invites the hearer to see through it another situation or reality. Because the point is not on the surface, understanding the parable demands insight; its point can be missed. Some of Jesus' parables assist the understanding by beginning as a simile: "the kingdom of Heaven is like a mustard seed which. . . ." (Matt. 13.31); others begin abruptly with the narrative itself: "A sower went out to sow" (Matt. 13.3). Either way, the story points beyond itself.

It is customary to distinguish parables from allegories, though a *mashal* can also be an allegory. In an allegory, each item in the story stands for something else, so that one can "decode" the story into its true religious or theological meaning. For example, in the noncanonical *Book of Enoch*, the story of Israel is told as the history of sheep who endure all sorts of bad experiences from wolves, bears, etc. The reader quickly translates the story by equating Israel with the sheep and the series of enemies with the marauding animals. It is generally believed that Jesus himself used parables but not allegories, but that the parables were later allegorized by the church. Thus, the parable of the abundant harvest (Mk. 4.3–8) was allegorized into the story of various kinds of soils (Mk. 4.14–20). This is a clear case where sensitivity to literary forms enables the reader to distinguish layers of tradition.

Earlier study insisted that the parable has but one point, a general truth, and subsequent study sought to relate each parable to a specific situation in Jesus' ministry in order to interpret it properly. Current interpretation, however, emphasizes the parable's use of language and its fiction-like capacity to convey a particular "world." The parable, in other words, is not a colorful way of making a point that can be expressed better as a principle or maxim; that would make the parable expendable once the idea is formulated. Rather, the point of the parable is in the story itself because its form and content cannot be separated. The parable's meaning, therefore, depends on the interaction between the story and the settings in which it is told, as can be seen in the Gospels themselves.

There are sermons in the Bible, but we must not confuse the New Testament "sermon" with what comes to mind when we use the term today. Rather, the biblical sermon generally was an extended religious discourse. Also, largely because the preaching of both Jesus and the earliest church was anchored in synagogue preaching, which was as much instruction as it was proclamation, it is difficult to distinguish New Testament preaching from teaching. That synagogue preaching in turn doubtless was rooted in Old Testament instructional preaching, as best represented by the addresses exhorting obedience in Deuteronomy and the prose speeches in the Book of Jeremiah. In any case, even though Christianity spread by preaching, and even though Jesus is reported to have preached in the synagogue, the New Testament contains no transcripts of any sermon. It does, however, include a number of discourses which have been called "sermons." On the one hand, the sermons of Jesus, including the Sermon on the Mount, are not real discourses but collections of sayings, clustered around certain themes. On the other hand, the speeches in Acts are not real sermons either but discourses composed by the author and placed at key points in the narrative in accord with the Hellenistic practice of having key figures say what the writer believed was important to have said at that point. This does not rule out the likelihood that the author used old traditions in composing these speeches. Interestingly, the New Testament possibly contains parts of sermons in the epistles; for example, it has sometimes been suggested that 1 Peter is basically a baptismal sermon, or a part of one, which has been given the appearance of a letter. Even without transcripts of preached sermons, some epistles convey certain aspects of early Christian preaching because their authors relied on their rhetorical skills as they dictated; besides, they knew that the letters would be read aloud in the congregation. Current scholarship's interest in rhetorical structures in the letters therefore complements the interest in epistolary conventions.

PRAYERS, HYMNS, AND RITUALS. Many biblical passages are prayers—words addressed to God. However, it is sometimes difficult to distinguish a prayer from a hymn because frequently both appear as poetry and are addressed to God. Hymns were presumably sung or chanted, probably by choirs, whereas prayers were spoken. While the Old Testament Psalms enshrine the hymns of the temple at various stages of its life, there is no comparable Christian collection in the New Testament.

The rich cultic life of ancient Israel gave rise to a great many different types of song and prayer, preserved for the most part in the Book of Psalms (see above, "Poetic books"). These types usually reflect use in various liturgies, though the festival occasions themselves are not named. Approximately one third of the psalms are songs of individual complaints (frequently called "Laments"), in which the sufferer petitions God for relief and deliverance. On the basis of the structure of such songs—in particular, changes in speaker—and allusions to worship, it has been suggested recently that the individual complaints were used in prayer services for persons in distress. Similar are songs of communal complaint (see Introduction to the Psalms). Closely related to these types are the songs of individual and communal thanksgiving, which were employed in celebrations of deliverance from particular difficulties. We also recognize a great many hymns of praise, which were associated primarily with the regularly scheduled services of worship. The hymns characteristically call to praise, expound God's acts or nature as reasons for praise, and conclude with the renewed summons to praise (see Psalm 113). The so-called "Enthronement Psalms" (e.g., Psalms 29–47, 93, 95–99) may have been developed for a New Year's festival when God's kingship was celebrated; these songs are characterized by the acclamation, "The LORD reigns!" There are also "Royal Psalms" which celebrate the king as the regent of God (e.g., Psalms 2, 20, 21, 45).

The variety of hymns and prayerlike poetry collected in the psalter is found in many other places in the Old Testament as well. For example, in Exodus ch. 15 we have two celebrations of the deliverance at the sea, a very old couplet in v. 21 (the Song of Miriam), and a more elaborate younger one in vv. 1–18. Second Samuel 1.19–27 is the lament of David over the death of Saul and Jonathan, while 2 Samuel ch. 22 (virtually identical with Psalm 18) contains a victory song.

In the New Testament, hymnic materials are of three kinds: the messianic hymns, the christological hymns, and hymns of the eschatological victory. In Luke chs. 1 and 2 the evangelist used messianic hymns inherited from certain Jewish circles to express the hope for the coming redemption. There are three passages which appear to be christological hymns. Embedded in the prologue of John (1.1–18) is an earlier hymn to the Word, the Creator; Phil. 2.5–11 celebrates the humiliation of the preexistent Christ and his subsequent exaltation; Col. 1.15–20 celebrates the relation of the preexistent Christ to the cosmos. Fragments of hymns (or possibly confessional pieces) appear also in Eph. 5.14 and 1 Tim. 3.16, for example. At key points in the Book of Revelation, the reader is apprised of hymns of deliverance being sung in heaven; these are usually considered to reflect the hymnody of the churches of Asia Minor.

In addition to poetic pieces used in ritual and liturgy, the Bible also contains narratives which were used in worship before they were included in the biblical text. By means of these narrative materials, the community recited fundamental events of its history and thereby celebrated its relation to God. Many scholars have seen in Joshua ch. 24 and other Old Testament texts the outlines of a covenant renewal ceremony by which the Israelite tribes recalled the Exodus and pledged their common fealty to God. These texts are for the most part narratives, but they mention either directly or indirectly the liturgical acts involved. Many of the steps in the liturgy of covenant renewal closely paralleled the points in ancient Near Eastern treaties.

In the New Testament, the accounts of the Lord's Supper (Matt. 26.17–29; Mk. 14.12–24; Lk. 22.7–38; 1 Cor. 11.23–25) differ from one another because they reflect the actual usages of the churches; but they all center in the words of Jesus concerning the bread and the wine. None of these accounts is as liturgically complete as the account of the first

Passover in Exodus ch. 12. Although the Book of Esther is traditionally associated with the Festival of Purim, the story itself does not refer explicitly to the festival. The books of Maccabees report the events that led up to the rededication of the temple, celebrated as Hanukkah, but there are no clear Hanukkah observance materials in the Bible, just as there are no observances linked with Pentecost. Centuries later, Christians associated both the stories of Jesus' wine miracle at Cana and the coming of the Magi with January 6 (Epiphany), but, of course, this belongs to the history of the interpretation of the Bible. These stories did not originate in connection with Epiphany.

This introduction to the literary forms of the Bible has, of necessity, been more illustrative than exhaustive. Many important modes of literary and oral expression have not been mentioned. But this basically literary approach, in addition to providing a description of some of the types of biblical literature, serves the serious reader of the Bible in several ways. In the first place, it opens up the historical depth of the biblical material. The Bible is a historical book not merely because it is preoccupied with history, but because its contents also have a history. This literary history of the materials has been recovered in large part because scholars have analyzed the individual literary genres and related these to the life of the communities in which they were used. In many cases we are able to reconstruct the history of the transmission of sayings and stories up to the way the text now reads. What emerges from such careful exploratory work is a keen appreciation of the fact that the Bible is the literary deposit of living tradition which reflects the beliefs and practices of real Israelite, Jewish, and Christian communities. So instead of reading the text in a "flat" way, simply for plot or for bare content, we can now recognize the texture of the matter, perceive its layers, and infer how the material functioned in various stages. Second, the concern with genres of literary and oral expression enables the reader to relate the stages of a text to the life of the communities which originated, used, and preserved it. Often particular genres can be located within certain social contexts, such as the worship in the temple, the practice of law, or the missionary activity of the early church. In the process we see that behind each text stand not primarily creative writers—though there were such—but communities of faith, for which certain genres and particular texts served very important purposes. Finally, this kind of study can facilitate fruitful dialogues with the texts themselves. Posing these literary questions— What kind of text is it? Where did it come from? How was it used?— enables the texts to speak to us, and not simply to reflect our own expectations of them. By looking at the Bible in this way our appreciation and understanding of it should be both broadened and deepened.

COMMUNITIES IN CONTEXT

Historical Contexts
of the Biblical Communities

W. LEE HUMPHREYS

Israel stands at the eastern end of the Mediterranean Sea, a location that is as crucial politically and historically as it is geographically. For its entire history—from the time before it was settled by the Hebrew people, through the political growth of the nation, up to the time it became the birthplace of the Christian faith, and beyond that to the present day—it has been powerfully affected by the play of political forces emanating from larger empires outside it, as well as subject to the stresses and strains of conflict within. The biblical communities existed within this dynamic matrix of forces, forces that were in uneasy tension with each other.

There were stresses within the communities themselves. These stresses included such matters as conflicts among the different classes of society; disputes between the central administration of the monarchy and those in outlying areas; and struggles between those who favored alliances with one or another of the great empires and those who opposed such alliances.

There were conflicts and alliances with near neighbors and competitors: the Canaanite peoples who had inhabited the land before the Hebrews; the Philistines, along the coast, who appear at about the same time as the Israelites and who controlled the five cities of Gath, Gaza, Ashkelon, Ashdod, and Ekron; the Arameans (Syrians), with their capital at Damascus; and other nomadic tribes and smaller kingdoms.

And there were the overshadowing effects of the great world powers. These were a succession of empires that dominated various parts of the eastern coast of the Mediterranean. To the south and west was the most stable of these, Egypt, in the Nile valley. It was already an old empire when the biblical story begins. Its political power, though declining overall during most of the life of Israel, grows and shrinks as its various ruling groups, called "dynasties," exert or lose control.

To the north and east, in the area of modern-day Syria, Iraq, and Iran, were other empires that followed one another in succession. These empires developed in the valleys of the Tigris and Euphrates rivers, an area called "Mesopotamia" from the Greek words for "between the rivers."

The Assyrian empire, the Babylonian empire, and the Medo-Persia empire each dominated the area for a time and then fell before the next conqueror. Often they were in conflict with Egypt, and Israel found itself caught in the middle.

Later there were dominant powers from further west in the Mediterranean. First the Greeks, under Alexander the Great and his successors, subdued the eastern Mediterranean and imposed Greek culture upon the conquered territories. Later the Romans replaced the Greek rulers and assimilated their empire.

Inside the biblical communities and outside as well, the balance of power would shift from one pole of tension to another, and sometimes the tensions became so severe that the matrix shattered and new configurations of world power, or new political arrangements, would emerge. Waves of historical change would dramatically alter the context in which the ancient nation of Israel, the early Jewish communities, and the early Christian churches sought to define themselves.

Moreover, at the heart of the religious confessions of ancient Israel, early Judaism, and early Christianity stood events that these groups understood to be firmly rooted in human history: the exodus from Egyptian bondage; the passion, death, and resurrection of Jesus of Nazareth. The historical contexts of these events, and the later, somewhat different contexts of the biblical communities that remembered them, provided the medium in which they perceived their God's self-revelation and in which they experienced distinctive relationships with this deity. Historical events that affected the lives of these communities would carry profound theological implications for the adherents of their faith. It was not enough for them to comprehend their world in the political, social, economic, cultural, or military terms that shape contemporary historical study. "What is God doing now?" "How can we respond faithfully to God in this historical moment?" These and other vital questions faced all believers. It is not too much to say that history from this perspective was a complex drama or conversation between the deity and the people. Understanding the historical contexts of the biblical communities is vital for an appreciation of their religious heritage.

The ancient nation of Israel lived most of its life, in its several forms, in a matrix of tension. It stood where three continents meet: Africa, Asia, and Europe. With some ebb and flow, Egyptian sway over this region gradually gave way first to Assyria and then to Babylon. With the triumph in the sixth century B.C.E. of the Babylonian Nebuchadnezzar II, before whose armies the last vestiges of an independent nation of Israel fell, a transformation of this power alignment was also in sight. Within decades, Persia, under the great king Cyrus and then his successors, claimed control of territory that stretched from India to Ethiopia (Esther 1.1). In the late fourth century this empire fell to Alexander the Great of Macedon. Upon his death in 323 B.C.E. his empire, which included much of the Aegean and eastern Mediterranean, was politically divided into three parts but would remain uniformly Hellenistic (Greek-influenced) in its dominant cultural traditions.

In this Persian and then Hellenistic context, the earliest Jewish communities emerged among the survivors of old Israel and sought to define a mode of life that would preserve an authentic identity as the people of God in alien if not always hostile settings. The old homeland in southern Palestine especially became a center of contention between segments of the empire Alexander shaped. Then in the last century B.C.E. Rome came increasingly to assert its control over this territory until, by the turn of the eras, it controlled both the Mediterranean basin and significant territories to the east. In this Roman empire, as well as further east, Rabbinic Judaism evolved and early Christian communities emerged.

This sketch provides a frame within which we can examine in more detail specific characteristics of these historical contexts of the biblical communities, as well as the complex interaction between them.

The Historical Context of Ancient Israel

Earliest Israel emerged in a world already old. The Sumerian civilization of ancient Mesopotamia had long vanished, leaving only traces of its legacy in the Assyrian and Babylonian states that followed it. Egypt as well had seen its "age of giants" disappear, its primary remains the grandeur of the colossal monuments and pyramids that endured. In the Late Bronze Age (ca. 1550–1200 B.C.E.) Egypt claimed at least nominal control of Syria-Palestine, control that was often contested and at times arbitrated in uneasy truces with the Hittite and Mitannian powers in eastern Asia Minor. By the thirteenth century this control was more assertion than fact, and new configurations of peoples moved into and emerged from the Canaanite city-states that jostled each other for space in southern Palestine.

Struggles between city-states in Canaan increased as Egyptian control of the area decreased. The Amarna Letters, a corpus of diplomatic exchanges from the reigns of Amenhotep III and IV (ca. 1403–1347 B.C.E.; the latter is better known as Akh-en-Aton), demonstrate that Egypt was losing control of this region and also that intercity warfare was on the increase, augmented by the presence of groups, called "Habiru," who were alienated from the established political structures. Their presence suggests that the increased turmoil in this part of the world was taking its toll on trade and the economy of the region, producing a most unstable situation.

It is not clear what forces and factors account for the emergence of a recognizable state of Israel toward the end of the thirteenth century B.C.E. Such a state is referred to, for example, by the Egyptian Pharaoh Mer-ne-Ptah in a victory stela—a stone slab with an inscription, erected as a monument—that has been dated to 1230 B.C.E. It is clear, however, that earliest Israel shaped itself in conscious contrast to both the royalist imperial structure of Egypt and the characteristic hierarchies of power in the Canaanite city-state system. Both were experienced as oppressive and dehumanizing.

Others as well moved into the area from the outside at this time, especially the so-called "Sea Peoples," whom the Egyptians were barely able to stop at their borders. Some of these Sea Peoples, known as Philistines, settled in five cities near the southern coast of Syria-Palestine, and within a century they were competing with Israel for control of the land. By the time of the death of Israel's first king, Saul of Benjamin, with his sons on Mount Gilboa, these Philistines, possibly in league with the Ammonites to the east of the Jordan river, seemed in control of most of the territory of the Israelite tribes. A note in 1 Samuel suggests that the Israelites had to rely on them for tools and weapons (13.19–22).

Seen more broadly, the waning of Egyptian authority in the area left a vacuum, disrupting trade as well as economic, social, and political structures. It was not to be the Philistines, however, but Israelites under the leadership of King David who would fill this vacuum. For a time, especially under David's son Solomon, Israel seemed the dominant power in the region. This brief interruption in external control of southern Palestine was a context in which emerged what later Israelites and Jews would view as that nation's "golden age." But a brief resurgence of Egyptian power in 935–934 B.C.E. under the Pharaoh Shishak I, who launched an attempt to reassert Egyptian control of the area, underscored the internal instability of Israel. This instability had been demonstrated a few years before, upon the death of Solomon, when the united country broke apart into two small kingdoms: Israel (also called Ephraim in some of the prophetic books) in the north and Judah in the south. Egypt would not be able, however, to follow up on Shishak's victories and would only be a sporadic player in the power struggles of the next several centuries.

Egypt would remain in Israel's memory, however, as the land of bondage and dehumanization from which Yahweh delivered the people with "signs and portents" (Deut. 26.8). This memory formed the basis of Israel's religious confession and self-understanding, and for those influenced by the Hebraic religious traditions Egypt and Pharaoh for centuries to come would symbolize oppressive structures and rulers. Ironically, a last small band of Israelite nationalists would flee back to Egypt, taking Jeremiah with them, when they were no longer able to live under Yahweh and the covenant in the land of promise (Jer. 42–44).

The Neo-Assyrian empire based in Mesopotamia would for a time be the dominant international force in the lives of the twin kingdoms of Israel and Judah, as well as of other small states in the land that linked Mesopotamia and Egypt. Among these smaller kingdoms, the Damascus-centered Arameans in particular were rivals with northern Israel for control of the region, especially the control of trade and the exchange of goods. Phoenicians to the north of Israel held the Palestinian coast above

Mount Carmel. But, since the Phoenician economy was built upon sea-faring trade throughout the Mediterranean basin, non-maritime nations like Israel and Aramea competed for the control of land trade and routes.

In fact, for their own benefit the Phoenicians needed to maintain mutually beneficial relations with those around them who might provide both goods for trade and a market for what came through the key port cities of Tyre and Sidon. In periods of relative stability Phoenicia would prosper as a link between land and sea trade, and through Phoenicia both basic and luxury items, as well as less tangible cultural influences, were dispersed throughout the Mediterranean basin. In the period of Israelite King Omri and his son Ahab, for example, relations with the Arameans of Damascus are depicted as tense at best, sometimes breaking into open hostility, while relations with the Phoenicians were sealed by the marriage of Jezebel (daughter of Ethbaal, king of the Phoenician city of Sidon) to King Ahab (1 Kgs. 16.31). Behind the quite hostile depiction of her and of this whole era in the books of Kings we can detect a period of prosperity and blending of cultures and religious traditions. Ivory carvings excavated at Samaria and the ivory houses and beds condemned by Amos (6.4) are physical evidence of pervasive foreign influences mediated by Phoenicia, which proved most attractive to the upper strata in the state of northern Israel. Samaria was no different from Jerusalem, whose temple was designed on Phoenician models by Phoenician architects and artists.

As the Neo-Assyrians consolidated power under a series of able kings in the ninth century B.C.E., it proved possible for the several states in Syria-Palestine to join together in a defense pact in an attempt to check Assyrian advance into their territory. At a battle fought at Qarqar in 853 B.C.E., such a coalition was successful, and we are told in Assyrian records that Ahab of Israel contributed significant military forces to the cause. Such coalitions were the exception rather than the rule, however, and more often than not relations between the states in the region were tense at best and sometimes openly hostile.

To the south, Judah and its capital Jerusalem were not as directly affected by these events, although they were not immune to either foreign influence or regional conflicts and power struggles. Jerusalem lay somewhat off the major routes of commerce, especially since Philistine cities to the west came to control the coastal routes, while Edom and Moab to the east of the Dead Sea and the Jordan river controlled the major trade routes that linked Arabia and Egypt through Damascus to the north and east. The Davidic kings of Jerusalem appear to have sat out the battle at Qarqar. Later, however, they found themselves on the defensive against a coalition that united northern Israel and Damascus in another attempt to forge an alliance to thwart Neo-Assyrian incursions into their territory. The siege of Jerusalem in 734–733 B.C.E. demonstrated that as Assyrian pressure increased in the region, even Judah and

Jerusalem would not be able to stand aloof from the transformations taking place in the larger contexts in which they lived.

By 722 B.C.E. northern Israel had been overrun by Assyria and incorporated fully into its expanding empire. Judah remained nominally independent but in vassalage to Assyria, responsible for annual payment of tribute and support of military expeditions into the region. Assyria wished to remain secure within the river valleys of the Tigris and Euphrates, which offered no natural protective frontiers (in contrast to the situation of Egypt in the Nile valley). It therefore became Assyrian policy to expand outward, conquering or making vassals of the peoples to the east, north, and west of them. To maintain this far-flung empire, to bolster an economy strained by extensive military expenditures, and especially to sustain the military forces it needed, Assyria had to set its sights on Egypt as a fundamental source of grain.

But for Assyria to secure Egypt, it had to control the corridor into Egypt that was Syria-Palestine. For those with keen foresight, like Amos, Hosea, Isaiah, and Micah, it seemed only a matter of time until all the states in this region came under Assyrian domination in some form, ranging from outright conquest and incorporation into its imperial system to some form of vassalage that allowed only nominal independence. These prophets of Yahweh could not rest content with an economic, political, and military analysis of Assyrian expansion; for them such incursions posed as well the fundamental challenge of interpreting these events in theological terms appropriate to Yahwism.

Egypt was not unaware of the Assyrian threat, and from the latter part of the eighth century B.C.E. until the middle decades of the seventh it attempted again and again to encourage the independence of the small states in Syria-Palestine, to serve as a buffer between it and Assyria. Often this support took the form of promises of aid for those who resisted Assyria, promises that were broken more often than they were honored. Egypt came to seem a "splintered cane" (Isa. 36.6), providing little support and a potential danger to those who might lean on it.

By the middle of the seventh century B.C.E. Assyria took control of Egypt. Ironically, with this success Assyria overreached itself and within decades it would fall to the combined armies of Media and Babylon. The impending collapse of the Assyrian empire so threatened to alter the configurations of power in the Near East that a somewhat revived Egypt under Pharaoh Neco even sought to come to Assyria's aid shortly before the fall of Nineveh. While the Pharaoh was able to alter the course of Judean political and religious history when he cut down the reforming King Josiah, he could not shore up the last traces of Assyrian rule.

Caught up again in changing balances of power in the Near East, kings of the Davidic dynasty, in Judah and its capital Jerusalem, would once more seek to play one power off against another, but this time they would be crushed in the process. In 598 and 587 B.C.E. Babylon's armies were outside Jerusalem's walls, and in the latter year the city fell, its temple was sacked, its rulers and leading citizens were either executed or exiled. The last vestige of the ancient nation of Israel was taken up into the Babylonian provincial system.

The nation Israel, ranging in form from federation to empire to twin kingdoms and then to one small state, thus lived its life in a shifting matrix of power defined by Egypt at one pole and Assyria and Babylon at the other. Caught between these powers, Israel came into being and then thrived for a brief period as an empire when each pole was relatively weak and unable to assert effective control over the region of Syria-Palestine. With the resurgence of Assyria the small states in the lands between Mesopotamia and the Nile valley attempted to survive as best they could by balancing one power against the other, preserving as much independence as possible. But it was a losing game in the long run for them all, even if the end brought the fall of Egypt to Assyria, Assyria to Babylon, and, as we shall see, Babylon to Persia and a new configuration of power.

Within this shifting matrix ancient Israel felt the impact of its historical context in many ways. While Israel emerged and first took shape in reaction against the Egyptian imperial and Canaanite city-state structures, which it found oppressive and dehumanizing, it adopted much from these structures. From its administrative system to personnel serving in the courts of David and Solomon (2 Sam. 8.16–18; 20.23–26), from the ivory houses and beds of northern royalty and nobility to the design and ornamentation of the temple in Jerusalem, ancient Israel was heavily influenced by its historical context. The way in which Israel drew on cultural, religious, economic, social, and political currents of that context is further discernible in important themes and motifs in the earlier (J) and later (P) strata of the Torah (Gen. 1–11), in ancient poetic forms preserved in the oldest material in the Bible (Exod. 15.1–8; Judges 5; Psalm 29), in early wisdom material (Prov. 22.17–24.22)—and even in the convenantal forms, terms, and themes that shaped the prophetic and deuteronomic understandings of Israel's relation with its God.

Influences from its near neighbors, and from the more distant and larger powers (often filtered through these nearer neighbors) affected ancient Israelite life and the Hebraic religious tradition in profound ways. Influences sometimes came through emulation and borrowing, as possibly in certain forms of covenant language, or through the adoption of traditions associated with the Canaanite high god El Elyon of Jerusalem, as legitimizing the transition from federation to kingship, especially the Davidic dynasty. The historical context also provided negative elements over against which Israelite tradition defined itself, as, for example, in the reaction against Canaanite traditions associated with the dying and rising fertility god Baal or divine kingship as found in Egypt. In general Israel's reactions to and interactions with its historical contexts were complex, different in distinct eras (a particular openness characterized the time of Solomon), and varied across social strata.

The Yahwism of old Israel was essentially a national religion like the religions of the states around it. It is true that the deity's power could be experienced elsewhere, in the midst of Egyptian oppression, for example, but to be a Yahwist was for all practical purposes to be an Israelite. With the death of the nation it was not inconceivable that the God of Israel had died or been rendered impotent as well, if indeed the people had not been abandoned because of God's anger at their misdeeds (see 2 Kgs. 19.22). The struggles of early Jewish communities to shape new lives in fundamentally new historical contexts would counter this theological assessment (see the following section). These communities would also shape new understandings of what it meant to live as the people of God in the larger and often alien world.

The Historical Context of Early Judaism

With the destruction of the ancient nation of Israel, followed within a few decades by the fall of the Babylonian empire responsible for its destruction, the historical contexts for the survivors of old Israel were dramatically changed, and consequently the communities of survivors took a very different shape. Persia, under the leadership of Cyrus the Great, brought the lands reaching from India to Ethiopia under an administration that was comparatively systematic and effective. Especially under those successors to Cyrus who were capable leaders, the diverse territories ruled by Persia knew peace and a level of stability that had not characterized the Near East for some time.

For the first time in many centuries non-Semitic peoples ruled the area. The policy of the new rulers seemed designed to win the allegiance of the diverse peoples within their empire through an appeal to enlightened self-interest rather than through fear. Broadly, the Babylonians and Assyrians had sought to compel the allegiance of captured or allied states through what has been described as a policy of "calculated frightfulness" (a policy depicted, for example, on Assyrian reliefs that graphically portrayed the fate of people who did not give full allegiance to Assyria). Persia replaced this by a policy that encouraged as much development of local cultural and religious interests and traditions as would not conflict with an empire at unity and at peace. Thus Cyrus depicted his capture of Babylon not as conquest (and, in fact, the city was handed over to his army by Babylonians disenchanted with Nabonidus, the last of the Babylonian kings), but as the grant of the Babylonian deity Marduk, who is said to have "grasped the right hand of Cyrus," thereby legitimating him as chosen king. Even the exiled prophet known as Second Isaiah (see chs. 40–55 of the book of Isaiah) could speak of Cyrus in royalist terms generally reserved for Davidic kings (Isa. 44.28–45.1).

In line with this encouragement of local diversity, Cyrus not only permitted exiled Judahites in Babylon to return to their homeland, but is reported even to have been willing to contribute to the rebuilding of a temple in Jerusalem. That this construction, as well as the later rebuilding of the walls of the city, took some time and came only with some struggle and effort was not because of a lack of support from the imperial center. Rather, it was the result of local opposition, conflicts over authority within the Palestinian Jewish community, and disputes with other regional groups. Persia sought to create conditions within its empire that would make it worthwhile for regional groups with local traditions to support the empire as a stable context within which they could thrive. As is demonstrated by the possible fate of the post-exilic leader Zerubbabel and the dashing of nationalistic and royalist hopes pinned on him, however, tolerance of cultural and religious diversity would extend only to a point short of attempts to gain political independence.

Not that conflict and threats to Jewish communities in Palestine and elsewhere were absent from the empire. Indeed, the book of Esther presents Jewish communities faced with a pogrom. Yet the point at issue between Haman and Mordecai seems more one of power and possessions than of clear anti-Jewish bias. Haman took advantage of existing anti-Jewish feeling in his struggle with Mordecai, but such feelings were not the reason for his pogrom. In fact, this same book demonstrates that positions at the very heights of power in the Persian capital and court were open to Jews. Esther is, after all, queen, and Mordecai is an official into whose hands remarkable authority and wealth fall by the end of the novella. On a level more historically secure, both Nehemiah, who restored the walls of Jerusalem and undertook reforms there, and Ezra, who undertook additional reforms and also established some form of the Torah as the constitution for Judaism in the city and vicinity, came armed with the power held by royal officials of the Persian court.

The fact that the situation of Jews after the fall of Jerusalem in 587 B.C.E. is more and more described as "diaspora" (dispersion) and less and less as "exile" reveals that the Persian setting for earliest Judaism was not uncongenial to the formation of religious communities and identities that were no longer limited to a particular nation or one's political identity. Certainly one of the most remarkable transformations in the biblical tradition and in the communities that produced and treasured it was that which led to the birth of early Judaism out of the old nation of Israel. It was by no means certain that a people could continue to exist and even thrive with a distinct religious identity that was not rooted in a nation-state. In fact, the policy of exile as practiced by Assyria and Babylon was precisely designed to destroy through attrition any religious allegiances and identities linked to the religion of a nation-state by removing people from their national homeland and setting them in new contexts into which they would most likely assimilate. The poignant cry, "How could we sing the LORD's song in a foreign land?" (Ps. 137.4) states the crisis faced by Israelite exiles in their new historical context. It was against all expectation that this religious tradition proved able to define and maintain itself in the form of communities that were generally small and scattered across the face of the Near East and eastern Mediterranean.

In the common view, the death of a nation was the effective death of that nation's deity, or at least a sign of the deity's impotence or lack of concern for its people. That ultimately Jewish heirs of old Israel could come to perceive that there were other ways to understand the death of their nation; that they could sing new songs to their God; that this God's authority transcended all national boundaries; and that ways could be found to be both Jewish and citizens of diverse nations—all this was due in part to the relatively stable and even congenial context these early Jewish communities found in the Persian empire. "Exile," a state of alienation and dislocation, became "diaspora," a situation in which the struggle for new identities, new forms of religious community, and new ways of being the people of Yahweh, could be explored.

The shapes of these explorations were diverse, some allowing more interaction with the historical context in which one found oneself than did others. A style of Judaism reflected in the lives of Esther and Mordecai allowed, and even encouraged, full and active involvement in the larger world, even at the highest levels of power. Others, fearing assimilation that would result in the loss of a distinctive Jewish identity, sought to develop a style of life that would distinguish Jews, both in their own eyes and in the eyes of others, from those among whom they lived. Characteristic Jewish practices, rooted in the Torah—such as the observance of the Sabbath, circumcision, dietary restrictions and regulations, and the celebration of an annual festival of Passover in each family unit—served the function of setting Jews apart. Whatever the roots of these practices in earlier Israelite tradition, such rules and observances distinguished Jews from their contexts and would, especially in the area of diet, restrict the extent of their full engagement in the social, political, economic, and cultural activities of the larger non-Jewish world. No one particular style of life characterized Jewish communities in the Persian world; this is shown, for example, by the fact that some later circles found it necessary to augment the book of Esther with additions, bringing it more into line with Judaism as defined in the Torah, while the unaugmented version of the book continued in use and was preserved in the canon of the Hebrew Bible. (The current edition of the Revised English Bible gives both versions of Esther in full, one in the Old Testament and one in the Apocrypha.)

In the last decades of the fourth century B.C.E. the Persian empire fell with remarkable rapidity to Alexander the Great. Upon Alexander's death a few years later, the empire was divided among three of his generals. One general, Ptolemy, gained control of Egypt and Palestine. A second, Seleucus, ruled the former Mesopotamian (Babylonian) empire and even, for a time, Alexander's conquests as far east as India. A third division of authority under Macedonian rule was subject to various wars of succession until the Romans conquered it in the second century B.C.E.

This political change once again transformed the context in which Jewish communities lived. These communities had been part of an empire where communication was made easy through a notable system of highways, so that Nehemiah in Susa, for instance, was well-informed of affairs in Jerusalem. On a political level, these communities were now separated from each other by often hostile borders. Jews in Egypt and Palestine, now under Ptolemaic rule, were cut off from Jews under Seleucid rule in Syria.

In fact, Jerusalem, with its walls restored and the second temple rebuilt, was in an area that was a focal point of contention between Seleucids and Ptolemies (the successors of the generals, who each founded a dynasty that bore his name). It appeared that the old poles of tension in the power alignments of the Near East, based in Egypt and Mesopotamia, had reasserted themselves. This further complicated the place of the old sacred city in the religious experience of Jews. Even for those in communities located far from Jerusalem and now cut off from it by contested boundaries, the sacred city was a focus of intense hope and interest. Yet for most Jews it was not a city they would personally visit even once in their lives. While the worship of Yahweh in the Jerusalem temple was supported by communities all across the diaspora, other more immediate modes of expressing allegiance to the deity were also developing in local settings. The synagogue and the family came to be the focal points.

Greek conquest of the Persian empire offered an even more profound challenge to early Judaism. While the power of the state was not used directly to enforce conformity to Hellenistic cultural standards or patterns of religious practice, Greeks had a fine sense of the superiority of their traditions and ways of life. In the areas over which they had control they established Greek enclaves that included theaters, gymnasiums, and temples, in all of which Greek ways flourished. Hellenism was a compelling alternative to all who sought to be at the creative edge of cultural and even religious affairs in this new historical context. Jewish communities in Palestine and in Egypt were not immune to this influence. Greek became the language of many Jews, in many cases the only language in which they were fluent. This led Jewish communities in Alexandria in Egypt, during the last centuries B.C.E., to translate the Hebrew religious texts into Greek. This translation, which included all of the texts now in the Hebrew Scriptures (Old Testament) but augmented them with a number of other works, comprises what has come to be known as the Septuagint, a collection of writings that was the Bible for some Jewish communities for a time and for early Christian communities as well.

Culturally as well as religiously Jews felt the pull of assimilation. Some adopted Greek dress and manners, sought to take part in Greek games, and studied Greek philosophical traditions, comparing and blending them with their own heritage. Some even attempted to mask certain signs of Jewish distinctiveness such as restrictive dietary practices or circumcision. Not a few found it possible to accommodate life in this larger context with their vision of Judaism. Others condemned these attempts as apostasy, a betrayal of their heritage and their God.

The degrees to which Jews accommodated to and interacted with the larger world, or remained more or less apart from it, varied. Works like the Wisdom of Solomon are built upon both Jewish and Greek foundations and seem designed to recommend each to the other. The idea that there is a life after death (Dan. 12.1–3) enters Judaism at this time, spurred by Hellenistic and other influences. Motifs in apocalyptic literature reveal creative contacts with the Gentile nations, the very ones often condemned in the apocalyptic visions.

In Palestine, however, under the Seleucid Antiochus IV in the middle decades of the second century B.C.E., there were increasing demands to adopt Greek ways and reject those aspects of Torah that set Judaism apart and distinguished it. Attempting to hold together an empire that in size and in ethnic and cultural diversity was unwieldy at best, Antiochus could not tolerate potentially separatist groups so near his contested border with the Ptolemaic empire centered in Egypt. It thus became his policy to outlaw salient marks of Torah Judaism—observance of sabbath, circumcision, special dietary practices, possession of a Torah scroll—and to enforce worship of Greek idols and even of the king. The power of the military was available to enforce these state attempts to stamp out the distinctive marks of Judaism, marks that for many Jews were at the core of Jewish identity.

For those Jews especially attracted to Hellenistic ways these Jewish practices were outmoded and anachronistic customs anyway and easily given up. But for those not inclined to assimilate, the choices could be cruel. Some submitted only to save their lives and livelihoods. Some others withdrew into hiding and exile in order to continue to live by their cherished customs, often losing all they possessed. Still others became martyrs, as recounted, for example, in 2 Maccabees 6–7. Among these latter groups we find the Hasidim, the "pious ones," whose purpose it was to remain faithful to their heritage as their way of carrying out the will of God. Finally, some Jews in Palestine were provoked into overt resistance, and under the leadership of the sons of a priest named Mattathias a guerilla war broke out against Seleucid rule. Taking their name from the nickname given the most distinguished of these sons, Judah who was called the "Maccabee" or "Hammer," this Maccabean resistance became a remarkably successful struggle for national independence. From about 165 to 63 B.C.E. the Maccabees and their Hasmonean descendants ruled a quasi-independent state centered in Jerusalem.

The situation remained unstable, however, both for Jews in Palestine and for the extensive Jewish communities in Egypt and Mesopotamia.

The specter of Rome hovered on the historical horizon; in fact, pressure from Rome was a significant factor that led the Seleucids to come to an accommodation with the Maccabees. Moreover, the Hasmonean descendants who ruled Palestine soon seemed to model themselves on the pattern of Hellenistic princes. For the Hasidim it must have appeared that they had won the war but lost the peace. Independence did not ensure the reinstatement of Torah Judaism as they understood it. Yet what to them must have seemed betrayal of the cause for which they had struggled quite likely appeared to others as necessary accommodation in the struggle to sustain a viable state in the complex context in which Rome was increasingly dominant. By 63 B.C.E. Rome assumed control of Palestine and from this point on it was governed by figures who owed their authority to Roman appointment and support.

Initially Rome's representative was the Hasmonean Hyrcanus II, whom Pompey named High Priest and whose minister was the politically shrewd Antipater from the province of Idumea (the territory of Edom). In 40 B.C.E. Antipater's son Herod was named king, a post to which he succeeded in 37. Following Herod's death in 4 B.C.E., Rome appointed his son Archelaus as "ethnarch" ("ruler of the people") of Judea and Samaria; Archelaus' competence was unequal to Rome's expectations and he was deposed in 6 C.E. After that time, except for one brief period, Judea was governed by procurators, Roman officials of whom few were capable of carrying out the sensitive task of understanding the unusual people they were sent to govern.

Out of these tensions emerged the several so-called "sects" or groups that characterized Palestinian Judaism from the last centuries B.C.E. through the Jewish revolt against Roman rule in 66–72 C.E. At stake in the disputes between these groups was the identity of Judaism and the extent to which that identity allowed engagement on all levels of life with its larger historical contexts. What some saw as necessary to survival in a complex world, or even as an opportunity to refine their faith, others saw as apostasy from one's people and one's God. Some Jews became powerful figures in the larger political, economic, and cultural contexts in which they found themselves. Others withdrew from that world, for example to Qumran on the northwest edge of the Dead Sea, to maintain their particular patterns of life and devotion to their God. Still others sought to live in but not to be a part of this larger world. Whether in engagement or withdrawal, the Judaism that entered the common era was profoundly shaped in its many forms by its larger historical context.

The Historical Context of the Early Christian Communities

One of the groups emerging within Judaism at the turn of the eras was, of course, the early Christian movement. Christian origins were intricately interwoven both with Jewish struggles for identity and with the larger Roman historical context. Jesus of Nazareth was executed on the authority of local Roman officials for crimes against ruling Roman authority. Within a very short time after the death of Jesus some small Jewish groups were claiming that Jesus had risen from the dead and that in his death and resurrection all men and women could overcome sin and death and find themselves in new relationships with God. They proclaimed that in the passion, death, and resurrection of this Jesus, now called the Christ (Greek for Messiah or "anointed," the Jewish title for the anticipated ruler), God had acted anew to reconcile all human beings to the divine being.

Soon this gospel moved beyond the confines of the Jewish communities of southern Palestine into the larger Gentile world. In fact, in Jewish contexts it had carried little conviction and gained few adherents. But it found a sympathetic and even enthusiastic hearing in certain circles of the larger Hellenistic and Roman context. The message proclaimed a new liberty and humanity offered in relation to God, and many, in all social strata, found it compelling. But it was especially compelling to those whom the existing political, social, and economic structures—structures that expressed the symbols and traditions of the dominant culture—had constrained and dehumanized. Furthermore, the scandal for Judaism in the death of this Messiah, this Christ, on a cross did not have the same impact on the larger Gentile world. For that world was not unacquainted with traditions about the death and return from the dead of a deity or offspring of a deity, a death and rebirth in which men and women could find their lives caught up and transformed as well. Roman cults that centered on such figures as Mithra, for example, were to be found throughout the historical context into which early Christianity moved, and they helped to set the stage for it.

This same message of transformation and liberation also entailed, however, a profound challenge to the rulers and ruling structures of that larger context. Allegiance to this God and Christ was generally understood, in line with the Christian's Jewish heritage, to prohibit allegiance to any other deity. In particular, this meant that one would not recognize the deities of the ruling Roman powers nor the emperor himself when claims were made that he too was divine. Christian and Roman perceptions of what was due Caesar and what was due God simply did not mesh. Roman divinities symbolized the established authority and structures that maintained the empire, and when Christians denied the divine status of the Roman deities, including the emperor, that denial could be interpreted as a denial of the political and social legitimacy of the established powers.

Christian communities nevertheless grew steadily during the course of the first two centuries of the common era. Especially after the failure of the Jewish revolt against Rome in 66–72 c.e. and the revolt in 132 c.e. under the insurgent nicknamed Bar Kochba ("son of a star"), Christianity was increasingly understood as separate from Judaism. Since Christianity was in fact often perceived as a destabilizing force in the Roman empire, some in authority made efforts to stamp it out or bring it into conformity with the established powers. Persecution and the possibility of martyrdom were constant threats, even if largely local, sporadic, and not very systematically organized.

Like the Jewish communities out of which they emerged, however, early Christian communities found themselves in tension with and even alienated from their larger historical context while at the same time they were influenced by it in many ways, often adopting much from it. These influences can be traced in many areas: in literary forms that are found in many New Testament and other early Christian writings; in organizational structures that were to shape Christian communities; in theological patterns by which Christian thinkers sought fuller understanding of the implications of God's act in Christ; and even in early Christian festivals and holy days. The early Christians put their own stamp on these practices, structures, and religious and philosophical traditions, but they nevertheless drew them from the larger world. In fact, several of the disputes that engaged the early Christian community mirrored disputes between religious and philosophical groups in the Roman world, the world in which these Christians sought to find their identity.

In these first centuries of the common era both Judaism and Christianity gave shape to and defined the authority of collections of writings that formed their respective Bibles or canons of sacred writings. For each this activity was not only a response to internal pressures and conflicts, important as these were, but it was also a response to the larger world in which Jewish and Christian communities lived. In their Bibles they aimed to construct at least the parameters within which they could define themselves and govern their interactions with that larger historical context.

Beyond that, many of the methods of interpretation by which both religious communities looked for meaning in their heritage, and the ways they appropriated the scriptures to address an ever-changing present, were often those used by others in the Hellenistic and Roman world as they also engaged their past in search of identity for the present and direction for the future. Authors who explained the Greek and Roman epics, as well as those who explicated the Jewish or Christian scriptures, were occupied with the discovery of typological patterns, those in which characters or events represent or foreshadow other characters and events in later writings. Such patterns were investigated across scriptures and between scriptures and contemporary situations. Likewise, the use of allegory to seek levels of meaning beneath the surface of a text, and the suggestion that distinct levels of meaning were to be found in texts, reflect Christian and Jewish engagement with interpretive strategies employed by Greeks, Romans, and others in working with their own heritage. Not only the books that came to comprise the Jewish Hebrew Bible and the Christian Old and New Testaments, but many of the ways they were kept living and enlivening, bear the clear imprint of the historical context of the biblical communities.

The Contributions
of Archaeology

CAROL MEYERS

Perhaps no other area on the surface of the earth has been so extensively and intensively explored and excavated as has been the heartland of the biblical world, ancient Palestine. The beginnings of the investigation of the material remains of the land in which the Bible took shape virtually coincided with the emergence of the western fascination with the lost civilizations of the ancient world. For centuries, travelers from Europe to the Mediterranean world, many of them pious pilgrims drawn to Bible lands, had brought back tales of the monuments and ruins they had seen in the general vicinity of places mentioned in holy texts. But it is barely more than a century and a half ago that the scientific recovery of the material remains of biblical antiquity began.

Archaeology, and in particular biblical archaeology, holds such a fascination in the western mind that the results of archaeological work have penetrated the popular culture in a way that relatively few scientific endeavors can claim. Magazine articles, television documentaries, newspaper reports, and even feature films have all presented wide audiences with data recovered from the biblical world. Because of the availability of such material, it is difficult to remember how different our perception of the Bible and its people was even a generation ago.

Without archaeology, the content of the biblical text is somehow flat, distant, and remote. Without a sense of the reality of the biblical world and of the authenticity of its peoples and places, the Bible seems almost like a mythical document, its content somehow isolated from the fabric of human experience. To be sure, many texts have their own inherent vitality; many passages transcend their distance in time and space from today's readers. Yet, unlike most religious documents, the Bible is not an abstract theological treatise. It is a story, or series of stories, set in the real world; it deals with particular human beings who moved about in specific places. Yet in its very focus on particular moments and persons, it is a selection and thus a distortion. It cannot possibly provide us with all the details of the ancient setting that could help us understand the dynamics of human existence in biblical antiquity and could thus enable us to grasp the reality of the life experiences that have been captured in the biblical word. Those life experiences have become the vehicles for expressing profound ideas about the relationship between God and the world, and therefore any means of further understanding them, and thereby increasing understanding of the biblical word, are of great importance to us.

What Is Biblical Archaeology and What Does It Do?

Strictly speaking, the word "archaeology" (derived from the Greek words *archaios,* "ancient," and *logos,* "knowledge") means the study of the past. However, the term is commonly used to describe a particular aspect of the study of the human past, namely, the material remains of ancient peoples. It deals with the realia, the physical objects, of everyday life—the buildings in which people lived and worked, the tools and vessels (containers) they used, the ways in which they earned their livelihood, the nature of their settlements, the clothes they wore, their implements of war and of worship, the manner in which they buried and memorialized the dead.

To this list of the tangible remnants of the people of the ancient world, one must also add the written remains of antiquity. In the case of biblical studies, such epigraphic discoveries have had a powerful impact upon our understanding of the Bible. Documents and inscriptions in abundance have been recovered from the lands surrounding the territory of ancient Israel. These materials have provided an invaluable perspective on the nature and content of biblical literature (see "Historical Contexts," p. * 33, and "Literature of the Ancient Near East," p. * 57). Although relatively few written sources have survived from ancient Palestine itself, the few scattered inscriptions, seals, and fragments of pottery with writing on them have all immeasurably enhanced our knowledge of certain features of ancient Israelite life. Most important and dramatic of all the epigraphic discoveries has been that of actual biblical scrolls. The collection of scrolls and fragments of scrolls that have survived in the area of the Dead Sea constitute an unprecedented and unparalleled source of information about the nature of the biblical canon and of its formation and transmission (see "Dead Sea Scrolls," p. * 101).

Thus, archaeology in its most inclusive sense involves all products, written and non-written, of human existence. In the case of written materials, the discoveries of texts in Near Eastern lands outside the biblical heartland have not been the result of archaeological work that could be characterized as "biblical archaeology." That term, therefore, has a special meaning that makes it different from any other "archaeology" preceded by an adjective.

Many scholars debate the very legitimacy of the designation "biblical archaeology," since it does not always have the direct relationship to field work that characterizes terms for archaeology in other parts of the world. In many ways, it makes more sense to refer to the archaeology of any area by a regional designation. So, for example, excavation of the large Mesopotamian cities that have yielded epigraphic remains so critical for biblical studies comes under the purview of "Mesopotamian archaeology." But it could also be called "biblical archaeology" in the sense that its discoveries do pertain to the Bible.

According to the system of regional designation, the archaeological recovery of materials from the holy land itself is called Syro-Palestinian archaeology. Such a term allows for the fact that the excavation of a site with even the most direct biblical connection can also provide materials that precede or postdate the biblical period. Hence the excavation of such a site in its entirety might not be properly called biblical archaeology. Similarly, despite the best advance planning and survey work, an archaeologist cannot possibly know what sort of discoveries lie beneath the surface of an ancient ruin. The discovery of remains of the biblical period or those relating to biblical texts may be the hope of an excavation team; but in scientific terms, field projects cannot be so specifically defined. Thus, the excavation of a site selected because of its explicitly biblical connections may yield much material that bears no relationship at all to biblical studies.

Because of such considerations, biblical archaeology is a term best applied to whatever material remains contribute to an understanding of biblical literature and life in biblical times, from wherever such data might be acquired. In that sense, biblical archaeology would not normally refer to the actual process of designing and carrying out an archaeological survey or excavation; that is the task of Syro-Palestinian archaeology. Instead, biblical archaeology is a specialized, interpretive discipline that seeks to relate material realia to places, persons, paraphernalia, and processes mentioned in or alluded to by a literary document, the Bible. Field archaeologists who have such an enterprise in mind are often called biblical archaeologists. But field archaeologists significantly removed from such considerations also may provide data for biblical archaeology. For example, the use of analogy is of considerable importance in reconstructing the past in any part of the world. Hence, the knowledge gained about an ancient society in as distant a place as South America or Australia could potentially contribute to our understanding of the biblical world.

Since its beginnings in holy land exploration by the American biblical scholar Edward Robinson in 1838 and 1852, biblical archaeology has historically been most valuable in establishing a context for the customs, events, beliefs, objects, and places recorded in the Bible. Context can refer to very simple matters, which we might call illumination of biblical texts. A given passage may refer, for example, to a certain musical instrument that is not part of our current repertoire of instruments. But if we can identify it with an excavated example, we will have a much better idea of its size, shape, and perhaps also of its musical capacity. We will know in a way not otherwise possible what the biblical author saw or imagined in reference to such an object. The biblical text gains a visual dimension, if not also an auditory dimension in this case, by recourse to an archaeological discovery.

Context, of course, can refer to much more complex issues. If we are to be rescued from the notion that the Bible somehow emerged all at once, fully formed, like Athena from the head of Zeus, we must learn as much as we can about the lives of the people whose experiences are reflected in the great diversity of literary genres that constitute the biblical corpus (see "Literary Forms," p. * 12). If we see the Bible as the collective work of countless and mostly nameless authors, whose identities are forever hidden from our view, we nonetheless can better understand their unique contributions to our western religious and cultural heritage by seeing them in social and political context. We gain access to this context in part by examining the settlements or cities in which they might have lived and by following the fate of such places over the course of the biblical period.

Indeed, much of biblical archaeology has been what we might call political archaeology. That is, it has served the traditional goals of political history; it has helped to chart the course of events mentioned in the great story of Israel that runs through the Hebrew Bible. To the extent that Palestinian sites can be identified with places mentioned in the Bible, biblical archaeologists have traced the development, frequent destruction, and habitual rebuilding of such sites and have sought to correlate the archaeological evidence of such aspects of a site's history with the biblical record. The destruction debris, for example, of a Palestinian *tell** can usually be quite accurately dated by the kind of artifacts (notably pottery) it contains. Such information is then juxtaposed with the biblical account of the conquest of the city in question.

The contextual dimension that such political history using archaeological data can provide, like the more simple, descriptive contextualizing functions of archaeology, has been a central goal of biblical archaeology since its inception. The reason for this prominent interest is that the correlations made between objects mentioned in the Bible and artifacts recovered from the debris of the millennia, as well as the connections made between events chronicled in the text and those that have left their mark in the long-buried remnants of biblical cities, serve to ground the biblical materials in a tangible reality. The texts themselves, in the written form in which we have them, are later by many centuries if not millennia than the events they purport to describe. How can we test the authenticity of the core life experiences reported about the individuals or peoples that form the central focus of the biblical story? Discovering that the details of the biblical stories ring true to the way of life in the time periods they signify validates the biblical text. Archaeology can provide an independent witness to the authenticity of the biblical experience.

As a source of information about the biblical world that is independent of the sacred texts produced by that world, archaeology has another important function. Not only does archaeology yield information about and background for what the text presents; it also provides data for dimensions of ancient life that the text ignores or even suppresses. Archaeology is thus an important corrective to the notion that the facts and features of life among biblical peoples as preserved in the Bible are ac-

---

*A *tell*, or city-mound, is an artificial hill resulting from the accumulated debris of successive settlements at a site over a long period of time.

curate reflections of the way all members of those groups actually acted or thought.

Social scientists have long pointed out that there is often a discrepancy or disjunction between what formal texts, such as scripture, contain and what daily reality was like. Texts may often be more a reflection of the ideal than the real. Archaeology along with the Bible can thus be seen as providing the two views that together give us a stereoscopic picture of the biblical past—two different angles of vision provide the depth that a single picture can never yield.

This is an important yet often unheralded function of archaeology, for it sometimes produces perspectives that are not congenial to those who hold the biblical text as the accepted norm, for antiquity as for the present. For example, a modest corpus of ancient Hebrew seals* has been recovered from Palestinian sites. A number of these seals, the use of which implies the right to transfer ownership of goods and to sign legal documents, belonged to women, thus apparently contradicting the impression one has from the Bible that such operations were male prerogatives. An even more controversial example regards the very nature of biblical monotheism. Was ancient Israel fully monotheistic before the period of the second temple (515 B.C.E. to 70 C.E.)? Various artistic and epigraphic remains, especially some apparently referring to a consort for Yahweh, seem to indicate a plurality of beliefs among the Israelites. Clearly, archaeologically recovered data allow for a much more nuanced view of the complexity of the society and beliefs of the biblical people than would otherwise be possible.

The Limitations of Biblical Archaeology

As rich with potential as is the enterprise of biblical archaeology, so also is it fraught with problems. For one thing, as an interpretive process, it is subject to the difficulties of interpretation that are intrinsic to methods of dealing both with artifactual materials and with the biblical text. By their very nature, non-epigraphic archaeological remains are mute. Establishing their function, date, relationship to other artifacts, indeed their very character, is often a complex and controversial task, on which agreement may not be reached even among the excavators themselves.

The existence of divergent views about the characteristics of many archaeological remains means that the utilization of such material in studying biblical texts is not necessarily the straightforward procedure that we might imagine. Because of the concrete nature of the artifacts and buildings recovered by field work, there is a tendency to view archaeological evidence as objective, "hard" data. Although this may be true on one level, at the interpretive level it is misleading. A destruction layer in an ancient *tell,* which the biblical archaeologist would like to relate to a bib-

*A seal is a small object made of a hard substance, bearing a design and/or inscription, which could be transferred to wax or clay, usually to mark ownership or authenticity.

lical narrative of military conquest, becomes a valid source of information only if its date can be successfully established.

But even then problems remain. An existing consensus on the date of virtually any archaeological materials is always subject to minor refinement, if not major revision, as new dating techniques as well as new materials become available. Furthermore, the evidence of destruction, to continue our example, even if securely located in a time period that can be related to events described in the Bible, never provides the identity of the perpetrator of the devastation. Thus an interpretive leap is involved in linking the debris in a *tell* with the details of a biblical narrative.

The problem of interpreting and reinterpreting material remains is often compounded by the existence of equally serious difficulties in understanding the evidence of the Bible itself. The plethora of biblical commentaries and the enormous body of scholarly literature dealing with scripture attest to the fact that the meaning of many biblical passages has not been clearly established. Again, to follow our hypothetical example of a city's destruction, scholars do not always agree on the dating of a biblical story. Furthermore, the date of the literary account itself may be far removed from the event being recounted. And to make matters even more complex, the apparently historical narratives in many parts of the Bible may be stylized, saga-like literature and not the eyewitness recording of contemporary events they seem to be. In short, the complexity of biblical interpretation provides as many potential pitfalls as does the complexity of archaeological interpretations for the task of the biblical archaeologist in bringing these two sets of data together.

The lesson of this dilemma of interpretation should be not to expect too much. Archaeology is clearly of enormous value in reconstructing the general biblical world. It is far less secure as a means of validating the specific biblical word. Archaeological evidence is more indirect than direct, and its extraordinary contributions to recapturing the realities of life in biblical antiquity rather than the verities of biblical texts should not be diminished by this realization.

At this point, one further misapprehension about what biblical archaeology can provide must be confronted. For many people, the fascination with archaeology in biblical lands derives from the expectation that archaeological materials will do more than provide general context for or even validate specific texts. That is, some believe that archaeology will "prove" the truth of the Bible. It may indeed be the case, though perhaps less common than we might expect, that archaeological data do confirm individual biblical passages. Yet what is meant by the truth of the Bible is not in fact subject to the kind of confirmation that archaeology can provide.

To illustrate this, let us again consider our example of a city's destruction. In the best of conditions the date of a conflagration level in a site that has been securely identified as the one mentioned in a biblical text can be convincingly related to the text's description of that site being razed at a specific point in biblical history. Archaeology might then be said to substantiate the historicity of the textual account. Yet it can never validate the textual claim. We must not forget that the Bible is not an ordinary chronicle of past events. Rather it tells its story to demonstrate its claim that God played an active role in the unfolding biblical story. The destruction of a city is thus ultimately ascribed to God's actions in delivering it into the hands of its conquerors.

The veracity of the Bible's claims about God's involvement in the world is of an order that can be neither proved nor disproved by archaeological information. Material remains can lead us into the world in which the ancients lived and in which they experienced the divine presence. But they cannot establish—nor can they contradict—the truth of the biblical claims about God. Dealing with the historical authenticity of biblical texts cannot be equated with revealing their spiritual truth.

The Future of Biblical Archaeology

Although biblical archaeology cannot verify the spiritual component of biblical materials, recent developments in the conceptualization of archaeology as a discipline may lead us somewhat closer to comprehending the religious dimension of biblical texts. Archaeology in general has changed markedly in recent decades as the result of the emergence in the New World of what is known as the "new archaeology." This development is not primarily an innovation in the process or method of excavation or exploration, although it does perhaps involve much closer attention to technological and ecological factors than has been traditionally characteristic of excavations, especially in Bible lands.

Rather, the new archaeology impinges on archaeological work more at the level of interpretation than at the primary level of the collection, description, and classification of material data. Its potential for biblical studies involves the broadening of the horizons of biblical archaeology. The task of biblical archaeology becomes more than a reconstruction of the material aspects of daily life in the ancient world. It becomes a challenging and ambitious integrative enterprise. It involves the combined use of archaeological data with all of its ecological facets, of biblical materials, and—and here is the "new" part for biblical archaeology—of comparative sociological and anthropological information and models.

The ultimate goals thus transcend the aims for historical and material reconstruction that characterized past generations of biblical archaeologists; they focus on the social existence of the various communities of people that appear in biblical texts, from the smallest communities (the family household), through clans, villages, towns, cities, and nations, to empires. The concern with sociopolitical dynamics is rooted in the attempt to understand why communities exist in the forms that they take, how those forms shift or stay the same in relation to historical and environmental variables, and how the mental life of any community—its self-awareness, its values, its belief system—serves both to reflect and to reinforce the social, political, and economic mechanisms by which it survives, or fails to survive, in the face of the vagaries of human existence.

The biblical archaeologists who have been most influenced by the advances in socio-archaeological theory in the past two decades are using the same archaeological and biblical data that their predecessors used. But they are asking different questions of the familiar material. They have new agendas, aimed at understanding individual and corporate life processes in the biblical world. In addition, they can also solve some problems in biblical studies that hitherto defied resolution.

As an example of the latter, the issue of whether or not there were scribal schools in monarchic Israel has long vexed biblical scholars. Such institutions are well attested in neighboring areas, but the epigraphic remains from Palestine and the biblical evidence are both indirect and inconclusive with respect to the question of the existence of such schools. Now, by using the wealth of material available from excavated sites and surveys, and by relating these data to what sociological research shows about contexts requiring a class of trained administrators, likely parameters for the existence of such literate personnel—scribes—can be posited. Specifically, the size and configuration of settlements, the construction of public works (e.g., water systems, city walls), and the appearance of luxury goods constitute a set of archaeological correlates to social patterns for which scribes would be necessary. For ancient Israel, the results are surprising: the training of scribes would not have been necessary until several centuries after the monarchy was established, and even then Jerusalem was the only urban center that might have warranted a formal school. (The question of literacy, it is to be noted, is quite separate, in a society using an easily learned alphabetic script, from the question of scribal schools.)

As for the new agendas—the attempts to understand the processes of human existence at all levels—here biblical archaeology has its richest potential. At its best, the new biblical archaeology can help us do more than envision the biblical world. Through the new analytical possibilities, it can also help us comprehend the dynamics of social, economic, and political life in biblical antiquity. In this way, perhaps we can come closer than ever before to reconstructing the life experiences that caused our biblical ancestors to draw their profound and powerful conclusions about the role of God in their lives and to make their compelling assertions about the ongoing relationship between God and humanity.

SUGGESTIONS FOR FURTHER READING

Dever, William G. *Archaeology and Biblical Studies. Retrospects and Prospects.* Evanston, Illinois: Seabury-Western Theological Seminary, 1974.
Dever, William G. "Syro-Palestinian Archaeology and Biblical Archaeology," pp. 31–74 in D. A. Knight and G. M. Tucker, eds., *The He-*

brew Bible and Its Modern Interpreters. Chico, California: Scholars Press, 1985.

Meyers, Carol, and Meyers, Eric. "Expanding The Frontiers of Biblical Archaeology," Eretz Israel 20 (1989): 140–147.

Lance, H. Darrell. The Old Testament and the Archaeologist. Philadelphia: Fortress Press, 1981.

Paul, Shalom M., and Dever, William G., eds., Biblical Archaeology. Jerusalem: Keter Publishing House, 1973.

DeVaux, Roland. "On Right and Wrong Uses of Archaeology," pp. 64–82 in J. A. Sanders, ed., Near Eastern Archaeology in the Twentieth Century. Garden City, NY: Doubleday and Company, 1970.

Wright, G. Ernest. Biblical Archaeology. Philadelphia: Westminster Press, 1962.

Literature of the Ancient Near East

CHOON-LEONG SEOW

Biblical literature grew out of the cradle of world literature, the ancient Near East. It was in this region that what is arguably humanity's earliest writings are found in the hieroglyphic texts of Egypt and ideographic writings of Sumer from the fourth millennium B.C.E. It was here, too, that the earliest alphabet, to which the English alphabet can ultimately be traced, was invented in the second millennium B.C.E. Although not even two centuries have passed since the world first became acquainted with the ancient languages and civilizations of the "fertile crescent," their discovery has forever transformed our understanding of the cultural milieu of biblical literature. The bulk of the texts have come from Egypt, Mesopotamia, and, to a lesser extent, Hatti, the home of the Hittites in Anatolia. A fortuitous discovery of an ancient tomb at a site on the Syrian coast, just across from the easternmost tip of Cyprus, led to the excavation of the Canaanite city of Ugarit (Ras Shamra) with its vast collection of texts. Epigraphic materials (inscriptions) have also been found throughout Syria-Palestine, although these are not nearly as impressive.

The number of extant ancient Near Eastern writings has become exceedingly large and diverse; multi-volume translations of the literature of Egypt and Mesopotamia have been produced. Less extensive editions for the Hittite and West-Semitic inscriptions (that is, those written in Ugaritic, Aramaic, Phoenician, Hebrew, and other Canaanite dialects) have also appeared, but other texts remain accessible only to those who read the original languages. The materials include graffiti, abecedaries (alphabets or alphabetically-arranged materials), stamps, seal impressions, tax receipts, lists of various sorts, letters, hymns, love songs, laments, prayers and various liturgical texts, votive and commemorative inscriptions, as well as comprehensive law codes, detailed annals, prophetic collections, and tales worthy of the designation "epic." The variety is noteworthy, but what is more remarkable is the sense that one is dealing not just with isolated texts, but literature. The people of the ancient Near East seem to have been aware of the value of their texts as literature, for they took great care to transmit and translate the "classics" of the region, adapting and adopting the apparently well-known works as they saw fit. So one finds evidence of interdependence in the writings of each civilization.

Myths and Legends

People in antiquity were as concerned as modern people are with the way the world functioned, and they expressed their understanding of the origin and preservation of world order through their stories about the primeval conflict between chaos and order. Such accounts, which give us insights into the cosmology of the ancient Near East, are commonly called "creation myths," even though in most cases creation is of secondary interest to the composers. The most famous of these myths is the Babylonian creation epic called *Enuma Elish* ("When on High"), a name derived from the opening line of the account. It begins with a time before heaven and earth were made, when only primeval fresh-water Apsu (English "abyss") and salt-water Tiamat (biblical Hebrew *tehom,* "Deep") existed. Soon after the gods came into existence, Tiamat conspired with Apsu to destroy them. Order was in jeopardy; chaos threatened to take over. Marduk, the patron god of Babylon, was summoned by the deities to rescue them. The god marched into battle against Tiamat and her monstrous entourage, killed her, and divided her body into two. With one half of her body the heavens were made, and with the other half the earth. Thereupon, Marduk was acknowledged by the gods as king and he ruled henceforth as the supreme deity in Babylon, the city of his choice.

Although the account tells of the creation of the world, its focus is not on the origins of the cosmos *per se.* The motivation behind the story was not scientific but ideological. Whereas in other creation stories from the region Marduk plays a subordinate role, or no role at all, he is the hero in this account. It was he who brought order out of chaos. The myth was recited annually at the New Year to celebrate the refurbishing of the temple of Marduk in Babylon. Its purpose was, in fact, to extol Babylon's role in the establishment and maintenance of world order.

Creation accounts in Egypt, likewise, are ideologically motivated. This was the case with the so-called "Theology of Memphis," a copy of which was inscribed on the Shabaka Stone. The text describes creation by the command of Ptah, the god of the sanctuary at Memphis; it stands in contrast to Atum's creation, which originated from primeval watery chaos. Memphis is regarded in this inscription as the center of life in all Egypt. The text thus argues for the superiority of the Memphite cultus over the more ancient one in Heliopolis. Atum, the creator god of Heliopolis, is said to have been created by Ptah and is portrayed as a mere functionary. According to this account, it was Ptah who made the souls of mortals and was responsible for the preservation of world order.

There are no indisputable creation texts from Ugarit, but there are conflict-myths that bear resemblance to the "creation myths" of Mesopotamia. Of course, the protagonist in these texts is Ugarit's deity, the storm-god, Baal. The most important texts occur in two variations, one concerning Baal's battles with Yamm, the deified Sea, and the other his conflict with Mot, Death. The enemies of Baal are accompanied by their entourage, which included one called Lothan (biblical "Leviathan"), a slithery dragon with seven heads. In the first variation, the messengers of Sea come before the divine assembly to demand the surrender of Baal. Thereupon, the gods of the council put "their heads on their knees," a gesture which may be associated with a mourning ritual in Egypt. Baal's demise is too readily conceded by his peers in the assembly; they are already mourning his death! But Baal ventures forth into combat, defeats Sea, and is declared king. Parallels with the Mesopotamian conflict-myths are obvious. The people of Ugarit were probably aware of this fact, as well, for a god list from the city explicitly identified Yamm (Sea) with Tiamat.

In the other variant of the conflict-myth, Death actually overcomes Baal and swallows him. Baal is declared dead and he descends into the netherworld where he remains for some time. But the initial setback is reversed when Baal is resurrected. Death is eventually defeated and it is proclaimed: "Baal lives!"

As in the conflict-myths elsewhere, the Baal stories are ideological. Some scholars think of the myths as reflecting the agricultural seasons of ancient Canaan, with the alternating dominance of death in the dry months of the summer and the revivification of nature during the rainy seasons. The myths are also political, inasmuch as they tell of the rise of Ugarit's primary deity to prominence. As in the *Enuma Elish*, Baal's victory over the forces of chaos resulted in the establishing of a temple from which Baal would rule and maintain order.

The dominant motifs and basic pattern of the Ugaritic conflict-myths are reflected in ancient Israel's psalmody (e.g., Pss. 24, 29, 74), where the God of Israel is presented as the divine warrior defeating the forces of chaos, resulting in the deity's enthronement as king in Jerusalem, the elect city. The motifs are also prominent in the apocalyptic passages of the Bible, where God appears as a warrior slaying the mythological monsters and ultimately scoring the decisive victory by swallowing death (Isa. chs. 24–27). But the mythic pattern is discernible in biblical narratives, too, as in the initial setback but ultimate victory for the Ark of the Covenant, which represented Israel's deity in conflict with the god of the Philistines (1 Sam. chs. 4–6).

The dragon-slaying theme is found elsewhere in the ancient Near East. In the Hittite "Myth of Illuyankas," the storm-god is initially bested by the sea-monster, but returns to defeat it. The theme of the repulsing of the dragon is also evident in Egyptian myth and ritual.

Apart from the conflict-myths there are stories in Mesopotamia about a great Flood that destroyed the world. There are several versions of the story, but the most well-known is the "Atrahasis Epic," named after the king who is the protagonist in the story. The legend is told in the context of primeval history and the establishing of order in the cosmos. Humanity had been created to be of service to the gods, but the fecundity of mortals proved to be a problem, contributing to disorder and chaos in the world. The god Enlil made several attempts to destroy humanity, but each time the plan was foiled through the intervention of another god, Enki. At last Enlil decided to wipe out the human race through a great Flood. But Enki advised Atrahasis to build a ship, in which a remnant of humanity escaped the destruction of the deluge. After the Flood had subsided, Atrahasis offered sacrifices to the gods, who, having been deprived of human care during the deluge, then swarmed about like flies. Thus the epic is ultimately an affirmation of the place of humanity in the cosmos, although measures had to be taken in the new order to control the unchecked growth of the human population: in the new order there would be sterile women in addition to the fertile, there would be a demon who would snatch away infants from their mothers, and there would be women who would never marry.

Like the "Atrahasis Epic," the biblical Flood account belongs with the creation of humanity in primeval history. But the Bible's assessment of humanity's function on earth differs significantly from that of Atrahasis. Moreover, the command to mortals at creation and after the Flood to "be fruitful and increase" (Gen. 1.28; 9.7) must be seen as a deliberate polemic against the perspective of Atrahasis that human fecundity is a problem for the deity.

Another version of the Flood story is found in the *Epic of Gilgamesh,* named after the legendary ruler of Uruk (biblical Erech) in Sumer who was "two-thirds god and one-third human." When his friend Enkidu died, Gilgamesh became despondent about his own mortality and obsessed with overcoming death. So he set forth to learn the secret of immortality from Utnapishtim, who had survived the great Flood long ago. Utnapishtim related the story of the Flood and how he received instructions to build a ship to save his family. When the Flood subsided and the ship landed on a mountain, Utnapishtim successively sent forth a dove, a swallow, and a raven to see if the water had indeed diminished. When the raven did not return, Utnapishtim went forth and sacrificed to the gods (cf. Gen. ch. 8). Utnapishtim and his wife were made "like gods" living at the source of the rivers. Immortality was a gift of the gods, however, and Gilgamesh was unable to receive it. Like all mortals, he had to face the stark reality of death.

There is a scene in the *Epic of Gilgamesh* where Ishtar, the goddess of war, tries to seduce the hero. When spurned by Gilgamesh, Ishtar wails before her father Anu, the chief deity of the pantheon. A similar scene is found in the Ugaritic "Tale of Aghat," where Anat the goddess of war tries to seduce Aghat by offering him immortality, among other things. When rejected by the hero, Anat complains to her father El, the Ugaritic equivalent of Anu in Mesopotamia. It is likely that some version of the *Epic of Gilgamesh* might have influenced the Ugaritic story, a possibility that is supported by the discovery of a fragment of the Mesopotamian story at Ugarit.

Law

Among the most impressive literary contributions of the ancient Near East are the law codes of Mesopotamia and Anatolia. These include the Sumerian Laws of Ur-Nammu and Lipit-Ishtar, certainly among the oldest law codes known to humanity. There are also the Old Babylonian law codes of Eshnunna and the famous Code of Hammurabi, as well as the Middle Assyrian codes, the Hittite laws, and fragments of a Neo-Babylonian collection from the late seventh century B.C.E. These laws cover a wide range of issues, including murder, theft, kidnapping, bearing false witness, striking one's parents, illicit sexual relations, rape, an ox goring another ox, and the manumission (freeing) of slaves. These have been compared with materials in the Bible: the Book of the Covenant (Exod. 21–23), the Holiness Code (Lev. 17–26), and the Deuteronomic Laws (Deut. 12–26). Indeed, there is so much in common in the content, language, and forms of the various law codes that one may speak of shared social ideals and aspirations of the people of the ancient Near East, if not a common legal tradition originating probably in Mesopotamia.

Besides the law codes, there are also the legal documents of international diplomacy: the treaties. The most well preserved of these are Hittite treaties of the second millennium B.C.E., the forms of which are, however, probably influenced by older Mesopotamian models. The treaties are of two types: (1) the parity treaty between two equal partners, and (2) the suzerainty treaty between a more powerful nation and its vassal. The first is best exemplified by the treaty between Hattusilis III of Hatti and Ramesses II of Egypt after the Battle of Kadesh in 1286 B.C.E. Such texts typically contain the self-laudatory titles of each party, a history of relationship between the two national partners, an affirmation of mutuality and friendship, a list of the terms of the treaty itself, a list of divine witnesses, and invocation of blessings on the partners if they keep their end of the deal and curses if they renege. The second type is exemplified by the treaty between Mursilis II of Hatti and Duppi Tessup of Amurru. These are typically sealed by an oath, with the terms set by the suzerain. Such treaties usually include (1) a preamble or titulary, (2) a historical prologue outlining the suzerain's benevolent deeds for the vassal, (3) stipulations of the treaty, (4) provisions for the deposit of the text and its public reading, (5) a list of divine witnesses to the treaty, and (6) blessings and curses. There are some variations in the order of the parts, however, and occasionally an element may be omitted from the treaty. One should also mention here the Assyrian documents such as the Vassal-Treaties of Esarhaddon and the Aramaic treaty between KTK and Arpad. There is evidence that the Assyrian treaties may have been modelled after those from Syria-Palestine.

Biblical scholars have used these treaty forms to explicate the Sinai covenant of Exodus chs. 19–24 and the covenant renewal ceremony in

Joshua ch. 24. As in the Hittite treaties, there is provision in the Bible for keeping the law in a sacred place and for public reading of it (Deut. 31.9–13).

In addition to law codes and treaties, there are many business and personal legal documents, such as the Hurrian legal texts from Nuzi and Alalakh that pertain to family law, adoption and business administration. From a later period we have a cache of fifth-century B.C.E. Aramaic papyri from a Jewish mercenary colony at Elephantine in Egypt, concerning loans, inheritance, marriage, sale of property, documents of manumission and adoption. Finally, there are the recently discovered Aramaic papyri from Wadi ed-Daliyeh, about halfway between Samaria and Jericho in the Jordan river valley. These fourth century B.C.E. documents are mainly contracts recording the sale of slaves which the owners had brought with them when fleeing the army of Alexander the Great in 331 B.C.E.

Historiography

The most abundant and widely attested of the ancient Near Eastern texts are those which are presented as deliberate records of history, whatever their ultimate purposes may have been. Among these historiographic texts are the king lists of Mesopotamia and Egypt. The best known of these is the "Sumerian King List," preserved in a number of copies from the first half of the second millennium. This document tells how kingship was "lowered from heaven" and first established at the city of Eridu. Then it names a series of kings, each with reigns of mythic lengths, before the great Flood swept the earth. The post-diluvian kings are given shorter reigns and kingship is said to have moved from city to city before finally being established in the city of Ur. In this way, the dynasties of the different Sumerian cities are consolidated into one common history that ends with Ur. According to this scheme, then, there was only one legitimate kingship for each period in the history of Sumer and Akkad.

The so-called "Assyrian King List" survives in three extant copies from different periods, with the succession of kings brought down to different periods, the latest one ending with Shalmaneser V in the eighth century B.C.E. Among the kings were the earliest "17 kings living in tents" and the subsequent "10 kings who were ancestors." Legitimate kingship is always associated with one place, the city of Asshur. Similar lists are found in Mesopotamia down to the Hellenistic period and the "Seleucid King List" that legitimated the transfer of power from Alexander the Great to the Seleucid rulers.

This type of literature is also found in Egypt, with a similar emphasis on unity and consolidation of dynastic data. It is exemplified by the Turin Papyrus with its list of kings dating to the Ramesside period around the thirteenth century B.C.E. The list tells how the rulers of the first dynasty descended from the gods and demigods, and kingship passed on to the later generations. This king list is thus presented as a history of the monarchy from its divine inception down to the time of the authors.

Among the types of historiographic literature are the dedicatory or commemorative inscriptions. Such works invariably present history from the perspectives of their sponsors and typically list the accomplishments of the rulers, especially their roles in assuring divine favor for their lands through the installation of the cult statues in their cities and their support for the cult. Indeed, some works are so strongly ideological that one must conclude that they were composed to bolster the dubious claims of the rulers in question. Examples include the Apology of Esarhaddon of Assyria and the Apology of Hattusilis III of Hatti, which some have compared with the History of David's Rise in 1 Samuel.

Far and away the most extensive and detailed of the royal inscriptions are the annals of Mesopotamia, Egypt, and Hatti. The Assyrian kings were particularly adept at the use of this genre to chronicle their military exploits, building projects, and support of the local temples. Included among these are the Monolith Inscription of Shalmaneser III that mentions the involvement of Israel's King Ahab in the battle of Qarqar in 853 B.C.E. and the Prism of Sennacherib that describes the events surrounding the siege of Jerusalem in 701 B.C.E.

The best examples from Egypt are the Annals of Thutmose III (fifteenth century B.C.E.), the most complete of which records the victory of the king over the Asiatics, including a detailed account of the victory at Megiddo. The record makes no pretense of being complete, suggesting that further details are "set down in the daybook of the palace."

Annals are well attested in Hittite literature, where they exhibit the same selectivity in the reporting of events. From the reign of Mursilis II (1330–1310 B.C.E.) come three major annalistic compositions, namely, the Deeds of Suppiluliumas (the father of Mursilis), the Ten Year Annals, and the Detailed Annals. Mursilis was the younger son of Suppiluliumas I and came to the throne at a very young age, succeeding a sickly older brother at a time of political uncertainty. The annals may, therefore, be seen as means for Mursilis to gain legitimacy. The Deeds of Suppiluliumas records the accomplishments of Mursilis' father and grandfather, while the Ten Year Annals and the Detailed Annals document the achievements of Mursilis himself. The documents speak repeatedly of the king's "manly deeds" and affirm the constant and unfailing support of the deities for him.

The chronicles of Mesopotamia are distinguished by their attention to detail and precision in dating. They are presented as archival texts, and not as inscriptions commissioned by specific regimes. The Assyrian Synchronistic Chronicles describe relations between Assyria and Babylon from about 1500 B.C.E. to 783 B.C.E. Each section of the text deals with an Assyrian king and his Babylonian counterpart. Kings who had no dealings with Babylon were excluded, but the report is otherwise comprehensive. Although not propagandistic in the same way as the royal inscriptions, these Chronicles are clearly written from the Assyrian point of view. Where disputes between the two nations are noted, Babylon is usually judged unfavorably; where skirmishes are reported, attention is usually on the victory of the Assyrians. For all their attention to historical details, these Chronicles cannot be seen as an objective presentation of data.

The Babylonian Chronicles deal with military and political affairs of the Babylonian kings from 747 B.C.E. to the Persian conquest in 539 B.C.E. They report on the events with remarkable objectivity and with only occasional recourse to explanations of divine causality. Even the demise of Babylon is reported with neither apology nor polemic. This is not to say, however, that these chronicles are presenting history for its own sake, only that the compilers saw no disadvantage for their purposes in laying out the historical data as they were.

It appears, then, that the historiographic works of the ancient Near East were purposeful documents written to lead one to certain conclusions. Even genealogies and chronicles were composed not for antiquarian and pedantic interests, but to persuade the readers to see the author's point of view. Thus, too, the historiographic materials of the Bible must be read, not as scientific presentation of data, but as purposeful—in most cases, theological—documents.

Prophecy

While the phenomenon of prophecy is mentioned in various texts, most notably in the Report of Wen Amun from the eleventh century B.C.E., the Hittite Prayer of Mursilis II from the fourteenth century B.C.E, the Annals of Ashurbanipal from the seventh century B.C.E., the inscription of Zakkur from the eighth century B.C.E., and various letters from Mari, relatively few literary texts may be taken as prophetic in the same manner as biblical prophecies.

The Admonitions of Ipu-wer from Egypt, for instance, has been regarded as a prophecy because of its social critique. The text reflects a concern that order was being threatened, as the nation was being torn asunder by civil strife and injustice was prevalent. But there is no claim in the text that the author was speaking by divine constraint. The gods do not speak through a prophet in these Admonitions; in fact, they do not intervene in any way.

The Prophecy of Neferti from Egypt is also commonly regarded as a prophetic text, but it is probably to be regarded as a propagandistic piece for Amenemhet I of Dynasty XII, usurper of the throne. The account is set in the time of Pharaoh Snefru of Dynasty IV. Seeking to be entertained, the Pharaoh summoned the sage Neferti to speak of the future.

The sage then proceeded to prophesy a series of disasters in the land which would come to an end only through the action of "Ameny" (i.e., Amenemhet I). The text is thus a "prophecy after the event" composed in the reign of Amenemhet to support the disputed claims of the king.

The function of this text is analogous to one from Mesopotamia dated to the reign of Nebuchadnezzar I in the twelfth century B.C.E. Written in the first person as a speech of Marduk to other gods, this Akkadian text speaks of Marduk's sojourn in Hatti, Assyria, and Elam, and "predicts" the rise of the new king in Babylon (Nebuchadnezzar I) who would return the cult statue of Marduk, restore the cult, and usher in a period of prosperity. This text, as well as the "Shulgi Prophecy" and "Uruk Prophecy" may be called prophecies only if one includes in one's definition of prophecy no necessary role for an intermediary through whom the inspired word is spoken.

Clear examples of prophetic texts are extant, however. A singular tablet preserves a collection of Akkadian oracles given in the name of the goddess Ishtar of Arbela to King Esarhaddon delivered through intermediaries. Each section of the tablet concludes with an identification formula: "from the mouth of So-and-So, the son/daughter of So-and-So of such and such a city." The prophets or prophetesses are specifically named to indicate their responsibilities for the words. There are no indications of the original settings for these prophecies, although the number of prophecies in favor of the king may indicate some connections with the royal court. Typically the oracle includes a "Fear Not" call to the king, which is followed by a command to wait for deliverance, an assurance of divine accompaniment, and a promise of victory over enemies.

Commonly associated with this collection of prophecies is another collection of sayings identified as "the word of Ishtar of Arbela to Esarhaddon king of Assyria." No mention is made of intermediaries, however, and elements in the collection suggest that these texts may have other, perhaps cultic, functions.

Yet another collection contains three oracles from the goddess Ninlil to Ashurbanipal with the repetition of the "Fear Not" assurance. An intermediary, called a *raggintu* ("proclaimer") is identified.

From the first half of the second millennium come Divine Revelations in a series of letters from Mari. These are reports of prophetic proclamations mainly to kings in the temple of Mari and elsewhere made on the basis of dreams, visions, auditions, and ecstatic activities. The content of the prophecies include prediction of military successes, admonitions concerning care of the sanctuaries, advice and warning about order in the society. In these letters, the intermediaries are variously called *muhhu/muhhūtu* ("ecstatic"), *āpilu/āpiltu* ("answerer"), and the unknown designation *assinnu/assinnatu*, although a few of the intermediaries are without titles. These intermediaries all speak in the first person under the constraint of the deity. Responsibility for the prophecies is indicated symbolically by the delivery of a lock of hair of the speaker and a piece of the hem from his or her garment.

Wisdom

There is perhaps no category of ancient writings more consciously composed and collected as literature than the didactic texts of Egypt and Mesopotamia. For their intense interests in the practical knowledge about the universe and their reflection on the nature of human life, these writings are sometimes described as "scientific" and "philosophical." On account of their affinities to the portions of the Bible that focus on the place of wisdom, they are together called "wisdom literature."

Subsumed under this category are the anthologies of pithy maxims that served to instruct people on the proper conduct of life. These collections, corresponding in many ways to modern manuals on etiquette, represent the collective wisdom of the communities based on their experience and observation of life. Whether the individual maxims first originated in the family, clan, or courts, it is certain that the large anthologies were made for instruction in formal settings. This was certainly the case in Egypt, where the *sebayit* ("instruction") was made for the training of potential rulers and bureaucrats. Not surprisingly, therefore, the collections were often gathered in the name of famous kings and other leaders from hoary antiquity. Some are presented in the form of "royal testaments," the legacy of departing kings for their successors, as is the Instruction for Merikare and the Instruction of Amenemhet I. The content and style of such instructional literature have led to comparison with the biblical Book of Proverbs, traditionally attributed to King Solomon. So suggestive in fact are some of the parallels that scholars sometimes speak of a dependence of portions of the Book of Proverbs on Egyptian didactic literature, such as the theory that Prov. 22.17–24.22 may have been translated directly from the Egyptian Instruction of Amenemope.

Similar types of collections are not widely attested in Mesopotamia, but there are anthologies of Sumerian and Akkadian proverbs. One may cite here the Instructions of Shuruppak and the Counsels of Wisdom, or even the Aramaic proverbs of Ahiqar from a story set in the time of Sennacherib of Assyria.

Besides the collections of maxims, there are a number of wisdom texts that reflect on the problem of human suffering. From Mesopotamia comes the text called *Ludlul Bel Nemeqi,* "I will Praise the Lord of Wisdom." This is the story of a righteous and pious noble who had been forsaken by the gods and afflicted with diseases, but was eventually restored to health by his god. The poem makes the point that the divine will is ultimately incomprehensible to mortals, for what mortals think is good may be an offense to the gods and what human beings regard as despicable may in fact be proper to the gods. The outline of the story is commonly recognized as corresponding to the story-line of the prose prologue and epilogue in the Book of Job.

Another text reminiscent of biblical Job is the so-called "Babylonian Theodicy." The text is an acrostic poem in the form of a dialogue between a sufferer who exposes the evils of injustice and a friend who tries to reconcile these facts with conventional views on divine justice.

The concern with the prevalence of evil and the lack of justice is also reflected in several Egyptian texts, including the Admonitions of Ipu-wer and the "Tale of the Eloquent Peasant."

Related to these texts are pieces of pessimistic literature. The Akkadian dialogical Counsels of a Pessimist, for instance, laments the transitory nature of human existence. The poet advises that one should accept things as they are and continue one's religious duties and daily chores. A similar satirical piece in the form of a dialogue between a master and his slave explores all the arguments regarding the meaningfulness of life, or the lack thereof. This literary device of a dialogue to present alternative views is also evident in the Egyptian text about a man's conversation with his soul, as well as the Complaint of Khakeperre-Sonb.

Conclusion

There is in antiquity no other region of comparable extent, with similar ethnic and linguistic diversity, that has produced a comparable amount and variety of literary texts, or shared so many traditions and ideals, as the ancient Near East. Through this immense literature one gains insight into the cultural milieu in which the authors of biblical literature lived and were inspired. It is no wonder, then, that the same literary richness and vitality are reflected in the Bible, the sacred scriptures for so many in so diverse a world.

SUGGESTIONS FOR FURTHER READING

Beyerlin, W., *Near Eastern Religious Texts Relating to the Old Testament.* Trans. John Bowden. OTL. Philadelphia, 1978.
Lichtheim, M., *Ancient Egyptian Literature.* 3 Volumes. Berkeley, 1975–80.
Pritchard, J. B., *Ancient Near Eastern Texts Relating to the Old Testament.* 3rd edition. Princeton, 1969.

The Social World
of the Old Testament

DAVID L. PETERSEN

The Old Testament presents a world full of compelling characters. Personages like Jacob, David, Jeremiah, Sarah, Miriam, and Abigail continue to capture the imagination of readers, so much so that the Old Testament has been understood as literature that focuses on characters as they carry out their lives in dialogue with God. That same Old Testament, however, conveys something less visible but equally important: a world of social realities which constitutes the matrix in which these characters act and which, in powerful ways, determines what can and cannot happen to them. There are, in fact, two social worlds of the Old Testament. There is a social world in the Old Testament, namely, the network of relationships depicted in the text, and a social world which produced the Old Testament, the "real" world of ancient Israel. Though obviously related, these worlds are not always identical.

Old Testament scholars have long recognized the importance of this latter social world. In recent years, however, there has been a virtual explosion of research devoted to the social world of ancient Israel. For example, scholars have recently argued that it is better to use the model of peasant culture than that of nomadism to understand certain features of early Israelite society. Further, it seems preferable to view Saul using the notion of a chief rather than a king. Finally, the very idea of family has now been subjected to a rigorous analysis that has distinguished the household unit (those who dwell together) from the lineage (those who share an ancestor) as distinct entities. Such redefinitions represent a refinement in social analysis which is a part of contemporary study of the social world of ancient Israel.

Whether one focuses on the social world depicted in the Old Testament or existing behind the Old Testament, it is clear that there are numerous subsidiary worlds: the world of genders (the different worlds of male and female behavior), the world of the household, the world of the extended family, the world of the local community (whether city or village), and the world of the state. And it is also clear that these worlds vary over time and according to region. The chronological period that has received special attention in social world studies is the time just before and then during the inception of monarchy. There has been a predominant regional focus as well, on the so-called central highlands, in part because it is relatively easy to identify material cultural remains of the aforementioned period in this area. This world was palpably different from that of the household located in Josiah's Jerusalem, from Ezekiel's house which was not far from Mesopotamian Nippur, or from Nehemiah's dwelling in rebuilt Jerusalem. The variables of region, chronology, and size of social unit require one to speak of various social worlds that lie behind the Old Testament.

The Family

THE HOUSEHOLD. Though there is much disagreement about the nature of early Israelite society, there is substantial agreement that the household—and not the clan or tribe—deserves attention as the primary or basic social unit. The Hebrew terms "house" (*bêt*) or "father's house" (*bêt 'āb*), as is the case with other such Hebrew terms, e.g., "clan" (*mišpāḥāh*), do not have singular or simple meanings. Moreover, the term "father's house" in the postexilic period develops an entirely new meaning, namely, a group whose forebears had been part of the Babylonian exile. For our purposes, the term will mean what it does mean in many Old Testament texts, the residential household. Literary, social scientific, and archaeological evidence help us understand this entity. To the reader of the Old Testament, the literary material will be the most familiar. For example, Gen. 36.6 provides a convenient description of a "house," in this case Esau's, in which lived Esau, "his wives, his sons and daughters and all the members of his household, his livestock, all the animals. . . ." Social scientists have determined that nuclear families in rural, peasant cultures would include, on average, five to seven members. Esau's household would be on the upper side of the average, but hardly abnormal, especially because of the high mortality rate of children. In this case, the two social worlds—in and behind the text—appear to coincide.

It might seem difficult to comprehend how seven or eight people might live as a residential unit, along with their livestock. Here data provided by archaeologists have helped us understand the physical setting of the household. One may speak of a typical house in non-urban Iron Age Israel. It was a rectangular structure, often, though not necessarily, with two stories, which fronted on a courtyard. The layout of the floor level is much clearer than is that of the upper level, which probably served as a sleeping area. There were three, sometimes four rooms, set apart from each other by pillars which could be hung with textiles. The small rooms apparently served multiple purposes, including use as stables for goats and sheep. By contrast, the large room, which extended the length of the back side of the house, included the hearth. This kitchen area would have served as the primary gathering place. The overall size of these houses would have been small for a "nuclear family," a grouping made up of one married couple, their children, and the rare grandparent who had survived or a stray sibling related to one member of the constitutive couple, along with their livestock. These buildings were truly multifunctional structures. Agricultural produce, both edible and dry goods (wool), was processed there; grain was stored; food was prepared and consumed.

Although certain goods such as weapons or pottery were probably obtained by trade, the notion of a "self-sufficient" economic unit is not wide of the mark.

Such households did not normally live in isolation. Two or three houses might be built together, sometimes, though not always, around a courtyard. These compounds may provide physical evidence for one type of extended family structure for which the term "lineage" is used (perhaps a better term than "clan"), the size of which provided the kind of labor pool appropriate to farming terraced land. A compound of four houses might provide a work force of between twenty and thirty individuals.

Early Israelites engaged in various agricultural practices appropriate to the land on which they resided, including the clearing of land by removing trees and moving rocks, the latter of which were used in the creation of terrace walls behind which soil was filled and leveled. Such terraces increased the amount of land available for agricultural purposes and also enabled the population to make better use of limited rainfall. When terracing was coupled with the use of cisterns cut into bedrock and lined with plaster to enhance their ability to keep water from dissipating, the hill country became a much more viable setting for human settlement, though one highly dependent on appropriate temperature and rainfall. These labor-intensive forms of agriculture exerted demands upon women to bear a relatively large number of children and also encouraged various households to work cooperatively to create and maintain the system of terracing.

The land itself was typically owned by the male member of the married couple. He inherited it from his father and would pass it on to one of his sons, though not always the eldest one, as seen in the inheritance of Isaac over Ishmael or Jacob over Esau (cf. Deut. 21.15–17). Should it become necessary to sell the land, members of the extended family had right of first refusal. To this extent it is possible to speak of land owned by the family as well as by its individual members. Such customs preserved land plots of a size large enough to sustain at least one household and thus insured the integrity both of individual land holdings and of the labor forces that "created" (by terracing) and farmed them. The sale of non-urban land (cf. Lev. 25.29–31) was more difficult than the sale of urban real estate. Numerous laws and customs assisted the lineage in maintaining agricultural real estate (see Jer. 32.6–14; Lev. 25.25).

The "household" depended upon a marriage, which was itself constrained by certain prerequisites. According both to genealogies and to narratives in Genesis, Israelite males married only certain females, those from the patrilineage of Terah. Marriages were endogamous, that is, they occurred within this patrilineage but outside the direct lineage or family compound. The marriages of both Isaac to Rebecca and Jacob to Rachel and Leah fit this pattern. By contrast, Esau married outside the patrilineage and in so doing created a household which was ineligible to participate in Israelite inheritance.

Various pictures of the household in the Old Testament, e.g., the family of Abraham with one wife, one concubine, two sons and numerous slaves, do not easily fit the picture of the central highlands in the pre-state period. Here the distinction between the social world in the text as opposed to the social world behind the text is important: the social world narrated in the text, though clear, cannot always be directly related to its would-be historical context in the Middle or Late Bronze Age. It is difficult to know when and where such conditions as those described in the narratives associated with Abraham and Sarah might have obtained, but they almost certainly postdate the inception of monarchy in Israel and likely reflect either urban residence or dependence on the mercantile activity of Iron Age cities.

SOCIAL STRUCTURE BEYOND THE HOUSEHOLD. Various terms—tribe (Hebrew, *šēbeṭ, māṭṭeh*) and clan (*mišpāḥāh*)—occur so regularly and are of such symbolic importance (e.g., the twelve tribes of Israel) that one is forced to think that Israelite society was, at some point, made up of groupings larger than the individual household (and clan—if that term refers to the multi-house compound) and different from the town or city. How can we best think about the nature of these social entities? It has recently become a commonplace to speak of segmentary society, a term which refers to a society in which a number of relatively similar entities, e.g., clans or the larger entities known as tribes, exist on a similar footing but without any centralized leadership. The clans or tribes may trace their heritage to a figure, e.g., Jacob, but one who does not symbolize a structure of political authority. In its ideal form, there is a branching structure, the connections of which are legitimated by the notion of blood and/or marriage ties. The traditional picture involves a symmetrical chart leading from families at the bottom to people or nation at top:

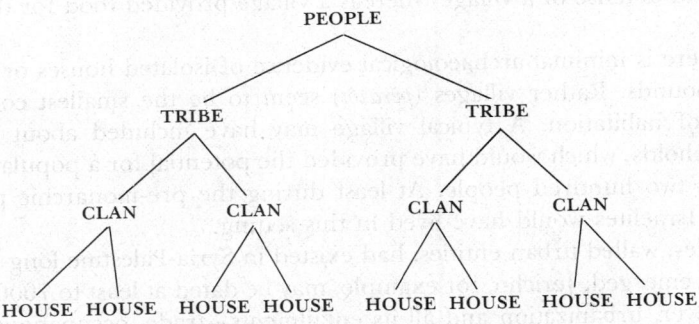

This chart, however, based on such texts as Josh. 7.16–18, does not reflect in a straightforward way the social world portrayed in the text. For example, the Hebrew phrase "house" or "father's house" may be used for various levels of social organization. In addition, there is both archaeological and literary evidence for a grouping larger than the household, the family compound, which some would call the lineage, but for which there is no single Hebrew noun. There is some, though ambiguous, literary evidence for an even larger grouping, which in Hebrew can be called a *mišpāḥāh* or clan. Scholars have suggested that this grouping had land ownership, defensive, religious, and economic functions.

The nature and function of the third level unit, the *šēbeṭ* or tribe, is even more ambiguous. They, like some "father's houses," were often associated with specific territories, e.g., Joshua 13–19. Alliances of tribes might provide for defense, relief during food shortages, and labor demands created by major agricultural tasks (terracing fields or harvesting). However, neither the internal functioning of the tribe nor the mechanisms of inter-tribal action are clear. Finally, the existence and character of "the people" or "Israel" is probably linked inextricably to the development of political and territorial identity under the monarchy, since there is minimal evidence for all Israelite tribes acting in concert before the tenth century. In sum, the chart above presents a highly idealized picture of the Israelite kinship structure.

The Village and/or City

Although the notion of village or town might seem totally different from that of family, the two can be integrally related since one lineage (one of the meanings of the father's house) could make up the population of a village. Put another way, villages could define themselves genealogically as well as geographically. The grouping of several households constitutes a small village, which, depending upon such factors as water supply, fertility of the land, and defensive position, could develop into a town or even a city. However, not all villages became cities; in fact, cities and villages functioned as complementary entities. A city provided a market for and defense of a village whereas a village provided food for those in a city.

There is minimal archaeological evidence of isolated houses or family compounds. Rather villages (*pĕrāzôt*) seem to be the smallest collective unit of habitation. A typical village may have included about twenty households, which would have provided the potential for a population of about two hundred people. At least during the pre-monarchic period, most Israelites would have lived in this setting.

Cities, walled urban entities, had existed in Syria-Palestine long before Israel emerged. Jericho, for example, may be dated at least to 7000 B.C.E. However, urbanization and all its entailments—trade, occupational specialization, social stratification, centralized political power—are normally associated with the political change from a loose agglomeration of families to a state; in Israel these developments are associated with the reigns of David and Solomon. There were two major moments of urbanization in ancient Israel, one accompanying the inception of monarchy, the other associated with the restoration of Judah in the late sixth and fifth centuries. Both served political administrative purposes, those of the Davidic and then of the Persian Empires respectively.

One may speak of a city's social structure. There was a ruling or elite class—merchants, military leaders, priests, political leaders, royalty, and administrators—who typically made up no more than ten percent of the population. The households of the elite class, in part because of their wealth, were larger in both size and population than those of the landed peasantry. The other inhabitants had a status in the larger society roughly similar to the peasants in villages outside the city, although they were more vulnerable to economic deprivation since they did not have direct access to the land and its produce.

Cities in Israel followed a basic plan. A roughly circular wall enclosed the whole. Houses were built up against this wall and fronted on a street that paralleled the lines of it. Other streets radiated off the main circular one. There were usually some large public buildings, e.g., temple and a residence for the ruler and/or aristocracy of the city. Immediately inside the city gate was a large, open area, which probably served as a place of public gathering, whether for economic (e.g., market), political, or religious purposes. If one assumes that one acre of a city can sustain upwards of two hundred individuals, Jerusalem during Solomon's reign would have had a population of about 6000 people.

The Nation or People

Questions such as when and why Israel became a people, a large social entity such as a nation, involve numerous subsidiary issues. The key questions are twofold: What forces impelled nascent Israel to become a state? and, How should the early nation be understood? The first question has elicited numerous answers: conflict with other Syro-Palestinian societies, especially the Sea Peoples (otherwise known as the Philistines); demand for increased land because of successful agricultural technologies and increased population density; an increasingly stratified society due to economic success, which in turn required a new form of political organization; a more complex system of economic production and distribution, which necessitated some form of centralized administration; and a more ethnically diverse population, which called for integration through political and religious means. Though it is difficult to assess the relative importance of these factors, it seems clear that both external and internal factors contributed to the development of the Israelite state. Some Old Testament texts suggest that the monarchic state was an improper intrusion (e.g., 1 Samuel 8). Careful attention to the social world of early Iron Age Israel, however, suggests that the chiefdom and then the monarchic state were appropriate adaptive responses to the situation that these early Israelites confronted. The centralization of power personified by the king corresponded to other centripetal forces—especially economic ones—at work in the society. The study of Israel's earliest monarchic period now includes topics such as urbanization, militarization, bureaucratization, economic stratification, and the change (called "latifundization") to a landholding system in which large estates, farmed by tenants while the owners often lived elsewhere, became more prevalent.

As to understanding the shape of the nation, a number of scholars would now claim that Saul ruled in the mode of a chieftain, whereas David ruled as king over a state. To use such language obviously suggests that a chief is different from a king and, more importantly, that the Israelite state developed quickly. The chief becomes necessary when complexities of various sorts (e.g., socio-economic stratification) require new forms of political leadership. The chiefdom rests on earlier forms of political organization, however, not on the centralized bureaucratic administration that was clearly present by the time of Solomon. The speed with which the transition from chief to king occurred in Israel was the result of numerous forces, among them the incredibly rapid acquisition of land and other economic resources by David, the development of trade routes on Israelite soil, and the need to integrate new populations into the pre-existing social system. David's military conquests required a state for proper administration of that which had been conquered. New administrative roles proliferated during the early years of the monarchy (see especially 1 Kings 4). The changes associated with the inception of monarchy proved formative for Israelite and Judahite society during the ensuing four centuries.

The social world of Israel changed significantly with the demise of the Judahite nation-state in 587 B.C.E. There were now numerous communities of those who worshiped the same God: some in Egypt, some in Mesopotamia, some on Cyprus, and, of course, some in Syria-Palestine. It would hardly be surprising for the social world of Machseiah, a mercenary living in Elephantine, to be markedly different from the social world of a priest (Ezekiel) living in exile in Mesopotamia. The situations were palpably different. Those in Elephantine consulted with authorities in Jerusalem about proper worship practices. However, those in Mesopotamian exile constituted a community which looked to itself for religious authority. That group possessed, as had earlier ones, priests, elders, and prophets, even a king in exile. And the elders continued to function there as had elders in urban contexts before the exile. No doubt, however, the means by which these various communities maintained their social and religious identities were similar, involving strategies of structural adaptation, like telling stories about heroes such as Esther, Daniel, and Joseph, all of whom flourished at foreign courts.

Exile became permanent for many, though some did return to territory in and around Jerusalem and attempt to recreate a community that stood in continuity with that of pre-monarchic times. Since the efforts of Zerubbabel and Joshua, Ezra and Nehemiah are typically associated with the advent of the second temple and the inception of Judaism, respectively, one must say both that something momentous did occur in the land and yet that return to the land would never again be a requirement either for the existence of Judean/Jewish communities or for the worship of their God.

The social world of those who lived in Judea after 520 B.C.E. was the world which saw the formal composition of much in the Old Testament. The Pentateuch was edited, the prophetical books collected and edited, much historical literature written. The political fortunes of this area were not under the control of those who worshiped the God of ancient Israel, though some may have had positions of importance as regional officials in the Persian empire. The narrowly circumscribed territory of Judah included new settlements and a number of military installations. Those who returned to the land competed for land ownership with those who had not gone into exile. Various means were used to determine who held power in the Judean community of the second temple. For example, during the fifth century it became important to trace one's genealogy to someone who had been in exile. In addition, there arose a new level of local officials, the "heads" of the father's houses, which were themselves different from groupings of the same name in the pre-exilic era.

In sum, the social worlds of Israel changed in marked ways both geographically and temporally, with the transition from village agriculture to urban statehood, from exiled communities to restored regional remnant.

Economic Life

During the monarchy, Israel's economy became much more diverse. Israel's agricultural activity now included the more fertile land of the coastal plain. Further, Israel could enter new markets because not only surpluses, but also goods in significant demand (e.g., wine and olive oil) were being produced. Instead of subsistence farming controlled by lineages, diverse modes of agricultural production were employed, including the use of larger estates, often controlled by royalty (so 1 Chr. 27.25–31), and sometimes by priests (Lev. 25.34; Joshua 21). In addition, new land was settled—particularly in the Negeb—and put into production using new strategies, i.e., runoff farming. Such developments presented the opportunity for the government to generate tax revenue, which was collected in the form of agricultural goods, thereby calling for storage systems owned not only by farmers but also by others, including the state.

Though trade-routes had developed in Syria-Palestine long before Israel emerged, the existence of the kingdoms would have facilitated the process of trade. Situated on the major north-south routes, whether inland or coastal, Syro-Palestinian cities such as Megiddo served and benefited from overland trade within that area and between the empires of

Egypt and Mesopotamia. First Kings 5–10 and Ezekiel 27–28 describe the sorts of goods conveyed in such trade activity, which, of course, included goods from naval commerce as well.

Perhaps no text serves as a better vignette of the new economic life of monarchic Israel than the one which depicts the vitality engendered by "a good wife" (Prov. 31.10–31). The household was still of primary importance as an economically productive entity, but it was now coupled with mercantile activity and capable of producing luxury goods.

The Social World of Israelite Religion

It has been a commonplace to think that theology or matters of faith are different from an individual's or a people's social world. That judgment is, however, erroneous. Attention to the most frequent form of psalm, the lament, demonstrates that the social world of friends and enemies as well as that of the legal system evoked considerable theological discourse in the Old Testament. Moreover, the literature of the Old Testament is rife with instances in which social conflict occurs over matters of what theology—one of peace or one of war—is appropriate to a particular occasion (see Jeremiah 28). In fact, the pivotal experience of liberation from slavery in Egypt enlivens a powerful theological tradition in which the God of Israel expresses concern for those who may be characterized with the stereotypic phrase, "the widow and orphan."

The Old Testament attests to a world in which the household was relatively self-sufficient, even as regards religious matters (so the shrine of Micah in Judg. 17.1–6). In the Iron Age, however, certain roles of religious specialists—such as the priest and the prophet—developed. Since not everyone exercised an official or priestly role, one may think of the general populace as a secular laity.

The social world of the priests during the Iron Age and Persian Period was one fraught with concerns about power and status. To be a priest was, at least in terms of public rhetoric, an ascribed, not an achieved status. A priest had to come from a family of priests, namely, the family which could trace its genealogy to Levi (Deut. 18.1–8; 33.8–9). Levites in the first temple period performed various tasks, including sacrifice as well as certain teaching and judicial work (Deut. 17.18). Moreover, the Levites lived throughout the land, although the nature of the so-called Levitical cities remains obscure (Josh. 21.1–42). According to Chronicles, the Levites had an important, though secondary, role, e.g., the service of song, carrying various ritual objects including the ark. It may well have been the case that families designated certain of their sons for priestly service and that they became priests; if so, they would have held an achieved, not an ascribed, status.

Though Levites had the status of priests, priestly power seems to have devolved on those priests who were associated with particular shrines or temples, and here again the association took the form of priestly "houses," which were defined in terms of patrilineal descent. (See, for example, the derogatory statements about Levites in Ezek. 44.10–14, a document that highlights the role of Zadokite priests. One may also theorize that Leviticus and Deuteronomy contain competing notions of priestly regulations.) Among the prominent houses were those of Eli at Shiloh, Amaziah at Bethel, and Zadok in Jerusalem. The house of Zadok, one of the two priestly houses associated with Jerusalem in the early monarchic period, gained power over the house of Abiathar, which was exiled to Anathoth (1 Kgs. 2.26). The "house of Aaron," unlike the other "houses," is a genealogical construct, which enables certain priests—probably Zadokites—to authenticate their status by tracing origins to Levi through Aaron (1 Chr. 24.1–19); a similar phenomenon may also have been at work in a priesthood that claimed Moses as its authenticating ancestor (Judg. 18.30). These were the priests who controlled the sacrificial system, particularly after the centralization of worship in Jerusalem associated with the reform of King Josiah. The high or chief priest is a role which became prominent in the second temple period; the term itself is used infrequently to describe a role in the first temple period.

The social world of ancient Israel was refracted in, as well as reinforced and revised by, the sacrificial system in which both priests and laity participated. Individual Israelites participated in the system according to their ability to pay; some would provide expensive offerings (a sheep), others something less valuable (a bird). The system provided rituals of two basic sorts: maintenance and integration. The first included sacrifices and offerings based on the calendar, viz., daily, weekly, monthly sacrifices (Numbers 28). Such regularity enhanced the notion of continuity in the life of the people. Non-calendrical sacrifices, e.g., guilt or sin offerings (Lev. 4.1–6.7), served the purpose of reintegrating the individual into the society after some infraction or misdeed had occurred. Sacrifices and other rituals constituted one important way in which Israel created a social identity that distinguished it from other peoples, as well as a way in which it addressed issues of internal social order.

Though priests could instruct the people in an authoritative way, whether by torah pronouncement or by the divine dice (*urim* and *thummim*), prophets provided another mode by means of which the deity could communicate with humanity. There was no absolute gap between prophet and priest; the prophets Ezekiel, Zechariah, and Jeremiah were priests. Prophets were intermediaries whose words and actions proclaimed the will of the deity to Israelites (and, in fact, other nations as well). Since communication includes both the proclamation and reception of a message, prophetic behavior was embedded in a social process, which involved people's reactions to prophets. The Old Testament makes it abundantly clear that prophets were not successful in swaying human economic or political behavior. They were, however, successful in delineating divine statements of judgment, which articulated the consequences of behavior that violated Israelite covenantal norms. Prophets, particularly those in the Neo-Babylonian period, announced radical changes in the social world of Israelites and Judahites: the end of a monarchic state and removal from the land.

Both priests and prophets represented a fairly orthodox religious viewpoint, which was not shared by all Israelites. One may gain some perspective on the popular religion by reading the prophetic literature or religiously prescriptive literature, e.g., Hosea or Deuteronomy 18, to see what behavior priests and prophets condemned, particularly the worship of other deities. Archaeologists have discovered amulets, household shrines, and inscriptions attesting veneration of such deities. In addition to popular or household religion, the Old Testament attests an upper class form of religious scepticism (Ecclesiastes).

In sum, the social world of Israelite religion was complex, including various institutions (e.g., numerous temples), various roles (e.g., priests and prophets), and various realms of religious behavior (e.g., the "official" religion of the state as well as the religious practices of the people, particularly as those addressed the concerns of the household).

SUGGESTIONS FOR FURTHER READING

Clements, Ronald, ed. *The World of Ancient Israel: Sociological, Anthropological and Political Perspectives.* Cambridge: Cambridge University Press, 1989.

Frick, Frank. *The City in Ancient Israel.* SBLDS, 36; Missoula, MT: Scholars Press, 1977.

Gottwald, Norman. *The Hebrew Bible: A Socio-Literary Introduction.* Philadelphia: Fortress Press, 1985.

Meyers, Carol. *Discovering Eve: Ancient Israelite Women in Context.* New York: Oxford University Press, 1988.

Overholt, Thomas. *Channels of Prophecy: The Social Dynamics of Prophetic Activity.* Minneapolis: Fortress, 1989.

Rogerson, John. *Anthropology of the Old Testament.* Oxford: Blackwell, 1978.

Wilson, Robert. *Sociological Approaches to the Old Testament.* Philadelphia: Fortress Press, 1984.

The Social World
of the New Testament

WAYNE A. MEEKS

Understanding the literature of any author or group requires identifying its appropriate social context. To ask about the social context within which the New Testament ought to be read is really to ask several different questions. First, we have to distinguish the social world of each document from the very different situations of Christians in the second to fourth centuries when the individual writings were being assembled into a "New Testament," not to mention the later contexts, down to the present, in which the resulting Bible has been read and understood. Second, the settings of the particular writings differ from one another. The Gospel of Mark, for example, addresses a situation quite different from that of the Gospel of John. Third, some of the documents describe a social world that is different from the social world of the author. Matthew, for example, describes the activities of Jesus in mostly rural parts of Galilee prior to the Jewish revolt of 66–72 c.e., but writes for a Greek-speaking audience, probably in Antioch or one of the smaller cities of Syria, at a time when Jewish life in Syria-Palestine has been devastated and transformed by the war and its aftermath. Matthew's world inevitably affects his description. Further, the way the author portrays the world may be different from the picture of the world that was in the minds of most of the original audience; that seems to be the case, for instance, with the Revelation of John. Finally, the image of the ancient world that we form with the help of historical research does not fully coincide with the world as seen by the people living in it then.

The generalizations that follow here apply for the most part to the first century of Christianity's existence. This description must be taken as a very large-scale map, wanting detailed adjustment to particular times and places.

City and Country

The division between rural and urban societies was sharp in the minds of many persons in antiquity, but that division was quite different from the separation between rural and urban people in modern industrial societies. The economy of the Roman empire was overwhelmingly agrarian. The wealth that counted most was invested in land, and the ownership of more and more was concentrated in the hands of fewer and fewer people. Ancient cities were much smaller than ours; no one was very far from the land. In the smallest cities a large part of the population worked farms outside the city. The institutions of modern commodity markets did not exist to separate urban consumer from rural producer. Nevertheless, there were strong emotional divisions between city and country people—the results of differences in wealth, status, language, and style. For the elite the cities were the places for learning and displaying the culture of privilege. Cities were thus the focal points of Hellenization and Romanization of the provinces, and the citizens looked down their noses at the more "backward" rustics. Rural people, on the other hand, had good reason to feel exploited by the city folk. Agents of an absentee landlord sent to collect the owner's share of the harvest—like those in Jesus' parable (Mk.12.1–9)—frequently met a violent reception. The world of Jesus may have been mostly rural (so Mark portrays it), but the Christian movement quickly established itself in the world of the Greek-speaking cities.

Levels of Status

There were two classes in Roman society: those few who had wealth, power, public offices, education, eloquence, and manners and the vast majority who did not. There was no middle class in our sense of the words. Legal codes of the second century distinguished the "more honorable" from the "more humble," formalizing older practice. The difference determined not only who had to swallow insults from whom, but what one could expect from a court of law. The same crime could bring crucifixion to the "insignificant" person, exile to one "more honorable." Dream manuals and divination texts give quite different interpretations of the same omens depending on whether the dreamer is rich or poor, slave or free, of a high or low occupation.

Within each class, there were further sharp divisions. At the very top were the formally defined "orders": the Roman senators, next the knights, below them the decurions or councilors of provincial cities. Superimposed on these old orders were the emperor and his household, who both manipulated the orders by patronage and limited their power. The "household of Caesar" under some of the emperors acted as almost the civil service of the empire—competing with the prerogatives of the knights and the decurions and even undermining the prestige of the senators. It especially galled members of the old aristocracy that a freed person (former slave) of the emperor might, as a member of the household, sometimes exercise power and influence greater than that of many a senator. The household of Caesar afforded one of the few opportunities for upward social mobility in ancient society.

Slave and Free

Even among the masses of the "more humble," people were ever conscious of differences of social level, though those differences were not so clearly marked as among the elite. The most fundamental difference was between slave and free. Most urban slaves could expect to be freed by around age thirty, but both they and their children would continue to carry a social stigma. The importance of that stigma varied, however. In a colony like Corinth, inscriptions show that many of the leading citizens were freed slaves or their descendants. Moreover, the slave of an important family, and above all of Caesar, might tower above an ordinary free worker. Tombstones of such slaves recorded their status with pride. In a large household, epitaphs of slaves often distinguished those who had more prestigious functions (nurse, doctor, valet). When Paul called himself "a slave of Christ," the title did not convey only humility to many members of his audience.

Slavery was a ubiquitous but varied factor in ancient society. The precise numbers of slaves are unknown; in Pergamum, one of the few cities for which there is specific evidence, they were about one-third of the population. The quality of a slave's life varied from the relatively happy state of managers of imperial offices or of businesses of wealthy families to the misery endured by gangs of laborers on rural estates or, even worse, in mines.

As an urban phenomenon, early Christianity did not include the most deprived groups of the society, rural workers both slave and free. The Christian groups did include both slaves and slave owners from the beginning, and there is some evidence that persons with the ambiguous status of "freedpersons" played a particularly large role in the movement's growth. A movement like Christianity was bound to experience some tensions, for it brought together members of different social levels and its baptismal ritual declared that for those who had "put on Christ" such old dichotomies as Jew-Greek, slave-free, male-female had been overcome (Gal. 3.28). Paul's eloquent appeal to Philemon to receive his slave Onesimus back "no longer as a slave but as more than a slave: as a dear brother" (Philem. 16) represents one possible resolution of those tensions. More commonly, the Christian groups reaffirmed the standard rules of the hierarchical household, insisting that slaves "give entire obedience to your earthly masters" (Col. 3.22; cf. Eph. 6.5; 1 Pet. 2.18). In the second century, Christians had to be warned occasionally not to use church money to purchase the freedom of slaves (Ignatius, *To Polycarp* 4.3), but some ascetic Christians urged emancipation on principle (*Acts of Thomas* 9.83; cf. *Acts of Peter* 28). For the most part, however, Christian attitudes toward slavery reflected those of the larger society.

Rich and Poor

The relative peace imposed on the Mediterranean basin by the Romans in the first two centuries of our era, together with the mobility made possible by Roman roads and comparatively safe sea routes, created conditions under which many people could enjoy some prosperity. The most visible consequence was that families already well off became still richer, while the poorest members of the society, especially peasants who had previously held small plots of their own, were driven into even greater extremes of dependency. Commercial ventures, however, produced new fortunes for some of the not-so-rich as well. Although the old elites disdained trade and crafts, they often engaged in commerce at arm's length, employing their slaves or freedpersons as agents. Money made in trade was often invested in land, which was thought to be a more proper as well as a more stable form of wealth. The distance, both economic and social, between the richest and the poorest grew steadily in the period around the time Christianity began.

Sympathy for the poor was not common in ancient society. Rich people felt obliged to spend, often lavishly, in gifts to their native cities and sometimes elsewhere as well. But these gifts were only very rarely devoted to projects that would directly aid disadvantaged members of the society. They rather produced conspicuous monuments, games, or spectacles that would redound to the honor of the donors. The Greek language distinguished the working poor, just able to eke out a living (penēs) from the destitute, who must beg (ptōchos). It is the latter term that is ordinarily used in the New Testament. Jesus' saying, "Happy are you poor" (Lk. 6.20, author's translation), would have seemed an absolute contradiction in terms to most ancient people. Christianity, however, inherited the vigorous Jewish tradition that God cared especially for the poor and judged the community by its attention to their needs. This tradition is voiced with special vividness in the Letter of James, but it echoes widely in early Christian literature—for example, in the Gospels, as a theme of the two-volume work Luke-Acts, and in Paul's extended effort to raise funds from the Gentile churches for "the poor among God's people at Jerusalem" (Rom. 15.26; cf. 1 Cor. 16.1–4; 2 Cor. 8–9; Gal. 2.10).

Men and Women

By the first century C.E., women in both the Greek and Latin cultural areas enjoyed more freedom and more legal rights than had been the case in classical Greece and Rome. Marriage came to be regarded more nearly as an agreement between equals, and the woman as well as the man could initiate divorce. Though single women still needed guardians in law, they were now free to choose them. Women owned property, conducted businesses, appeared in public, became benefactors of cities and patrons of clubs. Among the lower levels of society, women frequently labored alongside their husbands in crafts and trade, like the couple Prisca and Aquila so important as patrons of Paul's mission, or a husband-and-wife team of doctors commemorated in an inscription. A few philosophers, like the Roman Stoic Musonius Rufus, thought women ought to have the same education as men, even including training in philosophy. Still, the society remained fundamentally patriarchal in its organization and sentiments, and the changes just mentioned brought a backlash of extreme misogyny from some traditionalists, like the satirist Juvenal or the Jewish intellectual Philo.

Women appear among the first followers of Jesus, both as disciples and as financial supporters. Women leaders and patronesses were especially important in the Pauline communities, for Paul's letters frequently mention women as "fellow workers" or as benefactors. There were female prophets in local congregations as well as traveling missionaries, though sometimes their behavior provoked controversy (1 Cor. 11.2–16; Rev. 2.20–23). The importance of the household in the formation of urban Christianity led the Pauline groups and others to reaffirm the traditional role of women as "subordinate" to their husbands, just as they did in the case of slaves. Nevertheless, the wealthy female benefactor continued to be important for the growth of Christianity, as it frequently was for other cults and associations. Nor did the female charismatic leader entirely disappear in the second-century church, though the reaction to such figures grew more vehement. The apocryphal *Acts of Paul and Thecla* depicts a young, aristocratic woman who responds to Paul's preaching by assuming a celibate life, adopting the hairstyle and traveling garments of a man, and imitating Paul as a missionary. The author of the Pastoral Epistles warns against such women (1 Tim. 2.9–15). Female prophets would be important in the second-century millenarian movement (believing that Christ's rule, the millennium, would come soon) called Montanism, and women would also gain an honored place among the early martyrs, e.g., Blandina at Lyons, Perpetua and Felicitas in North Africa.

Friends and Patrons

It is remarkable that a society so egregiously unequal could have remained as stable as it did for so long. Open revolts are almost unknown in the period of our concern. In the case of the most obvious exception, the revolt in Judea and Galilee of 66–72 C.E., economic and social inequalities did play an important role, but they would hardly have led to war without the specific combination of resentment against Roman rule, exploitative taxation, and affronts to local religious sensibilities. By and large the masses of the population accepted their position at the bottom of the steep social pyramid.

The relative stability of the system is to be explained by its intricate network of reciprocity, which held its tensions in check. Between social equals, the exchange of favors and courtesies was carefully balanced by the conventions of friendship, which the Romans called *amicitia*. *Amicitia* set certain limits to the exuberant competitiveness that characterized society in the early empire. The ruling groups of a city consisted in a rather small circle of "friends," who jealously eyed one another's advantages but shared a common sense of dependence on their remote patrons in Rome and of superiority to those beneath them in their town.

Reciprocity between unequals was even more important for the stability of the social order. The powerful were linked with the weak through ties of patronage or *clientela*. Roman law had defined the relationship in the particular case of a freed slave, who remained under the protection of the former master, now patron, for life—in exchange for specific obligations ranging from daily appearances to salute the patron at an appointed time to political support, service in business enterprises, and other kinds of assistance. In the imperial age, analogous relations of protection and dependence extended to every corner of the society. At the top, the emperor and members of the Roman senate became patrons, and thus commanded the loyalty, of the local aristocracies of each of the thousand cities that made up the Roman Empire. Further down the scale, every person of some wealth and power used those advantages to put people of lesser status under obligation. At the bottom—indeed at every level except the very top—a person's welfare and any possible chance of improving one's position depended on the favor of someone higher up. The position and prestige of the person higher up, in turn, were enhanced by enlarging the number of dependents. Hence benefactions brought obligation, obligation yielded service and submission, service and submission earned protection.

Honor and Shame

"Discharge your obligations to everyone; pay tax and levy, reverence and respect, to those to whom they are due": the advice that Paul wrote to the Roman Christians (Rom. 13.7) sums up prudential rules for survival in the status-conscious society of the Roman empire. "Reverence and respect," more commonly translated "fear and honor," are pervasive indices of a person's, or a family's, place in a stratified system of relationships. One's welfare depended—and one's life might well depend—on knowing precisely whom one had better fear and to whom one was obliged to show honor.

"Honor" and "shame" in ancient society—and in many less-industrialized societies even today—do not refer primarily to private emotions but to public demonstrations of the behavior, the values, and the deserts deemed proper or improper for people, depending on their place in the society. A misbehaving child in a modern Greek village will be chided with "Aren't you ashamed!" An adult behaving improperly may be asked by an acquaintance, "Have you no *philotimo*?" *Philotimo* corresponds to the ancient Greek *philotimia*, "love of honor," which names the most powerful and pervasive root of ambition in ancient society. It was the pursuit of public honor by wealthy individuals that produced most of the grand monuments whose ruins still inspire our wonder at the cities of antiquity.

The monuments never lacked conspicuous inscriptions to tell passersby that So-and-so "erected this at [the donor's] own expense, in payment of a vow" or "in return for being elected" to some municipal office. Tombstones of the mighty recorded who they were, of what family, and what they had done—what offices they had held, how much they had spent on their home towns. Obviously the more wealthy and powerful one was, the "more honorable," as the second-century law codes mentioned above made clear.

Behaving in a way thought beneath one, on the other hand, brought shame, on both the individual and the family. The aristocrats of Rome were scandalized when the emperor Nero masqueraded as a charioteer, an actor, or a musician. To put on airs above one's position was risky, too, for failure to bring it off would make the person and his family a laughingstock. The Roman satirists delight in lampooning the manners of the newly rich. Any untoward public behavior might bring shame upon a person's family and clan; no wonder Jesus' family tried to restrain him when they thought, "He is out of his mind" (Mk. 3.21). To be unable to repay an obligation was also shameful, of course—unless the obligated person was obviously the social inferior of the other, or acknowledged the other as his patron. In that case the client renounced any claim to be the equal of the other and could enjoy the dim reflection of the patron's honor. For the lower classes, submissive modesty was a becoming virtue, as well as a practical necessity. For persons of higher status deliberately to lower themselves, on the other hand, was thought bizarre, or the political trickery of a demagogue. For "humility" to become a virtue, as it did in Christian moral discourse, required a new way of thinking about status and a new paradigm of power.

The new paradigm was the Christian story of the Messiah who was crucified, the one who was "in the form of God" but "made himself nothing, assuming the form of a slave . . ., humbled himself, and was obedient, even to the point of death, death on a cross" (Phil. 2.7–8), who "was rich, yet for your sake he became poor" (2 Cor. 8.9). Thus it was understandable to Christian readers, though it would have been astonishing to anyone else, that the apostles would be seen "rejoicing that they had been found worthy to suffer humiliation [lit., "to be dishonored"] for the sake of the name" (Acts 5.41). To be sure a Stoic philosopher, like Musonius Rufus, might urge the wise person to ignore insults, even a slap in the face—but because thus the philosopher won still greater honor by exhibiting his intellectual superiority to the insulter. The Christians were formulating a different sort of ideal, in which a person insulted by a slap on the cheek should turn the other. The Christian, too, expected to receive greater honor thereby, but in the form of the "glory" with which God would reward the faithful at the final judgment of the world.

In practice, not surprisingly, the ancient sentiments about honor and shame, integrally part of the positional society and households in which the Christian communities were embedded, lived on in the churches, in greater or less tension with the paradigm of humility. The churches, too, had to depend on the patronage of their wealthier members—sometimes even of non-members—for the housing and protection of their meetings, and those patrons would expect a certain deference in return. Conflicts between such traditional forms of benefaction and power and the claims of charismatic leaders, prophets and itinerant apostles, can be documented in the later church and may well lie behind some of the conflicts revealed in the letters of Paul. Some of the Corinthian Christians evidently felt, too, that Paul had shamed them by refusing to accept financial support from them (2 Cor. 11.7–8). As the institutional structure of the church became more formal in later centuries, it became common for bishops to be drawn from the "more honorable" levels of society, who could combine traditional forms of patronage with the power of office.

Kinship and Households

Kinship provides the basic structures of a society. In classical Greece and early Rome, the tribes, clans, families, and households were carefully organized and regulated—at least for the more prestigious segments of society. In the more mobile society of the Roman Principate, family ties, particularly of immigrants, were looser but still important. Both Greece and Rome were patrilineal societies; that is, inheritance and the lines of connection that counted most were strictly by the male line. In the Hellenistic age and in the period of the Roman empire, restrictions on inheritance by women were reduced, and in other ways as well kinship from the female side became more significant.

The early Christian groups were formed by conversion rather than by membership in existing units. Indeed, in any society the convert frequently finds that ties to family and friends are disrupted by the attachment to the new cult. This experience was familiar to proselytes to Judaism, and early Christian literature frequently acknowledges the sense of dislocation and hostility that the convert might encounter, for example in the saying of Jesus, "there is no one who has given up home, brothers or sisters, mother, father or children, or land, for my sake and for the gospel, who will not receive in this age a hundred times as much . . . and persecutions besides" (Mk. 10.29–30). The Christian communities used the language of kinship extensively to describe the new relationships within the movement: all who were baptized were "God's children" and thus called one another "brother" or "sister."

Nevertheless, existing kinship was not always simply disregarded for the sake of the new "family." Although there are several passages in the Gospels that suggest Jesus' own family opposed or misunderstood his mission, after his death James "the Lord's brother" quickly became the central leader of the Jerusalem circle of Jesus' followers (e.g., Gal. 1.19).

Further, we are told several times in the Acts of the Apostles about conversions of entire households (e.g., Acts 16.25–34).

The household was the fundamental unit of the Greek or Roman city. It was a larger and more complex entity than the modern family, constituted by lines of protection and dependence rather than kinship alone. A household of even moderate means might include not only relatives but also slaves, freedpersons, hired workers, and perhaps tenants and partners in trade or craft. The "household assembly," to which greetings are sent several times in the letters of Paul and his followers, was the basic cell of the Christian movement. In this respect the Christian movement followed a pattern that was common in the adaptation of religious groups and other kinds of association introduced into a city.

The household provided the place needed for the Christian meetings and a natural point of connection with other parts of urban society, for the Christian group could grow along the network of relationships to which the household belonged: kinship, friendship, and patronage. The household base limited the practical size of a meeting to a dozen or so at most, however, so expansion entailed the multiplication of separate household meetings in each city. One result would be that factions could easily emerge. There were also internal tensions, noted above, between the ethos of the household and novel paradigms of Christian belief and between the positional modes of power and charismatic leaders. Nevertheless, the household continued to be a fundamental organizing center of Christianity and the model for larger patterns of organization in its emerging institutions.

Citizens and Aliens

The cultural mixing of the Hellenistic age, followed by the mobility made possible by Roman roads and Roman pacification of the Mediterranean and lands around it, meant that large numbers of people settled in cities away from their places of birth. Immigrants from the same homeland formed associations, usually centering on the worship of the patron deities of their nations or home cities. The associations provided not only occasions for sociability and a continuing sense of identity, but also a base of power for negotiating with other groups. Resident aliens suffered legal disadvantages compared with citizens; *Roman* citizens, however, enjoyed special privileges anywhere in the empire. Gradually, under the Principate, Roman citizenship began to be extended to especially favored individuals in the provinces.

Jews living in the Greek and Roman cities followed a pattern of adaptation similar to that of other immigrant groups. In some respects their situation was more difficult than that of the others, however, for their exclusive monotheism prevented observant Jews from participating in the cultic acts that were a constant part of civic life. Most Jews were thus

barred from citizenship and its prerogatives, until legal changes in the
third century made their participation easier. Moreover, their scruples
about polytheistic worship were frequently regarded, in a society increasingly pluralistic, as signs of intolerance. In the competition for scarce
goods and privileges, Jews of the Greco-Roman cities thus frequently
suffered from prejudices and discrimination, which in a few instances led
to violence—like the attacks on the Jewish community of Alexandria in
38 c.e., described by Philo as an eye-witness. Beginning with Julius Caesar, however, the emperors of Rome had guaranteed the rights of the
Jews to maintain their distinctive customs, and Jewish communities
in trouble with local factions often appealed to the emperor for help, as
did the Alexandrian Jews. Jews living in Palestine, except for the local
aristocracies directly dependent on the Romans for protection and advancement, were much less likely to regard the Romans as allies. The
Romans tried to balance off the interests of the different groups in each
city in order to protect the tenuous peace of the public order. Most often
that put the emperor's agents on the side of the Jews when they were
under attack, but if the Jews initiated an attack, as in Judea in 66 c.e.,
in North Africa in the second decade of the second century, and in
Judea again in 132 c.e., the Roman response was ruthless military suppression.

The Social Forms of Early Christianity

The followers of Jesus were, in the beginning, a renewal movement
within Palestinian Judaism. The Roman governor Pilate perceived it as a
threat to the Roman order and undertook to stop it by crucifying its
leader, in the same way that he would crush a similar movement among
the Samaritans a half dozen years later. When the Christian movement
spread to the cities, it began among the Jewish communities. However, it
soon attracted Gentiles as well, probably beginning, as the Book of Acts
suggests, with those already attracted to Judaism. Its formation into
household groups facilitated its separation from the organized Jewish
communities, though in some places Christians continued to be found in
synagogues as late as the fifth century.

To outsiders, the Christian groups would have looked like the voluntary associations or clubs that were so popular in all parts of the empire.
Some of these clubs were neighborhood associations, some based on ethnic likeness, others on common crafts or trades, all with at least superficial religious ceremonies. In some ways the Christian groups resembled
religious cults, with their initiatory ritual of baptism and their sacred
meals. Yet they performed no sacrifices, staged no processions, and in
general had few of the outward rites typical of ancient religion. The
Christian practice of moral training and exhortation resembled some of
the more tightly organized philosophical schools, especially the Epicure-
ans, and so did their expectation of entry by conversion. Their sense of

being a single people, transcending local connections, was quite exceptional compared to these other models. That sense obviously came from the heritage of Israel, with its scriptural notions of covenant and election. The needs of the active missionary enterprise of first-century Christians incidentally gave to the concept of a universal People of God some very practical expressions, through the repeated visits of apostles or their delegates to new communities and through the exchange of letters. The social forms that evolved in the early decades of the Christian movement thus had many partial parallels in ancient society, but there emerged a combination that was in some respects unique.

SUGGESTIONS FOR FURTHER READING

Alföldy, Géza. *The Social History of Rome.* Trans. by David Braund and Frank Pollock. London: Routledge and Kegan Paul; Baltimore: Johns Hopkins University Press, 1988.

MacMullen, Ramsay. *Roman Social Relations 50 B.C. to A.D. 284.* New Haven and London: Yale University Press, 1974.

Malherbe, Abraham J. *Social Aspects of Early Christianity.* Second edition, enlarged. Philadelphia: Fortress Press, 1983.

Meeks, Wayne A. *The First Urban Christians: The Social World of the Apostle Paul.* New Haven and London: Yale University Press, 1983.

Shelton, Jo Ann. *As the Romans Did: A Sourcebook in Roman Social History.* New York: Oxford University Press, 1988.

Stambaugh, John E., and David L. Balch. *The New Testament in Its Social Environment.* Philadelphia: Westminster Press, 1986.

Theissen, Gerd. *Sociology of Early Palestinian Christianity.* Trans. by John Bowden. Philadelphia: Fortress Press, 1978.

THE LITERATURE OF
THE BIBLICAL COMMUNITIES

Communities and Canon

JAMES A. SANDERS

Contemporary Western Christians and Jews have in large part lost touch with the thought patterns of their early ancestors of biblical faith. Most think of religion as a personal matter and concern, something between them as individuals and God. Churches and synagogues are seen as groups of individuals who live in proximity to each other and find it convenient to get together for worship, religious education, and community service; and people imagine that it has always been so. Communities of faith are made up of individuals, and while the whole may indeed be more than the sum of those who belong to a particular church or synagogue, that whole is no more complex than other such community organizations.

Awareness of the historical dimension of Judaism or Christianity is often vague and hardly more compelling than with other apparently comparable social entities that had their origins before the present generation was born. Such lack of historical awareness is found especially in those Christian denominations and sects which stress the importance of a personal saving experience and individual decision-making, conjoined with insistence that their particular group takes all its cues for faith and order from the Bible only. This lack of historical awareness is fortunately less the case for most Jews whose nurture in Judaism of necessity stresses its historical dimensions and, in the past half century, its relation to Israel both past and present.

The Bible as a Community Book

The Bible is the churches' or the synagogues' book. It is a community book, was formed in ancient communities of faith, and was shaped to be read in community.

The recent tendency of most Westerners to think of the Bible as the book they should read privately and studiously if they are really serious about their faith makes for distance in thought pattern between them and those who passed along these texts. Moderns might even ask why the Bible is read aloud in community as a central part of worship. The priest or pastor might, instead, simply ask the people to read quietly and privately a particular passage or passages from Bibles provided in pew racks or brought to service individually. But, until the advent of widespread literacy in the last two centuries, the private alternative to communal reading was limited. Interestingly, the common Hebrew word for Scripture, *Miqra,* is not based on the verb "to write" (as is "scripture" from Latin) but on the Hebrew verb "to read aloud" or "to call out." The few literate members of a community would, whether in worship or study sessions, read Scripture aloud in manageable portions, in the hearing of the whole congregation, for interpretation and common understanding.

A good case in point might be Luke's congregation in the first century for whom he first gathered his sources for study of the work of God in Christ (the Gospel) and in the early churches (Acts of the Apostles). It is very clear from even a cursory reading of Luke and Acts that Luke and his largely gentile congregation must have been quite familiar with Hebrew Scripture in its early Greek translation (the Septuagint), since Luke constantly presupposes quite an in-depth knowledge of large portions of this material. In fact Scripture was just as important to the formation of Luke's two volumes as the Christian sectarian sources (Mark and the sayings source "Q") he undoubtedly also had available. Many of his most telling and subtle points are scored only if one knows Scripture quite well indeed. In our contemporary world, people are astonished by such evidence of comprehensive knowledge of the content of Scripture in a period prior to extensive literacy. Moreover, the shared reading-hearing of Scripture was critical to the individual's sense of identity and group membership.

Canon and Calendar

Enduring communities are characterized by marks of identity. A person or family, even in a foreign land or in a *polis* (city) of plural cultures, can be identified by observing or practicing such marks.

In Judaism and Christianity, as in most religions, there are two basic identity-giving marks: canon and calendar. If a neighbor celebrates Christmas in early January one immediately knows that he or she is a member of an Orthodox Christian community; if a neighbor celebrates Hanukkah rather than Christmas one knows that neighbor is a member of a Jewish community of faith; if a neighbor observes Ramadan one knows the neighbor is Muslim. But such marks are not primarily for the information of neighbors; they are first and foremost means whereby each new generation in a community may know who they are and what they stand for.

Knowledge of one's canon of Scripture gained in community provides in-depth faith identity. Knowledge of Scripture recited in community is a principal means whereby each new generation of that community may know who they are and what they stand for, wherever they happen to live or whatever may happen to them. On the other hand, if one's identity is primarily shaped by definitions acquired in the secular community, one's individual reading of Scripture may create distance between the reader and Scripture's story. Abraham and Sarah in such an individual reading may remain simply remote figures in history; and such reading is encouraged by the modern mind-set and supported to a large extent by the tenets and tendencies of western scholarship, with its concern for sources of the literature and the origins of individual biblical figures. By contrast, when the Abraham-Sarah story (and its Jewish and Christian sequels) are read in a faith community, they become primary marks of an individual's identity beyond any trait peculiar to the individual alone. The faith community becomes thereby the principal identity-giving force, and the individual knows herself or himself as a person within that community. Not only is the community more than the sum of its parts, it (rather than the individual) is the starting point for self-understanding.

The power of the community so perceived can be overwhelming and even abusive to the individual. The Westerner who travels for the first time to third-world nations is often impressed with how dehumanizing and oppressive such communities can be. But third-world citizens traveling to the West often perceive the opposite danger: the disintegration of any sense of community, the denigration of community values, and the abusive pursuit of "self-realization" which cares little or nothing for even the closest neighbors or their plight. The Renaissance in the West brought many correctives to the community's smothering of individual gifts and graces. But the loss of community brings its own pains and voids, including a lack of consciousness of identity by which the individual gains a sense of roots and of fulfillment which spans generations and even ages.

Within the Bible there is a rather poignant debate or dialogue about individual responsibility within the community of faith. The very concept of covenant, which pervades both testaments, stresses corporate or community responsibility. There are several forms of covenant manifest in the Hebrew Bible, but they all deal with God's relation with corporate Israel. That is basic, but within that relationship individual responsibility eventually became a conscious issue of faith and obedience. The basic statement of corporate responsibility may be found clearly stated in Exod. 34.6–7: ". . . the LORD, the LORD, a God . . . who punishes children and grandchildren to the third and the fourth generation for the iniquity of their fathers." And that concept is never completely abandoned. Somewhere between the defeat and destruction of the Northern Kingdom of Israel (722 B.C.E.) and that of the Southern Kingdom of Judah (586 B.C.E.) there was, however, considerable debate about the relation of individual to corporate responsibility (Jer. 31.29–34; Ezek. 18; Gen. 18.16–33). In the rise of Judaism out of the ashes of defeat, after the destruction of Jerusalem by Babylonia in 586 B.C.E., the notion of individual as well as corporate responsibility undoubtedly was very important in helping Jews scattered all over the Near East to survive in the belief that they could be obedient, could please God, and could avoid being punished again because of the manifold sins of their ancestors (Ps. 1; Ezra 9.6–15; Neh. 9.32–37; *et passim*). The covenant was still with Israel as a people, but within it individuals would express both faith and obedience. The classical understanding of Judaism arose out of this fruitful tension: "A Jew is called to the service of God and Judaism is the expression of that service."

Still today, by following weekly synagogue lessons, Jews throughout the world read in community the entire Pentateuch, or Torah, each year, just as Christians throughout the world read traditional lectionaries in cycle. Read in this way, Scripture as canon also provides each faith community with a common sense of values; members know what is expected of them as individuals and as a community. A canon provides answers to the two basic questions of life—"who are we?" and "what should we do?"—in ever-changing circumstances and situations.

Even while canon was only emerging (before Scripture had a particular structure), it had an identity-defining function in the community. Early oral traditions about what God had done for and with ancestors in the faith functioned in the precanonical period in much the same way oral recitations of Scripture in community function even yet. This steady and constant rehearsal of the roots of faith-identity keep that identity ever fresh, because the traditions are heard in ever-changing situations. This canonical process has provided a filtering factor, so that only those traditions survived which were adaptable to new situations and were truly life-giving. That is, the traditions which persisted were capable over and over again of reviving a sense of continuing identity in different situations. The same process of community recitation has provided the ongoing community with fresh strength to be obedient to the abiding principles of that identity even when the precise modes of obedience had to be altered and modified to fit new circumstances.

This on-going function of canon, whether in its early oral and fluid stages of repetition/recitation or in its later more stable stages of recitation of Scripture, is called *norma normans,* a Latin expression literally meaning "norm norming." It is Scripture as canon at work in the community, doing its thing again and again for each new generation, but marvelously never in quite precisely the same way each time. Each new set of circumstances brings a slightly different (or in the case of trauma a radically different) light to bear on hearing again the old story or stipulation. Traditionally this has been identified as the on-going work of God's *shekinah* or holy spirit. Believing communities that have survival power thus understand God to be giving continuing guidance through the past (Scripture) and in the present (the spirit). Word and spirit are the two power-giving elements of the faith of a believing community. Sometimes they have seemed to move together to provide the strength needed in given situations, sometimes they have seemed at odds.

At those times of crisis when new situations have seemed to demand new thinking and new departures have been indicated, word and spirit have sometimes seemed at odds. However, eventually Scripture has been found to contain within it the grounding needed for the community to "recapitulate and transcend" the crisis with identity intact, albeit reshaped for the new day. Is this experience of the flexibility of canon purely "eisegesis," that is, reading the new into the old? No. Scripture by its very nature and because of its history of formation in canonical *process* is adaptable for life. How so? Those traditions in which early communities found value for their continuing common lives, and which they recited again and again in ever-changing circumstances in their early histories, are the self-authenticating ones which make up Scripture. These traditions had the potential of becoming canonical because, from their first use, they were sufficiently multivalent to speak to different, changing situations.

But canon as *norma normata,* a Latin expression meaning "norm normed," or shaped in a certain way, is also pluralistic to a certain extent. When one speaks of "canon" one must specify of which canon and of which community one speaks. Community does affect the shape of canon. Though close to each other in content, the short Jewish canon of the Hebrew Bible, the Protestant first testament which has the same books but a different order, the longer Roman Catholic canon which includes books important to some pre-Christian Jewish sects, or the several Orthodox canons, do differ from each other in ways that are significant for each community. Yet, each of these collections is pluralistic within itself, to the extent of providing internal dialogues on many issues a community or an individual in the community might face. That is, even if one thinks of a canon as being a certain set of books, there is both considerable fluidity of order and content, according to which canon one addresses, and a certain amount of dialogue within each one. As a result of the historical process of canon formation, a community's canon has the voice or voices necessary to address new situations—whether a community is dealing with stability and the threats of prosperity or with discontinuity and the threats of trauma. If it was time to settle down, God was called on as God Most High; if it was time to move on to new ventures, forced or voluntary, God was called on as a guiding deity on the move and ready to accompany the community in pilgrimage. But because of the compression of so many views of God into one, it was eventually believed that even the most high God was capable of "going with" and "being with" the people whatever their fate (compare Exod. 33.16 and 1 Chr. 29.10–16).

The canonical process was thus parallel to the monotheizing process, the process of viewing Reality whole. Thus, there is movement from normal ancient belief in numerous deities, each with differing attributes and "job descriptions," to belief in the One God, with a heavenly council and heavenly hosts (made up undoubtedly of the many gods of normal polytheism but now denied all power in themselves). That God is seen as sole God of all creation, heaven, earth, and even the chthonian (under-world) regions—indeed, the God of risings and fallings, victory and defeat, life and death (e.g., Deut. 32.39; 1 Sam. 2.6–8; Lk. 1.52–53).

It was believed, even so, that the one God of all that is had a special relation to the Abraham-Sarah family and community (Deut. 32.8–9) for whom God had in mind a special mission and task toward all peoples (Gen. 12.1–3; Isa. 2.2–4 and 51.1–6). While even those passages noted can be matched by others for dialogue within the canon, there is clearly a monotheizing thrust to the whole epitomized in the first three of the Ten Commandments: no polytheism, no idolatry, and no co-opting of God's name for one particular view or agenda (Exod. 20.1–7; Deut. 5.6–11). The one God is God of all peoples. There is an integrity to Reality which is beyond description and proof but is the first article of biblical faith for all communities which find their identity in its basic story and shape their lives in its light.

The Stabilization of Text and Canon

The formation of the canon and the history of the text of the Bible are closely linked. The text of the Bible is based upon the numerous manuscripts of both testaments which have been inherited from ancient and medieval believing communities. We are directly dependent on those communities for the text we attempt to establish for reading and translation today. The manuscripts used for determining the most responsible and critical text include the original-language Hebrew, Aramaic, and Greek texts of the two testaments and also early translations or versions made in communities which spoke languages other than those of the originals. No two manuscripts are exactly the same; in fact, there are often thousands of differences among them, and the more ancient the manuscripts the more fluid they tend to be. For each testament there was a distinct period in which efforts at stabilization of the text began to be made. In the case of the Hebrew Bible, the work began apparently in the middle of the first century B.C.E. and was largely complete by the end of the first century C.E. In the case of the New Testament, standardization came about in the course of the fourth century, after the conversion of Constantine. Before those periods, for each testament, the manuscripts available exhibit a limited fluidity of text.

One needs to understand that all copyists and translators of biblical texts had two major responsibilities, to the past and to the present. That is, one responsibility was to the inherited text; the second was to the community of which the tradent (transmitter) was a member and which he or she served. All tradents wanted their communities to understand the text. And, obviously, that meant that each one wanted each particular community to have the tradent's understanding of the text. This very good intention often led to slight modifications and facilitations of the text, even in the original-language texts, all the more so in the versions where sanctity of the translated text had not yet been established in the community. This phenomenon of (limited) textual fluidity, especially in the precious older and more ancient manuscripts, eventually gave rise to attempts, as early as Luther in the sixteenth century, to establish dependable, standard texts. Since the seventeenth century, that effort to identify and evaluate differences in ancient texts has been called textual criticism.

Stabilization of the text of the Hebrew Bible, begun as noted in the first century B.C.E., reached phenomenal proportions in the work of the Masoretes near Tiberias by the ninth century of the common era. Like most good literature, canonical literature is highly multivalent, which was important to its survival of the canonical process described above. Consequently, single passages often can be read in quite different ways according to the concerns of the readers and the hermeneutics (rules of interpretation) they bring to the text. This is well-illustrated by the considerable fluidity in twentieth-century translations of almost any given passage.

Early in the history of Judaism, especially in the Hellenistic period, this fluidity and multivalency gave rise to many different ways of reading the texts. This led in turn to the considerable pluralism in the Judaism(s) of the time. Efforts needed to be made to provide constraints for such diverse readings. Parallel to the efforts at stabilization of the text itself were efforts to control the rules of interpretation brought to the text. There were apparently seven such rules by the end of the first century B.C.E., then thirteen by the end of the first century C.E., and eventually thirty-two.

The attempt to achieve a stable text was also pursued by Christian communities. In the case of Christianity, textual stabilization was attended by efforts in the several Christian communions, whether Catholicism in the west or the Orthodox communions in the east, to place ecclesiastical controls on biblical interpretation. And that was apparently fully accepted until Luther broke the linkage between Scripture and magisterium (ecclesiastical teaching authority). Protestantism insisted on providing translations for lay folk to hear in their own languages, and eventually to read for themselves.

By the ninth century C.E. the Masoretes had provided restraints within the text of the Hebrew Bible. The stabilization process of the first centuries B.C.E. and C.E. mentioned above dealt with the consonants of the Hebrew text only. The Masoretes inherited that consonantal text and inserted into it three different constraints: (a) vowels, or symbols for reading the text aloud; (b) accent or cantillation marks to guide the literate readers of the communities in their intonations and accentuations, along with markings of formal units of the text for reading aloud and translation at worship and study; and (c) scribal notations in the lateral, top and bottom margins (masorot) to guide subsequent copyists so that the text would be transmitted in as stabilized a form as possible.

The focus of these moves toward complete stabilization was on the Bible as sacred text. In fact, the masorot or marginal notations in many cases preserve anomalies in the text which do not simplify meanings but show their ambiguity. These notations also guard the pluralism that exists among doublets and triplets in the text (e.g., the numerous small differences between 2 Sam. 22 and Ps. 18 which are otherwise the same psalm; or between the two lists of Ten Commandments in Exod. 20 and Deut. 5). The tendency noted above for tradents to feel a responsibility for their communities' understanding of the text, and the tendency to harmonize the texts, were thus checked and put under considerable constraint.

Luther and many Christians since Luther, including many scholars today, have tended to belittle the authority of these constraints. Others, like the seventeenth century Buxtorfs in Germany and Richard Simon in France, and a growing number of scholars today, have tended to place considerable value on the traditions for reading and copying the text which the Masoretic notations transmitted. Christianity never developed such constraints, leaving stabilizing of the texts and understanding of their teachings to the several ecclesiastical bodies. Indeed, for the New Testament only a small number of manuscripts in Syriac translation have a few meager examples of such marginal notes.

There is no such thing as an autograph of a biblical book or unit of literature; that is, there are no originals in existence. All the many thousands of manuscripts extant today are apographs of Scripture; that is, they are copies of copies. Such an observation brings into focus another way of relating Scripture to communities of faith. The manuscripts available for establishing a responsibly critical text for reading and translation today are inherited from ancient communities, not from individuals. All tradents responsible for transmitting biblical texts across the centuries were serving their communities. Scribes, copyists, and translators did what they did out of a sense of service—not simply because they had literate skills or a profession to perform. And while they, being human, made mistakes, close study now indicates they were perhaps less error-prone than some text critics, eager to correct the text, have until recently thought. Again one has to think in terms of individuals within communities, not individuals in and of themselves in our typical western manner of thinking. This becomes an important observation which should limit the tendency of western minds to push behind inherited texts in search of supposed original forms of texts composed by ancient individuals.

Text, Canon, and Community

The Bible is largely pseudepigraphic. That is, most of the literature in it is anonymous either in initial composition or at points of community transmission; then, it is often attributed to one or another great, recognizable name in antiquity. In this manner unidentifiable individuals, even authors of truly great literary compositions, were caught up into community identity at the expense of their own. Attributions to former great figures often occurred rather late in the transmission process, many perhaps when the dialogue and debate in Early Judaism about corporate and individual responsibility had become widespread. Often the attribution was made in a late superscription or was passed on in oral transmission and does not occur in the manuscripts themselves. This is true of both testaments.

Many scholars today want to go behind the canonical stages of biblical texts inherited from ancient communities to a "recovered original" text. In some cases this effort may be based on some theory of authority (historical and/or theological) that impels the effort to reconstruct what ancient individuals said or wrote before the text became community property as canonical literature. In other cases, it is more of an intellectual exercise concerning the conjectured roots of variants or divergencies in extant manuscripts. In either case, one or more line(s) of textual transmission (e.g., the Septuagint in the case of the Old Testament) may be used in an attempt to reconstruct a more "original" form of the Hebrew text. The intent is to reach behind the early canonical stages of text exhibited in extant manuscripts. Such attempts are made even in the case of stories or accounts found in different stages of transmission which manifest quite distinctive cultural contexts—e.g., the stories of Hannah (in Hebrew, 1 Sam. 1) and Anna (in the Septuagint, 1 Kingdoms 1) or the books of Jeremiah (which are quite different in the Hebrew and Septuagint).

In contrast to this tendency, there is a growing interest among some scholars in preserving the differences (as the Masoretes did for the Hebrew text) and even translating two or more versions of the same story or accounts (as the Bible preserves both Ps. 18 and 2 Sam. 22). Some recent translations (including the REB) have the Hebrew Esther in the canonical Old Testament but also the full Greek Esther in its own integrity in the Apocrypha. Scholars as historians should be interested in probing back as far as possible toward the inception of all things biblical, but there is serious concern now that such probes not destroy the forms of the stories and accounts inherited from the tradents of the communities of the extant manuscript traditions. Indeed, scholars engaged in textual and canonical criticism can now usually reach agreement on the earliest canonical stage of a biblical text in antiquity and thus transmit the various text traditions responsibly to current believing communities. Such communities, scholars and lay folk together, are the heirs of centuries—even millennia—of textual tradition and are themselves now tradents in the continuing canonical process of these remarkable texts.

SUGGESTIONS FOR FURTHER READING

McDonald, Lee Martin, *The Formation of the Christian Biblical Canon*. Nashville: Abingdon Press, 1988.

Metzger, Bruce M., *The Canon of the New Testament*. Oxford: Clarendon Press, 1987.

Morgan, Donn F., *Between Text & Community: The "Writings" in Canonical Interpretation*. Minneapolis: Fortress, 1990.

Pokorny, Petr, "Das theologische Problem der neutestamentlichen Pseudepigraphie," *Evangelische Theologie* 44 (1984) 486–96.

Sanders, James A., *Canon and Community*. Philadelphia: Fortress, 1984.

———. *From Sacred Story to Sacred Text*. Philadelphia: Fortress, 1987.

———. "Deuteronomy," *The Books of the Bible*. Ed. B. W. Anderson. New York: Charles Scribner's Sons, 1989. Pp. 89–102.

———. "Canon (OT)," *Anchor Bible Dictionary*. Ed. D. N. Freedman. Garden City: Doubleday, forthcoming.

The Dead Sea Scrolls and Other Jewish Literature

CAROL A. NEWSOM

It would be a serious mistake to assume that the Bible contains all the literature produced by Israel in antiquity. The Bible itself occasionally makes reference to writings that no longer exist, works such as "the Book of Jashar" (Josh. 10.13). It is hardly surprising that much of the literature of ancient Israel has been lost. Texts written on leather or papyrus are highly perishable. But the process of recopying them by hand is expensive and extremely time consuming. As the needs and interests of Jewish communities changed over time, and as new texts continued to be written, many of the older writings ceased to be recopied and were ultimately lost. A small but significant number were preserved and copied by the early church, translated into Greek and ultimately into the languages of the various Christian communities: Latin, Syriac, Ethiopic, Armenian, Old Church Slavonic, etc. Often Christian scribes inserted passages referring to Christ or to distinctively Christian theological ideas into such works. Occasionally, it is uncertain whether a text is a Christian composition or a Jewish text adapted for Christian use.

Archaeological finds added spectacularly to our knowledge of ancient Jewish literature with the discovery in 1947 of the Qumran Scrolls in caves near the shore of the Dead Sea. Although most of the scrolls were preserved only in small fragments, it is estimated that these fragments come from some 800 different manuscripts, including over 500 nonbiblical texts. Although it is often difficult to establish the date a text was originally composed, virtually all of the surviving nonbiblical literature was probably written between 300 B.C.E. and 200 C.E.

The Dead Sea Scrolls

The ancient Roman writer Pliny (1st century C.E.) mentions a community of Jewish holy men who lived on the western shore of the Dead Sea. Not long after the discovery of the scrolls near the ruins known as Khirbet Qumran, scholars suggested that the scrolls had belonged to the community to which Pliny referred. The settlement was apparently connected with a larger religious movement known as the Essenes, a group described by the Jewish historian Josephus and by the Jewish philosopher Philo. The community, which was organized as a religious sect, probably arose as a reform movement during the first half of the second century B.C.E. Its members were concerned to live a life of strict obedience to the will of God as disclosed through their interpretation of the law. The

Qumran community's interpretation differed in important respects from that of many other Jewish groups, especially concerning the calendar that should be used in observing Sabbaths and holy days. These differences caused the Qumran community to reject the validity of the sacrifices as they were carried out by the priests in charge of the Jerusalem temple. They believed that their own lives of obedience, prayer, and praise would be an acceptable offering to God until such time as the temple service could be reformed. The Qumran community expected that God would soon intervene decisively to overthrow the gentile powers and other forces of evil and to allow for the reformation of Israel according to the sect's beliefs.

The scrolls that belonged to the Qumran community can be divided into three groups: (1) copies of biblical books; (2) sectarian texts, i.e., writings composed by and for the sect; and (3) nonsectarian texts, i.e., various religious writings that were of interest to the sect but not composed by them. Among the nonbiblical texts it is difficult to be certain in some cases whether a text was written by the community, although there is a general consensus concerning most of the major writings. The question is important because those texts that are not sectarian give us insight into the type of literature that circulated in a variety of circles in ancient Judaism.

COPIES OF BIBLICAL BOOKS. Every book of the Hebrew Bible with the exception of Esther is represented among the scrolls and fragments. The relatively large number of copies of Deuteronomy, Isaiah, and Psalms suggests that these books were especially influential. Biblical manuscripts from Qumran and other ancient sites (Muraba'at, Nahal Hever, and Masada) are important because they are almost a thousand years older than the earliest of the medieval manuscripts that provide the basis for modern editions and translations.

SECTARIAN TEXTS. Several of the texts that scholars call "Rules" were perhaps written as manuals of instruction for teachers and/or new members. The most important of these is the *Community Rule* (designated 1QS; sometimes called the *Manual of Discipline*). It describes the purposes for which the community was formed, gives an account of the yearly covenant renewal ceremony, and explains some of the distinctive religious beliefs of the sect. It also sets out procedures for the conduct of community meetings, for the admission of new members, and for disciplining those who break the society's rules. An appendix to the *Community Rule* describes the ideal organization of the community as it will exist in the end of days and gives the blessings to be pronounced over the community and its leaders.

Another Rule, usually called the *Damascus Covenant* (CD), seems to have been written not for the particular community that lived at Khirbet Qumran but for related groups that lived in towns and villages elsewhere in Judea. Although the *Damascus Covenant* contains a number of tantalizing references to the history of the sect, they are frustratingly obscure. It does appear, however, that the sect was in conflict with other Jewish groups about the proper interpretation of the law and the conduct of the temple service. The *Damascus Covenant* contains laws governing general behavior (e.g., concerning vows, Sabbath observance) as well as regulations relating to the internal life of the community.

The most unusual of the Rules is the *War Rule* (1QM). It describes the war of the end time, when the Children of Light will defeat the Children of Darkness and the proper forms of service will be restored in the temple. A considerable amount of this complex work is devoted to a minute description of the equipment to be used in the battles (banners, trumpets, weapons), military formations, the organization of the camp, and the leading role of the priests and Levites. The *War Rule* is not a scroll of practical instructions but a work of the imagination describing an event believed to be predetermined.

Not many of the scrolls found at Qumran deal primarily with the sect's distinctive interpretation of the law. One important text, entitled by its modern editors *Matters of the Law* (4QMMT; in Hebrew, *Miqsat Ma'aseh Ha-Torah*), appears to have been a letter sent by the sect to its opponents, outlining their differences in calendar and legal interpretation. Another legal text, the lengthy and well-preserved *Temple Scroll* (11Q Tem), presents itself as God's instructions to Moses. In large part the *Temple Scroll* is a systematic reworking of legal material from Exodus, Leviticus, Numbers, and Deuteronomy, with particular emphasis on laws pertaining to temple service. Extensive regulations are given concerning the construction of the temple and the procedures required to ensure its purity. The latter part of the scroll, drawn largely from Deuteronomy, concerns more general legal issues. Although the *Temple Scroll* was probably not written by a member of the Qumran community (its style and language are quite different from the sectarian writings), it has important similarities with the *Damascus Covenant* and the *War Rule*.

The Qumran community engaged in intensive study of scripture, not only in order to clarify the commandments but also to understand the history of the end time, in which the community believed it was then living. According to the Qumran community, the Psalms and the ancient writings of the prophets contained cryptic references to their sect, its struggles with its opponents, and the anticipated vindication of their community in the end of days. The results of their interpretations of scripture were embodied in a series of commentaries called "Interpretations" (in Hebrew, *Pesharim*). For the most part these *Pesharim* cite the text of a prophetic book section by section, accompanying each brief citation with an interpretation. In a few instances the sect wrote topical interpretations, selecting biblical texts from various books and interpreting them as prophetic references to the end time. The *Midrash on the Last Days* (4Q

Flor; also called the *Florilegium*) and the *Melchizedek Midrash* (11Q Melch) are the best examples of these topical *Pesharim*.

An important part of the life of the Qumran community consisted of acts of worship. Prayers, blessings, religious poetry, and liturgical texts of various kinds are abundantly represented among the scrolls. One large collection of hymns, the *Thanksgiving Scroll* (1QH), contains psalms of thanksgiving spoken by an individual. Most of the hymns could represent the religious experience of any member of the sect, but a few seem to be written from the perspective of a persecuted leader. Although the members of the Qumran community were to offer prayers to God at set times every day, it is not known whether they used prayers specially composed by someone within the sect. There are several collections of apparently nonsectarian prayer texts that may have served these purposes, including the *Daily Prayers, The Words of the Heavenly Lights,* and the *Prayers for the Festivals.* A text called *Blessings and Curses* may contain part of the annual ceremony of covenant renewal to which the *Community Rule* refers. Having separated themselves from participation in worship at the Jerusalem temple, the Qumran community developed a strong interest in the heavenly temple and its angelic priesthood, an interest reflected in the *Songs of the Sabbath Sacrifice.* Preoccupation with heavenly and demonic forces is also represented in a collection of songs of exorcism known as the *Songs of the Sage.*

NONSECTARIAN TEXTS. A type of literary activity that flourished during the second temple period was the practice of using a biblical character or narrative as the basis for a new composition. Some of these writings (often termed Pseudepigrapha) stick rather closely to the biblical text, while others have only a loose relationship to it. Many of the nonsectarian texts found in the Dead Sea caves are examples of this type of literary activity.

One fairly well preserved text, the *Genesis Apocryphon* (1Qap Gen) is a retelling and elaboration of narratives from Genesis, some of which are told in the first person. The book of *1 Enoch,* which is actually a compilation of various compositions, is an example of apocalyptic literature. In addition to expanding the biblical traditions about Enoch with additional legendary material, it presents this biblical character as a recipient of revelations concerning astronomical lore, the relationship between rebellious angels and the Flood, and the history of the world until its appointed end when the rebellious angels and other evildoers will be punished. The interest in the heavenly world and in the end time are prominent themes in apocalypses. Although only fragments of *1 Enoch* have been found in the Qumran caves, the complete text is known from medieval manuscripts in Greek and Ethiopic. Also found among the caves are very fragmentary copies of texts that appear to be testaments (i.e., death-bed farewell speeches) of Kohath and Amram, the great-grandfather and grandfather of Moses, respectively. All of these texts are written in Aramaic.

Several texts written in Hebrew are directly associated with Moses. One of these, the book of *Jubilees,* is preserved only in fragments at Qumran but was previously known from medieval manuscripts in Ethiopic and fragments in other languages. Although presented as an address to Moses by the angel of the Presence, the content of *Jubilees* is a reworking of the biblical material from Genesis 1 to Exodus 12. The author is very much concerned with calendar and chronology, advocating a calendar based on a solar rather than a lunar reckoning. Chronology is calculated on forty-nine year jubilee periods. The proper celebration of festivals and the importance of Levi, the ancestor of Israel's priests, are also major themes of the book.

Among the more fragmentary texts associated with Moses is one called *The Words of Moses.* Strongly influenced by the language and style of Deuteronomy, it appears to contain a speech by God and an address by Moses to the Israelites. Another text, also in the style of Deuteronomy, provides instructions for a ritual for distinguishing between true and false prophets (the so-called *Liturgy of the Three Tongues of Fire*). As mentioned above, the *Temple Scroll* also takes the form of a divine revelation to Moses. The various texts that are associated with Moses probably do not come from a single community. Their styles and contents are too different. They point to the relatively widespread literary technique of writing in the name of a famous figure of the past.

In addition to texts associated with Moses, there are rewritings of biblical narrative featuring Joshua (the so-called *Psalms of Joshua*), Samuel (published as *The Vision of Samuel*), and perhaps David. A very different adaptation of biblical material is characteristic of the work known as *Second Ezekiel.* That text, which presents itself as a series of dialogues between God and the prophet Ezekiel, appears to be concerned in part with the fate of the righteous in the end time. In this respect it has much in common with *1 Enoch.* Similarly, the fragmentary text of *Pseudo-Daniel* recounts history from the time of Noah to the end of days. Also related to the Daniel literature is the *Prayer of Nabonidus,* an Aramaic text that contains numerous parallels with the story of Daniel and Nebuchadnezzar in Daniel 4.

In addition to narratives and apocalyptic revelations, nonbiblical psalms and wisdom writings have been found in the Qumran caves. Although the proverb collections have not yet been published, several sermon-like compositions or admonitions and a poem based on Proverbs 7 have been. One well-preserved psalms scroll from Cave 11 contains both canonical and noncanonical psalms, all of which are attributed to David. Two other collections of noncanonical psalms, unfortunately very fragmentary, appear to have contained psalms attributed to various biblical figures, including Obadiah, Manasseh, a "man of God," and an unnamed king of Judah. As mentioned above, several collections of prayers and blessings that have been found in the caves were probably also of nonsectarian origin. The richness and variety of this literature is a clue to the wealth of literary production in the late second temple period.

Other Jewish Literature

It is useful to distinguish between Jewish literature written originally in Hebrew or Aramaic and that composed in Greek. Although some of the Greek compositions may have been written in Judea, most of them come from Jews living outside of Palestine, especially in the Egyptian Diaspora. Although Greek culture influenced Jews wherever they lived, the imprint of Greek literary and cultural values is more pronounced in the literature of the Diaspora.

WORKS COMPOSED IN HEBREW OR ARAMAIC. Works written originally in Hebrew or Aramaic tend to resemble the types of literature found among the nonsectarian texts from the Dead Sea caves. For example, the retelling and supplementing of biblical narrative is represented by a work known as the *Biblical Antiquities of Pseudo-Philo.* This text, traditionally but wrongly attributed to the Jewish philosopher Philo, retells the biblical story from Genesis through 1 Samuel. It is probably to be dated to the first century C.E. A contemporary work, *The Lives of the Prophets,* gives a brief account of "the names of the prophets, where they are from, where they died and how, and where they lie," supplemented in places with legendary accounts of their activities.

As with *1 Enoch,* described above, there are other texts that present figures from the past as recipients of revelations about the heavenly world and the end time. The *Testament of Moses* purports to be the private farewell speech of Moses to Joshua. Moses explains to Joshua what will be the course of history of the Israelites until, at the climax of an acute period of sin and oppression, a priest and his seven sons will be martyred. This event will trigger the intervention of the heavenly armies under an angelic leader and will secure for Israel a heavenly blessedness. The *Testament of Moses* was originally written during the persecution of Antiochus IV Epiphanes, about 165 B.C.E. The apocalypse of *2 Baruch* comes from a later period, after the destruction of the temple by the Romans in 70 C.E. Since the historical Baruch was a scribe who served Jeremiah at the time of the Babylonian destruction of the first temple, he is an especially suitable figure for an apocalypse concerned with the later destruction. As Baruch prays and laments, he is shown a vision of the history of the world, symbolized in alternating dark and bright rains, culminating in the final triumph of God's anointed. Another vision symbolically represents the overthrow of the Roman empire by the messiah. *Second Baruch* is roughly contemporary with the Apocryphal book 2 Esdras 3–14 (often known as *4 Ezra*). A third apocalypse that is probably from this period, the *Apocalypse of Abraham,* contains extensive legendary material about Abraham's conversion from idolatry as well as a description of Abraham's ascent to heaven, where he is shown a vision of the history of the world until its appointed end.

Religious poetry is represented in the collection known as the *Psalms of Solomon*. The title, which is not original, has nothing to do with the contents. Although most of the psalms are written in traditional language and refer in general terms to conflict between the righteous and the sinners, several of them refer specifically to the events of the mid-first century B.C.E., when the Romans captured Judea. The author of the *Psalms of Solomon* considered the native Hasmonean kings of Judea to be illegitimate but was even more appalled by the Roman occupation. The *Psalms of Solomon* look forward to a legitimate Davidic king who will restore the land.

WORKS COMPOSED IN GREEK. Although Jewish literature composed in Greek includes some genres developed originally in Hebrew and Aramaic, most of it reflects the cultural influence of the cosmopolitan Greek-speaking cities. The testament, or death-bed farewell speech, is an example of a literary type that was popular both in Hebrew/Aramaic and in Greek versions. The *Testaments of the Twelve Patriarchs* was probably composed in Greek but based on earlier Hebrew or Aramaic models. In this text each of Jacob's twelve sons tells his children the story of his life, using it as an example of a particular virtue or vice. The dying man urges his children to live a moral life according to his advice. He also predicts the future of the tribe, stressing the leading role of the tribes of Levi and Judah. The *Testament of Job* recasts the book of Job as a testament in which the dying Job gathers his children in order to recount his life. Unlike the *Testaments of the Twelve Patriarchs,* it contains little moral admonition and no prediction of the future. Casting the conflict as a struggle between Satan and Job, one of its central concerns is to condemn paganism and the worship of idols, while commending loyalty to God. Although the *Testament of Abraham* is not, properly speaking, a testament, it is a highly original and gently ironic piece of literature. When God sends an angel to require Abraham to prepare for his death, Abraham resists and tries to bargain for time. Part of the text concerns a heavenly journey during the course of which Abraham learns to value compassion over moral rigor. In the end Death takes Abraham's soul by a trick.

Although many Jewish apocalypses were translated into Greek, there are only a few surviving texts that were originally composed in Greek. The *Apocalypse of Zephaniah* and *3 Baruch* are probable examples. Hellenistic Jews also took up a form of pagan prophetic literature, the Sibylline oracle. According to tradition, the Sibyl was an aged woman who gave ecstatic prophecies. The Jewish Sybil is said to have been a daughter or daughter-in-law of Noah. Only brief fragments of pagan Sibylline oracles have survived, but some of the Jewish examples are simply Jewish adaptations of pagan oracles. Others are original Jewish compositions. The form was also used by Christians. In content the Sibylline oracles are strongly historical and political, with numerous predictions concerning the end time. Many of the oracles also contain ethical teachings.

In the cosmopolitan atmosphere of Hellenistic culture each ethnic community was self-conscious of its historical traditions and of the way in which these traditions related to those of other groups. Historiography, ranging from the scholarly to the unabashedly popular, became an important literary enterprise. The work of most of these historians exists now only in quotations and extracts in the writings of later Christian writers, so that the nature and extent of their histories is not always known. The earliest of these writers is Demetrius, who lived in Alexandria, Egypt, during the late third century B.C.E. Demetrius, who worked exclusively from the Septuagint, the Greek translation of the Hebrew Bible, was primarily interested in matters of chronology and in the explanation of apparent logical inconsistencies and moral lapses in the biblical narrative. In second century B.C.E. Palestine a bilingual, upper class Jew named Eupolemus wrote a history entitled *Concerning the Kings in Judea,* though its scope was actually much broader. Eupolemus, a friend of Judah the Maccabee, was concerned to glorify Israelite history and he elaborated the biblical narrative with additional legendary details. He presents Moses as a culture-bringer, specifically as the inventor of the alphabet, which was later borrowed by the Phoenicians and the Greeks. The influence and splendor of the Israelite kingdom under David and Solomon was a particular theme of Eupolemus. He describes the lavishness and superb construction of the temple, along with the contributions made by Hiram, king of Tyre, and Vaphres, king of Egypt. According to Eupolemus, Solomon responded to these contributions with extravagant gifts of his own, including a gold pillar for the temple of Zeus in Tyre.

An anonymous writer, probably a Samaritan, wrote a highly legendary history in which various details of Greek and Babylonian mythology are harmonized with biblical traditions. He identifies Enoch, for instance, with the Greek Atlas. Abraham is presented as the discoverer of astrology, which he taught to the Egyptians during his sojourn there. The correlation of biblical figures with pagan mythological and heroic figures is characteristic of several of these Hellenistic Jewish historians, most notably Artapanus. More a writer of historical romances than a historian, Artapanus recounts the stories of Abraham, Joseph, and Moses. Moses is presented as an inventor of basic technologies, a philosopher, a general in the Egyptian army, the organizer of Egyptian religion (!), and a man regarded as a virtual god by the Egyptians, who identified him with Hermes (the Greek equivalent of the Egyptian god Thoth). Moses also appears in Artapanus as the hero who rescues the Jews from the oppressions of the Egyptians.

The interest of Egyptian Jews in the figure of Joseph is reflected in a composition that is perhaps best described as a romantic novel, *Joseph and*

Asenath. Taking as its topic the marriage of Joseph to the Egyptian noblewoman Asenath, the story portrays Asenath as the model of a convert to Judaism. Both the plot and the depiction of characters reflect the complexity of Jewish-gentile relations in Hellenistic Egypt. Although biblical history was the most popular subject for Hellenistic Jewish writers, more recent periods sometimes provided topics. The book known as *3 Maccabees*, for instance, is a historical romance set in the time of Ptolemy IV Philopator, king of Egypt from 221 to 204 B.C.E. It has been suggested, though, that the book was actually written during the Roman period in the first century C.E. The story is one of persecution and miraculous deliverance for the Jewish community of Egypt. Although not reliable in its historical detail, the narrative reflects the vulnerability Egyptian Jews experienced with respect to their legal status and safety.

The more serious tradition of ancient Jewish historiography culminates in two figures from the first century C.E. who were bitter enemies: Justus of Tiberias and Josephus. The works of Justus have been completely lost, though it appears that he wrote two important books. One, a chronicle of world history, traced events from the time of Moses to the death of Agrippa II in 100 C.E. The other book was a history of the Jewish revolt against Rome, a work in which he explicitly criticized some of Josephus' actions during the war. Josephus' works, on the other hand, have been well preserved. In *Antiquities of the Jews* Josephus undertakes to retell the history of the Jewish people from Adam until his own time. Although much of the earlier part of the *Antiquities* consists of biblical paraphrase, Josephus' presentation of the material and his style reflect the influence of classical Greek historiography. In *The Jewish War* Josephus gives a detailed account of the revolt against Rome in which he participated. A brief work, the *Life*, is Josephus' reply to the criticism Justus of Tiberias directed at him in his history of the revolt. The other surviving work of Josephus, *Against Apion*, is a book devoted to refuting slanders leveled against Jews by gentile writers. It testifies to the competitive environment in which various ethnic groups interpreted their history and traditions in the Hellenistic and Roman periods.

Surviving fragments of Jewish poetic works composed in Greek are strongly influenced by Greek literary styles. Theodotus and Philo the Epic Poet wrote poems in hexameter verse about the cities of Shechem and Jerusalem, respectively. Such poetry, praising cities and countries, was popular in the Hellenistic period. Theodotus in particular seems to have been influenced by Homeric style, as can be seen in his account of the hand-to-hand combat between Jacob's sons Levi and Simeon and their opponents Hamor and Shechem (cf. Genesis 34). Unfortunately, very little of either poet's work is preserved. Much more extensive fragments remain of a tragic drama, *The Exodus*, written by Ezekiel the Tragedian. Moses is the hero of this drama, which probably covered the events of Exodus 1–15. Composed in iambic trimeter verse, the style of the play is influenced by that of the Greek dramatists Aeschylus and Euripides. Opinion remains divided as to whether these poets and playwrights lived in Palestine, in Egypt, or elsewhere in the Diaspora.

As early as the second century B.C.E. Alexandria produced a Jewish philosopher in the person of Aristobulus. Although his work survives only in quotations, he apparently wrote an extensive philosophical commentary on the Pentateuch. Aristobulus claimed that the law of Moses already contained what Greek philosophy later expounded. Indeed, he argued that Greek philosophers such as Pythagoras, Socrates, and Plato derived their ideas from the Jewish law.

Whether or not there was a tradition of Hellenistic Jewish philosophers, the Egyptian Diaspora produced a truly significant intellectual figure in Philo of Alexandria, who flourished around the turn of the era. Philo's thought shows the imprint of Greek philosophy, Stoic, Pythagorean, and especially Platonic. But to describe Philo simply in terms of philosophy would be misleading. Although he occasionally wrote philosophical treatises and dialogues in the Greek fashion, the largest part of Philo's extensive works are commentaries on the Pentateuch. In some of these works Philo retells the biblical narrative, incorporating his philosophical comments into the narrative. In others an allegorical and philosophical commentary takes the form of a verse by verse exposition of biblical texts. Throughout his writings, however, philosophy and biblical interpretation are always closely intertwined as Philo attempts to show that true philosophy is nothing other than the understanding of the Law of Moses.

Although there is no other Hellenistic Jewish philosopher comparable to Philo, a number of literary and rhetorical works show the extent to which a degree of philosophical knowledge can be assumed on the part of an educated Jewish audience of that era. The *Letter of Aristeas,* which dates from the second century B.C.E., is a fictional account of the translation of the Pentateuch into Greek. Aristeas is presented as a Greek member of the court of Ptolemy II, although the actual author of the work is unquestionably Jewish. In one section the High Priest presents Moses as a philosopher and interprets the laws allegorically in the spirit of Aristobulus. Later at a banquet with the king the Jewish translators discuss the nature and practice of kingship, a common topic in Hellenistic political philosophy. A later and more philosophically self-conscious work is the book of *4 Maccabees.* Perhaps composed as a speech commemorating the martyrs of the Maccabean persecutions, the work is a discourse on the topic of the sovereignty of reason over the passions. Its vocabulary and thought is closest to a type of Stoic philosophy, but the work has a thoroughly Jewish cast to it. The reason that is praised is religious reason, reason obedient to the law of God. Here, as with most of the Jewish literature written in Greek, one can see the concern to interpret the meaningfulness of ancestral traditions within a cultural context that was overwhelmingly gentile. The creative vitality with which the Jewish Diaspora met this challenge is reflected in the rich variety of literature it produced.

SUGGESTIONS FOR FURTHER READING

Modern translations of most of the texts discussed in this article can be found in the following books:

Vermes, G., *The Dead Sea Scrolls in English*, 3rd ed. Penguin: London, 1987.

Sparks, H., ed. *The Apocryphal Old Testament*. Oxford: Clarendon Press, 1984.

Charlesworth, J. H., *The Old Testament Pseudepigrapha*, 2 vols. Garden City, N.Y.: Doubleday, 1983, 1985.

Holladay, C., *Fragments from Hellenistic Jewish Authors, Volume 1: Historians*. Chico, CA: Scholars Press, 1983, *Volume 2: Poets*. Atlanta: Scholars Press, 1989.

Early Christian Literature

DENNIS R. MacDONALD

No writing survives from Jesus or his disciples. When early Christians transmitted their memories of him to others, they did so primarily by word of mouth, setting in motion a dynamic process of oral tradition whose energy still had not been spent until the end of the second century. There is good reason to presume, however, that many of Jesus' first followers, like many other Jews in first-century Palestine, were literate. One can easily imagine individuals recording Jesus' teachings, or writing up their interpretations of Jesus' life and tragic death in the light of the Jewish scriptures. Unfortunately if there were such writings, they no longer exist, except perhaps as sources absorbed into later documents.

During the centuries that followed, however, Christians composed hundreds of documents. In addition to those in the New Testament, the church preserved early letters, gospels, acts, apocalypses (books of revelations), church manuals, hymns, martyrologies, sermons, commentaries, and philosophical treatises. We also know of many other books, but only by their titles or through quotations by later authors. Fortunately, the arid sands of Egypt have protected fragments of many works, including the spectacular cache of thirteen fourth-century Coptic codices (or bound books) discovered at Nag Hammadi, Egypt, in 1945. Over a thousand pages of text contain some forty documents otherwise unknown, many of which had been composed by Christians centuries earlier. This wealth of documentation allows scholars to situate the New Testament more precisely in the context of early Christian literary activity. The story of Christian writing begins not in Palestine but in the Aegean basin (the region now occupied by Greece and Turkey) around the years 40–60 C.E. with the composition of letters, or epistles.

Letters

The letter is perhaps the form of literature closest to oral speech; the author of a letter, like a speaker, addresses a particular, known audience concerning circumstances germane to both parties. The first letters written by Christians may have been short letters of recommendation, written from one community to another, encouraging the recipients to welcome those who carried them. According to the Acts of the Apostles, Priscilla and Aquila wrote a letter introducing Apollos to the church at Corinth (18.27). Corinthian Christians requested Paul himself to obtain a letter from others in support of his mission (2 Cor. 3.1–3), and he expected the Corinthians to send him a letter commending those who were to deliver money to Jerusalem (1 Cor. 16.3, see also Acts 9.1–2 and 22.5). Philemon and Romans 16 (which seems originally to have been detached from the rest of Romans) are also letters of recommendation.

First Thessalonians is the earliest of all surviving Christian literature. Believers in Thessalonica had requested additional teaching from Paul, so he wrote them a letter, reluctantly, twice telling them he really did not need to write them because they already knew what they needed to know (4.9 and 5.1). Paul showed no such reluctance in his other letters. Indeed, he became more effective as a letter writer than as a speaker: " 'His letters,' so it is said, 'are weighty and powerful, but when he is present he is unimpressive, and as a speaker he is beneath contempt' " (2 Cor. 10.10, cf. 10.1).

No literary genre (or form of writing) became more widespread for the expression of early Christian thought than the letter. Of the twenty-seven books that comprise the New Testament, twenty-one might be called letters. At least three of Paul's letters probably are compilations of several, originally independent, pieces of correspondence. Romans probably is not one letter but two, Philippians not one letter but three, and 2 Corinthians not one but three or as many as six. Furthermore, the Book of Revelation contains seven letters in chapters 2–3, and Acts contains two (15.23–29 and 23.26–30). The total number of letters in the New Testament, then, is at least thirty-five, perhaps thirty-eight or more. This catalogue by no means includes all early Christian letters. Some of Paul's letters were lost (1 Cor. 5.9), and Paul received letters from others (e.g., 1 Cor. 7.1).

Many early Christian letters survive independent of the New Testament, several found in the collection called *The Apostolic Fathers*. For example, the church in Rome wrote a long letter (*1 Clement*) to Christians in Corinth. A bishop from Antioch, Ignatius, wrote letters to churches in Ephesus, Magnesia, Tralles, Rome, Philadelphia, and Smyrna, and to Polycarp, the bishop of Smyrna. Polycarp himself wrote to the church in Philadelphia. Clement, Ignatius, and Polycarp each had read some of Paul's letters and modeled their correspondence after them. *The Martyrdom of Polycarp,* in spite of its present title, is a letter to the church at Philomelium.

During the second century several authors used the letter to advance defenses, or "apologies," of the new faith. The apologists Quadratus and Aristeides wrote to the emperor Hadrian; Justin Martyr wrote to Antoninus Pius; Apollinaris, Melito, and Athenagoras to Marcus Aurelius. Though written to Roman emperors, these works seem to have been intended for other readers as well. *The Epistle to Diognetus* and Theophilus's *To Autolycus* likewise are apologetic letters. Such apologies provide valuable information concerning the emerging points of conflict between Christians and their pagan neighbors.

Early Christians also wrote letters in the names of others, a widespread ancient literary practice called "pseudepigraphy" (meaning "false attribution"). In some cases, authors wrote in the name of an apostle in order to enable the deceased hero to speak to conditions relevant to churches of a later date. In other cases, authors used pseudonymity to oppose objectionable causes for which the apostle's memory was (falsely) appropriated. The authors of 2 Thessalonians, Colossians, Ephesians, 1 and 2 Timothy, and Titus all imitate Pauline epistles. Letters outside the New Testament, too, made similar claims, such as *3 Corinthians, The Letter to the Laodiceans,* and letters supposedly exchanged between Paul and the Stoic philosopher Seneca. First and Second Peter claim Peter as their author, six letters of the fourth century present themselves as products of Ignatius' pen, and other letters pass themselves off as the work of Barnabas, Titus, James, Jude, and even Jesus. (Strictly speaking, Hebrews, 1 John, and *2 Clement* are not letters, even though they contain epistolary features.)

Christians with views later considered heretical also composed epistles, although few of them now survive. Among such Christians were Montanists (pneumatic [i.e., believing in certain spiritual gifts] and ascetic enthusiasts who promoted the idea of fresh revelations) and Gnostics (who claimed that by means of knowledge [Greek: *gnosis*] the soul could be freed from the body and from the wicked powers who created the world). The Montanist author Themiso composed a "catholic epistle" late in the second century. At about the same time, a certain Ptolemy wrote a letter to a woman named Flora, urging her to become a Gnostic Christian. The Nag Hammadi "library" contains four Gnostic letters: *The Letter of Peter to Philip, The Treatise on the Resurrection, The Apocryphon of James,* and *Eugnostos the Blessed.*

The popularity of the letter no doubt was due in part to its remarkable flexibility for meeting the various needs of early Christian communication. Sometimes the letters argued against rival groups (Galatians, 2 Cor. 10–13, and 2 Peter), treated complex theological topics (Romans, *3 Corinthians,* and *The Treatise on the Resurrection*), asked for money (2 Cor. 8 and 9), expressed thanks (Phil. 4.10–20), appealed for conversion (Ptolemy's *Letter to Flora*), established rules for church leadership (1 Timothy and Titus), communicated personal affection and concern (Philemon and Ignatius' *Polycarp*), responded to other letters (1 Corinthians), predicted future events (2 Thessalonians and 2 Timothy), defended the faith (the apologies), narrated martyrdoms (*The Martyrdom of Polycarp* and *The Martyrs of Lyons and Vienne*), interpreted scripture (*Barnabas*), opposed pagan philosophy (Paul to Seneca), shared the concerns of one church for another (*1 Clement*), warned of troublemakers (2 and 3 John), and revealed hidden, heavenly truths (*The Letter of Peter to Philip* and *The Apocryphon of James*).

Collections of Sayings and Miracle Stories

It is likely that as early as the fifth and sixth decades of the first century, Christian authors had composed documents recounting Jesus' teachings and activities. Although these writings *per se* no longer exist, the authors of the Gospels used some of them in creating their narratives. For example, it would appear that the authors of Matthew and Luke independently appropriated materials from a collection of Jesus' sayings, which scholars call Q or the Synoptic Sayings Source (see article, "The Gospels," pp. 1263–1265). Q seems to have derived from a circle of rigorist Christian prophets who wandered throughout Galilee and western Syria proclaiming Jesus' imminent return from heaven in judgment. Similar collections of Jesus' sayings may also lie behind Mark and John.

The collecting of Jesus' teachings continued well into the second century, when, for example, a bishop named Papias composed his five-volume *Interpretations of the Sayings of the Lord,* which he based on oral testimonies from those who had known the apostles. Clement of Alexandria, an intellectual who wrote around 200 C.E., quoted several sayings of Jesus from *The Gospel of the Egyptians,* which likewise may have been a collection of Jesus' teachings without extensive narrative or plot. Christians also collected alleged teachings of New Testament personalities other than Jesus. *The Preaching of Peter* purports to record sayings of Peter, and another claims to contain *The Teachings of Silvanus,* Paul's associate.

Among the codices found at Nag Hammadi was a document bearing the title *The Gospel of Thomas.* Like Q, this so-called gospel is a collection of Jesus' teachings with no framing narrative. A reader familiar with the New Testament will at once recognize similarities between the content of this gospel and sayings of Jesus recorded in the Synoptics. On the other hand, *The Gospel of Thomas* arranges material differently, differs significantly in wording, contains content unparalleled by the New Testament, and advances an alternative religious worldview. For instance, this gospel promises salvation through a proper understanding of its esoteric meanings, not through faith in Jesus as the crucified and risen one. Eschatological sayings of Jesus recorded in the Synoptics (that is, sayings which anticipate a radical intervention of God into human history) are used in *Thomas* to promote prudence, mystical self-reflection, or spatial dualism between the world and the realm of the divine. According to *Thomas,* the body is the tarnished, tragic, and temporary abode of the fallen, preexistent soul. By means of knowledge, this soul must put off its fleshly garment in order to recover its original, spiritual union with God.

Interpreters have long squabbled over the precise relationship of *The Gospel of Thomas* to the synoptics and Q or its historical value for understanding Jesus of Nazareth, and these debates show no signs of fatigue. Nonetheless, most scholars concur that even if the author of *Thomas* knew one or more of the canonical Gospels, such knowledge alone cannot account for its content. Not only does *Thomas* cite many sayings not found in the New Testament, it frequently preserves more primitive versions of sayings that are found there.

It would also appear that already in the first century some authors recorded stories of Jesus' miracles. Some of the stories in Mark and John may derive from such miracle collections. A second-century document, the so-called *Infancy Gospel of Thomas,* tells of Jesus' remarkable intelligence at school, his miracle-working helpfulness around the house and at the carpenter's shop, and his dangerous petulance with playmates.

Gospels

Prior to the destruction of Jerusalem in 70 C.E., the primary genres of Christian literature were letters and collections of Jesus' sayings and miracles. Early in the next decade, however, an unknown author composed a narrative about the life of Jesus that would forever transform Christian images of Jesus. Whether as a response to the Jewish war (66–70 C.E.), or to the deaths of the earliest followers of Jesus, or to the need for a definitive version of Jesus' life, or to objectionable theological trends, the author of the Gospel of Mark recast traditional materials into a dramatic narrative climaxing in Jesus' death. It is not clear precisely what kind of book the author set out to compose, insofar as no document written prior to Mark exactly conforms with its literary properties. Its themes of travel, conflict with supernatural foes, suffering, and secrecy resonate with Homer's *Odyssey* and Greek romantic novels. Its focus on the character, identity, and death of a single individual reminds one of ancient biographies. Its dialogues, tragic outcome, and peculiar ending call to mind Greek drama. Some have suggested that the author created a new, mixed genre for narrating the life and death of Jesus.

Be that as it may, Mark's story exerted enormous influence on subsequent Christian literature and theology. One of the first debtors to Mark was the author of the Gospel of Matthew, writing from Greek-speaking Syria late in the first century, who augmented Mark with content derived from oral tradition and written collections of sayings, most notably Q. Later, two Jewish gospels in turn modeled themselves after Matthew. *The Gospel of the Nazoreans* expanded Matthew (probably in Aramaic or Syriac), and *The Gospel of the Ebionites* borrowed extensively from Matthew, adding readings from Luke and perhaps Mark. Only a few citations from these gospels now survive. Of all the gospels, Matthew's was the most frequently quoted by early Christians.

The next most popular gospel was John's. The Fourth Gospel is the product of several stages of rewriting, or redaction. At some point John was influenced by one or more of the Synoptic Gospels (or by the written sources used by them). For the most part, however, the Gospel of John goes its own way. It seems to have come from an isolated community of Jewish-Christians who expressed their faith in Jesus with concepts more otherworldly than those in the Synoptics.

Sometime between 90 and 125 C.E. a Christian intellectual wrote a two-volume work, now known as the Gospel of Luke and the Acts of the

Apostles. Its unknown author announced his intention of providing an "orderly narrative" from the birth of Jesus to the last few months of Paul's life (Luke 1.1–4, Acts 1.1–5). Luke-Acts, then, is the first history of the church, but it is not a history in the modern sense. Ancient histories exhibit an astonishing freedom with traditions and sources. Historical accuracy mattered less than entertainment, plausibility, and persuasiveness. These histories typically promoted particular religious, political, or philosophical objectives. The author of Luke-Acts apparently sought to refashion the literature and traditions of the church into a triumphant narrative capable of providing the church with a heritage and an identity compatible with life in cities of the Roman Empire.

During the second century, several other authors compiled materials from earlier gospels and created new ones, such as *The Gospel of the Ebionites* mentioned above, which used Matthew and Luke, and *The Infancy Gospel of Thomas,* which expanded the childhood stories in Luke with folkloric themes. A four-page papyrus from the second century (*Papyrus Egerton 2*) shares episodes with Mark and John. Some scholars insist that this gospel was not a later combination of passages from Mark and John but a source known to both biblical authors. *The Gospel of the Hebrews* survives only in fragments, but they display unmistakable parallels with topics found also in other gospels, such as the birth of Jesus to Mary, his baptism, perhaps his temptation, dialogues with disciples, and a resurrection appearance (to James), followed by the Lord's Supper. *The Protevangelium of James,* dating probably to the middle of the second century, narrates the birth of Jesus, combining information from the infancy narratives of Matthew and Luke with motifs drawn from the Greek Bible. The book insists that even after birthing Jesus, Mary remained a virgin. Around the middle of the second century, a Syrian named Tatian wrote his *Diatessaron,* a gospel composed of readings taken from Matthew, Mark, Luke, and John, which by that time seem to have circulated together as a four-gospel collection.

Buried with the body of an eighth-century monk was a book containing a fragmentary narrative concerning Jesus' crucifixion and resurrection as told by the apostle Peter. Here Herod, not Pilate, takes responsibility for Jesus' execution. These pages almost certainly preserve a section of *The Gospel of Peter,* which enjoyed status as scripture for Christians in parts of western Syria at the end of the second century. Two small Greek papyrus fragments also preserve readings from this gospel. Several scholars have suggested that behind *The Gospel of Peter* lies a primitive Christian document available to the authors of the Gospels in the New Testament. These proposals have won few adherents. As the text now stands, it seems to be a melding together of readings from Matthew, Mark, Luke, and John into an original portrayal of the crucifixion and empty tomb. In addition, however, the author skillfully incorporated allusions to the Greek Old Testament, thereby strengthening the impression that Jesus' death conformed to divine purposes.

Revelatory Literature

As early as the second century B.C.E., Jews employed the "apocalypse" (from the Greek word for "unveiling" and therefore "revelation") to comfort and empower their readers by forecasting God's victory over wicked human and superhuman powers. Early Christians, too, were fascinated with prophetic predictions, especially predictions attributed to Jesus (see 1 Thess. 4.8–13). Q, for example, contains many such sayings, as does Mark 13 (the so-called "Synoptic Apocalypse," which may rely on an even earlier collection of prophetic sayings). Chapter 16 of a late first-century document known as The Didache (or "The Teaching," see below) likewise recorded predictions of imminent doom and salvation.

The most famous Christian example of this type of literature is The Apocalypse of John, or The Book of Revelation, in which the author claims to have visited heaven and seen visions of the future. Other such Christian apocalypses are The Apocalypse of Peter (which reports Peter's tour of heaven and hell), The Apocalypse of Paul (not the one from Nag Hammadi), The Epistula Apostolorum, The Shepherd of Hermas, 5 Ezra, 6 Ezra, and the Christian Sibylline Oracles. One particularly valuable example of early Christian prophecy is known as The Ascension of Isaiah, chs. 6–11 of which issue from circles of Christian prophets at the end of the first century or the beginning of the second.

Several Gnostic texts likewise present themselves as revelations of the risen Lord, but for the most part they refrain from speculating on future events. Instead, they purport to record post-resurrection visitations of Jesus to his followers, granting them secret instructions. The Apocryphon of James, which begins and ends as a letter (cf. The Letter of Peter to Philip), encourages its readers to endure martyrdom and to ascend with Christ to heaven. In The Book of Thomas the Contender, Jesus instructs Thomas concerning ascetic and spiritual practices. Jesus appears to the faithful in The Apocalypse of Peter (Nag Hammadi) warning them to beware of "those who are outside our number who name themselves bishop and also deacons, as if they have received their authority from God." Here Gnostics recruit Jesus to oppose "orthodox" Christian clergy. According to The Apocryphon of John, Jesus revealed to John through an elaborate myth how evil powers had created the physical world and how people may be saved from their domination. The Gospel of Mary claims that Jesus gave secret instructions to Mary that Andrew and Peter refused to accept because Mary was a woman. The Dialogue of the Savior, The Sophia of Jesus Christ, The (Second) Apocalypse of James, and Pistis Sophia also are Gnostic revelatory discourses.

Church Orders

The oldest surviving document delineating regulations for church life bears the title The Teaching of the Lord to the Gentiles through the Twelve

Apostles, but usually goes by the title *The Didache*. It probably dates to the first half of the second century. After establishing ethical expectations for the community, *The Didache* then prescribes the proper performance of Christian rituals, establishes rules for community organization and discipline, and concludes with apocalyptic prophecies. No document extant from this period provides a clearer window through which to observe the practices of baptism, eucharist, and fasting. *The Didache* also documents the transition of religious leadership from wandering missionaries, "prophets and teachers," to local clergy, "bishops and deacons." In the subsequent centuries, Christians wrote many similar "orders" for governing the life of the church.

Apostolic Legends

Between 160 and 225 C.E. Christians produced many narratives concerning the lives, teachings, and deaths of the apostles Peter, John, Paul, Andrew, and Thomas. Scholars have proposed various literary ancestors to these "acts," such as Luke's Acts of the Apostles, or Greek romantic novels, or lives of philosophers, but the closest parallels are found in gospels, especially in Matthew and John. Each of these acts begins with an apostle leaving Jerusalem after Jesus' resurrection to missionize various regions, where they, like Jesus, preach, heal, cast out demons, attract followers, and, with the exception of John, suffer martyrdom. According to *The Acts of Peter,* the apostle traveled to Rome in order to protect the church there from Simon Magus (mentioned also in Acts 8). After a series of magical contests between the two, Peter overcomes the magician, alienates a politician by persuading his lovers to cease sexual relations with him, and dies by crucifixion upside down.

According to *The Acts of John,* that apostle taught and performed wonders in Ephesus, where he died of old age. This composite document, rich in language and imagery drawn from the Gospel of John, suggests how Christians who denied Jesus' physical embodiment might have interpreted that Gospel.

The Acts of Paul sends Paul from Jerusalem to Rome through Asia Minor and Greece. Along the way he convinces many of his converts, including a young woman named Thecla, to reject sex. Thecla nearly dies twice for her decision to pursue celibacy, but in the end, Paul ordains her to teach and to care for the poor. In Rome, after teaching and raising Nero's cupbearer back to life, Paul is beheaded. The author seems to have recorded several of these stories from oral tradition which in some cases may derive from the first century. The story of Thecla was told to legitimate women's ministries of teaching and baptizing.

According to *The Acts of Thomas,* Thomas left Jerusalem for India. Thomas' radical insistence on chastity stirs up the anger of authorities. Thomas dies, stabbed by four soldiers. *The Acts of Thomas* provides valuable information concerning Christianity in bilingual Syria at the beginning of the third century. Apart from Luke's Acts, it is the only example of this genre still extant in its entirety.

The Acts of Andrew, unlike the other acts, is an elaborate product of early Christian philosophy fashioned to be a Christian *Odyssey* with Andrew as a new Odysseus, the hero of Homer's famous epic poem. The apostle fights demons and a monstrous serpent, endures shipwreck, and converts people who remind the reader of pagan heroes and gods. Andrew dies in Greece, lashed to his cross next to the sea, like Odysseus at the mast in Homer. With the possible exception of the writings of Clement of Alexandria, no document witnesses more extensively to early Christian attitudes toward classical mythology than *The Acts of Andrew.*

Other Literary Genres

Christians also composed sermons (perhaps Hebrews and *2 Clement*), theological treatises (e.g., Justin Martyr's *Dialogue with Trypho*), commentaries on Biblical books (e.g., Heracleon on John), stories of martyrdoms (e.g., *The Acts of Justin and Companions*), refutations of so-called heretical teachers (e.g., the lost *Syntagma* of Justin Martyr), and hymns (e.g., *The Odes of Solomon,* the hymns of Basilides, *The Manichaean Psalm-Book,* and hymns incorporated into *The Acts of John* and *The Acts of Thomas*).

Transmission and Collection

The documents surveyed here obviously represent great diversity in the literary life, beliefs, and practices of the early church. During the course of the first four centuries, the increasingly dominant form of Christianity became convinced that not all of this literature expressed the faith correctly. Lists of books to be included alongside the Jewish scriptures began circulating no later than the end of the second century, and by the end of the fourth, the supremacy of the twenty-seven books of the New Testament seems to have been assured. Other books, however, continued to be read, cherished, and scribally transmitted. Late in the seventeenth century several of these books came to be called the Apostolic Fathers, including the letters of Ignatius and Polycarp, *1* and *2 Clement,* and *The Shepherd of Hermas.* At about the same time other books, especially non-biblical gospels, acts, and apocalypses, came to be called "New Testament Apocrypha." The designation "apocryphal" ("hidden" or "secretive") had been used for centuries to describe literature considered dangerous to practicing Christians. Because of their questionable status, many of these books survive only as titles, as brief quotations, or in a single manuscript, often only in Latin, Syriac, Coptic, or Ethiopic translation. Other early apocrypha were rewritten into more orthodox recensions, promoting less objectionable theologies. There is no reason to think that the era of discovery of early Christian books has ended. Scholars continue searching

for overlooked manuscripts housed in monasteries or in library archives
and repeatedly add to our knowledge of early Christian composition.

SUGGESTIONS FOR FURTHER READING

Cameron, Ron, ed. *The Other Gospels: Non-Canonical Gospel Texts*. Phila-
    delphia: Westminster, 1982.

Hennecke, Edgar, and Schneemelcher, Wilhelm, eds. *New Testament Apoc-
    rypha*. 2 vols. English translation edited by Robert McL. Wilson.
    Philadelphia: Westminster, 1963 and 1965. Revised edition of vol.
    1. Westminster, 1990.

Lake, Kirsopp. *The Apostolic Fathers*. 2 vols. Loeb Classical Library.

Layton, Bentley. *The Gnostic Scriptures*. Garden City: Doubleday, 1987.

Quasten, Johannes. *Patrology*. Vol. 1. *The Beginnings of Patristic Literature*.
    Utrecht-Antwerp: Spectrum, 1950.

Robinson, James M. ed. *The Nag Hammadi Library*. Third edition. San
    Francisco: Harper & Row, 1988.

Hebrew Scriptures in Early Post-Biblical Judaism,

with Special Reference to the Rabbinic Tradition

ROBERT GOLDENBERG

At some point during the period that the Persian Empire ruled Judaea (538–332 B.C.E.), Ezra the priestly scribe came to Jerusalem and established "the law (Heb. *torah*, lit., "teaching") of Moses which the LORD the God of Israel had given them" (Ezra 7.6) as the law of the land. This law, along with some ancient stories and other miscellaneous material, was inscribed in a book which Scripture interchangeably calls "the book of the law of Moses" (Neh. 8.1) and "the book of the law of God" (Neh. 8.18). This book, often simply called the Torah, in turn became the basis of nearly all subsequent forms of Jewish religious life.

The Torah, or Pentateuch, forms the first, and for most of the history of Judaism the dominant, part of the larger collection of sacred texts known as the Hebrew Scriptures (which Christians call the Old Testament). In the Jewish tradition the collection as a whole received no single name, and has generally been viewed more as a collection or anthology of sacred writings, rather than as the unified canonical text that Christianity came to see in it. Both Judaism and Christianity have tended to affirm that all these texts are divine in origin and have a coherent content, though Jewish teaching has never insisted that these different books present a single message. Jews did not generally imagine that the collection as a whole contained fundamental disagreements or contradictions, but it was understood that different parts of the anthology were the work of different authors, all of whom had spoken with their own voices, expressing their own views on a great variety of questions.

An initial paradox is to be noted. Because all forms of Judaism have found it necessary to justify their particular rules and teachings through interpretation of the Torah, this text has served as the common bond linking all forms of Judaism and distinguishing them from other religious traditions. Ancient Judaism in all its variety was characterized by constant appeal to the Torah as the ultimate source of validation in religious life. By the same token, however, because each form of Judaism has found it necessary to justify its particular rules and teachings through interpretation of this one Torah, it has served also as the cause of religious disputes among the Jews. By putting forth its own way of life as the correct, uniquely valid fulfillment of the commands of the Torah, and its own views as the correct, uniquely valid interpretation of the message of the Torah, each particular Jewish group has implied (or sometimes openly stated) that every other Jewish group is wrong. Thus, the Torah has constituted both the common thread in the history of Judaism and also the most contentious issue. These two roles have sprung from the same set of factors: they can never be separated.

Classical Rabbinic Judaism, which will provide the main focus for this essay, assumed its mature shape during the early centuries of the Common Era, but proper understanding of rabbinic approaches to Scripture requires some attention to issues that had emerged even before that time. During the last centuries of its existence the Jerusalem temple was dominated by priests belonging to the party called Sadducees, a group notorious for its refusal to acknowledge the binding validity of any religious custom not explicitly ordained in Scripture. The Mishnah (*Sukkah* 4.9) reports that a riot once broke out in the temple on the festival of Tabernacles (*Sukkot*) when the High Priest rejected with contempt an annual water libation much beloved by the people, but not authorized in Scripture. The Mishnah (*Eruvin* 3.2; 6.1) also reveals that the widespread practice of *'eruv,* which was designed to ease the severity of Sabbath restrictions, but was likewise ungrounded in Scripture, was not acknowledged by all Jews. As these two examples illustrate, the validity of tradition as a source of religious authority alongside and equal to Scripture was a contentious issue early in the history of Judaism.

Another fundamental question concerned the relative importance of the surface meaning and possible deeper meanings of the Torah's narratives and rules. In this case surviving evidence provides more information about the nature of this debate among the Greek-speaking Jews of ancient Alexandria. The noted philosopher Philo, who taught in Alexandria during the first half of the first century c.e., developed an elaborate technique for interpreting the Torah as a complex allegory about the nature of virtue and religious experience. Throughout his writings Philo insists that the rules of the Torah must be followed, but he repeatedly emphasizes as well that the real value of the Torah lies in the sublime truths that can be uncovered once the key to its hidden meanings has been found. The knowledge thus obtained, he believes, is not only of immeasurable intellectual value, but also provides a mystical ecstasy available from no other source. Philo often argues against the "literalists" who are blind to this deeper layer of truth that Scripture can be made to yield, but he argues as well, and equally vehemently, against those who believe that once they have found the deeper meaning of the Torah's rules they are freed of the obligation to follow them. He compares such people to hermits living alone in the wilderness lacking all regard for the proper functioning of society, or to souls living without a body, that is, without connection to the concrete human relationships of everyday life (see *on the Migration of Abraham* 89–90). Philonic allegory did not survive among the Jews, but the fundamental issue that it represents continued to draw attention.

Some pre-rabbinic groups of Jews, for example the authors of certain Dead Sea Scrolls or the Christians who stand behind the Gospel of Matthew, took great care to present themselves, their respective doctrines, and their respective ways of life as the unique concrete fulfillment of biblical prophecy. Rabbinic thinking did not generally tend in this direction; the early rabbis instead developed a view of Judaism that in principle embraced the entire Jewish people and included all generations of Jews from the days of Moses to the end of history. This view was built on the most novel contribution of the early rabbis to the history of Jewish thought: the idea of Oral Torah.

The rabbinic concept of Oral Torah provided a new context for the questions just reviewed. Building on earlier notions and themes (see, for example, 2 Esd. 14.45–47), the rabbis of late antiquity developed the idea that from the very time it was revealed the "Torah of Moses" had been largely unwritten. In their innovative view, the book called by that name which Jews had revered for centuries was in reality but a small part of the divine revelation that underlies Jewish life. The book, in fact, was not regarded as sufficient by itself to serve as a guide to the will of God. In one telling passage in the Babylonian Talmud, a person who has learned Scripture but not undergone full rabbinic training is condemned by a series of rabbis as no better than an ignoramus, or a boor, or a Samaritan, or even a Magus (b. Sotah 22a). "Oral Torah" became the rabbis' name for everything they taught that went beyond simple restatement of Scripture. In principle the availability or absence of a Scriptural basis for any teaching of the rabbis—and thus for any aspect of Jewish religious life—was no longer of critical importance.

To be sure, rabbinic authorities continued to reserve for Scripture a special role in Jewish religious life. Perhaps most important, the centerpiece of Sabbath morning synagogue worship remained the weekly reading of the Pentateuch. Rabbinic law in fact required that the reading be letter perfect, and from a scroll written in the ancient way without vowel signs, punctuation, or other diacritical marks. The preservation of this ritual kept the text of the Pentateuch intimately familiar to those Jews who regularly attended a synagogue; it was repeatedly heard and studied, and it supplied raw material for homiletic elaboration week after week, and year after year.

Eventually, however, Jewish religious life paradoxically came to rest, not on the Bible, but rather on books in which early rabbis' "Oral Torah" got written down. Of these, the best known and most important are the Mishnah and the two Talmuds. The Mishnah is a compilation of mostly legal rabbinic teaching that first appeared around 200 c.e. The Talmuds, one Palestinian (ca. 425 c.e.) and one Babylonian (6th century c.e.), are vast collections of rabbinic discussion organized as commentary on the Mishnah but extremely wide-ranging in actual subject-matter. With respect to both form and content the Mishnah is a free-standing text; while it quotes Scripture from time to time, it does not aim to provide a systematic commentary on the Bible nor does it invoke the Bible as the basis of its own authority or status as a sacred text. The Talmuds do seek in varying degrees to link Mishnaic teaching to Scripture, but again not in a systematic fashion and not with any sense that rabbinic teaching depends on the Bible for its own validity. This central corpus of rabbinic literature thus makes clear that rabbinic Judaism in its own formative period assigned the sacred canon of Scripture an essentially marginal role in Jewish religious life.

Nevertheless, the early rabbis did study Scripture, and their own generic name for the hermeneutic methods underlying this activity was *midrash* ("inquiry"). Although lacking the systematic comprehensiveness of Philonic allegory, rabbinic midrash—the careful examination of Scripture in search of additional meanings alongside (or beyond, or beneath) the "plain" sense of the text—became a ubiquitous mode of discourse. Substantial portions of the Talmud take the form of attempts to associate with Scripture rabbinic teachings about all sorts of topics that have at first glance no particular connection to the passages adduced. Midrash thus served as a technique for overcoming the theoretical independence of Scripture and Oral Torah. Through skillful midrashic elaboration, virtually all of rabbinic teaching could be presented as interpretation of Scripture and all of Scripture could be understood as conforming to rabbinic teaching. To be sure, some rabbinic documents strive more energetically than others to achieve this synthesis of Scripture with tradition; the Mishnah, in particular, seems almost entirely uninterested in the question. In general, however, it became an important goal of later rabbinic inquiry to supply such links in cases where none had yet been found.

With respect to the second problem noted above, namely the relation between the surface meaning of Scripture and any additional significance that might be extracted from its text, midrash offered a technique for multiplying such extra interpretations virtually without limit while never losing track of the surface-level, contextually derived "simple meaning" (*pshat*) of the text. Midrash was unconcerned in principle with the plausibility of its exegesis or with the original context of its biblical raw materials; any meaning which any interpreter could derive from any detail in the biblical text could at least in theory be offered as a midrash on that text.

The power of midrash to extract unexpected meaning from the text of the Bible can best be understood through the following examples, which illustrate different applications of the procedure.

One frequent use of midrash was to solve a problem arising from the biblical text without explicitly acknowledging the force of that problem. The story of the "Binding of Isaac" in Genesis ch. 22 tells of God's command to Abraham that he offer his beloved son as a sacrifice; the story as told presents this command as a test of Abraham's obedience, but this idea is profoundly disturbing on both the moral and theological planes.

By juxtaposing Gen. 22.1 with Ps. 60.6, however, the verb *nissah* in Genesis, translated as "tested," can be linked to the noun *nes*, meaning "banner" or "standard," from the Psalm. This link allows the notoriously troublesome verse in Genesis to be translated "God put Abraham on display as one might a banner." The idea that God had tested Abraham through the cruel device of demanding the sacrifice of Isaac is thus removed from the text; it is replaced with the more gratifying notion that by pretending to make such a demand God had put Abraham's obedience on display for the whole world to see, and thus justified God's choice of Abraham as bearer of the covenant (see *Genesis Rabba* 55.1).

Midrash, however, was not used only to solve problems; it served as well to supply a scriptural basis for fundamental rabbinic teachings. Thus, by combining Gen. 1.1 with Prov. 8.22, each of which contains the word *reshit* (beginning), and by a novel interpretation of the one-letter preposition usually translated "in" with which the Torah begins, Rabbi Oshaia sought to demonstrate that the Torah—here identified with the "Wisdom" of Proverbs—existed before the world was created and in fact served as a kind of blueprint for its creation (see *Genesis Rabba* 1.1).

These two examples illustrate the points made above that midrash aims primarily at the discovery of new meaning in the biblical text and that midrash is normally uninterested in either the literary context of the verses (or even the words and letters) being interpreted or the exegetical plausibility of the interpretations reached. Midrash in principle aims at the endless production of new meaning, limited only by the ingenuity of the interpreter, and motivated by any imaginable consideration, from the fundamental to the superficial.

This unfettered approach to the words of Scripture was not without its problems, and efforts were made from an early time to subject midrash to various sorts of regulation. Hillel, the semilegendary proto-rabbi of the first century B.C.E., is said to have drawn up a set of seven norms by which the Torah might be interpreted, and a closely-related but expanded set of thirteen is somewhat more reliably attributed to the second-century Rabbi Ishmael. These norms did not function by way of dictating the interpretation that an exegete was expected to provide— even with such norms there was still no single correct interpretation of the Torah—but instead provided a list of acceptable types of argument. Anyone proposing a new interpretation for a given verse—in particular anyone seeking to derive new law (*halakhah*) from the text of Scripture— now had to be able to justify that interpretation or derive that new law through one of these types of argument.

These rules of interpretation themselves were not equally plausible by modern Western standards. In the lists of both Hillel and R. Ishmael the first norm is called *gal wa-homer,* and functions much like the argument *a fortiori* that is found in many logical systems. For instance, in the *Tosefta,* another collection of rabbinic material, the argument occurs that if God counts even an unintentional good deed as a good deed nonetheless, "how much more" will God count an intentional good deed as good (*T. Peah* 3.8). The validity of this mode of argument was beyond challenge, both on account of its intuitive cogency and also because examples of it could be found in the Scriptures themselves (e.g., Gen. 44.8, Exod. 6.12, Deut. 31.27). The second norm, however, is not strictly logical at all. Called *gezerah shawwah*, this type of argument is based on the idea that any two verses containing the same word must be linked in meaning as well, even if the word in question is no more than a common particle. To give one example, the religious obligations of women and of slaves were declared equal in a great variety of situations because biblical references to divorce and to manumission both contain the word "to her" (*b. Hagigah* 4a; see Lev. 19.20 and Deut. 24.1).

Now *gezerah shawwah* is unlike a more logical argument such as *gal wa-homer* in that there is no way such a demonstration can be refuted; in the hands of irresponsible practitioners this can lead to uncontrollably outlandish results. In recognition of this state of affairs, by the end of the Talmudic period (in the mid-sixth century C.E.) the rule had been established that no one could offer a new *gezerah shawwah* of his own invention, which is to say that no new laws could be derived from the Torah by means of this interpretive device (*b. Pesahim* 66a). In effect *gezerah shawwah* was removed by common consent from the repertoire of future interpreters of the Torah, although certain arguments from *gezerah shawwah* such as the one cited above that had the prestige of tradition behind them were allowed to stand.

Debate over the need for plausibility in midrash seems to have become most articulate in a set of disputes attributed to the second-century authorities Akiva and Ishmael. Rabbi Ishmael is repeatedly cited as having affirmed the principle that "the Torah speaks in the manner of human language" (*b. Berakhot* 31b); this means the Torah must not be interpreted in a manner that forces the biblical text into implausible or artificial constructions. Ishmael's great contemporary Akiva, however, approached the Torah as though every letter was a separate divine oracle. He was famed for his ability to find meaning in grammatical particles, in anomalies of spelling, in the sequence of topics, in the juxtaposition of apparently unrelated paragraphs. As later generations reported the debates between these two, the imaginative hermeneutics that Akiva championed aroused opposition: when Akiva interpreted the "and" (in Hebrew a single letter) of Lev. 21.9 ("[And] when a priest's daughter makes herself profane by becoming a prostitute, . . . she must be burnt.") to mean that a priest's betrothed daughter caught in adultery was to be executed by burning even if she was not yet married, Ishmael is said to have responded, "And because you interpret 'and's' shall we take this girl out for burning?" (*b. Sanhedrin* 51b).

Over the following generations, the techniques of Akiva gained wide acceptance, but attempts to ground Jewish law (*halakhah*) in this way never fully overcame the resistance of more sober-minded rabbis. As a result, two contrasting tendencies—one that read the Torah as though it was an ordinary though very important text; and one that read the Torah as though it was a product of divine perfection demanding imaginative elaboration of every detail—existed side by side for the rest of antiquity and beyond, through the Middle Ages and into the modern world.

It should be reiterated, however, that both sides in this debate were expressing rabbinic viewpoints. There was no dispute between them over the fundamental belief that in the long run the rabbis with their Oral Torah would determine the proper interpretation of Scripture; this was true for both the "simple meaning" of the text and also any midrashic elaboration that might be proposed. All rabbis agreed that Scripture could not be properly understood outside the framework of rabbinic tradition, and this meant that in theory, even if never fully in practice, the concept of Oral Torah made study of Scripture a second-rank activity in Jewish life. Rabbinic teaching as laid down in the great post-biblical texts, chiefly the Talmud, became the real foundation of Jewish law and the real fountainhead of Jewish thought. Scripture was not cast aside, needless to say; the education of children began with the Pentateuch, the public reading of the Torah in the synagogue remained a central feature of the liturgy, certain individuals studied the rest of Scripture as a kind of private interest, and some even prepared distinguished commentaries on post-Mosaic books of the Bible. Nevertheless, the center of gravity of Jewish religious life had shifted away from Scripture to something else. Under rabbinic tutelage the Jewish religious tradition continued to develop, neither fully independent of Scripture nor yet directly dependent on Scripture for its fundamental character; the history of Judaism is more a history of rabbinic thought (and later on, of responses to rabbinic thought) than a history of biblical interpretation.

Biblical Interpretation
in the Early Church

ELIZABETH A. CLARK

The Bible of the Early Christians

Christianity's entry to the world as a Jewish sect had profound consequences for its development. Possessing a distinctive body of texts, the Jewish Bible, was an important source of legitimacy for early Christians. Long after Christianity had acquired an almost exclusively "Gentile" constituency, it retained these Scriptures—yet claimed a monopoly on their interpretation. From the time of Paul onward, "the Law and the Prophets" (and soon, other books of Jewish Scripture) received extensive commentary by Christians. The "Old Testament," as Christians called it, was indeed *the* Bible for the earliest followers of Jesus. Even in the early second century, some Christians believed that if you could not find a teaching in the "charters" of the Old Testament, you should not believe it in the Gospel.

The formation of the New Testament took some time. Although Paul's letters, the Gospels, and several other Christian books later included in the New Testament were circulating by the late first century C.E., some Christians claimed that they preferred "the living and abiding voice" (i.e., the oral transmission of Christian teaching) to written documents. These issues were largely resolved in the course of the second century: Justin Martyr's account of a Christian worship service dating from the mid-second century reports that "on the day of the sun," Christians gather in assemblies where they hear read "the memoirs of the Apostles" (the Gospels, and perhaps Acts and the Pauline letters) as well as "the writings of the prophets."

Our earliest list of which Christian books were judged "Scripture"—the so-called Muratorian Canon—probably dates to the late second century. It lists the Gospels, Acts, Paul's letters (understood to include 1, 2 Timothy and Titus), Revelation, 1 and 2 John, and Jude, but several books of the modern canon are missing from the list: Hebrews, James, 3 John, and perhaps 1 and 2 Peter. Also surprising, the list of accepted books includes the Wisdom of Solomon and the *Apocalypse of Peter*. One criterion the anonymous author of the Muratorian Canon gives for whether a book is truly "Scriptural" is its suitability for public reading in church—although he does not tell us what determines such suitability. Nonetheless, here we glimpse the importance of Christian worship in constituting and interpreting Christian Scripture. Since it is probable that many early Christians, like their non-Christian neighbors, were illiterate (at least as far as their ability to read entire books was concerned), worship services might have been their only opportunity to hear the Bible.

It is not until 367 C.E. in Athanasius' *Festal Letter* that we find a list of Christian books that corresponds in every detail to the 27 now contained in the New Testament. Writing a few decades earlier, the church historian Eusebius of Caesarea reported that among the books disputed at his time were James, Jude, 2 Peter, and 2 and 3 John. Eusebius also tells what books had been rejected: among these stand several of the apocryphal gospels, Christian apocalypses, and several pieces of early Christian literature not included in our New Testament, such as the *Epistle of Barnabas,* the *Shepherd of Hermas,* and the *Teachings of the Apostles (The Didache).* He reports that there was considerable debate over the status of the Apocalypse of John (Revelation), a debate that we know continued throughout the fourth century. Moreover, a few Christian dissidents even questioned the then-settled canon of the Old Testament, arguing that such works as Job or the Song of Songs should not be included as genuine "Scripture." By the late fourth century, however, most Christians had accepted the 27 books we call the New Testament as well as the Jewish Scriptures in Greek translation (the Septuagint)—the latter including the books now designated as the Old Testament Apocrypha. Yet even within these accepted boundaries, many Scriptural verses required elaborate "sanitization" to make them useful and edifying for Christian consumption.

Although the church retained the Jewish Scriptures as part of its canon, its members, like most Jews throughout the Roman Empire, heard these Scriptures read to them in Greek (or later, in the West, Latin) translation. Only a handful of early Christian scholars had sufficient proficiency in Hebrew or Aramaic to consult the Old Testament in its languages of composition—and those scholars who did, such as Origen in the third century and Jerome in the fourth, often found themselves under attack for their "Jewish" predilections. What's the matter with the Septuagint?—as Augustine peevishly asked Jerome, whose Latin translation of the Hebrew Bible ("the Vulgate") was in process. Surely at this late date, Augustine protests, there is not anything to be found in the Hebrew text "which escaped so many translators who were perfectly acquainted with the language." His implication, of course, is that it would not be in accordance with Christian doctrine to imagine that the Greek translation was any less inspired by God than was the original Hebrew.

"Ownership" of Scripture

If emerging Catholic Christianity, institutionalized as the "Great Church," decided to retain Jewish Scripture as part of its canon, this did not mean that Christians accepted Jewish interpretations of those Scriptures. In the course of the second century, mainstream Christianity warred on two fronts. Against the Jews, Christian writers claimed that the "Old Testament" was *theirs,* was in essence a Christian book that contained hundreds of references to the coming of Jesus and the development of the Christian religion. Yet over against various Christian groups deemed heretical by the Great Church, Catholic Christians ferociously defended the importance of retaining these Jewish documents as "Scripture."

During Christianity's early expansion, many converts to the new faith either had no interest in preserving Jewish Scripture as part of the Christian sacred books, or believed that much in the Old Testament was inspired by a "lower" God who could not be identified with the Father of Jesus. For the most radical of these dissenters—such as Marcion, an important second-century critic of Catholic Christianity—it was best simply to dispense with the Hebrew Bible entirely: Jesus' teaching did not "fulfill" Jewish Scripture, but replaced it wholesale. Nor should Christians give their allegiance to the deity who supposedly inspired those writings. Marcion even went so far as to pit the words and deeds of the "lower" Creator God of the Old Testament against those of Jesus' Father, the true God. Yet if the Old Testament was rejected, what could serve as "Scripture" for Christians? Marcion made a "canon" of Christian documents—his was the first Christian attempt at formulating a canon—which consisted of ten letters of Paul plus an expurgated version of the Gospel of Luke, omitting references to the Creator God as Jesus' Father and to the birth stories of Jesus, which in Marcion's view subjected Jesus to disgusting material processes.

The teachers of the Great Church were outraged by Marcion's move. One outcry against Marcion's teaching issued from the late second-century bishop of Lyons, Irenaeus. Against Marcion, Irenaeus insisted that both Testaments proclaim one and the same God. The correctness of this belief, Irenaeus claimed, is guaranteed by the unbroken succession of bishops who transmitted the authoritative teaching from earliest Christian times—whereas Marcion was a latecomer upon the scene who had no privileged access to the ancient Christian traditions. But, as we can recognize from our vantage point, Irenaeus had no universally accepted canon of Scripture to replace the one that Marcion had given *his* followers. Indeed, it was in the struggle with second and third century dissidents that leaders of the Great Church slowly came to a consensus about which books should be included in the Christian canon.

If Marcion had resolved the problem of Jewish Scripture's relevance to Christianity by excising it, other second-century Christians adopted different approaches. In this period a variety of movements developed which we group under the umbrella term "Gnosticism." Common to many Gnostics was the view that the Creator of the world, also the giver of Old Testament Law, was a lesser deity whose ignorance of the High God, and of his own limited importance, led him to utter the embarrassing boast, "I am God and there is no other God beside me" (Exod. 20.2–3; Deut. 4.35). He was so ignorant that he had to ask Adam in the Garden of Eden, "Where are you?" (Gen. 3.9). His attempt to prevent Adam from eating of the tree of knowledge shows his envy, and the expulsion of Adam from Paradise to prevent his partaking of the tree of life shows this deity's malice. This is the God who says that he will visit the sins of the fathers upon the children to the third and fourth generations (Exod. 20.5), that he will make people's hearts thick and their minds blind so that they cannot understand (Isa. 6.10). What sort of a deity is this, that we should worship him, the Gnostic author of the *Testimony of Truth* asks scathingly? The valuations placed by "mainstream" Christians upon the Biblical stories could also be reversed by Gnostics: the wise serpent in Genesis 3 becomes a sympathetic character who helps Eve to achieve knowledge. In such ways, Gnostic authors referred to the Biblical text—but only to deprecate its authority or to reverse the moral values that Catholic Christians had read within its pages.

The approach to Hebrew Scripture of Ptolemy, a Gnostic teacher associated with the Valentinian school, is gentler. Writing to Flora, a potential follower, Ptolemy informs her that there has been much misunderstanding among Christians about the Mosaic Law: the truth is, it issued neither from the "perfect God" nor from the devil, but from an intermediary deity, a "just God." Parts of the Old Testament are divinely inspired and others are human creations that carry varying degrees of authority. Offensive legal injunctions such as the law of retaliation (Exod. 21.23–25), should be rejected. Other parts, such as the ritual laws, should be given a symbolic interpretation, not practiced literally. Yet, Ptolemy claims, even the "pure" laws, such as the Ten Commandments, are problematic: since Jesus is said to have fulfilled the law (Matt. 5.17), even the supposedly "pure" legislation must not have been perfect. Ptolemy, like many other Christian Gnostic writers, differentiated between the types of teachings which "ordinary" (i.e., Catholic) Christians accept and those appropriate for the spiritual elite, for those who are truly enlightened.

Except for his notion that a "lesser" God inspired the Old Testament, Ptolemy's view does not differ much from that of an "orthodox" second-century writer, the author of the *Epistle of Barnabas,* who uses a variety of interpretive devices to rescue the Old Testament for Christian use. For one, "Barnabas" (as we may call the anonymous author) believes that the Old Testament provides its own corrective interpretation: the prophets themselves railed against the Hebrews' ritual and sacrificial practices, thus showing that they, like Christians, advocated their abolition. Since some Hebrew practices such as circumcision were not unique to the Jews, they can safely be abandoned. The dietary laws were meant to symbolize moral virtues and vices: the prohibition against pork means that we should not associate with people who resemble swine; that against eating hare, that we should not be "corrupters of boys."

Barnabas also furnishes an early Christian example of typological interpretation, in which various details from the Old Testament are said to prefigure, or represe.. 'n advance, events fulfilled in the New Testament. Thus the scapegoat of Leviticus 16 who was sent into the desert bearing away the Israelites' sins is a "type" of Jesus, who suffered for human sinfulness. Likewise, when Moses stood upright with his arms outstretched surveying a battle (Exod. 17.8–13), he is a "type" of Jesus' cross.

Typological explanation was much developed by the mid-second-century author, Justin Martyr, in his *Dialogue with Trypho*. In this text, Justin stages a debate over correct interpretation of the Old Testament between a Jew and a Christian. In Justin's view, all features of the Jewish ritual rule pointed ahead to Christianity. Thus the Passover lamb is a "type" of Christ; the offering of fine flours, a "type" of the Eucharistic bread; the bells on the high priest's robe, "types" of the apostles. The Jewish interlocutor, Trypho, responds: Why then were such laws given to the Jews to be celebrated physically, not just understood typologically? Because of their sinfulness, Justin answers: Fleshly circumcision was ordained to separate the Jews from other nations and to make them suffer for their sins that culminated in their murder of Jesus. Dietary laws, sabbath observances, sacrifices—all these were for the hardness of the Jews' hearts as punishment for their wickedness. The only beneficial parts of Hebrew Scripture are thus those in which we can find a Christian referent. Just as "Barnabas" claimed that the covenant was "ours, not theirs" (i.e., that it belonged to the Christians, not to the Jews), so Justin argues against Trypho that the Scriptures are "ours, not yours." God's gift of prophecy has been taken away from the Jews and given to the Christians.

Pagan Critiques of Scripture

Christian commentators were also pushed by pagan scholars hostile to their religion to examine several problematic aspects of Scripture. Three pagan critics were particularly important for early Christian exegesis: Celsus, the late second-century author of a book entitled *The True Word;* the third-century Platonic critic of Christianity, Porphyry; and the mid-fourth-century pagan emperor, Julian "the Apostate."

Celsus debunked both the Old and the New Testaments. He claimed that the story of Jesus' virgin birth was a fabrication and that Jesus performed extraordinary deeds through the magical practices he had learned in Egypt. He compares the story of Adam and Eve unfavorably to the legends of human creation found in Greek writings. Some Christian teachings, Celsus argues, are just recycled versions of Greek philosophy: the injunction to "turn the other cheek" was derived from a passage in Plato's dialogue, the *Crito*. According to Celsus, both the ancient Jews and the present-day Christians were constituted from the lowest social classes and hence are highly superstitious—a point that makes ridiculous their claim that God cares for them alone. Nor does the Bible inculcate lofty morals, as the story of Lot's incestuous relations with his daughters demonstrates.

Porphyry, although his writings exist in even more fragmentary form than do Celsus', appears to have been a more serious scholar of the Bible. His criticism of the Old Testament focused especially on the Book of Daniel, and his general view is the one accepted by modern scholars: that the author of Daniel was not "foreseeing" Hebrew history from the vantage point of the sixth century B.C.E., but lived at the time of the Maccabean revolt four centuries later and described in "code" language the events of his own time. Christian writers of the fourth and fifth centuries, including the greatest Christian scholar of his age, Jerome, struck at Porphyry's revisionist thesis and opted for the traditional dating of Daniel.

Porphyry also attacked the New Testament, especially the inconsistencies in the Gospels, such as the discrepancies between the genealogies in Matthew and in Luke. He also notes the opposition between Peter and Paul (as reported in Galatians) as a means to discredit the apostles. Porphyry knew his Scripture so well that he could even point out passages in which the Gospel writers misidentified Scriptural quotations they took from the Old Testament.

The attack of Julian "the Apostate," titled *Against the Galileans,* centers on the Christian deviation from Old Testament teaching: how can Christians claim the Hebrew heritage for themselves and appropriate its Scriptures when they do not observe Jewish traditions and laws? Jesus' healings are worthy of mockery, his moral teaching is inadequate. His followers kill those who disagree with them and overturn their temples: this is the treatment received by those who refuse to "wail over the corpse" (of Jesus) as the Christians do. Julian also pinpoints differences among the Gospels: why does only the Gospel of John report that Jesus made heaven and earth? Why do Matthew and Luke differ on Jesus' genealogy? Although Moses said that the Law was for all time (e.g., in Exod. 12.14–15), Christians try to rationalize their non-observance of its precepts by falsely claiming that God meant the Law to remain in effect only for a short period of time.

Christian writers struggled to answer these critiques. In many cases, the pagan critics had spotted problems for which only the research of the past two centuries has provided explanations. Yet Christian authors tried to turn the pagan attacks to their own benefit. Thus, for example, Origen replies to Celsus that it is one of Christianity's marvels that even the ignorant (he specifies women and children) are cured of bad living through its precepts—while sophisticated intellectuals are also won over to the faith by its pure worship of God.

Augustine, in his *On the Harmony of the Gospels,* directed in part against Porphyry's criticism, labors to show that the discrepancies in the Gospels are only *apparent.* Thus, for Augustine, the divergent genealogies in Matthew and Luke are *both* true, since Joseph had both a "natural" and an adoptive father. Moreover, the discrepancies between what we call the Synoptics and John are not really that: the writers of Matthew, Mark, and Luke chose to speak more of Jesus' earthly life, not of his divinity, while John took a different approach. These variations do not represent "discrepancies," but merely the individual preferences of the Gospel writers.

According to Origen, the pagan critics mocked Christian Scripture because they adopted a strictly literal exegesis and refused to explore Scripture's mystical or allegorical meanings. Celsus put the point somewhat differently: intelligent Jews and Christians resort to allegorical interpretations "because they are ashamed" of the stories in the Bible. And he had a point: many texts had to be rendered more morally edifying and spiritually enlightening to be useful to the Church. Allegorical interpretation—the location of a "higher," non-literal meaning for Scriptural verses—thus loomed large on the agenda of the early church's approach to the Bible.

Allegorical Interpretation

Allegorical interpretation had a venerable history before Christian commentators appropriated it: both pagan commentators and philosophically-minded Jews such as Philo of Alexandria had employed allegorical exegesis to smooth over the problematic texts of their respective traditions. For sophisticated Hellenes, the ancient myths that portrayed deities as lying, fighting, and committing adultery were unacceptable as literal stories. The problem such intellectuals faced was how to retain the texts but give them different meanings. Likewise, the early Christian commentators struggled to affirm that both Testaments were morally and spiritually uplifting in all their parts through allegorical exegesis. Thus we see that the church's interests in interpreting the Bible were essentially practical.

The great master of allegorical interpretation in the early church was undoubtedly Origen. Book Four of his *On First Principles* contains the fullest defense of allegorical exegesis among early Christian writings. Since Origen believed that the "truth" of the Old Testament had been brought to light only with the coming of Jesus, it was important for his purpose to convince Christian audiences that the Hebrew Scriptures were enlightening. He argued against both the Jews, who denied that Old Testament prophecy referred to Christ, and the Gnostics, who mocked Biblical passages in which God was said to be angry or jealous, to repent, or to be responsible for evil. The problem of such opponents, Origen alleges, is that they employ only literal interpretations that damage the faith. Although all Scripture has a spiritual meaning, Origen believes, not all of it has a "bodily" sense. Some passages simply cannot be taken literally: for example, how could there have been "evening and morning" (Gen. 1.5, 8, 13) when there were not yet sun, moon, and stars? How can a thinking Christian believe that God "walked in Paradise in the cool of the day" (Gen. 3.8)? And in his Biblical commentaries, Origen was deeply concerned to answer the Gnostic charge that books such as Joshua showed the Old Testament God to be a bloodthirsty warmonger.

Nor did the Gospels escape Origen's relentless eye. Take, for example, the story of Jesus' temptation by the devil (Matt. 4.8). The Gospel writer reports that Jesus was taken to a high mountain from which he was told to view "the kingdoms of the whole world." How ridiculous, Origen writes, to think that from any mountain in Palestine you could see as far as Persia or India! And there are "thousands" of such passages whose hidden purpose is to convince Christians that not all the Bible can be read as historical truth.

Origen was not, of course, on a faith-smashing mission; he wanted to prove that such interpretive problems show up the deficiencies of a "historical" reading of the Bible. We should instead be encouraged, on such occasions, to search out the mystical or allegorical meaning of the passage, deliberately hidden under apparently offensive or meaningless texts. Thus the tale of earthly love and sexual desire found in the Song of Songs becomes for Origen an allegory of Christ's love for the church or for the individual Christian; the warfare of the Israelites to win the Promised Land becomes the Christian's struggle against the passions to win the Kingdom of Heaven.

Similar to Origen's struggle against the Gnostics was Augustine's battle with the Manicheans, whose beliefs and practices represented a more dangerous form of Gnostic teaching and posed a serious threat to the institutional church of the fourth century. For the brilliant young Augustine, the Bible seemed too crude to be worthy of acceptance. Only when he saw how Ambrose of Milan rendered Scripture palatable by allegorical exegesis did Augustine begin his conversion to the Christian religion. That he had been a Manichean for a long period in his young adulthood made his struggle against it, as a Catholic writer, especially intense.

Manichean leaders were close readers of the Bible. A formidable opponent of Augustine was the Manichean Faustus. Faustus' attack on the Bible was a three-pronged attempt to show that unworthy characteristics (such as ignorance and envy) are ascribed to God in the Old Testament; that the promises and blessings given to the Israelites were purely material (riches, land, progeny) and hence were unrelated to a spiritual salvation; and that the behavior of the Old Testament patriarchs was nothing short of disgusting. Who would want to sit at table in the Kingdom of Heaven with men like Jacob, who had "led the life of a goat" with his four wives? Since the Christian tradition aimed at a higher ideal—and North African Manicheans believed that they were the truest Christians—why accept the paltry offerings of the Jewish Bible?

Augustine's response to Faustus rests on the principle that *nothing* in the Bible is without meaning; throughout, God teaches us, if only we look to the symbolic meaning of the verses. Thus, Old Testament rituals serve as "types" of Christian truths, and the food laws contain allegories (once again, not eating pig meat becomes an injunction against swinish behavior). Nor should Jesus' teachings be interpreted as in opposition to the Old Testament. For example, his prohibition of divorce does not run counter to the Hebrew command that a man must write out a bill of divorce for his wife (Deut. 24.1), since the latter was intended to "prevent" divorce: the Old and the New Testament thus are in agreement.

Allegorical exegesis meant that contemporary audiences—Augustine's congregation, for example—would see the relevance of Biblical stories for their own moral lives. Thus the parable of the Good Samaritan is not a tale of how an "outsider's" charity overcame ancient Jewish exclusiveness, but provides theological instruction for Christians: the man is Adam, who falls among thieves (i.e., is overcome by sin); he is taken to an inn (the church), receives oil and wine (the Christian sacraments) and must remain there, a convalescent, until the day when he departs to acquire perfect health in the Kingdom of God. Thus, besides functioning to keep the Bible "Christian," allegory also rendered the text a tool for Christians' moral development and loyalty to the church.

Non-Allegorical Exegesis

Not all interpreters of Scripture in the early church were as devoted to allegorical exegesis as Origen and Augustine. For example, the second-century churchman Irenaeus of Lyons, who was concerned to combat fanciful interpretations of Scripture offered by Gnostic exegetes, advocated a "plainer" style of reading. Often the "anti-allegorists" are described as belonging to the "school of Antioch" and are hailed as forerunners of modern "literal" interpretation. Such a claim seems exaggerated, for even the figures who criticized the heavy use of allegorical interpretation by their contemporaries tended to explain Scripture along typological and spiritual lines, far removed from the kinds of literary and historical explication taught in classes on the Bible today at colleges and universities.

An important leader of the "anti-allegory" movement in the fourth century was Diodore of Tarsus, who apparently composed a (now lost) treatise entitled *On the Difference Between Theōria and Allegory*. From other writings of Diodore, we gather that he objected to the allegorists' erasure of the "plain sense" of historical accounts. By appealing to what Diodore and his colleagues called *theōria*, these "anti-allegorists" attempted to understand the spiritual vision that enabled the Biblical writers to penetrate the "deeper" meanings of texts and to foresee later developments of history. Diodore argued that when Paul in Galatians 4 spoke of the "allegory" of Sarah and Hagar, he was not referring to the type of exegesis practiced by Origen. Paul did not erase the status of Hagar and Sarah as real people who had lived in the past, but rather understood the two women to represent, respectively, unbelieving Jews and future Christian believers. Likewise, the events in Genesis 2 and 3 are better described under the rubric of "enigmas" than of "allegories": the serpent, an irrational animal who cannot speak, is used by the devil. Genesis 3 is thus truly historical, but contains a deeper explanation than what immediately meets the eye in the tale of a talking snake. And in Diodore's interpretation of the Psalms, he took care to point out the historical circumstances of the particular psalm's composition, whether it referred to a threat to Israel from the Assyrians, the Babylonian exile, or other historical events.

Similar concerns are present in the exegesis of Theodore of Mopsuestia, who had been Diodore's student. Unlike most church fathers Theodore took a free hand in rejecting books from the Old Testament canon that he thought had inappropriately been placed there: out went Job and the Song of Songs, Chronicles, Ezra and Nehemiah, and from the New Testament, the Catholic Epistles. For these and for other theological errors, he was condemned by a church council meeting in 553. Like his teacher, Theodore did not think that Paul's words in Galatians 4 gave a license for allegorical exegesis: Paul kept the historical referent of the study of Hagar and Sarah, very unlike those allegorists who can not distinguish history from "dreams in the night," and who use Scripture to serve their own ends. The "higher" meaning of a Biblical text is not, then, to be found in allegory, but in a spiritualized and typological reading that preserves the historicity of events. As an example of the latter, Theodore lists the story of Jonah's mission to the Ninevites, which prefigures Christ's stay in the tomb, his resurrection, and his appearance to all nations.

On some points, Theodore's interpretations seem modern, for example, his view that the chronology of the Gospel of John may sometimes be preferable to that of the other three gospels. Theodore was also unusual for his time in understanding that some difficulties in the interpretation of the Old Testament were occasioned by the Septuagint's translators' misunderstanding of the Hebrew. Hebrew, in any case, he notes, is very different in structure from Greek, and some features of Hebrew writing (such as the repetition of verbs) are inappropriate to Greek syntax.

In the late patristic period we find the first reference to a fourfold model of interpretation that was to become very popular in the Middle Ages: the monastic writer John Cassian appears to have been the first to distinguish allegorical exegesis not just from literal, but also from tropological (i.e., moral) and anagogical (i.e., relating to the heavenly afterlife). In this model, "Jerusalem" means a city of the Jews (literally), the church (allegorically), the soul (tropologically), and our heavenly home (anagogically).

Last, the later fourth century saw the production of a famous *Book of Rules* (for exegesis) by the North African churchman, Tyconius. Tyconius thought that the entire Bible, including the Old Testament, described the church—and hence, like many other early Christian interpreters, he insisted that all details of Scripture found their relevance in contemporary Christianity.

Later Theological Polemic and Scriptural Interpretation

It was not only in struggles with Gnostics, pagans, and Jews in the second and third centuries that exegesis was important: the doctrinal debates of the fourth and fifth centuries about God, Christ, sin, and ethics all proceeded by means of exegetical debate over particular Scriptural verses. Some verses became veritable "prooftexts" for one or another side of a controversy. Passages that earlier had been deemed useful for "orthodox" theological argument now became the site of embattled exegeses when the so-called "heretics" appropriated them to support their cause. Take the case of Prov. 8.22–31, a testimony to Wisdom's cooperative role alongside God in the production of the universe. In second-century ex-egesis, these verses were quoted to prove that the Son or the Holy Spirit, interpreted as "Wisdom," was always with God the Father. By the early fourth century, however, the verses had become highly suspect, since Arians used them to argue that the Son of God was a secondary and created being, not metaphysically equal to God the Father. Those who championed the decision of the Council of Nicaea in 325, on the other hand, held that the Father and the Son were "of one substance." Accordingly, for Nicaean orthodoxy, Prov. 8 could not be used to describe the relations of Father and Son within the Trinity; rather, they referred only to the period of Jesus' incarnation, when the eternal Son of God took on a created body that could hunger, thirst, and suffer.

Another notable controversy, this time waged among Latin Christians, concerned the proper interpretation of Rom. 5.12: "It was through one man that sin entered the world, and through sin death, and thus death pervaded the whole human race, inasmuch as all have sinned." In the early fifth century, Paul's words regarding the universality of human sinfulness were given a sharper edge in the battle between the followers of Pelagius and those of Augustine. Pelagius was a champion of human free will, God's gift lavished on human beings at creation and retained despite sin. Augustine, in contrast, thought that our free will (i.e., the freedom to choose the good) had been brought to an end by Adam's sinful deed. Augustine, reading a Latin translation of the verse, took Paul to mean that because of Adam's sin, sin and death passed to all other human beings through the mechanism of the lust that attends sexual intercourse. Pelagians preferred to interpret the verse to mean that Adam set a bad example in sinning that other human beings followed. And a Pelagian author of the 420s, Julian of Eclanum, went even further to challenge Augustine's interpretation: Augustine had no Scriptural grounds for claiming that it was through sexual intercourse that the sin passed to the fetus being conceived, for Rom. 5.12 reads, "through *one* man"—and everyone, even the foggy-headed Augustine, must know that sexual reproduction takes two!

Not all struggles over the use of Scripture involved human combatants. The desert ascetics, whose Christian commitment led them to staggering feats of bodily renunciation, believed that the ultimate Christian struggle lay against demons who, as agents of Satan, were old masters of Scriptural manipulation. Evagrius Ponticus supplies examples of the monks' struggles with demons who both quote Scripture and are defeated by Scripture. Thus the demon of lust could whisper verses from 1 Timothy on the goodness of marriage and childbearing, or the demon of gluttony might counsel you to drink a little wine "to help your digestion" (1 Tim. 5.23). Against these demonic Biblical experts, the desert monks armed themselves with verses of Scripture, much as Jesus is represented as withstanding the Tempter in Luke 4 and Matthew 4. Entire catalogs of Scriptural verses were drawn up corresponding to the vices that the monk must combat: gluttony, lust, avarice, and so forth. Thus a monk given to anger could repeat to himself, among many other verses, Eccles. 7.9, "Do not be quick to take offense, for it is fools who nurse resentment." A monk tempted by avarice when he recalled his parents' fine home, compared to his present miserable cell, was advised to repeat Ps. 84.10, "Better to linger by the threshold of God's house than to live in the dwellings of the wicked." Armed with these and hundreds of other verses, the desert ascetics employed Scripture they had memorized to fight the supreme enemy—much as Catholic polemicists used specific verses to defeat their "heretical" opponents.

Conclusion

We return to a dominant theme of this essay: the *practical* nature of the church's use of Scripture. The meaning of Scripture was developed through its use both to indoctrinate the Christian masses and to protect the church's power against its competitors. On the pastoral level, the Bible could instruct, exhort, and console. Beyond this, the Great Church used its Scriptural resources to counter the views of pagans, Jews, and "heretics." Thus Christians early tried to wrest exegetical control over the Old Testament from the Jews, and later, employed Scripture to pronounce definitive interpretations against rival Christian groups. To these ends, typological and allegorical exegesis played a decisive role. Allegorical interpretation is a means by which a community deals with and claims its sacred text; but it is also a way of securing that text against rivals. Early Christian Biblical interpretation did not arise in the ancient equivalent of an ivory tower, but on an ecclesiastical battleground. Then, as now, there was no such thing as disinterested interpretation.

SUGGESTIONS FOR FURTHER READING

Ackroyd, P. R., and C. F. Evans, eds. *The Cambridge History of the Bible. Volume I: From the Beginnings to Jerome.* Cambridge: University Press, 1970.

Dawson, John David. *Ancient Alexandrian Interpretation of Scripture.* Ph.D. dissertation, Yale University, 1988.

Froehlich, Karlfried. *Biblical Interpretation in the Early Church.* Philadelphia: Fortress Press, 1984.

Grant, Robert M., with David Tracy. *A Short History of the Interpretation of the Bible.* 2nd ed. Philadelphia: Fortress Press, 1984.

Greer, Rowan A. "The Christian Bible and Its Interpretation," in James L. Kugel and Rowan A. Greer, *Early Biblical Interpretation.* Library of Early Christianity 3. Philadelphia: Westminster Press, 1986.

Sadowski, Frank, ed. *The Church Fathers on the Bible: Selected Readings.* New York: Alba House, 1987.

Wilken, Robert L. "The Bible and Its Interpreters: Christian Biblical Interpretation." in *Harper's Bible Commentary.* San Francisco: Harper and Row, 1988.

THE COMMUNITIES'
EXPERIENCES OF GOD

Deity in the Biblical Communities and among their Neighbors

JOHN H. HAYES

The Apostle Paul, offering instructions to the Corinthians on the subject of eating consecrated meat derived from pagan sacrifices, quoted those to whom he writes: " 'A false god has no real existence, and there is no god but one.' " Paul responded, agreeing with their basic premise: "Even though there be so-called gods, whether in heaven or on earth—and indeed there are many such gods and many such lords—yet for us there is one God, the Father, from whom are all things, and we exist for him" (1 Cor. 8.4–6).

This text epitomizes the basic difference between biblical theology and practically all other theologies of the biblical world, namely, a monotheistic versus a polytheistic understanding of the divine. Simultaneously, the text alludes to the issue of the relationship between the biblical understanding of deity and those of the surrounding nations and communities.

Theological Thought in the Ancient World

The origins of theology and a belief in the divine date from pre-historic eras. By the time humans learned to record their thoughts in writing and to depict their speculations and imaginations in more than elementary art, deity was already an important element in their interpretation of existence and experience. The belief in deity was the way humans gave expression to their confrontation with and experience of the numinous. The numinous or the transcendent was experienced not only in the mysterious and the unusual which produced fear, fright, and anxiety but also was seen in the routine and the recurrent which produced awe, fascination, and praise. Deity was thus experienced and understood in both positive and negative categories, as both threatening and consoling.

The elemental reactions to the numinous were given theological expression in the thought of both the biblical communities and their neighbors. Based upon universal experiences, their theological thought developed many concepts which were shared by biblical and non-biblical communities. This underlying common theology consisted of many shared principles. (1) Deity was considered to be both transcendent and immanent to the world of experience, that is, the divine was understood as standing outside and above and yet as deeply involved in the natural and human worlds simultaneously. (2) The divine was seen as the source of world and human order. (3) The will of the deity for human life in the form of general societal and personal norms was made known to humans through various mediators and mediations, and obedience to these norms was believed to bring reward while disobedience was believed to bring judgment and punishment. (4) Deity was to be offered worship with regulated forms of ritual and with prayer that was both petition and praise. (5) Deity could and did intervene in the course of human history and in the lives of individuals for the purpose of redeeming and saving or judging and destroying.

The ancients not only shared a common store of theological positions but also frequently employed similar metaphorical language in speaking of deity. These metaphors were drawn from both the non-human and the human world. Deity could be spoken of as the power inherent in and manifested through natural phenomena such as wind, storm, vegetation, drought, pestilence, and so forth. With metaphors drawn from the human world, deity was often described in terms of family/household and political images. Parent-child, family-kin, and ruler-subject metaphors predominated, in describing both divine-human and divine-divine relationships.

Mesopotamian Deities

The religion of Mesopotamia presents a kaleidoscope of hundreds of deities and demons ever assuming new patterns in response to changing political fortunes. Its world of supernatural powers was rooted in two different cultures, a later Semitic deposit overlaying an older Sumerian level, the latter derived from a people resident in southern Mesopotamia but of unknown origin and employing a language without known affiliation. The oldest Sumerian deities were identified with the powers believed immanently manifested in natural phenomena and with economically important entities: Anu the god of heaven, Nanna the moon, Utu the sun, Ezen the goddess of grain, Enlil the lord of wind, Ninsuna mistress of wild cows, and so forth, each with their particular realm of power and special cult places. Most cities had their patron deities. With the gradual unification of the region, a loosely defined pantheon of gods developed, many associated with one another in terms of family relations or along the lines of political and administrative functions. In myths about the origins of divine beings and the cosmos found in the epic of creation (designated by its opening phrase, Enuma elish, "when above"), primordial beings such as Apsu (fresh water), Tiamat (sea water) and their immediate descendants functioned as ancestral parents of the gods but played no real role in the religious and cultic life of the people.

During the biblical period (after 1000 B.C.E.), the highest triad of Mesopotamian deities were Anu, god of the heavens and king and father of the gods (who functioned as a rather inactive background figure); Enlil, god of wind and storms (who embodied transcendental and judgmental aspects of divinity); and Ea or Enki, god of wisdom and magic and lord of underground fresh waters (who embodied immanental aspects of divinity). All three possessed consorts who were reflections of their male counterparts. The people's myths illustrate how they conceived of the deities and their interaction. In the Mesopotamian myth of Atrahasis, with its accounts of the deluge, Enlil decided on the destruction of humankind because of its noise-making. Enki, through cunning and scheming, saved the human race from total destruction in the flood while subsequently devising means (barrenness, childhood diseases, and so on) for population control. In *Enuma elish,* Enki saved the young gods from destruction by Apsu. Enki was conceived of as the source of world order, as the provider of the gifts of human civilization, and the source of power against demons.

Although goddesses played significant roles in early Sumerian religion, by the first millennium only two goddesses were prominent, Ereshkigal, queen of the underworld, and Inanna/Ishtar, identified with the planet Venus. With her husband/lover, Dumuzi (Tammuz), Ishtar was closely associated with fertility. The death of and search for Tammuz as part of the seasonal cycle was apparently even known in Judah (see Ezek. 8.14). In her many roles, predominantly as the morning and evening star, Ishtar was goddess of love and war. She may have been the deity known in the final days of Judah as the queen of heaven (Jer. 7.18; 44.18–19, 25) but this is not certain.

In addition to the star goddess Ishtar, other celestial bodies were considered deities: Sin, the moon-god, and Shamash, the sun-god. Since the sun, in its daily cycle across the heavens, witnessed everything happening on earth, Shamash was understood as the god of justice, the enemy of the wrongdoer and oppressor, and the defender of the just and the oppressed. On Hammurabi's stela, Shamash is shown commissioning the king to write down his laws which "caused the land to take the right way and have good government." Frequently associated with Shamash was the god Adad, a storm god, the source of life-giving rains.

With the development of the city-states of Babylon and Ashur into national states and subsequently into empires, the gods of the capital cities greatly increased in importance. Marduk, the chief god of Babylon, and Nabu, Marduk's son and patron of the nearby city of Borsippa (as well as of scribal art), played central roles in the state cult during Babylonian dominance, as did Ashur in the days of the Assyrian empire.

Many aspects and functions of other gods were absorbed by them. Marduk (whose name was replaced with Ashur in Assyria) became the supreme figure in the creation epic *Enuma elish*. In the myth, Marduk, a son of Ea, was appointed leader of the younger gods whom some of the older deities wished to destroy because their noisy commotion deprived the geriatric group of their rest. Empowered so his word would come true and with promises of reward if successful, Marduk took on the enemy. He slaughtered Tiamat, the primordial sea, and from her body created the universe, fashioning and ordering the constellations, stars, sun and moon, and the calendar. After the building of the city of Babylon, Marduk presided over Ea's creation of humans, fashioned from the remains of the slain rebel god Kingu. Humans were assigned the task of being servants to the gods so the latter might be at ease. The assembly of the deities hailed Marduk as eternal king of the gods and proclaimed his fifty names, each expressing some aspect of his power. The seven tablets of the *Enuma elish* (with the themes of the triumph of order over chaos, the greatness of Babylon, and the kingship of Marduk) were read on the fourth day of the annual eleven-day Babylonian new year festival, and its recital helped create the order it proclaimed.

Demons played a major role in Mesopotamian life, one that is unparalleled in ancient Near Eastern religion. Both good and bad demons existed and the latter were enemies of humans and gods. Demons lurked in any place fraught with danger and unfamiliarity and were especially active in crisis situations, such as childbirth. Evil demons who caused illnesses and other calamities were considered to have diverse origins: some were created by Anu, others came from the underworld, while others were the souls of dead human beings. Mesopotamian religion developed no concept of meaningful postmortem existence either in the underworld or beyond, so at best the deceased were not well off. Those who had died violent deaths or whose bodies were not properly buried might haunt the living. Numerous spells and incantation rituals existed to protect one from threatening demons or to rescue one from their clutches.

Often the worshiper had the sense of having "acquired a god," sometimes unnamed, who was the personal protector and object of devotion for an individual and the person's family. This personal religion was expressed especially in prayers similar to the penitential psalms of the Bible, but also in complaints like those of the Book of Job when individual worshipers considered their suffering unjustified.

Egyptian Deities

Egyptian religion was similar to that of Mesopotamia in several ways: polytheistic, genealogical relationships among the gods, major deities associated with principal cities, and pantheons that varied depending upon the political dominance of particular cities. In three basic ways the religions differed radically. While the Mesopotamians, like the early Israelites, developed no belief in meaningful life after death, this was a central concern in Egyptian religion, absorbing much of the energy and concern of the living. Secondly, theomachy, or strife among the gods, was not so prominent in Egypt as in Mesopotamia. This probably reflects two factors: Egyptian life was more tranquil, with the country less open to attack and invasion than Mesopotamia and the annual inundation of the Nile river, fed by rainfall in equatorial Africa, was far less tumultuous and disruptive than the floods of the Tigris and Euphrates. Thirdly, in Egypt, the reigning monarch, the pharaoh, was considered an incarnation of divinity, a deity in human flesh.

As in Mesopotamia, deities of various types were found in Egyptian religion: primordial gods whose roles were primarily limited to issues of divine and cosmic origins, cosmic and national gods whose activities sustained cosmic order and the normal flow of life, and particularistic gods related to specific places, events, or phenomena. The most important religious centers in Egypt each had their special cosmic gods: Ptah at Memphis, Re at Heliopolis, Amun at Thebes, Thoth at Hermopolis, Atum at Kheraha, and so on but often there was an intermingling of these. Solar deities and mythology were prominent throughout Egyptian history.

Various stories and allusions to the origins of the gods and creation of humans are found in Egyptian literature. In one form, nine gods (the Heliopolitan Ennead) played a role: Atum (the complete one) created the pair Shu (air) and Tefnut (moisture) from whom sprang Geb (earth) and Nut (watery sky) and a second generation consisting of Osiris and Seth with their sisters Isis and Nephthys. In the Hermopolitan Ogdoad, four pairs of primordial beings—hiddenness, darkness, formlessness, and watery abyss—represent the background of chaos and disorder against which the creator god emerged from an egg that appeared after the inundating waters subsided. In the myths, various means are used by the creator god to produce other divine beings: expectoration, ejaculation, and weeping. Humans were considered to be formed in the image of the divine and various myths suggested different means of their origin: from the tears of the sun-god Re's weeping, from a fashioning on the potter's wheel by Khnum, or by being spoken into existence by Ptah. Perhaps the closest to the Genesis account of creation is the so-called Memphis theology preserved on the Shabaka Stone (about 700 B.C.E.) in which Ptah thinks something in his heart and speaks it with his tongue and it comes into being.

The triad of deities—Osiris, Isis, and Horus—were venerated throughout Egyptian history and the worship associated with them spread into the Greco-Roman world. Osiris was god of both fertility-cultivation and the realm of the dead. Opposed by his brother Seth, the god of heat and desert, Osiris was killed and his dismembered body sought for by his sister-consort Isis. Having collected the body, Isis became pregnant by Osiris and gave birth to the male child Horus whose early days were spent in hiding in the marshes of the Nile. Horus eventually reclaimed the rights of his father and overcame the opposition of Seth to gain a favorable settlement from the other gods. The myth not only reflected the struggle of fertility versus aridity but also was a myth undergirding the pharaoh's claim to divinity. In this life, the pharaoh was identified with Horus and after death was identified and ruled in the "underworld" (originally in the heavens in Egyptian mythology) with Osiris.

The belief in and quest for life beyond death—originally a prerogative of royalty—produced some of the most notable Egyptian literature in the Pyramid and Coffin Texts and the *Book of Going Forth by Day* (previously designated the *Book of the Dead*). These texts contain spells, incantations, hymns, and confessions to get the deceased (whose body had to be preserved, thus the importance of embalming) past the forty-two deities of the judgment court. Although reflecting belief in magical powers to foil the gods, such material as section 125 of the *Book of Going Forth by Day* and the idea of weighing of the heart against the feather of truth (Maat) indicates that Egyptian gods expected their worshipers to live ethical lives in this world and to measure up to moral standards.

Egyptian religion was tolerant and syncretistic throughout its history, with the period of Akhenaton being a rare exception. Nubian, Lybian, and Syro-Palestinian deities and influence were present at various times. Some humans were deified, such as Imhotep, the architect of the step pyramid at Doser, who was later identified with the Greek god Asclepios. (Animals were not worshiped in Egypt, although many were sacred to particular deities and were mummified at death.)

Syro-Palestinian Deities

The religion of the eastern Mediterranean seaboard (the Levant), where ancient Israel was one population group, is known from a few scattered references in classical sources, some inscriptions set up for public display, a scattering of extant letters, but primarily from the so-called Ugaritic texts, artwork, and temples unearthed at modern Ras Shamra (ancient Ugarit) and Ras Ibn Hani on the coast of northern Syria opposite Cyprus. These fourteenth-thirteenth century B.C.E. texts, written mostly in alphabetic cuneiform, consist of legends, myths, letters, lists, and cultic texts. Since Ugarit was a cosmopolitan city, it was influenced by Egyptian, Mesopotamian, Hurrian, and Hittite cultures. Nonetheless, the texts present us with a glimpse of authentic Syro-Palestinian (often called Canaanite) religion. The names of over 200 gods appear in the texts, although in the god-lists only thirty or so gods are mentioned. Of these only about a dozen play significant roles in the mythological texts.

The rather well-organized pantheon was presided over by the patriarchal deity, El, with his consort Asherah. El was depicted as preeminent among the gods, a source of wisdom and counsel, and as beneficent and benign. He bore a number of titles and epithets: "bull," "father of years," "king," "father of the gods," and "creator of creatures." He may have been perceived as the creator of the world but this is uncertain. He seems to have represented deity in its transcendence, controlling but not directly involved in the governance of the world. Since the term El was a general Semitic word for "god," El may have been associated with various situations and sanctuaries where the numinous was experienced in a special way. In the myths, his abode was located at the source of the two deeps. His consort, Asherah, was the "mother of the gods."

Second to El in the lists is the god Dagan known from Mesopotamian texts and the Old Testament (as Dagon, associated with the Philistines; see Judg. 16.23; 1 Sam. 5.2–7). Although a temple was dedicated to him at Ugarit, Dagan plays no role in any of the known texts.

The most active of the gods was Baal, whose consort was Anat. Baal, identified with the Mesopotamian storm god, Adad, was the god of storms and rain and giver of fertility. He embodied deity in its immanent power. Baal, whose name means "lord, husband, owner," was widely worshiped throughout the region. He was described as the "powerful one," "king," "lord of the earth," and "rider of the clouds." Anat, like Ishtar a goddess of love and war, was the special protector of Baal.

In the myths, Baal's enemies were Yamm (the sea) and Mot (death). He struggled against Yamm for dominance among the gods, finally defeating Yamm and his cohorts, the sea monsters Litan (the biblical Leviathan) and Tunnan (the biblical Tannin). Baal's victory resulted in the reign of order over chaos, after which the gods constructed a house/temple for him. In his encounter with Mot, Baal was defeated and forced to go to the underworld. Fertility and vegetation disappeared during his stay. After Anat rescued the remains of Baal and defeated Mot, Baal was restored to life and fertility returned. This myth obviously reflected the seasonal and general climatic conditions in the region where a rainless summer when vegetation disappears is followed by a rainy season with new growth.

Other deities of some importance in the Ugaritic texts were Resheph, god of disease and pestilence, Shapash, the sun goddess, Yarih, the moon god, Shachar and Shalim, dawn and dusk, and Kothar wa-Hasis ("skilled and wise one"), the divine artisan.

Very little is known about the religion of Israel's near neighbors, the Edomites, Moabites, Ammonites, and Philistines. Only one major inscription from these nations is known, namely, an inscribed memorial stela erected by Mesha, the king of Moab in the ninth century B.C.E. In it Mesha made several references to the Moabite god Chemosh. The king noted that the Israelites had ruled over Moab "many days because Chemosh was angry at his land." This statement demonstrates that the Moabites held the view (also found in Israel) that the national god of a land acts in history to reward and punish.

Hellenistic Deities

Before Alexander the Great began the conquest of the East, in 334 B.C.E., contacts between the Greek and Jewish worlds had been limited and informal. Once Palestine became part of Alexander's empire, Jewish culture was exposed to the process of Hellenization and to Hellenistic views of deity. By this time in history, the older Greek religion with its worship of the Olympian deities had been exposed to new impulses and developments. Three of these are of background interest for understanding how some early Christian conceptions developed and were received.

First of all, the conquests of Alexander with their imposition of a common language and exposure to a common, potentially shared, culture which transcended national borders and other isolating boundaries ignited the sparks of ecumenicity. In limited ways, the idea of an all-encompassing religion based on a monotheistic theology and a concept of the universal commonalty of all humans began to be expressed.

Secondly, mystery cults, based on the worship of ancient deities such as the Egyptian Isis, the Greek Dionysius, and the Persian Mithras, became much more widespread. One joined these semi-secret groups voluntarily and underwent elaborate initiation rituals. Such associations provided their members with a sense of belonging and community, highly charged emotional experiences, the opportunity to devote themselves to a single deity, a realization of present salvation and a promise of future total redemption, and a sense of sharing in the life and fate of the deity, often in sacramental form.

Thirdly, ruler cults were characteristic of the eastern Mediterranean throughout the Greco-Roman period. Such cults were based on worship, sacrifice, and devotion offered to the ruler as divine. This veneration of a human figure paralleled the older Egyptian belief in the pharaoh as the god Horus, but there had not been a cult with sacrifice to and worship of the living pharaoh. In Greece, there was a history of hero cults venerating prominent figures, but only after their death, and Greek myths contained accounts of mortals having become divine after death. Alexander the Great played an important role in the development of the ruler cult. He was reportedly declared a "son of Zeus" at the oracle of Zeus-Amun in Libya and elsewhere and demanded that his divinity be acknowledged. Many of the rulers following Alexander proclaimed themselves as divine, imprinting their coins with such epithets as *epiphanes* ("[God] manifest") or even *theos epiphanes* ("God manifest"). The cults of these rulers as "man-god" required that they be treated as a traditional deity. The ruler cult was more widely prevalent in the eastern than the western Mediterranean world.

Deity in the Biblical Communities

Although the biblical communities shared many ideas about deity with their neighbors, they also developed some very distinctive features. First of all, among all the ancient nations of the Middle East, only Israel eventually moved to an explicit monotheism which concentrated all aspects of divinity into one being and denied the existence of other deities. The closest parallel to biblical monotheism was the short-lived exclusivistic worship of Aton (the sun disc) advocated by the Egyptian pharaoh Akhenaton (second quarter of the fourteenth century B.C.E.). Akhenaton sought to suppress the worship of other gods although he continued to view himself (and perhaps his wife Nefertiti) as an incarnation of divinity and as the intermediary between the Aton and the rest of creation. (His famous hymn to Aton has many parallels to Psalm 104.)

Second, in Israelite thought, the divine will was not subject to any higher order. In other major Near Eastern religions, deity operated within a system of order and fate to which deity could be and often was subservient. In Israelite monotheistic thought, the divine will stood above and beyond any order and, in fact, was the source of being for cosmic order.

Third, ancient Israel developed no theogony in the form of mythic narratives explaining the origin and descent of the divine. In biblical thought, the existence of the divine is accepted as a given and no effort is made to explain or narrate how deity came into being or to justify belief in the divine. Theogonic myths concerned with primordial conditions and how deity came into being are found in most of the non-biblical cultures from which any sizeable amount of literature has been preserved.

Fourth, the separation of the realm of the dead and the underworld from the divine realm was characteristic of official Israelite religion. Thus ancient Israel, unlike other cultures, developed no theory of underworld powers, and the realm of the dead was considered an arena of impurity. In early Israel, the dead were considered cut off from God (Pss. 6.5; 88.10–12; 115.17–18) and no reference is made to reward and punishment in the afterlife, to prayers for the dead, or to any hope of resurrection, although the dead could be consulted regarding the future (1 Sam. 28; Isa. 8.19) and food offerings could be made to the deceased (Deut. 26.14).

Finally, polytheistic religious systems tended to be both more conservative and more inclusively tolerant than monotheism, which could be both innovative and exclusive. In polytheism, new deities and new perspectives could be absorbed into the system through accretion. New deities were integrated into the pantheon, identified with other gods, or one deity could be stressed over against others without greatly disrupting the overall theological perspectives. Only innovations which threatened or called for the rejection of established concepts and practices were greeted with hostility. Reforms of religion and the cult which introduced new concepts or practices that required the rejection of traditional matters were attempted in Egypt by Akhenaton and in Mesopotamia by Shalmaneser V (726–722 B.C.E.) and Nabonidus (555–539 B.C.E.), but all encountered enormous opposition and were quickly reversed. Monotheistic religion tended to be very zealous and exclusive, generally opposing the accretion of radical new elements into the system. At the same time, however, monotheistic religion was more open to significant adjustments and reform than polytheistic systems since only one deity was involved in the change of theological perspectives.

Several historical and sociological factors contributed to the development of an exclusivistic monotheism in Israel. First of all, ancient Israel was a latecomer on the stage of history. Israel developed into a national state under Saul and David near the end of the eleventh century B.C.E., centuries after many other nations and city-states. These older political powers already possessed full-blown theological systems. Israel had to define itself and its beliefs over against these established political and religious entities. Israel began its history as a rather loosely defined tribal grouping and thus with only the rudimentary elements of a religious system. As such, it could evaluate and pick and choose in developing its theology. As a new entity without the baggage of a centuries-long inherited religious system and long venerated institutions and rituals and, therefore, without a strong reverence for tradition, Israel was fairly free to create, adopt, and modify. Thus an inherent critical stance was a strong influence in Israel from the very beginning. It was only relatively late in history that Israel described its origins to claim that a full-blown and unchallengeable "traditional" religious system existed from its earliest days (primarily found in the so-called "priestly material" of the Pentateuch).

Second, throughout its history, Israel remained a small state, generally both on the defensive against its neighbors and at the mercy of major foreign powers. The consequences of this posture were two-fold. On the one hand, Israel did not control an empire in which religious views had to undergo expansion and accretion in order to hold together a diverse constituency. On the other hand, Israel had to protect itself and express its faith in tension with, and even hostility toward, others. This contributed to the zeal and exclusiveness of Israelite religion. National identity and religious exclusivity went hand in hand.

Third, as a culture, Israel allowed and engaged in self-criticism to a degree unparalleled in ancient times. This willingness to question, challenge, and deny can be illustrated in various ways: by the prophets who called into question policies of state and religion, by such counter-culture groups as the Rechabites whose life-style opposed normal patterns of life (see Jeremiah 35), by the production of radical judgmental portrayals of Israelite history (especially Judges–2 Kings), and by such protest literature as Job and Ecclesiastes. (In other ancient Near Eastern cultures, most protest-questioning positions are limited to wisdom literature and to the theme of deity and human mortality and undeserved suffering.) This capacity for self-criticism gave to Israelite religion a dynamic quality that allowed for reform and made it possible for religious thought to adjust to changing times and changing concepts.

The biblical understanding and depiction of deity obviously developed and evolved over the years. An overt monotheism that proclaimed Yahweh, the God of Israel, to be the only deity was reasonably late in developing and represents the climax of the Old Testament understanding of God rather than the starting point of Israel's theological pilgrimage. The overall course of that pilgrimage is difficult to reconstruct for three reasons. First of all, the content and the shaping of much of the biblical material reporting on early Israelite history, especially in the Pentateuch, was produced in light of later stages of faith and thus is retouched history. Secondly, some of the highly judgmental literature in Judges–2 Kings probably presents the Israelites as being more inclined to worship other gods than actually was the case. Thirdly, the biblical material does not provide us with many depictions of the religious faith and practices of the general population since it is more concerned with state policies and practices than with the life of common folk.

The origins of the worship of Yahweh and the nature of early Israel's faith cannot be determined with any certainty. One stream of biblical tradition assumes that Yahweh was worshiped by the earliest humans (see Gen. 4.26) while another stream proposes that Yahweh was first revealed to Moses (see Exod. 6.3). The name Israel, which contains the element "el," may suggest that the Israelites were originally worshipers of El, but this is uncertain since "el" was not only the personal name for a god but also a word simply meaning "god." The patriarchs, Abraham, Isaac, and Jacob, are shown worshiping El (Gen. 14.18–20; 16.13; 17.1; 21.33; 31.13; 43.14; 48.3) and Jacob calls an altar erected at Shechem "El-elohey-israel" ("El, god of Israel," Gen. 33.20) and at Bethel El-Bethel ("God [of] Bethel," Gen. 35.7). In addition, in some texts the deity of the patriarchs is said to have been "the god of the father(s)" (Gen. 26.24; 28.13; 31.42; 32.9; 46.3; 49.25).

Biblical tradition associates Yahweh with the vicinity of Edom (Seir, Deut. 33.2; Judg. 5.4; Teman, Hab. 3.3–8), and the earliest appearance of the word Yahweh outside the Bible is an Egyptian inscription which refers to the same geographical region. Given present evidence, it is impossible to know where the worship of Yahweh originated or the meaning of the name (Exod. 3.13–15 offers a folk etymology). By the time of King Saul, the worship of Yahweh had become the national religion of Israel and remained so throughout its history.

Early Israel's national religion would have to be described as henotheism or monolatry, that is, belief in and worship focussed on one deity but without denying the existence of other gods (see Exod. 20.2–3). Although the editors of the history of Israel in Judges–2 Kings blamed the Israelites for worshiping other gods (see 2 Kgs. 17.7–12), this is probably an exaggeration if one assumes this means that some god other than Yahweh was worshiped as the state deity. The editors of this historical material used the charges of infidelity to Yahweh and the practice of polytheism to explain why Israel's history ended in tragedy and their account thus probably skewed actual conditions.

During three periods in Israel's history, the cults of other national gods seem to have been sponsored and participated in by the nation's leaders, but not as replacements for the national Yahwistic cult. During these times, the nation was a member of multi-national political coalitions organized against either the Assyrians or the Babylonians and "ecumenical" religious practices went hand in hand with "ecumenical" politics. The three periods were during the reigns of Omri-Ahab when there was close cooperation with Phoenicia and other states (see 1 Kgs. 16.23–33; 2 Kgs. 10.18–31; 11.17–18), the reign of Pekah (2 Kgs. 15.27–31; 16.5–9), and the reign of Zedekiah when Judah rebelled against Babylonia with the encouragement of the Egyptian pharaoh Psammetichus II in 592 (2 Kgs. 24.18–20; Ezek. 8). During these three periods Israelite rulers participated in foreign cults in the land of Israel. These "ecumenical" activities were condemned by such prophets as Elijah, Hosea, and Ezekiel. To deny that Israelite national religion was ever polytheistic does not mean that Israelites never worshiped gods other than Yahweh. This many of them certainly did as is evidenced by Jeremiah's condemnation of the worship of the queen of heaven (Jer. 7.18; 44.15–28).

Many of the aspects associated with other deities—creation, rule over the world as king, provider of fertility, and so on—and the forms and terminology in which these were expressed may have been borrowed by Israel, especially from the El and Baal cults. Like Baal, Yahweh smote the sea (Exod. 14) and like El ruled in the assembly of the gods (Ps. 82). Although Gen. 1–2 presuppose that God formed creation and cosmic order out of preexistent stuff, only poetic remnants have survived of any concept of opposition between Yahweh and cosmic forces or beings (see Isa. 27.1, 51.9; Pss. 74.12–17, 89.5–10; 104.26).

Three commonly used metaphors were employed to speak of Yahweh's relationship to Israel. First, and possibly oldest, was the language of parent-child. Israel/Judah was the adopted child of Yahweh. This imagery, also used to speak of the reigning monarch (Pss. 2.7; 89.26–29; Isa. 9.6–7) was dominant in the eighth-century prophets Isaiah and Hosea (see Isa. 1.2; Hos. 11.1; see Exod. 4.22), and as a child could be punished for wrongdoing but not destroyed without the hope and opportunity of repentance (see Deut. 21.18–21) so with Israel/Judah; thus the prophet's preaching of both judgment and hope. Second, the capital cities, Samaria and Jerusalem, were conceived, as was common in western Semitic cultures, as the spouses of Yahweh joined with him in marriage (see Hos. 1.10–2.23 where the wife is Samaria; Isa. 1.21–23; Ezek. 16, 23). Thirdly, the metaphor of ruler-subject, suzerain-vassal, Yahweh-people relationship, expressed in the form of treaty or covenant language, became the dominant metaphor (probably in the seventh century) and was used to shape the form and structure of the Hexateuch and the lives of Jews and Christians ever since.

In the Shema (Deut. 6.4) the oneness and unity of Yahweh was expressed in credal form and with the anonymous prophet of the exile,

Second Isaiah, Israelite monotheism found its poetic expression (Isa. 41.21–29; 43.10; 44.6–11).

The early Christian community inherited its views of deity from Israel, but modified these in some important ways. The parent-child metaphor was taken literally and applied to Jesus so as to understand him as the incarnation of deity. Christians could speak of Jesus as divine, not—as in the ruler cults—of man-God, but as God-man. Although the New Testament does not yet elaborate a doctrine of the Trinity, it certainly formulates the seeds of such a doctrine (see for example Matt. 28.19). The monotheism of Judaism was universalized so as to include Gentiles, by denying the eternal validity of the Mosaic Law (Gal. 3; Rom. 3), thus opening the way for universal community regardless of background. Finally, participation in the life and being of the deity and sacramental union with the divine, as in the mystery cults, was realized through the eucharist (Mk. 14.22–25 and parallels).

SUGGESTIONS FOR FURTHER READING

Grant, R. M. *Gods and the One God.* Philadelphia: Westminster Press, 1986.

Kaufmann, Y. *The Religion of Israel.* Chicago: University of Chicago Press, 1960.

Morenz, S. *Egyptian Religion.* Ithaca: Cornell University Press, 1973.

Saggs, H. W. F. *The Encounter with the Divine in Mesopotamia and Israel.* London: Athlone Press, 1978.

Smith, M. "The Common Theology of the Ancient Near East," *Journal of Biblical Literature* 71(1952)135–47.

Smith, M. S. *The Early History of God: Yahweh and the Other Deities in Ancient Israel.* San Francisco: Harper & Row, 1990.

Torah and Covenant

RICHARD ELLIOTT FRIEDMAN

"Torah" is the term used for the first five books of the Bible—Genesis, Exodus, Leviticus, Numbers, and Deuteronomy—also known as the Five Books of Moses or the Pentateuch. The Hebrew word *tôrāh* means "instruction," which, as in English, connotes both teaching and rules/law. And the Torah is indeed a teaching, a body of learning that is conveyed both through specific commandments and through the telling of a story. The Torah tells the story of the initiation of the relationship between the deity Yahweh and the human community. The relationship is expressed formally through covenants, which are binding contractual agreements between Yahweh and human beings.

The Torah is the heart of the Hebrew Bible. The rest continues from it, ultimately depends on it, responds to it, and is constructed within the structure that it builds, namely the covenantal structure. There are three primary covenants in the Torah: the covenant between the deity and Noah, between the deity and Abraham, and between the deity and the people of Israel at Mount Sinai. Each covenant comes at a climactic moment in the Torah's narrative, a moment that is understood to be a turning point in history. Each involves a divine promise, a particular name of the deity, and a sign.

The Noachic covenant, narrated in Genesis 9, follows the accounts of the creation and of the crisis in which the creation is nearly undone, as the "windows of the heavens" and the "springs of the great deep" open, allowing the cosmic waters to flood the habitable region (Gen. 6–8). It promises that the creation will not be so threatened again; the world is secure. The deity is identified in this covenant as "God" (*'ĕlōhǐm*). The sign is the rainbow.

The Abrahamic covenant, in Genesis 15 and 17, comes following Abraham's leaving his home and his settling in a new land at divine command, the act that narrows the focus of the story from the broad picture of the world in the primeval history (Gen. 1–11) to the more particular account of the destiny of a single family and the nation descended from it. The covenant promises that this land in which Abraham now resides will belong to his descendants, that Abraham will be the father of many nations, that kings will be descended from Abraham, and that the covenanting deity will be Abraham's and his descendants' God. The divine name that is explicitly associated with this covenant is *'ēl šadday*. Its sign is circumcision.

The covenant of Sinai (also known as the Mosaic covenant or the Israelite covenant; Exodus 19–20) follows the exodus from Egypt. It is the moment of Yahweh's greatest revelation to human beings, in which Yahweh speaks aloud from the heavens over Mount Sinai to an entire nation; and the words that the deity speaks are precisely the text of the covenant. Those words are the Ten Commandments, or Decalogue. The covenant also is understood to include other laws, revealed to Moses at Sinai, at the Tabernacle during the next forty years in the wilderness, and in the plains of Moab at the end of the forty years' journey. The covenant promise is well-being in the land that was promised in the Abrahamic covenant. The divine name that is pronounced in the first verse of this covenant is Yahweh. The sign is the sabbath.

One of the most fruitful products of twentieth century research into the Bible was the recognition that the Sinai/Israelite covenant was written according to the format of a common type of legal document in the ancient Near East: the suzerainty treaty. These treaties, authored by regional kings (suzerains) and imposed upon the local city kings under their dominion (vassals), are composed of a series of textual elements. Individual treaties may lack one or another of these elements or vary the order, but they all include enough of the basic framework to establish that this was a known, established legal form. The textual elements are:

1. *Preamble*. The suzerain is introduced by name.

2. *Historical Prologue*. There is an account of past actions of the suzerain, actions which were in the interest of the vassal but which were undeserved; they were, rather, gracious acts of the suzerain. This serves to justify the demands that the suzerain is about to make upon the vassal. The vassal must acknowledge a debt of future loyalty to the suzerain.

3. *Stipulations*. The nature of the vassal's future loyalty, i.e., the demands of the suzerain, are enumerated. These may be divided into (a) the prime stipulation, namely allegiance to the suzerain and to no other; and (b) the specific responsibilities of the vassal to the suzerain (e.g., contributing military support in time of war). The prime stipulation expresses the very essence of the treaty: a vassal cannot swear allegiance to more than one suzerain.

4. *Provision for the treaty document*. (a) The treaty is to be deposited in a sacred place (the sanctuary of the vassal). (b) The treaty is to be read in public periodically.

5. *Witnesses*. The treaty invokes as witnesses the gods of the suzerain and of the vassal as well as witnesses from the realm of nature, including heaven and earth and the seas.

6. *Blessings and curses*. Blessings are directed to the vassal as encouragement for loyalty. And, in order to discourage disloyalty, a remarkable collection of curses is listed in which illness, death, destruction, and degradation are heaped upon a vassal who would break the treaty.

In addition to these textual elements, the vassal swears an oath of fidelity to the suzerain and to the requirements of the treaty.

The Sinai covenant (Exod. 20.1–17) exhibits striking parallels to the preceding structure, containing several of the treaty elements:

Preamble: I am [Yahweh] your God

Historical Prologue: who brought you out of Egypt, out of the land of
    slavery.

Stipulations

  Prime: You must have no other god besides me.

  Specific: You must not make a carved image . . . Remember to keep
    the sabbath day holy . . . Honor your father and your mother . . .
    Do not commit murder . . .

In addition to these basic elements of the treaty formulation that appear in the text of the covenant at Sinai, the other treaty components
appear as well in subsequent texts of the Torah that relate to the Israelite
covenant. There is provision for the covenant document, comparable to
that component of the treaties. It is to be placed in a golden box (the
"ark") and kept in the nation's central sanctuary, the Tabernacle, or Tent
of Meeting (Exod. 25.10–16; 26.33; Deut. 10.1–5; 31.24–26). Also, it (or
at least a portion of it) is to be read publicly every seven years (Deut.
31.9–13).

Also comparable to the treaties, the Israelite covenant includes the
invocation of witnesses. Since the Torah's monotheism excludes the possibility of divine witnesses, heaven and earth are invoked as witnesses
(Deut. 4.26; 30.19; 31.28; 32.1).

Lengthy lists of blessings and curses, many of which are manifestly
similar to their counterparts in the treaties, are found in Leviticus 26 and
Deuteronomy 28.

Also, corresponding to the oath of loyalty taken by vassals, the Israelites declare that they will be obedient to the words of the covenant (Exod.
19.8; Deut. 29.9–28).

The Noachic and Abrahamic covenants function differently, in some
ways even in a manner which contrasts with the Israelite covenant. They
focus less on the deity's past actions for Noah and Abraham than on their
records of service to God. Further, it is the deity who makes a commitment to future action on behalf of Noah and Abraham rather than imposing codes of behavior upon them. Moreover, these two covenants
have the appearance of being unconditional; that is, their future standing
does not appear to depend on how the recipients or their descendants
behave. The cosmos is unconditionally secure from future deluges; the
land is at least eternally *available* (see below) to Abraham's descendants.
These covenants, like the Israelite covenant, have a prototype in ancient
Near Eastern practice, which helps to explain their special character. The
prototype is the royal grant. The royal grant was a transaction in which
a party, generally a suzerain, gave a gift of property and/or rule to some
weaker party, generally a vassal. It was in wide use in the second and first
millennia B.C.E. The elements of the grant almost all have counterparts
in the elements already described in the treaties. Where the two differ is
in the form that the elements take.

1. *Preamble.* The introduction of the donor of the grant by name and title is functionally the same in the grant document as in the preamble of the treaties.

2. *Historical Prologue.* The past relations of the donor and the recipient of the grant are described. The nature of the prologue depends on the reason for making the grant. If it is a case of a privileged vassal receiving the grant as a reward for having shown outstanding faithfulness, the prologue will deal with the meritorious record of the recipient. If it is a case of a suzerain making a grant for political purposes arising out of a specific situation, the prologue will deal with the beneficence of the donor.

3. *Stipulations.* The distinction between an ordinary grant and a grant to a privileged vassal plays an important role in the type of stipulations that appear as well. If the recipient is a privileged vassal, the stipulations are formulated in the vassal's own interest, e.g., prohibiting other persons from interfering with the recipient's holding. Most prominent of the stipulations written in the interest of the privileged vassal is the matter of conveyance in perpetuity. Having demonstrated outstanding loyalty through past actions, the privileged vassal is now rewarded with a tangible show of trust by the suzerain. The suzerain declares the grant to be the permanent possession of the recipient and the recipient's descendants. The grant to an ordinary recipient contains stipulations written to the advantage of the donor, including forfeiture in the event of betrayal; but, for the privileged recipient, conveyance in perpetuity is an explicit guarantee against forfeiture.

4. *Provision for the grant document.* (Comparable to treaties.)

5. *Witnesses.* (Comparable to treaties.)

6. *Blessings and curses.* This element in the grants is formulated in a way that protects the interest of the *recipient*. The curses thus may be formulated in either of two ways: (a) The text may curse any party who would interfere with the recipient of the grant. (b) The donor may even include a self-directed curse, to take effect in the event the donor violates the terms of the grant.

7. *Specification of granted territories.* The donor names the boundaries of the grant.

As in the case of the treaties, the royal grants are affirmed by the taking of an oath. What is strikingly different, however, is that the oath to uphold the terms of the grant is taken by the donor, i.e., the suzerain, rather than the vassal.

Much of this structure is to be found in the Abrahamic covenant. Thus:

Preamble. "I am Yahweh" (Gen. 15.7); "I am *'ēl šadday*" (Gen. 17.1). (The different names reflect the J (15.7) and P (17.1) strata.)

Historical Prologue. The Abrahamic covenant merges the language of grants to ordinary and privileged recipients. First, it deals with Abraham's record of loyalty, corresponding to the privileged recipient grant. In Gen. 15.6 we read, "Abram put his faith in Yahweh, who reckoned it to him as righteousness." Based on this the covenant text immediately follows. It begins, "I am Yahweh who brought you out from Ur of the Chaldees to give you this land as your possession," a wording that obviously resembles the prologue for an ordinary recipient (and, of course, Exod. 20.2); but the juxtaposition of v. 6 to this text still indicates that Abram's loyalty is the premise and prerequisite of the covenant. The presence of a statement of divine actions is not contradictory to this. Further, in Gen. 26.5 Yahweh tells Isaac that the reason for the grant of progeny and land is "because Abraham obeyed me and kept my charge, my commandments, statutes, and laws." Of particular interest here is the phrase "kept my charge," which is formal terminology that corresponds to terminology that is found in the grant texts. Therefore, both from the covenant text and from subsequent references to it in the biblical narrative, we should regard the Abrahamic covenant as most resembling the royal grant of the type made to a privileged recipient on the basis of proven loyalty. (The covenant text in Genesis 17 lacks a historical prologue and therefore sheds no light, at this point, on Abraham's status.)

Stipulations. The most common grant stipulations are those written in protection of "house" (i.e., descendants, dynasty) and land (i.e., property, rule). Thus we find in Gen. 15.4, 5, "your heir will be a child of your own body . . . Look up at the sky, and count the stars, if you can. So many will your descendants be." Here we have a grant of progeny, to which is added a gift of land, "I give to your descendants this land" (15.18). The narrative of the covenant in Genesis 17 also promises progeny and adds the element of dynasty: "I shall make you exceedingly fruitful; I shall make nations out of you, and kings shall spring from you" (17.6). The grant of land is also present: "I shall give you and your descendants after you the land . . . of Canaan" (17.8). Further, the grants of house and land to Abraham are attached to a stipulation of conveyance in perpetuity, as is found in the royal grants. The covenant narrative in Genesis 15 does not address this, but the Genesis 17 narrative emphasizes the eternality of the promise:

> And I shall maintain my covenant with you and your descendants after you, generation after generation, an *everlasting covenant* . . . As a possession *for all time* I shall give you and your descendants after you the land . . . .(17.7–8; cf. v. 19)

The things that are promised in the covenant are available forever. If Abraham's descendants turn away from their God for generations and thus encounter disaster, a later generation which returns may yet be reconciled once again under the terms of the covenant and recover the land, for a continued line of generations ("house") and possession of the land are conveyed in perpetuity.

The one stipulation that requires something of Abraham is the matter of circumcision (17.10–14). Since it is at the same time the formal sign of the covenant it has a singular status and need not be regarded as inconsistent with the notion that Abraham's status corresponds to that of a privileged recipient of a royal grant.

The elements of provision for a covenant document, witnesses, and blessings and curses are missing from the Abrahamic covenant. Their absence is most probably traceable to the essential difference between this covenant and the Near Eastern grants. The former is a theological document, regarding the deity not as merely a witness to the covenant but as a party to it. A written document with provision for deposit and public readings is unnecessary in a covenant between a God and a person who has already demonstrated trust in that God's word. In the royal grants the recipient's possession of a document was necessary protection against retraction by the suzerain's progeny after the suzerain's death. This is obviously not a factor in the case of a divine donor. (Provision for a document was necessary in the Israelite covenant, the Israelites having demonstrated anything but trust by their previous actions. Hence also their need for divine witnesses whereas none are needed in the Abrahamic covenant.) With regard to blessings and curses, in the royal grants these are either self-directed against the suzerain or aimed at those who would interfere with the recipient. In these texts blessings and curses as sanctions against Yahweh would have seemed ludicrous in biblical terms; and the cursing of third-party interference would be pointless in that foreign victories over Israel are regularly pictured as subject to divine control in any case.

Specification of granted territories. The Abrahamic equivalent of this grant element is found in Gen. 15.18–21, "I give to your descendants this land from the river of Egypt to the Great River, the river Euphrates." Genesis 17 states more generally, "I shall give you . . . the land . . . , the whole of Canaan" (v. 8).

In the Near Eastern grants the suzerain swears the oath rather than the vassal. In one such text the recipient provides a sacrificial animal whose neck is then cut in the oath ceremony taken by the donor. In Genesis 15 Abraham provides animals and prepares them, and the divine promise is made as a smoking brazier and a flaming torch pass between the pieces of the convenantal sacrifices. The sacrifices, the holding of a torch, and the association with a furnace are all characteristic elements of oath ceremonies elsewhere. Genesis 26.3, too, explicitly refers to God's having taken the oath on the occasion of giving the land to Abraham. In numerous particulars, therefore, the Abrahamic covenant coincides with a known legal form of the ancient Near East.

The Noachic covenant only occasionally coincides with this form. Its preamble does not name the deity, for the deity is identified only as God (*'ĕlōhîm*), not by name, at that point. It rather announces the covenant and specifies the recipients: Noah, his family, and their descendants (which is to say humankind), and all the animals who have been saved in the flood (Gen. 9.9–10). It has no historical prologue. Like the Abrahamic covenant, it has no witnesses, document, or blessings and curses (though it is preceded by a notation that God blesses Noah and his family, 9.1). It has no specification of territory since, after all, it covers the entire world. What it does contain are the stipulations that are the mark of the grant to a privileged recipient, i.e. stipulations that are formulated in the recipient's interest, namely: (1) The world will not be destroyed by the flood again. (2) Conveyance in perpetuity; like the Abrahamic covenant, this is declared to be an "everlasting covenant" (9.16). Arguably, the commandments given to Noah and his sons in 9.1–7 could be considered stipulations that require actions by the recipients, but this remains unclear because it is uncertain whether the covenant text properly begins at v. 1 or at v. 9, in which the deity actually declares that the covenant is being established. Overall, the point is that the nature of the Noachic covenant, applying to an extraordinary circumstance in the infancy of the creation, renders most of the conventional from inapplicable. Nonetheless, it has enough in common with the Abrahamic covenant (reward of a faithful individual, a sign, conveyance in perpetuity, common language) that we can still speak of the two as representing a common class, to be contrasted to the Israelite covenant, which represents another type.

The combination of the two types of covenant is intriguing and effective. The existence of each of the later covenants is based on the preceding covenants. The covenantal structure offers security in that the existence of the world and the availability of the land are guaranteed forever; but it also demands good behavior, on which immediate well-being depends, namely: fidelity to Yahweh, together with performance of the rituals and living according to the ethical standards commanded by Yahweh as giver of the covenant. The Noachic and Abrahamic covenants, in rewarding two individuals, implicitly identify these individuals as models. It would appear from the narrative contexts that the quality that these two individuals share and of which they are quintessential models is, above all, obedience. With these two covenants lauding obedience broadly, the Israelite covenant then comes detailing the specifics that constitute obedience to the God of Israel. The specifics number 617 commandments (according to tradition), covering a range of ritual and ethical behavior from sacrificing a goat to providing for the poor, from celebrating sabbaths and holidays to loving one's neighbor as oneself. In sum, the Abrahamic/Noachic (royal grant) type of covenant may be said to focus on divine commitment, whereas the covenant of Sinai (suzerainty treaty) type focuses on human obligation.

By using the mechanism of known legal forms, and then by setting these forms in the context of narrative, in which the deity and the human beings are pictured in the process of making these contracts, the Torah merges story and law. The result is that *law is grounded in history*. The Torah, thus, does not merely contain a large number of laws. Far more

pervasively, by the mechanism of covenant, in the Torah the very relationship between the deity and human beings is expressed in the legal
terms of that era. Law codes never appear as independent documents in
the Torah. They are always presented in the context of history. The
covenants are pictured as events, formalizing divine-human relationships,
stating explicitly what the deity expects of the human beings and what
they can expect of the deity. Law, theology, and history all meet in the
presentation of the covenants in the Torah, and that meeting is pivotal.
The central shrine of the people, the mark of their God's presence
among them, is the tent and box containing the covenant document. The
conclusion and culmination of the Torah in Deuteronomy comes following a lengthy corpus of covenantal material and pictures the people
poised on the edge of the promised land, prepared by virtue of the
covenant they possess to begin the story that will unfold in that land.

Torah and covenant then figure in a variety of ways in the other books
of the Hebrew Bible. In some cases the dependence of other biblical
books on the Torah's covenantal grounding is direct, as in the case of the
books of Kings, which allude to and involve the covenant of Sinai. In
some cases it is implicit; at the very least, human events in all the biblical
books are ultimately based in the Noachic covenant. With regard to the
biblical books of historical narrative subsequent to the Torah, the connection is particularly strong. The Deuteronomistic history (the books of
Joshua, Judges, 1 and 2 Samuel, and 1 and 2 Kings) and the Chronicler's
history (1 and 2 Chronicles, Ezra, and Nehemiah) base the destiny of the
nation on the Israelite covenant. The Davidic covenant, which appears in
the book of 2 Samuel, comes to figure in the nation's destiny as well, but
it stands in a complex and sometimes uncertain relationship with the
Torah's covenants, perhaps precisely because it comes later and is dependent upon those earlier covenants. Thus, for example, according to
the Deuteronomistic history the promises of the Davidic covenant include
the eternal security of the Davidic throne in Jerusalem (2 Sam. 7.13–16;
1 Kgs. 11.36), yet that history reports the demise of the kingship and of
Jerusalem at the end of 2 Kings. The Deuteronomistic historian recon-
ciles the seeming inconsistency by speaking of the fall of the kingdom in
terms of the nation's violation of the *Israelite* covenant (1 Kgs. 9.6–9;
2 Kgs. 21.8–15). That is, the throne and Jerusalem may unconditionally
belong to the royal family according to the terms of the Davidic covenant;
but without the secure existence of the people in the land, promised
conditionally in the terms of the Israelite covenant, the Davidic king has
no people over whom to rule and Jerusalem has no land for which it can
be capital.

Likewise in the books of the biblical prophets, covenant matters frequently and centrally in the prophets' oracles. A common genre of prophetic oracle is the covenant lawsuit (Heb., *rîb*), in which the prophet
brings Yahweh's case against the people for violation of the covenant
(e.g., Hosea 4; Micah 6). The form of the oracle resembles a litigation in

court based on an existing contract, with the notable difference that in this case the plaintiff is also the judge, who can bring the charge, rule on the people's culpability, and impose a penalty. Further, the prophet's choice of which covenant to emphasize varies according to the issue and the historical situation. The *rib* oracle is particularly suited to the Israelite covenant, which makes demands upon the human parties to the covenant. In general, when criticizing the nation or predicting a calamity the prophets are more likely to draw on the conditional terms of the Israelite covenant than on the guaranteed, assuring terms of the Abrahamic (or Noachic) covenant. Thus, notably, the prophets rarely, if ever, refer to the Abrahamic covenant prior to the defeat and exile of Judah by the Babylonians. Since the pre-exilic prophets are frequently pictured chastising the people or predicting a coming disaster, naturally their prophecies are grounded in the more conditional, Israelite covenant. They speak in terms of the covenant featuring human obligation when accusing Israel of a breach of obligation. But once the Babylonian army arrived on the scene, the people of Israel/Judah came to live with the reality of the curses of the Israelite covenant. From that time on, the Abrahamic covenant, the covenant featuring divine commitment, served as a source of hope, and so the Abrahamic tradition came to appear in the words of the prophets (Isa. 41.8–10; 51.2; Jer. 33.26).

Thus the combination of the two types of covenant in the Torah becomes a powerful mechanism in the subsequent books of the Bible and consequently in the life of the community thereafter. It provides security in that the existence of the world and the availability of the land are guaranteed forever. But it also demands good behavior—on which immediate well-being depends.

Most remarkably, the Torah itself comes to figure as an element in other books of the Bible. Not only is it referred to, alluded to, litigated upon, and quoted; the very document appears as an entity in the biblical account. In 2 Kings 22 (= 2 Chronicles 34), King Josiah of Judah has some portion of the Torah read publicly to the nation. In Nehemiah 8, Ezra reads the Torah (in its entirety, it would appear) to the community who have returned from the Babylonian exile, and it becomes the people's constitution thereafter. That is, the first five books of the Bible come to be an entity that figures in the other biblical books. The Hebrew Bible thus becomes, in a sense, a book about itself. And the Torah thus comes to acquire a singular literary place in the Hebrew Bible as it acquires a singular status historically in the life of the community. It was not only at the heart of the Hebrew Bible but at the heart of Judaism, first in the biblical world itself and for over two millennia thereafter. In post-biblical Judaism, living according to Torah comes to be what the religion is about.

Thus, despite a history filled with calamities and suffering, the Hebrew Bible concludes with possibilities and optimism, with the Jewish people in possession of a precious document that bears both their history and a constitution for their future. It revitalizes the possibility of the ultimate fulfillment of the promise made to Abraham both before and after the covenant, that through Abraham and his descendants all the world will be blessed (Gen. 12.3; 22.18).

The Phenomenon of Prophecy

JAMES L. MAYS

Prophets and prophecy played a crucial role in Israel's experience of God. In the Book of Amos there is a remarkable statement about the role of prophecy in God's relation to Israel: "The Lord GOD does nothing without revealing his plan to his servants the prophets" (3.7). God is viewed here as a sovereign who plans strategies to carry out the divine purpose in the world. The prophets are servants in the divine administration whose function is the promulgation of revelation. They are the agents who make known in the world what the Lord is going to do to maintain and advance the deity's sovereignty. The prophets made it possible for people to see their present situation and future prospects in light of God's purpose.

This high view of prophecy, incorporated by an editor in the Book of Amos, is the result of Israel's experience with the prophets. It is an assessment that looks back across centuries of history and takes certain figures in that past as norm and model of what a prophet was and did. This view led to the creation and inclusion of the books of Isaiah, Jeremiah, Ezekiel, and the twelve minor or shorter prophets in the Hebrew Scriptures. It is also the view that shaped many of the portrayals of prophets found in the books of Samuel and Kings.

It is through these books of Scripture that prophets and prophecy have become recognized as a constituent element of Judaism and Christianity, but the prophets were known and experienced through written presentation only in the latter part of Israel's history. Before that they were figures who played an established, though varied, role in Israel's society. They spoke and acted in performing their role, and it was through what they said and did that they became part of Israel's experience of God.

The institution of prophecy had a long and complex history in Israel. It emerged as part of the culture that Israel shared with other peoples of its time and region. Early Israelite prophecy is known from the accounts in the books of 1–2 Samuel and 1 Kings. In the eighth century B.C.E. the "canonical prophets" began to appear, so called because their careers resulted in books bearing their names that are now part of the biblical canon.

The Cultural Context of Biblical Prophecy

Prophecy in Israel is related to a background in the culture of the ancient Near East. The world in which Israel's history unfolded was thoroughly religious in the sense that belief in the reality of gods and spirits and demons was fundamental to the view of reality held by the nations and societies of the era. Corporate and individual human life was lived in an environment affected by the character and conduct, the actions and reactions of these other personal beings. It was important to be informed about what they had to do with what was happening to a person or a nation in the present, or would happen in the future. At times it was needful to communicate with them and seek to influence their purpose and power. The need was felt especially in times of crisis: sickness, conflict with others, economic distress, political upheavals, war.

In the nations who were Israel's neighbors, the need was met in a variety of ways. There were specialists who could divine the meaning of omens of different kinds, from accidental and astrological occurrences to patterns in the organs of sacrificial animals. There were persons who were able to communicate on behalf of a god through the help of trances, dreams, visions, or perhaps even rational reflection. Sometimes they spoke in response to inquiry, sometimes on their own initiative. Some of these persons had accepted, established roles in their society; others seem to have been marginal. Those about whom records have been preserved were mostly concerned with the organized worship of the god they represented, its performance and support, and with the decisions and destinies of leaders of their society. In Jer. 27.9 there is a list of the kinds of functionaries who informed the kings of Edom, Moab, Ammon, Tyre, and Sidon: prophets, diviners, women dreamers, soothsayers, and sorcerers.

In the popular religion of Israel, the situation was probably somewhat similar. But there is little information about the practices in the popular religion of the general population. There are only hints in the Old Testament story of what went on. Once King Saul, when the Lord did not answer by dreams or Urim (divination by lot) or prophet, sought the services of a medium who brought up the spirit of the dead Samuel for consultation (1 Sam. 28). The visit to the medium had to be secret because Saul himself had suppressed those who called up ghosts and spirits. The prohibition of some categories of divine-human communication became a feature of the religion of Israel; diviners, soothsayers, augurs, sorcerers, necromancers, and those who cast spells or traffic with ghosts and spirits are denounced in Israel's law as abominations that belong to the nations and not to those who worship the God of Israel (Deut. 18.9–14). The acceptable forms of mediation were dreams, Urim, and prophets (1 Sam. 28.6, 15). Of the three, prophets came to play the overwhelmingly major role in Israel's religion.

Prophecy in Early Israel

The title "prophet" refers to a role in Israel's society that was by no means uniform. Persons who were recognized as prophets performed in quite different ways. Indeed, the title "prophet" (Hebrew *nabi'*) itself was not consistent; persons we think of as prophets were called "seer" (Hebrew *roeh*), "visionary" (Hebrew *hozeh*), and "man of God," as well as "prophet." It is possible that in early Israel the different titles designated different roles, but according to 1 Sam. 9.9 "what is nowadays called a prophet used to be called a seer."

As one reads the story of Israel in the books of Samuel and Kings it becomes apparent in what different ways one could be a prophet in Israel. Some prophets were resident at holy places (1 Kgs. 13.11; 14.1–2). Others lived in ordinary surroundings in their homes or villages (2 Kgs. 22.14). Others were resident at the royal court (2 Sam. 24; 1 Kgs. 22). Some belonged to groups who lived a communal existence (1 Sam. 10; 2 Kgs. 2). Others were individual in playing their role (1 Kgs. 11.29–33). An Israelite might take the initiative to seek out a prophet to inquire about God's way with him or her in times of crisis; apparently prophets were frequently consulted about serious illness (1 Kgs. 14; 2 Kgs. 1). But prophets also received and brought revelations from God for persons who had not consulted them (1 Kgs. 12.22–24). Some prophets practiced prophecy in the form of group ecstasy induced by music and group excitement (1 Sam. 10.5; 2 Kgs. 3.15–16). Others spoke in formally-composed oracles containing clear and concise messages from God to people about their situation in the light of the deity's purpose (1 Kgs. 21.17–24).

The biblical story reflects all this variety without sorting out well-defined social roles for different types of prophets. To do so was not the purpose of the story of which prophets were a part. What seems to have held all this variety together under the category prophet is that all so named were recognized in Israel's society as intermediaries, persons who had the gift of being the medium of communication between the divine and human spheres. The story makes it clear at points that not all who were recognized as prophets in Israel's society played a positive role in the story (1 Kgs. 13 and 22). The focus is rather on a particular succession of prophets who at crucial stages in Israel's history played a significant role in guiding and maintaining the relation between Israel and its God.

Samuel is the introductory figure in two ways: He is the first prophet to play a prominent role in Israel's story, and his career provides a typical model of the prophetic role of those who followed him. (1) He became a prophet through the experience of a vision in which the Lord spoke to him. (2) In the vision he was given a message and a commission to deliver it. (3) The message took the form of "the word of the LORD." (4) The message was a rebuke and announcement of punishment for officials who perverted the relation between God and people, in this case the priestly clan who presided at the chief holy place. (5) His identity as one who had the gift of prophecy was claimed by the oracles or words which he spoke, and his authority by the fact that his oracles proved reliable. (For all the above, see 1 Sam. 3.)

Samuel as prophet dealt with two institutions that were of the highest importance in Israel's life: kingship and warfare. His relation to those institutions set the course for prophets who followed him. With respect to kingship, Samuel was the agent of the Lord in the inauguration of kingship in Israel and in the designation of Israel's first two kings, Saul and David (1 Sam. 9–10; 1 Sam. 16). He was the intermediary between God and king, concerned about the king's loyalty and obedience to the Lord as the real sovereign over Israel. At the appropriate times he brought word of the Lord's disapproval and rejection to the king (1 Sam. 15).

Samuel's role in relation to warfare was significant. In times of dire military crisis, Samuel was intercessor for the nation, seeking a word of salvation from God through his appeal (1 Sam. 7). He gave the king direct advice in military decisions (1 Sam. 15).

The prophets who are featured in the books of Samuel and Kings stand in the tradition of Samuel. The prophets Gad and Nathan belonged to David's retinue and guided his decisions and condemned his failures (1 Sam. 22.5; 2 Sam. 12). Nathan was the channel of the Lord's promise to establish David's house as the permanent dynasty in Israel (2 Sam. 7). Ahijah the Shilonite gave divine authorization to Jeroboam to lead the ten northern tribes in secession from the Davidic rule because of the failures of Solomon and Rehoboam (1 Kgs. 11.29–39). In the remaining history of the separate northern kingdom, prophets were active in designating kings, influencing military policy, and fomenting rebellion. Elijah the Tishbite fought an epochal battle against the introduction of the worship of the Canaanite deity Baal into Israel (1 Kgs. 18). Elisha was deeply involved in the wars of Israel with its neighbors (2 Kgs. 3).

The Canonical Prophets

In the eighth century B.C.E., a dramatic shift occurred in the course of prophecy in Israel. The performance of prophets and prophecy continued much as before, but now a sequence of prophets appeared whose sayings were carefully collected and preserved. The early prophets were remembered as actors in Israel's story. By contrast, these so-called "latter" prophets are remembered in terms of what they said. In their careers, the Word rises to such preeminence that they are presented in their books primarily through a collection of their sayings.

With these prophets, the message had a new audience, subject, and purpose. They continued to address the leaders of Israel and Judah, such as kings, officials, priests, and other prophets, but their primary audience was the nation itself. That is because their subject was the destiny of the people itself. The early prophets had dealt with the conduct of leaders, principally the kings, as it affected the people. These prophets are also concerned with the conduct of the whole people as it affected their destiny under God. The early prophets concentrated on the internal problems of the nation and on its conflicts with neighboring nations. For these prophets the arena of God's way with the elect people became international history. Their purpose was to bring to light the way in which God was working out the election of Israel to be the people of the Lord in the context of world history.

The background of the careers of the canonical prophets was a change in the historical conditions with which Judah and Israel had to cope. A series of empires with aggressive military policies dominated their region. Successively, Assyria, Babylon, and Persia, with Egypt always as a foil to the south, set the conditions under which the smaller nations in the Near East lived. The canonical prophets appeared and were active in the crises and changes provoked by the intrusion of these world powers. (See "Historical Contexts of the Biblical Communities," p. * 33.)

THE ASSYRIAN CRISIS. In the second half of the eighth century B.C.E., Assyrian armies and policy progressively weakened the northern state of Israel. The Assyrians finally overcame Israel and deported its population, and harassed Judah and brought it to the edge of defeat and ruin.

Years before the Assyrian threat was immediate, a Judean named Amos was called away from his flocks and herds to proclaim the word of God's judgment to Israel. He pointed to the failure of righteousness and justice in the courts, temples, and marketplaces, a failure that produced luxury for the powerful and oppression for the poor. Because of such violations of the divine will, the state of Israel with all its principal institutions would be brought to an end.

Amos was followed in the northern kingdom by Hosea, whose prophetic activity stretched across the tumultuous decades that led to the state's collapse. His rebukes were particularly aimed at Israel's involvement with the Canaanite god Baal, who was worshiped alongside of and confused with Israel's God. Because of unfaithfulness to their covenant with the Lord, Israel would be severely punished and restored to a new covenant relationship only after the most grievous suffering.

In the southern kingdom of Judah, Isaiah repeated and expanded Amos' charges against the primary institutions of the nation. He was concerned with the loyalty of Jerusalem and its resident kings to the Lord as the sole sovereign and savior, and opposed every policy and alliance that betrayed that preempting obligation. He portrayed the Assyrians as the rod of the Lord's anger to punish and purge the kingdom and restore it to its true righteousness and dependence on the Lord. For a brief period when the Assyrian threat to Judah was at its height, he was seconded and supported by Micah.

THE BABYLONIAN CRISIS. During the Assyrian crisis, Judah was invaded and despoiled, but Jerusalem did not fall, and its Davidic house was not displaced. The little kingdom, however, lived during much of the seventh century as a vassal state in the shadow of Assyrian power. When Assyria's dominance began to wane, a movement of independence and reform developed that brought changes in the institutional life of the nation. A prophet named Zephaniah had announced a day of the Lord's wrath against the religious pluralism and social unrighteousness prevalent in the population, a witness to the problems that called for reform. But the reform did not reshape the religious and social life in a radical way. When its principal sponsor, King Josiah, was killed in a battle to protect the new independence from a resurgent Egypt, the reform lost impetus.

About that time a Levite named Jeremiah was called by the Lord to disclose the true situation of the nation and reveal its future. Jeremiah adopted Hosea's theme of covenant unfaithfulness and expanded it in eloquent and passionate ways as the principal diagnosis of Israel's sinfulness. He charged that the unfaithfulness reached back to the beginning of his people's life in their land and had affected their very character. Only a total and radical repentance could renew their relation with the Lord. Failing that, the very character of the people would have to be transformed in a disastrous punishment that would create the conditions for a restoration that broke with the continuities of the past. The instrument of the Lord for judgment would be a foe from the north, a role filled by the new Babylonian Empire. Jeremiah persisted in his message in the face of royal opposition, persecution, imprisonment, while the terrible threat of his prophecy was being realized in the fall of the city, the exile of one king and the blinding of another, and a series of deportations of much of the population to a life of exile in Babylon.

During the climactic times of Babylon's invasion of Judah, another prophet named Habakkuk wrestled with the question of God's righteousness in using a wicked pagan nation as instrument of the divine purpose.

In the first group of Judeans exiled to Babylon there was a priest named Ezekiel who received in Babylon a visionary revelation of the Lord with a commission to be a prophet there. During the years that Babylon permitted Judah to exist as a vassal state, Ezekiel continually proclaimed that the Lord's punishment was not complete. When Judah rebelled and Jerusalem was subjected to a long and torturous siege, Ezekiel predicted its defeat and destruction. When news reached the exiles that Jerusalem had fallen, he began to foretell a restoration of the people of God to a new life around a rebuilt Jerusalem and temple.

THE PERSIAN PERIOD. In the middle of the sixth century B.C.E., the armies of the expanding Persian Empire swept to the west and south, overwhelming the nations in these regions and bringing a new policy of benevolence toward subject peoples. Concurrently, an unnamed prophet among the exiles in Babylon, whose sayings are preserved in chs. 40–55 of Isaiah, announced the end of the era of punishment and the beginning of the time of salvation. He proclaimed that the sovereignty of Israel's God would be revealed in a recapitulation of the exodus and wilderness journey that would conclude in a return of the exiles to Zion. His oracles portrayed the life of the restored community as a glorious existence of righteousness and blessing.

When Babylon was subdued by the Persian King Cyrus, he encouraged the displaced populations to return to their native lands and build religious and political communities under the Persian administration. Groups of Judeans began to return, but the conditions they found and the life they lived were in sorry contrast to the future portrayed by Ezekiel and the author of Isaiah 40–55. The oracles in Isaiah 56–66 are the sayings of a prophet who in those days looked for yet another judgment of God to bring about the righteous restoration that the residents of Jerusalem had failed to realize.

In the reconstructed community, the rebuilding of the ruined temple was a particularly important project. The prophets Haggai and Zechariah (chs. 1–8) linked the completion of the temple to the well-being of the community and announced encouraging visions of the future of the Judean people in the Lord's rule over human affairs.

The prophecies found in the books of Malachi, Joel, and Zechariah 9–14 probably belong to later times in the Persian era in the fifth century. In the sayings in these books, prophets continue to judge the life of the community by the standards of the Lord's will and to point to a divine intervention to set things right in Judah and the world. The prophecies in these books seem to represent the inconclusive conclusion of canonical prophecy. The canonical prophets had raised expectations of righteousness in their community and of fulfillment of the Lord's way in history that could not be realized in proximate and penultimate conditions and times. The way was open to another form of revelation, that of apocalyptic.

The Transition to Scripture

As the life of the community around the rebuilt temple developed and changed, the importance of prophecy diminished. The institution of prophecy gradually lost its place as a primary means by which communication between God and people occurred. There were no longer any kings to hear the rebukes and decisions of the divine sovereign. The nation no longer lived an independent existence with policies to be decided and wars to fight. The priesthood rose to an independence and authority that preempted the functions of other offices in the society. The conduct of society and individuals in it were judged in the light of the scriptures that had emerged as the authoritative source of the knowledge of God's way and will. The era of Samuel and Amos was succeeded by the era of Ezra and Nehemiah. Scripture and the scribe moved into the center.

Prophecy itself became scripture. The traditions of the early prophets had been incorporated in the history told in the books of Samuel and Kings. From the time of Amos, the sayings of the canonical prophets were collected, arranged, and expanded in the process that produced the prophetic books. The sayings were preserved, treasured, and interpreted because it was through the oracles of this group of prophets that Israel

could understand the tumultuous times through which it had passed—
the collapse of their national life, the exile, and the restoration—as their
God's way with them. The prophetic paradigm of judgment for sin with
salvation as the fulfillment of the divine promises became a permanent
witness to the Lord's sovereignty over their history.

The actual practice of prophecy during the second temple period declined until it eventually disappeared. In Judaism the prophets continued
to exist as books of scripture. In rabbinical literature prophecy was regarded as a means of revelation of a past dispensation that had come to
an end with the death of the last canonical prophet. Moses was held to
be the first and greatest of the prophets. All the rest were only successors
whose sayings expounded the *torah* that had been given through him.

Prophecy reappeared briefly in the early years of the Christian movement. John the Baptist is portrayed in the Gospels as a prophet, a second
Elijah announcing judgment and calling for repentance (Matt. 3.1–12;
17.10–13). Jesus was recognized as a prophet (Matt. 13.57; 21.11; Lk.
4.24). In some congregations, spirit-inspired prophets appeared and
spoke in assemblies for worship (1 Thess. 5.20; 1 Cor. 12.28–29; 14.26–
32). Lists of offices in the early church include prophets along with apostles and teachers as leaders of the congregation (Acts 11.27; 13.1; 15.32;
Eph. 2.20; 3.5; 4.11). But in Christianity as in Judaism it was through the
books of scripture that prophecy had, and still has, an enduring place in
the community's experience of God.

The Perspective of Wisdom

DIANNE BERGANT

Wisdom in Israel

Even a superficial survey of the religious traditions of biblical Israel shows that the predominant conviction of the people was that God was active in their history. God had chosen them, guided them, revealed the law to them, and rewarded and punished them according to their fidelity to that law. In effect, God was perceived as the principal actor in the drama of their history.

In addition to this view, some of the biblical literature provides a rather different perspective. It suggests that God can be known through the experiences of everyday life, experiences that do not necessarily contribute to the national story that many refer to as "salvation history." This additional perspective, known as "wisdom," is more interested in the unfolding of life in general and the successful living of that life in particular. Since the Israelites maintained that their God was responsible for the world and everything within it, they believed that living in harmony with this world and with others was both the basis for and the consequence of their relationship with God.

These two quite different perspectives flow from the same fundamental conviction, namely that God is involved both in nature and in human history and, through this involvement, is accessible to women and men. This means that human experience, whether within national events or the particular incidents in one's personal life, is the locus of an encounter with God. It also means that the circumstances of life influence the way God is perceived.

The wisdom literature includes the books of Job, Proverbs, Ecclesiastes, and the Song of Songs, as well as the deutero-canonical or apocryphal books, The Wisdom of Solomon and Ecclesiasticus. (Several psalms have been classified as wisdom psalms: 1, 37, 49, 73, 91, 112, 119, 127, 128, 133, 139.) The wisdom books deal with general questions of human welfare, human value, and human dignity, though the teachings relative to these humanistic concerns must be understood within the context of Israel's Yahwistic faith. The underlying presupposition of their message is that whatever benefits humankind is a good to be pursued and whatever is injurious should be avoided and condemned. Success or happiness is the criterion for evaluating any course of action and is also considered concrete evidence of the wisdom and the righteousness of the person who succeeds.

Reflection on life and observation of nature led the sages of Israel to conclude that there was some kind of order inherent in the world. They believed that, if they could discern how this order operated and harmonize their lives with it, they would live peacefully and fruitfully. Failure to identify and conform to this order would result in frustration, misfortune, and misery. The primary function of the wisdom tradition seems to have been instruction in a style of living that would assure one of well-being and prosperity. Since its emphasis was on education and training, the literary forms found in this tradition function pedagogically. These forms include: proverbs that describe particular life situations; parables, riddles and questions that tease the mind and lead to new insights; and stories that have a moral to teach.

A sapiential (wisdom) tradition is not unique to Israel. All cultures, both ancient and modern, have treasuries of wisdom that have been gleaned from experience, have passed the test of time, and have been handed down through the generations. It is by means of such a tradition that individuals learn the values, mores, and patterns of behavior expected of members of the group. That Israel was not alone in its quest for wisdom may be seen by pervasive biblical references to the sages of other nations, usually in passages that exalt the wisdom of an Israelite over that of a non-Israelite (e.g., Joseph in the court of Pharaoh, Gen. 41; Daniel in Babylon, Dan. 5). In fact, Israel's search for wisdom participated in a broad sapiential movement in the ancient Near Eastern world.

The Theology in Wisdom

Several theological themes dominate the wisdom teaching. While these themes are found within other biblical traditions as well (e.g., in the legal or prophetic writings), they are of fundamental importance to the wisdom tradition. Chief among these are: retribution, the theory that good will be rewarded and evil will be punished; concern for origins (creation) and ends (death); and the issue of the incomprehensible in life. Since these are fundamental questions, there is a universal and perennial dimension to them, which helps account for the similarity of so much of Israel's wisdom to the wisdom of other societies both ancient and contemporary. Despite the similarities, however, a dimension of this tradition is uniquely Israelite. This uniqueness resides in the distinctive way Israel understood these basic issues and dealt with them.

RETRIBUTION. The principle that discreet or virtuous behavior will yield happiness and well-being, while reckless or immoral conduct will beget adversity and grief, is derived from our reflective observation of occurrences in life. People learn from experience. They perceive certain patterns as working to their benefit and others as detrimental to their welfare. Often they preserve such insights in the form of proverbs. Such proverbs, which are really descriptions of circumstances in life, can also teach specific behaviors which will produce desired consequences. Eventually, such descriptive and didactic insights may well become the source of customs and even of regulations. The wisdom tradition, we should remember, is primarily interested in achieving peace and prosperity; the legal tradition, which is closely related to wisdom, governs the behavior that will ensure this peace and prosperity.

A careful examination of the literature of this tradition reveals several different yet related ways that wisdom is understood. First, the technical skill or dexterity of performance with which experts ply their trades or utilize their abilities is called wisdom. These people are able to perform with such expertise only because they have studied the rules governing their respective professions or crafts and have become accomplished in them (cf. 1 Kgs. 7.13–14; Ezek. 27.8–9). Although this meaning does not appear frequently, the focus on preparation in relation to accomplishment carries over to other meanings of wisdom.

A second arena wherein one can develop wisdom is the field of human interaction. There one learns to be tactful, shrewd, or sagacious. The wisdom books contain much instruction of this kind. In fact some interpreters maintain that such teaching originated from and was used within professional schools established to train official diplomats or scribal leaders of the court (cf. Prov. 25.1). Other commentators hold that this is too narrow an interpretation. They insist that the wisdom teaching is really a kind of training for life that is necessary for all. This training often takes place in the home, provided by both the father and the mother (cf. Prov. 1.8).

While both of these kinds of wisdom require the development of keen powers of observation in order to discover the inner workings of some aspect of life, the second wisdom seems to be more highly valued than the first. Human behavior is less predictable than the raw materials used by an artisan, and those who are able to steer themselves through the depths and shoals of human relations truly deserve to be called wise.

There is a way in which even those people who are bent on deception and wickedness might be considered wise. When they have insight into human limitation and frailty they often prey upon this weakness, take advantage of the unsuspecting, and benefit from their exploitation. Their wisdom might more accurately be termed cunning. The Book of Proverbs contains a recurrent warning to naive youth against such cunning (cf. 7.1–27 as well as the description of the serpent in Gen. 3.1).

Still another kind of wisdom is that attributed to those who demonstrate encyclopedic knowledge. Solomon is credited with a scope of knowledge and understanding unmatched in the world (cf. 1 Kgs. 4.29–34; Ecclus. 47.12–16; Wisd. 7.7–22).

Finally, it is in reverent obedience to the Lord that real wisdom is attained. "The first step to wisdom is the fear of the LORD" (Prov. 9.10). Such fear, based on the recognition of the holiness of God, is not merely an attitude of mind; it is the motivation of all conduct, launching every venture, sustaining it, and bringing it to conclusion. This religious mo-

tivation transforms the entire search for wisdom into a religious enterprise. The fruit of fear of the Lord is a wisdom that opens the person to
deeper reverence and, therefore, to broader wisdom. It is no wonder that
well-being and prosperity were regarded as rewards for fidelity to God.
Such thinking led the sages to the corollary conclusion that misfortune
and adversity were punishments for behavior that not only disregarded
the natural order established by God, but disdained fear of the Lord
itself.

Most of the instruction found in Proverbs, Ecclesiasticus, Wisdom and
the Wisdom Psalms is based on this theory of reward and punishment.
The teaching is quite practical and traditional. What in the past has
worked for the welfare of the individual and the community will work in
the present. Experience has proven the merit of this particular way of
life; wisdom dictates that it be followed. Adherence to the teaching assures the individual of acceptance in the group. It also supports established practices and strengthens the status quo, consequences that work
to the benefit of those in power.

On the other hand, both Job and Ecclesiastes question the universal
applicability of the theory of retribution. The unexplained tribulations of
the former and the discontent of the latter show that the righteous do not
always experience in this life the fulfillment that the theory of reward
and punishment promises, nor do the wicked always suffer misfortune.
While both books raise serious questions related to the issue of theodicy
(the vindication of divine justice in the face of innocent suffering), neither of them is able to offer answers to the dilemmas they describe. It was
apparently in the first century B.C.E. that the wisdom stream began to
develop a concept of retribution after death. The Wisdom of Solomon,
which shows the influence of Greek anthropology (e.g., an immaterial
soul that can survive death), speaks of immortality and the rewards that
the righteous will enjoy after this life.

CREATION AND DEATH. In awe of the wonders of nature, the Israelites came
to believe that their God was the great Creator-God, who was responsible
for the world, its organization, and everything within it. They perceived
this Creator not only as the primeval architect of the universe but also as
the provident sustainer of reality and the demanding judge safeguarding
the established order. They recognized that the splendor of creation
could have come only from One who was both powerful and wise. Elements of wisdom thinking pervade Israel's accounts of creation (e.g., the
order described in Genesis 1).

The wisdom books themselves contain traces of creation accounts
(Prov. 8.22–31; Ecclus. 24.1–12). What sets these passages apart from
other creation texts is the mysterious figure of Wisdom, personified as a
woman, found in this tradition. Although she herself does come from
God, this primeval woman clearly has an important role to play in the
creation. Some consider her simply the personification of a divine attri-

bute; others regard her as an hypostatization. A "personification" is an imaginative stylistic technique. An "hypostatization" treats what is normally merely a personal *trait* as a *person* with a distinct existence. In either case, one must ask: Why, if the Creator is usually characterized as male, is the personification or hypostatization female?

The Wisdom figure has been interpreted as an ancient deity. It is possible that the ancestors of Israel initially claimed to have many gods before they worshiped the Lord alone (cf. Gen. 31.25–30). They could have believed in a goddess of Wisdom on whom this figure is modelled. However, though primordial in origin and cosmic in influence, in Israelite literature this Wisdom figure is clearly a creature of God, which may tell against its derivation from a goddess. The representation does suggest that the wisdom human beings seek is somehow related not only to God but to the very first moments of creation.

Another description of creation is found in God's reply to Job (Job 38–41). These speeches are considered some of the most beautiful nature poetry of the ancient Near East. Here Job is closely questioned about the primeval events and the marvels of the natural world. His ability to exercise dominion over wild beasts or fathom some of the unique characteristics of the animal realm is contested. He can only stand in awe of the magnificent governing structure within the universe, one which far exceeds human comprehension or control. He is brought to acknowledge the wisdom and the power of the creator. Here creation, as primordial event and natural order, becomes the means for bringing Job to new insight. (The use of nature as a technique of instruction is a well established practice in folkloric traditions, e.g., Aesop's tales; cf. Prov. 6.6–11).

This same style of teaching is found in Ecclesiastes. Both the natural world (1.2–8) and the events in a person's life (3.1–8) follow a mysterious, yet evident, predetermined order. The regularity of nature in the first instance and the appropriate timing in life in the second are under the control of God, and God alone. As with Job, Ecclesiastes can only observe creation or life as it comes to him from the hand of the creator, try to discover the laws that are operative there, and live in harmony with them.

Both Job and Ecclesiastes see death as the end of all of life's possibilities. At the time of their composition Israel had no clear teaching about life after death. Hence the sages believed that this world and human history were the only stage on which the drama of life would unfold. If the curtain of death was lowered at a time and in a manner that prevented one from playing a role to the final scene, the conventional teaching of retribution would question the righteousness of that person. We have already seen how, each in its own way, these two books challenge this point of view.

It should be noted that, in the midst of his physical affliction and his anguish of mind and heart, Job longed for death only as a release from his torment—not as an opportunity for justification in an afterlife. That is, even when he did consider death as an option, it was only as a last resort and then only for a fleeting moment. He really did not despair of life. How could he if he clung to the hope that God would eventually vindicate him? With no doctrine of an afterlife, any vindication that he could enjoy would have to take place during his lifetime.

On the other hand, Ecclesiastes seems preoccupied with death. Since his life has not been difficult, death is not viewed as deliverance. Instead, it is almost seen as the final "futility." This wisdom teacher maintains that all of our striving for happiness and prosperity is in vain, for the same death comes to the successful and to the one who fails, to the wise and to the foolish. Death is truly the great leveler. Some have called this unjust; others have called it absurd. Ecclesiastes acknowledges it as a fact and teaches trust in God, for ultimately all things are in God's hands.

It was probably the untimely death of the righteous that prompted the author of the Wisdom of Solomon to look anew at the question of retribution. This book comes from a Jewish community that has been Hellenized (influenced by Greek culture) to a considerable degree. The philosophy and language of Greek civilization had profoundly challenged the ancient religious traditions. However, encounter with this prestigious culture had not been solely detrimental. Greek thinking provided new avenues for understanding traditional teaching and for broadening that teaching in new directions. The belief that each person has an immaterial soul that survives death was pivotal in the continuing development of the teaching regarding retribution (cf. Wisd. 3.1–9).

THE INCOMPREHENSIBLE IN LIFE. All of the theological themes already treated leave us standing before mystery. Both the wisdom tradition of ancient Israel and our own experience persuade us that there is much in life that we cannot comprehend. The sages taught that certain natural laws can be perceived and followed. They never taught that people would ever be in complete control of the world or of their lives in the world.

Despite the assurance about consequences presumed by a strict theory of reward and punishment such as is found in Proverbs, the sages acknowledged that the coveted prize of wisdom is often unattainable. In fact, that dimension of wisdom most desired, the wisdom that explains the universe and the inner workings of human life, is beyond human reach and resides with God alone. Most probably the mysterious figure of Wisdom, present and active at creation, represents the inaccessible dimension of wisdom that is always calling to us but ever eluding us.

Ecclesiastes also admits that often the answers to the questions that most plague us are beyond our comprehension (3.11). His advice in the face of such human limitation is to be satisfied with and to enjoy fully whatever happiness we may have received from the hand of God (2.24–25; 3.12–13; 5.18–20; 8.15; 9.7–9).

It is probably in Job that we find the most gripping realization of the immensity of life's incomprehensibility. Grounded in the theology of retributive justice and convinced of his own righteousness, Job issued the demand that God explain why he, Job, had become the victim of such calamity and why God had done nothing to remedy this situation. In one of his speeches to Job, Zophar reminded the tormented man of the immeasurable scope of the mystery of God (11.7–9), but neither Job nor his interlocutors seemed to give this point serious consideration. It was only after the speeches of God that Job returned to this thought.

Job had called for a court trial where God would be forced to account for Job's predicament (9.1–3; 16–18). Instead, his own knowledge and experience were put to the test. Question after question was put to him, each one challenging his understanding of some aspect of the universe or his control over it. All of the questions confronted Job with the limits of his own creaturehood. He was indeed rebuked by God but it was for the narrowness of his vision, not, as his interlocutors had warned, for any lack of integrity on his part. The scope of Job's experiential knowledge was challenged, not the uprightness of the man.

Job's ability to comprehend life had become the standard by which he measured the providence of God. By means of the pedagogical technique of the analogy of nature, he was brought to new insights as to the limits of human nature. If he could not even begin to imagine the many and diverse ways that God continues to sustain creation, how could he possibly fathom God's mysterious care in his own life? Through questions about nature, God led Job to concede that, just as there are mysteries here that are far beyond his comprehension, so there are mysteries in life that he will never be able to grasp.

Acknowledgment of the incomprehensible in life brought Job to a new realization of the mystery of God. The upheaval of his own life and his firm conviction of his own innocence had called into question the way he had perceived divine governance in his life in the days before misfortune engulfed him. Formerly, he had known of God through the testimony of the ancients as well as through the teaching of the sages (cf. 8.8; 15.18). Now, his unexpected, breathtaking encounter with the God of creation gave him experiential knowledge of his own, knowledge that assured him that God is indeed in charge even though he, Job, cannot comprehend how God governs.

Although Job had never intended to usurp any divine privilege or status, he expected, even demanded, an insight into reality far beyond what he as a human creature had a right to expect. God's questioning sought to correct this by pointing out time and again: God is God and Job is not. The splendor of creation transcended Job's comprehension and he could only stand in awe and wonder. The purpose of the theophany was not to silence him, but to reassure him of divine control over the universe and to inspire him to confidence in this wondrous yet incomprehensible God. Job's questions may not have been answered as they had been asked, but his fears were dissipated and his trust in this mysterious God was restored.

Wisdom in Early Christianity

In later Jewish literature, the continuing development of wisdom thought resulted in a heightened understanding of (heavenly) Wisdom as an active agent of creation, revelation and salvation—sometimes identified with Torah and sometimes viewed as Torah's source.

The evolved understanding of the mysterious Wisdom figure of Proverbs 8 provided the basis for an important development in Christology. Perhaps as early as Paul and Matthew and certainly in the Prologue of the Gospel of John (1.1–18), Jesus Christ was identified with Wisdom-Word and in that light was interpreted as involved in creation and salvation. The consequences of such Wisdom speculation for the subsequent course of theological thought were profound.

Other wisdom influences on early Christianity, especially those related to moral instruction, are also to be seen. The presentation of Jesus as teacher is strong in the early tradition. Sapiential materials are embedded in the Gospels, as may be seen in the Matthean Sermon on the Mount (Matt. 5–7). The teachings source "Q" used by Matthew and Luke may belong to the literary genre "Sayings of the Sages" (*logoi sophōn*) with origins in the wisdom collections of the Old Testament and Judaism. The forms of practical wisdom instruction persist: beatitudes commend behavior beneficial to the hearer; proverbs identify lessons found in life experience; parables introduce new insights or ways of viewing the world. Additionally, the Letter of James is made up primarily of instruction for leading a moral life and shows many similarities to Hellenistic wisdom literature.

Conclusion

The wisdom tradition has been variously described as: a humanistic outlook on life; a world view for coping with reality; a search for the underlying principles of causality and order for the purpose of conforming to them; an attempt to organize an otherwise chaotic existence. Each of these characterizations, though distinctly nuanced, highlights the primary concern of the movement. Wisdom thinking is interested in appropriate attitudes toward life and attendant behavior that will bring about happiness.

While it is true that proverbs preserve insights into life which have been gleaned from experience, each proverb depicts life only in a certain situation and under a specific set of circumstances. What is fitting in one context may be false in another. This explains why certain proverbs seem to contradict others. For instance, Prov. 10.19, "the prudent hold their tongues," and Prov. 10.31, "Wisdom flows from the mouth of the righteous," seem at the least to clash in emphasis. The wise person is not one who merely learns the teachings of the wisdom tradition and then applies them to another setting, but one who is able to decide what is appropriate in a new situation. Experience is both the originator of wisdom and the basis for criticism of its value. Wisdom is a dynamic reality. It takes seriously the tradition of the past, but is absorbed with the needs of the present, needs that may at times move believers beyond their traditional understandings. Though we may have "no comprehension of God's work from beginning to end" (Eccles. 3.11), still we are instructed to "Get wisdom!" (Prov. 4.5).

The Apocalyptic Vision

MARTHA HIMMELFARB

When the word "apocalypse" appears in the newspaper, it is usually in connection with the horrors of nuclear war or the threat of environmental pollution. The association of "apocalypse" with doom and disaster reflects the influence of the two canonical apocalypses, Daniel in the Hebrew Bible and Revelation in the New Testament. In these two works, as in 4 Ezra (2 Esd. 3–14) in the Apocrypha, the dominant theme is the imminent and cataclysmic end of the world and the reign of the righteous to follow, revealed through symbolic visions.

For some types of biblical literature, for example the prophetic books of the Hebrew Bible, no extra-biblical examples have survived. But a significant number of apocalypses have come down to us outside the canon. Some of these other apocalypses share with Daniel, Revelation, and 4 Ezra their concern for the coming end of the world and their use of symbolic visions as the medium of revelation. But the Greek *apokalypsis* means literally "uncovering," and thus, in the more extended sense relevant to ancient Judaism and Christianity, "revelation," without any necessary connection to the end of the world and the last judgment. Many apocalypses are as interested in the wonders of nature, the fate of souls after death, and the divine throne and its angelic entourage, as in collective eschatology. In these apocalypses the mode of revelation is not symbolic visions but ascent to heaven.

Jews and Christians continued to write apocalypses through the Middle Ages, but this essay will consider only the apocalypses that belong to the period relevant to the Bible, from the beginnings of apocalyptic literature in the third century B.C.E. through the second century C.E., a corpus of about twenty texts. It is worth noting that only four or five of these apocalypses are Christian. Thus despite their intense eschatological expectations, Christians of the first two centuries were not particularly inclined to express those hopes in apocalypses. All of the Jewish apocalypses concerned primarily with collective eschatology appear to have been written in Palestine. The other Jewish apocalypses that have survived were probably written in Egypt, where the Jews were thoroughly integrated into the culture of their Greek-speaking neighbors. In these apocalypses the final fate of the individual is a more central concern than the fate of the people, although collective eschatology is by no means absent. Of the clearly Christian apocalypses, one is from Egypt, one from Rome, one from Asia Minor or Syria, and the Book of Revelation surely from Asia Minor. The fact that Christians in Asia Minor were writing apocalypses centered on collective eschatology so early in the history of

Christianity may suggest a tradition of such apocalypses among the Jews of Asia Minor, from whom almost no literary evidence has survived.

The End of Prophecy and the Rise of Apocalyptic Literature

Apocalyptic literature is often viewed as the form in which visionary activity continued after the cessation of prophecy. But in fact prophecy never ceased. Although the last biblical prophets known to us by name were active around the time of the rebuilding of the temple at the end of the sixth century B.C.E., modern scholarship tells us that the prophetic books of the Hebrew Bible preserve under the names of earlier prophets the words of anonymous prophets who lived a century or two later. Prophets continue to appear in Jewish history to the turn of the era and beyond, but the behavior that characterizes people accepted as prophets is quite different from that of the classical prophets. Many of the later prophets claimed the title through the signs and wonders they performed, but some, like John the Baptist, engaged in preaching that places them in a certain continuity with the classical prophets. Still, there is considerable evidence that ancient Jews and Christians distinguished between the biblical type of prophecy, which they understood to have come to an end around the time of the rebuilding of the temple, and the prophecy of the period of the second temple, which did not attain the same exalted level.

A belief in the cessation of prophecy is often invoked to explain the pseudepigraphy, or false attributions, of the apocalypses. Because prophecy was understood to have come to an end, the argument goes, visions could no longer be presented in the author's own name, but instead had to be attached to the name of some ancient hero who lived before the end of prophecy. The willingness of John of Patmos, the seer of the Book of Revelation, and Hermas, the visionary of the *Shepherd of Hermas*, to use their own names reflects the Christian belief that the new age inaugurated by the appearance of Christ meant the restoration of prophecy, as promised by the biblical prophets themselves. There is considerable evidence for prophetic activity among early Christians, although of a form rather different from the prophecy of the Hebrew Bible or of the apocalypses.

For all the interest in apocalyptic literature in recent years, pseudepigraphy remains a poorly understood phenomenon. We have just seen that the assumption of this argument, that prophecy ceased, is problematic, but it is not entirely without value. The belief in the cessation of the old kind of prophecy in the second temple period may have been a contributing factor, but it is certainly not a complete explanation. Another suggestion that has some merit is that pseudepigraphy was intended to lend authority to visions by allowing the author to present a quite accurate account of the past as prophecy. In the Book of Daniel, for example, the author, who wrote in the middle of the second century

B.C.E., allows his hero, a seer in the court of the king of Babylonia, to see visions "predicting" the course of events from the fall of Babylonia to the author's own time. These relatively accurate "prophecies" promote the author's view that the course of history has been determined in advance and lend authority to the portions of the visions that are genuinely predictive.

But this motive for pseudepigraphy cannot serve for those apocalypses with little interest in the course of history. Given how little we know about how the apocalypses were understood by those who read them or heard them read, we may never come to a fully satisfying explanation of pseudepigraphy. Further, in light of their great diversity of content and historical context, it is unlikely that any single explanation will prove convincing for all the apocalypses. But any explanation must take into account the role of narrative in the apocalypses and thus the significance of the choice of pseudepigraphic hero. For unlike most of the oracles of the biblical prophets, the revelatory visions and ascents of the apocalypses appear in the context of narratives.

The stories, which are usually told in the first person, can be crucial to the understanding of the revelation. In light of the narrative of Abraham's rejection of idolatry that forms the first section of the *Apocalypse of Abraham,* for example, certain themes of the vision God shows Abraham after his ascent stand out more clearly. The seer is often chosen for the perspective his career offers on the issues with which the apocalypse is concerned. Thus several of the apocalypses concerned with the destruction of the second temple take as their hero Baruch, the scribe of the prophet Jeremiah, who prophesied and experienced the destruction of the first temple, or Ezra, the leader of the community of the Jews who returned from exile in the Persian period. Both choices implicitly equate the disaster of the author's time, the destruction of the second temple, with the destruction of the first temple, and thus suggest the expectation of a happy ending, the establishment of a new temple and the return of the Jews to their land, as occurred after the destruction of the first temple.

Apocalyptic Eschatology

The aspect of the apocalypses that has most shaped popular perception is their expectation of the imminent coming end of the world, although, as we have seen, such expectations are the dominant concern of only one group of apocalypses. Apocalyptic eschatology developed gradually from the eschatology of the prophets. The pre-exilic prophets believed that if Israel kept its end of the covenant with God, it would enjoy peace and prosperity in its own land under the rule of a king descended from David, established in the holy city of Jerusalem, seat of the temple in which God had chosen to let the divine glory dwell. Still, human life is understood to continue more or less as we know it; people will continue to grow old and die, although they will no longer die prematurely. Yet although there is nothing inherently supernatural about the new era, the prophetic descriptions of the harmony of all nature or of the wisdom of the Davidic king often have elements of the miraculous.

With the destruction of the first temple, the loss of independence, and the end of the Davidic line, the hopes of the prophets, which had once seemed not unrealistic, became more and more difficult to realize. Divine intervention began to seem the only possible way to achieve them. The Davidic king, now a figure of the future, begins to take on some of the characteristics of the later figure of the messiah. Many of the apocalypses look forward to a redeemer with supernatural powers who will defeat Israel's enemies. The expectation of such a redeemer contributes to the early Christian understanding of the figure of Jesus.

The prophets had claimed that God controlled not only the fate of Israel, but also the fate of all nations. First Assyria and then Babylonia triumphed not by their own might, but because God used them as instruments to punish the people of Israel for their wickedness. "The Assyrian! He is the rod I wield in my anger," Isaiah says of the most important enemy of his day (Isa. 10.5). So the claim of the apocalypses that the course of all history is in God's hands is nothing new. What is new is the claim that that course has already been determined once and for all. The prophets called on Israel to repent so that their punishment might be averted. The apocalypses issue no such call, for the end is approaching whatever human beings may do.

The importance of apocalyptic eschatology for our understanding of early Judaism cannot be underestimated, for these beliefs were by no means limited to the authors of the apocalypses. Indeed they had become a central part of popular expectations. While there was no agreement about the details for the scenario of the end, there was widespread belief, especially at times of persecution, that it was imminent and that it would entail a dramatic and terrible series of events. It was among Jews who held such expectations that Christianity first emerged, and it is in the context of such Jewish expectations that earliest Christianity must be understood.

Like the prophets, the authors of the apocalypses concerned with the end of history saw transcendent significance in historical events. Several apocalypses, including the Book of Daniel, appear in response to perhaps the greatest crisis of the second temple period, the decree of Antiochus IV prohibiting the practice of Judaism, the persecution of the pious and the ensuing martyrdoms, and finally the Maccabean Revolt in 167–62 B.C.E. The destruction of the second temple by the Romans in 70 C.E. also inspired a number of such apocalypses, including 4 Ezra. The Book of Revelation is usually associated with the sporadic persecutions experienced by Christians in the late first century C.E. The writing of some of the apocalypses, on the other hand, appears to have been motivated by on-going discontent rather than by specific events.

Although apocalyptic eschatology has its origins in the thought of Israel's prophets, there are some striking parallels to it in the ideologies that develop among other subject peoples of the Hellenistic Near East who saw their own kings deposed by Alexander the Great and his successors. In Egypt, for example, a body of oracular literature expresses the yearning for the restoration of native kingship, predicting the appearance of a new pharaoh who will rid Egypt of foreign invaders and restore order by cleansing the land of the pollution of foreigners. Themes typical of apocalyptic eschatology, then, appeared beyond Israel's borders as well as within.

Symbolic Visions

The central medium of revelation in the apocalypses concerned primarily with the end of history is the symbolic vision. In Daniel 8, for example, Daniel has a vision of a ram with two horns, one longer than the other, which overpowers all other beasts, but is finally overcome by a he-goat. At the height of the he-goat's power, its horn breaks, and in its place there come forth four horns. From one of these emerges a little horn, which tries to exalt itself above the heavenly host.

In the interpretation of this vision provided by the angel Gabriel, the two horns of the ram represent the two linked kingdoms of Media and Persia, the great horn of the he-goat is Alexander, referred to only as the first king, and the four horns that appear when the great horn is broken off are the kingdoms founded by Alexander's generals out of his empire upon his death (Dan. 8.20–22). The little horn is clearly Antiochus IV with his terrible persecution of the Jews. He is not mentioned by name either. Since the visionary is represented as a figure of the past, even the explanation of the vision must remain veiled. Although the identities of the great and little horns were surely intended to be obvious to the author's contemporaries, for Daniel, a seer in the court of the last kings of Babylonia, these names would be meaningless.

This mode of deciphering a vision by breaking it down into constituent parts has a long history in the dream and oracle interpretation of the ancient Near East. Joseph's interpretation of the dreams of his fellow prisoners and of Pharaoh stands squarely in this tradition (Gen. 40–41). Such visions have some precedents in the earlier prophets (Amos 7.1–8.3; Jer. 1.11–16; 24.1–10), and the visions of Zechariah in the late sixth century B.C.E. are quite similar in form to the complex visions of the apocalypses.

The appearance of these complex visions first in Zechariah and then in the apocalypses reflects the growing importance of interpretation in early Judaism. In the wake of the exile, the Torah first appears as a written document. With a written Torah comes a new type of religious functionary, the scribe, the skilled interpreter of the Torah. Zechariah, one of the last of the biblical prophets, no longer hears God's word, but rather sees

visions that require interpretation. The symbolic visions of the apocalypses, then, are a development of prophecy appropriate to an age of
interpretation.

Ascent to Heaven

The Hebrew Bible does not contain accounts of any ascents to heaven
beyond the brief mention of Elijah's departure for heaven in a whirlwind
(2 Kgs. 2.11), but the claim of the prophets to participate in the divine
council provides the seed for the growth of the ascents of the apocalypses. In Isaiah 6, for example, the prophet sees God enthroned in the
Jerusalem temple surrounded by angels. God is conducting a meeting,
seeking volunteers from among the heavenly host to deliver the divine
message of warning to Israel. In the end it is Isaiah who volunteers to
bear the message. The claim to have stood in the council of the Lord is
a central aspect of prophetic self-understanding, a mark of the prophet's
exalted status and a guarantee of the authenticity of the words spoken by
the prophet.

Isaiah (see ch. 6) found God's council meeting in the Jerusalem temple.
With the destruction of the first temple, God and the angelic attendants
lose their meeting place on earth. The prophet Ezekiel (see ch. 1), who
exercised a profound influence on the authors of the apocalypses, transforms the throne of cherubim, God's seat in the holy of holies in the
Jerusalem temple, into a wheeled chariot. In his visions he sees God
depart from the temple on the chariot-throne immediately before handing it over to the Babylonians for destruction.

In the concluding chapters of his book, Ezekiel sees the chariot once
again, returning its occupant to the new temple he visits in a vision. But
the temple that was finally built by the Jews who returned from exile was
not the eschatological temple for which Ezekiel longed. The second temple never enjoyed the prestige of the first temple, and many who were
unhappy with the conduct of the priests in charge came to view it as
polluted. Often these critics of the temple were themselves priests,
though outside the ruling circles.

The temple in Jerusalem had always been understood as modeled on
a heavenly prototype. For those dissatisfied with the earthly temple, the
heavenly temple becomes the focus of increasing attention. In the apocalypses, visionaries no longer enter God's presence by going to the Jerusalem temple. Rather they ascend to heaven and the heavenly temple.
In the *Book of the Watchers* (*1 Enoch* 1–36), the first apocalypse to contain
an ascent, Enoch passes through an awesome temple-like structure of
hailstones and fire to stand before God's cherubim throne; when he joins
the divine council, it consists of angels understood not so much as heavenly courtiers but as heavenly priests.

The *Book of the Watchers* was an extremely influential work. Several of
the later ascent-apocalypses are directly dependent on it. All show the

influence of its understanding of ascent and its picture of heaven, although some do not share its attitude toward the temple on earth.

The Sights of Heaven

At the culmination of the ascent in the *Book of the Watchers* and many other ascent-apocalypses, the visionary stands before the divine throne and receives a message or revelation from God. In the *Book of the Watchers,* the message is a message of doom to be delivered to the fallen Watchers. In *2 Enoch,* God reveals to Enoch the secret history of creation. In the *Ascension of Isaiah,* Isaiah is shown the descent and ascent of Christ.

But in at least one apocalypse the very contents of heaven constitute the message. In *3 Baruch,* in response to his lament about the fate of Israel, the angelic guide promises to show Baruch the glory of God. Baruch receives no revelation explicitly addressed to the injustice Israel has suffered, but the sights that he sees, from the punishment of wicked souls to the bliss of the righteous to the marvelous entourage of the sun as it travels its course, manifest both God's justice and glory and thus offer an indirect answer to Baruch's complaint.

Even in the apocalypses in which there is an explicit revelation before God's throne, the sights the visionary sees in the course of ascent are a central part of the message of the apocalypse. There is considerable diversity among the apocalypses in the details of their picture of heaven, although there are certain areas of broad agreement. The *Book of the Watchers* and some of the later apocalypses contain a single heaven, but most of the later works employ a schema of seven heavens. In some cases this allows for the ordering of sights by heavens.

One category of sights, which appears primarily in apocalypses directly indebted to the *Book of the Watchers,* is natural phenomena like the portals of the winds, the storehouses of rain, snow, and dew, and perhaps most prominent, the paths of the sun and moon. While the early wisdom literature of the Hebrew Bible understood nature as testifying to God's glory in a way that all could understand, this optimism faded in the wake of the exile. In the *Book of the Watchers* and the apocalypses that follow, these natural phenomena are understood as secrets not ordinarily accessible to humanity, but revealed by God to the righteous visionary. But the meaning of these phenomena is the same as in early wisdom: they are clear evidence of the greatness of their creator.

Another group of sights has to do with the fate of souls after death. The visionary sees the punishments that the wicked experience and the joy of the righteous. Frequently the righteous have become like the angels, and sometimes they enjoy a status even more exalted than that of the angels. In the *Ascension of Isaiah,* for example, Isaiah discovers that the righteous dead can look on God with steady gaze, while the angels can only glimpse the glory. It is obvious that such a vision serves to encourage the righteous on earth.

Finally, the visionary sees the angelic hosts and the divine presence itself. The angels perform a variety of tasks in heaven, but the most important is offering praise in their role as heavenly priests. Frequently the visionary does not simply observe the angels, but takes a place among them.

The awesome appearance of God's throne receives considerable attention in many of the apocalypses, and some of them even venture descriptions of the figure on the throne. These descriptions make the ability of the visionary to stand in God's presence all the more significant.

The description of the contents of heaven, then, delivers a message of its own, distinct from the explicit message God gives the visionary, although by no means in contradiction to it. The message of the sights is that however gloomy and chaotic things may appear on earth, God is in heaven, and the heavens at least are full of the glory of God.

God's Accessibility

What is more, according to these apocalypses, God is accessible to the righteous. By ascending, the visionary takes his place among the angels. Sometimes he (as a matter of historical fact, all of these visionaries were male) undergoes a physical transformation. In *2 Enoch,* after the angel Michael has clothed him in heavenly garments in a ceremony reminiscent of priestly investiture, Enoch reports, ". . . I looked at myself, and I was like one of the glorious ones, and there was no apparent difference" (*2 Enoch* 9.19).

Like the righteous dead, the visionary sometimes achieves a level above that of the angels. To take another example from *2 Enoch,* in the course of revealing the story of creation, God tells Enoch, "Not even to my angels have I revealed my secret" (*2 Enoch* 11.3). Enoch, though human, is worthy of a secret too great for the angels.

Discussion of the apocalypses has frequently emphasized the distance between God and humanity. After the destruction of the first temple and the exile, the argument goes, God comes to be seen as distant and inapproachable. This leads to the decline of prophecy and the emergence of a new form of great importance to the apocalypses: visions that need to be deciphered. The emphasis on God's dwelling place in the heavens rather than the divine presence on earth is another sign of distance, as are the angels who come to populate the heavens, standing between God and humanity, limiting humanity's access to God. But the ascent-apocalypses suggest something quite different. Rather than keeping humanity from God, the multiplication of angels there provides a means for human beings to come into contact with God, by joining the ranks of the angels, usually after death, but occasionally during life.

The apocalypses concerned primarily with apocalyptic eschatology offer one kind of hope: God is soon to bring an end to the world as we know it and to inaugurate a new world in which the righteous will find their just reward. Many of the ascent-apocalypses look forward to this new era, but they also offer a kind of daily encouragement. To live righteously is to achieve angelic heights, or even to surpass them. The righteous can expect to enjoy the company of the angels after death just as a few exceptionally righteous individuals were able to do during life.

SUGGESTIONS FOR FURTHER READING

Primary Texts

Most of the extra-biblical apocalypses discussed in this essay appear in two recent English translations of pseudepigrapha associated with figures from the Hebrew Bible:

The Old Testament Pseudepigrapha, vol. 1. James H. Charlesworth, ed. Garden City, N.Y.: Doubleday, 1983.

The Apocryphal Old Testament. H. F. D. Sparks, ed. Oxford: Clarendon Press, 1984.

Secondary Works

Collins, John J. *The Apocalyptic Imagination: An Introduction to the Jewish Matrix of Christianity.* New York: Crossroad, 1984. An excellent introduction to apocalyptic literature.

Himmelfarb, Martha. "From Prophecy to Apocalypse: The *Book of the Watchers* and Tours of Heaven." In Arthur Green, ed., *Jewish Spirituality: From the Bible through the Middle Ages,* pp. 145–65. New York: Crossroad, 1986. Treats the emergence of apocalyptic tours of heaven.

Nickelsburg, George W. E. *Jewish Literature Between the Bible and the Mishnah.* Philadelphia: Fortress, 1981. Excellent treatments of individual works considered here.

Stone, Michael E. *Scriptures, Sects and Visions.* Philadelphia: Fortress, 1980. Challenging discussion of varieties of early Judaism with particular interest in apocalyptic literature.

Relationship to God:
Public and Private Worship

BYRON E. SHAFER

Experiences of God as the source of life and deliverance, of blessing and hope, impelled and energized the worship of the biblical communities. Through ritual acts, both public and private, they sought—verbally, visually, dramatically—to maintain relationship with God, to draw on God's power, to learn of God's will, and to foster their own well-being.

Ancient Israel

A clear understanding of the development of Israel's worship eludes us. On the one hand, the priestly, Deuteronomistic, and prophetic traditions suggest that monotheism originated with Abraham; that centralized worship began with Moses; and that Canaanite elements in Israelite worship were syncretistic additions. On the other hand, archaeology and historical-critical textual study suggest that Israelite religion evolved out of Canaanite polytheism over many centuries in a number of stages; that only during the reign of Josiah, in the late seventh century B.C.E., was the public worship of God first limited to a single central sanctuary and "purged" of certain parts of its Canaanite heritage (e.g., "high places," fertility poles, and necromancy); and that monotheism, as we understand it, developed in the sixth century B.C.E.

A comprehensive understanding of Israel's worship also eludes us. First, most evidence comes from priests who officiated in the public cultus. Little is said in their writings, or in the rest of the Hebrew Bible, about the private practices of clans, families, and individuals; and only slightly more can be inferred from such artifacts as a few household shrines and numerous female figurines. Second, the priests' descriptions and prescriptions focus on ritual actions and materials and tell us nothing about accompanying words and music. While scholarly analysis of the psalms suggests that many were employed in liturgies, the texts are rarely explicit about the occasions for their use. Given what we currently know, we are unable to "reenact" so much as one Israelite ritual. Third, the authors of the Hebrew Bible were men, and the worship they describe comes from their world, Israel's public domain. They provide little information about worship in Israel's domestic domain, the women's world.

Acknowledging such limitations, much can nonetheless be said, or at least suggested, about Israel's worship, particularly about that in Judah during the late monarchic period.

PRIESTS AND WORSHIP. The office of priest was hereditary. Until the exile, there were at least several priestly families. In the post-exilic period, priesthood was limited to descendants of Aaron.

Among the priests, those serving the sanctuary or sanctuaries patronized by the king were of greatest authority and prestige. Headed by a chief priest, they were probably arranged into a system of orders—some performing or assisting at sacrifices, some composing liturgical texts, some singing and playing instruments at the various rituals. Lower in the hierarchy were priests who officiated at local sanctuaries or administered other shrines.

Service in a "house of God," as sanctuaries were called, required that priests be fit for God's presence—whole of body, ritually pure. Priests had to eat holy food, from the sacrifices, and to abstain from wine and strong drink before entering the sanctuary. They had to wear holy linen garments, to wash their hands and feet before approaching the courtyard altar, and to bathe and launder before entering the sanctuary proper.

Priests cared for God, guarding the sanctuary's integrity, keeping God's house in order, and mediating between God and people at the portal between the common and the sacred. Priests supervised entrances, officiated at purifications, received offerings, presided at sacrifices, pronounced blessings, led festival celebrations, functioned as oracles, taught laws, and assisted in private prayers and rituals.

Sanctuaries were divided into three zones of graduating purity, for sanctuaries were places both of access to God's immanence and of separation from God's holiness.

The first zone was the open-air courtyard where the altar of sacrifice stood. Purified laypersons could enter the courtyard with sacrifices and prayers but were not allowed to come within reach of the altar itself. There various types of sacrifice were offered on behalf of laypersons, priests, and community. The whole-offering was an unblemished animal immolated and sent upward to God as a gift of smoke and sweet savor (Lev. 1.3–17, 6.8–11). The grain-offering was a gift of choice unleavened flour mixed with olive oil and frankincense, seasoned with salt, and cooked (Lev. 2.1–16, 6.14–23, Num. 15.1–16). The purification-offering was an animal whose blood was used in rituals addressing the consequences of inadvertent sins, of certain deliberate sins confessed voluntarily, and of certain impurities associated with the power of death (Lev. 4.1–5.13, 6.24–30, Num. 15.22–31, 19.1–13). The reparation-offering was a sacrifice of expiation, most often for having caused material loss (Lev. 5.14–6.7, 7.1–6, Num. 5.5–8). The shared-offering was an animal apportioned between God, the family of the offerer, and the families of the priests (Lev. 3.1–17; 7.11–34). This sacrifice concluded with a festive meal that nurtured and strengthened the close relationship between God and people.

Sacrifices culminating in the consumption of flesh dramatized the mysterious cycle of life and death observable in the vegetable world: life rising from death; life nourished and perpetuated by death. Also, the falling axe, flowing blood, and festive eating would have produced that mixture of terror and ecstasy humans associate with experiences of the holy.

One theory of the origin of sacrifice holds that killing and consuming domesticated animals evoked human guilt and that ritual sacrifice was instituted to sanctify slaughter and meat-eating. It is noteworthy that the priests of Israel believed humans to have been created vegetarian and to have become carnivorous only later. When God granted human beings the right to eat meat, it was on condition that the animal's blood—its life-force—not be consumed (Gen. 9.2–4). Furthermore, Lev. 17.3–4 apparently forbade "secular" slaughter. Perhaps it was in order to limit human culpability before God and to prevent transgression of the blood taboo that the slaughter of animals was entrusted to specialists in the holy—the priests.

Beyond the sanctuary's courtyard and altar lay a second zone of greater purity—a covered room into which only priests could enter. Morning and evening the chief priest donned a special ephod (garment) and breastpiece with precious stones bearing the names of Israel's tribes, a mantle with a hem alternating golden bells and woolen pomegranates, and a turban with a gold medallion engraved, "Holy to the Lord." He entered the sanctuary, the bells alerting God to human presence, the stones presenting Israel for divine remembrance, the medallion reminding God of gifts offered on the altar. In the evening, the chief priest lit the lamps. In the morning, he cleaned and dressed them. Morning and evening he offered mixed spices, frankincense, and salt on the golden incense altar. Every day he placed a strong drink offering on the sanctuary table, and each sabbath he placed there twelve loaves of fresh bread. The bread of the previous sabbath was removed and consumed by priests in sacred precincts.

The third zone of the sanctuary, that of the greatest purity, was God's own chamber, the holy of holies. In Solomon's temple this held the Ark of the Covenant, which contained the tablets of the law and had a pure gold Cover. The Cover was God's throne; the Ark, God's footstool. Above them loomed two cherubim whose wings extended from wall to wall. The only person allowed to enter this chamber was the chief priest. He did so, in a condition of absolute purity, only once a year on the Day of Atonement.

LAYMEN, THEIR DEPENDENTS, AND WORSHIP. Laymen maintained the sanctuaries and their personnel through an annual tithe of grain and fruit and perhaps also of any increase in their livestock. The king probably supervised the collection of the tithe.

Beyond that, laymen had duties of pilgrimage and sacrifice. During most of the monarchic period, such duties could be performed at a local, regional, or national sanctuary. When worship was centralized, in the reign of Josiah and the post-exilic period, all pilgrims went to the Jerusalem temple.

Pilgrimage was prescribed for laymen three times a year. The full moon of the month Abib (April) inaugurated the feast of Unleavened Bread, which celebrated the start of the barley harvest. From early in Israel's history, Unleavened Bread was linked to the home-festival of Passover, which commemorated the deliverance of those enslaved in Egypt. According to one reconstruction, the layman slaughtered the Passover lamb outside his home in the late afternoon and presided over a family meal of lamb and unleavened bread that night. There followed seven days of eating unleavened bread and visiting the local sanctuary to present one's first sheaf of barley and to participate in public sacrifices and rituals. Harvesting continued through the intermediate days of the festival, the principal celebrations occurring at the beginning and end. When worship and sacrifice were centralized, most laymen and their dependents had to journey farther and interrupt harvesting, and the Passover lamb had to be slaughtered at the temple. Doubtless, fewer people participated.

The second pilgrimage-festival was called Harvest or Weeks and featured the offering of the first fruits of wheat, which matured four to six weeks later than barley. This one-day feast fell in one of the busiest parts of the agricultural cycle and was observed at the nearest sanctuary. One cultic calendar (Lev. 23.15–21) set the date fifty days after the elevation of the first barley sheaf and did *not* call the celebration a pilgrimage-feast. Perhaps it sought to permit local observance after cultic centralization. Post-exilic practice, however, accorded with Deut. 16.9–12, which required pilgrimage to Jerusalem for a day of sacrifice and feasting. At some point, Weeks also came to commemorate God's giving of the law on Mt. Sinai.

At the heart of Unleavened Bread and Harvest (or Weeks) was people's belief that crops could not be used for common purposes until their sacred (i.e., first) portion had been given to God, the rightful owner. First offerings also assured divine blessing on the remainder of the harvest.

Into and through the rainless summer months the drying, threshing, winnowing, measuring, and storing of grain took place. August and September saw the ingathering of fruit—grapes, figs, pomegranates, and olives. In October, agricultural work ended (except for gathering olives), and people awaited the coming of the fall and winter rains that would renew the cycle. There was time and reason to celebrate. With the full moon of Tishri came the biggest and best of the pilgrimage-feasts—Ingathering, or Booths. King Solomon dedicated his temple during this festival, and long before official centralization many made Jerusalem their Ingathering destination.

Laymen and their dependents assembled locally for the pilgrimage from the common to the sacred. During the journey, relationships were enhanced, and differences in wealth and social status were transcended.

Arriving in Jerusalem, pilgrims filled the night with singing (Isa. 30.29). Psalms 120–134 may be a collection of typical pilgrimage songs and prayers. With the dawn, people streamed toward the temple, lifting their voices in praise (Ps. 42.4), songs of Zion on their lips (Pss. 46, 48, 76, 84, 87, 121, 122). At the foot of the temple mount, priests and people re-called the ritual and ethical purity required for entering God's dwelling (Pss. 15, 24). Thus prepared, they ascended to the place where earth and heaven met; they entered Paradise (Ps. 36.8–9). They wandered Zion, and they experienced transforming closeness with God (Ps. 48.9–14). Then followed more feasting and music and dancing.

Sometime during the monarchy, the fall festival came to commemorate the sojourn of Moses and the people in the Sinai wilderness—thus the name Booths (temporary shelters). And for reasons that are obscure an eighth day of feasting was appended. Many scholars also associate with the festival in Jerusalem one or two celebrations posited on the basis of psalms believed to have been texts for the observances. The first is re-newal of the Sinai covenant (Pss. 81, 50); the second, celebration of God's victory over the cosmic waters (releasing the fertile power of the rains) and enthronement as King (Pss. 29, 65, 93, 96–99).

At some point, the priests of Jerusalem began observing two days of ritual preparation for the great festival of Booths. At the new moon of Tishri, the blasting of a horn signalled a day of complete rest for the people and of special sacrifices in the temple. On the tenth day of Tishri, the temple and its personnel were purified, and the sins of priests and laity were expiated. It was the Day of Atonement. Laypersons remained at home—fasting, praying, and abstaining from work. In Jerusalem, the chief priest purged the sanctuary of the pollution transferred to it as a result of the priests' and people's sins and impurities during the previous year. One crucial rite involved two he-goats. One, chosen by lot, was slaughtered. Its blood was taken into the holy of holies, and some was sprinkled on the Cover of the Ark to purge the pollution arising from the people's sins. The rest of the blood was taken to the courtyard and used to purify the altar. Afterward, the chief priest laid his hands on the head of the second animal, and he confessed Israel's sins, transferring them to the "scapegoat," which was then driven into the wilderness, never to re-turn. Thus was Israel spared the punishment it merited—exile. And by the end of the day, temple, priests, and laity were pure and holy, fit for God's presence.

Laymen and their dependents, in addition to celebrating the three pilgrimage-feasts, observed sabbaths and new moons. The sabbath was an institution unique to Israel, a rest from labor recurring every seventh day. Deuteronomic circles linked the day to remembrance of the Exodus and the Sinai covenant. The priests of Jerusalem linked the day to the creation of the world (Gen. 2.3). In the towns and settlements, the sab-bath was a day of family joy. Some people also visited a sanctuary, if it was nearby, for personal sacrifices or for consulting a prophet. In the post-exilic period, sabbath observance became an ever more important bulwark of Jewish identity against alien imperial cultures. New moons were observed similarly to sabbaths in people's homes. However, the public sacrifices prescribed for new moons were more costly and elaborate than those for sabbaths and included a purification-offering.

Laypeople—both men and women—prayed frequently, in a variety of circumstances. One may speak of three forms of lay prayer: cultic compositions recited by laypeople, or by priests or other ritual experts on their behalf; patterned, yet personal, expressions of thanks, petition, and confession responding to the events of daily life; and spontaneous exclamations responding to sudden or intense experiences of joy, sorrow, and pain. Perhaps prayers offered by laypeople outside the sanctuary helped prepare the way for a new religious institution, the synagogue.

The synagogue's origins are obscure and may never be understood. Many scholars think the institution developed during the sixth century B.C.E., when the Jerusalem temple lay in ruins and sacrifice was impossible. But the Hebrew Bible never mentions the synagogue, and no evidence for its existence antedates the Hellenistic period, when the institution co-existed with the second temple.

The synagogue was a local place for studying Torah and praying to God. It was unconsecrated space and needed no clergy. According to the Talmud, hundreds of synagogues existed in Jerusalem prior to the destruction of the temple in 70 C.E. Obviously the synagogue did not just serve those unable to travel to the temple. Priests were in charge of the temple. Laypeople were in charge of the synagogue. Perhaps much of the synagogue's popularity is explained as simply as that.

WOMEN AND WORSHIP. In Israel, as in pre-industrial agricultural societies generally, women's work was bearing, nursing, and nurturing children and caring for the household. Women could attend the public cultus, pray in the sanctuary, make vows in the name of God, consult oracles, and eat the food of shared-offerings. But their participation was *allowed*, not *required*. They could not be priests, and they apparently could not bring sacrifice. Women of priestly families and perhaps some women without families did perform domestic tasks connected with the sanctuary: cleaning vessels and living quarters, preparing meals, weaving textiles. They also took part in ritual music and dancing. Some texts associate Israelite women with foreign cultuses. By this the texts may mean that during the first temple period women played roles in the local sanctuaries and shrines of which those seeking to centralize worship disapproved. Because menstruation, pregnancy, nursing, and nurturing restricted Israelite women spatially, temporally, and functionally, the centralization of worship at a single, usually more distant, sanctuary further limited their participation.

The locus of women's worship was probably the home and the local shrine, and their rituals were probably connected to the life-cycle of birth, puberty, marriage, childbearing, and death. Perhaps the female figurines found in excavations of domestic areas relate to such rituals. Either Israelite men did not know women's rituals, or they did not care much about them. Perhaps both. In any event, the men who wrote the biblical texts said very little on the subject, leaving us largely ignorant.

New Testament Communities

The patterns of Israelite worship described above reflect a stage more than 500 years removed from Moses and Joshua. The books of the Hebrew Bible come not from nascent Israel but from monarchic and post-exilic Israel. In contrast, the New Testament comes from nascent Christianity. Most books were written during the second half of the first century c.e., and all were written by the mid-second century.

Early Christianity experienced dramatic cultural transformations as its locus and demography changed from Palestine and Jewish to Empire and Gentile. First-century Christian *communities* (for in truth there was no single community) were characterized by a variety of shifting, rather amorphous structures and patterns of worship, and such terms as "priest" and "sacrament" were not part of their vocabulary. Furthermore, no New Testament book describes worship directly. In short, our knowledge of Christian worship prior to the mid-second century is fragmentary.

Jesus and all his disciples were Jewish. The synoptic Gospels regularly portray Jesus at prayer and in the synagogue, and they narrate his final meal with the Twelve as a Passover celebration. John regularly describes Jesus at the temple during pilgrimage-feasts. However, the gospels also depict aspects of Jesus' worship life that are unique or unusual. He uses the intimate familial term "Abba" to address God in prayer; he interprets scriptural texts and festivals in terms of himself; he disagrees with the Pharisees on issues of sabbath-observance and purity, eliminating some conventionally accepted lines between sacred and common; and although his angry expulsion of the money changers shows zeal for temple reform, he does not bring sacrifices.

In the immediate aftermath of Jesus' death and resurrection, his followers were more a Messianic Jewish sect than a new religion. The Acts of the Apostles portrays them attending the temple for daily prayer, and Eusebius (ca. 260–340 c.e.) quotes a tradition that James, the brother of Jesus, prayed in the temple so frequently that his knees hardened like a camel's! As the sect opened to include Hellenistic Jews, then Samaritans, and finally Gentiles, tensions developed over the extent to which traditional Jewish practices were obligatory for non-Jewish followers of the Messiah/Christ. Apparently, a number of Jewish Christians continued to feel strongly connected to dietary laws, circumcision, the temple and its purity regulations, the calendar of sabbaths and festivals, and synagogues. Other Christians, both Jewish and non-Jewish, argued that Jewish piety was optional for Christians because Jesus, not Torah and temple, was the center of life. Belonging to Christ was sealed by baptism not circumcision, and Christian worship was principally conducted at the table not the temple.

In 70 C.E., the Romans destroyed the Jerusalem temple, and the residual attachment to it among Jewish Christians was broken. The Epistle to the Hebrews describes Jesus as the final high priest, who offers himself in the heavenly temple as the perfect sacrifice for sin. The Gospel of John understands the divine presence to be bound not to the temple but to the person of Christ, mediated through baptism and the Lord's Supper. Nonetheless, complex dynamics of continuity as well as contrast continued to shape worship as Christianity separated itself definitively from Judaism.

Baptism was in some ways continuous with Jewish rituals of purification. Like Jewish washings, it cleansed and set one apart from the common and impure for the holy, and it delivered one from evil powers. Like the Jewish immersion of proselytes (probably a pre-Christian custom), it marked one's incorporation into religious community. In other ways, however, baptism was discontinuous with Judaism. Almost all Jewish water rituals were self-administered, but baptism was not. And if the "households" baptized into Christianity included children, this too was a departure from Judaism. Furthermore, baptism came to symbolize such distinctly Christian meanings as dying and rising with Christ, being born anew, putting on Christ, and being enlightened. Finally, baptism was linked to God's bestowing of the Spirit on new Christians. Because of God's indwelling presence, Paul could refer to the community of Christian persons as "God's temple" (1 Cor. 3.16), a clear departure from Jewish tradition.

Paul's letters and the Acts of the Apostles suggest that early Christians gathered in a local home for prayer and worship, often in the context of a joyful meal. For example, the earliest communities celebrated a Passover meal, associating that season with the death and resurrection of Jesus. The Passover themes of freedom from Egyptian bondage and deliverance from the overseer's lash were interpreted by Christians as freedom from sin and deliverance from punishment for sin. Not until the second century was this Christian celebration dissociated from the Jewish date for Passover and developed into a special "Easter Sunday." It seems that first-century communities observed every first-day of the Jewish week by remembering the Lord's resurrection. Jewish-Christian house groups probably extended sabbath gatherings—devoted to praying, praising, and eating—through Saturday night, culminating in a Sunday-dawn meal. Later, non-Jewish house groups omitted the sabbath observance but, consonant with the Jewish seven-day week, retained a regularly recurring first-day observance, whether at dawn or in the evening or both. By the end of the first century, Christians began to call the first day "the Lord's Day."

Unfortunately, New Testament authors presume readers' knowledge of Christian house groups, and none offers a detailed description of their worship or leadership. Paul offers a set of disparate data about the meal and the worship that accompanied it (1 Cor. 11). Noteworthy components are: prayer, prophecy, and conversation; celebration of "the Lord's Supper" in unconsecrated space, with thanksgiving to God, the breaking and sharing of bread, and the blessing and drinking of a cup; recitation of a tradition about Jesus' institution of the meal; anticipation of Christ's return to earth; and participation by both women and men. Paul states that the meal (bread and cup as "body" and "blood") binds the community into one body through communion with Christ, the crucified and risen Lord. He also speaks approvingly of Jewish sacrificial meals, while forbidding Christians' participation in pagan sacrificial meals (1 Cor. 10.16–22). Perhaps Paul found the Jewish model of joyful communion with the invisible but vividly present God helpful in interpreting the Christian meal, even though blood—actual or symbolic—played no part in Jewish meals. The Johannine community understood the bread and wine to be the very flesh and blood of Christ, the sacred food and drink effecting unity with Christ and imparting eternal life (John 6.53–58).

Some communal meals may not have had eucharistic meaning. Some corporate worship may not have been connected to a meal. Paul does sum up components of community worship without connecting them to a meal (1 Cor. 14). Those he mentions include: singing, instruction (e.g., reading scripture and commenting on its meaning, or reading an apostolic letter), prayer, praise and thanksgiving, prophecy, and speaking in tongues if accompanied by interpretation. Paul seems to presuppose random expressions of the Spirit (albeit "decently and in order") rather than a fixed liturgical sequence.

By no later than the mid-second century, liturgical forms had developed. Baptismal liturgies seem to have included preparatory fasting, answering questions, renouncing evil, disrobing, professing faith, being immersed in the name of God the Father, Jesus Christ, and the Holy Spirit, donning a fresh garment, receiving chrismation, and breaking the fast (the Eucharist). First Timothy 4.13 mentions scripture reading, exhortation (preaching), and teaching as components of public worship. The lasting influence of synagogue patterns is visible here. A second-century book of church order, the *Didache* or "Teachings," urges Christians to gather every Lord's Day to break bread and give thanks. It requires confession of sin and reconciliation between persons before the Eucharist and prescribes words for prayers over the cup and the broken bread and at the end of the meal. As for private piety, the *Didache* urges Christians to pray the Lord's Prayer three times daily and prescribes fasting on Wednesdays and Fridays.

In the middle of the second century, Justin Martyr becomes the first to speak of a bread and cup ritual outside the context of an entire meal.

Performed at the Sunday gathering by the "president" (i.e., bishop), the ritual is preceded by reading from memoirs of the apostles or writings of the prophets, the president's exposition of the text, and group prayers; it is followed by an offering for the poor.

At the same time, in a different cultural world, a small Jewish-Christian community, the Ebionites, still observes the sabbath, practices circumcision, eats unleavened bread and water at the ritual meal, and faces Jerusalem when praying. Theirs, however, is not the way of the future.

The community of ancient Israel related to God in large part through media of worship associated with the *place* of God's immanence—the sanctuary. The Jewish canon of the Hebrew Bible ends, appropriately, with King Cyrus of Persia authorizing the building of the second temple (2 Chr. 36.23). New Testament communities related to God in large part through media of worship associated with the *person* of God's immanence—Jesus, the Christ. The Christian canon of the Old Testament concludes, appropriately, with the promise of the age of the Messiah (Mal. 4.5–6). And the New Testament closes with two elements of worship (Rev. 22.20b–21): an eschatological prayer used by some Christians at the end of the eucharistic meal, "Come, Lord Jesus!"; and a benediction, "The grace of the Lord Jesus be with all."

The Biblical Text with Annotations

THE OLD TESTAMENT

Introduction

The Old Testament consists of a collection of works composed at various times from the twelfth to the second century B.C.E. The books are written in classical Hebrew, except some brief portions (Ezra 4.8–6.18 and 7.12–26; Jeremiah 10.11; and Daniel 2.4–7.28) which are in Aramaic, a closely related and widely used language.

Very few manuscripts survived the destruction of Jerusalem in 70 C.E., and soon after that disaster the Jewish religious leaders set about defining the 'canon' (the scriptures accepted as authoritative) and finally standardizing the text. This was the Massoretic or 'traditional' text.

The original texts were written in a script which represents only a small proportion of the vowel sounds. In order to preserve the correct pronunciation in school and synagogue, and so to fix the meaning of words which could be read in more than one way, the Massoretic editors used vowel signs to modify the consonantal symbols. They were following a continuous tradition of reading the scriptures aloud; over the years errors had crept in, and so on occasion the present revisers, like the translators of The New English Bible, substituted other vowel signs where it seemed necessary.

In one case the Massoretes did not give the true vocalization. The divine name (*YHWH* in Hebrew characters) was probably pronounced 'Yahweh', but the name was regarded as ineffable, too sacred to be pronounced. The Massoretes, therefore, wrote in the vowel signs of the alternative words *adonai* ('Lord') or *elohim* ('God') to warn readers to use one of these in its place. Where the divine name occurs in the Hebrew text, this has been signalled in The Revised English Bible by using capital letters for 'LORD' or 'GOD', a widely accepted practice.

It is probable that the Massoretic Text remained substantially unaltered from the second century C.E. to the present time, and this text is reproduced in all Hebrew Bibles. The New English Bible translators used the third edition of R. Kittel's *Biblia Hebraica* (Stuttgart, 1937). A new and thoroughly revised edition, *Biblia Hebraica Stuttgartensia*, appeared in 1967/77, and is the most widely used modern edition. Both these take their text from a manuscript of the early eleventh century C.E. now preserved in Leningrad.

Despite the care used in the copying of the Massoretic Text, it contains errors, in the correction of which there are witnesses to be heard. None of them is throughout superior to the Massoretic Text, but in particular places their evidence may preserve the correct reading.

There are, firstly, Hebrew texts which are outside the Massoretic tradition: the Samaritan text and the Dead Sea Scrolls. The Samaritan text consists only of the Pentateuch (Genesis–Deuteronomy). It must date from a period before the secession of the Samaritans from Judaism (probably no later than the second century B.C.E.), but is preserved only in manuscripts the earliest of which is tentatively assigned to the eleventh century C.E. This is in effect the Hebrew text in Samaritan characters. Translators of the Old Testament may now make use of what are commonly known as the Dead Sea Scrolls, the discovery of which, in 1947 and after, revealed Hebrew manuscripts perhaps a thousand years older than those previously known.

The translators and revisers had in addition to the early Hebrew texts the evidence provided by the ancient versions in other languages. The earliest of these, the Greek translation made in Egypt in the third and second centuries B.C.E. and commonly called the Septuagint, is the major tool for recovering the original Hebrew text. In the early Christian era Lucian produced an edition of the Septuagint. Other Greek versions of the period were those of Aquila, Symmachus, and Theodotion.

When the need for a Latin Bible arose, the Old Latin version was produced by translating the Septuagint. The Vulgate, Jerome's translation into Latin of the Hebrew text, followed towards the end of the fourth century C.E.

As Hebrew had ceased to be commonly understood in Palestine, renderings into Aramaic known as Targums had been produced for synagogue use from the fourth century B.C.E. onwards. The early Christian church in Mesopotamia had its version in Syriac (a form of Aramaic); it is known as the Peshitta, a 'simple' or literal translation.

All these versions contribute in varying degrees to the recovery and understanding of the Hebrew.

Other contributions to the understanding of the Hebrew text have been made by archaeological discoveries and by the study of the cognate Semitic languages. This last method, used by medieval Jewish scholars and also by Christian scholars in the seventeenth and following centuries, has received fresh impetus from the decipherment of texts notably from Ras Shamra in Syria. It is a method which has led to valuable results, but its application demands both skill and particular caution; the revisers have been aware of the dangers of an over-zealous use of it.

The text is not infrequently uncertain and its meaning obscure, and after all the study of the texts and versions, the languages and culture of the ancient Near East, there remain a number of passages where the translator must either leave a blank in his version or, as the New English Bible translators and the present revisers have chosen to do, resort to conjectural emendation of the Hebrew text. This has been done as sparingly as possible, and attention is drawn to such cases in footnotes by the indicator *prob. rdg.*

Where exact identification of specialized terms such as 'Sheol' (the Hebrew word for the underworld) is required, these have been given as transliterations of the Hebrew, but where exact identification is less vital they have been rendered by some word or phrase approaching the original sense. The rendering of the terms for each kind of sacrifice has been revised and standardized in the statements of the Jewish legal codes, whereas they have been translated more freely in parts of the Old Testament where no technical problems are involved and strict consistency is not of overriding importance.

Where no exact equivalent exists for the original Hebrew, a somewhat expanded translation has been provided; on the other hand some abbreviation has been made when the Hebrew text seemed unduly repetitive by the normal standards of writing in English. Changes such as substituting nouns for pronouns have been made when clarity demanded it.

As elsewhere in The Revised English Bible, the guiding principle adopted has been to seek a fluent and idiomatic way of expressing biblical writing in contemporary English. Much emphasis has been laid on correctness and intelligibility, and at the same time on endeavouring to convey something of the directness and simplicity of the Hebrew original. All those who have been concerned with the production of this translation have done their work in the conviction that the Old Testament has contributed vitally to every tradition of Christian worship and culture, and that an accurate understanding of the Bible of the Jews is essential to the full appreciation of Christian doctrine and the events recorded in the New Testament.

The Pentateuch

The Pentateuch (literally, the "five scrolls"; popularly, the Five Books of Moses) is the final edition of traditions about Israel's early history which the community considered important for its self-identity. Beginning with creation and stories of primeval times, the story narrows in focus to Abraham and the stories of Israel's own ancestors (Genesis). The narrative continues with the story of Israel's deliverance from Egyptian slavery and acceptance of God's covenant offered at Sinai (Exodus and Leviticus). The subsequent period of wandering in the wilderness, punctuated by various acts of unfaithfulness, and military victory east of the Jordan (Numbers) comes to an end with the people poised across the river from Jericho to hear the farewell speeches of Moses (Deuteronomy).

Since it was Moses who relayed God's word to Israel at Sinai, much later generations (probably in the post-exilic era more than eight hundred years after the time of Moses) began to speak of "the law of Moses" in a sense that included not only the material revealed at Sinai but also the totality of the Pentateuch. This view that Moses authored the entire Pentateuch appears to have been well established by the time of Jesus. Christian and Jewish scholars raised questions about this tradition, however, beginning in the early centuries of the Common Era. They wondered, for instance, how Moses could have written about the details of his own death (Deut. 34) or why there were different commands to Noah about how many animals to take into the ark (two of every kind [Gen. 6.19] or one pair of some kinds and seven pairs of others [7.2–3]).

Today there is a wide consensus among biblical scholars that the Pentateuch is a composite work. This consensus has arisen out of observations of many differences in literary style, vocabulary, and theological themes that characterize various blocks of material in the Pentateuch. Scholars have also noticed that sometimes more than one version of a story seems to be included in the text (for example, two versions of the creation in Gen. 1 and 2; or three versions of a husband pretending to a king that his wife is really his sister, Gen. 12, 20, 26).

Various hypotheses have been proposed to account for these features of the text. The following paragraphs outline one widely accepted hypothesis, namely that three major sources, composed during different periods of Israel's history, are interwoven in the first four books (usually referred to as the "Tetrateuch," four scrolls). The Pentateuch was then formed by the addition of Deuteronomy, which represents another major tradition.

The J and E Sources

The stories of the ancestors and of the exodus and the wilderness experiences, long told orally, were perhaps first written down during the
time of Kings David and Solomon (tenth century B.C.E.), probably by
someone in Jerusalem who had connections with the royal court. Scholars
have designated this someone as the Yahwist or "J" (because the writer
used the name *Yahweh* [traditionally spelled *Jehovah*] for God in the book
of Genesis). This J source told the ancestral story in such a way as to
suggest that the newly established kingdom was the fulfillment of the
promises to Abraham and his descendants. After the reign of Solomon,
the northern tribes broke away. An alternative version of the old story,
usually called the Elohist or "E" source (because it uses *Elohim* for the
deity in Genesis), was handed down in the schismatic Northern Kingdom.
This version was eventually used to supplement J's narrative. Scholars
refer to this combined version as "JE."

The P Source

The Tetrateuch contains a great deal of material that does not belong
either to J or to E in terms of its literary style, subject matter, or theological interest. This material is usually designated "P" because of its high
degree of interest in matters relating to priesthood, worship, liturgy, sacrifice, ordination, etc. This third major source includes a very large
amount of legislation on these subjects, but also a considerable amount of
narrative.

P was composed sometime not long after the destruction of Jerusalem
and the first temple in 587 B.C.E. Drawing upon ancient traditions, the
priestly writer(s) sought to provide a theological response to the tragedy
of the end of the Kingdom and exile of the people to Babylon. P's emphasis on the tabernacle, a movable tent-sanctuary used in the wilderness
(Exod. 25–31, 35–40), reminded the people that God had once been
present with them in worship outside the land and without the Jerusalem
temple. By highlighting circumcision and sabbath, both of which could be
observed without regard for geographic location, P pointed the way toward the emergence of Jewish identity apart from a nation-state. Thus
P's work was foundational for the development of diaspora Judaism.

The Tetrateuch: JEP

Some scholars believe that JE was incorporated into P when P was first
composed; others argue that P first existed separately and was combined
with JE by a slightly later editor. In either case it is agreed that P material
furnishes the organizing structure of the Tetrateuch as we know it. The
narrative from creation through the Sinai revelation is organized by genealogies and by periods of history with their special signs and covenants:
the covenants with Noah, with Abraham, and with the people at Sinai,

and their respective covenantal signs of rainbow, circumcision, and sabbath. The wilderness story is organized around the theme of the first two generations of Israelites, of which the first illustrates disobedience and the second illustrates obedience to God's covenant.

Deuteronomy and the Pentateuch

The book of Deuteronomy exhorts the people to obedience to the Sinai covenant and contains much ancient legislation. A story in 2 Kings 22 reports that in the reign of King Josiah (621 B.C.E.) a forgotten lawbook was discovered during repairs to the Jerusalem temple. Scholars believe that the book which was found forms the core of Deuteronomy: chapters 5–26. Deuteronomy consists of this core plus a new preface which reviews the history of Moses' era, as well as supplemental material which emphasizes faithfulness to the commandments as the basis of a satisfying life for God's people. Under Josiah, the discovered book became the basis of a religious reform; it also provided a theological perspective for the writing of a history of the people from the time of Joshua up to Josiah's own time (Joshua–2 Kings).

Sometime in the postexilic era, when Jews developed an increasing interest in the role of Moses, the book of Deuteronomy was joined to the first four books to form what we now know as the Pentateuch, the "five books of Moses."

Although this hypothesis is complex, it can be helpful to the reader in various ways. It provides a way of accounting for inconsistencies and repetitions in the text, and it also draws attention to the diversity of theological viewpoints in the pentateuchal material. Here one may see how tradition was received and reappropriated in various new historical circumstances. As the story was retold in each context, the ancient Israelites were enabled to say of the story, "It is *our* story, not just the story of our ancestors." Awareness of this complexity or "depth dimension" of the Pentateuch makes the beauty of its final form all the more remarkable.

Genesis

Genesis, meaning "beginning," contains two major parts: the primeval history (chs. 1–11), which tells how human self-assertion brought the world to the brink of destruction; and the history of Israel's ancestors (chs. 12–50), which relates how the LORD, in an awesome and inexplicable act of grace, chose the clan of Abraham as the instrument for the rehabilitation of humankind. Yet for a variety of reasons, whether perceptible or hidden, the divine promise was not immediately realized. Even the existence of the next generation (i.e. Israel itself) was often uncertain. And as Genesis concludes, the clan has been delivered from famine through divine providence, only to become enslaved in Egypt.

When succeeding generations heard this part of their story freshly interpreted in light of new experiences, they understood that the crises of the present were not unique and were enabled to hope that the ancient promise would yet be realized.

The material concerning Abraham and Sarah and their descendants differs from the account of primeval time in that it can be placed within the context of the ancient Near Eastern culture of the second millennium B.C.E.

The creation of the universe

1 In the beginning God created the heavens and the earth. ² The earth was a vast waste, darkness covered the deep, and the spirit of God hovered over the surface of the water. ³ God said, 'Let there be light,' and there was light; ⁴ and God saw the light was good, and he separated light from darkness. ⁵ He called the light day, and the darkness night. So evening came, and morning came; it was the first day.

⁶ God said, 'Let there be a vault between the waters, to separate water from water.' ⁷ So God made the vault, and separated the water under the vault from the water above it, and so it was; ⁸ and God called the vault the heavens. Evening came, and morning came, the second day.

⁹ God said, 'Let the water under the heavens be gathered into one place, so that dry land may appear'; and so it was. ¹⁰ God called the dry land earth, and the gathering of the water he called sea; and God saw that it was good. ¹¹ Then God said, 'Let the earth produce growing things; let there be on the earth plants that bear seed, and trees bearing fruit each with its own kind of seed.' So it was; ¹² the earth produced growing things: plants bearing their own kind of seed and trees bearing fruit, each with its own kind of seed; and God saw that it was good. ¹³ Evening came, and morning came, the third day.

¹⁴ God said, 'Let there be lights in the vault of the heavens to separate day from night, and let them serve as signs both for festivals and for seasons and years. ¹⁵ Let them also shine in the heavens to give light on earth.' So it was; ¹⁶ God made two great lights, the greater to govern the day and the lesser to govern the night; he also made the stars. ¹⁷ God put these lights in the vault of the heavens to give light on earth, ¹⁸ to govern day and night, and to separate light from

1:1–2 **In . . . earth was:** or When God began to create the heavens and the earth, ²the earth was.   1:2 **the spirit . . . hovered:** or a great wind swept; or a wind from God swept.

1.1–2.3: **The creation account,** composed by priests. Order evolves from chaos by divine command, followed by God's resting, in example, on the sabbath. **1:** That creation arose out of nothing — that is, not out of materials at hand — became the usual understanding of this verse; see 2 Macc. 7.28. **2:** *Spirit:* the Heb. word also means "wind" or "breath." In Mesopotamian myth, wind was an instrument for destroying the watery *deep.* Genesis 1, by contrast, does not depict a battle between God and chaos. **5:** *Evening . . . morning:* day began at sundown and hence the order given here. **6:** *Vault:* a solid dome (Job 37.18), retaining the upper waters whence the rains come (Gen. 7.11–12). **14:** *Lights:* Israel's neighbors regarded the celestial bodies as deities

11

darkness; and God saw that it was good. [19] Evening came, and morning came, the fourth day.

[20] God said, 'Let the water teem with living creatures, and let birds fly above the earth across the vault of the heavens.' [21] God then created the great sea-beasts and all living creatures that move and swarm in the water, according to their various kinds, and every kind of bird; and God saw that it was good. [22] He blessed them and said, 'Be fruitful and increase; fill the water of the sea, and let the birds increase on the land.' [23] Evening came, and morning came, the fifth day.

[24] God said, 'Let the earth bring forth living creatures, according to their various kinds: cattle, creeping things, and wild animals, all according to their various kinds.' So it was; [25] God made wild animals, cattle, and every creeping thing, all according to their various kinds; and he saw that it was good. [26] Then God said, 'Let us make human beings in our image, after our likeness, to have dominion over the fish in the sea, the birds of the air, the cattle, all wild animals on land, and everything that creeps on the earth.'

[27] God created human beings in his own
    image;
   in the image of God he created them;
   male and female he created them.

[28] God blessed them and said to them, 'Be fruitful and increase, fill the earth and subdue it, have dominion over the fish in the sea, the birds of the air, and every living thing that moves on the earth.' [29] God also said, 'Throughout the earth I give you all plants that bear seed, and every tree that bears fruit with seed: they shall be yours for food. [30] All green plants I give for food to the wild animals, to all the birds of the air, and to every-

thing that creeps on the earth, every living creature.' So it was; [31] and God saw all that he had made, and it was very good. Evening came, and morning came, the sixth day.

2 Thus the heavens and the earth and everything in them were completed. [2] On the sixth day God brought to an end all the work he had been doing; on the seventh day, having finished all his work, [3] God blessed the day and made it holy, because it was the day he finished all his work of creation.

Adam and Eve

[4] THIS is the story of the heavens and the earth after their creation.

When the LORD God made the earth and the heavens, [5] there was neither shrub nor plant growing on the earth, because the LORD God had sent no rain; nor was there anyone to till the ground. [6] Moisture used to well up out of the earth and water all the surface of the ground.

[7] The LORD God formed a human being from the dust of the ground and breathed into his nostrils the breath of life, so that he became a living creature. [8] The LORD God planted a garden in Eden away to the east, and in it he put the man he had formed. [9] The LORD God made trees grow up from the ground, every kind of tree pleasing to the eye and good for food; and in the middle of the garden he set the tree of life and the tree of the knowledge of good and evil.

[10] There was a river flowing from Eden to water the garden, and from there it branched into four streams. [11] The name of the first is Pishon; it is the river which skirts

2:2 **sixth:** *so some Vss.; Heb.* seventh.   2:7 **human being:** *Heb.* adam. **ground:** *Heb.* adamah.

(see Deut. 4.19). Here, they are results of God's creation. **26:** The plural *us* (3.22; 11.7) may be a majestic plural, or else refer to the minor divine beings thought to surround God, like courtiers of a human king (1 Kgs. 22.19–22; Job 1.6). *Image:* in non-Israelite texts often refers to statues and other concrete representations of kings and deities. Its meaning here is not precisely stated. **28:** To *subdue* the earth is to be free from nature's tyranny and from idolizing mere objects.

   2.4–3.24: A second account of primeval time. This account is generally regarded as more ancient than 1.1–2.3. The first human beings do not accept the limits placed on their existence and thus disrupt God's intended harmony. **4:** *LORD God:* a compound designation largely confined to this section. **7:** A pun is present, linking *human being* ("earthling") and *ground* ("earth"); see Tfn. *Living creature:* not a duality of "body" and "soul" (a Greek idea), but rather a unity animated by God's creative act. The animals are also designated by the same term for "living" (1.20, 24). **8:** *Eden* is the fertile abode of God, as elaborated in Ezek. 28.13–19. Similar ideas appear in other ancient Near Eastern traditions. **9:** *Tree of life:* the notion that immortality could the whole land of Havilah, where gold is found. ¹²The gold of that land is good; gum resin and cornelians are also to be found there. ¹³The name of the second river is Gihon; this is the one which skirts the whole land of Cush. ¹⁴The name of the third is Tigris; this is the river which flows east of Asshur. The fourth river is the Euphrates.

¹⁵The LORD God took the man and put him in the garden of Eden to till it and look after it. ¹⁶'You may eat from any tree in the garden', he told the man, ¹⁷'except from the tree of the knowledge of good and evil; the day you eat from that, you are surely doomed to die.' ¹⁸Then the LORD God said, 'It is not good for the man to be alone; I shall make a partner suited to him.' ¹⁹So from the earth he formed all the wild animals and all the birds of the air, and brought them to the man to see what he would call them; whatever the man called each living creature, that would be its name. ²⁰The man gave names to all cattle, to the birds of the air, and to every wild animal; but for the man himself no suitable partner was found. ²¹The LORD God then put the man into a deep sleep and, while he slept, he took one of the man's ribs and closed up the flesh over the place. ²²The rib he had taken out of the man the LORD God built up into a woman, and he brought her to the man. ²³The man said:

'This one at last
is bone from my bones,
flesh from my flesh!
She shall be called woman,
for from man was she taken.'

²⁴That is why a man leaves his father and mother and attaches himself to his wife, and the two become one. ²⁵Both were naked, the man and his wife, but they had no feeling of shame.

3 THE serpent, which was the most cunning of all the creatures the LORD God had made, asked the woman, 'Is it true that God has forbidden you to eat from any tree in the garden?' ²She replied, 'We may eat the fruit of any tree in the garden, ³except for the tree in the middle of the garden. God has forbidden us to eat the fruit of that tree or even to touch it; if we do, we shall die.' ⁴'Of course you will not die,' said the serpent; ⁵'for God knows that, as soon as you eat it, your eyes will be opened and you will be like God himself, knowing both good and evil.' ⁶The woman looked at the tree: the fruit would be good to eat; it was pleasing to the eye and desirable for the knowledge it could give. So she took some and ate it; she also gave some to her husband, and he ate it. ⁷Then the eyes of both of them were opened, and they knew that they were naked; so they stitched fig-leaves together and made themselves loincloths.

⁸The man and his wife heard the sound of the LORD God walking about in the garden at the time of the evening breeze, and they hid from him among the trees. ⁹The LORD God called to the man, 'Where are you?' ¹⁰He replied, 'I heard the sound of you in the garden and I was afraid because I was naked, so I hid.' ¹¹God said, 'Who told you that you were naked? Have you eaten from the tree which I forbade you to eat from?' ¹²The man replied, 'It was the woman you gave to be with me who gave me fruit from the tree, and I ate it.' ¹³The LORD God said to the woman, 'What have you done?' The woman answered, 'It was the serpent who deceived me into eating it.' ¹⁴Then the LORD God said to the serpent:

'Because you have done this you are cursed

2:12 **gum resin:** or bdellium.   2:23 **woman:** Heb. ishshah. **man:** Heb. ish.   3:5 **God himself:** or gods. 3:6 **desirable . . . give:** or tempting to contemplate.

be attained by eating a magic plant is also found elsewhere in antiquity. **13:** Cush: elsewhere in the Old Testament usually refers to Ethiopia or Nubia, but here probably refers to the land of the Kassites, to the east, in Mesopotamia. **14:** The Tigris and Euphrates are the two major rivers that flow through Mesopotamia. The other two of the four "original" rivers are unidentifiable. **17:** The day: idiomatic for "when." Surely doomed to die: become mortal. **24:** A folk explanation is given for the origin of the sexual urge. **3.1:** Serpent: an ancient extrabiblical story tells how a serpent stole the plant which would have given immortality to human beings. It was believed that when the snake shed its skin, it was rejuvenated. Cunning: there is a pun in the Heb. words for cunning and naked (v. 7). Had made: a phrase deliberately used to show that the serpent was only one among God's many creatures. The idea of the serpent as a primeval adversary of God, indeed, the Devil, arose much later (see Wisd. 2.24); so too the fixing of blame on the woman arose at a much later time (Ecclus. 25.24). **7:** Naked: not intrinsically shameful, nakedness became so as the result of human sin and alienation from God.

alone of all cattle and the creatures of the wild.

'On your belly you will crawl,
and dust you will eat
all the days of your life.
15 I shall put enmity between you and the
woman,
between your brood and hers.
They will strike at your head,
and you will strike at their heel.'

16 To the woman he said:

'I shall give you great labour in
childbearing;
with labour you will bear children.
You will desire your husband,
but he will be your master.'

17 And to the man he said: 'Because you have listened to your wife and have eaten from the tree which I forbade you,

on your account the earth will be
cursed.
You will get your food from it only by
labour
all the days of your life;
18 it will yield thorns and thistles for you.
You will eat of the produce of the field,
19 and only by the sweat of your brow will
you win your bread
until you return to the earth;
for from it you were taken.
Dust you are, to dust you will return.'

20 The man named his wife Eve because she was the mother of all living beings. 21 The LORD God made coverings from skins for the man and his wife and clothed them. 22 But he said, 'The man has become like one of us, knowing good and evil; what if he now reaches out and takes fruit from the tree of life also, and eats it and lives for ever?' 23 So the LORD God banished him from the garden of Eden to till the ground from which he had been taken. 24 When he drove him out, God settled him to the east of the garden of Eden, and he stationed the cherubim and a sword whirling and flashing to guard the way to the tree of life.

4 The man lay with his wife Eve, and she conceived and gave birth to Cain. She said, 'With the help of the LORD I have brought into being a male child.' 2 Afterwards she had another child, Abel. He tended the flock, and Cain worked the land. 3 In due season Cain brought some of the fruits of the earth as an offering to the LORD, 4 while Abel brought the choicest of the first-born of his flock. The LORD regarded Abel and his offering with favour, 5 but not Cain and his offering. Cain was furious and he glowered. 6 The LORD said to Cain,

'Why are you angry? Why are you
scowling?
7 If you do well, you hold your head up;
if not, sin is a demon crouching at the
door;
it will desire you, and you will be
mastered by it.'

8 Cain said to his brother Abel, 'Let us go out into the country.' Once there, Cain attacked and murdered his brother. 9 The LORD asked Cain, 'Where is your brother Abel?' 'I do not know,' Cain answered. 'Am I my brother's keeper?' 10 The LORD said, 'What have you done? Your brother's blood is crying out to me from the ground. 11 Now you are ac-cursed and will be banished from the very ground which has opened its mouth to re-ceive the blood you have shed. 12 When you

3:20 **Eve:** *that is* Life.   4:7 **and you . . . it:** *or* but you must master it.   4:8 **Let us . . . country:** *so* Samar.; Heb. omits.

14–19: A series of originally independent folk explanations is woven together: Why do human beings feel hostile toward serpents? Why is childbirth painful? Why is women's social position subordinate? Why must men work? These explanations serve in context to show that the world as now encountered is of human making rather than remaining the divine ideal. **20:** The name *Eve* is thought to be related to a Heb. verb "to live"; see Tfn. **21:** The Heb. word *adam* occurs here as a personal name for the first time in the narrative, although the REB continues to translate it until 4.25. Up to this point its meaning has been "human being," as in 1.27; 2.7 and Tfn. there. **22:** *Us:* see 1.26 n. **24:** *Cherubim:* semidivine creatures, usually depicted as winged lions with human heads (Ezek. 41.19), often the guardians of sacred areas (1 Kgs. 8.6–7).

4.1–26: The first offspring. Cain and Abel may personify a culture conflict between the settled farmer and the seminomadic shepherd. **4–5:** The preference for Abel's offering reflects the view of the deity's full freedom till the ground, it will no longer yield you its produce. You shall be a wanderer, a fugitive on the earth.' 13 Cain said to the LORD, 'My punishment is heavier than I can bear; 14 now you are driving me off the land, and I must hide myself from your presence. I shall be a wanderer, a fugitive on the earth, and I can be killed at sight by anyone.' 15 The LORD answered him, 'No: if anyone kills Cain, sevenfold vengeance will be exacted from him.' The LORD put a mark on Cain, so that anyone happening to meet him should not kill him. 16 Cain went out from the LORD'S presence and settled in the land of Nod to the east of Eden.

17 Then Cain lay with his wife; and she conceived and gave birth to Enoch. Cain was then building a town which he named Enoch after his son. 18 Enoch was the father of Irad, Irad of Mehujael, Mehujael of Methushael, and Methushael of Lamech.

19 Lamech married two women, one named Adah, the other Zillah. 20 Adah gave birth to Jabal, the ancestor of tent-dwellers who raise flocks and herds. 21 His brother's name was Jubal; he was the ancestor of those who play the harp and pipe. 22 Zillah, the other wife, bore Tubal-cain, the master of all coppersmiths and blacksmiths, and Tubal-cain's sister was Naamah. 23 Lamech said to his wives:

'Adah and Zillah, listen to me;
wives of Lamech, mark what I say:
I kill a man for wounding me,
a young man for a blow.
24 If sevenfold vengeance was to be
exacted for Cain,
for Lamech it would be
seventy-sevenfold.'

25 Adam lay with his wife again. She gave birth to a son, and named him Seth, 'for', she said, 'God has granted me another son in place of Abel, because Cain killed him'. 26 Seth too had a son, whom he named Enosh. At that time people began to invoke the LORD by name.

From Adam to Noah

5 THIS is the list of Adam's descendants. On the day when God created human beings he made them in his own likeness. 2 He created them male and female, and on the day when he created them, he blessed them and called them man.

3 Adam was one hundred and thirty years old when he begot a son in his likeness and image, and named him Seth. 4 After the birth of Seth he lived eight hundred years, and had other sons and daughters. 5 He lived nine hundred and thirty years, and then he died.

6 Seth was one hundred and five years old when he begot Enosh. 7 After the birth of Enosh he lived eight hundred and seven years, and had other sons and daughters. 8 He lived nine hundred and twelve years, and then he died.

9 Enosh was ninety years old when he begot Kenan. 10 After the birth of Kenan he lived eight hundred and fifteen years, and had other sons and daughters. 11 He lived nine hundred and five years, and then he died.

12 Kenan was seventy years old when he begot Mahalalel. 13 After the birth of Mahalalel he lived eight hundred and forty years, and had other sons and daughters. 14 He lived nine hundred and ten years, and then he died.

4:16 **Nod:** *that is* Wandering.   4:25 **Seth:** *that is* Granted.   4:26 **LORD:** *this represents the Hebrew consonants YHWH; see Introduction, p. 3.*

(see Exod. 33.19). **10:** *Blood* was regarded as the seat of the life-force (see Deut. 12.23–24). **14:** *Anyone:* this passage presupposes an established society; possibly this account was once independent of 2.4–3.24 and only after the two accounts were joined were Cain and Abel regarded as the offspring of Adam and Eve (v. 1). **15:** *Mark:* devotees of deities wore distinctive emblems. Cain is designated here as a ward of the LORD. **17:** *Wife:* her mention is a surprise, for whence did she come? Perhaps we have here a fragment of a once independent tradition; see v. 14 n. **19–22:** The development of human culture is depicted. **23–24:** An ancient boast is used to illustrate the growing pride and callousness of humankind. **26:** *Enosh* is another word for "human being." This is possibly a fragment of a once separate, primitive genealogy. *At that time:* other biblical texts suggest the worship of the LORD by name began much later, within Israel (see Exod. 3.13–15; 6.3).

5.1–32: Adam's descendants. In form and content this section is a self-contained unit, related to 1.1–2.3, inserted here to bridge a narrative gap between earliest creation and the later deluge (6.5ff.). **4:** *Eight hundred:* ancient Near Eastern peoples attributed great longevity to their remote ancestors. The biblical writers steadily

15 Mahalalel was sixty-five years old when he begot Jared. 16 After the birth of Jared he lived eight hundred and thirty years, and had other sons and daughters. 17 He lived eight hundred and ninety-five years, and then he died.

18 Jared was one hundred and sixty-two years old when he begot Enoch. 19 After the birth of Enoch he lived eight hundred years, and had other sons and daughters. 20 He lived nine hundred and sixty-two years, and then he died.

21 Enoch was sixty-five years old when he begot Methuselah. 22 After the birth of Methuselah, Enoch walked with God for three hundred years, and had other sons and daughters. 23 He lived three hundred and sixty-five years. 24 Enoch walked with God, and then was seen no more, because God had taken him away.

25 Methuselah was one hundred and eighty-seven years old when he begot Lamech. 26 After the birth of Lamech he lived for seven hundred and eighty-two years, and had other sons and daughters. 27 He lived nine hundred and sixty-nine years, and then he died.

28 Lamech was one hundred and eighty-two years old when he begot a son. 29 He named him Noah, saying, 'This boy will bring us relief from our work, from the labour that has come upon us because of the LORD's curse on the ground.' 30 After the birth of Noah he lived for five hundred and ninety-five years, and had other sons and daughters. 31 Lamech lived seven hundred and seventy-seven years, and then he died. 32 Noah was five hundred years old when he begot Shem, Ham, and Japheth.

The flood and the tower of Babel

6 THE human race began to increase and to spread over the earth and daughters were born to them. 2 The sons of the gods saw how beautiful these daughters were, so they took for themselves such women as they chose. 3 But the LORD said, 'My spirit will not remain in a human being for ever; because he is mortal flesh, he will live only for a hundred and twenty years.'

4 In those days as well as later, when the sons of the gods had intercourse with the daughters of mortals and children were born to them, the Nephilim were on the earth; they were the heroes of old, people of renown.

5 When the LORD saw how great was the wickedness of human beings on earth, and how their every thought and inclination were always wicked, 6 he bitterly regretted that he had made mankind on earth. 7 He said, 'I shall wipe off the face of the earth this human race which I have created—yes, man and beast, creeping things and birds. I regret that I ever made them.' 8 Noah, however, had won the LORD's favour.

9 This is the story of Noah. Noah was a righteous man, the one blameless man of his time, and he walked with God. 10 He had three sons: Shem, Ham, and Japheth. 11 God saw that the world was corrupt and full of violence; 12 and seeing this corruption, for the life of everyone on earth was corrupt, 13 God said to Noah, 'I am going to bring the whole human race to an end, for because of them the earth is full of violence. I am about to destroy them, and the earth along with

6:4 Nephilim: or giants.

decrease the span of human life, symbolizing the consequences of sin. 29: Relief: by folk etymology, the name "Noah" is derived from the verb "to rest." Perhaps his cultivation of the vineyard and his wine making (9.20) are alluded to.

6.1–4: The birth of the Nephilim is an ancient fragment, a folk explanation for a race of giants. It is used here to illustrate the growing wickedness of humankind, to explain the decreasing life span, and to set the stage for the deluge. 2: Sons of the gods: a term of Canaanite origin for members of the pantheon ("assembly of the gods"). Later these were viewed as fallen angels (Jude 6–7). 3: Mortal: in ancient belief, sexual contact between gods and human beings transmitted the qualities of the former. Here, however, humanity has overstepped the bounds that God assigned to creatures, so that divine correction is needed; compare 11.1–9. A hundred and twenty years: a round number (Num. 7.86; 1 Kgs. 9.14; 10.10); see 5.4 n.

6.5–8.22: The great deluge. God's judgment takes the form of a punishing flood, while God's grace takes the form of preserving a remnant through whom a new beginning can take place. The story was adapted from the Babylonian Gilgamesh Epic, itself possibly the "explanation" of a local but catastrophic flood in the Tigris-Euphrates valley. 9–22: The story was transmitted in several versions; on being combined in the text them. 14 Make yourself an ark with ribs of cypress; cover it with reeds and coat it inside and out with pitch. 15 This is to be its design: the length of the ark is to be three hundred cubits, its breadth fifty cubits, and its height thirty cubits. 16 You are to make a roof for the ark, giving it a fall of one cubit when complete; put a door in the side of the ark, and build three decks, lower, middle, and upper. 17 I am about to bring the waters of the flood over the earth to destroy from under heaven every human being that has the spirit of life; everything on earth shall perish. 18 But with you I shall make my covenant, and you will go into the ark, you with your sons, your wife, and your sons' wives. 19 You are to bring living creatures of every kind into the ark to keep them alive with you, two of each kind, a male and a female; 20 two of every kind of bird, beast, and creeping thing are to come to you to be kept alive. 21 See that you take and store by you every kind of food that can be eaten; this will be food for you and for them.' 22 Noah carried out exactly all God had commanded him.

7 The LORD said to Noah, 'Go into the ark, you and all your household; for you alone in this generation have I found to be righteous. 2 Take with you seven pairs, a male and female, of all beasts that are ritually clean, and one pair, a male and female, of all beasts that are not clean; 3 also seven pairs, males and females, of every bird — to ensure that life continues on earth. 4 For in seven days' time I am going to send rain on the earth for forty days and forty nights, and I shall wipe off the face of the earth every living creature I have made.' 5 Noah did all that the LORD had commanded him. 6 He was six hundred years old when the water of the flood came on the earth.

7 So to escape the flood Noah went into the ark together with his sons, his wife, and his sons' wives. 8–9 And to him on board the ark went one pair, a male and a female, of all beasts, clean and unclean, of birds, and of everything that creeps on the ground, two by two, as God had commanded. 10 At the end of seven days the water of the flood came over

the earth. 11 In the year when Noah was six hundred years old, on the seventeenth day of the second month, that very day all the springs of the great deep burst out, the windows of the heavens were opened, 12 and rain fell on the earth for forty days and forty nights. 13 That was the day Noah went into the ark with his sons, Shem, Ham, and Japheth, his own wife, and his three sons' wives. 14 Wild animals of every kind, cattle of every kind, every kind of thing that creeps on the ground, and winged birds of every kind — 15 all living creatures came two by two to Noah in the ark. 16 Those which came were one male and one female of all living things; they came in as God had commanded Noah, and the LORD closed the door on him.

17 The flood continued on the earth for forty days, and the swelling waters lifted up the ark so that it rose high above the ground. 18 The ark floated on the surface of the swollen waters as they increased over the earth. 19 They increased more and more until they covered all the high mountains everywhere under heaven. 20 The water increased until the mountains were covered to a depth of fifteen cubits. 21 Every living thing that moved on earth perished: birds, cattle, wild animals, all creatures that swarm on the ground, and all human beings. 22 Everything on dry land died, everything that had the breath of life in its nostrils. 23 God wiped out every living creature that existed on earth, man and beast, creeping thing and bird; they were all wiped out over the whole earth, and only Noah and those who were with him in the ark survived.

24 When the water had increased over the 8 earth for a hundred and fifty days, 1 God took thought for Noah and all the beasts and cattle with him in the ark, and he caused a wind to blow over the earth, so that the water began to subside. 2 The springs of the deep and the windows of the heavens were stopped up, the downpour from the skies was checked. 3 Gradually the water receded from the earth, and by the end of a hundred and fifty days it had abated. 4 On the seven-

6:14 **cover . . . reeds:** *or* make compartments in it.

as we now have it, some duplication and divergence have ensued. **15:** *Cubits:* see p. xxvii. **7.2:** *Seven:* a round number (21.28; Num. 28.11). **4:** *Forty:* another round number (Exod. 16.35; 2 Sam. 5.4; Jonah 3.4). **11:** *Springs:* the earth was thought to be surrounded by water that could break through from below as well as from above. *Windows:* in the vault of heaven; see 1.6 n. The earth was threatened with a return to the pre-creation chaos (1.2). **24:** *A hundred and fifty days:* this precise number may reflect an effort to bind the events to a liturgical teenth day of the seventh month the ark grounded on the mountains of Ararat. ⁵The water continued to abate until the tenth month, and on the first day of the tenth month the tops of the mountains could be seen.

⁶At the end of forty days Noah opened the hatch that he had made in the ark, ⁷and sent out a raven; it continued flying to and fro until the water on the earth had dried up. ⁸Then Noah sent out a dove to see whether the water on the earth had subsided. ⁹But the dove found no place where she could settle because all the earth was under water, and so she came back to him in the ark. Noah reached out and caught her, and brought her into the ark. ¹⁰He waited seven days more and again sent out the dove from the ark. ¹¹She came back to him towards evening with a freshly plucked olive leaf in her beak. Noah knew then that the water had subsided from the earth's surface. ¹²He waited yet another seven days and, when he sent out the dove, she did not come back to him. ¹³So it came about that, on the first day of the first month of his six hundred and first year, the water had dried up on the earth, and when Noah removed the hatch and looked out, he saw that the ground was dry.

¹⁴By the twenty-seventh day of the second month the earth was dry, ¹⁵and God spoke to Noah. ¹⁶'Come out of the ark together with your wife, your sons, and their wives,' he said. ¹⁷'Bring out every living creature that is with you, live things of every kind, birds, beasts, and creeping things, and let them spread over the earth and be fruitful and increase on it.' ¹⁸So Noah came out with his sons, his wife, and his sons' wives, ¹⁹and all the animals, creeping things, and birds; everything that moves on the ground came out of the ark, one kind after another.

²⁰Noah built an altar to the LORD and, taking beasts and birds of every kind that were ritually clean, he offered them as whole-offerings on it. ²¹When the LORD smelt the soothing odour, he said within himself,

'Never again shall I put the earth under a curse because of mankind, however evil their inclination may be from their youth upwards, nor shall I ever again kill all living creatures, as I have just done.

²²'As long as the earth lasts,
  seedtime and harvest, cold and heat,
  summer and winter, day and night,
  they will never cease.'

9 GOD blessed Noah and his sons; he said to them, 'Be fruitful and increase in numbers, and fill the earth. ²Fear and dread of you will come on all the animals on earth, on all the birds of the air, on everything that moves on the ground, and on all fish in the sea; they are made subject to you. ³Every creature that lives and moves will be food for you; I give them all to you, as I have given you every green plant. ⁴But you must never eat flesh with its life still in it, that is the blood. ⁵And further, for your life-blood I shall demand satisfaction; from every animal I shall require it, and from human beings also I shall require satisfaction for the death of their fellows.

⁶'Anyone who sheds human blood,
  for that human being his blood will be
    shed;
  because in the image of God
  has God made human beings.

⁷'Be fruitful, then, and increase in number; people the earth and rule over it.'

⁸God said to Noah and his sons: ⁹'I am now establishing my covenant with you and with your descendants after you, ¹⁰and with every living creature that is with you, all birds and cattle, all the animals with you on earth, all that have come out of the ark. ¹¹I shall sustain my covenant with you: never again will all living creatures be destroyed by the waters of a flood, never again will there be a flood to lay waste the earth.'

9:7 **rule:** *prob. rdg, cp. 1:28; Heb.* increase.

---

calendar. **8.4:** *Ararat* was in upper Mesopotamia, an area from which some of Israel's ancestors migrated (11.27–12.5). **21:** *Again:* the earth had been cursed earlier (3.17–19). God's mercy will no longer depend upon human response.

9.1–17: The covenant with Noah. 1: The blessing given at creation (1.28) is renewed. **3–4:** The eating of meat is sanctioned but possibly regarded as undesirable (see 1.29–30). *Blood:* see 4.10 n. **6:** The violence of the preceding age is restrained by law basic to the creation (1.26) and enforced by punishment; the passage explains the origin of blood revenge, but without approving it. **8–9:** The covenant was made with all of

¹²God said, 'For all generations to come, this is the sign which I am giving of the covenant between myself and you and all living creatures with you:

¹³My bow I set in the clouds
to be a sign of the covenant
between myself and the earth.
¹⁴When I bring clouds over the earth,
the rainbow will appear in the clouds.

¹⁵'Then I shall remember the covenant which I have made with you and with all living creatures, and never again will the waters become a flood to destroy all creation. ¹⁶Whenever the bow appears in the cloud, I shall see it and remember the everlasting covenant between God and living creatures of every kind on earth.' ¹⁷So God said to Noah, 'This is the sign of the covenant which I have established with all that lives on earth.'

¹⁸The sons of Noah who came out of the ark were Shem, Ham, and Japheth; Ham was the father of Canaan. ¹⁹These three were the sons of Noah, and their descendants spread over the whole earth.

²⁰Noah, who was the first tiller of the soil, planted a vineyard. ²¹He drank so much of the wine that he became drunk and lay naked inside his tent. ²²Ham, father of Canaan, saw his father naked, and went out and told his two brothers. ²³Shem and Japheth took a cloak, put it on their shoulders, and, walking backwards, covered their father's naked body. They kept their faces averted, so that they did not see his nakedness. ²⁴When Noah woke from his drunkenness and learnt what his youngest son had done to him, ²⁵he said:

'Cursed be Canaan!
Most servile of slaves
shall he be to his brothers.'

²⁶And he went on:

'Bless, O LORD,
the tents of Shem;
may Canaan be his slave.
²⁷May God extend Japheth's boundaries,
let him dwell in the tents of Shem,
may Canaan be his slave.'

²⁸After the flood Noah lived for three hundred and fifty years; ²⁹he was nine hundred and fifty years old when he died.

10 These are the descendants of Noah's sons, Shem, Ham, and Japheth, the sons born to them after the flood. ²The sons of Japheth: Gomer, Magog, Madai, Javan, Tubal, Meshech, and Tiras. ³The sons of Gomer: Ashkenaz, Riphath, and Togarmah. ⁴The sons of Javan: Elishah, Tarshish, Kittim, and Rodanim. ⁵From these the peoples of the coasts and islands separated into their own countries, each with their own language, family by family, nation by nation.

⁶The sons of Ham: Cush, Mizraim, Put, and Canaan. ⁷The sons of Cush: Seba, Havilah, Sabtah, Raamah, and Sabtecha. The sons of Raamah: Sheba and Dedan. ⁸Cush was the father of Nimrod, who began to be known on earth for his might. ⁹He was outstanding as

9:26 **Bless . . . Shem:** *prob. rdg; Heb.* Blessed is the LORD the God of Shem.   9:27 **extend:** *Heb.* japht. 10:2 **Javan:** *or* Greece.   10:4 **Tarshish, Kittim:** *or* Tarshish of the Kittians. **Rodanim:** *so Samar.; Heb.* Dodanim.   10:6 **Mizraim:** *or* Egypt.

humankind (vv. 18–19); other covenants were with individuals or the Hebrew people. **13:** In ancient mythology the [rain]*bow* was a weapon of the deity (Hab. 3.9). Folk explanation regarded it as a sign of divine victory. Here it is reinterpreted as divine reassurance.

9.18–29: The curse upon Canaan. 20–21: The origin of *wine* making is attributed to Noah (5.29 n.). The story likely is an attack on the Canaanite farming life-style (see 4.1–26 n.). **25:** The story makes its point by shifting the blame from Ham to Canaan, the ancestor whose name signified his descendants; see 10.6 n. **26:** *Shem* is the eponymous ("name-giving") ancestor of the Semites, including Israel (10.21–25; 11.18–26); the verse attempts to explain the later conquest of Canaan (see Josh.–Judg.) in theological terms. The supposed sexual liberties of the later Canaanites offended the Israelites (see 19.5 n.; Lev. 18.3, 6–30). **27:** *Japheth:* the ancestor of peoples from the Aegean Sea; among these were the Philistines who settled in Palestine during the thirteenth century. **28–29:** Noah's death.

10.1–32: The "Table of the Nations." This chapter is a composite work, the latest editing of which intends it as a continuation of 5.32. By means of eponymous ("name-giving") ancestors, it shows the spread of humankind after the deluge. Chapter 11 offers a different explanation for the spread and diversity of humankind. **6:** *Ham:* the Egyptian political orbit; Canaan was under Egyptian control, about 1500–1200 B.C.E. *Cush:*

a mighty hunter—as the saying goes, 'like Nimrod, outstanding as a mighty hunter'. ¹⁰ At first his kingdom consisted of Babel, Erech, and Accad, all of them in the land of Shinar. ¹¹ From that land he migrated to Assyria and built Nineveh, Rehoboth-ir, Calah, ¹² and Resen, a great city between Nineveh and Calah. ¹³ From Mizraim sprang the Ludim, Anamites, Lehabites, Naphtuhites, ¹⁴ Pathrusites, Casluhites, and the Caphtorites, from whom the Philistines were descended.

¹⁵ Canaan was the father of Sidon, who was his eldest son, and Heth, ¹⁶ the Jebusites, the Amorites, the Girgashites, ¹⁷ the Hivites, the Arkites, the Sinites, ¹⁸ the Arvadites, the Zemarites, and the Hamathites. Later the Canaanites spread, ¹⁹ and then the Canaanite border ran from Sidon towards Gerar all the way to Gaza; then all the way to Sodom and Gomorrah, Admah, and Zeboyim as far as Lasha. ²⁰ These were the sons of Ham, by families and languages, with their countries and nations.

²¹ Sons were born also to Shem, elder brother of Japheth, the ancestor of all the sons of Eber. ²² The sons of Shem: Elam, Asshur, Arphaxad, Lud, and Aram. ²³ The sons of Aram: Uz, Hul, Gether, and Mash. ²⁴ Arphaxad was the father of Shelah, and Shelah the father of Eber. ²⁵ Eber had two sons: one was named Peleg, because in his time the earth was divided; and his brother's name was Joktan. ²⁶ Joktan was the father of Almodad, Sheleph, Hazarmoth, Jerah, ²⁷ Hadoram, Uzal, Diklah, ²⁸ Obal, Abimael, Sheba, ²⁹ Ophir, Havilah, and Jobab. All these were sons of Joktan. ³⁰ They lived in the eastern hill-country, from Mesha all the way to Sephar. ³¹ These were the sons of Shem, by families and languages, with their countries and nations.

³² These were the families of the sons of Noah according to their genealogies, nation by nation; and from them came the separate nations on earth after the flood.

11 There was a time when all the world spoke a single language and used the same words. ² As people journeyed in the east, they came upon a plain in the land of Shinar and settled there. ³ They said to one another, 'Come, let us make bricks and bake them hard'; they used bricks for stone and bitumen for mortar. ⁴ Then they said, 'Let us build ourselves a city and a tower with its top in the heavens and make a name for ourselves, or we shall be dispersed over the face of the earth.' ⁵ The Lord came down to see the city and tower which they had built, ⁶ and he said, 'Here they are, one people with a single language, and now they have started to do this; from now on nothing they have a mind to do will be beyond their reach. ⁷ Come, let us go down there and confuse their language, so that they will not understand what they say to one another.' ⁸ So the Lord dispersed them from there all over the earth, and they left off building the city. ⁹ That is why it is called Babel, because there the Lord made a babble of the language of the whole world. It was from that place the Lord scattered people over the face of the earth.

¹⁰ These are the descendants of Shem. Shem was a hundred years old when he begot Arphaxad, two years after the flood. ¹¹ After

10:14 **and the Caphtorites:** *transposed from end of verse; cp. Amos 9:7.*   10:15 **Heth:** *or the Hittites.*
10:25 **Peleg:** *that is* Division.   11:1 **the same:** *or* few.
11:9 **Babel:** *that is* Babylon.

sometimes this term denotes Ethiopia, as here, or else the land of the Kassites (v. 8; 2.13 n.). **21:** *Eber* is an eponymous ("name-giving") ancestor of the *'ibrim* (the "Hebrews"). This designation was used in Canaan ca. 1500–1200 b.c.e. to designate various groups on the margins of society. The Israelites came to understand it as a designation of themselves as a people.

11.1–9: The tower of Babel. An ancient story explaining the origin of diverse languages of humankind; here, it is another illustration of human refusal to accept limitations (2.4–3.24 n.; 6.3 n.). It sets the stage for the true climax of chs. 1–11, namely, the divine choice of Abram (12.1ff.). **2:** *Shinar:* Sumeria (see 10.10). **4:** *Tower:* the center of the Mesopotamian city was a complex of buildings including a pyramidal temple, extending upward toward a "gate" in the heavens through which the gods came down to reveal themselves. **8:** Probably the observation of vast temple ruins elicited this theological explanation by those to whom this culture was alien. **9:** *Babel:* this term, which for the Babylonians meant "the gate of the gods," is punned on through the verb *balal,* "to confuse," "make babble."

11.10–32: Abram's genealogy. This material connects the deluge and the call of Israel's ancestor. Its insertion the birth of Arphaxad he lived five hundred years, and had other sons and daughters. ¹²Arphaxad was thirty-five years old when he begot Shelah. ¹³After the birth of Shelah he lived four hundred and three years, and had other sons and daughters.

¹⁴Shelah was thirty years old when he begot Eber. ¹⁵After the birth of Eber he lived four hundred and three years, and had other sons and daughters.

¹⁶Eber was thirty-four years old when he begot Peleg. ¹⁷After the birth of Peleg he lived four hundred and thirty years, and had other sons and daughters.

¹⁸Peleg was thirty years old when he begot Reu. ¹⁹After the birth of Reu he lived two hundred and nine years, and had other sons and daughters.

²⁰Reu was thirty-two years old when he begot Serug. ²¹After the birth of Serug he lived two hundred and seven years, and had other sons and daughters.

²²Serug was thirty years old when he begot Nahor. ²³After the birth of Nahor he lived two hundred years, and had other sons and daughters.

²⁴Nahor was twenty-nine years old when he begot Terah. ²⁵After the birth of Terah he lived a hundred and nineteen years, and had other sons and daughters.

²⁶Terah was seventy years old when he begot Abram, Nahor, and Haran.

²⁷These are the descendants of Terah. Terah was the father of Abram, Nahor, and Haran. Haran was Lot's father. ²⁸Haran died in the land of his birth, Ur of the Chaldees, during his father's lifetime. ²⁹Abram and Nahor married wives; Abram's wife was called Sarai, and Nahor's Milcah. She was the daughter of Haran, father of Milcah and Iscah. ³⁰Sarai was barren; she had no child. ³¹Terah took his son Abram, his grandson Lot the son of Haran, and his daughter-in-law Sarai, Abram's wife, and they set out

from Ur of the Chaldees for Canaan. But when they reached Harran, they settled there. ³²Terah was two hundred and five years old when he died in Harran.

Abram's travels

12 The LORD said to Abram, 'Leave your own country, your kin, and your father's house, and go to a country that I will show you. ²I shall make you into a great nation; I shall bless you and make your name so great that it will be used in blessings:

³those who bless you, I shall bless;
  those who curse you, I shall curse.
All the peoples on earth
  will wish to be blessed as you are
  blessed.'

⁴Abram, who was seventy-five years old when he left Harran, set out as the LORD had bidden him, and Lot went with him. ⁵He took his wife Sarai, his brother's son Lot, and all the possessions they had gathered and the dependants they had acquired in Harran, and they departed for Canaan. When they arrived there, ⁶Abram went on as far as the sanctuary at Shechem, the terebinth tree of Moreh. (At that time the Canaanites lived in the land.) ⁷When the LORD appeared to him and said, 'I am giving this land to your descendants,' Abram built an altar there to the LORD who had appeared to him. ⁸From there he moved on to the hill-country east of Bethel and pitched his tent between Bethel on the west and Ai on the east. He built there an altar to the LORD whom he invoked by name. ⁹Thus Abram journeyed by stages towards the Negeb.

¹⁰The land was stricken by a famine so

11:32 **two hundred and five:** or, with Samar., one hundred and forty-five.   12:3 **will wish . . . are blessed:** or will be blessed because of you.

at this point heightens the effect of God's gracious but unexplained election of Abraham. **20–27:** Several of the names are personified cities. **28:** *Chaldees:* here the name is an anachronism; Chaldeans did not occupy lower Mesopotamia until much later.

12.1–9: The call of Abram. His migration may have been part of a population movement (known to modern scholars) in the early second millennium B.C.E. **3:** A traditional interpretation is: "Through you all the families of the earth will be blessed." The call of Abram marks a culmination of the deity's efforts to restore the harmony of creation. **7:** *Altar:* the account attributes to Israel's ancestor the founding of an ancient Canaanite sanctuary. **9:** *Negeb:* "south," the barren area between Beersheba and the Gulf of Aqaba.

12.10–20: Abram in Egypt. God's promise to Abram (vv. 2–3) encounters its first challenge. Abram is here found wanting, for he is willing to sacrifice the future ancestress of Israel for self-security. But God's grace does severe that Abram went down to Egypt to live there for a time. ¹¹ As he was about to enter Egypt, he said to his wife Sarai, 'I am well aware that you are a beautiful woman, and ¹² I know that when the Egyptians see you and think, "She is his wife," they will let you live but they will kill me. ¹³ Tell them you are my sister, so that all may go well with me because of you, and my life be spared on your account.'

¹⁴ When Abram arrived in Egypt, the Egyptians saw that Sarai was indeed very beautiful, ¹⁵ and Pharaoh's courtiers, when they saw her, sang her praises to Pharaoh. She was taken into Pharaoh's household, ¹⁶ and he treated Abram well because of her, and Abram acquired sheep and cattle and donkeys, male and female slaves, she-donkeys, and camels. ¹⁷ But when the LORD inflicted plagues on Pharaoh and his household on account of Abram's wife Sarai, ¹⁸ Pharaoh summoned Abram. 'Why have you treated me like this?' he said. 'Why did you not tell me she was your wife? ¹⁹ Why did you say she was your sister, so that I took her as a wife? Here she is: take her and go.' ²⁰ Pharaoh gave his men orders, and they sent Abram on his way with his wife and all that belonged to him.

Abram and Lot

13 FROM Egypt Abram went up into the Negeb, he and his wife and all that he possessed, and Lot went with him. ² Abram had become very rich in cattle and in silver and gold. ³ From the Negeb he journeyed by stages towards Bethel, to the place between Bethel and Ai where he had earlier pitched his tent, ⁴ and where he had previously set up an altar and invoked the LORD by name. ⁵ Since Lot, who was travelling with Abram, also possessed sheep and cattle and tents, ⁶ the land could not support them while they

were together. They had so much livestock that they could not settle in the same district, ⁷ and quarrels arose between Abram's herdsmen and Lot's. (The Canaanites and the Perizzites were then living in the land.) ⁸ Abram said to Lot, 'There must be no quarrelling between us, or between my herdsmen and yours; for we are close kinsmen. ⁹ The whole country is there in front of you. Let us part company: if you go north, I shall go south; if you go south, I shall go north.' ¹⁰ Lot looked around and saw how well watered the whole plain of Jordan was; all the way to Zoar it was like the Garden of the LORD, like the land of Egypt. This was before the LORD had destroyed Sodom and Gomorrah. ¹¹ So Lot chose all the Jordan plain and took the road to the east. They parted company: ¹² Abram settled in Canaan, while Lot settled among the cities of the plain and pitched his tent near Sodom. ¹³ Now the men of Sodom in their wickedness had committed monstrous sins against the LORD.

¹⁴ After Lot and Abram had parted, the LORD said to Abram, 'Look around from where you are towards north, south, east, and west: ¹⁵ all the land you see I shall give to you and to your descendants for ever. ¹⁶ I shall make your descendants countless as the dust of the earth; only if the specks of dust on the ground could be counted could your descendants be counted. ¹⁷ Now go through the length and breadth of the land, for I am giving it to you.' ¹⁸ Abram moved his tent and settled by the terebinths of Mamre at Hebron, where he built an altar to the LORD.

14 IN those days King Amraphel of Shinar, King Arioch of Ellasar, King Kedorlaomer of Elam, and King Tidal of Goyim ² went to war against King Bera of Sodom, King Birsha of Gomorrah, King Shi-

13:10 **the Garden of the LORD:** *or* a wonderful garden.

not depend upon human worthiness, so that Sarai is preserved anyway. That the incident is repeated in 20.1–18; 26.6–11 reflects the bringing together of independent traditions in the editorial growth of the Pentateuch.

13.1–18: Abram and Lot. 4: *Previously:* 12.8. **11:** *Chose:* through human freedom, God's promise of the land (12.7) begins to be fulfilled; i.e. by Lot's choice, the land of the promise was left to Abram. **18:** *Terebinth:* the exact species of tree is uncertain.

14.1–24: The defeat of the four eastern kings. Style and content indicate a one-time independent tradition. Its function may be to suggest that the Canaanite cult at Jerusalem, later assimilated and legitimized by David (2 Sam. chs. 6 and 24), had long previously been legitimized by Abram. **1–2:** Some of the personal names are attested in extrabiblical materials from the early second millennium B.C.E. This supports the basic historical nab of Admah, King Shemeber of Zeboyim, and the king of Bela, which is Zoar. ³These kings joined forces in the valley of Siddim, which is now the Dead Sea. ⁴For twelve years they had been subject to Kedorlaomer, but in the thirteenth year they rebelled. ⁵Then in the fourteenth year Kedorlaomer and the kings allied with him came and defeated the Rephaim in Ashteroth-karnaim, the Zuzim in Ham, the Emim in Shaveh-kiriathaim, ⁶and the Horites in their hill-country, Seir as far as El-paran on the edge of the wilderness. ⁷On their way back they came to En-mishpat, which is now Kadesh, and laid waste all the territory of the Amalekites as well as that of the Amorites who lived in Hazazon-tamar. ⁸Then the kings of Sodom, Gomorrah, Admah, Zeboyim, and Bela, which is now Zoar, marched out and drew up their forces against them in the valley of Siddim, ⁹against King Kedorlaomer of Elam, King Tidal of Goyim, King Amraphel of Shinar, and King Arioch of Ellasar, four kings against five. ¹⁰Now the valley of Siddim was full of bitumen pits, and when the kings of Sodom and Gomorrah fled, some of their men fell into them, but the rest made their escape to the hills. ¹¹The four kings captured all the flocks and herds of Sodom and Gomorrah and all their provisions, and withdrew, ¹²carrying off Abram's nephew, Lot, who was living in Sodom, and his flocks and herds.

¹³A fugitive brought the news to Abram the Hebrew, who at that time had his camp by the terebinths of Mamre the Amorite. This Mamre was the brother of Eshcol and Aner, allies of Abram. ¹⁴When Abram heard that his kinsman had been taken prisoner, he mustered his three hundred and eighteen retainers, men born in his household, and went in pursuit as far as Dan. ¹⁵Abram and his followers surrounded the enemy by night, routed them, and pursued them as far as Hobah, north of Damascus. ¹⁶He recovered all the flocks and herds and also his kinsman Lot with his flocks and herds, together with the women and all his company. ¹⁷On Abram's return from defeating Kedorlaomer and the allied kings, the king of Sodom came out to meet him in the valley of Shaveh, which is now the King's Valley.

Melchizedek blesses Abram

¹⁸THEN the king of Salem, Melchizedek, brought food and wine. He was priest of God Most High, ¹⁹and he pronounced this blessing on Abram:

'Blessed be Abram by God Most High,
Creator of the heavens and the earth.
²⁰And blessed be God Most High,
who has delivered your enemies into
your hand.'

Then Abram gave him a tithe of all the booty. ²¹The king of Sodom said to Abram, 'Give me the people, and you can take the livestock.' ²²But Abram replied, 'I lift my hand and swear by the LORD, God Most High, Creator of the heavens and the earth: ²³not a thread or a sandal-thong shall I accept of anything that is yours. You will never say, "I made Abram rich." ²⁴I shall accept nothing but what the young men have eaten and the share of the men who went with me, Aner, Eshcol, and Mamre; they must have their share.'

The Lord's covenant with Abram

15 AFTER this the word of the LORD came to Abram in a vision. He said, 'Do not be afraid, Abram; I am your shield. Your reward will be very great.' ²Abram replied, 'Lord GOD, what can you give me, seeing that I am childless? The heir to my household is Eliezer of Damascus. ³You have given me no children, and so my heir must be a slave born in my house.' ⁴The word of the LORD came to him: 'This man will not be your heir; your heir will be a child of your own body.' ⁵He brought Abram outside and said, 'Look up at the sky, and count the stars, if you can. So many will your descendants be.' ⁶Abram put his faith in the LORD, who reckoned it to him as righteousness, ⁷and

14:3 **Dead Sea:** *lit.* Salt Sea.

reliability of the account, although a specific date cannot be assigned. **13:** *Hebrew:* see 10.21 n. This passage may have played a role in giving the term its "ethnic" meaning. **18:** *Salem:* a variant name for Jerusalem (Ps. 76.2). *God Most High:* a divine name, attested in antiquity in both this and the shorter form, "the Most High" (Isa. 14.14; Ps. 9.2). Here the Most High is identified with the LORD (Yahweh) of Israel (v. 22).

15.1–21: The covenant with Abram. 2–3: The Nuzi Texts (from Mesopotamia, about fourteen censaid, 'I am the LORD who brought you out from Ur of the Chaldees to give you this land as your possession.' 8 Abram asked, 'Lord GOD, how can I be sure that I shall occupy it?' 9 The LORD answered, 'Bring me a heifer three years old, a she-goat three years old, a ram three years old, a turtle-dove, and a young pigeon.' 10 Abram brought him all these, cut the animals in two, and set the pieces opposite each other, but he did not cut the birds in half. 11 Birds of prey swooped down on the carcasses, but he scared them away. 12 As the sun was going down, Abram fell into a trance and great and fearful darkness came over him. 13 The LORD said to Abram, 'Know this for certain: your descendants will be aliens living in a land that is not their own; they will be enslaved and held in oppression for four hundred years. 14 But I shall punish the nation whose slaves they are, and afterwards they will depart with great possessions. 15 You yourself will join your forefathers in peace and be buried at a ripe old age. 16 But it will be the fourth generation who will return here, for till then the Amorites will not be ripe for punishment.' 17 The sun went down and it was dusk, and there appeared a smoking brazier and a flaming torch which passed between the divided pieces. 18 That day the LORD made a covenant with Abram, and said, 'I give to your descendants this land from the river of Egypt to the Great River, the river Euphrates, 19 the terri-

tory of the Kenites, Kenizzites, Kadmonites, 20 Hittites, Perizzites, Rephaim, 21 Amorites, Canaanites, Girgashites, and Jebusites.'

16 Abram's wife Sarai had borne him no children. She had, however, an Egyptian slave-girl named Hagar, 2 and Sarai said to Abram, 'The LORD has not let me have a child. Take my slave-girl; perhaps through her I shall have a son.' Abram heeded what his wife said; 3 so Sarai brought her slave-girl, Hagar the Egyptian, to her husband and gave her to Abram as a wife. When this happened Abram had been in Canaan for ten years. 4 He lay with Hagar and she conceived; and when she knew that she was pregnant, she looked down on her mistress. 5 Sarai complained to Abram, 'I am being wronged; you must do something about it. It was I who gave my slave-girl into your arms, but since she has known that she is pregnant, she has despised me. May the LORD see justice done between you and me.' 6 Abram replied, 'Your slave-girl is in your hands; deal with her as you please.' So Sarai ill-treated her and she ran away from her mistress.

7 The angel of the LORD came upon Hagar by a spring in the wilderness, the spring on the road to Shur, 8 and he said, 'Hagar, Sarai's slave-girl, where have you come from and where are you going?' She answered, 'I am running away from Sarai my mistress.' 9 The angel of the LORD said to her, 'Go back to your mistress and submit to ill-treatment

tury B.C.E.) stipulate that someone can be adopted in case of childlessness. **7:** A separate tradition now begins, concerned with the promise of land (12.7). The covenant ceremony has parallels in the Mari Texts from Mesopotamia, eighteenth century B.C.E. By means of it, the LORD replaces Abram's human associates. Abram has rejected the gifts of the king of Sodom (14.22–24) and now enters into alliance with the LORD. **10:** The covenanting parties walked between the sliced parts of the animals, swearing to keep the stipulations lest they likewise be dismembered; see Jer. 34.18, and compare, obliquely, 1 Sam. 11.7 and Judg. 19.29–30. **12:** Dreams were often regarded as the medium of divine revelation (20.3–7; Matt. 2.19–23). **13–14:** The period of oppression in Egypt is given as an illustration of how the "promise" may be delayed, and serves to exhort future generations to maintain their faith. **16:** The *punishment* was to be the conquest of the Amorites, who were Canaanites, in the time of Joshua. **17:** *Torch:* the presence of the deity is often symbolized by fire (Exod. 3.2; 13.21; 19.18). **18:** The boundaries given generally conform to those of the Davidic period (2 Sam. 8.1–12; 1 Kgs. 4.21; 8.65); this is an indication of the date at which this material was gathered. **21:** *Jebusites:* an ancient designation for the inhabitants of Jerusalem (2 Sam. 5.6).

16.1–16: The birth of Ishmael. 1: The gap between promise and realization (see Introduction) is here reflected for a didactic ("teaching") purpose. **2:** The Nuzi Texts (15.2–3 n.) stipulate that a barren wife could be required to provide her husband with a slave woman in order to insure his posterity (see 30.3, 9). **4–5:** Ancient law codes provide for punishment if a pregnant female slave claimed equality with her mistress. **6–14:** Sarai has exceeded the limit of justice, and the God of Israel, ever concerned with the oppressed (Exod. 3.7–10), gives Hagar a promise. **7:** *Angel:* a messenger of the divine council (1.26 n.). Depicted in human form, angels usually mediate between the deity and human beings, both symbolizing and mitigating the extreme loftiness at her hands.' 10 He also said, 'I shall make your descendants too many to be counted.' 11 The angel of the LORD went on:

'You are with child and will bear a son.
You are to name him Ishmael,
because the LORD has heard of your
   ill-treatment.
12 He will be like the wild ass;
his hand will be against everyone
and everyone's hand against him;
and he will live at odds with all his kin.'

13 Hagar called the LORD who spoke to her by the name El-roi, for she said, 'Have I indeed seen God and still live after that vision?' 14 That is why the well is called Beer-lahai-roi; it lies between Kadesh and Bered. 15 Hagar bore Abram a son, and he named the child she bore him Ishmael. 16 Abram was eighty-six years old when she bore Ishmael.

17 When Abram was ninety-nine years old, the LORD appeared to him and said, 'I am God Almighty. Live always in my presence and be blameless, 2 so that I may make my covenant with you and give you many descendants.' 3 Abram bowed low, and God went on, 4 'This is my covenant with you: you are to be the father of many nations. 5 Your name will no longer be Abram, but Abraham; for I shall make you father of many nations. 6 I shall make you exceedingly fruitful; I shall make nations out of you, and kings shall spring from you. 7 I shall maintain my covenant with you and your descendants after you, generation after generation, an everlasting covenant: I shall be your God, yours and your descendants'. 8 As a possession for all time I shall give you and your descendants after you the land in which you now are

aliens, the whole of Canaan, and I shall be their God.'

9 God said to Abraham, 'For your part, you must keep my covenant, you and your descendants after you, generation by generation. 10 This is how you are to keep this covenant between myself and you and your descendants after you: circumcise yourselves, every male among you. 11 You must circumcise the flesh of your foreskin, and it will be the sign of the covenant between us. 12 Every male among you in every generation must be circumcised on the eighth day, both those born in your house and any foreigner, not a member of your family but purchased. 13 Circumcise both those born in your house and those you buy; thus your flesh will be marked with the sign of my everlasting covenant. 14 Every uncircumcised male, everyone who has not had the flesh of his foreskin circumcised, will be cut off from the kin of his father; he has broken my covenant.'

15 God said to Abraham, 'As for Sarai your wife, you are to call her not Sarai, but Sarah. 16 I shall bless her and give you a son by her. I shall bless her and she will be the mother of nations; from her kings of peoples will spring.' 17 Abraham bowed low, and laughing said to himself, 'Can a son be born to a man who is a hundred years old? Can Sarah bear a child at ninety?' 18 He said to God, 'If only Ishmael might enjoy your special favour!' 19 But God replied, 'No; your wife Sarah will bear you a son, and you are to call him Isaac.

16:11 **Ishmael:** *that is* God heard.   16:13 **El-roi:** *that is* God of a vision. **God . . . live:** *prob. rdg; Heb.* hither. 16:14 **Beer-lahai-roi:** *that is* the Well of the Living One of Vision.   17:5 **Abram:** *that is* High Father. **Abraham:** *that is* Father of Many.   17:15 **Sarai:** *that is* Mockery. **Sarah:** *that is* Princess.   17:19 **Isaac:** *that is* He laughs.

of the deity. But sometimes "angel" is used as a direct manifestation of the deity, as here (v. 13). **12:** Ishmael is regarded as the ancestor of the Bedouin. **13–14:** *El-roi* is an epithet, or name, of the deity of this sacred spring; the writer identifies *El-roi* with Israel's God (14.18 n.).
   17.1–27: Second account of the covenant with Abram. In contrast to the earlier tradition (ch. 15), this late, Priestly account stresses the eternal nature of the covenant. **1:** *God Almighty:* lit. "the God of the Mountain(s)," an epithet possibly brought from Mesopotamia. It is here applied to the God of Israel (see Exod. 6.2–3). **5:** A person entering a new relationship or achieving a new status may receive an appropriate new name. Compare 32.28. Abram and Abraham are probably dialectical variants of the same name. **9–14:** Circumcision is an ancient rite; by it the writer seeks to give Israel a new sense of tradition and focus for identity, as the external *sign* of membership in the eternal covenant community. The Noachian covenant (9.9–17), which comes from the same tradition, was with all living creatures; the Abrahamic covenant is limited to Abraham's descendants **15:** Again, the names are dialectical variants. **19:** *Isaac:* see Tfn.; explanations of the name are also given in 18.12 and 21.6, which are part of older traditions. The meaning is joy, in that the parent rejoices at the newborn child.

With him I shall maintain my covenant as an everlasting covenant for his descendants after him. 20 But I have heard your request about Ishmael; I have blessed him and I shall make him fruitful. I shall give him many descendants; he will be father of twelve princes, and I shall raise a great nation from him. 21 But my covenant I shall fulfil with Isaac, whom Sarah will bear to you at this time next year.' 22 When he had finished talking with Abraham, God left him.

23 Then Abraham took Ishmael his son, everyone who had been born in his household and everyone he had bought, every male in his household, and that same day he circumcised the flesh of their foreskins as God had commanded him. 24 Abraham was ninety-nine years old when he was circumcised. 25 Ishmael was thirteen years old when he was circumcised. 26 Both Abraham and Ishmael were circumcised on the same day. 27 All the men of Abraham's household, born in the house or bought from foreigners, were circumcised with him.

18 THE LORD appeared to Abraham by the terebinths of Mamre, as he was sitting at the opening of his tent in the heat of the day. 2 He looked up and saw three men standing over against him. On seeing them, he hurried from his tent door to meet them. Bowing low 3 he said, 'Sirs, if I have deserved your favour, do not go past your servant without a visit. 4 Let me send for some water so that you may bathe your feet; and rest under this tree, 5 while I fetch a little food so that you may refresh yourselves. Afterwards you may continue the journey which has brought you my way.' They said, 'Very well, do as you say.' 6 So Abraham hurried into the tent to Sarah and said, 'Quick, take three measures of flour, knead it, and make cakes.' 7 He then hastened to the herd, chose a fine, tender calf, and gave it to a servant, who prepared it at once. 8 He took curds and milk and the calf which was now ready, set it all before them, and there under the tree waited on them himself while they ate.

9 They asked him where Sarah his wife was, and he replied, 'She is in the tent.' 10 One of them said, 'About this time next year I shall come back to you, and your wife Sarah will have a son.' Now Sarah was listening at the opening of the tent close by him. 11 Both Abraham and Sarah were very old, Sarah being well past the age of childbearing. 12 So she laughed to herself and said, 'At my time of life I am past bearing children, and my husband is old.' 13 The LORD said to Abraham, 'Why did Sarah laugh and say, "Can I really bear a child now that I am so old?" 14 Is anything impossible for the LORD? In due season, at this time next year, I shall come back to you, and Sarah will have a son.' 15 Because she was frightened, Sarah lied and denied that she had laughed; but he said, 'Yes, you did laugh.'

16 The men set out and looked down towards Sodom, and Abraham went with them to see them on their way. 17 The LORD had thought to himself, 'Shall I conceal from Abraham what I am about to do? 18 He will become a great and powerful nation, and all nations on earth will wish to be blessed as he is blessed. 19 I have singled him out so that he may charge his sons and family after him to conform to the way of the LORD and do what is right and just; thus I shall fulfil for him all that I have promised.' 20 The LORD said, 'How great is the outcry over Sodom and Gomorrah! How grave their sin must be! 21 I shall go down and see whether their deeds warrant the outcry reaching me. I must know the truth.' 22 When the men turned and went off towards Sodom, Abraham remained standing before the LORD. 23 Abraham drew near him and asked, 'Will you really sweep away innocent and wicked together? 24 Sup-

18:18 **will wish ... is blessed:** *or* will be blessed because of him.   18:22 **Abraham ... LORD:** *original reading was probably* the LORD remained standing before Abraham.

18.1–33: Abraham intercedes for Sodom. 2: Abraham addresses his visitors sometimes in the singular, sometimes in the plural, and the responses likewise shift in number. **11–12:** This tradition shows no knowledge of the similar one immediately before it (17.15–22); it abstains from explaining the name of the child as due to Sarah's laughter. **21:** The human qualities, including the lack of knowledge attributed to the deity, reflect a sophisticated dramatic literary style, and by no means a primitive stage of religious development. **23–33:** A basic ancient Near Eastern belief held that the wickedness of the few contaminated the entire community and rendered it liable to punishment. This account, applying the principle in reverse, marks a major development in Israel's religious thought. See 19.4 n.

pose there are fifty innocent in the city; will you really sweep it away, and not pardon the place because of the fifty innocent there? 25 Far be it from you to do such a thing — to kill innocent and wicked together; for then the innocent would suffer with the wicked. Far be it from you! Should not the judge of all the earth do what is just?' 26 The LORD replied, 'If I find in Sodom fifty innocent, I shall pardon the whole place for their sake.' 27 Abraham said, 'May I make so bold as to speak to the Lord, I who am nothing but dust and ashes: 28 suppose there are five short of fifty innocent? Will you destroy the whole city for the lack of five men?' 'If I find forty-five there,' he replied, 'I shall not destroy it.' 29 Abraham spoke again, 'Suppose forty can be found there?' 'For the sake of the forty I shall not do it,' he replied. 30 Then Abraham said, 'Let not my Lord become angry if I speak again: suppose thirty can be found there?' He answered, 'If I find thirty there, I shall not do it.' 31 Abraham continued, 'May I make so bold as to speak to the Lord: suppose twenty can be found there?' He replied, 'For the sake of the twenty I shall not destroy it.' 32 Abraham said, 'Let not my Lord become angry if I speak just once more: suppose ten can be found there?' 'For the sake of the ten I shall not destroy it,' said the Lord. 33 When the LORD had finished talking to Abraham, he went away, and Abraham returned home.

19 The two angels came to Sodom in the evening while Lot was sitting by the city gate. When he saw them, he rose to meet them and bowing low 2 he said, 'I pray you, sirs, turn aside to your servant's house to spend the night there and bathe your feet. You can continue your journey in the morning.' 'No,' they answered, 'we shall spend the night in the street.' 3 But Lot was so insistent that they accompanied him into his house. He prepared a meal for them, baking unleavened bread for them to eat.

4 Before they had lain down to sleep, the men of Sodom, both young and old, everyone without exception, surrounded the house. 5 They called to Lot: 'Where are the men who came to you tonight? Bring them out to us so that we may have intercourse with them.' 6 Lot went out into the doorway to them, and, closing the door behind him, 7 said, 'No, my friends, do not do anything so wicked. 8 Look, I have two daughters, virgins both of them; let me bring them out to you, and you can do what you like with them. But do nothing to these men, because they have come under the shelter of my roof.' 9 They said, 'Out of our way! This fellow has come and settled here as an alien, and does he now take it upon himself to judge us? We will treat you worse than them.' They crowded in on Lot and pressed close to break down the door. 10 But the two men inside reached out, pulled Lot into the house, and shut the door. 11 Then they struck those in the doorway, both young and old, with blindness so that they could not find the entrance.

12 The two men said to Lot, 'Have you anyone here, sons-in-law, sons, or daughters, or anyone else belonging to you in the city? Get them out of this place, 13 because we are going to destroy it. The LORD is aware of the great outcry against its citizens and has sent us to destroy it.' 14 So Lot went out and urged his sons-in-law to get out of the place at once. 'The LORD is about to destroy the city,' he said. But they did not take him seriously.

15 As soon as it was dawn, the angels urged Lot: 'Quick, take your wife and your two daughters who are here, or you will be destroyed when the city is punished.' 16 When he delayed, they grabbed his hand and the hands of his wife and two daughters, because the LORD had spared him, and they led him to safety outside the city. 17 After they had brought them out, one said, 'Flee for your lives! Do not look back or stop anywhere in the plain. Flee to the hills or you will be destroyed.' 18 Lot replied, 'No, sirs! 19 You have shown your servant favour, and even more by your unfailing care you have saved my life, but I cannot escape to the hills; I shall be overtaken by the disaster, and die. 20 Look, here is a town, only a small place, near enough for me to get to quickly. Let me escape to this small place and save my life.'

19.1–29: The destruction of Sodom and Gomorrah. This is a theological explanation of the ancient destruction of cities on the south shore of the Dead Sea; in Gen. 14.2, the cities number five. **4:** The entire population (see 18.23–33 n.) is here depicted as surrounding Lot's house. **5:** The intent is to illustrate sexual violence on the part of the Canaanites, warning Israel not to behave in such a way; see 9.26 n. **6–8:** In traditional fashion, Lot places the welfare of his guests above all else. Near Eastern hosts were obligated to

²¹ He said to him, 'I grant your request: I shall not overthrow the town you speak of. ²² But flee there quickly, because I can do nothing until you are there.' That is why the place was called Zoar. ²³ The sun had risen over the land as Lot entered Zoar, ²⁴ and the LORD rained down fire and brimstone from the skies on Sodom and Gomorrah. ²⁵ He overthrew those cities and destroyed all the plain, with everyone living there and everything growing in the ground. ²⁶ But Lot's wife looked back, and she turned into a pillar of salt.

²⁷ Early next morning Abraham went to the place where he had stood in the presence of the LORD. ²⁸ As he looked over Sodom and Gomorrah and all the wide extent of the plain, he saw thick smoke rising from the earth like smoke from a kiln. ²⁹ Thus it was, when God destroyed the cities of the plain, he took thought for Abraham by rescuing Lot from the total destruction of the cities where he had been living.

³⁰ Because Lot was afraid to stay in Zoar, he went up from there and settled with his two daughters in the hill-country, where he lived with them in a cave. ³¹ The elder daughter said to the younger, 'Our father is old and there is not a man in the country to come to us in the usual way. ³² Come now, let us ply our father with wine and then lie with him and in this way preserve the family through our father.' ³³ That night they gave him wine to drink, and the elder daughter came and lay with him, and he did not know when she lay down and when she got up. ³⁴ Next day the elder said to the younger, 'Last night I lay with my father. Let us ply him with wine again tonight; then you go in and lie with him. So we shall preserve the family through our father.' ³⁵ They gave their father wine to drink that night also; and the younger daughter went and lay with him, and he did not know when she lay down and when she got up. ³⁶ In this way both of Lot's daughters came to be pregnant by their father. ³⁷ The elder daughter bore a son and called him

Moab; he was the ancestor of the present-day Moabites. ³⁸ The younger also bore a son, whom she called Ben-ammi; he was the ancestor of the present-day Ammonites.

20 ABRAHAM journeyed by stages from there into the Negeb, and settled between Kadesh and Shur, living as an alien in Gerar. ² He said of Sarah his wife that she was his sister, and King Abimelech of Gerar had her brought to him. ³ But God came to Abimelech in a dream by night and said, 'You shall die because of this woman whom you have taken; she is a married woman.' ⁴ Abimelech, who had not gone near her, protested, 'Lord, will you destroy people who are innocent? ⁵ He told me himself that she was his sister, and she also said that he was her brother. It was in good faith and in all innocence that I did this.' ⁶ 'Yes, I know that you acted in good faith,' God replied in the dream. 'Indeed, it was I who held you back from committing a sin against me. That was why I did not let you touch her. ⁷ But now send back the man's wife; he is a prophet and will intercede on your behalf, and you will live. But if you do not give her back, I tell you that you are doomed to die, you and all your household.'

⁸ Next morning Abimelech rose early and called together all his court officials; when he told them the whole story, the men were terrified. ⁹ Abimelech then summoned Abraham. 'Why have you treated us like this?' he demanded. 'What harm have I done you that you should bring this great sin on me and my kingdom? You have done to me something you ought never to have done.' ¹⁰ And he asked, 'What was your purpose in doing this?' ¹¹ Abraham answered, 'I said to myself, "There is no fear of God in this place, and I shall be killed for the sake of my wife." ¹² She is in fact my sister, my father's daughter though not by my mother, and she became my wife. ¹³ When God set me wandering from my father's house, I said to her, "There

19:22 **Zoar:** *that is* Small.

guarantee the safety of their guests. See Judg. 19.16–24. **24:** *Brimstone:* sulphur, a flammable element found in the area. **26:** *Pillar:* a folk explanation for an oddly shaped column in the area, which is still today associated with Lot's wife.

19.30–38: The origin of the Moabites and Ammonites. The previous episode leads to this story of the unflattering origin of the two traditional enemies of Israel.

20.1–18: Abraham and Sarah at Gerar. God continues to deliver the ancestress of Israel, so that the promise can be realized (see 12.10–20 n.). **1:** *From there:* Mamre (18.1; 19.27); 19.30–38 seem to have been added is a duty towards me which you must loyally fulfil: wherever we go, you must say that I am your brother." ' ¹⁴Then Abimelech took sheep and cattle and male and female slaves and gave them to Abraham. He returned Sarah to him ¹⁵and said, 'My country is at your disposal; settle wherever you please.' ¹⁶To Sarah he said, 'I have given your brother a thousand pieces of silver to compensate you for all that has befallen you; you are completely cleared.' ¹⁷Then Abraham interceded with God, and he healed Abimelech, his wife, and his slave-girls, so that they could have children; ¹⁸for the LORD had made every woman in Abimelech's household barren on account of Sarah, Abraham's wife.

The early years of Isaac

21 THE LORD showed favour to Sarah as he had promised, and made good what he had said about her. ²She conceived and at the time foretold by God she bore a son to Abraham in his old age. ³The son whom Sarah bore to him Abraham named Isaac, ⁴and when Isaac was eight days old Abraham circumcised him, as decreed by God. ⁵Abraham was a hundred years old when his son Isaac was born. ⁶Sarah said, 'God has given me good reason to laugh, and everyone who hears will laugh with me.' ⁷She added, 'Whoever would have told Abraham that Sarah would suckle children? Yet I have borne him a son in his old age.' ⁸The boy grew and was weaned, and on the day of his weaning Abraham gave a great feast.

⁹Sarah saw the son whom Hagar the Egyptian had borne to Abraham playing with Isaac, ¹⁰and she said to Abraham, 'Drive out this slave-girl and her son! I will not have this slave's son sharing the inheritance with my son Isaac.' ¹¹Abraham was very upset at this because of Ishmael, ¹²but God said to him, 'Do not be upset for the boy and your slave-

girl. Do as Sarah says, because it is through Isaac's line that your name will be perpetuated. ¹³I shall make a nation of the slave-girl's son, because he also is your child.'

¹⁴Early next morning Abraham took some food and a full water-skin and gave them to Hagar. He set the child on her shoulder and sent her away, and she wandered about in the wilderness of Beersheba. ¹⁵When the water in the skin was finished, she thrust the child under a bush, ¹⁶then went and sat down some way off, about a bowshot distant. 'How can I watch the child die?' she said, and sat there, weeping bitterly. ¹⁷God heard the child crying, and the angel of God called from heaven to Hagar, 'What is the matter, Hagar? Do not be afraid: God has heard the child crying where you laid him. ¹⁸Go, lift the child and hold him in your arms, because I shall make of him a great nation.' ¹⁹Then God opened her eyes and she saw a well full of water; she went to it, filled the water-skin, and gave the child a drink. ²⁰God was with the child as he grew up. He lived in the wilderness of Paran and became an archer; ²¹and his mother got him a wife from Egypt.

²²About that time Abimelech, with Phicol the commander of his army, said to Abraham: 'God is with you in all that you do. ²³Here and now swear to me in the name of God, that you will not break faith with me or with my children and my descendants. As I have kept faith with you, so must you keep faith with me and with the country where you are living.' ²⁴Abraham said, 'I swear it.'

²⁵It happened that Abraham had a complaint to make to Abimelech about a well which Abimelech's men had seized. ²⁶Abimelech said, 'I do not know who did this. Up to this moment you never mentioned it, nor did I hear of it from anyone else.' ²⁷Then Abraham took sheep and cattle and gave them to Abimelech, and the two of them made a pact. ²⁸Abraham set seven ewe lambs apart, ²⁹and when Abimelech asked him why he had done

intrusively. **12:** Marriage to a half-sister (2 Sam. 13.13) was later forbidden (Lev. 18.11). **18:** Only in the final verse is the LORD identified with the deity of the story (see 14.18 n.; 16.13 n.; 17.1 n.).

21.1–8: The birth of Isaac. The extraordinary miracle of Israel's emergence and survival continues to be emphasized.

21.9–21: The expulsion of Ishmael. The account may be a variant of 16.1–12. **10:** Ancient Near Eastern law stipulated that the offspring of a slave wife could either inherit with the children of the free woman or be set free. Sarah demands the latter option. **17:** *God has heard:* a pun on the name Ishmael; see 16.11 and Tfn. there.

21.22–34: Abraham's dispute with Abimelech. The patriarch obtains property rights in the vicinity of so, [30] he said, 'Accept these seven lambs from me as a testimony on my behalf that I dug this well.' [31] This is why that place was called Beersheba, because there the two of them swore an oath. [32] When they had made the pact at Beersheba, Abimelech departed with Phicol the commander of his army and returned to the country of the Philistines. [33] Abraham planted a tamarisk tree at Beersheba, and there he invoked the LORD, the Everlasting God, by name. [34] He lived as an alien in the country of the Philistines for many years.

22 SOME time later God put Abraham to the test. 'Abraham!' he called to him, and Abraham replied, 'Here I am!' [2] God said, 'Take your son, your one and only son Isaac whom you love, and go to the land of Moriah. There you shall offer him as a sacrifice on one of the heights which I shall show you.' [3] Early in the morning Abraham saddled his donkey, and took with him two of his men and his son Isaac; and having split firewood for the sacrifice, he set out for the place of which God had spoken. [4] On the third day Abraham looked up and saw the shrine in the distance. [5] He said to his men, 'Stay here with the donkey while I and the boy go on ahead. We shall worship there, and then come back to you.'

[6] Abraham took the wood for the sacrifice and put it on his son Isaac's shoulder, while he himself carried the fire and the knife. As the two of them went on together, [7] Isaac spoke. 'Father!' he said. Abraham answered, 'What is it, my son?' Isaac said, 'Here are the fire and the wood, but where is the sheep for a sacrifice?' [8] Abraham answered, 'God will provide himself with a sheep for a sacrifice, my son.' The two of them went on together [9] until they came to the place of which God

had spoken. There Abraham built an altar and arranged the wood. He bound his son Isaac and laid him on the altar on top of the wood. [10] He reached out for the knife to slay his son, [11] but the angel of the LORD called to him from heaven, 'Abraham! Abraham!' He answered, 'Here I am!' [12] The angel said, 'Do not raise your hand against the boy; do not touch him. Now I know that you are a god-fearing man. You have not withheld from me your son, your only son.' [13] Abraham looked round, and there in a thicket he saw a ram caught by its horns. He went, seized the ram, and offered it as a sacrifice instead of his son. [14] Abraham named that shrine 'The LORD will provide'; and to this day the saying is: 'In the mountain of the LORD it was provided.'

[15] Then the angel of the LORD called from heaven a second time to Abraham [16] and said, 'This is the word of the LORD: By my own self I swear that because you have done this and have not withheld your son, your only son, [17] I shall bless you abundantly and make your descendants as numerous as the stars in the sky or the grains of sand on the seashore. Your descendants will possess the cities of their enemies. [18] All nations on earth will wish to be blessed as your descendants are blessed, because you have been obedient to me.'

[19] Abraham then went back to his men, and together they returned to Beersheba; and there Abraham remained.

[20] After this Abraham was told, 'Milcah has borne sons to your brother Nahor: [21] Uz his firstborn, then his brother Buz, and Kemuel father of Aram, [22] and Kesed, Hazo, Pildash, Jidlaph, and Bethuel; [23] and a daughter, Rebecca, has been born to Bethuel.' These eight Milcah bore to Abraham's brother Nahor. [24] His concubine, whose name was Reumah,

21:31 **Beersheba:** *that is* Well of Seven *and* Well of an Oath.   21:33 **tamarisk tree:** *or* strip of ground.

Beersheba, where the origin of an ancient sanctuary is attributed to him (see 12.7 n.). **31:** Two explanations for the name of the place have been combined; see Tfn. **32:** *Philistines:* an anachronism, for they settled in Palestine only later; see 9.27 n. **33:** *The Everlasting God:* an ancient epithet, probably from the pre-Israelite cult at Beersheba, is here applied to the LORD.

22.1–19: The testing of Abraham. At the very moment when the future of Israel seems finally established (21.1–8), it receives its most serious challenge, namely, can Israel continue to keep its identity despite adverse circumstance? **2:** The earliest form of this story may have been directed against child *sacrifice*, proposing that the deity desires the substitution of animals.

22.20–24: Abraham's Aramaean relatives. A league of twelve tribes paralleling the descendants of Ishmael (25.13–15) and Jacob (29.31–30.24; 35.16–20, 23–26) is presented. The list here differs from the Aramaean genealogy in 10.23.

also bore him sons: Tebah, Gaham, Tahash, and Maacah.

23 Sarah lived to be a hundred and twenty-seven years old, [2] and she died in Kiriath-arba (which is Hebron) in Canaan. Abraham went in to mourn over Sarah and to weep for her. [3] When at last he rose and left the presence of his dead one, he approached the Hittites: [4] 'I am an alien and a settler among you,' he said. 'Make over to me some ground among you for a burial-place, that I may bury my dead.' [5] The Hittites answered, [6] 'Listen to us, sir: you are a mighty prince among us; bury your dead in the best grave we have. There is not one of us who would deny you his grave or hinder you from burying your dead.' [7] Abraham rose and bowing low to the Hittites, the people of that region, [8] he said to them, 'If you have a mind to help me about the burial, then listen to me: speak to Ephron son of Zohar on my behalf, [9] and ask him to grant me the cave that belongs to him at Machpelah, at the far end of his land. In your presence let him make it over to me for the full price, so that I may take possession of it as a burial-place.' [10] Ephron was sitting with the other Hittites and in the hearing of all who had assembled at the city gate he gave Abraham this answer: [11] 'No, sir; hear me: I shall make you a gift of the land and also give you the cave which is on it. In the presence of my people I give it to you; so bury your dead.' [12] Abraham bowed low before the people [13] and said to Ephron in their hearing, 'Do you really mean it? But listen to me—let me give you the price of the land: take it from me, and I shall bury my dead there.' [14] Ephron answered, [15] 'Listen, sir: land worth four hundred shekels of silver, what is that between me and you! You may bury your dead there.' [16] Abraham closed the bargain with him and weighed out the amount that Ephron had named in the hearing of the Hittites, four hundred shekels of the standard recognized by merchants.

[17] So the plot of land belonging to Ephron at Machpelah to the east of Mamre, the plot, the cave that is on it, with all the trees in the whole area, became the [18] legal possession of Abraham, in the presence of all the Hittites who had assembled at the city gate. [19] After this Abraham buried his wife Sarah in the cave on the plot of land at Machpelah to the east of Mamre, which is Hebron, in Canaan. [20] Thus, by purchase from the Hittites, the plot and the cave on it became Abraham's possession as a burial-place.

Isaac and Rebecca

24 ABRAHAM was by now a very old man, and the LORD had blessed him in all that he did. [2] Abraham said to the servant who had been longest in his service and was in charge of all he owned, 'Give me your solemn oath: [3] I want you to swear by the LORD, the God of heaven and earth, that you will not take a wife for my son from the women of the Canaanites among whom I am living. [4] You must go to my own country and to my own kindred to find a wife for my son Isaac.' [5] 'What if the woman is unwilling to come with me to this country?' the servant asked. 'Must I take your son back to the land you came from?' [6] Abraham said to him, 'On no account are you to take my son back there. [7] The LORD the God of heaven who took me from my father's house and the land of my birth, the LORD who swore to me that he would give this land to my descendants—he will send his angel before you, and you will take a wife from there for my son. [8] If the woman is unwilling to come with you, then you will be released from your oath to me; only you must not take my son back there.' [9] The servant then put his hand under his master Abraham's thigh and swore that oath.

[10] The servant chose ten camels from his master's herds and, with all kinds of gifts from his master, he went to Aram-naharaim, to the town where Nahor lived. [11] Towards

24:2 **Give . . . oath:** *lit.* Put your hand under my thigh.

23.1–20: The tomb of the ancestors. 3: The *Hittites*, originally from Asia Minor, were part of the pre-Israelite population of Canaan (see 10.15 and Tfn. there). **11–18:** This marks another development in the ancestral claim to the land (see 21.22–34 n.).

24.1–67: Isaac and Rebecca. 2: The significance of Abraham's request that the servant place his hand under Abraham's thigh (see Tfn.) is not clear. The thigh may be a euphemism for the male organ. Such an act accompanied the making of a *solemn oath.* **3:** The fear is not that of the mixing of people but of religious deterioration; see Exod. 34.15–16; Deut. 7.3–4. **10:** *Aram-naharaim:* central Mesopotamia.

evening, the time when the women go out to draw water, he made the camels kneel down by the well outside the town. 12'Lord God of my master Abraham,' he said, 'give me good fortune this day; keep faith with my master Abraham. 13 Here I am by the spring, as the women of the town come out to draw water. 14 I shall say to a girl, "Please lower your jar so that I may drink"; and if she answers, "Drink, and I shall water your camels also," let that be the girl whom you intend for your servant Isaac. In this way I shall know that you have kept faith with my master.'

15 Before he had finished praying, he saw Rebecca coming out with her water-jar on her shoulder. She was the daughter of Bethuel son of Milcah, the wife of Abraham's brother Nahor. 16 The girl was very beautiful and a virgin guiltless of intercourse with any man. She went down to the spring, filled her jar, and came up again. 17 Abraham's servant hurried to meet her and said, 'Will you give me a little water from your jar?' 18'Please drink, sir,' she answered, and at once lowered her jar on to her hand to let him drink. 19 When she had finished giving him a drink, she said, 'I shall draw water for your camels also until they have had enough.' 20 She quickly emptied her jar into the water trough, and then hurrying again to the well she drew water and watered all the camels. 21 The man was watching quietly to see whether or not the Lord had made his journey successful, 22 and when the camels had finished drinking, he took a gold nose-ring weighing half a shekel, and two bracelets for her wrists weighing ten shekels, also of gold. 23'Tell me, please, whose daughter you are,' he said. 'Is there room in your father's house for us to spend the night?' 24 She answered, 'I am the daughter of Bethuel son of Nahor and Milcah; 25 we have plenty of straw and fodder and also room for you to spend the night.' 26 So the man bowed down and prostrated himself before the Lord 27 and said, 'Blessed be the Lord the God of my master Abraham. His faithfulness to my master has been constant and unfailing, for he has guided me to the house of my master's kinsman.'

28 The girl ran to her mother's house and told them what had happened. 29-30 Rebecca

had a brother named Laban, and, when he saw the nose-ring, and also the bracelets on his sister's wrists, and heard his sister Rebecca's account of what the man had said to her, he hurried out to the spring. When he got there he found the man still standing by the camels. 31'Come in,' he said, 'you whom the Lord has blessed. Why are you staying out here? I have prepared the house and there is a place for the camels.' 32 The man went into the house, while the camels were unloaded and provided with straw and fodder, and water was brought for him and his men to bathe their feet. 33 But when food was set before him, he protested, 'I will not eat until I have delivered my message.' Laban said, 'Let us hear it.'

34'I am Abraham's servant,' he answered. 35'The Lord has greatly blessed my master, and he has become a wealthy man: the Lord has given him flocks and herds, silver and gold, male and female slaves, camels and donkeys. 36 My master's wife Sarah in her old age bore him a son, to whom he has assigned all that he has. 37 My master made me swear an oath, saying, "You must not take a wife for my son from the women of the Canaanites in whose land I am living; 38 but go to my father's home, to my family, to get a wife for him." 39 I asked, "What if the woman will not come with me?" 40 He answered, "The Lord, in whose presence I have lived, will send his angel with you and make your journey successful. You are to take a wife for my son from my family and from my father's house; 41 then you will be released from the charge I have laid upon you. But if, when you come to my family, they refuse to give her to you, you will likewise be released from the charge."

42'Today when I came to the spring, I prayed, "Lord God of my master Abraham, if you will make my journey successful, let it turn out in this way: 43 here I am by the spring; when a young woman comes out to draw water, I shall say to her, 'Give me a little water from your jar to drink.' 44 If she answers, 'Yes, do drink, and I shall draw water for your camels as well,' she is the woman whom the Lord intends for my master's son." 45 Before I had finished praying, I saw Rebecca coming out with her water-jar on

14: It was a common ancient assumption that the will of the deity would be revealed through such possible incidents; see 1 Sam. 14.6–10; Judg. 6.36–37. 57–58: Nuzi Texts (see 15.2–3 n.) show that asking the her shoulder. She went down to the spring and drew water, and I said to her, "Will you please give me a drink?" 46 At once she lowered her jar from her shoulder and said, "Drink; and I shall also water your camels." So I drank, and she also gave the camels water. 47 I asked her whose daughter she was, and she said, "I am the daughter of Bethuel son of Nahor and Milcah." Then I put the ring in her nose and the bracelets on her wrists, 48 and I bowed low in worship before the Lord. I blessed the Lord, the God of my master Abraham, who had led me by the right road to take my master's niece for his son. 49 Now tell me if you mean to deal loyally and faithfully with my master. If not, say so, and I shall turn elsewhere.'

50 Laban and Bethuel replied, 'Since this is from the Lord, we can say nothing for or against it. 51 Here is Rebecca; take her and go. She shall be the wife of your master's son, as the Lord has decreed.' 52 When Abraham's servant heard what they said, he prostrated himself on the ground before the Lord. 53 Then he brought out silver and gold ornaments, and articles of clothing, and gave them to Rebecca, and he gave costly gifts to her brother and her mother. 54 He and his men then ate and drank and spent the night there.

When they rose in the morning, Abraham's servant said, 'Give me leave to go back to my master.' 55 Rebecca's brother and her mother replied, 'Let the girl stay with us for a few days, say ten days, and then she can go.' 56 But he said to them, 'Do not detain me, for it is the Lord who has granted me success. Give me leave to go back to my master.' 57 They said, 'Let us call the girl and see what she says.' 58 They called Rebecca and asked her if she would go with the man, and she answered, 'Yes, I will go.' 59 So they let their sister Rebecca and her maid go with Abraham's servant and his men. 60 They blessed Rebecca and said to her:

'You are our sister, may you be the
    mother of many children;
may your sons possess the cities of their
    enemies.'

61 Rebecca and her companions mounted their camels to follow the man. So the servant took Rebecca and set out.

62 Isaac meanwhile had moved on as far as Beer-lahai-roi and was living in the Negeb. 63 One evening when he had gone out into the open country hoping to meet them, he looked and saw camels approaching. 64 When Rebecca saw Isaac, she dismounted from her camel, 65 saying to the servant, 'Who is that man walking across the open country towards us?' When the servant answered, 'It is my master,' she took her veil and covered herself. 66 The servant related to Isaac all that had happened. 67 Isaac conducted her into the tent and took her as his wife. So she became his wife, and he loved her and was consoled for the death of his mother.

25 ABRAHAM married another wife, whose name was Keturah. 2 She bore him Zimran, Jokshan, Medan, Midian, Ishbak, and Shuah. 3 Jokshan became the father of Sheba and Dedan. The descendants of Dedan were the Asshurim, Letushim, and Leummim, 4 and the sons of Midian were Ephah, Epher, Enoch, Abida, and Eldaah. All these were descendants of Keturah.

5 Abraham had assigned all that he possessed to Isaac; 6 and he had already in his lifetime made gifts to his sons by his concubines and had sent them away eastwards, to a land of the east, out of his son Isaac's way. 7 Abraham had lived for a hundred and seventy-five years 8 when he breathed his last. He died at a great age, a full span of years, and was gathered to his forefathers. 9 His sons, Isaac and Ishmael, buried him in the cave at Machpelah, on the land of Ephron son of Zohar the Hittite, east of Mamre, 10 the plot which Abraham had bought from the Hittites. There Abraham was buried with his wife Sarah. 11 After the death of Abraham, God blessed his son Isaac, who settled close by Beer-lahai-roi.

12 This is the table of the descendants of Abraham's son Ishmael, whom Hagar the

24:63 **hoping to meet them:** *Heb. uncertain.*
24:67 **into the tent:** *prob. rdg; Heb. adds* Sarah his mother.

consent of the girl in such a situation was not unique among the people of this area. **62:** *Beer-lahai-roi:* see 16.13–14 n. and Tfn. at 16.14.

25.1–18: The death of Abraham. 1–6: This section may be out of place, for Abraham in 24.1 is already a very old man, and in 25.8 seems to be on his deathbed. **9–10:** *Machpelah:* see 23.8–20.

Egyptian, Sarah's slave-girl, bore to him.
[13] These are the names of the sons of Ishmael listed in order of their birth: Nebaioth, Ishmael's eldest son, then Kedar, Adbeel, Mibsam, [14] Mishma, Dumah, Massa, [15] Hadad, Tema, Jetur, Naphish, and Kedemah. [16] These are the sons of Ishmael, after whom their hamlets and encampments were named, twelve princes according to their tribes. [17] Ishmael had lived for a hundred and thirty-seven years when he breathed his last. So he died and was gathered to his forefathers. [18] Ishmael's sons inhabited the land from Havilah to Shur, which is east of Egypt on the way to Asshur; he himself had settled to the east of his brothers.

[19] This is an account of the descendants of Abraham's son Isaac. Isaac's father was Abraham. [20] When Isaac was forty years old he married Rebecca daughter of Bethuel, the Aramaean from Paddan-aram and sister of Laban the Aramaean. [21] Isaac appealed to the LORD on behalf of his wife because she was childless; the LORD gave heed to his entreaty, and Rebecca conceived. [22] The children pressed on each other in her womb, and she said, 'If all is well, why am I like this?' She went to seek guidance of the LORD, [23] who said to her:

> 'Two nations are in your womb,
>   two peoples going their own ways from
>   birth.
> One will be stronger than the other;
>   the elder will be servant to the
>   younger.'

[24] When her time had come, there were indeed twins in her womb. [25] The first to come out was reddish and covered with hairs like a cloak, and they named him Esau. [26] Imme-diately afterwards his brother was born with his hand grasping Esau's heel, and he was given the name Jacob. Isaac was sixty years old when they were born. [27] As the boys grew up, Esau became a skilful hunter, an outdoor man, while Jacob lived quietly among the tents. [28] Isaac favoured Esau because he kept him supplied with game, but Rebecca favoured Jacob. [29] One day Jacob was preparing broth when Esau came in from the country, exhausted. [30] He said to Jacob, 'I am exhausted; give me a helping of that red broth.' This is why he was called Edom. [31] Jacob retorted, 'Not till you sell me your rights as the firstborn.' [32] Esau replied, 'Here I am at death's door; what use is a birthright to me?' [33] Jacob said, 'First give me your oath!' So he gave him his oath and sold his birthright to Jacob. [34] Then Jacob gave Esau bread and some lentil broth, and he ate and drank and went his way. Esau showed by this how little he valued his birthright.

Isaac at Gerar and Beersheba

26 THE land was stricken by a famine — not the earlier famine which happened in Abraham's time — and Isaac went to Abimelech the Philistine king at Gerar. [2] The LORD appeared to Isaac and said, 'Do not go down to Egypt, but stay in this country as I bid you. [3] Stay here and I shall be with you and bless you, for to you and to your descendants I shall give all these lands, so fulfilling the oath which I swore to your father Abraham. [4] I shall make your descendants as numerous as the stars in the heavens, and give them all these lands. All the nations of the

25:26 **Jacob:** *that is* He caught by the heel *or* He supplanted.   25:30 **Edom:** *that is* Red.

16: The *sons* number *twelve*; see 22.20–24 n.
   25.19–34: The birth of Jacob (Israel) and his rivalry with Esau (Edom). **20:** *Paddan-aram:* a variant of Aram-naharaim; see 24.10 n. **21:** The repetition of the barrenness motif is another means of emphasizing the difficulties Israel would encounter in realizing the divine promise. **23:** The firstborn had exclusive rights of inheritance, and hence an unexpected reversal is here proposed. **25:** The Heb. word for *reddish* (*admoni*) is a play on Edom (v. 30), as *hairs* (*se'ar*) is on Seir (32.3). **26:** *Jacob* is explained by folk etymology. The name may actually have meant "Let (God) protect." **27:** The two typify the ways of life of the peoples whom they represent. **30:** In actuality, the name Edom may derive from the characteristic redness of the soil of the area. **31:** Specifically, the *rights* of the *firstborn* included a double share of the inheritance (Deut. 21.15–17). **33:** The intent is to explain how, in the mystery of God's providence, Israel flourished while their close kinsmen, the Edomites, did not. The latter, subdued by David (2 Sam. 8.13–14), were apparently securely established in their area before Israel (Num. 20.14–21; compare Gen. 36.31).

earth will wish to be blessed as they are blessed, [5] because Abraham obeyed me and kept my charge, my commandments, statutes, and laws.'

[6] Isaac settled in Gerar, and, [7] when the men of the place asked questions about his wife, he told them that she was his sister, for he was afraid to say Rebecca was his wife, in case they murdered him because of her; for she was very beautiful. [8] But when they had been there some considerable time, Abimelech the Philistine king looked down from his window and there was Isaac caressing his wife Rebecca. [9] He summoned Isaac and said, 'So she is your wife! What made you say she was your sister?' Isaac answered, 'I thought I should be put to death because of her.' [10] Abimelech said, 'Why have you treated us like this? One of the people might easily have lain with your wife, and then you would have made us incur guilt.' [11] Abimelech warned all the people that whoever harmed this man or his wife would be put to death.

[12] Isaac sowed seed in that land, and the same year he reaped a hundredfold. The LORD had blessed him, [13] and he became more and more wealthy, until he was very prosperous indeed. [14] He had flocks and herds and many slaves, so that the Philistines were envious of him. [15] They stopped up and filled with earth all the wells dug by the slaves in the days of Isaac's father Abraham. [18] Isaac reopened the wells which were dug in the lifetime of his father Abraham and stopped up by the Philistines after his death. He called them by the names which his father had given them.

[16] Then Abimelech said to him, 'Go, leave us; you have become too powerful for us.' [17] When Isaac left that place, he encamped in the wadi of Gerar, and stayed there. [19] Then Isaac's slaves dug in the wadi and found a spring of running water, [20] but the shepherds of Gerar quarrelled with Isaac's shepherds, claiming the water as theirs. He called the well Esek, because they made difficulties for him. [21] His men then dug another well, but a quarrel arose over that also, so he called it Sitnah. [22] He moved on from there and dug another well; over that there was no dispute, so he called it Rehoboth, saying, 'Now the LORD has given us room and our people will become more numerous in the land.'

[23] From there Isaac went up country to Beersheba; [24] that same night the LORD appeared to him. 'I am the God of your father Abraham,' he said; 'I am with you, so do not be afraid. I shall bless you and give you many descendants for the sake of my servant Abraham.' [25] Isaac built an altar there and invoked the LORD by name. He pitched his tent, and there also his slaves dug a well.

[26] Abimelech came to him from Gerar with Ahuzzath his friend and Phicol the commander of his army. [27] Isaac said to them, 'Why have you come here to me? You were ill-disposed towards me and sent me away from your midst.' [28] They answered, 'We have realized that the LORD is with you, and we propose that the two of us should bind each other by oath and make a pact. [29] You are to do us no harm, just as we have in no way molested you. We were always ready to do you a good turn and we let you go away peaceably. Now the LORD has prospered you.' [30] Isaac then gave a feast for them, and they ate and drank. [31] Early next morning they exchanged oaths, and after Isaac bade them farewell, they parted from him in peace. [32] The same day Isaac's slaves came and told him about a well they had dug: 'We have found water,' they told him. [33] He named the well Shibah; this is why the city is called Beersheba to this day.

[34] When Esau was forty years old he married Judith daughter of Beeri the Hittite, and Basemath daughter of Elon the Hittite; [35] this was a source of bitter grief to Isaac and Rebecca.

Jacob and Esau

27 WHEN Isaac grew old and his eyes had become so dim that he could not see, he called for his elder son Esau. 'My son!' he said. Esau answered, 'Here I am.' [2] Isaac said, 'Listen now: I am old and I do not know when I may die. [3] Take your hunting gear,

26:15–19 *Verse 18 transposed to follow 15.*
26:20 **Esek:** *that is* Difficulty.   26:21 **Sitnah:** *that is* Enmity.   26:22 **Rehoboth:** *that is* Roominess.
26:33 **Shibah:** *that is* Oath. **Beersheba:** *that is* Well of an Oath.

26.1–35: Isaac at Gerar. 1: *Earlier famine:* 12.10. **7–11:** Again, the ancestress is rescued, and the promise is kept alive; see 12.10–20 n. **28–31:** The promise of 12.3 is further realized in that the ancestral claim to the land is widened. **33:** *Shibah:* there is a duplicate tradition in 21.31.

your quiver and bow, and go out into the country and get me some game. 4 Then make me a savoury dish, the kind I like, and bring it for me to eat so that I may give you my blessing before I die.'

5 Now Rebecca had been listening as Isaac talked to his son Esau. When Esau went off into the country to hunt game for his father, 6 she said to her son Jacob, 'I have just overheard your father say to your brother Esau, 7 "Bring me some game and make a savoury dish for me to eat so that I may bless you in the presence of the LORD before I die." 8 Listen now to me, my son, and do what I tell you. 9 Go to the flock and pick me out two fine young kids, and I shall make them into a savoury dish for your father, the kind he likes. 10 Then take it in to your father to eat so that he may bless you before he dies.' 11 'But my brother Esau is a hairy man,' Jacob said to his mother Rebecca, 'and my skin is smooth. 12 Suppose my father touches me; he will know that I am playing a trick on him and I shall bring a curse instead of a blessing on myself.' 13 His mother answered, 'Let any curse for you fall on me, my son. Do as I say; go and fetch me the kids.' 14 So Jacob went and got them and brought them to his mother, who made them into a savoury dish such as his father liked. 15 Rebecca then took her elder son's clothes, Esau's best clothes which she had by her in the house, and put them on Jacob her younger son. 16 She put the goatskins on his hands and on the smooth nape of his neck. 17 Then she handed to her son Jacob the savoury dish and the bread she had made.

18 He went in to his father and said, 'Father!' Isaac answered, 'Yes, my son; which are you?' 19 Jacob answered, 'I am Esau, your elder son. I have done as you told me. Come, sit up and eat some of the game I have for you and then give me your blessing.' 20 Isaac said, 'How did you find it so quickly, my son?' Jacob answered, 'Because the LORD your God put it in my way.' 21 Isaac then said to Jacob, 'Come close and let me touch you, my son, to make sure that you are my son Esau.' 22 When Jacob came close to his father, Isaac felt him and said, 'The voice is Jacob's voice, but the hands are the hands of Esau.' 23 He did not recognize him, because his hands were hairy like Esau's, and so he blessed him.

24 He asked, 'Are you really my son Esau?' and when he answered, 'Yes, I am,' 25 Isaac said, 'Bring me some of the game to eat, my son, so that I may give you my blessing.' Jacob brought it to him, and he ate; he brought him wine also, and he drank it. 26 Then his father said to him, 'Come near, my son, and kiss me.' 27 So he went near and kissed him, and when Isaac smelt the smell of his clothes, he blessed him and said, 'The smell of my son is like the smell of open country blessed by the LORD.

28 'God give you dew from heaven
and the richness of the earth,
corn and new wine in plenty!
29 May peoples serve you
and nations bow down to you.
May you be lord over your brothers,
and may your mother's sons bow down
to you.
A curse on those who curse you,
but a blessing on those who bless you!'

30 Isaac finished blessing Jacob, who had scarcely left his father's presence when his brother Esau came in from hunting. 31 He too prepared a savoury dish and brought it to his father. He said, 'Come, father, eat some of the game I have for you, and then give me your blessing.' 32 'Who are you?' his father Isaac asked him. 'I am Esau, your elder son,' he replied. 33 Then Isaac, greatly agitated, said, 'Then who was it that hunted game and brought it to me? I ate it just before you came in, and I blessed him, and the blessing will stand.' 34 When Esau heard this, he lamented loudly and bitterly. 'Father, bless me too,' he begged. 35 But Isaac said, 'Your brother came full of deceit and took your blessing.' 36 'He is not called Jacob for nothing,' said Esau. 'This is the second time he has supplanted me. He took away my right as the firstborn, and now he has taken away my blessing. Have you kept back any blessing for me?' 37 Isaac answered, 'I have made him lord over you and set all his brothers under him. I have bestowed upon him grain and new wine for his sustenance. What is there left that I can do for you, my son?' 38 Esau asked, 'Had you

27:5 **for his father:** *so Gk; Heb.* to bring.
27:36 **Jacob:** *that is* He caught by the heel *or* He supplanted.

27.1–45: Jacob obtains his father's blessing. 4: Deathbed blessings play an important role in the literature then only one blessing, father? Bless me, too, my father.' Esau wept bitterly, ³⁹ and his father Isaac answered:

'Your dwelling will be far from the
    richness of the earth,
far from the dew of heaven above.
⁴⁰ By your sword you will live,
    and you will serve your brother.
But the time will come when you grow
    restive
and break his yoke from your neck.'

⁴¹ Esau harboured a grudge against Jacob because of the blessing which his father had given him, and he said to himself, 'The time of mourning for my father will soon be here; then I am going to kill my brother Jacob.' ⁴² When Rebecca was told what her elder son Esau was planning, she called Jacob, her younger son, and said to him, 'Your brother Esau is threatening to kill you. ⁴³ Now, my son, listen to me. Be off at once to my brother Laban in Harran, ⁴⁴ and stay with him for a while until your brother's anger cools. ⁴⁵ When it has died down and he has forgotten what you did to him, I will send and fetch you back. Why should I lose you both in one day?'

⁴⁶ Rebecca said to Isaac, 'I am weary to death of Hittite women! If Jacob marries a Hittite woman like those who live here, my
28 life will not be worth living.' ¹ So Isaac called Jacob, and after blessing him, gave him these instructions: 'You are not to marry a Canaanite woman. ² Go now to the home of Bethuel, your mother's father, in Paddan-aram, and there find a wife, one of the daughters of Laban, your mother's brother. ³ May God Almighty bless you; may he make you fruitful and increase your descendants until they become a community of nations. ⁴ May he bestow on you and your offspring the blessing given to Abraham, that you may possess the land where you are now living, and which God assigned to Abraham!' ⁵ Then Isaac sent Jacob away, and he went to

Paddan-aram to Laban, son of Bethuel the Aramaean and brother of Rebecca, the mother of Jacob and Esau.

⁶ Esau learnt that Isaac had given Jacob his blessing and had sent him away to Paddan-aram to find a wife there, that when he blessed him he had forbidden him to marry a Canaanite woman, ⁷ and that Jacob had obeyed his father and mother and gone to Paddan-aram. ⁸ Seeing that his father disliked Canaanite women, ⁹ Esau went to Ishmael, and, in addition to his other wives, married Mahalath sister of Nebaioth and daughter of Abraham's son Ishmael.

¹⁰ Jacob set out from Beersheba and journeyed towards Harran. ¹¹ He came to a certain shrine and, because the sun had gone down, he stopped for the night. He took one of the stones there and, using it as a pillow under his head, he lay down to sleep. ¹² In a dream he saw a ladder, which rested on the ground with its top reaching to heaven, and angels of God were going up and down on it. ¹³ The LORD was standing beside him saying, 'I am the LORD, the God of your father Abraham and the God of Isaac. This land on which you are lying I shall give to you and your descendants. ¹⁴ They will be countless as the specks of dust on the ground, and you will spread far and wide, to west and east, to north and south. All the families of the earth will wish to be blessed as you and your descendants are blessed. ¹⁵ I shall be with you to protect you wherever you go, and I shall bring you back to this land. I shall not leave you until I have done what I have promised you.'

¹⁶ When Jacob woke from his sleep he said, 'Truly the LORD is in this place, and I did not know it.' ¹⁷ He was awestruck and said, 'How awesome is this place! This is none other than the house of God; it is the gateway to heaven.' ¹⁸ Early in the morning, when Jacob awoke, he took the stone on which his head had rested, and set it up as a sacred pillar, pour-

28:13 **beside him:** or above it.

of ancient Israel (48.10–20; 49.1–27). **33–35:** Blessing or curse, once uttered, could not be revoked. **40:** During the Solomonic period (1 Kgs. 11.14–25), Edom revolted against Israelite domination.
27.46–28.22: Jacob's flight and dream at Bethel. The origin of this ancient Canaanite sanctuary is in this section traced to Israel's ancestor, Jacob (12.7 n.; 21.22–34 n.). **28.1–2:** See 24.3 n. **12:** In ancient belief, deities revealed themselves by dream at sacred sites (see 1 Sam. 3.1–14). Mesopotamians described their temple towers in similar terms; see 11.4 n. **13:** The LORD is here identified both as the traditional deity of the site and as the deity of the ancestors (see Exod. 3.15). **18:** The *pouring* of *oil* on an object or person conferred

ing oil over it. ¹⁹ He named that place Beth-el; but the earlier name of the town was Luz.

²⁰ Jacob made this vow: 'If God will be with me, if he will protect me on my journey and give me food to eat and clothes to wear, ²¹ so that I come back safely to my father's house, then the LORD shall be my God, ²² and this stone which I have set up as a sacred pillar shall be a house of God. And of all that you give me, I shall allot a tenth part to you.'

29 JACOB, continuing his journey, came to the land of the eastern tribes. ² There he saw a well in the open country with three flocks of sheep lying beside it, because flocks were watered from that well. Over its mouth was a huge stone, ³ and all the herdsmen used to gather there and roll it off the mouth of the well and water the flocks; then they would replace the stone over the well. ⁴ Jacob said to them, 'Where are you from, my friends?' 'We are from Harran,' they replied. ⁵ He asked them if they knew Laban the grandson of Nahor. They answered, 'Yes, we do.' ⁶ 'Is he well?' Jacob asked; and they answered, 'Yes, he is well, and there is his daughter Rachel coming with the flock.' ⁷ Jacob said, 'It is still broad daylight, and not yet time for penning the sheep. Water the flocks and then go and let them graze.' ⁸ But they replied, 'We cannot, until all the herdsmen have assembled and the stone has been rolled away from the mouth of the well; then we can water our flocks.' ⁹ While he was talking to them, Rachel arrived with her father's flock, for she was a shepherdess. ¹⁰ Immediately Jacob saw Rachel, the daughter of Laban his mother's brother, with Laban's flock, he went forward, rolled the stone off the mouth of the well and watered Laban's sheep. ¹¹ He kissed Rachel, and was moved to tears. ¹² When he told her that he was her father's kinsman, Rebecca's son, she ran and told her father. ¹³ No sooner had Laban heard the news of his sister's son Jacob, than he hurried to meet him, embraced and kissed him, and welcomed him to his home. Jacob told Laban all that had hap-

pened, ¹⁴ and Laban said, 'Yes, you are my own flesh and blood.'

After Jacob had stayed with him for a whole month, ¹⁵ Laban said to him, 'Why should you work for me for nothing simply because you are my kinsman? Tell me what wage you would settle for.' ¹⁶ Now Laban had two daughters: the elder was called Leah, and the younger Rachel. ¹⁷ Leah was dull-eyed, but Rachel was beautiful in both face and figure, and ¹⁸ Jacob had fallen in love with her. He said, 'For your younger daughter Rachel I would work seven years.' ¹⁹ Laban replied, 'It is better that I should give her to you than to anyone else; stay with me.' ²⁰ When Jacob had worked seven years for Rachel, and they seemed like a few days because he loved her, ²¹ he said to Laban, 'I have served my time. Give me my wife that I may lie with her.' ²² Laban brought all the people of the place together and held a wedding feast. ²³ In the evening he took his daughter Leah and brought her to Jacob, and he lay with her. ²⁴ At the same time Laban gave his slave-girl Zilpah to his daughter Leah. ²⁵ But when morning came, there was Leah! Jacob said to Laban, 'What is this you have done to me? It was for Rachel I worked. Why have you played this trick on me?' ²⁶ Laban answered, 'It is against the custom of our country to marry off the younger sister before the elder. ²⁷ Go through with the seven days' feast for the elder, and the younger shall be given you in return for a further seven years' work.' ²⁸ Jacob agreed, and completed the seven days for Leah.

Then Laban gave Jacob his daughter Rachel to be his wife; ²⁹ and to serve Rachel he gave his slave-girl Bilhah. ³⁰ Jacob lay with Rachel also; he loved her rather than Leah, and he worked for Laban for a further seven years. ³¹ When the LORD saw that Leah was unloved, he granted her a child, but Rachel remained childless. ³² Leah conceived and gave birth to a son; and she called him Reu-

28:19 **Beth-el:** *that is* House of God.   29:5 **grandson:** *lit.* son.   29:32 **Reuben:** *that is* See, a son.

extraordinary, often sacred, status. **19:** *Beth-el*, the name of an ancient Canaanite deity (Jer. 48.13), is likely the actual source of the place name, rather than the folk etymology given here.

29.1–31.55: Jacob at Harran. 1: *Eastern tribes:* a general designation for Mesopotamia. **8:** Bedouin custom demanded that all rightful parties be present when the well was opened, so that the water would be distributed fairly. **23:** Likely, the deception was possible because of a veil (24.65). **29.31–30.24:** The origin of the twelve tribes of Israel is presented in terms of the birth of Jacob's sons; see 22.20–24 n. Each name is explained by ben, for she said, 'The LORD has seen my humiliation, but now my husband will love me.' 33 Again she conceived and had a son and said, 'The LORD, hearing that I am unloved, has given me this child also'; and she called him Simeon. 34 She conceived again and had a son and said, 'Now that I have borne him three sons my husband will surely be attached to me.' So she called him Levi. 35 Once more she conceived and had a son, and said, 'Now I shall praise the LORD'; therefore she named him Judah. Then for a while she bore no more children.

30 When Rachel found that she bore Jacob no children, she became jealous of her sister and complained to Jacob, 'Give me sons, or I shall die!' 2 Jacob said angrily to Rachel, 'Can I take the place of God, who has denied you children?' 3 'Here is my slave-girl Bilhah,' she replied. 'Lie with her, so that she may bear sons to be laid upon my knees, and through her I too may build up a family.' 4 When she gave him her slave-girl Bilhah as a wife, Jacob lay with her, 5 and she conceived and bore him a son. 6 Then Rachel said, 'God has given judgement for me; he has indeed heard me and given me a son'; so she named him Dan. 7 Rachel's slave-girl Bilhah conceived again and bore Jacob another son. 8 Rachel said, 'I have devised a fine trick against my sister, and it has succeeded'; so she named him Naphtali.

9 When Leah found that she had stopped bearing children, she took her slave-girl Zilpah and gave her to Jacob as a wife, 10 and Zilpah, Leah's slave-girl, bore Jacob a son. 11 Leah said, 'Good fortune has come,' and she named him Gad. 12 Zilpah bore Jacob another son, 13 and Leah said, 'Happiness has come, for women will call me happy'; so she named him Asher.

14 Once at the time of the wheat harvest when Reuben was out in the open country he found some mandrakes and brought them to Leah his mother. Rachel asked Leah for some of her son's mandrakes, 15 but Leah said, 'Is it not enough to have taken away my husband, that you should take these mandrakes as well?' Rachel said, 'Very well, in exchange for your son's mandrakes let Jacob sleep with you tonight.' 16 In the evening, when Jacob came in from the country Leah went out to meet him. 'You are to sleep with me tonight,' she told him. 'I have hired you with my son's mandrakes.' He slept with her that night, 17 and God heard Leah's prayer, so that she conceived and bore a fifth son to Jacob. 18 Leah said, 'God has rewarded me, because I gave my slave-girl to my husband'; so she named him Issachar. 19 Leah conceived again and bore a sixth son. 20 She said, 'God has endowed me with a noble dowry. Now my husband will honour me like a princess, because I have borne him six sons'; so she named him Zebulun. 21 Later she bore a daughter whom she named Dinah. 22 Then God took thought for Rachel; he heard her prayer and gave her a child. 23 After she conceived and bore a son, she said, 'God has taken away my humiliation.' 24 She named him Joseph, saying, 'May the Lord add another son to me!'

25 After Rachel had given birth to Joseph, Jacob said to Laban, 'Send me on my way, for I want to return to my own home and country. 26 Give me my wives and children for whom I have served you, and I shall go; you know what service I have rendered you.' 27 Laban answered, 'I should like to say this— I have become prosperous and the LORD has blessed me through you. 28 So now tell me what wages I owe you, and I shall give you them.' 29 'You know how I have served you,' replied Jacob, 'and how your herds have prospered under my care. 30 The few you had when I came have increased beyond measure, and wherever I went the LORD brought you blessings. But is it not time for me to make provision for my family?' 31 Laban said, 'Then what shall I give you?' 'Nothing at all,' answered Jacob; 'I will tend your flocks and be in charge of them as before, if you will do what I suggest. 32 I shall go through your flocks today and pick out from them every black lamb, and all the brindled and the spotted goats, and they will be my

29:33 **Simeon:** *that is* Hearing.   29:34 **Levi:** *that is* Attachment.   29:35 **Judah:** *that is* Praise.
30:6 **Dan:** *that is* He has given judgement.
30:8 **Naphtali:** *that is* Trickery.   30:11 **Gad:** *that is* Good Fortune.   30:13 **Asher:** *that is* Happy.
30:18 **Issachar:** *that is* Reward.   30:20 **Zebulun:** *that is* Prince.   30:24 **Joseph:** *that is* May he add.
30:32 **from them:** *so Gk; Heb.* adds every spotted and brindled sheep and.

folk etymology involving a wordplay (see Tfns.). **30.14:** In antiquity these plants were widely regarded as aphrodisiacs, that is, they stimulated passion. The word in Heb. resembles the Heb. word for "love." **27:** *Through you:* possibly an echo of the promise in 12.3; see Tfn. at 12.3. **32:** Since sheep in the area are usually wages. ³³ This is a fair offer, and it will be to my own disadvantage later on, when we come to settling my wages: any goat amongst mine that is not spotted or brindled and any lamb that is not black will have been stolen.' ³⁴ Laban agreed: 'Let it be as you say.'

³⁵ But that same day Laban removed the he-goats that were striped and brindled and all the spotted and brindled she-goats, all that had any white on them, and every ram that was black, and he handed them over to his sons. ³⁶ Then he put a distance of three days' journey between himself and Jacob, while Jacob was tending the rest of Laban's flocks. ³⁷ So Jacob took fresh rods of poplar, almond, and plane trees, and peeled off strips of bark, exposing the white of the rods. ³⁸ He fixed the peeled rods upright in the troughs at the watering-places where the flocks came to drink, so that they were facing the she-goats that were in heat when they came to drink. ³⁹ They mated beside the rods and gave birth to young that were striped and spotted and brindled. ⁴⁰ The rams Jacob separated, and let the ewes run only with such of the rams in Laban's flocks as were striped and black; and thus he built up flocks for himself, which he did not add to Laban's sheep. ⁴¹ As for the goats, whenever the more vigorous were in heat, he set the rods in front of them at the troughs so that they mated beside the rods. ⁴² He did not put them there for the weaker goats, and in this way the weaker came to be Laban's and the stronger Jacob's. ⁴³ So Jacob's wealth increased more and more until he possessed great flocks, as well as male and female slaves, camels, and donkeys.

31 JACOB learnt that Laban's sons were saying, 'Jacob has taken everything that our father had, and all his wealth has come from our father's property.' ² He noticed also that Laban was not so well disposed to him as he had once been. ³ The LORD said to Jacob, 'Go back to the land of your fathers and to your kindred; I shall be with you,' ⁴ and Jacob sent word to Rachel and Leah to come out to where his flocks were in the country. ⁵ He said to them, 'I have been notic-

ing that your father is not so friendly to me as once he was. But the God of my father has been with me. ⁶ You yourselves know I have served your father to the best of my ability, ⁷ yet he has cheated me and changed my wages ten times over. But God did not let him do me any harm. ⁸ If your father said, "The spotted ones are to be your wages," then all the flock bore spotted young; and if he said, "The striped ones are to be your wages," then all the flock bore striped young. ⁹ It is God who has taken away your father's livestock and given them to me. ¹⁰ In the season when the flocks were in heat, I had a dream in which I saw that the he-goats which were mating were striped and spotted and dappled. ¹¹ The angel of God called to me in the dream, "Jacob!" and I replied, "Here I am!" ¹² He said, "See what is happening: all the he-goats mating are striped and spotted and dappled, for I have seen all that Laban has been doing to you. ¹³ I am the God of Bethel where you anointed a sacred pillar and made a vow to me. Now leave this country at once and return to your native land." ' ¹⁴ Rachel and Leah answered him, 'We no longer have any share in our father's house. ¹⁵ Does he not look on us as strangers, now that he has sold us and used the money paid for us? ¹⁶ All the wealth which God has saved from our father's clutches is surely ours and our children's. Now do whatever God has told you to do.' ¹⁷ At once Jacob put his sons and his wives on camels, ¹⁸ and he drove off all the cattle and other livestock which he had acquired in Paddan-aram, to go to his father Isaac in Canaan.

¹⁹ When Laban had gone to shear his sheep, Rachel stole the household gods belonging to her father. ²⁰ Jacob hoodwinked Laban the Aramaean and kept his departure secret; ²¹ he fled with all that he possessed, and soon was over the Euphrates and on the way to the hill-country of Gilead. ²² Three days later, when Laban heard that Jacob had fled, ²³ he took his kinsmen with him and pursued Jacob for seven days until he caught up with him in the hill-country of Gilead. ²⁴ But God came to Laban the Aramaean in

31:13 **the God of Bethel:** or the God Bethel.

white and goats are usually black, Laban quickly agreed to a deal so obviously to his advantage. **39:** Many people, ancient and modern, have believed that a fetus can be affected by the visual impressions of the mother. **31.14–16:** Ancient law, such as the Hurrian, provided for part of the bride payment to be reserved for the woman herself. **19:** Possession of the *household gods* insured safety and prosperity and possibly the right of a dream by night and said to him, 'Be careful to say nothing to Jacob, not a word.'

25 When Laban caught up with him, Jacob had pitched his tent in the hill-country of Gilead, and Laban encamped with his kinsmen in the same hill-country. 26 Laban said to Jacob, 'What have you done? You have deceived me and carried off my daughters as though they were captives taken in war. 27 Why did you slip away secretly without telling me? I would have set you on your way with songs and the music of tambourines and harps. 28 You did not even let me kiss my daughters and their children. In this you behaved foolishly. 29 I have it in my power to harm all of you, but last night the God of your father spoke to me; he told me to be careful to say nothing to you, not one word. 30 I expect that really you went away because you were homesick and pining for your father's house; but why did you steal my gods?'

31 Jacob answered, 'I was afraid; I thought you would take your daughters from me by force. 32 Whoever is found in possession of your gods shall die for it. In the presence of our kinsmen as witnesses, identify anything I have that is yours, and take it back.' Jacob did not know that Rachel had stolen the gods. 33 Laban went into Jacob's tent and Leah's tent and that of the two slave-girls, but he found nothing. After coming from Leah's tent he went into Rachel's. 34 In the mean time Rachel had taken the household gods and put them in the camel-bag and was sitting on them. Laban went through the whole tent but found nothing. 35 Rachel said, 'Do not take it amiss, father, that I cannot rise in your presence: the common lot of woman is upon me.' So for all his searching, Laban did not find the household gods.

36 Jacob heatedly took Laban to task. 'What have I done wrong?' he exclaimed. 'What is my offence, that you have come after me in hot pursuit 37 and have gone through all my belongings? Have you found a single article belonging to your household? If so, set it here in front of my kinsmen and yours, and let them decide between the two of us. 38 In all the twenty years I have been with you, your ewes and she-goats have never miscarried. I have never eaten rams from your flocks. 39 I have never brought to you the carcass of any animal mangled by wild beasts, but I bore the loss myself. You demanded that I should pay compensation for anything stolen by day or by night. 40 This was the way of it: the heat wore me down by day and the frost by night; I got no sleep. 41 For twenty years I have been in your household. I worked fourteen years for you to win your two daughters and six years for your flocks, and you changed my wages ten times over. 42 If the God of my father, the God of Abraham and the Fear of Isaac, had not been with me, you would now have sent me away empty-handed. But God saw my labour and my hardships, and last night he delivered his verdict.'

43 Laban answered Jacob, 'The daughters are my daughters, the children are my children, the flocks are my flocks; all you see is mine. But what am I to do now about my daughters and the children they have borne? 44 Come, let us make a pact, you and I, and let there be a witness between us.' 45 So Jacob chose a great stone and set it up as a sacred pillar. 46 Then he told his kinsmen to gather stones, and they took them and built a cairn, and there beside the cairn they ate together. 47 Laban called it Jegar-sahadutha, and Jacob called it Gal-ed. 48 'This cairn', said Laban, 'is a witness today between you and me.' That was why it was named Gal-ed; 49 it was also named Mizpah, for Laban said, 'May the LORD watch between you and me when we are absent from one another. 50 If you illtreat my daughters or take other wives besides them, then though no one is there as a witness, God will be the witness between us.'

51 Laban said to Jacob, 'Here is this cairn, and here the pillar which I have set up between us. 52 Both cairn and pillar are witnesses that I am not to pass beyond this cairn to your side with evil intent, and you must not pass beyond this cairn and this pillar to my side with evil intent. 53 May the God of Abraham and the God of Nahor judge between

31:47 **Jegar-sahadutha:** *Aram. for* Cairn of Witness. **Gal-ed:** *Heb. for* Cairn of Witness. 31:49 **Mizpah:** *that is* Watch-tower. 31:53 **between us:** *so Gk; Heb. adds* the God of their father.

inheritance. **35:** The ancient, humorous story now becomes a sarcastic attack on idolatry; the "gods" have been stolen, hidden, and soiled by menstrual blood (see Lev. 15.19–20). **39:** *Mangled:* on responsibility in such cases, see Exod. 22.10–13. **42:** *Fear of Isaac:* an unusual divine name. **43:** The custom of Laban's homeland is reflected, by which the husband moves into the wife's household. **46:** *Cairn:* a heap of stones.

us.' Jacob swore this oath in the name of the Fear of Isaac, the God of his father. ⁵⁴ He slaughtered an animal for sacrifice there in the hill-country, and summoned his kinsmen to the feast. They ate together and spent the night there.

⁵⁵ Laban rose early in the morning, kissed his daughters and their children, gave them his blessing, and then returned to his home.

32 As Jacob continued his journey he was met by angels of God. ² When he saw them, Jacob exclaimed, 'This is the company of God,' and he called that place Mahanaim.

³ Jacob sent messengers ahead of him to his brother Esau to the district of Seir in Edomite territory, ⁴ instructing them to say to Esau, 'My lord, your servant Jacob sends this message: I have been living with Laban and have stayed there till now. ⁵ I have acquired oxen, donkeys, and sheep, as well as male and female slaves, and I am sending to tell you this, my lord, so that I may win your favour.' ⁶ The messengers returned to Jacob and said, 'We went to your brother Esau and he is already on the way to meet you with four hundred men.' ⁷ Jacob, much afraid and distressed, divided the people with him, as well as the sheep, cattle, and camels, into two companies. ⁸ He reasoned that, if Esau should come upon one company and destroy it, the other might still survive.

⁹ Jacob prayed, 'God of my father Abraham, God of my father Isaac, LORD at whose bidding I came back to my own country and to my kindred, and who promised me prosperity, ¹⁰ I am not worthy of all the true and steadfast love which you have shown to me your servant. The last time I crossed the Jordan, I owned nothing but the staff in my hand; now I have two camps. ¹¹ Save me, I pray, from my brother Esau, for I am afraid that he may come and destroy me; he will spare neither mother nor child. ¹² But you said, "I shall make you prosper and your descendants will be like the sand of the sea, beyond all counting." '

¹³ After spending the night there Jacob chose a gift for his brother Esau from the herds he had with him: ¹⁴ two hundred she-goats, twenty he-goats, two hundred ewes and twenty rams, ¹⁵ thirty milch-camels with their young, forty cows and ten young bulls, twenty she-donkeys and ten donkeys. ¹⁶ He put each drove into the charge of a servant and said, 'Go on ahead of me, and leave gaps between one drove and the next.' ¹⁷ To the first servant he gave these instructions: 'When my brother Esau meets you and asks who your master is and where you are going and who owns these animals you are driving, ¹⁸ you are to say, "They belong to your servant Jacob, who sends them as a gift to my lord Esau; he himself is coming behind us." ' ¹⁹ He gave the same instructions to the second, to the third, and to all the drovers, telling each to say the same thing to Esau when they met him. ²⁰ And they were to add, 'Your servant Jacob is coming behind us.' Jacob thought, 'I shall appease him with the gift that I have sent on ahead, and afterwards, when we come face to face, perhaps he will receive me kindly.' ²¹ So Jacob's gift went on ahead of him, while he himself stayed that night at Mahaneh.

²² During the night Jacob rose, and taking his two wives, his two slave-girls, and his eleven sons, he crossed the ford of Jabbok. ²³ After he had sent them across the wadi with all that he had, ²⁴ Jacob was left alone, and a man wrestled with him there till daybreak. ²⁵ When the man saw that he could not get the better of Jacob, he struck him in the hollow of his thigh, so that Jacob's hip was dislocated as they wrestled. ²⁶ The man said, 'Let me go, for day is breaking,' but Jacob replied, 'I will not let you go unless you bless me.' ²⁷ The man asked, 'What is your name?' 'Jacob,' he answered. ²⁸ The man said, 'Your name shall no longer be Jacob but Israel, because you have striven with God and with mortals, and have prevailed.' ²⁹ Jacob said, 'Tell me your name, I pray.' He replied, 'Why do you ask my name?' but he gave him his blessing there. ³⁰ Jacob called the place

31:55 *In Heb. 32:1.*   32:2 **Mahanaim:** *that is* Two Companies.   32:24 **till daybreak:** *or* at daybreak. 32:28 **Israel:** *that is* God strove.   32:30 **Peniel:** *that is* Face of God (*elsewhere* Penuel).

32.1–33.20: Jacob's return and reconciliation with Esau. 1: *Angels of God:* see Ps. 91.11. **9:** *God of my father Abraham:* see 31.42. **20:** Compare Prov. 21.14. **24–26:** In keeping with much ancient folklore, the phantom visitor vanished with the sunrise. He may have been, in the earliest circulation of the story, either a border guardian or the "spirit" of the river. In context, his "blessing" helps to authenticate Jacob's right to the land. **27–32:** Folk explanations are given for the names *Israel* and *Peniel/Penuel,* and also for a food taboo

Peniel, 'because', he said, 'I have seen God face to face yet my life is spared'. ³¹ The sun rose as Jacob passed through Penuel, limping because of his hip. ³² That is why to this day the Israelites do not eat the sinew that is on the hollow of the thigh, because the man had struck Jacob on that sinew.

33 Jacob looked up and there was Esau coming with four hundred men. He divided the children between Leah and Rachel and the two slave-girls. ² He put the slave-girls and their children in front, Leah with her children next, and Rachel and Joseph in the rear. ³ He himself went on ahead of them, bowing low to the ground seven times as he approached his brother. ⁴ Esau ran to meet him and embraced him; he threw his arms round him and kissed him, and they both wept. ⁵ When Esau caught sight of the women and children, he asked, 'Who are these with you?' Jacob replied, 'The children whom God has graciously given to your servant.' ⁶ The slave-girls came near, each with her children, and they bowed low; ⁷ then Leah with her children came near and bowed low, and lastly Joseph and Rachel came and bowed low also. ⁸ Esau asked, 'What was all that company of yours that I met?' 'It was meant to win favour with you, my lord,' was the answer. ⁹ Esau said, 'I have more than enough. Keep what you have, my brother.' ¹⁰ But Jacob replied, 'No, please! If I have won your favour, then accept, I pray, this gift from me; for, as you see, I come into your presence as into that of a god, and yet you receive me favourably. ¹¹ Accept this gift which I bring you; for God has been gracious to me, and I have all I want.' Thus urged, Esau accepted it.

¹² Esau said, 'Let us set out, and I shall go at your pace.' ¹³ But Jacob answered him, 'You must know, my lord, that the children are small; the flocks and herds are suckling their young and I am concerned for them, and if they are overdriven for a single day, my beasts will all die. ¹⁴ I beg you, my lord, to go on ahead, and I shall move by easy stages at the pace of the livestock I am driving and

the pace of the children, until I come to my lord in Seir.' ¹⁵ Esau said, 'Let me detail some of my men to escort you,' but he replied, 'There is no reason why my lord should be so kind.' ¹⁶ That day Esau turned back towards Seir, ¹⁷ while Jacob set out for Succoth; there he built himself a house and made shelters for his cattle. Therefore he named that place Succoth.

¹⁸ So having journeyed from Paddan-aram, Jacob arrived safely at the town of Shechem in Canaan and pitched his tent to the east of it. ¹⁹ The piece of land where he had pitched his tent he bought from the sons of Hamor, Shechem's father, for a hundred sheep. ²⁰ He erected an altar there and called it El-elohey-israel.

34 Dinah, the daughter whom Leah had borne to Jacob, went out to visit women of the district, ² and Shechem, son of Hamor the Hivite, the local prince, saw her. He took her, lay with her, and violated her. ³ But Shechem was deeply attached to Jacob's daughter Dinah; he loved the girl and sought to win her affection. ⁴ Shechem said to Hamor his father, 'You must get me this girl as my wife.' ⁵ When Jacob learnt that his daughter Dinah had been dishonoured, his sons were with the herds in the open country, so he held his peace until they came home. ⁶ Meanwhile Shechem's father Hamor came out to Jacob to talk the matter over with him. ⁷ When they heard the news Jacob's sons came home from the country; they were distressed and very angry, because in lying with Jacob's daughter Shechem had done what the Israelites hold to be an intolerable outrage. ⁸ Hamor appealed to them: 'My son Shechem is in love with this girl; I beg you to let him have her as his wife. ⁹ Let us ally ourselves in marriage; you give us your daughters, and you take ours. ¹⁰ If you settle among us, the country is open before you; make your home in it, move about freely, and acquire land of your own.' ¹¹ Shechem said to

33:17 **Succoth:** *that is* Shelters.   33:19 **sheep:** *or* pieces of money.   33:20 **El-elohey-israel:** *that is* God the God of Israel.

(v. 32), mentioned only here. On a new name, see 17.5 n. **33.20:** *El* was the chief god of the Canaanites, apparently worshiped at Shechem before the introduction of the cult of the Lord.

34.1–31: The rape of Dinah. This is an ancient, once independent account of relations between the tribes of Simeon and Levi and their Canaanite neighbors, the tribes being represented by eponymous ("name-giving") ancestors. The episode is mentioned in 49.5–7, as the basis for the decline of these tribes in the tribal confederation. Simeon goes unmentioned in the list of tribes given in Deut. ch. 33, a passage from a later time.

the girl's father and brothers, 'I am eager to win your favour and I shall give whatever you ask. 12 Fix the bride-price and the gift as high as you like, and I shall give whatever you ask; only, give me the girl in marriage.'

13 Jacob's sons replied to Shechem and his father Hamor deceitfully, because Shechem had violated their sister Dinah: 14 'We cannot do this,' they said; 'we cannot give our sister to a man who is uncircumcised, for we look on that as a disgrace. 15 Only on one condition can we give our consent: if you follow our example and have every male among you circumcised, 16 we shall give you our daughters and take yours for ourselves. We will then live among you, and become one people with you. 17 But if you refuse to listen to us and be circumcised, we shall take the girl and go.' 18 Their proposal appeared satisfactory to Hamor and his son Shechem; 19 and the young man, who was held in respect above anyone in his father's house, did not hesitate to do what they had said, because his heart had been captured by Jacob's daughter.

20 Hamor and Shechem went to the gate of their town and addressed their fellow-townsmen: 21 'These men are friendly towards us,' they said; 'let them live in our country and move freely in it. The land has room enough for them. Let us marry their daughters and give them ours. 22 But on this condition only will these men agree to live with us as one people: every male among us must be circumcised as they are. 23 Their herds, their livestock, and all their chattels will then be ours. We need only agree to their condition, and then they are free to live with us.' 24 All the able-bodied men agreed with Hamor and his son Shechem, and every able-bodied male among them was circumcised. 25 Then two days later, while they were still in pain, two of Jacob's sons, Simeon and Levi, full brothers to Dinah, after arming themselves with swords, boldly entered the town and killed every male. 26 They cut down Hamor and his son Shechem and took Dinah from Shechem's house and went off. 27 Jacob's other sons came in over the dead bodies and plundered the town which had brought dishonour on their sister. 28 They seized flocks,

cattle, donkeys, whatever was inside the town and outside in the open country; 29 they carried off all the wealth, the women, and the children, and looted everything in the houses.

30 Jacob said to Simeon and Levi, 'You have brought trouble on me; you have brought my name into bad odour among the people of the country, the Canaanites and the Perizzites. My numbers are few; if they combine against me and attack, I shall be destroyed, I and my household with me.' 31 They answered, 'Is our sister to be treated as a common whore?'

35 GOD said to Jacob, 'Go up now to Bethel and, when you have settled there, erect an altar to the God who appeared to you when you fled from your brother Esau.' 2 Jacob said to his household and to all who were with him, 'Get rid of the foreign gods which you have; then purify yourselves, and put on fresh clothes. 3 We are to set off for Bethel, so that I can erect an altar there to the God who answered me when I was in distress; he has been with me wherever I have gone.' 4 They handed over to Jacob all the foreign gods in their possession and the ear-rings they were wearing, and he buried them under the terebinth tree near Shechem. 5 As they moved off, the towns round about were panic-stricken, so that they were unable to pursue Jacob's sons. 6 Jacob and all the people with him came to Luz, that is Bethel, in Canaan. 7 There he built an altar, and called the place El-bethel, because it was there that God had revealed himself to him when he was fleeing from his brother. 8 Rebecca's nurse Deborah died and was buried under the oak below Bethel, and Jacob called it Allon-bakuth.

9 God appeared again to Jacob after his return from Paddan-aram and blessed him. 10 God said: 'Jacob is now your name, but it is going to be Jacob no longer: your name is to be Israel.'

So Jacob was called Israel. 11 God said to him:

35:7 **El-bethel:** *that is* God of Bethel.
35:8 **Allon-bakuth:** *that is* Oak of Weeping.

35.1–15: Variant traditions about the founding of Bethel. Given Jacob's prior visit (28.18–19) and the importance of the place in Israel's religious heritage, some duplication and even misplacement have resulted. **2:** A change of garment was a necessary part of ceremonial purification (Exod. 19.10). **9–10:** A variant version of 32.24–28. **11–12:** An extension to Jacob of the promise to Abraham and Isaac. It might have been better

'I am God Almighty.
   Be fruitful and increase:
   a nation, a host of nations will come
      from you;
   kings also will descend from you.
¹²The land I gave to Abraham and Isaac
      I give to you;
   and to your descendants also I shall
      give this land.'

¹³When God left him, ¹⁴Jacob raised a sacred pillar of stone in the place where God had spoken with him, and he offered a drink-offering on it and poured oil over it. ¹⁵Jacob called the place where God had spoken with him Bethel.

¹⁶They moved from Bethel, and when there was still some distance to go to Ephrathah, Rachel went into labour and her pains were severe. ¹⁷While they were on her, the midwife said, 'Do not be afraid, for this is another son for you.' ¹⁸Then with her last breath, as she was dying, she named him Ben-oni, but his father called him Benjamin. ¹⁹So Rachel died and was buried by the side of the road to Ephrathah, that is Bethlehem. ²⁰Over her grave Jacob set up a sacred pillar; and to this day it is known as the Pillar of Rachel's Grave. ²¹Then continuing his journey Israel pitched his tent on the other side of Migdal-eder. ²²While Israel was living in that district, Reuben lay with his father's concubine Bilhah; and Israel came to hear of it.

The sons of Jacob were twelve. ²³The sons of Leah: Jacob's firstborn Reuben, then Simeon, Levi, Judah, Issachar, and Zebulun. ²⁴The sons of Rachel: Joseph and Benjamin. ²⁵The sons of Rachel's slave-girl Bilhah: Dan and Naphtali. ²⁶The sons of Leah's slave-girl Zilpah: Gad and Asher. These were Jacob's sons, born to him in Paddan-aram. ²⁷Jacob came to his father Isaac at Mamre near Kiriath-arba, that is Hebron, where Abraham and Isaac had stayed. ²⁸Isaac was a hundred and eighty years old when he breathed his

last. ²⁹He died and was gathered to his father's kin at this very great age, and his sons Esau and Jacob buried him.

36 THIS is an account of the descendants of Esau, that is Edom. ²Esau took Canaanite women in marriage: Adah daughter of Elon the Hittite and Oholibamah daughter of Anah son of Zibeon the Horite, ³and Basemath, Ishmael's daughter, sister of Nebaioth.

⁴Adah bore Eliphaz to Esau; Basemath bore Reuel, ⁵and Oholibamah bore Jeush, Jaalam, and Korah. These were Esau's sons, born to him in Canaan. ⁶Esau took his wives, his sons and daughters and all the members of his household, his livestock, all the animals, and all the possessions he had acquired in Canaan, and went to the district of Seir out of the way of his brother Jacob, ⁷because they had so much stock that they could not live together. The region where they were staying could not support them because of the numbers of their livestock. ⁸So Esau lived in the hill-country of Seir. (Esau is Edom.)

⁹This is an account of the descendants of Esau father of the Edomites in the hill-country of Seir.

¹⁰These are the names of the sons of Esau: Eliphaz was the son of Esau's wife Adah. Reuel was the son of Esau's wife Basemath. ¹¹The sons of Eliphaz were Teman, Omar, Zepho, Gatam, and Kenaz. ¹²Timna was the concubine of Esau's son Eliphaz, and she bore Amalek to him. These are the descendants of Esau's wife Adah. ¹³These are the sons of Reuel: Nahath, Zerah, Shammah, and Mizzah. These were the descendants of Esau's wife Basemath. ¹⁴These were the sons of Esau's wife Oholibamah daughter of Anah

35:18 **Ben-oni:** *that is* Son of my Grief. **Benjamin:** *that is* Son of the Right Hand *or* Son of Good Luck. 36:2 **son:** *so Samar.; Heb.* daughter. **Horite:** *prob. rdg (cp. verses 20,21); Heb.* Hivite.   36:6 **of Seir:** *so Syriac; Heb. omits.*

placed after Jacob's return from Harran and his new name. **13–15:** A variant of 28.16–19.

35.16–22: The birth of Benjamin. The name (see end of Tfn. at 35.18) likely refers to a geographical location south (i.e. "right") of Ephraim. **22:** An incomplete fragment, it explains the tribe's later loss of prestige (49.3–4) and of numbers (Deut. 33.6).

35.23–29: The death of Isaac. In 27.1, Isaac was already an old man at the point of death; this passage reflects an independent tradition.

36.1–43: The genealogy of Esau. Relations between Israel and Edom were usually better than between most neighbors in the area; the Edomites are never accused of idolatry. Perhaps that is why this non-Israelite material was preserved. **2:** This verse differs from a similar tradition in 26.34 and 28.9. **10:** The list is drawn from different son of Zibeon: she bore him Jeush, Jaalam, and Korah.

15 These are the chiefs descended from Esau. The sons of Esau's eldest son Eliphaz: Teman, Omar, Zepho, Kenaz, 16 Korah, Gatam, Amalek. These are the chiefs descended from Eliphaz in Edom. These are the descendants of Adah.

17 These are the sons of Esau's son Reuel who were chiefs: Nahath, Zerah, Shammah, Mizzah. These are the chiefs descended from Reuel in Edom. These are the descendants of Esau's wife Basemath.

18 These are the sons of Esau's wife Oholibamah: chief Jeush, chief Jaalam, chief Korah. These are the chiefs born to Oholibamah daughter of Anah and wife of Esau.

19 These are the sons of Esau, that is Edom, and these are their chiefs.

20 These are the sons of Seir the Horite, the original inhabitants of the land: Lotan, Shobal, Zibeon, Anah, 21 Dishon, Ezer, and Dishan. These are the chiefs of the Horites, the sons of Seir in Edom. 22 The sons of Lotan were Hori and Hemam, and Lotan had a sister named Timna.

23 These are the sons of Shobal: Alvan, Manahath, Ebal, Shepho, and Onam.

24 These are the sons of Zibeon: Aiah and Anah. He is the Anah who found hot springs in the wilderness while he was tending the donkeys of his father Zibeon. 25 These are the children of Anah: Dishon and Oholibamah daughter of Anah.

26 These are the children of Dishon: Hemdan, Eshban, Ithran, and Cheran. 27 These are the sons of Ezer: Bilhan, Zavan, and Akan. 28 These are the sons of Dishan: Uz and Aran.

29 These are the chiefs descended from the Horites: Lotan, Shobal, Zibeon, Anah, 30 Dishon, Ezer, Dishan. These are the chiefs that were descended from the Horites according to their clans in the district of Seir.

31 These are the kings who ruled over Edom before there were kings in Israel: 32 Bela son of Beor became king in Edom, and his city was named Dinhabah; 33 when he died, he was succeeded by Jobab son of Zerah of Bozrah. 34 When Jobab died, he was succeeded by Husham the Temanite. 35 When Husham died, he was succeeded by Hadad son of Bedad, who defeated Midian in Moabite country. His city was named Avith. 36 When Hadad died, he was succeeded by Samlah of Masrekah. 37 When Samlah died, he was succeeded by Saul of Rehoboth-on-the-Euphrates. 38 When Saul died, he was succeeded by Baal-hanan son of Akbor. 39 When Baal-hanan died, he was succeeded by Hadar. His city was named Pau; his wife's name was Mehetabel daughter of Matred a woman of Me-zahab.

40 These are the names of the chiefs descended from Esau, according to their families and places: Timna, Alvah, Jetheth, 41 Oholibamah, Elah, Pinon, 42 Kenaz, Teman, Mibzar, 43 Magdiel, and Iram: all chiefs of Edom according to their settlements in the land which they possessed. (Esau is the father of the Edomites.)

Joseph

37 JACOB settled in Canaan, the country in which his father had made his home, 2 and this is an account of Jacob's descendants.

When Joseph was a youth of seventeen, he used to accompany his brothers, the sons of Bilhah and Zilpah, his father's wives, when they were in charge of the flock, and he told tales about them to their father. 3 Because Joseph was a child of his old age, Israel loved him best of all his sons, and he made him a long robe with sleeves. 4 When his brothers saw that their father loved him best, it aroused their hatred and they had nothing but harsh words for him.

5 Joseph had a dream, and when he told it to his brothers, their hatred of him became still greater. 6 He said to them, 'Listen to this dream I had. 7 We were out in the field bind-

36:14 **son of Zibeon:** so Samar.; Heb. daughter of Zibeon.   36:24 **hot springs:** Heb. word of uncertain meaning.   36:39 **a woman of Me-zahab:** or daughter of Me-zahab.   37:3 **a long ... sleeves:** or an ornamental robe.

sources and repeats matters given in other verses; see v. 4. **31:** See 25.33 n.

37.1–36: Joseph is sold into Egypt. This material sets the stage for the Egyptian bondage, and hence for the people's deliverance and realization of the divine promise (12.1–3). Chapters 37, 39–47, 50 constitute a single literary unit, although composed out of earlier independent elements. Chapters 48–49 are later additions. Chapter 38 is an extraneous fragment. **7:** Bowed in homage: his future status in Egypt is foreshadowed (42.6;

ing sheaves, when all at once my sheaf rose and stood upright, and your sheaves gathered round and bowed in homage before my sheaf.' [8] His brothers retorted, 'Do you think that you will indeed be king over us and rule us?' and they hated him still more because of his dreams and what he had said. [9] Then he had another dream, which he related to his father and his brothers. 'Listen!' he said. 'I have had another dream, and in it the sun, the moon, and eleven stars were bowing down to me.' [10] When he told his father and his brothers, his father took him to task: 'What do you mean by this dream of yours?' he asked. 'Are we to come and bow to the ground before you, I and your mother and your brothers?' [11] His brothers were jealous of him, but his father did not forget the incident.

[12] Joseph's brothers had gone to herd their father's flocks at Shechem. [13] Israel said to him, 'Your brothers are herding the flocks at Shechem; I am going to send you to them.' Joseph answered, 'I am ready to go.' [14] Israel told him to go and see if all was well with his brothers and the flocks, and to bring back word to him. So Joseph was sent off from the vale of Hebron and came to Shechem, where [15] a man met him wandering in the open country and asked him what he was looking for. [16] 'I am looking for my brothers,' he replied. 'Can you tell me where they are herding the flocks?' [17] The man said, 'They have moved from here; I heard them speak of going to Dothan.' Joseph went after his brothers and came up with them at Dothan. [18] They saw him in the distance, and before he reached them, they plotted to kill him. [19] 'Here comes that dreamer,' they said to one another. [20] 'Now is our chance; let us kill him and throw him into one of these cisterns; we can say that a wild beast has devoured him. Then we shall see what becomes of his dreams.' [21] When Reuben heard, he came to his rescue, urging them not to take his life. [22] 'Let us have no bloodshed,' he said. 'Throw him into this cistern in the wilderness, but do him no injury.' Reuben meant to rescue him from their clutches in order to restore him to his father. [23] When Joseph reached his brothers, they stripped him of the long robe with sleeves which he was wearing, [24] picked him up, and threw him into the cistern. It was empty, with no water in it.

[25] They had sat down to eat when, looking up, they saw an Ishmaelite caravan coming from Gilead on the way down to Egypt, with camels carrying gum tragacanth and balm and myrrh. [26] Judah said to his brothers, 'What do we gain by killing our brother and concealing his death? [27] Why not sell him to these Ishmaelites? Let us do him no harm, for after all, he is our brother, our own flesh and blood'; his brothers agreed. [28] Meanwhile some passing Midianite merchants drew Joseph up out of the cistern and sold him for twenty pieces of silver to the Ishmaelites; they brought Joseph to Egypt. [29] When Reuben came back to the cistern, he found Joseph had gone. He tore his clothes [30] and going to his brothers he said, 'The boy is not there. Whatever shall I do?'

[31] Joseph's brothers took the long robe with sleeves, and dipped it in the blood of a goat which they had killed. [32] After tearing the robe, they brought it to their father and said, 'Look what we have found. Do you recognize it? Is this your son's robe or not?' [33] Jacob recognized it. 'It is my son's,' he said. 'A wild beast has devoured him. Joseph has been torn to pieces.' [34] Jacob tore his clothes; he put on sackcloth and for many days he mourned his son. [35] Though his sons and daughters all tried to comfort him, he refused to be comforted. He said, 'No, I shall go to Sheol mourning for my son.' Thus Joseph's father wept for him. [36] The Midianites meanwhile had sold Joseph in Egypt to Potiphar, one of Pharaoh's court officials, the captain of the guard.

38

ABOUT that time Judah parted from his brothers, and heading south he pitched his tent in company with an Adullamite named Hirah. [2] There he saw Bathshua the daughter of a Canaanite and

37:9 **his father and:** *so Gk; Heb. omits.*   37:35 **Sheol:** *or* the underworld.

50.18). **9:** *Eleven stars:* the zodiac is possibly meant, since the number of constellations in it agrees with that of the members of the tribal league. **18–30:** Variations from Reuben to Judah, and from Ishmaelites to Midianites, suggest that diverse accounts have been combined.

38.1–30: Judah and Tamar. After the tribe of Judah rose to prominence as the tribe of King David, its traditions received special preservation. The account here interrupts the flow of the Joseph narrative. When married her. He lay with her, ³and she conceived and bore a son, whom she called Er. ⁴She conceived again and bore a son, whom she called Onan. ⁵Once more she conceived and bore a son whom she called Shelah, and she was at Kezib when she bore him. ⁶Judah found a wife for his eldest son Er; her name was Tamar. ⁷But Judah's eldest son Er was wicked in the LORD's sight, and the LORD took away his life. ⁸Then Judah told Onan to sleep with his brother's wife, to do his duty as the husband's brother and raise up offspring for his brother. ⁹But Onan knew that the offspring would not count as his; so whenever he lay with his brother's wife, he spilled his seed on the ground so as not to raise up offspring for his brother. ¹⁰What he did was wicked in the LORD's sight, and the LORD took away his life also. ¹¹Judah said to his daughter-in-law Tamar, 'Remain as a widow in your father's house until my son Shelah grows up'; for he was afraid that Shelah too might die like his brothers. So Tamar went and stayed in her father's house.

¹²Time passed, and Judah's wife Bathshua died. When he had finished mourning, he and his friend Hirah the Adullamite went up to Timnath at sheep-shearing. ¹³When Tamar was told that her father-in-law was on his way to shear his sheep at Timnath, ¹⁴she took off her widow's clothes, covered her face with a veil, and then sat where the road forks on the way to Timnath. She did this because she saw that although Shelah was now grown up she had not been given to him as a wife. ¹⁵When Judah saw her he thought she was a prostitute, for she had veiled her face. ¹⁶He turned to her where she sat by the roadside and said, 'Let me lie with you,' not realizing she was his daughter-in-law. She said, 'What will you give to lie with me?' ¹⁷He answered, 'I shall send you a young goat from my flock.' She said, 'I agree, if you will give me a pledge until you send it.' ¹⁸He asked what pledge he should give her, and she replied, 'Your seal and its cord, and the staff which you are holding.' He handed them over to her and

lay with her, and she became pregnant. ¹⁹She then rose and went home, where she took off her veil and put on her widow's clothes again.

²⁰Judah sent the goat by his friend the Adullamite in order to recover the pledge from the woman, but he could not find her. ²¹When he enquired of the people of that place, 'Where is that temple-prostitute, the one who was sitting where the road forks?' they answered, 'There has been no temple-prostitute here.' ²²So he went back to Judah and reported that he had failed to find her and that the men of the place had said there was no such prostitute there. ²³Judah said, 'Let her keep the pledge, or we shall be a laughing-stock. After all, I did send the kid, even though you could not find her.'

²⁴About three months later Judah was told that his daughter-in-law Tamar had played the prostitute and got herself pregnant. 'Bring her out,' ordered Judah, 'so that she may be burnt.' ²⁵But as she was being brought out, she sent word to her father-in-law. 'The father of my child is the man to whom these things belong,' she said. 'See if you recognize whose they are, this seal, the pattern of the cord, and the staff.' ²⁶Judah identified them and said, 'She is more in the right than I am, because I did not give her to my son Shelah.' He did not have intercourse with her again.

²⁷When her time was come, she was found to have twins in her womb, ²⁸and while she was in labour one of them put out a hand. The midwife took a scarlet thread and fastened it round the wrist, saying, 'This one appeared first.' ²⁹No sooner had he drawn back his hand, than his brother came out and the midwife said, 'What! You have broken out first!' So he was named Perez. ³⁰Soon afterwards his brother was born with the scarlet thread on his wrist, and he was named Zerah.

38:5 **and she was:** *so Gk; Heb.* and he shall be.
38:14,21 **where . . . forks:** *or* by the gate of Enaim; *cp. Gk.*   38:29 **Perez:** *that is* Breaking out.
38:30 **Zerah:** *that is* Scarlet.

the latter resumes (ch. 39) Judah is still a member of his father's household. **7:** In the absence of alternatives, divine causation was assumed. **8:** *Duty:* levirate ("brother-in-law") marriage (Deut. 25.5–10), to insure the perpetuity of family name and property. **10:** The offense was in the unwillingness of Onan to insure posterity for the deceased. **21:** Hirah, to preserve Judah from embarrassment, suggests that the woman he seeks is not a common whore (v. 15) but one respected in the Canaanite worship. On sacred prostitutes, see 1 Kgs. 14.24; 2 Kgs. 23.7; Hos. 4.13–14. **26:** Since no brother was alive to carry out the levirate ("brother-in-law") obligation, the father-in-law might have done so, and hence Tamar acted quite legally. **28:** On the importance of

39 WHEN Joseph was taken down to Egypt by the Ishmaelites, he was bought from them by an Egyptian, Potiphar, one of Pharaoh's court officials, the captain of the guard. ²Joseph prospered, for the LORD was with him. He lived in the house of his Egyptian master, ³who saw that the LORD was with him and was giving him success in all that he undertook. ⁴Thus Joseph won his master's favour, and became his attendant. Indeed, his master put him in charge of his household, and entrusted him with everything he had. ⁵From the time that he put Joseph in charge of his household and all his property, the LORD blessed the household through Joseph; the LORD's blessing was on all that was his in house and field. ⁶Potiphar left it all in Joseph's care, and concerned himself with nothing but the food he ate.

Now Joseph was handsome in both face and figure, ⁷and after a time his master's wife became infatuated with him. 'Come, make love to me,' she said. ⁸But Joseph refused. 'Think of my master,' he said; 'he leaves the management of his whole house to me; he has trusted me with all he has. ⁹I am as important in this house as he is, and he has withheld nothing from me except you, because you are his wife. How can I do such a wicked thing? It is a sin against God.' ¹⁰Though she kept on at Joseph day after day, he refused to lie with her or be in her company.

¹¹One day when he came into the house to see to his duties, and none of the household servants was there indoors, ¹²she caught him by his loincloth, saying, 'Come, make love to me,' but he left the loincloth in her hand and ran from the house. ¹³When she saw that he had left his loincloth and run out of the house, ¹⁴she called to her servants, 'Look at this! My husband has brought in a Hebrew to bring insult on us. He came in here to rape me, but I gave a loud scream. ¹⁵When he heard me scream and call for help, he ran out, leaving his loincloth behind.' ¹⁶She kept it by her until his master came home, ¹⁷and then she repeated her tale: 'That Hebrew slave you brought in came to my room to make me an object of insult. ¹⁸But when I screamed for help, he ran out of the house,

leaving his loincloth behind.' ¹⁹Joseph's master was furious when he heard his wife's account of what his slave had done to her. ²⁰He had Joseph seized and thrown into the guardhouse, where the king's prisoners were kept; and there he was confined. ²¹But the LORD was with Joseph and kept faith with him, so that he won the favour of the governor of the guardhouse. ²²Joseph was put in charge of the prisoners, and he directed all their work. ²³The governor ceased to concern himself with anything entrusted to Joseph, because the LORD was with him and gave him success in all that he did.

40 Some time after these events it happened that the king's cupbearer and the royal baker gave offence to their lord, the king of Egypt. ²Pharaoh was displeased with his two officials, his chief cupbearer and chief baker, ³and put them in custody in the house of the captain of the guard, in the guardhouse where Joseph was imprisoned. ⁴The captain appointed Joseph as their attendant, and he waited on them.

They had been in prison in the guardhouse for some time, ⁵when one night the king's cupbearer and his baker both had dreams, each with a meaning of its own. ⁶Coming to them in the morning, Joseph saw that they looked dispirited, ⁷and asked these officials in custody with him in his master's house, why they were so downcast that day. ⁸They replied, 'We have each had a dream, but there is no one to interpret them.' Joseph said to them, 'All interpretation belongs to God. Why not tell me your dreams?' ⁹So the chief cupbearer told Joseph his dream: 'In my dream', he said, 'there was a vine in front of me. ¹⁰On the vine there were three branches, and as soon as it budded, it blossomed and its clusters ripened into grapes. ¹¹I plucked the grapes and pressed them into Pharaoh's cup which I was holding, and then put the cup into Pharaoh's hand.' ¹²Joseph said to him, 'This is the interpretation. The three branches are three days: ¹³within three days Pharaoh will raise your head and restore you to your post; then you will put the cup into Pharaoh's hand as you used to do when you were his cupbearer. ¹⁴When things go well with you, remember me and do me

determining the firstborn, see 25.31 n.

39.1–23: Joseph's temptation and imprisonment. The account follows on 37.36. The story has a very close Egyptian parallel, "The Story of the Two Brothers."

the kindness of bringing my case to Pharaoh's notice; help me to get out of this prison. [15] I was carried off by force from the land of the Hebrews, and here I have done nothing to deserve being put into this dungeon.'

[16] When the chief baker saw that the interpretation given by Joseph had been favourable, he said to him, 'I too had a dream, and in my dream there were three baskets of white bread on my head. [17] In the top basket there was every kind of food such as a baker might prepare for Pharaoh, but the birds were eating out of the top basket on my head.' [18] Joseph answered, 'This is the interpretation. The three baskets are three days: [19] within three days Pharaoh will raise your head off your shoulders and hang you on a tree, and the birds of the air will devour the flesh off your bones.'

[20] The third day was Pharaoh's birthday and he gave a banquet for all his officials. He had the chief cupbearer and the chief baker brought up where they were all assembled. [21] The cupbearer was restored to his position, and he put the cup into Pharaoh's hand; [22] but the baker was hanged. All went as Joseph had said in interpreting the dreams for them. [23] The cupbearer, however, did not bear Joseph in mind; he forgot him.

41 Two years later Pharaoh had a dream: he was standing by the Nile, [2] when there came up from the river seven cows, sleek and fat, and they grazed among the reeds. [3] Presently seven other cows, gaunt and lean, came up from the river, and stood beside the cows on the river bank. [4] The cows that were gaunt and lean devoured the seven cows that were sleek and fat. Then Pharaoh woke up.

[5] He fell asleep again and had a second dream: he saw seven ears of grain, full and ripe, growing on a single stalk. [6] Springing up after them were seven other ears, thin and shrivelled by the east wind. [7] The thin ears swallowed up the seven ears that were full and plump. Then Pharaoh woke up and found it was a dream.

[8] In the morning Pharaoh's mind was so troubled that he summoned all the dream-interpreters and wise men of Egypt, and told them his dreams; but there was no one who could interpret them for him. [9] Then Pharaoh's chief cupbearer spoke up. 'Now I must mention my offences,' he said: [10] 'Pharaoh was angry with his servants, and imprisoned me and the chief baker in the house of the captain of the guard. [11] One night we both had dreams, each requiring its own interpretation. [12] We had with us there a young Hebrew, a slave of the captain of the guard, and when we told him our dreams he interpreted them for us, giving each dream its own interpretation. [13] Things turned out exactly as the dreams had been interpreted to us: I was restored to my post, the other was hanged.'

[14] Pharaoh thereupon sent for Joseph, and they hurriedly brought him out of the dungeon. After he had shaved and changed his clothes, he came in before Pharaoh, [15] who said to him, 'I have had a dream which no one can interpret. I have heard that you can interpret any dream you hear.' [16] Joseph answered, 'Not I, but God, can give an answer which will reassure Pharaoh.' [17] Then Pharaoh said to him: 'In my dream I was standing on the bank of the Nile, [18] when there came up from the river seven cows, fat and sleek, and they grazed among the reeds. [19] After them seven other cows came up that were in poor condition, very gaunt and lean; in all Egypt I have never seen such gaunt creatures. [20] These lean, gaunt cows devoured the first cows, the seven fat ones. [21] They were swallowed up, but no one could have told they were in the bellies of the others, which looked just as gaunt as before. Then I woke up. [22] In another dream I saw seven ears of grain, full and ripe, growing on a single stalk. [23] Springing up after them were seven other ears, blighted, thin, and shrivelled by the east wind. [24] The thin ears swallowed up the seven ripe ears. When I spoke to the dream-interpreters, no one could tell me the meaning.'

[25] Joseph said to Pharaoh, 'Pharaoh's dreams are both the same; God has told Pharaoh what he is about to do. [26] The seven good cows are seven years, and the seven good ears of grain are seven years—it is all

---

40.1–23: The dreams of Pharaoh's servants. 19: *Will raise your head:* the expression is the same as in v. 13, but here it is given a gruesome turn.

41.1–57: Pharaoh's dreams, which provide the opportunity for Joseph to become an Egyptian official. **6:** *East wind:* a seasonal wind (*hamsin*) from the desert which destroys the vegetation (Ps. 103.15–16; Ezek. 17.10; 19.12). **8:** The scorn here of the Egyptian magicians becomes more fully developed in the account of the ten one dream. 27 The seven lean and gaunt cows that came up after them are seven years, and so also are the seven empty ears of grain blighted by the east wind; there are going to be seven years of famine. 28 It is as I have told Pharaoh: God has let Pharaoh see what he is about to do. 29 There are to be seven years of bumper harvests throughout Egypt. 30 After them will come seven years of famine; so that the great harvests in Egypt will all be forgotten, and famine will ruin the country. 31 The good years will leave no trace in the land because of the famine that follows, for it will be very severe. 32 That Pharaoh has dreamed this twice means God is firmly resolved on this plan, and very soon he will put it into effect.

33 'Let Pharaoh now look for a man of vision and wisdom and put him in charge of the country. 34 Pharaoh should take steps to appoint commissioners over the land to take one fifth of the produce of Egypt during the seven years of plenty. 35 They should collect all food produced in the good years that are coming and put the grain under Pharaoh's control as a store of food to be kept in the towns. 36 This food will be a reserve for the country against the seven years of famine which will come on Egypt, and so the country will not be devastated by the famine.'

37 The plan commended itself both to Pharaoh and to all his officials, 38 and Pharaoh asked them, 'Could we find another man like this, one so endowed with the spirit of God?' 39 To Joseph he said, 'Since God has made all this known to you, no one has your vision and wisdom. 40 You shall be in charge of my household, and all my people will respect your every word. Only in regard to the throne shall I rank higher than you.' 41 Pharaoh went on, 'I hereby give you authority over the whole land of Egypt.' 42 He took off his signet ring and put it on Joseph's finger; he had him dressed in robes of fine linen, and hung a gold chain round his neck. 43 He mounted him in his viceroy's chariot and men cried 'Make way!' before him. Thus Pharaoh made him ruler over all Egypt 44 and said to him, 'I am the Pharaoh, yet without your consent no one will lift hand or foot throughout Egypt.' 45 Pharaoh named him

Zaphenath-paneah, and he gave him as his wife Asenath daughter of Potiphera priest of On. Joseph's authority extended over the whole of Egypt.

46 Joseph was thirty years old at the time he entered the service of Pharaoh king of Egypt. When he left the royal presence, he made a tour of inspection through the land. 47 During the seven years of plenty when there were abundant harvests, 48 Joseph gathered all the food produced in Egypt then and stored it in the towns, putting in each the food from the surrounding country. 49 He stored the grain in huge quantities; it was like the sand of the sea, so much that he stopped measuring: it was beyond all measure.

50 Before the years of famine came, two sons were born to Joseph by Asenath daughter of Potiphera priest of On. 51 He named the elder Manasseh, 'for', he said, 'God has made me forget all my troubles and my father's family'. 52 He named the second Ephraim, 'for', he said, 'God has made me fruitful in the land of my hardships'. 53 When the seven years of plenty in Egypt came to an end, 54 the seven years of famine began, as Joseph had predicted. There was famine in every country, but there was food throughout Egypt. 55 When the famine came to be felt through all Egypt, the people appealed to Pharaoh for food and he ordered them to go to Joseph and do whatever he told them. 56 When the whole land was in the grip of famine, Joseph opened all the granaries and sold grain to the Egyptians, for the famine was severe. 57 The whole world came to Egypt to buy grain from Joseph, so severe was the famine everywhere.

42 WHEN Jacob learnt that there was grain in Egypt, he said to his sons, 'Why do you stand staring at each other? 2 I hear there is grain in Egypt. Go down there, and buy some for us to keep us alive and save us from starving to death.' 3 So ten of Joseph's brothers went down to buy grain from

41:43 **Make way:** *Egyptian word of uncertain meaning.*
41:51 **Manasseh:** *that is* Causing to forget.
41:52 **Ephraim:** *that is* Fruit. 41:56 **the granaries:** *so Gk; Heb.* which was in them.

plagues (Exod. chs. 7–12). **42:** The *ring* would give Pharaoh's authority to Joseph, since it could be used to stamp the Pharaoh's "signature." **45:** *Potiphera* is apparently a fuller form of Potiphar (37.36), but here the name refers to a different person.

Egypt, [4] but Jacob did not let Joseph's brother Benjamin go with them, for fear that he might come to harm.

[5] Thus the sons of Israel went with everyone else to buy grain because of the famine in Canaan. [6] Now Joseph was governor of the land, and it was he who sold the grain to all its people. Joseph's brothers came and bowed to the ground before him, [7] and when he saw his brothers he recognized them but, pretending not to know them, he greeted them harshly. 'Where do you come from?' he demanded. 'From Canaan to buy food,' they answered. [8] Although Joseph had recognized his brothers, they did not recognize him. [9] He remembered the dreams he had had about them and said, 'You are spies; you have come to spy out the weak points in our defences.' [10] 'No, my lord,' they answered; 'your servants have come to buy food. [11] We are all sons of one man. We are honest men; your servants are not spies.' [12] 'No,' he maintained, 'it is to spy out our weaknesses that you have come.' [13] They said, 'There were twelve of us, my lord, all brothers, sons of one man back in Canaan; the youngest is still with our father, and one is lost.' [14] But Joseph insisted, 'As I have already said to you: you are spies. [15] This is how you will be put to the test: unless your youngest brother comes here, I swear by the life of Pharaoh you shall not leave this place. [16] Send one of your number to fetch your brother; the rest of you will remain in prison. Thus your story will be tested to see whether you are telling the truth. If not, then by the life of Pharaoh you must be spies.' [17] With that he kept them in prison for three days.

[18] On the third day Joseph said to them, 'Do what I say and your lives will be spared, for I am a godfearing man: [19] if you are honest men, only one of you brothers shall be kept in prison, while the rest of you may go and take grain for your starving households; [20] but you must bring your youngest brother to me. In this way your words will be proved true, and you will not die.'

[21] They consented, and among themselves they said, 'No doubt we are being punished because of our brother. We saw his distress when he pleaded with us and we refused to listen. That is why this distress has come on us.' [22] Reuben said, 'Did I not warn you not to do wrong to the boy? But you would not listen, and now his blood is on our heads, and we must pay.' [23] They did not know that Joseph understood, since he had used an interpreter. [24] Joseph turned away from them and wept. Then he went back to speak to them, and took Simeon from among them and had him bound before their eyes. [25] He gave orders to fill their bags with grain, to put each man's silver back into his sack again, and to give them provisions for the journey. After this had been done, [26] they loaded their grain on their donkeys and set off. [27] When they stopped for the night, one of them opened his sack to give feed to his donkey, and there at the top was the silver. [28] He said to his brothers, 'My silver has been returned; here it is in my pack.' Bewildered and trembling, they asked one another, 'What is this that God has done to us?'

[29] When they came to their father Jacob in Canaan, they gave him an account of all that had happened to them. They said: [30] 'The man who is lord of the country spoke harshly to us and made out that we were spies. [31] But we said to him, "We are honest men, we are not spies. [32] There were twelve of us, all brothers, sons of the same father. One has disappeared, and the youngest is with our father in Canaan." [33] Then the man, the lord of the country, said to us, "This is how I shall discover if you are honest men: leave one of your brothers with me, take food for your starving households and go; [34] bring your youngest brother to me, and I shall know that you are honest men and not spies. Then I shall restore your brother to you, and you can move around the country freely." ' [35] But on emptying their sacks, each of them found his silver inside, and when they and their father saw the bundles of silver, they were afraid. [36] Their father Jacob said to them, 'You have robbed me of my children. Joseph is lost; Simeon is lost; and now you would take Benjamin. Everything is against me.' [37] Reuben said to his father, 'You may put both my sons to death if I do not bring him back to you. Entrust him to me, and I shall bring him back.' [38] But Jacob said, 'My son must not go with you, for his brother is dead and he alone is left. Should he come to any

42:33 **food:** *so Gk; Heb. omits.*

42.1–38: Joseph's brothers travel to Egypt. 6: *Bowed:* thus fulfilling Joseph's dreams (37.5–11). **15:** Joseph's purpose is to discomfit his half-brothers (see v. 21) by demanding to see Benjamin, his only full brother.

harm on the journey, you will bring down my grey hairs in sorrow to the grave.'

43 The famine was still severe in the land. ²When the grain they had brought from Egypt was all used up, their father said to them, 'Go again and buy some more grain for us to eat.' ³Judah replied, 'But the man warned us that we must not go into his presence unless our brother was with us. ⁴If you let our brother go with us, we will go down and buy you food. ⁵But if you will not let him, we cannot go, for the man declared, "You shall not come into my presence unless your brother is with you."' ⁶Israel said, 'Why have you treated me so badly by telling the man that you had another brother?' ⁷They answered, 'The man questioned us closely about ourselves and our family: "Is your father still alive?" he asked, "Have you a brother?" and we answered his questions. How were we to know he would tell us to bring our brother down?' ⁸Judah said to Israel his father, 'Send the boy with me; then we can start at once, and save everyone's life, ours, yours, and those of our children. ⁹I shall go surety for him, and you may hold me responsible. If I do not bring him back and restore him to you, you can blame me for it all my life. ¹⁰If we had not wasted all this time, we could have made the journey twice by now.'

¹¹Their father Israel said to them, 'If it must be so, then do this: in your baggage take, as a gift for the man, some of the produce for which our country is famous: a little balm and honey, with gum tragacanth, myrrh, pistachio nuts, and almonds. ¹²Take double the amount of silver with you and give back what was returned to you in your packs; perhaps there was some mistake. ¹³Take your brother with you and go straight back to the man. ¹⁴May God Almighty make him kindly disposed to you, and may he send back the one whom you left behind, and Benjamin too. As for me, if I am bereaved, I am bereaved.' ¹⁵So they took the gift and double the amount of silver, and accompanied by Benjamin they started at once for Egypt, where they presented themselves to Joseph.

¹⁶When Joseph saw Benjamin with them, he said to his steward, 'Bring these men indoors; then kill a beast and prepare a meal, for they are to eat with me at midday.' ¹⁷He brought the men into Joseph's house as he had been ordered. ¹⁸They were afraid because they had been brought there; they thought, 'We have been brought in here because of that affair of the silver which was replaced in our packs the first time. He means to make some charge against us, to inflict punishment on us, seize our donkeys, and make us his slaves.' ¹⁹So they approached Joseph's steward and spoke to him at the door of the house. ²⁰'Please listen, my lord,' they said. 'After our first visit to buy food, ²¹when we reached the place where we were to spend the night, we opened our packs and each of us found his silver, the full amount of it, at the top of his pack. We have brought it back with us, ²²and we have more silver to buy food. We do not know who put the silver in our packs.' ²³He answered, 'Calm yourselves; do not be afraid. It must have been your God, the God of your father, who hid treasure for you in your packs. I did receive the silver.' Then he brought Simeon out to them.

²⁴The steward conducted them into Joseph's house and gave them water to bathe their feet, and provided feed for their donkeys. ²⁵They had their gifts ready against Joseph's arrival at midday, for they had heard that they were to eat there. ²⁶When he came into the house, they presented him with the gifts which they had brought, bowing to the ground before him. ²⁷He asked them how they were and said, 'Is your father well, the old man of whom you spoke? Is he still alive?' ²⁸'Yes, my lord, our father is still alive and well,' they answered, bowing low in obeisance. ²⁹When Joseph looked around he saw his own mother's son, his brother Benjamin, and asked, 'Is this your youngest brother, of whom you told me?' and to Benjamin he said, 'May God be gracious to you, my son!' ³⁰Joseph, suddenly overcome by his feelings for his brother, was almost in tears, and he went into the inner room and wept. ³¹Then, having bathed his face, he came out and, with his feelings now under control, he ordered the meal to be served. ³²He was served by him-

---

42:38 **the grave:** *Heb.* Sheol.   43:14 **the one:** *so Samar.;* *Heb.* the other.   43:23 **father:** *or, with Samar.,* fathers.

43.1–34: The second journey to Egypt. Jacob reluctantly lets Benjamin accompany his brothers. **8–10:** Judah is here the spokesman; it was Reuben in 42.37. See 37.18–30 n. **26–28:** *Bowing:* 42.6 n. **32:** *Hebrews:* 10.21 n.

self, and the brothers by themselves; the Egyptians who were at the meal were also served separately, for to Egyptians it is abhorrent to eat with Hebrews. 33 When at his direction the brothers were seated, the eldest first and so on down to the youngest, they looked at one another in astonishment. 34 Joseph sent them each a portion from what was before him, but Benjamin's portion was five times larger than any of the others. So they feasted and drank with him.

44 Joseph gave the steward these instructions: 'Fill the men's packs with food, as much as they can carry, and put each man's silver at the top of his pack. 2 And put my goblet, the silver one, at the top of the youngest brother's pack along with the silver for the grain.' He did as Joseph had told him. 3 At first light the brothers were allowed to take their donkeys and set off; 4 but before they had gone very far from the city, Joseph said to his steward, 'Go after those men at once, and when you catch up with them, say, "Why have you repaid good with evil? 5 Why have you stolen the silver goblet? It is the one my lord drinks from, and which he uses for divination. This is a wicked thing you have done."' 6 When the steward overtook them, he reported his master's words. 7 But they replied, 'My lord, how can you say such things? Heaven forbid that we should do such a thing! 8 Look! The silver we found at the top of our packs we brought back to you from Canaan. Why, then, should we steal silver or gold from your master's house? 9 If any one of us is found with the goblet, he shall die; and, what is more, my lord, the rest of us shall become your slaves.' 10 He said, 'Very well; I accept what you say. Only the one in whose possession it is found will become my slave; the rest will go free.' 11 Each quickly lowered his pack to the ground and opened it, 12 and when the steward searched, beginning with the eldest and finishing with the youngest, the goblet was found in Benjamin's pack. 13 At this they tore their clothes; then one and all they loaded their donkeys and returned to the city.

14 Joseph was still in the house when Judah and his brothers arrived, and they threw themselves on the ground before him. 15 Joseph said, 'What is this you have done? You might have known that a man such as I am

uses divination.' 16 Judah said, 'What can we say, my lord? What can we plead, or how can we clear ourselves? God has uncovered our crime. Here we are, my lord, ready to be made your slaves, we ourselves as well as the one who was found with the goblet.' 17 'Heaven forbid that I should do such a thing!' answered Joseph. 'Only the one who was found with the goblet shall become my slave; the rest of you can go home to your father safe and sound.'

18 Then Judah went up to him and said, 'Please listen, my lord, and let your servant speak a word, I beg. Do not be angry with me, for you are as great as Pharaoh himself. 19 My lord, you asked us whether we had a father or a brother. 20 We answered, "We have an aged father, and he has a young son born in his old age; this boy's full brother is dead, and since he alone is left of his mother's children, his father loves him." 21 You said to us, your servants, "Bring him down to me so that I may set eyes on him." 22 We told you, my lord, that the boy could not leave his father; his father would die if he left him. 23 But you said, "Unless your youngest brother comes down with you, you shall not enter my presence again." 24 We went back to your servant my father, and reported to him what your lordship had said, 25 so when our father told us to go again and buy food, 26 we answered, "We cannot go down; for without our youngest brother we cannot enter the man's presence; but if our brother is with us, we will go." 27 Then your servant my father said to us, "You know that my wife bore me two sons. 28 One left me, and I said, 'He must have been torn to pieces.' I have not seen him since. 29 If you take this one from me as well, and he comes to any harm, then you will bring down my grey hairs in misery to the grave." 30 Now, my lord, if I return to my father without the boy — and remember, his life is bound up with the boy's — 31 what will happen is this: he will see that the boy is not with us and he will die, and your servants will have brought down our father's grey hairs in sorrow to the grave. 32 Indeed, my lord, it was I who went surety for the boy to my father. I said, "If I do not bring him back to you, then you can blame me for it all my life." 33 Now, my lord,

44:5 **Why ... goblet?:** *so Gk; Heb. omits.*

44.1–34: Joseph further discomfits his brothers. 15: He implies that the theft was discovered through *divination.* **17:** Joseph wants to see if his brothers will, as previously, sell one of their own into slavery.

let me remain in place of the boy as my lord's slave, and let him go with his brothers. ³⁴ How can I return to my father without the boy? I could not bear to see the misery which my father would suffer.'

45 Joseph was no longer able to control his feelings in front of all his attendants, and he called, 'Let everyone leave my presence!' There was nobody present when Joseph made himself known to his brothers, ²but he wept so loudly that the Egyptians heard him, and news of it got to Pharaoh's household. ³Joseph said to his brothers, 'I am Joseph! Can my father be still alive?' They were so dumbfounded at finding themselves face to face with Joseph that they could not answer. ⁴Joseph said to them, 'Come closer to me,' and when they did so, he said, 'I am your brother Joseph, whom you sold into Egypt. ⁵Now do not be distressed or blame yourselves for selling me into slavery here; it was to save lives that God sent me ahead of you. ⁶For there have now been two years of famine in the land, and there will be another five years with neither ploughing nor harvest. ⁷God sent me on ahead of you to ensure that you will have descendants on earth, and to preserve for you a host of survivors. ⁸It is clear that it was not you who sent me here, but God, and he has made me Pharaoh's chief counsellor, lord over his whole household and ruler of all Egypt. ⁹Hurry back to my father and give him this message from his son Joseph: "God has made me lord of all Egypt. Come down to me without delay. ¹⁰You will live in the land of Goshen and be near me, you, your children and grandchildren, your flocks and herds, and all that you have. ¹¹I shall provide for you there and see that you and your household and all that you have are not reduced to want; for there are still five years of famine to come." ¹²You can see for yourselves, and so can my brother Benjamin, that it is really Joseph himself who is speaking to you. ¹³Tell my father of all the honour which I enjoy in Egypt, tell him all you have seen, and bring him down here with all speed.' ¹⁴He threw his arms round his brother Benjamin and wept, and Benjamin

too embraced him weeping. ¹⁵He then kissed each of his brothers and wept over them; after that his brothers were able to talk with him.

¹⁶When the report reached the royal palace that Joseph's brothers had come, Pharaoh and his officials were pleased. ¹⁷Pharaoh told Joseph to say to his brothers: 'This is what you must do. Load your beasts and go straight back to Canaan. ¹⁸Fetch your father and your households and come to me. I shall give you the best region there is in Egypt, and you will enjoy the fat of the land.' ¹⁹He was also to tell them: 'Take wagons from Egypt for your dependants and your wives and fetch your father back here. ²⁰Have no regrets at leaving your possessions, for all the best there is in the whole of Egypt is yours.'

²¹Israel's sons followed these instructions, and Joseph supplied them with wagons, as Pharaoh had ordered, and provisions for the journey. ²²To each of them he gave new clothes, but to Benjamin he gave three hundred pieces of silver and five sets of clothes. ²³Moreover he sent his father ten donkeys carrying the finest products of Egypt, and ten she-donkeys laden with grain, bread, and other provisions for the journey. ²⁴He sent his brothers on their way, warning them not to quarrel among themselves on the road. ²⁵They set off, and went up from Egypt to their father Jacob in Canaan. ²⁶When they told him that Joseph was still alive and was ruler of the whole of Egypt, he was stunned at the news and did not believe them. ²⁷However when they reported to him all that Joseph had said to them, and when he saw the wagons which Joseph had provided to fetch him, his spirit revived. ²⁸Israel said, 'It is enough! Joseph my son is still alive; I shall go and see him before I die.'

The Israelites in Egypt

46 ISRAEL set out with all that he had and came to Beersheba, where he offered sacrifices to the God of his father Isaac.

45:8 **chief counsellor:** *lit.* father.

45.1–28: **Joseph discloses his identity. 5–8:** A central teaching of the Joseph story now unfolds: despite the evil intent of the brothers, God has worked to insure the realization of the divine promise. Thus, ultimate judgment cannot be passed upon momentarily unfavorable events. **16–20:** Ancient Egyptian sources relate the arrival of Asiatic nomads by such means.

46.1–47.12: **Jacob and his family settle in Egypt.** The stage is now set for the subsequent enslavement and

2 God called to Israel in a vision by night, 'Jacob! Jacob!' and he answered, 'I am here.' 3 God said, 'I am God, the God of your father. Do not be afraid to go down to Egypt, for there I shall make you a great nation. 4 I shall go down to Egypt with you, and I myself shall bring you back again without fail; and Joseph's will be the hands that close your eyes.' 5 So Jacob set out from Beersheba. Israel's sons conveyed their father Jacob along with their wives and children in the wagons which Pharaoh had sent to bring him. 6 They took their herds and the goods they had acquired in Canaan and came to Egypt, Jacob and all his family with him; 7 his sons and their sons, his daughters and his sons' daughters, he brought them all to Egypt.

8 These are the names of the Israelites, Jacob and his sons, who entered Egypt: Reuben, Jacob's eldest son, 9 and the sons of Reuben: Enoch, Pallu, Hezron, and Carmi. 10 The sons of Simeon: Jemuel, Jamin, Ohad, Jachin, Zohar, and Saul, who was the son of a Canaanite woman. 11 The sons of Levi: Gershon, Kohath, and Merari. 12 The sons of Judah: Er, Onan, Shelah, Perez, and Zerah; of these Er and Onan died in Canaan. The sons of Perez were Hezron and Hamul. 13 The sons of Issachar: Tola, Pua, Iob, and Shimron. 14 The sons of Zebulun: Sered, Elon, and Jahleel. 15 These are the sons of Leah whom she bore to Jacob in Paddan-aram, and there was also his daughter Dinah. His sons and daughters numbered thirty-three in all.

16 The sons of Gad: Ziphion, Haggi, Shuni, Ezbon, Eri, Arodi, and Areli. 17 The sons of Asher: Imnah, Ishvah, Ishvi, Beriah, and their sister Serah. The sons of Beriah: Heber and Malchiel. 18 These are the descendants of Zilpah whom Laban gave to his daughter Leah, sixteen in all, born to Jacob.

19 The sons of Jacob's wife Rachel: Joseph and Benjamin. 20 Manasseh and Ephraim were born to Joseph in Egypt; Asenath daughter of Potiphera priest of On bore them to him. 21 The sons of Benjamin: Bela, Becher, and Ashbel; and the sons of Bela: Gera, Naaman, Ehi, Rosh, Muppim, Huppim, and Ard. 22 These are the descendants of Rachel, fourteen in all, born to Jacob.

23 The son of Dan: Hushim. 24 The sons of Naphtali: Jahzeel, Guni, Jezer, and Shillem. 25 These are the descendants of Bilhah whom Laban had given to his daughter Rachel, seven in all, born to Jacob.

26 All the persons who came to Egypt with Jacob, his direct descendants, not including the wives of his sons, were sixty-six in all. 27 Two sons were born to Joseph in Egypt. Thus the whole house of Jacob numbered seventy when it entered Egypt.

28 Jacob sent Judah ahead to Joseph to advise him that he was on his way to Goshen. They entered Goshen, 29 and Joseph had his chariot yoked to go up there to meet Israel his father. When they met, Joseph threw his arms round him and wept on his shoulder for a long time. 30 Israel said to Joseph, 'I have seen for myself that you are still alive. Now I am ready to die.' 31 Joseph said to his brothers and to his father's household, 'I shall go up and inform Pharaoh; I shall tell him, "My brothers and my father's household who were in Canaan have come to me. 32 The men are shepherds with their own flocks and herds, and they have brought with them these flocks and herds and everything they possess." 33 So when Pharaoh summons you and asks what your occupation is, 34 you must answer, "My lord, we have herded flocks all our lives, as our fathers did before us." You must say this if you are to settle in Goshen, because shepherds are regarded as unclean by Egyptians.'

47 Joseph came and reported to Pharaoh, 'My father and my brothers have arrived from Canaan, with their flocks and herds and everything they possess, and they are now in Goshen.' 2 He had chosen five of his brothers, and he brought them into Pharaoh's presence. 3 When he asked them what their occupation was, they answered, 'We are shepherds like our fathers before us, 4 and we have come to stay in this country, because owing to the severe famine in Canaan there is no pasture there for our flocks. We ask your majesty's leave to settle now in Goshen.' 5 Pharaoh said to Joseph, 'As to your father and your brothers who have come to you, 6 the land of Egypt is at your disposal; settle them in the best part of it. Let them live

46:21 **and the sons of Bela:** *so Gk; Heb. omits.*

deliverance. **4:** *You:* here the "you" is the corporate Israel, not the single ancestor himself, for Jacob died in Egypt (49.33–50.3). **27:** *Seventy:* usually a round number (Exod. 15.27; 24.1; 2 Sam. 24.15; for other such numbers see 7.2 n.; 7.4 n.). The previous list (vv. 8–25) has undergone several adjustments and harmonizain Goshen, and if you know of any among them with the skill, make them chief herdsmen in charge of my cattle.'

⁷Then Joseph brought his father in and presented him to Pharaoh. Jacob blessed Pharaoh, ⁸who asked him his age, ⁹and he answered, 'The years of my life on earth are one hundred and thirty; few and hard have they been—fewer than the years my fathers lived.' ¹⁰Jacob then blessed Pharaoh and withdrew from his presence. ¹¹As Pharaoh had ordered, Joseph settled his father and his brothers, and allotted land to them in Egypt, in the best part of the country, the district of Rameses. ¹²He supported his father, his brothers, and his father's whole household with the food they needed.

¹³There was no food anywhere, so very severe was the famine; Egypt and Canaan were laid low by it. ¹⁴Joseph gathered in all the money in Egypt and Canaan in exchange for the grain which the people bought, and put it in Pharaoh's treasury. ¹⁵When the money in Egypt and Canaan had come to an end, the Egyptians all came to Joseph. 'Give us food,' they said, 'or we shall perish before your very eyes. Our money is all gone.' ¹⁶Joseph replied, 'If your money is all gone, hand over your livestock and I shall give you food in return.' ¹⁷So they brought their livestock to Joseph, who gave them food in exchange for their horses, their flocks of sheep, their herds of cattle, and their donkeys. He supported them that year with food in exchange for all their herds. ¹⁸The year came to an end, and in the following year they came to him and said, 'My lord, we cannot conceal from you that with our money finished and our herds of cattle made over to you, there is nothing left for your lordship but our bodies and our lands. ¹⁹Why should we perish before your eyes, we and our land as well? Take us and our land in payment for food, and we and our land alike will be in bondage to Pharaoh. Give us seed-corn to keep us alive, or we shall die and our land will become desert.'

²⁰So Joseph acquired for Pharaoh all the land in Egypt: because the Egyptians, hardpressed by the famine, sold all their fields, and the land became Pharaoh's. ²¹Joseph moved the people into the towns throughout the whole territory of Egypt. ²²Only the land which belonged to the priests Joseph did not buy; they had a fixed allowance from Pharaoh and lived on this, so that they did not have to sell their land.

²³Joseph said to the people, 'Listen; I have now bought you and your land for Pharaoh. Here is seed-corn for you. Sow the land, ²⁴but at harvest give one fifth of the crop to Pharaoh. Four fifths shall be yours to provide seed for your fields and food for yourselves, your households, and your dependants.' ²⁵'You have saved our lives,' the people said. 'If it please your lordship, we shall be Pharaoh's slaves.' ²⁶Joseph established it as a law in Egypt that one fifth of the produce should belong to Pharaoh, and so it has been from that day to this. It was only the priests' land that did not pass into Pharaoh's hands.

²⁷Thus Israel settled in Egypt, in Goshen, where they acquired land, and were fruitful, and increased greatly. ²⁸Jacob lived in Egypt for seventeen years and died at the age of a hundred and forty-seven. ²⁹When the hour of his death drew near, he summoned his son Joseph and said to him, 'I have a favour to ask: give me your solemn oath that you will deal loyally and faithfully with me; do not bury me in Egypt. ³⁰So that I may lie with my forefathers, you are to take me up from Egypt and bury me in their grave.' He answered, 'I shall do as you say.' ³¹'Swear that you will,' said Jacob. So he gave him his oath, and Israel bowed in worship by the head of his bed.

48 Some time later Joseph was informed that his father was ill, so he took his two sons, Manasseh and Ephraim, with him and came to Jacob. ²When Jacob heard that his son Joseph had come to him, he gathered

47:29 **give ... oath:** *lit.* put your hand under my thigh.   47:31 **head of his bed:** *or, with Gk,* top of his staff (*cp. Hebrews 11:21*).

tions. **47.9:** *One hundred and thirty:* Abraham lived to one hundred and seventy-five (25.7), Isaac to one hundred and eighty (35.28); see 5.4 n. **11:** *District of Rameses:* a synonym for Goshen (45.10), it is also the name of a city built by Hebrew slaves (see Exod. 1.11).

47.13–26: Joseph's economic policies. The story may reflect the actual affairs in Egypt (such as the Pharaoh's property rights at a given age) at the beginning of the New Kingdom.

47.27–48.22: Jacob's blessing of Ephraim and Manasseh. 29: *Solemn oath:* see 24.2 n. **48.5:** *My sons:* the his strength and sat up in bed. ³Jacob said to Joseph, 'God Almighty appeared to me at Luz in Canaan and blessed me; ⁴he said to me, "I shall make you fruitful and increase your descendants until they become a host of nations. I shall give this land to them after you as a possession for all time." ⁵Now,' Jacob went on, 'your two sons, who were born in Egypt before I came to join you here, will be counted as my sons; Ephraim and Manasseh will be mine as Reuben and Simeon are. ⁶But the children born to you after them will be counted as yours; in respect of their tribal territory they will be reckoned under their elder brothers' names. ⁷In Canaan on my return from Paddan-aram and while we were still some distance from Ephrath, your mother Rachel died on the way, and I buried her there by the road to Ephrath' (that is Bethlehem).

⁸When Israel saw Joseph's sons, he said, 'Who are these?' ⁹'They are my sons', replied Joseph, 'whom God has given me here.' Israel said, 'Then bring them to me, that I may bless them.' ¹⁰Now Israel's eyes were dim with age, and he could hardly see. Joseph brought the boys close to his father, and he kissed them and embraced them. ¹¹He said to Joseph, 'I had not expected to see your face again, and now God has let me see your sons as well.' ¹²Joseph removed them from his father's knees and bowed to the ground. ¹³Then he took the two of them and brought them close to Israel: Ephraim on the right, that is Israel's left; and Manasseh on the left, that is Israel's right. ¹⁴But Israel, crossing his hands, stretched out his right hand and laid it on Ephraim's head, although he was the younger, and laid his left hand on Manasseh's head, even though he was the firstborn. ¹⁵He blessed Joseph and said:

'The God in whose presence my
    forefathers lived,

my forefathers Abraham and Isaac,
    the God who has been my shepherd all
        my life to this day,
¹⁶the angel who rescued me from all
        misfortune,
may he bless these boys;
    they will be called by my name,
    and by the names of my forefathers,
        Abraham and Isaac;
may they grow into a great people on
    earth.'

¹⁷When Joseph saw his father laying his right hand on Ephraim's head, he was displeased and took hold of his father's hand to move it from Ephraim's head to Manasseh's. ¹⁸He said, 'That is not right, father. This is the firstborn; lay your right hand on his head.' ¹⁹But his father refused; he said, 'I know, my son, I know. He too will become a people, and he too will become great. Yet his younger brother will be greater than he, and his descendants will be a whole nation in themselves.' ²⁰So he blessed them that day and said:

'When a blessing is pronounced in
    Israel,
men shall use your names and say,
    "May God make you like Ephraim and
        Manasseh." '

So he set Ephraim before Manasseh. ²¹Then Israel said to Joseph, 'I am about to die, but God will be with you and bring you back to the land of your fathers, ²²where I assign you one ridge of land more than your brothers; I took it from the Amorites with sword and bow.'

48:7 **Paddan-aram:** *so Samar.; Heb.* Paddan. **your mother:** *so Samar.; Heb.* omits.   48:9 **bless them:** *or* take them on my knees.   48:22 **ridge of land:** *Heb.* shechem, *meaning* shoulder.

account seems to suggest that these two tribes were not among the early members of the league of twelve tribes specified in 49.1–27, but later came to be included (see Deut. 33.17). The prose account here is younger than the poem in ch. 49. The fading away of Simeon (see 34.1–31 n.) kept the total number at twelve. **9:** *Bless them:* receiving a child on one's knees (see Tfn.) was a formal part of an adoption procedure. **14:** The *firstborn* would be expected to occupy a position of military and tribal prominence (see Num. 26.28–37 n.). **17–19:** The later emergence of Ephraim to a position of great power in Israel is explained. It was, like events both before and after, a manifestation of God's mysterious freedom. **20:** The blessing seems to be another version of that in vv. 15–16. **21:** *Bring you back:* see Exod. 13.19. **22:** *Ridge:* in Heb., *sh'chem;* there is a pun here on the place name Shechem. There may be some obscure historical allusion which is at variance with the peaceful settlement suggested in 33.18–20.

49 Jacob summoned his sons. 'Come near,' he said, 'and I shall tell you what is to happen to you in days to come.

2 'Gather round me and listen, you sons of Jacob;
listen to Israel your father.

3 'Reuben, you are my firstborn,
my strength and the first fruit of my vigour,
excelling in pride, excelling in might.
4 Uncontrollable as a flood, you will excel no more,
because you climbed into your father's bed,
and defiled his concubine's couch.

5 'Simeon and Levi are brothers,
weapons of violence are their counsels.
6 My soul will not enter their council,
my heart will not join their assembly;
for in anger they killed men,
wantonly they hamstrung oxen.
7 A curse be on their anger, for it was fierce;
a curse on their wrath, for it was ruthless!
I shall scatter them in Jacob,
I shall disperse them in Israel.

8 'Judah, your brothers will praise you;
your hand will be on the neck of your enemies.
Your father's sons will bow to you in homage.
9 Judah, a lion's whelp,
you have returned from the kill, my son;
you crouch and stretch like a lion,
like a lion no one dares rouse.
10 The sceptre will not pass from Judah,
nor the staff from between his feet,

until he receives what is his due
and the obedience of the nations is his.
11 He tethers his donkey to the vine,
and its colt to the red vine;
he washes his cloak in wine,
his robe in the blood of grapes.
12 Darker than wine are his eyes,
whiter than milk his teeth.

13 'Zebulun lives by the seashore;
his coast is a haven for ships,
and his frontier touches Sidon.

14 'Issachar, a gelded donkey
lying down in the cattle pens,
15 saw that a settled home was good
and that the land was pleasant,
so he bent his back to the burden
and submitted to forced labour.

16 'Dan — his people will be strong
as any tribe in Israel!
17 Let Dan be a viper on the road,
a horned snake on the path,
that bites the horse's fetlock
so that the rider is thrown off backwards.

18 'I wait in hope for salvation from you, Lord.

19 'Gad is raided by raiders,
and he will raid them from the rear.

20 'Asher will feast every day,
and provide dishes fit for a king.

21 'Naphtali is a spreading terebinth
putting forth lovely boughs.

49:5 **counsels:** *Heb. word of uncertain meaning.*
49:10 **he receives . . . his due:** *or, as otherwise read,* Shiloh comes.   49:14 **gelded:** *so Samar.; or Heb.* bony.   49:16 **Dan . . . Israel:** *or* Dan will govern his people as one of the tribes of Israel.

49.1–27: The "Blessing of Jacob." The ancestor portrays the character and destiny of the tribes as these are represented by their ancestors. 3–4: A leading tribe in the early period, *Reuben* had acted indecisively (Judg. 5.15–16) and dwindled in numbers (Deut. 33.6). See 35.22 n. 5–7: On their attack against Shechem, here alluded to, see 34.1–31 n. *Simeon* was later absorbed into the tribe of Judah while the *Levites* assumed a religious status, losing their political character (Deut. 10.8–9). 8–12: The passage seems to allude to the reign of David; this provides a clue to the date of the composition of the chapter, which, however, uses earlier material. 14–15: The writer utilizes a folk etymology, whereby *Issachar* means "hired worker," in order to explain the tribe's subordination, possibly to Canaanites. The animal is a domesticated beast. 16–17: The Heb. word for "will govern" (see Tfn.), *yadin*, involves a play on the tribal name. 18: Possibly an invocation, used when the material was read in public. 19: Situated east of the Jordan river, *Gad* was often subject to raids from the east by desert tribes. 20: The fertile Mediterranean coast north of Carmel is meant (see Deut. 33.24). 21:

²²'Joseph is a fruitful tree by a spring,
  whose branches climb over the wall.
²³The archers savagely attacked him,
  shooting and assailing him fiercely,
²⁴but Joseph's bow remained unfailing
  and his arms were tireless
  by the power of the Strong One of
  Jacob,
  by the name of the Shepherd of Israel,
²⁵by the God of your father—so may he
  help you!
  By God Almighty—so may he bless you
  with the blessings of heaven above,
  and the blessings of the deep that lies
  below!
  The blessings of breast and womb
²⁶and the blessings of your father are
  stronger
  than the blessings of the eternal
  mountains
  and the bounty of the everlasting hills.
  May they rest on the head of Joseph,
  on the brow of him who was prince
  among his brothers.

²⁷'Benjamin is a ravening wolf:
  in the morning he devours the prey,
  in the evening he snatches a share of
  the spoil.'

²⁸These are the tribes of Israel, twelve in all,
and this was what their father said to them,
when he blessed them each in turn. ²⁹Then
he gave them his last charge and said, 'I am
about to be gathered to my ancestors; bury
me with my forefathers in the cave on the
plot of land which belonged to Ephron the
Hittite, ³⁰that is the cave on the plot of land
at Machpelah east of Mamre in Canaan, the
field which Abraham bought from Ephron
the Hittite for a burial-place. ³¹There Abraham was buried with his wife Sarah; there
Isaac and his wife Rebecca were buried; and
that is where I buried Leah. ³²The land and
the cave there were bought from the Hittites.' ³³When Jacob had finished giving
these instructions to his sons, he drew up his
feet on to the bed, breathed his last, and was
gathered to his ancestors.

50 Then Joseph threw himself upon his
father, weeping over him and kissing
him. ²He gave orders to the physicians in his
service to embalm his father, and they did so,
³finishing the task in forty days, the usual
time required for embalming. ⁴The Egyptians mourned Israel for seventy days.
⁵When the period of mourning was over,
Joseph spoke to members of Pharaoh's
household: 'May I ask a favour—please
speak for me to Pharaoh. Tell him that my
father on his deathbed made me swear that
I would bury him in the grave that he had
bought for himself in Canaan. Ask Pharaoh
to let me go up and bury my father; and
afterwards I shall return.' ⁶Pharaoh's reply
was: 'Go and bury your father in accordance
with your oath.' ⁷So Joseph went up to bury
his father, and with him went all Pharaoh's
officials, the elders of his household, and all
the elders of Egypt, ⁸as well as all Joseph's
own household, his brothers, and his father's
household; only their children, with the
flocks and herds, were left in Goshen. ⁹Char-
iots as well as horsemen went up with him, a
very great company.

¹⁰When they came to the threshing-floor
of Atad beside the river Jordan, they raised
a loud and bitter lamentation; and Joseph
observed seven days' mourning for his father. ¹¹When the Canaanites who lived there
saw this mourning at the threshing-floor of
Atad, they said, 'How bitterly the Egyptians
are mourning!' So they named the place beside the Jordan Abel-mizraim.

¹²Thus Jacob's sons did to him as he had
instructed them: ¹³they took him to Canaan
and buried him in the cave on the plot of land
at Machpelah, the land which Abraham had
bought as a burial-place from Ephron the
Hittite, to the east of Mamre. ¹⁴After burying
his father, Joseph returned to Egypt with his
brothers and all who had gone up with him
for the burial.

¹⁵Now that their father was dead, Joseph's

49:24 **Shepherd:** *prob. rdg; Heb. adds* stone.
50:5 **bought:** *or* dug.   50:11 **Abel-mizraim:** *that is*
Mourning of Egypt.

Naphtali was situated in the beautiful territory around Lake Tiberias. **22:** *Joseph:* this tradition is relatively early,
since Ephraim and Manasseh have not yet emerged as significant political entities (see 48.5 n.).

49.28–50.26: The deaths of Jacob and Joseph. 50.3: *Forty:* 7.4 n. **4:** *Seventy:* other sources say that the
Egyptians mourned their kings for seventy-two days. Because of Joseph's position, his father is given a royal

brothers were afraid, for they said, 'What if Joseph should bear a grudge against us and pay us back for all the harm we did to him?' 16 They therefore sent a messenger to Joseph to say, 'In his last words to us before he died, your father gave us this message: 17 "Say this to Joseph: I ask you to forgive your brothers' crime and wickedness; I know they did you harm." So now we beg you: forgive our crime, for we are servants of your father's God.' Joseph was moved to tears by their words. 18 His brothers approached and bowed to the ground before him. 'We are your slaves,' they said. 19 But Joseph replied, 'Do not be afraid. Am I in the place of God? 20 You meant to do me harm; but God meant to bring good out of it by preserving the lives of many people, as we see today. 21 Do not be

afraid. I shall provide for you and your dependants.' Thus he comforted them and set their minds at rest.

22 Joseph remained in Egypt, he and his father's household. He lived to be a hundred and ten years old, 23 and saw Ephraim's children to the third generation; he also recognized as his the children of Manasseh's son Machir. 24 He said to his brothers, 'I am about to die; but God will not fail to come to your aid and take you from here to the land which he promised on oath to Abraham, Isaac, and Jacob.' 25 He made the sons of Israel solemnly swear that when God came to their aid, they would carry his bones up with them from there. 26 So Joseph died in Egypt at the age of a hundred and ten, and he was embalmed and laid in a coffin.

funeral. **10–11:** *Atad:* an unknown location, seemingly not Machpelah of vv. 12–13 (see ch. 23). **18:** *Bowed to the ground:* the story concludes by hearkening back to a motif presented at its beginning (37.5–11). **20:** *God meant:* see 45.5–8 n. **23:** *Recognized as his:* lit. "were born upon the knees of Joseph." This adoption procedure (see 48.9 n.) signifies the admission of the clans of Machir (Judg. 5.14; Num. 32.39–40) into the Israelite confederation.

Exodus

The migration of Jacob's family to Egypt, undertaken with high expectation and understood as an act of God's grace (Gen. chs. 37–50), becomes the occasion for bondage to the Pharaoh. The promise (Gen. 12.1–3; 15.1–21; 17.1–8) now seemed but a delusion. Yet, the day arrived when Israel escaped and survived in the wilderness. At a sacred mountain the people reflected upon the meaning of God's past redemption, and pledged to become a community obedient only to the LORD's will. (The account was handed down in several versions, which were then combined into the present form; see Introduction to the Pentateuch). When subsequent generations heard the stirring story, they found parallels to the disappointments of their times, and also hope for the future.

The book has two major parts: chs. 1–18, relating the oppression, the manner of deliverance and the arrival at the sacred mountain under the leadership of Moses; and chs. 19–40, giving various accounts of the covenant regulations by means of which the community was to govern its life and worship.

Literary and archaeological evidence points to the period of the Nineteenth Egyptian Dynasty (about 1300 B.C.E.) as the most likely setting for the events.

The Israelites in Egypt

1 THESE are the names of the sons of Israel who, along with their households, accompanied Jacob to Egypt: ² Reuben, Simeon, Levi, and Judah; ³ Issachar, Zebulun, and Benjamin; ⁴ Dan and Naphtali, Gad and Asher. ⁵ All told there were seventy direct descendants of Jacob. Joseph was already in Egypt.

⁶ In course of time Joseph and all his brothers and that entire generation died. ⁷ The Israelites were prolific and increased greatly, becoming so numerous and strong that the land was full of them. ⁸ When a new king ascended the throne of Egypt, one who did not know about Joseph, ⁹ he said to his people, 'These Israelites have become too many and too strong for us. ¹⁰ We must take steps to ensure that they increase no further; otherwise we shall find that, if war comes, they will side with the enemy, fight against us, and become masters of the country.' ¹¹ So taskmasters were appointed over them to oppress them with forced labour. This is how Pharaoh's store cities, Pithom and Rameses,

were built. ¹² But the more oppressive the treatment of the Israelites, the more they increased and spread, until the Egyptians came to loathe them. ¹³ They ground down their Israelite slaves, ¹⁴ and made life bitter for them with their harsh demands, setting them to make mortar and bricks and to do all sorts of tasks in the fields. In every kind of labour they made ruthless use of them.

¹⁵ The king of Egypt issued instructions to the Hebrew midwives, of whom one was called Shiphrah, the other Puah. ¹⁶ 'When you are attending the Hebrew women in childbirth,' he told them, 'check as the child is delivered: if it is a boy, kill him; if it is a girl, however, let her live.' ¹⁷ But the midwives were godfearing women, and did not heed the king's words; they let the male children live. ¹⁸ Pharaoh summoned the midwives and, when he asked them why they had done this and let the male children live, ¹⁹ they answered, 'Hebrew women are not like Egyptian women; they go into labour and give birth before the midwife arrives.' ²⁰ God made the midwives prosper, and the people

1:10 **become ... country:** or escape from the country.

1.1–22: The bondage in Egypt begins. 5: Seventy: a round number (Gen. 46.27 n.). **7:** Were prolific: in keeping with the divine command at creation (Gen. 1.28) and with the promise to Abraham (Gen. 15.5; 17.5–6). **8:** The new king may be a member of the Nineteenth Dynasty, which came to power between 1320 and 1310 B.C.E. **10:** The new dynasty, hoping to recover an Asiatic empire, regarded the alien Hebrews (Gen. 10.21 n.) along its border as a security risk.

increased in numbers and strength; ²¹and because the midwives feared God he gave them families of their own. ²²Pharaoh then issued an order to all the Egyptians that every new-born Hebrew boy was to be thrown into the Nile, but all the girls were to be allowed to live.

Moses

2 A certain man, a descendant of Levi, married a Levite woman. ²She conceived and bore a son, and when she saw what a fine child he was, she kept him hidden for three months. ³Unable to conceal him any longer, she got a rush basket for him, made it watertight with pitch and tar, laid him in it, and placed it among the reeds by the bank of the Nile. ⁴The child's sister stood some distance away to see what would happen to him.

⁵Pharaoh's daughter came down to bathe in the river, while her ladies-in-waiting walked on the bank. She noticed the basket among the reeds and sent her slave-girl to bring it. ⁶When she opened it, there was the baby; it was crying, and she was moved with pity for it. 'This must be one of the Hebrew children,' she said. ⁷At this the sister approached Pharaoh's daughter: 'Shall I go and fetch you one of the Hebrew women to act as a wet-nurse for the child?' ⁸When Pharaoh's daughter told her to do so, she went and called the baby's mother. ⁹Pharaoh's daughter said to her, 'Take the child, nurse him for me, and I shall pay you for it.' She took the child and nursed him at her breast. ¹⁰Then, when he was old enough, she brought him to Pharaoh's daughter, who adopted him and called him Moses, 'because', said she, 'I drew him out of the water'.

¹¹One day after Moses was grown up, he went out to his own kinsmen and observed their labours. When he saw an Egyptian strike one of his fellow-Hebrews, ¹²he looked this way and that, and, seeing no one about, he struck the Egyptian down and hid his body in the sand. ¹³Next day when he went out, he came across two Hebrews fighting. He asked the one who was in the wrong, 'Why are you striking your fellow-countryman?' ¹⁴The man replied, 'Who set you up as an official and judge over us? Do you mean to murder me as you murdered the Egyptian?' Moses was alarmed and said to himself, 'The affair must have become known.' ¹⁵When it came to Pharaoh's ears, he tried to have Moses put to death, but Moses fled from his presence and went and settled in Midian.

As Moses sat by a well one day, ¹⁶the seven daughters of a priest of Midian came to draw water, and when they had filled the troughs to water their father's sheep, ¹⁷some shepherds came and drove them away. But Moses came to the help of the girls and watered the sheep. ¹⁸When they returned to Reuel, their father, he said, 'How is it that you are back so quickly today?' ¹⁹'An Egyptian rescued us from the shepherds,' they answered; 'he even drew water for us and watered the sheep.' ²⁰'Then where is he?' their father asked. 'Why did you leave him there? Go and invite him to eat with us.' ²¹So it came about that Moses agreed to stay with the man, and he gave Moses his daughter Zipporah in marriage. ²²She bore him a son, and Moses called him Gershom, 'because', he said, 'I have become an alien in a foreign land.'

²³Years passed, during which time the king of Egypt died, but the Israelites still groaned in slavery. They cried out, and their plea for rescue from slavery ascended to God. ²⁴He

2:10 **Moses:** *Heb.* Mosheh. **drew:** *Heb. verb* mashah.
2:22 **alien:** *Heb.* ger.

2.1–10: The birth of Moses. 3: The theme of the exposed child who is rescued and rises to a position of fame is attested elsewhere in the ancient world. Quite similar is the legend of Sargon, king of Akkad (about 2300 B.C.E.), who was rescued from a bitumen-sealed rush basket. **4:** *Sister:* Miriam (Num. 26.59). **7–10:** God uses Pharaoh's evil design to prepare for the deliverance of Israel. For a similar theme, see Gen. 45.5–8 n. **10:** A folk explanation for the child's name is given, in keeping with the details of the story. In reality, *Moses* is an Egyptian name meaning "has begotten a child." It may have been joined, originally, with the name of an Egyptian deity (as in Ra-moses, i.e. Rameses of 1.11).

2.11–22: Moses flees to Midian. 16: *Seven:* see Gen. 7.2 n. **18:** *Father:* see Judg. 1.16.

2.23–4.17: The call of Moses. 23: The *king* may be Seti I, the founder of the Nineteenth Dynasty (1.8 n.), who ruled about fifteen years. The oppressive building programs were continued by his successors, notably heard their groaning and called to mind his covenant with Abraham, Isaac, and Jacob; [25] he observed the plight of Israel and took heed of it.

3 While tending the sheep of his father-in-law Jethro, priest of Midian, Moses led the flock along the west side of the wilderness and came to Horeb, the mountain of God. [2] There an angel of the LORD appeared to him as a fire blazing out from a bush. Although the bush was on fire, it was not being burnt up, [3] and Moses said to himself, 'I must go across and see this remarkable sight. Why ever does the bush not burn away?' [4] When the LORD saw that Moses had turned aside to look, he called to him out of the bush, 'Moses, Moses!' He answered, 'Here I am!' [5] God said, 'Do not come near! Take off your sandals, for the place where you are standing is holy ground.' [6] Then he said, 'I am the God of your father, the God of Abraham, Isaac, and Jacob.' Moses hid his face, for he was afraid to look at God.

[7] The LORD said, 'I have witnessed the misery of my people in Egypt and have heard them crying out because of their oppressors. I know what they are suffering [8] and have come down to rescue them from the power of the Egyptians and to bring them up out of that country into a fine, broad land, a land flowing with milk and honey, the territory of Canaanites, Hittites, Amorites, Perizzites, Hivites, and Jebusites. [9] Now the Israelites' cry has reached me, and I have also seen how hard the Egyptians oppress them. [10] Come, I shall send you to Pharaoh, and you are to bring my people Israel out of Egypt.' [11] 'But who am I', Moses said to God, 'that I should approach Pharaoh and that I should bring the Israelites out of Egypt?' [12] God answered,

'I am with you. This will be your proof that it is I who have sent you: when you have brought the people out of Egypt, you will all worship God here at this mountain.'

[13] Moses said to God, 'If I come to the Israelites and tell them that the God of their forefathers has sent me to them, and they ask me his name, what am I to say to them?' [14] God answered, 'I AM that I am. Tell them that I AM has sent you to them.' [15] He continued, 'You are to tell the Israelites that it is the LORD, the God of their forefathers, the God of Abraham, Isaac, and Jacob, who has sent you to them. This is my name for ever; this is my title in every generation.

[16] 'Go and assemble the elders of Israel; tell them that the LORD, the God of their forefathers, the God of Abraham, Isaac, and Jacob, has appeared to you and said, "I have watched over you and have seen what has been done to you in Egypt, [17] and I have resolved to bring you up out of the misery of Egypt into the country of the Canaanites, Hittites, Amorites, Perizzites, Hivites, and Jebusites, a land flowing with milk and honey." [18] The elders will attend to what you say, and then you must go along with them to the king of Egypt and say to him, "The LORD the God of the Hebrews has encountered us. Now, we request you to give us leave to go a three days' journey into the wilderness to offer sacrifice to the LORD our God." [19] I know well that the king of Egypt will not allow you to go unless he is compelled. [20] I shall then stretch out my hand and assail the

---

3:2 **as a fire:** or in a fire.   3:12 **I am:** or I shall be.
3:14 **I AM . . . I am:** or I will be what I will be.
3:15 **the LORD:** the Hebrew consonants are YHWH, probably pronounced Yahweh, but traditionally read Jehovah.

Rameses II. **24:** Covenant: Gen. 12.1–3; 26.1–5; 28.13–15. **3.1:** Horeb seems to be a local Midianite shrine, and hence the alien Moses is unaware of its sacred nature (v. 5). It is later to be the site of the giving of the Law (18.5–20.21) and is called Sinai in another version of the tradition (19.1–2). Its location is unknown, but post-Christian tradition placed it in the Sinai Peninsula. **2:** On fire as a symbol for the divine presence, see Gen. 15.17 n. **5:** The removal of sandals before entering a sacred place was an ancient custom (Josh. 5.15), continued by Muslims until the present. **6:** The God of your father is an ancient designation for the deity of one's ancestors (Gen. 26.24; 49.25). Here, the ancestral god is identified with Yahweh, the LORD. **8:** Milk and honey were basic food for the seasonally nomadic Israelites, and hence the term describes the desirability of the land to them. **12:** I am: by folk explanation the divine name (Yahweh) is derived from the verb "to be." Thus, Israel understood the very essence of the deity to be expressed by the divine name. Actually, the form YHWH (see Tfn. at v. 15) would be third person ("he is"), but since the explanation of the name is given by the deity in the first person, the explanation becomes "I am." See also 6.3. **14–15:** The meaning of the divine name (v. 12) is repeated and expanded. God's freedom from and control of history are denoted by the phrase, "I will be what I will be" (see Tfn. at v. 14). For another paraphrase, which also expresses the divine freedom, see 33.19. **18:** Three: a

Egyptians with all the miracles I shall work among them. After that he will send you away. 21 What is more, I shall bring this people into such favour with the Egyptians that, when you go, you will not go empty-handed. 22 Every woman must ask her neighbour or any woman living in her house for silver and gold jewellery and for clothing; put them on your sons and daughters, and plunder the Egyptians.'

4 'But they will never believe me or listen to what I say,' Moses protested; 'they will say that it is untrue that the LORD appeared to me.' 2 The LORD said, 'What is that in your hand?' 'A staff,' replied Moses. 3 The LORD said, 'Throw it on the ground.' He did so, and it turned into a snake. Moses drew back hastily, 4 but the LORD said, 'Put your hand out and seize it by the tail.' When he took hold of it, it turned back into a staff in his hand. 5 'This', said the LORD, 'is to convince the people that the LORD the God of their forefathers, the God of Abraham, of Isaac, and of Jacob, did appear to you.'

6 Then the LORD said to him, 'Put your hand inside the fold of your cloak.' He did so, and when he drew his hand out the skin was white as snow with disease. 7 The LORD said, 'Put your hand in again'; he did so, and when he drew it out this time it was as healthy as the rest of his body. 8 'Now,' said the LORD, 'if they do not believe you and do not accept the evidence of the first sign, they may be persuaded by the second. 9 But if they are not convinced even by these two signs and will not accept what you say, then fetch some water from the Nile and pour it out on the dry land, and the water from the Nile will turn to blood on the ground.'

10 'But, LORD,' Moses protested, 'I have never been a man of ready speech, never in my life, not even now that you have spoken to me; I am slow and hesitant.' 11 The LORD said to him, 'Who is it that gives man speech? Who makes him dumb or deaf? Who makes him keen-sighted or blind? Is it not I, the LORD? 12 Go now; I shall help you to speak and show you what to say.' 13 Moses said, 'Lord, send anyone else you like.' 14 At this the LORD became angry with Moses: 'Do you not have a brother, Aaron the Levite? He, I know, will do all the speaking. He is already on his way out to meet you, and he will be overjoyed when he sees you. 15 You are to speak to him and put the words in his mouth; I shall help both of you to speak and tell you both what to do. 16 He will do all the speaking to the people for you; he will be the mouthpiece, and you will be the god he speaks for. 17 And take this staff in your hand; with it you are to work the signs.'

18 Moses then went back to Jethro his father-in-law and said, 'Let me return to Egypt and see whether my kinsfolk are still alive.' Jethro said, 'Go, and may you have a safe journey.'

19 THE LORD spoke to Moses in Midian. 'Go back to Egypt,' he said, 'for all those who wanted to kill you are now dead.' 20 Moses took his wife and children, mounted them on a donkey, and set out for Egypt with the staff of God in his hand. 21 The LORD said to Moses, 'While you are on your way back to Egypt, keep in mind all the portents I have given you power to show. You are to display these before Pharaoh, but I shall make him obstinate and he will not let the people go. 22 Then tell Pharaoh that these are the words of the LORD: Israel is my firstborn son. 23 I tell you, let my son go to worship me. Should you refuse to let him go, I shall kill your firstborn son.'

24 On the journey, while they were en-

4:20 children: or, possibly, son (cp. 2:22; 4:25).

commonly used round number (Gen. 30.36; 40.13; Exod. 2.2). 21–22: See 11.2–3; 12.35–36. 4.1–9: God supplies Moses with three signs of authentication. Israelite tradition presents Moses as able to compete with and triumph over the magicians of Egypt (see 7.11; 8.16–19; 9.10–11).

4.18–31: Moses returns to Egypt. 20: The staff of God: see 4.17. 21: Since, in ancient Israelite belief, a human being could hardly defy the divine will, Pharaoh's reluctance must ultimately be a part of the LORD's plan. 22: Firstborn son: an alternative way of expressing the election of Abraham (Gen. 11.10–32 n.). 24–26: This obscure passage seems to be a fragment of a once independent tradition about how a divine being, perhaps the god of the Midianite clan, sought the life of Moses' child because he was uncircumcised. Zipporah performs the rite, proclaiming that the child is now a blood-bridegroom (perhaps an initiated member of the religious community). The name "Moses" does not occur in the MT; only because the passage appears in its present context is it he who appears to be threatened.

camped for the night, the LORD met Moses and would have killed him, 25 but Zipporah picked up a sharp flint, cut off her son's foreskin, and touched Moses' genitals with it, saying, 'You are my blood-bridegroom.' 26 So the LORD let Moses alone. It was on that occasion she said, 'Blood-bridegroom by circumcision.'

27 Meanwhile the LORD had ordered Aaron to go and meet Moses in the wilderness. Aaron did so; he met him at the mountain of God and kissed him. 28 Moses told Aaron everything, the words the LORD had sent him to say and the signs he had commanded him to perform. 29 Moses and Aaron then went and assembled all the elders of Israel. 30 Aaron repeated to them everything that the LORD had said to Moses; he performed the signs before the people, 31 and they were convinced. When they heard that the LORD had shown his concern for the Israelites and seen their misery, they bowed to the ground in worship.

5 After this, Moses and Aaron came to Pharaoh and told him, 'These are the words of the LORD the God of Israel: Let my people go so that they may keep a pilgrim-feast in my honour in the wilderness.' 2 'Who is the LORD,' said Pharaoh, 'that I should listen to him and let Israel go? I do not acknowledge the LORD: and I tell you I will not let Israel go.' 3 They replied, 'The God of the Hebrews confronted us. Now we request leave to go three days' journey into the wilderness to offer sacrifice to the LORD our God, or else he may attack us with pestilence or sword.' 4 But the Egyptian king answered, 'What do you mean, Moses and Aaron, by distracting the people from their work? Back to your labours! 5 Your people already outnumber the native Egyptians; yet you would have them stop working!'

6 Pharaoh issued orders that same day to the people's slave-masters and their foremen 7 not to supply the people with the straw used in making bricks, as they had done hitherto. 'Let them go and collect their own straw, 8 but see that they produce the same tally of bricks as before; on no account reduce it. They are lazy, and that is why they are clamouring to go and offer sacrifice to their God. 9 Keep these men hard at work; let them attend to that. Take no notice of their lies.' 10 The slave-masters and foremen went out and said to the people, 'Pharaoh's orders are that no more straw is to be supplied. 11 Go and get it for yourselves wherever you can find it; but there is to be no reduction in your daily task.' 12 So the people scattered all over Egypt to gather stubble for the straw they needed, 13 while the slave-masters kept urging them on, demanding that they should complete, day after day, the same quantity as when straw had been supplied. 14 The Israelite foremen were flogged because they were held responsible by Pharaoh's slave-masters, who demanded, 'Why did you not complete the usual number of bricks yesterday or today?'

15 The foremen came and appealed to Pharaoh: 'Why does your majesty treat us like this?' they said. 16 'We are given no straw, yet they keep telling us to make bricks. Here are we being flogged, but the fault lies with your people.' 17 The king replied, 'You are lazy, bone lazy! That is why you keep on about going to offer sacrifice to the LORD. 18 Now get on with your work. You will not be given straw, but you must produce the full tally of bricks.' 19 When they were told that they must not let the daily number of bricks fall short, the Israelite foremen realized the trouble they were in. 20 As they came from Pharaoh's presence they found Moses and Aaron waiting to meet them, 21 and said, 'May this bring the LORD's judgement down on you! You have made us stink in the nostrils of Pharaoh and his subjects; you have put a sword in their hands to slay us.'

22 Moses went back to the LORD and said, 'Lord, why have you brought trouble on this people? And why did you ever send me? 23 Since I first went to Pharaoh to speak in your name he has treated your people cruelly, and you have done nothing at all to res-

4:25 **Moses' genitals:** *lit.* his feet.   4:26 **It was . . . said:** *or* Therefore women say.   5:5 **Your people . . . Egyptians:** *prob. rdg, cp. Samar.; Heb.* The people of the land are already many.

5.1–6.1: The first audience with Pharaoh. 1: *Pilgrim-feast:* see 3.18. **2:** The gods of powerless foreigners (Hebrews) command little respect from the Pharaoh, who is himself deified in Egyptian religion. **7:** Chopped *straw* was added to the wet clay to facilitate drying and bonding. **9:** The request to observe the festival is regarded as a pretext to leave the country permanently.

6 cue them.' [1] The LORD answered, 'Now you will see what I shall do to Pharaoh: he will be compelled to let them go, he will be forced to drive them from his country.'

[2] God said to Moses, 'I am the LORD. [3] I appeared to Abraham, Isaac, and Jacob as God Almighty; but I did not let myself be known to them by my name, the LORD. [4] I also established my covenant with them to give them Canaan, the land where for a time they settled as foreigners. [5] And now I have heard the groaning of the Israelites, enslaved by the Egyptians, and I am mindful of my covenant. [6] Therefore say to the Israelites, "I am the LORD. I shall free you from your labours in Egypt and deliver you from slavery. I shall rescue you with outstretched arm and with mighty acts of judgement. [7] I shall adopt you as my people, and I shall be your God. You will know that I, the LORD, am your God, the God who frees you from your labours in Egypt. [8] I shall lead you to the land which I swore with uplifted hand to give to Abraham, to Isaac, and to Jacob. I shall give it you for your possession. I am the LORD." ' [9] But when Moses repeated those words to the Israelites, they would not listen to him; because of their cruel slavery, they had reached the depths of despair.

[10] Then the LORD said to Moses, [11] 'Go and bid Pharaoh king of Egypt let the Israelites leave his country.' [12] Moses protested to the LORD, 'If the Israelites do not listen to me, how will Pharaoh listen to such a halting speaker as me?' [13] The LORD then spoke to both Moses and Aaron and gave them their commission concerning the Israelites and Pharaoh, which was that they should bring the Israelites out of Egypt.

[14] THESE were the heads of families. Sons of Reuben, Israel's eldest son: Enoch, Pallu, Hezron, and Carmi; these were the families of Reuben.

[15] Sons of Simeon: Jemuel, Jamin, Ohad, Jachin, Zohar, and Saul, who was the son of a Canaanite woman; these were the families of Simeon.

[16] These were the names of the sons of Levi in order of seniority: Gershon, Kohath, and Merari. Levi lived to be a hundred and thirty-seven.

[17] Sons of Gershon, family by family: Libni and Shimei.

[18] Sons of Kohath: Amram, Izhar, Hebron, and Uzziel. Kohath lived to be a hundred and thirty-three.

[19] Sons of Merari: Mahli and Mushi. These were the families of Levi in order of seniority. [20] Amram married his father's sister Jochebed, and she bore him Aaron and Moses. Amram lived to be a hundred and thirty-seven.

[21] Sons of Izhar: Korah, Nepheg, and Zichri.

[22] Sons of Uzziel: Mishael, Elzaphan, and Sithri.

[23] Aaron married Elisheba, who was the daughter of Amminadab and the sister of Nahshon, and she bore him Nadab, Abihu, Eleazar, and Ithamar.

[24] Sons of Korah: Assir, Elkanah, and Abiasaph; these were the Korahite families.

[25] Eleazar son of Aaron married one of the daughters of Putiel, and she bore him Phinehas. These were the heads of the Levite families, family by family.

[26] It was this Aaron, together with Moses, to whom the LORD said, 'Bring the Israelites out of Egypt, mustered in their tribal hosts.' [27] These were the men, this same Moses and Aaron, who told Pharaoh king of Egypt to let the Israelites leave Egypt.

6:3 **the LORD:** *see note on 3:15.*   6:12 **to such . . . me:** *lit. to me, seeing I am uncircumcised of lips.* 6:14–16 *Cp. Gen. 46:8–11; Num. 26:5,6,12,13.*

6.2–7.7: An alternative account of Moses' commission (compare 3.1–4.17), editorially placed so that it now serves as a reaffirmation of his call after Pharaoh's negative response. **3:** *God Almighty:* see Gen. 17.1 n.; 49.25. According to some modern interpreters, the Israelite twelve-tribal league (Gen. 29.31–30.24 n.) arose only after the conquest of Canaan, and included clans, escaped from Egypt, who previously had not worshiped the LORD (3.14–15 n.), and other clans who traced their worship of the LORD back to primeval time (Gen. 4.26). Later, all Israel accepted the Exod. tradition as their own (1.1–5) and identified Yahweh with their former deities (3.12 n.). **7:** *My people . . . your God:* the essence of the covenant relationship. **13–27:** There is an alternate account of the commission of Moses in vv. 13, 26–27; this brief account reflects almost nothing of the elaborate narrative in the preceding and ensuing chapters. The genealogy (vv. 14–25), which seems pointed toward emphasizing the role of Aaron and his relation to Moses, was apparently once independent and self-contained.

The struggle with Pharaoh

28 WHEN the LORD spoke to Moses in Egypt he said, 29 'I am the LORD. Report to Pharaoh king of Egypt all that I say to you.' 30 Moses protested to the LORD, 'I am a halting speaker; how will Pharaoh listen to me?'

7 1 The LORD answered, 'See now, I have made you like a god for Pharaoh, with your brother Aaron as your spokesman. 2 Tell Aaron all I command you to say, and he will tell Pharaoh to let the Israelites leave his country. 3 But I shall make him stubborn, and though I show sign after sign and portent after portent in the land of Egypt, 4 Pharaoh will not listen to you. Then I shall assert my power in Egypt, and with mighty acts of judgement I shall bring my people, the Israelites, out of Egypt in their tribal hosts. 5 When I exert my power against Egypt and bring the Israelites out from there, then the Egyptians will know that I am the LORD.' 6 Moses and Aaron did exactly as the LORD had commanded. 7 At the time when they spoke to Pharaoh, Moses was eighty years old and Aaron eighty-three.

8 The LORD said to Moses and Aaron, 9 'If Pharaoh demands some portent from you, then you, Moses, must say to Aaron, "Take your staff and throw it down in front of Pharaoh," and it will turn into a serpent.' 10 When Moses and Aaron came to Pharaoh, they did as the LORD had told them; Aaron threw down his staff in front of Pharaoh and his courtiers, and it turned into a serpent. 11 At this, Pharaoh summoned the wise men and the sorcerers, and the Egyptian magicians did the same thing by their spells: 12 every man threw his staff down, and each staff turned into a serpent. But Aaron's staff swallowed up theirs. 13 Pharaoh, however, was obstinate; as the LORD had foretold, he would not listen to Moses and Aaron.

14 The LORD said to Moses, 'Pharaoh has been obdurate: he has refused to let the people go. 15 In the morning go to him on his way out to the river. Stand on the bank of the Nile to meet him, and take with you the staff that turned into a snake. 16 Say to him: "The LORD the God of the Hebrews sent me with this message for you: Let my people go in order to worship me in the wilderness. So far you have not listened. 17 Now the LORD says: By this you will know that I am the LORD. With this rod I hold in my hand, I shall strike the water of the Nile and it will be changed into blood. 18 The fish will die and the river will stink, and the Egyptians will be unable to drink water from the Nile." '

19 The LORD told Moses to say to Aaron, 'Take your staff and stretch your hand out over the waters of Egypt, its rivers and its canals, and over every pool and cistern, to turn them into blood. There will be blood throughout the whole of Egypt, blood even in their wooden bowls and stone jars.' 20 Moses and Aaron did as the LORD had commanded. In the sight of Pharaoh and his courtiers Aaron lifted his staff and struck the water of the Nile, and all the water was changed to blood. 21 The fish died and the river stank, so that the Egyptians could not drink water from the Nile. There was blood everywhere in Egypt.

22 But the Egyptian magicians did the same

7:1 **spokesman:** *lit.* prophet.

7.3: *Stubborn:* see 4.21 n.

7.8–13: An alternative account of the first audience with Pharaoh, varying considerably in detail from 5.1–6.1. The miracles used to authenticate Moses to the people of Israel (4.1–9) are here understood as the means of his authentication to Pharaoh. As it now stands, the passage serves as introduction to the account of the even greater miracles (the ten plagues). It took its final shape when the Aaronite priesthood ruled Israel, and hence it enhances the role of Aaron.

7.14–11.10: The ten plagues. This section, inspired by and meant to serve as a preface for Israel's miraculous departure from Egypt (chs. 12–15), presents dramatic episodes in which Pharaoh alternately agrees and refuses to let Israel realize its destiny, typifying the reversals which Israel would experience throughout its history and encouraging the belief that the promise to the ancestors will ultimately be realized. Although each plague may rest upon a natural phenomenon enhanced through cultic recitation, the literary purpose here is to ridicule the deities of Egypt as forces of nature under the LORD's control.

7.14–25: The first plague is directed against the deified Nile upon which all life in Egypt depends. Its annual inundation replenishes (and fertilizes) the soil. **17:** Pharaoh has professed no such knowledge in 5.2. **19:** On Aaron's role, see 7.8–13 n. **22:** The feat of the magicians is an embellishment meant to heighten the contest thing by their spells. So Pharaoh still remained obstinate, as the LORD had foretold, and he did not listen to Moses and Aaron. 23 He turned and went into his palace, dismissing the matter from his mind. 24 The Egyptians all dug for drinking water round about the river, because they could not drink from the waters of the Nile itself. 25 This lasted for seven days from the time when the LORD struck the Nile.

8 The LORD then told Moses to go to Pharaoh and say, 'These are the words of the LORD: Let my people go in order to worship me. 2 If you refuse, I shall bring a plague of frogs over the whole of your territory. 3 The Nile will swarm with them. They will come up from the river into your palace, into your bedroom and onto your bed, into the houses of your courtiers and your people, into your ovens and your kneading troughs. 4 The frogs will clamber over you, your people, and all your courtiers.'

5 The LORD told Moses to say to Aaron, 'Take your staff in your hand and stretch it out over the rivers, canals, and pools, to bring up frogs on the land of Egypt.' 6 When Aaron stretched his hand over the waters of Egypt, the frogs came up and covered the land. 7 But the magicians did the same thing by their spells: they too brought up frogs on the land of Egypt.

8 Pharaoh summoned Moses and Aaron. 'Pray to the LORD', he said, 'to remove the frogs from me and my people, and I shall let the people go to sacrifice to the LORD.' 9 Moses said, 'I give your majesty the choice of a time for me to intercede for you, your courtiers, and your people, to rid you and your houses of the frogs; none will be left except in the Nile.' 10 'Tomorrow,' said Pharaoh. 'It will be as you say,' replied Moses, 'so that you may know there is no one like our God, the LORD. 11 The frogs will leave you, your houses, courtiers, and people: none will be left except in the Nile.' 12 Moses and Aaron

left Pharaoh's presence, and Moses asked the LORD to remove the frogs which he had brought on Pharaoh. 13 The LORD granted the request, and in house, farmyard, and field all the frogs perished. 14 They were piled into countless heaps and the land stank. 15 But when Pharaoh found that he was given relief he became obdurate; as the LORD had foretold, he would not listen to Moses and Aaron.

16 The LORD told Moses to say to Aaron, 'Stretch out your staff and strike the dust on the ground, and it will turn into maggots throughout the whole of Egypt.' 17 They obeyed, and when Aaron stretched out his hand with his staff in it and struck the dust, it turned into maggots on man and beast. Throughout Egypt all the dust turned into maggots. 18 The magicians tried to produce maggots in the same way by their spells, but they failed. The maggots were everywhere, on man and beast. 19 'It is the hand of God,' said the magicians to Pharaoh, but Pharaoh remained obstinate; as the LORD had foretold, he would not listen.

20 The LORD told Moses to rise early in the morning and stand in Pharaoh's path as he went out to the river, and to say to him, 'These are the words of the LORD: Let my people go in order to worship me. 21 If you refuse, I shall send swarms of flies on you, your courtiers, your people, and your houses; the houses of the Egyptians will be filled with the swarms and so will all the land they live in. 22 But on that day I shall make an exception of Goshen, the land where my people live: there will be no swarms there. Thus you will know that I, the LORD, am here in the land. 23 I shall make a distinction between my people and yours. Tomorrow this sign will appear.' 24 The LORD did this; dense swarms of flies infested Pharaoh's palace and the houses of his courtiers; throughout Egypt

8:1 *In Heb. 7:26.*　　8:5 *In Heb. 8:1.*
8:23 **distinction:** *so Gk; Heb.* redemption.

between Yahweh and the gods of Egypt.

8.1–15: The second plague is directed against the frog-goddess Heqet. It follows naturally upon the first, since the mud of the Nile's overflow could serve as a breeding place. **8:** Thus Pharaoh indirectly acknowledges the LORD's existence for the first time.

8.16–19: The third plague follows naturally from the previous plague, since vermin could breed in the decaying carcasses of the frogs. **18:** The failure of the magicians heightens the drama and leads us toward the LORD's ultimate victory. **19:** The *hand of God* is an ancient Near Eastern idiom for a manifestation of divine power.

8.20–32: The fourth plague may represent the mature larvae of the previous plague. **22:** The exemption the land was threatened with ruin by the swarms. 25 Pharaoh summoned Moses and Aaron and said to them, 'Go and sacrifice to your God, but in this country.' 26 'That is impossible,' replied Moses, 'because the victim we are to sacrifice to the LORD our God is an abomination to the Egyptians. If the Egyptians see us offer such an animal, they will surely stone us to death. 27 We must go a three days' journey into the wilderness to sacrifice to the LORD our God, as he commands us.' 28 'I shall let you go,' said Pharaoh, 'and you may sacrifice to your God in the wilderness; only do not go far. Now intercede for me.' 29 Moses answered, 'As soon as I leave you I shall intercede with the LORD. Tomorrow the swarms will depart from Pharaoh, his courtiers, and his people. Only your majesty must not trifle any more with the people by preventing them from going to sacrifice to the LORD.'

30 Then Moses left Pharaoh and interceded with the LORD. 31 The LORD did as Moses had promised; he removed the swarms from Pharaoh, his courtiers, and his people; not one was left. 32 But once again Pharaoh became obdurate and would not let the people go.

9 The LORD said to Moses, 'Go in to Pharaoh and tell him, "The LORD the God of the Hebrews says: Let my people go in order to worship me. 2 If you refuse to let them go, if you still keep them in subjection, 3 the LORD will strike your livestock out in the country, the horses and donkeys, camels, cattle, and sheep with a devastating pestilence. 4 But the LORD will make a distinction between Israel's livestock and the livestock of the Egyptians. Of all that belong to Israel not a single one will die." ' 5 The LORD fixed a time and said, 'Tomorrow I shall do this throughout the land.' 6 The next day the LORD struck. All the livestock of Egypt died, but from Israel's livestock not one single beast died. 7 Pharaoh made enquiries and was told that from Israel's livestock not an animal had died; and yet he remained obdurate and would not let the people go.

8 The LORD said to Moses and Aaron, 'Take handfuls of soot from a kiln, and when Moses tosses it into the air in Pharaoh's sight, 9 it will turn into a fine dust over the whole of Egypt. Throughout the land it will produce festering boils on man and beast.' 10 They took the soot from the kiln and when they stood before Pharaoh, Moses tossed it into the air, and it produced festering boils on man and beast. 11 The magicians were no match for Moses because of the boils, which attacked them and all the Egyptians. 12 But the LORD made Pharaoh obstinate; as the LORD had foretold to Moses, he would not listen to Moses and Aaron.

13 The LORD then told Moses to rise early and confront Pharaoh, saying to him, 'The LORD the God of the Hebrews has said: Let my people go in order to worship me. 14 This time I shall strike home with all my plagues against you yourself, your courtiers, and your people, so that you may know that there is none like me in all the world. 15 By now I could have stretched out my hand, and struck you and your people with pestilence, and you would have vanished from the earth. 16 I have let you live only to show you my power and to spread my fame all over the world. 17 Since you still obstruct my people and will not let them go, 18 tomorrow at this time I shall cause a violent hailstorm to come, such as has never been in Egypt from its first beginnings until now. 19 Send now and bring your herds under cover, and everything you have out in the open field. Anything which happens to be left out in the open, whether

of Goshen demonstrates that the plagues are not natural catastrophes, and heightens the drama. **26–27:** Whether the *abomination* represents an unstated Egyptian taboo, or whether it is a literary embellishment for dramatic effect, is unclear. Compare Gen. 43.32; 46.34. **28:** For Pharaoh's suspicions of Moses' true intent, see 5.9 n.

9.1–7: The fifth plague is directed, in part, against the bovine-deities Hathor and Apis. It may be connected with the previous one as a disease spread by flies. **4:** *Distinction:* see 8.22 n.

9.8–12: The sixth plague. This account may be a variant of the previous one. In any case, this plague does not seem to be depicted as immediately consecutive; beasts presumably killed by the fifth plague are here afflicted as if anew.

9.13–35: The seventh plague. 15–16: An explanation for the persistence of the oppression is offered, meant to comfort later Israel in similar circumstances. **19:** That *herds* abound, despite the fifth plague (see 9.8–12 n.), man or beast, will die when the hail falls on it.' 20 Those of Pharaoh's subjects who feared the warning of the LORD hurried their slaves and livestock into shelter; 21 but those who did not take it to heart left them in the open.

22 The LORD said to Moses, 'Stretch your hand towards the sky to bring down hail on the whole land of Egypt, on man and beast and every growing thing throughout the land.' 23 As Moses stretched his staff towards the sky, the LORD sent thunder and hail, with fire flashing to the ground. The LORD rained down hail on the land of Egypt, 24 hail and fiery flashes through the hail, so heavy that there had been nothing like it in all Egypt from the time that Egypt became a nation. 25 Throughout Egypt the hail struck down everything in the fields, both man and beast; it beat down every growing thing and shattered every tree. 26 Only in the land of Goshen, where the Israelites lived, was there no hail.

27 Pharaoh summoned Moses and Aaron. 'This time I have sinned,' he said; 'the LORD is in the right; I and my people are in the wrong. 28 Intercede with the LORD, for we can bear no more of this thunder and hail. I shall let you go; you need stay no longer.' 29 Moses said, 'As soon as I leave the city I shall spread out my hands in prayer to the LORD. The thunder will cease, and there will be no more hail, so that you may know that the earth is the LORD's. 30 But you and your subjects, I know, do not yet fear the LORD God.' 31 (The flax and barley were destroyed because the barley was in the ear and the flax in bud, 32 but the wheat and vetches were not destroyed because they come later.) 33 Moses left Pharaoh's presence and went out of the city, where he lifted up his hands to the LORD in prayer: the thunder and hail ceased, and no more rain fell. 34 When Pharaoh saw that the downpour, the hail, and the thunder had ceased, he went back to his sinful obduracy, he and his courtiers. 35 Pharaoh remained obstinate; as the LORD had foretold through Moses, he would not let the people go.

10 The LORD said to Moses, 'Go in to Pharaoh. I have made him and his courtiers obdurate, so that I may show these signs among them, 2 and so that you can tell your children and grandchildren the story: how I toyed with the Egyptians, and what signs I showed among them. Thus you will know that I am the LORD.'

3 Moses and Aaron went to Pharaoh and said to him, 'The LORD the God of the Hebrews has said: How long will you refuse to humble yourself before me? Let my people go in order to worship me. 4 If you refuse to let them go, tomorrow I am going to bring locusts into your country. 5 They will cover the face of the land so that it cannot be seen. They will eat up the last remnant left you by the hail. They will devour every tree that grows in your countryside. 6 Your houses and your courtiers' houses, every house in Egypt, will be full of them; your fathers never saw the like, nor their fathers before them; such a thing has not happened from their time until now.' With that he turned and left Pharaoh's presence.

7 Pharaoh's courtiers said to him, 'How long must we be caught in this man's toils? Let their menfolk go and worship the LORD their God. Do you not know by now that Egypt is ruined?' 8 So Moses and Aaron were brought back to Pharaoh, and he said to them, 'Go, worship the LORD your God; but who exactly is to go?' 9 'Everyone,' said Moses, 'young and old, boys and girls, sheep and cattle; for we have to keep the LORD's pilgrim-feast.' 10 Pharaoh replied, 'The LORD be with you if I let you and your dependants go! You have some sinister purpose in mind. 11 No, your menfolk may go and worship the LORD, for that is what you were asking for.' And they were driven from Pharaoh's presence.

12 The LORD said to Moses, 'Stretch out your hand over Egypt so that locusts may come and invade the land and devour all the vegetation in it, whatever the hail has left.' 13 When Moses stretched out his staff over

10:12 **so that . . . come:** *so Gk; Heb.* with the locusts.

suggests that we do not have a unified chronicle of consecutive historical events. **20:** Elements of the Egyptian people begin to acknowledge Yahweh's lordship, emphasizing Pharaoh's stubbornness and setting the stage for the climactic plague. **27:** The narrative is advanced by the initial confession of failure by Pharaoh. **31–32:** This comment, perhaps editorial, explains how, in the following plague, there was something left for the locusts to devour.

10.1–20: The eighth plague. Swarms of locusts were known and feared throughout the ancient Near East.

the land of Egypt, the LORD sent a wind roaring in from the east all that day and all that night; and when morning came the east wind had brought the locusts. [14] They invaded the whole land of Egypt, and settled on all its territory in swarms so dense that the like of them had never been seen before, nor ever will be again. [15] They covered the surface of the whole land till it was black with them; they devoured all the vegetation and all the fruit of the trees that the hail had spared; there was no green left on tree or plant throughout all Egypt.

[16] Pharaoh hastily summoned Moses and Aaron. 'I have sinned against the LORD your God and against you,' he said. [17] 'Forgive my sin, I pray, just this once, and intercede with the LORD your God to remove this deadly plague from me.' [18] When Moses left Pharaoh and interceded with the LORD, [19] the wind was changed by the LORD into a westerly gale, which carried the locusts away and swept them into the Red Sea. Not one locust was left within the borders of Egypt. [20] But the LORD made Pharaoh obstinate, and he would not let the Israelites go.

[21] Then the LORD said to Moses, 'Stretch out your hand towards the sky so that over the land of Egypt there may be a darkness so dense that it can be felt.' [22] Moses stretched out his hand towards the sky, and for three days pitch darkness covered the whole land of Egypt. [23] People could not see one another, and for three days no one stirred from where he was. But where the Israelites were living there was no darkness.

[24] Pharaoh summoned Moses. 'Go, worship the LORD,' he said. 'Your dependants may go with you; but your flocks and herds must remain here.' [25] But Moses said, 'No, you yourself must supply us with animals for sacrifice and whole-offering to the LORD our God; [26] and our own livestock must go with us too—not a hoof must be left behind. We may need animals from our own flocks to worship the LORD our God; we ourselves cannot tell until we are there how we are to worship the LORD.' [27] The LORD made Pharaoh obstinate, and he refused to let them go. [28] 'Be off! Leave me!' he said to Moses. 'Mind you do not see my face again, for on the day you do, you die.' [29] 'You are right,' said Moses; 'I shall not see your face again.'

11 The LORD said to Moses, 'One last plague I shall bring on Pharaoh and Egypt. When he finally lets you go, he will drive you out forcibly as a man might dismiss a rejected bride. [2] Tell the people that everyone, men and women, should ask their neighbours for silver and gold jewellery.' [3] The LORD made the Egyptians well disposed towards them and, moreover, in Egypt Moses was a very great man in the eyes of Pharaoh's courtiers and of the people.

[4] Moses said, 'The LORD said: At midnight I shall go out among the Egyptians. [5] All the firstborn in Egypt shall die, from the firstborn of Pharaoh on his throne to the firstborn of the slave-girl at the handmill, besides the firstborn of the cattle. [6] From all over Egypt there will go up a great cry, the like of which has never been heard before, nor ever will be again. [7] But throughout all Israel no sound will be heard from man or beast, not even a dog's bark. Thus you will know that the LORD distinguishes between Egypt and Israel. [8] All these courtiers of yours will come down to me, prostrate themselves, and cry, "Go away, you and all the people who follow at your heels." When that time comes I shall go.' In hot anger, Moses left Pharaoh's presence.

[9] The LORD said to Moses, 'Pharaoh will not listen to you; I shall therefore show still more portents in the land of Egypt.' [10] Moses and Aaron had shown all these portents in the presence of Pharaoh, and yet the LORD made him obstinate, and he would not let the Israelites leave his country.

10:19 **Red Sea:** *or* sea of Reeds.

10.21–29: The ninth plague is possibly directed against the sun-god. **21:** *A darkness so dense that it can be felt* adequately describes a *"hamsin,"* a hot, dust-laden wind from the desert, covering the land with an eerie gloom during which breathing becomes difficult. But that there was no darkness where the Israelites dwelled (v. 23) suggests something supernatural. **28:** With Pharaoh's threat, on the day you see my face again *you die,* it is obvious that the plagues are not endless; rather their climax is now at hand.

11.1–10: The announcement of a final plague. 8: Up to this point, the context suggests that Moses' speech is to the Hebrews. Here, however, the Pharaoh is addressed, despite 10.28. Apparently, we have a second account of the final confrontation between the two leaders. **10:** Probably an editorial summary of the plague accounts, not a direct continuation of 11.1–9.

The institution of the Passover

12 THE LORD said to Moses and Aaron in Egypt: ²'This month is to be for you the first of the months; you are to make it the first month of the year. ³Say to the whole community of Israel: On the tenth day of this month let each man procure a lamb or kid for his family, one for each household, ⁴but if a household is too small for one lamb or kid, then, taking into account the number of persons, the man and his nearest neighbour may take one between them. They are to share the cost according to the amount each person eats. ⁵Your animal, taken either from the sheep or the goats, must be without blemish, a yearling male. ⁶Have it in safe keeping until the fourteenth day of this month, and then all the assembled community of Israel must slaughter the victims between dusk and dark. ⁷They must take some of the blood and smear it on the two doorposts and on the lintel of the houses in which they eat the victims. ⁸On that night they must eat the flesh roasted on the fire; they must eat it with unleavened bread and bitter herbs. ⁹You are not to eat any of it raw or even boiled in water, but roasted: head, shins, and entrails. ¹⁰You are not to leave any of it till morning; anything left over until morning must be destroyed by fire.

¹¹'This is the way in which you are to eat it: have your belt fastened, sandals on your feet, and your staff in your hand, and you must eat in urgent haste. It is the LORD's Passover. ¹²On that night I shall pass through the land of Egypt and kill every first-born of man and beast. Thus I shall execute judgement, I the LORD, against all the gods of Egypt. ¹³As for you, the blood will be a sign on the houses in which you are: when I see the blood I shall pass over you; when I strike Egypt, the mortal blow will not touch you.

¹⁴'You are to keep this day as a day of remembrance, and make it a pilgrim-feast, a festival of the LORD; generation after generation you are to observe it as a statute for all time. ¹⁵For seven days you are to eat unleavened bread. On the very first day you must rid your houses of leaven; from the first day to the seventh anyone who eats leavened bread is to be expelled from Israel. ¹⁶On the first day there is to be a sacred assembly and on the seventh day a sacred assembly: on these days no work is to be done, except what must be done to provide food for everyone; only that will be allowed. ¹⁷You are to observe the feast of Unleavened Bread because it was on this very day that I brought you out of Egypt in your tribal hosts. Observe this day from generation to generation as a statute for all time.

¹⁸'You are to eat unleavened bread in the first month from the evening which begins the fourteenth day until the evening which begins the twenty-first day. ¹⁹For seven days no leaven must be found in your houses; anyone who eats anything fermented is to be expelled from the community of Israel, be he foreigner or native. ²⁰You must eat nothing fermented; wherever you live, you must eat unleavened bread.'

²¹Moses summoned all the elders of Israel and said, 'Go at once, procure lambs for your families, and slaughter the Passover. ²²Then take a bunch of marjoram, dip it in the blood in the basin, and smear some blood from the

12:6 **between . . . dark:** *lit.* between the two evenings. 12:11 **belt fastened:** *lit.* loins girt.   12:13 **pass over:** *or* stand guard over.   12:22 **marjoram:** *or* hyssop. **in the basin:** *or* on the threshold. **from the basin:** *or* from the threshold.

12.1–27: Preparation for the Passover. 2: *The first month of the year* is reckoned as at Passover time, the month of Nisan (March–April), in keeping with the late, postexilic calendar. Thus, vv. 1–20 belong to a late stage of the tradition; in the preexilic calendar, the new year began in autumn (23.16 n.; 34.22). **3–6:** This annual sacrifice of a lamb or a goat at the coming of spring may have had its origins in a pre-Mosaic shepherds' festival, meant both to insure fertility and to preserve the newborn lambs during the nomadic pasturing. Indeed, it may have been this traditional festival which Moses demanded that the people be allowed to observe (5.1; 10.9). **11–13:** The origin of the old festival is now connected with Israel's history: the people must be ready to move, not to new pasture, but to the realization of God's promise in the land of Canaan. The name *Passover*, whose original meaning is uncertain, is now connected with the impending deliverance from Egypt. **12:** *Against all the gods of Egypt:* see 7.14–11.10 n. **15:** The festival of *unleavened bread*, probably an ancient Canaanite agricultural rite to celebrate the barley harvest, is here joined to the pastoral Passover festival and is connected in origin with Israel's impending departure. The absence of leaven, originally prohibited because it was basin on the lintel and the two doorposts. Nobody may go out through the door of his house till morning. ²³ The LORD will go throughout Egypt and strike it, but when he sees the blood on the lintel and the two doorposts, he will pass over that door and not let the destroyer enter to strike you. ²⁴ You are to observe this as a statute for you and your children for all time; ²⁵ when you enter the land which the LORD will give you as he promised, you are to observe this rite. ²⁶ When your children ask you, "What is the meaning of this rite?" ²⁷ you must say, "It is the LORD's Passover, for he passed over the houses of the Israelites in Egypt when he struck the Egyptians and spared our houses." ' The people bowed low in worship. ²⁸ The Israelites went and did exactly as the LORD had commanded Moses and Aaron; ²⁹ and by midnight the LORD had struck down all the firstborn in Egypt, from the firstborn of Pharaoh on his throne to the firstborn of the prisoner in the dungeon, besides the firstborn of cattle. ³⁰ Before night was over Pharaoh rose, he and all his courtiers and all the Egyptians, and there was great wailing, for not a house in Egypt was without its dead.

³¹ Pharaoh summoned Moses and Aaron while it was still night and said, 'Up with you! Be off, and leave my people, you and the Israelites. Go and worship the LORD, as you request; ³² take your sheep and cattle, and go; and ask God's blessing on me also.' ³³ The Egyptians urged on the people and hurried them out of the country, 'or else', they said, 'we shall all be dead'. ³⁴ The people picked up their dough before it was leavened, wrapped their kneading troughs in their cloaks, and slung them on their shoulders. ³⁵ Meanwhile, as Moses had told them, the Israelites had asked the Egyptians for silver and gold jewellery and for clothing. ³⁶ Because the LORD had made the Egyptians well disposed towards them, they let the Israelites have whatever they asked; in this way the Egyptians were plundered.

The exodus from Egypt

³⁷ THE Israelites set out from Rameses on the way to Succoth, about six hundred thousand men on foot, as well as women and children. ³⁸ With them too went a large company of others, and animals in great numbers, both flocks and herds. ³⁹ The dough they had brought from Egypt they baked into unleavened loaves of bread, because there was no leaven; for they had been driven out of Egypt and had had no time even to get food ready for themselves.

⁴⁰ The Israelites had been settled in Egypt for four hundred and thirty years. ⁴¹ At the end of the four hundred and thirty years to the very day, all the tribes of the LORD came out of Egypt. ⁴² This was the night when the LORD kept vigil to bring them out of Egypt. It is the LORD's night, a vigil for all Israelites generation after generation.

⁴³ The LORD said to Moses and Aaron: 'This is the statute for the Passover: No foreigner may partake of it; ⁴⁴ any bought slave may partake provided you have circumcised him; ⁴⁵ no visitor or hired man may partake of it. ⁴⁶ Each Passover victim must be eaten inside one house, and you must not take any of the flesh outside. You must not break any of its bones. ⁴⁷ The whole community of Israel is to keep this feast.

⁴⁸ 'If aliens settled among you keep the Passover to the LORD, every male among them must first be circumcised, and then he can take part; he will rank as native-born. No male who is uncircumcised may eat of it. ⁴⁹ The same law will apply both to the native-born and to the alien who is living among you.'

⁵⁰ All the Israelites did exactly as the LORD had commanded Moses and Aaron; ⁵¹ and on

considered ritually impure, is now attributed to the need for haste. **22:** *Marjoram:* an aromatic plant often used for ritual purposes (Lev. 14.4; Num. 19.6). **23:** The *destroyer,* the death-demon of the old shepherds' festival, is reinterpreted as an agent of the LORD.

12.28–36: The tenth plague, continuing the account of 11.1–10.

12.37–13.22: Israel moves to the border of Egypt. 37: *Rameses:* one of the store-cities which the Hebrews had built (1.11). *Six hundred thousand:* for how the figure was derived, see Num. 1.17–46. **40:** *Four hundred and thirty:* this length of stay differs from Gen. 15.13 (four hundred years) and from Gen. 15.16 (four generations; compare 6.16–20, which lists only four generations between Jacob and Moses). **43–49:** Supplementary regulations about the Passover, related to 12.1–27. The mention of *bought slave, hired man,* and *native-born* presupposes social conditions after the later settlement in the agricultural setting of Canaan.

2[a[co

that very day the LORD brought the Israelites out of Egypt mustered in their tribal hosts.

13 The LORD spoke to Moses. He said, 2'Every firstborn, the first birth of every womb among the Israelites, you must dedicate to me, both man and beast; it belongs to me.'

3 Then Moses said to the people, 'Remember this day, the day on which you have come out of Egypt, the land of slavery, because the LORD by the strength of his hand has brought you out. Nothing leavened may be eaten this day, 4 for today, in the month of Abib, is the day of your exodus. 5 When the LORD has brought you into the land of the Canaanites, Hittites, Amorites, Hivites, and Jebusites, the land which he swore to your forefathers to give you, a land flowing with milk and honey, then in this same month you must observe this rite: 6 for seven days you are to eat unleavened bread, and on the seventh day there is to be a pilgrim-feast of the LORD. 7 Only unleavened bread is to be eaten during the seven days; nothing fermented or leavened must be seen throughout your territory. 8 On that day you are to tell your son, "This is because of what the LORD did for me when I came out of Egypt." 9 You must have the record of it as a sign upon your hand, and as a reminder on your forehead to make sure that the law of the LORD is always on your lips, because the LORD with a strong hand brought you out of Egypt. 10 This is a statute to be kept by you at the appointed time from year to year.

11 'After the LORD has brought you into the land of the Canaanites and given it to you, as

he swore to you and to your forefathers, 12 you are to make over to the LORD the first birth of every womb; and of all firstborn offspring of your animals the males belong to the LORD. 13 Every firstborn male donkey you may redeem with a kid or lamb, but if you do not redeem it, you must break its neck. Every firstborn among your sons you must redeem. 14 'When in time to come your son asks you what this means, say to him, "By the strength of his hand the LORD brought us out of Egypt, out of the land of slavery. 15 Pharaoh stubbornly refused to let us go, and the LORD killed all the firstborn in Egypt, both man and beast. That is why I sacrifice to the LORD the first birth of every womb if it is a male, and why I redeem every firstborn of my sons. 16 You must have the record of it as a sign on your hand, and as a phylactery on your forehead, because by the strength of his hand the LORD brought us out of Egypt." '

17 WHEN Pharaoh let the people go, God did not guide them by the road leading towards the Philistines, although that was the shortest way; for he said, 'The people may change their minds when war confronts them, and they may turn back to Egypt.' 18 So God made them go round by way of the wilderness towards the Red Sea. Thus the fifth generation of Israelites departed from Egypt.

19 Moses took the bones of Joseph with him, because Joseph had exacted an oath from the Israelites: 'Some day', he said, 'God will show his care for you, and then, as you leave, you must take my bones with you.'

20 They set out from Succoth and en-

13.1–16: Additional Passover regulations, not directly related to those in ch. 12. **2:** The *firstborn* of animals must be sacrificed in thanksgiving and in recognition of the LORD's rule; so too, the first yield of the harvest (Deut. 26.1–2). For the exclusion of humans, see v. 13. **4:** *Abib:* the name of the month during which Passover fell according to the preexilic calendar (contrast 12.2 n.). This way of dating suggests a relatively early age for the formulation of this unit of material. **8:** *Me . . . I:* when the story of the LORD's deliverance is related annually in the cult, it becomes a personal and contemporary experience. **9:** *Sign:* an old practice of placing a mark on the hand or an amulet on the forehead as a sign of tribal membership is reinterpreted as a reminder of the LORD's deliverance from Egypt. Compare Gen. 4.15 n.; Deut. 6.6–8. **13:** Human sacrifice, particularly of the firstborn, was practiced in the ancient Near East (Deut. 12.31; 1 Kgs. 16.34; 2 Kgs. 16.3), but Israel was commanded to substitute an animal. See Gen. 22.2 n. **14–15:** The explanation of the ancient practice of substitution is here based on the events of the Passover in an attempt to make the prohibition more authoritative. **16:** *Phylactery:* a small leather case containing a verse of Scripture, worn originally as a reminder of one's identity (v. 9 n.). **17:** *Philistines:* Gen. 9.27 n.; the main route to Canaan, here avoided, was along the seacoast, and would have been guarded by garrisons of Egyptian troops. **18:** *Red Sea:* lit. "Sea of Reeds," and hence a shallow papyrus marsh on the border of Egypt. The Red Sea is the name of the "Gulf of Elath, much farther east. **19:** See Gen. 50.25.

camped at Etham on the edge of the wilderness. 21 And all the time the LORD went before them, by day a pillar of cloud to guide them on their journey, by night a pillar of fire to give them light; so they could travel both by day and by night. 22 The pillar of cloud never left its place in front of the people by day, nor did the pillar of fire by night.

14 The LORD spoke to Moses. 2 'Tell the Israelites', he said, 'they are to turn back and encamp before Pi-hahiroth, between Migdol and the sea to the east of Baal-zephon; your camp shall be opposite, by the sea. 3 Pharaoh will then think that the Israelites are finding themselves in difficult country, and are hemmed in by the wilderness. 4 I shall make Pharaoh obstinate, and he will pursue them, so that I may win glory for myself at the expense of Pharaoh and all his army; and the Egyptians will know that I am the LORD.' The Israelites did as they were ordered.

5 When it was reported to the Egyptian king that the Israelites had gone, he and his courtiers had a change of heart and said, 'What is this we have done? We have let our Israelite slaves go free!' 6 Pharaoh had his chariot yoked, and took his troops with him, 7 six hundred picked chariots and all the other chariots of Egypt, with a commander in each. 8 Then, made obstinate by the LORD, Pharaoh king of Egypt pursued the Israelites as they marched defiantly away. 9 The Egyptians, all Pharaoh's chariots and horses, cavalry and infantry, went in pursuit, and overtook them encamped beside the sea by Pi-hahiroth to the east of Baal-zephon.

10 Pharaoh was almost upon them when the Israelites looked up and saw the Egyptians close behind, and in terror they clamoured to the LORD for help. 11 They said to Moses, 'Were there no graves in Egypt, that you have

brought us here to perish in the wilderness? See what you have done to us by bringing us out of Egypt! 12 Is this not just what we meant when we said in Egypt, "Leave us alone; let us be slaves to the Egyptians"? Better for us to serve as slaves to the Egyptians than to perish in the wilderness.' 13 But Moses answered, 'Have no fear; stand firm and see the deliverance that the LORD will bring you this day; for as sure as you see the Egyptians now, you will never see them again. 14 The LORD will fight for you; so say no more.'

15 The LORD said to Moses, 'What is the meaning of this clamour? Tell the Israelites to strike camp, 16 and you are to raise high your staff and hold your hand out over the sea to divide it asunder, so that the Israelites can pass through the sea on dry ground. 17 For my part I shall make the Egyptians obstinate and they will come after you; thus I shall win glory for myself at the expense of Pharaoh and his army, chariots and cavalry all together. 18 The Egyptians will know that I am the LORD when I win glory for myself at the expense of their Pharaoh, his chariots and horsemen.'

19 The angel of God, who had travelled in front of the Israelites, now moved away to the rear. The pillar of cloud moved from the front and took up its position behind them, 20 thus coming between the Egyptians and the Israelites. The cloud brought on darkness and early nightfall, so that contact was lost throughout the night.

21 Then Moses held out his hand over the sea, and the LORD drove the sea away with a strong east wind all night long, and turned the seabed into dry land. The waters were divided asunder, 22 and the Israelites went through the sea on the dry ground, while the

14:2 **before Pi-hahiroth:** *or* where the desert tracks begin.

13.21: It is uncertain whether the *cloud* and *fire* derive from ordinary practices in travel (such as the ancient custom of carrying a burning brazier at the head of a caravan) or are, instead, symbols of the divine presence (Gen. 15.17 n.); the latter seems preferable, for the intent is to suggest the supernatural. The Canaanites personified the clouds on the fringes of a storm as minor deities (messengers) who announced the impending arrival of the storm-god.

14.1–31: The deliverance at the sea. At the moment when the LORD's promise of deliverance (3.7–8) is about to be realized, Pharaoh attempts to reassert his power. For a somewhat similar challenge to Israel's faith, see Gen. 22.1–19 n. **12:** Compare 5.20–21. **13–14:** Israel is exhorted to believe that, even in its darkest hour, the promise will yet be realized. **19:** *Angel of God* and *pillar of cloud* are used as synonyms. See 13.21 n. **21–29:** The story may be based upon natural phenomena, and enhanced through ages of recital: the *east wind* (v. 21) drives back the waters of the shallow marsh (13.18 n.), but later generations ascribed this to direct divine intervention, as in v. 30.

waters formed a wall to right and left of them. ²³ The Egyptians, all Pharaoh's horse, his chariots and cavalry, followed in pursuit into the sea. ²⁴ In the morning watch the LORD looked down on the Egyptian army through the pillar of fire and cloud, and he threw them into a panic. ²⁵ He clogged their chariot wheels and made them drag along heavily, so that the Egyptians said, 'It is the LORD fighting for Israel against Egypt; let us flee.'

²⁶ Then the LORD said to Moses, 'Hold your hand out over the sea, so that the water may flow back on the Egyptians, their chariots and horsemen.' ²⁷ Moses held his hand out over the sea, and at daybreak the water returned to its usual place and the Egyptians fled before its advance, but the LORD swept them into the sea. ²⁸ As the water came back it covered all Pharaoh's army, the chariots and cavalry, which had pressed the pursuit into the sea. Not one survived. ²⁹ Meanwhile the Israelites had passed along the dry ground through the sea, with the water forming a wall for them to right and to left. ³⁰ That day the LORD saved Israel from the power of Egypt. When the Israelites saw the Egyptians lying dead on the seashore, ³¹ and saw the great power which the LORD had put forth against Egypt, the people were in awe of the LORD and put their faith in him and in Moses his servant.

15 Then Moses and the Israelites sang this song to the LORD:

'I shall sing to the LORD, for he has
    risen up in triumph;
horse and rider he has hurled into the
    sea.
² The LORD is my refuge and my
    defence;
he has shown himself my deliverer.
He is my God, and I shall glorify him;
my father's God, and I shall exalt him.
³ The LORD is a warrior; the LORD is his
    name.
⁴ Pharaoh's chariots and his army
he has cast into the sea;
the flower of his officers
are engulfed in the Red Sea.
⁵ The watery abyss has covered them;

they sank to the depths like a stone.
⁶ Your right hand, LORD, is majestic in
    strength;
your right hand, LORD, shattered the
    enemy.
⁷ In the fullness of your triumph
you overthrew those who opposed you:
you let loose your fury;
it consumed them like stubble.
⁸ At the blast of your anger the sea piled
    up;
the water stood up like a bank;
out at sea the great deep congealed.

⁹ 'The enemy boasted, "I shall pursue, I
    shall overtake;
I shall divide the spoil,
I shall glut my appetite on them;
I shall draw my sword,
I shall rid myself of them."
¹⁰ You blew with your blast; the sea
    covered them;
they sank like lead in the swelling
    waves.

¹¹ 'LORD, who is like you among the gods?
Who is like you, majestic in holiness,
worthy of awe and praise, worker of
    wonders?
¹² You stretched out your right hand;
the earth engulfed them.

¹³ 'In your constant love you led the
    people
whom you had redeemed:
you guided them by your strength
to your holy dwelling-place.
¹⁴ Nations heard and trembled;
anguish seized the dwellers in Philistia.
¹⁵ The chieftains of Edom were then
    dismayed,
trembling seized the leaders of Moab,
the inhabitants of Canaan were all
    panic-stricken;
¹⁶ terror and dread fell upon them;
through the might of your arm
they stayed stone-still

14:25 **clogged:** *so Samar.; Heb.* removed.
15:2 **defence:** *or* song.   15:11 **among the gods:** *or*
in might.

15.1–21: **Songs of victory,** attributed to Moses (vv. 1–18) and Miriam (v. 21). These two extremely old hymns, possibly used in an ancient liturgy memorializing the deliverance, are depicted as originating immediately after the event. **11:** *Among the gods:* see Gen. 1.26 n. **13–18:** The allusions seem to assume Israel's settlement in Canaan, and to mark the age when this part of the hymn was composed.

while your people passed, Lord,
while the people whom you made your
  own passed by.
17 You will bring them in and plant them
in the mount that is your possession,
the dwelling-place, Lord, of your own
  making,
the sanctuary, Lord, which your own
  hands established.
18 The Lord will reign for ever and for
  ever.'

19 When Pharaoh's horse, both chariots and cavalry, went into the sea, the Lord brought back the waters over them; but Israel had passed through the sea on dry ground. 20 The prophetess Miriam, Aaron's sister, took up her tambourine, and all the women followed her, dancing to the sound of tambourines; 21 and Miriam sang them this refrain:

'Sing to the Lord, for he has risen up
  in triumph;
horse and rider he has hurled into the
  sea.'

In the wilderness

22 Moses led Israel from the Red Sea out into the wilderness of Shur, where for three days they travelled through the wilderness without finding water. 23 When they came to Marah, they could not drink the water there because it was bitter; that is why the place was called Marah. 24 The people complained to Moses, asking, 'What are we to drink?' 25 Moses cried to the Lord, who showed him a log which, when thrown into the water, made the water sweet.

It was there that the Lord laid down a statute and rule of life; there he put the people to the test. 26 He said, 'If only you will obey the Lord your God, if you will do what is right in his eyes, if you will listen to his commands and keep all his statutes, then I shall never bring on you any of the sufferings

which I brought on the Egyptians; for I the Lord am your healer.'
27 They came to Elim, where there were twelve springs and seventy palm trees, and there they encamped beside the water.

16 The whole Israelite community, setting out from Elim, arrived at the wilderness of Sin, which lies between Elim and Sinai. This was on the fifteenth day of the second month after they left Egypt.
2 The Israelites all complained to Moses and Aaron in the wilderness. 3 They said, 'If only we had died at the Lord's hand in Egypt, where we sat by the fleshpots and had plenty of bread! But you have brought us out into this wilderness to let this whole assembly starve to death.' 4 The Lord said to Moses, 'I shall rain down bread from heaven for you. Each day the people are to go out and gather a day's supply, so that I can put them to the test and see whether they follow my instructions or not. 5 But on the sixth day, when they prepare what they bring in, it should be twice as much as they gather on other days.' 6 Moses and Aaron said to all the Israelites, 'In the evening you will know that it was the Lord who brought you out of Egypt, 7 and in the morning you will see the glory of the Lord, because he has listened to your complaints against him. Who are we that you should bring complaints against us?' 8 'You will know this', Moses said, 'when in answer to your complaints the Lord gives you flesh to eat in the evening, and in the morning bread in plenty. What are we? It is against the Lord that you bring your complaints, not against us.'
9 Moses told Aaron to say to the whole community of Israel, 'Come into the presence of the Lord, for he has listened to your complaints.' 10 While Aaron was addressing the whole Israelite community, they looked towards the wilderness, and there was the glory of the Lord appearing in the cloud. 11 The Lord spoke to Moses: 12 'I have heard the

15:16 **made your own:** or created.

15.22–17.7: **Complaints in the wilderness.** Common to Israel's history are moments of exhilaration followed by challenges and despair (compare 7.14–11.10 n.; 14.1–31 n.). **25:** The idea that water may be made drinkable by casting pieces of wood into it is elsewhere attested in antiquity. **16.1:** The precise chronology reflects the concern of later generations. Here the motive is to bind the events of the Exodus to a liturgical calendar. See Gen. 7.24 n. **4:** The *test* is to determine whether Israel is willing to continue into the wilderness, with food available only on a daily basis. **5:** The double portion for the sabbath is to make labor on that day unnecessary. **6–8:** Here, the blessings of *bread* (manna) and *flesh* (quails) are both given, whereas in another version (Num. 11.4–34) the quails are provided only when the people grow tired of the manna. **10:** *Glory:*

complaints of the Israelites. Say to them: Between dusk and dark you will have flesh to eat and in the morning bread in plenty. You will know that I the LORD am your God.'

13 That evening a flock of quails flew in and settled over the whole camp; in the morning a fall of dew lay all around it. 14 When the dew was gone, there over the surface of the wilderness fine flakes appeared, fine as hoarfrost on the ground. 15 When the Israelites saw it, they said one to another, 'What is that?' because they did not know what it was. Moses said to them, 'That is the bread which the LORD has given you to eat. 16 Here is the command the LORD has given: Each of you is to gather as much as he can eat: let every man take an omer apiece for every person in his tent.' 17 The Israelites did this, and they gathered, some more, some less, 18 but when they measured it by the omer, those who had gathered more had not too much, and those who had gathered less had not too little. Each had just as much as he could eat. 19 Moses said, 'No one is to keep any of it till morning.' 20 Some, however, did not listen to him; they kept part of it till morning, and it became full of maggots and stank, and Moses was angry with them.

21 Each morning every man gathered as much as he needed; it melted away when the sun grew hot. 22 On the sixth day they gathered twice as much food, two omers each, and when the chiefs of the community all came and told Moses, 23 'This', he answered, 'is what the LORD has said: Tomorrow is a day of sacred rest, a sabbath holy to the LORD. So bake what you want to bake now, and boil what you want to boil; what remains over put aside to be kept till morning.' 24 So they put it aside till morning as Moses had commanded, and it neither stank nor became infested with maggots. 25 'Eat it today,' said Moses, 'because today is a sabbath of the LORD. Today you will find none outside. 26 For six days you may gather it, but on the seventh day, the sabbath, there will be none.' 27 Some of the people did go out to gather

it on the seventh day, but they found nothing. 28 The LORD said to Moses, 'How long will you Israelites refuse to obey my commands and instructions? 29 You are aware the LORD has given you the sabbath, and so he gives you two days' food every sixth day. Let everyone stay where he is; no one may stir from his home on the seventh.' 30 So the people kept the sabbath on the seventh day.

31 Israel called the food manna; it was like coriander seed, but white, and it tasted like a wafer made with honey.

32 'This', said Moses, 'is the command which the LORD has given: Take a full omer of it to be kept for future generations, so that they may see the bread with which I fed you in the wilderness when I brought you out of Egypt.' 33 Moses said to Aaron, 'Take a jar and fill it with an omer of manna, and store it in the presence of the LORD to be kept for future generations.' 34 Aaron did as the LORD had commanded Moses, and stored it before the Testimony for safe keeping. 35 The Israelites ate the manna for forty years until they came to a land where they could settle; they ate it until they came to the border of Canaan. 36 (An omer is one tenth of an ephah.)

17 The whole community of Israel set out from the wilderness of Sin and travelled by stages as the LORD directed. They encamped at Rephidim, but there was no water for the people to drink, 2 and a dispute arose between them and Moses. When they said, 'Give us water to drink,' Moses said, 'Why do you dispute with me? Why do you challenge the LORD?' 3 The people became so thirsty there that they raised an outcry against Moses: 'Why have you brought us out of Egypt with our children and our herds to let us die of thirst?' 4 Moses appealed to the LORD, 'What shall I do with these people? In a moment they will be stoning me.' 5 The LORD answered, 'Go forward ahead of the people; take with you some of the elders of Israel and bring along the staff with which

16:15 **What is that:** Heb. man-hu (cp. verse 31).

radiance, a light, like fire (Gen. 15.17 n.), serves as a symbol of the divine presence. **14–15:** The bread (manna) may be the "honey-dew" secretion of the tamarisk tree which drops to the ground and solidifies during the cool of the night. It is still gathered today by inhabitants of the area. **18:** Omer: see p. xxviii. **31:** Manna: the original meaning of the term cannot be ascertained; the tradition here supplies a folk explanation (v. 15). Elsewhere (Ps. 78.25) it is called "the bread of angels." **34:** Testimony: a technical term probably referring to a record of God's actions and requirements, including a copy of the Ten Commandments; see 25.16; 31.18; Deut. 10.1–5. **35:** Forty: see Gen. 7.4 n. **17.6:** Horeb: announced as the goal of the journey in 3.12.

you struck the Nile. Go, ⁶you will find me waiting for you there, by a rock in Horeb. Strike the rock; water will pour out of it for the people to drink.' Moses did this in the sight of the elders of Israel. ⁷He named the place Massah and Meribah, because the Israelites had disputed with him and put the LORD to the test with their question, 'Is the LORD in our midst or not?'

⁸The Amalekites came and attacked Israel at Rephidim. ⁹Moses said to Joshua, 'Pick men for us, and march out tomorrow to fight against Amalek; and I shall stand on the hilltop with the staff of God in my hand.' ¹⁰Joshua did as Moses commanded and fought against Amalek, while Moses, Aaron, and Hur climbed to the top of the hill. ¹¹Whenever Moses raised his hands Israel had the advantage, and when he lowered his hands the advantage passed to Amalek. ¹²When his arms grew heavy they took a stone and put it under him and, as he sat, Aaron and Hur held up his hands, one on each side, so that his hands remained steady till sunset. ¹³Thus Joshua defeated Amalek and put its people to the sword.

¹⁴The LORD said to Moses, 'Record this in writing, and tell it to Joshua in these words: I am resolved to blot out all memory of Amalek from under heaven.' ¹⁵Moses built an altar, and named it 'The LORD is my Banner' and said, ¹⁶'My oath upon it: the LORD is at war with Amalek generation after generation.'

18 JETHRO priest of Midian, father-in-law of Moses, heard all that God had done for Moses and for Israel his people, and how the LORD had brought Israel out of Egypt. ²When Moses had sent away his wife Zipporah, Jethro his father-in-law had received her ³and her two sons. The name of the one was Gershom, 'for', said Moses, 'I have become an alien living in a foreign land'; ⁴the other's name was Eliezer, 'for', he said, 'the God of my father was my help and saved me from Pharaoh's sword.'

⁵Jethro, Moses' father-in-law, now came to him with his sons and his wife, to the wilderness where he was encamped at the mountain of God. ⁶Moses was told, 'Here is Jethro, your father-in-law, coming to you with your wife and her two sons.' ⁷Moses went out to meet his father-in-law, bowed low to him, and kissed him. After they had greeted one another and come into the tent, ⁸Moses told him all that the LORD had done to Pharaoh and to Egypt for Israel's sake, and about all their hardships on the journey, and how the LORD had saved them. ⁹Jethro rejoiced at all the good the LORD had done for Israel in saving them from the power of Egypt.

¹⁰⁻¹¹He said, 'Blessed be the LORD who has delivered you from the power of Egypt and of Pharaoh. Now I know that the LORD is the greatest of all gods, because he has delivered the people from the Egyptians who dealt so arrogantly with them.' ¹²Jethro, Moses' father-in-law, brought a whole-offering and sacrifices for God; and Aaron and all the elders of Israel came and shared the meal with Jethro in the presence of God.

¹³The next day Moses took his seat to settle disputes among the people, and he was surrounded from morning till evening. ¹⁴At the sight of all that he was doing for the people, Jethro asked, 'What is this you are doing for the people? Why do you sit alone with all of them standing round you from morning till evening?' ¹⁵'The people come to me to seek God's guidance,' Moses answered. ¹⁶'Whenever there is a dispute among them, they come to me, and I decide between one party

17:7 **Massah:** *that is* Test. **Meribah:** *that is* Dispute.
17:16 **My oath upon it:** *so Samar.; lit.* Hand upon buttock; *Heb. unintelligible.* 18:3 **an alien:** *cp. 2:22.*
18:4 **Eliezer:** *that is* God is help. 18:6 **Here is:** *so Gk; Heb.* I am.

17.7: Despite the previous evidence of God's guidance, Israel's trust vanished at the first difficulty.

17.8–16: War with the Amalekites. A once-independent story, its function here is to explain and justify the continued animosity between Israel and a strong desert-dwelling tribe from the vicinity of Kadesh (Num. 24.20; Deut. 25.17–19; 1 Sam. 15.2–3; 1 Chr. 4.43). **9:** *Joshua's* sudden appearance here suggests that this story once belonged in another context.

18.1–27: Israel arrives at the sacred mountain. 1: *Jethro:* in 2.16–21, the name of the priest of Midian is Reuel. **2:** Moses may have left his family in Midian on leaving for Egypt. **5:** *Mountain of God:* Horeb (3.1), thus fulfilling the sign given to Moses (3.12). **13–26:** The judicial system of Israel is traced back to Mosaic authority. To limit the power of civil courts ("officers over units": v. 25), the ultimate decision remains in the hands of religious leadership (Moses).

and the other. I make known the statutes and laws of God.' [17] His father-in-law said to him, 'This is not the best way to do it. [18] You will only wear yourself out and wear out the people who are here. The task is too heavy for you; you cannot do it alone. [19] Now listen to me: take my advice, and God be with you. It is for you to be the people's representative before God, and bring their disputes to him, [20] to instruct them in the statutes and laws, and teach them how they must behave and what they must do. [21] But you should search for capable, godfearing men among all the people, honest and incorruptible men, and appoint them over the people as officers over units of a thousand, of a hundred, of fifty, or of ten. [22] They can act as judges for the people at all times; difficult cases they should refer to you, but decide simple cases themselves. In this way your burden will be lightened, as they will be sharing it with you. [23] If you do this, then God will direct you and you will be able to go on. And, moreover, this whole people will arrive at its destination in harmony.'

[24] Moses heeded his father-in-law and did all he had suggested. [25] He chose capable men from all Israel and appointed them leaders of the people, officers over units of a thousand, of a hundred, of fifty, or of ten. [26] They sat as a permanent court, bringing the difficult cases to Moses but deciding simple cases themselves. [27] When his father-in-law went back to his own country, Moses set him on his way.

Israel at Mount Sinai

19 IN the third month after Israel had left Egypt, they came to the wilderness of Sinai. [2] They set out from Rephidim and, entering the wilderness of Sinai, they encamped there, pitching their tents in front of the mountain. [3] Moses went up to God, and the LORD called to him from the mountain and said, 'This is what you are to say to the house of Jacob and tell the sons of Israel: [4] You yourselves have seen what I did to Egypt, and how I have carried you on eagles' wings and brought you here to me. [5] If only you will now listen to me and keep my covenant, then out of all peoples you will become my special possession; for the whole earth is mine. [6] You will be to me a kingdom of priests, my holy nation. Those are the words you are to speak to the Israelites.'

[7] Moses went down, and summoning the elders of the people he set before them all these commands which the LORD had laid on him. [8] As one the people answered, 'Whatever the LORD has said we shall do.' When Moses brought this answer back to the LORD, [9] the LORD said to him, 'I am coming to you in a thick cloud, so that I may speak to you in the hearing of the people, and so their faith in you may never fail.'

When Moses reported to the LORD the pledge given by the people, [10] the LORD said to him, 'Go to the people and hallow them today and tomorrow and have them wash their clothes. [11] They must be ready by the third day, because on that day the LORD will descend on Mount Sinai in the sight of all the people. [12] You must set bounds for the people, saying, "Take care not to go up the mountain or even to touch its base." Anyone who touches the mountain shall be put to death. [13] No hand may touch him; he is to be stoned to death or shot: neither man nor beast may live. But when the ram's horn sounds, they may go up the mountain.' [14] Moses came down from the mountain to the people. He hallowed them and they washed their clothes. [15] He said, 'Be ready by the

19:1 **after . . . Egypt:** *prob. rdg; Heb. adds* on this day.
19:13 **shot:** *or* hurled to his death.

19.1–25: Moses prepares the people to enter into covenant with the LORD. 1: *Sinai:* see 3.1 n. **2:** This version of the conclusion of Israel's wandering omits the meeting with Jethro (18.1–12) as the initial event at the sacred mountain. **3:** The idea that gods dwell upon or reveal themselves upon high mountains is attested throughout the ancient world. The LORD was believed to dwell in heaven and to come down to the mountain top (v. 20) to meet with Moses. **9:** The association of a *cloud* with the divine presence may have originated in the observation of mists surrounding the tops of high mountains (see v. 3 n.) or may have been borrowed from Canaanite mythology (see 13.21 n.). Here, the cloud serves to obscure God from mortal eyes (see 33.20 for a reason why) and to avoid the impression that the LORD exists in bodily form (Deut. 4.11–12). **10:** A change of clothing was a regular prescription for preparation for rituals (Gen. 35.2). **12–13:** The place at which the deity is revealed is holy (Gen. 28.16–17; Exod. 3.5), and holiness was regarded as a mysterious energy transmittable by touch (Lev. 6.24–27), which is sometimes fatal (2 Sam. 6.6–7). **15:** The prohibition against third day; do not go near a woman.' ¹⁶At dawn on the third day there were peals of thunder and flashes of lightning, dense cloud on the mountain, and a loud trumpet-blast; all the people in the camp trembled.

¹⁷Moses brought the people out from the camp to meet God, and they took their stand at the foot of the mountain. ¹⁸Mount Sinai was enveloped in smoke because the Lord had come down on it in fire; the smoke rose like the smoke from a kiln; all the people trembled violently, ¹⁹and the sound of the trumpet grew ever louder. Whenever Moses spoke, God answered him in a peal of thunder. ²⁰The Lord came down on the top of Mount Sinai and summoned Moses up to the mountaintop. ²¹The Lord said to him, 'Go down; warn the people solemnly that they must not force their way through to the Lord to see him, or many of them will perish. ²²Even the priests, who may approach the Lord, must hallow themselves, for fear that the Lord may break out against them.' ²³Moses answered the Lord, 'The people cannot come up Mount Sinai, because you solemnly warned us to set bounds to the mountain and keep it holy.' ²⁴The Lord said, 'Go down; then come back, bringing Aaron with you, but let neither priests nor people force their way up to the Lord, for fear that he may break out against them.' ²⁵So Moses went down to the people and spoke to them.

20 God spoke all these words: ²I am the Lord your God who brought you out of Egypt, out of the land of slavery.

³You must have no other god besides me.

⁴You must not make a carved image for yourself, nor the likeness of anything in the heavens above, or on the earth below, or in the waters under the earth.

⁵You must not bow down to them in worship; for I, the Lord your God, am a jealous God, punishing the children for the sins of the parents to the third and fourth generation of those who reject me. ⁶But I keep faith with thousands, those who love me and keep my commandments.

⁷You must not make wrong use of the name of the Lord your God; the Lord will not leave unpunished anyone who misuses his name.

⁸Remember to keep the sabbath day holy. ⁹You have six days to labour and do all your work; ¹⁰but the seventh day is a sabbath of the Lord your God; that day you must not do any work, neither you, nor your son or your daughter, your slave or your slave-girl, your cattle, or the alien residing among you; ¹¹for in six days the Lord made the heavens and the earth, the sea, and all that is in them, and on the seventh day he rested. Therefore the Lord blessed the sabbath day and declared it holy.

¹²Honour your father and your mother, so that you may enjoy long life in the land which the Lord your God is giving you.

¹³Do not commit murder.

¹⁴Do not commit adultery.

¹⁵Do not steal.

¹⁶Do not give false evidence against your neighbour.

¹⁷Do not covet your neighbour's household: you must not covet your neighbour's wife, his slave, his slave-girl, his ox, his donkey, or anything that belongs to him.

19:18 **the people:** *so some MSS; others* the mountain. 19:19 **in . . . thunder:** *or* by voice. 20:3 **god:** *or* gods. 20:6 **with thousands:** *or* for a thousand generations with.

sexual intercourse in the context of divine worship may be an attempt to distinguish the cult of the Lord from that of the gods of Canaan; see Lev. 15.16–18 n. **16:** The *trumpet-blast* was the means of summoning the people to an assembly (Ps. 81.3).

20.1–21: The Ten Commandments are the basic requirements if Israel is to enter into covenant with the Lord and become God's "holy nation" (19.6). In adopting them to regulate its internal affairs, Israel renounces all other loyalties, divine or human. Other versions in various stages of expansion are recorded (34.14–26; Deut. 5.6–21). **2:** As in recorded secular alliances of the time, a great king recited his gracious deeds on behalf of formerly oppressed peoples, inviting them to respond with gratitude and to formalize the relationship. **4:** The prohibition is not against all plastic art, but only the use of such items in the cult of the Lord, since they tend to reduce the Lord of all the world (19.5) to a physical object (Isa. 44.9–17). **5:** Inherited guilt, a common assumption in the ancient world, was rejected by some biblical writers (Jer. 31.29–30; Ezek. 18.19–20) though it continued to hold sway with the populace (Jn. 9.1–2). **7:** Lev. 19.12 specifies one such *wrong use of the name:* in a false oath. **13:** That *murder* does not include capital punishment or killing in war is suggested by

18 WHEN all the people saw how it thundered and the lightning flashed, when they heard the trumpet sound and saw the mountain in smoke, they were afraid and trembled. They stood at a distance 19 and said to Moses, 'Speak to us yourself and we will listen; but do not let God speak to us or we shall die.' 20 Moses answered, 'Do not be afraid. God has come only to test you, so that the fear of him may remain with you and preserve you from sinning.' 21 So the people kept their distance, while Moses approached the dark cloud where God was.

22 THE LORD said to Moses, Say this to the Israelites: You know now that I have spoken from heaven to you. 23 You must not make gods of silver to be worshipped besides me, nor may you make yourselves gods of gold. 24 The altar you make for me is to be of earth, and you are to sacrifice on it both your whole-offerings and your shared-offerings, your sheep and goats and your cattle. Wherever I cause my name to be invoked, I will come to you and bless you. 25 If you make an altar of stones for me, you must not build it of hewn stones, for if you use a tool on them, you profane them. 26 You must not mount up to my altar by steps, in case your private parts are exposed over against it.

21 These are the laws you are to set before them:

2 When you purchase a Hebrew as a slave, he will be your slave for six years; in the seventh year he is to go free without paying anything.

3 If he comes to you alone, he is to go away alone; but if he is already a married man, his wife is to go away with him.

4 If his master gives him a wife, and she bears him sons or daughters, the woman with her children belongs to her master, and the man must go away alone. 5 But if the slave should say, 'I am devoted to my master and my wife and children; I do not wish to go free,' 6 then his master must bring him to God: he is to be brought to the door or the doorpost, and his master will pierce his ear with an awl; the man will then be his slave for life.

7 When a man sells his daughter into slavery, she is not to go free as male slaves may. 8 If she proves unpleasing to her master who had designated her for himself, he must let her be redeemed; he has treated her unfairly, and therefore he has no right to sell her to foreigners. 9 If he assigns her to his son, he must allow her the rights of a daughter. 10 If he takes another woman, he must not deprive the first of meat, clothes, and conjugal rights; 11 if he does not provide her with these three things, she is to go free without payment.

12 Whoever strikes another man and kills him must be put to death. 13 But if he did not act with intent, but it came about by act of God, the slayer may flee to a place which I shall appoint for you. 14 But if a man wilfully kills another by treachery, you are to take him even from my altar to be put to death.

15 Whoever strikes his father or mother must be put to death.

16 Whoever kidnaps an Israelite must be put to death, whether he has sold him, or the man is found in his possession.

20:24 **shared-offerings:** *exact meaning of Heb. uncertain.*
21:6 **God:** *or the gods or the judges.*

21.12–17 and Deut. 20.10–18. **18–21:** This section, a logical continuation of 19.25, is the bridge between the Commandments and the loosely related material which follows.

20.22–23.33: The Book of the Covenant: See 24.7. Several earlier collections are recognizable by topical similarity and similar structure. Portions presuppose settled agrarian life, suggesting secular legislation operative in the land of Canaan, or even borrowed from the Canaanites. Israel, however, came to regard the legislation as an extension of the covenant requirements (20.2–17) and hence given at Sinai.

20.22–26: Cultic regulations. 24: This verse seems to sanction a variety of sanctuaries, in contrast to limitations encountered elsewhere, e.g. Deut. 12.5. **25:** The altars of the LORD must remain distinct from those of the gods of Canaan.

21.1–22.17: Social and economic regulations. These rules are introduced by "when" or "if," and represent an origin different from those in 22.18–23.13. **2:** *Hebrew:* see Gen. 10.21 n. Contrast Deut. 15.12, where the term has become synonymous with "Israelite." **6:** This extremely old law may be a relic of belief in household gods (Gen. 31.19) who dwell at the *doorpost*. **7–11:** The regulation offers some protection for a female slave, but there is no limit on her term of service (contrast v. 4). In Deut. 15.12–16, a passage from a later period, male and female slaves are to be treated equally. **13:** See Num. 35.9–12.

¹⁷Whoever reviles his father or mother must be put to death.

¹⁸When men quarrel and one hits another with a stone or with his fist, and the man is not killed but takes to his bed, ¹⁹and if he recovers so as to walk about outside with his staff, then the one who struck him has no liability, except that he must pay compensation for the other's loss of time and see that his recovery is complete.

²⁰When a man strikes his slave or his slave-girl with a stick and the slave dies on the spot, he must be punished. ²¹But he is not to be punished if the slave survives for one day or two, because the slave is his property.

²²When, in the course of a brawl, a man knocks against a pregnant woman so that she has a miscarriage but suffers no further injury, then the offender must pay whatever fine the woman's husband demands after assessment. ²³But where injury ensues, you are to give life for life, ²⁴eye for eye, tooth for tooth, hand for hand, foot for foot, ²⁵burn for burn, bruise for bruise, wound for wound.

²⁶When a man strikes his slave or slave-girl in the eye and destroys it, he must let the slave go free in compensation for the eye. ²⁷When he knocks out the tooth of a slave or a slave-girl, he must let the slave go free in compensation for the tooth.

²⁸When an ox gores a man or a woman to death, the ox must be put to death by stoning, and its flesh is not to be eaten; the owner of the ox will be free from liability. ²⁹If, however, the ox has for some time past been a vicious animal, and the owner has been duly warned but has not kept it under control, and the ox kills a man or a woman, then the ox must be stoned to death, and the owner put to death as well. ³⁰If, however, the penalty is commuted for a money payment, he must pay in redemption of his life whatever is imposed upon him. ³¹If the ox gores a son or a daughter, the same ruling applies. ³²If the ox gores a slave or slave-girl, its owner must pay thirty shekels of silver to their master, and the ox must be stoned to death.

³³When a man removes the cover of a cistern or digs a cistern and leaves it uncovered, then if an ox or a donkey falls into it, ³⁴the owner of the cistern must make good the loss; he must pay the owner the price of the animal, and the dead beast will be his.

³⁵When one man's ox butts another's and kills it, they must sell the live ox, share the price, and also share the dead beast. ³⁶But if it is known that the ox has for some time past been vicious and the owner has not kept it under control, he must make good the loss, ox for ox, but the dead beast is his.

22 When a man steals an ox or a sheep and slaughters or sells it, he must repay five beasts for the ox and four sheep for the sheep. ²⁻⁴He must pay in full; if he has no means, he is to be sold to pay for the theft. But if the animal is found alive in his possession, be it ox, donkey, or sheep, he must repay two for each one stolen.

If a burglar is caught in the act and receives a fatal injury, it is not murder; but if he breaks in after sunrise and receives a fatal injury, then it is murder.

⁵When a man burns off a field or a vineyard and lets the fire spread so that it burns another man's field, he must make restitution from his own field according to the yield expected; and if the whole field is laid waste, he must make restitution from the best part of his own field or vineyard.

⁶When a fire starts and spreads to a thorn hedge, so that sheaves, or standing grain, or a whole field is destroyed, whoever started the fire must make full restitution.

⁷When someone gives another silver or chattels for safe keeping, and they are stolen from that person's house, the thief, if apprehended, must restore twofold. ⁸But if the thief is not apprehended, the owner of the house will have to appear before God for it to be ascertained whether or not he has laid hands on his neighbour's property. ⁹In every case of misappropriation involving an ox, a donkey, or a sheep, a cloak, or any lost property which may be claimed, each party must bring his case before God; the one whom

21:18 **fist:** or hoe.   21:33 **cistern:** or pit.   22:1 In Heb. 21:37.   22:2–4 Verses rearranged thus: 3b,4,2,3a. 22:2–4 **If a burglar:** in Heb. the beginning of 22:1. 22:5 **When ... man's field:** or When a man uses his field or vineyard for grazing, and lets his beast loose, and it feeds in another man's field. **he must ... waste:** so Samar.; Heb. omits.   22:8,9 **God:** or the judges.

17: Reviles: a curse was expected; see Gen. 27.33–35 n. **23–25:** The punishment must not exceed the crime and must be equitably applied (Lev. 24.19–22). **22.8:** Before God: at the sanctuary, where the priests will decide the case (1 Kgs. 8.31–32).

God declares to be in the wrong will have to restore double to his neighbour.

[10] When someone gives a donkey, an ox, a sheep, or any beast into a neighbour's keeping, and it dies or is injured or is carried off, there being no witness, [11] then by swearing by the LORD it will have to be settled between them whether or not the neighbour has laid hands on the other's property. If not, no restitution is to be made and the owner must accept this. [12] If it has been stolen from the neighbour, he must make restitution to its owner. [13] If it has been mauled by a wild beast, he must bring it in as evidence; he will not have to make restitution for what has been mauled.

[14] When a man borrows a beast from his neighbour and it is injured or dies while its owner is not present, the borrower must make full restitution; [15] but if the owner is with it, the borrower does not have to make restitution. If it was hired, only the hire is due.

[16] When a man seduces a virgin who is not yet betrothed, he must pay the bride-price for her to be his wife. [17] If her father refuses to give her to him, the seducer must pay in silver a sum equal to the bride-price for virgins.

[18] You must not allow a witch to live.

[19] Whoever has sexual intercourse with a beast must be put to death.

[20] Whoever sacrifices to any god but the LORD must be put to death under solemn ban.

[21] You must not wrong or oppress an alien; you were yourselves aliens in Egypt.

[22] You must not wrong a widow or a fatherless child. [23] If you do, and they appeal to me, be sure that I shall listen; [24] my anger will be roused and I shall kill you with the sword; your own wives will become widows and your children fatherless.

[25] If you advance money to any poor man amongst my people, you are not to act like a moneylender; you must not exact interest from him.

[26] If you take your neighbour's cloak in pawn, return it to him by sunset, [27] because it is his only covering. It is the cloak in which he wraps his body; in what else can he sleep? If he appeals to me, I shall listen, for I am full of compassion.

[28] You must not revile God, nor curse a chief of your own people.

[29] You must not hold back the first of your harvest, whether grain or wine. You must give me your firstborn sons. [30] You must do the same with your oxen and your sheep. They should stay with the mother for seven days; on the eighth day you are to give them to me.

[31] You must be holy to me: you are not to eat the flesh of anything killed by beasts in the open country; you are to throw it to the dogs.

23 You must not spread a baseless rumour, nor make common cause with a wicked man by giving malicious evidence. [2] You must not be led into wrongdoing by the majority, nor, when you give evidence in a lawsuit, should you side with the majority to pervert justice; [3] nor should you show favouritism to a poor person in his lawsuit.

[4] Should you come upon your enemy's ox or donkey straying, you must take it back to him. [5] Should you see the donkey of someone who hates you lying helpless under its load, however unwilling you may be to help, you must lend a hand with it.

[6] You must not deprive the poor man of justice in his lawsuit. [7] Avoid all lies, and do not cause the death of the innocent and guiltless; for I the LORD will never acquit the guilty. [8] Do not accept a bribe, for bribery makes the discerning person blind and the just person give a crooked answer.

[9] Do not oppress the alien, for you know how it feels to be an alien; you yourselves were aliens in Egypt.

[10] For six years you may sow your land and gather its produce; [11] but in the seventh year you must let it lie fallow and leave it alone. Let it provide food for the poor of your people, and what they leave the wild animals may eat. You are to do likewise with your vineyard and your olive grove.

[12] For six days you may do your work, but

22:14 **a beast:** *so Scroll; Heb. omits.*   22:29 **the first . . . wine:** *mng of Heb. words uncertain.*   23:2 **justice:** *so Gk; Heb. omits.*

22.18–23.13: Social and economic regulations, introduced by "You must not"; see 21.1–22.17 n. **20:** *Ban:* compare Deut. 13.12–16 and see Josh. 6.17. **23:** *I shall listen:* see 3.7–10. **29–30:** See 13.2 n. **31:** Such food was forbidden because it was impossible to remove the blood from it (Lev. 17.13–14; see Gen. 4.10 n.). **23.9:** This repeats 22.21; such repetitions suggest that materials have been compiled from diverse sources.

on the seventh day abstain from work, so that your ox and your donkey may rest, and your home-born slave and the alien may refresh themselves.

¹³ Be attentive to every word of mine. You must not invoke other gods: their names are not to cross your lips.

¹⁴ Three times a year you are to keep a pilgrim-feast to me. ¹⁵ You are to celebrate the pilgrim-feast of Unleavened Bread: for seven days, as I have commanded you, you are to eat unleavened bread at the appointed time in the month of Abib, for in that month you came out of Egypt; and no one is to come into my presence without an offering. ¹⁶ You are to celebrate the pilgrim-feast of Harvest, with the firstfruits of your work in sowing the land, and the pilgrim-feast of Ingathering at the end of the year, when you gather the fruits of your work in from the land. ¹⁷ Those three times a year all your males are to come into the presence of the Lord GOD.

¹⁸ Do not offer the blood of my sacrifice at the same time as anything leavened.

The fat of my festal offering is not to remain overnight till morning.

¹⁹ You must bring the choicest firstfruits of your soil to the house of the LORD your God.

Do not boil a kid in its mother's milk.

²⁰ And now I am sending an angel before you to guard you on your way and to bring you to the place I have prepared. ²¹ Heed him and listen to his voice. Do not defy him; he will not pardon your rebelliousness, for my authority rests in him. ²² If you will only listen to his voice and do all I tell you, then I shall be an enemy to your enemies, and I shall harass those who harass you. ²³ My angel will go before you and bring you to the Amorites,

the Hittites, the Perizzites, the Canaanites, the Hivites, and the Jebusites, and I will make an end of them. ²⁴ You are not to bow down to their gods; you are not to worship them or observe their rites. Rather, you must tear down all their images and smash their sacred pillars. ²⁵ You are to worship the LORD your God, and he will bless your bread and your water. I shall take away all sickness out of your midst. ²⁶ No woman will miscarry or be barren in your land. I shall grant you a full span of life.

²⁷ I shall send terror of me ahead of you and throw into panic every people you find in your path. I shall make all your enemies turn their backs towards you. ²⁸ I shall spread panic before you to drive out the Hivites, the Canaanites, and the Hittites in front of you. ²⁹ I shall not drive them out all in one year, or the land would become waste and the wild beasts too many for you, ³⁰ but I shall drive them out little by little until you have grown numerous enough to take possession of the country. ³¹ I shall establish your frontiers from the Red Sea to the sea of the Philistines, and from the wilderness to the river Euphrates. I shall give the inhabitants of the land into your power, and you will drive them out before you. ³² You are not to make any alliance with them and their gods. ³³ They must not stay in your land, for fear they make you sin against me by ensnaring you into the worship of their gods.

24 THE LORD said to Moses, 'Come up to the LORD, you and Aaron, Nadab and Abihu, and seventy of the Israelite el-

23:15 **come . . . presence:** *lit.* see my face.
23:16 **end:** *or* beginning; *lit.* going out.   23:17 **come . . . of:** *lit.* see the face of.

23.14–19: Cultic regulations. 15: Since there is no mention of Passover, this section may reflect a time before the *pilgrim-feast of Unleavened Bread* and Passover were joined; see 12.15 n. **16:** The *pilgrim-feast of Harvest,* also called the pilgrim-feast of Weeks (34.22), came fifty days after Passover (Lev. 23.16; hence its Greek name, "Pentecost"); it celebrated the wheat harvest. The *Ingathering,* also called Booths and Tabernacles, celebrated the harvest of grapes and olives which, in the preexilic calendar, ended the year; on the postexilic calendar, see 12.2 n. **19:** *Boil a kid in its mother's milk:* a Canaanite ritual, here forbidden to Israel.

23.20–33: Instructions for the entry into Canaan. While this section presupposes that the giving of the Law is now complete and Israel is ready to depart from the sacred mountain, much more legislation appears in the ensuing chapters. This suggests that several old traditions have been combined, but with little regard for precise sequence. **20:** *Angel:* compare the previous symbol of divine leadership in the wilderness (13.21 n.). **31:** *Red Sea:* here, the Gulf of Elath (see 13.18 n.). *Euphrates:* see Gen. 15.18 n.

24.1–11: Israel accepts the covenant obligations. Two old traditions have been combined. In vv. 3–8 the ceremony takes place at the foot of the mountain, with all the people participating; in vv. 1–2, 9–11, it takes place on the mountain in the presence only of the leaders. **1:** The abrupt mention of *Nadab and Abihu* ders. While you are still at a distance, you are to bow down; [2] then Moses is to approach the LORD by himself, but not the others. The people must not go up with him.'

[3] Moses went and repeated to the people all the words of the LORD, all his laws. With one voice the whole people answered, 'We will do everything the LORD has told us.' [4] Moses wrote down all the words of the LORD. Early in the morning he built an altar at the foot of the mountain, and erected twelve sacred pillars for the twelve tribes of Israel. [5] He sent the young men of Israel and they sacrificed bulls to the LORD as whole-offerings and shared-offerings. [6] Moses took half the blood and put it in basins, and the other half he flung against the altar. [7] Then he took the Book of the Covenant and read it aloud for the people to hear. They said, 'We shall obey, and do all that the LORD has said.' [8] Moses then took the blood and flung it over the people, saying, 'This is the blood of the covenant which the LORD has made with you on the terms of this book.'

[9] Moses went up with Aaron, Nadab, and Abihu, and seventy of the elders of Israel, [10] and they saw the God of Israel. Under his feet there was, as it were, a pavement of sapphire, clear blue as the very heavens; [11] but the LORD did not stretch out his hand against the leaders of Israel. They saw God; they ate and they drank. [12] The LORD said to Moses, 'Come up to me on the mountain, stay there, and let me give you the stone tablets with the law and commandment I have written down for their instruction.' [13] Moses with Joshua his assistant set off up the mountain of God;

[14] he said to the elders, 'Wait for us here until we come back to you. You have Aaron and Hur; if anyone has a dispute, let him go to them.'

[15] So Moses went up the mountain and a cloud covered it. [16] The glory of the LORD rested on Mount Sinai, and the cloud covered the mountain for six days; on the seventh day he called to Moses out of the cloud. [17] To the Israelites the glory of the LORD looked like a devouring fire on the mountaintop. [18] Moses entered the cloud and went up the mountain; there he stayed forty days and forty nights.

25 THE LORD spoke to Moses and said: [2] Tell the Israelites to set aside a contribution for me; you are to accept whatever contribution each man freely offers. [3] You may accept any of the following: gold, silver, copper; [4] violet, purple, and scarlet yarn; fine linen and goats' hair; [5] tanned rams' skins and dugong-hides; acacia-wood; [6] oil for the lamp, spices for the anointing oil and for the fragrant incense; [7] cornelians and other stones ready for setting on the ephod and the breastpiece.

[8] Make me a sanctuary, and I shall dwell among the Israelites. [9] Make it exactly according to the design I show you, the design for the Tabernacle and for all its furniture. This is how you must make it: [10] Make an Ark, a chest of acacia-wood two and a half cubits long, one and a half cubits wide, and

24:6 **against:** *or* upon.   24:10 **they saw:** *or* they were afraid of. **sapphire:** *or* lapis lazuli.
24:11 **They saw:** *or* They stayed before.
25:7 **breastpiece:** *or* pouch.

emphasizes the fragmentary nature of this account and suggests that it once belonged to another context (compare 17.9 n.). **3:** The *words:* Ten Commandments (see 20.1–21 n.); the *laws* are the regulations of 20.22–23.33. **6–8:** The *altar* represents the deity. **10:** Back of this account lies the older notion that a high mountain could reach into the heavens (Gen. 11.4 n.), into the domain of the deity. This idea, though present in passing clues, was superseded in the developing thought. **11:** *Stretch out his hand:* to slay. But contrast 33.20. *Ate and . . . drank:* a meal formalized a covenant; see Gen. 31.54.

24.12–18: Moses prepares to receive the stone tablets, upon which the Ten Commandments are written. Chronologically, this segment of tradition should come before ch. 20. **18:** *Forty:* on the number, see Gen. 7.4 n. This verse prepares for ch. 32, which once followed immediately.

25.1–31.17: The sanctuary and its personnel. This material, inserted during the last (priestly) stage of tradition collection and information, ascribes the cultic practices of the postexilic period to the Sinai period. The wealth (and technology) required for such a structure as described would have been an intolerable strain during the wilderness period.

25.1–40: Furnishings for the Tabernacle. 7: *Ephod:* here a garment; see 28.6–12; 1 Sam. 2.18. **8:** The abiding presence of the deity, who was formerly thought to dwell in heaven and to appear especially upon sacred mountains (3.1; 19.3 n.), is symbolized through the erection of the portable sanctuary. **10:** The *Ark:*

one and a half cubits high. [11] Overlay it with pure gold both inside and out, and put a band of gold all round it. [12] Cast four gold rings for it, and fasten them to its four feet, two rings on each side. [13] Make poles of acacia-wood and overlay them with gold, [14] and insert the poles in the rings at the sides of the Ark to lift it. [15] The poles are to remain in the rings of the Ark and never be removed. [16] Put into the Ark the Testimony which I shall give you.

[17] Make a cover of pure gold two and a half cubits long and one and a half cubits wide. [18] Make two gold cherubim of beaten work at the ends of the cover, [19] one at each end; make each cherub of one piece with the cover. [20] They are to be made with wings spread out and pointing upwards to screen the cover with their wings. They will be face to face, looking inwards over the cover. [21] Place the cover on the Ark, and put into the Ark the Testimony that I shall give you. [22] It is there that I shall meet you; from above the cover, between the two cherubim over the Ark of the Testimony, I shall deliver to you all my commands for the Israelites.

[23] Make a table of acacia-wood two cubits long, one cubit wide, and one and a half cubits high. [24] Overlay it with pure gold, and put a band of gold all round it. [25] Make a rim round it a hand's breadth wide, and a gold band round the rim. [26] Make four gold rings for the table, and put the rings at the four corners by the four legs. [27] The rings, which are to receive the poles for carrying the table, must be adjacent to the rim. [28] Make the poles of acacia-wood and overlay them with gold; they are to be used for carrying the table. [29] Make dishes and saucers for it, and flagons and bowls from which drink-offerings may be poured; make them of pure gold. [30] Put the Bread of the Presence on the table, to be always before me.

[31] Make a lampstand of pure gold. The lampstand, stem and branches, shall be of beaten work: its cups, both calyxes and petals, shall be of one piece with it. [32] There are to be six branches springing from the sides of the lampstand, three branches from one side and three branches from the other. [33] There shall be three cups shaped like almond blossoms with calyx and petals on the first branch, three cups shaped like almond blossoms with calyx and petals on the next branch, and similarly for all six branches springing from the lampstand. [34] On the main stem of the lampstand there are to be four cups shaped like almond blossoms with calyx and petals, [35] and there shall be calyxes of one piece with it under the six branches which spring from the lampstand, a single calyx under each pair of branches. [36] The calyxes and the branches are to be of one piece with it, all a single piece of beaten work of pure gold. [37] Make seven lamps for this and mount them to shed light over the space in front of the lampstand. [38] Its tongs and firepans are to be of pure gold. [39] The lampstand and all these fittings are to be made from one talent of pure gold. [40] See that you work to the design shown to you on the mountain.

26 Make the Tabernacle itself of ten hangings of finely woven linen, and violet, purple, and scarlet yarn, with cherubim worked on them, all made by a seamster. [2] The length of each hanging is to be twenty-eight cubits and the breadth four cubits; all are to be of the same size. [3] Five of the hangings are to be joined together, and similarly the other five. [4] Make violet loops along the outer edge of the last hanging in each set, [5] fifty for each set; they must be opposite one another. [6] Make fifty gold fasteners, join the hangings one to another with them, and the Tabernacle will form a single whole.

[7] Make hangings of goats' hair, eleven in all, to form a tent over the Tabernacle; [8] each

25:30 **Bread of the Presence:** or Shewbread.

a portable wooden chest. *Cubit:* see p. xxvii. **16:** *Testimony:* see 16.34 n. **18:** *Cherubim:* see Gen. 3.24 n. **22:** It is in the presence of the *Ark of the Testimony,* as the people reflect upon the LORD's requirements and gracious acts (20.2 n.), that God's commands will be communicated to Israel. **30:** *Bread:* see Lev. 24.5–9. **40:** Ancient Near Eastern temples and their furnishings were believed to be based upon celestial models rather than human design (compare the developed idea in Rev. 21.2).

26.1–37: The design of the Tabernacle. Two conceptions of the portable sanctuary are here combined: the Tent of Meeting (33.7–10; Num. 11.16–17), which is seemingly simple and unadorned, and the ornate Tabernacle. In v. 7 the two are so combined that the former covers the latter. Although the Tabernacle and its adornments are presented as forerunners of the temple in Jerusalem, it is more likely that the temples of Solomon (1 Kgs. ch. 6) or Zerubbabel (Hag. ch. 1) provided the priestly author's view of the structure and hanging is to be thirty cubits long and four cubits wide; all eleven are to be of the same size. ⁹ Join five of the hangings together, and similarly the other six; then fold the sixth hanging double at the front of the tent. ¹⁰ Make fifty loops on the edge of the last hanging in the first set and make fifty loops on the joining edge of the second set. ¹¹ Make fifty bronze fasteners, insert them into the loops, and join up the tent to make it a single whole. ¹² The additional length of the tent hanging is to fall over the back of the Tabernacle. ¹³ On each side there will be an additional cubit in the length of the tent hangings; this must fall over the two sides of the Tabernacle to cover it. ¹⁴ Make for the tent a cover of tanned rams' skins and an outer covering of dugong-hides.

¹⁵ Make for the Tabernacle frames of acacia-wood as uprights, ¹⁶ each frame ten cubits long and one and a half cubits wide, ¹⁷ and two tenons for each frame joined to each other. Do the same for all the frames of the Tabernacle. ¹⁸ Arrange the frames thus: twenty frames for the south side, facing southwards, ¹⁹ with forty silver sockets under them, two sockets under each frame for its two tenons; ²⁰ and for the second or northern side of the Tabernacle twenty frames ²¹ with forty silver sockets, two under each frame. ²² Make six frames for the far end of the Tabernacle on the west. ²³ Make two frames for the corners of the Tabernacle at the far end; ²⁴ at the bottom they are to be alike, and at the top, both alike, they are to fit into a single ring. Do the same for both of them; they will be for the two corners. ²⁵ There will be eight frames with their silver sockets, sixteen sockets in all, two sockets under each frame.

²⁶ Make bars of acacia-wood: five for the frames on one side of the Tabernacle, ²⁷ five for the frames on the other side, and five for the frames on the far side of the Tabernacle on the west. ²⁸ The middle bar is to run along from end to end half-way up the frames. ²⁹ Overlay the frames with gold, make rings of gold on them to hold the bars, and overlay the bars with gold. ³⁰ Set up the Tabernacle according to the design you were shown on the mountain.

³¹ Make a curtain of finely woven linen and violet, purple, and scarlet yarn, with cherubim worked on it, all made by a seamster. ³² Fasten it with hooks of gold to four posts of acacia-wood overlaid with gold, standing in four silver sockets. ³³ Hang the curtain below the fasteners and bring the Ark of the Testimony inside the curtain. Thus the curtain will make a clear separation for you between the Holy Place and the Holy of Holies. ³⁴ Place the cover over the Ark of the Testimony in the Holy of Holies. ³⁵ Put the table outside the curtain and the lampstand at the south side of the Tabernacle, opposite the table which you are to put at the north side.

³⁶ For the entrance of the tent make a screen of finely woven linen, embroidered with violet, purple, and scarlet. ³⁷ Make five posts of acacia-wood for the screen and overlay them with gold; make golden hooks for them and cast five bronze sockets for them.

27 Make the altar of acacia-wood; it is to be square, five cubits long by five cubits broad, and its height is to be three cubits. ² Make horns at the four corners and let them be of one piece with it; then overlay it with bronze. ³ Make for it pots to take away the fat and the ashes, with shovels, tossing-bowls, forks, and firepans, all of bronze. ⁴ Make a grating for it of bronze network, and fit bronze rings on the network, one at each of its four corners. ⁵ Put it below the ledge of the altar, so that the network comes half-way up the altar. ⁶ Make poles of acacia-wood for the altar and overlay them with bronze. ⁷ They are to be inserted in the rings at either side of the altar to carry it. ⁸ Leave the altar hollow inside its boards. As you were shown on the mountain, so must it be made.

⁹ Make the court of the Tabernacle. On the south side facing southwards, the court is to have hangings of finely woven linen a hundred cubits long, ¹⁰ with twenty posts and twenty bronze sockets; the hooks and bands on the posts will be of silver. ¹¹ Similarly along the north side there will be hangings of a

26:11 **bronze:** *or* copper *and so throughout the descriptions of the Tabernacle.*   26:12 **The additional . . . hanging:** *prob. rdg; Heb. adds* half the hanging which remains over.   26:24 **both alike:** *so Samar.; Heb.* both perfect.

adornments of the Tabernacle. See 25.1–31.17 n. **33:** *Holy Place:* the outer shrine, containing incense-altar (30.1–6), lampstand, and table. *Holy of Holies:* the inner shrine containing the Ark. See 1 Kgs. 6.14–17.

27.1–21: The court of the Tabernacle. 1: The *altar,* for animals, was the main object in the court. **2:** *Horns:* elevations at each corner, creating a shallow depression atop the altar onto which the sacrifice was placed.

hundred cubits, with twenty posts and twenty bronze sockets; the hooks and bands on the posts will be of silver. 12 For the breadth of the court, on the west side, there are to be hangings fifty cubits long, with ten posts and ten sockets. 13 On the east side, towards the sunrise, which will be fifty cubits, 14 hangings will extend fifteen cubits from one corner, with three posts and three sockets, 15 and hangings will extend fifteen cubits from the other corner, with three posts and three sockets. 16 At the gateway of the court, there will be a screen twenty cubits long of finely woven linen embroidered with violet, purple, and scarlet, with four posts and four sockets. 17 The posts all round the court are to have bands of silver, with silver hooks and bronze sockets. 18 The length of the court is to be a hundred cubits, and the breadth fifty, and the height five cubits, with hangings of finely woven linen and with bronze sockets throughout. 19 All the equipment needed for serving the Tabernacle, all its pegs and those of the court, will be of bronze.

20 You are to order the Israelites to bring you pure oil of pounded olives ready for the regular mounting of the lamp. 21 In the Tent of Meeting outside the curtain that conceals the Testimony, Aaron and his sons must keep the lamp in trim from dusk to dawn before the LORD. This is a rule binding on their descendants among the Israelites for all time.

28 Out of all the Israelites you are to summon to your presence your brother Aaron and his sons to serve as my priests: Aaron and his sons Nadab and Abihu, Eleazar and Ithamar. 2 For your brother Aaron make sacred vestments, to give him dignity and grandeur. 3 To all the craftsmen whom I have endowed with skill give instructions for making the vestments for the consecration of Aaron as my priest. 4 These are the vestments they are to make: a breastpiece, an ephod, a mantle, a chequered tunic, a turban, and a sash. For Aaron your brother and his sons to wear when they serve as my priests they are to make sacred vestments, 5 using gold, violet, purple, and scarlet yarn, and fine linen.

6 The ephod will be made of gold, and with violet, purple, and scarlet yarn, and with finely woven linen worked by a seamster. 7 It will have two shoulder-pieces joined back and front. 8 The waistband on it will be of the same workmanship and material as the fabric of the ephod, and will be of gold, with violet, purple, and scarlet yarn, and finely woven linen. 9 You are to take two cornelians and engrave on them the names of the sons of Israel: 10 six of their names on one stone, and the six other names on the second, all in order of seniority. 11 With the skill of a craftsman, a seal-cutter, you are to engrave the two stones with the names of the sons of Israel; set them in gold rosettes, 12 and fasten them on the shoulder-pieces of the ephod, as reminders of the sons of Israel. Aaron will bear their names on his shoulders as a reminder before the LORD. 13 Make gold rosettes 14 and two chains of pure gold worked into the form of cords, which you will fix on the rosettes.

15 Make the breastpiece of judgement; it is to be made in gold, like the ephod, by a seamster, with violet, purple, and scarlet yarn, and finely woven linen. 16 It will form a square when folded double, a span long and a span wide. 17 Arrange on it four rows of precious stones: the first row, sardin, chrysolite, and green feldspar; 18 the second row, purple garnet, sapphire, and jade; 19 the third row, turquoise, agate, and jasper; 20 the fourth row, topaz, cornelian, and green jasper, all set in gold rosettes. 21 The stones will correspond to the twelve sons of Israel name by name, each stone bearing the name of one of the twelve tribes engraved as on a seal.

22 Make for the breastpiece chains of pure gold worked into a cord. 23 Make two gold rings, and fix them on the two upper corners of the breastpiece. 24 Fasten the two gold cords to the two rings at those corners of the breastpiece, 25 and the other ends of the ropes to the two rosettes, thus binding the breastpiece to the shoulder-pieces on the front of the ephod. 26 Make two gold rings and put them at the two lower corners of the breastpiece on the inner side next to the ephod. 27 Make two gold rings and fix them

27:18 **the breadth fifty:** *so Samar.; Heb. adds* by fifty.

The horns were regarded as especially sacred (29.12; 1 Kgs. 1.50). **20:** The *lamp* was located inside the Tabernacle (25.31–40).
 28.1–43: Instructions for making the priestly garments. *Sons of Israel:* the tribal names. **15:** The *breastpiece of judgement* contained *the Urim and Thummim* (v. 30), the two sacred lots by which the priests could

on the two shoulder-pieces of the ephod, low down in front, along its seam above the waistband of the ephod. 28 Then the breastpiece is to be bound by its rings to the rings of the ephod with violet braid, just above the waistband of the ephod, so that the breastpiece does not become loosened from the ephod. 29 So, when Aaron enters the Holy Place, he will bear over his heart in the breastpiece of judgement the names of the sons of Israel, as a constant reminder before the LORD.

30 Finally, put the Urim and the Thummim into the breastpiece of judgement, and they will be over Aaron's heart when he enters the presence of the LORD. So Aaron will bear these symbols of judgement upon the sons of Israel over his heart constantly before the LORD.

31 Make the mantle of the ephod a single piece of violet stuff. 32 Make an opening for the head in the middle of it. All round the opening there will be a hem of woven work, with an oversewn edge, to prevent it tearing. 33 On its hem make pomegranates of violet, purple, and scarlet stuff, with golden bells between them, 34 a golden bell and a pomegranate alternately the whole way round the hem of the mantle. 35 Aaron is to wear it when he ministers, and the sound of it will be heard when he enters the Holy Place before the LORD and when he comes out; and so he will not die.

36 Make a medallion of pure gold and engrave on it as on a seal: 'Holy to the LORD'. 37 Fasten it on a violet braid and set it on the front of the turban. 38 It is to be on Aaron's forehead; he has to bear the blame for defects in the rites with which the Israelites offer their sacred gifts, and the medallion will be always on his forehead so that they may be acceptable to the LORD.

39 Make the chequered tunic and the turban of fine linen, but the sash of embroidered work. 40 For Aaron's sons make tunics and sashes; and make tall headdresses to give

them dignity and grandeur. 41 With these invest your brother Aaron and his sons, anoint them, install them, and consecrate them; so they will serve me as priests. 42 Make for them linen shorts reaching to the thighs to cover their private parts; 43 and Aaron and his sons must wear them when they enter the Tent of Meeting or approach the altar to minister in the sanctuary. Thus they will not incur guilt and die. This is a statute binding on him and his descendants for all time.

29 In their consecration to be my priests this is the rite to be observed. Take a young bull and two rams without blemish. 2 Take unleavened bread, unleavened loaves mixed with oil, and unleavened wafers smeared with oil, all made of wheaten flour; 3 put them in a basket and bring them in it. Bring also the bull and the two rams. 4 When you have brought Aaron and his sons to the entrance of the Tent of Meeting, wash them with water. 5 Take the vestments and dress Aaron in the tunic, the mantle of the ephod, the ephod itself, and the breastpiece, and fasten the ephod to him with its waistband. 6 Set the turban on his head, and attach the symbol of holy dedication to the turban. 7 Take the anointing oil, pour it on his head, and anoint him. 8 Then bring his sons forward, dress them in tunics, 9 gird them with the sashes, and tie their tall headdresses on them. They will hold the priesthood by a statute binding for all time.

Next install Aaron and his sons. 10 Bring the bull to the front of the Tent of Meeting, where they must lay their hands on its head. 11 Slaughter the bull before the LORD at the entrance to the Tent. 12 Take some of its blood, and smear it with your finger on the horns of the altar. Pour the rest of it at the

28:32 **with . . . edge:** *lit.* like the opening of a womb.
28:36 **as . . . LORD:** *or* 'YHWH' as on a seal in sacred characters.   28:41 **install them:** *lit.* fill their hands.
29:9 **gird them:** *so Gk; Heb. adds* Aaron and his sons.
29:12 **the rest:** *so Gk; Heb. omits.*

determine the divine will (compare 1 Sam. 14.38–42). **33–35:** *Bells:* their purpose is uncertain, but possibly derived from an ancient practice of ringing bells to frighten away demons.

29.1–46: Instructions for the installation of the priests. The passage ascribes the origin of the Aaronite priesthood to the Mosaic period (see 25.1–31.17 n.). However, in early Israelite history, eligibility for serving as a priest was not confined to a tribe, or to a clan within a tribe (see Judg. ch. 17). As history unfolded, the Levites came to be recognized as the priestly tribe (Deut. 33.8–11). Later (namely in the postexilic period) a subgroup, supposedly descended from Aaron, a Levite, became the only priests. **4:** The *Tent of Meeting:* see 26.1–37 n. **10:** By touching the sacrificial victim, the worshiper identified with it. **12:** *Blood,* the life-force (Gen. 9.4), was sacred to God. The blood was to be used to add to the sense of communion with the deity which base of the altar. [13] Then take all the fat covering the entrails, the long lobe of the liver, and the two kidneys with the fat upon them, and burn them on the altar; [14] but the flesh of the bull, and its skin and offal, you must destroy by fire outside the camp. It is a purification-offering.

[15] Take one of the rams and, after Aaron and his sons have laid their hands on its head, [16] slaughter it; take its blood, and fling it against the sides of the altar. [17] Cut up the ram; wash its entrails and its shins, lay them with the pieces and the head, [18] and burn the whole ram on the altar: it is a whole-offering to the LORD; it is a soothing odour, a food-offering to the LORD.

[19] Take the second ram and, after Aaron and his sons have laid their hands on its head, [20] slaughter it; take some of its blood, and put it on the lobes of the right ears of Aaron and his sons, and on their right thumbs and the big toes of their right feet. Fling the rest of the blood against the sides of the altar. [21] Take some of the blood which is on the altar and some of the anointing oil, and sprinkle it on Aaron and his vestments, and on his sons and their vestments. So he, his sons, and the vestments will become sacred.

[22] Take the fat from the ram, the fat-tail, the fat covering the entrails, the long lobe of the liver, the two kidneys with the fat upon them, and the right leg: for it is a ram of installation. [23] Take also one round loaf of bread, one cake cooked with oil, and one wafer from the basket of unleavened bread that is before the LORD. [24] Place all these on the hands of Aaron and of his sons and present them as a special gift before the LORD. [25] Then receive them back from their hands, and burn them on the altar with the whole-offering for a soothing odour to the LORD: it is a food-offering to the LORD.

[26] Take the breast of Aaron's ram of installation and present it as a special gift before the LORD; it is to be your perquisite. [27] Hallow the breast of the special gift and the leg of the contribution, that which is presented and that which is set aside from the ram of instal-

lation, that which is for Aaron and that which is for his sons; [28] they are to belong to Aaron and his sons, by a statute binding for all time, as a gift from the Israelites, for it is a contribution set aside from their shared-offerings, their contribution to the LORD.

[29] Aaron's sacred vestments must be kept for the anointing and installation of his sons after him. [30] The priest appointed in his stead from among his sons, the one who enters the Tent of Meeting to minister in the Holy Place, is to wear them for seven days.

[31] Take the ram of installation and boil its flesh in a sacred place; [32] Aaron and his sons are to eat the ram's flesh and the bread left in the basket, at the entrance to the Tent of Meeting. [33] They are to eat the things with which expiation was made at their installation and their consecration. No lay person may eat them, for they are holy. [34] If any of the flesh of the installation, or any of the bread, is left over till morning, you must destroy it by fire; it is not to be eaten, for it is holy.

[35] Do this with Aaron and his sons as I have commanded you, spending seven days over their installation.

[36] Offer a bull each day, a purification-offering as expiation for sin; offer the purification-offering on the altar when you make expiation for it, and consecrate it by anointing. [37] For seven days you are to purify the altar and consecrate it; it will be most holy. Whoever touches the altar must be treated as holy.

[38] This is what you have to offer on the altar: two yearling rams regularly every day. [39] Offer one ram at dawn, and the second between dusk and dark. [40] With the first lamb offer a tenth of an ephah of flour mixed with a quarter of a hin of pure oil of pounded olives, and a drink-offering of a quarter of a hin of wine. [41] Offer the second ram between dusk and dark, and with it the same grain-offering and drink-offering as at dawn, for a soothing odour: it is a food-offering to the

29:30 **the one who enters:** or when he enters.
29:37 **Whoever:** or Whatever.

the sacrifice brought about. **18:** *Soothing odour:* an idiom meaning "acceptable sacrifice" (Gen. 8.21). In earlier polytheistic times, the gods were believed attracted by the smell. **26:** *Perquisite:* a gift equivalent to wages, or beyond the stipulated wage. The officiating priest was to receive an agreed portion of the sacrifice; see Lev. 7.31–36; Deut. 18.3. An abuse is related in 1 Sam. 2.12–17. **27–28:** In subsequent times portions of some sacrifices were to be preserved perpetually for Aaron's descendants. **36–42:** The daily sacrificial ritual of the postexilic temple is here ascribed to the period of Aaron's consecration.

LORD, [42] a regular whole-offering generation after generation for all time; you are to make the offering at the entrance to the Tent of Meeting before the LORD, where I meet you and speak to you. [43] I shall meet the Israelites there, and the place will be hallowed by my glory. [44] I shall consecrate the Tent of Meeting and the altar; and Aaron and his sons I shall consecrate to serve me as priests. [45] I shall dwell in the midst of the Israelites, I shall become their God, [46] and by my dwelling among them they will know that I am the LORD their God who brought them out of Egypt. I am the LORD their God.

30 Make an altar on which to burn incense; make it of acacia-wood. [2] It is to be square, a cubit long by a cubit broad, and stand two cubits high; its horns are to be of one piece with it. [3] Overlay it with pure gold, the top, all the sides, and the horns; and put round it a band of gold. [4] Make pairs of gold rings for it; put them under the gold band at the two corners on both sides to receive the poles by which it is to be carried. [5] The poles are to be of acacia-wood overlaid with gold. [6] Put the altar before the curtain which is in front of the Ark of the Testimony where I shall meet you. [7] On it Aaron must burn fragrant incense; every morning when he trims the lamps he is to burn the incense, [8] and when he tends the lamps between dusk and dark he is to burn the incense; so let there be a regular burning of incense before the LORD for all time. [9] You must not offer on it any unauthorized incense, nor any whole-offering or grain-offering; and you must not pour a drink-offering over it. [10] Once a year Aaron is to make expiation with blood on its horns; this must be done for all time with blood from the purification-offering of the yearly expiation for it. It is most holy to the LORD.

[11] The LORD said to Moses: [12] When you take a census of the Israelites, each man is to give a ransom for his life to the LORD, to avert

plague among them during the registration. [13] As each man crosses over to those already counted he must give half a shekel by the sacred standard at the rate of twenty gerahs to the shekel, as a contribution levied for the LORD. [14] Everyone aged twenty or more who has crossed over to those already counted will give a contribution for the LORD. [15] The rich man will give no more than the half-shekel, and the poor man no less, when you give the contribution for the LORD to make expiation for your lives. [16] The money received from the Israelites for expiation you are to apply to the service of the Tent of Meeting. The expiation for your lives is to be a reminder of the Israelites before the LORD.

[17] The LORD said to Moses: [18] Make a bronze basin for ablution with its stand of bronze; place it between the Tent of Meeting and the altar, and fill it with water [19] with which Aaron and his sons are to wash their hands and feet. [20] When they enter the Tent of Meeting they must wash with water, lest they die. Likewise when they approach the altar to minister, to burn a food-offering to the LORD, [21] they must wash their hands and feet, lest they die. It is to be a statute for all time binding on him and his descendants in every generation.

[22] The LORD said to Moses: [23] Take spices as follows: five hundred shekels of sticks of myrrh, half that amount, that is two hundred and fifty shekels, of fragrant cinnamon, two hundred and fifty shekels of aromatic cane, [24] five hundred shekels of cassia by the sacred standard, and a hin of olive oil. [25] From these prepare sacred anointing oil, a perfume compounded by the perfumer's art. This will be the sacred anointing oil. [26] Anoint with it the Tent of Meeting and the Ark of the Testimony, [27] the table and all its vessels, the lamp-

30:6 **Put ... Testimony:** *so Samar.; Heb. adds* before the cover over the Testimony. 30:10 **expiation:** *or* atonement. 30:12 **to the LORD:** *so Gk; Heb. adds* because of the registration.

30.1–10: The construction of the incense-altar. The *altar* for *incense* was part of the furnishings of the outer shrine (v. 6; 26.33 n.). This section logically belongs with 25.1–40. **10:** The *yearly expiation:* the Day of Atonement; see Lev. ch. 16.

30.11–16: The financial support of the cult. The census for military and financial purposes, introduced possibly under the monarchy, was considered offensive to God (2 Sam. 24.10). The tax paid by the worshipers was a *ransom* (v. 12) to protect them from the offense to the deity. **13:** *Shekel:* see p. xxvii.

30.17–21: The basin for ritual washing. The *basin* stood in the Tabernacle court. This section logically belongs with 27.1–21. Compare the Sea in Solomon's temple, 1 Kgs. 7.23–26.

30.22–38: Formulas for the sacred oil and incense. 23: *Myrrh:* a fragrant resin. **24:** *Cassia:* an aromatic bark.

stand and its fittings, the altar of incense, 28 the altar of whole-offering and all its vessels, the basin and its stand. 29 Consecrate them, and they will be most holy; whoever touches them will be treated as holy. 30 Anoint Aaron and his sons, and consecrate them to be my priests. 31 Speak to the Israelites and say: This will be the holy anointing oil for my service in every generation. 32 It must not be used for anointing the human body, and you must not prepare any oil like it after the same prescription. It is holy, and you are to treat it as holy. 33 The man who compounds perfume like it, or who puts any of it on any lay person, will be cut off from his father's kin.

34 The LORD said to Moses, Take fragrant spices: gum resin, aromatic shell, galbanum; add clear frankincense to the spices in equal proportions. 35 Make it into incense, perfume made by the perfumer's craft, salted and pure, a holy thing. 36 Pound some of it into fine powder, and put it in front of the Testimony in the Tent of Meeting, where I shall meet you; you are to treat it as most holy. 37 The incense you prepared according to this prescription you must not make for your personal use; you are to treat it as holy to the LORD. 38 The man who makes any like it for his own enjoyment will be cut off from his father's kin.

31 THE LORD said to Moses, 2 Take note that I have specially chosen Bezalel son of Uri, son of Hur, of the tribe of Judah. 3 I have filled him with the spirit of God, making him skilful and ingenious, expert in every craft, 4 and a master of design, whether in gold, silver, copper, 5 or cutting precious stones for setting, or carving wood, for workmanship of every kind. 6 Further, I have appointed Aholiab son of Ahisamach of the tribe of Dan to be his assistant, and I have endowed every skilled craftsman with the

skill which he has. They are to make everything that I have commanded you: 7 the Tent of Meeting, the Ark for the Testimony, the cover over it, and all the furnishings of the tent; 8 the table and its vessels, the pure lampstand and all its fittings, the altar of incense, 9 the altar of whole-offering and all its vessels, the basin and its stand; 10 the stitched vestments, that is the sacred vestments for Aaron the priest and the vestments for his sons when they minister as priests, 11 the anointing oil, and the fragrant incense for the Holy Place. They are to carry it all out as I commanded you.

12 The LORD said to Moses, 13 Say to the Israelites: Above all you must keep my sabbaths, for the sabbath is a sign between me and you in every generation that you may know that I am the LORD who hallows you. 14 You are to keep the sabbath, because for you it is a holy day. If anyone profanes it he must be put to death. Anyone who does work on it is to be cut off from his father's kin. 15 Work may be done for six days, but on the seventh day there is a sabbath of solemn abstinence from work, holy to the LORD. Whoever does any work on the sabbath day shall be put to death. 16 The Israelites must keep the sabbath, observing it in every generation as a covenant for ever. 17 It is a sign for ever between me and the Israelites, for in six days the LORD made the heavens and the earth, but on the seventh day he ceased work and refreshed himself.

18 When he had finished speaking with Moses on Mount Sinai, the LORD gave him the two tablets of the Testimony, stone tablets written with the finger of God.

32 WHEN the people saw that Moses was so long in coming down from the mountain, they congregated before Aaron

30:29 **whoever:** or whatever.   30:34 **gum resin:** or mastic.   31:6 **Aholiab:** or Oholiab.

Hin: see p. xxviii. **34:** *Aromatic shell:* derived from a mollusk found in the Red Sea. *Galbanum . . . frankincense:* resinous (vegetable) gums.

31.1–11: The appointment of craftsmen.

31.12–17: The sabbath, the sign of the covenant. This strong emphasis on the sabbath observance may reflect the exilic period when the great pilgrim festivals (23.14–17) could not be kept; if so, its intent was to give the community a deeper sense of corporate identity.

31.18–32.35: The breach of the covenant. The ancient narrative strand, last met in 24.18, is resumed here. Aaron is seriously involved in the idolatrous incident of the golden calf; the effect of the intervening priestly material (25.1–31.17) centering on him softens the account of the sin. **32.1:** *So long:* forty days (24.18). Despite earlier enthusiasm for the covenant (24.7), Israel's faith in the LORD wavers at the delay. *Gods:* the Heb. noun and said, 'Come, make us gods to go before us. As for this Moses, who brought us up from Egypt, we do not know what has become of him.' ²Aaron answered, 'Take the gold rings from the ears of your wives and daughters, and bring them to me.' ³So all the people stripped themselves of their gold earrings and brought them to Aaron. ⁴He received them from their hands, cast the metal in a mould, and made it into the image of a bull-calf; then they said, 'Israel, these are your gods that brought you up from Egypt.' ⁵Seeing this, Aaron built an altar in front of it and announced, 'Tomorrow there is to be a feast to the LORD.' ⁶Next day the people rose early, offered whole-offerings, and brought shared-offerings. After this they sat down to eat and drink and then gave themselves up to revelry.

⁷The LORD said to Moses, 'Go down at once, for your people, the people you brought up from Egypt, have committed a monstrous act. ⁸They have lost no time in turning aside from the way which I commanded them to follow, and cast for themselves a metal image of a bull-calf; they have prostrated themselves before it, sacrificed to it, and said, "Israel, these are your gods that brought you up from Egypt."' ⁹The LORD said to Moses, 'I have considered this people, and I see their stubbornness. ¹⁰Now, let me alone to pour out my anger on them, so that I may put an end to them and make a great nation spring from you.'

¹¹Moses set himself to placate the LORD his God: 'LORD,' he said, 'why pour out your anger on your people, whom you brought out of Egypt with great power and a strong hand? ¹²Why let the Egyptians say, "He meant evil when he took them out, to kill them in the mountains and wipe them off the face of the earth"? Turn from your anger, and think better of the evil you intend against your people. ¹³Remember Abraham, Isaac, and Israel, your servants, to whom you swore by your own self: "I shall make your descendants countless as the stars in the heavens, and all this land, of which I have spoken, I shall give to them, and they will possess it for ever."' ¹⁴So the LORD thought better of the evil with which he had threatened his people.

¹⁵Moses went back down the mountain holding the two tablets of the Testimony, inscribed on both sides, on the front and on the back. ¹⁶The tablets were the handiwork of God, and the writing was God's writing, engraved on the tablets. ¹⁷Joshua, hearing the uproar the people were making, said to Moses, 'Listen! There is fighting in the camp.' ¹⁸Moses replied,

'This is not the sound of warriors,
    nor the sound of a defeated people;
    it is the sound of singing that I hear.'

¹⁹As he approached the camp, Moses saw the bull-calf and the dancing, and in a burst of anger he flung down the tablets and shattered them at the foot of the mountain. ²⁰He took the calf they had made and burnt it; he ground it to powder, sprinkled it on water, and made the Israelites drink it.

²¹He demanded of Aaron, 'What did this people do to you that you should have brought such great guilt upon them?' ²²Aaron replied, 'Please do not be angry, my lord. You know how wicked the people are. ²³They said to me, "Make us gods to go ahead of us, because, as for this Moses, who brought us up from Egypt, we do not know what has become of him." ²⁴So I said to them, "Those of you who have any gold, take it off." They gave it to me, I threw it in the fire, and out came this bull-calf.'

²⁵Moses saw that the people were out of control and that Aaron had laid them open to the secret malice of their enemies. ²⁶He took his place at the gate of the camp and said, 'Who is on the LORD's side? Come here to me'; and the Levites all rallied to him. ²⁷He said to them, 'The LORD the God of Israel has said: Arm yourselves, each of you, with his sword. Go through the camp from gate to gate and back again. Each of you kill brother, friend, neighbour.' ²⁸The Levites obeyed, and about three thousand of the people died that day. ²⁹Moses said, 'You have been in-

32:2 **wives:** *so Gk; Heb. adds* and sons.

is plural in form, but has a singular meaning (as in Gen. 1.1) throughout the chapter. **4:** The *bull-calf* was to serve as a visible symbol of the presence of the deity. See 1 Kgs. 12.28 n. **9–14:** God continues to accept Israel, not because of its merits, but as another manifestation of the mystery of divine grace. **19:** Moses' action symbolizes the state of the covenant at that moment. **21–24:** This may be a priestly attempt to bring out the role of the people and thus minimize Aaron's guilt. **25–29:** The Levites here earn recognition as the LORD's stalled as priests to the LORD today, because you have turned each against his own son and his own brother and so have brought a blessing this day upon yourselves.'

30 The next day Moses said to the people, 'You have committed a great sin. Now I shall go up to the LORD; perhaps I may be able to secure pardon for your sin.' 31 When he went back to the LORD he said, 'Oh, what a great sin this people has committed: they have made themselves gods of gold.

32 'Now if you will forgive them, forgive; but if not, blot out my name, I pray, from your book which you have written.' 33 The LORD answered Moses, 'Whoever has sinned against me, him I shall blot out from my book. 34 Now go, lead the people to the place of which I have told you. My angel will go ahead of you, but a day will come when I shall punish them for their sin.' 35 Then the LORD punished the people who through Aaron made the bull-calf.

33 THE LORD spoke to Moses: 'Set out, you and the people you have brought up from Egypt, go from here to the land which I swore to Abraham, Isaac, and Jacob that I would give to their descendants. 2 I shall send an angel ahead of you, and drive out the Canaanites, the Amorites and the Hittites and the Perizzites, the Hivites and the Jebusites. 3 I shall bring you to a land flowing with milk and honey, but I shall not journey in your company, for fear that I should destroy you on the way, for you are a stubborn people.' 4 When the people heard this harsh sentence they went about like mourners, and no one put on his ornaments. 5 The LORD said to Moses, 'Tell the Israelites: You are a stubborn people; at any moment, if I journeyed in your company, I might destroy you. Put away your ornaments now, and I shall determine what to do to you.' 6 So the Israelites stripped off their ornaments, and wore them no more from Mount Horeb onwards.

7 Moses used to take the Tent and set it up outside the camp some distance away. He called it the Tent of Meeting, and everyone who sought the LORD would go outside the camp to the Tent of Meeting. 8 Whenever Moses went out to the Tent, all the people would rise and stand, each at the door of his tent, and follow Moses with their eyes until he had entered the Tent. 9 When Moses entered it, the pillar of cloud came down, and stayed at the entrance to the Tent while the LORD spoke with Moses. 10 As soon as the people saw the pillar of cloud standing at the entrance to the Tent, they would all prostrate themselves, each at the door of his tent. 11 The LORD used to speak with Moses face to face, as one man speaks to another, and Moses then returned to the camp, but his attendant, Joshua son of Nun, never moved from inside the Tent.

12 Moses said to the LORD, 'You tell me to lead up this people without letting me know whom you will send with me, even though you have said to me, "I know you by name, and, what is more, you have found favour with me." 13 If I have indeed won your favour, then teach me to know your ways, so that I can know you and continue in favour with you, for this nation is your own people.' 14 The LORD answered, 'I shall go myself and set your mind at rest.' 15 Moses said to him, 'Indeed if you do not go yourself, do not send us up from here; 16 for how can it ever be known that I and your people have found favour with you, except by your going with us? So we shall be distinct, I and your people, from all the peoples on earth.' 17 The LORD said to Moses, 'I shall do what you have asked, because you have found favour with me, and I know you by name.'

18 But Moses prayed, 'Show me your glory.' 19 The LORD answered, 'I shall make all my goodness pass before you, and I shall pro-

33:3 **I shall bring you:** so Gk; Heb. omits.
33:16 **peoples:** so Gk; Heb. people.
33:19 **goodness:** or character. **LORD:** see note on 3:15.

priests by demonstrating a loyalty higher than that to family and people. **33:** *My book:* see Mal. 3.16. The allusion is to a belief of a record of human merits or trespasses, kept in heaven; late Judaism embroidered this theme.

33.1–23: Israel prepares to leave the sacred mountain. Another tradition has already been related; see 23.20–33 n. The inclusion of various ancient traditions about Sinai (24.1–32.35) creates a sense of some delay. **7–11:** This seems an old tradition, originally independent, about the *Tent of Meeting* (29.4; see 26.1–37 n.). Why the material was placed in this particular context is not clear. **19:** *The name "LORD":* see 3.15 and Tfn. there. It is only because the LORD is *gracious* and compassionate that Israel is not rejected because of its nounce in your hearing the name "LORD". I shall be gracious to whom I shall be gracious, and I shall have compassion on whom I shall have compassion.' ²⁰But he added, 'My face you cannot see, for no mortal may see me and live.' ²¹The LORD said, 'Here is a place beside me. Take your stand on the rock ²²and, when my glory passes by, I shall put you in a crevice of the rock and cover you with my hand until I have passed by. ²³Then I shall take away my hand, and you will see my back, but my face must not be seen.'

34 The LORD said to Moses, 'Cut for yourself two stone tablets like the former ones, and I shall write on them the words which were on the first tablets which you broke. ²Be ready by morning, and then go up Mount Sinai, and present yourself to me there on the top. ³No one is to go up with you, no one must even be seen anywhere on the mountain, nor must flocks or herds graze within sight of that mountain.' ⁴So Moses cut two stone tablets like the first, and early in the morning he went up Mount Sinai as the LORD had commanded him, taking the two stone tablets in his hands. ⁵The LORD came down in the cloud, and, as Moses stood there in his presence, he pronounced the name 'LORD'. ⁶He passed in front of Moses and proclaimed: 'The LORD, the LORD, a God compassionate and gracious, long-suffering, ever faithful and true, ⁷remaining faithful to thousands, forgiving iniquity, rebellion, and sin but without acquitting the guilty, one who punishes children and grandchildren to the third and fourth generation for the iniquity of their fathers!' ⁸At once Moses bowed to the ground in worship. ⁹He said, 'If I have indeed won your favour, Lord, then please go in our company. However stubborn a people they are, forgive our iniquity and our sin, and take us as your own possession.'

¹⁰The LORD said: Here and now I am making a covenant. In full view of all your people I shall do such miracles as have never been performed in all the world or in any nation.

All the peoples among whom you live shall see the work of the LORD, for it is an awesome thing that I shall do for you. ¹¹Observe all I command you this day; and I for my part shall drive out before you the Amorites, Canaanites, Hittites, Perizzites, Hivites, and Jebusites. ¹²Beware of making an alliance with the inhabitants of the land against which you are going, or they will prove a snare in your midst. ¹³You must demolish their altars, smash their sacred pillars, and cut down their sacred poles. ¹⁴You are not to bow in worship to any other god, for the LORD's name is the Jealous God, and a jealous God he is. ¹⁵Avoid any alliance with the inhabitants of the land, or, when they go wantonly after their gods and sacrifice to them, you, any one of you, may be invited to partake of their sacrifices, ¹⁶and marry your sons to their daughters, and when their daughters go wantonly after their gods, they may lead your sons astray too.

¹⁷Do not make yourselves gods of cast metal.

¹⁸You are to celebrate the pilgrim-feast of Unleavened Bread: for seven days, as I have commanded you, you are to eat unleavened bread at the appointed time in the month of Abib, because it was in Abib that you came out from Egypt.

¹⁹The first birth of every womb belongs to me, the males of all your herds, both cattle and sheep. ²⁰The first birth of a donkey you may redeem with a lamb, but if you do not redeem it, you must break its neck. Every firstborn among your sons you must redeem, and no one is to come into my presence without an offering.

²¹For six days you may work, but on the seventh abstain from work; even at ploughing time and harvest you must cease work.

²²You are to observe the pilgrim-feast of Weeks, the firstfruits of the wheat harvest,

34:13 **sacred poles:** *Heb.* asherim.   34:19 **the males:** *so Gk; Heb. unintelligible.*   34:20 **come ... presence:** *lit.* see my face.

disobedience in the episode of the calf (ch. 32).

34.1–35: The renewal of the covenant. The episodes of the shattering of the tablets (32.19) and of Moses' request for a theophany or divine self-manifestation (33.18–23) provide the narrator with an opportunity to relate still other ancient Sinaitic traditions, including a (somewhat different) list of Ten Commandments (vv. 14–26; see 20.1–21 n.), under the theme of a covenant renewal. Israel's departure is again apparently delayed. **6–7:** This seems to be an extremely ancient cultic confession, and it is repeated many times (Num. 14.18; Neh. 9.17; Ps. 103.8; Joel 2.13; Jonah 4.2). **13:** *Sacred pillars* and *poles* were a central feature of Canaanite shrines, symbolizing the presence of the fertility gods Baal and Asherah. **14–26:** The covenant and the pilgrim-feast of Ingathering at the turn of the year. 23 Those three times a year all your males are to come into the presence of the Lord, the LORD the God of Israel; 24 for after I have dispossessed the nations before you and extended your frontiers, there will be no danger from covetous neighbours when you go up those three times to enter the presence of the LORD your God.

25 Do not offer the blood of my sacrifice at the same time as anything leavened; nor is any portion of the victim of the pilgrim-feast of Passover to remain overnight till morning.

26 You must bring the choicest firstfruits of your soil to the house of the LORD your God.

Do not boil a kid in its mother's milk.

27 The LORD said to Moses, 'Write these words down, because the covenant I make with you and with Israel is on those terms.' 28 So Moses remained there with the LORD forty days and forty nights without food or drink. The LORD wrote down the words of the covenant, the Ten Commandments, on the tablets.

29 At length Moses came down from Mount Sinai with the two stone tablets of the Testimony in his hands, and when he came down, he did not know that the skin of his face shone because he had been talking with the LORD. 30 When Aaron and the Israelites saw how the skin of Moses' face shone, they were afraid to approach him. 31 He called out to them, and Aaron and all the chiefs in the community turned towards him. Moses spoke to them, 32 and after that all the Israelites drew near. He gave them all the commands with which the LORD had charged him on Mount Sinai.

33 When Moses finished what he had to say, he put a veil over his face. 34 But whenever he went in before the LORD to speak with him, he left the veil off until he came out. Then he would go out and tell the Israelites all the commands he had received. 35 The Israelites would see how the skin of Moses' face shone, and he would put the veil back over his face until he went in again to speak with the LORD.

35 MOSES called the whole community of Israelites together: 'These', he said, 'are the LORD's commands to you: 2 Work may be done for six days, but the seventh you are to keep as a sabbath of solemn abstinence from work, holy to the LORD. Whoever does any work on that day is to be put to death. 3 Wherever you live, you are not even to light your fire on the sabbath day.'

4 Moses said to the whole Israelite community: 'This is the command the LORD has given: 5 Each of you is to set aside a contribution to the LORD. Let all who wish bring a contribution to the LORD: gold, silver, copper; 6 violet, purple, and scarlet yarn; fine linen and goats' hair; 7 tanned rams' skins and dugong-hides; and acacia-wood; 8 oil for the lamp, spices for the anointing oil and for the fragrant incense; 9 cornelians and other stones ready for setting on the ephod and the breastpiece.

10 'Let all the skilled craftsmen among you come and make everything the LORD has commanded: 11 the Tabernacle, its tent and covering, fasteners, planks, bars, posts, and sockets, 12 the Ark and its poles, the cover and the curtain of the screen, 13 the table, its poles and all its vessels, and the Bread of the Presence; 14 the lampstand for the light, its fittings, lamps, and the lamp oil; 15 the altar of incense and its poles, the anointing oil, the fragrant incense, and the screen for the entrance of the Tabernacle, 16 the altar of whole-offering, its bronze grating, poles, and all appurtenances, the basin and its stand; 17 the hangings of the court, its posts and sockets, and the screen for the gateway of the court; 18 the pegs of the Tabernacle and court and their cords, 19 the stitched vestments for ministering in the Holy Place, that is the sacred vestments for Aaron the priest and the vestments for his sons when they minister as priests.'

34:28 **Ten Commandments:** *lit.* Ten Words.

regulations, paralleled in 20.3–6, 8–11; 22.29–30; 23.14–19. **29:** God's "glory," which Moses has requested to see (33.18, 22), is ofttimes described as a visible radiance (16.10). Because of the unique revelation accorded Moses, his face is now said to "shine." The Vulgate, the Latin translation prepared by Jerome, mistranslated "Moses' face had horns" (hence Michelangelo's horned Moses); the mistranslation arises from the fact that Heb. *qeren* means both "ray of light" and "horn" and may be related to the way ancient priests were sometimes depicted with a horned headpiece which symbolized their semidivine status.

35.1–40.38: The erection of the Tabernacle. The priestly narrative now continues from 31.17, showing how the instructions which began in 25.1 were carried out.

20 The whole community of the Israelites went out from Moses' presence, 21 and everyone who was so minded brought of his own free will a contribution to the LORD for the making of the Tent of Meeting and for all its service, and for the sacred vestments. 22 Men and women alike came and freely brought clasps, ear-rings, finger-rings, and pendants, gold ornaments of every kind, every one of them presenting a special gift of gold to the LORD. 23 Every man brought what he possessed of violet, purple, and scarlet yarn, fine linen and goats' hair, tanned rams' skins, and dugong-hides. 24 Every man, setting aside a contribution of silver or copper, brought it as a contribution to the LORD, and all who had acacia-wood suitable for any part of the work brought it. 25 Every woman with the skill spun and brought the violet, purple, and scarlet yarn, and fine linen. 26 The women, all whose skill moved them, spun the goats' hair. 27 The chiefs brought cornelians and other stones ready for setting in the ephod and the breast-piece, 28 the spices and oil for the lamp, for the anointing oil, and for the fragrant incense. 29 Every Israelite man and woman who was minded to bring offerings to the LORD for all the work which he had commanded through Moses did so freely.

30 Moses said to the Israelites, 'Take note that the LORD has specially chosen Bezalel son of Uri, son of Hur, of the tribe of Judah. 31 He has filled him with the spirit of God, making him skilful and ingenious, expert in every craft, 32 and a master of design, whether in gold, silver, and copper, 33 or cutting precious stones for setting, or carving wood, in every kind of design. 34 He has inspired both him and Aholiab son of Ahisamach of the tribe of Dan to instruct 35 workers and designers of every kind, engravers, seamsters, embroiderers in violet, purple, and scarlet yarn and fine linen, and weavers, fully endowing them with skill to

36 execute all kinds of work. 1 Bezalel and Aholiab are to work exactly as the LORD has commanded, and so also is every craftsman whom the LORD has made skilful and ingenious in these matters so that they may know how to execute every kind of work for the service of the sanctuary.'

2 Moses summoned Bezalel, Aholiab, and every other craftsman to whom the LORD had given skill and who was willing, to come forward and set to work. 3 They took from before Moses all the contributions which the Israelites had brought for the work of the service of the sanctuary, but the people still brought freewill-offerings morning after morning. 4 The craftsmen at work on the sanctuary therefore left what they were doing, every one of them, 5 and came to Moses and said, 'The people are bringing much more than we need for doing the work which the LORD has commanded.' 6 So Moses sent word round the camp that no man or woman should prepare anything more as a contribution for the sanctuary. The people stopped bringing gifts; 7 what was there already was more than enough for all the work they had to do.

8 So all the skilled craftsmen among the workers made the Tabernacle of ten hangings of finely woven linen, and violet, purple, and scarlet yarn, with cherubim worked on them, all made by a seamster. 9 The length of each hanging was twenty-eight cubits and the breadth four cubits, all of the same size. 10 They joined five of the hangings together, and similarly the other five. 11 They made violet loops along the outer edge of one set of hangings and they did the same for the outer edge of the other set of hangings. 12 They made fifty loops for each hanging; they made also fifty loops for the end hanging in the second set, the loops being opposite each other. 13 They made fifty gold fasteners, with which they joined the hangings one to another, and the Tabernacle became a single whole.

14 They made hangings of goats' hair, eleven in all, to form a tent over the Tabernacle; 15 each hanging was thirty cubits long and four cubits wide, all eleven of the same size. 16 They joined five of the hangings together, and similarly the other six. 17 They made fifty loops on the edge of the last hanging in the first set and fifty loops on the joining edge of the second set, 18 and fifty bronze fasteners to join up the tent and make it a single whole. 19 They made for the tent a cover of tanned rams' skins and an outer covering of dugong-hides.

35:22 **pendants:** *Heb. word of uncertain meaning.*

35.4–36.7: The obtaining of finances and craftsmen. 4–29: This is an expansion of 25.1–7. **35.30–36.7:** See 31.1–11.

20 They made for the Tabernacle frames of acacia-wood as uprights, 21 each frame ten cubits long and one and a half cubits wide, 22 and two tenons for each frame joined to each other. They did the same for all the frames of the Tabernacle. 23 They arranged the frames thus: twenty frames for the south side facing southwards, 24 with forty silver sockets under them, two sockets under each frame for its two tenons; 25 and for the second or northern side of the Tabernacle twenty frames 26 with forty silver sockets, two under each frame. 27 They made six frames for the far end of the Tabernacle on the west. 28 They made two frames for the corners of the Tabernacle at the far end; 29 at the bottom they were alike, and at the top, both alike, they fitted into a single ring. They did the same for both of them at the two corners. 30 There were eight frames with their silver sockets, sixteen sockets in all, two sockets under each frame.

31 They made bars of acacia-wood: five for the frames on one side of the Tabernacle, 32 five bars for the frames on the second side of the Tabernacle, and five bars for the frames on the far end of the Tabernacle on the west. 33 They made the middle bar to run along from end to end half-way up the frames. 34 They overlaid the frames with gold and made rings of gold on them to hold the bars, which were also overlaid with gold.

35 They made the curtain of finely woven linen and violet, purple, and scarlet yarn, with cherubim worked on it, all made by a seamster. 36 They made for it four posts of acacia-wood overlaid with gold, with gold hooks, and cast four silver sockets for them. 37 For the entrance of the tent a screen of finely woven linen was made, embroidered with violet, purple, and scarlet, 38 and five posts of acacia-wood with their hooks. They overlaid the tops of the posts and the bands round them with gold; the five sockets for them were of bronze.

37 Bezalel then made the Ark, a chest of acacia-wood two and a half cubits long, one and a half cubits wide, and one and a half cubits high. 2 He overlaid it with pure gold both inside and out, and put a band of gold all round it. 3 He cast four gold rings to be on its four feet, two rings on each side. 4 He made poles of acacia-wood and overlaid them with gold, 5 and inserted the poles in the rings at the sides of the Ark to lift it. 6 He made a cover of pure gold two and a half cubits long and one and a half cubits wide. 7 He made two gold cherubim of beaten work at the ends of the cover, 8 one at each end; he made each cherub of one piece with the cover. 9 They had wings spread out and pointing upwards, screening the cover with their wings; they stood face to face, looking inwards over the cover.

10 He made the table of acacia-wood two cubits long, one cubit wide, and one and a half cubits high. 11 He overlaid it with pure gold and put a band of gold all round it. 12 He made a rim round it a hand's breadth wide, and a gold band round the rim. 13 He cast four gold rings for it, and put the rings at the four corners by the four legs. 14 The rings, which were to receive the poles for carrying the table, were adjacent to the rim. 15 These poles he made of acacia-wood and overlaid them with gold. 16 He made the vessels for the table, its dishes and saucers, and its flagons and bowls from which drink-offerings were to be poured; he made them of pure gold.

17 He made the lampstand of pure gold. The lampstand, stem and branches, was of beaten work, its cups, both calyxes and petals, being of one piece with it. 18 There were six branches springing from the sides of the lampstand, three branches from one side and three branches from the other. 19 There were three cups shaped like almond blossoms with calyx and petals on the first branch, three cups shaped like almond blossoms with calyx and petals on the next branch, and similarly for all six branches springing from the lampstand. 20 On the main stem of the lampstand there were four cups shaped like almond blossoms with calyx and petals, 21 and there were calyxes of one piece with it under the six branches which sprang from the lampstand, a single calyx under each pair of branches. 22 The calyxes and the branches were of one piece with it, all a single piece of beaten work of pure gold. 23 He made its seven lamps, its tongs, and firepans of pure gold. 24 The lampstand and all these fittings were made from one talent of pure gold.

25 He made the altar of incense of acacia-wood; it was square, a cubit long by a cubit

36:29 **both alike:** so Samar.; Heb. both perfect.

broad, and it stood two cubits high, its horns of one piece with it. [26] He overlaid it with pure gold, the top, all the sides, and the horns, and he put round it a band of gold. [27] He made pairs of gold rings for it; he put them under the gold band at the two corners on both sides to receive the poles by which it was to be carried. [28] He made the poles of acacia-wood and overlaid them with gold.

[29] He prepared the sacred anointing oil and the fragrant incense, pure, compounded by the perfumer's art.

38 He made the altar of whole offering from acacia-wood; it was square, five cubits long by five cubits broad, and its height was three cubits. [2] Its horns at the four corners were of one piece with it, and he overlaid it with bronze. [3] He made all the vessels for the altar, its pots, shovels, tossing-bowls, forks, and firepans, all of bronze. [4] He made for the altar a grating of bronze network under the ledge, coming half-way up. [5] He cast four rings for the four corners of the bronze grating to receive the poles, [6] and he made the poles of acacia-wood and overlaid them with bronze. [7] He inserted the poles in the rings at the sides of the altar to carry it. The altar was made of boards and left hollow.

[8] The basin and its stand of bronze he made out of the bronze mirrors of the women waiting at the entrance to the Tent of Meeting.

[9] He made the court. On the south side facing southwards the hangings of the court were of finely woven linen a hundred cubits long, [10] with twenty posts and twenty bronze sockets; the hooks and bands on the posts were of silver. [11] Along the north side there were hangings of a hundred cubits, with twenty posts and twenty bronze sockets; the hooks and bands on the posts were of silver. [12] On the west side there were hangings fifty cubits long, with ten posts and ten sockets; the hooks and bands on the posts were of silver. [13] On the east side, towards the sunrise, fifty cubits; [14-15] there were hangings on either side of the gateway of the court; they extended fifteen cubits to one corner, with their three posts and three sockets, and fifteen cubits to the second corner, with their

three posts and three sockets. [16] The hangings of the court all round were of finely woven linen. [17] The sockets for the posts were of bronze; the hooks were of silver as were the bands on the posts, the tops of them overlaid with silver, and all the posts of the court were bound with silver. [18] The screen at the gateway of the court was of finely woven linen, embroidered with violet, purple, and scarlet, twenty cubits long and five cubits high to correspond to the hangings of the court, [19] with four posts and four sockets of bronze, their hooks of silver, and the tops of them and their bands overlaid with silver. [20] All the pegs for the Tabernacle and those for the court were of bronze.

[21] These were the appointments of the Tabernacle, that is the Tabernacle of the Testimony which was assigned by Moses to the charge of the Levites under Ithamar son of Aaron the priest. [22] Bezalel son of Uri, son of Hur, of the tribe of Judah, made everything the LORD had commanded Moses. [23] He was assisted by Aholiab son of Ahisamach of the tribe of Dan, an engraver, a seamster, and an embroiderer in fine linen with violet, purple, and scarlet yarn.

[24] The gold of the special gift used for the work of the sanctuary amounted in all to twenty-nine talents seven hundred and thirty shekels by the sacred standard. [25] The silver contributed by the community when registered was one hundred talents one thousand seven hundred and seventy-five shekels by the sacred standard.

[26] This amounted to a beka a head, that is half a shekel by the sacred standard, for every man aged twenty years or more, who had been registered, a total of six hundred and three thousand five hundred and fifty men. [27] The hundred talents of silver were for casting the sockets for the sanctuary and those for the curtain, a hundred sockets to a hundred talents, a talent to a socket. [28] With the one thousand seven hundred and seventy-five shekels he made hooks for the posts, overlaid the tops of the posts, and put bands round them. [29] The bronze of the special gift came to seventy talents two thousand four hundred shekels; [30] with this he made sockets

25.23–30; here, too, execution follows the instructions previously given. **17–24:** See 25.31–40. **25–28:** See 30.1–10. **29:** See 30.22–38. **38.1–7:** See 27.1–8. **8:** See 30.17–21. **9–20:** See 27.9–19; there is no deviation here from the instructions given there. A single court is presumed; some temples often had two courts. **21:** *Testimony:* see 25.16 and 16.34 n. **26:** The figure is the same as that in the census recorded in Num. 1.46.

for the entrance to the Tent of Meeting, the bronze altar and its bronze grating, all the vessels for the altar, ³¹ the sockets all round the court, the sockets for the posts at the gateway of the court, all the pegs for the Tabernacle, and the pegs all round the court.

39 They used violet, purple, and scarlet yarn in making the stitched vestments for ministering in the sanctuary and in making the sacred vestments for Aaron, as the LORD had commanded Moses.

² They made the ephod of gold, with violet, purple, and scarlet yarn, and finely woven linen. ³ The gold was beaten into thin plates, cut and twisted into braid to be worked in by a seamster with the violet, purple, and scarlet yarn, and fine linen. ⁴ They made shoulder-pieces for it, joined back and front. ⁵ The waistband on it was of the same workmanship and material as the fabric of the ephod; it was gold, with violet, purple, and scarlet yarn, and finely woven linen, as the LORD had commanded Moses.

⁶ They prepared the cornelians, fixed in gold rosettes, engraved by the art of a seal-cutter with the names of the sons of Israel, ⁷ and fastened them on the shoulder-pieces of the ephod as reminders of the sons of Israel, as the LORD had commanded Moses.

⁸ They made the breastpiece; it was worked in gold like the ephod by a seamster, with violet, purple, and scarlet yarn, and finely woven linen. ⁹ They made the breastpiece square when folded double, a span long and a span wide. ¹⁰ They set in it four rows of precious stones: the first row, sardin, chrysolite, and green feldspar; ¹¹ the second row, purple garnet, sapphire, and jade; ¹² the third row, turquoise, agate, and jasper; ¹³ the fourth row, topaz, cornelian, and green jasper, all set in gold rosettes. ¹⁴ The stones corresponded to the twelve sons of Israel, name by name, each stone bearing the name of one of the twelve tribes engraved as on a seal.

¹⁵ They made for the breastpiece chains of pure gold worked into a cord. ¹⁶ They made two gold rosettes and two gold rings, and they fixed the two rings on the two corners of the breastpiece. ¹⁷ They fastened the two gold cords to the two rings at those corners of the breastpiece, ¹⁸ and the other ends of the two cords to the two rosettes, thus binding them to the shoulder-pieces on the front of the ephod. ¹⁹ They made two gold rings and put them at the two corners of the breastpiece on the inner side next to the ephod.

²⁰ They made two gold rings and fixed them on the two shoulder-pieces of the ephod, low down and in front, close to its seam above the waistband of the ephod. ²¹ They bound the breastpiece by its rings to the rings of the ephod with a violet braid, just above the waistband on the ephod, so that the breastpiece would not become loosened from the ephod; so the LORD had commanded Moses.

²² They made the mantle of the ephod a single piece of woven violet stuff, ²³ with an opening in the middle of it which had a hem round it, with an oversewn edge to prevent it from tearing. ²⁴ On its hem they made pomegranates of violet, purple, and scarlet stuff, and finely woven linen. ²⁵ They made bells of pure gold and put them all round the hem of the mantle between the pomegranates, ²⁶ a bell and a pomegranate alternately the whole way round the hem of the mantle, to be worn when ministering, as the LORD had commanded Moses.

²⁷ They made the tunics of fine linen, woven work, for Aaron and his sons, ²⁸ the turban of fine linen, the tall headdresses and their bands all of fine linen, the shorts of finely woven linen, ²⁹ and the sashes of finely woven linen, embroidered in violet, purple, and scarlet, as the LORD had commanded Moses.

³⁰ They made a medallion of pure gold as the symbol of their holy dedication and inscribed on it as the engraving on a seal, 'Holy to the LORD', ³¹ and they fastened on it a violet braid to fix it on the turban at the top, as the LORD had commanded Moses.

³² Thus all the work of the Tabernacle of the Tent of Meeting was completed, and the Israelites did everything exactly as the LORD had commanded Moses. ³³ They brought the Tabernacle to Moses, the tent and all its furnishings, its fasteners, frames, bars, posts, and sockets, ³⁴ the covering of tanned rams' skins and the outer covering of dugong-hides, the curtain of the screen, ³⁵ the Ark of the Testimony and its poles, the cover, ³⁶ the table and its vessels, and the Bread of the Presence, ³⁷ the pure lampstand with its lamps in a row and all its fittings, and the lamp oil, ³⁸ the gold altar, the anointing oil, the fragrant incense, and the screen at the

39:8 **They:** *so Gk; Heb.* He.   39:23 **oversewn edge:** *see* 28:32.   39:24 **linen:** *so Samar.; Heb. omits.* 39:30 **on it . . . LORD:** *or* 'YHWH' *on it in sacred characters as engraved on a seal.*

entrance of the tent, ³⁹ the bronze altar, the bronze grating attached to it, its poles and all its furnishings, the basin and its stand, ⁴⁰ the hangings of the court, its posts and sockets, the screen for the gateway of the court, its cords and pegs, and all the equipment for the service of the Tabernacle for the Tent of Meeting, ⁴¹ the stitched vestments for ministering in the sanctuary, that is the sacred vestments for Aaron the priest and the vestments for his sons when ministering as priests. ⁴² As the LORD had commanded Moses, so the Israelites carried out the whole work. ⁴³ Moses inspected all the work, and saw that they had carried it out according to the command of the LORD; and he blessed them.

40 THE LORD said to Moses: ² On the first day of the first month you are to set up the Tabernacle of the Tent of Meeting. ³ Put the Ark of the Testimony in it and screen the Ark with the curtain. ⁴ Bring in the table and lay it; then bring in the lampstand and mount its lamps. ⁵ Then set the gold altar of incense in front of the Ark of the Testimony and put the screen of the entrance of the Tabernacle in place. ⁶ Place the altar of whole-offering in front of the entrance of the Tabernacle of the Tent of Meeting, ⁷ and the basin between the Tent of Meeting and the altar, and put water in it. ⁸ Set up the court all round, and put in place the screen at the entrance of the court.

⁹ With the anointing oil anoint the Tabernacle and everything in it, thus consecrating it and all its furnishings; it will then be holy. ¹⁰ Anoint the altar of whole-offering and all its vessels, thus consecrating it; it will be most holy. ¹¹ Anoint the basin and its stand and consecrate it.

¹² Bring Aaron and his sons to the entrance of the Tent of Meeting and wash them with the water. ¹³ Then clothe Aaron with the sacred vestments, anoint him, and consecrate him to be my priest. ¹⁴ Then bring forward his sons, clothe them in tunics, ¹⁵ and anoint them as you anointed their father; and they will be my priests. Their anointing inaugurates a hereditary priesthood for all time. ¹⁶ Moses did everything exactly as the LORD had commanded him. ¹⁷ In the first month of

the second year, on the first day of that month, the Tabernacle was set up.

¹⁸ Moses erected the Tabernacle: he put the sockets in place, inserted the frames, fixed the crossbars, and set up the posts. ¹⁹ He spread the tent over the Tabernacle and fixed the covering of the tent on top of that, as the LORD had commanded him.

²⁰ He took the Testimony and put it into the Ark, inserted the poles in the Ark, and put the cover over the top of the Ark. ²¹ He brought the Ark into the Tabernacle, set up the curtain of the screen, and so screened the Ark of the Testimony, as the LORD had commanded him.

²² He put the table in the Tent of Meeting on the north side of the Tabernacle outside the curtain ²³ and arranged bread on it before the LORD, as the LORD had commanded him. ²⁴ He set the lampstand in the Tent of Meeting opposite the table at the south side of the Tabernacle ²⁵ and mounted the lamps before the LORD, as the LORD had commanded him. ²⁶ He set up the gold altar in the Tent of Meeting in front of the curtain ²⁷ and burnt fragrant incense on it, as the LORD had commanded him.

²⁸ He set up the screen at the entrance of the Tabernacle, ²⁹ fixed the altar of whole-offering at the entrance of the Tabernacle of the Tent of Meeting, and offered on it whole-offerings and grain-offerings, as the LORD had commanded him. ³⁰ He set up the basin between the Tent of Meeting and the altar and put water there for washing. ³¹ Moses and Aaron and Aaron's sons used to wash their hands and feet ³² when they entered the Tent of Meeting or approached the altar, as the LORD had commanded Moses. ³³ He set up the court all round the Tabernacle and the altar, and put the screen at the entrance of the court.

Moses completed the work, ³⁴ and the cloud covered the Tent of Meeting, and the glory of the LORD filled the Tabernacle. ³⁵ Moses was unable to enter the Tent of Meeting, because the cloud had settled on it and the glory of the LORD filled the Tabernacle. ³⁶ At every stage of their journey, when the cloud lifted from the Tabernacle, the Israelites used to break camp; ³⁷ but if the cloud

39.1–31: See 28.1–43. **32–43:** A summary of the completed work. **43:** *Inspected:* to be sure of precise workmanship.

40.1–38: The erection of the Tabernacle. 2: For the purpose of the chronological references, see 16.1. n.

did not lift from the Tabernacle, they used not to break camp until such time as it did lift. ³⁸ For the cloud of the LORD was over the Tabernacle by day, and there was fire in the cloud by night, and all the Israelites could see it at every stage of their journey.

34: *Cloud:* see 14.19; 19.9 n. *Glory:* see 34.29 n. **35:** See also 1 Kgs. 8.10–11. **38:** See 13.21–22.

104

Leviticus

This segment of Israel's tradition is part of a larger priestly account of the origins of the sanctuary, its personnel and rituals, which begins in Exodus chs. 25–31, 35–40 and continues into Numbers chs. 1–10 (see Introduction to the Pentateuch). Despite the probability that the account assumed its present form early in the postexilic age, it contains many units and even collections of material handed down from a much earlier time.

The title, Leviticus, supplied in the Greek and Latin translations, arose from the emphasis upon the duties of the tribe of Levi as priests. The concerns of the book, however, are much wider than the title suggests, and may be classified as follows: (1) guidelines for worshipers bringing offerings of animals or grain (chs. 1–7); (2) the ordination of the Aaronite priests (chs. 8–10); (3) legislation concerning uncleanness (chs. 11–15); (4) the annual Day of Atonement (ch. 16); (5) the exhortation to be a holy people (chs. 17–26, the section being called the "Holiness Code"); (6) regulations for the fulfillment of religious vows (ch. 27).

During the postexilic age, an impoverished, harassed Israel lived under the domination of the Persian Empire. With its identity as a monarchical political state no longer secure or adequate, Israel sought to recover its ancient identity as a worshiping community ruled by the LORD. Accordingly, Leviticus stresses the antiquity of the Aaronite priestly leadership and of the attendant rituals. In a time of uncertainty about Israel's election and of a tendency to assimilate to the culture of its neighbors, Leviticus placed great stress on the uniqueness of Israel's socio-economic legislation and encouraged the observance of even the smallest details of the cultic regulations. In contrast to the unrestrained social and economic abuses of the late monarchic and exilic periods, it reasserted the ancient prohibition against absolute human domination of persons and physical property. Thus, in spite of the failures of the past and the hardships of the present, Israel could once again recover its identity as a "holy people" in whose midst the LORD dwelled.

Offerings and sacrifices

1 THE LORD summoned Moses and spoke to him from the Tent of Meeting. He told him 2 to say to the Israelites: When anyone among you presents an animal as an offering to the LORD, it may be chosen either from the herd or from the flock.

3 If his offering is a whole-offering from the herd, he must present a male without blemish; he must present it at the entrance to the Tent of Meeting so as to secure acceptance before the LORD. 4 He must lay his hand on the head of the victim and it will be ac- cepted on his behalf to make expiation for him. 5 He must then slaughter the bull before the LORD, and the Aaronite priests are to present the blood and fling it against the sides of the altar at the entrance of the Tent of Meeting. 6 He must flay the victim and dismember it. 7 The sons of Aaron the priest, having kindled a fire on the altar and ar- ranged wood on the fire, 8 are to arrange the pieces, including the head and the suet, on the wood on the altar-fire; 9 the entrails and shins must be washed in water, and the priest

1:4 **on his behalf:** or by him (the LORD). 1:9 **shins:** or hind legs.

1.1–17: **The whole-offering of an animal by fire** (also called a "holocaust" or "burnt offering"). **1:** Moses: the transmitter of these sacrificial regulations assigned their origin to the LORD at Sinai. Tent of Meeting: see Exod. 26.1–37 n. **2:** When: these are not requirements for specific occasions, but voluntary offerings by individuals. **4:** Originally an offering of praise and gratitude, this ancient sacrifice was increasingly used as a rite of expiation, by means of which atonement with God was effected. **5:** Aaronite priests: see Exod. 29.1–46 n. Present the blood: see Exod. 29.12 n. **9:** The shins are washed to remove dirt and dung (compare Exod. 29.14),

105

is to burn it all on the altar as a whole-offering, a food-offering of soothing odour to the LORD.

¹⁰ If his whole-offering is from the flock, from either the rams or the goats, he must present a male without blemish. ¹¹ He must slaughter it before the LORD at the north side of the altar, and the Aaronite priests are to fling the blood against the sides of the altar. ¹² He must cut it up in pieces, and the priests are to arrange the pieces, together with the head and the suet, on the wood on the altar-fire; ¹³ the entrails and shins must be washed in water, and the priest is to present and burn it all on the altar: it is a whole-offering, a food-offering of soothing odour to the LORD.

¹⁴ If his offering to the LORD is a whole-offering of birds, he is to present a turtle-dove or pigeon as his offering. ¹⁵ The priest must present it at the altar and wrench off the head, which he is to burn on the altar; the blood is to be drained out against the side of the altar. ¹⁶ He must remove the crop and its contents in one piece, and throw it to the east side of the altar, where the ashes are. ¹⁷ Having torn it open by its wings without severing it completely, the priest is to burn it on the altar, on top of the wood of the altar-fire: it is a whole-offering, a food-offering of soothing odour to the LORD.

2 When someone presents a grain-offering to the LORD, his offering must be of flour. Having poured oil on it and added frankincense, ² he must bring it to the Aaronite priests, one of whom is to scoop up a handful of the flour and oil with all the frankincense. The priest must burn this as a token on the altar, a food-offering of soothing odour to the LORD. ³ The remainder of the grain-offering belongs to Aaron and his sons: it is most holy, taken from the food-offerings of the LORD.

⁴ When you present as a grain-offering something baked in an oven, it is to take the form either of unleavened cakes of flour mixed with oil or of unleavened wafers smeared with oil. ⁵ If your offering is a grain-offering cooked on a griddle, let it be an unleavened cake of flour mixed with oil. ⁶ Crumble it and pour oil over it. This is a grain-offering. ⁷ If your offering is a grain-offering cooked in a pan, the flour is to be prepared with oil.

⁸ Bring an offering prepared in any of these ways to the LORD and present it to the priest, who will take it to the altar. ⁹ He must set aside part of the grain-offering as a token and burn it on the altar, a food-offering of soothing odour to the LORD. ¹⁰ The remainder of the grain-offering belongs to Aaron and his sons: it is most holy, taken from the food-offerings of the LORD.

¹¹ No grain-offering which you present to the LORD must be made of anything that ferments; you are not to burn any leaven or any honey as a food-offering to the LORD. ¹² You may present them to the LORD as an offering of firstfruits, but they are not to be offered up at the altar as a soothing odour. ¹³ Every offering of yours which is a grain-offering is to be salted; you must not fail to put the salt of your covenant with God on your grain-offering. Salt must accompany all offerings.

¹⁴ If you present to the LORD a grain-offering of first-ripe grain, you must present fresh grain roasted, crushed meal from fully ripened grain; ¹⁵ add oil to it and put frankincense on it. This is a grain-offering, ¹⁶ and the priest is to burn as its token some of the crushed meal and some of the oil, together with all the frankincense, as a food-offering to the LORD.

3 If someone's offering is a shared-offering from the cattle, whether a male or a female, what he presents before the LORD must be without blemish. ² He must lay his hand on the head of the victim and slaughter it at the entrance to the Tent of Meeting. The Aaronite priests must fling the blood against the sides of the altar. ³ One of them is to

impediments to sacrifices. *Soothing odour:* see Exod. 29.18 n. **14–17:** The poor, unable to afford cattle or sheep, are given this equally acceptable option.

2.1–16: Grain-offerings by fire as a gift to God. Three types are mentioned: flour (vv. 1–3), cakes (vv. 4–7), or roasted meal (vv. 14–16). **2:** *Oil:* of the olive. *Frankincense:* see Exod. 30.34 n. **3:** *Most holy:* hence to be eaten by the priests only, in the sanctuary area (compare 6.25–26). **11:** *Honey,* like *leaven,* caused fermentation, which was regarded as ritually impure. **12:** *Firstfruits:* see Deut. 26.1–11. **13:** *Salt* symbolized sharing. Possibly, too, its purifying (2 Kgs. 2.21) and preserving properties made it desirable for the meal which sealed a covenant (Num. 18.19). **14:** *Grain:* barley or wheat.

3.1–17: The shared-offering for deity, priests and worshipers. Only the preparation of the victim is dealt present part of the shared-offering as a food-offering to the LORD: he must remove the fat covering the entrails and all the fat upon the entrails, ⁴both kidneys with the fat on them near the loins, and the long lobe of the liver with the kidneys. ⁵The Aaronites are to burn it on the altar on top of the whole-offering which is upon the wood on the fire, a food-offering of soothing odour to the LORD.

⁶If someone's offering as a shared-offering to the LORD is from the flock, whether a male or a female, what he presents must be without blemish. ⁷If he is presenting a ram as his offering, he must present it before the LORD, ⁸lay his hand on the head of the victim, and slaughter it in front of the Tent of Meeting. The Aaronites must then fling its blood against the sides of the altar. ⁹He is to present part of the shared-offering as a food-offering to the LORD: he is to remove its fat, the entire fat-tail cut off close by the spine, the fat covering the entrails and all the fat upon the entrails, ¹⁰both kidneys with the fat on them beside the loins, and the long lobe of the liver with the kidneys. ¹¹The priest is to burn it at the altar, as food offered to the LORD.

¹²If someone's offering is a goat, he must present it before the LORD, ¹³lay his hand on its head, and slaughter it in front of the Tent of Meeting. The Aaronites must then fling its blood against the sides of the altar. ¹⁴He is to present part of the victim as a food-offering to the LORD; he is to remove the fat covering the entrails and all the fat upon the entrails, ¹⁵both kidneys with the fat on them near the loins, and the long lobe of the liver with the kidneys. ¹⁶The priest is to burn this at the altar as a food-offering of soothing odour. All fat belongs to the LORD.

¹⁷This is a rule for all time from generation to generation wherever you live: that you must consume neither fat nor blood.

4 THE LORD told Moses ²to say to the Israelites, When anyone sins inadvertently by doing anything forbidden by any of the LORD's commandments: ³If it is the anointed priest who sins, thus bringing guilt on the people, then for the sin he has committed he must present to the LORD a young bull without blemish as a purification-offering. ⁴He must bring the bull to the entrance of the Tent of Meeting before the LORD, lay his hand on its head, and slaughter it before the LORD. ⁵The anointed priest must then bring some of its blood into the Tent of Meeting, ⁶dip his finger in the blood, and sprinkle it in front of the sanctuary curtain seven times before the LORD. ⁷The priest must then smear some of the blood on the horns of the altar where fragrant incense is burnt before the LORD in the Tent of Meeting; the rest of the bull's blood he is to pour out at the base of the altar of whole-offering, which is at the entrance of the Tent of Meeting. ⁸He must set aside all the fat from the bull of the purification-offering; he must set aside the fat covering the entrails and all the fat upon the entrails, ⁹both kidneys with the fat on them beside the loins, and the long lobe of the liver with the kidneys. ¹⁰It is to be set aside as was done with the fat from the bull at the shared-offering. The priest must burn the pieces of fat on the altar of whole-offering; ¹¹but the hide of the bull and all its flesh, as well as its head, its shins, its entrails and offal, ¹²the whole of it, he must take away outside the camp to a

---

with here (see also 7.11–36). **1**: *Male or female:* for the whole-offering only a male was permitted. **3**: Since *part* is offered *to the LORD,* the ritual departs from that of the whole-offering because the priests and worshipers share in the "meal." *Fat,* considered a source of great vitality and delicacy, was, like blood (17.10–16), to be reserved for the deity alone (vv. 16–17). **5**: The whole-offering, made afresh each day (6.9), would already be on the altar when the shared-offering was being prepared.

4.1–5.13: The purification-offering for inadvertent transgression. For deliberate sin, see Num. 15.30. **3**: *Bringing guilt:* compare Gen. 18.23–33 n. Since *the priest* represents the entire community before God and vice versa, any sin on his part contaminates the people and excludes his offering an atoning sacrifice in their behalf. *A young bull:* the most expensive sacrificial animal. **5–6**: Unlike the previously mentioned rituals, part of this more serious sacrifice is offered *in the Tent.* Sins of the whole community were regarded as equally as grave as those of priests (vv. 13–21), whereas those of individuals were less serious (vv. 22–35). **6**: *Curtain:* see Exod. 26.31–33. **7**: *Horns:* see Exod. 27.2 n. *Altar . . . incense:* see Exod. 30.1–10. *Blood:* the locus of the life-force and forbidden for human consumption, blood was especially effective in expiation (17.10–12; Heb. 9.22). **11–12**: Although part of other sacrifices was reserved for the priests (2.10; 7.14; Exod.

ritually clean place, where the ash-heap is, and destroy it on a wood fire on top of the ash-heap.

13 If it is the whole Israelite community that sins inadvertently by doing what is forbidden by any of the LORD's commandments, and so incurs guilt, and the matter is not known to the assembly, 14 then, when the sin they have committed is brought to their notice, the assembly must present a young bull as a purification-offering and bring it in front of the Tent of Meeting. 15 The elders of the community must lay their hands on the victim's head before the LORD, and it must be slaughtered before the LORD. 16 The anointed priest must then bring some of the blood into the Tent of Meeting, 17 dip his finger in it, and sprinkle it in front of the curtain seven times before the LORD. 18 He must smear some of the blood on the horns of the altar which is before the LORD in the Tent of Meeting, and pour all the rest at the base of the altar of whole-offering, which is at the entrance of the Tent of Meeting. 19 He must set aside all the fat from the bull and burn it on the altar. 20 He is to deal with this bull as he deals with the bull of the purification-offering; in this way the priest makes expiation for the people's guilt and they are forgiven. 21 He is then to have the bull taken outside the camp to be burnt as the other bull was burnt. This is a purification-offering for the assembly.

22 When a leader sins by doing inadvertently what is forbidden by any of the commandments of the LORD his God, thereby incurring guilt, 23 and the sin he has committed is made known to him, he must bring a he-goat without blemish as his offering. 24 He must lay his hand on the goat's head and slaughter it before the LORD in the place where the whole-offering is slaughtered. It is a purification-offering. 25 The priest must then take some of the blood of the victim with his finger and smear it on the horns of the altar of whole-offering; the rest of the blood he is to pour out at the base of the altar of whole-offering. 26 He must burn all the fat at the altar in the same way as the fat of the shared-offering. Thus the priest is to make

expiation for that person's sin, and it will be forgiven him.

27 If anyone among the ordinary lay people sins inadvertently and does what is forbidden in any of the LORD's commandments, thereby incurring guilt, 28 and the sin he has committed is made known to him, he must bring as his offering for the sin which he has committed a she-goat without blemish. 29 He must lay his hand on the head of the victim and slaughter it at the place where the whole-offering is slaughtered. 30 The priest must then take some of its blood with his finger and smear it on the horns of the altar of whole-offering; the rest of the blood he is to pour out at the base of the altar. 31 He must remove all its fat as the fat is removed from the shared-offering, and burn it on the altar as a soothing odour to the LORD. Thus the priest is to make expiation for that person's guilt, and it will be forgiven him.

32 If it is a sheep he brings as his offering for sin, it must be a ewe without blemish. 33 He must lay his hand on the head of the victim and slaughter it as a purification-offering at the place where the whole-offering is slaughtered. 34 The priest must then take some of the blood of the victim with his finger and smear it on the horns of the altar of whole-offering; the rest of the blood he is to pour out at the base of the altar. 35 He must remove all its fat, as the fat of the sheep is removed from the shared-offering. He must burn the pieces of fat at the altar on top of the food-offerings to the LORD; thus the priest is to make expiation on account of the sin that the person has committed, and it will be forgiven him.

5 If a person sins in that he hears a solemn adjuration to give evidence as a witness to something he has seen or heard, but does not declare what he knows, he must bear the consequences; 2 or if a person touches anything ritually unclean, such as the dead body of an unclean animal, whether wild or domestic, or of an unclean swarming creature, and it is unremembered by him, and then

5:2,3,4 **unremembered:** *or* concealed.

29.27–28 n.), they could not eat of one offered for their own sin (compare 6.29–30). **13–21:** Community-wide sin also requires that the inner altar be purified with sacrificial blood. **22–35:** For those less serious individual offenses there is permission to use cheaper sacrificial animals (vv. 23, 28, 32), to conduct the rite at the outer altar only (v. 25), and to omit the burning of the nonfat portions which are to go to the priest (6.26). **5.1–4:** An appendix illustrating situations for which a purification-offering is required. **2–3:** For details concerning being unclean he realizes his guilt; ³or if he touches any human uncleanness of whatever kind, and it is unremembered by him, and becoming aware of it he realizes his guilt; ⁴or if a person utters an oath to bring about evil or good, in any matter in which such a person may swear a rash oath, and it is unremembered by him, and becoming aware of it he realizes his guilt in such cases: ⁵when he realizes his guilt in any of these cases, he must confess how he has sinned, ⁶and bring to the LORD in reparation for the sin that he has committed a female of the flock, either a ewe or a she-goat, to be a purification-offering, and the priest is to offer expiation for his sin on his behalf, and he will be pardoned.

⁷If he cannot afford as much as a young animal, he must bring to the LORD in reparation for his sin two turtle-doves or two pigeons, one to be a purification-offering and the other to be a whole-offering. ⁸He must bring them to the priest, who is to present first the one intended for the purification-offering. He must wrench its head back without severing it. ⁹He must sprinkle some of the blood of the victim against the side of the altar, and what is left of the blood is to be drained out at the base of the altar: it is a purification-offering. ¹⁰He must deal with the second bird as a whole-offering in the prescribed way. Thus the priest is to offer expiation for the sin the person has committed, and it will be forgiven him.

¹¹If anyone cannot afford two turtle-doves or two pigeons, for his sin he must bring as his offering a tenth of an ephah of flour as a purification-offering. He must add no oil to it nor put frankincense on it, because it is a purification-offering. ¹²He must bring it to the priest, who is to scoop up a handful from it as a token and burn it on the altar on the food-offerings to the LORD: it is a purification-offering. ¹³The priest is to offer expiation for the sin the person has committed in any one of these cases, and it will be forgiven him. As with the grain-offering, the remainder belongs to the priest.

¹⁴The LORD spoke to Moses and said: ¹⁵When any person commits an offence by inadvertently defaulting in dues sacred to the LORD, he must bring to the LORD as his reparation-offering a ram without blemish from the flock; the value is to be determined by you in silver shekels by the sacred standard, for a reparation-offering; ¹⁶he must make good his default in sacred dues, adding one fifth of the value. He must give it to the priest, who is to offer expiation for his sin with the ram of the reparation-offering, and it will be forgiven him.

¹⁷If and when any person sins unwittingly and does what is forbidden by any commandment of the LORD, thereby incurring guilt, he must bear the consequences. ¹⁸He must bring to the priest as a reparation-offering a ram without blemish from the flock, valued by you, and the priest is to offer expiation for the error into which he has unwittingly fallen, and it will be forgiven him. ¹⁹It is a reparation-offering; he has been guilty of an offence against the LORD.

6 When the LORD spoke to Moses he said: ²When any person sins by false use of the LORD's name, whether the person lies to a fellow-countryman about a deposit or contract, or a theft, or wrongs him by extortion, ³or finds lost property and then lies about it, and swears a false oath in regard to any sin of this sort that he commits — ⁴if he does this and realizes his guilt, he must restore what he has stolen or gained by extortion, or the deposit entrusted to him, or the lost property which he found, ⁵or anything at all concerning which he swore a false oath. He must make full restitution, adding one fifth of the value to it, and give it back to the aggrieved party on the day when he realizes his guilt. ⁶He must bring to the priest as his reparation-offering to the LORD a ram without blemish from the flock, valued by you, as a reparation-offering. ⁷When the priest makes expiation for his guilt before the LORD, he

5:13 **the remainder:** *so Gk; Heb. omits.*　　6:1 *In Heb.* 5:20.

uncleanness, see chs. 11–15. **7–13:** Less expensive but equally acceptable sin-offerings are listed (see 1.14–17 n.). **11:** *Ephah:* see p. xxviii.

5.14–6.7: The reparation-offering, a special designation for the purification-offering when it must be accompanied by reparation to an offended party. **15:** *Sacred standard:* see p. xxvii. **6.1–7:** Whereas the previous section has been concerned with offenses strictly against the deity, here the focus is offenses against other persons. Only when the *aggrieved party* has been satisfied may one then bring a reparation-offering to the deity.

will be forgiven for any act for which he has realized his guilt.

8 THE LORD told Moses 9 to give these commands to Aaron and his sons: This is the law of the whole-offering. The whole-offering is to remain on the altar-hearth overnight till morning, and the altar-fire is to be kept burning there. 10 The priest, having donned his linen robe and put on linen shorts to cover himself, must remove the ashes to which the fire reduces the whole-offering on the altar and put them beside the altar. 11 Then having changed into other garments he is to take the ashes outside the camp to a place which is ritually clean.

12 The fire on the altar is to be kept burning; it must never go out. Every morning the priest must add fresh wood, arrange the whole-offering on it, and on top burn the fat from the shared-offerings. 13 Fire must always be kept burning on the altar; it must not go out.

14 This is the law of the grain-offering. The Aaronites must present it before the LORD in front of the altar. 15 The priest must set aside a handful of the flour from it, with the oil of the grain-offering, and all the frankincense on it, and burn this token of it on the altar as a soothing odour to the LORD. 16 Aaron and his sons are to eat the rest; it is to be eaten in the form of unleavened cakes and in a holy place, the court of the Tent of Meeting. 17 It must not be baked with leaven. I have allotted this to them as their share of my food-offerings. Like the purification and the reparation-offerings, it is most holy. 18 Only Aaron's descendants may eat it, as a due from the food-offerings to the LORD, for generation after generation for all time. Whoever touches it is to be treated as holy.

19 When the LORD spoke to Moses he said: 20 This is the offering which Aaron and his sons are to present to the LORD: one tenth of an ephah of flour, the usual grain-offering, half of it in the morning and half in the evening. 21 It is to be cooked with oil on a griddle. Bring it well-mixed, and present it crumbled in small pieces as a grain-offering, a soothing odour to the LORD. 22 The priest in the line of Aaron anointed to succeed him is to offer it. This is a rule binding for all time; it must be burnt in sacrifice to the LORD as a complete offering. 23 Every grain-offering of a priest shall be a complete offering; it must not be eaten.

24 The LORD told Moses 25 to say to Aaron and his sons: This is the law of the purification-offering. This offering is to be slaughtered before the LORD in the place where the whole-offering is slaughtered; it is most holy. 26 The priest who officiates is to eat of the flesh; it must be eaten in a sacred place, in the court of the Tent of Meeting. 27 Whoever touches its flesh is to be treated as holy, and if any of the blood is splashed on clothing, it must be washed in a sacred place. 28 Any earthenware vessel in which the purification-offering is boiled must be broken; if it has been boiled in a copper vessel, that must be scoured and rinsed with water. 29 Any male of priestly family may eat of this offering; it is most holy. 30 If, however, part of the blood is brought to the Tent of Meeting to make expiation in the holy place, the offering must not be eaten; it must be destroyed by fire.

7 This is the law of the reparation-offering. It is most holy; 2 the reparation vic-

6:8 In Heb. 6:1.   6:18 Whoever: or Whatever.
6:20 This ... LORD: prob. rdg; Heb. adds on the day when he is anointed.   6:21 crumbled: Heb. word of uncertain meaning.   6:27 Whoever: or Whatever.
must be washed: so Gk; Heb. you must wash.

6.8–7.38: The role of the Aaronite priests in the sacrifices previously mentioned (1.1–6.7). To this point, the directions are primarily for the lay person who has brought the animal (see 1.2 n.); here the directions are for the priests. **9:** A *whole-offering* for the entire people is to be offered twice daily and to consist of a ram (Exod. 29.38–39; Num. 28.3–4). In the preexilic period it was required but once daily (2 Kgs. 16.15). **12–13:** The undying *fire on the altar* symbolizes Israel's unceasing obedience to the will of the LORD. **14:** *Grain-offering:* the lay person's voluntary sacrifice (2.1–16). **16:** Since the priests share in a portion of this offering made to God, it must be eaten in *the court,* not in a profane area (compare v. 11; 4.12; 2.3 n.). **19–23:** This special *grain-offering* by the priests must, unlike the previous one, be burned entirely. See 4.11–12 n. **27–28:** Holiness, regarded almost like a fluid substance, and transmitted by contact (see Exod. 19.12–13 n.), must be washed from a garment, scoured from a copper vessel, and released from a porous vessel by smashing it. **30:** The distinction here is between the purification-offering for priest or community (4.3–21) and that for individuals (4.22–35). See 4.5–6 n.; 4.22–35 n. **7.1–10:** The ritual for the *reparation-offering,* omitted in 5.14–6.7

tim must be slaughtered in the place where the whole-offering is slaughtered, and its blood flung against the sides of the altar. ³The priest must present all the fat from it: the fat-tail and the fat covering the entrails, ⁴both kidneys with the fat on them beside the loins, and the long lobe of the liver with the kidneys. ⁵The priest must burn those pieces on the altar as a food-offering to the LORD: it is a reparation-offering. ⁶Only males belonging to the priestly family may eat it. It is to be eaten in a sacred place; it is most holy. ⁷There is one law for both purification-offering and reparation-offering: they belong to the priest who performs the rite of expiation. ⁸The hide of anyone's whole-offering belongs to the priest who presents it. ⁹Every grain-offering baked in an oven and everything that is cooked in a pan or on a griddle belong to the priest who presents them. ¹⁰Every grain-offering, whether mixed with oil or dry, is to be shared equally among all the Aaronites.

¹¹This is the law of the shared-offering presented to the LORD. ¹²If someone presents it as a thank-offering, then, in addition to the thank-offering, he must present unleavened bread mixed with oil, wafers of unleavened flour smeared with oil, and flat bread-cakes of well-mixed flour moistened with oil. ¹³He must present flat cakes of leavened bread in addition to his shared thank-offering. ¹⁴One part of every offering he is to present as a contribution for the LORD: it is to belong to the priest who flings the blood of the shared-offering against the altar. ¹⁵The flesh must be eaten on the day it is presented; none of it may be put aside till morning.

¹⁶If, however, anyone's sacrifice is a votive offering or a freewill-offering, it may be eaten on the day it is presented or on the next day; ¹⁷but any flesh left over on the third day must be destroyed by fire. ¹⁸If any flesh of his shared-offering is eaten on the third day, the one who has presented it will not be ac-

cepted. It will not be counted to his credit, but will be reckoned as tainted, and the person who eats any of it must accept responsibility.

¹⁹If the flesh comes into contact with anything unclean it must not be eaten; it must be destroyed by fire. Flesh may be eaten by anyone who is clean, ²⁰but the person who, while unclean, eats flesh from a shared-offering presented to the LORD is to be cut off from his father's kin. ²¹When any person is contaminated by contact with anything unclean, be it man, beast, or swarming creature, and then eats any of the flesh from the shared-offerings presented to the LORD, that person is to be cut off from his father's kin.

²²The LORD told Moses ²³to say to the Israelites: You must not eat the fat of any ox, sheep, or goat. ²⁴The fat of an animal that has died a natural death or has been mauled by wild beasts may be put to any other use, but you are not to eat it. ²⁵Everyone who eats fat from a beast from which food-offerings are presented to the LORD is to be cut off from his father's kin.

²⁶You are not to consume any of the blood, whether of bird or of beast, wherever you may live. ²⁷Anyone consuming any of the blood is to be cut off from his father's kin.

²⁸The LORD told Moses ²⁹to say to the Israelites: Whoever comes to present a shared-offering must set aside part of it as an offering to the LORD. ³⁰With his own hands he is to bring the food-offerings to the LORD. He must also bring the fat together with the breast which is to be presented as a dedicated portion before the LORD. ³¹The priest must burn the fat on the altar, but the breast is to belong to Aaron and his descendants. ³²Give the right hind leg of your shared-offerings as a contribution for the priest; ³³it will be the perquisite of the Aaronite who presents the blood and the fat of the shared-offering. ³⁴I

7:16 **next day:** *so Gk; Heb. adds* and the rest of it must be eaten.   7:21 **swarming creature:** *so some MSS; others* noxious thing.

because of its similarity to the preceding purification-offering, is here outlined. Since it is prescribed for individuals only, the blood is not applied to the incense-altar and hence the meat is available for consumption by the priests (6.30 n.). **11–18:** Various occasions for a *shared-offering* (3.1–17) are mentioned, with minor accompanying procedures. **16:** *A votive offering:* one vowed to be given to the deity in return for the granting of a special request; see ch. 27. *A freewill-offering:* presented without special reason or occasion. **19–20:** *Eaten by anyone:* that is, except for the portions reserved for the priests (vv. 31–36). *Clean . . . unclean:* for the relevant rules, see chs. 11–15. **21:** It is unclear here whether *cut off* means execution by the community or death by divine causation; compare 20.1–8. **24:** *Fat:* see 3.3 n. *Mauled:* see Exod. 22.31 n. **28–36:** This is have taken from the Israelites the breast of the dedicated portion and the leg of the contribution made out of the shared-offerings, and have given them as a due from the Israelites to Aaron the priest and his descendants for all time. 35 This is the portion allotted to Aaron and his descendants out of the LORD's food-offerings, appointed on the day when they were presented as priests to the LORD; 36 and on the day when they were anointed, the LORD commanded that these prescribed portions should be given to them by the Israelites. This is a rule binding on their descendants for all time.

37 Such, then, is the law concerning the whole-offering, the grain-offering, the purification-offering, the reparation-offering, the ordination-offering, and the shared-offering, 38 with which the LORD charged Moses on Mount Sinai on the day when he commanded the Israelites to present their offerings to the LORD in the wilderness of Sinai.

The priesthood

8 WHEN the LORD spoke to Moses he said: 2 Bring Aaron and his sons, along with the vestments, the anointing oil, the bull for a purification-offering, the two rams, and the basket of unleavened bread, 3 and assemble all the community at the entrance to the Tent of Meeting. 4 Moses did as the LORD commanded him, and when the community assembled at the entrance to the Tent of Meeting, 5 he told them that this was what the LORD had ordered to be done.

6 Moses brought forward Aaron and his sons and washed them with water. 7 He invested Aaron with the tunic, girded him with the sash, robed him with the mantle, put the ephod on him, tied it with its waistband, and fastened the ephod to him with the band. 8 He put the breastpiece on him and set the Urim and Thummim in it. 9 He placed the turban on his head, with the gold medallion as a symbol of holy dedication on the front of the turban, as the LORD had commanded him.

10 Moses then took the anointing oil, and anointed the Tabernacle and all that was in it, so consecrating them. 11 With some of the oil he sprinkled the altar seven times, anointing it and all its vessels, along with the basin with its stand, to consecrate them, 12 and poured some of the anointing oil on Aaron's head to consecrate him. 13 Moses brought Aaron's sons forward and, as the LORD had commanded him, he invested them with tunics, girded them with sashes, and tied their headdresses.

14 Moses had the bull for the purification-offering brought, and Aaron and his sons laid their hands on its head. 15 Moses slaughtered it, and taking some of the blood he smeared it with his finger on the horns at the corners of the altar to purify it. He poured out the remaining blood at the base of the altar, which he consecrated by purifying it. 16 He took all the fat on the entrails, the long lobe of the liver, and both kidneys with their fat, and burnt them on the altar, 17 but the rest of the bull with its hide, flesh, and offal he destroyed by fire outside the camp, as commanded by the LORD.

18 Moses then had the ram of the whole-offering brought, and Aaron and his sons laid their hands on the ram's head. 19 Moses slaughtered it, and flung its blood against the

8:8 **breastpiece:** or pouch.   8:13 **sashes:** so Samar.; *Heb.* sash.   8:15 **some of:** so Gk; *Heb.* omits. 8:18 **Moses:** so Gk; *Heb. omits.*

a supplement to vv. 11–21, specifying or expanding the priestly share of the sacrificial meat. **35–36:** The obligation to support the priesthood in the specified ways is integrated into the very foundation of the cult at Sinai (see 1.1 n.; compare Exod. 29.36–42 n.).

8.1–36: The ordination of the Aaronite priesthood, following the instructions of Exod. 29.1–46 (see also Exod. 40.12–15). The instructions for the sanctuary and its personnel are given in Exod. 25.1–31.17 and the carrying out in Exod. 35.1–40.38. The delay in the ordination of the priesthood (despite the wording of Exod. 40.16) is logical: the cultic activity can only begin when the Tabernacle is completed. Accordingly, the instructions for sacrifice (Lev. chs. 1–7) interrupt the flow of the narrative. **2:** *Aaron:* for the development of the priesthood, see Exod. 29.1–46 n. The *vestments* are described in Exod. ch. 28. *Anointing oil:* see Exod. 30.22–33 for the formula. *Bull . . . rams . . . unleavened bread:* Exod. 29.1–3. **6:** *Washed them with water:* see Exod. 29.4; compare Exod. 30.17–21 for the more general ritual. **7:** *Ephod:* see Exod. 28.6–14. **8:** *Urim and Thummim:* see Exod. 28.15 n. **10–11:** The instructions for anointing the furniture and vessels of the Tabernacle are contained in Exod. 30.26–29; 40.9–11. **15:** For the instructions for purification of the altar, sides of the altar. ²⁰ He cut the ram into pieces and burnt the head, the pieces, and the suet. ²¹ He washed the entrails and the shins in water and burnt the whole on the altar. This was a whole-offering, to be a food-offering of soothing odour to the Lord, as the Lord had commanded Moses.

²² Moses had the second ram brought forward, the ram for the ordination of priests, and Aaron and his sons laid their hands on its head. ²³ Moses slaughtered it, and taking some of its blood he put it on the lobe of Aaron's right ear, on his right thumb, and on the big toe of his right foot. ²⁴ He then brought forward the sons of Aaron and put some of the blood on the lobes of their right ears, on their right thumbs, and on the big toes of their right feet. The rest of the blood he flung against the sides of the altar. ²⁵ He took the fat, the fat-tail, the fat covering the entrails, the long lobe of the liver, both kidneys with their fat, and the right leg. ²⁶ From the basket of unleavened bread before the Lord he took one unleavened cake, one cake of bread made with oil, and one wafer, and laid them on the fatty parts and the right leg. ²⁷ He put it all on the hands of Aaron and of his sons, presenting it as a dedicated portion before the Lord. ²⁸ Moses then took it from their hands and burnt it on the altar on top of the whole-offering. This was an ordination-offering, a food-offering of soothing odour to the Lord. ²⁹ He took the breast and presented it as a dedicated portion before the Lord; it was his portion of the ram of ordination, as the Lord had commanded him.

³⁰ Moses took some of the anointing oil and some of the blood on the altar and sprinkled it on Aaron and his vestments, and also on his sons and their vestments. Thus he consecrated Aaron and his vestments, along with his sons and their vestments.

³¹ Moses said to Aaron and his sons, 'Boil the flesh of the ram at the entrance to the Tent of Meeting, and eat it there, together with the bread that is in the ordination-bas-ket, in accordance with the command: "Aaron and his sons are to eat it." ³² What remains of the flesh and bread you are to destroy by fire. ³³ You are not to go outside the entrance to the Tent of Meeting for seven days, until the day which completes the period of your ordination, for it lasts seven days. ³⁴ What was done this day followed the Lord's command to make expiation for you. ³⁵ Stay by the entrance to the Tent of Meeting day and night for seven days, keeping vigil to the Lord, so that you do not die, for so I was commanded.'

³⁶ Aaron and his sons did everything that the Lord had commanded through Moses.

9 On the eighth day, when Moses had summoned Aaron and his sons and the Israelite elders, ² he said to Aaron, 'Take for yourself a bull-calf for a purification-offering and a ram for a whole-offering, both without blemish, and present them before the Lord. ³ Then bid the Israelites take a he-goat for a purification-offering, a calf and a lamb, both yearlings without blemish, for a whole-offering, ⁴ and a bull and a ram for shared-offerings to be sacrificed before the Lord, together with a grain-offering mixed with oil. For today the Lord will appear to you.'

⁵ They brought what Moses had commanded to the front of the Tent of Meeting, and the whole community approached and stood before the Lord. ⁶ Moses said, 'This is what the Lord has commanded you to do, so that the glory of the Lord may appear to you.' ⁷ Moses said to Aaron, 'Approach the altar; sacrifice your purification-offering and your whole-offering, making expiation for yourself and for your household. Then sacrifice the offering of the people and make expiation for them, as the Lord has commanded.'

⁸ So Aaron approached the altar and slaughtered the calf, which was his purifica-

8:27 **presenting:** or, with Lat., who presented.
9:7 **for your household:** so Gk; Heb. for the people.

see Exod. 29.36–37; on the use of blood, see 4.7 n. **22:** The *ram for the ordination* is a shared-offering (3.1–17; 7.11–36), and hence consumed by God (v. 28), by Moses as the officiating priest (v. 29), and by the Aaronites as the community (v. 31). **23:** *Ear . . . thumb . . . toe:* the significance of this act is uncertain (compare 14.14, 17, 25, 28), but the parts chosen may be extremities representative of the whole person. **24:** The *blood,* put on the priests' bodies and the *altar* (representing the deity: see Exod. 29.12 n.), expresses the special relationship between the priesthood and the Lord. **30:** *Sprinkled . . . his vestments:* see Exod. 29.21.

9.1–24: The priests assume their sacrificial duties, which have been described in 6.8–7.38. **1:** *The eighth day:* at the conclusion of the ordination (8.33–35). **5–6:** The function of the sacrificial ritual is to bring about tion-offering. [9] His sons presented the blood to him, and he dipped his finger in the blood and smeared it on the horns of the altar; the rest of the blood he poured out at the base of the altar. [10] Part of the purification-offering, namely the fat, the kidneys, and the long lobe of the liver, he burnt on the altar as the LORD had commanded Moses; [11] the flesh and the hide he destroyed by fire outside the camp. [12] Then Aaron slaughtered the whole-offering. His sons handed him the blood, and he flung it against the sides of the altar; [13] they handed him the pieces of the whole-offering and the head, and he burnt them on the altar. [14] He washed the entrails and the shins and burnt them on the altar, on top of the whole-offering.

[15] Next he brought forward the offering of the people. He took the he-goat, the people's purification-offering, slaughtered it, and performed the rite of the purification-offering as he had previously done for himself. [16] He presented the whole-offering and sacrificed it in the manner prescribed. [17] He brought forward the grain-offering, took a handful of it, and burnt it on the altar, in addition to the morning whole-offering.

[18] He slaughtered the bull and the ram, the shared-offerings of the people. His sons handed him the blood, and he flung it against the sides of the altar. [19] But the portions of fat from the bull, the fat-tail of the ram, the fat covering the entrails, and both kidneys with the fat upon them, and the long lobe of the liver, [20] all this fat they first put on the breasts of the animals and then Aaron burnt it on the altar. [21] He presented the breasts and the right leg as a dedicated por-

tion before the LORD, as Moses had been commanded.

[22] Aaron lifted up his hands towards the people and pronounced the blessing over them. After performing the rites of the purification-offering, the whole-offering, and the shared-offerings, he came down, [23] and Moses and Aaron entered the Tent of Meeting. When they came out, they blessed the people, and the glory of the LORD appeared to all the people. [24] Fire came out from before the LORD and consumed the whole-offering and the portions of fat on the altar. At the sight, all the people shouted joyfully and prostrated themselves.

10 AARON's sons Nadab and Abihu took their censers, put fire in them, threw incense on the fire, and presented before the LORD illicit fire, such as he had not commanded them to present. [2] Fire came out from before the LORD and destroyed them; so they died in the presence of the LORD. [3] Moses said to Aaron, 'This is what the LORD meant when he said:

Among those who approach me I must
    be treated as holy;
in the presence of all the people I must
    be given honour.'

Aaron kept silent.

[4] Moses sent for Mishael and Elzaphan, the sons of Aaron's uncle Uzziel, and said to them, 'Come and carry your cousins outside the camp away from the sanctuary.' [5] They

9:19 **the fat covering ... upon them:** *so Gk; Heb.* and the covering and the kidneys. 10:1 **illicit:** *or* alien.

an awareness of the divine presence. **8–11:** Aaron begins with a purification-offering for priests (4.3–12), following that already offered by Moses (8.14–17), so that he will be sinless when he ministers before the congregation (compare 4.3 n.). **15:** The sacrificial animal differs from that of 4.13–21, and this suggests that the practice changed from time to time. **22:** *The blessing:* Num. 6.22–27. *Came down:* from the altar. **23:** *Glory:* Exod. 16.10 n.

10.1–20: Deviation from prescribed ritual and its consequences. It is in part through precise ritual that postexilic Israel maintained its identity and distinctiveness, and a specific episode is here cited in order to encourage strict obedience (vv. 1–7). This then presented a suitable occasion for the transmitters of the traditions to append related warnings (vv. 8–20). **1:** *Nadab and Abihu* were the oldest of Aaron's sons who once played an important role in Israel's traditions (see Exod. 6.23 and 24.1–10). What exactly is meant by *illicit fire* is unclear, although the plain lesson of the incident is to warn against unauthorized ritual acts. **2:** The story may perhaps be based on a struggle for power between different priestly groups (compare Num. ch. 16; see Exod. 29.1–46 n.), which resulted in a defeat for the descendants of these two men, so that the priesthood descended through the next oldest son, Eleazar (Num. 20.25–28). **3:** *Those who approach me:* the priests. **4:** *Outside the camp:* where the sacrificial remains were burned and the altar ashes deposited (4.12).

came and carried them away in their tunics out of the camp, as Moses had told them. ⁶Moses said to Aaron and to his sons Eleazar and Ithamar, 'You are not to let your hair hang loose or tear your clothes in mourning, or you may die and the LORD be angry with the whole community. Your kinsmen, all the house of Israel, shall weep for the destruction by fire which the LORD has kindled. ⁷You must not leave the entrance to the Tent of Meeting; otherwise you may die, because the LORD's anointing oil is on you.' They did as Moses had said.

⁸WHEN the LORD spoke to Aaron he said: ⁹You and your sons with you must not drink wine or strong drink when you are to enter the Tent of Meeting, that you may not die. This is a rule binding on your descendants for all time, ¹⁰to make a distinction between sacred and profane, between clean and unclean, ¹¹and to teach the Israelites all the decrees which the LORD has spoken to them through Moses.

¹²Moses said to Aaron and his surviving sons, Eleazar and Ithamar, 'Take what is left over of the grain-offering out of the food-offerings of the LORD, and eat it unleavened beside the altar; it is most holy. ¹³Eat it in a sacred place; it is your due and that of your sons out of the LORD's food-offerings, for so I was commanded. ¹⁴You and your sons and daughters must eat in a clean place the breast of the dedicated portion and the leg which is a contribution for the priests, for they have

been given to you and your children as your due out of the shared-offerings of the Israelites. ¹⁵The leg of the contribution and the breast of the dedicated portion must be brought, along with the food-offerings of fat, to be presented as a dedicated portion before the LORD; it will belong to you and your children as a due for all time; for so the LORD has commanded.'

¹⁶When Moses made searching enquiry about the goat of the purification-offering and found it had been burnt, he was angry with Eleazar and Ithamar, Aaron's surviving sons, and said, ¹⁷'Why did you not eat the purification-offering in the sacred place? It is most holy. It was given to you to take away the guilt of the community by making expiation for them before the LORD. ¹⁸Since the blood was not brought within the sacred precincts, you should have eaten the purification-offering there as I was commanded.' ¹⁹But Aaron replied to Moses, 'See, they have today presented their purification-offering and their whole-offering before the LORD, and this is what has happened to me! If I had eaten a purification-offering today, would the LORD have considered it right?' ²⁰When Moses heard this, he considered Aaron was right.

Purification and atonement

11 The LORD told Moses and Aaron ²to say to the Israelites: These are the creatures you may eat: Of all the larger land

6: *Hair . . . clothes:* these funeral actions were forbidden to the chief priest; see 21.10–11. **7:** To prevent contamination, the priest must remain within the temple-complex (21.12; for the consequences, see 4.3 n.). **9:** The warning against alcoholic beverage may rest upon two bases: to ensure the ability to observe the fine details of the ritual (compare Isa. 28.7–8), and to avoid the cultic practices of Israel's neighbors. It also probably reflects the persistence of an anti-alcohol ethic of eastern nomads, an ethic that disappeared among the laity as Israel emerged as an agricultural society. **12–13:** See 6.16–18. **14–15:** See 7.28–34. **16–20:** On the sacrificial animal (v. 16), see 9.15 n. According to 4.13–21, the blood should have been sprinkled inside the sanctuary and applied to the incense-altar there. This Aaron apparently failed to do (9.15; compare 9.8–9), applying the blood rather to the sacrificial altar in the court. Thus the meat should have been eaten by the priests (6.25–30). A discrepancy in such precise and central material (10.1–20 n.) called for explanation, and those who collected the priestly materials saw in the Nadab and Abihu episode the opportunity to provide Aaron with an excuse which would not create a precedent for future deviations. Since Aaron shared in his sons' guilt (compare 4.3 n.), it would be inappropriate for him to consume a purification-offering (compare 4.11–12 n.). However, the occasion for the excuse creates a chronological difficulty: the erroneous purification-offering occurred before the sins of Aaron's sons!

11.1–47: Clean and unclean animals. The priestly theologians believed that God had intended for humankind to be vegetarian (Gen. 1.29), but had approved the eating of meat from the time of Noah onward (Gen. 9.3–4). But now Israel's distinctiveness as a "holy nation" (vv. 43–45; Exod. 19.6) is enforced and a focus for animals ³you may eat any hoofed animal which has cloven hoofs and also chews the cud; ⁴those which only have cloven hoofs or only chew the cud you must not eat. These are: the camel, because though it chews the cud it does not have cloven hoofs, and is unclean for you; ⁵the rock-badger, because though it chews the cud it does not have cloven hoofs, and is unclean for you; ⁶the hare, because though it chews the cud it does not have a parted foot; it is unclean for you; ⁷the pig, because although it is a hoofed animal with cloven hoofs it does not chew the cud, and is unclean for you. ⁸You are not to eat the flesh of these or even touch their dead carcasses; they are unclean for you.

⁹Of creatures that live in water these may be eaten: all, whether in salt water or fresh, that have fins and scales; ¹⁰but all, whether in salt or fresh water, that have neither fins nor scales, including both small creatures in shoals and larger creatures, you are to regard as prohibited. ¹¹They are prohibited to you; you must not eat their flesh, and their dead bodies you are to treat as prohibited. ¹²Every creature in the water that has neither fins nor scales is prohibited to you.

¹³These are the birds you are to regard as prohibited, and for that reason they must not be eaten: the griffon-vulture, the black vulture, and the bearded vulture; ¹⁴the kite and every kind of falcon; ¹⁵every kind of crow, ¹⁶the desert-owl, the short-eared owl, the long-eared owl, and every kind of hawk; ¹⁷the tawny owl, the fisher-owl, and the screech-owl; ¹⁸the little owl, the horned owl, the osprey, ¹⁹the stork, the various kinds of cormorant, the hoopoe, and the bat.

²⁰All winged creatures that swarm and go on all fours are prohibited to you, ²¹except those which have legs jointed above their feet for leaping on the ground. ²²Of these you may eat every kind of great locust, every kind of long-headed locust, every kind of green locust, and every kind of desert locust. ²³Every other swarming winged creature that has four legs is prohibited to you.

²⁴These are the creatures that will make you unclean: whoever touches their dead bodies will be unclean till evening, ²⁵and whoever picks up the dead body of any of them must wash his clothes and remain unclean till evening. ²⁶Every animal which has hoofs but not cloven hoofs and does not chew the cud is to be unclean to you: whoever touches them will be unclean. ²⁷You are to regard as unclean all four-footed wild animals that walk on flat paws; whatever touches their dead bodies will be unclean till evening, ²⁸and whoever takes up their dead bodies must wash his clothes and remain unclean till evening. They are to be unclean to you.

²⁹The following creatures that swarm on the ground are to be unclean to you: the mole-rat, the jerboa, and every kind of thorn-tailed lizard; ³⁰the gecko, the sand-gecko, the wall-gecko, the great lizard, and the chameleon. ³¹Those among swarming creatures are to be unclean to you; whoever touches them when they are dead will be unclean till evening. ³²Anything on which any of them falls when dead will be unclean, any article of wood, any garment or hide or sacking, any article which may be put to use; it must be immersed in water and remain unclean till evening, when it will be clean. ³³If any of the creatures falls into an earthenware vessel, its contents will be unclean, and you must break the vessel. ³⁴Any food which is fit for eating and then comes in contact with water from such a vessel will be unclean, and any drink in such a vessel will be unclean. ³⁵Anything on which the dead body of such a creature falls will be unclean; a clay oven or pot must be broken, for they are unclean and you must treat them as such; ³⁶but a spring or a cistern where water collects will remain clean, though whoever touches the dead body will be unclean. ³⁷When any of their

11:5 **rock-badger:** *or* rock-rabbit.
11:13 **griffon-vulture:** *or* eagle. **bearded vulture:** *or* ossifrage. 11:15 **crow:** *or* raven. 11:19 **stork:** *or* heron. 11:24,26 **whoever:** *or* whatever.
11:29 **mole-rat:** *or* weasel. 11:31 **whoever:** *or* whatever. 11:36 **whoever:** *or* whatever.

identity provided, by severely restricting the creatures which the people might consume. This would be especially important during the exilic (Dan. ch. 1) and postexilic periods (compare Exod. 31.12–17 n.), although it is here suggested that the origins of the prohibition lie in the Mosaic Age (see Exod. 25.1–31.17 n.). A similar but shorter account is found in Deut. 14.3–21. **3–4:** The original basis for this distinction is obscure: it may perhaps be related to the sacredness of the animals to the deities of Israel's neighbors (see Exod. 23.19 n.). **5–6:** The *rock-badger* and the *hare* do not really chew the cud, but only appear to do so. **24–25:** Uncleanness, like holiness (6.27–28 n.), can be transferred from one object to another. **33:** *Break the vessel:* compare 6.28.

dead bodies falls on seed intended for sowing, the seed remains clean; ³⁸ but if the seed has been soaked in water and any dead body falls on it, it will be unclean for you.

³⁹ When any animal allowed as food dies, anyone who touches the carcass will be unclean till evening. ⁴⁰ Whoever eats any of the carcass must wash his clothes and remain unclean till evening, and whoever takes up the carcass must wash his clothes and be unclean till evening.

⁴¹ All creatures that swarm on the ground are prohibited; they must not be eaten. ⁴² All creatures that swarm on the ground, whether they crawl on their bellies or go on all fours or have many legs, you must not eat, because they are prohibited. ⁴³ You must not contaminate yourselves through any creatures that swarm; you must not defile yourselves with them and make yourselves unclean by them. ⁴⁴ For I am the LORD your God; you are to make yourselves holy and keep yourselves holy, because I am holy. You must not defile yourselves with any creatures that swarm and creep on the ground. ⁴⁵ I am the LORD who brought you up from Egypt to become your God. You are to keep yourselves holy, because I am holy.

⁴⁶ Such, then, is the law concerning beast and bird, every living creature that moves in the water, and all living creatures that swarm on the land, ⁴⁷ the purpose of the law being to make a distinction between the unclean and the clean, between living creatures that may be eaten and those that may not be eaten.

12 The LORD told Moses ² to say to the Israelites: When a woman becomes pregnant and gives birth to a male child, she will be unclean for seven days, as in the period of her impurity through menstruation. ³ On the eighth day, the child is to have the flesh of his foreskin circumcised. ⁴ The woman must then wait for thirty-three days because her blood requires purification; she must touch nothing that is holy, and must not enter the sanctuary till her days of purification are completed. ⁵ If she bears a female child, she will be unclean as in menstruation for fourteen days and must wait for sixty-six days because her blood requires purification.

⁶ When her days of purification are completed for either son or daughter, she must bring a yearling ram for a whole-offering and a pigeon or a turtle-dove for a purification-offering to the priest at the entrance to the Tent of Meeting. ⁷ He will present it before the LORD and offer expiation for her, and she will be clean from her issue of blood. This is the law for the woman who gives birth to a child, whether male or female. ⁸ If she cannot afford a ram, she is to bring two turtle-doves or two pigeons, one for a whole-offering and the other for a purification-offering. The priest then offers expiation for her, and she will be clean.

13 When the LORD spoke to Moses and Aaron he said: ² When anyone has a discoloration on the skin of his body, a pustule or inflammation, and it may develop into the sores of a virulent skin disease, that person is to be brought to the priest, either to Aaron or to one of his sons. ³ The priest is to examine the sore on the skin; if the hairs on the affected part have turned white and it appears to be more than skin deep, it must be considered the sore of a virulent skin disease, and, after examination, the priest will pronounce the person ritually unclean. ⁴ But if the inflammation on his skin is white and

---

36: Basic sources of water (*spring* or *cistern*) were, like *seed* (v. 37), exempt because of their value to the community. **38:** The reason for the exclusion of *soaked* seed is not made clear, but it may have been that "uncleanness" could then permeate it more thoroughly.

12.1–8: Uncleanness from childbirth. The mysterious power at work in childbirth was regarded with awe throughout the ancient world. The "uncleanness" was ritual rather than literal or hygienic. **2:** *Menstruation:* see 15.19–24. **4:** On the frequent use of the number forty (thirty-three plus the seven of v. 2), see Gen. 7.4 n. *Purification:* the loss of blood marked an imperfection, a blemish, and hence cultic unacceptability (compare the sacrifices "without blemish": 1.3, 10; and the limitations of priests with bodily blemishes: 21.16–23). **5:** The longer delay after the birth of a daughter may reflect the view that daughters were considered less desirable than sons. **6:** On the need for a purification-offering, compare 4.1–5.13 n.

13.1–46; 14.1–32: Uncleanness from skin disease. Illness, when it produced marked imperfection, rendered the person cultically "unclean" (see 12.4 n.). **4–5:** The *isolation* was to prevent the inadvertent transfer of cultic impurity (see 11.24–25 n.) by one's touching of the impure.

seems no deeper than the skin, and not a single hair has turned white, the priest must isolate the affected person for seven days. ⁵ If, when he examines him on the seventh day, the sore remains as it was and has not spread in the skin, he is to keep him in isolation for a further seven days. ⁶ When on the seventh day the priest examines him again, if he finds that the sore has faded and has not spread on the skin, the priest will pronounce him ritually clean. It is only a scab; after washing his clothes, he will be clean. ⁷ But if the scab spreads on the skin after he has been to the priest to be pronounced ritually clean, he must show himself a second time to the priest, ⁸ who must examine him again. If it continues to spread, the priest will pronounce him ritually unclean; it is a virulent skin disease.

⁹ When anyone has the sores of a virulent skin disease, he is to be brought to the priest, ¹⁰ who then examines him. If there is a white mark on the skin, turning hairs white, and an ulceration appears in the mark, ¹¹ it is a chronic skin disease on the body, and the priest must pronounce him ritually unclean; there is no need for isolation because he is unclean already. ¹² If the skin disease spreads and covers the affected person from head to foot as far as the priest can see, ¹³ the priest is to examine him, and if he finds the condition covers the whole body, he must pronounce him ritually clean. It has all gone white; he is clean. ¹⁴ But as soon as raw flesh appears, he must be considered unclean. ¹⁵ The priest, when he sees it, must pronounce him unclean. Raw flesh is to be considered unclean; it is a virulent skin disease. ¹⁶ On the other hand, when the raw flesh heals and turns white, he is to go to the priest, ¹⁷ who will examine him, and if the sores have gone white, he will pronounce him clean. He is ritually clean.

¹⁸ When a fester appears on the skin and heals up, ¹⁹ but is followed by a white mark or reddish-white inflammation on the site of the fester, the person affected must show himself to the priest. ²⁰ The priest will examine him, and if it seems to be beneath the skin and the hairs have turned white, the priest must pronounce him ritually unclean; it is a virulent skin disease which has broken out on the site of the fester. ²¹ But if the priest on examination finds that it has no white hairs, is not beneath the skin, and has faded, he must isolate him for seven days. ²² If the affection

has spread at all in the skin, then the priest must pronounce him unclean; for it is a virulent skin disease. ²³ But if the inflammation is no worse and has not spread, it is only the scar of the fester, and the priest will pronounce him ritually clean.

²⁴ Again, in the case of a burn on the skin, if the raw spot left by the burn becomes a reddish-white or white inflammation, ²⁵ the priest is to examine it. If hair on the inflammation has turned white and it is deeper than the skin, it is a virulent skin disease which has broken out at the site of the burn. The priest must pronounce the person ritually unclean; it is a virulent skin disease. ²⁶ But if the priest on examination finds that there are no white hairs on the inflammation and it is not beneath the skin and has faded, he must keep him in isolation for seven days. ²⁷ When the priest examines him on the seventh day, if the inflammation has spread at all in the skin, the priest must pronounce him unclean; it is a virulent skin disease. ²⁸ But if the inflammation is no worse, has not spread, and has faded, it is only a mark from the burn. The priest will pronounce him ritually clean because it is the scar of the burn.

²⁹ When a man, or woman, has a sore on the head or chin, ³⁰ the priest is to examine it, and if it seems deeper than the skin and the hair is yellow and sparse, the priest must pronounce the person ritually unclean; it is a scale, a virulent skin disease of the head or chin. ³¹ But when the priest sees the sore, if it appears to be no deeper than the skin and yet there are no yellow hairs on the place, the priest must isolate the affected person for seven days. ³² When the priest examines the sore on the seventh day, if the scale has not spread and there are no yellow hairs on it and it seems no deeper than the skin, ³³ the person must be shaved except for the scurfy part, and be kept in isolation for another seven days. ³⁴ When the priest examines it again on the seventh day, if the scale has not spread on the skin and appears to be no deeper than the skin, the priest will pronounce the person clean. After washing his clothes the person will be ritually clean. ³⁵ But if the scale spreads at all in the skin after the person has been pronounced clean, ³⁶ the priest must make a further examination. If it has spread in the skin, the priest need not even look for yellow hairs; the person is un-

13:22 **virulent skin disease:** *so one MS; others* sore.
13:31 **yellow:** *so Gk; Heb.* black.

clean. [37] If, however, the scale remains as it was but black hair has begun to grow on it, it has healed. The person is ritually clean and the priest will pronounce this.

[38] When a man, or woman, has inflamed patches on the skin and they are white, [39] the priest is to examine them. If they are white and fading, it is vitiligo that has broken out on the skin. The person is ritually clean.

[40] When someone's hair falls out from his head, he is bald but not ritually unclean. [41] If the hair falls out from the front of the scalp, he is bald on the forehead but clean. [42] But if on the bald patch on his head or forehead there is a reddish-white sore, it is a virulent skin disease breaking out on those parts. [43] The priest must examine him, and if the discoloured sore on the bald patch on his head or forehead is reddish-white, similar in appearance to a virulent skin disease on the body, [44] the person is suffering from such a disease; he is ritually unclean and the priest must not fail to pronounce him so. The symptoms are in this case on his head.

[45] Anyone who suffers from a virulent skin disease must wear torn clothes and have his hair all dishevelled; he must conceal his upper lip, and call out, 'Unclean, unclean.' [46] So long as the sore persists, he is to be considered ritually unclean, and live alone, staying outside the camp.

[47] When there is a stain of mould, whether on a garment of wool or linen, [48] or on the threads or woven piece of linen or wool, or on a hide or anything made of hide; [49] if the stain is greenish or reddish in colour on the garment or hide, or on the threads or woven piece of cloth, or on anything made of hide, it is a stain of mould which must be shown to the priest. [50] The priest must examine it and put the stained material aside by itself for seven days. [51] On the seventh day he must examine it again. If the stain has spread on the garment, threads, piece of cloth, or hide, whatever the use of the hide, the stain is a rotting mould: it is ritually unclean. [52] He must burn the garment or the threads or woven piece, whether wool or linen, or anything of hide which is stained; because it is a rotting mould, it must be destroyed by fire.

[53] But if the priest sees that the stain has not spread on the garment, threads, or piece of woven cloth, or anything made of hide, [54] he is to give orders for the stained material to be washed, and then put it aside for another seven days. [55] After it has been washed the priest must examine the stain; if it has not changed its appearance, even though it has not spread, it is unclean and you must destroy it by fire, whether the rot is on the right side or the wrong. [56] If the priest examines it and finds the stain faded after being washed, he is to tear it out of the garment, or the hide, or the threads, or woven piece. [57] If, however, the stain reappears in the garment, threads, or woven piece, or in anything made of hide, it is breaking out afresh and you must destroy by fire whatever is stained. [58] If you wash the garment, threads, piece of woven cloth, or the article made of hide and the stain disappears, it must be washed a second time and then it will be ritually clean.

[59] Such is the law concerning stain of mould on a garment of wool or linen, on threads or a piece of woven cloth, or on anything made of hide; by it they will be pronounced ritually clean or unclean.

14 When the LORD spoke to Moses he said: [2] This is the law concerning anyone suffering from a virulent skin disease. On the day when he is to be cleansed he is to be brought to the priest, [3] who will go outside the camp and examine him. If the person has recovered from his disease, [4] then the priest is to order two ritually clean small birds to be brought alive for the person who is to be cleansed, together with cedar-wood, scarlet thread, and marjoram. [5] He must order one of the birds to be killed over an earthenware bowl containing fresh water. [6] He will then take the live bird together with the cedar-wood, scarlet thread, and marjoram and dip them all in the blood of the bird that has been killed over the fresh water. [7] He must sprinkle the blood seven times on the one who is to be cleansed from the skin disease and so cleanse him; the live bird he will release to fly

13:39 **vitiligo:** *or* dull-white leprosy.
14:4 **marjoram:** *or* hyssop.

14.2: *Cleansed:* The ritual is not for healing (since that is here assumed), but for the removal of impurity (vv. 4–20) for reentry into the community. **4:** The color *scarlet* was regarded as effective in the exorcism of demons. *Marjoram:* see Exod. 12.22 n. **5–7:** On the effectiveness of *blood* as a cleansing agent, see 4.7 n. The flight of the *live bird* symbolizes the person's freedom from impurity, the uncleanness perhaps having been away over the open country. 8 The person to be cleansed must wash his clothes, shave off all his hair, bathe in water, and so be ritually clean. He may then enter the camp, but must stay outside his tent for seven days. 9 On the seventh day he must shave off all the hair on his head, his beard, and his eyebrows, and then shave the rest of his hair, wash his clothes, and bathe in water; then he will be ritually clean.

10 On the eighth day he must bring two yearling rams and one yearling ewe, all three without blemish, a grain-offering of three tenths of an ephah of flour mixed with oil, and one log measure of oil. 11 The officiating priest must place the person to be cleansed and his offerings before the LORD at the entrance to the Tent of Meeting.

12 The priest must take one of the rams and offer it with the log of oil as a reparation-offering, presenting them as a dedicated portion before the LORD. 13 The ram must be slaughtered where the purification-offerings and the whole-offerings are slaughtered, within the sacred precincts, because the reparation-offering, like the purification-offering, belongs to the priest. It is most holy. 14 The priest must then take some of the blood of the reparation-offering and put it on the lobe of the right ear of the person to be cleansed, and on his right thumb and the big toe of his right foot. 15 He must next take the log of oil and pour some of it on the palm of his own left hand, 16 dip his right forefinger into the oil on his left palm, and sprinkle some of it with his finger seven times before the LORD. 17 He must then put some of the oil remaining on his palm on the lobe of the right ear of the person to be cleansed, on his right thumb, and on the big toe of his right foot, on top of the blood of the reparation-offering. 18 The remainder of the oil on the priest's palm is to be put upon the head of the person to be cleansed, and thus the priest makes expiation for him before the LORD. 19 The priest will then offer the purification-offering and make expiation for the uncleanness of the person who is to be cleansed. After this he must slaughter the whole-of-

fering 20 and offer it and the grain-offering on the altar. Thus the priest makes expiation for him, and he will be clean.

21 If the person is poor and cannot afford these offerings, he must bring one young ram as a reparation-offering to be a dedicated portion making expiation for him, and a grain-offering of a tenth of an ephah of flour mixed with oil, and a log measure of oil, 22 also two turtle-doves or two pigeons, whichever he can afford, one for a purification-offering and the other for a whole-offering. 23 He must bring them on the eighth day to the priest for his cleansing, at the entrance to the Tent of Meeting before the LORD. 24 The priest will take the ram for the reparation-offering and the log of oil, and present them as a dedicated portion before the LORD. 25 The ram for the reparation-offering must then be slaughtered, and the priest must take some of the blood of the reparation-offering, and put it on the lobe of the right ear of the man to be cleansed and on his right thumb and on the big toe of his right foot. 26 The priest must pour some of the oil on the palm of his own left hand 27 and sprinkle some of it with his right forefinger seven times before the LORD. 28 He will then put some of the oil remaining on his palm on the lobe of the right ear of the man to be cleansed, and on his right thumb and on the big toe of his right foot exactly where the blood of the reparation-offering was put. 29 The remainder of the oil on the priest's palm is to be put upon the head of the person to be cleansed to make expiation for him before the LORD. 30–31 Of the birds which the person has been able to afford, turtle-doves or pigeons, whichever it may be, the priest must deal with one as a purification-offering and with the other as a whole-offering and make the grain-offering with them. Thus the priest makes expiation before the LORD for the person who is to be cleansed. 32 Such is the law for anyone with a virulent skin disease who cannot afford the regular offering for his cleansing.

33 When the LORD spoke to Moses and

14:10 **yearling rams:** *so Samar.; Heb. omits* yearling.

transferred to it (compare 16.20–22). **8:** *Wash . . . shave . . . bathe:* thus cleansing all places to which the impurity might cling. **10:** *Ephah; log:* see p. xxviii. **12:** *Reparation-offering:* see 5.14–6.7. **13:** *To the priest:* 6.29; 10.16–18. **14–17:** See 8.23 n. **19:** The *purification-offering:* the ewe (4.32–35). The *whole-offering:* the second ram (1.10–13). **21–32:** Regulations allowing less valuable animals are given in 1.14–17 (whole-offering) and 5.7–13 (purification-offering).

Aaron he said: ³⁴ When you have entered Canaan, which I am giving you to occupy, if I inflict a fungous infection upon a house in the land you have occupied, ³⁵ the owner must come and report to the priest that there appears to him to be a patch of infection in his house. ³⁶ The priest must order the house to be emptied before he goes in to examine the infection, or everything in it will become unclean. After this the priest must go in to inspect the house. ³⁷ If on inspection he finds the patch on the walls consists of greenish or reddish depressions, apparently going deeper than the surface, ³⁸ he is to go out of the house, and at the entrance put it in quarantine for seven days. ³⁹ On the seventh day he must return and inspect the house, and if the patch has spread in the walls, ⁴⁰ he must order the infected stones to be pulled out and thrown away outside the town in an unclean place. ⁴¹ He must then have the house scraped inside throughout, and all the daub they have scraped off is to be tipped outside the town in an unclean place. ⁴² They must take fresh stones to replace the others and replaster the house with fresh daub.

⁴³ If the infection reappears in the house and spreads after the stones have been pulled out and the house scraped and re-daubed, ⁴⁴ the priest must come and inspect it. If the infection has spread in the house, it is a corrosive growth; the house is unclean. ⁴⁵ The house must be demolished, stones, timber, and daub, and everything must be taken away outside the town to an unclean place. ⁴⁶ Anyone who has entered the house during the time it has been in quarantine will be unclean till evening. ⁴⁷ Anyone who has slept or eaten a meal in the house must wash his clothes.

⁴⁸ If, when the priest goes into the house and inspects it, he finds that the infection has not spread after the redaubing, then he must pronounce the house ritually clean, because the infection has been cured. ⁴⁹ In order to rid the house of impurity, the priest must take two small birds along with cedar-wood, scarlet thread, and marjoram. ⁵⁰ He must kill one of the birds over an earthenware bowl containing fresh water. ⁵¹ He must then take the cedar-wood, marjoram, and scarlet thread, together with the live bird, dip them in the blood of the bird that has been killed and in the fresh water, and sprinkle the house seven times. ⁵² Thus he must purify the house, using the blood of the bird, the fresh water, the live bird, the cedar-wood, the marjoram, and the scarlet thread. ⁵³ He is to set the live bird free outside the town to fly away over the open country. So he will purify the house, and it will be clean.

⁵⁴ Such is the law for all virulent skin diseases, and for scale, ⁵⁵ for mould in clothes and fungus in houses, ⁵⁶ for a discoloration of the skin, scab, and inflammation, ⁵⁷ in deciding when these are pronounced unclean and when clean. It is the law for skin disease, mould, and fungus.

15 The LORD told Moses and Aaron ² to say to the Israelites: When anyone has a discharge from his private parts, the discharge is ritually unclean. ³ This is the law concerning the uncleanness due to his discharge whether it continues or has been stopped; in either case he is unclean.

⁴ All bedding on which anyone with such a discharge lies will be ritually unclean, and everything on which he sits will be unclean. ⁵ Anyone who touches the bedding must wash his clothes, bathe in water, and remain unclean till evening. ⁶ Whoever sits on anything on which the person with this discharge has sat must wash his clothes, bathe in water, and remain unclean till evening. ⁷ Whoever touches the body of a person with the discharge must wash his clothes, bathe in water, and remain unclean till evening. ⁸ If the person with such a discharge spits on one who is ritually clean, the latter must wash his clothes, bathe in water, and remain unclean till evening. ⁹ Everything on which this person sits when riding will be unclean. ¹⁰ Whoever touches anything that has been under

14:41 **daub:** *or* mud. **have scraped off:** *so Syriac; Heb.* have brought to an end.   14:43 **scraped:** *so Gk; Heb.* brought to an end.   15:3 **the law concerning:** *so Gk; Heb. omits.*

13.47–59; 14.33–53: Uncleanness in fabric or buildings. *Mould* (13.47) or *fungous infection* (14.34), like fermentation (2.11 n.), are corruptions not to be introduced into the cultic sphere.

14.54–57: A formulaic conclusion to the regulations concerning skin disease and uncleanness in fabric or buildings.

15.1–33: Uncleanness from genital discharge. 2: The condition referred to is likely gonorrhea.

him will be unclean till evening, and whoever handles such things must wash his clothes, bathe in water, and remain unclean till evening. ¹¹ Anyone whom the person with the discharge touches without having rinsed his hands in water must wash his clothes, bathe in water, and remain unclean till evening. ¹² Every earthenware bowl touched by the person must be broken, and every wooden bowl be rinsed with water.

¹³ When such a person is cleansed from his discharge, he must reckon seven days to his cleansing, then wash his clothes, bathe his body in fresh water, and be ritually clean. ¹⁴ On the eighth day he must obtain two turtle-doves or two pigeons, come before the LORD at the entrance to the Tent of Meeting, and give them to the priest. ¹⁵ The priest must deal with one as a purification-offering and with the other as a whole-offering, and offer for him before the LORD the expiation on account of the discharge.

¹⁶ When a man has emitted semen, he must bathe his whole body in water and be unclean till evening. ¹⁷ Every piece of clothing or leather on which there is any semen is to be washed and remain unclean till evening. ¹⁸ This applies also to the woman with whom a man has had intercourse; both must bathe in water and remain unclean till evening.

¹⁹ When a woman has her discharge of blood, her impurity will last for seven days; anyone who touches her will be unclean till evening. ²⁰ Everything on which she lies or sits during her impurity will be unclean, ²¹ and whoever touches her bedding must wash his clothes, bathe in water, and remain unclean till evening. ²² Whoever touches anything on which she sits must wash his clothes, bathe in water, and remain unclean till evening. ²³ If it is the bed or seat where she is sitting, by touching it he will become unclean till evening. ²⁴ If a man goes so far as to have intercourse with her and any of her dis-

charge gets on to him, then he will be unclean for seven days, and any bedding on which he lies down will be unclean.

²⁵ If a woman has a prolonged discharge of blood not at the time of her menstruation, or if her discharge continues beyond the period of menstruation, her impurity will last all the time of her discharge; she will be unclean as during the period of her menstruation. ²⁶ Any bedding on which she lies during the time of her discharge will be like that which she used during menstruation, and everything on which she sits will be unclean as in her menstrual uncleanness. ²⁷ Anyone who touches them will be unclean; he must wash his clothes, bathe in water, and remain unclean till evening. ²⁸ If she becomes cleansed from her discharge, she must reckon seven days and after that she will be ritually clean. ²⁹ On the eighth day she is to obtain two turtle-doves or two pigeons and bring them to the priest at the entrance to the Tent of Meeting. ³⁰ The priest must deal with one as a purification-offering and with the other as a whole-offering, and offer for her before the LORD the expiation on account of her unclean discharge.

³¹ In this way you must warn the Israelites against uncleanness, in order that they may not die by bringing uncleanness upon the Tabernacle where I dwell among them.

³² Such is the law for the man who has a discharge, for him who has an emission of semen and is thereby unclean, ³³ and for the woman who is suffering her menstruation — for everyone, male or female, who has a discharge, and for the man who has intercourse with a woman who is unclean.

16 THE LORD spoke to Moses after the death of Aaron's two sons, who died when they offered illicit fire before the LORD.

16:1 when ... LORD: *so Gk; Heb.* when they came near before the LORD.

16–18: The intent is to effect a complete separation between sexual activity and cult worship; the unclean person could not approach the sanctuary. This separation is in sharp contrast to some forms of religious expression among ancient peoples, for whom fertility rites were not uncommon. Compare Gen. 19.5 n.; 20.26; Exod. 28.42–43. **19–24:** Regulations concerning menstruation.

16.1–34: The annual purification ritual purges the sanctuary and forgives the community of the accumulated transgressions which voluntary purification-offerings (4.1–5.13) have not covered. The origin of this regular ritual (v. 29) of the postexilic period is ascribed to the Mosaic Age (compare Exod. 20.22–23.33 n.; 25.1–31.17 n.; Lev. 1.1 n.). The combination of the sins of Nadab and Abihu (10.1–7) plus the presence of their corpses in the sanctuary (v. 1; compare ch. 21) created the need for a special ritual of purification. This section logically follows ch. 10, and the insertion of the laws on uncleanness (chs. 11–15) has served to

2 He said to him: Tell your brother Aaron that on pain of death he must not enter the sanctuary behind the curtain, which is in front of the cover over the Ark, except at the appointed time; for I appear in the cloud above the cover. 3 When Aaron enters the sanctuary, this is what he must do. He must bring a young bull for a purification-offering and a ram for a whole-offering; 4 he is to wear a sacred linen tunic and linen shorts to cover himself, and he is to put a linen sash round his waist and wind a linen turban round his head; all these are sacred vestments, and he must bathe in water before putting them on. 5 He is to receive from the community of the Israelites two he-goats for a purification-offering and a ram for a whole-offering.

6 He must offer the bull reserved for his purification-offering and make expiation for himself and his household. 7 Then he must take the two he-goats and set them before the LORD at the entrance to the Tent of Meeting. 8 He must cast lots over the two goats, one to be for the LORD and the other for Azazel. 9 He must present the goat on which the lot for the LORD has fallen and deal with it as a purification-offering; 10 but the goat on which the lot for Azazel has fallen is to be made to stand alive before the LORD, for expiation to be made over it, before it is driven away into the wilderness to Azazel.

11 Aaron must present his bull as a purification-offering, making expiation for himself and his household. He is to slaughter the bull as a purification-offering, 12 and then take a censer full of glowing embers from the altar before the LORD, and a double handful of powdered fragrant incense, and bring them behind the curtain. 13 He is to put the incense on the fire before the LORD, and the cloud of incense will hide the cover over the Tokens so that he may not die. 14 He must take some of the bull's blood and sprinkle it with his finger both on the surface of the cover, eastwards, and seven times in front of the cover. 15 He must then slaughter the goat for the

people's purification-offering, bring its blood behind the curtain, and do with its blood as he did with the bull's blood, sprinkling it on the cover and in front of it. 16 So is he to purge the sanctuary of the ritual uncleanness of the Israelites and their acts of rebellion, that is, of all their sins; and he must do the same for the Tent of Meeting, which is present among them in the midst of their uncleanness. 17 No one else must be within the Tent of Meeting from the time when he goes in to effect cleansing in the sanctuary until he comes out. So is he to make expiation for himself, his household, and the whole assembly of Israel.

18 Then he is to come out to the altar which is before the LORD and purify it, take some of the bull's blood and some of the goat's blood, and smear them over each of the horns of the altar; 19 he is to sprinkle some of the blood on the altar with his finger seven times. So he will purify it from all the uncleanness of the Israelites and hallow it.

20 When Aaron has finished the purification of the sanctuary, the Tent of Meeting, and the altar, he is to bring forward the live goat. 21 Laying both his hands on its head he must confess over it all the iniquities of the Israelites and all their acts of rebellion, that is all their sins; he is to lay his hands on the head of the goat and send it away into the wilderness in the charge of a man who is waiting ready. 22 The goat will carry all their iniquities upon itself into some barren waste, where the man will release it, there in the wilderness.

23 Aaron is then to enter the Tent of Meeting, take off the linen clothes which he had put on when he entered the sanctuary, and leave them there. 24 He must bathe in water in a consecrated place and, after putting on his vestments, he is to go out and perform his own whole-offering and that of the people, thus making expiation for himself and for

16:8 **for Azazel:** or for the Precipice.

heighten the need for a regular ritual such as that here described. **2:** *Death:* see Exod. 33.20. Only on this occasion does the sacrifice take the priest *behind the curtain;* previously mentioned purification-offerings took place either at the sacrificial altar in the Tabernacle court (Exod. 27.1 n.) or at the incense-altar in the outer part of the structure (Exod. 26.33 n.). See 4.6, 17, 25, 30. *Ark:* see Exod. 25.10 n. *Appointed time:* see vv. 29–30. *Cloud:* see Exod. 19.9 n. **5:** *He-goats:* see 9.15 n. **8:** *Azazel:* possibly the name of a demon who, in earlier times, was thought to be exorcised from the community. **9:** *Lot:* see Exod. 28.15 n. **11:** *For himself:* see 9.8–11 n. **14:** *Eastwards:* the direction of the desert (wilderness: v. 21), where demons were thought to dwell. **16:** *Purge the sanctuary:* see 4.13–21 n. **20–22:** The idea of transferring sin to animals is found in many the people. ²⁵ He must burn the fat of the purification-offering upon the altar.

²⁶ The man who drove the goat away to Azazel must wash his clothes and bathe in water, and not till then may he enter the camp. ²⁷ The two purification-offerings, the bull and the goat, the blood of which was brought behind the curtain to purge the sanctuary of ritual uncleanness, must be taken outside the camp and destroyed by fire —hide, flesh, and offal. ²⁸ The man who burns them must wash his clothes and bathe in water, and not till then may he enter the camp.

²⁹ This is to be a rule binding on you for all time: on the tenth day of the seventh month you must fast; you, whether native Israelite or alien settler among you, must do no work, ³⁰ because on this day expiation will be made on your behalf to cleanse you, and so make you clean before the LORD from all your sins. ³¹ This is a sabbath of solemn abstinence from work for you, and you must mortify yourselves; it is a rule binding for all time.

³² Expiation is to be made by the priest duly anointed and ordained to serve in succession to his father; he is to put on the sacred linen clothes ³³ and purify of ritual uncleanness the holy sanctuary, the Tent of Meeting, and the altar, on behalf of the priests and the whole assembly of the people. ³⁴ This is to become a rule binding on you for all time, to offer for the Israelites once a year the expiation required by all their sins.

It was carried out as the LORD commanded Moses.

Law of holiness

17 THE LORD told Moses ² to say to Aaron, his sons, and all the Israelites: This is what the LORD has commanded. ³ Any Israelite who slaughters an ox, a sheep, or a goat, either inside or outside the camp, ⁴ and has not brought it to the entrance of the Tent of Meeting to present it as an offering to the LORD before his Tabernacle is to be held guilty of bloodshed: he has shed blood and will be cut off from his people. ⁵ The purpose is that the Israelites should bring to the LORD the animals which they have been slaughtering in the open country; they must bring them to the priest at the entrance to the Tent of Meeting and offer them as shared-offerings to the LORD. ⁶ The priest will fling the blood against the altar of the LORD at the entrance to the Tent of Meeting, and burn the fat as a soothing odour to the LORD. ⁷ No longer are they to offer their slaughtered beasts to the demons whom they wantonly follow. This is to be a rule binding on them and their descendants for all time.

⁸ You must warn them: Any Israelite or alien settled in Israel who offers a whole-offering or a sacrifice ⁹ and does not bring it to the entrance of the Tent of Meeting to offer it to the LORD is to be cut off from his father's kin.

¹⁰ If any Israelite or alien settled in Israel consumes any blood, I shall set my face against him and cut him off from his people,

16:29 **This:** *so Gk; Heb. omits.*   17:7 **demons:** *or satyrs.*

societies. Here, the action may only symbolize the community's freedom from sin. Compare 14.5–7 n. **27:** *Destroyed by fire:* in keeping with the requirements of 4.12, 21. **29:** The *tenth day* is near the autumnal equinox, which marked the new year in the older preexilic solar calendar (see Exod. 12.2 n.; Ezek. 40.1 n.). In 23.27 and 25.9 it is called "the Day of Atonement." Throughout the ancient world, the days of the equinox were marked by rites of mortification (v. 29), purgation (v. 30), and renewal.

17.1–26.46: The Law of Holiness, by means of which Israel is to be holy because God is holy (19.2; 20.7–8). This collection of regulations and exhortations, once independent, serves here to stress the obligations of the community, rather than those of the priests. The section gets its name, Holiness Code, from the repeated refrain, "You must be holy."

17.1–16: Regulations concerning the slaughter of animals. 3: *Slaughters:* the animals are here intended for food. **4:** Contrast the regulations in Deut. 12.15, 20–21, written earlier, which exempted food animals from this requirement. The Holiness Code envisages proximity to Jerusalem, while Deut. supposes possible residence in places far distant from it. *Cut off:* see 7.21 n. **5:** *Bring to the LORD:* i.e. to the temple in Jerusalem. This mandate reflects a time directly before or shortly after the Babylonian Exile (see Introduction), when there was a Judean community, but small and confined to the immediate environs of Jerusalem. **7:** According to 2 Kgs. 23.8, a cult of *demons* was widespread in Judah before the Babylonian Exile. The need to exterminate it seemed sufficient justification for the requirement in vv. 3–6. **8:** *Aliens* were increasingly common in Judah during the

[11] because the life of a creature is the blood, and I appoint it to make expiation on the altar for yourselves: it is the blood, which is the life, that makes expiation. [12] Therefore I have told you Israelites that neither you, nor any alien settled among you, is to consume blood.

[13] Any Israelite or alien settled in Israel who hunts beasts or birds that may lawfully be eaten must drain out the blood and cover it with earth, [14] because the life of every living creature is its blood, and I have forbidden the Israelites to consume the blood of any creature, because the life of every creature is its blood: whoever eats it is to be cut off.

[15] Every person, native or alien, who eats something which has died a natural death or has been mauled by wild beasts must wash his clothes and bathe in water, and remain ritually unclean till evening; then he will be clean. [16] But if he does not wash his clothes and bathe his body, he must accept responsibility.

18 THE LORD told Moses [2] to say to the Israelites: I am the LORD your God. [3] You must not do as they do in Egypt where once you dwelt, nor may you do as they do in Canaan to which I am bringing you; you must not conform to their customs. [4] You must keep my laws and conform faithfully to my statutes: I am the LORD your God. [5] Observe my statutes and my laws: whoever keeps them will have life through them. I am the LORD.

[6] No man may approach a blood relation for intercourse. I am the LORD. [7] You must not bring shame on your father by intercourse with your mother: she is your mother; do not bring shame on her. [8] You must not have intercourse with a wife of your father: that is to bring shame upon your father.

[9] You must not have intercourse with your sister, either your father's daughter or your mother's daughter, whether brought up in the family or in another home; you must not bring shame on them. [10] You must not have intercourse with your son's daughter or your daughter's daughter: that is to bring shame on yourself. [11] You must not have intercourse with a daughter of a wife of your father, begotten by your father, because she is your sister; do not bring shame on her. [12] You must not have intercourse with your father's sister; she is a blood relation of your father. [13] You must not have intercourse with your mother's sister: she is a blood relation of your mother. [14] You must not bring shame on your father's brother by approaching his wife, because she is your aunt. [15] You must not have intercourse with your daughter-in-law, because she is your son's wife; you must not bring shame on her. [16] You must not have intercourse with your brother's wife: that is to bring shame on him. [17] You must not have intercourse with both a woman and her daughter, nor may you take her son's daughter or her daughter's daughter to have intercourse with them: they are blood relations, and such conduct is lewdness. [18] You must not take a woman who is your wife's sister to make her a rival wife, and to have intercourse with her during her sister's lifetime.

[19] You must not approach a woman to have intercourse with her during her period of menstruation. [20] Do not have sexual intercourse with the wife of your fellow-countryman and so make yourself unclean with her. [21] You must not surrender any of your children to Molech and thus profane the name of your God: I am the LORD. [22] You must not lie with a man as with a woman: that is an abomination. [23] You must not have sexual intercourse with any animal to make yourself

---

Babylonian Exile and shortly thereafter. **10:** *Blood:* see also Deut. 12.23–25. **11:** *Expiation:* see 4.7 n., and for the rites involved, 4.1–6.7; ch. 16. **13:** *Beasts or birds:* nonsacrificial animals. *Lawfully be eaten:* see ch. 11. Every meal involving meat thus became an opportunity for Israel to remember its special identity, a task which became increasingly difficult during the exilic and postexilic periods (see Introduction to Lev. and 11.1–47 n.).

18.1–30: Prohibited sexual relations. 2: *I am the* LORD *your God:* the introductory words of the covenant ceremony (Exod. 20.2), calling to mind the LORD's gracious deeds for Israel, and Israel's need of obedience. **3:** *In Canaan:* the Canaanites were traditionally believed to practice improper sexual relations; see Gen. 9.26 n. **11:** Marriage to a half-sister was previously allowable (Gen. 20.12 n.). **12:** Marriage to an aunt was apparently acceptable at an earlier time. Indeed, Moses and Aaron were the product of such a union (Exod. 6.20). **16:** *Brother's wife:* while he is alive. After his death, however, such a marriage could become an obligation (Deut. 25.5–10 n.). **18:** Marriage to women who were sisters was allowable at an earlier time (Gen. 29.1–30). **21:** The Ammonite god was offered child sacrifices by fire (Jer. 32.35).

unclean with it, nor may a woman submit herself to intercourse with an animal: that is a violation of nature.

24 You must not make yourselves unclean in any of those ways; for in such ways the nations, whom I am driving out before you, made themselves unclean. 25 That is how the land became unclean, and I punished it for its iniquity so that it spewed out its inhabitants. 26 You, unlike them, must observe my statutes and my laws: none of you, whether natives or aliens settled among you, may do any of those abominable things. 27 The people who were there before you did those abominable things and the land became unclean. 28 So do not let the land spew you out for making it unclean as it spewed them out; 29 for anyone who does any of those abominable things will be cut off from his people. 30 Observe my charge, therefore, and follow none of the abominable institutions customary before your time; do not make yourselves unclean with them. I am the LORD your God.

19 THE LORD told Moses 2 to say to the whole Israelite community: You must be holy, because I, the LORD your God, am holy. 3 Each one of you must revere his mother and father. You must keep my sabbaths. I am the LORD your God. 4 Do not resort to idols or make for yourselves gods of cast metal. I am the LORD your God.

5 When you sacrifice a shared-offering to the LORD, you are to slaughter it so as to win acceptance for yourselves. 6 It must be eaten on the day of your sacrifice or on the next day. Anything left over till the third day must be destroyed by fire; 7 it is tainted, and if any of it is eaten on the third day, it will not be acceptable. 8 He who eats it must accept responsibility, because he has profaned the holy-gift to the LORD: that person will be cut off from his father's kin.

9 When you reap the harvest in your land, do not reap right up to the edges of your field, or gather the gleanings of your crop. 10 Do not completely strip your vineyard, or pick up the fallen grapes; leave them for the poor and for the alien. I am the LORD your God.

11 You must not steal; you must not cheat or deceive a fellow-countryman. 12 You must not swear in my name with intent to deceive and thus profane the name of your God. I am the LORD. 13 You are not to oppress your neighbour or rob him. Do not keep back a hired man's wages till next morning. 14 Do not treat the deaf with contempt, or put an obstacle in the way of the blind; you are to fear your God. I am the LORD.

15 You are not to pervert justice, either by favouring the poor or by subservience to the great. You are to administer justice to your fellow-countryman with strict fairness. 16 Do not go about spreading slander among your father's kin; do not take sides against your neighbour on a capital charge. I am the LORD. 17 You are not to nurse hatred towards your brother. Reprove your fellow-countryman frankly, and so you will have no share in his guilt. 18 Never seek revenge or cherish a grudge towards your kinsfolk; you must love your neighbour as yourself. I am the LORD.

19 You must observe my statutes. You may not allow two different kinds of animal to mate together. You are not to plant your field with two kinds of seed, nor to wear a garment woven with two kinds of yarn.

20 When a man has intercourse with a slave-girl who has been assigned to another but has been neither redeemed nor given her freedom, enquiry should be made. They are not to be put to death, because she has not been freed. 21 The man is to bring his reparation-offering, a ram, to the LORD to the entrance of the Tent of Meeting, 22 and with it the priest will make expiation for him before the LORD for his sin, and he will be forgiven the sin he has committed.

23 When you enter the land, and plant any kind of tree for food, you are to treat it as

19:17 **and . . . guilt:** or and for that you will incur no blame.

25–29: That Israel has already settled in Canaan seems clearly presupposed. Compare Exod. 20.22–23.33 n.

19.1–37: Diverse social and cultic regulations, possibly constructed around a version of part of the Ten Commandments (vv. 3–4, 11–12; see Exod. 20.1–21 n.). The importance of these guidelines is emphasized by the repeated remark, "I am the LORD" (18.2 n.). **2:** The theme of human obedience as imitation of God's holiness is stressed here. **6:** See 7.16–18. **18:** See Mk. 12.28–31. This love is to be extended to the alien as well (vv. 33–34). See Lk. 10.29–37. **20:** Assigned: chosen for marriage. **21:** Since a reparation-offering would be accompanied by compensation for damages (see 6.1–7), the law is concerned not only with the sin of illicit bearing forbidden fruit. For three years it is forbidden and may not be eaten. ²⁴ In the fourth year all its fruit is to be holy for a praise-offering to the LORD, a festal jubilation. ²⁵ In the fifth year you may eat its fruit. Thus the yield it gives you will be increased. I am the LORD your God.

²⁶ Never eat meat with the blood in it. You must not practise divination or soothsaying. ²⁷ You are not to cut off your hair from your temples or shave the edge of your beards. ²⁸ You must not gash yourselves in mourning for the dead or tattoo yourselves. I am the LORD.

²⁹ Do not debase your daughter by making her become a prostitute. The land is not to play the prostitute and be full of lewdness. ³⁰ You must keep my sabbaths and revere my sanctuary. I am the LORD.

³¹ Do not resort to ghosts and spirits or make yourselves unclean by seeking them out. I am the LORD your God.

³² Rise in the presence of grey hairs, give honour to the aged, and fear your God. I am the LORD.

³³ When an alien resides with you in your land, you must not oppress him. ³⁴ He is to be treated as a native born among you. Love him as yourself, because you were aliens in Egypt. I am the LORD your God.

³⁵ You are not to falsify measures of length, weight, or quantity. ³⁶ You must use true scales and weights, true dry and liquid measures. I am the LORD your God who brought you out of Egypt. ³⁷ You must observe all my statutes and all my laws and carry them out. I am the LORD.

20 The LORD told Moses ² to say to the Israelites: Anyone, whether Israelite or alien settled in Israel, who gives any of his children to Molech must be put to death: the people are to stone him. ³ I for my part shall set my face against that man and cut him off from his people, for by giving a child of his to Molech he has made my sanctuary unclean and profaned my holy name. ⁴ If the people connive at it when a man has given a child of his to Molech and do not put him to death, ⁵ I shall set my face against that man and his family, and cut off from their people both him and all who follow him in his wanton worship of Molech.

⁶ I shall set my face against anyone who wantonly resorts to ghosts and spirits, and I shall cut that person off from his people. ⁷ Hallow yourselves and be holy, because I am the LORD your God. ⁸ Observe my statutes and obey them: I am the LORD who hallows you.

⁹ When anyone reviles his father and his mother, he must be put to death. Since he has reviled his father and his mother, let his blood be on his own head. ¹⁰ If a man commits adultery with another's wife, that is with the wife of a fellow-countryman, both adulterer and adulteress must be put to death. ¹¹ The man who has intercourse with his father's wife has brought shame on his father. Both must be put to death; their blood be on their own heads! ¹² If a man has intercourse with his daughter-in-law, both must be put to death. Their deed is a violation of nature; their blood be on their own heads! ¹³ If a man has intercourse with a man as with a woman, both commit an abomination. They must be put to death; their blood be on their own

19:23 **forbidden:** *lit.* uncircumcised.

---

intercourse but also with the damages to the owner who could not sell her as a virgin. **23–25:** The purpose behind this legislation is obscure; perhaps the Canaanites regarded the *tree* as a new creation of the fertility gods. Here, it is enjoined simply as the demand of the LORD, although the language of MT in v. 23 (lit. "you will leave its foreskin, namely its fruit, uncircumcised") draws on the analogy of the male child who can only be dedicated after circumcision. **26:** *Divination or soothsaying:* methods of determining the divine will, practiced in the cults of Israel's neighbors. **27–28:** These actions are possibly forbidden because of their role in the cult of Canaanite gods. **29:** Sacred, rather than ordinary, prostitution is meant. See Gen. 38.21 n. **31:** The dead were supposed to have knowledge of the future. See 1 Sam. ch. 28.

20.1–27: Transgressions punishable by death. The subject matter is essentially that of ch. 18, but now with penalties attached. Perhaps the two chapters were once independent, self-contained units. **2:** *Molech:* see 18.21 n. **3:** *Cut him off:* see 7.21 n. *Sanctuary unclean:* compare 4.13–21 n. **10–16:** The community is to apply the death penalty for these sexual offenses, as opposed to those in vv. 17–21 where retribution is seemingly left to the deity. Since these relationships (in vv. 17–21) had been practiced in an earlier age (18.11–12 nn., 18.18 n.), their prohibition was likely regarded as unenforceable.

heads! 14 If a man takes both a woman and her mother, that is lewdness. Both he and they must be burnt, so that there may be no lewdness in your midst. 15 A man who has sexual intercourse with an animal must be put to death, and you are to kill the beast. 16 If a woman approaches an animal to mate with it, you must kill both woman and beast. They must be put to death; their blood be on their own heads! 17 If a man takes his sister, whether his father's daughter or his mother's daughter, and they see one another naked, it is an infamous disgrace. They are to be cut off in the presence of their people. The man has had intercourse with his sister and he must be held responsible. 18 If a man lies with a woman during her monthly period, uncovering her body, he has exposed her discharge and she has uncovered the source of her discharge; they are both to be cut off from their people. 19 You must not have intercourse with your mother's sister or your father's sister: it is the exposure of a blood relation. Both must accept responsibility. 20 A man who has intercourse with his uncle's wife has brought shame on his uncle. They must accept responsibility for their sin and be proscribed and put to death. 21 If a man takes his brother's wife, it is impurity. He has brought shame on his brother; they are to be proscribed.

22 You are to observe my statutes and my laws and carry them out, so that the land into which I am bringing you to live may not spew you out. 23 You must not conform to the institutions of the nations whom I am driving out before you: they did all these things and I abhorred them, 24 and I told you that you should occupy their land, and I would give you possession of it, a land flowing with milk and honey. I am the LORD your God: I have made a clear separation between you and the nations, 25 and you are to make a clear separation between clean beasts and unclean beasts and between unclean and clean birds. You must not contaminate yourselves through beast or bird or anything that creeps on the ground, for I have made a clear separation between them and you, declaring them unclean. 26 You must be holy to me, because I the LORD am holy. I have made a clear separation between you and the heathen, that you

may belong to me. 27 Any man or woman among you who calls up ghosts or spirits must be put to death. The people are to stone them; their blood be on their own heads!

21 THE LORD told Moses to say to the priests, the sons of Aaron: A priest is not to render himself unclean for the death of any of his kin 2 except for a near blood relation, that is for mother, father, son, daughter, brother, 3 or full sister who is unmarried and a virgin; 4 nor is he to make himself unclean for any married woman among his father's kin, and so profane himself.

5 Priests are not to make bald patches on their heads as a sign of mourning, or cut the edges of their beards, or gash their bodies. 6 They must be holy to their God, and must not profane the name of their God, because they present the food-offerings of the LORD, the food of their God, and they must be holy. 7 A priest must not marry a prostitute or a girl who has lost her virginity, or marry a woman divorced from her husband; for he is holy to his God. 8 You must keep him holy because he presents the food of your God; you are to regard him as holy, because I the LORD, I who hallow them, am holy. 9 When a priest's daughter makes herself profane by becoming a prostitute, she profanes her father. She must be burnt.

10 The high priest, the one among his fellows who has had the anointing oil poured on his head and has been ordained to wear the priestly vestments, must neither let his hair hang loose nor tear his clothes. 11 He must not enter the place where any dead body lies; not even for his father or his mother may he render himself unclean. 12 He must not go out of the sanctuary, for fear that he dishonour the sanctuary of his God, because the consecration of the anointing oil of his God is on him. I am the LORD. 13 He is to marry a woman who is still a virgin. 14 He is not to marry a widow, a divorced woman, a woman who has lost her virginity, or a prostitute, but only a virgin from his father's kin; 15 he must not dishonour his descendants among his father's kin, for I am the LORD who hallows him.

21:4 **for any married woman:** *prob. rdg; Heb.* husband.
21:8 **them:** *so Samar. (cp. verse 23); Heb.* you.

21.1–24: The preservation of priestly sanctity. On the importance of this, see 4.3 n. **1:** *Render himself unclean:* by participating in the funeral rites (see Num. 19.11–19). **5:** See 19.27–28 n. **10–12:** See 10.6 n.;

16 The LORD told Moses 17 to say to Aaron: No man among your descendants for all time who has any physical defect is to come and present the food of his God. 18 No man with a defect is to come, whether a blind man, a lame man, a man stunted or overgrown, 19 a man deformed in foot or hand, 20 or with misshapen brows or a film over his eye or a discharge from it, a man who has a scab or eruption or has had a testicle ruptured. 21 No descendant of Aaron the priest who has any defect in his body may approach the altar to present the food-offerings of the LORD; because he has a defect he must not approach the altar to present the food of his God. 22 He may eat the bread of God both from the holy-gifts and from the holiest of holy-gifts, 23 but not come up to the curtain or approach the altar, because he has a defect in his body; he is not to profane my sanctuaries, for I am the LORD who hallows them.

24 Thus Moses spoke to Aaron and his sons and to all the Israelites.

22 The LORD told Moses 2 to say to Aaron and his sons: You must be scrupulous in your handling of the holy-gifts of the Israelites which you hallow to me, so that you do not profane my holy name. I am the LORD. 3 Say to them: Any man of your descent for all time who in a state of uncleanness approaches the holy-gifts which the Israelites hallow to the LORD is to be cut off from my presence. I am the LORD. 4 No man descended from Aaron who suffers from a virulent skin disease, or has a bodily discharge, may eat of the holy-gifts until he is cleansed. A man who touches anything which makes him unclean, or who has an emission of semen, 5 a man who touches any creature which makes him unclean or any human being who makes him unclean: 6 any person who touches such a thing is unclean till sunset and unless he has washed his body he must not eat of the holy-gifts. 7 When the sun goes down, he will be clean, and after that he may eat from the holy-gifts, because they are his food.

8 He must not eat an animal that has died a natural death or has been mauled by wild beasts, thereby making himself unclean. I am the LORD. 9 The priests must observe my charge, lest they make themselves guilty and die for profaning my name. I am the LORD who hallows them.

10 No lay person may eat a holy-gift; neither a stranger who is a priest's guest nor a priest's hired man may eat it. 11 A slave bought by a priest with his own money may do so, and slaves born in his household may also share his food. 12 When a priest's daughter marries a layman, she may not eat any of the contributions of holy-gifts; 13 but if she is widowed or divorced and is childless and returns to live in her father's house as in her youth, she may share her father's food. No lay person may eat any of it.

14 When anyone inadvertently eats a holy-gift, he must make good the holy-gift to the priest, adding one fifth to its value. 15 The priests must not profane the holy-gifts of the Israelites which they set aside for the LORD; 16 they are not to let anyone eat their holy-gifts and so incur guilt and its penalty, for I am the LORD who hallows them.

17 The LORD said to Moses: 18 Tell Aaron, his sons, and all the Israelites that whenever anyone belonging to the Israelite community or any alien settled in Israel presents, whether as a votive offering or as a freewill-offering, an offering such as is presented to the LORD for a whole-offering 19 so as to win acceptance for yourselves, it must be a male without defect from the cattle, sheep, or goats. 20 You are not to present anything which has a defect, because it will not be acceptable on your behalf. 21 When a man presents a shared-offering to the LORD, whether cattle or sheep, to fulfil a special vow or as a freewill-offering, if it is to be acceptable it must be perfect; there must be no defect in it. 22 You are to present to the LORD nothing blind, disabled, mutilated, with a running sore, scab, or eruption, nor are you to set any such creature on the altar as a food-offering to the LORD. 23 If a bull or a sheep is overgrown or stunted, you may make of it a freewill-offering, but it will not be acceptable in fulfilment of a vow. 24 If its

21:20 film ... discharge: *the Heb. words are of uncertain meaning.* 22:21 fulfil a special: *or* discharge a.

10.7 n. **16–23:** Compare 12.4 n.; 13.1–46 n.

22.1–33: Preservation of the sanctity of sacrificial gifts. These rules concern those who may consume the parts of the sacrifice reserved for priests (2.3; 5.13; 6.16–18, 29–30; 7.6–10). **3:** *Uncleanness:* as defined by the regulations in chs. 11–15. **16:** The priest is forbidden to give or sell the sacrificial food to unsuspecting testicles have been crushed or bruised, torn or cut, do not present it to the LORD; this is forbidden in your own land, 25 and you must not procure any such creature from a foreigner and present it as food for your God. Their deformity is inherent in them, a permanent defect, and they will not be acceptable on your behalf.

26 When the LORD spoke to Moses he said: 27 When a calf, a lamb, or a kid is born, it must not be taken from its mother for seven days. From the eighth day onwards it will be acceptable when offered as a food-offering to the LORD. 28 You must not slaughter a cow or a sheep at the same time as its young. 29 When you make a thank-offering to the LORD, you must sacrifice it so as to win acceptance for yourselves; 30 it is to be eaten that same day, and none must be left over till morning. I am the LORD.

31 Observe my commandments and perform them. I am the LORD. 32 You must not profane my holy name; I am to be hallowed among the Israelites. I am the LORD who hallows you, 33 who brought you out of Egypt to become your God. I am the LORD.

23 THE LORD told Moses 2 to say to the Israelites: These are the appointed seasons of the LORD, and you are to proclaim them as sacred assemblies; these are my appointed seasons. 3 On six days work may be done, but every seventh day is a day of solemn abstinence from work, a day of sacred assembly, on which you must do no work. Wherever you live, it is the LORD's sabbath.

4 These are the appointed seasons of the LORD, the sacred assemblies which you are to proclaim in their appointed order. 5 In the first month on the fourteenth day between dusk and dark is the LORD's Passover. 6 On the fifteenth day of the same month begins the LORD's pilgrim-feast of Unleavened Bread; for seven days you are to eat unleavened bread. 7 On the first day there will be a sacred assembly; you are not to do your daily work. 8 For seven days you must present your

food-offerings to the LORD. On the seventh day also there will be a sacred assembly; you are not to do your daily work.

9 The LORD told Moses 10 to say to the Israelites: When you enter the land which I am giving you, and you reap its harvest, you are to bring the first sheaf of your harvest to the priest. 11 He will present the sheaf as a dedicated portion before the LORD on the day after the sabbath, so as to gain acceptance for you. 12 On the day you present the sheaf, you are to prepare a perfect yearling ram for a whole-offering to the LORD, 13 together with the proper grain-offering, two tenths of an ephah of flour mixed with oil, as a food-offering to the LORD, of soothing odour, and also with the proper drink-offering, a quarter of a hin of wine. 14 You are to eat neither bread nor roasted or fully ripened grain until that day, the day on which you bring your God his offering; this is a rule binding on your descendants for all time wherever you live.

15 From the day after the sabbath, the day on which you bring your sheaf as a dedicated portion, you are to count off seven full weeks. 16 The day after the seventh sabbath will make fifty days, and then you will present to the LORD a grain-offering from the new crop. 17 Bring from your homes two loaves as a dedicated portion; they are to contain two tenths of an ephah of flour and be baked with leaven. They are the LORD's firstfruits. 18 In addition to the bread you are to present seven perfect yearling sheep, one young bull, and two rams. They will be a whole-offering to the LORD with the proper grain-offering and the proper drink-offering, a food-offering of soothing odour to the LORD. 19 You must also prepare one he-goat as a purification-offering and two yearling sheep as a shared-offering, 20 and the priest will present the two sheep in addition to the bread of the firstfruits as a dedicated

23:11 **on the day:** or from the day.   23:20 **before the LORD:** so Lat.; Heb. adds in addition to the two sheep.

lay persons and then collect fines from them (v. 15). **26–27:** Compare 19.23–25 n. **28:** Such may have been a Canaanite cult practice. **29–30:** See 7.11–15. **31–33:** See 18.2 n.

23.1–44: The calendar of the sacred days. 2: The entire community is addressed, since it is the obligation of every individual to observe the sacred occasions. **4:** Assemblies: festivals requiring pilgrimage to the sanctuary. See Deut. 16.16. **5:** Passover: see Exod. 12.1–27 and the notes. **6:** Unleavened Bread: Exod. 12.15 n. **9:** This second introduction suggests that a once independent regulation about Passover has been joined to the context. **10:** The first sheaf was of barley, which ripened in April. **16:** Fifty days (Gk. "Pentecost"): see Exod.

portion before the LORD. They are a holy-gift
to the LORD for the priest. ²¹On that same
day you are to proclaim a sacred assembly for
yourselves; you must not do your daily work.
This is a rule binding on your descendants
for all time wherever you live.

²²When you reap the harvest in your land,
do not reap right up to the edges of your
field or gather the gleanings of your crop.
Leave them for the poor and for the alien. I
am the LORD your God.

²³When the LORD spoke to Moses he said:
²⁴Tell the Israelites that in the seventh
month they are to keep the first day as a day
of solemn abstinence from work, a day of
remembrance and acclamation, of sacred assembly. ²⁵They must not do their daily work,
but are to present a food-offering to the
LORD.

²⁶When the LORD spoke to Moses he said:
²⁷Further, the tenth day of this seventh
month is the Day of Atonement. There is to
be a sacred assembly; you yourselves must
fast and present a food-offering to the LORD.
²⁸On that day you are to do no work because
it is a day of expiation, on which expiation is
made for you before the LORD your God.
²⁹Everyone who does not fast on that day
must be cut off from his father's kin, ³⁰and
everyone who does any work on that day I
shall root out from among them. ³¹Do no
work whatsoever; it is a rule binding on your
descendants for all time wherever you live.
³²It is for you a day of solemn abstinence
from work, and you must fast. From the evening of the ninth day to the following evening you are to keep your sabbath rest.

³³The LORD told Moses ³⁴to say to the Israelites: On the fifteenth day of this seventh
month the LORD's pilgrim-feast of Booths begins, and it lasts for seven days. ³⁵On the first
day there is to be a sacred assembly; you are
not to do your daily work. ³⁶For seven days
present a food-offering to the LORD; on the
eighth day there will be a sacred assembly,

and you are to present a food-offering to the
LORD. It is the closing ceremony; you must
not do your daily work.

³⁷These are the appointed seasons of the
LORD which you are to proclaim as sacred
assemblies for presenting food-offerings to
the LORD, whole-offerings and grain-offerings, shared-offerings and drink-offerings,
each on its day, ³⁸besides the LORD's sabbaths
and all your gifts, your votive offerings and
your freewill-offerings to the LORD.

³⁹Further, from the fifteenth day of the
seventh month, when the harvest has been
gathered, you are to keep the LORD's pilgrim-
feast for seven days. The first day is a day of
solemn abstinence from work and so is the
eighth day. ⁴⁰On the first day take the fruit
of citrus trees, palm-fronds, and leafy
branches, and willows from the riverside,
and rejoice before the LORD your God for
seven days. ⁴¹You are to keep this as a pilgrim-feast in the LORD's honour for seven
days every year. It is a rule binding for all
time on your descendants; in the seventh
month you are to hold this pilgrim-feast.
⁴²You are to live in booths for seven days, all
who are native Israelites, ⁴³so that your descendants may be reminded how I made the
Israelites live in booths when I brought them
out of Egypt. I am the LORD your God.

⁴⁴Thus Moses announced to the Israelites
the appointed seasons of the LORD.

24 WHEN the LORD spoke to Moses he
said: ²Order the Israelites to bring
pure oil of pounded olives ready for the regular mounting of the lamp ³outside the curtain of the Testimony in the Tent of Meeting.
Aaron must keep the lamp in trim regularly
from dusk to dawn before the LORD: this is
a rule binding on your descendants for all
time. ⁴The lamps on the lampstand, ritually

23:27 **Atonement:** or Expiation.   23:34 **Booths:** or
Tabernacles.   23:40 **willows:** or poplars.

23.16 n. This observance was of the wheat harvest in May or June. **22:** See 19.9–10. **23:** See v. 9 n. **24–25:**
The new year day. It varies in biblical calendars, at times in the fall, and at times in the spring (see Exod. 12.2 n.).
26–32: The ritual is outlined in ch. 16. **34:** *Booths:* see Exod. 23.16 n. **43:** An old Canaanite agricultural festival
is here connected with the LORD's gracious deliverance of Israel: the harvester's temporary shelter imitates the
dwellings in the wilderness (compare Exod. 12.11–13 n., 15 n.). Thus, that great event was to be "relived"
annually (compare Exod. 13.8 n.).
   24.1–9: Regulations concerning the sanctuary. This belongs topically with the instructions to the priests
found in chs. 21–22; the concern with the calendar (ch. 23) resumes in ch. 25. Chapter 24 is possibly a priestly
addition to the Holiness Code (see 17.1–26.46 n.). **3:** *From dusk to dawn:* may reflect a change from an earlier

clean, must be regularly kept trimmed by him before the LORD.

5 You are to take flour and bake it into twelve loaves, two tenths of an ephah to each. 6 Arrange them in two rows, six to a row on the table, ritually clean, before the LORD. 7 Sprinkle pure frankincense on the rows, and this will be a token of the bread, offered to the LORD as a food-offering. 8 Regularly, sabbath after sabbath, it is to be arranged before the LORD as a gift from the Israelites. This is a covenant for ever; 9 it is the privilege of Aaron and his sons, and they are to eat the bread in a holy place, because it is the holiest of holy-gifts. It is his due out of the food-offerings of the LORD for all time.

10–11 In the Israelite camp there was a certain man whose mother was an Israelite and his father an Egyptian; his mother's name was Shelomith daughter of Dibri of the tribe of Dan. He went out and, becoming involved in a brawl with an Israelite of pure descent, he uttered the holy name in blasphemy. He was brought to Moses, 12 and put in custody until the LORD's will should be made clear to them.

13 When the LORD spoke to Moses he said: 14 The man who blasphemed is to be taken outside the camp, and let everyone who heard him lay a hand on his head, and let the whole community stone him to death. 15 Say to the Israelites: When anyone, whoever he is, blasphemes his God, he must accept responsibility for his sin. 16 Whoever utters the name of the LORD must be put to death. The whole community must stone him; whether alien or native, if he utters the name, he must be put to death.

17 If one person strikes another and kills him, he must be put to death. 18 Whoever strikes an animal and kills it is to make restitution, life for life. 19 If anyone injures and disfigures a fellow-countryman, it must be done to him as he has done: 20 fracture for fracture, eye for eye, tooth for tooth; the injury and disfigurement that he has inflicted on another must in turn be inflicted on him.

21 Whoever strikes and kills an animal is to make restitution, but whoever strikes a man and kills him must be put to death. 22 You must have one and the same law for resident alien and native Israelite. For I am the LORD your God.

23 Moses spoke thus to the Israelites, and they took the man who had blasphemed out of the camp and stoned him to death. The Israelites did as the LORD had commanded Moses.

25 WHEN the LORD spoke to Moses on Mount Sinai he told him 2 to say to the Israelites: When you enter the land which I am giving you, the land must keep sabbaths to the LORD. 3 For six years you may sow your fields and prune your vineyards and gather the harvest, 4 but in the seventh year the land is to have a sabbatical rest, a sabbath to the LORD. You are not to sow your field or prune your vineyard; 5 you are not to harvest the crop that grows from fallen grain, or gather in the grapes from the unpruned vines. It is to be a year of rest for the

---

practice in which the lamp did not burn to dawn (1 Sam. 3.4). **5:** *Twelve:* one for each of the twelve tribes of Israel. **7:** *Token:* and hence to be burned at the weekly renewal of the bread (compare 2.1–3). Topically, vv. 5–9 belong with the instructions for the priests in 6.14–23.

24.10–16: An instance of contempt for God (blasphemy). The intent is not only to provide legislation through a precedent-setting case, but also to recall how aliens were protected under law, and their near equality to the native (16.29; 17.8–16; 19.33–34). **11:** *Blasphemy* was cursing God, or showing contempt for the deity by word or action (see Num. 15.30–31; compare Isa. 36.18–20; 37.6). Blasphemy is extended in v. 16 to the mere pronunciation of the divine name, Yahweh. **13–15:** Compare Deut. 17.2–7.

24.17–22: The law of retaliation, topically related to vv. 10–16 by the theme of capital punishment and equality under the law. **19–20:** See Exod. 21.23–25 n.

25.1–55: The sabbatical and jubilee years. The former celebration (vv. 2–7) symbolizes the LORD's ultimate ownership of the land; the latter (vv. 8–34) attempts to prevent the growth of economic classes. **1:** That this legislation is allocated to *Sinai,* rather than to the Tent of Meeting (1.1 and subsequent chapter headings), suggests not only its original independence of the present context but also its importance in the opinion of those who transmitted it. The legislation assumes the settlement of Israel in Canaan and subsequent economic abuses. **4:** The application of the *sabbatical rest* notion to the *sabbath* of the *land* introduces a dimension absent from land. ⁶Yet what the land itself produces in the sabbath year will be food for you, for your male and female slaves, for your hired man, and for the stranger lodging under your roof, ⁷for your cattle and for the wild animals in your country. Everything it produces may be used for food.

⁸You are to count off seven sabbaths of years, that is seven times seven years, forty-nine years, ⁹and in the seventh month on the tenth day of the month, on the Day of Atonement, you are to send the ram's horn throughout your land to sound a blast. ¹⁰Hallow the fiftieth year and proclaim liberation in the land for all its inhabitants. It is to be a jubilee year for you: each of you is to return to his holding, everyone to his family. ¹¹The fiftieth year is to be a jubilee for you: you are not to sow, and you are not to harvest the self-sown crop, or gather in the grapes from the unpruned vines, ¹²for it is a jubilee, to be kept holy by you. You are to eat the produce direct from the land.

¹³In this year of jubilee every one of you is to return to his holding. ¹⁴When you sell or buy land amongst yourselves, neither party must exploit the other. ¹⁵You must pay your fellow-countryman according to the number of years since the jubilee, and he must sell to you according to the remaining number of annual crops. ¹⁶The more years there are to run, the higher the price; the fewer the years, the lower, because what he is selling you is a series of crops. ¹⁷You must not victimize one another, but fear your God, because I am the LORD your God. ¹⁸Observe my statutes, keep my judgements, and carry them out; and you will live without any fear in the land. ¹⁹The land will yield its harvest; you will eat your fill and live there secure. ²⁰If you ask what you are to eat during the seventh year, seeing that you will neither sow nor gather the harvest,

²¹I shall ordain my blessing for you in the sixth year and the land will produce a crop sufficient for three years. ²²When you sow in the eighth year, you will still be eating from the earlier crop; you will eat the old until the new crop is gathered in the ninth year.

²³No land may be sold outright, because the land is mine, and you come to it as aliens and tenants of mine. ²⁴Throughout the whole land you hold, you must allow a right of redemption over land which has been sold.

²⁵If one of you is reduced to poverty and sells part of his holding, his next-of-kin who has the duty of redemption may come and redeem what his kinsman has sold. ²⁶When a man has no such next-of-kin and himself becomes able to afford its redemption, ²⁷he must take into account the years since the sale and repay the purchaser the balance up to the jubilee. Then he may return to his holding. ²⁸But if the man cannot afford to buy back the property, it remains in the hands of the purchaser till the jubilee year. It then reverts to the original owner, and he can return to his holding.

²⁹When a man sells a dwelling-house in a walled town, he must retain the right of redemption till a full year has elapsed after the sale; for that time he has the right of redemption. ³⁰If it is not redeemed before a full year is out, the house in the walled town will belong for ever to the buyer and his descendants; it does not revert to its former owner at the jubilee. ³¹But houses in unwalled hamlets are to be treated as property in the open country: the right of redemption will hold good, and in any case the house reverts at the jubilee.

³²Levites are to have the perpetual right to

25:9 **Atonement:** *or* Expiation.   25:30 **walled:** *so Gk; Heb.* unwalled.

the form of the regulation given in Exod. 23.10–11. **6:** Permission for the owner to benefit from the land also differs from Exod. 23.10–11 and may be a concession to economic necessity or to the impossibility of strict enforcement. **8–12:** A brief summary of the jubilee regulation. **9:** *Day of Atonement:* see 16.29 n. *Ram's horn:* in Heb. *yobhel,* whence the English word "jubilee." The horn was blown to announce the celebration (compare Exod. 19.16 n.). **10:** "Sale" or "lease" of land was not in perpetuity; rather, land was to return to the original owner at the jubilee. This is expanded in vv. 23–28. **15–16:** In addition to area and fertility, the value of land to be leased depended on the duration of the contract, the maximum being until the next jubilee. **23:** The LORD had given the land to Israel freely, not through merit (Deut. 9.1–6) and hence Israel may not use it for unrestrained personal gain. The people are only *tenants* dependent upon the LORD's land. **29–31:** City property is exempted from the law of redemption. **32–34:** The Levites, having no tribal territory of their own (Num. 18.20–24; 35.1–8; Deut. 10.8–9; see Gen. 34.1–31 n.), must be protected from dispossession more rigidly redeem houses which they hold in towns belonging to them. [33] If one of the Levites does not redeem his house in such a town, then it will still revert to him at the jubilee, because the houses in Levite towns are their holding in Israel. [34] The common land surrounding their towns cannot be sold, because it is their property in perpetuity.

[35] If your brother-Israelite is reduced to poverty and cannot support himself in the community, you must assist him as you would an alien or a stranger, and he will live with you. [36] You must not charge him interest on a loan, either by deducting it in advance from the capital sum, or by adding it on repayment. Fear your God, and let your brother live with you; [37] do not deduct interest when advancing him money, or add interest to the payment due for food supplied on credit. [38] I am the LORD your God who brought you out of Egypt to give you Canaan and to become your God.

[39] If your fellow-countryman is reduced to poverty and sells himself to you, you must not use him to work for you as a slave. [40] His status will be that of a hired man or a stranger lodging with you; he will work for you only until the jubilee year. [41] He will then leave your service, with his children, and go back to his family and to his ancestral property: [42] because they are my slaves whom I brought out of Egypt, they must not be sold as slaves are sold. [43] You must not work him ruthlessly, but you are to fear your God. [44] Such slaves as you have, male or female, should come from the nations round about you; from them you may buy slaves. [45] You may also buy the children of those who have settled and lodge with you and such of their family as are born in your land. These may become your property, [46] and you may leave them to your sons after you; you may use them as slaves permanently. But your fellow-Israelites you must not work ruthlessly.

[47] If an alien or a stranger living among you becomes rich, and one of your fellow-countrymen becomes poor and sells himself to the alien or stranger or to a member of some alien family, [48] he is to keep the right of redemption after he has sold himself. One of his brothers may redeem him, [49] or his uncle, his cousin, or any blood relation of his family, or, if he has the means, he may redeem himself. [50] He and his purchaser together must reckon from the year when he sold himself to the year of jubilee, and the price will be adjusted to the number of years. His period of service with his owner will be reckoned at the rate of a hired man. [51] If there are still many years to run to the year of jubilee, he must pay for his redemption a proportionate amount of the sum for which he sold himself; [52] if there are only a few, he is to reckon and repay accordingly. [53] He will have the status of a labourer hired from year to year, and you must not let him be worked ruthlessly by his owner. [54] If the man is not redeemed in the intervening years, he and his children must be released in the year of jubilee; [55] for it is to me that the Israelites are slaves, my slaves whom I brought out of Egypt. I am the LORD your God.

26 You MUST not make idols for yourselves or erect carved images or sacred pillars; you must not put a stone carved figure on your land to worship, because I am the LORD your God. [2] You must keep my sabbaths and revere my sanctuary. I am the LORD.

[3] If you conform to my statutes, if you observe and carry out my commandments, [4] I shall give you rain at the proper season; the land will yield its produce and the trees of the countryside their fruit. [5] Threshing will last till vintage, and vintage till sowing; you will eat your fill and live secure in your land.

[6] I shall give peace in the land, and you will lie down to sleep with none to terrify you. I shall rid the land of beasts of prey and it will not be ravaged by the sword. [7] You will put

---

25:33 **does not redeem:** so Lat.; Heb. redeems. **in such a town:** so Gk; Heb. and such a town.   25:35 **as you would:** Gk as; Heb. omits.

---

than the general population. **38:** Just as the LORD aided the landless, alien Hebrews in Egypt, so must they respond to the needs of those around them. See 18.2 n.; Deut. 5.12–15. **42–43:** Members of the community are, like land (v. 23 n.), the possession of the LORD. **44–46:** There are striking differences between the legislation here and that of Exod. 21.1–11. **47–48:** On the status of aliens under Israelite law, see 24.10–16 n.

26.1–46: The consequence of obedience or disobedience. This conclusion of the Holiness Code (see 17.1–26.46 n.) is patterned after ancient Near Eastern contracts which conclude with a list of curses against those who disregard their stipulations. **1–2:** This appears to be either an isolated fragment or the conclusion your enemies to flight and they will fall in battle before you. ⁸ Five of you will give chase to a hundred and a hundred of you chase ten thousand; so will the enemy fall by your sword. ⁹ I shall look upon you with favour, making you fruitful and increasing your numbers; I shall give full effect to my covenant with you. ¹⁰ Your harvest will last you in store until you have to clear out the old to make room for the new. ¹¹ I shall establish my Tabernacle among you and never spurn you. ¹² I shall be ever present among you; I shall become your God and you will become my people. ¹³ I am the Lord your God who brought you out of Egypt to be slaves there no longer; I broke the bars of your yoke and enabled you to walk erect.

¹⁴ But if you do not listen to me, if you fail to keep all these commandments, ¹⁵ if you reject my statutes, spurn my judgements, and fail to obey all my commandments, and if you break my covenant, ¹⁶ then assuredly this is what I shall do to you: I shall bring upon you sudden terror, wasting disease, recurrent fever, and plagues that dim the sight and cause the appetite to fail. You will sow your seed to no purpose, for your enemies will eat the crop. ¹⁷ I shall set my face against you, and you will be routed by your enemies. Those that hate you will hound you, and you will run when there is no one pursuing.

¹⁸ If after all this you will not listen to me, I shall go on to punish you seven times over for your sins. ¹⁹ I shall break down your stubborn pride. I shall make the sky above you like iron, the earth beneath you like bronze. ²⁰ Your strength will be spent in vain; your land will not yield its produce, nor the trees in it their fruit.

²¹ If you still defy me and refuse to listen, I shall increase your calamities seven times, as your sins deserve. ²² I shall send wild beasts in among you; they will tear your children from you, destroy your cattle, and bring your numbers low, until your roads are deserted. ²³ If after all this you have not learnt discipline but still defy me, ²⁴ I in turn shall show hostility to you and scourge you seven times over for your sins. ²⁵ I shall bring the sword against you to avenge the covenant; you will

be herded into your cities, where I shall send pestilence among you, and you will be given into the clutches of the enemy. ²⁶ I shall cut short your daily bread until ten women can bake your bread in a single oven; they will dole it out by weight, and though you eat, you will not be satisfied.

²⁷ If in spite of this you do not listen to me and still oppose me, ²⁸ I shall oppose you in anger, and I myself shall punish you seven times over for your sins. ²⁹ Instead of meat you will eat your sons and your daughters. ³⁰ I shall destroy your shrines and demolish your incense-altars. I shall pile your corpses on your lifeless idols, and I shall spurn you. ³¹ I shall make your cities desolate and lay waste your sanctuaries; I shall not accept the soothing odour of your offerings. ³² I shall destroy your land, and the enemies who occupy it will be appalled. ³³ I shall scatter you among the heathen, pursue you with drawn sword; your land will be desert and your cities heaps of rubble. ³⁴ Then, all the time that it lies desolate, while you are in exile among your enemies, your land will enjoy its sabbaths to the full. ³⁵ All the time of its desolation it will have the sabbath rest which it did not have while you were living there. ³⁶ And I shall make those of you who are left in the land of your enemies so fearful that, when a leaf rustles behind them in the wind, they will run as if it were a sword after them; they will fall with no one in pursuit. ³⁷ Though no one pursues them they will stumble over one another, as if a sword were after them, and you will be helpless to make a stand against the enemy. ³⁸ You will meet your end among the heathen, and your enemies' land will swallow you up. ³⁹ Those who survive will pine away in an enemy land because of their iniquities, and also because of their forefathers' iniquities they will pine away just as they did.

⁴⁰ But though they confess their iniquity, their own and that of their forefathers, their treachery and their opposition to me, ⁴¹ I in my turn shall oppose them and carry them off into their enemies' land. If then their stubborn spirit is broken and they accept

26:26 I . . . daily bread: lit. I shall break your stick of bread.　　26:41 stubborn: lit. uncircumcised.

of ch. 25. 9: *Covenant*: see Exod. 20.1–21 n.; Gen. chs 15 and 17. 11–13: A summary of the fundamental goal of the foregoing legislation. See 9.5–6 n. 18: The Lord uses only that amount of discipline necessary to accomplish the task. On progressive intensification, see Amos 4.6–12. 21–39: See 26.1–46 n. While the language, in keeping with this form of document, seems extreme, it may, in part, be based upon the observation their punishment in full, [42] I shall remember my covenant with Jacob, my covenant also with Isaac, and my covenant with Abraham, and I shall remember the land. [43] The land, deserted by its people, will enjoy in full its sabbaths while it lies desolate; they will pay the penalty in full because they rejected my judgements and spurned my statutes. [44] Yet even then while they are in their enemies' land, I shall not have so rejected and spurned them as to bring them to an end and break my covenant with them, because I am the LORD their God. [45] I shall remember on their behalf the covenant with the former generation whom I brought out of Egypt in full sight of the nations, that I might be their God. I am the LORD.

[46] These are the statutes, the judgements, and the laws which the LORD established between himself and the Israelites through Moses on Mount Sinai.

27 WHEN the LORD spoke to Moses he said, [2] Speak to the Israelites and tell them: When anyone makes a special vow to the LORD which requires your valuation of living persons, [3] a male between twenty and sixty years old is to be valued at fifty silver shekels by the sacred standard. [4] If it is a female, she is to be valued at thirty shekels. [5] If it is someone between five years old and twenty, the valuation will be twenty shekels for a male and ten for a female. [6] If it is someone between a month and five years old, the valuation will be five silver shekels for a male and three for a female. [7] If it is someone over sixty and a male, the valuation will be fifteen shekels, but if a female, ten shekels. [8] If the person who is making the vow is too poor to pay the amount of your valuation, the person to be valued must be set before the priest, who will then set the value according to what the person who makes the vow

can afford: the priest will make the valuation. [9] If the vow concerns an animal acceptable as an offering to the LORD, then such a gift is holy to the LORD. [10] It must not be exchanged or substituted for another, whether good for bad or bad for good. But if a substitution is in fact made of one animal for another, then both the original animal and its substitute are holy. [11] If the vow concerns an unclean animal unacceptable as an offering to the LORD, then the animal is to be brought before the priest, [12] and he must value it whether good or bad. The priest's valuation is decisive; [13] in case of redemption the payment must be increased by one fifth.

[14] When a man dedicates his house as holy to the LORD, the priest is to judge whether it is good or bad, and the priest's valuation must be decisive. [15] If the donor redeems his house, he must pay the amount of the valuation increased by one fifth, and the house then reverts to him.

[16] If someone dedicates to the LORD part of his ancestral land, you are to value it according to the amount of seed-corn it can carry, at the rate of fifty shekels of silver for a homer of barley seed. [17] If he dedicates his land from the year of jubilee, it stands at your valuation; [18] but if he dedicates it after the year of jubilee, the priest must estimate the price in silver according to the number of years remaining until the next year of jubilee, and this will be deducted from your valuation. [19] If the one who dedicates his field should redeem it, he has to pay the amount of your valuation in silver, increased by one fifth, and it then reverts to him. [20] If he does not redeem it but sells the land to another, it is no longer redeemable; [21] when the land reverts at the year of jubilee, it will be like land that has been dedicated, holy to the

27:2 **makes a special:** or discharges a.

27.1–34: The fulfillment of religious vows. In return for success (Judg. 11.29–31) or recovery from misfortune (Ps. 66.13–15), a person would make a *special vow* of a sacrifice or donation to the sanctuary. **2:** *Valuation:* persons dedicated to perform minor cultic services (compare 1 Sam. 1.11, 21–28) could be released through a payment of money. **11:** The *unclean animal*, since it cannot be sacrificed, may be redeemed by the person who vowed it, but only at the expense of a penalty. **16:** The value of the land depends upon its productivity (the annual yield of barley). *Homer:* see p. xxviii. **17–19:** Priests, like lay persons (25.8–34) cannot gain permanent possession of others' land and thus impoverish them, even though the land has been vowed to the LORD. The land may be redeemed at penalty, or received back at the jubilee. This is in contrast to other ancient Near Eastern religions which allowed the temples to accumulate vast estates. **20–21:** If someone seeks to disregard a vow to the LORD by selling dedicated property, the punishment is forfeiture of any right to the

LORD. It will belong to the priest as his holding.

22 If someone dedicates to the LORD land which he has bought, land which is not part of his ancestral land, 23 the priest must estimate the amount of the value for the period until the year of jubilee, and the person must give the amount fixed as at that day; it is holy to the LORD. 24 At the year of jubilee the land reverts to the person from whom it was bought, whose holding it is. 25 Every valuation you make is to be made by the sacred standard at the rate of twenty gerahs to the shekel.

26 No one may dedicate to the LORD the firstborn of an animal which in any case has to be offered as a firstborn, whether from the herd or the flock. It is the LORD's. 27 If it is an unclean animal, he may redeem it at your valuation and add one fifth; but if it is not redeemed, it is to be sold at your valuation. 28 Nothing, however, which anyone devotes to the LORD irredeemably from his own property, whether a human being, an animal, or ancestral land, may be sold or redeemed. Everything so devoted is most holy to the LORD. 29 No human being thus devoted may be redeemed; he must be put to death.

30 Every tithe on land, whether from grain or from the fruit of a tree, belongs to the LORD; it is holy to the LORD. 31 If anyone wishes to redeem any of his tithe, he must pay its value increased by one fifth. 32 Every tenth creature that passes under the counting rod is holy to the LORD; this applies to all tithes of cattle and sheep. 33 There is to be no enquiry whether it is good or bad, and no substitution. If any substitution is made, then the tithe-animal and its substitute are both forfeit as holy; they cannot be redeemed.

34 These are the commandments which the LORD gave to Moses on Mount Sinai for the Israelites.

---

property. **25:** *Gerahs:* see p. xxvii. **26:** *Firstborn:* one cannot vow to the LORD that which already belongs to God (Exod. 13.11–13). **27:** *Unclean animal:* compare Exod. 13.13 for the case of a male donkey. Here, however, the beast may be kept by the sanctuary for sale. "Clean" firstborn could not be redeemed (Num. 18.17). **30:** The *tithe,* used to support the priesthood (Num. 18.21, 24; compare Lev. 25.32–34 n.) and the poor (Deut. 26.12), cannot be a vowed donation, for it is already an obligation. **31:** *Redeem any of his tithe:* the opportunity is here provided to pay in money rather than in kind. **32–33:** *Cattle and sheep:* these tithes are regarded as "devoted" to the LORD, and whatever was devoted (see v. 28) could not be "redeemed," that is, cash could not be substituted. (What was "devoted" was deemed as thereafter unsuitable for normal human use.) Moreover, the actual tenth animal was to be given; probably the intent was to prevent the gift of a sickly or emaciated animal rather than a healthy one. **32:** *Counting rod:* compare Jer. 33.13 for the method of counting the flock.

Numbers

This segment of Israel's early story is known in the Hebrew Bible as "In the wilderness" (a phrase occurring in the initial verse), a title more characteristic of the whole book than is "Numbers." The latter, found in the Greek and Latin translations, is derived from the various censuses and general arithmetical precision which characterize the work.

The book may be topically divided as follows: (1) preparation for departure from the sacred mountain, Sinai (1.1–10.10); (2) the journey to the oasis at Kadesh where, according to the priestly chronology, most of the "forty years" (33.38) in the wilderness were spent (10.11–12.16; compare 13.26); (3) the stay at Kadesh (13.1–20.21); (4) an abortive attempt to enter Canaan from the south (14.39–45; 21.1–3); (5) the detour around Edom through Transjordan to the eastern border of Canaan (20.22–36.13). With the departure from Sinai, the place of divine revelation shifts from the mountain to the movable Tent of Meeting.

The theme is repeated that the community was willing to shun its destiny through exchanging the perils of the wilderness journey for a return to the supposed safety of Egypt. Yet Israel was preserved by the grace of God in order that the ancient promise to the ancestors (see Introduction to the Pentateuch) would be realized.

Israel in the wilderness of Sinai

1 On the first day of the second month in the second year after the Israelites came out of Egypt, the LORD spoke to Moses in the Tent of Meeting in the wilderness of Sinai. He said: ²'Make a census of the whole community of Israel by families in the father's line, recording the name of every male person ³aged twenty years and upwards fit for military service. You and Aaron are to make a list of them by their tribal hosts, ⁴and to assist you you will have one head of family from each tribe. ⁵These are their names:

from Reuben, Elizur son of Shedeur;
⁶from Simeon, Shelumiel son of Zurishaddai;
⁷from Judah, Nahshon son of Amminadab;
⁸from Issachar, Nethanel son of Zuar;
⁹from Zebulun, Eliab son of Helon;
¹⁰from Joseph: of Ephraim, Elishama son of Ammihud;

of Manasseh, Gamaliel son of Pedahzur;
¹¹from Benjamin, Abidan son of Gideoni;
¹²from Dan, Ahiezer son of Ammishaddai;
¹³from Asher, Pagiel son of Ochran;
¹⁴from Gad, Eliasaph son of Reuel;
¹⁵from Naphtali, Ahira son of Enan.'
¹⁶These were the representatives of the community, chiefs of their fathers' tribes and heads of Israelite clans. ¹⁷Moses and Aaron took those men who had been indicated by name, ¹⁸and on the first day of the second month they summoned the whole community, and recorded every male person aged twenty years and upwards, registering their descent by families in the father's line, ¹⁹as the LORD had commanded Moses. He drew up the lists as follows in the wilderness of Sinai.

²⁰The tribal list of Reuben, Israel's eldest son, by families in the father's line, with the name of every male person aged twenty years

1:14 **Reuel:** *so Gk (cp. 2:14); Heb.* Deuel *(so also 7:42,47).*

1.1–54: A census of the tribes. In anticipation of departure from Sinai (10.11) and of armed opposition by the Canaanites (chs. 13–14), a survey of military potential is conducted. 1: *Second month:* one month since the construction of the Tabernacle (Exod. 40.2); on the priestly chronology, see Gen. 7.24 n. 5–15: Although Israel as a league of twelve tribes took shape only after the conquest of Canaan (Exod. 6.3 n.), here each tribe is represented as part of a united Israel in the wilderness. On the omission of Levi, see vv. 47–49 n. 6: *Simeon:* see Gen. 34.1–31 n. 10: *Joseph* is subdivided (Gen. 48.5 n.) in order to keep the total number of tribes at twelve and upwards fit for service, [21] the number in the list of the tribe of Reuben being forty-six thousand five hundred.

[22] The tribal list of Simeon, by families in the father's line, with the name of every male person aged twenty years and upwards fit for service, [23] the number in the list of the tribe of Simeon being fifty-nine thousand three hundred.

[24] The tribal list of Gad, by families in the father's line, with the names of all men aged twenty years and upwards fit for service, [25] the number in the list of the tribe of Gad being forty-five thousand six hundred and fifty.

[26] The tribal list of Judah, by families in the father's line, with the names of all men aged twenty years and upwards fit for service, [27] the number in the list of the tribe of Judah being seventy-four thousand six hundred.

[28] The tribal list of Issachar, by families in the father's line, with the names of all men aged twenty years and upwards fit for service, [29] the number in the list of the tribe of Issachar being fifty-four thousand four hundred.

[30] The tribal list of Zebulun, by families in the father's line, with the names of all men aged twenty years and upwards fit for service, [31] the number in the list of the tribe of Zebulun being fifty-seven thousand four hundred.

[32] The tribal lists of Joseph: that of Ephraim, by families in the father's line, with the names of all men aged twenty years and upwards fit for service, [33] the number in the list of the tribe of Ephraim being forty thousand five hundred; [34] that of Manasseh, by families in the father's line, with the names of all men aged twenty years and upwards fit for service, [35] the number in the list of the tribe of Manasseh being thirty-two thousand two hundred.

[36] The tribal list of Benjamin, by families in the father's line, with the names of all men aged twenty years and upwards fit for service, [37] the number in the list of the tribe of Benjamin being thirty-five thousand four hundred.

[38] The tribal list of Dan, by families in the father's line, with the names of all men aged twenty years and upwards fit for service, [39] the number in the list of the tribe of Dan being sixty-two thousand seven hundred.

[40] The tribal list of Asher, by families in the father's line, with the names of all men aged twenty years and upwards fit for service, [41] the number in the list of the tribe of Asher being forty-one thousand five hundred.

[42] The tribal list of Naphtali, by families in the father's line, with the names of all men aged twenty years and upwards fit for service, [43] the number in the list of the tribe of Naphtali being fifty-three thousand four hundred.

[44] These were the numbers recorded in the lists by Moses, Aaron, and the twelve chiefs of Israel, each representing one tribe and being the head of a family. [45] The total number of Israelites aged twenty years and upwards fit for service, recorded in the lists of fathers' families, [46] was six hundred and three thousand five hundred and fifty.

[47] A list of the Levites by their fathers' families was not made. [48] The LORD said to Moses, [49] 'You are not to record the total number of the Levites or make a census of them among the Israelites. [50] You are to put the Levites in charge of the Tabernacle of the Testimony with all its equipment and everything in it. They will carry the Tabernacle and all its equipment; they alone will be its attendants and pitch their tents round it. [51] The Levites will take the Tabernacle down when it is due to move and put it up when it halts; any lay person who comes near it must be put to death. [52] The other Israelites will pitch their tents, each tribal host in its proper camp and under its own standard. [53] But the Levites are to encamp round the Tabernacle of the Testimony, so that divine wrath may not come on the community of Israel; the Tabernacle of the Testimony will be in their charge.'

[54] The Israelites did everything exactly as the LORD had commanded Moses.

1:44 **each . . . family:** *prob. rdg (cp. Samar. and Gk);* *Heb.* each representing a family.

(compare Gen. 22.20–24 n.). **20–46:** A preserved ancient census, possibly taken well after the conquest of Canaan (Exod. 30.11–16 n.), is here presented as conducted at Sinai, for the wilderness could scarcely have supported this aggregate (v. 46) of persons for a sustained period (33.38). **47–49:** Contrast 3.14–39, where a census for nonmilitary purposes is taken. On the lack of a *list . . .*, see Gen. 49.5–7 n. **50–53:** On the duties of the Levites, see ch. 3.

2 The LORD said to Moses and Aaron, ²'The Israelites are to encamp each under his own standard by the emblems of his father's family; they are to pitch their tents round the Tent of Meeting, facing it.

³'In front of it, on the east, the division of Judah is to be stationed under the standard of its camp by tribal hosts. The chief of Judah will be Nahshon son of Amminadab. ⁴His host, with its members as listed, numbers seventy-four thousand six hundred men. ⁵Next to Judah the tribe of Issachar is to be stationed. Its chief will be Nethanel son of Zuar; ⁶his host, with its members as listed, numbers fifty-four thousand four hundred. ⁷Then the tribe of Zebulun; its chief will be Eliab son of Helon; ⁸his host, with its members as listed, numbers fifty-seven thousand four hundred. ⁹The number listed in the camp of Judah, by hosts, is one hundred and eighty-six thousand four hundred. They will be the first to march.

¹⁰'To the south the division of Reuben is to be stationed under the standard of its camp by tribal hosts. The chief of Reuben will be Elizur son of Shedeur; ¹¹his host, with its members as listed, numbers forty-six thousand five hundred. ¹²Next to him the tribe of Simeon is to be stationed. Its chief will be Shelumiel son of Zurishaddai; ¹³his host, with its members as listed, numbers fifty-nine thousand three hundred. ¹⁴Then the tribe of Gad: its chief will be Eliasaph son of Reuel; ¹⁵his host, with its members as listed, numbers forty-five thousand six hundred and fifty. ¹⁶The number listed in the camp of Reuben, by hosts, is one hundred and fifty-one thousand four hundred and fifty. They will be the second to march.

¹⁷'When the Tent of Meeting moves, the camp of the Levites must keep its station in the centre of the other camps; let them move in the order of their encamping, each man in his proper place under his standard.

¹⁸'To the west the division of Ephraim is to be stationed under the standard of its camp by tribal hosts. The chief of Ephraim will be Elishama son of Ammihud; ¹⁹his host, with its members as listed, numbers forty thousand five hundred. ²⁰Next to him the tribe of Manasseh is to be stationed. Its chief will be Gamaliel son of Pedahzur; ²¹his host, with its members as listed, numbers thirty-two thousand two hundred. ²²Then the tribe of Benjamin: its chief will be Abidan son of Gideoni; ²³his host, with its members as listed, numbers thirty-five thousand four hundred. ²⁴The number listed in the camp of Ephraim, by hosts, is one hundred and eight thousand one hundred. They will be the third to march.

²⁵'To the north the division of Dan is to be stationed under the standard of its camp by tribal hosts. The chief of Dan will be Ahiezer son of Ammishaddai; ²⁶his host, with its members as listed, numbers sixty-two thousand seven hundred. ²⁷Next to him the tribe of Asher is to be stationed. Its chief will be Pagiel son of Ochran; ²⁸his host, with its members as listed, numbers forty-one thousand five hundred. ²⁹Then the tribe of Naphtali: its chief will be Ahira son of Enan; ³⁰his host, with its members as listed, numbers fifty-three thousand four hundred. ³¹The number listed in the camp of Dan is one hundred and fifty-seven thousand six hundred. They will march last, under their standards.'

³²Those were the Israelites listed by their fathers' families. The total number in the camp, recorded by tribal hosts, was six hundred and three thousand five hundred and fifty.

³³The Levites were not included in the lists

2.1–34: The arrangement of the tribes for encampment or march. The model for this conception may possibly have been encampments around the sanctuary at one of the pilgrimage festivals (Deut. 16.16). **3:** The preferential position assigned to *Judah* may reflect its eminence in later times (compare Gen. 38.1–30 n.), especially its survival after other tribes had been overrun and exiled by the Assyrians in 721 B.C.E. *Nahshon:* his name is found in the list in 1.5–15. **4:** The numbers throughout this chapter conform with those in 1.20–46. **17:** The central position of the *Tent* reflected its importance as well as insured its protection. In an old version of the tradition (Exod. 33.7–11), it was located outside the encampment. **18:** On the position of *Ephraim* and Manasseh (v. 20), contrast the preferential place of Judah (v. 3 n.). Ephraim was the seat of the "apostate" cult of the golden calves (1 Kgs. 12.25–33) and Manasseh contained the capital city (Samaria) from which the "evil" kings of the northern tribes reigned (2 Kgs. 17.5–17). In the postexilic period, the Samaritans were regarded as racially impure by the priestly leadership of Judah (see 2 Kgs. 17.24).

with their fellow-Israelites, for so the LORD had commanded Moses. 34 The Israelites did everything just as the LORD had commanded Moses, pitching and breaking camp standard by standard, each man according to his family in his father's line.

3 THESE were the descendants of Aaron and Moses at the time when the LORD spoke to Moses on Mount Sinai. 2 The names of the sons of Aaron were Nadab the eldest, Abihu, Eleazar, and Ithamar. 3 These were the names of Aaron's sons, the anointed priests who had been installed in the priestly office. 4 Nadab and Abihu fell dead before the LORD because they had presented illicit fire before the LORD in the wilderness of Sinai; they left no sons. Eleazar and Ithamar continued to perform the priestly office during their father's lifetime. 5 The LORD said to Moses, 6 'Bring forward the tribe of Levi and appoint them to serve Aaron the priest and to minister to him. 7 They are to be in attendance on him and on the whole community before the Tent of Meeting, undertaking the service of the Tabernacle. 8 They are to be in charge of all the equipment in the Tent of Meeting, and be in attendance on the Israelites, undertaking the service of the Tabernacle. 9 You are to assign the Levites to Aaron and his sons as especially dedicated to him out of all the Israelites. 10 Commit the priestly office to Aaron and his line, and they are to perform its duties; any lay person who encroaches on it must be put to death.' 11 The LORD said to Moses, 12 'I take for myself, out of all the Israelites, the Levites as a substitute for the eldest male child of every woman; the Levites are to be mine. 13 For every eldest child, if a boy, became mine when I destroyed all the eldest sons in Egypt. So I have consecrated to myself all the firstborn in Israel, both man and beast. They are to be mine. I am the LORD.'

14 The LORD said to Moses in the wilderness of Sinai, 15 'Make a list of all the Levites by their families in the father's line, every male aged one month or more.'

16 Moses made a list of them in accordance with the command given him by the LORD. 17 Now these were the names of the sons of Levi.

Gershon, Kohath, and Merari. 18 Descendants of Gershon, by families: Libni and Shimei. 19 Descendants of Kohath, by families: Amram, Izhar, Hebron, and Uzziel. 20 Descendants of Merari, by families: Mahli and Mushi.

These were the families of Levi, by fathers' families.

21 Gershon: the family of Libni and the family of Shimei. These were the families of Gershon, 22 and the number of males in their list as drawn up, aged one month or more, was seven thousand five hundred. 23 The families of Gershon were stationed on the west, behind the Tabernacle. 24 Their chief was Eliasaph son of Lael, 25 and in the service of the Tent of Meeting they were in charge of the Tabernacle and the Tent, its covering, and the screen at the entrance to the Tent of Meeting, 26 the hangings of the court, the screen at the entrance to the court all round

3.1–51: The appointment and enumeration of the Levites. 4: See Lev. 10.1–7 and the notes. **6:** *To serve Aaron:* The differentiation between Aaron's family and the rest of the Levites arose historically in the postexilic period; here the priestly (Aaronite) writers ascribe it as commanded at Sinai. See Exod. 29.1–46 n. **10:** *Be put to death:* the warning about the unqualified persons who may be put to death is directed to Levitical groups who might become dissatisfied with the custodial duties here assigned to them, especially so since other ancient traditions know nothing of exclusive eminence for the family of Aaron (Deut. 33.8–11). For a controversy over this eminence, see ch. 16. **11–13:** This positive view of the Levites, seemingly old, is here placed in a context of subordination to the Aaronites. See also vv. 40–51 and the repetition in 8.15–19. **12:** Regulations concerning the *eldest male* are found in Exod. 13.2, 11–15 but there it is suggested that an animal *substitute* is in order (Exod. 13.13 n.). **13:** *When I destroyed:* see Exod. 13.14–15 n. **15:** Those below the age of *one month* are possibly excluded because of a high infant mortality rate. On the reason for the census, see vv. 40–48. **17–20:** See also Exod. 6.16–19. This division of Levi is functional, providing for a group for each of the four sides of the Tabernacle (vv. 23, 29, 35, 38). The Aaronites (v. 38) make a fifth group. See also 26.58. **23:** The reason for the unfavorable position given the descendants of *Gershon* is obscure (compare 2.18 n.). See Judg. 18.30–31, the idolatrous service instituted by the sons of Jonathan (son of Gershom), a group possibly to be the Tabernacle and the altar, and of all else needed for its maintenance.

27 Kohath: the family of Amram, the family of Izhar, the family of Hebron, the family of Uzziel. These were the families of Kohath, 28 and the number of males aged one month or more was eight thousand six hundred. They were the guardians of the holy things. 29 The families of Kohath were stationed on the south, at the side of the Tabernacle. 30 Their chief was Elizaphan son of Uzziel; 31 they were in charge of the Ark, the table, the lampstands and the altars, together with the sacred vessels used in their service, and the screen with everything needed for its maintenance. 32 The chief over all the chiefs of the Levites was Eleazar son of Aaron the priest, who was appointed overseer of those in charge of the sanctuary.

33 Merari: the family of Mahli, the family of Mushi. These were the families of Merari, 34 and the number of males in their list as drawn up, aged one month or more, was six thousand two hundred. 35 Their chief was Zuriel son of Abihail; they were stationed on the north, at the side of the Tabernacle. 36 The Merarites were in charge of the planks, bars, posts, and sockets of the Tabernacle, together with its vessels and all the equipment needed for its maintenance, 37 the posts, sockets, pegs, and cords of the surrounding court.

38 In front of the Tabernacle on the east, Moses was stationed, with Aaron and his sons, in front of the Tent of Meeting eastwards. They were in charge of the sanctuary on behalf of the Israelites; any lay person who came near would be put to death. 39 The number of Levites recorded by Moses on the list by families at the command of the LORD was twenty-two thousand males aged one month or more.

40 The LORD said to Moses, 'Make a list of all the male firstborn in Israel aged one month or more, and count the number of persons. 41 You are to reserve the Levites for me—I am the LORD—in substitution for the eldest sons of the Israelites, and in the same way the Levites' cattle in substitution for the firstborn cattle of the Israelites.' 42 As the LORD had commanded him, Moses made a list of all the eldest sons of the Israelites, 43 and the total number of firstborn males recorded by name in the register, aged one month or more, was twenty-two thousand two hundred and seventy-three.

44 The LORD said to Moses, 45 'Take the Levites as a substitute for all the eldest sons in Israel and the cattle of the Levites as a substitute for their cattle. The Levites are to be mine. I am the LORD. 46 The eldest sons in Israel will outnumber the Levites by two hundred and seventy-three. 47 This remainder must be redeemed, and for each of them you are to accept five shekels by the sacred standard, at the rate of twenty gerahs to the shekel; 48 give the money with which they are redeemed to Aaron and his sons.'

49 Moses took the money paid to redeem those who remained over when the substitution of Levites was complete. 50 The amount received was one thousand three hundred and sixty-five shekels of silver by the sacred standard. 51 In accordance with what the LORD had said, he gave the money to Aaron and his sons, doing what the LORD had commanded him.

4 The LORD said to Moses and Aaron, 2-3 'Among the Levites, make a count of the descendants of Kohath between the ages of thirty and fifty, by families in the father's line, comprising everyone who comes to take duty in the service of the Tent of Meeting. 4 'This is the service to be rendered by the Kohathites in the Tent of Meeting; it is most holy. 5 When the camp is due to move, let Aaron and his sons come and take down the curtain of the screen, and cover the Ark of the Testimony with it; 6 over this they are to

3:39 **Moses:** *so some MSS; others add* and Aaron.

identified with Gershonites. **29:** The descendants of *Kohath* are given charge of *the holy things* because they are the nearest relatives of the Aaronites (Exod. 6.18, 20). **32:** *Eleazar:* see Lev. 10.2 n. **39:** For a possible origin of this census figure, compare 1.20–46 n. The numbers given in vv. 22, 28, 34 actually total 22,300. In v. 46, the excess of firstborn sons in Israel over Levites is derived from the figure in v. 39. **40–48:** See vv. 11–13 n., 12 n. **41:** The substitution of the Levites' cattle is elsewhere unattested, and was not always practiced (18.17). **49–51:** Financial support of the cult rests on Mosaic authority. **50:** *Shekels:* see p. xxvii.

4.1–49: An alternative account of the assignment of Levitical duties, particularly in relation to preparation of the Tent for travel. **2–3:** On the priority of *Kohath,* see 3.29 n. The minimum age for service varied from time to time (8.24). **5:** *Curtain:* see Exod. 26.31–35. *Ark:* see Exod. 25.10 n. *Testimony:* see Exod. 25.16 n.

put a covering of dugong-hide and over that again a violet cloth all of one piece; they will then put its poles in place. 7 Over the table of the Bread of the Presence they are to spread a violet cloth and lay on it the dishes, saucers, and flagons, and the bowls for drink-offerings; the Bread regularly presented will also lie on it; 8 then they are to spread over them a scarlet cloth and over that a covering of dugong-hide, and put the poles in place. 9 They are to take a violet cloth and cover the lampstand, its lamps, tongs, firepans, and all the containers for the oil used in its service; 10 they are to put it with all its equipment in a sheet of dugong-hide slung from a pole. 11 Over the gold altar let them spread a violet cloth, cover it with a dugong-hide covering, and put its poles in place. 12 They are to take all the articles used for the service of the sanctuary, put them on a violet cloth, cover them with a dugong-hide covering, and sling them from a pole. 13 They are to clear the altar of the fat and ashes, spread a purple cloth over it, 14 and then lay on it all the equipment used in its service, the firepans, forks, shovels, tossing-bowls, and all the equipment of the altar, spread a covering of dugong-hide over it, and put the poles in place. 15 Once Aaron and his sons have finished covering the sanctuary and all the sacred equipment, when the camp is due to move, the Kohathites are to do the carrying; they must not touch the sacred objects, on pain of death. Those things are the load to be carried by the Kohathites, the things connected with the Tent of Meeting.

16 'Eleazar son of Aaron the priest is to have charge of the lamp oil, the fragrant incense, the regular grain-offering, and the anointing oil, with the general oversight of the whole Tabernacle and its contents, the sanctuary and its equipment.'

17 The LORD said to Moses and Aaron, 18 'You must not let the families of Kohath be wiped out and lost to the tribe of Levi. 19 If they are to live and not die when they approach the most holy things, this is what you

must do: let Aaron and his sons come and set each man to his appointed task and to his load, 20 but the Kohathites themselves must not enter to cast even a passing glance at the sanctuary, on pain of death.'

21 The LORD said to Moses, 22 'Number the Gershonites by families in the father's line. 23 Make a list of all those between the ages of thirty and fifty who come on duty to perform service in the Tent of Meeting.

24 'This is the service to be rendered by the Gershonite families, comprising their general duty and their loads. 25 They are to transport the hangings of the Tabernacle, the Tent of Meeting, its covering, that is the covering of dugong-hide which is over it, the screen at the entrance to the Tent of Meeting, 26 the hangings of the court, the screen at the entrance to the court surrounding the Tabernacle and the altar, their cords, and all the equipment for their service; and they are to perform all the tasks connected with them. These are the acts of service they have to render. 27 All the service of the Gershonites, their loads and their other duties, will be directed by Aaron and his sons; you will assign them the loads for which they will be responsible. 28 That is the service assigned to the Gershonite families in connection with the Tent of Meeting; Ithamar son of Aaron the priest is to be in charge of them.

29 'Make a list of the Merarites by families in the father's line, 30 all those between the ages of thirty and fifty, who come on duty to perform service in the Tent of Meeting.

31 'These are the loads for which they are to be responsible in virtue of their service in the Tent of Meeting: the planks of the Tabernacle with its bars, posts, and sockets, 32 the posts of the surrounding court with their sockets, pegs, and cords, and all that is needed for the maintenance of them; you should assign to each man by name the load for which he is responsible. 33 Those are the duties of the Merarite families in virtue of their service in the Tent of Meeting. Ithamar

4:20 **to cast . . . glance:** *lit.* to look as they swallow.

7: *Bread:* Exod. 25.30; Lev. 24.5–9. 9: *Lampstand:* see Exod. 25.31–40. 11: *Gold altar:* for incense (see Exod. 30.1–10). 13: *The altar:* for whole-offerings (Lev. 1.1–17), located in the court (Exod. 27.1–8). 15: It is only after the Aaronites have packed the furniture of the sanctuary and insulated it from touch and view with bags of skin that their nearest relatives (3.29 n.) are allowed to approach it. 17–20: The repeated warnings against the Kohathites' approaching the sacred objects (v. 15; compare 3.10, 38) possibly reflect an obscure power struggle within the priesthood (compare Lev. 10.2 n. and Exod. 32.26–29 n.); this section anticipates the challenge in ch. 16. 25: *Hangings:* see Exod. 26.1–6. *Tent:* see Exod. 26.1–37 n. 31: *Planks:* see Exod.

son of Aaron the priest shall be in charge of them.'

34 Moses and Aaron and the chiefs of the community made a list of the Kohathites by families in the father's line, 35 taking all between the ages of thirty and fifty who came on duty to perform service in the Tent of Meeting. 36 The number recorded by families in the lists was two thousand seven hundred and fifty. 37 This was the total number in the lists of the Kohathite families who did duty in the Tent of Meeting; they were recorded by Moses and Aaron as the LORD had commanded them through Moses.

38-39 The Gershonites between the ages of thirty and fifty, who came on duty for service in the Tent of Meeting, were recorded in lists by families in the father's line. 40 Their number, by families in the father's line, was two thousand six hundred and thirty. 41 This was the total recorded in the lists of the Gershonite families who came on duty in the Tent of Meeting and were recorded by Moses and Aaron as the LORD had commanded them.

42-43 The families of Merari, between the ages of thirty and fifty, who came on duty to perform service in the Tent of Meeting, were recorded in lists by families in the father's line. 44 Their number by families was three thousand two hundred. 45 These were recorded in the Merarite families by Moses and Aaron as the LORD had commanded them through Moses.

46 Thus Moses and Aaron and the chiefs of Israel made a list of all the Levites by families in the father's line, 47 between the ages of thirty and fifty years; these were all who came to perform their various duties and carry their loads in the service of the Tent of Meeting. 48 Their number was eight thousand five hundred and eighty. 49 They were recorded one by one by Moses at the command of the LORD, according to their general

duty and the loads they carried. For so the LORD had commanded Moses.

5 THE LORD said to Moses: 2 'Command the Israelites to expel from the camp everyone who suffers from a ritually unclean skin disease or a discharge, and everyone ritually unclean through contact with a corpse. 3 Put them outside the camp, both male and female, so that they do not defile your camps in which I dwell among you.' 4 The Israelites did this: they expelled them from the camp, doing exactly as the LORD had said when he spoke to Moses.

5 The LORD told Moses 6 to say to the Israelites: 'When anyone, man or woman, wrongs another and thereby breaks faith with the LORD, that person has incurred guilt which demands reparation. 7 He must confess the sin he has committed, make restitution in full with the addition of one fifth, and give it to the one to whom compensation is due. 8 If there is no next-of-kin to whom compensation can be paid, the compensation payable in that case is to be the LORD's, for the use of the priest, in addition to the ram of expiation with which the priest makes expiation for him.

9 'Every contribution made by way of holy-gift which the Israelites bring to the priest is to be the priest's. 10 The priest is to have the holy-gifts which a man gives; whatever is given to him is to be his.'

11 The LORD told Moses 12 to say to the Israelites: 'When a married woman goes astray and is unfaithful to her husband 13 by having sexual intercourse with another man, and this happens without the husband's knowledge, and without the woman being detected because, though she has been defiled, there is no direct evidence against her and she was

4:49 according ... carried: *prob. rdg; Heb. adds* and his registered ones. 5:3 your camps ... you: *so Syriac; Heb.* their camps ... among them.

26.15–30. 48: For a possible origin of this figure, compare 1.20–46 n.

5.1–6.27: An appendix of unrelated regulations, most of which clarify prior legislation. The Sinai narrative is nearing its completion: the writers here assemble all remaining material understood to have had its origin there. 2: *Skin disease:* see Lev. 13.1–46. *Discharge:* see Lev. 15.1–33. *Contact with a corpse:* 19.11–22; compare Lev. 21.1–12. 3: *Put them outside:* although earlier legislation commanded the unclean to "stay outside" (Lev. 13.46), it made no provision for their failure to do so. *Defile:* see Lev. 11.24–25 n. 5–8: Lev. 6.1–7 does not cover the case in which no one is present to receive compensation for property damage. Even if the injured party has no next-of-kin, the guilty person cannot escape obligation: payment must be made to the sanctuary. 11–31: Lev. 20.10 presupposes the presence of witnesses with evidence to prove adultery and justify the death penalty. Here, in the absence of such evidence, a divine indication of guilt or innocence was not caught in the act, [14] and when in such a case a fit of jealousy comes over the husband which makes him suspect his wife, whether she is defiled or not; [15] then the husband must bring his wife to the priest together with the prescribed offering for her, a tenth of an ephah of barley-meal. He must not pour oil on it or put frankincense on it, because it is a grain-offering for jealousy, a grain-offering of protestation conveying an imputation of guilt.

[16] 'The priest must bring her forward and set her before the LORD. [17] He is to take holy water in an earthenware vessel, and take dust from the floor of the Tabernacle and add it to the water. [18] He must set the woman before the LORD, uncover her head, and place the grain-offering of protestation in her hands; it is a grain-offering for jealousy. Holding in his own hand the ordeal-water which tests under pain of curse, [19] the priest must put the woman on oath and say to her, "If no man has had intercourse with you, if you have not gone astray and let yourself become defiled while owing obedience to your husband, then may your innocence be established by the ordeal-water. [20] But if, while owing him obedience, you have gone astray and let yourself become defiled, if any man other than your husband has had intercourse with you," [21] (the priest shall here put the woman on oath with an adjuration, and shall continue) "may the LORD make an example of you among your people in adjurations and in swearing of oaths by bringing upon you miscarriage and untimely birth; [22] and let this ordeal-water that tests under pain of curse enter your body, bringing upon you miscarriage and untimely birth." The woman must respond, "Amen, Amen."

[23] 'The priest is to write these curses on a scroll, wash them off into the ordeal-water, [24] and make the woman drink the ordeal-water; it will enter her body to test her. [25] The priest is to take the grain-offering for jealousy from the woman's hand, present it as a special gift before the LORD, and offer it at the altar. [26] He is to take a handful from the grain-offering by way of token, and burn it

at the altar. Finally he must make the woman drink the water. [27] If she has let herself become defiled and has been unfaithful to her husband, then, when the priest makes her drink the ordeal-water and it enters her body to test her, she will suffer a miscarriage or untimely birth, and her name will become an example in adjuration among her kin. [28] But if the woman has not let herself become defiled and is pure, then her innocence is established and she will bear her child.

[29] 'Such is the law for cases of jealousy, where a woman, owing obedience to her husband, goes astray and lets herself become defiled, [30] or where a fit of jealousy comes over a man which causes him to suspect his wife. When he sets her before the LORD, the priest must deal with her as this law prescribes. [31] No guilt will attach to the husband, but the woman must bear the penalty of her guilt.'

6 The LORD told Moses [2] to say to the Israelites: 'When anyone, man or woman, makes a special vow dedicating himself to the LORD as a Nazirite, [3] he is to abstain from wine and strong drink. These he must not drink, nor anything made from the juice of grapes; nor is he to eat grapes, fresh or dried. [4] During the whole term of his vow he must eat nothing that comes from the vine, nothing whatever, skin or seed. [5] During the whole term of his vow no razor is to touch his head; he must let his hair grow in long locks until he has completed the term of his dedication: he is to keep himself holy to the LORD. [6] During the whole term of his vow to the LORD he must not go near a dead person, [7] not even when it is his father or mother, brother or sister who has died; he must not make himself ritually unclean for them, because the Nazirite vow to his God is on his head. [8] He must keep himself holy to the LORD during the whole term of his Nazirite vow.

5:21 **by bringing ... birth:** *lit.* by making your thigh to fall and your belly to melt away; *similarly in verses 22 and 27.* 6:2 **Nazirite:** *that is* separated one *or* dedicated one. 6:4 **skin or seed:** *the two Heb. words are of uncertain meaning.*

sought through "trial by ordeal" (vv. 16–28). Such "ordeals" were widely practised in the ancient world. **15:** See Lev. 5.11. **17:** *Dust from the . . . Tabernacle:* a holy ingredient, meant to enhance respect for the oath to be taken (vv. 19–22). **18:** *Uncover her head:* a custom otherwise connected with mourning (Lev. 10.6). **6.3:** *Wine* may have been avoided because it could induce drunkenness, unbecoming in a holy person; see also Lev. 2.11 n.; 10.9 n. **5:** See, for example, Judg. 13.5 and 16.15–19. **6–7:** Compare Lev. 21.1–12.

9 'If someone suddenly falls dead by his side, touching him and thereby making his hair, which has been dedicated, ritually unclean, he must shave his head on the day when he becomes clean; he shall shave it on the seventh day. 10 On the eighth day he must bring two turtle-doves or two pigeons to the priest at the entrance to the Tent of Meeting. 11 The priest will offer one as a purification-offering and the other as a whole-offering and so make expiation for him for the sin he has incurred through contact with the dead body; he must consecrate his head afresh on that day. 12 The man must rededicate himself to the LORD for the full term of his vow and bring a yearling ram as a guilt-offering. The previous period is not to be included, because the hair which he dedicated became unclean.

13 'The law for the Nazirite, when the term of his dedication is complete, is this. He is to be brought to the entrance to the Tent of Meeting 14 and present his offering to the LORD: one yearling ram without blemish as a whole-offering, one yearling ewe without blemish as a purification-offering, one ram without blemish as a shared-offering, 15 and a basket of bread made of flour mixed with oil, and of wafers smeared with oil, both unleavened, together with the proper grain-offerings and drink-offerings. 16 The priest will present all these before the LORD and offer the man's purification-offering and whole-offering; 17 the ram he offers is a shared-offering to the LORD, together with the basket of unleavened bread and the proper grain-offering and drink-offering. 18 The Nazirite will shave his head at the entrance to the Tent of Meeting, take the hair which had been dedicated, and put it on the fire where the shared-offering is burning. 19 The priest will take the shoulder of the ram, after boiling it, and take also one unleavened loaf from the basket and one unleavened wafer, and put them on the palms of the Nazirite's hands, his

hair which had been dedicated having been shaved. 20 The priest will then present them as a dedicated portion before the LORD; these, together with the breast of the dedicated portion and the leg of the contribution, are holy and belong to the priest. When this has been done, the Nazirite is again free to drink wine.

21 'Such is the law for the Nazirite who has made his vow. Such is the offering he must make to the LORD for his dedication, apart from anything else that he can afford. He must carry out his vow in full according to the law governing his dedication.'

22 The LORD said to Moses, 23 'Say this to Aaron and his sons: These are the words with which you are to bless the Israelites:

24 May the LORD bless you and guard you;
25 may the LORD make his face shine on
   you and be gracious to you;
26 may the LORD look kindly on you and
   give you peace.

27 'So they are to invoke my name on the Israelites, and I shall bless them.'

7 ON the day that Moses completed the setting up of the Tabernacle, he anointed and consecrated it and all its equipment, along with the altar and all its vessels. 2 The chief men of Israel, heads of families — that is the tribal chiefs in charge of the enrolled men — came forward 3 and brought their offering before the LORD, six covered wagons and twelve oxen, one wagon from every two chiefs and from every chief one ox. These they brought forward before the Tabernacle; 4 and the LORD said to Moses, 5 'Accept these from them: they are for use in the service of the Tent of Meeting. Assign them to the Levites as their several duties require.'

6 So Moses accepted the wagons and oxen and assigned them to the Levites. 7 He gave two wagons and four oxen to the Gershonites as required for their service; 8 four wagons

9: The elapse of *seven days* is normal (19.11). 10: The sacrificial animals correspond to those required in some other cases of recovery from uncleanness (Lev. 12.8 and 14.22). 22–26: This blessing was likely part of the regular temple service (see Lev. 9.22). 25: *Make his face shine* is alternatively expressed in v. 26 as *look kindly on*. See Pss. 31.16 and 80.3.

7.1–89: Offerings of the tribal leaders at the consecration of the Tabernacle. Topically, this once independent unit belongs with Exod. ch. 40 which describes the completion of the sanctuary. The narrative in Lev. chs. 8–9, where the sacrificial ritual was initiated, does not reflect it; in the priestly chronology (see 1.1 n.), a month has now passed. The placement here is logical: this unit presupposes rules for lay persons bringing sacrifices (Lev. chs. 1–7) and the presence of Aaronites (Lev. chs. 8–9) and Levites (Num. ch. 3) to receive the and eight oxen to the Merarites as required for their service, in charge of Ithamar the son of Aaron the priest. 9 He gave none to the Kohathites because the service laid upon them was that of the holy things: these they had to carry on their shoulders.

10 When the altar was anointed, the chiefs brought their gift for its dedication and presented their offering before it. 11 The LORD said to Moses, 'Let the chiefs present their offering for the dedication of the altar one by one, on consecutive days.'

12 The chief who presented his offering on the first day was Nahshon son of Amminadab of the tribe of Judah. 13 His offering was one silver dish weighing a hundred and thirty shekels by the sacred standard, and one silver tossing-bowl weighing seventy, both full of flour mixed with oil as a grain-offering; 14 one gold saucer weighing ten shekels, filled with incense; 15 one young bull, one full-grown ram, and one yearling ram, as a whole-offering; 16 one he-goat as a purification-offering; 17 and two bulls, five full-grown rams, five he-goats, and five yearling rams, as a shared-offering. This was the offering of Nahshon son of Amminadab.

18 On the second day Nethanel son of Zuar, chief of Issachar, brought his offering. 19 He brought one silver dish weighing a hundred and thirty shekels by the sacred standard, and one silver tossing-bowl weighing seventy, both full of flour mixed with oil as a grain-offering; 20 one gold saucer weighing ten shekels, filled with incense; 21 one young bull, one full-grown ram, and one yearling ram, as a whole-offering; 22 one he-goat as a purification-offering; 23 and two bulls, five full-grown rams, five he-goats, and five yearling rams, as a shared-offering. This was the offering of Nethanel son of Zuar.

24 On the third day the chief of the Zebulunites, Eliab son of Helon, came. 25 His offering was one silver dish weighing a hundred and thirty shekels by the sacred standard, and one silver tossing-bowl weighing seventy, both full of flour mixed with oil as a grain-offering; 26 one gold saucer weighing ten shekels, filled with incense; 27 one young bull, one full-grown ram, and one yearling ram, as a whole-offering; 28 one he-goat as a purification-offering; 29 and two

bulls, five full-grown rams, five he-goats, and five yearling rams, as a shared-offering. This was the offering of Eliab son of Helon.

30 On the fourth day the chief of the Reubenites, Elizur son of Shedeur, came. 31 His offering was one silver dish weighing a hundred and thirty shekels by the sacred standard, and one silver tossing-bowl weighing seventy, both full of flour mixed with oil as a grain-offering; 32 one gold saucer weighing ten shekels, filled with incense; 33 one young bull, one full-grown ram, and one yearling ram, as a whole-offering; 34 one he-goat as a purification-offering; 35 and two bulls, five full-grown rams, five he-goats, and five yearling rams, as a shared-offering. This was the offering of Elizur son of Shedeur.

36 On the fifth day the chief of the Simeonites, Shelumiel son of Zurishaddai, came. 37 His offering was one silver dish weighing a hundred and thirty shekels by the sacred standard, and one silver tossing-bowl weighing seventy, both full of flour mixed with oil as a grain-offering; 38 one gold saucer weighing ten shekels, filled with incense; 39 one young bull, one full-grown ram, and one yearling ram, as a whole-offering; 40 one he-goat as a purification-offering; 41 and two bulls, five full-grown rams, five he-goats, and five yearling rams, as a shared-offering. This was the offering of Shelumiel son of Zurishaddai.

42 On the sixth day the chief of the Gadites, Eliasaph son of Reuel, came. 43 His offering was one silver dish weighing a hundred and thirty shekels by the sacred standard, and one silver tossing-bowl weighing seventy, both full of flour mixed with oil as a grain-offering; 44 one gold saucer weighing ten shekels, filled with incense; 45 one young bull, one full-grown ram, and one yearling ram, as a whole-offering; 46 one he-goat as a purification-offering; 47 and two bulls, five full-grown rams, five he-goats, and five yearling rams, as a shared-offering. This was the offering of Eliasaph son of Reuel.

48 On the seventh day the chief of the Ephraimites, Elishama son of Ammihud, came. 49 His offering was one silver dish weighing a hundred and thirty shekels by the sacred standard, and one silver tossing-bowl weighing seventy, both full of flour mixed

offerings. **2**: *Enrolled*: in the census of ch. 1. **9**: *Holy things*: see 4.1–15. **11**: *Consecutive days*: the length and detail of the narrative which follows (12–83) suggest the importance of financial support for the cult and with oil as a grain-offering; [50] one gold saucer weighing ten shekels, filled with incense; [51] one young bull, one full-grown ram, and one yearling ram, as a whole-offering; [52] one he-goat as a purification-offering; [53] and two bulls, five full-grown rams, five he-goats, and five yearling rams, as a shared-offering. This was the offering of Elishama son of Ammihud.

[54] On the eighth day the chief of the Manassites, Gamaliel son of Pedahzur, came. [55] His offering was one silver dish weighing a hundred and thirty shekels by the sacred standard, and one silver tossing-bowl weighing seventy, both full of flour mixed with oil as a grain-offering; [56] one gold saucer weighing ten shekels, filled with incense; [57] one young bull, one full-grown ram, and one yearling ram, as a whole-offering; [58] one he-goat as a purification-offering; [59] and two bulls, five full-grown rams, five he-goats, and five yearling rams, as a shared-offering. This was the offering of Gamaliel son of Pedahzur.

[60] On the ninth day the chief of the Benjamites, Abidan son of Gideoni, came. [61] His offering was one silver dish weighing a hundred and thirty shekels by the sacred standard, and one silver tossing-bowl weighing seventy, both full of flour mixed with oil as a grain-offering; [62] one gold saucer weighing ten shekels, filled with incense; [63] one young bull, one full-grown ram, and one yearling ram, as a whole-offering; [64] one he-goat as a purification-offering; [65] and two bulls, five full-grown rams, five he-goats, and five yearling rams, as a shared-offering. This was the offering of Abidan son of Gideoni.

[66] On the tenth day the chief of the Danites, Ahiezer son of Ammishaddai, came. [67] His offering was one silver dish weighing a hundred and thirty shekels by the sacred standard, and one silver tossing-bowl weighing seventy, both full of flour mixed with oil as a grain-offering; [68] one gold saucer weighing ten shekels, filled with incense; [69] one young bull, one full-grown ram, and one yearling ram, as a whole-offering; [70] one he-goat as a purification-offering; [71] and two bulls, five full-grown rams, five he-goats, and five yearling rams, as a shared-offering. This was the offering of Ahiezer son of Ammishaddai.

[72] On the eleventh day the chief of the Asherites, Pagiel son of Ochran, came. [73] His offering was one silver dish weighing a hundred and thirty shekels by the sacred standard, and one silver tossing-bowl weighing seventy, both full of flour mixed with oil as a grain-offering; [74] one gold saucer weighing ten shekels, filled with incense; [75] one young bull, one full-grown ram, and one yearling ram, as a whole-offering; [76] one he-goat as a purification-offering; [77] and two bulls, five full-grown rams, five he-goats, and five yearling rams, as a shared-offering. This was the offering of Pagiel son of Ochran.

[78] On the twelfth day the chief of the Naphtalites, Ahira son of Enan, came. [79] His offering was one silver dish weighing a hundred and thirty shekels by the sacred standard, and one silver tossing-bowl weighing seventy, both full of flour mixed with oil as a grain-offering; [80] one gold saucer weighing ten shekels, filled with incense; [81] one young bull, one full-grown ram, and one yearling ram, as a whole-offering; [82] one he-goat as a purification-offering; [83] and two bulls, five full-grown rams, five he-goats, and five yearling rams, as a shared-offering. This was the offering of Ahira son of Enan.

[84] This was the gift from the chiefs of Israel for the dedication of the altar when it was anointed: twelve silver dishes, twelve silver tossing-bowls, and twelve gold saucers; [85] each silver dish weighed a hundred and thirty shekels, each silver tossing-bowl seventy shekels. The total weight of the silver vessels was two thousand four hundred shekels by the sacred standard. [86] There were twelve gold saucers full of incense, ten shekels each by the sacred standard: the total weight of the gold of the saucers was a hundred and twenty shekels. [87] The number of beasts for the whole-offering was twelve bulls, twelve full-grown rams, and twelve yearling rams, with the prescribed grain-offerings, and twelve he-goats for the purification-offering. [88] The number of beasts for the shared-offering was twenty-four bulls, sixty full-grown rams, sixty he-goats, and sixty yearling rams. This was the gift for the dedication of the altar when it was anointed. [89] When Moses entered the Tent of Meeting to speak with the LORD, he heard the voice

encourage imitation of the generosity of the tribal leaders. **89:** This appears to be a fragment with no relation to its present context. See Exod. 25.22.

8.1–9.14: Another collection of miscellaneous materials (see 5.1–6.27 n. for the reason). **1–4:** Belonging speaking from above the cover over the Ark of the Testimony from between the two cherubim: the voice spoke to him.

8 The LORD told Moses [2] to say to Aaron: 'When you put the seven lamps in position, see that they shed their light forwards in front of the lampstand.' [3] Aaron did this: he positioned the lamps so as to shed light forwards in front of the lampstand, as the LORD had instructed Moses. [4] The lampstand was made of beaten work in gold from stem to petals, made to match the pattern the LORD had shown Moses.

[5] The LORD said to Moses: [6] 'Separate the Levites from the rest of the Israelites and cleanse them ritually. [7] This is how the cleansing is to be done. Sprinkle lustral water over them; they are then to shave their whole bodies, wash their clothes, and so be cleansed. [8] Next, they must take a young bull as a whole-offering with its prescribed grain-offering, flour mixed with oil, while you take a second young bull as a purification-offering. [9] Bring the Levites before the Tent of Meeting and, when you have called the whole community of Israelites together, [10] bring the Levites before the LORD, and let the Israelites lay their hands on the Levites' heads. [11] Aaron must present the Levites before the LORD as a special gift from the Israelites, and they will be dedicated to the service of the LORD. [12] The Levites must lay their hands on the heads of the bulls, one bull to be offered as a purification-offering and the other as a whole-offering to the LORD, to make expiation for the Levites. [13] Then stand the Levites before Aaron and his sons, presenting them to the LORD as a special gift. [14] You thus separate the Levites from the rest of the Israelites, and they are to be mine.

[15] 'After this, the Levites may enter the Tent of Meeting to serve in it, ritually cleansed and presented as a special gift; [16] for out of all the Israelites they are assigned and dedicated to me. I have accepted them as mine in place of all that comes first from the womb, every first child among the Israelites;

[17] for every firstborn male creature, man or beast, among the Israelites is mine. On the day when I struck down every firstborn creature in Egypt, I consecrated all the firstborn of the Israelites to myself, [18] and I have accepted the Levites in their place. [19] I have assigned the Levites to Aaron and his sons, dedicated among the Israelites to perform the service of the Israelites in the Tent of Meeting and to make expiation for them; then no calamity will befall the Israelites should they come close to the sanctuary.'

[20] Moses and Aaron and the whole community of Israelites carried out all the commands the LORD had given to Moses for the dedication of the Levites. [21] The Levites purified themselves of sin and washed their clothes, and Aaron presented them as a dedicated gift before the LORD and made expiation for them, to cleanse them. [22] Then at last they went in to perform their service in the Tent of Meeting, before Aaron and his sons. Thus the commands the LORD had given to Moses concerning the Levites were all carried out.

[23] The LORD said to Moses, [24] 'As regards the Levites, they are to begin their active work in the service of the Tent of Meeting at the age of twenty-five. [25] At the age of fifty a Levite must retire from regular service and serve no longer. [26] He may continue to assist his fellow-Levites in attendance in the Tent of Meeting, but no longer perform regular service. That is how you are to arrange the duties of the Levites.'

9 In the first month of the second year after they came out of Egypt, the LORD spoke to Moses in the wilderness of Sinai. He said, [2] 'Let the Israelites prepare the Passover at the time appointed for it. [3] This is to be between dusk and dark on the fourteenth day of this month; keep it at this appointed time, observing every rule and custom proper to it.' [4] So Moses told the Israelites to prepare the Passover, [5] and they prepared it on the fourteenth day of the first month,

8:8 **as a whole-offering:** *prob. rdg; Heb. omits.*

topically with Exod. 25.31–40 and 37.17–24, this section specifies the orientation of the lamps. **5–26:** The consecration of the Levites. The material of ch. 3 is enlarged as the story moves from appointment to ordination. The procedure is similar to that for the Aaronites in Lev. ch. 8. **7:** *Shave . . . wash:* see Lev. 14.8 n. **10:** *Lay their hands:* thus the Levites become an offering brought by the people, a variation upon the theme that they are a substitute for the firstborn (vv. 16–18; 3.11–13). **13:** *Before Aaron:* see 3.6 n. **24:** *Twenty-five:* see 4.2–3 n. **9.1–14:** Provision for a delayed Passover celebration. **1:** *First month:* chronologically, this material, like ch. 7, belongs before 1.1 which is dated to the second month. **2–3:** See Exod. 12.1–10. **6:** For seven days between dusk and dark, in the wilderness of Sinai. The Israelites did everything exactly as the LORD had instructed Moses.

6 It happened that some men were ritually unclean through contact with a dead body and so could not keep the Passover on the right day. They came that day before Moses and Aaron 7 and said, 'We are unclean through contact with a dead body. Must we therefore be debarred from presenting the LORD's offering at its appointed time with the rest of the Israelites?' 8 Moses answered, 'Wait, and let me hear what command the LORD has for you.'

9 The LORD told Moses 10 to say to the Israelites: 'If any one of you or of your descendants is ritually unclean through contact with a dead body, or if he is far away on a journey, he must keep a Passover to the LORD none the less. 11 But in that case he is to prepare the victim in the second month, between dusk and dark on the fourteenth day. It must be eaten with unleavened bread and bitter herbs; 12 let nothing be left over till morning, and let no bone of it be broken. The Passover is to be kept exactly as the law prescribes. 13 The man who, being ritually clean and not absent on a journey, neglects to keep the Passover, will be cut off from his father's kin, because he has not presented the LORD's offering at its appointed time. That man must accept responsibility for his sin.

14 'When an alien is settled among you, he also is to keep the Passover to the LORD, observing every rule and custom proper to it. The same statute applies to you all, to alien and native-born alike.'

The journey from Sinai to Edom

15 ON the day when they set up the Tabernacle, that is the Tent of the Testimony, cloud covered it, and in the evening a brightness like fire appeared over it till morning. 16 So it was always: the cloud covered it by day and a brightness like fire by night. 17 Whenever the cloud lifted from the tent, the Israelites struck camp, and at the place where the cloud settled, there they pitched their camp. 18 At the command of the LORD they struck camp, and at his command they encamped again, and continued in camp as long as the cloud rested over the Tabernacle. 19 When the cloud stayed long over the Tabernacle, the Israelites kept the LORD's injunction and did not move; 20 and it was the same when the cloud continued over the Tabernacle only a few days: at the command of the LORD they remained in camp, and at his command they struck camp. 21 There were also times when the cloud continued only from evening till morning, and in the morning, when the cloud lifted, they moved on. Whether by day or by night, they moved as soon as the cloud lifted. 22 Whether it was for a day or two, for a month or longer, whenever the cloud stayed long over the Tabernacle, the Israelites remained where they were and did not move on; they did so only when the cloud lifted. 23 At the command of the LORD they encamped, and at his command they struck camp. They kept the LORD's injunction at the LORD's command, given through Moses.

10 The LORD said to Moses: 2 'Make two trumpets of beaten silver and use them for summoning the community and for breaking camp. 3 When both are sounded, the whole community is to muster before you at the entrance to the Tent of Meeting. 4 If a single trumpet is sounded, the chiefs who are heads of the Israelite clans will muster. 5 When a fanfare is sounded, those encamped on the east side are to move off. 6 When a second fanfare is sounded, those encamped on the south are to move off. A fanfare is the signal to move off. 7 When you convene the assembly, a trumpet-call must be sounded, not a fanfare. 8 This sounding of the trumpets is the duty of the Aaronite priests; let it be a rule binding for all time on your descendants.

9 'When you go into battle against an in-

9:16 **by day:** *so Gk; Heb. omits.*

after *contact with a dead body,* a person could not approach the Tabernacle (19.11–22). **6–8:** The tension between the laws of uncleanness and the command for each person to observe the Passover (Exod. 12.3) is resolved by a precedent placed in the time of Moses. **10:** *Away:* a possibility not covered by previous legislation. For similar extensions or liberalizations, indicative of the flexibility with which later generations viewed their laws, see 5.3 n., 5–8 n., 11–31 n. **13:** *Cut off:* see Lev. 7.21 n. **14:** See Exod. 12.43–49.

9.15–10.36: Preparation and departure from Sinai. The narrative has reached this point twice previously (see Exod. 23.20–33 n. and 33.1–23 n., plus Exod. 34.1–35 n.): it resumes from Exod. 40.38. **16:** *Cloud . . .*

vader and are hard pressed by him, sound a fanfare on the trumpets, and this will serve as a reminder of you before the LORD your God and you will be delivered from your enemies. 10 On your festal days and at your appointed seasons and on the first day of every month, sound the trumpets over your whole-offerings and your shared-offerings; the trumpets will be a reminder on your behalf before your God. I am the LORD your God.'

11 In the second year, on the twentieth day of the second month, the cloud lifted from the Tabernacle of the Testimony, 12 and the Israelites moved by stages from the wilderness of Sinai, until the cloud came to rest in the wilderness of Paran. 13 The first time that they broke camp at the command of the LORD given through Moses, 14 the standard of the division of Judah moved off in the lead with its tribal hosts: the host of Judah under Nahshon son of Amminadab, 15 the host of Issachar under Nethanel son of Zuar, 16 and the host of Zebulun under Eliab son of Helon. 17 Then the Tabernacle was taken down, and its bearers, the sons of Gershon and Merari, moved off.

18 Secondly, the standard of the division of Reuben moved off with its tribal hosts: the host of Reuben under Elizur son of Shedeur, 19 the host of Simeon under Shelumiel son of Zurishaddai, 20 and the host of Gad under Eliasaph son of Reuel. 21 The Kohathites, the bearers of the holy objects, moved off next, and on their arrival found the Tabernacle set up.

22 Thirdly, the standard of the division of Ephraim moved off with its tribal hosts: the host of Ephraim under Elishama son of Ammihud, 23 the host of Manasseh under Gamaliel son of Pedahzur, 24 and the host of Benjamin under Abidan son of Gideoni.

25 Lastly, the standard of the division of Dan, the rearguard of all the divisions, moved off with its tribal hosts: the host of Dan under Ahiezer son of Ammishaddai, 26 the host of Asher under Pagiel son of Och-

ran, 27 and the host of Naphtali under Ahira son of Enan.

28 This was the order of march for the Israelites, mustered in their hosts, and in this order they broke camp.

29 Moses said to Hobab his brother-in-law, son of Reuel the Midianite, 'We are setting out for the place which the LORD promised to give us. Come with us, and we shall deal generously with you, for the LORD has given an assurance of prosperity for Israel.' 30 But he replied, 'No, I would rather go to my own country and my own people.' 31 Moses said, 'Do not leave us, I beg you; for you know where we ought to camp in the wilderness, and you will be our guide. 32 If you will go with us, then all the prosperity with which the LORD favours us we shall share with you.'

33 Then they moved off from the mountain of the LORD and journeyed for three days, and the Ark of the Covenant of the LORD kept three days' journey ahead of them to find them a place to rest. 34 The cloud of the LORD was over them by day when they moved camp. 35 Whenever the Ark set out, Moses said,

'Arise, LORD, and may your enemies be
    scattered;
  may those hostile to you flee at your
    approach.'

36 Whenever it halted, he said,

'Rest, LORD of the countless thousands
    of Israel.'

11 THE people began complaining loudly to the LORD about their hardships, and when he heard he became angry. Fire from the LORD broke out among them, and raged on the outskirts of the camp. 2 Moses, when appealed to by the people, interceded with the LORD, and the fire died down. 3 They named that place Taberah, because

10:20 **Reuel:** *so Gk (cp. 2:14); Heb.* Deuel.
10:21 **holy objects:** *so Gk; Heb.* sanctuary.
11:3 **Taberah:** *that is* Burning.

fire: see Exod. 13.21 n. **10.13–27:** The order of the march follows the prescription of 2.3–31 and the responsibilities follow that of 4.1–33. **29:** The tradition here, different from later priestly versions, continues from Exod. 34.35. *Reuel:* see Exod. 18.1 n.

11.1–34: Rebellion in the wilderness. Despite Israel's certainty of God's presence and graciousness in granting the covenant (Exod. chs. 20–24) and in renewing it (Exod. ch. 34), doubts and complaints nevertheless arose at the first new difficulty. **1:** On *fire* as a means or symbol of divine punishment, see Lev. 10.1–2. **4:**

fire from the LORD had burned among them.

4 A mixed company of strangers had joined the Israelites, and these people began to be greedy for better things. Even the Israelites themselves with renewed weeping cried out, 'If only we had meat! 5 Remember how in Egypt we had fish for the asking, cucumbers and water-melons, leeks and onions and garlic. 6 Now our appetite is gone; wherever we look there is nothing except this manna.' 7 (The manna looked like coriander seed, the colour of bdellium. 8 The people went about collecting it to grind in handmills or pound in mortars; they cooked it in a pot and made it into cakes, which tasted like butter-cakes. 9 When dew fell on the camp at night, the manna would fall with it.) 10 Moses heard all the people lamenting in their families at the opening of their tents. The LORD became very angry, and Moses was troubled, 11 and said to the LORD, 'Why have you brought trouble on your servant? How have I displeased the LORD that I am burdened with all this people? 12 Am I their mother? Have I brought them into the world, and am I called on to carry them in my arms, like a nurse with a baby, to the land promised by you on oath to their fathers? 13 Where am I to find meat to give them all? They pester me with their wailing and their "Give us meat to eat." 14 This whole people is a burden too heavy for me; I cannot carry it alone. 15 If that is your purpose for me, then kill me outright: if I have found favour with you, spare me this trouble afflicting me.'

16 The LORD answered Moses, 'Assemble for me seventy of Israel's elders, men known to you as elders and officers in the community; bring them to the Tent of Meeting, and there let them take their place with you. 17 I shall come down and speak with you there. I shall withdraw part of the spirit which is conferred on you and bestow it on them, and they will share with you the burden of the people; then you will not have to bear it alone. 18 And say to the people: Sanctify yourselves in readiness for tomorrow; you will have meat to eat. You wailed in the LORD's hearing; you said, "If only we had meat! In Egypt we lived well." The LORD will give you meat and you will eat it. 19 Not for one day only, nor for two days, nor five, nor ten, nor twenty, 20 but for a whole month you will eat it until it comes out at your nostrils and makes you sick; because you have rejected the LORD who is in your midst, wailing in his presence and saying, "Why did we ever come out of Egypt?" '

21 Moses said, 'Here am I with six hundred thousand men on the march around me, and you promise them meat to eat for a whole month! 22 How can the sheep and oxen be slaughtered that would be enough for them? If all the fish in the sea could be caught, would they be enough?' 23 The LORD replied, 'Is there a limit to the power of the LORD? You will now see whether or not my words come true.'

24 Moses went out and told the people what the LORD had said. He assembled seventy men from the elders of the people and stationed them round the Tent. 25 Then the LORD descended in the cloud and spoke to him. He withdrew part of the spirit which had been conferred on Moses and bestowed it on the seventy elders; as the spirit alighted on them, they were seized by a prophetic ecstasy, for the first and only time.

26 Two men, one named Eldad and the other Medad, who had been enrolled with the seventy, were left behind in the camp. Though they had not gone out to the Tent, the spirit alighted on them none the less, and they were seized by prophetic ecstasy there in the camp. 27 A young man ran and told Moses that Eldad and Medad were in an ecstasy in the camp, 28 whereupon Joshua son of Nun, who had served since boyhood with Moses, broke in, 'Moses my lord, stop them!' 29 But

11:7 **bdellium:** *or* gum resin.

Strangers: see Exod. 12.38. *Greedy:* see Ps. 78.18. **6:** *Manna:* see Exod. 16.14–15, 31 nn. In another version, placed after the escape from Egypt (Exod. ch. 16), manna and meat (quails) are the LORD's response to a single demand for food. In its present setting, however, the story depicts Israel as increasingly inappreciative: the quails are granted only when the manna is declared insufficient. See Exod. 16.6–8 n. **14–17, 24b–30:** The intensification of the rebellion provides the opportunity for introduction of a new theme: the sharing of Moses' responsibility as leader. The elders, who must have exercised tribal leadership since antiquity, are here said to derive their power from and to remain under the authority of the community's religious leadership. Compare Exod. 18.13–26 n. **16:** *Seventy:* as in Exod. 24.1; see Gen. 46.27 n. **18–24a, 31–34:** Continuation of the food tradition. **26:** *Out to the Tent:* see 2.17 n. for various traditions as to its location. **27–30:** *Prophets,* deriving

Moses said to him, 'Are you jealous on my account? I wish that all the LORD's people were prophets and that the LORD would bestow his spirit on them all!' ³⁰ Moses then rejoined the camp with the elders of Israel.

³¹ There sprang up a wind from the LORD, which drove quails in from the west, and they were flying all round the camp for the distance of a day's journey, three feet above the ground. ³² The people were busy gathering quails all that day and night, and all next day, and even those who got least gathered ten homers of them. They spread them out to dry all about the camp. ³³ But the meat was scarcely between their teeth, and they had not so much as bitten it, when the LORD's anger flared up against the people and he struck them with a severe plague. ³⁴ That place came to be called Kibroth-hattaavah, because there they buried the people who had been greedy for meat.

³⁵ From Kibroth-hattaavah the Israelites went on to Hazeroth, and while they were

12 there, ¹ Miriam and Aaron began to find fault with Moses. They criticized him for his Cushite wife (for he had married a Cushite woman), ²⁻³ and they complained, 'Is Moses the only one by whom the LORD has spoken? Has he not spoken by us as well?' — though Moses was a man of great humility, the most humble man on earth. But the LORD heard them ⁴ and at once said to Moses, Aaron, and Miriam, 'Go out all three of you to the Tent of Meeting.' When they went out, ⁵ the LORD descended in a pillar of cloud and, standing at the entrance to the tent, he summoned Aaron and Miriam. The two of them came forward, ⁶ and the LORD said,

'Listen to my words.
If he were your prophet and nothing

more,
I would make myself known to him in a vision,
I would speak with him in a dream.
⁷ But my servant Moses is not such a prophet;
of all my household he alone is faithful.
⁸ With him I speak face to face,
openly and not in riddles.
He sees the very form of the LORD.
How dare you speak against my servant Moses?'

⁹ With his anger still hot against them, the LORD left them; ¹⁰ and as the cloud moved from the tent, there was Miriam, her skin diseased and white as snow. When Aaron, turning towards her, saw her skin diseased, ¹¹ he said to Moses, 'My lord, do not make us pay the penalty of sin, foolish and wicked though we have been. ¹² Let her not be like something stillborn, whose flesh is half eaten away when it comes from the womb.' ¹³ So Moses cried, 'LORD, not this! Heal her, I pray.' ¹⁴ The LORD answered, 'Suppose her father had spat in her face, would she not have to remain in disgrace for seven days? Let her be confined outside the camp for seven days and then be brought back.' ¹⁵ So Miriam was shut outside for seven days, and the people did not strike camp until she was brought back. ¹⁶ After that they moved on from Hazeroth and pitched camp in the wilderness of Paran.

13 THE LORD said to Moses, ² 'Send men out to explore Canaan, the land which I am going to give to the Israelites;

11:31 **three feet:** *lit.* two cubits.
11:34 **Kibroth-hattaavah:** *that is* the Graves of Greed.
12:2–3 **by:** *or* with.   12:6 **If he were:** *prob. rdg; Heb.* If the LORD were.

their inspiration directly from God, were a challenge to all established forms of religious authority. Here, the later prophetic movement is traced back to Moses and receives sanction from his blessing. **31:** *Quails:* see Exod. 16.6–8 n. **32:** *Homer:* see p. xxviii.

11.35–12.16: A challenge to Moses' authority. 12.1: *Cushite:* possibly another designation for Midianite (Hab. 3.7), and hence Zipporah (Exod. 2.16–22). Compare 25.6–18; 31.1–18. For other possibilities, see Gen. 10.6 n. **2–3:** *By us:* Miriam is called a "prophetess" and recognized as a leader in Exod. 15.20. **8:** *Face to face:* Exod. 33.11. *Form:* Exod. 33.18–23. **14:** Spit is mentioned as causing uncleanness in Lev. 15.8. *Seven days:* the prescribed period following recovery from skin disease (Lev. 14.8–9). **16:** The itinerary does not accord with 10.12.

13.1–33: Spying out the land of Canaan. With this account, the theme of the conquest of the promised land begins to rise, to reach its climax in the Book of Josh. Various memories have here been combined, with from each ancestral tribe send one man, a man of high rank.' ³ So at the LORD's command Moses sent them out from the wilderness of Paran, all of them leading men among the Israelites. ⁴ These were their names:

from the tribe of Reuben, Shammua son of Zaccur;

⁵ from the tribe of Simeon, Shaphat son of Hori;

⁶ from the tribe of Judah, Caleb son of Jephunneh;

⁷ from the tribe of Issachar, Igal son of Joseph;

⁸ from the tribe of Ephraim, Hoshea son of Nun;

⁹ from the tribe of Benjamin, Palti son of Raphu;

¹⁰ from the tribe of Zebulun, Gaddiel son of Sodi;

¹¹ from the tribe of Joseph (that is from the tribe of Manasseh), Gaddi son of Susi;

¹² from the tribe of Dan, Ammiel son of Gemalli;

¹³ from the tribe of Asher, Sethur son of Michael;

¹⁴ from the tribe of Naphtali, Nahbi son of Vophsi;

¹⁵ from the tribe of Gad, Geuel son of Machi.

¹⁶ Those are the names of the men whom Moses sent to explore the land. But Moses named the son of Nun Joshua, instead of Hoshea.

¹⁷ When Moses sent them to explore Canaan, he said, 'Make your way up by the Negeb, up into the hill-country, ¹⁸ and see what the land is like, and whether the people who live there are strong or weak, few or many. ¹⁹ See whether the country in which they live is easy or difficult, and whether their towns are open or fortified. ²⁰ Is the land fertile or barren, and is it wooded or not? Go boldly in and bring some of its fruit.' It was the season when the first grapes were ripe.

²¹ They went up and explored the country from the wilderness of Zin as far as Rehob by Lebo-hamath. ²² Going up by the Negeb they came to Hebron, where Ahiman, Sheshai, and Talmai, the descendants of Anak, were living. (Hebron was built seven years before Zoan in Egypt.) ²³ They came to the wadi Eshcol, and there they cut a branch with a single bunch of grapes, which they carried on a pole between two of them; they also picked pomegranates and figs. ²⁴ That place was named the wadi Eshcol from the bunch of grapes the Israelites cut there.

²⁵ After forty days they returned from exploring the country ²⁶ and, coming back to Moses and Aaron and the whole community of Israelites at Kadesh in the wilderness of Paran, they made their report, and showed them the fruit of the country. ²⁷ They gave Moses this account: 'We made our way into the land to which you sent us. It is flowing with milk and honey, and here is the fruit it grows; ²⁸ but its inhabitants are formidable, and the towns are fortified and very large; indeed, we saw there the descendants of Anak. ²⁹ We also saw the Amalekites who live in the Negeb, Hittites, Jebusites, and Amorites who live in the hill-country, and the Canaanites who live by the sea and along the Jordan.'

³⁰ Caleb silenced the people for Moses. 'Let us go up at once and occupy the country,' he said; 'we are well able to conquer it.' ³¹ But the men who had gone with him said, 'No, we cannot attack these people; they are too strong for us.' ³² Their report to the Israelites about the land which they had explored was discouraging: 'The country we explored', they said, 'will swallow up any who go to live in it. All the people we saw there are men of gigantic stature. ³³ When we set eyes on the Nephilim (the sons of Anak belong to the Nephilim) we felt no bigger than grasshoppers; and that is how we must have been in their eyes.'

14 At this the whole Israelite community cried out in dismay and the

13:19 **are . . . fortified:** *prob. rdg; cp. Samar. MSS; Heb.* are in camps or in walled towns.
13:22 **descendants of Anak:** *or* tall men.
13:23 **Eshcol:** *that is* Bunch of Grapes.
13:29 **Hittites:** *or, with Samar.,* Hivites.
13:33 **Nephilim:** *or* giants. **sons of Anak:** *or* tall men.

duplications and variations. **16:** *Joshua, instead of Hoshea:* the two names, however, come from the same Heb. verb. Hoshea means "save"; Joshua, "the LORD saves." "Jesus" is a much later form of Joshua. **21:** *Lebo-hamath:* this tradition, at variance with a shallow exploration in v. 22, may be based on the northern boundaries of the Solomonic kingdom (1 Kgs. 8.65). Compare Gen. 15.18 n. **25:** *Forty days:* see Gen. 7.4 n. **26:** *Kadesh:* the setting for the events until 20.22, forty years later (14.32–33). **33:** *Nephilim:* see Gen. 6.1–4 n.

people wept all night long. ²Everyone complained against Moses and Aaron: 'If only we had died in Egypt or in the wilderness!' they said. ³'Why should the LORD bring us to this land, to die in battle and leave our wives and our dependants to become the spoils of war? It would be better for us to go back to Egypt.' ⁴And they spoke of choosing someone to lead them back there.

⁵Then Moses and Aaron flung themselves on the ground before the assembled community of the Israelites, ⁶and two of those who had explored the land, Joshua son of Nun and Caleb son of Jephunneh, tore their clothes, ⁷and encouraged the whole community: 'The country we travelled through and explored', they said, 'is a very good land indeed. ⁸If the LORD is pleased with us, he will bring us into this land, a land flowing with milk and honey, and give it to us. ⁹But you must not act in defiance of the LORD. You need not fear the people of the country, for we shall devour them. They have lost the protection that they had: the LORD is with us. You have nothing to fear from them.' ¹⁰As the whole assembly threatened to stone them, the glory of the LORD appeared in the Tent of Meeting to all the Israelites.

¹¹The LORD said to Moses, 'How much longer will this people set me at naught? How much longer will they refuse to trust me in spite of all the signs I have shown among them? ¹²I shall strike them with pestilence. I shall deny them their heritage, and you and your descendants I shall make into a nation greater and more numerous than they.' ¹³But Moses answered the LORD, 'What if the Egyptians hear of it? You brought this people out of Egypt by your might. ¹⁴What if they tell the inhabitants of this land? They too have heard of you, LORD, that you are with this people and are seen face to face, that your cloud stays over them, and that you go before them in a pillar of cloud by day and in a pillar of fire by night. ¹⁵If then you do put them all to death at one blow, the nations who have heard these reports about you will say, ¹⁶"The LORD could not bring this people

into the land which he promised them by oath; and so he destroyed them in the wilderness."

¹⁷'Now let the LORD's might be shown in its greatness, true to your proclamation of yourself—¹⁸"The LORD, long-suffering, ever faithful, who forgives iniquity and rebellion, and punishes children to the third and fourth generation for the iniquity of their fathers, though he does not sweep them clean away." ¹⁹You have borne with this people from Egypt all the way here; forgive their iniquity, I beseech you, as befits your great and constant love.'

²⁰The LORD said, 'Your prayer is answered, and I pardon them. ²¹But as I live, and as the glory of the LORD fills the whole earth, ²²⁻²³not one of all those who have seen my glory and the signs which I wrought in Egypt and in the wilderness shall see the country which I promised on oath to their fathers. Ten times they have challenged me and not obeyed my voice. None of those who have set me at naught shall see this land. ²⁴⁻²⁵But my servant Caleb showed a different spirit and remained loyal to me. Because of this, I shall bring him into the land in which he has already set foot, the territory of the Amalekites and the Canaanites who dwell in the Vale, and I shall put his descendants in possession of it. Tomorrow you must turn back and set out for the wilderness by way of the Red Sea.'

²⁶The LORD said to Moses and Aaron, ²⁷'How long must I tolerate the complaints of this wicked community? I have heard the Israelites making complaints against me. ²⁸Tell them that this is the word of the LORD: As I live, I shall do to you the very things I have heard you say. ²⁹Here in this wilderness your bones will lie, every one of you on the register aged twenty or more, because you have made these complaints against me. ³⁰Not one of you will enter the land which I swore with uplifted hand should be your home, except

14:24–25 **Red Sea:** *or* sea of Reeds.　　14:27 **must I tolerate:** *prob. rdg; Heb.* for.

14.1–45: Israel's response to the report of the spies. The theme of "rebellion" (11.1–34; Exod. 15.22–17.7) here reaches a climax with a theological explanation for "forty" years of wandering in the wilderness. The combination of variant traditions evident in ch. 13 continues in ch. 14. **18:** See Exod. 34.6–7 n. The LORD's sovereignty is evident in graciousness as well as in power. **24–25:** *Vale:* the coastal plain. *Turn back:* from direct entry from the south, and detour to the east by way of Elath (*the Red Sea:* Exod. 13.18 n.). See 21.4. Part of the group disregarded this directive (vv. 39–45). **26–38:** This is an alternative version of vv. 11–25.

only Caleb son of Jephunneh and Joshua son of Nun. ³¹Your dependants, who, you said, would become the spoils of war, those dependants I shall bring into the land you have rejected, and they will enjoy it. ³²But as for the rest of you, your bones will lie in this wilderness; ³³your children will be wanderers in the wilderness forty years, paying the penalty of your wanton faithlessness till the last one of you dies there. ³⁴Forty days you spent exploring the country, and forty years, a year for each day, you will spend paying the penalty of your iniquities. You will know what it means to have me against you. ³⁵I, the LORD, have spoken. This I swear to do to all this wicked community who have combined against me. There will be an end of them here in this wilderness; here they will die.'

³⁶The men whom Moses had sent to explore the land, and who came back and by their report set all the community complaining against him, ³⁷died of a plague before the LORD; they died of plague because they had made a bad report. ³⁸Of those who went to explore the land, Joshua son of Nun and Caleb son of Jephunneh alone survived.

³⁹When Moses reported the LORD's words to all the Israelites, there was great lamentation. ⁴⁰Early next morning they set out and made for the heights of the hill-country, saying, 'Look, we are on our way up to the place the LORD spoke of. We admit that we have been wrong.' ⁴¹But Moses replied, 'Must you persist in disobeying the LORD's command? No good will come of this. ⁴²Go no farther; you will not have the LORD with you, and your enemies will defeat you. ⁴³For in front of you are the Amalekites and Canaanites, and you will fall by the sword, because you have ceased to follow the LORD, and he will no longer be with you.' ⁴⁴But they went on recklessly towards the heights of the hill-country, though neither the Ark of the Covenant of the LORD nor Moses moved from the camp; ⁴⁵and the Amalekites and Canaanites who lived in those hills came down to the attack and inflicted a crushing defeat on them at Hormah.

15 THE LORD told Moses ²to say to the Israelites: 'When you enter the land which I am giving you to live in, ³make food-offerings to the LORD; they may be whole-offerings or any sacrifice made in fulfilment of a special vow or by way of freewill-offering or at one of the appointed seasons. When you thus make an offering of soothing odour from herd or flock to the LORD, ⁴whoever presents the offering should add a grain-offering consisting of a tenth of an ephah of flour mixed with a quarter of a hin of oil. ⁵Add to the whole-offering or shared-offering a quarter of a hin of wine as a drink-offering with each lamb sacrificed.

⁶'If the animal is a ram, the grain-offering should consist of two tenths of an ephah of flour mixed with a third of a hin of oil, ⁷and the wine for the drink-offering a third of a hin; in this way you will make an offering of soothing odour to the LORD.

⁸'When you offer to the LORD a young bull, whether as a whole-offering or as a sacrifice to fulfil a special vow, or as a shared-offering, ⁹add a grain-offering of three tenths of an ephah of flour mixed with half a hin of oil, ¹⁰and for the drink-offering, half a hin of wine; the whole will thus be a food-offering of soothing odour to the LORD. ¹¹This is what must be done in each case, for every bull or ram, lamb or kid, ¹²whatever the number of each that you offer. ¹³Every native Israelite must observe these rules whenever he offers a food-offering of soothing odour to the LORD.

¹⁴'When an alien residing with you or permanently settled among you offers a food-offering of soothing odour to the LORD, he should do as you do. ¹⁵There is one and the same statute for you and for the resident alien, a rule binding for all time on your descendants; before the LORD you and the alien are alike. ¹⁶There must be one law and one custom for you and for the alien residing among you.'

¹⁷The LORD told Moses ¹⁸to say to the Isra-

14:34 **to have ... you:** *or* to thwart me.   15:14 **as you do:** *so Syriac; Heb. adds* the assembly.

15.1–41: A collection of miscellaneous cultic regulations. It possibly was placed here, rather than with the Sinai legislation, because it was to be operative after the conquest of Canaan (v. 2), and that theme makes its appearance only in chs. 13–14. Possibly, though, it was placed here because the episode of vv. 32–36 occurred in the wilderness. **1–16:** Grain and wine, products common in Canaan as opposed to the wilderness, must then accompany the previously specified animal sacrifice (Lev. chs. 1–7). **4:** *Ephah; hin:* see p. xxviii. The quantities of grain and wine are set according to the kind of animal sacrificed. **14:** *Alien:* see Lev.

elites: 'After you have entered the land into which I am bringing you, 19 whenever you eat the bread of the country, set aside a contribution for the LORD. 20 Set aside a loaf made of your first kneading of dough, as you set aside the contribution from the threshing-floor. 21 You must give a contribution to the LORD from your first kneading of dough; this rule is binding on your descendants.

22 'When through inadvertence you omit to carry out any of these commands which the LORD gave to Moses — 23 any command whatever that the LORD gave you through Moses on that first day and thereafter and made binding on your descendants — 24 if it be done inadvertently, unnoticed by the community, then the whole community must offer one young bull as a whole-offering, a soothing odour to the LORD, with its proper grain-offering and drink-offering according to custom; and they are to add one he-goat as a purification-offering. 25 The priest must make expiation for the whole Israelite community, and they will be forgiven. The omission was inadvertent; and they have brought their offering, a food-offering to the LORD; they have made their purification-offering before the LORD for their inadvertence; 26 the whole community of Israelites and the aliens residing among you will be forgiven. The inadvertence was shared by the whole people.

27 'If it is an individual who sins inadvertently, he should present a yearling she-goat as a purification-offering, 28 and the priest will make expiation before the LORD for that person, who will then be forgiven. 29 For anyone who sins inadvertently, there must be one law for all, whether native Israelite or resident alien.

30 'But the person, be he native or alien, who sins presumptuously, insults the LORD; that person is to be cut off from the people. 31 Because he has brought the word of the LORD into contempt and violated his command, that person will be cut off completely; the guilt will be on his head alone.'

32 During the time that the Israelites were in the wilderness, a man was found gathering sticks on the sabbath day. 33 Those who had caught him in the act brought him to Moses and Aaron and all the community, 34 and they kept him in custody, because it was not clearly known what was to be done with him. 35 The LORD said to Moses, 'The man must be put to death; he must be stoned by the whole community outside the camp.' 36 So the whole community took him outside the camp, where he was stoned to death, as the LORD had commanded Moses.

37 The LORD told Moses 38 to say to the Israelites: 'Make tassels on the corners of your garments, you and your children's children. Into this tassel you are to work a violet thread, 39 and whenever you see this in the tassel, you will remember all the LORD's commands and obey them, and not go your own wanton ways, led astray by your own hearts and eyes. 40 This token is to ensure that you remember and obey all my commands, and keep yourselves holy, consecrated to your God.

41 'I am the LORD your God who brought you out of Egypt to become your God. I am the LORD your God.'

16 KORAH son of Izhar, son of Kohath, son of Levi, along with the Reubenites Dathan and Abiram sons of Eliab and On son of Peleth, challenged the authority of Moses. 2 Siding with them in their revolt were two hundred and fifty Israelites, all chiefs of the community, conveners of assembly and men of good standing. 3 They confronted Moses and Aaron and said, 'You take too much on yourselves. Each and every member of the community is holy and the LORD is among them. Why do you set yourselves up

24.10–15 n. **17–21:** This seems to be an extension of Lev. 23.9–14 and Deut. 26.1–4, which required an offering of cakes in addition to the first sheaf. **22–31:** The expanded requirements of vv. 1–16 are here applied to the purification-offering (Lev. 4.1–5.13). **22–29:** Expiation in the case of sin by *inadvertence*. **32–36:** The law about "presumptuous" sin (vv. 30–31) is concretely illustrated. **37–40:** An ancient custom of dress (*tassels*) is here reinterpreted as a reminder of religious identity. Compare Gen. 17.9–14 n. **41:** See Lev. 18.2 n.

16.1–17.13: The wilderness revolt. Two different accounts are seen blended together. One is between factions of Levites (3.6 n.; compare Lev. 10.2 n.); this account is anticipated in previous warnings (3.10 n.), especially those directed against the descendants of Kohath (4.17–20 n.). The other account is non-Levite. Possibly the older, non-Levite revolt by Dathan and Abiram (compare Deut. 11.6; Ps. 106.16–18) is here expanded by the priestly writers so as to include the Levite Korah as a rebel (vv. 1a, 2b–11, 16–24, 27a, 32b, above the assembly of the LORD?' 4 When Moses heard this, he prostrated himself, 5 and he said to Korah and all his company, 'Tomorrow morning the LORD will declare who is his, who is holy and who may present offerings to him. The man whom the LORD chooses may present them. 6 This is what you must do, you, Korah, and all your company: you must take censers, 7 and put fire in them and place incense on them before the LORD tomorrow. The man whom the LORD then chooses is the man who is holy. You take too much on yourselves, you Levites.'

8 Moses said to Korah, 'Listen, you Levites. 9 Is it not enough for you that the God of Israel has set you apart from the community of Israel, bringing you near him to maintain the service of the Tabernacle of the LORD and to stand before the community as their ministers? 10 He has had you come near him, and all your brother Levites with you; now do you seek the priesthood as well? 11 That is why you and all your company have combined together against the LORD. What is Aaron that you should make these complaints against him?'

12 Moses sent to fetch Dathan and Abiram sons of Eliab, but they answered, 'We will not come. 13 Is it not enough that you have brought us away from a land flowing with milk and honey to let us die in the wilderness? Must you also set yourself up as prince over us? 14 What is more, you have not brought us into a land flowing with milk and honey, nor have you given us fields and vineyards to inherit. Do you think you can hoodwink men like us? We are not coming.' 15 Moses became very angry, and said to the LORD, 'Take no notice of their murmuring. I have not taken from them so much as a single donkey; I have not wronged any of them.'

16 Moses said to Korah, 'Present yourselves before the LORD tomorrow, you and all your company, you and they and Aaron. 17 Each man of you is to take his censer and put incense on it. Then you shall present them before the LORD with their two hundred and fifty censers, and you and Aaron shall also bring your censers.' 18 So each man took his censer, put fire in it, and placed incense on it. Moses and Aaron took their stand at the entrance to the Tent of Meeting, 19 and Korah gathered his whole company together and faced them at the entrance to the Tent of Meeting.

Then the glory of the LORD appeared to the whole community, 20 and the LORD said to Moses and Aaron, 21 'Stand apart from them, so that I may make an end of them in a single moment.' 22 But Moses and Aaron prostrated themselves and said, 'God, you God of the spirits of all mankind, if one man sins, will you be angry with the whole community?' 23 But the LORD said to Moses, 24 'Tell them all to stand back from the dwellings of Korah, Dathan, and Abiram.'

25 Moses rose and went to Dathan and Abiram, and the elders of Israel followed him. 26 He said to the whole community, 'Stand well away from the tents of these wicked men; touch nothing of theirs, or you will be swept away because of all their sins.' 27 So they moved away from the dwellings of Korah, Dathan, and Abiram. Dathan and Abiram had come out and were standing at the entrance of their tents with their wives, their children, and their dependants. 28 Moses said, 'By this you shall know that it is the LORD who sent me to do all I have done, and it was not my own heart that prompted me. 29 If these men die a natural death, merely sharing the common fate of man, then the LORD has not sent me; 30 but if the LORD works a miracle, and the ground opens its mouth and swallows them and all that is theirs, and they go down alive to Sheol, then you will know that these men have set the LORD at naught.'

31 Hardly had Moses spoken when the ground beneath them split apart; 32 the earth opened its mouth and swallowed them and their homes — all the followers of Korah and all their property. 33 They went down alive into Sheol with all that they had; the earth closed over them, and they vanished from the assembly. 34 At their cries all the Israelites around them fled. 'Look out!' they shouted. 'The earth might swallow us.' 35 Fire came out from the LORD and consumed the two hundred and fifty men presenting the incense.

36 Then the LORD said to Moses, 37 'Order Eleazar son of Aaron the priest to set aside the censers from the burnt remains, and scatter the fire from them a long way off, because they are holy. 38 The censers of these men

---

16:14 **hoodwink:** *lit.* gouge out the eyes of.
16:18 **Moses . . . Meeting:** *so some MSS; others* They stood at the entrance to the Tent of Meeting, and Moses and Aaron.   16:19 **his:** *so Gk; Heb.* the.
16:30 **works a miracle:** *lit.* creates a creation.
16:30,33 **Sheol:** *or* the underworld.   16:36 *In Heb. 17:1.*

who sinned at the cost of their lives you shall make into beaten plates to overlay the altar; they are holy, because they have been presented before the LORD. Let them be a sign to the Israelites.' 39 Eleazar the priest took the bronze censers which the victims of the fire had presented, and they were beaten into plates to cover the altar, 40 to be a reminder to the Israelites that no lay person, no one not descended from Aaron, should come forward to burn incense before the LORD, or his fate would be that of Korah and his company. All this was done as the LORD commanded Eleazar through Moses.

41 Next day the whole Israelite community raised complaints against Moses and Aaron and taxed them with causing the death of some of the LORD's people. 42 As they gathered against Moses and Aaron, they turned towards the Tent of Meeting and saw that the cloud covered it, and the glory of the LORD appeared. 43 When Moses and Aaron came to the front of the Tent of Meeting, 44 the LORD said to them, 45 'Stand well clear of this community, so that in a single moment I may make an end of them.' They prostrated themselves, 46 and then Moses said to Aaron, 'Take your censer, put fire from the altar in it, set incense on it, and go with it quickly to the assembled community to make expiation for them. Wrath has gone forth already from the presence of the LORD; the plague has begun.' 47 As Moses had directed him, Aaron took his censer, ran into the midst of the assembly, and found that the plague had indeed begun among the people. He put incense on the censer and made expiation for the people, 48 standing between the dead and the living, and the plague was stopped. 49 Fourteen thousand seven hundred died of it, in addition to those who had died for Korah's offence. 50 When Aaron came back to Moses at the entrance to the Tent of Meeting, the plague had stopped.

17 The LORD said to Moses, 2 'Speak to the Israelites and get from them a staff for each tribe, one from every tribal chief, twelve in all, and write each man's name on his staff. 3 On Levi's staff write Aaron's name, for there must be one staff for each head of a tribe. 4 Put them all in the Tent of Meeting before the Testimony, where I meet you, 5 and the staff of the man whom I choose will put forth buds. I shall rid myself of the complaints of these Israelites, who keep on complaining against you.'

6 Moses gave those instructions to the Israelites, and each of their chiefs handed him a staff for his tribe, twelve in all, and Aaron's staff among them. 7 Moses laid them before the LORD in the Tent of the Testimony, 8 and next day when he entered the tent, he found that Aaron's staff, the staff for the tribe of Levi, had budded. Indeed, it had put forth buds, blossomed, and produced ripe almonds. 9 Moses then brought out the staffs from before the LORD and showed them to all the Israelites; they saw for themselves, and each man took his own staff. 10 The LORD said to Moses, 'Put back Aaron's staff in front of the Testimony to be kept as a warning to rebels, so that you may rid me of their complaints, and then they will not die.' 11 Moses did this, doing exactly as the LORD had commanded him.

12 THE Israelites said to Moses, 'This is the end of us! We must perish, one and all! 13 Everyone who goes near the Tabernacle of the LORD will die. Is this to be our final end?'

18 The LORD said to Aaron: 'You and your sons, together with the members of your father's tribe, are to be fully answerable for the sanctuary. You and your sons alone will be answerable for your priestly office; 2 but admit your kinsmen of

16:39 **bronze:** *or* copper.   17:1 *In Heb.* 17:16.

35–50). **15:** Compare 1 Sam. 12.3. **30:** *Sheol:* the underworld, domain of the dead. **37:** *A long way off:* compare Lev. 10.4 n. **39–40:** But see Exod. 27.2 and 38.2, according to which the *plates* covering the *altar* were attached earlier at Sinai. (See Exod. 25.1–31.17 n.) **41–50:** The larger community is warned never to assist the Levites in their aspiration for the priesthood, and informed that only Aaron's expiatory activity can prevent catastrophe. **17.1–11:** In a final attempt to secure recognition for the Aaronite priesthood, God chooses Aaron's *staff* from among those of the tribes. Levites other than the descendants of Aaron are here ignored. The motif of a flowering rod as a sign of divine election is found in many parts of the world. **12–13:** These verses fit more logically after 16.34. They now form a conclusion to the entire passage, 16.1–17.11.

18.1–32: The duties and rights of the priests and Levites. The catastrophes of chs. 16–17, caused by neglect and violation of guidelines for the Levites, provided an appropriate setting for the repetition and expansion of

Levi, your father's tribe, to be attached to you and assist you while you and your sons are before the Tent of the Testimony. ³Let them be in attendance on you and fulfil all the duties of the Tent, but they must not go near the sacred vessels or the altar, otherwise they will die and you with them. ⁴They will be attached to you and be responsible for the maintenance of the Tent of Meeting in every detail. No lay person is to come near you, ⁵for you by yourselves will be responsible for the duties of the sanctuary and the altar, so that wrath may not fall again on the Israelites. ⁶It is I who have selected the Levites your kinsmen out of all the Israelites as a gift for you, made over to the LORD for the maintenance of the Tent of Meeting. ⁷But only you and your sons may fulfil the duties of your priestly office that concern the altar or lie within the curtain. This duty is yours; I bestow on you this gift of priestly service. Any person who is not a priest and who usurps it must be put to death.'

⁸The LORD said to Aaron: 'I, the LORD, commit to your control the contributions made to me, that is all the holy-gifts of the Israelites. I give them to you and to your sons for your allotted portion due to you for all time. ⁹Out of the most holy gifts kept back from the altar-fire this part is to belong to you: every offering, whether grain-offering, purification-offering, or reparation-offering, rendered to me as a most holy gift, belongs to you and to your sons. ¹⁰You must eat it in a most holy place; every male may eat it. You are to regard it as holy.

¹¹'This also is yours: the contribution from all such of their gifts as are presented as offerings dedicated by the Israelites. I give it to you and to your sons and daughters with you as a due for all time. Every person in your household who is ritually clean may eat it.

¹²'I give you all the choicest of the oil, the choicest of the new wine and the corn, the firstfruits which are given to the LORD. ¹³The first-ripe fruits of all produce in the land which are brought to the LORD are to be yours. Everyone in your household who is ritually clean may eat them.

¹⁴'Everything in Israel which has been devoted to God is to be yours.

¹⁵'All the firstborn of man or animal which are brought to the LORD are to be yours. Notwithstanding, you must accept payment in redemption of every firstborn of man and of unclean beasts: ¹⁶at the end of one month you may redeem it at the fixed price of five shekels of silver by the sacred standard, at the rate of twenty gerahs to the shekel. ¹⁷You must not, however, allow the redemption of the firstborn of a cow, sheep, or goat; they are holy. You must fling their blood against the altar and burn their fat in sacrifice as a food-offering of soothing odour to the LORD; ¹⁸their flesh is yours, as are the breast of the dedicated portion and the right leg.

¹⁹'All the dedicated portions, which the Israelites set aside for the LORD, I give to you and to your sons and daughters with you as a due for all time. This is a perpetual covenant of salt before the LORD with you and your descendants also.'

²⁰The LORD said to Aaron: 'You are to have no holding in Israel, no share of land among them; I am your holding in Israel, I am your share.

²¹'To the Levites I give every tithe in Israel to be their share, in return for the service they render in maintaining the Tent of Meeting. ²²In order that the Israelites may not henceforth approach the Tent and thus incur the penalty of death, ²³the Levites alone are to perform the service of the Tent and accept full responsibility for it. This rule is binding on your descendants for all time. They are to have no share of land among the Israelites, ²⁴because as their holding I give them the tithe which the Israelites set aside as a contribution to the LORD. Therefore I say concerning them: They are to have no holding among the Israelites.'

²⁵The LORD told Moses ²⁶to say to the Levites: 'When you receive from the Israelites the tithe which I give you from them as your share, you are to set aside from it the contribution to the LORD, a tithe of the tithe. ²⁷Your contribution will count for you as if it were corn from the threshing-floor and juice

material previously related. **1–7:** See 3.5–10. **8–10:** For the kinds of offerings, see Lev. chs. 1–7. **12–13:** On the offering of *firstfruits*, see 15.17–21 n. **15:** See Exod. 13.11–13 for the redemption of the firstborn. **16:** Compare 3.44–48. **17:** Compare Lev. 27.9–10, 26–27. **18:** See Lev. 7.28–36. **19:** *Covenant of salt:* see Lev. 2.13 n. **21:** *Tithe:* see Lev. 27.30–33. In older legislation (Deut. 26.12–13), the Levites were not the sole recipients. **24:** See Lev. 25.32–34 n.

from the wine vat. ²⁸ In this way you too will set aside the contribution due to the LORD out of all tithes which you receive from the Israelites, and you will give the LORD's contribution to Aaron the priest. ²⁹ Out of all the gifts you receive you are to set aside the contribution due to the LORD; and the gift which you consecrate must be taken from the choicest of them.

³⁰ 'Say to them also: When you have set aside the choicest part of your portion, what remains will count for you as the produce of the threshing-floor and the wine vat, ³¹ and you may eat it anywhere, you and your households. It is your payment for service in the Tent of Meeting. ³² When you have set aside its choicest part, you will incur no penalty in respect of it, and you will not be profaning the holy-gifts of the Israelites; so you will escape death.'

19 THE LORD said to Moses and Aaron: ² 'This is a statute of the law which the LORD has ordained. Tell the Israelites to bring you a red cow without blemish or defect, one which has never borne a yoke. ³ Give it to Eleazar the priest, to be taken outside the camp and slaughtered to the east of it. ⁴ Eleazar the priest is to take some of the blood on his finger and sprinkle it seven times towards the front of the Tent of Meeting. ⁵ The cow must be burnt in his sight, skin, flesh, and blood, together with the offal. ⁶ The priest must then take cedar-wood, marjoram, and scarlet thread, and throw them into the heart of the fire in which the cow is burning. ⁷ He must wash his clothes and bathe his body in water; after which he may enter the camp, but he remains ritually unclean till sunset. ⁸ The man who burnt the cow must wash his clothes and bathe his body in water; he also remains unclean till sunset. ⁹ Then a man who is clean is to collect the ashes of the cow and deposit them outside the camp in a clean place. They shall be reserved for use by the Israelite community in the water of ritual purification; for the cow is a purification-of-

fering. ¹⁰ The man who collected the ashes of the cow must wash his clothes, and he remains unclean till sunset. This statute is to be binding for all time on the Israelites and on the alien living among them.

¹¹ 'Whoever touches a dead body is ritually unclean for seven days. ¹² He must get himself purified with the water of ritual purification on the third day and on the seventh day, and then he is clean. If he is not purified both on the third day and on the seventh, he is not clean. ¹³ Anyone who touches a dead person, that is the body of a person who has died, and does not purify himself, defiles the Tabernacle of the LORD; he is to be cut off from Israel. The water of purification has not been flung over him; he remains unclean, and his impurity is still upon him.

¹⁴ 'When someone dies in a tent, this is the law: everyone who enters the tent and everyone already in it is ritually unclean for seven days, ¹⁵ and every open vessel which has no covering tied over it is unclean. ¹⁶ In the open, anyone who touches someone killed with a weapon or someone who has died naturally, or anyone who touches a human bone or a grave, is unclean for seven days. ¹⁷ For such uncleanness, they must take some of the ash from the burnt mass of the purification-offering and add fresh water to it in a vessel. ¹⁸ Then a person who is clean should take marjoram, dip it in the water, and sprinkle the tent and all the vessels in it and all the people who were there, or anyone who has touched a human bone, a corpse (whether the person was killed or died naturally), or a grave. ¹⁹ The one who is clean must sprinkle the one who is unclean on the third day and on the seventh; on the seventh day he is to purify him; then the one who is unclean must wash his clothes and bathe in water, and at sunset he will be clean. ²⁰ If anyone who is unclean does not get himself purified, that person is to be cut off from the assembly, because he has defiled the sanctuary of the LORD. As long as the water of purification has

18:29 **you consecrate:** *prob. rdg; Heb. obscure.*

19.1–22: Purification after contact with a dead body. This ritual is related here, rather than with the other regulations regarding uncleanness (Lev. chs. 11–15), possibly because of the large number of fatalities reported in chs. 16–17. **2:** *Red:* compare Lev. 14.4 n. **3:** *East:* see Lev. 16.14 n. **5:** The burning of the *skin, blood,* and *offal* is here unique. **6:** *Cedar-wood, marjoram,* and *scarlet thread* are also used in the ritual of purification after recovery from skin disease (Lev. 14.1–9). **7:** *Wash . . . bathe:* see Lev. 14.8 n. **13:** *Cut off:* see Lev. 7.21 n. **15:** The uncleanness of an *open vessel* may have originated from the fear that a demon which caused the death or disease might have taken refuge in the vessel.

not been flung over him, he is unclean. [21]This rule is to be binding on you for all time. The man who sprinkles the water of purification must also wash his clothes, and whoever touches the water is unclean till sunset. [22]Whatever the unclean man touches is unclean, and anyone who touches it will be unclean till sunset.'

20 IN the first month the whole community of Israel arrived in the wilderness of Zin and stayed some time at Kadesh. Miriam died and was buried there.

[2]As the community was without water, the people gathered against Moses and Aaron. [3]They disputed with Moses. 'If only we had perished when our brothers perished before the LORD!' they said. [4]'Why have you brought the LORD's assembly into this wilderness for us and our livestock to die here? [5]Why did you make us come up from Egypt to land us in this terrible place, where nothing will grow, neither grain nor figs nor vines nor pomegranates? There is not even water to drink.'

[6]Moses and Aaron went from the assembly to the entrance of the Tent of Meeting, where they prostrated themselves, and the glory of the LORD appeared to them. [7]The LORD said to Moses, [8]'Take your staff, and then with Aaron your brother assemble the community, and in front of them all command the rock to yield its waters. Thus you will produce water for the community out of the rock, for them and their livestock to drink.' [9]Moses took his staff from before the LORD, as he had been ordered. [10]He with Aaron assembled the people in front of the rock, and said to them, 'Listen, you rebels. Must we get water for you out of this rock?' [11]Moses raised his hand and struck the rock twice with his staff. Water gushed out in abundance and they all drank, men and animals. [12]But the LORD said to Moses and Aaron, 'You did not trust me so far as to uphold my holiness in the sight of the Israelites; therefore you will not lead this assembly into the land I am giving them.' [13]Such were the waters of Meribah, where the people disputed with the LORD and through which his holiness was upheld.

The approach to the promised land

[14]FROM Kadesh Moses sent envoys to the king of Edom: 'This message is from your brother Israel. You know all the hardships we have encountered, [15]how our ancestors went down to Egypt, and we lived there for many years. The Egyptians ill-treated us and our fathers before us, [16]and we cried to the LORD for help. He listened to us, sent an angel, and brought us out of Egypt.

'Now we are here at Kadesh, a town on your frontier. [17]Grant us, we ask, passage through your country. We shall not trespass on field or vineyard, nor drink from your wells. We shall keep to the king's highway, not turning off to right or left until we have crossed your territory.' [18]But the Edomites answered, 'You shall not cross our land. If you do, we shall march out and attack you.' [19]The Israelites said, 'But we shall keep to the main road. If we and our flocks drink your water, we shall pay you for it. Ours is a trifling request: we would simply cross your land on foot.' [20]But the Edomites refused, and marched out to oppose them with a large army in full strength. [21]Since the Edomites would not allow Israel to cross their frontier, Israel turned and went a different way.

[22]The whole community of Israel set out from Kadesh and came to Mount Hor. [23]There, near the frontier of Edom, the LORD said to Moses and Aaron, [24]'Aaron is now to be gathered to his father's kin. He will

19:21 **you:** *so some MSS; others* them.
20:13 **Meribah:** *that is* Dispute.

20.1–13: The demand for water at Meribah. Exodus 17.1–7 places this event, in slightly different form, before the arrival at Sinai. **1:** This account was once independent of the present context, for in 13.26, the people have already arrived at Kadesh. The precise year is here missing, but the context requires that it be toward the end of the "forty" years of wandering (see 13.26 n.). **12:** The reason given for the LORD's anger is not clear. It may have been because Moses, by acting himself, high-handedly, thereby impedes a miracle dependent on divine grace. See also Deut. 32.48–52. The episode reflects the knowledge of later generations that Joshua, not Moses, led Israel into Canaan, for Moses had died before the conquest. See Deut. 1.37. The account is placed here because of Aaron's death in vv. 22–29.

20.14–29: Preparation and departure from Kadesh. 14: A detour through *Edom* was necessary because an attempt at direct entry had failed (14.39–45). *Brother:* see Gen. 25.24–30. **17:** The *king's highway* was the not enter the land which I am giving to the Israelites, because over the waters of Meribah you both rebelled against my command. 25 Take Aaron and his son Eleazar, and go up Mount Hor. 26 Strip Aaron of his robes and invest Eleazar his son with them, for Aaron is to be taken from you: he will die there.' 27 Moses did as the LORD had commanded: in full view of the whole community they went up Mount Hor, 28 where Moses stripped Aaron of his robes and invested his son Eleazar with them. Aaron died there on the mountaintop. When Moses and Eleazar came down from the mountain, 29 the whole Israelite community saw that Aaron had died, and all the people mourned for thirty days.

21 When the Canaanite king of Arad, who lived in the Negeb, heard that the Israelites were coming by way of Atharim, he gave battle and took some of the Israelites prisoner. 2 Israel made this vow to the LORD, 'If you deliver this people into our power, we will utterly destroy their towns.' 3 The LORD listened to Israel and delivered up the Canaanites to them. Israel destroyed them and their towns, and the place became known as Hormah.

4 From Mount Hor they left by way of the Red Sea to march round the flank of Edom. But on the way the people grew impatient 5 and spoke against God and Moses. 'Why have you brought us up from Egypt', they said, 'to die in the desert where there is neither food nor water? We are heartily sick of this miserable fare.' 6 Then the LORD sent venomous snakes among them, and they bit the Israelites so that many of them died. 7 The people came to Moses and said, 'We sinned when we spoke against the LORD and you. Plead with the LORD to rid us of the snakes.' Moses interceded for the people, 8 and the LORD told him to make a serpent and erect it as a standard, so that anyone who had been bitten could look at it and recover.

9 So Moses made a bronze serpent and erected it as a standard, in order that anyone bitten by a snake could look at the bronze serpent and recover.

10 The Israelites continued their journey and encamped at Oboth. 11 From there they moved on and encamped at Iye-abarim in the wilderness on the eastern frontier of Moab. 12 When they moved from there they encamped by the wadi Zared. 13 From the Zared they moved on and encamped by the farther side of the Arnon in the wilderness which extends into Amorite territory, for the Arnon was the Moabite frontier, the frontier between Moab and the Amorites. 14 That is why the Book of the Wars of the LORD speaks of Waheb in Suphah and the wadis:

> Arnon 15 and the watershed of the
> wadis
> that falls away towards the dwellings at
> Ar
> and slopes towards the frontier of
> Moab.

16 From there they went on to Be-er: this is the well where the LORD said to Moses, 'Gather the people together and I shall give them water.' 17 It was then that Israel sang this song:

> Spring up, O well! Greet it with song,
> 18 the well dug by the princes,
> laid open by the leaders of the people
> with sceptre and staff,
> a gift from the wilderness.

19 From Be-er they proceeded to Nahaliel,

21:3 **to them:** *so Samar.; Heb. omits.* **Hormah:** *that is* Destruction.　　21:6 **venomous:** *lit.* burning. 21:8 **a serpent:** *lit.* a burning thing.　　21:14 **Waheb:** *name meaning* Watershed.　　21:16 **Be-er:** *name meaning* Water-hole.　　21:18 **a gift from:** *so Samar.; Heb.* and from.　　21:19 **From Be-er:** *prob. rdg; Heb.* From a gift.

main route from Elath (14.25 n.) northward to Syria. **24:** *Gathered to his father's kin* is a common biblical idiom for death, reflecting the ancient practice of a burial in a family tomb (Gen. 49.29–33).

21.1–35: From the border of Edom to the plains of Moab. 1–3: This seems to be an originally independent unit, interrupting the continuity between 20.29 and 21.4. It tells how Israel later avenged the defeat at Hormah (14.39–45), and suggests that it happened just before the detour around Edom. Judges 1.16–17, however, places the event at a later time. **4–9:** An idol in the temple at Jerusalem (2 Kgs. 18.4) was later traced back to this episode. Unlike previous protests because of lack of food or water (chs. 11, 20; Exod. 15.22–17.7), this protest brings no relief. **13:** *Amorites:* an alternative name for the Canaanites. **14–15:** *The Book of the Wars of the LORD* has not been preserved beyond this quotation. **17–18:** Since the custom of music and dance at the clearing of a well is widely attested in the Near East, this likely was a traditional chant for such an occasion.

and from Nahaliel to Bamoth; [20] then from Bamoth to the valley in the Moabite country below the summit of Pisgah overlooking Jeshimon.

[21] Israel sent envoys to Sihon the Amorite king with this request: [22] 'Grant us passage through your country. We shall not trespass on field or vineyard, nor drink from your wells. We shall keep to the king's highway until we have crossed your territory.' [23] But Sihon refused Israel passage through his territory; he mustered his whole army and marched out to oppose Israel in the wilderness. He advanced as far as Jahaz and gave battle, [24] but Israel put them to the sword, and occupied their land from the Arnon to the Jabbok, the territory of the Ammonites, where the country became difficult. [25] Israel seized all those Amorite towns and settled in them, that is in Heshbon and all its dependent villages.

[26] Heshbon was the capital of the Amorite king Sihon, who had fought against the former king of Moab, and stripped him of all his territory as far as the Arnon. [27] Therefore the bards say:

> Come to Heshbon! Let it be rebuilt!
> Let Sihon's capital be restored!
> [28] For fire blazed out from Heshbon
> and flames from Sihon's city.
> It devoured Ar of Moab,
> and swept the heights of Arnon.
>
> [29] Woe betide you, Moab;
> people of Kemosh, it is the end of you.
> He has made his sons fugitives
> and his daughters captives
> of Sihon the Amorite king.
> [30] From Heshbon to Dibon
> their very embers are burnt out
> and they are extinct,
> while the fire spreads onward to
> Medeba.

[31] Thus Israel occupied the territory of the Amorites.

[32] After Moses had sent men to reconnoitre Jazer, the Israelites captured it together with its dependent villages and drove out the Amorites there.

[33] They then turned and advanced along the road to Bashan. King Og of Bashan, with his whole army, took the field against them at Edrei, [34] but the LORD said to Moses, 'Do not be afraid of him. I have delivered him into your hands, with all his people and his land. Deal with him as you dealt with Sihon the Amorite king living in Heshbon.' [35] So they put him to the sword with his sons and all his people, until there was no survivor left, and they took possession of his land.

Israel in the plains of Moab

22 THE Israelites moved on and encamped in the lowlands of Moab on the farther side of the Jordan opposite Jericho.

[2] Balak son of Zippor saw all that Israel had done to the Amorites, [3] and Moab was in terror of the people because there were so many of them. The Moabites were overcome with fear at the sight of them; [4] and they said to the elders of Midian, 'This horde will soon eat up everything round us as an ox eats up the new grass in the field.' Balak son of Zippor, who was at that time king of Moab, [5] sent a deputation to summon Balaam son of Beor, who was at Pethor by the Euphrates in the land of the Amavites, with this message, 'A whole nation has just arrived from Egypt: they cover the face of the country and are settling at my very door. [6] Come at once and lay a curse on them, because they are too many for me. I may then be able to defeat them and drive them out of the country. I know that those whom you bless are blessed, and those whom you curse are cursed.' [7] The elders of Moab and Midian took the fees for augury with them, and coming to

---

21:30 **while the fire:** *so Samar.; Heb.* which.
21:32 **captured ... villages:** *so Gk; Heb.* captured its dependent villages.

27–30: An Amorite victory ballad is cited, in order to enhance the subsequent victory of Israel. *Kemosh* (v. 29) was the chief god of the Moabites (1 Kgs. 11.33). **33–35:** See Deut. 3.1–7.

22.1–40: Balaam is summoned to curse Israel. 6: *Lay a curse:* see Gen. 27.33–35 n. The use of professional cursers, regarded as having special rapport with the deity, is well attested from antiquity. **7–20:** This is one version of the next phase of the story, the other being vv. 21–35. According to the first, Balaam consults the LORD and is forbidden (vv. 7–14), then allowed (vv. 15–20), to accept Balak's invitation. According to the second, he does not consult the LORD and learns of divine opposition only after an angel has threatened his

Balaam they gave him Balak's message. ⁸'Spend this night here,' he replied, 'and I shall give you whatever answer the LORD gives me.' So the Moabite chiefs stayed with Balaam. ⁹God came to Balaam and asked him, 'Who are these men with you?' ¹⁰Balaam replied, 'Balak son of Zippor king of Moab has sent them to me and he says, ¹¹"A people which has just come out of Egypt is covering the face of the country. Come at once and put a curse on them for me; then I may be able to give battle and drive them away."' ¹²God said to Balaam, 'You are not to go with them or curse the people, because they are to be blessed.' ¹³So when Balaam rose in the morning he said to Balak's chiefs, 'Go back to your own country; the LORD has refused to let me go with you.' ¹⁴The Moabite chiefs took their leave and went back to Balak, and reported to him that Balaam had refused to come with them.

¹⁵Balak sent a second embassy, larger and more high-powered than the first. ¹⁶When they came to Balaam they said, 'This is the message from Balak son of Zippor: "Let nothing stand in the way of your coming to me. ¹⁷I shall confer great honour upon you and do whatever you ask me. But you must come and put a curse on this people for me."' ¹⁸Balaam gave this answer to Balak's messengers: 'Even if Balak were to give me all the silver and gold in his palace, I could not disobey the command of the LORD my God in anything, small or great. ¹⁹But stay here for this night, as the others did, that I may learn what more the LORD may have to say to me.' ²⁰During the night God came to Balaam and said to him, 'If these men have come to summon you, then rise and go with them, but do only what I tell you.' ²¹When morning came Balaam rose, saddled his donkey, and went with the Moabite chiefs.

²²But God was angry because Balaam was going, and as he came riding on his donkey, accompanied by his two servants, the angel of the LORD took his stand in the road to bar his way. ²³When the donkey saw the angel standing in the road with his sword drawn, she turned off the road into the fields, and Balaam beat her to bring her back on to the road. ²⁴The angel of the LORD then stood

where the road ran through a hollow, with enclosed vineyards on either side. ²⁵The donkey saw the angel and, squeezing herself against the wall, she crushed Balaam's foot against it, and again he beat her. ²⁶The angel of the LORD moved on farther and stood in a narrow place where there was no room to turn to either right or left. ²⁷When the donkey saw the angel, she lay down under Balaam. At that Balaam lost his temper and beat the donkey with his staff.

²⁸The LORD then made the donkey speak, and she said to Balaam, 'What have I done? This is the third time you have beaten me.' ²⁹Balaam answered, 'You have been making a fool of me. If I had had a sword with me, I should have killed you on the spot.' ³⁰But the donkey answered, 'Am I not still the donkey which you have ridden all your life? Have I ever taken such a liberty with you before?' He said, 'No.' ³¹Then the LORD opened Balaam's eyes: he saw the angel of the LORD standing in the road with his sword drawn, and he bowed down and prostrated himself. ³²The angel said to him, 'What do you mean by beating your donkey three times like this? I came out to bar your way, but you made straight for me, ³³and three times your donkey saw me and turned aside. If she had not turned aside, I should by now have killed you, while sparing her.' ³⁴'I have done wrong,' Balaam replied to the angel of the LORD. 'I did not know that you stood confronting me in the road. But now, if my journey displeases you, I shall turn back.' ³⁵The angel of the LORD said to Balaam, 'Go with the men; but say only what I tell you.' So Balaam went on with Balak's chiefs.

³⁶When Balak heard that Balaam was coming, he went out to meet him as far as Ar of Moab by the Arnon on his frontier. ³⁷Balak said to Balaam, 'Did I not send time and again to summon you? Why did you not come? Did you think that I could not do you honour?' ³⁸Balaam replied, 'I have come, as you see. But now that I am here, what power have I of myself to say anything? It is only whatever word God puts into my mouth that I can speak.' ³⁹So Balaam went with Balak till

22:12 **are to be blessed:** or are blessed.   22:33 **If she had not:** so Gk; Heb. Perhaps she had.

life. He is then allowed to proceed. **7:** Augury is the so-called science of determining the divine will through omens. **15–17:** Balak's insistence is ironic in view of the final result of Balaam's services: he is unknowingly arranging his own defeat. **21–35:** See vv. 7–20 n.

they came to Kiriath-huzoth, [40] and Balak slaughtered cattle and sheep and sent portions to Balaam and to the chiefs who were with him.

[41] In the morning Balak took Balaam and led him up to Bamoth-baal, from where he could see the full extent of the Israelite host.

23 [1] Then Balaam said to Balak, 'Build me here seven altars and prepare for me seven bulls and seven rams.' [2] Balak followed Balaam's instructions; after offering a bull and a ram on each altar, [3-4] he said to him, 'I have prepared the seven altars, and I have offered the bull and the ram on each altar.' Balaam answered, 'You stand here beside your sacrifice, and let me go off by myself. It may be that the LORD will meet me. Whatever he reveals to me, I shall tell you.' He went off to a height, where God met him. [5] The LORD put words into Balaam's mouth and said, 'Go back to Balak, and speak as I tell you.' [6] He went back, and found Balak standing by his sacrifice, and with him all the Moabite chiefs. [7] Then Balaam uttered his oracle:

'From Aram, from the mountains of
the east,
Balak king of Moab has brought me:
"Come, lay a curse on Jacob for me,"
he said.
"Come, denounce Israel."
[8] How can I curse someone God has not
cursed,
how denounce someone the LORD has
not denounced?
[9] From the rocky heights I see them,
I watch them from the rounded hills.
I see a people that dwells apart,
that has not made itself one with the
nations.
[10] Who can count the host of Jacob
or number the myriads of Israel?
Let me die as those who are righteous
die;
grant that my end may be as theirs!'

[11] Balak said, 'What is this you have done? I

sent for you to put a curse on my enemies, and what you have done is to bless them.' [12] Balaam replied, 'I can but keep to the words which the LORD puts into my mouth.' [13] Balak then said to him, 'Come with me now to another place from which you will see them, though not the full extent of them; you will not see them all. Curse them for me from there.' [14] So he took him to the Field of the Watchers on the summit of Pisgah, where he built seven altars and offered a bull and a ram on each altar. [15] Balaam said to Balak, 'You stand beside your sacrifice; I shall meet the LORD over there.' [16] The LORD met Balaam and put words into his mouth, and said, 'Go back to Balak, and speak as I tell you.' [17] He went, and found him standing beside his sacrifice with the Moabite chiefs. Balak asked what the LORD had said, [18] and Balaam uttered his oracle:

'Up, Balak, and listen:
hear what I am charged to say, son of
Zippor.
[19] God is not a mortal that he should lie,
not a man that he should change his
mind.
Would he speak, and not make it good?
What he proclaims, will he not fulfil?
[20] I have received a command to bless;
I shall bless, and I cannot gainsay it.
[21] He has discovered no iniquity in Jacob
and has seen no mischief in Israel.
The LORD their God is with them,
acclaimed among them as King.
[22] What its curving horns are to the wild
ox,
God is to them, who brought them out
of Egypt.
[23] Surely there is no divination in Jacob,
and no augury in Israel;
now it is said to Jacob
and to Israel, "See what God has
wrought!"

23:2 **after offering:** so some MSS; others and Balak and Balaam offered.   23:7 **Aram:** or Syria.
23:14 **Field of the Watchers:** or Field of Zophim.
23:19 **change his mind:** or feel regret.   23:20 **I shall bless:** so Samar.; Heb. he blessed.

22.41–24.25: The oracles of Balaam. 23.1–2: Balaam may have desired the sacrifices in order to examine the markings of the livers for omens (compare Ezek. 21.21). **3–5:** Balaam looks for omens which will reveal the divine will. **9:** Israel's distinctiveness is emphasized in much of the legislation contained in Exod.-Num. **10:** *Myriads:* thus fulfilling the promise to the ancestors (Gen. 15.5). Since it is obvious from their numbers that God has blessed Israel, Balaam concludes that he must do likewise (v. 8). **14:** *Watchers:* the term is sometimes used in the ancient Near East for observers of astrological omens. **19:** *Change his mind:* from that

24 Behold a people rearing up like a
    lioness,
  rampant like a lion;
  he will not couch till he has devoured
    the prey
  and drunk the blood of the slain.'

25 Then Balak said to Balaam, 'You will not
put a curse on them; then at least do not bless
them.' 26 He answered, 'Did I not warn you
that I must do whatever the LORD tells me?'
27 Balak said, 'Come, let me take you to
another place; perhaps God will be pleased
to let you curse them for me there.' 28 So he
took Balaam to the summit of Peor overlooking Jeshimon, 29 and Balaam told him to
build seven altars for him there and prepare
seven bulls and seven rams. 30 Balak did as
Balaam had said, and he offered a bull and
a ram on each altar.

24 But now that Balaam knew that the
LORD wished him to bless Israel, he
did not go and resort to divination as before.
He turned towards the desert, 2 and before
his eyes he saw Israel encamped tribe by
tribe; and, the spirit of God coming on him,
3 he uttered his oracle:

'The word of Balaam son of Beor,
  the word of the man whose sight is
    clear,
4 the word of him who hears the words
    of God,
who with opened eyes sees in a
    trance
  the vision from the Almighty:
5 Jacob, how fair are your tents,
Israel, your encampments,
6 like long palm groves,
  like gardens by a river,
like aloe trees planted by the LORD,
  like cedars beside the waters!
7 The water in his vessels shall overflow,
  and his seed shall be like great waters
so that his king may be taller than
    Agag,
  and his kingdom lifted high.
8 What its curving horns are to the wild
    ox,

God is to him, who brought him out of
    Egypt;
he will devour hostile nations,
  crunch their bones, and break their
    backs.
9 When he reclines he couches like a lion
  or like a lioness; who dares to rouse
    him?
Blessed be those who bless you,
  and let them who curse you be
    accursed!'

10 At that Balak's anger was aroused against
Balaam; beating his hands together, he cried,
'It was to curse my enemies that I summoned
you, and three times you have persisted in
blessing them. 11 Off with you at once to your
own place! I promised to confer great honour upon you, but now the LORD has kept this
honour from you.' 12 Balaam answered, 'But
I said to your messengers: 13 "Were Balak to
give me all the silver and gold in his palace,
I could not disobey the command of the
LORD by doing anything of my own will, good
or bad. What the LORD says to me, that is
what I must say." 14 Now I am going to my
own people; but first, let me warn you what
this people will do to yours in the days to
come.' 15 Then he uttered his oracle:

'The word of Balaam son of Beor,
  the word of the man whose sight is
    clear,
16 the word of him who hears the words
    of God,
who shares the knowledge of the Most
    High,
who with opened eyes sees in a trance
  the vision from the Almighty:
17 I see him, but not now;
I behold him, but not near:
a star will come forth out of Jacob,
a comet will arise from Israel.
He will smite the warriors of Moab,
and beat down all the sons of Sheth.
18 Edom will be his by conquest
and Seir, his enemy, will become his.
Israel will do valiant deeds;

24:8 **backs:** *prob. meaning; Heb.* arrows.

of the first oracle. **23:** The techniques which Balak desires are ineffective against Israel. **27:** Balak's increasing
desperation continues to add to his ultimate defeat (22.15–17 n.). **24.4:** *Almighty:* See Gen. 17.1 n. **7:** *Agag:*
if this is the king of the Amalekites of Saul's time (1 Sam. 15.8), this part of the blessing was composed much
later than the time of Balaam. **16:** *Most high:* see Gen. 14.18 n. **17–19:** The Davidic conquest of Moab and
Edom (2 Sam. 8.2, 13–14) seems referred to; this may be an indication of the period of authorship of this oracle

¹⁹ Jacob will trample them down,
   the last survivor from Ar will he
      destroy.'

²⁰ He saw Amalek and uttered his oracle:

'First of all the nations was Amalek,
but his end will be utter destruction.'

²¹ He saw the Kenites and uttered his oracle:

'Your refuge, though it seems secure,
your nest, though set on the mountain
      crag,
²² is doomed, Cain, to be burnt,
   when Asshur takes you captive.'

²³ He uttered his oracle:

'Alas, who are these assembling in the
      north,
²⁴ invaders from the region of Kittim?
   They will lay waste Asshur; they will lay
      Eber waste:
   he too will perish utterly.'

²⁵ Then Balaam arose and returned home,
and Balak also went on his way.

25 WHEN the Israelites were in Shittim,
the men began to have intercourse
with Moabite women, ² who invited them to
the sacrifices offered to their gods. The Israelites ate the sacrificial food and prostrated
themselves before the gods of Moab; ³ they
joined in the worship of the Baal of Peor.
This aroused the anger of the LORD, ⁴ who
said to Moses, 'Take all the leaders of the
people and hurl them down to their death

before the LORD in the full light of day, that
the fury of my anger may turn away from
Israel.' ⁵ Moses gave this order to the judges
of Israel: 'Each of you put to death those of
his tribe who have joined in the worship of
the Baal of Peor.'

⁶ One of the Israelites brought a Midianite
woman into his family in open defiance of
Moses and all the community of Israel, while
they were weeping by the entrance of the
Tent of Meeting. ⁷ When Phinehas son of Eleazar, son of Aaron the priest, saw him, he
got up from the assembly and took a spear,
⁸ and went into the nuptial tent after the Israelite, where he transfixed the two of them,
the Israelite and the woman, pinning them
together. Then the plague which had attacked the Israelites was brought to a stop;
⁹ but twenty-four thousand had already died.

¹⁰ The LORD said to Moses, ¹¹ 'Phinehas son
of Eleazar, son of Aaron the priest, has
turned my wrath away from the Israelites; he
displayed among them the same jealous anger that moved me, and therefore I did not
exterminate the Israelites in my jealous anger. ¹² Make known that I hereby grant him
my covenant pledge of prosperity: ¹³ he and
his descendants after him shall enjoy the
priesthood under a covenant for all time, because he showed his zeal for his God and
made expiation for the Israelites.' ¹⁴ The
name of the Israelite struck down with the
Midianite woman was Zimri son of Salu, a
chief in a Simeonite family, ¹⁵ and the Midianite woman's name was Cozbi daughter of
Zur, who was the tribal head of an ancestral
house in Midian.

24:24 **invaders:** *so Gk; Heb. obscure.*   25:8 **together:**
lit. into her belly.

(compare v. 7 n.). **20:** See Exod. 17.8–16 n. This may also refer to the time of Saul (1 Sam. ch. 15) or David
(1 Sam. ch. 30). **21–22:** On the *Kenites,* see Judg. 1.16 n. In Heb. Kenite is *qēni; nest* (Heb. *qēn*) is a pun on
qēni, and on the name Cain (Heb. *qayyin,* "smith"). The smith will himself be smelted. **23–24:** The text is
obscure at every point. *Kittim* is Cyprus (see Gen. 10.4).

   25.1–18: Apostasy to the Moabite gods. Israel's rebellion against the LORD (11.1–34; ch. 14; 20.1–13; Exod.
14.10–14; 15.22–17.7) continues even after survival in the wilderness and arrival at the border of the promised
land. That it occurs again just after the blessing of Balaam (chs. 23–24) is meant as ironic. **2:** The charge is
religious disloyalty, not sexual immorality, although in the fertility cults of Canaan sexual activity was part of
the ritual. Compare Gen. 24.3 n. *Sacrificial food:* see Lev. 3.3 n. and 7.20 n.; 1 Cor. ch. 8. **3:** *Baal:* see Exod.
34.13 n. *Peor:* a place (23.28). **4:** The *leaders* are responsible for the activity. **5:** This seems to be an alternative
account of the punishment. **6:** Another story may begin here, since the topic switches from Moabite women
to Midianite ones. **8:** That the plague has not been mentioned previously supports the possibility that a new
unit began in v. 6. **13:** Phinehas is specifically granted the priesthood for zealous deeds (compare Exod.
32.26–29), though he was entitled to this through his descent from Aaron (Exod. 6.25), to whose descendants

16 The LORD said to Moses, 17–18 'Make the Midianites suffer as they made you suffer with their wiles, and strike them down; their wiles were your undoing at Peor and in the affair of Cozbi their sister, the daughter of a Midianite chief, who was struck down at the time of the plague that resulted from Peor.'

26 AFTER the plague the LORD said to Moses and Eleazar the priest, son of Aaron, 2 'Make a census of the whole community of Israel by fathers' families, recording everyone in Israel aged twenty years and upwards fit for military service.' 3 Moses and Eleazar the priest collected them all in the lowlands of Moab by the Jordan near Jericho, 4 all who were twenty years of age and upwards, as the LORD had commanded Moses.

These were the Israelites who came out of Egypt.

5 Reubenites (Reuben was Israel's eldest son): Enoch, the Enochite family; Pallu, the Palluite family; 6 Hezron, the Hezronite family; Carmi, the Carmite family. 7 These were the Reubenite families: the number in their list was forty-three thousand seven hundred and thirty. 8 Son of Pallu: Eliab. 9 Sons of Eliab: Nemuel, Dathan, and Abiram. These were the same Dathan and Abiram, conveners of the community, who defied Moses and Aaron and joined the company of Korah in defying the LORD. 10 Then the earth opened its mouth and swallowed them up with Korah, and so their company died, while fire burnt up the two hundred and fifty men, and they became a warning. 11 The Korahites, however, did not die.

12 Simeonites, by their families: Nemuel, the Nemuelite family; Jamin, the Jaminite family; Jachin, the Jachinite family; 13 Zerah, the Zarhite family; Saul, the Saulite family. 14 These were the Simeonite families; the number in their list was twenty-two thousand two hundred.

15 Gadites, by their families: Zephon, the Zephonite family; Haggi, the Haggite family; Shuni, the Shunite family; 16 Ozni, the Oznite family; Eri, the Erite family; 17 Arod, the Arodite family; Areli, the Arelite family. 18 These were the Gadite families; the number in their list was forty thousand five hundred.

19 The sons of Judah were Er, Onan, Shelah, Perez, and Zerah; Er and Onan died in Canaan. 20 Judahites, by their families: Shelah, the Shelanite family; Perez, the Perezite family; Zerah, the Zarhite family. 21 Perezites: Hezron, the Hezronite family; Hamul, the Hamulite family. 22 These were the families of Judah; the number in their list was seventy-six thousand five hundred.

23 Issacharites, by their families: Tola, the Tolaite family; Pua, the Puite family; 24 Jashub, the Jashubite family; Shimron, the Shimronite family. 25 These were the families of Issachar; the number in their list was sixty-four thousand three hundred.

26 Zebulunites, by their families: Sered, the Sardite family; Elon, the Elonite family; Jahleel, the Jahleelite family. 27 These were the Zebulunite families; the number in their list was sixty thousand five hundred.

28 Josephites, by their families: Manasseh and Ephraim. 29 Manassites: Machir, the Machirite family. Machir was the father of Gilead: Gilead, the Gileadite family. 30 Gileadites: Jeezer, the Jeezerite family; Helek, the Helekite family; 31 Asriel, the Asrielite family; Shechem, the Shechemite family; 32 Shemida, the Shemidaite family; Hepher, the Hepherite family. 33 Zelophehad son of Hepher had no sons, only daughters; their names were Mahlah, Noah, Hoglah, Milcah, and Tirzah. 34 These were the families of Ma-

26:3 **Jericho:** *prob. rdg; Heb. adds* saying.   26:14 **in their list:** *so Gk; Heb. omits.*   26:19 **Er . . . Zerah:** *so some Gk MSS (cp. Gen. 46:12); Heb.* Er and Onan. 26:23 **Puite:** *so Samar.; Heb.* Punite.

the office was promised forever (Exod. 29.9). **16–18:** These verses, possibly the latest part of the chapter, shift the blame from the Israelites (vv. 1–5) to the Midianites (vv. 6–15) and anticipate the events of ch. 31.

26.1–65: The second census, taken in anticipation of the invasion of the promised land. It seeks to show that, despite the hardships of the wilderness and the deaths from divine punishment (11.1–3, 33–34; 14.44–45; 16.1–35, 45–50; 21.1–3, 6), the population remained constant. For a possible origin of the census, see 1.20–46 n. **7:** Contrast 1.21. Reuben evidently continued to decline in number. See the prayer in Deut. 33.6. **9:** *Dathan and Abiram:* see 16.1–40. **14:** On Simeon's drastic decline, compare Gen. 49.5–7 n. **28–37:** Manasseh is listed first, in keeping with the order of birth given in Gen. 41.50–52. This reflects tribal and military prominence (Gen. 48.14 n.) which was later reversed (Gen. 48.17–19 n.), in keeping with the order nasseh; the number in their list was fifty-two thousand seven hundred.

35 Ephraimites, by their families: Shuthelah, the Shuthalhite family; Becher, the Bachrite family; Tahan, the Tahanite family. 36 Shuthalhites: Eran, the Eranite family. 37 These were the Ephraimite families; the number in their list was thirty-two thousand five hundred. These were the Josephites, by families.

38 Benjamites, by their families: Bela, the Belaite family; Ashbel, the Ashbelite family; Ahiram, the Ahiramite family; 39 Shupham, the Shuphamite family; Hupham, the Huphamite family. 40 Belaites: Ard and Naaman. Ard, the Ardite family; Naaman, the Naamite family. 41 These were the Benjamite families; the number in their list was forty-five thousand six hundred.

42 Danites, by their families: Shuham, the Shuhamite family. These were the families of Dan by their families; 43 the number in the list of the Shuhamite family was sixty-four thousand four hundred.

44 Asherites, by their families: Imna, the Imnite family; Ishvi, the Ishvite family; Beriah, the Beriite family. 45 Beriite families: Heber, the Heberite family; Malchiel, the Malchielite family. 46 The daughter of Asher was named Serah. 47 These were the Asherite families; the number in their list was fifty-three thousand four hundred.

48 Naphtalites, by their families: Jahzeel, the Jahzeelite family; Guni, the Gunite family; 49 Jezer, the Jezerite family; Shillem, the Shillemite family. 50 These were the Naphtalite families by their families; the number in their list was forty-five thousand four hundred.

51 The total in the Israelite lists was six hundred and one thousand seven hundred and thirty.

52 The LORD said to Moses, 53 'The land is to be apportioned among these tribes according to the number of names recorded. 54 To the larger group give a larger share of territory and to the smaller a smaller; a share will be given to each in proportion to its size as shown in the census. 55 The land, however, is to be apportioned by lot, the lots being cast for the territory by families in the father's line, 56 and shares apportioned by lot between the larger families and the smaller.'

57 The lists of Levi, by families: Gershon, the Gershonite family; Kohath, the Kohathite family; Merari, the Merarite family. 58 These were the families of Levi: the Libnite, Hebronite, Mahlite, Mushite, and Korahite families.

Kohath was the father of Amram; 59 Amram's wife was named Jochebed daughter of Levi, born to him in Egypt. She bore to Amram Aaron, Moses, and their sister Miriam. 60 Aaron's sons were Nadab, Abihu, Eleazar, and Ithamar. 61 Nadab and Abihu died because they had presented illicit fire before the LORD.

62 In the lists of Levi the number of males, aged one month and upwards, was twenty-three thousand. They were recorded separately from the other Israelites because no holding was allotted to them among the Israelites.

63 These were the lists prepared by Moses and Eleazar the priest when they made a census of the Israelites in the lowlands of Moab by the Jordan near Jericho. 64 Among them there was not a single one of the Israelites whom Moses and Aaron the priest had recorded in the wilderness of Sinai; 65 for the LORD had said they should all die in the wilderness. None of them was still living except Caleb son of Jephunneh and Joshua son of Nun.

27 A claim was presented by the daughters of Zelophehad son of Hepher, son of Gilead, son of Machir, son of Manasseh, son of Joseph. Their names were Mahlah, Noah, Hoglah, Milcah, and Tirzah. 2 They appeared before Moses, Eleazar the priest, the chiefs, and all the community at the entrance of the Tent of Meeting, and spoke as follows: 3 'Our father died in the

26:39 **Shupham:** *so some MSS; others* Shephupham.
26:40 **Ard, the:** *so Samar.; Heb. omits* Ard.
27:1 **Manasseh:** *so Lat.; Heb. adds* of the families of Manasseh.

of 1.32–35. (Accordingly, the present census may be older than that of ch. 1.) **55–56:** Since *lots* were thought to reveal the divine will (see Exod. 28.15 n.), such apportionment confessed the LORD's sovereignty over the land (compare Lev. 25.1–55 n., 23 n.). **57–62:** See 3.14–39.

27.1–11: Women's right to receive property in the promised land. This precedent-setting case is anticipated in 26.33 and clarified in ch. 36. Similar concern for preserving family property is expressed in Lev. ch. 25; 1 Kgs. 21.1–3.

wilderness. But he was not among the company of Korah which combined together against the Lord; he died for his own sin and left no sons. ⁴Is it right that, because he had no son, our father's name should disappear from his family? Give us our holding on the same footing as our father's brothers.'

⁵Moses brought their case before the Lord, ⁶who said to him, ⁷'The claim of the daughters of Zelophehad is good: you must allow them to inherit on the same footing as their father's brothers, and let their father's holding pass to them. ⁸Intimate this to the Israelites: When a man dies leaving no son, his holding is to pass to his daughter. ⁹If he has no daughter, give it to his brothers. ¹⁰If he has no brothers, give it to his father's brothers. ¹¹If his father had no brothers, then give possession to the nearest survivor in his family, and he will inherit. This is to be a legal precedent for the Israelites, as the Lord has commanded Moses.'

¹²The Lord said to Moses, 'Go up this mountain, Mount Abarim, and view the land which I have given to the Israelites. ¹³Then, when you have seen it, you too will be gathered to your father's kin as was your brother Aaron; ¹⁴for you and Aaron disobeyed my command when the community disputed with me in the wilderness of Zin: you did not uphold my holiness before them at the waters.' These were the waters of Meribah-by-Kadesh in the wilderness of Zin.

¹⁵Then Moses said to the Lord, ¹⁶'Let the Lord, the God of the spirits of all mankind, appoint a man over the community ¹⁷to go out and come in at their head, to lead them out and bring them home, so that the community of the Lord may not be like sheep without a shepherd.' ¹⁸The Lord answered, 'Take Joshua son of Nun, a man powerful in spirit; lay your hand on him ¹⁹and have him stand before Eleazar the priest and all the community. Give him his commission in their presence, ²⁰and delegate some of your authority to him, so that the entire Israelite community will obey him. ²¹He must present himself before Eleazar the priest, who will obtain a decision for him by consulting the Urim before the Lord; at his word they are to go out and come home, both Joshua and the whole community of the Israelites.'

²²Moses did as the Lord had commanded him. He took Joshua, presented him to Eleazar the priest and the whole community, ²³laid his hands on him, and gave him his commission, as instructed by the Lord.

28 The Lord told Moses ²to say to the Israelites: See that my offerings, the food for the food-offering of soothing odour, are presented to me at the appointed time. ³Tell them: This is the food-offering which you are to present to the Lord: the regular daily whole-offering of two yearling rams without blemish; ⁴one you must sacrifice in the morning and the second between dusk and dark. ⁵The grain-offering is to be a tenth of an ephah of flour mixed with a quarter of a hin of oil of pounded olives. ⁶(This was the regular whole-offering instituted at Mount Sinai, a soothing odour, a food-offering to the Lord.) ⁷The wine for the proper drink-offering is to be a quarter of a hin to each ram; you are to pour out this strong drink in the holy place as an offering to the Lord. ⁸You are to sacrifice the second ram between dusk and dark, with the same grain-offering as at the morning sacrifice and with the proper drink-offering; it is a food-offering of soothing odour to the Lord.

⁹For the sabbath day: two yearling rams without blemish, a grain-offering of two tenths of an ephah of flour mixed with oil, and the proper drink-offering. ¹⁰This whole-offering, presented every sabbath, is in addition to the regular whole-offering and the proper drink-offering.

¹¹On the first day of every month present a whole-offering to the Lord, consisting of

28:7 **The wine:** *so Gk; Heb. omits.*

27.12–23: Moses' successor is appointed. 13: See 20.22–29. **14:** See 20.1–13. **17:** *Go out and come in:* at the head of the army. **19–21:** In the postexilic community, the priesthood retained ultimate authority over military affairs (see Introduction to Lev.); thus Joshua *must present himself before Eleazar . . . who will obtain a decision. Urim:* see Exod. 28.15 n.

28.1–29.40: The sacrificial calendar. This is a summary of all the sacrifices to be made by the community and is an expansion of Lev. ch. 23 (and of Ezek. 45.18–46.15). (For offerings by individuals, see 29.39 and Lev. chs. 1–7.) The definitive statement on the subject, it is placed just after the note of Moses' impending death (27.12–23). **2:** *Soothing odour:* see Exod. 29.18 n. **3–8:** See Exod. 29.38–42; Lev. 6.8–13. **9–10:** Ezek. 46.4–5 two young bulls, one ram, and seven yearling rams without blemish. ¹² The grain-offering is to be three tenths of flour mixed with oil for each bull, two tenths of flour mixed with oil for the full-grown ram, ¹³ and one tenth of flour mixed with oil for each young ram. This is a whole-offering, a food-offering of soothing odour to the LORD. ¹⁴ The proper drink-offering is half a hin of wine for each bull, a third for the full-grown ram, and a quarter for each young ram. This is the whole-offering to be made, month by month, throughout the year. ¹⁵ Further, one he-goat is to be sacrificed as a purification-offering to the LORD, in addition to the regular whole-offering and the proper drink-offering.

¹⁶ The Passover of the LORD is to be held on the fourteenth day of the first month, ¹⁷ and on the fifteenth day there is to be a pilgrim-feast; for seven days you must eat only unleavened bread. ¹⁸ On the first day there must be a sacred assembly; you must not do your daily work. ¹⁹ As a food-offering, a whole-offering to the LORD, you will present two young bulls, one ram, and seven yearling rams, all without blemish. ²⁰ Offer the proper grain-offerings of flour mixed with oil, three tenths for each bull, two tenths for the ram, ²¹ and one tenth for each of the seven young rams; ²² and as a purification-offering, one he-goat to make expiation for you. ²³ All these you must offer in addition to the morning whole-offering, which is the regular sacrifice. ²⁴ Repeat this daily till the seventh day, presenting food as a food-offering of soothing odour to the LORD, in addition to the regular whole-offering and the proper drink-offering. ²⁵ On the seventh day there will be a sacred assembly; you must not do your daily work.

²⁶ On the day of Firstfruits, when you bring to the LORD your grain-offering from the new crop at your feast of Weeks, there is to be a sacred assembly; you must not do your daily work. ²⁷ Bring a whole-offering as a soothing odour to the LORD: two young bulls, one full-grown ram, and seven yearling rams. ²⁸ The proper grain-offering will be of flour mixed with oil, three tenths for each

bull, two tenths for the one ram, ²⁹ and a tenth for each of the seven young rams, ³⁰ and there must be one he-goat as a purification-offering to make expiation for you; ³¹ they must all be without blemish. All these are to be offered in addition to the regular whole-offering with the proper grain-offering and drink-offering.

29 On the first day of the seventh month hold a sacred assembly; you must not do your daily work. It is to be a day of acclamation. ² You are to sacrifice a whole-offering as a soothing odour to the LORD: one young bull, one full-grown ram, and seven yearling rams, without blemish. ³ Their proper grain-offering is flour mixed with oil, three tenths for the bull, two tenths for the one ram, ⁴ and one tenth for each of the seven young rams, ⁵ and there will be one he-goat as a purification-offering to make expiation for you. ⁶ This is in addition to the monthly whole-offering and the regular whole-offering with their proper grain-offerings and drink-offerings according to custom; it is a food-offering of soothing odour to the LORD.

⁷ On the tenth day of this seventh month hold a sacred assembly, when you are to mortify yourselves. You must do no work. ⁸ You are to bring a whole-offering to the LORD as a soothing odour: one young bull, one full-grown ram, and seven yearling rams, everything without blemish. ⁹ The proper grain-offering is flour mixed with oil, three tenths for the bull, two tenths for the one ram, ¹⁰ and one tenth for each of the seven young rams, ¹¹ and there will be one he-goat as a purification-offering, in addition to the expiatory sin-offering and the regular whole-offering, with the proper grain-offering and drink-offering.

¹² On the fifteenth day of the seventh month hold a sacred assembly. You must not do your daily work, but for seven days keep a pilgrim-feast to the LORD. ¹³ As a whole-offering, a food-offering of soothing odour to the LORD, you are to bring thirteen young

28:30 **as a purification-offering:** *so Samar.; Heb.* omits.
29:11 **drink-offering:** *so Gk; Heb.* drink-offerings.

differs considerably. **11–15:** The lunar calendar, with these sacrifices at the new moon, was dominant in postexilic times. Compare 10.10; Isa. 1.14; Amos 8.5. **16–25:** See Exod. 12.1–27; 13.3–10; Lev. 23.5–8. **26–31:** See Exod. 23.16; 34.22; Lev. 23.15–21. **29.1–6:** This day is called the "new year" in the calendar in Lev. ch. 23 (see Lev. 23.24–25 n.). **7–11:** The Day of Atonement (see Lev. ch. 16; 23.26–32). **12–38:** The pilgrim-feast of Ingathering (see Exod. 23.16; Lev. 23.34–36).

bulls, two full-grown rams, and fourteen yearling rams, everything without blemish. ¹⁴ The proper grain-offering is flour mixed with oil, three tenths for each of the thirteen bulls, two tenths for each of the two rams, ¹⁵ and one tenth for each of the fourteen young rams, ¹⁶ and there will be one he-goat as a purification-offering, in addition to the regular whole-offering with the proper grain-offering and drink-offering.

¹⁷ On the second day: twelve young bulls, two full-grown rams, and fourteen yearling rams, without blemish, ¹⁸ together with the proper grain-offerings and drink-offerings for bulls, full-grown rams, and young rams, as prescribed according to their number, ¹⁹ and there will be one he-goat as a purification-offering, in addition to the regular whole-offering with the proper grain-offering and drink-offering.

²⁰ On the third day: eleven bulls, two full-grown rams, and fourteen yearling rams, without blemish, ²¹ together with the proper grain-offerings and drink-offerings for bulls, full-grown rams, and young rams, as prescribed according to their number, ²² and there will be one he-goat as a purification-offering, in addition to the regular whole-offering with the proper grain-offering and drink-offering.

²³ On the fourth day: ten bulls, two full-grown rams, and fourteen yearling rams, without blemish, ²⁴ together with the proper grain-offerings and drink-offerings for bulls, full-grown rams, and young rams, as prescribed according to their number, ²⁵ and there will be one he-goat as a purification-offering, in addition to the regular whole-offering with the proper grain-offering and drink-offering.

²⁶ On the fifth day: nine bulls, two full-grown rams, and fourteen yearling rams, without blemish, ²⁷ together with the proper grain-offerings and drink-offerings for bulls, full-grown rams, and young rams, as prescribed according to their number, ²⁸ and there will be one he-goat as a purification-offering, in addition to the regular whole-offering with the proper grain-offering and drink-offering.

²⁹ On the sixth day: eight bulls, two full-grown rams, and fourteen yearling rams,

without blemish, ³⁰ together with the proper grain-offerings and drink-offerings for bulls, full-grown rams, and young rams, as prescribed according to their number, ³¹ and there will be one he-goat as a purification-offering, in addition to the regular whole-offering with the proper grain-offering and drink-offering.

³² On the seventh day: seven bulls, two full-grown rams, and fourteen yearling rams, without blemish, ³³ together with the proper grain-offerings and drink-offerings for bulls, full-grown rams, and young rams, as prescribed according to their number, ³⁴ and there will be one he-goat as a purification-offering, in addition to the regular whole-offering with the proper grain-offering and drink-offering.

³⁵ The eighth day keep as a closing ceremony; you must not do your daily work. ³⁶ As a whole-offering, a food-offering of soothing odour to the LORD, you must bring one bull, one full-grown ram, and seven yearling rams, without blemish, ³⁷ together with the proper grain-offerings and drink-offerings for bulls, full-grown rams, and young rams, as prescribed according to their number, ³⁸ and there will be one he-goat as a purification-offering, in addition to the regular whole-offering with the proper grain-offering and drink-offering.

³⁹ These are the sacrifices which you are to offer to the LORD at the appointed seasons, in addition to the votive offerings, the free-will-offerings, the whole-offerings, the grain-offerings, the drink-offerings, and the shared-offerings.

⁴⁰ Moses passed everything on to the Israelites exactly as the LORD had commanded him.

30 MOSES spoke to the heads of the Israelite tribes and said: 'This is the LORD's command: ² When a man makes a vow to the LORD or by an oath puts himself under a binding obligation, he must not break his word. Every word he has spoken, he must make good. ³ When a woman, still young and

29:19 **drink-offering:** *so some MSS; others* drink-offerings.   29:31 **drink-offering:** *so some MSS; others* drink-offerings.   29:40 *In Heb.* 30:1.

30.1–16: Vows taken by women. Israel's cultic obligations were mandatory only on adult males (Exod. 23.17), but women were to be present at worship (Deut. 12.12; 31.12) and might volunteer to undertake sacrificial obligations within the limits specified. For other regulations concerning vows, see 6.1–21; Lev.

living in her father's house, makes a vow to the LORD or puts herself under a binding obligation, 4 if her father hears of it and keeps silence, then any such vow or obligation is valid. 5 But if her father disallows it when he hears of it, none of her vows or her obligations is valid; the LORD will absolve her, because her father has disallowed it. 6 If the woman is married when she is under a vow or a binding obligation rashly uttered, 7 then if her husband hears of it and keeps silence when he hears, her vow or her obligation by which she has bound herself is valid. 8 If, however, her husband disallows it when he hears of it and repudiates the vow which she has taken upon herself or the rash utterance with which she has bound herself, then the LORD will absolve her. 9 Every vow by which a widow or a divorced woman has bound herself is valid. 10 But if it is in her husband's house that a woman makes a vow or puts herself under a binding obligation by an oath, 11 and her husband, hearing of it, keeps silence and does not disallow it, then every vow and every obligation under which she has put herself is valid; 12 but if her husband clearly repudiates them when he hears of them, then nothing that she has uttered, whether it is a vow or an obligation, is valid. Her husband has repudiated them, and the LORD will absolve her.

13 'The husband can confirm or repudiate any vow or any oath by which a woman binds herself to mortification. 14 If he maintains silence day after day, he thereby confirms any vow or any obligation under which she has put herself: he confirms them, because he kept silence at the time when he heard them. 15 If he repudiates them some time after he has heard them, he is to be held responsible for her default.'

16 Such are the decrees which the LORD gave to Moses concerning a husband and his wife, and a father and his daughter still young and living in her father's house.

31 THE LORD said to Moses, 2 'You are to exact vengeance for Israel on the

Midianites. After that you will be gathered to your father's kin.'

3 Moses addressed the people: 'Let men among you be drafted for active service; they are to fall on Midian and exact vengeance in the LORD's name. 4 Send out a thousand men from each of the tribes of Israel.' 5 So men were called up from the clans of Israel, a thousand from each tribe, twelve thousand in all, drafted for active service. 6 Moses sent out this force, a thousand from each tribe, with Phinehas son of Eleazar the priest, who was in charge of the sacred equipment and of the trumpets to give the signal for the battle cry. 7 They made war on Midian as the LORD had commanded Moses, and slew every male. 8 In addition to those slain in battle they killed the five kings of Midian — Evi, Rekem, Zur, Hur, and Reba — and they put to death also Balaam son of Beor. 9 The Israelites took the Midianites' women and dependants captive, and carried off all their herds, flocks, and property. 10 They set fire to all the towns in which they lived, and all their encampments. 11 They collected the spoil and plunder, both man and beast, 12 and brought it all — captives, plunder, and spoil — to Moses and Eleazar the priest and to the whole Israelite community at the camp in the lowlands of Moab by the Jordan over against Jericho.

13 Moses and Eleazar the priest and all the chiefs of the community went to meet them outside the camp. 14 Moses spoke angrily to the officers of the army, the commanders of units of a thousand and of a hundred, who were returning from the campaign: 15 'Have you spared all the women?' he said. 16 'Remember, it was they who, on Balaam's departure, set about seducing the Israelites into disloyalty to the LORD in the affair at Peor, so that the plague struck the community of the LORD. 17 Now kill every male child, and kill every woman who has had intercourse with a man, 18 but you may spare for yourselves every woman among them who has not had intercourse. 19 You yourselves, every one of you who has taken life and every one who has touched the dead, must remain outside the

ch. 27; Deut. 23.21–23. **2:** On observing such vows, see Eccles. 5.4–5. **13:** *Mortification:* fasting.

31.1–54: Vengeance against the Midianites. The chapter is a sequel to 25.16–18 and illustrates the rules for "holy" war. For another instance, see 1 Sam. 15.2–33, and for a statement of guidance, see Deut. 13.12–18. **6:** Phinehas serves here as priest both because of his valor in the previous episode (25.7–13) and because the high priest (Eleazar) must avoid contact with dead bodies (Lev. 21.10–12). **8:** Why Balaam should have been in the Midianite camp (contrast 24.25) or been blamed for the incident at Shittim (ch. 25) is unclear. He is camp for seven days. Purify yourselves and your captives on the third day and on the seventh day, 20 and purify also every piece of clothing, every article made of hide, everything woven of goats' hair, and everything made of wood.'

21 Eleazar the priest said to the soldiers returning from battle, 'This is a statute of the law which the LORD has ordained through Moses. 22–23 Anything which will stand fire, whether gold, silver, copper, iron, tin, or lead, you must pass through fire and then it will be clean. Other things must be purified by the water of ritual purification; whatever cannot stand fire is to be passed through the water. 24 On the seventh day wash your clothes and be clean; after that you may re-enter the camp.'

25 The LORD said to Moses, 26 'You and Eleazar the priest and the heads of families in the community must count everything that has been captured, whether human beings or animals, 27 and divide them equally between the fighting men who went on the campaign and the rest of the community. 28 Levy a tribute for the LORD: from the combatants it is to be one out of every five hundred, whether human beings, cattle, donkeys, or sheep, 29 to be taken out of their share and given to Eleazar the priest as a contribution for the LORD. 30 Out of the Israelites' share it is to be one out of every fifty taken, whether human beings or cattle, donkeys, or sheep, all the animals, to be given to the Levites who are in charge of the LORD's Tabernacle.' 31 Moses and Eleazar the priest did as the LORD had commanded Moses.

32 These were the spoils which remained of the plunder taken by the fighting men: six hundred and seventy-five thousand sheep, 33 seventy-two thousand cattle, 34 sixty-one thousand donkeys; 35 and of persons, thirty-two thousand young women who had had no intercourse with a man.

36 The half share of those who took part in the campaign was thus three hundred and thirty-seven thousand five hundred sheep, 37 the tribute for the LORD from these being six hundred and seventy-five; 38 thirty-six thousand cattle, the tribute being seventy-two; 39 thirty thousand five hundred donkeys, the tribute being sixty-one; 40 and sixteen thousand persons, the tribute being thirty-two. 41 Moses gave to Eleazar the priest the tribute levied for the LORD, as the LORD had commanded him.

42–43 The share of the community, being the half share for the Israelites which Moses separated from that of the combatants, was three hundred and thirty-seven thousand five hundred sheep, 44 thirty-six thousand cattle, 45 thirty thousand five hundred donkeys, 46 and sixteen thousand persons. 47 Moses took one out of every fifty, whether man or animal, from the half share of the Israelites, and gave it to the Levites who were in charge of the LORD's Tabernacle, as the LORD had commanded him.

48 Then the officers who had commanded the forces on the campaign, the commanders of units of a thousand and of a hundred, came to Moses 49 and said to him, 'Sir, we have checked the roll of the fighting men who were under our command, and not one of them is missing. 50 So we have brought the gold ornaments, the armlets, bracelets, signet rings, ear-rings, and pendants that each man has found, to offer them before the LORD as expiation for our lives.'

51 Moses and Eleazar the priest received this gold from the commanders of units of a thousand and of a hundred, all of it craftsman's work, 52 and the gold thus given as a contribution to the LORD weighed sixteen thousand seven hundred and fifty shekels; 53 for every man in the army had taken plunder. 54 Moses and Eleazar the priest received the gold from the commanders of units of a thousand and of a hundred, and brought it to the Tent of Meeting that the LORD might remember Israel.

32 The Reubenites and the Gadites owned a very large amount of live-

31:50 **pendants:** *Heb. word of uncertain meaning.*

viewed negatively also in 2 Pet. 2.15–16; Jude 11; Rev. 2.14. **19–20:** See ch. 19 for the obligatory ritual of purification. **21–24:** The various items of booty must likewise be purified (see 19.14–18; Lev. 11.24–25 n.); fire as the means of doing so has not been specified previously. **50:** An *expiation* was needed because taking a census, even of men returning from battle, was offensive to God (see Exod. 30.11–16 n.).

32.1–42: The distribution of the territory east of the Jordan. Possibly the story was preserved in order to encourage future generations east of the Jordan to participate in the military actions of the larger whole. (For an instance of such failure to do so, see Judg. 5.15–17.) The episode is reviewed in Deut. 3.12–20 and the stock, and when they saw that the land of Jazer and Gilead was good grazing country, [2] they came to Moses and Eleazar the priest and to the chiefs of the community and said, [3] 'Ataroth, Dibon, Jazer, Nimrah, Heshbon, Elealeh, Sebam, Nebo, and Beon, [4] the region which the LORD has subdued before the advance of the Israelite community, is grazing country, and livestock is our main possession. [5] If we have found favour with you, sir, then let this country be given to us as our possession, and do not make us cross the Jordan.' [6] Moses demanded, 'Are your kinsmen to go into battle while you Gadites and Reubenites stay here? [7] How dare you discourage the Israelites from crossing over to the land which the LORD has given them? [8] This is what your fathers did when I sent them out from Kadesh-barnea to view the land. [9] They went up as far as the wadi Eshcol and viewed the land, and on their return so discouraged the Israelites that they would not enter the land which the LORD had given them. [10] The LORD's anger was aroused that day, and he solemnly swore: [11] "Because they have not loyally followed me, none of the men aged twenty or more who came up out of Egypt will see the land which I promised on oath to Abraham, Isaac, and Jacob." [12] This meant all except Caleb son of Jephunneh the Kenizzite and Joshua son of Nun; they followed the LORD with their whole heart. [13] In his anger the LORD made Israel wander in the wilderness for forty years until that whole generation was gone which had done what was wrong in his eyes. [14] You are now following in your fathers' footsteps, a fresh brood of sinful men to fire the LORD's anger once more against Israel. [15] If you refuse to follow him, he will again abandon this whole people in the wilderness and you will be the cause of their destruction.'

[16] Presently they came forward with this offer: 'We shall build pens for our livestock here and towns for our dependants. [17] Then we can be drafted as a fighting force to go at the head of the Israelites until we have brought them to their destination. Meanwhile our dependants can live in the fortified towns, safe from the natives of the land. [18] We shall not return to our homes until every Israelite is settled in possession of his own holding; [19] we shall not claim any share of the land with them over the Jordan and beyond, because our holding has already been allotted to us on this side, east of Jordan.' [20] Moses answered, 'If you stand by your promise, if in the presence of the LORD you are drafted for battle, [21] and the whole draft crosses the Jordan in front of the LORD and remains there until the LORD has driven out his enemies, [22] and the land has been subdued before him, then you may come back and be quit of your obligation to the LORD and to Israel; and this land will be your holding in the sight of the LORD. [23] But I warn you, if you fail to do all this, you will have sinned against the LORD, and your sin will find you out. [24] Build towns for your dependants and folds for your sheep; but carry out your promise.'

[25] The Gadites and Reubenites answered Moses, 'Sir, we are your servants and shall do as you command. [26] Our dependants and wives, our flocks and all our animals will remain here in the towns of Gilead; [27] but we, all who have been drafted for active service with the LORD, shall cross the river and fight, according to your command.'

[28] Moses gave instructions to Eleazar the priest and Joshua son of Nun and to the heads of the families in the Israelite tribes. [29] He said, 'If the Gadites and Reubenites, all who have been drafted for battle before the LORD, cross the Jordan with you, then when the land falls into your hands, you are to give them Gilead for their holding. [30] But if they fail to cross as drafted troops with you, then they will have to acquire land alongside you in Canaan.' [31] The Gadites and Reubenites said in response, 'Sir, the LORD has spoken, and we shall obey. [32] Once we have been drafted, we shall cross over before the LORD into Canaan; but we shall have our holding here on this side of Jordan.'

[33] So Moses assigned to the Gadites, the Reubenites, and half the tribe of Manasseh son of Joseph the kingdoms of Sihon king of the Amorites and King Og of Bashan, the whole land with its towns and the country round them. [34] The Gadites rebuilt Dibon, Ataroth, Aroer, [35] Atroth-shophan, Jazer, Jogbehah, [36] Beth-nimrah, and Beth-haran,

32:3 **Sebam:** Sibmah *in verse 38.* 32:17 **as . . . force:** *so Gk; Heb. obscure.*

boundaries involved are outlined in Josh. 13.8–32. **8–13:** See chs. 13–14. **33:** *Half the tribe:* for the settlement of the remainder west of the Jordan, see Josh. 17.1–6.

all of them fortified towns with folds for their sheep. ³⁷The Reubenites rebuilt Heshbon, Elealeh, Kiriathaim, ³⁸Nebo, Baal-meon (whose names were changed), and Sibmah; these were the names they gave to the towns they restored.

³⁹The sons of Machir son of Manasseh invaded Gilead, took it, and drove out the Amorite inhabitants; ⁴⁰Moses then assigned Gilead to Machir son of Manasseh, and he made his home there. ⁴¹Jair son of Manasseh attacked and took the tent-villages of Ham and called them Havvoth-jair. ⁴²Nobah attacked and took Kenath and its villages, and gave it his own name, Nobah.

33 THESE are the stages in the journey of the Israelites, when they were led by Moses and Aaron in their tribal hosts out of Egypt. ²Moses recorded their starting-points stage by stage as the LORD commanded him. These are their stages from one starting-point to the next.

³The Israelites left Rameses on the fifteenth day of the first month, the day after the Passover; they marched out defiantly in full view of all the Egyptians, ⁴while the Egyptians were burying all the firstborn struck down by the LORD as a judgement on their gods.

⁵The Israelites left Rameses and encamped at Succoth.

⁶They left Succoth and encamped at Etham on the edge of the wilderness.

⁷They left Etham, turned back near Pi-hahiroth on the east of Baal-zephon, and encamped before Migdol.

⁸They left Pi-hahiroth, and passed through the Sea into the wilderness; they marched for three days through the wilderness of Etham, and encamped at Marah.

⁹They left Marah and came to Elim; in Elim there were twelve springs of water and seventy palm trees, so they encamped there.

¹⁰They left Elim and encamped by the Red Sea.

¹¹They left the Red Sea and encamped in the wilderness of Sin.

¹²They left the wilderness of Sin and encamped at Dophkah.

¹³They left Dophkah and encamped at Alush.

¹⁴They left Alush and encamped at Rephidim, where there was no water for the people to drink.

¹⁵They left Rephidim and encamped in the wilderness of Sinai.

¹⁶They left the wilderness of Sinai and encamped at Kibroth-hattaavah.

¹⁷They left Kibroth-hattaavah and encamped at Hazeroth.

¹⁸They left Hazeroth and encamped at Rithmah.

¹⁹They left Rithmah and encamped at Rimmon-parez.

²⁰They left Rimmon-parez and encamped at Libnah.

²¹They left Libnah and encamped at Rissah.

²²They left Rissah and encamped at Kehelathah.

²³They left Kehelathah and encamped at Mount Shapher.

²⁴They left Mount Shapher and encamped at Haradah.

²⁵They left Haradah and encamped at Makheloth.

²⁶They left Makheloth and encamped at Tahath.

²⁷They left Tahath and encamped at Tarah.

²⁸They left Tarah and encamped at Mithcah.

²⁹They left Mithcah and encamped at Hashmonah.

³⁰They left Hashmonah and encamped at Moseroth.

³¹They left Moseroth and encamped at Bene-jaakan.

³²They left Bene-jaakan and encamped at Hor-haggidgad.

³³They left Hor-haggidgad and encamped at Jotbathah.

³⁴They left Jotbathah and encamped at Ebronah.

32:37,38 *Cp. verse 3.*   32:41 **the tent-villages of Ham:** *prob. rdg; Heb.* their tent-villages. **Havvoth-jair:** *that is* Tent-villages of Jair.   33:7 **Pi-hahiroth:** *see Exod.* 14:2.   33:8 **They left Pi-hahiroth:** *so Samar.; Heb.* They left from before Hahiroth. 33:12,13 **Dophkah:** *or, with Gk,* Rophkah.

33.1–49: A review of Israel's itinerary from Egypt to the lowlands of Moab. It has been shaped so as to contain forty stages before the mountains overlooking the promised land are reached (v. 47), in keeping with the forty years in the wilderness (14.32–33). Relics of older sources have been used, as is evident from several omissions from and additions to the basic account in Exod.–Num. **5–15:** See Exod. 12.37–19.2. **16–36:** See

35 They left Ebronah and encamped at Ezion-geber.

36 They left Ezion-geber and encamped in the wilderness of Zin, that is Kadesh.

37 They left Kadesh and encamped on Mount Hor on the frontier of Edom.

38 Aaron the priest went up Mount Hor at the command of the LORD and there he died, on the first day of the fifth month in the fortieth year after the Israelites came out of Egypt; 39 when he died there he was a hundred and twenty-three years old.

40 The Canaanite king of Arad, who lived in the Canaanite Negeb, heard that the Israelites were coming.

41 They left Mount Hor and encamped at Zalmonah.

42 They left Zalmonah and encamped at Punon.

43 They left Punon and encamped at Oboth.

44 They left Oboth and encamped at Iye-abarim on the frontier of Moab.

45 They left Iyim and encamped at Dibon-gad.

46 They left Dibon-gad and encamped at Almon-diblathaim.

47 They left Almon-diblathaim and encamped in the mountains of Abarim east of Nebo.

48 They left the mountains of Abarim and encamped in the lowlands of Moab by the Jordan near Jericho. 49 Their camp beside the Jordan extended from Beth-jeshimoth to Abel-shittim in the lowlands of Moab.

50 In the lowlands of Moab by the Jordan opposite Jericho the LORD told Moses 51 to say this to the Israelites: 'You will soon be crossing the Jordan to enter Canaan. 52 You must drive out all its inhabitants as you advance, destroy all their stone carved figures and their images of cast metal, and lay their shrines in ruins. 53 You are to take possession of the land and settle there, for I have given the land for you to occupy. 54 You must divide it by lot among your families, each taking its own share of territory, the larger family a larger share and the small family a smaller. It will be assigned to them according to the fall of the lot, each tribe and family taking its own territory. 55 But if you do not drive out the inhabitants of the land as you advance, any whom you leave in possession will become like a barbed hook in your eye and a thorn in your side. They will continually dispute your possession of the land, 56 and what I meant to do to them I shall do to you.'

34 The LORD said to Moses, 2 'Give these instructions to the Israelites: Soon you will be entering Canaan. This is the land assigned to you as your portion, the land of Canaan thus defined by its frontiers. 3 Your southern border will start from the wilderness of Zin, where it marches with Edom, and run southwards from the end of the Dead Sea on its eastern side. 4 It will then turn from the south up the ascent of Akrabbim and pass by Zin, and its southern limit will be Kadesh-barnea. It will proceed by Hazar-addar to Azmon 5 and from Azmon turn towards the wadi of Egypt, and its limit will be the sea. 6 Your western frontier will be the Great Sea and the seaboard; this will be your frontier to the west. 7 This will be your northern frontier: you will draw a line from the Great Sea to Mount Hor 8 and from Mount Hor to Lebo-hamath, and the limit of the frontier will be Zedad. 9 From there it will run to Ziphron, and its limit will be Hazar-enan; this will be your frontier to the north. 10 To the east you will draw a line from Hazar-enan to Shepham; 11 it will run down from Shepham to Riblah east of Ain, continuing until it strikes the ridge east of the sea of Kinnereth. 12 The frontier will then run down to the Jordan and its limit will be the Dead Sea. The land defined by these frontiers will be your land.'

13 Moses gave these instructions to the Israelites: 'This is the land which you are to assign by lot as holdings; it is the land which the LORD has commanded to be given to nine tribes and a half tribe. 14 For the Reubenites, the Gadites, and the half tribe of Manasseh have already taken possession of their holdings, family by family. 15 These two and a half tribes have received their holding here beyond the Jordan, east of Jericho, towards the sunrise.'

16 The LORD said to Moses, 17 'These are the men who are to assign the land for you: Eleazar the priest and Joshua son of Nun. 18 You

10.11–20.1. **37–49:** See 20.22–22.1.

33.50–34.29: Directions for the distribution of territory west of the Jordan. 54: Lot: see 26.55–56 n. for the reason. **55–56:** For a slightly different reason for expelling the Canaanites, see Deut. 7.1–6. **34.8:**

must also take one chief from each tribe to assign the land. ¹⁹These are their names:

from the tribe of Judah: Caleb son of Je-phunneh;

²⁰from the tribe of Simeon: Samuel son of Ammihud;

²¹from the tribe of Benjamin: Elidad son of Kislon;

²²from the tribe of Dan: the chief Bukki son of Jogli;

²³from the Josephites: from Manasseh, the chief Hanniel son of Ephod;

²⁴and from Ephraim, the chief Kemuel son of Shiphtan;

²⁵from Zebulun: the chief Elizaphan son of Parnach;

²⁶from Issachar: the chief Paltiel son of Azzan;

²⁷from Asher: the chief Ahihud son of Shelomi;

²⁸from Naphtali: the chief Pedahel son of Ammihud.'

²⁹These were the men whom the LORD appointed to assign the holdings in the land of Canaan.

35 THE LORD spoke to Moses in the lowlands of Moab by the Jordan near Jericho. He said: ²'Tell the Israelites to set aside towns in their holdings as homes for the Levites, and give them also the common land surrounding the towns. ³They are to live in the towns, and keep their animals, their herds, and all their livestock on the common land. ⁴The land of the towns which you give the Levites will extend from the centre of the town outwards for a thousand cubits in each direction. ⁵Starting from the town the eastern boundary will measure two thousand cubits, the southern two thousand, the western two thousand, and the northern two thousand, with the town in the centre. They will have this as the common land adjoining their towns.

⁶'When you give the Levites their towns,

six of them are to be cities of refuge, in which the homicide may take sanctuary; and you are to give them forty-two other towns. ⁷The total number of towns to be given to the Levites, each with its common land, is forty-eight. ⁸When you set aside these towns out of the territory of the Israelites, you should allot more from a larger tribe and less from a smaller; each tribe must give towns to the Levites in proportion to the portion assigned to it.'

⁹The LORD told Moses ¹⁰to say to the Israelites: 'When you cross the Jordan into Canaan, ¹¹you are to designate certain cities to be places of refuge, in which the homicide who has inadvertently killed a man may take sanctuary. ¹²These cities will be places of refuge from the dead man's next-of-kin, so that the homicide is not put to death without a trial before the community. ¹³The cities appointed as places of refuge are to be six in number, ¹⁴three east of the Jordan and three in Canaan. ¹⁵These six cities will be places of refuge, so that any man who has taken life inadvertently, whether he be Israelite, resident alien, or temporary settler, may take sanctuary in one of them.

¹⁶'If anyone strikes his victim with anything made of iron, and he dies, then he is a murderer: the murderer must be put to death. ¹⁷If a man has a stone in his hand capable of causing death and strikes another man and he dies, he is a murderer: the murderer must be put to death. ¹⁸If a man has a wooden thing in his hand capable of causing death, and strikes another man and he dies, he is a murderer: the murderer must be put to death. ¹⁹The dead man's next-of-kin is to put the murderer to death; he is to put him to death because he attacked his victim. ²⁰If the homicide sets upon a man openly and deliberately or aims a missile at him of set purpose and he dies, ²¹or if in enmity he falls upon him with his bare hands and he dies,

35:4 **centre:** *meaning of Heb. uncertain in context.*

Lebo-hamath: see 13.21 n. **14–15:** See ch. 32. **19–28:** The order is roughly that of the geographical position of the tribes from south to north after the conquest, under Joshua, thus reflecting the date of its composition; however, Judah unexpectedly appears before Simeon (see 2.3 n.; Gen. 34.1–31 n.).

35.1–34: Levitical cities and cities of refuge. 2–8: The *Levites,* having been set aside for special duties at the sanctuary, are not given a separate allotment of territory (Deut. 10.8–9). In compensation, they receive tithes (Num. 18.21–24), spoils of war (31.30), special rights at the jubilee (Lev. 25.32–34), and now cities scattered throughout the tribes. See Josh. ch. 21; 1 Chr. 6.54–81. For another perspective on the decline of the tribe of Levi, see Gen. 34.1–31 n. **11:** *Places of refuge:* see Exod. 21.13; Deut. 19.1–13; Josh. ch. 20. **12:** *From the dead man's next-of-kin:* see Josh. 20.3.

then the assailant must be put to death; he is a murderer. The next-of-kin is to put the murderer to death because he attacked his victim.

22'If the homicide has attacked anyone on the spur of the moment, not being his enemy, 23 or has hurled a missile at him not of set purpose, or if without looking he has thrown a stone capable of causing death and it hits someone, then if that person dies, provided the attacker was not his enemy and was not harming him of set purpose, 24 the community is to judge between the attacker and the next-of-kin according to these rules. 25 The community must protect the homicide from the vengeance of the kinsman and take him back to the city of refuge where he had taken sanctuary. He must stay there till the death of the duly anointed high priest. 26 If the homicide ever goes beyond the boundaries of the city where he has taken sanctuary, 27 and the next-of-kin finds him outside and kills him, then the next-of-kin is not guilty of murder. 28 The homicide must remain in the city of refuge till the death of the high priest; after the death of the high priest he may go back to his own holding. 29 These will be for you legal precedents for all time wherever you live.

30 'The homicide may be put to death as a murderer only on the testimony of witnesses; the testimony of a single witness is not enough to bring him to his death. 31 You should not accept payment for the life of a homicide guilty of a capital offence; he must be put to death. 32 You should not accept a payment from a man who has taken sanctuary in a city of refuge, allowing him to go back before the death of the high priest and live at large. 33 You must not defile your land by bloodshed. Blood defiles the land; no expiation can be made on behalf of the land for blood shed on it, except by the blood of him who shed it. 34 You must not make the land which you inhabit unclean, the land in which I dwell; for I, the LORD, dwell among the Israelites.'

36 THE heads of the fathers' families of Gilead son of Machir, son of Manasseh, one of the families of the sons of Joseph, approached Moses and the chiefs, heads of families in Israel, and addressed them. 2 'The LORD commanded you, sir,' they said, 'to distribute the land by lot to the Israelites, and you were also commanded to give the portion of our brother Zelophehad to his daughters. 3 Now if any of them should be married to a husband from another Israelite tribe, her share would be lost to the portion of our fathers and be added to that of the tribe into which she marries, and so part of our allotted portion would be lost. 4 When the jubilee year comes round in Israel, her share would be added to the share of the tribe into which she marries, and it would be permanently lost to the portion of our fathers' tribe.'

5 Instructed by the LORD, Moses gave the Israelites this ruling: 'The tribe of the sons of Joseph is right. 6 This is the LORD's command for the daughters of Zelophehad: They may marry whom they please, but only within a family of their father's tribe. 7 No portion in Israel shall pass from one tribe to another, but every Israelite shall retain his father's portion. 8 Any woman of an Israelite tribe who is an heiress may marry a man from any family in her father's tribe. Thus each of the Israelites shall retain the portion of his forefathers. 9 No portion shall pass from one tribe to another, but every tribe in Israel shall retain its own share.'

10 The daughters of Zelophehad acted in accordance with the LORD's command to Moses; 11 Mahlah, Tirzah, Hoglah, Milcah, and Noah, the daughters of Zelophehad, married sons of their father's brothers. 12 They married within the families of the sons of Manasseh son of Joseph, and their portion remained with the tribe of their father's family.

13 These are the commandments and the decrees which the LORD issued to the Israelites through Moses in the lowlands of Moab by the Jordan near Jericho.

24: *Community is to judge:* see v. 12. **28:** Perhaps now the *high priest,* functioning as the monarch in the postexilic community (see Introduction to Lev.), could grant amnesty to all such homicides at the beginning of his rule; or perhaps such amnesty was automatic. **31:** This is in contrast to some ancient Near Eastern codes.
  36.1–13: An appendix on women's right to receive property. The basic legislation is contained in 27.1–11. **4:** It is difficult to understand precisely how the jubilee legislation (Lev. ch. 25) applies. **13:** The concluding statement refers back to chs. 22–36.

Deuteronomy

Deuteronomy means "second law," a name appropriate because chs. 12–26 repeat much of the legislation found in Exodus–Leviticus–Numbers. In Deuteronomy Moses speaks in the first person in three addresses (1.6–4.40; 5.1–28.68; and 29.1–30.20) given in the plains of Moab, as his farewell to his people. Chapters 31–34 resume in the third person the narrative found at the end of Numbers.

The first address is a review of the wilderness experience as the basis for exhorting Israel to fidelity in its forthcoming invasion of Canaan. The tone of the legal section is hortatory rather than legislative. The climactic third address (chs. 29–30), in the renewal of the covenant, joins the beckoning future to the record of God's gracious action in the past.

Within the repetition of the laws, a theme recurs that there is to be only one valid sanctuary, this in order for Israel to avoid contamination by the paganism lurking in a multiplicity of local shrines. Since the early nineteenth century, modern scholarship has associated this theme, and hence the Book of Deuteronomy, with the religious reformation in 621 B.C.E. of King Josiah (2 Kgs. chs. 22–23), by which the temple of Jerusalem became the only legitimate shrine. The writing of Deuteronomy is attributed to the age of Josiah, though older traditions are embodied and later materials apparently added. The exhortation seems addressed specifically to the kingdom of Judah so as to enable it to escape the fate of conquest and exile suffered by the kingdom of Israel which fell to Assyria in 721 B.C.E.

In addressing the people assembled before Moses just prior to his death, the Book of Deuteronomy is meant to speak to all future generations.

Moses' first discourse

1 THESE are the words that Moses addressed to all Israel in the wilderness beyond the Jordan, that is to say, in the Arabah opposite Suph, between Paran on the one side and Tophel, Laban, Hazeroth, and Dizahab on the other. ² (The journey from Horeb through the hill-country of Seir to Kadesh-barnea takes eleven days.)

³ On the first day of the eleventh month of the fortieth year, Moses repeated to the Israelites all the commands that the LORD had given him for them. ⁴ This was after the defeat of Sihon king of the Amorites who ruled in Heshbon, and the defeat at Edrei of King Og of Bashan who ruled in Ashtaroth, ⁵ and it was beyond the Jordan, in Moab, that Moses resolved to expound this law.

These were his words.

⁶ The LORD our God speaking to us at Horeb said, 'You have stayed at this mountain long enough; ⁷ up, break camp, and make for the hill-country of the Amorites, and pass on to all their neighbours in the Arabah, in the hill-country, in the Shephelah, in the Negeb, and on the coast: in short, all Canaan and the Lebanon as far as the Great River, the Euphrates. ⁸ I have laid the land open before you; go in and occupy it, the land which the LORD swore to give to your forefathers Abraham, Isaac, and Jacob, and to their descendants after them.'

⁹ At that time I said to you, 'You are too

1.1–3.29: A review of Israel's journey from Horeb (Sinai) to the plains of Moab. See 4.44–49 n. The LORD's graciousness, despite repeated rebellion, is stressed in order to instruct future generations. 1.1–5: The setting of Moses' final addresses. 2: Kadesh-barnea: Kadesh (Num. 20.1). 3: Eleventh month: see Gen. 7.24 n. 4: See Num. 21.21–35. 5: This law: chs. 12–26, which contain both a review of previous legislation and much that is new. See 5.22–31 n. 6–7: See Exod. 33.1–2. Amorites: see Num. 21.13 n. Euphrates: see Gen. 15.18 n. 8: Forefathers: Gen. 12.1–3; 15.12–21; 26.1–5; 28.10–15. 9–18: Elements of Num. 11.14–17 (in vv. 9–12) heavy a burden for me to bear unaided. [10] The LORD your God has so increased you that today you are as numerous as the stars in the heavens. [11] May the LORD, the God of your forefathers, increase your numbers a thousand times and bless you as he promised! [12] How can I bear unaided the heavy burden you are to me, and put up with your complaints? [13] Choose men of wisdom, understanding, and repute for each of your tribes, and I shall set them in authority over you.' [14] Your answer was, 'What you propose to do is good.' [15] So I took leading men of your tribes, men of wisdom and repute, and set them in authority over you, some as commanders over units of a thousand, of a hundred, of fifty, or of ten, and others as officers, for each of your tribes. [16] At that time also I gave your judges this command: 'Hear the cases that arise among your kinsmen and judge fairly between one person and another, whether fellow-countryman or resident alien. [17] You must be impartial and listen to high and low alike: have no fear of your fellows, for judgement belongs to God. But should any case be too difficult for you, refer it to me and I shall hear it.' [18] At the same time I instructed you in all your duties.

[19] We set out from Horeb, in obedience to the orders of the LORD our God, and made our way through that vast and terrible wilderness, as you found it to be, on the way to the hill-country of the Amorites. When we came to Kadesh-barnea, [20] I said to you, 'You have reached the hill-country of the Amorites which the LORD our God is giving us. [21] The LORD your God has now laid the land open before you. Go forward and occupy it in fulfilment of the promise which the LORD the God of your forefathers made you; do not be afraid or discouraged.' [22] But you all came to me and said, 'Let us send men ahead to explore the country and report back to us about the route we should take and the towns we shall find.' [23] I approved of the plan and picked twelve of your number, one from each tribe. [24] They set out and made their way up into the hill-country which they reconnoitred as far as the wadi of Eshcol. [25] They collected samples of the fruit of the country to bring back to us, and in their report they said: 'It is a rich land that the LORD our God is giving us.'

[26] However, you refused to go up, rebelling against the command of the LORD your God, [27] muttering treason in your tents and saying, 'It was because the LORD hated us that he brought us out of Egypt to hand us over to the Amorites to be wiped out. [28] What shall we find up there? Our kinsmen have discouraged us by their report of a people bigger and taller than we are, and of great cities with fortifications towering to the sky. Besides, they saw the descendants of the Anakim there.'

[29] I said to you, 'You must not dread them or be afraid. [30] The LORD your God, who goes at your head, will fight for you; he will do again what you saw him do for you in Egypt [31] and in the wilderness. You saw there how the LORD your God carried you all the way to this place, as a father carries his son.' [32] In spite of this you persisted in not trusting the LORD your God, [33] who went ahead on the journey to find a place for your camp. He went in fire by night and in a cloud by day to show you the route you should take.

[34] When the LORD heard your complaints, he was angry and solemnly swore: [35] 'Not one of these men, this wicked generation, will see the good land which I swore to give your forefathers, [36] none except Caleb son of Jephunneh; he will see it, and to him and his descendants I shall give the land on which he has set foot, because he followed the LORD loyally.'

[37] On your account the LORD was angry with me also and said, 'Neither will you yourself go in there; [38] only Joshua son of Nun, who is in attendance on you, will go. Support him, for he will put Israel in possession of that land. [39] Your dependants who, you thought, would become spoils of war, and your children who do not yet know good from evil, they will enter; I shall give it to them, and they are to occupy it. [40] You yourselves must turn and set out for the wilderness making towards the Red Sea.'

[41] You answered me, 'We have sinned against the LORD; we ourselves shall go up

1:28 **descendants . . . Anakim:** or giants.   1:40 **Red Sea:** or sea of Reeds.

and Exod. 18.13–27 (in vv. 13–17) have been combined. **19:** See Num. 10.11–13.26; 20.1. **20–46:** See Num. 13.1–14.45. Here, rather than the LORD (Num. 13.1–2), it is the people who request spies (v. 22); this is indicative of their lack of faith. **28:** *Towering:* built atop hills for defensive purposes. **30:** See Exod. 14.13–14.

and make the attack just as the LORD our God commanded us.' Every man of you, thinking it an easy thing to invade the hill-country, fastened on his weapons. [42] But the LORD said to me, 'Warn them not to go up and fight, for I shall not be with them, and the enemy will defeat them.' [43] I told you this, but you would not listen; you rebelled against the LORD's command and defiantly went up to the hill-country. [44] Then the Amorites living there came out against you and swarmed after you like bees; they crushed you at Hormah in Seir. [45] When you came back you wept before the LORD, but he would not hear you or listen to you. [46] That is why you remained in Kadesh as long as you did.

2 When we turned and set out for the wilderness, making towards the Red Sea as the LORD had instructed me, we spent many days marching round the hill-country of Seir. [2] Then the LORD said to me, [3] 'You have been marching round these hills long enough; turn northwards. [4] Give the people this charge: You are about to pass through the territory of your kinsmen, the descendants of Esau, who live in Seir. Although they are afraid of you, be very careful [5] not to quarrel with them; for I shall not give you any of their land, not so much as a foot's breadth: I have given the hill-country of Seir to Esau as a possession. [6] You may purchase food from them to eat and buy water to drink.' [7] The LORD your God has blessed you in everything you have undertaken. He has watched over your journey through this great wilderness; these forty years the LORD your God has been with you, and you have gone short of nothing.

[8] So we went on past our kinsmen, the descendants of Esau who live in Seir, and along the road of the Arabah which comes from Elath and Ezion-geber, and we turned and went in the direction of the wilderness of Moab. [9] There the LORD warned me, 'Do not harass the Moabites or provoke them to battle, for I shall not give you any of their land as a possession. I have given Ar to the descendants of Lot as a possession.' [10] (Formerly the Emim lived there — [11] a great and numerous people, as tall as the Anakim. The Rephaim also were reckoned as Anakim, but the Moabites called them Emim. [12] The Horites lived in Seir at one time, but the descendants of Esau occupied their territory: they exterminated them as they advanced and settled in their place, just as Israel did in the territory which the LORD gave them.) [13] 'Come, cross the wadi of the Zared,' said the LORD. So we went across. [14] The journey from Kadesh-barnea to the crossing of the Zared lasted thirty-eight years, until the entire generation of fighting men had passed away, as the LORD had sworn that they would. [15] The LORD's hand was against them, and he rooted them out of the camp to the last man.

[16] When the last of the fighting men among the people had died, [17] the LORD spoke to me. [18] 'Today', he said, 'you are to cross by Ar which lies on the frontier of Moab, [19] and when you reach the territory of the Ammonites, you must not harass them or provoke them to battle, for I shall not give you any Ammonite land as a possession; I have assigned it to the descendants of Lot.' [20] (This also is reckoned as the territory of the Rephaim, who lived there at one time; but the Ammonites called them Zamzummim. [21] They were a great and numerous people, as tall as the Anakim, but the LORD destroyed them as the Ammonites advanced and occupied their territory, [22] just as he had done for Esau's descendants who lived in Seir. As they advanced, he destroyed the Horites so that they occupied their territory and took possession instead of them: so it is to this day. [23] It was Caphtorites from Caphtor who destroyed the Avvim who lived in the hamlets near Gaza, and settled in the land instead of them.) [24] 'Come, move on and cross the wadi of the Arnon, for I have delivered Sihon the Amorite, king of Heshbon, and his territory into your hands. Begin the conquest; engage him in battle. [25] Today I shall start to put the fear and dread of you into all the peoples under heaven; if they so much as hear a rumour of you, they will quake and tremble before you.'

2:6 **buy:** *or* dig for.   2:8 **along:** *so Gk; Heb.* past.

33: See Exod. 13.21 n. 37: *On your account:* compare Num. 25.4 n.; contrast Num. 20.12 n. **2.1–25:** From Kadesh to the Amorite border (Num. 20.14–21.15). **1:** Towards *the Red Sea:* see Num. 14.25 n. **4:** *Pass through:* contrast Num. 20.14–21. **7:** *Short of nothing:* contrast Num. chs. 11; 20. **9:** The *Moabites* and Ammonites (v. 19) were relatives of Israel (Gen. 19.30–38; 11.27). **14:** *Thirty-eight:* this is a different tradition from v. 7, which places this span of time at Kadesh (see Num. 13.26 n.). **23:** *Caphtor:* Crete (or possibly Asia Minor);

26 From the wilderness of Kedemoth I sent envoys to King Sihon of Heshbon with the following overtures: 27 'Grant us passage through your country: we shall keep to the highway, trespassing neither to right nor to left, 28 and we shall pay you the full price for the food we eat and the water we drink. 29 The descendants of Esau who live in Seir granted us passage, and so did the Moabites in Ar. We shall simply pass through your land on foot, until we cross the Jordan to the land which the LORD our God is giving us.' 30 But King Sihon of Heshbon refused to grant us passage; for the LORD your God had made him stubborn and obstinate, in order that he and his land might become subject to you, as it is to this day.

31 The LORD said to me, 'Come, I have begun to deliver Sihon and his territory into your hands. Begin the conquest; occupy his land.' 32 When Sihon with all his people marched out to oppose us in battle at Jahaz, 33 the LORD our God delivered him into our hands; we killed him along with his sons and all his army. 34 We captured all his towns at that time and put to death under solemn ban everyone in them, men, women, and dependants; we left no survivors. 35 We carried off the cattle as spoil and plundered the towns we captured. 36 From Aroer on the edge of the wadi of the Arnon and the town in the wadi, as far as Gilead, no town had walls too lofty for us; the LORD our God laid everything open to us. 37 But you avoided the territory of the Ammonites, both the parts along the wadi of the Jabbok and their towns in the hills, thus fulfilling all that the LORD our God had commanded.

3 Next we turned and advanced along the road to Bashan. King Og of Bashan came out with his whole army to give battle at Edrei. 2 The LORD assured me, 'Do not be afraid of him, for I have delivered him into your hands, with all his people and his land. Deal with him as you dealt with King Sihon of the Amorites who lived in Heshbon.' 3 So the LORD our God also delivered King Og of Bashan into our hands, with all his people. We slaughtered them and left him no survivor, 4 and at the same time we captured all his towns; there was not one town that we did not

take from them. In all we captured sixty towns, the whole region of Argob, the kingdom of Og in Bashan; 5 all these were fortified towns with high walls and barred gates; in addition we took a great many open settlements. 6 In every town we put to death under solemn ban all the men, women, and dependants, as we did to King Sihon of Heshbon. 7 All the cattle and the spoil from the towns we carried off for ourselves.

8 At that time we seized from the two Amorite kings beyond the Jordan the territory that runs from the wadi of the Arnon to Mount Hermon 9 (the mountain that the Sidonians call Sirion and the Amorites Senir), 10 all the towns of the tableland, and the whole of Gilead and Bashan as far as Salcah and Edrei, towns in the kingdom of Og in Bashan. 11 (Only King Og of Bashan remained, as the sole survivor of the Rephaim. His sarcophagus of basalt was over thirteen feet long and six feet wide, and it may still be seen in the Ammonite town of Rabbah.)

12 When at that time we occupied this territory, I assigned to the Reubenites and Gadites the land beyond Aroer on the wadi of the Arnon and half the hill-country of Gilead with its towns, 13 while the rest of Gilead and the whole of Bashan the kingdom of Og, all the region of Argob, I assigned to half the tribe of Manasseh. (All Bashan used to be called the land of the Rephaim. 14 Jair son of Manasseh captured all the region of Argob as far as the Geshurite and Maacathite border. There are tent-villages in Bashan still bearing his name, Havvoth-jair.) 15 To Machir I assigned Gilead, 16 and to the Reubenites and the Gadites I assigned land from Gilead to the wadi of the Arnon, that is to the middle of the wadi; its territory ran to the wadi of the Jabbok, the Ammonite frontier, 17 and included the Arabah, with the Jordan and land adjacent, from Kinnereth to the sea of the Arabah, that is the Dead Sea, below the watershed of Pisgah on the east.

2:37 **thus . . . all:** *so Gk; Heb.* and all. 3:11 **basalt:** *or* iron. **over . . . wide:** *lit.* nine cubits long and four cubits wide by the common standard.
3:14 **Havvoth-jair:** *that is* Tent-villages of Jair.
3:16 **that is . . . ran:** *or* including the bed of the wadi and the adjacent strip of land. **its territory ran:** *prob. rdg; Heb.* and territory and.

the Philistine invasion is meant (Amos 9.7; Gen. 9.27 n.). **2.26–3.11:** Victory over the Amorites (Num. 21.21–35). **30:** *Made him stubborn:* see Exod. 4.21 n. **34:** *No survivors:* on "holy" war, see 20.1–20. **3.11:** *Sarcophagus:* such stone coffins were widely used in the area. **12–20:** Distribution of the Amorite territory

18 At that time I gave you this command: 'Since the LORD your God has given you this land to occupy, let all your fighting men be drafted and cross at the head of their fellow-Israelites. 19 Only your wives and dependants and your livestock—I know you have much livestock—may remain in the towns I have given you. 20 This you are to do until the LORD gives your kinsfolk security as he has given it to you, and until they too occupy the land which the LORD your God is giving them on the other side of the Jordan; then you may each return to the possession I have given you.'

21 Also at that time I gave Joshua this charge: 'You have seen for yourself all that the LORD your God has done to these two kings; he will do the same to all the kingdoms into which you are about to cross. 22 Do not be afraid of them, for the LORD your God himself will fight for you.'

23 It was then I made this plea to the LORD: 24 'LORD God,' I said, 'you have begun to show to your servant your great power and your strong hand: what god is there in heaven or on earth who can match your works and mighty deeds? 25 Let me cross over, I beg, and see that good land which lies on the other side of the Jordan, and the fine hill-country and the Lebanon.' 26 But because of you the LORD angrily brushed me aside and would not listen. 'Enough!' he answered. 'Say no more about this. 27 Go to the top of Pisgah and look west and north, south and east; look well at what you see, for you will not cross this river Jordan. 28 Give Joshua his commission, support and strengthen him, for he will lead this people across, and he will put them in possession of the land you see before you.'

29 So we remained in the glen opposite Beth-peor.

4 AND now, Israel, listen to the statutes and laws which I am about to teach you; obey them, so that you may live and go in to occupy the land which the LORD the God of your forefathers is giving you. 2 You must not add anything to the charge I decree or take anything away from it; you must carry out the commandments of the LORD your God which I lay upon you.

3 You saw for yourselves what the LORD did at Baal-peor; the LORD your God destroyed from among you everyone who went over to the Baal of Peor, 4 but you who held fast to the LORD your God are all alive today. 5 I have taught you statutes and laws, as the LORD my God commanded me; see that you keep them when you go into and occupy the land. 6 Observe them carefully, for thereby you will display your wisdom and understanding to other peoples. When they hear about all these statutes, they will say, 'What a wise and understanding people this great nation is!' 7 What great nation has a god close at hand as the LORD our God is close to us whenever we call to him? 8 What great nation is there whose statutes and laws are so just, as is all this code of laws which I am setting before you today?

9 But take care: keep careful watch on yourselves so that you do not forget the things that you have seen with your own eyes; do not let them pass from your minds as long as you live, but teach them to your children and to your children's children. 10 You must never forget the day when you stood before the LORD your God at Horeb, and the LORD said to me, 'Assemble the people for me; I shall make them hear my words and they will learn to fear me all their lives in the land, and they will teach their children to do so.' 11 Then you came near and stood at the foot of the mountain, which was ablaze with fire to the very skies, and there was dark cloud and thick mist. 12 When the LORD spoke to you from the heart of the fire you heard a voice speaking, but you saw no form; there was only a voice. 13 He announced to you the terms of his covenant, bidding you observe the Ten Commandments, which he wrote on two stone tablets. 14 At the same time the LORD charged me to teach you statutes and laws which you should observe in the land

4:13 **Commandments:** *lit.* Words.

(Num. ch. 32). **21–28:** Moses' successor (see 31.1–29 n.). **26:** *Because of you:* see 1.37 n. **27:** See 34.1–4.
   4.1–43: An exhortation to obey the law after the settlement in Canaan. **1:** *And now . . . listen:* the LORD's previous gracious acts should motivate obedience. Compare Exod. 20.2 n.; Lev. 18.2 n. **2:** The prohibition against altering the wording follows ancient Near Eastern legislative custom and is motivated by fear that the new situation in Canaan would lead to deviation. **3:** An illustration of the consequences of disobedience, taken from Num. ch. 25. **8:** *Today:* on possible liturgical reenactment of the past, see 5.1–3 n.; Exod. 13.8 n. **10–11:**

into which you are about to cross to occupy it.

15 On the day when the LORD spoke to you from the heart of the fire at Horeb, you saw no form of any kind; so take good care 16 not to fall into the infamous practice of making for yourselves carved images in the form of any statue of a man or woman, 17 or of any animal on earth or bird that flies in the air, 18 or of anything that creeps on the ground or of any fish in the waters under the earth. 19 Nor must you raise your eyes to the heavens and look up to the sun, the moon, and the stars, all the host of heaven, and be led astray to bow down to them in worship; the LORD your God assigned these for all the peoples everywhere under heaven. 20 But you are the people whom the LORD brought out of Egypt, from the smelting furnace, and took for his own possession, as you are to this day.

21 The LORD was angry with me on your account and solemnly swore that I should not cross the Jordan or enter the good land which the LORD your God is about to give you as your holding. 22 I myself am to die in this country; I shall not cross the Jordan, but you are about to cross and occupy that good land. 23 Take care that you do not forget the covenant which the LORD your God made with you; do not make for yourselves a carved image in any form; the LORD your God has forbidden it. 24 For the LORD your God is a devouring fire, a jealous God.

25 When you have children and grandchildren and have grown old in the land, if you then fall into the infamous practice of making carved images in any form, doing what is wrong in the eyes of the LORD your God and provoking him to anger, 26 I summon heaven and earth to witness against you this day: you will soon perish from upon the land which you are to occupy after crossing the Jordan. You will not enjoy long life in it; you will be swept away. 27 The LORD will scatter you among the peoples, and you will be left few in number among the nations to which the LORD will lead you. 28 There you will serve gods made by human hands out of wood and stone, gods that can neither see nor hear, eat nor smell. 29 But should you from there seek the LORD your God, you will find him, if it is with all your heart and soul that you search. 30 When you are in distress and all those things happen to you, you will in days to come turn back to the LORD your God and obey him. 31 The LORD your God is a merciful God; he will never fail you or destroy you; he will not forget the covenant with your forefathers which he guaranteed by oath.

32 Search into days gone by, long before your time, beginning at the day when God created man on earth; search from one end of heaven to the other, and ask if any deed as mighty as this has been seen or heard. 33 Did any people ever hear the voice of a god speaking from the heart of the fire, as you heard it, and remain alive? 34 Or did a god ever attempt to come and take a nation for himself away from another nation, with a challenge, and with signs, portents, and wars, with a strong hand and an outstretched arm, and with great deeds of terror, like all you saw the LORD your God do for you in Egypt? 35 You have had sure proof that the LORD is God; there is none other. 36 From heaven he let you hear his voice for your instruction, and on earth he let you see his great fire, and from the heart of the fire you heard his words. 37 Because he loved your fathers and chose their children after them, he in his own person brought you out of Egypt by his great strength, 38 so that he might drive out before you nations greater and more powerful than you and bring you in to give you their land in possession, as it is to this day.

39 Be sure to bear in mind this day that the LORD is God in heaven above and on earth below; there is none other. 40 You must keep his statutes and his commands which I give you today; so all will be well with you and with your children after you, and you will enjoy long life in the land which the LORD your God is giving you for all time.

41 Then Moses set apart three cities in the

See Exod. 19.10–19. **17–19**: Compare Exod. 20.4 n.; Gen. 1.14 n. **21**: See 1.37 n. **26**: *Summon heaven and earth*: This is very old covenant (legal) terminology, originating in a polytheistic environment, and surviving in later times. The gods of those domains served as witnesses to an agreement between parties, and their testimony was invoked in case of violation (Deut. 30.19 n.; 31.28; see Isa. 1.2; Mic. 6.1–2). **32–33**: See Exod. 20.18–21. **32**: See 32.7. **34**: See Exod. chs. 1–15. **37**: Here, for the first time, the LORD's election of Israel is explained as the result of love (see 7.7–8). It should evoke a responding love which results in obedience (6.5). **41–43**: A once independent fragment whose relationship to the present context is not clear. *Places of refuge:*

east beyond the Jordan [42] to be places of refuge for the homicide who kills someone without malice aforethought. If he took sanctuary in one of these cities his life would be safe. [43] The cities were: Bezer-in-the-wilderness on the tableland for the Reubenites, Ramoth in Gilead for the Gadites, and Golan in Bashan for the Manassites.

[44] This is the code of laws which Moses laid down for the Israelites. [45] These are the precepts, the statutes, and the laws which Moses proclaimed to the Israelites, when they had come out of Egypt [46] and were beyond the Jordan in the valley opposite Beth-peor in the land of Sihon king of the Amorites who lived in Heshbon. Moses and the Israelites had defeated him when they came out of Egypt [47] and had occupied his territory and the territory of King Og of Bashan, the two Amorite kings east of the Jordan. [48] The territory ran from Aroer on the wadi of the Arnon to Mount Sirion, that is Hermon; [49] it included all the Arabah beyond the Jordan, as far as the sea of the Arabah below the watershed of Pisgah.

Moses' second discourse

5 Moses summoned all Israel and said to them: Israel, listen to the statutes and the laws which I proclaim to you this day. Learn them, and be careful to observe them. [2] The Lord our God made a covenant with us at Horeb. [3] It was not with our forefathers that the Lord made this covenant, but with us, all of us who are alive and are here this day. [4] The Lord spoke with you face to face on the mountain out of the heart of the fire. [5] I stood between the Lord and you at that time to report the words of the Lord; for you were afraid of the fire and did not go up the mountain. The Lord said:

[6] I am the Lord your God who brought you out of Egypt, out of that land where you lived as slaves.

[7] You must have no other gods beside me. [8] You are not to make a carved image for yourself, nor the likeness of anything in the heavens above, or on the earth below, or in the waters under the earth. [9] You must not worship or serve them; for I am the Lord your God, a jealous God, punishing children for the sins of their parents to the third and fourth generations of those who reject me. [10] But I keep faith with thousands, those who love me and keep my commandments.

[11] You shall not make wrong use of the name of the Lord your God; the Lord will not leave unpunished anyone who misuses his name.

[12] Observe the sabbath day and keep it holy as the Lord your God commanded you. [13] You have six days to labour and do all your work; [14] but the seventh day there is a sabbath of the Lord your God; that day you must not do any work, neither you, nor your son or your daughter, your slave or your slave-girl, your ox, your donkey, or any of your cattle, or the alien residing among you, so that your slaves and slave-girls may rest as you do. [15] Bear in mind that you were slaves in Egypt, and the Lord your God brought you out with a strong hand and an outstretched arm, and for that reason the Lord your God has commanded you to keep the sabbath day.

[16] Honour your father and your mother, as the Lord your God commanded you, so that you may enjoy long life, and it will be well with you in the land which the Lord your God is giving you.

[17] Do not commit murder.

[18] Do not commit adultery.

4:48 **Sirion:** *so Syriac, cp. 3:9; Heb.* Sion.
5:5 **words:** *so Samar.; Heb.* word.   5:7 **gods:** *or* god.
5:8 **nor:** *so many MSS; others omit.*   5:10 **with thousands:** *or* for a thousand generations with.

compare 19.1–13; Num. 35.9–34.

4.44–49: An older historical preface. At one stage in the collection and writing of materials attributed to Moses in the plains of Moab, this section may have been the opening. At a later stage, these verses provided the setting for 4.1–43; the brief historical review of vv. 46b–49 was expanded into 2.24–3.17, which was preceded by an account summarizing the journey from Sinai (Horeb) onward (1.6–2.23); thereafter a new introduction (1.1–5) was written.

5.1–31: A review of the covenant at Sinai. 1–3: Israel's past acceptance of the covenant obligations is to turn out to be of no consequence unless the covenant becomes the contemporary experience of the present generation. The passage may be part of a liturgy by means of which the relationship was regularly renewed. See 31.9–13; Josh. 24.1–28. **6–21:** This version of the Ten Commandments (see Exod. 20.1–21 n.) is substan-

¹⁹ Do not steal.

²⁰ Do not give baseless evidence against your neighbour.

²¹ Do not lust after your neighbour's wife; do not covet your neighbour's household, his land, his slave, his slave-girl, his ox, his donkey, or anything that belongs to him.

²² These commandments the LORD spoke in a loud voice to your whole assembly on the mountain out of the fire, the cloud, and the thick mist; then he said no more. He wrote them on two stone tablets, which he gave to me.

²³ When you heard the voice out of the darkness, while the mountain was ablaze with fire, all the heads of your tribes and the elders came to me ²⁴ and said, 'The LORD our God has indeed shown us his glory and his great power, and we have heard his voice from the heart of the fire: today we have seen that people may still live after God has spoken with them. ²⁵ But why should we now risk death, for this great fire will devour us? If we hear the voice of the LORD our God again, we shall die. ²⁶ Is there any creature like us who has heard the voice of the living God speaking out of the fire and remained alive? ²⁷ Go near and listen to all that the LORD our God says to you, and report to us whatever the LORD our God says; we shall listen and obey.'

²⁸ When the LORD heard these words which you spoke to me, he said, 'I have heard what this people has said to you; every word they have spoken is right. ²⁹ Would that they may always be of a mind to fear me and observe my commandments, so that all will be well with them and their children for ever! ³⁰ Go, and tell them to return to their tents, ³¹ but you yourself stand here beside me; I will set forth to you all the commandments, statutes, and laws which you are to teach them to observe in the land which I am about to give them to occupy.'

³² You must be careful to do as the LORD your God has commanded you; do not deviate from it to right or to left. ³³ You must conform to all the LORD your God commands you, if you would live and prosper and remain long in the land you are to occupy.

6 These are the commandments, statutes, and laws which the LORD your God commanded me to teach you to observe in the land into which you are crossing to occupy it, a land flowing with milk and honey, ² so that you may fear the LORD your God and keep all his statutes and commandments which I am giving you, both you, your children, and your descendants all your days, that you may enjoy long life. ³ If you listen, Israel, and are careful to observe them, you will prosper and increase greatly as the LORD the God of your forefathers promised you.

⁴ Hear, Israel: the LORD is our God, the LORD our one God; ⁵ and you must love the LORD your God with all your heart and with all your soul and with all your strength. ⁶ These commandments which I give you this day are to be remembered and taken to heart; ⁷ repeat them to your children, and speak of them both indoors and out of doors, when you lie down and when you get up. ⁸ Bind them as a sign on your hand and wear them as a pendant on your forehead; ⁹ write them on the doorposts of your houses and on your gates.

¹⁰ The LORD your God will bring you into

6:1 **a land . . . honey:** *transposed from verse 3.*
6:4 **LORD:** *see note on Exod. 3:15.*

tially that of Exod. 20.2–17, except for the added motivation for sabbath observance. **22–31:** The purpose in the prefatory verses (4.44–49) and the review (5.1–33) here become specific: the fear exhibited by the people (Exod. 20.18–21) necessitated that Moses act as mediator. Thus, some of the legislation received while he was alone atop the mountain has not yet been conveyed to the people; now the laws for the new life in Canaan are to be disclosed.

5.32–11.32: Exhortations and warnings to revere the law after the settlement in Canaan.

6.1–25: Fidelity to the one LORD. Much of the chapter may be viewed as an elaboration of the first commandment (5.7). **1:** *Commandments* is singular in MT, and possibly refers to vv. 4–5. The specific *statutes and laws* are delayed until ch. 12. *Milk and honey:* see Exod. 3.8 n. **4–9:** These verses are a standard preface to private and public prayer in the Jewish tradition. They are called the Shema, from the initial word which means "Hear!" The Shema is virtually a Jewish "creed." **4–5:** These verses are described as the greatest commandment in Mk. 12.28–34. **4:** *One God:* the only God (4.35, 39; Isa. 45.18). **5:** *Heart:* intellect, will. *Soul:* self, total being. Compare Gen. 2.7 n. *Strength:* determination. See 4.37 n. **8:** *Sign:* see Exod. 13.9 n. *Pendant:* or phylactery; see Exod. 13.16 n. **10–15:** This theme, central to the entire book, is expanded in ch. 8.

the land which he swore to your forefathers Abraham, Isaac, and Jacob that he would give you, a land of large, fine towns which you did not build, [11] houses full of good things which you did not provide, cisterns hewn from the rock but not by you, and vineyards and olive groves which you did not plant. When he brings you in and you have all you want to eat, [12] see that you do not forget the LORD who brought you out of Egypt, out of that land of slavery. [13] You are to fear the LORD your God; serve him alone, and take your oaths in his name. [14] You must not go after other gods, gods of the nations around you; [15] if you do, the anger of the LORD your God who is among you will be roused against you, and he will sweep you off the face of the earth, for the LORD your God is a jealous God.

[16] You must not put the LORD your God to the test as you did at Massah. [17] You must diligently keep the commandments of the LORD your God and the precepts and statutes which he gave you. [18] You must do what is right and good in the eyes of the LORD, so that all may go well with you, and you may enter and occupy the good land which the LORD promised on oath to your forefathers; [19] then, as the LORD promised, you will drive out all your enemies before you.

[20] When in time to come your son asks you, 'What is the meaning of the precepts, statutes, and laws which the LORD our God gave you?' [21] say to him, 'We were Pharaoh's slaves in Egypt, and the LORD brought us out of Egypt with his strong hand. [22] He harrowed the Egyptians including Pharaoh and all his court with mighty signs and portents, as we saw for ourselves. [23] But he led us out from there to bring us into the land and give it to us as he had promised to our forefathers. [24] The LORD commanded us to observe all these statutes and to fear the LORD our God; it will be for our own good at all times, and he will continue to preserve our lives. [25] For us to be in the right we should keep all these commandments before the LORD our God, as he has commanded us to do.'

7 WHEN the LORD your God brings you into the land which you are about to enter to occupy it, when he drives out many nations before you — Hittites, Girgashites, Amorites, Canaanites, Perizzites, Hivites, and Jebusites, seven nations more numerous and powerful than you — [2] and when the LORD your God delivers them into your power for you to defeat, you must exterminate them. You must not make an alliance with them or spare them. [3] You must not intermarry with them, giving your daughters to their sons or taking their daughters for your sons, [4] because if you do, they will draw your children away from the LORD to serve other gods. Then the anger of the LORD will be roused against you and he will soon destroy you. [5] But this is what you must do to them: pull down their altars, break their sacred pillars, hack down their sacred poles, and burn their idols, [6] for you are a people holy to the LORD your God, and he has chosen you out of all peoples on earth to be his special possession.

[7] It was not because you were more numerous than any other nation that the LORD cared for you and chose you, for you were the smallest of all nations; [8] it was because the LORD loved you and stood by his oath to your forefathers, that he brought you out with his strong hand and redeemed you from the place of slavery, from the power of Pharaoh king of Egypt. [9] Know then that the LORD your God is God, the faithful God; with those who love him and keep his commandments he keeps covenant and faith for a thousand generations, [10] but those who defy and reject him he repays with destruction: he will not be slow to requite any who reject him.

6:16 **Massah:** *that is* Test.   7:4 **from the LORD:** *prob. rdg; Heb.* from me.   7:5 **sacred poles:** *Heb.* asherim.

16: *Massah:* see Exod. 17.2–7. To *put . . . to the test* means to require the granting of material blessings as a prerequisite for worshiping God. **20–25:** These verses may be part of the ancient Passover liturgy (Exod. 12.26–27 and 13.8–9; compare Exod. 15.1–21 n.).

7.1–26: The inhabitants of Canaan. The reason for the injunctions in the chapter is given in v. 4. Compare Exod. 20.1–21 n. **2:** *Exterminate:* on rules for "holy" war, see 20.1–20. Those who gathered the Deuteronomic traditions believed that the kingdom of Israel had suffered defeat through succumbing to Canaanite influence (compare 2 Kgs. 17.1–23). The measures described here are meant to protect the kingdom of Judah from a similar catastrophe. *Not make an alliance:* this is in marked contrast to earlier attitudes (Gen. 21.22–32 and 26.26–31). **5:** *Pillars; poles:* see Exod. 34.13 n. **9–10:** See Exod. 34.6–7 n.

11 You are to observe these commandments, statutes, and laws which I give you this day, and keep them.

12 Because you listen to these laws and are careful to observe them, the LORD your God will observe the sworn covenant he made with your forefathers and will keep faith with you. 13 He will love you, bless you, and increase your numbers. He will bless the fruit of your body and the fruit of your soil, your grain and new wine and oil, the young of your herds and lambing flocks, in the land which he swore to your forefathers he would give you. 14 You will be blessed above every other nation; neither among your people nor among your cattle will there be an impotent male or a barren female. 15 The LORD will keep you free from all sickness; he will not bring on you any of the foul diseases of Egypt which you have experienced; but he will bring them on all who are hostile to you. 16 You are to devour all the nations which the LORD your God is giving over to you. Show none of them mercy, so that you do not serve their gods; that is the snare which awaits you.

17 You may say to yourselves, 'These nations outnumber us; how can we drive them out?' 18 You need have no fear of them; only bear in mind what the LORD your God did to Pharaoh and the whole of Egypt, 19 the great challenge which you yourselves witnessed, the signs and portents, the strong hand and the outstretched arm by which the LORD your God brought you out. So will he deal with all the nations of whom you are afraid. 20 Moreover he will spread panic among them until all who are left and are in hiding will perish before you.

21 Feel no dread of them, for the LORD your God is among you, a great and terrible God. 22 Little by little he will drive out these nations before you. You cannot exterminate them quickly, for fear the wild beasts become too numerous for you. 23 The LORD your God will deliver these nations over to you and throw them into utter confusion until they are wiped out. 24 He will put their kings into your hands, and you must wipe out their name from under heaven. No one will be able to withstand you; you will destroy them. 25 Their idols you must destroy by fire; you are not to covet the silver and gold on them and take it for yourselves; you might be ensnared by it, and these things are an abomination to the LORD your God. 26 You must not introduce any abominable idol into your houses and thus bring yourselves under solemn ban along with it. You shall hold it loathsome and abominable, for it is proscribed under the ban.

8 You must carefully observe every command I give you this day so that you may live and increase in numbers and enter and occupy the land which the LORD promised on oath to your forefathers. 2 Remember the whole way by which the LORD your God has led you these forty years in the wilderness to humble and test you, and to discover whether or not it was in your heart to keep his commandments. 3 So he afflicted you with hunger and then fed you on manna which neither you nor your fathers had known before, to teach you that people cannot live on bread alone, but that they live on every word that comes from the mouth of the LORD. 4 The clothes on your backs did not wear out, nor did your feet blister, all these forty years. 5 Take to heart this lesson: that the LORD your God was disciplining you as a father disciplines his son. 6 Keep the commandments of the LORD your God, conforming to his ways and fearing him.

7 The LORD your God is bringing you to a good land, a land with streams, springs, and underground waters gushing out in valley and hill, 8 a land with wheat and barley, vines, fig trees, and pomegranates, a land with olive oil and honey. 9 It is a land where you will never suffer any scarcity of food to eat, nor want for anything, a land whose stones are iron ore and from whose hills you will mine

---

12: *Forefathers:* see 1.8 n. **13–14:** The emphasis upon the LORD as the source of material blessings is a polemic against the Canaanite gods of fertility. **26:** *Ban:* the state of being accursed (see Exod. 22.20 n.).

8.1–20: Injunction for life in the promised land. The lesson learned through hardship, that "people cannot live on bread alone" (v. 3), must not be forgotten amidst the abundance of Canaan. **2:** The hardships of the *wilderness,* against which Israel rebelled and was punished (see Num. 25.1–18 n.), are reinterpreted as discipline in preparation for life in "a good land" (v. 7). **3:** *Manna:* see Num. 11.6 n. It was given, not alone to satisfy physical hunger, but to remind Israel of its dependence upon God. **4:** This tradition is not found outside Deut. **15:** *Snakes:* see Num. 21.4–9. *Rock:* see Num. 20.2–11.

copper. 10When you have plenty to eat, bless the LORD your God for the good land he has given you.

11See that you do not forget the LORD your God by failing to keep his commandments, laws, and statutes which I give you this day. 12When you have plenty to eat and live in fine houses of your own building, 13when your herds and flocks, your silver and gold, and all your possessions increase, 14do not become proud and forget the LORD your God who brought you out of Egypt, out of that land of slavery; 15he led you through the vast and terrible wilderness infested with venomous snakes and scorpions, a thirsty, waterless land where he caused water to flow for you from the flinty rock; 16he fed you in the wilderness with manna which your fathers had never known, to humble and test you, and in the end to make you prosper. 17Nor must you say to yourselves, 'My own strength and energy have gained me this wealth.' 18Remember the LORD your God; it is he who gives you strength to become prosperous, so fulfilling the covenant guaranteed by oath with your forefathers, as he does to this day.

19If you forget the LORD your God and go after other gods, serving them and bowing down to them, I give you a solemn warning this day that you will certainly be destroyed. 20Because of your disobedience to the LORD your God, you will be destroyed as surely as were the nations whom the LORD destroyed at your coming.

9 Hear, Israel; this day you will be crossing the Jordan to go in and occupy the territory of nations greater and more powerful than you, and great cities with fortifications towering to the sky. 2They are a great and tall people, the descendants of the Anakim, of whom you know, for you have heard it said, 'Who can withstand the sons of Anak?' 3Know then this day that it is the LORD your God himself who crosses at your head as a devouring fire; it is he who will subdue them and destroy them as you advance; you will drive them out and soon overwhelm them, as he promised you.

4When the LORD your God drives them out before you, do not say to yourselves, 'It is because of our merits that the LORD has brought us in to occupy this land.' 5It is not because of your merit or your integrity that you are entering their land to occupy it; it is because of the wickedness of these nations that the LORD your God is driving them out before you, and to fulfil the promise which the LORD made on oath to your forefathers, Abraham, Isaac, and Jacob.

6Know that it is not because of any merit of yours that the LORD your God is giving you this good land to occupy; indeed, you are a stubborn people. 7Remember, and never forget, how you angered the LORD your God in the wilderness: from the day you left Egypt until you came to this place you have defied the LORD. 8Even at Horeb you roused the LORD's anger, and the LORD in his wrath was ready to destroy you. 9When I went up the mountain to receive the stone tablets, the tablets of the covenant which the LORD made with you, I remained on the mountain forty days and forty nights without food or drink. 10Then the LORD gave me the two stone tablets written with the finger of God, and on them were all the words the LORD had spoken to you from the heart of the fire, on the mountain during the day of the assembly. 11At the end of forty days and forty nights the LORD gave me the two stone tablets, the tablets of the covenant, 12and said to me, 'Go down from the mountain at once, because your people whom you brought out of Egypt have committed a monstrous act: they have lost no time in turning from the way which I commanded them to follow, and have cast for themselves a metal image.'

13The LORD said to me, 'I have observed this people and I find them a stubborn people. 14Let me be, and I shall destroy them and blot out their name from under heaven; and I shall make you a nation more powerful and numerous than they.'

15I went back down the mountain; it was ablaze, and I had the two tablets of the covenant in my hands. 16When I saw how you had sinned against the LORD your God and had made for yourselves a cast image of a bull-

9:4 **this land:** *so Gk; Heb. adds* and because of the wickedness of these nations the LORD is driving them out before you.

9.1–10.11: The basis for the granting of the land. It was the wickedness of the Canaanites that led to their displacement, not the merit of Israel. Indeed, the latter would have been entirely destroyed in the wilderness were it not for the intercession of Moses. **2:** *Anakim:* see 1.28; Num. 13.22, 27–28. **9:** See Exod. 24.12–18.

calf, losing no time in turning from the way the Lord had told you to follow, 17 I flung down the two tablets which I held and shattered them in the sight of you all. 18 Then, as before, I lay prostrate before the Lord, forty days and forty nights without food or drink, on account of all the sin that you had committed, and because, in doing what was wrong in the eyes of the Lord, you had provoked him to anger. 19 I was in dread of the Lord's anger and the wrath with which he threatened to destroy you; but once again the Lord listened to me. 20 The Lord was greatly incensed with Aaron also and would have killed him; so I interceded for him at that time. 21 I took the calf, that sinful object you had made, and burnt it and pounded it, grinding it until it was as fine as dust; then I flung its dust into the torrent that flowed down from the mountain.

22 At Taberah also you roused the Lord's anger, and at Massah, and at Kibroth-hattaavah. 23 Again, when the Lord sent you from Kadesh-barnea with orders to advance and occupy the land which he was giving you, you defied the Lord your God and did not trust him or obey him. 24 You were defiant from the day that the Lord first knew you. 25 Forty days and forty nights I lay prostrate before the Lord because he had threatened to destroy you; 26 I prayed to the Lord and said, 'Lord God, do not destroy your people, your own possession, whom you redeemed by your great power and brought out of Egypt by your strong hand. 27 Remember your servants, Abraham, Isaac, and Jacob, and overlook the stubbornness of this people, their wickedness, and their sin; 28 otherwise the people in the land from which you led us will say, "It is because the Lord was not able to bring them into the land which he promised

them and because he hated them, that he has led them out to let them die in the wilderness." 29 But they are your people, your own possession, whom you brought out by your great strength, by your outstretched arm.'

10 At that time the Lord said to me, 'Cut for yourself two stone tablets like the former ones, and make also a wooden chest, an ark. Come up to me on the mountain, 2 and I shall write on the tablets the words that were on the first tablets, which you broke; you are to put them into the ark.' 3 When I had made an ark of acacia-wood and cut two stone tablets like the first, I went up the mountain taking the tablets in my hands. 4 Then in the same writing as before, the Lord wrote down the Ten Commandments which he had spoken to you from the heart of the fire, at the mountain on the day of the assembly, and the Lord gave them to me. 5 I came back down the mountain, and as the Lord had commanded I put the tablets in the ark I had made, and there they have remained ever since.

6 (The Israelites journeyed by stages from Beeroth-bene-jaakan to Moserah. Aaron died and was buried there; and his son Eleazar succeeded him as priest. 7 From there they travelled to Gudgodah and from Gudgodah to Jotbathah, a land of many wadis. 8 At that time the Lord set apart the tribe of Levi to carry the Ark of the Covenant of the Lord, to be in attendance on the Lord and minister to him, and to bless in his name, as they have done to this day. 9 That is why the Levites have no holding of ancestral land like

9:24 **the Lord:** *so Samar.; Heb.* I. 9:28 **the people in:** *so Samar.; Heb. omits.* 10:4 **Commandments:** *lit.* Words.

11–21: See Exod. ch. 32. **20:** The prayer for Aaron is not recorded in Exod. ch. 32. **21:** *Into the torrent:* contrast Exod. 32.20. **22–24:** These verses interrupt the context and logically belong before the post-Sinai itinerary in 10.6–7. They heighten the need for the intercessory prayer which follows. **22:** *Taberah:* Num. 11.1–3. *Massah:* Exod. 17.1–7; compare Num. 20.2–13. *Kibroth-hattaavah:* Num. 11.4–34. **23:** See Num. chs. 13–14. **25–29:** This prayer is prior to the breaking of the tablets in Exod. 32.11–13. **10.1–11:** The renewal of the covenant. The theme of Israel's unworthiness to inherit the land is resumed only in vv. 10–11. **1:** See Exod. 34.1, which contains no mention of the Ark. **6–7:** Since these verses, like 9.22–24, cover the itinerary after the departure from Sinai (Num. 33.16, 30–33), they logically belong after v. 11. They may allude to examples of Israel's unworthiness which have not been preserved in the OT. Placed here, they emphasize that Israel would not have entered the land but for the prayers of Moses (vv. 10–11). *Beeroth-bene-jaakan:* the Bene-jaakan of Num. 33.30–31, where the order is reversed. Aaron died on Mount Hor according to Num. 20.22–29; 33.37–39. *Gudgodah:* possibly the (Hor-hag)gidgad of Num. 33.32. **8–9:** This event should follow 9.29, according to Exod. 32.26–29. The point that the Levites did not share in Aaron's sin is emphasized by their being set apart their kinsmen; the LORD is their holding, as he promised them.)

[10] I remained on the mountain forty days and forty nights, as I did before, and once again the LORD listened to me; he consented not to destroy you. [11] The LORD said to me, 'Set out now at the head of the people so that they may enter and occupy the land which I swore to give to their forefathers.'

[12] What then, Israel, does the LORD your God ask of you? Only this: to fear the LORD your God, to conform to all his ways, to love him, and to serve him with all your heart and soul. [13] This you will do by observing the commandments of the LORD and his statutes which I give you this day for your good. [14] To the LORD your God belong heaven itself, the highest heaven, the earth and everything in it; [15] yet the LORD was attached to your forefathers by his love for them, and he chose their descendants after them. Out of all nations you were his chosen people, as you are this day. [16] So now you must circumcise your hearts and not be stubborn any more, [17] for the LORD your God is God of gods and Lord of lords, the great, mighty, and terrible God. He is no respecter of persons; he is not to be bribed; [18] he secures justice for the fatherless and the widow, and he shows love towards the alien who lives among you, giving him food and clothing. [19] You too must show love towards the alien, for you once lived as aliens in Egypt. [20] You are to fear the LORD your God, serve him, hold fast to him, and take your oaths in his name. [21] He is your proud boast, your God who has done for you these great and terrible things which you saw for yourselves. [22] When your forefathers went down into Egypt they were only seventy strong, but now the LORD your God has made you as countless as the stars in the heavens.

11 Love the LORD your God and keep for all time the charge he laid upon you, his statutes, laws, and commandments. [2] This day you know the discipline of the LORD, though your children who have neither known nor experienced it do not; you know his great power, his strong hand and

outstretched arm, [3] the signs he worked and his deeds in Egypt against Pharaoh the king and his whole country, [4] and what he did to the Egyptian army, its horses and chariots, when he caused the waters of the Red Sea to engulf them as they pursued you. In this way the LORD completely destroyed them, and so things remain to this day. [5] You know what he did for you in the wilderness as you journeyed to this place, [6] and what he did to Dathan and Abiram, sons of Eliab the Reubenite, when the earth opened its mouth and swallowed them in the midst of all Israel, together with their households, their tents, and every living thing in their company. [7] It was you who saw for yourselves all the great work which the LORD did.

[8] Observe all the commands I give you this day, so that you may have the strength to enter and occupy the land into which you are about to cross, [9] and so that you may enjoy long life in the land which the LORD swore to your forefathers to give them and their descendants, a land flowing with milk and honey.

[10] The land which you are about to enter and occupy is not like the land of Egypt from which you have come, where, after sowing your seed, you regulated the water by means of your foot as in a vegetable garden. [11] But the land into which you are about to cross to occupy it is a land of mountains and valleys watered by the rain of heaven. [12] It is a land which the LORD your God tends and on which his eye rests from one year's end to the next. [13] If you pay heed to the commandments which I give you this day, to love the LORD your God and serve him with all your heart and soul, [14] then I shall send rain for your land in season, both autumn and spring rains, and you will gather your corn and new wine and oil, [15] and I shall provide pasture in the fields for your cattle: you will have all you want to eat. [16] Take care not to be led astray in your hearts, and not to turn aside and serve and worship other gods, [17] or the

11:12 **which ... tends:** *or* whose soil the LORD your God has made firm.

after his death. **10:** The narrative resumes from v. 5.

10.12–11.32: A final exhortation to future obedience. 12: *What then* refers to the conclusions to be drawn from the historical review (9.7–10.11). Compare 4.1 n.; Mic. 6.4–8. The answer is summarized in a single sentence, repeating 6.4–5 (see 6.1 n.). **12–13:** One keeps the commandments not for fear or desire of reward, but as an expression of love and gratitude. **16:** *Circumcise . . . your hearts:* see Jer. 4.3–4 n. **22:** *Seventy:* see Exod. 1.5 n. **11.2:** *This day:* see 5.1–3 n. *Discipline:* see 8.5; Lev. 26.18 n. **6:** *Dathan and Abiram:* see Num.

LORD's anger will be roused against you: he will shut up the heavens and there will be no rain, your soil will not yield its harvest, and you will quickly perish from upon the good land which the LORD is giving you.

¹⁸ Take these commandments of mine to heart and keep them in mind. Bind them as a sign on your hands and wear them as a pendant on your foreheads. ¹⁹ Teach them to your children, and speak of them indoors and out of doors, when you lie down and when you get up. ²⁰ Write them on the doorposts of your houses and on your gates. ²¹ Then you will live long, you and your children, in the land which the LORD swore to your forefathers to give them, for as long as the heavens are above the earth.

²² If you diligently keep all these commandments that I now charge you to observe, loving the LORD your God, conforming to his ways, and holding fast to him, ²³ the LORD will drive out all these nations before you and you will occupy the territory of nations greater and more powerful than you are. ²⁴ Every place where you set foot will be yours. Your borders will run from the wilderness to the Lebanon, and from the river, the Euphrates, to the western sea. ²⁵ No one will be able to withstand you; the LORD your God will put the fear and dread of you on the whole land on which you set foot, as he promised you.

²⁶ See, this day I offer you the choice of a blessing or a curse: ²⁷ the blessing if you obey the commandments of the LORD your God which I give you this day; ²⁸ the curse if you do not obey the commandments of the LORD your God, but turn from the way that I command you this day and go after other gods of whom you have had no experience.

²⁹ When the LORD your God brings you into the land which you are entering to oc-cupy, there on Mount Gerizim you shall pronounce the blessing and on Mount Ebal the curse. ³⁰ (These mountains are on the other side of the Jordan, close to Gilgal beside the terebinth of Moreh, beyond the road to the west which lies in the territory of the Canaanites of the Arabah.) ³¹ You are about to cross the Jordan to enter and occupy the land which the LORD your God is giving you. Occupy it and settle in it, ³² and be careful to observe all the statutes and laws which I have set before you this day.

Laws delivered by Moses

12 THESE are the statutes and laws which you must be careful to observe in the land which the LORD the God of your forefathers is giving you to occupy all your earthly life.

² You are to demolish completely all the sanctuaries where the nations whom you are dispossessing worship their gods, whether on high mountains or on hills or under every spreading tree. ³ Pull down their altars, break their sacred pillars, burn their sacred poles, and hack down the idols of their gods, and thus blot out the name of them from the place.

⁴ You must not adopt such practices in the worship of the LORD your God; ⁵ instead you are to resort to the place which the LORD your God will choose out of all your tribes to receive his name that it may dwell there. Come there ⁶ and bring your whole-offerings and sacrifices, your tithes and contributions, your vows and freewill-offerings, and the first-born of your herds and flocks. ⁷ You are to eat there before the LORD your God; so you

11:24 **to the Lebanon:** *prob. rdg; Heb.* and the Lebanon.   11:30 **terebinth:** *so Gk; Heb.* terebinths.

16.1–17.13 n.; note here the absence of mention of Korah. **17:** If Israel worships the gods of Canaan (idolizes material property), nature will fail and demonstrate their powerlessness (see 8.1–20 n.). **18–21:** See 6.6–9. **24:** *Your borders:* for the LORD's covenant with Abraham, see Gen. 15.18 and note there. **26–28:** Examples of *blessing* and *curse* are given in vv. 16–17, 22–25; on their place in the covenant ceremony, see Lev. 26.1–46 n. **29:** See 27.11–28.68.

12.1–32: The one legitimate sanctuary. The command for centralization of worship, presented under three aspects (vv. 2–7, 8–12, 13–28), was intended to prevent the Canaanite influence and practices at local shrines (vv. 29–31). **1:** Here begin the laws, continuing to 26.15. See 1.5 n. **2–3:** See ch. 7. **4:** Israel's uniqueness is enhanced in the sanctuary. Compare Exod. 20.25 n.; 23.19 n.; Lev. 15.16–18 n. **5:** *The place:* Jerusalem. Prior to 621 B.C.E. (see Introduction), worship had been conducted throughout the land without criticism (Josh. 18.1; 24.1; 1 Sam. 1.3; 10.8; see Deut. 27.5 n.). The LORD, although present in the sanctuary where the divine *name* is invoked, is not bound to the sanctuary. **6:** For the various kinds of *offerings*, see Lev. chs. 1–7; *vows,* Lev.

will find joy in whatever you undertake, you and your families, because the LORD your God has blessed you.

8 You are not to act as we act here today, everyone doing as he pleases, 9 for till now you have not reached the resting-place, the territory which the LORD your God is giving you. 10 When you cross the Jordan and settle in the land which the LORD your God allots you as your holding, when he grants you peace from all your enemies on every side, and you live in security, 11 then you must bring everything that I command you to the place which the LORD your God chooses as a dwelling for his name — your whole-offerings and sacrifices, your tithes and contributions, and all the choice gifts that you have vowed to the LORD. 12 You will rejoice in the presence of the LORD your God with your sons and daughters, your male and female slaves, and the Levites who live in your settlements because they have no holding, no ancestral portion among you.

13 See that you do not offer your whole-offerings in any sanctuary at random, 14 but offer them only at the place which the LORD will choose in one of your tribes, and there you must do all I command you. 15 On the other hand, you may freely slaughter for food in any of your settlements, as the LORD your God blesses you. Clean and unclean alike may eat it, as they would eat the meat of gazelle or deer. 16 But on no account may you partake of the blood; you are to pour it out on the ground like water.

17 In your settlements you may not eat the tithe of your grain and new wine and oil, any of the firstborn of your cattle and sheep, any of the gifts that you vow, or any of your freewill-offerings and contributions; 18 these you must eat in the presence of the LORD your God in the place that the LORD your God will choose — you, your sons and daughters, your male and female slaves, and the Levites living in your settlements; so you will find joy before the LORD your God in all that you undertake. 19 Be careful not to neglect the Levites as long as you live in your land.

20 When the LORD your God enlarges your territory, as he has promised, and you say to yourselves, 'I should like to eat meat,' because you have a craving for it, then you may freely eat it. 21 If the place where the LORD your God will choose to set his name is too far away, then you may slaughter a beast from the herds or flocks which the LORD has given you and freely eat it in your settlements as I command you. 22 You may eat it as you would the meat of gazelle or deer; both clean and unclean alike may eat it. 23 But you must strictly refrain from partaking of the blood, because the blood is the life; you must not eat the life with the flesh. 24 You must not consume it; you must pour it out on the ground like water. 25 If you abstain from it, all will be well with you and your children after you; for you will be doing what is right in the eyes of the LORD.

26 But such holy-gifts as you may have and the gifts you have vowed you must bring to the place which the LORD will choose. 27 You must present your whole-offerings, both the flesh and the blood, on the altar of the LORD your God; but of your shared-offerings you are to eat the flesh, while the blood is to be poured on the altar of the LORD your God.

28 See that you listen, and do all that I command you, and then it will go well with you and your children after you for ever; for you will be doing what is good and right in the eyes of the LORD your God.

29 When, as you advance, the LORD your God exterminates the nations whose country you are entering to occupy, you will take their place and settle in their land. 30 After they have been destroyed, take care that you are not ensnared into their ways. Do not enquire about their gods, saying, 'How used these nations to serve their gods? I too shall do the same.' 31 You must not do for the LORD your God what they do, for all that they do for their gods is hateful and abominable to the LORD. Even their sons and their daughters they burn in honour of their gods.

12:12 **settlements:** *lit.* gates.   12:28 **and do:** *so Samar.; Heb. omits.*

ch. 27; *tithes,* Num. 18.21–32. **12:** *Levites:* see Num. 35.1–8. **13–28:** In earlier periods, every slaughter of an animal was a religious act, to be performed at the local sanctuary. With centralization, a distinction is drawn between sacrifice and slaughter for food. The distinction, however, is absent from the priestly code, which came at a later time (Lev. 17.4, 5 nn.). **15:** An *unclean* person, however, could not participate in a sacrifice (compare Lev. 7.20–21; Num. 18.11). For the rules governing uncleanness, see Lev. chs. 11–15; Num. ch. 19. **16:** *Blood:* see Lev. 17.10–12. **31:** On child sacrifice, see Exod. 13.13 n.; Lev. 18.21 n.

³²See that you carry out exactly what I command you: you must not add anything to it or take anything away from it.

13 Should a prophet or a pedlar of dreams appear among you and offer you a sign or a portent, ²and call on you to go after other gods whom you have not known and to worship them, even if the sign or portent should come true ³do not heed the words of that prophet or dreamer. The LORD your God is testing you to discover whether you love him with all your heart and soul. ⁴It is the LORD your God you must follow and him you must fear; you must keep his commandments and obey him, serve him and hold fast to him. ⁵As for that prophet or dreamer, he must be put to death for preaching rebellion against the LORD your God who brought you out of Egypt and redeemed you from that land of slavery; he has tried to lead you astray from the path which the LORD your God commanded you to take. You must get rid of this wickedness from your midst.

⁶If your brother, your father's son or your mother's son, or your son or daughter, your beloved wife, or your dearest friend should entice you secretly to go and serve other gods —gods of whom neither you nor your fathers have had experience, ⁷gods of the people round about you, near or far, at one end of the land or the other—⁸then you must not consent or listen. Show none of them mercy, neither spare nor shield them; ⁹you are to put them to death, your own hand being the first to be raised against them, and then all the people are to follow. ¹⁰Stone them to death, because they tried to lead you astray from the LORD your God who brought you out of Egypt, out of that land where you were slaves. ¹¹All Israel when they hear of it will be afraid; never again will anything as wicked as this be done among you.

¹²⁻¹³When you hear that miscreants have appeared in any of the towns which the LORD your God is giving you to occupy, and have led its inhabitants astray by calling on them to serve other gods whom you have not known, ¹⁴then you are to investigate the matter carefully. If, after diligent examination, the report proves to be true and it is confirmed that this abominable thing has been done among you, ¹⁵you must put the inhabitants of that town to the sword, and lay the town under solemn ban together with everything in it. ¹⁶Gather all its goods into the public square and burn both town and goods as a complete offering to the LORD your God; and let it remain a mound of ruins and never be rebuilt. ¹⁷Nothing out of all that has been laid under the ban must be found in your possession; in this way the LORD may turn from his fierce anger and show you compassion; and in his compassion he will make you grow as he swore to your forefathers, ¹⁸provided that you obey the LORD your God and keep all his commandments which I give you this day, doing only what is right in the eyes of the LORD your God.

14 YOU ARE the children of the LORD your God: you must not gash yourselves or shave your forelocks in mourning for the dead. ²You are a people holy to the LORD your God, and he has chosen you out of all peoples on earth to be his special possession.

³You must not eat any abominable thing. ⁴These are the animals you may eat: ox, sheep, goat, ⁵buck, gazelle, roebuck, ibex, white-rumped deer, long-horned antelope, and rock-goat. ⁶You may eat any hoofed animal which has cloven hoofs and also chews the cud; ⁷those which only chew the cud or only have cloven hoofs you must not eat. These are: the camel, the hare, and the rock-badger, because they chew the cud but do not have cloven hoofs; they are unclean for you; ⁸and the pig, because it has cloven hoofs but

12:32 *In Heb. 13:1.* 13:6 **your father's son or:** *so Samar.; Heb. omits.* 13:12–13 **miscreants:** *lit.* sons of Belial. 13:15 **in it:** *so Gk; Heb. adds* and the cattle to the sword. 14:1 **your forelocks:** *lit.* between your eyes. 14:7 **rock-badger:** *or* rock-rabbit.

13.1–18: The treatment of enticers to apostasy. For a reason behind such extreme measures, see 7.2 n. **1:** Throughout the ancient world dreams were regarded as a medium of divine communication (Gen. 15.12 n.; 41.25; Num. 12.6). **3:** *Testing:* a divine action continuing from the wilderness experience (8.2). **6–11:** No loyalty may be placed ahead of that which belongs to the LORD. See 7.1–26 n.; compare Matt. 10.34–39.

14.1–21: Restrictions on mourning custom and diet. This was intended to stress Israel's uniqueness and to prevent participation in the cult of the Canaanite gods. **1:** Possibly these rites were connected with the worship of the dead (26.14) or of the fertility gods who were thought to "die" and "arise" with the cycle of vegetation. Compare Ezek. 8.14; Zech. 12.11. **3–20:** See Lev. 11.1–23; see also Lev. 11.1–47 n. on eating does not chew the cud, it is unclean for you. You are not to eat their flesh or even touch their dead carcasses. ⁹Of creatures that live in water these may be eaten: all that have fins and scales; ¹⁰but you may not eat any that have neither fins nor scales; they are unclean for you. ¹¹You may eat any clean bird. ¹²These are the birds you may not eat: the griffon-vulture, the black vulture, the bearded vulture, ¹³the kite, every kind of falcon, ¹⁴every kind of crow, ¹⁵the desert-owl, the short-eared owl, the long-eared owl, every kind of hawk, ¹⁶the tawny owl, the screech-owl, the little owl, ¹⁷the horned owl, the osprey, the fisher-owl, ¹⁸the stork, the various kinds of cormorant, the hoopoe, and the bat.

¹⁹All swarming winged creatures are unclean for you; they may not be eaten. ²⁰You may eat any clean winged creature.

²¹You must not eat anything that has died a natural death. You may give it to aliens residing among you, and they may eat it, or you may sell it to a foreigner; but you are a people holy to the LORD your God.

Do not boil a kid in its mother's milk.

²²Year by year you are to set aside a tithe of all the produce of your sowing, of everything that grows on the land. ²³You must eat it in the presence of the LORD your God in the place which he will choose as a dwelling for his name—the tithe of your grain and new wine and oil, and the firstborn of your cattle and sheep, so that for all time you may learn to fear the LORD your God. ²⁴When the LORD your God has blessed you with prosperity, and the place where he will choose to set his name is too far away and the journey too great for you to carry your tithe, ²⁵then you may convert it into money. Tie up the money and take it with you to the place which the LORD your God will choose. ²⁶There you may spend it as you choose on cattle or sheep, wine or strong drink, or anything else you please, and there feast with rejoicing, both you and your family, in the presence of the LORD your God.

²⁷Also, the Levites who live in your settlements must not suffer neglect at your hands, for they have no holding of ancestral land among you. ²⁸At the end of every third year you are to bring out all the tithe of your produce for that year and leave it in your settlements ²⁹so that the Levites, who have no holding of ancestral land among you, and the aliens, orphans, and widows in your settlements may come and have plenty to eat. If you do this the LORD your God will bless you in everything to which you set your hand.

15 At the end of every seventh year you must make a remission of debts. ²This is how it is to be made: everyone who holds a pledge shall return the pledge of the person indebted to him. He must not press a fellow-countryman for repayment, for the LORD's year of remission has been declared. ³You may press foreigners; but if it is a fellow-countryman that holds anything of yours, you must renounce all claim on it.

⁴⁻⁵There will never be any poor among you if only you obey the LORD your God by carefully keeping these commandments which I lay upon you this day; for the LORD your God will bless you with great prosperity in the land which he is giving you to occupy as your holding. ⁶When the LORD your God blesses you, as he promised, you will lend to people of many nations, but you yourselves will borrow from none; you will rule many nations, but none will rule you.

⁷When in any of your settlements in the land which the LORD your God is giving you one of your fellow-countrymen becomes poor, do not be hard-hearted or close-fisted towards him in his need. ⁸Be open-handed towards him and lend him on pledge as much as he needs. ⁹See that you do not harbour the villainous thought that the seventh year, the year of remission, is near, and look askance

14:12 **griffon-vulture:** *or* eagle. **bearded vulture:** *or* ossifrage.   14:13 **kite:** *so Samar., cp. Lev. 11:14; Heb. has an unknown word.* **falcon:** *so some MSS; others add* kite.   14:14 **crow:** *or* raven.   14:18 **stork:** *or* heron.   15:2 **has been declared:** *or* has come. 15:9 **villainous thought:** *lit.* thought of Belial.

clean and unclean animals. **21:** *A natural death:* see Lev. 17.15; compare Exod. 22.31 n. On boiling a *kid,* see Exod. 23.19 n.

14.22–29: Tithing and centralization. 23–26: One intent was to deprive local sanctuaries of support. **27–29:** Since it was not possible for all of the abundance of Levites to serve at the central sanctuary (18.6–8), many continued to live throughout the land (Num. 35.1–8) and to receive tithes like the poor.

15.1–23: The sabbatical year. The rest granted the land every seventh year in acknowledgment of the LORD's ownership (Lev. 25.2–7) or for the use of the poor (Exod. 23.10–11) must now be accompanied by a at your needy countryman and give him nothing. If you do, he will appeal to the LORD against you, and you will be found guilty of sin. ¹⁰ Give freely to him and do not begrudge him your bounty, because it is for this very bounty that the LORD your God will bless you in everything that you do or undertake. ¹¹ The poor will always be with you in your land, and that is why I command you to be open-handed towards any of your countrymen there who are in poverty and need.

¹² Should a fellow-Hebrew, be it a man or a woman, sell himself to you as a slave, he is to serve you for six years. In the seventh year you must set him free, ¹³ and when you set him free, do not let him go empty-handed. ¹⁴ Give to him lavishly from your flock, from your threshing-floor and your winepress. Be generous to him, as the LORD your God has blessed you. ¹⁸ Do not resent it when you have to set him free, for his six years' service to you has been worth twice the wage of a hired man. Then the LORD your God will bless you in everything you do. ¹⁵ Bear in mind that you were slaves in Egypt and the LORD your God redeemed you; that is why I am giving you this command today.

¹⁶ If, however, a slave is content to be with you and says, 'I shall not leave you; I love you and your family,' ¹⁷ then take an awl and pierce through his ear to the door, and he will be your slave for life. Treat a slave-girl in the same way.

¹⁹ You must dedicate to the LORD your God every male firstborn of your herds and flocks. You must not plough with the firstborn of your cattle or shear the firstborn of your sheep. ²⁰ Year by year you and your household must eat them in the presence of the LORD your God, in the place which the LORD will choose. ²¹ If any animal has a defect, if it is lame or blind or has any other serious defect, you may not sacrifice it to the LORD your God. ²² Eat it in your settlements;

both clean and unclean alike may eat it as they would the meat of gazelle or deer. ²³ But on no account may you partake of its blood; you must pour it out on the ground like water.

16 OBSERVE the month of Abib and celebrate the Passover to the LORD your God, for it was in that month that the LORD your God brought you out of Egypt by night. ² Slaughter an animal from flock or herd as a Passover victim to the LORD your God in the place which he will choose as a dwelling for his name. ³ You must eat nothing leavened with it; for seven days you must eat unleavened bread, the bread of affliction, because you came out of Egypt in urgent haste. Thus as long as you live you are to commemorate the day of your coming out of Egypt. ⁴ No leaven must be seen in all your territory for seven days, nor must any of the flesh which you have slaughtered in the evening of the first day remain overnight till morning.

⁵ You may not slaughter the Passover victim in any of the settlements which the LORD your God is giving you, ⁶ but only in the place which he will choose as a dwelling for his name; there you are to slaughter the Passover victim in the evening as the sun goes down, the time of your coming out of Egypt. ⁷ Cook it and eat it in the place which the LORD your God will choose, and then next morning set off back to your tents. ⁸ For six days you must eat unleavened loaves, and on the seventh day hold a closing ceremony in honour of the LORD your God; you must do no work.

⁹ Seven weeks should be counted off: start counting them from the time when the sickle is put to the standing grain; ¹⁰ then celebrate the pilgrim-feast of Weeks to the LORD your God and offer a freewill-offering in propor-

15:14–19 *Verse 18 transposed to follow verse 14.*
15:18 **worth twice:** *or* equivalent to.

cancellation of debts. Compare the termination of sale or lease of property at the jubilee (Lev. 25.8–34). **12–17:** Compare Exod. 21.2–11. *Woman:* see Exod. 21.7 n. **13–14:** This was not required by an earlier law (Exod. 21.1–4). **17:** *To the door:* see Exod. 21.6 n. **19:** *Firstborn:* see Exod. 13.2 n. **20:** *Year by year:* the centralization of worship and hence great distance from Jerusalem made sacrifice on the eighth day (Exod. 22.30) impractical. **21:** *Defect:* see Lev. 12.4 n.

16.1–17: The annual pilgrim-feasts, hereafter to be celebrated only at the central sanctuary. Formerly, with the exception of Passover (which was kept in the home: Exod. 12.21–27), they had been observed at the local shrines. Other special days which do not require the bringing of offerings, such as the New Year and the Day of Atonement (Lev. 23.23–32; Num. 29.1–11), are not mentioned here. **1:** *Abib:* see Exod. 13.4 n. *Passover:* see (Exod. 12.1–27; 13.1–16. **3:** *Unleavened bread:* see Exod. 12.15 n. **9–12:** *The pilgrim-feast of Weeks:*

tion to the blessing that the Lord your God has given you. [11] Rejoice before the Lord your God, with your sons and daughters, your male and female slaves, the Levites who live in your settlements, and the aliens, fatherless, and widows among you. Rejoice in the place which the Lord your God will choose as a dwelling for his name [12] and keep in mind that you were slaves in Egypt. You are to be careful to observe all these statutes.

[13] After you bring in the produce from your threshing-floor and winepress, you are to celebrate the pilgrim-feast of Booths for seven days. [14] Rejoice at your feast with your sons and daughters, your male and female slaves, the Levites, aliens, fatherless, and widows living in your settlements. [15] For seven days you are to celebrate this feast to the Lord your God in the place which he will choose, when the Lord your God gives you his blessing in all your harvest and in all your work; you shall keep the feast with joy.

[16] Three times a year all your males must come into the presence of the Lord your God in the place which he will choose: at the pilgrim-feasts of Unleavened Bread, of Weeks, and of Booths. No one may come into the presence of the Lord without an offering; [17] each of you is to bring such a gift as he can in proportion to the blessing which the Lord your God has given you.

[18] In every settlement which the Lord your God is giving you, you must appoint for yourselves judges and officers, tribe by tribe, and they will dispense true justice to the people. [19] You must not pervert the course of justice or show favour or accept a bribe; for bribery makes the wise person blind and the just person give a crooked answer. [20] Justice, and justice alone, must be your aim, so that you may live and occupy the land which the Lord your God is giving you.

[21] Do not plant any kind of tree as a sacred pole beside the altar of the Lord your God which you will build, [22] nor erect a sacred pillar; for all such are hateful to the Lord your God.

17 You must not sacrifice to the Lord your God a bull or sheep that has any defect or serious blemish, for that would be abominable to the Lord your God.

[2] Should there be found among you, in any of the settlements which the Lord your God is giving you, a man or woman who does what is wrong in the eyes of the Lord your God, by violating his covenant [3] and going to serve other gods, prostrating himself before them or before the sun and moon and all the host of heaven—a thing that I have forbidden— [4] then, if it is reported to you or you hear of it, make careful enquiry. If the report proves to be true, and it is confirmed that this abominable thing has been done in Israel, [5] then bring the man or woman who has done this wicked deed to the gate of the town to be stoned to death. [6] Sentence of death is to be carried out on the testimony of two or of three witnesses: no one must be put to death on the testimony of a single witness. [7] The first stones are to be thrown by the witnesses and then all the people must follow; so you will get rid of the wickedness in your midst.

[8] When the issue in any lawsuit that is disputed in your courts is beyond your competence, whether it be a case of accidental or premeditated homicide, civil rights, or personal injury, then resort without delay to the place which the Lord your God will choose. [9] Appear before the levitical priests or the judge then in office and seek guidance; they will give you the verdict. [10] Act on the pronouncement which they make from the place chosen by the Lord, and see that you carry out all their instructions. [11] Act on the instruction they give you, or on the precedent they cite; do not deviate from the decision they hand down to you, either to right or to left. [12] Anyone who presumes to reject the decision either of the priest ministering there to the Lord your God, or of the judge, is to be put to death; thus you will purge Israel of

---

16:21 **sacred pole:** *Heb.* asherah. *Heb. adds* the man or the woman.   17:5 **town:** *so Gk*; 17:8 **in your courts:** *lit.* in your gates.

---

see Exod. 23.16 n.; Lev. 23.15–21. **13–15:** *The pilgrim-feast of Booths:* see Exod. 23.16 n.; Lev. 23.33–35, 39–43.

16.18–17.13: Centralization of the judicial system. 18: Guidance for the local courts. **21–22:** *Pole; pillar:* see Exod. 34.13 n. The verses belong topically with 12.30–31. **17.1:** *Blemish:* see Lev. 12.4 n. **2–5:** See ch. 13 for similar instances; for the reason, see 7.2 n. **6:** So also 19.15; Num. 35.30. For a procedure in the absence of witnesses, see Num. 5.11–31. **8–13:** The ultimate authority in case of litigation (1.17; see Exod. 18.13–26 n.).

wickedness. ¹³ Then all the people when they hear of it will be afraid, and never again show such presumption.

¹⁴ After you come into the land which the LORD your God is giving you, and have occupied it and settled there, if you then say, 'Let us appoint a king over us, as all the surrounding nations do,' ¹⁵ you must appoint as king the man whom the LORD your God will choose. You must appoint over you a man of your own people; you must not appoint a foreigner, one who is not of your own people. ¹⁶ He must not acquire numerous horses, or send men to Egypt to obtain more horses, for the LORD said to you: 'You are never to go back that way.' ¹⁷ Your king must not acquire numerous wives and so be led astray, or amass for himself silver and gold in great quantities.

¹⁸ When he has ascended the throne of the kingdom, he is to make a copy of this law in a book at the dictation of the levitical priests. ¹⁹ He is to have it by him and read from it all his life, so that he may learn to fear the LORD his God and keep all the words of this law and observe these statutes. ²⁰ Thus he will avoid alienation from his fellow-countrymen through pride, and not deviate from these commandments to right or to left; then he and his sons will reign long in Israel.

18 The levitical priests, the whole tribe of Levi, are to have no holding of ancestral land in Israel; they are to eat the food-offerings of the LORD as their share. ² They will have no holding among their fellow-countrymen; the LORD is their holding, as he promised them.

³ This is to be the customary due of the priests from those of the people who offer sacrifice, whether a bull or a sheep: the shoulder, the cheeks, and the stomach are to be given to the priests. ⁴ Give them also the firstfruits of your grain and new wine and oil, and the first fleece at the shearing of your flock. ⁵ For it was they whom the LORD your God chose from all your tribes to attend on the LORD and to minister in the name of the LORD, both they and their sons for all time. ⁶ When a Levite from any settlement in Israel where he may be resident comes to the place which the LORD will choose, if he comes in the eagerness of his heart ⁷ and ministers in the name of the LORD his God, like all his fellow-Levites who attend on the LORD there, ⁸ he is to have an equal share of food with them, besides what he may inherit from his father's family.

⁹ After you come into the land which the LORD your God is giving you, do not learn to imitate the abominable practices of those other nations. ¹⁰ Let no one be found among you who makes his son or daughter pass through fire, no augur or soothsayer or diviner or sorcerer, ¹¹ no one who casts spells or traffics with ghosts and spirits, and no necromancer. ¹² Those who do such things are abominable to the LORD, and it is on account of these abominable practices that the LORD your God is driving them out before you.

18:5 **on the LORD:** *so Samar.; Heb. omits.*

17.14–20: Regulations concerning kingship. This office had been established during the eleventh century, accompanied by both positive and negative attitudes (1 Sam. chs. 8–12; see also Judg. 8.22–23; 9.1–21). The point here is that the role of the king must not be patterned after those of the surrounding nations. **15:** *God will choose:* legitimate kings must be divinely approved and anointed, as were Saul (1 Sam. chs. 9–10) and David (1 Sam. chs. 15–16). See Hos. 8.4. *Foreigner:* possibly an allusion to Queen Jezebel (a Phoenician from the city of Sidon, 1 Kgs. 16.31), who violated the customs of Israel by introducing the worship of her foreign god (1 Kgs. chs. 18.19; 21). **16–17:** The economic and military policies of Solomon (1 Kgs. 10.26–29), as well as his many marriages to foreign women (1 Kgs. 11.1–8), may be alluded to here. **18:** *This law:* namely, chs. 12–26.

18.1–8: Support for the centralized priesthood. For the early history of the tribe of Levi, see Gen. 34.1–31 n.; for their rise to the priestly office, see Exod. 32.26–29 n. Here, the entire tribe serves as priests, but in the postexilic period the descendants of Aaron received special designation (Num. 16.1–17.13 n.). **3–5:** See Num. 35.2–8 n. **6:** *Any settlement:* local sanctuary (14.28–29 n.). Those Levites unable or unwilling to transfer to the central shrine (2 Kgs. 23.8–9) remained in their cities (12.18–19; 14.27, 29) or moved to the cities set aside for them (Num. 35.1–8).

18.9–22: The office of prophet. 9–14: Various Canaanite ways of seeking the divine will are contrasted with the LORD's initiative in speaking through a prophet (vv. 15–19). **10:** *Pass through fire:* see Lev. 18.21 n.; 2 Kgs. 16.3; 21.6. *Augur:* see Num. 22.7 n. *Soothsayer:* see Lev. 19.26 n. **11:** *Necromancer:* one who consults

13 You must be undivided in your service of the LORD your God. 14 These nations whose place you are taking listen to soothsayers and augurs, but the LORD your God does not permit you to do this.

15 The LORD your God will raise up for you a prophet like me from among your own people; it is to him you must listen. 16 All this follows from your request to the LORD your God at Horeb on the day of the assembly. There you said, 'Let us not hear again the voice of the LORD our God, nor see this great fire again, or we shall die.' 17 Then the LORD said to me, 'What they have said is right. 18 I shall raise up for them a prophet like you, one of their own people, and I shall put my words into his mouth. He will declare to them whatever I command him; 19 if anyone refuses to listen to the words which he will speak in my name I shall call that person to account. 20 But the prophet who presumes to utter in my name what I have not commanded him, or who speaks in the name of other gods — that prophet must be put to death.'

21 If you wonder, 'How are we to recognize a word that the LORD has not uttered?' 22 here is the answer: When a word spoken by a prophet in the name of the LORD is not fulfilled and does not come true, it is not a word spoken by the LORD. The prophet has spoken presumptuously; have no fear of him.

19 WHEN the LORD your God exterminates the nations whose land he is giving you, and you take their place and settle in their towns and houses, 2 you are to set apart three cities in the land which he is giving you to occupy. 3 Divide into three districts the territory which the LORD your God is giving you as a holding, and determine where each city shall lie. These are to be places in which homicides may take sanctuary.

4 This is the kind of homicide who may take sanctuary there and save his life: one who strikes another accidentally and with no malice aforethought; 5 for instance, the man who goes into a wood with another to fell trees, and as he swings the axe to cut a tree the head glances off the tree, hits the other man, and kills him. The homicide may take sanctuary in any one of these cities, and his life is to be safe. 6 Otherwise, when the dead man's next-of-kin on whom lies the duty of vengeance pursued him in the heat of temper, he might overtake him if the distance were great, and take his life, although the homicide was not liable to the death penalty because there had been no previous enmity on his part. 7 That is why I command you to set apart three cities.

8 If the LORD your God enlarges your territory, as he promised on oath to your forefathers, and gives you the whole land which he promised to them, 9 because you keep all the commandments that I am laying down today and carry them out by loving the LORD your God and by conforming to his ways for all time, then you shall add three more cities of refuge to these three. 10 Let no innocent blood be shed in the land which the LORD your God is allotting to you, or blood-guilt will fall on you.

11 When one person has a feud with another, and lies in wait for him, attacks him, and strikes him a fatal blow, and then takes sanctuary in one of these cities, 12 the elders of his own town must send to fetch him and hand him over to the next-of-kin to be put to death. 13 You are to show him no mercy, but rid Israel of the guilt of innocent blood; then all will be well with you.

14 Do not move your neighbour's boundary stone, fixed by the men of former times in the holding which you will occupy in the land

18:22 **fear of him:** *or* fear of it.

the dead for oracles (see Lev. 19.31 n.). **15:** On the origin of the prophetic office in Moses' time, see Num. 11.27–30 n. **16:** *You said:* see Exod. 20.18–21. **17–18:** The people's fear of God is interpreted as a permanent state and hence the office of mediator (5.22–31 n.) is necessary in every succeeding age. For the development in much later times of the idea of a prophet like Moses, see Jn. 6.14 n.; 7.40. Acts 3.17–24 applies the passage to Jesus. **20:** See 13.1–5. **21–22:** History is to be the final judge of the truth of uttered prophecies. On "false prophets" see Jer. ch. 28 and 1 Kgs. 22.1–28.

19.1–13: Cities of refuge for the accidental homicide. They must be conveniently located throughout the land, since the local altars which served the purpose (Exod. 21.14; 1 Kgs. 1.50–53) were to be closed (ch. 12). See also Num. 35.9–34.

19.14–21: Boundary markers and witnesses. This is related topically to the previous section by the mention the LORD your God is giving you for your possession.

15 A single witness may not give evidence against anyone in the matter of any crime or sin which he may have committed: a charge must be established on the evidence of two or of three witnesses.

16 When a malicious witness comes forward to accuse a person of a crime, 17 the two parties to the dispute must appear in the presence of the LORD, before the priests or the judges then in office; 18 if, after careful examination by the judges, he is proved to be a false witness giving false evidence against his fellow, 19 treat him as he intended to treat his fellow. You must rid yourselves of this wickedness. 20 The rest of the people when they hear of it will be afraid, and never again will anything as wicked as this be done among you. 21 You must show no mercy: life for life, eye for eye, tooth for tooth, hand for hand, foot for foot!

20 WHEN you take the field against your enemies and are faced by horses and chariots, a force greater than yours, you need have no fear of them, for the LORD your God, who brought you up from Egypt, will be with you. 2 Then when fighting impends, the priest must come forward and address the army in these words: 3 'Hear, Israel! Now that you are about to join battle with your enemy, do not lose heart or be afraid; do not let alarm affect you, and do not give way to panic in face of them. 4 The LORD your God accompanies you to fight for you against your enemy and give you the victory.' 5 The officers are to say to the army: 'Any man who has built a new house and has not dedicated it should go back to his house; otherwise he may die in battle and another man dedicate it. 6 Any man who has planted a vineyard and has not begun to use it should go back home; otherwise he may die in battle and another man get the use of it. 7 Any man who has pledged himself to take a woman in marriage

and has not taken her should go back home; otherwise he may die in battle and another man take her.' 8 The officers must also say to the army: 'Let anyone who is afraid and has lost heart go back home; or his faint-heartedness may affect his comrades.' 9 When the officers have finished addressing the army, commanders will assume command.

10 When you advance on a town to attack it, make an offer of peace. 11 If the offer is accepted and the town opens its gates to you, then all the people who live there are to be put to forced labour and work for you. 12 If the town does not make peace with you but gives battle, you are to lay siege to it 13 and, when the LORD your God delivers it into your hands, put every male in it to the sword; 14 but you may take the women, the dependants, and the livestock for yourselves, and plunder everything else in the town. You may enjoy the use of the spoil from your enemies which the LORD your God gives you.

15 That is how you are to deal with towns at a great distance, as opposed to those which belong to nations near at hand. 16 In the towns of these nations whose land the LORD your God is giving you as your holding, you must not leave a soul alive. 17 As the LORD your God commanded you, you must destroy them under solemn ban — Hittites, Amorites, Canaanites, Perizzites, Hivites, Jebusites — 18 so that they may not teach you to imitate the abominable practices they have carried on for their gods, and so cause you to sin against the LORD your God.

19 When in the course of war you lay siege to a town for a long time in order to take it, do not destroy its trees by taking an axe to them, for they provide you with food; you must not cut them down. The trees of the field are not people, that you should besiege them. 20 But you may destroy or cut down any trees that you know do not yield food, and use them in siege-works against the town that is at war with you, until it falls.

of districts (v. 3) and territory (v. 8). **14:** On the preservation of ancestral property, see Num. 27.1–11 n. **15:** See 17.6 n. **18:** The giving of *false evidence* is forbidden in Exod. 20.16, but no penalty is given there. **21:** See Exod. 21.23–25 n.

20.1–20: Rules for warfare. 5–7: The reluctance of such individuals to participate enthusiastically would, like fear (v. 8), infect the other troops. **6:** A *vineyard* could not be harvested until the fifth year (Lev. 19.23–25). **7:** The exemption of the newlywed was for one year (24.5). **10–15:** Procedure for remote cities which offer little danger of cultic contamination. For an illustration, see Num. ch. 31. **16–18:** Procedure for nearby cities (7.1–5). For an illustration, see Josh. 6.15–27.

21 When a murder victim is found lying in open country, in the land which the LORD your God is giving you to occupy, and it is not known who struck the blow, ² your elders and your judges are to come out and measure the distance to the surrounding towns to establish which is nearest. ³ The elders of that town are to take a heifer that has never been put to work or worn a yoke, ⁴ and bring it down to a wadi where there is a stream that never runs dry and the ground is never tilled or sown, and there in the wadi they are to break its neck. ⁵ The priests, the sons of Levi, are then to come forward; for the LORD your God has chosen them to minister to him and to bless in the name of the LORD, and their voice shall be decisive in all cases of dispute and assault. ⁶ All the elders of the town nearest to the dead body will then wash their hands over the heifer whose neck has been broken in the wadi, ⁷ and solemnly declare: 'Our hands did not shed this blood, nor did we witness the bloodshed. ⁸ Accept expiation, O LORD, for your people Israel whom you redeemed, and do not let the guilt of innocent blood rest upon your people Israel: let this bloodshed be expiated on their behalf.' ⁹ Thus, by doing what is right in the eyes of the LORD, you will rid yourselves of the guilt of innocent blood.

¹⁰ When you go to battle against your enemies and the LORD your God delivers them into your hands and you take some of them captive, ¹¹ then if you see a comely woman among the prisoners and are attracted to her, you may take her as your wife. ¹² Bring her into your house; there she must shave her head, pare her nails, ¹³ and discard the clothes which she had when captured. For a full month she is to stay in your house mourning for her father and mother. After that you may have intercourse with her, and be man and wife. ¹⁴ But if you no longer find her pleasing, let her go free. You must not sell her or treat her harshly, since you have had your will with her.

¹⁵ When a man has two wives, one loved and the other unloved, if they both bear him sons, and the son of the unloved wife is the elder, ¹⁶ then, when the day comes for him to divide his property among his sons, he must not treat the son of the loved wife as his firstborn in preference to his true firstborn, the son of the unloved wife. ¹⁷ He must recognize the rights of his firstborn, the son of the unloved wife, and give him a double share of all that he possesses; for he was the firstfruits of his manhood, and the right of the firstborn is his.

¹⁸ When a man has a son who is rebellious and out of control, who does not obey his father and mother, or take heed when they punish him, ¹⁹ then his father and mother are to lay hold of him and bring him out to the elders of the town at the town gate, ²⁰ and say, 'This son of ours is rebellious and out of control; he will not obey us, he is a wastrel and a drunkard.' ²¹ Then all the men of the town must stone him to death, and you will thereby rid yourselves of this wickedness. All Israel when they hear of it will be afraid.

²² When someone is convicted of a capital offence and is put to death, and you hang him on a gibbet, ²³ his body must not remain there overnight; it must be buried on the same day. Anyone hanged is accursed in the sight of God, and the land which the LORD your God is giving you as your holding must not be polluted.

22 SHOULD you see a fellow-countryman's ox or sheep straying, do not ignore it; you must take it back to him. ² If the owner is not a near neighbour and you do not know who he is, bring the animal to your own house and keep it with you until he claims it; then give it back to him. ³ Do the same with

21.1–25.19: **A collection of civil laws** unrelated to centralization.

21.1–9: **Expiation for an unsolved murder.** Topically, the unit belongs with 19.1–13. Since the blood of the murderer is not available for expiation (Num. 35.33) and the land is hence polluted, an animal substitute is used. The removal of guilt is symbolized by the washing of hands and by the blood being carried away by the stream (compare Lev. 14.5–7 n.). The earliest form of this ritual may have been a Canaanite sacrifice to the gods of the underworld. **4:** *Wadi:* a ravine or valley. These were traditional places of sacrifice to underworld deities (2 Chr. 33.6; Isa. 57.5–6). *Never tilled:* barren ground was once thought to be the domain of demons. **7–9:** The ritual act is largely only a formality, and is made effective by prayer to the LORD.

21.10–22.12: **Miscellaneous laws. 10–14:** This belongs topically with 20.1–20. **18–21:** Execution of an incorrigible son. The complaint must be lodged by both parents and evaluated by legal authorities. **22.1–4:**

his donkey or his cloak or anything else that your fellow-countryman loses. You may not ignore it.

⁴Should you see your fellow-countryman's donkey or ox lying on the road, do not ignore it; you must help him to raise it to its feet.

⁵No woman may wear an article of man's clothing, nor may a man put on woman's dress; for those who do these things are abominable to the LORD your God.

⁶When you come upon a bird's nest by the road, in a tree or on the ground, with fledgelings or eggs in it and the mother bird on the nest, do not take both mother and young. ⁷Let the mother bird go free, and take only the young; then you will prosper and enjoy long life.

⁸When you build a new house, put a parapet along the roof, or you will bring the guilt of bloodshed on your house if anyone should fall from it.

⁹You are not to sow two kinds of seed between your vine rows, or the full yield will be forfeit, both the yield of the seeds you sow and the fruit of the vineyard. ¹⁰You are not to plough with an ox and a donkey yoked together. ¹¹You are not to wear clothes woven with two kinds of yarn, wool and flax together.

¹²Make twisted tassels on the four corners of the garment which you wrap round you.

¹³When a man takes a wife and, after intercourse, turns against her ¹⁴and brings trumped-up charges against her, giving her a bad name and saying, 'I took this woman and slept with her and did not find proof of virginity in her,' ¹⁵then the girl's father and mother should take the proof of her virginity to the elders of the town at the town gate. ¹⁶The girl's father will say to the elders, 'I gave my daughter in marriage to this man, and he has turned against her. ¹⁷He has trumped up a charge and said, "I have not found proofs of virginity in your daughter." Here are the proofs.' They must then spread the cloth before the elders of the town. ¹⁸The elders must take the man and punish him: ¹⁹they are to fine him a hundred pieces of silver because he has given a bad name to a virgin of Israel, and the money is to be handed over to the girl's father. She will remain his wife: he will not be free to divorce her all his days.

²⁰If, on the other hand, the accusation turns out to be true, no proof of the girl's virginity being found, ²¹then they must bring her out to the door of her father's house and the men of her town will stone her to death. She has committed an outrage in Israel by playing the prostitute in her father's house: you must rid yourselves of this wickedness.

²²When a man is discovered lying with a married woman, both are to be put to death, the woman as well as the man who lay with her: you must purge Israel of this wickedness.

²³When a virgin is pledged in marriage to a man, and another man encounters her in the town and lies with her, ²⁴bring both of them out to the gate of that town and stone them to death; the girl because, although she was in the town, she did not cry for help, and the man because he violated another man's wife: you must rid yourselves of this wickedness.

²⁵But if it is out in the country that the man encounters and rapes such a girl, then the man alone is to be put to death because he lay with her. ²⁶Do nothing to the girl; no guilt deserving of death attaches to her: this case is like that of a man who attacks another and murders him: ²⁷the man came upon her in the country, and, though the girl may have cried for help, there was no one to come to her rescue.

²⁸When a man encounters a virgin who is not yet betrothed and forces her to lie with him, and they are discovered, ²⁹then the man who lies with her must give the girl's father fifty pieces of silver, and she will be his wife because he has violated her. He is not free to divorce her all his days.

³⁰A man must not take his father's wife: he must not bring shame on his father.

23 No man whose testicles have been crushed or whose organ has been cut

22:30 *In Heb. 23:1.*

See Exod. 23.4–5. **9–11:** The origin of these prohibitions is obscure. **12:** *Tassels:* see Num. 15.37–40.

22.13–30: Sexual relations. 15: *Proof:* a bloodstained sheet. **19:** On *divorce,* compare 24.1–4. **22:** See Lev. 20.10. The Ten Commandments (Exod. 20.14) do not specify a penalty. **23–27:** The violation is more against one's neighbor than against the girl, as the next regulation makes clear. **28–29:** See Exod. 22.16–17. **30:** See 27.20; Lev. 18.8; 20.11.

23.1–14: Exclusion from the community worship. Since the initial categories are sexual, this unit logically off may become a member of the assembly of the LORD.

2 No descendant of an irregular union, even down to the tenth generation, may become a member of the assembly of the LORD. 3 No Ammonite or Moabite, even down to the tenth generation, may become a member of the assembly of the LORD. They must never become members of the assembly of the LORD 4 because they did not meet you with food and water on your journey from Egypt, and because they hired Balaam son of Beor from Pethor in Aram-naharaim to curse you. 5 The LORD your God refused to listen to Balaam and turned the curse into a blessing for you, because the LORD your God loved you. 6 As long as you live you are not to seek their welfare or their good.

7 Do not regard an Edomite as an abomination, for he is your own kin; nor an Egyptian, for you were aliens in his land. 8 The third generation of children born to them may become members of the assembly of the LORD.

9 When you are encamped against an enemy, you must be careful to avoid any foulness. 10 When one of your number is unclean because of an emission of seed at night, he must go outside the camp; he may not come into it. 11 Towards evening he is to wash himself in water, and at sunset he may re-enter the camp. 12 You must have a sign outside the camp showing where you can withdraw to relieve yourself. 13 As part of your equipment you are to have a trowel, and when you squat outside, you are to scrape a hole with it and then turn and cover your excrement. 14 For the LORD your God moves with your camp, to keep you safe and to hand over your enemies as you advance, and your camp must be kept holy for fear that he should see something offensive and go with you no farther.

15 You must not surrender to his master a slave who has taken refuge with you. 16 Let him stay with you anywhere he chooses in any one of your settlements, wherever suits him best; you must not force him.

17 No Israelite woman may become a temple-prostitute, nor may an Israelite man. 18 You must not allow a common prostitute's fee, or the pay of a male prostitute, to be brought into the house of the LORD your God in fulfilment of any vow, for both of them are abominable to the LORD your God.

19 You are not to exact interest on anything you lend to a fellow-countryman, whether money or food or anything else on which interest can be charged. 20 You may exact interest on a loan to a foreigner but not on a loan to a fellow-countryman, and then the LORD your God will bless you in all you undertake in the land which you are entering to occupy.

21 When you make a vow to the LORD your God, do not put off its fulfilment; otherwise the LORD your God will require satisfaction from you and you will be guilty of sin. 22 If you choose not to make a vow, you will not be guilty of sin; 23 but if you voluntarily make a vow to the LORD your God, mind what you say and do what you have promised.

24 When you go into another man's vineyard, you may eat as many grapes as you wish to satisfy your hunger, but you may not put any into your basket.

25 When you go into another man's standing grain, you may pluck ears to rub in your hands, but you may not put a sickle to the standing crop.

24 If a man has taken a woman in marriage, but she does not win his favour because he finds something offensive in her,

23:4 **Aram-naharaim:** *that is* Aram of Two Rivers.

follows the previous one. **1:** For more general regulations concerning imperfection, see Lev. 12.4 n.; 13.1–46 n. **2:** *Irregular union:* possibly those described in Lev. 18.6–18. **3–6:** The basis for exclusion shifts from sexual irregularities to ancestry and historical events. Recurring warfare with Ammonites and Moabites lies behind this prohibition. **4:** Numbers chs. 22–24 do not mention Ammonite participation in the Balaam episode. **7:** *Your own kin:* Gen. 25.24–26. That the Edomites are here accepted, despite their one-time hostility to Israel (see Num. 20.14–21), suggests that this passage is very late in origin, reflecting a time when the age-old hostilities had ceased. The basis for the view of the Egyptians here is unknown. **9–14:** These supplements to the rules for "holy" warfare (20.1–20) are included here because they deal with temporary disqualification from the sacred assembly. **10–11:** See Lev. 15.16–17.

23.15–25.19: Miscellaneous laws. 15–16: In contrast, other ancient Near Eastern codes provided the death penalty for harboring a fugitive slave. **17–18:** See Gen. 38.21 n. **19–20:** See Exod. 22.25; Lev. 25.35–38. **21–23:** See Lev. ch. 27; Num. ch. 30. **24–25:** See 24.19–22. *Rub in your hands:* to remove the husks before eating. See Matt. 12.1. **24.1–4:** The intent is to prevent impulsive divorce. **1:** *Offensive:* probably not adultery, and he writes her a certificate of divorce, gives it to her, and dismisses her, ²and if after leaving his house she goes off to become the wife of another man, ³and this second husband turns against her and writes her a certificate of divorce, gives it to her, and dismisses her, or dies after making her his wife, ⁴then her first husband who had dismissed her is not free to take her to be his wife again; for him she has become unclean. This would be abominable to the LORD, and you must not bring sin upon the land which the LORD your God is giving you as your holding.

⁵When a man is newly married, he is not to be liable for military service or any other public duty. He must remain at home exempt from service for one year and be happy with the wife he has taken.

⁶No one may take millstones, or even the upper millstone alone, in pledge; that would be taking a life in pledge.

⁷When a man is found to have kidnapped a fellow-countryman, an Israelite, and to have treated him harshly or sold him, he must suffer the death penalty, and so you will rid yourselves of this wickedness.

⁸Be careful how you act in all cases of virulent skin disease; be careful to observe all that the levitical priests tell you; you must obey the instructions I gave them. ⁹Keep in mind what the LORD your God did to Miriam as you journeyed from Egypt.

¹⁰When you make any loan to anyone, do not enter his house to take a pledge from him. ¹¹Wait outside, and the person whose creditor you are must bring the pledge out to you. ¹²If he is a poor man, do not sleep in the cloak he has pledged. ¹³Return it to him at sunset so that he may sleep in it and bless you; then it will be counted to your credit in the sight of the LORD your God.

¹⁴You must not keep back the wages of a man who is poor and needy, whether a fellow-countryman or an alien living in your country in one of your settlements. ¹⁵Pay him his wages on the same day before sunset, for

he is poor and he relies on them: otherwise he may appeal to the LORD against you, and you will be guilty of sin.

¹⁶Parents are not to be put to death for their children, nor children for their parents; each one may be put to death only for his own sin.

¹⁷You must not deprive aliens and the fatherless of justice or take a widow's cloak in pledge. ¹⁸Bear in mind that you were slaves in Egypt and the LORD your God redeemed you from there; that is why I command you to do this.

¹⁹When you reap the harvest in your field and overlook a sheaf, do not go back to pick it up; it is to be left for the alien, the fatherless, and the widow, so that the LORD your God may bless you in all that you undertake.

²⁰When you beat your olive trees, do not strip them afterwards; what is left is for the alien, the fatherless, and the widow.

²¹When you gather the grapes from your vineyard, do not glean afterwards; what is left is for the alien, the fatherless, and the widow. ²²Keep in mind that you were slaves in Egypt; that is why I command you to do this.

25 When two go to law and present themselves for judgement, the judges are to try the case; they must acquit the innocent and condemn the guilty. ²If the guilty party is sentenced to be flogged, the judge is to have him lie down and be beaten in his presence; the number of lashes will correspond to the gravity of the offence. ³They may give him forty strokes, but not more; otherwise, if they go farther and exceed this number, your fellow-countryman will have been publicly degraded.

⁴You are not to muzzle an ox while it is treading out the grain.

⁵When brothers live together and one of them dies without leaving a son, his widow is not to marry outside the family. Her hus-

---

24:14 **keep . . . man:** *so Scroll; Heb.* oppress a hired man.   24:17 **and:** *so Gk; Heb. omits.*

which carried the death penalty (22.22). **5:** See 20.5–7. **6:** *Millstones:* used to grind grain, the dietary staple. **7:** See Exod. 21.16. **8:** See Lev. chs. 13–14. **9:** See Num. ch. 12. **12–13:** The regulation made loans available to those least able to provide surety. **14–15:** See Lev. 19.13; Jer. 22.13. **16:** Inherited guilt (5.9–10) must not be punished by human agents (for instances to the contrary, see Josh. 7.24–26; 2 Sam. 21.1–9). On the rejection of inherited guilt, see Exod. 20.5 n. **19–22:** See Lev. 19.9–10; 23.22; for related legislation, see Exod. 23.10–11. **20:** See also 10.18; 14.29. **25.2:** The presence of the *judge* assures that punishment is not exceeded. **4:** For similar concern for animals, see 5.14; 22.4, 6–7; Exod. 23.11. **5–10:** The *duty* of levirate marriage (from band's brother is to have intercourse with her; he should take her in marriage and do his duty by her as her husband's brother. 6 The first son she bears will perpetuate the dead brother's name so that it may not be blotted out from Israel.

7 But if the man is unwilling to take his brother's wife, she must go to the elders at the town gate and say, 'My husband's brother refuses to perpetuate his brother's name in Israel; he will not do his duty by me.' 8 At this the elders of the town should summon him and reason with him. If he still stands his ground and says, 'I refuse to take her,' 9 his brother's widow must go up to him in the presence of the elders, pull his sandal off his foot, spit in his face, and declare: 'Thus we requite the man who will not build up his brother's family.' 10 His family will be known in Israel as the house of the unsandalled man.

11 When two men are fighting and the wife of one of them intervenes to drag her husband clear of his opponent, if she puts out her hand and catches hold of the man by the genitals, 12 you must cut off her hand and show her no mercy.

13 You must not have unequal weights in your bag, one heavy, the other light. 14 You must not have unequal measures in your house, one large, the other small. 15 You must have true and correct weights and true and correct measures, so that you may enjoy long life in the land which the LORD your God is giving you. 16 All who do such things, all who deal dishonestly, are abominable to the LORD your God.

17 Bear in mind what the Amalekites did to you on your journey from Egypt, 18 how they fell on you on the road when you were faint and weary and cut off those at the rear, all who were lagging behind exhausted: they showed no fear of God. 19 When the LORD your God gives you peace from your enemies on every side, in the land which he is giving you to occupy as your holding, you must

without fail blot out all memory of Amalek from under heaven.

26 AFTER you come into the land which the LORD your God is giving you to occupy as your holding and settle in it, 2 you are to take some of the firstfruits of all the produce of the soil, which you harvest from the land which the LORD your God is giving you, and, having put them in a basket, go to the place which the LORD your God will choose as a dwelling for his name. 3 When you come to the priest, whoever he is at that time, say to him, 'I acknowledge this day to the LORD your God that I have entered the land which the LORD swore to our forefathers to give us.' 4 The priest will receive the basket from your hand and set it down before the altar of the LORD your God. 5 Then you must solemnly recite before the LORD your God: 'My father was a homeless Aramaean who went down to Egypt and lived there with a small band of people, but there it became a great, powerful, and large nation. 6 The Egyptians treated us harshly and humiliated us; they imposed cruel slavery on us. 7 We cried to the LORD the God of our fathers for help, and he listened to us, and, when he saw our misery and hardship and oppression, 8 the LORD led us out of Egypt with a strong hand and outstretched arm, with terrifying deeds, and with signs and portents. 9 He brought us to this place and gave us this land, a land flowing with milk and honey. 10 Now I have brought here the firstfruits of the soil which you, LORD, have given me.' You are then to set the basket before the LORD your God and bow in worship before him. 11 You are to rejoice, you and the Levites and the aliens living among you, in all the good things which the LORD your God has bestowed on you and your household.

12 In the third year, the tithe-year, when you have finished taking the tithe of your

25:14,15 **measures:** *Heb.* ephahs.   26:5 **homeless:** *or* wandering.

the Latin *levir*, "brother-in-law") was adopted not only to preserve the family name, but to keep the property intact (compare Num. 27.1–11 n.). See Gen. 38.8, 10, 26 nn.; Ruth 4.1–13 and notes. **11–12:** The wish to avoid causing an inability to beget offspring links this unit topically with the previous one. **13–16:** See Lev. 19.35–36. **17–19:** See Exod. 17.8–16 n.

26.1–15: Liturgies for the bringing of firstfruits and tithes. 2: *Firstfruits* were offered at the pilgrim-feasts (16.1–17) of Unleavened Bread (Lev. 23.6–14), Weeks (16.9–12; Num. 28.26–31), and Booths-Ingathering (16.13–15; Exod. 23.16). *The place:* Jerusalem; see 12.5 n. **5–10:** A liturgical summary of Israel's history. **5:** *Father:* Jacob. **6:** *Us:* see 5.1–3 n.; Exod. 13.8 n. **10:** *Now:* see 4.1 n. **12–15:** See 14.28–29.

produce and have given it to the Levites and to the aliens, the fatherless, and the widows, so that they may eat it in your settlements and be well fed, [13] then declare before the LORD your God: 'I have rid my house of the tithe that was holy to you and given it to the Levites, to the aliens, the fatherless, and the widows, according to all the commandments which you laid on me. I have not infringed or forgotten any of your commandments. [14] I have not eaten any of the tithe while in mourning, nor have I got rid of any of it while unclean, nor offered any to the dead. I have obeyed the LORD my God, doing all that you commanded me. [15] Look down from heaven, your holy dwelling-place, and bless your people Israel and the soil which you have given to us as you promised on oath to our forefathers, a land flowing with milk and honey.'

[16] This day the LORD your God commands you to keep these statutes and laws: be careful to observe them with all your heart and soul. [17] You have recognized the LORD this day as your God; you are to conform to his ways, to keep his statutes, his commandments, and his laws, and to obey him. [18] The LORD has recognized you this day as his special possession, as he promised you, and you are to keep all his commandments; [19] high above all the nations which he has made he will raise you, to bring him praise and fame and glory, and to be a people holy to the LORD your God, according to his promise.

Moses' closing discourse

27 Moses, with the elders of Israel, gave the people this charge: Keep all the commandments that I now lay upon you.

[2] On the day you cross the Jordan to the land which the LORD your God is giving you, you are to set up great stones. Coat them with plaster, [3] and inscribe on them all the words of this law, when you have crossed over to enter the land which the LORD your God is giving you, a land flowing with milk and honey, as the LORD the God of your forefathers promised you.

[4] When you have crossed the Jordan you are to set up these stones on Mount Ebal, as I instruct you this day, and coat them with plaster. [5] Build an altar there to the LORD your God, an altar of stones on which no iron tool is to be used. [6] Build the altar of the LORD your God with blocks of undressed stone, and offer whole-offerings on it to the LORD your God. [7] Slaughter shared-offerings and eat them there, and rejoice before the LORD your God. [8] Inscribe on the stones all the words of this law, engraving them clearly and carefully.

[9] Moses and the levitical priests said to all Israel: Be silent, Israel, and listen; this day you have become a people belonging to the LORD your God. [10] Obey the LORD your God, and observe his commandments and statutes that I now lay upon you.

[11] That day Moses gave the people this command: [12] When you have crossed the Jordan those who are to stand on Mount Gerizim to bless the people are: Simeon, Levi, Judah, Issachar, Joseph, and Benjamin. [13] Those who are to stand on Mount Ebal to pronounce the curse are: Reuben, Gad, Asher, Zebulun, Dan, and Naphtali. [14] The Levites, in the hearing of all Israel,

26:14 nor have ... unclean: *mng of Heb. obscure.* **to the dead:** *or* for the dead. **27:4 Ebal:** Gerizim *in Samar.*

14: *While in mourning:* that is, while "unclean" from contact with the dead body (Num. 19.11–16) and able to transfer "uncleanness" to the sacred tithe (Hag. 2.12–13; Lev. 11.24–25 n.). *To the dead:* see 14.1 n.; 21.1–9 n.

26.16–30.20: Ratification of the covenant in Moab. The covenant stipulations given (Exod. ch. 20) and received (Exod. ch. 24) at Sinai are viewed as extended to the end of the wilderness period. The present generation now accepts the expansions (29.1) and is urged to renew its dedication regularly thereafter (31.9–13).

26.16–19: A fragment of the covenant renewal ceremony. The section is a part of a larger liturgy connected with covenant renewal. It included the recitation of the LORD's demands (v. 16; chs. 12–26), reaffirmation of the LORD as Israel's only God (v. 17; 6.1–25), and proclamation of the promise that Israel remains God's people (vv. 18–19), as a prelude to the close (28.68) of the second of Moses' three addresses. On the terminology involved, see Exod. 6.7 n.

27.1–28.68: Provision for the renewal of the covenant at Shechem, an event anticipated in 11.29–32 and are to intone these words: [15]'A curse on any-one who carves an image or casts an idol, anything abominable to the LORD, a crafts-man's handiwork, and sets it up in secret': the people must all respond, 'Amen.'

[16]'A curse on anyone who slights his father or his mother': the people must all say, 'Amen.'

[17]'A curse on anyone who moves his neigh-bour's boundary stone': the people must all say, 'Amen.'

[18]'A curse on anyone who misdirects a blind man': the people must all say, 'Amen.'

[19]'A curse on anyone who withholds justice from the alien, the fatherless, and the widow': the people must all say, 'Amen.'

[20]'A curse on anyone who lies with his fa-ther's wife, for he brings shame upon his father': the people must all say, 'Amen.'

[21]'A curse on anyone who lies with any animal': the people must all say, 'Amen.'

[22]'A curse on anyone who lies with his sis-ter, whether his father's daughter or his mother's daughter': the people must all say, 'Amen.'

[23]'A curse on anyone who lies with his wife's mother': the people must all say, 'Amen.'

[24]'A curse on anyone who strikes another in secret': the people must all say, 'Amen.'

[25]'A curse on anyone who accepts payment for killing an innocent person': the people must all say, 'Amen.'

[26]'A curse on anyone who does not fulfil this law by doing all that it prescribes': the people must all say, 'Amen.'

28
If you faithfully obey the LORD your God by diligently observing all his commandments which I lay on you this day, then the LORD your God will raise you high above all nations of the earth, [2]and the fol-lowing blessings will all come and light on you, because you obey the LORD your God.

[3]A blessing on you in the town; a blessing on you in the country.

[4]A blessing on the fruit of your body, the fruit of your land and cattle, the offspring of your herds and lambing flocks.

[5]A blessing on your basket and your kneading trough.

[6]A blessing on you as you come in, and a blessing on you as you go out.

[7]May the LORD deliver up to you the ene-mies who attack you, and let them be put to rout before you. Though they come out against you one way, they will flee before you by seven.

[8]May the LORD grant you a blessing in your granaries and on all your labours; may the LORD your God bless you in the land which he is giving you.

[9]The LORD will establish you as his own holy people, as he swore to you, provided you keep the commandments of the LORD your God and conform to his ways. [10]All people on earth seeing that the LORD has named you as his very own will go in fear of you. [11]The LORD will make you prosper greatly in the fruit of your body and of your cattle, and in the fruit of the soil in the land which he swore to your forefathers to give you. [12]May the LORD open the heavens for you, his rich storehouse, to give your land rain at the proper time and bless everything to which you turn your hand. You may lend to many nations, but borrow from none; [13]the LORD

27:14 **intone:** *lit.* recite in a high-pitched voice.

found in Josh. 8.30–35. Joshua ch. 24 may be intended as an example for the regular observance of the ceremony at Shechem. **4:** *Mount Ebal:* opposite Mount Gerizim (v. 12) and near Shechem. **5:** *Altar:* perhaps this may have been the earliest location of the central sanctuary demanded in ch. 12. If so, after the Assyrian conquest in 721 B.C.E., the "chosen" place was understood as not here, but Jerusalem (12.5 n.). **6:** *Undressed stone:* see Exod. 20.25 n. **9–10:** These verses interrupt the ceremony prescribed for Shechem and continue the account of covenant renewal in Moab (26.16–19), resumed again in 29.1. **11–13:** The ceremony of blessing and cursing. Their content is amplified in ch. 28. For their role in contracts, see Lev. 26.1–46 n.; Deut. 11.26–28 n. **14–26:** An ancient list of twelve brief curses. Since most of them are directed against violations of covenant stipulations, they have been added to the present ceremony. They are announced by Levites rather than the six tribes of v. 13. **15:** See 5.8; compare 12.1–4. **16:** Compare 5.16; 21.18–21. **17:** See 19.14. **18:** See Lev. 19.14. **19:** See 24.17. **20:** See 22.30. **21:** See Exod. 22.19. **22–23:** See 23.2 n. **24:** See 5.17; 21.1–9. **28:1** The ceremony continues from 27.13. **3–6:** Six blessings are given, in agreement with the number of tribes in 27.12. They emphasize that the LORD is the source of fertility of flock and soil, rather than the Canaanite gods (see 7.13–14 n.). **7–14:** Amplification of the blessings. **7:** *By seven:* compare Lev. 26.18 n.

will make you the head and not the tail: you will always be at the top and never at the bottom, if you listen to the commandments of the LORD your God, which I give you this day to keep and to fulfil. 14 Deviate neither to right nor to left from all the things which I command you this day, and do not go after other gods to serve them.

15 BUT if you will not obey the LORD your God by diligently observing all his commandments and statutes which I lay upon you this day, then all the following curses will come and light upon you.

16 A curse on you in the town, a curse in the country.

17 A curse on your basket and your kneading trough.

18 A curse on the fruit of your body, the fruit of your land, the offspring of your herds and your lambing flocks.

19 A curse on you as you come in, and a curse on you as you go out.

20 May the LORD send on you cursing, confusion, and rebuke in whatever you are doing, until you are destroyed and soon perish for the evil you have done in forsaking him. 21 May the LORD cause pestilence to haunt you until he has exterminated you out of the land which you are entering to occupy; 22 may the LORD afflict you with wasting disease and recurrent fever, ague, and eruptions; with drought, and black blight and red; and may these plague you until you perish. 23 May the skies above you be brazen, and the earth beneath you iron. 24 May the LORD turn the rain in your country to fine sand, and may dust descend on you from the sky until you are blotted out.

25 May the LORD put you to rout before your enemies. Though you go out against them by one way, you will flee before them by seven. May you be repugnant to all the kingdoms on earth. 26 May your bodies become food for all the birds of the air and all the wild beasts, with no one to scare them off.

27 May the LORD strike you with Egyptian boils and with tumours, scabs, and itch, for which you will find no cure. 28 May the LORD strike you with madness, blindness, and stupefaction; 29 so that you will grope about in broad daylight, just as a blind man gropes in darkness, and you will fail to find your way. You will be oppressed and robbed, day in, day out, with no one to save you. 30 A woman will be betrothed to you, but someone will ravish her; you will build a house but not live in it; you will plant a vineyard but not enjoy its fruit. 31 Your ox will be slaughtered before your eyes, but you will not eat any of it; and while you watch your donkey will be stolen and will not come back to you; your sheep will be given to the enemy, and there will be no one to recover them. 32 Your sons and daughters will be given to another people with you looking on; your eyes will strain after them all day long, but you will be powerless. 33 A nation which you do not know will eat the products of your land and of all your toil, and your lot will be nothing but grievous oppression. 34 The sights you see will drive you mad. 35 May the LORD strike you on knee and leg with severe boils for which you will find no cure; they will spread from the sole of your foot to the crown of your head.

36 May the LORD give you up, you and the king whom you have appointed, to a nation which neither you nor your fathers have known, and there you will serve other gods, gods of wood and stone. 37 You will become a horror, a byword, and an object-lesson to all the peoples amongst whom the LORD disperses you.

38 You will carry plentiful seed to your fields, but you will harvest little, for locusts will devour it. 39 You will plant vineyards and cultivate them, but you will not drink the wine or gather the grapes, for the grub will eat them. 40 You will have olive trees everywhere in your territory, but you will not anoint yourselves with the oil, for your olives will drop off. 41 You will have sons and daughters, but they will not remain yours, for they will go into captivity. 42 All your trees and the fruit of the ground will be infested with the mole-cricket. 43 The alien who lives with you will raise himself higher and higher, and you will sink lower and lower. 44 He will lend to you but you will not lend to him: he will be the head and you the tail. 45 All these curses will come on you; they will pursue and overtake you until you are destroyed, be-

28:20 **cursing . . . rebuke:** or starvation, burning thirst, and dysentery. **him:** prob. rdg; Heb. me.
28:27 **tumours:** or, as otherwise read, haemorrhoids.

16–19: Six curses that are the reverse of the blessings. **20–46:** Amplification of the curses. **22:** Seven afflictions (Lev. 26.18 n.). **27:** The plague once directed toward the Egyptians (Exod. 9.8–12) would now strike Israel. **30:**

cause you did not obey the LORD your God by keeping the commandments and statutes which he gave you. 46 They will be a sign and a portent to you and your descendants for ever.

47 You have not served the LORD your God, rejoicing in gladness of heart over all your blessings; 48 therefore in hunger and thirst, in nakedness and extreme want, you will have to serve the enemies whom the LORD will send against you. He will put a yoke of iron on your neck until you are subdued.

49 May the LORD bring against you from afar, from the end of the earth, a nation which will swoop upon you like a vulture, a nation whose language you will not understand, 50 a nation of grim aspect with no regard for the old, no pity for the young. 51 When you have been subdued, they will devour the offspring of your cattle and the fruit of your land. They will leave you neither grain nor new wine nor oil, neither calves from your herds nor lambs from your flocks, until you are brought to ruin. 52 They will besiege you in all your towns until they overthrow your high fortifications, those walls throughout your land in which you trust. They will besiege you within all your towns, throughout the land which the LORD your God has given you. 53 Then, because of the dire straits to which you will be reduced when your enemy besieges you, you will eat your own children, the flesh of your sons and daughters whom the LORD your God has given you. 54 The most delicately bred and sensitive man will not share with his brother, or with the wife he loves, or with his own remaining children 55 any of the meat which he is eating, the flesh of his own children. He is left with nothing else because of the dire straits to which you will be reduced within all your towns when the enemy besieges you. 56 The most delicately bred and sensitive woman, so delicate and sensitive that she would never venture to put a foot to the ground, will not share with her own husband or her son or her daughter 57 the afterbirth which she expels, or any boy or girl that she may bear. During the siege she herself will eat them secretly in her extreme want, in the dire straits to which

the enemy will reduce you in your towns.

58 If you do not observe and fulfil all the law written down in this book, if you do not revere this honoured and dreaded name, this name 'the LORD your God', 59 then the LORD will strike you and your descendants with unimaginable plagues, virulent and chronic, and with lingering and severe sickness. 60 He will bring on you once again all the diseases of Egypt which you dreaded, and they will cling to you. 61 The LORD will bring upon you sickness and plague of every kind, even those not recorded in this book of the law, until you are destroyed. 62 Then you who were countless as the stars in the heavens will be left few in number, because you did not obey the LORD your God. 63 Just as the LORD took delight in you, prospering you and increasing your numbers, so now it will be his delight to ruin and exterminate you, and you will be uprooted from the land which you are entering to occupy.

64 The LORD will disperse you among all peoples from one end of the earth to the other, and there you will serve other gods of whom neither you nor your forefathers have had experience, gods of wood and stone. 65 Among those nations you will find no peace, no resting-place for the sole of your foot. Then the LORD will give you an unquiet mind, dim eyes, and failing appetite. 66 Your life will hang continually in suspense, fear will beset you night and day, and you will find no security all your life long. 67 Every morning you will say, 'Would God it were evening!' and every evening, 'Would God it were morning!' because of the terror that fills your heart and because of the sights you see. 68 The LORD will bring you back sorrowing to Egypt by that very road of which I said to you, 'You shall not see that road again'; there you will offer yourselves for sale as slaves to your enemies, but there will be no buyer.

29 These are the terms of the covenant which the LORD commanded Moses to make with the Israelites in Moab, in addition to the covenant which he made with them on Horeb.

28:52 towns: lit. gates.   28:58 LORD: see note on Exod. 3:15.   29:1 In Heb. 28:69.

Contrast 20.5–7. 47–68: An expansion of the curses, possibly alluding to the fate of the kingdom of Israel in 721 B.C.E., when the Assyrians destroyed the country and took most of its population into captivity (2 Kgs. 17.1–6). 62: Few in number: a reversal of the promise to Abraham (Gen. 15.5). 68: Of which I said: compare 17.16.

29.1–30.20: The third address of Moses. 1: The covenant is a renewal of the Sinai covenant. For its

2 MOSES summoned all the Israelites and addressed them: You have seen for yourselves all that the LORD did in Egypt to Pharaoh, to all his courtiers, and to his whole land, 3 the great challenge which you yourselves witnessed, those great signs and portents, 4 but to this day the LORD has not given you a mind to understand or eyes to see or ears to hear.

5 I led you for forty years in the wilderness; the clothes on your back did not wear out, nor did your sandals become worn and fall off your feet; 6 you ate no bread and drank no wine or strong drink, in order that you might learn that I am the LORD your God. 7 When you reached this place King Sihon of Heshbon and King Og of Bashan launched an attack on us. We defeated them, 8 took their land, and gave it as a holding to the Reubenites, the Gadites, and half the tribe of Manasseh. 9 Observe the provisions of this covenant and keep them so that you may be successful in all you do.

10 You are standing here today before the LORD your God, all of you leaders of tribes, elders, and officers, all the men of Israel, 11 with your dependants, your wives, the aliens who live in your camp—all of them, from those who cut wood for you to those who draw water—12 and you are ready to accept the oath and enter into the covenant which the LORD your God is making with you now. 13 The covenant is to constitute you his people this day, and he will be your God, as he promised you and as he swore to your forefathers, Abraham, Isaac, and Jacob. 14 It is not with you alone that I am making this covenant and this oath, 15 but with all those who stand here with us today before the LORD our God and also with those who are not here with us today.

16 You know how we lived in Egypt and how we and you, as we passed through the nations, 17 saw their loathsome idols and the false gods they had, gods made of wood and stone, of silver and gold. 18 If there should be among you a man or woman, family or tribe, who is moved today to turn from the LORD our God and to go and serve the gods of those nations—if there is among you such a root from which springs gall and wormwood, 19 then any such person on hearing the terms

of this oath may inwardly flatter himself and think, 'All will be well with me even if I follow the promptings of my stubborn heart'; but this will bring sweeping disaster. 20 The LORD will not be willing to forgive him; but his anger and resentment will overwhelm this person, and the curses described in this book will fall heavily on him, and the LORD will blot out his name from under heaven. 21 The LORD will single him out from all the tribes of Israel for disaster to fall on him, according to the oath required by the covenant and prescribed in this book of the law.

22 The next generation, your children who follow you, and the foreigners who come from distant countries, will see the plagues of this land and the diseases which the LORD has brought upon its people, 23 the whole land burnt up with brimstone and salt, nothing sown, nothing growing, not a plant in sight. It will be as desolate as Sodom and Gomorrah, Admah and Zeboyim, when the LORD overthrew them in raging anger. 24 Then they, and all the nations with them, will ask, 'Why has the LORD so afflicted this land? Why this great outburst of anger?' 25 The answer will be: 'Because they forsook the covenant of the LORD the God of their forefathers which he made with them when he brought them out of Egypt. 26 They began to serve other gods and to bow down to them, gods of whom they had no experience and whom the LORD had not assigned to them. 27 The anger of the LORD was roused against that land, so that he brought on it all the curses described in this book. 28 The LORD uprooted them from their soil in anger, in rage and great fury, and banished them to another land, where they are to this day.'

29 There are things hidden, and they belong to the LORD our God, but what is revealed belongs to us and our children for ever; it is for us to observe all that is prescribed in this law.

30 When all these things have happened to you, the blessing and the curse of which I have offered you the choice, if you take them to heart there among all the na-

29:2 In Heb. 29:1.   29:19 but ... disaster: lit. to the sweeping away of moist and dry.   29:22 diseases: or ulcers.

conditions, see 28.1, 15, 63; 30.1, 5, 7, 9. 2–8: Recitation of previous history (for the reason, see 4.1 n.). 5: See 8.4; 2.7. 7–8: A summary of 2.26–3.17. 9: Chapters 12–26. 13: His people; your God: 26.17–18; Exod. 6.7 n. Forefathers: see 1.8 n. 15: Today: see 5.1–3 n. 18: Wormwood: a bitter drug. 23: Brimstone: sulphur. Admah and Zeboyim: see Gen. 10.19. 26: Assigned: see 32.8–9 n. 30.1–10: Exile and return. An expansion tions to which the LORD your God has banished you, ²if you and your children turn back to him and obey him heart and soul in all that I command you this day, ³then the LORD your God will restore your fortunes. In compassion for you he will gather you again from all the peoples to which he has dispersed you. ⁴Even though he has banished you to the ends of the earth, the LORD your God will gather you from there, and from there he will fetch you home. ⁵The LORD your God will bring you into the land which your forefathers occupied, and you will occupy it again; then he will bring you prosperity and make you more numerous than your forefathers were.

⁶The LORD your God will circumcise your hearts and the hearts of your descendants, so that you will love him with all your heart and soul and you will live. ⁷The LORD your God will turn all these curses against your enemies and the foes who persecute you. ⁸Then you will obey the LORD once more and keep all his commandments which I give you this day. ⁹⁻¹⁰The LORD your God will make you more than prosperous in all that you do, in the fruit of your body and of your cattle and in the fruits of your soil; for, when you obey the LORD your God by keeping his commandments and statutes, as they are written in this book of the law, and when you turn back to the LORD your God with all your heart and soul, he will again rejoice over you and be good to you, as he rejoiced over your forefathers.

¹¹This commandment that I lay on you today is not too difficult for you or beyond your reach. ¹²It is not in the heavens, that you should say, 'Who will go up to the heavens for us to fetch it and tell it to us, so that we can keep it?' ¹³Nor is it beyond the sea, that you should say, 'Who will cross the sea for us to fetch it and tell it to us, so that we can keep it?' ¹⁴It is a thing very near to you, on your lips and in your heart ready to be kept.

¹⁵Today I offer you the choice of life and good, or death and evil. ¹⁶If you obey the commandments of the LORD your God which I give you this day, by loving the LORD your God, conforming to his ways, and keeping his commandments, statutes, and laws, then you will live and increase, and the LORD your God will bless you in the land which you are about to enter to occupy. ¹⁷But if in your heart you turn away and do not listen, and you are led astray to worship other gods and serve them, ¹⁸I tell you here and now that you will perish, and not enjoy long life in the land which you will enter to occupy after crossing the Jordan. ¹⁹I summon heaven and earth to witness against you this day: I offer you the choice of life or death, blessing or curse. Choose life and you and your descendants will live; ²⁰love the LORD your God, obey him, and hold fast to him: that is life for you and length of days on the soil which the LORD swore to give to your forefathers, Abraham, Isaac, and Jacob.

31 Moses, finishing this address to all Israel, ²went on to say: At a hundred and twenty years old, I am no longer able to lead the campaign; and the LORD has told me that I shall not cross the Jordan. ³It is the LORD your God who will cross over at your head and destroy these nations before your advance, and you will occupy their lands; and, as he directed, Joshua will lead you across. ⁴The LORD will do to these nations as he did to Sihon and Og, kings of the Amorites, and to their lands, when he destroyed them. ⁵The LORD will deliver them into your power, and you are to do to them as I have commanded you. ⁶Be strong and resolute; you must not dread them or be afraid, for the LORD your God himself accompanies you; he will not let you down or forsake you.

⁷Moses summoned Joshua and in the sight of all Israel said to him: Be strong and reso-

30:16 **If you … of the LORD your God:** *so Gk; Heb. omits.*　31:1 **finishing this address:** *so Scroll; Heb.* went and spoke.

of 4.29–31, possibly written either during the Exile of Israel (721 B.C.E.; see 28.47–68 n.) or Judah (587 B.C.E.) in order to encourage those whose situation then appeared hopeless. **15–18:** The passage gives the precise blessing and curse pronounced after the acceptance of the covenant (as in 27.11–28.68; see 27.11–13 n.). **19:** The summoning of witnesses closes the covenant ceremony (4.26 n.).

31.1–29: The appointment of Moses' successor (vv. 1–8, 14–23; compare Num. 27.12–23) alternates with the provisions for writing, preserving, and reciting the law (vv. 9–13, 24–27). **2:** *Hundred and twenty:* eighty (Exod. 7.7) plus the forty in the wilderness (2.7). *I shall not cross:* see 1.37 n. **3:** *At your head and destroy:* see 9.3. As he directed: 3.23–28. **4:** See Num. 21.21–35. **10:** *Year of remission:* see 15.1–18. *Booths:* see lute, for it is you who will lead this people into the land which the LORD swore to give their forefathers; you are to bring them into possession of it. [8] The LORD himself goes at your head; he will be with you; he will not let you down or forsake you. Do not be afraid or discouraged.

[9] Moses wrote down this law and gave it to the priests, the sons of Levi, who carried the Ark of the Covenant of the LORD, and to all the elders of Israel. [10] Moses gave them this command: At the end of every seven years, at the appointed time for the year of remission, at the pilgrim-feast of Booths, [11] when all Israel comes to appear before the LORD your God in the place which he will choose, this law is to be read in the hearing of all Israel. [12] Assemble the people, men, women, and dependants, together with the aliens residing in your settlements, so that they may listen, and learn to fear the LORD your God and observe all these laws with care. [13] Their children, too, who do not know the laws, will hear them, and learn to fear the LORD your God all their lives in the land which you will occupy after crossing the Jordan.

[14] THE LORD said to Moses, 'The time of your death is drawing near. Summon Joshua, and present yourselves in the Tent of Meeting so that I may give him his commission.' When Moses and Joshua went and presented themselves in the Tent of Meeting, [15] the LORD appeared in a pillar of cloud, which stood over the entrance of the Tent.

[16] The LORD said to Moses, 'You are about to die and join your forefathers, and then this people, when they come into the land and live among foreigners, will wantonly worship their gods; they will abandon me and break the covenant which I have made with them. [17] My anger will be roused against them on that day, and I shall abandon them and hide my face from them. They will be an easy prey, and many terrible disasters will come upon them. On that day they will say,

"These disasters have come because our God is not among us." [18] On that day I shall hide my face because of all the evil they have done in turning to other gods.

[19] 'Now write down this song and teach it to the Israelites; make them repeat it, so that it may be a witness for me against them. [20] When I have brought them into the land which I swore to give to their forefathers, a land flowing with milk and honey, and they have plenty to eat and are thriving, then they will turn to other gods and serve them, spurning me and breaking my covenant; [21] and many terrible disasters will follow. Then this song will confront them as a witness, for it will not be forgotten by their descendants. For even before I bring them into the land which I swore to give them, I already know which way their thoughts incline.'

[22] That day Moses wrote down this song and taught it to the Israelites. [23] The LORD gave Joshua son of Nun his commission in these words: 'Be strong and resolute; for you are to lead the Israelites into the land which I swore to give them, and I shall be with you.'

[24] When Moses had finished writing down these laws from beginning to end in a book, [25] he gave this command to the Levites who carried the Ark of the Covenant of the LORD: [26] Take this book of the law and put it beside the Ark of the Covenant of the LORD your God, and let it be there as a witness against you. [27] For I know how defiant and stubborn you are; even during my lifetime you have defied the LORD; how much more, then, will you do so after my death! [28] Assemble for me all the elders of your tribes and your officers; I shall say all these words in their hearing and summon heaven and earth to witness against them. [29] For I know that, when I am dead, you will take to infamous practices and turn

31:11 **appear before:** *lit.* see the face of.
31:13 **their lives:** *so Samar.; Heb.* your lives.
31:19 **song:** *or* rule of life.   31:23 **The LORD:** *prob. rdg; Heb.* He.

16.13–15 n. **11–13:** Provision for public reading was a regular part of ancient Near Eastern treaties (covenants), and the festival would be the occasion for renewal (27.1–28.68 n.). **14–15:** These verses are conceptually and linguistically related to Exod. 33.7–11; Num. 11.16–17, 24–25. **16–22:** These verses intrude; they anticipate ch. 32, the "Song of Moses" (vv. 19, 30), which may have been sung as part of the covenant renewal ceremony. Thus the Song, like the "book of the law" (vv. 24–27), would serve as a "witness" to God's graciousness in the past and as a challenge to Israel's life in the future. **23:** This verse is a sequel to vv. 14–15. **26:** *Beside the Ark:* symbolizing its authority and making it accessible for public reading (vv. 10–11). Compare 10.1–5. **28:** *Witness:* see 30.19 n.

aside from the way which I told you to follow. In days to come disaster will befall you, for in doing what is wrong in the eyes of the LORD you provoked him to anger.

30 MOSES recited this song from beginning to end in the hearing of the whole assembly of Israel:

32 Give ear, you heavens, to what I say;
listen, earth, to the words I speak.
2 May my teaching fall like raindrops,
my words distil like dew,
like fine rain on tender grass,
like lavish showers on growing plants.

3 When I proclaim the name of the
LORD,
you will respond: 'Great is our God,
4 the Creator, whose work is perfect,
for all his ways are just,
a faithful God who does no wrong;
how righteous and true is he!'

5 Perverted and crooked generation
whose faults have proved you no
children of his,
6 is this how you repay the LORD,
you senseless, stupid people?
Is he not your father who formed you?
Did he not make you and establish you?
7 Remember the days of old,
think of the years, age upon age;
ask your father to inform you,
the elders to tell you.

8 When the Most High gave each nation
its heritage,
when he divided all mankind,
he laid down the boundaries for
peoples
according to the number of the sons of
God;
9 but the LORD's share was his own
people,

Jacob was his allotted portion.

10 He found his people in a desert land,
in a barren, howling waste.
He protected and trained them,
he guarded them as the apple of his
eye.
11 As an eagle watches over its nest,
hovers above its young,
spreads its pinions and takes them up,
and bears them on its wings,
12 the LORD alone led his people,
no alien god at his side.

13 He made them ride over the heights of
the earth
and fed them on the harvest of the
fields;
he satisfied them with honey from the
crags
and oil from the flinty rock,
14 curds from the cattle, milk from the
herd,
the fat of lambs' kidneys,
of Bashan rams, and of goats,
with the finest flour of wheat;
and you, his people, drank red wine
from the juice of the grape.

15 Jacob ate and was well fed,
Jeshurun grew fat and unruly,
they grew fat and bloated and sleek.
They forsook God their Maker
and dishonoured the Rock of their
salvation.
16 They roused his jealousy with alien
gods
and provoked him to anger with
abominable practices.
17 They sacrificed to demons that are no
gods,
to gods who were strangers to them;

32:4 **Creator:** *or* Rock.   32:8 **sons of God:** *so Scroll; Heb.* sons of Israel.   32:14 **kidneys:** *transposed from fourth line.*   32:15 **Jacob . . . fed:** *so Samar.; Heb. omits.* **unruly:** *or* kicked.

31.30–32.47: The "Song of Moses." See 31.16–22 n. The Song is linked to the previous chapter by the summoning of heaven and earth (31.28 and 32.1). In reality, it is an appended psalm, perhaps older than Deut. itself. **32.1–4: Invocation. 5–6: An accusation of ingratitude** (see 4.1 n.). **7: A call to consider the past.**
    32.8–14: Recitation of the LORD's gracious deeds. 8–9: *The sons of God* are minor figures in the divine council (Gen. 1.26 n.) to whom *the Most High* has assigned governorship of the nations, while Israel is retained as God's own. **10:** This may be part of a tradition that Israel became the LORD's people in the wilderness (see also Hos. 9.10), against the dominant view, e.g. Gen. ch. 12. **15–18: Israel's ungrateful response. 15:** *Jeshurun:* an occasional, ancient name for Israel (33.5, 26).

they consorted with upstart gods from
their neighbours,
gods whom your fathers did not
acknowledge.
18 You forsook the Creator who begot you
and ceased to care for God who
brought you to birth.

19 The LORD saw and spurned them;
his own sons and daughters provoked
his anger.
20 'I shall hide my face from them,' he
said;
'let me see what their end will be,
for they are a subversive generation,
children not to be trusted.
21 They roused my jealousy with a god of
no account,
with their worthless idols they provoked
me to anger,
so I shall rouse their jealousy with a
people of no account,
with a foolish nation I shall provoke
them.
22 For fire is set ablaze by my anger,
it burns to the depths of Sheol;
it devours earth and its harvest
and the flames reach the very roots of
the mountains.

23 'I shall heap on them one disaster after
another,
and expend my arrows on them:
24 pangs of hunger, ravages of plague,
and bitter pestilence.
I shall harry them with the fangs of
wild beasts
and the poison of creatures that crawl
in the dust.
25 The sword will make orphans in the
streets,
make widows in their homes;
it will take toll of young men and girls,
of babes in arms as well as of the aged.
26 I had resolved to strike them down

and to destroy all memory of them,
27 but I feared that I should be provoked
by their foes,
that their enemies would take the
credit,
saying, "It was not the LORD,
but we who got the upper hand." '

28 They are a nation devoid of good
counsel,
that lacks all understanding.
29 If only they had the wisdom to discern
this
and understand what their end is to be!
30 How could one man rout a thousand of
them,
how could two put ten thousand to
flight,
if their Rock had not sold them to their
enemies,
if the LORD had not handed them over?
31 For the enemy have no Rock like ours;
in themselves they are mere fools.
32 Their vines are from the vines of
Sodom,
grown on the terraces of Gomorrah;
their grapes are poisonous,
the clusters bitter to the taste.
33 Their wine is the venom of serpents,
the cruel poison of asps;
34 all this I have in reserve,
sealed up in my storehouses
35 till the day of punishment and
vengeance,
till the moment when their foot slips;
for the day of their downfall is near,
their doom is fast approaching.
36 The LORD will judge his people
and have compassion on his servants;
for he will see that their strength is
gone,
no one, either fettered or free, is left.

32:18 **Creator:** *or* Rock. 32:22 **Sheol:** *or* the
underworld. 32:31 **fools:** *so Gk; Heb.* judges.
32:35 **till the day of:** *so Samar.; Heb.* for me.

32.19–47: God's judgment. 19: The historical event to which *spurned them* refers is uncertain; the allusion
is meant as a warning for future generations. **22:** *Sheol:* Num. 16.30 n. Destruction of the *harvest* demonstrates
the powerlessness of the gods of fertility (7.13–14 n.). In all, seven evils are enumerated (28.22 n.). **26–35:**
God's reflections upon the divine judgment. It cannot be a final one, lest Israel's neighbors misunderstand the
cause. When Israel is restored, God's sovereignty over both punishment and deliverance will be evident. The
passage 30.1–10, however, demands repentance as the prerequisite for restoration. **27:** Compare Isa.
10.12–15. **28:** *They:* the enemies who have defeated Israel. **30:** *One man:* of the enemy. *Thousand:* of Israel.
That such a small force defeated Israel indicates that it was God's will. *Rock:* a common ancient Near Eastern
divine title denoting permanence. **31:** The speaker shifts from God to the congregation. **36–42:** The renuncia-

37 He will ask, 'Where are your gods,
　　the rock in which you sought refuge,
38 the gods who ate the fat of your
　　　sacrifices
　　and drank the wine of your
　　　drink-offerings?
　　Let them rise to help you!
　　Let them be your protection!
39 See now that I, I am He,
　　and besides me there is no god:
　　I put to death and I keep alive,
　　I inflict wounds and I heal;
　　there is no rescue from my grasp.
40 I raise my hand towards heaven
　　and swear: As I live for ever,
41 when I have whetted my flashing
　　　sword,
　　when I have set my hand to judgement,
　　then I shall punish my adversaries
　　and wreak vengeance on my foes.
42 I shall make my arrows drunk with
　　　blood,
　　my sword will devour flesh,
　　blood of slain and captives,
　　the heads of the enemy princes.'

43 Rejoice with him, you heavens,
　　bow down, all you gods, before him;
　　for he will avenge the blood of his sons
　　and take vengeance on his adversaries;
　　he will punish those who hate him
　　and cleanse his people's land.

44 These are the words of the song that Moses, when he came with Joshua son of Nun, recited in full in the hearing of the people.

45 When Moses had finished reciting all these words to Israel 46 he said: Take to heart all the warnings which I give you this day: command your children to be careful to observe all the words of this law. 47 For you they are no empty words; they are your very life, and by them you will enjoy long life in the land which you are to occupy after crossing the Jordan.

48 That same day the LORD said to Moses, 49 'Go up the mountain of the Abarim, Mount Nebo in Moab, to the east of Jericho, and view the land of Canaan that I am giving to the Israelites for their possession. 50 On this mountain you will die and be gathered to your father's kin, just as Aaron your brother died on Mount Hor and was gathered to his father's kin. 51 This is because both of you broke faith with me at the waters of Meribah-kadesh in the wilderness of Zin, when you did not uphold my holiness among the Israelites. 52 You may see the land from a distance, but you may not enter the land I am giving to the Israelites.'

Moses' final words and death

33 THIS is the blessing that Moses, the man of God, pronounced on the Israelites before his death:

2 The LORD came from Sinai
　　and shone forth from Seir.
　　He appeared from Mount Paran,
　　and with him were myriads of holy
　　　ones
　　streaming along at his right hand.
3 Truly he loves his people
　　and blesses his holy ones.
　　They sit at his feet
　　and receive his instruction,
4 the law which Moses laid upon us,
　　as a possession for the assembly of
　　　Jacob.
5 Then a king arose in Jeshurun,
　　when the chiefs of the people were
　　　assembled
　　together with all the tribes of Israel.

6 Of Reuben he said:

32:43 **Rejoice ... before him:** so Scroll, cp. Gk; Heb. Cause his people to rejoice, you nations. **sons:** so Scroll; Heb. servants. **he will punish ... land:** so Scroll; Heb. and make expiation for his land, his people. 32:44 **Joshua:** Heb. Hoshea (cp. Num. 13:16). 33:2 **and with ... ones:** prob. rdg; Heb. and he came from myriads of holiness. 33:3 **his people:** so Gk; Heb. peoples. **blesses:** so Syriac; Heb. in your hand. **his feet ... his instruction:** so Lat.; Heb. your feet ... your instruction. 33:5 **a king arose:** or there was a king. 33:6 **Of Reuben he said:** prob. rdg; Heb. omits.

tion of foreign gods and the anticipation of deliverance. **43:** Closing hymn of praise. **45–47:** The insertion of the "Song of Moses" seems to sever these verses from the context in 31.29.
　　32.48–52: Moses prepares for his death. For related materials, see 3.23–28; Num. 20.1–13.
　　33.1–29: The "Blessing of Moses," a second psalm appended to Deut. (see 31.30–32.47 n.). **1:** Pronounced ... before his death: see Gen. 27.4 n., 33–35 n. for deathbed blessing or curse. **5:** Jeshurun: see 32.15 n. **6:** On the decline of Reuben as a tribal power (May Reuben live . . . but . . . be few in number), see Gen. 49.3–4 n.;

May Reuben live and not die out,
but may he be few in number.

[7] And of Judah he said this:

Hear, Lord, the cry of Judah
and join him to his people;
strengthen his hands for him,
be his helper against his adversaries.

[8] Of Levi he said:

Give your Thummim to Levi,
your Urim to your loyal servant
whom you tested at Massah,
for whom you pleaded at the waters of
Meribah,
[9] who said of his parents, 'I do not know
them,'
who did not acknowledge his brothers,
who disowned his children.
But they observe your word
and keep your covenant;
[10] they teach your precepts to Jacob,
your law to Israel.
They furnish you with the smoke of
sacrifice
and offerings on your altar.
[11] Bless his powers, Lord,
and accept the work of his hands.
Strike his adversaries hip and thigh,
and may those hostile to him rise no
more.

[12] Of Benjamin he said:

The Lord's beloved dwells securely,
the High God shields him all the day
long,
and he dwells under his protection.

[13] Of Joseph he said:

May the Lord's blessing be on his land
with choice fruit watered from heaven
above
and from the deep that lies below,
[14] with choice fruit ripened by the sun,

choice fruit, the produce of the months,
[15] with all good things from the ancient
mountains,
the choice fruit of the everlasting hills,
[16] the choice fruits of earth and its
fullness,
by the favour of him who dwells in the
burning bush.
May this rest on the head of Joseph,
on the brow of him who was prince
among his brothers.
[17] In majesty he shall be like a firstborn
bull,
his horns those of a wild ox
with which he will gore nations
and drive them to the ends of the
earth.
Such will be the myriads of Ephraim,
and such the thousands of Manasseh.

[18] Of Zebulun he said:

Rejoice, Zebulun, when you set forth,
rejoice in your tents, Issachar.
[19] They will summon peoples to the
mountain;
there they will offer true sacrifices,
for they will draw from the abundance
of the sea,
from the hidden wealth of the sand.

[20] Of Gad he said:

Blessed be Gad, in his wide domain;
he couches like a lion
tearing an arm or a scalp.
[21] He chose the best for himself,
for to him was allotted a ruler's
portion,
when the chiefs of the people were
assembled together.

33:8 **Give ... servant:** *so Gk; Heb.* Your Thummim
and Urim belong to your loyal servant.
33:11 **powers:** *or* skill.   33:12 **the High God:** *prob.
rdg; Heb.* upon him. **under his protection:** *lit.* between
his shoulders.   33:13 **above:** *so some MSS; others with*
dew.   33:16 **May this rest:** *prob. rdg, cp. Gen. 49:26;
Heb. has an unintelligible form.*   33:17 **and drive:** *prob.
rdg; Heb.* together.   33:21 **were assembled together:**
so Gk; Heb. obscure.

Num. 26.7 n. That Simeon is not mentioned at all suggests that it had ceased to exist as a tribe and hence the
present passage was composed later than the "Blessing of Jacob" (see Gen. 49.5–7 n.). **8:** *Levi:* see 18.1–8 n.
for references to the development of the tribe and priesthood. *Thummim; Urim:* see Exod. 28.15 n. *Massah;
Meribah:* for the loyalty of the Levites see Exod. 32.25–29. The Massah-Meribah incidents lack specific mention
of the Levites. **12:** *High God:* see Gen. 14.18 n. **16:** *Burning bush:* see Exod. 3.2. **17:** *Ephraim; Manasseh:* see
Gen. 49.22 n. **19:** *Mountain:* possibly Mount Tabor (Judg. 4.12–14; Hos. 5.1). **20:** *Tearing an arm:* see Gen.

He did what the Lord deemed right,
observing his ordinances for Israel.

22 Of Dan he said:

Dan is a lion's cub
springing out from Bashan.

23 Of Naphtali he said:

Naphtali is richly favoured
and full of the blessings of the Lord;
his domain stretches to the sea and
southward.

24 Of Asher he said:

Asher is the most blest of sons;
may he be the favourite among his
brothers
and bathe his feet in oil!
25 May your bolts be of iron and bronze,
and your strength last as long as you
live.

26 There is none like the God of Jeshurun
who rides on the heavens to your aid,
on the clouds in his glory,
27 who humbled the gods of old
and subdued the ancient powers;
who drove out the enemy before you
and gave the command to destroy.
28 Israel lives in security,
and Jacob dwells alone
in a land of grain and wine
where the skies drip with dew.
29 Happy are you, Israel, peerless, set
free!
The Lord is the shield that guards you,
the Blessed One is your glorious sword.
When your enemies come cringing to
you,

you will trample their backs underfoot.

34 Moses went up from the lowlands of Moab to Mount Nebo, to the top of Pisgah eastwards from Jericho, and the Lord showed him the whole land, from Gilead to Dan; 2 the whole of Naphtali; the territory of Ephraim and Manasseh, and all Judah as far as the western sea; 3 the Negeb and the plain; the valley of Jericho, city of palm trees, as far as Zoar. 4 The Lord said to him, 'This is the land which I swore to Abraham, Isaac, and Jacob that I would give to their descendants. I have let you see it with your own eyes, but you will not cross over into it.'

5 There in the Moabite country Moses the servant of the Lord died, as the Lord had said. 6 He was buried in a valley in Moab opposite Beth-peor; but to this day no one knows his burial-place. 7 Moses was a hundred and twenty years old when he died, his sight undimmed, his vigour unimpaired. 8 The Israelites wept for Moses in the lowlands of Moab for thirty days. The time of mourning for Moses came to an end. 9 Joshua son of Nun was filled with the spirit of wisdom, for Moses had laid his hands on him. The Israelites listened to him and did what the Lord had commanded Moses.

10 There has never yet risen in Israel a prophet like Moses, whom the Lord knew face to face: 11 remember all the signs and portents which the Lord sent him to show in Egypt to Pharaoh and all his servants and the whole land; 12 remember the strong hand of Moses and the awesome deeds which he did in the sight of all Israel.

33:24 **among:** *or* of.   33:27 **subdued:** *prob. rdg; Heb.* under.   33:28 **dwells:** *prob. rdg; Heb.* fountain. **wine:** *or* new wine.   33:29 **the Blessed One:** *Heb.* Asher.

49.19 n. **23:** *Sea:* of Galilee.
34.1–12: The death of Moses, which resumes the narrative from 32.52. Verses 1–6 may once have concluded the account of the division of the territory east of the Jordan (Num. ch. 32) and have become separated from it by the later insertion of other traditions. **1:** *Nebo* (32.49); *Pisgah* (3.27): either variant traditions have been combined, or *Pisgah* is the very peak of *Nebo*. **4:** See Gen. 12.7; 28.13. **5:** See 32.50; Josh. 1.1–2. **7:** *A hundred and twenty years:* see 31.2 n. **9:** See 31.7–8, 14–15, 23. **10:** *Face to face:* See Exod. 33.11 and Num. 12.6–8. While on the surface the meaning is that Moses was able to see the invisible Deity, it is likely that this is not the intent; the intent, rather, is to speak of the unique stature of Moses. The thought that a Moses could see the Deity is a relic of early times, before the view matured that the Deity is invisible.

THE BOOK OF
Joshua

This book, the story of the conquest of Canaan, follows on the wanderings in the wilderness. Modern criticism considers Joshua to be part of a unique and extensive history, a writing that carried on the account of the wilderness period in Deuteronomy and that included Joshua, Judges, Samuel, and Kings; the entirety is known as the "Deuteronomic history." Joshua begins with the crossing of the Jordan river and the destruction of Jericho (chs. 1–6). The conquest of the south through battles and alliances is next described (chs. 7–10). A final battle at Hazor in the north completes the conquest (ch. 11). After a short summary of Joshua's triumphs (ch. 12), the account deals with the division of the land among the tribes (chs. 13–22). The final two chapters present Joshua's farewell discourse, the covenant ceremony at Shechem, and the death of Joshua (chs. 23–24). God is pictured as closely involved in the events as a God of Battles, whose power is clearly manifested in the conquest.

Comparison with the Book of Judges indicates that the story of the conquest in Joshua is very much idealized and that the conquest was, in fact, quite complicated and much less decisive and less complete (see 13.1–6 and 17.12–18) than the book repeatedly suggests.

Prelude to the conquest of Canaan

1 AFTER the death of Moses the LORD's servant, the LORD said to Joshua son of Nun, Moses' assistant, 2 'Now that my servant Moses is dead, get ready to cross the Jordan, you and all this people, to the land which I am giving to the Israelites. 3 Every place where you set foot is yours: I have given it to you, as I promised Moses. 4 From the desert and this Lebanon to the great river, the Euphrates, and across all the Hittite country westwards to the Great Sea, all of it is to be your territory. 5 As long as you live no one will be able to stand against you: as I was with Moses, so shall I be with you; I shall not fail you or forsake you. 6 Be strong, be resolute; it is you who are to put this people in possession of the land which I swore to their forefathers I would give them. 7 Only be very strong and resolute. Observe diligently all

the law which my servant Moses has given you; if you would succeed wherever you go, you must not swerve from it either to right or to left. 8 This book of the law must never be off your lips; you must keep it in mind day and night so that you may diligently observe everything that is written in it. Then you will prosper and be successful in everything you do. 9 This is my command: be strong, be resolute; do not be fearful or discouraged, for wherever you go the LORD your God is with you.'

10 Then Joshua instructed the officers 11 to pass through the camp and give this order to the people: 'Get food ready to take with you, for within three days you will be crossing this Jordan to occupy the country which the LORD your God is giving you to possess.'

12 To the Reubenites, the Gadites, and the half tribe of Manasseh, Joshua said, 13 'Re-

1:4 **Great Sea:** *or* Mediterranean Sea.

1.1–12.24: Israel's entry into the promised land.

1.1–9: The command to conquer the land. The invasion of Canaan came *after the death of Moses:* he had been forbidden to lead it (Num. 20.12). *Joshua* was from the tribe of Ephraim (Num. 13.8, 16). **2:** *Jordan:* this river was the eastern boundary of Canaan. **4:** The extent of the promised land (see Gen. 15.18; Deut. 1.7) is here: the *desert* to the south; the *Lebanon* mountains to the northwest; *the river Euphrates* to the east; *the Hittite country,* northern Syria, at one time part of the Hittite empire; *westwards to the Great Sea,* the Mediterranean. This extent exceeds considerably the boundaries indicated by chs. 13–19 and Judg. 20.1. **7–8:** *This book of the law* refers to the Book of Deut., which teaches that fidelity to the law brings prosperity (see Deut. ch. 6).

1.10–18: Preparations for the invasion. 12: *The Reubenites, the Gadites, and the half tribe of Manasseh* member what Moses the servant of the LORD commanded when he said, "The LORD your God will grant you security here and will give you this territory." 14 Your wives and dependants and your livestock may stay east of the Jordan in the territory which Moses has assigned you; but as for yourselves, all the warriors among you must cross over as a fighting force at the head of your kinsmen. You are to assist them, 15 until the LORD grants them security like you have, and they too take possession of the land which the LORD your God is giving them. You may then return and occupy the land which is your possession, the territory which Moses the servant of the LORD has assigned you east of the Jordan.' 16 They answered Joshua, 'Whatever you tell us, we shall do; wherever you send us, we shall go. 17 As we obeyed Moses in all things, so shall we obey you; and may the LORD your God be with you as he was with Moses! 18 Anyone who rebels against your command, and fails to carry out all your orders, is to be put to death. Only be strong and resolute.'

In central Canaan

2 JOSHUA son of Nun sent out two spies secretly from Shittim with orders to reconnoitre the land and especially Jericho. The two men set off and came to the house of a prostitute named Rahab to spend the night there. 2 When it was reported to the king of Jericho that some Israelites had arrived that night to explore the country, 3 he sent word to Rahab: 'Bring out the men who have come to you and are now in your house, for they have come to spy out the whole country.' 4 The woman, who had taken the two men and hidden them, replied, 'True, the men did come to me, but I did not know where they came from; 5 and at nightfall when it was time to shut the gate, they had gone. I do not know where they were going,

but if you hurry after them you may overtake them.' 6 In fact, she had brought them up on to the roof and concealed them among the stalks of flax which she had laid out there in rows. 7 The messengers went in pursuit of them in the direction of the fords of the Jordan, and as soon as they had gone out the gate was closed.

8 The men had not yet settled down, when Rahab came up to them on the roof, 9 and said, 'I know that the LORD has given the land to you; terror of you has fallen upon us, and the whole country is panic-stricken. 10 We have heard how the LORD dried up the waters of the Red Sea before you when you came out of Egypt, and what you did to Sihon and Og, the two Amorite kings beyond the Jordan, for you destroyed them. 11 When we heard this, our courage failed; your coming has left no spirit in any of us; for the LORD your God is God in heaven above and on earth below. 12 Swear to me by the LORD that you will keep faith with my family, as I have kept faith with you. Give me a token of good faith; 13 promise that you will spare the lives of my father and mother, my brothers and sisters, and all who belong to them, and preserve us from death.' 14 The men replied, 'Our lives for yours, so long as you do not betray our business. When the LORD gives us the country, we shall deal loyally and faithfully by you.'

15 She then let them down through a window by a rope; for the house where she lived was on an angle of the wall. 16 'Make for the hills,' she said, 'or the pursuers will come upon you. Hide there for three days until they return; then go on your way.' 17 The men warned her that, unless she did what they told her, they would be free from the oath she had made them take. 18 'When we invade the land,' they said, 'you must fasten

2:4 **them:** *prob. rdg; Heb.* him.   2:10 **Red Sea:** *or* sea of Reeds.

were Transjordanian tribes (see Num. ch. 32 and 32.1–42 n.), who would return home after the conquest (v. 15). The conquest, according to the Book of Joshua, is the work of the entire people; in Judg. it is the work of isolated tribes.

2.1–24: The spies at Jericho and Rahab. Since Rahab was a prostitute, visitors to her could fail to arouse attention. **1:** *Shittim:* the Israelite camp, in the lowlands of Moab just east of the Jordan (Num. 33.49). *Jericho* was the main city in the lower Jordan valley and guarded the westward way to the central highlands. Archaeologists have not yet succeeded in finding any definite remains of the Jericho of Joshua's time. **10:** *Sihon and Og:* see Num. 21.21–35. **11:** Rahab's profession of faith has a Deuteronomic ring to it; see Deut. 4.39. Hebrews 11.31 emphasizes Rahab's faith; Jas. 2.25, her works. **17–21:** These verses are considered by some to be a fragment from a separate tradition. **18:** The *scarlet cord* is not mentioned after v. 21.

this strand of scarlet cord in the window through which you have lowered us, and get everybody together here inside the house, your father and mother, your brothers, and all your family. 19 Should anybody go out of doors into the street, his blood will be on his own head; we shall be free of the oath. But if a hand is laid on anyone who stays indoors with you, his blood be on our heads! 20 Remember too that, if you betray our business, then we shall be free of the oath you have made us take.' 21 'It shall be as you say,' she replied, and sent them on their way. When they had gone, she fastened the strand of scarlet cord in the window.

22 The men made their way into the hills and stayed there for three days until the pursuers returned. They had searched all along the road, but had not found them. 23 The two men then came down from the hills and crossed the river. When they joined up with Joshua son of Nun, they reported all that had happened to them. 24 'The LORD has delivered the whole country into our hands,' they said; 'the inhabitants are all panic-stricken at our approach.'

3 Early in the morning Joshua and all the Israelites set out from Shittim and came to the Jordan, where they encamped before crossing. 2 At the end of three days the officers passed through the camp, 3 giving the people these instructions: 'When you see the Ark of the Covenant of the LORD your God being carried forward by the levitical priests, then you too must leave your positions and set out. Follow it, 4 but do not go close to it; keep some distance behind, about two thousand cubits. It will show you the route you are to follow, for you have not travelled this way before.' 5 Joshua said to the people, 'Consecrate yourselves, for tomorrow the LORD will perform a great miracle among you.' 6 To the priests he said, 'Lift the Ark of the Covenant

and move ahead of the people.' So they lifted it up and went at the head of the people.

7 The LORD said to Joshua, 'Today I shall begin to exalt you in the eyes of all Israel, and they will know that I shall be with you as I was with Moses. 8 Give this order to the priests who carry the Ark of the Covenant: When you come to the edge of the waters of the Jordan, you are to take your stand in the river.'

9 Joshua said to the Israelites, 'Draw near and listen to the words of the LORD your God.' 10 He went on, 'By this you will know that the living God is among you and that he will without fail drive out before you the Canaanites, Hittites, Hivites, Perizzites, Girgashites, Amorites, and Jebusites: 11 the Ark of the Covenant of the Lord of all the earth is to cross the Jordan at your head. 12 Choose now twelve men from the tribes of Israel, one from each tribe. 13 As soon as the priests carrying the Ark of the LORD, the Lord of all the earth, set foot in the waters of the Jordan, then the waters of the Jordan will be cut off; the water coming down from upstream will stand piled up like a bank.'

14 The people set out from their encampment to cross the Jordan, with the priests in front carrying the Ark of the Covenant. 15 Now the Jordan is in full flood in all its reaches throughout the time of harvest, but as soon as the priests reached the Jordan and their feet touched the water at the edge, 16 the water flowing down from upstream was brought to a standstill; it piled up like a bank for a long way back, as far as Adam, a town near Zarethan. The water coming down to the sea of the Arabah, the Dead Sea, was completely cut off, and the people crossed

2:22 **three days ... found them:** or three days while the pursuers scoured the land and searched all along the road, but did not find them.   3:16 **Dead Sea:** lit. Salt Sea.

3.1–17: The crossing of the Jordan. In 3.1–5.12 there is a deliberate general parallelism with the account of the crossing of the Red Sea in Exod. 3: *The Ark of the Covenant* was a sign of the presence of God (Exod. 25.8, 10 nn.); it was carried into battle as a war palladium, a "safeguard" (see Num. 10.35–36; 1 Sam. 4.3–22). *Levitical priests:* see Num. 3.6–10. 4: *Keep some distance behind:* to show reverence to the Ark and to the presence of God; see 2 Sam. 6.6–7. 5: *Consecrate yourselves:* refers to a ritual purification before a religious ceremony; see Exod. 19.10, 15. 10: On these peoples, see Deut. 7.1; Gen. 10.15–20. 13: *Piled up like a bank* recalls Exod. 14.22; see 4.23. Some scholars regard this incident as a ceremony commemorating the crossing of the Red Sea. 15: *Throughout the time of harvest:* in the spring, the melting snow of Mount Hermon brings the Jordan to full flood. 16: *Adam* is about eighteen miles north of Jericho; *Zarethan* is about twelve miles farther north. *Arabah:* the extensive geological depression in which the Jordan and the Dead Sea, and areas further south, were situated. It is often rendered "desert."

over opposite Jericho. [17] The priests carrying the Ark of the Covenant of the LORD stood firmly on the dry bed in the middle of the river, and all Israel passed over on dry ground, until the whole nation had completed the crossing of the Jordan.

4 WHEN the whole nation had completed the crossing of the Jordan, the LORD said to Joshua, [2] 'Choose twelve men from the people, one from each tribe, [3] and order them to take up twelve stones from this place in the middle of the Jordan, where the priests have taken their stand. They are to carry the stones across and place them in the camp where you spend the night.' [4] Joshua summoned the twelve Israelites whom he had appointed, one man from each tribe, [5] and said to them, 'Go over in front of the Ark of the LORD your God as far as the middle of the Jordan, and let each of you take up a stone on his shoulder, one for each of the tribes of Israel. [6] These stones are to stand as a memorial among you: in days to come, when your children ask what these stones mean, [7] you will tell them how the waters of the Jordan were cut off before the Ark of the Covenant of the LORD; when it crossed the Jordan the waters of the Jordan were cut off. These stones will always be a reminder to the Israelites.' [8] The Israelites did as Joshua had commanded: they took up twelve stones from the middle of the Jordan, as the LORD had instructed Joshua, one for each of the tribes of Israel, carried them across to the camp, and placed them there. [9] Joshua also erected twelve stones in the middle of the Jordan at the place where the priests who carried the Ark of the Covenant had stood; they are there to this day. [10] The priests carrying the Ark remained standing in the middle of the Jordan until every command which the LORD had told Joshua to give the people was fulfilled. The people crossed hurriedly, [11] and when they had all got across, then the Ark of the LORD crossed, and the priests with it to lead the people. [12] At the head of the Israelites, there crossed over the Reubenites, the Gadites, and the half tribe of Manasseh, as a fighting force, as Moses had told them to do; [13] about forty thousand strong, drafted for active service, they crossed over to the lowlands of Jericho in the presence of the LORD to do battle.

[14] That day the LORD exalted Joshua in the eyes of all Israel, and the people revered him, as they had revered Moses all his life.

[15] The LORD said to Joshua, [16] 'Command the priests carrying the Ark of the Testimony to come up from the Jordan.' [17] Joshua passed the command to the priests; [18] and no sooner had the priests carrying the Ark of the Covenant of the LORD come up from the river bed, and set foot on dry land, than the waters of the Jordan returned to their course and filled up all its reaches as before.

[19] On the tenth day of the first month the people went up from the Jordan and encamped in Gilgal in the district east of Jericho, [20] and there Joshua set up these twelve stones they had taken from the Jordan. [21] He said to the Israelites, 'In days to come, when your descendants ask their fathers what these stones mean, [22] you are to explain to them that Israel crossed this Jordan on dry land, [23] for the LORD your God dried up the waters of the Jordan in front of you until you had gone across, just as the LORD your God did at the Red Sea when he dried it up for us until we had crossed. [24] Thus all people on earth will know how strong is the hand of the LORD; and thus you will always stand in awe of the LORD your God.'

5 When all the Amorite kings to the west of the Jordan and all the Canaanite kings by the sea-coast heard how the LORD had dried up the waters of the Jordan before the advance of the Israelites until they had crossed, their courage failed them; there was no more spirit left in them because of the Israelites.

[2] At that time the LORD said to Joshua,

4:10 **fulfilled:** *so Gk; Heb. adds* according to all that Moses commanded Joshua.

4.1–5.1: Twelve memorial stones. There are traces of two traditions: one speaks of twelve stones to be set up at Gilgal (4.1–8), the other of twelve stones set up in the Jordan (9–13). **12:** The Transjordanian tribes crossed first. **19:** *The first month* was Abib (March–April), later called Nisan (Exod. 12.2 n.). *Gilgal* was somewhere near Jericho; later it became an important sanctuary in the tribe of Benjamin (see 1 Sam. 11.15; 2 Sam. 19.15, 40). Amos (4.4; 5.5) and Hosea (4.15; 9.15; 12.11) spoke against the worship there.

5.2–9: Circumcision of Israelites at Gilgal. Circumcision was primitively a rite of initiation for marriage and for admission into full membership in the community; in the later traditions of Israel it became a sign of God's

'Fashion knives out of flint, and make Israel a circumcised people again.' ³So Joshua made knives of flint, and the Israelites were circumcised at Gibeath-haaraloth. ⁴This is why he had them circumcised: all the males who came out of Egypt, all the fighting men, had died in the wilderness on the journey from Egypt. ⁵The people who came out of Egypt had all been circumcised, but not those who had been born in the wilderness during the journey. ⁶The Israelites had travelled in the wilderness for forty years, until the whole generation, all the fighting men in the nation, died, all who came out of Egypt and had disobeyed the LORD. The LORD swore that he would not allow any of these to see the land which he had sworn to their fathers to give us, a land flowing with milk and honey. ⁷So it was their sons, whom the LORD had raised up in their place, that Joshua circumcised; they were uncircumcised because they had not been circumcised on the journey. ⁸When the circumcision of the whole nation was complete, they stayed where they were in camp until they had recovered. ⁹The LORD then said to Joshua, 'Today I have rolled away from you the reproaches of the Egyptians.' Therefore the place is called Gilgal to this day.

¹⁰While the Israelites were encamped in Gilgal, at sunset on the fourteenth day of the month they kept the Passover in the lowlands of Jericho. ¹¹On the day after the Passover they ate of the produce of the country, roasted grain and loaves made without leaven. ¹²It was from that day, when they first ate the produce of the country, that the manna ceased. The Israelites got no more manna; that year they ate what had grown in the land of Canaan.

¹³When Joshua was near Jericho he looked up and saw a man standing in front of him with a drawn sword in his hand. Joshua approached him and asked, 'Are you for us or for our enemies?' ¹⁴The man replied, 'Neither! I am here as captain of the army of the LORD.' Joshua prostrated himself in homage, and said, 'What have you to say to your servant, my lord?' ¹⁵The captain of the LORD's army answered, 'Remove your sandals, for the place where you are standing is holy'; and Joshua did so.

6 JERICHO was bolted and barred against the Israelites; no one could go out or in. ²The LORD said to Joshua, 'See, I am delivering Jericho, its king, and his warriors into your hands. ³You are to march round the city with all your fighting men, making the circuit of it once a day for six days. ⁴Seven priests carrying seven trumpets made from rams' horns are to go ahead of the Ark. On the seventh day you are to march round the city seven times with the priests blowing their trumpets. ⁵At the blast of the rams' horns, when you hear the trumpet sound, the whole army must raise a great shout; the city wall will collapse and the army will advance, every man straight ahead.'

⁶Joshua son of Nun summoned the priests and gave them instructions: 'Take up the Ark of the Covenant; let seven priests with seven trumpets of ram's horn go ahead of the Ark of the LORD.' ⁷Then he gave orders to the army: 'Move on, march round the city,

5:3 **Gibeath-haaraloth:** *that is* the Hill of Foreskins.
5:9 **Gilgal:** *that is* Rolling Stones.   5:14 **The man . . .**
I: *so some MSS; others* The man said, 'No, I.

covenant relationship with the people (Gen. 17.9–14 n.); it took on its full importance with the Babylonian Exile. **2:** *Knives of flint:* used because religious ceremonies tend to preserve ancient ways of doing things; the Israelites were already familiar with the use of metal. *A circumcised people again:* see vv. 4–7. **3:** *Gibeath-haaraloth* means "the hill of the foreskins." **6:** *Until the whole nation, all the fighting men, had passed away:* see Num. 14.20–38. **9:** *Reproaches:* the allusion is unclear; possibly the reproaches were for being uncircumcised. The Heb. contains a pun, *Gilgal* and *rolled away*. The meaning of Gilgal is "circle" (of stones), a circle recalling a wheel which can roll.

5.10–12: Passover at Gilgal. 10: The first Passover in Canaan. **12:** On *manna* see Exod. ch. 16 and notes.

5.13–15: A theophany. Joshua meets *the captain of the army of the* LORD (compare Num. 22.22; 2 Kgs. 6.17). The story is fragmentary, for a sequel seems expected, but is not given (compare Exod. 3.5–12).

6.1–27: The capture of Jericho. The divine mandate was for the Israelites to march around the city once a day for six days, carrying the Ark and blowing trumpets. On the seventh day the procession moved around the city seven times; then, the shout of the Israelites was enough to overthrow the walls; on Jericho see 2.1 n. **4:** *Seven,* often a sacred number, occurs repeatedly in this chapter. **5:** The *shout* is part of the ritual of the Ark and let the men who have been drafted go in front of the Ark of the LORD.'

8 After Joshua had issued this command to the army, the seven priests carrying the seven trumpets of ram's horn before the LORD moved on and blew the trumpets; the Ark of the Covenant of the LORD followed them. 9 The drafted men marched in front of the priests who blew the trumpets, and the rearguard came behind the Ark, the trumpets sounding as they marched. 10 But Joshua commanded the army not to shout, or to raise their voices or even utter a word, till the day when he would tell them to shout; then they were to give a mighty shout. 11 Thus he made the Ark of the LORD go round the city, making the circuit of it once, and then they returned to the camp and spent the night there. 12 Joshua rose early next morning, and the priests took up the Ark of the LORD. 13 The seven priests carrying the seven trumpets of ram's horn marched in front of the Ark of the LORD, blowing the trumpets as they went, with the drafted men in front of them and the rearguard following the Ark, the trumpets sounding as they marched. 14 They marched round the city once on the second day and returned to the camp; this they did for six days.

15 On the seventh day they rose at dawn and marched seven times round the city in the same way; that was the only day on which they marched round seven times. 16 The seventh time, as the priests blew the trumpets, Joshua said to the army, 'Shout! The LORD has given you the city. 17 The city is to be under solemn ban: everything in it belongs to the LORD. No one is to be spared except the prostitute Rahab and everyone who is with her in the house, because she hid the men we sent. 18 And you must beware of coveting anything that is forbidden under the ban; you must take none of it for yourselves, or else you will put the Israelite camp itself under the ban and bring disaster on it. 19 All silver and gold, all the vessels of copper and iron, are to be holy; they belong to the LORD and must go into his treasury.'

20 So the trumpets were blown, and when the army heard the trumpets sound, they raised a great shout, and the wall collapsed. The army advanced on the city, every man straight ahead, and they captured it. 21 Under the ban they destroyed everything there; they put everyone to the sword, men and women, young and old, as well as the cattle, the sheep, and the donkeys.

22 The two men who had been sent out to reconnoitre the land were told by Joshua to go to the prostitute's house and bring out the woman and all who belonged to her, as they had sworn to do. 23 The young men went and brought out Rahab, her father and mother, her brothers, and all who belonged to her; they brought the whole family and placed them outside the Israelite camp. 24 The city and everything in it were then set on fire, except that the silver and gold and the vessels of copper and iron were deposited in the treasury of the LORD's house. 25 Thus Joshua spared the lives of Rahab the prostitute, her household, and all who belonged to her, because she had hidden the men whom Joshua had sent to reconnoitre Jericho; she and her family settled permanently among the Israelites.

26 At that time Joshua pronounced this curse:

'May the LORD's curse light on anyone
  who comes forward to rebuild this
  city of Jericho:
  the laying of its foundations shall cost
    him his eldest son,
  the setting up of its gates shall cost him
    his youngest.'

27 THE LORD was with Joshua, and his fame spread throughout the country.

7 In a perfidious act, however, Israelites violated the ban: Achan son of Carmi, son of Zabdi, son of Zerah, of the tribe of Judah, took some of the forbidden things,

6:18 **coveting:** *so Gk; Heb.* putting under the ban.
6:20 **So:** *so Gk; Heb. adds* the people shouted and.

(see 1 Sam. 4.5; 2 Sam. 6.15). **17:** *Solemn ban* is a technical term meaning that the city and all that is in it is to be offered as a holocaust to God (see v. 21); no booty is allowed to be taken (but see 8.2) and any deviation would be a sacrilege to be severely punished (see v. 18; 7.1; 1 Sam. 15.14–23); the only exception is mentioned in vv. 19 and 24. **24:** *The LORD's house* is an anachronism, since the temple did not yet exist. **26:** The fulfillment of this curse is narrated in 1 Kgs. 16.34.

7.1–26: The setback at Ai. 1: This verse foreshadows the narrative in vv. 6–21.

and the LORD's anger blazed out against Israel.

2 Joshua sent men from Jericho with orders to go up to Ai, near Beth-aven, east of Bethel, and reconnoitre the land. The men went and explored Ai, 3 and on their return reported to Joshua that there was no need for the whole army to move: 'Let some two or three thousand men advance to attack Ai. Do not have the whole army toil up there; the population is small.' 4 About three thousand troops went up, but they were routed by the men of Ai, 5 who killed some thirty-six of them; they chased the rest all the way from the gate to the Quarries and killed them on the pass. At this the courage of the people melted and flowed away like water.

6 Joshua and the elders of Israel tore their clothes and flung themselves face downwards to the ground; throwing dust on their heads, they lay in front of the Ark of the LORD till evening. 7 Joshua cried, 'Alas, Lord GOD, why did you bring this people across the Jordan just to hand us over to the Amorites to be destroyed? If only we had been content to settle on the other side of the Jordan! 8 I beseech you, Lord; what can I say, now that Israel has been routed by the enemy? 9 When the Canaanites and all the other natives of the country hear of this, they will close in upon us and wipe us off the face of the earth. What will you do then for the honour of your great name?'

10 The LORD answered, 'Stand up; why lie prostrate on your face? 11 Israel has sinned: they have violated the covenant which I laid upon them; they have taken things forbidden under the ban; they have stolen them; they have concealed them by putting them among their own possessions. 12 That is why the Israelites cannot stand against their enemies: they are defeated because they have brought themselves under the ban. Unless you Israelites destroy every single thing among you that is forbidden under the ban, I shall be with you no longer.

13 'Get up and consecrate the people; tell them they must consecrate themselves for tomorrow. Say to them that these are the words of the LORD the God of Israel: You have among you forbidden things, Israel, and you will not be able to stand against your enemies until you have rid yourselves of these things. 14 In the morning come forward tribe by tribe, and the tribe which the LORD takes must come forward clan by clan; the clan which the LORD takes must come forward family by family, and the family which the LORD takes must come forward man by man. 15 The man who is taken as the harbourer of forbidden things must be burnt, he and all that is his, because he has violated the covenant of the LORD and committed an outrage in Israel.'

16 Early next morning Joshua rose and had Israel come forward tribe by tribe, and the tribe of Judah was taken; 17 he brought forward the clans of Judah, and the clan of Zerah was taken; then the clan of Zerah family by family, and the family of Zabdi was taken. 18 He had that family brought forward man by man, and Achan son of Carmi, son of Zabdi, son of Zerah, of the tribe of Judah, was taken.

19 Then Joshua said to Achan, 'My son, give honour to the LORD the God of Israel and make your confession to him. Tell me what you have done; hide nothing from me.' 20 Achan answered, 'It is true; I have sinned against the LORD the God of Israel. This is what I did: 21 among the booty I saw a fine mantle from Shinar, two hundred shekels of silver, and a bar of gold weighing fifty shekels; I coveted them and I took them. You will find them hidden in the ground inside my tent, with the silver underneath.' 22 Joshua sent messengers, who went straight to the tent, and there it was hidden in the tent with the silver underneath. 23 They took the things from the tent, brought them to Joshua and all the Israelites, and laid them out before the LORD.

24 Then Joshua and all Israel with him took Achan son of Zerah, with the silver, the man-

7:5 **the Quarries:** *or* Shebarim.   7:17 **family by family:** *so some MSS; others* man by man. **the family of:** *so Gk; Heb. omits.*

7.2: *Ai* was in the central highlands northwest of Jericho. Archaeology indicates that it was in ruins (for Ai means "ruin") in Joshua's time, yet these ruins could have served as an outpost for Bethel (MT adds Bethel in 8.17). Many scholars think that there was behind this story a battle for the important site, *Bethel,* and not for Ai; the Book of Joshua, otherwise, has no account of the capture of Bethel (but see Judg. 1.22–26). *Beth-aven* means "house of wickedness," referring to Bethel in Hos. 4.15 (see Amos 5.5); some regard *near Beth-aven* as a gloss. **11:** That *Israel has sinned* because one person (see v. 1) has trespassed reflects the ancient unitary view tle, and the bar of gold, together with his sons and daughters, his oxen, his donkeys, and his sheep, his tent, and everything he had, and they brought them up to the vale of Achor. 25 Joshua said, 'What trouble you have brought on us! Now the LORD will bring trouble on you.' Then all the Israelites stoned him to death; 26 and they raised over him a great cairn of stones which is there to this day. So the LORD's anger was abated. That is why to this day the place is called the vale of Achor.

8 THE LORD said to Joshua, 'Do not be afraid or discouraged; take the whole army with you and go and attack Ai. I am delivering the king of Ai into your hands, along with his people, his city, and his territory. 2 Deal with Ai and its king as you dealt with Jericho and its king, except that you may keep for yourselves the cattle and any other spoil you take. Set an ambush for the city to the west of it.'

3 Joshua and the army prepared for the assault on Ai. He chose thirty thousand warriors and dispatched them by night, 4 with these orders: 'Lie in ambush to the west of the city, not far distant from it, and hold yourselves in readiness, all of you. 5 I myself will advance on the city with the rest of the army, and when the enemy come out to meet us as they did last time, we shall turn and flee before them. 6 They will come in pursuit until we have drawn them away from the city, for they will think we are in flight as before. While we are retreating, 7 rise from your ambush and occupy the city; the LORD your God will deliver it into your hands. 8 When you have taken it, set it on fire. Thus you will do what the LORD commands; these are my orders to you.' 9 After Joshua sent them off, they went to the place of ambush and lay in wait between Bethel and Ai to the west of Ai, while Joshua spent the night with the army. 10 Early in the morning Joshua mustered

the army and, with Joshua himself and the elders of Israel at its head, they marched against Ai. 11 All the armed forces with him marched on until they came within sight of the city, where they encamped north of Ai, with the valley between them and the city. 12 Joshua took some five thousand men and set them in ambush between Bethel and Ai to the west of the city. 14 When the king of Ai saw them, he and the citizens set off hurriedly and marched out to do battle against Israel, being unaware that an ambush had been prepared for him to the west of the city. 15 Joshua and the Israelites made as if they were worsted by them and fled towards the wilderness, 16 while all the people of the city were called out in pursuit. In pursuing Joshua they were drawn away from the city, 17 until not a man was left in Ai; they had all gone out in pursuit of the Israelites and thus had left the place wide open.

18 The LORD then said to Joshua, 'Point towards Ai with the dagger you are holding, for I will deliver the city into your hands.' Joshua pointed with his dagger towards Ai 19 and, at his signal, the men in ambush rose quickly from their position; dashing into the city, they captured it and at once set it on fire. 20 The men of Ai looked back and saw the smoke from the city already going up to the sky; they were powerless to make their escape in any direction.

The Israelites who had feigned flight towards the wilderness now turned on their pursuers, 21 for when Joshua and all the Israelites with him saw that the men in ambush had seized the city and that smoke from it was

7:24 **Achor:** *that is* Trouble.   7:25 **to death:** *so Gk; Heb. adds* and they burnt them with fire and pelted them with stones.   8:12 **the city:** *so Gk; Heb. adds* 13 So the army pitched camp to the north of the city, and the rearguard to the west, while Joshua went that night into the valley.   8:14 **Israel:** *so Gk; Heb. adds* for the appointed time, before the Arabah. 8:17 **Ai:** *so Gk; Heb. adds* or Bethel.

of society. **14:** *The LORD takes:* probably by the casting of lots; on sacred lots see Exod. 28.15 n.; 1 Sam. 14.40–42. **24–25:** The unitary concept of society required that Achan and all he had be purged from Israel (see Num. 16.16–35). *Achor:* a pun, for it is from the same root as the Heb. word for *trouble* (see Hos. 2.15). **26:** *A great cairn of stones* marked the burial places of criminals (see 8.29; 10.27; 2 Sam. 18.17). *To this day:* a fixed formula in stories told to explain curious surviving facts, names, and institutions (see 4.9; 8.28–29; 9.27; 10.27).

8.1–29: Victory at Ai. Israel, now free from Achan's guilt, easily captures and destroys Ai by a clever stratagem. **9:** *Bethel,* later one of the chief shrines of the Northern Kingdom (1 Kgs. 12.28–30; see also Gen. 28.10–22), is about one and one-quarter miles northwest of Ai; see 7.2 n. **12:** *Five thousand:* thirty thousand is the figure in v. 3. **13:** See Tfn. **15:** *Towards the wilderness:* eastward. **18:** *Point towards Ai with the dagger:* this is obviously not an ordinary signal (see v. 26) but a symbolic gesture (see Exod. 17.8–13; 2 Kgs. 13.14–19).

already going up, they faced about and attacked the men of Ai. ²² Those who had come out to contend with the Israelites were now hemmed in by Israelites on both sides of them, and the Israelites cut them down until there was not a single survivor; no one escaped. ²³ Only the king of Ai was taken alive and brought to Joshua.

²⁴ When the Israelites had slain all the inhabitants of Ai in the open country and the wilderness where they had pursued them, and the massacre was complete, they all went back to Ai and put it to the sword. ²⁵ The number who fell that day, men and women, was twelve thousand, the whole population of Ai. ²⁶ Joshua held out his dagger and did not draw back his hand until all who lived in Ai had been destroyed; ²⁷ but the Israelites kept for themselves the cattle and any other spoil that they took, following the LORD's instructions given to Joshua.

²⁸ So Joshua burnt Ai to the ground, and left it the desolate ruined mound it remains to this day. ²⁹ He hanged the king of Ai on a gibbet and left him there till evening. At sunset they cut down the body on Joshua's orders and flung it on the ground at the entrance of the city gate. Over it they raised a great cairn of stones, which is there to this day.

³⁰ At that time Joshua built an altar to the LORD the God of Israel on Mount Ebal. ³¹ The altar was of blocks of undressed stone on which no iron tool had been used; this followed the commands given to the Israelites by Moses the servant of the LORD, as is described in the book of the law of Moses. On the altar they offered whole-offerings to the LORD, and slaughtered shared-offerings. ³² There in the presence of the Israelites Joshua engraved on blocks of stone a copy of the law of Moses. ³³ All Israel, native-born and resident alien alike, with the elders, officers, and judges, took their stand on either side of the Ark, facing the levitical priests who carried the Ark of the Covenant of the LORD. Half of them stood facing Mount Gerizim and half facing Mount Ebal, to fulfil the command of Moses the servant of the LORD that the blessing should be pronounced first. ³⁴ Then Joshua recited the whole of the blessing and the cursing word by word, as they are written in the book of the law; ³⁵ there was not a single word of all that Moses had commanded which Joshua did not read aloud in the presence of the whole congregation of Israel, including the women and dependants and the aliens resident among them.

⁹ News of these happenings reached all the kings west of the Jordan, in the hill-country, in the Shephelah, and in all the coast of the Great Sea running up to the Lebanon, and the kings of the Hittites, Amorites, Canaanites, Perizzites, Hivites, and Jebusites ² agreed to join forces and fight against Joshua and Israel.

³ When the inhabitants of Gibeon heard how Joshua had dealt with Jericho and Ai, ⁴ they resorted to a ruse: they set out after disguising themselves, with old sacks on their donkeys, old wineskins split and mended, ⁵ old and patched sandals for their feet, old clothing to wear, and by way of provisions nothing but dry and crumbling bread. ⁶ They came to Joshua in the camp at Gilgal, where they said to him and the Israelites, 'We have come from a distant country to ask you now to grant us a treaty.' ⁷ The Israelites said to these Hivites, 'But it may be that you live in our neighbourhood: if so, how can we grant you a treaty?' ⁸ They said to Joshua, 'We are your slaves.'

Joshua asked them who they were and where they came from. ⁹ 'Sir,' they replied, 'our country is very far away, and we have come because of the renown of the LORD

8:32 **on blocks:** or on the blocks. **Moses:** so Gk; Heb. adds which he had engraved.

8.30–35: Mount Ebal: the building of an altar and reading of the Law. These verses interrupt the story of the conquest and probably are not in their original position here (see ch. 24 for events in the same area). Joshua here carries out the prescriptions of Deut. 27.4–13 (see also Deut. 11.29–30). The events take place just west of Shechem, about twenty miles north of Ai, with Mount Ebal to the north and Mount Gerizim (v. 33) to the south.

9.1–27: The stratagem of the Gibeonites. 1: The victories at Jericho and Ai lead to a coalition against Israel. **3–15:** The inhabitants of Gibeon gained a treaty by pretending to be from a distant country; in Deut. 20.10–18, Israel was permitted to make peace only with those who lived at a great distance; those near at hand were to be annihilated. Gibeon is modern El-Jib, about seven miles southwest of Ai; but the Gibeonites also dwelt in three neighboring cities (v. 17). **7:** The Gibeonites are called Hivites (see 11.19); they were possibly an your God. We have heard the report of all that he did to Egypt [10] and to the two Amorite kings east of the Jordan, King Sihon of Heshbon and King Og of Bashan who lived at Ashtaroth. [11] Our elders and all the people of our country told us to take provisions for the journey and come to meet you, and say, "We are your slaves; please grant us a treaty." [12] Look at our bread; it was hot from the oven when we packed it at home on the day we came away. Now, as you see, it is dry and crumbling. [13] Here are our wineskins; they were new when we filled them, and now they are all split; look at our clothes and our sandals, worn out by the very long journey.' [14] Without seeking guidance from the LORD, the leaders of the community accepted some of their provisions. [15] Joshua received them peaceably and granted them a treaty, promising to spare their lives, and the leaders ratified it on oath.

[16] However, within three days of granting them the treaty the Israelites learnt that these people were in fact neighbours, living nearby. [17] The Israelites then set out and on the third day they reached their towns, Gibeon, Kephirah, Beeroth, and Kiriath-jearim. [18] The Israelites did not attack them, because of the oath which the chief men of the community had sworn to them by the LORD the God of Israel. When the whole community was indignant with the leaders, [19] they all made this reply: 'We swore an oath to them by the LORD the God of Israel; so now we cannot touch them. [20] What we shall do is this: we shall spare their lives so that the oath which we swore to them may bring down no wrath on us. [21] But though their lives must be spared, they will be set to cut wood and draw water for the community.' The people agreed to do as their chiefs had said.

[22] Joshua summoned the Gibeonites and said to them, 'Why did you play this trick on us? You told us that you live a long way off, when in fact you are near neighbours. [23] From now there is a curse on you: for all time you shall provide us with slaves, to cut

wood and draw water for the house of my God.' [24] They answered Joshua, 'We were told, sir, that the LORD your God had commanded his servant Moses to give you the whole country and to wipe out its inhabitants; so because of you we were in terror of our lives, and that is why we did this. [25] We are in your hands: do with us whatever you think right and proper.' [26] What he did was this: he saved them from death at the hands of the Israelites, and they did not kill them; [27] but from that day he assigned them to cut wood and draw water for the community and for the altar of the LORD. And to this day they do so at the place which the LORD chose.

The conquest of the south

10 WHEN King Adoni-zedek of Jerusalem heard that Joshua had captured and destroyed Ai, dealing with Ai and its king as he had dealt with Jericho and its king, and also that the inhabitants of Gibeon had come to terms with Israel and were living among them, [2] he was greatly alarmed; for Gibeon was a large place, like a royal city: it was larger than Ai, and its men were all good fighters. [3] So King Adoni-zedek of Jerusalem sent this message to King Hoham of Hebron, King Piram of Jarmuth, King Japhia of Lachish, and King Debir of Eglon: [4] 'Come up and assist me to attack Gibeon, because it has come to terms with Joshua and the Israelites.'

[5] The five Amorite kings, the kings of Jerusalem, Hebron, Jarmuth, Lachish, and Eglon, advanced with their united forces to take up position for the attack on Gibeon. [6] The Gibeonites sent word to Joshua in the camp at Gilgal: 'Do not abandon your slaves; come quickly to our relief. Come and help us, for all the Amorite kings in the hill-country have

9:14 **the leaders:** *so Gk; Heb.* the men.   9:21 **But though:** *so Gk; Heb.* prefixes And the chiefs said to them. **will be:** *so Gk; Heb.* were. **The people ... do:** *so some Gk MSS; Heb.* omits.   10:2 **he was:** *so Syriac; Heb.* they were.

isolated non-Canaanite group. Their towns are listed in v. 17. **10:** *Sihon and Og:* Num. 21.21–35. **14:** Sharing in the *provisions* would constitute a treaty. **20:** An *oath* once made, even in error, could not be broken. **21:** The Gibeonites were to perform menial services at the temple (see 1 Kgs. 9.20–21; Ezek. 44.7 n.). **27:** *The place ... chose:* a conventional allusion to Jerusalem in Deut. (e.g. 12.5) and related books.

10.1–27: Israel's victory over the five kings. Joshua comes to the rescue of the Gibeonites when they are attacked by a coalition of five Amorite cities; the Israelite capture of Jericho and Ai impelled that coalition. **3:** *Hebron:* twenty miles south of Jerusalem. The other three places are about fifteen to thirty-five miles joined forces against us.' 7 When Joshua went up from Gilgal followed by his whole force, all his warriors, 8 the LORD said to him, 'Do not be afraid; I have delivered these kings into your hands, and not one of them will be able to withstand you.' 9 After a night march from Gilgal, Joshua launched a surprise assault on the five kings, 10 and the LORD threw them into confusion before the Israelites. Joshua utterly defeated them at Gibeon; he pursued them down the pass of Beth-horon and kept up the attack as far as Azekah and Makkedah. 11 As they fled from Israel down the pass, the LORD hurled great hailstones at them out of the sky all the way to Azekah, and they perished: more died from the hailstones than were slain by the swords of the Israelites.

12 On that day when the LORD delivered up the Amorites into the hands of Israel, Joshua spoke with the LORD, and in the presence of Israel said:

'Stand still, you sun, at Gibeon;
 you moon, at the vale of Aijalon.'

13 The sun stood still and the moon halted until the nation had taken vengeance on its enemies, as indeed is written in the Book of Jashar. The sun stayed in mid-heaven and made no haste to set for almost a whole day. 14 Never before or since has there been such a day as that on which the LORD listened to the voice of a mortal. Surely the LORD fought for Israel! 15 Then Joshua returned with all the Israelites to the camp at Gilgal.

16 The five kings fled and hid in a cave at Makkedah, 17 and Joshua was told that they had been found hiding there. 18 Joshua replied, 'Roll large stones against the mouth of the cave, and post men there to keep watch over the kings. 19 But you yourselves must not stay. Keep up the pursuit, attack your enemies from the rear and do not let them reach

their towns; the LORD your God has delivered them into your hands.'

20 When Joshua and the Israelites had completed the work of slaughter and everyone had been put to the sword — all except a few survivors who escaped into the fortified towns — 21 the whole army returned safely to Joshua at Makkedah; not one of the Israelites suffered so much as a scratch.

22 Joshua gave the order: 'Open up the mouth of the cave, and bring out those five kings to me.' 23 This was done; the five kings, the kings of Jerusalem, Hebron, Jarmuth, Lachish, and Eglon, were taken from the cave 24 and brought to Joshua. When he had summoned all the Israelites he said to the commanders of the troops who had served with him, 'Come forward and put your feet on the necks of these kings.' They did so, 25 and Joshua said to them, 'Do not be afraid or discouraged; be strong and resolute; for the LORD will do this to every enemy whom you fight.' 26 He fell on the kings and slew them; then he hung their bodies on five gibbets, where they remained hanging till evening. 27 At sunset they were taken down on Joshua's orders and thrown into the cave in which they had hidden; large stones were piled against its mouth, where they remain to this very day.

28 On that same day Joshua captured Makkedah and put both king and people to the sword, destroying under the ban both them and every living thing in the city. He left no survivor, and he dealt with the king of Makkedah as he had dealt with the king of Jericho. 29 Then Joshua with all the Israelites marched on from Makkedah to Libnah and attacked it. 30 The LORD delivered the city and its king to the Israelites, and they put its

10:13 **Book of Jashar:** *or* Book of the Upright.
10:21 **returned:** *so Gk; Heb. adds* to the camp. **not one**
. . . scratch: *Heb. adds* on his tongue; *or* no one raised his voice against the Israelites.

---

southwest of Jerusalem. **10:** *The pass of Beth-horon* led westward to the coastal plain. **11:** *More died from the hailstones . . .* expresses the writer's belief that the victories were miracles accomplished by God's intervention rather than by military skill. **12:** *Aijalon* is about ten miles west of Gibeon. **13:** *Jashar:* "upright." *The Book of Jashar* was an ancient collection of Heb. poetry now lost (compare 2 Sam. 1.18 and 1 Kgs. 8.12–13 n.). The poetic imagery of *Stand still, you Sun . . .* is repeated literally in the prose to glorify the LORD, and Joshua too. **16–27:** The fugitive kings are captured, humiliated, and killed; their bodies were then returned to the caves in which they had hidden.

10.28–43: Summary of Joshua's conquests in the south. After the defeat of the five kings, Israel had no difficulty in conquering the whole of southern Palestine (but see 13.1–6).

people and every living thing in it to the sword; they left no survivor there, and dealt with its king as they had dealt with the king of Jericho. [31] From Libnah Joshua and all the Israelites marched on to Lachish, where they took up their positions against it and attacked it. [32] The LORD delivered Lachish into their hands; they took it on the second day and put every living thing in it to the sword, as they had done at Libnah.

[33] Meanwhile King Horam of Gezer had advanced to the relief of Lachish; but Joshua attacked him and his army until not a survivor was left to him. [34] From Lachish Joshua and all the Israelites marched on to Eglon, took up their positions against it, and attacked it; [35] that same day they captured it and put its inhabitants to the sword, destroying every living thing in it as they had done at Lachish. [36] From Eglon Joshua and all the Israelites advanced to Hebron and attacked it. [37] They captured it and put its king to the sword together with every living thing in it and in all its villages; as at Eglon, he left no survivor, destroying it and every living thing in it. [38] Then Joshua and all the Israelites wheeled round towards Debir and attacked it. [39] They captured the king, the city, and all its villages, put them to the sword, and destroyed every living thing; they left no survivor. They dealt with Debir and its king as they had dealt with Hebron and with Libnah and its king.

[40] So Joshua conquered the whole region—the hill-country, the Negeb, the Shephelah, the watersheds—and all its kings. He left no survivor, destroying everything that drew breath, as the LORD the God of Israel had commanded. [41] Joshua's conquests extended from Kadesh-barnea to Gaza, over the whole land of Goshen, and as far as Gibeon. [42] All these kings he captured at the same time, and their country with them, for the LORD the God of Israel fought for Israel. [43] Then Joshua returned with all the Israelites to the camp at Gilgal.

2/21/10

The conquest of the north

11 WHEN King Jabin of Hazor heard of these events, he sent to King Jobab of Madon, to the kings of Shimron and Akshaph, [2] to the northern kings in the hill-country, in the Arabah opposite Kinnereth, in the Shephelah, and in the district of Dor on the west, [3] the Canaanites to the east and the west, the Amorites, Hittites, Perizzites, and Jebusites in the hill-country, and the Hivites below Hermon in the land of Mizpah. [4] They took the field with all their forces, a great host countless as the grains of sand on the seashore, among them a very large number of horses and chariots. [5] All these kings, making common cause, came and encamped at the waters of Merom to fight against Israel. [6] The LORD said to Joshua, 'Do not be afraid of them, for at this time tomorrow I shall deliver them to Israel all dead men; you are to hamstring their horses and burn their chariots.' [7] Joshua with his whole army launched a surprise attack on them by the waters of Merom, [8] and the LORD delivered them into the hands of Israel, who defeated them, cutting down the fugitives the whole way to Greater Sidon, Misrephoth on the west, and the vale of Mizpah on the east. They cut them down until they had left not a single survivor. [9] Joshua dealt with them as the LORD had commanded: he hamstrung their horses and burnt their chariots.

[10] At this point, Joshua turned his forces against Hazor, formerly the leader among all these kingdoms. He captured the city and put its king to death with the sword. [11] They put under the ban and killed every living thing in it; they spared nothing that drew breath, and Hazor itself was destroyed by fire.

[12] So Joshua captured these kings and their cities and put them to the sword, destroying them all, as Moses the servant of the LORD had commanded. [13] The cities whose ruined

11:2 **opposite:** *so Gk; Heb.* south of.

11.1–23: The conquest of the north. The northern Canaanite rulers, hearing of Israel's victories in the south, field a united opposing force, but they are overwhelmingly defeated. **1:** *Hazor* was one of the largest cities of Galilee. Excavations have shown its importance in antiquity, and confirm a capture of the city at about the period of time indicated in this narrative. The other three places in this verse are all between the Sea of Galilee and the Mediterranean. **2:** *Arabah:* see 3.16 n. *Kinnereth:* the ancient name for the Sea of Galilee. *Shephelah:* the low hill country immediately east of the Mediterranean plain. *Dor:* on the coast, west of Megiddo. *Hivites:* see 9.7 n. **5:** *The waters of Merom:* probably the brook which flows from Merom (modern Meiron) into the Sea of Galilee at its northwest corner. **8:** *Sidon:* the great Phoenician seaport to the north of Palestine.

mounds are still standing were not burnt by the Israelites; it was Hazor alone that Joshua burnt. [14] The Israelites plundered all these cities and kept for themselves the cattle and any other spoil they took; but they put every living soul to the sword until they had destroyed everyone; they did not leave alive anyone that drew breath. [15] The LORD had laid his commands on his servant Moses, and Moses laid these same commands on Joshua, and Joshua carried them out. Not one of the commands laid on Moses by the LORD was left unfulfilled.

[16] Thus Joshua took the whole land, the hill-country, all the Negeb, all the land of Goshen, the Shephelah, the Arabah, and the Israelite hill-country with the adjoining lowlands. [17] His conquests extended from the bare mountain which leads up to Seir as far as Baal-gad in the vale of Lebanon under Mount Hermon. He captured all their kings, struck them down, and put them to death. [18] It was a lengthy campaign he waged against all those kingdoms; [19] except for the Hivites who lived in Gibeon, not one of their towns or cities came to terms with the Israelites; all had to be taken by storm. [20] It was the LORD's purpose that they should offer stubborn resistance to the Israelites, and thus be annihilated and utterly destroyed without mercy, as the LORD had commanded Moses.

[21] It was then that Joshua proceeded to wipe out the Anakim from the hill-country, from Hebron, Debir, Anab, all the hill-country of Judah, and all the hill-country of Israel, destroying both them and their towns. [22] No Anakim were left in the land taken by the Israelites; they survived only in Gaza, Gath, and Ashdod.

[23] Joshua took the whole land, fulfilling all the commands that the LORD had laid on Moses; he assigned it to Israel, allotting to each tribe its share. Then the land was at peace.

12 These are the names of the kings of the land whom the Israelites slew,

and whose territory they occupied beyond the Jordan towards the sunrise from the wadi of the Arnon as far as Mount Hermon and all the Arabah on the east. [2] Sihon the Amorite king who lived in Heshbon: his rule extended from Aroer, which is on the edge of the wadi of the Arnon, along the middle of the wadi and over half Gilead as far as the wadi of the Jabbok, the Ammonite frontier; [3] along the Arabah as far as the eastern side of the sea of Kinnereth and as far as the eastern side of the sea of the Arabah, the Dead Sea, by the road to Beth-jeshimoth and from Teman under the watershed of Pisgah. [4] King Og of Bashan, one of the survivors of the Rephaim, who lived in Ashtaroth and Edrei: [5] he ruled over Mount Hermon, Salcah, all Bashan as far as the Geshurite and Maacathite borders, and half Gilead as far as the boundary of King Sihon of Heshbon. [6] Moses the servant of the LORD put them to death, he and the Israelites, and he assigned their land to the Reubenites, the Gadites, and half the tribe of Manasseh.

[7] These are the kings whom Joshua and the Israelites put to death on the west side of Jordan, from Baal-gad in the vale of Lebanon as far as the bare mountain that leads up to Seir; Joshua assigned their land to the Israelite tribes according to their allotted shares, [8] in the hill-country, the Shephelah, the Arabah, the watersheds, the wilderness, and the Negeb; lands of the Hittites, Amorites, Canaanites, Perizzites, Hivites, and Jebusites: [9] the king of Jericho; the king of Ai which is beside Bethel; [10] the king of Jerusalem; the king of Hebron; [11] the king of Jarmuth; the king of Lachish; [12] the king of Eglon; the king of Gezer; [13] the king of Debir; the king of Geder; [14] the king of Hormah; the king of Arad; [15] the king of Libnah; the king of Adullam; [16] the king of Makkedah; the king of Bethel; [17] the king of Tappuah; the

12:3 **Dead Sea:** *lit.* Salt Sea.   12:4 **King Og:** *so Gk; Heb.* The boundary of King Og.   12:5 **Gilead as far as:** *so Gk (Luc.); Heb. omits* as far as.

Misrephoth: on the Mediterranean coast, west of Hazor. *Mizpah:* see v. 3. **16–20:** A summary of the victories in the south and the north. **17:** *Seir:* a synonym for Edom. **20:** *The LORD's purpose:* see Deut. 7.2–6; 20.16–18. **21:** *Anakim* were reputed to be of gigantic size (see Num. 13.33; Deut. 2.10–11). In Josh. they seem to be an aristocracy in the hill country around Hebron and in the coastal towns; in 14.12–15 and 15.13–15 Caleb, not Joshua, is their conqueror. **23:** Nothing remained to be done but to divide the land among the tribes.

12.1–24: Summary of Israel's victories. 1–6: Moses' victories in Transjordan (see Deut. 2.26–3.11). **6:** On the land of the Transjordan tribes, see Deut. 3.12–17. **7–24:** Joshua's conquests west of the Jordan. Some of these names were not mentioned previously. The "kings" were merely local chieftains.

king of Hepher; 18 the king of Aphek; the king of Aphek-in-Sharon; 19 the king of Madon; the king of Hazor; 20 the king of Shimron-meron; the king of Akshaph; 21 the king of Taanach; the king of Megiddo; 22 the king of Kedesh; the king of Jokneam-in-Carmel; 23 the king of Dor in the district of Dor; the king of Gaiam-in-Galilee; 24 the king of Tirzah: thirty-one kings in all, one of each town.

13 By this time Joshua had become very old, and the LORD said to him, 'You are now a very old man, and much of the country still remains to be occupied. 2 The remaining territory is this: all the districts of the Philistines and all the Geshurite country 3 (this is reckoned as Canaanite territory from Shihor to the east of Egypt as far north as Ekron; and it belongs to the five lords of the Philistines, those of Gaza, Ashdod, Ashkelon, Gath, and Ekron); all the districts of the Avvim 4 on the south; all the Canaanite country from Mearah which belongs to the Sidonians as far as Aphek, the Amorite frontier; 5 the land of the Gebalites and all the Lebanon to the east from Baal-gad under Mount Hermon as far as Lebo-hamath. 6 I shall drive out in favour of the Israelites all the inhabitants of the hill-country from the Lebanon as far as Misrephoth on the west, and all the Sidonians. In the mean time, following my command, you are to allot all this to the Israelites as their holding. 7 Distribute this country now to the nine tribes and the half tribe of Manasseh as their holding.'

Land distributed east of Jordan

8 HALF the tribe of Manasseh, and with them the Reubenites and the Gadites, had taken the holding which Moses gave them east of

the Jordan, as Moses the servant of the LORD had ordained. 9 It started from Aroer which is on the edge of the wadi of the Arnon, and the level land half-way along the wadi, and included all the tableland from Medeba as far as Dibon; 10 all the towns of Sihon, the Amorite king who ruled in Heshbon, as far as the Ammonite frontier; 11 and it also included Gilead and the Geshurite and Maacathite territory, and all Mount Hermon and the whole of Bashan as far as Salcah, 12 all the kingdom of Og which he ruled from both Ashtaroth and Edrei in Bashan. He was a survivor from the remnant of the Rephaim, but Moses put both kings to death and occupied their lands. 13 But the Israelites failed to drive out the Geshurites and the Maacathites, and they live among Israel to this day. 14 The tribe of Levi, however, received no holding; the LORD the God of Israel is their portion, as he promised them.

15 So Moses allotted territory to the tribe of the Reubenites family by family. 16 Their territory started from Aroer which is on the edge of the wadi of the Arnon, and the level land half-way along the wadi, and included all the tableland as far as Medeba; 17 Heshbon and all its towns on the tableland, Dibon, Bamoth-baal, Beth-baal-meon, 18 Jahaz, Kedemoth, Mephaath, 19 Kiriathaim, Sibmah, Zereth-shahar on the hill in the valley, 20 Beth-peor, the watershed of Pisgah, and Beth-jeshimoth, 21 all the towns of the tableland, all the kingdom of Sihon the Amorite king who ruled in Heshbon, whom Moses put to death together with the princes of

12:18 **of Aphek-in-Sharon:** *prob. rdg; Heb. omits* Aphek.
12:20 **Shimron-meron:** *in 11:1* Shimron.
12:23 **Gaiam-in-Galilee:** *prob. rdg, cp. Gk; Heb.* nations to Gilgal. 13:8 **Half . . . Manasseh, and:** *prob. rdg; Heb. omits.* 13:14 **holding:** *so Gk; Heb. adds* the food-offerings of.

13.1–33: The beginning of the distribution of the land. The distribution continues through ch. 18. **2–7:** These territories were still unconquered, even though ideally they were to be part of Israel according to 1.4 and Num. 34.1–12. **2:** *The Philistines* came from Caphtor (Deut. 2.23 n.). They settled on the coast of Palestine (which gets its name from them) shortly after 1200 B.C.E.; their five districts are listed in v. 3. Not Semites, they did not practice circumcision. They were mortal enemies of Israel for over 200 years. *Geshurite country:* south of the Philistine cities; see 1 Sam. 27.7–8. **3:** *Avvim* lived around Gaza. **4–6:** This is unconquered territory on the northern edges of Palestine. **7:** This is done in chs. 14–19. **8–32:** The land east of the Jordan is allotted to Reuben, Gad, and half of Manasseh; see Num. ch. 32 and Deut. 3.12–17. The boundaries of Reuben and Gad were pushed back when the Ammonite and Moabite kingdoms developed. The origins of the half tribe of Manasseh are obscure. **13:** That *the Israelites did not drive out the Geshurites . . .* is the first of several passages (14.6–13; 15.13–19, 63; 16.10; 17.12–18; Judg. 1.19, 21, 27–35) derived from an ancient source, which indicate that the conquest was less complete than the late editor of Joshua usually states. **14:** *Levi:* see ch. 21.

Midian: Evi, Rekem, Zur, Hur, and Reba, the vassals of Sihon who dwelt in the country. [22] Balaam son of Beor, who practised augury, was among those whom the Israelites put to the sword. [23] The boundary of the Reubenites was the Jordan and the land adjacent: this is the holding of the Reubenites family by family, both the towns and their hamlets.

[24] Moses allotted territory to the Gadites family by family. [25] Their territory was Jazer, all the towns of Gilead, and half the Ammonite country as far as Aroer which is east of Rabbah. [26] It reached from Heshbon as far as Ramath-mizpeh and Betonim, and from Mahanaim as far as the boundary of Lo-debar; [27] it included, in the valley, Beth-haram, Beth-nimrah, Succoth, and Zaphon, the rest of the kingdom of King Sihon of Heshbon. The boundary was the Jordan and the adjacent land as far as the end of the sea of Kinnereth east of the Jordan. [28] This is the holding of the Gadites family by family, both the towns and their hamlets.

[29] Moses allotted territory to the half tribe of Manasseh: it was for half the tribe of the Manassites family by family. [30] Their territory ran from Mahanaim and included all Bashan, all the kingdom of King Og of Bashan, and all Havvoth-jair in Bashan — sixty towns. [31] Half Gilead, and Ashtaroth and Edrei, the royal cities of Og in Bashan, belong to the sons of Machir son of Manasseh on behalf of half the Machirites family by family. [32] These are the territories which Moses allotted to the tribes as their holdings in the lowlands of Moab east of the Jordan. [33] But to the tribe of Levi he gave no holding: the LORD the God of Israel is their portion, as he promised them.

Land distributed west of Jordan

14 THE following are the possessions which the Israelites acquired in the land of Canaan, as Eleazar the priest, Joshua son of Nun, and the heads of the families of the Israelite tribes allotted them. [2] They were assigned by lot, following the LORD's command given through Moses, to the nine and a half tribes. [3] To two and a half tribes Moses had given holdings beyond the Jordan; but he gave none to the Levites as he did to the other tribes. [4] The tribe of Joseph formed the two tribes of Manasseh and Ephraim. The Levites were given no share in the land, only towns to live in, with their common land for flocks and herds. [5] So the Israelites assigned the land according to the LORD's command given to Moses.

[6] The tribe of Judah had come to Joshua at Gilgal, and Caleb son of Jephunneh the Kenizzite said to him, 'You remember what the LORD said to Moses the man of God concerning you and me at Kadesh-barnea. [7] I was forty years old when Moses the servant of the LORD sent me from there to reconnoitre the land, and I brought back an honest report. [8] The others who went up with me discouraged the people, but I loyally carried out the purpose of the LORD my God. [9] Moses swore an oath that day: "The land on which you have set foot", he said, "is to be your holding and your sons' after you as a possession for ever; for you have loyally carried out the purpose of the LORD my God." [10] Well, the LORD has spared my life as he promised; it is forty-five years since he made this promise to Moses, at the time when Israel was journeying in the wilderness. Now here I am at eighty-five, [11] still as strong as I was on the day when Moses sent me out; I am as fit now for war as I was then and am ready to take the field again. [12] Give me today this hill-country which the LORD then promised me. You yourself heard on that day that the Anakim were there and their towns were large and fortified. Perhaps the LORD will be with me, and I shall drive them out as he promised.'

[13] Joshua blessed Caleb and gave him Hebron for his holding, [14] and that is why He-

13:24 **allotted:** *so Gk; Heb. adds* to the tribe of Gad.
13:32 **Jordan:** *so Syriac; Heb. adds* Jericho.

14.1–5: General introduction to the allotment of land.

14.6–15: Hebron assigned to Caleb. Caleb in Num. 13.6; 34.19 is of the tribe of Judah, but is here and in Num. 32.12 a Kenizzite, therefore a non-Israelite (see v. 14; Gen. 15.19); he receives land *within the tribe of Judah* as had been promised (see Num. 14.24) because he "showed a different spirit" than the others sent to explore the land (Num. 13.30; 14.6–9). Some scholars think that Caleb and some other non-Israelite elements had penetrated Canaan from the south along with some elements of Judah and Simeon; this opinion is based on a comparison of Judg. 1.16–17 and Num. 21.3 as well as Judg. 1.9–15 and Josh. 15.13–19.

bron remains to this day in the possession of Caleb son of Jephunneh the Kenizzite. It is because he loyally carried out the purpose of the LORD the God of Israel. 15 Formerly the name of Hebron was Kiriath-arba; this Arba was the chief man of the Anakim.

The land was now at peace.

15 This is the territory allotted to the tribe of the sons of Judah family by family. It started from the Edomite frontier at the wilderness of Zin and ran as far as the Negeb at its southern end, 2 and it had a common border with the Negeb at the end of the Dead Sea, where an inlet of water bends towards the Negeb. 3 It continued from the south by the ascent of Akrabbim, passed by Zin, went up from the south of Kadesh-barnea, passed by Hezron, went on to Addar, and turned round to Karka. 4 It then passed along to Azmon, reached the wadi of Egypt, and its limit was the sea. This was their southern boundary.

5 The eastern boundary is the Dead Sea as far as the mouth of the Jordan and the adjacent land northwards from the inlet of the sea, at the mouth of the Jordan. 6 The boundary goes up to Beth-hoglah; it passes north of Beth-arabah and thence to the stone of Bohan son of Reuben, 7 thence to Debir from the vale of Achor, and then turns north to the districts in front of the ascent of Adummim south of the wadi. The boundary then passes the waters of En-shemesh and the limit there is Enrogel. 8 It then goes up by the valley of Ben-hinnom to the southern slope of the Jebusites (that is Jerusalem). Thence it goes up to the top of the hill which faces the valley of Hinnom on the west; this is at the northern end of the vale of Rephaim. 9 The boundary then bends round from the top of the hill to the spring of the waters of Nephtoah and runs round to the cities of Mount Ephron and to Baalah, that is Kiriath-jearim. 10 It then continues westwards from Baalah to Mount Seir, passes on to the north side of the slope of Mount Jearim, that is Kesalon, down to Beth-shemesh and on to Timnah. 11 The

boundary then goes north to the slope of Ekron, bends round to Shikkeron, crosses to Mount Baalah, and reaches Jebneel; its limit is the sea. 12 The western boundary is the Great Sea and the land adjacent. This is the whole circuit of the boundary of the tribe of Judah family by family.

13 Caleb son of Jephunneh received his share of the land within the tribe of Judah as the LORD had told Joshua. It was Kiriath-arba, that is Hebron; this Arba was the ancestor of the Anakim. 14 Caleb drove out the three Anakim, Sheshai, Ahiman, and Talmai, descendants of Anak. 15 From there he attacked the inhabitants of Debir, formerly called Kiriath-sepher. 16 Caleb announced that whoever should attack and capture Kiriath-sepher would receive his daughter Achsah in marriage. 17 It was captured by Othniel, son of Caleb's brother Kenaz, and Caleb gave him his daughter Achsah. 18 When she became his wife, he induced her to ask her father for a piece of land. She dismounted from her donkey, and Caleb asked her, 'What do you want?' 19 She replied, 'Grant me this favour: you have put me in this arid Negeb; you must give me pools of water as well.' So Caleb gave her the upper pool and the lower pool.

20 This is the holding of the tribe of the sons of Judah family by family. 21 These are the towns belonging to the tribe of Judah, the full count. By the Edomite frontier in the Negeb: Kabzeel, Eder, Jagur, 22 Kinah, Dimonah, Ararah, 23 Kedesh, Hazor, Ithnan, 24 Ziph, Telem, Bealoth, 25 Hazor-hadattah, Kerioth-hezron, 26 Amam, Shema, Moladah, 27 Hazar-gaddah, Heshmon, Beth-pelet, 28 Hazar-shual, Beersheba and its villages,

15:4 **their:** *so Gk; Heb.* your.   15:7 **to the districts:** *prob. rdg, cp. 18:17; Heb.* to Gilgal.   15:18 **he induced her:** *so some Gk MSS; Heb.* she induced him. 15:22 **Ararah:** *prob. rdg; Heb.* Adadah. 15:23, 24 **Hazor** *and* **Ziph** *omitted by Gk.* 15:25 **Hazor-hadattah:** *omitted by Gk.* **Kerioth-hezron:** *so Syriac; Heb. adds* that is, Hazor.   15:27 **Heshmon:** *omitted by Gk.*   15:28 **its villages:** *so Gk; Heb.* Biziothiah.

15.1–63: The territory allotted to Judah. In this and the following sections the boundaries of each tribe are described as they existed before the rise of the monarchy. **1–12:** These are the boundaries of Judah: vv. 2–4, the southern, from the Dead Sea to the Mediterranean; vv. 5–11, the eastern, the Dead Sea; and the northern, from the mouth of the Jordan to the Mediterranean, passing just south of Jerusalem; v. 12, the western, the Mediterranean. **13–19:** Another reference to Caleb (compare 14.6–15); vv. 15–19 are almost identical with Judg. 1.11–15. **20–63:** A list of Judah's towns by districts. Many think this list was taken from an official register of the subdivisions of the kingdom of Judah, either after the division of Judah and Israel in 922 B.C.E., or perhaps

29 Baalah, Iyim, Ezem, 30 Eltolad, Kesil, Hormah, 31 Ziklag, Madmannah, Sansannah, 32 Lebaoth, Shilhim, Ain, and Rimmon: in all, twenty-nine towns with their hamlets.

33 In the Shephelah: Eshtaol, Zorah, Ashnah, 34 Zanoah, En-gannim, Tappuah, Enam, 35 Jarmuth, Adullam, Socoh, Azekah, 36 Shaaraim, Adithaim, Gederah, namely both parts of Gederah: fourteen towns with their hamlets. 37 Zenan, Hadashah, Migdal-gad, 38 Dilan, Mizpeh, Joktheel, 39 Lachish, Bozkath, Eglon, 40 Cabbon, Lahmas, Kithlish, 41 Gederoth, Beth-dagon, Naamah, and Makkedah: sixteen towns with their hamlets. 42 Libnah, Ether, Ashan, 43 Jiphtah, Ashnah, Nezib, 44 Keilah, Achzib, and Mareshah: nine towns with their hamlets. 45 Ekron, with its villages and hamlets, 46 and from Ekron westwards, all the towns near Ashdod and their hamlets. 47 Ashdod with its villages and hamlets, Gaza with its villages and hamlets as far as the wadi of Egypt and the Great Sea and the land adjacent.

48 In the hill-country: Shamir, Jattir, Socoh, 49 Dannah, Kiriath-sannah, that is Debir, 50 Anab, Eshtemoh, Anim, 51 Goshen, Holon, and Giloh: eleven towns in all with their hamlets. 52 Arab, Dumah, Eshan, 53 Janim, Beth-tappuah, Aphek, 54 Humtah, Kiriath-arba, that is Hebron, and Zior: nine towns in all with their hamlets. 55 Maon, Carmel, Ziph, Juttah, 56 Jezreel, Jokdeam, Zanoah, 57 Kain, Gibeah, and Timnah: ten towns in all with their hamlets. 58 Halhul, Beth-zur, Gedor, 59 Maarath, Beth-anoth, and Eltekon: six towns in all with their hamlets. Tekoa, Ephrathah, that is Bethlehem, Peor, Etam, Culom, Tatam, Sores, Carem, Gallim, Baither, and Manach: eleven towns in all with their hamlets. 60 Kiriath-baal, that is Kiriath-jearim, and Rabbah: two towns with their hamlets.

61 In the wilderness: Beth-arabah, Middin, Secacah, 62 Nibshan, Irmelach, and En-gedi: six towns with their hamlets.

63 At Jerusalem, the men of Judah failed to drive out the Jebusites living there, and to this day Jebusites and men of Judah live together in Jerusalem.

16 This is the lot that fell to the sons of Joseph: the boundary runs from the Jordan at Jericho, east of the waters of Jericho by the wilderness, and goes up from Jericho into the hill-country to Bethel. 2 It runs on from Bethel to Luz and crosses the Archite border at Ataroth. 3 Westwards it descends to the boundary of the Japhletites as far as the boundary of Lower Beth-horon and Gezer; its limit is the sea. 4 Here Manasseh and Ephraim the sons of Joseph received their holding.

5 This was the boundary of the Ephraimites family by family: their eastern boundary ran from Ataroth-addar up to Upper Beth-horon. 6 It continued westwards to Michmethath on the north, going round by the east of Taanath-shiloh and passing by it on the east of Janoah. 7 It descends from Janoah to Ataroth and Naarath, touches Jericho and continues to the Jordan, 8 and from Tappuah it goes westwards by the wadi of Kanah; and its limit is the sea. This is the holding of the tribe of Ephraim family by family. 9 There were also towns reserved for the Ephraimites within the holding of the Manassites, each of these towns with its hamlets. 10 They did not however drive out the Canaanites who lived in Gezer; the Canaanites have lived among the Ephraimites to the present day but have been subject to forced labour.

17 This is the territory allotted to the tribe of Manasseh, Joseph's eldest son. Machir was Manasseh's eldest son and father of Gilead, a fighting man; Gilead and Bashan were allotted to him.

2 The rest of the Manassites family by family were the sons of Abiezer, the sons of Helek, the sons of Asriel, the sons of Shechem, the sons of Hepher, and the sons of Shemida; these were the male offspring of Manasseh son of Joseph family by family.

3 Zelophehad son of Hepher, son of Gilead, son of Machir, son of Manasseh, had no sons but only daughters: their names were Mahlah, Noah, Hoglah, Milcah, and Tirzah.

15:29 **Iyim:** *omitted in 19:3 (cp. 1 Chr. 4:29).*
15:42 **Ether:** *or, with 1 Sam. 30:30,* Athak.
15:53 **Aphek:** *or* Aphekah. 15:59 **Tekoa …
hamlets:** *so Gk; Heb. omits.*

in the time of King Josiah (626–609). **63:** See 2 Sam. 5.6–9.

16.1–17.18: The territory allotted to the Joseph tribes. The two tribes of Ephraim and Manasseh receive the central highlands. **1–4:** The southern boundary ran roughly from the Jordan at Jericho to Bethel, then slightly south toward Gezer and on to the Mediterranean. **5–10:** The boundaries of Ephraim were south of Manasseh, but some Ephraimite cities were within Manasseh (v. 9). **17.1–6:** Arrangements for Manasseh. **2:** *The rest of*

4 They presented themselves before Eleazar the priest and Joshua son of Nun, and before the leaders, and said, 'The LORD commanded Moses to allow us to inherit on the same footing as our kinsmen.' They were therefore given a holding on the same footing as their father's brothers according to the commandment of the LORD.

5 There fell to Manasseh's lot ten shares, apart from the country of Gilead and Bashan beyond the Jordan, 6 because Manasseh's daughters had received a holding on the same footing as his sons. The country of Gilead belonged to the rest of Manasseh's sons.

7 The boundary of Manasseh reached from Asher as far as Michmethath, which is to the east of Shechem, and thence southwards towards Jashub by Entappuah. 8 The territory of Tappuah belonged to Manasseh, but Tappuah itself was on the border of Manasseh and belonged to Ephraim. 9 The boundary then followed the wadi of Kanah to the south of the wadi (these towns belong to Ephraim, although they lie among the towns of Manasseh), the boundary of Manasseh being on the north of the wadi; its limit was the sea. 10 The southern side belonged to Ephraim and the northern to Manasseh, and their boundary was the sea. They marched with Asher on the north and Issachar on the east. 11 But in Issachar and Asher, Manasseh possessed Bethshean and its villages, Ibleam and its villages, the inhabitants of Dor and its villages, the inhabitants of En-dor and its villages, the inhabitants of Taanach and its villages, and the inhabitants of Megiddo and its villages. (The third is the district of Dor.) 12 The Manassites were unable to occupy these towns; the Canaanites maintained their hold on that part of the country. 13 When the Israelites grew stronger, they put the Canaanites to forced labour, but did not drive them out.

14 The sons of Joseph appealed to Joshua: 'Why have you given us only one lot and one share as our holding? We are a numerous people; so far the LORD has blessed us.' 15 Joshua replied, 'If you are so numerous, go up into the forest in the territory of the Perizzites and the Rephaim and clear it for yourselves. You are their near neighbours in the hill-country of Ephraim.' 16 The sons of Joseph contended, 'The hill-country is not enough for us; besides, all the Canaanites have iron-clad chariots, both those who inhabit the valley beside Beth-shean and its villages and also those in the valley of Jezreel.' 17 Joshua said to the house of Joseph, that is Ephraim and Manasseh: 'You are a numerous people of great vigour. You shall not have one lot only. 18 The hill-country is to be yours. It is forest land; clear it and it will be yours to its farthest limits. The Canaanites may be powerful and equipped with iron-clad chariots, but you will be able to drive them out.'

18 THE whole Israelite community assembled at Shiloh and established the Tent of Meeting there. The country now lay subdued at their feet; 2 but there remained seven tribes among the Israelites who had not yet taken possession of the holdings which would fall to them. 3 Joshua therefore said to them, 'How much longer will you neglect to take possession of the land which the LORD the God of your fathers has assigned to you? 4 Appoint three men from each tribe, and I shall send them out to travel throughout the country. They are to make a survey of it showing the holding suitable for each tribe, and come back to me, 5 and then it can be shared out among you in seven portions. Judah will retain his boundary in the south, and the house of Joseph their boundary in the north. 6 Survey the land in seven portions, and bring your findings to me, and I shall cast lots for you in the presence of the LORD our God. 7 Levi has no share among you, because his share is the priesthood of the LORD; and Gad, Reuben, and the half tribe of Manasseh have each taken possession of their holding east of the Jordan, which Moses the servant of the LORD assigned to them.'

17:7 **Jashub by:** *prob. rdg; Heb.* the inhabitants of.
17:9 **these towns:** *prob. reading.*   17:10 **their:** *so Gk; Heb.* his.   17:11 **The third . . . Dor:** *prob. rdg; Heb.* The three districts.   17:15 **You are . . . neighbours:** *prob. rdg; Heb. obscure.*

---

the Manassites: those not already settled east of the Jordan (vv. 1, 5–6; 13.29–31). **7–13:** The boundaries of Manasseh. **11–13:** These verses closely parallel Judg. 1.27–28. **14–18:** The Joseph tribes ask for and receive a double portion.

18.1–19.51: The territory of the seven other tribes. 1–10: Preparations for the further division of the land. **1:** *Shiloh,* in Ephraim, ten miles north of Bethel, was the new religious center, replacing Gilgal; see 19.51; 21.2;

8 The men set out on their journey. Joshua ordered the emissaries to survey the country: 'Go through the whole country,' he said, 'survey it, and return to me, and I shall cast lots for you here before the LORD in Shiloh.' 9 So the men went and passed through the country; they recorded the survey on a scroll, town by town, in seven portions. Then they came to Joshua in the camp at Shiloh; 10 he cast lots for them in Shiloh before the LORD, and apportioned the land there to the Israelites in their proper shares.

11 This is the lot which fell to the tribe of the Benjamites family by family. The territory allotted to them lay between the territories of Judah and Joseph. 12 Their boundary at its northern corner starts from the Jordan; it goes up the slope on the north side of Jericho, continuing westwards into the hill-country, and its limit there is the wilderness of Beth-aven. 13 From there it runs on to Luz, to the southern slope of Luz, that is Bethel, and down to Ataroth-addar over the hill-country south of Lower Beth-horon. 14 The boundary then bends round at the west corner southwards from the hill-country above Beth-horon, and its limit is Kiriath-baal, that is Kiriath-jearim, which belongs to Judah. This is the western side. 15 The southern side starts from the edge of Kiriath-jearim and ends at the spring of the waters of Nephtoah. 16 It goes down to the edge of the hill to the east of the valley of Ben-hinnom, north of the vale of Rephaim, down the valley of Hinnom, to the southern slope of the Jebusites and so to En-rogel. 17 It then bends round north and comes out at En-shemesh, goes on to the districts in front of the ascent of Adummim and thence down to the stone of Bohan son of Reuben. 18 It passes to the northern side of the slope facing the Arabah and goes down to the Arabah, 19 passing the northern slope of Beth-hoglah, and its limit is the northern inlet of the Dead Sea, at the southern mouth of the Jordan. This forms the southern boundary. 20 The Jordan is the boundary on the east side. This is the holding of the Benjamites, the complete circuit of their boundaries family by family.

21 The towns belonging to the tribe of the Benjamites family by family are: Jericho, Beth-hoglah, Emek-keziz, 22 Beth-arabah, Zemaraim, Bethel, 23 Avvim, Parah, Ophrah, 24 Kephar-ammoni, Ophni, and Geba: twelve towns in all with their hamlets. 25 Gibeon, Ramah, Beeroth, 26 Mizpah, Kephirah, Mozah, 27 Rekem, Irpeel, Taralah, 28 Zela, Eleph, Jebus, that is Jerusalem, Gibeah, and Kiriath-jearim: fourteen towns in all with their hamlets. This is the holding of the Benjamites family by family.

19 The second lot cast was for Simeon, the tribe of the Simeonites family by family. Their holding was included in that of Judah. 2 For their holding they had Beer-sheba, Moladah, 3 Hazar-shual, Balah, Ezem, 4 Eltolad, Bethul, Hormah, 5 Ziklag, Beth-marcaboth, Hazar-susah, 6 Beth-lebaoth, and Sharuhen: in all, thirteen towns and their hamlets. 7 They had Ain, Rimmon, Ether, and Ashan: four towns and their hamlets, 8 all the hamlets round these towns as far as Baalath-beer and Ramath-negeb. This was the holding of the tribe of Simeon family by family. 9 The holding of the Simeonites was part of the land allotted to the men of Judah, because their share was larger than they needed. The Simeonites therefore had their holding within the territory of Judah.

10 The third lot fell to the Zebulunites family by family. The boundary of their holding extended to Shadud. 11 Their boundary went up westwards as far as Maralah and touched Dabbesheth and the wadi east of Jokneam. 12 It turned back from Shadud eastwards towards the sunrise up to the border of Kisloth-tabor, on to Daberath and up to Japhia. 13 From there it crossed eastwards towards the sunrise to Gath-hepher, to Ittah-kazin, out to Rimmon, and bent round to Neah. 14 The northern boundary went round to Hannathon, and its limits were the valley of Jiphtah-el, 15 Kattath, Nahalal, Shimron, Idalah, and Bethlehem: twelve towns in all with their hamlets. 16 These towns and their ham-

18:15 **ends:** *prob. rdg; Heb. adds* westwards and ends.
18:28 **Jebus:** *so Gk; Heb.* the Jebusite. **Kiriath-jearim:** *so Gk; Heb.* Kiriath. 19:2 **Beersheba:** *prob. rdg, cp. 1 Chr. 4:28; Heb. adds* and Sheba. 19:10 **Shadud:** *prob. rdg; Heb.* Sarid *(similarly in verse 12)*.
19:13 **and bent round:** *prob. rdg; Heb.* which stretched.

22.9, 12; Judg. 18.31; 1 Sam. 1.3; 4.3–4. *Tent of Meeting:* see Exod. 26.1–37 n. **11–28:** The territory of Benjamin, between Judah and Joseph. **19.1–9:** The territory of Simeon lay within Judah, because the Judahite *share was larger than they needed* (v. 9). Simeon had once been powerful (see Gen. 34.1–31 n.; 49.5–7 n.); it seems secondary to Judah here and is not mentioned in the blessings of Deut. ch. 33. Some scholars believe lets were the holding of Zebulun family by family.

17 The fourth lot cast was for the sons of Issachar family by family. 18 Their boundary included Jezreel, Kesulloth, Shunem, 19 Hapharaim, Shion, Anaharath, 20 Rabbith, Kishon, Ebez, 21 Remeth, En-gannim, En-haddah, and Beth-pazzez. 22 The boundary touched Tabor, Shahazumah, and Beth-shemesh, and its limit was the Jordan: sixteen towns with their hamlets. 23 This was the holding of the tribe of the sons of Issachar family by family, both towns and hamlets.

24 The fifth lot cast was for the tribe of the Asherites family by family. 25 Their boundary included Helkath, Hali, Beten, Akshaph, 26 Alammelech, Amad, and Mishal; it touched Carmel on the west and the swamp of Libnath. 27 It then turned back towards the east to Beth-dagon, touched Zebulun and the valley of Jiphtah-el on the north at Beth-emek and Neiel, and reached Cabul on its northern side, 28 and Abdon, Rehob, Hammon, and Kanah as far as Greater Sidon. 29 The boundary turned at Ramah, going as far as the fortress city of Tyre, and then back again to Hosah, and its limits to the west were Mehalbeh, Achzib, 30 Acco, Aphek, and Rehob: twenty-two towns in all with their hamlets. 31 This was the holding of the tribe of Asher family by family, these towns and their hamlets.

32 The sixth lot cast was for the sons of Naphtali family by family. 33 Their boundary started from Heleph and from Elon-bezaanannim and ran past Adami-nekeb and Jabneel as far as Lakkum, and its limit was the Jordan. 34 The boundary turned back westwards to Aznoth-tabor and from there on to Hukok. It touched Zebulun on the south, Asher on the west, and the low-lying land by the Jordan on the east. 35 Their fortified towns were Ziddim, Zer, Hamath, Rakkath, Kinnereth, 36 Adamah, Ramah, Hazor, 37 Kedesh, Edrei, En-hazor, 38 Iron, Migdal-el, Horem, Beth-anath, and Beth-shemesh: nineteen towns with their hamlets. 39 This was the holding of the tribe of Naphtali

family by family, both towns and hamlets.

40 The seventh lot cast was for the tribe of the sons of Dan family by family. 41 The boundary of their holding was Zorah, Eshtaol, Ir-shemesh, 42 Shaalabbin, Aijalon, Jithlah, 43 Elon, Timnah, Ekron, 44 Eltekeh, Gibbethon, Baalath, 45 Jehud, Bene-berak, and Gath-rimmon; 46 and on the west, Jarkon was the boundary opposite Joppa. 47 But the Danites, when they lost this territory, marched against Leshem, which they attacked and captured. They put its people to the sword, occupied it, and settled there; and they renamed the place Dan after their ancestor Dan. 48 This was the holding of the tribe of the sons of Dan family by family, these towns and their hamlets.

49 So the Israelites finished allocating the land and marking out its frontiers; and they gave Joshua son of Nun a holding within their territory. 50 They followed the commands of the LORD and gave him the town for which he asked, Timnath-serah in the hill-country of Ephraim; he rebuilt it and settled there.

51 These are the holdings which Eleazar the priest and Joshua son of Nun and the heads of families assigned by lot to the Israelite tribes at Shiloh before the LORD at the entrance of the Tent of Meeting. Thus they completed the distribution of the land.

Cities of refuge

20 THE LORD spoke to Joshua 2 and commanded him to say this to the Israelites: 'You must now appoint your cities of refuge, of which I spoke to you through Moses. 3 They are to be places where the homicide, the man who kills another inadvert-

19:28 **Abdon:** *so some MSS, cp. 21:30, 1 Chr. 6:74; others* Ebron.　　19:29 **Mehalbeh:** *in Judg. 1:31* Ahlab. 19:29-30 **Mehalbeh ... Acco:** *prob. rdg; Heb.* from the district of Achzib and Ummah.　　19:33 **from Heleph and:** *prob. rdg, cp. Gk; Heb.* omits.　　19:46 **and on ... boundary:** *so Gk; Heb.* Me-jarkon and Rakkon were on the boundary.　　19:50 **Timnath-serah:** *in Judg. 2:9* Timnath-heres.

it disappeared as a separate tribe. **10–48:** The territory of the Galilee tribes. **10–16:** *Zebulun.* **17–23:** *Issachar.* **24–31:** *Asher.* **32–39:** *Naphtali.* **40–48:** *Dan* never conquered these southern lands west of Benjamin (vv. 41–46); after being forced out, by the Amorites (Judg. 1.34–35) or by the Philistines (Judg. chs. 13–16), they then emigrated north (v. 47) to Leshem (Laish); see Judg. 18.27. **49–51:** These verses conclude the distribution of land to the tribes.

20.1–9: Cities of refuge. These are cities to which an accused murderer might flee until the case was judged;

ently and without intent, may take sanctuary. Single them out as cities of refuge from the vengeance of the dead man's next-of-kin. ⁴When a man takes sanctuary in one of them, he must stop at the entrance of the city gate and present his case in the hearing of the elders of that city; if they admit him into the city, they will grant him a place where he may live as one of themselves. ⁵When the next-of-kin comes in pursuit, they are not to surrender him: he struck down his fellow without intent and had not previously been at enmity with him. ⁶The homicide may stay in that city until he stands trial before the community. On the death of the ruling high priest, he may return to the town and home from which he has fled.' ⁷They dedicated Kedesh in Galilee in the hill-country of Naphtali, Shechem in the hill-country of Ephraim, and Kiriath-arba, that is Hebron, in the hill-country of Judah. ⁸Across the Jordan eastwards from Jericho they appointed these cities: from the tribe of Reuben, Bezer-in-the-wilderness on the tableland, from the tribe of Gad, Ramoth in Gilead, and from the tribe of Manasseh, Golan in Bashan. ⁹These were the appointed cities where any Israelite or any alien residing among them might take sanctuary. They were intended for any man who killed another inadvertently, to ensure that no one should die at the hand of the next-of-kin until he had stood trial before the community.

21 The heads of the Levite families approached Eleazar the priest and Joshua son of Nun and the heads of the families of the tribes of Israel. ²They came before them at Shiloh in Canaan and said, 'The LORD gave his command through Moses that we were to receive towns to live in, together with the common land belonging to them for our cattle.' ³The Israelites, therefore, in obedience to the LORD's command, assigned to the Levites out of their own holdings the following towns with their common land.

⁴When lots were cast the first fell to the Kohathite family. Those Levites who were descended from Aaron the priest received thirteen towns chosen by lot from the tribes of Judah, Simeon, and Benjamin; ⁵the rest of the Kohathites were allotted family by family ten towns from the tribes of Ephraim, Dan, and half Manasseh.

⁶The Gershonites were allotted family by family thirteen towns from the tribes of Issachar, Asher, Naphtali, and the half tribe of Manasseh in Bashan.

⁷The Merarites were allotted family by family twelve towns from the tribes of Reuben, Gad, and Zebulun.

⁸So the Israelites gave the Levites these towns with their common land, allocating them by lot as the LORD had commanded through Moses.

⁹The Israelites designated the following towns out of the tribes of Judah and Simeon ¹⁰for those sons of Aaron who were of the Kohathite families of the Levites, because their lot came out first. ¹¹They gave them Kiriath-arba (Arba was the father of Anak), that is Hebron, in the hill-country of Judah, and the common land round it, ¹²but they gave the open country near the town, and its hamlets, to Caleb son of Jephunneh as his holding.

¹³To the sons of Aaron the priest they gave Hebron, a city of refuge for the homicide, Libnah, ¹⁴Jattir, Eshtemoa, ¹⁵Holon, Debir, ¹⁶Ashan, Juttah, and Beth-shemesh, each with its common land: nine towns from these two tribes. ¹⁷They also gave towns from the tribe of Benjamin, Gibeon, Geba, ¹⁸Anathoth, and Almon, each with its common land: four towns. ¹⁹The number of the towns with their common land given to the sons of Aaron, the priests, was thirteen.

21:5 **family by family:** *prob. rdg; Heb.* from the families *(similarly in verse 6).*   21:7 **were allotted:** *so Gk; Heb.* omits.   21:13–39 *Cp. 1 Chr. 6:57–81.* 21:16 **Ashan:** *prob. rdg, cp. 1 Chr. 6:59; Heb.* Ain.

see Exod. 21.12–13; Num. 35.12; Deut. 4.41–43; 19.1–13. **3:** The dead person's *next-of-kin* had the obligation of avenging the death; the word "next-of-kin" is translated "avenger" or "vindicator" by some; it is "redeemer" when used of God in Isa. 41.14, and "Guardian" in Prov. 23.11. **4:** *The city gate* was the place where the *elders* of the city met; business was also normally transacted there; see Ruth 4.1. The gate was not merely an entrance, but also a building, often containing several rooms and more than one story.

21.1–42: The cities allotted to the tribe of Levi. This tribe, because of its religious functions, did not receive an allotment of territory; see 13.14, 33; 18.7. It was given the six cities of refuge of ch. 20 and forty-two others in all the tribes with rights to pasture land nearby; see Num. 35.1–34 n. The disapproval of Levi in Gen. 49.5–7 does not seem to be reflected here.

20 The towns which the rest of the Kohathite families of the Levites received by lot were from the tribe of Ephraim. 21 They gave them Shechem, a city of refuge for the homicide in the hill-country of Ephraim, Gezer, 22 Kibzaim, and Beth-horon, each with its common land: four towns. 23 From the tribe of Dan, they gave them Eltekeh, Gibbethon, 24 Aijalon, and Gath-rimmon, each with its common land: four towns. 25 From the half tribe of Manasseh, they gave them Taanach and Gath-rimmon, each with its common land: two towns. 26 The number of the towns belonging to the rest of the Kohathite families with their common land was ten.

27 The Gershonite families of the Levites received, out of the share of the half tribe of Manasseh, Golan in Bashan, a city of refuge for the homicide, and Be-ashtaroth, each with its common land: two towns. 28 From the tribe of Issachar they received Kishon, Daberath, 29 Jarmuth, and En-gannim, each with its common land: four towns. 30 From the tribe of Asher they received Mishal, Abdon, 31 Helkath, and Rehob, each with its common land: four towns. 32 From the tribe of Naphtali they received Kedesh in Galilee, a city of refuge for the homicide, Hammoth-dor, and Kartan, each with its common land: three towns. 33 The number of the towns of the Gershonite families with their common land was thirteen.

34 From the tribe of Zebulun the rest of the Merarite families of the Levites received Jokneam, Kartah, 35 Rimmon, and Nahalal, each with its common land: four towns. 36 East of the Jordan at Jericho, from the tribe of Reuben they were given Bezer-in-the-wilderness on the tableland, a city of refuge for the homicide, Jahaz, 37 Kedemoth, and Mephaath, each with its common land: four towns. 38 From the tribe of Gad they received Ramoth in Gilead, a city of refuge for the homicide, Mahanaim, 39 Heshbon, and Jazer, each with its common land: four towns in all. 40 Twelve towns in all fell by lot to the rest of the Merarite families of the Levites.

41 The towns of the Levites within the Israelite holdings numbered forty-eight in all, with their common land. 42 Each town had its common land round it, and it was the same for all of them.

43 Thus the LORD gave Israel all the land which he had sworn to give to their forefathers; they occupied it and settled in it. 44 The LORD gave them security on every side as he had sworn to their forefathers. Of all their enemies not a man could withstand them; the LORD delivered all their enemies into their hands. 45 Not a word of the LORD's promises to the house of Israel went unfulfilled; they all came true.

22 At that time Joshua summoned the Reubenites, the Gadites, and the half tribe of Manasseh, 2 and said to them, 'You have observed all the commands of Moses the servant of the LORD, and you have obeyed me in every command I laid on you. 3 All this time you have not deserted your kinsmen; right up to the present day you have faithfully observed the charge laid on you by the LORD your God. 4 The LORD your God has now given your kinsmen security as he promised them. Now you may return to your homes, to your own land which Moses the servant of the LORD assigned to you east of the Jordan. 5 But be very careful to keep the commands and the law which Moses the servant of the LORD gave you: to love the LORD your God; to conform to all his ways; to observe his commandments; to hold fast to him; to serve him with your whole heart and soul.' 6 Joshua blessed them and dismissed them, and they went to their homes. 7-8 When he sent them away with his blessing, he said: 'Go to your homes richly laden, with great herds, with silver and gold, copper and iron, and with large stores of clothing. See that you share with your kinsmen the spoil you have taken from your enemies.'

To one half of the tribe of Manasseh Moses had given territory in Bashan; to the other half Joshua gave territory west of the Jordan among their kinsmen.

9 So at Shiloh in Canaan the Reubenites, the Gadites, and the half tribe of Manasseh parted from the rest of the Israelites to go into Gilead, the land which belonged to them according to the decree of the LORD given through Moses. 10 When these tribes came to

21:27 **Be-ashtaroth:** *prob. rdg; Heb.* Be-eshterah.
21:29 **Jarmuth:** *or, with Gk,* Remeth, *cp. 19:21.*
21:35 **Rimmon:** *prob. rdg, cp. 19:13, 1 Chr. 6:77; Heb.* Dimnah.   21:36–37 *Some important Heb. MSS omit these verses.*

21.43–22.34: The return of the Transjordan tribes. The conquest complete, the two and one-half tribes were

Geliloth by the Jordan, they built there by the river a great altar for all to see. ¹¹ The Israelites heard that the Reubenites, the Gadites, and the half tribe of Manasseh had built the altar facing the land of Canaan, at Geliloth by the Jordan opposite the Israelite side, ¹² and, at the news, the whole Israelite community assembled at Shiloh to march against them.

¹³ At the same time the Israelites sent Phinehas son of Eleazar the priest into the land of Gilead, to the Reubenites, the Gadites, and the half tribe of Manasseh; ¹⁴ he was accompanied by ten leading men, one from each of the tribes of Israel, all of them heads of households among the clans of Israel. ¹⁵ They came to the Reubenites, the Gadites, and the half tribe of Manasseh in the land of Gilead, and remonstrated with them: ¹⁶ 'We speak for the whole community of the LORD,' they declared. 'What is this treachery you have committed against the God of Israel? Are you ceasing to follow the LORD, and are you building your own altar this day in defiance of the LORD? ¹⁷ Remember our offence at Peor, for which a plague struck the community of the LORD; to this day we have not been purified from it. Was that offence so slight ¹⁸ that you dare cease to follow the LORD today? If today you defy the LORD, tomorrow he will be angry with the whole community of Israel. ¹⁹ If the land you have taken is unclean, then cross over to the LORD's own land, where the Tabernacle of the LORD now rests, and take a share of it with us. But do not defy the LORD and involve us in your defiance by building an altar of your own besides the altar of the LORD our God. ²⁰ Remember the treachery of Achan son of Zerah, who defied the ban, and the whole community of Israel suffered for it; he was not the only one who paid with his life for that sin.'

²¹ In reply the Reubenites, the Gadites, and the half tribe of Manasseh said to the heads of the clans of Israel: ²² 'The LORD the God of gods, the LORD the God of gods, he knows, and Israel must know: if this had been an act of defiance or treachery against the LORD, you could not save us today. ²³ If we had built ourselves an altar and meant to forsake the

LORD, or had offered whole-offerings and grain-offerings on it, or had presented shared-offerings, the LORD himself would exact punishment. ²⁴ The truth is that we have done this for fear that the day may come when your children will say to ours, "What have you to do with the LORD, the God of Israel? ²⁵ The LORD put the Jordan as a boundary between us and you. You have no share in the LORD, you Reubenites and Gadites." So your children would prevent ours from worshipping the LORD.

²⁶ 'We resolved to build an altar, not for whole-offerings and sacrifices, ²⁷ but as a witness between us and you, and between the generations to come. Thus we shall be able to perform service before the LORD, as we do now, with our whole-offerings, our sacrifices, and our shared-offerings; and your children will never be able to say to our children in time to come, "You have no share in the LORD." ²⁸ And we thought, if ever they do say this to us and to our descendants, we will point to this copy of the altar of the LORD which we have made, not for whole-offerings and not for sacrifices, but as a witness between us and you. ²⁹ God forbid that we should defy the LORD and forsake him now by building another altar for whole-offerings, grain-offerings, and sacrifices, in addition to the altar of the LORD our God which stands in front of his tabernacle.'

³⁰ When Phinehas the priest and the leaders of the community, the heads of the Israelite clans, who were with him, heard what the Reubenites, Gadites, and Manassites had to say, they were satisfied. ³¹ Phinehas son of Eleazar the priest said to the Reubenites, Gadites, and Manassites, 'Now we know that the LORD is in our midst; you have not acted treacherously against the LORD, but have preserved all Israel from punishment at his hand.'

³² Phinehas son of Eleazar the priest and the leaders left the Reubenites and the Gadites in Gilead and made their report to the

22:10 **Geliloth . . . Jordan:** *prob. rdg; Heb. adds* which was in Canaan.   22:24 **for fear:** *so Syriac; Heb. adds* from a word.

free to go home (1.12–18). **22.12:** *Shiloh* was the place of the Ark of the Covenant and the Tent of Meeting and its adherents would be opposed to the multiplication of altars. **17:** *Offence at Peor:* Num. 25.3–5. **20:** *Treachery of Achan:* see 7.1. **22–29:** The altar is considered only a memorial, *a witness* between the tribes on the two sides of the Jordan; see v. 34.

Israelites in Canaan. ³³The Israelites were satisfied, and they blessed God and thought no more of attacking and ravaging the land where Reuben and Gad had settled. ³⁴The Reubenites and Gadites declared, 'The altar is a witness between us that the LORD is God,' and they named it 'Witness'.

Joshua's farewell and death

23 A LONG time had passed since the LORD had given Israel security from all their enemies around them, and Joshua was now very old. ²He summoned all Israel, their elders and heads of families, their judges and officers, and said to them, 'I am now an old man, far advanced in years. ³You have seen for yourselves everything the LORD your God has done to all these peoples for your sake; it was the LORD God himself who fought for you. ⁴I have allotted to you tribe by tribe your holdings, the land of all the peoples that I have wiped out and of all these that remain between the Jordan and the Great Sea which lies towards the setting sun. ⁵The LORD your God himself drove them out at your approach; he dispossessed them to make way for you, and you occupied their land, as the LORD your God had promised you.

⁶'Be very resolute therefore to observe and perform everything written in the book of the law of Moses, without swerving either to the right or to the left. ⁷You must not associate with these peoples that are still here among you; you must not invoke their gods or swear by them or bow down to them in worship. ⁸You must hold fast to the LORD your God as you have done up to this day.

⁹'The LORD has driven out great and powerful nations before you; to this day not a man of them has withstood you. ¹⁰One of you can rout a thousand, because the LORD your God fights for you, as he promised. ¹¹For your own sakes be very careful to love the LORD your God. ¹²But if you do turn away

and attach yourselves to the peoples still remaining among you, and intermarry with them and associate with them and they with you, ¹³then be sure that the LORD will not continue to drive out those peoples from before you. They will be snares to entrap you, whips for your backs, and barbed hooks in your eyes, until you perish from this good land which the LORD your God has given you.

¹⁴'Now, as you see, I am going the way of all mortals. You know in your heart of hearts, all of you, that nothing the LORD your God promised you has failed to come true, not one word of it. ¹⁵But the same LORD God who has kept his word to you to such good effect can equally bring every kind of evil on you, until he has rooted you out from this good land which he has given you. ¹⁶If you violate the covenant which the LORD your God has laid upon you and go and serve other gods and worship them, then the LORD's anger will be roused against you and the good land he has given you will soon see you no more.'

24 Joshua assembled all the tribes of Israel at Shechem. He summoned the elders of Israel, the heads of families, the judges and officers. When they presented themselves before God, ²Joshua said to all the people: 'This is the word of the LORD the God of Israel: Long ago your forefathers, including Terah the father of Abraham and Nahor, lived beyond the Euphrates and served other gods. ³I took your ancestor Abraham from beside the Euphrates and led him through the length and breadth of Canaan. I gave him many descendants: I gave him Isaac, ⁴and to Isaac I gave Jacob and Esau. I assigned the hill-country of Seir to Esau as his possession; Jacob and his sons went down to Egypt.

⁵'Later I sent Moses and Aaron, and I struck the Egyptians with plagues—you know well what I did among them—and af-

22:34 **'Witness':** *so some MSS; others omit.*

23.1–16: Joshua's farewell and death. See Moses' farewell, Deut. ch. 31.

24.1–33: The covenant at Shechem. The generation born in the wilderness makes a covenant with the LORD similar to the one which their ancestors had entered into at Sinai; see Exod. 24.1–11; 34.27–28; compare Josh. 8.30–35. Some scholars think that involved here were clans related to Israel who had not taken part in the Exodus events. **1:** *Shechem,* in the center of the country, was ideally located for a gathering of the tribes; see 1 Kgs. ch. 12. Its religious history, too, made it ideal for the making of a covenant: see Gen. 12.6–7;

ter that I brought you out; [6] I brought your forefathers out of Egypt, but at the Red Sea the Egyptians sent their chariots and cavalry to pursue them. [7] When they appealed to the LORD, he put a screen of darkness between you and the Egyptians, and brought the sea down on them to engulf them; you saw for yourselves what I did to Egypt.

'For a long time you lived in the wilderness, [8] and then I brought you into the land of the Amorites who lived east of the Jordan. They fought against you, but I delivered them into your power; you took possession of their country, when I destroyed them before you. [9] The king of Moab, Balak son of Zippor, took the field against Israel. He sent for Balaam son of Beor to lay a curse on you, [10] but I would not listen to Balaam. Instead of that he was constrained to bless you, and so I saved you from Balak's clutches. [11] Then you crossed the Jordan and came to Jericho. Its people fought against you, but I delivered them into your hands. [12] I spread panic before your advance, and it was this, not your sword or your bow, that drove out the two kings of the Amorites. [13] I gave you land on which you had not laboured, towns which you had not built; you have settled in those towns and you eat the produce of vineyards and olive groves which you did not plant.

[14] 'Now hold the LORD in awe, and serve him in loyalty and truth. Put away the gods your fathers served beyond the Euphrates and in Egypt, and serve the LORD. [15] But if it does not please you to serve the LORD, choose here and now whom you will serve: the gods whom your forefathers served beyond the Euphrates, or the gods of the Amorites in whose land you are living. But I and my family, we shall serve the LORD.'

[16] The people answered, 'God forbid that we should forsake the LORD to serve other gods!' They declared: [17] 'The LORD our God it was who brought us and our forefathers up from Egypt, that land of slavery; it was he who displayed those great signs before our eyes, who guarded us on all our wanderings

among the many peoples through whose lands we passed. [18] The LORD drove out before us the Amorites and all the peoples who lived in that country. We too shall serve the LORD; he is our God.'

[19] Joshua said to the people, 'You may not be able to serve the LORD. He is a holy God, a jealous God, and he will not forgive your rebellion and your sins. [20] If you forsake the LORD and serve foreign deities, he will turn and bring disaster on you and make an end of you, even though he once brought you prosperity.' [21] The people answered, 'No; we shall serve the LORD.' [22] He said to them, 'You are witnesses against yourselves that you have chosen the LORD and will serve him.' 'Yes,' they answered, 'we are witnesses.' [23] 'Then here and now banish the foreign gods that are among you,' he said to them, 'and turn your hearts to the LORD the God of Israel.' [24] The people replied, 'We shall serve the LORD our God and his voice we shall obey.'

[25] So Joshua made a covenant for the people that day; he drew up a statute and an ordinance for them in Shechem [26] and recorded its terms in the book of the law of God. He took a great stone and set it up there under the terebinth in the sanctuary of the LORD. [27] He said to all the people, 'You see this stone — it will be a witness against us; for it has heard all the words which the LORD has spoken to us. If you renounce your God, it will be a witness against you.' [28] Then Joshua dismissed the people, each man to his allotted holding.

[29] After these events, Joshua son of Nun, the servant of the LORD, died at the age of a hundred and ten. [30] They buried him within his own holding in Timnath-serah to the north of Mount Gaash in the hill-country of Ephraim. [31] Israel served the LORD throughout the lifetime of Joshua and of the elders

24:6 **Red Sea:** *or* sea of Reeds.
24:11 **against you:** *prob. rdg; Heb. adds* Amorites, Perizzites, Canaanites, Hittites, Girgashites, Hivites, and Jebusites.

33.18–20. **2–13:** Joshua recalls the LORD's interventions in favor of Israel; see Deut. 6.21–23; 26.5–9. **14–24:** Israel pledges loyalty to the LORD. **25–28:** The covenant is established. **25:** The Canaanite god worshiped at Shechem was called Baal-berith or El-berith, "god of the covenant" (see Judg. 9.4, 46); hence the city had covenant associations for the Canaanites too. **26:** Sacred trees were often connected with ancient sanctuaries (Gen. 12.6; 13.18; 35.4, 8; Judg. 9.6), as were stone pillars (Gen. 28.18; Exod. 24.4). **29–31:** Death and burial

who outlived him and who knew all that the
LORD had done for Israel.

³² The bones of Joseph, which the Israelites
had brought up from Egypt, were buried in
Shechem, in the plot of land which Jacob had
bought from the sons of Hamor father of
Shechem for a hundred sheep; and they
passed into the ancestral holding of the
house of Joseph.

³³ Eleazar son of Aaron died and was bur-
ied in the hill which had been assigned to
Phinehas his son in the hill-country of
Ephraim.

24:32 **sheep:** *or* pieces of money.

of Joshua. **30:** *Timnath-serah:* see 19.49–50. **32–33:** The burial of Joseph and Eleazar. *Brought up from Egypt:*
see Exod. 13.19. *Which Jacob bought:* Gen. 33.19.

THE BOOK OF
Judges

Whereas the Book of Joshua deals with the conquest of Canaan, Judges deals with the subsequent settlement. Largely an account of battles lasting through several generations before the country was securely in Israel's hands, Judges preserves traditions of various tribes and the exploits of their particular heroes, the "judges" (see 2.16 n.).

The opening section (1.1–2.5) describes the settlement of the tribes. It implies that much of Canaan was not yet subjugated, despite the view in Joshua of a complete conquest. The main part of the book, after a moralizing introduction (2.6–3.6), recalls the contribution of the individual judges who are given as a total of twelve, though long narratives are about only five: Ehud (3.12–30); Deborah (chs. 4–5); Gideon (chs. 6–8), ch. 9 treats his wicked son, Abimelech; Jephthah (10.6–12.7); and Samson (chs. 13–16). The other seven are to be found in 3.7–11, 31; 10.1–5; and 12.8–15. An appendix contains an account of the migration of Dan (chs. 17–18) and the trespass of the Benjaminites (chs. 19–21).

The final editor, in preserving these colorful stories, was concerned with the moral lesson that loyalty to God brings national success and disloyalty guarantees disaster. This is the theme also of Deuteronomy, especially Deut. ch. 28. Modern criticism considers Judges to be part of the "Deuteronomic history" (see Introduction to Josh.).

Completing the conquest of Canaan

1 AFTER the death of Joshua the Israelites enquired of the LORD which tribe should go up first to attack the Canaanites. ²The LORD answered, 'Judah is to go up; I have delivered the country into their power.' ³The Judahites said to their kinsmen, the Simeonites, 'Go up with us into the territory allotted to us, and let us do battle with the Canaanites, and we in turn shall go with you into your territory.' So the Simeonites went with them. ⁴Judah advanced to the attack, and the LORD delivered the Canaanites and the Perizzites into their hands, so that they slaughtered ten thousand of them at Bezek. ⁵At Bezek they came upon Adoni-bezek, en-

gaged him in battle, and defeated the Canaanites and Perizzites. ⁶Adoni-bezek fled, but they pursued him, and having taken him prisoner cut off his thumbs and his big toes. ⁷Adoni-bezek said, 'I once had seventy kings with their thumbs and big toes cut off who were picking up the scraps under my table. What I have done, God has done to me.' He was brought to Jerusalem, and he died there.

⁸The men of Judah made an assault on Jerusalem and captured it; they put its people to the sword, and set fire to the city. ⁹Then they turned south to fight the Canaanites living in the hill-country, the Negeb, and the Shephelah. ¹⁰Judah attacked the Canaanites in Hebron, formerly called Kiriath-arba, and defeated Sheshai, Ahiman, and

1.1–2.5: The conquest of Canaan completed. This historical prologue, considered by most scholars to be an ancient document, or derived from one, describes the arduous attempts at conquest by isolated tribes, with the native inhabitants being subjugated rather than exterminated; contrast Josh. chs. 10–11; see Josh. 13.13 n. **1.1–21: The course of conquests.** Compare Josh. ch. 15. Many scholars hold that the ancient document (1.1–2.5 n.) has been shaped to enhance Judah, in which territory Jerusalem lay. **1:** *After the death of Joshua* is probably added so as to accord with Josh. 24.29; it contradicts the ensuing narrative; see 2.6–8. They *enquired of the LORD,* probably by using sacred lots; see Exod. 28.15 n. **3:** *Simeon:* see Josh. 19.1–9 n. **4:** *Perizzites:* see Gen. 13.7; Deut. 7.1. The location of *Bezek* is uncertain. **5:** *Adoni-bezek* is possibly the same as the Adoni-zedek, king of Jerusalem, of Josh. 10.1–3. **8:** *Jerusalem* is portrayed as captured at a later time by David in 2 Sam. 5.6–9. **9:** *Negeb:* the southern desert. *Shephelah:* see Josh. 11.2 n. **10:** *Hebron:* see Josh.

Talmai. [11] From there they marched against the inhabitants of Debir, formerly called Kiriath-sepher.

[12] Caleb said, 'I shall give my daughter Achsah in marriage to the man who attacks and captures Kiriath-sepher.' [13] Othniel, son of Caleb's younger brother Kenaz, captured it, and Caleb gave him his daughter Achsah. [14] When she became his wife, Othniel induced her to ask her father for a piece of land. She dismounted from her donkey, and Caleb asked her, 'What do you want?' [15] She replied, 'Grant me this favour: you have put me in this arid Negeb; you must give me pools of water as well.' So Caleb gave her the upper pool and the lower pool.

[16] The descendants of the Kenite, Moses' father-in-law, went up with the Judahites from the city of palm trees to the wilderness of Judah which is in the Negeb of Arad, and they settled among the Amalekites. [17] The Judahites then set out with their kinsmen the Simeonites, attacked the Canaanites in Zephath, and utterly destroyed it; hence the town was given the name Hormah. [18] Judah took Gaza, Ashkelon, and Ekron, along with the territory of each. [19] As the LORD was with the Judahites, they occupied the hill-country; but they failed to drive out the inhabitants of the plain because they had iron-clad chariots. [20] As Moses had directed, Hebron was given to Caleb, who drove out the three Anakim.

[21] But the Benjamites failed to drive out the Jebusite inhabitants of Jerusalem, and the Jebusites have lived on in Jerusalem alongside the Benjamites to this day.

[22] The men of Joseph also attacked Bethel, and the LORD was with them. [23] They reconnoitred Bethel, formerly called Luz, [24] and when the spies saw a man coming out of the town they said to him, 'Show us a way into the town, and we will see that you come to no harm.' [25] When he showed them how to enter, they put the town to the sword, but let the man and his family go unscathed. [26] The man went into Hittite country, where he built a town, which he called Luz, the name it bears to this day.

[27] Manasseh failed to drive out the inhabitants of Beth-shean, Taanach, Dor, Ibleam, and Megiddo and their villages; the Canaanites maintained their hold on that region. [28] Later, when Israel became strong, they put them to forced labour, but never completely drove them out.

[29] Ephraim failed to drive out the Canaanites who lived in Gezer; the Canaanites lived among them there.

[30] Zebulun failed to drive out the inhabitants of Kitron and Nahalol; the Canaanites lived among them and were put to forced labour.

[31] Asher failed to drive out the inhabitants of Acco and Sidon, of Ahlab, Achzib, Helbah, Aphik, and Rehob. [32] Thus the Asherites lived among the Canaanite inhabitants and did not drive them out.

[33] Naphtali failed to drive out the inhabitants of Beth-shemesh and of Beth-anath, and lived among the Canaanite inhabitants, putting the inhabitants of Beth-shemesh and Beth-anath to forced labour.

[34] The Amorites pressed the Danites back into the hill-country and did not allow them to come down into the plain. [35] The Amorites maintained their hold on Mount Heres and on Aijalon and Shaalbim, but the Joseph tribes increased their pressure on them until they reduced them to forced labour.

[36] The boundary of the Edomites ran from the ascent of Akrabbim, upwards from Sela.

1:14 **Othniel induced her:** *so Gk; Heb.* she induced him. **dismounted:** *or* made a noise.
1:16 **Amalekites:** *so some Gk MSS; Heb.* people.
1:17 **Hormah:** *that is* Destruction.   1:31 **Ahlab:** Mehalbeh *in Josh.* 19:29.   1:36 **Edomites:** *so one form of Gk; Heb.* Amorites.

10.36–37. According to v. 20 and Josh. 14.6–15 and 15.13–14, it was given to the clan of Caleb. **11–15:** This story occurs also in Josh. 15.15–19. **11:** *Debir:* probably the modern Tell Beit Mirsim, southwest of Hebron. **16:** The Kenites, a nomadic tribe, here mentioned as allies of Judah during the invasion of Canaan, settled among the Amalekites. Because of their aid to Israel, they are spared by Saul (1 Sam. 15.6). *Amalekites:* see Exod. 17.8 n. **17:** *Zephath:* a city in the Negeb; *Hormah* means "destruction." Some scholars think this reference is the same as the incident in Num. 21.3. **18:** Gaza, Ashkelon, and Ekron are three of the five Philistine cities; see Josh. 13.2 n. This account of their capture seems to anticipate 2 Sam. 8.1; Sept., however, says specifically that Judah "did not" take them; the negative may have been omitted from the MT by a copyist. **19–21:** See Josh. 13.13 n. **19:** The Philistines had a monopoly on iron; see 1 Sam. 13.19–22.

1.22–29: Conquests of the Joseph tribes. See Josh. chs. 16–17 and 13.13 n. **22–26:** See Josh. 7.2 n.

Result of disobedience

2 THE angel of the LORD went up from Gilgal to Bokim, and said, 'I brought you up out of Egypt and into the country which I promised on oath I would give to your forefathers. I said: I shall never annul my covenant with you, ²and you in turn must make no covenant with the inhabitants of this country; you must pull down their altars. But you did not obey me, and look what you have done! ³So I said, I shall not drive them out before you; they will entice you astray, and their gods will become a snare for you.' ⁴When the angel of the LORD said this to the Israelites, they all broke into loud lamentation. ⁵They called the place Bokim and offered sacrifices there to the LORD.

⁶JOSHUA dismissed the people, and the Israelites went off to occupy the country, each to his allotted holding. ⁷The people served the LORD as long as Joshua and the elders who outlived him were alive—everyone, that is, who had witnessed all the great deeds the LORD had done for Israel. ⁸At the age of a hundred and ten Joshua son of Nun, the servant of the LORD, died, ⁹and was buried within his own holding in Timnath-heres to the north of Mount Gaash in the hill-country of Ephraim.

¹⁰When that whole generation was gathered to its forefathers, and was succeeded by another generation, who did not acknowledge the LORD and did not know what he had done for Israel, ¹¹then the Israelites did what was wrong in the eyes of the LORD by serving the baalim. ¹²They forsook the LORD, their fathers' God who had brought them out of Egypt, and went after other gods, the gods of the peoples among whom they lived; by bowing down before them they provoked the LORD to anger; ¹³they forsook the LORD and served the baalim and the ashtaroth. ¹⁴In his anger the LORD made them the prey of bands of raiders and plunderers; he sold them into the power of their enemies around them, so that they could no longer stand against them. ¹⁵Every time they went out to do battle the LORD brought disaster on them, as he had said when he gave them his solemn warning; and they were in dire straits.

The first judges

¹⁶THEN the LORD raised up judges to rescue them from the marauding bands, ¹⁷yet even to their judges they did not listen. They prostituted themselves by worshipping other gods and bowed down before them; all too soon they abandoned the path of obedience to the LORD's commands which their forefathers had followed. They did not obey the LORD. ¹⁸Whenever the LORD set up a judge over them, he was with that judge, and kept them safe from their enemies so long as the judge lived. The LORD would relent when he heard them groaning under oppression and tyranny. ¹⁹But on the death of the judge they would relapse into corruption deeper than that of their predecessors and go after other gods; serving them and bowing before them, they would give up none of their evil practices and wilful ways. ²⁰So the LORD's anger was roused against Israel and he said, 'Because this nation has violated the covenant which I laid upon their forefathers, and has not obeyed me, ²¹I for my part shall not drive

2:1 **I brought:** *prob. rdg; Heb.* I will bring.
2:5 **Bokim:** *that is* Weepers.

1.30–36: The conquests of the Galilee area. See Josh. chs. 18–19 and 13.13 n. **36:** Boundary of Edom and Judah; see Num. 34.3–5.

2.1–5: The moral reason for the delay in the conquest is Israel's infidelity. See Deut. ch. 28. In 1.28–35 the reason was the enemies' strength. **1:** *The angel:* the words that follow, *I brought you up out of Egypt,* indicate God rather than an angel as the speaker; see Gen. 16.7 n. *Gilgal:* see Josh. 4.19 n. *Bokim* is probably Bethel; the word means "weepers" (vv. 4–5).

2.6–3.6: Second introduction. An editor explains the whole history of the age in terms of recurring cycles of prosperity, apostasy, punishment, repentance, and deliverance; "judges" are the deliverers who bring the people back from idolatry (vv. 16–18); deprived of judges the people relapse (v. 19). **8:** Joshua's death: see Josh. 24.29. **11–13:** *Baalim:* male Canaanite deities; *Ashtaroth,* female Canaanite deities. **15:** *The LORD brought disaster on them:* all is attributed to God; secondary causes are passed over. **16:** The *judges* were military heroes who defended and delivered the people from oppression and then continued to govern them; a divine impulse moves them (see 3.10). **22–23:** The native population is allowed to survive to *test* Israel's loyalty to God; see out before them one individual of all the nations which Joshua left at his death. 22 Through them I shall test Israel, to see whether or not they will keep strictly to the way of the LORD as their forefathers did.' 23 So the LORD left those nations alone and made no haste to drive them out or give them into Joshua's hands.

3 As a means of testing all the Israelites who had not taken part in the battles for Canaan, the LORD left these nations, 2 his purpose being to train succeeding generations of Israel in the art of warfare, or those at least who had not learnt it in former times. 3 They were: the five lords of the Philistines, all the Canaanites, the Sidonians, and the Hivites who lived in Mount Lebanon and from Mount Baal-hermon as far as Lebo-hamath. 4 His purpose also was to test whether the Israelites would obey the commandments which the LORD had given to their forefathers through Moses. 5 Thus the Israelites lived among the Canaanites, the Hittites, the Amorites, the Perizzites, the Hivites, and the Jebusites; 6 they took their daughters in marriage and gave their own daughters to their sons; and they served their gods.

7 The Israelites did what was wrong in the eyes of the LORD: forgetting the LORD their God, they served the baalim and the asheroth. 8 The anger of the LORD was roused against Israel and he sold them into the power of King Cushan-rishathaim of Aramnaharaim, who kept them in subjection for eight years. 9 Then the Israelites cried to the LORD for help, and to deliver them he raised up Othniel son of Caleb's younger brother Kenaz, and he set them free. 10 The spirit of the LORD came upon him and he became judge over Israel. He took the field, and the LORD delivered King Cushan-rishathaim of Aram into his hands; Othniel was too strong for

him. 11 Thus the land was at peace for forty years until Othniel son of Kenaz died.

12 Once again the Israelites did what was wrong in the eyes of the LORD, and because of this he roused King Eglon of Moab against Israel. 13 Eglon mustered the Ammonites and the Amalekites, attacked Israel, and took possession of the city of palm trees. 14 The Israelites were subject to King Eglon of Moab for eighteen years.

15 Then they cried to the LORD for help, and to deliver them he raised up Ehud son of Gera the Benjamite; he was left-handed. The Israelites sent him to hand over their tribute to King Eglon. 16 Ehud had made himself a two-edged sword, about eighteen inches long, which he fastened on his right side under his clothes 17 when he brought the tribute to King Eglon. Eglon was a very fat man. 18 After Ehud had finished presenting the tribute, he sent on the men who had carried it, 19 while he himself turned back from the Carved Stones at Gilgal. 'My lord king,' he said, 'I have a message for you in private.' Eglon called for silence and dismissed all his attendants. 20 Ehud then approached him as he sat in the roof-chamber of his summer palace. He said, 'Your majesty, I have a message from God for you.' As Eglon rose from his seat, 21 Ehud reached with his left hand, drew the sword from his right side, and drove it into Eglon's belly. 22 The hilt went in after the blade and the fat closed over the blade, for he did not draw the sword out but left it protruding behind. 23 Ehud then went out to the porch, where he shut the door on him and fastened it.

24 After he had gone, Eglon's servants came and, finding the doors fastened, they said, 'He must be relieving himself in the

3:16 **about . . . long:** *lit.* a short cubit in length.
3:22 **behind:** *Heb. word of uncertain meaning.*
3:23 **porch:** *Heb. word of uncertain meaning.*

3.1–4. **3.3:** See Josh. 13.2–5. **4:** See Deut. 8.2; Judg. 2.22. **5:** See Deut. 7.1.

3.7–11: Othniel. The first judge is from Judah, a tribe of special interest to the author; see 1.1–21 n. The story may be related to 1.12–13. **7:** *Asheroth* is the plural of Asherah, the name of a goddess; see 2.11–13 n. **8:** *Sold:* see 2.15 n. *Cushan-rishathaim* is unknown elsewhere. *Aram-naharaim,* "Aram of Two Rivers," is a name for Mesopotamia. The geographical improbability of an invasion from Mesopotamia leads some to conjecture that "Aram" should be emended to the more probable "Edom." **10:** *The Spirit of the LORD came upon him:* the judges were impelled or inspired as the prophets were. **11:** *Land was at peace:* an editorial formula frequent in Judg.

3.12–30: Ehud and delivery from the Moabites. 12: *Moab* was immediately east of the Dead Sea, *Ammon* just north of Moab. *Amalek:* see Exod. 17.8–16 n. **13:** *City of palm trees:* this is usually considered to allude to Jericho; see 1.16. **19:** *Carved Stones at Gilgal:* see Josh. 4.1–5.1 n.

closet of his summer palace.' 25 They waited until they became alarmed and, when he still did not open the door of the roof-chamber, they took the key and opened the door; and there was their master lying dead on the floor.

26 While they had been waiting, Ehud had made good his escape; he passed the Carved Stones and escaped to Seirah. 27 Once there, he sounded the trumpet in the hill-country of Ephraim, and the Israelites went down from the hills with him at their head. 28 He said to them, 'Follow me, for the LORD has delivered your enemies, the Moabites, into your hands.' They went down after him, and held the fords of the Jordan against the Moabites, allowing no one to cross. 29 They killed at that time some ten thousand Moabites, all of them stalwart and valiant fighters; not one escaped. 30 Moab became subject to Israel on that day, and the land was at peace for eighty years.

31 After Ehud there was Shamgar son of Anath. He killed six hundred Philistines with an ox-goad, and he too delivered Israel.

Deborah

4 AFTER Ehud's death the Israelites once again did what was wrong in the eyes of the LORD, 2 and he sold them into the power of Jabin, the Canaanite king who ruled in Hazor. The commander of his forces was Sisera, who lived in Harosheth-of-the-Gentiles. 3 The Israelites cried to the LORD for help, because Sisera with his nine hundred iron-clad chariots had oppressed Israel harshly for twenty years.

4 At that time Deborah wife of Lappidoth, a prophetess, was judge in Israel. 5 It was her custom to sit under the Palm Tree of Deborah between Ramah and Bethel in the hill-country of Ephraim, and Israelites seeking a judgement went up to her. 6 She sent for Barak son of Abinoam from Kedesh in Naphtali and said to him, 'This is the command of the LORD the God of Israel: Go and lead out ten thousand men from Naphtali and Zebulun and bring them with you to Mount Tabor. 7 I shall draw out to you at the wadi Kishon Jabin's commander Sisera, along with his chariots and troops, and deliver him into your power.' 8 Barak answered, 'If you go with me, I shall go, but if you will not go, neither shall I.' 9 'Certainly I shall go with you,' she said, 'but this venture will bring you no glory, because the LORD will leave Sisera to fall into the hands of a woman.' Deborah set off with Barak and went to Kedesh. 10 Barak mustered Zebulun and Naphtali to Kedesh and marched up with ten thousand followers; Deborah went up with him.

11 Now Heber the Kenite had parted company with the Kenites, the descendants of Hobab, Moses' brother-in-law, and he had pitched his tent at Elon-bezaanannim near Kedesh.

12 When it was reported to Sisera that Barak son of Abinoam had gone up to Mount Tabor, 13 he mustered all nine hundred of his iron-clad chariots, along with all the troops he had, and marched from Harosheth-of-the-Gentiles to the wadi Kishon. 14 Deborah said to Barak, 'Up! This day the LORD is to give Sisera into your hands. See, the LORD has marched out at your head!' Barak came down from Mount Tabor with ten thousand men at his back, 15 and the LORD threw Sisera and all his chariots and army into panic-stricken rout before Barak's onslaught; Sisera himself dismounted from his chariot and fled on foot. 16 Barak pursued the chariots and the troops as far as Harosheth, and the whole army was put to the sword; not a man was left alive.

28: The Moabites had been occupying an area west of the Jordan. 29: The massacre of the Moabites.

3.31: **Shamgar.** This notably brief passage is to be found in some manuscripts after 16.31; Shamgar is mentioned in 5.6. The verse separates the stories of Ehud and Deborah, linked together in 4.1. The allusion here to the Philistines also points to a later period; see Josh. 13.2 n.

4.1–5.31: **Deborah.** The victory of Deborah and Barak over the Canaanites is told twice, in prose (ch. 4), and in poetry (ch. 5). Chapter 5 is far older than ch. 4. **2:** *Jabin* is not mentioned in ch. 5; in Josh. 11.1–5 he organizes a coalition against Joshua. *Hazor:* see Josh. 11.1 n. *Harosheth-of-the-Gentiles* is tentatively identified with Tell Amr on the river Kishon; see v. 7 n. **3:** *Iron-clad chariots:* the Hebrews as yet were unskilled in working in iron (1.19 n.; Josh. 17.16; 1 Sam. 13.19–22) and lacked such chariots. **6:** *Naphtali* and *Zebulun* were two of the Galilean tribes; see 1.30, 33. *Mount Tabor:* in Galilee north of the plain of Esdraelon. **7:** *Wadi Kishon:*

¹⁷ Meanwhile Sisera fled on foot to the tent of Jael wife of Heber the Kenite, because King Jabin of Hazor and the household of Heber the Kenite were on friendly terms. ¹⁸ Jael came out to greet Sisera and said, 'Come in, my lord, come in here; do not be afraid.' He went into the tent, and she covered him with a rug. ¹⁹ He said to her, 'Give me some water to drink, for I am thirsty.' She opened a skin of milk, gave him a drink, and covered him again. ²⁰ He said to her, 'Stand at the tent door, and if anyone comes and asks if there is a man here, say "No."' ²¹ But as Sisera lay fast asleep through exhaustion Jael took a tent-peg, picked up a mallet, and, creeping up to him, drove the peg into his temple, so that it went down into the ground, and Sisera died. ²² When Barak came by in pursuit of Sisera, Jael went out to meet him. 'Come,' she said, 'I shall show you the man you are looking for.' He went in with her, and there was Sisera lying dead with the tent-peg in his temple. ²³ That day God gave victory to the Israelites over King Jabin of Canaan, ²⁴ and they pressed home their attacks upon him until he was destroyed.

The song of Deborah and Barak

5 On that day Deborah and Barak son of Abinoam sang this song:

² 'For the leaders, the leaders in Israel,
  for the people who answered the call,
  bless the LORD.
³ Hear, you kings; princes, give ear!
  I shall sing, I shall sing to the LORD,
  making music to the LORD, the God of
    Israel.

⁴ 'LORD, when you set forth from Seir,
  when you marched from the land of
    Edom,
  earth trembled; heaven quaked;
  the clouds streamed down in torrents.
⁵ Mountains shook in fear before the
    LORD, the Lord of Sinai,
  before the LORD, the God of Israel.

⁶ 'In the days of Shamgar son of Anath,
  in the days of Jael, caravans plied no
    longer;
  travellers who had followed the high
    roads
  went round by devious paths.
⁷ Champions there were none,
  none left in Israel,
  until you, Deborah, arose,
  arose as a mother in Israel.
⁸ They chose new gods,
  they consorted with demons.
  Not a shield was to be seen, not a lance
  among forty thousand Israelites.

⁹ 'My heart goes out to you, the marshals
    of Israel;
  you among the people that answered
    the call,
  bless the LORD.
¹⁰ You that sit on saddle-cloths
  riding your tawny she-donkeys,
  and you that take the road on foot,
  ponder on this.
¹¹ Hark, the sound of the merrymakers
  at the places where they draw water!
  There they commemorate the victories
    of the LORD,
  his triumphs as the champion of Israel.

'Down to the gates came the LORD's
    people:
¹² "Rouse yourself, rouse yourself,
    Deborah,
  rouse yourself, break into song.
  Up, Barak! Take prisoners in plenty,
  you son of Abinoam."

¹³ 'Then down marched the column and
    its chieftains,
  the people of the LORD marching down
    like warriors.

4:21 **it went down:** *prob. mng; Heb. obscure.*   5:2 **For
. . . Israel:** *or* For those who had flowing locks in
Israel.   5:7 **you:** *or* I.   5:11 **merrymakers:** *prob.
rdg; Heb. obscure.*   5:13 **column:** *prob. rdg; Heb.
survivor.* **marching down:** *prob. rdg; Heb. adds to me.*

a valley with a westward-flowing stream, north of Mount Carmel. **11:** *Kenite:* see 1.16 n. **5.1–31:** This song is the oldest surviving extended fragment of Heb. literature. At places the text is corrupt and almost unintelligible. **2:** See Tfn. The unbinding of the hair was a war ritual. **4:** The LORD is pictured as coming *from Seir* and *Edom* to help the people; it is the route of the Exodus; note the reference to Sinai in v. 5. The *torrents* here and in v. 21 may refer to a rainstorm which enabled Israelite foot soldiers to overcome the chariots of 4.3, 15. For Israel the storm (v. 21) manifested the presence of the LORD. **6:** *Caravans plied no longer:* it was a time

14 The men of Ephraim rallied in the
vale,
crying, "We are with you, Benjamin!
Your clansmen are here!"
Down came the marshals from Machir,
from Zebulun the bearers of the
musterer's staff.
15 The princes of Issachar were with
Deborah,
Issachar with Barak;
down into the valley they rushed in
pursuit.

'Reuben however was split into factions;
great were their heart-searchings.
16 Why did you linger by the sheepfolds
to listen to the shrill calling of the
shepherds?
17 Gilead stayed beyond Jordan;
and Dan, why did he tarry by the
ships?
Asher remained by the seashore,
by its creeks he stayed.
18 The people of Zebulun risked their
lives;
so did Naphtali on the heights of the
battlefield.

19 'Kings came, they fought;
then fought the kings of Canaan
at Taanach by the waters of Megiddo;
no plunder of silver did they take.
20 The stars fought from heaven,
the stars in their courses fought against
Sisera.
21 The torrent of Kishon swept him away,
the torrent barred his flight, the torrent
of Kishon.
March on in might, my soul!
22 Then hammered the hoofs of his
horses,
his chargers galloped, galloped away.

23 'A curse on Meroz, said the angel of
the LORD;
a curse, a curse on its inhabitants,
because they did not come to the help
of the LORD,
to the help of the LORD and the
fighting men.

24 'Blest above women be Jael
wife of Heber the Kenite;
blest above all women in the tents.
25 He asked for water: she gave him milk,
she offered him curds in a bowl fit for
a chieftain.
26 She reached out her hand for the
tent-peg,
her right hand for the workman's
hammer.
With the hammer she struck Sisera,
crushing his head;
with a shattering blow she pierced his
temple.
27 At her feet he sank, he fell, he lay
prone;
at her feet he sank down and fell.
Where he sank down, there he fell,
done to death.

28 'The mother of Sisera peered through
the lattice,
through the window she peered and
cried,
"Why is his chariot so long in coming?
Why is the clatter of his chariots so
delayed?"
29 The wisest of her ladies answered her,
yes, she found her own answer:

5:14 **rallied:** *prob. rdg; Heb.* their root. **the vale:** *so Gk; Heb.* Amalek.   5:15 **heart-searchings:** *so some MSS; others have an unknown word.*   5:16 **shepherds:** *prob. rdg; Heb. adds* Reuben was split into factions; great were their heart-searchings.

of anarchy. **14:** *Machir:* part of the tribe of Manasseh, established in Gilead east of the Jordan; see Gen. 50.23 and Josh. 13.31. However, because Gilead took no part in this war (v. 17), some scholars think that here Machir is the part of Manasseh west of the Jordan. **15–17:** The distant tribes of *Reuben, Gilead, Dan,* and *Asher* stayed at home. Judah, Simeon, and Levi go unmentioned. *Gilead* may refer to the part of Manasseh east of the Jordan; see v. 14 n. and Josh. 13.29–32, or it may refer to the tribe of Gad; see Josh. 13.24–28. *Dan* appears to be associated with Asher in the north, yet the mention of *ships* suggests Dan's earlier effort to settle near the Philistine coast; see Josh. 19.40–47 n. **19:** *Taanach* and *Megiddo* guarded the passes through the Carmel range. Some scholars think that the mention of *the waters of Megiddo* rather than the city itself indicates that Megiddo was unoccupied at this time; using archaeological evidence they then date the battle here about 1125 B.C.E. **21:** See v. 7 n. **23:** *Meroz* is probably a nearby town which took no part in the battle. **24–27:** Jael kills *Sisera,* the commander of the Canaanite forces; compare 4.17–22. **29–30:** The Canaanite women are ironically pictured as waiting for the *spoil.*

30 "They must be finding spoil, taking
    their shares,
a damsel for each man, two damsels,
booty of dyed stuffs for Sisera,
booty of dyed stuffs,
dyed stuff and brocade, two lengths of
    brocade
to grace the victor's neck."

31 'So perish all your enemies, LORD;
    but let those who love you be like the
    sun rising in strength.'

The land was at peace for forty years.

Gideon

6 THE Israelites did what was wrong in the
eyes of the LORD and he delivered them
into the hands of Midian for seven years.
2 The Midianites were too strong for the Israelites, who were forced to find themselves
hollow places in the mountains, in caves and
fastnesses. 3 If the Israelites had sown seed,
the Midianites and the Amalekites and other
eastern tribes would come up and attack Israel, 4 pitching their camps in the country
and destroying the crops as far as the outskirts of Gaza. They left nothing to support
life in Israel, neither sheep nor ox nor donkey. 5 They came up with their herds and
their tents, swarming like locusts; they and
their camels were past counting. They would
come into the land and lay it waste. 6 The
Israelites, brought to destitution by the Midianites, cried to the LORD for help.

7 When the Israelites cried to the LORD because of what they were suffering from the
Midianites, 8 he sent them a prophet who said
to them, 'These are the words of the LORD
the God of Israel: I brought you up from
Egypt, that land of slavery. 9 I rescued you
from the Egyptians and from all your oppressors, whom I drove out before you to
give you their lands. 10 I said to you, "I am the
LORD your God: do not worship the gods of

the Amorites in whose country you are settling." But you did not listen to me.'
11 The angel of the LORD came to Ophrah
and sat under the terebinth which belonged
to Joash the Abiezrite. While Gideon son of
Joash was threshing wheat in the winepress,
so that he might keep it out of sight of the
Midianites, 12 the angel of the LORD appeared
to him and said, 'You are a brave man, and
the LORD is with you.' 13 'Pray, my lord,' said
Gideon, 'if the LORD really is with us, why has
all this happened to us? What has become of
all those wonderful deeds of his, of which we
have heard from our forefathers, when they
told us how the LORD brought us up from
Egypt? But now the LORD has cast us off and
delivered us into the power of the Midianites.'
14 The LORD turned to him and said, 'Go
and use this strength of yours to free Israel
from the Midianites. It is I who send you.'
15 Gideon said, 'Pray, my lord, how can I save
Israel? Look at my clan: it is the weakest in
Manasseh, and I am the least in my father's
family.' 16 The LORD answered, 'I shall be
with you, and you will lay low all Midian as
one man.' 17 He replied, 'If I stand so well
with you, give me a sign that it is you who
speak to me. 18 Do not leave this place, I beg
you, until I come with my gift and lay it before you.' He answered, 'I shall stay until you
return.'
19 So Gideon went in, and prepared a
young goat and made an ephah of flour into
unleavened bread. He put the meat in a basket, poured the broth into a pot, and brought
it out to the angel under the terebinth. As he
approached, 20 the angel of God said to him,
'Take the meat and the bread, and put them
here on the rock and pour out the broth.'
When he did so, 21 the angel of the LORD
reached out the staff in his hand and touched
the meat and bread with the tip of it. Fire
sprang up from the rock and consumed the
meat and the bread. Then the angel of the
LORD vanished from his sight. 22 Gideon real-

5:31 you: so Syriac; Heb. him.

6.1–8.35: Gideon and delivery from the Midianites, a kindred people (Gen. 25.1–6) who were desert
nomads. **3–4:** These nomadic raiders were pasturing their flocks on Israelite crops. **8:** The appearance of a
prophet, as here, is frequent in the Deuteronomic books, especially Kgs. **10:** You did not listen to me: the
Israelites had adopted the worship of the Baalim who, the native Amorites thought, guaranteed good crops;
see vv. 25–32 and 2.11–13. **11:** The angel of the LORD: see 2.1 n. In v. 14 it is the LORD, not an angel, who
speaks. Terebinth refers to a sacred tree; see Gen. 12.6. The location of Ophrah is not known beyond its being

ized it was the angel of the LORD and said, 'Alas, Lord GOD! Then it is true: I have seen the angel of the LORD face to face.' 23 But the LORD said to him, 'Peace be with you! Do not be afraid; you shall not die.' 24 Gideon built an altar there to the LORD and named it The LORD is Peace. It stands to this day at Oph-rah-of-the-Abiezrites.

25 That night the LORD said to Gideon, 'Take a young bull of your father's, the year-ling bull; tear down the altar of Baal belong-ing to your father, and cut down the sacred pole which stands beside it. 26 Then build an altar of the proper pattern to the LORD your God on the top of this earthwork; take the yearling bull and offer it as a whole-offering with the wood of the sacred pole that you cut down.' 27 Gideon took ten of his servants and did as the LORD had told him; but because he was afraid of his father's family and the peo-ple of the town, he did it by night and not by day. 28 When the people rose early next morning, they found the altar of Baal over-turned, the sacred pole which had stood be-side it cut down, and the yearling bull offered up as a whole-offering on an altar which had been built. 29 They asked among themselves who had done it, and, after searching enqui-ries, they declared it was Gideon son of Jo-ash. 30 The townspeople said to Joash, 'Bring out your son. He has overturned the altar of Baal and cut down the sacred pole beside it; he must die.' 31 But as they crowded round him Joash retorted, 'Are you pleading Baal's cause then? Do you think it is for you to save him? Whoever pleads his cause shall be put to death at dawn. If Baal is a god, and some-one has torn down his altar, let him take up his own cause.' 32 That day Joash named Gid-eon Jerubbaal, saying, 'Let Baal plead his own cause against this man, for he has torn down his altar.'

33 When all the Midianites, the Amalekites, and the eastern tribes joined forces, crossed the river, and encamped in the valley of Jez-reel, 34 the spirit of the LORD took possession of Gideon. He sounded the trumpet to call out the Abiezrites to follow him, 35 and sent messengers all through Manasseh; and they too rallied to him. He sent messengers to Asher, Zebulun, and Naphtali, and they ad-vanced to meet the others.

36 Gideon said to God, 'If indeed you are going to deliver Israel through me as you promised, 37 I shall put a fleece of wool on the threshing-floor, and if there is dew on the fleece while all the ground is dry, then I shall be sure that it is through me you will deliver Israel as you promised.' 38 And that is what happened. When he rose early next day and wrung out the fleece, he squeezed enough dew from it to fill a bowl with water. 39 Gid-eon then said to God, 'Do not be angry with me, but give me leave to speak once again. Allow me, I pray, to make one more test with the fleece. This time let the fleece be dry, and all the ground be covered with dew.' 40 God let it be so that night: the fleece alone was dry, and all over the ground there was dew.

7 Early next morning Jerubbaal, that is Gideon, with all his troops pitched camp at En-harod; the Midianite encampment was in the valley to the north of his by the hill at Moreh. 2 The LORD said to Gideon, 'Those with you are more than I need to deliver Midian into their hands: Israel might claim the glory for themselves and say that it is their own strength that has given them the victory. 3 Make a proclamation now to the army to say that anyone who is afraid or anx-ious is to leave Mount Galud at once and go home.' Twenty-two thousand of them went, and ten thousand remained.

4 'There are still too many,' said the LORD

6:25 the yearling bull: prob. rdg; Heb. the second bull seven years old. beside: or on. 6:26 of ... pattern: or with the stones in rows. earthwork: or stronghold or refuge. 6:32 Jerubbaal: that is Let Baal plead. 6:34 took possession of: lit. clothed itself with. 7:1 En-harod: that is Spring of Fright. 7:3 Mount Galud: prob. rdg; Heb. Mount Gilead.

in Manasseh. The Abiezrites were a small clan within Manasseh; see v. 15. **25–32:** Gideon destroys the altar of Baal. **25:** *The sacred pole:* the object which symbolized the goddess Asherah; see 3.7 n. **32:** This popular explanation of *Jerubbaal, "Let Baal plead,"* is not the natural one; a person with this name, which really means "May Baal take action," would be a worshiper of Baal, not a foe. Other difficulties in the Gideon stories indicate that several different sources have not been perfectly fused; vv. 25–32 are unrelated to the context. **33–40:** Gideon's military preparations. **33:** *Valley of Jezreel* was at the eastern end of the valley of Esdraelon. **34:** *The Spirit of the LORD:* compare 3.10 n. **36–40:** The incident of the *fleece* is a sign additional to that of vv. 17–21.

7.1–8.35: Gideon routs the Midianites. 1: *En-harod* was on the northern slopes of Mount Gilboa. It means "spring of fright"; see v. 3. *The hill of Moreh* was in the plain between Mount Tabor and Mount Gilboa. **4–7:**

to Gideon. 'Bring them down to the water, and I shall separate them for you there. If I say to you, "This man shall go with you," he shall go; and if I say, "This man shall not go," he shall not go.' 5 When Gideon brought the men down to the water, the LORD said to him, 'Make every man who laps the water with his tongue like a dog stand on one side, and on the other every man who kneels down and drinks.' 6 The number of those who lapped, putting their hands to their mouths, was three hundred; all the rest had gone down on their knees to drink. 7 The LORD said, 'By means of the three hundred men who lapped I shall save you and give Midian into your power; the rest may go home.' 8 Gideon sent all these Israelites home, but he kept the three hundred, and they took with them the jars and the trumpets which the people had.

The Midianite camp was below him in the valley, 9 and that night the LORD said to Gideon, 'Go down at once and attack the camp, for I have delivered it into your hands. 10 If you are afraid to do so, then go down first with your servant Purah, 11 and when you hear what they are saying, that will give you courage to attack the camp.' So he and his servant Purah went down to the outposts of the camp where the fighting men were stationed. 12 The Midianites, the Amalekites, and all the eastern tribes were so many that they lay there in the valley like a swarm of locusts; there was no counting their camels, which in number were like grains of sand on the seashore. 13 As Gideon came close, there was a man telling his comrades about a dream. He said, 'I dreamt that I saw a barley loaf rolling over and over through the Midianite camp; it came to a tent, struck it, and the tent collapsed and turned upside down.' 14 The other answered, 'This can be none other than the sword of Gideon son of Joash the Israelite. God has delivered Midian and the whole army into his hands.'

15 When Gideon heard the account of the dream and its interpretation, he bowed down in worship. Then going back to the Israelite camp he said, 'Let us go! The LORD has deliv-

ered the camp of the Midianites into our hands.' 16 He divided the three hundred men into three companies, and furnished every man with a trumpet and an empty jar, with a torch inside each jar. 17 'Watch me,' he said to them. 'When I come to the edge of the camp, do exactly as I do. 18 When I and those with me blow our trumpets, you too all round the camp blow your trumpets and shout, "For the LORD and for Gideon!"'

19 Gideon and the hundred men who were with him reached the outskirts of the camp at the beginning of the middle watch, just after the posting of the sentries. They blew the trumpets and smashed the jars they were holding. 20 All three companies blew their trumpets and smashed their jars; then, grasping the torches in their left hands and the trumpets in their right, they shouted, 'A sword for the LORD and for Gideon!' 21 Every man stood where he was, all round the camp, and the whole camp leapt up in a panic and took flight. 22 When the three hundred blew their trumpets, the LORD set all the men in the camp fighting against each other. They fled as far as Beth-shittah in the direction of Zererah, as far as the ridge of Abel-meholah near Tabbath.

23 The Israelites from Naphtali and Asher and all Manasseh were called out to pursue the Midianites. 24 Gideon also sent messengers throughout the hill-country of Ephraim to say: 'Come down and cut off the Midianites. Hold the fords of the Jordan against them as far as Beth-barah.' So all the Ephraimites when called out held the fords of the Jordan as far as Beth-barah. 25 They captured the two Midianite princes, Oreb and Zeeb. Oreb they killed at the Rock of Oreb, and Zeeb by the Winepress of Zeeb, and they kept up the pursuit of the Midianites; afterwards they brought the heads of Oreb and Zeeb to Gideon on the other side of Jordan.

8 The men of Ephraim said to Gideon, 'Why have you treated us like this? Why

7:5 **on the other:** *so Gk; Heb. omits.*   7:8 **jars:** *prob. rdg; Heb.* provisions.   7:13 **struck it:** *prob. rdg; Heb. adds* and it fell.

The test as presented is a literary device; the number of Gideon's warriors is reduced in order to make clear that the victory belongs to the LORD. **8:** *The jars and the trumpets:* see vv. 16–22. Lighted torches are concealed in the jars. **10–15:** Another sign of victory for Gideon. **13–14:** The *barley loaf* symbolizes settled farmers, the *tent* the nomadic Midianites. **22:** *Bethshittah . . . Tabbath:* all the places mentioned here are east of the Jordan. **24–25:** *Oreb* and *Zeeb* are captured and executed by the Ephraimites. The summons to Ephraim to hold *the fords of the Jordan,* after the Midianites had already fled across it, is another example of imperfectly fused did you not summon us when you went to fight Midian?' and they upbraided him fiercely. ²But he replied, 'What have I now accomplished compared with you? Are not Ephraim's gleanings better than the whole grape harvest of Abiezer? ³God delivered Oreb and Zeeb, the princes of Midian, into your hands. What have I been able to accomplish compared with you?' At that their anger against him died down.

⁴Gideon came to the Jordan, and he and his three hundred men crossed over to continue the pursuit, exhausted though they were. ⁵He said to the people of Succoth, 'Will you give my followers some bread? They are exhausted, and I am pursuing Zebah and Zalmunna, the kings of Midian.' ⁶But the chief men of Succoth replied, 'Are Zebah and Zalmunna already in your hands, that we should give bread to your troops?' ⁷Gideon said, 'For that, when the Lord delivers Zebah and Zalmunna into my hands, I shall thresh your bodies with desert thorns and briars.' ⁸He went on from there to Penuel and made the same request; the people of Penuel gave the same answer as had the people of Succoth. ⁹He said to them, 'When I return victorious, I shall pull down your tower.'

¹⁰Zebah and Zalmunna were at Karkor with an army of about fifteen thousand men. Those were all that remained of the entire host of the eastern tribes, a hundred and twenty thousand warriors having fallen in battle. ¹¹Gideon advanced along the track used by the tent-dwellers east of Nobah and Jogbehah, and his attack caught the enemy off guard. ¹²Zebah and Zalmunna fled; but he went in pursuit of the Midianite kings and captured them both; and their whole army melted away.

¹³As Gideon son of Joash was returning from battle by the ascent of Heres, ¹⁴he caught a young man from Succoth. When questioned the young man listed for him the names of the rulers of Succoth and its elders, seventy-seven in all. ¹⁵Gideon then came to

the people of Succoth and said, 'Here are Zebah and Zalmunna, about whom you taunted me. "Are Zebah and Zalmunna already in your hands," you said, "that we should give your exhausted men bread?"' ¹⁶Then he took the elders of Succoth and inflicted punishment on them with desert thorns and briars. ¹⁷He also pulled down the tower of Penuel and put the men of the town to death.

¹⁸He said to Zebah and Zalmunna, 'What sort of men did you kill in Tabor?' They answered, 'They were like you; every one had the look of a king's son.' ¹⁹'They were my brothers,' he said, 'my mother's sons. I swear by the Lord, if you had let them live I would not have killed you.' ²⁰Then he said to his eldest son Jether, 'Stand up and kill them.' But he was still only a lad, and did not draw his sword, because he was afraid. ²¹Zebah and Zalmunna said, 'Rise up yourself and dispatch us, for you have a man's strength.' So Gideon got up and killed them both, and he took the crescents from the necks of their camels.

²²The Israelites said to Gideon, 'You have saved us from the Midianites; now you be our ruler, you and your son and your grandson.' ²³But Gideon replied, 'I shall not rule over you, nor will my son; the Lord will rule over you.' ²⁴He went on, 'I have a request to make: will every one of you give me an ear-ring from his booty?'—for the enemy, being Ishmaelites, wore gold ear-rings. ²⁵They said, 'Of course we shall give them.' So a cloak was spread out and every man threw on to it a gold ear-ring from his booty. ²⁶The ear-rings he asked for weighed seventeen hundred shekels of gold; this was in addition to the crescents and pendants and the purple robes worn by the Midianite kings, and not counting the chains on the necks of their camels. ²⁷Gideon made the gold into an ephod which he set up in his own town of Ophrah. All the Israelites went astray by worshipping it, and

8:21 **you have:** *so Gk; Heb.* he has.

accounts; see 6.32 n. **8.2–3:** Gideon placates the Ephraimites by assuring them that their *gleanings,* that is, their accomplishments, are more important and valuable than his own, the *grape harvest of Abiezer* (6.11 n.). This is probably a proverbial saying. **4–12:** Gideon asks for supplies, continues the pursuit of the Midianites, and kills their kings, *Zebah* and *Zalmunna*. This seems to be a somewhat different version of 7.24–8.3. **5–17:** The other places mentioned in this section were east of the Jordan. **10:** The numbers seem exaggerated. **18–19:** That Gideon's *brothers* had been killed at Mount Tabor by Midianites is not recorded in the account in ch. 6, nor is the personal motive given there. On blood vengeance, see Josh. 20.3. **21:** *Crescents:* ornaments, possibly amulets. **22–23:** Gideon refuses hereditary kingship. **24–27:** Here the *ephod* is some kind of image; elsewhere it became a snare for Gideon and his household. [28] Thus the Midianites were subdued by the Israelites; they could no longer hold up their heads. For forty years the land was at peace, all the lifetime of Gideon, [29] that is Jerubbaal son of Joash; and he retired to his own home. [30] Gideon had seventy sons, his own offspring, for he had many wives. [31] He had a concubine who lived in Shechem, and she also bore him a son, whom he named Abimelech. [32] Gideon son of Joash died at a ripe old age and was buried in his father's grave at Ophrah-of-the-Abiezrites.

[33] After Gideon's death the Israelites again went astray: they worshipped the baalim and made Baal-berith their god. [34] They were unmindful of the LORD their God who had delivered them from all their enemies around them, [35] nor did they show to the family of Jerubbaal, that is Gideon, the loyalty that was due to them for all the good he had done Israel.

Abimelech and his successors

9 ABIMELECH son of Jerubbaal went to Shechem to his mother's brothers, and spoke with them and with the rest of the clan of his mother's family. [2] 'I beg you,' he said, 'whisper a word in the ears of all the people of Shechem. Ask them which is better for them: that seventy men, all the sons of Jerubbaal, should rule over them, or one man. Tell them to remember that I am their own flesh and blood.' [3] When his mother's kinsfolk repeated all this to every Shechemite on his behalf, they were moved to come over to Abimelech's side, because, as they said, he was their kinsman. [4] They gave him seventy pieces of silver from the temple of Baal-berith, and with these he hired good-for-nothing, reckless fellows as his followers. [5] He went to his father's house in Ophrah and butchered his seventy brothers, the sons of Jerubbaal, on a single stone block, all but Jotham, the youngest, who survived because he had gone into hiding. [6] Then all the inhabitants of Shechem and all Beth-millo came together and made Abimelech king beside the propped-up terebinth at Shechem.

[7] When this was reported to Jotham, he climbed to the summit of Mount Gerizim, and standing there he cried at the top of his voice: 'Listen to me, you people of Shechem, and may God listen to you.

[8] 'Once upon a time the trees set out to anoint a king over them. They said to the olive tree: "Be king over us." [9] But the olive tree answered: "What, leave my rich oil by which gods and men are honoured, to go and hold sway over the trees?"

[10] 'So the trees said to the fig tree: "Then will you come and be king over us?" [11] But the fig tree answered: "What, leave my good fruit and all its sweetness, to go and hold sway over the trees?"

[12] 'So the trees said to the vine: "Then will you come and be king over us?" [13] But the vine answered: "What, leave my new wine which gladdens gods and men, to go and hold sway over the trees?"

[14] 'Then all the trees said to the thorn bush: "Will you come and be king over us?" [15] The thorn answered: "If you really mean to anoint me as your king, then come under the protection of my shadow; if not, fire will come out of the thorn and burn up the cedars of Lebanon." '

[16] Jotham said, 'Now have you acted fairly and honourably in making Abimelech king? Have you done the right thing by Jerubbaal and his household? Have you given my father his proper due — [17] who fought for you, and risked his life to deliver you from the Midianites? [18] Today you have risen against my father's family, butchered his sons, seventy on a single stone block, and made Abimelech, the son of his slave-girl, king over the inhabitants of Shechem just because he is your kinsman. [19] In this day's work have you acted fairly and honourably by Jerubbaal and his family? If so, I wish you joy in Abimelech and wish him joy in you! [20] If not, may fire come out of Abimelech and devour the inhabitants of Shechem and all Beth-millo;

it is a sacred garment (Exod. 25.7 n.). It brought disaster to Gideon's family. **28–35:** The section in part seems misplaced. Perhaps vv. 28–29, at least, belong after v. 23.

9.1–57: Abimelech, son of Jerubbaal (Gideon). **1:** *Jerubbaal:* see 6.32 n. *Shechem:* see Josh. 24.1 n. It guarded the important highway between Mount Ebal and Mount Gerizim. **4:** *Baal-berith:* see Josh. 24.25 n. **6:** *Beth-millo* probably refers to the fortified section of Shechem, the tower of vv. 46, 49. *Terebinth:* see Josh. 24.26. **7–21:** Jotham denounces Abimelech. **8–15:** In this antimonarchic parable, the useless thorn bush may fire also come out from the inhabitants of Shechem and Beth-millo to devour Abimelech.' 21 Jotham then slipped away and made his escape; he came to Be-er, and there he settled, to be out of reach of his brother Abimelech.

22 After Abimelech had been prince over Israel for three years, 23 God sent an evil spirit to create a breach between Abimelech and the inhabitants of Shechem, and they broke faith with him. 24 This was done in order that the violent murder of the seventy sons of Jerubbaal might recoil on their brother Abimelech who did the murder, and on the people of Shechem who encouraged him to do it. 25 The people of Shechem set men to lie in wait for him on the hilltops, and they robbed all who passed that way. But Abimelech had word of it.

26 Gaal son of Ebed came with his kinsmen to Shechem, and the people of Shechem gave him their allegiance. 27 They went out into the countryside, picked the early grapes in their vineyards, trod them in the winepress, and made merry. They went into the temple of their god, where they ate and drank and reviled Abimelech. 28 'Who is Abimelech,' said Gaal son of Ebed, 'and who are the Shechemites, that we should be his subjects? Have not this son of Jerubbaal and his lieutenant Zebul been subjects of the men of Hamor the father of Shechem? Why indeed should we be subject to him? 29 If only this people were in my charge I should know how to get rid of Abimelech! I should say to him, "Muster your force and come out."'

30 When Zebul the governor of the city heard what Gaal son of Ebed said, he was furious. 31 He resorted to a ruse and sent messengers to report to Abimelech, 'Gaal son of Ebed and his kinsmen have come to Shechem and are turning the city against you. 32 Set off by night, you and the people with you, and lie in wait out in the country. 33 Then in the morning start at sunrise, and advance with all speed on the city. When he and his people come out to you, do to him what the situation demands.'

34 So Abimelech and all the troops with him set out under cover of night, and lay in wait in four companies to attack Shechem. 35 Gaal son of Ebed came out and stood in the entrance of the city gate. When Abimelech and his men rose from their hiding-place, 36 and Gaal saw them, he said to Zebul, 'There are people coming down from the tops of the hills,' but Zebul replied, 'What you see that looks like men is the shadow of the hills.' 37 Once more Gaal said, 'There are people coming down from the central ridge, and another group is advancing along the road of the Soothsayers' Terebinth.' 38 Then Zebul said to him, 'Where are your brave words now? You said, "Who is Abimelech that we should be subject to him?" Are not these the people you despised? Go out and fight him.' 39 Gaal led out the men of Shechem and attacked Abimelech, 40 but Abimelech routed him and he fled. The ground was strewn with corpses all the way to the entrance of the gate. 41 Abimelech established himself in Arumah, and Zebul drove out Gaal and his kinsmen and allowed them no place in Shechem.

42 Next day the people came out into the open country, and this was reported to Abimelech. 43 He took his supporters, divided them into three companies, and lay in wait in the open country; when he saw the people coming out of the city, he rose and attacked them. 44 Abimelech and the company with him advanced rapidly and took up position at the entrance of the city gate, while the other two companies made a dash against all those who were in the open and struck them down. 45 Abimelech kept up the attack on the city all that day and, when he captured it, he slaughtered the people inside, razed the city to the ground, and sowed it with salt. 46 When news of this reached the occupants of the tower of Shechem, they took refuge in the crypt of the temple of Elberith. 47 It was reported to Abimelech that all the occupants of the tower of Shechem had flocked together, 48 and he and all his men went up Mount Zalmon, where with an axe he cut brushwood. He took it and, hoisting it on his shoulder, he said to his men, 'You see what I am doing; quick, do the same.' 49 Each man cut brushwood and then following

9:29 **I should say:** *so Gk; Heb.* And he said.
9:37 **central ridge:** *lit.* navel of the land.
9:44 **company:** *so Lat.; Heb.* companies.

aspires to be king, but useful trees do not. **22–25:** A quarrel between Abimelech and the Shechemites. **26–41:** Abimelech crushes Gaal's rebellion. **28:** Abimelech lived at Arumah (v. 41); Shechem was governed by his deputy *Zebul*. **42–49:** Shechem destroyed. **45:** *Salt* would destroy fertility, implying total destruction.

Abimelech they laid the brushwood on the crypt. They burnt it over the heads of the occupants of the tower, and they all died, about a thousand men and women.

⁵⁰ Abimelech proceeded to Thebez, which he besieged and captured. ⁵¹ There was a strong tower in the middle of the town, and all the townspeople, men and women, took refuge there. They shut themselves in and went up on the roof. ⁵² Abimelech came up to the tower and attacked it, and as he approached the entrance to set fire to it, ⁵³ a woman threw a millstone down on his head and fractured his skull. ⁵⁴ He called hurriedly to his armour-bearer and said, 'Draw your sword and dispatch me, or it will be said of me: A woman killed him.' So the young man ran him through, and he died. ⁵⁵ When the Israelites saw that Abimelech was dead, they all went back to their homes. ⁵⁶ In this way God repaid the crime which Abimelech had committed against his father by the murder of his seventy brothers, ⁵⁷ and brought all the wickedness of the men of Shechem on their own heads. The curse of Jotham son of Jerubbaal overtook them.

10 After Abimelech there came forward to deliver Israel Tola son of Pua, son of Dodo, a man of Issachar who lived at Shamir in the hill-country of Ephraim. ² He was judge over Israel for twenty-three years, and when he died he was buried in Shamir.

³ After him came Jair the Gileadite; he was judge over Israel for twenty-two years. ⁴ He had thirty sons, who rode on thirty donkeys; they had thirty towns in the land of Gilead, which to this day are called Havvoth-jair. ⁵ When Jair died, he was buried in Kamon.

⁶ Once more the Israelites did what was wrong in the eyes of the LORD, serving the baalim and the ashtaroth, the deities of Aram and of Sidon and of Moab, of the Ammonites and of the Philistines. They forsook the LORD and did not serve him. ⁷ The anger of the LORD was roused against Israel, and he sold them into the power of the Philistines and the

Ammonites, ⁸ who for eighteen years harassed and oppressed all those Israelites who lived beyond the Jordan in Amorite territory in Gilead. ⁹ The Ammonites also crossed the Jordan to attack Judah, Benjamin, and Ephraim, so that Israel was in dire straits.

¹⁰ Then the Israelites cried to the LORD: 'We have sinned against you; we have forsaken our God and served the baalim.' ¹¹ The LORD answered, 'The Egyptians, the Amorites, the Ammonites, the Philistines, ¹² the Sidonians too, and the Amalekites and the Midianites — all these oppressed you and you cried to me for help; and did I not deliver you? ¹³ But you have forsaken me and served other gods; therefore I shall come to your rescue no more. ¹⁴ Go and cry for help to the gods you have chosen; let them save you in your day of distress.' ¹⁵ But the Israelites said to the LORD, 'We have sinned. Deal with us as you please; only save us this day, we implore you.' ¹⁶ They banished their foreign gods and served the LORD; and he could no longer bear the plight of Israel.

¹⁷ The Ammonites were called to arms and encamped in Gilead, while the Israelites assembled and encamped in Mizpah. ¹⁸ The people of Gilead and their chief men said to one another, 'Whoever strikes the first blow at the Ammonites shall be head over all the inhabitants of Gilead.'

Jephthah and his successors

11 JEPHTHAH the Gileadite was an intrepid warrior; he was the son of Gilead by a prostitute. ² Gilead's wife also bore him sons, and when they grew up they drove Jephthah away, saying to him, 'You have no inheritance in our father's house; you are another woman's son.' ³ To escape his brothers, Jephthah fled and settled in the land of Tob, and a number of good-for-nothing fel-

10:4 **Havvoth-jair:** *that is* Tent-villages of Jair.
10:8 **who for eighteen years:** *prob. rdg; Heb. adds* in that year.   10:12 **the Midianites:** *so Gk; Heb.* Maon.

10.1–5: **Two minor judges. 1:** *Tola:* no more is known about him. **3–5:** No more is known about *Jair;* he is mentioned, curiously enough, in Num. 32.41, raising the problem of whether he belonged to the age of Moses and Joshua, or the judges.

10.6–12.7: **Jephthah and delivery from the Ammonites. 10–16:** Here it is the LORD, rather than a prophet, who directly rebukes the sinning Israelites. In 11–12, the allusions are broader than to the contents of Judges. The Masoretic Text has Maonites for *Midianites.* The Maonites may be the same as the Meunites of 2 Chr. 20.1; 26.7. **10.17–11.11:** Jephthah, exiled by his own family, is summoned from Tob, in northeastern Gilead, to command the Israelite forces. **11.1:** *Gilead* is ordinarily a geographical name; it is possibly used here because lows rallied to him and became his followers.

⁴The time came when the Ammonites launched an offensive against Israel ⁵and, when the fighting began, the elders of Gilead went to fetch Jephthah from the land of Tob. ⁶'Come and be our commander so that we can fight the Ammonites,' they said to him. ⁷But Jephthah answered, 'You drove me from my father's house in hatred. Why come to me now when you are in trouble?' ⁸'It is because of that', they replied, 'that we have turned to you now. Come with us, fight the Ammonites, and become head over all the inhabitants of Gilead.' ⁹Jephthah said to them, 'If you ask me back to fight the Ammonites and if the LORD delivers them into my hands, then I must become your head.' ¹⁰The Gilead elders said to him, 'We swear by the LORD, who will be witness between us, that we will do what you say.' ¹¹Jephthah then went with the elders of Gilead, and the people made him their head and commander. And at Mizpah, in the presence of the LORD, Jephthah repeated the terms he had laid down.

¹²Jephthah sent a mission to the king of Ammon to ask what quarrel he had with them that made him invade their country. ¹³The king replied to the messengers: 'When the Israelites came up from Egypt, they seized our land all the way from the Arnon to the Jabbok and the Jordan. Now return these lands peaceably.' ¹⁴Jephthah sent a second mission to the king of Ammon ¹⁵to say, 'This is Jephthah's answer: Israel took neither Moabite nor Ammonite territory. ¹⁶When they came up from Egypt, the Israelites passed through the wilderness to the Red Sea, and on to Kadesh. ¹⁷They then sent envoys to the king of Edom asking him to grant them passage through his country, but the king of Edom would not consent. They sent also to the king of Moab, but he would not agree; so Israel remained at Kadesh. ¹⁸'They then journeyed through the wilderness, skirting Edom and Moab, and kept

to the east of Moab. They encamped beside the Arnon, but they did not enter Moabite territory, because the Arnon is the frontier of Moab. ¹⁹Israel then sent envoys to the king of the Amorites, King Sihon of Heshbon, asking him to give them free passage through his country to their destination. ²⁰But Sihon refused to grant Israel passage through his territory; he mustered all his people, and from his camp in Jahaz he launched an attack on Israel. ²¹But the LORD the God of Israel delivered Sihon and his whole army into the hands of Israel, who defeated the Amorites and occupied all their territory in that region. ²²They took possession of the entire Amorite country from the Arnon to the Jabbok and from the wilderness to the Jordan. ²³The LORD the God of Israel drove out the Amorites for the benefit of his people Israel. And do you now propose to take their place? ²⁴It is for you to possess whatever Kemosh your god gives you; and all that the LORD our God gave us as we advanced is ours.

²⁵'For that matter, are you any better than Balak son of Zippor, king of Moab? Did he ever pick a quarrel with Israel or attack them? ²⁶For three hundred years Israelites have lived in Heshbon and its dependent villages, in Aroer and its villages, and in all the towns by the Arnon. Why did you not retake them during all that time? ²⁷We have done you no wrong; it is you who are doing us wrong by attacking us. The LORD who is judge will decide this day between the Israelites and the Ammonites.' ²⁸But the king of the Ammonites would not listen to the message Jephthah sent him.

²⁹Then the spirit of the LORD came upon Jephthah, who passed through Gilead and Manasseh, by Mizpeh of Gilead, and from Mizpeh over to the Ammonites. ³⁰Jephthah made this vow to the LORD: 'If you will deliver the Ammonites into my hands, ³¹then the first creature that comes out of the door of my house to meet me when I return from

11:16 **Red Sea:** *or* sea of Reeds.

the name of Jephthah's father was unknown. **3:** *Good-for-nothing fellows:* probably brigands. **10:** The words recall Gen. 31.49, and reflect a covenant between Jephthah and the elders. **11:** This *Mizpah* (there was one in Benjamin) was in Gilead, probably south of the Jabbok river. **12–28:** Negotiations with the king of Ammon fail. The passage echoes Num. chs. 20–24. **17:** See Num. 20.14–21. **19–23:** See Num. 21.21–31. **24:** A nation has a right to the land its god gives it. Usually *Kemosh* is god of the Moabites, Milcom (or Molech) god of the Ammonites; compare 1 Kgs. 11.5, 7. **25:** *Balak:* see Num. chs. 22–24. **26:** *Three hundred years:* the supposed time between Moses and Jephthah. The number is scarcely precise. **29–33:** Jephthah's foolish vow. **29:** *The spirit:* see 3.10 n. **31:** *Creature:* possibly a human being, but animals also shared the house. The Israelites them safely shall be the LORD's; I shall offer that as a whole-offering.'

³² So Jephthah crossed over to attack the Ammonites, and the LORD delivered them into his hands. ³³ He routed them with very great slaughter all the way from Aroer to near Minnith, taking twenty towns, and as far as Abel-keramim. Thus Ammon was subdued by Israel.

³⁴ When Jephthah arrived home in Mizpah, it was his daughter who came out to meet him with tambourines and dancing. She was his only child; apart from her he had neither son nor daughter. ³⁵ At the sight of her, he tore his clothes and said, 'Oh, my daughter, you have broken my heart! Such calamity you have brought on me! I have made a vow to the LORD and I cannot go back on it.'

³⁶ She replied, 'Father, since you have made a vow to the LORD, do to me as your vow demands, now that the LORD has avenged you on the Ammonites, your enemies. ³⁷ But, father, grant me this one favour: spare me for two months, that I may roam the hills with my companions and mourn that I must die a virgin.' ³⁸ 'Go,' he said, and he let her depart for two months. She went with her companions and mourned her virginity on the hills. ³⁹ At the end of two months she came back to her father, and he fulfilled the vow he had made; she died a virgin. It became a tradition ⁴⁰ that the daughters of Israel should go year by year and commemorate for four days the daughter of Jephthah the Gileadite.

12 The Ephraimites mustered their forces and, crossing over to Zaphon, said to Jephthah, 'Why did you march against the Ammonites and not summon us to go with you? We shall burn your house over your head.' ² Jephthah answered, 'I and my people had a grave feud with the Ammonites, and had I appealed to you for help, you would not have saved us from them. ³ When I saw that we were not to look for help

from you, I took my life in my hands and marched against the Ammonites, and the LORD delivered them into my power. So why do you now attack me?' ⁴ Jephthah then mustered all the men of Gilead and fought Ephraim, and the Gileadites defeated them. ⁵ The Gileadites seized the fords of the Jordan and held them against Ephraim. When any Ephraimite who had escaped wished to cross, the men of Gilead would ask, 'Are you an Ephraimite?' and if he said, 'No,' ⁶ they would retort, 'Say "Shibboleth."' He would say 'Sibboleth,' and because he could not pronounce the word properly, they seized him and killed him at the fords. At that time forty-two thousand men of Ephraim lost their lives.

⁷ Jephthah was judge over Israel for six years; when he died he was buried in his own town in Gilead. ⁸ After him Ibzan of Bethlehem was made judge over Israel. ⁹ He had thirty sons and thirty daughters. He gave away the thirty girls in marriage and brought in thirty girls for his sons. He was judge over Israel for seven years, ¹⁰ and when he died he was buried in Bethlehem.

¹¹ After him Elon the Zebulunite was judge over Israel for ten years. ¹² When he died, he was buried in Aijalon in Zebulun territory.

¹³ Next Abdon son of Hillel the Pirathonite was judge over Israel. ¹⁴ He had forty sons and thirty grandsons, each of whom rode on his own donkey. He was judge over Israel for eight years; ¹⁵ and when he died he was buried in Pirathon in Ephraim territory on the hill of the Amalekite.

Samson and the Philistines

13 ONCE more the Israelites did what was wrong in the eyes of the LORD,

11:37 **that ... roam:** or that I may go down country to.   12:4 **defeated them:** so some Gk MSS; Heb. adds for they said, 'You are fugitives from Ephraim, Gilead, in the midst of Ephraim, in the midst of Manasseh.'

generally abhorred and ultimately prohibited human sacrifice (Lev. 18.21; Gen. 22.2 n.; Exod. 13.13 n.); for an example of its practice, see 2 Kgs. 21.6. **34–40:** Jephthah fulfills his vow. **37:** In Israelite society, it was regarded as a great tragedy for a woman to die unmarried and childless; she therefore mourns her virginity. **40:** This mourning ceremony is not mentioned elsewhere. **12.1–7:** Jephthah's war with the Ephraimites; see also 8.1–3. **6:** *Shibboleth* means "ear of corn" or "flood water." The Ephraimites betrayed themselves by their inability to pronounce the "sh" sound.

12.8–15: Ibzan, Elon, and Abdon. These minor judges are otherwise unknown.

13.1–16.31: Israel oppressed by the Philistines. The emphasis is on Samson the man, rather than on tribal and he delivered them into the hands of the Philistines for forty years.

2 There was a certain man from Zorah of the tribe of Dan whose name was Manoah and whose wife was barren; she had no child. 3 The angel of the LORD appeared to her and said, 'Though you are barren and have no child, you will conceive and give birth to a son. 4 Now be careful to drink no wine or strong drink, and to eat no forbidden food. 5 You will conceive and give birth to a son, and no razor must touch his head, for the boy is to be a Nazirite, consecrated to God from birth. He will strike the first blow for Israel's freedom from the power of the Philistines.'

6 The woman went and told her husband. 'A man of God came to me,' she said to him; 'his appearance was that of an angel of God, most terrible to see. I did not ask him where he came from, nor did he tell me his name, 7 but he said to me, "You are going to conceive and give birth to a son. From now on drink no wine or strong drink and eat no forbidden food, for the boy is to be a Nazirite, consecrated to God from his birth to the day of his death."'

8 Manoah prayed to the LORD, 'If it is pleasing to you, Lord, let the man of God whom you sent come again to tell us what we are to do for the boy that is to be born.' 9 God heard Manoah's prayer, and the angel of God came again to the woman, as she was sitting in the field. Her husband not being with her, 10 the woman ran quickly and said to him, 'The man who came to me the other day has appeared to me again.' 11 Manoah went with her at once and approached the man and said, 'Are you the man who talked with my wife?' 'Yes,' he replied, 'I am.' 12 'Now when your words come true,' Manoah said, 'what kind of boy will he be and what will he do?' 13 The angel of the LORD answered, 'Your wife must be careful to do all that I told her: 14 she must

not taste anything that comes from the vine; she must drink no wine or strong drink, and she must eat no forbidden food. She must do whatever I say.'

15 Manoah said to the angel of the LORD, 'May we urge you to stay? Let us prepare a young goat for you.' 16 The angel replied, 'Though you urge me to stay, I shall not eat your food; but prepare a whole-offering if you will, and offer that to the LORD.' Manoah did not know that he was the angel of the LORD, 17 and said to him, 'What is your name? For we shall want to honour you when your words come true.' 18 The angel of the LORD said to him, 'How can you ask my name? It is a name of wonder.' 19 Manoah took a young goat with the proper grain-offering, and offered it on the rock to the LORD, to him whose works are full of wonder. While Manoah and his wife were watching, 20 the flame went up from the altar towards heaven, and the angel of the LORD ascended in the flame. Seeing this, Manoah and his wife fell face downward to the ground.

21 The angel of the LORD did not appear again to Manoah and his wife. When Manoah realized that it had been the angel of the LORD, 22 he said to his wife, 'We are doomed to die, for we have seen God.' 23 But she replied, 'If the LORD had wanted to kill us, he would not have accepted a whole-offering and a grain-offering at our hands; he would not now have let us see and hear all this.'

24-25 The woman gave birth to a son and named him Samson. The boy grew up in Mahaneh-dan between Zorah and Eshtaol, and the LORD blessed him, and the spirit of the LORD began to move him.

14 Samson went down to Timnah, and there a woman, one of the Philistines,

13:4 **forbidden:** *lit.* unclean.   13:6 **an angel:** *or* the angel.

---

or national difficulties. Modern criticism considers these stories choice examples of early Israelite folklore. The tribe of *Dan* at this time lived in the southwest, near the Philistine plain; later they moved north (ch. 18). **1–25:** Samson's wondrous birth. The chapter seems a late composition, serving as a prologue to the ancient folktales which follow; it is kindred more with the ending, 16.28–31, than with the folktales. The account influences Lk. chs. 1–2. **1:** *Philistines:* see Josh. 13.2 n. **2:** *Zorah* was about twelve miles west of Jerusalem. **3:** *Angel of the* LORD: see 2.1 n. **5:** A *Nazirite* was consecrated to God by these special vows, whether for a time or for life; compare Num. 6.1–21. Samson is consecrated for life (v. 7). Since the folktales attributed Samson's strength to his hair, these stories were linked to the Nazirite vow. **13–14:** Samson's mother must also observe special prohibitions, since he is consecrated even in the womb. **17–18:** On the request to know the name, see Gen. 32.29 and Exod. 3.13. **22:** Compare Exod. 33.20–23. **25:** See 3.10 n.

14.1–20: Samson's first wife. **1:** *Timnah,* possibly at one time a Philistine town, was in Dan (Josh. 19.40) caught his notice. ²On his return he told his father and mother that he had seen this Philistine woman in Timnah and asked them to get her for him as his wife. ³His parents protested, 'Is there no woman among your cousins or in all our own people? Must you go to the uncircumcised Philistines to find a wife?' But Samson said to his father, 'Get her for me, because she pleases me.' ⁴Neither his father nor his mother knew that the LORD was at work in this, seeking an opportunity against the Philistines, who at that time held Israel in subjection.

⁵Samson went down to Timnah and, when he reached the vineyards there, a young lion came at him growling. ⁶The spirit of the LORD suddenly seized him and, without any weapon in his hand, Samson tore the lion to pieces as if it were a kid. He did not tell his parents what he had done. ⁷Then he went down and spoke to the woman, and she pleased him.

⁸When, after a time, he went down again to make her his wife, he turned aside to look at the carcass of the lion, and saw there was a swarm of bees in it, and honey. ⁹He scraped the honey into his hands and went on, eating as he went. When he came to his father and mother, he gave them some and they ate it; but he did not tell them that he had scraped the honey out of the lion's carcass.

¹⁰His father went down to see the woman, and Samson gave a feast there as the custom of young men was. ¹¹When the people saw him, they picked thirty companions to escort him. ¹²Samson said to them, 'Let me ask you a riddle. If you can solve it during the seven days of the feast, I shall give you thirty lengths of linen and thirty changes of clothing; ¹³but if you cannot guess the answer, then you will give me thirty lengths of linen and thirty changes of clothing.' 'Tell us your riddle,' they said; 'let us hear it.' ¹⁴So he said to them:

'Out of the eater came something to
    eat;
out of the strong came something
    sweet.'

At the end of three days they had failed to guess the answer. ¹⁵On the fourth day they said to Samson's wife, 'Coax your husband and make him explain the riddle to you, or we shall burn you and your father's house. Did you invite us here to beggar us?' ¹⁶So Samson's wife wept on his shoulder and said, 'You only hate me, you do not love me. You have asked my kinsfolk a riddle and you have not told it to me.' He said to her, 'I have not told it even to my father and mother; and am I to tell it to you?' ¹⁷But she wept on his shoulder every day until the seven feast days were ended, and on the seventh day, because she pestered him so, he told her, and she told the riddle to her kinsfolk. ¹⁸So on the seventh day the men of the city said to Samson just before he entered the bridal chamber:

'What is sweeter than honey?
What is stronger than a lion?'

He replied, 'If you had not ploughed with my heifer, you would not have solved my riddle.' ¹⁹Then the spirit of the LORD suddenly seized him, and he went down to Ashkelon, where he killed thirty men, took their belts, and gave their clothes to the men who had answered his riddle; then in a furious temper he went off to his father's house. ²⁰Samson's wife was given in marriage to the one who had been his groomsman.

15 After a while, during the time of wheat harvest, Samson went to visit his wife, taking a young goat as a present for her. He said, 'I am going to my wife in our bridal chamber,' but her father would not let him in. ²He said, 'I was sure that you were really hostile to her, so I gave her in marriage to your groomsman. Her young sister is better than she is—take her instead.' ³Samson said, 'This time I shall settle my score with the Philistines; I shall do them some real harm.' ⁴He went and caught three hundred jackals and got some torches; he tied the jackals tail to tail and fastened a torch between each pair

14:5 **Samson:** *prob. rdg; Heb. adds* and his father and mother. **he reached:** *so Gk; Heb.* they reached.
14:15 **fourth:** *so Gk; Heb.* seventh. **here:** *so some MSS; others* or not.   14:18 **he entered ... chamber:** *prob. rdg; Heb.* the sun went down.

near the border of Judah (Josh. 15.10). **3:** *Uncircumcised:* see Josh. 13.2 n. **4:** *Held Israel in subjection:* partly because of their higher level of material culture; see 1.19 n. **5–6:** The Asian *lion* was smaller than the African lion, but Samson's feat is still impressive. **15–18:** The motif of a woman wheedling a secret from Samson appears again in 16.4–18. **19:** *Ashkelon:* see Josh. 13.3.

of tails. 5 He then lit the torches and turned the jackals loose in the standing grain of the Philistines, setting fire to standing grain and sheaves, as well as to vineyards and olive groves.

6 'Who has done this?' the Philistines demanded, and when they were told that it was Samson, because the Timnite, his father-in-law, had taken his wife and given her to his groomsman, they came and burnt her and her father to death. 7 Samson said to them, 'If you do things like that, I swear I will be revenged on you before I have done.' 8 He smote them hip and thigh, causing great slaughter; and after that he went down to live in a cave in the Rock of Etam.

9 The Philistines came up and pitched camp in Judah, and overran Lehi. 10 The Judahites said, 'Why have you attacked us?' They answered, 'We have come to take Samson prisoner, and do to him as he did to us.' 11 Then three thousand men from Judah went down to the cave in the Rock of Etam, where they said to Samson, 'Surely you know that the Philistines are our masters? Now look what you have done to us.' He answered, 'I only did to them as they had done to me.' 12 They told him, 'We have come down to bind you and hand you over to the Philistines.' 'Swear to me that you will not set upon me yourselves,' he said. 13 'No, we shall not kill you,' they answered; 'we shall only bind you and hand you over to them.' They bound him with two new ropes and brought him up from the cave in the Rock.

14 When Samson came to Lehi, the Philistines met him with shouts of triumph; but the spirit of the LORD suddenly seized him, the ropes on his arms became like burnt tow, and his bonds melted away. 15 He came on the fresh jaw-bone of a donkey, and seizing it he slew a thousand men. 16 He made up this saying:

'With the jaw-bone of a donkey I have
    flayed them like donkeys;
with the jaw-bone of a donkey I have
    slain a thousand men.'

17 Having said this he threw away the jaw-bone; and he called that place Ramath-lehi.

18 He began to feel very thirsty and cried aloud to the LORD, 'You have let me, your servant, win this great victory, and must I now die of thirst and fall into the hands of the uncircumcised?' 19 God split open the Hollow of Lehi and water came out of it. Samson drank, his strength returned, and he revived. This is why to this day the spring in Lehi is called En-hakkore.

20 Samson was judge over Israel for twenty years in the days of the Philistines.

16 Samson went to Gaza, and seeing a prostitute there he lay with her. 2 The people of Gaza heard that Samson had come, and they gathered round and lay in wait for him all night at the city gate. During the night, however, they took no action, saying to themselves, 'When dawn comes we shall kill him.' 3 Samson stayed in bed till midnight; but then he rose, took hold of the doors of the city gate and the two gateposts, and pulled them out, bar and all; he hoisted them on his shoulders, and carried them to the top of the hill east of Hebron.

4 Afterwards Samson fell in love with a woman named Delilah, who lived by the wadi of Sorek. 5 The lords of the Philistines went up to her and said, 'Cajole him and find out what gives him his great strength, and how we can overpower and bind him and render him helpless. We shall each give you eleven hundred pieces of silver.'

6 Delilah said to Samson, 'Tell me, what gives you your great strength? How could you be bound and made helpless?' 7 'If I were bound with seven fresh bowstrings not yet dry,' replied Samson, 'then I should become no stronger than any other man.' 8 The lords of the Philistines brought her seven fresh bowstrings not yet dry, and she bound him with them. 9 She had men concealed in the inner room, and she cried, 'Samson, the Phil-

15:5 **and olive groves:** *so Gk; Heb.* omits and.
15:17 **Ramath-lehi:** *that is* Jaw-bone Hill.
15:19 **Hollow:** *lit.* Mortar. **En-hakkore:** *that is* the Crier's Spring.   16:2 **The people ... heard:** *so Gk; Heb.* To the people of Gaza.

15.1–8: Samson's revenge. 8: *Hip and thigh* is a proverbial expression whose original significance is unknown.

15.9–20: Samson's further revenge. 9: The location of *Lehi* is unknown; see 2 Sam. 23.11. It has the same spelling as the word for "jawbone" (vv. 15–17). **14:** *Tow* or flax. **17:** *Ramath-lehi:* see Tfn. **19:** *En-hakkore:* see Tfn.

16.1–3: Samson's escape. 1: *Gaza:* see Josh. 13.3. **3:** *Hebron* was forty miles east of Gaza.

istines are upon you!' Thereupon he snapped the bowstrings as a strand of tow snaps at the touch of fire, and his strength was not impaired.

10 Delilah said to Samson, 'You have made a fool of me and lied to me. Now tell me this time how you can be bound.' 11 He said to her, 'If I were tightly bound with new ropes that have never been used, then I should become no stronger than any other man.' 12 Delilah took new ropes and bound him with them. Then, with men concealed in the inner room, she cried, 'Samson, the Philistines are upon you!' But he snapped the ropes off his arms like thread.

13 Delilah said to him, 'You are still making a fool of me, still lying to me. Tell me: how can you be bound?' He said, 'Take the seven loose locks of my hair, weave them into the warp, and drive them tight with the beater; then I shall become no stronger than any other man.' So she lulled him to sleep, wove the seven loose locks of his hair into the warp, 14 drove them tight with the beater, and cried, 'Samson, the Philistines are upon you!' He woke from sleep and pulled away the warp and the loom with it.

15 She said to him, 'How can you say you love me when you do not confide in me? This is the third time you have made a fool of me and have not told me what gives you your great strength.' 16 She so pestered him with these words day after day, pressing him hard and wearying him to death, 17 that he told her the whole secret. 'No razor has touched my head,' he said, 'because I am a Nazirite, consecrated to God from the day of my birth. If my head were shaved, then my strength would leave me, and I should become no stronger than any other man.'

18 Delilah realized that he had told her his secret, and she sent word to the lords of the Philistines: 'Come up at once,' she said; 'he has told me his secret.' The lords of the Philistines came, bringing the money with them. 19 She lulled Samson to sleep on her lap, and then summoned a man to shave the seven locks of his hair. She was now making him helpless. When his strength had left him,

20 she cried, 'Samson, the Philistines are upon you!' He woke from his sleep and thought, 'I will go out as usual and shake myself'; he did not know that the LORD had left him. 21 Then the Philistines seized him, gouged out his eyes, and brought him down to Gaza. There they bound him with bronze fetters, and he was set to grinding grain in the prison. 22 But his hair, after it had been shaved, began to grow again.

23 The lords of the Philistines assembled to offer a great sacrifice to their god Dagon, and to rejoice and say,

'Our god has delivered into our hands
Samson our enemy.'

24 The people, when they saw him, praised their god, chanting:

'Our god has delivered our enemy into
our hands,
the scourge of our land who piled it
with our dead.'

25 When they grew merry, they said, 'Call Samson, and let him entertain us.' When Samson was summoned from prison, he was a source of entertainment to them. They then stood him between the pillars, 26 and Samson said to the boy who led him by the hand, 'Put me where I can feel the pillars which support the temple, so that I may lean against them.' 27 The temple was full of men and women, and all the lords of the Philistines were there, and there were about three thousand men and women on the roof watching the entertainment.

28 Samson cried to the LORD and said, 'Remember me, Lord GOD, remember me: for this one occasion, God, give me strength, and let me at one stroke be avenged on the Philistines for my two eyes.' 29 He put his arms round the two central pillars which supported the temple, his right arm round one and his left round the other and, bracing

16:13 **and drive . . . warp:** *so Gk; Heb. omits.*
16:14 **the warp . . . with it:** *prob. rdg; Heb. adds an unintelligible word.*

16.4–22: **Samson and Delilah. 4:** *The wadi of Sorek* led into the northern end of the Philistine plain. **13:** *Warp* and *beater* are weaving terms. **17:** See 13.5 n. **20:** *LORD had left him:* the Nazirite vow had been broken by the cutting of the hair.

16.23–31: **Samson's heroic death. 23:** *Dagon:* Semitic grain deity, adopted by the Philistines; see 1 Sam. 5.2–5.

himself, [30] he said, 'Let me die with the Philistines.' Then Samson leaned forward with all his might, and the temple crashed down on the lords and all the people who were in it. So the dead whom he killed at his death were more than those he had killed in his life. [31] His brothers and all his father's family came down, carried him up to the grave of his father Manoah between Zorah and Eshtaol, and buried him there. He had been judge over Israel for twenty years.

17 Once there was a man named Micah from the hill-country of Ephraim [2] who said to his mother, 'You remember the eleven hundred pieces of silver which were stolen from you, and how in my hearing you called down a curse on the thief? I have the money; I took it, and now I give it back to you.' His mother said, 'May the LORD bless you, my son!' [3] He gave back the eleven hundred pieces of silver to his mother, and she said, 'I now solemnly dedicate this silver to the LORD for the benefit of my son, to make a carved image and a cast idol.' [4] When he returned the money to his mother, she handed two hundred of the pieces of silver to a silversmith, who made them into an image and an idol, which were placed in Micah's house. [5] This man Micah had a shrine, and he made an ephod and teraphim and installed one of his sons to be his priest. [6] In those days there was no king in Israel and everyone did what was right in his own eyes.

[7] There was a young man from Bethlehem in Judah, from the clan of Judah, a Levite named Ben-gershom. [8] He had left the city of Bethlehem to go and find somewhere to live. On his way he came to Micah's house in the hill-country of Ephraim. [9] Micah asked him, 'Where have you come from?' and he replied, 'I am a Levite from Bethlehem in Judah, and I am looking for somewhere to live.' [10] 'Stay with me and be a father and priest to me,' Micah said. 'I shall give you ten pieces of silver a year, and provide you with food and clothes.' [11] The Levite agreed to stay with the man, who treated him as one of his own family. [12] Micah installed the Levite, and the young man became his priest and a member of his household. [13] Micah said, 'Now I know that the LORD will make me prosper, because I have a Levite as my priest.'

The Danites settle in Laish

18 In those days when Israel had no king, the tribe of Dan was looking for territory to occupy, because they had not so far come into possession of the territory allotted to them among the tribes of Israel. [2] The Danites therefore sent out five of their valiant fighters from Zorah and Eshtaol, instructing them to reconnoitre and explore the land. As they followed their instructions, they came to Micah's house in the hill-country of Ephraim and spent the night there. [3] While at the house, they recognized the speech of the young Levite, and turning they said, 'Who brought you here, and what are you doing? What is your business here?' [4] He explained, 'Micah did such and such: he hired me and I have become his priest.' [5] They said to him, 'Then enquire of God on our behalf whether our mission will be successful.' [6] The priest replied, 'Go and prosper. The LORD looks favourably on the mission you have undertaken.'

[7] The five men went on their way and came to Laish. There they found the inhabitants living free of care in the same way as the Sidonians, quiet and carefree with nothing lacking in the country. They were a long way

17:2 **and now ... to you:** *transposed from verse 3.* 17:5 **teraphim:** *or* household gods.   17:7 **named Ben-gershom:** *prob. rdg, cp. 18:30; Heb.* he lodged there.   17:10 **food and clothes:** *so Lat.; Heb. adds* and the Levite went.   18:1 **they had ... territory:** *so Gk; Heb. obscure.*   18:7 **with nothing ... country:** *prob. rdg; Heb. obscure.* **Aramaeans:** *so some Gk MSS; Heb.* men.

17.1–21.25: Years of lawlessness. The two tales in these chapters are not concerned with "judges"; they describe anarchy which the authors regard as necessitating the rise of the monarchy.

17.1–18.31: The origin of the cult of Dan. 1–6: The laws forbidding images (Exod. 20.4, 23; 34.17) seem here unknown. **5:** *Ephod:* see 8.24–27 n. *Teraphim:* see Tfn. **6:** On this verse (compare 21.25) see 17.1–21.25 n. **7–13:** *Levite* here probably means a priest, not a member of a tribe; in v. 13, the word has a tribal meaning, unless the intention there is to explain that "levite" once meant "priest." **7:** *Bethlehem:* five miles south of Jerusalem.

18.1–31: The migration of the Danites. The reason for the move northward by the tribe of Dan is not mentioned here; see 13.1–16.31 n. **5:** To *enquire of God:* probably by casting lots; see Josh. 7.14 n. **7:** *Laish,* from the Sidonians, and had no contact with the Aramaeans.

8 On their return to Zorah and Eshtaol, the five men were asked by their kinsmen for their report, 9 and they replied, 'Go and attack them at once. The land that we saw was very good. Why hang back? Do not hesitate to go there and take possession. 10 When you get there, you will find a people living a carefree life in a wide expanse of open country. It is a place where nothing on earth is lacking, and God has delivered it into your hands.'

11 Six hundred fully armed men from the Danite clan set out from Zorah and Eshtaol, 12 and went up country, where they encamped in Kiriath-jearim in Judah, which is why that place is called Mahaneh-dan to this day; it lies west of Kiriath-jearim. 13 From there they passed on to the hill-country of Ephraim until they came to Micah's house. 14 The five men who had been sent to reconnoitre the country round Laish addressed their kinsmen. 'Do you know', they said, 'that in one of these houses there are an ephod and teraphim, an image and an idol? Now consider what you had best do.'

15 They turned aside to Micah's house and greeted him. 16 As the six hundred armed Danites took their stand at the entrance of the gate, 17 the five men who had gone to explore the country went indoors to take the image and the idol, the ephod and the teraphim; the priest meanwhile was standing at the entrance with the six hundred armed men. 18 When the five men entered Micah's house and laid hands on the image and the idol, the ephod and the teraphim, the priest asked them what they were doing. 19 They said to him, 'Be quiet; not a word. Come with us and be to us a father and priest. Which is better, to be priest in the household of one man or to be priest to a tribe and clan in Israel?' 20 This pleased the priest, and carrying off the ephod and the teraphim, the image and the idol, he went with the people. 21 They set out on their way, putting their dependants, herds, and possessions in front. 22 The Danites had gone some distance from Micah's house, when his neighbours

were called out in pursuit. As they caught up with them, 23 they shouted, and the Danites turned round and said to Micah, 'What is the matter with you that you have called out your men?' 24 'You have taken the gods which I made for myself and have taken the priest,' he answered; 'you have gone off and left me nothing. How can you ask, "What is the matter with you?"' 25 The Danites said to him, 'Not another word from you! We are desperate men and if we set about you it will be the death of you and your family.' 26 With that the Danites went on their way, and Micah, seeing that they were too strong for him, turned and went home.

27 Carrying off the things which Micah had made for himself along with his priest, the Danites then attacked Laish, whose people were quiet and carefree. They put the people to the sword and set fire to their town. 28 There was no one to save them, for it was a long way from Sidon and they had no contact with the Aramaeans; the town was in the valley near Beth-rehob. They rebuilt the town and settled in it, 29 naming it Dan after their forefather Dan, a son of Israel; its original name was Laish. 30 The Danites set up the image, and Jonathan son of Gershom, son of Moses, and his sons were priests to the tribe of Dan until the exile. 31 They set up for themselves the image which Micah had made, and it was there as long as the house of God was at Shiloh.

19 IN those days when Israel had no king, a Levite residing in the heart of the hill-country of Ephraim had taken himself a concubine from Bethlehem in Judah. 2 In a fit of anger she had left him and gone to her father's house in Bethlehem in Judah. When she had been there four months, 3 her husband set out after her, with his servant

18:12 **Mahaneh-dan:** *that is* the Camp of Dan. 18:15 **turned aside to:** *so Gk (Luc.); Heb. adds* the house of the young Levite.   18:18 **the image . . . teraphim:** *prob. rdg; Heb.* the idol of the ephod, and teraphim and image.   18:20 **and the idol:** *so Gk; Heb. omits.*   18:28 **Aramaeans:** *prob. rdg, cp. verse 7; Heb.* men.   19:2 **In . . . anger:** *so Gk; Heb.* She was unfaithful.

near the sources of the Jordan, was allied with *the Sidonians,* who were, however, far away. **11–26:** The theft of Micah's priest and images. **12:** *Mahaneh-dan:* see Tfn. **30–31:** On the two great shrines of the later Northern Kingdom, see 1 Kgs. 12.29. **30:** *Son of Moses:* the Heb. may also be read as Manasseh. The thrust of the verse is to give the priest's name for the first time.

19.1–21.25: The crime of the Benjaminites at Gibeah and the war against them. 1: *No king:* see and two donkeys, to appeal to her and bring her back. She brought him into the house of her father, who was delighted to see him and made him welcome. 4 Being pressed by his father-in-law, the girl's father, he stayed there three days, and they were regaled with food and drink during their visit. 5 On the fourth day, they rose early in the morning, and the Levite prepared to leave, but the father said to his son-in-law, 'Have a bite of something to sustain you before you go,' 6 and the two of them sat down and ate and drank together. The girl's father said to the man, 'Why not spend the night and enjoy yourself?' 7 The man, however, rose to go, but his father-in-law urged him to stay, and again he stayed for the night. 8 He rose early in the morning on the fifth day to depart, but the girl's father said, 'Have something to eat first.' So they lingered till late afternoon, eating and drinking together. 9 Then the man stood up to go with his concubine and his servant, but his father-in-law said, 'Look, the day is wearing on towards sunset. Spend the night here and enjoy yourself, and tomorrow rise early and set out for home.' 10 But the man would not stay the night; he set off on his journey.

He reached a point opposite Jebus, that is Jerusalem, with his two laden donkeys and his concubine. 11 Since they were close to Jebus and the day was nearly gone, the servant said to his master, 'Do let us turn into this Jebusite town for the night.' 12 His master replied, 'No, not into a strange town where the people are not Israelites; let us go on to Gibeah. 13 Come, we will go and find some other place, Gibeah or Ramah, to spend the night.' 14 So they went on until sunset overtook them; they were then near Gibeah which belongs to Benjamin. 15 They turned in there to spend the night, and went and sat down in the open square of the town; but nobody took them into his house for the night.

16 At nightfall an old man was coming home from his work in the fields. He was from the hill-country of Ephraim, though he lived in Gibeah, where the people were Benjamites. 17 When his eye lighted on the travel-ler in the town square, he asked him where he was going and where he came from. 18 He answered, 'We are travelling from Bethlehem in Judah to the heart of the hill-country of Ephraim. I come from there; I have been to Bethlehem in Judah and I am going home, but nobody has taken me into his house. 19 I have straw and provender for our donkeys, food and wine for myself, the girl, and the young man; we have all we need.' 20 The old man said, 'You are welcome. I shall supply all your wants; you must not spend the night in the open.' 21 He took him inside, where he provided fodder for the donkeys. Then, having bathed their feet, they all ate and drank.

22 While they were enjoying themselves, some of the most depraved scoundrels in the town surrounded the house, beating the door violently and shouting to the old man whose house it was, 'Bring out the man who has come to your house, for us to have intercourse with him.' 23 The owner of the house went outside to them and said, 'No, my friends, do nothing so wicked. This man is my guest; do not commit this outrage. 24 Here are my daughter, who is a virgin, and the man's concubine; let me bring them out to you. Abuse them and do what you please; but you must not commit such an outrage against this man.' 25 When the men refused to listen to him, the Levite took his concubine and thrust her outside for them. They raped and abused her all night till the morning; only when dawn broke did they let her go. 26 The woman came at daybreak and collapsed at the entrance of the man's house where her husband was, and lay there until it was light.

27 Her husband rose in the morning and opened the door of the house to be on his way, and there was his concubine lying at the door with her hands on the threshold. 28 He said to her, 'Get up and let us be off'; but there was no answer. So he lifted her on to his donkey and set off for home.

29 When he arrived there, he picked up a

19:8 **and drinking:** *so some Gk MSS; Heb. omits.*
19:9 **towards sunset:** *so Gk; Heb. adds* Spend the night: behold the camping of the day.   19:18 **home:** *so Gk; Heb.* to the house of the LORD.

17.1–21.25 n.; compare 17.6 and 21.25. **10–12:** *Jerusalem* was as yet unconquered by the Hebrews; contrast 1.8 but compare 2 Sam. 5.6–9. (Extrabiblical sources always refer to it as Jerusalem, never as Jebus.) *Gibeah*, about five miles north of Jerusalem, was later the home of Saul (1 Sam. 10.26). **22–26:** Compare Gen. 19.4–9. Gibeah became proverbial as a place of shameful wickedness; see Hos. 9.9; 10.9. **27–30:** The summons to knife, took hold of his concubine, and cut her limb by limb into twelve pieces, which he then sent through the length and breadth of Israel. 30 He told the men he sent with them to say to every Israelite, 'Has the like of this happened or been seen from the time the Israelites came up from Egypt till today? Consider among yourselves and speak your minds.' Everyone who saw them said, 'Since that time no such thing has ever happened or been seen.'

The Benjamites

20 ALL the Israelites, the whole community from Dan to Beersheba and also from Gilead, left their homes and as one man assembled before the LORD at Mizpah. 2 The leaders of the people and all the tribes of Israel presented themselves in the assembly of God's people, four hundred thousand foot-soldiers armed with swords. 3 That the Israelites had gone up to Mizpah became known to the Benjamites.

The Israelites asked how this wicked crime happened, 4 and the Levite, to whom the murdered woman belonged, answered, 'I and my concubine arrived at Gibeah in Benjamin to spend the night. 5 The townsmen of Gibeah rose against me that night and surrounded the house where I was, intending to kill me; and they raped my concubine so that she died. 6 I took her and cut her in pieces, and sent the pieces through the length and breadth of Israel, because of the abominable outrage they had committed in Israel. 7 It is for you, the whole of Israel, to come to a decision as to what action should be taken.'

8 As one man all the people stood up and declared, 'Not one of us will go back to his tent, not one will return home. 9 But this is what we shall do to Gibeah: we shall draw lots for the attack, 10 and in all the tribes of Israel we shall take ten men out of every hundred, a hundred out of every thousand, and a thousand out of every ten thousand, and they will collect provisions for the army, for those who have taken the field against Gibeah in Benjamin to avenge the outrage committed in Israel.' 11 Thus all the Israelites,

united to a man, were massed against the town.

12 The tribes of Israel sent messengers throughout the tribe of Benjamin saying, 'What crime is this that has taken place among you? 13 Hand over to us now those scoundrels in Gibeah; we shall put them to death and purge Israel of this wickedness.' The Benjamites, however, refused to listen to their fellow-Israelites. 14 They flocked from their towns to Gibeah to do battle with the Israelites, 15 and that day they mustered out of their towns twenty-six thousand men armed with swords. There were also seven hundred picked men from Gibeah, 16 left-handed men, who could sling a stone and not miss by a hair's breadth. 17 The Israelites, without the Benjamites, numbered four hundred thousand men armed with swords, every one a warrior. 18 The Israelites at once moved on to Bethel and there sought an oracle from God. 'Which of us is to lead the attack on the Benjamites?' they enquired, and the LORD's answer was, 'Judah is to lead the attack.'

19 The Israelites set out at dawn and encamped opposite Gibeah. 20 They advanced to do battle with the Benjamites and drew up their forces before the town. 21 The Benjamites sallied out from Gibeah and laid low twenty-two thousand of Israel on the field that day. 23 The Israelites went up to Bethel, where they lamented before the LORD until evening, and enquired whether they should again attack their kinsmen the Benjamites. The LORD said, 'Go up to the attack.'

22 The Israelite army took fresh courage and formed up again on the same ground as the first day. 24 So on the second day they advanced against the Benjamites, 25 who sallied out from Gibeah to meet them and laid

19:30 **He told ... been seen from:** *prob. rdg, cp. Gk; Heb. omits* He ... seen.   20:2 **and:** *so Gk; Heb. omits.* 20:9 **we shall draw ... attack:** *so Gk; Heb.* against it by lot.   20:10 **who have ... to avenge:** *prob. rdg, cp. Gk; Heb.* to do when they come to Geba in Benjamin. 20:15 **from Gibeah:** *so Gk; Heb. adds* out of all this army there were seven hundred picked men. 20:22,23 *These verses transposed.*   20:23 **to Bethel:** *prob. rdg, cp. verses 18,26; Heb. omits.*

vengeance. **29:** Compare 1 Sam. 11.7.

20.1–48: The tribes assemble against the Benjamites. 1: *Dan to Beersheba:* that is, all Israel, from the extreme north to the extreme south. This *Mizpah* was on the northern border of Benjamin (see 11.11 n.). Some scholars believe the assembly (see v. 18) was at Bethel in Ephraim. **12–36a:** The Israelites suffer two setbacks, and then by a ruse defeat the Benjaminites. **17:** The numbers are greatly exaggerated. **18:** On seeking *an oracle,* low on the field another eighteen thousand armed men.

²⁶ The Israelites, the whole army, went back to Bethel, where they sat before the LORD lamenting and fasting until evening, and they offered whole-offerings and shared-offerings before the LORD. ²⁷⁻²⁸ In those days the Ark of the Covenant of God was there, and Phinehas son of Eleazar, son of Aaron, served before the LORD. The Israelites enquired of the LORD, 'Shall we again march out to battle against Benjamin our kin, or shall we desist?' The LORD answered, 'Attack! Tomorrow I shall deliver him into your hands.'

²⁹ The Israelites posted men in ambush all round Gibeah, ³⁰ and on the third day they advanced against the Benjamites and drew up their forces at Gibeah as before. ³¹ The Benjamites sallied out to meet them, and were drawn away from the town. They began the attack as before by killing a few Israelites, about thirty, on the highways which led across open country, one to Bethel and the other to Gibeon. ³² They thought that once again they were inflicting a defeat, but the Israelites had planned a retreat to draw them out on the highways away from the town. ³³⁻³⁴ Meanwhile the main body of Israelites left their positions and re-formed at Baal-tamar, while those in ambush, ten thousand picked men all told, burst out from their position in the neighbourhood of Gibeah and came in on the east of the town. There was soon heavy fighting; yet the Benjamites did not suspect the disaster threatening them. ³⁵ So the LORD put Benjamin to flight before Israel, and on that day the Israelites killed twenty-five thousand one hundred Benjamites, all armed with swords.

³⁶ The men of Benjamin now saw that they had suffered a defeat, for all that the Israelites, trusting in the ambush which they had set by Gibeah, had given ground before them. ³⁷ The men in ambush made a sudden dash on Gibeah, fell on the town from all sides, and put all the inhabitants to the sword. ³⁸ The agreed signal between the Israelites and those in ambush was to be a column of smoke sent up from the town, ³⁹ and the Israelites would then face about in the battle.

Benjamin began to cut down the Israelites, killing about thirty of them, in the belief that they were defeating the enemy as they had done in the first encounter. ⁴⁰ But as the column of smoke began to go up from the town, the Benjamites looked back and thought the whole town was in flames. ⁴¹ Then the Israelites faced about, and the Benjamites saw that disaster had overtaken them. They were seized with panic, ⁴² and turned in flight before the Israelites in the direction of the wilderness; but the fighting caught up with them, and soon those from the town were among them, cutting them down. ⁴³ They hemmed in the Benjamites, pursuing them without respite, and overtook them at a point to the east of Gibeah. ⁴⁴ Eighteen thousand of the Benjamites fell, all of them valiant warriors. ⁴⁵ The survivors turned and fled into the wilderness towards the Rock of Rimmon. The Israelites picked off the stragglers on the roads, five thousand of them, and continued the pursuit until they had cut down two thousand more. ⁴⁶ Twenty-five thousand armed men of Benjamin fell in battle that day, all valiant warriors. ⁴⁷ The six hundred who survived made off into the wilderness as far as the Rock of Rimmon, and there they remained for four months. ⁴⁸ The Israelites then turned back to deal with the other Benjamites, and put to the sword the people in the towns and the cattle, every creature that they found; they also set fire to every town within their reach.

21 The Israelites had taken an oath at Mizpah that none of them would give his daughter in marriage to a Benjamite. ² The people now came to Bethel and remained there in God's presence till sunset, raising their voices in bitter lamentation. ³ 'LORD God of Israel,' they cried, 'why has it happened among us that one tribe should this day be lost to Israel?' ⁴ Early next morning the people built an altar there and of-

20:31 **a few . . . thirty:** *or* about thirty wounded men. **Gibeon:** *prob. rdg; Heb.* Gibeah.   20:33–34 **Gibeah:** *prob. rdg, cp. Gk; Heb.* Geba.   20:38 **those in ambush:** *prob. rdg; Heb. adds an unintelligible word.* 20:39 **to cut . . . of them:** *or* to kill about thirty wounded men among the Israelites.   20:42 **town:** *so Lat.; Heb.* towns.   20:43 **without respite:** *or* from Nohah.

see 18.5 n. **27–28:** Since only here in Judg. is the Ark mentioned, these verses are often regarded as a late insertion. *Phinehas:* see Num. 25.6–13. **36b–48:** This is a second, fuller account of the ambush and victory of vv. 29–36.

fered whole-offerings and shared-offerings. ⁵At that the Israelites asked themselves whether among all the tribes of Israel there was any who did not go up to the assembly before the LORD; for under the terms of the weighty oath they had sworn, anyone who had not gone up to the LORD at Mizpah was to be put to death. ⁶The Israelites felt remorse over their kinsmen the Benjamites, because, as they said, 'This day one whole tribe has been lopped off Israel.'

⁷They asked, 'What shall we do to provide wives for those who are left, as we ourselves have sworn to the LORD not to give any of our daughters to them in marriage? ⁸Is there anyone in all the tribes of Israel who did not go up to the LORD at Mizpah?' Now it happened that no one from Jabesh-gilead had come to the camp for the assembly; ⁹so when they held a roll-call of the people, they found that none of the inhabitants of Jabesh-gilead was present. ¹⁰The community therefore sent off twelve thousand valiant fighting men with orders to go and put the inhabitants of Jabesh-gilead to the sword, men, women, and dependants. ¹¹'This is what you are to do,' they said: 'put to death every male person, and every woman who has had intercourse with a man, but spare any who are virgins.' This they did. ¹²Among the inhabitants of Jabesh-gilead they found four hundred young women who were virgins and had not had intercourse with a man, and they brought them to the camp at Shiloh in Canaan. ¹³The whole community sent messengers to the Benjamites at the Rock of Rimmon to parley with them, and peace was proclaimed. ¹⁴The Benjamites came back then, and were given those of the women of Jabesh-gilead who had been spared; but these were not enough.

¹⁵The people were still full of remorse

over Benjamin because the LORD had made this gap in the tribes of Israel. ¹⁶The elders of the community said, 'What can we do for wives for those who are left, as all the women in Benjamin have been wiped out?' ¹⁷They said, 'Heirs there must be for the surviving Benjamites! Then Israel will not see one of its tribes destroyed. ¹⁸Yet we cannot give them our own daughters in marriage, because we have sworn that there shall be a curse on the man who gives a wife to a Benjamite.'

¹⁹They bethought themselves of the pilgrimage in honour of the LORD, made every year to Shiloh, the place which lies to the north of Bethel, on the east side of the highway from Bethel to Shechem and to the south of Lebonah. ²⁰They told the Benjamites to go and hide in the vineyards. ²¹'Keep watch,' they said, 'and when the girls of Shiloh come out to take part in the dance, come from the vineyards, and each of you seize one of them for his wife; then be off to the territory of Benjamin. ²²If their fathers or brothers come and complain to us, we shall say to them, "Let them keep them with your approval, for none of us has captured a wife in battle. Had you yourselves given them the women, you would now have incurred guilt." '

²³The Benjamites did this; they carried off as many wives as they needed, snatching them from the dance; then they went their way back to their own territory, where they rebuilt their towns and settled in them. ²⁴The Israelites also dispersed by tribes and families, and every man returned to his own holding.

²⁵In those days there was no king in Israel; everyone did what was right in his own eyes.

21:11 **but spare . . . they did:** *so Gk; Heb. omits.*

21.1–25: The rehabilitation of Benjamin. Two accounts (vv. 1–15 and 16–25) are blended. **5–15:** *Jabesh-gilead* was east of the Jordan. **12:** On the sparing of *virgins* in warfare, compare Num. 31.17–18. **15–25:** No other biblical data are available about this festival which was perhaps the occasion of agricultural fertility rites. **19:** On *Shiloh* pilgrimages see 1 Sam. 1.3, 21.

Ruth

Ruth was a Moabite woman who, after the death of her Judean husband, chose to give up the security of her homeland to return to Judah with her mother-in-law, Naomi (ch. 1). There Ruth's loyalty and devotion to Naomi brought her to the notice of Boaz, a relative of her late husband. Boaz married Ruth (2.1–4.12), and through this marriage she became the great-grandmother of David (4.13–22).

The opening verse sets the story in the period of the Judges. Some scholars consider Ruth a postexilic literary creation, though perhaps based on an older tale; on this view, it was intended to counteract the harsh decrees of Ezra and Nehemiah against foreign wives (Ezra 10.1–5; Neh. 13.23–27). Others, however, date it much earlier, during the reigns of the first kings of Judah, before bitter enmity toward Moab had developed; furthermore, Davidic connections with Moab are indicated by 1 Sam. 22.3–4, and it is argued that a foreign extraction would hardly have been attributed to David without any basis.

In the Hebrew Bible this book is found in the Writings, in some MSS. in first place; it is placed after Judges in the Sept. and Vg. In the synagogue traditions, Ruth, one of the five Megilloth ("Scrolls"), is read in public at the pilgrim-feast of Weeks ("Pentecost").

Ruth and Naomi

1 ONCE, in the time of the Judges when there was a famine in the land, a man from Bethlehem in Judah went with his wife and two sons to live in Moabite territory. ² The man's name was Elimelech, his wife was Naomi, and his sons were Mahlon and Chilion; they were Ephrathites from Bethlehem in Judah. They came to Moab and settled there.

³ Elimelech died, and Naomi was left a widow with her two sons. ⁴ The sons married Moabite women, one of whom was called Orpah and the other Ruth. They had lived there about ten years ⁵ when both Mahlon and Chilion died. Then Naomi, bereaved of her two sons as well as of her husband, ⁶ got ready to return to her own country with her daughters-in-law, because she heard in Moab that the LORD had shown his care for his people by giving them food. ⁷ Accompanied by her two daughters-in-law she left the place where she had been living, and they took the road leading back to Judah.

⁸ Naomi said to her daughters-in-law, 'Go back, both of you, home to your own mothers. May the LORD keep faith with you, as you have kept faith with the dead and with me; ⁹ and may he grant each of you the security of a home with a new husband.' And she kissed them goodbye. They wept aloud ¹⁰ and said, 'No, we shall return with you to your people.' ¹¹ But Naomi insisted, 'Go back, my daughters. Why should you come with me? Am I likely to bear any more sons to be husbands for you? ¹² Go back, my daughters, go; for I am too old to marry again. But if I could say that I had hope of a child, even if I were to be married tonight and were to bear sons, ¹³ would you, then, wait until they grew up? Would you on their account remain unmarried? No, my daughters! For your sakes I feel bitter that the LORD has inflicted such misfortune on me.' ¹⁴ At this they wept still more. Then Orpah kissed her mother-in-law and took her leave, but Ruth clung to her.

1:13 For ... that: or My lot is more bitter than yours, because.

1.1–22: Naomi and Ruth. 1–5: Introduction. 1: *Bethlehem in Judah* distinguishes it from Bethlehem in the tribe of Zebulun (Josh. 19.15). *Moab:* east of the Dead Sea. In the late biblical period the Moabites were regarded as special enemies of the Israelites; see Deut. 23.3–6 n. 2: *Ephrathites from Bethlehem:* they belonged to a Judean clan settled in Bethlehem; see 1 Chr. 2.50–51. 6–18: Ruth chooses to return to Judah with Naomi. 11: *More sons to be husbands for you:* according to levirate law; see Deut. 25.5–10. 15–18: Orpah goes back

15 'Look,' said Naomi, 'your sister-in-law has gone back to her people and her god. Go, follow her.' 16 Ruth answered, 'Do not urge me to go back and desert you. Where you go, I shall go, and where you stay, I shall stay. Your people will be my people, and your God my God. 17 Where you die, I shall die, and there be buried. I solemnly declare before the LORD that nothing but death will part me from you.' 18 When Naomi saw that Ruth was determined to go with her, she said no more.

19 The two of them went on until they came to Bethlehem, where their arrival set the whole town buzzing with excitement. The women cried, 'Can this be Naomi?' 20 'Do not call me Naomi,' she said; 'call me Mara, for the Almighty has made my life very bitter. 21 I went away full, and the LORD has brought me back empty. Why call me Naomi? The LORD has pronounced against me, the Almighty has brought me misfortune.'

22 That was how Naomi's daughter-in-law, Ruth the Moabite, returned with her from Moab; they arrived in Bethlehem just as the barley harvest was beginning.

Ruth and Boaz

2 NAOMI had a relative on her husband's side, a prominent and well-to-do member of Elimelech's family; his name was Boaz. 2 One day Ruth the Moabite asked Naomi, 'May I go to the harvest fields and glean behind anyone who will allow me?' 'Yes, go, my daughter,' she replied. 3 So Ruth went gleaning in the fields behind the reapers. As it happened, she was in that strip of the fields which belonged to Boaz of Elimelech's family, 4 and there was Boaz himself coming out from Bethlehem. He greeted the reapers, 'The LORD be with you!' and they responded, 'The LORD bless you!' 5 'Whose girl is this?' he asked the servant in charge of the reapers.

The servant answered, 6 'She is a Moabite girl who has come back with Naomi from Moab. 7 She asked if she might glean, gathering among the sheaves behind the reapers. She came and has been on her feet from morning till now; she has hardly had a moment's rest in the shelter.'

8 Boaz said to Ruth, 'Listen, my daughter: do not go to glean in any other field. Do not look any farther, but stay close to my servant-girls. 9 Watch where the men reap, and follow the gleaners; I have told the men not to molest you. Any time you are thirsty, go and drink from the jars they have filled.' 10 She bowed to the ground and said, 'Why are you so kind as to take notice of me, when I am just a foreigner?' 11 Boaz answered, 'I have been told the whole story of what you have done for your mother-in-law since the death of your husband, how you left father and mother and homeland and came among a people you did not know before. 12 The LORD reward you for what you have done; may you be richly repaid by the LORD the God of Israel, under whose wings you have come for refuge.' 13 She said: 'I hope you will continue to be pleased with me, sir, for you have eased my mind by speaking kindly to me, though I am not one of your slave-girls.'

14 When mealtime came round, Boaz said to Ruth, 'Come over here and have something to eat. Dip your piece of bread in the vinegar.' She sat down beside the reapers, and he passed her some roasted grain. She ate all she wanted and still had some left. 15 When she got up to glean, Boaz instructed the men to allow her to glean right among the sheaves. 'Do not find fault with her,' he added; 16 'you may even pull out some ears of grain from the handfuls as you cut, and leave them for her to glean; do not check her.'

1:20 **Naomi:** *that is* Pleasure. **Mara:** *that is* Bitter.

---

to *her god,* the god of Moab, i.e. Kemosh, the chief god of Moab. Ruth chooses Israel and Israel's God. However, Orpah is not being condemned here; there are no villains in the Book of Ruth. Though the setting is in the time of the judges, the characters seem unmarked by the violent spirit manifested in the Book of Judg. Verses 16–17 are poetic prose, and reflect a meter found in Hebrew poetry. **19–22:** Naomi and Ruth arrive in Bethlehem. **22:** *The barley harvest* usually began in April.

2.1–4.22: Ruth and Boaz. 1–3: While gleaning, Ruth happens to come to the field owned by Boaz, a relative of her father-in-law Elimelech (1.2). **2:** Hebrew law allowed the poor to *glean,* i.e. to pick up the grain left in the fields after the reapers had finished (Lev. 19.9–10; Deut. 24.19–22). **4–7:** Ruth meets Boaz. **5:** In the Orient every woman belonged to someone: to father, husband, brother, or master. **8–16:** The kindliness of Boaz. **15–16:** Boaz goes beyond the requirement of Hebrew law (see v. 2).

17 Ruth gleaned in the field until sunset, and when she beat out what she had gathered it came to about a bushel of barley. 18 She carried it into the town and showed her mother-in-law how much she had got; she also brought out and handed her what she had left over from the meal. 19 Her mother-in-law asked, 'Where did you glean today? Which way did you go? Blessings on the man who took notice of you!' She told her mother-in-law in whose field she had been working. 'The owner of the field where I worked today', she said, 'is a man called Boaz.' 20 Naomi exclaimed, 'Blessings on him from the LORD, who has kept faith with the living and the dead! This man', she explained, 'is related to us; he is one of our very near kinsmen.' 21 'And what is more,' Ruth said, 'he told me to stay close to his workers until they had finished all his harvest.' 22 Naomi said, 'My daughter, it would be as well for you to go with his girls; in another field you might come to harm.' 23 So Ruth kept close to them, gleaning with them till the end of both barley and wheat harvests; but she lived with her mother-in-law.

3 One day Naomi, Ruth's mother-in-law, said to her, 'My daughter, I want to see you settled happily. 2 Now there is our kinsman Boaz, whose girls you have been with. 3 Tonight he will be winnowing barley at the threshing-floor. Bathe and anoint yourself with perfumed oil, then get dressed and go down to the threshing-floor; but do not make yourself known to the man until he has finished eating and drinking. 4 When he lies down make sure you know the place where he is. Then go in, turn back the covering at his feet and lie down. He will tell you what to do.' 5 'I will do everything you say,' replied Ruth.

6 She went down to the threshing-floor and did exactly as her mother-in-law had told her. 7 When Boaz had eaten and drunk, he felt at peace with the world and went and lay down to sleep at the far end of the heap of grain. Ruth came quietly, turned back the covering at his feet and lay down. 8 About midnight the man woke with a start; he turned over, and there, lying at his feet, was a woman! 9 'Who are you?' he said. 'Sir, it is I, Ruth,' she replied. 'Spread the skirt of your cloak over me, for you are my next-of-kin.' 10 Boaz said, 'The LORD bless you, my daughter! You are proving yourself more devoted to the family than ever by not running after any young man, whether rich or poor. 11 Set your mind at rest, my daughter: I shall do all you ask, for the whole town knows what a fine woman you are. 12 Yes, it is true that I am a near kinsman; but there is one even closer than I am. 13 Stay tonight, and then in the morning, if he is willing to act as your next-of-kin, well and good; but if he is not, then as sure as the LORD lives, I shall do so. Now lie down till morning.'

14 She lay at his feet till next morning, but rose before it was light enough for one man to recognize another; Boaz had it in mind that no one should know that the woman had been to the threshing-floor. 15 He said to her, 'Take the cloak you are wearing, and hold it out.' When she did so, he poured in six measures of barley and lifted it for her to carry, and she went off to the town.

16 When she came to her mother-in-law, Naomi asked, 'How did things go with you, my daughter?' Ruth related all that the man had done for her, 17 and she added, 'He gave me these six measures of barley; he would not let me come home to my mother-in-law empty-handed.' 18 Naomi said, 'Wait, my daughter, until you see what will come of it;

2:17 **bushel:** *Heb.* ephah.
3:15 **she went:** *so many MSS; others* he went.

2.17–23: Ruth relates her experiences to Naomi. **20:** *Very near kinsman:* Heb. go'el, a technical term for one who had certain rights and obligations: to restore the property which an impoverished relative had lost (Lev. 25.25; see Ruth 4.3–4) and to marry the widow of a relative without male offspring (see 1.11–13; 4.5–6; Deut. 25.5–10). It is also the term for a blood avenger (Num. 35.12). Boaz, however (3.12–13), is not the nearest next-of-kin. **23:** These *harvests* ended in June.

3.1–18: The threshing-floor incident. 1–5: Naomi's instructions. These relate to ordinary bridal customs. **6–13:** Carried out, Naomi's instructions win the assent of Boaz. **9:** To *spread* one's *skirt over* someone symbolizes marriage; compare Ezek. 16.8. *Next-of-kin:* Heb. go'el; see 2.20 n. **14–18:** Boaz's concern for Ruth's good name.

he will not rest till he has settled the matter this very day.'

4 Boaz meanwhile had gone up to the town gate and was sitting there when the next-of-kin of whom he had spoken came past. Calling him by name, Boaz cried, 'Come over here and sit down.' He went over and sat down. ²Boaz also stopped ten of the town's elders and asked them to sit there. When they were seated, ³he addressed the next-of-kin: 'You will remember the strip of field that belonged to our kinsman Elimelech. Naomi is selling it, now that she has returned from Moab. ⁴I promised to open the matter with you, to ask you to acquire it in the presence of those sitting here and in the presence of the elders of my people. If you are going to do your duty as next-of-kin, then do so; but if not, someone must do it. So tell me, and then I shall know, for I come after you as next-of-kin.' He answered, 'I shall act as next-of-kin.' ⁵Boaz continued: 'On the day you take over the field from Naomi, I take over the widow, Ruth the Moabite, so as to perpetuate the name of the dead man on his holding.' ⁶'Then I cannot act,' said the next-of-kin, 'lest it should be detrimental to my own holding; and as I cannot act, you yourself must take over my duty as next-of-kin.'

⁷Now it used to be the custom when ratifying any transaction by which property was redeemed or transferred for a man to take off his sandal and give it to the other party; this was the form of attestation in Israel. ⁸Accordingly when the next-of-kin said to Boaz, 'You must take it over,' he drew off his sandal and handed it over. ⁹Then Boaz addressed the elders and all the other people there: 'You are witnesses this day that I have taken over from Naomi all that belonged to Elime-lech and all that belonged to Chilion and Mahlon; ¹⁰and, further, that I have taken over Mahlon's widow, Ruth the Moabite, to be my wife, in order to keep alive the dead man's name on his holding, so that his name may not be missing among his kindred and at the gate of his native town. You are witnesses this day.' ¹¹All who were at the gate, including the elders, replied, 'We are witnesses. May the LORD make this woman, who is about to come into your home, to be like Rachel and Leah, the two who built up the family of Israel. May you do a worthy deed in Ephrathah by keeping this name alive in Bethlehem. ¹²Through the offspring the LORD gives you by this young woman may your family be like the family of Perez, whom Tamar bore to Judah.'

¹³So Boaz took Ruth and she became his wife. When they had come together the LORD caused her to conceive, and she gave birth to a son. ¹⁴The women said to Naomi, 'Blessed be the LORD, who has not left you this day without next-of-kin. May the name of your dead son be kept alive in Israel! ¹⁵The child will give you renewed life and be your support and stay in your old age, for your devoted daughter-in-law, who has proved better to you than seven sons, has borne him.' ¹⁶Naomi took the child and laid him in her own lap, and she became his foster-mother. ¹⁷Her women neighbours gave him a name: 'Naomi has a son; we shall call him Obed,' they said. He became the father of Jesse, David's father.

4:8 **and handed it over:** *so Gk; Heb. omits.*
4:14 **May . . . son:** *lit.* May his name.   4:15 **The child:** *lit.* He.

4.1–12: The nearer relative foregoes his right. 1: *The city gate:* the customary place for commerce and public transactions. **2:** *Ten elders* were to give a legal decision, as well as witness the settlement of business affairs. **3–4:** The *strip of field* is hitherto unmentioned. Compare 2.20 n. **5:** Boaz at first mentions only the field and not Ruth; a masterful storyteller is here keeping his audience in suspense about whether Ruth will become the wife of Boaz. Ruth is referred to as *the dead man's wife,* although it is Elimelech, and not his son, who has been mentioned in v. 3. **6:** *Risk:* the matter is not completely clear. **7–8:** The procedure is somewhat different from Deut. 25.7–10. There the woman herself shows her contempt for the man unwilling to marry her; here the first next-of-kin is only publicly surrendering his right and obligation. The two passages possibly represent quite different stages in the development of Hebrew law, with Ruth an earlier one. **9–12:** Boaz assumes the obligations, both to the property and to Ruth. **11–12:** Like *Rachel and Leah;* see Gen. 35.23–26. *Ephrathah:* another name for Bethlehem (1.2). *Perez:* see Gen. 38.6–30. Tamar (Gen. ch. 38) was also involved in a levirate marriage. *Perez* is mentioned here as part of the tracing of the ancestry of David in the next verses.
4.13–17: Naomi's new line. The climax of 4.11–17 is in the words *Jesse, David's father.*

The ancestry of David

18 THIS is the genealogy of Perez: Perez was the father of Hezron, 19 Hezron of Ram, Ram of Amminadab, 20 Amminadab of Nah-shon, Nahshon of Salmon, 21 Salmon of Boaz, Boaz of Obed, 22 Obed of Jesse, and Jesse of David.

4:20 **Salmon:** *so some MSS; others* Salmah.

4.18–22: The genealogy from Perez. Some commentators regard this *genealogy* as a later addition to the Book of Ruth. Earlier concern was that Elimelech and Mahlon have an heir; here attention is directed to the line into which Boaz and David fitted. A genealogy, with similar names spelled differently, is found in 1 Chr. 2.5, 9–15. The genealogy here is not needed; its inclusion suggests a reflection of a view of its high importance. These genealogies are used in Matt. 1.2–6; Lk. 3.31–33. **18:** *Perez:* see 4.12; Gen. 38.29.

THE FIRST BOOK OF
Samuel

In the ancient Greek Bible, the books of Samuel and Kings formed a single work (in four books) entitled "Concerning the Kingdoms," an arrangement and title appropriate for several reasons. First, Samuel appears only in parts of 1 Samuel; David is much more the hero of the total narrative. Second, the division in the Hebrew Bible between 2 Samuel and 1 Kings, ascribable only to the length, unduly separates the account of David's reign in 2 Samuel from the important narrative of the succession of his throne in 1 Kings 1.1–2.12. Third, the materials of Samuel and Kings are organized around the topic of kingship: how it came to be established in Israel (1 Sam. chs. 1–14); how the Davidic dynasty received divine sanction (1 Sam. ch. 15–2 Sam. ch. 7); and how the destiny of Israel in the land was shaped by the conduct of the subsequent kings, especially in relation to the Jerusalem temple (1 Kgs. 1.1–2 Kgs. 25.30).

The establishment of David's dynasty (2 Sam. ch. 7) and the consecration of the Solomonic temple (1 Kgs. 8.1–9.9) are the two subjects that give a unique content to the entire so-called "Deuteronomic history." This history begins in Deuteronomy, there as if stating a theme, and continues, in fidelity to the theme, through Joshua, Judges, and Samuel-Kings. A special viewpoint, appearing in Deuteronomy, expresses concern more with prophetic exhortation and judgment than with precision respecting laws (the latter marks the Priestly Code). The Deuteronomists stress fidelity to God, contending that to worship other gods, such as the Canaanite Baal, is to forsake the God of Israel. At many junctures in Samuel-Kings, both named and anonymous prophets arise to pass judgment on the people, and especially on the rulers, in the light of the covenant obligations. In the Book of Deuteronomy, the view recurs that only one sanctuary was to be valid in the future; the Deuteronomic historians credit Solomon with building the valid sanctuary, and hence the welfare of Solomon's temple is treated as of paramount importance after Solomon's time. Furthermore, since Israel is God's people by covenant, recurring attention is given to the covenant and, because of it, to Israel as God's unique people.

A variety of older sources were incorporated into the Deuteronomic history, sometimes untouched but sometimes retouched or rewritten by the Deuteronomic historians. Such older sources are particularly clear in Samuel: the Ark narrative in 1 Samuel chs. 4–6 and 2 Samuel ch. 6; the two conflicting strands concerning the origin of kingship in 1 Samuel chs. 8–14; the collection of stories about David's rise to kingship in 1 Samuel ch. 16–2 Samuel ch. 5; and the magnificent history of the succession to David's throne in 2 Samuel chs. 9–20; 1 Kings chs. 1–2. In addition to such longer sources, individual narratives (e.g. 1 Sam. 2.1–10) and early Deuteronomic speeches (e.g. 1 Sam. 12.6–15) were included. The events of 1 Samuel cover approximately the period 1050–1010 B.C.E. See also Introduction to 1 Kings.

Samuel's birth and childhood

1 THERE was a certain man from Rama-thaim, a Zuphite from the hill-country of Ephraim, named Elkanah son of Jeroham, son of Elihu, son of Tohu, son of Zuph an Ephraimite. ² He had two wives, Hannah and Peninnah; Peninnah had children, but Hannah was childless. ³ Every year this man went

1:1 **a Zuphite:** *so Gk; Heb.* Zophim.

1.1–4.1a: **Samuel at Shiloh.** This section establishes Samuel's legitimacy in Israel's history. Two themes are interwoven: the positive role of Samuel, and, negatively, the condemnation of the priestly family of Eli. Two up from his town to worship and offer sacrifice to the LORD of Hosts at Shiloh, where Eli's two sons, Hophni and Phinehas, were priests of the LORD.

⁴When Elkanah sacrificed, he gave several shares of the meat to his wife Peninnah with all her sons and daughters; ⁵but to Hannah he gave only one share; the LORD had not granted her children, yet it was Hannah whom Elkanah loved. ⁶Hannah's rival also used to torment and humiliate her because she had no children. ⁷This happened year after year when they went up to the house of the LORD; her rival used to torment her, until she was in tears and would not eat. ⁸Her husband Elkanah said to her, 'Hannah, why are you crying and eating nothing? Why are you so miserable? Am I not more to you than ten sons?'

⁹⁻¹⁰After they had finished eating and drinking at the sacrifice at Shiloh, Hannah rose in deep distress, and weeping bitterly stood before the LORD and prayed to him. Meanwhile Eli the priest was sitting on his seat beside the door of the temple of the LORD. ¹¹Hannah made this vow: 'LORD of Hosts, if you will only take notice of my trouble and remember me, if you will not forget me but grant me offspring, then I shall give the child to the LORD for the whole of his life, and no razor shall ever touch his head.'

¹²For a long time she went on praying before the LORD, while Eli watched her lips. ¹³Hannah was praying silently; her lips were moving although her voice could not be heard, and Eli took her for a drunken woman. ¹⁴'Enough of this drunken behav-

iour!' he said to her. 'Leave off until the effect of the wine has gone.' ¹⁵'Oh, sir!' she answered, 'I am a heart-broken woman; I have drunk neither wine nor strong drink, but I have been pouring out my feelings before the LORD. ¹⁶Do not think me so devoid of shame, sir; all this time I have been speaking out of the depths of my grief and misery.' ¹⁷Eli said, 'Go in peace, and may the God of Israel grant what you have asked of him.' ¹⁸Hannah replied, 'May I be worthy of your kindness.' And no longer downcast she went away and had something to eat.

¹⁹Next morning they were up early and, after prostrating themselves before the LORD, returned to their home at Ramah. Elkanah had intercourse with his wife Hannah, and the LORD remembered her; ²⁰she conceived, and in due time bore a son, whom she named Samuel, 'because', she said, 'I asked the LORD for him'.

²¹Elkanah with his whole household went up to make the annual sacrifice to the LORD and to keep his vow. ²²Hannah did not go; she said to her husband, 'After the child is weaned I shall come up with him to present him before the LORD; then he is to stay there always.' ²³Her husband Elkanah said to her, 'Do what you think best; stay at home until you have weaned him. Only, may the LORD indeed see your vow fulfilled.' So the woman stayed behind and nursed her son until she had weaned him.

1:7 **they:** *so Lat.; Heb.* she.   1:9–10 **stood before the LORD:** *so Gk; Heb. omits.*   1:22 **come up ... he is to:** *or* bring him up, and he will come into the presence of the LORD and.   1:23 **your:** *so Gk; Heb.* his.

narratives (Samuel's birth, ch. 1, and his first prophetic word, ch. 3), form the core of the section. Other materials are present to supplement the section which foreshadows Samuel's later activity as kingmaker.

1.1–28: Samuel's birth story. Birth stories are a response to curiosity about important historical figures, as may be seen in the cases of Moses (Exod. 2.1–10), Samson (Judg. 13.2–25), and Jesus (Matt. 1.18–2.23; Lk. chs. 1–2). The barrenness of a favored wife is a repeated motif of such stories (Gen. 18.1–15; 29.29–32; Judg. 13.2–5; Lk. 1.5–17). The birth story here is regarded by some as originally being about Saul rather than about Samuel; in v. 28 the Heb. word for *lent* is the same word as Saul, whose name is derived from the same Heb. roots in *asked* (1.20) and *make over* (1.28). **1:** *Ramathaim* is a variant of the Ramah mentioned as Samuel's home village at 1.19. **3:** *Lord of Hosts* occurs here for the first time in the OT; the "hosts" may be either heavenly powers or the forces of the Israelites (see 17.45). This phrase apparently arose in *Shiloh,* an important center before the monarchic period, but little is known about Shiloh from the monarchy on (see Josh. 18.1; Judg. 21.19; 1 Kgs. 11.29; 14.2; Jer. 7.12; Ps. 78.60). *Phinehas,* a name of Egyptian origin, was probably a descendant of the zealous priest of Num. 25.6–15. **9–10:** *Before the LORD* is a ritual position in front of the temple. **11:** Not cutting the hair is a mark of consecration to the LORD, combined in Nazirite vows with abstinence from wine (see Num. 6.1–21 and Judg. 13.3–5). **20:** *Samuel* means "he who is from God"; curiously, the verse explains the name "Saul"; see 1.1–28 n.

24 When she had weaned him, she took him up with her. She took also a bull three years old, an ephah of flour, and a skin of wine, and she brought him, child as he was, into the house of the LORD at Shiloh. 25 When the bull had been slaughtered, Hannah brought the boy to Eli 26 and said, 'Sir, as sure as you live, I am the woman who stood here beside you praying to the LORD. 27 It was this boy that I prayed for and the LORD has granted what I asked. 28 Now I make him over to the LORD; for his whole life he is lent to the LORD.' And they prostrated themselves there before the LORD.

2 Then Hannah offered this prayer:

'My heart exults in the LORD,
in the LORD I now hold my head high;
I gloat over my enemies;
I rejoice because you have saved me.
2 There is none but you,
none so holy as the LORD,
none so righteous as our God.

3 'Cease your proud boasting,
let no word of arrogance pass your lips,
for the LORD is a God who knows;
he governs what mortals do.
4 Strong men stand in mute dismay,
but those who faltered put on new strength.
5 Those who had plenty sell themselves for a crust,
and the hungry grow strong again.
The barren woman bears seven children,
and the mother of many sons is left to languish.

6 'The LORD metes out both death and life:
he sends down to Sheol, he can bring the dead up again.

7 Poverty and riches both come from the LORD;
he brings low and he raises up.
8 He lifts the weak out of the dust
and raises the poor from the refuse heap
to give them a place among the great,
to assign them seats of honour.

'The foundations of the earth are the LORD's,
and he has set the world upon them.
9 He will guard the footsteps of his loyal servants,
while the wicked will be silenced in darkness;
for it is not by strength that a mortal prevails.

10 'Those who oppose the LORD will be terrified
when from the heavens he thunders against them.
The LORD is judge even to the ends of the earth;
he will endow his king with strength
and raise high the head of his anointed one.'

11 Then Elkanah went home to Ramah, but the boy remained behind in the service of the LORD under Eli the priest.

12 Eli's sons were scoundrels with little regard for the LORD. 13 The custom of the priests in their dealings with the people was this: when anyone offered a sacrifice, the priest's servant would come while the flesh was stewing 14 and would thrust a three-pronged fork into the cauldron or pan or

1:24 **a bull ... old:** *so Gk; Heb.* three bulls. 1:28 **they ... themselves:** *so Syriac; Heb.* he ... himself.   2:2 **righteous:** *so Gk; Heb.* rock.   2:4 **in mute:** *prob. rdg; Heb.* obscure.   2:6 **Sheol:** *or the* underworld.

2.1–10: The song of Hannah. Hannah's *prayer* is quite different from the idyllic narrative of ch. 1. The motifs of reversal of fortune (vv. 4–8) and the *barren woman* (v. 5) relate it to Hannah's story. A relatively old composition, it was incorporated into the Samuel story late in literary growth; see Introduction. **1:** The *I* is originally a king, recently victorious; the language, however, is quite stereotyped. **6:** *Sheol* is the underworld, abode of the dead; compare Isa. 14.9–11. **10:** The verse uses frequently found motifs to express the divine sanction of the king; see, in fuller form, 2 Sam. 22.5–18. *Anointed:* see 10.1 n.
2.11–36: Samuel and Eli's sons contrasted. A series of connective units precedes the second narrative of chs. 1–3. The positive theme of Samuel's future rise and the negative theme of the condemnation of Eli's sons alternate and culminate in the call of Samuel (ch. 3). **11, 18–21:** The barren woman theme (1.1–28 n.) has its conclusion here, in the birth of other children. **12–17:** The sins of Eli's sons consist both in greed (v. 15)

kettle or pot; and the priest would take whatever the fork brought out. This should have been their practice whenever Israelites came to sacrifice at Shiloh; but now, 15 even before the fat was burnt, the priest's servant would come and say to the person who was sacrificing, 'Give me meat to roast for the priest; he will not accept what has been already stewed, only raw meat.' 16 And if the man protested, 'Let them burn the fat first, and then take what you want,' the servant would say, 'No, hand it over now, or I shall take it by force.' 17 The young men's sin was very great in the LORD's sight, for they caused what was offered to him to be brought into general contempt.

18 Samuel continued in the service of the LORD, a mere boy with a linen ephod fastened round him. 19 Every year his mother made him a little cloak and took it to him when she went up with her husband to offer the annual sacrifice. 20 Eli would give his blessing to Elkanah and his wife and say, 'The LORD grant you children by this woman in place of the one whom you made over to the LORD.' Then they would return home.

21 The LORD showed his care for Hannah, and she conceived and gave birth to three sons and two daughters; meanwhile the boy Samuel grew up in the presence of the LORD.

22 When Eli, now a very old man, heard a detailed account of how his sons were treating all the Israelites, and how they lay with the women who were serving at the entrance to the Tent of Meeting, 23 he said to them, 'Why do you do such things? I hear from every quarter how wickedly you behave. 24 Do stop it, my sons; for this is not a good report that I hear spreading among the LORD's people. 25 If someone sins against another, God will intervene; but if someone sins against the LORD, who can intercede for him?' They would not listen, however, to their father's rebuke, for the LORD meant to bring about their death. 26 The young Samuel, as he grew up, increasingly commended himself to the LORD and to the people.

27 A man of God came to Eli and said, 'This is the word of the LORD: You know that I revealed myself to your forefather's house when he and his family were in Egypt in slavery to the house of Pharaoh. 28 You know that I chose your forefather out of all the tribes of Israel to be my priest, to go up to my altar, to burn incense, and to carry the ephod before me; and that I assigned all the food-offerings of the Israelites to your family. 29 Why then do you show disrespect for my sacrifices and the offerings which I have ordained? What makes you resent them? Why do you honour your sons more than me by letting them batten on the choicest offerings of my people Israel? 30 The LORD's word was: I promise that your house and your father's house will serve before me for all time. But now his word is: I shall have no such thing; I shall honour those who honour me, and those who despise me will meet with contempt. 31 The time is coming when I shall lop off every limb of your own and of your father's family, so that no one in your house will attain old age. 32 You will even resent the prosperity I give to Israel; never again will anyone in your house live to old age. 33 If I allow any to survive to serve my altar, his eyes will grow dim, his appetite fail, and his issue will be weaklings and die off. 34 The fate of your two sons will be a proof to you; Hophni and Phinehas will both die on the same day. 35 I shall appoint for myself a priest who will be faithful, who will do what I have in my mind and in my heart. I shall establish his family to serve in perpetual succession before my anointed king. 36 Any of your family still left will come and bow humbly before him to

2:27 **in slavery:** *so Gk; Heb. omits.*   2:28 **carry:** *or wear.*   2:29 **What ... them?:** *so Gk; Heb. a dwelling-place.*   2:32 **You ... resent:** *prob. rdg; Heb. obscure.* **I give:** *so Aram. (Targ.); Heb. he gives.* 2:33 **his:** *so Gk; Heb. your.*

and in cultic violations (v. 16, although the details here are obscure). **18:** *Ephod:* see Exod. 25.7 n. **22–26:** Eli here reproves his sons, in contrast to 3.13 where he is charged with laxity. **22:** *Serving:* the nature of the service of *the women* is not known, but may reflect a sexual and perhaps fertility cult aspect of Canaanite and early Israelite religion. Such women may also be referred to in Exod. 38.8. *Tent* is a traditional term, not taken literally, since it is clear that Shiloh had a temple as its sanctuary (ch. 3). **27–36:** An anonymous *man of God,* rather than Samuel, prophesies against Eli; this preserves 3.11–14 as the climax of the section. **27–28:** The *forefather* is presumably Aaron, to whose grandson Phinehas the promise was given; Num. 25.13. **34–36:** This passage appears to have been written in the light of these subsequent events: (1) The deaths of Hophni and Phinehas in ch. 4; and (2) the Solomonic priestly establishment (see 1 Kgs. 2.27).

beg for a piece of silver and a loaf of bread, and ask for a turn of priestly duty to earn a crust.'

3 The boy Samuel was in the LORD's service under Eli. In those days the word of the LORD was rarely heard, and there was no outpouring of vision. ² One night Eli, whose eyes were dim and his sight failing, was lying down in his usual place, ³ while Samuel slept in the temple of the LORD where the Ark of God was. Before the lamp of God had gone out, ⁴ the LORD called him, and Samuel answered, 'Here I am!' ⁵ and ran to Eli saying, 'You called me: here I am.' 'No, I did not call you,' said Eli; 'lie down again.' So he went and lay down. ⁶ The LORD called Samuel again, and he got up and went to Eli. 'Here I am!' he said. 'Surely you called me.' 'I did not call, my son,' he answered; 'lie down again.' ⁷ Samuel had not yet come to know the LORD, and the word of the LORD had not been disclosed to him. ⁸ When the LORD called him for the third time, he again went to Eli and said, 'Here I am! You did call me.' Then Eli understood that it was the LORD calling the boy; ⁹ he told Samuel to go and lie down and said, 'If someone calls once more, say, "Speak, LORD; your servant is listening."' So Samuel went and lay down in his place.

¹⁰ Then the LORD came, and standing there called, 'Samuel, Samuel!' as before. Samuel answered, 'Speak, your servant is listening.' ¹¹ The LORD said, 'Soon I shall do something in Israel which will ring in the ears of all who hear it. ¹² When that day comes I shall make good every word from beginning to end that I have spoken against Eli and his family. ¹³ You are to tell him that my judgement on his house will stand for ever because he knew of his sons' blasphemies against God and did not restrain them. ¹⁴ Therefore I have sworn to the family of Eli that their abuse of sacrifices and offerings will never be expiated.'

¹⁵ Samuel lay down till morning, when he opened the doors of the house of the LORD; but he was afraid to tell Eli about the vision. ¹⁶ Eli called Samuel: 'Samuel, my son!' he said; and Samuel answered, 'Here I am!' ¹⁷ Eli asked, 'What did the LORD say to you? Do not hide it from me. God's curse upon you if you conceal from me one word of all that he said to you.' ¹⁸ Then Samuel told him everything, concealing nothing. Eli said, 'The LORD must do what is good in his eyes.'

¹⁹ As Samuel grew up, the LORD was with him, and none of his words went unfulfilled. ²⁰ From Dan to Beersheba, all Israel recognized that Samuel was attested as a prophet of the LORD. ²¹ So the LORD continued to appear in Shiloh, because he had revealed himself there to Samuel. ¹ Samuel's word had authority throughout Israel.

The struggle with the Philistines

THE time came when the Philistines mustered for battle against Israel, and the Israel-

3:13 **You are to:** *prob. rdg; Heb.* I shall. **because:** *prob. rdg; Heb.* in guilt. **against God:** *prob. original reading, altered in Heb. to* to them.   3:21 **because . . . Samuel:** *prob. rdg; Heb. adds* according to the word of the LORD. 4:1 **The time . . . Israel:** *so Gk; Heb. omits.*

3.1–4.1a: Samuel becomes a prophet. Chapter 1 explains Samuel's priestly role. This narrative explains his prophetic role. The account of the wonder child (vv. 4–9) is lighthearted compared with the somber seriousness of the divine message (vv. 11–14). **3:** How and when the *Ark of God* came to be based at Shiloh is not known (but see Josh. 18.1). **4:** *The lamp of God* was a regular feature of sanctuaries; see Exod. 27.21; Lev. 24.1–4; 1 Kgs. 7.48–49. **4–9:** The artfulness of the story should not lead to regarding this as a primitive stage of the religion of Israel. **13:** This prophecy, not entirely compatible with 2.27–36, exhibits a view of Eli earlier than that in 2.22–25. **15–18:** Eli is here a tragic figure, in contrast to vv. 11–14.

4.1b–7.1: The Ark of the Lord and its movements. Chapters 1–3 prepare for ch. 4; however, Samuel does not appear in chs. 4–6, where the focus is on the Ark, that box-throne object upon which the presence of the Lord of Israel was made manifest; see Exod. 25.22; Num. 7.89; 10.33–36; and Josh. chs. 3–4. The narrative of chs. 4–6 has a conclusion in 2 Sam. ch. 6, with the Ark finally brought to David's Jerusalem. The primary point of the total Ark story is that the LORD (not merely the Ark) moved from Shiloh to Jerusalem; the narrative here is as mythical (that is, a story of the activities of a god) as is any section in the historical books of the OT.

4.1b–22: The Philistine defeat of Israel. This chapter could be called "the departure of the Ark," since the LORD here permits the defeat of Israel and withdraws from the people. This is the sequel toward which chs. 2–3 look.

4.1b–11: The battles. 1b: *The Philistines* were based in five main cities on the southwestern coastal plain ites, marching out to meet them, encamped near Eben-ezer, while the Philistines' camp was at Aphek. ²The Philistines drew up their lines facing the Israelites, and when battle was joined the Israelites were defeated by the Philistines, who killed about four thousand men on the field. ³When their army got back to camp, the Israelite elders asked, 'Why did the Lord let us be defeated today by the Philistines? Let us fetch the Ark of the Covenant of the Lord from Shiloh to go with us and deliver us from the power of our enemies.' ⁴The army sent to Shiloh and fetched the Ark of the Covenant of the Lord of Hosts, who is enthroned upon the cherubim; Eli's two sons, Hophni and Phinehas, were there with the Ark.

⁵When the Ark came into the camp it was greeted with such a great shout by all the Israelites that the earth rang. ⁶The Philistines, hearing the noise, asked, 'What is this great shouting in the camp of the Hebrews?' When they learned that the Ark of the Lord had come into the camp, ⁷they were alarmed. 'A god has come into the camp,' they cried. 'We are lost! No such thing has ever happened before. ⁸We are utterly lost! Who can deliver us from the power of this mighty god? This is the god who broke the Egyptians and crushed them in the wilderness. ⁹Courage, act like men, you Philistines, or you will become slaves to the Hebrews as they were to you. Be men, and fight!' ¹⁰The Philistines then gave battle, and the Israelites were defeated and fled to their homes. It was a great defeat, and thirty thousand Israelite foot-soldiers fell. ¹¹The Ark of God was captured, and Eli's two sons, Hophni and Phinehas, perished.

¹²A Benjamite ran from the battlefield and reached Shiloh on the same day, his clothes torn and dust on his head. ¹³When he arrived Eli was sitting on a seat by the road to Mizpah, for he was deeply troubled about the Ark of God. The man entered the town with his news, and all the people cried out in horror. ¹⁴When Eli heard the uproar, he asked, 'What does it mean?' The man hurried to Eli and told him. ¹⁵Eli was ninety-eight years old and sat staring with sightless eyes. ¹⁶The man said to him, 'I am the one who has just come from the battle. I fled from the field this very day.' Eli asked, 'What is the news, my son?' ¹⁷The runner answered, 'The Israelites have fled before the Philistines; the army has suffered severe losses; your two sons, Hophni and Phinehas, are dead; and the Ark of God is taken.' ¹⁸At the mention of the Ark of God, Eli fell backwards from his seat by the gate and broke his neck, for he was an old man and heavy. So he died; he had been judge over Israel for forty years.

¹⁹His daughter-in-law, the wife of Phinehas, was pregnant and near her time, and when she heard of the capture of the Ark and the deaths of her father-in-law and her husband, she went into labour and she crouched down and was delivered. ²⁰As she lay dying, the women who attended her said, 'Do not be afraid; you have a son.' But she did not answer or heed what they said. ²¹She named the boy Ichabod, saying, 'Glory has departed from Israel,' referring to the capture of the Ark of God and the deaths of her father-in-law and her husband; ²²'Glory has departed from Israel,' she said, 'because the Ark of God is taken.'

4:21 Ichabod: *that is* No-glory.

of Palestine. The events reflected here occurred around 1050 B.C.E. and were part of a Philistine move to rule all of Palestine. The battle occurs at the base of a pass leading up to the hill country around Shiloh. **3:** Compare Josh. 7.2–9. **4:** The throne character of the Ark is clear here. The Lord was understood to be seated invisibly between two winged creatures, the *cherubim;* compare Exod. 25.10–22. **5–9:** This second Israelite effort, with the sacred object now with them, should have succeeded; instead the Ark's presence increases the dramatic tension. **6:** *Hebrews:* this term originally designated a social status rather than an ethnic group; (see 14.21 and Gen. 14.13; 39.14; Exod. 1.15–22). **8:** The Philistines are portrayed as garbling the Israelite sacred history.

4.12–22: The fall of Eli's house. The prophecies in chs. 2.27–54 and 3.11–14 are here fulfilled. **12:** *Clothes torn and dust on his head* indicates mourning. **13:** *Seat* can also be translated "throne," which, if an elevated seat, could explain why Eli's fall breaks his neck in v. 18. **18:** *Judge over Israel* is a comment by a later writer bringing Eli into the system of judges presented by Deuteronomic historians; see 7.15; Judg. 2.6–23. **21:** A popular etymology for the name *Ichabod* is based on the loss of the Ark. Though the Philistines captured and destroyed Shiloh at this time, some members of Eli's house escaped.

5 After the Philistines had captured the Ark of God, they brought it from Eben-ezer to Ashdod, ²where they carried it into the temple of Dagon and set it beside the god. ³When the people of Ashdod rose next morning, there was Dagon fallen face downwards on the ground before the Ark of the LORD. They lifted him up and put him back in his place. ⁴But next morning when they rose, Dagon had again fallen face downwards on the ground before the Ark of the LORD, with his head and his two hands lying broken off beside his platform; only Dagon's body remained on it. ⁵That is why to this day the priests of Dagon and all who enter the temple of Dagon at Ashdod do not set foot on Dagon's platform.

⁶The LORD's hand oppressed the people of Ashdod. He threw them into despair; he plagued them with tumours, and their territory swarmed with rats. There was death and destruction all through the city. ⁷Seeing this, the men of Ashdod decided, 'The Ark of the God of Israel must not stay here, for his hand is pressing on us and on Dagon our god.' ⁸When they called together all the Philistine lords to ask what should be done with the Ark, they were told, 'Let the Ark of the God of Israel be taken across to Gath.' They moved it there, ⁹and after its removal there the LORD caused great havoc in that city; he plagued everybody, high and low alike, with the tumours which broke out. ¹⁰So the Ark of God was sent on to Ekron, and when it arrived there, the people cried, 'They have moved the Ark of the God of Israel over to us, to kill us and our families.' ¹¹Summoning all the Philistine lords they said, 'Send the Ark of the God of Israel away; let it go back to its own place, or it will be the death of us all.' There was death and destruction all through the city; for the hand of God lay heavy upon it. ¹²Those who did not die were plagued with tumours, and the cry of the city ascended to heaven.

6 When the Ark of the LORD had been in their territory for seven months, ²the Philistines summoned the priests and soothsayers and asked, 'What shall we do with the Ark of the LORD? Tell us how we ought to send it back to its own place.' ³Their answer was, 'If you send the Ark of the God of Israel back, do not let it go empty, but send it back with an offering by way of compensation; if you are then healed you will know why his hand had not been lifted from you.' ⁴When they were asked, 'What should we send to him?' they answered, 'Send five tumours modelled in gold and five gold rats, one for each of the Philistine lords, for the same plague afflicted all of you and your lords. ⁵Make models of your tumours and of the rats which are ravaging the land, and give honour to the God of Israel; perhaps he will relax the pressure of his hand on you, your god, and your land. ⁶Why be stubborn like Pharaoh and the Egyptians? Remember how this God made sport of them until they let Israel go.

⁷'Now make ready a new wagon with two milch cows which have never been yoked; harness the cows to the wagon, but take their calves away and keep them in their stall. ⁸Fetch the Ark of the LORD and put it on the wagon, place beside it in a casket the gold offerings that you are sending to him, and let it go where it will. ⁹Watch: if it goes up towards its own territory to Beth-shemesh, then it was the LORD who has inflicted this great injury on us; but if not, then we shall

5:4 **beside his platform:** or upon the threshold. **Dagon's body:** prob. rdg, cp. Gk; Heb. Dagon. 5:6 **tumours:** or, as otherwise read, haemorrhoids. **and their ... city:** so Gk; Heb. Ashdod and its territory. **rats:** or mice.   6:4 **you:** so some MSS; others them.

5.1–5: The LORD defeats Dagon. The action is presented realistically in terms of what the Philistines did and found, not in terms of what the gods did; it is nevertheless mythical (see 4.1b–7.1 n.). **1:** Ashdod was one of the five Philistine cities; see 6.17. The others were Ashkelon, Ekron, Gath, and Gaza. **2:** Dagon was a god of grain worshiped in Palestine before the Philistines arrived (about 1200 B.C.E.) and adopted the worship of him.

5.6–12: The LORD plagues the Philistines. An epidemic of bubonic plague may lie behind this artistic presentation of the power of the God of Israel.

6.1–7.1: The Ark proceeds to Judah. 1–5: The golden tumours and rats represent sympathetic magic, i.e. ritual imitations of what is to be removed. **6:** The entire Ark story seems to reflect the influence of the account of the plagues on Egypt (Exod. chs. 7–11). **7–12:** This action shows that the LORD alone determined the movement. Possibly old rituals for moving the Ark are reflected here. **7:** A new wagon was needed to avoid any contamination from previous use. **9:** Beth-shemesh, much further south than Shiloh and Eben-ezer, was know that it was not his hand that struck us, but that we have been the victims of chance.' ¹⁰ They did this: they took two milch cows and harnessed them to a wagon, meanwhile shutting up their calves in the stall; ¹¹ they placed the Ark of the LORD on the wagon together with the casket containing the gold rats, and the models of their tumours. ¹² The cows went straight in the direction of Beth-shemesh; they kept to the road, lowing as they went and turning neither right nor left, while the Philistine lords followed them as far as the territory of Beth-shemesh.

¹³ The people of Beth-shemesh, busy harvesting their wheat in the valley, looked up and saw the Ark, and they rejoiced at the sight. ¹⁴ The wagon came to the field of Joshua of Beth-shemesh and halted there, close by a great stone. The people chopped up the wood of the wagon and offered the cows as a whole-offering to the LORD. ¹⁵ The Levites who lifted down the Ark of the LORD and the casket containing the gold offerings laid them on the great stone; and the men of Beth-shemesh offered whole-offerings and shared-offerings that day to the LORD. ¹⁶ The five lords of the Philistines watched all this, and returned to Ekron the same day.

¹⁷ These golden tumours which the Philistines sent back as an offering to the LORD were for Ashdod, Gaza, Ashkelon, Gath, and Ekron, one for each city. ¹⁸ The gold rats were for all the towns of the Philistines governed by the five lords, both fortified towns and open settlements. The great stone where they deposited the Ark of the LORD stands witness on the farm of Joshua of Beth-shemesh to this day.

¹⁹ But the sons of Jeconiah did not rejoice with the rest of the men of Beth-shemesh when they welcomed the Ark of the LORD, and he struck down seventy of them. The people mourned because the LORD had struck them so heavy a blow, ²⁰ and the men

of Beth-shemesh said, 'No one is safe in the presence of the LORD, this holy God. To whom can we send the Ark, to be rid of him?' ²¹ So they sent this message to the inhabitants of Kiriath-jearim: 'The Philistines have returned the Ark of the LORD; come down and take charge of it.' ¹ The men of Kiriath-jearim came and took the Ark of the LORD away; they brought it into the house of Abinadab on the hill and consecrated his son Eleazar as its custodian.

Samuel judge over Israel

² FOR a long while, some twenty years in all, the Ark was housed in Kiriath-jearim. Then there was a movement throughout Israel to follow the LORD, ³ and Samuel addressed these words to the whole nation: 'If your return to the LORD is whole-hearted, banish the foreign gods and the ashtaroth from your shrines; turn to the LORD with heart and mind, and worship him alone, and he will deliver you from the Philistines.' ⁴ So the Israelites banished the baalim and the ashtaroth, and worshipped the LORD alone.

⁵ Samuel summoned all Israel to an assembly at Mizpah, so that he might intercede with the LORD for them. ⁶ When they had assembled, they drew water and poured it out before the LORD and fasted all day, confessing that they had sinned against the LORD. It was at Mizpah that Samuel acted as judge over Israel.

⁷ When the Philistines heard that the Israelites had assembled at Mizpah, their lords marched against them. The Israelites heard that the Philistines were advancing, and they were afraid ⁸ and begged Samuel, 'Do not

6:18 **The great stone:** *so Gk; Heb.* Abel-haggedolah.
6:19 **But . . . seventy of them:** *prob. rdg, cp. Gk; Heb.* And he struck down some of the men of Beth-shemesh because they had gazed upon the Ark of the LORD; he struck down seventy men among the people, fifty thousand men.

situated in a pass leading up from Ekron toward Jerusalem. **13–18:** A local sanctuary at Beth-shemesh is here reflected. The cows go directly to the *great stone,* and sacrifices are first offered to the LORD there. **15:** This verse is a later correction to introduce *the Levites* as functionaries in accordance with subsequent practice. **17–18:** *Golden tumours . . . rats:* the passage is old, as if the writer witnessed the events and saw these things. **6:19–7:1:** This passage provides a transition from the end of the Philistine story (6.18) to the later movement of the Ark from Kiriath-jearim to Jerusalem (2 Sam. ch. 6).

7.2–17: Samuel judges at Mizpah. This passage portrays Samuel as a "judge," conforming to the schematic formula of the Deuteronomic authors; see 4.18 n. **4:** *Baalim* and *Ashtaroth* were cult objects representing the Canaanite fertility deities Baal and Astarte. **5:** *Mizpah,* in the vicinity of Bethel, Gilgal, and Ramah (vv. 15–16), was in Benjaminite territory, considerably further south than Shiloh; this reflects the continued encroachment cease to pray for us to the LORD our God to save us from the power of the Philistines.' ⁹Samuel took a sucking-lamb, offered it up complete as a whole-offering, and prayed aloud to the LORD on behalf of Israel, and the LORD answered his prayer. ¹⁰As Samuel was offering the sacrifice and the Philistines were advancing to the attack, the LORD with mighty thunder threw the Philistines into confusion. They fled in panic before the Israelites, ¹¹who set out from Mizpah in pursuit and kept up the slaughter of the Philistines till they reached a point below Beth-car.

¹²There Samuel took a stone and set it up as a monument between Mizpah and Jeshanah, naming it Eben-ezer. 'This is a witness', he said, 'that the LORD has helped us.' ¹³Thus the Philistines were subdued and no longer encroached on the territory of Israel; as long as Samuel lived, the hand of the LORD was against them. ¹⁴The towns they had captured were restored to Israel, and from Ekron to Gath the borderland was freed from Philistine control. Between Israel and the Amorites also peace was maintained.

¹⁵Samuel acted as judge in Israel as long as he lived, ¹⁶and every year went on circuit to Bethel, Gilgal, and Mizpah; he dispensed justice at all these places. ¹⁷But always he went back to Ramah; that was his home and the place from which he governed Israel, and there he built an altar to the LORD.

Establishment of the monarchy

8 WHEN Samuel grew old, he appointed his sons to be judges in Israel. ²The eldest son was called Joel and the second Abiah; they acted as judges in Beersheba. ³His sons did not follow their father's ways but were intent on their own profit, taking bribes and perverting the course of justice. ⁴So all the elders of Israel met, and came to Samuel at Ramah. ⁵They said to him, 'You are now old and your sons do not follow your ways; appoint us a king to rule us, like all the other nations.' ⁶But their request for a king displeased Samuel. He prayed to the LORD, ⁷and the LORD told him, 'Listen to the people and all that they are saying; they have not rejected you, it is I whom they have rejected, I whom they will not have to be their king. ⁸They are now doing to you just what they have done to me since I brought them up from Egypt: they have forsaken me and worshipped other gods. ⁹Hear what they have to say now, but give them a solemn warning and tell them what sort of king will rule them.'

¹⁰Samuel reported to the people who were asking him for a king all that the LORD had said to him. ¹¹'This will be the sort of king who will bear rule over you,' he said. 'He will take your sons and make them serve in his chariots and with his cavalry, and they will

7:12 **Jeshanah:** *prob. rdg (cp. 2 Chr. 13:19); Heb. the tooth.* **Eben-ezer:** *that is* Stone of Help.

of the Philistines. **6:** Pouring out water (rather than wine) is not a common ritual in the OT. **13–14:** This period of peace conforms to the view of the Deuteronomic historians regarding the achievements of the judges; see Judg. 2.18. **15–17:** This more modest view of Samuel is probably an accurate glimpse of him. Here he is based at Ramah, a local sanctuary, as is seen in ch. 9.

8.1–15.35: Israel becomes a kingdom. In chs. 1–7, Samuel was established as prophet, as judge, and as successor to the Shiloh priestly establishment, these achievements qualifying him to be kingmaker. Moreover, the LORD moved south from Shiloh to Judah, as symbolized by the movement of the Ark. The scene is now set for kingship. Kingship is a topic with two parts: the question of the legitimacy of kingship itself (chs. 8–14); and the establishment of the house of David in place of the house of Saul (ch. 15–2 Sam. ch. 7).

8.1–22: The negative view of kingship. One strand of material (ch. 8; 10.17–27; ch. 12) regards human kingship as the rejection of the kingship of the LORD; this strand may be read as a single account without a gap. The positive strand begins in ch. 9. The negative, with some affinities with the Deuteronomic historians' views, is the later of the two strands, even though the basic attitude may go back to opposition to monarchy in principle in early Israel. **1:** *Judges* are not the military heroes of the Book of Judges, but only those persons responsible for administering justice (see Exod. 18.13–27 and 2 Chr. 19.4–11). **2:** *Beersheba,* in southern Judah, was an important sanctuary; see Amos 5.5 and 8.14. **3:** *Taking bribes* was a recurrent problem; see Exod. 23.6–8; Isa. 5.22–23; Deut. 16.19. **4:** *Ramah* is probably the city of Samuel's parents (see 1.1 n.) and is Samuel's base from here on, especially in the strand favorable to kingship. **11–18:** This is mostly a portrayal of typical ancient Near Eastern monarchy. The portrayal may be based on practices of Solomon which generated resentment as in 1 Kgs. 12.4.

run before his chariot. 12 Some he will appoint officers over units of a thousand and units of fifty. Others will plough his fields and reap his harvest; others again will make weapons of war and equipment for the chariots. 13 He will take your daughters for perfumers, cooks, and bakers. 14 He will seize the best of your fields, vineyards, and olive groves, and give them to his courtiers. 15 He will take a tenth of your grain and your vintage to give to his eunuchs and courtiers. 16 Your slaves, both men and women, and the best of your cattle and your donkeys he will take for his own use. 17 He will take a tenth of your flocks, and you yourselves will become his slaves. 18 There will come a day when you will cry out against the king whom you have chosen; but the LORD will not answer you on that day.'

19 The people, however, refused to listen to Samuel. 'No,' they said, 'we must have a king over us; 20 then we shall be like other nations, with a king to rule us, to lead us out to war and fight our battles.' 21 When Samuel heard what the people had decided, he told the LORD, 22 who said, 'Take them at their word and appoint them a king.' Samuel then dismissed all the Israelites to their homes.

9 There was a man from the territory of Benjamin, whose name was Kish son of Abiel, son of Zeror, son of Bechorath, son of Aphiah a Benjamite. He was a man of substance, 2 and had a son named Saul, a young man in his prime; there was no better man among the Israelites than he. He stood a head taller than any of the people.

3 One day some donkeys belonging to Saul's father Kish had strayed, so he said to his son Saul, 'Take one of the servants with you, and go and look for the donkeys.' 4 They crossed the hill-country of Ephraim and went through the district of Shalisha but did not find them; they passed through the district of Shaalim but they were not there; they passed through the district of Benjamin but again did not find them. 5 When they reached the district of Zuph, Saul said to the servant who was with him, 'Come, we ought to turn back, or my father will stop thinking about the donkeys and begin to worry about us.' 6 The servant answered, 'There is a man of God in this town who has a great reputation, because everything he says comes true. Suppose we go there; he may tell us which way to take.' 7 Saul said, 'If we go, what shall we offer him? There is no food left in our packs and we have no present to give the man of God, nothing at all.' 8 The servant answered him again, 'Wait! I have here a quarter-shekel of silver. I can give that to the man, to tell us the way.' 10 Saul said, 'Good! Let us go to him.' So they went to the town where the man of God lived. 9 (In Israel in days gone by, when someone wished to consult God, he would say, 'Let us go to the seer.' For what is nowadays called a prophet used to be called a seer.)

11 As they were going up the ascent to the town they met some girls coming out to draw water and asked them, 'Shall we find the seer there?' 12 'Yes,' they answered, 'he is ahead of you; hurry now, for he has just arrived in the town because there is a feast at the shrine today. 13 As you enter the town you will meet him before he goes up to the shrine to eat; the people will not start until he comes, for he has to bless the sacrifice before the invited company can eat. Go up now, and you will find him at once.' 14 So they went up to the town and, just as they were going in, there was Samuel coming towards them on his way up to the shrine.

15 The day before Saul's arrival there, the LORD had disclosed his intention to Samuel: 16 'At this time tomorrow', he said, 'I shall send you a man from the territory of Benjamin, and you are to anoint him prince over my people Israel. He will deliver my people from the Philistines; for I have seen the sufferings of my people, and their cry has reached my ears.' 17 The moment Saul ap-

8:16 **your cattle:** *so Gk; Heb.* your picked men.
9:9–10 *Verses 9 and 10 transposed.*   9:16 **the sufferings of:** *so Gk; Heb. omits.*

9.1–10.16: The anointing of Saul. 2: The words *a young man* are suited to this hero story, but see 13.1. **4:** The *district*(s) mentioned here have not been identified with certainty in biblical geography. **5:** *Zuph:* see 1.1. **6:** *Everything he says comes true:* this repeats the substance of 3.19–21. **9:** The term *seer* was no longer used in the time of the writer, when a seer was *called a prophet*. **12:** *Shrine:* in early Israel no stigma applied to the local sanctuaries, but later Israelite tradition condemned them without qualification; see 1 Kgs. 3.2; 2 Kgs. 12.3; 14.4. **15–16:** Kingship here is a gracious benefit bestowed by the LORD. In the strand (see 8.1–22 n.) favorable to kingship, *prince* is used rather than "king"; king is used in the negative strand. Compare 10.1;

peared the LORD said to Samuel, 'Here is the man of whom I spoke to you. This man will govern my people.' 18 Saul came up to Samuel in the gateway and said, 'Tell me, please, where the seer lives.' 19 Samuel replied, 'I am the seer. Go on ahead of me to the shrine and eat with me today; in the morning I shall set you on your way, after telling you what you have on your mind. 20 Trouble yourself no more about the donkeys lost three days ago; they have been found. To whom does the tribute of all Israel belong? It belongs to you and to your whole ancestral house.' 21 'But I am a Benjamite,' said Saul, 'from the smallest of the tribes of Israel, and my family is the least important of all the families of the tribe of Benjamin. Why do you say this to me?'

22 Samuel brought Saul and his servant into the dining-hall and gave them a place at the head of the invited company, about thirty in number. 23 He said to the cook, 'Bring the portion that I gave you and told you to put on one side.' 24 The cook took up the whole haunch and leg and put it before Saul; and Samuel said, 'Here is the portion of meat kept for you. Eat it: it has been reserved for you at this feast to which I have invited the people.'

Saul dined with Samuel that day, 25 and when they came down from the shrine to the town a bed was spread on the roof for Saul, and he stayed there that night. 26 At dawn Samuel called to Saul on the roof, 'Get up, and I shall set you on your way.' When Saul rose, he and Samuel went outside together, 27 and as they came to the edge of the town, Samuel said to Saul, 'Tell the boy to go on ahead.' He did so; then Samuel said, 'Stay here a moment, and I shall tell you what God has said.'

10 Samuel took a flask of oil and poured it over Saul's head; he kissed him and said, 'The LORD anoints you prince over his people Israel. You are to rule the people of the LORD and deliver them from the enemies round about. You will receive a sign that the LORD has anointed you prince to govern his

possession: 2 when you leave me today, you will meet two men by Rachel's tomb at Zelzah in the territory of Benjamin. They will tell you that the donkeys you set out to look for have been found and that your father is concerned for them no longer; he is anxious about you and keeps saying, "What shall I do about my son?" 3 From there go across country as far as the terebinth of Tabor, where three men going up to Bethel to worship God will meet you. One of them will be carrying three young goats, the second three loaves, and the third a skin of wine. 4 They will greet you and offer you two loaves, which you will accept. 5 Then when you reach the hill of God, where the Philistine governor resides, you will meet a company of prophets coming down from the shrine, led by lute, drum, fife, and lyre, and filled with prophetic rapture. 6 The spirit of the LORD will suddenly take possession of you, and you too will be rapt like a prophet and become another man. 7 When these signs happen, do whatever the occasion demands; God will be with you. 8 You are to go down to Gilgal ahead of me, and I shall come to you to sacrifice whole-offerings and shared-offerings. Wait seven days until I join you; then I shall tell you what to do.'

9 As Saul turned to leave Samuel, God made him a different person. On that same day all these signs happened. 10 When they reached the hill there was a company of prophets coming to meet him, and the spirit of God suddenly took possession of him, so that he too was filled with prophetic rapture. 11 When people who had known him previously saw that he was rapt like the prophets, they said to one another, 'What can have happened to the son of Kish? Is Saul also among the prophets?' 12 One of the men of that place said, 'And whose sons are they?' Hence the proverb, 'Is Saul also among the prophets?'

9:24 **the portion of meat:** *prob. rdg; Heb.* what is left over. **to which:** *so Lat.; Heb.* saying.   9:25 **a bed ... and he:** *so Gk; Heb.* he spoke with Saul on the roof and they.   10:1 **The LORD anoints ... sign:** *so Gk; Heb.* omits.   10:5 **governor:** *or* garrison.

13.14. ("King" in 10.16 translates the Heb. for "kingship.") **10.1:** *Anointing:* the rite which raised a commoner to kingship in Israel. Saul and David were anointed in secret; compare 16.1–13. Later it was a more formal and public act; see 1 Kgs. 1.32–40. **2:** *Rachel's tomb* was especially associated with Benjamin; see Gen. 35.16–20. **6–8:** *Another man:* prophecy in early times was marked by a frantic dance which altered the prophet's mental state. Compare 19.23–24. **8:** This verse is an addition, preparing for the rupture between Samuel and Saul in 13.8–14. *Gilgal* seems to have had special importance for kingship (11.14–15; 13.7–14; 15.10–33; 2 Sam. 19.15, 39–40), but why is not clear. **11–12:** In 19.19–24 the origin of the proverb about

13 When the prophetic rapture had passed, he went home. 14 Saul's uncle said to him and the boy, 'Where have you been?' Saul answered, 'To look for the donkeys, and when we could not find them, we went to Samuel.' 15 His uncle said, 'Tell me what Samuel said.' 16 'He told us that the donkeys had been found,' replied Saul; but he did not repeat what Samuel had said about his being king.

17 Samuel summoned the Israelites to the LORD at Mizpah 18 and said to them, 'This is the word of the LORD the God of Israel: I brought Israel up from Egypt; I delivered you from the Egyptians and from all the kingdoms that oppressed you. 19 But today you have rejected your God who saved you from all your misery and distress; you have said, "No, set a king over us." Therefore take up your positions now before the LORD tribe by tribe and clan by clan.'

20 Samuel presented all the tribes of Israel, and Benjamin was picked by lot. 21 Then he presented the tribe of Benjamin, family by family, and the family of Matri was picked. He presented the family of Matri, man by man, and Saul son of Kish was picked; but when search was made he was not to be found. 22 They went on to ask the LORD, 'Will the man be coming?' The LORD answered, 'There he is, hiding among the baggage.' 23 So some ran and fetched him out, and as he took his stand among the people, he was a head taller than anyone else. 24 Samuel said to the people, 'Look at the man whom the LORD has chosen; there is no one like him in this whole nation.' They all acclaimed him, shouting, 'Long live the king!'

25 Samuel explained to the people the nature of a king, and made a written record of it on a scroll which he deposited before the LORD. He then dismissed them to their homes. 26 Saul too went home to Gibeah, and with him went some fighting men whose hearts God had moved. 27 But there were scoundrels who said, 'How can this fellow deliver us?' They thought nothing of him and brought him no gifts.

11 About a month later Nahash the Ammonite attacked and besieged Jabesh-gilead. The men of Jabesh said to Nahash, 'Grant us terms and we will be your subjects.' 2 Nahash answered, 'On one condition only shall I grant you terms: that I gouge out the right eye of every one of you and bring disgrace on all Israel.' 3 The elders of Jabesh-gilead said, 'Give us seven days' respite to send messengers throughout Israel and then, if no one relieves us, we shall surrender to you.' 4 The messengers came to Gibeah, where Saul lived, and delivered their message, and all the people broke into lamentation and weeping. 5 Saul was just coming from the field, driving in the oxen, and asked why the people were lamenting; and they told him what the men of Jabesh had said. 6 When Saul heard this, the spirit of God suddenly seized him; in anger 7 he took a pair of oxen, cut them in pieces, and sent messengers with the pieces all through Israel to proclaim that the same would be done to the oxen of any man who did not follow Saul and Samuel to battle. The fear of the LORD fell upon the people and they came out to a man. 8 Saul mustered them in Bezek, three hun-

10:13 **home:** *prob. rdg; Heb.* to the shrine.
10:19 **said, "No:** *so many MSS; others* said to him.
10:21 **He... by man:** *so Gk; Heb.* omits.   10:22 **the man:** *so Gk; Heb.* a man.   10:26 **some fighting men:** *so Gk; Heb.* the army.   11:1 **About ... later:** *so Scroll; Heb.* But he was silent.

Saul is explained differently. **14:** *Saul's uncle* was probably Ner; see 14.50.

10.17–27: Saul is acclaimed as king. Continuing the negative strand on kingship (see 8.1–22 n.) from ch. 8, the LORD here grudgingly provides the best man for kingship. **17:** *Mizpah* is the place of assembly in the negative strand, Gilgal in the positive. **20–21:** This method of divine selection is seen also in the Achan story in Josh. ch. 7. **22:** The verse is puzzling. Perhaps it is meant to stress Saul's passivity or modesty. **23–24:** Samuel's positive view here is surprising. **25:** This *scroll* apparently did more than repeat the substance of 8.11–18, but probably proceeded to put some limitations on the king's prerogatives.

11.1–15: Saul's victory over the Ammonites. In the positive strand (see 8.1–22 n.) on kingship, this spectacular victory was the occasion for Saul's public establishment as king; see 10.7. **1:** Ammon, east of the Jordan, was the territory of the upper Jabbok river. *Jabesh-gilead* was a city on the lower Jabbok near the Jordan. The Ammonites were probably seeking to control the entirety of the Jabbok basin. **6:** *The spirit of God:* here it is not the ecstasy and frenzy as in 10.10–12; rather, it was the power to act with determination and effectiveness. **7:** The phrase *and Samuel* is probably a later addition to harmonize the different strands; Samuel dred thousand men from Israel and thirty thousand from Judah. [9] He said to the messengers, 'Tell the men of Jabesh-gilead, "Victory will be yours tomorrow by the time the sun is hot." '

When they received this message, the men of Jabesh took heart; [10] but they said to Nahash, 'Tomorrow we shall surrender to you, and then you may deal with us as you think fit.' [11] Next day Saul with his men in three columns forced a way right into the enemy camp during the morning watch and massacred the Ammonites until the day grew hot; those who survived were scattered until no two of them were left together.

[12] The people said to Samuel, 'Who said that Saul should not reign over us? Hand the men over to us to be put to death.' [13] But Saul said, 'No man is to be put to death on a day when the LORD has won such a victory in Israel.' [14] Samuel said to the people, 'Let us now go to Gilgal and there establish the kingship anew.' [15] So they all went to Gilgal and invested Saul there as king in the presence of the LORD. They sacrificed shared-offerings before the LORD, and Saul and all the Israelites celebrated with great joy.

12 SAMUEL thus addressed the assembled Israelites: 'I have listened to your request and installed a king to rule over you. [2] The king is now your leader, while I am old and white-haired and my sons are with you; but I have been your leader from my youth to the present. [3] Here I am! Cite your complaints against me in the presence of the LORD and of his anointed one. Whose ox have I taken, whose donkey have I taken? Whom have I wronged, whom have I oppressed? From whom have I taken a bribe to turn a blind eye? Tell me, and I shall make restitution to you.' [4] They answered, 'You have not wronged us, you have not oppressed us, nor have you taken anything

from anyone.' [5] Samuel said to them, 'This day the LORD is witness among you, his anointed king is witness, that you have found nothing in my hands.' They said, 'He is witness.'

[6] Samuel said to the people, 'The LORD is witness, the LORD who appointed Moses and Aaron and brought your fathers up from Egypt. [7] Now stand up, and here in the presence of the LORD I shall put the case against you and recite all the victories which he has won for you and for your forefathers. [8] After Jacob and his sons had gone down to Egypt and suffered at the hands of the Egyptians, your forefathers appealed to the LORD for help, and he sent Moses and Aaron, who brought them out of Egypt and settled them in this place. [9] But they forgot the LORD their God, and he abandoned them to Sisera, commander-in-chief of King Jabin of Hazor, to the Philistines, and to the king of Moab, and they had to fight against them. [10] Then your forefathers cried to the LORD for help: "We have sinned in forsaking the LORD and worshipping the baalim and the ashtaroth. But now, deliver us from our enemies, and we shall worship you." [11] The LORD sent Jerubbaal and Barak, Jephthah and Samson, and delivered you from your enemies on every side; and you lived in security.

[12] 'Yet when you saw Nahash king of the Ammonites coming against you, you said to me, "No, let us have a king to rule over us," although the LORD your God was your king. [13] Now here is the king you chose; you asked for a king, and the LORD has set one over you. [14] If you will revere the LORD and give true and loyal service, if you do not rebel against his commands, and if you and the king who

11:9 **He:** *so Gk; Heb.* They.   12:6 **is witness:** *so Gk; Heb. omits.*   12:7 **and recite:** *so Gk; Heb. omits.* 12:8 **and his sons:** *so Gk; Heb. omits.* **suffered . . . Egyptians:** *so Gk; Heb. omits.*   12:9 **King Jabin of:** *so Gk; Heb. omits.*   12:11 **Barak:** *so Gk; Heb.* Bedan. **Samson:** *so Gk (Luc.); Heb.* Samuel.

is not a war leader elsewhere in the positive strand. **8:** *Bezek:* north of Shechem and west of the Jordan. **11:** *The morning watch:* the last third of the night. **14–16:** The people of Jabesh-gilead later show their gratitude to Saul (1 Sam. 31.11–13). **14:** *Anew:* in the sense of a public proclamation.

12.1–25: Samuel's farewell address. The speech reviews past deeds of God for Israel and turns to the present situation, with the initiation of kingship. Views of late Deuteronomic writers are present, especially in the contention that the people have rejected the kingship of God by asking for a human king. See 8.1–22 n. **1:** Here it is the people who are held culpable for turning away from the LORD; by contrast, 1 and 2 Kgs. hold the kings responsible for infidelity against the LORD. **7:** A recitation of the saving deeds of God for Israel is part of other addresses, e.g. Josh. 24.2–13. **9–11:** *Sisera:* Judg. chs. 4–5. *Philistines:* Judg. chs. 13–16. *King of Moab:* Judg. 3.12–30. *Jerubbaal:* Gideon, Judg. chs. 6–8. *Barak:* Judg. 4.6–5.11. *Samson:* Judg. chs. 13–16.

reigns over you are faithful to the LORD your God, well and good; 15 but if you do not obey the LORD, and if you rebel against his commands, then his hand will be against you and against your king.

16 'Stand now, and witness the great wonder which the LORD will perform before your eyes. 17 It is now wheat harvest. When I call upon the LORD and he sends thunder and rain, you will know and see how displeasing it was to the LORD for you to ask for a king.' 18 So Samuel called to the LORD and he sent thunder and rain that day; and all the people were in great fear of the LORD and of Samuel.

19 The people all said to Samuel, 'Pray for us your servants to the LORD your God, to save us from death; for we have added to all our other sins the great wickedness of asking for a king.' 20 Samuel answered, 'Do not be afraid; although you have been so wicked, do not give up the worship of the LORD, but serve him with all your heart. 21 Do not turn to the worship of sham gods which can neither help nor save, because they are a sham. 22 For his great name's sake the LORD will not cast you off, because he has resolved to make you his own people.

23 'As for me, God forbid that I should sin against the LORD by ceasing to pray for you. I shall show you what is right and good: 24 to revere the LORD and worship him faithfully with all your heart; for consider what great things he has done for you. 25 But if you persist in wickedness, both you and your king will be swept away.'

Campaign against the Philistines

13 SAUL was thirty years old when he became king, and he reigned over Israel for twenty-two years.

2 Saul picked three thousand men from Israel, two thousand to be with him in Michmash and the hill-country of Bethel and a thousand to be with Jonathan in Gibeah of Benjamin; the rest of the army he dismissed to their homes.

3 Jonathan defeated the Philistine garrison in Geba, and the news spread among the Philistines that the Hebrews were in revolt. Saul sounded the trumpet all through the land; 4 and when the Israelites heard that Saul had defeated a Philistine garrison and that the very name of Israel was offensive among the Philistines, they answered the call to arms and rallied to Saul at Gilgal.

5 The Philistines mustered to attack Israel; they had thirty thousand chariots and six thousand horse, with infantry as countless as sand on the seashore. They went up and camped at Michmash, to the east of Bethaven. 6 The Israelites found themselves in sore straits, for the army was hard pressed, so they hid themselves in caves and holes and among the rocks, in pits and cisterns. 7 Some of them crossed the Jordan into the district of Gad and Gilead, but Saul remained at Gilgal, and all his followers were in a state of alarm. 8 He waited seven days for his meeting with Samuel, but Samuel failed to appear, and when the people began to drift away, 9 Saul said, 'Bring me the whole-offering and the shared-offerings,' and he offered up the whole-offering. 10 Saul had just finished the sacrifice, when Samuel arrived, and he went

12:15 **your king:** so Gk; Heb. your fathers.
13:1 **thirty years:** so some Gk MSS; Heb. a year.
twenty-two: prob. rdg; Heb. two.   13:2 **Gibeah:** Geba in verse 3.   13:3 **garrison:** or governors. **that . . . revolt:** prob. rdg; Heb. has saying, Let the Hebrews hear after through the land.   13:4 **they . . . Gilgal:** or they were summoned to follow Saul to Gilgal.   13:7 **but . . . alarm:** or but Saul was still at Gilgal, and all the army joined him there.

17–18: *Wheat harvest* was in early summer when it never rained. 19–25: The passage strikes a delicate balance between reproving the people and admitting a divine sanction for kingship in Israel. 22: *For his name's sake:* a major motif in Israelite reflections; see Ezek. ch. 20; also Ps. 23.3. 23: Samuel is viewed as a renowned intercessor in Jer. 15.1 and Ps. 99.6–9.

13.1–14.46: Saul's victory over the Philistines. The action is now in the central hill country where the Philistines have virtually secured control. 1: See Tfn. The Heb. text lacks numbers, due to faulty copying. 2: *Michmash* was in central Benjaminite territory, as were most of the places named in this account. *Jonathan* was Saul's warrior son and later (18.1–4) David's bosom friend. *Gibeah* and *Geba* (v. 3) are at times interchanged in this passage. 3: *Hebrews:* see 4.6 n. and 14.21. 4: *Gilgal:* see 10.17 n. 5: The numbers here, as often in OT narratives, are intended to give an impression of vastness rather than an exact count. *Chariots* would have been quite impractical in this terrain (14.4). **7b–15:** This section is a later addition; it is pro-David apologetic, and anti-Saul. Its condemnation of Saul (recurrent in such additions) is rather arbitrary. See 10.8.

out to greet him. [11] Samuel said, 'What have you done?' Saul answered, 'I saw that the people were drifting away from me, and you yourself had not come at the time fixed, and the Philistines were mustering at Michmash; [12] and I thought, "The Philistines will now fall on me at Gilgal, and I have not ensured the LORD's favour"; so I felt compelled to make the whole-offering myself.' [13] Samuel said to Saul, 'You have acted foolishly! You have not kept the command laid on you by the LORD your God; if you had, he would have established your dynasty over Israel for all time. [14] But now your line will not endure; the LORD will seek out a man after his own heart, and appoint him prince over his people, because you have not kept the LORD's command.'

[15] Without more ado Samuel left Gilgal and went on his way. The rest of the people followed Saul, as he moved from Gilgal towards the enemy. At Gibeah of Benjamin he mustered his followers; they were about six hundred men. [16] Saul, his son Jonathan, and their men took up their quarters in Gibeah of Benjamin, while the Philistines were encamped in Michmash. [17] Raiding parties went out from the Philistine camp in three directions. One party headed towards Ophrah in the district of Shual, [18] another towards Beth-horon, and the third towards the range of hills overlooking the valley of Zeboim and the wilderness beyond.

[19] No blacksmith was to be found in the whole of Israel, for the Philistines were determined to prevent the Hebrews from making swords and spears. [20] The Israelites had all to go down to the Philistines for their ploughshares, mattocks, axes, and sickles to be sharpened. [21] The charge was two thirds of a shekel for ploughshares and mattocks, and one third of a shekel for sharpening the axes and pointing the goads. [22] So when war broke out the followers of Saul and Jonathan had neither sword nor spear; only Saul and Jonathan carried arms.

[23] The Philistines had posted a company of troops to hold the pass of Michmash,

14 [1] and one day Saul's son Jonathan said to his armour-bearer, 'Come, let us go over to the Philistine outpost across there.' He did not tell his father, [2] who at the time had his tent under the pomegranate tree at Migron on the outskirts of Gibeah; with him were about six hundred men. [3] The ephod was carried by Ahijah son of Ahitub, Ichabod's brother, son of Phinehas son of Eli, the priest of the LORD at Shiloh. Nobody knew that Jonathan had gone. [4] On either side of the pass through which Jonathan sought to make his way to the Philistine post stood two sharp columns of rock, called Bozez and Seneh; [5] one of them was on the north towards Michmash, and the other on the south towards Geba. [6] Jonathan said to his armour-bearer, 'Let us go and pay a visit to the post of the uncircumcised yonder. Perhaps the LORD will do something for us. Nothing can stop him from winning a victory, by many or by few.' [7] The armour-bearer answered, 'Do what you will, go ahead; I am with you whatever you do.' [8] Jonathan said, 'We shall cross over and let the men see us. [9] If they say, "Stay there till we come to you," then we shall stay where we are and not go up to them. [10] But if they say, "Come up to us," we shall go up; that will be the proof that the LORD has given them into our power.' [11] The two showed themselves to the Philistine outpost. 'Look!' said the Philistines. 'Hebrews coming out of the holes where they have been hiding!' [12] And they called across to Jonathan and his armour-bearer, 'Come up to us; we shall show you something.' Jonathan said to the armour-bearer, 'Come on, the LORD has put them into Israel's power.' [13] Jonathan climbed up on hands and feet, and the armour-bearer followed him. The Philistines fell before Jonathan, and the armour-bearer, coming be-

13:15 **and went . . . enemy:** *prob. rdg, cp. Gk; Heb. omits.*
13:16 **Gibeah:** *so Aram. (Targ.); Heb. Geba.*
13:20 **and sickles:** *so Gk; Heb. and ploughshares.*
13:21 **one third . . . goads:** *prob. rdg; Heb. obscure.*
14:4 **Bozez:** *that is* Shining. **Seneh:** *that is* Bramble Bush.

19–22: This period was the beginning of the iron age. The Philistines had a monopoly on the new metal. **14.1:** *The armour-bearer* accompanied the heavily armored, elite warrior, as in the Homeric epics; see also ch. 17. **3:** This *ephod* is a box (see v. 41) containing lots, and not the linen garment, "cloak," in 2.18. *Ahijah's* lineage is given (probably by a later editor) so as to make his priestly descent clear. **6:** *Uncircumcised* was a term of reproach. Like their Semitic neighbors, the Israelites practiced circumcision, while the Philistines, deriving from Asia Minor and the Aegean, did not; compare Jer. 9.25–26. **9–12:** Jonathan tests divine support for his hind, dispatched them. ¹⁴ In that first attack Jonathan and his armour-bearer killed about twenty of them, like men cutting a furrow across a half-acre field. ¹⁵ Terror spread throughout the army in the camp and in the field; the men at the post and the raiding parties were terrified. The very ground quaked, and there was great panic.

¹⁶ Saul's men on the watch in Gibeah of Benjamin saw the mob of Philistines surging to and fro in confusion. ¹⁷ Saul ordered his forces to call the roll to find out who was missing and, when it was called, they found that Jonathan and his armour-bearer were absent. ¹⁸ Saul said to Ahijah, 'Bring forward the ephod,' for it was he who at that time carried the ephod before Israel. ¹⁹ While Saul was speaking, the confusion in the Philistine camp kept increasing, and he said to the priest, 'Hold your hand.' ²⁰ Then Saul and all his men made a concerted rush for the battlefield, where they found the enemy in complete disorder, every man's sword against his fellow. ²¹ Those Hebrews who up to now had been under the Philistines, and had been with them in camp, changed sides and joined the Israelites under Saul and Jonathan. ²² When all the Israelites in hiding in the hill-country of Ephraim heard that the Philistines were in flight, they also joined in and set off in close pursuit. ²³ That day the LORD delivered Israel, and the fighting passed on beyond Beth-aven.

²⁴ The Israelites had been driven to exhaustion on that day. Saul had issued this warning to the troops: 'A curse on any man who takes food before nightfall and before I have taken vengeance on my enemies.' So no one tasted any food. ²⁵ There was honeycomb in the countryside; ²⁶ but when his men came upon it, dripping with honey though it was, not one of them put his hand to his mouth for fear of the curse. ²⁷ Jonathan, however, had not heard his father's interdict to the

army, and he stretched out the stick that was in his hand, dipped the end of it in the honeycomb, put it to his mouth, and was refreshed. ²⁸ One of the people said to him, 'Your father strictly forbade this, saying, "A curse on the man who eats food today!" And the men are faint.' ²⁹ Jonathan said, 'My father has done the people great harm; see how I am refreshed by this mere taste of honey. ³⁰ How much better if the army had eaten today whatever they took from their enemies by way of spoil! Then there would indeed have been a great slaughter of Philistines.'

³¹ Israel defeated the Philistines that day, and pursued them from Michmash to Aijalon. But the troops were so faint with hunger ³² that they turned to plunder and seized sheep, cattle, and calves; they slaughtered them on the bare ground, and ate the meat with the blood in it. ³³ Someone told Saul that the people were sinning against the LORD by eating meat with the blood in it. 'This is treacherous behaviour!' cried Saul. 'Roll a great stone here at once.' ³⁴ He then said, 'Go about among the troops and tell them to bring their oxen and sheep, and to slaughter and eat them here; and so they will not sin against the LORD by eating meat with the blood in it.' So as night fell each man came, driving his own ox, and slaughtered it there. ³⁵ Thus Saul came to erect an altar to the LORD, and this was the first altar to the LORD that he erected.

³⁶ Saul said, 'Let us go down and make a night attack on the Philistines and harry them till daylight; we will not spare a single

14:14 **like men cutting:** *so Syriac; Heb.* as in half of.
14:16 **to and fro:** *so Gk; Heb.* and he went thither.
14:18 **'Bring . . . Israel:** *so Gk; Heb.* 'Bring forward the Ark of God,' for the Ark of God was on that day and the Israelites.   14:21 **changed sides:** *so Gk; Heb.* round and also.   14:25 **There was honeycomb:** *prob. rdg; Heb.* All the land went into the forest, and there was honey.

enterprise; compare Gen. 24.12–14; Judg. 6.36–40. **14–15:** The panic that produces victory is not here ascribed simply to divine intervention, but to heroic and surprising action; contrast 7.10–11; see 7.7–10 n. **16–23:** Haste was required to take advantage of Jonathan's stroke. Consulting the oracle involved careful and time-consuming steps by the priest, and Saul (v. 19) sees that he cannot wait. **21:** In Scripture *Hebrews* has various meanings, ranging from merchants through an ethnic group related to, but separate from, the Israelites, and also the Israelites themselves. This verse suggests that not all Hebrews were Israelites. **24–30:** Abstinences of various kinds were thought to enhance the sacred force of the soldiers; see 21.4–5. **31–35:** Indulging in their plunder, the people ignore cult requirements, which Saul is very solicitous to observe. **33:** On the *blood* in the *meat,* see Lev. 19.26. **35:** It is assumed here, in contrast to 13.8–15, that *Saul* could exercise priestly functions. **36–46:** Night having come, Saul wished to press the advantage against the Philistines. The inadverone of them.' His men answered, 'Do what you think best,' but the priest said, 'Let us first consult God.' [37] Saul enquired of God, 'Shall I pursue the Philistines? Will you put them into Israel's power?' But this time he received no answer. [38] So he said, 'Let all the leaders of the people come forward and let us find out where the sin lies this day. [39] As the LORD, the deliverer of Israel, lives, even if the sin lies in my son Jonathan, he shall die.' Not a soul answered him. [40] Then he said to the Israelites, 'All of you stand on one side, and I and my son Jonathan will stand on the other.' His men answered, 'Do what you think best.' [41] Saul said to the LORD the God of Israel, 'Why have you not answered your servant today? LORD God of Israel, if this guilt lies in me or in my son Jonathan, let the lot be Urim; if it lies in your people Israel, let it be Thummim.' Jonathan and Saul were taken, and the people were cleared. [42] Then Saul said, 'Cast lots between me and my son Jonathan'; and Jonathan was taken.

[43] Saul said to Jonathan, 'Tell me what you have done.' Jonathan told him, 'True, I did taste a little honey on the tip of my stick. Here I am; I am ready to die.' [44] Then Saul swore a solemn oath that Jonathan should die. [45] But his men said to Saul, 'Shall Jonathan die, Jonathan who has won this great victory in Israel? God forbid! As the LORD lives, not a hair of his head shall fall to the ground, for he has been at work with God today.' So the army delivered Jonathan and he did not die. [46] Saul broke off the pursuit of the Philistines, who then made their way home.

[47] When Saul had made his throne secure in Israel, he gave battle to his enemies on every side, the Moabites, the Ammonites, the Edomites, the king of Zobah, and the Philistines; and wherever he turned he met with victory. [48] He displayed his strength by de-

feating the Amalekites and freeing Israel from hostile raids.

[49] Saul's sons were: Jonathan, Ishyo, and Malchishua. These were the names of his two daughters: Merab the elder and Michal the younger. [50] His wife was Ahinoam daughter of Ahimaaz, and his commander-in-chief was Abner, son of Saul's uncle, Ner; [51] Saul's father Kish and Abner's father Ner were sons of Abiel.

[52] There was bitter warfare with the Philistines throughout Saul's lifetime; any strong man and any brave man that he found he took into his service.

Saul and David

15 SAMUEL said to Saul, 'The LORD sent me to anoint you king over his people Israel. Now listen to the voice of the LORD: [2] this is the very word of the LORD of Hosts: I shall punish the Amalekites for what they did to Israel, when they opposed them on their way up from Egypt. [3] Go now, fall upon the Amalekites, destroy them, and put their property under ban. Spare no one; put them all to death, men and women, children and babes in arms, herds and flocks, camels and donkeys.'

[4] Saul called out the levy and reviewed them at Telaim: there were two hundred thousand foot-soldiers and another ten thousand from Judah. [5] When he reached the city of Amalek, he halted for a time in the valley. [6] Meanwhile he sent word to the Kenites to leave the Amalekites and come down, 'or', he said, 'I shall destroy you as well as them; but

14:41 **Why ... people Israel:** *so Gk; Heb. omits.*
14:47 **king:** *so Gk; Heb.* kings. 14:49 **Ishyo:** *so Gk (Luc.); Heb.* Ishvi (Ishbosheth *in 2 Sam. 2:8;* Eshbaal *in 1 Chr. 8:33).* 14:51 **sons:** *prob. rdg; Heb.* son.
15:4 **another ... Judah:** *prob. rdg; Heb.* ten thousand with the men of Judah.

tent violation of the curse by Jonathan prevented the proper divine approval. **45:** *Delivered:* probably with an animal sacrifice.

14.47–52: Summaries from Saul's reign. These lists indicate that Saul's reign was of some length and had positive effect. There is no hint (as elsewhere) of condemnation of him.

15.1–35: Saul's final condemnation. This narrative is in some continuity with the negative strand in chs. 8, 10, and 12 (see 8.1–22 n.). Here, however, it is only Saul that is condemned, not kingship. As in the positive strand, however, Gilgal is the scene of the great decisions about kingship. **1–9:** Saul conducts a successful campaign against the Amalekites. **2:** *Amalekites:* see Exod. 17.8–16. Saul's campaign did not end the old enmity; compare 1 Sam. ch. 30. **3:** The *ban,* making a battle an absolute, relentless struggle, was a powerful psychological force in holy war; see Josh. chs. 6–7. **4:** The numbers are impressionistic; see 13.5 n. *Judah* was a group of clans south of, and separated from, the central Israelite tribes. **5:** *The city of Amalek,* otherwise you were friendly to Israel as they came up from Egypt'. So the Kenites left the Amalekites.

[7] Saul inflicted defeat on the Amalekites all the way from Havilah to Shur on the borders of Egypt. [8] Agag king of the Amalekites he took alive, but he destroyed all the people, putting them to the sword. [9] Saul and his army spared Agag and the best of the sheep and cattle, the fat beasts and the lambs, and everything worth keeping; these they were unwilling to destroy, but anything that was useless and of no value they destroyed.

[10] The word of the LORD came to Samuel: [11] 'I repent of having made Saul king, for he has turned away from me and has not obeyed my instructions.' Samuel was angry; all night long he cried aloud to the LORD. [12] Early next morning he went to meet Saul, but was told that he had gone to Carmel, for he had set up a monument to himself there, and then had turned and gone on down to Gilgal. [13] There Samuel found him, and Saul greeted him with the words, 'The LORD's blessing on you! I have carried out the LORD's instructions.' [14] 'What then is this bleating of sheep in my ears?' demanded Samuel. 'How do I come to hear the lowing of cattle?' [15] Saul answered, 'The troops have taken them from the Amalekites. These are what they spared, the best of the sheep and cattle, to sacrifice to the LORD your God; the rest we completely destroyed.' [16] Samuel said to Saul, 'Be quiet! Let me tell you what the LORD said to me last night.' 'Tell me,' said Saul. [17] So Samuel went on, 'Once you thought little of yourself, but now you are head of the tribes of Israel. The LORD, who anointed you king over Israel, [18] charged you with the destruction of that wicked nation, the Amalekites; you were to go and wage war against them until you had wiped them out. [19] Why then did you not obey the LORD? Why did you swoop on the spoil, so doing what was wrong in the eyes of the LORD?' [20] Saul answered, 'But I did obey the LORD; I went where the LORD sent me, and I have brought back Agag king of the Amalekites. [21] The rest of them I destroyed.

Out of the spoil the troops took sheep and oxen, the choicest of the animals laid under ban, to sacrifice to the LORD your God at Gilgal.' [22] Samuel then said:

'Does the LORD desire whole-offerings
   and sacrifices
as he desires obedience?
To obey is better than sacrifice,
and to listen to him better than the fat
   of rams.
[23] Rebellion is as sinful as witchcraft,
   arrogance as evil as idolatry.
Because you have rejected the word of
   the LORD,
he has rejected you as king.'

[24] Saul said to Samuel, 'I have sinned. I have not complied with the LORD's command or with your instructions: I was afraid of the troops and gave in to them. [25] But now forgive my sin, I implore you, and come back with me, and I shall bow in worship before the LORD.' [26] Samuel answered, 'I shall not come back with you; you have rejected the word of the LORD and therefore the LORD has rejected you as king over Israel.' [27] As he turned to go, Saul caught the corner of his cloak and it tore. [28] And Samuel said to him, 'The LORD has torn the kingdom of Israel from your hand today and will give it to another, a better man than you. [29] God who is the Splendour of Israel does not deceive, nor does he change his mind, as a mortal might do.' [30] Saul pleaded, 'I have sinned; but honour me this once before the elders of my people and before Israel and come back with me, and I will bow in worship before the LORD your God.' [31] Samuel went back with Saul, and Saul worshipped the LORD.

[32] Samuel said, 'Bring Agag king of the Amalekites.' So Agag came to him with faltering step and said, 'Surely the bitterness of death has passed.' [33] Samuel said,

15:9 **the fat ... lambs:** so Aram. (Targ.); Heb. obscure. 15:23 **as evil as:** prob. rdg; Heb. evil and. **idolatry:** lit. household gods; Heb. teraphim.   15:32 **with faltering step:** prob. rdg, cp. Gk; Heb. delicately.

unknown, was far south of Judah. **6:** Kenites: see Judg. 1.16. **11:** The OT does not view the LORD as governed by immutable plans; therefore, the LORD could repent of a decision. Angry: compare Jer. 20.7–9. **22:** This is a classic statement of the prophetic motif as opposed to the priestly. **29:** That God's mind does not change is not entirely right (see v. 11); here it means that the decision about Saul was final. **31:** Samuel keeps up appearances; this is consistent with the secrecy of the anointing of David, 16.1–13. **32–33:** The ban (v. 3 n.) demanded unrelieved violence.

'As your sword has made women
  childless,
so your mother will be childless among
  women.'

Then Samuel hewed Agag in pieces before
the LORD at Gilgal.

³⁴ Saul went to his own home at Gibeah,
and Samuel went to Ramah; ³⁵ and he never
saw Saul again to his dying day, but he
grieved for him, because the LORD had repented of having made him king over Israel.

16 THE LORD said to Samuel, 'How long
will you grieve because I have rejected Saul as king of Israel? Fill your horn
with oil and take it with you; I am sending
you to Jesse of Bethlehem; for I have chosen
myself a king from among his sons.' ² Samuel
answered, 'How can I go? If Saul hears of it,
he will kill me.' 'Take a heifer with you,' said
the LORD; 'say you have come to offer a sacrifice to the LORD, ³ and invite Jesse to the sacrifice; then I shall show you what you must do.
You are to anoint for me the man whom I
indicate to you.' ⁴ Samuel did as the LORD had
told him, and went to Bethlehem, where the
elders came in haste to meet him, saying,
'Why have you come? Is all well?' ⁵ 'All is well,'
said Samuel; 'I have come to sacrifice to the
LORD. Purify yourselves and come with me to
the sacrifice.' He himself purified Jesse and
his sons and invited them to the sacrifice.
⁶ When they came, and Samuel saw Eliab,
he thought, 'Surely here, before the LORD, is
his anointed king.' ⁷ But the LORD said to
him, 'Pay no attention to his outward appearance and stature, for I have rejected him.
The LORD does not see as a mortal sees; mortals see only appearances but the LORD sees
into the heart.' ⁸ Then Jesse called Abinadab
and had him pass before Samuel, but he said,
'No, the LORD has not chosen this one.' ⁹ Next
he presented Shammah, of whom Samuel

said, 'Nor has the LORD chosen him.' ¹⁰ Seven
of his sons were presented to Samuel by
Jesse, but he said, 'The LORD has not chosen
any of these.'

¹¹ Samuel asked, 'Are these all the sons you
have?' 'There is still the youngest,' replied
Jesse, 'but he is looking after the sheep.' Samuel said to Jesse, 'Send and fetch him; we will
not sit down until he comes.' ¹² So he sent and
fetched him. He was handsome, with ruddy
cheeks and bright eyes. The LORD said, 'Rise
and anoint him: this is the man.' ¹³ Samuel
took the horn of oil and anointed him in the
presence of his brothers, and the spirit of the
LORD came upon David and was with him
from that day onwards. Then Samuel set out
on his way to Ramah.

¹⁴ The spirit of the LORD had forsaken
Saul, and at times an evil spirit from the LORD
would seize him suddenly. ¹⁵ His servants
said to him, 'You see how an evil spirit from
God seizes you; ¹⁶ sir, why do you not command your servants here to go and find
someone who can play on the lyre? Then,
when an evil spirit from God comes on you,
he can play and you will recover.' ¹⁷ Saul said
to his servants, 'Find me someone who can
play well and bring him to me.' ¹⁸ One of his
attendants said, 'I have seen a son of Jesse of
Bethlehem who can play; he is a brave man
and a good fighter, wise in speech and handsome, and the LORD is with him.' ¹⁹ Saul
therefore dispatched messengers to ask Jesse
to send him his son David, who was with the
sheep. ²⁰ Jesse took a batch of bread, a skin of
wine, and a kid, and sent them to Saul by his
son David. ²¹ David came to Saul and entered
his service; Saul loved him dearly, and David
became his armour-bearer. ²² Saul sent word

16:3 **to the sacrifice:** *so Gk; Heb.* with the sacrifice.
16:5 **me to the sacrifice:** *so Lat.; Heb.* me with the
sacrifice.   16:7 **The LORD . . . mortal sees:** *so Gk;
Heb.* For not what a mortal sees.   16:12 **and bright
eyes:** *prob. rdg; Heb. obscure.*   16:20 **batch:** *Heb.*
homer.

16.1–2 Sam. 5.25: David becomes king of Israel. In chs. 8–15 kingship was established as legitimate in
Israel, but the house of Saul was rejected for that office. The rejection, however, was as yet only a divine
decision and still to be worked out in events, as portrayed in 1 Sam. chs. 16–31; afterward David's rise is
inevitable (2 Sam. chs. 1–5).

    16.1–17.58: The introduction of David. After the secret anointing of David, varying ways in which he was
introduced to Saul's court are reported.

    16.1–13: The anointing of David. 8: *Jesse's* action indicates that those present for the sacrifice understood
the significance of the occasion. **11:** The selection of the least probable is a motif also in the anointing of Saul
in 9.21.

    16.14–23: David as harpist and warrior. Saul's ecstatic powers now take an *evil* turn, causing periods of to Jesse: 'Allow David to stay in my service, for I am pleased with him.' 23 And whenever an evil spirit from God came upon Saul, David would take his lyre and play it, so that relief would come to Saul; he would recover and the evil spirit would leave him alone.

17 The Philistines mustered their forces for war; they massed at Socoh in Judah and encamped between Socoh and Azekah at Ephes-dammim. 2 Saul and the Israelites also mustered, and they encamped in the valley of Elah. They drew up their lines of battle facing the Philistines, 3 the Philistines occupying a position on one hill and the Israelites on another, with a valley between them.

4 A champion came out from the Philistine camp, a man named Goliath, from Gath; he was over nine feet in height. 5 He had a bronze helmet on his head, and he wore plate armour of bronze, weighing five thousand shekels. 6 On his legs were bronze greaves, and one of his weapons was a bronze dagger. 7 The shaft of his spear was like a weaver's beam, and its head, which was of iron, weighed six hundred shekels. His shield-bearer marched ahead of him.

8 The champion stood and shouted to the ranks of Israel, 'Why do you come out to do battle? I am the Philistine champion and you are Saul's men. Choose your man to meet me. 9 If he defeats and kills me in fair fight, we shall become your slaves; but if I vanquish and kill him, you will be our slaves and serve us. 10 Here and now I challenge the ranks of Israel. Get me a man, and we will fight it out.' 11 When Saul and the Israelites heard what the Philistine said, they were all shaken and deeply afraid.

12 David was the son of an Ephrathite called Jesse, who had eight sons, and who by Saul's time had become old, well advanced in years. 13 His three eldest sons had followed Saul to the war; the eldest was called Eliab, the next Abinadab, and the third Shammah; 14 David

was the youngest. When the three eldest followed Saul, 15 David used to go from attending Saul to minding his father's flocks at Bethlehem.

16 Morning and evening for forty days the Philistine came forward and took up his stance. 17 Then one day Jesse said to his son David, 'Take your brothers an ephah of this roasted grain and these ten loaves of bread, and go with them as quickly as you can to the camp. 18 These ten cream-cheeses are for you to take to their commanding officer. See if your brothers are well and bring back some token from them.' 19 Saul and the brothers and all the Israelites were in the valley of Elah, fighting the Philistines.

20 Early next morning David, having left someone in charge of the sheep, set out on his errand and went as Jesse had told him. He reached the lines just as the army was going out to take up position and was raising the war cry. 21 The Israelites and the Philistines drew up their ranks opposite each other. 22 David left his things in the charge of the quartermaster, ran to the line, and went up to his brothers to greet them. 23 While he was talking with them the Philistine champion, Goliath from Gath, came out from the Philistine ranks and issued his challenge in the same words as before; and David heard him. 24 When the Israelites saw the man they fell back before him in fear.

25 'Look at this man who comes out day after day to defy Israel,' they said. 'The king is to give a rich reward to the man who kills him; he will also give him his daughter in marriage and will exempt his family from service due in Israel.' 26 David asked the men near him, 'What is to be done for the man who kills this Philistine and wipes out this disgrace? And who is he, an uncircumcised Philistine, to defy the armies of the living

17:4 over ... feet: lit. six cubits and a span.
17:12 Ephrathite: prob. rdg; Heb. adds Is this the man from Bethlehem in Judah?

deep depression. 21: A well-rounded courtier could be an accomplished musician and also conduct himself expertly in battle. This narrative is inconsistent with parts of ch. 17 but stands here because of the close connection of the spirit of the LORD passing to David (16.13) from Saul (16.14).

17.1–58: David slays Goliath. This story assumes an entry by David into Saul's court quite different from the preceding narrative, and it is not entirely consistent within itself. The story is legendary, in the sense that it is intended to enhance the reputation of a famous figure; in 2 Sam. 21.19, the slaying of Goliath, ascribed by legend to David, was the deed of his warriors. **1–2:** *Socoh, Azekah,* and the *valley of Elah* were farther south than any previous Philistine action. This perhaps represents a different strategy by the Philistines, after their defeat in the region of Benjamin, ch. 14. **12–31:** This section seems to be a later insertion. Without it,

God?' 27 The soldiers, repeating what had been said, told him what was to be done for the man who killed him.

28 David's elder brother Eliab overheard him talking with the men and angrily demanded, 'What are you doing here? And whom have you left to look after those few sheep in the wilderness? I know you, you impudent young rascal; you have only come to see the fighting.' 29 David answered, 'Now what have I done? I only asked a question.' 30 He turned away from him to someone else and repeated his question, but everybody gave him the same answer.

31 David's words were overheard and reported to Saul, who sent for him. 32 David said to him, 'Let no one lose heart! I shall go and fight this Philistine.' 33 Saul answered, 'You are not able to fight this Philistine; you are only a lad, and he has been a fighting man all his life.' 34 David said to Saul, 'Sir, I am my father's shepherd; whenever a lion or bear comes and carries off a sheep from the flock, 35 I go out after it and attack it and rescue the victim from its jaws. Then if it turns on me, I seize it by the beard and batter it to death. 36 I have killed lions and bears, and this uncircumcised Philistine will fare no better than they; he has defied the ranks of the living God. 37 The LORD who saved me from the lion and the bear will save me from this Philistine.' 'Go then,' said Saul; 'and the LORD be with you.'

38 He put his own tunic on David, placed a bronze helmet on his head, and gave him a coat of mail to wear; 39 he then fastened his sword on David over his tunic. But David held back, because he had not tried them, and said to Saul, 'I cannot go with these, because I am not used to them.' David took them off, 40 then picked up his stick, chose five smooth stones from the wadi, and put them in a shepherd's bag which served as his pouch, and, sling in hand, went to meet the Philistine.

41 The Philistine, preceded by his shield-bearer, came on towards David. 42 He looked David up and down and had nothing but disdain for this lad with his ruddy cheeks and bright eyes. 43 He said to David, 'Am I a dog that you come out against me with sticks?' He cursed him in the name of his god, 44 and said, 'Come, I shall give your flesh to the birds and the beasts.' 45 David answered, 'You have come against me with sword and spear and dagger, but I come against you in the name of the LORD of Hosts, the God of the ranks of Israel which you have defied. 46 The LORD will put you into my power this day; I shall strike you down and cut your head off and leave your carcass and the carcasses of the Philistines to the birds and the wild beasts; the whole world will know that there is a God in Israel. 47 All those who are gathered here will see that the LORD saves without sword or spear; the battle is the LORD's, and he will put you all into our power.'

48 When the Philistine began moving closer to attack, David ran quickly to engage him. 49 Reaching into his bag, he took out a stone, which he slung and struck the Philistine on the forehead. The stone sank into his head, and he fell prone on the ground. 50 So with sling and stone David proved the victor; though he had no sword, he struck down the Philistine and gave him a mortal wound. 51 He ran up to the Philistine and stood over him; then, grasping his sword, he drew it out of the scabbard, dispatched him, and cut off his head.

When the Philistines saw the fate of their champion, they turned and fled. 52 The men of Israel and Judah at once raised the war cry and closely pursued them all the way to Gath and up to the gates of Ekron. The road that runs to Shaaraim, Gath, and Ekron was strewn with their dead. 53 On their return from the pursuit of the Philistines, the Israelites plundered their camp. 54 David took Goliath's head and carried it to Jerusalem, but he put Goliath's weapons in his own tent.

55 As Saul watched David go out to meet the Philistine, he said to Abner his commander-in-chief, 'That youth there, Abner, whose son is he?' 'By your life, your majesty,' replied Abner, 'I do not know.' 56 The king said, 'Go and find out whose son the stripling is.'

17:39 **he then . . . on David:** *so Gk; Heb.* David fastened on his sword.   17:40 **which . . . pouch:** *so Gk; Heb.* which was his and in the pouch.   17:42 **lad . . . eyes:** *prob. rdg; Heb.* obscure.   17:46 **leave . . . Philistines:** *so Gk; Heb.* leave the carcass of the Philistines.   17:52 **to Gath:** *so Gk; Heb.* to a valley.

the narrative would otherwise be largely compatible with 16.14–23. **54:** *Jerusalem* was then still an independent city-state; David, a Bethlehemite, had grown up in the shadow of its walls and may have had an intimate relation to it. **55–58:** As in vv. 12–31, David is hitherto unknown to Saul.

57 When David came back after killing the Philistine, Abner took him and presented him to Saul with the Philistine's head still in his hand. 58 Saul asked him, 'Whose son are you, young man?' and David answered, 'I am the son of your servant Jesse of Bethlehem.'

18 1-2 That same day, when Saul had finished talking with David, he kept him and would not let him return any more to his father's house, for he saw that Jonathan had given his heart to David and had grown to love him as himself. 3 Jonathan and David made a solemn compact because each loved the other as dearly as himself. 4 Jonathan stripped off the cloak and tunic he was wearing, and gave them to David, together with his sword, his bow, and his belt.

5 David succeeded so well in every venture on which Saul sent him that he was given command of the fighting forces, and his promotion pleased all ranks, even the officials round Saul.

6 At the homecoming of the army and the return of David from slaying the Philistine, the women from all the cities and towns of Israel came out singing and dancing to meet King Saul, rejoicing with tambourines and three-stringed instruments. 7 The women as they made merry sang to one another:

'Saul struck down thousands,
but David tens of thousands.'

8 Saul was furious, and the words rankled. He said, 'They have ascribed to David tens of thousands and to me only thousands. What more can they do but make him king?' 9 From that time forward Saul kept a jealous eye on David.

10 Next day an evil spirit from God seized on Saul. He fell into a frenzy in the house, and David played the lyre to him as he had done before. Saul had a spear in his hand, 11 and he hurled it at David, meaning to pin him to the wall; but twice David dodged

aside. 12 After this Saul was afraid of David, because he saw that the LORD had forsaken him and was with David. 13 He therefore removed David from his household and appointed him to the command of a thousand men. David led his men into action, 14 and succeeded in everything that he undertook, because the LORD was with him. 15 When Saul saw how successful he was, he was more afraid of him than ever. 16 But all Israel and Judah loved David because he took the field at their head.

17 Saul said to David, 'Here is my elder daughter Merab; I shall give her to you in marriage, but in return you must serve me valiantly and fight the LORD's battles.' For Saul meant David to meet his end not at his hands but at the hands of the Philistines. 18 David answered Saul, 'Who am I and what are my father's people, my kinsfolk, in Israel, that I should become the king's son-in-law?' 19 However, when the time came for Saul's daughter Merab to be married to David, she had already been given to Adriel of Meholah.

20 But Michal, Saul's other daughter, fell in love with David, and when Saul was told of this, he saw that it suited his plans. 21 He said to himself, 'I will give her to him; let her be the bait that lures him to his death at the hands of the Philistines.' So Saul proposed a second time to make David his son-in-law, 22 and ordered his courtiers to say to David privately, 'The king is well disposed to you and you are dear to us all; now is the time for you to marry into the king's family.' 23 When they spoke in this way to David, he said to them, 'Do you think that marrying the king's daughter is a matter of so little consequence that a poor man of no account, like myself, can do it?'

24 The courtiers reported what David had said, 25 and Saul replied, 'Tell David this: all the king wants as the bride-price is the fore-

18:6 **singing:** or watching.   18:10 **a frenzy:** or prophetic rapture.

18.1–20.42: **David's vicissitudes at Saul's court.** The sequence of episodes here is rapid and complex. Each chapter begins with an episode involving Jonathan and David (18.1–4; 19.1–7; 20.1–42) followed in chs. 18 and 19 by notices of David's successes against the Philistines (18.5, 14–16, 30; 19.8), and Saul's jealous attacks upon David with his spear (18.10–13; 19.9–10). The three passages concerning Jonathan and David show a gradual disillusionment on Jonathan's part. Chapters 18 and 19 also relate David's marriage to Saul's daughter Michal (18.17–29) and her aid in his escape from Saul (19.11–17). **4:** The exchange of garments and weapons effected a bond of souls. **7:** This old poetic refrain may have originally had no suggestion of invidious comparison between Saul and David, the second line being simply a poetic parallel to the first. In later times, this song was used to account for the jealousy on Saul's part. The saying was well known; see 21.11; 29.5.

skins of a hundred Philistines, by way of vengeance on his enemies.' Saul was counting on David's death at the hands of the Philistines. 26 The courtiers told David what Saul had said, and marriage with the king's daughter on these terms pleased him well. Before the appointed time, 27 David went out with his men and slew two hundred Philistines; he brought their foreskins and counted them out to the king in order to be accepted as his son-in-law. Saul then married his daughter Michal to David. 28 He saw clearly that the LORD was with David, and knew that Michal his daughter had fallen in love with him; 29 and he grew more and more afraid of David and was his enemy for the rest of his life.

30 The Philistine commanders continued to make forays, but whenever they took the field David had more success against them than all the rest of Saul's men, and he won a great name for himself.

19 SAUL incited Jonathan his son and all his household to kill David. 2 But Jonathan was devoted to David and told him that his father Saul was seeking to kill him. 'Be on your guard tomorrow morning,' he said; 'conceal yourself, and remain in hiding. 3 I shall come out and join my father in the open country where you are and speak to him about you, and if I discover anything I shall tell you.'

4 Jonathan spoke up for David to his father Saul and said to him, 'Sir, do not wrong your servant David; he has not wronged you; his achievements have all benefited you greatly. 5 Did he not take his life in his hands when he killed the Philistine, and the LORD brought about a great victory for all Israel? You saw it and shared in the rejoicing. Why should you wrong an innocent man and put David to death without cause?' 6 Saul heeded Jonathan's plea and swore solemnly by the LORD that David should not be put to death. 7 Jonathan called David and reported all this; then he brought him to Saul to be in attendance on the king as before.

8 When hostilities broke out again and David advanced to the attack, he inflicted such a severe defeat on the Philistines that they fled before him.

9 An evil spirit from the LORD came on Saul as he was sitting in the house with a spear in his hand; and David was playing on the lyre. 10 Saul tried to pin David to the wall with the spear, but he dodged the king's thrust so that Saul drove the spear into the wall. David escaped and got safely away.

That night 11 Saul sent servants to keep watch on David's house, intending to kill him in the morning. But David's wife Michal warned him to get away that night, 'or tomorrow', she said, 'you will be a dead man'. 12 She let David down through a window and he slipped away and escaped. 13 Michal then took their household god and put it on the bed; at its head she laid a goat's-hair rug and covered it all with a cloak. 14 When the men arrived to arrest David she told them he was ill. 15 Saul, however, sent them back to see David for themselves. 'Bring him to me, bed and all,' he ordered, 'so that I may kill him.' 16 When they came, there was the household god on the bed and the goat's-hair rug at its head. 17 Saul said to Michal, 'Why have you played this trick on me and let my enemy get away?' Michal answered, 'He said to me, "Help me to escape or I shall kill you."'

18 Meanwhile David made good his escape, and coming to Samuel at Ramah, he described how Saul had treated him. He and Samuel went to Naioth and stayed there. 19 When Saul was told that David was at Naioth, 20 he sent a party of men to seize him. But at the sight of the company of prophets in a frenzy, with Samuel standing at their head, the spirit of God came upon them and they fell into prophetic frenzy. 21 When this was reported to Saul he sent another party; these also fell into a frenzy, and when he sent men a third time, they did the same. 22 Saul himself then set out for Ramah and came to the great cistern in Secu. He asked where Samuel and David were and was told that they were at Naioth in Ramah. 23 On his way there the spirit of God came upon him too and he went on, in a prophetic frenzy as he went, till he

19:13 **household god:** *Heb.* teraphim.

25: Since the Philistines were uncircumcised, *foreskins* made a grisly trophy of battle. **19.1–7:** Jonathan's intercession delays Saul's open hostility to David. **3:** The meeting in the *open country* is notably similar to the narrative of ch. 20. **9–10:** The king's jealousy breaks out again. **17:** Saul is defeated in his attempts on David by both his son and his daughter, an indirect effect of divine favor toward David. **18–24:** This legend of the great force of Samuel's charismatic power is peripheral to the main narrative but supplies another explanation came to Naioth in Ramah. ²⁴There he too stripped off his clothes and like the rest fell into a frenzy before Samuel and lay down naked all that day and throughout that night. That is the reason for the saying, 'Is Saul also among the prophets?'

20 David made his escape from Naioth in Ramah and came to Jonathan. 'What have I done?' he asked. 'What is my offence? What wrong does your father think I have done, that he seeks my life?' ²Jonathan answered, 'God forbid! There is no thought of putting you to death. I am sure my father will not do anything whatever without telling me. Why should my father hide such a thing from me? I cannot believe it!' ³David said, 'I am ready to swear to it: your father has said to himself, "Jonathan must not know this or he will resent it," because he knows that you have a high regard for me. As the LORD lives, your life upon it, I am only a step away from death.' ⁴Jonathan said to David, 'What do you want me to do for you?' ⁵David answered, 'It is new moon tomorrow, and I am to dine with the king. But let me go and lie hidden in the fields until the third evening, ⁶and if your father misses me, say, "David asked me for leave to hurry off on a visit to his home in Bethlehem, for it is the annual sacrifice there for the whole family." ⁷If he says, "Good," it will be well for me; but if he flies into a rage, you will know that he is set on doing me harm. ⁸My lord, keep faith with me; for you and I have entered into a solemn compact before the LORD. Kill me yourself if I am guilty, but do not let me fall into your father's hands.' ⁹'God forbid!' cried Jonathan. 'If I find my father set on doing you harm, I shall tell you.' ¹⁰David answered Jonathan, 'How will you let me know if he answers harshly?' ¹¹Jonathan said, 'Let us go into the fields,' and so they went there together.

¹²Jonathan said, 'I promise you, David, in the sight of the LORD the God of Israel, this time tomorrow I shall sound my father for the third time and, if he is well disposed to you, I shall send and let you know. ¹³If my father means mischief, may the LORD do the same to me and more, if I do not let you know and get you safely away. The LORD be with

you as he has been with my father! ¹⁴I know that as long as I live you will show me faithful friendship, as the LORD requires; and if I should die, ¹⁵you will continue loyal to my family for ever. When the LORD rids the earth of all David's enemies, ¹⁶may the LORD call him to account if he and his house are no longer my friends.' ¹⁷Jonathan pledged himself afresh to David because of his love for him, for he loved him as himself.

¹⁸Jonathan said, 'Tomorrow is the new moon, and you will be missed when your place is empty. ¹⁹So the day after tomorrow go down at nightfall to the place where you hid on the day when the affair started; stay by the mound there. ²⁰I shall shoot three arrows towards it as though aiming at a target. ²¹Then I shall send my boy to find the arrows. If I say to him, "Look, the arrows are on this side of you; pick them up," then you can come out of hiding. You will be quite safe, I swear it, for there will be nothing amiss. ²²But if I say to him, "Look, the arrows are on the other side of you, farther on," then the LORD has said that you must go; ²³the LORD stands witness between us for ever to the pledges we have exchanged.'

²⁴David hid in the fields, and when the new moon came the king sat down to eat at mealtime. ²⁵Saul took his customary seat by the wall, and Abner sat beside him; Jonathan too was present, but David's place was empty. ²⁶That day Saul said nothing, for he thought that David was absent by some chance, perhaps because he was ritually unclean. ²⁷But on the second day, the day after the new moon, David's place was still empty, and Saul said to his son Jonathan, 'Why has the son of Jesse not come to the feast, either yesterday or today?' ²⁸Jonathan answered, 'David asked permission to go to Bethlehem. ²⁹He asked my leave and said, "Our family is holding a sacrifice in the town and my brother himself has told me to be there. Now, if you have any regard for me, let me slip away to

20:12 **I promise . . . LORD:** *so Syriac; Heb.* David, the LORD.   20:16 **him:** *so Gk (Luc.); Heb.* David's enemies. **he . . . friends:** *so Gk; Heb. obscure.* 20:17 **pledged . . . David:** *so Gk; Heb.* made David swear.   20:19 **by . . . there:** *prob. rdg, cp. Gk; Heb.* by the Azel stone.   20:27 **on the second day:** *so Gk; Heb.* the second.

for the popular proverb about Saul among the prophets; compare 10.11–12. **20.1–42:** This is the fullest elaboration of Saul's deviousness and of Jonathan's loyalty to David. **18–23:** These plans assume that someone will be with Jonathan, so that he must use signals.

see my brothers." That is why he has not come to the king's table.' ³⁰Saul's anger blazed up against Jonathan and he said, 'You son of a crooked and rebellious mother! I know perfectly well you have made a friend of the son of Jesse only to bring shame on yourself and dishonour on your mother. ³¹But as long as Jesse's son remains alive on the earth, neither you nor your kingdom will be established. Send at once and fetch him; he deserves to die.' ³²Jonathan answered his father, 'Deserves to die? Why? What has he done?' ³³At that, Saul picked up his spear and threatened to kill him; and Jonathan knew that his father was bent on David's death. ³⁴He left the table in a rage and ate nothing on the second day of the festival; for he was indignant on David's behalf and because his father had humiliated him.

³⁵Next morning Jonathan, accompanied by a young boy, went out into the fields to keep the appointment with David. ³⁶He said to the boy, 'Run ahead and find the arrows I shoot.' As the boy ran on, he shot the arrows over his head. ³⁷When the boy reached the place where the arrows had fallen, Jonathan called out after him, 'Look, the arrows are beyond you. ³⁸Hurry! Go quickly! Do not delay.' The boy gathered up the arrows and brought them to his master; ³⁹but only Jonathan and David knew what this meant; the boy knew nothing. ⁴⁰Jonathan handed his weapons to the boy and told him to take them back to the town.

⁴¹When the boy had gone, David got up from behind the mound and bowed humbly three times. Then they kissed one another and shed tears together, until David's grief was even greater than Jonathan's. ⁴²Jonathan said to David, 'Go in safety; we have pledged each other in the name of the LORD who is witness for ever between you and me and between your descendants and mine.' David went off at once, while Jonathan returned to the town. ¹David made his **21** way to Nob to the priest Ahimelech, who hurried out to meet him and asked, 'Why are you alone and unattended?' ²David

answered Ahimelech, 'I am under orders from the king: I was to let no one know about the mission on which he was sending me or what these orders were. When I took leave of my men I told them to meet me in such and such a place. ³Now, what have you got by you? Let me have five loaves, or as many as you can find.' ⁴The priest answered David, 'I have no ordinary bread available. There is only the sacred bread; but have the young men kept themselves from women?' ⁵David answered the priest, 'Women have been denied us as hitherto when I have been on campaign, even an ordinary campaign, and the young men's bodies have remained holy; and how much more will they be holy today!' ⁶So, as there was no other bread there, the priest gave him the sacred bread, the Bread of the Presence, which had just been taken from the presence of the LORD to be replaced by freshly baked bread on the day that the old was removed. ⁷One of Saul's servants happened to be there that day, detained before the LORD; his name was Doeg the Edomite, and he was the chief of Saul's herdsmen. ⁸David said to Ahimelech, 'Have you a spear or sword here at hand? I have no sword or other weapon with me, because the king's business was urgent.' ⁹The priest answered, 'There is the sword of Goliath the Philistine whom you slew in the valley of Elah; it is wrapped up in a cloak behind the ephod. If you want to take that, take it; there is no other weapon here.' David said, 'There is no sword like it; give it to me.'

¹⁰That day David went on his way, fleeing from Saul, and came to King Achish of Gath. ¹¹The servants of Achish said to him, 'Surely this is David, the king of his country, the man of whom they sang as they danced:

"Saul struck down thousands,
  but David tens of thousands." '

¹²These comments were not lost on David, and he became very much afraid of King

20:41 **the mound:** *prob. rdg, cp. Gk; Heb.* the Negeb.
20:42 **David went off:** *in Heb.* 21:1 *begins here.*
21:1 *In Heb.* 21:2.

21.1–23.13: David becomes a fugitive. Several episodes here form a transition from David at Saul's court to David as leader of an outlaw band in the Judean wilderness. **1–9:** David gets assistance from Ahimelech, a descendant of the priestly line of Shiloh (22.9; 14.3). **2:** Ahimelech does not knowingly assist a fugitive. **6:** *The Bread of the Presence* was set before God in the sanctuary and periodically replaced. Only priests could eat it; compare Lev. 24.5–9. **7:** *Doeg the Edomite* was to prove an informer and executioner; 22.9–23. **10–15:** David's fugitive period is opened and closed by stays with Achish of Gath; see 27.1–6. **11:** On the song see

Achish of Gath. ¹³ So he altered his behaviour in public and acted like a madman in front of them all, scrabbling on the double doors of the city gate and dribbling down his beard. ¹⁴ Achish said to his servants, 'The man is insane! Why bring him to me? ¹⁵ Am I short of madmen that you bring this one to plague me? Must I have this fellow in my house?'

David as outlaw captain

22 DAVID stole away from there and went to the cave of Adullam, and, when his brothers and all the members of his family heard where he was, they went down and joined him there. ² Everyone in any kind of distress or in debt or with a grievance gathered round him, about four hundred in number, and he became their chief. ³ From there David went to Mizpeh in Moab and said to the king of Moab, 'Let my father and mother come and take shelter with you until I know what God will do for me.' ⁴ He left them at the court of the king of Moab, and they stayed there as long as David remained in his stronghold.

⁵ The prophet Gad said to David, 'You must not stay in your stronghold; go at once into Judah.' David went as far as the forest of Hareth. ⁶ News that the whereabouts of David and his men was known reached Saul while he was in Gibeah, sitting under the tamarisk tree on the hilltop with his spear in his hand and all his retainers standing about him. ⁷ He said to them, 'Listen to me, you Benjamites: do you expect the son of Jesse to give you all fields and vineyards, or make you all officers over units of a thousand and a hundred? ⁸ Is that why you have all conspired against me? Not one of you told me when my son made a compact with the son of Jesse; none of you spared a thought for me or told me that my son had set against me my own servant, who is lying in wait for me now.'

⁹ Doeg the Edomite, who was standing with Saul's servants, spoke up: 'I saw the son of Jesse coming to Nob, to Ahimelech son of Ahitub. ¹⁰ Ahimelech consulted the LORD on his behalf, then gave him food and handed over to him the sword of Goliath the Philistine.' ¹¹ The king sent for Ahimelech the priest and his whole family, who were priests at Nob, and they all came to him. ¹² Saul said, 'Now listen, you son of Ahitub,' and the man answered, 'Yes, my lord?' ¹³ Saul said to him, 'Why have you and the son of Jesse plotted against me? You gave him food and a sword, and consulted God on his behalf; and now he has risen against me and is at this moment lying in wait for me.' ¹⁴ 'And who among all your servants', answered Ahimelech, 'is like David, a man to be trusted, the king's son-in-law, appointed to your staff and holding an honourable place in your household? ¹⁵ Have I on this occasion done something profane in consulting God on his behalf? God forbid! I trust that my lord the king will not accuse me or my family; for I know nothing whatever about it.' ¹⁶ But the king said, 'Ahimelech, you shall die, you and all your family.' ¹⁷ He then said to the bodyguard attending him, 'Turn on the priests of the LORD and kill them; for they are in league with David, and, though they knew that he was a fugitive, they did not inform me.' The king's men, however, were unwilling to raise a hand against the priests of the LORD. ¹⁸ The king therefore said to Doeg the Edomite, 'You, Doeg, go and fall on the priests'; so Doeg went and fell upon the priests, killing that day with his own hand eighty-five men who wore the linen ephod. ¹⁹ He put to the sword every living thing in Nob, the town of the priests: men and women, children and babes in arms, oxen, donkeys, and sheep.

²⁰ One of Ahimelech's sons named Abiathar made his escape and joined David. ²¹ He told David how Saul had killed the priests of the LORD, ²² and David said to him, 'When Doeg the Edomite was there that day, I knew that he would certainly tell Saul. I have brought this on all the members of your father's house. ²³ Stay here with me, have no fear; he who seeks your life seeks mine, and you will be safe with me.'

23 The Philistines had launched an assault on Keilah and were plundering the threshing-floors. When this was reported to David, ² he consulted the LORD and asked whether he should go and attack these Philistines. The LORD answered, 'Go, attack them, and relieve Keilah.' ³ But David's men said to

18.7 n. **22.1–5:** David accepts his situation as fugitive, organizes a band of outlaws, and secures his family against Saul. **5:** *The prophet Gad* appears also in 2 Sam. 24.11–14, rather suddenly in both cases. **6–23:** Saul avenges himself on Ahimelech, brother of his own priest Ahijah (14.3). **23.1–13:** David's band begins to be a force in the south. He carefully consults the LORD concerning all his movements. **1:** *Keilah* was an independent him, 'Here in Judah we are afraid. How much worse if we challenge the Philistine forces at Keilah!' 4 David consulted the LORD once again and got the answer, 'Go down at once to Keilah; I shall give the Philistines into your hands.' 5 David and his men marched to Keilah, fought the Philistines, and carried off their livestock; they inflicted a heavy defeat on them and relieved the inhabitants of Keilah.

6 When Abiathar son of Ahimelech fled and joined David at Keilah, he brought an ephod with him. 7 It was reported to Saul that David had entered Keilah, and he said, 'God has put him into my hands; for he has walked into a trap by entering a walled town with its barred gates.' 8 He called out all the army to march on Keilah and besiege David and his men.

9 When David learnt how Saul planned his overthrow, he told Abiathar the priest to bring the ephod, 10 and then he prayed, 'LORD God of Israel, I your servant have heard that Saul intends to come to Keilah and destroy the town because of me. 11 Will the townspeople of Keilah surrender me to him? Will Saul come down as I have heard? LORD God of Israel, I pray you, tell your servant.' The LORD answered, 'He will come.' 12 David asked, 'Will the citizens of Keilah surrender me and my men to Saul?' and the LORD answered, 'They will.' 13 At once David left Keilah with his men, who numbered about six hundred, and moved about from place to place. When it was reported to Saul that David had escaped from Keilah, he called off the operation.

14 David was living in the fastnesses of the wilderness of Ziph, in the hill-country, and though Saul went daily in search of him, God did not put him into his power. 15 David was at Horesh in the wilderness of Ziph, when he learnt that Saul had come out to seek his life. 16 Saul's son Jonathan came to David at Horesh and gave him fresh courage in God's name: 17 'Do not be afraid,' he said; 'my fa-

ther's hand will not touch you. You will become king of Israel and I shall rank after you. This my father knows.' 18 After the two of them had made a solemn compact before the LORD, David remained in Horesh and Jonathan went home.

19 The Ziphites brought to Saul at Gibeah the news that David was in hiding among them in the fastnesses of Horesh on the hill of Hachilah, south of Jeshimon. 20 'Let your majesty come down whenever you will,' they said, 'and it will be our business to surrender him to you.' 21 Saul replied, 'The LORD's blessing on you; you have rendered me a service. 22 Go now and make further enquiry, and find out exactly where he is and who saw him there. They tell me that he is crafty enough to outwit me. 23 Find out which of his hiding-places he is using; then come back to me at such and such a place, and I shall go with you. So long as he stays in this country, I shall hunt him down, if I have to go through all the clans of Judah one by one.' 24 They left for Ziph without delay, ahead of Saul.

David and his men were in the wilderness of Maon in the Arabah to the south of Jeshimon. 25 Saul set off with his men to look for him; but David got word of it and went down to a refuge in the rocks, and there he stayed in the wilderness of Maon. On hearing this, Saul went into the wilderness after him; 26 he was on one side of the hill, David and his men on the other. While David and his men were trying desperately to get away, and Saul and his followers were closing in for the capture, 27 a runner brought a message to Saul: 'Come at once! The Philistines are invading the land.' 28 Saul called off the pursuit of David and turned back to face the Philistines. This is why that place is called the Dividing Rock. 29 David went up from there and lived in the fastnesses of En-gedi.

24
On his return from the pursuit of the Philistines, Saul learnt that David was

23:29 *In Heb. 24:1.*

town southwest of Judah. **11–12:** The oracle answered one question at a time, yes or no.

23.14–24.22: The chase in the wilderness. David's wilderness period was a popular narrative topic. **14:** *Ziph* was a rough region a few miles south and east of Hebron. **16–18:** *Jonathan,* now fully aware of his father's intent, here predicts and consents to David's future establishment as king. Several other speeches in these chapters view David's kingship as the inevitable outcome of these events. **26–28:** The pressure of the *Philistines* continued, interrupting Saul in the nick of time. *The Dividing Rock* was later said to be named for this escape. **29:** *En-gedi* was in the most barren part of Judah, just west of the Dead Sea. **24.1:** The *Philistines* are treated here as no more than a brief interlude in Saul's real enterprise.

in the wilderness of En-gedi. ²Taking three thousand men picked from the whole of Israel, he went in search of David and his followers to the east of the Rocks of the Mountain Goats. ³There beside the road were some sheepfolds, and nearby was a cave, in the inner recesses of which David and his men were concealed. Saul came to the cave and went in to relieve himself. ⁴⁻⁷David's men said to him, 'The day has come: the LORD has put your enemy into your hands, as he promised he would. You may do what you please with him.' David said to his men, 'God forbid that I should harm my master, the LORD's anointed, or lift a hand against him. He is after all the LORD's anointed.' So David reproved his men and would not allow them to attack Saul. He himself got up stealthily and cut off a piece of Saul's cloak; but after he had cut it off, he was struck with remorse.

Saul left the cave and went on his way; ⁸whereupon David also came out of the cave and called after Saul, 'My lord king!' When Saul looked round, David prostrated himself in obeisance ⁹and said to him, 'Why do you listen to those who say that David means to do you harm? ¹⁰Today you can see for yourself that the LORD put you into my power in the cave. Though urged to kill you, I spared your life. "I cannot lift my hand against my master," I said, "for he is the LORD's anointed." ¹¹Look, my dear lord, see this piece of your cloak in my hand. I cut it off, but I did not kill you. This shows that I have no thought of violence or treachery against you, and that I have done you no wrong. Yet you are resolved to take my life. ¹²May the LORD judge between us! But though he may take vengeance on you for my sake, my hand will not be against you. ¹³As the old proverb has it, "One wrong begets another"; yet my hand will not be against you. ¹⁴Against whom has the king of Israel come out? What are you pursuing? A dead dog? A flea? ¹⁵May the LORD be judge and decide between us; let

him consider my cause; he will plead for me and acquit me.'

¹⁶When David had finished speaking, Saul said, 'Is that you, David my son?' and he burst into tears. ¹⁷He said, 'The right is on your side, not mine: you have treated me so well; I have treated you so badly. ¹⁸You have made plain today the good you have done me; the LORD put me at your mercy, but you did not kill me. ¹⁹Not often does a man find his enemy and let him go unharmed. May the LORD reward you well for what you have done for me today! ²⁰I know now that you will surely become king, and that the kingdom of Israel will flourish under your rule. ²¹Swear to me now by the LORD that you will not exterminate my descendants and blot out my name from my father's house.' ²²David swore this on oath to Saul. Then Saul went to his home, while David and his men went up to their fastness.

25 SAMUEL died, and all Israel gathered to mourn for him, and they buried him at his home in Ramah. Afterwards David went down to the wilderness of Paran.

²There was a man in Maon who had property at Carmel and owned three thousand sheep and a thousand goats; and he was shearing his flocks in Carmel. ³His name was Nabal and his wife's name Abigail; she was a beautiful and intelligent woman, but her husband, a Calebite, was surly and mean. ⁴David heard in the wilderness that Nabal was shearing his flocks, ⁵and sent ten of his young men, saying to them, 'Go up to Carmel, find Nabal, and give him my greetings. ⁶You are to say, "All good wishes for the year ahead! Prosperity to yourself, your household, and all that is yours! ⁷I hear that you are shearing. Your shepherds have been with us lately and we did not molest them; nothing of

24:4–7 *These verses are rearranged as follows: 4a,6,7a, 4b,5,7b.*   24:18 **You have made . . . done me:** *or* Your goodness to me this day has passed all bounds.

24.3: The narrative which begins here verges on the burlesque. **4–7:** David's speech moves from irony into a serious statement of *the LORD's anointed*. The sanctity of that office was not to be violated under any circumstances, according to the view of the writers toward the kingship in Jerusalem. **8–22:** The tone changes from the humor of the opening in v. 3. **20:** See 23.16–18 n.

25.1–44: David and Abigail. This delightful narrative stands in the midst of the wilderness period to convey the flavor of David's life there. **1:** Samuel's king-making work has been done since ch. 16, but he will appear yet once more (ch. 28). **2:** *Maon* was a few miles south of Ziph. It was a region where grazing lands bordered on agricultural lands. **3:** *Nabal* is the noun "fool" used as a name; see v. 25. **6–8:** David's speech is very theirs was missing all the time they were in Carmel. 8 Ask your own men and they will tell you. Receive my men kindly, for this is an auspicious day with us, and give what you can to David your son and your servant."'

9 David's servants came and delivered this message to Nabal in David's name. When they paused, 10 Nabal answered, 'Who is David? Who is this son of Jesse? In these days there are many slaves who break away from their masters. 11 Am I to take my food and my wine and the meat I have provided for my shearers, and give it to men who come from I know not where?' 12 David's servants turned and made their way back to him and told him all this. 13 He said to his followers, 'Buckle on your swords, all of you.' So they buckled on their swords, as did David, and they followed him, four hundred of them, while two hundred stayed behind with the baggage.

14 One of Nabal's servants said to Abigail, Nabal's wife, 'David sent messengers from the wilderness to ask our master politely for a present, and he flared up at them. 15 The men have been very good to us and have not molested us, nor did we miss anything all the time we were going about with them in the open country. 16 They were as good as a wall round us, night and day, while we were minding the flocks. 17 Consider carefully what you had better do, for it is certain ruin for our master and his whole house; he is such a wretched fellow that it is no good talking to him.'

18 Abigail hastily collected two hundred loaves and two skins of wine, five sheep ready dressed, five measures of roasted grain, a hundred bunches of raisins, and two hundred cakes of dried figs, and loaded them on donkeys, 19 but told her husband nothing about it. She said to her servants, 'Go on ahead, I shall follow you.' 20 As she made her way on her donkey, hidden by the hill, there were David and his men coming down towards her, and she met them. 21 David had said, 'It was a waste of time to protect this fellow's property in the wilderness so well that nothing of his was missing. He has repaid me evil for good.' 22 David swore a sol-

emn oath: 'God do the same to me and more if I leave him a single mother's son alive by morning!'

23 When Abigail saw David she dismounted in haste and prostrated herself before him, bowing low to the ground 24 at his feet, and said, 'Let me take the blame, my lord, but allow your humble servant to speak out, and let my lord give me a hearing. 25 How can you take any notice of this wretched fellow? He is just what his name Nabal means: "Churl" is his name, and churlish his behaviour. Sir, I did not myself see the men you sent. 26 And now, sir, the LORD has restrained you from starting a blood feud and from striking a blow for yourself. As the LORD lives, your life upon it, your enemies and all who want to see you ruined will be like Nabal. 27 Here is the present which I, your humble servant, have brought; give it to the young men under your command. 28 Forgive me, my lord, if I am presuming; for the LORD will establish your family for ever, because you have fought his battles. No calamity will overtake you as long as you live. 29 If anyone tries to pursue you and take your life, the LORD your God will wrap your life up and put it with his own treasure, but the lives of your enemies he will hurl away like stones from a sling. 30 When the LORD has made good all his promises to you, and has made you ruler of Israel, 31 there will be no reason why you should stumble or your courage should falter because you have shed innocent blood or struck a blow for yourself. Then when the LORD makes all you do prosper, remember me, your servant.'

32 David said to Abigail, 'Blessed be the LORD the God of Israel who today has sent you to meet me. 33 A blessing on your good sense, a blessing on you because you have saved me today from the guilt of bloodshed and from striking a blow for myself. 34 For I swear by the life of the LORD the God of

25:11 **wine:** *so Gk; Heb.* water.　　25:14 **flared up:** *or* railed.　　25:17 **wretched fellow:** *lit.* son of Belial. 25:18 **measures:** *Heb.* seahs.　　25:22 **David:** *so Gk; Heb.* David's enemies.　　25:31 **because . . . shed:** *so some MSS; others* or you should shed.

courteous, but the request for a "protection" payment is clear. **10:** David was apparently renowned as a rebel against Saul. **16:** David is depicted as a kind of Robin Hood whose band constituted an informal peace keeping force. On those terms, there would be some justice in his request of gifts from Nabal. **19:** Abigail understands both her husband's character and the crisis of the moment. **24–35:** Abigail argues (v. 26) that if David kills Nabal, the *blood feud* can imperil the sanctity of his future kingship (on such speeches see 23.16–18 n.). David

Israel who has kept me from doing you wrong: if you had not come at once to meet me, not a man of Nabal's household, not a single mother's son, would have been left alive by morning.' 35 Then David accepted from her what she had brought him and said, 'Go home in peace; I have listened to you and I grant your request.'

36 On her return she found Nabal holding a right royal banquet in his house. He grew merry and became very drunk, so drunk that his wife said nothing at all to him till daybreak. 37 In the morning, when the wine had worn off, she told him everything, and he had a seizure and lay there like a log. 38 Some ten days later the LORD struck him and he died.

39 When David heard that Nabal was dead he said, 'Blessed be the LORD, who has himself punished Nabal for his insult, and has kept me his servant from doing wrong. The LORD has made Nabal's wrongdoing recoil on his own head.' David then sent a message to Abigail proposing that she should become his wife. 40 His servants came to her at Carmel and said, 'David has sent us to fetch you to be his wife.' 41 She rose and prostrated herself with her face to the ground, and said, 'I am his slave to command; I would wash the feet of my lord's servants.' 42 Abigail made her preparations with all speed and, with her five maids in attendance and accompanied by David's messengers, she set out on a donkey; and she became David's wife. 43 David had also married Ahinoam of Jezreel; both these women became his wives. 44 Saul meanwhile had given his daughter Michal, David's wife, to Palti son of Laish from Gallim.

26 THE Ziphites came to Saul at Gibeah with the news that David was in hiding on the hill of Hachilah overlooking Jeshimon. 2 Saul went down at once to the wilderness of Ziph, taking with him three thousand picked men, to search for David there. 3 He encamped beside the road on the hill of Hachilah overlooking Jeshimon, while David was still in the wilderness. As soon as

David learnt that Saul had come to the wilderness in pursuit of him, 4 he sent out scouts and found that Saul had reached such and such a place. 5 He went at once to the place where Saul had pitched his camp, and observed where Saul and Abner son of Ner, the commander-in-chief, were lying. Saul lay within the lines with his troops encamped in a circle round him. 6 David turned to Ahimelech the Hittite and Abishai son of Zeruiah, Joab's brother, and said, 'Who will venture with me into the camp to Saul?' Abishai answered, 'I will.'

7 David and Abishai entered the camp at night, and there was Saul lying asleep within the lines with his spear thrust into the ground beside his head. Abner and the army were asleep all around him. 8 Abishai said to David, 'God has put your enemy into your power today. Let me strike him and pin him to the ground with one thrust of the spear. I shall not have to strike twice.' 9 David said to him, 'Do him no harm. Who has ever lifted his hand against the LORD's anointed and gone unpunished? 10 As the LORD lives,' David went on, 'the LORD will strike him down; either his time will come and he will die, or he will go down to battle and meet his end. 11 God forbid that I should lift my hand against the LORD's anointed! But now let us take the spear which is by his head, and the water-jar, and go.' 12 So David took the spear and the water-jar from beside Saul's head, and they left. The whole camp was asleep; no one saw him, no one knew anything, no one woke. A deep sleep sent by the LORD had fallen on them.

13 Then David crossed over to the other side and stood on the top of a hill at some distance; there was a wide stretch between them. 14 David shouted across to the army and hailed Abner son of Ner, 'Answer me, Abner!' He answered, 'Who are you to shout to the king?' 15 David said to Abner, 'Do you call yourself a man? Is there anyone like you in Israel? Why, then, did you not keep watch over your lord the king, when someone came to harm your lord the king? 16 This was not

---

agrees and is grateful to Abigail for restraining him from the *guilt of bloodshed* (v. 33). **39:** In these stories God is understood to be working out the destiny leading to David's kingship, including his royal family (see 2 Sam. 3.3). **44:** *Michal,* first supportive of David (19.11–17), later changed (2 Sam. 3.14–16; 6.20–23).

    26.1–25: David again spares Saul's life. This narrative was originally an alternative version of 23.14–24.22. **9–11:** On David's speech, see 24.4–7 n. Saul's *spear* is recurrently prominent; see 18.10–11; 19.9–10; 22.6. **12:** The *deep sleep* introduces a miraculous element not really required by the story.

well done. As the Lord lives, you deserve to die, all of you, because you have not kept watch over your master the Lord's anointed. Look! Where are the king's spear and the water-jar that were by his head?'

17 Saul recognized David's voice and said, 'Is that you, David my son?' 'Yes, your majesty, it is,' said David. 18 'Why must my lord pursue me? What have I done? What mischief am I plotting? 19 Listen, my lord king, to what I have to say. If it is the Lord who has set you against me, may an offering be acceptable to him; but if it is mortals, a curse on them in the Lord's name! For they have ousted me today from my share in the Lord's possession and have banished me to serve other gods! 20 Do not let my blood be shed on foreign soil, far from the presence of the Lord, just because the king of Israel came out to look for a flea, as one might hunt a partridge over the hills.'

21 Saul said, 'I have done wrong; come back, David my son. You have held my life precious this day, and I will never harm you again. I have been a fool, I have been sadly in the wrong.' 22 David answered, 'Here is the king's spear; let one of your men come across and fetch it. 23 The Lord who rewards uprightness and loyalty will reward the man into whose power he put you today, for I refused to lift my hand against the Lord's anointed. 24 As I held your life precious today, so may the Lord hold mine precious and deliver me from every distress.' 25 Saul said to David, 'A blessing on you, David my son! You will do great things and be triumphant.' With that David went on his way and Saul returned home.

David among the Philistines

27 DAVID thought to himself, 'One of these days I shall be killed by Saul. The best thing for me to do will be to escape into Philistine territory; then Saul will give up all further hope of finding me anywhere in Israel, search as he may, and I shall escape his clutches.' 2 So David and his six hundred men set out and crossed the frontier to Achish son of Maoch, king of Gath. 3 David settled in Gath with Achish, taking with him his men and their families and his two wives, Ahinoam of Jezreel and Abigail of Carmel, Nabal's widow. 4 Saul was told that David had escaped to Gath, and he abandoned the search.

5 David said to Achish, 'If I stand well in your opinion, grant me a place in one of your country towns where I may settle. Why should I remain in the royal city with your majesty?' 6 Achish granted him Ziklag on that day: that is why Ziklag still belongs to the kings of Judah.

7 David spent a year and four months in Philistine country. 8 He and his men would sally out and raid the Geshurites, the Gizrites, and the Amalekites, for it was they who inhabited the country from Telaim all the way to Shur and Egypt. 9 When David raided any territory he left no one alive, man or woman; he took flocks and herds, donkeys and camels, and clothes too, and then came back again to Achish. 10 Achish would ask, 'Where was your raid today?' and David would answer, 'The Negeb of Judah' or 'The Negeb of the Jerahmeelites' or 'The Negeb of the Kenites'. 11 He let neither man nor woman survive to be brought back to Gath, for fear that they might denounce him and his men for what they had done. This was his practice as long as he remained with the Philistines. 12 Achish trusted him, thinking that David had made himself so obnoxious among his own people the Israelites that he would remain his vassal all his life.

28 AT that time the Philistines mustered their army for an attack on Israel, and Achish said to David, 'You know that you and your men must take the field with me.' 2 David answered, 'Good, you will learn what your servant can do.' Achish said, 'I will make you my bodyguard for life.'

3 By this time Samuel was dead, and all Israel had mourned for him and buried him

27:8 **from Telaim:** *prob. rdg; Heb.* from of old.

27.1–28.2: David becomes a vassal of Achish of Gath. The narrow escapes in the wilderness finally drive David (again) to the protection of the Philistines; see 21.10–15. **5–6:** David had a feudal relation to Achish; he owed certain military duties (28.1) in return for the benefits of the territory of *Ziklag.* **7–8:** David's raids were in regions south of Judah. **10:** *Jerahmeelites* and *Kenites* were clans eventually absorbed into the tribe of Judah; see 1 Chr. 2.25, 55. *Negeb* means "dry country"; here it is applied to a small local region.

28.3–25: Saul and the ghost of Samuel. The collapse of Saul's personality and character reaches its climax.

in Ramah, his own town; and Saul had banished from the land all who trafficked with ghosts and spirits. 4 The Philistines mustered and encamped at Shunem, and Saul mustered all the Israelites and encamped at Gilboa. 5 At the sight of the Philistine forces, Saul was afraid, indeed struck to the heart by terror. 6 He enquired of the Lord, but the Lord did not answer him, neither by dreams, nor by Urim, nor by prophets. 7 So he said to his servants, 'Find a woman who has a familiar spirit, and I will go and enquire through her.' They told him that there was such a woman at En-dor.

8 Saul put on different clothes and went in disguise with two of his men. He came to the woman by night and said, 'Tell me my fortune by consulting the dead, and call up the man I name to you.' 9 The woman answered, 'Surely you know what Saul has done, how he has made away with those who call up ghosts and spirits; why do you press me to do what will lead to my death?' 10 Saul swore her an oath: 'As the Lord lives, no harm shall come to you for this.' 11 The woman asked whom she should call up, and Saul answered, 'Samuel.' 12 When the woman saw Samuel appear, she shrieked and said to Saul, 'Why have you deceived me? You are Saul!' 13 The king said to her, 'Do not be afraid. What do you see?' The woman answered, 'I see a ghostly form coming up from the earth.' 14 'What is it like?' he asked; she answered, 'Like an old man coming up, wrapped in a cloak.' Then Saul knew it was Samuel, and he bowed low with his face to the ground, and prostrated himself.

15 Samuel said to Saul, 'Why have you disturbed me and raised me?' Saul answered, 'I am in great trouble; the Philistines are waging war against me, and God has turned away; he no longer answers me through prophets or through dreams, and I have summoned you to tell me what I should do.' 16 Samuel said, 'Why do you ask me, now that the Lord has turned from you and become

your adversary? 17 He has done what he foretold through me. He has wrested the kingdom from your hand and given it to another, to David. 18 You have not obeyed the Lord, or executed the judgement of his fierce anger against the Amalekites; that is why he has done this to you today. 19 For the same reason the Lord will let your people Israel fall along with you into the hands of the Philistines. What is more, tomorrow you and your sons will be with me. I tell you again: the Lord will give the Israelite army into the power of the Philistines.' 20 Saul was overcome, and terrified by Samuel's words he fell full length to the ground. He had no strength left, for he had eaten nothing all day and all night.

21 The woman went to Saul and, seeing how deeply shaken he was, she said, 'I listened to what you said and I risked my life to obey you. 22 Now listen to me: let me set before you a little food to give you strength for your journey.' 23 He refused to eat anything, but when his servants joined the woman in pressing him, he yielded, rose from the ground, and sat on the couch. 24 The woman had a fattened calf at home, which she quickly slaughtered; she also took some meal, kneaded it, and baked unleavened loaves. 25 She set the food before Saul and his servants, and when they had eaten they set off that same night.

29 The Philistines mustered their entire army at Aphek; the Israelites encamped at En-harod in Jezreel. 2 While the Philistine lords were advancing with their troops in units of a hundred and a thousand, David and his men were in the rear of the column with Achish. 3 The Philistine commanders asked, 'What are those Hebrews doing here?' Achish answered, 'This is David, the servant of King Saul of Israel who has been with me now for a year or more. Ever since he came over to me I have had no fault

28:23 in pressing: prob. rdg, cp. Gk; Heb. in breaking out on.   29:1 at En-harod: prob. rdg; Heb. at the spring.

3: Consultation of ghosts and spirits of the dead was consistently opposed in Israelite religious practice; see Lev. 19.31; 20.6, 27; Deut. 18.10–11; 2 Kgs. 23.24. 4: The movement of the Philistines anticipates ch. 29. 6: To be auspicious, important decisions needed divine sanction; compare 14.18, 36–37; 23.1–13. 13: Coming up from the earth means up from Sheol, the underground abode of the dead; see 2.6 n. 17–18: This may be a later writer's harmonization with ch. 15. There (15.28) the man was anonymous; here he is named as David.

29.1–11: David's exclusion by the Philistines from the war against Saul. 1: The Philistines aimed at occupying the valley of Jezreel that cuts across from the Mediterranean to the Jordan valley. Saul seeks to stop to find with him.' ⁴The commanders were indignant and said, 'Send the man back to the place you allotted to him. He must not fight side by side with us, for he may turn traitor in the battle. What better way to buy his master's favour, than at the price of our lives? ⁵This is that David of whom they sang, as they danced:

"Saul struck down thousands,
　but David tens of thousands."'

⁶Achish summoned David and said to him, 'As the LORD lives, you are an upright man and your service on my campaigns has well satisfied me. I have had no fault to find with you ever since you joined me, but the lords are not willing to accept you. ⁷Now go home in peace, and you will then be doing nothing that they can regard as wrong.' ⁸David protested, 'What have I done, or what fault have you found in me from the day I first entered your service till now, that I should not come and fight against the enemies of my lord the king?' ⁹Achish answered, 'I agree that you have been as true to me as an angel of God, but the Philistine commanders insist that you are not to fight alongside them. ¹⁰Now rise early tomorrow with those of your lord's subjects who have followed you, and go to the town which I allotted to you; harbour no resentment, for I am well satisfied with you. Be up early and start as soon as it is light.' ¹¹So in the morning David and his men made an early start to go back to the land of the Philistines, while the Philistines went on to Jezreel.

30 On the third day David and his men reached Ziklag. In the mean time the Amalekites had made a raid into the Negeb, attacked Ziklag, and set it on fire. ²They had taken captive all the women, young and old. They did not put any to death, but carried them off as they continued their march. ³When David and his men came to the town, they found it destroyed by fire, and their wives, their sons, and their daughters taken captive. ⁴David and the people with him wept aloud until they could weep no more. ⁵David's two wives, Ahinoam of Jezreel and Abigail widow of Nabal of Carmel, were among the captives. ⁶David was in a desperate position because the troops, embittered by the loss of their sons and daughters, threatened to stone him.

David sought strength in the LORD his God, ⁷and told Abiathar the priest, son of Ahimelech, to bring the ephod. When Abiathar had brought the ephod, ⁸David enquired of the LORD, 'Shall I pursue these raiders? And shall I overtake them?' The answer came, 'Pursue them: you will overtake them and rescue everyone.' ⁹David and his six hundred men set out and reached the wadi of Besor. ¹⁰Two hundred of them who were too exhausted to cross the wadi stayed behind, and David with four hundred pressed on in pursuit.

¹¹In the open country they came across an Egyptian and took him to David. They gave him food to eat and water to drink, ¹²also a lump of dried figs and two bunches of raisins. When he had eaten he revived; for he had had nothing to eat or drink for three days and nights. ¹³David asked him, 'Whose slave are you, and where have you come from?' 'I am an Egyptian,' he answered, 'the slave of an Amalekite, but my master left me behind because three days ago I fell ill. ¹⁴We had raided the Negeb of the Kerethites, part of Judah, and the Negeb of Caleb; we also burned down Ziklag.' ¹⁵David asked, 'Can you guide me to the raiders?' 'Swear to me by God', he answered, 'that you will not put me to death or hand me back to my master, and I shall guide you to them.' ¹⁶He led him down, and there they found the Amalekites scattered everywhere, eating and drinking and celebrating the great mass of spoil taken from the Philistine and Judaean territories.

¹⁷David attacked from dawn to dusk and continued till next day; only four hundred young men mounted on camels got away.

29:10 **and go . . . with you:** *so Gk; Heb. omits.*
30:9 **Besor:** *prob. rdg; Heb. adds* those who were left over remained.

them at the narrowest part of that valley. **3–6:** The Philistines mistrust David. On *Hebrews,* see 14.21 n. **5:** See 18.7 n.

　30.1–31: David's reprisal against the Amalekites. Saul's campaign (15.1–9) did not prevent the Amalekites from harassing the southern Judean clans. **6:** Compare David's situation here with that of Moses in Exod. 17.4. **7–8:** David is again scrupulous in consulting the LORD; see 23.1–13. **14:** The *Kerethites* were Cretans, closely related to the Philistines; see Zeph. 2.5 and Ezek. 25.16. The *Negeb of Caleb* was in the vicinity of Hebron;

¹⁸David rescued all those whom the Amalekites had taken captive, including his two wives. ¹⁹No one was missing, young or old, sons or daughters, nor was any of the spoil missing, anything they had seized for themselves: David recovered everything. ²⁰They took all the flocks and herds, drove the cattle before him and said, 'This is David's spoil.'

²¹When David returned to the two hundred men who had been too exhausted to follow him and whom he had left behind at the wadi of Besor, they came forward to meet him and his men. David greeted them all, enquiring how things were with them. ²²But some of those who had gone with David, rogues and scoundrels, broke in and said, 'These men did not go with us; we will not allot them any of the spoil that we have recaptured, except that each of them may take his wife and children and go.' ²³'That', said David, 'you must not do, considering what the LORD has given us, and how he has kept us safe and given the raiding party into our hands. ²⁴Who could agree with what you propose? Those who stayed with the stores are to have the same share as those who went into battle. All must share and share alike.' ²⁵From that time onwards, this has been the established custom in Israel down to this day.

²⁶When David reached Ziklag, he sent some of the spoil to the elders of Judah and to his friends, with this message: 'This is a present for you out of the spoil taken from the LORD's enemies.' ²⁷He sent to those in Bethuel, in Ramoth-negeb, in Jattir, ²⁸in Ararah, in Siphmoth, in Eshtemoa, ²⁹in Rachal, in the cities of the Jerahmeelites, in the towns of the Kenites, ³⁰in Hormah, in Borashan, in Athak, ³¹in Hebron, and in all the places over which he and his men had ranged.

31 The Philistines engaged Israel in battle, and the Israelites were routed, leaving their dead on Mount Gilboa. ²The Philistines closely pursued Saul and his sons, and Jonathan, Abinadab, and Malchishua, the sons of Saul, were killed. ³The battle went hard for Saul, and when the archers caught up with him they wounded him severely. ⁴He said to his armour-bearer, 'Draw your sword and run me through, so that these uncircumcised brutes may not come and taunt me and make sport of me.' But the armour-bearer refused; he dared not do it. Thereupon Saul took his own sword and fell on it. ⁵When the armour-bearer saw that Saul was dead, he too fell on his sword and died with him. ⁶So they died together on that day, Saul, his three sons, and his armour-bearer, as well as all his men. ⁷When the Israelites in the neighbourhood of the valley and of the Jordan saw that the other Israelites had fled and that Saul and his sons had perished, they fled likewise, abandoning their towns; and the Philistines moved in and occupied them.

⁸Next day, when the Philistines came to strip the slain, they found Saul and his three sons lying dead on Mount Gilboa. ⁹They cut off his head and stripped him of his armour; then they sent messengers through the length and breadth of their land to carry the good news to idols and people alike. ¹⁰They deposited his armour in the temple of Ashtoreth and nailed his body on the wall of Beth-shan. ¹¹When the inhabitants of Jabesh-gilead heard what the Philistines had done to Saul, ¹²all the warriors among them set out and journeyed through the night to recover the bodies of Saul and his sons from the wall of Beth-shan. They brought them back to Jabesh and burned them; ¹³they took the bones and buried them under the tamarisk tree in Jabesh, and for seven days they fasted.

30:20 **They ... before him:** *prob. rdg; Heb.* David took all the flocks and herds; they drove before that cattle. 30:22 **us:** *so some MSS; others* me. 30:23 **considering:** *prob. rdg, cp. Gk; Heb.* my brothers. 30:26 **and;** *so Gk; Heb. omits.*   30:28 **Ararah:** *prob. rdg; Heb.* Aroer.   31:1–13 *Cp. 1 Chr. 10:1–12.* 31:9 **idols:** *so Gk; Heb.* house of idols.   31:11 **heard:** *so Gk; Heb. adds* to him.   31:12 **They brought them:** *so Gk, cp. 1 Chr. 10:12; Heb.* they came.

see Josh. 15.13–19. **26–31:** David is currying favor preparatory to becoming king. On the *Jerahmeelites* and *Kenites;* see 27.10 n.

31.1–13: The death of Saul. Saul had made some headway against the Philistines and here sought to prevent their occupation of the central valley; see 29.1 n. The result, however, was disastrous. **10:** *Ashtoreth;* see 7.4 n. *Beth-shan:* probably the Canaanite city in the eastern part of the valley, near Mount Gilboa (v. 8). **11–13:** The inhabitants of *Jabesh-gilead* were grateful to Saul for his rescue of them; see ch. 11.

THE SECOND BOOK OF
Samuel

Without a break, the story begun in 1 Samuel continues in 2 Samuel (see Introduction to 1 Samuel). The focus of the narrative is on David the king, first (chs. 1–8) on the establishment of his rule in Judah and in Israel, then (chs. 9–20) on events largely related to the issue of succession to the throne. Chapters 21–24 appear to be an intrusive appendix concerning David's reign (see 21.1–24.25 n.), but the throne succession narrative is concluded in 1 Kings chs. 1–2.

Beginning with 8.1–18, the relationship of the report in 2 Samuel to that in the books of Chronicles is such that the annotations which cross-reference to the latter work deserve special attention.

David installed as king

1 AFTER Saul's death David returned from his victory over the Amalekites and spent two days in Ziklag. ² On the third day a man came from Saul's camp; his clothes were torn and there was dust on his head. Coming into David's presence he fell to the ground and did obeisance. ³ David asked him where he had come from, and he replied, 'I have escaped from the Israelite camp.' ⁴ David said, 'What is the news? Tell me.' 'The army has been driven from the field,' he answered, 'many have fallen in battle, and Saul and Jonathan his son are dead.' ⁵ David said to the young man who brought the news, 'How do you know that Saul and Jonathan are dead?' ⁶ He answered, 'It so happened that I was on Mount Gilboa and saw Saul leaning on his spear with the chariots and horsemen closing in on him. ⁷ He turned and, seeing me, called to me. I said, "What is it, sir?" ⁸ He asked me who I was, and I said, "An Amalekite." ⁹ He said to me, "Come and stand over me and dispatch me. I still live, but the throes of death have seized me." ¹⁰ So I stood over him and dealt him the death blow, for I knew that, stricken as he was, he could not live. Then I took the crown from his head and the armlet from his arm, and I have brought them here to you, my lord.' ¹¹ At that David and all the men with him took hold of their clothes and tore them. ¹² They mourned and wept, and they fasted till evening because Saul and Jonathan his son and the army of the LORD and the house of Israel had fallen in battle.

¹³ David said to the young man who brought him the news, 'Where do you come from?' and he answered, 'I am the son of an alien, an Amalekite.' ¹⁴ 'How is it', said David, 'that you were not afraid to raise your hand to kill the LORD's anointed?' ¹⁵ Summoning one of his own young men he ordered him to fall upon the Amalekite. The young man struck him down and he died. ¹⁶ David said, 'Your blood be on your own head; for out of your own mouth you condemned yourself by saying, "I killed the LORD's anointed." '

¹⁷ David raised this lament over Saul and Jonathan his son; ¹⁸ and he ordered that this dirge over them should be taught to the peo-

1.1–5.25: David acquires the kingship. This is the concluding section of the history of the rise of David (see 1 Sam. 16.1–2 Sam. 5.25 n.). Though strongly favorable toward David, it is a fine piece of balanced historical writing.

1.1–27: David learns of Saul's death. Throughout the account of his rise David is viewed as maintaining scrupulous loyalty toward Saul. That emphasis here reaches its strongest expression. **1:** The narrative resumes from the end of 1 Sam. ch. 30. **2:** Compare the messenger in 1 Sam. 4.12. **6:** On Saul's *spear,* see 1 Sam. 26.9–11 n. **8:** The *Amalekite* was a mercenary in the Israelite army. **14:** On *the LORD's anointed,* see 1 Sam. 24.4–7 n. **17–27:** Since David was a harpist (1 Sam. 16.14–23) this *dirge* may indeed go back to him. It is lyric poetry without any particular religious aspect.

ple of Judah. It was written down and may be found in the Book of Jashar:

19 Israel, upon your heights your beauty
   lies slain!
   How are the warriors fallen!

20 Do not tell it in Gath
   or proclaim it in the streets of Ashkelon,
   in case the Philistine maidens rejoice,
   and the daughters of the uncircumcised
   exult.

21 Hills of Gilboa, let no dew or rain fall
   on you,
   no showers on the uplands!
   For there the shields of the warriors lie
   tarnished,
   and the shield of Saul, no longer bright
   with oil.

22 The bow of Jonathan never held back
   from the breast of the foeman, from
   the blood of the slain;
   the sword of Saul never returned
   empty to the scabbard.

23 Beloved and lovely were Saul and
   Jonathan;
   neither in life nor in death were they
   parted.
   They were swifter than eagles,
   stronger than lions.

24 Daughters of Israel, weep for Saul,
   who clothed you in scarlet and rich
   embroideries,
   who spangled your attire with jewels of
   gold.

25 How are the warriors fallen on the field
   of battle!

Jonathan lies slain on your heights.
26 I grieve for you, Jonathan my brother;
   you were most dear to me;
   your love for me was wonderful,
   surpassing the love of women.

27 How are the warriors fallen,
   and their armour abandoned on the
   battlefield!

2 Afterwards David enquired of the LORD, 'Shall I go up into one of the towns of Judah?' The LORD answered, 'Go.' David asked, 'Where shall I go?' and the answer was, 'To Hebron.' 2 So David went up there with his two wives, Ahinoam of Jezreel and Abigail widow of Nabal of Carmel. 3 David also brought the men who had joined him, with their families, and they settled in Hebron and the neighbouring towns. 4 The men of Judah came, and there they anointed David king over the house of Judah.

It was reported to David that the men of Jabesh-gilead had buried Saul, 5 and he sent them this message: 'The LORD bless you because you kept faith with Saul your lord and buried him. 6 For this may the LORD keep faith and truth with you, and I for my part will show you favour too, because you have done this. 7 Be strong, be valiant, now that Saul your lord is dead, and the people of Judah have anointed me to be king over them.'

8 Meanwhile Saul's commander-in-chief, Abner son of Ner, had taken Saul's son Ishbosheth, brought him across to Mahanaim,

1:18 **Book of Jashar:** or Book of the Upright.
1:21 **showers on the uplands:** prob. rdg; Heb. fields of offerings.

18: Jashar: "Upright." On the Book of Jashar see Josh. 10.13 n. Its contents may have been taught to the people, probably by recitation at assemblies and festivals. **20:** Uncircumcised: see 1 Sam 14.6 n. **21:** The place of Saul's death should be afflicted with drought. The leather shields were kept in good condition with oil.

2.1–7: David becomes king of Judah. 1–3: David again carefully consults the LORD about his movements; see 1 Sam. 23.1–13; 30.7–8. With Saul gone, the Judahites take their own steps against the Philistines. **4b–7:** David's message to Jabesh-gilead had its political motivations, for it was in the territory of the remnant kingdom of Saul's son.

2.8–5.5: All Israel comes to David. There is a twofold concern throughout this narrative: to show how events worked inevitably toward David's becoming king of all Israel, but also that he himself remained blameless of bloodshed and other offenses in the process. **8:** Ishbosheth: The name literally means "man (ish) of shame (bosheth)"; the bosheth was originally "baal," and then the name meant "man of Baal." Late editors eliminated here the abhorred name of the Canaanite deity; the change was not made in Chr. ("Eshbaal," 1 Chr. 8.33; 9.39). Mahanaim was a prominent city in Gilead. It also served as a refuge for David when he had to flee to the east

⁹and made him king over Gilead, the Asherites, Jezreel, Ephraim, and Benjamin, and all Israel. ¹⁰Ishbosheth was forty years old when he became king over Israel, and he reigned for two years. The tribe of Judah, however, followed David. ¹¹David's rule over Judah in Hebron lasted seven and a half years.

¹²Abner son of Ner, with the troops of Saul's son Ishbosheth, marched out from Mahanaim to Gibeon, ¹³and Joab son of Zeruiah marched out with David's troops from Hebron. They met at the pool of Gibeon and took up their positions, one force on one side of the pool and the other on the opposite side. ¹⁴Abner said to Joab, 'Let the young men come forward and join in single combat before us.' Joab agreed. ¹⁵So they came up, one by one, and took their places, twelve for Benjamin and Ishbosheth and twelve from David's men. ¹⁶Each man seized his opponent by the head and thrust his sword into his opponent's side; and thus they fell together. That is why that place, which lies in Gibeon, was called the Field of Blades.

¹⁷There ensued a very hard-fought battle that day, and Abner and the men of Israel were defeated by David's troops. ¹⁸All three sons of Zeruiah were there, Joab, Abishai, and Asahel. Asahel, who was swift as a gazelle of the plains, ¹⁹chased after Abner, swerving to neither right nor left in his pursuit. ²⁰Abner glanced back and said, 'Is it you, Asahel?' Asahel answered, 'It is.' ²¹Abner said, 'Turn aside to right or left; tackle one of the young men and win his belt for yourself.' But Asahel would not abandon the pursuit. ²²Abner again urged him to give it up. 'Why should I kill you?' he said. 'How could I look Joab your brother in the face?' ²³When he still refused to turn away, Abner struck him in the belly with a back-thrust of his spear so that the spear came out through his back, and he fell dead in his tracks. All who came to the place where Asahel lay dead stopped there. ²⁴But Joab and Abishai kept up the pursuit of Abner, until, at sunset, they reached the hill of Ammah, opposite Giah on the road leading to the pastures of Gibeon.

²⁵The Benjamites rallied to Abner and, forming themselves into a single group, took their stand on the top of a hill. ²⁶Abner called to Joab, 'Must the slaughter go on for ever? Can you not see the bitterness that will result? How long before you recall the troops from the pursuit of their kinsmen?' ²⁷Joab answered, 'As God lives, if you had not spoken, they would not have given up the pursuit till morning.' ²⁸Then Joab sounded the trumpet, and the troops all halted; they abandoned the pursuit of the Israelites, and the fighting ceased.

²⁹Abner and his men moved along the Arabah all that night, crossed the Jordan, and continued all morning till they reached Mahanaim. ³⁰After Joab returned from the pursuit of Abner, he mustered his troops and found that, besides Asahel, nineteen of David's men were missing. ³¹David's forces had routed the Benjamites and the followers of Abner, killing three hundred and sixty of them. ³²They took up Asahel and buried him in his father's tomb at Bethlehem. Joab and his men marched all night, and as day broke they reached Hebron.

3 THE war between the house of Saul and the house of David was long drawn out, David growing steadily stronger while the house of Saul became weaker.

²Sons were born to David at Hebron. His eldest was Amnon, whose mother was Ahinoam from Jezreel; ³his second Cileab, whose mother was Abigail widow of Nabal from Carmel; the third Absalom, whose mother was Maacah daughter of Talmai king of Geshur; ⁴the fourth Adonijah, whose mother was Haggith; the fifth Shephatiah, whose mother was Abital; ⁵and the sixth Ithream, whose mother was David's wife Eglah. These were born to David at Hebron.

⁶As the war between the houses of Saul and David went on, Abner gradually strengthened his position in the house of Saul. ⁷Now Saul had had a concubine named

2:23 **a back-thrust of his spear:** *prob. rdg; Heb. obscure.*
3:2–5 *Cp. 1 Chr. 3:1–4.*

(17.24). **9:** That *Ishbosheth* actually ruled over *all Israel* is an exaggeration, an instance of court etiquette. **10–11:** The chronology here is difficult. But if Ishbosheth reigned only two years, and then David became king of all Israel, David's wars with the Philistines (5.17–25) probably preceded his conquest of Jerusalem (5.6–10); thereby we can possibly understand the *seven years and a half* of his reign at Hebron. **16:** The exact nature of this combat is obscure. **22:** *Abner* wishes to avoid a blood feud with his respected opponent. **29:** *Arabah,* "dry place," is the southern Jordan valley. **3.2–5:** This is an editorial addition to the main narrative.

Rizpah daughter of Aiah. Ishbosheth challenged Abner, 'Why have you slept with my father's concubine?' [8] Abner, angered by this, exclaimed, 'Do you take me for a Judahite dog? Up to now I have been loyal to the house of your father Saul, to his brothers and friends, and I have not betrayed you into David's hands; yet you choose this moment to charge me with an offence over a woman. [9] But now, so help me God, I shall do all I can to bring about what the LORD swore to do for David: [10] I shall set to work to overthrow the house of Saul and to establish David's throne over Israel and Judah from Dan to Beersheba.' [11] Ishbosheth dared not say another word; he was too much afraid of Abner.

[12] Abner sent envoys on his own behalf to David with the message, 'Who is to control the land? Let us come to terms, and you will have my support in bringing the whole of Israel over to you.' [13] David's answer was: 'Good, I will come to terms with you, but on one condition: that you do not come into my presence without bringing Saul's daughter Michal to me.' [14] David also sent messengers to Saul's son Ishbosheth with the demand: 'Hand over to me my wife Michal for whom I gave a hundred Philistine foreskins as the bride-price.' [15] Thereupon Ishbosheth sent and took her from her husband, Paltiel son of Laish. [16] Her husband followed her as far as Bahurim, weeping all the way, until Abner ordered him back, and he went.

[17] Abner conferred with the elders of Israel: 'For some time past', he said, 'you have wanted David for your king. [18] Now is the time to act, for this is the word of the LORD about David: "By the hand of my servant David I shall deliver my people Israel from the Philistines and from all their enemies."' [19] Abner spoke also to the Benjamites and then went to report to David at Hebron all that the Israelites and the Benjamites had agreed. [20] When Abner, attended by twenty men, arrived, David gave a feast for him and his men. [21] Abner said to David, 'I shall now

go and bring the whole of Israel over to your majesty. They will make a covenant with you, and you will be king over a realm after your own heart.' David dismissed Abner, granting him safe conduct.

[22] Just then David's men and Joab returned from a raid, bringing a great quantity of plunder with them. Abner, having been dismissed, was no longer with David in Hebron. [23] Joab and the whole force with him were greeted on their arrival with the news that Abner son of Ner had been with the king and had departed under safe conduct.

[24] Joab went in to the king and said, 'What have you done? You have had Abner here with you. How could you let him go and get clean away? [25] You know Abner son of Ner: his purpose in coming was to deceive you, to learn about your movements, and to find out everything you are doing.'

[26] Leaving David's presence, Joab sent messengers after Abner, and they brought him back from the Pool of Sirah; but David knew nothing of this. [27] On Abner's return to Hebron, Joab drew him aside in the gateway, as though to speak privately with him, and there, in revenge for his brother Asahel, he stabbed him in the belly, and he died.

[28] When David heard the news he said, 'In the sight of the LORD I and my kingdom are for ever innocent of the blood of Abner son of Ner. [29] May it recoil on the head of Joab and on all his family! May the house of Joab never be free from running sore or foul disease, nor lack a son fit only to ply the distaff or doomed to die by the sword or beg his bread!' [30] Joab and Abishai his brother slew Abner because he had killed their brother Asahel in battle at Gibeon. [31] Then David ordered Joab and all the troops with him to tear their clothes, put on sackcloth, and mourn for Abner, and the king himself walked behind the bier. [32] They buried Abner in Hebron and the king wept aloud at the tomb, while all the people wept with him. [33] The king made this lament for Abner:

7: To take a king's concubine was an act of treason; compare 16.20–22; 1 Kgs. 2.13–24. 14: David's interest in *Michal* was for a claim, as son-in-law, of continuity with Saul. 19: In this entire narrative the *Benjamites* are depicted as remarkably independent, probably because they were Saul's tribe. 22–27: Joab's killing of Abner threatened to undo David's plans to become king of all Israel; hence David's great anger. 28–39: The violent outbreak and conspicuous mourning over *Abner* reflect David's need to persuade the Israelites of his own innocence. David may curse *Joab* (v. 29), but Joab is far too valuable to execute, as had been done to the Amalekite (1.15) and was to be done to the assassins of Ishbosheth (4.12). 29: A *distaff* was an instrument used in spinning

Must Abner die so base a death?
34 Your hands were not bound,
   your feet not fettered;
you fell as one who falls at the hands of
   a criminal.

The people all wept again for him.
35 They came to urge David to eat something; but it was still day and he took an oath,
'So help me God! I refuse to touch food of
any kind before sunset.' 36 The people noted
this with approval; indeed, everything the
king did pleased them all. 37 It was then
known throughout Israel that the king had
had no hand in the murder of Abner son of
Ner. 38 The king said to his servants, 'You
must know that a warrior, a great man, has
fallen this day in Israel. 39 Anointed king
though I am, I feel weak and powerless in
face of these ruthless sons of Zeruiah; they
are too much for me. May the LORD requite
the wrongdoer as his wrongdoing deserves.'

4 When Saul's son Ishbosheth heard that
Abner had met his death in Hebron, his
courage failed him, and all Israel was
alarmed. 2 Ishbosheth had two officers, who
were captains of raiding parties, and whose
names were Baanah and Rechab; they were
Benjamites, sons of Rimmon of Beeroth, Beeroth being reckoned part of Benjamin; 3 but
the Beerothites had sought refuge in Gittaim, where they have lived as aliens ever
since.

4 (Saul's son Jonathan had a son lame in
both feet. He was five years old when word
of the death of Saul and Jonathan came from
Jezreel. His nurse had picked him up and
fled, but as she hurried to get away he fell
and was crippled. His name was Mephibosheth.)

5 Rechab and Baanah, the sons of Rimmon
of Beeroth, came to Ishbosheth's house in
the heat of the day, while he was taking his
midday rest. 6 The door-keeper had been
sifting wheat, but she had grown drowsy and
fallen asleep, so Rechab and his brother Baanah slipped past, 7 found their way to the

room where Ishbosheth was asleep on the
bed, and attacked and killed him. They cut
off his head and took it with them and, making their way along the Arabah all night,
came to Hebron. 8 They brought Ishbosheth's head to David there and said to the
king, 'Here is the head of Ishbosheth son of
Saul, your enemy, who sought your life. The
LORD has avenged your majesty today on
Saul and on his family.' 9 David answered Rechab and his brother Baanah: 'As the LORD
lives, who has delivered me from all my troubles, 10 I seized the man who brought me
word that Saul was dead and thought he was
bringing good news; I killed him in Ziklag.
That was how I rewarded him for his news!
11 How much more shall I reward wicked
men who have killed an innocent man on his
bed in his own house! Am I not to take vengeance on you now for the blood you have
shed, and rid the earth of you?' 12 David gave
the word, and the young men killed them;
they cut off their hands and feet and hung
them up beside the pool in Hebron; but the
head of Ishbosheth they took and buried in
Abner's tomb at Hebron.

5 ALL the tribes of Israel came to David at
Hebron and said to him, 'We are your
own flesh and blood. 2 In the past, while Saul
was still king over us, it was you that led the
forces of Israel on their campaigns. To you
the LORD said, "You are to be shepherd of my
people Israel; you are to be their prince."'
3 The elders of Israel all came to the king at
Hebron; there David made a covenant with
them before the LORD, and they anointed
David king over Israel.

4 David came to the throne at the age of
thirty and reigned for forty years. 5 In Hebron he had ruled over Judah for seven and
a half years, and in Jerusalem he reigned

4:2 **had:** *prob. rdg; Heb. omits.*   4:6 **The door-keeper**
... past: *prob. rdg, cp. Gk; Heb.* They came right into
the house carrying wheat, and they struck him in the
belly; Rechab and his brother Baanah were acting
stealthily. They.   5:1–3,6–10 *Cp. 1 Chr. 11:1–9.*

thread from wool, a task ordinarily done by women. **4.2:** *Beeroth* was a village of the old city-state of Gibeon
(Josh. 9.17), with which Saul had some kind of feud (21.1), and which may have led to *Beeroth being reckoned*
part of Benjamin. **4:** Another editorial addition; it prepares for ch. 9. *Mephibosheth* is a distortion of the original
Meribbaal; see 2.8 n. **11:** David does not speak of Ishbosheth as the Lord's anointed, as he did of Saul (1 Sam.
24.4–7 n.), but only as an *innocent man!* **5.2:** On *prince,* see 1 Sam. 9.15–16 n. **3:** In contrast to David's rule
of Jerusalem, this is a kingship by *covenant,* not by conquest. **4–5:** The *forty years* of David's reign may be a
round number, but it is approximately correct. His conquest of Jerusalem occurred very near the year 1000 B.C.E.

over Israel and Judah combined for thirty-three years.

6 The king and his men went to Jerusalem to attack the Jebusites, the inhabitants of that region. The Jebusites said to David, 'You will never come in here, not till you have disposed of the blind and the lame,' stressing that David would never come in. 7 None the less David did capture the stronghold of Zion, and it is now known as the City of David. 8 On that day David had said, 'Everyone who is eager to attack the Jebusites, let him get up the water-shaft to reach the lame and the blind, David's bitter enemies.' That is why they say, 'No one who is blind or lame is to come into the LORD's house.'

9 David took up his residence in the stronghold and called it the City of David. He built up the city around it, starting at the Millo and working inwards. 10 David steadily grew more and more powerful, for the LORD the God of Hosts was with him.

David's achievements

11 KING Hiram of Tyre sent envoys to David with cedar logs, and with them carpenters and stonemasons, who built David a house. 12 David knew by now that the LORD had confirmed him as king over Israel and had enhanced his royal power for the sake of his people Israel.

13 After he had moved from Hebron he took more concubines and wives in Jerusalem, and more sons and daughters were born to him. 14 These are the names of the children born to him in Jerusalem: Shammua, Shobab, Nathan, Solomon, 15 Ibhar, Elishua,

Nepheg, Japhia, 16 Elishama, Eliada, and Eliphelet.

17 When the Philistines learnt that David had been anointed king over Israel, they came up in force to seek him out. David, getting wind of this, went down to the stronghold for refuge. 18 When the Philistines had come and overrun the valley of Rephaim, 19 David enquired of the LORD, 'If I attack the Philistines, will you deliver them into my hands?' The LORD answered, 'Go, I shall deliver the Philistines into your hands.' 20 He went and attacked and defeated them at Baal-perazim. 'The LORD has broken through my enemies' lines', David said, 'as a river breaks its banks.' That is why the place was named Baal-perazim. 21 The Philistines abandoned their idols there, and David and his men carried them off.

22 The Philistines made another attack and overran the valley of Rephaim. 23 David enquired of the LORD, who said, 'Do not attack now but make a detour and come on them towards the rear opposite the aspens. 24 As soon as you hear a rustling sound in the treetops, move at once; for then the LORD will have gone out before you to defeat the Philistine army.' 25 David did as the LORD had commanded, and drove the Philistines in flight all the way from Geba to Gezer.

6 David again summoned the picked men of Israel, thirty thousand in all, 2 and

5:8 **the LORD's house:** *lit.* the house.   5:9 **the city:** *prob. rdg, cp.* 1 Chr. 11:8; *Heb.* omits.   5:11–25 *Cp.* 1 Chr. 14:1–16.   5:14–16 *Cp.* 1 Chr. 3:5–8; 14:4–7. 5:20 **Baal-perazim:** *that is* Baal of Break-through. 5:25 **Geba:** *or, with* 1 Chr. 14:16 *and Gk,* Gibeon. 6:2–11 *Cp.* 1 Chr. 13:6–14.

5.6–10: Jerusalem becomes the City of David. *Jerusalem* was a very ancient settlement or city, as much as a thousand years older than the era of David. Biblical traditions about it vary. In Judg. 19.10 its name is Jebus, and it is there a Jebusite city; in Josh. 10.1–10 its forces are defeated; it is captured in Judg. 1.8 and then burned. The account here seems unaware of the capture of Jerusalem in Judg. 1.8. David was seeking a base that had no previous alliance with either Israel to the north or Judah to the south. By capturing the city in the way he did it became his private property, the *City of David*. He did not destroy the city or kill its population (for contrast, see 1 Kgs. 9.16). **7:** *Zion:* a hill crest in Jerusalem, it is a poetic term for the city, frequent in the Psalms and prophetic writings but rare in prose texts. The name Zion became attached to the area where Solomon's temple was built.

5.11–25: David secures his kingdom. 11: That *King Hiram of Tyre* took these measures indicates that David, after defeating the Philistines, became a power to be reckoned with. **17–25:** These two notices of defeats of *the Philistines* are regrettably laconic, interested primarily in David's guidance by the LORD. No narrative develops this topic in the way that was done with another of David's wars, that against the Ammonites and the Arameans (ch. 10 and 12.26–31).

6.1–23: David brings the Ark to Jerusalem. The account of the Ark was suspended at 1 Sam. 7.1, giving went with the whole army that was then with him to Baalath-judah to fetch from there the Ark of God which bore the name of the LORD of Hosts, who is enthroned upon the cherubim. ³They mounted the Ark of God on a new cart and conveyed it from Abinadab's house on the hill, with Uzzah and Ahio, sons of Abinadab, guiding the cart. ⁴They led it with the Ark of God upon it from Abinadab's house on the hill, with Ahio walking in front. ⁵David and all Israel danced for joy before the LORD with all their might to the sound of singing, of lyres, lutes, tambourines, castanets, and cymbals.

⁶When they came to a certain threshing-floor, the oxen stumbled, and Uzzah reached out and held the Ark of God. ⁷The LORD was angry with Uzzah and struck him down for his imprudent action, and he died there beside the Ark of God. ⁸David was vexed because the LORD's anger had broken out on Uzzah, and he called the place Perez-uzzah, the name it still bears.

⁹David was afraid of the LORD that day and said, 'How can the Ark of the LORD come to me?' ¹⁰He felt he could not take the Ark of the LORD with him to the City of David; he turned aside and carried it to the house of Obed-edom the Gittite. ¹¹The Ark of the LORD remained at Obed-edom's house for three months, and the LORD blessed Obed-edom and his whole household.

¹²When David was informed that the LORD had blessed Obed-edom's family and all that he possessed because of the Ark of God, he went and brought the Ark of God from the house of Obed-edom up to the City of David amid rejoicing. ¹³When the bearers of the Ark of the LORD had gone six steps he sacrificed a bull and a buffalo. ¹⁴He was wearing a linen ephod, and he danced with abandon before the LORD, ¹⁵as he and all the Israelites brought up the Ark of the LORD with acclamation and blowing of trumpets. ¹⁶As the Ark of the LORD was entering the City of David, Saul's daughter Michal looked down from a window and saw King David leaping and whirling before the LORD, and she despised him in her heart.

¹⁷After they had brought the Ark of the LORD, they put it in its place inside the tent that David had set up for it, and David offered whole-offerings and shared-offerings before the LORD. ¹⁸Having completed these sacrifices, David blessed the people in the name of the LORD of Hosts, ¹⁹and distributed food to them all, a flat loaf of bread, a portion of meat, and a cake of raisins, to every man and woman in the whole gathering of the Israelites. Then all the people went home.

²⁰David returned to greet his household, and Michal, Saul's daughter, came out to meet him. She said, 'What a glorious day for the king of Israel, when he made an exhibition of himself in the sight of his servants' slave-girls, as any vulgar clown might do!' ²¹David answered her, 'But it was done in the presence of the LORD, who chose me instead of your father and his family and appointed me prince over Israel, the people of the LORD. Before the LORD I shall dance for joy, yes, ²²and I shall earn yet more disgrace and demean myself still more in your eyes; but those slave-girls of whom you speak, they will hold me in honour for it.'

²³To her dying day Michal, Saul's daughter, was childless.

7 Once the king was established in his palace and the LORD had given him security

6:2 **to Baalath-judah:** *prob. rdg, cp. 1 Chr. 13:6; Heb.* from the lords of Judah.   6:5 **with . . . singing:** *prob. rdg, cp. 1 Chr. 13:8; Heb.* to the beating of batons.   6:8 **Perez-uzzah:** *that is* Outbreak on Uzzah.   6:12–19 *Cp. 1 Chr. 15:25—16:3.*   6:19 **portion of meat:** *meaning of Heb. word uncertain.*   6:22 **your:** *so Gk; Heb.* my. 7:1–29 *Cp. 1 Chr. 17:1–27.*

way to the topic of kingship; see 1 Sam. 4.1b–7.1 n. and 8.1–15.35 n. The Ark here moves from the outskirts of Judah to the great sacred city of the future, Jerusalem. **1:** *Thirty thousand* is another number that gives an impression rather than a report; see 1 Sam. 13.5 n. **2:** *Ark . . . enthroned:* see 1 Sam. 4.4 n. **3:** The *new cart* was a ritual requirement; see 1 Sam. 6.7 n. **7:** The uncontrollable and dangerous aspect of the deity is prominent in the Ark story; see 1 Sam. 6.19–20. **10:** *Obed-edom* was a *Gittite,* that is, a man of Gath, the Philistine city. **12–19:** The occasion was one of great festivity. In addition to the procession, dancing, and shouting, the many sacrifices supplied meat for banquets, and David concluded the event with gifts to all the people. **20:** David was apparently dressed only in the linen ephod (v. 14), a kind of priestly apron.

7.1–29: The establishment of the house of David. This is the climax to all that precedes in the books of Samuel. After the legitimacy of kingship was established through Samuel and Saul (1 Sam. chs. 8–14), what remained to establish was the legitimacy of the Davidic dynasty. **1–7:** David proposes to build a temple. An from his enemies on all sides, ²he said to Nathan the prophet, 'Here I am living in a house of cedar, while the Ark of God is housed in a tent.' ³Nathan answered, 'Do whatever you have in mind, for the LORD is with you.' ⁴But that same night the word of the LORD came to Nathan: ⁵'Go and say to David my servant, This is the word of the LORD: Are you to build me a house to dwell in? ⁶Down to this day I have never dwelt in a house since I brought Israel up from Egypt; I lived in a tent and a tabernacle. ⁷Wherever I journeyed with Israel, did I ever ask any of the judges whom I appointed shepherds of my people Israel why they had not built me a cedar house?

⁸'Then say this to my servant David: This is the word of the LORD of Hosts: I took you from the pastures and from following the sheep to be prince over my people Israel. ⁹I have been with you wherever you have gone, and have destroyed all the enemies in your path. I shall bring you fame like the fame of the great ones of the earth. ¹⁰I shall assign a place for my people Israel; there I shall plant them to dwell in their own land. They will be disturbed no more; never again will the wicked oppress them as they did in the past, ¹¹from the day when I appointed judges over my people Israel; and I shall give you peace from all your enemies.

'The LORD has told you that he would build up your royal house. ¹²When your life ends and you rest with your forefathers, I shall set up one of your family, one of your own children, to succeed you, and I shall establish his kingdom. ¹³It is he who is to build a house in honour of my name, and I shall establish his royal throne for all time. ¹⁴I shall be a father to him, and he will be my son. When he does wrong, I shall punish him as any father might, and not spare the rod. ¹⁵But my love will never be withdrawn from him as I withdrew it from Saul, whom I removed from your path. ¹⁶Your family and your kingdom will be established for ever in my sight; your throne will endure for all time.'

¹⁷Nathan recounted to David all that had been said to him and all that had been revealed. ¹⁸Then King David went into the presence of the LORD and, taking his place there, said, 'Who am I, Lord GOD, and what is my family, that you have brought me thus far? ¹⁹It was a small thing in your sight, Lord GOD, to have planned for your servant's house in days long past. ²⁰What more can I say? Lord GOD, you yourself know your servant David. ²¹For the sake of your promise and in accordance with your purpose you have done all this great thing to reveal it to your servant.

²²'Lord GOD, you are great. There is none like you; there is no God but you, as everything we have heard bears witness. ²³And your people Israel, to whom can they be compared? Is there any other nation on earth whom you, God, have set out to redeem from slavery to be your people? You have won renown for yourself by great and awesome deeds, driving out other nations and their gods to make way for your people whom you redeemed from Egypt. ²⁴You have established your people Israel as your own for ever, and you, LORD, have become their God.

²⁵'Now, LORD God, perform for all time what you have promised for your servant and his house; make good what you have promised. ²⁶May your fame be great for evermore, and let people say, "The LORD of Hosts is God over Israel"; and may the house of your servant David be established before you. ²⁷LORD of Hosts, God of Israel, you have shown me your purpose, in saying to your servant, "I shall build up your house"; and therefore I have made bold to offer this prayer to you. ²⁸Now, Lord GOD, you are God and your promises will come true; you have made these noble promises to your servant. ²⁹Be pleased now to bless your servant's house so that it may continue always before

7:7 **judges:** *prob. rdg, cp. 1 Chr. 17:6; Heb.* tribes.
7:16 **my:** *so some MSS; others* your.　7:19 **long past:** *Heb. adds* This, Lord GOD, is a law for men.
7:23 **any other:** *so Gk; Heb.* one. **driving ... people:** *so Gk, cp. 1 Chr. 17:21; Heb. unintelligible.*

old tradition about the LORD not dwelling in a permanent house is drawn upon to oppose that plan. That the Ark dwelt in a temple at Shiloh (1 Sam. 3.3) is ignored. **2:** *Nathan the prophet* first appears here. Since he always appears in Jerusalem and was a close associate of the priest Zadok (1 Kgs. 1.32), he may have been a native of Jerusalem. **8–16:** There is a deliberate wordplay on *house:* David will not build the LORD a house (the temple), but the LORD will build David a house (dynasty). **12–15:** These verses, concerned with the conduct of later kings, are probably a late expansion of the passage. **17–29:** The prayer is often regarded as reflecting a time later than that of David, for it deals with David's *house,* that is, the dynasty of his descendants.

you; you, Lord GOD, have promised, and may your blessing rest on your servant's house for ever.'

8 After this David attacked and subdued the Philistines, and took from them Metheg-ha-ammah. ² He defeated the Moabites and made them lie along the ground, where he measured them off with a length of cord; for every two lengths that were to be put to death one full length was spared. The Moabites became subject to him and paid tribute.

³ David also defeated Hadadezer the Rehobite, king of Zobah, who was on his way to restore his monument of victory by the river Euphrates. ⁴ From him David captured seventeen hundred horse and twenty thousand foot-soldiers; he hamstrung all the chariot-horses, except a hundred which he retained. ⁵ When the Aramaeans of Damascus came to the aid of King Hadadezer of Zobah, David destroyed twenty-two thousand of them, ⁶ and stationed garrisons among these Aramaeans; they became subject to him and paid tribute. Thus the LORD gave David victory wherever he went. ⁷ David took the gold shields borne by Hadadezer's attendants and brought them to Jerusalem; ⁸ he also removed from Hadadezer's cities, Betah and Berothai, a great quantity of bronze.

⁹ When King Toi of Hamath heard that David had defeated Hadadezer's entire army, ¹⁰ he sent his son Joram to King David to greet him and to congratulate him on his victory over Hadadezer, for Hadadezer had been at war with Toi; Joram brought with him vessels of silver, gold, and bronze. ¹¹ These King David dedicated to the LORD,

along with the silver and gold taken from all the nations he had subdued, ¹² from Edom and Moab, from the Ammonites, the Philistines, and Amalek, as well as part of the spoil taken from Hadadezer the Rehobite, king of Zobah.

¹³ David made a great name for himself by the slaughter of eighteen thousand Edomites in the Valley of Salt. ¹⁴ He stationed garrisons throughout Edom, and all the Edomites became subject to him. The LORD gave David victory wherever he went.

¹⁵ David ruled over the whole of Israel and maintained law and justice among all his people. ¹⁶ Joab son of Zeruiah was in command of the army; Jehoshaphat son of Ahilud was secretary of state; ¹⁷ Zadok and Abiathar son of Ahimelech, son of Ahitub, were priests; Seraiah was adjutant-general; ¹⁸ Benaiah son of Jehoiada commanded the Kerethite and Pelethite guards. David's sons were priests.

9 David enquired, 'Is any member of Saul's family left, to whom I can show kindness for Jonathan's sake?' ² A servant of Saul's family named Ziba was summoned to David, who asked, 'Are you Ziba?' He answered, 'Your servant, sir.' ³ The king asked, 'Is there any member of Saul's family still alive to whom I may show the kindness that

8:1–14 *Cp. 1 Chr. 18:1–13.*   8:3 **restore ... victory by:** *or* recover control of the crossings of.
8:7 **shields:** *or* quivers.   8:8,10 **bronze:** *or* copper.
8:12 **Edom:** *so some MSS; others* Aram.
8:13 **Edomites:** *so some MSS; others* Aramaeans.
8:15–18 *Cp. 20:23–26; 1 Kgs. 4:2–6; 1 Chr. 18:14–17.*
8:17 **and Abiathar ... Ahitub:** *prob. rdg, cp. 1 Sam. 22:11,20; 2 Sam. 20:25; Heb.* son of Ahitub and Ahimelech son of Abiathar.   8:18 **commanded:** *so Lat., cp. 2 Sam. 20:23; 1 Chr. 18:17; Heb.* and.

8.1–18: David's wars and administration. This list of notices stands between the long narrative of David's rise to power (1 Sam. ch. 16–2 Sam. ch. 5) and the dramatic narrative of David's sons and the succession to the throne (chs. 9–20, concluded in 1 Kgs. chs. 1–2). (From this point on, cross-references to the books of Chronicles should be noted.) **1:** *Metheg-ha-ammah* is probably not a proper name. First Chronicles 18.1 reads "Gath with its villages," a reading appropriate here, too. **2:** No reason for the severity here toward the *Moabites* is given; it is surprising in view of 1 Sam. 22.3–4. **3–10:** These conquests were all to the north and east, subduing the *Aramaeans,* who were, however, to remain a thorn in Israel's side until the Assyrian conquest in the eighth century. **4:** Unlike his son Solomon (1 Kgs. 10.26–29), David did not exploit chariot warfare. **17:** *Zadok and Abiathar* represented two priestly traditions, Abiathar the old line of Eli at Shiloh (1 Sam. 23.6; 22.9; 14.3), Zadok the priestly line of Jerusalem. **18:** *The Kerethite and Pelethite guards* were mercenaries, sometimes more loyal to the king than his own people; compare 15.17–22. Kerethites and Pelethites were, in origin, from Mediterranean islands.

9.1–20.22: David's children and the succession to the throne. Many regard this narrative of court intrigue and rebellion, which has its conclusion in 1 Kgs. chs. 1–2, as the finest piece of historical writing in the OT.

9.1–13: David cares for Jonathan's son. The king's kindness probably was motivated by political wisdom as well as friendship. By keeping Saul's heir under control, David was assured that no rebellion could form

God requires?' 'Yes,' said Ziba, 'there is still a son of Jonathan alive; he is a cripple, lame in both feet.' [4]'Where is he?' said the king, and Ziba answered, 'He is staying with Machir son of Ammiel in Lo-debar.'

[5] The king had him fetched from Lodebar, from the house of Machir son of Ammiel, [6] and when Mephibosheth, son of Jonathan and grandson of Saul, entered David's presence, he prostrated himself and did obeisance. David said to him, 'Mephibosheth!' and he answered, 'Your servant, sir.' [7] Then David said, 'Do not be afraid; I mean to show you kindness for your father Jonathan's sake; I shall restore to you the whole estate of your grandfather Saul and you will have a regular place at my table.' [8] Mephibosheth prostrated himself again and said, 'Who am I that you should spare a thought for a dead dog like me?'

[9] David summoned Saul's servant Ziba and said, 'I assign to your master's grandson all the property that belonged to Saul and his family. [10] You and your sons and your slaves must cultivate the land and bring in the harvest to provide for your master's household, but Mephibosheth your master's grandson shall have a regular place at my table.' Ziba, who had fifteen sons and twenty slaves, [11] answered: 'I shall do all that your majesty commands.' So Mephibosheth took his place in the royal household like one of the king's sons. [12] He had a young son, named Mica; and the members of Ziba's household were all Mephibosheth's servants, [13] while Mephibosheth lived in Jerusalem and had his regular place at the king's table, crippled as he was in both feet.

10 Some time afterwards the king of the Ammonites died and was succeeded by his son Hanun. [2] David said, 'I must keep up the same loyal friendship with Hanun son of Nahash as his father showed me,' and he sent a mission to condole with him on the death of his father.

When David's envoys entered the country of the Ammonites, [3] the Ammonite princes said to Hanun their lord, 'Do you suppose David means to do honour to your father when he sends envoys to condole with you? These men of his are spies whom he has sent to find out how to overthrow the city.' [4] So Hanun took David's servants, shaved off half their beards and cut off half their garments up to the buttocks, and then dismissed them. [5] Hearing how they had been treated, David ordered them to be met, for they were deeply humiliated; he told them to wait in Jericho and not return until their beards had grown again.

[6] The Ammonites, realizing they had given offence to David, hired the Aramaeans of Beth-rehob and of Zobah to come to their help with twenty thousand infantry; they hired also the king of Maacah with a thousand men, and twelve thousand men from Tob. [7] When this was reported to David, he sent Joab out with all the fighting men. [8] The Ammonites came on and took up their position at the entrance to the city gate, while the Aramaeans of Zobah and of Rehob and the men of Tob and Maacah took up theirs in the open country. [9] When Joab saw that he was threatened from both front and rear, he detailed some picked Israelite troops and drew them up facing the Aramaeans. [10] The rest of his forces he put under his brother Abishai, who took up a position facing the Ammonites. [11] 'If the Aramaeans prove too strong for me,' he said, 'you must come to my relief; and if the Ammonites prove too strong for you, I shall come to yours. [12] Courage! Let us fight bravely for our people and for the cities of our God. And may the LORD's will be done.'

[13] Joab and his men engaged the Aramaeans closely and put them to flight; [14] and when the Ammonites saw them in flight, they too fled before Abishai and withdrew into the city. Then Joab returned from the battle against the Ammonites and came to Jerusalem.

[15] The Aramaeans, reviewing their defeat

9:7 **grandfather:** *lit.* father.   9:9,10 **grandson:** *lit.* son.   9:10 **household:** *so some Gk MSS; Heb.* son. 9:11 **the royal:** *so Gk (Luc.); Heb.* my.   10:1–19 *Cp. 1 Chr.* 19:1–19.

around Mephibosheth. **1:** *For Jonathan's sake:* see 1 Sam. 20.42. **3:** *Cripple:* see 4.4. **4:** *Lo-debar* was east of the Jordan: see 17.27. **6:** For *Mephibosheth,* see 4.4 n.

10.1–11.1: The Ammonite war. Though this seems to be a digression, it provides the setting and the occasion for David's relation to Bathsheba in ch. 11. **2:** *Nahash* was the Ammonite king defeated by Saul (1 Sam. ch. 11). Perhaps David's earlier friendship was based on their mutual enmity toward Saul. **6:** *Aramaeans:* see 8.3–10. They wished to prevent David from gaining control of the north-south trade routes east of the Jordan, a source by Israel, rallied their forces, 16and Hadadezer sent to summon other Aramaeans from the Great Bend of the Euphrates, and they advanced to Helam under Shobach, commander of Hadadezer's army. 17Their movement was reported to David, who immediately mustered all the forces of Israel, crossed the Jordan, and advanced to Helam. The Aramaeans took up positions facing David and engaged him, 18but were put to flight by Israel. David slew seven hundred Aramaeans in chariots and forty thousand horsemen, mortally wounding Shobach, who died on the field. 19When all the vassal kings of Hadadezer saw that they had been worsted by Israel, they sued for peace and submitted to the Israelites. The Aramaeans never dared to help the Ammonites again.

David's crimes

11 AT the turn of the year, when kings go out to battle, David sent Joab out with his other officers and all the Israelite forces, and they ravaged Ammon and laid siege to Rabbah.

David remained in Jerusalem, 2and one evening, as he got up from his couch and walked about on the roof of the palace, he saw from there a woman bathing, and she was very beautiful. 3He made enquiries about the woman and was told, 'It must be Bathsheba daughter of Eliam and wife of Uriah the Hittite.' 4He sent messengers to fetch her, and when she came to him, he had intercourse with her, though she was still purifying herself after her period, and then she went home. 5She conceived, and sent word to David that she was pregnant.

6David ordered Joab to send Uriah the Hittite to him. Joab did so, 7and when Uriah arrived, David asked him for news of Joab and the troops and how the campaign was going, 8and then said to him, 'Go down to your house and wash your feet after your journey.' As he left the palace, a present from the king followed him. 9Uriah, however, did not return to his house; he lay down by the palace gate with all the king's servants. 10David, learning that Uriah had not gone home, said to him, 'You have had a long journey; why did you not go home?' 11Uriah answered, 'Israel and Judah are under canvas, and so is the Ark, and my lord Joab and your majesty's officers are camping in the open; how can I go home to eat and drink and to sleep with my wife? By your life, I cannot do this!' 12David then said to Uriah, 'Stay here another day, and tomorrow I shall let you go.' So Uriah stayed in Jerusalem that day. 13On the following day David invited him to eat and drink with him and made him drunk. But in the evening Uriah went out to lie down in his blanket among the king's servants and did not go home.

14In the morning David wrote a letter to Joab and sent it with Uriah. 15In it he wrote, 'Put Uriah opposite the enemy where the fighting is fiercest and then fall back, and leave him to meet his death.' 16So Joab, during the siege of the city, stationed Uriah at a point where he knew the enemy had expert troops. 17The men of the city sallied out and engaged Joab, and some of David's guards fell; Uriah the Hittite was also killed. 18Joab sent David a dispatch with all the news of the battle 19and gave the messenger these instructions: 'When you have finished your report to the king, 20he may be angry and ask, "Why did you go so near the city during the fight? You must have known there would be shooting from the wall. 21Remember who killed Abimelech son of Jerubbesheth. Was it

11:1 **when . . . battle:** *so some MSS, cp. 1 Chr. 20:1; others* when messengers set out.   11:11 **under canvas:** *or* at Succoth.   11:13 **in his blanket:** *or* on his pallet.

of considerable wealth. **7:** *The fighting men:* the professional army. In v. 17 David drafts additional forces. **19:** The *vassal kings* were often little more than chiefs of tribes; see 1 Kgs. 20.1. **11.1:** Having won the battles in the field, David now seeks to capture *Rabbah* itself, the capital city of the Ammonites.

11.2–27: David, Bathsheba, and Uriah. The story of intrigue and violence in David's family now begins in earnest. His ensuing setbacks are interpreted as the fruit of his sin here. **2–5:** The relation to *Bathsheba* is passed over briefly; it is the relation to *Uriah,* her husband, that forms the real drama. **4:** On menstrual purification, see Lev. 15.19–24. **6–13:** David tries to get Uriah to spend a night at home with his wife, to cover up his deed. There is both sardonic humor and pathos in Uriah's stubborn loyalty to duty. **9:** Uriah avoids his wife in order to remain qualified for battle, for which sexual abstinence was required; see 1 Sam. 21.5. **14–25:** David's general, Joab, was ever ready to shed blood in David's behalf; see 3.26–30; 18.9–15. **21:** *Abimelech:*

not a woman who threw down an upper millstone on him from the wall of Thebez and killed him? Why did you go near the wall?"—if he asks this, then tell him, "Your servant Uriah the Hittite also is dead." '

²² The messenger set out and, when he came to David, he made his report as Joab had instructed him. David, angry with Joab, said to the messenger, 'Why did you go so near the city during the fight? You must have known you would be struck down from the wall. Remember who killed Abimelech son of Jerubbesheth. Was it not a woman who threw down an upper millstone on him from the wall of Thebez and killed him? Why did you go near the wall?' ²³ He answered, 'The enemy massed against us and sallied out into the open; we drove them back as far as the gateway. ²⁴ There the archers shot down at us from the wall and some of your majesty's men fell; and your servant Uriah the Hittite is dead.' ²⁵ David told the messenger to say this to Joab: 'Do not let the matter distress you—there is no knowing where the sword will strike. Press home your attack on the city, take it, and raze it to the ground'; and to tell him to take heart.

²⁶ When Uriah's wife heard that her husband was dead, she mourned for him. ²⁷ Once the period of mourning was over, David sent for her and brought her into the palace; she became his wife and bore him a son. But what David had done was wrong in the eyes of the LORD.

12 The LORD sent Nathan the prophet to David, and when he entered the king's presence, he said, 'In a certain town there lived two men, one rich, the other poor. ² The rich man had large flocks and herds; ³ the poor man had nothing of his own except one little ewe lamb he had bought. He reared it, and it grew up in his home together with his children. It shared his food, drank from his cup, and nestled in his arms; it was like a daughter to him. ⁴ One day a traveller came to the rich man's house, and he, too mean to take something from his own flock or herd to

serve to his guest, took the poor man's lamb and served that up.'

⁵ David was very angry, and burst out, 'As the LORD lives, the man who did this deserves to die! ⁶ He shall pay for the lamb four times over, because he has done this and shown no pity.'

⁷ Nathan said to David, 'You are the man! This is the word of the LORD the God of Israel to you: I anointed you king over Israel, I rescued you from the power of Saul, ⁸ I gave you your master's daughter and his wives to be your own, I gave you the daughters of Israel and Judah; and, had this not been enough, I would have added other favours as well. ⁹ Why then have you flouted the LORD's word by doing what is wrong in my eyes? You have struck down Uriah the Hittite with the sword; the man himself you murdered by the sword of the Ammonites, and you have stolen his wife. ¹⁰ Now, therefore, since you have despised me and taken the wife of Uriah the Hittite to be your own wife, your family will never again have rest from the sword. ¹¹ This is the word of the LORD: I shall bring trouble on you from within your own family. I shall take your wives and give them to another man before your eyes, and he will lie with them in broad daylight. ¹² What you did was done in secret; but I shall do this in broad daylight for all Israel to see.' ¹³ David said to Nathan, 'I have sinned against the LORD.' Nathan answered, 'The LORD has laid on another the consequences of your sin: you will not die, ¹⁴ but, since by this deed you have shown your contempt for the LORD, the child who will be born to you shall die.'

¹⁵ After Nathan had gone home, the LORD struck the boy whom Uriah's wife had borne to David, and he became very ill. ¹⁶ David prayed to God for the child; he fasted and went in and spent the nights lying in sack-

11:22 **David, angry . . . near the wall:** so *Gk; Heb.* omits.   12:1 **the prophet:** *so some MSS; others omit.* 12:8 **daughter:** *prob. rdg; Heb.* house. **daughters:** *so Syriac; Heb.* house.   12:14 **the enemies of the LORD:** *prob. rdg; Heb.* the enemies of the LORD.   12:16 **in sackcloth:** *so Scroll; Heb.* omits.

The account is in Judg. ch. 9. *Jerubbesheth* is a distorted form of Jerubbaal; see 2.8 n. and Judg. 9.1. Apparently Joab took unwise risks in order to carry out David's plot. **26:** The period of mourning was apparently short enough that Bathsheba's pregnancy could be attributed to her new marriage. **27:** The narrator's observation is most laconic and thereby the more forceful.

12.1–14: Nathan's rebuke and prophecy. An effective courtier had to know how to lead a king into judging himself; compare 14.1–23. Nathan's parable achieves this exceedingly well. **7–12:** This prophecy is the narrator's statement of the theme of the following chapters.

cloth on the ground. ¹⁷The older men of his household tried to get him to rise, but he refused and would eat no food with them. ¹⁸On the seventh day the child died, and David's servants were afraid to tell him. 'While the boy was alive', they said, 'we spoke to him, and he did not listen to us; how can we now tell him that the boy is dead? He may do something desperate.' ¹⁹David saw his servants whispering among themselves and realized that the boy was dead. He asked, 'Is the child dead?' and they answered, 'Yes, he is dead.'

²⁰David then rose from the ground, bathed and anointed himself, and put on fresh clothes; he entered the house of the Lord and prostrated himself there. Afterwards he returned home; he ordered food to be brought and, when it was set before him, ate it. ²¹His servants asked him, 'What is this? While the boy lived you fasted and wept for him, but now that he is dead you rise and eat.' ²²'While the boy was still alive', he answered, 'I fasted and wept, thinking, "It may be that the Lord will be gracious to me, and the boy will live." ²³But now that he is dead, why should I fast? Can I bring him back again? I shall go to him; he will not come back to me.' ²⁴David consoled Bathsheba his wife; he went to her and had intercourse with her, and she gave birth to a son and called him Solomon. And because the Lord loved him, ²⁵he sent word through Nathan the prophet that for the Lord's sake he should be given the name Jedidiah.

²⁶Joab attacked the Ammonite city of Rabbah and took the King's Pool. ²⁷He sent this report to David: 'I have attacked Rabbah and have taken the pool. ²⁸Now muster the rest of the army, besiege the city, and take it; otherwise I myself shall take the city and the name to be proclaimed over it will be mine.'

²⁹David accordingly mustered his whole force, marched on Rabbah, and attacked and captured it. ³⁰The crown, which weighed a talent of gold and was set with a precious stone, was taken from the head of Milcom and placed on David's head; David also removed a vast quantity of booty from the city. ³¹He brought out its inhabitants and set them to work with saws and other iron tools, sharp and toothed, and made them labour at the brick-kilns. David did this to all the Ammonite towns; then he and all his army returned to Jerusalem.

Conflict in David's family

13 The following occurred some time later. David's son Absalom had a beautiful sister named Tamar, and David's son Amnon fell in love with her. ²Amnon was so tormented that he became ill with love for his half-sister; for he thought it an impossible thing to approach her since she was a virgin. ³But Amnon had a friend, a very shrewd man named Jonadab, son of David's brother Shimeah, ⁴and he said to Amnon, 'Why are you, the king's son, so low-spirited morning after morning? Will you not tell me?' Amnon told him that he was in love with Tamar, his brother Absalom's sister. ⁵Jonadab said to him, 'Take to your bed and pretend to be ill. When your father comes to visit you, say to him, "Please let my sister Tamar come and give me my food. Let her prepare it in front of me, so that I may watch her and then take it from her own hands."' ⁶So Amnon lay down and pretended to be ill. When the king came to visit him, he said, 'Sir, let my sister

12:24 **and called:** *or, as otherwise read,* and he called.
12:25 **Jedidiah:** *that is* Beloved of the Lord.
12:26–31 *Cp. 1 Chr. 20:1–3.*   12:30 **was set with:** *so Syriac; Heb.* omits. **Milcom:** *or* their king.
12:31 **labour at:** *prob. rdg; Heb.* pass through.

12.15–25: Death of the first son and birth of Solomon. 16: *Lying on the ground:* possibly at an altar. **23:** The child would go down to Sheol (1 Sam. 2.6 n.) from which he would not return (Job 7.9–10). **24–25:** The second son lived and was *loved* by the Lord. Solomon's second name reflects the practice of assuming a throne name at the accession; see 2 Kgs. 23.34; 24.17.

12.26–31: The conclusion of the Ammonite war. 26: *The King's Pool* was probably the city's water supply. After its capture, the city would shortly have to capitulate. **28:** Joab was constantly more solicitous of David's interests than his own. **30:** *Milcom* was the god of the Ammonites. A *talent* was over sixty pounds; this makes it hard to imagine on David's *head.*

13.1–22: The rape of Tamar. The drama now turns to David's oldest sons, those from among whom the next king would presumably come. *Amnon* was the eldest son, Absalom the third, but the second son Cileab seems to have dropped from the scene, probably by an early death; compare 3.2–3. Verse 13 indicates that

Tamar come and make a few bread-cakes in front of me, and serve them to me with her own hands.'

7 David sent a message to Tamar in the palace: 'Go to your brother Amnon's quarters and prepare a meal for him.' 8 Tamar came to her brother and found him lying down. She took some dough, kneaded it, and made cakes in front of him; having baked them, 9 she took the pan and turned them out before him. But Amnon refused to eat and ordered everyone out of the room. When they had all gone, 10 he said to Tamar, 'Bring the food over to the recess so that I may eat from your own hands.' Tamar took the cakes she had made and brought them to Amnon her brother in the recess. 11 When she offered them to him, he caught hold of her and said, 'Sister, come to bed with me.' 12 She answered, 'No, my brother, do not dishonour me. Such things are not done in Israel; do not behave so infamously. 13 Where could I go and hide my disgrace? You would sink as low as the most infamous in Israel. Why not speak to the king for me? He will not refuse you leave to marry me.' 14 But he would not listen; he overpowered and raped her.

15 Then Amnon was filled with intense revulsion; his revulsion for her was stronger than the love he had felt; he said to her, 'Get up and go.' 16 She answered, 'No, this great wrong, your sending me away, is worse than anything else you have done to me.' He would not listen to her; 17 he summoned the servant who attended him and said, 'Rid me of this woman; put her out and bolt the door after her.' 18 The servant turned her out and bolted the door. She had on a long robe with sleeves, the usual dress of unmarried princesses. 19 Tamar threw ashes over her head, tore the robe that she was wearing, put her hand on her head, and went away, sobbing as she went.

20 Her brother Absalom asked her, 'Has your brother Amnon been with you? Keep this to yourself; he is your brother. Do not

take it to heart.' Forlorn and desolate, Tamar remained in her brother Absalom's house. 21 When King David heard the whole story he was very angry; but he would not hurt Amnon because he was his eldest son and he loved him. 22 Absalom did not speak a single word to Amnon, friendly or unfriendly, but he hated him for having dishonoured his sister Tamar.

23 Two years later Absalom invited all the king's sons to his sheep-shearing at Baal-hazor, near Ephron. 24 He approached the king and said, 'Sir, I am shearing; will your majesty and your servants come?' 25 The king answered, 'No, my son, we must not all come and be a burden to you.' Absalom pressed him, but David was still unwilling to go and dismissed him with his blessing. 26 Absalom said, 'If you will not come, may my brother Amnon come with us?' 'Why should he go with you?' the king asked; 27 but Absalom pressed him again, so he let Amnon and all the other princes go with him.

28 Absalom prepared a feast fit for a king, and gave this order to his servants: 'Watch your chance, and when Amnon is merry with wine and I say to you, "Strike Amnon," then kill him. You have nothing to fear; these are my orders. Be bold and resolute.' 29 Absalom's servants did to Amnon as Absalom had ordered, whereupon all the king's sons immediately mounted their mules and fled.

30 While they were on their way, a rumour reached David that Absalom had murdered all the royal princes and that not one was left alive. 31 The king stood up and tore his clothes and then threw himself on the ground; all his servants were standing round him with their clothes torn. 32 Then Jonadab, son of David's brother Shimeah, said, 'My lord must not think that all the young princes have been murdered; only Amnon is dead.

13:18 **long . . . sleeves:** or ornamental robe.
13:21 **but he . . . loved him:** so Gk; Heb. omits.
13:23 **Ephron:** prob. rdg; Heb. Ephraim.
13:25 **pressed:** so Gk; Heb. omits.
13:28 **Absalom . . . king:** so Gk; Heb. omits.

marriage to a half-sister was not yet generally prohibited, as it was later; see Lev. 18.9,11; Deut. 27.22. **6:** The Heb. word for *bread-cakes* is related to the noun "heart." Some special healing powers may have been attributed to them. **9:** *Amnon* might claim that the conditions for the healing ritual were not right until *everyone* was *out of the room.* **15–19:** The anguish of Tamar is contrasted to Amnon's callous treatment of her.

13.23–39: Absalom's revenge. 23: *Absalom* waits *two years* to allay suspicion, though David may still suspect something; see v. 26. The princes, who are clearly adult men here, would have received possessions in the realm from their father. Thus, Absalom has a farm *at Baal-hazor.* The *sheep-shearing* was a time of festivity and potential violence; see Gen. 31.19–54; 38.12–26; 1 Sam. 25.4–13, 36–38. **32:** *Jonadab,* having had a

Absalom has gone about with a scowl on his face ever since Amnon ravished his sister Tamar. 33 Your majesty must not pay attention to what is no more than a rumour that all the princes are dead; only Amnon is dead.' 34 Absalom meanwhile had made good his escape.

The sentry on duty saw a crowd of people coming down the hill from the direction of Horonaim. He came and reported to the king, 'I see men coming down the hill from Horonaim.' 35 Jonadab said to the king, 'Here come the royal princes, just as I said they would.' 36 As he finished speaking, the princes came in and broke into loud lamentations; the king and all his servants also wept bitterly.

37 Absalom went to take refuge with Talmai son of Ammihud king of Geshur; and for a long while the king mourned for Amnon. 38 Absalom, having escaped to Geshur, stayed there for three years; 39 and David's heart went out to him with longing, as he became reconciled to the death of Amnon.

14 Joab son of Zeruiah saw that the king longed in his heart for Absalom, 2 so he sent for a wise woman from Tekoah and said to her, 'Pretend to be a mourner; put on mourning garb, go without anointing yourself, and behave like a woman who has been bereaved these many days. 3 Then go to the king and repeat what I tell you.' He told her exactly what she was to say.

4 When the woman from Tekoah came into the king's presence, she bowed to the ground in homage and cried, 'Help, your majesty!' 5 The king asked, 'What is it?' She answered, 'Sir, I am a widow; my husband is dead. 6 I had two sons; they came to blows out in the country where there was no one to part them, and one struck the other and killed him. 7 Now, sir, the kinsmen have confronted me with the demand, "Hand over the one who killed his brother, so that we can put him to death for taking his brother's life, and so cut

off the succession." If they do this, they will stamp out my last live ember and leave my husband without name or descendant on the earth.' 8 'Go home,' said the king to the woman, 'and I shall settle your case.'

9 But the woman continued, 'The guilt be on me, your majesty, and on my father's house; let the king and his throne be blameless.' 10 The king said, 'If anyone says anything more to you, bring him to me and he will not trouble you again.' 11 Then the woman went on, 'Let your majesty call upon the LORD your God, to prevent the next-of-kin from doing their worst and destroying my son.' The king swore, 'As the LORD lives, not a hair of your son's head shall fall to the ground.'

12 The woman then said, 'May I add one word more, your majesty?' 'Say on,' said the king. 13 So she continued, 'How then could it enter your head to do this same wrong to God's people? By the decision you have pronounced, your majesty, you condemn yourself in that you have refused to bring back the one you banished. 14 We shall all die; we shall be like water that is spilt on the ground and lost; but God will spare the man who does not set himself to keep the outlaw in banishment.

15 'I came to say this to your majesty because the people have threatened me: I thought, "If I can only speak to the king, perhaps he will attend to my case; 16 for he will listen, and he will save me from anyone who is seeking to cut off me and my son together from God's own possession." 17 I thought too that the words of my lord the king would be a comfort to me; for your

13:34 **from the direction of Horonaim:** *prob. rdg; Heb.* from a road behind him. **He came . . . from Horonaim:** *so Gk; Heb. omits.* 13:39 **David's heart:** *so Aram. (Targ.); Heb.* David. 14:4 **came . . . presence:** *so some MSS; others* said to the king. 14:8 *See note on verses 15–17.* 14:15–17 *Probably these verses are misplaced and should follow verse 7.* 14:16 **who is seeking:** *so Gk; Heb. omits.*

hand in the original deed of *Amnon,* vv. 3–5, understands the situation and is not misled by rumors. **34:** *Horonaim* means "the two horons," Upper Beth-horon and Lower Beth-horon, a few miles northwest of Jerusalem. **37:** *Talmai* was Absalom's maternal grandfather; see 3.3. **39:** David's favor shifted to whichever son was in line for the throne.

14.1–24: Joab secures Absalom's return. The king is induced to give in to his true feelings toward Absalom and recall the prince to Jerusalem. **1:** *A wise woman* was skilled in speech, especially in decision making; see the important position of the wise woman in 20.14–22. **8:** David is reluctant to use his royal authority to override tribal customs concerning bloodshed. The woman persists in vv. 9–11, and the king finally swears to protect the son. **12–17:** In a series of hints and flattery, the woman reveals to David that her case was a parable of Absalom and Amnon; see v. 20; 12.1–14 n.; 19.27.

majesty is like the angel of God and can decide between right and wrong. May the LORD your God be with you!'

18 The king said to the woman, 'Tell me no lies: I shall now ask you a question.' 'Let your majesty speak,' she said. 19 The king asked, 'Is the hand of Joab behind you in all this?' 'Your life upon it, sir!' she answered. 'When your majesty asks a question, there is no way round it, right or left. Yes, your servant Joab did prompt me; it was he who put the whole story into my mouth. 20 He did it to give a new turn to this affair. Your majesty is as wise as the angel of God and knows all that goes on in the land.'

21 The king said to Joab, 'You have my consent; go and bring back the young man Absalom.' 22 Then Joab humbly prostrated himself, took leave of the king with a blessing, and said, 'Now I know that I have found favour with your majesty, because you have granted my humble petition.' 23 Joab went at once to Geshur and brought Absalom to Jerusalem. 24 But the king said, 'Let him go to his own quarters; he shall not come into my presence.' So Absalom repaired to his own quarters and did not enter the king's presence.

25 In all Israel no man was so much admired for his beauty as Absalom; from the crown of his head to the sole of his foot he was without flaw. 26 When he cut his hair (as had to be done every year, for he found it heavy), it weighed two hundred shekels by the royal standard. 27 Three sons were born to Absalom, and a daughter named Tamar, who became a very beautiful woman.

28 Absalom lived in Jerusalem for two whole years without entering the king's presence. 29 Then he summoned Joab, intending to send a message by him to the king, but Joab refused to come; he sent for him a second time, but he still refused. 30 Absalom said to his servants, 'You know that Joab has a field next to mine with barley growing in it; go and set fire to it.' When Absalom's servants set fire to the field, 31 Joab promptly

came to Absalom in his own quarters and demanded, 'Why have your servants set fire to my field?' 32 Absalom answered, 'I had sent for you to come here, so that I could ask you to give the king this message from me: "Why did I leave Geshur? It would be better for me if I were still there. Let me now come into your majesty's presence and, if I have done any wrong, put me to death."' 33 When Joab went to the king and told him, he summoned Absalom, who came and prostrated himself humbly, and the king greeted him with a kiss.

Absalom's rebellion

15 AFTER this Absalom provided himself with a chariot and horses and fifty outrunners. 2 He made it a practice to rise early and stand by the road leading through the city gate, and would hail everyone who had a case to bring before the king for judgement and ask him which town he came from. When he answered, 'I come, sir, from such and such a tribe of Israel,' 3 Absalom would say to him, 'I can see that you have a very good case, but you will get no hearing from the king.' 4 He would add, 'If only I were appointed judge in the land, it would be my business to see that everyone with a lawsuit or a claim got justice from me.' 5 Whenever a man approached to prostrate himself, Absalom would stretch out his hand, take hold of him, and kiss him. 6 By behaving like this to every Israelite who sought justice from the king, Absalom stole the affections of the people.

7 At the end of four years, Absalom said to the king, 'Give me leave to go to Hebron to fulfil a vow there that I made to the LORD. 8 When I lived at Geshur in Aram, I vowed, "If the LORD brings me back to Jerusalem, I shall worship the LORD in Hebron."' 9 The king answered, 'You may go'; so he set off and went to Hebron.

10 Absalom sent runners through all the

15:7 **four:** so Gk (Luc.); Heb. forty.   15:8 **in Hebron:** so Gk (Luc.); Heb. omits.

14.25–33: Absalom's restoration. Absalom finds a way to regain full standing in David's court. **26:** *Two hundred shekels* would be just over four pounds. **28–33:** *Absalom* is, if anything, even more strongheaded than Amnon was. The now aged *king* gives in.

15.1–12: Absalom's rebellion. Absalom would have become king on David's death. He either became too impatient or was embittered by the circumstances of the preceding years. **1:** Absalom's *chariot, horses,* and *outrunners* give him the airs of a king-to-be. **7–12:** These *four years* extend the Absalom story over eleven years; see 13.23, 38; 14.28. By making his bid for kingship from *Hebron,* the former capital of Judah, Absalom made tribes of Israel with this message: 'As soon as you hear the sound of the trumpet, then say, "Absalom has become king in Hebron."' ¹¹ Two hundred men accompanied Absalom from Jerusalem; they were invited as guests and went in all innocence, knowing nothing of the affair. ¹² Absalom also sent to summon Ahithophel the Gilonite, David's counsellor, from Giloh his town, where he was offering the customary sacrifices. The conspiracy gathered strength, and Absalom's supporters increased in number.

¹³ A messenger brought the news to David that the men of Israel had transferred their allegiance to Absalom. ¹⁴ The king said to those who were with him in Jerusalem, 'We must get away at once, or there will be no escape from Absalom for any of us. Make haste, or else he will soon be upon us, bringing disaster and putting the city to the sword.' ¹⁵ The king's servants said to him, 'Whatever your majesty thinks best; we are ready.' ¹⁶ The king set out, and all his household followed him except ten concubines whom he left in charge of the palace.

¹⁷ At the Far House the king and all the people who were with him halted. ¹⁸ His own servants then stood at his side, while the Kerethite and Pelethite guards and Ittai with the six hundred Gittites under him marched past the king. ¹⁹ The king said to Ittai the Gittite, 'Why should you come with us? Go back and stay with the new king, for you are a foreigner and, what is more, an exile from your own country. ²⁰ You came only yesterday, and must you today be compelled to share my wanderings when I do not know where I am going? Go back home and take your countrymen with you; and may the LORD ever be your steadfast friend.' ²¹ Ittai answered, 'As the LORD lives, your life upon it, wherever you may be whether for life or death, I, your servant, shall be there.' ²² David said to Ittai, 'It is well, march on!' And Ittai the Gittite marched on with his whole

company and all the dependants who were with him. ²³ The whole countryside resounded with their weeping. The king remained standing while all the people crossed the wadi of the Kidron before him, by way of the olive tree in the wilderness.

²⁴ Zadok also was there and all the Levites with him, carrying the Ark of the Covenant of God. They set it down beside Abiathar until all the army had passed out of the city. ²⁵ The king said to Zadok, 'Take the Ark of God back into the city. If I find favour with the LORD, he will bring me back and let me see the Ark and its dwelling-place again. ²⁶ But if he says he does not want me, then here I am; let him do what he pleases with me.' ²⁷ The king went on to say to Zadok the priest, 'Are you not a seer? You may safely go back to the city, you and Abiathar, and take with you the two young men, Ahimaaz your son and Abiathar's son Jonathan. ²⁸ I shall wait at the Fords of the Wilderness until you can send word to me.' ²⁹ Then Zadok and Abiathar took the Ark of God back to Jerusalem and remained there.

³⁰ David wept as he went up the slope of the mount of Olives; he was bareheaded and went barefoot. The people with him all had their heads uncovered and wept as they went. ³¹ David had been told that Ahithophel was among the conspirators with Absalom, and he prayed, 'LORD, frustrate the counsel of Ahithophel.'

³² As David was approaching the top of the ridge where it was the custom to prostrate oneself to God, Hushai the Archite was there to meet him with his tunic torn and dust on his head. ³³ David said to him, 'If you come

15:18 **stood:** *prob. rdg; Heb.* passed. **and Ittai:** *prob. rdg; Heb. omits.*   15:20 **and may ... friend:** *so Gk; Heb.* constant love and truth.   15:23 **standing:** *prob. rdg; Heb.* passing. **by way ... wilderness:** *prob. rdg; Heb. obscure.*   15:24 **beside Abiathar:** *prob. rdg; Heb.* and Abiathar went up.   15:27 **you and Abiathar:** *prob. rdg, cp. verse 29; Heb. omits.*   15:31 **David ... told:** *so Gk; Heb.* David told.

sure David would not have his old territory to retreat to. **10:** *The trumpet* was normally sounded at the coronation of a new king; see 1 Kgs. 1.39. **12:** *Giloh* was a village near Hebron.

15.13–16.14: David's flight from Jerusalem. The narrative dwells at some length on this action. The question of loyalty to David is developed through a series of scenes. **16:** On the *ten concubines,* see 16.21–23. **17:** *The Far House* was a boundary point of the city. **18:** The international makeup of the royal court is conspicuous here. *Kerethite:* Cretan; *Pelethite:* Philistine; *Ittai:* a Philistine banished from his own city, as was David in the period of Saul's reign. **24:** *All the Levites* is a later addition to conform to the theory that only Levites carried the Ark; see 1 Chr. 15.12–15. **30:** David leads a mourning procession up *the mount of Olives.* **32:** This sanctuary on the south side of the mount of Olives was later regarded as idolatrous; compare 1 Kgs. 11.7; 2 Kgs.

with me you will only be a hindrance; [34] but you can help me to frustrate Ahithophel's plans if you go back to the city and say to Absalom, "I shall be your majesty's servant. In the past I was your father's servant; now I shall be yours." [35] You will have with you, as you know, the priests Zadok and Abiathar; report to them everything that you hear in the royal palace. [36] They have with them Zadok's son Ahimaaz and Abiathar's son Jonathan, and through them you may pass on to me everything you hear.' [37] So Hushai, David's Friend, came to the city as Absalom was entering Jerusalem.

16 When David had moved on a little from the top of the ridge, he was met by Ziba the servant of Mephibosheth, who had with him a pair of donkeys saddled and loaded with two hundred loaves of bread, a hundred clusters of raisins, a hundred bunches of summer fruit, and a skin of wine. [2] The king asked, 'What are you doing with these?' Ziba answered, 'The donkeys are for the king's family to ride on, the bread and the summer fruit are for his servants to eat, and the wine for anyone who becomes exhausted in the wilderness.' [3] The king asked, 'Where is your master's grandson?' 'He is staying in Jerusalem,' said Ziba, 'for he thought that the Israelites might now restore to him his grandfather's kingdom.' [4] The king said to Ziba, 'You shall have everything that belongs to Mephibosheth.' Ziba said, 'I am your humble servant, sir; may I always find favour with your majesty.'

[5] As King David approached Bahurim, a man of Saul's family, whose name was Shimei son of Gera, came out, cursing all the while. [6] He showered stones right and left on David and on all the king's servants and on everyone, soldiers and people alike. [7] With curses Shimei shouted: 'Get out, get out, you murderous scoundrel! [8] The LORD has taken vengeance on you for the blood of the house of Saul whose throne you took, and he has given the kingdom to your son Absalom. You murderer, see how your crimes have overtaken you!'

[9] Abishai son of Zeruiah said to the king, 'Why let this dead dog curse your majesty? I will go across and strike off his head.' [10] But the king said, 'What has this to do with us, you sons of Zeruiah? If he curses because the LORD has told him to curse David, who can question it?' [11] David said to Abishai and to all his servants, 'If my very own son is out to kill me, who can wonder at this Benjamite? Let him be, let him curse; for the LORD has told him to. [12] Perhaps the LORD will mark my sufferings and bestow a blessing on me in place of the curse laid on me this day.' [13] David and his men continued on their way, and Shimei kept abreast along the ridge of the hill parallel to David's path, cursing as he went and hurling stones across the valley at him and covering him with dust. [14] When the king and all the people with him reached the Jordan, they rested there, for they were worn out.

[15] By now Absalom and all his Israelites had reached Jerusalem, and Ahithophel was with him. [16] When Hushai the Archite, David's Friend, met Absalom he said, 'Long live the king! Long live the king!' [17] But Absalom retorted, 'Is this your loyalty to your friend? Why did you not go with him?' [18] Hushai answered, 'Because I mean to attach myself to the man chosen by the LORD and by this people and by all the men of Israel, and with him I shall stay. [19] After all, whom ought I to serve? Should I not serve the son? I shall serve you as I have served your father.'

[20] Absalom said to Ahithophel, 'Give us your advice: how shall we act?' [21] Ahithophel answered, 'Lie with your father's concubines whom he left in charge of the palace. Then all Israel will come to hear that you have given great cause of offence to your father, and this will confirm the resolution of your followers.' [22] So they set up a tent for Absalom on the roof, and he lay with his father's concubines in the sight of all Israel.

[23] In those days a man would seek counsel of Ahithophel as if he were making an en-

16:12 **sufferings:** *so Gk; Heb.* wickedness.   16:14 **the Jordan:** *so Gk (Luc.); Heb. omits.*

23.13–14. **37:** *Friend:* in Heb., a term for a royal official; see 1 Kgs. 4.5. **16.1:** *Ziba:* see ch. 9. **3–4:** This conflicts with *Mephibosheth's* own story in 19.24–30, where David allows him the benefit of the doubt. **8:** The *blood* Shimei refers to may be that of 21.1–14. **10–12:** See David's attitude in 15.25–26.

16.15–17.23: Absalom forms a strategy. The king judged between alternative courses of action proposed by wise counselors. *Hushai,* actually still loyal to David (15.32–34), and *Ahithophel* compete as counselors. **16–19:** Such deceit was assumed and not particularly condemned in court intrigues of this kind. **20–22:** On quiry of the word of God; that was how Ahithophel's counsel was esteemed by both

17 David and Absalom. [1] Ahithophel said to Absalom, 'Let me pick twelve thousand men to go in pursuit of David tonight. [2] If I overtake him when he is tired and dispirited I shall cut him off from his people and they will all scatter; I shall kill no one but the king. [3] I shall bring all the people over to you as a bride is brought to her husband. It is only one man's life that you are seeking; the rest of the people will be unharmed.' [4] Absalom and all the elders of Israel approved of Ahithophel's advice; [5] but Absalom said, 'Now summon Hushai the Archite and let us also hear what he has to say.' [6] When Hushai came, Absalom told him what Ahithophel had said and asked him, 'Shall we do as he advises? If not, speak up.'

[7] Hushai said to Absalom, 'For once the counsel that Ahithophel has given is not good. [8] You know', he went on, 'that your father and the men with him are hardened warriors and savage as a bear in the wilds robbed of her cubs. Your father is an old campaigner and will not spend the night with the main body; [9] even now he will be lying hidden in a pit or in some such place. Then if any of your men are killed at the outset, whoever hears the news will say, "Disaster has overtaken Absalom's followers." [10] The courage of the most resolute and lion-hearted will melt away, for all Israel knows that your father is a man of war and has seasoned warriors with him.

[11] 'Here is my advice. Wait until the whole of Israel, from Dan to Beersheba, is gathered about you, countless as grains of sand on the seashore, and then march to battle with them in person. [12] When we come on him somewhere, wherever he may be, and descend on him like dew falling on the ground, not a man of his family or of his followers will be left alive. [13] If he retreats into a town, all Israel will bring ropes to that town, and we shall drag it into a ravine until not a stone can be found on the site.' [14] Absalom and all the Israelites said, 'Hushai the Archite has given us better advice than Ahithophel.' It was the LORD's purpose to frustrate Ahithophel's

good advice and so bring disaster on Absalom.

[15] Hushai told Zadok and Abiathar the priests all the advice that Ahithophel had given to Absalom and the elders of Israel, and also what he himself had advised. [16] 'Now send quickly to David', he said, 'and warn him not to spend the night at the Fords of the Wilderness but to cross the river at once, before an overwhelming blow can be launched at the king and his followers.' [17] Jonathan and Ahimaaz were waiting at En-rogel, and a servant-girl used to go and tell them what happened and they would pass it on to King David; for they dared not risk being seen entering the city. [18] But a lad saw them and told Absalom; so the two of them hurried to Bahurim to the house of a man who had a cistern in his courtyard, and they climbed down into it. [19] The man's wife took a covering, spread it over the mouth of the cistern, and scattered grain over it, so that nothing would be noticed. [20] Absalom's servants came to the house and asked the woman, 'Where are Ahimaaz and Jonathan?' She answered, 'They went past the pool.' The men searched, but not finding them they returned to Jerusalem. [21] As soon as they had gone the two climbed out of the cistern and went off to report to King David. They said to him, 'Get over the water at once, and with all speed!' and they told him Ahithophel's plan against him. [22] So David and all his company began at once to cross the Jordan; by daybreak there was not one who had not reached the other bank.

[23] When Ahithophel saw that his advice had not been taken he saddled his donkey, went straight home to his own town, gave his last instructions to his household, and then hanged himself. So he died and was buried in his father's grave.

[24] By the time that Absalom had crossed the Jordan with the Israelites, David was already at Mahanaim. [25] Absalom had appointed Amasa as commander-in-chief in Joab's place; he was the son of a man named

17:3 **as a bride ... seeking:** *so Gk; Heb.* as the whole returns, so is the man you are seeking.   17:20 **pool:** *Heb. word of uncertain meaning.*

the importance of royal concubines, see 3.7 n. **17.1–14:** Ahithophel's advice was best, but Hushai's prevailed, since it was *the LORD's purpose* (v. 14) to defeat Absalom. **15–22:** David's escape is made good by those still loyal to him at Jerusalem. **23:** *Ahithophel's* suicide is mentioned immediately after David has made good his escape, since that was the final frustration of his counsel.

Ithra, an Ishmaelite, by Abigal daughter of Nahash and sister to Joab's mother Zeruiah. [26] The Israelites and Absalom camped in the district of Gilead.

[27] When David came to Mahanaim, he was met by Shobi son of Nahash from the Ammonite town Rabbah, Machir son of Ammiel from Lo-debar, and Barzillai the Gileadite from Rogelim, [28] bringing mattresses and blankets, bowls, and jugs. They brought also wheat and barley, flour and roasted grain, beans and lentils, [29] honey and curds, sheep and fat cattle, and offered them to David and his people to eat, knowing that the people must be hungry and thirsty and weary in the wilderness.

18 David reviewed the troops who were with him, and appointed officers over units of a thousand and of a hundred. [2] He divided his army in three, one division under the command of Joab, one under Joab's brother Abishai son of Zeruiah, and the third under Ittai the Gittite. The king announced to the troops that he himself was coming out with them. [3] But they said, 'No, you must not; if we take to flight, no one will care, nor will they even if half of us are killed; but you are worth ten thousand of us, and it would be better now for you to remain in the town in support.' [4] The king answered, 'I shall do what you think best.' He stood beside the gate, while all the army marched past by hundreds and by thousands, [5] and he gave this order to Joab, Abishai, and Ittai: 'Deal gently with the young man Absalom for my sake.' The whole army heard the king giving each of the officers the order about Absalom.

[6] The army took the field against the Israelites, and a battle was fought in the forest of Ephron. [7] There the Israelites were routed before the onslaught of David's men, and the loss of life was great, for twenty thousand fell. [8] The fighting spread over the whole countryside, and the forest took toll of more people that day than the sword.

[9] Some of David's men caught sight of Absalom; he was riding his mule and, as it passed beneath a large oak, his head was caught in its boughs; he was left in mid-air, while the mule went on from under him. [10] One of the men who saw this told Joab, 'I saw Absalom hanging from an oak.' [11] While the man was telling him, Joab broke in, 'You saw him? Why did you not strike him to the ground then and there? I would have given you ten pieces of silver and a belt.' [12] The man answered, 'If you were to put into my hands a thousand pieces of silver, I would not lift a finger against the king's son; we all heard the king giving orders to you and Abishai and Ittai to take care of the young man Absalom. [13] If I had dealt him a treacherous blow, the king would soon have known, and you would have kept well out of it.' [14] 'That is a lie!' said Joab. 'I will make a start and show you.' He picked up three javelins and drove them into Absalom's chest while he was held fast in the tree and still alive. [15] Then ten young men who were Joab's armour-bearers closed in on Absalom, struck at him, and killed him. [16] Joab sounded the trumpet, and the army came back from the pursuit of Israel, because he had called on them to halt. [17] They took Absalom's body and flung it into a large pit in the forest, and raised over it a great cairn of stones. The Israelites all fled to their homes.

[18] The pillar in the King's Valley had been set up by Absalom in his lifetime, for he said, 'I have no son to carry on my name.' He had named the pillar after himself, and to this day it is called Absalom's Monument.

[19] Ahimaaz son of Zadok said, 'Let me run and take the news to the king that the LORD has avenged him and delivered him from his enemies.' [20] But Joab replied, 'This is no day for you to be the bearer of news. Another day

17:25 **Ishmaelite:** *so one form of Gk, cp. 1 Chr. 2:17; Heb.* Israelite.   17:28 **bringing . . . jugs:** *prob. rdg; Heb.* a couch, bowls, and a potter's vessel. **lentils:** *so Gk; Heb. adds* and roasted grain.   18:3 **but you:** *so Gk; Heb.* but now. **in the town:** *so Gk; Heb.* from a town.   18:6 **Ephron:** *prob. rdg; Heb.* Ephraim.   18:9 **oak:** *or* terebinth. 18:14 **I . . . show you:** *or* I can waste no more time on you like this. **javelins:** *so Gk; Heb.* clubs.

17.24–19.8: The battle in Gilead and Absalom's death. 27: Many of David's supporters were non-Israelites. On *Nahash*, see 10.2 n.; on *Machir*, see 9.4; on *Barzillai*, see 19.31–39. **18.1–4:** The king's safety was decisive; compare 21.15–17. **5:** David showed strong attachment to successive favorite sons; see 13.21, 39. **6:** *Forest:* in ancient times there were forests on the Gilead highlands. **9:** Absalom's great head of hair (14.26) may have helped get him caught in the tree. **14:** *Into Absalom's chest,* more literally rendered, is "in Absalom's heart." Joab, in direct opposition to David's public orders, dispatched Absalom without hesitation. **18:** This verse reflects popular tradition about a *pillar in the King's Valley,* the Kidron valley just east of Jerusalem (contrast you may have news to carry, but not today, because the king's son is dead.' ²¹Joab told a Cushite to go and report to the king what he had seen. The Cushite bowed to Joab and set off running. ²²Ahimaaz pleaded again with Joab, 'Come what may,' he said, 'let me run after the Cushite.' 'Why should you, my son?' asked Joab. 'You will get no reward for your news.' ²³'Come what may,' he said, 'let me run.' 'Go, then,' said Joab. So Ahimaaz ran by the road through the plain of the Jordan and outstripped the Cushite.

²⁴David was sitting between the inner and outer gates and the watchman had gone up to the roof of the gatehouse by the wall of the town. Looking out and seeing a man running alone, ²⁵the watchman called to the king and told him. 'If he is alone,' said the king, 'then he is bringing news.' The man continued to approach, ²⁶and then the watchman saw another man running. He called down into the gate, 'Look, there is another man running alone.' The king said, 'He too brings news.' ²⁷The watchman said, 'I see by the way he runs that the first runner is Ahimaaz son of Zadok.' The king said, 'He is a good man and shall earn the reward for good news.'

²⁸Ahimaaz called out to the king, 'All is well!' He bowed low before him and said, 'Blessed be the LORD your God who has given into your hands the men who rebelled against your majesty.' ²⁹The king asked, 'Is all well with the young man Absalom?' Ahimaaz answered, 'Sir, when your servant Joab sent me, I saw a great commotion, but I did not know what had happened.' ³⁰The king told him to stand on one side; so he turned aside and waited there.

³¹Then the Cushite came in and said, 'Good news for my lord the king! The LORD has avenged you this day on all those who rebelled against you.' ³²The king said to the Cushite, 'Is all well with the young man Absalom?' The Cushite answered, 'May all the king's enemies and all rebels intent on harming you be as that young man is.' ³³The king was deeply moved and went up to the roof-chamber over the gate and wept, crying out

as he went, 'O, my son! Absalom my son, my son Absalom! Would that I had died instead of you! O Absalom, my son, my son.'

19 Joab was told that the king was weeping and mourning for Absalom; ²and that day's victory was turned for the whole army into mourning, because the troops heard how the king grieved for his son; ³they stole into the city like men ashamed to show their faces after fleeing from a battle. ⁴The king covered his face and cried aloud, 'My son Absalom; O Absalom, my son, my son.'

⁵Joab came into the king's quarters and said to him, 'All your servants, who have saved you and your sons and daughters, your wives and your concubines, you have covered with shame this day ⁶by showing love for those who hate you and hate for those who love you. Today you have made it clear to officers and men alike that we are nothing to you; I realize that if Absalom were still alive and all of us dead, you would be content. ⁷Now go at once and give your servants some encouragement; if you refuse, I swear by the LORD that by nightfall not a man will remain with you, and that would be a worse disaster than any you have suffered since your earliest days.' ⁸At that the king rose and took his seat by the gate; and when the army was told that the king was sitting at the gate, they assembled before him there.

MEANWHILE the Israelites had scattered to their homes. ⁹Throughout all the tribes of Israel people were discussing it among themselves and saying, 'The king has saved us from our enemies and freed us from the power of the Philistines, and now he has fled the country because of Absalom. ¹⁰But Absalom, whom we anointed king, has fallen in battle; so now why have we no plans for bringing the king back?'

¹¹What all Israel was saying came to the

18:29 **Sir ... sent me:** *prob. rdg; Heb.* At the sending of Joab the king's servant and your servant.
18:33 *In Heb.* 19:1.   19:11 **What ... ears:** *prob. rdg; Heb. has these words after* back to his palace *and adds to* his palace.

14.27). **19:** *Ahimaaz:* see 15.27; 17.17–21. **21:** That a *Cushite,* from Ethiopia or Nubia, was in David's army is further evidence of its international character. **29:** *Ahimaaz* was more discreet about Absalom's death than the Cushite (v. 32). **19.1–8:** Joab persuaded David to take a realistic attitude. David did not reward Joab very graciously; see v. 13.
   19.9–43: Bringing David back. Once it was clear that Absalom's rebellion had failed, the issue became the reconciliation of the warring factions. Israel and Judah — here treated as two distinct groups — and also individ-

king's ears, and he sent word to Zadok and Abiathar the priests: 'Ask the elders of Judah why they should be the last to bring the king back to his palace. 12 Tell them, "You are my brothers, my own flesh and blood; why are you last to bring me back?" 13 And say to Amasa, "You are my own flesh and blood. So help me God, you shall be my commander-in-chief for the rest of your life in place of Joab." ' 14 Thus David swayed the hearts of all in Judah, and one and all they sent to the king, urging him and his men to return.

15 When on his way back the king reached the Jordan, the men of Judah came to Gilgal to meet him and escort him across the river. 16 Shimei son of Gera the Benjamite from Bahurim hastened down among the men of Judah to meet King David 17 with a thousand men from Benjamin; Ziba was there too, the servant of Saul's family, with his fifteen sons and twenty servants. They rushed into the Jordan under the king's eyes 18 and crossed to and fro conveying his household in order to win his favour. Shimei son of Gera, when he had crossed the river, threw himself down before the king 19 and said, 'I beg your majesty not to remember how disgracefully your servant behaved when your majesty left Jerusalem; do not hold it against me. 20 I humbly acknowledge that I did wrong, and today I am the first of all the house of Joseph to come down to meet your majesty.' 21 Abishai son of Zeruiah objected. 'Ought not Shimei to be put to death', he said, 'because he cursed the LORD's anointed prince?' 22 David answered, 'What right have you, you sons of Zeruiah, to oppose me today? Should anyone be put to death this day in Israel? I know now that I am king of Israel.' 23 The king said to Shimei, 'You shall not die,' and he confirmed it with an oath.

24 Saul's grandson Mephibosheth also went down to meet the king. He had not bathed his feet, trimmed his beard, or washed his clothes, from the day the king went away until he returned victorious. 25 When he came from Jerusalem to meet the king, David said to him, 'Why did you not go with me,

Mephibosheth?' 26 He answered, 'Sir, my servant deceived me; I did intend to harness my donkey and ride with the king (for I am lame), 27 but his stories set your majesty against me. Your majesty is like the angel of God; you must do what you think right. 28 My father's whole family, one and all, deserved to die at your majesty's hands, but you gave me, your servant, my place at your table. What further favour can I expect of the king?' 29 The king answered, 'You have said enough. My decision is that you and Ziba are to share the estate.' 30 Mephibosheth said, 'Let him have it all, now that your majesty has come home victorious.'

31 Barzillai the Gileadite too had come down from Rogelim, and he went as far as the Jordan with the king to escort him on his way. 32 Barzillai was very old, eighty years of age; it was he who had provided for the king while he was at Mahanaim, for he was a man of great wealth. 33 The king said to Barzillai, 'Cross over with me and I shall provide for you in my household in Jerusalem.' 34 Barzillai answered, 'Your servant is far too old to go up with your majesty to Jerusalem. 35 I am now eighty years old. I cannot tell what is pleasant and what is not; I cannot taste what I eat or drink; I can no longer listen to the voices of men and women singing. Why should I be a further burden on your majesty? 36 Your servant will attend the king for a short way across the Jordan; and why should the king reward me so handsomely? 37 Let me go back and end my days in my own town near the grave of my father and mother. Here is my son Kimham; let him cross over with your majesty, and do for him what you think best.' 38 The king answered, 'Let Kimham cross with me, and I shall do for him whatever you think best; and I shall do for you whatever you ask.'

39 All the people crossed the Jordan while the king waited. The king then kissed Barzillai and gave him his blessing. Barzillai re-

19:25 from: *so some Gk MSS; Heb.* to.   19:37 my son: *so Gk; Heb. omits.*   19:39 waited: *so Gk (Luc.); Heb.* crossed.

ual petitioners had to make their peace with the king who was clearly going to regain his throne. 11–15: David takes the side of Judah against Israel. 13: David bribes *Amasa,* Absalom's commander-in-chief; see 17.25. 16–39: David makes very lenient settlements with those whose loyalty during the rebellion was questionable: *Shimei son of Gera,* who had cursed David at his departure (16.5–13), vv. 16–23; *Mephibosheth,* son of Jonathan, whose loyalty had been challenged by his servant *Ziba* (16.1–4), vv. 24–36; for his old friend *Barzillai,* the only question was how to reward his loyalty (17.27), vv. 31–39.

332

turned home; [40] the king crossed to Gilgal, Kimham with him.

The whole army of Judah had escorted the king over the river, as had also half the army of Israel. [41] But the Israelites all kept coming to the king and saying, 'Why should our brothers of Judah have got possession of the king's person by joining King David's own men and then escorting him and his household across the Jordan?' [42] The answer of all the men of Judah to the Israelites was, 'Because his majesty is our near kinsman. Why should you resent it? Have we eaten at the king's expense? Have we received any gifts?' [43] The men of Israel answered, 'We have ten times your interest in the king and, what is more, we are senior to you; why do you disparage us? Were we not the first to speak of bringing the king back?' The men of Judah used language even fiercer than the men of Israel.

20 A scoundrel named Sheba son of Bichri, a man of Benjamin, happened to be there. He sounded the trumpet and cried out:

'We have no share in David,
  no lot in the son of Jesse.
Every man to his tent, O Israel!'

[2] All the men of Israel deserted David to follow Sheba son of Bichri, but the men of Judah stood by their king and followed him from the Jordan to Jerusalem.

[3] When David went up to his palace in Jerusalem he took the ten concubines whom he had left in charge of the palace and put them in a house under guard; he maintained them but did not have intercourse with them. They were kept in seclusion, living as if they were widows until the day of their death.

[4] The king said to Amasa, 'Call up the men of Judah and appear before me again in three days' time.' [5] Amasa went to call up the men of Judah, but he took longer than the time fixed by the king. [6] David said to Abishai, 'Sheba son of Bichri will give us more trouble than Absalom; take the royal bodyguard and follow him closely in case he occupies some fortified cities and escapes us.'

[7] Joab, along with the Kerethite and Pelethite guards and all the fighting men, marched out behind Abishai, and left Jerusalem in pursuit of Sheba son of Bichri.

[8] When they reached the great stone in Gibeon, Amasa came to meet them. Joab was wearing his tunic and over it a belt supporting a sword in its scabbard. He came forward, concealing his treachery, [9] and said to Amasa, 'I hope you are well, my brother,' and with his right hand he grasped Amasa's beard to kiss him. [10] Amasa was not on his guard against the sword in Joab's hand. Joab struck him with it in the belly and his entrails poured out to the ground; he did not have to strike a second blow, for Amasa was dead. Joab with his brother Abishai went on in pursuit of Sheba son of Bichri. [11] One of Joab's men stood over Amasa and called out, 'Follow Joab, all who are for Joab and for David!' [12] Amasa's body lay soaked in blood in the middle of the road, and when the man saw how all the people stopped, he rolled him off the road into the field and threw a cloak over him; for everyone who came by stopped at the sight of the body. [13] When it had been removed from the road, they all went on and followed Joab in pursuit of Sheba son of Bichri.

[14] Sheba passed through all the tribes of Israel until he came to Abel-beth-maacah, and all the clan of Bichri rallied to him and followed him into the city. [15] Joab's forces came up and besieged him in Abel-beth-maacah, raised a siege-ramp against it, and began undermining the wall to bring it down. [16] Then a wise woman stood on the rampart and called from the city, 'Listen, listen! Tell Joab to come here and let me speak with him.' [17] When he came forward the woman said, 'Are you Joab?' He answered, 'I am.' 'Listen to what I have to say, sir,' she said. 'I am listening,' he replied. [18] 'In the old days', she went on, 'there was a saying, "Go to Abel for the answer," and that settled the matter.

19:43 **senior:** *so Gk; Heb.* in David.   20:7 **behind Abishai:** *prob. rdg; Heb.* after him men.
20:14 **Abel-beth-maacah:** *prob. rdg, cp. verse 15; Heb.* Abel and Beth-maacah. **Bichri:** *prob. rdg; Heb.* Beri.
20:16 **stood . . . rampart:** *transposed from verse 15.*

20.1–22: Another rebellion of Israel. A rebellion of the Israelite tribes, called for by the Benjaminite *Sheba*, is portrayed as a sequel to the disagreements over the return of David. **1:** This call to rebellion is used again in 1 Kgs. 12.16. **8–13:** Joab again resorts to bloodshed, this time to regain his position as head of the army. **14:** *Sheba* either lacked the time to gather sufficient forces for an engagement, or else Israelites, other than *the*

19 My town is known to be one of the most peaceable and loyal in Israel; she is like a watchful mother in Israel, and you are seeking to kill her. Would you destroy the LORD's own possession?' 20 Joab answered, 'God forbid, far be it from me to ruin or destroy! 21 That is not our aim; but a man from the hill-country of Ephraim named Sheba son of Bichri has raised a revolt against King David. Surrender this one man, and I shall retire from the city.' The woman said to Joab, 'His head will be thrown over the wall to you.' 22 Then the woman went to the people, who, persuaded by her wisdom, cut off Sheba's head and threw it to Joab. He then sounded the trumpet, and the whole army withdrew from the town; they dispersed to their homes, while Joab went back to the king in Jerusalem.

Stories of David's reign

23 JOAB was in command of the whole army in Israel, and Benaiah son of Jehoiada commanded the Kerethite and Pelethite guards. 24 Adoram was in charge of the forced levy, and Jehoshaphat son of Ahilud was secretary of state. 25 Sheva was adjutant-general, and Zadok and Abiathar were priests; 26 Ira the Jairite was David's priest.

21 IN David's reign there was a famine that lasted for three successive years. David consulted the LORD, who answered, 'Blood-guilt rests on Saul and on his family because he put the Gibeonites to death.' 2 (The Gibeonites were not of Israelite de-

scent; they were a remnant of Amorite stock whom the Israelites had sworn that they would spare. Saul, however, in his zeal for Israel and Judah had sought to exterminate them.) King David summoned the Gibeonites, therefore, and said to them, 3 'What can be done for you? How can I make expiation, so that you may have cause to bless the LORD's own people?' 4 The Gibeonites answered, 'Our feud with Saul and his family cannot be settled in silver or gold, and there is no other man in Israel whose death would content us.' 'Then what do you want me to do for you?' asked David. 5 They answered, 'Let us make an end of the man who caused our undoing and ruined us, so that he will never again have his place within the borders of Israel. 6 Hand over to us seven of that man's descendants, and we shall hurl them down to their death before the LORD in Gibeah of Saul, the LORD's chosen one.' The king agreed to hand them over. 7 He spared Mephibosheth son of Jonathan, son of Saul, because of the oath that had been taken in the LORD's name by David and Saul's son Jonathan, 8 but the king took the two sons whom Rizpah daughter of Aiah had borne to Saul, Armoni and Mephibosheth, and the five sons whom Merab, Saul's daughter, had borne to Adriel son of Barzillai of Meholah. 9 He handed them over to the Gibeonites, and they flung them down from the mountain before the LORD; the seven of them fell together. They were put to

20:19 My town ... loyal: *prob. rdg; Heb.* I am the requited ones of the loyal ones.   20:23–26 *Cp. 8:16–18; 1 Kgs. 4:2–6; 1 Chr. 18:15–17.* 21:6 **before:** *or* for.   21:8 **Merab:** *so some MSS; others* Michal.

---

clan of Bichri, failed to respond. *Abel-beth-maacah* was in the far north, near Dan. **19:** Cities were often spoken of as *mothers* and their dependent villages as "daughters." The term "metropolis" (mother city) still reflects this idiom. **22:** The people of the city had consented to give Sheba refuge. Faced with Joab's ultimatum, they recanted.

20.23–26: David's officers. This is a parallel to 8.16–18.

21.1–24.25: A miscellany of David's reign. This is a group of items pertaining to David's reign that collectors did not want to lose. They are arranged in an "envelope form": (1) a cultic narrative (21.1–14), (2) heroic anecdotes (21.15–22), (3) a royal song (22.1–51), (3') a royal song (23.1–7), (2') more heroic anecdotes (23.8–39), and (1') another cultic narrative (24.1–25). The whole miscellany forms an appendix to the throne succession narrative of chs. 9–20.

21.1–14: Expiation of Saul's blood-guilt. The ancient notion that *famine,* drought, or other disasters indicated some divine wrath to be assuaged long persisted. **1:** Nothing is otherwise known of Saul's action against *the Gibeonites,* but see 4.2 n. **2:** See Josh. ch. 9. **4–6:** Since the offense to be expiated was sacral, it was the priests of Gibeon who laid down these terms. The sanctuary of Gibeon was highly venerated by Jerusalemites; see 1 Kgs. 3.4. **8:** On *Rizpah,* see 3.7. *Merab* appears in 1 Sam. 18.17–19; her children are not otherwise mentioned. **9:** This was a ritual execution carried out *before the LORD. The first days of harvest* were around death in the first days of harvest at the beginning of the barley harvest.

¹⁰ Rizpah daughter of Aiah took sackcloth and spread it out as a bed for herself on the rock, from the beginning of harvest until the rains came and fell from the heavens on the bodies. She kept the birds away from them by day and the wild beasts by night. ¹¹ When David was told what Rizpah the concubine of Saul had done, ¹² he went and got the bones of Saul and his son Jonathan from the citizens of Jabesh-gilead, who had carried them off from the public square at Beth-shan, where the Philistines had hung them on the day they defeated Saul at Gilboa. ¹³ He removed the bones of Saul and Jonathan from there and gathered up the bones of the men who had been hurled to death. ¹⁴ They buried the bones of Saul and his son Jonathan at Zela in Benjamin, in the grave of his father Kish. Everything was done as the king ordered, and thereafter the LORD was willing to accept prayers offered for the country.

¹⁵ Once again war broke out between the Philistines and Israel. David and his men went down to the battle, but as he fought with the Philistines he fell exhausted. ¹⁶ When Benob, one of the race of the Rephaim, whose bronze spear weighed three hundred shekels and who wore a belt of honour, was about to kill David, ¹⁷ Abishai son of Zeruiah came to the king's aid; he struck the Philistine down and killed him. Then David's officers swore that he should never again go out with them to war, for fear that the lamp of Israel might be extinguished.

¹⁸ Some time later war with the Philistines broke out again in Gob: it was then that Sibbechai from Hushah killed Saph, a descendant of the Rephaim. ¹⁹ In another campaign against the Philistines in Gob, Elhanan son of Jair of Bethlehem killed Goliath of Gath,

whose spear had a shaft like a weaver's beam. ²⁰ In yet another campaign in Gath there appeared a giant with six fingers on each hand and six toes on each foot, twenty-four in all. He too was descended from the Rephaim; ²¹ when he defied Israel, Jonathan son of David's brother Shimeai killed him. ²² These four giants were the descendants of the Rephaim in Gath, and they all fell at the hands of David and his men.

Songs of David

22 THESE are the words of the song David sang to the LORD on the day when the LORD delivered him from the power of all his enemies and from the power of Saul:

²The LORD is my lofty crag,
  my fortress, my champion,
³ my God, my rock in whom I find
    shelter,
  my shield and sure defender, my strong
    tower,
  my refuge, my deliverer who saves me
    from violence.
⁴ I shall call to the LORD to whom all
    praise is due;
  then I shall be made safe from my
    enemies.

⁵ When the waves of death encompassed
    me
  and destructive torrents overtook me,
⁶ the bonds of Sheol tightened about me,
  the snares of death were set to catch
    me.

21:16 **shekels:** *prob. rdg; Heb.* weight. **a belt of honour:** *lit.* a new belt.   21:18–22 Cp. 1 Chr. 20:4–7.
21:19 **Jair:** *prob. rdg, cp. 1 Chr. 20:5; Heb.* Jaare-oregim.   22:2–51 Cp. Ps. 18:2–50.
22:6 **Sheol:** *or* the underworld.

April. **10:** *Rizpah* had to keep her vigil for some months, until the autumn rains. The coming of the rains showed that the expiation was complete. **11–14:** David's action suggests some ambivalence on his part about consenting to the Gibeonite demand.

21.15–22: Anecdotes from the Philistine wars. These events were earlier than those of the throne succession narrative (chs. 9–20). **16:** *The Rephaim,* legendary inhabitants of southern and eastern Canaan, were remarkable for their unusual stature. **17:** See 18.2–4. This seems to have been an earlier occasion. **19:** The slaying of *Goliath* was romanticized in later times as a deed of David himself; see 1 Sam. 17.1–58 n.

22.1–51: The song of David. See 1.17–27 n. This song also appears as Ps. 18; see the annotations there. The speaker is a king who was first delivered from cosmic powers by a theophany of the LORD (vv. 1–20), who then celebrates the character of the LORD and his own righteousness (vv. 21–31), and who finally achieves spectacular victory because the LORD is his support (vv. 32–51).

7 When in anguish of heart I cried to the
   LORD
 and called to my God,
 he heard me from his temple,
 and my cry reached his ears.

8 The earth shook and quaked.
 Heaven's foundations trembled,
 shaking because of his anger.
9 Smoke went up from his nostrils,
 devouring fire from his mouth,
 glowing coals and searing heat.
10 He parted the heavens and came down;
 thick darkness lay under his feet.
11 He flew on the back of a cherub;
 he swooped on the wings of the wind.
12 He made darkness around him his
   covering,
 dense vapour his canopy.
13 Thick clouds came from the radiance
   before him;
 glowing coals burned brightly.
14 GOD thundered from the heavens;
 the Most High raised his voice.
15 He loosed arrows, he sped them far
   and wide,
 his lightning shafts, and sent them
   echoing.
16 The channels of the sea were exposed,
 earth's foundations laid bare
 at the LORD's rebuke,
 at the blast of breath from his nostrils.

17 He reached down from on high and
   took me,
 he drew me out of mighty waters,
18 he delivered me from my enemies,
   strong as they were,
 from my foes when they grew too
   powerful for me.
19 They confronted me in my hour of
   peril,
 but the LORD was my buttress.
20 He brought me into untrammelled
   liberty;
 he rescued me because he delighted in
   me.

21 The LORD repaid me as my
   righteousness deserved;
 because my conduct was spotless he
   rewarded me,
22 for I have kept to the ways of the LORD
 and have not turned from my God to
   wickedness.
23 All his laws I keep before me,

and have never failed to follow his
   decrees.
24 In his sight I was blameless
 and kept myself from wrongdoing;
25 because I was spotless in his eyes
 the LORD rewarded me as my
   righteousness deserved.

26 To the loyal you show yourself loyal
 and blameless to the blameless.
27 To the pure you show yourself pure,
 but skilful in your dealings with the
   perverse.
28 You bring humble folk to safety,
 but humiliate those who look so high
   and mighty.
29 LORD, you are my lamp;
 my God will lighten my darkness.
30 With your help I storm a rampart;
 by my God's aid I leap over a wall.

31 The way of God is blameless;
 the LORD's word has stood the test;
 he is the shield of all who take refuge
   in him.
32 What god is there but the LORD?
 What rock but our God:
33 the God who girds me with strength
 and makes my way free from blame,
34 who makes me swift as a hind
 and sets me secure on the heights,
35 who trains my hands for battle
 so that my arms can aim a
   bronze-tipped bow?

36 You have given me the shield of your
   salvation;
 you stoop down to make me great.
37 You made room for my steps;
 my feet have not slipped.
38 I pursue and destroy my enemies,
 until I have made an end of them I do
   not turn back.
39 I make an end of them, I strike them
   down;
 they rise no more, but fall prostrate at
   my feet.
40 You gird me with strength for the
   battle
 and subdue my assailants beneath me.
41 You set my foot on my enemies' necks,

22:11 **swooped:** *prob. rdg, cp. Ps. 18:10; Heb. was seen.*
22:33 **who girds me:** *prob. rdg, cp. Ps. 18:32; Heb. my
refuge or my strength.* **and makes . . . blame:** *prob. rdg,
cp. Ps. 18:32; Heb. unintelligible.* 22:34 **the heights:**
Heb. my heights. 22:41 **You set:** *prob. rdg, cp. Ps.
18:40; Heb. unintelligible.*

and I wipe out those who hate me.
42 They cry, but there is no one to save
   them;
   they cry to the LORD, but he does not
   answer.
43 I shall beat them fine as dust on the
   ground,
   like mud in the streets I shall trample
   them.
44 You set me free from the people who
   challenge me,
   and make me master of nations.
   A people I never knew will be my
   subjects.
45 Foreigners will come fawning to me;
   as soon as they hear tell of me, they will
   submit.
46 Foreigners will be disheartened
   and come trembling from their
   strongholds.
47 The LORD lives! Blessed is my rock!
   High above all is God, my safe refuge.

48 You grant me vengeance, God,
   laying nations prostrate at my feet;
49 you free me from my enemies,
   setting me over my assailants;
   you are my deliverer from violent men.
50 Therefore, LORD, I shall praise you
   among the nations
   and sing psalms to your name,
51 to one who gives his king great victories
   and keeps faith with his anointed,
   with David and his descendants for
   ever.

23 These are the last words of David:

   The word of David son of Jesse,
   the word of the man whom the High
      God raised up,
   the anointed of the God of Jacob
   and the singer of Israel's psalms:

2 The spirit of the LORD has spoken
   through me,
   and his word is on my lips.

3 The God of Israel spoke,
   the Rock of Israel said of me:
   'He who rules people in justice,
   who rules in the fear of God,
4 is like the light of morning at sunrise,
   a morning that is cloudless after rain
   and makes the grass from the earth
   sparkle.'

5 Surely my house is true to God;
   for he has made an everlasting
   covenant with me,
   its terms spelled out and faithfully kept;
   that is my whole salvation, all my
   delight.

6 But the ungodly put forth no shoots,
   they are all like briars thrown aside;
   none dare put out his hand to pick
   them up,
7 none touch them but with a tool of iron
   or wood;
   they are fit only for burning where
   they lie.

David's heroes

8 THESE are the names of David's heroes. First
came Ishbosheth the Hachmonite, chief of
the three; it was he who brandished his spear
over eight hundred, all slain at one time.
9 Next to him was Eleazar son of Dodo the
Ahohite, one of the heroic three. He was with
David at Pas-dammim where the Philistines
had gathered for battle. When the Israelites

22:42 **cry, but:** *prob. rdg, cp. Ps. 18:41; Heb.* look, but.
22:43 **trample them:** *prob. rdg, cp. Ps. 18:42; Heb. adds*
I will stamp them down.   22:44 **people who**
challenge me: *so Gk and Ps. 18:43; Heb. obscure.* **make:**
so Gk (Luc.) and Ps. 18:43; Heb. keep.   22:47 **God:**
Heb. adds rock.   23:7 **but:** *prob. rdg; Heb.* he shall be
filled.   23:8–39 *Cp. 1 Chr. 11:10–41.*
23:8 **Ishbosheth the Hachmonite:** *prob. rdg; Heb.*
Josheb-basshebeth a Tahchemonite. **three:** *so Gk (Luc.);*
Heb. third. **who . . . spear:** *prob. rdg, cp. 1 Chr. 11:11;*
Heb. unintelligible.   23:9 **the Ahohite:** *prob. rdg, cp.*
1 Chr. 11:12; Heb. son of Ahohi. **He . . . Philistines:**
prob. rdg, cp. 1 Chr. 11:13; Heb. With David they
taunted them among the Philistines.

23.1–7: The last words of David. The text of this song is rather uncertain; it has a good claim to be from
David himself. **1:** *High God:* A divine epithet or name. It appears as "Most High" in 2 Sam. 22.14 and, in a
longer form, in Gen. 14.18–19 and elsewhere. It derived from pre-Israelite traditions and eventually applied
to Yahweh, the God of Israel. **3:** *Rock* is a forceful metaphor, common in poetic texts; see Deut. 32.30. **5:** This
may be the earliest reference to the *everlasting covenant* between the LORD and David; compare ch. 7.
   23.8–39: David's warriors. The heroic deeds are probably touched up, but David commanded the loyalty
of a powerful following. The organization in *the three* and *the thirty* reflects a ten-to-one ratio that often appears

fell back, [10] he stood his ground and rained blows on the Philistines until, from sheer weariness, his hand stuck to his sword. The LORD brought about a great victory that day. Afterwards the people rallied to him, but it was only to strip the dead. [11] Next to him was Shammah son of Agee a Hararite. The Philistines had gathered at Lehi, where there was a field with a fine crop of lentils; and, when the Philistines put the people to flight, [12] he stood his ground in the field, defended it, and defeated the foe. So the LORD brought about a great victory.

[13] Towards the beginning of the harvest three of the thirty went down to join David at the cave of Adullam, while a band of Philistines was encamped in the valley of Rephaim. [14] David was then in the stronghold, and a Philistine garrison held Bethlehem. [15] One day David exclaimed with longing, 'If only I could have a drink of water from the well by the gate at Bethlehem!' [16] At this the heroic three made their way through the Philistine lines and drew water from the well by the gate of Bethlehem and brought it to David. But he refused to drink it; he poured it out to the LORD [17] saying, 'The LORD forbid that I should do such a thing! Can I drink the blood of these men who went at the risk of their lives?' So he would not drink it. Such were the exploits of the heroic three.

[18] Abishai the brother of Joab son of Zeruiah was chief of the thirty; he it was who brandished his spear over three hundred dead. He was famous among the thirty, [19] and some think he surpassed in reputation the rest of the thirty; he became their captain, but he did not rival the three. [20] Benaiah son of Jehoiada, from Kabzeel, was a hero of many exploits. It was he who slew the two champions of Moab, and who once went down into a pit and killed a lion on a snowy day. [21] He also killed an Egyptian, a man of striking appearance armed with a spear. Benaiah went to meet him with a club, wrested the spear out of the Egyptian's hand, and killed him with his own weapon. [22] Such were the exploits of Benaiah son of Jehoiada, famous among the heroic thirty. [23] He was more famous than the rest of the thirty, but

he did not rival the three. David appointed him to his household.

[24] Asahel the brother of Joab was one of the thirty; Elhanan son of Dodo from Bethlehem; [25] Shammah from Harod; Elika from Harod; [26] Helez from a place unknown; Ira son of Ikkesh from Tekoa; [27] Abiezer from Anathoth; Mebunnai from Hushah; [28] Zalmon the Ahohite; Maharai from Netophah; [29] Heled son of Baanah from Netophah; Ittai son of Ribai from Gibeah of Benjamin; [30] Benaiah from Pirathon; Hiddai from the wadis of Gaash; [31] Abi-albon from Beth-arabah; Azmoth from Bahurim; [32] Eliahba from Shaalbon; Hashem the Gizonite; Jonathan son of [33] Shammah the Hararite; Ahiam son of Sharar the Hararite; [34] Eliphelet son of Ahasbai son of the Maacathite; Eliam son of Ahithophel the Gilonite; [35] Hezrai from Carmel; Paarai the Arbite; [36] Igal son of Nathan from Zobah; Bani the Gadite; [37] Zelek the Ammonite; Naharai from Beeroth, armour-bearer to Joab son of Zeruiah; [38] Ira the Ithrite; Gareb the Ithrite; [39] Uriah the Hittite: there were thirty-seven in all.

David's census

24 ONCE again the Israelites felt the LORD's anger, when he incited David against them and instructed him to take a census of Israel and Judah. [2] The king commanded Joab and the officers of the army with him to go round all the tribes of Israel, from Dan to Beersheba, and make a record of the people and report back the number to him. [3] Joab answered, 'Even if the LORD your God should increase the people a hundredfold and your majesty should live to see it, what pleasure would that give your majesty?'

23:17 **I drink:** *prob. rdg, cp. 1 Chr. 11:19; Heb. omits.*
23:18 **thirty:** *so Syriac; Heb.* three.   23:19,22 **thirty:** *prob. rdg; Heb.* three.   23:24 **from:** *so some MSS; others omit.*   23:29 **Heled:** *so many MSS; others* Heleb.
23:31 **Beth-arabah:** *prob. rdg, cp. Josh. 18:22; Heb.* Arabah. **Bahurim:** *prob. rdg, cp. 1 Chr. 11:33; Heb.* Barhum.   23:32 **Hashem ... son of:** *prob. rdg, cp. 1 Chr. 11:34; Heb.* the sons of Jashen, Jonathan.
23:33 **Sharar the Hararite:** *prob. rdg, cp. 1 Chr. 11:35; Heb.* Sharar the Ararite.   24:1–25 *Cp. 1 Chr. 21:1–27.*   24:2 **Joab ... army:** *prob. rdg, cp. 1 Chr. 21:2; Heb.* Joab the officer of the army.

in military, labor force, and cultic groups. **24–39:** There are thirty-one names here, plus *Abishai* and *Benaiah* in vv. 18–23. The list may include names of men who belonged to the elite *thirty* at different times, some replacing others.

24.1–25: David's census and the Jerusalem altar. This "sacred story" sanctions the site of the altar of the

4 But Joab and the officers, being overruled by the king, left his presence in order to take the census.

5 They crossed the Jordan and began at Aroer and the town at the wadi, proceeding towards Gad and Jazer. 6 They came to Gilead and to the land of the Hittites, to Kadesh, and then to Dan and Iyyon and so round towards Sidon. 7 They went as far as the walled city of Tyre and all the towns of the Hivites and Canaanites, and then went on to the Negeb of Judah at Beersheba. 8 They covered the whole country and arrived back at Jerusalem after nine months and twenty days. 9 Joab reported to the king the numbers recorded: the number of able-bodied men, capable of bearing arms, was eight hundred thousand in Israel and five hundred thousand in Judah.

10 After he had taken the census, David was overcome with remorse, and said to the LORD, 'I have acted very wickedly: I pray you, LORD, remove your servant's guilt, for I have been very foolish.' 11 When he rose next morning, the command of the LORD had come to the prophet Gad, David's seer, 12 to go and tell David: 'This is the word of the LORD: I offer you three things; choose one and I shall bring it upon you.' 13 Gad came to David and reported this to him and said, 'Is it to be three years of famine in your land, or three months of flight with the enemy in close pursuit, or three days of pestilence in your land? Consider carefully now what answer I am to take back to him who sent me.' 14 David said to Gad, 'This is a desperate plight I am in; let us fall into the hands of the LORD, for his mercy is great; and let me not fall into the hands of men.'

15 The LORD sent a pestilence throughout Israel from the morning till the end of the appointed time; from Dan to Beersheba seventy thousand of the people died. 16 The angel stretched out his arm towards Jerusalem to destroy it; but the LORD repented of the

evil and said to the angel who was destroying the people, 'Enough! Stay your hand.' At that moment the angel of the LORD was at the threshing-floor of Araunah the Jebusite.

17 When David saw the angel who was striking down the people, he said to the LORD, 'It is I who have sinned, I who committed the wrong; but these poor sheep, what have they done? Let your hand fall on me and on my family.'

18 Gad came to David that day and said, 'Go and set up an altar to the LORD on the threshing-floor of Araunah the Jebusite.' 19 David obeyed Gad's instructions, and went up as the LORD had commanded. 20 When Araunah looked down and saw the king and his servants coming towards him, he went out and, prostrating himself before the king, 21 said, 'Why has your majesty come to visit his servant?' David answered, 'To buy the threshing-floor from you so that I may build an altar to the LORD, and the plague which has attacked the people may be stopped.' 22 Araunah answered, 'I beg your majesty to take it and sacrifice what you think fit. See, here are the oxen for the whole-offering, and the threshing-sledges and the ox-yokes for fuel.' 23 Araunah gave it all to the king for his own use and said to him, 'May the LORD your God accept you.' 24 But the king said to Araunah, 'No, I shall buy it from you; I am not going to offer up to the LORD my God whole-offerings that have cost me nothing.' So David bought the threshing-floor and the oxen for fifty shekels of silver. 25 He built an altar to the LORD there and offered whole-offerings and shared-offerings. Then the LORD yielded to his prayer for the land, and the plague in Israel stopped.

24:5 began . . . Gad: *prob. rdg; Heb.* encamped in Aroer on the right of the level land of the wadi Gad. 24:6 of the . . . Kadesh: *so Gk (Luc.); Heb.* of Tahtim, Hodshi. Iyyon: *prob. rdg, cp. 1 Kgs. 15:20; Heb.* Yaan. round: *so Gk; Heb. obscure.*   24:13 three years: *so Gk, cp. 1 Chr. 21:12; Heb.* seven years.   24:23 Araunah: *prob. rdg; Heb. adds* the king.

Solomonic temple. **1:** *The LORD's anger* must be assuaged, as in 21.1–14. **4:** David insists on the census; it was a step toward effective government of his realm, but intruded upon the independence of tribal groups. **9:** The numbers are improbable, even for David's time. **10:** The interest of the narrative is cultic; hence, consistency of conduct on David's part is sacrificed to that interest. **11:** *The prophet Gad:* see 1 Sam. 22.5. **17:** David's piety is similar to that expressed in the throne succession narrative; compare 15.25–26; 16.10–12. **18:** That *the threshing-floor of Araunah* became the place of the altar of the temple is only implicit here, but is made explicit in 1 Chr. 21.28–22.1.

THE FIRST BOOK OF
Kings

First and Second Kings are a single book in Hebrew, related to 1 and 2 Samuel and the whole "Deuteronomic history" (see Introduction to 1 Sam.). The establishment of David's dynasty and the building of Solomon's temple bring to a completion the LORD's work of establishing Israel in Canaan (1 Kgs. chs. 1–10).

Israel's prosperity has a condition, however: that the LORD's commandments be carefully obeyed. Hence, the rest of Kings tells how disaster finally came upon the Israelite kingdoms through their failure to meet that condition. While individual kings were guilty of various offenses, two particular violations of the LORD's cultic requirements condemned the two kingdoms. In the Northern Kingdom of Israel, the violation was the "sin" of Jeroboam I, namely, his establishment of the cult of the golden calves at Bethel; this constituted a worship of the LORD, but an improper one (see 1 Kgs. 12.25–33; 2 Kgs. 17.21–23). In Judah, the violation was permitting the local sanctuaries, called the shrines, to continue after the temple was built (see, e.g. 1 Kgs. 3.2–3; 22.41–43).

Only two kings of the late period, Hezekiah and Josiah, are fully approved, this because they removed the shrines (2 Kgs. 18.3–4; 23.8).

First Kings opens with the conclusion (chs. 1–2) of the narrative of the succession to David's throne; earlier parts of that same source are in 2 Sam. chs. 9–20. At different points some other literary sources are referred to: "the annals of Solomon" (1 Kgs. 11.41), "the annals of the kings of Israel" (14.19), and "the annals of the kings of Judah" (14.29). Data from these annals are given in regular formulas for each king (see e.g. 14.21–22; 15.25–26). Also drawn upon, without explicit reference, were various traditions about the history of the temple (e.g. 6.2–36; 2 Kgs. 12.4–16; 16.10–18) and collections of prophetic legends (e.g. 1 Kgs. chs. 13; 17–19; 2 Kgs. chs. 2–8; 18.17–20.19). Also, the Deuteronomic historians contributed speeches and reflections in their distinctive style (e.g. 1 Kgs. 8.14–61; 2 Kgs. 17.7–23).

A "first edition" of these materials may have been composed during Josiah's reign, before his death (609 B.C.E.). The point of that edition would have been to show that the previous history of the kings justified Josiah's religious reform (see 2 Kgs. 22.3–23.24). Later (about 550 B.C.E.), after the kingdom of Judah had fallen, a "second edition" of Kings, extending the account, was incorporated into the larger Deuteronomic history.

Solomon succeeds David

1 KING David was now a very old man, and, though they wrapped clothes round him, he could not keep warm. ²His attendants said to him, 'Let us find a young virgin for your majesty, to attend you and take care of you; and let her lie in your arms, sir, and make you warm.' ³After searching throughout Israel for a beautiful maiden, they found Abishag, a Shunammite, and brought her to the king. ⁴She was a very beautiful girl. She took care of the king and waited on him, but he did not have intercourse with her.

⁵Adonijah, whose mother was Haggith,

1.1–2.46: Solomon's succession to the throne. This is the conclusion of the throne succession narrative in 2 Sam. chs. 9–20.

1.1–53: Two parties struggle for the kingship. 1: *Very old*: about seventy at this time. 5–6: *Adonijah*, as

340

was boasting that he was to be king. He provided himself with chariots and horses and fifty outrunners. [6] His father never corrected him or asked why he behaved as he did. He was next in age to Absalom, and was a very handsome man too. [7] He took counsel with Joab son of Zeruiah and with Abiathar the priest, and they assured him of their support; [8] but Zadok the priest, Benaiah son of Jehoiada, Nathan the prophet, Shimei, Rei, and David's bodyguard of heroes did not take his side. [9] Adonijah then held a sacrifice of sheep, oxen, and buffaloes at the stone Zoheleth beside En-rogel; he invited all his royal brothers and all those officers of the household who were of the tribe of Judah, [10] but he did not invite Nathan the prophet, Benaiah and the bodyguard, or Solomon his brother.

[11] Nathan said to Bathsheba, Solomon's mother, 'Have you not heard that Adonijah son of Haggith has become king, without the knowledge of our lord David? [12] Now come, let me advise you what to do for your own safety and for the safety of your son Solomon. [13] Go in at once to the king and say to him, "Did not your majesty swear to me, your servant, that my son Solomon should succeed you as king, and that it was he who should sit on your throne? Why then has Adonijah become king?" [14] While you are still there speaking to the king, I shall come in after you and confirm your words.'

[15] Bathsheba went to the king in his private chamber; he was now very old, and Abishag the Shunammite was waiting on him. [16] Bathsheba bowed before the king and did obeisance. 'What is your request?' asked the king. [17] She answered, 'My lord, you yourself swore to me your servant, by the LORD your God, that my son Solomon should succeed you as king and sit on your throne. [18] But now, here is Adonijah become king, all unknown to

your majesty. [19] He has sacrificed great numbers of oxen, buffaloes, and sheep, and has invited to the feast all the king's sons, with Abiathar the priest and Joab the commander-in-chief, but he has not invited your servant Solomon. [20] Your majesty, all Israel is now looking to you to announce your successor on the throne. [21] Otherwise, when you, sir, rest with your forefathers, my son Solomon and I will be treated as criminals.'

[22] Bathsheba was still addressing the king when Nathan the prophet arrived. [23] The king was informed that Nathan was there; he came into the king's presence and prostrated himself. [24] 'My lord,' he said, 'has your majesty declared that Adonijah should succeed you and sit on your throne? [25] He has today gone down and sacrificed great numbers of oxen, buffaloes, and sheep, and has invited to the feast all the king's sons, the commanders of the army, and Abiathar the priest; and at this very moment they are eating and drinking in his presence and shouting, "Long live King Adonijah!" [26] But he has not invited me your servant, Zadok the priest, Benaiah son of Jehoiada, or your servant Solomon. [27] Has this been done by your majesty's authority? You have not told us your servants who should succeed you on the throne.'

[28] King David said, 'Call Bathsheba,' and when she came into his presence and stood before him, [29] the king swore an oath to her: 'As the LORD lives, who has delivered me from all my troubles, [30] I swore by the LORD the God of Israel that Solomon your son should succeed me and that he should sit on my throne; this day I give effect to my oath.' [31] Bathsheba bowed low to the king, did obeisance, and said, 'May my lord King David live for ever!'

[32] King David said, 'Summon Zadok the priest, Nathan the prophet, and Benaiah son of Jehoiada,' and, when they came into the

next in age to Absalom (now dead), had good reason to suppose he would succeed David; compare 2 Sam. 15.1. **7–10:** Adonijah was born during David's Hebron period and was therefore supported by David's leading men of that time, *Joab,* commander of the army (2 Sam. 2.13 is his first appearance), and *Abiathar,* the priest who escaped Saul's wrath and dwelt with David during the fugitive years in the wilderness (1 Sam. 22.20; 23.6). Solomon's support, on the other hand, came from leaders who only appeared after David's settlement in Jerusalem: *Zadok,* the other leader of the priests (2 Sam. 8.17 n.), *Nathan* the prophet (see 2 Sam. 7.2 n.; 12.1–14 n.), and *Benaiah,* commander of David's Philistine palace guard (2 Sam. 8.18; 20.23). *Solomon* was, of course, born in David's Jerusalem period to a Jerusalemite mother (2 Sam. 12.24–25). The two parties represented a tension that would persist through the centuries (see 2 Kgs. 21.23–24) between the old city-state of Jerusalem and the new kingdom of Judah. **9:** *En-rogel:* a spring southeast of the city (2 Sam. 17.17). **11–31:** *Nathan* sees the crisis and knows that through *Bathsheba* a counter-stroke can be effected.

king's presence, ³³ he gave them this order: 'Take the officers of the household with you; mount my son Solomon on the king's mule and escort him down to Gihon. ³⁴ There let Zadok the priest and Nathan the prophet anoint him king over Israel. Then sound the trumpet and shout, "Long live King Solomon!" ³⁵ When you escort him home again let him come and sit on my throne and reign in my place; for he is the man that I have designated to be prince over Israel and Judah.' ³⁶ Benaiah son of Jehoiada answered the king, 'It will be done. And may the LORD, the God of my lord the king, confirm it! ³⁷ As the LORD has been with your majesty, so may he be with Solomon; may he make his throne even greater than the throne of my lord King David.'

³⁸ Zadok the priest, Nathan the prophet, and Benaiah son of Jehoiada, together with the Kerethite and Pelethite guards, went down and, mounting Solomon on King David's mule, they escorted him to Gihon. ³⁹ Zadok the priest took the horn of oil from the Tent of the LORD and anointed Solomon; they sounded the trumpet and all the people shouted, 'Long live King Solomon!' ⁴⁰ Then all the people escorted him home in procession, with great rejoicing and playing of pipes, so that the very earth split with the noise.

⁴¹ Adonijah and his guests had just finished their banquet when the noise reached their ears. On hearing the sound of the trumpet, Joab exclaimed, 'What is the meaning of this uproar in the city?' ⁴² Even as he was speaking, Jonathan son of Abiathar the priest arrived. 'Come in,' said Adonijah. 'You are an honourable man and must be a bringer of good news.' ⁴³ 'Far from it,' Jonathan replied; 'our lord King David has made Solomon king. ⁴⁴ He has sent with him Zadok the priest, Nathan the prophet, and Benaiah son

of Jehoiada, together with the Kerethite and Pelethite guards, and they have mounted Solomon on the king's mule, ⁴⁵ and Zadok the priest and Nathan the prophet have anointed him king at Gihon. They have now escorted him home rejoicing, and the city is in an uproar. That was the noise you heard. ⁴⁶ More than that, Solomon has taken his seat on the royal throne. ⁴⁷ Yes, and the officers of the household have been to our lord, King David, and greeted him in this fashion: "May your God make the name of Solomon your son more famous than your own and his throne even greater than yours," and the king bowed upon his couch. ⁴⁸ What is more, he said this: "Blessed be the LORD the God of Israel who has set a successor on my throne this day while I am still alive to see it."'

⁴⁹ Adonijah's guests all rose in panic and dispersed. ⁵⁰ Adonijah himself, in fear of Solomon, went at once to the altar and grasped hold of its horns. ⁵¹ A message was sent to Solomon: 'Adonijah, in his fear of King Solomon, is clinging to the horns of the altar; he says, "Let King Solomon swear to me here and now that he will not put his servant to the sword."' ⁵² Solomon said, 'If he proves himself an honourable man, not a hair of his head will fall to the ground; but if he is found making trouble, he must die.' ⁵³ Then King Solomon sent and had him brought down from the altar. He came in and prostrated himself before the king, and Solomon said to him, 'Go to your house.'

2 As the time of David's death drew near, he gave this charge to his son Solomon: ² 'I am about to go the way of all the earth. Be strong and show yourself a man. ³ Fulfil your duty to the LORD your God; conform to his ways, observe his statutes and his commandments, his judgements and his solemn pre-

1:39 **the Tent ... LORD:** *lit.* the tent, *cp.* 2:28.

33: *Gihon* was a sacred spring to the east of the city, in the Kidron Valley. **36–37:** *Benaiah,* as commander of the guard, occupied the key position here. **38:** *The Kerethite and Pelethite guards* were Cretan and Philistine mercenaries. The king's *mule* had special significance in the royal rituals of the city; compare Zech. 9.9. **39:** The city *priest* anoints the new king with *oil* preserved in the sanctuary for ritual purposes. On anointing *oil,* see Exod. 30.22–33. For *the Tent of the LORD,* see 2 Sam. 6.17; 7.1–7. **40:** The *procession* went to the royal palace where Solomon was seated on the throne, the decisive conclusion to the coronation; see v. 46. **41–53:** When it was clear that Solomon's supporters had carried out their coup and that the king fully concurred (v. 48), Adonijah and his followers fled in panic (v. 49). **52–53:** Solomon wished to avoid an open confrontation between the two parties. He would subsequently find ways to secure his own party.

2.1–46: David's death and the securing of Solomon's throne. 1–9: Old scores and debts, which for various reasons David had not settled, were bequeathed to Solomon. **3–4:** This reflects the piety of the Deuteronomic cepts, as they are written in the law of Moses, so that you may prosper in whatever you do and whichever way you turn, [4] and that the LORD may fulfil this promise that he made about me: "If your descendants are careful to walk faithfully in my sight with all their heart and with all their soul, you shall never lack a successor on the throne of Israel."

[5] 'You know how Joab son of Zeruiah treated me and what he did to two commanders-in-chief in Israel, Abner son of Ner and Amasa son of Jether. He killed them both, breaking the peace by bloody acts of war; and with that blood he stained the belt about his waist and the sandals on his feet. [6] Act as your wisdom prompts you, and do not let his grey hairs go down to the grave in peace. [7] Show constant friendship to the family of Barzillai of Gilead; let them have their place at your table; they rallied to me when I was a fugitive from your brother Absalom. [8] Do not forget Shimei son of Gera, the Benjamite from Bahurim, who cursed me bitterly the day I went to Mahanaim. True, he came down to meet me at the Jordan, and I swore by the LORD that I would not put him to death. [9] But you do not need to let him go unpunished now; you are a wise man and will know how to deal with him; bring down his grey hairs in blood to the grave.'

[10] So David rested with his forefathers and was buried in the city of David, [11] having reigned over Israel for forty years, seven in Hebron and thirty-three in Jerusalem; [12] and Solomon succeeded his father David as king and was firmly established on the throne.

[13] THEN Adonijah son of Haggith came to Bathsheba, Solomon's mother. 'Do you come as a friend?' she asked. 'As a friend,' he answered; [14] 'I have something to discuss with you.' 'Tell me,' she said. [15] 'You know', he went on, 'that the throne was mine and that all Israel was looking to me to be king; but I

was passed over and the throne has gone to my brother; it was his by the will of the LORD. [16] Now I have one request to make of you; do not refuse me.' 'What is it?' she said. [17] He answered, 'Will you ask King Solomon (he will never refuse you) to give me Abishag the Shunammite in marriage?' [18] 'Very well,' said Bathsheba, 'I shall speak to the king on your behalf.'

[19] When Bathsheba went in to King Solomon to speak for Adonijah, the king rose to meet her and do obeisance to her. Then he seated himself on his throne, and a throne was set for the king's mother at his right hand. [20] She said, 'I have one small request to make of you; do not refuse me.' 'What is it, mother?' he replied. 'I will not refuse you.' [21] 'It is this,' she said, 'that Abishag the Shunammite be given in marriage to your brother Adonijah.' [22] At that King Solomon answered, 'Why do you ask that Abishag the Shunammite be given to Adonijah? You might as well ask the kingdom for him; he is my elder brother and has both Abiathar the priest and Joab son of Zeruiah on his side.' [23] Then he swore by the LORD: 'So help me God, Adonijah must pay for this with his life. [24] As the LORD lives, who has established me and set me on the throne of David my father and has founded a house for me as he promised, this very day Adonijah must be put to death!' [25] King Solomon sent Benaiah son of Jehoiada with orders to strike him down; so Adonijah died.

[26] Abiathar the priest was told by the king to go to Anathoth to his estate. 'You deserve to die,' he said, 'but in spite of this day's work I shall not put you to death, for you carried the Ark of the Lord GOD before my father David, and you shared in all the hardships he endured.' [27] Solomon deposed Abiathar from his office as priest of the LORD, so ful-

2:6,9 **the grave:** *lit.* Sheol *(the underworld).*

historians. **5–6:** *Joab* had slain *Abner* (2 Sam. 3.22–27) and *Amasa* (2 Sam. 20.8–10), both of whom were commanders who had previously opposed David (2 Sam. 2.8–10, 12–13; 17.25; 19.13). It is striking, however, that David does not here blame *Joab* for killing Absalom (2 Sam. 18.9–17). That Joab always labored in behalf of David is beyond question, even when bloodshed was required. A Solomonic viewpoint, however, has condemned him. **7:** On *Barzillai*, see 2 Sam. 17.27 and 19.31–39. **8:** On *Shimei*, see 2 Sam. 16.5–14 and 19.15–23. **17:** As v. 22 shows, Adonijah's request for David's concubine *Abishag* would have serious political implication; see 2 Sam. 3.7 n. **19:** The king's mother may have occupied a very important position in Jerusalem and thus had a *throne* at her son's *right hand*. **24:** Adonijah's assassination was the first in a series of executions intended to remove dangerous antagonists from the scene. **26–27:** *Abiathar* the *priest* was next to be removed. The prophet Jeremiah was descended from these priests at *Anathoth* (Jer. 1.1). *The sentence pronounced by* filling the sentence pronounced by the LORD against the house of Eli in Shiloh. 28 When news of all this reached Joab, he fled to the Tent of the LORD and laid hold of the horns of the altar; for he had sided with Adonijah, though not with Absalom. 29 When King Solomon was told that Joab had fled to the Tent of the LORD and was beside the altar, he sent Benaiah son of Jehoiada with orders to strike him down. 30 Benaiah came to the Tent of the LORD and ordered Joab in the king's name to come away. But he said, 'No, I will die here.' Benaiah reported Joab's answer to the king, 31 and the king said, 'Let him have his way; strike him down and bury him, and so rid me and my father's house of the guilt for the blood that he wantonly shed. 32 The LORD will hold him responsible for his own death, because he struck down two innocent men who were better men than he, Abner son of Ner, commander of the army of Israel, and Amasa son of Jether, commander of the army of Judah, and ran them through with the sword, without my father David's knowledge. 33 Let the guilt of their blood recoil on Joab and his descendants for all time; but may David and his descendants, his house and his throne, enjoy perpetual prosperity from the LORD.' 34 Benaiah son of Jehoiada went up to the altar and struck Joab down and killed him, and he was buried at his house out in the country. 35 The king appointed Benaiah to command the army in place of Joab, and installed Zadok the priest in the place of Abiathar.

36 Next the king sent for Shimei and said to him, 'Build yourself a house in Jerusalem and stay there; you are not to leave the city for any other place. 37 If ever you leave and cross the wadi Kidron, know for certain that you will die. Your blood will be on your own head.' 38 Shimei replied, 'I accept your sentence; I shall do as your majesty commands.'

For a long time Shimei remained in Jerusalem. 39 But when three years later two of his slaves ran away to Achish son of Maacah, king of Gath, and this was reported to Shimei, 40 he at once saddled his donkey and went to Achish in search of his slaves; he reached Gath and brought them back. 41 When King Solomon was informed that Shimei had gone from Jerusalem to Gath and back, 42 he sent for him and said, 'Did I not require you to swear by the LORD? Did I not give you this solemn warning: "If ever you leave this city for any other place, know for certain that you will die"? You said, "I accept your sentence; I shall obey." 43 Why then have you not kept the oath which you swore by the LORD, and the order which I gave you? 44 Shimei, you know in your heart what mischief you did to my father David; the LORD is now making that mischief recoil on your own head. 45 But King Solomon is blessed, and the throne of David will be secure before the LORD for all time.' 46 The king then gave orders to Benaiah son of Jehoiada, who went out and struck Shimei down, and he died. Thus Solomon's royal power was securely established.

3 Solomon allied himself to Pharaoh king of Egypt by marrying his daughter. He

the LORD concerning Eli appears in 1 Sam 2.35–36. **28–35:** No new high-handed action by *Joab* is reported, but he too had to die; see vv. 5–6 n. **34:** *Out in the country:* near Bethlehem, where Joab's father and brother were buried (2 Sam. 2.32). **36–46:** *Three years* passed before *Shimei,* the last opponent, slipped; with his death Solomon's *royal power was . . . established.*

3.1–11.43: The reign of Solomon. This complex section, which has little affinity with the two preceding chs., is based on three kinds of material: popular narratives of Solomon's character, annalistic materials concerning his administration and works, and statistics and speeches concerning the establishment of the temple. The whole is arranged in an "envelope" (1,2,3,2,1) structure: (1) narratives of Solomon's divine favor, ch. 3; (2) details of his administration and wisdom, ch. 4; (3) the temple, 5.1–9.9; (2') details of administration, wisdom, and wealth, 9.10–10.29; and (1') Solomon's divine disfavor, ch. 11. The resulting impression—that the building of the temple was the great and central work of the reign and that it was only late in the reign that Solomon took foreign wives and supported foreign religious establishments—is the viewpoint of later interpreters primarily interested in the exclusive claims of the Jerusalem temple.

3.1–28: Solomon chooses wisdom and uses it. After brief introductory comments, two popular narratives of Solomon's surpassing wisdom introduce his reign. **1:** The *Pharaoh* whose *daughter* was Solomon's wife must have belonged to the weak twenty-first dynasty, since Shishak (about 935–914 B.C.E.), the first king of the twenty-second dynasty, was hostile to Judah (14.25). *The City of David* was the old city. Solomon, through brought her to the City of David, until he had finished building his palace and the house of the LORD and the wall round Jerusalem. [2] The people however continued to sacrifice at the shrines, for up to that time no house had been built for the name of the LORD. [3] Solomon himself loved the LORD, conforming to the precepts laid down by his father David; but he too slaughtered and burnt sacrifices at the shrines.

[4] The king went to Gibeon to offer a sacrifice, for that was the chief shrine, where he used to offer a thousand whole-offerings on the altar. [5] That night the LORD appeared to Solomon there in a dream. God said, 'What shall I give you? Tell me.' [6] He answered, 'You have shown great and constant love to your servant David my father, because he walked before you in loyalty, righteousness, and integrity of heart; and you have maintained this great and constant love towards him and now you have given him a son to succeed him on the throne.

[7] 'Now, LORD my God, you have made your servant king in place of my father David, though I am a mere child, unskilled in leadership. [8] Here I am in the midst of your people, the people of your choice, too many to be numbered or counted. [9] Grant your servant, therefore, a heart with skill to listen, so that he may govern your people justly and distinguish good from evil. Otherwise who is equal to the task of governing this great people of yours?'

[10] The Lord was well pleased that this was what Solomon had asked for, [11] and God said, 'Because you have asked for this, and not for long life, or for wealth, or for the lives of your enemies, but have asked for discernment in administering justice, [12] I grant your request; I give you a heart so wise and so understanding that there has been none like you before your time, nor will there be after you. [13] What is more, I give you those things

for which you did not ask, such wealth and glory as no king of your time can match. [14] If you conform to my ways and observe my ordinances and commandments, as your father David did, I will also give you long life.' [15] Then Solomon awoke, and realized it was a dream.

Solomon came to Jerusalem and stood before the Ark of the Covenant of the Lord, where he sacrificed whole-offerings and brought shared-offerings, and gave a banquet for all his household.

[16] Two women who were prostitutes approached the king at that time, and as they stood before him [17] one said, 'My lord, this woman and I share a house, and I gave birth to a child when she was there with me. [18] On the third day after my baby was born she too gave birth to a child. We were alone; no one else was with us in the house; only the two of us were there. [19] During the night this woman's child died because she lay on it, [20] and she got up in the middle of the night, took my baby from my side while I, your servant, was asleep, and laid it on her bosom, putting her dead child on mine. [21] When I got up in the morning to feed my baby, I found him dead; but when I looked at him closely, I found that it was not the child that I had borne.' [22] The other woman broke in, 'No, the living child is mine; yours is the dead one,' while the first insisted, 'No, the dead child is yours; mine is the living one.' So they went on arguing before the king.

[23] The king thought to himself, 'One of them says, "This is my child, the living one; yours is the dead one." The other says, "No, it is your child that is dead and mine that is alive." ' [24] Then he said, 'Fetch me a sword.' When a sword was brought, [25] the king gave the order: 'Cut the living child in two and give half to one woman and half to the other.' [26] At this the woman who was the mother of

3:5–13 *Cp. 2 Chr. 1:7–12.*

his building campaigns, was to double its size. **2–3:** From the late compilers' viewpoint, *shrines* (including local city sanctuaries) were legitimate sanctuaries of the LORD before the Jerusalem temple was built, but not afterward. Failure to eliminate these shrines is to be the basis for the Deuteronomic historian's criticism of most of the kings of Judah. **4–15:** *Gibeon:* a Canaanite city that tricked the Israelites into a treaty during the time of Joshua (Josh. 9.3–27). Saul's violation of the treaty required cultic expiation; see 2 Sam. 21.1–14 n. *A thousand whole-offerings* is either a great exaggeration or covers a considerable period of time. **6–9:** Solomon as imagined in seventh-century piety speaks here. **15:** This late comment is designed to reassert the religious importance of *Jerusalem* after the reference to Gibeon as "the chief shrine" (v. 4). **16–28:** The wisdom bestowed by the LORD results in judgments manifestly just; see Isa. 11.2–5. **19:** *She lay on it:* accidentally smothering the baby.

the living child, moved with love for her child, said to the king, 'Oh, sir, let her have the baby! Whatever you do, do not kill it.' The other said, 'Let neither of us have it; cut it in two.' 27 The king then spoke up: 'Give the living baby to the first woman,' he said; 'do not kill it. She is its mother.' 28 When Israel heard the judgement which the king had given, they all stood in awe of him; for they saw that he possessed wisdom from God for administering justice.

4 KING Solomon reigned over Israel. 2 His officers were as follows:
In charge of the calendar: Azariah son of Zadok the priest.
3 Adjutant-general: Ahijah son of Shisha. Secretary of state: Jehoshaphat son of Ahilud.
4 Commander of the army: Benaiah son of Jehoiada.
Priests: Zadok and Abiathar.
5 Superintendent of the regional governors: Azariah son of Nathan.
King's Friend: Zabud son of Nathan.
6 Comptroller of the household: Ahishar. Superintendent of the forced levy: Adoniram son of Abda.

7 Solomon had twelve regional governors over Israel and they supplied the food for the king and the royal household, each being responsible for one month's provision in the year. 8 These were their names:
Ben-hur in the hill-country of Ephraim.
9 Ben-dekar in Makaz, Shaalbim, Beth-shemesh, Elon, and Beth-hanan.
10 Ben-hesed in Aruboth; he had charge also of Socoh and all the land of Hepher.
11 Ben-abinadab, who had married Solomon's daughter Taphath, in all the district of Dor.
12 Baana son of Ahilud in Taanach and Megiddo, all Beth-shean as far as Abel-meholah beside Zartanah, and from Beth-shean below Jezreel as far as Jokmeam.

13 Ben-geber in Ramoth-gilead, including the tent-villages of Jair son of Manasseh in Gilead and the region of Argob in Bashan, sixty large walled towns with bronze gate-bars.
14 Ahinadab son of Iddo in Mahanaim.
15 Ahimaaz in Naphtali; he also had married a daughter of Solomon, Basmath.
16 Baanah son of Hushai in Asher and Aloth.
17 Jehoshaphat son of Paruah in Issachar.
18 Shimei son of Elah in Benjamin.
19 Geber son of Uri in Gilead, the country of Sihon king of the Amorites and of Og king of Bashan.
In addition, one governor over all the governors in the land.

20 THE people of Judah and Israel were countless as the sands of the sea; they ate and drank and enjoyed life. 21 Solomon ruled over all the kingdoms from the river Euphrates to Philistia and as far as the frontier of Egypt; they paid tribute and were subject to him all his life.

22 Solomon's provisions for one day were thirty kor of flour and sixty kor of meal, 23 ten fat oxen and twenty oxen from the pastures and a hundred sheep, as well as stags, gazelles, roebucks, and fattened fowl. 24 For he was paramount over all the region west of the Euphrates from Tiphsah to Gaza, ruling all the kings west of the river; and he enjoyed peace on all sides. 25 All through his reign the people of Judah and Israel lived in peace, everyone from Dan to Beersheba under his own vine and his own fig tree.

26 Solomon had forty thousand chariot-horses in his stables and twelve thousand cavalry horses.

4:2–6 Cp. 2 Sam. 8:16–18; 20:23–26; 1 Chr. 18:15–17.
4:2 In . . . calendar: prob. rdg; Heb. Elihoreph (verse 3).
4:3 Adjutant-general: prob. rdg, cp. 1 Chr. 18:16; Heb. Adjutants-general. son of Shisha: prob. rdg; Heb. sons of Shisha.   4:5 Zabud . . . Nathan: so Gk; Heb. adds priest.   4:9 Elon, and Beth-hanan: so some MSS; others Elon-beth-hanan.   4:19 over . . . governors: prob. rdg; Heb. omits.   4:21 In Heb. 5:1.

4.1–34: Solomon's administration and wisdom. 1–6: Compare 2 Sam. 8.16–18 and 20.23–26. **7–19:** The division of the northern part of the kingdom (Israel) replaced local tribal leadership with more dependable regional governors and resulted in more efficient support of the large palace establishment (vv. 27–28). **20–28:** The extent of his empire, the magnitude of his daily provisions, and the peace of his reign confer praise on Solomon and his wisdom. **22–23:** Kor: five bushels. These supplies may have been for royal service in several cities (see 9.15–19). **26:** Solomon maintained a large military force (compare 10.26) with which he preserved peace throughout his reign. Unlike David (compare 2 Sam. 8.4), Solomon made extensive use of chariotry,

²⁷The regional governors, each for a month in turn, supplied provisions for King Solomon and all who came to his table; they never fell short in their deliveries. ²⁸They provided also barley and straw, each according to his duty, for the horses and chariot-horses where it was required.

²⁹God gave Solomon deep wisdom and insight, and understanding as wide as the sand on the seashore, ³⁰so that Solomon's wisdom surpassed that of all the men of the east and of all Egypt. ³¹For he was wiser than any man, wiser than Ethan the Ezrahite, and Heman, Calcol, and Darda, the sons of Mahol; his fame spread among all the surrounding nations. ³²He propounded three thousand proverbs, and his songs numbered a thousand and five. ³³He discoursed of trees, from the cedar of Lebanon down to the marjoram that grows out of the wall, of beasts and birds, of reptiles and fish. ³⁴People of all races came to listen to the wisdom of Solomon, and he received gifts from all the kings in the world who had heard of his wisdom.

Building of the temple

5 WHEN Hiram king of Tyre heard that Solomon had been anointed king in his father's place, he sent envoys to him, because he had always been friendly with David. ²Solomon sent this message to Hiram: ³'You know that my father David could not build a house for the name of the LORD his God, because of the armed nations surrounding him, until the LORD made them subject to him. ⁴But now on every side the LORD my God has given me peace; there is no one to oppose me, I fear no attack. ⁵So I propose to build a house for the name of the LORD my God, following the promise given by the LORD to my father David: "Your son whom I shall set on the throne in your place will build the house for my name." ⁶If therefore you will now give orders that cedars be felled and brought from Lebanon, my men will work with yours, and I shall pay you for your men whatever sum you fix; for, as you know, we have none so skilled at felling trees as your Sidonians.'

⁷Hiram was greatly pleased to receive Solomon's message, and said, 'Blessed be the LORD today who has given David a wise son to rule over this great people.' ⁸He sent Solomon this reply: 'I have received your message. In this matter of timber, both cedar and pine, I shall do all you wish. ⁹My men will bring down the logs from Lebanon to the sea and I shall make them up into rafts to be floated to the place you appoint; I shall have them broken up there and you can remove them. You, for your part, will meet my wishes if you provide the food for my household.' ¹⁰So Hiram kept Solomon supplied with all the cedar and pine that he wanted, ¹¹and Solomon supplied Hiram with twenty thousand kor of wheat as food for his household and twenty kor of oil of pounded olives; Solomon gave this yearly to Hiram. ¹²The LORD bestowed wisdom on Solomon as he had promised him; there was peace between Hiram and Solomon and they concluded a treaty.

¹³King Solomon raised a forced levy from the whole of Israel amounting to thirty thousand men. ¹⁴He sent them to Lebanon in monthly relays of ten thousand, so that the men spent one month in Lebanon and two at home; Adoniram was superintendent of the levy. ¹⁵Solomon had also seventy thousand hauliers and eighty thousand quarrymen, ¹⁶apart from the three thousand three hundred foremen in charge of the work who superintended the labourers. ¹⁷By the king's orders they quarried huge, costly blocks for

4:34 **he received gifts:** *so Gk (Luc.); Heb. omits.*
5:1 *In Heb. 5:15.*   5:2–11 *Cp. 2 Chr. 2:3–16.*

as the Canaanite city-state kings had done before him (see Judg. 4.12–16; Josh. 11.1–9). **29–34:** Solomon's reputation for wisdom made him the hero of Wisdom literature (Prov. 1.1) as David was of the Psalms. **30:** *Of the east:* from Mesopotamia or north Arabia; see Job 1.3.

5.1–9.9: The building and dedication of the temple. This central part of the presentation of Solomon's reign is drawn from old court records (in "the annals of Solomon," 11.41) and temple records, with inserted speeches expressing the viewpoint of the late monarchic period.

5.1–18: Preparing the materials. When *Hiram* ruled in Tyre (about 969–936 B.C.E.), Phoenicia began its great commercial success in the Mediterranean. Alliances between Tyre and land powers that controlled trade routes with the east and with Arabia were necessary for its commercial policies. **2–6:** This speech depends on 2 Sam. ch. 7. **13:** On *forced* labor see 9.20–23. **16:** *Three thousand three hundred foremen:* a foreman laying the foundation of the Lord's house in hewn stone. 18 The builders supplied by Solomon and Hiram, together with the Gebalites, shaped the blocks and prepared both timber and stone for the building of the house.

6 It was in the four hundred and eightieth year after the Israelites had come out of Egypt, in the fourth year of Solomon's reign over Israel, in the second month of that year, the month of Ziv, that he began to build the house of the Lord.

2 The house which King Solomon built for the Lord was sixty cubits long by twenty cubits broad, and its height was thirty cubits. 3 The vestibule in front of the sanctuary was twenty cubits long, spanning the whole breadth of the house, while it projected ten cubits in front of the house; 4 and he fitted the house with embrasures. 5 Then he built a terrace against its wall round both the sanctuary and the inner shrine. He made arcades all round: 6 the lowest arcade was five cubits in depth, the middle six, and the highest seven; for he made rebatements all round the outside of the main wall so that the bearer beams might not be fixed into the walls. 7 In the building of the house, only blocks of stone dressed at the quarry were used; no hammer or axe or any iron tool whatever was heard in the house while it was being built.

8 The entrance to the lowest arcade was in the right-hand corner of the house; there was access by a spiral stairway from that to the middle arcade, and from the middle arcade to the highest. 9-10 So Solomon built the house and finished it, having constructed the terrace five cubits high against the whole building, braced the house with struts of cedar, and roofed it with beams and coffering of cedar.

11 Then the word of the Lord came to Solomon, saying, 12 'As for this house which you are building, if you are obedient to my ordinances and conform to my precepts and loyally observe all my commands, then I will fulfil my promise to you, the promise I gave to your father David, 13 and I will dwell among the Israelites and never forsake my people Israel.'

14 So Solomon built the Lord's house and finished it. 15 He panelled the inner walls of the house with cedar boards, covering the interior from floor to rafters with wood; the floor he laid with boards of pine. 16 In the innermost part of the house he partitioned off a space of twenty cubits with cedar boards from floor to rafters and made of it an inner shrine, to be the Most Holy Place. 17 The sanctuary in front of this was forty cubits long. 18 The cedar inside the house was carved with open flowers and gourds; all was cedar, no stone was left visible.

19 He prepared an inner shrine in the farthest recesses of the house to receive the Ark of the Covenant of the Lord. 20 This inner shrine was twenty cubits square and it stood

6,7 *In these chapters there are several Hebrew technical terms whose meaning is not certain and has to be determined, as well as may be, from the context.* 6:1–3 *Cp. 2 Chr. 3:2–4.* 6:5 **against its wall:** *so Gk; Heb. adds* round the walls of the house. 6:6 **arcade:** *so Gk; Heb.* platform. **the bearer beams:** *so Aram. (Targ.); Heb. omits.* 6:8 **lowest:** *so Gk; Heb.* middle. 6:15 **rafters:** *so Gk; Heb.* walls. 6:17 **The sanctuary ... this:** *so Gk; Heb.* The house, that is the sanctuary, before me. 6:20 **This inner:** *so Lat.; Heb. prefixes* Before.

served over ten men, with a supervisor over ten foremen, and so on to higher officials. **18:** *Gebalites:* from the old Phoenician city Gebal; Greeks called it Byblos, the Gk. term for papyrus. Byblos, altered in spelling, yields "bible" and the prefix "biblio-."

6.1–13: The external structure of the temple. 1: *Four hundred and eightieth:* this number is artificial, equaling twelve generations of forty years each. *The fourth year of Solomon's reign* was 957 B.C.E. or shortly after. *Ziv:* the old Canaanite name for *the second month* (April–May). **2:** *Cubit:* eighteen inches. **3:** *Vestibule:* an enclosed porch. **4:** *Embrasures:* openings in thick walls with sides slanting outward. **5:** *Terrace:* a platform built around the sides and rear of the temple upon which the *arcades* were built. *The sanctuary:* the large main room of the temple (vv. 33–35). *The inner shrine:* the holiest place of the temple, a small chamber at the rear where the Ark would rest (see vv. 19–22; 8.6–8). The arcades were three stories high, the chambers of the lower stories narrower because their thicker walls provided support for the upper ones. The chambers in the arcades were for storage (see Neh. 13.4–5). **7:** A long-standing tradition prohibited the use of *iron tools* in constructing an altar; see Deut. 27.5; Josh. 8.31. **11–13:** This brief oracle anticipates 9.1–9.

6.14–38: The internal structure of the temple. The inside of the temple was seen only by priests, some prophets, and royalty. The description here may be idealized. That *cedar* covered all the *stone* is doubtful, and twenty cubits high; he overlaid it with red gold and made an altar of cedar. [21] Solomon overlaid the inside of the house with red gold and drew a veil with golden chains across in front of the inner shrine. [22] The whole house he overlaid with gold until it was all covered; and the whole of the altar by the inner shrine he overlaid with gold.

[23] In the inner shrine he carved two cherubim of wild olive wood, each ten cubits high. [24] Each wing of the cherubim was five cubits long, and from wingtip to wingtip was ten cubits. [25] Similarly, the second cherub measured ten cubits; the two cherubim were alike in size and shape, [26] and each ten cubits high. [27] He put the cherubim within the inner shrine and their wings were spread, so that a wing of one cherub touched the wall on one side and a wing of the other touched the wall on the other side, and their other wings met in the middle; [28] he overlaid the cherubim with gold.

[29] Round all the walls of the house he carved figures of cherubim, palm trees, and open flowers, both in the inner chamber and in the outer. [30] The floor of the house he overlaid with gold, both in the inner chamber and in the outer. [31] At the entrance to the inner shrine he made a double door of wild olive wood; the pilasters and the doorposts were pentagonal. [32] The doors were of wild olive, and he carved cherubim, palms, and open flowers on them, overlaying them with gold and hammering the gold upon the cherubim and the palms. [33] Similarly for the doorway of the sanctuary he made a square frame of wild olive [34] and a double door of pine, each leaf having two swivel-pins. [35] On them he carved cherubim, palms, and open flowers, overlaying them evenly with gold over the carving.

[36] He built the inner court with three courses of dressed stone and one course of lengths of cedar.

[37] In the fourth year of Solomon's reign, in the month of Ziv, the foundation of the house of the LORD was laid; [38] and in the eleventh year, in the month of Bul, which is the eighth month, the house was finished in all its details according to the specification. It had taken seven years to build.

7 By the time he had finished, Solomon had been engaged on building for thirteen years. [2] He built the House of the Forest of Lebanon, a hundred cubits long, fifty broad, and thirty high, constructed of four rows of cedar columns, on top of which were laid lengths of cedar. [3] It had a cedar roof, extending over the beams, which rested on the columns, fifteen in each row; and the number of the beams was forty-five. [4] There were three rows of window-frames, and the windows corresponded to each other at three levels. [5] All the doorways and the windows had square frames, and window corresponded to window at three levels.

[6] Solomon made also the portico, fifty cubits long and thirty broad, with a cornice above.

[7] He built the Portico of Judgement, the portico containing the throne where he was to give judgement; this was panelled in cedar from floor to rafters.

[8] His own house where he was to reside, in another courtyard set back from the portico, and the house he made for Pharaoh's daughter whom he had married, were constructed like this portico.

[9] All these were made of costly blocks of stone, hewn to measure and trimmed with the saw on the inner and outer sides, from foundation to coping and from the court of the house as far as the great court. [10] At the base were costly stones, huge blocks, some ten and some eight cubits in size, [11] and above were costly stones dressed to measure, and cedar. [12] The great court had three courses of dressed stone all around and a course of lengths of cedar; so had the inner court of

6:20 **made:** *so Gk; Heb.* overlaid.   6:21 **a veil:** *prob. rdg; Heb. omits.* **inner shrine:** *prob. rdg; Heb. adds* and overlaid it with gold.   6:23–28 *Cp. 2 Chr. 3:10–13.*   6:29,30 **inner chamber:** *so Gk; Heb.* inwards.   6:31 **and the:** *prob. rdg; Heb. omits.* **pentagonal:** *so Gk; Heb.* fifth.   6:33 **a square:** *so Gk; Heb.* from with a fourth.   7:5 **windows:** *so Gk; Heb.* doorposts.   7:6 **fifty...broad:** *prob. rdg; Heb. adds* and a colonnade and pillars in front of them.   7:7 **rafters:** *so Lat.; Heb.* floor.   7:9 **from the...house:** *prob. rdg, cp. verse 12; Heb.* from outside.

that all important parts were *overlaid . . . with red gold* may be a later glorification. **23:** *Cherubim:* compare Exod. 25.18–22. **38:** *Bul:* another old Canaanite month name, *the eighth month* (October–November); see also v. 1.

7.1–12: The rest of the palace complex. The temple was only one part of the entire palace. *The great court* of v. 9 enclosed the whole, within which "the inner court" of the temple was only one area (6.36).

the house of the LORD, and so had the vestibule of the house.

[13] King Solomon fetched from Tyre Hiram, [14] the son of a widow of the tribe of Naphtali. His father, a native of Tyre, had been a worker in bronze, and he himself was a man of great skill and ingenuity, versed in every kind of craftsmanship in bronze. After he came to King Solomon, Hiram carried out all his works.

[15] He cast in a mould the two bronze pillars. One stood eighteen cubits high and it took a cord of twelve cubits long to go round it; it was hollow, and the metal was four fingers thick. The second pillar was the same. [16] He made two capitals of solid bronze to set on the tops of the pillars, each capital five cubits high. [17] He made two bands of ornamental network, in festoons of chain-work, for the capitals on the tops of the pillars, a band of network for each capital. [18] He made pomegranates in two rows all round on top of the ornamental network of the one pillar; he did the same with the other capital. [19] The capitals at the tops of the pillars in the vestibule were shaped like lilies and were four cubits high. [20] On the capitals at the tops of the two pillars, immediately above the cushion, extending beyond the network upwards, were two hundred pomegranates in rows all round on the two capitals. [21] Then he erected the pillars at the vestibule of the sanctuary. When he had erected the pillar on the right side, he named it Jachin; and when he had erected the one on the left side, he named it Boaz. [22] On the tops of the pillars was lily-work. Thus the work of the pillars was finished.

[23] He made the Sea of cast metal; it was round in shape, the diameter from rim to rim being ten cubits; it stood five cubits high, and it took a line thirty cubits long to go round it. [24] All round the Sea on the outside under its rim, completely surrounding the thirty cubits of its circumference, were two rows of gourds, cast in one piece with the Sea itself. [25] It was mounted on twelve oxen, three facing north, three west, three south, and three east, their hindquarters turned inwards; the Sea rested on top of them. [26] Its thickness was a hand's breadth; its rim was made like that of a cup, shaped like the calyx of a lily; it held two thousand bath.

[27] Hiram also made the ten trolleys of bronze; each trolley was four cubits long, four wide, and three high. [28] This was the construction of the trolleys: they had panels set in frames; [29] on these panels were portrayed lions, oxen, and cherubim, and the same on the frames; above and below the lions, oxen, and cherubim were fillets of hammered work of spiral design. [30] Each trolley had four bronze wheels with bronze axles; it also had four flanges and handles beneath the laver, and these handles were of cast metal with a spiral design on their sides. [31] The opening for the basin was set within a crown which projected one cubit; the opening was round with a level edge, and it had decorations in relief. The panels of the trolleys were square, not round. [32] The four wheels were beneath the panels, and the wheel-forks were made in one piece with the trolleys; the height of each wheel was one and a half cubits. [33] The wheels were constructed like those of a chariot, their axles, hubs, spokes, and felloes being all of cast metal. [34] The four handles were at the four corners of each trolley, of one piece with the trolley. [35] At the top of the trolley there was a circular band half a cubit high; the struts and panels on the trolley were of one piece with it. [36] On the plates, that is on the panels, he carved cherubim, lions, and palm trees, wherever there was a blank space, with spiral work all round it. [37] This is how the ten trolleys were made; all of them were cast alike, having the same size and the same shape.

[38] Hiram then made ten bronze basins, each holding forty bath and measuring four

7:15–21 *Cp. 2 Chr. 3:15–17.* 7:15 **it was ... thick:** *prob. rdg, cp. Jer. 52:21; Heb. omits.* **the same:** *so Gk; Heb. omits.* 7:17 **He made two:** *so Gk; Heb. omits.* **a band of network:** *so Gk; Heb.* seven. 7:18 **pomegranates:** *so some MSS; others* pillars. **one pillar:** *so Gk; Heb. adds* to cover the capitals on the top of the pomegranates. 7:20 **the two capitals:** *prob. rdg; Heb.* the second capital. 7:21 **Jachin:** *that is* He shall establish. **Boaz:** *that is* In him is strength. 7:23–26 *Cp. 2 Chr. 4:2–5.* 7:24 **thirty:** *prob. rdg; Heb.* ten. 7:29 **and cherubim were fillets:** *prob. rdg; Heb. omits* and cherubim. 7:31 **level edge:** *prob. rdg; Heb. adds* one and a half cubits (*cp. verse 32*). 7:35 **on:** *prob. rdg; Heb. adds* the head of. 7:36 **the panels:** *prob. rdg; Heb. adds* its struts.

7.13–51: The bronze fixtures of the temple court. These are again parts of the temple complex visible to the lay worshiper. The bronze *trolleys* (v. 27), *basins* (v. 38), *pots, shovels,* and *tossing-bowls* (v. 40) were used in the preparation of various sacrificial materials and in the daily work of maintaining the altar.

cubits; there was a basin for each of the ten trolleys. ³⁹He put five trolleys on the right side of the house and five on the left side; and he placed the Sea in the south-east corner of it.

⁴⁰Hiram made the pots, the shovels, and the tossing-bowls. With them he finished all the work which he had undertaken for King Solomon in the house of the LORD: ⁴¹the two pillars; the two bowl-shaped capitals on the tops of the pillars; the two ornamental networks to cover the two bowl-shaped capitals on the tops of the pillars; ⁴²the four hundred pomegranates for the two networks, two rows of pomegranates for each network, to cover the bowl-shaped capitals on the two pillars; ⁴³the ten trolleys and the ten basins on the trolleys; ⁴⁴the one Sea and the twelve oxen which supported it; ⁴⁵the pots, the shovels, and the tossing-bowls—all these objects in the house of the LORD which Hiram made for King Solomon being of burnished bronze. ⁴⁶The king cast them in the foundry between Succoth and Zarethan in the plain of the Jordan.

⁴⁷Solomon put all these objects in their places; so great was the quantity of bronze used in their making that the weight of it was beyond all reckoning. ⁴⁸He made also all the furnishings for the house of the LORD: the golden altar and the golden table upon which was set the Bread of the Presence; ⁴⁹the lampstands of red gold, five on the right side and five on the left side of the inner shrine; the flowers, lamps, and tongs of gold; ⁵⁰the cups, snuffers, tossing-bowls, saucers, and firepans of red gold; and the panels for the doors of the inner sanctuary, the Most Holy Place, and for the doors of the house, of gold. ⁵¹When all the work which King Solomon did for the house of the LORD was completed, he brought in the sacred treasures of his father David, the silver, the gold, and the vessels, and deposited them in the treasuries of the house of the LORD.

Temple worship

8 THEN Solomon summoned to him at Jerusalem the elders of Israel, all the heads of the tribes who were chiefs of families in Israel, in order to bring up the Ark of the Covenant of the LORD from the City of David, which is called Zion. ²All the men of Israel assembled in King Solomon's presence at the pilgrim-feast in the month Ethanim, the seventh month. ³When the elders of Israel had all arrived, the priests lifted the Ark of the LORD ⁴and carried it up; the Tent of Meeting and all the sacred furnishings of the Tent were carried by the priests and the Levites. ⁵King Solomon and the whole congregation of Israel assembled with him before the Ark sacrificed sheep and oxen in numbers past counting or reckoning.

⁶The priests brought in the Ark of the

7:40–51 *Cp. 2 Chr. 4:11–5:1.* 7:40 **pots:** *so many MSS; others* basins. 7:42 **on the two:** *so Gk; Heb.* on the surface of. 7:50 **the house:** *prob. rdg; Heb. adds* for the temple. 8:1–9 *Cp. 2 Chr. 5:2–10.*

8.1–66: The dedication of the temple. This chapter (together with the LORD's response in 9.1–9) presents the second great development in the LORD's relation to Israel as the Deuteronomic historians viewed it. The first was the emergence of kingship, approved by the LORD in the form of the Davidic dynasty; see 2 Sam. 7.8–16. There was also a tradition in the older period that the LORD did not dwell in a house of cedar (2 Sam. 7.5–7). The Deuteronomic historians show as the second development how the LORD agreed to a change in the mode of divine dwelling; that change reaches its climax here with the dedication of the temple of Solomon. This chapter consists of elements of an old report of Solomon's transfer of the Ark to the new temple, of some Deuteronomic and priestly glosses added to that report, and of extensive speeches from a Deuteronomic viewpoint put into Solomon's mouth. **1–13:** *The Ark of the Covenant* represented the presence of the LORD. Its movement from one sanctuary to another was an awesome, even hazardous, operation (compare 2 Sam. ch. 6). **1:** The writer emphasizes that all the leaders of *Israel* participated in the ceremonies of the movement of the Ark. *The City of David* was the old city, greatly expanded on the north side by Solomon's building activities. **2:** A *pilgrim-feast* was a time when Israelites were required to appear before the LORD with offerings (Exod. 23.14–17; 34.18, 22–24; Deut. 16.1–17). This pilgrim-feast is identified with Tabernacles (Booths), set in the later Israelite calendars at full moon of *the seventh month* (Sept.–Oct.), the old Canaanite name of which was *Ethanim.* This feast is explained as derived from a Canaanite new year festival at which the kingship of God over the powers of chaos and drought was symbolically celebrated; some associate Pss. 93, 97 with the festival. Eleven months elapsed between the completion (6.38) and the dedication. **4:** This mention of *the Tent*

Covenant of the LORD to its place in the inner shrine of the house, the Most Holy Place, beneath the wings of the cherubim. ⁷The cherubim, whose wings were spread over the place of the Ark, formed a canopy above the Ark and its poles. ⁸The poles projected, and their ends were visible from the Holy Place immediately in front of the inner shrine, but from nowhere else outside; they are there to this day. ⁹There was nothing inside the Ark but the two stone tablets which Moses had deposited there at Horeb, when the LORD made the covenant with the Israelites after they left Egypt.

¹⁰The priests came out of the Holy Place, since the cloud was filling the house of the LORD, ¹¹and they could not continue to minister because of it, for the glory of the LORD filled his house. ¹²Then Solomon said:

'The LORD has caused his sun to shine
    in the heavens,
but he has said he would dwell in thick
    darkness.
¹³I have built you a lofty house,
a dwelling-place for you to occupy for
    ever.'

¹⁴While the whole assembly of Israelites stood, the king turned and blessed them: ¹⁵'Blessed be the LORD the God of Israel who spoke directly to my father David and has himself fulfilled his promise. For he said, ¹⁶"From the day when I brought my people Israel out of Egypt, I chose no city out of all the tribes of Israel where I should build a house for my name to be, but I chose Jerusalem where my name should be, and David to be over my people Israel." ¹⁷'My father David had it in mind to build a house for the name of the LORD the God of Israel, ¹⁸but the LORD said to him, "You purposed to build a house for my name, and your purpose was good. ¹⁹Nevertheless, you

are not to build it; but the son who is to be born to you, he is to build the house for my name." ²⁰The LORD has now fulfilled his promise: I have succeeded my father David and taken his place on the throne of Israel, as the LORD promised; and I have built the house for the name of the LORD the God of Israel. ²¹I have assigned a place in it for the Ark containing the covenant of the LORD, which he made with our forefathers when he brought them out of Egypt.'

²²Standing in front of the altar of the LORD in the presence of the whole assembly of Israel, Solomon spread out his hands towards heaven ²³and said, 'LORD God of Israel, there is no God like you in heaven above or on earth beneath, keeping covenant with your servants and showing them constant love while they continue faithful to you with all their hearts. ²⁴You have kept your promise to your servant David my father; by your deeds this day you have fulfilled what you said to him in words. ²⁵Now, therefore, LORD God of Israel, keep this promise of yours to your servant David my father, when you said: "You will never want for a man appointed by me to sit on the throne of Israel, if only your sons look to their ways and walk before me as you have done." ²⁶God of Israel, let the promise which you made to your servant David my father be confirmed.

²⁷'But can God indeed dwell on earth? Heaven itself, the highest heaven, cannot contain you; how much less this house that I have built! ²⁸Yet attend, LORD my God, to the prayer and the supplication of your servant; listen to the cry and the prayer which your servant makes before you this day, ²⁹that your eyes may ever be on this house night and day, this place of which you said, "My name will be there." Hear your servant when

8:12–50 *Cp. 2 Chr. 6:1–39.*   8:12 **has caused . . . but he:** *prob. rdg, cp. Gk; Heb. omits.*   8:16 **Jerusalem . . . and:** *so Gk; Heb. omits.*

of *Meeting* and *the Levites* is regarded as a late priestly gloss. **8:** The formula *to this day* was often employed in popular explanations and here may reflect a time earlier than the writer of the Deuteronomic history. **9:** A relatively late tradition combined the much older separate traditions of the *stone tablets* (Exod. 24.12; 34.1, 27–29) and of the *Ark* (Num. 10.35–36; 1 Sam. 4.3–5); see Deut. 10.1–5. *Horeb* is the usual Deuteronomic name for the mountain of God (Deut. 1.6; 5.2, etc.), though it was also used in earlier traditions (Exod. 3.1; 1 Kgs. 19.8). **10–11:** *The cloud* of *the glory of the LORD* here is modeled after the tradition in Exod. 40.34–35; compare Ezek. chs. 9–11 and 43.1–5. **12–13:** This is a piece from one of the very old Israelite collections of songs, perhaps the "Book of Jashar"; see Josh. 10.13 n. and 2 Sam. 1.18 n. **14–21:** In this blessing Solomon speaks in the light of 2 Sam. 7.1–16. **27–53:** A Deuteronomic theology of the temple. A finely wrought meditation on the spatial relation of the LORD to the temple (vv. 27–30) is followed by petitions that the LORD he prays towards this place. ³⁰ Hear the supplication of your servant and your people Israel when they pray towards this place. Hear in heaven your dwelling and, when you hear, forgive.

³¹ 'Should anyone wrong a neighbour and be adjured to take an oath, and come to take the oath before your altar in this house, ³² then hear in heaven and take action: be your servants' judge, condemning the guilty person and bringing his deeds on his own head, acquitting the innocent and rewarding him as his innocence may deserve.

³³ 'Should your people Israel be defeated by an enemy because they have sinned against you, and then turn back to you, confessing your name and making their prayer and supplication to you in this house, ³⁴ hear in heaven; forgive the sin of your people Israel and restore them to the land which you gave to their forefathers.

³⁵ 'Should the heavens be shut up and there be no rain, because your servant and your people Israel have sinned against you, and they then pray towards this place, confessing your name and forsaking their sin when they feel your punishment, ³⁶ hear in heaven and forgive their sin; so teach them the good way which they are to follow, and grant rain on your land which you have given to your people as their own possession.

³⁷ 'Should there be famine in the land, or pestilence, or blight either black or red, or locusts developing or fully grown, or should their enemies besiege them in any of their cities, or plague or sickness befall them, ³⁸ then hear the prayer or supplication of everyone among your people Israel, as each, prompted by the remorse of his own heart, spreads out his hands towards this house: ³⁹ hear it in heaven your dwelling-place, forgive, and take action. As you know a person's heart, reward him according to his deeds, for you alone know the hearts of all; ⁴⁰ and so they will fear you throughout their lives in the land you gave to our forefathers.

⁴¹ 'The foreigner too, anyone who does not belong to your people Israel, but has come from a distant land because of your fame ⁴² (for your great fame and your strong hand and outstretched arm will be widely known), when such a one comes and prays towards this house, ⁴³ hear in heaven your dwelling-place and respond to the call which the foreigner makes to you, so that like your people Israel all the peoples of the earth may know your fame and fear you, and learn that this house which I have built bears your name.

⁴⁴ 'When your people go to war against an enemy, wherever you send them, and when they pray to the LORD, turning towards this city which you have chosen and towards this house which I have built for your name, ⁴⁵ then hear in heaven their prayer and supplication, and maintain their cause.

⁴⁶ 'Should they sin against you (and who is free from sin?) and should you in your anger give them over to an enemy who carries them captive to his own land, far or near, ⁴⁷ and should they then in the land of their captivity have a change of heart and make supplication to you there and say, "We have sinned and acted perversely and wickedly," ⁴⁸ and turn back to you wholeheartedly in the land of their enemies who took them captive, and pray to you, turning towards their land which you gave to their forefathers and towards this city which you chose and this house which I have built for your name, ⁴⁹ then in heaven your dwelling-place hear their prayer and supplication, and maintain their cause. ⁵⁰ Forgive your people their sins and transgressions against you; put pity for them in their captors' hearts. ⁵¹ For they are your possession, your people whom you brought out of Egypt, from the smelting furnace. ⁵² Let your eyes be ever open to the entreaty of your servant and of your people Israel, and hear whenever they call to you. ⁵³ You yourself have singled them out from all the peoples of the earth to be your possession; so, Lord GOD, you promised through your servant Moses when you brought our forefathers from Egypt.'

⁵⁴ As Solomon finished all this prayer and supplication to the LORD, he rose from be-

8:35 **servant**: *so Gk; Heb.* servants.   8:37 **in any:** *so Gk; Heb.* in the land.

---

will hearken when the faithful will pray *towards* it in times of typical human crises. **46–53:** This passage deals with Exile. It is commonly viewed as an addition from the time of the Exile to Babylonia after 587. Yet the possibility of exile (and the terms of return) were issues of importance from shortly after the fall of the Northern Kingdom (722 B.C.E.). Hence, though the present form of vv. 46–53 may come after 587, its leading ideas are probably much older, possibly as old as Hezekiah, about 715–687 B.C.E.; see 2 Kgs. 18.3–8; 2 Chr. 30.1–31.1.

fore the altar of the LORD, where he had been kneeling with his hands spread out to heaven; 55 he stood up and in a loud voice blessed the whole assembly of Israel: 56 'Blessed be the LORD who has given his people Israel rest, as he promised: not one of the promises he made through his servant Moses has failed. 57 May the LORD our God be with us as he was with our forefathers; may he never leave us or forsake us. 58 May he turn our hearts towards him, so that we may conform to all his ways, observing his commandments, statutes, and judgements, as he commanded our forefathers. 59 And may the words of my supplication to the LORD be with the LORD our God day and night, that, as the need arises day by day, he may maintain the cause of his servant and of his people Israel. 60 So all the peoples of the earth will know that the LORD is God, he and no other, 61 and you will be perfect in loyalty to the LORD our God as you are this day, conforming to his statutes and observing his commandments.'

62 The king and all Israel with him offered sacrifices before the LORD; 63 Solomon offered as shared-offerings to the LORD twenty-two thousand oxen and a hundred and twenty thousand sheep. Thus the king and the Israelites dedicated the house of the LORD. 64 On that day also the king consecrated the centre of the court which lay in front of the house of the LORD; there he offered the whole-offering, the grain-offering, and the fat portions of the shared-offerings, because the bronze altar which stood before the LORD was too small to accommodate the whole-offering, the grain-offering, and the fat portions of the shared-offerings. 65 So Solomon and with him all Israel, a great assembly from Lebo-hamath to the wadi of Egypt, celebrated the pilgrim-feast at that time before the LORD our God for seven days. 66 On the eighth day he dismissed the people; and they blessed the king, and went home happy and glad at heart for all the

prosperity granted by the LORD to his servant David and to his people Israel.

The reign of Solomon

9 WHEN Solomon had completed the house of the LORD and the palace and all the plans for building on which he had set his heart, 2 the LORD again appeared to him, as he had appeared to him at Gibeon, 3 and said, 'I have heard the prayer and supplication which you have offered me. I have consecrated this house which you have built to receive my name for all time, and my eyes and my heart will be fixed on it for ever. 4 If you, for your part, live in my sight as your father David lived, in integrity and uprightness, doing all I command you and observing my statutes and my judgements, 5 then I shall establish the throne of your kingdom over Israel for ever, as I promised your father David when I said, "You shall never want for a man on the throne of Israel." 6 But if you or your sons turn away from following me and do not observe my commandments and my statutes which I have set before you, and if you go and serve other gods and bow down before them, 7 then I shall cut off Israel from the land which I gave them; I shall renounce this house which I have consecrated to my name, and Israel will become a byword and an object-lesson among all peoples. 8 This house will become a ruin; every passer-by will be appalled and gasp at the sight of it; and they will ask, "Why has the LORD so treated this land and this house?" 9 The answer will be, "Because they forsook the LORD their God, who brought their forefathers out of Egypt, and they clung to other gods, bowing down before them and serving them; that is

8:64–66 Cp. 2 Chr. 7:7–10.   8:64 **in front:** or to the east.   8:65 **for seven days:** so Gk; Heb. adds and seven days, fourteen days.   9:1–9 Cp. 2 Chr. 7:11–22.   9:8 **become a ruin:** so Syriac; Heb. be high. **gasp:** lit. hiss.

For other passages anticipating exile, see Lev. 26.32–45; Deut. 4.25–31; 30.1–10. **54–61:** A second benediction refers to the promises through . . . Moses rather than those to David; see vv. 14–21. **62–66:** The numbers in v. 63 are exaggerated. The bronze altar (v. 64) is curiously lacking from the description of the temple court fixtures in 7.13–46. **65:** Lebo-hamath was north of the Lebanon mountain range in Syria.

9.1–9: The LORD sanctions the temple. Of all the kings treated in this history, it is only to Solomon that the LORD speaks directly; otherwise God speaks through prophets. The Deuteronomic historians portray the LORD's approval of the Jerusalem temple, and the conditions on which that approval is given. They saw the meaning of the history of the kingdoms epitomized in the recurrent failures to meet those conditions. **2:** Gibeon: see 3.4–15. **5:** For the promise to David, see 2 Sam. 7.8–16.

why the LORD has brought all this misfortune on them."'

¹⁰At the end of the twenty years it had taken Solomon to build the two houses, the house of the LORD and the palace, ¹¹he made over to Hiram king of Tyre twenty towns in Galilee, for Hiram had supplied him with the timber, both cedar and pine, and the gold, all he requested. ¹²But when Hiram went from Tyre to inspect the towns, they did not satisfy him, ¹³and he said, 'My brother, what kind of towns are these you have given me?' And so he called them the Land of Cabul, the name they still bear. ¹⁴Hiram had sent a hundred and twenty talents of gold to the king.

¹⁵This is the record of the forced labour which King Solomon conscripted to build the house of the LORD, his own palace, the Millo, the wall of Jerusalem, and Hazor, Megiddo, and Gezer. ¹⁶Gezer had been attacked and captured by Pharaoh king of Egypt, who had burnt it to the ground, put its Canaanite inhabitants to death, and given it as a marriage gift to his daughter, Solomon's wife. ¹⁷Solomon rebuilt it. He also built Lower Beth-horon, ¹⁸Baalath, and Tamar in the wilderness, ¹⁹as well as all his store-cities, and the towns where he quartered his chariots and horses; and he carried out all his cherished plans for building in Jerusalem, in the Lebanon, and throughout his whole dominion. ²⁰All the survivors of the Amorites, Hittites, Perizzites, Hivites, and Jebusites who did not belong to Israel—²¹that is those of their descendants who survived in the land, wherever the Israelites had been unable to exterminate them—all were employed by Solomon on perpetual forced labour, as they still are. ²²None of the Israelites were put to forced labour; they were his fighting men, his captains and lieutenants, and the commanders of his chariots and of his cavalry. ²³The number of officers in charge of the foremen over Solomon's work was five hundred and fifty; these superintended the people engaged on the work.

²⁴Solomon brought Pharaoh's daughter up from the City of David to her own house which he had built for her; later he built the Millo.

²⁵Three times a year Solomon used to offer whole-offerings and shared-offerings on the altar which he had built to the LORD, burning the offerings before the LORD. So he completed the house.

²⁶King Solomon built a fleet of ships at Ezion-geber, near Eloth on the shore of the Red Sea, in Edom. ²⁷Hiram sent men of his own to serve with the fleet, experienced seamen, to work with Solomon's men. ²⁸They went to Ophir and brought back four hundred and twenty talents of gold, which they delivered to King Solomon.

10 THE queen of Sheba heard of Solomon's fame and came to test him with enigmatic questions. ²She arrived in Jerusalem with a very large retinue, camels laden with spices, gold in vast quantity, and precious stones. When she came to Solomon, she talked to him about everything she had on her mind. ³Solomon answered all her questions; not one of them was too hard for the king to answer. ⁴When the queen of Sheba observed all the wisdom of Solomon, the palace he had built, ⁵the food on his table, the courtiers sitting around him, and his attendants standing behind in their livery, his cupbearers, and the whole-offerings which he used to offer in the house of the LORD, she was overcome with amazement. ⁶She said to the king, 'The account which I heard in my own country about your achievements and

9:10–28 Cp. 2 Chr. 8:1–18.   9:13 **Cabul:** that is Sterile.   9:18 **Tamar:** or, as otherwise read, Tadmor. **wilderness:** so Gk; Heb. adds in the land.
9:19 **horses:** or cavalry.   9:22 **fighting men:** prob. rdg; Heb. adds and his servants.   9:24 **Solomon . . . up:** so Gk; Heb. However, Pharaoh's daughter had gone up.   9:25 **the offerings:** so Gk; Heb. adds with it which.   9:26 **Red Sea:** or sea of Reeds.
10:1–25 Cp. 2 Chr. 9:1–24.   10:1 **The queen . . . fame:** prob. rdg, cp. 2 Chr. 9:1; Heb. adds to the name of the LORD.

9.10–10.29: Solomon's works, wisdom, and wealth. The materials of this section balance those of ch. 4; see 3.1–11.43 n. **10–14:** The reasons for Solomon's sale of *towns* (actually only villages) are unknown, though overexpenditure in building programs is a likely explanation. A playful folk etymology explains the town name *Cabul* (v. 13) as meaning "like nothing." **15–23:** *The forced labour* for Solomon's projects was probably drawn largely from non-Israelite inhabitants of Canaan, but some Israelites were apparently also drawn upon; see 5.13; 11.28; 12.4. From a later viewpoint, the continued presence of non-Israelites in the promised land required special explanation; see Josh. 9.22–27; Judg. 2.20–3.6. **24:** See 3.1 n. **25:** *Three times a year:* see 8.2 n. **26–28:** Commerce rather than conquest was the key to Solomon's wealth. **10.1–13:** This narrative is a popular your wisdom was true, [7] but I did not believe what they told me until I came and saw for myself. Indeed I was not told half of it; your wisdom and your prosperity far surpass all I had heard of them. [8] Happy are your wives, happy these courtiers of yours who are in attendance on you every day and hear your wisdom! [9] Blessed be the LORD your God who has delighted in you and has set you on the throne of Israel; because he loves Israel unendingly, he has made you king to maintain law and justice.' [10] She presented the king with a hundred and twenty talents of gold, spices in great abundance, and precious stones. Never again did such a quantity of spices come as the queen of Sheba gave to King Solomon.

[11] Besides all this, Hiram's fleet of ships, which had brought gold from Ophir, brought also from Ophir huge cargoes of almug wood and precious stones. [12] The king used the wood to make stools for the house of the LORD and for the palace, as well as lyres and lutes for the singers. No such quantities of almug wood have ever been imported or even seen since that time.

[13] King Solomon gave the queen of Sheba whatever she desired and asked for, in addition to all that he gave her of his royal bounty. Then she departed with her retinue and went back to her own land.

[14] The weight of gold which Solomon received in any one year was six hundred and sixty-six talents, [15] in addition to the tolls levied by the customs officers, the profits on foreign trade, and the tribute of the kings of Arabia and the regional governors.

[16] King Solomon made two hundred shields of beaten gold, and six hundred shekels of gold went to the making of each one; [17] he also made three hundred bucklers of beaten gold, and three minas of gold went to the making of each buckler. The king put these into the House of the Forest of Lebanon.

[18] The king also made a great throne inlaid with ivory and overlaid with fine gold. [19] Six

steps led up to the throne; at the back of the throne there was the head of a calf. There were armrests on each side of the seat, with a lion standing beside each of them, [20] while twelve lions stood on the six steps, one at either end of each step. Nothing like it had ever been made for any monarch. [21] All Solomon's drinking vessels were of gold, and all the plate in the House of the Forest of Lebanon was of red gold; no silver was used, for it was reckoned of no value in the days of Solomon. [22] The king had a fleet of merchantmen at sea with Hiram's fleet; once every three years this fleet of merchantmen came home, bringing gold and silver, ivory, apes, and monkeys.

[23] Thus King Solomon outdid all the kings of the earth in wealth and wisdom, [24] and the whole world courted him to hear the wisdom with which God had endowed his mind. [25] Each one brought his gift with him, vessels of silver and gold, garments, perfumes and spices, horses and mules in annual tribute.

[26] Solomon amassed chariots and horses; he had fourteen hundred chariots and twelve thousand horses; he stationed some in the chariot-towns, while others he kept at hand in Jerusalem. [27] He made silver as common in Jerusalem as stone, and cedar as plentiful as the sycomore-fig is in the Shephelah. [28] Horses were imported from Egypt and Kue for Solomon; the merchants of the king obtained them from Kue by purchase. [29] Chariots were imported from Egypt for six hundred silver shekels each, and horses for a hundred and fifty; in the same way the merchants obtained them for export from all the kings of the Hittites and the kings of Aram.

11 King Solomon loved many foreign women; in addition to Pharaoh's

10:8 **wives:** *so Gk; Heb.* men.   10:12 **stools:** *meaning of Heb. word uncertain.*   10:15 **tolls levied by:** *so Gk; Heb.* men of. **and the tribute of:** *prob. rdg; Heb.* and all. 10:22 **merchantmen:** *lit.* ships of Tarshish. 10:26 **horses:** *or* cavalry.   10:26–29 *Cp. 2 Chr. 1:14–17; 9:25–28.*   10:28 **Kue:** *or* Cilicia.

magnification of Solomon's wisdom. *Sheba* was a region in Arabia, renowned for wisdom; see 4.30 n. **11:** *Almug wood:* sandalwood, used for ornamental carving and incense. **13:** The Ethiopian tradition of their king's descent from David is based on interpreting *whatever she desired* as including an heir. **14–29:** These verses indicate the sources and the uses of Solomon's great wealth. **28:** *Kue:* Cilicia, in southern Asia Minor.

11.1–43: Solomon's divine disfavor. This chapter is a special construction of the Deuteronomic historians. They balanced a positive view of Solomon as wise ruler and devout temple builder with a negative view of him as taking foreign wives, sponsoring foreign cults, and beginning the process of apostasy that was eventually daughter there were Moabite, Ammonite, Edomite, Sidonian, and Hittite women, [2] from the nations with whom the LORD had forbidden the Israelites to intermarry, 'because', he said, 'they will entice you to serve their gods'. But Solomon was devoted to them and loved them dearly. [3] He had seven hundred wives, all princesses, and three hundred concubines, and they influenced him, [4] for as he grew old, his wives turned his heart to follow other gods, and he did not remain wholly loyal to the LORD his God as his father David had been. [5] He followed Ashtoreth, goddess of the Sidonians, and Milcom, the loathsome god of the Ammonites. [6] Thus Solomon did what was wrong in the eyes of the LORD, and was not wholehearted in his loyalty to the LORD as his father David had been. [7] He built a shrine for Kemosh, the loathsome god of Moab, on the heights to the east of Jerusalem, and one for Milcom, the loathsome god of the Ammonites. [8] These things he did for the gods to whom all his foreign wives burnt offerings and made sacrifices.

[9] The LORD was angry with Solomon because his heart had turned away from the LORD the God of Israel, who had appeared to him twice [10] and had strictly commanded him not to follow other gods; but he disobeyed the LORD's command. [11] The LORD therefore said to Solomon, 'Because you have done this and have not kept my covenant and my statutes as I commanded you, I will tear the kingdom from you and give it to your servant. [12] Nevertheless, for the sake of your father David I will not do this in your day; I will tear it out of your son's hand. [13] Even so not the whole kingdom; I will leave him one tribe for the sake of my servant David and for the sake of Jerusalem, my chosen city.'

[14] The LORD raised up an adversary for Solomon, Hadad the Edomite, of the royal house of Edom. [15] At the time when David reduced Edom, his commander-in-chief Joab had destroyed every male in the country when he went into it to bury the slain. [16] He and the Israelite armies remained there for six months, until he had slain every male in Edom. [17] But Hadad, who was still a boy, fled the country with some of his father's Edomite servants; their goal was Egypt. [18] They set out from Midian, made their way to Paran, and, taking some men from there, came to Pharaoh king of Egypt, who assigned Hadad a house and maintenance and made him a grant of land. [19] Hadad found great favour with Pharaoh, who gave him in marriage a sister of his wife, Queen Tahpenes. [20] She bore him his son Genubath; Tahpenes weaned the child in Pharaoh's palace, and he lived there with Pharaoh's sons.

[21] When Hadad heard in Egypt that David rested with his forefathers and that his commander-in-chief Joab was also dead, he said to Pharaoh, 'Give me leave to go, so that I may return to my own country.' [22] 'What is it that you find wanting in my country', said Pharaoh, 'that you want to go back to your own?' 'Nothing,' replied Hadad, 'but do let me go.' [25] He remained an adversary for Israel all through Solomon's reign. This is the harm that Hadad caused: he maintained a stranglehold on Israel and became king of Edom.

[23] Another adversary God raised up against Solomon was Rezon son of Eliada, who had fled from his master Hadadezer king of Zobah. [24] He gathered men about him and became a captain of freebooters; he went to Damascus, occupied it, and became king there.

11:7 **Milcom:** *so Gk; Heb.* Molech.   11:22–26 *Verse 25 transposed to follow verse 22.*   11:25 **This:** *so Gk; Heb. obscure.* **maintained . . . on:** *so Syriac; Heb.* loathed. **Edom:** *so Gk; Heb.* Aram.   11:24 **freebooters:** *so Gk; Heb. adds* when David killed them. **he:** *so Gk; Heb.* they.

---

to undo Israel (compare Deut. 17.14–20; 7.1–4). The view here is that the apostasy resulting from his foreign wives arose only late in his reign. However, his son and successor Rehoboam was born of an Ammonite wife one year before Solomon came to the throne, for Rehoboam was forty-one (14.21) when he succeeded Solomon, who reigned forty years (11.42). Solomon married his Egyptian wife during the first twenty years of his reign (3.1; 6.1; 9.10). The Deuteronomic historians suggest that rebellions against Solomon reflected the LORD's abandoning him (vv. 14–40). **5–7:** *Milcom* is a variant of *melek,* "king," used as a name for the Ammonite god. These shrines remained for more than three hundred years; see 2 Kgs. 23.13. **13:** *David* and *Jerusalem* are the primary objects of interest in the Deuteronomic history. **14–25:** All that is known of *Hadad the Edomite* is related here. Though *Edom* was not a serious threat during Solomon's reign, a resistance group may have arisen there. **18:** The change of dynasties in Egypt (see 3.1 n.) almost certainly affected Solomon's political relations; see also v. 40. **23:** *Hadadezer:* see 2 Sam. 10.15–19. *Rezon* was probably only a rebellious

²⁶Jeroboam son of Nebat, one of Solomon's courtiers, an Ephrathite from Zeredah, whose widowed mother was named Zeruah, rebelled against the king. ²⁷This is the story of his rebellion. When Solomon built the Millo and closed the breach in the wall of the city of his father David, ²⁸he saw how the young man worked, for Jeroboam was a man of great ability, and the king put him in charge of all the labour-gangs in the tribal district of Joseph. ²⁹On one occasion when Jeroboam left Jerusalem, the prophet Ahijah from Shiloh met him on the road. The prophet was wearing a new cloak and, when the two of them were alone out in the open country, ³⁰Ahijah, taking hold of the new cloak he was wearing, tore it into twelve pieces, ³¹and said to Jeroboam, 'Take for yourself ten pieces, for the LORD the God of Israel has declared that he is about to tear the kingdom from the hand of Solomon and give you ten tribes. ³²But, says the LORD, one tribe will remain Solomon's, for the sake of my servant David and for the sake of Jerusalem, the city I have chosen out of all the tribes of Israel. ³³I shall do this because Solomon has forsaken me; he has bowed down before Ashtoreth goddess of the Sidonians, Kemosh god of Moab, and Milcom god of the Ammonites, and has not conformed to my ways. He has not done what is right in my eyes or observed my statutes and judgements as David his father did.

³⁴'Nevertheless I shall not take the whole kingdom from him, but shall maintain his rule as long as he lives, for the sake of my chosen servant David, who did observe my commandments and statutes. ³⁵But I shall take the kingdom, that is the ten tribes, from his son and give it to you. ³⁶To his son I shall give one tribe, that my servant David may always have a lamp burning before me in Jerusalem, the city which I chose to receive my name. ³⁷I shall appoint you to rule over all that you can desire, and to be king over Israel. ³⁸If you pay heed to all my commands, if you conform to my ways and do what is right in my eyes, observing my statutes and commandments as my servant David did, then I shall be with you. I shall establish your family for ever as I did for David; I shall give Israel to you, ³⁹and punish David's descendants as they have deserved, but not for ever.'

⁴⁰After this Solomon sought to kill Jeroboam, but he fled to King Shishak in Egypt and remained there till Solomon's death.

⁴¹The other acts and events of Solomon's reign, and all his wisdom, are recorded in the annals of Solomon. ⁴²The reign of King Solomon in Jerusalem over the whole of Israel lasted forty years. ⁴³Then he rested with his forefathers and was buried in the city of David his father; he was succeeded by his son Rehoboam.

The kingdom divided

12 REHOBOAM went to Shechem, for all Israel had gone there to make him king. ²When Jeroboam son of Nebat, who was still in Egypt, heard of it, he remained there, having taken refuge in Egypt to escape King Solomon. ³The people now recalled him, and he and all the assembly of Israel came to Rehoboam and said, ⁴'Your father laid a harsh yoke upon us; but if you will now lighten the harsh labour he imposed and the heavy yoke he laid on us, we shall serve you.'

11:33 **has forsaken ... has bowed down ... has not conformed:** *so Gk; Heb. has plural.* 12:1–19 *Cp. 2 Chr. 10:1–19.*

vassal of Solomon. **29–39:** Here appears the first instance of a pattern repeated throughout Kgs.: The LORD sends a prophet to announce in advance a change in dynasty, thus giving a divine sanction to the change and to the new dynasty. Thus, the northern dynasties of Jeroboam, Baasha, and Jehu had divine sanction; the dynasty of Omri did not, nor did any of the kings who ruled after the fall of the Jehu dynasty. This theory of legitimacy is presented in 14.7–11, 14; 15.25–29; 16.1–4, 9–12; 19.15–18; 21.17–22; 2 Kgs. 9.1–10; 10.30–31; 15.8–12. **30–32:** *Twelve* was the traditional number of the tribes; but by this time Judah had absorbed Simeon and the two were spoken of as only *one tribe.*

12.1–16.34 The first period of the two kingdoms. Here the compilers of Kgs. begin their parallel account of the two kingdoms. The sources drawn upon are the royal annals of Judah and Israel (14.19, 29) and collections of prophetic legends.

12.1–24: The division of two kingdoms. 1: David ruled over (north) Israel by covenant (2 Sam. 5.3); apparently their acceptance of that kingship had to be renewed at the beginning of each reign. **3:** More than

5'Give me three days,' he said, 'and then come back.'

When the people had gone, 6 King Rehoboam consulted the elders who had been in attendance during the lifetime of his father Solomon: 'What answer do you advise me to give to this people?' 7 They said, 'If today you are willing to serve this people, show yourself their servant now and speak kindly to them, and they will be your servants ever after.' 8 But he rejected the advice given him by the elders, and consulted the young men who had grown up with him, and were now in attendance; 9 he asked them, 'What answer do you advise me to give to this people's request that I should lighten the yoke which my father laid on them?' 10 The young men replied, 'Give this answer to the people who say that your father made their yoke heavy and ask you to lighten it; tell them: "My little finger is thicker than my father's loins. 11 My father laid a heavy yoke on you, but I shall make it heavier. My father whipped you, but I shall flay you." '

12 Jeroboam and the people all came to Rehoboam on the third day, as the king had ordered. 13 The king gave them a harsh answer; he rejected the advice which the elders had given him 14 and spoke to the people as the young men had advised: 'My father made your yoke heavy, but I shall make it heavier. My father whipped you, but I shall flay you.' 15 The king would not listen to the people; for the LORD had given this turn to the affair in order that the word he had spoken by Ahijah of Shiloh to Jeroboam son of Nebat might be fulfilled.

16 When all Israel saw that the king would not listen to them, they answered:

'What share have we in David?
We have no lot in the son of Jesse.
Away to your tents, Israel!
Now see to your own house, David!'

With that Israel went off to their homes. 17 Rehoboam ruled only over those Israelites who lived in the cities and towns of Judah.

18 King Rehoboam sent out Adoram, the commander of the forced levies, but when the Israelites stoned him to death, the king hastily mounted his chariot and fled to Jerusalem. 19 From that day to this Israel has been in rebellion against the house of David. 20 When the men of Israel heard that Jeroboam had returned, they sent and called him to the assembly and made him king over the whole of Israel. The tribe of Judah alone stayed loyal to the house of David.

21 When Rehoboam reached Jerusalem, he mustered the tribes of Judah and Benjamin, a hundred and eighty thousand chosen warriors, to fight against Israel and recover his kingdom. 22 But this word of God came to Shemaiah the man of God: 23 'Say to Rehoboam son of Solomon, king of Judah, and to all Judah and Benjamin and the rest of the people, 24 This is the word of the LORD: You are not to go up to make war on your kinsmen the Israelites. Return to your homes, for this is my doing.' They listened to the word of the LORD and went back, as the LORD had told them.

25 JEROBOAM rebuilt Shechem in the hill-country of Ephraim and took up residence there; from there he went out and built Penuel. 26 'As things now stand', he said to himself, 'the kingdom will revert to the house of David. 27 If these people go up to sacrifice in the house of the LORD in Jerusalem, it will revive their allegiance to their lord King Rehoboam of Judah, and they will kill me and return to King Rehoboam.' 28 After taking counsel about the matter he made two calves of gold and said to the people, 'You have gone up to Jerusalem long enough; here are your gods, Israel, that brought you up from Egypt.' 29 One he set up at Bethel and the other he put at Dan, 30 and this thing became a sin in Israel; the people went to Bethel to worship the one, and all the way to Dan to

12:21–24 *Cp. 2 Chr. 11:1–4.*   12:30 **in Israel ... one, and:** *so Gk (Luc.); Heb.* the people went.

one account of *Jeroboam* has been drawn upon; this verse conflicts with v. 20. **15:** *Ahijah:* see 11.29–39. **16:** See the similar summons in 2 Sam. 20.1. **19:** *From that day to this:* a formula not always used literally; see 8.8 n. **21–24:** A prophetic oracle forces *Rehoboam* to accept the division of the kingdoms.

12.25–33: Jeroboam's religious establishment. Jeroboam, to secure his kingdom, fortified *Shechem*, making it his capital city west of the Jordan, and then securing a similar military base east of the Jordan, at *Penuel* in Gilead. Dan and Bethel (vv. 29–30) were at the northern and southern extremes of his kingdom. **28:** Images of *calves* or bulls were associated with worship of the Canaanite deity Baal. Tradition also traced such an image worship the other. [31] He also erected temple buildings at shrines and appointed priests who did not belong to the Levites, from every class of the people. [32] He instituted a pilgrim-feast on the fifteenth day of the eighth month like that in Judah, and he offered sacrifices on the altar. This he did at Bethel, sacrificing to the calves that he had made and compelling the priests of the shrines, which he had set up, to serve at Bethel. [33] He went up on the fifteenth day of the eighth month to the altar that he had made at Bethel; there, in a month of his own choosing, he instituted for the Israelites a pilgrim-feast and himself went up to the altar to burn the sacrifice.

13 As Jeroboam stood by the altar to burn the sacrifice, a man of God from Judah, moved by the word of the LORD, appeared at Bethel. [2] He inveighed against the altar in the LORD's name, crying out, 'O altar, altar! This is the word of the LORD: Listen! To the house of David a child shall be born named Josiah. On you he will sacrifice the priests of the shrines who make offerings on you, and he will burn human bones on you.' [3] He gave a sign the same day: 'This is the sign which the LORD has ordained: This altar will be split asunder and the ashes on it will be scattered.' [4] When King Jeroboam heard the sentence which the man of God pronounced against the altar at Bethel, he pointed to him from the altar and cried, 'Seize him!' Immediately the hand which he had pointed at him became paralysed, so that he could not draw it back. [5] The altar too was split asunder and the ashes were scattered, in fulfilment of the sign that the man of God had given at the LORD's command. [6] The king appealed to the man of God to placate the LORD his God and pray for him that his hand might be restored. The man of God did as he asked; the king's hand was restored and became as it had been before. [7] He said to the man of God, 'Come home with me and have some refreshment, and let me give you a reward.' [8] But he answered, 'If you were to give me half your house, I would not enter it with you: I will eat and drink nothing in this place,

[9] for the LORD's command to me was to eat and drink nothing, and not to go back by the way I came.' [10] So he went back another way, not returning by the road he had taken to Bethel.

[11] At that time there was an aged prophet living in Bethel. His sons came and told him all that the man of God had done there that day, and what he had said to the king. [12] Their father asked, 'Which road did he take?' They pointed out the direction taken by the man of God who had come from Judah. [13] He said to his sons, 'Saddle the donkey for me.' They saddled the donkey, and, mounted on it, [14] he went after the man of God.

He came on him seated under a terebinth and asked, 'Are you the man of God who came from Judah?' 'I am,' he replied. [15] 'Come home and eat with me,' said the prophet. [16] 'I may not go back with you or enter your house,' said the other; 'I may neither eat nor drink with you in this place, [17] for it was told me by the word of the LORD: You are to eat and drink nothing there, nor are you to go back the way you came.' [18] The old man urged him, 'I also am a prophet, as you are; and an angel commanded me by the word of the LORD to bring you to my home to eat and drink with me.' He was lying; [19] but the man of Judah went back with him and ate and drank in his house. [20] While they were still seated at table the word of the LORD came to the prophet who had brought him back, [21] and he cried out to the man of God from Judah, 'This is the word of the LORD: You have defied the word of the LORD your God and have not obeyed his command; [22] you have gone back to eat and drink in the place where he forbade it; therefore your body will not be laid in the grave of your forefathers.'

[23] After the man of God had eaten and drunk, the prophet who had brought him back saddled the donkey for him. [24] As he rode on his way a lion met him and killed him, and his body was left lying in the road,

13:2 **he will burn:** *so Gk; Heb.* they will burn.
13:11 **His sons came:** *so Gk; Heb.* His son came.

---

to Aaron, however; see Exod. 32.1–6. Speaking of *gods* in the plural is intended to express an alien viewpoint. **31–33:** Besides the cultic objects and sanctuaries, Jeroboam established his own priesthood, his own pilgrim-feast (one month later than in Jerusalem; see 8.2 n.), and he himself offered the sacrifices.

13.1–34: The man of God from Judah. A prophetic legend reflects divine condemnation of Jeroboam's altar and anticipates Josiah's destruction of it over three hundred years later. **2:** See 2 Kgs. 23.15. **4–6:** On such prophetic miracles, compare 2 Kgs. 2.19–25; 4.38–44.

with the donkey and the lion both standing beside it. ²⁵ Some passers-by saw the body lying in the road and the lion standing beside it, and they brought the news to the town where the old prophet lived. ²⁶ When the prophet who had caused him to break his journey heard it, he said, 'It is the man of God who defied the word of the LORD. The LORD has given him to the lion, and it has broken his neck and killed him in fulfilment of the word of the LORD.' ²⁷ He told his sons to saddle the donkey and, when they did so, ²⁸ he set out and found the body lying in the road with the donkey and the lion standing beside it; the lion had neither devoured the body nor broken the back of the donkey. ²⁹ The prophet lifted the body of the man of God, laid it on the donkey, and brought it back to his own town to mourn over it and bury it. ³⁰ He laid the body in his own grave and they mourned for him, saying, 'Oh, my brother!' ³¹ After burying him, he said to his sons, 'When I die, bury me in the grave where the man of God lies buried; lay my bones beside his; ³² for the sentence which he pronounced at the LORD's command against the altar in Bethel and all the temples at shrines throughout Samaria will surely come true.'

³³ After this Jeroboam still did not abandon his evil ways, but went on appointing priests for the shrines from all classes of the people; any man who offered himself he would consecrate to be priest of a shrine. ³⁴ By doing this he brought guilt on his own house and doomed it to utter destruction.

14 At that time Jeroboam's son Abijah fell ill, ² and Jeroboam said to his wife, 'Go at once to Shiloh, but disguise yourself so that people will not recognize you as my wife. Ahijah the prophet is there, he who said I was to be king over this people. ³ Take with you ten loaves, some raisins, and a jar of honey. Go to him and he will tell you what will happen to the boy.' ⁴ Jeroboam's wife did so; she set off at once for Shiloh and came to Ahijah's house. Now as Ahijah could not see, for his eyes were fixed in the blindness of old age, ⁵ the LORD had said to him, 'Jeroboam's

wife is on her way to consult you about her son, who is ill; you are to give her such and such an answer.'

When she came in, concealing who she was, ⁶ and Ahijah heard her footsteps at the door, he said, 'Come in, wife of Jeroboam. Why conceal who you are? I have heavy news for you. ⁷ Go, tell Jeroboam: "This is the word of the LORD the God of Israel: I raised you out of the people and appointed you prince over my people Israel; ⁸ I tore the kingdom from the house of David and gave it to you. But you have not been like my servant David, who kept my commands and followed me with his whole heart, doing only what was right in my eyes. ⁹ You have outdone all your predecessors in wickedness; you have provoked me to anger by making for yourself other gods and images of cast metal; and you have turned your back on me. ¹⁰ For this I am going to bring disaster on the house of Jeroboam; I shall destroy them all, every mother's son, whether still under the protection of the family or not, and I shall sweep away the house of Jeroboam in Israel, as one sweeps away dung until none is left. ¹¹ Those of that house who die in the town shall be food for the dogs, and those who die in the country shall be food for the birds. It is the word of the LORD."

¹² 'Go home now; the moment you set foot in the town, the child will die. ¹³ All Israel will mourn for him and bury him; he alone of all Jeroboam's family will have proper burial, because in him alone could the LORD the God of Israel find anything good.

¹⁴ 'The LORD will set up a king over Israel who will put an end to the house of Jeroboam. This first; and what next? ¹⁵ The LORD will strike Israel, till it trembles like a reed in the water; he will uproot its people from this good land which he gave to their forefathers and scatter them beyond the Euphrates, because they have made their sacred poles, thus provoking the LORD's anger. ¹⁶ He will abandon Israel because of the sins that Jeroboam has committed and has led Israel to commit.'

14:14 **next:** *so Aram. (Targ.); Heb.* now.
14:15 **sacred poles:** *Heb.* asherim.

14.1–20: Prophetic condemnation of Jeroboam. This legend enhances the prophets (vv. 4–6, 12, 17); it is used here to convey a second stage of the Deuteronomic theory about northern kingship (vv. 7–11; compare 11.29–39 n.). **1:** *Jeroboam* sends to the prophet who had originally sanctioned his kingship (11.29–39). **11:** The stereotyped curse here means that no member of the family would have an honorable burial; compare v. 13. **14b–16:** This Deuteronomic comment anticipates the exile of the leading citizens of the Northern

17 Jeroboam's wife went away back to Tirzah and, as she crossed the threshold of the house, the boy died. 18 They buried him, and all Israel mourned over him; and thus the word of the LORD was fulfilled which he had spoken through his servant Ahijah the prophet.

19 The other events of Jeroboam's reign, in war and peace, are recorded in the annals of the kings of Israel. 20 After reigning for twenty-two years, he rested with his forefathers and was succeeded by his son Nadab.

21 In Judah Rehoboam son of Solomon had become king. He was forty-one years old when he came to the throne, and he reigned for seventeen years in Jerusalem, the city where the LORD had chosen, out of all the tribes of Israel, to set his name. Rehoboam's mother was a woman of Ammon called Naamah. 22 Judah did what was wrong in the eyes of the LORD, rousing his jealous indignation by the sins they committed, which were beyond anything that their forefathers had done. 23 They erected shrines, sacred pillars, and sacred poles on every high hill and under every spreading tree. 24 Worse still, all over the country there were male prostitutes attached to the shrines, and the people adopted all the abominable practices of the nations whom the LORD had dispossessed in favour of Israel.

25 In the fifth year of Rehoboam's reign King Shishak of Egypt attacked Jerusalem, 26 and carried away the treasures of the house of the LORD and of the king's palace; he seized everything, including all the gold shields made for Solomon. 27 King Rehoboam replaced them with bronze shields and entrusted them to the officers of the escort who guarded the entrance of the palace. 28 Whenever the king entered the house of the LORD, the escort carried them; afterwards they returned them to the guardroom.

29 The other acts and events of Rehoboam's reign are recorded in the annals of the kings of Judah. 30 There was continual fighting between him and Jeroboam. 31 He rested with his forefathers and was buried with them in the city of David. Rehoboam's mother was an Ammonite called Naamah. He was succeeded by his son Abijam.

15 In the eighteenth year of the reign of Jeroboam son of Nebat, Abijam became king of Judah. 2 He reigned in Jerusalem for three years; his mother was Maacah granddaughter of Abishalom. 3 All the sins that his father before him had committed he also committed, nor was he faithful to the LORD his God as his ancestor David had been. 4 But for David's sake the LORD his God gave him a lamp to burn in Jerusalem, by establishing his dynasty and making Jerusalem secure, 5 because David had done what was right in the eyes of the LORD and had not disobeyed any of his commandments all his life, except in the matter of Uriah the Hittite. 7 The other acts and events of Abijam's reign are recorded in the annals of the kings of Judah. There was war between Abijam and Jeroboam. 8 Abijam rested with his forefathers and was buried in the city of David; his son Asa succeeded him.

9 In the twentieth year of King Jeroboam of Israel, Asa became king of Judah. 10 He reigned in Jerusalem for forty-one years; his grandmother was Maacah granddaughter of Abishalom. 11 Asa did what was right in the eyes of the LORD, as his ancestor David had done. 12 He expelled from the land the male prostitutes attached to the shrines and removed all the idols which his predecessors had made. 13 He even deprived Maacah his grandmother of her rank as queen mother because she had an obscene object made for the worship of Asherah; Asa cut it down and burnt it in the wadi Kidron. 14 Although the shrines were allowed to remain, Asa himself

14:25–28 *Cp. 2 Chr. 12:9–11.* 14:29–31 *Cp. 2 Chr. 12:13–16.* 15:2 **granddaughter:** *lit.* daughter. 15:5 **except . . . Hittite:** *prob. rdg; Heb. adds* 6 There was war between Rehoboam and Jeroboam all his days *(cp. 14:30).* 15:10 **grandmother:** *lit.* mother. **granddaughter:** *lit.* daughter. 15:13–15 *Cp. 2 Chr. 15:16–18.*

Kingdom in 722 B.C.E. **17:** For an unknown reason Jeroboam had moved his capital to *Tirzah,* a few miles northeast of Shechem.

14.21–31: The reign of Rehoboam of Judah. The usual condemnation in Kgs. for cultic offenses is well illustrated here. **25–26:** On *Shishak,* first king of the twenty-second Egyptian dynasty, see 3.1 n. and 11.40. Shishak also conquered several cities in Israel at this time.

15.1–24: The reigns of Abijam and Asa in Judah. 1–8: *Abijam* was a son of *Maacah,* who is here identified as *granddaughter of Abishalom,* the latter probably David's son Absalom (see, on Maacah, 2 Sam. 3.3). This

remained faithful to the LORD all his life.
15 He brought into the house of the LORD all
his father's votive offerings and his own, the
silver and gold and the sacred vessels.

16 There was war between Asa and King
Baasha of Israel all through their reigns.
17 King Baasha invaded Judah and fortified
Ramah to prevent anyone leaving or entering the kingdom of Asa of Judah. 18 Asa took
all the silver and gold that remained in the
treasuries of the house of the LORD and the
palace, and sent his servants with them to
Ben-hadad son of Tabrimmon, son of He-
zion, king of Aram, whose capital was Damascus, with instructions to say, 19 'Let there
be an alliance between us, as there was between our fathers. Herewith I send you a
present of silver and gold; break off your
alliance with King Baasha of Israel, so that he
will abandon his campaign against me.'
20 Ben-hadad listened with approval to King
Asa; he ordered his army commanders to
move against the towns of Israel, and they
attacked Iyyon, Dan, Abel-beth-maacah, and
that part of Kinnereth which marches with
the land of Naphtali. 21 When Baasha heard
of it, he discontinued the fortifying of Ramah and fell back on Tirzah. 22 Then King
Asa issued a proclamation requiring every
man in Judah without exception to join in
removing the stones of Ramah and the timbers with which Baasha had fortified it, and
he used them to fortify Geba of Benjamin
and Mizpah.

23 All the other events of Asa's reign, his
exploits and achievements, and the towns he
built, are recorded in the annals of the kings
of Judah. But in his old age he was afflicted
with disease in his feet. 24 He rested with his
forefathers and was buried with them in the
city of his ancestor David; he was succeeded
by his son Jehoshaphat.

25 Nadab son of Jeroboam became king of
Israel in the second year of King Asa of Judah, and he reigned for two years. 26 He did
what was wrong in the eyes of the LORD and
followed in his father's footsteps, repeating
the sin which Jeroboam had led Israel to
commit. 27 Baasha son of Ahijah, of the house

of Issachar, conspired against him and attacked him at Gibbethon, a Philistine town
which Nadab was besieging with all his
forces. 28 Baasha slew him and usurped the
throne in the third year of King Asa of Judah. 29 As soon as he became king, he struck
down the whole family of Jeroboam, destroying every living soul and leaving not one survivor. Thus the word of the LORD was
fulfilled which he spoke through his servant
Ahijah the Shilonite. 30 This happened because of the sins of Jeroboam and the sins
which he led Israel to commit, and because
he had provoked the anger of the LORD the
God of Israel. 31 The other events of Nadab's
reign and all his acts are recorded in the
annals of the kings of Israel. 32 There was war
between Asa and King Baasha of Israel
throughout their reigns.

33 In the third year of King Asa of Judah,
Baasha son of Ahijah became king of all Israel in Tirzah and reigned for twenty-four
years. 34 He did what was wrong in the eyes
of the LORD and followed in Jeroboam's footsteps, repeating the sin which Jeroboam had
16 led Israel to commit. 1 This word of
the LORD against Baasha came to
Jehu son of Hanani: 2 'I raised you from the
dust and made you a prince over my people
Israel, but you have followed in the footsteps
of Jeroboam and have led my people Israel
into sin, so provoking me to anger with their
sins. 3 Therefore I am about to sweep away
Baasha and his house and deal with it as I
dealt with the house of Jeroboam son of Nebat. 4 Those of Baasha's family who die in a
town will be food for the dogs, and those who
die in the country will be food for the birds.'
5 The other events of Baasha's reign, his
achievements and his exploits, are recorded
in the annals of the kings of Israel. 6 Baasha
rested with his forefathers and was buried in
Tirzah; he was succeeded by his son Elah.

7 The word of the LORD concerning Baasha
and his family came also through the
prophet Jehu son of Hanani, because of all

15:17–22 *Cp. 2 Chr. 16:1–6,*   15:23–24 *Cp. 2 Chr.*
16:11–14.

Maacah was a woman of great influence; see vv. 11–13; 2 Chr. 13.2 n. **14:** *Asa* is the first of several Judean
kings who are approved of by the compilers, except that they did not remove the *shrines*. **16–24:** Once the
two Hebrew kingdoms were at odds rather than coordinated under one king, *Damascus* became an independent and threatening power in the northeast.

15.25–16.7: Nadab and Baasha of Israel. These two kings are treated in stereotyped terms; see 11.29–39 n.

the wrong that he had done in the eyes of the LORD, thereby provoking his anger: he had not only sinned like the house of Jeroboam, but had also brought destruction upon it.

8 In the twenty-sixth year of King Asa of Judah, Elah son of Baasha became king of Israel and he reigned in Tirzah for two years. 9 Zimri, who was in his service commanding half the chariotry, plotted against him. The king was in Tirzah drinking himself into insensibility in the house of Arza, comptroller of the household there, 10 when Zimri broke in, attacked and assassinated him, and made himself king. This took place in the twenty-seventh year of King Asa of Judah.

11 As soon as Zimri had become king and was enthroned, he struck down all the household of Baasha; he left him not a single mother's son alive, neither kinsman nor friend. 12 By destroying the whole household of Baasha he fulfilled the word of the LORD concerning Baasha, spoken through the prophet Jehu. 13 This was what came of all the sins which Baasha and his son Elah had committed and the sins into which they had led Israel, provoking the anger of the LORD the God of Israel with their worthless idols. 14 The other events and acts of Elah's reign are recorded in the annals of the kings of Israel.

15 In the twenty-seventh year of King Asa of Judah, Zimri reigned in Tirzah for seven days. At the time the army was investing the Philistine city of Gibbethon. 16 When the Israelite troops in the camp heard of Zimri's conspiracy and the murder of the king, there and then they made their commander Omri king of Israel by common consent. 17 Omri and his whole force then withdrew from Gibbethon and laid siege to Tirzah. 18 As soon as Zimri saw that the city had fallen, he retreated to the keep of the royal palace, set the

whole of it on fire over his head, and so perished. 19 This was what came of the sin he had committed by doing what was wrong in the eyes of the LORD and following in the footsteps of Jeroboam, repeating the sin into which he had led Israel. 20 The other events of Zimri's reign, and his conspiracy, are recorded in the annals of the kings of Israel.

21 Thereafter the people of Israel were split into two factions: one supported Tibni son of Ginath, determined to make him king; the other supported Omri. 22 Omri's party proved the stronger; Tibni lost his life, and Omri became king.

23 It was in the thirty-first year of King Asa of Judah that Omri became king of Israel and he reigned for twelve years, six of them in Tirzah. 24 He bought the hill of Samaria from Shemer for two talents of silver, and built a city on it which he named Samaria after Shemer the owner of the hill. 25 Omri did what was wrong in the eyes of the LORD; he outdid all his predecessors in wickedness. 26 He followed in the footsteps of Jeroboam son of Nebat, repeating the sins which he had led Israel to commit, so that they provoked the anger of the LORD their God with their worthless idols. 27 The other events of Omri's reign, and his exploits, are recorded in the annals of the kings of Israel. 28 So Omri rested with his forefathers and was buried in Samaria; he was succeeded by his son Ahab.

Ahab and Elijah

29 AHAB son of Omri became king of Israel in the thirty-eighth year of King Asa of Judah, and he reigned over Israel in Samaria for twenty-two years. 30 More than any of his predecessors he did what was wrong in the eyes of the LORD. 31 As if it were not enough for him to follow the sinful ways of Jeroboam

16.8–34: The establishment of the dynasty of Omri. Though this was the greatest dynasty of the north, its founder receives little attention from the Deuteronomic historians. 13: See 11.29–39 n. 15–20: The episode of *Zimri* was no more than a palace revolt. 21–22: The following six years witnessed a genuine civil war, which the compilers of Kgs. pass over in a phrase. 23–34: *Omri* and his son *Ahab* devised a new policy for the Northern Kingdom. Whereas the two Hebrew kingdoms had been at war with each other for fifty years after Solomon's death (14.30; 15.32), the dynasty of Omri made peace with the kingdom of Judah and even established a marriage tie between the two royal houses (2 Kgs. 8.26). The two kingdoms then collaborated in wars to dominate the kingdoms east of the Jordan (see 1 Kgs. ch. 22 and 2 Kgs. ch. 3), probably to control the inland trade routes. The policy of Omri and Ahab also included peaceful relations with the maritime power of Tyre, strengthened by the marriage of *Jezebel* to Ahab (16.31). This alliance introduced into Israel strong influences from the religious practices of Tyre, especially the worship of Baal. From the later historians' viewpoint, Baal worship was the worst kind of apostasy, and they judge the leading kings of the dynasty of son of Nebat, he took as his wife Jezebel daughter of King Ethbaal of Sidon, and went and served Baal; he prostrated himself before him ³² and erected an altar to him in the temple of Baal which he built in Samaria. ³³ He also set up a sacred pole; indeed he did more to provoke the anger of the LORD the God of Israel than all the kings of Israel before him.

³⁴ During Ahab's reign Hiel of Bethel rebuilt Jericho; laying its foundations cost him his eldest son Abiram, and the setting up of its gates cost him Segub his youngest son. Thus was fulfilled what the LORD had spoken through Joshua son of Nun.

17 Elijah the Tishbite from Tishbe in Gilead said to Ahab, 'I swear by the life of the LORD the God of Israel, whose servant I am, that there will be neither dew nor rain these coming years unless I give the word.' ² Then the word of the LORD came to him: ³ 'Leave this place, turn eastwards, and go into hiding in the wadi of Kerith east of the Jordan. ⁴ You are to drink from the stream, and I have commanded the ravens to feed you there.' ⁵ Elijah did as the LORD had told him: he went and stayed in the wadi of Kerith east of the Jordan, ⁶ and the ravens brought him bread and meat morning and evening, and he drank from the stream.

⁷ After a while the stream dried up, for there had been no rain in the land. ⁸ Then the word of the LORD came to him: ⁹ 'Go now to Zarephath, a village of Sidon, and stay there; I have commanded a widow there to feed you.' ¹⁰ He went off to Zarephath, and when he reached the entrance to the village, he saw a widow gathering sticks. He called to her, 'Please bring me a little water in a pitcher to drink.' ¹¹ As she went to fetch it, he called after her, 'Bring me, please, a piece of bread as well.' ¹² But she answered, 'As the LORD your God lives, I have no food baked, only a handful of flour in a jar and a little oil in a flask. I am just gathering two or three sticks to go and cook it for my son and myself before we die.' ¹³ 'Have no fear,' said Elijah; 'go and do as you have said. But first make me a small cake from what you have and bring it out to me, and after that make something for your son and yourself. ¹⁴ For this is the word of the LORD the God of Israel: The jar of flour will not give out, nor the flask of oil fail, until the LORD sends rain on the land.' ¹⁵ She went and did as Elijah had said, and there was food for him and her and her family for a long time. ¹⁶ The jar of flour did not give out, nor did the flask of oil fail, as the word of the LORD foretold through Elijah.

¹⁷ Afterwards the son of the woman, the owner of the house, fell ill and was in a very bad way, until at last his breathing stopped. ¹⁸ The woman said to Elijah, 'What made you interfere, you man of God? You came here to bring my sins to light and cause my son's death!' ¹⁹ 'Give me your son,' he said. He took

Omri accordingly (16.26, 30–33). **23–24:** A new capital city *Samaria* was to symbolize the new policy. **32:** *The temple of Baal* was certainly a part of Omri's original plan for the city (the city was less than six years old at the time of Omri's death). **34:** A direct reference to Josh. 6.26.

17.1–2 Kgs. 10.36: The religious crisis of the ninth century. During the two generations of the prophets Elijah and Elisha a sharp conflict of greatest importance arose between partisans of the LORD (Yahweh), the God of old Israel, and of the Baal, the god of Canaan and Phoenicia. Elijah led the fight for the LORD; Jezebel, the Phoenician wife of Ahab, Omri's son, with her group of prophets, fought for the Baal. The conflict led finally to the overthrow of the Omri dynasty. The account in Kgs. draws on a cycle of Elijah stories (1 Kgs. chs. 17–19, 21; 2 Kgs. ch. 1), a cycle of Elisha stories (2 Kgs. 2.1–8.15), more selections from royal annals (e.g. 1 Kgs. 22.39–53; 2 Kgs. 8.16–27), and historical narratives about Ahab's wars with Damascus (1 Kgs. chs. 20, 22) and Jehu's overthrow of the Omri dynasty (2 Kgs. chs. 9–10).

17.1–19.21: Elijah's work. A series of stories about Elijah relates the first stage of the overthrow of the dynasty of Omri. The parallels between Elijah and Moses, and between Elisha and Joshua, are deliberate. In chs. 17–19 three groups of materials have been combined: episodes concerning the drought that Elijah announced and ended (17.1–18.16, 41–46); the contest with the prophets of Baal on Mount Carmel (18.17–40); and the pilgrimage to Horeb, the mountain of God (ch. 19).

17.1–18.16: Elijah brings a severe drought. The issue was which of the two gods controls the rain. **1:** The compilers used only parts of their older source; hence the abruptness of the appearance of Elijah here. **2–16:** The drought soon leads to famine. Where the holy man goes, there is miraculous provision of food; compare 2 Kgs. 4.1–7. **17–24:** The *woman* thinks the holy man's presence causes punishment for her *sins*. Compare the boy from her arms and carried him up to the roof-chamber where his lodging was, and laid him on his bed. ²⁰He called out to the LORD, 'LORD my God, is this your care for the widow with whom I lodge, that you have been so cruel to her son?' ²¹Then he breathed deeply on the child three times and called to the LORD, 'I pray, LORD my God, let the breath of life return to the body of this child.' ²²The LORD listened to Elijah's cry, and the breath of life returned to the child's body, and he revived.

²³Elijah lifted him and took him down from the roof-chamber into the house, and giving him to his mother he said, 'Look, your son is alive.' ²⁴She said to Elijah, 'Now I know for certain that you are a man of God and that the word of the LORD on your lips is truth.'

18 Time went by, and in the third year the word of the LORD came to Elijah: 'Go, appear before Ahab, and I shall send rain on the land.' ²So Elijah went to show himself to Ahab.

At this time the famine in Samaria was at its height, ³and Ahab summoned Obadiah, the comptroller of his household, a devout worshipper of the LORD. ⁴When Jezebel massacred the prophets of the LORD, he had taken a hundred of them, hidden them in caves, fifty by fifty, and sustained them with food and drink. ⁵Ahab said to Obadiah, 'Let us go throughout the land to every spring and wadi; if we can find enough grass we may keep the horses and mules alive and not lose any of our animals.' ⁶They divided the land between them for their survey, Ahab himself going one way and Obadiah another.

⁷As Obadiah was on his journey, Elijah suddenly confronted him. Obadiah recognized Elijah and prostrated himself before him. 'Can it really be you, my lord Elijah?' he said. ⁸'Yes,' he replied, 'it is I. Go and tell your master that Elijah is here.' ⁹'What wrong have I done?' protested Obadiah. 'Why should you give me into Ahab's hands?

He will put me to death. ¹⁰As the LORD your God lives, there is no region or kingdom to which my master has not sent in search of you. If they said, "He is not here," he made that kingdom or region swear on oath that you could not be found. ¹¹Yet now you say, "Go and tell your master that Elijah is here." ¹²What will happen? As soon as I leave you, the spirit of the LORD will carry you away, who knows where? I shall go and tell Ahab, and when he fails to find you, he will kill me. Yet I, your servant, have been a worshipper of the LORD from boyhood. ¹³Have you not been told, my lord, what I did when Jezebel put the LORD's prophets to death, how I hid a hundred of them in caves, fifty by fifty, and kept them alive with food and drink? ¹⁴And now you say, "Go and tell your master that Elijah is here"! He will kill me.' ¹⁵Elijah answered, 'As the LORD of Hosts lives, whose servant I am, I swear that I shall show myself to him this day.' ¹⁶So Obadiah went to find Ahab and gave him the message, and Ahab went to confront Elijah.

¹⁷As soon as Ahab saw Elijah, he said to him, 'Is it you, you troubler of Israel?' ¹⁸'It is not I who have brought trouble on Israel,' Elijah replied, 'but you and your father's family, by forsaking the commandments of the LORD and following Baal. ¹⁹Now summon all Israel to meet me on Mount Carmel, including the four hundred and fifty prophets of Baal and the four hundred prophets of the goddess Asherah, who are attached to Jezebel's household.' ²⁰So Ahab sent throughout the length and breadth of Israel and assembled the prophets on Mount Carmel.

²¹Elijah stepped forward towards all the people there and said, 'How long will you sit on the fence? If the LORD is God, follow him; but if Baal, then follow him.' Not a word did they answer. ²²Then Elijah said, 'I am the

17:21 **breathed deeply:** *or* stretched himself.
18:5 **Let ... throughout:** *so Gk; Heb.* Go into.
18:21 **sit on the fence:** *lit.* bestride two branches.

---

2 Kgs. 4.18–37. **24:** The compilers were particularly interested in showing the power of *the word of the* LORD through the prophets. **18.3–4:** The intensity of the religious conflict is shown by the slaughtering of prophets on both sides (v. 40). **7–16:** *Elijah* had a reputation for elusiveness; *Obadiah* tactfully seeks assurance that he will remain.

18.17–46: The contest on Mount Carmel. 17–18: When *Ahab* introduced the worship of *Baal* into the Northern Kingdom he did not cease to worship the LORD; see 22.5–6. It was such religious tolerance or pluralism that *Elijah* was attacking. From Ahab's viewpoint, therefore, Elijah was a *troubler of Israel*. **19:** *Prophets* throughout these narratives usually means followers or disciples, living at court or in separate only prophet of the LORD still left, but there are four hundred and fifty prophets of Baal. 23 Bring two bulls for us. Let them choose one for themselves, cut it up, and lay it on the wood without setting fire to it, and I shall prepare the other and lay it on the wood without setting fire to it. 24 Then invoke your god by name and I shall invoke the LORD by name; the god who answers by fire, he is God.' The people all shouted their approval.

25 Elijah said to the prophets of Baal, 'Choose one of the bulls and offer it first, for there are more of you; invoke your god by name, but do not set fire to the wood.' 26 They took the bull provided for them and offered it, and they invoked Baal by name from morning until noon, crying, 'Baal, answer us'; but there was no sound, no answer. They danced wildly by the altar they had set up. 27 At midday Elijah mocked them: 'Call louder, for he is a god. It may be he is deep in thought, or engaged, or on a journey; or he may have gone to sleep and must be woken up.' 28 They cried still louder and, as was their custom, gashed themselves with swords and spears until the blood flowed. 29 All afternoon they raved and ranted till the hour of the regular offering, but still there was no sound, no answer, no sign of attention.

30 Elijah said to the people, 'Come here to me,' and they all came to him. He repaired the altar of the LORD which had been torn down. 31 He took twelve stones, one for each tribe of the sons of Jacob, him who was named Israel by the word of the LORD. 32 With these stones he built an altar in the name of the LORD, and dug a trench round it big enough to hold two measures of seed; 33 he arranged the wood, cut up the bull, and laid it on the wood. 34 Then he said, 'Fill four jars with water and pour it on the whole-offering and on the wood.' They did so; he said, 'Do it again.' They did it again; he said,

'Do it a third time.' They did it a third time, 35 and the water ran all round the altar and even filled the trench.

36 At the hour of the regular offering the prophet Elijah came forward and prayed, 'LORD God of Abraham, of Isaac, and of Israel, let it be known today that you are God in Israel and that I am your servant and have done all these things at your command. 37 Answer me, LORD, answer me and let this people know that you, LORD, are God and that it is you who have brought them back to their allegiance.' 38 The fire of the LORD fell, consuming the whole-offering, the wood, the stones, and the earth, and licking up the water in the trench. 39 At the sight the people all bowed with their faces to the ground and cried, 'The LORD is God, the LORD is God.' 40 Elijah said to them, 'Seize the prophets of Baal; let not one of them escape.' They were seized, and Elijah took them down to the Kishon and slaughtered them there in the valley.

41 Elijah said to Ahab, 'Go back now, eat and drink, for I hear the sound of heavy rain.' 42 He did so, while Elijah himself climbed to the crest of Carmel, where he bowed down to the ground and put his face between his knees. 43 He said to his servant, 'Go and look toward the west.' He went and looked; 'There is nothing to see,' he said. Seven times Elijah ordered him back, and seven times he went. 44 The seventh time he said, 'I see a cloud no bigger than a man's hand, coming up from the west.' 'Now go', said Elijah, 'and tell Ahab to harness his chariot and be off, or the rain will stop him.' 45 Meanwhile the sky grew black with clouds, the wind rose, and heavy rain began to fall. Ahab mounted his chariot and set off for Jezreel; 46 and the power of the LORD was on

18:32 measures: *the Heb. measure called seah.*
18:34 They did so: *so Gk; Heb. omits.*   18:43 and
seven . . . went: *so Gk; Heb. omits.*

communities; see e.g. 2 Kgs. 6.1–3. **21:** Ahab's policy was to avoid this alternative. **22:** *Elijah* was not *the only prophet of the LORD still left,* but he may have been the only one willing to come forward as such. **23–24:** The contest is cast in terms of a tradition about the holy fire of the altar; see Lev. 9.24; 1 Chr. 21.26; 2 Chr. 7.1–3; 2 Macc. 1.18–22. **26:** The dancing was a ritual action consisting of limping motions. **27:** This fierce satire may be even stronger if, as is likely, *engaged* is a euphemism for seeing to bodily needs. **28:** *Gashed themselves:* a ritual action done in an ecstatic state (compare Hos. 7.14), usually associated with mourning for the dead (Jer. 16.6), a practice forbidden to Israelites (Deut. 14.1). **29:** *The hour of the regular sacrifice* was roughly 3:00 P.M. **30–35:** Much symbolism is involved here; the *twelve stones* and twelve *jars* of *water,* and the complex of *altar* (land) and the *trench* (water) probably symbolize the cosmic order. **38:** *The fire of the LORD;* see vv. 23–24 n. **41–46:** The narrative of the drought, dropped at v. 16, is concluded here. **46:** The distance to

Elijah: he tucked up his robe and ran before Ahab all the way to Jezreel.

19 When Ahab told Jezebel all that Elijah had done and how he had put all the prophets to the sword, 2 she sent this message to Elijah, 'The gods do the same to me and more, unless by this time tomorrow I have taken your life as you took theirs.' 3 In fear he fled for his life, and when he reached Beersheba in Judah he left his servant there, 4 while he himself went a day's journey into the wilderness. He came to a broom bush, and sitting down under it he prayed for death: 'It is enough,' he said; 'now, LORD, take away my life, for I am no better than my fathers before me.' 5 He lay down under the bush and, while he slept, an angel touched him and said, 6 'Rise and eat.' He looked, and there at his head was a cake baked on hot stones, and a pitcher of water. He ate and drank and lay down again. 7 The angel of the LORD came again and touched him a second time, saying, 'Rise and eat; the journey is too much for you.' 8 He rose and ate and drank and, sustained by this food, he went on for forty days and forty nights to Horeb, the mount of God. 9 There he entered a cave where he spent the night.

The word of the LORD came to him: 'Why are you here, Elijah?' 10 'Because of my great zeal for the LORD the God of Hosts,' he replied. 'The people of Israel have forsaken your covenant, torn down your altars, and put your prophets to the sword. I alone am left, and they seek to take my life.' 11 To this the answer came: 'Go and stand on the mount before the LORD.' The LORD was passing by: a great and strong wind came, rending mountains and shattering rocks before him, but the LORD was not in the wind; and after the wind there was an earthquake, but the LORD was not in the earthquake; 12 and after the earthquake fire, but the LORD was not in the fire; and after the fire a faint murmuring sound. 13 When Elijah heard it, he wrapped his face in his cloak and went out and stood at the entrance to the cave. There came a voice: 'Why are you here, Elijah?' 14 'Because of my great zeal for the LORD the God of Hosts,' he replied. 'The people of Israel have forsaken your covenant, torn down your altars, and put your prophets to the sword. I alone am left, and they seek to take my life.'

15 The LORD said to him, 'Go back by way of the wilderness of Damascus, enter the city, and anoint Hazael to be king of Aram; 16 anoint also Jehu son of Nimshi to be king of Israel, and Elisha son of Shaphat of Abel-meholah to be prophet in your place. 17 Whoever escapes the sword of Hazael Jehu will slay, and whoever escapes the sword of Jehu Elisha will slay. 18 But I shall leave seven thousand in Israel, all who have not bowed the knee to Baal, all whose lips have not kissed him.'

19 Elijah departed and found Elisha son of Shaphat ploughing; there were twelve pair of oxen ahead of him, and he himself was with the last of them. As Elijah passed, he threw his cloak over him. 20 Elisha, leaving his oxen, ran after Elijah and said, 'Let me kiss my father and mother goodbye, and then I shall follow you.' 'Go back,' he replied; 'what have I done to prevent you?' 21 He followed him no farther but went home, took his pair of oxen, slaughtered them, and burnt the wooden yokes to cook the flesh, which he gave to the people to eat. He then followed Elijah and became his disciple.

20 KING Ben-hadad of Aram, having mustered all his forces, and taking with him thirty-two kings with their horses and chariots, marched up against Samaria to take it by siege and assault. 2 He sent envoys into the city to King Ahab of Israel to say, 'Hear what Ben-hadad says: 3 Your silver and

19:16 **son of Nimshi:** or grandson of Nimshi (cp. 2 Kgs. 9:2).

Jezreel was over fifteen miles.

19.1–21: Elijah at Mount Horeb. 1–4: *Elijah's* triumph was only momentary; *Jezebel* still has the balance of power. Elijah flees, therefore, and then falls into a mood of depression. **5–8:** *At his head . . . cake . . . and water:* on food and water in the wilderness, see Exod. chs. 16–17. **11–14:** Compare with the natural phenomena of Exod. ch. 19. **12:** The *faint murmuring sound:* possibly the experience of prophetic inspiration. **15–18:** A program and divine sanction are here provided for overthrowing the dynasty of Omri; see vv. 19–21; 2 Kgs. 8.7–15; 9.1–13. **19–21:** The third part of Elijah's three-fold commission (vv. 15–16) is carried out first.

20.1–43: Episodes of the Syrian wars. Verses 1–34 present Ahab in quite a different light from the Elijah materials (see 17.1–2 Kgs. 10.36 n.). Ahab is here a popular king supported by the prophets of the LORD. **1:**

gold are mine, your wives and fine children are mine.' [4] The king of Israel answered, 'As you say, my lord king, I and all that I have are yours.' [5] The envoys came again and said, 'Hear what Ben-hadad says: I demand that you hand over your silver and gold, your wives and your children. [6] This time tomorrow I shall send my servants to ransack your palace and your subjects' houses to take possession of everything you prize, and carry it off.'

[7] The king of Israel summoned all the elders of the land and said, 'You can see the man is bent on picking a quarrel; for I did not demur when he sent to claim my wives and my children, my silver and gold.' [8] The elders and people all answered, 'Do not listen to him; you must not consent.' [9] So he gave this reply to Ben-hadad's envoys: 'Say to my lord the king: I accepted your majesty's demands on the first occasion; but what you now ask I cannot do.' The envoys went away and reported to their master, [10] and Ben-hadad sent back word: 'The gods do the same to me and more, if enough dust is left in Samaria to provide a handful for each of my men.' [11] The king of Israel made reply, 'Tell him of the saying: "The time for boasting is after the battle."' [12] This message reached Ben-hadad while he and the kings were feasting in their quarters, and he at once ordered his men to position themselves for an attack on the city, and they did so.

[13] Meanwhile a prophet had come to King Ahab of Israel and announced, 'This is the word of the LORD: You see this great host? Today I shall give it into your hands and you will know that I am the LORD.' [14] 'Whom will you use for that?' asked Ahab. 'The LORD says: The young men who serve the district officers,' was the answer. 'Who will launch the attack?' asked the king. 'You,' said the prophet. [15] Then Ahab mustered these young men, two hundred and thirty-two all told, and behind them the people of Israel, seven thousand in all.

[16] They marched out at midday, while Ben-hadad and his allies, those thirty-two kings, were drinking themselves into insensibility in their quarters. [17] The young men sallied out first, and word was sent to Ben-hadad that men had come out of Samaria. [18] 'If they have come out for peace,' he said, 'take them alive; if for battle, take them alive.'

[19] With the army following behind them, the young men went out from the city; [20] each struck down his man, and the Aramaeans fled, with the Israelites in pursuit. Ben-hadad the king of Aram escaped on horseback with some of the cavalry. [21] The king of Israel advanced and captured the horses and chariots, inflicting a heavy defeat on the Aramaeans.

[22] The prophet came to the king of Israel and advised him, 'Build up your forces; you know what you must do. At the turn of the year the king of Aram will renew the attack.' [23] The ministers of the king of Aram gave him this advice: 'Their gods are gods of the hills; that is why they are too strong for us. Let us fight them in the plain, and then we shall have the upper hand. [24] What you must do is to relieve the kings of their command and appoint other officers in their place. [25] Raise another army like the one you have lost. Bring your cavalry and chariots up to their former strength, and then let us fight Israel in the plain; then assuredly we shall have the upper hand.' He listened to their advice and acted on it.

[26] At the turn of the year Ben-hadad mustered the Aramaeans and advanced to Aphek to launch their attack on Israel. [27] The Israelites too were mustered and formed into companies, and then went to meet the enemy. When the Israelites encamped opposite them, they seemed no better than a pair of new-born goats, while the Aramaeans covered the countryside. [28] The man of God came to the king of Israel and said, 'This is the word of the LORD: The Aramaeans may think that the LORD is a god of the hills and not a god of the valleys; but I shall give all this great host into your hands and you will know that I am the LORD.'

[29] They lay in camp opposite one another

20:16 **in their quarters:** *or* at Succoth.
20:21 **captured:** *so Gk; Heb.* destroyed.   20:23 **gods are gods:** *or* God is a god.

Minor rulers of small cities or tribes could be called *kings*. **2–9:** *Ahab* responds to *Ben-hadad's* demand with the formality proper to one king as vassal of another. Ben-hadad insists on more than formality, and Ahab is incited to serious resistance. **13–28:** The prophets are portrayed as playing a large role in the struggle against Damascus. **24–25:** The administration of the military force had to be made more professional; compare 4.7–19 n. **26:** In the next year, the battle is around *Aphek,* east of the Sea of Galilee. **29–30:** The numbers for seven days; on the seventh day battle was joined and the Israelites destroyed a hundred thousand of the Aramaean infantry in one day. ³⁰ The survivors fled to Aphek, into the citadel, and the city wall fell upon the twenty-seven thousand men who were left. Ben-hadad took refuge in the citadel, retreating into an inner room.

³¹ His attendants said to him, 'We have heard that the Israelite kings are men to be trusted. Let us therefore put sackcloth round our waists and wind rough cord round our heads and go out to the king of Israel. It may be that he will spare your life.' ³² So they fastened on the sackcloth and the cord, and went to the king of Israel and said, 'Your servant Ben-hadad pleads for his life.' 'My royal cousin,' he said, 'is he still alive?' ³³ The men, taking the word for a favourable omen, caught it up at once and said, 'Your cousin Ben-hadad, yes.' 'Go and fetch him,' he said. When Ben-hadad came out Ahab invited him into his chariot. ³⁴ Ben-hadad said to him, 'I shall give back the towns which my father took from your father, and you may establish for yourself a trading quarter in Damascus, as my father did in Samaria.' 'On these terms', said Ahab, 'I shall let you go.' So he granted him a treaty and let him go.

³⁵ One of a company of prophets, at the command of the LORD, ordered a certain man to strike him, but the man refused. ³⁶ 'Because you have not obeyed the LORD,' said the prophet, 'when you leave me a lion will attack you.' When the man left, a lion did come upon him and attack him. ³⁷ The prophet met another man and ordered him to strike him. This man struck and wounded him. ³⁸ The prophet went off, with a bandage over his eyes, and thus disguised waited by the wayside for the king. ³⁹ As the king was passing, he called out to him, 'Sir, I went into the thick of the battle, and a soldier came over to me with a prisoner and said, "Take charge of this fellow. If by any chance he gets away, your life will be forfeit, or you must pay a talent of silver." ⁴⁰ While I was busy with one thing and another, sir, he disappeared.' The king of Israel said to him, 'You have

passed sentence on yourself.' ⁴¹ At that the prophet tore the bandage from his eyes, and the king saw that he was one of the prophets. ⁴² He said to the king, 'This is the word of the LORD: Because you let that man go when I had put him under a ban, your life shall be forfeit for his life, your people for his people.' ⁴³ The king of Israel went off home and entered Samaria sullen and angry.

21 SOME time later there occurred an incident involving Naboth of Jezreel, who had a vineyard in Jezreel adjoining the palace of King Ahab of Samaria. ² Ahab made a proposal to Naboth: 'Your vineyard is close to my palace; let me have it for a garden, and I shall give you a better vineyard in exchange for it or, if you prefer, I shall give you its value in silver.' ³ But Naboth answered, 'The LORD forbid that I should surrender to you land which has always been in my family.' ⁴ Ahab went home sullen and angry because Naboth had refused to let him have his ancestral holding. He took to his bed, covered his face, and refused to eat. ⁵ When his wife Jezebel came in to him and asked, 'Why this sullenness, and why do you refuse to eat?' ⁶ he replied, 'I proposed that Naboth of Jezreel should let me have his vineyard at its value or, if he liked, in exchange for another; but he refused to let me have it.' ⁷ 'Are you or are you not king in Israel?' retorted Jezebel. 'Come, eat and take heart; I shall make you a gift of the vineyard of Naboth of Jezreel.'

⁸ She wrote letters in Ahab's name, sealed them with his seal, and sent them to the elders and notables of Naboth's city, who sat in council with him. ⁹ She wrote: 'Proclaim a fast and give Naboth the seat of honour among the people. ¹⁰ Opposite him seat two unprincipled rogues to charge him with cursing God and the king; then take him out and stone him to death.' ¹¹ The elders and notables of Naboth's city carried out the instructions Jezebel had sent them in her letter: ¹² they proclaimed a fast and gave Naboth the seat of honour. ¹³ The two unprincipled

21:10,13 **cursing:** *lit.* bidding farewell to.

---

are exaggerated. **32:** *My royal cousin:* not a family tie but their common royalty. **35–43:** Some prophets took a more hostile view of Ahab. **40:** The king must be induced to pass *sentence* on himself unwittingly; see 2 Sam. 12.1–6.

21.1–29: The crime of Naboth's vineyard. This story of the abuse of royal authority is the occasion for Elijah's condemnation of Ahab's dynasty. **3:** *Always been in my family:* by religious law Naboth could not permanently rogues came in, sat opposite him, and charged him publicly with cursing God and the king. He was then taken outside the city and stoned, 14 and word was sent to Jezebel that Naboth had been stoned to death.

15 As soon as Jezebel heard of the death of Naboth, she said to Ahab, 'Get up and take possession of the vineyard which Naboth refused to sell you, for he is no longer alive; Naboth of Jezreel is dead.' 16 On hearing that Naboth was dead, Ahab got up and went to the vineyard to take possession.

17 The word of the LORD came to Elijah the Tishbite: 18 'Go down at once to King Ahab of Israel, who is in Samaria; you will find him in Naboth's vineyard, where he has gone to take possession. 19 Say to him, "This is the word of the LORD: Have you murdered and seized property?" Say to him, "This is the word of the LORD: Where dogs licked the blood of Naboth, there dogs will lick your blood."' 20 Ahab said to Elijah, 'So you have found me, my enemy.' 'Yes,' he said, 'because you have sold yourself to do what is wrong in the eyes of the LORD. 21 I shall bring disaster on you; I shall sweep you away and destroy every mother's son of the house of Ahab in Israel, whether under protection of the family or not. 22 I shall deal with your house as I dealt with the house of Jeroboam son of Nebat and that of Baasha son of Ahijah, because you have provoked my anger and led Israel into sin.' 23 The LORD went on to say of Jezebel, 'Jezebel will be eaten by dogs near the rampart of Jezreel. 24 Of the house of Ahab, those who die in the city will be food for the dogs, and those who die in the country food for the birds.'

25 (Never was there a man who sold himself to do what is wrong in the LORD's eyes as Ahab did, and all at the prompting of Jezebel his wife. 26 He committed gross abominations in going after false gods, doing everything that had been done by the Amorites, whom the LORD dispossessed in favour of Israel.)

27 When Ahab heard Elijah's words, he tore his clothes, put on sackcloth, and fasted; he lay down in his sackcloth and went about moaning. 28 The word of the LORD came to Elijah the Tishbite: 29 'Have you seen how Ahab has humbled himself before me? Because he has thus humbled himself, I shall not bring disaster on his house in his own lifetime, but in that of his son.'

22 FOR three years there was no war between the Aramaeans and the Israelites. 2 In the third year King Jehoshaphat of Judah went down to visit the king of Israel, 3 who had said to his ministers, 'You know that Ramoth-gilead belongs to us, and yet we do nothing to recover it from the king of Aram'; 4 and to Jehoshaphat he said, 'Will you join me in attacking Ramoth-gilead?' Jehoshaphat replied, 'What is mine is yours: myself, my people, and my horses,' 5 but he said to the king of Israel, 'First let us seek counsel from the LORD.'

6 The king of Israel assembled the prophets, some four hundred of them, and asked, 'Shall I attack Ramoth-gilead or not?' 'Attack,' was the answer; 'the Lord will deliver it into your majesty's hands.' 7 Jehoshaphat asked, 'Is there no other prophet of the LORD here through whom we may seek guidance?' 8 'There is one more', the king of Israel answered, 'through whom we may seek guidance of the LORD, but I hate the man, because he never prophesies good for me, never anything but evil. His name is Micaiah son of Imlah.' Jehoshaphat exclaimed, 'My lord king, let no such word pass your lips!' 9 So the king of Israel called one of his eunuchs and told him to fetch Micaiah son of Imlah with all speed.

10 The king of Israel and King Jehoshaphat of Judah in their royal robes were seated on their thrones at the entrance to the gate of

21:20–21 **he said . . . LORD. I shall bring:** *or* he said. 'Because you . . . LORD, I am bringing.   21:23 **near the rampart of:** *or, with some MSS,* in the plot of ground at *(cp. 2 Kgs. 9:36).*   22:2–35 *Cp. 2 Chr. 18:2–34.*

alienate his land; see Lev. 25.10, 13. **13:** See Exod. 22.28. *Two* witnesses were required; see Deut. 17.6–7. **27–29:** The Deuteronomic historians offer Ahab's repentance as the reason the dynasty did not fall immediately.

22.1–40: Ahab's last campaign and Micaiah the prophet. The *king of Israel* is understood to be Ahab, although his name never appears in vv. 1–38. **1:** Assyrian records establish that Ahab was in alliance with *the Aramaeans* against the Assyrians at the battle of Qarqar in 853 B.C.E.; later in 853 Israel and Damascus were again at war. **2:** On *Jehoshaphat,* see vv. 41–53 n. **3:** *Ramoth-gilead* was the key to control of important trade routes in northern Transjordan. **6:** The issue here is between true and false prophets of Yahweh (unlike

Samaria, and all the prophets were prophesying before them. ¹¹One of them, Zedekiah son of Kenaanah, made himself iron horns and declared, 'This is the word of the LORD: With horns like these you will gore the Aramaeans and make an end of them.' ¹²In the same vein all the prophets prophesied, 'Attack Ramoth-gilead and win the day; the LORD will deliver it into your hands.'

¹³The messenger sent to fetch Micaiah told him that the prophets had unanimously given the king a favourable answer. 'And mind you agree with them,' he added. ¹⁴'As the LORD lives,' said Micaiah, 'I shall say only what the LORD tells me to say.' ¹⁵When he came into the king's presence, the king asked, 'Micaiah, shall I attack Ramoth-gilead, or shall I refrain?' 'Attack and win the day,' he replied; 'the LORD will deliver it into your hands.' ¹⁶'How often must I adjure you', said the king, 'to tell me nothing but the truth in the name of the LORD?' ¹⁷Then Micaiah said,

'I saw all Israel scattered on the
    mountains,
like sheep without a shepherd;
and I heard the LORD say, "They have
    no master;
let them go home in peace." '

¹⁸The king of Israel said to Jehoshaphat, 'Did I not tell you that he never prophesies good for me, never anything but evil?' ¹⁹Micaiah went on, 'Listen now to the word of the LORD: I saw the LORD seated on his throne, with all the host of heaven in attendance on his right and on his left. ²⁰The LORD said, "Who will entice Ahab to go up and attack Ramoth-gilead?" One said one thing and one said another, ²¹until a spirit came forward and, standing before the LORD, said, "I shall entice him." ²²"How?" said the LORD. "I shall go out", he answered, "and be a lying spirit in the mouths of all his prophets." "Entice him; you will succeed," said the LORD. "Go and do it." ²³You see, then, how the LORD has put a lying spirit in the mouths of all these prophets of yours, because he has decreed disaster for you.'

²⁴At that, Zedekiah son of Kenaanah came

up to Micaiah and struck him in the face: 'And how did the spirit of the LORD pass from me to speak to you?' he demanded. ²⁵Micaiah retorted, 'That you will find out on the day when you run into an inner room to hide.' ²⁶The king of Israel ordered Micaiah to be arrested and committed to the custody of Amon the governor of the city and Joash the king's son. ²⁷'Throw this fellow into prison,' he said, 'and put him on a prison diet of bread and water until I come home in safety.' ²⁸Micaiah declared, 'If you do return in safety, the LORD has not spoken by me.'

²⁹The king of Israel and King Jehoshaphat of Judah marched on Ramoth-gilead. ³⁰The king of Israel went into battle in disguise, for he had said to Jehoshaphat, 'I shall disguise myself to go into battle, but you must wear your royal robes.' ³¹The king of Aram had ordered the thirty-two captains of his chariots not to engage all and sundry, but the king of Israel alone. ³²When the captains saw Jehoshaphat, they thought he was the king of Israel and turned to attack him, but Jehoshaphat cried out, ³³and when the captains saw that he was not the king of Israel, they broke off the attack on him. ³⁴One man, however, drew his bow at random and hit the king of Israel where the breastplate joins the plates of the armour. The king said to his driver, 'Turn about and take me out of the line; I am wounded.' ³⁵When the day's fighting reached its height, the king was facing the Aramaeans, propped up in his chariot, and the blood from his wound flowed down to the floor of the chariot; and in the evening he died. ³⁶At sunset the herald went through the ranks, crying, 'Every man to his city, every man to his country.' ³⁷Thus the king died. He was brought to Samaria and buried there. ³⁸The chariot was swilled out at the pool of Samaria where the prostitutes washed themselves, and dogs licked up the blood, in fulfilment of the word the LORD had spoken.

³⁹The other acts and events of Ahab's reign, the palace he decorated with ivory and all the towns he built, are recorded in the

22:15 I: *so Gk; Heb.* we.   22:26 **son:** *or* deputy.
22:28 **by me:** *so Gk; Heb. adds* and he said, 'Listen, peoples, all together.'

18.17–40, where it is between Yahweh and Baal). **11:** *Horns:* symbols of military power; see Deut. 33.17; Zech. 1.18–21. Compare Jeremiah's dramatic action in Jer. chs. 27–28. **17–23:** Micaiah's speech is an effort to dissuade the king, not simply to prophesy his death. **19:** Compare Isa. ch. 6. **20–23:** This is one of several instances of the theme of divine enticement to sin or disaster; compare 2 Sam. 24.1; 1 Chr. 21.1. **38:** If by *the* annals of the kings of Israel. ⁴⁰ Ahab rested with his forefathers and was succeeded by his son Ahaziah.

⁴¹ Jehoshaphat son of Asa had become king of Judah in the fourth year of King Ahab of Israel. ⁴² He was thirty-five years old when he came to the throne, and he reigned in Jerusalem for twenty-five years; his mother was Azubah daughter of Shilhi. ⁴³ He followed in the footsteps of Asa his father and did not deviate from them; he did what was right in the eyes of the LORD. But the shrines were allowed to remain; the people continued to sacrifice and burn offerings there. ⁴⁴ Jehoshaphat remained at peace with the king of Israel. ⁴⁵ The other events of Jehoshaphat's reign, his exploits and his wars, are recorded in the annals of the kings of Judah. ⁴⁶ He expelled from the land such of the male prostitutes attached to the shrines as were still left from the days of Asa his father.

⁴⁷ There was no king in Edom, only a viceroy of Jehoshaphat; ⁴⁸ he built merchantmen to sail to Ophir for gold, but they never made the voyage because they were wrecked at Ezion-geber. ⁴⁹ Ahaziah son of Ahab proposed to Jehoshaphat that his men should go to sea with Jehoshaphat's; but Jehoshaphat would not agree.

⁵⁰ Jehoshaphat rested with his forefathers and was buried with them in the city of David his father; he was succeeded by his son Joram.

⁵¹ Ahaziah son of Ahab became king of Israel in Samaria in the seventeenth year of King Jehoshaphat of Judah, and reigned over Israel for two years. ⁵² He did what was wrong in the eyes of the LORD, following in the footsteps of his father and mother and in those of Jeroboam son of Nebat, who had led Israel into sin. ⁵³ He served Baal and worshipped him, and provoked the anger of the LORD the God of Israel, as his father had done.

22:41–43 *Cp. 2 Chr. 20:31–33.*   22:43 **But . . . there:** *verse 44 in Heb.*   22:47 **only:** *prob. rdg; Heb. omits.*   22:48 **merchantmen:** *lit. ships of Tarshish.*

word of the LORD 21.21–24 is meant, the details are treated rather loosely. **39:** As with Omri (16.8–34 n.), much of Ahab's activity is quickly passed over, in keeping with the compilers' bent.

22.41–53: Jehoshaphat of Judah and Ahaziah of Israel. Jehoshaphat was the first new king of Judah after the dynasty of Omri came to power in Israel. He cooperated with Omri's and Ahab's master policy to control Syria-Palestine (see 16.23–34 n.), and accordingly married his son and heir to Ahab's daughter Athaliah (2 Kgs. 8.16–18, 25–28) and cooperated with the military campaigns of Ahab (vv. 1–38) and his successors (2 Kgs. ch. 3). **43–46:** Jehoshaphat's open collaboration with the Northern Kingdom does not preclude his approval by the historian. **50–53:** On *Ahaziah,* see 2 Kgs. ch. 1.

THE SECOND BOOK OF
Kings

Second Kings is not actually a second book but the continuation of 1 Kings. Here, the violations of the requirements of the LORD lead to the end which the Deuteronomic historian sees as inevitable: the fall of Israel (ch. 17) and of Judah (ch. 25). See the Introduction to 1 Kings.

Elisha and the house of Ahab

1 AFTER Ahab's death Moab rebelled against Israel.

2 When Ahaziah fell through a latticed window in his roof-chamber in Samaria and injured himself, he sent messengers to enquire of Baal-zebub the god of Ekron whether he would recover from this injury. 3 The angel of the LORD ordered Elijah the Tishbite to go and meet the messengers of the king of Samaria and say to them, 'Is there no God in Israel, that you go to consult Baal-zebub the god of Ekron? 4 For what you have done the word of the LORD to your master is this: You will not rise from the bed where you are lying; you will die.' With that Elijah departed.

5 When the messengers returned to the king, he asked them why they had come back. 6 They answered that a man had come to meet them and had ordered them to return to the king who had sent them and say, 'This is the word of the LORD: Is there no God in Israel, that you send to enquire of Baal-zebub the god of Ekron? In consequence, you will not rise from the bed where you are lying; you will die.' 7 The king asked them what kind of man it was who had come to meet them and given them this message. 8 'A hairy man', they answered, 'with a leather belt round his waist.' 'It is Elijah the Tishbite,' said the king.

9 The king sent a captain with his company of fifty men to Elijah. He went up to the prophet, who was sitting on a hilltop, and said, 'Man of God, the king orders you to come down.' 10 Elijah answered, 'If I am a man of God, may fire fall from heaven and consume you and your company!' Fire fell from heaven and consumed the officer and his fifty men.

11 The king sent another captain of fifty with his company, and he went up and said to the prophet, 'Man of God, this is the king's command: Come down at once.' 12 Elijah answered, 'If I am a man of God, may fire fall from heaven and consume you and your company!' Fire from God fell from heaven and consumed the man and his company.

13 The king sent the captain of a third company with his fifty men, and this third captain went up the hill to Elijah and knelt down before him. 'Man of God,' he pleaded, 'consider me and these fifty servants of yours, and have some regard for our lives. 14 Fire fell from heaven and consumed the other two captains of fifty and their companies; but now have regard for my life.' 15 The angel of the LORD said to Elijah, 'Go down with him; do not be afraid.' At that he rose and went down with him to the king, 16 to whom he said, 'This is the word of the LORD: You have sent to consult Baal-zebub the god of Ekron. Is that because there is no God in Israel you could consult? For what you have done you will not rise from the bed where you are ly-

1:11 **went up:** *so Gk (Luc.); Heb.* answered.

1.1–10.36: The climax of the religious crisis. Further materials (chs. 1–2; 8–10) relevant to the religious crisis of the ninth century are arranged around a collection of miracle stories about Elisha (chs. 3–7). See 1 Kgs. 17.1–2 Kgs. 10.36 n.

1.1–18: Elijah condemns Ahaziah. Two prophetic legends (vv. 2–8, 16–17 and vv. 9–15) are merged; compare vv. 9–15 with 1 Sam. 19.18–24 and vv. 2–8, 16–17 with 1 Kgs. 14.1–18. **1:** This verse, here apparently misplaced by a copyist, is repeated in 3.5. **2:** *Baal-zebub*, meaning "lord of flies," is a distorted, contemptuous alteration of Baal-zebul, "Baal the Prince." **9–14:** *Elijah* has heavenly fire at his disposal; Samuel, ing; you will die.' 17 Ahaziah's death fulfilled the word of the LORD which Elijah had spoken. Because Ahaziah had no son, his brother Jehoram succeeded him; that was in the second year of Joram son of King Jehoshaphat of Judah.

18 The other events of Ahaziah's reign are recorded in the annals of the kings of Israel.

2 When the LORD was about to take Elijah up to heaven in a whirlwind, Elijah and Elisha had set out from Gilgal. 2 Elijah said to Elisha, 'Stay here; for the LORD has sent me to Bethel.' Elisha replied, 'As the LORD lives, your life upon it, I shall not leave you.' They went down country to Bethel, 3 and there a company of prophets came out to Elisha and said to him, 'Do you know that the LORD is going to take your lord and master from you today?' 'I do know,' he replied; 'say nothing.'

4 Elijah said to him, 'Stay here, Elisha; for the LORD has sent me to Jericho.' He replied, 'As the LORD lives, your life upon it, I shall not leave you.' So they went to Jericho, 5 and there a company of prophets came up to Elisha and said to him, 'Do you know that the LORD is going to take your lord and master from you today?' 'I do know,' he replied; 'say nothing.'

6 Then Elijah said to him, 'Stay here; for the LORD has sent me to the Jordan.' The other replied, 'As the LORD lives, your life upon it, I shall not leave you.' So the two of them went on. 7 Fifty of the prophets followed, and stood watching from a distance as the two of them stopped by the Jordan. 8 Elijah took his cloak, rolled it up, and struck the water with it. The water divided to right and left, and both crossed over on dry ground.

9 While they were crossing, Elijah said to Elisha, 'Tell me what I can do for you before I am taken from you.' Elisha said, 'Let me inherit a double share of your spirit.' 10 'You have asked a hard thing,' said Elijah. 'If you see me taken from you, your wish will be granted; if you do not, it will not be granted.'

11 They went on, talking as they went, and suddenly there appeared a chariot of fire and horses of fire, which separated them from one another, and Elijah was carried up to heaven in a whirlwind. 12 At the sight Elisha cried out, 'My father, my father, the chariot and the horsemen of Israel!' and he saw him no more.

He clutched hold of his mantle and tore it in two. 13 He picked up the cloak which had fallen from Elijah, and went back and stood on the bank of the Jordan. 14 There he struck the water with Elijah's cloak, saying as he did so, 'Where is the LORD, the God of Elijah?' As he too struck the water, it divided to right and left, and he crossed over.

15 The prophets from Jericho, who were watching, said, 'The spirit of Elijah has settled on Elisha.' They came to meet him, bowed to the ground before him, 16 and said, 'Your servants have fifty stalwart men. Let them go and search for your master; perhaps the spirit of the LORD has lifted him up and cast him on some mountain or into some valley.' But he said, 'No, you must not send them.' 17 They pressed him, however, until he had not the heart to refuse. So they sent out the fifty men but, though they searched for three days, they did not find him. 18 When they came back to Elisha, who had remained at Jericho, he said to them, 'Did I not tell you not to go?'

19 The people of the city said to Elisha, 'Lord, you can see how pleasantly situated our city is, but the water is polluted and the country is sterile.' 20 He said, 'Fetch me a new, unused bowl and put salt in it.' When they had brought it, 21 he went out to the spring and, throwing the salt into it, he said, 'This is the word of the LORD: I purify this water. It shall no longer cause death or sterility.' 22 The water has remained pure till this day, in fulfilment of Elisha's word.

23 From there he went up to Bethel and, as

1:17 **his brother:** *so Gk (Luc.); Heb. omits.*

---

in a similar situation, employed only prophetic ecstasy, 1 Sam. 19.18–24. **17:** The Deuteronomic emphasis on the fulfillment of the prophetic *word* continues; see also 1 Kgs. 17.24. The chronological data of 1.17 and 3.1 are inconsistent.

2.1–25: Elisha succeeds Elijah. Elijah is taken up by God in the same geographical locale in which Moses was buried (see Deut. 34.5–6), and Elisha recrosses the Jordan even as Joshua led Israel across; compare vv. 13–15 with Josh. 3.9–4.14. **2:** This *Gilgal* was in Ephraim, different from the one near Jericho. **3:** *A company of prophets:* see 1 Kgs. 18.19 n. **19–25:** These two miracle stories are brief versions of the types that appear in chs. 4–7. These legends stress the power and holiness of the prophet, occasionally even (v. 24) at the cost of humaneness.

he was on his way, some small boys came out of the town and jeered at him, saying, 'Get along with you, bald head, get along.' ²⁴ He turned round, looked at them, and cursed them in the name of the Lord; and two she-bears came out of a wood and mauled forty-two of them. ²⁵ From there he went on to Mount Carmel, and thence back to Samaria.

3 In the eighteenth year of King Jehoshaphat of Judah, Jehoram son of Ahab became king of Israel in Samaria, and he reigned for twelve years. ² He did what was wrong in the eyes of the Lord, though not as his father and his mother had done; he did remove the sacred pillar of the Baal which his father had made. ³ Yet he persisted in the sins into which Jeroboam son of Nebat had led Israel, and did not give them up.

⁴ King Mesha of Moab was a sheep-breeder, and he had to supply the king of Israel regularly with the wool of a hundred thousand lambs and a hundred thousand rams. ⁵ When Ahab died, the king of Moab rebelled against the king of Israel, ⁶ and King Jehoram marched out from Samaria and mustered all Israel. ⁷ He also sent this message to King Jehoshaphat of Judah: 'The king of Moab has rebelled against me. Will you join me in a campaign against Moab?' 'I will join you,' he replied; 'what is mine is yours: myself, my people, and my horses.' ⁸ 'From which direction shall we attack?' he asked. 'Through the wilderness of Edom,' replied the other.

⁹ The king of Israel set out with the king of Judah and the king of Edom, and when they had been seven days on the indirect route they were following, they had no water left for the army or their pack-animals. ¹⁰ The king of Israel cried, 'Alas, the Lord has brought together three kings, only to put us at the mercy of the Moabites.' ¹¹ Jehoshaphat said, 'Is there not a prophet of the Lord here through whom we may seek the Lord's guidance?' One of the officers of the king of Israel answered, 'Elisha son of Shaphat is here, the man who poured water on Elijah's hands.' ¹² 'The word of the Lord is with him,' said Jehoshaphat. When the king of Israel and Jehoshaphat and the king of Edom went down to Elisha, ¹³ he said to the king of Israel, 'Why do you come to me? Go to your father's prophets or your mother's.' 'No,' answered the king of Israel; 'it is the Lord who has called us three kings out to put us at the mercy of the Moabites.' ¹⁴ 'As the Lord of Hosts lives, whom I serve,' said Elisha, 'I would not spare a look or a glance for you, if it were not for my regard for King Jehoshaphat of Judah. ¹⁵ But now fetch me a minstrel'; and while the minstrel played, the power of the Lord came on Elisha, ¹⁶ and he said, 'This is the word of the Lord: Pools will form all over this wadi. ¹⁷ The Lord has decreed that you will see neither wind nor rain, yet this wadi will be filled with water for you and your army and your pack-animals to drink. ¹⁸ That is a mere trifle in the sight of the Lord; what he will also do is to put Moab at your mercy. ¹⁹ You will raze to the ground every fortified town and every noble city; you will cut down all their fine trees; you will stop up all the springs of water; and you will spoil every good piece of land by littering it with stones.' ²⁰ In the morning at the hour of the regular offering they saw water flowing in from the direction of Edom, and the land was flooded.

²¹ Meanwhile all Moab had heard that the kings had come up to wage war against them, and every man, young and old, who could bear arms was called out and stationed on the frontier. ²² When they got up next morning and the sun was shining over the water, the Moabites saw the water in front of them red like blood ²³ and cried out, 'It is blood! The kings must have quarrelled and attacked one another. Now to the plunder, Moab!' ²⁴ But when they came to the Israelite camp, the Israelites sallied out and attacked them, driving the Moabites in headlong flight. The Israelites pushed forward into Moab, destroying as they went. ²⁵ They razed the towns to the ground; they littered every good

3:17 **army:** *so Gk (Luc.); Heb.* cattle.   3:24 **pushed . . . into:** *so Gk; Heb.* destroyed.

3.1–27: Israel's campaign against Mesha of Moab. In the alliance of Israel and Judah that was a part of Omri's policy (see 1 Kgs. 16.23–34 n.), Judah dominated Edom (1 Kgs. 22.47) while Israel dominated Moab (vv. 4–5), and the two cooperated in maintaining their dominance. **2:** *The sacred pillar* Jehoram removed was presumably in Samaria. **5:** A Moabite account of the successful revolt by *Mesha,* carved in stone, was discovered in 1868. **7:** See similar words in 1 Kgs. 22.4. **8:** The strategy was to circle the south side of the Dead Sea. **15:** The *minstrel* suggests the use of music to induce the ecstatic state in which the *power of the Lord* was experienced. **22:**

piece of land with stones, each man casting a stone on it; they stopped up every spring of water; they cut down all the fine trees; and they harried Moab until only in Kir-hareseth were any buildings left standing, and even this city the slingers surrounded and attacked.

26 When the Moabite king saw that the war had gone against him, he took with him seven hundred men armed with swords to cut a way through to the king of Aram, but the attempt failed. 27 Then he took his eldest son, who would have succeeded him, and offered him as a whole-offering on the city wall. There was such great consternation among the Israelites that they struck camp and returned to their own land.

4 The wife of one of the prophets appealed to Elisha. 'My husband, your servant, has died,' she said, 'and you know that he was a man who feared the LORD. Now a creditor has come to take away my two boys as slaves.' 2 Elisha asked her, 'How can I help you? Tell me what you have in the house.' 'Nothing at all,' she answered, 'except a flask of oil.' 3 'Go out', he said, 'and borrow vessels from everyone in the neighbourhood; get as many empty ones as you can. 4 When you come home, shut yourself in with your sons; then pour from the flask into all the vessels and, as they are filled, set them aside.' 5 She left him and shut herself indoors with her sons. As they brought her the vessels she filled them. 6 When they were all full, she said to one of her sons, 'Bring me another.' 'There are none left,' he replied. Then the flow of oil ceased. 7 She came out and told the man of God, and he said, 'Go, sell the oil and pay off your debt, and you and your sons can live on what is left.'

8 IT happened once that Elisha went over to Shunem. There was a well-to-do woman there who pressed him to accept hospitality, and afterwards whenever he came that way, he stopped there for a meal. 9 One day she said to her husband, 'I know that this man who comes here regularly is a holy man of God. 10 Why not build up the wall to make him a small roof-chamber, and put in it a bed, a table, a seat, and a lamp, and let him stay there whenever he comes to us?'

11 One time when he arrived there and went to this roof-chamber to lie down, 12 he said to Gehazi, his servant, 'Call this Shunammite woman.' When he called her and she appeared before the prophet, 13 Elisha said to his servant, 'Say to her, "You have taken all this trouble for us. What can I do for you? Shall I speak for you to the king or to the commander-in-chief?"' But she replied, 'I am content where I am, among my own people.' 14 He said, 'Then what can be done for her?' Gehazi said, 'There is only this: she has no child and her husband is old.' 15 'Call her back,' Elisha said. When she was called and appeared in the doorway, 16 he said, 'In due season, this time next year, you will have a son in your arms.' But she said, 'No, no, my lord, you are a man of God and would not lie to your servant.' 17 Next year in due season the woman conceived and bore a son, as Elisha had foretold.

18 When the child was old enough, he went out one day to his father among the reapers. 19 All of a sudden he cried out to his father, 'Oh, my head, my head!' His father told a servant to carry the child to his mother, 20 and when he was brought to her, he sat on her lap till midday, and then he died. 21 She went up, laid him on the bed of the man of God, shut

3:25 **and . . . Moab:** *so Gk (Luc.); Heb. omits.*
3:26 **Aram:** *so Old Latin; Heb. Edom.*

The *red* seen by *the Moabites* arises from the red sandstone common in Edom. **25:** Elisha's prophecy (v. 19) is nearly fulfilled here, but the Israelites do not gain final victory. **26:** *The king of Aram* (Damascus) was always interested in aiding rebels against Israel. **27:** The sacrifice of a prince was a last extreme step. On human sacrifice see Exod. 22.29–30; Judg. 11.30–39; 1 Kgs. 16.34.

4.1–8.6: Various miracles of Elisha. This collection of stories (see also 2.19–25) magnifies the prophetic power of Elisha. Not until the Gospels does a comparable collection of miracle stories appear in biblical literature.

4.1–37: Elisha's prophetic powers. 1–7: This story is parallel to Elijah's first miracle during the drought (1 Kgs. 17.8–16). **8–37:** Elisha is related to the *well-to-do woman* of *Shunem* in several episodes (the concluding one is in 8.1–6). **8–17:** The childless woman eventually bears a child; compare Gen. 18.1–15; 1 Sam. ch. 1. **18–37:** The child miraculously born to the woman is later revived after an accidental death. The story parallels 1 Kgs. 17.17–24.

the door, and went out. 22 She called her husband and said, 'Send me one of the servants and a she-donkey; I must go to the man of God as fast as I can, and come straight back.' 23 'Why go to him today?' he asked. 'It is neither new moon nor sabbath.' 'Never mind that,' she answered. 24 When the donkey was saddled, she said to her servant, 'Lead on and do not slacken pace unless I tell you.' 25 So she set out and came to the man of God on Mount Carmel.

The man of God spied her in the distance and said to Gehazi, his servant, 'That is the Shunammite woman coming. 26 Run and meet her, and ask, "Is all well with you? Is all well with your husband? Is all well with the boy?" ' She answered, 'All is well.' 27 When she reached the man of God on the hill, she clutched his feet. Gehazi came forward to push her away, but the man of God said, 'Let her alone; she is in great distress, and the LORD has concealed it from me and not told me.' 28 'My lord,' she said, 'did I ask for a son? Did I not beg you not to raise my hopes and then dash them?' 29 Elisha turned to Gehazi: 'Hitch up your cloak; take my staff with you and run. If you meet anyone on the way, do not stop to greet him; if anyone greets you, do not answer. Lay my staff on the boy's face.' 30 But the mother cried, 'As the LORD lives, your life upon it, I shall not leave you.' So he got up and followed her.

31 Gehazi went on ahead and laid the staff on the boy's face, but there was no sound or sign of life, so he went back to meet Elisha and told him that the boy had not stirred. 32 When Elisha entered the house, there was the dead boy, where he had been laid on the bed. 33 He went into the room, shut the door on the two of them, and prayed to the LORD. 34 Then, getting on to the bed, he lay upon the child, put his mouth to the child's mouth, his eyes to his eyes, and his hands to his hands; as he crouched upon him, the child's body grew warm. 35 Elisha got up and walked once up and down the room; getting on to the bed again, he crouched upon him and breathed into him seven times, and the boy opened his eyes. 36 The prophet summoned Gehazi and said, 'Call the Shunammite woman.' She answered his call and the

prophet said, 'Take up your child.' 37 She came in and prostrated herself before him. Then she took up her son and went out.

38 ELISHA returned to Gilgal at a time when there was a famine in the land. One day, when a group of prophets was sitting at his feet, he said to his servant, 'Set the big pot on the fire and prepare broth for the company.' 39 One of them went out into the fields to gather herbs and found a wild vine, and filled the skirt of his garment with wild gourds. He came back and sliced them into the pot, not knowing what they were. 40 The broth was poured out for the men to eat but, on tasting it, they cried out, 'Man of God, there is death in the pot,' and they could not eat it. 41 The prophet said, 'Fetch some meal.' He threw it into the pot and said, 'Now pour out for the people to eat.' This time there was no harm in the pot.

42 A MAN came from Baal-shalisha, bringing the man of God some of the new season's bread, twenty barley loaves, and fresh ripe ears of grain. Elisha said, 'Give this to the people to eat.' 43 His attendant protested, 'I cannot set this before a hundred people.' Still he insisted, 'Give it to the people to eat; for this is the word of the LORD: They will eat and there will be some left over.' 44 So he set it before them, and they ate and had some left over, as the LORD had said.

5 NAAMAN, commander of the king of Aram's army, was a great man and highly esteemed by his master, because through him the LORD had given victory to Aram; he was a mighty warrior, but he was a leper. 2 On one of their raids the Aramaeans brought back as a captive from the land of Israel a young girl, who became a servant to Naaman's wife. 3 She said to her mistress, 'If only my master could meet the prophet who lives in Samaria, he would cure him of the leprosy.' 4 Naaman went and reported to his master what the Israelite girl had said. 5 'Certainly you may go,' said the king of

4:35 **and breathed into him:** or and the boy sneezed.
4:42 **fresh . . . grain:** prob. rdg; Heb. unintelligible.
5:1 **he was a leper:** or his skin was diseased.

4.38–44: Two food miracles. Elisha here does with food what he did with water in 2.19–22. The multiplying of the loaves of *bread* is echoed in the later miracles of Jesus (Matt. 14.13–21; 15.32–38).

5.1–27: Elisha cures Naaman's leprosy. The narrative speaks simply of *the king of Aram* and *the king of*

Aram, 'and I shall send a letter to the king of Israel.'

Naaman set off, taking with him ten talents of silver, six thousand shekels of gold, and ten changes of clothing. 6 He delivered the letter to the king of Israel; it read: 'This letter is to inform you that I am sending to you my servant Naaman, and I beg you to cure him of his leprosy.' 7 When the king of Israel read the letter, he tore his clothes and said, 'Am I God to kill and to make alive, that this fellow sends to me to cure a man of his disease? See how he picks a quarrel with me.' 8 When Elisha, the man of God, heard how the king of Israel had torn his clothes, he sent him this message: 'Why did you tear your clothes? Let the man come to me, and he will know that there is a prophet in Israel.' 9 When Naaman came with his horses and chariots and halted at the entrance to Elisha's house, 10 Elisha sent out a messenger to say to him, 'If you go and wash seven times in the Jordan, your flesh will be restored and you will be clean.'

11 At this Naaman was furious and went away, saying, 'I thought he would at least have come out and stood and invoked the LORD his God by name, waved his hand over the place, and cured me of the leprosy. 12 Are not Abana and Pharpar, rivers of Damascus, better than all the waters of Israel? Can I not wash in them and be clean?' So he turned and went off in a rage.

13 But his servants came to him and said, 'If the prophet had told you to do something difficult, would you not do it? How much more should you, then, if he says to you, "Wash and be clean"!' 14 So he went down and dipped himself in the Jordan seven times as the man of God had told him, and his flesh was restored so that it was like a little child's, and he was clean.

15 Accompanied by his retinue he went back to the man of God and standing before him said, 'Now I know that there is no god anywhere in the world except in Israel. Will you accept a token of gratitude from your servant?' 16 'As the LORD lives, whom I serve,' said the prophet, 'I shall accept nothing.'

Though pressed to accept, he refused. 17 'Then if you will not,' said Naaman, 'let me, sir, have two mules' load of earth, for I shall no longer offer whole-offering or sacrifice to any god but the LORD. 18 In one matter only may the LORD pardon me: when my master goes to the temple of Rimmon to worship, leaning on my arm, and I worship in the temple of Rimmon when he worships there, for this let the LORD pardon me.' 19 Elisha bade him go in peace.

Naaman had gone only a short distance on his way, 20 when Gehazi, the servant of Elisha the man of God, said to himself, 'Has my master let this Aramaean, Naaman, go without accepting what he brought? As the LORD lives, I shall run after him and get something from him.' 21 So Gehazi hurried after Naaman. When Naaman saw him running after him, he alighted from his chariot to meet him saying, 'Is anything wrong?' 22 'Nothing,' replied Gehazi, 'but my master sent me to say that two young men of the company of prophets from the hill-country of Ephraim have just arrived. Could you provide them with a talent of silver and two changes of clothing?' 23 Naaman said, 'By all means; take two talents.' He pressed him to take them; then he tied up the two talents of silver in two bags, and the two changes of clothing, and gave them to two of his servants, and they walked ahead carrying them. 24 When Gehazi came to the citadel he took them from the two servants, deposited them in the house, and dismissed the men; and they went away.

25 When he went in and stood before his master, Elisha said, 'Where have you been, Gehazi?' 'Nowhere,' said Gehazi. 26 But he said to him, 'Was I not present in spirit when the man turned and got down from his chariot to meet you? Was it a time to get money and garments, olive trees and vineyards, sheep and oxen, slaves and slave-girls? 27 Naaman's leprosy will fasten on you and on your descendants for ever.' Gehazi left Elisha's

5:7 **Am I God:** or Am I a god.   5:18 **he worships:** so Gk; Heb. I worship.   5:23 **pressed:** prob. rdg; Heb. broke out on.   5:24 **citadel:** or hill.

Israel without names, a usual mark of legendary materials. **5:** The money amounts to an enormous sum. **7:** The narrative assumes that Damascus dominated Israel; this would be after the overthrow of the Omri dynasty; see 10.32–33; 13.3. **15–19:** This viewpoint is on the verge of explicit monotheism; yet, Naaman needs Israelite soil in order to worship the LORD at home in Aram. *Rimmon*, a title of Hadad, the god of Damascus, was also known in Canaan (Zech. 12.11). **22:** A *talent* (over sixty pounds) *of silver* (see p. xxvii) was an extravagant amount for *two* needy *young men*. **25–27:** The prophet's divine powers enforced justice among his adherents.

presence, his skin diseased, white as snow.

6 The company of prophets who were with Elisha said to him, 'As you see, this place where we live with you is too cramped for us. ²Let us go to the Jordan and each fetch a log, and make ourselves a place to live in.' The prophet said, 'Yes, go.' ³One of them said, 'Please, sir, come with us.' 'I shall come,' he said, ⁴and he went with them. When they reached the Jordan and began cutting down trees ⁵it chanced that, as one of them was felling a trunk, the head of his axe flew off into the water. 'Oh, master!' he exclaimed. 'It was borrowed.' ⁶'Where did it fall?' asked the man of God. When shown the place, he cut off a piece of wood and threw it into the water and made the iron float. ⁷Elisha said, 'Lift it out.' So he reached down and picked it up.

⁸Once, when the king of Aram was at war with Israel, he held a conference with his staff at which he said, 'I mean to attack in such and such a direction.' ⁹The man of God warned the king of Israel: 'Take care to avoid this place, for the Aramaeans are going down there.' ¹⁰The king of Israel sent word to the place about which the man of God had given him this warning; and the king took special precautions every time he found himself near that place. ¹¹The king of Aram was greatly incensed at this and, summoning his staff, he said to them, 'Tell me, which of us is for the king of Israel?' ¹²'There is no one, my lord king,' said one of his staff; 'but Elisha, the prophet in Israel, tells the king of Israel the very words you speak in your bedchamber.' ¹³'Go, find out where he is,' said the king, 'and I shall send and seize him.' It was reported to him that the prophet was at Dothan, ¹⁴and he sent a strong force there with horses and chariots. They came by night and surrounded the town.

¹⁵When the attendant of the man of God rose and went out early next morning, he saw a force with horses and chariots surrounding the town. 'Oh, master,' he said, 'which way are we to turn?' ¹⁶Elisha answered, 'Do not be afraid, for those on our side are more than those on theirs.' ¹⁷He offered this prayer: 'Lord, open his eyes and let him see.' The Lord opened the young man's eyes, and he saw the hills covered with horses and chariots of fire all around Elisha. ¹⁸As the Aramaeans came down towards him, Elisha prayed to the Lord: 'Strike this host, I pray, with blindness'; and they were struck blind as Elisha had asked. ¹⁹Elisha said to them, 'You are on the wrong road; this is not the town. Follow me and I will lead you to the man you are looking for.' And he led them to Samaria.

²⁰As soon as they had entered Samaria, Elisha prayed, 'Lord, open the eyes of these men and let them see again.' He opened their eyes, and they saw that they were inside Samaria. ²¹When the king of Israel saw them, he said to Elisha, 'My father, am I to destroy them?' ²²'No, you must not do that,' he answered. 'Would you destroy those whom you have not taken prisoner with your own sword and bow? As for these men, provide them with food and water, and let them eat and drink and go back to their master.' ²³So he prepared a great feast for them; they ate and drank and then were sent back to their master. From that time Aramaean raids on Israel ceased.

²⁴But later, Ben-hadad king of Aram mustered his whole army and marched to the siege of Samaria. ²⁵The city was near starvation, and they were besieging it so closely that a donkey's head was sold for eighty shekels of silver, and a quarter of a kab of locust-beans for five shekels. ²⁶One day, as the king of Israel was walking along the city wall, a woman called to him, 'Help, my lord king!'

6:2 **make ourselves:** *so Syriac; Heb. adds* there.
6:22 **[have] not:** *so Gk (Luc.); Heb. omits.*

6.1–7: The floating axe head. This episode, showing only the prophet's miraculous power, is like those in 2.19–25 and ch. 4.

6.8–23: Elisha foils Aramaean raids. 8–10: As 8.7 shows, prophets could come and go between Israel and Damascus. The story does not mean, however, that Elisha conducted an efficient spy network. His knowledge was due to his supernatural powers. **17:** *Horses and chariots of fire* are often motifs in the Elijah-Elisha stories; see 2.11; 1.9–14 n. **22–23:** The prisoners captured by supernatural means are evidence that divine power resists the *Aramaean raids.*

6.24–7.20: Episodes in a siege of Samaria. 24: *Ben-hadad:* there were several kings of *Aram* who bore this name. The name of the Israelite king is not given. Prophetic legends tend to lack precise historical references.

27 He said, 'If the LORD does not bring you help, where can I find help for you? From threshing-floor or from winepress? 28 What is your trouble?' She replied, 'This woman said to me, "Give up your child for us to eat today, and we will eat mine tomorrow." 29 So we cooked my son and ate him; but when I said to her the next day, "Now give up your child for us to eat," she had hidden him.' 30 When he heard the woman's story, the king tore his clothes. He was walking along the wall at the time, and, when the people looked, they saw that he had sackcloth underneath, next to his skin. 31 He said, 'The LORD do the same to me and more, if the head of Elisha son of Shaphat stays on his shoulders today.'

32 Elisha was sitting at home, the elders with him. The king had dispatched one of those at court, but, before the messenger arrived, Elisha said to the elders, 'See how this son of a murderer has sent to behead me! When the messenger comes, be sure to close the door and hold it fast against him. Can you not hear his master following on his heels?' 33 While he was still speaking, the king arrived and said, 'Look at our plight! This is the LORD's doing. Why should I wait any longer

7 for him to help us?' 1 Elisha answered, 'Hear this word from the LORD: By this time tomorrow a shekel will buy a measure of flour or two measures of barley at the gate of Samaria.' 2 The officer on whose arm the king leaned said to the man of God, 'Even if the LORD were to open windows in the sky, such a thing could not happen!' He answered, 'You will see it with your own eyes, but you will not eat any of it.'

3 At the city gate were four lepers. They said to one another, 'Why should we stay here and wait for death? 4 If we say we will go into the city, the famine is there, and we shall die; if we stay here, we shall die. Well then, let us go to the camp of the Aramaeans and give ourselves up: if they spare us, we shall live; if they put us to death, we can but die.' 5 At dusk they set out for the Aramaean camp, and when they reached the outskirts, they found no one there. 6 The LORD had caused the Aramaean army to hear a sound like that of chariots and horses and a great host, so that the word went round: 'The king of Israel has hired the kings of the Hittites

and the kings of Egypt to attack us.' 7 They had taken to flight in the dusk, abandoning their tents, horses, and donkeys. Leaving the camp as it stood, they had fled for their lives. 8 Those lepers came to the outskirts of the camp, where they went into a tent. They ate and drank, looted silver and gold and clothing, and made off and hid them. Then they came back, went into another tent and rifled it, and made off and hid the loot.

9 But they said to one another, 'What we are doing is not right. This is a day of good news and we are keeping it to ourselves. If we wait till morning, we shall be held to blame. We must go now and give the news to the king's household.' 10 So they went and called to the watch at the city gate and described how they had gone to the Aramaean camp and found not one man in it and had heard no human voice: nothing but horses and donkeys tethered, and the tents left as they were. 11 The watch called out and announced the news to the king's household in the palace.

12 The king rose in the night and said to his staff, 'I shall tell you what the Aramaeans have done. They know we are starving, so they have left their camp to go and hide in the open country, expecting us to come out, and then they can take us alive and enter the city.' 13 One of his staff said, 'Send out a party of men with some of the horses that are left; if they live, they will be as well off as all the other Israelites who are still left; if they die, they will be no worse off than all those who have already perished. Let them go and see what has happened.' 14 They picked two mounted men, and the king dispatched them in the track of the Aramaean army with the order to go and find out what had happened. 15 Having followed as far as the Jordan and found the whole road littered with clothing and equipment which the Aramaeans had discarded in their haste, the messengers returned and made their report to the king.

16 The people went out and plundered the Aramaean camp, and a measure of flour was

6:27 **If the LORD does not:** *so Aram. (Targ.); Heb.* Let the LORD not.   6:33 **king:** *prob. rdg; Heb.* messenger. 7:1 **measure:** *Heb.* seah.   7:3 **lepers:** *or* men suffering from skin disease.   7:13 **if they live ... if they die:** *prob. rdg; Heb.* obscure.   7:14 **two mounted men:** *so Gk; Heb.* two horse-chariots.

25: The prices were extremely high; see p. xxvii. **30:** The king's *sackcloth* showed how much he was concerned with the distress of his people. **31:** Possibly Elisha was blamed because he was thought to embody anti-Ara-sold for a shekel and two measures of barley for a shekel, so that the word of the LORD came true. 17 The king had appointed the officer on whose arm he leaned to take charge of the gate, and the crowd trampled him to death there, just as the man of God had foretold when the king visited him. 18 For when the man of God said to the king, 'By this time tomorrow a shekel will buy two measures of barley or one measure of flour at the gate of Samaria,' 19 the officer had answered, 'Even if the LORD were to open windows in the sky, such a thing could not happen!' And the man of God had said, 'You will see it with your own eyes, but you will not eat any of it.' 20 This is what happened to him: he was trampled to death at the gate by the crowd.

8 Elisha said to the woman whose son he had restored to life, 'Go away at once with your household and find lodging where you can, for the LORD has decreed a seven years' famine and it has already come on the land.' 2 The woman acted at once on the word of the man of God and went away with her household to Philistine territory, where she stayed for seven years. 3 On her return at the end of that time she sought an audience of the king to beg for her house and land. 4 The king was questioning Gehazi, the servant of the man of God, about all the great things Elisha had done; 5 and, as he was describing to the king how he had brought the dead to life, the selfsame woman began her appeal to the king for her house and land. 'My lord king,' said Gehazi, 'this is the woman, and this is her son whom Elisha restored to life.' 6 The king questioned the woman, and she told him about it. Then he entrusted her case to an official, ordering him to restore all her property to her, together with all the revenues from her land from the time she left till that day.

7 Elisha came to Damascus, at a time when King Ben-hadad of Aram was ill; and when the king was told that the man of God had arrived, 8 he ordered Hazael to take a gift with him and go to the man of God and through him enquire of the LORD whether he would recover from his illness. 9 Hazael went, taking with him as a gift forty camel-loads of all kinds of Damascus wares. When he came into the prophet's presence, he said, 'Your son King Ben-hadad of Aram has sent me to you to ask whether he will recover from his illness.' 10 'Go and tell him that he will recover,' he answered; 'but the LORD has revealed to me that in fact he will die.' 11 The man of God stood staring with set face until Hazael became disconcerted; then the man of God wept. 12 'Why do you weep, sir?' said Hazael. He answered, 'Because I know the harm you will do to the Israelites: you will set their fortresses on fire and put their young men to the sword; you will dash their children to the ground and rip open their pregnant women.' 13 Hazael said, 'But I am a dog, a mere nobody; how can I do this great thing?' Elisha answered, 'The LORD has revealed to me that you will become king of Aram.' 14 Hazael left Elisha and returned to his master, who asked what Elisha had said. 'He told me that you would recover,' he replied. 15 But the next day he took a blanket and, after dipping it in water, laid it over the king's face, so that he died; and Hazael succeeded him.

16 In the fifth year of Jehoram son of King Ahab of Israel, Joram son of King Jehoshaphat of Judah became king. 17 He was thirty-two years old when he came to the throne, and he reigned in Jerusalem for eight years. 18 He followed the practices of the kings of Israel as the house of Ahab had done, for he had married Ahab's daughter; he did what

7:17 **had foretold:** *so Syriac; Heb. adds* which he had foretold. 8:16 **King ... Israel:** *so some Gk MSS; Heb. adds* and Jehoshaphat king of Judah. 8:17–22 *Cp. 2 Chr. 21:5–10.*

maean policies that had reduced Samaria to dire straits. **7.17:** Elisha's prophecies always come true, even if somewhat grimly.

8.1–6: The Shunammite woman as witness. This episode resumes the story of Elisha and the Shunammite woman from 4.37. **4:** As yet *Gehazi* does not seem to have suffered the leprosy of 5.25–27.

8.7–15: Elisha and revolution in Damascus. The Elisha stories now return to the larger account of the overthrow of the dynasty of Omri. The second of the three commissions given to Elijah at Mount Horeb (1 Kgs. 19.15–16, 19–21 n.) is here carried out. **10:** The deception of Ben-hadad is God's will. **12:** Elisha foresees the events of 10.32–33 and 13.3.

8.16–29: The last years of the Omri dynasty. *Joram* of *Judah* followed the policy of collaboration with the Northern Kingdom and the religious tolerance involved in that policy (v. 18). The power of the two kingdoms was wrong in the eyes of the LORD. ¹⁹Yet for his servant David's sake the LORD was unwilling to destroy Judah, as he had promised to give him and his descendants a lamp for all time.

²⁰During Joram's reign Edom revolted against Judah and set up its own king. ²¹Joram with all his chariots pushed on to Zair. When the Edomites encircled him and his chariot-commanders he made a sortie by night, and broke out; his main force, however, fled to their homes. ²²To this day Edom has remained independent of Judah. Libnah also revolted at the same time. ²³The other acts and events of Joram's reign are recorded in the annals of the kings of Judah. ²⁴Joram rested with his forefathers and was buried with them in the city of David. His son Ahaziah succeeded him.

²⁵In the twelfth year of Jehoram son of Ahab king of Israel, Ahaziah son of King Joram of Judah became king. ²⁶Ahaziah was twenty-two years old when he came to the throne, and he reigned in Jerusalem for one year; his mother was Athaliah granddaughter of King Omri of Israel. ²⁷He followed the practices of the house of Ahab and did what was wrong in the eyes of the LORD like the house of Ahab, for he was connected with that house by marriage. ²⁸He allied himself with Jehoram son of Ahab to fight against King Hazael of Aram at Ramoth-gilead. But King Jehoram was wounded by the Arameans, ²⁹and retired to Jezreel to recover from the wounds inflicted on him at Ramoth in battle with King Hazael. Because of Jehoram's injury Ahaziah son of Joram king of Judah went down to Jezreel to visit him.

9 ELISHA the prophet summoned one of the company of prophets and said to him, 'Get ready for the road; take this flask of oil with you and go to Ramoth-gilead. ²When you arrive, look there for Jehu son of Jehoshaphat, son of Nimshi; go in and call him aside from his fellow-officers, and lead him through to an inner room. ³Take the flask and pour the oil on his head and say, "This is the word of the LORD: I anoint you king over Israel." After that open the door and flee for your life.'

⁴The young prophet went to Ramoth-gilead, ⁵and when he arrived, he found the officers sitting together. He said, 'Sir, I have a word for you.' 'For which of us?' asked Jehu. 'For you, sir,' he said. ⁶Jehu rose and went into the house, where the prophet poured the oil on his head, saying, 'This is the word of the LORD the God of Israel: I anoint you king over Israel, the people of the LORD. ⁷You are to strike down the house of Ahab your master, and I shall take vengeance on Jezebel for the blood of my servants the prophets and for the blood of all the LORD's servants. ⁸The entire house of Ahab will perish; I shall destroy every mother's son of his house in Israel, whether under the protection of the family or not. ⁹I shall make Ahab's house like the house of Jeroboam son of Nebat and the house of Baasha son of Ahijah. ¹⁰Jezebel will be devoured by dogs in the plot of ground at Jezreel and no one will bury her.' With that he opened the door and fled.

¹¹When Jehu rejoined the king's officers, they said to him, 'Is all well? What did this crazy fellow want with you?' 'You know him and his ideas,' he said. ¹²'That is no answer!' they replied. 'Tell us what happened.' 'I shall tell you exactly what he said: "This is the word of the LORD: I anoint you king over Israel." ' ¹³They snatched up their cloaks and spread them under him at the top of the steps, and they sounded the trumpet and shouted, 'Jehu is king.'

¹⁴Jehu son of Jehoshaphat, son of Nimshi, organized a conspiracy against Jehoram, while Jehoram and all the Israelites were defending Ramoth-gilead against King Hazael of Aram. ¹⁵King Jehoram had returned to Jezreel to recover from the wounds inflicted on him by the Arameans in his battle against

8:19 **him and:** *so many MSS; others omit.*
8:25–29 *Cp. 2 Chr. 22:1–6.*　　8:26 **grand-daughter:** *lit.* daughter.　　8:29 **Ramoth:** *so Gk; Heb.* Ramah.

was declining; Israel had lost control of Moab (3.27), and now *Judah* loses control of *Edom* (vv. 20–22). **26:** *Athaliah,* daughter of Jezebel, was to prove much more powerful than her son *Ahaziah;* see ch. 11.

9.1–10.36: Jehu overthrows the dynasty of Omri. The third and last commission to Elijah at Horeb (1 Kgs. 19.15–18) is carried out here. This fine piece of historical writing is without legendary coloring.

9.1–13: The anointing of Jehu. 1: *Elisha* must work in secret; therefore, he sends one of his disciples to anoint Jehu. **6–7:** On the LORD's sanction of Jehu's dynasty, see 1 Kgs. 11.29–39 n.

9.14–37: Jehu kills the reigning kings. 15: *Jezreel* served as a second capital of the Northern Kingdom, nearer

Hazael. Jehu said to his colleagues, 'If you are on my side, see that no one escapes from the city to carry the news to Jezreel.' ¹⁶ He mounted his chariot and drove to Jezreel, for Jehoram was laid up there and King Ahaziah of Judah had gone down to visit him.

¹⁷ The watchman standing on the watchtower in Jezreel saw Jehu's troops approaching and called out, 'I see a troop of men.' Jehoram said, 'Fetch a horseman and send to meet them and ask if they come peaceably.' ¹⁸ The horseman went to meet him and said, 'The king asks, "Is it peace?"' Jehu said, 'Peace? What is that to do with you? Fall in behind me.' The watchman reported, 'The messenger has met them but is not coming back.' ¹⁹ A second horseman was sent; when he met them, he also said, 'The king asks, "Is it peace?"' 'Peace?' said Jehu. 'What is that to do with you? Fall in behind me.' ²⁰ The watchman reported, 'He has met them but is not coming back. The driving is like the driving of Jehu son of Nimshi, for he drives furiously.'

²¹ 'Harness my chariot,' said Jehoram. When it was ready King Jehoram of Israel and King Ahaziah of Judah went out each in his own chariot to meet Jehu, and they met him by the plot of Naboth of Jezreel. ²² When Jehoram saw Jehu, he said, 'Is it peace, Jehu?' He replied, 'Do you call it peace while your mother Jezebel keeps up her obscene idol-worship and monstrous sorceries?' ²³ Jehoram wheeled about and fled, crying out, 'Treachery, Ahaziah!' ²⁴ Jehu drew his bow and shot Jehoram between the shoulders; the arrow pierced his heart and he slumped down in his chariot. ²⁵ Jehu said to Bidkar, his lieutenant, 'Pick him up and throw him into the plot of land belonging to Naboth of Jezreel; remember how, when you and I were riding side by side behind Ahab his father, the LORD pronounced this sentence against him: ²⁶ "It is the word of the LORD: as surely as I saw yesterday the blood of Naboth and

the blood of his sons, I will requite you on this plot of land." Pick him up, therefore, and throw him into the plot and so fulfil the word of the LORD.' ²⁷ When King Ahaziah of Judah saw this he fled by the road to Beth-haggan. Jehu pursued him and said, 'Get him too.' They shot him down in his chariot on the road up the valley near Ibleam, but he escaped to Megiddo and died there. ²⁸ His servants conveyed his body to Jerusalem by chariot and buried him in his tomb with his forefathers in the city of David.

²⁹ It was in the eleventh year of Jehoram son of Ahab that Ahaziah became king over Judah.

³⁰ Then Jehu came to Jezreel. When Jezebel heard what had happened she painted her eyes and adorned her hair, and she stood looking down from a window. ³¹ As Jehu entered the gate, she said, 'Is it peace, you Zimri, you murderer of your master?' ³² He looked up at the window and said, 'Who is on my side? Who?' Two or three eunuchs looked out to him, ³³ and he said, 'Throw her down.' They threw her down, and some of her blood splashed on to the wall and the horses, which trampled her underfoot. ³⁴ Jehu went in and ate and drank. 'See to this accursed woman,' he said, 'and bury her; for she is a king's daughter.' ³⁵ But when they went to bury her they found nothing of her but the skull, the feet, and the palms of her hands. ³⁶ When they went back and told him, Jehu said, 'It is the word of the LORD which his servant Elijah the Tishbite spoke, when he said, "In the plot of ground at Jezreel the dogs will devour the flesh of Jezebel, ³⁷ and Jezebel's corpse will lie like dung on the ground in the plot at Jezreel so that no one will be able to say: This is Jezebel."'

10 There were seventy sons of Ahab left in Samaria. Jehu therefore sent a let-

9:15 **on my side:** *so Gk; Heb. omits.*   9:20 **son:** *or* grandson (*cp. verse 2*).   9:27 **They ... down:** *so Syriac; Heb. omits.* **the valley:** *prob. rdg; Heb. to* Gur.

the war front than Samaria. **17:** *Jezreel* was about forty miles from Ramoth-gilead. It overlooked the valley going down to the Jordan river. **18–22:** *Jehoram* is concerned here about news from the war front. **25–26:** The prophecy of 1 Kgs. 21.19–29 is fulfilled. **27:** *Ahaziah,* though *king of Judah,* was both grandson of Jezebel and ally of Jehoram. **30–37:** *Jezebel* was now an elderly queen mother. **31:** On *Zimri,* see 1 Kgs. 16.8–12. **36–37:** See 1 Kgs. 21.23.

10.1–14: The execution of the royal families. The whole dynasty of Israel and its Judean allies had to be removed or else the religious issue would not be settled. **1:** The *seventy sons of Ahab:* leading members of the royal family, not literally sons of Ahab; see similar groups in Judg. 8.30; 9.5; 12.13; Num. 11.16–17, 24–30. **9:** Jehu wished it to appear that not he alone was guilty of shedding royal blood.

ter to Samaria, addressed to the rulers of the city, the elders, and the guardians of Ahab's sons, in which he wrote: ²'You have in your care your master's family as well as his chariots and horses, fortified cities, and weapons; therefore, whenever this letter reaches you, ³choose the best and the most suitable of your master's sons, set him on his father's throne, and fight for your master's house.' ⁴They were panic-stricken and said, 'If two kings could not stand against him, what hope is there that we can?' ⁵Therefore the comptroller of the household and the governor of the city, with the elders and the children's guardians, sent this message to Jehu: 'We are your servants. Whatever you tell us we shall do; but we shall not make anyone king. Do as you think fit.'

⁶So in a second letter to them Jehu wrote: 'If you are on my side and will obey my orders, then bring the heads of your master's sons to me at Jezreel by this time tomorrow.' The royal princes, seventy in all, were with the nobles of the city who had charge of their upbringing. ⁷When the letter arrived, they took the royal princes and killed all seventy; they piled their heads in baskets and sent the heads to Jehu in Jezreel. ⁸When the messenger came to him and reported that they had brought the heads of the royal princes, he ordered them to be piled in two heaps and left till morning at the entrance to the city gate.

⁹In the morning Jehu went out, and standing there said to all the people, 'You are fairminded judges. I conspired against my master and killed him, but who put all these to death? ¹⁰Be sure then that every word which the Lord has spoken against the house of Ahab will be fulfilled, and that the Lord has now done what he promised through his servant Elijah.' ¹¹So Jehu put to death all who were left of the house of Ahab in Jezreel, as well as all Ahab's nobles, his close friends, and priests, until he had left not one survivor.

¹²Then he set out for Samaria, and on the way there, when he had reached a shepherds' shelter, ¹³he came upon the kinsmen of King Ahaziah of Judah and demanded to know who they were. 'We are kinsmen of Ahaziah,' they replied, 'and we have come down to pay

our respects to the families of the king and of the queen mother.' ¹⁴'Take them alive,' he said. They were taken alive, all forty-two of them, then slain, and flung into a pit that was there; he did not leave a single survivor.

¹⁵When he had left that place, he found Jehonadab son of Rechab coming to meet him. Jehu greeted him and said, 'Are you with me wholeheartedly, as I am with you?' 'I am,' replied Jehonadab. 'Then if you are,' said Jehu, 'give me your hand,' and he did so. Jehu had him come up into his chariot. ¹⁶'Come with me,' he said, 'and you will see my zeal for the Lord.' So he took him with him in his chariot. ¹⁷When he came to Samaria, he put to death all of Ahab's house who were left there and so blotted it out, in fulfilment of the word which the Lord had spoken to Elijah.

¹⁸Jehu called all the people together and said to them, 'Ahab served the Baal a little; Jehu will serve him much. ¹⁹Now summon all the prophets of Baal, all his ministers and priests; not one must be missing. For I am holding a great sacrifice to Baal, and no one who is missing from it shall live.' In this way Jehu outwitted the ministers of Baal in order to destroy them. ²⁰Jehu gave the order, 'Proclaim a sacred ceremony for Baal.' This was done, ²¹and Jehu himself sent word throughout Israel. All the ministers of Baal came; there was not a man left who did not come, and when they went into the temple of Baal, it was filled from end to end. ²²Jehu said to the person who had charge of the wardrobe, 'Bring out robes for all the ministers of Baal'; and he brought them out. ²³Then Jehu and Jehonadab son of Rechab went into the temple of Baal and said to the ministers, 'Look carefully and make sure that there are no servants of the Lord here with you, but only the ministers of Baal.' ²⁴Then they went in to offer sacrifices and whole-offerings.

Jehu had stationed eighty of his men out-

10:1 **of the city:** *so Gk (Luc.); Heb.* of Jezreel. **Ahab's sons:** *so some Gk MSS; Heb. omits* sons. 10:2 **cities:** *so some MSS; others* city.　10:6 **the heads of:** *so Gk (Luc.); Heb. adds* the men of.　10:12 **a shepherds' shelter:** *or* Beth-eked of the Shepherds. 10:15 **said Jehu:** *so Gk; Heb. omits.*　10:16 **he took:** *so Gk; Heb.* they took.

10.15–36: Jehu's religious purge. Overt, and official, Baalism was destroyed in Israel. **15:** *Jehonadab son of Rechab:* the leader of a religious order bound by vows of abstinence from certain features of settled life in Canaan; see Jer. 35.1–11. **21:** *The temple of Baal* was built by Ahab (1 Kgs. 16.32). **22:** The *robes* were ritual side and warned them, 'I shall hold you responsible for these men, and if anyone of you lets one of them escape he will pay for it with his own life.' 25 When he had finished offering the whole-offering, Jehu ordered the guards and officers to go in and cut them all down, and let not one of them escape. They were slain without quarter, and the guard and the officers threw them out. Then going into the keep of the temple of Baal, 26 they brought out the sacred pole from the temple and burnt it; 27 they overthrew the sacred pillar of the Baal and pulled down the temple itself and made a privy of it — as it is today. 28 Thus Jehu stamped out the worship of Baal in Israel. 29 He did not however abandon the sins of Jeroboam son of Nebat who led Israel into sin: he maintained the worship of the golden calves of Bethel and Dan.

30 The LORD said to Jehu, 'You have done well in carrying out what is right in my eyes, and you have done to the house of Ahab all that it was in my mind to do. Therefore your sons to the fourth generation will occupy the throne of Israel.' 31 But Jehu was not careful to follow the law of the LORD the God of Israel with all his heart; he did not abandon the sins of Jeroboam who led Israel into sin.

Kings of Israel and Judah

32 In those days the LORD began to cut down Israel. Hazael struck at them in every corner of their territory 33 eastwards from the Jordan: all the land of Gilead, Gad, Reuben, and Manasseh, from Aroer which is by the wadi of the Arnon, including Gilead and Bashan.

34 The other events of Jehu's reign, his achievements and his exploits, are recorded in the annals of the kings of Israel. 35 Jehu

rested with his forefathers and was buried in Samaria. His son Jehoahaz succeeded him. 36 Jehu had reigned over Israel in Samaria for twenty-eight years.

11 As SOON as Athaliah mother of Ahaziah saw that her son was dead, she set out to destroy the whole royal line. 2 But Jehosheba, the daughter of King Joram, the sister of Ahaziah, took Ahaziah's son Joash and stole him away from among the princes who were being murdered; she put him and his nurse in a bedchamber where he was hidden from Athaliah and escaped death. 3 He remained concealed with her in the house of the LORD for six years, while Athaliah ruled the country.

4 In the seventh year Jehoiada sent for the captains of units of a hundred, both of the Carites and of the guards, and he brought them to him in the house of the LORD, where he made a compact with them and put them on oath; he showed them the king's son, 5 and gave them these orders: 'One third of you who are on duty on the sabbath are to be on guard in the palace; 6 the rest of you are to be on special duty in the house of the LORD, one third at the Sur Gate and the other third at the gate with the outrunners. 7 Your two companies who are off duty on the sabbath are to be on duty for the king in the house of the LORD. 8 Mount guard round the king, each man holding his weapons, and anyone who comes near the ranks is to be put to death. You are to stay with the king wherever he goes.'

9 The captains carried out the orders of

10:26 **sacred pole:** *prob. rdg;* Heb. sacred pillars. 11:1–20 *Cp. 2 Chr. 22:10–23:21.* 11:2 **she put:** *prob. rdg, cp. 2 Chr. 22:11;* Heb. omits. 11:5 **are to . . . guard:** *so Syriac;* Heb. who keep guard.

garments kept in the holy precincts. **27:** *The sacred pillar of the Baal:* 3.2 reports it as removed by Jehoram; apparently it had been re-erected. **30:** See 1 Kgs. 11.29–39 n. **32–33:** Jehu's revolution meant the complete breakdown of Omri's policy and the dissolution of alliances with Phoenicia and Judah (see 1 Kgs. 16.23–34 n.). Isolated thereby, Israel had no hope of holding Transjordan against Damascus.

11.1–17.41: The second period of the two kingdoms. From the viewpoint of the compilers, the period of Elijah and Elisha had settled the question that Yahweh, not the Baal, was the god of Israel. The question that remained was the persistence of the cult of the golden calves of Bethel and Dan; see 1 Kgs. 12.25–33; 2 Kgs. 10.31.

11.1–20: Athaliah overthrown in Jerusalem. The revolution in Israel against the house of Omri was not immediately effective in the kingdom of Judah. **1:** After *Ahaziah* was killed in the north (9.27) his mother *Athaliah,* daughter of Jezebel, determined to hold power in Jerusalem. No other queen is known to have ruled without a king in the two Hebrew kingdoms. **2:** *Jehosheba* was wife of the priest Jehoiada according to 2 Chr. 22.11; thus, she had access to the temple chambers. **4:** *Carites:* foreign mercenaries; see 2 Sam. 8.18 n. **6:** The

Jehoiada the priest to the letter: each took his men, both those who came on duty on the sabbath and those who went off, and they reported to Jehoiada. [10] The priest handed out to the captains King David's spears and shields, which were kept in the house of the LORD. [11] The guards took up their stations round the king, each man holding his weapons, from corner to corner of the house to north and south. [12] Then Jehoiada brought out the king's son, put the crown on his head, handed him the testimony, and anointed him king. The people clapped their hands and shouted, 'Long live the king.'

[13] When Athaliah heard the noise made by the guards and the people, she came into the house of the LORD where the people were; [14] she found the king standing by the pillar, as was the custom, amidst outbursts of song and fanfares of trumpets in his honour; all the populace were rejoicing and blowing trumpets. Athaliah tore her clothes and cried, 'Treason! Treason!' [15] Jehoiada the priest gave orders to the captains in command of the troops: 'Bring her outside the precincts and put to the sword anyone in attendance on her'; for the priest said, 'Let her not be put to death in the house of the LORD.' [16] They took her and brought her out by the entry for horses to the palace, and there she was put to death.

[17] Jehoiada made a covenant, between the LORD on one side and the king and people on the other, that they should be the LORD's people, and a covenant also between the king and the people. [18] The people all went to the temple of Baal and pulled it down; they smashed to pieces its altars and images, and they slew Mattan the priest of Baal before the altars.

Jehoiada set a guard over the house of the LORD; [19] he took the captains of units of a hundred, the Carites and the guards, and all the people, and they escorted the king from the house of the LORD through the Gate of the Guards to the palace, and seated him on the royal throne. [20] The whole people rejoiced and the city had quiet. That is how Athaliah was put to the sword in the palace.

[21] Joash was seven years old when he became king. [1] It was in the seventh year of Jehu that Joash became king, and he reigned in Jerusalem for forty years; his mother was Zibiah from Beersheba. [2] He did what was right in the eyes of the LORD all his days, as Jehoiada the priest had taught him. [3] The shrines, however, were allowed to remain; the people continued to sacrifice and burn offerings there.

[4] Joash ordered that all the silver brought as holy-gifts into the house of the LORD, the silver for which each man was assessed, the silver for the persons assessed under his name, and any silver brought voluntarily to the house of the LORD, [5] should be taken by the priests, each receiving it from a treasurer; he also ordered them to repair the house wherever it was found necessary. [6] But in the twenty-third year of Joash's reign the priests had still not carried out the repairs. [7] The king summoned Jehoiada the priest along with the other priests and asked, 'Why are you not repairing the house? Henceforth you need not receive the money from your treasurers, but hand it over for the repair of the house.' [8] The priests agreed neither to receive money from the people nor to undertake the repairs of the house themselves.

[9] Jehoiada the priest took a chest, bored a hole in the lid, and put it beside the sacrificial slaughtering-place on the right side going

11:10 **spears:** *so Gk, cp. 2 Chr. 23:9; Heb.* spear. 11:11 **north and south:** *prob. rdg; Heb. adds of the altar and the house.* 11:12 **The people:** *so Gk (Luc.); Heb. omits.* 11:13 **and the people:** *so Syriac; Heb. omits and.* 11:14 **by the pillar:** *or on the dais (cp. Lat.).* 11:21 *In Heb. 12:1.* 11:21—12:15 *Cp. 2 Chr. 24:1—14.* 12:4 **all the silver . . . assessed:** *prob. rdg; Heb. obscure.* 12:9 **sacrificial slaughtering-place:** *prob. rdg; Heb.* altar.

location of these gates is uncertain. **12:** The *testimony* was probably a document giving the king's royal titles and divine sanction, a usage derived from Egypt. **14:** *The populace* is literally "the people of the land," a phrase designating refugees from the Judean countryside who moved to Jerusalem because of military upheaval and from time to time exerted political influence. They were to play an increasingly important role in the late history of Judah; see vv. 18–20; 15.5 n.; 16.15; 21.24; 23.30, 35; 25.3, 19. **17:** The *covenant* established the same religious policy for Judah as Jehu had established in the north.

12.1–21: Joash of Judah. 1: *Forty years:* about 835–796 B.C.E. **3:** Just as the failure to remove Jeroboam's golden calves was the great fault of northern kings, so the failure to remove *the shrines* was the fault of the kings of Judah, until Hezekiah (18.4) and Josiah (23.4–20). **4–16:** This section comes from a source concerned into the house of the LORD. The priests on duty at the entrance put in it all the money brought to the house of the LORD. ¹⁰ Whenever they saw that the chest was well filled, the king's secretary and the high priest came and melted down the silver found in the house of the LORD and weighed it. ¹¹ When it had been checked, they handed over the silver to those supervising the work in the house of the LORD, and they paid the carpenters and the builders working there ¹² and the masons and the stone-cutters; they used it also to purchase timber and hewn stone for the repairs and for all other expenses connected with them. ¹³ They did not use the money brought into the house of the LORD to make silver cups, snuffers, tossing-bowls, trumpets, or any gold or silver vessels; ¹⁴ but they used it for paying the workmen and for the repairs. ¹⁵ No account was asked from the men to whom the money was given for the payment of the workers; they were acting on trust. ¹⁶ Money from reparation-offerings and purification-offerings was not brought into the house of the LORD: it belonged to the priests.

¹⁷ King Hazael of Aram came up at that time and attacked Gath, and after its capture he moved on against Jerusalem. ¹⁸ Thereupon King Joash of Judah took all the holy-gifts that Jehoshaphat, Joram, and Ahaziah his forefathers, kings of Judah, had dedicated, and his own holy-gifts, and all the gold that was in the treasuries of the house of the LORD and in the royal palace, and sent them to Hazael; and he withdrew from Jerusalem.

¹⁹ The other acts and events of the reign of Joash are recorded in the annals of the kings of Judah. ²⁰ His servants rose against him in a conspiracy and assassinated him in the house of Millo on the descent to Silla; ²¹ it was his servants Jozachar son of Shimeath and Jehozabad son of Shomer who struck the fatal blow. He was buried with his forefathers in the city of David. His son Amaziah succeeded him.

13 In the twenty-third year of Joash son of Ahaziah king of Judah, Jehoahaz son of Jehu became king over Israel in Samaria and he reigned for seventeen years. ² He did what was wrong in the eyes of the LORD and continued the sinful practices of Jeroboam son of Nebat who led Israel into sin, and did not give them up. ³ This roused the anger of the LORD against Israel, and he made them subject for some years to King Hazael of Aram and Ben-hadad his son. ⁴ When Jehoahaz sought to placate the LORD, the LORD heard his prayer, for he saw how the king of Aram oppressed Israel. ⁵ The LORD appointed a deliverer for Israel, and they escaped from the power of Aram and settled down again in their own homes. ⁶ But they did not give up the sinful practices of the house of Jeroboam who led Israel into sin, but continued in them; the goddess Asherah remained in Samaria. ⁷ Hazael had left Jehoahaz no armed force except fifty horsemen, ten chariots, and ten thousand infantry; all the rest the king of Aram had destroyed and made like dust under foot.

⁸ The other events of the reign of Jehoahaz, and all his achievements and exploits, are recorded in the annals of the kings of Israel. ⁹ He rested with his forefathers and was buried in Samaria. His son Jehoash succeeded him.

¹⁰ In the thirty-ninth year of King Joash of Judah, Jehoash son of Jehoahaz became king over Israel in Samaria and reigned for sixteen years. ¹¹ He did what was wrong in the eyes of the LORD; he did not give up any of the sinful practices of Jeroboam son of Nebat who led Israel into sin, but continued in them. ¹² The other events of the reign of Jehoash, all his achievements, his exploits, and his war with King Amaziah of Judah, are recorded in the annals of the kings of Israel.

12:20–21 *Cp. 2 Chr. 24:25–27.* 12:21 **Jozachar:** *so some MSS; others* Jozabad. 13:6 **but continued:** *so Gk; Heb.* he continued. **the goddess Asherah:** *or the sacred pole.* 13:10 **thirty-ninth:** *so some Gk MSS; Heb.* thirty-seventh.

with the history of the temple; see 22.3–7. **17–18:** Judah also suffered from the breakdown of the alliance by Omri (1 Kgs. 16.23–34 n.). It was oppressed by Hazael, as was the kingdom of Israel (10.32–33 n.). **20–21:** The issues behind Joash's assassination are unknown. The crown prince was already of age (14.2).

13.1–25: Jehoahaz and Jehoash of Israel. These two reigns covered (roughly) 814–782 B.C.E. Israel was still suffering under the power of Damascus, but under Jehoash a recovery began, largely because Damascus was severely pressed by renewed Assyrian power. **4–5:** The shift in power is attributed to Jehoahaz's contriteness. The *deliverer* is probably Adad-nirari III of Assyria (811–783 B.C.E.), who decisively defeated Damascus in 802 B.C.E. **6:** The *goddess Asherah* was not purged, even from the public cult, to the same degree Baal had

13 Jehoash rested with his forefathers and was buried in Samaria with the kings of Israel. Jeroboam ascended the throne.

14 When Elisha fell ill and lay on his deathbed, King Jehoash of Israel went down to him and, weeping over him, said, 'My father! My father! The chariots and horsemen of Israel!' 15 Elisha said, 'Take a bow and arrows,' and he did so. 16 'Put your hand to the bow,' said the prophet. He did so, and Elisha laid his hands on those of the king. 17 Then he said, 'Open the window towards the east'; he opened it and Elisha told him to shoot, and he did so. Then the prophet said, 'An arrow for the LORD's victory, an arrow for victory over Aram! You will utterly defeat Aram at Aphek.' 18 He went on, 'Now take up your arrows.' When he did so, Elisha said, 'Strike the ground with them.' He struck three times and stopped. 19 The man of God was angry with him and said, 'You should have struck five or six times; then you would have defeated Aram utterly; as it is, you will strike Aram three times and no more.'

20 Elisha died and was buried.

Year after year Moabite raiders used to invade the land. 21 Once some men were burying a dead man when they caught sight of the raiders, and they threw the body into the grave of Elisha and made off. When the body touched the prophet's bones, the man came to life and rose to his feet.

22 All through the reign of Jehoahaz, King Hazael of Aram oppressed Israel. 23 But the LORD was gracious and took pity on them; because of his covenant with Abraham, Isaac, and Jacob, he looked on them with favour and was unwilling to destroy them; nor has he even yet banished them from his sight. 24 When King Hazael of Aram died and was succeeded by his son Ben-hadad, 25 Jehoash son of Jehoahaz recaptured the towns which Ben-hadad had taken in war from Jehoahaz his father; three times Jehoash defeated him and so recovered the towns of Israel.

14 In the second year of Jehoash son of Jehoahaz king of Israel, Amaziah son

of King Joash of Judah succeeded his father. 2 He was twenty-five years old when he came to the throne, and he reigned in Jerusalem for twenty-nine years; his mother was Jehoaddin from Jerusalem. 3 He did what was right in the eyes of the LORD, yet not as his ancestor David had done; he followed his father Joash in everything. 4 The shrines were not abolished; the people continued to sacrifice and burn offerings there. 5 As soon as the royal power was firmly in his grasp, he put to death those of his servants who had murdered the king his father; 6 but he spared the murderers' children in obedience to the LORD's command written in the law of Moses: 'Parents are not to be put to death for their children, nor children for their parents; each one may be put to death only for his own sin.' 7 He defeated ten thousand Edomites in the valley of Salt and captured Sela; he gave it the name Joktheel, which it still bears.

8 Amaziah sent envoys to Jehoash son of Jehoahaz, son of Jehu, king of Israel, to propose a confrontation. 9 King Jehoash of Israel sent back this answer to King Amaziah of Judah: 'A thistle in Lebanon sent to a cedar in Lebanon to say, "Give your daughter in marriage to my son." But a wild beast in Lebanon, passing by, trampled on the thistle. 10 You have defeated Edom, it is true; but it has gone to your head. Stay at home and enjoy your triumph. Why should you involve yourself in disaster and bring yourself to the ground, and drag down Judah with you?'

11 When, however, Amaziah would not listen, King Jehoash of Israel marched out, and he and King Amaziah of Judah clashed at Beth-shemesh in Judah. 12 The men of Judah were routed by Israel and fled to their homes. 13 King Jehoash of Israel captured Amaziah king of Judah, son of Joash, son of Ahaziah, at Beth-shemesh. He marched on Jerusalem, where he broke down the city wall from the Ephraim Gate to the Corner Gate,

13:21 **and made off:** *so Gk (Luc.); Heb.* and he made off.   14:1–6 *Cp. 2 Chr. 25:1–4.*   14:8–14 *Cp. 2 Chr. 25:17–24.*

been. **12:** On *Jehoash's* war with *Amaziah king of Judah,* see 14.8–14. **14–20:** Two brief prophetic legends about Elisha are allocated to Jehoash's reign. *Three* Israelite victories against *Aram* (Damascus) are attributed to magical rituals performed by Elisha; see vv. 24–25. **23:** *Even yet:* the late compilers hold out some hope that both Israel and Judah can return from exile; compare 1 Kgs. 8.27–53 n. and Jer. chs. 30–31.

14.1–22: Amaziah of Judah. This was one of the more aggressive kings. **6:** *The law of Moses:* see Deut. 24.16. **7:** Amaziah moved to reestablish Judean power in the south; compare 8.20–22. **8:** *Confrontation:* a face-to-face encounter; a trial of strength. **9–10:** *Jehoash* knew that the two kingdoms could be powerful only a distance of four hundred cubits. [14] He took all the gold and silver and all the vessels found in the house of the LORD and in the treasuries of the palace, as well as hostages, and then returned to Samaria.

[15] The other events of the reign of Jehoash, and all his achievements, his exploits, and his wars with King Amaziah of Judah, are recorded in the annals of the kings of Israel. [16] He rested with his forefathers and was buried in Samaria with the kings of Israel. His son Jeroboam succeeded him.

[17] Amaziah son of Joash, king of Judah, outlived Jehoash son of Jehoahaz, king of Israel, by fifteen years. [18] The other events of Amaziah's reign are recorded in the annals of the kings of Judah. [19] A conspiracy was formed against him in Jerusalem and he fled to Lachish; but the conspirators sent after him to Lachish and put him to death there. [20] His body was conveyed on horseback to Jerusalem, and there he was buried with his forefathers in the city of David.

[21] The people of Judah, acting together, took Azariah, now sixteen years old, and made him king in succession to his father Amaziah. [22] It was he who built Elath and restored it to Judah after the king rested with his forefathers.

[23] In the fifteenth year of Amaziah son of Joash, king of Judah, Jeroboam son of Jehoash, king of Israel, became king in Samaria and reigned for forty-one years. [24] He did what was wrong in the eyes of the LORD; he did not give up the sinful practices of Jeroboam son of Nebat who led Israel into sin. [25] He re-established the frontiers of Israel from Lebo-hamath to the sea of the Arabah, in fulfilment of the word of the LORD the God of Israel spoken by his servant the prophet Jonah son of Amittai, from Gath-hepher. [26] For the LORD had seen how bitterly Israel had suffered; no one was safe, whether under the protection of his family or not, and Israel was left defenceless. [27] But the LORD had made no threat to blot out the name of Israel under heaven, and he saved them through Jeroboam son of Jehoash.

[28] The other events of Jeroboam's reign, and all his achievements, his exploits, the wars he fought, and how he recovered Damascus and Hamath in Jaudi for Israel, are recorded in the annals of the kings of Israel. [29] Jeroboam rested with his forefathers the kings of Israel, and he was succeeded by his son Zechariah.

15 In the twenty-seventh year of King Jeroboam of Israel, Azariah son of King Amaziah of Judah became king. [2] He was sixteen years old when he came to the throne, and he reigned in Jerusalem for fifty-two years; his mother was Jecoliah from Jerusalem. [3] He did what was right in the eyes of the LORD, as Amaziah his father had done. [4] But the shrines were not abolished; the people still continued to sacrifice and burn offerings there. [5] The LORD struck the king with leprosy, which he had till the day of his death; he was relieved of all duties and lived in his palace, while his son Jotham was comptroller of the household and regent over the country. [6] The other acts and events of Azariah's reign are recorded in the annals of the kings of Judah. [7] He rested with his forefathers and was buried with them in the city of David. His son Jotham succeeded him.

[8] In the thirty-eighth year of King Azariah of Judah, Zechariah son of Jeroboam became king over Israel in Samaria and reigned for six months. [9] He did what was wrong in the eyes of the LORD, as his forefathers had done; he did not give up the sinful practices of Jeroboam son of Nebat who led Israel into sin. [10] Shallum son of Jabesh formed a conspiracy against him, attacked and killed him in Ibleam, and usurped the throne. [11] The other events of Zechariah's reign are re-

14:17–22 *Cp.* 2 *Chr.* 25:25—26:2.   14:28 **in Jaudi for:** *prob. rdg; Heb.* to Judah in.   15:1 **Azariah:** Uzziah *in verses* 13,30,32,34.   15:2–3 *Cp.* 2 *Chr.* 26:3–4.   15:5–7 *Cp.* 2 *Chr.* 26:21–23. 15:5 **leprosy:** *or* a skin disease.   15:10 **in Ibleam:** *so Gk (Luc.); Heb.* before people.

when allied. **15–16:** This repeats 13.12–13. **19–21:** The reasons for the *conspiracy* are not known.

14.23–15.7: Jeroboam II of Israel and Azariah (Uzziah) of Judah. Under these two kings the Israelite kingdoms attained, for the third and last time, a dominance over Syria-Palestine. As in the case of Omri, some kings of great historical significance receive scant treatment by the compilers of Kgs. **28:** *Jaudi* may have been a minor kingdom in Syria. **15.2:** *Fifty-two years:* These include several years of coregency by Azariah with his father before the latter's assassination. Azariah's death (compare Isa. 6.1) brought an era to an end. **5:** *Regent:* lit. "he judged the people of the land"; see 11.14 n.

15.8–38: The decline of Israel. After Jeroboam II's long reign, the dynasty of Jehu was overthrown. No stable

corded in the annals of the kings of Israel.
¹²Thus the word of the LORD spoken to Jehu
was fulfilled: 'Your sons to the fourth generation will occupy the throne of Israel.'

¹³Shallum son of Jabesh became king in
the thirty-ninth year of King Uzziah of Judah, and he reigned for one full month in
Samaria. ¹⁴Menahem son of Gadi came up
from Tirzah to Samaria, attacked Shallum
son of Jabesh there, killed him, and usurped
the throne. ¹⁵The other events of Shallum's
reign and the conspiracy that he formed are
recorded in the annals of the kings of Israel.

¹⁶Then Menahem, starting out from Tirzah, destroyed Tappuah and everything in it
and ravaged its territory; he ravaged it because it had not opened its gates to him, and
he ripped open every pregnant woman
there.

¹⁷In the thirty-ninth year of King Azariah
of Judah, Menahem son of Gadi became king
over Israel and he reigned in Samaria for ten
years. ¹⁸⁻¹⁹He did what was wrong in the eyes
of the LORD; he did not give up the sinful
practices of Jeroboam son of Nebat who led
Israel into sin. In Menahem's time King Pul
of Assyria invaded the country, and Menahem gave him a thousand talents of silver to
obtain his help in strengthening his hold on
the kingdom. ²⁰Menahem laid a levy on all
the men of wealth in Israel; each had to give
the king of Assyria fifty silver shekels, and he
withdrew without occupying the country.
²¹The other acts and events of Menahem's
reign are recorded in the annals of the kings
of Israel. ²²He rested with his forefathers,
and was succeeded by his son Pekahiah.

²³In the fiftieth year of King Azariah of
Judah, Pekahiah son of Menahem became
king over Israel in Samaria and reigned for
two years. ²⁴He did what was wrong in the
eyes of the LORD; he did not give up the
sinful practices of Jeroboam son of Nebat
who led Israel into sin. ²⁵Pekah son of Rema-

liah, his lieutenant, formed a conspiracy
against him and, with the help of fifty Gileadites, attacked and killed him in the citadel of
the royal palace in Samaria, and usurped the
throne. ²⁶The other acts and events of Pekahiah's reign are recorded in the annals of the
kings of Israel.

²⁷In the fifty-second year of King Azariah
of Judah, Pekah son of Remaliah became
king over Israel in Samaria and reigned for
twenty years. ²⁸He did what was wrong in the
eyes of the LORD; he did not give up the
sinful practices of Jeroboam son of Nebat
who led Israel into sin. ²⁹In the days of King
Pekah of Israel, King Tiglath-pileser of Assyria came and seized Iyyon, Abel-beth-maacah, Janoah, Kedesh, Hazor, Gilead, and
Galilee, with all the land of Naphtali, and
deported the people to Assyria. ³⁰Then Hoshea son of Elah formed a conspiracy against
Pekah son of Remaliah, attacked and killed
him, and usurped the throne in the twentieth
year of Jotham son of Uzziah. ³¹The other
acts and events of Pekah's reign are recorded
in the annals of the kings of Israel.

³²In the second year of Pekah son of Remaliah, king of Israel, Jotham son of King Uzziah of Judah became king. ³³He was
twenty-five years old when he came to the
throne, and he reigned in Jerusalem for sixteen years; his mother was Jerusha daughter
of Zadok. ³⁴He did what was right in the eyes
of the LORD, as his father Uzziah had done;
³⁵but the shrines were not abolished and the
people continued to sacrifice and burn offerings there. It was he who constructed the
Upper Gate of the house of the LORD. ³⁶The
other acts and events of Jotham's reign are
recorded in the annals of the kings of Judah.
³⁷In those days the LORD began to send King
Rezin of Aram and Pekah son of Remaliah to

15:16 **Tappuah:** *so Gk (Luc.); Heb.* Tiphsah.
15:25 **the citadel ... palace:** *prob. rdg; Heb. adds* Argob
and Arieh.   15:33–38 *Cp.* 2 Chr. 27:1–9.

regime was again established in the north. **12:** See 10.31 and 1 Kgs. 11.29–39 n. **19:** *Pul:* the Babylonian throne
name of the Assyrian king Tiglath-pileser III (745–727 B.C.E.). *Menahem* represented a policy of vassalage to
Assyria; his contemporary opponent Pekah pursued an anti-Assyrian policy; see v. 27 n. **25:** *Gileadites* disturbed the Israelite throne more than once; see 1 Kgs. 17.1. **27:** Pekah's *twenty years* are counted from the
death of Zechariah, the last king of the Jehu dynasty. He was a claimant to the throne throughout the reigns
of Shallum, Menahem, and Pekahiah. His victory was the signal for an uprising in alliance with Damascus
against Assyria; see v. 37; Isa. 7.1–9. **29–30:** The rebellion against Tiglath-pileser was a great failure, and Israel
lost all its northern territory. Such a disaster invited yet another coup by a leader willing to come to terms with
Assyria. **30:** *The twentieth year of Jotham:* v. 33 gives *Jotham* only sixteen years; he must have reigned for some
years as coregent with his father.

attack Judah. ³⁸ Jotham rested with his fore-fathers and was buried with them in the city of David his forefather. His son Ahaz suc-ceeded him.

Downfall of the northern kingdom

16 In the seventeenth year of Pekah son of Remaliah, Ahaz son of King Jo-tham of Judah became king. ² Ahaz was twenty years old when he came to the throne, and he reigned in Jerusalem for sixteen years. He did not do what was right in the eyes of the LORD his God like his forefather David, ³ but followed in the footsteps of the kings of Israel; he even passed his son through the fire according to the abominable practice of the nations whom the LORD had dispossessed in favour of the Israelites. ⁴ He sacrificed and burned offerings at the shrines and on the hilltops and under every spreading tree.

⁵ Then King Rezin of Aram and Pekah son of Remaliah, king of Israel, attacked Jerusa-lem and besieged Ahaz but could not bring him to battle. ⁶ At that time the king of Edom recovered Elath by driving the Judaeans out of it; the Edomites entered the city and have occupied it to this day. ⁷ Ahaz sent messen-gers to King Tiglath-pileser of Assyria to say, 'I am your servant and your son. Come and save me from the king of Aram and from the king of Israel, who are attacking me.' ⁸ Ahaz took the silver and gold found in the house of the LORD and in the treasuries of the royal palace and sent them as a gift to the king of Assyria, ⁹ who listened to him; he advanced on Damascus, captured it, deported its in-habitants to Kir, and put Rezin to death.

¹⁰ When King Ahaz went to meet King Tig-lath-pileser of Assyria at Damascus, he saw there an altar of which he sent a sketch and a detailed plan to Uriah the priest. ¹¹ Accord-ingly, Uriah built an altar, following all the instructions that the king had sent him from Damascus, and had it ready against the king's

return. ¹² When the king came back from Da-mascus, he saw the altar, approached it, and mounted the steps; ¹³ there he burnt his whole-offering and his grain-offering and poured out his drink-offering, and he flung the blood of his shared-offerings against it. ¹⁴ The bronze altar that was before the LORD he removed from the front of the house, from between this new altar and the house of the LORD, and put it on the north side of this altar.

¹⁵ King Ahaz gave these instructions to Uriah the priest: 'Burn on the great altar the morning whole-offering and the evening grain-offering, and the king's whole-offering and his grain-offering, and the whole-of-fering of all the people of the land, their grain-offering and their drink-offerings, and fling against it all the blood of the sacri-fices. But the bronze altar shall be for me, to offer morning sacrifice.' ¹⁶ Uriah the priest carried out all the king's orders.

¹⁷ King Ahaz stripped the trolleys and re-moved the panels, and he took down the ba-sin and the Sea of bronze from the oxen which supported it and put it on a stone base. ¹⁸ In the house of the LORD he removed the structure they had erected for use on the sabbath, and the outer gate for the king, to satisfy the king of Assyria. ¹⁹ The other acts and events of the reign of Ahaz are recorded in the annals of the kings of Judah. ²⁰ Ahaz rested with his forefathers and was buried with them in the city of David. His son Heze-kiah succeeded him.

17 In the twelfth year of King Ahaz of Judah, Hoshea son of Elah became king over Israel and he reigned in Samaria for nine years. ² He did what was wrong in the eyes of the LORD, but not as previous kings of Israel had done. ³ King Shalmaneser of Assyria marched up against Hoshea, who

16:2–4 *Cp. 2 Chr. 28:1–4.* 16:6 **the king of Edom:** *prob. rdg; Heb.* Rezin king of Aram.
16:18 **structure:** *meaning uncertain.* 16:19–20 *Cp. 2 Chr. 28:26–27.*

16.1–20: Ahaz of Judah. 3: In the late monarchic period some very primitive cult practices were revived; compare 3.27; Jer. 7.30–31. 5–9: Compare Isa. 7.1–9. 6: Because of pressure on Judah from the north, *Edom* was able again (see 8.20–22) to escape its domination. *Elath:* the harbor on the Gulf of Aqaba. 10–18: This passage is taken from a source about the history of the temple; see 12.4–16. *Ahaz* had to make these changes because he became a vassal of Assyria. 14: *The bronze altar* was from Solomon's time; see 1 Kgs. 8.64. 15: On *the people of the land,* see 11.14 n.

17.1–41: The fall of Israel. The Deuteronomist attributes the fall of the Northern Kingdom to apostasy, heaping scorn on the syncretistic religious practices of the population of the conquered area. 3: *Shalmaneser* V had been tributary to him, ⁴but when the king of Assyria discovered that Hoshea was being disloyal to him, sending envoys to the king of Egypt at So, and withholding the annual tribute which he had been paying, the king of Assyria seized and imprisoned him. ⁵He overran the whole country and, reaching Samaria, besieged it for three years. ⁶In the ninth year of Hoshea he captured Samaria and deported its people to Assyria, and settled them in Halah and on the Habor, the river of Gozan, and in the towns of Media.

⁷All this came about because the Israelites had sinned against the Lord their God who brought them up from Egypt, from the despotic rule of Pharaoh king of Egypt; they paid homage to other gods ⁸and observed the laws and customs of the nations whom the Lord had dispossessed before them, ⁹and uttered blasphemies against the Lord their God; they built shrines for themselves in all their settlements, from watch-tower to fortified city; ¹⁰they set up for themselves sacred pillars and sacred poles on every high hill and under every spreading tree, ¹¹and burnt offerings at all the shrines there, as the nations did whom the Lord had displaced before them. By this wickedness of theirs they provoked the Lord's anger. ¹²They worshipped idols, a thing which the Lord had forbidden them to do.

¹³Still the Lord solemnly charged Israel and Judah by every prophet and seer, saying, 'Give up your evil ways; keep my commandments and statutes given in all the law which I enjoined on your forefathers and delivered to you through my servants the prophets.' ¹⁴They would not listen, however, but were as stubborn and rebellious as their forefathers had been, for they too refused to put their trust in the Lord their God. ¹⁵They rejected his statutes and the covenant which he had made with their forefathers and the solemn warnings which he had given to them. Following worthless idols they became worthless themselves and imitated the nations round about them, which the Lord had forbidden them to do. ¹⁶Forsaking every

commandment of the Lord their God, they made themselves images, two calves of cast metal, and also a sacred pole. They prostrated themselves to all the host of heaven and worshipped Baal; ¹⁷they made their sons and daughters pass through the fire. They practised augury and divination; they sold themselves to do what was wrong in the eyes of the Lord and so provoked his anger.

¹⁸Thus it was that the Lord was incensed against Israel and banished them from his presence; only the tribe of Judah was left. ¹⁹Even Judah did not keep the commandments of the Lord their God but followed the practices adopted by Israel; ²⁰so the Lord rejected all the descendants of Israel and punished them and gave them over to plunderers and finally flung them out from his presence. ²¹When he tore Israel from the house of David, they made Jeroboam son of Nebat king, and he seduced Israel from their allegiance to the Lord and led them into grave sin. ²²The Israelites persisted in all the sins that Jeroboam had committed and did not give them up, ²³until finally the Lord banished the Israelites from his presence, as he had threatened through all his servants the prophets, and they were deported from their own land to exile in Assyria; and there they are to this day.

²⁴Then the king of Assyria brought people from Babylon, Cuthah, Avva, Hamath, and Sepharvaim, and settled them in the towns of Samaria in place of the Israelites; so they occupied Samaria and lived in its towns. ²⁵In the early years of their settlement they did not pay homage to the Lord, so the Lord sent lions among them to prey on them. ²⁶The king of Assyria was told that the deported peoples whom he had settled in the towns of Samaria did not know the established usage of the God of the country, and that he had sent lions among them which were preying on them because they did not know this. ²⁷The king, therefore, gave orders that one of the priests taken captive

17:4 **to the . . . So:** *prob. rdg; Heb.* to So king of Egypt. 17:8 **before them:** *so Syriac; Heb. adds* and those of the kings of Egypt which they practised.

(727–722 B.C.E.) began the siege of Samaria but the conquest was completed under Sargon II (722–705 B.C.E.). **6:** In his own inscriptions, Sargon claims to have deported 27,290 Israelites. **7–23:** Here the Deuteronomic compilers speak as commentators; usually they put a speech into the mouth of a famous leader or prophet. **19–20:** At the time of the writing (see Introduction to 1 Kgs.) Judah has also fallen. **24–41:** The imported population possessed a mixture of religious identities and practices that later marked the *Samaritans* (v. 29);

from Samaria should be sent back to live there and teach the people the usage of the God of the country. 28 So one of the deported priests came and lived at Bethel, and taught them how to worship the LORD.

29 But each of the nations went on making its own god. They set them up in niches at the shrines which the Samaritans had made, each nation in its own settlements. 30 Succoth-benoth was worshipped by the men of Babylon, Nergal by the men of Cuth, Ashima by the men of Hamath, 31 Nibhaz and Tartak by the Avvites; and the Sepharvites burnt their children as offerings to Adrammelech and Anammelech, the gods of Sepharvaim. 32 While still paying homage to the LORD, they appointed all sorts of people to act as priests of the shrines and they resorted to them there. 33 They paid homage to the LORD, while at the same time they served their own gods, according to the custom of the nations from which they had been carried into exile.

34 They keep up these old practices to this day; they do not pay homage to the LORD, for they do not keep his statutes and his judgements, the law and commandment, which he enjoined on the descendants of Jacob whom he named Israel. 35 When the LORD made a covenant with them, he gave them this commandment: 'Do not pay homage to other gods or bow down to them or serve them or sacrifice to them, 36 but pay homage to the LORD who brought you up from Egypt with great power and with outstretched arm; to him alone you are to bow down, to him alone you are to offer sacrifice. 37 You must faithfully keep the statutes, the judgements, the law, and the commandments which he wrote for you; you must not pay homage to other gods. 38 Do not forget the covenant which I made with you; do not pay homage to other gods. 39 But to the LORD your God you are to

pay homage; it is he who will preserve you from all your enemies.' 40 However, they would not listen but continued their former practices. 41 While these nations paid homage to the LORD they continued to serve their images, and their children and their children's children have maintained the practice of their forefathers to this day.

Judah under Hezekiah

18 In the third year of Hoshea son of Elah, king of Israel, Hezekiah son of King Ahaz of Judah became king. 2 He was twenty-five years old when he came to the throne, and he reigned in Jerusalem for twenty-nine years; his mother was Abi daughter of Zechariah. 3 He did what was right in the eyes of the LORD, as his ancestor David had done. 4 It was he who suppressed the shrines, smashed the sacred pillars, cut down every sacred pole, and broke up the bronze serpent that Moses had made, for up to that time the Israelites had been in the habit of burning sacrifices to it; they called it Nehushtan. 5 He put his trust in the LORD the God of Israel; there was nobody like him among all the kings of Judah who succeeded him or among those who had gone before him. 6 He remained loyal to the LORD and did not fail in his allegiance to him, and he kept the commandments which the LORD had given to Moses. 7 The LORD was with him and he prospered in all that he undertook. He rebelled against the king of Assyria and was no longer subject to him; 8 he conquered the Philistine country as far as Gaza and its boundaries, from watch-tower to fortified city.

9 In the fourth year of Hezekiah's reign,

17:34 *his: prob. rdg; Heb.* their.   18:1-3 *Cp. 2 Chr. 29:1-2.*

the practices were improper from the standpoint of later Judean norms. **41:** *To this day:* the time of the Judean exile.

18.1–20.21: The reign of Hezekiah. The dating of Hezekiah's reign is one of the most difficult chronological problems in Kgs. According to 18.1 it began in 729 B.C.E.; according to 18.14, in 716/715, for Sennacherib's siege is known to have occurred in 701 B.C.E. The account of the reign consists of annalistic data (18.1–8, 13–16) and stories involving the prophet Isaiah at the siege of Jerusalem in 701 B.C.E. (18.17–20.21).

18.1–16: Hezekiah in the annals. When the Assyrian king Sargon II died in 705, Hezekiah timed his rebellion to coincide with that of Merodach-baladan in Babylonia (see 20.12). The religious purge included removing local sanctuaries (the shrines) in Judah in favor of the sole sanctuary in Jerusalem and purging venerated but superstitious practices from the cult at Jerusalem itself (v. 4). **4:** The *shrines* are suppressed for the first time; compare 1 Kgs. 3.2 and e.g. 1 Kgs. 22.43. *The bronze serpent that Moses had made* was which was the seventh year of Hoshea son of Elah, king of Israel, King Shalmaneser of Assyria marched up against Samaria, laid siege to it, [10] and captured it at the end of three years; it was in the sixth year of Hezekiah, that is the ninth year of King Hoshea of Israel, that Samaria was captured. [11] The king of Assyria deported the Israelites to Assyria and settled them in Halah and on the Habor, the river of Gozan, and in the cities of Media, [12] because they did not obey the LORD their God but violated his covenant and every commandment that Moses the servant of the LORD had given them; they would not listen and they would not obey.

[13] In the fourteenth year of King Hezekiah's reign, King Sennacherib of Assyria attacked and captured all the fortified towns of Judah. [14] Hezekiah sent a message to the king of Assyria at Lachish: 'I have done wrong; withdraw from me, and I shall pay any penalty you impose upon me.' The king of Assyria laid on Hezekiah king of Judah a penalty of three hundred talents of silver and thirty talents of gold; [15] and Hezekiah gave him all the silver found in the house of the LORD and in the treasuries of the palace. [16] At that time Hezekiah stripped of their gold the doors of the temple of the LORD and the door-frames which he himself had plated, and gave it to the king of Assyria.

[17] From Lachish the king of Assyria sent the commander-in-chief, the chief eunuch, and the chief officer with a strong force to King Hezekiah at Jerusalem. They marched up and when they reached Jerusalem they halted by the conduit of the Upper Pool on the causeway leading to the Fuller's Field. [18] When they called for the king, the comptroller of the household, Eliakim son of Hilkiah, came out to them with Shebna, the adjutant-general, and Joah son of Asaph, the secretary of state.

[19] The chief officer said to them, 'Tell Hezekiah that this is the message of the Great King, the king of Assyria: "What ground have you for this confidence of yours? [20] Do you think words can take the place of skill and military strength? On whom then do you rely for support in your rebellion against me? [21] On Egypt? Egypt is a splintered cane that will run into a man's hand and pierce it if he leans on it. That is what Pharaoh king of Egypt proves to all who rely on him. [22] And if you tell me that you are relying on the LORD your God, is he not the god whose shrines and altars Hezekiah has suppressed, telling Judah and Jerusalem they must worship at this altar in Jerusalem?"

[23] 'Now, make a deal with my master the king of Assyria: I shall give you two thousand horses if you can find riders for them. [24] How then can you reject the authority of even the least of my master's servants and rely on Egypt for chariots and horsemen? [25] Do you think that I have come to attack this place and destroy it without the consent of the LORD? No; the LORD himself said to me, "Go up and destroy this land."'

[26] Eliakim son of Hilkiah, Shebna, and Joah said to the chief officer, 'Please speak to us in Aramaic, for we understand it; do not speak Hebrew to us within earshot of the people on the city wall.' [27] The chief officer answered, 'Is it to your master and to you that my master has sent me to say this? Is it not to the people sitting on the wall who, like you, will have to eat their own dung and drink their own urine?'

[28] Then he stood and shouted in Hebrew, 'Hear the message of the Great King, the king of Assyria! [29] These are the king's words: "Do not be taken in by Hezekiah. He is powerless to save you from me. [30] Do not let him persuade you to rely on the LORD, and tell you that the LORD will surely save you and that this city will never be surrendered to the king of Assyria." [31] Do not listen to Hezekiah, for this is what the king of Assyria says: "Make your peace with me, and surrender.

18:13–37 *Cp. Isa. 36:1–22; 2 Chr. 32:1–19.*
18:17 **the commander-in-chief ... officer:** *or* Tartan, Rab-saris, and Rab-shakeh. **reached Jerusalem:** *so Gk; Heb. adds* and went up and came.

destroyed; the story of its supposed origin is preserved in Num. 21.4–9. **9–12:** A brief summary of ch. 17. **13–16:** This realistic report is contradicted in Sennacherib's own inscription only by his claim to have received eight hundred instead of *three hundred talents of silver* (v. 14).

18.17–19.37: The siege and deliverance of Jerusalem. Within the totality of the Deuteronomic history (Deut.–2 Kgs.), this is the last time the LORD intervenes by prophecy and marvelous action on Israel's behalf. **17:** For more details about *the conduit of the Upper Pool* see Isa. 7.3. **18:** *Shebna:* see Isa. 22.15–19. **26:** *Aramaic* was becoming the common language of commerce and diplomacy.

Then every one of you will eat the fruit of his own vine and of his own fig tree, and drink the water of his own cistern, ³² until I come and take you to a land like your own, a land of grain and new wine, of bread and vineyards, of olives, fine oil, and honey—life for you all, instead of death. Do not listen to Hezekiah; he will only mislead you by telling you that the LORD will save you. ³³ Did any god of the nations save his land from the king of Assyria's power? ³⁴ Where are the gods of Hamath and Arpad? Where are the gods of Sepharvaim, Hena, and Ivvah? Where are the gods of Samaria? Did they save Samaria from me? ³⁵ Among all the gods of the nations is there one who saved his land from me? So how is the LORD to save Jerusalem?"'

³⁶ The people remained silent and said not a word in reply, for the king had given orders that no one was to answer him. ³⁷ Eliakim son of Hilkiah, comptroller of the household, Shebna the adjutant-general, and Joah son of Asaph, secretary of state, came to Hezekiah with their clothes torn and reported the words of the chief officer.

19 When King Hezekiah heard their report, he tore his clothes, put on sackcloth, and went into the house of the LORD. ² He sent Eliakim comptroller of the household, Shebna the adjutant-general, and the senior priests, all wearing sackcloth, to the prophet Isaiah son of Amoz, ³ to give him this message from the king: 'Today is a day of trouble for us, a day of reproof and contumely. We are like a woman who has no strength to bring to birth the child she is carrying. ⁴ It may be that the LORD your God will give heed to all the words of the chief officer whom his master the king of Assyria sent to taunt the living God, and will confute the words which the LORD your God heard. Offer a prayer for those who still survive.'

⁵ When King Hezekiah's servants came to Isaiah, ⁶ they were given this answer for their master: 'Here is the word of the LORD: Do not be alarmed at what you heard when the Assyrian king's minions blasphemed me. ⁷ I

shall sap his morale till at a mere rumour he will withdraw to his own country; and there I shall make him fall by the sword.'

⁸ Meanwhile the chief officer went back, and having heard that the king of Assyria had moved camp from Lachish, he found him attacking Libnah. ⁹ But when the king learnt that King Tirhakah of Cush was on the way to engage him in battle, he sent messengers again to King Hezekiah of Judah ¹⁰ to say to him, 'How can you be deluded by your God on whom you rely when he promises that Jerusalem will not fall into the hands of the king of Assyria? ¹¹ You yourself must have heard what the kings of Assyria have done to all countries: they utterly destroyed them. Can you then hope to escape? ¹² Did their gods save the nations which my predecessors wiped out: Gozan, Harran, Rezeph, and the people of Eden living in Telassar? ¹³ Where are the kings of Hamath, of Arpad, and of Lahir, Sepharvaim, Hena, and Ivvah?'

¹⁴ Hezekiah received the letter from the messengers and, having read it, he went up to the house of the LORD and spread it out before the LORD ¹⁵ with this prayer: 'LORD God of Israel, enthroned on the cherubim, you alone are God of all the kingdoms of the world; you made heaven and earth. ¹⁶ Incline your ear, LORD, and listen; open your eyes, LORD, and see; hear the words that Sennacherib has sent to taunt the living God. ¹⁷ LORD, it is true that the kings of Assyria have laid waste the nations and their lands ¹⁸ and have consigned their gods to the flames. They destroyed them, because they were no gods but the work of men's hands, mere wood and stone. ¹⁹ Now, LORD our God, save us from his power, so that all the kingdoms of the earth may know that you alone, LORD, are God.'

²⁰ Isaiah son of Amoz sent Hezekiah the following message: 'This is the word of the

---

18:34 **Where are the gods of Samaria?:** *so Gk (Luc.)*; *Heb. omits.*   19:1–37 *Cp. Isa. 37:1–38; 2 Chr. 32:20–22.*   19:7 **I shall sap his morale:** *lit.* I shall put a spirit in him.

19.1: The penitent attitude is to gain the LORD's favor. **6–7:** Isaiah's prophecy is fulfilled inexactly in what follows; it does not include striking down the Assyrian army; compare vv. 35–37. **8–13:** This second ultimatum to Hezekiah, plus the fact that *Tirhakah* did not become king of Egypt before 690 B.C.E., has led some to think there were two different sieges of Jerusalem by Sennacherib, the second taking place around 689–688 B.C.E. A duplication of reports of the same siege is more likely. **14–19:** Hezekiah's *prayer* here is much less related to the immediate situation than vv. 3–4. **15:** *Enthroned on the cherubim:* see 1 Sam. 4.4 n. **20–28:** Isaiah's taunt song against Sennacherib is similar to the prophecy in Isa. 10.5–19, probably delivered on the occasion

LORD the God of Israel: I have heard your prayer to me concerning King Sennacherib of Assyria, ²¹and this is the word which the LORD has spoken against him:

The virgin daughter of Zion disdains you,
she laughs you to scorn;
the daughter of Jerusalem tosses her head
as you retreat.
²²Whom have you taunted and blasphemed?
Against whom did you raise an outcry,
casting haughty glances at the Holy One of Israel?
²³You sent your messengers to taunt the Lord, and said:
"I have mounted my chariot and performed mighty deeds;
I have ascended the mountain heights,
gone to the remote recesses of Lebanon.
I have felled its tallest cedars,
the finest of its pines;
I have reached its farthest corners,
the most luxuriant forest.
²⁴I have dug wells
and drunk the waters of a foreign land,
and with the sole of my foot I have dried up
all the streams of Egypt."

²⁵'Have you not heard?
Long ago I did it all.
In days gone by I planned it
and now I have brought it about,
till your fortified cities have crashed into heaps of rubble.
²⁶Their inhabitants, shorn of strength,
disheartened and put to shame,
were but as plants in the field, frail as green herbs,
as grass on the rooftops blasted by the east wind.
²⁷I know your rising up and your sitting down,
your going out and your coming in.
²⁸The frenzy of your rage against me
and your arrogance have come to my ears.

I shall put a ring in your nose
and a bridle in your mouth,
and I shall take you back
by the way on which you came.

²⁹'This will be the sign for you: this year you will eat the leavings of the grain and in the second year what is self-sown; but in the third year you will sow and reap, plant vineyards and eat their fruit. ³⁰The survivors left in Judah will strike fresh root below ground and yield fruit above ground, ³¹for a remnant will come out of Jerusalem and survivors from Mount Zion. The zeal of the LORD will perform this.

³²'Therefore, this is the word of the LORD about the king of Assyria:

He will not enter this city
or shoot an arrow there,
he will not advance against it with shield
or cast up a siege-ramp against it.
³³By the way he came he will go back;
he will not enter this city.
This is the word of the LORD.
³⁴I shall shield this city to deliver it
for my own sake and for the sake of my servant David.'

³⁵That night the angel of the LORD went out and struck down a hundred and eighty-five thousand in the Assyrian camp; when morning dawned, there they all lay dead. ³⁶King Sennacherib of Assyria broke camp and marched away; he went back to Nineveh and remained there. ³⁷One day, while he was worshipping in the temple of his god Nisroch, Adrammelech and Sharezer his sons assassinated him and made their escape to the land of Ararat. His son Esarhaddon succeeded him.

20 At this time Hezekiah became mortally ill, and the prophet Isaiah son of

19:23 **and performed mighty deeds:** *so Gk (Luc.); Heb. omits.* 19:25 **heaps of rubble:** *prob. rdg, cp. Isa. 37:26; Heb. obscure.* 19:26 **by the east wind:** *prob. rdg, cp. Isa. 37:27; Heb. before it is mature.* 19:27 **your rising up:** *prob. rdg, cp. Isa. 37:28; Heb. omits.* 19:28 **against me:** *prob. rdg, cp. Isa. 37:29; Heb. repeats* the frenzy of your rage against me. 19:33 **came:** *so some MSS; others* comes. 20:1–11 *Cp. Isa. 38:1–8,21,22.*

of Sennacherib's siege of Jerusalem in 701 B.C.E. **21:** *Zion:* the city is personified as a woman. **27–28:** The LORD speaks again, to Assyria. **32–34:** This oracle speaks to a situation prior to the last desperate siege. **35:** This miracle has neither been prepared for nor is it referred to elsewhere. **37:** Sennacherib died in 681 B.C.E., twenty years after the siege of Jerusalem.

Amoz came to him with this message from the LORD: 'Give your last instructions to your household, for you are dying; you will not recover.' ²Hezekiah turned his face to the wall and offered this prayer to the LORD: ³'LORD, remember how I have lived before you, faithful and loyal in your service, doing always what was pleasing to you.' And he wept bitterly. ⁴But before Isaiah had left the citadel, the word of the LORD came to him: ⁵'Go back and say to Hezekiah, the prince of my people: This is the word of the LORD the God of your father David: I have heard your prayer and seen your tears; I shall heal you, and on the third day you will go up to the house of the LORD. ⁶I shall add fifteen years to your life and deliver you and this city from the king of Assyria. I shall protect this city for my own sake and for the sake of my servant David.'

⁷Isaiah told them to prepare a fig-plaster; when it was made and applied to the inflammation, Hezekiah recovered. ⁸He asked Isaiah what proof there was that the LORD would cure him and that he would go up to the house of the LORD on the third day. ⁹Isaiah replied, 'This will be your proof from the LORD that he will do what he has promised; will the shadow go forward ten steps or back ten steps?' ¹⁰Hezekiah answered, 'It is an easy thing for the shadow to move forward ten steps; rather let it go back ten steps.' ¹¹Isaiah the prophet called to the LORD, and he made the shadow go back ten steps where it had advanced down the stairway of Ahaz.

¹²At that time the king of Babylon, Merodach-baladan son of Baladan, sent envoys with a gift to Hezekiah, for he heard that he had been ill. ¹³Hezekiah welcomed them and showed them all his treasury, the silver and gold, the spices and fragrant oil, his armoury, and everything to be found among his treasures; there was nothing in his palace

or in his whole realm that Hezekiah did not show them.

¹⁴The prophet Isaiah came to King Hezekiah and asked, 'What did these men say? Where did they come from?' 'They came from a distant country,' Hezekiah answered, 'from Babylon.' ¹⁵'What did they see in your palace?' Isaiah demanded. 'They saw everything,' was the reply; 'there was nothing among my treasures that I did not show them.' ¹⁶Isaiah said to Hezekiah, 'Hear the word of the LORD: ¹⁷The time is coming, says the LORD, when everything in your palace, and all that your forefathers have amassed till the present day, will be carried away to Babylon; not a thing will be left. ¹⁸And some of your sons, your own offspring, will be taken from you to serve as eunuchs in the palace of the king of Babylon.' ¹⁹Hezekiah answered, 'The word of the LORD which you have spoken is good,' for he was thinking to himself that peace and security would last out his lifetime.

²⁰The other events of Hezekiah's reign, his exploits, and how he made the pool and the conduit and brought water into the city, are recorded in the annals of the kings of Judah. ²¹Hezekiah rested with his forefathers, and his son Manasseh succeeded him.

21 MANASSEH was twelve years old when he came to the throne, and he reigned in Jerusalem for fifty-five years; his mother was Hephzibah. ²He did what was wrong in the eyes of the LORD, in following the abominable practices of the nations which the LORD had dispossessed in favour of the Israelites. ³He rebuilt the shrines which his father Hezekiah had destroyed, he

20:9 **will the shadow go:** *so Aram. (Targ.); Heb.* has the shadow gone.   20:12–19 *Cp. Isa. 39:1–8.*
20:12 **Merodach:** *so some MSS, cp. Isa. 39:1; others* Berodach.   20:13 **welcomed:** *so some MSS, cp. Isa. 39:2; others* heard.   21:1–9 *Cp. 2 Chr. 33:1–9.*

20.1–21: Two legends of Isaiah. 6: That *fifteen years* are added to Hezekiah's life is probably related to the problem of the chronology in Hezekiah's reign; compare 18.1–20.21 n. **8–11:** The *sign* given is the backward movement of the sun's shadow on some stairs; this was a normal time-keeping device. **12–19:** *Merodach-baladan* rebelled against Sennacherib at the same time as Hezekiah; see 18.1–16 n. An actual eighth-century embassy to coordinate the rebellion is here combined with a more legendary prophetic story about Isaiah, which reflects a much later time (after 605 B.C.E.) when Babylon became a threat to, rather than an ally of, Judean independence. **18:** None of Hezekiah's *sons* became Babylonian prisoners; Babylon as well as Judah was subject to Assyria.

21.1–18: Manasseh and Judah. The Northern Kingdom had fallen because the sins of Jeroboam were never removed. Manasseh's *fifty-five years* began with a coregency with Hezekiah (697 B.C.E.), not long after erected altars to the Baal, made a sacred pole as Ahab king of Israel had done, and prostrated himself before all the host of heaven and served them. ⁴He built altars in the house of the LORD, that house of which the LORD had said, 'I shall set my name in Jerusalem.' ⁵He built altars for all the host of heaven in the two courts of the house of the LORD; ⁶he made his son pass through the fire, he practised soothsaying and divination, and dealt with ghosts and spirits. He did much wrong in the eyes of the LORD and provoked his anger. ⁷He made an image of the goddess Asherah and set it up in the house of which the LORD had said to David and Solomon his son, 'In this house and Jerusalem, which I chose out of all the tribes of Israel, I shall establish my name for all time. ⁸I shall not again make Israel outcasts from the land which I gave to their forefathers, if only they are careful to observe all my commands and all the law that my servant Moses gave them.' ⁹But they did not obey, and Manasseh led them astray into wickedness far worse than that of the nations which the LORD had exterminated in favour of the Israelites.

¹⁰The LORD spoke through his servants the prophets: ¹¹'Because King Manasseh of Judah has done these abominable things, outdoing the Amorites before him in wickedness, and because he has led Judah into sin with his idols, ¹²this is the word of the LORD the God of Israel: I am about to bring such disaster on Jerusalem and Judah that it will ring in the ears of all who hear of it. ¹³I shall use against Jerusalem the measuring line used against Samaria and the plummet used against the house of Ahab. I shall wipe Jerusalem as one wipes a plate and turns it upside down. ¹⁴I shall cast off what is left of my people, my own possession, and hand them over to their enemies. They will be plundered, a prey to all their enemies, ¹⁵for they have done what is wrong in my eyes and have provoked my anger from the day their fore-

fathers left Egypt up to the present day. ¹⁶This Manasseh shed so much innocent blood that he filled Jerusalem with it from end to end, not to mention the sin into which he led Judah by doing what is wrong in my eyes.'

¹⁷The other events and acts of Manasseh's reign, and the sin that he committed, are recorded in the annals of the kings of Judah. ¹⁸Manasseh rested with his forefathers and was buried in the garden-tomb of his family, in the garden of Uzza. His son Amon succeeded him.

¹⁹Amon was twenty-two years old when he came to the throne, and he reigned in Jerusalem for two years; his mother was Meshullemeth daughter of Haruz from Jotbah. ²⁰He did what was wrong in the eyes of the LORD as his father Manasseh had done. ²¹Following in his father's footsteps he served the idols that his father had served and prostrated himself before them. ²²He forsook the LORD the God of his forefathers and did not conform to the LORD's ways. ²³Amon's courtiers conspired against him and assassinated him in the palace; ²⁴but the people of the land killed all the conspirators and made his son Josiah king in his place. ²⁵The other events of Amon's reign are recorded in the annals of the kings of Judah. ²⁶He was buried in his grave in the garden of Uzza. His son Josiah succeeded him.

Josiah's reform

22 JOSIAH was eight years old when he came to the throne, and he reigned in Jerusalem for thirty-one years; his mother was Jedidah daughter of Adaiah of Bozkath. ²He did what was right in the eyes of the LORD, following in the footsteps of his forefather David and deviating neither to the right nor to the left.

³In the eighteenth year of his reign, Josiah

21:19–24 *Cp. 2 Chr. 33:21–25.* 22:1–2 *Cp. 2 Chr. 34:1–2.* 22:3–23:3 *Cp. 2 Chr. 34:8–32.*

Sennacherib's defeat of the rebellion. **7:** *Asherah:* see 13.6. **10–16:** The condemnation is anonymous, spoken simply by the LORD's *servants the prophets.* **11:** *Amorites:* see Gen. 15.16 n.

21.19–26: Amon of Judah. 19: Amon's *mother,* Manasseh's most important wife, was from *Jotbah.* **23:** This assassination probably had some relation to the policy toward Assyria. **24:** *The people of the land:* see 11.14 n.

22.1–23.30: Josiah. With this king the Deuteronomic history reached its climax. *Josiah* carries out what all earlier kings are blamed for failing to do. He removes the shrines in Judah and destroys the cult center in Bethel. Religiously, his program was deemed entirely correct, but—from the final viewpoint of Kgs.—he came one generation too late, for the divine decision about Judah had been made; see 21.10–15; 23.26–27. **3–7:** *Josiah* sent Shaphan son of Azaliah, son of Meshullam, the adjutant-general, to the house of the Lord. 4 'Go to the high priest Hilkiah,' he said, 'and tell him to melt down the silver that has been brought into the house of the Lord, which those on duty at the entrance have received from the people; 5 tell him to hand it over to those supervising in the house of the Lord, to pay the workmen who are carrying out repairs in it, 6 the carpenters, builders, and masons, and to purchase timber and hewn stones for its repair. 7 They are not to be asked to account for the money that has been given them; they are acting on trust.'

8 The high priest Hilkiah told Shaphan the adjutant-general that he had discovered the scroll of the law in the house of the Lord, and he gave it to him to read. 9 When Shaphan came to report to the king that his servants had melted down the silver in the house of the Lord and handed it over to those supervising there, 10 he told the king of the scroll the high priest Hilkiah had given him, and he read it in the king's presence. 11 When the king heard what was written in the book of the law, he tore his clothes. 12 He ordered the priest Hilkiah, Ahikam son of Shaphan, Akbor son of Micaiah, Shaphan the adjutant-general, and Asaiah the king's attendant 13 to go and seek guidance of the Lord for himself, for the people, and for all Judah, about the contents of this book that had been discovered. 'Great must be the wrath of the Lord', he said, 'that has been kindled against us, because our forefathers did not obey the commands in this scroll and do all that is laid on us.'

14 Hilkiah the priest, Ahikam, Akbor, Shaphan, and Asaiah went to Huldah the prophetess, wife of Shallum son of Tikvah, son of Harhas, the keeper of the wardrobe, and consulted her at her home in the Second Quarter of Jerusalem. 15 'This is the word of the Lord the God of Israel,' she answered: 'Tell the man who sent you to me, 16 that this is what the Lord says: I am about to bring disaster on this place and its inhabitants as foretold in the scroll which the king of Judah has read, 17 because they have forsaken me

and burnt sacrifices to other gods, provoking my anger with all the idols they have made with their own hands; for this my wrath is kindled against this place and will not be quenched. 18 Tell the king of Judah who sent you to seek guidance of the Lord that this is what the Lord the God of Israel says: You have listened to my words 19 and shown a willing heart and humbled yourself before the Lord when you heard me say that this place and its inhabitants would become objects of loathing and scorn, and have torn your clothes and wept before me. Because of this, I for my part have listened to you. This is the word of the Lord. 20 Therefore I shall gather you to your forefathers, and you will be gathered to your grave in peace; you will not live to see all the disaster which I am bringing on this place.' They brought back this answer to the king.

23 At the king's summons all the elders of Judah and Jerusalem were assembled, 2 and he went up to the house of the Lord, taking with him all the men of Judah, the inhabitants of Jerusalem, the priests, and the prophets, the entire population, high and low. There he read out to them the whole scroll of the covenant which had been discovered in the house of the Lord. 3 Then, standing by the pillar, the king entered into a covenant before the Lord to obey him and keep his commandments, his testimonies, and his statutes, with all his heart and soul, and so carry out the terms of the covenant written in the scroll. All the people pledged themselves to the covenant.

4 The king ordered the high priest Hilkiah, the deputy high priest, and those on duty at the entrance to remove from the house of the Lord all the objects made for Baal, for Asherah, and for all the host of heaven, and he burnt these outside Jerusalem on the slope by the Kidron, and carried the ashes to Bethel. 5 He suppressed the heathen priests whom the kings of Judah had appointed to burn sacrifices at the shrines in the towns of

22:4 **melt down:** *so Gk (Luc.); Heb.* complete.
23:4 **deputy high priest:** *prob. rdg; Heb.* deputy high priests.   23:5 **to burn:** *so Gk (Luc.); Heb.* and he burnt.

instructs *Shaphan* to institute the temple repairs; compare 12.4–16. **8–13:** The king's response to the *scroll* implies that it contained divine requirements not previously known. **14–20:** The punishment promised in the book is inescapable, but because of the faithfulness of Josiah it is to be postponed until after his death. **23.1–3:** *The scroll of the covenant* becomes authorized as the law of the land; the *scroll* is often taken to be the central portion of Deuteronomy, chs. 5–28. **4–14:** The cult objects and sites of temples were regarded as illicit both

Judah and in the neighbourhood of Jerusalem, as well as those who burnt sacrifices to Baal, to the sun and moon, to the planets and all the host of heaven. 6 He took the Asherah from the house of the LORD to the wadi of the Kidron outside Jerusalem, burnt it there, and pounded it to dust, which was then scattered over the common burial-ground. 7 He also pulled down the quarters of the male prostitutes attached to the house of the LORD, where the women wove vestments in honour of Asherah.

8 The king brought in all the priests from the towns of Judah and desecrated the shrines where they had burnt sacrifices, from Geba to Beersheba, and dismantled the shrines of the demons in front of the gate of Joshua, the city governor, which is to the left of the city gate. 9 These priests, however, never came up to the altar of the LORD in Jerusalem but used to eat unleavened bread with the priests of their clan. 10 He desecrated Topheth in the valley of Ben-hinnom, so that no one might make his son or daughter pass through the fire for Molech. 11 He did away with the horses that the kings of Judah had set up in honour of the sun at the entrance to the house of the LORD, beside the room of the eunuch Nathan-melech in the colonnade, and he burnt the chariots of the sun. 12 He demolished the altars made by the kings of Judah on the roof by the upper chamber of Ahaz and the altars made by Manasseh in the two courts of the house of the LORD; he pounded them to dust and threw it into the wadi of the Kidron. 13 Also, on the east of Jerusalem, to the south of the mount of Olives, the king desecrated the shrines which Solomon the king of Israel had built for Ashtoreth the loathsome goddess of the Sidonians, and for Kemosh the loathsome god of Moab, and for Milcom the abominable god of the Ammonites; 14 he smashed the sacred pillars and cut down the sacred poles and filled the places where they had stood with human bones.

15 At Bethel he dismantled the altar by the shrine made by Jeroboam son of Nebat who led Israel into sin, together with the shrine itself; he broke its stones in pieces, crushed them to dust, and burnt the sacred pole. 16 When Josiah saw the graves which were there on the hill, he sent and had the bones taken from them, and he burnt them on the altar to desecrate it, thus fulfilling the word of the LORD announced by the man of God when Jeroboam stood by the altar at the feast. When Josiah saw the grave of the man of God who had foretold these things, 17 he asked, 'What is that monument I see?' The people of the town answered, 'It is the grave of the man of God who came from Judah and foretold all that you have done to the altar at Bethel.' 18 'Leave it alone,' he said; 'let no one disturb his bones.' So they spared his bones along with those of the prophet who came from Samaria. 19 Josiah also suppressed all the temples at the shrines in the towns of Samaria, which the kings of Israel had set up and thereby provoked the LORD's anger, and he did to them what he had done at Bethel. 20 He slaughtered on the altars all the priests of the shrines who were there, and he burnt human bones on them. Then he went back to Jerusalem.

21 The king ordered all the people to keep the Passover to the LORD their God, as this scroll of the covenant prescribed; 22 no Passover like it had been kept either when the judges were ruling Israel or during the times of the kings of Israel and of Judah, 23 until in the eighteenth year of Josiah's reign this Passover was kept to the LORD in Jerusalem.

24 Further, Josiah got rid of all who called up ghosts and spirits, and of all household gods and idols and all the loathsome objects to be seen in the land of Judah and in Jerusalem, so that he might fulfil the requirements of the law written in the scroll which the priest Hilkiah had discovered in the house of

23:6 **Asherah:** *or* sacred pole.   23:13 **mount of Olives:** *so Aram. (Targ.); Heb.* mount of the Destroyer. 23:15 **by the shrine:** *prob. rdg; Heb.* omits by. **he broke . . . pieces:** *so Gk; Heb.* he burnt the shrine. 23:16 **when Jeroboam . . . man of God:** *so Gk; Heb.* omits.   23:19 **the LORD's:** *so Gk; Heb.* omits. 23:24 **household gods:** *Heb.* teraphim.

from the viewpoint of Josiah and of those who in postexilic times were faithful to the norms here set forth. **8–9:** While *shrines* were eliminated, their *priests* were incorporated into a more complex Jerusalemite priesthood. **13:** Compare 1 Kgs. 11.7. **15–20:** Later in his reign, after Assyria had collapsed, Josiah moved to take over the territory of the former Northern Kingdom. He defended that territory against Pharaoh Necho II, at the cost of his life (vv. 29–30; compare 2 Chr. 35.20–25). **16–18:** See 1 Kgs. 13.2, 30–32. **21–23:** The *Passover* observance was the occasion on which the people reconstituted themselves as the people of God; compare the LORD. 25 No king before him had turned to the LORD as he did, with all his heart and soul and strength, following the whole law of Moses; nor did any king like him appear again.

26 Yet the LORD did not abate his fierce anger; it still burned against Judah because of all the provocation which Manasseh had given him. 27 'Judah also I shall banish from my presence', he declared, 'as I banished Israel; and I shall reject this city of Jerusalem which once I chose, and the house where I promised that my name should be.'

28 The other events and acts of Josiah's reign are recorded in the annals of the kings of Judah. 29 It was in his reign that Pharaoh Necho king of Egypt set out for the river Euphrates to help the king of Assyria. King Josiah went to meet him; and when they met at Megiddo, Pharaoh Necho slew him. 30 His attendants conveyed his body in a chariot from Megiddo to Jerusalem and buried him in his own burial-place. Then the people of the land took Josiah's son Jehoahaz and anointed him king in place of his father.

Downfall of the southern kingdom

31 JEHOAHAZ was twenty-three years old when he came to the throne, and he reigned in Jerusalem for three months; his mother was Hamital daughter of Jeremiah from Libnah. 32 He did what was wrong in the eyes of the LORD, as his forefathers had done. 33 Pharaoh Necho removed him from the throne in Jerusalem, and imposed on the land an indemnity of a hundred talents of silver and one talent of gold. 34 He made Josiah's son Eliakim king in place of his father and changed his name to Jehoiakim. He carried Jehoahaz away to Egypt, where he died. 35 Jehoiakim handed over the silver and gold to Pharaoh, taxing the country to meet Pharaoh's demands; he exacted it from the peo-ple, from every man according to his assessment, so that he could pay Pharaoh Necho.

36 Jehoiakim was twenty-five years old when he came to the throne, and he reigned in Jerusalem for eleven years; his mother was Zebidah daughter of Pedaiah of Rumah. 37 He did what was wrong in the eyes of the

24 LORD as his forefathers had done. 1 During his reign an attack was launched by King Nebuchadnezzar of Babylon, and Jehoiakim became his vassal; three years later, however, he broke with him and revolted. 2 The LORD sent against him raiding parties of Chaldaeans, Aramaeans, Moabites, and Ammonites, letting them range through Judah and ravage it, as the LORD had foretold through his servants the prophets. 3 All this happened to Judah in fulfilment of the LORD's purpose, to banish them from his presence because of all the sin Manasseh had committed 4 and because of the innocent blood he had shed; he had flooded Jerusalem with innocent blood, and the LORD would not forgive him. 5 The other events and acts of Jehoiakim's reign are recorded in the annals of the kings of Judah. 6 He rested with his forefathers, and his son Jehoiachin succeeded him. 7 The Egyptian king did not leave his own land again, because the king of Babylon had stripped him of all he possessed from the wadi of Egypt to the river Euphrates.

8 JEHOIACHIN was eighteen years old when he came to the throne, and he reigned in Jerusalem for three months; his mother was Nehushta daughter of Elnathan from Jerusalem. 9 He did what was wrong in the eyes of the LORD, as his father had done.

23:30–34 *Cp. 2 Chr. 36:1–4.*   23:33 **removed ...** **throne:** *prob. rdg, cp. 2 Chr. 36:3; Heb.* bound him at Riblah in the land of Hamath when he was king. 24:8–17 *Cp. 2 Chr. 36:9–10.*

2 Chr. ch. 30 and Ezra 6.19–22. **26–27:** See 21.10–15; 22.16–20. **29–30:** By the account in 2 Chr. 35.20–25 Josiah was moving to impede Necho's aid for the Assyrians at Carchemish. The Babylonians took and held that city, thanks, perhaps, to Josiah's delaying tactics against the Egyptians. **30:** *The people of the land* were Josiah's primary support; see 11.14 n.

23.31–24.20: The last kings of Judah. 31–35: *Jehoahaz* was Josiah's second son, born to his second wife (vv. 31.36). After Josiah's death he, rather than Jehoiakim, the eldest son, was put on the throne by *the people of the land* (v. 30). Accordingly, Necho put the older son on the throne (609 B.C.E.) and imposed a heavy fine on the people of the land, who had been the mainstay of Josiah's movement; see 11.14 n. **24.1:** *Nebuchadnezzar* won the battle of Carchemish in 605 (see Jer. 46.2), driving Egyptian forces out of Syria. *Jehoiakim* took the first opportunity, however, to rebel against the new Babylonian master. **2:** See Jer. 25.9. **3–4:** See 21.10–15.

¹⁰ At that time the troops of King Nebuchadnezzar of Babylon advanced on Jerusalem and the city came under siege. ¹¹ Nebuchadnezzar arrived while his troops were besieging it, ¹² and King Jehoiachin of Judah, along with his mother, his courtiers, his officers, and his eunuchs surrendered to the king of Babylon. The king of Babylon, now in the eighth year of his reign, made him a prisoner; ¹³ and, as the LORD had foretold, he carried off all the treasures of the house of the LORD and of the palace and broke up all the vessels of gold which King Solomon of Israel had made for the temple of the LORD. ¹⁴ He took into exile the people of Jerusalem, the officers and all the fighting men, ten thousand in number, together with all the craftsmen and smiths; only the poorest class of the people was left. ¹⁵ He deported Jehoiachin to Babylon; he also took into exile from Jerusalem to Babylon the king's mother and his wives, his eunuchs, and the foremost men of the land. ¹⁶ He took also all the people of substance, seven thousand in number, and a thousand craftsmen and smiths, all of them able-bodied men and skilled armourers. ¹⁷ He made Mattaniah, uncle of Jehoiachin, king in his place and changed his name to Zedekiah.

¹⁸ Zedekiah was twenty-one years old when he came to the throne, and he reigned in Jerusalem for eleven years; his mother was Hamital daughter of Jeremiah from Libnah. ¹⁹ He did what was wrong in the eyes of the LORD, as Jehoiakim had done. ²⁰ Jerusalem and Judah so angered the LORD that in the end he banished them from his sight.

Zedekiah rebelled against the king of Babylon. **25** ¹ In the ninth year of his reign, on the tenth day of the tenth month, King Nebuchadnezzar of Babylon advanced with his whole army against Jerusalem, invested it, and erected siege-towers against it on every side; ² the siege lasted till the eleventh year of King Zedekiah. ³ In the fourth month of that year, on the ninth day of the month, when famine was severe in the city

and there was no food for the people, ⁴ the city capitulated. When King Zedekiah of Judah saw this, he and all his armed escort left the city and, fleeing by night through the gate called Between the Two Walls, near the king's garden, they made their escape towards the Arabah, although the Chaldaeans were surrounding the city. ⁵ The Chaldaean army pursued the king and overtook him in the lowlands of Jericho. His men all forsook him and scattered, ⁶ and the king was captured and, having been brought before the king of Babylon at Riblah, he was put on trial and sentenced. ⁷ Zedekiah's sons were slain before his eyes; then his eyes were put out, and he was brought to Babylon bound in bronze fetters.

⁸ In the fifth month, on the seventh day of the month, in the nineteenth year of King Nebuchadnezzar of Babylon, Nebuzaradan, captain of the king of Babylon's bodyguard, came to Jerusalem. ⁹ He set fire to the house of the LORD and the royal palace, indeed all the houses in the city; every notable's house was burnt down. ¹⁰ The whole Chaldaean force which was with the captain of the guard razed to the ground the walls on every side of Jerusalem. ¹¹ Nebuzaradan captain of the guard deported the people who were left in the city, those who had deserted to the king of Babylon, and any remaining artisans. ¹² He left only the poorest class of the people, to be vine-dressers and labourers.

¹³ The Chaldaeans broke up the bronze pillars in the house of the LORD, the trolleys, and the bronze Sea, and took the metal to Babylon. ¹⁴ They took also the pots, shovels, snuffers, saucers, and all the bronze vessels used in the service of the temple. ¹⁵ The cap-

24:18—25:21 *Cp. Jer. 52:1–27.*   25:1–12 *Cp. Jer. 39:1–10; verses 1–17, cp. 2 Chr. 36:17–20.*   25:3 **In ... year:** *prob. rdg, cp. Jer. 52:6; Heb. omits.* 25:4 **When ... this:** *prob. rdg, cp. Jer. 39:4; Heb. omits.* **left ... fleeing:** *so Syriac, cp. Jer. 52:7; Heb. omits.* 25:10 **The ... was with:** *so many MSS, cp. Jer. 52:14; others omit.*   25:11 **any ... artisans:** *prob. rdg, cp. Jer. 52:15; Heb. the remaining crowd.*

10–17: Jehoiakim had rebelled against *Nebuchadnezzar,* but he died before the inevitable surrender. His young son *Jehoiachin* thus bore the brunt of the anti-Babylonian policy. **18–20:** *Zedekiah* appears repeatedly in the Book of Jer., e.g. Jer. 21.1–7; 38.14–28; 39.1–10.

25.1–30: The destruction of Jerusalem. 2–4: *Jerusalem* fell on July 29, 587 B.C.E.; some scholars, assuming an autumn new year, give the year as 586. The city was destroyed one month later (v. 8). Some records were seemingly removed during that month and were thus available to the Deuteronomic historians. *The people* (v. 4) were "the people of the land"; see 11.14 n. **13–17:** The *bronze* work of the temple court is described tain of the guard took away the precious metal, whether gold or silver, of which the firepans and the tossing-bowls were made. 16 The bronze of the two pillars, the one Sea, and the trolleys, which Solomon had made for the house of the LORD, was beyond weighing. 17 One pillar was eighteen cubits high and its capital was bronze; the capital was three cubits high, and a decoration of network and pomegranates ran all round it, wholly of bronze. The other pillar, with its network, was exactly like it.

18 The captain of the guard took Seraiah the chief priest, Zephaniah the deputy chief priest, and the three on duty at the entrance; 19 he took also from the city a eunuch who was in charge of the fighting men, five of those with right of access to the king who were still in the city, the adjutant-general whose duty was to muster the people for war, and sixty men of the people who were still there. 20 These Nebuzaradan captain of the guard brought to the king of Babylon at Riblah. 21 There, in the land of Hamath, the king had them flogged and put to death. So Judah went into exile from her own land.

22 King Nebuchadnezzar of Babylon appointed Gedaliah son of Ahikam, son of Shaphan, governor over the people whom he had left in Judah. 23 When the captains of the armed bands and their men heard that the king of Babylon had appointed Gedaliah governor, they all gathered to him at Mizpah: Ishmael son of Nethaniah, Johanan son of Kareah, Seraiah son of Tanhumeth of Netophah, and Jaazaniah of Beth-maacah. 24 Gedaliah gave them and their men this assurance: 'Have no fear of the Chaldaean officers. Settle down in the land and serve the king of Babylon; and all will be well with you.' 25 But in the seventh month Ishmael son of Nethaniah, son of Elishama, who was a member of the royal house, came with ten men and assassinated Gedaliah and the Jews and Chaldaeans who were with him at Mizpah. 26 Thereupon all the people, high and low, and the captains of the armed forces, fled to Egypt for fear of the Chaldaeans.

27 In the thirty-seventh year of the exile of King Jehoiachin of Judah, on the twenty-seventh day of the twelfth month, King Evil-merodach of Babylon in the year of his accession showed favour to King Jehoiachin. He released him from prison, 28 treated him kindly, and gave him a seat at table above the kings with him in Babylon. 29 Jehoiachin, discarding his prison clothes, lived as a pensioner of the king for the rest of his life. 30 For his maintenance as long as he lived a regular daily allowance was given him by the king.

25:19 **adjutant-general:** *prob. rdg; Heb. adds* commander-in-chief.   25:27–30 *Cp. Jer. 52:31–34.* 25:27 **He released him:** *so Gk, cp. Jer. 52:31; Heb. omits.*

in 1 Kgs. 7.15–46 and 7.13–51 n. **19:** That there was an officer responsible for mustering the people ("the people of the land"; see 11.14 n.) *for war* indicates the dependence of the Judean monarchy on a draft in its later years. **22:** It should be noted that *Gedaliah* was the grandson of Josiah's adjutant-general (22.3), sharing a pro-Babylonian orientation with Josiah. **23–26:** Compare Jer. chs. 41–44. **27–30:** Compare Jer. 52.31–34. This last hopeful word of the Deuteronomic history may be a later appendix. It reaffirms a motif of the whole work, that the LORD will not forever abandon the house of David.

THE FIRST BOOK OF THE
Chronicles

The books of 1 and 2 Chronicles are the first and larger part of a comprehensive work continued in the books of Ezra and Nehemiah. The entire work is concerned with the proper service of the LORD at the temple in Jerusalem: how that service was established by David (1 Chr.), how it was finally lost through the folly of the kings of Judah (2 Chr.), and how it was restored by Ezra and Nehemiah. The writing was completed some time during the fourth century B.C.E.

The Chronicler made extensive use of the books of Samuel and Kings, often taking over long passages without major change; the annotations to those books can be consulted. The author also made use of historical sources not otherwise known (see e.g. 2 Chr. 11.5–12; 26.11–13) and reproduced genealogical lists which probably reflect earlier conditions (see e.g. 1 Chr. chs. 23–27).

David is the center of attention in 1 Chronicles. After a genealogical survey of history until David (chs. 1–9), David is treated in four blocks of material: his accession to the throne (chs. 10–12), his bringing the Ark into Jerusalem (chs. 13–16), his military achievements (chs. 18–20), and his elaborate preparation for the building of the temple before his death (chs. 21–29). Second Chronicles carries on the account of David's dynasty.

While some of the sources used have great historical value, the Chronicler's work itself should not be read as precise history. It presents, rather, a liturgical history of the City of David, with a prevalent mood and atmosphere of joyful veneration of a sacred past, centered in the temple. Most of the numbers given and the battles described are more like figures in stained-glass windows than in real life. The heroes of this work are the faithful servants of the sanctuary, the Levites, and especially the singers. It is usually thought that the Chronicler was one of these singers.

From Adam to Saul

1 ADAM, Seth, Enosh, ²Kenan, Mahalalel, Jared, ³Enoch, Methuselah, Lamech, ⁴Noah.

The sons of Noah: Shem, Ham, and Japheth.

⁵The sons of Japheth: Gomer, Magog, Madai, Javan, Tubal, Meshech, and Tiras. ⁶The sons of Gomer: Ashkenaz, Diphath, and Togarmah. ⁷The sons of Javan: Elishah, Tarshish, Kittim, and Rodanim.

⁸The sons of Ham: Cush, Mizraim, Put, and Canaan. ⁹The sons of Cush: Seba, Havilah, Sabta, Raama, and Sabtecha. The sons of Raama: Sheba and Dedan. ¹⁰Cush was the

1:2–4 Cp. Gen. 5:9–32.   1:4 **The sons of:** so Gk; Heb. omits.   1:5–7 Cp. Gen. 10:2–4.   1:5 **Javan:** or Greece.   1:6 **Diphath:** or, with many MSS, Riphath (cp. Gen. 10:3).   1:7 **Tarshish, Kittim:** or Tarshish of the Kittians. **Rodanim:** or, with many MSS, Dodanim (cp. Gen. 10:4).   1:8–10 Cp. Gen. 10:6–8.
1:8 **Mizraim:** or Egypt.

1.1–9.44: Genealogical prologues. To the liturgical history of the City of David, the Chronicler gave a universal setting by assembling the genealogies of 1 Chr. chs. 1–9, recording the line from Adam to David, with whom the liturgical history really began. Within this overall plan, some of the sources utilized had their own purposes, as is noted. A striking feature is the almost total absence of narrative here; world history simply moves through the families of humankind until it reaches David.

1.1–54: From Adam to Israel. Here the materials are from Genesis; special materials from the Chronicler's own circle (see Introduction) either were not required or were not available. **1–4:** The Chronicler provides only the briefest list of the names of the antediluvians, omitting data, such as their ages at the birth of their sons given in Gen. 5.3–31. **5–23:** This is a catalogue of nations rather than simply a genealogy; compare Gen.

father of Nimrod, who began to show himself a man of might on earth. [11] From Mizraim sprang the Lydians, Anamites, Lehabites, Naphtuhites, [12] Pathrusites, Casluhites, and the Caphtorites, from whom the Philistines were descended.

[13] Canaan was the father of Sidon, who was his eldest son, and Heth, [14] the Jebusites, the Amorites, the Girgashites, [15] the Hivites, the Arkites, the Sinites, [16] the Arvadites, the Zemarites, and the Hamathites.

[17] The sons of Shem: Elam, Asshur, Arphaxad, Lud, and Aram. The sons of Aram: Uz, Hul, Gether, and Mash. [18] Arphaxad was the father of Shelah, and Shelah the father of Eber. [19] Eber had two sons: one was named Peleg, because in his time the earth was divided, and his brother's name was Joktan. [20] Joktan was the father of Almodad, Sheleph, Hazarmoth, Jerah, [21] Hadoram, Uzal, Diklah, [22] Ebal, Abimael, Sheba, [23] Ophir, Havilah, and Jobab. All these were sons of Joktan.

[24] The line of Shem: Arphaxad, Shelah, [25] Eber, Peleg, Reu, [26] Serug, Nahor, Terah, [27] Abram, also known as Abraham, [28] whose sons were Isaac and Ishmael.

[29] The sons of Ishmael in the order of their birth: Nebaioth the eldest, then Kedar, Adbeel, Mibsam, [30] Mishma, Dumah, Massa, Hadad, Teman, [31] Jetur, Naphish, and Kedemah. These were Ishmael's sons.

[32] The sons of Keturah, Abraham's concubine: she bore him Zimran, Jokshan, Medan, Midian, Ishbak, and Shuah. The sons of Jokshan: Sheba and Dedan. [33] The sons of Midian: Ephah, Epher, Enoch, Abida, and

Eldaah. All these were descendants of Keturah.

[34] Abraham was the father of Isaac, and Isaac's sons were Esau and Israel. [35] The sons of Esau: Eliphaz, Reuel, Jeush, Jaalam, and Korah. [36] The sons of Eliphaz: Teman, Omar, Zephi, Gatam, Kenaz, Timna, and Amalek. [37] The sons of Reuel: Nahath, Zerah, Shammah, and Mizzah.

[38] The sons of Seir: Lotan, Shobal, Zibeon, Anah, Dishon, Ezer, and Dishan. [39] The sons of Lotan: Hori and Homam; and Lotan had a sister named Timna. [40] The sons of Shobal: Alvan, Manahath, Ebal, Shephi, and Onam. The sons of Zibeon: Aiah and Anah. [41] The son of Anah: Dishon. The sons of Dishon: Hamran, Eshban, Ithran, and Cheran. [42] The sons of Ezer: Bilhan, Zaavan, and Akan. The sons of Dishan: Uz and Aran.

[43] These are the kings who ruled over Edom before there were kings in Israel: Bela

1:11–16 *Cp. Gen. 10:13–18.* 1:12 **and the Caphtorites:** *transposed from end of verse; cp. Amos 9:7.* 1:13 **Heth:** *or* the Hittites. 1:17–23 *Cp. Gen. 10:22–29.* 1:17 **Lud:** *or* the Lydians. **The sons of Aram:** *so one MS, cp. Gen. 10:23; others omit.* **Mash:** *so some MSS, cp. Gen. 10:23; others* Meshech. 1:19 **Peleg:** *that is* Division. 1:22 **Ebal:** *so some MSS; others* Obal. 1:24–27 *Cp. Gen.11:10–26.* 1:24 **The line of:** *prob. rdg; Heb. omits.* 1:29–31 *Cp. Gen. 25:13–16.* 1:29 **The sons of:** *prob. rdg, cp. Gen. 25:13; Heb. omits.* 1:30 **Hadad:** *or, possibly,* Hadar *(cp. Gen. 25:15).* **Teman:** *so Gk; Heb.* Tema. 1:32–33 *Cp. Gen. 25:1–4.* 1:35–37 *Cp. Gen. 36:4–5,9–13.* 1:38–42 *Cp. Gen. 36:20–28.* 1:40 **Alvan:** *so many MSS, cp. Gen. 36:23; others* Alian. 1:41 **son:** *prob. rdg; Heb.* sons; *the same correction is made in several other places in chapters 1–9.* 1:42 **and Akan:** *so many MSS, cp. Gen. 36:27; others* Jaakan. 1:43–54 *Cp. Gen. 36:31–43.*

ch. 10. **24–27:** The genealogy from *Shem* through *Abraham* is given. Just as there were ten generations before the flood, so there were ten from the flood to Abraham. **29–54:** Here the Chronicler rearranges the genealogies found in Genesis by consistently listing first the descendants who do not lead to David. **29–34:** The offspring of Abraham are given in three groups; each son was from a different wife, Hagar, Keturah, and Sarah. See v. 32 n. **31:** The Chronicler does not comment here (as does Gen. 25.16) that the twelve names of 1.29–30 were tribal and territorial groups. The twelve tribes of *Ishmael* at some time formed a union like that of the twelve tribes of Israel. **32:** The Chronicler mentions specifically *Keturah,* but not Hagar or Sarah. **33:** Genesis 25.3 includes two sons of *Dedan,* omitted here, probably inadvertently. **34:** The Chronicler regularly uses the name *Israel* rather than Jacob. **35–54:** The longer treatment given to the descendants of *Esau* is probably due to the extent of the materials available in Gen. 36.1–43 rather than to any special importance of their own. **35–37:** The Chronicler greatly abbreviates Gen. 36.1–14, mainly by eliminating some repetitions and the references to the Canaanite wives of *Esau.* **36:** The Chronicler, or an underlying source, mistakes *Timna* for a son instead of a concubine; see Gen. 36.12. **38–42:** The Chronicler skips the lists of chiefs of the tribes of Edom (Gen. 36.15–19). Instead, surprisingly, lists are given of the clans of pre-Edomite inhabitants, *the sons of Seir* (Seir was a mountainous region south of Judah), called Horites in the Genesis source. **43–50:** It is remarkable that Israelites should have preserved this careful list of *the kings* of *Edom.* The form of the Edomite son of Beor, whose city was named Dinhabah. 44 When he died, he was succeeded by Jobab son of Zerah from Bozrah. 45 When Jobab died, he was succeeded by Husham from Teman. 46 When Husham died, he was succeeded by Hadad son of Bedad, who defeated Midian in Moabite country. His city was named Avith. 47 When Hadad died, he was succeeded by Samlah from Masrekah. 48 When Samlah died, he was succeeded by Saul from Rehoboth on the River. 49 When Saul died, he was succeeded by Baal-hanan son of Akbor. 50 When Baal-hanan died, he was succeeded by Hadad. His city was named Pai; his wife's name was Mehetabel daughter of Matred, a woman of Me-zahab.

51 After Hadad died the chiefs in Edom were: Timna, Aliah, Jetheth, 52 Oholibamah, Elah, Pinon, 53 Kenaz, Teman, Mibzar, 54 Magdiel, and Iram. These were the chiefs of Edom.

2 These were the sons of Israel: Reuben, Simeon, Levi, Judah, Issachar, Zebulun, 2 Dan, Joseph, Benjamin, Naphtali, Gad, and Asher.

3 The sons of Judah: Er, Onan, and Shelah; the mother of these three was a Canaanite woman, Bathshua. Er, Judah's eldest son, displeased the LORD and the LORD slew him.

4 Then Tamar, Judah's daughter-in-law, bore him Perez and Zerah, making in all five sons of Judah. 5 The sons of Perez: Hezron and Hamul. 6 The sons of Zerah: Zimri, Ethan, Heman, Calcol, and Darda, five in all. 7 The son of Zimri: Carmi. The son of Carmi: Achar, who brought trouble on Israel by his violation of the sacred ban. 8 The son of Ethan: Azariah. 9 The sons of Hezron: Jerahmeel, Ram, and Caleb. 10 Ram was the father of Amminadab, Amminadab father of Nahshon, prince of Judah. 11 Nahshon was the father of Salma, Salma father of Boaz, 12 Boaz father of Obed, Obed father of Jesse. 13 The eldest son of Jesse was Eliab, the second Abinadab, the third Shimea, 14 the fourth Nethanel, the fifth Raddai, 15 the sixth Ozem, the seventh David; 16 their sisters were Zeruiah and Abigail. The sons of Zeruiah: Abishai, Joab, and Asahel, three in all. 17 Abigail was the mother of Amasa; his father was Jether the Ishmaelite.

18 Caleb son of Hezron had Jerioth by Azubah his wife; these were her sons: Jesher,

1:50 **woman of Me-zahab:** or daughter of Mezahab.
2:3 **Bathshua:** or daughter of Shua.   2:6 **Darda:** so many MSS; others Dara.   2:7 **The son of Zimri: Carmi:** prob. rdg (cp. Josh. 7:1,18); Heb. omits.
2:9 **Caleb:** so Gk; Heb. Celubai.   2:18 **his wife:** prob. rdg; Heb. a woman and.

monarchy apparently required that the kingship pass from one family to another, as no dynastic principle was observed. Since the city of each king is also listed, that too was apparently a point of importance. **51–54:** The Chronicler makes these *chiefs* successors to the kings; in Gen. 36.51–54 they simply form an alternative list of earlier chiefs; the significance of this alternative list is no longer clear.

2.1–55: The offspring of Judah. The details of the lists provided here present complexities. **1–2:** There is considerable variety in the sequence in which the twelve *sons of Israel* are listed in Scripture; see e.g. Gen. 29.32–30.24 (Benjamin in 35.16–18); 35.23–25; and 46.8–25. The list here is close to Gen. 35.23–25 and Exod. 1.2–4, though *Dan* could well be linked with *Naphtali*, as sons of the same mother. **3–17:** An initial genealogy carries the main line from *the sons of Judah* to the generation of *David* and his contemporary relatives; no part of the genealogies was more important to the Chronicler. **3–5:** For the names and events referred to here, see Gen. ch. 38. **5:** The *Perez-Hezron* line is most important; see vv. 9–15. **6:** Here some traditional names of wise men and singers are incorporated into the minor Judean line of *Zerah;* see *Ethan* and *Heman* as inspired musicians in 15.17–18 and 25.1 (Jeduthun = Ethan). Compare 1 Kgs. 4.31 (which has no mention of *Zimri*). **7:** *Zimri* is included here as a son of Zerah (see v. 6 n.), in order to link the Judahite genealogy of the "troubler" *Achar* with the minor Judean clan of Zerah; compare Josh. 7.1, 18. Achar and Achan, and Zimri and Zabdi (of Josh. 7.1, etc.) are pronunciation or copyist variants of the same names. **9–12:** The three *sons of Hezron* are particularly important because the rest of this genealogy of Judah traces their descendants separately: *Ram* (vv. 10–17), *Caleb* (vv. 18–24), and *Jerahmeel* (vv. 25–41). **11–12:** *Nahshon* is listed as a Judahite assistant to Moses and Aaron during Israel's wilderness sojourn (Num. 1.7). On *Boaz, Obed,* and *Jesse,* the immediate ancestors of David, see Ruth 4.13–17. **13:** On the sons of *Jesse,* see 1 Sam. 16.1–13. **16:** The main account of *the sons of Zeruiah* and their role in the rise of David is in 2 Sam. chs. 2–3; see especially 2 Sam. 2.18–24. **18–24:** *Caleb* was a name claimed as an ancestor by many clans in Judah with Hebron as their major city; see Josh. 14.6–15; 15.13–19. Several different lists of Calebite clans and villages arranged

Shobab, and Ardon. 19 When Azubah died, Caleb married Ephrath, who bore him Hur. 20 Hur was the father of Uri, and Uri father of Bezalel. 21 Later, Hezron, then sixty years of age, married and had intercourse with the daughter of Machir, father of Gilead, and she bore Segub. 22 Segub was the father of Jair, who had twenty-three towns in Gilead. 23 Geshur and Aram took from them Havvoth-jair, and Kenath and its dependent villages, a total of sixty places. All these were descendants of Machir father of Gilead. 24 After the death of Hezron, Caleb had intercourse with Ephrathah and she bore him Ashhur the founder of Tekoa.

25 The sons of Jerahmeel, eldest son of Hezron by Ahijah, were Ram the eldest, Bunah, Oren, and Ozem. 26 Jerahmeel had another wife, whose name was Atarah; she was the mother of Onam. 27 The sons of Ram, eldest son of Jerahmeel: Maaz, Jamin, and Eker. 28 The sons of Onam: Shammai and Jada. The sons of Shammai: Nadab and Abishur. 29 The name of Abishur's wife was Abihail; she bore him Ahban and Molid. 30 The sons of Nadab: Seled and Ephraim; Seled died without children. 31 Ephraim's son was Ishi, Ishi's son Sheshan, Sheshan's son Ahlai. 32 The sons of Jada brother of Shammai: Jether and Jonathan; Jether died without children. 33 The sons of Jonathan: Peleth and Zaza. These were the descendants of Jerahmeel.

34 Sheshan had daughters but no sons. He had an Egyptian servant named Jarha; 35 he gave his daughter in marriage to this Jarha, and she bore him Attai. 36 Attai was the father of Nathan, Nathan father of Zabad, 37 Zabad father of Ephlal, Ephlal father of Obed, 38 Obed father of Jehu, Jehu father of Azariah, 39 Azariah father of Helez, Helez father of Elasah, 40 Elasah father of Sisamai, Sisamai father of Shallum, 41 Shallum father of Jekamiah, and Jekamiah father of Elishama.

42 The sons of Caleb brother of Jerahmeel: Mesha the eldest, founder of Ziph, and Mareshah, founder of Hebron. 43 The sons of Hebron: Korah, Tappuah, Rekem, and Shema. 44 Shema was the father of Raham father of Jorkoam, and Rekem was the father of Shammai. 45 The son of Shammai was Maon, and Maon was the founder of Bethzur. 46 Ephah, Caleb's concubine, was the mother of Haran, Moza, and Gazez; Haran was the father of Gazez. 47 The sons of Jahdai: Regem, Jotham, Geshan, Pelet, Ephah, and Shaaph. 48 Maacah, Caleb's concubine, was the mother of Sheber and Tirhanah; 49 she bore also Shaaph, founder of Madmannah, and Sheva, founder of Machbenah and Gibea. Caleb also had a daughter named Achsah.

50 The descendants of Caleb: the sons of Hur, the eldest son of Ephrathah: Shobal the founder of Kiriath-jearim, 51 Salma the founder of Bethlehem, and Hareph the founder of Beth-gader. 52 Shobal the founder of Kiriath-jearim was the father of Reaiah and the ancestor of half the Manahethites.

53 The clans of Kiriath-jearim: Ithrites, Puthites, Shumathites, and Mishraites, from whom were descended the Zorathites and the Eshtaulites.

54 The descendants of Salma: Bethlehem, the Netophathites, Ataroth, Beth-joab, half the Manahethites, and the Zorites.

55 The clans of Sophrites living at Jabez: Tirathites, Shimeathites, and Suchathites.

2:24 **Caleb had intercourse:** *so Gk; Heb.* in Caleb. **Ephrathah:** *so Syriac; Heb. adds* and Abiah Hezron's wife. **founder:** *lit.* father *and similarly several times in chapters 2–4.*   2:25 **by:** *prob. rdg; Heb. omits.* 2:30 **Ephraim:** *so one MS; others* Appaim.   2:42 **and:** *prob. rdg; Heb. adds* the sons of.   2:50 **sons:** *so Gk; Heb.* son.   2:52 **Reaiah:** *prob. rdg, cp. 4:2; Heb.* the seer. **Manahethites:** *prob. rdg, cp. verse 54; Heb.* Menuhoth.   2:55 **Sophrites:** *or* secretaries. **Kenites:** *lit.* Kinites.

as family trees were seemingly available to the Chronicler, who used them even though they were not fully consistent; see vv. 42–55 and 4.15. **18:** The different wives of an ancestor stand for different groupings of clans or villages within the one tribe or tribal division. **20:** On *Bezalel*, artisan of the Tabernacle, see Exod. 31.2. **21–23:** The area of northeastern Transjordan (*Gilead*) was partially colonized by Israelites from west of the Jordan, though the colonists are not otherwise identified as Judeans; see Josh. 13.29–31. **25–41:** *The sons of Jerahmeel* were another group of clans that were eventually absorbed into Judah by taking a place in the genealogy of *Hezron* alongside Ram and Caleb (see v. 9). **34–41:** A mixture of Canaanite and *Egyptian* (slave) people in southern Palestine is historically probable. **42–54:** The additional *Caleb* genealogies show special interest in place names (used as if they were personal names) and in the founding of towns. *Hebron*, for example, appears as the city in v. 42 and as an ancestor in v. 43, while *Bethlehem* appears as a son of *Salma*

These were Kenites who were connected by marriage with the ancestor of the Rechabites.

3 These were the sons of David who were born at Hebron: the eldest Amnon, whose mother was Ahinoam from Jezreel; the second Daniel, whose mother was Abigail from Carmel; ²the third Absalom, whose mother was Maacah daughter of Talmai king of Geshur; the fourth Adonijah, whose mother was Haggith; ³the fifth Shephatiah, whose mother was Abital; the sixth Ithream, whose mother was David's wife Eglah. ⁴These six were born at Hebron, where David reigned for seven years and six months.

In Jerusalem he reigned for thirty-three years, ⁵and there the following sons were born to him: Shimea, Shobab, Nathan, and Solomon; these four were sons of Bathsheba daughter of Ammiel. ⁶⁻⁸There were nine others: Ibhar, Elishama, Eliphelet, Nogah, Nepheg, Japhia, Elishama, Eliada, and Eliphelet. ⁹These were all the sons of David, with their sister Tamar, in addition to his sons by concubines.

¹⁰Solomon's son was Rehoboam, his son Abijah, his son Asa, his son Jehoshaphat, ¹¹his son Joram, his son Ahaziah, his son Joash, ¹²his son Amaziah, his son Azariah, his son Jotham, ¹³his son Ahaz, his son Hezekiah, his son Manasseh, ¹⁴his son Amon, and his son Josiah. ¹⁵The sons of Josiah: the eldest was Johanan, the second Jehoiakim, the third Zedekiah, the fourth Shallum. ¹⁶The sons of Jehoiakim: Jeconiah and Zedekiah. ¹⁷The sons of Jeconiah, a prisoner: Shealtiel, ¹⁸Malchiram, Pedaiah, Shenazzar, Jekamiah, Hoshama, and Nedabiah. ¹⁹The sons of Pedaiah: Zerubbabel and Shimei. The sons of Zerubbabel: Meshullam and Hananiah; they had a sister, Shelomith. ²⁰There were five others: Hashubah, Ohel, Berechiah, Hasadiah, and Jushab-hesed. ²¹The sons of Hananiah: Pelatiah and Isaiah; his son was Rephaiah, his son Arnan, his son Obadiah, his son Shecaniah. ²²The sons of Shecaniah: Shemaiah, Hattush, Igal, Bariah, Neariah, and Shaphat, six in all. ²³The sons of Neariah: Elioenai, Hezekiah, and Azrikam, three in all. ²⁴The sons of Elioenai: Hodaiah, Eliashib, Pelaiah, Akkub, Johanan, Delaiah, and Anani, seven in all.

4 The sons of Judah: Perez, Hezron, Carmi, Hur, and Shobal. ²Reaiah son of

3:1–4 *Cp. 2 Sam.* 3:2–5.   3:5–8 *Cp.* 14:4–7; *2 Sam.* 5:14–16.   3:5 **Bathsheba:** *so Lat.; Heb.* Bathshua. 3:17 **Jeconiah, a prisoner:** *or* Jeconiah: Assir. **Shealtiel:** *so Gk; Heb. adds* his son.   3:19 **sons of Zerubbabel:** *so some MSS; others* son of Zerubbabel. 3:21 **his son was:** *so Gk, throughout verse; Heb.* the sons of.   3:22 **Shemaiah:** *prob. rdg; Heb. adds* and the sons of Shemaiah.

in v. 54. **55:** By mentioning *Sophrites* ("scribes"), the Chronicler may be drawing on a list of professional accountants, in effect, lawyers. Compare the function of Baruch, the scribe, in Jer. 32.9–12. *The Rechabites* presumably refers to the sons of Rechab who appear in 2 Kgs. 10.15–16 and Jer. 35.1–11. This verse suggests a link between the old *Kenite* clan to which Moses' father-in-law belonged (Judg. 1.16) and the Rechabites of later times.

3.1–24: The line of David. This is a continuation of the line of Ram from 2.17. **1–9:** *The sons of David* are listed as in 2 Sam. 3.2–5 and 5.14–16. A comparison of minor differences in the three lists of David's sons born at Jerusalem (2 Sam. 5.14–16; 1 Chr. 3.5–8; 14.4–7) is instructive for the difficulties facing ancient writers in transmitting such lists. **10–14:** The kings of Judah from *Solomon* to *Josiah* are listed without reference to brothers or other members of the royal family. Athaliah (2 Kgs. ch. 11), the one queen to rule over Judah, is omitted. **14–16:** The order and number of the *sons of Josiah* are confused. No *Johanan* is otherwise known; *Jehoiakim* was the eldest son, though *Shallum* (with the throne name Jehoahaz) reigned three months before *Jehoiakim* came to the throne; see 2 Kgs. 23.28–37. Also, *Zedekiah* was *Jehoiakim's* younger brother, not his son; see 2 Kgs. 24.17–18. **17–24:** For the descendants of David after *Jeconiah* (Jehoiachin), the Chronicler is the only extant source, though *Shealtiel* is mentioned in Ezra 3.2, and *Zerubbabel* is known to have been governor when the temple was rebuilt in Jerusalem; see Hag. 1.1, 12; 2.2 (see also Sheshbazzar in Ezra 1.8). The number of generations listed here after *Jeconiah* may be significant for the date of the final form of the book; eleven are listed. If twenty years is calculated between the birth of first sons, the list will come down to about 375 B.C.E., a probable date on other grounds for the Chronicler's work.

4.1–23: Further lists of the clans of Judah. The tribes were very fluid entities, constantly absorbing and losing smaller clan or family units. Consequently, enumerations of the families of the same tribe would vary at different times. In the time of the Chronicler, only the tribe of *Judah* was still organized in anything like the old

Shobal was the father of Jahath, Jahath father of Ahumai and Lahad. These were the clans of the Zorathites.

³⁻⁴ The sons of Etam: Jezreel, Ishma, Idbash, Penuel the founder of Gedor, and Ezer the founder of Hushah; they had a sister named Hazelelponi. These were the sons of Hur: Ephrathah the eldest, the founder of Bethlehem.

⁵ Ashhur the founder of Tekoa had two wives, Helah and Naarah. ⁶ Naarah bore him Ahuzzam, Hepher, Temeni, and Haahashtari. These were the sons of Naarah. ⁷ The sons of Helah: Zereth, Jezoar, Ethnan, and Coz. ⁸ Coz was the father of Anub and Zobebah and the clans of Aharhel son of Harum.

⁹ Jabez ranked higher than his brothers; his mother called him Jabez because, as she said, she had borne him in pain. ¹⁰ Jabez called to the God of Israel, 'I pray you, bless me and grant me wide territories. May your hand be with me; do me no harm, I pray you, and let me be free from pain'; and God granted his petition.

¹¹ Kelub brother of Shuah was the father of Mehir the father of Eshton. ¹² Eshton was the father of Beth-rapha, Paseah, and Tehinnah father of Irnahash. These were the men of Rechah.

¹³ The sons of Kenaz: Othniel and Seraiah. The sons of Othniel: Hathath and Meonothai.

¹⁴ Meonothai was the father of Ophrah.

Seraiah was the father of Joab founder of Ge-harashim, for they were craftsmen.

¹⁵ The sons of Caleb son of Jephunneh: Iru, Elah, and Naam. The son of Elah: Kenaz.

¹⁶ The sons of Jehallelel: Ziph and Ziphah, Tiria, and Asarel.

¹⁷⁻¹⁸ The sons of Ezra: Jether, Mered, Epher, and Jalon. These were the sons of Bithiah daughter of Pharaoh, whom Mered had married; she conceived and gave birth to Miriam, Shammai, and Ishbah founder of Eshtemoa. His Jewish wife was the mother of Jered founder of Gedor, Heber founder of Soco, and Jekuthiel founder of Zanoah. ¹⁹ The sons of his wife Hodiah sister of Naham were Daliah father of Keilah the Garmite, and Eshtemoa the Maacathite. ²⁰ The sons of Shimon: Amnon, Rinnah, Ben-hanan, and Tilon.

The sons of Ishi: Zoheth and Ben-zoheth. ²¹ The sons of Shelah son of Judah: Er founder of Lecah, Laadah founder of Mareshah, the clans of the guild of linen-workers at Ashbea, ²² Jokim, the men of Kozeba, Joash, and Saraph who fell out with Moab and came back to Bethlehem. (The records are ancient.) ²³ They were the potters, and those who lived at Netaim and Gederah were there on the king's service.

²⁴ The sons of Simeon: Nemuel, Jamin, Jarib, Zerah, Saul, ²⁵ his son Shallum, his son Mibsam, and his son Mishma. ²⁶ The sons of Mishma: his son Hammuel, his son Zaccur, and his son Shimei. ²⁷ Shimei had sixteen sons and six daughters, but others of his family had fewer children, and the clan as a whole did not increase as much as the tribe of Judah. ²⁸ They lived at Beersheba, Moladah, Hazar-shual, ²⁹ Bilhah, Ezem, Tolad, ³⁰ Bethuel, Hormah, Ziklag, ³¹ Beth-marcaboth, Hazar-susim, Beth-biri, and Shaaraim. These were their towns until David came to the throne. ³² Their settlements were Etam, Ain, Rimmon, Tochen, and Ashan, five towns in all. ³³ They had also hamlets round these towns as far as Baal. These were the places where they lived.

³⁴ The names on their register were: Meshobab, Jamlech, Joshah son of Amaziah, ³⁵ Joel, Jehu son of Joshibiah, son of Seraiah, son of Asiel, ³⁶ Elioenai, Jaakobah, Jeshohaiah, Asaiah, Adiel, Jesimiel, Benaiah, ³⁷ Ziza son of Shiphi, son of Allon, son of Jedaiah, son of Shimri, son of Shemaiah, ³⁸ whose names are recorded as princes in their clans, and their families had greatly increased. ³⁹ They then went from the approaches to Gedor east of the valley in search of pasture for their flocks. ⁴⁰ They found rich and good pasture in a wide stretch of open country where everything was quiet and peaceful; before then it had been occupied by Hamites.

4:3–4 **sons of Etam:** *so Gk; Heb.* father of Etam. 4:6 **Temeni, and Haahashtari:** *or* the Temanite and the Ahashtarite. 4:7 **and Coz:** *so Aram. (Targ.); Heb. omits.* 4:13 **The sons of Othniel . . . Meonothai:** *so Lat.; Heb.* The sons of Othniel: Hathath. 4:14 **Ge-harashim:** *or* the valley of Craftsmen. 4:15 **Kenaz:** *so some MSS; others* and Kenaz. 4:17–18 **and gave birth to:** *prob. rdg; Heb. omits.* 4:19 **his:** *prob. rdg; Heb. omits.* **Daliah:** *so Gk; Heb. omits.* 4:22 **and came . . . Bethlehem:** *prob. rdg; Heb. unintelligible.* 4:32 **settlements:** *prob. rdg; Heb.* hamlets.

fashion. For that tribe many materials were available, but they were not reducible to a coherent picture.

4.24–43: The sons of Simeon. *Simeon* had ceased to be a separate tribe long before the Chronicler's time.

41 During the reign of King Hezekiah of Judah those whose names are written above came and destroyed the tribes of Ham and the Meunites whom they found there. They annihilated them so that no trace of them has remained to this day; and they occupied the land in their place, for there was pasture for their flocks. 42 Of their number five hundred Simeonites invaded the hill-country of Seir, led by Pelatiah, Neariah, Rephaiah, and Uzziel, the sons of Ishi. 43 They destroyed all who were left of the surviving Amalekites; and they live there still.

5 The sons of Reuben, the eldest of Israel's sons. (He had been, in fact, the first son born, but because he committed incest with a wife of his father's the status of the eldest was transferred to the sons of Joseph, Israel's son, who, however, could not be registered as the eldest son. 2 Judah held the leading place among his brothers because he fathered a ruler, and the status of the eldest was his, not Joseph's.) 3 The sons of Reuben, the eldest of Israel's sons: Enoch, Pallu, Hezron, and Carmi. 4 The sons of Joel: his son Shemaiah, his son Gog, his son Shimei, 5 his son Micah, his son Reaia, his son Baal, 6 his son Beerah, whom King Tiglath-pileser of Assyria carried away into exile; he was a prince of the Reubenites. 7 His kinsmen, family by family, as registered in their tribal lists: Jeiel the chief, Zechariah, 8 Bela son of Azaz, son of Shema, son of Joel. They lived in Aroer, and their lands stretched as far as Nebo and Baal-meon. 9 Eastwards they occupied territory as far as the edge of the desert which stretches from the river Euphrates, for they had large numbers of cattle in Gilead. 10 During Saul's reign they made war on the Hagarites, whom they conquered, occupying their encampments over all the territory east of Gilead.

11 Adjoining them were the Gadites, occupying the district of Bashan as far as Salcah: 12 Joel the chief; second in rank, Shapham; then Jaanai and Shaphat in Bashan. 13 Their fellow-tribesmen belonged to the families of Michael, Meshullam, Sheba, Jorai, Jachan, Zia, and Heber, seven in all. 14 These were the sons of Abihail son of Huri, son of Jaroah, son of Gilead, son of Michael, son of Jeshishai, son of Jahdo, son of Buz. 15 Ahi son of Abdiel, son of Guni, was head of their family; 16 they lived in Gilead, in Bashan and its villages, in all the common land of Sharon as far as it stretched. 17 These registers were all compiled in the reigns of King Jotham of Judah and King Jeroboam of Israel.

18 The sons of Reuben, Gad, and half the tribe of Manasseh: of their fighting men armed with shield and sword, their archers and their battle-trained soldiers, forty-four thousand seven hundred and sixty were ready for active service. 19 They made war on the Hagarites, Jetur, Nephish, and Nodab. 20 They were given help against them, for they cried to their God for help in the battle, and because they trusted him he listened to their prayer, and the Hagarites and all their allies surrendered to them. 21 They drove off their cattle, fifty thousand camels, two hundred and fifty thousand sheep, and two thousand donkeys, and they took a hundred thousand captives. 22 Many Hagarites had been killed, for the war was of God's making, and they occupied their land until the exile.

23 Half the tribe of Manasseh lived in the land from Bashan to Baal-hermon, Senir, and Mount Hermon, and were numerous also in Lebanon. 24 The heads of their families were: Epher, Ishi, Eliel, Azriel, Jeremiah,

4:41 **the tribes of Ham:** *prob. rdg, cp. verse 40; Heb.* their tribes. 5:2 **his, not:** *prob. rdg; Heb. omits.* 5:6 **Tiglath-pileser:** *so Gk (Luc.); Heb.* Tilgath-pilneser. 5:16 **as far as:** *so Gk; Heb.* upon. 5:20 **They were . . . to them:** *or* They attacked them boldly, and the Hagarites and all their allies surrendered to them, for they cried . . . to their prayer. 5:23 **in Lebanon:** *so Gk; Heb. omits.* 5:24 **Epher:** *so Gk; Heb.* and Epher.

41–43: The military actions and migrations suggested here are not otherwise known.

5.1–26: The tribes east of the Jordan. After three chapters on the descendants of Judah, attention is given much more briefly to the other sons of Israel. **1–10:** Verses 2–3 explain the order in which the first genealogies are given. The firstborn son (*Reuben*) would normally be given first; but *Judah* had *fathered a ruler*, David, and therefore his genealogy was given first. **4–7:** There are two lists, one giving the succession of sons (vv. 4–6) and one the three contemporary *families* (v. 7). **10:** *Hagarites:* see vv. 18–22. **11–17:** *Gadites:* there are again two lists, one of *families* and one of generations. **17:** These genealogies are brought down to the time of the exile of the Northern Kingdom, the late eighth century; see vv. 6, 22, 26. The lists are, in fact, not long enough to cover such a period of time. **18–22:** The tribes east of the Jordan had conflicts with north Arabian tribes, *Hagarites,* related to Hagar, Abraham's servant wife; see Gen. ch. 16 and 21.9–21. **23–24:** Eastern *Manasseh:*

Hodaviah, and Jahdiel, all men of ability and repute, heads of their families. 25 But they sinned against the God of their fathers, and turned wantonly to worship the gods of the peoples whom God had destroyed before them. 26 So the God of Israel stirred up King Pul of Assyria, that is King Tiglath-pileser of Assyria, and he carried away Reuben, Gad, and half the tribe of Manasseh. He took them to Halah, Habor, Hara, and the river Gozan, where they are to this day.

6 THE sons of Levi: Gershon, Kohath, and Merari. 2 The sons of Kohath: Amram, Izhar, Hebron, and Uzziel. 3 The children of Amram: Aaron, Moses, and Miriam. The sons of Aaron: Nadab, Abihu, Eleazar, and Ithamar. 4 Eleazar was the father of Phinehas, Phinehas father of Abishua, 5 Abishua father of Bukki, Bukki father of Uzzi, 6 Uzzi father of Zerahiah, Zerahiah father of Meraioth, 7 Meraioth father of Amariah, Amariah father of Ahitub, 8 Ahitub father of Zadok, Zadok father of Ahimaaz, 9 Ahimaaz father of Azariah, Azariah father of Johanan, 10 and Johanan father of Azariah, the priest who officiated in the LORD's house which Solomon built at Jerusalem. 11 Azariah was the father of Amariah, Amariah father of Ahitub, 12 Ahitub father of Zadok, Zadok father of Shallum, 13 Shallum father of Hilkiah, Hilkiah father of Azariah, 14 Azariah father of Seraiah, and Seraiah father of Jehozadak. 15 Jehozadak was deported when the LORD sent Judah and Jerusalem into exile under Nebuchadnezzar.

16 The sons of Levi: Gershom, Kohath, and Merari. 17 The sons of Gershom: Libni and Shimei. 18 The sons of Kohath: Amram, Izhar, Hebron, and Uzziel. 19 The sons of Merari: Mahli and Mushi. The clans of Levi,

family by family: 20 Gershom: his son Libni, his son Jahath, his son Zimmah, 21 his son Joah, his son Iddo, his son Zerah, his son Jeaterai. 22 The sons of Kohath: his son Amminadab, his son Korah, his son Assir, 23 his son Elkanah, his son Ebiasaph, his son Assir, 24 his son Tahath, his son Uriel, his son Uzziah, his son Saul. 25 The sons of Elkanah: Amasai and Ahimoth, 26 his son Elkanah, his son Zophai, his son Nahath, 27 his son Eliab, his son Jeroham, his son Elkanah. 28 The sons of Samuel: Joel the eldest and Abiah the second. 29 The sons of Merari: his son Mahli, his son Libni, his son Shimei, his son Uzza, 30 his son Shimea, his son Haggiah, his son Asaiah.

31 These are the men whom David appointed to take charge of the music in the house of the LORD when the Ark should be deposited there. 32 They performed their musical duties at the front of the Tent of Meeting before Solomon built the house of the LORD in Jerusalem; they took their turns of duty as was laid down for them. 33 The following, with their descendants, took this duty. Of the line of Kohath: Heman the musician, son of Joel, son of Samuel, 34 son of Elkanah, son of Jeroham, son of Eliel, son of Toah, 35 son of Zuph, son of Elkanah, son of Mahath, son of Amasai, 36 son of Elkanah, son of Joel, son of Azariah, son of Zephaniah, 37 son of Tahath, son of Assir, son of Ebiasaph, son of Korah, 38 son of Izhar, son of Kohath, son of Levi, son of Israel. 39 Heman's colleague Asaph stood at his right hand. He

5:26 **Tiglath-pileser:** *so Syriac; Heb.* Tilgath-pilneser.
6:1 *In Heb. 5:27.* **Gershon:** Gershom *in verses 16,17,20.*
6:4–8 *Cp. verses 50–53.*   6:16 *In Heb. 6:1.*
6:16–19 *Cp. Exod. 6:16–19.*   6:20–21 *Cp. verses 41–43.*   6:22–28 *Cp. verses 33–38.*   6:26 **his son Elkanah:** *so Gk; Heb.* Elkanah, the sons of Elkanah. 6:28 **Joel . . . second:** *so Gk (Luc.); Heb.* the eldest Vashni and Abiah.   6:29 **his son Mahli:** *so Syriac; Heb. omits* his son.

only *families* are given here; the main genealogy is in 7.14–18. **26:** On the conquest (in 733 B.C.E.), see 2 Kgs. 15.29. *Pul* and *Tiglath-pileser* are different names for the same king.

6.1–81: The genealogies and settlements of the Levites. The genealogies of the clans of the Levites were of as great interest to the Chronicler as the ancestry of David. Among *the sons of Levi, the sons of Aaron* occupied a special place as priests; the rest of the three main clans had other liturgical functions. These lists are genealogies, giving the succession of generations. In chs. 23–26, lists of the same clans are given according to contemporary family groups. **3–15:** The Aaronites are listed to the time of the Judean Exile in 587 B.C.E. **8:** *Zadok* was not originally an Aaronite, but came to be regarded as such in the late monarchic period; see 2 Sam. 8.17 n.; Ezek. 44.9–16. **16–30:** Though the organization of the Levites into these three clans was postexilic (with, however, older beginnings), these lists go down only to the time of David. See 23.8–23 n. for other lists of Levites. **23–27:** The fourth *Elkanah* is intended as *Samuel's* father, though it is clear from 1 Sam. 1.1 that he was not a Levite. **31–48:** The genealogies of the Chronicler's favorite Levites, the musicians, are full and was the son of Berechiah, son of Shimea, [40] son of Michael, son of Baaseiah, son of Malchiah, [41] son of Ethni, son of Zerah, son of Adaiah, [42] son of Ethan, son of Zimmah, son of Shimei, [43] son of Jahath, son of Gershom, son of Levi. [44] On their left stood their colleague of the line of Merari: Ethan son of Kishi, son of Abdi, son of Malluch, [45] son of Hashabiah, son of Amaziah, son of Hilkiah, [46] son of Amzi, son of Bani, son of Shemer, [47] son of Mahli, son of Mushi, son of Merari, son of Levi. [48] Their kinsmen the Levites were dedicated to all the service of the Tabernacle, the house of God.

[49] But it was Aaron and his descendants who burnt the sacrifices on the altar of whole-offering and the altar of incense, in fulfilment of all the duties connected with the most sacred gifts, and to make expiation for Israel, exactly as Moses the servant of God had commanded. [50] The sons of Aaron: his son Eleazar, his son Phinehas, his son Abishua, [51] his son Bukki, his son Uzzi, his son Zerahiah, [52] his son Meraioth, his son Amariah, his son Ahitub, [53] his son Zadok, his son Ahimaaz.

[54] These are their settlements in encampments in the districts assigned to the descendants of Aaron, to the clan of Kohath, for it was to them that the lot had fallen: [55] they were given Hebron in Judah, with the common land round it, [56] but to Caleb son of Jephunneh were assigned the open country belonging to the town and its hamlets. [57] To the sons of Aaron were given: Hebron the city of refuge, Libnah, Jattir, Eshtemoa, [58] Hilen, Debir, [59] Ashan, and Beth-shemesh, each with its common land. [60] And from the tribe of Benjamin: Geba, Alemeth, and Anathoth, each with its common land, making thirteen towns in all by their clans.

[61] To the remaining clans of the sons of Kohath ten towns were allotted from the half tribe of Manasseh. [62] To the sons of Gershom according to their clans they gave thirteen towns from the tribes of Issachar, Asher, Naphtali, and Manasseh in Bashan. [63] To the sons of Merari according to their clans they gave by lot twelve towns from the tribes of Reuben, Gad, and Zebulun. [64] Israel gave these towns, each with its common land, to the Levites. [65] (The towns mentioned above, from the tribes of Judah, Simeon, and Benjamin, were assigned by lot.)

[66] Some of the clans of Kohath had towns allotted to them. [67] They gave them the city of refuge Shechem in the hill-country of Ephraim, Gezer, [68] Jokmeam, Beth-horon, [69] Aijalon, and Gath-rimmon, each with its common land. [70] From the half tribe of Manasseh, Aner and Bileam, each with its common land, were given to the rest of the clans of Kohath.

[71] To the sons of Gershom they gave from the half tribe of Manasseh: Golan in Bashan, and Ashtaroth, each with its common land. [72] From the tribe of Issachar: Kedesh, Daberath, [73] Ramoth, and Anem, each with its common land. [74] From the tribe of Asher: Mashal, Abdon, [75] Hukok, and Rehob, each with its common land. [76] From the tribe of Naphtali: Kedesh in Galilee, Hammon, and Kiriathaim, each with its common land.

[77] To the rest of the sons of Merari they gave from the tribe of Zebulun: Rimmon and Tabor, each with its common land. [78] On the east of Jordan, opposite Jericho, from the tribe of Reuben: Bezer-in-the-wilderness, Jahaz, [79] Kedemoth, and Mephaath, each with its common land. [80] From the tribe of Gad: Ramoth in Gilead, Mahanaim, [81] Heshbon, and Jazer, each with its common land.

7 The sons of Issachar: Tola, Pua, Jashub, and Shimron, four. [2] The sons of Tola: Uzzi, Rephaiah, Jeriel, Jahmai, Jibsam, and Samuel, all able men and heads of families by paternal descent from Tola according to their tribal lists; their number in David's time was twenty-two thousand six hundred. [3] The

6:41–43 *Cp. verses 20–21.*   6:50–53 *Cp. verses 4–8.*
6:57–81 *Cp. Josh. 21:13–39.*   6:57 **city:** *prob. rdg, cp.
Josh. 21:13; Heb.* cities.   6:58 **Hilen:** *so many MSS;
others* Hilez.   6:61 **half tribe:** *so Lat.; Heb. adds* half.
6:66 **allotted:** *prob. rdg, cp. Josh. 21:20; Heb. of their
frontier.*   6:67 **city:** *prob. rdg, cp. Josh. 21:21; Heb.*
cities.   6:77 **Rimmon:** *so Gk; Heb.* his Rimmon.
7:1,6,13,30 and 8:1–5 *Cp. Gen. 46:13,17,21–24.*
7:1 **The sons of:** *so Syriac; Heb.* To the sons of.

careful; compare 15.16–22; 16.4–42; ch. 25. **49–53:** A second genealogy of *Aaron* shows that the special sacrificial duties passed down to *Zadok.* **54–81:** The Chronicler draws materials concerning the Levite settlements from Josh. ch. 21. In theory there were forty-eight Levite cities (see the numbers in vv. 60–65), but forty-eight names are not given.

7.1–40: The northern tribes. For the remaining tribes, except Benjamin, the Chronicler gives a few generations for each tribe, emphasizing their military strength at the time David became king; compare ch. 12. As son of Uzzi: Izrahiah, and the sons of Izrahiah — Michael, Obadiah, Joel, and Isshiah — making a total of five, all of them chiefs. ⁴In addition there were bands of fighting men recorded by families according to the tribal lists to the number of thirty-six thousand, for they had many wives and children. ⁵Their fellow-tribesmen in all the clans of Issachar were able men, eighty-seven thousand; every one of them was registered.

⁶The sons of Benjamin: Bela, Becher, and Jediael, three. ⁷The sons of Bela: Ezbon, Uzzi, Uzziel, Jerimoth, and Iri, five. They were heads of their families and able men; the number registered was twenty-two thousand and thirty-four. ⁸The sons of Becher: Zemira, Joash, Eliezer, Elioenai, Omri, Jeremoth, Abijah, Anathoth, and Alemeth; all these were sons of Becher ⁹according to their tribal lists, heads of their families and able men; and the number registered was twenty thousand two hundred. ¹⁰The son of Jediael: Bilhan. The sons of Bilhan: Jeush, Benjamin, Ehud, Kenaanah, Zethan, Tarshish, and Ahishahar. ¹¹All these were descendants of Jediael, heads of families and able men. The number was seventeen thousand two hundred men, fit for active service in war.

¹²The sons of Dan: Hushim and the sons of Aher.

¹³The sons of Naphtali: Jahziel, Guni, Jezer, Shallum. These were sons of Bilhah.

¹⁴The sons of Manasseh, born of his concubine, an Aramaean: Machir father of Gilead. ¹⁵Machir married a woman whose name was Maacah. The second son was named Zelophehad, and Zelophehad had daughters. ¹⁶Maacah wife of Machir had a son whom she named Peresh. His brother's name was Sheresh, and his sons were Ulam and Rakem. ¹⁷The son of Ulam: Bedan. These were the sons of Gilead son of Machir, son of Manasseh. ¹⁸His sister Hammoleketh was the mother of Ishhod, Abiezer, and Mahlah. ¹⁹The sons of Shemida: Ahian, Shechem, Likhi, and Aniam.

²⁰The sons of Ephraim: Shuthelah, his son Bered, his son Tahath, his son Eladah, his son Tahath, ²¹his son Zabad, his son Shuthelah. Ephraim's other sons Ezer and Elead were killed by the native Gittites when they came down to lift their cattle. ²²Their father Ephraim mourned for them a long while, and his kinsmen came to comfort him. ²³Then he had intercourse with his wife; she conceived and had a son whom he named Beriah (because disaster had come on his family). ²⁴He had a daughter named Sherah; she built Lower and Upper Beth-horon and Uzzen-sherah. ²⁵He also had a son named Rephah; his son was Resheph, his son Telah, his son Tahan, ²⁶his son Laadan, his son Ammihud, his son Elishama, ²⁷his son Nun, his son Joshua.

²⁸Their lands and settlements were: Bethel and its dependent villages, to the east Naaran, to the west Gezer, Shechem, and Gaza, with their villages. ²⁹In the possession of Manasseh were Beth-shean, Taanach, Megiddo, and Dor, with their villages. In all of these lived the descendants of Joseph the son of Israel.

³⁰The sons of Asher: Imnah, Ishvah, Ishvi, and Beriah, together with their sister Serah. ³¹The sons of Beriah: Heber and Malchiel father of Birzavith. ³²Heber was the father of Japhlet, Shomer, Hotham, and their sister Shua. ³³The sons of Japhlet: Pasach, Bimhal, and Ashvath. These were the sons of Japhlet. ³⁴The sons of Shomer: Ahi, Rohgah, Jehubbah, and Aram. ³⁵The sons of his brother Hotham: Zophah, Imna, Shelesh, and Amal. ³⁶The sons of Zophah: Suah, Harnepher, Shual, Beri, Imrah, ³⁷Bezer, Hod, Shamma, Shilshah, Ithran, and Beera. ³⁸The sons of Jether: Jephunneh, Pispah, and Ara. ³⁹The sons of Ulla: Arah, Hanniel, and Rezia. ⁴⁰All

7:6 **The sons of:** *so some MSS; others omit.*
7:11 **heads of:** *prob. rdg; Heb.* to the heads of.
7:12 **The sons of Dan:** *prob. rdg, cp. Gen. 46:23; Heb.* And Shuppim and Huppim, the sons of Ir. **Aher:** *or* another. 7:14–19 *Cp. Num. 26:29–33.*
7:14 **Manasseh:** *prob. rdg; Heb.* adds Asriel.
7:15 **whose name was:** *prob. rdg; Heb.* to Huppim and Shuppim, and his sister's name was. **The second . . . daughters:** *possibly to be transposed to follow* Gilead *at the end of verse 14.* 7:23 **disaster:** *Heb.* beraah.
7:25 **his son was:** *so Gk (Luc.); Heb.* omits.
7:28 **Gaza:** *so some MSS; others* Aiah. 7:35 **Hotham:** *prob. rdg, cp. verse 32; Heb.* Helem.

is mostly the case, the numbers are exaggerated. **6:** Instead of *Benjamin*, this is the list for Zebulun, otherwise the only tribe missing. Benjamin is given in ch. 8. **12–13:** Apparently little tradition survived about *Dan* and *Naphtali*. **14:** *Manasseh* is regarded as the grandfather of *Gilead* because of an early colonization of Gilead east of the Jordan by settlers from Manasseh west of it. *Machir* had an *Aramaean* mother because *Gilead* often shared territory with the Aramaeans.

these were descendants of Asher, heads of families, picked men of ability, leading princes. They were enrolled among the fighting troops; the total number was twenty-six thousand men.

8 The sons of Benjamin were: the eldest Bela, the second Ashbel, the third Aharah, ²the fourth Nohah, and the fifth Rapha. ³The sons of Bela: Addar, Gera father of Ehud, ⁴Abishua, Naaman, Ahoah, ⁵Gera, Shephuphan, and Huram. ⁶These were the sons of Ehud, heads of families living in Geba, who were removed to Manahath: ⁷Naaman, Ahiah, and Gera—he it was who removed them; he was the father of Uzza and Ahihud. ⁸Shaharaim had sons born to him in Moabite country, after putting away his wives Mahasham and Baara. ⁹By his wife Hodesh he had Jobab, Zibia, Mesha, Malcham, ¹⁰Jeuz, Sachiah, and Mirmah. These were his sons, heads of families. ¹¹By Mahasham he had had Abitub and Elpaal. ¹²The sons of Elpaal: Eber, Misham, Shamed who built Ono and Lod with its villages, ¹³also Beriah and Shema who were heads of families living in Aijalon, having cleared out the inhabitants of Gath. ¹⁴Ahio, Shashak, Jeremoth, ¹⁵Zebadiah, Arad, Eder, ¹⁶Michael, Ishpah, and Joha were sons of Beriah; ¹⁷Zebadiah, Meshullam, Hizki, Heber, ¹⁸Ishmerai, Jezliah, and Jobab were sons of Elpaal; ¹⁹Jakim, Zichri, Zabdi, ²⁰Elienai, Zillethai, Eliel, ²¹Adaiah, Beraiah, and Shimrath were sons of Shimei; ²²Ishpan, Heber, Eliel, ²³Abdon, Zichri, Hanan, ²⁴Hananiah, Elam, Antothiah, ²⁵Iphedeiah, and Penuel were sons of Shashak; ²⁶Shamsherai, Shehariah, Athaliah, ²⁷Jaareshiah, Elijah, and Zichri were sons of Jeroham. ²⁸These were enrolled in the tribal lists as heads of families, chiefs living in Jerusalem.

²⁹Jehiel founder of Gibeon lived at Gibeon; his wife's name was Maacah. ³⁰His eldest son was Abdon, followed by Zur, Kish, Baal, Nadab, ³¹Gedor, Ahio, Zecher, and Mikloth. ³²Mikloth was the father of Shimeah; they lived alongside their kinsmen in Jerusalem.

³³Ner was the father of Kish, Kish father of Saul, Saul father of Jonathan, Malchishua, Abinadab, and Eshbaal. ³⁴Jonathan's son was Meribbaal, who was the father of Micah. ³⁵The sons of Micah: Pithon, Melech, Tarea, and Ahaz. ³⁶Ahaz was the father of Jehoaddah, Jehoaddah father of Alemeth, Azmoth, and Zimri. Zimri was the father of Moza, ³⁷and Moza father of Binea; his son was Raphah, his son Elasah, and his son Azel. ³⁸Azel had six sons, whose names were Azrikam, Bocheru, Ishmael, Sheariah, Obadiah, and Hanan. All these were sons of Azel. ³⁹The sons of his brother Eshek: the eldest Ulam, the second Jeush, the third Eliphelet. ⁴⁰The sons of Ulam were able men, archers, and they had many sons and grandsons, a hundred and fifty. All these were descendants of Benjamin.

The restored community

9 ALL Israel were registered and recorded in the book of the kings of Israel; but Judah for their sins were carried away to exile in Babylon. ²The first to occupy their ancestral land in their towns were lay Israelites, priests, Levites, and temple servitors. ³Jerusalem was occupied partly by Judahites, partly by Benjamites, and partly by men of Ephraim and Manasseh. ⁴Judahites: Uthai son of Ammihud, son of Omri, son of Imri, son of Bani, a descendant of Perez son of Judah. ⁵Shelanites: Asaiah the eldest and his sons. ⁶The sons of Zerah: Jeuel and six hundred and ninety of their kinsmen. ⁷Benjamites: Sallu son of Meshullam, son of

8:3 **father of Ehud**: *prob. rdg, cp. Judg. 3:15; Heb.* Abihud.   8:8 **Mahasham:** *prob. rdg, cp. Gk (Luc.) in verse 11; Heb.* Hushim.   8:11 **Mahasham:** *prob. rdg, cp. Gk (Luc.); Heb.* Hushim.   8:29–38 *Cp. 9:35–44.* 8:29 **Jehiel:** *so Gk (Luc.), cp. 9:35; Heb. omits.* 8:31 **and Mikloth:** *so Gk, cp. 9:37; Heb. omits.* 8:32 **in Jerusalem:** *so Syriac; Heb. adds with their kinsmen.*   9:2–22 *Cp. Neh. 11:3–22.*   9:2 **temple servitors:** *Heb.* Nethinim.   9:4 **Judahites:** *prob. rdg; Heb. omits.*

8.1–40: Benjamin. The Chronicler's materials show greater interest in *Benjamin* than in any other of the tribes except Judah and Levi. In the postexilic period much of the former territory of Benjamin was attached to Judah; thus Benjaminites were prominent in the postexilic community around Jerusalem; see 9.7–9 and Neh. 11.7–9. **33–40:** The mention of *Saul* (v. 33) prepares for ch. 10; the Chronicler, however, carries the genealogy through the monarchic period.

9.1–44: The restored community. This chapter forms an appendix to chs. 1–8. It lists the families, especially of the temple personnel, resettled after the Exile. Lists were compiled from sources such as Neh. ch. 11. **1:** *The book of the kings of Israel:* this probably refers to chs. 1–8, understanding that the official tribal lists were once

Hodaviah, son of Hassenuah, [8] Ibneiah son of Jeroham, Elah son of Uzzi, son of Micri, Meshullam son of Shephatiah, son of Reuel, son of Ibnijah, [9] and their recorded kinsmen numbering nine hundred and fifty-six, all heads of families.

[10] Priests: Jedaiah, Jehoiarib, Jachin, [11] Azariah son of Hilkiah, son of Meshullam, son of Zadok, son of Meraioth, son of Ahitub, the official in charge of the house of God, [12] Adaiah son of Jeroham, son of Pashhur, son of Malchiah, Maasai son of Adiel, son of Jahzerah, son of Meshullam, son of Meshillemith, son of Immer, [13] and their colleagues, heads of families numbering one thousand seven hundred and sixty, men of substance with responsibility for the work connected with the service of the house of God.

[14] Levites: Shemaiah son of Hasshub, son of Azrikam, son of Hashabiah, a descendant of Merari, [15] Bakbakkar, Heresh, Galal, Mattaniah son of Mica, son of Zichri, son of Asaph, [16] Obadiah son of Shemaiah, son of Galal, son of Jeduthun, and Berechiah son of Asa, son of Elkanah, who lived in the hamlets of the Netophathites.

[17] The door-keepers were Shallum, Akkub, Talmon, and Ahiman; their brother Shallum was the chief. [18] Until then they had all been door-keepers in the quarters of the Levites at the King's Gate, on the east. [19] Shallum son of Kore, son of Ebiasaph, son of Korah, and his kinsmen of the Korahite family were responsible for service as guards of the thresholds of the Tabernacle; their ancestors had performed the duty of guarding the entrances to the camp of the LORD. [20] Phinehas son of Eleazar had been their overseer in the past—the LORD was with him. [21] Zechariah son of Meshelemiah was the door-keeper of the Tent of Meeting.

[22] Those picked to be door-keepers numbered two hundred and twelve in all, registered in their hamlets. David and Samuel the seer had installed them because they were trustworthy. [23] They and their sons had charge, by watches, of the gates of the house, the tent-dwelling of the LORD. [24] The door-keepers were to be on four sides, east, west, north, and south. [25] Their kinsmen from their hamlets had to come on duty with them for seven days at a time in turn. [26] The four principal door-keepers were chosen for their trustworthiness; they were Levites and had charge of the rooms and the stores in the house of God. [27] They always slept in the precincts of the house of God (for the watch was their duty) and they had charge of the key for opening the gates every morning.

[28] Some of them had charge of the vessels used in the service of the temple, keeping count of them as they were brought in and taken out. [29] Some of them were detailed to take charge of the furniture and all the sacred vessels, the flour, the wine, the oil, the incense, and the spices. [30] Some of the priests compounded the ointment for the perfumes. [31] Mattithiah the Levite, the eldest son of Shallum the Korahite, was in charge of the preparation of the wafers because he was trustworthy. [32] Some of their Kohathite kinsmen were in charge of setting out the rows of the Bread of the Presence every sabbath.

[33] These are the musicians, heads of Levite families, who were lodged in rooms set apart for them, because they were liable for duty by day and by night.

[34] These are the heads of Levite families, chiefs according to their tribal lists, living in Jerusalem.

[35] Jehiel founder of Gibeon lived at Gibeon; his wife's name was Maacah, [36] and his sons were Abdon the eldest, Zur, Kish, Baal, Ner, Nadab, [37] Gedor, Ahio, Zechariah, and Mikloth. [38] Mikloth was the father of Shimeam; they lived alongside their kinsmen in Jerusalem. [39] Ner was the father of Kish, Kish father of Saul, Saul father of Jonathan, Malchishua, Abinadab, and Eshbaal. [40] The son of Jonathan was Meribbaal, and Meribbaal was the father of Micah. [41] The sons of Micah: Pithon, Melech, Tahrea, and Ahaz. [42] Ahaz was the father of Jarah, Jarah father of Alemeth, Azmoth, and Zimri; Zimri father of Moza, [43] and Moza father of Binea; his son was Rephaiah, his son Elasah, his son Azel. [44] Azel had six sons, whose names were Azri-

9:19 **Tabernacle:** *lit.* Tent.   9:22 **numbered:** *so Syriac; Heb.* at the thresholds.   9:35–44 *Cp. 8:29–38.* 9:38 **in Jerusalem:** *prob. rdg; Heb adds* with their kinsmen.   9:41 **and Ahaz:** *so Gk (Lac.), cp. 8:35; Heb. omits.*

the particular concern of kings. **17–32:** This attention to *the door-keepers* is out of proportion to that given to the other groups. The Chronicler esteemed very highly their functions as well as their trustworthiness; compare ch. 26. **35–44:** A repetition of 8:29–38; it prepares for ch. 10.

kam, Bocheru, Ishmael, Sheariah, Obadiah, and Hanan. These were the sons of Azel.

David succeeds Saul

10 THE Philistines engaged Israel in battle, and the Israelites were routed, leaving their dead on Mount Gilboa. ²The Philistines closely pursued Saul and his sons, and Jonathan, Abinadab, and Malchishua, the sons of Saul, were killed. ³The battle went hard for Saul, and when the archers caught up with him they wounded him. ⁴He said to his armour-bearer, 'Draw your sword and run me through, so that these uncircumcised brutes may not come and make sport of me.' But the armour-bearer refused; he dared not. Thereupon Saul took his own sword and fell on it. ⁵When the armour-bearer saw that Saul was dead, he too fell on his sword and died. ⁶Thus Saul and his three sons died; his whole house perished together. ⁷When all the Israelites in the valley saw that their army had fled and that Saul and his sons had perished, they fled likewise, abandoning their towns; and the Philistines moved in and occupied them.

⁸Next day, when the Philistines came to strip the slain, they found Saul and his sons lying dead on Mount Gilboa. ⁹They stripped him, cut off his head, and took away his armour; then they sent messengers through the length and breadth of their land to carry the good news to idols and people alike. ¹⁰They deposited his armour in the temple of their god, and nailed up his skull in the temple of Dagon. ¹¹When the people of Jabesh-gilead heard everything the Philistines had done to Saul, ¹²all the warriors among them set out to recover the bodies of Saul and his sons. They brought them back to Jabesh and buried their bones under the oak tree there, and for seven days they fasted. ¹³Thus Saul paid with his life for his unfaithfulness: he had disobeyed the word of the LORD and had resorted to ghosts for guidance. ¹⁴He had not sought guidance of the LORD, who therefore destroyed him and transferred the kingdom to David son of Jesse.

11 ALL Israel assembled and came to David at Hebron. 'We are your own flesh and blood,' they said. ²'In the past, while Saul was still king, it was you that led the forces of Israel on their campaigns. To you the LORD your God said, "You are to be shepherd of my people Israel; you are to be their prince."' ³The elders of Israel all came to the king at Hebron; there David made a covenant with them before the LORD, and they anointed David king over Israel, as the LORD had said through the lips of Samuel.

⁴David and all Israel went to Jerusalem, that is Jebus, where the Jebusites, the inhabitants of the region, lived. ⁵The people of Jebus said to David, 'You will never come in here'; none the less David did capture the stronghold of Zion, and it is now known as the City of David. ⁶David had said, 'The first man to kill a Jebusite will become a commander or an officer,' and the first man to go up was Joab son of Zeruiah; so he was given the command.

⁷David took up his residence in the stronghold: that is why it was called the City of

10:1–12 *Cp. 1 Sam. 31:1–13.*   10:10 **god:** *or* gods.
11:1–9 *Cp. 2 Sam. 5:1–3, 6–10.*

10.1–12.40: David established as king. The first block of David materials (see Introduction) shows how Israel unanimously acknowledged David's kingship. Materials drawn from 1 and 2 Sam. were reorganized to give the following sequence: death of Saul; David made king of Israel at Hebron; the capture of Jerusalem, which becomes David's capital; and an enumeration of the chiefs and heroes who made David king (chs. 10–11). Additional lists of warriors and of military contingents from the twelve tribes (ch. 12) are given from sources other than 1 and 2 Sam.

10.1–14: Saul is removed. The account of Saul's death is taken from 1 Sam. ch. 31. The circumstances leading to the death scene, so richly developed there, are ignored by the Chronicler here. Saul is treated only as an obstacle to David's kingship. **6:** Saul's *whole house* did not perish at the battle of Gilboa (2 Sam. 2.8–10; ch. 9). However, the Chronicler does not narrate the subsequent demise of that house (see 2 Sam. 21.1–14). **13–14:** This is the Chronicler's succinct summary of Saul's misdeeds recorded in 1 Sam. chs. 15 and 28.

11.1–9: David, as king, takes Jerusalem. Chronicles retains excerpts from 2 Sam. in the order in which they appear in that book (5.1–3, 6–10; 23.8–39), even though the author's own additions (ch. 12) pertain to slightly earlier events. The material is organized more by topic than by chronology. **3:** The reference to *Samuel's* prophecy is an addition to the excerpt from 2 Sam. **5–6:** The text simplifies some textual problems

David. [8] He built the city around it: David started at the Millo and included its neighbourhood, while Joab reconstructed the rest of the city. [9] David steadily grew more and more powerful, for the LORD of Hosts was with him.

[10] These were the chief of David's heroes, men who lent their full strength to his government and, with all Israel, joined in making him king; such was the LORD's decree for Israel. [11] First came Jashobeam the Hachmonite, chief of the three; it was he who brandished his spear over three hundred, all slain at one time. [12] Next to him was Eleazar son of Dodo the Ahohite, one of the heroic three. [13] He was with David at Pas-dammim where the Philistines had gathered for battle in a field carrying a good crop of barley. When the people had fled from the Philistines [14] he stood his ground in the field, defended it, and defeated them. So the LORD brought about a great victory.

[15] Three of the thirty chiefs went down to the rock to join David at the cave of Adullam, while the Philistines were encamped in the valley of Rephaim. [16] David was then in the stronghold, and a Philistine garrison held Bethlehem. [17] One day David exclaimed with longing, 'If only I could have a drink of water from the well by the gate at Bethlehem!' [18] At this the three made their way through the Philistine lines and drew water from the well by the gate of Bethlehem and brought it to David. But he refused to drink it; he poured it out to the LORD, [19] saying, 'God forbid that I should do such a thing! Can I drink the blood of these men? They have brought it at the risk of their lives.' So he would not drink it. Such were the exploits of the heroic three.

[20] Abishai the brother of Joab was chief of the thirty; he it was who brandished his spear over three hundred dead. He was famous among the thirty. [21] He surpassed in reputation the rest of the thirty; he became their captain, but he did not rival the three. [22] Benaiah son of Jehoiada, from Kabzeel, was a hero of many exploits. It was he who slew the two champions of Moab, and who once went down into a pit and killed a lion on a snowy day. [23] He also killed an Egyptian, a giant seven and a half feet high armed with a spear as big as the beam of a loom. Benaiah went to meet him with a club, wrested the spear out of the Egyptian's hand, and killed him with his own weapon. [24] Such were the exploits of Benaiah son of Jehoiada, famous among the heroic thirty. [25] He was more famous than the rest of the thirty, but he did not rival the three. David appointed him to his household.

[26] These were his valiant heroes: Asahel the brother of Joab; Elhanan son of Dodo from Bethlehem; [27] Shammoth from Harod; Helez from a place unknown; [28] Ira son of Ikkesh from Tekoa; Abiezer from Anathoth; [29] Sibbechai from Hushah; Ilai the Ahohite; [30] Maharai from Netophah; Heled son of Baanah from Netophah; [31] Ithai son of Ribai from Gibeah of Benjamin; Benaiah from Pirathon; [32] Hurai from the wadis of Gaash; Abiel from Beth-arabah; [33] Azmoth from Bahurim; Eliahba from Shaalbon; [34] Hashem the Gizonite; Jonathan son of Shage the Hararite; [35] Ahiam son of Sacar the Hararite; Eliphal son of Ur; [36] Hepher from Mecherah; Ahijah from a place unknown; [37] Hezro from Carmel; Naarai son of Ezbai; [38] Joel brother of Nathan; Mibhar son of Hageri; [39] Zelek the Ammonite; Naharai from Beroth, armour-bearer to Joab son of Zeruiah; [40] Ira the Ithrite; Gareb the Ithrite; [41] Uriah the Hittite; Zabad son of Ahlai.

11:10–41 *Cp. 2 Sam. 23:8–39.* 11:11 **Jashobeam:** *some Gk MSS have Ishbaal.* **the three:** *so Gk (Luc.); Heb.* the thirty *or* the lieutenants. 11:14 **he . . . ground:** *so Gk, cp. 2 Sam. 23:12; Heb.* they stood their ground. 11:17 **well:** *or* cistern. 11:19 **these men:** *so Lat.; Heb. adds* at the risk of their lives. 11:20,21 **thirty:** *so Syriac; Heb.* three. 11:22 **Kabzeel, was:** *so Syriac; Heb. adds* the son of. 11:23 **seven . . . feet:** *lit.* five cubits. 11:24 **thirty:** *prob. rdg; Heb.* three. 11:27 **Harod:** *prob. rdg, cp. 2 Sam. 23:25; Heb.* Haror. 11:34 **Hashem:** *so some Gk MSS, cp. 2 Sam. 23:32; Heb.* the sons of Hashem.

in 2 Sam. 5.6–8. **8:** *Joab:* an addition to the Samuel source.

11.10–47: David's warrior heroes. The Chronicler uses the list of David's heroes from 2 Sam. ch. 23 without significant change but with a new purpose, expressed in v. 10. **10–14:** The Chronicler omits the third of *the three,* Shammah (2 Sam. 23.11). **15–19:** The confusion as to whether these were *three of the thirty chiefs* (v. 15) or *the heroic three* (v. 19) derives from the source in 2 Sam. 23.13–17. *The heroic three* is most likely meant. **20–21:** The *thirty* and *three* reflect a ten-to-one ratio among commanders, similar to that employed in the administration of the labor forces; compare 1 Kgs. 5.16 n. **25:** David's *household* is enumerated in 18.14–17. **26–41:** *Valiant heroes:* thirty-one names are from 2 Sam. 23.24–39, where it is said (v. 39) that there were

42 Adina son of Shiza the Reubenite, a chief of the Reubenites, was over these thirty. 43 Also Hanan son of Maacah, and Joshaphat the Mithnite; 44 Uzzia from Ashtaroth, Shama and Jeiel the sons of Hotham from Aroer; 45 Jediael son of Shimri, and his brother Joha the Tizite; 46 Eliel the Mahavite, and Jeribai and Joshaviah sons of Elnaam, and Ithmah the Moabite; 47 Eliel and Obed, and Jaasiel from Zobah.

12 These are the men who joined David at Ziklag while he was banned from the presence of Saul son of Kish. They ranked among the warriors valiant in battle; 2 they carried bows and could sling stones or shoot arrows with the left hand or the right. They were Benjamites, kinsmen of Saul. 3 The foremost were Ahiezer and Joash, the sons of Shemaah of Gibeah; Jeziel and Pelet, men of Beth-azmoth; Berakah and Jehu from Anathoth; 4 Ishmaiah the Gibeonite, a hero among the thirty and a chief among them; Jeremiah, Jahaziel, Johanan, and Jozabad from Gederah; 5 Eluzai, Jerimoth, Bealiah, Shemariah, and Shephatiah the Hariphite; 6 Elkanah, Isshiah, Azarel, Joezer, Jashobeam, the Korahites; 7 and Joelah and Zebadiah sons of Jeroham from Gedor.

8 Some Gadites also joined David at the stronghold in the wilderness, valiant men trained for war, experts with the heavy shield and spear, grim as lions and swift as gazelles on the mountains. 9 Ezer was their chief, Obadiah the second, Eliab the third; 10 Mishmannah the fourth and Jeremiah the fifth; 11 Attai the sixth and Eliel the seventh; 12 Johanan the eighth and Elzabad the ninth; 13 Jeremiah the tenth and Machbanai the eleventh. 14 These were chiefs of the Gadites in the army, the least of them a match for a hundred, the greatest a match for a thousand. 15 These were the men who in the first month crossed the Jordan, which was in full flood in all its reaches; they cleared the valleys, east and west.

16 Some men of Benjamin and Judah came to David at the stronghold. 17 David went out to them and said, 'If you come as friends to help me, join me and welcome; but if you come to betray me to my enemies, innocent though I am of any crime of violence, may the God of our fathers see and judge.' 18 At that a spirit took possession of Amasai, the chief of the thirty, and he said:

'We are on your side, David!
We are with you, son of Jesse!
All prosperity to you
and to him who helps you,
for your God is your helper.'

So David welcomed them and attached them to the columns of his raiding parties.

19 Some men of Manasseh had deserted to David when he went with the Philistines to war against Saul, though he did not, in fact, fight on the side of the Philistines. Their lords dismissed him, saying to themselves that he would desert them for his master Saul, and that would cost them their heads. 20 The men of Manasseh who deserted to him when he went to Ziklag were these: Adnah, Jozabad, Jediael, Michael, Jozabad, Elihu, and Zillethai, each commanding his thou-

11:42 **was ... thirty:** *so Syriac; Heb.* had thirty over him.   11:47 **from Zobah:** *prob. rdg; Heb. obscure.*
12:3 **men of Beth-azmoth:** *lit.* sons of Azmoth.
12:4 *In Heb. verses 4 and 5.*   12:5 *In Heb. verse 6.*
12:18 **took possession of:** *lit.* clothed itself with. **and he said:** *so Gk; Heb. omits.*

---

thirty-seven heroes in all. **42–47:** Sixteen names are added by the Chronicler from another source. If a group of thirty leading warriors was maintained constantly over a period of many years, far more than just thirty men would have been required. The longer list may reflect that fact.

12.1–40: The contingents that came to David. The Chronicler's purpose is to show a progressive transfer of allegiance to David on the part of Israel's military forces. There are five stages in the process; the Chronicler supplies a list of warriors for each, except the third. **1–7:** The first contingent. While David was at *Ziklag* (as a vassal of Achish, king of Gath; see 1 Sam. ch. 27), some of Saul's own best warriors joined him. **8–15:** The second contingent. *The stronghold* where David was a fugitive (1 Sam. 22.4) was near Moab. The territory of the *Gadites* was north of Moab in Transjordan. **15:** The Gadites had to cross *the Jordan* to reach Judah. On the flood in *the first month*, see Josh. 3.15; 4.19. **16–18:** The third contingent: *men of Benjamin and Judah.* No list is given here, but the unqualified devotion of the new supporters is emphasized. **19–22:** The fourth contingent. When the crisis between Saul and the Philistines reached its height (1 Sam. ch. 29), more of Saul's followers, in this case *men of Manasseh,* went over to David at *Ziklag* and aided against *the raiders;*

sand in Manasseh. ²¹It was they who stood valiantly by David against the raiders, for they were all good fighters, and they were given commands in his forces. ²²Day by day men came in to help David, until he had gathered an immense army.

²³These are the numbers of the armed bands which joined David at Hebron to transfer the sovereignty to him in succession to Saul, as the LORD had said: ²⁴men of Judah, bearing heavy shield and spear, six thousand eight hundred drafted for active service; ²⁵of Simeon, fighting men drafted for active service, seven thousand one hundred; ²⁶of Levi, four thousand six hundred, ²⁷together with Jehoiada prince of the house of Aaron and three thousand seven hundred men, ²⁸and Zadok, a valiant fighter, with twenty-two officers of his own clan; ²⁹of Benjamin, Saul's kinsmen, three thousand, though most of them had hitherto remained loyal to the house of Saul; ³⁰of Ephraim, twenty thousand eight hundred fighting men, famous in their own clans; ³¹of the half tribe of Manasseh, eighteen thousand, who had been nominated to come and make David king; ³²of Issachar, whose tribesmen were skilled in reading the signs of the times to discover what course Israel should follow, two hundred chiefs with all their kinsmen under their command; ³³of Zebulun, fifty thousand troops well-drilled for battle, armed with every kind of weapon, bold and single-minded; ³⁴of Naphtali, a thousand officers with thirty-seven thousand men equipped with heavy shield and spear; ³⁵of the Danites, twenty-eight thousand six hundred well-drilled for battle; ³⁶of Asher, forty thousand troops well-drilled for battle; ³⁷of the Reubenites and the Gadites and the half tribe of Manasseh east of Jordan, a hundred and twenty thousand armed with every kind of weapon.

³⁸All these valiant men trained for war came to Hebron, fully determined to make David king over the whole of Israel; the rest of Israel, too, were of one mind to make him king. ³⁹They spent three days there with David, eating and drinking, for their kinsmen made provision for them. ⁴⁰Also their neighbours round about, as far away as Issachar, Zebulun, and Naphtali, brought food on donkeys and camels, on mules and oxen: supplies of meal, fig-cakes, raisin-cakes, wine and oil, oxen and sheep in plenty; for there was rejoicing in Israel.

13 DAVID consulted the officers over units of a thousand and a hundred on every matter brought forward. ²Then he said to the whole assembly of Israel, 'If you approve, and if the LORD our God opens a way, let us send to our kinsmen who have stayed behind in all the districts of Israel, and also to the priests and Levites in the cities and towns where they have common lands, bidding them join us. ³Let us fetch the Ark of our God, for while Saul lived we never resorted to it.' ⁴With the approval of the whole nation the assembly resolved unanimously to do this.

⁵So David assembled all Israel from the Shihor in Egypt to Lebo-hamath, in order to fetch the Ark of God from Kiriath-jearim. ⁶David and all Israel went up to Baalah, to Kiriath-jearim, which belonged to Judah, to fetch from there the Ark of God, the LORD enthroned upon the cherubim, the Ark

12:22 **an immense army:** *lit.* a great army like the army of God.   12:28 **of:** *so Gk; Heb. omits.*
13:2 **and if . . . let us:** *or* and if it is from the LORD our God, let us seize the opportunity and.
13:6–14 Cp. 2 Sam. 6:2–11.

see 1 Sam. ch. 30. **23–37:** The fifth contingent. After Saul's death, all Israel came over to *David at Hebron* (see 2 Sam. 5.1–5). Thus, the Chronicler gives a list of forces from all twelve tribes (plus contingents of Levites and priests, vv. 26–28). Old data from muster lists of Israelite militia (possibly in the time of Josiah) probably lie behind the list. The terms *thousand* and *hundred* were originally conventional terms for military units, not actual numbers.

13.1–16.43: The Ark is established in Jerusalem. The second block of Davidic material (see Introduction) turns to David's establishing the proper service of the LORD in Jerusalem. In 2 Sam. ch. 6 the two movements of the Ark are related successively. The Chronicler retains the first movement without change (13.5–14) but inserts other materials from 2 Sam. ch. 5 before the second movement (chs. 15–16). The second movement is elaborated with special materials of particular interest to the Chronicler.

13.1–14: The first movement of the Ark. The Chronicler adds an introduction, vv. 1–4, which emphasizes the unison of Israel's action; the main account, however, simply follows 2 Sam. 6.2–11.

which bore his name. 7They mounted the Ark on a new cart and conveyed it from the house of Abinadab, with Uzza and Ahio guiding the cart. 8David and all Israel danced for joy before God with all their might to the sound of singing, of lyres, lutes, tambourines, cymbals, and trumpets. 9When they came to the threshing-floor of Kidon, the oxen stumbled, and Uzza reached out his hand to hold the Ark. 10The LORD was angry with Uzza and struck him down because he had put out his hand to the Ark. So he died there before God. 11David was vexed because the LORD's anger had broken out on Uzza, and he called the place Perez-uzza, the name it still bears.

12David was afraid of God that day and said, 'How can the Ark of God come to me?' 13So he did not take the Ark with him into the City of David; he turned aside and carried it to the house of Obed-edom the Gittite. 14The Ark of God remained in its tent beside Obed-edom's house for three months, and the LORD blessed the family of Obed-edom and all that he had.

14 King Hiram of Tyre sent envoys to David with cedar logs, and with them masons and carpenters to build him a house. 2David knew by now that the LORD had confirmed him as king over Israel and had enhanced his royal power for the sake of his people Israel.

3David married more wives in Jerusalem, and more sons and daughters were born to him. 4These are the names of the children born to him in Jerusalem: Shammua, Shobab, Nathan, Solomon, 5Ibhar, Elishua, Elpelet, 6Nogah, Nepheg, Japhia, 7Elishama, Beeliada, and Eliphelet.

8When the Philistines learnt that David had been anointed king over the whole of Israel, they came up in force to seek him out. David, getting wind of this, went out to face them. 9When the Philistines came and raided the valley of Rephaim, 10David enquired of God, 'If I attack the Philistines, will you de-

liver them into my hands?' The LORD answered, 'Go, I shall deliver them into your hands.' 11He went up and attacked and defeated them at Baal-perazim. 'God has used me to break through my enemies' lines', David said, 'as a river breaks through its banks.' That is why the place was named Baal-perazim. 12The Philistines abandoned their gods there, and by David's orders these were burnt.

13The Philistines made another raid on the valley. 14Again David enquired of God, who said to him, 'No, you must attack towards their rear; make a detour without making contact and come upon them opposite the aspens. 15As soon as you hear a rustling sound in the treetops, then give battle at once, for God will have gone out before you to defeat the Philistine army.' 16David did as God had commanded, and the Philistine army was driven in flight all the way from Gibeon to Gezer. 17David's fame spread through every land, and the LORD inspired all nations with dread of him.

15 DAVID built himself quarters in the City of David, and prepared a place for the Ark of God and pitched a tent for it. 2He decreed that only Levites should carry the Ark of God, since they had been chosen by the LORD to carry it and to serve him for ever. 3David assembled all Israel at Jerusalem to bring up the Ark of the LORD to the place he had prepared for it. 4He gathered together the descendants of Aaron and the Levites: 5of the descendants of Kohath, Uriel the chief with a hundred and twenty of his kinsmen; 6of the descendants of Merari, Asa-

13:6 **which bore his name:** *prob. rdg; Heb. obscure.*
13:11 **Perez-uzza:** *that is* Outbreak on Uzza.
13:14 **its:** *or* his.　　14:1–16 *Cp. 2 Sam. 5:11–25.*
14:2 **and:** *so Aram.* (Targ.), *cp. 2 Sam. 5:12; Heb. omits.*
14:4–7 *Cp. 3:5–8.*　　14:11 **He:** *so Gk, cp. 2 Sam. 5:20; Heb.* They. **Baal-perazim:** *that is* Baal of Break-through.　　14:14 **No ... contact and:** *or* Do not go up to the attack; withdraw from them and then.　　15:2 **him:** *or* it.

14.1–17: David secures his position. This chapter is mostly drawn from 2 Sam. 5, but the Chronicler inserts it between the two Ark movements. **4–7:** Compare 3.1–9 n.

15.1–16.43: The Ark and its Levitical service. The account of the bringing up of the Ark in 2 Sam. 6.12–19 is greatly expanded by the Chronicler's interest in the Levites, and especially the Levitical musicians. **1–15:** In the Chronicler's view, the outbreak of the LORD against Uzza in 13.7–11 was because the Levites were not carrying the Ark; see v. 13. Therefore, on the second attempt to bring up the Ark, the Levites had to carry it. **4–10:** Normally there are only three families of Levites, not six; compare 6.16–30; 23.6–23. *Hebron* and *Uzziel* appear as sons of *Kohath*, 6.18; 23.12; and, more rarely, *Elizaphan* is listed as a son of Uzziel, Lev.

iah the chief with two hundred and twenty of his kinsmen; ⁷of the descendants of Gershom, Joel the chief with a hundred and thirty of his kinsmen; ⁸of the descendants of Elizaphan, Shemaiah the chief with two hundred of his kinsmen; ⁹of the descendants of Hebron, Eliel the chief with eighty of his kinsmen; ¹⁰of the descendants of Uzziel, Amminadab the chief with a hundred and twelve of his kinsmen.

¹¹David summoned Zadok and Abiathar the priests, together with the Levites Uriel, Asaiah, Joel, Shemaiah, Eliel, and Amminadab, ¹²and said to them, 'You are heads of families of the Levites; hallow yourselves, you and your kinsmen, and bring up the Ark of the LORD the God of Israel to the place which I have prepared for it. ¹³It was because you were not present the first time that the LORD our God broke out upon us. For we had not sought his guidance as we should have done.' ¹⁴The priests and the Levites then hallowed themselves to bring up the Ark of the LORD the God of Israel, ¹⁵and the Levites carried the Ark of God, bearing it on their shoulders with poles as Moses had ordered on instructions from the LORD.

¹⁶David ordered the chiefs of the Levites to install as musicians those of their kinsmen who were players skilled in making joyful music on their instruments—lutes, lyres, and cymbals. ¹⁷The Levites installed Heman son of Joel and, from his kinsmen, Asaph son of Berechiah; and from their kinsmen the Merarites, Ethan son of Kushaiah, ¹⁸together with their kinsmen of the second degree Zechariah, Jaaziel, Shemiramoth, Jehiel, Unni, Eliab, Benaiah, Maaseiah, Mattithiah, Eliphelehu, and Mikneiah, and the door-keepers Obed-edom and Jeiel. ¹⁹They installed the musicians Heman, Asaph, and Ethan to sound the bronze cymbals; ²⁰Zechariah, Jaaziel, Shemiramoth, Jehiel, Unni, Eliab, Maaseiah, and Benaiah to play on lutes; ²¹Mattithiah, Eliphelehu, Mikneiah, Obed-edom, Jeiel, and Azaziah to play on lyres. ²²Kenaniah, officer of the Levites, was

precentor in charge of the music because of his proficiency.

²³Berechiah and Elkanah were door-keepers for the Ark, ²⁴while the priests Shebaniah, Joshaphat, Nethanel, Amasai, Zechariah, Benaiah, and Eliezer sounded the trumpets before the Ark of God; and Obed-edom and Jehiah also were door-keepers for the Ark.

²⁵Then David and the elders of Israel and the captains of units of a thousand went to bring up the Ark of the Covenant of the LORD with much rejoicing from the house of Obed-edom. ²⁶Because God had helped the Levites who carried the Ark of the Covenant of the LORD, they sacrificed seven bulls and seven rams.

²⁷David and all the Levites who carried the Ark, and the musicians, and Kenaniah the precentor, were arrayed in robes of fine linen; and David had on a linen ephod. ²⁸All Israel escorted the Ark of the Covenant of the LORD with acclamation, blowing on horns and trumpets, clashing cymbals, and playing on lutes and lyres. ²⁹As the Ark of the Covenant of the LORD was entering the City of David, Saul's daughter Michal looked down from a window and saw King David dancing and making merry, and she despised him in her heart.

16 After they had brought the Ark of God, they put it inside the tent that David had set up for it, and they offered whole-offerings and shared-offerings before God. ²Having completed these sacrifices, David blessed the people in the name of the LORD ³and distributed food, a loaf of bread, a portion of meat, and a cake of raisins, to each Israelite, man or woman. ⁴He appointed certain Levites to serve before the

15:18 **Zechariah:** *so some MSS, cp. verse 20; others add* a son.   15:20 **on lutes:** *prob. rdg; Heb. adds* al alamoth, *possibly a musical term.*   15:21 **on lyres:** *prob. rdg; Heb. adds* al hashsheminith lenasseah, *probably musical terms.*   15:25–29 *Cp. 2 Sam. 6:12–16.*   15:27 **the precentor:** *prob. rdg; Heb. obscure.*   16:1–3 *Cp. 2 Sam. 6:17–19.*   16:3 **portion of meat:** *meaning of Heb. word uncertain.*

10.4 (here spelled "Elzaphan"); Num. 3.30. **16–24:** The provision for carefully defined groups of musicians is a late development, mostly from the postexilic organization of the temple, though based on older monarchic practice. Verses 17–18 give the basic list, vv. 19–24 supplementary lists and comments. The lists are not completely consistent with each other. **15.25–16.3:** After the liturgical arrangements, the Ark is brought in. Second Samuel 6.12–19 is revised. **26:** The Chronicler makes *the Levites* the reason for the sacrifices. **27:** In the Chronicler's version, all the officiants wear ritual garments. **29:** *Michal's* motives are eliminated here; compare 2 Sam. 6.20. **16.4–36:** There were three guilds of Levitical musicians; those of Heman, *Asaph,* and

Ark of the LORD, to celebrate, to give thanks, and to praise the LORD the God of Israel. 5 Their leader was Asaph; second to him was Zechariah; then came Jaaziel, Shemiramoth, Jehiel, Mattithiah, Eliab, Benaiah, Obed-edom, and Jeiel, with lutes and lyres; Asaph, who sounded the cymbals; 6 and Benaiah and Jahaziel the priests, who blew the trumpets regularly before the Ark of the Covenant of God.

A song of thanksgiving

7 IT was then that David first ordained the offering of thanks to the LORD by Asaph and his kinsmen:

8 Give thanks to the LORD, invoke him by name,
make known his deeds among the peoples.
9 Pay him honour with song and psalm and tell of all his marvellous deeds.
10 Exult in his hallowed name;
let those who seek the LORD be joyful in heart.
11 Look to the LORD and be strong;
at all times seek his presence.
12 Remember the marvels he has wrought, his portents and the judgements he has given,
13 you descendants of Israel, his servants, you children of Jacob, his chosen ones!

14 He is the LORD our God;
his judgements cover the whole world.
15 He is ever mindful of his covenant, the promise he ordained for a thousand generations,
16 the covenant made with Abraham, his oath given to Isaac,
17 and confirmed as a statute for Jacob, as an everlasting covenant for Israel:
18 'I shall give you the land of Canaan', he said,
'as your allotted holding.'

19 A small company it was,

few in number, strangers in that land,
20 wandering from nation to nation, from one kingdom to another;
21 but he let no one oppress them;
on their account he rebuked kings:
22 'Do not touch my anointed servants,' he said;
'do no harm to my prophets.'

23 Sing to the LORD, all the earth, proclaim his victory day by day.
24 Declare his glory among the nations, his marvellous deeds to every people.
25 Great is the LORD and most worthy of praise;
he is more to be feared than all gods.
26 For the gods of the nations are idols every one;
but the LORD made the heavens.
27 Majesty and splendour attend him, might and joy are in his dwelling.

28 Ascribe to the LORD, you families of nations,
ascribe to the LORD glory and might;
29 ascribe to the LORD the glory due to his name.
Bring an offering and come before him.
Worship the LORD in holy attire.
30 Tremble before him, all the earth.
He has established the earth immovably.

31 Let the heavens rejoice and the earth be glad;
let it be declared among the nations, 'The LORD is king.'

16:5 **Jaaziel:** *prob. rdg, cp. 15:18,20; Heb.* Jeiel. 16:8–22 *Cp. Ps. 105:1–15.*   16:11 **and be strong:** *or* the symbol of his strength; *lit.* and his strength. 16:13 **servants:** *so Gk; Heb.* servant.   16:15 **He is ... covenant:** *so some Gk MSS, cp. Ps. 105:8; Heb.* For ever call his covenant to mind.   16:19 **it was:** *so some MSS, cp. Ps. 105:12; others* you were. 16:23–33 *Cp. Ps. 96:1–13.*

Ethan or Jeduthun (6.33–47; 15.17–18; 25.1–8). Only that of *Asaph*, however, was assigned to the service of the Ark because, from the Chronicler's viewpoint, the other two guilds were still serving at the Tabernacle in Gibeon; see vv. 39–42. **5–6:** Including the two *priests, who blew trumpets,* twelve musicians are listed. On the *trumpets,* see Num. 10.1–10. **7:** The Chronicler is familiar with a regular order of *offering of thanks* at the temple, an order attributed to David. **8–36:** The Chronicler includes a hymn of praise, composed by drawing on parts of hymns now contained in the canonical book of Psalms, especially Pss. 105 and 96. Only a

³²Let the sea resound and everything in
it,
let the fields exult and all that is in
them;
³³let the trees of the forest shout for joy
before the Lord, when he comes to
judge the earth.

³⁴It is good to give thanks to the Lord,
for his love endures for ever.
³⁵Cry, 'Deliver us, God our saviour;
gather us in and save us from the
nations
that we may give thanks to your holy
name
and make your praise our pride.'

³⁶Blessed be the Lord, the God of Israel,
from everlasting to everlasting.

And all the people said 'Amen' and 'Praise
the Lord.'
³⁷David left Asaph and his kinsmen there
before the Ark of the Covenant of the Lord,
to perform regular service before the Ark as
each day's duty required. ³⁸As door-keepers
he left Obed-edom son of Jeduthun, and Hosah. Obed-edom and his kinsmen were sixty-
eight in number. ³⁹He left Zadok the priest
and his kinsmen the priests before the Tabernacle of the Lord at the shrine in Gibeon,
⁴⁰to make offerings there to the Lord upon
the altar of whole-offering regularly morning and evening, exactly as it is written in the
law enjoined by the Lord on Israel. ⁴¹With
them he left Heman and Jeduthun and the
other men chosen by name to give thanks to
the Lord, 'for his love endures for ever'.
⁴²They had trumpets and cymbals for the
players, and the instruments used for sacred
song. The sons of Jeduthun kept the
gate.
⁴³So all the people went home, and David
returned to greet his household.

David's plan to build a temple

17 Once David was established in his
palace, he said to Nathan the
prophet, 'Here I am living in a house of cedar, while the Ark of the Covenant of the
Lord is housed in a tent.' ²Nathan answered,
'Do whatever you have in mind, for God is
with you.' ³But that same night the word of
God came to Nathan: ⁴'Go and say to David
my servant, This is the word of the Lord: It
is not you who are to build me a house to
dwell in. ⁵Down to this day I have never
dwelt in a house since I brought Israel up
from Egypt; I lived in a tent and a tabernacle.
⁶Wherever I journeyed with Israel, did I ever
ask any of the judges whom I appointed
shepherds of my people why they had not
built me a cedar house?

⁷'Then say this to my servant David: This
is the word of the Lord of Hosts: I took you
from the pastures and from following the
sheep to be prince over my people Israel. ⁸I
have been with you wherever you have gone,
and have destroyed all the enemies in your
path. I shall bring you fame like the fame of
the great ones of the earth. ⁹I shall assign a
place for my people Israel; there I shall plant
them to dwell in their own land. They will be
disturbed no more; never again will the
wicked wear them down as they did ¹⁰in the
past from the day when I appointed judges
over my people Israel; and I shall subdue all
your enemies.

'But I shall make you great and the Lord
will build up your royal house. ¹¹When your
life ends and you go to join your forefathers,
I shall set up one of your family, one of your
own sons, to succeed you, and I shall establish
his kingdom. ¹²It is he who will build me a

16:34 *Cp. Ps. 107:1.* 16:35–36 *Cp. Ps. 106:47–48.*
16:38 **his:** *so Gk; Heb.* their. 16:42 **They:** *so Gk;
Heb. adds* Heman and Jeduthun. 17:1–27 *Cp.
2 Sam. 7:1–29.* 17:5 **I lived … tabernacle:** *prob.
rdg; Heb.* I have been from tent to tent and from a
tabernacle.

concluding note of lamentation (v. 35) suggests a different mood. **37–42:** From the Chronicler's viewpoint, the
service of the Mosaic *Tabernacle* was still in *Gibeon* while the new Davidic service of *the Ark* was in Jerusalem.
The two services were to be merged in Solomon's time; see 2 Chr. 1.2–6; 5.4–5.

17.1–27: The Lord establishes David's house. The remaining two blocks of material concerning David
(chs. 18–20, 21–29) are introduced by ch. 17. Second Samuel ch. 7 is drawn on to show that David was a
man of war (the motif presented in chs. 18–20) and that, consequently, not he but his son would build the
Lord's house. Nevertheless, David makes all the preparations for the temple (chs. 21–29). This latter view is
stated explicitly in the Chronicler's speech in 22.7–10.

house, and I shall establish his throne for all time. ¹³ I shall be a father to him, and he will be my son. I shall never withdraw my love from him as I withdrew it from your predecessor. ¹⁴ But I shall give him a sure place in my house and kingdom for all time, and his throne will endure for ever.'

¹⁵ Nathan recounted to David all that had been said to him and all that had been revealed. ¹⁶ Then King David went into the presence of the LORD and, taking his place there, said, 'Who am I, LORD God, and what is my family, that you have brought me thus far? ¹⁷ It was a small thing in your sight, God, to have planned for your servant's house in days long past, and now you look on me as a man already embarked on a high career, LORD God. ¹⁸ What more can David say to you of the honour you have done your servant? You yourself know your servant. ¹⁹ For the sake of your servant, LORD, in accordance with your purpose, you have done this great thing and revealed all the great things to come.

²⁰ 'There is none like you, LORD; there is no God but you, as everything we have heard bears witness. ²¹ And your people Israel, to whom can they be compared? Is there any other nation on earth whom you, God, have set out to redeem from slavery to be your people? You have won renown for yourself by great and awesome deeds, driving out nations to make way for your people whom you redeemed from Egypt. ²² You have made your people Israel your own for ever, and you, LORD, have become their God.

²³ 'But now, LORD, let what you have promised for your servant and his house stand fast for all time; make good what you have promised. ²⁴ Let it stand fast, that your fame may be great for evermore, and let people say, "The LORD of Hosts, the God of Israel, is Israel's God"; and may the house of your servant David be established before you. ²⁵ You, my God, have shown me your purpose, to build up your servant's house; therefore I have been able to pray before you. ²⁶ LORD, you are God, and you have made these noble promises to your servant. ²⁷ Be pleased now to bless your servant's house, so that it may continue always before you; you

it is who have blessed it, and it shall be blessed for ever.'

David's campaigns

18 AFTER this David attacked and subdued the Philistines, and took from them Gath with its villages. ² He defeated the Moabites, and they became subject to him and paid him tribute. ³ He also defeated King Hadadezer of Zobah-hamath, who was on his way to set up his monument of victory by the river Euphrates. ⁴ From him David captured a thousand chariots, seven thousand horsemen, and twenty thousand foot-soldiers; he hamstrung all the chariot-horses, except a hundred which he retained. ⁵ When the Aramaeans of Damascus came to the aid of King Hadadezer of Zobah, David destroyed twenty-two thousand of them, ⁶ and stationed garrisons among these Aramaeans; they became subject to him and paid him tribute. Thus the LORD gave David victory wherever he went. ⁷ David took the gold shields borne by Hadadezer's servants and brought them to Jerusalem; ⁸ he also removed from Hadadezer's cities Tibhath and Kun a great quantity of bronze, from which Solomon made the bronze Sea, the pillars, and the bronze vessels.

⁹ When King Tou of Hamath heard that David had defeated the entire army of King Hadadezer of Zobah, ¹⁰ he sent his son Hadoram to King David to greet him and to congratulate him on his victory over Hadadezer in battle, for Hadadezer had been at war with Tou; Hadoram brought with him vessels of gold, silver, and bronze. ¹¹ These King David dedicated to the LORD, along with the silver and gold which he had carried away from all the nations, from Edom and Moab, from the Ammonites and Philistines, and from Amalek.

¹² Abishai son of Zeruiah killed eighteen thousand of the Edomites in the valley of Salt; ¹³ he stationed garrisons throughout Edom, and all the Edomites became subject

17:21 **any other:** *so Gk; Heb.* one.   18:1–13 *Cp. 2 Sam. 8:1–14.*   18:7 **shields:** *or* quivers.
18:10 **Hadoram brought with him:** *so Syriac and 2 Sam. 8:10; Heb. omits.* **vessels:** *so Syriac and 2 Sam. 8:10; Heb.* all vessels.

18.1–20.8: David's imperial victories. The Chronicler includes the accounts of David's victories from 2 Sam. chs. 8, 10, 12, and 21. Omitted, however, are the stories of David's court life related in 2 Sam. chs. 11–20. **4:** The numbers differ from those of 2 Sam. 8.4. **8:** The Chronicler infers that this *bronze* must have been put to David. The LORD gave David victory wherever he went.

14 David ruled over the whole of Israel and maintained law and justice among all his people. 15 Joab son of Zeruiah was in command of the army; Jehoshaphat son of Ahilud was secretary of state; 16 Zadok and Abiathar son of Ahimelech, son of Ahitub, were priests; Shavsha was adjutant-general; 17 Benaiah son of Jehoiada commanded the Kerethite and Pelethite guards. The eldest sons of David were in attendance on the king.

19 Some time afterwards Nahash king of the Ammonites died and was succeeded by his son. 2 David said, 'I must keep up the same loyal friendship with Hanun son of Nahash as his father showed me,' and he sent a mission to condole with him on the death of his father.

When David's envoys entered the country of the Ammonites to condole with Hanun, 3 the Ammonite princes said to Hanun, 'Do you suppose David means to do honour to your father when he sends envoys to condole with you? These men of his are spies whom he has sent to find out how to overthrow the country.' 4 So Hanun took David's servants, shaved them, and cut off half their garments up to the buttocks, and then dismissed them. 5 Hearing how they had been treated, David ordered them to be met, for they were deeply humiliated; he told them to wait in Jericho and not return until their beards had grown again.

6 The Ammonites realized that they had given offence to David, so Hanun and the Ammonites sent a thousand talents of silver to hire chariots and horsemen from Aram-naharaim, Maacah, and Aram-zobah. 7 They hired thirty-two thousand chariots and the king of Maacah and his people, who came and encamped before Medeba, while the Ammonites came from their cities and mustered for battle. 8 When this was reported to David, he sent Joab out with all the fighting men. 9 The Ammonites came on and took up their position at the entrance to the city, while the allied kings took up theirs in the open country. 10 When Joab saw that he was threatened from both front and rear, he detailed some picked Israelite troops and drew them up facing the Aramaeans. 11 The rest of his forces he put under his brother Abishai, who took up a position facing the Ammonites. 12 'If the Aramaeans prove too strong for me,' he said, 'you must come to my relief; and if the Ammonites prove too strong for you, I shall come to yours. 13 Courage! Let us fight bravely for our people and for the cities of our God. And may the LORD's will be done.'

14 Joab and his men engaged with the Aramaeans closely and put them to flight; 15 and when the Ammonites saw them in flight, they too fled before his brother Abishai and withdrew into the city. Then Joab came to Jerusalem.

16 The Aramaeans, reviewing their defeat by Israel, sent messengers to summon other Aramaeans from the Great Bend of the Euphrates under Shophach, commander of Hadadezer's army. 17 Their movement was reported to David, who immediately mustered all the forces of Israel, crossed the Jordan, and advanced against them and took up battle positions. The Aramaeans likewise took up positions facing David and engaged him, 18 but were put to flight by Israel. David slew seven thousand Aramaeans in chariots and forty thousand infantry, killing Shophach the commander of the army. 19 When Hadadezer's men saw that they had been worsted by Israel, they sued for peace and submitted to David. The Aramaeans were never willing to help the Ammonites again.

20 AT the turn of the year, when kings go out to battle, Joab led the army out

18:14–17 Cp. 2 Sam. 8:15–18; 20:23–26; 1 Kgs. 4:2–4.
18:16 **and Abiathar ... Ahitub:** prob. rdg, cp. 2 Sam. 8:17; Heb. son of Ahitub and Abimelech son of Abiathar.   19:1–19 Cp. 2 Sam. 10:1–19.
19:6 **Aram-naharaim:** that is Aram of Two Rivers.
Maacah, and Aram-zobah: prob. rdg; Heb. Aram-maacah, and Zobah.   19:13 **cities:** or altars.
19:17 **The Aramaeans ... him:** so Gk; Heb. When David had taken up positions facing the Aramaeans, they engaged him.   20:1–3 Cp. 2 Sam. 11:1; 12:26–31.

to a good use, i.e. the making of such objects as Solomon's bronze Sea. **17:** The Chronicler has views of priesthood that prohibit David's sons from being priests, as they are in 2 Sam. 8.18; therefore, here they are only in attendance on the king.

    20.1–8: War with the Ammonites and Philistines. While the dramatic military action of ch. 19 is unchanged from its source (2 Sam. ch. 10), care is taken to avoid any hint of the Bathsheba-Uriah story (2 Sam. chs. 11–12), and even of Joab's efforts to insure that David was the conqueror of Rabbah in person; compare 2 Sam.

and ravaged the Ammonite country, while David remained in Jerusalem. Joab came to Rabbah and laid siege to it, and after reducing it he razed it to the ground. 2 David took the crown from the head of Milcom and found that it weighed a talent of gold and was set with a precious stone, and it was placed on David's head; he also removed a vast quantity of booty from the city. 3 He brought out its inhabitants and set them to work with saws and other iron tools, sharp and toothed. David did this to all the Ammonite towns; then he and all his army returned to Jerusalem.

4 Some time later war with the Philistines broke out in Gezer; it was then that Sibbechai from Hushah killed Sippai, a descendant of the Rephaim, and the Philistines were reduced to submission. 5 In another campaign against the Philistines, Elhanan son of Jair killed Lahmi brother of Goliath of Gath, whose spear had a shaft like a weaver's beam. 6 In yet another campaign in Gath there appeared a giant with six fingers on each hand and six toes on each foot, twenty-four in all. He too was descended from the Rephaim; 7 when he defied Israel, Jonathan son of David's brother Shimea killed him. 8 These giants were the descendants of the Rephaim in Gath, and they all fell at the hands of David and his men.

David's census

21 Now SATAN, setting himself against Israel, incited David to make a census of the people. 2 The king commanded Joab and the officers of the army to go out and number Israel from Beersheba to Dan, and to report back the number to him. 3 Joab answered, 'Even if the LORD should increase his people a hundredfold, would not your majesty still be king and all the people your slaves? Why should your majesty want to do this? It will only bring guilt on Israel.' 4 But Joab was overruled by the king; he set out and went up and down the whole country. He then came to Jerusalem 5 and reported to David the numbers recorded: those capable of bearing arms were one million one hundred thousand in Israel, and four hundred and seventy thousand in Judah. 6 Levi and Benjamin were not counted by Joab, so deep was his repugnance against the king's order.

7 God also was displeased with the order, and he proceeded to punish Israel. 8 David said to God, 'I have acted very wickedly: I pray you remove your servant's guilt, for I have been very foolish.' 9 The LORD said to Gad, David's seer, 10 'Go and tell David, This is the word of the LORD: I offer three things; choose one and I shall bring it on you.' 11 Gad came to David and said, 'This is the word of the LORD: Make your choice: 12 three years of famine, three months of harrying by your foes and close pursuit by the sword of your enemy, or three days of the LORD's own sword, bringing pestilence throughout the land, and the LORD's angel working destruction in all the territory of Israel. Consider now what answer I am to take back to him who sent me.' 13 David said to Gad, 'This is a desperate plight I am in; let me fall into the hands of the LORD, for his mercy is very great; and let me not fall into the hands of man.'

14 The LORD sent a pestilence throughout Israel, and seventy thousand Israelites died. 15 God sent an angel to Jerusalem to destroy it; but, as he was destroying it, the LORD saw and repented of the evil, and said to the destroying angel at the moment when he was

20:3 **toothed:** *so one MS, cp. 2 Sam. 12:31; others* saws. 20:4–8 *Cp. 2 Sam. 21:18–22.*   21:1–27 *Cp. 2 Sam. 24:1–25.*

12.26–29. **4–8:** Materials about the exploits of David's heroes not previously used by the Chronicler find their appropriate place here. **4:** *The Rephaim:* legendary inhabitants of southern and eastern Palestine noted for their unusual stature. **5:** The Chronicler does not narrate the David and Goliath story; however, the inconsistency between that story and 2 Sam. 21.19 is eliminated by making *Elhanan* the slayer of the *brother of Goliath* rather than of Goliath himself. **6:** *Gath:* see 1 Sam. 5.8. **7:** *Shimea:* Shammah of 1 Sam. 16.9.

21.1–22.1: The consecration of the temple site. This is taken from the story of the altar site of the Solomonic temple (2 Sam. ch. 24). The story serves here as the introduction to David's preparations for the temple that Solomon would build (chs. 22–29), after the empire will have been secured; see 17.1–27 n. **1:** *Satan* means "the Adversary." See the role played by this figure in the heavenly court in Job 1.6–12; compare 1 Kgs. 22.19–23; Zech. 3.1–2; and, in a poetic context, Ps. 82. **5:** Compare the numbers in 2 Sam. 24.9. **6:** *Levi* was not a tribal territory; to count Levites (local priests) was not the same as to count the other tribes. Why *Benjamin* standing at the threshing-floor of Ornan the Jebusite, 'Enough! Stay your hand.'

16 When David looked up and saw the angel of the LORD standing between earth and heaven, and in his hand a drawn sword stretched out over Jerusalem, he and the elders, clothed in sackcloth, fell prostrate to the ground. 17 David said to God, 'It was I who gave the order to count the people. It is I who have sinned, I, the shepherd, who have committed the wrong; but these poor sheep, what have they done? LORD my God, let your hand fall on me and on my family, but check this plague on the people.'

18 The angel of the LORD, speaking through the lips of Gad, commanded David to go to the threshing-floor of Ornan the Jebusite and to set up there an altar to the LORD. 19 David went up as Gad had bidden him in the LORD's name. 20 Ornan's four sons who were with him hid themselves, but he was busy threshing his wheat when he turned and saw the angel. 21 As David approached, Ornan looked up and, seeing the king, came out from the threshing-floor and prostrated himself before him. 22 David said to Ornan, 'Let me have the site of the threshing-floor, so that I may build on it an altar to the LORD; sell it to me at the full price, so that the plague which has attacked the people may be stopped.' 23 Ornan answered, 'Take it and let your majesty do as he thinks fit; see, here are the oxen for whole-offerings, the threshing-sledges for the fuel, and the wheat for the grain-offering; I give you everything.' 24 But King David said to Ornan, 'No, I shall pay the full price; I am not going to present to the LORD what is yours, or offer a whole-offering which has cost me nothing.' 25 So David gave Ornan six hundred shekels of gold for the site. 26 He built an altar to the LORD there, and offered whole-offerings and shared-offerings. He called to the LORD, who answered him with fire falling from heaven on the altar

of whole-offering. 27 Then, at the LORD's command, the angel sheathed his sword.

28 It was when David saw that the LORD had answered him at the threshing-floor of Ornan the Jebusite that he offered sacrifice there. 29 The Tabernacle of the LORD and the altar of whole-offering which Moses had made in the wilderness were then at the shrine in Gibeon; 30 but David had been unable to go there and seek God's guidance, so shocked and shaken was he at the sight of the

22 angel's sword. 1 Then David said, 'This is to be the house of the LORD God, and this is to be an altar of whole-offering for Israel.'

Preparation for the temple

2 DAVID now gave orders to assemble the aliens resident in Israel, and he set them as masons to dress hewn stones for building the house of God. 3 He laid in a great store of iron to make nails and clamps for the doors, and more bronze than could be weighed, 4 and cedar-wood without limit; the men of Sidon and Tyre brought David an ample supply of cedar. 5 David said, 'My son Solomon is a boy of tender years, and the house that is to be built for the LORD must be exceedingly magnificent, renowned and celebrated in every land; therefore I must make provision for it myself.' So David before his death made abundant provision.

6 He sent for Solomon his son and charged him with building a house for the LORD the God of Israel. 7 'Solomon, my son,' he said, 'it was my intention to build a house for the name of the LORD my God; 8 but the LORD forbade me and said, "You have shed much blood in my sight and waged great wars; for this reason you are not to build a house for

21:17 **I, the shepherd:** *prob. rdg; Heb.* doing wrong. **check . . . people:** *prob. rdg; Heb.* among your people, not for a plague.

should be omitted is not clear. **22–25:** Compare David's refusal to take the site as a gift, for religious reasons, with Abram's response to the king of Sodom in Gen. 14.21–24. **26:** On the tradition of the *fire . . . from heaven,* see 1 Kgs. 18.23–24 n. **21.28–22.1:** This is the Chronicler's own comment on the episode taken from 2 Sam.

    22.2–29.30: The preparations for the temple. These materials are derived from different sources preserved in the Chronicler's circle. Chapter 22 is mostly repeated in chs. 28–29; the two sections are probably two renderings of the same topic. Chapters 23–27, lists of Levites and other groups are not closely connected to the speeches in the surrounding chs. Such lists probably existed separately in the Chronicler's circle.

    22.2–19: A survey of the preparations. David assembles the workers and materials, addresses Solomon (see 28.20–21), and gives a charge to the officers of Israel (see 28.1–10). **2:** On the *aliens* as a source of labor, see 1 Kgs. 9.15–23 n. **8:** In 17.4–6 the Chronicler has already given a reason (quoted unaltered from my name. ⁹But you will have a son who will be a man of peace; I shall give him peace from all his enemies on every side; his name will be Solomon, 'Man of Peace', and I shall grant peace and quiet to Israel in his days. ¹⁰It is he who will build a house for my name; he will be my son and I shall be a father to him, and I shall establish his royal throne over Israel for ever."

¹¹'Now, my son, may the LORD be with you! May you prosper and build the house of the LORD your God as he promised you would. ¹²May the LORD grant you insight and understanding, so that when he gives you authority in Israel you may keep the law of the LORD your God. ¹³You will prosper only if you are careful to observe the decrees and ordinances which the LORD enjoined upon Moses for Israel; be strong and resolute, neither faint-hearted nor dismayed.

¹⁴'At the cost of some trouble, I have here ready for the house of the LORD a hundred thousand talents of gold and a million talents of silver, with great quantities of bronze and iron, more than can be weighed; timber and stone, too, I have got ready; and you may add to them. ¹⁵Besides, you have at your disposal a large force of workmen, masons, sculptors, and carpenters, and every kind of skilled craftsmen ¹⁶in gold and silver, bronze and iron. Set to work, and the LORD be with you!'

¹⁷David ordered all the officers of Israel to help Solomon his son: ¹⁸'Is not the LORD your God with you? Will he not give you

peace on every side? For he has given the inhabitants of the land into my power; the land will be subdued before the LORD and his people. ¹⁹Devote yourselves, therefore, heart and soul, to seeking guidance of the LORD your God, and set about building his sanctuary, so that the Ark of the Covenant of the LORD and God's holy vessels may be brought into the house built for his name.'

23 David was now an old man, weighed down with years, and he appointed Solomon his son king over Israel. ²He assembled all the officers of Israel, the priests, and the Levites. ³The Levites were enrolled from the age of thirty upwards, their males being thirty-eight thousand in all. ⁴Of these, twenty-four thousand were to be responsible for the maintenance and service of the house of the LORD, six thousand to act as officers and magistrates, ⁵four thousand to be doorkeepers, and four thousand to praise the LORD with the musical instruments which David had produced for the service of praise. ⁶David organized them in divisions, called after Gershon, Kohath, and Merari, the sons of Levi.

⁷The sons of Gershon: Laadan and Shimei. ⁸The sons of Laadan: Jehiel the chief, Zetham, and Joel, three. ⁹These were the heads of the families grouped under Laa-

22:9 *Cp. 1 Kgs. 5:4.* **peace:** *Heb.* shalom.
23:5 **David:** *so Gk; Heb.* I.　　23:8 **three:** *prob. rdg; Heb. adds* The sons of Shimei: Shelomith, Haziel, and Haran, three.

2 Sam. 7) that the LORD *forbade* David to build a temple. Here the Chronicler gives a different reason: that David shed much blood in the conquest of his empire. **9:** In contrast to David, *Solomon* was a *"Man of Peace"*; the Heb. Solomon (*Shelōmōh*) is related to the noun *peace* (*shālōm*). **14:** The *trouble* may have been the acute family problems and rebellions related in 2 Sam. chs. 12–20 but omitted by the Chronicler.

23.1–26.32: The divisions of the religious personnel. Other than the genealogies of chs. 1–10, this is the most "technical" section of 1 and 2 Chr., and important to the Chronicler's circle in that the family lists of Levites and priests established the legitimacy of and the priorities for the many personnel involved in the service and benefits of the postexilic temple.

23.1–32: The Levites. 3–6: These statements apply to all the Levitical groups to be listed. Here, the Levites did not begin active service until *the age of thirty*. Later, when more were needed in active service, the age was lowered to twenty-five (Num. 8.24), and even to twenty (23.24, 27). **8–23:** For other genealogies of the Levites, see Exod. 6.16–25; Num. 3.17–39; 1 Chr. 6.16–30; 24.20–30. The three main clans, *Gershon, Kohath,* and *Merari,* are firm in all lists. The third generation is also very consistent, though *Gershon*'s first son otherwise appears as Libni instead of *Laadan*. Except for the genealogies of Aaron (see ch. 24), only Chr. gives names beyond the third generation, and those names differ in each list. This list gives the families active at one time within the several Levitical clans. The list in 1 Chr. 6.16–30 on the other hand, traces the lineage of each clan through several generations. When one of the sons is referred to as *chief,* it means he was the leader for that group in carrying out its temple duties. If only the last generation of each family is counted, twenty-one families are listed. However, two families were merged because neither was large enough to carry dan. ¹⁰The sons of Shimei: Jahath, Ziza, Jeush, and Beriah, four. ¹¹Jahath was the chief and Ziza the second, but Jeush and Beriah, having few children, were reckoned for duty as a single family.

¹²The sons of Kohath: Amram, Izhar, Hebron, and Uzziel, four. ¹³The sons of Amram: Aaron and Moses. Aaron was set apart, he and his sons in perpetuity, to dedicate the most holy gifts, to burn sacrifices before the LORD, to serve him, and to give the blessing in his name for ever, ¹⁴but the sons of Moses, the man of God, were to keep the name of Levite. ¹⁵The sons of Moses: Gershom and Eliezer. ¹⁶The sons of Gershom: Shubael the chief. ¹⁷The sons of Eliezer: Rehabiah the chief. Eliezer had no other sons, but Rehabiah had very many. ¹⁸The sons of Izhar: Shelomoth the chief. ¹⁹The sons of Hebron: Jeriah the chief, Amariah the second, Jahaziel the third, and Jekameam the fourth. ²⁰The sons of Uzziel: Micah the chief and Isshiah the second.

²¹The sons of Merari: Mahli and Mushi. The sons of Mahli: Eleazar and Kish. ²²When Eleazar died, he left daughters but no sons, and their cousins, the sons of Kish, married them. ²³The sons of Mushi: Mahli, Eder, and Jeremoth, three.

²⁴Such were the Levites, grouped by families in the father's line whose heads were named in the detailed list; they performed duties in the service of the house of the LORD, from the age of twenty upwards. ²⁵For David said, 'The LORD the God of Israel has given his people peace and has made his dwelling in Jerusalem for ever. ²⁶The Levites will no longer have to carry the Tabernacle or any of the vessels for its service.' ²⁷According to these last instructions of David the Levites were enrolled from the age of twenty upwards. ²⁸Their duty was to help the descendants of Aaron in the service of the house of the LORD: they were responsible for the care of the courts and the rooms, for the cleansing of all holy things, and for the general service

of the house of God; ²⁹for the rows of the Bread of the Presence, the flour for the grain-offerings, unleavened wafers, cakes baked on the griddle, and pastry, and for the weights and measures. ³⁰They were to be on duty continually before the LORD every morning and evening, giving thanks and praise to him, ³¹and whenever whole-offerings were presented to the LORD, on sabbaths, new moons, and at the appointed seasons, according to their prescribed number. ³²The Levites were to have charge of the Tent of Meeting and of the sanctuary, but Aaron's descendants, their kinsmen, were charged with the service of worship in the house of the LORD.

24 The divisions of the sons of Aaron: his sons were Nadab and Abihu, Eleazar and Ithamar. ²Nadab and Abihu died before their father, leaving no sons; therefore Eleazar and Ithamar held the office of priest. ³David, acting with Zadok of the sons of Eleazar and with Ahimelech of the sons of Ithamar, organized them in divisions for the discharge of the duties of their office. ⁴The male heads of families proved to be more numerous in the line of Eleazar than in that of Ithamar, so that sixteen heads of families were grouped under the line of Eleazar and eight under that of Ithamar. ⁵He organized them by drawing lots among them, for there were sacred officers and officers of God in the line of Eleazar and in that of Ithamar.

⁶Shemaiah the clerk, a Levite, son of Nethanel, wrote down the names in the presence of the king, the officers, Zadok the priest, and Ahimelech son of Abiathar, and of the heads of the priestly and levitical families, one priestly family being taken from the line of Eleazar and one from that of Ithamar.

23:10 **Ziza:** *so Gk; Heb.* Zina.   23:13 **to dedicate …gifts:** *or* to be hallowed as most holy.
23:16 **Shubael:** *so Gk; Heb.* Shebuel.
23:18 **Shelomoth:** *so one MS; others* Shelomith.
24:5 **sacred officers:** *or* officers of the sanctuary.
24:6 **one from that:** *so some MSS; others* taken from that.

out its duties separately (v. 11), and one family had no male descendants (v. 22). **25–26:** On the earlier duties of the Levites, see Num. chs. 3–4. **27:** On the age, see vv. 3–6 n. The *last instructions* here are meant to acknowledge that though *David* once said thirty years, his last word was *twenty*.

24.1–31: The divisions of the priests. The genealogy of Aaron, tracing the line of the chief priests, is given in 6.1–15. Here, the names of the priestly families who alternated in service at the temple are given. The twenty-four families probably each served from sabbath to sabbath according to an established order; see 9.25 and Lk. 1.5–10. The income from the altar service went partly to all *the sons of Aaron* and partly to the priests who were presiding at any given time; compare Lev. 2.3, 10; 7.14, 32–35. **6:** Solemn measures were taken

7 The first lot fell to Jehoiarib, the second to Jedaiah, 8 the third to Harim, the fourth to Seorim, 9 the fifth to Malchiah, the sixth to Mijamin, 10 the seventh to Hakkoz, the eighth to Abijah, 11 the ninth to Jeshua, the tenth to Shecaniah, 12 the eleventh to Eliashib, the twelfth to Jakim, 13 the thirteenth to Huppah, the fourteenth to Jeshebeab, 14 the fifteenth to Bilgah, the sixteenth to Immer, 15 the seventeenth to Hezir, the eighteenth to Aphses, 16 the nineteenth to Pethahiah, the twentieth to Jehezkel, 17 the twenty-first to Jachin, the twenty-second to Gamul, 18 the twenty-third to Delaiah, and the twenty-fourth to Maaziah. 19 This was their order of duty for the discharge of their service when they entered the house of the LORD, according to the rule prescribed for them by their ancestor Aaron, who had received his instructions from the LORD the God of Israel.

20 Of the remaining Levites: of the sons of Amram: Shubael. Of the sons of Shubael: Jehdeiah. 21 Of Rehabiah: Isshiah, the chief of Rehabiah's sons. 22 Of the line of Izhar: Shelomoth. Of the sons of Shelomoth; Jahath. 23 The sons of Hebron: Jeriah the chief, Amariah the second, Jahaziel the third, and Jekameam the fourth. 24 The sons of Uzziel: Micah. Of the sons of Micah: Shamir; 25 Micah's brother: Isshiah. Of the sons of Isshiah: Zechariah. 26 The sons of Merari: Mahli and Mushi and also Jaaziah his son. 27 The sons of Merari: of Jaaziah: Beno, Shoham, Zaccur, and Ibri. 28 Of Mahli: Eleazar, who had no sons; 29 of Kish: the sons of Kish: Jerahmeel; 30 and the sons of Mushi: Mahli, Eder, and Jerimoth. These were the Levites by families. 31 These also, side by side with their kinsmen the descendants of Aaron, cast lots in the presence of King David, Zadok, Ahimelech, and the heads of the priestly and levitical families, the senior and junior houses casting lots side by side.

25 David and his chief officers assigned special duties to the sons of Asaph, of Heman, and of Jeduthun, leaders in inspired prophecy to the accompaniment of lyres, lutes, and cymbals; the list of those who performed this work in the temple was as follows. 2 Of the sons of Asaph: Zaccur, Joseph, Nethaniah, and Asarelah; these were under Asaph, a leader in inspired prophecy under the king. 3 Of the sons of Jeduthun: Gedaliah, Izri, Isaiah, Shimei, Hashabiah, Mattithiah, these six under their father Jeduthun, a leader in inspired prophecy to the accompaniment of the lyre, giving thanks and praise to the LORD. 4 Of the sons of Heman: Bukkiah, Mattaniah, Uzziel, Shubael, Jerimoth, Hananiah, Hanani, Eliathah, Giddalti, Romamti-ezer, Joshbekashah, Mallothi, Hothir, and Mahazioth; 5 all these were sons of Heman the king's seer, given to him through the promises of God for his greater glory. God had given Heman fourteen sons and three daughters, 6 and they all served under their father for the singing in the house of the LORD; they took part in the service of the house of God, with cymbals, lutes, and lyres, while Asaph, Jeduthun, and Heman were under the king. 7 Reckoned with their kinsmen, trained singers of the LORD, they brought the total number of skilled musicians up to two hundred and eighty-eight. 8 They cast lots for their duties, young and old, master-singer and apprentice side by side.

9 The first lot fell to Joseph: he and his brothers and his sons, twelve. The second to

24:13 **Jeshebeab:** *one form of Gk has* Ishbaal. 24:23 **Hebron:** *so one MS; others omit.* **the chief:** *so Gk (Luc.); Heb. omits.* 24:26 **and also:** *prob. rdg; Heb.* the sons of. 25:3 **Izri:** *prob. rdg, cp. verse 11; Heb.* Zeri. **Shimei:** *so one MS; others omit.* 25:4 **Shubael:** *so Gk, cp. verse 20; Heb.* Shebuel. **Hananiah ... Mahzioth:** *these nine proper names may have been originally the words of a prayer:* Be gracious to me, LORD, be gracious to me; you are my God; I will magnify and exalt you, my helper. Lingering in hardship, I faint. Grant me vision after vision. 25:9 **fell:** *prob. rdg; Heb. adds* to Asaph. **Joseph: he and his brothers and his sons, twelve:** *prob. rdg; Heb. omits* he . . . twelve.

to assure a proper priestly service and to give each family its due. **20–31:** An appendix containing an alternative list to 23.16–23.

25.1–31: The singers and musicians. 1: The name of the third guild varies: it is Ethan in 6.31–48 and 15.16–24, but Jeduthun in 16.41; 25.3, 6; 2 Chr. 5.12; 29.14; and Neh. 11.17. The two names became identified; it is unknown whether originally they reflected two separate clans. *Asaph* appears in the Heb. headings of Pss. 50, 73–83; Ethan, Ps. 89; and *Jeduthun*, Pss. 39, 62, 77. *Prophecy*: see v. 5 n. **5:** *Seer:* there is reflected the kinship between music and prophecy; compare 2 Chr. 20.14 and 2 Kgs. 3.14–16. **7:** *Two hundred and eighty-eight:* twelve singers for each of the twenty-four divisions, matching the divisions of the priests in ch. 24. A different number, four thousand, is given in 23.5. **9–31:** The twenty-four names are given

Gedaliah: he and his brothers and his sons, twelve. [10] The third to Zaccur: his sons and his brothers, twelve. [11] The fourth to Izri: his sons and his brothers, twelve. [12] The fifth to Nethaniah: his sons and his brothers, twelve. [13] The sixth to Bukkiah: his sons and his brothers, twelve. [14] The seventh to Asarelah: his sons and his brothers, twelve. [15] The eighth to Isaiah: his sons and his brothers, twelve. [16] The ninth to Mattaniah: his sons and his brothers, twelve. [17] The tenth to Shimei: his sons and his brothers, twelve. [18] The eleventh to Azarel: his sons and his brothers, twelve. [19] The twelfth to Hashabiah: his sons and his brothers, twelve. [20] The thirteenth to Shubael: his sons and his brothers, twelve. [21] The fourteenth to Mattithiah: his sons and his brothers, twelve. [22] The fifteenth to Jeremoth: his sons and his brothers, twelve. [23] The sixteenth to Hananiah: his sons and his brothers, twelve. [24] The seventeenth to Joshbekashah: his sons and his brothers, twelve. [25] The eighteenth to Hanani: his sons and his brothers, twelve. [26] The nineteenth to Mallothi: his sons and his brothers, twelve. [27] The twentieth to Eliathah: his sons and his brothers, twelve. [28] The twenty-first to Hothir: his sons and his brothers, twelve. [29] The twenty-second to Giddalti: his sons and his brothers, twelve. [30] The twenty-third to Mahazioth: his sons and his brothers, twelve. [31] The twenty-fourth to Romamti-ezer: his sons and his brothers, twelve.

26 The divisions of the door-keepers: Korahites: Meshelemiah son of Kore, son of Ebiasaph. [2] Sons of Meshelemiah: Zechariah the eldest, Jediael the second, Zebadiah the third, Jathniel the fourth, [3] Elam the fifth, Jehohanan the sixth, Eliehoenai the seventh. [4] Sons of Obed-edom: Shemaiah the eldest, Jehozabad the second, Joah the third, Sacar the fourth, Nethanel the fifth, [5] Ammiel the sixth, Issachar the seventh, Peulthai the eighth (for God had blessed him). [6] Shemaiah, his son, was the father of sons who had authority in their family, for they were men of great ability. [7] Sons

of Shemaiah: Othni, Rephael, Obed, Elzabad, and his brothers Elihu and Semachiah, men of ability. [8] All these belonged to the family of Obed-edom; they, their sons and brothers, were men of ability, fit for service in the temple; total: sixty-two. [9] Sons and brothers of Meshelemiah, all men of ability, eighteen. [10] Sons of Hosah, a Merarite: Shimri the chief (he was not the eldest, but his father had made him chief), [11] Hilkiah the second, Tebaliah the third, Zechariah the fourth. Total of Hosah's sons and brothers: thirteen.

[12] The male heads of families constituted the divisions of the door-keepers; their duty was to serve in the house of the LORD side by side with their kinsmen. [13] Young and old, family by family, they cast lots for the gates. [14] The lot for the east gate fell to Shelemiah; then lots were cast for his son Zechariah, a prudent counsellor, and he was allotted the north gate. [15] To Obed-edom was allotted the south gate, and the gatehouse to his sons. [16] Hosah was allotted the west gate, together with the Shallecheth gate on the ascending causeway. Guard corresponded to guard. [17] Six Levites were on duty daily on the east side, four on the north and four on the south, and two at each gatehouse; [18] at the western colonnade there were four at the causeway and two at the colonnade itself. [19] These were the divisions of the door-keepers, Korahites and Merarites.

[20] Fellow-Levites were in charge of the stores of the house of God and of the stores of sacred gifts. [21] Of the children of Laadan, descendants of the Gershonite line through Laadan, heads of families in the group of Laadan the Gershonite: Jehiel [22] and his brothers Zetham and Joel were in charge of the stores of the house of the LORD. [23] Of the

25:14 **Asarelah:** *so one form of Gk, cp. verse 2; Heb.* Yesarelah. 26:1 **son of Ebiasaph:** *prob. rdg; Heb.* from the sons of Asaph. 26:7 **Elzabad, and:** *so some MSS; others omit* and. 26:10 **the chief:** *or the* fratriarch. 26:16 **Hosah:** *prob. rdg; Heb.* Shuppim and Hosah. 26:20 **Fellow-Levites:** *so Gk; Heb.* Levites, Ahijah. 26:21–22 **Jehiel and:** *prob. rdg; Heb.* Jehieli. The sons of Jehieli.

in the order of their duty as determined by lot (see the same for the priests in 24.5–6).

26.1–32: The door-keepers and other Levites. Compare 9.17–32; 15.23–24; 16.37–42. **1–11:** The leaders of the clans of *door-keepers — Meshelemiah* (v. 1), *Obed-edom* (v. 4), and *Hosah* (v. 10) — are only minor figures in Levite lists. The overlap of names with those of musical clans perhaps suggests a close relationship between gatekeepers and musicians. **12–19:** The structure of the temple as reflected in these guard posts envisions the postexilic age of the Chronicler, not Solomon's temple; compare 9.17–27. **20–32:** The Levites families of Amram, Izhar, Hebron, and Uzziel, 24 Shubael son of Gershom, son of Moses, was overseer of the stores. 25 The line of Eliezer his brother: his son Rehabiah, his son Isaiah, his son Joram, his son Zichri, and his son Shelomoth. 26 This Shelomoth and his kinsmen were in charge of all the stores of the sacred gifts dedicated by King David, the heads of families, the officers over units of a thousand and a hundred, and other officers of the army. 27 They had dedicated some of the spoils taken in the wars for the upkeep of the house of the LORD. 28 Everything which Samuel the seer, Saul son of Kish, Abner son of Ner, and Joab son of Zeruiah had dedicated, in short every sacred gift, was under the charge of Shelomoth and his kinsmen. 29 Of the family of Izhar: Kenaniah and his sons acted as clerks and magistrates in the secular affairs of Israel. 30 Of the family of Hebron: Hashabiah and his kinsmen, men of ability to the number of seventeen hundred, had the oversight of Israel west of the Jordan, both in the work of the LORD and in the service of the king. 31 Also of the family of Hebron, Jeriah was the chief. (In the fortieth year of David's reign search was made in the family histories of the Hebronites, and men of great ability were found among them at Jazer in Gilead.) 32 His kinsmen, all men of ability, two thousand seven hundred of them, heads of families, were charged by King David with the oversight of the Reubenites, the Gadites, and the half tribe of Manasseh, in religious and civil affairs alike.

27 THE number of the Israelites — that is to say, of the heads of families, the officers over units of a thousand and a hundred, and the clerks who had their share in the king's service in the various divisions which took monthly turns of duty throughout the year — was twenty-four thousand in each division.

2 First, Jashobeam son of Zabdiel commanded the division for the first month with twenty-four thousand in his division; 3 a member of the house of Perez, he was chief officer of the temple staff for the first month. 4 Eleazar son of Dodai the Ahohite commanded the division for the second month with twenty-four thousand in his division. 5 Third, Benaiah son of Jehoiada the chief priest, commander of the army, was the officer for the third month with twenty-four thousand in his division 6 (he was the Benaiah who was one of the thirty warriors and was a chief among the thirty); but his son Ammizabad commanded his division. 7 Fourth, Asahel, the brother of Joab, was the officer commanding for the fourth month with twenty-four thousand in his division; and his successor was Zebadiah his son. 8 Fifth, Shamhuth the Zerahite was the officer commanding for the fifth month with twenty-four thousand in his division. 9 Sixth, Ira son of Ikkesh, a man of Tekoa, was the officer commanding for the sixth month with twenty-four thousand in his division. 10 Seventh, Helez, an Ephraimite from a place unknown, was the officer commanding for the seventh month with twenty-four thousand in his division. 11 Eighth, Sibbechai from Hushah, of the family of Zerah, was the officer commanding for the eighth month with twenty-four thousand in his division. 12 Ninth, Abiezer, from Anathoth in Benjamin, was the officer commanding for the ninth month with twenty-four thousand in his division. 13 Tenth, Maharai the Netophathite, of the family of Zerah, was the officer commanding for the tenth month with twenty-four thousand in his division. 14 Eleventh, Benaiah the Pirathonite, from Ephraim, was the officer commanding for the eleventh month with twenty-four thousand in his division. 15 Twelfth, Heldai the Netophathite, of the family of Othniel, was the officer commanding for the twelfth

26:24 **Shubael:** *so Lat.; Heb.* Shebuel.   26:25 **The line . . . brother:** *so Gk; Heb. obscure.*   27:4 **Eleazar son of:** *prob. rdg, cp. 11:12; Heb. omits.* **the Ahohite:** *so Gk; Heb. adds* and his division and Mikloth the prince.   27:6 **commanded:** *so Gk; Heb. omits.*   27:8 **the Zerahite:** *prob. rdg; Heb.* the Izrah.

engaged in administrative tasks. **21–22:** Three officials were *in charge of the stores* in the temple. **23–24:** The overseer(s) *of the stores* were from different families, perhaps to insure fairness in handling them. **26:** A still different family was *in charge of . . . the sacred gifts.* **29–32:** Three other groups of Levites conducted secular judicial and administrative tasks outside of Jerusalem: *clerks and magistrates* (v. 29); administrators *west of the Jordan* (v. 30); and administrators *east of the Jordan* (vv. 31–32). Compare 2 Chr. 19.8–11 and Deut. 17.8–13.

27.1–34: Officials of the realm. 1–15: In his own time, David was in no position to rule through such a schematic arrangement; also, the postexilic period offered no opportunity for such exaggerated numbers as month with twenty-four thousand in his division.

16 The following were the principal officers in charge of the tribes of Israel: of Reuben, Eliezer son of Zichri; of Simeon, Shephatiah son of Maacah; 17 of Levi, Hashabiah son of Kemuel; of Aaron, Zadok; 18 of Judah, Elihu a kinsman of David; of Issachar, Omri son of Michael; 19 of Zebulun, Ishmaiah son of Obadiah; of Naphtali, Jerimoth son of Azriel; 20 of Ephraim, Hoshea son of Azaziah; of the half tribe of Manasseh, Joel son of Pedaiah; 21 of the half of Manasseh in Gilead, Iddo son of Zechariah; of Benjamin, Jaasiel son of Abner; 22 of Dan, Azarel son of Jeroham. These were the officers in charge of the tribes of Israel.

23 David took no census of those under twenty years of age, for the LORD had promised to make the Israelites as many as the stars in the sky. 24 Joab son of Zeruiah did begin to take a census but he did not finish it; the census brought down wrath on Israel, and it was not entered in the annals of King David's reign.

25 Azmoth son of Adiel was in charge of the king's stores; Jonathan son of Uzziah was in charge of the stores in the country, in the cities, in the villages, and in the fortresses. 26 Ezri son of Kelub had oversight of the workers on the land; 27 Shimei from Ramah was in charge of the vine-dressers, while Zabdi from Shephem had charge of the produce of the vineyards for the wine cellars. 28 Baal-hanan the Gederite supervised the wild olives and the sycomore-figs in the Shephelah; Joash was in charge of the oil stores. 29 Shitrai from Sharon was in charge of the herds grazing in Sharon, Shaphat son of Adlai of the herds in the valleys. 30 Obil the Ishmaelite was in charge of the camels, Jehdeiah the Meronothite of the donkeys. 31 Jaziz the Hagarite was in charge of the flocks. All these were the officers in charge of King David's possessions. 32 David's favourite nephew Jonathan, a counsellor, a discreet and learned man, and Jehiel the Hachmonite, were tutors to the king's sons. 33 Ahithophel was a king's

counsellor; Hushai the Archite was the king's Friend. 34 Ahithophel was succeeded by Jehoiada son of Benaiah and by Abiathar. Joab was commander of the army.

28 DAVID assembled at Jerusalem all the officers of Israel, the officers over the tribes, over the divisions engaged in the king's service, over the units of a thousand and a hundred, and officials in charge of all the property and the cattle of the king and of his sons, as well as the eunuchs, the heroes, and all the men of ability.

2 King David stood up and addressed them: 'Hear me, my kinsmen and my people. I had it in mind to build a house as a resting-place for the Ark of the Covenant of the LORD which might serve as a footstool for our God, and I made preparations to build it. 3 But God said to me, "You are not to build a house for my name, because you have been a fighting man and you have shed blood." 4 Nevertheless, the LORD the God of Israel chose me out of all my father's family to be king over Israel for ever. For it was Judah that he chose as ruling tribe, and, out of the house of Judah, my father's family; and among my father's sons it was I whom he was pleased to make king over all Israel. 5 And out of all my sons—for the LORD gave me many sons—he has chosen Solomon to sit on the throne of the LORD's sovereignty over Israel; 6 he said to me, "It is Solomon your son who is to build my house and my courts, for I have chosen him to be a son to me and I shall be a father to him. 7 I shall establish his sovereignty for ever, if he steadfastly obeys my commandments and my laws as he now does."

8 'Now therefore, in the sight of all Israel, the assembly of the LORD, and in the hearing of our God, I say to you: Study carefully all the commandments of the LORD your God, in order that you may possess this good land and hand it down as an inheritance for all time to your children after you.

9 'And you, Solomon my son, acknowledge your father's God and serve him with whole

twenty-four thousand people in each of the twelve divisions. **16–22:** The tribe of Asher is omitted, yet *Aaron* is included (v. 17) as if a tribe; contrast 12.26–27, where Aaron is listed but not counted as a tribe. **23–24:** On the census, see 21.1–6. **32–34:** This *Jonathan* is elsewhere unmentioned, as is the case with *Jehiel*. On *Ahithophel* see 2 Sam. 15.31; 16.23; 17.23. On *Hushai*, 2 Sam. 15.32–37; 16.16–19; 17.5–16. On *Abiathar*, 1 Sam. 22.20–23; on *Joab*, 2 Sam. 2.12–17.

28.1–29.30: David's farewell addresses and his death. This whole block of material is an elaboration of heart and willing mind, for the Lord searches all hearts and discerns whatever plan may be devised. If you search for him, he will let you find him, but if you forsake him, he will cast you off for ever. 10 Remember, then, that the Lord has chosen you to build a house as a sanctuary: be steadfast and do it.'

11 David gave Solomon his son the plan of the porch of the temple and its buildings, strong-rooms, roof-chambers and inner courts, and the shrine of expiation; 12 also the plans of all he had in mind for the courts of the house of the Lord and for all the rooms around it, for the stores of God's house, and for the stores of the sacred gifts. 13 He gave directions for the divisions of the priests and Levites, for all the work connected with the service of the house of the Lord, and for all the vessels used in its service. 14 He prescribed the weight of gold for all the gold vessels used in the various services, and the weight of silver for all the silver vessels used in the various services; 15 and the weight of gold for the gold lampstands and their lamps; and the weight of silver for the silver lampstands, the weight required for each lampstand and its lamps according to the use of each; 16 and the weight of gold for each of the tables for the rows of the Bread of the Presence, and of silver for the silver tables. 17 He prescribed also the weight of pure gold for the forks, tossing-bowls, and cups, the weight of gold for each of the golden dishes, and of silver for each of the silver dishes; 18 the weight also of refined gold for the altar of incense, and of gold for the model of the chariot, that is the cherubim with their wings spread to screen the Ark of the Covenant of the Lord. 19 'All this was drafted by the Lord's own hand,' said David; 'my part was to consider the detailed working out of the plan.'

20 Then David said to Solomon his son, 'Be steadfast and resolute and carry it out; be neither faint-hearted nor dismayed, for the Lord God, my God, will be with you; he will neither fail you nor forsake you, until you have finished all the work needed for the service of the house of the Lord. 21 Here are the divisions of the priests and the Levites, ready for all the service of the house of God. In all the work you will have the help of every willing craftsman for any task; and the officers and all the people are entirely at your command.'

Solomon succeeds David as king

29 King David said to the whole assembly, 'My son Solomon is the one chosen by God, Solomon alone, a boy of tender years; and this is a great work, for it is a habitation not for man but for the Lord God. 2 Now to the best of my ability I have made ready for the house of my God gold for the gold work, silver for the silver, bronze for the bronze, iron for the iron, and wood for the woodwork, together with cornelian and other gems for setting, stones for mosaic work, precious stones of every sort, and marble in plenty. 3 Further, because I delight in the house of my God, I have given my own private store of gold and silver for the house of my God—over and above all the store which I have collected for the sanctuary— 4 namely three thousand talents of gold from Ophir, and seven thousand talents of fine silver for overlaying the walls of the buildings, 5 for providing gold for the gold work, silver for the silver, and for any work to be done by skilled craftsmen. Now who is willing to give with open hand to the Lord today?'

6 Then the heads of families, the officers administering the tribes of Israel, the officers over units of a thousand and a hundred, and the officers in charge of the king's service, responded willingly 7 and gave for the work of the house of God five thousand talents of gold, ten thousand darics, ten thousand talents of silver, eighteen thousand talents of bronze, and a hundred thousand talents of

28:11 **of the temple:** *prob. rdg; Heb. omits.* **the shrine of expiation:** *or* the place for the Ark with its cover. 28:14 **for . . . gold vessels:** *prob. rdg; Heb.* for gold. **of silver:** *prob. rdg; Heb. omits.*   28:17 **of silver:** *prob. rdg; Heb. omits.*

David as founder of the dynasty and the preparer for the temple, but not its builder. **11–19:** Just as Moses received a divine plan for the first sanctuary (Exod. 25.9), so David is the recipient of a divine pattern for the temple (v. 19). **18:** *The Ark* with *cherubim* is called a *chariot* because originally it was understood as a mobile place of enthronement for the invisible deity; see 1 Sam. 4.4. **21:** These farewell words take account of the lists in chs. 23–27, as the speeches in ch. 22 do not. **29.1–5:** Compare David's provisions in 22.3–4, 14–15. **6–9:** On the extravagant generosity by the people, compare Exod. 35.4–29. **7:** *Darics* were Persian coins, iron. 8 Further, those who possessed precious stones gave them to the treasury of the house of the LORD, into the charge of Jehiel the Gershonite. 9 The people rejoiced at this willing response, because in the loyalty of their hearts they had given willingly to the LORD; King David also was full of joy.

10 David blessed the LORD in the presence of all the assembly, saying:

'Blessed are you, LORD God of our
   father Israel,
from of old and for ever.
11 Yours, LORD, is the greatness and the
   power,
the glory, the splendour, and the
   majesty;
for everything in heaven and on earth
   is yours;
yours, LORD, is the sovereignty,
and you are exalted over all as head.
12 Wealth and honour come from you;
   you rule over all;
might and power are of your disposing;
yours it is to give power and strength to
   all.
13 Now, our God, we give you thanks
and praise your glorious name.

14 'But who am I, and who are my people, that we should be able to give willingly like this? For everything comes from you, and it is only of your gifts that we give to you. 15 We are aliens before you and settlers, as were all our fathers; our days on earth are like a shadow, and we have no abiding place. 16 LORD our God, from you comes all this wealth that we have laid up to build a house in honour of your holy name, and it is all yours. 17 I know that you test the heart and that integrity pleases you, my God; with an honest heart I have given all these gifts willingly, and have rejoiced now to see your people who are here present give willingly to you. 18 LORD God of Abraham, Isaac, and Israel, our forefathers,

maintain this purpose for ever in your people's thoughts and direct their hearts toward yourself. 19 Grant that Solomon my son may loyally keep your commandments, your solemn charge, and your statutes, that he may fulfil them all, and build the palace for which I have made provision.'

20 Turning to the whole assembly, David said, 'Now bless the LORD your God.' Then all the assembly blessed the LORD the God of their forefathers, bowing low and prostrating themselves before the LORD and the king. 21 The next day they sacrificed to the LORD and offered whole-offerings to him: a thousand oxen, a thousand rams, a thousand lambs, with the prescribed drink-offerings, and abundant sacrifices for all Israel. 22 So they ate and drank before the LORD that day with great rejoicing.

They then appointed Solomon, David's son, king a second time and anointed him as the LORD's prince, and Zadok as priest. 23 So Solomon sat on the LORD's throne as king in place of his father David, and he prospered and all Israel obeyed him. 24 All the officers and the warriors, as well as all the sons of King David, swore fealty to King Solomon. 25 The LORD made Solomon stand very high in the eyes of all Israel, and bestowed upon him sovereignty such as no king in Israel had had before him.

26 David son of Jesse had ruled over the whole of Israel, 27 and the length of his reign over Israel was forty years, seven years in Hebron and thirty-three in Jerusalem. 28 He died in ripe old age, full of years, wealth, and honour; and Solomon his son ruled in his stead. 29 The events of King David's reign from first to last are recorded in the books of Samuel the seer, of Nathan the prophet, and of Gad the seer, 30 with a full account of his reign, his prowess, and of the times through which he and Israel and all the kingdoms of the world had passed.

29:11 **is yours:** *prob. rdg; Heb. omits.*

indicating a date of origin of the passage not earlier than 400 B.C.E. **8:** *Jehiel:* see 26.21. **10–19:** The speech of an ideal king, from the postexilic perspective. Such a speech by David is found in the Deuteronomic history in 2 Sam. 7.18–29. **18:** *God of Abraham, Isaac and Israel:* a phrasing favored by the Chronicler; see 2 Chr. 30.6 (also Elijah's prayer in 1 Kgs. 18.36). **22–25:** The enthronement of Solomon; see 23.1. **22:** The high priest Zadok was *anointed* because in postexilic practice, the high priest had the civil functions which in preexilic times belonged to the king. **29:** *The books of Samuel* and *Nathan* may be 1 Sam. and most of 2 Sam. respectively; the book of *Gad* could be 2 Sam. chs. 21–24, used by the Chronicler in 1 Chr. chs. 11, 20, and 21.

THE SECOND BOOK OF THE
Chronicles

Second Chronicles is part of an idealized history of the elect people, especially of the kingdom of Judah (see Introduction to 1 Chronicles). The segment of that history encompassed in 2 Chronicles extends from Solomon to the Babylonian Exile.

The most distinctive feature of 2 Chronicles is the speeches attributed to faithful kings and prophets (see e.g. 13.5–12 and ch. 20). Such speeches were often placed in the mouths of worthy figures of the monarchic age by the later period in which they were composed.

The Chronicler frequently interprets the past history of the monarchy in the light of the piety that flourished at Jerusalem after the Exile.

The reign of Solomon

1 KING Solomon, David's son, strengthened his hold on the kingdom, for the LORD his God was with him and made him very great.

2 Solomon addressed all Israel, the officers over units of a thousand and of a hundred, the judges, and all the leading men of Israel, the heads of families. 3 Then he, together with all the assembled people, went to the shrine at Gibeon, for the Tent of Meeting, which Moses the LORD's servant had made in the wilderness, was there. 4 (The Ark of God had been brought up from Kiriath-jearim by David to the place which he had prepared for it; he had pitched a tent for it in Jerusalem.) 5 The bronze altar also, which Bezalel son of Uri, son of Hur, had made, was at Gibeon in front of the Tabernacle of the LORD; and Solomon and the assembly resorted to it. 6 Solomon went up to this bronze altar before the LORD in the Tent of Meeting and offered on it a thousand whole-offerings.

7 God appeared to Solomon that night and said, 'What shall I give you? Tell me.' 8 He answered, 'You have shown great and constant love to David my father and you have made me king in his place. 9 Now, LORD God, let your promise to David my father be confirmed, for you have made me king over a people as numerous as the dust on the earth; 10 now grant me wisdom and knowledge, that I may lead this people; otherwise who can govern this great people of yours?'

11 God said to Solomon, 'Because this is what you desire, because you have not asked for wealth or possessions or honour, or the lives of those hostile to you, or even long life for yourself, but have asked for wisdom and knowledge to govern my people over whom I have made you king, 12 wisdom and knowledge are granted to you; I shall also give you wealth and possessions and glory, such as no king before you has had, and none after you shall have.' 13 Then Solomon returned to Jerusalem from before the Tent of Meeting at the shrine at Gibeon, and reigned over Israel.

14 Solomon amassed chariots and horses;

1:5 **was at Gibeon:** *lit.* was there; *some MSS read* he placed. **resorted to it:** *or* worshipped him.
1:7–12 *Cp. 1 Kgs. 3:5–14.*   1:14 **horses:** *or* cavalry.
1:14–17 *Cp. 9:25–28; 1 Kgs. 10:26–29.*

1.1–9.31: Solomon and the temple. The Chronicler draws most of the material concerning *Solomon* from 1 Kgs. chs. 3–10, omitting the struggle for David's throne in 1 Kgs. chs. 1–2, and thereby moving quickly to the building and dedication of the temple.

1.1–17: Solomon's wisdom and wealth. *Solomon's* dream at *Gibeon* (vv. 7–13) is abbreviated from the 1 Kgs. 3.4–15 source; an excerpt is also given (14–17) to document Solomon's *wealth* which God said would be given as well as *wisdom* (1 Kgs. 10.26–29). **3–4:** Because a *shrine* was normally pagan, and it could appear unseemly for Solomon to have gone to a pagan shrine, v. 3 mentions the Mosaic *Tent of Meeting;* yet v. 4 then comments that the Ark was not in this tent, but on hand at Jerusalem! The Tent of Meeting and the Ark come he had fourteen hundred chariots and twelve thousand horses; he stationed some in the chariot-towns, while others he kept at hand in Jerusalem. ¹⁵ The king made silver and gold as common in Jerusalem as stone, and cedar as plentiful as the sycomore-fig is in the Shephelah. ¹⁶ Horses were imported from Egypt and Kue for Solomon; the merchants of the king obtained them from Kue by purchase. ¹⁷ Chariots were imported from Egypt for six hundred silver shekels each, and horses for a hundred and fifty; in the same way the merchants obtained them for export from all the kings of the Hittites and the kings of Aram.

2 Solomon resolved to build a house for the name of the LORD and a royal palace for himself. ² He engaged seventy thousand bearers and eighty thousand quarrymen, and three thousand six hundred men to superintend them. ³ He sent this message to King Huram of Tyre: 'You were so good as to send my father David cedar-wood to build his royal residence. ⁴ Now I am about to build a house for the name of the LORD my God and to consecrate it to him, so that I may burn fragrant incense in it before him, and present the rows of the Bread of the Presence regularly, and whole-offerings morning and evening, on the sabbaths and at the new moons and appointed festivals of the LORD our God; for this is a duty laid on Israel for ever. ⁵ The house I am about to build must be great, because our God is greater than all gods. ⁶ But who is able to build a house for him when heaven itself, the highest heaven, cannot contain him? Who am I that I should build him a house, except to burn sacrifices before him? ⁷ Send me now a skilled craftsman, one able to work in gold and silver, bronze, and iron, and in purple, crimson, and violet yarn, one who is also an expert engraver and will work in Judah and in Jerusalem with my skilled workmen who were provided by David my father. ⁸ Send me also cedar, pine, and algum timber from Lebanon, for I know that your men are expert at

felling the trees of Lebanon; my men will work with yours ⁹ to get an ample supply of timber ready for me, for the house which I shall build will be great and wonderful. ¹⁰ I shall supply provisions for your servants, the woodmen who fell the trees: twenty thousand kor of wheat and twenty thousand kor of barley, with twenty thousand bath of wine and twenty thousand bath of oil.'

¹¹ King Huram of Tyre sent this letter in reply: 'It is because of the love which the LORD has for his people that he has made you king over them.' ¹² The letter continued, 'Blessed be the LORD the God of Israel, maker of heaven and earth, who has given to King David a wise son, endowed with insight and understanding, to build a house for the LORD and a royal palace for himself.

¹³ 'I now send you my expert Huram, a skilful and experienced craftsman. ¹⁴ He is the son of a Danite woman and a Tyrian father; he is an experienced worker in gold and silver, bronze and iron, stone and wood, as well as in purple, violet, and crimson yarn, and in fine linen; he is also a trained engraver who will be able to work with your own skilled craftsmen and those of my lord David your father, to any design submitted to him. ¹⁵ Now let my lord send his servants the wheat and the barley, the oil and the wine, which he promised; ¹⁶ we shall fell all the timber in Lebanon that you need and float it as rafts to the roadstead at Joppa; you can convey it up to Jerusalem.'

¹⁷ Solomon took a census of all the aliens resident in Israel, similar to the census which David his father had taken; these were found to be a hundred and fifty-three thousand six hundred. ¹⁸ He made seventy thousand of them bearers, and eighty thousand quarrymen, and three thousand six hundred superintendents to make the people work.

1:16 **Kue:** *or* Cilicia.   2:1 *In Heb. 1:18.*   2:2 *In Heb. 2:1*   2:3–16 *Cp. 1 Kgs. 5:2–11.*   2:7 **bronze:** *or* copper.   2:8 **algum:** almug *in 1 Kgs. 10:11.*   2:10 **provisions:** *so Lat., cp. 1 Kgs. 5:11; Heb.* plagues.   2:14 **bronze:** *or* copper.

together in 5.4–5. **14–17:** This passage on Solomon's wealth also occurs in 9.25–28.

2.1–18: Preparation for building the temple. 4–6: The Chronicler's own view of the religious service is added to the source material; compare 1 Kgs. 5.1–6. **3:** *Huram* here and Hiram of Kgs. are the same man. **11–12:** The Chronicler heightens Huram's praise of *the LORD* and of Solomon (1 Kgs. 5.7). **17–18:** The source, 1 Kgs. 5.13–18, makes no mention of these *aliens;* rather, it is Israelites there who do the work.

3.1–5.1: The construction of the temple. The Chronicler greatly reduces from 1 Kgs. 6.1–7.22 the description of the basic structure of the temple; the building of Solomon's palace (1 Kgs. 7.1–12) is omitted altogether.

3 Then Solomon began to build the house of the LORD in Jerusalem on Mount Moriah, where the LORD had appeared to his father David; it was the site which David had prepared on the threshing-floor of Ornan the Jebusite. ²He began to build in the second month of the fourth year of his reign. ³These are the foundations which Solomon laid for building the house of God: according to the old standard of measurement the length was sixty cubits and the breadth twenty. ⁴The vestibule in front of the house was twenty cubits long, spanning the whole breadth of the house, and its height was twenty; on the inside he overlaid it with pure gold. ⁵He panelled the large chamber with pine, covered it with fine gold, and carved on it palm trees and chain-work. ⁶He adorned the house with precious stones for decoration and with gold from Parvaim. ⁷He overlaid the whole house with gold, its rafters and frames, its walls and doors; and he carved cherubim on the walls.

⁸He made the Most Holy Place twenty cubits long, corresponding to the breadth of the house, and twenty cubits broad. He overlaid it all with six hundred talents of fine gold, ⁹and the weight of the gold nails was fifty shekels. He also covered the upper chambers with gold.

¹⁰In the Most Holy Place he carved two images of cherubim and overlaid them with gold. ¹¹The total span of the wings of the cherubim was twenty cubits. A wing of one cherub extended five cubits to touch the wall of the house, while its other wing reached out five cubits to meet a wing of the other cherub. ¹²Similarly, a wing of the second cherub extended five cubits to touch the other wall of the house, while its other wing met a wing of the first cherub. ¹³The wings of these cherubim extended twenty cubits; they stood with their feet on the ground, facing the outer chamber. ¹⁴He made the veil of violet, purple, and crimson yarn, and fine linen, and embroidered cherubim on it.

¹⁵In front of the house he erected two pillars eighteen cubits high, with a capital five cubits high on top of each. ¹⁶He made chain-work like a necklace and set it round the tops of the pillars, and he carved a hundred pomegranates and set them in the chain-work. ¹⁷He erected the pillars in front of the temple, one on the right and one on the left; the one on the right he named Jachin and the one on the left Boaz.

4 He made an altar of bronze, twenty cubits long, twenty cubits broad, and ten cubits high. ²He made the Sea of cast metal; it was round in shape, the diameter from rim to rim being ten cubits; it stood five cubits high, and it took a line thirty cubits long to go round it. ³Under the Sea, on every side, completely surrounding the thirty cubits of its circumference, were what looked like gourds, two rows of them, cast in one piece with the Sea itself. ⁴It was mounted on twelve oxen, three facing north, three west, three south, and three east, their hindquarters turned inwards; the Sea rested on top of them. ⁵Its thickness was a hand's breadth; its rim was made like that of a cup, shaped like the calyx of a lily; when full it held three thousand bath. ⁶He also made ten basins for washing, setting five on the left side and five on the right; in these they rinsed everything

3:1 **it was . . . prepared:** *so Gk; Heb.* which he had prepared on David's site.   3:2–4 *Cp. 1 Kgs.* 6:1–3.   3:2 **in . . . month:** *so some MSS; others add* on the second.   3:4 **house was:** *prob. rdg; Heb.* length was. **height was twenty:** *so Gk; Heb.* heights was a hundred and twenty.   3:9 **gold . . . shekels:** *prob. rdg; Heb.* nails was fifty shekels of gold.   3:10–13 *Cp. 1 Kgs.* 6:23–28.   3:10 **images:** *mng of Heb. word uncertain.*   3:15–17 *Cp. 1 Kgs.* 7:15–21.   3:15 **eighteen:** *so Syriac, cp. 1 Kgs.* 7:15; Heb. thirty-five.   3:16 **necklace:** *prob. rdg; Heb. obscure.*   3:17 **Jachin:** *or* Jachun, *that is* It shall stand. **Boaz:** *or* Booz, *that is* In Strength.   4:2–5 *Cp. 1 Kgs.* 7:23–26.   4:3 **thirty:** *prob. rdg; Heb.* ten. **gourds:** *prob. rdg, cp. 1 Kgs.* 7:24; Heb. oxen.

1: *Moriah:* Rabbinic tradition uses the mention here of Moriah to identify it with Mount Zion; compare too Gen. 22.2. Possibly this rabbinic identification is as old as the age of the Chronicler. **4:** *Its height was twenty* (see Tfn.): note that the figure is taken from the Sept., but the MT reads "a hundred and twenty"; this latter is either an error or else an exaggeration characteristic of the Chronicler. The source, 1 Kgs. 6.2, reads "thirty." **5:** *Pine* is given here instead of the cedar of 1 Kgs. 6.18. That all the wood was *covered with fine gold* (six hundred talents' worth, see v. 8) is an embroidered exaggeration. **14:** *The veil* is possibly the Chronicler's own contribution, reflecting the postexilic temple; the source (1 Kgs. 6.31) speaks of doors, though the wilderness Tabernacle had a curtain (Exod. 36.35). See Matt. 27.51; Mk. 15.38; Lk. 23.45. **17:** See Tfn. **4.1:** *The altar of bronze* is not directly mentioned in 1 Kgs. ch. 7, but see 1 Kgs. 8.64 and n. there. **6:** *Basins:* See 1 Kgs. 7.38–39. That *the Sea* was used *for washing* is the Chronicler's contribution.

used for the whole-offering. The Sea was for the priests to wash in.

7 He made ten gold lampstands in the prescribed manner and set them in the temple, five on the right side and five on the left. 8 He also made ten tables and placed them in the temple, five on the right and five on the left; and he made a hundred gold tossing-bowls. 9 He made the court of the priests and the great precinct and the doors for it, and overlaid the doors of both with copper; 10 he put the Sea at the right side, at the south-east corner of the temple.

11 Huram made the pots, the shovels, and the tossing-bowls. With them he finished the work which he had undertaken for King Solomon on the house of God: 12 the two pillars; the two bowl-shaped capitals on the tops of the pillars; the two ornamental networks to cover the two bowl-shaped capitals on the tops of the pillars; 13 the four hundred pomegranates for the two networks, two rows of pomegranates for each network, to cover the two bowl-shaped capitals on the two pillars; 14 the ten trolleys and the ten basins on the trolleys; 15 the one Sea and the twelve oxen which supported it; 16 the pots, the shovels, and the tossing-bowls — all these objects Master Huram made of burnished bronze for King Solomon for the house of the LORD. 17 The king cast them in the foundry between Succoth and Zeredah in the plain of Jordan. 18 Solomon made great quantities of all these objects; the weight of the bronze used was beyond reckoning.

19 Solomon made also all the furnishings for the house of God: the golden altar, the tables upon which was set the Bread of the Presence, 20 the lampstands of red gold whose lamps burned before the inner shrine in the prescribed manner, 21 the flowers, lamps, and tongs of solid gold, 22 the snuffers, tossing-bowls, saucers, and firepans of red gold, and, at the entrance to the house, the inner doors leading to the Most Holy Place and those leading to the sanctuary, of gold.

5 When all the work which Solomon did for the house of the LORD was completed, he brought in the treasures dedicated by his father David, the silver, the gold, and the vessels, and deposited them in the treasuries of the house of God.

2 THEN Solomon summoned the elders of Israel, and all the heads of the tribes who were chiefs of families in Israel, to assemble in Jerusalem, in order to bring up the Ark of the Covenant of the LORD from the City of David, which is called Zion. 3 All the men of Israel were assembled in the king's presence at the pilgrim-feast in the seventh month. 4 When the elders of Israel had all arrived, the Levites lifted the Ark 5 and carried it up; the Tent of Meeting and all the sacred furnishings of the Tent were carried by the priests and the Levites. 6 King Solomon and the whole congregation of Israel assembled with him before the Ark sacrificed sheep and oxen in numbers past counting or reckoning.

7 The priests brought in the Ark of the Covenant of the LORD to its place, in the inner shrine of the house, the Most Holy Place, beneath the wings of the cherubim. 8 The cherubim, whose wings were spread over the place of the Ark, formed a canopy above the Ark and its poles. 9 The poles projected, and their ends were visible from the Holy Place immediately in front of the inner shrine, but from nowhere else outside; they are there to this day. 10 There was nothing inside the Ark but the two tablets which Moses had put there at Horeb, when the LORD made the covenant with the Israelites after they left Egypt.

11 When the priests came out of the Holy Place (for all the priests who were present had hallowed themselves without keeping to their divisions), 12 all the levitical singers, Asaph, Heman, and Jeduthun, their sons,

4:11–5:1 Cp. 1 Kgs. 7:40–51.   4:12 **bowl-shaped capitals:** prob. rdg, cp. 1 Kgs. 7:41; Heb. the bowls and the capitals.   4:13 **two pillars:** prob. rdg, cp. 1 Kgs. 7:42; Heb. surface of the pillars.   4:14 **the ten:** prob. rdg, cp. 1 Kgs. 7:43; Heb. he made the.   4:16 **tossing-bowls:** prob. rdg, cp. 1 Kgs. 7:45; Heb. forks. **these:** prob. rdg, cp. 1 Kgs. 7:45; Heb. their.   4:18 **bronze:** or copper.   4:21 **solid:** mng of Heb. word uncertain.   5:2–10 Cp. 1 Kgs. 8:1–9.   5:5 **priests and:** so some MSS; others omit and.   5:9 **Holy Place:** so Gk; Heb. Ark. **they are:** so many MSS; others it is.

5.2–7.22: The dedication and divine acceptance of the temple. The source is 1 Kgs. 8.1–9.9. **2–14:** The Ark is brought into the temple. See 11–13 n. **3–4:** The Chronicler omits Ethanim (1 Kgs. 8.2), the Canaanite name of the seventh month (September-October), and replaces priests (1 Kgs. 8.3) with Levites as the bearers of the Ark; see 1 Chr. 15.1–15. **11–13:** The Chronicler adds the role of Levites and the musicians here as and their kinsmen, attired in fine linen, stood with cymbals, lutes, and lyres to the east of the altar, together with a hundred and twenty priests who blew trumpets. 13 Now the trumpeters and the singers joined in unison to sound forth praise and thanksgiving to the LORD, and the song was raised with trumpets, cymbals, and musical instruments, in praise of the LORD, because 'it is good, for his love endures for ever'; and the house was filled with the cloud of the glory of the LORD. 14 The priests could not continue to minister because of the cloud, for the glory of the LORD filled the house of God. 1 Then

6 Solomon said:

'The LORD has caused the sun to shine
    in the heavens;
but he has said he would dwell in thick
    darkness.
2 I have built you a lofty house,
    a dwelling-place for you to occupy for
    ever.'

3 While the whole assembly of Israelites stood, the king turned and blessed them. 4 Blessed be the LORD the God of Israel who spoke directly to my father David and has himself fulfilled his promise. For he said, 5 "From the day when I brought my people out of Egypt, I chose no city out of all the tribes of Israel where I should build a house for my name to be, nor did I choose any man to be prince over my people Israel. 6 But I chose Jerusalem where my name should be, and David to be over my people Israel."

7 'My father David had it in mind to build a house for the name of the LORD the God of Israel, 8 but the LORD said to him, "You purposed to build a house for my name, and your purpose was good. 9 Nevertheless you are not to build it; but the son who is to be born to you, he is to build the house for my name." 10 The LORD has now fulfilled his promise: I have succeeded my father David and taken his place on the throne of Israel, as the LORD promised; and I have built the house for the name of the LORD the God of Israel. 11 I have installed there the Ark containing the covenant of the LORD, which he made with Israel.'

12 Standing in front of the altar of the LORD in the presence of the whole assembly of Israel, Solomon spread out his hands. 13 He had made a bronze platform, five cubits long, five cubits broad, and three cubits high, and had placed it in the centre of the precinct. He mounted it and knelt down in the presence of the assembly and, spreading out his hands towards heaven, 14 he said, 'LORD God of Israel, there is no God like you in heaven or on earth, keeping covenant with your servants and showing them constant love while they continue faithful to you with all their heart. 15 You have kept your promise to your servant David my father; by your deeds this day you have fulfilled what you said to him in words. 16 Now, therefore, LORD God of Israel, keep this promise of yours to your servant David my father, when you said: "You will never want for a man appointed by me to sit on the throne of Israel, if only your sons look to their ways and conform to my law, as you have walked before me." 17 LORD God of Israel, let the promise which you made to your servant David be now confirmed.

18 'But can God indeed dwell with mortals on earth? Heaven itself, the highest heaven, cannot contain you; how much less this house that I have built! 19 Yet attend, LORD my God, to the prayer and the supplication of your servant; listen to the cry and the prayer which your servant makes before you, 20 that your eyes may ever be on this house day and night, this place where you said you would set your name. Hear your servant when he prays towards this place. 21 Hear the supplications of your servant and of your people Israel when they pray towards this place. Hear from heaven your dwelling and, when you hear, forgive.

22 'Should anyone wrong a neighbour and be adjured to take an oath, and come to take the oath before your altar in this house, 23 then hear from heaven and take action: be your servants' judge, requiting the guilty person and bringing his deeds on his own head, acquitting the innocent and rewarding him as his innocence may deserve.

24 'Should your people Israel be defeated by an enemy because they have sinned

5:13 **it:** *or* he. **glory:** *so Gk; Heb.* house.   6:1-39 *Cp. 1 Kgs. 8:12-50.*   6:1 **The LORD ... heavens:** *prob. rdg, cp. 1 Kgs. 8:12.*

previously at David's bringing up of the Ark in 1 Chr. 15.16–22; 16.4–6. **14:** *The cloud of the glory:* see 1 Kgs. 8.10–11 n. **6.1–42:** The Chronicler makes few alterations in the benediction and prayer of *Solomon* as given against you, and then turn back to you, confessing your name and making their prayer and supplication before you in this house, 25 hear from heaven; forgive the sin of your people Israel and restore them to the land which you gave to them and to their forefathers.

26 'Should the heavens be shut up and there be no rain, because your servant and your people Israel have sinned against you, and they then pray towards this place, confessing your name and forsaking their sin when they feel your punishment, 27 hear in heaven and forgive their sin; so teach them the good way which they are to follow, and grant rain on your land which you have given to your people as their own possession.

28 'Should there be famine in the land, or pestilence, or black blight or red, or locusts developing or fully grown, or should their enemies besiege them in any of their cities, or plague or sickness befall them, 29 then hear the prayer or supplication of everyone among your people Israel, as each, prompted by his own suffering and misery, spreads out his hands towards this house; 30 hear it from heaven your dwelling-place and forgive. As you know a person's heart, reward him according to his deeds, for you alone know the hearts of all; 31 and so they will fear and obey you throughout their lives in the land you gave to our forefathers.

32 'The foreigner too, anyone who does not belong to your people Israel, but has come from a distant land because of your great fame and your strong hand and outstretched arm, when such a one comes and prays towards this house, 33 hear from heaven your dwelling-place and respond to the call which the foreigner makes to you, so that like your people Israel all the peoples of the earth may know your fame and fear you, and learn that this house which I have built bears your name.

34 'When your people go to war against their enemies, wherever you send them, and when they pray to you, turning towards this city which you have chosen and towards this house which I have built for your name,

35 then hear from heaven their prayer and supplication, and maintain their cause.

36 'Should they sin against you (and who is free from sin?) and should you in your anger give them over to an enemy who carries them captive to a land far or near; 37 and should they then in the land of their captivity have a change of heart and turn back and make supplication to you there and say, "We have sinned and acted perversely and wickedly," 38 and turn back to you wholeheartedly in the land of their captivity to which they have been taken, and pray, turning towards their land which you gave to their forefathers and towards this city which you chose and this house which I have built for your name; 39 then from heaven your dwelling-place hear their prayer and supplications and maintain their cause. Forgive your people their sins against you. 40 Now, my God, let your eyes be open and your ears attentive to the prayer made in this place.

41 'Arise now, Lord God, and come to
    your resting-place,
    you and your powerful Ark.
Let your priests, Lord God, be clothed
    with salvation
and your loyal servants rejoice in
    prosperity.
42 Lord God, do not reject your anointed
    one;
    remember the loyal service of David
    your servant.'

7 As Solomon finished this prayer, fire came down from heaven and consumed the whole-offering and the sacrifices, while the glory of the Lord filled the house. 2 The priests were unable to enter the house of the Lord because the glory of the Lord had filled it. 3 All the Israelites witnessed the fire coming down with the glory of the Lord on the house, and where they were on the paved court they bowed low to the ground and wor-

6:26 **servant:** *so Syriac; Heb.* servants.   6:27 **in:** *or,* *with Gk,* from.   6:28 **in any:** *prob. rdg; Heb.* in the land.   6:42 **one:** *so many MSS; others* ones. **the loyal . . . servant:** *or* your constant love for David your servant.   7:3 **it** *or* he.

in 1 Kgs. 8.12–53. **13:** The *bronze platform,* added by the Chronicler, is not mentioned in 1 Kgs. **40–42:** These verses follow not the Kgs. source, but Ps. 132.8–10. Verse 42 reverts to David; see 1 Chr. 28.1–29.30 n. Solomon is the *anointed one.* **7.1–3:** First Kings 8.54–61 has a second benediction instead of an immediate divine response to Solomon's *prayer.* The Chronicler gives a second divine sign, drawing on the tradition of *fire from heaven* to consecrate an altar; compare Lev. 9.24; 1 Kgs. 18.38; 1 Chr. 21.26. The *glory* sanctioned shipped and gave thanks to the Lord, because 'it is good, for his love endures for ever'.

4 The king and all the people offered sacrifice before the Lord; 5 King Solomon offered a sacrifice of twenty-two thousand oxen and a hundred and twenty thousand sheep. Thus the king and all the people dedicated the house of God. 6 The priests stood at their appointed posts; so too the Levites with their musical instruments for the Lord's service, which King David had made for giving thanks to the Lord — 'for his love endures for ever' — whenever he rendered praise with their help; opposite them, the priests sounded their trumpets, while all the Israelites were standing. 7 Then Solomon consecrated the centre of the court which lay in front of the house of the Lord; there he offered the whole-offerings and the fat portions of the shared-offerings, because the bronze altar which he had made could not accommodate the whole-offering, the grain-offering, and the fat portions.

8 So Solomon and with him all Israel, a very great assembly from Lebo-hamath to the wadi of Egypt, celebrated the pilgrim-feast at that time for seven days. 9 On the eighth day they held a closing ceremony; for they had celebrated the dedication of the altar for seven days, and the pilgrim-feast lasted seven days. 10 On the twenty-third day of the seventh month he dismissed the people to their homes, happy and glad at heart for all the prosperity granted by the Lord to David, to Solomon, and to his people Israel.

11 When Solomon had completed the house of the Lord and the palace and had carried out successfully all that he had planned for the house of the Lord and the palace, 12 the Lord appeared to him by night and said: 'I have heard your prayer and I have chosen this place to be my house of sacrifice. 13 When I shut up the heavens and there is no rain, or command the locusts to consume the land, or send a pestilence on my people, 14 and then my people whom I have named my own submit and pray to me and seek me and turn back from their evil ways, I shall hear from heaven and forgive their sins and restore their land. 15 Now my eyes will be open and my ears attentive to the prayers which are made in this place. 16 I have chosen and consecrated this house, so that my name may be there for all time and my eyes and my heart may be fixed on it for ever. 17 If you, for your part, live in my sight as your father David lived, doing all I command you, and observing my statutes and my judgements, 18 then I shall establish the throne of your kingdom, as I promised by a covenant granted to your father David when I said, "You will never want for a man to rule Israel." 19 But if you turn away and forsake my statutes and my commandments which I have set before you, and if you go and serve other gods and bow down before them, 20 then I shall uproot you from my land which I gave you; I shall reject this house which I have consecrated to my name, and make it a byword and an object-lesson among all peoples. 21 This house will become a ruin; every passer-by will be appalled at the sight of it, and they will ask, "Why has the Lord so treated this land and this house?" 22 The answer will be, "Because they forsook the Lord the God of their forefathers, who brought them out of Egypt, and they clung to other gods, bowing down before them and serving them; that is why the Lord has brought all this misfortune on them." '

8 At the end of the twenty years Solomon had taken to build the house of the Lord and his own palace, 2 he rebuilt the towns which Huram had given him and he settled Israelites in them. 3 He went to Hamath-zo-

7:7–22 Cp. 1 Kgs. 8:64–9:9.		7:7 in front: or to the east.	7:20 you: so Gk; Heb. them.	7:21 will become a ruin: so Syriac; Heb. which was high.
8:1–18 Cp. 1 Kgs. 9:10–28.

the house; the fire sanctioned the altar. 7–8: Compare 1 Kgs. 8.64–65. 9–10: The Chronicler is concerned to make clear the different sacred times involved; see 1 Kgs. 8.66. According to the Chronicler, there were two seven-day periods, one to dedicate the altar (compare Ezek. 43.18–27) and one to observe the regular autumn festival of Tabernacles (Booths), which lasted from the fifteenth through the twenty-first day of the seventh month. The eighth day of the Tabernacles festival was to be specially consecrated (Lev. 23.36). Only on the twenty-third day of the month, therefore, were the people dismissed. 11–22: From 1 Kgs. 9.1–9; but vv. 13–15 are here added to furnish hope.

8.1–9.31: Solomon's works, wisdom, and wealth. The Chronicler makes only slight changes in the source material. 1–28: Compare 1 Kgs. 9.10–28. 2–4: In 1 Kgs. 9.10–11 it was Solomon who gave cities to Huram, bah and seized it. 4 He strengthened Tadmor in the wilderness and all the store-cities which he had built in Hamath. 5 He also built Upper Beth-horon and Lower Beth-horon as fortified cities with walls and barred gates, 6 and Baalath, as well as all his store-cities, and all the towns where he quartered his chariots and horses. He carried out all his cherished plans for building in Jerusalem, in the Lebanon, and throughout his whole dominion. 7 All the survivors of the Hittites, Amorites, Perizzites, Hivites, and Jebusites, who did not belong to Israel— 8 that is those of their descendants who survived in the land, wherever the Israelites had been unable to exterminate them—all were employed by Solomon on forced labour, as they still are. 9 None of the Israelites were put to forced labour for his public works; they were his fighting men, his captains and lieutenants, and the commanders of his chariots and of his cavalry. 10 These were King Solomon's officers, two hundred and fifty of them, in charge of the foremen who superintended the people.

11 Solomon brought Pharaoh's daughter up from the City of David to the house he had built for her, for he said, 'No wife of mine shall live in the house of King David of Israel, because this place which the Ark of the LORD has entered is holy.'

12 Then Solomon offered whole-offerings to the LORD on the altar which he had built to the east of the vestibule, 13 according to what was required for each day, making offerings according to the law of Moses for the sabbaths, the new moons, and the three annual appointed feasts—the pilgrim-feasts of Unleavened Bread, of Weeks, and of Booths. 14 Following the practice of his father David, he drew up the roster of service for the priests and that for the Levites for leading the praise and for waiting upon the priests, as each day required, and that for the doorkeepers at each gate; for such was the instruction which David the man of God had given. 15 The instructions which David had given concerning the priests and the Levites and concerning the treasuries were never disregarded.

16 By this time all Solomon's work was achieved, from the foundation of the house of the LORD to its completion; the house of the LORD was completed. 17 Then Solomon went to Ezion-geber and to Eloth on the coast of Edom, 18 and Huram sent ships under the command of his own officers and manned by crews of experienced seamen; and these, in company with Solomon's servants, went to Ophir and brought back four hundred and fifty talents of gold, which they delivered to King Solomon.

9 THE queen of Sheba heard of Solomon's fame and came to test him with enigmatic questions. She arrived in Jerusalem with a very large retinue, camels laden with spices, much gold, and precious stones. When she came to Solomon, she talked to him about everything she had on her mind. 2 Solomon answered all her questions; not one of them was too hard for him to answer. 3 When the queen of Sheba observed the wisdom of Solomon, the palace he had built, 4 the food on his table, the courtiers sitting around him, his attendants and his cupbearers in their livery standing behind, and the stairs by which he went up to the house of the LORD, she was overcome with amazement. 5 She said to the king, 'The account which I heard in my own country about your achievements and your wisdom was true, 6 but I did not believe what they told me until I came and saw for myself. Indeed, I was not told half of the greatness of your wisdom; you surpass all I had heard of you. 7 Happy are your wives, happy these courtiers of yours who are in attendance on you every day and hear your wisdom! 8 Blessed be the LORD your God who has delighted in you and has set you on his throne as his king; because in his love your God has elected Israel to make it endure for ever, he has made you king over it to maintain law and justice.' 9 She presented

8:6 **horses:** or cavalry.   8:9 **his captains and lieutenants:** *so Gk; Heb.* the captains of his lieutenants. 8:11 **this place which ... is:** *prob. rdg; Heb.* those which ... are.   8:13 **Booths:** *or* Tabernacles. 9:1–24 *Cp. 1 Kgs. 10:1–25.*   9:4 **stairs ... up to:** *or,* *with Gk,* whole-offerings which he used to offer in. 9:7 **wives:** *so Gk (Luc.); Heb.* men.

not the reverse. The source did not mention the campaign to the north (vv. 3–4). **11:** Compare 1 Kgs. 9.24. Solomon's comment is added by the Chronicler. **13:** The Chronicler adds the occasions on which the sacrifices are to be offered according to Mosaic legislation; see Lev. ch. 23 and Num. chs. 28–29. **14–15:** The priestly and Levitical organizations ascribed to *David* in 1 Chr. chs. 23–26 are referred to. **9.1–28:** These reports are the king with a hundred and twenty talents of gold, spices in great abundance, and precious stones. There had never been any spices to equal those which the queen of Sheba gave to King Solomon.

¹⁰ Besides all this, the servants of Huram and of Solomon, who had brought gold from Ophir, brought also cargoes of algum-wood and precious stones. ¹¹ The king used the wood to make stands for the house of the LORD and for the palace, as well as lyres and lutes for the singers. The like of them had never before been seen in the land of Judah.

¹² King Solomon gave the queen of Sheba whatever she desired and asked for, in addition to his gifts in return for what she had brought him. Then she departed with her retinue and went back to her own land.

¹³ The weight of gold which Solomon received in any one year was six hundred and sixty-six talents, ¹⁴ in addition to the tolls levied on merchants and on traders who imported goods; all the kings of Arabia and the regional governors also brought gold and silver to the king.

¹⁵ King Solomon made two hundred shields of beaten gold, and six hundred shekels of gold went to the making of each one; ¹⁶ he also made three hundred bucklers of beaten gold, and three hundred shekels of gold went to the making of each buckler. The king put these into the House of the Forest of Lebanon.

¹⁷ The king also made a great throne inlaid with ivory and overlaid with pure gold. ¹⁸ Six steps and a footstool for the throne were all encased in gold. There were armrests on each side of the seat, with a lion standing beside each of them, ¹⁹ while twelve lions stood on the six steps, one at either end of each step. Nothing like it had ever been made for any monarch. ²⁰ All Solomon's drinking vessels were of gold, and all the plate in the House of the Forest of Lebanon was of red gold; silver was reckoned of no value in the days of Solomon. ²¹ The king had a fleet of ships plying to Tarshish with Huram's men;

once every three years this fleet of merchantmen came home, bringing gold and silver, ivory, apes, and monkeys.

²² Thus King Solomon outdid all the kings of the earth in wealth and wisdom, ²³ and all the kings of the earth courted him, to hear the wisdom with which God had endowed his mind. ²⁴ Each one brought his gift with him, vessels of silver and gold, garments, perfumes and spices, horses and mules in annual tribute.

²⁵ Solomon had standing for four thousand horses and chariots, and twelve thousand cavalry horses; he stationed some in the chariot-towns, while others he kept at hand in Jerusalem. ²⁶ He ruled over all the kings from the Euphrates to the land of the Philistines and the border of Egypt. ²⁷ He made silver as common in Jerusalem as stone, and cedar as plentiful as the sycomore-fig is in the Shephelah. ²⁸ Horses were imported from Egypt and from all countries for Solomon.

²⁹ The rest of the acts of Solomon's reign, from first to last, are recorded in the history of Nathan the prophet, in the prophecy of Ahijah of Shiloh, and in the visions of Iddo the seer concerning Jeroboam son of Nebat. ³⁰ Solomon ruled in Jerusalem over the whole of Israel for forty years. ³¹ Then he rested with his forefathers and was buried in the city of David his father; he was succeeded by his son Rehoboam.

Kings of Judah

10 REHOBOAM went to Shechem, for all Israel had gone there to make him king. ² When Jeroboam son of Nebat heard of it in Egypt, where he had taken refuge to escape Solomon, he returned from Egypt.

9:11 **stands:** *mng of Heb. word uncertain.* 9:12 **his gifts ... for:** *prob. rdg; Heb. omits.* 9:14 **tolls:** *so Syriac; Heb.* men. **all ... also:** *or* and on all the kings of Arabia and the regional governors who. 9:21 **merchantmen:** *lit.* ships of Tarshish. 9:25–28 *Cp. 1:14–17; 1 Kgs. 10:26–29.* 9:29–31 *Cp. 1 Kgs. 11:41–43.* 10:1–19 *Cp. 1 Kgs. 12:1–19.*

taken over almost unchanged from 1 Kgs. 10.1–25. **29–31:** The Chronicler omits the entire negative side of Solomon's reign as given in 1 Kgs. 11.1–40. None of the prophetic sources listed is mentioned in 1 Kgs. 11.41; see 1 Chr. 29.29 n. *Ahijah of Shiloh* is included even though the Chronicler omits the account of his prophecy; compare 1 Kgs. 11.29–39. *Iddo the seer* is also mentioned in 12.15 and 13.22, but is otherwise unknown.

10.1–28.27: The kings of Judah from Rehoboam to Ahaz. 10.1–11.4: The beginning of the reign of *Rehoboam.* The account here is taken over without change from 1 Kgs. 12.12–19, 21–24. The crowning of Jeroboam (1 Kgs. 12.20) is omitted; the event was distasteful to the Chronicler.

³The people now recalled him, and he and all Israel came to Rehoboam and said, ⁴'Your father laid a harsh yoke upon us; but if you will now lighten the harsh labour he imposed and the heavy yoke he laid on us, we shall serve you.' ⁵'Give me three days,' he said, 'and then come back.'

When the people had gone, ⁶King Rehoboam consulted the elders who had been in attendance during the lifetime of his father Solomon: 'What answer do you advise me to give to this people?' ⁷They said, 'If you show yourself well-disposed to this people and gratify them by speaking kindly to them, they will be your servants ever after.' ⁸But rejecting the advice given him by the elders he consulted the young men who had grown up with him and were now in attendance; ⁹he asked them, 'What answer do you advise me to give to this people's request that I should lighten the yoke which my father laid on them?' ¹⁰The young men replied, 'Give this answer to the people who say that your father made their yoke heavy and ask you to lighten it; tell them: "My little finger is thicker than my father's loins. ¹¹My father laid a heavy yoke on you; but I shall make it heavier. My father whipped you; but I shall flay you."'

¹²Jeroboam and the people all came to Rehoboam on the third day, as the king had ordered. ¹³The king gave them a harsh answer; he rejected the advice which the elders had given him ¹⁴and spoke to the people as the young men had advised: 'My father made your yoke heavy; but I shall make it heavier. My father whipped you; but I shall flay you.' ¹⁵The king would not listen to the people, for the LORD had given this turn to the affair in order that the word he had spoken by Ahijah of Shiloh to Jeroboam son of Nebat might be fulfilled.

¹⁶When all Israel saw that the king would not listen to them, they answered:

'What share have we in David?
We have no lot in the son of Jesse.
Away to your tents, Israel!
Now see to your own house, David.'

With that all Israel went off to their homes.

¹⁷Rehoboam ruled only over those Israelites who lived in the cities and towns of Judah. ¹⁸King Rehoboam sent out Hadoram, the commander of the forced levies, but when the Israelites stoned him to death, the king hastily mounted his chariot and fled to Jerusalem. ¹⁹From that day to this Israel has been in rebellion against the house of David.

11 When Rehoboam reached Jerusalem, he mustered the tribes of Judah and Benjamin, a hundred and eighty thousand chosen warriors, to fight against Israel and recover his kingdom. ²But this word of the LORD came to Shemaiah the man of God: ³'Say to Rehoboam son of Solomon, king of Judah, and to all the Israelites in Judah and Benjamin, ⁴This is the word of the LORD: You are not to go up to make war on your kinsmen. Return to your homes, for this is my doing.' They listened to the word of the LORD and abandoned their campaign against Jeroboam.

⁵Rehoboam resided in Jerusalem and built up the defences of certain towns in Judah. ⁶The towns in Judah and Benjamin which he fortified were Bethlehem, Etam, Tekoa, ⁷Beth-zur, Soco, Adullam, ⁸Gath, Mareshah, Ziph, ⁹Adoraim, Lachish, Azekah, ¹⁰Zorah, Aijalon, and Hebron. ¹¹He strengthened the defences of these fortified towns, and put governors in them, as well as supplies of food, oil, and wine. ¹²Also he stored shields and spears in each of them, and made them very strong. Thus he retained possession of Judah and Benjamin.

¹³The priests and the Levites throughout the whole of Israel resorted to Rehoboam from all their territories; ¹⁴for the Levites had left all their common land and their own property and had gone to Judah and Jerusalem, because Jeroboam and his successors rejected their services as priests of the LORD, ¹⁵and he appointed his own priests for the shrines, for the demons, and for the calves which he had made. ¹⁶Out of all the tribes of Israel, those who were resolved to seek the LORD the God of Israel followed the Levites

10:14 **My father made:** *so some MSS; others* I shall make. 10:16 **saw:** *prob. rdg, cp. 1 Kgs. 12:16; Heb. omits.* 11:1–4 *Cp. 1 Kgs. 12:21–24.* 11:15 **demons:** *or* satyrs.

11.5–12.16: The rest of the reign of Rehoboam. The Chronicler proceeds (vv. 5–12) to use a source otherwise unknown but quite credible historically (with the exception, at times, of the numbers given). **13–16:** The Chronicler portrays the faithfulness of *the Levites;* they abandon the apostate Northern Kingdom. Historically, circles of *Levites* remained in the Northern Kingdom until its fall in 722/21; after that they became to Jerusalem to sacrifice to the LORD the God of their fathers. 17 They strengthened the kingdom of Judah and for three years made Rehoboam son of Solomon secure, because he followed the example of David and Solomon during that time.

18 Rehoboam married Mahalath, whose father was Jerimoth son of David and whose mother was Abihail daughter of Eliab son of Jesse. 19 His sons by her were: Jeush, Shemariah, and Zaham. 20 Next he married Maacah granddaughter of Absalom, who bore him Abijah, Attai, Ziza, and Shelomith. 21 Of all his wives and concubines, Rehoboam loved Maacah most; he had in all eighteen wives and sixty concubines and became the father of twenty-eight sons and sixty daughters. 22 He appointed Abijah son of Maacah chief among his brothers, making him crown prince and planning to make him his successor on the throne. 23 He showed prudence in detailing his sons to take charge of all the fortified towns throughout the whole territory of Judah and Benjamin; he also made generous provision for them and obtained wives for them.

12 When Rehoboam's kingdom was firmly established and he grew powerful, he along with all Israel forsook the law of the LORD. 2 In the fifth year of Rehoboam's reign, because of this disloyalty to the LORD, King Shishak of Egypt attacked Jerusalem 3 with twelve hundred chariots and sixty thousand horsemen; he also brought with him from Egypt an innumerable following of Libyans, Sukkites, and Cushites. 4 He captured the fortified towns of Judah and reached Jerusalem. 5 Then Shemaiah the prophet came to Rehoboam and the leading men of Judah, who had collected together at Jerusalem in the face of the advance of Shishak, and said, 'This is the word of the LORD: You have abandoned me; therefore I now abandon you to Shishak.' 6 The princes of Israel and the king submitted and said, 'The LORD is just.' 7 When the LORD saw that they had submitted, there came from him this word to Shemaiah: 'Because they have submitted I shall not destroy them; I shall grant them some measure of relief: my wrath will not be poured out on Jerusalem by means of Shishak, 8 but they will become his servants; then they will know the difference between serving me and serving the rulers of other countries.' 9 King Shishak of Egypt in his attack on Jerusalem carried away the treasures of the house of the LORD and of the king's palace, and seized everything, including the gold shields made for Solomon. 10 King Rehoboam replaced them with bronze shields and entrusted them to the officers of the escort who guarded the entrance of the palace. 11 Whenever the king entered the house of the LORD, the escort entered, carrying the shields; afterwards they returned them to the guardroom. 12 Because Rehoboam submitted, the LORD's wrath was averted from him, and he was not utterly destroyed; Judah enjoyed prosperity.

13 King Rehoboam increased his power in Jerusalem. He was forty-one years old when he came to the throne, and he reigned for seventeen years in Jerusalem, the city which the LORD had chosen out of all the tribes of Israel as the place to receive his name. Rehoboam's mother was an Ammonite woman called Naamah. 14 He did what was wrong; he did not make a practice of seeking guidance of the LORD. 15 The events of Rehoboam's reign, from first to last, are recorded in the histories of Shemaiah the prophet and Iddo the seer. There was continual fighting be-

11:17 **he:** *so Gk; Heb.* they.　　11:20 **granddaughter:** *lit.* daughter.　　11:22 **planning:** *so Lat.; Heb.* omits. 11:23 **obtained . . . them:** *prob. rdg; Heb.* asked for a multitude of wives.　　12:3 **Cushites:** *or* Nubians. 12:9–11 *Cp. 1 Kgs. 14:25–28.*　　12:13–16 *Cp. 1 Kgs. 14:29–31.*　　12:15 **and . . . seer:** *prob. rdg; Heb. adds* to be enrolled by genealogy.

important in reform movements in the surviving Southern Kingdom. **14:** See 1 Kgs. 12.31. **17:** *Rehoboam* was first faithful to the LORD in the manner of *David and Solomon;* afterward he was unfaithful and brought trouble upon himself. Thus is established a pattern also exemplified by other kings; see Asa, 16.7–10; Joash, 24.1–24; Amaziah, 25.14–24; and Uzziah, 26.16–21. **18–23:** The source is unknown. The Chronicler gives here the abundance of Rehoboam's wives, but Solomon's abundance, 1 Kgs. 11.3, has previously been omitted. **12.1–12:** First Kings treated the invasion of *Shishak* as simply an event of Rehoboam's reign; the Chronicler sees it as a punishment for some fault and explains that it is a result of *Rehoboam's* forsaking the LORD. **4–8:** The repentance of the Judeans and the consequent limitation of the punishment are characteristic motifs of the Chronicler's history. **15:** The Chronicler tends to cite sources written by prophets rather than court annals; contrast 1 Kgs. 14.29.

447

tween Rehoboam and Jeroboam. ¹⁶Rehoboam rested with his forefathers and was buried in the city of David. His son Abijah succeeded him.

13 In the eighteenth year of King Jeroboam's reign Abijah became king of Judah. ²He reigned in Jerusalem for three years; his mother was Maacah daughter of Uriel of Gibeah.

When war broke out between Abijah and Jeroboam, ³Abijah drew up his army of four hundred thousand picked troops in order of battle, while Jeroboam formed up against him with eight hundred thousand picked troops. ⁴Abijah stood up on the slopes of Mount Zemaraim in the hill-country of Ephraim and called out, 'Jeroboam and all Israel, hear me: ⁵Do you not know that the LORD the God of Israel gave the kingship over Israel to David and his descendants for ever by a covenant of salt? ⁶Yet Jeroboam son of Nebat, a servant of Solomon son of David, rose in rebellion against his lord, ⁷and certain worthless scoundrels gathered round him, who stubbornly opposed Solomon's son Rehoboam when he was young and inexperienced, and he was no match for them.

⁸'Now you propose to match yourselves against the kingdom of the LORD as ruled by David's sons, you with your mob of supporters and the golden calves which Jeroboam has made to be your gods. ⁹Have you not dismissed from office the Aaronites, priests of the LORD, and the Levites, and followed the practice of other lands in appointing your own priests? If any man comes for ordination with an offering of a young bull and seven rams, you accept him as a priest to a god who is no god.

¹⁰'But as for us, the LORD is our God and we have not forsaken him. We have Aaronites as priests ministering to the LORD with the Levites, duly discharging their office. ¹¹Morning and evening, these burn whole-offerings and fragrant incense to the LORD and offer the Bread of the Presence arranged in rows on a table ritually clean; they also kindle the lamps on the gold lampstand every evening. Thus we do indeed keep the charge of the LORD our God, whereas you have forsaken him. ¹²God is with us at our head, and his priests stand there with trumpets to signal the battle cry against you. Men of Israel, do not fight the LORD the God of your forefathers; you will have no success.'

¹³Jeroboam sent a detachment of his troops to go round and lay an ambush in the rear, so that his main body faced Judah while the ambush lay behind them. ¹⁴The men of Judah turned to find that they were engaged front and rear. They cried to the LORD for help; the priests sounded their trumpets, ¹⁵and the men of Judah raised their battle cry; and when they shouted, God put Jeroboam and all Israel to rout before Abijah and Judah. ¹⁶The Israelites fled before the men of Judah, and God delivered them into their power. ¹⁷Abijah and his men defeated them

13:2 **Maacah:** *so Gk, cp. 1 Kgs. 15:2; Heb.* Micaiah.
13:10 **duly ... office:** *so Gk; Heb.* in the work.

13.1–14.1: The reign of Abijah. A longer account is given here than the brief mention in 1 Kgs. 15.1–8 (there Abijah's name is spelled Abijam). **2:** Here Abijah's mother is a daughter of *Uriel of Gibeah* whereas in 1 Kgs. 15.2 the Heb. calls her the daughter (probably meaning granddaughter) of Abishalom, who was probably David's rebellious son Absalom (2 Sam. chs. 13–18). The Chronicler may have wanted to avoid having Absalom an ancestor of later kings. The mother's name is given both as Micaiah and *Maacah.* In 15.16, the Heb. calls her mother of Asa, with mother probably to be understood as grandmother. **3:** The Chronicler shows interest in the numbers of Judean armies and the armies of their enemies, usually to glorify the Judean kings or their God. The numbers are unreliable. **5–12:** The speech presents the two motifs of greatest concern to the Chronicler: the validity of the dynasty of *David* as the one proper kingship in *Israel,* and the validity of the *Aaronite* priesthood and the service of *the Levites* at Jerusalem. Compare 1 Chr. 29.10–19. The Northern Kingdom, given more serious treatment in the Book of Kings, is dealt with negatively and only partially by the Chronicler. **5:** A *covenant of salt* was an eternal agreement (Num. 18.19) sealed by both parties eating of the same food. **8:** The origin of the *golden calves* (1 Kgs. 12.26–30) was deliberately omitted; the mention here is therefore strange. **11:** The ritual service assumed here is that of the Mosaic Tabernacle; compare 2.4–6 and Exod. 25.23–40; 29.38–42; 30.1–10. **13–20:** This battle account expresses the Chronicler's view of battles; see also 20.22–27. The LORD throws the enemy army into panic or confusion, and the (smaller) army of the righteous is victorious because of divine intervention. The numbers involved are typical of the Chronicler's with very heavy losses: five hundred thousand picked men of Israel fell in the battle. [18] On that occasion the Israelites had to submit; Judah prevailed because they relied on the LORD the God of their forefathers. [19] Abijah pressed home his victory over Jeroboam by capturing from him the cities of Bethel, Jeshanah, and Ephron with their villages. [20] Jeroboam did not regain his power all the days of Abijah; finally the LORD struck him down and he died.

[21] But Abijah established his position; he married fourteen wives and became the father of twenty-two sons and sixteen daughters. [22] The other events of Abijah's reign, both what he said and what he did, are recorded in the discourse of the prophet Iddo.

14 [1] Abijah rested with his forefathers and was buried in the city of David. His son Asa succeeded him, and in his time the land had peace for ten years.

[2] Asa did what was good and right in the eyes of the LORD his God. [3] He suppressed the foreign altars and the shrines, smashed the sacred pillars and hacked down the sacred poles, [4] and ordered Judah to seek guidance of the LORD the God of their forefathers and to keep the law and the commandments. [5] In all the towns he suppressed the shrines and the incense-altars, and the kingdom was at peace under him. [6] He built fortified towns in Judah, for the land was at peace. He had no war on his hands during those years, because the LORD had given him security. [7] Asa said to the men of Judah, 'Let us build these towns and fortify them, with walls round them, and towers and barred gates. The land still lies open before us. Because we have sought guidance of the LORD our God, he has sought us and given us security on every side.' So they built and prospered.

[8] Asa had an army equipped with large shields and with spears; three hundred thousand men came from Judah, and two hundred and eighty thousand from Benjamin, archers carrying bucklers; all were valiant warriors. [9] Zerah the Cushite marched out against them with an army a million strong and three hundred chariots. When he reached Mareshah, [10] Asa came out to meet him and they took up position in the valley of Zephathah at Mareshah. [11] Asa called to the LORD his God and said, 'There is none like you, LORD, to help men, whether strong or weak; help us, LORD our God, for on you we rely and in your name we have come out against this horde. LORD, you are our God; no mere mortal can vie with you.' [12] The LORD gave Asa and Judah victory over the Cushites, who fled, [13] with Asa and his men in pursuit as far as Gerar. The Cushites broke before the LORD and his army, and many of them fell mortally wounded. Judah carried off great loads of spoil. [14] They destroyed all the towns around Gerar, for the LORD had struck the people with panic; and they plundered the towns, finding rich spoil in them all. [15] They also killed the herdsmen and seized many sheep and camels, and then they returned to Jerusalem.

15 The spirit of God came upon Azariah son of Oded. [2] He went out to meet Asa and said, 'Hear me, Asa and all Judah and Benjamin. The LORD is with you when you are with him; if you seek him, he will let himself be found, but if you forsake

14:1 *In Heb.* 13:23.   14:2 *In Heb.* 14:1.

exaggerations. **20:** Actually, Jeroboam survived Abijah (1 Kgs. 15.8–9). **21:** The statistics of *Abijah's* family are quite credible for a Judean king. **22:** *Iddo:* see 9.29–31 n. **14.1:** The *ten years* of *peace* refer to the first ten years of Asa's reign.

14.2–16.14: The reign of Asa. Two main occurrences were reported concerning Asa in 1 Kgs.: his religious reform (1 Kgs. 15.9–15) and his successful war against Baasha of Israel (1 Kgs. 15.16–22). These lead the Chronicler to a lengthy account (chs. 14–16), absent from Kgs., of Asa's faithfulness to the LORD, including a divinely given military victory (14.8–15; see 13.13–20 n.), and a shorter period of warfare (16.1–14) in which his reliance on foreign alliances instead of the LORD brings him suffering from disease (16.12). **2–7:** The Chronicler sees the reform of religious practice as the cause of the period of peace. **5:** Contrast 15.17, and its source (1 Kgs. 15.14). **9:** *Zerah the Cushite:* his identity is uncertain. Cush is sometimes Ethiopia, but also an Arabian tribe, as is probable here. This account is another example of the stylized combat in which the LORD intervenes for the victory of the righteous people; see 13.13–20 n.

15.1–19: Asa's religious reform. 1–7: One of the typical speeches developed within the Chronicler's circle; see Introduction to 2 Chr. **1:** *Azariah son of Oded* is otherwise unknown. A prophet Oded is mentioned in 28.9.

him, he will forsake you. ³For a long time Israel was without the true God, without a priest to interpret the law, and without law. ⁴But when, in their distress, they turned to the LORD the God of Israel and sought him, he let himself be found by them. ⁵At those times there was no safety for people as they went about their business; the inhabitants of every land had their fill of trouble; ⁶there was ruin on every side, nation at odds with nation, city with city, for God harassed them with every kind of distress. ⁷But now you must be strong and not let your courage fail; for your work will be rewarded.'

⁸When Asa heard these words, this prophecy of Oded the prophet, he resolutely suppressed the loathsome idols in all Judah and Benjamin and in the towns which he had captured in the hill-country of Ephraim, and he repaired the altar of the LORD which stood before the vestibule of the LORD's house. ⁹Then he assembled all the people of Judah and Benjamin and all who had come from Ephraim, Manasseh, and Simeon to reside among them, for great numbers had come over to him from Israel, when they saw that the LORD his God was with him.

¹⁰They assembled at Jerusalem in the third month of the fifteenth year of Asa's reign, ¹¹and that day they sacrificed to the LORD seven hundred oxen and seven thousand sheep from the spoil which they had brought. ¹²They entered wholeheartedly into a covenant to seek guidance of the LORD the God of their fathers; ¹³all who would not seek the LORD the God of Israel were to be put to death, whether young or old, men and women alike. ¹⁴Then they bound themselves by an oath to the LORD, with loud shouts of acclamation while trumpets and horns sounded. ¹⁵All Judah rejoiced at the oath, because they had bound themselves with all their heart and had sought the LORD earnestly; he had let himself be found by them, and he gave them security on every side. ¹⁶King Asa even deprived Maacah his grandmother of her rank as queen mother because she had an obscene object made for the worship of Asherah; Asa cut it down, ground it

to powder, and burnt it in the wadi of the Kidron. ¹⁷Although the shrines were allowed to remain in Israel, Asa himself remained faithful all his life. ¹⁸He brought into the house of God all his father's votive offerings and his own, gold and silver and sacred vessels. ¹⁹And there was no more war until the thirty-fifth year of Asa's reign.

16 In the thirty-sixth year of the reign of Asa, King Baasha of Israel invaded Judah and fortified Ramah to prevent anyone leaving or entering the kingdom of Asa of Judah. ²Asa brought out silver and gold from the treasuries of the house of the LORD and the king's palace, and sent them to Ben-hadad king of Aram, whose capital was Damascus, with this request: ³'Let there be an alliance between us, as there was between our fathers. Herewith I send you silver and gold; break off your alliance with King Baasha of Israel, so that he may abandon his campaign against me.' ⁴Ben-hadad listened with approval to King Asa; he ordered his army commanders to move against the towns of Israel, and they attacked Iyyon, Dan, Abel-mayim, and all the store-cities of Naphtali. ⁵When Baasha heard of it, he discontinued the fortifying of Ramah and stopped all work on it. ⁶Then King Asa took with him all the men of Judah and they removed the stones of Ramah and the timbers with which Baasha had fortified it, and he used them to fortify Geba and Mizpah.

⁷At that time the seer Hanani came to King Asa of Judah and said to him, 'Because you relied on the king of Aram and not on the LORD your God, the army of the king of Israel has escaped. ⁸Did not the Cushites and the Libyans have a great army with a vast number of chariots and horsemen? Yet, because you relied on the LORD, he delivered them into your power. ⁹The eyes of the LORD range through the whole world, to bring aid and comfort to those whose hearts are loyal to him. You have acted foolishly in this affair; you will have wars from now on.' ¹⁰Asa was

15:3 **without law:** *or* without the law.   15:8 **house:** *prob. rdg; Heb. omits.*   15:16–18 *Cp. 1 Kgs. 15:13–15.* 15:16 **grandmother:** *lit.* mother.   16:1–6 *Cp. 1 Kgs. 15:17–22.*   16:7 **Israel:** *so Gk (Luc.); Heb.* Aram.

10: *The third month* (Sivan) was June-July, the time of the grain harvest. The reference may be to the early summer pilgrim-feast, called Harvest, or Weeks (Exod. 23.16; 34.22). **11:** The sacrificial *sheep* often have a ten-to-one ratio to the *oxen.*

   16.1–14: War and apostasy. 1–6: There is little change from 1 Kgs. 15.17–22. **7–10:** The Chronicler adds a homily to the source material. It prepares for v. 12. *Hanani* figures only here; his son, the prophet Jehu, figures vexed with the seer and had him put in the stocks; for those words had made the king very indignant. At the same time he treated some of the people with great brutality.

11 The events of Asa's reign, from beginning to end, are recorded in the annals of the kings of Judah and Israel. 12 In the thirty-ninth year of his reign Asa became gravely affected with disease in his feet; he did not seek guidance of the LORD but resorted to physicians. 13 He rested with his forefathers, in the forty-first year of his reign, 14 and was buried in the tomb which he had bought for himself in the city of David, being laid on a bier which had been heaped with all kinds of spices skilfully compounded; and a great fire was kindled in his honour.

17 ASA was succeeded by his son Jehoshaphat, who strengthened his position against Israel, 2 posting troops in all the fortified towns of Judah and stationing garrisons throughout Judah and in the towns of Ephraim which his father Asa had captured. 3 The LORD was with Jehoshaphat, for he followed the example his father had set in his early years and did not resort to the baalim; 4 he sought guidance of the God of his father and obeyed his commandments and did not follow the practices of Israel. 5 The LORD established the kingdom under his control; all Judah brought him gifts, and his wealth and fame became very great. 6 He took pride in the service of the LORD; he again suppressed the shrines and the sacred poles in Judah.

7 In the third year of his reign he sent his officers Ben-hayil, Obadiah, Zechariah, Nethanel, and Micaiah to teach in the towns of Judah, 8 together with the Levites Shemaiah, Nethaniah, Zebadiah, Asahel, Shemiramoth, Jehonathan, Adonijah, Tobiah, and Tob-adonijah, accompanied by the priests Elishama

and Jehoram. 9 They taught in Judah, having with them the scroll of the law of the LORD; they went round the towns of Judah teaching the people.

10 The dread of the LORD fell upon all the rulers of the lands surrounding Judah, and they did not make war on Jehoshaphat. 11 Certain Philistines brought him a gift of a great quantity of silver; the Arabs too brought him seven thousand seven hundred rams and seven thousand seven hundred he-goats. 12 Jehoshaphat grew ever more powerful. He built fortresses and store-towns in Judah, 13 and was engaged on much work in her towns.

He kept regular, seasoned troops in Jerusalem, 14 enrolled according to their clans in this way: of Judah, the officers over units of a thousand: Adnah the commander, together with three hundred thousand seasoned troops; 15 next to him the commander Johanan, with two hundred and eighty thousand; 16 next to him Amasiah son of Zichri, who had volunteered for the service of the LORD, with two hundred thousand seasoned troops; 17 and of Benjamin: an experienced soldier Eliada, with two hundred thousand men armed with bows and shields; 18 next to him Jehozabad, with a hundred and eighty thousand fully armed men. 19 These were the men who served the king, apart from those whom the king had posted in the fortified towns throughout Judah.

18 When Jehoshaphat had become very wealthy and famous, he allied himself with Ahab by marriage. 2 Some years afterwards he went down to Samaria to visit

16:11–14 *Cp. 1 Kgs. 15:23–24.*   16:14 **bought:** *or* dug. **on a bier:** *or* in a niche.   17:2 **garrisons:** *or* officers.   17:3 **father:** *so some MSS; others add* David. **the baalim:** *or* Baal.   17:5 **fame:** *or* riches. 17:8 **Tob-adonijah:** *prob. rdg; Heb. adds* the Levites. 18:1 **famous:** *or* rich.   18:2–34 *Cp. 1 Kgs. 22:2–35.*

in 19.2; 20.34 and 1 Kgs. 16.1, 7. *The eyes that range through the whole world* recall Zech. 4.4–5. **11–14:** The Chronicler adds here to 1 Kgs. 15.23–24 the comments about *physicians, the tomb, the bier,* and the *great fire.* **14:** An unusually full funeral description.

17.1–20.37: The reign of Jehoshaphat. The only incident of *Jehoshaphat's* reign related at any length in Kgs. is the battle in which Ahab was killed, presented here in ch. 18. Jehoshaphat was one of the great kings of Judah, however, and the Chronicler greatly expands the account of him.

17.1–19.11: Organizing the righteous kingdom. The account of Jehoshaphat's alliance with Ahab (ch. 18) is placed between descriptions of Jehoshaphat's good administration of the kingdom. **1b–6:** This is not in Kgs. **6:** Yet according to 20.33 *the shrines* were not removed. **7–9:** The king's instruction of the people here is an added element. **10–19:** Again this is an added element. The *troops* attributed to *Jehoshaphat* add up to 1,160,000 men. The numbers reflect the exaggerations usual in the Chronicler's writing. **18.1–34:** The affairs of the Northern Kingdom are usually neglected by the Chronicler, but the dramatic narrative of *Ahab's* death

Ahab, who slaughtered many sheep and oxen for him and his retinue, and incited him to attack Ramoth-gilead. ³ What King Ahab of Israel said to King Jehoshaphat of Judah was: 'Will you join me in attacking Ramoth-gilead?' Jehoshaphat replied, 'What is mine is yours: myself and my people; I shall join you in the war,' ⁴ but he said to the king of Israel, 'First let us seek counsel from the LORD.'

⁵ The king of Israel assembled the prophets, some four hundred of them, and asked them, 'Shall we attack Ramoth-gilead or not?' 'Attack,' was the answer; 'God will deliver it into your majesty's hands.' ⁶ Jehoshaphat asked, 'Is there no other prophet of the LORD here through whom we may seek guidance?' ⁷ 'There is one more,' the king of Israel answered, 'through whom we may seek guidance of the LORD, but I hate the man, because he never prophesies good for me, never anything but evil. His name is Micaiah son of Imla.' Jehoshaphat exclaimed, 'Let your majesty say no such thing!' ⁸ The king of Israel called one of his eunuchs and told him to fetch Micaiah son of Imla with all speed.

⁹ The king of Israel and King Jehoshaphat of Judah, clothed in their royal robes and in shining armour, were seated on their thrones at the entrance to the gate of Samaria, and all the prophets were prophesying before them. ¹⁰ One of them, Zedekiah son of Kenaanah, made himself iron horns and declared, 'This is the word of the LORD: "With horns like these you will gore the Aramaeans and make an end of them."' ¹¹ In the same vein all the prophets prophesied, 'Attack Ramoth-gilead and win the day; the LORD will deliver it into your hands.'

¹² The messenger sent to fetch Micaiah told him that the prophets had unanimously given the king a favourable answer. 'And mind you agree with them,' he added. ¹³ 'As the LORD lives,' said Micaiah, 'I shall say only what my God tells me to say.' ¹⁴ When he came into the king's presence, the king asked him, 'Micaiah, shall we attack Ramoth-gilead or not?' 'Attack and win the day,' he replied; 'it will fall into your hands.' ¹⁵ 'How often must I adjure you', said the king, 'to tell me nothing but the truth in the name of the LORD?' ¹⁶ Then Micaiah said,

'I saw all Israel scattered on the
   mountains,
like sheep without a shepherd;
and I heard the LORD say: "They have
   no master;
let them go home in peace."'

¹⁷ The king of Israel said to Jehoshaphat, 'Did I not tell you that he never prophesies good for me, never anything but evil?' ¹⁸ Micaiah went on, 'Listen now to the word of the LORD: I saw the LORD seated on his throne, with all the host of heaven in attendance on his right and on his left. ¹⁹ The LORD said, "Who will entice King Ahab of Israel to go up and attack Ramoth-gilead?" One said one thing and one said another, ²⁰ until a spirit came forward and, standing before the LORD, said, "I shall entice him." "How?" said the LORD. ²¹ "I shall go out", he answered, "and be a lying spirit in the mouths of all his prophets." "Entice him; you will succeed," said the LORD. "Go and do it." ²² You see, then, how the LORD has put a lying spirit in the mouths of all these prophets of yours, because he has decreed disaster for you.'

²³ At that Zedekiah son of Kenaanah came up to Micaiah and struck him in the face: 'And how did the spirit of the LORD pass from me to speak to you?' he demanded. ²⁴ Micaiah retorted, 'That you will find out on the day when you run into an inner room to hide.' ²⁵ The king of Israel ordered Micaiah to be arrested and committed to the custody of Amon the governor of the city and Joash the king's son. ²⁶ 'Throw this fellow into prison,' he said, 'and put him on a prison diet of bread and water until I come home in safety.' ²⁷ Micaiah declared, 'If you do return in safety, the LORD has not spoken by me.'

²⁸ The king of Israel and King Jehoshaphat of Judah marched on Ramoth-gilead. ²⁹ The king of Israel went into battle in disguise, for he had said to Jehoshaphat, 'I shall disguise myself to go into battle, but you must wear your royal robes.' ³⁰ The king of Aram had ordered the captains of his chariots not to engage all and sundry, but the king of Israel alone. ³¹ When the captains saw Jehoshaphat,

18:25 **son:** or deputy.   18:27 **the LORD . . . me:** prob. rdg; Heb. adds and he said, 'Listen, peoples, all together.'

is here included for the sake of *Jehoshaphat*'s part in it. Apart from vv. 1–2, the material is mostly from 1 Kgs. 22.1–35. **1:** See 2 Kgs. 8.18, 25–27. **2:** The verse expands 1 Kgs. 22.2. **31:** The LORD's overt intervention is they thought he was the king of Israel and wheeled to attack him, but Jehoshaphat cried out, and the LORD came to his help; God drew them away from him. [32] When the captains saw that he was not the king of Israel, they broke off the attack on him. [33] One man, however, drew his bow at random and hit the king of Israel where the breastplate joins the plates of the armour. The king said to his driver, 'Turn about and take me out of the line; I am wounded.' [34] When the day's fighting reached its height, the king of Israel was facing the Aramaeans, propped up in his chariot; he remained so till evening, and at sunset he died.

19 As King Jehoshaphat of Judah returned in safety to his palace in Jerusalem, [2] Jehu son of Hanani, the seer, went out to meet him and said, 'Do you take delight in helping the wicked and befriending the enemies of the LORD? For this the LORD's wrath will strike you. [3] Yet there is some good in you, for you have swept away the sacred poles from the land and have made a practice of seeking guidance of God.'

[4] Jehoshaphat had his residence in Jerusalem, but he went out again among his people from Beersheba to the hill-country of Ephraim and brought them back to the LORD the God of their forefathers. [5] He appointed judges throughout the land, one in each of the fortified towns of Judah, [6] and said to them, 'Be careful what you do; you are there as judges, to please not man but the LORD, who is with you when you pass sentence. [7] Now let the dread of the LORD be on you; take care what you do, for the LORD our God will not tolerate injustice, partiality, or bribery.'

[8] In Jerusalem Jehoshaphat appointed some of the Levites and priests and some heads of Israelite families by paternal descent to administer the law of the LORD and to arbitrate in lawsuits among the inhabitants of the towns. [9] He gave them these instructions: 'You must at all times act in the fear of

the LORD, faithfully and with singleness of mind. [10] In every suit which comes before you from your kinsmen, in whatever town they live, whether cases of bloodshed or offences against the law or the commandments, against statutes or regulations, you must warn them to commit no offence against the LORD; otherwise the LORD's wrath will strike you and your kinsmen. If you act thus, you will be free of all offence. [11] Your authority in all matters which concern the LORD is Amariah the chief priest, and in those which concern the king it is Zebadiah son of Ishmael, the prince of the house of Judah; the Levites are your officers. Be strong and resolute, and may the LORD be on the side of the good!'

20 It happened some time afterwards that the Moabites, the Ammonites, and some of the Meunites came to make war on Jehoshaphat. [2] News was brought to him of an attack by a great horde from beyond the Dead Sea, from Edom; they were already at Hazazon-tamar, which is En-gedi. [3] Jehoshaphat in alarm resolved to seek guidance of the LORD, and proclaimed a fast for all Judah. [4] The Judahites gathered to ask counsel of the LORD, coming from every town in the land to consult him.

[5] Jehoshaphat stood in the assembly of Judah and Jerusalem in the house of the LORD in front of the new court, [6] and said, 'LORD God of our forefathers, are you not the God who is in heaven? You rule over all the kingdoms of the nations; in your hand are strength and power, and there is none who can withstand you. [7] You, our God, dispossessed the inhabitants of this land in favour of your people Israel, and gave it for ever to the descendants of your friend Abraham. [8] They have lived in it and built a sanctuary in it for your name, saying, [9] "Should any disaster befall us, whether war or flood, pes-

19:8 **in . . . inhabitants:** *prob. rdg, cp. Gk; Heb. obscure.*
20:1 **Meunites:** *prob. rdg, cp. Gk; Heb.* Ammonites.
20:2 **Edom:** *so one MS; others* Aram.   20:9 **flood:** *prob. rdg; Heb.* judgement.

the Chronicler's addition; see 1 Kgs. 22.33. **19.1–3:** *Jehoshaphat* is reprimanded in this expansion by a prophet, Jehu, for collaborating with the Northern Kingdom, as was his father Asa; see 16.7–10 n. **5–7:** This is an expansion by the Chronicler. On instruction to the *judges,* compare Deut. 1.16–17. **8–11:** The Chronicler adds that supreme courts were appointed *in Jerusalem* with highest authority for both religious and civil cases. **8:** *Israel* here is the entire people, not just the Northern Kingdom.

20.1–37: Jehoshaphat's great victory. This full narrative is typical of the Chronicler's expansions. They are, as usual, the religious speech (vv. 5–12, 20) made by the king or else a prophet (vv. 15–17), and are ascribed to successive stages of the action. **1:** *Meunites* were an Arab tribe. The Heb. reads "Ammonites," but is tilence or famine, we shall stand before this house and before you, for in this house is your name, and we shall cry to you in our distress, and you will hear and save." [10] You did not allow the Israelites, when they came out of Egypt, to enter the land of the Ammonites, the Moabites, and the people of the hill-country of Seir, so they turned aside and left them alone and did not destroy them. [11] Now see how these people repay us: they are coming to drive us out of your possession which you gave to us. [12] Judge them, God our God, for we have not the strength to face this great host which is invading our land; we do not know what we ought to do, but our eyes look to you.'

[13] As all the men of Judah stood before the LORD, with their dependants, their wives, and their children, [14] there, in the midst of the assembly, the spirit of the LORD came upon Jahaziel son of Zechariah, son of Benaiah, son of Jeiel, son of Mattaniah, a Levite of the line of Asaph, [15] and he said, 'Pay attention, all Judah and you inhabitants of Jerusalem and King Jehoshaphat; this is the word of the LORD to you: Do not fear or be dismayed by this great horde, for the battle is in God's hands, not yours. [16] Go down to engage them tomorrow as they come up by the ascent of Ziz; you will find them at the end of the wadi, east of the wilderness of Jeruel. [17] It is not you who will fight this battle; stand firm and wait, and you will see the deliverance worked by the LORD for you, Judah and Jerusalem. Do not fear or be dismayed; go out tomorrow to face them, for the LORD is with you.' [18] Jehoshaphat bowed low to the ground, and all Judah and the inhabitants of Jerusalem fell down before the LORD in obeisance to him. [19] Then the Levites of the lines of Kohath and Korah stood up and praised the LORD the God of Israel with mighty voice.

[20] They rose early next morning to go out to the wilderness of Tekoa. As they were about to start, Jehoshaphat stood up and said, 'Hear me, Judah and you inhabitants of Jerusalem: hold firmly to your faith in the LORD your God and you will be upheld; have faith in his prophets and you will succeed.' [21] After consulting with the people, he ap-

pointed men to sing to the LORD and praise the splendour of his holiness as they marched out before the armed troops, singing:

'Give thanks to the LORD,
    for his love endures for ever.'

[22] As soon as their loud shouts of praise were heard, the LORD misled the Ammonites and Moabites and the men of the hill-country of Seir who were invading Judah, and they were defeated. [23] It turned out that the Ammonites and Moabites had taken up a position against the men of the hill-country of Seir, and set themselves to annihilate and destroy them; and when they had exterminated the men of Seir, they savagely attacked one another.

[24] When Judah came to the watch-tower in the wilderness and looked towards the enemy host, there they were all lying dead on the ground; none had escaped. [25] Jehoshaphat and his men, coming to collect the booty, found many cattle and a large quantity of equipment, clothing, and articles of value, which they plundered until they could carry away no more. They spent three days gathering the booty, there was so much of it. [26] On the fourth day they assembled in the valley of Berakah, the name that it bears to this day because there they blessed the LORD. [27] Afterwards, with Jehoshaphat at their head, all the men of Judah and Jerusalem returned home to the city in triumph; for the LORD had given them cause to triumph over their enemies. [28] They entered Jerusalem with lutes, lyres, and trumpets playing, and went into the house of the LORD. [29] The dread of God fell upon the rulers of every country, when they heard that the LORD had fought against the enemies of Israel. [30] With God giving Jehoshaphat security on all sides, his realm enjoyed peace.

[31] Thus Jehoshaphat reigned over Judah.

20:21 **men . . . holiness:** *or* singers in sacred vestments to praise the LORD.   20:25 **cattle:** *so Gk; Heb.* among them. **clothing:** *so some MSS; others* effigies. 20:26 **Berakah:** *that is* Blessing.   20:31–33 *Cp. 1 Kgs. 22:41–43.*

corrected, as in other modern translations, from 26.7. **10:** Compare Deut. 2.1–19. *Seir* is the area from which the Meunites came; here it does not mean Edom, as elsewhere it does. **17:** See 13.13–20 n. **22, 28:** Note the music before and after the battle. **23:** Some internal dissension seems to have arisen. The Meunites are slain by their erstwhile allies. **31–35:** The passage is rewritten from 1 Kgs. 22.41–49, *Israel* here strangely replacing

He was thirty-five years old when he came to the throne, and he reigned in Jerusalem for twenty-five years; his mother was Azubah daughter of Shilhi. 32 He followed in the footsteps of Asa his father and did not deviate from them; he did what was right in the eyes of the LORD. 33 But the shrines were allowed to remain, and the people did not set their hearts on the God of their forefathers. 34 The other events of Jehoshaphat's reign, from first to last, are recorded in the history of Jehu son of Hanani, which is included in the annals of the kings of Israel.

35 Later King Jehoshaphat of Judah allied himself with King Ahaziah of Israel: he did wrong 36 in joining with him to build ships for trade with Tarshish; these were built in Ezion-geber. 37 But Eliezer son of Dodavahu of Mareshah denounced Jehoshaphat with this prophecy: 'Because you have joined with Ahaziah, the LORD will bring your work to nothing.' So the ships were wrecked and could not make the voyage to Tarshish.

21 JEHOSHAPHAT rested with his forefathers and was buried with them in the city of David. He was succeeded by his son Joram, 2 whose brothers, sons of Jehoshaphat, were Azariah, Jehiel, Zechariah, Azariah, Michael, and Shephatiah. All of them were sons of King Jehoshaphat of Judah, 3 and their father gave them many gifts, silver and gold and other costly things, as well as fortified towns in Judah; the kingship he gave to Joram because he was the eldest. 4 When Joram was firmly established on his father's throne, he put to the sword all his brothers, as well as some of the leading figures in Israel. 5 He was thirty-two years old when he came to the throne, and he reigned in Jerusalem for eight years. 6 He followed the practices of the kings of Israel as the house of Ahab had done, for he had married Ahab's daughter; he did what was wrong in the eyes of the LORD. 7 Yet for the sake of the covenant which he had made with David, the LORD was unwilling to destroy the house of David, as he had promised to give him and his descendants a lamp for all time.

8 During Joram's reign Edom revolted against Judah and set up its own king. 9 Joram, with his commanders and all his chariots, pushed on into Edom. When the Edomites encircled him and his chariot-commanders he made a sortie by night and broke out. 10 To this day Edom has remained independent of Judah. Libnah revolted against him at the same time, because he had forsaken the LORD the God of his fathers, 11 and because he had built shrines in the hill-country of Judah and had seduced the inhabitants of Jerusalem into idolatrous practices and corrupted Judah.

12 A letter reached Joram from Elijah the prophet, which read: 'This is the word of the LORD the God of David your father: You have not followed in the footsteps of Jehoshaphat your father and of King Asa of Judah, 13 but have followed the kings of Israel and have led astray Judah and the inhabitants of Jerusalem, as the house of Ahab did; and you have murdered your own brothers, sons of your father's house, men better than yourself. 14 Because of all this, the LORD is about to strike a heavy blow at your people, your children, your wives, and all your possessions; 15 you yourself will suffer from a chronic disease of the bowels, so that they prolapse and become severely ulcerated.'

16 The LORD aroused against Joram the hostility of the Philistines and of the Arabs who live near the Cushites, 17 and they invaded Judah. Overrunning it, they carried off all the property which they found in the

21:2 **Judah:** *so many MSS; others* Israel.   21:5–10 *Cp. 2 Kgs. 8:17–22.*

Judah there in the reference to *annals* (v. 34). **35–37:** Here the motif is added that Jehoshaphat's alliance with *Ahaziah* was evil, and caused the *ships* to be *wrecked*. *Eliezer* is mentioned only here. *Ezion-geber* (v. 36) is identified with Elath on the Gulf of Aqaba, which gave access to the Red Sea. *Tarshish* is often identified with Spain (possibly correctly; see Jonah 1.3), but Spain is hardly possible here, since it is on the Mediterranean.

21.1–24.27: A period of failures. The Chronicler now deals with a succession of four reigns disastrous to Judah. At points the source material (2 Kgs. 8.16–12.21) is greatly amplified to increase the wickedness of the kings, but an abundance of material is also omitted. **1–20:** *Joram's* reign. **2–4:** Joram's killing of his *brothers* is not otherwise attested; it is hard to know whether the material is historical, or whether the Chronicler has increased Joram's misdeeds, and thereby his consequent punishment. **10–11:** The reasons given for *Libnah's* revolt are the Chronicler's own contribution. **12–20:** The letter from *Elijah* and the ensuing defeats were added by the Chronicler. Apparently the figure of Elijah, magnified in later legend, was already a commanding one.

king's palace, as well as his sons and wives; not a son was left to him except the youngest, Jehoahaz. 18 After this the LORD struck down the king with an incurable disease of the bowels. 19 It continued for some time, and towards the end of the second year the disease caused his bowels to prolapse, and the painful ulceration brought on his death. But his people kindled no fire in his honour as they had done for his fathers.

20 Joram was thirty-two years old when he became king, and he reigned in Jerusalem for eight years. His passing went unsung, and he was buried in the city of David, but not in the burial-place of the kings.

22 Then the inhabitants of Jerusalem made Ahaziah, his youngest son, king in his place, for the raiders who had joined the Arabs in the campaign had killed all the older sons. So Ahaziah son of Joram became king of Judah. 2 He was twenty-two years old when he came to the throne, and he reigned in Jerusalem for one year; his mother was Athaliah granddaughter of Omri. 3 He too followed the practices of the house of Ahab, for his mother was his counsellor in wickedness. 4 He did what was wrong in the eyes of the LORD like the house of Ahab, for they had been his counsellors after his father's death, to his undoing. 5 He followed their counsel in the alliance he made with Jehoram son of Ahab king of Israel, to fight against King Hazael of Aram at Ramoth-gilead. But Jehoram was wounded by the Aramaeans, 6 and retired to Jezreel to recover from the wounds inflicted on him at Ramoth in battle with King Hazael.

Because of Jehoram's injury Ahaziah son of Joram king of Judah went down to Jezreel to visit him. 7 It was God's will that the visit of Ahaziah to Jehoram should be the occasion of his downfall. During the visit he went out with Jehoram to meet Jehu son of Nimshi, whom the LORD had anointed to bring the house of Ahab to an end. 8 So it came about that Jehu, who was then at variance with the house of Ahab, found the officers of Judah and the kinsmen of Ahaziah who were his attendants, and killed them. 9 He then searched out Ahaziah himself, and his men captured him in Samaria, where he had gone into hiding. They brought him to Jehu and put him to death; they gave him burial, for they said, 'He was descended from Jehoshaphat who sought the guidance of the LORD with his whole heart.' There was no one left of the house of Ahaziah strong enough to rule.

10 As soon as Athaliah mother of Ahaziah saw that her son was dead, she set out to get rid of the whole royal line of the house of Judah. 11 But Jehosheba the daughter of King Joram took Ahaziah's son Joash and stole him away from among the princes who were being murdered; she put him and his nurse in a bedchamber. Thus Jehosheba daughter of King Joram and wife of Jehoiada the priest, because she was Ahaziah's sister, hid Joash from Athaliah so that she did not put him to death. 12 He remained concealed with them in the house of God for six years, while Athaliah ruled the country.

23 In the seventh year Jehoiada felt himself strong enough to make an agreement with Azariah son of Jeroham, Ishmael son of Jehohanan, Azariah son of Obed, Maaseiah son of Adaiah, and Elishaphat son of Zichri, all captains of units of a hundred. 2 They went throughout Judah and gathered to Jerusalem the Levites from all the cities of Judah and the heads of clans in Israel, and they came to Jerusalem. 3 The whole assembly made a compact with the king in the house of God, and Jehoiada said to them, 'Here is the king's son! He will be king, as the LORD promised that David's descendants should be. 4 This is what you must do: one third of you, priests and Levites, as you come on duty on the sabbath, are to be on guard at the threshold gates, 5 another third are to be in the royal palace, and another third are to be at the Foundation Gate, while all the people will be in the courts of the house of the LORD. 6 No one must enter the house of the LORD except the priests and the

22:1–6 *Cp. 2 Kgs. 8:25–29.* 22:1 **campaign:** *lit.* camp. 22:2 **twenty-two:** *prob. rdg, cp. 2 Kgs. 8:26; Heb.* forty-two. **granddaughter:** *lit.* daughter. 22:6 **from:** *so some MSS; others* because. **Ramoth:** *so Gk (Luc.); Heb.* Ramah. **Ahaziah:** *so some MSS, cp. 2 Kgs. 8:29; others* Azariah. 22:8 **Judah and:** *so Gk; Heb. adds* the sons of. 22:10–23:21 *Cp. 2 Kgs. 11:1–20.* 22:11 **Jehosheba:** *so Gk, cp. 2 Kgs. 11:2; Heb.* Jehoshabeath.

22.1–12: Ahaziah. 2: He was twenty-two (2 Kgs. 8.26), not *forty-two*, at his accession. **7:** The comment about *God's will* is the Chronicler's addition. The account of *Jehu's* revolution (2 Kgs. 9.1–10.31) is here greatly compressed, with much of the material in Kgs. omitted.

attendant Levites; they may enter, for they are holy, but all the people must continue to keep the LORD's charge. 7 The Levites must mount guard round the king, each man holding his weapons, and anyone who tries to enter the house is to be put to death. They are to stay with the king wherever he goes.'

8 The Levites and all Judah carried out the orders of Jehoiada the priest to the letter: each captain took his men, both those who came on duty on the sabbath and those who went off, for Jehoiada the priest had not released the outgoing divisions. 9 Jehoiada the priest handed out to the captains King David's spears, shields, and bucklers, which were kept in the house of God. 10 He stationed all the troops round the king, each man holding his weapon, from corner to corner of the house to north and south. 11 Then they brought out the king's son, put the crown on his head, handed him the testimony, and proclaimed him king. When Jehoiada and his sons anointed him, a shout went up: 'Long live the king.'

12 When Athaliah heard the noise made by the people as they ran and cheered the king, she came into the house of the LORD where the people were, 13 and found the king standing by the pillar at the entrance, amidst outbursts of song and fanfares of trumpets in his honour; all the populace were rejoicing and blowing trumpets, and singers with musical instruments were leading the celebrations. Athaliah tore her clothes and cried, 'Treason! Treason!' 14 Jehoiada the priest gave orders to the captains in command of the troops: 'Bring her outside the precincts and put to the sword anyone in attendance on her'; for the priest said, 'Do not kill her in the house of the LORD.' 15 They took her and brought her to the royal palace and there at the passage to the Horse Gate they put her to death.

16 Jehoiada made a covenant between the LORD on one side and the whole people and the king on the other, that they should be the LORD's people. 17 The people all went to the temple of Baal and pulled it down; they smashed its altars and images, and they slew Mattan the priest of Baal before the altars. 18 Jehoiada committed the supervision of

the house of the LORD to the charge of the priests and the Levites whom David had allocated to the house of the LORD, to offer whole-offerings to the LORD as prescribed in the law of Moses, with the singing and rejoicing as handed down from David. 19 He stationed the door-keepers at the gates of the house of the LORD, to prevent anyone entering who was in any way unclean. 20 Then he took the captains of units of a hundred, the nobles, and the governors of the people, and all the people of the land, and they escorted the king from the house of the LORD through the Upper Gate to the palace, and seated him on the royal throne. 21 The whole people rejoiced and the city had quiet. That is how Athaliah was put to the sword.

24 Joash was seven years old when he became king, and he reigned in Jerusalem for forty years; his mother was Zibiah from Beersheba. 2 He did what was right in the eyes of the LORD as long as Jehoiada the priest was alive. 3 Jehoiada chose him two wives, and he had a family of sons and daughters.

4 Some time afterwards, Joash decided to renovate the house of the LORD. 5 He assembled the priests and Levites and said to them, 'Go through the cities and towns of Judah and collect without delay the annual tax from all the Israelites for the restoration of the house of your God.' But the Levites did not act quickly. 6 The king summoned Jehoiada the chief priest and asked him, 'Why have you not required the Levites to bring in from Judah and Jerusalem the tax imposed by Moses the servant of the LORD and by the assembly of Israel for the Tent of the Testimony?' 7 For the wicked Athaliah and her adherents had broken into the house of God and had even devoted all its holy things to the service of the baalim.

8 The king ordered a chest to be made

23:9 **bucklers:** *mng of Heb. word uncertain.*
23:10 **north and south:** *prob. rdg; Heb. adds* of the altar and the house.   23:13 **by the pillar:** *prob. rdg, cp.* 2 *Kgs.* 11:14; *Heb.* on the dais.   23:14 **gave orders to:** *prob. rdg, cp.* 2 *Kgs.* 11:15; *Heb.* brought out.
23:16 **the LORD:** *prob. rdg, cp.* 2 *Kgs.* 11:17; *Heb.* him.
23:18 **priests and:** *so some MSS; others omit* and.
24:1–14 *Cp.* 2 *Kgs.* 11:21—12:15.   24:7 **Athaliah and:** *so Gk; Heb. omits* and. **her adherents:** *lit.* her sons.

23.1–21: Athaliah. 1–3: The Chronicler added proper names as well as all references to *the Levites.* **18–19:** Some revision of, and addition to, the source, 2 Kgs. 11.1–16, brings the account into line with Chronicler's view of *Levites,* singers, *door-keepers,* and *the law of Moses.*

24.1–27: Joash. The source is 2 Kgs. ch. 12.

and placed outside the gate of the house of the LORD; ⁹and proclamation was made throughout Judah and Jerusalem that the people should bring to the LORD the tax imposed on Israel in the wilderness by Moses the servant of God. ¹⁰All the leaders and the people gladly brought their taxes and dropped them into the chest until it was full. ¹¹Whenever the chest was brought by the Levites to the king's officers and they saw that it was well filled, the king's secretary and the chief priest's officer would come to empty it, after which it was returned to its place. This they did daily, and a large sum of money was collected. ¹²The king and Jehoiada handed it over to those responsible for carrying out the work in the house of the LORD, and they hired masons and carpenters to do the renovation, as well as craftsmen in iron and copper to restore the house. ¹³The workmen got on with their task and the work progressed under their hands; they restored the house of God according to its original design and strengthened it. ¹⁴When they had finished, they brought what was left of the money to the king and Jehoiada, and it was made into vessels for the house of the LORD, both for service and for sacrificing, saucers and other articles of gold and silver. During Jehoiada's lifetime whole-offerings were offered regularly in the house of the LORD.

¹⁵Jehoiada, now old and weighed down with years, died at the age of a hundred and thirty ¹⁶and was buried with the kings in the city of David, because he had done good in Israel in the service of God and of his house.

¹⁷After the death of Jehoiada the leading men of Judah came and made obeisance to the king. He listened to them, ¹⁸and they forsook the house of the LORD the God of their forefathers and worshipped sacred poles and idols. For this wickedness Judah and Jerusalem suffered. ¹⁹The LORD sent prophets to bring them back to himself, prophets who denounced them but were not heeded. ²⁰Then the spirit of God took possession of Zechariah son of Jehoiada the priest. Taking his stance looking down on the people he declared, 'This is the word of God: Why do you disobey the commands of the LORD and court disaster? Because you have forsaken the LORD, he has forsaken you.' ²¹But they made common cause against him, and on orders from the king they stoned him to death in the court of the house of the LORD. ²²King Joash, forgetful of the loyalty of Zechariah's father Jehoiada, killed his son. As he was dying he said, 'May the LORD see this and exact the penalty.'

²³At the turn of the year a force of Aramaeans advanced against Joash; they invaded Judah and Jerusalem and massacred all the officers of the army, so that it ceased to exist, and they sent all their spoil to the king of Damascus. ²⁴Although the Aramaeans had invaded with a small force, the LORD delivered a very great army into their power, because the people had forsaken the LORD the God of their forefathers; and Joash suffered just punishment.

²⁵When the Aramaeans had withdrawn, leaving the king severely wounded, his servants conspired against him to avenge the death of the son of Jehoiada the priest, and they murdered him on his bed. Thus he died and was buried in the city of David, but not in the burial-place of the kings. ²⁶The conspirators were Zabad son of Shimeath an Ammonite woman and Jehozabad son of Shimrith a Moabite woman. ²⁷His children, the many oracles about him, and his reconstruction of the house of God are all on record in the discourse given in the annals of the kings. His son Amaziah succeeded him.

25 AMAZIAH was twenty-five years old when he came to the throne, and he

24:12 **copper:** or bronze.   24:20 **took possession of:** lit. clothed itself with.   24:25–27 Cp. 2 Kgs. 12:20–21.   24:25 **son:** so Gk; Heb. sons. 25:1–4 Cp. 2 Kgs. 14:1–6.

15–22: This is entirely from the Chronicler. As elsewhere, a good king turns bad toward the end of his reign and receives punishment; compare 11.17 n. **23–24:** This revision of 2 Kgs. 12.17–18 adds the motif of punishment. **26:** That the two assassins were sons of an *Ammonite woman* and a *Moabite woman* is the Chronicler's own comment, suggesting that evil influence is likely to come from foreigners.

25.1–28.27: Four kings assessed concerning their faithfulness. The Chronicler continues recasting the source, 2 Kgs. 14.1–16.20, sometimes drastically adding incidents to show that only faithfulness to the LORD leads to welfare and peace. The first two kings, Amaziah and Uzziah, are faithful at first and then unfaithful; the third, Jotham, is faithful, the fourth, Ahaz, completely unfaithful.

reigned in Jerusalem for twenty-nine years; his mother was Jehoaddan from Jerusalem. [2] He did what was right in the eyes of the LORD, yet not wholeheartedly. [3] As soon as the royal power was firmly in his grasp, he put to death those of his servants who had murdered the king his father; [4] but he spared their children, in obedience to the LORD's command written in the law of Moses: 'Parents are not to be put to death for their children, nor children for their parents; each one may be put to death only for his own sin.'

[5] Amaziah assembled the men of Judah and drew them up by families, and Benjamin as well as all Judah, under officers over units of a thousand and a hundred. He mustered those of twenty years old and upwards and found their number to be three hundred thousand, all picked troops ready for service, able to handle spear and shield. [6] He also hired a hundred thousand seasoned troops from Israel for a hundred talents of silver. [7] But a man of God came to him and said, 'My lord king, do not let the Israelite army march with you; the LORD is not with Israel—all these Ephraimites! [8] For, if you make these people your allies in the war, God will overthrow you in battle, for God has the power to help or to overthrow.' [9] Amaziah said to the man of God, 'What am I to do about the hundred talents which I have spent on the Israelite army?' The man answered, 'It is in the LORD's power to give you much more than that.' [10] Amaziah detached the troops which had come to him from Ephraim and sent them home; that made them furious against Judah and they went home in a rage.

[11] Amaziah led his men with resolution to the valley of Salt and there killed ten thousand men of Seir. [12] The men of Judah captured another ten thousand men alive, brought them to the top of a cliff, and hurled them over so that they were all dashed to pieces. [13] Meanwhile the troops which Amaziah had sent home without allowing them to take part in the battle raided the towns of Judah from Samaria to Beth-horon, massa-

cred three thousand people in them, and carried off rich spoil.

[14] After Amaziah had returned from the defeat of the Edomites, he brought the gods of the people of Seir and, setting them up as his own gods, worshipped them and burnt sacrifices to them. [15] The LORD was angry with Amaziah for this and sent a prophet who said to him, 'Why have you resorted to gods who could not save their own people from you?' [16] While he was speaking, the king said to him, 'Have we appointed you counsellor to the king? Stop! Why risk your life?' The prophet did stop, but first he said, 'I know that God has determined to destroy you because you do this and do not listen to my counsel.'

[17] King Amaziah of Judah, after consultation, sent envoys to Jehoash son of Jehoahaz son of Jehu, king of Israel, to propose a confrontation. [18] King Jehoash of Israel sent back this answer to King Amaziah of Judah: 'A thistle in Lebanon sent to a cedar in Lebanon to say, "Give your daughter in marriage to my son." But a wild beast in Lebanon, passing by, trampled on the thistle. [19] You have defeated Edom, I see, but it has gone to your head. Stay at home and enjoy your triumph. Why should you involve yourself in disaster and bring yourself to the ground, and drag down Judah with you?'

[20] Amaziah, however, would not listen; and this was God's doing in order to give Judah into the power of Jehoash, because they had resorted to the gods of Edom. [21] So King Jehoash of Israel marched out, and he and King Amaziah of Judah clashed at Beth-shemesh in Judah. [22] The men of Judah were routed by Israel and fled to their homes. [23] King Jehoash of Israel captured Amaziah king of Judah, son of Joash, son of Jehoahaz, at Beth-shemesh. He brought him to Jerusalem, where he broke down the city wall from the Ephraim Gate to the Corner Gate, a distance of four hundred cubits. [24] He took all

25:8 **these people:** *prob. rdg; Heb. obscure.*   25:12 **a cliff:** *or Sela.*   25:17–24 *Cp. 2 Kgs. 14:8–14.*
25:20 **of Jehoash:** *so Gk (Luc.); Heb. omits.*
25:24 **He took:** *prob. rdg, cp. 2 Kgs. 14:14; Heb. omits.*

25.1–28: Amaziah. The source is 2 Kgs. 14.1–20. The brief report of *Amaziah*'s Edomite campaign in the source is here expanded by the Chronicler in four respects: the king's military force is listed (vv. 5–6); a prophet dissuades him from employing northern mercenaries (vv. 7–10); the military destruction is increased (vv. 11–13); and *Amaziah*'s veneration of the captured Edomite idols becomes the occasion of divine disfavor (vv. 14–16). **20:** The Chronicler adds the comment that *Amaziah*'s rashness was God's punishment for the apostasy referred to in vv. 14–16.

the gold and silver and all the vessels found in the house of God, in the care of Obed-edom, and the treasures of the palace, as well as hostages, and then returned to Samaria.

25 Amaziah son of Joash, king of Judah, outlived Jehoash son of Jehoahaz, king of Israel, by fifteen years. 26 The other events of Amaziah's reign, from first to last, are recorded in the annals of the kings of Judah and Israel. 27 From the time when he turned away from the LORD, a conspiracy was formed against him in Jerusalem, and he fled to Lachish; the conspirators sent after him to Lachish and put him to death there. 28 His body was conveyed on horseback to Jerusalem, and there he was buried with his forefathers in the city of David.

26 The people of Judah, acting together, took Uzziah, now sixteen years old, and made him king in succession to his father Amaziah. 2 It was he who built Eloth and restored it to Judah after the king rested with his forefathers.

3 Uzziah was sixteen years old when he came to the throne, and he reigned in Jerusalem for fifty-two years; his mother was Jecoliah from Jerusalem. 4 He did what was right in the eyes of the LORD, as Amaziah his father had done. 5 He set himself to seek the guidance of God in the days of Zechariah, who instructed him in the fear of God; as long as he sought guidance from the LORD, God caused him to prosper.

6 He took the field against the Philistines. He broke down the walls of Gath, Jabneh, and Ashdod, and built towns in the territory of Ashdod and among the Philistines. 7 God aided him against them, as well as against the Arabs who lived in Gur-baal, and against the Meunites. 8 The Ammonites brought tribute to Uzziah and his fame spread to the borders of Egypt, for he had become very powerful. 9 He erected towers in Jerusalem at the Corner Gate, at the Valley Gate, and at the escarpment, and fortified them. 10 He erected other towers in the wilderness and dug many cisterns, for he had large herds of cattle both in the Shephelah and in the plain. He also had farmers and vine-dressers in the hill-country and in the fertile lands, for he loved the soil.

11 Uzziah had an army of soldiers trained and ready for service, mustered in divisions according to the numbering made by Jeiel the adjutant-general and Maaseiah the clerk, under the direction of Hananiah, one of the king's commanders. 12 The total number of heads of families which supplied seasoned warriors was two thousand six hundred. 13 Under their command was an army of three hundred and seven thousand five hundred, a powerful fighting force to aid the king against his enemies. 14 Uzziah provided for the whole army shields, spears, helmets, coats of armour, bows, and sling-stones. 15 In Jerusalem he had machines designed by engineers for use on towers and battlements to discharge arrows and large stones. His fame spread far and wide, for he was so wonderfully gifted that he became very powerful.

16 But when he grew powerful his pride became great and led to his own undoing: he offended against the LORD his God by entering the temple of the LORD to burn incense on the incense-altar. 17 Azariah the priest and eighty others of the LORD's priests, courageous men, went in after King Uzziah, 18 confronted him, and said, 'It is not for you, Uzziah, to burn incense to the LORD, but for the Aaronite priests who have been consecrated for that office. Leave the sanctuary; for you have offended, and that will certainly bring you no honour from the LORD God.' 19 The king, who had a censer in his hand ready to burn incense, was enraged; but while he was raging at the priests, leprosy broke out on his forehead in the presence of the priests, there in the house of the LORD, beside the altar of incense. 20 When Azariah the chief priest and the other priests looked towards him, they saw that his forehead was leprous. They hurried him out of the temple, and indeed he himself hastened to leave, be-

25:25—26:2 *Cp. 2 Kgs. 14:17–22.*   25:28 **David:** *so some MSS; others* Judah.   26:3–4 *Cp. 2 Kgs. 15:2–3*
26:5 **in the fear of:** *so some MSS; others* on seeing.
26:14 **and:** *prob. rdg; Heb. adds* for.   26:16 **his pride ... undoing:** *or* he became so proud that he acted corruptly.

26.1–23: Uzziah. In 2 Kgs. 15.1–34 he is usually called Azariah; one name may be personal, the other a throne name. 2: *Eloth:* Elath. 6–15: The Chronicler expands here, following sources other than 2 Kgs. Those sources gave an accurate view, however, of *Uzziah*'s historical importance. 12–13: This is one of the few instances in which the numbers given by the Chronicler are not artificial and schematic, but are apparently based upon older, written sources. 16–23: The source simply reported *Uzziah*'s *leprosy;* the Chronicler here cause the LORD had struck him with the disease. [21] King Uzziah remained a leper till the day of his death; he lived in his palace as a leper, relieved of all duties and excluded from the house of the LORD, while his son Jotham was comptroller of the household and regent over the country. [22] The other events of Uzziah's reign, from first to last, are recorded by the prophet Isaiah son of Amoz. [23] He rested with his forefathers and was buried with them, but in the field adjoining the royal tombs, for they said, 'He is a leper.' His son Jotham succeeded him.

27 Jotham was twenty-five years old when he came to the throne, and he reigned in Jerusalem for sixteen years; his mother was Jerushah daughter of Zadok. [2] He did what was right in the eyes of the LORD, as his father Uzziah had done, but unlike him he did not enter the temple of the LORD; the people, however, continued their corrupt practices. [3] He constructed the Upper Gate of the house of the LORD and built extensions on the wall at Ophel. [4] He built towns in the hill-country of Judah, and forts and towers on the wooded hills. [5] He made war on the king of the Ammonites and defeated him; and that year the Ammonites delivered to him a hundred talents of silver, ten thousand kor of wheat, and ten thousand of barley. They paid him the same tribute in the second and third years. [6] Jotham became very powerful because he maintained a steady course of obedience to the LORD his God. [7] The other events of Jotham's reign, all that he did in war and in peace, are recorded in the annals of the kings of Israel and Judah. [8] He was twenty-five years old when he came to the throne, and he reigned in Jerusalem for sixteen years. [9] He rested with his forefathers and was buried in the city of David. His son Ahaz succeeded him.

28 AHAZ was twenty years old when he came to the throne, and he reigned in Jerusalem for sixteen years. He did not do what was right in the eyes of the LORD like his forefather David, [2] but followed in the footsteps of the kings of Israel, and cast metal images for the baalim. [3] He also burnt sacrifices in the valley of Ben-hinnom; he even

burnt his sons in the fire according to the abominable practice of the nations whom the LORD had dispossessed in favour of the Israelites. [4] He sacrificed and burned offerings at the shrines and on the hilltops and under every spreading tree.

[5] The LORD his God let Ahaz suffer at the hands of the king of Aram: the Aramaeans defeated him, took many captives, and brought them to Damascus. He was also made to suffer at the hands of the king of Israel, who inflicted a severe defeat on him. [6] This was Pekah son of Remaliah, who killed in one day a hundred and twenty thousand men of Judah, seasoned troops, for they had forsaken the LORD the God of their forefathers. [7] Zichri, an Ephraimite hero, killed Maaseiah the king's son and Azrikam the comptroller of the household and Elkanah the king's chief minister. [8] The Israelites took captive from their kinsmen two hundred thousand women and children; they also removed a large amount of booty and brought it to Samaria.

[9] A prophet of the LORD was there, Oded by name; he went out to meet the army as it returned to Samaria and said to them, 'It is because the LORD the God of your forefathers is angry with Judah that he has given them into your power. But you have massacred them in a rage that has towered up to heaven. [10] You now propose to force the people of Judah and Jerusalem, male and female, into slavery. Are you not also guilty men before the LORD your God? [11] Now listen to me. Send back those you have taken captive from your kinsmen, for the anger of the LORD is roused against you.'

[12] Next, some Ephraimite chiefs, Azariah son of Jehohanan, Berechiah son of Meshillemoth, Hezekiah son of Shallum, and Amasa son of Hadlai, met those who were returning from the war [13] and said to them, 'You must not bring these captives into our country; what you are proposing would make us guilty before the LORD and add to our sins and transgressions. We are guilty

---

27:1–9 *Cp. 2 Kgs. 15:33–38.*   28:1–4 *Cp. 2 Kgs. 16:2–4.*   28:7 **son:** or deputy.   28:12 **Hezekiah:** or Jehizkiah.

---

explains it as a result of a cultic offense on Uzziah's part. **22:** *Isaiah:* 2 Kgs. 15.6 speaks rather of the "annals of the kings of Judah." *From first to last* exaggerates the attention to Uzziah found in Isaiah.

27.1–28.27: Jotham and Ahaz. *Jotham* receives only favorable treatment (27.1–9); *Ahaz* (28.1–27) only unfavorable. **2:** The king is portrayed as faithful; the infidelity is on the part of the people. This latter is added enough already, and there is fierce anger against Israel.' ¹⁴So the armed men left the captives and the spoil with the officers and the assembled people. ¹⁵The captives were put in the charge of men nominated for this duty, who found clothes from the spoil for all who were naked; they clothed and shod them, gave them food and drink, and anointed them. All who were tottering on their last legs they mounted on donkeys, and took them to their kinsmen in Jericho, the city of palm trees. Then they themselves returned to Samaria.

¹⁶At that time King Ahaz sent to the king of Assyria for help. ¹⁷The Edomites had invaded again and defeated Judah and carried away prisoners, ¹⁸while the Philistines had raided towns of the Shephelah and of the Negeb of Judah; they had captured and occupied Beth-shemesh, Aijalon, and Gederoth, as well as Soco, Timnah, and Gimzo with their villages. ¹⁹The LORD had reduced Judah to submission because of Ahaz king of Judah; for his actions in Judah had been unbridled and he had been grossly unfaithful to the LORD. ²⁰Then King Tiglath-pileser of Assyria came to him and, far from assisting him, pressed him hard. ²¹Ahaz stripped the house of the LORD, the king's palace, and the houses of his officers, and gave the plunder to the king of Assyria; but all to no purpose.

²²This king, Ahaz, when hard pressed, became more and more unfaithful to the LORD; ²³he sacrificed to the gods of Damascus who had defeated him, for he said, 'The gods of the kings of Aram helped them; I shall sacrifice to them so that they may help me.' But in fact they caused his downfall and that of all Israel. ²⁴Then Ahaz gathered together the vessels of the house of God and broke them up, and shut up the doors of the house of the LORD; he made himself altars at every

corner in Jerusalem, ²⁵and at every town of Judah he made shrines to burn sacrifices to other gods and provoked the anger of the LORD the God of his forefathers.

²⁶The other acts and all the events of his reign, from first to last, are recorded in the annals of the kings of Judah and Israel. ²⁷Ahaz rested with his forefathers and was buried in the city of Jerusalem, but he was not given burial with the kings of Judah. His son Hezekiah succeeded him.

Hezekiah and his successors

29 HEZEKIAH was twenty-five years old when he came to the throne, and he reigned in Jerusalem for twenty-nine years; his mother was Abijah daughter of Zechariah. ²He did what was right in the eyes of the LORD, as his ancestor David had done.

³In the first year of his reign, in the first month, he opened and repaired the doors of the house of the LORD. ⁴He brought in the priests and Levites and, assembling them in the square on the east side, ⁵said to them, 'Levites, listen to me. Hallow yourselves now, hallow the house of the LORD the God of your forefathers, and remove all defilement from the sanctuary. ⁶For our forefathers were unfaithful and did what was wrong in the eyes of the LORD our God: they forsook him, they faced about, and they turned their backs on his dwelling-place. ⁷They shut the doors of the porch and extinguished the lamps; they ceased to burn incense and offer whole-offerings in the sanctuary to the God of Israel. ⁸Therefore the anger of the LORD fell on Judah and Jerusalem and he made them re-

28:16 **the king:** *so Gk; Heb.* the kings.   28:19 **king of Judah:** *so some MSS; others* king of Israel.
28:20 **Tiglath-pileser:** *so Syriac; Heb.* Tilgath-pilneser.
28:26–27 *Cp. 2 Kgs. 16:19–20.*   28:27 **Judah:** *so Syriac; Heb.* Israel.   29:1–2 *Cp. 2 Kgs. 18:2–3.*

by the Chronicler. **28.6–15:** This episode is the Chronicler's own contribution. **16–21:** The Chronicler eliminates the positive assistance the Assyrian king rendered *Ahaz* found in 2 Kgs. 16.5–9, giving instead the viewpoint found in Isa. 7.1–17.

29.1–32.33: The reign of Hezekiah. *Hezekiah* is portrayed in Kgs. as one of the most faithful kings; the Chronicler greatly elaborates the account of his reign, adding all of chs. 29–31. Chapter 32, on the other hand, is an abbreviated version of 2 Kgs. 18.13–20.21. In the Chronicler's account, Hezekiah gave more attention to the temple and its service than any king since Solomon; see 30.26.

29.1–36: Restoration of the temple service. After the apostasy of Ahaz (28.24), *Hezekiah*'s first act was to restore the proper temple service. The Chronicler's special interest in *the Levites* and *singers* reappears (vv. 12–14, 25–26, 34). After sixteen days of renovating the temple (vv. 3–19), the renewal of service consisted of sacrifices by the king and leaders (vv. 20–30) and then by all the assembled people (vv. 31–36).

pugnant, an object of horror and derision, as you see for yourselves. [9] That is why our fathers fell by the sword, why our sons and daughters and our wives are in captivity. [10] Now I intend that we should pledge ourselves to the LORD the God of Israel, in order that his anger may be averted from us. [11] My sons, let no time be lost; for the LORD has chosen you to serve him and to minister to him, to be his ministers and to burn sacrifices.'

[12] The Levites set to work; they were Mahath son of Amasai and Joel son of Azariah of the family of Kohath; of the family of Merari, Kish son of Abdi and Azariah son of Jehallelel; of the family of Gershon, Joah son of Zimmah and Eden son of Joah; [13] of the family of Elizaphan, Shimri and Jeiel; of the family of Asaph, Zechariah and Mattaniah; [14] of the family of Heman, Jehiel and Shimei; and of the family of Jeduthun, Shemaiah and Uzziel. [15] They assembled their kinsmen and hallowed themselves, and then went in, as at the LORD's command the king had instructed them, to purify the house of the LORD. [16] The priests went inside to purify the house of the LORD; they removed all defilement they found in the temple into the court of the house of the LORD, where the Levites received it and carried it outside to the wadi of the Kidron. [17] They began the rites on the first day of the first month, and on the eighth day they reached the porch; then for eight days they consecrated the house of the LORD, and on the sixteenth day of the first month they finished.

[18] When they went into the palace they reported to King Hezekiah, 'We have purified the whole of the house of the LORD, the altar of whole-offering with all its vessels, and the table of the Bread of the Presence arranged in rows with all its vessels. [19] We have also put in order and consecrated all the vessels which King Ahaz cast aside during his reign, when he was unfaithful. They are now in place before the altar of the LORD.'

[20] Early next morning King Hezekiah assembled the officers of the city and went up to the house of the LORD. [21] They brought seven bulls, seven rams, and seven lambs for the whole-offering, and seven he-goats as a purification-offering for the kingdom, for the sanctuary, and for Judah; these he commanded the priests of Aaron's line to offer on the altar of the LORD. [22] When the bulls were slaughtered, the priests took the blood

and flung it against the altar; the rams were slaughtered, and their blood was flung against the altar; the lambs were slaughtered, and their blood was flung against the altar. [23] The he-goats for the purification-offering were brought before the king and the assembly, who laid their hands on them; [24] and the priests slaughtered them and used their blood as a purification-offering on the altar to make expiation for all Israel. For the king had commanded that the whole-offering and the purification-offering should be made for all Israel.

[25] He stationed the Levites in the house of the LORD with cymbals, lutes, and lyres, according to the rule prescribed by David, by Gad the king's seer, and Nathan the prophet; for this rule had come from the LORD through his prophets. [26] The Levites stood ready with the instruments of David, and the priests with the trumpets. [27] Hezekiah gave the order that the whole-offering should be offered on the altar. At the moment when the whole-offering began, the song to the LORD began too, with the trumpets, led by the instruments of David king of Israel. [28] The whole assembly prostrated themselves, the singers sang, and the trumpeters sounded; all this continued until the whole-offering was complete. [29] When the offering was complete, the king and all his company bowed down and prostrated themselves. [30] King Hezekiah and his officers commanded the Levites to praise the LORD in the words of David and of Asaph the seer. They praised him most joyfully and bowed down and prostrated themselves.

[31] Hezekiah said, 'Now that you are consecrated to the LORD, approach with your sacrifices and thank-offerings for the house of the LORD.' So the assembly brought sacrifices and thank-offerings; and everyone of willing spirit brought whole-offerings. [32] The number of whole-offerings which the assembly brought was seventy bulls, a hundred rams, and two hundred lambs; all these made a whole-offering to the LORD. [33] The consecrated offerings were six hundred bulls and three thousand sheep. [34] But the priests were too few and could not flay all the whole-offerings; so their colleagues the Levites helped them until the work was completed and all the priests had hallowed themselves — for the Levites had been more scrupulous than the priests in hallowing themselves.

29:21 **for the whole-offering:** *prob. rdg; Heb. omits.*

35 There were indeed whole-offerings in abundance, besides the fat of the shared-offerings and the drink-offerings for the whole-offerings. In this way the service of the house of the LORD was restored; 36 and Hezekiah and all the people rejoiced over what God had done for the people and because it had come about so speedily.

30 Hezekiah sent word to all Israel and Judah, and also wrote letters to Ephraim and Manasseh, inviting them to come to the house of the LORD in Jerusalem to keep the Passover of the LORD the God of Israel. 2 The king and his officers and all the assembly in Jerusalem had agreed to keep the Passover in the second month, 3 but they had not been able to keep it at that time, because not enough priests had hallowed themselves and the people had not assembled in Jerusalem. 4 The proposal being acceptable to the king and the whole assembly, 5 they resolved to make a proclamation throughout all Israel, from Beersheba to Dan, that the people should come to Jerusalem to keep the Passover of the LORD the God of Israel. Never before had so many kept it according to the prescribed form. 6 Couriers went throughout all Israel and Judah with letters from the king and his officers, proclaiming the royal command: 'Turn back, you Israelites, to the LORD the God of your forefathers, Abraham, Isaac, and Israel, so that he may turn back to those of you who escaped capture by the kings of Assyria. 7 Do not be like your forefathers and your kinsmen, who were unfaithful to the LORD the God of their fathers, so that he made them an object of horror, as you yourselves saw. 8 Do not be stubborn as your forefathers were; submit yourselves to the LORD and enter his sanctuary which he has sanctified for ever, and worship the LORD your God, so that his anger may be averted from you. 9 For when you turn back to the LORD, your kinsmen and your children will win compassion from their captors and return to this land. The LORD your God is gracious and compassionate, and

he will not turn away from you if you turn back to him.'

10 As the couriers passed from town to town throughout the land of Ephraim and Manasseh and as far as Zebulun, they were treated with scorn and ridicule. 11 However, a few people from Asher, Manasseh, and Zebulun submitted and came to Jerusalem. 12 Further, the hand of God moved the people in Judah with one accord to carry out what the king and his officers had ordered at the LORD's command.

13 It was a very large assembly that gathered in Jerusalem to keep the pilgrim-feast of Unleavened Bread in the second month. 14 They began by removing the altars in Jerusalem, and the incense-altars they removed and threw into the wadi of the Kidron. 15 They killed the Passover lamb on the fourteenth day of the second month. The priests and the Levites were bitterly ashamed, and they hallowed themselves and brought whole-offerings to the house of the LORD. 16 They took their accustomed places, according to the direction laid down for them in the law of Moses the man of God, and the priests flung against the altar the blood which they received from the Levites.

17 Because many in the assembly had not hallowed themselves, the Levites had to kill Passover lambs for all who were unclean, in order to hallow them to the LORD. 18 For a majority of the people, many from Ephraim, Manasseh, Issachar, and Zebulun, had not kept themselves ritually clean, and therefore kept the Passover irregularly. But Hezekiah prayed for them, saying, 'May the good LORD grant pardon to everyone 19 who makes a practice of seeking guidance of God, the LORD the God of his forefathers, even if he has not observed the rules of purification for the sanctuary.' 20 The LORD heard Hezekiah and healed the people.

21 The Israelites who were present in Jerusalem kept the feast of Unleavened Bread for seven days with great rejoicing, and the Levites and the priests praised the LORD every

30.1–27: Hezekiah's great Passover in Jerusalem. The Chronicler did not relate the fall of the Northern Kingdom (compare 2 Kgs. 18.9–12); this chapter reflects *Hezekiah*'s effort to unite the divided kingdoms into a single one centered in the Davidic monarchy and the Jerusalem temple; see his appeal in vv. 6–9. None of this material is in 2 Kgs. **2:** A *Passover in the second month:* compare Num. 9.1–14. The festival of *Unleavened Bread* (v. 13) was not normally held in the second month. **14:** In the first month (ch. 29) the temple was purified; now the city is cleansed. **15–20:** Only the daytime Passover rituals are reported; the nocturnal meal (see Exod. 12.1–14) is not relevant to the Chronicler's purpose.

day with unrestrained fervour. ²²Hezekiah spoke encouragingly to all the Levites who had shown true insight in the service of the Lord. The seven days of the festival they spent sacrificing shared-offerings and making confession to the Lord the God of their forefathers.

²³The whole assembly agreed to keep the feast for another seven days, and they kept it with general rejoicing. ²⁴For Hezekiah king of Judah set aside for the assembly a thousand bulls and seven thousand sheep, and his officers set aside for the assembly a thousand bulls and ten thousand sheep; and priests hallowed themselves in great numbers. ²⁵The whole assembly of Judah, including the priests and the Levites, rejoiced along with all who had assembled from Israel, and the resident aliens from Israel as well as those who lived in Judah. ²⁶There was great rejoicing in Jerusalem, the like of which had not been known there since the days of Solomon son of David king of Israel. ²⁷The priests and the Levites stood to bless the people, and their voice was heard when their prayer reached God's holy dwelling-place in heaven.

31 When this was over, all the Israelites present went out into the towns and cities of Judah and smashed the sacred pillars, hacked down the sacred poles, and demolished the shrines and the altars throughout Judah and Benjamin, and in Ephraim and Manasseh, until they had made an end of them all. That done, the Israelites returned, each to his own holding in his own town.

²Hezekiah installed the priests and the Levites in office, division by division, allotting to each priest and each Levite his own particular duty, for whole-offerings or shared-offerings, to serve, to give thanks, and to sing praise at the gates of the several quarters in the Lord's house.

³The king provided from his own resources, as the share due from him, the whole-offerings for both morning and evening, and for sabbaths, new moons, and appointed seasons, as prescribed in the law of the Lord. ⁴He ordered the people living in Jerusalem to provide the share due to the priests and the Levites, so that these might devote themselves entirely to the law of the Lord. ⁵As soon as the king's order was issued to the Israelites, they gave generously from the firstfruits of their grain, new wine, oil, and honey, all the produce of their land; they brought a full tithe of everything. ⁶The Israelites and Judaeans living in the towns of Judah also brought a tithe of cattle and sheep, and a tithe of all produce as offerings dedicated to the Lord their God, and they stacked the produce in heaps. ⁷They began to deposit the heaps in the third month and completed them in the seventh.

⁸When Hezekiah and his officers came and saw the heaps, they praised the Lord and his people Israel. ⁹Hezekiah consulted the priests and the Levites about these heaps, ¹⁰and Azariah the chief priest, who was of the line of Zadok, answered, 'From the time when the people began to bring their contribution into the house of the Lord, they have had enough to eat, enough and to spare; indeed, the Lord has so greatly blessed them that they have this great store left over.'

¹¹Hezekiah gave orders for storerooms to be prepared in the house of the Lord, and when this was done ¹²the people faithfully brought in their contributions, the tithe, and their dedicated gifts. The overseer in charge of them was Conaniah the Levite, with Shimei his brother as his deputy; ¹³Jehiel, Azaziah, Nahath, Asahel, Jerimoth, Jozabad, Eliel, Ismachiah, Mahath, and Benaiah were appointed by King Hezekiah and Azariah, the chief overseer of the house of God, to assist Conaniah and Shimei his brother. ¹⁴Kore son of Imnah the Levite, keeper of the East Gate, was in charge of the freewill-offerings to God, to apportion the contributions made to the Lord and the most sacred offerings. ¹⁵Eden, Miniamin, Jeshua, She-

30:21 **with unrestrained fervour:** *prob. rdg; Heb.* with powerful instruments.   30:22 **making confession to:** *or* confessing.   30:27 **and the Levites:** *so many MSS; others omit* and.   31:2 **in the Lord's house:** *so Gk; Heb.* of the Lord.   31:15 **young and old:** *or* high and low.

31.1–21: The support of the temple service. Hezekiah's first act had prepared the temple (ch. 29) and his second, the city as the center for all Israel (ch. 30); here his third act prepares the land for the support of the proper service of the Lord. The land is first cleansed of offensive religious objects (v. 1), then its abundant produce is amassed for support of the temple (vv. 2–10), and finally the king reorganizes the temple personnel for a just distribution of that produce (vv. 11–19).

maiah, Amariah, and Shecaniah in the priestly cities and towns assisted him in the fair distribution of portions to their kinsmen, young and old alike, by divisions. 16 Irrespective of their registration, shares were distributed to all males three years of age and upwards who would enter the house of the LORD to take their daily part in the service, according to their divisions, as their office demanded. 17 The priests were registered by families, the Levites of twenty years of age and upwards by their offices in their divisions. 18 They were registered with all their dependants, their wives, their sons, and their daughters, the whole company of them, because in virtue of their permanent standing they had to keep themselves duly hallowed. 19 As for the priests of Aaron's line in the common lands attached to their cities and towns, in every place men were nominated to distribute portions to every male among the priests and to everyone among the Levites who was on the register.

20 Such was the action taken by Hezekiah throughout Judah; he did what was good and right and loyal in the sight of the LORD his God. 21 Whatever he undertook in the service of the house of God and in obedience to the law and the commandment to seek guidance of his God, he did with all his heart, and he prospered.

32 It was after these events and this example of loyal conduct that King Sennacherib of Assyria invaded Judah and encamped against the fortified towns, believing that he could gain entry and secure them for himself. 2 When Hezekiah saw that he had come determined to attack Jerusalem, 3 he consulted his civil and military officers about blocking up the springs outside the city; and they supported him. 4 They brought together a large number of people to block up all the springs and the stream which flowed through the land. 'Why should Assyrian kings come here and find plenty of water?' they said. 5 Acting with resolution the king made good every breach in the city wall, erecting towers on it and building another wall outside it. He strengthened the Millo of the city of David, and got together a large quantity of weapons and shields.

6 He appointed military commanders over the people and, assembling them in the public square by the city gate, he spoke these

words of encouragement: 7 'Be strong; be brave. Do not let the king of Assyria or the rabble he has brought with him strike terror or panic into your hearts, for we have more on our side than he has. 8 He has human strength; but we have the LORD our God to help us and to fight our battles.' The people were buoyed up by the speech of King Hezekiah.

9 After this, while King Sennacherib of Assyria and his high command were at Lachish, he sent envoys to Jerusalem to deliver this message to King Hezekiah of Judah and to all the Judaeans in Jerusalem: 10 'King Sennacherib of Assyria says, "What gives you the confidence to stay in Jerusalem under siege? 11 Hezekiah is deluding you into risking death by famine or thirst where you are, when he tells you that the LORD your God will save you from the clutches of the Assyrian king. 12 Was it not Hezekiah himself who suppressed the LORD's shrines and altars and told the people of Judah and Jerusalem that they must worship at one altar only and burn sacrifices there?

13 ' "You know very well what I and my forefathers have done to all the peoples of other lands. Were the gods of these nations able to save their lands from me? 14 Not one of the gods of these nations, which my predecessors exterminated, was able to save his people from me. Much less will your God save you! 15 Now, can you let Hezekiah deceive and delude you like this? Can you put any trust in him, for no god of any nation or kingdom has been able to save his people from me or my forefathers? Much less will your gods save you!" '

16 Sennacherib's envoys spoke still more against the LORD God and against his servant Hezekiah. 17 The king also wrote a letter insulting the LORD the God of Israel in these terms: 'Just as the gods of other nations could not save their people from me, so Hezekiah's God cannot save his people from me.' 18 Then they shouted in Hebrew at the tops of their voices at the people of Jerusalem on the wall, to strike them with fear and terror, hoping thus to capture the city. 19 They described the God of Jerusalem as being like

32:1–19 Cp. 2 Kgs. 18:13–37; Isa. 36:1–22.
32:5 towers on it: so Aram. (Targ.); Heb. on the towers.
32:15 gods: or, with some MSS, God.   32:19 God: or gods.

32.1–33: Sennacherib's assault and Hezekiah's response. The Chronicler shortens the account in 2 Kgs.

the gods of the other peoples of the earth — things made by the hands of men. [20] In this plight King Hezekiah and the prophet Isaiah son of Amoz cried to heaven in prayer. [21] So the LORD sent an angel who cut down every fighting man, leader, and commander in the camp of the king of Assyria, so that he withdrew disgraced to his own land. When he entered the temple of his god, certain of his own sons put him to the sword. [22] Thus the LORD saved Hezekiah and the inhabitants of Jerusalem from King Sennacherib of Assyria and from all their enemies; he gave them respite on every side. [23] Many people brought to Jerusalem offerings for the LORD and costly gifts for King Hezekiah of Judah. From then on he was held in high honour by all the nations.

[24] In those days Hezekiah fell dangerously ill and prayed to the LORD, who said, 'I shall heal you,' and granted him a sign. [25] But, being a proud man, he was not grateful for the good done to him, and the LORD's wrath fell on him and on Judah and Jerusalem. [26] Then, proud though he was, Hezekiah submitted, and the people of Jerusalem with him, and the LORD's anger did not fall on them again in Hezekiah's time.

[27] Hezekiah enjoyed great wealth and fame. He built treasuries for silver, gold, precious stones, spices, shields, and other costly things; [28] and barns for the harvests of grain, new wine, and oil; and stalls for various kinds of cattle, as well as sheepfolds. [29] He amassed a great many flocks and herds; God had indeed given him vast riches. [30] It was this same Hezekiah who blocked the upper outflow of the waters of Gihon and directed them downwards and westwards to the city of David. In fact, Hezekiah was successful in everything he attempted, [31] even in the affair of the envoys sent by the king of Babylon, the envoys who came to enquire about the portent which had been seen in the land at the time when God left him to himself, in order to test him and to discover all that was in his mind.

[32] The other events of Hezekiah's reign, and his works of piety, are recorded in the vision of the prophet Isaiah son of Amoz and in the annals of the kings of Judah and Israel. [33] Hezekiah rested with his forefathers and was buried in the upper part of the graves of David's sons; all Judah and the people of Jerusalem paid him honour when he died. His son Manasseh succeeded him.

33

[33] MANASSEH was twelve years old when he came to the throne, and he reigned in Jerusalem for fifty-five years. [2] He did what was wrong in the eyes of the LORD, in following the abominable practices of the nations which the LORD had dispossessed in favour of the Israelites. [3] He rebuilt the shrines which his father Hezekiah had demolished, he erected altars to the baalim, made sacred poles, and prostrated himself before all the host of heaven and served them. [4] He built altars in the house of the LORD, that house of which the LORD had said, 'In Jerusalem my name will be for ever.' [5] He built altars for all the host of heaven in the two courts of the house of the LORD; [6] he made his sons pass through the fire in the valley of Ben-hinnom, he practised soothsaying, divination, and sorcery, and dealt with ghosts and spirits. He did much wrong in the eyes of the LORD and provoked his anger. [7] The image that he had had carved in relief he set up in the house of God, of which God had said to David and Solomon his son, 'In this house and Jerusalem, which I chose out of all the tribes of Israel, I shall establish my name for all time. [8] I shall not again displace Israel from the land which I assigned to their forefathers, if only they are careful to observe all that I commanded them through Moses, all the law, the statutes, and the rules.' [9] But Manasseh led Judah and the inhabitants of Jerusalem astray into wickedness far worse than that of the nations which the

32:20–22 *Cp. 2 Kgs. 19:1–37; Isa. 37:1–38.*   32:24 **I . . . you:** *prob. rdg, cp. 2 Kgs. 20:5; Heb. omits.*
32:28 **sheepfolds:** *so Gk; Heb.* sheep for the folds.
32:29 **He amassed:** *prob. rdg; Heb. adds* cities.
32:31 **king:** *prob. rdg, cp. 2 Kgs. 20:12; Heb.* officers.
32:32 **and in:** *so Gk; Heb. omits* and.   33:1–9 *Cp. 2 Kgs. 21:1–9.*

18.13–20.19 but also adds new comments, e.g. vv. 3–8, 22–23, and 27–31. **24–26:** The verses abridge 2 Kgs. 20.1–9, to suggest that worthy Hezekiah was less than perfect; compare Isa. 38.1–39.8.

33.1–25: Manasseh and Amon. In 2 Kgs. *Manasseh* is the worst king of the Davidic dynasty. It was during his reign that the LORD finally gave up on Jerusalem and Judah (2 Kgs. 21.10–16). Here, however, Manasseh repents and is restored. This theme possibly arises from the very long reign of *fifty-five years*, which the

LORD had exterminated in favour of the Israelites.

10 The LORD spoke to Manasseh and his people, but when they paid no heed, 11 he brought against them the commanders of the army of the king of Assyria; they captured Manasseh with spiked weapons, put him in bronze fetters, and brought him to Babylon. 12 In his distress he prayed to the LORD his God and sought to placate him, and made his humble submission before the God of his forefathers. 13 When he prayed, God accepted his petition and heard his supplication; he brought him back to Jerusalem and restored him to the throne. Thus Manasseh learnt that the LORD was God.

14 After this he built an outer wall for the city of David, west of Gihon in the valley, and extended it to the entrance by the Fish Gate, enclosing Ophel; and he raised it to a great height. He also stationed military commanders in all the fortified towns of Judah. 15 He removed the foreign gods and the carved image from the house of the LORD as well as all the altars which he had erected on the temple mount and in Jerusalem, and threw them out of the city. 16 He repaired the altar of the LORD and sacrificed at it shared-offerings and thank-offerings, and commanded Judah to serve the LORD the God of Israel. 17 But the people still continued to sacrifice at the shrines, though only to the LORD their God.

18 The rest of the acts of Manasseh, his prayer to his God, and the discourses of the seers who spoke to him in the name of the LORD the God of Israel, are recorded in the chronicles of the kings of Israel. 19 His prayer and the answer to it he received, all his sin and unfaithfulness, and the places where he built shrines and set up sacred poles and carved idols before he submitted, are recorded in the chronicles of the seers. 20 Manasseh rested with his forefathers and was buried in the garden-tomb of his family. His son Amon succeeded him.

21 Amon was twenty-two years old when he came to the throne, and he reigned in Jerusalem for two years. 22 He did what was wrong in the eyes of the LORD as his father Manasseh had done. He sacrificed to all the images that his father Manasseh had made, and worshipped them. 23 He was not submissive before the LORD like his father Manasseh; his guilt was much greater. 24 His courtiers conspired against him and assassinated him in the palace; 25 but the people of the land killed all the conspirators and made his son Josiah king in his place.

Josiah's reforms

34 JOSIAH was eight years old when he came to the throne, and he reigned in Jerusalem for thirty-one years. 2 He did what was right in the eyes of the LORD, following in the footsteps of his forefather David, and deviating neither to the right nor to the left. 3 In the eighth year of his reign, when he was still a youth, he began to seek guidance of the God of his forefather David; and in the twelfth year he began to purge Judah and Jerusalem of the shrines and the sacred poles, and the carved idols and the metal images. 4 He saw to it that the altars for the baalim were destroyed and he hacked down the incense-altars which stood above them; he broke in pieces the sacred poles and the carved and metal images, grinding them to powder and scattering it on the graves of those who had sacrificed to them. 5 He burnt the bones of the priests on their altars and purged Judah and Jerusalem. 6 In the towns of Manasseh, Ephraim, and Simeon, and as far as Naphtali, he burnt down their houses wherever he found them; 7 he destroyed the altars and the sacred poles, ground the idols to powder, and hacked down the incense-altars throughout the land of Israel. Then he returned to Jerusalem.

8 In the eighteenth year of his reign, after he had purified the land and the house of the LORD, Josiah sent Shaphan son of Azaliah

33:15 **temple mount:** *lit.* mount of the house of the LORD. 33:19 **the seers:** *so one MS; others* my seers. 33:20 **the garden-tomb of:** *prob. rdg, cp. 2 Kgs. 21:18; Heb. omits.* 33:21–25 *Cp. 2 Kgs. 21:19–24.* 34:1–2 *Cp. 2 Kgs. 22:1–2.* 34:8–32 *Cp. 2 Kgs. 22:3–23:3.*

Chronicler may have thought was due to some good on the king's part. **18:** The Gk. translation adds the penitential prayer of Manasseh, found in the Apocrypha.

34.1–35.27: Josiah, the faithful king (2 Kgs. chs. 22–23). In 2 Kgs. *Josiah's* great religious reform was a concentrated event after the discovery of the *scroll of the law;* here his purge of pagan practices preceded that discovery (vv. 14–18) and, indeed, lasted six years (vv. 3–7). The Chronicler's view is probably correct. **8–13:**

and Maaseiah the governor of the city and Joah son of Joahaz the secretary of state to repair the house of the LORD his God. [9] They came to Hilkiah the high priest and delivered to him the silver that had been brought to the house of God, the silver which the Levites, on duty at the threshold, had received from Manasseh, Ephraim, and all the rest of Israel, as well as from Judah and Benjamin and the inhabitants of Jerusalem. [10] It was then handed over to those supervising the work in the house of the LORD, and these men, working in the house, used it for repairing and strengthening the fabric; [11] they gave it also to the carpenters and builders to purchase hewn stone, and timber for rafters and beams, for the buildings which the kings of Judah had allowed to fall into disrepair. [12-13] The men did their work faithfully under the supervision of Jahath and Obadiah, Levites of the line of Merari, and Zechariah and Meshullam, members of the family of Kohath. These also had control of the bearers and directed the workmen of every trade. The Levites were all skilled musicians, and some of them were secretaries, clerks, or door-keepers.

[14] When they were fetching out the silver which had been brought to the house of the LORD, the priest Hilkiah discovered the scroll of the law of the LORD which had been given through Moses. [15] Hilkiah told Shaphan the adjutant-general that he had discovered the scroll of the law in the house of the LORD; [16] he gave the scroll to Shaphan, who brought it to the king and reported to him: 'Your servants are doing all that was entrusted to them. [17] They have melted down the silver in the house of the LORD and have handed it over to the supervisors of the work and the workmen.'

[18] Shaphan the adjutant-general also told the king of the scroll that the priest Hilkiah had given him; and he read from it in the king's presence. [19] When the king heard what was written in the scroll of the law, he tore his clothes. [20] He ordered Hilkiah, Ahikam son of Shaphan, Abdon son of Micah, Shaphan the adjutant-general, and Asaiah the king's attendant [21] to go and seek guidance of the LORD for himself and for all who still remained in Israel and Judah, about the con-

tents of the scroll that had been discovered. 'Great must be the wrath of the LORD,' he said, 'and it has been poured out on us, because our forefathers did not observe the LORD's command and do all that is written in this scroll.'

[22] Hilkiah and those whom the king had instructed went to Huldah the prophetess, wife of Shallum son of Tikvah, son of Hasrah, the keeper of the wardrobe, and consulted her at her home in the Second Quarter of Jerusalem. [23] 'This is the word of the LORD the God of Israel,' she answered: 'Tell the man who sent you to me [24] that this is what the LORD says: I am about to bring disaster on this place and its inhabitants, fulfilling all the imprecations recorded in the scroll which was read in the presence of the king of Judah, [25] because they have forsaken me and burnt sacrifices to other gods, provoking my anger with all the idols they have made with their own hands; for this my wrath will be poured out on this place and will not be quenched. [26] Tell the king of Judah who sent you to seek guidance of the LORD that this is what the LORD the God of Israel says: You have listened to my words [27] and shown a willing heart and humbled yourself before God when you heard what I said about this place and its inhabitants; you humbled yourself and tore your clothes and wept before me. Because of this, I for my part have listened to you. This is the word of the LORD. [28] Therefore I shall gather you to your forefathers, and you will be gathered to your grave in peace; you will not live to see all the disaster which I am bringing on this place and its inhabitants.' They brought back this answer to the king.

[29] At the king's summons all the elders of Judah and Jerusalem were assembled, [30] and he went up to the house of the LORD, taking with him all the men of Judah, the inhabitants of Jerusalem, the priests, and the Levites, the entire population, high and low. There he read out to them the whole scroll of the covenant which had been discovered in the house of the LORD. [31] Then, standing by the pillar, the king entered into a covenant

34:22 **had instructed:** *so Gk; Heb. omits.* **Tikvah:** *prob. rdg, cp. 2 Kgs. 22:14; Heb.* Tokhath.　　34:31 **by the pillar:** *or* on the dais.

Greater attention is paid here to the Levites and temple workers than in the source, 2 Kgs. 22.3–7. **29–33:** This is based on 2 Kgs. 23.1–20.

before the LORD to obey him and keep his commandments, his testimonies, and his statutes with all his heart and soul, and so carry out the terms of the covenant written in the scroll. 32 Then he took an oath, swearing with all who were present in Jerusalem to keep the covenant. Thereafter the inhabitants of Jerusalem did obey the covenant of God, the God of their forefathers. 33 Josiah removed all the abominable idols from the whole territory of the Israelites, so that everyone living in Israel might serve the LORD his God. As long as he lived they did not fail in their allegiance to the LORD the God of their forefathers.

35 Josiah kept a Passover to the LORD in Jerusalem, the Passover lamb being killed on the fourteenth day of the first month. 2 He appointed the priests to their offices and encouraged them in the service of the house of the LORD. 3 He said to the Levites, who instructed Israel and were dedicated to the LORD, 'Put the sacred Ark in the house which Solomon son of David king of Israel built. As it is not to be carried about on your shoulders, you are now to serve the LORD your God and his people Israel: 4 prepare yourselves by families according to your divisions, following the written instructions of David king of Israel and those of Solomon his son. 5 Stand in the Holy Place as representatives of the family groups of the lay people, your brothers, one division of Levites to each family group. 6 Kill the Passover lamb and hallow yourselves, and prepare for your brothers to fulfil the word of the LORD given through Moses.'

7 Josiah contributed on behalf of all the lay people present thirty thousand small livestock, that is young rams and goats, for the Passover, in addition to three thousand bulls; all these were from the king's own resources. 8 His officers contributed willingly for the people, the priests, and the Levites. Hilkiah, Zechariah, and Jehiel, the chief officers of the house of God, gave on behalf of the priests two thousand six hundred small livestock for the Passover, in addition to three hundred bulls. 9 Conaniah, Shemaiah and Nethanel his brothers, and Hashabiah, Jeiel, and Jozabad, the chiefs of the Levites, gave on behalf of the Levites for the Passover five thousand small livestock in addition to five hundred bulls.

10 When the service had been arranged, the priests stood in their places and the Levites in their divisions according to the king's command. 11 The Levites killed the Passover victims, and the priests flung the blood against the altar, while the Levites flayed the animals. 12 Then they removed the fat flesh, which they allocated to the people by groups of families for them to offer to the LORD, as prescribed in the book of Moses; and so with the bulls. 13 They cooked the Passover victims over the fire according to custom, and boiled the holy offerings in pots, cauldrons, and pans, and served them quickly to all the people.

14 After that they made the necessary preparations for themselves and the priests, because the priests of Aaron's line were engaged till nightfall in offering whole-offerings and the fat portions; so the Levites made the necessary preparations for themselves and for the priests of Aaron's line. 15 The Asaphite singers were in their places according to the rules laid down by David and by Asaph, Heman, and Jeduthun, the king's seers. The door-keepers stood, each at his gate; there was no need for them to leave their posts, because their kinsmen the Levites had made the preparations for them.

16 In this manner all the service of the LORD was arranged that day, to keep the Passover and to offer whole-offerings on the altar of the LORD, according to the command of King Josiah. 17 The people of Israel who were present kept the Passover at that time and the

34:32 to keep the covenant: *prob. rdg, cp. 2 Kgs. 23:3; Heb.* and Benjamin.   35:11 the blood: *so Syriac; Heb.* from their hand.   35:12 fat flesh: *or* whole-offering. 35:15 seers: *so some MSS; others* seer.

35.1–19: The Chronicler expands the brief report of a *Passover* observance in 2 Kgs. 23.21–23. As usual, the part of *the Levites* and the *singers* is emphasized. **3:** The statement here seems to imply that the *Ark* had been regularly moved for religious ceremonies prior to Josiah's time. The exact function of the *Ark* in the older temple service is obscure; see Jer. 3.16. **4:** *Written instructions of David:* see 1 Chr. chs. 23–26. **10–15:** Characteristically, the Chronicler reports the importance, absent from the source material, of the Levites and other temple workers. **16–19:** Based on 2 Kgs. 23.22–23. **18:** *Since the days of the prophet Samuel:* the meaning is, since the beginning of the monarchy; compare 2 Kgs. 23.22. This unique pilgrim-feast of Unleavened Bread for seven days. [18] No Passover like it had been kept in Israel since the days of the prophet Samuel; none of the kings of Israel had ever kept such a Passover as Josiah kept, with the priests and Levites and all Judah and Israel who were present and the inhabitants of Jerusalem. [19] This Passover was kept in the eighteenth year of Josiah's reign.

[20] Some time after Josiah had thus organized the entire service of the house of the LORD, King Necho marched up from Egypt to attack Carchemish on the Euphrates; Josiah went out to confront him. [21] Necho sent envoys, saying, 'King of Judah, what do you want with me? I have no quarrel with you today, only with those with whom I am at war. God has purposed, to speed me on my way, and God is on my side. Do not stand in his way, or he will destroy you.' [22] Josiah would not be deflected from his purpose but determined to fight; he refused to listen to Necho's words spoken at God's command, and he sallied out to join battle in the vale of Megiddo. [23] The archers shot at him; he was severely wounded and told his bodyguard to take him away. [24] They lifted him out of his chariot and conveyed him in his viceroy's chariot to Jerusalem. There he died and was buried among the tombs of his ancestors, and all Judah and Jerusalem mourned for him. [25] Jeremiah also made a lament for Josiah; and to this day the minstrels, both men and women, commemorate Josiah in their lamentations. Such laments have become traditional in Israel, and they are found in the written collections.

[26] The other events of Josiah's reign, and his works of piety, all performed in accordance with what is laid down in the law of the LORD, [27] and his acts from first to last are recorded in the annals of the kings of Israel and Judah.

The last kings of Judah

36 THE people of the land took Josiah's son Jehoahaz and made him king at Jerusalem in place of his father. [2] He was twenty-three years old when he came to the throne, and he reigned in Jerusalem for three months. [3] Then Necho king of Egypt removed him from the throne in Jerusalem and imposed on the land an indemnity of a hundred talents of silver and one talent of gold. [4] He made Jehoahaz's brother Eliakim king over Judah and Jerusalem in his place, and changed his name to Jehoiakim. He carried away his brother Jehoahaz to Egypt.

[5] Jehoiakim was twenty-five years old when he came to the throne, and he reigned in Jerusalem for eleven years. He did what was wrong in the eyes of the LORD his God. [6] King Nebuchadnezzar of Babylon launched an attack against him, put him in bronze fetters, and took him to Babylon. [7] Nebuchadnezzar also removed to Babylon some of the vessels of the house of the LORD and put them into his own palace there. [8] The other events of Jehoiakim's reign, including the abominations he committed, and everything of which he was held guilty, are recorded in the annals of the kings of Israel and Judah. His son Jehoiachin succeeded him.

[9] Jehoiachin was eight years old when he came to the throne, and he reigned in Jerusalem for three months and ten days. He did what was wrong in the eyes of the LORD. [10] At the turn of the year King Nebuchadnezzar sent and brought him to Babylon, together with the choicest vessels of the house of the LORD, and made his father's brother Zedekiah king over Judah and Jerusalem.

[11] Zedekiah was twenty-one years old when

36:1–4 *Cp. 2 Kgs. 23:30–34.*   36:9–10 *Cp. 2 Kgs. 24:8–17.*   36:10 **father's brother:** *so Gk; Heb.* brother.

Passover expressed the unity of all *Israel,* otherwise lacking throughout the monarchic period. **20–22:** Historically, *Josiah*'s policy of resistance to *Necho* arose from his collaboration with the Babylonians; see 2 Kgs. 23.29–30 n. Here that collaboration is viewed as a violation of God's will, expressed by the foreign king himself. This addition, by the Chronicler, explains how the otherwise righteous Josiah fell in battle. **25:** *Jeremiah* goes unmentioned in Kgs. Compare Jer. 22.10–11, 15.

36.1–23: The end of the Judean monarchy. The Chronicler condenses the account in 2 Kgs. 23.30–24.15, yet also adds to it, for example, v. 14. **1–4:** The brief reign of Jehoahaz, a condensation of 2 Kgs. 23.30–34. *Jehoiakim:* see 2 Kgs. 23.36–24.6. **6:** *Jehoiakim* actually died before the Babylonian king could capture and exile him; compare 2 Kgs. 24.1–6. **7:** This has been added by the Chronicler, see v. 10. **9–10:** *Jehoiachin:* again condensation (of 2 Kgs. 24.8–17) is present. **9:** *Eight:* The correct number is eighteen, as in 2 Kgs. 24.8. **11–13:** *Zedekiah:* This is much changed from 2 Kgs. 24.18–20, with the names of his mother and grandfather he came to the throne, and he reigned in Jerusalem for eleven years. [12] He did what was wrong in the eyes of the LORD his God; he did not defer to the guidance of the prophet Jeremiah, the spokesman of the LORD. [13] He also rebelled against King Nebuchadnezzar, who had laid on him a solemn oath of allegiance. He was stubborn and obstinate and refused to return to the LORD the God of Israel. [14] All the chiefs of Judah and the priests and the people became more and more unfaithful, following all the abominable practices of the other nations; and they defiled the house of the LORD which he had hallowed in Jerusalem.

[15] The LORD God of their forefathers had warned them time and again through his messengers, for he took pity on his people and on his dwelling-place; [16] but they never ceased to deride his messengers, scorn his words, and scoff at his prophets, until the anger of the LORD burst out against his people and could not be appeased. [17] He brought against them the king of the Chaldaeans, who put their young men to the sword in the sanctuary and spared neither young man nor maiden, neither the old nor the weak; God gave them all into his power.

[18] Nebuchadnezzar took all the vessels of the house of God, great and small, and the treasures of the house of the LORD and of the king and his officers—all these he took to Babylon. [19] They set fire to the house of God, razed to the ground the city wall of Jerusalem, and burnt down all its stately mansions and all the cherished possessions in them until everything was destroyed. [20] Those who escaped the sword he carried captive to Babylon, and they became slaves to him and his sons until the sovereignty passed to the Persians, [21] while the land of Israel ran the full term of its sabbaths. All the time that it lay desolate it kept the sabbath rest, to complete seventy years in fulfilment of the word of the LORD by the prophet Jeremiah.

[22] In the first year of King Cyrus of Persia, the LORD, to fulfil his word spoken through Jeremiah, inspired the king to issue throughout his kingdom the following proclamation, which he also put in writing:

[23] The decree of King Cyrus of Persia: The LORD the God of heaven has given me all the kingdoms of the earth, and he himself has charged me to build him a house at Jerusalem in Judah. Whoever among you belongs to his people, may the LORD his God be with him, and let him go up.

36:14 **Judah and:** *so Gk; Heb. omits.*   36:17–20 *Cp. 2 Kgs. 25:1–17.*   36:22–23 *Cp. Ezra 1:1–3.* 36:23 **be:** *prob. rdg, cp. Ezra 1:3; Heb. omits.*

omitted. **12:** See 35.25 n. On the reference here to *Jeremiah,* see Jer. 32.1–5; 37.1–10; 38.28. **14:** In the source, the blame for the end of the monarchy was placed on the wicked kings, not, as here, on *chiefs, priests,* and the *people.* Note that the Levites go unmentioned here. **15–16:** The ignoring of the *prophets* appears repeatedly, e.g. 12.5–8; 15.1–8; 19.1–3; and elsewhere. **17–21:** The account of the fall of Jerusalem and the beginning of the Exile is greatly abridged from 2 Kgs. 25.1–21. **21:** On *the sabbath rest,* see Lev. 26.33–45 and Jer. 25.11–12. **22–23:** These verses appear also in Ezra 1.1–3, an indication that the single book Ezra-Neh. was the continuation of Chr. Apparently the verses were the first written, but later they were repeated and incorporated here to abstain from an ending so negative as v. 21. In the MT, 2 Chr. is the last book; it was characteristic of later rabbinic thought that even passages of doom must end in hope.

THE BOOK OF
Ezra

The books of Chronicles, Ezra, and Nehemiah were originally a single unit which came to be separated (see Introduction to 1 Chronicles). The Book of Ezra deals with several episodes of the return to Zion by Judeans after the Babylonian Exile (587–539 B.C.E.); these episodes took place in both the sixth and the fifth centuries, and focus on Sheshbazzar, Zerubbabel, Ezra (who made two trips), and Nehemiah (who made two trips).

The book poses a number of historical and literary problems, the chief of which is that of sources and the sequence of materials. Two main sources used by the author, usually called the Chronicler, are the "Memoirs of Ezra" and the "Memoirs of Nehemiah" (narratives using first person forms). But some of the Nehemiah material appears in the Book of Ezra and some of the Ezra material is in the Book of Nehemiah, suggesting that materials were dislocated in the course of their transmission.

As a consequence, uncertainty attends the effort to determine whether Ezra and Nehemiah were contemporaries. If they were not, then problems arise as to whose career came first. In the order of the books in the Hebrew Bible, the Book of Ezra precedes the Book of Nehemiah, and the general impression suggests that priority belonged to Ezra. But serious doubts have been raised; for example, if Ezra came first, why does Nehemiah seem to ignore him? (See also 10.6 n.) Hence a frequent view adopted here concludes that Nehemiah preceded Ezra. Accordingly, the king of 7.1 is likely Artaxerxes II (404–359 B.C.E.); the king at the time of Nehemiah was Artaxerxes I (464–424 B.C.E.).

On the date of composition, probably the fourth century B.C.E. is to be adopted; see Introduction to 1 Chronicles.

Chapters 1–6 are not about Ezra but deal with a return from Babylonia led by Sheshbazzar (about 538 B.C.E.), and with further events of the time of Zerubbabel (about 516 B.C.E.); some scholars term these early chapters "The Book of Zerubbabel."

The material on Ezra himself is in Ezra chs. 7–10 and Neh. chs. 8–9.

Despite the problems, the prevailing interest in the book is clear. The returned exiles represent to the author the remnant of Israel who must exhibit fullest fidelity to, and conformity with, the Law of Moses. Hence, the community needed to reconstruct Jerusalem and the temple, and to maintain its sanctity in the midst of foreign peoples.

Return of exiles to Jerusalem

1 IN the first year of King Cyrus of Persia the LORD, to fulfil his word spoken through Jeremiah, inspired the king to issue throughout his kingdom the following proclamation, which he also put in writing:

2 The decree of King Cyrus of Persia.
The LORD the God of the heavens has

1.1–11: The return of the exiles to Jerusalem under Sheshbazzar. 1–3: These verses duplicate 2 Chr. 36.22–23; see annotation there. **1:** *The first year of Cyrus* was 538 B.C.E. Cyrus II's rule over Persia actually began in 557 B.C.E.; 538 is the date from the perspective of the Babylonians. The *word spoken through Jeremiah:* what to the Persians was undoubtedly an act of political expediency was to the Jews the fulfillment of God's promise as taught by Jeremiah (see Jer. 25.11–14; 29.10; compare Isa. 44.28; 45.1). Notices *in writing* were posted in public places. **2–4:** Compare the decree of Cyrus in vv. 2–4, which is in Heb., with the Aram. parallel in 6.3–5. The somewhat different versions both conform with what is known of the diplomatic policies given me all the kingdoms of the earth, and he himself has charged me to build him a house at Jerusalem in Judah. [3] Whoever among you belongs to his people, may his God be with him; and let him go up to Jerusalem in Judah, and build the house of the LORD the God of Israel, the God who is in Jerusalem. [4] Let every Jew left among us, wherever he is settled throughout the country, be helped by his neighbours with silver and gold, goods and livestock, in addition to the voluntary offerings for the house of God in Jerusalem.

[5] Thereupon the heads of families of Judah and Benjamin came forward, along with the priests and the Levites, all whom God had moved to go up and rebuild the house of the LORD in Jerusalem. [6] Their neighbours all supported them with gifts of every kind, silver and gold, goods and livestock and valuable gifts in abundance, in addition to everything given as a freewill-offering. [7] Moreover, King Cyrus brought out the vessels of the house of the LORD which Nebuchadnezzar had removed from Jerusalem and placed in the temple of his gods. [8] When King Cyrus of Persia brought them out he gave them into the charge of Mithredath the treasurer, who made an inventory of them for Sheshbazzar the ruler of Judah. [9] The list was as follows: thirty gold basins, a thousand silver basins, twenty-nine vessels of various kinds, [10] thirty gold dishes, four hundred and ten silver dishes of various types, and a thousand other vessels. [11] In all there were five thousand four hundred gold and silver vessels; and Sheshbazzar took them all up to Jerusalem, when the exiles were brought back there from Babylon.

2 Of the captives whom King Nebuchadnezzar of Babylon had taken into exile in Babylon, these were the people of the province who returned to Jerusalem and Judah, each to his own town. [2] They were led by Zerubbabel, Jeshua, Nehemiah, Seraiah, Re-elaiah, Mordecai, Bilshan, Mispar, Bigvai, Rehum, and Baanah.

The number of the men of the Israelite nation: [3] the line of Parosh two thousand one hundred and seventy-two; [4] the line of Shephatiah three hundred and seventy-two; [5] the line of Arah seven hundred and seventy-five; [6] the line of Pahath-moab, namely the lines of Jeshua and Joab, two thousand eight hundred and twelve; [7] the line of Elam one thousand two hundred and fifty-four; [8] the line of Zattu nine hundred and forty-five; [9] the line of Zaccai seven hundred and sixty; [10] the line of Bani six hundred and forty-two; [11] the line of Bebai six hundred and twenty-three; [12] the line of Azgad one thousand two hundred and twenty-two; [13] the line of Adonikam six hundred and sixty-six; [14] the line of Bigvai two thousand and fifty-six; [15] the line of Adin four hundred and fifty-four; [16] the line of Ater, namely that of Hezekiah, ninety-eight; [17] the line of Bezai three hundred and twenty-three; [18] the line of Jorah one hundred and twelve; [19] the line of Hashum two hundred and twenty-three; [20] the line of Gibbar ninety-five. [21] The men of Bethlehem one hundred and twenty-three; [22] the men of Netophah fifty-six; [23] the men of Anathoth one hundred and twenty-eight; [24] the men of Beth-azmoth forty-two; [25] the men of Kiriath-jearim, Kephirah, and Beeroth seven hundred and forty-three; [26] the men of Ramah and Geba six hundred and twenty-one; [27] the men of Michmas one hundred and twenty-two; [28] the men of Bethel and Ai two hundred and twenty-three; [29] the men of Nebo fifty-two; [30] the

1:4,6 **goods:** *or* pack-animals.   1:6 **with gifts ...**
silver: *prob. rdg, cp. 1 Esd. 2:9; Heb.* with vessels of
silver. **in abundance:** *prob. rdg, cp. 1 Esd. 2:9; Heb.*
apart.   2:1–70 *Cp. Neh. 7:6–73.*   2:6 **and Joab:**
prob. rdg, cp. Neh. 7:11; Heb. omits and.   2:21 **men:**
prob. rdg, cp. Neh. 7:26; Heb. line.   2:24 **the men of**
Beth-azmoth: *prob. rdg, cp. Neh. 7:28; Heb.* the line of
Azmoth.   2:25 **the men of Kiriath-jearim:** *prob. rdg,*
cp. Neh. 7:29; Heb. the line of Kiriath-arim.
2:26 **men:** *prob. rdg, cp. Neh. 7:30; Heb.* line.
2:29–35 **men:** *prob. rdg; Heb.* line.

of the early Persian Achaemenid kings (sixth–fourth centuries B.C.E.). **4:** *Left among us:* surviving (2 Chr. 36.20). **8:** *Mithredath:* Cyrus' treasurer. *Sheshbazzar* may be identical with a son of Jeconiah whose name in 1 Chr. 3.18 is given as Shenazzar and elsewhere as Shenabasar or Sheshbazzar. *Ruler:* leader. **11:** *In all:* see 1 Esd. 2.13–15.

2.1–70: The census of returnees, paralleled in Neh. 7.6–73. **2:** Possibly a composite list of those who at different times led groups of exiles home. **3–67:** Enumeration of the heads of families of Israel (Judah and Benjamin, see 1.5), various temple officials and servants (vv. 36–63), and animals (vv. 66–67). Some returnees are listed according to the name of the father, others according to place of origin. **41–42:** *Singers and* men of Magbish one hundred and fifty-six; [31] the men of the other Elam one thousand two hundred and fifty-four; [32] the men of Harim three hundred and twenty; [33] the men of Lod, Hadid, and Ono seven hundred and twenty-five; [34] the men of Jericho three hundred and forty-five; [35] the men of Senaah three thousand six hundred and thirty.

[36] The priests: the line of Jedaiah, of the house of Jeshua, nine hundred and seventy-three; [37] the line of Immer one thousand and fifty-two; [38] the line of Pashhur one thousand two hundred and forty-seven; [39] the line of Harim one thousand and seventeen.

[40] The Levites: the lines of Jeshua and Kadmiel, of the house of Hodaviah, seventy-four. [41] The singers: the line of Asaph one hundred and twenty-eight. [42] The guild of doorkeepers: the line of Shallum, the line of Ater, the line of Talmon, the line of Akkub, the line of Hatita, and the line of Shobai, one hundred and thirty-nine in all.

[43] The temple servitors: the line of Ziha, the line of Hasupha, the line of Tabbaoth, [44] the line of Keros, the line of Siaha, the line of Padon, [45] the line of Lebanah, the line of Hagabah, the line of Akkub, [46] the line of Hagab, the line of Shamlai, the line of Hanan, [47] the line of Giddel, the line of Gahar, the line of Reaiah, [48] the line of Rezin, the line of Nekoda, the line of Gazzam, [49] the line of Uzza, the line of Paseah, the line of Besai, [50] the line of Asnah, the line of the Meunim, the line of the Nephusim, [51] the line of Bakbuk, the line of Hakupha, the line of Harhur, [52] the line of Bazluth, the line of Mehida, the line of Harsha, [53] the line of Barkos, the line of Sisera, the line of Temah, [54] the line of Neziah, and the line of Hatipha.

[55] The descendants of Solomon's servants: the line of Sotai, the line of Hassophereth, the line of Peruda, [56] the line of Jaalah, the line of Darkon, the line of Giddel, [57] the line of Shephatiah, the line of Hattil, the line of Pochereth-hazzebaim, and the line of Ami.

[58] The temple servitors and the descendants of Solomon's servants amounted to three hundred and ninety-two in all.

[59] The following returned from Tel-melah, Tel-harsha, Kerub, Addan, and Immer, but could not prove by their father's line or their descent that they were Israelites: [60] the line of Delaiah, the line of Tobiah, and the line of Nekoda, six hundred and fifty-two. [61] Also of the priests: the line of Hobaiah, the line of Hakkoz, and the line of Barzillai who had married a daughter of Barzillai the Gileadite and went by his name. [62] When these searched for their names among those enrolled in the genealogies, they could not be traced, and so they were deemed disqualified and debarred from officiating. [63] The governor forbade them to partake of the most sacred food until there should be a priest able to consult the Urim and Thummim.

[64] The whole assembled people numbered forty-two thousand three hundred and sixty, [65] apart from their slaves, male and female, of whom there were seven thousand three hundred and thirty-seven; and they had two hundred male and female singers. [66] Their horses numbered seven hundred and thirty-six, their mules two hundred and forty-five, [67] their camels four hundred and thirty-five, and their donkeys six thousand seven hundred and twenty.

[68] On their arrival at the house of the LORD in Jerusalem, certain of the heads of families offered to rebuild the house of God on its original site. [69] According to their ability they gave to the treasury for the fabric a total of sixty-one thousand drachmas of gold, five thousand minas of silver, and one hundred priestly vestments.

[70] The priests, the Levites, and some of the people stayed in Jerusalem and the neighbourhood; the singers, the door-keepers and the temple servitors, and all the rest of the Israelites, lived in their own towns.

2:46 **Shamlai:** *or* Shalmai *(cp. Neh. 7:48).*   2:70 **in ... neighbourhood:** *prob. rdg, cp. 1 Esd. 5:46; Heb. omits.* **temple servitors:** *prob. rdg; Heb. adds* in their towns.

door-keepers: functionaries among the Levites. **43:** *Servitors:* Heb. *nethinim.* **63:** *Governor:* Sheshbazzar (1.8). The statement *until there should be a priest able to consult the Urim and the Thummin* (see 1 Sam. 14.41) refers ostensibly to the future when the use of the sacred lot would be reinstated, but the author apparently knew that that ancient practice was never reintroduced, as is clear from later rabbinic sources. **64:** The figure for *the whole assembled people* apparently included those from tribes not specified above. **65:** The *two hundred* were not the temple singers of v. 41, but entertainers (see 2 Sam. 19.35 or 2 Chr. 35.25), here morale boosters for the long journey. **69:** *Treasury for the fabric:* a reserve fund for building maintenance and repair. For a contrasting version of the quantities contributed, see Neh. 7.70–71.

Restoration of altar and temple

3 WHEN the seventh month came, the Israelites now being settled in their towns, the people came together with one accord to Jerusalem, 2 and Jeshua son of Jozadak along with his fellow-priests, and Zerubbabel son of Shealtiel, with his colleagues, set to work to build the altar of the God of Israel, in order to offer on it whole-offerings as prescribed in the law of Moses, the man of God. 3 They put the altar in place first, because they lived in fear of the foreign population; and they offered on it whole-offerings to the LORD, both morning and evening offerings. 4 They kept the pilgrim-feast of Booths as decreed, and offered whole-offerings every day in the number prescribed for each day; 5 in addition to these, they made the regular whole-offerings and the offerings for sabbaths, for new moons, and for all the sacred seasons appointed by the LORD, and all voluntary offerings made to the LORD. 6 The presentation of whole-offerings began from the first day of the seventh month, although the foundations of the temple of the LORD had not yet been laid. 7 Money was contributed for the masons and carpenters; the Sidonians and the Tyrians were supplied with food and drink and oil for bringing cedar trees from the Lebanon to the roadstead at Joppa. This was done by authority of King Cyrus of Persia.

8 In the second month of the second year, after they came to the house of God in Jerusalem, Zerubbabel son of Shealtiel and Jeshua son of Jozadak began the work. They were aided by all their fellow-Israelites, the priests and the Levites and all who had returned to Jerusalem from captivity. Levites who were aged twenty years and upwards were appointed to supervise the work of the house of the LORD. 9 Jeshua, with his sons and his kinsmen Kadmiel, Binnui, and Hodaviah, together assumed control of those doing the work on the house of God.

10 When the builders had laid the foundation of the temple of the LORD, the priests in their robes took their places with their trumpets, and the Levites, the sons of Asaph, with cymbals, to praise the LORD in the manner prescribed by King David of Israel. 11 They chanted praises and thanksgiving to the LORD, singing, 'It is good to give thanks to the LORD, for his love towards Israel endures for ever.' The whole people raised a great shout of praise to the LORD because the foundation of the LORD's house had been laid. 12 Many of the priests and Levites and heads of families, who were old enough to have seen the former house, wept and wailed aloud when they saw the foundation of this house laid, while many others shouted for joy at the tops of their voices. 13 The people could not distinguish the sound of the shout of joy from that of the weeping and wailing, so great was the shout which the people were raising, and the sound could be heard a long way off.

4 When those who were hostile to Judah and Benjamin heard that the returned exiles were building a temple to the LORD the God of Israel, 2 they approached Zerubbabel and Jeshua and the heads of families. 'Let us build with you,' they said, 'for like you we seek your God, and have sacrificed to him ever since the days of King Esarhaddon of Assyria who brought us here.' 3 But Zerubbabel and Jeshua and the rest of the heads of the Israelite families replied, 'It is not for you to share in building the house for our God;

3:5 **for sabbaths:** *prob. rdg, cp. 1 Esd. 5:52; Heb. omits.*
3:9 **Binnui, and Hodaviah:** *prob. rdg; Heb.* and his sons the line of Judah. **house of God:** *prob. rdg; Heb. adds* the line of Henadad, their sons, and their kinsmen the Levites. 3:11 **to give thanks to the LORD:** *prob. rdg, cp. Ps. 106:1; Heb. omits.*

3.1–13: Worship restored and the temple rebuilt. 1: *The seventh month:* Tishri (September–October); the date is regarded by some as 538 B.C.E., the first year of Cyrus (see 1.1 n.), but by others as 520, the second year of Darius. **3:** After *they put the altar in place,* the sacrifices for the sacred days could be offered (vv. 3–6). **7:** *Sidonians* and *Tyrians:* Phoenicians. Compare the account of Solomon's building of the temple in 2 Chr. 2.1–16. **8:** *The second month:* Iyyar (April–May). **10:** *Prescribed by King David:* see 2 Chr. 29.25–30.

4.1–6.23: Opposition to the efforts to rebuild. Verses 4.1–5 record opposition to rebuilding the *temple,* but vv. 6–23 to rebuilding the *walls* of Jerusalem. Verses 4.1–5 reflect the reigns of Cyrus, Cambyses (not mentioned in the book), and Darius I (though only the beginning), that is, the period 538–520 B.C.E. Verses 4.6–23, however, reflect the reign of Artaxerxes, namely, 464–424, and intrude into and interrupt the account in 4.1–6.22. **1:** *Those . . . hostile:* the Samaritans. **2:** See 2 Kgs. 17.24–28 on the non-Jewish origin of the we alone are to build it for the LORD the God of Israel, as his majesty King Cyrus of Persia commanded us.'

⁴Then the people of the land caused the Jews to lose heart and made them afraid to continue building; ⁵and, in order to thwart the purpose of the Jews, those people bribed officials at court to act against them. This continued throughout the lifetime of King Cyrus of Persia and into the reign of King Darius.

⁶At the beginning of the reign of Ahasuerus, the people of the land brought a charge in writing against the inhabitants of Judah and Jerusalem. ⁷In the days of King Artaxerxes of Persia, Tabeel and all his colleagues, with the agreement of Mithredath, wrote to the king; the letter was written in Aramaic and translated. (The following text is in Aramaic.)

⁸Rehum the high commissioner and Shimshai the secretary wrote a letter to King Artaxerxes concerning Jerusalem as follows:

⁹From Rehum the High Commissioner, Shimshai the Secretary, and all their colleagues, the judges, the commissioners, the overseers and chief officers, the men of Erech and Babylon, and the Elamites in Susa, ¹⁰and the other peoples whom the great and renowned Asnappar deported and settled in the city of Samaria and in the rest of the province of Beyond-Euphrates.

¹¹Here follows a copy of their letter:

To King Artaxerxes from his servants, the men of the province of Beyond-Euphrates. ¹²Be it known to your majesty that the Jews who left you to come here have arrived in Jerusalem. They are rebuilding that rebellious and wicked city; they are restoring the walls and repairing the foundations of the temple. ¹³Be it known to your majesty that, if their city is rebuilt and the walls are completed, they will pay nei-

ther general levy, nor poll tax, nor land tax, and in the end your royal house will suffer harm. ¹⁴Now, because we eat the king's salt and it is not right that we should witness the king's dishonour, therefore we have sent to bring it to your majesty's notice, ¹⁵in order that search may be made in the records left by your predecessors. You will discover by searching the records that this has been a rebellious city, harmful to the royal house and to the provinces, and that from earliest times sedition has been rife within its walls. For that reason it was laid in ruins. ¹⁶We submit to your majesty that, if this city is rebuilt and its walls are completed, the result will be that you will be denied a footing in the province of Beyond-Euphrates.

¹⁷The king sent this reply:

To Rehum the High Commissioner, Shimshai the Secretary, and all your colleagues resident in Samaria and in the rest of the province of Beyond-Euphrates. Greeting.

¹⁸The letter which you sent to me has now been translated and read in my presence. ¹⁹I ordered search to be made and that city, it was discovered, has a long history of opposition to the royal house, and rebellion and sedition have been rife in it. ²⁰There have been powerful kings ruling in Jerusalem and exercising authority over the whole province of Beyond-Euphrates; and general levy, poll tax, and land tax have been paid to them. ²¹Therefore, issue orders that these men must desist; this city is not to be rebuilt until a decree to that effect is issued by me. ²²See that you do not neglect your duty in this matter, lest more damage and harm result to the royal house.

²³When the copy of the letter from King Ar-

4:8 *The text in Aramaic continues to 6:18.*

Samaritans. **6:** *Ahasuerus:* Xerxes I (485–465). The verse, not part of vv. 7–23, seems out of place, but where it may belong is uncertain. **7–23:** The section appears to be misplaced, but it is no longer possible to determine its proper location. **7:** *Mithredath:* not to be confused with the man mentioned in 1.8. *With the agreement of:* Heb. *bishlam,* regarded by some as a proper name of a man to be associated with Mithredath and Tabeel. *Written in Aramaic:* probably the letter was both in the Aramaic language and also written in the Aramaic script (rather than in another alphabet). Aramaic was the official diplomatic language of the Persian Empire. **9:** The terms *judges, commissioners, overseers, and chief officers* translate words of uncertain meaning; they may be names of local peoples (such as *Erech* and *Babylon*) rather than official titles. **10:** *Asnappar:* probably Ashurbataxerxes was read before Rehum the high commissioner, Shimshai the secretary, and their colleagues, they went at once to Jerusalem and forcibly compelled the Jews to stop work. 24 From then onwards the work on the house of God in Jerusalem ceased; it remained at a standstill till the second year of the reign of King Darius of Persia.

5 The prophets Haggai and Zechariah son of Iddo prophesied to the Jews in Judah and Jerusalem, rebuking them in the name of the God of Israel. 2 Then Zerubbabel son of Shealtiel and Jeshua son of Jozadak, with the prophets of God at their side to help them, began at once to rebuild the house of God in Jerusalem. 3 Immediately Tattenai, governor of the province of Beyond-Euphrates, Shethar-bozenai, and their colleagues came to them and asked, 'Who has given you authority to rebuild this house and complete its furnishings?' 4 They also asked for the names of the men engaged in the building. 5 But the elders of the Jews were under God's watchful eye, and they were not prevented from continuing the work, until such time as a report should reach Darius and an official reply should be received.

6 Here follows a copy of the letter to King Darius sent by Tattenai, governor of the province of Beyond-Euphrates, Shethar-bozenai, and his colleagues, the inspectors in the province of Beyond-Euphrates. 7 This is the written report that they sent:

To King Darius.
  All greetings.
  8 Be it known to your majesty that we went to the province of Judah and found the house of the great God being rebuilt, with massive stones and beams set in the walls. The work was being done energetically and was making rapid headway under the direction of the elders. 9 We then enquired of them by whose authority they were building this house and completing the furnishings. 10 We also asked them for

their names, so that we might provide for your information a list of those in charge. 11 Their reply was as follows: 'We are servants of the God of heaven and earth, and we are rebuilding the house first erected many years ago; it was built and completed by a great king of Israel. 12 But because our forefathers provoked the anger of the God of heaven, he delivered them into the power of the Chaldaean, King Nebuchadnezzar of Babylon. The house was demolished and the people carried away captive to Babylon.

13 'But King Cyrus of Babylon in the first year of his reign issued a decree that this house of God should be rebuilt. 14 He brought out from the temple in Babylon the gold and silver vessels of the house of God, which Nebuchadnezzar had taken from the temple in Jerusalem and put in the temple in Babylon, and he delivered them to a man named Sheshbazzar, whom he had appointed governor. 15 He said to him, "Take these vessels; go and restore them to the temple in Jerusalem, and let the house of God be rebuilt on its original site." 16 Then this Sheshbazzar came and laid the foundations of the house of God in Jerusalem; and from that time until now the rebuilding has continued, and is still not completed.'

17 Now, therefore, if it please your majesty, let search be made in the royal treasury in Babylon, to discover whether a decree was issued by King Cyrus for the rebuilding of the house of God in Jerusalem, and let the king convey to us his wishes in the matter.

6 King Darius ordered search to be made in the archives where treasures were deposited in Babylon, 2 and there was found in Ecbatana, in the royal residence in the province of Media, a scroll on which was written the following memorandum:

3 In the first year of his reign King Cyrus

nipal (668–627 B.C.E.). **11–22:** The complaint (vv. 11–16) and the royal reply (vv. 17–22). **23:** The cessation of building.

4.24–5.17: The resumption of rebuilding. 24: See 4.1–6.23 n. **5.1:** *Haggai and Zechariah:* prophets whose books are preserved in Scripture. **8–17:** The report to the king seeks to ascertain whether proper channels have been consulted and proper authorization obtained. We are in the realm of bureaucracy, not hostility. **11:** *Great king:* Solomon. **12–14:** The conduct of the Chaldeans, who had destroyed the temple, and the Persian Achaemenids, who allowed its rebuilding, is skillfully contrasted.

6.1–22: Completion of the temple and celebration of Passover. 2: *Ecbatana,* modern Hamadan, was the issued this decree concerning the house of God in Jerusalem: Let the house be rebuilt as a place where sacrifices are offered and fire-offerings brought. Its height is to be sixty cubits and its breadth sixty cubits, 4 with three courses of massive stones to one course of timber, the cost to be defrayed from the royal treasury. 5 Also the gold and silver vessels of the house of God, which Nebuchadnezzar carried away from the temple in Jerusalem and brought to Babylon, are to be returned; they are all to be taken back to the temple in Jerusalem, and restored each to its place in the house of God.

6 Then King Darius issued this instruction:

Now, Tattenai, governor of the province of Beyond-Euphrates, Shethar-bozenai, and your colleagues, the inspectors in the province of Beyond-Euphrates, you are to keep away from the place, 7 and to leave the governor of the Jews and their elders free to rebuild this house of God; let them rebuild it on its original site. 8 I also issue an order prescribing what you are to do for these elders of the Jews, so that the said house of God may be rebuilt. Their expenses are to be defrayed in full from the royal funds accruing from the taxes of the province of Beyond-Euphrates, so that the work may not be brought to a standstill. 9 Let there be provided for them daily without fail whatever they need, young bulls, rams, and lambs as whole-offerings for the God of heaven, and wheat, salt, wine, and oil, as the priests in Jerusalem require, 10 so that they may offer soothing sacrifices to the God of heaven, and pray for the life of the king and his sons. 11 Furthermore, I decree that whoever tampers with this edict will have a beam torn out of his house, and he will be fastened erect to it and flogged; in addition, his house is to be razed to the ground. 12 May the God who made that place a dwelling for his name overthrow any king or people that presumes to tamper with

this edict or to destroy this house of God in Jerusalem.

I Darius have decreed it; let it be strictly obeyed.

13 Then Tattenai, governor of the province of Beyond-Euphrates, Shethar-bozenai, and their colleagues carried out to the letter the instructions which King Darius had sent them, 14 and the elders of the Jews went on with the rebuilding. Good progress was made with the sacred works, as the result of the prophecies of Haggai and Zechariah son of Iddo, and they finished the rebuilding as commanded by the God of Israel and according to the decrees of Cyrus and Darius and King Artaxerxes of Persia. 15 The house was completed on the third day of the month of Adar, in the sixth year of the reign of King Darius.

16 Then the Israelites, priests, Levites, and all the other exiles who had returned, celebrated the rededication of this house of God with great rejoicing. 17 At its rededication they offered one hundred bulls, two hundred rams, and four hundred lambs, and as a purification-offering for all Israel twelve he-goats, corresponding to the number of the tribes of Israel. 18 They re-established the priests in their groups and the Levites in their divisions for the service of God in Jerusalem, as prescribed in the book of Moses.

19 On the fourteenth day of the first month the returned exiles observed the Passover. 20 The priests and the Levites, one and all, had purified themselves; all of them were ritually clean, and they killed the Passover lamb for all the exiles who had returned, for their fellow-priests, and for themselves. 21 It was eaten by the Israelites who had returned from exile and by all who had held aloof from the peoples of the land and their uncleanness, and had sought the LORD the God of Israel. 22 They observed the pilgrim-feast of Unleavened Bread for seven days with rejoicing; for the LORD had given them cause

6:4 **one:** *prob. rdg; cp. 1 Esd. 6:25; Aram.* new.
6:6 **Then . . . instruction:** *prob. rdg, cp. 1 Esd. 6:27; Aram. omits.*

summer residence of the Persian kings. **4:** *Stones . . . timber:* such construction was usual. **7:** *Governor:* possibly Zerubbabel (see Hag. 2.21). **14:** Artaxerxes is mentioned in error, for he ruled after Darius I, and hence subsequent to the completion of the temple. **15:** The date corresponds to late March, 516 B.C.E. **16–18:** Compare 1 Kgs. ch. 8. **18:** No provision exists in the Pentateuch for the *priests in their groups* and *Levites in their divisions.* **19:** *First month:* Nisan, corresponding to March–April. Passover (the fourteenth of Nisan) falls for joy by changing the disposition of the Assyrian king towards them, so that he supported them in the work of the house of God, the God of Israel.

Ezra's mission to Jerusalem

7 IT was after these events, in the reign of King Artaxerxes of Persia, that Ezra came. He was the son of Seraiah son of Azariah, son of Hilkiah, ²son of Shallum, son of Zadok, son of Ahitub, ³son of Amariah, son of Azariah, son of Meraioth, ⁴son of Zerahiah, son of Uzzi, son of Bukki, ⁵son of Abishua, son of Phinehas, son of Eleazar, son of Aaron the chief priest. ⁶Ezra had come up from Babylon; he was a scribe, expert in the law of Moses which the LORD the God of Israel had given them. The king granted him everything he requested, for the favour of the LORD his God was with him.

⁷He was accompanied to Jerusalem by some Israelites, priests, Levites, temple singers, door-keepers, and temple servitors in the seventh year of King Artaxerxes. ⁸They reached Jerusalem in the fifth month, in the seventh year of the king. ⁹On the first day of the first month Ezra fixed the day for departure from Babylon, and on the first day of the fifth month he arrived at Jerusalem; the favour of God was with him, ¹⁰for he had devoted himself to the study and observance of the law of the LORD and to teaching statute and ordinance in Israel.

¹¹This is a copy of the letter which King Artaxerxes had given to Ezra the priest and scribe, a scribe versed in questions concerning the commandments and the statutes of the LORD laid upon Israel:

¹²Artaxerxes, King of Kings, to Ezra the priest and scribe learned in the law of the God of heaven.

This is my decision. ¹³I hereby issue a decree that any of the people of Israel or of its priests or Levites in my kingdom who volunteer to go to Jerusalem may go with you. ¹⁴You are sent by the king and his seven counsellors to consider the situation in Judah and Jerusalem with regard to the law of your God with which you are entrusted. ¹⁵You are also to convey the silver and gold which the king and his counsellors have freely offered to the God of Israel whose dwelling is in Jerusalem, ¹⁶together with any silver and gold that you may find throughout the province of Babylon, and the voluntary offerings of the people and of the priests which they freely offer for the house of their God in Jerusalem. ¹⁷In pursuance of this decree you are to expend the money solely on the purchase of bulls, rams, and lambs, and the proper grain-offerings and drink-offerings, to be offered on the altar in the house of your God in Jerusalem. ¹⁸Further, should any silver and gold be left over, it may be put to such use as you and your colleagues think fit, according to the will of your God. ¹⁹In the presence of the God of Jerusalem you are to hand over the vessels which have been given you for the service of the house of your God. ²⁰Any other expenses you may incur for the needs of the house of your God will be defrayed from the royal treasury.

²¹I, King Artaxerxes, hereby issue an order to all treasurers in the province of Beyond-Euphrates, to supply exactly to Ezra the priest, a scribe learned in the law of the God of heaven, whatever he may request of you, ²²up to one hundred talents of silver, one hundred kor of wheat, one hundred bath of wine, one hundred bath of oil, and salt without a set limit. ²³Let all the commands of the God of heaven be diligently fulfilled for the house of the God of

7:12–26 *The text of verses 12–26 is in Aramaic.*

six weeks after the third of Adar mentioned in v. 15. **22:** The end of "The Book of Zerubbabel"; see Introduction. *Assyrian king* is anachronistic, for Assyria had fallen in 612 B.C.E., about a hundred years earlier; but the phrase may simply mean a distant emperor ruling over what had been Assyria.

7.1–10.44: Ezra's mission to Jerusalem. "The Memoirs of Ezra" seem extracted from the personal diaries of Ezra himself; see Introduction. The entire biblical book received its name from these chapters. It is likely that this section belongs chronologically after Neh. chs. 1–7; the "Memoirs" continue in Neh. chs. 8–10. **1:** *Artaxerxes:* see Introduction. **6:** *Scribe* means teacher, rather than copyist. **9:** *The first month* was Nisan (March–April); *the fifth month* was Ab (July–August).

7.11–26: Artaxerxes' letter. Scholars disagree as to the precise nature and extent of Ezra's authority here granted, whether it was restricted to religious matters pertaining only to the returnees, or whether it included heaven; otherwise wrath may befall the realm of the king and his sons. 24 You are informed that you have no authority to impose a general levy, poll tax, or land tax on any of the priests, Levites, musicians, door-keepers, temple servitors, or other servants of this house of God.

25 You, Ezra, in accordance with the wisdom of your God with which you are entrusted, are to appoint arbitrators and judges to administer justice for all your people in the province of Beyond-Euphrates, all who acknowledge the laws of your God, and you with them are to instruct those who do not know those laws. 26 Whoever will not obey the law of your God and the law of the king, let judgement be rigorously executed on him, be it death, banishment, confiscation of property, or imprisonment.

27 Then Ezra the scribe said, 'Blessed is the LORD the God of our fathers who has put such a thing as this into the king's mind, to glorify the house of the LORD in Jerusalem, 28 and has made the king and his counsellors and all his high officers well disposed towards me!'

Encouraged by the help of the LORD my God, I gathered leading men out of Israel to 8 go up with me. 1 These are the heads of families, as registered, family by family, of those who went up with me from Babylon in the reign of King Artaxerxes: 2 of the line of Phinehas, Gershom; of the line of Ithamar, Daniel; of the line of David, Hattush 3 son of Shecaniah; of the line of Parosh, Zechariah, and with him a hundred and fifty males in the register; 4 of the line of Pahathmoab, Elihoenai son of Zerahiah, and with him two hundred males; 5 of the line of Zattu, Shecaniah son of Jahaziel, and with him three hundred males; 6 of the line of Adin, Ebed son of Jonathan, and with him fifty males; 7 of the line of Elam, Isaiah son of Athaliah, and with him seventy males; 8 of the

line of Shephatiah, Zebadiah son of Michael, and with him eighty males; 9 of the line of Joab, Obadiah son of Jehiel, and with him two hundred and eighteen males; 10 of the line of Bani, Shelomith son of Josiphiah, and with him a hundred and sixty males; 11 of the line of Bebai, Zechariah son of Bebai, and with him twenty-eight males; 12 of the line of Azgad, Johanan son of Hakkatan, and with him a hundred and ten males. 13 The last were the line of Adonikam, and these were their names: Eliphelet, Jeiel, and Shemaiah, and with them sixty males; 14 and the line of Bigvai, Uthai and Zabbud, and with them seventy males.

15 I assembled them by the river which flows towards Ahava, and we encamped there for three days. I checked the people and the priests, and finding no one there who was a Levite, 16 I sent to Eliezer, Ariel, Shemaiah, Elnathan, Jarib, Elnathan, Nathan, Zechariah, and Meshullam, prominent men, and Joiarib and Elnathan, men of discretion, 17 and instructed them to go to Iddo, the head of the settlement at Casiphia; and I gave them a message for him and his colleagues, the temple servitors there, asking that there should be sent to us men to serve in the house of our God. 18 Under the providence of God they sent us Sherebiah, a man of discretion, of the line of Mahli son of Levi, son of Israel, together with his sons and kinsmen, eighteen men in all; 19 also Hashabiah, together with Isaiah of the line of Merari, his kinsmen and their sons, twenty men; 20 besides two hundred and twenty temple servitors, an order instituted by David and his officers to assist the Levites. These were all indicated by name.

7:25 **to administer . . . your God:** *or* all of them versed in the laws of your God, to judge all the people in the province of Beyond-Euphrates.   7:27 **Then . . . said:** *prob. rdg; Heb. omits.*   **8:3 son of:** *prob. rdg; Heb. of the family of.*   **8:5 of Zattu:** *prob. rdg, cp. 1 Esd. 8:32; Heb. omits.*   **8:10 of Bani:** *prob. rdg, cp. 1 Esd. 8:36; Heb. omits.*   **8:14 Zabbud:** *or, as otherwise read,* Zaccur.

broad political powers over the entire province. **24:** The tax exemption of temple functionaries. **25:** *Laws of your God* hearkens back to vv. 6 and 14.

7.27–28: Ezra's thanksgiving prayer.

8.1–14: A list of returnees is given here, just as one is also given in ch. 2 for earlier returnees.

8.15–20: Recruitment of Levites. The locations of the canal/*river* and *Ahava* cannot be ascertained. **15:** *No . . . Levite:* in the list of earlier returnees the Levites (2.40) appear to have been few. **16:** There may be an erroneous duplication of the same names; *Elnathan* surprisingly occurs three times. **17:** *Casiphia:* its location is unknown.

²¹ I proclaimed a fast there by the river Ahava, so that we might mortify ourselves before our God and ask him for a straightforward journey for ourselves, our dependants, and all our possessions. ²² I was ashamed to apply to the king for an escort of infantry and cavalry to protect us against enemies on the way, for we had told him that the might of our God would ensure a successful outcome for all those who looked to him; but his fierce anger is on all who forsake him. ²³ So we fasted and asked our God for a safe journey, and he answered our prayer.

²⁴ Then I set apart twelve of the chiefs of the priests, together with Sherebiah and Hashabiah and ten of their kinsmen. ²⁵ I weighed out for them the silver and gold and the vessels, the contribution for the house of our God presented by the king, his counsellors and officers, and by all the Israelites there present, as their contribution to the house of our God. ²⁶ After weighing it, I handed over to them six hundred and fifty talents of silver, a hundred silver vessels weighing two talents, a hundred talents of gold, ²⁷ twenty gold dishes worth a thousand darics, and two vessels of a fine red copper, precious as gold. ²⁸ I said, 'Just as you are consecrated to the Lord, so too are the sacred vessels; the silver and gold are a voluntary offering to the Lord the God of your fathers. ²⁹ Guard them with all vigilance until you weigh them at Jerusalem in the rooms of the Lord's house in the presence of the chiefs of the priests, the Levites, and the heads of the families of Israel.' ³⁰ So the priests and the Levites received the consignment of silver and gold and vessels, to be taken to the house of God in Jerusalem.

³¹ On the twelfth day of the first month we struck camp at the river Ahava and set out for Jerusalem. Under the protection of our God, who saved us from enemy attack and ambush on the way, ³² we reached Jerusalem and rested there for three days. ³³ On the fourth day the silver and gold and vessels were weighed and handed over in the house

of our God into the charge of Meremoth son of Uriah the priest, with whom was Eleazar son of Phinehas; present with them were the Levites Jozabad son of Jeshua and Noadiah son of Binnui. ³⁴ Everything was counted and weighed and every weight recorded then and there.

³⁵ Those who had returned from captivity offered as whole-offerings to the God of Israel twelve bulls for all Israel, ninety-six rams, and seventy-seven lambs, with twelve he-goats as a purification-offering; all these were offered as a whole-offering to the Lord. ³⁶ They also delivered the king's commission to the royal satraps and governors in the province of Beyond-Euphrates; and these gave support to the people and the house of God.

Measures against mixed marriages

9 Once this business had been concluded, the leaders came to me and said, 'The people of Israel, including even priests and Levites, have not kept themselves apart from the alien population and from the abominable practices of the Canaanites, Hittites, Perizzites, Jebusites, Ammonites, Moabites, Egyptians, and Amorites. ² They have taken women of these nations as wives for themselves and their sons, so that the holy race has become mixed with the alien population; and the leaders and magistrates have been the chief offenders.'

³ At this news I tore my robe and mantle; I plucked tufts from my beard and the hair of my head and sat appalled. ⁴ All who went in fear of the words of the God of Israel gathered round me because of the offence of these exiles; and I sat appalled until the evening sacrifice. ⁵ Then, at the evening sacrifice, with my robe and mantle torn, I rose from my self-abasement and, kneeling down, held out my hands in prayer to the Lord my God.

8:24 **together with:** *prob. rdg; cp. 1 Esd. 8:54; Heb. omits.*

8.21–36: The preparation for leaving (vv. 21–30); **the journey** (31–32); **the arrival in Jerusalem** (33–36). **21–23:** The *fast* and prayer were usual devotional preparations for a new venture. **22:** *Ashamed to apply:* Ezra, a priest, believed that God would protect the people, without need of soldiers; Nehemiah, designated the governor (Neh. 12.26), went to Jerusalem with an escort of army officers with cavalry (Neh. 2.9). **26–27:** The amounts here are regarded as exaggerated. **31–32:** See 7.9; the journey took four months. **36:** *The king's commission* presumably spelled out to the local rulers the precise extent of Ezra's authority.

9.1–15: Mixed marriages. 2: *Holy race:* see v. 11–12.

⁶'I am humiliated, my God,' I said, 'I am ashamed, my God, to lift my face to you. Our sins tower above us, and our guilt is so great that it reaches high heaven. ⁷From the days of our forefathers down to this present day our guilt has been great. Because of our iniquities we and our kings and priests have been given into the power of foreign rulers to be killed, taken captive, pillaged, and humiliated to this very day. ⁸But now, for a brief moment, the LORD our God has been gracious to us, leaving us some survivors and giving us a foothold in his holy place; our God has brought light to our eyes again and given us some chance to renew our lives in our slavery. ⁹For slaves we are; nevertheless, our God has not forsaken us in our slavery, but has secured for us the favour of the kings of Persia: they have provided us with the means of renewal, so that we may repair the house of our God and rebuild its ruins, thereby giving us a wall of defence for Judah and Jerusalem.

¹⁰'Now, our God, in the face of this, what are we to say? For we have neglected your commandments, ¹¹given us through your servants the prophets. You said: "The land which you are going to occupy is a land defiled with the pollution of its heathen population and their abominable practices; they have filled it with their impure ways from end to end. ¹²Now therefore do not marry your daughters to their sons or take their daughters for your sons; nor must you ever seek their welfare or prosperity. Only thus will you be strong and enjoy the good things of the land, and hand it on as an everlasting possession to your descendants." ¹³After all that has come upon us through our evil deeds and great guilt—although you, our God, have punished us less than our iniquities deserved and have allowed us to survive as now we do—¹⁴shall we once again disobey your commands and intermarry with peoples who indulge in such abominable practices? Would you not be so angry with us as to

destroy us till no remnant, no survivor was left? ¹⁵LORD God of Israel, you are just; for we today are a remnant that has survived. In all our guilt we are here before you; because of it we can no longer stand in your presence.'

10 While Ezra was praying and making confession, prostrate in tears before the house of God, there gathered round him a vast throng of Israelites, men, women, and children, and there was widespread lamentation among the crowd. ²Shecaniah son of Jehiel, one of the family of Elam, spoke up and said to Ezra, 'We have broken faith with our God in taking foreign wives from the peoples of the land. But in spite of this, there is still hope for Israel. ³Let us now pledge ourselves to our God to get rid of all such wives with their children, according to your counsel, my lord, and the counsel of those who go in fear of the command of our God; and let the law take its course. ⁴Rise up, the matter is in your hands; and we are with you. Take strong action!' ⁵Ezra got up and put the chiefs of the priests, the Levites, and all the Israelites on oath to act in this way, and they took the oath. ⁶Ezra then left the forecourt of the house of God and went to the room of Jehohanan grandson of Eliashib. He stayed there, eating no bread and drinking no water, for he was still mourning for the unfaithfulness of the returned exiles.

⁷A proclamation was issued throughout Judah and Jerusalem directing all the returned exiles to assemble at Jerusalem. ⁸If any failed to arrive within three days, as decided by the chief officers and the elders, they were to have all their property confiscated and would themselves be excluded from the community that had come from exile.

⁹Three days later, on the twentieth day of the ninth month, all the men of Judah and Benjamin had assembled in Jerusalem, where they all sat in the open space before

10:6 **stayed:** *prob. rdg, cp. 1 Esd. 9:2; Heb.* went.

9.10–15: Ezra's prayer for forgiveness. 11–12: *You said:* an exact quotation from Scripture is expected, but does not appear, as is the case too in Neh. 1.8–9; only an echo of general ideas (e.g. Lev. 18.24–30 or Deut. 7.1–3) is given. **11:** The Heb. word for *pollution* is used in Lev. ch. 15 (and elsewhere) for sexual impurity, a result of the *abominable practices* of the natives.

10.1–44: The divorce of Gentile wives. The drastic step was deemed necessary to preserve the Hebrew faith unadulterated (compare also 1 Kgs. 11.1–13). **6:** The Heb. *ben* can mean grandson as well as son. Despite some uncertainties, it would seem from Neh. 13.28 that *Jehohanan* was the grandson of *Eliashib* and son of Jehoiada. In Neh. 3.1, Eliashib is identified as contemporaneous with Nehemiah. Here the grandson is the house of God, full of apprehension and shivering in the heavy rain. 10 Ezra the priest stood up and addressed them: 'You have broken faith in marrying foreign women,' he said 'and have added to Israel's guilt. 11 Now, make confession to the LORD the God of your fathers; do his will, cut yourselves off from the peoples of the land and from your foreign wives.'

12 The whole company assented loudly, saying, 'We shall do as you say! 13 But', they added, 'our numbers are great; it is the rainy season and we cannot stay out in the open. Besides, this is not the work of one or two days only, for the offence is rife amongst us. 14 Let our leading men act for the whole assembly, and let all those who have married foreign wives present themselves at stated times, accompanied by the elders and judges for each town, until our God's fierce anger at what has been done is averted from us.' 15 Only Jonathan son of Asahel and Jahzeiah son of Tikvah, supported by Meshullam and Shabbethai the Levite, opposed this.

16 The returned exiles duly put this into effect, and Ezra the priest selected, each by name, certain men, heads of households representing their families. They met in session to investigate the matter on the first day of the tenth month, 17 and by the first day of the first month the enquiry into all the marriages with foreign women was brought to a conclusion.

18 Among the members of priestly families who had married foreign women were found Maaseiah, Eliezer, Jarib, and Gedaliah, of the line of Jeshua son of Jozadak, and his brothers. 19 They pledged themselves to dismiss their wives, and to offer a ram from the flock as a reparation-offering for their offence. 20 Of the line of Immer: Hanani and Zebadiah. 21 Of the line of Harim: Maaseiah, Elijah, Shemaiah, Jehiel, and Uzziah. 22 Of the line of Pashhur: Elioenai, Maaseiah, Ishmael, Nethanel, Jozabad, and Elasah.

23 Of the Levites: Jozabad, Shimei, Kelaiah (that is Kelita), Pethahiah, Judah, and Eliezer. 24 Of the singers: Eliashib. Of the doorkeepers: Shallum, Telem, and Uri.

25 And of Israel: of the line of Parosh: Ramiah, Izziah, Malchiah, Mijamin, Eleazar, Malchiah, and Benaiah. 26 Of the line of Elam: Mattaniah, Zechariah, Jehiel, Abdi, Jeremoth, and Elijah. 27 Of the line of Zattu: Elioenai, Eliashib, Mattaniah, Jeremoth, Zabad, and Aziza. 28 Of the line of Bebai: Jehohanan, Hananiah, Zabbai, and Athlai. 29 Of the line of Bani: Meshullam, Malluch, Adaiah, Jashub, Sheal, and Jeremoth. 30 Of the line of Pahath-moab: Adna, Kelal, Benaiah, Maaseiah, Mattaniah, Bezalel, Binnui, and Manasseh. 31 Of the line of Harim: Eliezer, Isshiah, Malchiah, Shemaiah, Simeon, 32 Benjamin, Malluch, and Shemariah. 33 Of the line of Hashum: Mattenai, Mattattah, Zabad, Eliphelet, Jeremai, Manasseh, and Shimei. 34 Of the line of Bani: Maadai, Amram and Uel, 35 Benaiah, Bedeiah and Keluhi, 36 Vaniah, Meremoth, Eliashib, 37 Mattaniah, Mattenai, and Jaasau. 38 Of the line of Binnui: Shimei, 39 Shelemiah, Nathan and Adaiah, 40 Maknadebai, Shashai and Sharai, 41 Azarel, Shelemiah and Shemariah, 42 Shallum, Amariah, and Joseph. 43 Of the line of Nebo: Jeiel, Mattithiah, Zabad, Zebina, Jaddai, Joel, and Benaiah. 44 All these had married foreign women, and they dismissed them, together with their children.

10:16 **and . . . selected:** *prob. rdg, cp. 1 Esd. 9:16; Heb. obscure.* 10:38 **Of the line of:** *prob. rdg, cp. 1 Esd. 9:34; Heb.* and Bani and. 10:44 **and they . . . children:** *prob. rdg, cp. 1 Esd. 9:36; Heb.* and some of them were women; and they had borne sons.

contemporaneous with Ezra. **9:** *The ninth month* was Kislev (November–December), a rainy period. **15:** These opponents (*Jonathan, Jahzeiah, Meshullam, Shabbethai*) are not otherwise identified. **16:** *Tenth month:* Tebeth (December–January). **17:** *The first month* was Nisan (March–April). **18–43:** The list numbers over one hundred offenders, a fraction of the total populace. Perhaps only the names of the prominent persons are given, but others too were implicated. **19:** *A reparation-offering* is not specifically prescribed in Scripture for marriage to a non-Israelite spouse; it could have been an ad hoc decision by the leaders of v. 16. **44:** *Children:* see Tfn.

THE BOOK OF
Nehemiah

The books of Ezra and Nehemiah are part of the same writing; the Introduction to Ezra treats literary and chronological problems of Nehemiah too.

The events described in the Book of Nehemiah (except chs. 8–9) took place during the reign of the Persian king, Artaxerxes I (464–424 B.C.E.). Nehemiah, who lived in Susa, the Persian capital, made two visits to Jerusalem. The first was in 445/444 B.C.E. (1.1; 2.1), and lasted for twelve years (until 433/432); see 5.14. The second visit was some time after this, but before the death of Artaxerxes I (13.6–7).

The material here, like that in Ezra, consists of several distinct genres. Nehemiah's memoirs provide personal reflections on the events of the day, a number of prayers, and accounts of his determination to ameliorate the position of the downtrodden Judeans. In addition, there are census lists, a psalm of confession and repentance, and a record of rededication to the service of God.

Nehemiah's mission

1 THE narrative of Nehemiah son of Hacaliah.

In the month of Kislev in the twentieth year, when I was in Susa the capital city, it happened [2] that one of my brothers, Hanani, arrived with some other Judaeans. I asked them about Jerusalem and about the Jews, the families still remaining of those who survived the captivity. [3] They told me that those who had survived the captivity and still lived in the province were facing dire trouble and derision; the wall of Jerusalem was broken down and its gates had been destroyed by fire.

[4] When I heard this news, I sat and wept, mourning for several days, fasting and praying before the God of heaven. [5] This was my prayer: 'LORD God of heaven, great and terrible God faithfully keeping covenant with those who love him and observe his commandments, [6] let your ear be attentive and your eyes open to my humble prayer, which now day and night I make in your presence on behalf of your servants, the people of Israel. I confess the sins which we Israelites have committed against you, and of which my father's house and I are also guilty. [7] We have acted very wrongly towards you and have not observed the commandments, statutes, and rules which you enjoined on your servant Moses.

[8] 'Remember what you impressed on him when you said: "If you are unfaithful, I shall scatter you among the nations; [9] but if you return to me and observe my commandments and fulfil them, I shall gather those of you who have been scattered to the far corners of the world and bring you to the place

1.1–2.10: Nehemiah's commission: *Susa* was the winter residence of the Persian kings after 521 B.C.E. Nehemiah, the royal cupbearer (1.11), was an influential court figure. **1:** *Kislev:* November–December. *The twentieth year* alludes to the reign of Artaxerxes I (mentioned in 2.1) and would be 445/444 B.C.E. Nisan (March–April) is described as still "in the twentieth year" in 2.1, where we would expect the twenty-first, for the Babylonian year ran from spring to spring. But possibly the years here are reckoned from Tishri (September–October) and are regnal years, differing from ordinary calendar years. **2:** While *brothers* can mean friends or colleagues, 7.2 suggests that Hanani was a real brother. *The families still remaining* had continued in Jerusalem when substantial parts of the population went into exile after 587 B.C.E. **3:** *Broken down . . . destroyed:* this seems to allude to an obscure disaster after the time of Cyrus (538–529 B.C.E.); Nehemiah has had no prior knowledge of it. **5–11:** The structure of Nehemiah's prayer is praise, supplication, confession, supplication. **8–9:** An exact quotation from the Pentateuch is expected but does not appear; perhaps Deut.

I have chosen as a dwelling for my name."

10 'They are your servants and people, whom you have redeemed with your great might and your strong hand. 11 Lord, let your ear be attentive to my humble prayer, and to the prayer of your servants who delight to revere your name. Grant me success this day, and put it into this man's heart to show me kindness.' I was then cupbearer to the king.

2 One day, in the month of Nisan, in the twentieth year of King Artaxerxes, when his wine was ready, I took it and handed it to the king, and as I stood before him my face revealed my unhappiness. 2 The king asked, 'Why do you look so unhappy? You are not ill; it can be nothing but a feeling of unhappiness.' I was very much afraid, 3 but I answered, 'May the king live for ever! But how can I help looking unhappy when the city where my forefathers are buried lies in ruins with its gates burnt down?' 4 'What then do you want?' asked the king. With a prayer to the God of heaven, 5 I answered, 'If it please your majesty, and if I enjoy your favour, I beg you to send me to Judah, to the city where my forefathers are buried, so that I may rebuild it.' 6 The king, with the queen consort sitting beside him, asked me, 'How long will the journey last, and when will you return?' When I told him how long I should be, the king approved the request and let me go.

7 I then said to him, 'If it please your majesty, let letters be given me for the governors in the province of Beyond-Euphrates, with orders to grant me safe passage until I reach Judah. 8 Let me have also a letter for Asaph, the keeper of your royal forests, instructing him to supply me with timber to make beams for the gates of the citadel, which adjoins the temple, and for the city wall, and for the temple which is the object of my journey.' The king granted my requests, for the gracious hand of my God was upon me.

The city walls rebuilt

9 I CAME in due course to the governors in the province of Beyond-Euphrates and presented the king's letters to them; the king had given me an escort of army officers with cavalry. 10 But when Sanballat the Horonite and the slave Tobiah, an Ammonite, heard this, they were greatly displeased that someone should have come to promote the interests of the Israelites.

11 WHEN I arrived in Jerusalem, I waited three days. 12 Then I set out by night, taking a few men with me, but without telling anyone what my God was prompting me to do for Jerusalem. Taking no beast with me except the one on which I myself rode, 13 I went out by night through the Valley Gate towards the Dragon Spring and the Dung Gate; and I inspected the places where the walls of Jerusalem had been broken down, and its gates, which had been destroyed by fire. 14 Then I passed on to the Fountain Gate and the King's Pool; but there was no room for me to ride through. 15 I went up the valley by night and inspected the city wall; then I re-entered the city through the Valley Gate. So I arrived back 16 without the magistrates knowing where I had been or what I was doing, for I had not yet told the Jews, neither the priests, the nobles, the magistrates, nor any of those who would be responsible for the work.

17 Then I said to them, 'You see what trouble we are in: Jerusalem lies in ruins, its gates destroyed by fire. Come, let us rebuild the wall of Jerusalem and suffer derision no more.' 18 I told them also how the gracious hand of my God had been upon me and also what the king had said to me. They replied, 'Let us start the rebuilding,' and they set about the work vigorously and to good purpose.

19 But when Sanballat the Horonite, To-

30.1–5 is being echoed. **11:** *Let your ear be attentive* is not a needless repetition of the same phrase in v. 6, but, rather, climaxes Nehemiah's prayer. *This man's heart* refers to Artaxerxes I. See 2.1.

2.1–10: Beginning of Nehemiah's mission in Jerusalem. 1: On the date, see 1.1 n. Note the similarity in the cupbearer of 2.1 to Gen. 40.1, and "Why do you look so unhappy?" (2.2) to Gen. 40.7. **8:** The *citadel* is mentioned again in 7.2. **10:** *Sanballat, Tobiah:* see 2.19 n.

2.11–3.32: The walls of Jerusalem rebuilt. 12: *By night:* a secret inspection. **13:** Nehemiah begins at the *Valley Gate,* apparently at the southwest corner of the walled city, and proceeds eastward, then northward. **19:** The three opponents were very influential men. *Sanballat the Horonite* (mentioned in the Elephantine papyri of the late fifth century B.C.E.) was governor of Samaria; he was related by marriage to the High Priest, biah the Ammonite slave, and Geshem the Arab heard of it, they jeered at us, asking contemptuously, 'What is this you are doing? Is this a rebellion against the king?' 20 But I answered, 'The God of heaven will grant us success. We, his servants, are making a start with the rebuilding. But you have no stake, or claim, or traditional right in Jerusalem.'

3 Eliashib the high priest and his fellow-priests set to work and rebuilt the Sheep Gate. They laid its beams and put its doors in place; they carried the work as far as the Tower of the Hundred and the Tower of Hananel, and consecrated it. 2 The men of Jericho worked next to Eliashib; and next to them Zaccur son of Imri.

3 The Fish Gate was built by the sons of Hassenaah; they laid its tie-beams and put its doors in place with their bolts and bars. 4 Next to them Meremoth son of Uriah, son of Hakkoz, repaired his section; next to them Meshullam son of Berechiah, son of Meshezabel; next to them Zadok son of Baana did the repairs; 5 and next again the men of Tekoa did the repairs, but their nobles would not demean themselves to serve their governor.

6 The Jeshanah Gate was repaired by Joiada son of Paseah and Meshullam son of Besodeiah; they laid its tie-beams and put its doors in place with their bolts and bars. 7 Next to them Melatiah the Gibeonite and Jadon the Meronothite, the men of Gibeon and Mizpah, did the repairs in the service of the governor of the province of Beyond-Euphrates. 8 Next to them Uzziel son of Harhaiah, a goldsmith, did the repairs, and next Hananiah of the perfumers' guild; they reconstructed Jerusalem as far as the Broad Wall. 9 Next to them Rephaiah son of Hur, ruler of half the district of Jerusalem, did the repairs. 10 Next to them Jedaiah son of Harumaph did the repairs opposite his own house; and next Hattush son of Hashabniah. 11 Malchiah son of Harim and Hasshub son of Pahath-moab repaired a second section including the Tower of the Ovens. 12 Next to them Shallum son of Hallohesh, ruler of half

the district of Jerusalem, did the repairs with the help of his daughters.

13 The Valley Gate was repaired by Hanun and the inhabitants of Zanoah; they rebuilt it and put its doors in place with their bolts and bars, and they repaired a thousand cubits of the wall as far as the Dung Gate. 14 The Dung Gate itself was repaired by Malchiah son of Rechab, ruler of the district of Beth-hakkerem; he rebuilt it and put its doors in place with their bolts and bars. 15 The Fountain Gate was repaired by Shallun son of Col-hozeh, ruler of the district of Mizpah; he rebuilt and roofed it and put its doors in place with their bolts and bars; and he built the wall of the Pool of Shelah next to the king's garden and onwards as far as the steps leading down from the City of David.

16 After him Nehemiah son of Azbuk, ruler of half the district of Beth-zur, did the repairs as far as a point opposite the burial-place of David, as far as the artificial pool and the barracks. 17 After him the Levites did the repairs: Rehum son of Bani and next to him Hashabiah, ruler of half the district of Keilah, did the repairs for his district. 18 After him their kinsmen did the repairs: Binnui son of Henadad, ruler of half the district of Keilah; 19 next to him Ezer son of Jeshua, ruler of Mizpah, repaired a second section opposite the point at which the ascent meets the escarpment; 20 after him Baruch son of Zabbai repaired a second section, from the escarpment to the door of the house of Eliashib the high priest. 21 After him Meremoth son of Uriah, son of Hakkoz, repaired a second section, from the door of Eliashib's house to the end of his house.

22 After him the priests of the neighbourhood of Jerusalem did the repairs. 23 Next Benjamin and Hasshub did the repairs opposite their own house; and next Azariah son of

3:1 **laid its beams:** *prob. rdg; Heb.* consecrated it. 3:6 **Jeshanah Gate:** *or* gate of the Old City. 3:8 **a goldsmith:** *so Syriac; Heb.* goldsmiths. 3:14 **rebuilt:** *prob. rdg; Heb.* will rebuild. 3:15 **rebuilt:** *prob. rdg; Heb.* will rebuild. 3:20 **son of Zabbai:** *so some MSS; others add* inflamed.

Eliashib (13.28). *Tobiah* was a *slave,* not to Sanballat, but to the Persian king; *the Ammonite slave* here probably means agent (perhaps even governor), with jurisdiction in Ammon.

3.1–32: The reconstruction of the wall. The description indicates that the construction began at the northern part of the city and moved in a counterclockwise direction. **1:** *Eliashib* was the grandson of the high priest Jeshua (12.10; see Zech. 3.1) and grandfather of Jehohanan, a later high priest (Ezra 10.6). **3–32:** The groupings of the builders are according to priestly or levitical identity, place of origin, or membership in a craft guild.

Maaseiah, son of Ananiah, did the repairs beside his house. 24 After him Binnui son of Henadad repaired a second section, from the house of Azariah as far as the escarpment and the corner. 25 Palal son of Uzai worked opposite the escarpment and the upper tower which projects from the king's house and belongs to the court of the guard. After him Pedaiah son of Parosh 26 worked as far as a point on the east opposite the Water Gate and the projecting tower. 27 Next the men of Tekoa repaired a second section, from a point opposite the great projecting tower as far as the wall of Ophel.

28 Above the Horse Gate the priests did the repairs opposite their own houses. 29 After them Zadok son of Immer did the repairs opposite his own house; after him Shemaiah son of Shecaniah, the keeper of the East Gate, did the repairs. 30 After him Hananiah son of Shelemiah, along with Hanun, sixth son of Zalaph, repaired a second section. After him Meshullam son of Berechiah did the repairs opposite his room. 31 After him Malchiah, a goldsmith, did the repairs as far as the house of the temple servitors and the merchants, opposite the Mustering Gate, as far as the roof-chamber at the corner. 32 Between the roof-chamber at the corner and the Sheep Gate the goldsmiths and merchants did the repairs.

4 THE news that we were rebuilding the wall roused the indignation of Sanballat, and angrily he jeered at the Jews, 2 saying in front of his companions and of the garrison in Samaria, 'What do these feeble Jews think they are doing? Do they mean to reconstruct the place? Do they hope to offer sacrifice and finish the work in a day? Can they make stones again out of heaps of rubble, and burnt rubble at that?' 3 Tobiah the Ammonite, who was beside him, said, 'Whatever it is they are building, if a fox climbs up their stone walls, it will break them down.'

4 Hear, our God, how we are treated with contempt. Make their derision recoil on their own heads; let them become objects of contempt in a land of captivity. 5 Do not condone their guilt or let their sin be struck off the record, for they have openly provoked the builders.

6 We built up the wall until it was continuous all round up to half its height; and the people worked with a will. 7 But when Sanballat and Tobiah, and the Arabs and Ammonites and Ashdodites, heard that the new work on the walls of Jerusalem had made progress and that the closing up of the breaches had gone ahead, they were furious, 8 and all banded together to launch an attack on Jerusalem and create confusion. 9 So we prayed to our God, and posted a guard against them day and night.

10 In Judah it was said:

'The labourers' strength has failed,
and there is too much rubble;
by ourselves we shall never be able
to rebuild the wall.'

11 Our adversaries said, 'Before they know it or see anything, we shall be upon them, killing them and putting an end to the work.' 12 When the Jews living nearby came into the city, they warned us a dozen times that our adversaries would gather from every place where they lived to attack us, 13 and that they would station themselves on the lowest levels below the wall, on patches of open ground. Accordingly I posted my people by families, armed with swords, spears, and bows. 14 Then having surveyed the position I addressed the nobles, the magistrates, and the rest of the people. 'Do not be afraid of them,' I said. 'Remember the Lord, great and terrible, and fight for your brothers, your sons and daughters, your wives and your homes.' 15 When our enemies heard that everything was known to us, and that God had frustrated their plans, we all returned to the wall, each to his task.

16 From that day forward half the men under me were engaged in the actual building, while the other half stood by holding their spears, shields, and bows, and wearing coats of mail; and officers supervised all the people of Judah 17 who were engaged on the wall. The porters carrying the loads held their load with one hand and a weapon with the other. 18 The builders had their swords attached to their belts as they built. The trumpeter stayed beside me, 19 and I said to the

3:25 son of Parosh: prob. rdg; Heb. adds and the temple servitors lodged on Ophel (cp. 11:21).
4:1 In Heb. 3:33.   4:7 In Heb. 4:1.
4:12–13 where … themselves: so Gk; Heb. which you return against us and I stationed.

4.1–23: The attempts to impede. 4–5: The narrative is interrupted by a curse pronounced against the nobles, the magistrates, and all the people: 'The work is great and extends over much ground, and we are widely separated on the wall, each man at some distance from his neighbour. 20 Wherever you hear the trumpet sound, rally to us there, and our God will fight for us.' 21 So with half the men holding spears we continued the work from daybreak until the stars came out. 22 At the same time I had said to the people, 'Let every man and his servant remain all night inside Jerusalem, to act as a guard for us by night and a working party by day.' 23 Neither I nor my kinsmen nor the men under me nor my bodyguard ever took off our clothes; each one kept his right hand on his spear.

Nehemiah's social reforms

5 THERE came a time when the common people, both men and women, raised a great outcry against their fellow-Jews. 2 Some complained that they had to give their sons and daughters as pledges for food to eat to keep themselves alive; 3 others that they were mortgaging their fields, vineyards, and homes to buy grain during the famine; 4 still others that they were borrowing money on their fields and vineyards to pay the king's tax. 5 'But', they said, 'our bodily needs are the same as other people's, our children are as good as theirs; yet here we are, forcing our sons and daughters into slavery. Some of our daughters are already enslaved, and there is nothing we can do, because our fields and vineyards now belong to others.'

6 When I heard their outcry and the story they told, I was greatly incensed, 7 but I controlled my feelings and reasoned with the nobles and the magistrates. I said to them, 'You are holding your fellow-Jews as pledges for debt.' I rebuked them severely 8 and said, 'As far as we have been able, we have bought back our fellow-Jews who had been sold to foreigners; but you are now selling your own

fellow-countrymen, and they will have to be bought back by us!' They were silent and had not a word to say.

9 I went on, 'What you are doing is wrong. You ought to live so much in the fear of our God that you are above reproach in the eyes of the nations who are our enemies. 10 Speaking for myself, I and my kinsmen and the men under me are advancing them money and grain. Let us give up this taking of pledges for debt. 11 This very day give them back their fields and vineyards, their olive groves and houses, as well as the income in money, in grain, new wine, and oil.' 12 'We shall give them back', they promised, 'and exact nothing more. We shall do as you say.' Then after summoning the priests I put the offenders on oath to do as they had promised. 13 Also I shook out the fold of my robe and said, 'So may God shake out from house and property every man who fails to keep this promise. May he be shaken out like this and emptied!' All the assembled people said 'Amen' and praised the LORD; and they did as they had promised.

14 Moreover, from the twentieth year of King Artaxerxes, the time when I was appointed governor in Judah, until his thirty-second year, a period of twelve years, neither I nor my kinsmen drew the governor's allowance of food. 15 Former governors, my predecessors, had laid a heavy burden on the people, exacting from them a daily toll of bread and wine to the value of forty shekels of silver, while the men under them had also tyrannized over the people. But, because I feared God, I did not behave like this. 16 Further, I put all my energy into working on the

---

4:23 kept ... on: *prob. rdg; Heb. obscure.*   5:2 **that they ... pledges:** *prob. rdg; Heb.* that they, their sons and daughters were many.   5:4 **on:** *so Gk (Luc.); Heb. omits.*   5:7 **I rebuked ... severely:** *or* I called a great assembly to deal with them.   5:11 **income:** *prob. rdg; Heb.* hundredth.   5:15 **a daily toll:** *prob. rdg; Heb. obscure.*

---

enemies. **10–15:** Even some Jews join against the builders. **16–23:** The protection of the workers. **18:** *The trumpeter stayed beside me:* presumably others were also stationed around the wall to give the alarm from any quarter.

5.1–13: The plight of the poor. The chapter seems out of place and not directly connected with the building of the wall, which it interrupts. **1–5:** The exploitation of the poor by the rich. **6–13:** Nehemiah's response. **7–10:** The charging of interest is prohibited in Deut. 23.20. **13:** *Shook out:* a symbolic gesture meant to reinforce the oath of the offenders.

5.14–19: Nehemiah defends his governorship. The section emphasizes his concern not to harass the poor through personal demands. The occasion for the apologia is not known.

wall; I acquired no land, and all my men were gathered there for the work. 17 At my table I had as guests a hundred and fifty Jews, including the magistrates, as well as men who came to us from the surrounding nations. 18 The provision which had to be made each day was an ox and six prime sheep; fowls also were prepared for me, and every ten days skins of wine in abundance. Yet even so I did not draw the governor's allowance, because the people were so heavily burdened.

19 God, remember me favourably for all that I have done for this people!

6 When it was reported to Sanballat, Tobiah, Geshem the Arab, and the rest of our enemies that I had rebuilt the wall and not a single gap remained in it—although I had not yet set up the gates in the gateways— 2 Sanballat and Geshem sent me an invitation to come and confer with them at Hakkephirim in the plain of Ono; their intention was to do me some harm. 3 So I sent messengers to them with this reply: 'I have important work on my hands at the moment and am unable to come down. Why should the work be brought to a standstill while I leave it and come down to you?' 4 Four times they sent me a similar invitation, and each time I gave them the same answer. 5 On a fifth occasion Sanballat made a similar approach, but this time his servant came with an open letter. 6 It ran as follows: 'It is reported among the nations, and Gashmu confirms it, that you and the Jews are plotting rebellion, and that is why you are building the wall; it is further reported that you yourself want to be king, 7 and have even appointed prophets to make this proclamation concerning you in Jerusalem: "Judah has a king!" Such matters will certainly get to the king's notice; so come at once and let us talk them over.' 8 I sent this reply: 'No such thing as you allege has taken place; your imagination has invented the whole story.' 9 They were all trying to intimidate us, in the hope that we should then relax our efforts and that the work would never be

completed. Strengthen me for the work, was my prayer.

10 One day I went to the house of Shemaiah son of Delaiah, son of Mehetabel, for he was confined to his house. He said,

'Let us meet in the house of God,
within the sanctuary,
and let us shut the doors,
for they are coming to kill you,
and they will come to do it by night.'

11 But I said, 'Should a man like me run away? Can a man like me go into the sanctuary to save his life? I will not go.' 12 Then it dawned on me: God had not sent him. His prophecy aimed at harming me, and Tobiah and Sanballat had bribed him to utter it. 13 He had been bribed to frighten me into compliance and into committing sin; then they could give me a bad name and discredit me.

14 God, remember Tobiah and Sanballat for what they have done, and also the prophetess Noadiah and all the other prophets who tried to intimidate me!

15 On the twenty-fifth day of the month of Elul the wall was finished; it had taken fifty-two days. 16 When all our enemies heard of it, and all the surrounding nations saw it, they thought it a very wonderful achievement, and recognized it was by the help of our God that this work had been accomplished.

17 In those days the nobles in Judah kept sending letters to Tobiah, and receiving replies from him, 18 for many in Judah were in league with him, because he was a son-in-law of Shecaniah son of Arah, and his son Jehohanan had married a daughter of Meshullam son of Berechiah. 19 They were always praising him in my presence and repeating to him what I said. Tobiah also wrote to me to intimidate me.

6:6 **Gashmu:** Geshem *elsewhere.*

6.1–19: The plots of the enemy. 2: *Hakkephirim* is an unknown village; *the plain of Ono* is located near the seacoast, some distance from Jerusalem. **5–9:** Accusation of rebellion. **5:** The *open letter,* if recorded on a clay tablet, had no clay envelope; if on papyrus or parchment, it was not folded or sealed. In either case, the senders obviously intended no secrecy. Compare Jer. 32.14. **10–14:** *Shemaiah* plots against Nehemiah. **11:** *A man like me:* a political leader must neither show cowardice nor commit sacrilege (see Num. 3.10; 18.7). **15–19:** Completion of the wall. **15:** *Elul:* August–September, 444 B.C.E. **16:** The verse reflects understandable exaggeration. **17–19:** For further data on *Tobiah* and his Jewish connections—his chamber in the temple—see 13.4–9.

7 WHEN the wall had been rebuilt, and I had put the gates in place and the gate-keepers had been appointed, ²I gave the charge of Jerusalem to my brother Hanani and to Hananiah, the governor of the citadel, for he was trustworthy and godfearing above other men. ³I said to them, 'The entrances to Jerusalem are not to be left open during the heat of the day; the gates must be kept shut and barred while the gate-keepers are standing at ease. Appoint guards from among the inhabitants of Jerusalem, some on sentry duty and others posted in front of their own homes.'

⁴The city was large and spacious; there were few people in it and no houses had yet been rebuilt. ⁵Then God prompted me to assemble the nobles, the magistrates, and the people, to be enrolled family by family. I discovered the register of the genealogies of those who had been the first to come back, and this is what I found written in it:

⁶Of the captives whom King Nebuchadnezzar of Babylon had taken into exile, these are the people of the province who have returned to Jerusalem and Judah, each to his own town, ⁷led by Zerubbabel, Jeshua, Nehemiah, Azariah, Raamiah, Nahamani, Mordecai, Bilshan, Mispereth, Bigvai, Nehum, and Baanah.

The roll of the men of the people of Israel: ⁸the line of Parosh two thousand one hundred and seventy-two; ⁹the line of Shephatiah three hundred and seventy-two; ¹⁰the line of Arah six hundred and fifty-two; ¹¹the line of Pahath-moab, namely the lines of Jeshua and Joab, two thousand eight hundred and eighteen; ¹²the line of Elam one thousand two hundred and fifty-four; ¹³the line of Zattu eight hundred and forty-five; ¹⁴the line of Zaccai seven hundred and sixty; ¹⁵the line of Binnui six hundred and forty-eight; ¹⁶the line of Bebai six hundred and twenty-eight; ¹⁷the line of Azgad two thousand three hundred and twenty-two; ¹⁸the line of Adonikam six hundred and sixty-seven; ¹⁹the line of Bigvai two thousand and sixty-seven; ²⁰the line of Adin six hundred and fifty-five; ²¹the line of Ater, namely that of Hezekiah, ninety-eight;

²²the line of Hashum three hundred and twenty-eight; ²³the line of Bezai three hundred and twenty-four; ²⁴the line of Hariph one hundred and twelve; ²⁵the line of Gibeon ninety-five. ²⁶The men of Bethlehem and Netophah one hundred and eighty-eight; ²⁷the men of Anathoth one hundred and twenty-eight; ²⁸the men of Beth-azmoth forty-two; ²⁹the men of Kiriath-jearim, Kephirah, and Beeroth seven hundred and forty-three; ³⁰the men of Ramah and Geba six hundred and twenty-one; ³¹the men of Michmas one hundred and twenty-two; ³²the men of Bethel and Ai one hundred and twenty-three; ³³the men of Nebo fifty-two; ³⁴the men of the other Elam one thousand two hundred and fifty-four; ³⁵the men of Harim three hundred and twenty; ³⁶the men of Jericho three hundred and forty-five; ³⁷the men of Lod, Hadid, and Ono seven hundred and twenty-one; ³⁸the men of Senaah three thousand nine hundred and thirty.

³⁹Priests: the line of Jedaiah, of the house of Jeshua, nine hundred and seventy-three; ⁴⁰the line of Immer one thousand and fifty-two; ⁴¹the line of Pashhur one thousand two hundred and forty-seven; ⁴²the line of Harim one thousand and seventeen.

⁴³Levites: the lines of Jeshua and Kadmiel, of the house of Hodvah, seventy-four. ⁴⁴Singers: the line of Asaph one hundred and forty-eight. ⁴⁵Door-keepers: the line of Shallum, the line of Ater, the line of Talmon, the line of Akkub, the line of Hatita, and the line of Shobai, one hundred and thirty-eight in all.

⁴⁶Temple servitors: the line of Ziha, the line of Hasupha, the line of Tabbaoth, ⁴⁷the line of Keros, the line of Sia, the line of Padon, ⁴⁸the line of Lebanah, the line of Hagabah, the line of Shalmai, ⁴⁹the line of Hanan, the line of Giddel, the line of Gahar, ⁵⁰the line of Reaiah, the line of Rezin, the line of Nekoda, ⁵¹the line of Gazzam, the line of Uzza, the line of Paseah, ⁵²the

7:1 gate-keepers: *prob. rdg; Heb. adds* the singers and the Levites.   7:6–73 *Cp. Ezra 2:1–70.*   7:33 the men of: *prob. rdg, cp. Ezra 2:29; Heb. adds* the other. 7:34 men: *prob. rdg; Heb.* line *(also in verses 35–38).* 7:43 and: *prob. rdg, cp. Ezra 2:40; Heb.* to.

7.1–73a: Guards and patrols. 2: *Hanani:* see 1.2 n. *Citadel:* mentioned in 2.8. **4–5:** The taking of a census. **6–73a:** This list of returning Judeans duplicates, with slight variations, that of Ezra 2.1–70.

line of Besai, the line of the Meunim, the line of the Nephishesim, ⁵³ the line of Bakbuk, the line of Hakupha, the line of Harhur, ⁵⁴ the line of Bazlith, the line of Mehida, the line of Harsha, ⁵⁵ the line of Barkos, the line of Sisera, the line of Temah, ⁵⁶ the line of Neziah, and the line of Hatipha.

⁵⁷ Descendants of Solomon's servants: the line of Sotai, the line of Sophereth, the line of Perida, ⁵⁸ the line of Jaalah, the line of Darkon, the line of Giddel, ⁵⁹ the line of Shephatiah, the line of Hattil, the line of Pochereth-hazzebaim, and the line of Amon.

⁶⁰ The temple servitors and the descendants of Solomon's servants amounted to three hundred and ninety-two in all.

⁶¹ The following were those who returned from Tel-melah, Tel-harsha, Kerub, Addon, and Immer, but could not establish their father's line nor whether by descent they belonged to Israel: ⁶² the line of Delaiah, the line of Tobiah, the line of Nekoda, six hundred and forty-two. ⁶³ Also of the priests: the line of Hobaiah, the line of Hakkoz, and the line of Barzillai who had married a daughter of Barzillai the Gileadite and went by his name. ⁶⁴ These searched for their names among those enrolled in the genealogies, but they could not be found; they were disqualified for the priesthood as unclean, ⁶⁵ and the governor forbade them to partake of the most sacred food until there should be a priest able to consult the Urim and the Thummim.

⁶⁶ The whole assembled people numbered forty-two thousand three hundred and sixty, ⁶⁷ apart from their slaves, male and female, of whom there were seven thousand three hundred and thirty-seven; and they had two hundred and forty-five singers, men and women. ⁶⁸ Their horses numbered seven hundred and thirty-six, their mules two hundred and forty-five, ⁶⁹ their camels four hundred and thirty-five, and their donkeys six thousand seven hundred and twenty.

⁷⁰ Some of the heads of families gave contributions for the work. The governor gave to the treasury a thousand gold drachmas, fifty tossing-bowls, and five hundred and thirty priestly vestments. ⁷¹ Some of the heads of families gave for the fabric fund twenty thousand gold drachmas and two thousand two hundred silver minas. ⁷² What the rest of the people gave us was twenty thousand gold drachmas, two thousand silver minas, and sixty-seven priestly vestments.

⁷³ The priests and Levites, with some of the people, lived in Jerusalem and its neighbourhood; the door-keepers, the singers, the temple servitors, and all other Israelites lived in their own towns.

The reading of the law and the people's response

8 WHEN the seventh month came, and the Israelites were now settled in their towns, ¹ all the people assembled with one accord in the broad space in front of the Water Gate, and requested Ezra the scribe to bring the book of the law of Moses, which the LORD had enjoined upon Israel. ² On the first day of the seventh month, Ezra the priest brought the law before the whole assembly, both men and women, and all who were capable of understanding what they heard. ³ From early morning till noon he read aloud from it, facing the square in front of the Water Gate, in the presence of the men and the women, and those who could understand; the people all listened attentively to the book of the law.

⁴ Ezra the scribe stood on a wooden platform which had been made for this purpose; beside him stood Mattithiah, Shema, Anaiah, Uriah, Hilkiah, and Maaseiah on his right hand, and on his left Pedaiah, Mishael, Malchiah, Hashum, Hashbaddanah, Zechariah, and Meshullam. ⁵ Then Ezra opened the book in the sight of all the people, for he was standing above them; and when he opened it, they all stood. ⁶ Ezra blessed the LORD, the

---

7:68 **Their horses . . . forty-five:** *so some MSS; others omit.* 7:73 **in . . . neighbourhood:** *prob. rdg, cp. 1 Esd. 5:46; Heb. omits.* 8:1 **scribe:** *or doctor of the law.*

7.73b–8.12: The law read by Ezra and the covenant renewed. The section 7.73b–9.37 is misplaced (see Introduction to Ezra); it is about Ezra. Perhaps it should follow directly after Ezra chs. 9–10. **8.1:** *The book of the law of Moses:* not the entire Pentateuch as we now know it, but selections from it. **2:** *The first day of the seventh month:* Tishri (September–October); compare Lev. 23.24 and Num. 29.1. The first day of Tishri great God, and all the people raised their hands and responded, 'Amen, Amen'; then they bowed their heads and prostrated themselves before the LORD. 7 Jeshua, Bani, Sherebiah, Jamin, Akkub, Shabbethai, Hodiah, Maaseiah, Kelita, Azariah, Jozabad, Hanan, and Pelaiah, the Levites, expounded the law to the people while the people remained in their places. 8 They read from the book of the law of God clearly, made its sense plain, and gave instruction in what was read.

9 Then Nehemiah the governor and Ezra the priest and scribe, and the Levites who instructed the people, said to them all, 'This day is holy to the LORD your God; do not mourn or weep'; for the people had all been weeping while they listened to the words of the law. 10 'Go now,' he continued, 'feast yourselves on rich food and sweet drinks, and send a share to all who cannot provide for themselves, for the day is holy to our Lord. Let there be no sadness, for joy in the LORD is your strength.' 11 The Levites calmed the people, saying, 'Be quiet, for this day is holy; let there be no sadness.' 12 So all the people went away to eat and to drink, to send shares to others, and to celebrate the day with great rejoicing, because they had understood what had been explained to them.

13 On the second day the heads of families of the whole people, with the priests and the Levites, assembled before Ezra the scribe to study the law. 14 They found written in the law that the LORD had given commandment through Moses that the Israelites were to live in booths during the feast of the seventh month; 15 they should issue this proclamation throughout all their towns and in Jerusalem: 'Go out to the hills and fetch branches of olive and wild olive, myrtle and palm, and other leafy boughs, to make booths as prescribed.' 16 So the people went and fetched branches and made booths for themselves, each on his own roof, and in their courtyards and in the precincts of the house of God, and in the square at the Water Gate and the square at the Ephraim Gate. 17 The whole community of those who had returned from the captivity made booths and lived in them, a thing that the Israelites had not done from the days of Joshua son of Nun until that day; and there was very great rejoicing. 18 The book of the law of God was read day by day, from the first day to the last. They kept the feast for seven days, and on the eighth day there was a closing ceremony, according to the rule.

9 ON the twenty-fourth day of this month the Israelites, clothed in sackcloth and with dust on their heads, assembled for a fast. 2 Those who were of Israelite descent separated themselves from all who were foreigners; they stood and confessed their sins and the iniquities of their forefathers. 3 Then, while they stood up where they were, the book of the law of the LORD their God was read for one quarter of the day, and another quarter of the day they spent in confession and in worshipping the LORD their God. 4 On the steps assigned to the Levites stood Jeshua, Bani, Kadmiel, Shebaniah, Bunni, Sherebiah, Bani, and Kenani, and they cried aloud to the LORD their God. 5 Then the Levites, Jeshua, Kadmiel, Bani, Hashabniah, Sherebiah, Hodiah, Shebaniah, and Pethahiah, said, 'Stand up and bless the LORD your God in these words: From everlasting to everlasting may your glorious name be blessed and exalted above all blessing and praise.

6 'You alone are the LORD;
    you created the heavens,

8:7 **the Levites**: *prob. rdg; Heb.* and the Levites.

---

is observed by Jews as the new year day, a term rare in the OT. **7–8:** The law was in Heb.; the language of the Judeans after the sixth century B.C.E. was Aram. Hence the Levites, after reading in Heb., *expounded* in the Aram, giving *instruction in what was read.*

8.13–18: Renewal of the celebration of the pilgrim-feast of Booths. 14: *Booths:* compare Lev. 23.33–43. **15:** Five species of plants are prescribed here; Lev. 23.40 prescribes four species; only two species are common; the differences seem due to varying practices concerning this pilgrim-feast. Both family and community booths seem described.

9.1–5: A day of fasting. This cannot be the Day of Atonement, which fell on the tenth day of the seventh month (Lev. 23.26–32; Num. 29.7–9). Indeed, the Day of Atonement is not mentioned; some speculate that its introduction came at a later time.

9.6–37: The confession and prayer, a skillfully designed tapestry of historical reminiscence, an acknowledgment of backsliding, and an appeal to God's compassion, was probably once an independent psalm. **6:** The

493

the highest heavens with all their
host,
the earth and all that is on it,
the seas and all that is in them.
You give life to them all,
and the heavenly host worships you.

7'You are the LORD,
the God who chose Abram,
who brought him from Ur of the
Chaldees
and named him Abraham.
8Finding him faithful you made a
covenant with him
to give to his descendants
the land of the Canaanites,
Hittites, Amorites, and Perizzites,
Jebusites, and Girgashites;
you fulfilled your promise,
for you are just.

9'You saw the misery of our forefathers
in Egypt
and heard their cry at the Red Sea.
10You worked signs and portents against
Pharaoh,
against all his courtiers and the people
of his land,
for you knew how arrogantly
they treated our forefathers;
and you won for yourself renown
that lives to this day.
11You divided asunder the sea before
them,
and they passed through on dry
ground;
but their pursuers you flung into the
depths,
like a stone flung into turbulent
waters.
12By a pillar of cloud you guided them in
the daytime,
and at night by a pillar of fire
to light the road they were to travel.
13You came down on Mount Sinai
and spoke to them from heaven;
you gave them right judgements and
true laws,
statutes and commandments which
were good.
14You made known to them your holy
sabbath,
and through Moses your servant

you gave them commandments,
statutes, and laws.
15You gave them bread from heaven to
stay their hunger
and brought water out from a rock to
quench their thirst.
You bade them enter and take
possession of the land
which you had solemnly sworn to give
them.

16'But they, our forefathers, were
arrogant;
stubbornly they flouted your
commandments.
17They refused to listen,
forgetful of the miracles you had
accomplished among them.
In their stubbornness they appointed a
leader
to bring them back to slavery in Egypt.
But you are a forgiving God,
gracious and compassionate,
long-suffering and ever constant,
and you did not abandon them.

18'Even when they made for themselves
the metal image of a bull-calf
and said, "This is your god
who brought you up from Egypt,"
and were guilty of gross blasphemies,
19you in your great compassion
did not abandon them in the
wilderness.
The pillar of cloud never failed
to guide them on their journey by day,
nor did the pillar of fire fail by night
to light the road they were to travel.
20You gave your good spirit to instruct
them;
you did not withhold your manna,
and you gave them water for their
thirst.
21During forty years you sustained them;
in the wilderness they lacked nothing,
their clothes did not wear out,
and their feet were not swollen.

22'You gave them kings and their people
as spoils of war.
They took possession
of the land of King Sihon of Heshbon

9:9 **Red Sea:** *or* sea of Reeds.   9:17 **in Egypt:** *so
some MSS; others* in their rebellion.

Gk. has the words, "And Ezra said," before the opening line of the prayer, *You . . . the* LORD.

494

and the land of King Og of Bashan.
23 You made their descendants numerous,
  countless as the stars in the sky,
  and brought them into the land
  you had promised their forefathers
  they would enter and possess.
24 When their descendants came into the
    land
  to take possession of it,
  you subdued the Canaanite inhabitants
    before them,
  giving kings and peoples into their
    hands
  to do with them as they pleased.
25 They captured fortified towns and
    fertile land,
  taking possession of houses
  filled with all good things,
  of rock-hewn cisterns, vineyards, olive
    groves,
  and fruit trees in abundance.
  They ate and were satisfied and grew
    fat;
  they found delight in your great
    goodness.

26 'In growing defiance, they rebelled
  and turned their backs on your law.
  They killed your prophets,
  who with warnings admonished them
  to bring them again to you;
  they were guilty of great blasphemies.
27 You handed them over to enemies to
    be oppressed.
  But when they, under oppression,
    appealed to you,
  from heaven you heard them
  and in your great compassion sent
    saviours
  to save them from their enemies.
28 After some respite
  again they did what was wrong in your
    eyes,
  and you abandoned them to their
    enemies,
  who held them in subjection.
  Yet once more they appealed to you,
  and time after time you heard them
    from heaven
  and in your compassion saved them.
29 To bring them back to your law
  you solemnly warned them,
  but arrogantly they flouted your
    commandments,
  sinning against the ordinances

which bring life to those who keep
    them.
  Stubbornly they turned aside;
  in their obstinacy they would not obey.
30 For many years you were patient
  and your spirit admonished them
    through the prophets.
  Still they would not listen,
  and so you handed them over
  to the peoples of other countries.
31 Nevertheless in your great compassion
  you did not make an end of them or
    forsake them;
  for you are a gracious and
    compassionate God.

32 'Now, great and mighty and terrible
    God,
  faithfully keeping covenant, our God,
  do not regard as a small thing the
    hardships
  that have befallen us, our kings and
    princes,
  our priests, our prophets, our
    forefathers,
  and all your people from the time of
    the kings of Assyria
  up to the present day.
33 In all that has come upon us
  you have been just,
  for you have kept faith
  while we have done wrong.
34 Our kings, our princes, our priests, and
    our forefathers
  did not keep your law;
  they paid no heed to your
    commandments
  and the warnings you gave them.
35 Even in their own kingdom,
  while they were enjoying
  the great prosperity you gave them,
  and the broad, fertile land you
    bestowed on them,
  they did not serve you or renounce
    their evil ways.

36 'Today we are slaves,
  slaves here in the land
  which you gave to our forefathers
  so that they might eat its fruits
  and enjoy its good things.
37 All its produce now goes to the kings
  whom you have set over us
  because of our sins.
  They have power over our bodies,

and they do as they please with our livestock:

we are in dire distress.

38 'Because of all this we make a binding declaration in writing, and our princes, our Levites, and our priests witness the sealing.

10 'Those who witness the sealing are Nehemiah the governor, son of Hacaliah, Zedekiah, 2 Seraiah, Azariah, Jeremiah, 3 Pashhur, Amariah, Malchiah, 4 Hattush, Shebaniah, Malluch, 5 Harim, Meremoth, Obadiah, 6 Daniel, Ginnethon, Baruch, 7 Meshullam, Abiah, Mijamin, 8 Maaziah, Bilgai, Shemaiah; these are the priests. 9 The Levites: Jeshua son of Azaniah, Binnui of the line of Henadad, Kadmiel; 10 and their brethren, Shebaniah, Hodiah, Kelita, Pelaiah, Hanan, 11 Mica, Rehob, Hashabiah, 12 Zaccur, Sherebiah, Shebaniah, 13 Hodiah, Bani, Beninu. 14 The chiefs of the people: Parosh, Pahath-moab, Elam, Zattu, Bani, 15 Bunni, Azgad, Bebai, 16 Adonijah, Bigvai, Adin, 17 Ater, Hezekiah, Azzur, 18 Hodiah, Hashum, Bezai, 19 Hariph, Anathoth, Nebai, 20 Magpiash, Meshullam, Hezir, 21 Meshezabel, Zadok, Jaddua, 22 Pelatiah, Hanan, Anaiah, 23 Hoshea, Hananiah, Hasshub, 24 Hallohesh, Pilha, Shobek, 25 Rehum, Hashabnah, Maaseiah, 26 Ahiah, Hanan, Anan, 27 Malluch, Harim, Baanah.

28 'The rest of the people, the priests, the Levites, the door-keepers, the singers, the temple servitors, with their wives, their sons, and their daughters, all who are capable of understanding, all who for the sake of the law of God have kept themselves apart from the foreign population, 29 join with the leading brethren, when the oath is put to them, in swearing to obey God's law given by Moses the servant of God, and to observe and fulfil all the commandments of the LORD our Lord, his rules and his statutes.

30 'We shall not give our daughters in marriage to the foreign population or take their daughters for our sons. 31 If on the sabbath these people bring in merchandise or grain for sale, we shall not buy from them on the sabbath or on any holy day. We shall forgo the crops of the seventh year and release every person still held as a pledge for debt.

32 'We hereby undertake the duty of giving yearly one third of a shekel for the service of the house of our God: 33 for the rows of the Bread of the Presence, the regular grain-offering and whole-offering, the sabbaths, the new moons, the appointed seasons, the holygifts, and the purification-offerings to make expiation on behalf of Israel, and for all else that has to be done in the house of our God. 34 We, the priests, the Levites, and the people, have cast lots for the wood-offering, so that it may be brought into the house of our God by each family in turn, at appointed times, year by year, to burn upon the altar of the LORD our God, as prescribed in the law. 35 We undertake to bring the firstfruits of our land and the firstfruits of every fruit tree, year by year, to the house of the LORD; 36 also to bring to the house of our God, to the priests who minister in the house of our God, the firstborn of our sons and of our cattle, as prescribed in the law, and the firstborn of our herds and of our flocks; 37 and to bring to the priests the first kneading of our dough, and the first of the fruit of every tree, of the new wine and of the oil, to the storerooms in the house of our God; and to bring to the Levites the tithes from our land, for it is the Levites who collect the tithes in all our farming villages. 38 An Aaronite priest must be with the Levites when they collect the tithes; and the Levites are to bring up one tenth of the tithes to the house of our God, to the appropriate rooms in the storehouse. 39 For the Israelites

9:38 *In Heb. 10:1.*   10:9 **Jeshua:** *prob. rdg; Heb.* and Jeshua.   10:37 **our dough:** *so Gk; Heb. adds* and our contributions.

9.38–10.39: Renewal of the covenant, and its obligations. The structure resembles that of similar stipulations of loyalty found in clay tablets: writing and sealing, list of witnesses, oath, and enumeration of particulars. The stress against intermarriage in this "covenant renewal" (it is mentioned first) should be seen against the background of the harassment of the surrounding nations and the pressing security needs of the small Jerusalem community. Later ages introduced proselytizing. **10.30–31:** For the prohibition of intermarriage, see Deut. 7.3; of work on the sabbath day, see Exod. 20.8–11; of planting during the release year, see Exod. 23.10–11; for the release of pledges, Deut. 15.2. **32:** The offering of *the third of a shekel* for the temple seems voluntary; the legislation of Exod. 30.13 stipulated a compulsory half shekel, to which the voluntary was added. **34:** On *wood* for *the altar,* see Lev. 6.12, which does not mention the casting of lots found here. **35–37:** *Firstfruits:* see Exod. 23.19. *Firstborn:* see Exod. 13.13. *Tithes,* see Lev. 27.30–33 and Num. 18.25–32.

and the Levites must bring the contribution of grain, new wine, and oil to the rooms where the vessels of the sanctuary are kept, and where the ministering priests, the door-keepers, and the singers are lodged. We shall not neglect the house of our God.'

11 THE leaders of the people settled in Jerusalem; and the rest of the people cast lots to bring one in every ten to live in Jerusalem, the Holy City, while the remaining nine lived in other towns. 2 The people invoked a blessing on all those who volunteered to settle in Jerusalem.

3 These are the chiefs of the province who lived in Jerusalem; but, in the towns of Judah, other Israelites, priests, Levites, temple servitors, and descendants of Solomon's servants lived on their own property, in their own towns. 4 Some members of the tribes of Judah and Benjamin lived in Jerusalem. Of Judah: Athaiah son of Uzziah, son of Zechariah, son of Amariah, son of Shephatiah, son of Mahalalel of the line of Perez, 6 all of whose family, to the number of four hundred and sixty-eight men of substance, lived in Jerusalem; 5 and Maaseiah son of Baruch, son of Col-hozeh, son of Hazaiah, son of Adaiah, son of Joiarib, son of Zechariah of the Shelanite family.

7 These were the Benjamites: Sallu son of Meshullam, son of Joed, son of Pedaiah, son of Kolaiah, son of Maaseiah, son of Ithiel, son of Isaiah, 8 and his kinsmen Gabbai and Sallai, nine hundred and twenty-eight in all. 9 Joel son of Zichri was their overseer, and Judah son of Hassenuah was second over the city.

10 Of the priests: Jedaiah son of Joiarib, son of 11 Seraiah, son of Hilkiah, son of Meshullam, son of Zadok, son of Meraioth, son of Ahitub, supervisor of the house of God, 12 and his brethren responsible for the work in the temple, eight hundred and twenty-two in all; and Adaiah son of Jeroham, son of Pelaliah, son of Amzi, son of Zechariah, son of Pashhur, son of Malchiah, 13 and his brethren, heads of fathers' houses, two hundred and forty-two in all; and Amashai son of Azarel, son of Ahzai, son of Meshillemoth, son of Immer, 14 and his brethren, men of substance, a hundred and twenty-eight in all; their overseer was Zabdiel son of Haggedolim.

15 And of the Levites: Shemaiah son of Hasshub, son of Azrikam, son of Hashabiah, son of Bunni; 16 and Shabbethai and Jozabad of the chiefs of the Levites, who had charge of the external business of the house of God; 17 and Mattaniah son of Micah, son of Zabdi, son of Asaph, who as precentor led the prayer of thanksgiving, and Bakbukiah who held the second place among his brethren; and Abda son of Shammua, son of Galal, son of Jeduthun. 18 The number of Levites in the Holy City was two hundred and eighty-four in all.

19 The gate-keepers who kept guard at the gates were Akkub, Talmon, and their brethren, a hundred and seventy-two. 20 The rest of the Israelites were in all the towns of Judah, each man on his own inherited property. 21 But the temple servitors lodged on Mount Ophel, and Ziha and Gishpa were in charge of them.

22 The overseer of the Levites in Jerusalem was Uzzi son of Bani, son of Hashabiah, son of Mattaniah, son of Mica, of the line of Asaph, the singers, for the supervision of the business of the house of God. 23 For they were under the king's orders, and there was obligatory duty for the singers every day. 24 Pethahiah son of Meshezabel, of the line of Zerah son of Judah, was the king's adviser on all matters affecting the people.

25 As for the hamlets with their surrounding fields: some of the men of Judah lived in Kiriath-arba and its villages, in Dibon and its villages, and in Jekabzeel and its hamlets, 26 in Jeshua, Moladah, and Bethpelet, 27 in Hazarshual, and in Beersheba and its villages, 28 in Ziklag and in Meconah and its villages, 29 in Enrimmon, Zorah, and Jarmuth, 30 in Zanoah, Adullam, and their hamlets, in Lachish and its fields, and Azekah and its villages.

11:8 **his kinsmen:** *so Gk (Luc.); Heb. after him.*
11:10 **son of [Seraiah]:** *prob. rdg; Heb. obscure.*
11:20 **The rest . . . Israelites:** *prob. rdg; Heb. adds the levitical priests.*

11.1–24: Repopulation of Jerusalem. A parallel list, 1 Chr. ch. 9, provides a similar order: chiefs, priests, Levites, and people with other functions. Some scholars connect this chapter with Neh. 7.5a as continuing the "Memoirs of Nehemiah."

11.25–36: Population of the surrounding Judean area. The borders of Judea extend to *Beersheba* in the south, and *Lachish* and *Ziklag,* towns closer to the coast in the southwest.

Thus they occupied the country from Beer-sheba to the valley of Hinnom.

31 The men of Benjamin lived in Geba, Michmash, Aiah, and Bethel with its villages, 32 in Anathoth, Nob, and Ananiah, 33 in Hazor, Ramah, and Gittaim, 34 in Hadid, Zeboim, and Neballat, 35 in Lod, Ono, and Ge-harashim. 36 Certain divisions of the Levites in Judah were attached to Benjamin.

12 These are the priests and the Levites who came back with Zerubbabel son of Shealtiel, and with Jeshua: Seraiah, Jeremiah, Ezra, 2 Amariah, Malluch, Hattush, 3 Shecaniah, Rehum, Meremoth, 4 Iddo, Ginnethon, Abiah, 5 Mijamin, Maadiah, Bilgah, 6 Shemaiah, Joiarib, Jedaiah, 7 Sallu, Amok, Hilkiah, Jedaiah. These were the chiefs of the priests and of their brethren in the days of Jeshua.

8 And the Levites: Jeshua, Binnui, Kadmiel, Sherebiah, Judah, and Mattaniah, who with his brethren was in charge of the songs of thanksgiving. 9 And Bakbukiah and Unni their brethren stood opposite them in the service. 10 And Jeshua was the father of Joiakim, Joiakim the father of Eliashib, Eliashib of Joiada, 11 Joiada the father of Jonathan, and Jonathan the father of Jaddua. 12 And in the days of Joiakim the priests who were heads of families were: of Seraiah, Meraiah; of Jeremiah, Hananiah; 13 of Ezra, Meshullam; of Amariah, Jehohanan; 14 of Melichu, Jonathan; of Shebaniah, Joseph; 15 of Harim, Adna; of Meraioth, Helkai; 16 of Iddo, Zechariah; of Ginnethon, Meshullam; 17 of Abiah, Zichri; of Miniamin; of Moadiah, Piltai; 18 of Bilgah, Shammua; of Shemaiah, Jehonathan; 19 of Joiarib, Mattenai; of Jedaiah, Uzzi; 20 of Sallu, Kallai; of Amok, Eber; 21 of Hilkiah, Hashabiah; of Jedaiah, Nethanel.

22 The heads of the priestly families in the days of Eliashib, Joiada, Johanan, and Jaddua were recorded down to the reign of Darius the Persian. 23 The heads of the levitical families were recorded in the annals only down to the days of Johanan the grandson of Eliashib. 24 And the chiefs of the Levites: Hashabiah, Sherebiah, Jeshua, Binnui, Kadmiel, with their brethren in the other turn of duty, to praise and to give thanks, according to the commandment of David the man of God, turn by turn. 25 Mattaniah, Bakbukiah, Obadiah, Meshullam, Talmon, and Akkub were gate-keepers standing guard at the gatehouses. 26 This was the arrangement in the days of Joiakim son of Jeshua, son of Jozadak, and in the days of Nehemiah the governor and of Ezra the priest and scribe.

27 At the dedication of the wall of Jerusalem the Levites, wherever they had settled, were sought out and brought to the city to celebrate the dedication with rejoicing, with thanksgiving and song, to the accompaniment of cymbals, harps, and lyres. 28 The Levites, the singers, were assembled from the district round Jerusalem and from the hamlets of the Netophathites, 29 also from Bethgilgal and the region of Geba and Beth-azmoth; for the singers had built themselves hamlets in the neighbourhood of Jerusalem. 30 When the priests and the Levites had purified themselves, they purified the people, the gates, and the wall.

31 Then I assembled the leading men of Judah on the city wall, and appointed two large choirs to give thanks. One went in procession to the right, going along the wall to the Dung Gate; 32 and after it went Hoshaiah with half the leading men of Judah, 33 and Azariah, Ezra, Meshullam, 34 Judah, Benjamin, Shemaiah, and Jeremiah; 35 and certain of the priests with trumpets: Zechariah son of Jonathan, son of Shemaiah, son of Matta-

11:31 lived in: *prob. rdg; Heb.* from.
12:11 Jonathan: Johanan *in verse 22.*   12:17 of Miniamin: *a name is missing here.*   12:20 Sallu: *prob. rdg, cp. verse 7; Heb.* Sallai.   12:22 The heads: *prob. rdg; Heb. prefixes* The Levites. heads . . . families: *prob. rdg; Heb.* heads of the families and the priests.
12:24 Jeshua, Binnui: *prob. rdg; Heb.* and Jeshua son of.   12:28 The Levites: *prob. rdg; Heb.* The sons of.
12:29 Beth-azmoth: *prob. rdg, cp. 7:28; Heb.* Azmoth.
12:31 One . . . procession: *prob. rdg; Heb.* Processions.

11.31–36: The towns of Benjamin. These are located north and west of Jerusalem; the farthest of these (Ono) was about thirty miles away.

12.1–26: List of priests and Levites. A later hand has appended this additional list. 10–11: The genealogy of high priests. *Jonathan* is often regarded as an error for Jehohanan; see Ezra 10.6 n. 22: The historian Josephus tells that *Jaddua* was high priest in 332 B.C.E., in the time of the conquest by Alexander the Great. *Darius* may be Darius III who ruled 335–331 B.C.E.

12.27–43: Dedication of the walls. 33: The mentions of *Ezra* here and in v. 36 are regarded as interpolations; see Introduction to Ezra on dislocations of materials.

niah, son of Micaiah, son of Zaccur, son of Asaph, 36 and his kinsmen, Shemaiah, Azarel, Milalai, Gilalai, Maai, Nethanel, Judah, and Hanani, with the musical instruments of David the man of God; and Ezra the scribe led them. 37 They went past the Fountain Gate and thence straight forward by the steps up to the City of David, by the ascent to the city wall, past the house of David, and on to the Water Gate on the east.

38 The other thanksgiving choir went to the left, and I followed it with half the leading men of the people, continuing along the wall, past the Tower of the Ovens to the Broad Wall, 39 and past the Ephraim Gate, and over the Jeshanah Gate, and over the Fish Gate, taking in the Tower of Hananel and the Tower of the Hundred, as far as the Sheep Gate; and they halted at the Guardhouse Gate.

40 Then the two thanksgiving choirs took their place in the house of God, and I and half the magistrates with me; 41 and the priests Eliakim, Maaseiah, Miniamin, Micaiah, Elioenai, Zechariah, and Hananiah, with trumpets; 42 Maaseiah, Shemaiah, Eleazar, Uzzi, Jehohanan, Malchiah, Elam, and Ezer. The singers, led by Izrahiah, raised their voices. 43 A great sacrifice was celebrated that day, and they all rejoiced because God had given them great cause for rejoicing; the women and children rejoiced with them. And the rejoicing in Jerusalem was heard a long way off.

44 Men were appointed at that time to take charge of the storerooms for the contributions, the firstfruits, and the tithes, to gather in the portions required by the law for the priests and Levites according to the extent of the farmlands round the towns; for all Judah was full of rejoicing at the ministry of the priests and Levites, 45 who performed the service of their God and the service of purification, as did the singers and the door-keepers, according to the rules laid down by David and his son Solomon. 46 For it was in the days of David that Asaph took the lead as chief of the singers and director of praise and

thanksgiving to God, 47 and in the days of Zerubbabel and of Nehemiah all Israel gave the portions for the singers and the door-keepers as each day required; they set apart the portion for the Levites, and the Levites set apart the portion for the Aaronites.

Nehemiah's religious reforms

13 On that day at the public reading from the book of Moses, it was found to be laid down that no Ammonite or Moabite should ever enter the assembly of God, 2 because they did not welcome the Israelites with food and water but hired Balaam to curse them, though our God turned the curse into a blessing. 3 When the people heard the law, they separated off from Israel all who were of mixed blood.

4 But before this, Eliashib the priest, who was appointed over the storerooms of the house of our God, and who was connected by marriage with Tobiah, 5 had provided for his use a large room where formerly they had kept the grain-offering, the frankincense, the temple vessels, the tithes of grain, new wine, and oil prescribed for the Levites, singers, and door-keepers, and the contributions for the priests. 6 All this while I was not in Jerusalem because, in the thirty-second year of King Artaxerxes of Babylon, I had gone to the king. Some time later, however, having asked permission from him, 7 I returned to Jerusalem and there discovered the outrageous thing that Eliashib had done for Tobiah's benefit in providing him with a room in the courts of the house of God. 8 I was greatly displeased and threw all Tobiah's belongings out of the room. 9 I then gave orders that the room should be purified, and that the vessels of the house of God, with the grain-offering and frankincense, should be put back into it.

12:38 **to the left:** *prob. rdg; Heb.* to the front. **the leading men of:** *prob. rdg; Heb.* omits.
12:39 **Jeshanah Gate:** *or* gate of the Old City.
12:46 **director:** *prob. rdg; Heb.* song.

12.44–47: The admirable functioning of the cult. 45: See also 2 Chr. 8.14, dependent on 1 Chr. chs. 23–26. **47:** The mention of Zerubbabel instead of Ezra has influenced scholars to conclude that Ezra was not contemporaneous with Nehemiah. See Introduction to Ezra.

13.1–31: Nehemiah's reforms. 1–3: These verses connect the chapter with 8.18. **1:** See Deut. 23.3–5. **2:** *Balaam:* see Num. chs. 22–24. **4–9:** The expulsion of *Tobiah* the Ammonite (2.10) is important to the author, so that the community could maintain an unadulterated worship of God. **6:** *Some time later:* Nehemiah was

10 I also learnt that the Levites had not been given their portions; both they and the singers, who were responsible for their respective duties, had made off to their farms. 11 I remonstrated with the magistrates: 'Why is the house of God deserted?' I demanded. I recalled the men and restored them to their places. 12 Then all Judah brought the tithes of grain, new wine, and oil into the storehouses. 13 Over the stores I set Shelemiah the priest, Zadok the accountant, and Pedaiah a Levite, with Hanan son of Zaccur, son of Mattaniah, as their assistant, for they were considered trustworthy men; their duty was the distribution of their shares to their brethren.

14 God, remember this to my credit, and do not wipe out of your memory the devotion which I have shown in the house of my God and in his service!

15 In those days I saw men in Judah treading winepresses on the sabbath, collecting quantities of produce and loading it on donkeys — wine, grapes, figs, and every kind of load, which they brought into Jerusalem on the sabbath. I warned them against the selling of food on that day. 16 Tyrians living in Jerusalem were also bringing fish and all kinds of merchandise and selling them on the sabbath to the people of Judah, even in Jerusalem. 17 I complained to the nobles of Judah and said to them, 'How dare you profane the sabbath in this wicked fashion? 18 Is not this just what your forefathers did, so that our God has brought all this evil on us and on this city? Now you are bringing more wrath on Israel by profaning the sabbath.'

19 When the entrances to Jerusalem had been cleared in preparation for the sabbath, I gave orders that the gates should be shut and not opened until after the sabbath; and I posted some of my men at the gates to ensure that no load came in on the sabbath. 20 Then on one or two occasions the merchants and all kinds of traders spent the night just outside Jerusalem, 21 but I warned them: 'Why are you spending the night in front of the city wall? Do it again, and I shall take action against you.' After that they did not come on the sabbath. 22 I instructed the Levites to purify themselves and take up duty as guards at the gates, to ensure that the sabbath was kept holy.

God, remember this also to my credit, and spare me in your great love!

23 In those days also I saw that some Jews had married women from Ashdod, Ammon, and Moab. 24 Half their children spoke the language of Ashdod or of one of the other peoples but could not speak the language of the Jews. 25 I argued with them and reviled them, I beat some of them and tore out their hair; and I made them swear in the name of God: 'We shall not marry our daughters to their sons, or take any of their daughters in marriage for our sons or for ourselves.' 26 'Was it not because of such women', I said, 'that King Solomon of Israel sinned? Among all the nations there was no king like him; he was loved by his God, and God made him king over all Israel; nevertheless even he was led by foreign women into sin. 27 Are we then to follow your example and commit this grave offence, breaking faith with our God by marrying foreign women?' 28 One of the sons of Joiada son of Eliashib the high priest had married a daughter of Sanballat the Horonite; therefore I drove him out of my presence.

29 God, remember to their discredit that they have defiled the priesthood and the covenant of the priests and the Levites.

30 Thus I purified them from everything foreign, and I made the Levites and the priests resume the duties of their office; 31 I also made provision for the delivery of the wood at appointed times, and for the first-fruits.

God, remember me favourably!

in Susa from 433 to 424 B.C.E. The king is Artaxerxes I, 464–424/3. **10–14:** The *tithes:* contrast 12.47, where tithes seem given freely. **15–22:** *The sabbath:* disregard for the sabbath law was considered to be the cause for exile and enslavement to foreign kings. Compare Jer. 17.19–27, possibly hearkened back to in v. 18. **23–29:** On mixed marriages, see 10.30 and Ezra 9.1–5; 10.2. **26:** *Solomon:* see 1 Kgs. 11.1–8. **28:** *Sanballat* was a personal foe; see 2.10; 4.1–2, 7–8; 6.1–14. **30–31:** Closing verses and prayer.

Esther

This book tells how Esther, a young Jewish girl, delivers the Jews in Persia when they are threatened with extermination by Haman, the chief minister of the Persian king. Esther, who has become queen, acts on the advice of her cousin, Mordecai, the principal object of Haman's anger. A complete reversal of positions results; Haman is hanged, Mordecai assumes his office, and the Jews massacre their enemies. To commemorate this victory, the annual feast of Purim is instituted.

Esther is often considered to have been written in the Persian period (538–333 B.C.E.), though some view it as much later, perhaps even in the Maccabean period. Although Persian customs are familiar to the author and details about the city of Susa and the palace are confirmed by archaeology, it is impossible to find historical confirmation of the events recounted. However, an official at Susa under King Xerxes I is named Marduka, which is close to Mordecai. In the Hebrew Bible, Esther is the last of the five Megilloth, or Scrolls, for reading at the great festivals; it is read on Purim.

Although God's name is not mentioned, there is an obvious implicit trust in divine guidance, as 4.13–17 makes clear. Because religious themes are not explicitly stressed, some ancient rabbis opposed the book's reception into Scripture. In the Greek some additions are found which modify the secular tone of the Hebrew; see "The Rest of the Chapters of the Book of Esther" in the Apocrypha.

King Ahasuerus's banquet

1 THE events here related happened in the days of Ahasuerus, that Ahasuerus who ruled from India to Ethiopia, a hundred and twenty-seven provinces, ²at the time when he was settled on the royal throne in Susa, the capital city. ³In the third year of his reign he gave a banquet for all his officers and his courtiers; the Persians and Medes in full force, along with his nobles and provincial rulers, were in attendance. ⁴He put on display for many days, a hundred and eighty in all, the dazzling wealth of his kingdom and the pomp and splendour of his realm. ⁵At the end of that time the king gave a banquet for all the people present in Susa the capital city, both high and low; it lasted for seven days and was held in the garden court of the royal pavilion. ⁶There were white curtains and violet hangings fastened to silver rings by cords of fine linen with purple thread; the pillars were of marble, and gold and silver couches were placed on a mosaic pavement of malachite, marble, mother-of-pearl, and turquoise. ⁷Wine was served in golden goblets, each of a different design: the king's wine flowed in royal style, ⁸and the drinking was according to no fixed rule, for the king had laid down that all the palace stewards should respect the wishes of each guest. ⁹Queen Vashti too gave a banquet for the women inside the royal palace of King Ahasuerus.

¹⁰On the seventh day, when he was merry with wine, the king ordered Mehuman, Biztha, Harbona, Bigtha, Abagtha, Zethar, and Carcas, the seven eunuchs who were in attendance on the king's person, ¹¹to bring Queen Vashti into his presence wearing her royal diadem, in order to display her beauty to the people and to the officers; for she was indeed a beautiful woman. ¹²But when the royal command was conveyed to her by the eu-

1:1 **Ethiopia:** *Heb.* Cush.   1:6 **thread:** *prob. mng;* *Heb. omits.*

1.1–9: Ahasuerus' banquet. 1: *Ahasuerus* (see Ezra 4.6; Dan. 9.1) seems to be Xerxes I (485–465 B.C.E.), whose empire extended from *India* to *Ethiopia,* and included some twenty satrapies, subdivided into *provinces.* **2:** *Susa,* in Elam, was the king's winter residence; Persepolis was the capital of Persia. **3:** Greek authors mention the great banquets given by Persian kings. **5:** Archaeologists have uncovered such a *court* at Susa. **9:** Xerxes' queen was Amestris; *Vashti* was perhaps a royal concubine. No mention of Vashti or Esther is to be found outside this book.

nuchs, Queen Vashti refused to come. This greatly incensed the king, and his wrath flared up. ¹³ He conferred with wise men versed in precedents, for it was his custom to consult all who were expert in law and usage. ¹⁴ Those closest to the king were Carshena, Shethar, Admatha, Tarshish, Meres, Marsena, and Memucan, the seven vicegerents of Persia and Media; they had access to the king and occupied the premier positions in the kingdom. ¹⁵ 'What', he asked, 'does the law require to be done with Queen Vashti for disobeying my royal command conveyed to her by the eunuchs?'

¹⁶ In the presence of the king and the vicegerents, Memucan declared: 'Queen Vashti has done wrong, not to the king alone, but also to all the officers and to all the peoples in every province of King Ahasuerus. ¹⁷ The queen's conduct will come to the ears of all women and embolden them to treat their husbands with disrespect; they will say, "King Ahasuerus ordered Queen Vashti to be brought before him, but she would not come!" ¹⁸ The great ladies of Persia and Media, who have heard what the queen has said, will quote this day to all the king's officers, and there will be no end to the disrespect and discord!

¹⁹ 'If it please your majesty, let a royal decree be issued by you, and let it be inscribed among the laws of the Persians and Medes, never to be revoked, that Vashti shall not again appear before King Ahasuerus; and let your majesty give her place as queen to another who is more worthy of it than she. ²⁰ When the edict made by the king is proclaimed throughout the length and breadth of the kingdom, all women, high and low alike, will give honour to their husbands.' ²¹ The advice pleased the king and the vicegerents, and the king did as Memucan had proposed. ²² Dispatches were sent to all the king's provinces, to every province in its own script and to every people in their own language, in order that each man, whatever language he spoke, should be master in his own house.

Esther becomes queen

2 SOME time later, when the anger of King Ahasuerus had died down, he called Vashti to mind, remembering what she had done and what had been decreed against her. ² The king's attendants said: 'Let there be sought out for your majesty beautiful young virgins; ³ let your majesty appoint commissioners in every province of your kingdom to assemble all these beautiful young virgins and bring them to the women's quarters in the capital Susa. Have them placed under the care of Hegai, the king's eunuch who has charge of the women, and let him provide the cosmetics they need. ⁴ The girl who is most acceptable to the king shall become queen in place of Vashti.' The advice pleased the king, and he acted on it.

⁵ In Susa the capital there lived a Jew named Mordecai son of Jair, son of Shimei, son of Kish, a Benjamite; ⁶ he had been taken into exile from Jerusalem among those whom King Nebuchadnezzar of Babylon had carried away with King Jeconiah of Judah. ⁷ He had a foster-child Hadassah, that is, Esther, his uncle's daughter, who had neither father nor mother. She was a beautiful and charming girl, and after the death of her parents, Mordecai had adopted her as his own daughter.

⁸ When the king's order and decree were proclaimed and many girls were brought to Susa the capital to be committed to the care of Hegai, who had charge of the women, Esther too was taken to the palace to be entrusted to him. ⁹ He found her pleasing, and

1.10–2.4: **Vashti deposed. 13:** The *wise men* are possibly his seven counselors (Ezra 7.14). **19:** Reference to laws *never to be revoked* is also made in 8.8 and in Dan. 6.8, 12, 15. There may be some irony in the allusion that in both Esther and Daniel the irrevocable decrees against the Jews are ineffective. **22:** The verse seems to be exaggeration.

2.5–23: **The selection of Esther.** Mordecai and Esther have names derived from the Babylonian deities Marduk and Ishtar, who also were cousins. That Mordecai, like Saul, was a Benjaminite is stressed to foreshadow the enmity of Haman, an Amalekite of the Agag family, Saul's enemy, 1 Sam. 15.1–9. **5:** On these remote ancestors see 2 Sam. 16.5–8, *Shimei;* and 1 Sam. 9.1–2, *Kish,* the father of Saul. **6:** *Jeconiah* is also known as Jehoiachin (2 Kgs. 24.6). Modern critics regard the author as unconcerned with precise chronology, for Mordecai's age here would appear to be at least one hundred and fifteen years. **7:** *Hadassah* is a Heb. word she received his special favour: he promptly supplied her with her cosmetics and her allowance of food, and also with seven specially chosen maids from the king's palace. She and her maids were marked out for favourable treatment in the women's quarters.

¹⁰ Esther had not disclosed her race or family, because Mordecai had forbidden her to do so. ¹¹ Every day Mordecai would walk past the forecourt of the women's quarters to learn how Esther fared and what was happening to her.

¹² The full period of preparation before a girl went to King Ahasuerus was twelve months: six months' treatment with oil of myrrh, and six months' with perfumes and cosmetics. At the end of this each girl's turn came, ¹³ and, when she went from the women's quarters to the king's palace, she was allowed to take with her whatever she asked. ¹⁴ She would enter the palace in the evening and return in the morning to another part of the women's quarters, to be under the care of Shaashgaz, the king's eunuch in charge of the concubines. She would not go again to the king unless he expressed a wish for her and she was summoned by name.

¹⁵ When the turn came for Esther, the girl Mordecai had adopted, the daughter of his uncle Abihail, to go in to the king, she asked for nothing to take with her except what was advised by Hegai, the king's eunuch in charge of the women. Esther charmed all who saw her, ¹⁶ and when she was brought to King Ahasuerus in the royal palace, in the tenth month, the month of Tebeth, in the seventh year of his reign, ¹⁷ the king loved her more than any of his other women. He treated her with greater favour and kindness than all the rest of the virgins, and placed a royal diadem on her head, making her queen in place of Vashti. ¹⁸ Then in Esther's honour the king gave a great banquet, to which were invited all his officers and courtiers. He also proclaimed a holiday throughout his provinces and distributed gifts worthy of a king.

Mordecai and Haman

¹⁹ MORDECAI was in attendance in the court. ²⁰ On his instructions Esther had not disclosed her family or her race, obeying Mordecai in this as she used to do when she was his ward. ²¹ One day when Mordecai was at court, two of the king's eunuchs, Bigthan and Teresh, keepers of the threshold who were disaffected, were plotting to assassinate King Ahasuerus. ²² This became known to Mordecai, who told Queen Esther; and she, on behalf of Mordecai, informed the king. ²³ The matter was investigated and, the report being confirmed, the two men were hanged on the gallows. All this was recorded in the court chronicle in the king's presence.

3 IT was after those events that King Ahasuerus promoted Haman son of Hammedatha the Agagite, advancing him and giving him precedence above all his fellow-officers. ² Everyone in attendance on the king at court bowed down and did obeisance to Haman, for so the king had commanded; but Mordecai would not bow or do obeisance. ³ The courtiers said to him, 'Why do you flout his majesty's command?' ⁴ They challenged him day after day, and when he refused to listen they informed Haman, in order to discover if Mordecai's conduct would be tolerated, for he had told them that he was a Jew. ⁵ Haman was furious when he saw that Mordecai was not bowing down or doing obeisance to him; ⁶ but having learnt who Mordecai's people were, he scorned to lay hands on him alone; he looked for a way to exterminate not only Mordecai but all the Jews throughout the whole kingdom.

⁷ In the twelfth year of King Ahasuerus, in the first month, Nisan, they cast lots — Pur as it is called — in the presence of Haman, taking the days and months one by one, and the

2:18 **a holiday:** *or* an amnesty.　　2:19 **in the court:** *so Gk; Heb. adds* when the virgins were brought together a second time.　　3:7 **and the lot . . . twelfth month:** *prob. rdg, cp. Gk and verse 13; Heb.* the twelfth.

meaning "myrtle." **10:** The requirement of the plot in ch. 6 is the likely reason why *Esther had not disclosed her race or her family.* **11:** We are not told precisely how Mordecai received information. See also vv. 19–23. **16:** *Tebeth* (December–January) is a Babylonian month name. **18:** A *holiday:* see Tfn. **21:** The *keepers of the threshold* guarded the king's private apartment. Xerxes died by assassination in just such a plot. **23:** The delay in a reward for Mordecai foreshadows 6.1–13. *Court chronicle:* see 10.2.

3.1–5.14: Haman's plot against the Jews. 3.1: The identification of Haman as an Agagite (see 2.5–23 n.) subtly emphasizes the hostility between Mordecai and Haman. **7:** *Pur* is a Babylonian word meaning *lot.* The lot fell on the thirteenth day of the twelfth month, the month of Adar.

8 Haman said to King Ahasuerus: 'Dispersed in scattered groups among the peoples throughout the provinces of your realm, there is a certain people whose laws are different from those of every other people. They do not observe the king's laws, and it does not befit your majesty to tolerate them. 9 If it please your majesty, let an order be drawn up for their destruction; and I shall hand over to your majesty's officials the sum of ten thousand talents of silver, to be deposited in the royal treasury.' 10 The king drew off the signet ring from his finger and gave it to Haman son of Hammedatha the Agagite, the enemy of the Jews. 11 'Keep the money,' he said, 'and deal with the people as you think best.'

12 On the thirteenth day of the first month the king's secretaries were summoned and, in accordance with Haman's instructions, a writ was issued to the king's satraps and the governors of every province, and to the rulers over each separate people. It was drawn up in the name of King Ahasuerus and sealed with the king's signet, and transcribed for each province in its own script and for each people in their own language. 13 Dispatches were sent by courier to all the king's provinces with orders to destroy, slay, and exterminate all Jews, young and old, women and children, in one day, the thirteenth day of the twelfth month, the month of Adar; their goods were to be treated as spoil. 14 A copy of the writ was to be issued as a decree in every province and to be publicly displayed to all the peoples, so that they might be ready for that day. 15 At the king's command the couriers set off post-haste, and the decree was issued in Susa the capital city. The king and Haman sat down to carouse, but in the city of Susa confusion reigned.

Esther plans to rescue the Jews

4 WHEN Mordecai learnt of all that had been done, he tore his clothes and put on sackcloth and ashes. He went out through the city, lamenting loudly and bitterly, 2 until he came right in front of the palace gate; no one wearing sackcloth was allowed to pass through that gate. 3 In every province reached by the royal command and decree there was great mourning among the Jews, with fasting and weeping and beating of the breast; most of them lay down on beds of sackcloth and ashes. 4 When Queen Esther's maids and eunuchs came in and told her, she was greatly distraught. She sent clothes for Mordecai to wear instead of his sackcloth; but he would not accept them.

5 Esther then summoned Hathach, one of the king's eunuchs appointed to wait on her, and ordered him to find out from Mordecai what was the trouble and the reason for it. 6 Hathach went out to Mordecai in the city square opposite the palace, 7 and Mordecai told him all that had happened to him and how much money Haman had offered to pay into the royal treasury for the destruction of the Jews. 8 He also gave him a copy of the writ for their extermination, which had been issued in Susa, so that he might show it to Esther and tell her about it, directing her to go to the king to implore his favour and intercede for her people. 9 When Hathach came in and informed Esther of what Mordecai had said, 10 she told him to take back this message: 11 'All the courtiers and the people in the king's provinces know that if any person, man or woman, enters the royal presence in the inner court without being summoned, there is but one law: that person shall be put to death, unless the king extends to him the gold sceptre; only then may he live. What is more, I have not been summoned to the king for the last thirty days.'

12 When Mordecai was told what Esther had said, 13 he sent this reply, 'Do not imagine, Esther, that, because you are in the royal palace, you alone of all the Jews will escape. 14 If you remain silent at such a time as this, relief and deliverance for the Jews will appear from another quarter; but you and your father's family will perish. And who knows whether it is not for a time like this that you have become queen?' 15 Esther sent this an-

swer back to Mordecai: [16]'Go and assemble all the Jews that are in Susa, and fast on my behalf; for three days, night and day, take neither food nor drink, and I also will fast with my maids. After that, in defiance of the law, I shall go to the king; if I perish, I perish.' [17]Mordecai then went away and did exactly as Esther had bidden him.

5 On the third day Esther arrayed herself in her royal robes and stood in the inner court, facing the palace itself; the king was seated on his royal throne in the palace, opposite the entrance. [2]When he caught sight of Queen Esther standing in the court, he extended to her the gold sceptre he held, for she had obtained his favour. Esther approached and touched the tip of the sceptre. [3]The king said to her, 'What is it, Queen Esther? Whatever you request, up to half my kingdom, it shall be granted you.' [4]'If it please your majesty,' she answered, 'will you come today, my lord, and Haman with you, to a banquet I have prepared for you?' [5]The king gave orders for Haman to be brought with all speed to meet Esther's wishes; and the king and Haman went to the banquet she had prepared.

[6]Over the wine the king said to Esther, 'Whatever you ask will be given you; whatever you request, up to half my kingdom, will be granted.' [7]Esther replied, 'What I ask and request is this: [8]If I have found favour with your majesty, and if it please you, my lord, to give me what I ask and to grant my request, will your majesty and Haman come again tomorrow to the banquet that I shall prepare for you both? Tomorrow I shall do as your majesty says.'

[9]Haman left the royal presence that day overjoyed and in the best of spirits, but as soon as he saw Mordecai in the king's court

and observed that he did not rise or defer to him, he was furious; [10]yet he kept control of himself. When he arrived home, he sent for his friends and for Zeresh his wife [11]and held forth to them about the splendour of his wealth and his many sons, and how the king had promoted him and advanced him above the other officers and courtiers. [12]'Nor is that all,' Haman went on; 'Queen Esther had no one but myself come with the king to the banquet which she had prepared; and I am invited by her again tomorrow with the king. [13]Yet all this gives me no satisfaction so long as I see that Jew Mordecai in attendance at the king's court.' [14]His wife Zeresh and all his friends said to him, 'Have a gallows set up, seventy-five feet high, and in the morning propose to the king that Mordecai be hanged on it. Then you can go with the king to the banquet and enjoy yourself.' This advice seemed good to Haman, and he set up the gallows.

Haman executed

6 THAT night sleep eluded the king, so he ordered the chronicle of memorable events to be brought, and it was read to him. [2]There it was found recorded how Mordecai had furnished information about Bigthana and Teresh, the two royal eunuchs among the keepers of the threshold who had plotted to assassinate King Ahasuerus. [3]When the king asked what honour or dignity had been conferred on Mordecai for this, his attendants said, 'Nothing has been done for him.' [4]'Who is in the court?' said the king. As Haman had just then entered the outer court of

5:8 **again tomorrow:** *so Gk; Heb.* omits.
5:14 **seventy-five feet:** *lit.* fifty cubits.
6:2 **Bigthana:** *or* Bigthan; *cp. 2:21.*

famous Persian post service; see 8.10 n.
   4.1–17: Mordecai appeals to Esther. 11: Prohibition to enter without a summons was possibly for security reasons. **14:** *Another quarter* seems to be a veiled allusion to God. The question *"who knows whether . . .?"* implies that Esther's position is providential. See The Rest of the Chapters of the Book of Esther in the Apocrypha. **16:** To *fast* has long been regarded as a pious act which wins divine favor.
   5.1–8: Esther before the king. 2: The gesture of *extending to her the golden sceptre* is explained in 4.11. **3:** *Up to half my kingdom* is gross exaggeration. **4–8:** The early banquets with Haman the only guest, and Esther passing up two opportunities to intercede for her people, are literary devices necessary for working out the plot of the story. **8:** For additional details, see 6.14; 7.3; 8.5.
   5.9–14: Haman's gallows. 14: The height of the *gallows* seems exaggerated, unless it was on a high building or hill for all to see. *Haman . . . set up the gallows,* all the while gleefully thinking it was intended for *Mordecai.*
   6.1–14: Haman's downfall and Mordecai's triumph. 1: The insomnia of kings, a common theme in eastern

the palace to propose to the king that Mordecai should be hanged on the gallows he had prepared for him, [5] the king's attendants replied, 'Haman is standing there in the court.' 'Let him enter!' commanded the king. [6] When he came in, the king asked him, 'What should be done for the man whom the king wishes to honour?' Haman thought to himself, 'Whom, other than myself, would the king wish to honour?' [7] So he answered, 'For the man whom the king wishes to honour, [8] let there be brought a royal robe which the king himself has worn, and a horse on which the king rides, with a royal diadem on its head. [9] Let the robe and the horse be handed over to one of the king's noble officers, and let him invest the man whom the king wishes to honour and lead him mounted on the horse through the city square, proclaiming as he goes: "This is what is done for the man whom the king wishes to honour." ' [10] The king said to Haman, 'Take the robe and the horse at once, as you have said, and do this for Mordecai the Jew who is present at court. Let nothing be omitted of all you have proposed.' [11] Haman took the robe and the horse, invested Mordecai, and led him on horseback through the city square, proclaiming before him: 'This is what is done for the man whom the king wishes to honour.'

[12] Mordecai then returned to court, while Haman in grief hurried off home with his head veiled. [13] When he told his wife Zeresh and all his friends everything that had happened to him, the response he got from his advisers and Zeresh was: 'If you have begun to fall before Mordecai, and he is a Jew, you cannot get the better of him; your downfall before him is certain.'

[14] While they were still talking with him, the king's eunuchs arrived and Haman was hurried off to the banquet Esther had prepared.

7 So the king and Haman went to Queen Esther's banquet, [2] and again on that second day over the wine the king said, 'What-ever you ask will be given you, Queen Esther. Whatever you request, up to half my kingdom, it will be granted.' [3] She answered, 'If I have found favour with your majesty, and if it please you, my lord, what I ask is that my own life and the lives of my people be spared. [4] For we have been sold, I and my people, to be destroyed, slain, and exterminated. If it had been a matter of selling us, men and women alike, into slavery, I should have kept silence; for then our plight would not have been such as to injure the king's interests.' [5] King Ahasuerus demanded, 'Who is he, and where is he, who has dared to do such a thing?' [6] 'A ruthless enemy,' she answered, 'this wicked Haman!' Haman stood aghast before the king and queen. [7] In a rage the king rose from the banquet and went into the garden of the pavilion, while Haman remained where he was to plead for his life with Queen Esther; for he saw that in the king's mind his fate was determined. [8] When the king returned from the pavilion garden to the banqueting hall, Haman had flung himself on the couch where Esther was reclining. The king exclaimed, 'Will he even assault the queen in the palace before my very eyes?' The words had no sooner left the king's lips than Haman's face was covered. [9] Harbona, one of the eunuchs in attendance on the king, said, 'There is a gallows seventy-five feet high standing at Haman's house; he had it erected for Mordecai, whose evidence once saved your majesty.' 'Let Haman be hanged on it!' said the king. [10] So they hanged Haman on the gallows he had prepared for Mordecai. Then the king's anger subsided.

8 That same day King Ahasuerus gave Queen Esther the property of Haman, the enemy of the Jews, and Mordecai came into the king's presence, for Esther had revealed his relationship to her. [2] The king drew off his signet ring, which he had taken

---

7:9 **seventy-five feet:** *lit.* fifty cubits.

literature, is here treated comically. **5:** That *Haman* was *standing there* (during the night!) is a necessity of the plot. **8:** The bestowal of *a royal robe* was common in ancient times; see Gen. 41.42. Horses wearing royal crowns are pictured on Persian monuments. **13:** The *response* to Haman here is another reference to Providence; see 4.14 n. **14:** It was Oriental custom for the guests to be escorted.

7.1–10: Haman's end. 4: *Sold:* a reference to the bribe (3.9–10); Esther could tolerate *slavery* occasioned by the bribe, but *to be destroyed, slain, and exterminated* was intolerable. **9:** *Mordecai, whose evidence once saved your majesty:* Haman has tried to kill a benefactor of the king, and hence all the more merits hanging.

8.1–17: The calamity averted. 2: The transfer of the *signet ring* gives Mordecai the same powers as Haman back from Haman, and gave it to Mordecai. Esther put Mordecai in charge of Haman's property.

The triumphant Jews destroy their enemies

³ ONCE again Esther addressed the king, falling at his feet and imploring him with tears to thwart the wickedness of Haman the Agagite and frustrate his plot against the Jews. ⁴ The king extended his gold sceptre towards her, and she rose and stood before him. ⁵ 'May it please your majesty,' Esther said; 'if I have found favour with you, and if what I propose seems right to your majesty and I have won your approval, let a writ be issued to recall the dispatches which Haman son of Hammedatha the Agagite wrote in pursuance of his plan to destroy the Jews in all the royal provinces. ⁶ For how can I bear to witness the disaster which threatens my people? How can I bear to witness the destruction of my kindred?' ⁷ King Ahasuerus said to Queen Esther and to Mordecai the Jew, 'I have given Haman's property to Esther, and he has been hanged on the gallows because he threatened the lives of the Jews. ⁸ Now you may issue a writ in my name concerning the Jews, in whatever terms you think fit, and seal it with the royal signet; no order written in the name of the king and sealed with the royal signet can be rescinded.'

⁹ On the twenty-third day of the third month, the month of Sivan, the king's secretaries were summoned, and a writ exactly as Mordecai directed was issued to the Jews, and to the satraps, the governors, and the rulers of the hundred and twenty-seven provinces from India to Ethiopia; it was issued for each province in its own script and for each people in their own language, and also for the Jews in their script and language. ¹⁰ The writ was drawn up in the name of King Ahasuerus and sealed with the royal signet, and dispatches were sent by couriers

mounted on horses from the royal stables. ¹¹ By these dispatches the king granted permission to the Jews in each and every city to assemble in self-defence, and to destroy, slay, and exterminate every man, woman, and child, of any people or province which might attack them, and to treat their goods as spoil, ¹² throughout all the provinces of King Ahasuerus, in one day, the thirteenth day of Adar, the twelfth month. ¹³ A copy of the writ was to be issued as a decree in every province and published to all peoples, and the Jews were to be ready for that day, the day of vengeance on their enemies. ¹⁴ Couriers, mounted on horses from the royal stables, set off posthaste at the king's urgent command; and the decree was proclaimed also in Susa the capital.

¹⁵ When Mordecai left the king's presence in a royal robe of violet and white, wearing an imposing gold crown and a cloak of fine linen with purple thread, the city of Susa shouted for joy. ¹⁶ All was light and joy, gladness and honour for the Jews; ¹⁷ in every province and city reached by the royal command and decree there was joy and gladness for the Jews, feasting and holiday. And many of the peoples of the world professed Judaism, because fear of the Jews had fallen on them.

9 ON the thirteenth day of Adar, the twelfth month, the time came for the king's command and decree to be carried out. That very day on which the enemies of the Jews had hoped to triumph over them was to become the day when the Jews should triumph over those who hated them. ² Throughout all the provinces of King Ahasuerus, the Jews assembled in their cities to attack those who had sought to bring disaster on them. None could offer resistance, because fear of them had fallen on all the peoples. ³ The rulers of the provinces, the satraps and the governors, and the royal officials all aided the Jews, out of fear of Mordecai, ⁴ for

8:15 **thread:** *prob. mng; Heb. omits.*

had; see 3.10 n. **5:** Esther emphasizes that the edict against the Jews was from Haman, not the king. **8–17:** Note the general similarity of this passage to 3.9–4.3. The wording in 9–14 is very similar to 3.12–15; the main difference is that it is aimed at the enemies of the Jews. A Persian king would hardly have allowed such a slaughter of his people; this section is not history but theology, legend, emphasizing retributive justice. **9:** *Sivan* is May–June. **10:** Greek writers mention the *horses* of the Persian postal system. **12:** The date is given precisely since it helps date the Purim festival. **15:** The *crown* is the turban of the vizier. **17:** Some interpret the verse to mean conversion to Judaism; some think not conversion, but only association with the Jews took place; see 9.27. Still others regard the verse as just a literary enhancement of the story.

he had become a person of great power in the royal palace, and as the power of the man increased, his fame spread throughout every province. ⁵ The Jews put all their enemies to the sword. There was great slaughter and destruction, and they worked their will on those who hated them.

⁶ In Susa the capital the Jews slaughtered five hundred men; ⁷ and they also put to death Parshandatha, Dalphon, Aspatha, ⁸ Poratha, Adalia, Aridatha, ⁹ Parmashta, Arisai, Aridai, and Vaizatha, ¹⁰ the ten sons of Haman son of Hammedatha, the persecutor of the Jews; but they took no plunder.

¹¹ That day when the number of those killed in Susa was reported to the king, ¹² he said to Queen Esther, 'In Susa the capital the Jews have slaughtered five hundred men; they have killed the ten sons of Haman; what will they have done in the rest of the provinces of the kingdom? Whatever you ask will be given you; whatever further request you have, it will be granted.' ¹³ Esther replied, 'If it please your majesty, let the Jews in Susa be permitted tomorrow also to take action according to this day's decree; and let the bodies of Haman's ten sons be hung up on the gallows.' ¹⁴ The king gave orders for this to be done; the decree was issued in Susa, and Haman's ten sons were hung up on the gallows. ¹⁵ The Jews in Susa assembled again on the fourteenth day of the month of Adar and killed there three hundred men; but they took no plunder.

¹⁶ The rest of the Jews throughout the king's provinces rallied in self-defence and so had respite from their enemies; they slaughtered seventy-five thousand of those who hated them, but they took no plunder. ¹⁷ That was on the thirteenth day of the month of Adar; on the fourteenth day they rested and made it a day of feasting and joy. ¹⁸ The Jews in Susa had assembled on both the thirteenth and fourteenth days of the month; they rested on the fifteenth day and made that a day of feasting and joy. ¹⁹ This explains why Jews in the countryside who live in remote villages observe the fourteenth day of Adar with joy and feasting as a holiday, sending presents of food to one another.

The feast of Purim

²⁰ MORDECAI put these things on record, and he sent letters to all the Jews throughout the provinces of King Ahasuerus, both near and far, ²¹ requiring them to observe annually the fourteenth and fifteenth days of the month of Adar ²² as the days on which the Jews had respite from their enemies; that was the month which was changed for them from sorrow into joy, from a time of mourning to a holiday. They were to observe them as days of feasting and joy, days for sending presents of food to one another and gifts to the poor.

²³ The Jews undertook to continue the practice that they had begun in accordance with Mordecai's letter. ²⁴ This they did because Haman son of Hammedatha the Agagite, the enemy of all the Jews, had plotted to destroy them and had cast lots — Pur as it is called — with intent to crush and destroy them. ²⁵ But when the matter came before the king, he issued written orders that the wicked plot which Haman had devised against the Jews should recoil on his own head, and that he and his sons should be hanged on the gallows. ²⁶ This is why these days were named Purim, from the word Pur. Accordingly, because of all that was written in this letter, because of all they had seen and experienced in this affair, ²⁷ the Jews resolved and undertook, on behalf of themselves, their descendants, and all who might join them, to observe without fail these two days as a yearly festival in the prescribed manner and at the appointed time; ²⁸ further, that these days were to be remembered and celebrated throughout all generations, in every family, province, and city, so that the observance of the days of Purim should

---

9.1–32: The inauguration of the feast of Purim. 7: In MT manuscripts the names of Haman's sons are written in a column one under the other, a peculiar arrangement (similar to Josh. 12.9–23); the reason is unknown, but may reflect triumphalism. **10:** The emphasis here and in vv. 15–16 that *they took no plunder,* despite the permission of 8.11, seems to be a deliberate echo of, and dissent from, 1 Sam. 15.9–35, the Agag story, in which Israel took plunder, to their harm. **15–19:** These verses explain different customs in the observance of Purim, city Jews having a two-day celebration but village Jews only one day. **20–32:** This summary of how Purim became part of the Jewish religious calendar seems to be an addition to the book. It is comprised of Mordecai's letter (vv. 20–22), the deliberate resolve of the Jews (vv. 23–28), and the confirmatory letter of never lapse among the Jews, and the commemoration of them should never cease among their descendants.

²⁹Queen Esther daughter of Abihail gave full authority in writing to Mordecai the Jew, to confirm this second letter about Purim. ³⁰Letters to ensure peace and security were sent to all the Jews in the one hundred and twenty-seven provinces of King Ahasuerus, ³¹requiring the observance of these days of Purim at their appointed time, as Mordecai the Jew and Queen Esther had prescribed for them, and in the same way as regulations for fasts and lamentations were prescribed for themselves and for their descendants. ³²By the command of Esther these regulations for Purim were confirmed and put in writing.

10 King Ahasuerus exacted tribute from the land and the coasts and islands. ²All his acts of might and power, and the high dignities which he conferred on Mordecai, are recorded in the annals of the kings of Media and Persia. ³Mordecai the Jew ranked second only to King Ahasuerus himself; he was a great man among the Jews and popular with all his many countrymen, for he sought the good of his people and promoted the welfare of all their descendants.

9:29 **to Mordecai:** *prob. rdg; Heb.* and Mordecai.
10:1 **tribute:** *or* forced labour.

Esther and Mordecai (vv. 29–32). **31:** *Fasts:* the date is not specified here, but the thirteenth of Adar, set by Haman for the pogrom (3.13), naturally suggests itself; this date is known in the Jewish calendar as "the fast of Esther."

10.1–3: Conclusion. These verses, also an addition (see 9.20–32 n.), exalt the power of Xerxes and his high elevation of Mordecai.

THE BOOK OF
Job

In the Book of Job, a gifted poet and theologian examines the problem of a just God allowing the innocent to suffer. While the literary form may be modeled after the Babylonian "discussion literature"—rather than after Greek tragedy, as is sometimes suggested—the story itself possibly derives from an ancient folktale about an Edomite. External similarities to the Mesopotamian literary works, "The Babylonian Theodicy," "I Will Praise the Lord of Wisdom," and "Man and His God," are worthy of notice, but Job surpasses them in theological depth, human insight, and literary skill.

The structure of the book is as follows: (1) Introduction: a mythological presentation of a meeting in the heavenly court between God and the angels, among whom is the Adversary (chs. 1–2). (2) Poetic dialogue: the central poem containing three cycles of speeches (chs. 3–31). Into this core has been inserted a hymn on the inaccessibility of Wisdom (ch. 28); and speeches by an extraneous character, Elihu, a spokesman for a later orthodoxy that found the arguments of Job blasphemous (chs. 32–37), supplement the dialogue. (3) Divine resolution (chs. 38–42.6) and an epilogue (42.7–17). An alternative reading posits a drama about a hidden conflict (1.1–2.10), a conflict explored (2.11–31.40), and a conflict resolved (32.1–42.17).

The poet boldly challenges the Deuteronomistic theology that goodness is rewarded with material prosperity and wickedness is punished with temporal suffering. While the merit of this position is acknowledged, the poet creates a dialogue in which Job maintains that integrity in the face of disaster must not be sacrificed to social convention, nor even to its established concepts of the deity as upheld by the friends. In the end, Job discovers that his own God as well as that of his friends is too small. Nevertheless, because of his integrity, Job is exonerated and stands before God as intercessor for his friends. And perhaps the key to the book is the view that the suffering righteous individual stands in the presence of God.

The date of the writing is most uncertain. The poet used an old folktale (without the figure of the Adversary or the three friends) as the basic material for the prologue and epilogue. The core dialogue (chs. 3.1–31.40; 38.1–42.6) was probably written in the sixth or fifth century B.C.E. The Elihu material (32.1–37.24) is often viewed as a later addition, along with ch. 28.

Prologue

1 THERE lived in the land of Uz a man of blameless and upright life named Job, who feared God and set his face against wrongdoing. ²He had seven sons and three daughters; ³and he owned seven thousand sheep, three thousand camels, five hundred yoke of oxen, and five hundred she-donkeys, together with a large number of slaves. Thus Job was the greatest man in all the East.

⁴His sons used to meet together and give,

1.1–2.13: The prologue. Job, a devout and prosperous man, is tested for his integrity by calamity and disaster. **1:** *Uz* probably means Edom, although northern Transjordan is possible (see Gen. 36.28 and Jer. 25.20 for the former and Gen. 10.23; 22.21, and 1 Chr. 1.17 for the latter). *Blameless:* lit. whole; the import is not sinless perfection. The name Job occurs widely in the ancient world meaning "Where is my father?" It may also mean "inveterate foe" or else the "penitent one," thus indicating the role of Job and the content of the book. **2:** A family consisting of *seven sons and three daughters* (see Ruth 4.15) was deemed ideal. **3:** The wealth described is that of a seasonally nomadic sheik (note the absence of such items as precious stones or metal). **4:** The each in turn, a banquet in his own house, and they would send and invite their three sisters to eat and drink with them. ⁵Then, when a round of banquets was over, Job would send for his children and sanctify them, rising early in the morning and sacrificing a whole-offering for each of them; for he thought that they might somehow have sinned against God and committed blasphemy in their hearts. This Job did regularly.

⁶The day came when the members of the court of heaven took their places in the presence of the LORD, and the Adversary, Satan, was there among them. ⁷The LORD asked him where he had been. 'Ranging over the earth', said the Adversary, 'from end to end.' ⁸The LORD asked him, 'Have you considered my servant Job? You will find no one like him on earth, a man of blameless and upright life, who fears God and sets his face against wrongdoing.' ⁹'Has not Job good reason to be godfearing?' answered the Adversary. ¹⁰'Have you not hedged him round on every side with your protection, him and his family and all his possessions? Whatever he does you bless, and everywhere his herds have increased beyond measure. ¹¹But just stretch out your hand and touch all that he has, and see if he will not curse you to your face.' ¹²'Very well,' said the LORD. 'All that he has is in your power; only the man himself you must not touch.' With that the Adversary left the LORD's presence.

¹³On the day when Job's sons and daughters were eating and drinking in the eldest brother's house, ¹⁴a messenger came to Job and said, 'The oxen were ploughing and the donkeys were grazing near them, ¹⁵when the Sabaeans swooped down and carried them off, after putting the herdsmen to the sword; only I have escaped to bring you the news.' ¹⁶While he was still speaking, another mes-senger arrived and said, 'God's fire flashed from heaven, striking the sheep and the shepherds and burning them up; only I have escaped to bring you the news.' ¹⁷While he was still speaking, another arrived and said, 'The Chaldaeans, three bands of them, have made a raid on the camels and carried them off, after putting those tending them to the sword; only I have escaped to bring you the news.' ¹⁸While this man was speaking, yet another arrived and said, 'Your sons and daughters were eating and drinking in their eldest brother's house, ¹⁹when suddenly a whirlwind swept across from the desert and struck the four corners of the house, which fell on the young people. They are dead, and only I have escaped to bring you the news.' ²⁰At this Job stood up, tore his cloak, shaved his head, and threw himself prostrate on the ground, ²¹saying:

'Naked I came from the womb,
naked I shall return whence I came.
The LORD gives and the LORD takes
    away;
blessed be the name of the LORD.'

²²Throughout all this Job did not sin, nor did he ascribe any fault to God.

2 Once again the day came when the members of the court of heaven took their places in the presence of the LORD, and the Adversary was there among them. ²The LORD enquired where he had been. 'Ranging over the earth', said the Adversary, 'from end to end.' ³The LORD asked, 'Have you considered my servant Job? You will find no one like him on earth, a man of blameless and upright life, who fears God and sets his face against wrongdoing. You incited me to ruin him without cause, but he still holds fast to his

1:6 **members . . . heaven:** *lit.* sons of God.

---

banquet is possibly to be understood as an annual festival celebration. **5:** *Sanctity:* a ceremonial removal of ritual uncleanness in preparation for worship; see Exod. 19.15; Lev. 11.39–47; Num. 11.18. **6:** For the ancients, human events were decided in divine councils; see 1 Kgs. 22.19–22; Isa. 6.8. *Adversary:* Heb. "the satan," accuser, apparently a legal term (Ps. 109.6), and not yet the proper name for an evil being it was to become later. This title and function possibly derive from the Persian secret police, and the duties would compare to those of a district attorney in the United States. The Adversary is the enemy of human beings, not of God. **10:** *Hedged him round:* the barrier of thorns would keep adversity away from Job's territory (see Hos. 2.6 for the figure). **15:** *Sabaeans:* nomads from Arabia. **16:** The author makes skillful use of a refrain, "Only I have escaped . . ." here and in the following verses. *God's fire:* lightning. **17:** *Chaldaeans:* the biblical word for Babylonians. The import here is wandering marauders, not invaders. **19:** *Whirlwind:* a wind much more violent than the sirocco (*hamsin*). **21:** *The womb* is likened to mother earth. *Whence I came:* lit. there, a euphemism for Sheol, integrity.' ⁴The Adversary replied, 'Skin for skin! To save himself there is nothing a man will withhold. ⁵But just reach out your hand and touch his bones and his flesh, and see if he will not curse you to your face.' ⁶The LORD said to the Adversary, 'So be it. He is in your power; only spare his life.'

⁷When the Adversary left the LORD's presence, he afflicted Job with running sores from the soles of his feet to the crown of his head, ⁸and Job took a piece of a broken pot to scratch himself as he sat among the ashes. ⁹His wife said to him, 'Why do you still hold fast to your integrity? Curse God, and die!' ¹⁰He answered, 'You talk as any impious woman might talk. If we accept good from God, shall we not accept evil?' Throughout all this, Job did not utter one sinful word.

¹¹When Job's three friends, Eliphaz of Teman, Bildad of Shuah, and Zophar of Naamah, heard of all these calamities which had overtaken him, they set out from their homes, arranging to go and condole with him and comfort him. ¹²But when they first saw him from a distance, they did not recognize him; they wept aloud, tore their cloaks, and tossed dust into the air over their heads. ¹³For seven days and seven nights they sat beside him on the ground, and none of them spoke a word to him, for they saw that his suffering was very great.

Job's complaint to God

3 ¹⁻²AFTER this Job broke his silence and cursed the day of his birth:

³Perish the day when I was born,
and the night which said, 'A boy is conceived'!

⁴May that day turn to darkness;
may God above not look for it,
nor light of dawn shine on it.
⁵May gloom and deep darkness claim it again;
may cloud smother that day, blackness eclipse its sun.

⁶May blind darkness swallow up that night!
May it not be counted among the days of the year
or reckoned in the cycle of the months.
⁷May that night be barren for ever,
may no cry of joy be heard in it.
⁸Let it be cursed by those whose spells bind the sea monster,
who have the skill to tame Leviathan.
⁹May no star shine out in its twilight;
may it wait for a dawn that never breaks,
and never see the eyelids of the morning,
¹⁰because it did not shut the doors of the womb that bore me
and keep trouble away from my sight.

¹¹Why was I not stillborn,
why did I not perish when I came from the womb?
¹²Why was I ever laid on my mother's knees
or put to suck at her breasts?
¹⁶Or why was I not concealed like an untimely birth,
like an infant who never saw the light?
¹³For now I should be lying in the quiet grave,

3:8 **sea monster:** *prob. rdg; Heb.* day.   3:12–17 *Verse 16 transposed to follow verse 12.*

the netherworld. **2.4:** *Skin for skin:* a proverbial expression meaning "value for value." **7:** It is impossible to determine the illness; some sort of skin boil is suggested. **9:** Death was not an immediate result of cursing God: the hope here is that death may soon follow. **11:** *Teman:* see Jer. 49.7 n. *Shuah:* perhaps Edom or Arabia (see Gen. 25.2; 1 Chr. 1.32). *Naamah:* an unknown place (but see Josh. 15.41).

3.1–26: Job's complaint to God. Two subtle links unite the poetry with the folk narrative, namely the curse (which is against Job's day of birth rather than God) and an ironic reference to God's hedging in of Job on all sides (1.10), now no longer a sign of favor (v. 23). **1:** Compare Jer. 20.14–18. **8:** Astrologers and magicians were reputed to have dominance, by means of incantations, over the dragon of chaos, *Leviathan;* the mythological monster, mentioned frequently in Canaanite literature, plays a prominent role in Israelite poetry as the embodiment of disorder (Job 7.12; 9.13 n.; 26.12–13; Pss. 74.13–14; 104.26; Isa. 27.1, etc.). In the Babylonian creation story, the god Marduk slays the monster. **12:** The repeated *why* (vv. 12, 16, 20, 23) shows Job confused over the meaning of his suffering but not questioning the justice of God. His friends raise that issue (4.7–9). **13:** The positive attitude toward Sheol (see 1.21 n.) as providing anticipated rest is in contrast to the

asleep in death, at rest
14 with kings and their earthly counsellors
who built for themselves cities now laid
waste,
15 or with princes rich in gold
whose houses were replete with silver.

17 There the wicked chafe no more,
there the tired labourer takes his ease;
18 the captive too finds peace there,
no slave-driver's voice reaches him;
19 high and low alike are there,
even the slave, free from his master.
20 Why should the sufferer be born to see
the light?
Why is life given to those who find it so
bitter?
21 They long for death but it does not
come,
they seek it more eagerly than hidden
treasure.
22 They are glad when they reach the
grave;
when they come to the tomb they exult.
23 Why should a man be born to wander
blindly,
hedged about by God on every side?

24 Sighing is for me all my food;
groans pour from me in a torrent.
25 Every terror that haunted me has
caught up with me;
what I dreaded has overtaken me.
26 There is no peace of mind, no quiet for
me;
trouble comes, and I have no rest.

First cycle of speeches

4 THEN Eliphaz the Temanite spoke up:

2 If one should venture a word with you,
would you lose patience?

Yet who could curb his tongue any
longer?
3 Think how you once encouraged many,
how you braced feeble arms,
4 how a word from you upheld those
who stumbled
and put strength into failing knees.
5 But now adversity comes on you, and
you are impatient;
it touches you, and you are dismayed.
6 Does your piety give you no assurance?
Does your blameless life afford you no
hope?
7 For consider, has any innocent person
ever perished?
Where have the upright ever been
destroyed?
8 This is what I have seen:
those who plough mischief and sow
trouble
reap no other harvest.
9 They perish at the blast of God;
they are shrivelled by the breath of his
nostrils.
10 The roar of the lion, the whimpering
of his cubs, fall silent;
the teeth of the young lions are broken;
11 the lion perishes for lack of prey
and the whelps of the lioness are
abandoned.

12 A word came to me stealthily,
so that my ear caught a mere whisper
of it.
13 In the anxious visions of the night
when everyone sinks into deepest sleep,
14 terror seized me and shuddering;
it made my whole frame tremble with
fear.
15 A wind brushed across my face
and made the hairs of my body stand
on end.

3:15 whose . . . replete: or who filled their final
resting-places. 4:15 wind: or breath.

Semite's usual fear of the underworld and underlines Job's present misery. **23:** *Hedged about:* see 3.1–26 n.

4.1–14.22: First cycle of speeches.

4.1–5.27: Eliphaz's first speech. Gently Eliphaz broaches the central ideas that will recur throughout the friends' speeches: people cannot be more righteous than God, and even celestial beings have no claim to purity in God's sight. **2:** Note the courtesy here. "The Babylonian Theodicy," a somewhat similar work, is replete with politeness, even while the argument is vehement. Eliphaz is not above harsh innuendo (vv. 5–7) and even open attack (vv. 8–9). **7:** The view expressed that the righteous do not suffer is an implied slur, a vicious one, and Job is later (12.4) portrayed responding to it. (See the similar formulations in Ps. 37.25, Prov. 12.21, Ecclus. 2.10, etc.) **12–21:** The appeal to subjective *visions of the night* is a subtle admission that the Wisdom tradition which drew its conclusions from empirical evidence had no cogent answer to suffering. The *visions* are in the

¹⁶A figure halted there, whose shape I
could not discern,
an apparition loomed before me,
and I heard a voice murmur:
¹⁷'Can a human being be righteous
before God,
a mere mortal pure before his Maker?
¹⁸If God mistrusts his own servants
and finds his messengers at fault,
¹⁹how much more those who dwell in
houses of clay,
whose foundations are in the dust,
which can be crushed like a bird's nest,
²⁰torn down between dawn and dusk.
How much more shall they perish
unheeded for ever,
²¹die without ever finding wisdom!'

5 Call if you will; is there any to answer
you?
To whom among the holy ones will you
turn?
²Fools are destroyed by their own angry
passion,
and the end of childish resentment is
death.
³I have seen it for myself: fools
uprooted,
their homes in sudden ruin,
⁴their children cut off from help,
browbeaten in court with none to come
to their defence.
⁵Their rich possessions are snatched
from them;
what they have harvested others
hungrily devour;
panting, thirsting for their wealth,
stronger men seize it from the
panniers.
⁶Mischief does not grow out of the
ground,
nor does trouble spring from the
soil;
⁷yet man is born to trouble,
as surely as birds fly upwards.

⁸For my part, I would make my appeal
to God;
I would lay my plea before him
⁹who does great and unsearchable
things,
marvels beyond all reckoning.
¹⁰He gives rain to the earth
and sends water over the fields;
¹¹he raises the lowly on high,
and the mourners are lifted to safety;
¹²he frustrates the plots of the crafty,
and they achieve no success;
¹³he traps the cunning in their own
craftiness,
and the schemers' plans are thrown into
confusion.
¹⁴By day they encounter darkness,
and grope their way at noon as in the
night;
¹⁵he saves the destitute from their greed,
and the needy from the clutches of the
strong.
¹⁶So the poor have hope again,
to the outrage of the unjust.

¹⁷Happy indeed are they whom God
rebukes!
Therefore do not reject the Almighty's
discipline.
¹⁸For, though he wounds, he will bind
up;
the hands that harm will heal.
¹⁹You may meet disaster six times, and
he will rescue you;
seven times, and no harm will touch
you.
²⁰In famine he will deliver you from
death,

4:17 **righteous before:** *or* more righteous than. **pure
before:** *or* more pure than.   4:19 **bird's nest:** *or*
moth.   4:21 **die ... wisdom:** *prob. rdg, transposing*
Their rich possessions are snatched from them *to follow*
5:4.   5:3 **ruin:** *prob. rdg; Heb. obscure.*   5:4 **in
court:** *lit.* in the gate.   5:5 **Their ... them:** *line
transposed from 4:21.*   5:7 **birds:** *or* sparks.
5:15 **greed:** *lit.* mouths.

tradition of professional prophecy which was at this time in disrepute. See Ezek. 13.6–16; Zech. 13.2–6. **18:**
Messengers: angels. **19:** *Houses:* the human body. In later literature, e.g. Wisd. 9.15, there is development of
the idea in this verse, there influenced by strands of Greek thought in which anything material was devalued.
5.1: *Holy ones:* members of the heavenly court; see 1.6 n. **2:** This verse quotes or paraphrases a proverb like
29.11. **4:** The word translated *court* means "gates"; justice was administered at the gates of the city. **7:** See
Tfn. **17–18:** Divine *discipline* of human beings, *musar* in Heb., is emphasized by Elihu in 33.14–30; 36.7–15.
The theme of discipline as a means of education and correction is frequent in Wisdom literature; see Ecclus.
4.17; 32.14. The *Almighty* will heal Job if he does *not reject* his suffering as a correction for his evil-doing.
19: *Six ... seven:* a frequent numerical device meaning "totality." It originates from the pattern of poetic

in battle from the menace of the sword.
21 You will be shielded from the scourge
  of slander,
  unafraid when violence comes.
22 You will laugh at violence and famine
  and need not fear any beast on earth;
23 for you will be in league with the stones
  of the fields,
  and the wild animals have been
  constrained to leave you at peace.
24 You will know that all is well with your
  household,
  you will look round your home and
  find nothing amiss;
25 you will know that your descendants
  will be many
  and your offspring like grass, thick on
  the earth.
26 You will come to the grave in sturdy
  old age
  as sheaves come in due season to the
  threshing-floor.
27 We have enquired into all this, and so
  it is;
  this we have heard, and know it to be
  true for you.

6 Job answered:

2 If only the grounds for my resentment
  might be weighed,
  and my misfortunes placed with them
  on the scales!
3 For they would outweigh the sands of
  the sea:
  what wonder if my words are frenzied!
4 The arrows of the Almighty find their
  mark in me,
  and their poison soaks into my spirit;
  God's onslaughts wear me down.
5 Does a wild ass bray when it has
  grass
  or an ox low when it has fodder?
6 Is tasteless food eaten unseasoned,

or is there any flavour in the juice of
  mallows?
7 Such food sticks in my throat,
  and my bowels rumble like an echo.

8 If only I might have my request
  and God would grant what I hope for:
9 that he would be pleased to crush me,
  to sever with his hand and cut me off!
10 That would bring me relief,
  and in the face of unsparing anguish I
  would leap for joy,
  for I have never denied the words of
  the Holy One.
11 Have I the strength to go on waiting?
  What end have I to expect, that I
  should be patient?
12 Is my strength the strength of stone,
  or is my flesh made of bronze?
13 Oh how shall I find help within myself
  now that success has been put beyond
  my reach?

14 Devotion is due from his friends
  to one who despairs and loses faith in
  the Almighty;
15 but my brothers have been deceptive as
  a torrent,
  like the watercourses of torrents that
  run dry.
16 They turn dark with ice
  and are hidden with piled-up snow;
17 but they vanish the moment they are in
  spate,
  dwindle in the heat and are gone.
18 Caravans, winding hither and thither,
  go up into the desert and perish;
19 the caravans of Tema look for the
  water,
  the travelling merchants of Sheba rely
  on it;
20 but they are disappointed, for all their
  confidence,
  they arrive, only to be frustrated.

parallelism. **23:** Job's acceptance of correction will insure a *league,* i.e. harmony, with the *stones* and *wild animals* since they too obey God. Stones are the bane of the Palestinian fields whose soil is very shallow. **27:** Eliphaz here reinforces his earlier mention of God's way and discipline (vv. 10–17) by an appeal to what he has learned from experience.

6.1–7.21: Job's answer. His distress has come from God, unjustly. He will not abstain from expressing his bitterness. **3–12:** Job's *frenzied words* are as involuntary and physical as the lowing of an ox when hungry, for his flesh is not *bronze.* **4:** While fire *arrows* were used in the ancient Near East, there is no OT evidence of poison arrows outside this verse. The metaphor of God as an archer occurs frequently (Deut. 32.23; Ezek. 5.16; Ps. 7.13). **15–20:** Streams in Palestine rush into the plain filled with water from mountain rain and *snow* but quickly lose themselves as they *run dry* in the *heat* and sand of the desert. Those who follow their banks

21 Just so unreliable have you now been to
   me:
   you felt dismay and took fright.
22 Did I ever say, 'Give me this or that,'
   or say, 'Use your wealth to save my
   life'?
23 Did I say, 'Rescue me from my enemy's
   grip,'
   or, 'Ransom me from the clutches of
   ruthless people'?
24 Tell me plainly, and I shall listen in
   silence;
   show me where I have been at fault.
25 How harsh are the words of the
   upright!
   But what do your arguments prove?
26 Do you mean to argue about mere
   words?
   Surely such despairing utterance is
   mere wind.
27 Would you assail an orphan?
   Would you make attacks on your
   friend?
28 So now, I beg you, turn and look at
   me:
   am I likely to lie to your faces?
29 Think again, let me have no more
   injustice;
   think again, for my integrity is in
   question.
30 Do I ever give voice to injustice?
   Have I not the sense to discern when
   my words are wild?

7 Does not every mortal have hard
   service on earth,
   and are not his days like those of a
   hired labourer,
2 like those of a slave longing for the
   shade
   or a servant kept waiting for his wages?
3 So months of futility are my portion,
   troubled nights are my lot.
4 When I lie down, I think,
   'When will it be day, that I may rise?'

But the night drags on,
and I do nothing but toss till dawn.
5 My body is infested with worms,
and scabs cover my skin;
it is cracked and discharging.
6 My days pass more swiftly than a
weaver's shuttle
and come to an end as the thread of
life runs out.

7 Remember that my life is but a breath
of wind;
I shall never again see good times.
8 The eye that now sees me will behold
me no more;
under your very eyes I shall vanish.
9 As a cloud breaks up and disperses,
so no one who goes down to Sheol ever
comes back;
10 he never returns to his house,
and his abode knows him no more.

11 But I cannot hold my peace;
I shall speak out in my anguish of spirit
and complain in my bitterness of soul.
12 Am I the monster of the deep, am I
the sea serpent,
that you set a watch over me?
13 When I think that my bed will comfort
me,
that sleep will relieve my complaint,
14 you terrify me with dreams
and affright me through visions.
15 I would rather be choked outright;
death would be better than these
sufferings of mine.
16 I am in despair, I have no desire to
live;
let me alone, for my days are but a
breath.
17 What is man, that you make much of
him

6:21 **Just ... to me:** *prob. rdg; Heb. obscure.*
6:27 **orphan:** *or* blameless person.   7:4 **day, that:** *so
Gk; Heb. omits.*   7:6 **as ... out:** *or* without hope.
7:9 **Sheol:** *or* the underworld.   7:15 **sufferings:**
prob. rdg; Heb. bones.

in security suddenly find themselves without water. **22–23:** Job does not ask his friend to take any risks to *save*
his *life*, he asks only for compassion. **26–27:** Job accuses his friends of being heartless with a man in despair
and of a power play against an *orphan*, a helpless *friend*. **29:** *Think again:* lit. turn back. **7.1–6:** Job universalizes
his experience. **1:** *Service:* the image seems to derive from military duty. **6:** As a shuttle runs out of thread,
so Job's life is being emptied of hope. **9:** *Sheol:* the netherworld. **12:** Job, here addressing God, in effect is
saying: "Am I a threat to divine order like the chaos *monster* (see 3.8 n.) who requires constant surveillance?"
17–18: The traditional sublime celebration of God's concern for people (see Ps. 8) here becomes a parody,
for Job wishes God to abstain from taking thought of him; beneficent providence has been replaced by divine

and turn your thoughts towards him,

18 only to punish him morning after morning
or to test him every hour of the day?

19 Will you not look away from me for an instant,
leave me long enough to swallow my spittle?

20 If I have sinned, what harm can I do you,
you watcher of the human heart?
Why have you made me your target?
Why have I become a burden to you?

21 Why do you not pardon my offence
and take away my guilt?
For soon I shall lie in the dust of the grave;
you may seek me, but I shall be no more.

8 Then Bildad the Shuhite spoke up:

2 How long will you go on saying such things,
those long-winded ramblings of an old man?

3 Does God pervert justice?
Does the Almighty pervert what is right?

4 If your sons sinned against him,
he has left them to be victims of their own iniquity.

5 If only you yourself will seek God
and plead for the favour of the Almighty,

6 if you are pure and upright,
then indeed he will watch over you
and see your just intent fulfilled.

7 Then, though your beginnings were humble,
your future will be very great.

8 Enquire now of older generations
and consider the experience of their forefathers;

9 for we are but of yesterday and know nothing;
our days on earth are but a passing shadow.

10 Will they not teach you and tell you
and pour out the wisdom of their minds?

11 Can rushes thrive where there is no marsh?
Can reeds flourish without water?

12 While still in flower and not ready for cutting,
they would wither before any green plant.

13 Such is the fate of all who forget God;
the life-thread of the godless breaks off;

14 his confidence is gossamer,
and the basis of his trust a spider's web.

15 He leans against his house, but it does not stand;
he clutches at it, but it does not hold firm.

16 His is the lush growth of a plant in the sun,
pushing out shoots over the garden;

17 but its roots become entangled in a stony patch
and run against a bed of rock.

18 Then someone uproots it from its place,
which disowns it, saying, 'I have never known you.'

19 That is how its life withers away,
and other plants spring up from the earth.

7:20 **heart:** *so Gk; Heb.* omits. **to you:** *so Gk; Heb.* to me.
8:6 **see . . . fulfilled:** *or* restore your rightful habitation.   8:13 **life-thread:** *or* hope.
8:18 **which:** *or* and.

---

harassment. **19–21:** Job finds even God's gaze oppressive. He declares that it is unworthy of God to punish fragile human beings, even though they be guilty, since they do not *harm* God. **20:** *Watcher of the human heart* is meant as a rebuke, not as adoration.

8.1–22: Bildad's first speech, an appeal not to his own experience, but to that of the human race. **4:** Compare the accusation against Job's children with their innocence in 1.4–5. **5–7:** Picking up Job's mention of God's watchfulness (7.19), Bildad assures Job that innocence coupled with repentance will lead to restoration. **8–10:** Lessons, distilled from experience, that have stood the test of time and the scrutiny of the ancients are more worthy to be considered *wisdom* than the subjective experience that is still in flux like a *passing shadow.* **8–9:** See 8.1–22 n. Lessons derived from experience are preserved by the wise. **11–13:** The law of retribution is as certain as the order of nature. **14–19:** Neither the root nor the fruit, i.e. house, of a wicked person's life has sufficient substance to give security. **17:** The metaphor of plants growing in stony ground is also used in

20 Be sure, God will not spurn the
　　blameless man,
　nor will he clasp the hand of the
　　wrongdoer.
21 He will yet fill your mouth with
　　laughter,
　and shouts of joy will be on your lips;
22 your enemies will be wrapped in
　　confusion,
　and the dwellings of the wicked will
　　vanish away.

9 Job answered:

2 Indeed, this I know for the truth:
　that no one can win his case against
　　God.
3 If anyone does choose to argue with
　　him,
　God will not answer one question in a
　　thousand.
4 He is wise, he is all-powerful;
　who has stood up to him and remained
　　unscathed?
5 It is God who moves mountains before
　　they know it,
　overturning them in his wrath;
6 who makes the earth start from its
　　place
　so that its pillars are shaken;
7 who commands the sun not to rise
　and shuts up the stars under his seal;
8 who by himself spread out the heavens
　and trod on the back of the sea
　　monster;
9 who made Aldebaran and Orion,

the Pleiades and the circle of the
　　southern stars;
10 who does great, unsearchable things,
　marvels beyond all reckoning.
11 He goes by me, and I do not see him;
　he moves on his way undiscerned by
　　me.
12 If he hurries on, who can bring him
　　back?
　Who will ask him what he is doing?
13 God does not turn back his wrath;
　the partisans of Rahab lie prostrate at
　　his feet.
14 How much less can I answer him
　or find words to dispute with him?
15 Though I am in the right, I get no
　　answer,
　even if I plead with my accuser for
　　mercy.
16 If I summoned him to court and he
　　responded,
　I do not believe that he would listen to
　　my plea;
17 for he strikes at me for a trifle
　and rains blows on me without cause;
18 he leaves me no respite to recover my
　　breath,
　but sates me with bitter thoughts.
19 If the appeal is to force, see how
　　mighty he is;

9:3 **If anyone ... thousand:** *or* If God is pleased to
argue with him, no one can answer one question in a
thousand.　　9:8 **on ... monster:** *or* on the crests of
the waves.　　9:12 **hurries on:** *so some MSS; others*
seizes.　　9:17 **trifle:** *lit.* hair.

Mk. 4.3–9. **20:** To *clasp the hand* is a symbol of divine election to a favored position and of support in it; see Isa. 42.6; 51.18. **21–22:** God *will yet fill your mouth with laughter . . . and the dwellings of the wicked will vanish away.* Thus, after his earlier harsh criticism of Job, Bildad softens his tone and assures him that God will be just after all if he, Job, will change his attitude.

9.1–10.22: Job's response. The praise of God's majesty (vv. 5–10) gives way (9.11–10.22) to an accusation of divine malice of intent; Job feels the necessity (9.33–35) of calling in an arbitrator between himself and God. **3:** The phrase "one in a thousand" is a hyperbole; see also Eccles. 7.28. **5–10:** The so-called "doxologies" in Amos 4.13; 5.8–9; 9.5–6 are strikingly similar to this hymn. **5:** *Moves mountains:* earthquake. These are often described as accompanying a theophany, e.g. Judg. 5.4. **6:** *Pillars:* the seven columns supporting the cosmic house (see Prov. 9.1). **7:** The *sun* does *not rise* and the *stars* are *under* a *seal* at God's command in an overcast sky. **8:** Note Tfn., "crests of the waves." **9:** The precise identity of these constellations is uncertain. **10:** See 5.9. Job's praise of God's grandeur here seems to surpass that of Eliphaz in a similar hymn in 5.9–16. **11–12:** God cannot be accosted or called into question in any way. **13:** *Rahab:* in folklore the mythological ocean-chaos monster, elsewhere called Leviathan or Tannin, slain by the deity (compare 26.12; Isa. 51.9; Ps. 89.10). In Isa. 30.7 and Ps. 87.4 Rahab and Egypt are identified. **14–20:** An imaginary courtroom, with God pictured as judge and prosecuting attorney. **15:** *Right:* innocent. That is, even when the verdict of innocence is pronounced, Job must beg for mercy. **19:** Here the crucial point is made that God is not subject to human

if to justice, who can compel him to
give me a hearing?
²⁰Though I am in the right, he
condemns me out of my own mouth;
though I am blameless, he makes me
out to be crooked.
²¹Blameless, I say; of myself
I reck nothing, I hold my life cheap.
²²But it is all one; therefore I declare,
'He destroys blameless and wicked
alike.'
²³When a sudden flood brings death,
he mocks the plight of the innocent.
²⁴When a country is delivered into the
power of the wicked,
he blindfolds the eyes of its judges.

²⁵My days have passed more swiftly than
a runner,
they have slipped away without ever
seeing prosperity;
²⁶they have glided by like reed-built
skiffs,
swift as an eagle swooping on its prey.
²⁷If I think, 'I shall forget my complaints,
I shall show a cheerful face and smile,'
²⁸I still dread all I must suffer;
I know that you will not acquit me.
²⁹If I am to be accounted guilty,
why do I waste my labour?
³⁰Though I were to wash myself with
soap
and cleanse my hands with lye,
³¹you would thrust me into the miry pit
and my clothes would render me
loathsome.

³²God is not as I am, not someone I can
challenge,
and say, 'Let us confront one another
in court.'
³³If only there were one to arbitrate
between us
and impose his authority on us
both,

³⁴so that God might take his rod from
my back,
and terror of him might not come on
me suddenly.
³⁵I should then speak out without fear of
him,
for I know I am not what I am thought
to be.

10 I am sickened of life;
I shall give free rein to my
complaints,
speaking out in the bitterness of my
soul.
²I shall say to God, Do not condemn me,
but let me know the charge against me.
³Do you find any advantage in
oppression,
in spurning the work of your own
hands
while smiling on the policy of the
wicked?
⁴Have you the eyes of flesh?
Do you see as a mortal sees?
⁵Are your days as those of a mortal
or your years as his lifespan?
⁶Is that why you look for guilt in me
and seek in me for sin,
⁷though you know that I am guiltless
and have none to save me from your
power?

⁸Your hands shaped and fashioned me;
and will you at once turn and destroy
me?
⁹Recall that you moulded me like clay;
and would you reduce me to dust
again?
¹⁰Did you not pour me out like milk
and curdle me like cheese,
¹¹clothe me with skin and flesh
and knit me together with bones and
sinews?

9:19 **him:** *so Gk; Heb.* me.   9:24 **blindfolds . . .
judges:** *prob. rdg; Heb. adds* if not he, then who?

laws (Jer. 12.1). **20–24:** These bitter verses indict God's governing of the universe as callous indifference, if
not malevolence. Job here abandons the basic premise of all ancient wisdom, namely, an order sustained by
the Creator. **20:** Job, despite his innocence, has no defense against God's power. **30–31:** The image of sin as
filth is frequent, e.g. Zech. 3.3–5. **32–35:** Job pleads that he be allowed to present his case as a human being
without being compared to God and without having to deal with God's awesome might and holiness which
he acknowledges. An arbitrator could bring this about and Job will call for this helper again; see 16.21. **34:**
The divine *rod* is here no comfort; contrast Ps. 23.4. **10.2:** *Charge:* that is, a lawsuit. This figure of speech is
common, especially in prophetic literature. **4–7:** For God to hunt for sin in Job is to act like another human
being who sees only the externals without understanding the depths of earthly existence. God should try to

12 You granted me life and continuing
favour,
   and your providence watched over my
spirit.
13 Yet this was the secret purpose of your
heart,
   and I know what was your intent:
14 that, if I sinned, you would be watching
me
   and would not absolve me of my guilt.
15 If indeed I am wicked, all the worse for
me!
   If I am upright, I cannot hold up my
head;
   I am filled with shame and steeped in
my affliction.
16 If I am proud as a lion, you hunt me
down
   and confront me again with marvellous
power;
17 you renew your onslaught on me,
   and with mounting anger against
me
   bring fresh forces to the attack.

18 Why did you bring me out of the
womb?
   Better if I had expired and no one had
set eyes on me,
19 if I had been carried from womb to
grave
   and were as though I had not been
born.
20 Is not my life short and fleeting?
   Let me be, that I may be happy for a
moment,
21 before I depart to a land of gloom,
   a land of deepest darkness, never to
return,
22 a land of dense darkness and
disorder,
   increasing darkness lit by no ray of
light.

11 Then Zophar the Naamathite spoke
up:

2 Is this spate of words to go
unanswered?
   Must the glib of tongue always be
right?
3 Is your endless talk to reduce others to
silence?
   When you speak irreverently, is no one
to take you to task?
4 You claim that your opinions are
sound;
   you say to God, 'I am spotless in your
sight.'
5 But if only God would speak
   and open his lips to reply,
6 to expound to you the secrets of
wisdom,
   for wonderful are its achievements!
   Know then that God exacts from you
less than your sin deserves.
7 Can you fathom the mystery of God,
   or attain to the limits of the Almighty?
8 They are higher than the heavens.
What can you do?
   They are deeper than Sheol. What can
you know?
9 In extent they are longer than the
earth
   and broader than the ocean.
10 If he passes by, he may keep secret his
passing;
   if he proclaims it, who can turn him
back?
11 He surely knows who are false,
   and when he sees iniquity, does he not
take note of it?
12 A fool will attain to understanding
   when a wild ass's foal is born a human
being!

13 If only you had directed your heart
rightly
   and spread out your hands in prayer to
him!

10:16 **If I am:** *so* Gk; *Heb.* If he is.
10:22 **increasing ... light:** *cp.* Gk; *Heb. obscure.*
11:8 **Sheol:** *or* the underworld.

understand human limitations and predicaments. **13–22:** God, in granting people life, constantly scrutinizes them for their guilt or innocence. So relentlessly does God punish individuals that it seems better for them not to have been born — unless God gives some respite.

11.1–20: Zophar's first speech. He rebukes Job for presuming to understand God's unfathomable character, and exhorts Job to repent. **11:** In Exod. 32.32 and Mal. 3.16–18 the mention of divine record keeping is quite explicit. Late Judaism embellished this idea. **12:** Apparently a popular proverb. Some scholars suggest a change of MT, altering *born a human being* to "come to learn." **13–20:** The rewards for repentance are great; hence, Job should repent for his sins.

¹⁴Any wrongdoing you have in hand,
  thrust it far away,
and do not let iniquity make its home
  with you.
¹⁵Then you could hold up your head
  without fault;
you would be steadfast and fearless.
¹⁶Then you will forget trouble,
  remembering it only as floodwaters that
    have passed.
¹⁷Life will be lasting, radiant as noon,
  and darkness will be turned to
    morning.
¹⁸You will be confident, because there is
  hope;
  sure of protection, you will rest in
    confidence
¹⁹and lie down unafraid.
  The great will court your favour.
²⁰But blindness will fall on the wicked;
  to them the ways of escape are closed,
  and their only hope is death.

12 Job answered:

²No doubt you are intelligent people,
  and when you die, wisdom will
    perish!
³But I have sense, as well as you;
  in no way do I fall short of you;
  what gifts indeed have you that others
    have not?
⁴Yet I am a laughing-stock to my
  friends—
  a laughing-stock, though I am innocent
    and blameless:
  one that called upon God, but he
    afflicted me.
⁵Those at ease look down on misfortune,
  on the blow that fells one who is
    already reeling,
⁶while the marauders' tents are left
  undisturbed
  and those who provoke God live safe
    and sound.

⁷But ask the beasts, and they will teach
  you;
  ask the birds of the air to inform you,
⁸or tell the creatures that crawl to teach
  you,
  and the fish of the sea to instruct you.
⁹Who does not come to know from all
  these
  that the hand of the LORD has done
    this?
¹⁰In his hand are the souls of all that live,
  the spirits of every human being.
¹¹Does not the ear test words
  as the palate savours food?
¹²'Is wisdom with the aged?
  Does long life bring understanding?'

¹³'With God are wisdom and power,
  to him belong counsel and
    understanding.'
¹⁴If he pulls down, there is no
  rebuilding;
  if he imprisons, there is no release.
¹⁵If he holds back the waters, there is
  drought;
  if he lets them loose, the earth is
    overwhelmed.
¹⁶Strength and success belong to him,
  deceived and deceiver are his to use.
¹⁷He makes counsellors behave like
  madmen
  and turns judges crazy;
¹⁸he looses the bonds imposed by kings
  and removes the girdle of office from
    their waists;
¹⁹he makes priests behave like idiots
  and overthrows those long in office;
²⁰trusted counsellors he strikes with
  dumbness,
  he robs the old of their judgement;

12:2 **intelligent:** *prob. rdg; Heb. omits.*   12:4 **but . . .
me:** *or* and he answered.   12:6 **those . . . sound:**
prob. rdg; Heb. adds into whose hands God brings.
12:18 **removes . . . from:** *or* binds a loincloth on.
12:19 **those . . . office:** *or* temple servitors.

12.1–14.22: Job's response. He is no less wise than his friends, for even dumb animals understand shallow matters. To lie on behalf of God is wrong, and will be punished no less. Let God directly confront Job and let Job speak. People are frail and have only one life to live; why, then, is God so severe? **2:** *Intelligent people . . . wisdom:* the words are sarcastic. See also 13.2. **4–6:** As in society everywhere it is much easier to make a scapegoat of a helpless person for some trivial fault than to confront a powerful person for a serious wrong. **7–9:** Job observes that such profound knowledge as his visitors have shown is known to the lowest creatures. **9:** LORD: Nowhere else in Job (except perhaps at 28.28) does the poetry use the divine name Yahweh, whereas the prose prologue and epilogue employ it regularly. *Hand has done this:* compare Isa. 41.20. **12:** An ironic question. **13–25:** The fate which God decrees for humankind or nations is not subject to alteration, and divine

²¹ he pours scorn on princes
and abates the arrogance of nobles.
²² He unveils mysteries deep in obscurity
and into thick darkness he brings light.
²³ He leads peoples astray and destroys
them,
he lays them low, and there they lie.
²⁴ He deprives the nations' rulers of their
wits
and leaves them wandering in a
trackless desert;
²⁵ without light they grope their way in
darkness
and are left to wander like drunkards.

13 All this I have seen with my own
eyes,
with my own ears I have heard and
understood it.
² What you know, I also know;
in no way do I fall short of you.
³ Nevertheless I would speak with the
Almighty;
I am ready to argue with God,
⁴ while you go on smearing truth with
your falsehoods,
one and all stitching a patchwork of
lies.
⁵ If only you would be silent
and let silence be your wisdom!

⁶ Listen, now, to my arguments;
attend while I put my case.
⁷ Is it on God's behalf that you speak so
wickedly,
in his defence that you voice what is
false?
⁸ Must you take God's part,
putting his case for him?
⁹ Will all go well when he examines you?
Can you deceive him as you could a
human being?
¹⁰ He will most surely expose you
if you take his part by falsely accusing
me.
¹¹ Will not God's majesty strike you with
dread,
and fear of him overcome you?

¹² Your moralizing talk is so much dross,
your arguments crumble like clay.

¹³ Be silent, leave me to speak my mind,
and let what may come upon me!
¹⁴ Why do I expose myself to danger
and take my life in my hands?
¹⁵ If he wishes to slay me, I have nothing
to lose;
I shall still defend my conduct to his
face.
¹⁶ This at least assures my deliverance:
that no godless person may appear
before him.
¹⁷ Listen closely, then, to my words,
and give a hearing to my statement.
¹⁸ Be sure of this: once I have stated my
case
I know that I shall be acquitted.
¹⁹ Who is there that can make a case
against me
so that I should be reduced to silence
and death?

²⁰ God, grant me these two conditions
only,
and then I shall not hide out of your
sight:
²¹ remove your hand from upon me
and let not fear of you strike me with
dismay.
²² Then summon me, and I shall respond;
or let me speak first, and you answer
me.
²³ How many crimes and sins are laid to
my charge?
Let me know my offence and my sin.
²⁴ Why do you hide your face
and treat me as your enemy?
²⁵ Will you harass a wind-driven leaf
and pursue dry chaff,
²⁶ that you draw up bitter charges against
me,
making me heir to the iniquities of my
youth,
²⁷ putting my feet in the stocks,

13:12 **your arguments ... clay:** *lit.* the bosses of your
shields are bosses of clay.　　13:14 **expose ... danger:**
lit. take my flesh in my teeth.

causality is all-pervasive. **13.5:** In Egyptian Wisdom literature "the silent one" is an epithet for the sage, as over
against "the passionate one." **7–12:** Job's friends are accused of defending God with lies. **10:** Job here argues
on the basis of a just God, an idea he has previously rejected. **15:** An older (and traditional) translation
incorrectly renders the verse as expressive of unflagging trust in God: "Though God slay me, I shall wait for
the deity." **15–16:** Some interpreters view this passage as the key to the book, namely, confidence that no sinner
can stand before God; since God later appears to him, Job is vindicated. **27:** For purposes of tracking runaway

keeping a close watch on all I do,
and setting a slave-mark on my instep?

14 Every being born of woman is
short-lived and full of trouble.
[2] He blossoms like a flower and withers
away;
fleeting as a shadow, he does not
endure;
he is like a wineskin that perishes
or a garment that moths have eaten.
[3] It is on such a creature you fix your
eyes,
and bring him into court before you!
[5] Truly the days of such a one's life are
determined,
and the number of his months is
known to you;
you have laid down a limit, which
cannot be exceeded.
[6] Look away from him therefore and
leave him
to count off the hours like a hired
labourer.

[7] If a tree is cut down,
there is hope that it will sprout again
and fresh shoots will not fail.
[8] Though its root becomes old in the
earth,
its stump dying in the ground,
[9] yet when it scents water it may break
into bud
and make new growth like a young
plant.
[10] But when a human being dies all his
power vanishes;
he expires, and where is he then?
[11] As the waters of a lake dwindle,
or as a river shrinks and runs dry,
[12] so mortal man lies down, never
to rise
until the very sky splits open.
If a man dies, can he live again?

He can never be roused from this
sleep.

[13] If only you would hide me in Sheol,
conceal me until your anger is past,
and only then fix a time to recall me to
mind!
[14] I would not lose hope, however long
my service,
waiting for my relief to come.
[15] You would summon me, and I would
answer;
you would long to see the creature you
have made,
[16] whereas now you count my every step,
watching all my errant course.
[17] Every offence of mine is stored in your
bag,
where you keep my iniquity under seal.
[18] Yet as a falling mountainside is swept
away,
and a rock is dislodged from its place,
[19] as water wears away stone,
and a cloudburst scours the soil from
the land,
so you have wiped out the hope of frail
man;
[20] finally you overpower him, and he is
gone;
with changed appearance he is
banished from your sight.
[21] His sons may rise to honour, but he is
unaware of it;
they may sink into obscurity, but he
knows it not.

13:27 **setting ... instep:** *prob. rdg; Heb. adds verse 28,*
he is like ... have eaten, *now transposed to follow 14:2.*
14:2 **he is ... eaten:** *13:28 transposed here.*
14:3 **into ... you:** *so one MS; others add* [4]Who can
produce pure out of unclean? No one. 14:6 **and
leave him:** *so one MS; others that he may cease.*
14:12 **If ... again:** *line transposed from beginning of verse
14.* 14:13 **Sheol:** *or the underworld.* 14:14 *See
note on verse 12.*

slaves, a *mark* was cut on the bottoms of their feet. **14.1–22:** Human life is limited and death is the end. **12:**
Until the very sky splits open is here a symbol of the hopelessness of a person ever returning from Sheol. It
is not an apocalyptic symbol for the end of the world and the resurrection from the dead. **13:** Job sees his plight
as a temporary *anger* on God's part which would abate if he could but escape God's sight. Since in some circles
of Israelite belief God was absent from Sheol, Job asks to be hidden there for a fixed time, rather than in death
from which he can *never be roused*. **15:** Job recognizes that God could love him since the deity could long
to see him, *a creature;* therefore the underlying principle of the relationship to God is not justice but love. **17:**
Bag: tiny stones may have been used for counting sheep; the bag, then, connotes tabulation and recording
(see 11.11 n.). **20:** A person's changed appearance indicated anger, fear, or consternation; compare Dan. 5.6,
9, 10.

22 His kinsfolk are grieved for him
   and his slaves mourn his loss.

Second cycle of speeches

15 Then Eliphaz the Temanite answered:

2 Would a sensible person give vent to
   such hot-air arguments
   or puff himself up with an east wind?
3 Would he bandy useless words
   and speeches so unprofitable?
4 Why! You even banish the fear of God
   from your mind,
   cutting off all communication with him.
5 Your iniquity dictates what you say,
   and deceit is your chosen language.
6 You are condemned out of your own
   mouth, not by me;
   your own lips testify against you.

7 Were you the firstborn of mankind,
   brought forth before the hills?
8 Do you listen in God's secret council
   or usurp all wisdom for yourself alone?
9 What do you know that we do not
   know?
   What insight have you that we do not
   share?
10 We have age and white hairs in our
   company,
   men older than your father.
11 Does not consolation from God suffice
   you,
   a word whispered quietly in your ear?
12 What makes you so bold at heart,
   and why do your eyes flash,
13 that you vent your anger on God
   and pour out such mouthfuls of words?
14 What is any human being, that he
   should be innocent,

or any child of woman, that he should
   be justified?
15 If God puts no trust in his holy ones,
   and the heavens are not innocent in his
   sight,
16 how much less so are human beings,
   who are loathsome and corrupt
   and lap up evil like water!

17 I shall tell you, if only you will listen;
   I shall recount what I have seen —
18 what has been handed down by wise
   men
   and was not concealed from them by
   their forefathers,
19 to whom alone the land was given,
   and no foreigner moved among them:
20 the wicked through all their days are
   racked with anxiety;
   so it is with the tyrant through all the
   years allotted to him.
21 The noise of the hunter's scare rings in
   his ears;
   even in time of peace the marauder
   swoops down on him;
22 he cannot hope to escape from dark
   death;
   he is marked down for the sword;
23 he is flung out as food for vultures;
   he knows that his destruction is certain.
24 Suddenly a black day comes upon him,
   distress and anxiety overwhelm him
   like a king about to fall;
25 for he has lifted his hand against God
   and pits himself against the Almighty,
26 running at him head lowered,
   with the full weight of his bossed
   shield.

27 Heavy though his jowl is and gross,
   and though his sides bulge with fat,
28 the city where he lives will lie in ruins,

15.1–21.34: Second cycle of speeches.

15.1–35: Eliphaz's second speech. Offended by Job's contentions, Eliphaz asserts that the apparent prosperity of the wicked is only temporary, and then disaster strikes them. Job is accused of despising the three basic institutions of Israel's religious life: wisdom (vv. 2–3), priestly piety (vv. 4–5), and prophecy (v. 11). **4:** There is no Heb. term for "religion." *Fear of God* is a near equivalent. **8:** *Council:* see 1.6 n. **10:** Job is apparently younger than his visitors; he has not reached the age of a grandfather. **11:** Suffering is seen as an occasion for a mystical experience of a message from God, bringing its own *consolation*. **14:** This verse is not directly related to the later doctrine of original sin but maintains that human beings are already subject to sin at birth. **16:** Perhaps this is a proverb describing humankind's evil propensity. **18:** In the Egyptian "Instructions" also much is made of the necessity of handing down the teachings of the wise from one generation to another. **20–24:** Pangs of conscience and fear of *dark death* were considered to be the hidden punishments of the wicked

his house will be deserted,
destined to crumble in a heap of
rubble.
29 He will be rich no longer, his wealth
will not endure,
and he will strike no root in the earth;
30 scorching heat will shrivel his shoots,
and his blossom will be shaken off by
the wind.
31 He deceives himself, trusting in his
high rank,
for all his dealings will come to
nothing.
32 His palm trees will wither unseasonably,
and his branches will not be luxuriant;
33 he will be like a vine that sheds its
grapes unripened,
like an olive tree that drops its blossom.
34 For the godless, one and all, are
barren,
and their homes, enriched through
bribery, are destroyed by fire;
35 they conceive mischief and give birth to
trouble,
and the child of their womb is deceit.

16 Job answered:

2 I have heard such things so often
before!
You are trouble-makers one and all!
3 You say, 'Will this windbag never have
done?'
or 'What makes him so stubborn in
argument?'
4 If you and I were to change places, I
could talk as you do;
how I could harangue you and wag my
head at you!
5 But no, I would speak words of
encouragement,
and my condolences would be
unrestrained.
6 If I speak, my pain is not eased;
if I am silent, it does not leave me.
7 Meanwhile, my friend wearies me with
his gloating;

he and his fellows seize me.
8 He has come forward to give evidence
against me;
the liar testifies against me to my face,
9 in his wrath he tears me and assaults
me angrily;
he gnashes at me with his teeth.

My enemies look daggers at me,
10 they bare their teeth at me,
they strike me on the cheek and taunt
me;
they are all in league against me.
11 God has left me at the mercy of
malefactors,
he has cast me into the power of the
wicked.
12 I was at ease, but he savaged me,
seized me by the neck, and worried me.
He set me up as his target;
13 his arrows rained on me from every
side;
pitiless, he pierced deep into my vitals,
he spilt my gall on the ground.
14 He made breach after breach in my
defences;
like a warrior he rushed on me.

15 I stitched sackcloth together to cover
my body
and laid my forehead in the dust;
16 my cheeks were inflamed with weeping
and dark shadows were round my eyes.
17 Yet my hands were free from violence
and my prayer was sincere.

18 Let not the earth cover my blood,
and let my cry for justice find no rest!
19 For now my witness is in heaven;

15:29 **root:** *prob. rdg, cp. Lat.; Heb. unintelligible.* **in the earth:** *prob. rdg; Heb. adds* he will not escape from darkness. 15:30 **blossom:** *so Gk; Heb.* mouth. 15:32 **His palm trees:** *prob. rdg, cp. Gk; Heb. omits.* **wither:** *so Gk; Heb.* be filled. 16:5 **unrestrained:** *so Gk; Heb.* restrained. 16:7 **his fellows:** *prob. rdg; Heb.* my fellows. 16:8 **the liar:** *so Lat.; Heb.* my falsehood.

who seemed to prosper. **29–34:** The traditional teaching held that the wicked who seemed to prosper would *strike no root in the earth* either by being *barren* or through losing their children by sudden death, like a *blossom . . . shaken off by the wind;* see Ps. 109.12–13.
   16.1–17.16: Job's answer laments the lack of sympathy and understanding in his friends and repeats that his disaster has come from God. **4:** To *wag the head* was a sign of gloating over the misfortune of another; see Matt. 27.39–40. **9:** *Gnashes teeth:* a sign of scornful hatred and hostility; see Lam. 2.16; Pss. 35.16; 37.12. **15:** *Sackcloth . . . and dust:* signs of grief and mourning; see Ezek. 27.30–31. **18:** According to Gen. 4.10–11

there is One on high ready to answer
for me.
20 My appeal will come before God,
while my eyes turn anxiously to him.
21 If only there were one to arbitrate
between man and God,
as between a man and his neighbour!
22 For there are but few years to come
before I take the road from which
there is no return.

17

My mind is distraught, my days are
numbered,
and the grave awaits me.
2 Wherever I turn, I am taunted,
and my eye meets nothing but sneers.
3 Be my surety with yourself,
for who else will pledge himself for
me?
4 You will not let those triumph
whose minds you have sunk in
ignorance;
5 if such a one denounces his friends to
their ruin,
his sons' eyes will fail.

6 I am held up as a byword in every
land,
a marvel for all to see;
7 my eyes are dimmed by grief,
my limbs wasted to a shadow.
8 The upright are bewildered at this,
and at my downfall the innocent are
indignant.

9 In spite of all, one who is righteous
maintains his course;
he goes from strength to strength
whose hands are clean.
10 But come on, one and all, try again!
I shall not find one who is wise among
you.
11 My days die away like an echo;
my heart-strings are snapped.
12 Night is turned into day,
and morning light is darkened before
me.

13 If I measure Sheol for my house,
if I spread my couch in the darkness,
14 if I call the grave my father
and the worm my mother or my sister,
15 where, then, will my hope be,
and who will take account of my piety?
16 I cannot take them with me down to
Sheol,
nor shall we descend together to the
dust.

18

Then Bildad the Shuhite answered:

2 How soon will you bridle your tongue?
Show some sense, and then we can talk.
3 What do you mean by treating us as no
more than cattle?
Are we nothing but brute beasts to
you?
4 Is the earth to be deserted to prove you
right,
or the rocks to be moved from their
place?

5 No, it is the evildoer whose light is
extinguished,
from whose fire no flame will rekindle;
6 the light in his tent fades,
his lamp beside him dies down.
7 His vigorous stride is shortened,
and he is tripped by his own policy;
8 he rushes headlong into a net
and his feet are entangled in its
meshes;
9 his heel is caught in a snare,
the thong grips him tightly;
10 a noose lies hidden for him in the
ground
and a trap in his path.
11 Terror of death suddenly besets him
so that he cannot hold back his urine.

16:20 **My . . . come:** *so Gk; Heb.* My friends are my
scorners.   17:12 **morning:** *prob. rdg; Heb.* near.
17:13 **Sheol:** *or* the underworld.   17:16 **with . . .
Sheol:** *so Gk; Heb.* obscure.   18:2 **bridle:** *prob. rdg;*
Heb. unintelligible.   18:3 **Are we . . . to you?:** *prob.*
rdg; Heb. adds (4)rending himself in his anger.

spilled *blood* of an innocent victim cries out to the Lord of Justice (see also Jonah 1.14). **17.3:** This is a key
sentence in which Job shows his faith by asking God to be Job's pledge with the deity, as he had stated in
16.19–20. **9:** Some interpreters view this verse as a later pious addition, others as a sarcastic quotation of his
friends' view. **15–16:** A bitter comment that both hope and piety disappear at death.
     18.1–21: Bildad's second speech. The sinner, dying horribly, leaves neither positive memory nor progeny.
2: The *you* is plural in the MT, as if the author is addressing the wicked in general. **4:** The allegation is that
Job seeks an alteration in the order of nature just to vindicate him. **5–6:** *Light* here is a figure for the human

¹²For all his vigour he is paralysed with
fear;
  strong as he is, disaster awaits him.
¹³Disease eats away his skin,
  death's firstborn devours his limbs.
¹⁴He is plucked from the safety of his
home,
  and death's terrors escort him to their
king.
¹⁵Fire settles on his tent,
  and brimstone is strewn over his
dwelling.
¹⁶His roots beneath dry up,
  and above, his branches wither.
¹⁷All memory of him vanishes from the
earth
  and he leaves no name in the inhabited
world.
¹⁸He is thrust out from light into
darkness
  and banished from the land of the
living.
¹⁹He leaves no issue or offspring among
his people,
  no survivor where once he lived.
²⁰In the west people are appalled at his
end;
  in the east they shudder with horror.
²¹Such is the fate of the dwellings of
evildoers,
  of the homes of those who care nothing
for God.

19 Job answered:

²How long will you grieve me
  and crush me with words?
³You have insulted me now a dozen
times
  and shamelessly wronged me.
⁴If in fact I had erred,
  the error would still be mine alone.
⁵Will you indeed claim to excel me
  and put forward my disgrace as an
argument against me?
⁶I tell you, God himself has put me in
the wrong

and drawn his net about me.
⁷If I shout 'Violence!' no one answers;
  if I appeal for help, I get no justice.
⁸He has blocked my path so that I
cannot go forward,
  he has planted a hedge across my way.
⁹He has stripped me of all honour
  and taken the crown from my head.
¹⁰On every side he beats me down till I
am gone;
  he has uprooted my hope like a tree.
¹¹His anger is hot against me
  and he regards me as his enemy.
¹²His raiders gather in force,
  raising their siege-ramps against me
  and encamping about my tent.

¹³My kinsfolk hold aloof,
  my acquaintances are wholly estranged
from me;
¹⁴⁻¹⁵my relatives and friends fall away.
  My retainers have forgotten me;
  my slave-girls treat me as a stranger;
  I have become an alien in their eyes.
¹⁶I summon my slave, but he does not
answer,
  though I ask him directly as a favour.
¹⁷My breath is offensive to my wife,
  and I stink in the nostrils of my own
family.
¹⁸The very children despise me
  and, when I rise, turn their backs on
me.
¹⁹All my close companions abhor me,
  and those whom I love have turned
against me.
²⁰My bones stand out under my skin,
  and I gnaw my under-lip with my
teeth.

²¹Pity me, have pity on me, you that are
my friends,
  for the hand of God has touched me.
²²Must you pursue me as God pursues
me?

18:15 **Fire:** *prob. rdg; Heb. obscure.*   19:3 **wronged
me:** *so some MSS; others* are astonished at me.

life-force (see also Prov. 13.9; 20.20; 24.20). **13–14:** Far from being a place of rest and even solace, Sheol
can be a constant terror; see 26.5–6. *Death's firstborn:* this seems to reflect mythology and to allude to Mot,
the Canaanite god of death. Perhaps, though, *firstborn* is a fatal illness, or the fear of dying. **15:** Such practices,
to cure diseases, or restore ritual purity, are familiar from Canaanite and Mesopotamian texts. The verse seems
to hearken back to v. 13.
   19.1–29: Job's reply. He describes eloquently the wrongs done him by God (vv. 1–20), yet a vindicator,
God, will emerge to defend him. **3:** *A dozen times:* "ten times" in Heb. **17:** The allusion to family, if taken

Have you not had your teeth in me
long enough?

23 Would that my words might be written
down,
that they might be engraved in an
inscription,

24 incised with an iron tool and filled with
lead,
carved in rock as a witness!

25 But I know that my vindicator lives
and that he will rise last to speak in
court;

26 I shall discern my witness standing at
my side
and see my defending counsel, even
God himself,

27 whom I shall see with my own eyes,
I myself and no other.

My heart sank within me 28 when you
said,
'What a series of misfortunes befalls
him,
and the root of the trouble lies in
himself!'

29 Beware of the sword that points at you,
the sword that sweeps away all iniquity;
then you will know that there is a
judge.

20 Then Zophar the Naamathite answered:

2 My distress of mind forces me to reply,
and this is why I hasten to speak.

3 I have heard arguments that are an
outrage to me,
but a spirit beyond my understanding
gives me the answers.

4 Surely you know that since time began,
since mortals were first set on the
earth, this has been true:

5 the triumph of a wicked person is
short-lived,

the glee of one who is godless lasts but
a moment!

6 Though in his pride he stands high as
the heavens,
and his head touches the clouds,

7 he will be swept utterly away like his
own dung,
and those used to seeing him will say,
'Where is he?'

8 He will fly away like a dream and be
found no more,
gone like a vision of the night;

9 eyes which glimpsed him will do so no
more
and never again will they see him in his
place.

11 The youthful vigour which filled his
bones
will lie with him in the earth.

10 His sons will curry favour with the
poor;
his children will give back his wealth.

12 Though evil tastes sweet in his mouth,
and he savours it, rolling it round his
tongue,

13 though he lingers over it and will not
let it go,
and holds it back on his palate,

14 yet his food turns in his stomach,
changing to asps' venom within him.

15 He gulps down wealth, then spews it
up;
God makes him vomit it from his
stomach.

16 He sucks the poison of asps,
and the tongue of the viper kills him.

17 Not for him to swill down rivers of
cream

19:24 **as a witness:** *or* for ever.   19:26 **my witness
. . . side:** *prob. rdg; Heb. unintelligible.*   19:28 **himself:**
so many MSS; others me.   19:29 **judge:** *or* judgement.
20:2 **this is why:** *prob. rdg; Heb. obscure.*
20:10–11 *Verses 10 and 11 transposed.*
20:10 **children:** *prob. rdg; Heb.* hands.   20:17 **rivers
of cream:** *prob. rdg; Heb. obscure.*

literally, stands in tension with the earlier passage (1.18–19) reporting the death of his children. **23–24:** Job
wants his words to be *engraved* on a *rock* so that his case may be judged by others who are more honest than
his friends. For *inscription . . . filled with lead,* compare Behistun stone. **25:** In ancient *court* trials the witness
for the defense stood at the accused person's right *side* and the accuser stood at the left; compare Ps. 109.31.
The rendering here, *in court,* is an interpretation of the MT "on the dust." **26–27:** These verses are so poorly
preserved that it is impossible to discern the exact meaning. It is clear, however, that Job expresses his certainty
that somehow and somewhere he will be shown to have been innocent. **28–29:** His friends will in time be
punished for their false accusations. See 42.7.

20.1–29: Zophar's second speech. The bad fate of the wicked is certain, with short-lived triumph giving
way to extreme punishment. **2–3:** *Beyond my understanding:* not human experience or that of the race (5.27

or torrents of honey and curds;
18 he must give back his gains
    unswallowed,
and spew out his profit undigested;
19 for he has oppressed and harassed the
    poor,
he has seized houses which he did not
    build.
20 Because his appetite gave him no rest,
he let nothing he craved escape him;
21 because nothing survived his greed,
therefore his wellbeing does not last.
22 With every need satisfied his troubles
    begin,
and the full force of hardship strikes
    him.
23 Let that fill his belly!
God vents his anger upon him
and rains on him cruel blows.
24 He is wounded by an iron weapon
and pierced by a bronze-tipped arrow;
25 the point comes out at his back,
the gleaming tip from his gall-bladder.
Terrors threaten him,
26 darkness unrelieved awaits him;
a fire that needs no fanning will
    consume him.
Woe betide any survivor in his tent!
27 The heavens will lay bare his guilt,
and earth will rise up to condemn him.
28 A flood will sweep away his house,
rushing waters on the day of wrath.
29 Such is God's reward for the wicked,
the God-ordained portion for the rebel.

21 Job answered:

2 Give careful heed to my words,
and let that be the comfort you offer
    me.
3 Bear with me while I have my say;
after I have spoken, you may mock.
4 My complaint is not about mortals,
so have I not cause to be impatient?
5 Look at my plight, and be aghast;
clap your hand to your mouth.
6 When I stop to think, I am filled with
    horror,

and my whole body shudders.

7 Why do the wicked live on,
hale in old age, and great and
    powerful?
8 They see their children settled around
    them,
their descendants flourishing,
9 their households secure and safe;
the rod of God's justice does not reach
    them.
10 Their bull breeds without fail;
their cow calves and does not cast her
    calf.
11 Like flocks they produce babes in
    droves,
and their little ones skip and dance;
12 they rejoice with tambourine and lyre
and make merry to the sound of the
    flute.
13 They live out their days in prosperity,
and they go down to Sheol in peace.
14 They say to God, 'Leave us alone;
we do not want to know your ways!
15 What is the Almighty that we should
    worship him,
or what should we gain by entreating
    his favour?'
16 Is not the prosperity of the wicked in
    their own hands?
Are not their purposes very different
    from God's?
17 How often is the lamp of the wicked
    snuffed out,
how often does ruin come upon them?
How often does God in his anger deal
    out suffering?
18 How often are they like a wisp of straw
    before the wind,
like chaff which the storm whirls away?
19 You say, 'The trouble a man earns,
God reserves for his sons';
no, let him be paid for it in full and be
    punished.

20:26 **awaits him:** *so Gk; Heb.* awaits his stored things.
20:29 **the rebel:** *prob. rdg; Heb.* his word.
21:12 **with:** *so some MSS; others* as to.   21:13 **Sheol:**
or the underworld.   21:16 **God's:** *prob. rdg; Heb.*
mine.

and 8.8–10), but a supernatural *spirit* is said to guide his words. **16:** *Poison:* a figure of speech. **26:** For a similar
threat on *darkness,* see 18.18. On a punishing *fire,* see Pss. 21.9 and 140.10. **27:** Compare Deut. 31.28.
 21.1–34: Job's answer. Against his friends' arguments, Job asserts that the wicked do prosper, and only rarely
undergo misfortune. **14–15:** The wicked presume to scorn God. **16:** Job appears to quote his friends' words
(e.g. 18.5–21) only to refute them. **19–20:** Against Zophar's argument (20.10, echoing Exod. 34.7) that the
punishment of the wicked is visited on *his sons,* Job demands a justice in which the wicked *drink* the *cup* of

20 Let his own eyes witness the
    condemnation come on him;
    may the wrath of the Almighty be the
      cup he drinks.
21 What joy will he have in his children
    after him,
    if his months are numbered?
22 Can any human being teach God,
    when it is he who judges even those in
      heaven above?

23 I tell you this: one man dies crowned
    with success,
    lapped in security and comfort,
24 his loins full of vigour
    and the marrow juicy in his bones;
25 another dies in bitterness of soul,
    never having tasted prosperity.
26 Side by side they are laid in the
    earth,
    and worms are the shroud of both.

27 I know well what you are thinking
    and the arguments you are marshalling
      against me;
28 I know you will ask, 'Where now is the
    great man's house,
    what has become of the dwelling of the
      wicked?'
29 Have you never questioned travellers?
    Do you not accept the evidence they
      bring:
30 that a wicked person is spared when
    disaster comes
    and conveyed to safety before the day
      of wrath?
31 Who will denounce his conduct to his
    face?
    Who will requite him for what he has
      done?
32–33 When he is borne to the grave,

all the world escorts him, before and
    behind;
the dust of earth is sweet to him,
and thousands keep watch at his tomb.
34 How futile, then, is the comfort you
    offer me!
How false your answers ring!

Third cycle of speeches

22 THEN Eliphaz the Temanite an-
    swered:

2 Can anyone be any benefit to God?
Can he benefit even from the wise?
3 Is it an advantage to the Almighty if
    you are righteous?
What gain to him if your conduct is
    perfect?
4 Does he arraign you for your piety—
is it on this count he brings you to trial?
5 No: it is because your wickedness is so
    great,
and your depravity passes all bounds.

6 Without cause you exact pledges from
    your brothers,
leaving them stripped of their clothes
    and naked.
7 To the weary you give no water to
    drink
and you withhold bread from the
    starving.
8 Is the earth, then, the preserve of the
    strong,
a domain for the favoured few?
9 You have sent widows away
    empty-handed,
the fatherless you have left without
    support.

21.27 **you are marshalling:** *so Syriac; Heb.* you do
violence.

their own punishment; see Jer. 31.29; Ezek. 18.2–4. **22:** Perhaps this verse is a gloss, or else irony. It could,
however, be an expression of despair over the necessity to instruct God in elementary human justice. **27–34:**
Arguments: their syllogism is that God is pleased with goodness; God favors the good person; therefore, the
good fare well. The broadest human experience refutes such arguments, so that their comfort of him (v. 34)
is futile. **28:** See 8.22. **30:** Contrast 20.28; Prov. 16.4; Rom. 2.5.

22.1–27.23: Third cycle of speeches.

22.1–30: Eliphaz's third speech. He insists that Job has definitely trespassed, perhaps in mistreating the
hungry, *widows,* and *the fatherless* (vv. 5–9) and has thought that a thick cloud shielded him from God's eyes
(vv. 12–14). Hence Job must repent (vv. 21–30). **2–3:** God has no need of anyone, even the *wise* or the
righteous (see 35.7), and hence can have no ulterior motive for punishing Job. **6:** *Clothes:* a poor person's outer
garment taken in pledge had to be returned by nightfall, since it was protection from the cold (Exod. 22.26–27;
Deut. 24.10–13). **9:** *Widows* and *the fatherless* are frequently linked together in the OT; their cause is also

¹⁰No wonder there are pitfalls in your
    path,
  scares to fill you with sudden terror!
¹¹No wonder light is turned to darkness,
    so that you cannot see,
  and a deluge of rain envelops you!

¹²Surely God is at the zenith of the
    heavens
  and looks down on the topmost stars,
    high as they are.
¹³Yet you say, 'What can God know?
  Can he see through thick darkness to
    judge?
¹⁴His eyes cannot pierce the curtain of
    the clouds
  as he moves to and fro on the vault of
    heaven.'
¹⁵Consider the course of the wicked,
  the path the miscreants tread;
¹⁶see how they are snatched off before
    their time,
  their very foundation flowing away like
    a river.
¹⁷They said to God, 'Leave us alone.
  What can the Almighty do to us?'
¹⁸Yet it was he who filled their houses
    with good things,
  although their purposes and his were
    very different.
¹⁹The righteous see and exult,
  the innocent make game of them;
²⁰for their riches are swept away,
  the profusion of their wealth is
    consumed by fire.

²¹Come to terms with God and you will
    prosper;
  that is the way to mend your fortune.
²²Accept instruction from his lips
  and take his words to heart.
²³If you come back to the Almighty in
    sincerity,
  if you banish wrongdoing from your
    home,
²⁴if you treat your precious metal as dust
  and the gold of Ophir as stones from
    the stream,

²⁵then the Almighty himself will be your
    precious metal;
  he will be your silver in double
    measure.
²⁶Then, with sure trust in the Almighty,
  you will raise your face to God;
²⁷you will pray to him, and he will hear
    you,
  and you will fulfil your vows.
²⁸In all your decisions you will have
    success,
  and on your path light will shine;
²⁹but God brings down the pride of the
    haughty
  and keeps safe those who are humble.
³⁰He will deliver the innocent,
  and you will be delivered, because your
    hands are pure.

23 Job answered:

²Even today my thoughts are
    embittered,
  for God's hand is heavy on me in my
    trouble.
³If only I knew how to reach him,
  how to enter his court,
⁴I should state my case before him
  and set out my arguments in full;
⁵then I should learn what answer he
    would give
  and understand what he had to say to
    me.
⁶Would he exert his great power to
    browbeat me?
  No; God himself would never set his
    face against me.
⁷There in his court the upright are
    vindicated,
  and I should win from my judge an
    outright acquittal.

22:11 **light:** *so Gk; Heb.* or.   22:17 **to us:** *so Gk; Heb.*
to them.   22:18 **his:** *so Gk; Heb.* mine.
22:20 **riches:** *so Gk; Heb. word unknown.*   22:24 **If
. . . dust:** *prob. rdg; Heb.* if you put your precious metal
on dust.   22:26 **with . . . in:** *or* delighting in.
22:29 **but . . . haughty:** *prob. rdg; Heb. obscure.*
22:30 **the innocent:** *prob. rdg; Heb.* the not innocent.
23:2 **God's:** *so Gk; Heb.* my.

championed in the Hammurabi code, Canaanite texts, Egyptian wisdom literature (Amen-em-ope). **14:** The
vault of heaven was regarded as if it were solid; see Ezek. 1.22 n.; Gen. 1.6. **21:** *Come to terms:* be reconciled.
24: *Ophir:* the proverbial source of *gold,* identified differently as India, south Arabia, or South Africa.
    23.1–24.25: Job's answer. If only it were possible to encounter God in a court of law, Job would emerge
vindicated by God, for he is innocent; in such a court, the wicked are convicted. **2:** *God's hand* was thought
heavy when a person was struck with disease or other tragedy; see 1 Sam. 5.6–7; Ps. 32.3–4. **3–6:** The view

8 If I go to the east, he is not there;
  if west, I cannot find him;
9 when I turn north, I do not descry
  him;
  I face south, but he is not to be seen.
10 Yet he knows me in action and at rest;
  when he tests me, I shall emerge like
  gold.
11 My feet have kept to the path he has
  set me;
  without deviating I have kept to his
  way.
12 I do not neglect the commands he
  issues,
  I have treasured in my heart all he
  says.
13 When he decides, who can turn him
  from his purpose?
  What he desires, he does.
14 Whatever he determines for me, that
  he carries out;
  his mind is full of plans like these.
15 That is why I am fearful of meeting
  him;
  when I think about it, I am afraid;
16 it is God who makes me faint-hearted,
  the Almighty who fills me with fear,
17 yet I am not reduced to silence by the
  darkness
  or by the mystery which hides him.

24 The day of reckoning is no secret
   to the Almighty,
  though those who know him have no
  hint of its date.
2 The wicked move boundary stones,
  and pasture flocks they have stolen.
6 In the field they reap what is not theirs,
  and filch the late grapes from the rich
  man's vineyard.
3 They drive off the donkey belonging to
  the fatherless,
  and lead away the widow's ox with a
  rope.
9 They snatch the fatherless infant from
  the breast
  and take the poor person's child in
  pledge.
4 They jostle the poor out of the way;
  the destitute in the land are forced into
  hiding together.

5 The poor rise early like the wild ass,
  when it scours the wilderness for food;
  but though they work till nightfall,
  their children go hungry.
7 Without clothing, they pass the night
  naked
  and with no cover against the cold.
8 Drenched by rainstorms from the hills,
  they cling to the rock, their only
  shelter.
10 Naked and bare they go about their
  work;
  those who carry the sheaves go hungry;
11 they press the oil in the shade where
  two walls meet,
  they tread the winepress but themselves
  go thirsty.
12 Far from the city, they groan as if
  dying,
  and like those mortally wounded they
  cry out;
  but God remains deaf to their prayer.

13 Some there are who rebel against the
  light,
  who know nothing of its ways
  and do not stay in its paths.
14–15 Before daylight the murderer rises
  to kill some miserable wretch.
  The seducer watches eagerly for
  twilight,
  thinking, 'No one will set eyes on me.'
  In the night the thief prowls about,
  his face covered with a mask;
16 in the darkness he breaks into houses
  which he has marked down during the
  day.

23:8 **to the east:** *or* forward. **west:** *or* backward.
23:9 **I turn:** *prob. rdg; Heb.* he turns. **north:** *or* left. **I
face:** *so Syriac; Heb.* he faces. **south:** *or* right.
23:10 **me ... rest:** *so Syriac; Heb.* a way with me.
23:12 **in my heart:** *so Gk; Heb.* from my allotted
portion.   23:13 **he decides:** *prob. rdg; Heb.* he in
one.   23:17 **yet I am not ... or:** *or* indeed I am ...
and.   24:1 **The ... reckoning:** *prob. rdg; Heb.* prefixes
Why.   24:2 **The wicked:** *prob. rdg, cp. Gk; Heb.*
obscure.   24:2–10 *Verses 3–9 rearranged to restore the
natural order.*   24:6 **theirs:** *lit.* his. **rich:** *or* wicked.
24:3 **with a rope:** *or* in pledge.   24:5 **but ...
nightfall:** *prob. rdg; Heb.* obscure. **go hungry:** *prob. rdg;
Heb.* to it food.   24:14–15 **the thief prowls about:**
prob. rdg; Heb. let him be like a thief.   24:16 **he has:**
so Syriac; Heb. they have.

that God is hidden or is hiding is a frequent theme in the OT; see e.g. Ps. 22.1–2. **17:** *Mystery:* lit. thick darkness.
24.1–17: The misdeeds of the wicked. **24.1:** Only God knows when the *day of reckoning*, that is, the death,
of each individual is to come. **13:** *Light* is a sign of uprightness having a real connection with one's existence;

One and all, they are strangers to the
  daylight,
[17] but dark night is morning to them;
  and amid the terrors of night they are
  at home.
[18] Such men are scum on the surface of
  the water;
  throughout the land their fields are
  accursed,
  and no labourer will go near their
  vineyards.
[19] As drought and heat make away with
  snow,
  so the waters of Sheol make away with
  sinners.
[20] The womb forgets them, the worm
  sucks them dry;
  they will not be remembered ever after.
  Iniquity is snapped like a stick!
[21] They may have wronged the barren
  childless woman
  and been no help to the widow;
[22] yet God in his strength carries off the
  mighty;
  they may rise, but they have no firm
  hope of life.
[23] He lulls them into security and
  confidence;
  but his eyes are fixed on their ways.
[24] For a moment they rise to the heights,
  but they are soon gone.
  Laid low they wilt like a mallow-flower;
  they droop like an ear of grain on the
  stalk.

[25] If this is not so, who will prove me
  wrong
  and make nonsense of my argument?

25 Then Bildad the Shuhite answered:

[2] Authority and awe are with him

who has established peace in his realm
  on high.
[3] His squadrons are without number;
  at whom will they not spring from
  ambush?
[4] How then can a mere mortal be
  justified in God's sight,
  or one born of woman be regarded as
  virtuous?
[5] If the circling moon is found wanting,
  and the stars are not innocent in his
  eyes,
[6] much more so man, who is but a
  maggot,
  mortal man, who is a worm.

26 Job answered:

[2] What a help you have been to one
  without resource!
  What deliverance you have brought to
  the powerless!
[3] What counsel you offer to one bereft of
  wisdom,
  what sound advice to the simple!
[4] Who has prompted you to utter such
  words,
  and whose spirit is expressed in your
  speech?

[5] The shades below writhe in fear,
  the waters and all that inhabit them are
  afraid.
[6] Sheol is laid bare before him;
  Abaddon lies uncovered.
[7] God spreads the canopy of the sky over
  chaos

24:16 **One and all:** *transposed from after* but *in next verse.*
24:19 **snow ... Sheol:** *prob. rdg; Heb.* snow-water,
Sheol. **Sheol:** *or* the underworld.   24:21 **They ...
wronged:** *so Aram. (Targ.); Heb.* shepherd.   25:3 **at
... ambush:** *so Gk; Heb.* on whom does his light not
rise?   26:5 **are afraid:** *prob. rdg; Heb.* omits.
26:6 **Sheol:** *or* the underworld.

see Ps. 97.11; Prov. 4.18–19. **18–25:** Some interpreters believe these verses belong with 27.11–23; see
27.11–23 n. The third cycle of speeches is apparently preserved in great disorder. **21:** *Barren childless:* see
the similar repetition intoned in Isa. 54.1, this to intensify the poetic effect of the passage. **23:** God is often
pictured as leading individuals into mistaken confidence in themselves (compare Jer. 20.7; Isa. 6.9–10),
especially through false prophets (Ezek. 14.9).

25.1–6: Bildad's third speech. So brief is this speech, and so little new is in it, that some interpreters believe
that a part of it has been lost, or that 26.5–14 continues it. **3:** *Squadrons:* of angels.

26.1–27.10: Job's reply. Anger moves Job to wish upon his friends the fate of the wicked; again he reminds
them that a sinner would never challenge God to a trial. **2–4:** The irony here is remarkably bitter. **5–14:** Perhaps
Bildad's speech. See 25.1–6 n. **6:** *Abaddon:* another name for Sheol, meaning place of "destruction" (see Prov.
15.11). **7:** *Canopy:* lit. *zaphon,* i.e. the north, the mythological dwelling of heavenly beings, especially those

and suspends earth over the void.
8 He keeps the waters penned in dense
cloud masses,
yet no cloud bursts open under their
weight.
9 He veils the face of the full moon,
unrolling his clouds across it.
10 He has fixed the horizon on the surface
of the waters
at the boundary between light and
darkness.
11 The pillars of heaven quake,
aghast at the thunder of his voice.
12 With his strong arm he cleft the sea
monster;
he struck down Rahab by his skill.
13 Winds from him clear the skies,
and his hand slays the twisting sea
serpent.
14 These are but the fringes of his power,
and how faint the whisper that we hear
of him!
Who could comprehend the thunder of
his might?

27

Then Job resumed his discourse:

2 I swear by the living God, who has
denied me justice,
by the Almighty, who has filled me with
bitterness,
3 that so long as there is any life left in
me
and the breath of God is in my
nostrils,
4 no untrue word will pass my lips,
nor will my tongue utter any falsehood.
5 Far be it from me to concede that you
are right!
Till I cease to be, I shall not abandon
my claim of innocence.
6 I maintain and shall never give up the
rightness of my cause;
so long as I live, I shall not change.
7 Let my enemy meet the fate of the
wicked,

and my antagonist the doom of the
wrongdoer!
8 What hope has a godless man, when he
is cut off,
when God takes away his life?
9 Will God listen to his cry
when trouble overtakes him?
10 Will he trust himself to the Almighty?
Will he call upon God at all times?
11 I shall teach you what is in God's
power,
and not conceal the purpose of the
Almighty.
12 If all of you have seen these things,
why then do you talk such empty
nonsense?

13 Such is God's reward for the wicked
man,
the Almighty's portion for him who is
ruthless.
14 Though his sons be many, they will fall
by the sword,
and his offspring will never have
enough to eat;
15 the survivors will be brought to the
grave by plague,
and no widows will weep for them.
16 He may heap up silver like dirt
and get himself stacks of clothes;
17 he may get them, but the righteous will
wear them,
and his silver will be shared among the
innocent.
18 The house he builds is flimsy as a bird's
nest
or a shelter put up by a watchman.
19 He may lie down rich one day, but
never again;
he opens his eyes, to find his wealth is
gone.
20 Disaster overtakes him like a flood,

26:9 **He veils ... moon:** or He overlays the surface of
his throne.   26:13 **twisting:** or primeval.
27:10 **trust ... to:** or delight in.   27:19 **but ...
again:** so Gk; Heb. but he is not gathered in.

hostile to Israel; compare Isaiah 14.13; Ezek. 39.2. **27.1:** *Resumed:* only here is a speech interrupted. Perhaps
this verse is a consequence of the disorder in the third cycle of speeches and is a copyist's note identifying
what ensues as a continuation of 26.1–4. **2:** Despite his accusations, Job swears by the accused deity.
27.11–23: The lot of the wicked. Some interpreters believe that this section is part, or all, of Zophar's speech;
if not, then strangely there is no third speech by him. Note that ch. 28 is almost universally regarded as an
interpolation into the book, indicative of disorder in the text. The description of the fate of the wicked comes
very close to Job's own situation. **20:** *Flood* (Heb. *kamayim*): a slight change in the Heb. would substitute
yōmān, "by day," yielding a better parallel for *in the night.*

and a storm snatches him away in the
night;
²¹ an east wind lifts him up and he is
gone;
it sweeps him far from his home;
²² it hurls itself at him without mercy,
and he is battered and buffeted by its
force;
²³ it snaps its fingers at him
and whistles over him wherever he may
be.

God's unfathomable wisdom

28 THERE are mines for silver
and places where gold is refined.
² Iron is won from the earth
and copper smelted from the ore.
³ Men master the darkness;
to the farthest recesses they seek
ore in gloom and deep darkness.
⁴ Foreigners cut the shafts;
forgotten, suspended without foothold,
they swing to and fro, far away from
anyone.
⁵ While grain is springing from the earth
above,
what lies beneath is turned over like a
fire,
⁶ and out of its rocks comes lapis lazuli,
dusted with flecks of gold.
⁷ No bird of prey knows the path there;
the falcon's keen eye cannot descry it;
⁸ proud beasts do not set foot on it,
and no lion passes there.
⁹ Man sets his hand to the granite rock
and lays bare the roots of the
mountains;
¹⁰ he cuts galleries in the rocks,
and gems of every kind meet his eye;
¹¹ he dams up the sources of the streams
and brings the hidden riches of the
earth to light.

¹² But where can wisdom be found,
and where is the source of
understanding?
¹³ No one knows the way to it,
nor is it to be found in the land of the
living.

¹⁴ 'It is not in us,' declare the ocean
depths;
the sea declares, 'It is not with me.'
¹⁵ Red gold cannot buy it,
nor can its price be weighed out in
silver;
¹⁶ gold of Ophir cannot be set in the
scales against it,
nor precious cornelian nor sapphire;
¹⁷ gold and crystal are not to be matched
with it,
no work in fine gold can be bartered
for it;
¹⁸ black coral and alabaster are not worth
mention,
and a parcel of wisdom fetches more
than red coral;
¹⁹ chrysolite from Ethiopia is not to be
matched with it,
pure gold cannot be set in the scales
against it.
²⁰ Where, then, does wisdom come from?
Where is the source of understanding?
²¹ No creature on earth can set eyes on it;
even from birds of the air it is
concealed.
²² Destruction and Death declare,
'We know of it only by hearsay.'

²³ God alone understands the way to it,
he alone knows its source;
²⁴ for he can see to the ends of the earth
and observe every place under heaven.
²⁵ When he regulated the force of the
wind
and measured out the waters in
proportion,
²⁶ when he laid down a limit for the rain
and cleared a path for the thunderbolt,
²⁷ it was then he saw wisdom and took
stock of it,
he considered it and fathomed its very
depths.
²⁸ And he said to mankind:

27:22 **and he ... force:** *or* and he flees headlong from
its force. 28:4 **Foreigners ... shafts:** *prob. rdg; Heb.*
obscure. 28:13 **knows ... to it:** *so Gk; Heb.* knows its
value. 28:16 **sapphire:** *or* lapis lazuli.
28:17 **crystal:** *lit.* glass. 28:22 **Destruction:** *Heb.*
Abaddon. 28:27 **considered:** *so some MSS; others*
established.

28.1–28: God's unfathomable wisdom. This poem is probably a later addition; it marvels at human ingenuity
in extracting precious ore hidden in the heart of the earth but the inability to find even a trace of wisdom. **12:**
This refrain recurs in v. 20 in slightly different form. **28:** The verse is a sort of motto; compare Prov. 1.7. It
probably postdates the poem itself. *Lord:* Heb., *adonai*, not Yahweh; only here is *adonai* used in Job.

'The fear of the Lord is wisdom,
and to turn from evil, that is
understanding!'

Job's final survey of his case

29 THEN Job resumed his discourse:

2 If only I could go back to the old days,
to the time when God was watching
over me,
3 when his lamp shone above my head,
and by its light I walked through the
darkness!
4 If I could be as in the days of my
prime,
when God protected my home,
5 while the Almighty was still there at my
side,
and my servants stood round me,
6 while my path flowed with milk,
and the rocks poured forth streams of
oil for me!
7 When I went out of my gate up to the
town
to take my seat in the public square,
8 young men saw me and kept back out
of sight,
old men rose to their feet,
9 men in authority broke off their talk
and put their hands to their lips;
10 the voices of the nobles died away,
and every man held his tongue.
21 They listened to me expectantly
and waited in silence for my counsel.
22 After I had spoken, no one spoke
again;
my words fell gently on them;
23 they waited for me as for rain,
open-mouthed as for spring showers.
24 When I smiled on them, they took
heart;
when my face lit up, they lost their
gloomy looks.
25 I presided over them, planning their
course,
like a king encamped with his troops,
like one who comforts mourners.

11 Whoever heard of me spoke favourably
of me,
and those who saw me bore witness to
my merit,
12 how I saved the poor who appealed for
help,
and the fatherless and him who had no
protector.
13 He who was threatened with ruin
blessed me,
and I made the widow's heart sing for
joy.
14 I put on righteousness as a garment
and it clothed me;
justice, like a cloak and turban, adorned
me.
15 I was eyes to the blind
and feet to the lame;
16 I was a father to the needy,
and I took up the stranger's cause.
17 I broke the fangs of the miscreant
and wrested the prey from his teeth.
18 I thought, 'I shall die with my powers
unimpaired
and my days uncounted as the grains of
sand,
19 with my roots spreading out to the
water
and the dew lying on my branches,
20 with the bow always new in my grasp
and the arrow ever ready to my hand.'

30 But now I am laughed to scorn
by men of a younger generation,
men whose fathers I would have
disdained
to put with the dogs guarding my flock.
2 What use to me was the strength of
their arms,
since their vigour had wasted away?
3 Gaunt with want and hunger,
they gnawed roots in the desert,
4 they plucked saltwort and wormwood

29:10 *Verses 21–25 transposed to follow this verse.*
29:18 **as . . . sand:** *or as those of the phoenix.*
29:20 *Verses 21–25 transposed to follow verse 10.*
30:3 **Gaunt . . . desert:** *prob. rdg; Heb. adds* yesterday
ruin and ruination. **roots:** *prob. rdg; Heb. omits.*

29.1–31.40: Job's final survey of his case. Remembering his gratifying life before God's blow fell (ch. 29),
Job describes the contrast of his decline and the attendant scorn (30.1–19). Piteously he pleads with God
(30.20–31; 31.2–4) and sets forth his past ethical conduct (31.5, 1, 6–37). **4:** *Prime:* lit. "autumn days." The
meaning is clearly the prime period of fruitful harvest, not one's fading years. **7–10, 21–25, 11–20:** The
erstwhile prestige of Job described here surpasses that of the prologue, 1.1–3. The translators' rearrangement
should be noted. **11–17:** The good deeds Job claims here contradict the accusations made by Eliphaz in

and for warmth the root of broom.
5 Driven out from human society,
    pursued like thieves with hue and cry,
6 they made their homes in gullies and
        ravines,
    in holes in the ground and rocky clefts;
7 they howled like beasts among the
        bushes,
    huddled together beneath the scrub,
8 vile, disreputable wretches,
    outcasts from the haunts of men.

9 Now I have become the target of their
        taunts;
    my name is a byword among them.
10 They abhor me, they shun me,
    they dare to spit in my face.
11 They run wild and savage me;
    at sight of me they throw off all
        restraint.
12 On my right flank they attack in a mob;
    they raise their siege-ramps against me;
13 to destroy me they tear down my
        crumbling defences,
    and scramble up against me
        unhindered;
14 they burst in as through a gaping
        breach;
    at the moment of the crash they come
        in waves.
15 Terror after terror overwhelms me;
    my noble designs are swept away as by
        the wind,
    and my hope of deliverance vanishes
        like a cloud.
16 So now my life ebbs away;
    misery has me daily in its grip.
17 By night pain pierces my very bones,
    and there is ceaseless throbbing in my
        veins;
18 my garments are all bespattered with
        my phlegm,
    which chokes me like the collar of a
        garment.
19 God himself has flung me down in the
        mud;
    I have become no better than dust or
        ashes.

20 I call out to you, God, but you do not
        answer,
    I stand up to plead, but you keep aloof.
21 You have turned cruelly against me;
    with your strong hand you persecute
        me.
22 You snatch me up and mount me on
        the wind;
    the tempest tosses me about.
23 I know that you will hand me over to
        death,
    to the place appointed for all mortals.

24 Yet no beggar held out his hand to me
        in vain
    for relief in his distress.
25 Did I not weep for the unfortunate?
    Did not my heart grieve for the
        destitute?
26 Yet evil has come though I expected
        good,
    and when I looked for light, darkness
        came.
27 My bowels are in ferment and know no
        peace;
    days of misery stretch out in front of
        me.
28 I go about dejected and comfortless;
    I rise in the assembly, only to appeal
        for help.
29 The wolf is now my brother,
    the desert-owls have become my
        companions.
30 My blackened skin peels off,
    and my body is scorched by the heat.
31 My lyre has been tuned for a dirge,
    my flute to the sound of weeping.

31 2 What is the lot prescribed by God
        above,
    the portion from the Almighty on high?

30:4 **warmth:** *or* food.   30:5 **human society:** *prob.
rdg; Heb. obscure.*   30:12 **they ... mob:** *prob. rdg;
Heb. adds* they let loose my feet.   30:24 **for relief:**
prob. rdg; Heb. unintelligible.   30:28 **comfortless:**
prob. rdg; Heb. without heat.   31:2 *Verse 1 transposed
to follow verse 5.*

22.5–9. **18:** The fabled phoenix (see Tfn.) arose to new life from the ashes of its funeral pyre. **20:** The *bow*
and *arrow* may here and in Ecclus. 26.12 have overtones of sexual potency. **30.22:** Irony is intended, Job being
punished by having to *mount* the wind, a role elsewhere deemed the great prerogative of the LORD (see Ps.
18.9–10) and also of the Canaanite Baal. **24–28:** Job's claim is that no needy person was ever refused help
by him, yet now no one, not even God, listens to his *appeal for help;* thereby God is less compassionate than
Job. Compare 32.2–3. **31.1–37:** Job's record of ethical conduct.

3 Is not ruin prescribed for the
    miscreant,
  disaster for the wrongdoer?
4 Yet does not God himself see my ways
  and take account of my every step?

5 I swear I have had no dealings with
    falsehood
  and have not gone hotfoot after deceit.
1 I have taken an oath
  never to let my eyes linger on a girl.
6 Let God weigh me in the scales of
    justice,
  and he will know that I am blameless!
7 If my steps have wandered from the
    way,
  if my heart has followed my eyes,
  or any dirt has stuck to my hands,
8 then may another eat what I sow,
  and may my crops be uprooted!

9 If my heart has been enticed by a
    woman
  or I have lurked by my neighbour's
    door,
10 may my wife be another man's slave,
  and may other men enjoy her.
11 For that would have been a heinous
    act,
  an offence before the law:
12 it would be a consuming and
    destructive fire
  raging among my crops.

13 If I ever rejected the plea of my slave
    or slave-girl
  when they brought a complaint against
    me,
14 what shall I do if God appears?
  What shall I answer if he intervenes?
15 Did not he who made me in the belly
    make them?
  Did not the same God create us in the
    womb?
16 If I have withheld from the poor what
    they needed
  or made the widow's eye grow dim with
    tears;
17 if I have eaten my portion of food by
    myself,

and the fatherless child has not shared
    it with me—
18 the boy who said, 'From my youth he
    brought me up,'
  or the girl who claimed that from her
    birth I guided her—
19 if I have seen anyone perish for lack of
    clothing
  or a poor man with nothing to cover
    him;
20 if his body had no cause to bless me,
  because he was not kept warm with a
    fleece from my flock;
21 if I have raised my hand against the
    innocent,
  knowing that those who would side with
    me were in court:
22 then may my shoulder-blade be torn
    from my shoulder,
  my arm wrenched out of its socket!
23 But the fear of God was heavy upon
    me;
  because of his majesty I could do none
    of these things.

24 If I have put my faith in gold
  and my trust in the gold of Nubia;
25 if I have rejoiced in my great wealth
  and in the increase of riches in my
    possession;
26 if I ever looked on the sun in
    splendour
  or the moon moving in her glory,
27 and was led astray in my secret heart
  and kissed my hand in homage:
28 this would have been an offence before
    the law,
  for I should have been unfaithful to
    God on high.

38 If my land has cried out in reproach at
    me,
  and its furrows have joined in weeping;
39 If I have eaten its produce without
    payment

31:5 *Verse 1 transposed to follow this verse.*   31:10 **be
... slave:** *lit.* grind corn for another.   31:12 **raging:**
prob. rdg; Heb. uprooting.   31:21 **innocent:** *or*
fatherless. **in court:** *lit.* in the gate.   31:23 **the fear
... me:** *prob. rdg; Heb.* fear towards me is a disaster
from God.   31:28 *Verses 38, 39, and part of verse 40
transposed to follow this verse.*

1: See also Ecclus. 9.5. It might be useful to compare Matt. 5.27–28 to note that the NT is not the sole
repository of interior ethics, as is sometimes claimed. **7:** *Dirt:* perhaps an allusion to land-grabbing practices
(see Amos 2.7). **11–12:** The verses are probably a gloss to reject the content of vv. 9–10. **18:** *Her:* Heb. "my."
24: *Nubia:* Ethiopia. **38:** *Land has cried out:* see Gen. 4.10.

and left my creditors to languish:
⁴⁰may thistles spring up instead of
    wheat,
and noxious weeds instead of barley!

²⁹Have I rejoiced at the ruin of anyone
    who hated me
or been filled with glee when
    misfortune overtook him,
³⁰even though I did not allow my tongue
    to sin
by laying his life under a curse?
³¹The men of my household have indeed
    said:
'Who has eaten of his food and not
    been satisfied?'
³²No stranger has had to spend the night
    in the street,
for I have kept open house for the
    traveller.
³³Have I ever concealed my misdeeds as
    others do,
keeping my guilt hidden within my
    breast,
³⁴⁻³⁵because I feared the gossip of the
    town
or dreaded the scorn of my
    fellow-citizens?
Let me but call a witness in my
    defence!
Let the Almighty state his case against
    me!
If my accuser had written out his
    indictment,
I should not keep silence and remain
    indoors.
³⁶No! I should flaunt it on my shoulder
    and wear it like a crown on my head;
³⁷I should plead the whole record of my
    life

and present that in court as my
    defence.

⁴⁰Job's speeches are finished.

Speeches of Elihu

32 THESE three men gave up answering
Job, for he continued to think him-
self righteous. ²Then Elihu son of Barakel
the Buzite, of the family of Ram, became
angry: angry because Job had made himself
out to be more righteous than God, ³and
angry with his three friends because they had
found no answer to Job and so let God appear wrong. ⁴Now Elihu had hung back
while they were talking with Job because they
were older than he was; ⁵but, when he saw
that the three had no answer to give, he could
no longer contain his anger. ⁶So Elihu son of
Barakel the Buzite began to speak:

I am young in years, while you are old;
    that is why I held back and shrank
    from expressing my opinion in front of
        you.
⁷I said to myself, 'Let age speak,
    and length of years expound wisdom.'
⁸But it is a spirit in a human being,
    the breath of the Almighty, that gives
        him understanding;
⁹it is not only the old who are wise,
    not only the aged who understand what
        is right.
¹⁰Therefore I say: Listen to me;

31:39 **creditors:** *or* tenants.   31:31 **household:** *lit.*
tent.   31:33 **others do:** *or* Adam did.   31:37 *Verses*
38, 39, and part of verse 40 transposed to follow verse 28.
32:2 **had . . . God:** *or* had justified himself with God.
32:3 **and so . . . wrong:** *prob. original rdg; altered in*
Heb. to and had not proved Job wrong.

32.1–37.24: The speeches of Elihu. These chapters interrupt the context, introduce a new character unmentioned elsewhere, and repeat many of the friends' arguments, while addressing themselves more directly to
Job's objections. Probably a later addition to the poetic text, they emphasize the disciplinary nature of suffering
and life as divine gift.

32.1–6a: Prose introduction. 1: The three had earlier been called "friends," but here *men*, suggesting a
different author. **2:** *Elihu* means "That one is my God." *Barakel* means "God has blessed," a frequent name
in Akkadian texts, possibly indicating some connection with Babylonian literature. *Buzite:* perhaps a clan living
on the Persian gulf (Gen. 22.21). *Ram:* see Ruth 4.19; 1 Chr. 2.9, 25, 27. It is usual in OT narrative patterns
to record the father's name and that of the clan. *Had . . . God:* See Tfn. at v. 2. **3:** *God:* See Tfn. at v. 3. The
substitution of *Job* for God in the MT is one of the eighteen recorded alterations by ancient Jewish scribes.

32.6b–37.24: The poems of Elihu. 6b–22: Elihu feels that he must speak in order to make up for the
ineffectiveness of the friends. The tone here appears to be comic. **10:** The imperative *listen* is in the singular
as if addressed to Job alone as in 33.1, but the friends are addressed in the plural in *your words* and in *not*

I too want to express an opinion.

11 Here I have been waiting for what you
    had to say,
listening to your reasoning,
    while you picked your words;
12 I have been giving thought to those
    conclusions,
but not one of you convicts Job or
    refutes his arguments.
13 See then that you do not claim to have
    found wisdom;
or say 'God will rebut him, not man.'
14 I shall not string words together like
    you
or answer him in the way you have
    done.

15 If these men are confounded and are
    stuck for an answer,
if words fail them,
16 am I to wait because they do not
    speak,
because they stand there, stuck for an
    answer?
17 I, too, have a furrow to plough;
I am going to express my opinion,
18 for I am bursting with words,
as if wind in my belly were griping me.
19 My belly is distended as if with wine,
about to burst open like a new
    wineskin;
20 I must speak and find relief,
I must open my lips and answer;
21 I shall show no favour to anyone;
I shall flatter no one,
22 for I cannot use flattering titles,
or my Maker would soon do away with
    me.

33 But now, Job, listen to my words,
attend carefully to everything I say.
2 I am ready with my answer as you see;
the words are on the tip of my tongue.
3 My heart assures me that I speak with
    knowledge,
that my lips speak with sincerity.
4 For the spirit of God made me,

the breath of the Almighty gave me
    life.
5 Answer me, if you can,
marshal your arguments and confront
    me.
6 In God's sight I am just what you are;
I too am only a handful of clay.
7 Fear of me need not abash you,
nor any pressure from me overawe you.

8 You have said your say in my hearing;
I have listened to the words you spoke:
9 'I am innocent', you said, 'and free
    from offence,
blameless and without guilt.
10 Yet God finds occasions to put me in
    the wrong
and counts me his enemy;
11 he puts my feet in the stocks
and keeps a close watch on all my
    conduct.'

12 You are not in the right—that is my
    answer;
for God is greater than any mortal.
13 Why then plead your case with him,
for no one can answer his arguments?
14 Indeed, once God has spoken
he does not speak a second time to
    confirm it.
15 In dreams, in visions of the night,
when deepest slumber falls on mortals,
while they lie asleep in bed
16 God imparts his message,
and as a warning strikes them with
    terror.
17 To turn someone from his evil deeds,
to check human pride,
18 at the edge of the pit he holds him
    back alive
and stops him from crossing the river
    of death.
19 Or again, someone learns his lesson on
    a bed of pain,

32:14 **I ... string:** *prob. rdg; Heb.* He has not strung.
like you: *prob. rdg; Heb.* towards me.   33:6 **In God's
sight:** *or* In strength.   33:10 **finds ... wrong:** *so
Syriac; Heb.* finds ways of thwarting me.
33:17 **pride:** *prob. rdg; Heb.* obscure.

one of you in vv. 11–12 and other instances. **22:** "The Babylonian Theodicy" (see Introduction) makes generous
use of *flattering titles,* though it has sharp verbal retorts.

33.1–35.16: A reply to Job. The passage cites Job's assertions (vv. 9–11) in a context of refuting him. **1:**
The three friends never addressed Job by name as Elihu does here and in v. 31. **7:** Pointedly, Elihu asserts that,
unlike God, he cannot *overawe* Job. **12:** Elihu's argument is: "If you admit that *God is greater than any mortal*
(which Job has admitted, 9.1–14; 12.13–25), then how can you bring a law *case* against the deity?" **15:** This

tormented by a ceaseless ague in his
bones;
20 he turns from his food with loathing
and has no relish for the choicest
dishes;
21 his flesh hangs loose on him,
his bones are loosened and out of joint,
22 his soul draws near to the pit,
his life to the waters of death.

23 Yet if an angel, one of a thousand,
stands by him,
a mediator between him and God,
to expound God's righteousness to man
and to secure mortal man his due;
24 if he speaks on behalf of him and says,
'Reprieve him from going down to the
pit;
I have the price of his release':
25 then his body will grow sturdier than it
was in his youth;
he will return to the days of his prime.

26 If he entreats God to show him favour,
to let him enter his presence with joy;
27 if he affirms before everyone, 'I have
sinned,
turned right into wrong without a
thought':
28 then he saves himself from going down
to the pit,
he lives and sees the light.
29 All these things God may do to
someone
again and yet again,
30 bringing him back from the pit
to enjoy the full light of life.

31 Listen, Job, and attend to me;
be silent, and let me speak.
32 If you have anything to say, answer me;
speak, for I shall gladly find you
proved right.
33 But if you have nothing, then listen to
me:
be silent, and I shall teach you wisdom.

34 Then Elihu went on to say:

2 Mark my words, you master-minds!

You that know so much, listen to me!
3 For the ear tests words
as the palate savours food.
4 Let us then examine for ourselves what
is right;
let us together establish the true good.

5 Job has said, 'I am innocent,
but God has denied me justice,
6 he has falsified my case;
my state is desperate, yet I have done
no wrong.'
7 Was there ever a man like Job
with his thirst for irreverent talk,
8 choosing bad company to share his
journeys,
a fellow-traveller with wicked men?
9 For he says that it brings no profit to
anyone
to find favour with God.

10 But listen to me, you men of good
sense.
Far be it from God to do evil,
from the Almighty to play false!
11 For he requites everyone according to
his actions
and sees that each gets the reward his
conduct deserves.
12 The truth is, God would never do
wrong,
the Almighty does not pervert justice.
13 Who committed the earth to his
keeping?
Who but he established the whole
world?
14 If he were to turn his thoughts inwards
and withdraw his life-giving spirit,
15 all flesh would perish on the instant,
all mortals would turn again to dust.

16 Now Job, if you have the wit, consider
this;
listen to what I am saying:

33:22 **waters:** *Heb.* killers.   33:23 **and to . . . due:**
line transposed from verse 26.   33:24 **Reprieve:** *so some
MSS; others have an unknown word.*   33:25 **will grow
sturdier:** *prob. rdg; Heb. unintelligible.*   33:26 *See note
on verse 23.*   34:6 **he has falsified:** *so Gk; Heb.* am I
falsifying.

verse cites the words of Eliphaz in 4.13; Elihu often quotes portions of earlier speeches. **22–28:** Angels as
ministers of death appear early in Israelite literature; see 2 Sam. 24.16. Angels as *mediators* who *expound* God's
will and intercede also appear; see Josh. 5.13–14; Dan. 8.15–17. **34.1–37:** Job is wrong in imputing injustice
to God. **3:** Repeats 12.11 almost verbatim. **5–6:** These verses echo 27.2 and 33.9.

17 Can it be that a hater of justice is in
control?
Do you disparage a sovereign whose
rule is so fair,
18 who says to a prince, 'You scoundrel,'
and calls the nobles blackguards to their
faces;
19 who shows no special respect to those
in office
and favours the rich no more than the
poor?
All alike are God's creatures,
20 who may die in a moment, in the
middle of the night;
at his touch the rich are no more,
and he removes the mighty without
lifting a finger!

21 His eyes are on the ways of everyone,
and he watches each step they take;
22 there is nowhere so dark, so deep in
shadow,
that wrongdoers may hide themselves.
25 Therefore he repudiates all that they
do;
he turns on them in the night, and they
are crushed.
23 There are no appointed days for
people
to appear before God for judgement.
24 Without holding an enquiry, he breaks
the powerful
and sets others in their place.
26 For their crimes he strikes them down
as a public spectacle,
27 because they have ceased to obey him,
and pay no heed to any of his ways,
28 but have caused the cry of the poor to
reach his ears,
so that he hears the distressed when
they cry.

29-30 Even if he is silent, who can condemn
him?
If he looks away, who can find fault?
What though he makes a godless man
king
over a stubborn nation and all its
people?

31 But suppose you were to say to God,
'I have overstepped the mark, but shall
do no more mischief.
32 I am contemptible; grant me guidance;
whatever wrong I have done, I shall do
no more.'
33 Will he, at these words, condone your
rejection of him?
It is for you, Job, to decide, not me:
but what can you answer?
34 Men of good sense will say,
any intelligent hearer will tell me,
35 'Job is talking without knowledge,
and there is no sense in his words.
36 If only Job could be put to the test
once and for all
for answering like a mischief-maker!
37 He is a sinner and a rebel as well
with his endless ranting against God.'

35

Elihu went on to say:

2 Do you reckon this to be a sound plea,
to maintain that you are in the right
against God
3 if you say, 'What would be the
advantage to me?
How much should I gain from sinning'?
4 I shall bring arguments myself in reply
to you
and to your three friends as well.

5 Look up at the sky and then consider,
observe the rain-clouds towering above
you.
6 How does it touch God if you have
sinned?
However many your misdeeds, how
does it affect him?
7 If you do right, what good do you
bring him,
what does he receive at your hand?

34:22–26 *Verse 25 transposed to follow verse 22.*
34:23 **appointed days:** *prob. rdg; Heb.* still.
34:29–30 **a stubborn:** *so Gk; Heb.* the snares of a.
34:31 **more:** *prob. rdg; Heb.* obscure.　34:37 **He is . . .
well:** *prob. rdg; Heb.* adds between us it is enough.
35:4 **three:** *so Gk; Heb.* omits.

21: See 24.23 and 31.4. **25, 23–24:** Since God observes everything under the sun, the deity does not need to go through a legal process such as Job demands, i.e. *enquiry* or *appointed days . . . for judgement* in court, but Job's sentence is sudden, out of *the night*. **31–37:** Elihu states that Job's violent language is a *ranting rejection* of God that will merit further punishment even if he were now to repent of it. Job will repent (42.6) but the punishment does not follow, which may be a key to the whole story. **35.4:** Elihu attacks the three friends

8 Your wickedness touches only your
fellow-creatures;
any right you do affects none but other
mortals.

9 People cry out under the weight of
oppression
and call for help against the power of
the great;
10 but none of them asks, 'Where is God,
my Maker,
who gives protection by night,
11 who grants us more knowledge than
the beasts of the earth
and makes us wiser than the birds of
the air?'
12 So, when they cry out, he does not
answer,
because they are proud and wicked.
13 All to no purpose! God does not listen,
the Almighty takes no notice.

14 The worse for you when you say you
do not see him!
Humble yourself in his presence and
wait for his word.
15 But now, because God does not grow
angry and punish,
because he lets folly pass unheeded,
16 Job gives vent to windy nonsense;
he babbles a stream of empty
words.

36 Then Elihu went on to say:

2 Be patient a little longer, and let me
enlighten you;
there is still more to be said on God's
behalf.
3 I shall search far and wide to support
my conclusions,
as I ascribe justice to my Maker.
4 There are, I claim, no flaws in my
reasoning;
before you stands one whose
conclusions are sound.

5 God, I say, repudiates the high and
mighty
6 and does not let the wicked prosper,
but bestows justice on the wronged.
7 He does not deprive sufferers of their
due,
but on the throne with kings
he seats them in eminence, for ever
exalted.
8 Next you may see them loaded with
fetters,
held fast in chains like captives:
9 he denounces their conduct to them,
showing how, puffed with pride, they
lapsed into sin.
10 With his warnings sounding in their
ears
he directs them back from their evil
courses.
11 If they listen and serve him,
they will live out their days in
prosperity
and their years in comfort.
12 But, if they do not listen, they cross the
river of death,
dying with their lesson unlearnt.
13 The proud rage against him
and do not cry to him for help when
caught in his toils;
14 so they die in their prime,
short-lived as male prostitutes.
15 Those who suffer he rescues through
suffering
and teaches them by the discipline of
affliction.

16 Beware, if you are tempted to exchange
hardship for comfort,
with unlimited plenty spread before
you and a generous table;
17 if you eat your fill of a rich man's fare

35:14 **Humble yourself:** *prob. rdg; Heb. Judge.*
36:5 **God:** *prob. rdg; Heb. adds* a mighty one and not.
and: *prob. rdg; Heb. omits.*   36:7 **deprive . . . due:** *or*
take his eyes off the righteous.   36:16 **for comfort:**
prob. rdg; Heb. omits. **before you:** *so one MS; others*
before her.

not because they agree with Job, but because their arguments against him are so feeble. **9–16:** This passage replies to Job's contention that God does not reply to Job's challenge to come to a trial (13.20–24; 30.20).
In due time God responds to human beings.

36.1–19, 21: God does not allow the wicked to prosper forever. Those who learn from suffering attain
contentment. **14:** *Male prostitutes* had a role in the fertility rites of Canaanite temples. In times of religious
decline they were attached to the Israelite temple and shrines; see Deut. 23.17, also 2 Kgs. 23.7. It seems that
the writer believed sexual excess led to an early death.

when you are occupied with the
business of the law,
18 do not be led astray by lavish gifts of
wine
and do not let bribery warp your
judgement.
19 Will that wealth of yours, however
great, avail you,
or all the resources of your high
position?
21 Take care not to turn to mischief,
for that is why you are tried by
affliction.

20 Have no fear if in the breathless terrors
of the night
you see nations vanish where they
stand.
22 God is pre-eminent in majesty;
who wields such sovereign power as he?
23 Who has prescribed his course for him
or said to him, 'You have done wrong'?
24 Remember, then, to sing the praises of
his work,
as mortals have always sung them.
25 All mankind gazes at him;
the race of mortals look on from afar.
26 Consider: God is so great that we
cannot know him;
the number of his years is past
searching out.
27 He draws up drops of water from the
sea
and distils rain from the flood;
28 the rain-clouds pour down in torrents,
they descend in showers on the
ground;
31 thus he sustains the nations
and provides food in plenty.

29 Can anyone read the secret of the
billowing clouds,
spread like a carpet under his pavilion?
30 See how he scatters his light about him,
and its rays cover the sea.
32 He charges the thunderbolts with flame
and launches them straight at the mark;
33 in his anger he calls up the tempest,
and the thunder is the herald of its
coming.

37 This too makes my heart beat
wildly
and start from its place.

2 Just listen to the thunder of God's
voice,
the rumbling of his utterance!
3 Under the vault of heaven he lets it
roll,
and his lightning flashes to the ends of
the earth.
4 There follows a sound, a roaring
as he thunders with majestic voice.
5 At God's command wonderful things
come to pass;
great deeds beyond our knowledge are
done by him.
6 For he says to the snow, 'Fall over the
earth';
to the rainstorms he says, 'Be violent,'
and at his voice the rains pour down
unchecked.
7 He shuts everyone fast indoors,
and all whom he has made are quiet;
8 beasts withdraw into their lairs
and take cover in their dens.
9 The hurricane bursts from its prison,
and the rain-winds bring bitter cold.
10 By the breath of God the ice is formed,
and the wide waters are frozen hard.
11 He hurls lightning from the dense
clouds,
and the clouds spread his light,
12 as they travel round in their courses,
directed by his guiding hand
to do his bidding
all over the habitable world;
13 whether for punishment or for love
he brings them forth.

14 Listen, Job, to this argument;
stop and consider God's wonderful
works.
15 Do you know how God assigns them
their tasks,

36:19–22 Verses 20 and 21 transposed.   36:25 him: or
it.   36:27 from the sea: prob. rdg; Heb. omits.
36:28 in torrents: prob. rdg; Heb. which.
36:28–32 Verse 31 transposed to follow verse 28.
36:29 spread . . . under: prob. rdg; Heb. crashing
noises.   36:30 its rays: prob. rdg; Heb. the roots of.
36:32 and . . . straight: prob. rdg; Heb. and gives orders
concerning it.   36:33 in his anger . . . coming: prob.
rdg; Heb. obscure.   37:4 See note on verse 6.
37:5 come to pass: prob. rdg; Heb. he thunders.
37:6 and . . . unchecked: prob. rdg; some words in this
line transposed from verse 4.   37:7 indoors: prob. rdg;
Heb. obscure.   37:13 punishment: prob. rdg; Heb. adds
or for his land.

36.20, 22–37.24: God's power over nature is such that mere mortals cannot truly understand the deity; they

how he sends light flashing from his
clouds?

¹⁶ Do you know how the clouds hang
poised overhead,
a wonderful work of his consummate
skill?

¹⁷ Sweltering there in your stifling clothes,
when the earth lies sultry under the
south wind,

¹⁸ can you as he does beat out the vault of
the skies,
hard as a mirror of cast metal?

¹⁹ Teach us then what to say to him;
for all is dark, and we cannot marshal
our thoughts.

²⁰ Can anyone dictate to God when he is
to speak,
or command him to make
proclamation?

²¹ At one moment the light is not seen,
being overcast with cloud;
then the wind passes by and clears it
away,

²² and a golden glow comes from the
north.

²³ But the Almighty we cannot find;
his power is beyond our ken,
yet in his great righteousness he does
not pervert justice.

²⁴ Therefore mortals pay him reverence,
and all who are wise fear him.

God's answer and Job's submission

38 Then the Lord answered Job out of
the tempest:

² Who is this who darkens counsel
with words devoid of knowledge?

³ Brace yourself and stand up like a
man;
I shall put questions to you, and you
must answer.

⁴ Where were you when I laid the earth's
foundations?
Tell me, if you know and understand.

⁵ Who fixed its dimensions? Surely you
know!
Who stretched a measuring line over it?

⁶ On what do its supporting pillars rest?
Who set its corner-stone in place,

⁷ while the morning stars sang in chorus
and the sons of God all shouted for
joy?

⁸ Who supported the sea at its birth,
when it burst in flood from the
womb—

⁹ when I wrapped it in a blanket of cloud
and swaddled it in dense fog,

¹⁰ when I established its bounds,
set its barred doors in place,

¹¹ and said, 'Thus far may you come but
no farther;
here your surging waves must halt'?

¹² In all your life have you ever called up
the dawn
or assigned the morning its place?

¹³ Have you taught it to grasp the fringes
of the earth
and shake the Dog-star from the sky;

37:20 **he is:** *prob. rdg; Heb.* I am.   37:22 **golden . . .
north:** *prob rdg; Heb. adds* this refers to God, terrible in
majesty.   37:24 **fear him:** *so Gk; Heb.* fear not.
38:8 **Who . . . birth:** *prob. rdg; Heb.* And he held back
the sea with two doors.   38:13 **the Dog-star . . . sky:**
lit. the Dog-stars from it.

can only marvel at God's greatness. (Note transposition of vv. 20 and 21.) **37.22:** *North:* Heb., *zaphon,* the
mountain habitation of the gods (see 26.7 n.).

38.1–42.6: God's speeches and Job's submission.

38.1–40.2: God's speech from the whirlwind. God's argument seems to be that in the beauty, majesty,
power, and wonder of the world, Job's situation cannot be the one thing out of joint. Surely Job cannot deny
that his condition must fit into the mysteries of the universe which Job cannot penetrate and yet cannot blame
God for making them incomprehensible. The form of the passage is derived from nature wisdom, encyclopedic
data under the care of the sages (in Egypt especially). The passage ignores the accusations made against God,
and focuses on Job's inevitable, human ignorance. **1:** Whereas *the tempest* had brought Job's calamity in the
beginning (1.19, *whirlwind*), it is now the occasion for his vindication. The passage ensues directly on 31.37,
abstaining from comment on the Elihu speeches (see 32.1–37.24 n.). **3:** *Brace:* the word means to prepare for
warfare, and may derive from belt wrestling. **7:** Light is a symbol of rejoicing; compare Ps. 97.11–12. Because
of their brilliance in the surrounding darkness, the heavenly bodies are often personified as rejoicing and

¹⁴to bring up the horizon in relief as clay
under a seal,
until all things stand out like the folds
of a cloak,
¹⁵when the light of the Dog-star is
dimmed
and the stars of the Navigator's Line go
out one by one?

¹⁶Have you gone down to the springs of
the sea
or walked in the unfathomable deep?
¹⁷Have the portals of death been revealed
to you?
Have you seen the door-keepers of the
place of darkness?
¹⁸Have you comprehended the vast
expanse of the world?
Tell me all this, if you know.

¹⁹Which is the way to the home of light,
and where does darkness dwell?
²⁰Can you then take each to its appointed
boundary
and escort it on its homeward path?
²¹Doubtless you know, for you were
already born.
So long is the span of your life!

²²Have you visited the storehouses of the
snow
or seen the arsenal where hail is stored,
²³which I have kept ready for the day of
calamity,
for war and for the hour of battle?
²⁴By what paths is the heat spread
abroad
or the east wind dispersed world-wide?
²⁵Who has cut channels for the
downpour
and cleared a path for the thunderbolt,
²⁶for rain to fall on land devoid of
people,
on the uninhabited wilderness,
²⁷clothing waste and derelict lands with
green
and making grass spring up on thirsty
ground?

²⁸Does the rain have a father?

Who sired the drops of dew?
²⁹Whose womb gave birth to the ice,
and who was the mother of the
hoar-frost in the skies,
³⁰which lays a stony cover over the waters
and freezes the surface of the deep?

³¹Can you bind the cluster of the Pleiades
or loose Orion's belt?
³²Can you bring out the signs of the
zodiac in their season
or guide Aldebaran and its satellite
stars?
³³Did you proclaim the rules that govern
the heavens
or determine the laws of nature on the
earth?
³⁴Can you command the clouds
to envelop you in a deluge of rain?

³⁵If you bid lightning speed on its way,
will it say to you, 'I am ready'?
³⁶Who put wisdom in depths of darkness
and veiled understanding in secrecy?
³⁷Who is wise enough to marshal the
rain-clouds
and empty the cisterns of heaven,
³⁸when the dusty soil sets in a dense
mass,
and the clods of earth stick fast
together?

³⁹Can you hunt prey for the lioness
and satisfy the appetite of young lions,
⁴⁰as they crouch in the lair
or lie in wait in the covert?
⁴¹Who provides the raven with its quarry
when its fledgelings cry aloud,
croaking for lack of food?

39 Do you know when the mountain
goats give birth?
Do you attend the wild doe when she is
calving?
²Can you count the months that they
carry their young
or know the time of their delivery,

38:27 **thirsty ground:** *prob. rdg; Heb.* source.
38:36 **secrecy:** *prob. rdg; Heb.* word unknown.
38:37 **empty the cisterns:** *lit.* tilt the water-skins.
38:41 **cry aloud:** *prob. rdg; Heb.* adds to God.

praising God; see Pss. 19.1–6; 148.3–4. **21:** Further irony: Job may be comparing himself to Wisdom, which
existed in the beginning with God (see Prov. 8.22 n.). **22–23:** *Hail:* compare Josh. 10.11 and Ecclus. 46.6. **30:**
The surface of the deep: any body of water such as the Sea of Galilee. **32:** This verse seems to allude to the
Great Bear and Little Bear. **36:** The text is disturbed here. Perhaps the meaning is that even *darkness* of which

3 when they crouch down to open their
   wombs
 and deliver their offspring,
4 when the fawns growing and thriving in
   the open country
 leave and do not return?

5 Who has let the Syrian wild ass range at
   will
 and given the Arabian wild ass its
   freedom?
6 I have made its haunts in the
   wilderness
 and its home in the saltings;
7 it disdains the noise of the city
 and does not obey a driver's shout;
8 it roams the hills as its pasture
 in search of a morsel of green.

9 Is the wild ox willing to serve you
 or spend the night in your stall?
10 Can you harness its strength with
   ropes;
 will it harrow the furrows after
   you?
11 Can you depend on it, strong as it is,
 and leave your heavy work to it?
12 Can you rely on it to come,
 bringing your grain to the
   threshing-floor?

13 The wings of the ostrich are stunted;
 her pinions and plumage being so
   scanty
14 she leaves her eggs on the ground
 and lets them be kept warm by the
   sand.
15 She is unmindful that a foot may crush
   them,
 or a wild animal trample on them;
16 she treats her chicks heartlessly
 as if they were not her own,
 not caring if her labour is wasted.
17 For God has denied her wisdom
 and left her without sense,
18 while like a cock she struts over the
   uplands,
 scorning both horse and rider.

19 Do you give the horse his strength?
 Have you clothed his neck with a
   mane?

20 Do you make him quiver like a locust's
   wings,
 when his shrill neighing strikes terror?
21 He shows his mettle as he paws and
   prances;
 in his might he charges the armoured
   line.
22 He scorns alarms and knows no dismay;
 he does not shy away before the sword.
23 The quiver rattles at his side,
 the spear and sabre flash.
24 Trembling with eagerness, he devours
   the ground
 and when the trumpet sounds there is
   no holding him;
25 at the trumpet-call he cries 'Aha!'
 and from afar he scents the battle,
 the shouting of the captains, and the
   war cries.

26 Does your skill teach the hawk to use its
   pinions
 and spread its wings towards the south?
27 Do you instruct the eagle to soar aloft
 and build its nest high up?
28 It dwells among the rocks and there it
   has its nest,
 secure on a rocky crag;
29 from there it searches for food,
 keenly scanning the distance,
30 that its brood may be gorged with
   blood;
 wherever the slain are, it is there.

41 Can you lift out the whale with a
   gaff
 or slip a noose round its tongue?
2 Can you pass a rope through its nose
 or pierce its jaw with a hook?
3 Will it take to pleading with you for
   mercy
 or beg for its life with soft words?
4 Will it enter into an agreement with
   you
 to become your slave for life?

39:10 **its . . . furrows:** *prob. rdg; Heb. transposes* strength
and furrows.   39:12 **grain to:** *so Gk; Heb.* grain and.
39:13 **ostrich:** *Heb. word of uncertain meaning.* **are
stunted:** *prob. rdg; Heb. unintelligible.* **her pinions:** *prob.
rdg; Heb. prefixes* if. **scanty:** *prob. rdg; Heb. obscure.*
39:16 **as if they:** *so Lat.; Heb.* those that.
39:18 **while . . . struts:** *lit.* while she plays the male.
39:21 **he paws:** *so Gk; Heb.* they paw.   39:30 **41:1–6**
(*in Heb.* 40:25–30) *transposed to follow this verse.*

the Israelite was afraid had a purpose. **39.13–18:** Perhaps this means that God could be no less compassionate
to Job than to the *ostrich.* **19–25:** The *horse* was considered extremely valuable in warfare, as Canaanite texts

5 Will you toy with it as with a bird
  or keep it on a leash for your girls?
6 Do partners in the fishing haggle over
  it
  or merchants share it out?

40 The LORD then said to Job:

2 Is it for a man who disputes with the
  Almighty to be stubborn?
  Should he who argues with God answer
  back?

3 Job answered the LORD:

4 What reply can I give you, I who carry
  no weight?
  I put my finger to my lips.
5 I have spoken once; I shall not answer
  again;
  twice have I spoken; I shall do so no
  more.

6 Then the LORD answered Job out of the
tempest:

7 Brace yourself and stand up like a
  man;
  I shall put questions to you, and you
  must answer.
8 Would you dare deny that I am just,
  or put me in the wrong to prove
  yourself right?
9 Have you an arm like God's arm;
  can you thunder with a voice like his?
10 Deck yourself out, if you can, in pride
  and dignity,
  array yourself in pomp and splendour.
11 Unleash the fury of your wrath,
  look on all who are proud, and humble
  them;
12 look on all who are proud, and bring
  them low,
  crush the wicked where they stand;

13 bury them in the earth together,
  and shroud them in an unknown grave.
14 Then I in turn would acknowledge
  that your own right hand could save
  you.

15 But consider the chief of beasts, the
  crocodile,
  who devours cattle as if they were
  grass:
16 what strength is in his loins!
  What power in the muscles of his belly!
17 His tail is rigid as a cedar,
  the sinews of his flanks are tightly knit;
18 his bones are like tubes of bronze,
  his limbs like iron bars.
19 He is the chief of God's works,
  made to be a tyrant over his
  fellow-creatures;
20 for he takes the cattle of the hills for
  his prey
  and in his jaws he crunches all beasts of
  the wild.
21 There under the thorny lotus he lies,
  hidden among the reeds in the swamp;
22 the lotus conceals him in its shade,
  the poplars of the stream surround
  him.
23 If the river is in spate, that does not
  perturb him;
  he sprawls at his ease though
  submerged in the torrent.
24 Can anyone blind his eyes and take him
  or pierce his nose with the teeth of a
  trap?

41 7 Can you fill his skin with
  harpoons
  or his head with fishing spears?

40:15 **chief ... crocodile:** *prob. rdg; Heb.* beasts
(*behemoth*) which I have made with you. **cattle ...
grass:** *prob. rdg; Heb.* grass like cattle.
40:19 **fellow-creatures:** *prob. rdg; Heb.* sword.
40:24 **Can ... blind:** *prob. rdg; Heb.* obscure.
41:7–8 *In Heb. 40:31–32; 41:1–6 transposed to follow
39:30.*

indicate. **40.2:** Two interpretations of the text are possible, namely, (a) that for Job to *answer back* would be further impudence; or (b) an invitation to Job to answer God if he can.

40.3–5: Job's reply is that he is moved to silence.

40.6–41.34: God's second speech. In the REB translation 41.1–6 has been moved to the context of the first speech. In the Hebrew order the second speech focuses on two animals. In addition to human ignorance, no one is able to humble the proud person or to master the *crocodile* and *whale* (41.1, or hippopotamus) as God has done. The subdued animal is to be understood both literally and as recalling the primeval sea monster of mythology (3.8 and 26.12–13; compare Ps. 74.13–14). **6:** See 38.1. **7:** See 38.3 n. **15:** Behemoth in Heb. (see Tfn.) is an intensive plural for majesty, but denotes a singular, as in older translations. **17:** The reference to *his tail* suggests a crocodile, rather than the hippopotamus found in some older commentaries.

⁸If ever you lift your hand against him,
   think of the struggle that awaits you,
   and stop!
⁹Anyone who tackles him has no hope
   of success,
   but is overcome at the very sight of
   him.
¹⁰How fierce he is when roused!
   Who is able to stand up to him?
¹¹Who has ever attacked him and come
   out of it safely?
   No one under the wide heaven.
¹²I shall not pass over in silence his limbs,
   his prowess, and the grace of his
   proportions.
¹³Who has ever stripped off his outer
   garment
   or penetrated his doublet of hide?
¹⁴Who has ever prised open the portals
   of his face
   where terror lies in the circuits of his
   teeth?
¹⁵His back is row upon row of shields,
   enclosed in a wall of flints;
¹⁶one presses so close on the next
   that no air can pass between them,
¹⁷each so firmly clamped to its neighbour
   that they hold and cannot be parted.
¹⁸His sneezing sends out sprays of light,
   and his eyes gleam like the shimmer of
   dawn.
¹⁹Firebrands shoot from his mouth,
   and sparks come flying out;
²⁰his nostrils gush forth steam
   like a cauldron on a fire fanned to full
   heat.
²¹His breath sets coals ablaze,
   and flames issue from his mouth.
²²Strength resides in his neck,
   and dismay dances ahead of him.
²³Close-knit is his underbelly,
   no pressure will make it yield.
²⁴His heart is firm as a rock,
   firm as the nether millstone.

²⁵When he rears up, strong men are
   afraid,

panic-stricken at the lashings of his tail.
²⁶Sword or spear, dart or javelin
   may touch him, but all without effect.
²⁷Iron he counts as straw,
   and bronze as rotted wood.
²⁸No arrow can pierce him,
   and for him sling-stones are so much
   chaff;
²⁹to him a cudgel is but a reed,
   and he laughs at the swish of the sabre.
³⁰Armoured beneath with jagged sherds,
   he sprawls on the mud like a
   threshing-sledge.
³¹He makes the deep water boil like a
   cauldron,
   he churns up the lake like ointment in
   a mixing bowl.
³²He leaves a shining trail behind him,
   and in his wake the great river is like
   white hair.
³³He has no equal on earth,
   a creature utterly fearless.
³⁴He looks down on all, even the highest;
   over all proud beasts he is king.

42 Job answered the LORD:

²I know that you can do all things
   and that no purpose is beyond you.
³You ask: Who is this obscuring counsel
   yet lacking knowledge?
   But I have spoken of things
   which I have not understood,
   things too wonderful for me to know.
⁴Listen, and let me speak. You said:
   I shall put questions to you, and you
   must answer.
⁵I knew of you then only by report,
   but now I see you with my own eyes.

41:9 *In Heb. 41:1.*   41:10 **him:** *some MSS; others* me.
41:11 **him:** *prob. rdg; Heb.* me. **and . . . safely:** *so Gk;
Heb.* and I am safe. **No one:** *prob. rdg; Heb.* He is mine.
41:15 **back:** *prob. rdg; Heb.* pride. **wall:** *prob. rdg; Heb.*
seal.   41:18 **shimmer of dawn:** *lit.* eyelids of the
morning.   41:20 **full heat:** *so Syriac; Heb.* rushes.
41:25 **strong men:** *or* leaders *or* gods.

42.1–6: Job's repentance. Job's silence (40.3–5) now gives way to the immediacy of God's presence and brings him to repentance. Job quotes from God's initial speech (38.2–3) to admit the validity of the divine charge. **5–6:** Job's knowledge of God was a conceptual one acquired from tradition *by report;* now he has a vivid personal encounter. As a consequence he recognizes not only his limitations in understanding but comes to acknowledge that God's actions in ordering the universe go beyond a system of justice as human beings know it. Job experienced God as bounty (38.41–39.12), beauty (38.12–15), freedom (38.5–6), and grace (41.9–31).

⁶Therefore I yield,
  repenting in dust and ashes.

Epilogue

⁷WHEN the LORD had finished speaking to Job, he said to Eliphaz the Temanite, 'My anger is aroused against you and your two friends, because, unlike my servant Job, you have not spoken as you ought about me. ⁸Now take seven bulls and seven rams, go to my servant Job and offer a whole-offering for yourselves, and he will intercede for you. I shall surely show him favour by not being harsh with you because you have not spoken as you ought about me, as he has done.' ⁹Then Eliphaz the Temanite and Bildad the Shuhite and Zophar the Naamathite went and carried out the LORD's command, and the LORD showed favour to Job ¹⁰when he had interceded for his friends.

The LORD restored Job's fortunes, and gave him twice the possessions he had before. ¹¹All Job's brothers and sisters and his acquaintance of former days came and feasted with him in his home. They consoled and comforted him for all the misfortunes which the LORD had inflicted on him, and each of them gave him a sheep and a gold ring. ¹²Thus the LORD blessed the end of Job's life more than the beginning: he had fourteen thousand sheep and six thousand camels, a thousand yoke of oxen, and as many she-donkeys. ¹³He also had seven sons and three daughters; ¹⁴he named his eldest daughter Jemimah, the second Keziah, and the third Keren-happuch. ¹⁵There were no women in all the world so beautiful as Job's daughters; and their father gave them an inheritance with their brothers.

¹⁶Thereafter Job lived another hundred and forty years; he saw his sons and his grandsons to four generations, ¹⁷and he died at a very great age.

42:7 **unlike . . . me:** *so some MSS; others* you have not spoken as you ought to me about my servant Job.
42:8 **about . . . done:** *so some MSS; others* to me about him.   42:9 **and Zophar:** *so many MSS; others* omit and.   42:11 **sheep:** *or* piece of money.
42:13 **seven:** *or* fourteen.

42.7–17: Epilogue. Job is restored to his former glory. The epilogue, like the prologue (chs. 1–2), is in prose. **10:** The suffering righteous one stands before God as intercessor. **12:** The *gold ring* was for the ear or the nose. **13:** More than three daughters may have been viewed as a liability. See Ecclus. 26.10–12; 42.9–11. Several manuscripts read fourteen sons (see Tfn.), in line with the doubling of his property. **14:** *Jemimah:* dove (S. of S. 2.14). *Keziah:* cinnamon (Prov. 7.17). *Keren-happuch:* horn of eye cosmetics. **15:** The specific mention of daughters receiving an inheritance is unique in the OT, but see Num. 26.33; 27.1–8; 36.1–12. **16–17:** Job's life span becomes double the usual expectation (Ps. 90.10). *Four generations:* compare Ps. 128.6. The language here is reminiscent of descriptions of the ancestors in Gen. 25.8; 35.29; 50.23, for the story is set in that time.

Psalms

In the psalms there are many voices, from various times and places, from Joshua to Ezra, and from Jerusalem to Babylon. Gathered by unknown persons, often called "the sages of Israel," the psalms were used in ancient worship as they have continued to live in both synagogue and church.

When Israel came to Canaan it encountered and absorbed a living poetic tradition; hence many psalms reveal much that Israel had in common with its predecessors and neighbors. At times, however, some of Israel's poets skillfully shaped the language with intuitive insight greater even than the very language itself; these are the occasions which are always exciting for the student who is interested in the singular thrust of Israel's creative literary achievement. But the historian must also recognize that the less striking aspects, the common elements themselves, could be of great significance too in the late biblical age.

Some of the poetic voices seem muffled by our own world view, yet others break through such barriers, for in many passages the Hebrew poets sang of a reality which is only on the horizon of our comprehension.

The Book of Psalms is divided into five books. In the Hebrew Masoretic Text, there is a superscription or heading for many psalms. These superscriptions are relatively early additions to the psalms, identifying them with particular persons, for example, David, connecting them with historical events, as in Pss. 51, 56, and 57, or giving musical or liturgical notations, as in Pss. 4–8. Two recurrent words, "Selah" and "Amen," appear at times in the body of a psalm. These words appear to be instructions inserted when the psalms were used liturgically. Perhaps Selah, whose meaning is unclear, was a signal for an instrumental interlude. Amen (e.g. 41.13), likewise uncertain in its original use, seems to instruct the participants in the liturgy to assent to the passage read to them.

The classification of each psalm is to be regarded as summary, and meant to be useful rather than complete. Thus, the "Laments" are not here classified into subcategories such as "individual" and "group" Laments. The procedure in the notes is to designate the following types: Lament, Thanksgiving, Hymn, Enthronement Hymn, Royal Psalm, Wisdom Psalm, Prophetic Judgment, Vow, Liturgy, and Benediction. Some psalms are really only fragments of known types and others are impossible to classify at all.

A Lament, the most abundant type, was sung in time of great trouble. It usually contains a statement of the poet's distress, a word of trust, an appeal to God, a declaration about the poet's obedience, and a vow to sing a Thanksgiving (see Pss. 22 and 26; also compare 56.8, 12; 107.22). A Thanksgiving Psalm gives thanks for what God has done in specific historical circumstances to save an individual or the nation. A Hymn praises God for what God is accustomed to do in nature or history for the welfare of humankind. An Enthronement Hymn was used to celebrate the kingship of God. Royal Psalms dealt with the human king; many were used at the time of his coronation and one is a Wedding Song. The Wisdom Psalms reflect the teaching of the sages of Israel. Other types are rather rare, and are explained in the notes.

Tradition ascribes the Book of Psalms to David (2 Sam. 23.1); about half are so ascribed in the superscriptions. Modern scholarship rejects a view held some generations ago which supposed that no psalms were as early as David; indeed, some were written even before his time. The Psalter is a collection, indeed, probably a collection of collections, of poems from all periods of Israel's history. It has, with justice, been called "the prayer book of the second temple," for in that later period (after 520 B.C.E.) the psalms were used in the liturgy.

Book 1

1 ¹ HAPPY is the one
who does not take the counsel of the
wicked for a guide,
or follow the path that sinners tread,
or take his seat in the company of
scoffers.
² His delight is in the law of the LORD;
it is his meditation day and night.
³ He is like a tree
planted beside water channels;
it yields its fruit in season
and its foliage never fades.
So he too prospers in all he does.

⁴ The wicked are not like this;
rather they are like chaff driven by the
wind.
⁵ When judgement comes, therefore,
they will not stand firm,
nor will sinners in the assembly of the
righteous.

⁶ The LORD watches over the way of the
righteous,
but the way of the wicked is doomed.

2 ¹ WHY are the nations in turmoil?
Why do the peoples hatch their futile
plots?
² Kings of the earth stand ready,
and princes conspire together
against the LORD and his anointed king.
³ 'Let us break their fetters,' they cry,

'let us throw off their chains!'

⁴ He who sits enthroned in the heavens
laughs,
the Lord derides them;
⁵ then angrily he rebukes them,
threatening them in his wrath.
⁶ 'I myself have enthroned my king', he
says,
'on Zion, my holy mountain.'

⁷ I shall announce the decree of the
LORD:
'You are my son,' he said to me;
'this day I become your father.
⁸ Ask of me what you will:
I shall give you nations as your domain,
the earth to its farthest ends as your
possession.
⁹ You will break them with a rod of iron,
shatter them like an earthen pot.'

¹⁰ Be mindful, then, you kings;
take warning, you earthly rulers:
¹¹⁻¹² worship the LORD with reverence;
tremble, and pay glad homage to the
king,
for fear the LORD may become angry
and you may be struck down in
mid-course;
for his anger flares up in a moment.
Happy are all who find refuge in him!

2:11–12 **tremble . . . king:** *poss. mng; Heb.* and rejoice
with trembling; kiss the son.

Ps. 1: The LORD watches over the way of the righteous. This Wisdom Psalm (see Introduction) contrasts the two ways of life — good and evil — and their consequences — happiness and misery. Thus, it is a summary of the moral teaching of the Psalter; hence, its place at the beginning of the Psalms. **1–3:** *Happy is the one:* a common Wisdom phrase; see Ps. 41.1 and the beatitudes of Jesus (Matt. 5.1–12). See also Prov. 3.13 n. *A tree . . . beside water channels* is a symbol of the fullness of life in arid Palestine where trees are generally dwarfed for lack of moisture; compare Ezek. 47.1–12; Ecclus. 24.13–31. **6:** The confident assertion that the LORD *watches over the way of the righteous* is found in many psalms, especially Wisdom Psalms. Even though in the Laments the psalmist recognizes the paradox of the just suffering, the one praying trusts that deliverance always comes; see Ps. 22.

Ps. 2: I have enthroned my king on Zion. A Royal Psalm used at the time of coronation. For comparable psalms see Pss. 72, 101, 110, and 132. **1–2:** The accession of a new emperor was the time usually picked by subject *kings* to revolt. Because the emperor-king was considered chosen by God, for subjects to *conspire* against him was to conspire against the LORD. The word *king* is not found here in the Heb. The Heb. word for *anointed* is *messiah*. This word, in later tradition, came to stand for the ideal king who would accomplish God's purposes and Israel's destiny. Perhaps because of this connotation this psalm is placed here at the head of the Psalter. The passage is cited in Acts 4.25–26. **7:** *You are my son:* a formula apparently used at the time of the coronation (see 2 Sam. 7.14; Ps. 89.26–27). For Christian interpretation, see Lk. 3.22 and, more explicitly, Acts 13.33.

3 A psalm: for David (when he fled from his son
Absalom)

¹ LORD, how numerous are my enemies!
How many there are who rise against
me,
² how many who say of me,
'He will not find safety in God!'   [Selah

³ But you, LORD, are a shield to cover
me:
you are my glory, you raise my head
high.
⁴ As often as I cry aloud to the LORD,
he answers from his holy mountain.
    [Selah

⁵ I lie down and sleep,
and I wake again, for the LORD
upholds me.
⁶ I shall not fear their myriad forces
ranged against me on every side.

⁷ Arise, LORD; save me, my God!
You strike all my foes across the face;
you break the teeth of the wicked.
⁸ Yours is the victory, LORD;
may your blessing rest on your people.
    [Selah

4 For the leader: with stringed instruments: a
psalm: for David

¹ ANSWER me when I call,
God, the upholder of my right!
When I was hard pressed you set me
free;
be gracious to me and hear my prayer.
² Men of rank, how long will you
dishonour my glorious one,
setting your heart on empty idols and
resorting to false gods?   [Selah
³ Know that the LORD has singled out for
himself his loyal servant;

the Lord hears when I call to him.
⁴ Let awe restrain you from sin;
while you rest, meditate in silence:
    [Selah
⁵ offer your due of sacrifice,
and put your trust in the LORD.

⁶ There are many who say, 'If only we
might see good times!
Let the light of your face shine on us,
LORD.'
⁷ But you have put into my heart a
greater happiness
than others had from grain and wine in
plenty.
⁸ Now in peace I shall lie down and
sleep;
for it is you alone, LORD, who let me
live in safety.

5 For the leader: with the flutes: a psalm: for
David

¹ LISTEN to my words, LORD,
consider my inmost thoughts;
² heed my cry for help, my King and God.
³ When I pray to you, LORD,
in the morning you will hear me.
I shall prepare a morning sacrifice
and keep watch.
⁴ For you are not a God who welcomes
wickedness;
evil can be no guest of yours.
⁵ The arrogant will not stand in your
presence;
you hate all evildoers,
⁶ you make an end of liars.
The LORD abhors those who are violent
and deceitful.

⁷ But through your great love I may
come into your house,

Ps. 3: I cry aloud to the LORD. A Lament, this psalm has characteristics usually found in all psalms of this category: (a) a cry to God (v. 1); (b) narration of trouble or complaint (vv. 1–2); (c) expression of trust in God (vv. 3–6); (d) a plea for God's help (vv. 7–8). The superscription (see Introduction) ascribes this psalm to David when he fled from his rebellious son Absalom (2 Sam. 15.13–16). Psalms 3–41 are all ascribed to, or are about, David. **4:** *Holy mountain:* Mount Zion, the place of the temple, symbolic of God's heavenly abode.

Ps. 4: Answer me when I call. Partly a Lament, and partly exultation on delivery from distress. **4–5:** The virtue of obedience. Note the mention of sacrifices; the obedience advised is ritual as well as ethical. **6:** *Face:* an idiom, originally royal, often applied to God. A king could show pleasure by allowing his subjects to "seek his face," or by making his face shine on someone; as used of God see Pss. 31.16; 67.1 and Num. 6.25.

Ps. 5: Listen to my words, LORD. A Lament. A *sacrifice* was prescribed for various sins (see Lev. 4.27–6.7), here possibly after a vigil in the temple. To *keep watch* meant to look for signs of God's forgiveness and approval in the events of life. **4–6:** *The arrogant . . .* may be the enemies of the psalmist. **7:** The psalmist, through the

and at your holy temple bow down in
  awe.
⁸ Lead me and protect me, LORD,
  because I am beset by enemies;
  give me a straight path to follow.
⁹ Nothing they say is true;
  they are bent on complete destruction.
  Their throats are gaping tombs;
  smooth talk runs off their tongues.
¹⁰ God, bring ruin on them;
  let their own devices be their downfall.
  Cast them out for their many
    rebellions,
  for they have defied you.

¹¹ But let all who take refuge in you
    rejoice,
  let them for ever shout for joy;
  shelter those who love your name,
  that they may exult in you.
¹² For you, LORD, will bless the righteous;
  you will surround them with favour as
    with a shield.

6 For the leader: with stringed instruments: ac-
    cording to the sheminith: a psalm: for David
¹ LORD, do not rebuke me in your anger,
  do not punish me in your wrath.
² Show favour to me, LORD, for my
    strength fails;
  LORD, heal me, for my body is racked
    with pain;
³ I am utterly distraught.
  When will you act, LORD?
⁴ Return, LORD, deliver me;
  save me, for your love is steadfast.
⁵ Among the dead no one remembers
    you;
  in Sheol who praises you?

⁶ I am wearied with my moaning;
  all night long my pillow is wet with
    tears,
  I drench my bed with weeping.
⁷ Grief dims my eyes;
  they are worn out because of all my
    adversaries.

⁸ Leave me alone, you workers of evil,
  for the LORD has heard my weeping!
⁹ The LORD has heard my entreaty;
  the LORD will accept my prayer.
¹⁰ All my enemies will be confounded,
    stricken with terror;
  they will turn away in sudden
    confusion.

7 A shiggaion: for David (which he sang to the
    LORD because of Cush, a Benjamite)
¹ LORD my God, in you I find refuge;
  rescue me from all my pursuers and
    save me
² before they tear at my throat like a lion
  and drag me off beyond hope of
    rescue.
³ LORD my God, if I have done any of
    these things —
  if I have stained my hands with guilt,
⁴ if I have repaid a friend evil for good
  or wantonly despoiled an adversary —
⁵ let an enemy come in pursuit and
    overtake me,
  let him trample my life to the ground
  and lay my honour in the dust!   [Selah

⁶ Arise, LORD, in your anger,
  rouse yourself in wrath against my
    adversaries.

6:5 **Sheol:** or the underworld.

grace of God, may enter the *house* of the LORD, the temple; see Ps. 15 for conditions to be fulfilled before
entering the sanctuary. Compare Isa. 6.5–7. **11–12:** Transition from cry of sorrow to *shout* of *joy* is a sign of
God's *love* and *favour.*

   Ps. 6: Show favour to me, LORD. A Lament (see Introduction), one of seven "Penitential Psalms" (see Ps.
130 n.), seemingly to be uttered in the time of a severe illness (vv. 2–7). **1–3:** *Body is racked . . . utterly
distraught:* possibly symptoms of a sickness. Illness was considered a sign of God's *anger* and a punishment
for sin; compare Jn. 9.2–3. **5:** The motive for God's healing is that death would mean the end of praising God,
for there is no worship of God in *Sheol,* the place of the dead. **9–10:** The psalm ends with a usual note of
confidence.

   Ps. 7: Rescue me from all my pursuers. A Lament (see Introduction). The background seems to be that of
a prisoner awaiting trial, or of an innocent person falsely accused. **5:** The crime of which the psalmist is accused
seems to demand payment with *life. Lay honour in the dust:* to die in dishonor; compare Isa. 53.9–12. **6–9:**
This section has the flavor of the Book of Job. **6:** Compare 44.23 n. In the face of manifest injustice, God is

My God who ordered justice to be
   done, awake.
[7] Let the peoples assemble around you;
   take your seat on high above them.
[8] The LORD passes sentence on the
   nations.
   Uphold my cause, LORD, as my
      righteousness deserves,
   for I am clearly innocent.
[9] Let the wicked do no more harm,
   but grant support to the righteous,
   you searcher of heart and mind,
   you righteous God.

[10] I rely on God to shield me;
   he saves the honest of heart.
[11] God is a just judge,
   constant in his righteous anger.

[12] The enemy sharpens his sword again,
   strings his bow and makes it ready.
[13] It is against himself he has prepared his
      deadly shafts
   and tipped his arrows with fire.
[14] He is in labour with iniquity;
   he has conceived mischief and given
      birth to lies.
[15] He has made a pit and dug it deep,
   but he himself will fall into the hole he
      was making.
[16] His mischief will recoil upon him,
   and his violence fall on his own head.

[17] I shall praise the LORD for his
      righteousness
   and sing to the name of the LORD Most
      High.

8 *For the leader: according to the gittith: a
      psalm: for David*
   [1] LORD our sovereign,

how glorious is your name throughout
   the world!
Your majesty is praised as high as the
   heavens,
[2] from the mouths of babes and infants
   at the breast.
You have established a bulwark against
   your adversaries
to restrain the enemy and the avenger.

[3] When I look up at your heavens, the
      work of your fingers,
   at the moon and the stars you have set
      in place,
[4] what is a frail mortal, that you should
      be mindful of him,
   a human being, that you should take
      notice of him?

[5] Yet you have made him little less than a
      god,
   crowning his head with glory and
      honour.
[6] You make him master over all that you
      have made,
   putting everything in subjection under
      his feet:
[7] all sheep and oxen, all the wild beasts,
[8] the birds in the air, the fish in the sea,
   and everything that moves along ocean
      paths.

[9] LORD our sovereign,
   how glorious is your name throughout
      the world!

9-10 *For the leader: set to 'Muth
         labben': a psalm: for David*
   [1] I SHALL give praise to you, LORD, with
      my whole heart,

seen as one who needs to *awake* from sleep. **7-8:** God here is asked to vindicate the psalmist's innocence before the peoples. **15:** The theme of a wicked person falling into the very *pit* that person has *dug* is frequent in Wisdom literature. **17:** Many Laments end with a vow to praise or thank the LORD for what God will surely do.

Ps. 8: How glorious is your name throughout the world. This Hymn, drawing its inspiration from the beauties of the night, glorifies God's majesty and power (v. 3). **1:** God's *name* is *glorious* when God's power is manifest and acknowledged. **4-5:** The poet is here affirmative about humankind; elsewhere (144.3-4) the mood is one of discouragement about humanity and its estate; compare Job 7.17-19. **6-8:** The verses echo the idea of Gen. 1.26-29. **9:** The repetition of v. 1 is the literary device known as "Inclusion," designed to extend the idea of God's glory to all that is between the two statements.

Pss. 9-10: Show me favour, LORD. A Lament (see Introduction). Most scholars take these two psalms as a single poem, as in the Sept. It is an alphabetic acrostic, though not perfectly so preserved; see Ps. 111 n. The

I shall recount all your marvellous
   deeds.
2 I shall rejoice and exult in you, the
   Most High;
I shall sing praise to your name
3 because my enemies turn back;
at your presence they fall headlong and
   perish.

4 For seated on your throne, a righteous
   judge,
you have upheld my right and my
   cause;
5 you have rebuked the nations and
   overwhelmed the ungodly,
blotting out their name for all time.
6 The enemy are finished, ruined for
   evermore.
You have overthrown their cities; all
   memory of them is lost.

7 The LORD sits enthroned for ever:
he has established his throne for
   judgement.
8 He it is who will judge the world with
   justice,
who will try the cause of peoples with
   equity.

9 May the LORD be a tower of strength
   for the oppressed,
a tower of strength in time of trouble.
10 Those who acknowledge your name will
   trust in you,
for you, LORD, do not abandon those
   who seek you.

11 Sing to the LORD enthroned in Zion;
proclaim his deeds among the nations.
12 For the avenger of blood keeps the
   afflicted in mind;
he does not ignore their cry.

13 Show me favour, LORD; see how my
   foes afflict me;
you raise me from the gates of death,
14 that I may declare all your praise

and in the gates of Zion exult at this
   deliverance.

15 The nations have plunged into a pit of
   their own making;
their feet are entangled in the net they
   have hidden.
16 The LORD makes himself known, and
   justice is done:
the wicked are trapped in their own
   devices.   [Higgaion. Selah
17 The wicked depart to Sheol,
all the nations who are heedless of God.

18 But the poor will not always be
   unheeded,
nor the hope of the destitute be always
   vain.
19 Arise, LORD, restrain the power of
   mortals;
let the nations be judged in your
   presence.
20 Strike them with fear, LORD;
let the nations know that they are but
   human beings.   [Selah

[10] 1 Why stand far off, LORD?
Why hide away in times of trouble?
2 The wicked in their arrogance hunt
   down the afflicted:
may their crafty schemes prove their
   undoing!
3 The wicked boast of the desires they
   harbour;
in their greed they curse and revile the
   LORD.
4 The wicked in their pride do not seek
   God;
there is no place for God in any of
   their schemes.
5 Their ways are always devious;
your judgements are beyond their
   grasp,
and they scoff at all their adversaries.
6 Because they escape misfortune,
they think they will never be shaken.

9:17 **Sheol:** or the underworld.

nations (9.5, 15–19; 10.16) may possibly be interpreted as personal enemies. The vow (9.1–2) and expression
of confidence (vv. 3–12), normally in the midst of Laments, are here at the beginning. **4:** The LORD's rule is
stressed in 9.7 and 10.16. **7–9:** God is enthroned to vindicate the rights of the oppressed. **12:** The duty of
avenging a murdered or wronged person fell upon the next-of-kin. God is the *avenger of blood of the afflicted*;
compare Gen. 4.10; Num. 35.23–29. **13:** *Gates of death:* Sheol, the place of the dead, under the image of
a fortified city; compare Tfn. at Matt. 16.18. **15–16:** See 7.15. **10.2–6:** The *wicked* act as if God does not matter
and does not have to be reckoned with. **4:** *Place for God:* not atheists, but those who deny all moral force

7 The wicked person's mouth is full of
cursing, deceit, and violence;
mischief and wickedness are under his
tongue.
8 He lurks in ambush near settlements
and murders the innocent by stealth.
Ever on the watch for some
unfortunate wretch,
9 he seizes him and drags him away in
his net.
He crouches stealthily, like a lion in its
lair
crouching to seize its victim;
10 he strikes and lays him low.
Unfortunate wretches fall into his toils.
11 He says to himself, 'God has forgotten;
he has hidden his face and seen
nothing.'

12 Arise, Lord, set your hand to the task;
God, do not forget the afflicted.
13 Why have the wicked rejected you,
God,
and said that you will not call them to
account?

14 You see that mischief and grief are
their companions;
you take the matter into your own
hands.
The hapless victim commits himself to
you;
in you the fatherless finds a helper.

15 Break the power of the wicked and evil
person;
hunt out his wickedness until you can
find no more.
16 The Lord is king for ever and ever;
the nations have vanished from his
land.

17 Lord, you have heard the lament of
the humble;

you strengthen their hearts, you give
heed to them,
18 bringing redress to the fatherless and
the oppressed,
so that no one on earth may ever again
inspire terror.

11 *For the leader: for David*
1 In the Lord I take refuge. How
can you say to me,
'Flee like a bird to the mountains;
2 for see, the wicked string their bows
and fit the arrow to the bowstring,
to shoot from the darkness at honest
folk'?
3 When foundations are undermined,
what can the just person do?

4 The Lord is in his holy temple;
the Lord's throne is in heaven.
His gaze is upon mankind, his
searching eye tests them.
5 The Lord weighs just and unjust,
and he hates all who love violence.
6 He will rain fiery coals and brimstone
on the wicked;
scorching winds will be the portion they
drink.
7 For the Lord is just and loves just
dealing;
his face is turned towards the upright.

12 *For the leader: according to the shemi-
nith: a psalm: for David*
1 Save us, Lord, for no one who is loyal
remains;
good faith between people has
vanished.
2 One lies to another:
both talk with smooth words, but with
duplicity in their hearts.
3 May the Lord make an end of such
smooth words
and the tongue that talks so boastfully!

or scrutiny. See v. 13; 14.1 n. **11:** Here the *face of God* is *hidden* in order not to see; see 4.6 n. and 11.7 for
a different use of *face*.

Ps. 11: The Lord is just. Some scholars classify this poem as a Song of Trust; it is kindred to the statement
of confidence contained in most Laments (see Introduction). **1:** The mountains are often considered a place
of refuge in calamity; see Gen. 19.17; Mk. 13.14. **4:** *Holy temple . . . throne in heaven:* not a contradiction
to the psalmist. That God is in Zion (9.11), the site of the Jerusalem temple, does not exclude a dwelling in
heaven from whence God can look upon humanity. **6:** *Scorching winds* brought death from the desert,
considered a punishment from God; see Hos. 13.15.

Ps. 12: Save us Lord, for no one who is loyal remains. A Lament (see Introduction). This psalm may have
been spoken in drama form in the temple liturgy. **1–3:** Possibly spoken by a chorus.

4 They say, 'By our tongues we shall
    prevail.
  With words as our ally, who can master
    us?'
5 'Now I will arise,' says the LORD,
  'for the poor are plundered, the needy
    groan;
  I shall place them in the safety for
    which they long.'

6 The words of the LORD are unalloyed:
    silver refined in a crucible,
  gold purified seven times over.
7 LORD, you are our protector
  and will for ever guard us from such
    people.
8 The wicked parade about,
  and what is of little worth wins general
    esteem.

13 For the leader: a psalm: for David
    1 How LONG, LORD, will you leave
      me forgotten,
  how long hide your face from me?
2 How long must I suffer anguish in my
    soul,
  grief in my heart day after day?
  How long will my enemy lord it over
    me?

3 Look now, LORD my God, and answer
    me.
  Give light to my eyes lest I sleep the
    sleep of death,
4 lest my enemy say, 'I have overthrown
    him,'
  and my adversaries rejoice at my
    downfall.

5 As for me, I trust in your unfailing
    love;
  my heart will rejoice when I am
    brought to safety.
6 I shall sing to the LORD, for he has
    granted all my desire.

14 For the leader: for David
    1 THE impious fool says in his
      heart,
  'There is no God.'
  Everyone is depraved, every deed is
    vile;
  no one does good!
2 The LORD looks out from heaven
  on all the human race
  to see if any act wisely,
  if any seek God.
3 But all are unfaithful, altogether
    corrupt;
  no one does good, no, not even one.

4 Have they no understanding,
  all those evildoers who devour my
    people
  as if eating bread,
  and never call to the LORD?
5 They will be in dire alarm,
  for God is in the assembly of the
    righteous.
6 Though you would frustrate the
    counsel of the poor,
  the LORD is their refuge.
7 If only deliverance for Israel might
    come from Zion!

12:6 gold: prob. rdg; Heb. to the earth.   12:7 our: so
some MSS; others their.   13:2 day after day: prob.
rdg; Heb. by day.

12:4: *They say:* possibly a cue, to bring on another group of voices. **5:** *I will arise:* this expression, and others
like it, is found repeatedly to depict the action of the LORD, as in Num. 10.35; see Ps. 44.23 n. *Says the LORD:*
could be spoken by a priest. **6–8:** Another chorus, indicated by the word *our*. **6:** *Pure words:* in contrast to
human *smooth words* (v. 2).

  Ps. 13: How long, LORD? A very typical Lament (see Introduction) with distress (vv. 1–2), request (vv. 3–4),
trust (v. 5), and vow (v. 6). Note the force of the repetition of *How long*. **1:** *Hide your face:* compare 10.11 n.

  Ps. 14: If only deliverance might come from God. This Lament (see Introduction) is almost identical with
Ps. 53. The poet says in despair (vv. 1–3) that everyone is *corrupt;* the psalmist experiences a deep and rampant
wickedness. **1:** *Impious fool:* a single word in Heb. In biblical language *the fool* is the *wicked. Says in his heart:*
secretly thinks to be able to act as if there is *no* God. See 10.4 n. **2–6:** God's help enables the godly to resist
the wicked. **2:** To *seek God* is to *act wisely:* a theme of Wisdom literature; see Wisd. 1.1. **4:** *Devour my people:*
to exploit them; see Ezek. 34.9–10. *Call to the LORD:* worship God. **7:** *Zion:* Mount Zion, the location of the
temple; hence it means deliverance from God. *Jacob . . . Israel:* the two names of the ancestor of the Hebrews
are each applied to the nation; see Gen. 32.27–28.

When the LORD restores his people's
fortunes,
let Jacob rejoice, let Israel be glad.

15 *A psalm: for David*
¹ LORD, who may lodge in your
tent?
Who may dwell on your holy
mountain?
² One of blameless life, who does what is
right
and speaks the truth from his heart;
³ who has no malice on his tongue,
who never wrongs his fellow,
and tells no tales against his neighbour;
⁴ who shows his scorn for those the LORD
rejects,
but honours those who fear the LORD;
who holds to his oath even to his own
hurt,
⁵ who does not put his money out to
usury,
and never accepts a bribe against the
innocent.
He who behaves in this way will remain
unshaken.

16 *A miktam: for David*
¹ KEEP me, God, for in you have I
found refuge.
² I have said to the LORD, 'You are my
Lord;
from you alone comes the good I enjoy.
³ All my delight is in the noble ones,
the godly in the land.
⁴ Those who run after other gods find
endless trouble;
I shall never offer libations of blood to
such gods,

never take their names on my lips.
⁵ LORD, you are my allotted portion and
my cup;
you maintain my boundaries:
⁶ the lines fall for me in pleasant places;
I am well content with my inheritance.'

⁷ I shall bless the LORD who has given me
counsel:
in the night he imparts wisdom to my
inmost being.
⁸ I have set the LORD before me at all
times:
with him at my right hand I cannot be
shaken.
⁹ Therefore my heart is glad
and my spirit rejoices,
my body too rests unafraid;
¹⁰ for you will not abandon me to Sheol
or suffer your faithful servant to see
the pit.
¹¹ You will show me the path of life;
in your presence is the fullness of joy,
at your right hand are pleasures for
evermore.

17 *A prayer: for David*
¹ LORD, hear my plea for justice,
give heed to my cry;
listen to the prayer from my lips,
for they are innocent of all deceit.
² Let your judgement be given in my
favour;
let your eyes discern what is right.
³ You have tested my heart and watched
me all night long;

15:4 **even ... hurt:** *prob. rdg; Heb.* to do evil.
16:10 **Sheol:** *or* the underworld.

Ps. 15: Who may dwell on your holy mountain? This psalm, difficult to classify (see Introduction), is best considered a poem describing requirements for participating in the temple worship. **1:** *Who . . . who:* possibly this was connected with the liturgy of entrance into the temple, the questions being asked by pilgrims and the answer given by a priest. *Lodge . . . dwell:* the words are to be taken as hyperbole, not literally. **2–5:** The descriptive statements number ten; hence, they are often regarded as related in some way to the Ten Commandments.

Ps. 16: Keep me, God. This psalm is difficult to classify (see Introduction). The word *miktam* in the superscription may suggest that the psalm was inscribed on a wall or monument. **3–4:** A curse on idolators. **4:** *Blood* of animals was poured upon the altar as part of sacrificial ritual. To *take* the name of a god on the *lips* meant to call on that deity in worship; see Gen. 13.4. **5:** *My cup:* destiny, here in an infrequent pleasant sense. *Maintain my boundaries:* a figure of speech for abundant blessings. **6–11:** The blessedness of the faithful. **6:** *Lines:* a surveyor's measure. **8:** In a trial the defendants of an accused person stood at that one's *right hand;* here it is God. *Cannot be shaken:* the Heb. is the same as 15.5, there rendered "be brought low." **10:** *Sheol* and *pit* are synonymous; they refer to the place of the dead.

Ps. 17: Listen to the prayer of my lips. A Lament (see Introduction). **1–5:** In courtroom language the psalmist

you have assayed me and found no
malice in me.
4 Guided by the words of your lips,
I have observed the deeds of mortals,
their violent ways.
5 My steps have held steadily to your
paths;
my feet have not faltered.

6 God, I call upon you, for you will
answer me.
Bend down your ear to me, listen to my
words.
7 Show me how marvellous is your
unfailing love:
your right hand saves
those who seek sanctuary from their
assailants.
8 Guard me like the apple of your eye;
hide me in the shadow of your wings
9 from the wicked who do me violence,
from deadly foes who throng around
me.
10 They have stifled all compassion;
their mouths utter proud words;
11 they press me hard, now they hem me
in,
on the watch to bring me to the
ground.
12 The enemy is like a lion hungry for
prey,
like a young lion crouching in ambush.

13 Arise, LORD, confront them and bring
them down.
Save my life from the wicked;
make an end of them with your sword.
14 With your hand, LORD, make an end of
them;
thrust them out of this world from
among the living.
May those whom you cherish have food
in plenty,
may their children be satisfied
and their little ones inherit their wealth.

15 My plea is just: may I see your face
and be blest with a vision of you when I
awake.

18 *For the leader: for the* LORD's *servant:
for David (who recited the words of this
song to the* LORD *on the day when the* LORD *rescued him from the power of all his enemies and
from the hand of Saul. He said:)*
1 I LOVE you, LORD, my strength.
2 The LORD is my lofty crag, my fortress,
my champion,
my God, my rock in whom I find
shelter,
my shield and sure defender, my strong
tower.
3 I shall call to the LORD to whom all
praise is due;
then I shall be made safe from my
enemies.

4 The bonds of death encompassed me
and destructive torrents overtook me,
5 the bonds of Sheol tightened about me,
the snares of death were set to catch
me.
6 When in anguish of heart I cried to the
LORD
and called for help to my God,
he heard me from his temple,
and my cry reached his ears.

7 The earth shook and quaked,
the foundations of the mountains
trembled,
shaking because of his anger.
8 Smoke went up from his nostrils,
devouring fire from his mouth,

17:4–5 **Guided ... faltered:** *or* I shall not speak of the
deeds of men; /I have taken good note of all your
sayings. /⁵I have not strayed from the course you
commanded; /I have followed your path and never
faltered.   17:11 **they press me hard:** *prob. rdg; Heb.*
our footsteps.   17:14 **make an end of them:** *prob.
rdg; Heb. unintelligible.*   18:2–50 *Cp.* 2 Sam. 22:2–51.
18:5 **Sheol:** *or* the underworld.

claims to be innocent and calls on the LORD for justice and help. **8:** *Apple:* lit. the pupil, the most essential
part of the eye. *Shadow of your wings:* the image is of an eagle hovering over its young, with a reference to
God's protection of Israel in the Exodus; compare Deut. 32.10–11. **15:** Darkness is viewed as a time of trial,
when evil is on the loose and God is absent; the dawn brings a new *vision* of God's presence.

Ps. 18: The LORD **delivers the ruler.** A Thanksgiving. This psalm is also found in 2 Sam. ch. 22. There, and
in the superscription (see Introduction), it is said that David sang this psalm when the LORD delivered him from
all his enemies and from Saul. **1–3:** The poem begins by praising the LORD. **4–6:** Next, as in such psalms, the
poet refers to troubles which were encountered. **4:** *Bonds of death* is similar in meaning to *bonds of Sheol*,
i.e. some mortal danger. **7–19:** God appears in response. The description of the appearance of the Deity reflects

glowing coals and searing heat.
9 He parted the heavens and came down;
thick darkness lay under his feet.
10 He flew on the back of a cherub;
he swooped on the wings of the wind.
11 He made darkness around him his
covering,
dense vapour his canopy.
12 Thick clouds came from the radiance
before him,
hail and glowing coals.
13 The LORD thundered from the
heavens;
the Most High raised his voice
amid hail and glowing coals.
14 He loosed arrows, he sped them far
and wide,
he hurled forth lightning shafts and
sent them echoing.
15 The channels of the waters were
exposed,
earth's foundations laid bare
at the LORD's rebuke,
at the blast of breath from his nostrils.

16 He reached down from on high and
took me,
he drew me out of mighty waters,
17 he delivered me from my enemies,
strong as they were,
from my foes when they grew too
powerful for me.
18 They confronted me in my hour of
peril,
but the LORD was my buttress.
19 He brought me into untrammelled
liberty;
he rescued me because he delighted in
me.

20 The LORD repaid me as my
righteousness deserved;
because my conduct was spotless he
rewarded me,
21 for I have kept to the ways of the LORD
and have not turned from my God to
wickedness.
22 All his laws I keep before me,

and have never failed to follow his
decrees.
23 In his sight I was blameless
and kept myself from wrongdoing;
24 because my conduct was spotless in his
eyes,
the LORD rewarded me as my
righteousness deserved.

25 To the loyal you show yourself loyal
and blameless to the blameless.
26 To the pure you show yourself pure,
but skilful in your dealings with the
perverse.
27 You bring humble folk to safety,
but humiliate those who look so high
and mighty.
28 LORD, you make my lamp burn bright;
my God will lighten my darkness.
29 With your help I storm a rampart,
and by my God's aid I leap over a wall.

30 The way of God is blameless;
the LORD's word has stood the test;
he is a shield to all who take refuge in
him.
31 What god is there but the LORD?
What rock but our God?
32 It is God who girds me with strength
and makes my way free from blame,
33 who makes me swift as a hind
and sets me secure on the heights,
34 who trains my hands for battle
so that my arms can aim a
bronze-tipped bow.

35 You have given me the shield of your
salvation;
your right hand sustains me;
you stoop down to make me great.
36 You made room for my steps;
my feet have not slipped.
37 I pursue and overtake my enemies;
until I have made an end of them I do
not turn back.

18:11 **dense:** *prob. rdg, cp. 2 Sam. 22:12; Heb.* dark.
18:29 **rampart:** *prob. rdg; Heb.* troop.   18:33 **the
heights:** *so Gk; Heb.* my heights.

words and terms of Canaanite mythological language. **9–14:** The LORD is viewed as the storm god; see also
Ps. 29. **10:** *On the back of a cherub:* compare 68.4 and 104.3, where God rides on the clouds. **13–19:** In
mythology thunder and lightning are the symbols of the storm god's power over the forces of chaos which God
subdues on the way to becoming the Creator-King. Israelite poets borrowed such motifs (see Introduction). The
LORD defeats the powers of chaos, delivering the king in distress. **20–29:** The deliverance was merited because
God is just. **30–45:** The LORD trains the ruler for battle.

38 I strike them down and they can rise
    no more;
  they fall prostrate at my feet.
39 You gird me with strength for the
    battle
  and subdue my assailants beneath me.
40 You set my foot on my enemies' necks,
  and I wipe out those who hate me.
41 They cry, but there is no one to save
    them;
  they cry to the LORD, but he does not
    answer.
42 I shall beat them as fine as dust before
    the wind,
  like mud in the streets I shall trample
    them.
43 You set me free from the people who
    challenge me,
  and make me master of nations.
  A people I never knew will be my
    subjects.
44 Foreigners will come fawning to me;
  as soon as they hear tell of me they will
    submit.
45 Foreigners will be disheartened
  and come trembling from their
    strongholds.

46 The LORD lives! Blessed is my rock!
  High above all is God, my safe refuge.

47 You grant me vengeance, God,
  laying nations prostrate at my feet;
48 you free me from my enemies,
  setting me over my assailants;
  you are my deliverer from violent men.
49 Therefore, LORD, I shall praise you
    among the nations
  and sing psalms to your name,
50 to one who gives his king great victories
  and keeps faith with his anointed,
  with David and his descendants for
    ever.

19 *For the leader: a psalm: for David*
  1 THE heavens tell out the glory of
    God,
  heaven's vault makes known his

handiwork.
2 One day speaks to another,
  night to night imparts knowledge,
3 and this without speech or language
  or sound of any voice.
4 Their sign shines forth on all the earth,
  their message to the ends of the world.
  In the heavens an abode is fixed for
    the sun,
5 which comes out like a bridegroom
    from the bridal chamber,
  rejoicing like a strong man to run his
    course.
6 Its rising is at one end of the heavens,
  its circuit reaches from one end to the
    other,
  and nothing is hidden from its heat.

7 The law of the LORD is perfect and
    revives the soul.
  The LORD's instruction never fails;
  it makes the simple wise.
8 The precepts of the LORD are right
  and give joy to the heart.
  The commandment of the LORD is pure
  and gives light to the eyes.
9 The fear of the LORD is unsullied; it
    abides for ever.
  The LORD's judgements are true and
    righteous every one,
10 more to be desired than gold, pure
    gold in plenty,
  sweeter than honey dripping from the
    comb.
11 It is through them that your servant is
    warned;
  in obeying them is great reward.

12 Who is aware of his unwitting sins?
  Cleanse me of any secret fault.
13 Hold back your servant also from wilful
    sins,
  lest they get the better of me.
  Then I shall be blameless,
  innocent of grave offence.

18:42 **I shall trample them:** *prob. rdg, cp. 2 Sam. 22:43;*
Heb. I shall empty them out.

46–50: This is an additional praise and vow. **50:** *His anointed* is *David.*

  Ps. 19: The glory of God. A Hymn. All creation reveals God's handiwork. Indeed, nature, law, history, and
the personal problems of the individual must be combined in terms of God's kingdom. **4:** In Wisdom literature
the *sun* is a symbol of justice and of wisdom itself; see Wisd. 5.6; 7.29. **7–11:** The *law* is wisdom itself; and
these *give* (v. 11) a more important *light* (v. 8) than the sun. **12–14:** Even when inspired and guided, the psalmist
may still sin. Hence, the worshiper asks forgiveness of God.

14 May the words of my mouth and the
thoughts of my mind
be acceptable to you,
LORD, my rock and my redeemer!

20 *For the leader: a psalm: for David*
1 MAY the LORD answer you in time
of trouble.
May the name of Jacob's God be your
tower of strength.
2 May he send you help from the
sanctuary,
and give you support from Zion.
3 May he remember all your offerings
and look with favour on your sacrifices.
[*Selah*

4 May he give you your heart's desire,
and grant success to all your plans.
5 Let us sing aloud in praise of your
victory,
let us do homage to the name of our
God!
May the LORD grant your every
request!

6 Now I know that the LORD has given
victory to his anointed one:
he will answer him from his holy
heaven
with the victorious might of his right
hand.
7 Some boast of chariots and some of
horses,
but our boast is the name of the LORD
our God.
8 They totter and fall,
but we rise up and stand firm.
9 LORD, save the king,
and answer us when we call.

21 *For the leader: a psalm: for David*
1 LORD, the king rejoices in your
might:
well may he exult in your victory.
2 You have granted him his heart's desire
and have not refused what he
requested.
[*Selah*

3 You welcome him with blessings and
prosperity
and place a crown of finest gold on his
head.
4 He asked of you life, and you gave it to
him,
length of days for ever and ever.
5 Your victory has brought him great
glory;
you invest him with majesty and
honour,
6 for you bestow everlasting blessings on
him,
and make him glad with the joy of your
presence,
7 for the king puts his trust in the LORD;
the loving care of the Most High keeps
him unshaken.

8 Your hand will reach all your enemies,
your right hand all who hate you;
9 at your coming you will set them in a
fiery furnace;
in his anger the LORD will engulf them,
and fire will consume them.
10 It will destroy their offspring from the
earth
and rid mankind of their posterity.
11 For they have aimed wicked blows at
you;
in spite of their plots they could not
prevail;
12 but you will aim at their faces with your
bows
and force them to turn in flight.

13 Be exalted, LORD, in your might;
we shall sing a psalm of praise to your
power.

22 *For the leader: set to 'Hind of the Dawn':
a psalm: for David*
1 MY God, my God, why have you
forsaken me?

20:9 **LORD . . . answer us:** *so Gk; Heb.* Save, LORD: let
the king answer us.   21:10 **It:** *or You.*

Ps. 20: LORD, save the king. A psalm, possibly Royal, of public supplication used in the temple liturgy before
a battle. **1–5:** A prayer for God's support of the king. **2:** *The sanctuary* and *Zion* are synonymous. **5:** Choral
response to the petitions. **6:** Possibly an oracle pronounced by a priest or cult prophet. **7–9:** Choral response.
Ps. 21: The LORD gives life. A Royal Psalm of thanksgiving, as if in gratitude for the victory prayed for in Ps.
20. It is very similar in structure and content to Ps. 18, though much briefer. **1–7:** Motives for thanksgiving.
8–12: Perhaps an oracle by a priest or a cultic prophet. **13:** Antiphonal acclamation by the bystanders. For
such recurring expressions, see Ps. 57.5, 11.

Why are you so far from saving me,
so far from heeding my groans?
2 My God, by day I cry to you, but there
is no answer;
in the night I cry with no respite.
3 You, the praise of Israel,
are enthroned in the sanctuary.
4 In you our fathers put their trust;
they trusted, and you rescued them.
5 To you they cried and were delivered;
in you they trusted and were not
discomfited.

6 But I am a worm, not a man,
abused by everyone, scorned by the
people.
7 All who see me jeer at me,
grimace at me, and wag their heads:
8 'He threw himself on the LORD for
rescue;
let the LORD deliver him, for he holds
him dear!'

9 But you are he who brought me from
the womb,
who laid me at my mother's breast.
10 To your care I was entrusted at birth;
from my mother's womb you have been
my God.
11 Do not remain far from me,
for trouble is near and I have no
helper.
12 A herd of bulls surrounds me,
great bulls of Bashan beset me.
13 Lions ravening and roaring
open their mouths wide against me.
14 My strength drains away like water
and all my bones are racked.
My heart has turned to wax
and melts within me.
15 My mouth is dry as a potsherd,
and my tongue sticks to my gums;
I am laid low in the dust of death.
16 Hounds are all about me;
a band of ruffians rings me round,
and they have bound me hand and
foot.

17 I tell my tale of misery,
while they look on gloating.
18 They share out my clothes among them
and cast lots for my garments.

19 But do not remain far away, LORD;
you are my help, come quickly to my
aid.
20 Deliver me from the sword,
my precious life from the axe.
21 Save me from the lion's mouth,
this poor body from the horns of the
wild ox.

22 I shall declare your fame to my
associates,
praising you in the midst of the
assembly.
23 You that fear the LORD, praise him;
hold him in honour, all you
descendants of Jacob,
revere him, you descendants of Israel.
24 For he has not scorned him who is
downtrodden,
nor shrunk in loathing from his plight,
nor hidden his face from him,
but he has listened to his cry for help.
25 You inspire my praise in the great
assembly;
I shall fulfil my vows in the sight of
those who fear you.

26 Let the humble eat and be satisfied.
Let those who seek the LORD praise
him.
May you always be in good heart!
27 Let all the ends of the earth remember
and turn again to the LORD;
let all the families of the nations bow
before him.
28 For kingly power belongs to the LORD;

22:15 **mouth:** *prob. rdg; Heb.* strength. **I am laid:** *prob.
rdg; Heb.* you will lay me.   22:16 **and . . . bound me:**
prob. rdg; Heb. like a lion.   22:20 **axe:** *or* dog.
22:21 **this poor body:** *prob. rdg; Heb.* you have
answered me.

Ps. 22: My God, my God, why have you forsaken me? The classic example of a Lament. **1:** Introduction:
invocation of the divine name; see Mk. 15.34. **2–19:** Motives for deliverance, apparently from serious illness:
(a) God's deliverance of ancestors (vv. 2–5); (b) the poet's present abject and helpless state. **3:** God was
considered *enthroned* above the Ark of the Covenant in the temple; see Isa. 6.1–3. **7:** *Wag their heads:* sign
of derision. **8:** The poet's enemies deride the psalmist's call for God's help since illness was considered a
punishment from God for sin. **12:** *Bashan:* grazing area south of Damascus noted for its large cattle. **14–15:**
Symptoms of an illness accompanied by a severe fever are suggested. **18:** The enemies divide the poet's

dominion over the nations is his.
29 How can those who sleep in the earth
do him homage,
how can those who go down to the
grave do obeisance?
But I shall live for his sake;
30 my descendants will serve him.
The coming generation will be told of
the LORD;
31 they will make known his righteous
deeds,
declaring to a people yet unborn:
'The LORD has acted.'

23 A psalm: for David

1 THE LORD is my shepherd; I lack
for nothing.
2 He makes me lie down in green
pastures,
he leads me to water where I may rest;
3 he revives my spirit;
for his name's sake he guides me in the
right paths.
4 Even were I to walk through a valley of
deepest darkness
I should fear no harm, for you are with
me;
your shepherd's staff and crook afford
me comfort.

5 You spread a table for me in the
presence of my enemies;
you have richly anointed my head with
oil,
and my cup brims over.
6 Goodness and love unfailing will follow
me

all the days of my life,
and I shall dwell in the house of the
LORD
throughout the years to come.

24 For David: a psalm

1 To THE LORD belong the earth
and everything in it,
the world and all its inhabitants.
2 For it was he who founded it on the
seas
and planted it firm on the waters
beneath.

3 Who may go up the mountain of the
LORD?
Who may stand in his holy place?
4 One who has clean hands and a pure
heart,
who has not set his mind on what is
false
or sworn deceitfully.
5 Such a one shall receive blessing from
the LORD,
and be vindicated by God his saviour.
6 Such is the fortune of those who seek
him,
who seek the presence of the God of
Jacob.   [Selah

7 Lift up your heads, you gates,
lift yourselves up, you everlasting
doors,

22:29 **How . . . homage:** *prob. rdg; Heb.* All the prosperous ones in the land have eaten and worshipped. **I:** *so Gk; Heb.* he.   22:30 **my:** *so Gk; Heb. omits.*   24:6 **the presence . . . Jacob:** *so Gk; Heb.* your face, Jacob.

possessions. **22–27:** A hymn of praise anticipating the healing and the fulfillment of a *vow* (v. 25). **29:** See 6.5 n.
Ps. 23: The LORD is my shepherd and host. A Psalm of Confidence or a Psalm of Thanksgiving, or possibly of pilgrimage to the temple. **1:** God is often considered a *shepherd;* see Ezek. ch. 34. **2:** *Green pastures* are scarce in Palestine. **3:** *Name's sake:* the "name" gives the nature of a person or a god. **4:** *Darkness* reflects deep ravines of Judean hills. A Palestinian shepherd sometimes has a *staff,* a cudgel, to ward off wild animals, as well as a *crook* for guiding sheep. **5:** *The table* was probably where a sacrifice was eaten in the temple in the *presence of . . . enemies. Cup brims over:* abundant blessing and joy. The head of an honored guest was anointed with oil in the Near East; see Lk. 7.46. **6:** The joy and *goodness* experienced in the temple will carry over into daily *life.* The poet will continue to *dwell* in the temple in desire and in worship.
Ps. 24: The LORD is Creator-King. A Liturgy used in the temple worship. **1–2:** As the pilgrims go through the countryside they observe that the LORD is the possessor and creator of the earth. Myth in the ancient Near East viewed God as defeating the sea, or chaos, in order to build the earth on the sea. *Waters beneath:* underground reservoir of water from which springs arise; compare Gen. 7.11. **3:** As pilgrims approach the temple they ask who is worthy to *stand in* the *holy place.* **4:** Conditions for entry are moral rather than ritual cleanliness. **6:** *Seek the presence of . . . God:* visit the temple. **7–10:** This seems to reflect a processional liturgy with the Ark of the Covenant, in which antiphonal singing takes place. **7:** The procession with the Ark stops

that the king of glory may come in.
⁸Who is this king of glory?
The LORD strong and mighty,
the LORD mighty in battle.

⁹Lift up your heads, you gates,
lift them up, you everlasting doors,
that the king of glory may come in.
¹⁰Who is he, this king of glory?
The LORD of Hosts, he is the king of
glory. [*Selah*

25 *For David*
¹LORD my God, to you I lift my
heart.
²In you I trust: do not let me be put to
shame,
do not let my enemies exult over me.
³No one whose hope is in you is put to
shame;
but shame comes to all who break faith
without cause.
⁴Make your paths known to me, LORD;
teach me your ways.
⁵Lead me by your faithfulness and teach
me,
for you are God my saviour;
in you I put my hope all day long.
⁶Remember, LORD, your tender care and
love unfailing,
for they are from of old.
⁷Do not remember the sins and offences
of my youth,
but remember me in your unfailing
love,
in accordance with your goodness,
LORD.

⁸The LORD is good and upright;
therefore he teaches sinners the way
they should go.
⁹He guides the humble in right conduct,
and teaches them his way.
¹⁰All the paths of the LORD are loving
and sure

to those who keep his covenant and his
solemn charge.
¹¹LORD, for the honour of your name
forgive my wickedness, great though it
is.
¹²Whoever fears the LORD
will be shown the path he should
choose.
¹³He will enjoy lasting prosperity,
and his descendants will inherit the
land.
¹⁴The LORD confides his purposes to
those who fear him;
his covenant is for their instruction.
¹⁵My eyes are ever on the LORD,
who alone can free my feet from the
net.

¹⁶Turn to me and show me your favour,
for I am lonely and oppressed.
¹⁷Relieve the troubles of my heart
and lead me out of my distress.
¹⁸Look on my affliction and misery
and forgive me every sin.
¹⁹Look at my enemies, see how many
they are,
how violent their hatred of me.
²⁰Defend me and deliver me;
let me not be put to shame, for in you
I find refuge.
²¹Let integrity and uprightness protect
me;
in you, LORD, I put my hope.
²²God, deliver Israel from all their
troubles.

26 *For David*
¹LORD, uphold my cause,
for I have led a blameless life,
and put unfaltering trust in you.
²Test me, LORD, and try me,
putting my heart and mind to the
proof;
³for your constant love is before my
eyes,

in front of the closed doors of the temple; hence the dramatic request, *Lift*. **8a:** This question comes from within. **8b–9:** The answer comes from those bearing the Ark. **10:** Question and answer repeated.
    Ps. 25: Defend me and deliver me. A Lament (see Introduction): an alphabetical acrostic, each verse beginning with a successive letter of the Heb. alphabet (see Ps. 111 n.). **1–3:** The poet's distress. **4–14:** The psalmist prays for God's guidance and help as in the past (vv. 4–9) for those faithful to God's covenant (vv. 10–14). **13–14:** To *inherit the land* was a sign of God's blessing, especially after the return from Babylonian Exile of 587 B.C.E., and was a reward for keeping the *covenant*. **16–22:** The psalmist pleads for deliverance from affliction.
    Ps. 26: Deliver me, LORD. A Lament (see Introduction). **1–3:** A cry for justice. **4–7:** A protestation of

and I live by your faithfulness.

⁴I have not sat among the worthless,
  nor do I associate with hypocrites;
⁵I detest the company of evildoers,
  nor shall I sit among the ungodly.
⁶I wash my hands free from guilt
  to go in procession round your altar,
  LORD,
⁷recounting your marvellous deeds,
  making them known with thankful
  voice.
⁸LORD, I love the house where you
  dwell,
  the place where your glory resides.
⁹Do not sweep me away with sinners,
  nor cast me out with those who thirst
  for blood,
¹⁰whose fingers are active in mischief,
  whose right hands are full of bribes.

¹¹But I lead a blameless life;
  deliver me and show me your favour.
¹²My feet are planted on firm ground;
  I shall bless the LORD in the full
  assembly.

27 *For David*
¹THE LORD is my light and my
  salvation;
  whom should I fear?
  The LORD is the stronghold of my life;
  of whom then should I go in dread?
²When evildoers close in on me to
  devour me,
  it is my adversaries, my enemies,
  who stumble and fall.
³Should an army encamp against me,
  my heart would have no fear;
  if armed men should fall upon me,
  even then I would be undismayed.
⁴One thing I ask of the LORD,
  it is the one thing I seek:
  that I may dwell in the house of the
  LORD

all the days of my life,
  to gaze on the beauty of the LORD
  and to seek him in his temple.
⁵For he will hide me in his shelter
  in the day of misfortune;
  he will conceal me under cover of his
  tent,
  set me high on a rock.
⁶Now my head will be raised high
  above the enemy all about me;
  so I shall acclaim him in his tent with
  sacrifice
  and sing a psalm of praise to the LORD.

⁷Hear, LORD, when I call aloud;
  show me favour and answer me.
⁸'Come,' my heart has said,
  'seek his presence.'
  I seek your presence, LORD;
⁹do not hide your face from me,
  nor in your anger turn away your
  servant,
  whose help you have been;
  God my saviour, do not reject me or
  forsake me.
¹⁰Though my father and my mother
  forsake me,
  the LORD will take me into his care.
¹¹⁻¹²Teach me your way, LORD;
  do not give me up to the greed of my
  enemies;
  lead me by a level path
  to escape the foes who beset me:
  liars breathing malice come forward
  to give evidence against me.
¹³Well I know that I shall see the
  goodness of the LORD
  in the land of the living.

¹⁴Wait for the LORD; be strong and
  brave,
  and put your hope in the LORD.

27:5 **shelter:** *or* arbour.   27:8 **seek his presence:**
prob. rdg; Heb. seek my presence.   27:13 **Well I**
know: *so some MSS; others* Had I not well known.

innocence. **5:** To *sit among the ungodly:* to be identified with their values. **6–7:** To *wash the hands* was a dramatic protestation of innocence, possibly a condition for joining a temple procession; compare Deut. 21.6–7. **9:** *Your glory:* the sense of God's majesty. **12:** The usual vow.

Ps. 27: Hear, LORD, when I call aloud. The classification of this psalm is difficult; perhaps it is a Lament or Hymn (see Introduction). **1–6:** Such a statement of trust could be a part of either a Lament or a Thanksgiving. **5–6:** *Tent:* poetic word for temple alluding to the Tabernacle used for worship in the wilderness. **7–14:** A plea to God. The tone is more typical of the Lament than of the Hymn. **8:** To *seek* the LORD's *presence* originally meant to consult God by means of an oracle; see 2 Sam. 21.1. Later it meant to seek the LORD by faithful service and hence to seek God's favor. See 4.6 n.

28 *For David*
¹To you, Lord, I call;
my Rock, do not be deaf to my
    cry,
lest, if you answer me with silence,
I become like those who go down to the
    abyss.
²Hear my voice as I plead for mercy,
as I call to you for help
with hands uplifted towards your holy
    shrine.
³Do not drag me away with the ungodly,
with evildoers who speak civilly to their
    fellows,
though with malice in their hearts.
⁴⁻⁵Requite them for their works, their evil
    deeds;
repay them for what their hands have
    done,
because they do not discern the works
    of the Lord
or what his hands have done.
May they be given their deserts;
may he strike them down and never
    restore them!

⁶Blessed be the Lord,
for he has heard my voice as I plead
    for mercy.
⁷The Lord is my strength and my
    shield;
in him my heart trusts.
I am sustained, and my heart leaps for
    joy,
and with my song I praise him.
⁸The Lord is strength to his people,
a safe refuge for his anointed one.

⁹Save your people and bless those who
    belong to you,
shepherd them and carry them for
    ever.

29 *A psalm: for David*
¹Ascribe to the Lord, you angelic
    powers,
ascribe to the Lord glory and might.
²Ascribe to the Lord the glory due to
    his name;
in holy attire worship the Lord.

³The voice of the Lord echoes over the
    waters;
the God of glory thunders;
the Lord thunders over the mighty
    waters,
⁴the voice of the Lord in power,
the voice of the Lord in majesty.
⁵The voice of the Lord breaks the cedar
    trees,
the Lord shatters the cedars of
    Lebanon.
⁶He makes Lebanon skip like a calf,
Sirion like a young wild ox.

⁷The voice of the Lord makes flames of
    fire burst forth;
⁸the voice of the Lord makes the
    wilderness writhe in travail,
the Lord makes the wilderness of
    Kadesh writhe.
⁹The voice of the Lord makes the hinds
    calve;
he strips the forest bare,
and in his temple all cry, 'Glory!'
¹⁰The Lord is king above the flood,
the Lord has taken his royal seat as
    king for ever.

¹¹The Lord will give strength to his
    people;
the Lord will bless his people with
    peace.

28:8 **to his people:** *so some MSS; others* to them.
29:9 **strips . . . bare:** *or* brings young goats early to
birth.

Ps. 28: Hear my voice as I plead for mercy. A Lament (see Introduction), including Thanksgiving to be sung
when the Lord has heard the cry of the psalmist. **1–3:** The appeal to God. **4–5:** Let God punish the wicked.
6–9: The Thanksgiving.

Ps. 29: The God of glory thunders. This hymn describes an awesome storm as it rises over the Mediterranean,
crosses the Lebanon mountains in Phoenicia, the Anti-Lebanon in Syria, and spends itself in the desert. This
poem is often viewed by modern students as an ancient Canaanite poem written originally to the storm god,
Baal, and adapted by Israel with the necessary change in the divine name and other alterations. **3:** *Mighty
waters:* possibly the Mediterranean Sea. **4:** *Voice of the Lord:* thunder. **6:** *Sirion:* Mount Hermon in Syria. *Skip
like a calf:* reverberation of the thunder. **8:** *Kadesh:* the desert east of the Syrian city of Kadesh. **9:** *The hinds
calve* prematurely from fright. **10:** *Above the flood:* God subdues the waters and claims rule over them by being
enthroned above them.

30 *A psalm (a song for the dedication of the temple): for David*

1 I SHALL exalt you, LORD;
you have lifted me up
and have not let my enemies be jubilant
over me.

2 LORD my God, I cried to you and you
healed me.

3 You have brought me up, LORD, from
Sheol,
and saved my life as I was sinking into
the abyss.

4 Sing a psalm to the LORD, all you his
loyal servants;
give thanks to his holy name.

5 In his anger is distress, in his favour
there is life.
Tears may linger at nightfall,
but rejoicing comes in the morning.

6 I felt secure and said,
'I can never be shaken.'

7 LORD, by your favour you made my
mountain strong;
when you hid your face, I was struck
with dismay.

8 To you, LORD, I called
and pleaded with you for mercy:

9 'What profit is there in my death,
in my going down to the pit?
Can the dust praise you?
Can it proclaim your truth?

10 Hear, LORD, and be gracious to me;
LORD, be my helper.'

11 You have turned my laments into
dancing;
you have stripped off my sackcloth and
clothed me with joy,

12 that I may sing psalms to you without
ceasing.

LORD my God, I shall praise you for
ever.

31 *For the leader: a psalm: for David*

1 IN you, LORD, I have found
refuge;
let me never be put to shame.
By your saving power deliver me,

2 bend down and hear me,
come quickly to my rescue.
Be to me a rock of refuge,
a stronghold to keep me safe.

3 You are my rock and my stronghold;
lead and guide me for the honour of
your name.

4 Set me free from the net that has been
hidden to catch me;
for you are my refuge.

5 Into your hand I commit my spirit.
You have delivered me, LORD, you God
of truth.

6 I hate all who worship worthless idols;
I for my part put my trust in the LORD.

7 I shall rejoice and be glad in your
unfailing love,
for you have seen my affliction
and have cared for me in my distress.

8 You have not abandoned me to the
power of the enemy,
but have set me where I have
untrammelled liberty.

9 Be gracious to me, LORD, for I am in
distress
and my eyes are dimmed with grief.

10 My life is worn away with sorrow
and my years with sighing;

30:3 **Sheol:** *or* the underworld. **and saved . . . abyss:** *or* and rescued me alive from among those who go down to the abyss.   30:5 **In his anger . . . life:** *or* His anger is for a moment, his favour lifelong.
31:9 **grief:** *prob. rdg; Heb. adds* my throat and my belly.

Ps. 30: You have turned my laments into dancing. A Thanksgiving, or a "declarative" Hymn of praise. Perhaps it reflects recovery from serious illness. **3:** The entrance to *Sheol* was viewed as an opening to a well into which the poet was already falling when pulled out by God. **11:** The transition from sickness to health is expressed in a change from *sackcloth*, the clothing of penance and grief, to festive garments of *joy*.

Ps. 31: Be gracious to me, LORD. A Lament, or, indeed, two separate Laments, the one vv. 1–8, and the other vv. 9–24. Each Lament (see Introduction) contains Thanksgivings to ensue after God has delivered the distressed (vv. 5–8 and 21–24). **2:** Solid *rock* is the only secure foothold on the shallow and pebbly or sandy soil of Palestine; compare Matt. 7.24. **7:** *Unfailing love:* a single word, *ḥesed,* in Heb. *Ḥesed* is a key word in the OT. At times translated as "steadfast love" or "loving kindness," it has the connotation of a love arising out of a covenant or a bond, and manifested in concrete action; see also vv. 16 and 21. **9–13:** Compare with this passage Job 30.1–15. The distress is the loneliness of having fallen from heights to a low estate, and being

through misery my strength falters
and my bones waste away.
11 I am scorned by all my enemies,
my neighbours find me burdensome,
my friends shudder at me;
when they see me on the street they
turn away quickly.
12 Like the dead I have passed out of
mind;
I have become like some article thrown
away.
13 For I hear many
whispering threats from every side,
conspiring together against me
and scheming to take my life.

14 But in you, LORD, I put my trust;
I say, 'You are my God.'
15 My fortunes are in your hand;
rescue me from the power of my
enemies
and those who persecute me.
16 Let your face shine on your servant;
save me in your unfailing love.
17 LORD, do not humiliate me when I call
to you;
let humiliation be for the wicked,
let them sink into Sheol.
18 May lying lips be struck dumb,
lips speaking with contempt against the
righteous
in pride and arrogance.

19 How great is your goodness,
stored up for those who fear you,
made manifest before mortal eyes
for all who turn to you for shelter.
20 You will hide them under the cover of
your presence
from those who conspire together;
you keep them in your shelter,
safe from contentious tongues.

21 Blessed be the LORD,
whose unfailing love for me was
wonderful
when I was in sore straits.

22 In sudden alarm I said,
'I am shut out from your sight.'
But you heard my plea
when I called to you for help.
23 Love the LORD, all you his loyal
servants.
The LORD protects the faithful,
but the arrogant he repays in full.
24 Be strong and stout-hearted,
all you whose hope is in the LORD.

32 *For David: a maskil*
1 HAPPY is he whose offence is
forgiven,
whose sin is blotted out!
2 Happy is he to whom the LORD imputes
no fault,
in whose spirit there is no deceit.

3 While I refused to speak, my body
wasted away
with day-long moaning.
4 For day and night
your hand was heavy upon me;
the sap in me dried up as in summer
drought. [*Selah*
5 When I acknowledged my sin to you,
when I no longer concealed my guilt,
but said, 'I shall confess my offence to
the LORD,'
then you for your part remitted the
penalty of my sin. [*Selah*
6 So let every faithful heart pray to you
in the hour of anxiety;
when great floods threaten
they shall not touch him.
7 You are a hiding-place for me from
distress;
you guard me and enfold me in
salvation. [*Selah*

8 I shall teach you and guide you in the
way you should go.

31:10 **misery:** *prob. rdg; Heb.* iniquity.
31:17 **Sheol:** *or* the underworld. 31:21 **when . . .
straits:** *lit.* in a city besieged. 32:6 **of anxiety:** *prob.
rdg; Heb. unintelligible.* 32:7 **you guard me:** *prob.
rdg; Heb. adds an unintelligible word.*

fearful of plots against one's life. The latter possibly is to be taken figuratively, but compare Jer. 20.10. **16:** *Let
your face shine:* see 4.6 n. **20:** Compare 27.5.
Ps. 32: Happy is the one who is forgiven. A Thanksgiving Psalm, probably used as a Wisdom Psalm (see
Introduction). One of seven "Penitential Psalms" (see Ps. 130 n.). An ancient idea that sickness was a consequence of sin is clearly implied (vv. 3–5). The poem proceeds (vv. 6–11) to commend to others the poet's
experience of forgiveness and recovery from illness. **3:** *Refused to speak:* a refusal to acknowledge or confess
sin, a condition for healing in traditional Israelite theology; see Prov. 28.13. **4:** The *hand* of God is *heavy,*

I shall keep you under my eye.
⁹Do not behave like a horse or a mule,
    unreasoning creatures
whose mettle must be curbed with bit
    and bridle,
so that they do not come near you.
¹⁰Many are the torments for the ungodly,
    but unfailing love enfolds those who
    trust in the LORD.
¹¹Rejoice in the LORD and be glad, you
    righteous ones;
sing aloud, all you of honest heart.

33 *For David*
    ¹SHOUT for joy in the LORD, you
        that are righteous;
praise comes well from the upright.
²Give thanks to the LORD on the lyre;
    make music to him on the ten-stringed
    harp.
³Sing to him a new song;
    strike up with all your skill and shout in
    triumph,
⁴for the word of the LORD holds true,
    and all his work endures.
⁵He is a lover of righteousness and
    justice;
the earth is filled with the LORD's
    unfailing love.

⁶The word of the LORD created the
    heavens;
all the host of heaven was formed at his
    command.
⁷He gathered into a heap the waters of
    the sea,
he laid up the deeps in his
    store-chambers.
⁸Let the whole world fear the LORD
    and all earth's inhabitants stand in awe
    of him.

⁹For he spoke, and it was;
    he commanded, and there it stood.
¹⁰The LORD frustrates the purposes of
    nations;
he foils the plans of the peoples.
¹¹But the LORD's own purpose stands for
    ever,
and the plans he has in mind endure
    for all generations.
¹²Happy is the nation whose God is the
    LORD,
the people he has chosen for his own.
¹³The LORD looks out from heaven;
    he sees the whole race of mortals,
¹⁴he surveys from his dwelling-place
    all the inhabitants of the earth.
¹⁵It is he who fashions the hearts of them
    all,
who discerns everything they do.

¹⁶No king is saved by a great army,
    no warrior delivered by great strength.
¹⁷No one can rely on his horse to save
    him,
nor for all its power can it be a means
    of escape.
¹⁸The LORD's eyes are turned towards
    those who fear him,
towards those who hope for his
    unfailing love
¹⁹to deliver them from death,
    and in famine to preserve them alive.

²⁰We have waited eagerly for the LORD;
    he is our help and our shield.
²¹In him our hearts are glad,
    because we have trusted in his holy
    name.
²²LORD, let your unfailing love rest on us,

33:heading *So Gk; Heb. omits.*

---

especially with calamity, when God touches someone's life. **8–11:** Possibly an oracle spoken by a priest in the temple. **10:** *Unfailing love:* see 31.7 n.

Ps. 33: Shout for joy. A Hymn (see Introduction), in praise and description of God. The praise (vv. 1–3) turns into praise of God as creator and ruler (4–11). **3:** *Shout in triumph:* one word in Heb., the battle cry of an attacking army (Josh. 6.5); later it meant a liturgical acclamation of God as king of Israel and of the nations (as here; compare Num. 23.21), and as savior (compare Isa. 44.23). **4–5:** The four terms, *holds true* (i.e. is faithful), *righteousness, justice,* and *unfailing love,* are used most consistently in the OT to describe God and God's activities; compare Hos. 2.19. **6:** *His command:* lit. "the wind of his mouth." **7:** Out of chaos (the combat in which God defeats the sea), there comes order. **8:** *Fear:* that is, worship for which creation is the basis. **10–19:** God's universal rule. **10:** *Plans of the peoples:* human wisdom and diplomacy. **12:** Israel in the context of many nations. In virtue of the mighty deeds at the Exodus by which God redeemed Israel from Egypt, Israel is God's *possession.* **20–22:** God alone is the hope of Israel.

as we have put our hope in you.

34 *For David (when he feigned madness in Abimelech's presence; Abimelech then drove him away, and he departed)*

¹I SHALL bless the LORD at all times;
his praise will be ever on my lips.
²In the LORD I shall glory;
the humble will hear and be glad.
³Glorify the LORD with me;
let us exalt his name together.
⁴I sought the LORD's help; he answered me
and set me free from all my fears.
⁵They who look to him are radiant with joy;
they will never be put out of countenance.
⁶Here is one who cried out in his affliction;
the LORD heard him and saved him from all his troubles.
⁷The angel of the LORD is on guard round those who fear him, and he rescues them.
⁸Taste and see that the LORD is good.
Happy are they who find refuge in him!
⁹Fear the LORD, you his holy people;
those who fear him lack for nothing.
¹⁰Princes may suffer want and go hungry,
but those who seek the LORD lack no good thing.

¹¹Come, children, listen to me;
I shall teach you the fear of the LORD.
¹²Which of you delights in life

and desires a long life to enjoy prosperity?
¹³Then keep your tongue from evil
and your lips from telling lies;
¹⁴shun evil and do good;
seek peace and pursue it.
¹⁵The eyes of the LORD are on the righteous;
his ears are open to their cry.
¹⁶The LORD sets his face against wrongdoers
to cut off all memory of them from the earth.
¹⁷When the righteous cry for help, the LORD hears
and sets them free from all their troubles.
¹⁸The LORD is close to those whose courage is broken;
he saves those whose spirit is crushed.
¹⁹Though the misfortunes of one who is righteous be many,
the LORD delivers him out of them all.
²⁰He guards every bone of his body,
and not one of them will be broken.
²¹Misfortune will bring death to the wicked,
and punishment befalls those who hate the righteous.
²²The LORD delivers the lives of his servants,
and no punishment befalls those who seek refuge in him.

35 *For David*
¹STRIVE against those who strive against me, LORD;

34:10 **Princes:** *or* Unbelievers.

Ps. 34: The LORD ransoms the lives of God's servants. A Thanksgiving, and an alphabetic acrostic (see Ps. 111 n.). Both this psalm and Ps. 25, also an acrostic, provide, after the alphabet is complete, an extra verse which begins with the Heb. word for "deliver" or "redeem." Such acrostic psalms were useful in instruction, and were connected to the experiences of Israel's kings. Thus, the superscription (see Introduction) connects it with a time when David feigned madness (compare 1 Sam. 21.11–16). **1–3:** The praise of God. **4–8:** God's deliverance. **7:** An *angel* to *guard* it was promised to Israel at the Exodus; see Exod. 23.20, 23. The theme was developed extensively during the persecution of the Maccabean period; compare Tob. 5.4–22; 2 Macc. 11.6–8. **8:** To *taste* is to surrender to God's care and to distinguish true *good* from the apparent; compare Job 34.3–4. **9–22:** The way of God with the righteous. **10:** *Princes:* Heb. literally reads "young lions," which may be metaphorical for leaders or nobles. *Lack no good thing:* compare 23.1.

Ps. 35: LORD, be not far aloof from me. A Lament (see Introduction). Some would see three Laments in this psalm (vv. 1–10, 11–18, 19–28), yet the structure of the Lament was never so firm as to bar the variations found here. Rather, the whole psalm seems to be a single Lament, but with a three-fold vow. The first part contains a cry for deliverance and vengeance (vv. 1–8), plus the first vow (vv. 9–10); the second, a cry of innocence and a plea for help (vv. 11–17), plus the second vow (v. 18); and the third, a complaint and a cry

fight those who fight against me.
² Grasp shield and buckler,
and rise to my aid.
³ Brandish spear and axe
against my pursuers.
Let me hear you declare,
'I am your salvation.'

⁴ May shame and disgrace cover those
who seek my life;
may those who plan my downfall
retreat in dismay!
⁵ May they be like chaff before the
wind,
driven away by the angel of the LORD!
⁶ Let their path be dark and slippery
with the angel of the LORD pursuing
them!
⁷ For unprovoked they have hidden a net
to catch me,
unprovoked they have dug a pit to trap
me.
⁸ May destruction unforeseen come upon
them;
may the net which they hid catch them;
may they fall into the pit and be
destroyed!

⁹ Then I shall rejoice in the LORD
and delight in his salvation.
¹⁰ My whole frame cries out,
'LORD, who is there like you,
saviour of the oppressed from those too
strong for them,
of the oppressed and poor from those
who prey on them?'
¹¹ Malicious witnesses come forward
and question me on matters of which I
know nothing.
¹² They return me evil for good,
lying in wait to take my life.
¹³ Yet when they were ill, I put on
sackcloth,
I mortified myself with fasting.
When my prayer came back
unanswered,
¹⁴ I walked with head bowed in grief as if
for a brother;
as one in sorrow for his mother I lay
prostrate in mourning.

¹⁵ But when I stumbled, they crowded
round rejoicing,
they crowded about me;
unknown assailants jeered at me
and nothing would stop them.
¹⁶ When I slipped, they mocked and
derided me,
grinding their teeth at me.
¹⁷ Lord, how long will you look on?
Rescue me from those who would
destroy me,
save my precious life from the
powerful.
¹⁸ Then I shall praise you in the great
assembly,
I shall extol you in a large
congregation.

¹⁹ Let no treacherous enemy gloat over
me;
let not those who hate me for no
reason leer at me.
²⁰ Their words are hostile
and against the peaceful they hatch
intrigues.
²¹ They open their mouths and shout at
me:
'Hurrah! What a sight for us to see!'

²² You have seen all this, LORD; do not
keep silence.
Lord, be not far aloof from me.
²³ Awake, rouse yourself, my God, my
Lord,
to vindicate me and plead my cause.
²⁴ Judge me, LORD my God, as you are
righteous;
do not let them gloat over me.
²⁵ Do not let them say to themselves,
'Hurrah! We have got our wish,
we have swallowed him up!'
²⁶ Let all who rejoice at my downfall
be discomfited and dismayed;
let those who glory over me

35:3 **axe:** *so Scroll; Heb.* bar the way.   35:7 **a net:**
prob. rdg, transposing a pit *from this line to follow* have
dug.   35:12 **lying . . . life:** *prob. rdg; Heb.*
bereavement for me.   35:15 **unknown assailants:** *or*
assailants who give me no rest.   35:16 **and derided
me:** *so Gk; Heb. obscure.*

for justice (vv. 19–27), plus the third vow (v. 28). **5:** *Angel of the LORD:* see Ps. 34.7 n. **13:** *Sackcloth:* sign of
grief. *Fasting:* expression of supplication; compare Joel 1.13–14. **16:** *Grinding their teeth:* sign of hatred and
malicious aggressiveness; compare Lam. 2.16; Acts 7.54. **23–24:** *Vindicate . . . Judge . . . righteous:* aspects
of God's character and action to save the oppressed.

be covered with shame and dishonour.

27 But let all who want to see me
   vindicated shout for joy,
let them cry continually,
'All glory to the Lord
who wants to see his servant prosper!'
28 And I shall declare your saving power
   and your praise all the day long.

36

*For the leader: for the Lord's servant:
for David*

1 A wicked person's talk is prompted by
   sin in his heart;
he sees no need to fear God.
2 For it flatters and deceives him
and, when his iniquity is found out, he
   does not change.
3 Everything he says is mischievous and
   false;
he has lost all understanding of right
   conduct;
4 he lies in bed planning the mischief he
   will do.
So set is he on his evil course
that he rejects no wickedness.

5 Lord, your unfailing love reaches to
   the heavens,
your faithfulness to the skies.
6 Your righteousness is like the lofty
   mountains,
your justice like the great deep;
Lord who saves man and beast,
7 how precious is your unfailing love!
Gods and frail mortals seek refuge in
   the shadow of your wings.
8 They are filled with the rich plenty of
   your house,
and you give them to drink from the
   stream of your delights;
9 for with you is the fountain of life,
and by your light we are enlightened.

10 Continue your love unfailing to those
   who know you,
and your saving power towards the
   honest of heart.
11 Let not the foot of the proud come
   near me,
let no wicked hand disturb me.
12 There they lie, the evildoers,
flung down and not able to rise.

37

For David

1 Do not be vexed because of
   evildoers
or envy those who do wrong.
2 For like the grass they soon wither,
and like green pasture they fade away.

3 Trust in the Lord and do good;
settle in the land and find safe pasture.
4 Delight in the Lord,
and he will grant you your heart's
   desire.
5 Commit your way to the Lord;
trust in him, and he will act.
6 He will make your righteousness shine
   clear as the day
and the justice of your cause like the
   brightness of noon.

7 Wait quietly for the Lord, be patient
   till he comes;
do not envy those who gain their ends,
or be vexed at their success.

8 Be angry no more, have done with
   wrath;
do not be vexed: that leads to evil.
9 For evildoers will be destroyed,
while they who hope in the Lord will
   possess the land.

36:1 **his:** *so some MSS; others* my.   36:2 **he ...
change:** *prob. rdg; Heb. unintelligible.*   36:6 **lofty
mountains:** *lit.* mountains of God.

Ps. 36: Continue your love unfailing. Perhaps a Lament, though a common element, the vow, is missing
(see Introduction); it might be classified as a Wisdom Psalm, depicting the two ways, the lonely way of evil
and the union with God, the way of the good. **1:** *Fear* of *God* is the beginning of wisdom, according to the
sages, and the sinner is a fool; see Prov. 1.7. **5–6:** God's *faithfulness, righteousness, justice* are qualities by
which God saves human beings and animals. **8–9:** A *fountain* of water in arid Palestine is a symbol of God's
life-giving qualities; compare Jer. 2.13; Ezek. 47.1–12.

Ps. 37: The righteous will possess the land. A Wisdom Psalm, in acrostic form (see Ps. 111 n.). Verse 40
has the idea, but not the identical words, found in 25.22 and 34.22, that the Lord will save. Just as some
Laments can be related to the challenging speeches of Job, so a psalm such as this can be related to the
"orthodox" view of Job's "friends," that the righteous will be rewarded but the wicked perish (compare vv. 20
and 25). Because the psalm is an acrostic, it presents a variety of views, rather than a single, well-developed

¹⁰A little while, and the wicked will be no
 more;
  however hard you look, you will find
   their place empty.
¹¹But the humble will possess the land
 and enjoy untold prosperity.

¹²The wicked plot against the righteous
 and grind their teeth at the sight of
  them.
¹³The Lord will laugh at the wicked,
 for he sees that their day of judgement
  is coming.

¹⁴They have drawn their swords
 and strung their bows
  to lay low the oppressed and poor,
  and to slaughter those who are honest.
¹⁵Their swords will pierce their own
  hearts
 and their bows will be shattered.

¹⁶Better is the little which the righteous
  person has
 than all the wealth of the wicked;
¹⁷for the power of the wicked will be
  broken,
 but the Lord upholds the righteous.

¹⁸The Lord watches over the upright all
  their days,
 and their inheritance will last for ever.
¹⁹When times are bad, they will not be
  distressed,
 and in a period of famine they will
  have enough.
²⁰But the wicked will perish;
 the enemies of the Lord, like fuel in a
  furnace,
 will go up in smoke.

²¹The wicked borrow and do not repay;
 the righteous give generously.
²²Those whom the Lord has blessed will
  possess the land,
 and those who are cursed by him will
  be cut off.

²³It is the Lord who directs a person's
  steps;
 he holds him firm and approves of his
  conduct.

²⁴Though he may fall, he will not go
  headlong,
 for the Lord grasps him by the hand.

²⁵I have been young and now have
  grown old,
 but never have I seen the righteous
  forsaken
 or their children begging bread.
²⁶Day in, day out, such a one lends
  generously,
 and his children become a blessing.

²⁷If you shun evil and do good,
 you will live at peace for ever;
²⁸for the Lord is a lover of justice
 and will not forsake his loyal servants.

 The lawless are banished for ever
 and the children of the wicked cut off,
²⁹while the righteous will possess the land
 and live there for ever.

³⁰A righteous person speaks words of
  wisdom
 and justice is always on his lips.
³¹The law of his God is in his heart;
 his steps do not falter.

³²The wicked watch out for the righteous
 and seek to put them to death;
³³but the Lord will not leave them in
  their power,
 nor let them be condemned if they are
  brought to trial.

³⁴Wait for the Lord and hold to his way;
 he will raise you to be master of the
  land.
 When the wicked are destroyed, you
  will be there to watch.

³⁵I have seen a wicked man inspiring
  terror,
 flourishing as a spreading tree in its
  native soil.
³⁶But one day I passed by and he was
  gone;
 for all that I searched for him, he was
  not to be found.

37:20 **like . . . furnace:** *prob. rdg; Heb.* like the worth of
rams.   37:28 **The lawless:** *prob. rdg, cp. Gk; Heb.*
omits.   37:36 **I passed:** *so Gk; Heb.* he passed.

view. **11:** Compare Matt. 5.5. **12:** *Grind their teeth:* see 35.16 n. **22:** For the significance of a curse see Num.
22.6. **36–38:** In a number of biblical books, the view occurs that the scandal of seeing the wicked prospering

37 Observe the good man, watch him who
is honest,
for the man of peace leaves
descendants;
38 but transgressors are wiped out one
and all,
and the descendants of the wicked are
cut off.

39 Deliverance for the righteous comes
from the LORD,
their refuge in time of trouble.
40 The LORD will help them and deliver
them,
he will keep them safe from the
wicked;
he will save them because they seek
shelter in him.

38 A psalm: for David: for commemoration
1 LORD, do not rebuke me in anger
or punish me in your wrath.
2 For your arrows have rained down on
me,
and your hand on me has been heavy.
3 Your indignation has left no part of my
body unscathed;
because of my sin there is no health in
my whole frame.
4 For my iniquities tower above my head;
they are a heavier load than I can bear.
5 My wounds fester and stink because of
my folly.
6 I am bowed down and utterly prostrate.
All day long I go about as if in
mourning,
7 for my loins burn with fever,
and there is no wholesome flesh in me.
8 Faint and badly crushed
I groan aloud in anguish of heart.

9 All my longing lies open before you,
Lord,
and my sighing is no secret to you.
10 My heart throbs, my strength is spent,

and the light has faded from my eyes.
11 My friends and companions shun me in
my sickness,
and my kinsfolk keep far off.
12 Those who seek my life set their traps,
those who mean to injure me threaten
my destruction;
they plot all the day long.
13 But I am like a deaf man, hearing
nothing,
like a dumb man who cannot open his
mouth.
14 I behave like one who does not hear,
whose tongue offers no defence.
15 On you, LORD, I fix my hope;
you, LORD my God, will answer.
16 I said, 'Let them never rejoice over me
who exult when my foot slips.'

17 I am on the brink of disaster,
and pain is constantly with me.
18 I make no secret of my iniquity;
I am troubled because of my sin.
19 But many are my enemies, all without
cause,
and numerous are those who hate me
without reason,
20 who repay good with evil,
opposing me because my purpose is
good.
21 But, LORD, do not forsake me;
my God, be not far aloof from me.
22 Lord my deliverer, hasten to my aid.

39 For the leader: for Jeduthun: a psalm: for
David
1 I SAID: 'I shall keep watch over my
conduct,
that what I say may be free from sin.
I shall keep a muzzle on my mouth,
so long as the wicked confront me.'

38:19 all ... cause: prob. rdg; Heb. living.

would be removed by the sudden death of the wicked or the extermination of their descendants.

Ps. 38: LORD, do not forsake me. A Lament (see Introduction). One of seven "Penitential Psalms" (see Ps. 130 n.). The sickness of the psalmist (v. 3) is seen to be the result of sin and folly. **2:** God's hand is heavy upon a person in bringing affliction and trial; compare 32.4 and see n. **3:** The poet attributes loss of health to sin and to God's consequent indignation. **10:** Heart throbs, etc.: symptoms of the illness. **18:** In traditional theology restoration to health required the confession of sin. Compare 32.3–5.

Ps. 39: Do not be deaf to my weeping. A Lament (see Introduction), but a rather strange one, for it begins by asserting that the poet had earlier stifled a complaint (vv. 1–3). Indeed, the agony is increased by the silence. Aware that life is short (span is a measurement, about three inches, v. 5) and riches unyielding (v. 6), the psalmist

² I kept utterly silent,
 I refrained from speech.
 My agony was quickened,
³ and my heart burned within me.
 As I pondered my mind was inflamed,
 and I began to speak:

⁴ 'LORD, let me know my end and the
   number of my days;
 tell me how short my life is to be.
⁵ I know you have made my days a mere
   span long,
 and my whole life is as nothing in your
   sight.
 A human being, however firm he
   stands, is but a puff of wind,   [Selah
⁶ his life but a passing shadow;
 the riches he piles up are no more than
   vapour,
 and there is no knowing who will enjoy
   them.'

⁷ Now, Lord, what do I wait for?
 My hope is in you.
⁸ Deliver me from all who do me wrong;
 make me no longer the butt of fools.
⁹ I am dumb, I shall not open my
   mouth,
 because it is your doing.
¹⁰ Rain no more blows on me;
 I am exhausted by your hostility.
¹¹ When you rebuke anyone to punish his
   sin,
 you make what he desires melt away;
 every mortal being is only a breath of
   wind.   [Selah

¹² Hear my prayer, LORD;
 listen to my cry,
 do not be deaf to my weeping;
 for I find shelter with you;
 I am a passing guest, as all my
   forefathers were.
¹³ Frown on me no more; let me look
   cheerful
 before I depart and cease to be.

40 *For the leader: for David: a psalm*
¹ PATIENTLY I waited for the LORD;
 he bent down to me and listened to my
   cry.
² He raised me out of the miry pit,
 out of the mud and clay;
 he set my feet on rock
 and gave me a firm footing.
³ On my lips he put a new song,
 a song of praise to our God.
 Many will look with awe
 and put their trust in the LORD.
⁴ Happy is he who puts his trust in the
   LORD
 and does not look to the arrogant and
   treacherous.
⁵ LORD my God, great things you have
   done;
 your wonders and your purposes are
   for our good;
 none can compare with you.
 I would proclaim them and speak of
   them,
 but they are more than I can tell.

⁶ You have not desired sacrifice or
   offering,
 you have not demanded
   whole-offerings or purifying
   offerings;
 you have given me receptive ears.
⁷ Then I said, 'Here I am,'
 as is prescribed for me in a written
   scroll.
⁸ God, my desire is to do your will;
 your law is in my heart.
⁹ In the great assembly I have
   proclaimed what is right;
 I do not hold back my words,
 as you know, LORD.
¹⁰ I have not kept your goodness hidden
   in my heart;
 I have proclaimed your faithfulness and
   saving power,

39:6 **the riches:** *prob. rdg; Heb.* they murmur.

prays for healing from sickness, even if that may bring only a brief respite (vv. 7–13). **12–13:** It was the duty of a host, here God, to defend one's *guest* against any avenger and even to hold back one's own vengeance, if it were deserved, until the guest went away.

Ps. 40: God, my desire is to do your will. A Thanksgiving, though ending with a Lament (vv. 12–17); see Introduction. Verses 13–17 are almost identical with Ps. 70. Like other psalms at the end of Book 1 (see Introduction), this psalm echoes Wisdom poems, as in v. 4, *happy is . . . .* **2:** The psalmist is viewed as already sinking into the *pit,* i.e. Sheol, when God reaches down and pulls the petitioner out on to a *rock.* **6–8:** The righteous one esteems God's *will* above ritual sacrifice. This passage is quoted in Heb. 10.5–7.

and have not concealed your unfailing
    love and truth
from the great assembly.
11 You, Lord, will not withhold
    your tender care from me;
may your love and truth for ever guard
    me.

12 For misfortunes beyond counting
    press on me from all sides;
my iniquities have overtaken me,
    and I cannot see;
they are more in number than the hairs
    of my head;
my courage fails.
13 Show me favour, Lord, and save me;
    Lord, come quickly to my help.
14 Let all who seek to take my life
    be discomfited and dismayed;
let those who desire my hurt be turned
    back in disgrace;
15 let those who cry 'Hurrah!' at my
    downfall
be horrified at their shame.
16 But let all who seek you
    be jubilant and rejoice in you;
and may those who long for your
    saving aid
for ever cry, 'All glory to the Lord!'

17 But I am poor and needy;
    may the Lord think of me.
You are my help and my deliverer;
    my God, do not delay.

41 *For the leader: a psalm: for David*
1 Happy is anyone who has a
    concern for the helpless!
The Lord will save him in time of
    trouble;
2 the Lord protects him and gives him
    life,
making him secure in the land;
the Lord never leaves him to the will of
    his enemies.
3 On his sick-bed he nurses him,

transforming his every illness to health.

4 I said, 'Lord, be gracious to me!
    Heal me, for I have sinned against
    you.'
5 'His case is desperate,' my enemies say;
    'when will he die and his name perish?'
6 All who visit me speak from hearts
    devoid of sincerity;
they are keen to gather bad news
    and go out to spread it abroad.
7 All who hate me whisper together
    about me,
imputing the worst to me:
8 'An evil spell is cast on him,' they say;
    'he is laid on his bed, and will never
    rise again.'
9 Even the friend whom I trusted, who
    ate at my table,
exults over my misfortune.

10 Lord, be gracious and restore me
    that I may repay them in full.
11 Then shall I know that you delight in
    me
and that my enemy will not triumph
    over me.
12 But I am upheld by you because of my
    innocence;
you keep me for ever in your presence.

13 Praise be to the Lord, the God of
    Israel,
from everlasting to everlasting.
    Amen and Amen.

Book 2

42-43 *For the leader: a maskil: for the Korahites*
1 As a hind longs for the running
    streams,

40:13–17 *Cp. Ps. 70:1–5.*   41:2 **never leaves him:**
prob. rdg; Heb. do you not give him up.   41:9 **who
. . . table:** *or* who slanders me.   41:10 **in full:**
transposed from end of verse 9.

Ps. 41: You keep me forever in your presence. A mixture of Thanksgiving and Lament; see Introduction.
Possibly the psalm has been reworked as a conclusion to Book 1 (see Introduction). It begins in the same way
as Ps. 1: *Happy is the one.* **4–9:** The Lament, possibly of some king, often interpreted as David; the *friend* (v. 9)
has been seen traditionally as Ahithophel (2 Sam. 15.12, 30–31). **5:** The extinction of one's *name* or lineage
was the greatest tragedy and punishment from God that could befall a person. **9:** *Ate at my table:* the height
in betrayal; see Jn. 13.18. **13:** This verse, not truly a part of the psalm, marks the end of Book 1. Compare
72.18–20; 89.52; 106.48, which end, respectively, Books 2, 3, and 4.

Pss. 42–43: Send out your light. These two psalms make up a single Lament which has three parts. (Note

so I long for you, my God.
2 I thirst for God, the living God;
when shall I come to appear in his
presence?
3 Tears are my food day and night,
while all day long people ask me,
'Where is your God?'
4 As I pour out my soul in distress, I call
to mind
how I marched in the ranks of the
great to God's house,
among exultant shouts of praise, the
clamour of the pilgrims.
5 How deep I am sunk in misery,
groaning in my distress!
I shall wait for God; I shall yet praise
him,
my deliverer, my God.

6 I am sunk in misery, therefore I shall
remember you
from the springs of Jordan and from
the Hermons,
and from the hill of Mizar.
7 Deep calls to deep in the roar of your
cataracts,
and all your waves, all your breakers,
sweep over me.
8 By day the LORD grants his unfailing
love;
at night his praise is upon my lips,
a prayer to the God of my life.

9 I shall say to God, my Rock, 'Why have
you forgotten me?'
Why must I go like a mourner because
my foes oppress me?
10 My enemies taunt me with crushing
insults:
the whole day long they ask, 'Where is
your God?'
11 How deep I am sunk in misery,

groaning in my distress!
I shall wait for God; I shall yet praise
him,
my deliverer, my God.

[43] 1 Uphold my cause, God, and give
judgement for me
against a godless nation;
rescue me from liars and evil men.
2 For you are my God, my refuge; why
have you rejected me?
Why must I go like a mourner,
oppressed by my foes?
3 Send out your light and your truth to
be my guide;
let them lead me to your holy hill, to
your dwelling-place.
4 Then I shall come to the altar of God,
the God of my joy and delight,
and praise you with the lyre, God my
God.
5 How deep I am sunk in misery,
groaning in my distress!
I shall wait for God; I shall yet praise
him,
my deliverer, my God.

44 *For the leader: for the Korahites: a maskil*
1 WE have heard for ourselves,
God,
our forefathers have told us
what deeds you did in their time,
2 all your hand accomplished in days of
old.
To plant them in the land, you drove
out the nations;
to settle them, you laid waste the
inhabitants.

42:4 **of the great:** *so some MSS; others have an obscure
word.*   42:5 **my deliverer:** *so some MSS; others* his
deliverer.   42:6 **springs:** *lit.* land.   42:10 **with ...
insults:** *lit.* with a breaking in my bones.

the repeated refrain, vv. 5, 11; 43.5. Compare the three-part structure of Ps. 35.) The psalmist, who lives in
the far north, near the sources of the Jordan (42.6), is sick and cannot join the pilgrims on their way to Jerusalem
but hopes to do so in the future (43.3–4). The poems in Book 2 (see Introduction) emphasize the importance
of Jerusalem and the temple, and hence this psalm is an appropriate beginning. **2:** God's presence was
considered especially realized above the Ark of the Covenant in the temple; see 1 Chr. 13.6. **3:** *Where is your
God?:* the rhetorical question is intended as a reproach to someone in distress, as if to imply that sin-caused
illness means being forsaken by God. See the repetition in v. 10. See Job 35.10. **6:** *Hermons:* A mountain in
northern Palestine, usually written Hermon, but here in the plural because of its three peaks. *Mizar:* a hill
probably near Hermon; its exact location is unknown. **43.3:** *Holy hill:* this is the site of the temple, where the
psalmist prays to be sent.
    Ps. 44: Arise and come to our aid. A collective Lament, after a bitter military defeat suffered by the nation.
2: Compare Exod. 15.17. **3:** That God fought and won the victory for Israel at the time of the Exodus is a frequent

3 It was not our fathers' swords that won
  them the land,
nor did their strong arm give them
  victory,
but your right hand and your arm
and the light of your presence; such
  was your favour to them.

4 God, you are my King;
command victory for Jacob.
5 By your help we shall throw back our
  enemies,
in your name we shall trample down
  our assailants.
6 My trust is not in my bow,
nor will my victory be won by my
  sword;
7 for you deliver us from our foes,
you put to confusion those hostile to us.
8 In God have we gloried all day long,
and we shall praise your name for ever.
                                  [Selah

9 Yet you have rejected and humbled us
and no longer lead our armies to battle.
10 You have forced us to retreat before
  the foe,
and our enemies have plundered us at
  will.
11 You have given us up to be slaughtered
  like sheep
and scattered us among the nations.
12 You sold your people for next to
  nothing
and had no profit from the sale.
13 You have exposed us to the contempt
  of our neighbours,
to the gibes and mockery of those
  about us.
14 You have made us a byword among the
  nations,
and the peoples toss their heads at us;

15 so all day long my disgrace confronts
  me,
and I am covered with shame
16 at the shouts of those who taunt and
  abuse me
as the enemy takes his revenge.

17 Though all this has befallen us, we do
  not forget you
and have not been false to your
  covenant;
18 our hearts have not been unfaithful,
nor have our feet strayed from your
  path.
19 Yet you have crushed us as the sea
  serpent was crushed,
and covered us with deepest darkness.
20 Had we forgotten the name of our God
and spread our hands in prayer to alien
  gods,
21 would not God have found out,
for he knows the secrets of the heart?
22 For your sake we are being done to
  death all day long,
treated like sheep for slaughter.

23 Rouse yourself, Lord; why do you
  sleep?
Awake! Do not reject us for ever.
24 Why do you hide your face,
heedless of our misery and our
  sufferings?
25 For we sink down to the dust
and lie prone on the ground.
26 Arise and come to our aid;
for your love's sake deliver us.

45 For the leader: set to 'Lilies': for the Korahites: a maskil: a love song
1 My heart is astir with a noble theme;
in honour of a king I recite the song I

44:19 **sea serpent:** *so Syriac; Heb.* wolves.

theme; compare Josh. 24.5–13. **9:** Perhaps this is a reference to the time when the Ark of the Covenant was taken by *armies into battle;* compare 1 Sam. 4.1–11. The Ark was lost during the destruction of Jerusalem in 587 B.C.E. **10–16:** The conditions described here may fit the period after the destruction of Jerusalem when Israel was scattered *among the nations.* **12:** God received *no profit* from handing over Israel into captivity because the nations gave credit for it to their gods, not to the LORD. See Isa. 52.3. **17–22:** The conditions described here may fit the Maccabean period (about 165 B.C.E.) when Israel was persecuted because of its loyalty to the Covenant; see 1 Macc. 1.20–64. **19:** With the Babylonian Exile Israel ceased to exist as a nation and was lost in the *deepest darkness.* **23:** The poet believed so strongly in the justice of Israel's cause and in God's power to deliver it that no other reason suited the human emotions except that the LORD was in *sleep* even though only alien gods were considered to slumber; see 7.6; 35.23; Isa. 51.9. Contrast Ps. 121.4. **24:** *Hide your face:* see 10.11 n.

have composed,
and my tongue runs swiftly like the pen
    of an expert scribe.

2 You surpass all others in beauty;
gracious words flow from your lips,
for you are blessed by God for ever.
3 Gird on your sword at your side, you
    warrior king,
4 advance in your pomp and splendour,
ride on in the cause of truth and for
    justice.
Your right hand will perform awesome
    deeds:
5 your arrows are sharp; nations lie
    beneath your feet.
The hearts of the king's enemies fail.

6 God has enthroned you for all eternity;
your royal sceptre is a sceptre of equity.
7 You love right and hate wrong;
therefore God, your God, has anointed
    you
above your fellows with oil, the token
    of joy.
8 Your robes are all fragrant with myrrh
    and powdered aloes,
and you are made glad by string music
from palaces panelled with ivory.
9 Princesses are among your noble ladies,
your consort takes her place at your
    right hand
in gold of Ophir.

10 Listen, my daughter, hear my words
    and consider them:
forget your own people and your
    father's house;
11 let the king desire your beauty,
for he is your lord.

12 Do him obeisance, daughter of Tyre.
The richest in the land will court you
    with gifts.

13 Within the palace the royal bride is
    adorned,
arrayed in cloth-of-gold.
14 She will be brought to the king in all
    her finery.
Virgins who are her companions
will be brought to you in her retinue,
15 escorted with the noise of revels and
    rejoicing
as they enter the king's palace.

16 You will have sons to succeed your
    forefathers,
and you will make them princes
    throughout the land.
17 I shall declare your fame through all
    generations;
therefore nations will praise you for
    ever and ever.

46 For the leader: for the Korahites: accord-
    ing to alamoth: a song
1 GOD is our refuge and our stronghold,
a timely help in trouble;
2 so we are not afraid though the earth
    shakes
and the mountains move in the depths
    of the sea,
3 when its waters seethe in tumult
and the mountains quake before his
    majesty.   [Selah

4 There is a river whose streams bring
    joy to the city of God,

45:4 **advance:** *or* prosper. **and for:** *prob. rdg; Heb.
obscure.*

Ps. 45: Blessed by God forever. A Royal Psalm, a wedding song for a king and his bride. It is a unique psalm. It consists of an introduction (v. 1), words about the king (vv. 2–9), words about the queen (vv. 10–15), and the conclusion (vv. 16–17). **2–9:** This section may have been used before the wedding at a feast for the king and his friends (see Gen. 29.22). **6:** It was the king's duty to establish the righteousness of God; see 1 Sam. 10.1. **8:** The *palaces* of the kings of the Northern Kingdom are described as *ivory* either because they abounded in ivory utensils and decoration or because the stone of which they were made resembled ivory. **10–15:** This passage may have traditionally been read to the bride and her friends before she was brought to the king.

Ps. 46: The LORD of Hosts is with us. A Hymn, probably glorifying God's power as it will be manifested in the final judgment over the world. The vision of the future is based on the mythology of creation borrowed from non-Israelite sources. The centrality of Jerusalem in the poem (vv. 4–5) has prompted a phrase, "songs of Zion," from 137.3, to allude to this and other psalms emphasizing Jerusalem. **1–3:** God will abide in the upheavals to take place at the end of time. **1:** This verse inspired Luther's hymn, "A Mighty Fortress." **4–5:** *The city of God:* Jerusalem. Here it is apparently under siege, but God will deliver it as the climax to history. **4:** *A river:* that is, the place of the divine throne. In the mythology of the ancient Near East, God, after defeating

the holy dwelling of the Most High;
5 God is in her midst; she will not be
overthrown,
and at the break of day he will help
her.
6 Nations are in tumult, kingdoms
overturned;
when he thunders, the earth melts.
7 The LORD of Hosts is with us;
the God of Jacob is our fortress.   [*Selah*
8 Come, see what the LORD has done,
the astounding deeds he has wrought
on earth;
9 in every part of the wide world he puts
an end to war:
he breaks the bow, he snaps the spear,
he burns the shields in the fire.
10 'Let be then; learn that I am God,
exalted among the nations, exalted in
the earth.'
11 The LORD of Hosts is with us;
the God of Jacob is our fortress.   [*Selah*

47 *For the leader: for the Korahites: a psalm*
1 CLAP your hands, all you nations,
acclaim God with shouts of joy.
2 How awesome is the LORD Most High,
great King over all the earth!
3 He subdues nations under us,
peoples under our feet;
4 he chooses for us our heritage,
the pride of Jacob whom he loves.

[*Selah*

5 To the shout of triumph God has gone
up,
the LORD has gone up at the sound of
the horn.
6 Praise God, praise him with psalms;

praise our King, praise him with
psalms,
7 for God is King of all the earth;
sing psalms with all your skill.

8 Seated on his holy throne,
God reigns over the nations.
9 The princes of the nations assemble
with the people of the God of
Abraham;
for the mighty ones of earth belong to
God,
and he is exalted on high.

48 *A song: a psalm: for the Korahites*
1 GREAT is the LORD and most
worthy of praise
in the city of our God.
His holy mountain 2 is fair and lofty,
the joy of the whole earth.
The mountain of Zion, the far recesses
of the north,
is the city of the great King.
3 God in her palaces
is revealed as a tower of strength.

4 See, the kings assemble;
they advance together.
5 They look, and are astounded;
filled with alarm they panic.
6 Trembling has seized them there;
they toss in pain like a woman in
labour,
7 like the ships of Tarshish
when an east wind wrecks them.
8 What we had heard we saw now with

46:9 **shields:** *or* wagons.   47:7 **with . . . skill:**
meaning of Heb. word uncertain.   47:9 **with:** *prob. rdg;*
Heb. omits. **mighty ones:** *lit.* shields.   48:2 **the north:**
or Zaphon.

chaos, sits upon the sea or water (see 29.10). Also, a river or some kind of water is often mentioned in
connection with God's throne or temple (see Ezek. 47.1–12; Zech. 14.8–9; or Rev. 22.1–2). **8–11:** A vision
of universal peace, after the punishing upheavals.

Ps. 47: God is King of all the earth. An Enthronement Hymn, celebrating the rule of God. Enthronement
Hymns are believed to have been sung during a festival, probably Booths. Other such hymns are Pss. 93, 95–99.
5–9: The passage has a liturgical ring. **5–7:** The Ark of the Covenant was carried in liturgical procession with
shouts, psalms, clapping of *hands* (v. 1) and fanfare of trumpets; see 2 Sam. 6.12–19. **9:** God is the true King,
and hence the King of kings.

Ps. 48: The joy of the whole earth is Zion's hill. A Hymn, a "Song of Zion" (see Ps. 46 n.). The psalm exultantly
expresses confidence in the formidable power of Jerusalem as a fortress city. **2:** *North:* lit. Zaphon (see Tfn.),
to be identified with Mount Casius, north of the ancient city of Ugarit, site of a temple of Baal, where the
Canaanite pantheon dwelled. To Zion are ascribed the majestic qualities which mythology ascribed to Zaphon.
7: *The ships of Tarshish* were used for the transport of metals from the western Mediterranean to Phoenicia.

our own eyes
in the city of the Lord of Hosts,
in the city of our God;
God will establish it for evermore.

[*Selah*

⁹God, within your temple
we meditate on your steadfast love.
¹⁰God, the praise your name deserves
is heard at earth's farthest bounds.
Your right hand is full of victory.
¹¹The hill of Zion rejoices
and Judah's cities are glad,
for you redress their wrongs.

¹²Go round Zion in procession,
count the number of her towers,
¹³take note of her ramparts,
pass her palaces in review,
that you may tell generations yet to
come
¹⁴that such is God,
our God for ever;
he will be our guide for evermore.

49 *For the leader: for the Korahites: a psalm*
¹Hear this, all you peoples;
listen, all you inhabitants of the world,
²both high and low,
rich and poor,
³for the words that I have to speak are
wise;
my thoughts provide understanding.
⁴I listen with care to the parable
and interpret a mystery to the music of
the lyre.

⁵Why should I be afraid in evil times
when beset by the wickedness of
treacherous foes,
⁶trusting in their wealth
and boasting of their great riches?
⁷Alas! No one can ever ransom himself,
nor pay God the price for his release;
⁸the ransom would be too high,
for ever beyond his power to pay,

⁹the ransom that would let him live on
for ever
and not see death's pit.
¹⁰For we see that the wise die,
as the stupid and senseless all perish,
leaving their wealth to others.
¹¹Though they give their names to
estates,
the grave is their eternal home,
their dwelling for all time to come.
¹²For human beings like oxen are
short-lived;
they are like beasts whose lives are cut
short.

¹³Such is the fate of the foolish
and of those after them who approve
their words.   [*Selah*
¹⁴Like sheep they head for Sheol;
with death as their shepherd,
they go straight down to the grave.
Their bodies, stripped of all honour,
waste away in Sheol.
¹⁵But God will ransom my life
and take me from the power of Sheol.
[*Selah*
¹⁶Do not envy anyone though he grows
rich,
when the wealth of his family increases;
¹⁷at his death he can take nothing,
for his wealth will not go down with
him.
¹⁸Though in his lifetime he counts
himself happy
and he is praised in his prosperity,
¹⁹he will go to join the company of his
forefathers
who will never again see the light.

48:14 **evermore:** *poss. meaning; Heb. word uncertain.*
49:7 **Alas! . . . himself:** *or* No one can ever ransom
anyone else.   49:11 **the grave:** *so Gk; Heb.* their
inward parts.   49:12 **like oxen:** *prob. rdg; Heb.* in
honour.   49:14 **the grave:** *prob. rdg; Heb.* the
morning.   49:14,15 **Sheol:** *or* the underworld.
49:18 **and he . . . in his:** *prob. rdg; Heb.* and you are
praised in your.   49:19 **he:** *prob. rdg; Heb.* you.

Tarshish is often supposed to have been in southern Spain. *East wind:* a violent wind arising in the desert.

Ps. 49: No one can ever ransom oneself. A Wisdom Psalm. Quite beyond the usual Wisdom theme of the merits of the righteous, this meditation asserts that not only is life short but also no one can buy salvation. One need not fear the rich, for they too die. A refrain occurs twice (vv. 12, 20). **11:** The giving of *names to estates* was a common practice. **15:** *Take me from the power of Sheol:* most scholars hold that this passage speaks only about deliverance from present trouble. *Sheol* is the place of the dead; hence, to some interpreters it seems quite possible that the psalmist here speaks of an afterlife with God. But compare v. 19.

20 For human beings like oxen are
    short-lived;
  they are like beasts whose lives are cut
    short.

50 A psalm: for Asaph
  ¹ GOD, the LORD God, has spoken
    and summoned the world
  from the rising of the sun to its setting.
  ² God shines out from Zion, perfect in
    beauty.
  ³ Our God is coming and will not keep
    silence;
  consuming fire runs ahead of him
  and round him a great storm rages.
  ⁴ The heavens above and the earth
  he summons to the judging of his
    people:
  ⁵ 'Gather to me my loyal servants,
    those who by sacrifice made a covenant
    with me.'
  ⁶ The heavens proclaim his justice,
    for God himself is judge.   [Selah

  ⁷ Listen, my people, and I shall speak;
  I shall bear witness against you, Israel:
  I am God, your God.
  ⁸ Not for your sacrifices do I rebuke you,
  your whole-offerings always before me;
  ⁹ I need take no young bull from your
    farmstead,
  no he-goat from your folds;
  ¹⁰ for all the living creatures of the forest
    are mine
  and the animals in their thousands on
    my hills.
  ¹¹ I know every bird on those mountains;
  the teeming life of the plains is my
    care.
  ¹² If I were hungry, I would not tell you,
  for the world and all that is in it are
    mine.
  ¹³ Do I eat the flesh of bulls
  or drink the blood of he-goats?
  ¹⁴ Offer to God a sacrifice of thanksgiving

and fulfil your vows to the Most High;
  ¹⁵ then if you call to me in time of
    trouble,
  I shall come to your rescue, and you
    will honour me.

  ¹⁶ God's word to a wicked person is this:
  What right have you to recite my
    statutes,
  to take the words of my covenant on
    your lips?
  ¹⁷ For you hate correction
  and cast my words out of your sight.
  ¹⁸ If you meet a thief, you choose him as
    your friend,
  and you make common cause with
    adulterers;
  ¹⁹ freely you employ your mouth for evil
  and harness your tongue to deceit.
  ²⁰ You are forever talking against your
    brother,
  imputing faults to your own mother's
    son.
  ²¹ When you have done these things, and
    kept silence,
  you thought that I was someone like
    yourself;
  but I shall rebuke you and indict you to
    your face.
  ²² You forget God, but think well on this,
  lest I tear you in pieces and there be no
    one to save you:
  ²³ he honours me who offers a sacrifice of
    thanksgiving,
  and to him who follows my way
  I shall show the salvation of God.

51 For the leader: a psalm: for David (when
Nathan the prophet came to him after he
had taken Bathsheba)
  ¹ GOD, be gracious to me in your faithful
    love;

49:20 **like oxen:** *prob. rdg; Heb.* in honour.
50:23 **him . . . way:** *prob. rdg; Heb.* him who puts a
way.

Ps. 50: God has summoned the world. A prophetic judgment. The prophets often used the figure of the courtroom. Here, God, the judge, will summon the world to the courtroom and there present the case against God's people, indicting them on two counts: (a) formalism in worship (vv. 8–15); and (b) transgression of the moral law (vv. 16–22). **1:** *God, the LORD God:* lit. God of gods is the LORD (compare Josh. 22.22 and Ps. 136.1–3). **8:** *Sacrifices* in general are not the basis for the relationship with God. **12:** Animal sacrifices satisfied no need of God, such as hunger, as was thought in pagan sacrifices. **14, 23:** *Sacrifice of thanksgiving:* it is possible that Thanksgiving Psalms were used in accompaniment of thanksgiving sacrifices at the temple. **16:** While the indictment for ritualism applied to the whole nation, what follows is addressed only to the *wicked*. **21:** God, in effect, keeps silence if the evil is left unpunished.

in the fullness of your mercy blot out
   my misdeeds.
2 Wash away all my iniquity
   and cleanse me from my sin.
3 For well I know my misdeeds,
   and my sins confront me all the time.
4 Against you only have I sinned
   and have done what displeases;
   you are right when you accuse me
   and justified in passing sentence.
5 From my birth I have been evil,
   sinful from the time my mother
   conceived me.

6 You desire faithfulness in the inmost
   being,
   so teach me wisdom in my heart.
7 Sprinkle me with hyssop, so that I may
   be cleansed;
   wash me, and I shall be whiter than
   snow.
8 Let me hear the sound of joy and
   gladness;
   you have crushed me, but make me
   rejoice again.
9 Turn away your face from my sins
   and wipe out all my iniquity.

10 God, create a pure heart for me,
   and give me a new and steadfast spirit.
11 Do not drive me from your presence
   or take your holy spirit from me.
12 Restore to me the joy of your
   deliverance
   and grant me a willing spirit to uphold
   me.
13 I shall teach transgressors your ways,

and sinners will return to you.

14 My God, God my deliverer, deliver me
   from bloodshed,
   and I shall sing the praises of your
   saving power.
15 Lord, open my lips,
   that my mouth may proclaim your
   praise.
16 You have no delight in sacrifice;
   if I were to bring a whole-offering you
   would not accept it.
17 God, my sacrifice is a broken spirit;
   you, God, will not despise a chastened
   heart.

18 Show favour to Zion and grant her
   prosperity;
   rebuild the walls of Jerusalem.
19 Then you will delight in the appointed
   sacrifices;
   then young bulls will be offered on
   your altar.

52 *For the leader: a maskil: for David (when
Doeg the Edomite came and told Saul that
David had gone to Abimelech's house)*
1 YOU MIGHTY man, why do you boast all
   the day
   of your infamy against God's loyal
   servant?

51:6 **You ... being:** *or* You have hidden the truth in
darkness. **in my heart:** *or* in secret.   51:7 **hyssop:** *or*
marjoram.   51:17 **chastened:** *so Syriac; Heb.* broken
and wounded.   51:19 **Then ... sacrifices:** *prob. rdg;
Heb. adds* a whole-offering and one completely
consumed.   52:1 **against:** *prob. rdg, cp. Syriac; Heb.
omits.*

Ps. 51: God, be gracious to me. A Lament, in confession of sin, one of seven "Penitential Psalms" (see Ps.
130 n.). The superscription (see Introduction) gives the occasion for the psalm as the time when Nathan came
to David after his affair with Bathsheba (2 Sam. 12.1–14). Illness was a token of sin, confessed to in a general
way in vv. 1–9, followed by a plea for forgiveness and restoration (vv. 10–12) in terms of genuine contrition
(vv. 13–17); an addition (vv. 18–19) validates worthy sacrifices seemingly deemed worthless in v. 16. **7:**
Hyssop: leaves of an aromatic plant, used in ceremonies for purging guilt; see Tfn. at Exod. 12.22. Here the
request is that God figuratively purge the sinner. **8:** *You have crushed me* seems to refer to a physical illness
which will give way to *joy,* the transition from guilt to forgiveness. **10:** Creation of a *pure heart* and a *new
. . . spirit* meant a total transformation which could be accomplished only by God; compare Ezek. 36.25–27.
16: *You have no delight in sacrifice:* the statement is sweeping, and is modified in the last verses. **17:** *Broken
spirit:* afflicted and humbled. **18–19:** This modification of v. 16 is probably an addition. **18:** *Rebuild the walls:*
see Neh. chs. 1–3, which rebuilding is possibly alluded to here.

   Ps. 52: I am like a spreading olive tree. A psalm difficult to classify (see Introduction) and a Lament only
in that a righteous person is denouncing a wicked one, and it ends in the typical vow (v. 9). The tone is righteous,
even vindictive (vv. 5–6). *Mighty man* (vv. 1 and 7) is unclear, but is surely someone highly placed and wealthy,
accused of slander and falsehood (vv. 3–4).

2 You plan destruction;
  your slanderous tongue is sharp as a
    razor.
3 You love evil rather than good,
  falsehood rather than truthful speech;
                                    [Selah
4 you love all malicious talk and slander.
5 So may God fling you to the ground,
  sweep you away, leave you ruined and
    homeless,
  uprooted from the land of the living.
                                    [Selah
6 The righteous will look on, awestruck,
  then laugh at his plight:
7 'This is the man', they say,
  'who would not make God his refuge,
  but trusted in his great wealth
  and took refuge in his riches.'

8 But I am like a spreading olive tree in
    God's house,
  for I trust in God's faithful love for
    ever and ever.
9 I shall praise you for ever for what you
    have done,
  and glorify your name among your
    loyal servants,
  for that is good.

53 *For the leader: set to 'Mahalath': a mas-
      kil: for David*
1 THE impious fool says in his heart,
  'There is no God.'
  Everyone is depraved, every deed is
    vile;
  no one does good!
2 God looks out from heaven
  on all the human race
  to see if any act wisely,
  if any seek God.
3 But all are unfaithful, altogether
    corrupt;
  no one does good, no, not even one.

4 Have they no understanding,
  those evildoers who devour my people
  as if eating bread,

and never call to God?
5 They will be in dire alarm
  when God scatters the bones of the
    godless,
  confounded when God rejects them.
6 If only deliverance for Israel might
    come from Zion!
  When God restores his people's
    fortunes,
  let Jacob rejoice, let Israel be glad.

54 *For the leader: with stringed instruments:
      a maskil: for David (when the Ziphites
came and said to Saul, 'David is in hiding among
us.')*
1 SAVE me, God, by the power of your
    name,
  and vindicate me through your might.
2 God, hear my prayer,
  listen to my supplication.
3 Violent men rise to attack me,
  ruthless men seek my life;
  they give no thought to God.   [Selah

4 But God is my helper,
  the Lord the sustainer of my life.
5 May their own malice recoil on the foes
    who beset me!
  Show yourself faithful and destroy
    them.
6 Freely I shall offer you a sacrifice
  and praise your name, LORD, as is most
    seemly;
7 God has rescued me from every
    trouble;
  I look with delight on the downfall of
    my enemies.

55 *For the leader: on stringed instruments: a
      maskil: for David*
1 LISTEN, God, to my prayer:

52:5 **So may God:** *or* So God will.   52:7 **in his
riches:** *so Syriac; Heb.* in his destruction.   53:1–6 *Cp.
Ps. 14:1–7.*   53:5 **They . . . alarm:** *so some MSS;
others add* there was no fear. **when God scatters:** *or*
when God has scattered. **the godless:** *prob. rdg, cp. Gk;
Heb.* one who encamps against you.   54:3 **Violent
men:** *so some MSS; others* Strangers.

Ps. 53: If only deliverance for Israel might come from Zion. A Lament, with the usual vow (v. 6). See Ps.
14, with which this psalm is almost identical. They differ in that the divine name here is *Elohim* (God), and
in Ps. 14 it is *Yahweh* (LORD).
    Ps. 54: God, hear my prayer. A Lament (see Introduction), possibly the prayer of a king as in Ps. 20. **1–2:**
A plea for help. **3–4:** The distress caused by evildoers. **5:** Against the foe. **6–7:** The vow usual in a Lament.
6: *Freely . . . sacrifice:* see Num. 15.3.
    Ps. 55: Hear me and answer. A Lament (see Introduction), with a vindictive tone. **1–2:** A plea for God's

do not hide yourself from my pleading.
2 Hear me and give me an answer,
  for my cares leave me no peace.
3 I am panic-stricken at the hostile
    shouts,
  at the shrill clamour of the wicked;
  for they heap trouble on me
  and revile me in their fury.
4 My heart is torn with anguish
  and the terrors of death bear down on
    me.
5 Fear and trembling assail me
  and my whole frame shudders.
6 I say: 'Oh that I had the wings of a
    dove
  to fly away and find rest!'
7 I would escape far away
  to a refuge in the wilderness.   [*Selah*

8 Soon I would find myself a shelter
  from raging wind and tempest.

9 Frustrate and divide their counsels,
    Lord!
  I have seen violence and strife in the
    city;
10 day and night they encircle it,
  all along its walls;
  it is filled with trouble and mischief,
11 destruction is rife within it;
  its public square is never free
  from oppression and deceit.

12 It was no enemy that taunted me,
  or I should have avoided him;
  no foe that treated me with scorn,
  or I should have kept out of his way.
13 It was you, a man of my own sort,
  a comrade, my own dear friend;
14 we held pleasant converse together
  walking with the throng in the house of
    God.

15 May death strike them,
  may they go down alive into Sheol;
  for their homes are haunts of evil!

16 But I appeal to God,
  and the LORD will save me.
17 Evening and morning and at noonday

I make my complaint and groan.
18 He will hear my cry and deliver me
  and give me security
  so that none may attack me,
  for many are hostile to me.
19 God hears, and he humbles them,
  he who is enthroned from of old. [*Selah*
  They have no respect for an oath,
  nor any fear of God.
20 Such men do violence to those at peace
    with them
  and break their solemn word;
21 their speech is smoother than butter,
  but their thoughts are of war;
  their words are softer than oil,
  but they themselves are like drawn
    swords.

22 Commit your fortunes to the LORD,
  and he will sustain you;
  he will never let the righteous be
    shaken.
23 But you will cast them down, God,
  into the pit of destruction;
  bloodthirsty and treacherous,
  they will not live out half their days.
  For my part, LORD, I shall put my trust
    in you.

56 *For the leader: set to 'The Dove of the Distant Oaks': for David: a miktam (when the Philistines seized him in Gath)*
1 BE gracious to me, God, for I am
    trampled underfoot;
  assailants harass me all the day.
2 All day long foes beset and oppress me,
  for numerous are those who assail me.
3 In my day of fear
  I put my trust in you, the Most High,
4 in God, whose promise is my boast,
  in God I trust and shall not be afraid;
  what can mortals do to me?
5 All day long they wound me with
    words;
  every plan they make is aimed at me.
6 In malice they band together and watch
    for me,

55:15 **Sheol:** *or* the underworld.   56:5 **with words:** *prob. rdg; Heb.* my words.

response. **3–15:** The poet's distress. **3–9a:** The impulse to flee. **7:** *A refuge in the wilderness:* see Jer. 9.2. **9b–11:** The vice in the city. **12–15a:** On such betrayal, compare 41.9 n. **15b:** A curse. **16–21:** God's deliverance. **22–23:** The word of trust.

  Ps. 56: Be gracious to me, God. A Lament (see Introduction), similar to the others (Pss. 51–61), but somewhat less plaintive. The distress is in vv. 1–2 and 5–6, the expression of trust in vv. 3–4, and the vow in v. 12. The

they dog my footsteps;
but, while they lie in wait for me,
7 there is no escape for them because of
their iniquity.
God, in your anger overthrow the
nations.

8 You have noted my grief;
store my tears in your flask.
Are they not recorded in your book?
9 Then my enemies will turn back
on the day when I call to you.
This I know, that God is on my side.
10 In God, whose promise is my boast,
in the LORD, whose promise is my
boast,
11 in God I trust and shall not be afraid;
what can mortals do to me?

12 I have bound myself with vows made to
you, God,
and will redeem them with due
thank-offerings;
13 for you have rescued me from death
and my feet from stumbling,
to walk in the presence of God,
in the light of life.

57 *For the leader: set to 'Destroy not': for
David: a miktam (when he was a fugitive
from Saul in the cave)*
1 GOD, be gracious to me; be gracious,
for I have made you my refuge.
I shall seek refuge in the shadow of
your wings
until the storms are past.
2 I shall call to God Most High,
to the God who will fulfil his purpose
for me.
3 He will send from heaven and save me,

and my persecutors he will put to
scorn. [*Selah*
May God send his love, unfailing and
sure.
4 I lie prostrate among lions, man-eaters
whose teeth are spears and arrows,
whose tongues are sharp swords.
5 God, be exalted above the heavens;
let your glory be over all the earth.

6 Some have prepared a net to catch me
as I walk,
but they themselves were brought low;
they have dug a pit in my path
but have themselves fallen into it. [*Selah*

7 My heart is steadfast, God,
my heart is steadfast.
I shall sing and raise a psalm.
8 Awake, my soul,
awake, harp and lyre;
I shall awake at dawn.
9 I shall praise you among the peoples,
Lord,
among the nations I shall raise a psalm
to you,
10 for your unfailing love is as high as the
heavens;
your faithfulness reaches to the skies.
11 God, be exalted above the heavens;
let your glory be over all the earth.

58 *For the leader: set to 'Destroy not': for
David: a miktam*
1 YOU RULERS, are your decisions really
just?

56:7 **there is no:** *prob. rdg; cp. Gk.*   56:10 **whose
promise:** *prob. rdg; Heb.* a promise.   57:6 **they
themselves:** *prob. rdg; Heb.* I myself.   57:7–11 *Cp.
Ps. 108:1–5.*   58:1 **rulers:** *or* gods.

latter part of v. 7 is a plea for God's vengeance. **8:** On a heavenly record *book,* see Exod. 32.33. **12:**
Thank-offerings: see Ps. 50.14, 23 n. **13:** God's *presence* is the *light* that gives meaning and value to *life.*

Ps. 57: God, be gracious to me. A Lament (see Introduction), the poet's plea to God and trust in God. **1–6:**
The poet's distress. **1:** The figure of an eagle protecting her young under her *wings* to represent God giving
refuge to the innocent goes back to the trials of the Exodus from Egypt; see Exod. 19.4; Deut. 32.11–12. **3–4:**
The poet, having been attacked by slanderous *tongues,* asks God's *unfailing love* to ward off the evil. Teeth
biting flesh is the symbol of slander; compare Job 19.22. **5:** A refrain. **7–11:** A combined vow and utterance
of thanks, virtually identical with Ps. 108.1–5. **7:** *Raise a psalm:* see Ps. 50.14, 23 n. **8:** The poet's confidence
in God is so great that restoration can be anticipated by a thanksgiving on lyre and *harp* at the earliest
opportunity, i.e. *dawn.* **11:** A refrain.

Ps. 58: God, break the teeth in their mouths. A Lament (see Introduction), violent in its outburst of wrath.
The curse uttered in v. 6 is often viewed as responsive to a curse that enemies have put on the poet, alluded
to in the word "charmer" in v. 5. It is uncertain, however, just who the enemies are in vv. 1–5, which allude
to them. The curse (vv. 6–9) is followed by an assurance of vengeance (vv. 10–11). **1:** *Rulers:* gods (see Tfn.);

Do you judge your people with equity?
2 No! Your hearts devise wickedness
   and your hands mete out violence in
      the land.

3 The wicked go astray from birth:
   liars, no sooner born than they take to
      wrong ways.
4 Venomous with the venom of serpents,
   they are like the deaf asp which stops
      its ears
5 and will not listen to the sound of the
      charmer,
   however skilfully he may play.

6 God, break the teeth in their mouths;
   LORD, shatter the fangs of the
      oppressors.
7 May they vanish like water that runs
      away;
   may he aim his arrows, may they perish
      by them;
8 may they be like an abortive birth
      which melts away
   or a stillborn child which never sees the
      sun!
9 Before they know it, may they be
   rooted up like a thorn bush,
   like weeds which a man angrily clears
      away!

10 The righteous will rejoice at the sight
      of vengeance done;
   they will bathe their feet in the blood of
      the wicked.
11 It will be said,
   'There is after all reward for the
      righteous;
   there is after all a God who dispenses
      justice on earth.'

59 *For the leader: set to 'Destroy not': for*
David: a miktam (when Saul sent men to
keep watch on David's house to kill him)
1 RESCUE me, my God, from my enemies;

be my strong tower against those who
      assail me.
2 Rescue me from evildoers;
   deliver me from the bloodthirsty.
3 Violent men lie in wait for me,
   they lie in ambush ready to attack me;
   for no fault or guilt of mine, LORD,
4-5 innocent though I am, they rush to
      oppose me.
But you, LORD God of Hosts, Israel's
      God,
   arouse yourself to come to me and
      keep watch:
   awake, and punish all the nations.
   Have no mercy on these treacherous
      evildoers,   [*Selah*
6 who come out at nightfall,
   snarling like dogs as they prowl about
      the city.
7 From their mouths comes a stream of
      abuse,
   and words that wound are on their lips;
   for they say, 'Who will hear us?'
8 But you laugh at them, LORD,
   mocking all the nations.

9 My strength, I look to you;
   for God is my strong tower.
10 My God, in his unfailing love, will go
      before me;
   with God's help, I shall gloat over the
      foes who beset me.
11 Will you not kill them, lest my people
      be tempted to forget?
   Scatter them by your might and bring
      them to ruin,
   Lord, my shield.
12 Their every word is a sinful utterance.
   Let them be taken in their pride,
   by the curses and falsehoods they utter.
13 In wrath bring them to an end,

58:7 **by them:** *prob. rdg; Heb.* like.   58:9 **may ... up**
like: *prob. rdg; Heb.* your pots. **angrily:** *prob. rdg; Heb.*
like anger.   59:4–5 **though I am:** *prob. rdg, cp. Aram.*
(Targ.); Heb. omits.   59:9 **My strength:** *so Gk; Heb.*
His strength. **strength:** *or* refuge.

in either case the translation rests on a usual correction of the Heb. **10:** *Bathe their feet in the blood of the*
wicked: the Canaanite goddess Anat is described after a battle with her enemies, in a text from Ugarit, as
follows: "She washes her hands of the blood of warriors, her fingers of the gore of troops."
Ps. 59: Rescue me, my God, from my enemies. A Lament, which seems to veer from the personal (vv. 1–4a)
to the national (4b–7), unless "nations" is a figure of speech for personal enemies. The usual trust is in vv. 8–10,
the plea for vengeance in 11–13, and the vow in 16–17. **4–5:** *Arouse yourself . . . awake:* compare Ps. 44.23 n.
8: *Laugh:* compare Ps. 2.4. **9:** The parts of the city walls that were the weakest, e.g. gates, were furnished with
strong towers from which defenders could repel the attackers; see v. 17.

and they will be no more;
then it will be known to earth's farthest
  limits
that God is ruler in Jacob.   [*Selah*
14 They come out at nightfall,
snarling like dogs as they prowl about
  the city;
15 they roam here and there in search of
  food,
and howl if they are not satisfied.
16 But I shall sing of your strength,
and acclaim your love when morning
  comes;
for you have been my strong tower
and a refuge in my day of trouble.
17 I shall raise a psalm to you, my
  strength;
for God is my strong tower.
He is my gracious God.

60 *For the leader: set to 'The Lily of Testimony': a miktam: for David: for instruction (when he fought against Aram-naharaim and
Aram-zobah, and Joab returned and struck twelve
thousand Edomites in the valley of Salt)*
1 You HAVE rejected and crushed us,
  God.
You have been angry; restore us.
2 You have made the land quake and
  caused it to split open;
repair its ruins, for it is shattered.
3 You have made your people drunk with
  a bitter draught,
you have given us wine that makes us
  stagger.
4 But to those who fear you, you have
  raised a banner
to which they may escape from the
  bow.   [*Selah*
5 Save with your right hand and respond,

that those dear to you may be
  delivered.
6 God has spoken from his sanctuary:
'I will go up now and divide Shechem;
I will measure off the valley of Succoth;
7 Gilead and Manasseh are mine;
Ephraim is my helmet, Judah my
  sceptre;
8 Moab is my washbowl, on Edom I fling
  my sandals;
Philistia, shout and acclaim me.'

9 Who will bring me to the fortified city?
Who will guide me to Edom?
10 Have you rejected us, God,
and do you no longer lead our armies
  to battle?
11 Grant us help against the foe;
in vain we look to any mortal for
  deliverance.
12 With God's help we shall fight valiantly,
and God himself will tread our foes
  under foot.

61 *For the leader: on stringed instruments:
for David*
1 GOD, hear my cry; listen to my prayer.
2 From the end of the earth I call to you
  with fainting heart;
lift me up and set me high on a rock.
3 For you have been my shelter,
a tower of strength against the enemy.
4 In your tent I shall make my home for
  ever
and find shelter under the cover of
  your wings.   [*Selah*

60:5–12 *Cp. Ps. 108:6–13.*   60:6 **from his
sanctuary:** *or in his holiness.* **go up now:** *or exult.*
61:2 **lift me up:** *prob. rdg, cp. Gk; Heb. obscure.*

Ps. 60: Save with your right hand. A Lament, after a national humiliation. **1a:** The Lament begins, as usual,
with an invocation of the divine name. **1b–3:** The national tribulation, a military humiliation, is depicted in
the apocalyptic imagery of a cosmic catastrophe; compare Isa. 24.19–20. **5:** The supplication for deliverance
asks for God to *respond* in the form of an oracle. **6–8:** In the oracle, *spoken* probably by a priest, assurance
is given that even though the lands of *Shechem, Succoth, Gilead* and *Manasseh* are in the hands of foreigners,
they belong to God who will *measure* them out again as an inheritance to the LORD's people; compare Jer.
32.42–44. The cause of *Ephraim* and *Judah* is God's cause for they are God's instruments of judgment and
warfare, *helmet* and *sceptre. Moab, Edom* and *Philistia,* which now oppress the land, are objects of scorn and
anger. The conditions fit the period after the destruction of Jerusalem in 587 B.C.E.; compare Ezek. 25.8–17.
9: *Me:* probably the king is meant. **10:** Perhaps an allusion to the fact that the Ark of the Covenant was lost
after 587 B.C.E. and no longer taken to battle as in early days; see 1 Sam. 4.3–11.

   Ps. 61: God, hear my cry. A Lament (see Introduction) by someone far from Judea, who yearns for the temple
in Jerusalem, possibly a Levite or a priest who had been attached to the temple. **2:** *End of the earth:* outside
the Holy Land. **4:** *Tent:* an ancient word for tabernacle or temple; see 27.6. *Cover of your wings:* see Ps. 57.1 n.

5 For you, God, will hear my vows
and grant the wish of those who revere
your name.

6 To the king's life add length of days;
prolong his years for many generations.
7 May he abide in God's presence for
ever;
may true and constant love preserve
him.

8 So I shall ever sing psalms in honour of
your name
as I fulfil my vows day after day.

62 *For the leader: according to Jeduthun: a*
psalm: for David
1 For God alone I wait silently;
my deliverance comes from him.
2 He only is my rock of deliverance,
my strong tower, so that I stand
unshaken.
3 How long will you assail with your
threats,
all beating against your prey
as if he were a leaning wall, a toppling
fence?
4 They aim to topple him from his
height.
They take delight in lying;
they bless him with their lips,
but curse him in their hearts.   [Selah
5 For God alone I wait silently;
my hope comes from him.
6 He alone is my rock of deliverance,
my strong tower, so that I am
unshaken.
7 On God my safety and my honour
depend,
God who is my rock of refuge and my
shelter.
8 Trust in him at all times, you people;
pour out your hearts before him;
God is our shelter.   [Selah

9 The common people are mere empty
air,
while people of rank are a sham;
when placed on the scales they rise,
all of them lighter than air.

10 Put no trust in extortion,
no false confidence in robbery;
though wealth increases, do not set
your heart on it.
11 One thing God has spoken,
two things I have learnt:
'Power belongs to God'
12 and 'Unfailing love is yours, Lord';
you reward everyone according to what
he has done.

63 *A psalm: for David (when he was in the*
wilderness of Judah)
1 God, you are my God; I seek you
eagerly
with a heart that thirsts for you
and a body wasted with longing for
you,
like a dry land, parched and devoid of
water.
2 With such longing I see you in the
sanctuary
and behold your power and glory.

3 Your unfailing love is better than life;
therefore I shall sing your praises.
4 Thus all my life I bless you;
in your name I lift my hands in prayer.
5 I am satisfied as with a rich feast
and there is a shout of praise on my
lips.

6 I call you to mind on my bed
and meditate on you in the night
watches,
7 for you have been my help

61:5 **wish:** *prob. rdg; Heb.* heritage.   61:7 **preserve:**
so some MSS; others add an unintelligible word.

6–7: The prayer for the king appears to be an interpolation; it recalls Nathan's prophecy in 2 Sam. 7.16.
Ps. 62: Power belongs to God. A poem of trust, kindred to a Wisdom Psalm, though echoing the Lament.
Its theme is that not human power and wealth, but only God can help. The distress of the poet (vv. 3–4) comes
in between two assertions of trust in God (vv. 1–2 and 5–7), followed by the counsel to others also to trust
in God (vv. 8–12). **10:** Wisdom literature often warns against setting the heart on riches. **11:** *One thing . . .*
two things: compare Prov. 6.16; 30.15–31. This numerical progression is common in Wisdom literature.
Ps. 63: I seek you, God. A Wisdom Psalm emphasizing the poet's *longing* for God. **1:** A thirst for God and
for wisdom is a frequent theme in Wisdom literature. See Ecclus. 24.23–34; Isa. 55.1. **5:** Wisdom, as a quality
of God, is presented as a *rich feast;* see Prov. 9.1–5. **6:** *Night watches* were divided into three shifts. **7:** *Shadow*

and I am safe in the shadow of your
  wings.
8 I follow you closely
  and your right hand upholds me.

9 May those who seek my life themselves
  be destroyed,
  may they sink into the depths of the
  earth;
10 may they be given over to the sword,
  and become carrion for jackals.

11 The king will rejoice in God;
  all who swear by God's name will exult,
  while the mouths of liars will be
  stopped.

64 For the leader: a psalm: for David
  1 GOD, hear me as I make my
  lament;
keep me safe from the terror of the
  enemy.
2 Protect me from the intrigues of the
  wicked,
  from the mob of evildoers.
3 They sharpen their tongues like swords
  and aim venomous words like arrows
4 to shoot down the innocent from cover,
  shooting suddenly, themselves unseen.
5 They confirm their wicked resolves;
  they talk of hiding snares
  and say, 'Who will see us?'
6 They hatch their evil plots;
  they conceal the schemes they have
  devised,
  deep in their inmost heart.

7 But God with his arrow shoots them
  down,
  and sudden is their overthrow.
8 He will make them fall, using their own
  words against them.
All who see them will flee in horror,
9 every one terrified.
'This is God's work,' they declare;

they understand what he has done.
10 The righteous rejoice and seek refuge
  in the LORD,
  and all the upright in heart exult.

65 For the leader: a psalm: for David: a song
  1 IT is fitting to praise you in Zion,
  God;
  vows should be paid to you.
2 Hearer of prayer,
  to you everyone should come.
3 Evil deeds are too heavy for me;
  only you can wipe out our offences.

4 Happy are those whom you choose
  and bring near to remain in your
  courts.
Grant us in abundance the bounty of
  your house,
  of your holy temple.
5 Through dread deeds you answer us
  with victory,
God our deliverer,
  in whom all put their trust
at the ends of the earth and on distant
  seas.

6 By your might you fix the mountains in
  place;
  you are girded with strength;
7 you calm the seas and their raging
  waves,
  and the tumult of the nations.
8 The dwellers at the ends of the earth
  are overawed by your signs;
  you make east and west sing aloud in
  triumph.

9 You care for the earth and make it
  fruitful;
  you enrich it greatly,
  filling its great channels with rain.

64:5 us: prob. rdg; Heb. them.   65:6 your: prob. rdg;
Heb. his.   65:9 filling . . . rain: lit. the channel of
God is full of water.

---

of your wings: see Ps. 57.1 n. 11: Especially in need of wisdom is the king; see Wisd. 1.1.
  Ps. 64: God, hear me. A Lament on the evil of the wicked. A plea (vv. 1–2) is followed by a description
of the wicked (vv. 5–6), whom God overthrows (vv. 7–9), to the gratification of the righteous (v. 10). 3:
Venomous words: either slander, or else curses believed to have magical force. 6: The poet is the object of
backbiting and calumny.
  Ps. 65: Praise of God is fitting. A Thanksgiving Hymn because it offers praise for God's creative work and
provision of care (vv. 6–10). It was recited in the context of a pilgrimage to the temple (v. 4) which probably
took place at the pilgrim-feast of Weeks; see Deut. 16.9–12. Hence, it can also be classified as a pilgrimage
psalm. 6–8: One of frequent allusions to God the warrior who at creation defeated chaos; compare 24.1–2 n.

In this way you prepare the earth
and provide grain for its people.
10 You water its furrows, level its ridges,
soften it with showers, and bless its
growth.
11 You crown the year with your good
gifts;
places where you have passed drip with
plenty;
12 the open pastures are lush
and the hills wreathed in happiness;
13 the meadows are clothed with sheep
and the valleys decked with grain,
so that with shouts of joy they break
into song.

66 *For the leader: a song: a psalm*
1 LET all the earth acclaim God.
2 Sing to the glory of his name,
make his praise glorious.
3 Say to God, 'How awesome are your
deeds!
Your foes cower before the greatness of
your strength.
4 The whole world bows low in your
presence;
they praise your name in song.'   [*Selah*
5 Come and see what God has done,
his awesome dealings with mankind.
6 He changed the sea into dry land;
his people passed over the river on
foot;
there we rejoiced in him
7 who rules for ever by his power.
His eyes keep watch on the nations;
let no rebel rise in defiance.   [*Selah*

8 Bless our God, you nations;
let the sound of his praise be heard.
9 He preserves us in life;

he keeps our feet from stumbling.
10 For you, God, have put us to the test
and refined us like silver.
11 You have brought us into the net,
you have bound our bodies fast;
12 you have let men ride over our heads.
We went through fire and water,
but you have brought us out into a
place of plenty.

13 I shall bring whole-offerings into your
house
and fulfil to you vows
14 which my lips have made
and my mouth promised on oath
during my distress.
15 I shall offer you fat beasts as
whole-offerings
and burn rams as a soothing offering;
I shall make ready bulls and he-goats.
[*Selah*

16 Come, listen, all who fear God,
and I shall tell you what he has done
for me;
17 I lifted up my voice in prayer,
his praise was on my tongue.
18 If I had cherished evil thoughts,
the Lord would not have listened;
19 but in truth God did listen
and paid heed to my plea.
20 Blessed is God
who has not withdrawn from me his
love and care.

67 *For the leader: on stringed instruments: a*
psalm: a song
1 MAY God be gracious to us and bless us,

66:6 **his people:** *Heb.* they.   66:20 **who ...**
withdrawn: *prob. rdg; Heb. adds* my prayer and.

7: *Their raging waves:* compare Ps. 74.12–14. **8:** *East and west sing aloud:* the psalmist joins the chorus of
all creation in praise of the creator. **9:** The much needed *rain* is a blessing to the crops. See Pss. 68.9, 10;
104.13–15. **11–13:** As the pilgrims go through the fields teeming with life just before the harvest, they are
overwhelmed with joy and a feeling of thanksgiving.

Ps. 66: Let all the earth acclaim God. Verses 1–12 are a corporate Thanksgiving Hymn (see vv. 1–4),
vv. 13–20 a personal, private one. The two portions are fused together, both beginning with the invitation
"come" (vv. 5, 16). **1:** The invitation to *all the earth* to *acclaim God* is the typical beginning of a Hymn. **6:**
This verse recalls the Exodus from Egypt and the entry into the land of Canaan. **10–12:** Perhaps these verses
echo the Babylonian Exile or some other experience of national oppression. **13–15:** The large numbers of
sacrifices referred to are such as would be offered by a prince or a ruler; see Ezek. 46.4–7. **16–20:** The verses
seem to hearken back to vv. 1–2. **16:** *Fear:* the word reflects not fright but dutiful worship. To fear God or to
love God are synonymous in the Heb. Bible. **18:** The prayers of even the devout will not be answered if *evil
thoughts* are *cherished*.

Ps. 67: Let all peoples praise you. A Hymn of Praise, kindred to a blessing (compare Num. 6.24–27 which

may he cause his face to shine on us,
　　　　　　　　　　　　　　　[*Selah*

2 that your purpose may be known on
　　earth,
your saving power among all nations.
3 Let the peoples praise you, God;
let all peoples praise you.

4 Let nations rejoice and shout in
　　triumph;
for you judge the peoples with equity
and guide the nations of the earth.
　　　　　　　　　　　　　　　[*Selah*

5 Let the peoples praise you, God;
let all peoples praise you.

6 The earth has yielded its harvest.
May God, our God, bless us.
7 God grant us his blessing,
that all the ends of the earth may fear
　　him.

68 *For the leader: for David: a psalm: a song*
1 MAY God arise and his enemies be
　　scattered,
and those hostile to him flee at his
　　approach.
2 You disperse them like smoke;
you melt them like wax near fire.
The wicked perish at the presence of
　　God,
3 but the righteous are joyful;
they exult before God
with gladness and rejoicing.
4 Sing the praises of God, raise a psalm
　　to his name;
extol him who rides on the clouds.
The LORD is his name, exult before
　　him,
5 a father to the fatherless, the widow's
　　defender —

God in his holy dwelling-place.
6 God gives the friendless a home
and leads the prisoner out in all safety,
but rebels must remain in the scorching
　　desert.

7 God, when at the head of your people
you marched out through the barren
　　waste,　　　　　　　　　　　　[*Selah*
8 earth trembled, rain poured from the
　　heavens
before God the Lord of Sinai, before
　　God the God of Israel.

9 You, God, send plenteous rain;
when your own land languishes you
　　restore it.
10 There your people settled;
in your goodness, God, you provide for
　　the poor.

11 The Lord speaks the word;
the women with the good news are a
　　mighty host.
12 Kings with their armies are in headlong
　　flight,
while the women at home divide the
　　spoil.
13 Though you linger among the
　　sheepfolds
the dove's wings are covered with silver
and its pinions with yellow gold.
14 When the Almighty routs the kings in
　　the land
snow falls on Zalmon.

15 The hill of Bashan is a lofty hill,
a hill of many peaks is Bashan's hill.
16 But, you hill of many peaks, why gaze
　　so enviously

is here echoed). **1:** *Cause . . . face to shine:* compare Ps. 4.6 n. **6–7:** The occasion seems to be a rich harvest; compare Ps. 65.11–13.

Ps. 68: Sing the praises of God. The psalm is a Hymn in which God is praised for the liberation of Israel from Egypt, their establishment in the Land, and victories over their attackers in later history. Since different historical events are alluded to in poetic form, the impression is given of disconnected fragments which some scholars see collected here. **1–3:** Narrative of what God is accustomed to do in behalf of the *righteous.* **4–10:** Allusion to the Exodus and the conquest of the Land. **4:** "Rider of the clouds" is a phrase used also of the Canaanite god Baal; see v. 33. **11–14:** The allusion is to the victory over the Canaanite *kings* after much hesitation on the part of some tribes to leave their *sheepfolds;* see Judg. 5.16–20. **15–18:** The allusion seems to be to the victory over the Ammonites either by Jephthah (Judg. 11.4–33), or by Saul (1 Sam. 11.1–11), or by David (2 Sam. 10.1–12.31). **15:** The Syrians from the territory of *Bashan* joined the Ammonites in the fight against David; see 2 Sam. 10.6. Mount Hermon with its three *peaks* personifies the Syrian rulers. **21:** The desert warriors left their hair *flowing* loose when they went to battle; see Judg. 5.2 and Tfn. there. **23:** Compare 58.10

at the hill where the LORD delights to
dwell,
where the LORD himself will stay for
ever?
17 There were myriads of God's chariots,
thousands upon thousands,
when the Lord came in holiness from
Sinai.
18 You went up to your dwelling-place on
high
taking captives into captivity;
everyone brought you tribute;
no rebel could live in the presence of
the LORD God.

19 Blessed is the Lord:
he carries us day by day,
God our salvation.   [Selah
20 Our God is a God who saves;
to the LORD God belongs all escape
from death.
21 God himself smites the heads of his
enemies,
those proud sinners with their flowing
locks.
22 The Lord says, 'I shall fetch them back
from Bashan,
I shall fetch them from the depths of
the sea,
23 that you may bathe your feet in blood,
while the tongues of your dogs are
eager for it.'

24 Your processions, God, come into view,
the processions of my God, my King in
the sanctuary:
25 in front the singers, with minstrels
following,
and in their midst girls beating
tambourines.
26 Bless God in the great congregation;
let the assembly of Israel bless the
LORD.
27 There is the little tribe of Benjamin
leading them,

there the company of Judah's princes,
the princes of Zebulun and of Naphtali.

28 God, set your might to work,
the divine might which you have
wielded for us.
29 Kings will bring you gifts
for the honour of your temple in
Jerusalem.
30 Rebuke those wild beasts of the reeds,
that herd of bulls, the bull-calf warriors
of the nations,
who bring bars of silver and prostrate
themselves.
Scatter these nations which delight in
war.
31 Envoys will come from Egypt;
Nubia will stretch out her hands to
God.

32 You kingdoms of the world, sing
praises to God,
make music to the Lord,   [Selah
33 to him who rides on the heavens, the
ancient heavens.
Listen! He speaks in the mighty
thunder.
34 Ascribe might to God, whose majesty is
over Israel,
Israel's pride and might throned in the
skies.
35 Awesome is God in your sanctuary;
he is Israel's God.
He gives might and power to his
people.
Praise be to God.

69 For the leader: set to 'Lilies': for David
1 SAVE me, God,
for the water has risen to my neck.

68:18 **no rebel . . . God:** so Syriac; Heb. unintelligible.
68:23 **bathe:** so Gk; Heb. smite. **are eager:** prob. rdg;
Heb. obscure.   68:26 **assembly:** prob. rdg; Heb. obscure.
68:28 **God . . . your might:** so Gk; Heb. Your God has
directed.

and see n. **24–35:** A liturgical celebration in which the victories of God are reenacted in a temple procession,
possibly with the Ark of the Covenant at its head. **27:** The *tribe of Benjamin* is first in the procession, either
because of its role in the victory over the Canaanites (Judg. 5.14) or because Saul of Benjamin was victorious
over the Ammonites (1 Sam. 11.1–11). David of *Judah* defeated the Ammonites; see vv. 15–18 n. *Zebulun* and
Naphtali were the leading tribes in the victory over the Canaanites; see Judg. 4.6–7. **30:** *Beasts of the reeds:*
Egyptians. *Herd of bulls:* warriors (Syrians) from Bashan, a place known for its cattle. **31:** *Nubia* adjoined Egypt.
32–35: A Hymn of praise; compare Ps. 29. **33:** See v. 4 n.

Ps. 69: Save me, God. A Lament, probably written by an exile (in Babylon) in the sixth century B.C.E., as
suggested by v. 35. The figure of a person sunken into the mire is most vivid. **1–6:** The poet's distress. The

2 I sink in muddy depths where there is
   no foothold;
   I have come into deep water, and the
   flood sweeps me away.
3 I am exhausted with crying, my throat
   is sore,
   my eyes are worn out with waiting for
   God.
4 Those who hate me without reason
   are more than the hairs of my head;
   my persecutors are strong,
   my foes are treacherous.
   How can I restore what I have not
   stolen?

5 God, you know how foolish I am,
   and my guilty deeds are not hidden
   from you.
6 Lord GOD of Hosts,
   let none of those who hope in you be
   discouraged through me;
   God of Israel,
   let none who seek you be humiliated
   through me.
7 For your sake I have suffered
   reproach;
   I dare not show my face for shame.
8 I have become a stranger to my
   brothers,
   an alien to my mother's sons.
9 Zeal for your house has consumed me;
   the insults aimed at you have landed on
   me.
10 I wept bitterly while I fasted
   and I exposed myself to insults.
11 I have made sackcloth my clothing
   and become a byword among the
   people.
12 Those who sit by the town gate gossip
   about me;
   I am the theme of drunken songs.

13 At an acceptable time
   I lift my prayer to you, LORD.
   In your great and enduring love
   answer me, God, with sure deliverance.
14 Rescue me from the mire, do not let
   me sink;
   let me be rescued from my enemies

and from the watery depths.
15 Let no billows sweep me away,
   no abyss swallow me up,
   no deep close over me.
16 Answer me, LORD, in the goodness of
   your unfailing love,
   in your great compassion turn towards
   me.
17 Do not hide your face from me, your
   servant;
   answer me without delay, for I am in
   dire straits.
18 Come near to me and redeem me;
   deliver me from my enemies.

19 You know what insults I bear,
   my shame and my ignominy;
   all who distress me are well known to
   you.
20 Insults have broken my heart
   and I am in despair;
   I looked for consolation, but received
   none,
   for comfort, but did not find any.
21 They put poison in my food
   and when I was thirsty they gave me
   vinegar to drink.

22 May their table be a snare to them
   and a trap when they feel secure!
23 May their eyes be darkened so that they
   do not see;
   let a continual ague shake their loins!
24 Vent your indignation on them
   and let your burning anger overtake
   them.
25 Let their settlements be desolate,
   their tents without inhabitant,
26 for they pursue him whom you have
   struck down
   and multiply the torments of those
   whom you have wounded.
27 Heap punishment after punishment on
   them;
   grant them no vindication;
28 let them be blotted out from the book
   of the living;

69:26 **multiply:** so Gk; Heb. recount.

mire (vv. 1–3) is figurative; it is repeated in vv. 14–15. **7–21:** The experience of humiliation. **9:** The allusion
is uncertain. The verse is cited in Jn. 2.17. **13–18:** An intervening prayer. **17:** *Hide your face:* compare 10.11
and 27.9. **21:** Compare Matt. 27.34, 48; Mk. 15.36; Lk. 23.36; Jn. 19.29. **22–28:** A curse. **25:** See Acts 1.20.

let them not be enrolled among the
innocent.

29 I am afflicted and in pain;
let your saving power, God, set me
securely on high.
30 I shall praise God's name in song
and glorify him with thanksgiving;
31 that will please the LORD more than the
offering of a bull,
a young bull with horns and cloven
hoofs.

32 When the humble see this let them
rejoice.
Take heart, you seekers after God,
33 for the LORD listens to the poor
and does not despise his captive people.
34 Let sky and earth praise him,
the seas and all that moves in them,
35 for God will deliver Zion
and rebuild the cities of Judah;
his people will settle there and possess
it.
36 The children of those who serve him
will inherit it,
and those who love his name will live
there.

70 *For the leader: for David: for commemoration*
1 MAKE haste and save me, God;
LORD, come quickly to my help.
2 Let those who seek my life
be discomfited and dismayed,
let those who desire my hurt be turned
back in disgrace;
3 let those who cry 'Hurrah!'
withdraw in their shame.
4 But let all who seek you
be jubilant and rejoice in you;
and may those who long for your
saving aid
forever cry, 'All glory to God!'

5 But I am oppressed and poor;
God, come quickly to me.

You are my help and my deliverer;
LORD, do not delay.

71 1 IN you, LORD, I have found
refuge;
let me never be put to shame.
2 By your saving power rescue and
deliver me;
hear me and save me!
3 Be to me a rock of refuge
to which at all times I may come;
you have decreed my deliverance,
for you are my rock and stronghold.
4 Keep me safe, my God, from the power
of the wicked,
from the clutches of the pitiless and
unjust.

5 You are my hope, Lord GOD,
my trust since my childhood.
6 On you I have leaned from birth;
you brought me from my mother's
womb;
to you I offer praise at all times.
7 I have become like a portent to many;
but you are my strong refuge.
8 My mouth will be full of your praises,
I shall tell of your splendour all day
long.
9 Do not cast me off when old age comes
or forsake me as my strength fails,
10 for my enemies whisper against me
and those who spy on me intrigue
together,
11 saying, 'God has forsaken him;
harry him and seize him;
there is no one to come to his rescue.'
12 God, do not stand aloof from me;
come quickly, my God, to my help.
13 Let my accusers be put to shame and
perish;
let those intent on harming me be
covered with scorn and dishonour.

70:1–5 *Cp. Ps. 40:13–17.*

28: *The book of the living:* compare 56.8 n.; 109.15. **29–31:** A prayer and vow. Normally the vow is favorable
to animal sacrifice. **32–36:** The psalmist's trust in God. **35:** An allusion to the situation after the Babylonian
conquest (597 B.C.E.) and the Exile (587–520).

Ps. 70: LORD, **do not delay.** A Lament (see Introduction) almost identical to Ps. 40.13–17.

Ps. 71: **Do not forsake me, God.** A Lament (see Introduction), possibly of an old person in serious trouble
who reminds God of all God's past faithfulness. **7–11:** The general belief of the OT, that troubles were due
to a rejection by God because of some sin, made the psalmist's troubled life (v. 20) *like a portent* or warning

14 But as for me, I shall wait in continual
hope,
I shall praise you again and yet again;
15 I shall declare your vindicating power,
declare all day long your saving acts,
although I lack the skill to recount
them.
16 I shall come declaring your mighty acts,
Lord GOD,
and proclaim your sole power to
vindicate.
17 You have taught me from childhood,
God,
and all my life I have proclaimed your
marvellous works.
18 Now that I am old and my hair is grey,
do not forsake me, God,
until I have extolled your strength
to generations yet to come,
19 your might and vindicating power to
highest heaven;
for great are the things you have done.
Who is there like you, my God?
20 You have made me suffer many
grievous hardships,
yet you revive me once more
and lift me again from earth's watery
depths.
21 Restore me to honour, and comfort me
again;
22 then I shall praise you on the harp
for your faithfulness, my God;
on the lyre I shall sing to you,
the Holy One of Israel.
23 Songs of joy will be on my lips;
I shall sing to you because you have
redeemed me.
24 All day long my tongue will tell of your
vindicating power,
for those who seek my hurt are shamed
and disgraced.

72 For Solomon

1 GOD, endow the king with your
own justice,
his royal person with your
righteousness,
2 that he may govern your people rightly
and deal justly with your oppressed
ones.
3 May hills and mountains provide your
people
with prosperity in righteousness.
4 May he give judgement for the
oppressed among the people
and help to the needy;
may he crush the oppressor.
5 May he fear you as long as the sun
endures,
and as the moon throughout the ages.
6 May he be like rain falling on early
crops,
like showers watering the earth.
7 In his days may righteousness flourish,
prosperity abound until the moon is no
more.
8 May he hold sway from sea to sea,
from the Euphrates river to the ends of
the earth.
9 May desert tribes bend low before him,
his enemies lick the dust.
10 May the kings of Tarshish and of the
isles bring gifts,
the kings of Sheba and Seba present
their tribute.
11 Let all kings pay him homage,
all nations serve him.
12 For he will rescue the needy who
appeal for help,

72:7 **righteousness:** *so some MSS; others* a righteous
person.

to would-be sinners. **14–24:** The vow here to *praise* as a motive for God's favorable action is longer than usual.
20: The *earth's watery depths* are the underground place of the dead into which the psalmist seems already
sunk. **22:** Though not a poet (v. 15), the psalmist offers this musical praise as the content of his vow.
   Ps. 72: May the king live long. A Royal Psalm. The superscription (see Introduction) describes this as a psalm
of Solomon. Verses 18–20 are an editorial addition to close Book 2 (see Ps. 41.13 n. for other closings). Royal
or Wisdom psalms are common at the beginnings and at the ends of the five books (see Pss. 1, 2, 41, 73, 89,
90, 91). This psalm could have been used at a coronation or at its annual celebration. **1–2:** The word *justice*
(Sept.) is "judgments" in the MT. To *judge* meant to vindicate the rights of the poor and to relieve suffering.
Thus, the king was also a judge, and therefore needed to be just. **6–7:** *Early crops* were those that matured
before the drought of summer came and hence needed much rain. In Near Eastern ideas of the king, even the
fertility of the land depended on him. **8–11:** The king was envisioned as having a universal dominion; see
2.10–11. *To lick dust* was a symbol of utter defeat. **10:** *Tarshish:* probably in Spain. *Sheba and Seba:* in South

the distressed who have no protector.
13 He will have pity on the poor and the
   needy,
and deliver the needy from death;
14 he will redeem them from oppression
   and violence
and their blood will be precious in his
   eyes.

15 May the king live long!
May gifts of gold from Sheba be given
   him.
May prayer be made for him
   continually;
blessings be his all the day long.
16 May there be grain in plenty
   throughout the land,
growing thickly over the heights of the
   hills;
may its crops flourish like Lebanon,
and the sheaves be plenteous as blades
   of grass.
17 Long may the king's name endure,
may it remain for ever like the sun;
then all will pray to be blessed as he
   was;
all nations will tell of his happiness.

18 Blessed be the LORD God, the God of
   Israel,
who alone does marvellous things;
19 blessed be his glorious name for ever;
may his glory fill the whole earth.
Amen and Amen.

20 Here end the prayers of David son of Jesse.

Book 3

73 A psalm: for Asaph
1 ASSUREDLY God is good to the
   upright,

to those who are pure in heart!

2 My feet had almost slipped,
my foothold had all but given way,
3 because boasters roused my envy
when I saw how the wicked prosper.
4 No painful suffering for them!
They are sleek and sound in body;
5 they are not in trouble like ordinary
   mortals,
nor are they afflicted like other folk.
6 Therefore they wear pride like a
   necklace
and violence like a robe that wraps
   them round.
7 Their eyes gleam through folds of fat,
while vain fancies flit through their
   minds.
8 Their talk is all mockery and malice;
high-handedly they threaten
   oppression.
9 Their slanders reach up to heaven,
while their tongues are never still on
   earth.
10 So the people follow their lead
and find in them nothing blameworthy.
11 They say, 'How does God know?
Does the Most High know or care?'
12 Such are the wicked;
unshakeably secure, they pile up
   wealth.

13 Indeed it was all for nothing I kept my
   heart pure
and washed my hands free from guilt!
14 For all day long I suffer affliction
and every morning brings new
   punishment.
15 Had I thought to speak as they do,

72:15 **gold:** or frankincense.   72:16 **the sheaves:**
prob. rdg; Heb. from a city.   73:1 **to the upright:**
prob. rdg; Heb. to Israel.   73:10 **and find . . .**
blameworthy: prob. rdg; Heb. obscure.

Arabia. **12–14:** The king, like God (v. 1), was to *redeem* people from *oppression*. The absolute kings of the Near East often shed the blood of the weak with little remorse; see Ezek. 24.1–13. **15–17:** A prayer on behalf of the king. **17:** Many kings in the ancient Near East were called "the Sun" and still more were compared to the sun. **18–19:** A prayer, not part of the original psalm, but added by an editor to close (v. 20) the second collection of psalms.

   Ps. 73: Assuredly God is good to the upright. A Wisdom Psalm, used as the introduction to Book 3 (see Introduction). The psalm falls into two major divisions. The first (vv. 2–15) asks why the wicked prosper and the righteous suffer; the second (vv. 16–28) asserts that after a visit to the temple, the psalmist learned that the prosperity of the wicked is only temporary and that the righteous enjoy the constant guidance of God. **6–7:** *Fat* connotes an insensitive heart which indulges in *violence*. **11:** The assertion of the wicked, that God is indifferent to human behavior, is a practical "atheism." **13–15:** The claim that a *pure heart*, i.e. upright life,

I should have been false to your
people.
16 I set my mind to understand this
but I found it too hard for me,
17 until I went into God's sanctuary,
where I saw clearly what their destiny
would be.

18 Indeed you place them on slippery
ground
and drive them headlong into utter
ruin!
19 In a moment they are destroyed,
disasters making an end of them,
20 like a dream when one awakes, Lord,
like images dismissed when one rouses
from sleep!

21 My mind was embittered,
and I was pierced to the heart.
22 I was too brutish to understand,
in your sight, God, no better than a
beast.
23 Yet I am always with you;
you hold my right hand.
24 You guide me by your counsel
and afterwards you will receive me with
glory.
25 Whom have I in heaven but you?
And having you, I desire nothing else
on earth.
26 Though heart and body fail,
yet God is the rock of my heart, my
portion for ever.
27 Those who are far from you will
perish;
you will destroy all who are unfaithful
to you.
28 But my chief good is to be near you,
God;
I have chosen you, Lord GOD, to be my
refuge,
and I shall recount all your works.

Why do you fume with anger at the
flock you used to shepherd?
2 Remember the assembly of your
people,
taken long since for your own,
redeemed to be your own tribe.
Remember Mount Zion, which you
made your dwelling-place.
3 Restore now what has been altogether
ruined,
all the destruction that the foe has
brought on your sanctuary.

4 The shouts of your enemies filled your
temple;
they planted their standards there as
tokens of victory.
5 They brought it crashing down,
like woodmen plying their axes in the
forest;
6 they ripped out the carvings,
they smashed them with hatchet and
pick.
7 They set fire to your sanctuary,
tore down and polluted the abode of
your name.
8 They said to themselves, 'Let us
together oppress them,'
and they burnt every holy place
throughout the land.
9 We cannot see any sign for us, we have
no prophet now;
no one amongst us knows how long this
is to last.
10 How long, God, will the foe utter his
taunts?
Will the enemy pour scorn on your
name for ever?
11 Why do you hold back your hand,
why keep your right hand within your
bosom?

74

A maskil: for Asaph
1 GOD, why have you cast us off?
And is it for ever?

74:3 **now**: *prob. rdg; Heb.* your steps.   74:5 **They . . .
forest**: *prob. rdg; Heb.* unintelligible.   74:6 **they
ripped out**: *so Gk; Heb.* and now.

is *all for nothing* is an attack on the foundation of Israel's existence and so a betrayal of its hopes; see Deut.
6.1–3. **22–23**: A *brutish* person is moved only by physical force in pain and is insensitive to God's touch in
leading by the *hand*; compare Ps. 32.8–10. **24–27**: The final reward of the just is to be in dialogue with God
and to receive God's counsel; compare Job 38.1–42.6; Pss. 27.4; 32.8; 63.1–11.

Ps. 74: Do not forget for ever the sufferings of your servants. A Lament over the destruction of the temple
by a foreign invader. **9**: The people have lost all confidence in the prophetic word. The confirming signs of
the prophets have not come to pass, and prophetic efforts to set a limit of duration to God's punishment have

¹²God, my King from of old,
  whose saving acts are wrought on
    earth,
¹³by your power you cleft the sea
    monster in two
  and broke the sea serpent's heads in
    the waters;
¹⁴you crushed the heads of Leviathan
  and threw him to the sharks for food.
¹⁵You opened channels for spring and
    torrent;
  you dried up streams never known to
    fail.
¹⁶The day is yours, yours also is the
    night;
  you ordered the light of moon and sun.
¹⁷You have fixed all the regions of the
    earth;
  you created both summer and winter.

¹⁸Remember, LORD, the taunts of the
    enemy,
  the scorn a barbarous nation pours on
    your name.
¹⁹Do not cast to the beasts the soul that
    confesses you;
  do not forget for ever the sufferings of
    your servants.
²⁰Look upon your creatures: they are
    filled with dark thoughts,
  and the land is a haunt of violence.
²¹Let not the oppressed be shamed and
    turned away;
  may the poor and the downtrodden
    praise your name.

²²Rise up, God, defend your cause;
  remember how fools mock you all day
    long.
²³Ignore no longer the uproar of your
    assailants,
  the ever-rising clamour of those who
    defy you.

75 *For the leader: set to 'Destroy not': a
  psalm: for Asaph: a song*
¹WE give thanks to you, God, we give
    you thanks;
  your name is brought very near to us
  in the account of your wonderful
    deeds.

²I shall seize the appointed time
  and then judge mankind with equity.
³When the earth quakes, and all who
    live on it,
  it is I who hold its pillars firm.   [*Selah*
⁴To the boastful I say, 'Boast no more,'
  and to the wicked, 'Do not vaunt your
    strength:
⁵do not vaunt yourself against heaven
  or speak arrogantly against the Rock.'

⁶No power from the east or from the
    west,
  no power from the wilderness, can raise
    anyone up.
⁷For God is ruler;
  he puts one down, another he raises up.

⁸For the LORD holds a cup in his hand,
  and the wine foams in it, richly spiced;
  he pours out this wine,
  and all the wicked on earth must drain
    it to the dregs.

⁹But I shall confess him for ever;
  I shall sing praises to the God of Jacob.
¹⁰He will break down the strength of the
    wicked,
  but the strength of the righteous will be
    raised high.

74:14 **to the sharks:** *prob. rdg; Heb.* to a people,
desert-dwellers.   74:19 **that confesses you:** *so Gk;
Heb.* of your turtle-dove.   74:20 **your creatures:**
prob. rdg; Heb. the covenant, because.   75:5 **Rock:**
prob. rdg; Heb. neck.   75:10 **He:** *prob. rdg; Heb.* I.

failed. **11:** *Hold back your hand:* refrain from acting in behalf of Israel. **12–17:** God's power in restoring
dispersed Israel is often compared to the creation of the universe and described in mythological imagery of
the ancient Near East; compare Isa. 51.9–16. God is here a great warrior who defeats primitive chaos identified
as the *sea monster, sea serpent, Leviathan,* to bring about a benevolent order of *day* and *night,* etc. **18–23:**
A prayer for deliverance, the motive being to end the *taunts of the enemy* against God. The vow usual in a
Lament is absent, perhaps because it involved a sacrifice which was impossible because the temple was in
ruins.

  Ps. 75: We give thanks to you, God. This is classified by some as a Thanksgiving but by others as a Wisdom
Psalm of exhortation. **1:** Gratitude due God. **2–5:** God is the speaker. **6–9:** God alone is the true judge, whose
judgment is sure to come. **8:** On the *cup* of judgment, compare Isa. 51.22–23; Jer. 25.15; Lk. 22.42.

76 *For the leader: on stringed instruments: a psalm: for Asaph: a song*

1 IN Judah God is known,
his name is great in Israel;
2 his tent is in Salem,
his dwelling in Zion.
3 There he has broken the flashing arrows,
shield and sword and weapons of war.
[*Selah*

4 You are awesome, Lord,
more majestic than the everlasting mountains.
5 The bravest are despoiled,
they sleep their last sleep,
and the strongest cannot lift a hand.
6 At your rebuke, God of Jacob,
rider and horse lie prostrate.

7 You are awesome, Lord;
when you are angry, who can stand in your presence?
8 You gave sentence out of heaven;
the earth was afraid and kept silence
9 when you rose in judgement, God,
to deliver all the afflicted in the land.
[*Selah*

10 Edom, for all his fury, will praise you
and the remnant left in Hamath will dance in worship.

11 Make vows to the LORD your God, and keep them;
let the peoples all around him bring their tribute;
12 for he curbs the spirit of princes,
he fills the kings of the earth with awe.

77 *For the leader: according to Jeduthun: for Asaph: a psalm*

1 I CRIED aloud to God,
I cried to God and he heard me.

2 In the day of my distress I sought the Lord,
and by night I lifted my hands in prayer.
My tears ran unceasingly,
I refused all comfort.
3 When I called God to mind, I groaned;
as I pondered, faintness overwhelmed me.
[*Selah*
4 My eyelids were tightly closed;
I was distraught and could not speak.
5 My thoughts went back to times long past,
I remembered distant years;
6 all night long I meditated,
I pondered and examined my heart.

7 Will the Lord always reject me
and never again show favour?
8 Has his love now failed utterly?
Will his promise never be fulfilled?
9 Has God forgotten to be gracious?
Has he in anger withheld his compassion?
[*Selah*
10 'Has his right hand grown weak?' I said.
'Has the right hand of the Most High changed?'

11 I call to mind the deeds of the LORD;
I recall your wonderful acts of old;
12 I reflect on all your works
and consider what you have done.
13 Your way, God, is holy;
what god is as great as our God?
14 You are a God who works miracles;

76:4 **awesome:** *so Gk (Theod.); Heb.* illuminated.
76:10 **Edom ... worship:** *poss. meaning; Heb.* obscure.
76:11 **their tribute:** *prob. rdg; Heb.* adds for the terror.
77:2 **I lifted:** *prob. rdg; Heb.* omits.   77:6 **I meditated:** *so Gk; Heb.* my song.   77:8 **his promise:** *so Syriac; Heb.* omits his.   77:10 **grown weak:** *prob. rdg; Heb.* my suffering. **changed:** *prob. rdg; Heb.* the years of.

Ps. 76: You are awesome, Lord. A Hymn, after a military victory (v. 3). The introduction (vv. 1–3) is followed by allusions to an unknown battle (vv. 6–10), and ended by an exhortation to thank God (vv. 11–12). This is one of the songs of Zion (see Ps. 46 n.). **2:** *Salem:* mentioned in Gen. 14.18; tradition, as here, identifies it with Jerusalem. **10:** *Edom* to the southeast and *Hamath* to the north. This translation is based on minor corrections of the MT. **11:** *Vows:* in Laments, the poet usually vows to express gratitude through offering a sacrifice.

Ps. 77: I recall your wonderful acts of old. A Lament that has a hymn of praise (vv. 11–20), in place of the usual vow, as a motive in eliciting God's saving action. **2–4:** *Groaning* and *faintness* indicate either a physical illness or great anxiety of spirit. **9–10:** Two questions about God arise in the face of human suffering: (a) Is God *gracious*, i.e. good and concerned enough to want to help? (b) Is God able to help? **11–15:** A Hymn,

you have shown the nations your
   power.
¹⁵ With your strong arm you rescued your
   people,
the descendants of Jacob and Joseph.
                              [*Selah*

¹⁶ The waters saw you, God,
they saw you and writhed in anguish;
the ocean was troubled to its depths.
¹⁷ The clouds poured down water, the
   skies thundered,
your arrows flashed hither and thither.
¹⁸ The sound of your thunder was in the
   whirlwind,
lightning-flashes lit up the world,
the earth shook and quaked.
¹⁹ Your path was through the sea,
your way through mighty waters,
and none could mark your footsteps.
²⁰ You guided your people like a flock
shepherded by Moses and Aaron.

78
A maskil: for Asaph
¹ My people, mark my teaching,
listen to the words I am about to speak.
² I shall tell you a meaningful story;
I shall expound the riddle of things
   past,
³ things that we have heard and know,
things our forefathers have recounted
   to us.
⁴ They were not hidden from their
   descendants,
who will repeat them to the next
   generation:
the praiseworthy acts of the LORD
and the wonders he has done.

⁵ He laid on Jacob a solemn charge

and established a rule in Israel,
which he commanded our forefathers
to teach their descendants,
⁶ so that it might be known to a future
   generation,
to children yet to be born,
and they in turn would repeat it to
   their children.
⁷ They were charged to put their trust in
   God,
to hold his great acts ever in mind
and to keep his commandments,
⁸ and not to do as their forefathers did,
a disobedient and rebellious generation,
a generation with no firm purpose,
with hearts not fixed steadfastly on
   God.

⁹ The Ephraimites, bowmen all and
   marksmen,
turned tail in the hour of battle.
¹⁰ They had not kept God's covenant;
they had refused to live by his law;
¹¹ they forgot the things he had done,
the wonders he had shown them.

¹² As their fathers witnessed he
   performed wonderful deeds
in Egypt, the region of Zoan:
¹³ he divided the sea and brought them
   through;
he heaped up the waters on either side.
¹⁴ He led them with a cloud by day,
and all night long with a glowing fire.
¹⁵ He split the rock in the wilderness
and gave them water to drink,
   abundant as the deep;
¹⁶ he brought streams out of the crag
and made water run down like torrents.

---

extolling God's *way* as *holy* in redeeming the *people* in the past, affirms God's goodness. **16–19:** An ancient
Hymn describing creation to mythological images — the sea serpent writhes *in anguish* — affirms God's power
to help. See 74.13–14. **20:** Since God's goodness and power were manifested to the *people* in the Exodus,
they need to be displayed again now.

Ps. 78: From Moses to David. A historical psalm (see also Pss. 105, 106, 135, 136). Israel's story was
undoubtedly told again and again by her poets and for various reasons. An emphasis here is the condemnation
of Ephraim (vv. 9–11, 67), the leading tribe of the Northern Kingdom. The historical allusions are quite clear,
especially in the light of information in the Pentateuch. Perhaps the psalm was used on a festival day. **1–4:**
This introduction is kindred to Wisdom writings (see 49.1–4); the *teaching* is offered so that the present
generation will perpetuate its legacy. **2:** This verse is paraphrased in Matt. 13.35. **5–8:** The Sinai episode, Exod.
chs. 19–24. **6:** Compare Deut. 6.7. **9–11:** The allusion to *in the hour of battle* is obscure. The major denunciation, though, is in vv. 10–11. **12–53:** A review of the Exodus and the wilderness experience emphasizes God's
wondrous deeds related in Exod. and Num. The usual trespasses of Israel (vv. 17–20 and 32–40) balanced
God's great deeds with Israel's deficiencies. **12:** *Zoan:* called Rameses in Exod. 1.11. **15–16:** See Exod. 17.6

17 But they sinned against him yet again:
in the desert they defied the Most
High,
18 trying God's patience wilfully
by demanding the food they craved.
19 They spoke against God and said,
'Can God spread a table in the
wilderness?'
20 When he struck a rock, water gushed
out
until the wadis overflowed;
'But can he give bread as well?' they
demanded.
'Can he provide meat for his people?'
21 When the Lord heard this, he was
infuriated:
fire raged against Jacob,
anger blazed up against Israel,
22 because they put no faith in God,
no trust in his power to save.

23 Then he gave orders to the skies above
and threw open heaven's doors;
24 he rained down manna for them to eat
and gave them the grain of heaven.
25 So everyone ate the bread of angels;
he sent them food in plenty.
26 He let loose the east wind from heaven
and drove the south wind by his power;
27 he rained meat down on them like a
dust storm,
birds flying thick as the sand of the
seashore.
28 He made them fall within the camp,
all around their tents.
29 The people ate and were well filled,
for he had given them what they
wanted.
30 But still they wanted more,
even while the food was in their
mouths.
31 Then the anger of God blazed up
against them;
he spread death among their strongest
men
and laid low the young men of Israel.

32 In spite of all, they persisted in their
sin
and had no faith in his wonders.
33 So he made their days end in emptiness
and their years in terror.
34 When he brought death among them,
they began to seek him,

and look eagerly for God once more;
35 they remembered that God was their
rock,
that God Most High was their
redeemer.
36 But still they sought to beguile him
with words
and deceive him with their tongues;
37 but they were not loyal to him in their
hearts,
nor were they faithful to his covenant.
38 Yet he was merciful,
wiping out guilt and not destroying.
Time and again he restrained his wrath
and did not give vent to his anger.
39 He remembered that they were but
mortal,
a breath of air which passes by and
does not return.

40 How often they defied him in the
wilderness
and grieved him in the desert!
41 Again and again they tried God's
patience
and provoked the Holy One of Israel.
42 They did not keep in mind his power
or the day when he delivered them
from the enemy,
43 how he displayed his signs in Egypt,
his portents in the region of Zoan.
44 He turned their streams into blood,
and they could not drink the running
water.
45 He sent swarms of flies which devoured
them,
and frogs which brought devastation;
46 he gave their harvest over to locusts,
their produce to the grubs;
47 he devastated their vines with
hailstones,
their fig trees with torrents of rain;
48 he abandoned their cattle to the plague,
their animals to attacks of pestilence.
49 He unleashed his blazing anger on
them,
wrath and enmity and rage,
launching those messengers of evil.
50 He opened a way for his fury;
he did not spare them from death,

78:48 **plague:** *so one MS; others* hail.

and Num. 20.10–13. **17–31:** See Exod. 16.1–17.7; Num. 11.1–9, 31–34. **24:** See Jn. 6.31–35. **42–53:** The

but gave them up to the plague.
51 He struck down all the firstborn in
   Egypt,
the firstfruits of their manhood in the
   tents of Ham.

52 He led out his own people like sheep
and guided them like a flock in the
   wilderness.
53 He led them in safety and they were
   not afraid,
but their enemies were engulfed by the
   sea.
54 He brought his people to his holy land,
to the hill-country which his right hand
   had won.
55 He drove out nations before them,
allotting their lands to Israel as a
   possession
and settling the tribes in their
   dwellings.

56 Yet they provoked and defied God
   Most High,
refusing to keep his solemn charges;
57 they were renegades, faithless like their
   fathers,
unreliable like a bow gone slack.
58 They provoked him to anger with their
   shrines
and roused his jealousy with their
   carved images.
59 God heard and was enraged;
he utterly rejected Israel.
60 He forsook his dwelling at Shiloh,
the tabernacle in which he dwelt among
   mortals;
61 he surrendered his strength to captivity,
his pride into enemy hands;
62 he gave his people to the sword,
he was enraged with his own
   possession.
63 Fire devoured their young men,
and their maidens could raise no
   lament for them;

64 their priests fell by the sword,
and the widows among them could not
   weep.

65 Then the Lord awoke as a sleeper
   wakes
or a warrior flushed with wine;
66 he struck his foes and drove them back,
bringing perpetual shame upon them.

67 He rejected the clan of Joseph
and did not choose the tribe of
   Ephraim;
68 but he chose the tribe of Judah,
Mount Zion which he loved.
69 He built his sanctuary high as the
   mountains,
founded like the earth to last for ever.
70 He chose David to be his servant
and took him from the sheepfolds;
71 he brought him from minding the ewes
to be the shepherd of his people Jacob
and of Israel his possession;
72 he shepherded them in singleness of
   heart
and guided them with a skilful hand.

79 *A psalm: for Asaph*
¹ THE heathen have invaded your
      domain, God;
they have defiled your holy temple
and laid Jerusalem in ruins.
² The dead bodies of your servants they
   have thrown out
as food for the birds;
everyone loyal to you they have made
   carrion for wild beasts.
³ All round Jerusalem their blood is spilt
   like water,
and there is no one to give them burial.
⁴ We suffer the taunts of our neighbours,
the gibes and mockery of those about
   us.

78:66 **and . . . back:** *or* in the back.

---

sequence of the plagues differs from that of Exod. chs. 7–12. **54–64:** These vv. deal with the conquest of the land of Canaan and the age of the Judges. God gave Israel the land, but infidelity did not cease. **55:** Joshua chs. 13–17. **60:** *Shiloh:* See Josh. 18.1; Judg. 18.31; 1 Sam. chs. 1–4. On its abandonment, see Jer. 7.12–14; 26.6. **61:** *His strength:* the Ark of the Covenant, captured by the Philistines; see 1 Sam. 4.1–7.1. **65–72:** Perhaps this section refers to the destruction of the Northern Kingdom in 721 B.C.E., 2 Kgs. 17.3–6; perhaps, as some suggest, it reflects the Samaritan schism of the age of Ezra and Nehemiah. **65:** *The Lord awoke:* compare 44.23 n. and 59.5. **68:** *Judah:* the tribe to which David belonged. **69:** 1 Kgs. chs. 6–8. **70–71:** 1 Sam. 16.1–14.

Ps. 79: How long, LORD. A national Lament after invaders have defiled the temple and devastated Jerusalem. **3:** An unburied corpse was a great indignity to the dead person (Tob. 1.17–19) and made the whole place

5 How long, LORD, will you be roused to
  such fury?
  How long will your indignation blaze
    like a fire?
6 Pour out your wrath on nations that do
    not acknowledge you,
  on kingdoms that do not call on you by
    name,
7 for they have devoured Jacob and left
    his homeland a waste.
8 Do not remember against us the guilt
    of past generations;
  rather let your compassion come swiftly
    to meet us,
  for we have been brought so low.

9 Help us, God our saviour, for the
    honour of your name;
  for your name's sake rescue us and
    wipe out our sins.
10 Why should the nations ask, 'Where is
    their God?'
  Before our very eyes may those nations
    know
  your vengeance for the slaughter of
    your servants.

11 Let the groaning of the captives reach
    your presence
  and in your great might save those
    under sentence of death.
12 Turn back sevenfold on their own
    heads, Lord,
  the contempt our neighbours pour on
    you.
13 Then we, your people, the flock which
    you shepherd,
  will give you thanks for ever
  and repeat your praise to all
    generations.

80 *For the leader: set to 'Lilies': a testimony:
    for Asaph: a psalm*
1 HEAR us, Shepherd of Israel,
  leading Joseph like a flock.

Shine forth, as you sit enthroned on
  the cherubim.
2 Leading Ephraim, Benjamin, and
    Manasseh,
  rouse your might and come to our
    rescue.
3 God, restore us,
  and make your face shine on us, that
    we may be saved.

4 LORD God of Hosts,
  how long will you fume at your
    people's prayer?
5 You have made sorrow their daily
    bread
  and copious tears their drink.
6 You have made us an object of
    contempt to our neighbours,
  and a laughing-stock to our enemies.
7 God of Hosts, restore us,
  and make your face shine on us, that
    we may be saved.

8 You brought a vine from Egypt;
  you drove out nations and planted it;
9 you cleared the ground for it,
  so that it struck root and filled the
    land.
10 The mountains were covered with its
    shade,
  and its branches were like those of
    mighty cedars.
11 It put out boughs all the way to the sea,
  its shoots as far as the river.
12 Why have you broken down the
    vineyard wall
  so that every passer-by can pluck its
    fruit?
13 The wild boar from the thicket gnaws
    it,
  and wild creatures of the countryside
    feed on it.

80:5 **copious:** *Heb.* threefold.

unclean; see Num. 19.11–16. **5:** Israel aroused God to *indignation*, literally "jealousy," by their acceptance
of other gods and religious practices; see Deut. 4.23–24; 5.9. **7:** *Jacob*, the father of the twelve patriarchs, is
the ancestor of the Israelites and here a symbol for the nation.
  Ps. 80: Hear us, Shepherd of Israel. A group Lament, possibly composed shortly after the fall of the Northern
Kingdom in 721 B.C.E. The parts are indicated by the refrain found three times (vv. 3, 7, 19); for the phrase *make
your face shine,* see Ps. 4.6 n. **1:** *Cherubim:* see 1 Sam. 4.4. **2:** *Ephraim* and *Manasseh* were the sons of Joseph
who gave their names to the two principal tribes of the Northern Kingdom. The tribe of *Benjamin,* Joseph's
younger brother, was often associated with them. **8–16:** Israel is the *vine,* a frequent figure; see Hos. 10.1 and
compare Isa. 5.1–7. **11:** *The sea:* the Mediterranean. *The river:* the Euphrates. **12:** *The vineyard wall* serves

14 God of Hosts, turn to us, we pray;
    look down from heaven and see.
    Tend this vine,
15 this stock which your right hand has
    planted.
16 May those who set it on fire and cut it
    down
    perish before your angry look.
17 Let your hand rest on the one at your
    right side,
    the one whom you have made strong
    for your service.
18 Then we shall not turn back from you;
    grant us new life, and we shall invoke
    you by name.
19 LORD God of Hosts, restore us,
    and make your face shine on us, that
    we may be saved.

81 *For the leader: according to the gittith: for
    Asaph*
1 SING out in praise of God our refuge,
    acclaim the God of Jacob.
2 Raise a melody; beat the drum,
    play the tuneful lyre and harp.
3 At the new moon blow the ram's horn,
    and blow it at the full moon on the day
    of our pilgrim-feast.
4 This is a law for Israel,
    an ordinance of the God of Jacob,
5 laid as a solemn charge on Joseph
    at the exodus from Egypt.

    I hear an unfamiliar voice:
6 I lifted the load from his shoulders;
    his hands let go the builder's basket.
7 When you cried to me in distress, I
    rescued you;
    I answered you from the
    thunder-cloud.

    I put you to the test at the waters of
    Meribah.   [*Selah*
8 Listen, my people, while I give you a
    solemn charge —
    O that you would listen to me, Israel:
9 you shall have no foreign god
    nor bow down to an alien deity;
10 I am the LORD your God
    who brought you up from Egypt.
    Open your mouth, and I shall fill it.

11 But my people did not listen to my
    voice,
    Israel would have none of me;
12 so I let them go with their stubborn
    hearts
    to follow their own devices.

13 If my people would but listen to me,
    if Israel would only conform to my
    ways,
14 I should soon bring their enemies to
    their knees
    and turn my hand against their foes.
15 Those hostile to the LORD would come
    cringing to him,
    and meet with everlasting punishment,
16 while Israel would be fed with the
    finest flour
    and satisfied with honey from the
    rocks.

82 *A psalm: for Asaph*
1 GOD takes his place in the court
    of heaven
    to pronounce judgement among the
    gods:

80:15 **this stock . . . planted:** *prob. rdg; Heb. adds* and
on the son whom you have made strong for your
service (*cp. verse 17*).   81:1 **refuge:** *or* strength.

as God's protection. **17:** This may be a prayer for the king, or else *the one* is a figure for Israel. **18:** The vow usual in a Lament is here a promise to invoke God's name. It is overshadowed by the refrain in v. 19.

Ps. 81: Acclaim the God of Jacob. A Didactic Psalm used for a festival (possibly Passover or Booths), consisting of ritual prescriptions (vv. 1–5) and prophetic exhortation (vv. 6–15). **3:** It is not clear which *pilgrim-feast* is meant of the three ordained in the Pentateuch: Passover, Booths, or Weeks (Deut. 16.16). The first two fit the *full moon* prescription. **6–12:** The divine words were possibly spoken as an exhortation by a cultic prophet in a liturgical recitation. **7:** *When you cried to me:* see Exod. 3.7. *Thunder-cloud:* i.e. at Sinai. *Meribah:* see Exod. 17.7 and Ps. 95.8. **9–10:** *No foreign god:* the first of the Ten Commandments; Exod. 20.2–3. **13–15:** God's benefits to Israel are conditional on Israel's obedience and fidelity; compare 95.7–11.

Ps. 82: Arise and judge the earth. A Lament, or a Wisdom Psalm, possibly in a liturgical setting, in which a prophetic judgment against the unjust rulers of the world is given. **1:** *Court of heaven* as an assembly of *gods* (Heb. *elohim*), superhuman beings lesser than God, is found also in 89.5–7; Job 1.6 and elsewhere. Some scholars interpret "gods" (here and in v. 6) literally as a mythological motif taken over from Canaanite literature.

2 'How much longer will you judge
  unjustly
and favour the wicked? [*Selah*

3 Uphold the cause of the weak and the
  fatherless,
and see right done to the afflicted and
  destitute.

4 Rescue the weak and the needy,
and save them from the clutches of the
  wicked.'

5 But these gods know nothing and
  understand nothing,
they walk about in darkness;
meanwhile earth's foundations are all
  giving way.

6 'This is my sentence: Though you are
  gods,
all sons of the Most High,

7 yet you shall die as mortals die,
and fall as any prince does.'

8 God, arise and judge the earth,
for all the nations are yours.

83 *A song: a psalm: for Asaph*
¹ Do NOT keep silent, God;
be neither quiet, God, nor still,

2 for your enemies raise an uproar,
and those who are hostile to you carry
  their heads high.

3 They devise a cunning plot against your
  people
and conspire against those whom you
  treasure:

4 'Let us wipe them out as a nation,' they
  say;
'let the name of Israel be remembered
  no more.'

5 With one mind they have conspired

to form a league against you:

6 the families of Edom, the Ishmaelites,
  Moabites and Hagar's people,

7 Gebal, Ammon, and Amalek,
  Philistia and the citizens of Tyre.

8 Asshur too is their ally,
  lending aid to the descendants of Lot.
[*Selah*

9 Deal with them as with Sisera,
  as with Jabin by the wadi of Kishon,

10 who were vanquished and fell, as
  Midian fell at En-harod,
  and became manure on the ground.

11 Make their princes like Oreb and Zeeb,
  make all their nobles like Zebah and
  Zalmunna,

12 who said, 'We will seize for ourselves
  the territory of God's people.'

13 Scatter them, my God, like thistledown,
  like chaff blown before the wind.

14 As a fire raging through the forest,
  as flames which blaze across the hills,

15 so pursue them with your tempest,
  terrify them with your storm-wind.

16 Heap shame on their heads
  until, LORD, they seek your name.

17 Let them be humiliated, and live in
  constant terror;
  let them suffer disgrace and perish.

18 So let it be known that you, whose
  name is the LORD,
  are alone Most High over all the earth.

84 *For the leader: according to the gittith: for
the Korahites: a psalm*
¹ LORD of Hosts,

83:10 **as Midian:** *transposed from previous verse.*
En-harod: *prob. rdg; cp. Judg. 7:1; Heb. Endor.*

Others see it as a reference to human judges, as in Jn. 10.34. **2–7:** One explanation of evil in the world was that heavenly beings abused the power over the world given them by God. The divine words, possibly spoken by a prophet in a temple ceremony, contain a condemnation of these beings by God; this takes the place of the lamentation and the vow usual in a Lament.

Ps. 83: Do not keep silent, God. A Lament calling for vengeance on the nations which intended to destroy Israel. The exact historic situation is unclear; a loose connection with Ps. 79 is possible. A call for help (v. 1) arises from the aggressive plans of the nations (vv. 2–8); a plea follows for their destruction (vv. 9–18) as other foes were once destroyed (vv. 9–11). **6–7:** The enemies are neighboring nations, often mentioned in Scripture, except for the unclear *Hagar's people*. Since the Ishmaelites were descended from Hagar (Gen. 16.15), the name may be a synonym for Ishmaelites, a desert people. *Gebal* probably means the Phoenician city Byblos. An interesting variant from Masada reads "the gods of Edom" instead of *the families of Edom*. **8:** *Asshur* is clearly Assyria, but the allusion is not clear. Lot's *descendants* were Ammon and Moab (Gen. 19.30–38). **9:** *Sisera and Jabin:* see Judg. chs. 4–5. **10:** *Midian:* compare Judg. chs. 6–8. **11:** *Oreb . . . Zeeb:* Judg. 7.25. *Zebah and Zalmunna:* Judg. 8.21. **13–19:** A characteristic curse.

how dearly loved is your dwelling-place!
2 I pine and faint with longing
for the courts of the LORD's temple;
my whole being cries out with joy
to the living God.
3 Even the sparrow finds a home,
and the swallow has her nest
where she rears her brood beside your
altars,
LORD of Hosts, my King and God.

4 Happy are those who dwell in your
house;
they never cease to praise you!   [Selah
5 Happy those whose refuge is in you,
whose hearts are set on the pilgrim
ways!
6 As they pass through the waterless
valley
the LORD fills it with springs,
and the early rain covers it with pools.
7 So they pass on from outer wall to
inner,
and the God of gods shows himself in
Zion

8 LORD God of hosts, hear my prayer;
God of Jacob, listen.   [Selah
9 God, look upon our shield the king
and accept your anointed one with
favour.

10 Better one day in your courts
than a thousand days in my home;
better to linger by the threshold of
God's house
than to live in the dwellings of the
wicked.
11 The LORD God is a sun and shield;
grace and honour are his to bestow.
The LORD withholds no good thing
from those whose life is blameless.

12 O LORD of Hosts,
happy are they who trust in you!

85
For the leader: for the Korahites: a psalm
1 LORD, you have been gracious to
your land
and turned the tide of Jacob's fortunes.
2 You have forgiven the guilt of your
people
and put all their sins away.   [Selah
3 You have withdrawn all your wrath
and turned from your hot anger.

4 God our saviour, restore us
and abandon your displeasure towards
us.
5 Will you be angry with us for ever?
Must your wrath last for all
generations?
6 Will you not give us new life
that your people may rejoice in you?
7 LORD, show us your love
and grant us your deliverance.

8 Let me hear the words of God the
LORD:
he proclaims peace to his people and
loyal servants;
let them not go back to foolish ways.
9 Deliverance is near to those who
worship him,
so that glory may dwell in our land.
10 Love and faithfulness have come
together;
justice and peace have embraced.
11 Faithfulness appears from earth
and justice looks down from heaven.
12 The LORD will grant prosperity,
and our land will yield its harvest.
13 Justice will go in front of him,
and peace on the path he treads.

86
A prayer: for David
1 LISTEN, LORD, and give me an
answer,

84:10 **in my home:** *prob. rdg; Heb. obscure.*
85:13 **and peace . . . treads:** *prob. rdg; Heb. so that he
may put his feet to a way.*

Ps. 84: Happy are those who dwell in your house. A Hymn, probably sung by a pilgrim at the temple on
a festival. A prayer for the king (vv. 8–9) may be an addition. The praise of the temple (vv. 1–4) is followed
by an allusion to the pilgrim's journey (vv. 5–7), and an exaltation of the temple (vv. 10–12) closes the psalm.
6: *Waterless:* older translations interpreted the Heb. to mean "valley of weeping."

Ps. 85: Will you not give us new life? A national Lament (see Introduction), possibly composed during the
difficult times following the return from the Exile (see Neh. 5.1–5), as seems indicated by v. 2. **9:** *Glory* may
refer to the presence of God in the temple. God's presence left Jerusalem at the Exile and returned with the
captives; see Ezek. 11.23–24; 43.1–2. **10–11:** God's *love* and Israel's *faithfulness* are seen as a dialogue
between heaven and earth.

for I am oppressed and poor.
2 Guard me, for I am faithful;
save your servant who puts his trust in
  you.
You are my God. 3 Show me your
  favour, Lord;
I call to you all day long.
4 Fill your servant's heart with joy,
for to you, Lord, I lift up my heart.
5 Lord, you are kind and forgiving,
full of love towards all who cry to you.
6 LORD, listen to my prayer
and hear my pleading.
7 In the day of my distress I call to you,
for you will answer me.

8 Among the gods not one is like you,
  Lord;
no deeds compare with yours.
9 All the nations you have made
will come to bow before you, Lord,
and honour your name,
10 for you are great, and your works are
  wonderful;
you alone are God.

11 LORD, teach me your way,
that I may walk in your truth.
Let me worship your name with
  undivided heart.
12 I shall praise you, Lord my God, with
  all my heart
and give honour to your name for ever.
13 For your love towards me is great,
and you have rescued me from the
  depths of Sheol.
14 Violent men rise to attack me,
a band of ruthless men seeks my life;
they give no thought to you, my God.
15 But you, Lord, are God, compassionate
  and gracious,
long-suffering, ever faithful and true.
16 Turn to me and show me your favour;
grant your servant protection
and rescue your slave-girl's son.
17 Give me a sign of your favour;

let those who hate me see it and be
  abashed,
for you, LORD, have been my help and
  comfort.

87 *For the Korahites: a psalm: a song*
1 THE city the LORD founded stands
    on the holy hills.
2 He loves the gates of Zion
more than all the dwellings of Jacob.
3 Glorious things are spoken about you,
city of God.   [Selah

4 I shall count Rahab and Babylon
among those who acknowledge me;
of Philistines, Tyrians, and Nubians
it will be said, 'Such a one was born
  there.'
5 Of Zion it will be said,
'This one and that one were born
  there.'
The Most High himself establishes her.
6 The LORD will record in the register of
  the peoples:
this one was born there.   [Selah
7 Singers and dancers alike say,
'The source of all good is in you.'

88 *A song: a psalm: for the Korahites: for the*
     leader: set to 'Mahalath le-annoth': a
maskil: for Heman the Ezrahite
1 LORD, my God, by day I call for help,
by night I cry aloud in your presence.
2 Let my prayer come before you,
hear my loud entreaty;
3 for I have had my fill of woes,
which have brought me to the brink of
  Sheol.
4 I am numbered with those who go
  down to the abyss;
I have become like a man beyond help,
5 abandoned among the dead,
like the slain lying in the grave

86:13 **Sheol:** *or* the underworld.   87:1 **The city ...**
founded: *lit.* His foundation.   87:7 **The source ...**
good: *lit.* All my springs.   88:1 **I call for help:** *prob.*
rdg; Heb. my deliverance.   88:3 **Sheol:** *or* the
underworld.

Ps. 86: LORD, listen to my prayer. A Lament. **1:** *Oppressed:* perhaps to be taken literally, but more likely
the usual language of self-abasement. **13:** *Rescued me from the depths of Sheol:* saved my life from death. **16:**
Your slave-girl's son is the psalmist. See Ps. 116.5 n.

Ps. 87: City of God. A Hymn. *Zion,* the city of God, is the mother of the faithful of all the world. **4:** *Rahab:*
the sea dragon, a frequent figure for Egypt.

Ps. 88: Hear my loud entreaty. An extremely bitter Lament of a person desperately ill, perhaps from a life-long
sickness (v. 15). **3–5:** The psalmist considers life to be all but ended, *Sheol* and *abyss* being the place of the

whom you hold in mind no more,
who are cut off from your care.
6 You have plunged me into the lowest
abyss,
into the darkest regions of the depths.
7 Your wrath bears heavily on me,
you have brought on me all your fury.
                                    [Selah
8 You have removed my friends far from
me
and made me utterly loathsome to
them.
I am shut in with no escape;
9 my eyes are dim with anguish.
LORD, every day I have called to you
and stretched out my hands in prayer.

10 Will it be for the dead you work
wonders?
Or can the shades rise up and praise
you?   [Selah
11 Will they speak in the grave of your
love,
of your faithfulness in the tomb?
12 Will your wonders be known in the
region of darkness,
your victories in the land of oblivion?

13 But as for me, LORD, I cry to you,
my prayer comes before you in the
morning.
14 LORD, why have you cast me off,
why do you hide your face from me?
15 From childhood I have suffered and
been near to death;
I have borne your terrors, I am numb.
16 Your burning fury has swept over me,
your onslaughts have overwhelmed me;
17 all the day long they surge round me
like a flood,
from every side they close in on me.
18 You have taken friend and neighbour
far from me;
darkness is now my only companion.

89 A maskil: for Ethan the Ezrahite
1 I SHALL sing always of the loving
deeds of the LORD;

throughout every generation I shall
proclaim your faithfulness.
2 I said: Your love will stand firm for
ever;
in the heavens you have established
your faithfulness.

3 I have made a covenant with the one I
have chosen,
I have sworn on oath to my servant
David:
4 'I shall establish your line for ever,
I shall make your throne endure for all
generations.'   [Selah

5 Let the heavens praise your wonders,
LORD;
let the assembly of the angels exalt your
faithfulness.
6 In the skies who is there like the LORD,
who like the LORD in the court of
heaven,
7 a God dreaded in the council of the
angels,
great and terrible above all who stand
about him?
8 LORD God of Hosts, who is like you?
Your strength and faithfulness, LORD,
are all around you.
9 You rule the raging of the sea,
calming the turmoil of its waves.
10 You crushed and slew the monster
Rahab
and scattered your enemies with your
strong arm.

11 The heavens are yours, the earth yours
also;
you founded the world and all that is in
it.
12 You created the north and the south;
Tabor and Hermon echo your name.
13 Strength of arm and valour are yours;
your hand is mighty, your right hand
lifted high;

88:7 **fury:** *or* waves.   88:11 **the tomb:** *Heb.*
Abaddon.   88:15 **I am numb:** *prob. rdg; Heb.*
unintelligible.   89:7 **great:** *so Gk; Heb.* greatly.
89:8 **Your strength:** *prob. rdg; Heb. obscure.*

dead. **10–12:** A classic description of Sheol. The motive for securing God's healing is that no one can *praise*
God in the *grave*. **13:** The usual vow is the promise of *prayer*.

Ps. 89: How long will your wrath blaze like a fire? A Lament with a complicated structure, including a hymn
and a royal prayer for a lasting line (v. 36). **1–8:** A hymn of praise to the Creator-King. **5–7:** See 82.1 n. *Terrible:*
inspires terror. **9–10:** On the mythical language of creation see 74.12–17 n.; Isa. 51.9–10. **12:** *Tabor* is in
northern Israel, and *Hermon* in Syria, near Damascus. They were considered sacred in ancient myths as

14 your throne is founded on
  righteousness and justice;
love and faithfulness are in attendance
  on you.

15 Happy the people who have learnt to
  acclaim you,
who walk in the light of your
  countenance, LORD!
16 In your name they rejoice all day long;
  your righteousness will lift them up.
17 You are yourself the strength in which
  they glory;
through your favour we hold our heads
  high.
18 To the LORD belongs our shield,
  to the Holy One of Israel our king.

19 A time came when you spoke in a
  vision,
declaring to your faithful servant:
I have granted help to a warrior;
I have exalted one chosen from the
  people.
20 I have found David my servant
  and anointed him with my sacred oil.
21 My hand will be ready to help him,
  my arm to give him strength.
22 No enemy will outwit him,
  no wicked person will oppress him;
23 I shall crush his adversaries before him
  and strike down those who are hostile
  to him.
24 My faithfulness and love will be with
  him
and through my name he will hold his
  head high.
25 I shall establish his rule over the sea,
  his dominion over the rivers.
26 He will call to me, 'You are my father,
  my God, my rock where I find safety.'
27 I shall give him the rank of firstborn,
  highest among the kings of the earth.
28 I shall maintain my love for him for
  ever
and be faithful in my covenant with
  him.
29 I shall establish his line for ever

and his throne as long as the heavens
  endure.

30 If his children forsake my law
  and do not conform to my judgements,
31 if they violate my statutes
  and do not observe my commandments,
32 then I shall punish their disobedience
  with the rod,
their iniquity with lashes.
33 Yet I shall not deprive him of my love,
  nor swerve from my faithfulness;
34 I shall not violate my covenant,
  nor alter what I have promised.
35 I have sworn by my holiness once and
  for all,
I shall not break my word to David:
36 his posterity will continue for ever,
  his throne before me like the sun;
37 like the moon it will endure for ever,
  a faithful witness in the sky.   [Selah

38 Yet you have spurned your anointed
  one,
you have rejected him and raged
  against him,
39 you have renounced the covenant with
  your servant,
defiled his crown and flung it to the
  ground.
40 You have breached all his walls
  and laid his fortresses in ruins;
41 every passer-by plunders him,
  and he suffers his neighbours' taunts.
42 You have increased the power of his
  adversaries
and brought joy to all his foes;
43 you have driven back his drawn sword
  and left him without support in battle.
44 You have put an end to his splendour
  and hurled his throne to the ground;
45 you have cut short the days of his
  youth
and covered him as with a cloak of
  shame.   [Selah

46 How long, LORD, will you hide yourself
  from sight?

residences of the gods. **14:** *Righteousness, justice, love,* and *faithfulness* are the most characteristic attributes of God's covenant dealing with Israel. **18:** *Shield:* protector. **19–37:** God's words which proclaimed an eternal dynasty for David and his descendants, even should the latter fall into *disobedience* (v. 32); see 2 Sam. 7.12–16. **26–27:** *Firstborn:* the position of highest favor. **38–45:** A military defeat seems to have ended the king's rule and nullified *the covenant.* **46:** God's *wrath blazes* in hiding from human *sight,* i.e. experience.

How long will your wrath blaze like a
  fire?
47 Remember how fleeting is our life!
  Have you created all mankind to no
  purpose?
48 Who can live and not see death?
  Who can save himself from the power
  of Sheol?   [*Selah*
49 Where are your former loving deeds,
  Lord,
  which you promised faithfully to David?
50 Remember, Lord, the taunts hurled at
  your servant,
  how I have borne in my heart the
  calumnies of the nations;
51 for your enemies have taunted us,
  LORD,
  taunted your anointed king at every
  step.

52 Blessed be the LORD for ever.
  Amen and Amen.

Book 4

90 *A prayer: ascribed to Moses, the man of
God*
1 LORD, you have been our refuge
  throughout all generations.
2 Before the mountains were brought
  forth
  or the earth and the world were born,
  from age to age you are God.

3 You turn mortals back to dust,
  saying, 'Turn back, you children of
  mortals,'
4 for in your sight a thousand years
  are as the passing of one day
  or as a watch in the night.
5 You cut them off;
  they are asleep in death.
  They are like grass which shoots up;
6 though in the morning it flourishes and
  shoots up,
  by evening it droops and withers.

7 We are brought to an end by your
  anger,
  terrified by your wrath.
8 You set out our iniquities before you,
  our secret sins in the light of your
  presence.
9 All our days pass under your wrath;
  our years die away like a murmur.
10 Seventy years is the span of our life,
  eighty if our strength holds;
  at their best they are but toil and
  sorrow,
  for they pass quickly and we vanish.
11 Who feels the power of your anger,
  who feels your wrath like those who
  fear you?
12 So make us know how few are our
  days,
  that our minds may learn wisdom.

13 LORD, how long?
  Turn and show compassion to your
  servants.
14 Satisfy us at daybreak with your love,
  that we may sing for joy and be glad all
  our days.
15 Grant us days of gladness for the days
  you have humbled us,
  for the years when we have known
  misfortune.
16 May your saving acts appear to your
  servants,
  and your glory to their children.
17 May the favour of the Lord our God be
  on us.
  Establish for us all that we do,
  establish it firmly.

91 1 HE who lives in the shelter of the
  Most High,
  who lodges under the shadow of the
  Almighty,

89:48 **Sheol:** *or* the underworld.   89:50 **the
calumnies . . . nations:** *prob. rdg; Heb.* all of many
peoples.   90:1 **refuge:** *so some MSS; others*
dwelling-place.

47–51: Human fragility and God's faithfulness to the *promises* are motives for deliverance.
  Ps. 90: Make us know how few are our days. A Lament of the community in which the description of the
grievance is a wisdomlike reflection on the transient condition of human life (vv. 3–12) and God's involvement
in that condition to judge and deliver. **13–17:** The petition for deliverance has as its motive the prolonged
suffering of the past.
  Ps. 91: The shelter of the Most High. A psalm of trust in the Wisdom tradition. **1:** *Most High, Almighty, LORD,
God* represent different Heb. names for God. To know the name of a person indicates a deep knowledge of,

2 says of the LORD, 'He is my refuge and
      fortress,
   my God in whom I put my trust.'

3 He will rescue you
      from the fowler's snare and from
      deadly pestilence.
4 He will cover you with his wings;
      you will find refuge beneath his
      pinions.
   His truth will be a shield and buckler.
5 You will not fear the terrors abroad at
      night
   or the arrow that flies by day,
6 the pestilence that stalks in darkness
   or the plague raging at noonday.
7 A thousand may fall at your side,
      ten thousand close at hand,
   but you it will not touch.
8 With your own eyes you will observe
      this;
   you will see the retribution on the
      wicked.
9 Surely you are my refuge, LORD.

   You have made the Most High your
      dwelling-place;
10 no disaster will befall you,
    no calamity touch your home.
11 For he will charge his angels
    to guard you wherever you go,
12 to lift you on their hands
    for fear you strike your foot against a
      stone.
13 You will tread on asp and cobra,
    you will trample on snake and serpent.

14 Because his love holds fast to me, I
      shall deliver him;
    I shall lift him to safety, for he knows
      my name.

15 When he calls to me, I shall answer;
    I shall be with him in time of trouble;
    I shall rescue him and bring him to
      honour.
16 I shall satisfy him with long life
    and show him my salvation.

92   *A psalm: a song: for the sabbath day*
      1 IT is good to give thanks to the
         LORD,
   to sing psalms to your name, Most
      High,
2 to declare your love in the morning
   and your faithfulness every night
3 to the music of a ten-stringed harp,
   to the sounding chords of the lyre.
4 Your acts, LORD, fill me with exultation;
   I shout in triumph at your mighty
      deeds.
5 How great are your deeds, LORD,
   how very deep are your thoughts!

6 Anyone who does not grasp this is a
      stupid person,
   and a fool does not understand it:
7 that though the wicked grow like grass
   and every evildoer prospers,
   they will be finally destroyed,
8 while you, LORD, reign for ever.
9 Your enemies, LORD, your enemies will
      perish;
   all evildoers will be scattered.

10 You have raised my head high
    like the horns of a wild ox;
    I am anointed richly with oil.
11 I look on my enemies' ruin,
    I hear the downfall of my wicked foes.
12 The righteous flourish like a palm tree,
    they grow tall as a cedar on Lebanon;
13 planted in the house of the LORD,

and access to, the person; see v. 14. **6:** *Pestilence* and *plague:* considered demonic powers in Israelite belief.
11–12: Used in Matt. 4.6; Lk. 4.10–11. **14–16:** The words are God's, perhaps in an oracle spoken by a priest
in the temple; they reflect the Wisdom teaching that God tests the virtuous by their suffering, but in the end
will *deliver* them.

   Ps. 92: It is good to give thanks. A Thanksgiving Psalm which has a hymn of praise for introduction (vv. 1–5)
and a Wisdom-tradition description of the "two ways of human life," good rewarded and evil punished. **8–9:**
God, Creator-King, having defeated the cosmic powers, reigns forever. This is one of several echoes in Psalms
of a common ancient myth. Many scholars view the tripartite structure of v. 9 as a parallel to a "tricolon" found
in a Ugaritic text (68.8–9) describing Baal's defeat of the Sea: "Lo, your enemies, O Baal, Lo your enemies
you will smite, Lo, you will vanquish your foes." **10:** *Horns of a wild ox:* symbol of strength; *anointed with
oil:* symbol of well-being and prosperity. **13:** Other passages (e.g. 52.8; Exod. 15.17) speak of righteous people
as *planted* in God's house.

and flourishing in the courts of our
God,
14 they still bear fruit in old age;
they are luxuriant, wide-spreading
trees.
15 They declare that the Lord is just:
my rock, in him there is no
unrighteousness.

93 ¹ THE LORD has become King,
clothed with majesty;
the LORD is robed, girded with might.

The earth is established immovably;
² your throne is established from of old;
from all eternity you are God.
³ LORD, the great deep lifts up,
the deep lifts up its voice;
the deep lifts up its crashing waves.
⁴ Mightier than the sound of great
waters,
mightier than the breakers of the sea,
mighty on high is the LORD.

⁵ Your decrees stand firm,
and holiness befits your house,
LORD, throughout the ages.

94 ¹ GOD of vengeance, LORD,
God of vengeance, show yourself!
² Rise, judge of the earth;
repay the arrogant as they deserve.
³ LORD, how long will the wicked,
how long will the wicked exult?
⁴ Evildoers are all full of bluster,
boasting and bragging.

⁵ They crush your people, LORD,
and oppress your chosen nation;
⁶ they murder the widow and the
stranger
and put the fatherless to death.

⁷ They say, 'The LORD does not see,
the God of Jacob pays no heed.'
⁸ Take heed yourselves, most stupid of
people;
you fools, when will you be wise?
⁹ Can he who implanted the ear not
hear,
he who fashioned the eye not see?
10 Will he who instructs the nations not
correct them?
The teacher of mankind, has he no
knowledge?
11 The LORD knows that the thoughts of
everyone
are but a puff of wind.

12 Happy the one whom you, LORD,
instruct
and teach from your law,
13 giving him respite from misfortune
until a pit is dug for the wicked.
14 The LORD will not abandon his people
or forsake his chosen nation;
15 for justice will again be joined to right,
and all who are upright in heart will
follow it.

16 Who is on my side against the wicked?
Who will stand up for me against the
evildoers?
17 Had the LORD not been my helper,
I should soon have dwelt in the silent
grave.
18 If I said that my foot was slipping,
your love, LORD, continued to hold me
up.
19 When anxious thoughts filled my heart,
your comfort brought me joy.
20 Will corrupt justice win you as an ally,
contriving mischief under cover of law?

93:2 **God:** *so Aram. (Targ.); Heb. omits.*

Ps. 93: The LORD has become King. An Enthronement Hymn, as are also Pss. 95–99 and 47; see 47 n. The theme of enthronement (vv. 1–2) moves (3–4) to a recollection of the cosmic warfare (symbolized by the control of the sea); see 74.12–17; 104.7–9; Job 38.8–11. **1:** *Girded with might:* as if to say that God is valiant in warfare; compare Exod. 15.3; Isa. 42.13. "King," "warrior," and "creator" are many times synonymous, and all are implied in this Hymn. **2–4:** God controls the sea, and hence secures order in all creation. **5:** *Holiness* is the divine quality of being removed from and beyond the profane and human.

Ps. 94: Rise, judge of the earth. It is difficult to say whether this psalm is a Thanksgiving in which former trials are described, or a Lament in which deliverance and thanksgiving are anticipated. There is an invocation of God to help (vv. 1–3); the description of the trials (if a Lament) is in the Wisdom motif of the "two ways" — the evil and their punishment (vv. 4–11) and the virtuous being tested and their reward (vv. 12–15). **20–21:** Under pious pretense of carrying out God's *law,* the powerful oppress the innocent weak; see 1 Kgs. 21.1–14.

21 They conspire to take the life of the
  righteous
and condemn the innocent to death.
22 But the LORD has been my strong
  tower,
and my God is my rock and refuge.
23 He will repay the wicked for their
  injustice;
the LORD our God will destroy them for
  their misdeeds.

95 ¹ COME! Let us raise a joyful song
    to the LORD,
a shout of triumph to the rock of our
  salvation.
² Let us come into his presence with
  thanksgiving
and sing psalms of triumph to him.

³ For the LORD is a great God,
a great King above all gods.
⁴ The depths of the earth are in his
  hands,
and the peaks of the mountains belong
  to him;
⁵ the sea is his, for he made it,
and the dry land which his hands
  fashioned.

⁶ Enter in! Let us bow down in worship,
let us kneel before the LORD who made
  us,
⁷ for he is our God,
we the people he shepherds, the flock
  in his care.

If only you would listen to him now!
⁸ Do not be stubborn, as you were at
  Meribah,
as on that day at Massah in the
  wilderness,

⁹ when your forefathers made trial of
  me,
tested me, though they had seen what I
  did.
¹⁰ For forty years I abhorred that
  generation
and said: 'They are a people whose
  hearts are astray,
who do not discern my ways.'
¹¹ Therefore I vowed in my anger:
'They shall never enter my rest.'

96 ¹ SING a new song to the LORD.
    Sing to the LORD, all the earth.
² Sing to the LORD and bless his name;
day by day proclaim his victory.
³ Declare his glory among the nations,
his marvellous deeds to every people.
⁴ Great is the LORD and most worthy of
  praise;
he is more to be feared than all gods.
⁵ For the gods of the nations are idols
  every one;
but the LORD made the heavens.
⁶ Majesty and splendour attend him,
might and beauty are in his sanctuary.

⁷ Ascribe to the LORD, you families of
  nations,
ascribe to the LORD glory and might;
⁸ ascribe to the LORD the glory due to his
  name.
Bring an offering and enter his courts;
⁹ in holy attire worship the LORD;
tremble before him, all the earth.
¹⁰ Declare among the nations, 'The LORD
  is King;
the world is established immovably;
he will judge the peoples with equity.'

95:8 **Meribah:** *that is* Dispute. **Massah:** *that is* Trial.

Ps. 95: The LORD is a great God. An Enthronement Hymn (see Ps. 47 n.) with the motif of God as king, expressed in a liturgical ceremony. **1:** God is the *rock of our salvation.* This may be in reference to the rock which gave water in the wilderness (Exod. 17.1–7) or the rock on which the temple stood; or it may be a metaphor for the sure faithfulness of God that gives security in the face of threats. **3–7:** God is *King* in virtue of being the Creator. **3:** *Gods:* see 82.1 n. **7:** Israel listened to God's voice speaking in nature and in the covenant. Verses 7b–11 are quoted in Heb. 3.7–11; 4.3–11. **8–9:** For the event at *Meribah* see Exod. 17.1–7; Num. 20.1–13. **10:** *Forty years* is usually symbolic of one *generation;* see Num. 14.33. **11:** *My rest:* land of Canaan; see Deut. 3.20; 12.10.

  Ps. 96: Sing a new song to the LORD. An Enthronement Hymn; see Ps. 47 n. It is found also in 1 Chr. 16.23–33 in a slightly different form. There it appears as used on the occasion of the movement of the Ark of the Covenant to Jerusalem. **4–6:** *Than all gods:* see 82.1 n.; 89.6–7. God as Creator is a usual motif in Enthronement psalms, as is God's *sanctuary.* **10–13:** A description of God as the divine *King,* Creator, and *judge.*

¹¹ Let the heavens rejoice and the earth
be glad,
let the sea resound and everything in it,
¹² let the fields exult and all that is in
them;
let all the trees of the forest shout for
joy
¹³ before the LORD when he comes,
when he comes to judge the earth.
He will judge the world with justice
and peoples by his faithfulness.

97 ¹ THE LORD has become King; let
the earth be glad,
let coasts and islands all rejoice.
² Cloud and thick mist enfold him,
righteousness and justice
are the foundation of his throne.
³ Fire goes ahead of him
and consumes his enemies all around.
⁴ His lightning-flashes light up the world;
the earth sees and trembles.
⁵ Mountains melt like wax at the LORD's
approach,
the Lord of all the earth.
⁶ The heavens proclaim his
righteousness,
and all peoples see his glory.
⁷ May those who worship images, those
who vaunt their idols,
may they all be put to shame.
Bow down, all you gods, before him!

⁸ Zion heard and rejoiced, LORD;
Judah's cities were glad at your
judgements.
⁹ For you, LORD, are Most High over all
the earth,
far exalted above all gods.

¹⁰ The LORD loves those who hate evil;
he keeps his loyal servants safe
and rescues them from the power of
the wicked.

¹¹ A harvest of light has arisen for the
righteous,
and joy for the upright in heart.
¹² You that are righteous, rejoice in the
LORD
and praise his holy name.

98 *A psalm*
¹ SING a new song to the LORD,
for he has done marvellous deeds;
his right hand and his holy arm have
won him victory.
² The LORD has made his victory known;
he has displayed his saving
righteousness to all the nations.
³ He has remembered his love for Jacob,
his faithfulness towards the house of
Israel.
All the ends of the earth have seen
the victory of our God.

⁴ Acclaim the LORD, all the earth;
break into songs of joy, sing psalms.
⁵ Sing psalms in the LORD's honour with
the lyre,
with the lyre and with resounding
music,
⁶ with trumpet and echoing horn
acclaim the presence of the LORD our
King.
⁷ Let the sea resound and everything in
it,
the world and those who dwell there.
⁸ Let the rivers clap their hands,
let the mountains sing aloud together
⁹ before the LORD; for he comes
to judge the earth.
He will judge the world with justice
and the peoples with equity.

97:10 **The LORD loves:** *prob. rdg; Heb.* Lovers of the
LORD.   97:11 **has arisen:** *so Gk; Heb.* is sown.
98:3 **for Jacob:** *so Gk; Heb.* omits.

Ps. 97: The LORD has become King. An Enthronement Hymn with motifs of God's future final victory and rule over all peoples (vv. 1–7); see Ps. 47 n. **2–6:** The images employed here occur in other psalms; see 18.7–15; 50.1–3. **9:** *Above all gods:* see 82.1 n.; 89.6–7.

Ps. 98: The LORD our King. An Enthronement Hymn (Ps. 47 n.) with motifs of God's final judgment and establishment of "peoples with equity" (v. 9). The themes in this and other Enthronement psalms are frequent in Isa. chs. 40–55, e.g. 41.1–5. **1:** *God's right hand ... won ... victory,* both initially and most decisively, over chaos at the time of creation. **2–3:** God's creative power is continued by characteristic qualities in dealing with Israel: *righteousness, love, faithfulness,* justice (v. 9). **5–6:** A flourish of *trumpets* accompanies God's enthronement here as it did at the making of the covenant on Sinai (Exod. 19.16), in the manner of the coronation of the kings of Israel; see 2 Sam. 15.10; 1 Kgs. 1.34. **7–9:** Compare, e.g. 96.7–13 and Isa. 55.12–13.

99

¹THE LORD has become King; let
peoples tremble.
He is enthroned on the cherubim; let
the earth shake.
²The LORD is great in Zion;
he is exalted above all the peoples.
³Let them extol your great and terrible
name.
Holy is he.

⁴The King in his might loves justice.
You have established equity;
you have dealt justly and righteously in
Jacob.
⁵Exalt the LORD our God
and bow down at his footstool.
Holy is he.

⁶Moses and Aaron were among his
priests,
and Samuel was among those who
invoked his name;
they called to the LORD, and he
answered them.
⁷He spoke to them in a pillar of cloud;
they kept his decrees and the statute he
gave them.

⁸O LORD our God, you answered them;
you were a God who forgave them,
yet you called them to account for their
misdeeds.
⁹Exalt the LORD our God,
and bow down towards his holy
mountain;
for holy is the LORD our God.

100

A psalm: for thanksgiving
¹LET all the earth acclaim the
LORD!
²Worship the LORD in gladness;
enter his presence with joyful songs.
³Acknowledge that the LORD is God;
he made us and we are his,
his own people, the flock which he
shepherds.

⁴Enter his gates with thanksgiving,
his courts with praise.
Give thanks to him and bless his name;
⁵for the LORD is good and his love is
everlasting,
his faithfulness endures to all
generations.

101

For David: a psalm
¹I SHALL sing of loyalty and
justice,
as I raise a psalm to you, LORD.

²I shall lead a wise and blameless life;
when will you come to me?
My conduct among my household will
be blameless.
³I shall not set before my eyes any
shameful thing;
I hate apostasy, and will have none of
it.
⁴I shall banish all crooked thoughts,
and will have no dealings with evil.
⁵I shall silence those who whisper
slanders;
I cannot endure the proud and the
arrogant.
⁶I shall choose for my companions the
faithful in the land;
my servants will be those whose lives
are blameless.
⁷No treacherous person will live in my
household;
no liar will establish himself in my
presence.
⁸Morning after morning I shall reduce
all the wicked to silence,
ridding the LORD's city of all evildoers.

102

*A prayer: for the afflicted one when he
is faint and pours out his complaint
before the LORD*
¹LORD, hear my prayer
and let my cry for help come to you.
²Do not hide your face from me
when I am in dire straits.

Ps. 99: Holy is the LORD our God. An Enthronement Hymn (see 47 n.) with emphasis on God's holiness (vv. 4, 5, and 9). **1:** *Cherubim:* see Exod. 25.18–22. **4:** God's holiness is demonstrated in the moral or social sphere. **6–8:** *Moses* (Exod. 32.30–35), *Aaron* (Num. 16.46–50), and *Samuel* (1 Sam. 7.8–9) interceded with God and were favorably answered.

Ps. 100: The LORD is God. Some regard it as a deliberate close of the collection of Enthronement hymns: Pss. 93, 95–99. It carries on the themes of these other, longer psalms.

Ps. 101: A wise and blameless life. A Royal Psalm. It may represent the king's vow at the time of the coronation. In much biblical thought, the king is viewed as God's representative on earth. Hence, a proper

Listen to my prayer
and, when I call, be swift to reply;
3 for my days vanish like smoke,
my body is burnt up as in an oven.
4 I am stricken, withered like grass;
I neglect to eat my food.
5 I groan aloud;
I am just skin and bone.

6 I am like a desert-owl in the wilderness,
like an owl that lives among ruins.
7 I lie awake and have become like a bird
solitary on a rooftop.
8 My enemies taunt me the whole day
long;
mad with rage, they conspire against
me.
9 I have eaten ashes for bread
and mingled tears with my drink.
10 In furious anger
you have taken me up only to fling me
aside.
11 My days decline like shadows
lengthening;
I wither away like grass.

12 But you, LORD, are enthroned for ever;
your fame will endure to all
generations.
13 You will arise and have mercy on Zion,
for it is time to pity her;
the appointed time has come.
14 Her very stones are dear to your
servants,
and even her dust moves them to pity.
15 The nations will revere your name,
LORD,
and all earthly kings your glory,
16 when the LORD builds Zion again
and shows himself in his glory,
17 when he turns to hear the prayer of the
destitute

and does not spurn their prayer.

18 This will be written down for future
generations,
that people yet unborn may praise the
LORD:
19 'The LORD looks down from his
sanctuary on high;
from heaven he surveys the earth
20 to hear the groaning of the prisoners
and set free those under sentence of
death.'
21 So shall the LORD's name be declared in
Zion
and his praise told in Jerusalem,
22 when peoples are assembled together,
and kingdoms, to serve the LORD.

23 He has broken my strength before my
course is run;
he has cut short the time allotted me.
24 I say, 'Do not carry me off before half
my days are done,
for your years extend through all
generations.'
25 Long ago you laid earth's foundations,
and the heavens were your handiwork.
26 They will pass away, but you remain;
like clothes they will all wear out;
you will cast them off like a cloak
and they will vanish.
27 But you are the same and your years
will have no end.
28 The children of those who serve you
will continue,
and their descendants will be
established in your presence.

103 For David
1 BLESS the LORD, my soul;
with all my being I bless his holy name.
2 Bless the LORD, my soul,

king needed to display the qualities attributed to God. Here the king offers such assurance. **8:** *The LORD's city:* probably Jerusalem, but it can refer more restrictively to the temple and palace quarter.

Ps. 102: Let my cry for help come to you. A Lament (see Introduction). One of seven "Penitential Psalms" (see Ps. 130 n.). The first section (vv. 1–11) contains an individual's cry for deliverance from sickness and loneliness; next (vv. 12–22) there is an appeal to God to have mercy on and rebuild Zion. Finally (vv. 23–28) there is another individual cry for help, as from someone who is ill; it contrasts the brevity of human life with the eternity of God in the manner of Wisdom literature (see Ecclus. ch. 17). **2:** *Do not hide your face:* see 4.6 n. and 10.11. **14:** *Stones . . . dust:* possibly an allusion to the temple lying in ruins. **19:** *Sanctuary on high:* God's abode in heaven. **25–27:** These verses are taken up in Heb. 1.10–12. **27:** *The same:* lit. "You are the one." **28:** Assurance, at least to the children of the one praying.

Ps. 103: Bless the LORD, all created things. A Hymn in which the poet's thanksgiving for healing (vv. 3–5) overflows into a universal praise for all God's goodness to Israel (vv. 6–10) and to everyone (vv. 11–18). **1:**

and forget none of his benefits.
³ He pardons all my wrongdoing
and heals all my ills.
⁴ He rescues me from death's pit
and crowns me with love and
compassion.
⁵ He satisfies me with all good in the
prime of life,
and my youth is renewed like an
eagle's.

⁶ The LORD is righteous in all he does;
he brings justice to all who have been
wronged.
⁷ He revealed his ways to Moses,
his mighty deeds to the Israelites.
⁸ The LORD is compassionate and
gracious,
long-suffering and ever faithful;
⁹ he will not always accuse
or nurse his anger for ever.
¹⁰ He has not treated us as our sins
deserve
or repaid us according to our misdeeds.
¹¹ As the heavens tower high above the
earth,
so outstanding is his love towards those
who fear him.
¹² As far as east is from west,
so far from us has he put away our
offences.
¹³ As a father has compassion on his
children,
so the LORD has compassion on those
who fear him;
¹⁴ for he knows how we were made,
he remembers that we are but dust.

¹⁵ The days of a mortal are as grass;
he blossoms like a wild flower in the
meadow:

¹⁶ a wind passes over him, and he is gone,
and his place knows him no more.
¹⁷ But the LORD's love is for ever on those
who fear him,
and his righteousness on their posterity,
¹⁸ on those who hold fast to his covenant,
who keep his commandments in mind.

¹⁹ The LORD has established his throne in
heaven,
his kingly power over the whole world.
²⁰ Bless the LORD, you his angels,
mighty in power, who do his bidding
and obey his command.
²¹ Bless the LORD, all you his hosts,
his ministers who do his will.
²² Bless the LORD, all created things,
everywhere in his dominion.

Bless the LORD, my soul.

104

¹ BLESS the LORD, my soul.
LORD my God, you are very
great,
clothed in majesty and splendour,
² and enfolded in a robe of light.
You have spread out the heavens like a
tent,
³ and laid the beams of your dwelling on
the waters;
you take the clouds for your chariot,
riding on the wings of the wind;
⁴ you make the winds your messengers,
flames of fire your servants;
⁵ you fixed the earth on its foundation
so that it will never be moved.
⁶ The deep covered it like a cloak,
and the waters stood above the
mountains.
⁷ At your rebuke they fled,

Bless the LORD: give praise and thanks. **3:** *Wrongdoing* and *ills* were linked together in a causal relationship.
5: An *eagle's* strength was thought to be renewed with molting. **6–8:** These verses contain the heart of OT
piety, for they show the characteristic qualities of God's dealing with Israel as revealed to Moses: *righteous,
compassionate, gracious, long-suffering, ever faithful,* bringing *justice* to the *wronged;* see Exod. 34.6. **16:** The
hot *wind* from the desert wilts all vegetation in its path. **19:** *Throne in heaven:* compare 102.19.
    Ps. 104: By your wisdom you have made them all. A creation Hymn often compared to the Egyptian "Hymn
to Aton" and to the Mesopotamian Creation Epic since it uses similar mythological language. Perhaps Pss.
104–105 were used together in the temple liturgy, providing a sequence of movement from God's majesty
in the universe (Ps. 104) to God's historic deeds on behalf of Israel (105.5–45); see vv. 31–35 n. **3:** The *beams*
of God's *dwelling,* were thought to rest above the reservoir of water contained in the vault of heaven (29.10),
just as the earth is established on the waters below it; see Gen. 1.6–8. **6–9:** God controls the sea, having fixed
a *boundary* for it, making Leviathan, the wild sea monster who symbolizes the unruly sea of the original chaos,

at the sound of your thunder they
　rushed away,
8 flowing over the hills,
　pouring down into the valleys
　to the place appointed for them.
9 You fixed a boundary which they were
　not to pass;
　they were never to cover the earth
　again.

10 You make springs break out in the
　wadis,
　so that water from them flows between
　the hills.
11 The wild beasts all drink from them,
　the wild donkeys quench their thirst;
12 the birds of the air nest on their banks
　and sing among the foliage.

13 From your dwelling you water the hills;
　the earth is enriched by your provision.
14-15 You make grass grow for the cattle
　and plants for the use of mortals,
　producing grain from the earth,
　food to sustain their strength,
　wine to gladden the hearts of the
　people,
　and oil to make their faces shine.
16 The trees of the LORD flourish,
　the cedars of Lebanon which he
　planted;
17 birds build their nests in them,
　the stork makes her home in their tops.
18 High hills are the haunt of the
　mountain goat,
　and crags a cover for the rock-badger.

19 He created the moon to mark the
　seasons,
　and makes the sun know when to set.
20 You bring darkness, and it is night,
　when all the beasts of the forest go
　prowling;
21 the young lions roar for prey,
　seeking their food from God;
22 when the sun rises, they slink away
　and seek rest in their lairs.
23 Man goes out to his work
　and his labours until evening.

24 Countless are the things you have
　made, LORD;
　by your wisdom you have made them
　all;
　the earth is full of your creatures.
25 Here is the vast immeasurable sea,
　in which move crawling things beyond
　number,
　living creatures great and small.
26 Here ships sail to and fro;
　here is Leviathan which you have made
　to sport there.

27 All of them look to you in hope
　to give them their food when it is due.
28 What you give them they gather up;
　when you open your hand, they eat
　their fill of good things.
29 When you hide your face, they are
　dismayed.
　When you take away their spirit, they
　die
　and return to the dust from which they
　came.
30 When you send forth your spirit, they
　are created,
　and you give new life to the earth.

31 May the glory of the LORD stand for
　ever,
　and may the LORD rejoice in his works!
32 When he looks at the earth, it quakes;
　when he touches the mountains, they
　pour forth smoke.

33 As long as I live I shall sing to the
　LORD;
　I shall sing psalms to my God all my
　life long.
34 May my meditation be acceptable to
　him;
　I shall delight in the LORD.
35 May sinners be banished from the earth
　and may the wicked be no more!

Bless the LORD, my soul.
Praise the LORD.

104:17 **in their tops:** *prob. rdg; Heb.* the pine trees.

into a plaything (v. 26); compare 74.12–17 n. **10–26:** The order God brought out of chaos is marvelous and
benign. **27–30:** God's continued creative presence prevents a return to chaos. **30:** God's *spirit,* or breath, is
the source of all *life* (v. 30); see Gen. 1.2; 2.7. **31–35:** A prayer that all may continue beneficently for the
righteous. It ends with *Bless the LORD, my soul,* thus beginning and closing in the same way. The final phrase,
praise the LORD (in Heb. *Hallelujah*), may belong to Ps. 105 at its beginning.

105

¹Give thanks to the Lord,
invoke him by name;
make known his deeds among the
peoples.
²Pay him honour with song and psalm
and tell of all his marvellous deeds.
³Exult in his hallowed name;
let those who seek the Lord be joyful
in heart.
⁴Look to the Lord and be strong;
at all times seek his presence.

⁵⁻⁶You offspring of Abraham his servant,
the children of Jacob, his chosen ones,
remember the marvels he has wrought,
his portents, and the judgements he has
given.

⁷He is the Lord our God;
his judgements cover the whole world.
⁸He is ever mindful of his covenant,
the promise he ordained for a thousand
generations,
⁹the covenant made with Abraham,
his oath given to Isaac,
¹⁰and confirmed as a statute for Jacob,
as an everlasting covenant for Israel:
¹¹'I shall give you the land of Canaan', he
said,
'as your allotted holding.'

¹²A small company it was,
few in number, strangers in that land,
¹³roaming from nation to nation,
from one kingdom to another;
¹⁴but he let no one oppress them;
on their account he rebuked kings:
¹⁵'Do not touch my anointed servants,' he
said;
'do no harm to my prophets.'

¹⁶He called down famine on the land
and cut off their daily bread.
¹⁷But he had sent on a man before them,
Joseph, who was sold into slavery,
¹⁸where they thrust his feet into fetters

and clamped an iron collar round his
neck.
¹⁹He was tested by the Lord's command
until what he foretold took place.
²⁰The king sent and had him released,
the ruler of peoples set him free
²¹and made him master of his household,
ruler over all his possessions,
²²to correct his officers as he saw fit
and teach his counsellors wisdom.

²³Then Israel too went down into Egypt,
Jacob came to live in the land of Ham.
²⁴There God made his people very
fruitful,
too numerous for their enemies,
²⁵whose hearts he turned to hatred of his
people,
to double-dealing with his servants.

²⁶He sent his servant Moses
and Aaron whom he had chosen.
²⁷They were appointed to announce his
signs,
his portents in the land of Ham.
²⁸He sent darkness, and all was dark,
but still the Egyptians resisted his
commands.
²⁹He turned all the water to blood,
so causing the fish to die.
³⁰Their land swarmed with frogs,
even in the royal apartments.
³¹At his command there came swarms of
flies
and maggots throughout their land.
³²He sent showers of hail,
and lightning flashing over their
country.
³³He blasted their vines and their fig
trees
and shattered the trees throughout
their territory.
³⁴At his command the locusts came,
hoppers past all numbering;

105:4 **be strong:** *so Gk; Heb.* his strength.

Ps. 105: Remember the marvels that God has wrought. A Hymn celebrating God's action in Israel's history.
It could have been used at any of the major festivals; vv. 1–15 are used in 1 Chr. 16.8–22 for the transfer of
the Ark of the Covenant to Jerusalem. While nothing is mentioned specifically of the events at Sinai, the themes
of *covenant* (v. 8) and of *laws* and *statutes* (v. 45) presuppose Sinai and form the framework of the historical
recital. **5:** *Judgements:* God's decisive actions in behalf of Israel, the *sons of Jacob.* **8–15:** The *roaming* of
Abraham, Isaac and *Jacob from nation to nation* is narrated in Gen. 12.1–37.1. **15:** The ancestors are called
anointed servants inasmuch as they were filled with the spirit of the Lord, like the *prophets;* compare Isa. 61.1.
16–23: The story of *Joseph;* see Gen. chs. 37, 39–50. **24–43:** The Exodus and God's guidance in the

35 they devoured every green thing in the
  land,
 eating up all the produce of the soil.
36 Then he struck down all the firstborn
  in the land,
 the firstfruits of all their manhood.

37 He led his people out, laden with silver
  and gold,
 and among all their tribes not one
  person fell.
38 The Egyptians were glad to see them
  go,
 for fear of Israel had seized them.
39 He spread a cloud as a screen for them,
 and fire to light up the night.
40 When they asked, he sent them quails;
 he gave them bread of heaven in
  plenty.
41 He opened a rock and water gushed
  out,
 flowing in a stream through a parched
  land;
42 for he was mindful of his solemn
  promise
 to his servant Abraham.

43 He led out his people rejoicing,
 his chosen ones in triumph.
44 He gave them the lands of heathen
  nations;
 they took possession where others had
  toiled,
45 so that they might keep his statutes
 and obey his laws.

Praise the LORD.

106   1 PRAISE the LORD.

It is good to give thanks to the LORD,
 for his love endures for ever.
2 Who can tell of the LORD's mighty acts
 and make all his praises heard?
3 Happy are they who act justly,
 who do what is right at all times!

4 Remember me, LORD, when you show
  favour to your people;
 look on me when you save them,
5 that I may see the prosperity of your
  chosen ones,
 that I may rejoice in your nation's joy
 and exult with your own people.

6 Like our forefathers we have sinned,
 we have gone astray and done wrong.
7 Our forefathers in Egypt disregarded
  your marvels;
 they were not mindful of your many
  acts of love,
 and on their journey they rebelled by
  the Red Sea.
8 Yet the LORD delivered them for his
  name's sake
 and so made known his mighty power.
9 He rebuked the Red Sea, and it dried
  up;
 he led his people through the deep as
  through a desert.
10 He delivered them from those who
  hated them,
 and rescued them from the enemy's
  hand.
11 The waters closed over their
  adversaries;
 not one of them survived.
12 Then they believed what he had said
 and sang his praises.

13 But they soon forgot all he had done
 and would not wait to hear his counsel;
14 their greed was insatiable in the
  wilderness,
 there in the desert they tried God's
  patience.
15 He gave them what they asked,
 but followed it with a wasting sickness.

16 In the camp they were envious of
  Moses,

106:7 **on their journey:** *so Gk; Heb.* by the sea. **Red Sea:** *or* sea of Reeds.

wilderness; see Exod. 1.1–17.6. **27:** *Ham:* Egypt, as in 78.51; see Gen. 10.6. **44–45:** The settlement in the land.

Ps. 106: Deliver us, LORD our God. A Lament (see Introduction) of the community, in a liturgical setting, in which the recitation of the adversity is a national confession of sins which brought on various punishments, ending in the crowning adversity of being scattered among the nations in the Exile. The psalm closes Book 4. **1–5:** The invitation to *praise the LORD* seems to be in the course of a worship. **6:** To have *sinned* against God is the greatest calamity to have befallen Israel; this is the theme of the psalm. **7–12:** Story of the Exodus; see 105.24–43 n. **13–15:** Manna and the quails: Num. 11.4–15, 31–34. **16–18:** *Dathan* and *Abiram:* Num.

and of Aaron, who was consecrated to
the LORD.
17 The earth opened and swallowed
Dathan;
it closed over the company of Abiram.
18 Fire raged through their company;
the wicked perished in flames.

19 At Horeb they made a calf
and worshipped this image;
20 they exchanged their God
for the image of a bull that feeds on
grass.
21 They forgot God their deliverer,
who had done great things in Egypt,
22 such marvels in the land of Ham,
awesome deeds at the Red Sea.
23 So he purposed to destroy them,
but Moses, the man he had chosen,
stood before him in the breach
to prevent his wrath from destroying
them.

24 Disbelieving his promise,
they rejected the pleasant land.
25 They muttered treason in their tents,
and would not obey the LORD.
26 So with hand uplifted against them he
made an oath
to strike them down in the wilderness,
27 to scatter their descendants among the
nations
and disperse them throughout the
lands.

28 They joined in worshipping the Baal of
Peor
and ate meat sacrificed to lifeless gods.
29 Their deeds provoked the LORD to
anger,
and plague broke out amongst them;
30 but Phinehas stood up and intervened,
and the plague was checked.
31 This was counted to him as
righteousness
throughout the generations ever
afterwards.

32 They roused the LORD's anger at the
waters of Meribah,

and it went ill with Moses because of
them;
33 for when they had embittered his spirit
he spoke rashly.
34 They did not destroy the nations
as the LORD had commanded them to
do,
35 but they associated with the people
and learnt their ways;
36 they worshipped their idols
and were ensnared by them.
37 Their sons and their daughters
they sacrificed to foreign deities;
38 they shed innocent blood,
the blood of sons and daughters
offered to the gods of Canaan,
and the land was polluted with blood.
39 Thus they defiled themselves by their
actions
and were faithless in their conduct.

40 Then the LORD became angry with his
people
and, though they were his own chosen
nation, he loathed them;
41 he handed them over to the nations,
and they were ruled by their foes;
42 their enemies oppressed them
and kept them in subjection to their
power.
43 Time and again he came to their
rescue,
but they were rebellious in their
designs,
and so were brought low by their
wrongdoing.
44 Yet when he heard them wail and cry
aloud
he looked with pity on their distress;
45 he called to mind his covenant with
them
and, in his boundless love, relented;
46 he roused compassion for them
in the hearts of all their captors.

47 Deliver us, LORD our God,
and gather us in from among the
nations,

106:20 **their God:** *Heb.* their glory.   106:22 **Red
Sea:** *or* sea of Reeds.

ch. 16. **19–23:** *Horeb:* Sinai; for the golden *calf* incident, see Exod. ch. 32. **24–27:** Refusal to enter the
promised land shows lack of trust; Num. ch. 14. **28–31:** In Num. ch. 25, Phinehas slays the offending Israelite;
the episode is embellished here. **32–33:** The incident of the *waters of Meribah* has also been embellished;
see Num. 20.2–13. **34–46:** Summary of the events in the Book of Judges. **34:** *The LORD had commanded:*

that we may give thanks to your holy
    name
and make your praise our pride.

48 Blessed be the LORD, the God of Israel,
    from everlasting to everlasting.
Let all the people say 'Amen.'

Praise the LORD.

Book 5

107 ¹ It is good to give thanks to the
        LORD,
for his love endures for ever.
² So let them say who were redeemed by
    the Lord,
redeemed by him from the power of
    the enemy
³ and gathered out of the lands,
from east and west, from north and
    south.

⁴ Some lost their way in desert waste
    lands;
they found no path to a city to live in.
⁵ They were hungry and thirsty,
and their spirit was faint within them.
⁶ So they cried to the LORD in their
    trouble,
and he rescued them from their
    distress;
⁷ he led them by a straight and easy path
until they came to a city where they
    might live.
⁸ Let them give thanks to the LORD for
    his love
and for the marvellous things he has
    done for mankind;
⁹ he has satisfied the thirsty
and filled the hungry with good things.

¹⁰ Some sat in the dark, in deepest
    darkness,
prisoners bound fast in iron fetters,
¹¹ because they had defied God's
    commands
and flouted the purpose of the Most
    High.
¹² Their spirit was subdued by hard
    labour;
they stumbled and fell with none to
    help.
¹³ So they cried to the LORD in their
    trouble,
and he saved them from their distress;
¹⁴ he brought them out of the dark, the
    deepest darkness,
and burst their chains.
¹⁵ Let them give thanks to the LORD for
    his love
and for the marvellous things he has
    done for mankind;
¹⁶ he has shattered bronze gates,
and cut through iron bars.

¹⁷ Some were fools, who took to rebellious
    ways,
and for their transgression suffered
    punishment.
¹⁸ Revulsion seized them at the sight of
    food;
they were at the very gates of death.
¹⁹ So they cried to the LORD in their
    trouble,
and he saved them from their distress;
²⁰ he sent his word to heal them
and snatch them out of the pit of
    death.
²¹ Let them give thanks to the LORD for
    his love

107:3 **and south:** *prob. rdg; cp. Aram. (Targ.); Heb.* and
west.   107:20 **out … death:** *prob. rdg; Heb. obscure.*

compare Exod. 23.23–33; Deut. 7.1–5. **38:** For a typical incident of child sacrifice, see 1 Kgs. 16.34. **47:** This
verse seems to indicate that the psalm was written during the Babylonian Exile, i.e. after 587 B.C.E. **48:** *Let all
the people say* seems to be a liturgical prescription. This verse appears to be an addition to the psalm, either
to adapt it to public worship or to close the collection of psalms in Book 4.

Ps. 107: Let them give thanks to the LORD. A Thanksgiving of the community sung either by captives returning
from the Babylonian Exile or by pilgrims to Jerusalem who had been delivered from various dangers. Wisdom
motifs are prominent (vv. 33–43) as in other psalms which stand at the beginning of collections: Pss. 1 (Book 1),
73 (Book 3) and 90 (Book 4). **1:** A frequent exclamation of praise in the liturgy of the temple; see 118.1; 1 Chr.
16.34; 1 Macc. 4.24. **2–3:** A universal gathering out of all nations of those whom God calls and delivers;
compare Isa. 43.5–6; 49.12. The four sections that follow perhaps symbolize the four quarters of the earth.
4–32: Thanksgiving of those delivered from perils of the desert (vv. 4–9), from prison (vv. 10–16), from sickness
(vv. 17–22), from the dangers of the sea (vv. 23–32). **8–9:** A refrain that is repeated and adapted to each

and for the marvellous things he has
   done for mankind.
22 Let them offer sacrifices of thanksgiving
   and tell of his deeds with joyful shouts.

23 Others there are who go to sea in ships,
   plying their trade on the wide ocean.
24 These have seen what the LORD has
   done,
   his marvellous actions in the deep.
25 At his command the storm-wind rose
   and lifted the waves high.
26 The seamen were carried up to the
   skies,
   then plunged down into the depths;
   they were tossed to and fro in peril,
27 they reeled and staggered like
   drunkards,
   and all their skill was of no avail.
28 So they cried to the LORD in their
   trouble,
   and he brought them out of their
   distress.
29 The storm sank to a murmur
   and the waves of the sea were stilled.
30 They rejoiced because it was calm,
   and he guided them to the harbour
   they were making for.
31 Let them give thanks to the LORD for
   his enduring love
   and for the marvellous things he has
   done for mankind.
32 Let them exalt him in the assembly of
   the people
   and praise him in the elders' council.

33 He turns rivers into desert,
   springs of water into parched ground;
34 he turns fruitful land into salt-marsh,
   because the people who live there are
   so wicked.
35 Desert he changes to standing pools,
   arid land into springs of water.
36 There he gives the hungry a home
   and they build themselves a town to live
   in;
37 they sow fields and plant vineyards
   which yield a good harvest.
38 He blesses them and their numbers

grow,
   and he does not let their herds
   decrease.
39 Tyrants lose their strength and are
   brought low
   in the grip of misfortune and sorrow;
40 he brings princes into contempt
   and leaves them to wander in a
   trackless waste.
41 But the poor man he lifts clear of his
   troubles
   and makes families increase like flocks
   of sheep.
42 The upright see it and are glad,
   while evildoers are reduced to silence.

43 Whoever is wise, let him lay these
   things to heart,
   and ponder the loving deeds of the
   LORD.

108   *A song: a psalm: for David*
         1 My heart is steadfast, God,
my heart is steadfast.
I shall sing and raise a psalm.
Awake, my soul.
2 Awake, harp and lyre;
   I shall awake at dawn.
3 I shall praise you among the peoples,
   LORD,
   among the nations I shall raise a psalm
   to you;
4 for your unfailing love is high above
   the heavens;
   your faithfulness reaches to the skies.
5 God, be exalted above the heavens;
   let your glory be over all the earth.
6 Save with your right hand and respond,
   that those dear to you may be delivered.

7 God has spoken from his sanctuary:
   'I will go up now and divide Shechem;

107:26 **they were tossed . . . peril:** *or* their courage
melted in the face of peril.   107:39 **Tyrants:** *prob.
rdg; Heb. omits.*   108:1–5 *Cp. Ps. 57:7–11.*
108:1 **my heart is steadfast:** *so some MSS; others omit.*
Awake: *prob. rdg; Heb. also.*   108:6–13 *Cp. Ps.
60:5–12.*   108:7 **from his sanctuary:** *or* in his
holiness. **go up now:** *or* exult.

situation; see vv. 15–16; 21–22; 31–32. **22:** *Sacrifices:* probably to fulfill vows made during distress. **33–43:**
The Wisdom themes of the two ways, "good and evil," and the reversal of situations in rewarding the *upright*
and humiliating the *evildoers* are elaborated.

   Ps. 108: I shall raise a psalm to you. A vow; vv. 1–5 are almost identical with 57.7–11 and vv. 6–13 with
60.5–12. See the annotations to those passages.

I will measure off the valley of Succoth;
8 Gilead and Manasseh are mine;
Ephraim is my helmet, Judah my
    sceptre;
9 Moab is my washbowl, on Edom I fling
    my sandals;
I shout my war cry against Philistia.'

10 Who will bring me to the impregnable
    city?
Who will guide me to Edom?
11 Have you rejected us, God,
and do you no longer lead our armies
    to battle?
12 Grant us help against the foe;
for in vain we look to any mortal for
    deliverance.
13 With God's help we shall fight valiantly,
and God himself will tread our foes
    under foot.

109 *For the leader: for David: a psalm*
1 GOD to whom I offer praise,
    do not be silent,
2 for the wicked have heaped calumnies
    upon me.
They have lied to my face
3 and encompassed me on every side with
    words of hatred.
They have assailed me without cause;
4 in return for my love they denounced
    me,
though I have done nothing wrong.
5 They have repaid me evil for good,
hatred in return for my love.
6 They say, 'Put up some rogue to
    denounce him,
an accuser to confront him.'
7 But when judgement is given that
    rogue will be exposed
and his wrongdoing accounted a sin.

8 May his days be few;
may his hoarded wealth be seized by

another!
9 May his children be fatherless,
his wife a widow!
10 May his children be vagrants and
    beggars,
driven from their ruined homes!
11 May the creditor distrain on all his
    goods
and strangers run off with his earnings!
12 May none remain loyal to him,
and none pity his fatherless children!
13 May his line be doomed to extinction,
may his name be wiped out within a
    generation!
14 May the sins of his forefathers be
    remembered
and his own mother's wickedness never
    be wiped out!
15 May they remain on record before the
    LORD,
but may he cut off all memory of them
    from the earth!
16 For that man never set himself
to be loyal to his friend,
but persecuted the downtrodden and
    the poor
and hounded the broken-hearted to
    their death.
17 He loved to curse: may the curse recoil
    on him!
He took no pleasure in blessing: may
    no blessing be his!
18 He clothed himself in cursing like a
    garment:
may it seep into his body like water
and into his bones like oil!
19 May it wrap him round like the clothes
    he puts on,
like the belt which he wears every day!
20 May the LORD so repay my accusers,

109:4 **though . . . wrong:** *prob. rdg; Heb. obscure.*
109:6 **to confront him:** *Heb.* to stand at his right hand.
109:8 **hoarded wealth:** *or* charge, *cp. Acts 1:20.*
109:14 **remembered:** *so Syriac; Heb. adds* before the
LORD.

Ps. 109: Help me, LORD my God. A Lament (see Introduction) of an individual who may be falsely accused
of a crime. It is divided into three distinct sections; the first (vv. 1–5) and the third (vv. 20–31) are supplications
for deliverance, the second (vv. 6–19) is a series of curses against an individual by that one's enemies. **6–19:**
These verses seem to be spoken by the poet's enemies, for there is a profound emotional change—from
meekness of vv. 1–5 into hatred, as well as a pronominal change from "they" of vv. 1–5, to *his*. The curses
all seek the destruction of the accused. **6:** Ordinarily the accuser stood at the left of the accused and the defender
of the accused at the right: see v. 31; 110.5; 121.5. **8:** See Tfn. **13:** For one's *name to be wiped out* in one
generation was the Israelite's greatest tragedy. **16–17:** It seems that the psalmist was accused of accomplishing
someone's *death* by a *curse*. **20:** Other translations of this verse are possible; in this one the psalmist invokes

those who speak evil against me!

21 You, LORD my God,
deal with me as befits your honour;
in the goodness of your love deliver
me,
22 for I am downtrodden and poor,
and my heart within me is distraught.
23 I fade like a passing shadow,
I am shaken off like a locust.
24 My knees are weak for want of food
and my flesh wastes away, so meagre is
my fare.
25 I have become the object of their
taunts;
when they see me they wag their heads.

26 Help me, LORD my God;
save me by your love,
27 that all may know this is your doing
and you alone, LORD, have done it.
28 They may curse, but you will bless;
let my opponents be put to shame,
but may your servant rejoice!
29 May my accusers be clothed with
dishonour,
wrapped in their shame as in a cloak!

30 I shall lift up my voice to extol the
LORD,
before a great company I shall praise
him.
31 For he stands at the right hand of the
poor
to save them from those who bring
them to trial.

110 For David: a psalm
1 THIS is the LORD's oracle to my
lord:
'Sit at my right hand,
and I shall make your enemies your

footstool.'

2 The LORD extends the sway of your
powerful sceptre, saying,
'From Zion reign over your enemies.'
3 You gain the homage of your people
on the day of your power.
Arrayed in holy garments, a child of
the dawn,
you have the dew of your youth.
4 The LORD has sworn an oath and will
not change his mind:
'You are a priest for ever,
a Melchizedek in my service.'
5 The Lord is at your right hand;
he crushes kings on the day of his
wrath.
6 In glorious majesty he judges the
nations,
shattering heads throughout the wide
earth.

7 He will drink from the stream on his
way;
therefore he will hold his head high.

111 1 PRAISE the LORD.

With all my heart I shall give thanks to
the LORD
in the congregation, in the assembly of
the upright.
2 Great are the works of the LORD,
pondered over by all who delight in
them.
3 His deeds are full of majesty and
splendour;
his righteousness stands sure for ever.

109:28 **let my . . . shame:** so *Gk; Heb.* they rose up and
were put to shame.   110:4 **a Melchizedek . . .**
service: *or* in the succession of Melchizedek, *cp.*
Hebrews 5:6.   110:6 **In glorious majesty:** *prob. rdg;*
Heb. Full of corpses.

the law of the talion, i.e. "an eye for an eye" against the accusers. **23:** Locusts were either *shaken off* to the
ground and killed or swept away by the wind; see Exod. 10.19. **25:** To *wag* the head was a sign of derision
and hostility.

Ps. 110: Sit at my right hand. A Royal Psalm, probably used at the coronation ceremonies for kings (compare
Ps. 2). **1:** *The LORD:* Yahweh. *My lord:* the king who is taking office. *Footstool:* a figure for complete domination.
4: *A Melchizedek in my service:* the king will also serve as priest, like a predecessor Melchizedek, the Canaanite
priest-king of Jerusalem (Gen. 14.18–20). The verse is quoted in Heb. 5.6 and 7.17. **5:** *Right hand:* chief
support, as in v. 1.

Ps. 111: The beginning of wisdom. A Hymn with Wisdom themes. It is an acrostic; hence each of the
twenty-two half-verses begins with a successive letter of the Heb. alphabet. The opening phrase, *Praise the*
LORD (Heb. *Hallelujah*), is not part of the alphabetic structure; Pss. 112 and 113 also begin with this ritual

⁴He has won renown for his marvellous
deeds;
the LORD is gracious and
compassionate.
⁵He provides food for those who fear
him;
he keeps his covenant always in mind.
⁶He showed his people how powerfully
he worked
by bestowing on them the lands of the
nations.
⁷His works are truth and justice;
all his precepts are trustworthy,
⁸established to endure for ever,
enacted in faithfulness and truth.
⁹He sent and redeemed his people;
he decreed that his covenant should
endure for ever.
Holy and awe-inspiring is his name.
¹⁰The fear of the LORD is the beginning
of wisdom,
and they who live by it grow in
understanding.
Praise will be his for ever.

112   ¹PRAISE the LORD.

Happy is he who fears the LORD,
who finds deep delight in obeying his
commandments.
²His descendants will be powerful in the
land,
a blessed generation of upright people.
³His house will be full of riches and
wealth;
his righteousness will stand sure for
ever.
⁴A beacon in darkness for the upright,

he is gracious, compassionate, good.
⁵It is well with one who is gracious in his
lending,
ordering his affairs with equity.
⁶Nothing will ever shake him;
his goodness will be remembered for all
time.
⁷News of misfortune will have no terrors
for him,
because his heart is steadfast, trusting
in the LORD.
⁸His confidence is well established, he
has no fears,
and in the end he will see the downfall
of his enemies.
⁹He lavishes his gifts on the needy;
his righteousness will stand sure for
ever;
in honour he carries his head high.
¹⁰The wicked will see it with rising anger
and grind their teeth in despair;
the hopes of the wicked will come to
nothing.

113   ¹PRAISE the LORD.

Praise the LORD, you that are his
servants,
praise the name of the LORD.
²Blessed be the name of the LORD
now and evermore.
³From the rising of the sun to its setting
may the LORD's name be praised!

⁴High is the LORD above all nations,
high his glory above the heavens.
⁵⁻⁶There is none like the LORD our God

111:10 **beginning:** *or* chief part. **it:** *so Gk; Heb.* them.

proclamation. **10:** Compare Prov. 1.7 and Job 28.28.

Ps. 112: Happy is the one who fears the LORD. A Wisdom Psalm in acrostic form; see Ps. 111 n. It continues
the previous psalm, being linked to it by the phrase "fear of the LORD" (v. 1; 111.10), which it elaborates and
applies to practical life. Attributes assigned to God in Ps. 111 are here ascribed to the virtuous one who acts
as God does (v. 4). **1:** *Praise the LORD:* see Ps. 111 n. **3–5:** *Righteousness,* graciousness, compassion, goodness,
equity are all attributes that are applied ordinarily to God's relation to humanity and in particular to Israel; see
111.3–4; 103.6–8, 13, 17. **3:** *Righteousness* here is the state of being in proper order with God and of
possessing the happiness that flows from it. **5:** To act *with equity* is to work for truth and justice (111.7) by
delivering the oppressed, giving freely to the poor (v. 9) to bring about righteousness. **8:** *Well established:*
compare 111.8. **10:** *Grind teeth:* an expression of extreme and malicious anger and/or frustration; see Lam.
2.16; Matt. 8.12; Acts 7.54.

Ps. 113: Praise the LORD. A Hymn, the first of a collection (Pss. 113–118) known as the "Hallel" (praise).
This collection (often called the "Egyptian Hallel") was used on the great festivals: Booths, Passover, and Weeks.
At the Passover seder service, Pss. 113–114 are sung before the meal and Pss. 115–118 after it. See Matt. 26.30;
Mk. 14.26. **2–4:** The response of an assembly to the call to praise the LORD (v. 1). **5–6:** A key concept in Israel's

in heaven or on earth,
who sets his throne so high
but deigns to look down so low;
7 who lifts the weak out of the dust
and raises the poor from the rubbish
heap,
8 giving them a place among princes,
among the princes of his people;
9 who makes the woman in a childless
house
a happy mother of children.

114 1 PRAISE the LORD.

When Israel came out of Egypt,
the house of Jacob from a barbaric
people,
2 Judah became God's sanctuary,
Israel his domain.
3 The sea fled at the sight;
Jordan turned back.
4 The mountains skipped like rams,
the hills like lambs of the flock.
5 What made you, the sea, flee away?
Jordan, what made you turn back?
6 Why did you skip like rams, you
mountains,
and like lambs, you hills?
7 Earth, dance at the presence of the
Lord,
at the presence of the God of Jacob,
8 who turned the rock into a pool of
water,
the flinty cliff into a welling spring.

115 1 NOT to us, LORD, not to us,
but to your name give glory
for your love, for your faithfulness!

2 Why should the nations ask,
'Where, then, is their God?'
3 Our God is high in heaven;
he does whatever he wills.

4 Their idols are silver and gold,
made by human hands.
5 They have mouths, but cannot speak,
eyes, but cannot see;
6 they have ears, but cannot hear,
nostrils, but cannot smell;
7 with their hands they cannot feel,
with their feet they cannot walk,
and no sound comes from their throats.
8 Their makers become like them,
and so do all who put their trust in
them.
9 But Israel trusts in the LORD:
he is their help and their shield.
10 The house of Aaron trusts in the LORD:
he is their help and their shield.
11 Those who fear the LORD trust in the
LORD:
he is their help and their shield.

12 The LORD who has been mindful of us
will bless us,
he will bless the house of Israel,
he will bless the house of Aaron.
13 The LORD will bless those who fear
him,
both high and low.

14 May the LORD give you increase,

113:9 **children:** *Heb. adds* Praise the LORD, *transposed to
the beginning of Ps. 114 as Gk.* 114:1 **Praise the
LORD:** *transposed from end of Ps. 113; so Gk.* **barbaric
people:** *or* people of alien speech. 114:7 **dance:** *or*
tremble.

relation to God was that God was exalted *so high* as to be beyond reach, yet came *so low* as to live in their
midst; see Ezek. 48.35. **7:** *Rubbish heap:* sign of abject rejection and ritual uncleanness. **9:** Barrenness was
considered a curse and disgrace; see Gen. 16.4–5; 1 Sam. 1.6.

   Ps. 114: Judah became God's sanctuary. A Thanksgiving, although some classify it as a Hymn. This psalm,
which continues the Hallel, is a psalm of praise proclaiming how God saved Israel at the Exodus. **2:** *Judah:*
name of the southern portion; *Israel:* name of the northern portion. **3–6:** Wondrous events accompanied the
Exodus at the Red *sea* (Exod. ch. 14), at the *Jordan* river (Josh. ch. 3) and at Sinai (Exod. 19.16–20). **7–8:** The
entire world is to enter into the joy of vv. 3–6. **8:** See Exod. 17.6 and Num. 20.11.

   Ps. 115: To your name give glory. A Liturgy, part of the Hallel (Ps. 113 n.), contrasts the invisible God with
the idols of the heathen. **1:** God's glory is God's *love;* compare 1 Jn. 4.7–9. **2–8:** Israel's God is invisible to
the *nations* but God's actions of constant love are evident; the idols are visible but their actions are not. **9–11:**
These verses perhaps were sung antiphonally, i.e. one chorus said the first part of the verse and another the
second. Three classes of people take part: *Israel* are all the lay people; *house of Aaron* are the priestly class;
those who fear the LORD are either the converts from the nations or the first two classes combined. **12–13:** An
oracle perhaps pronounced by a temple prophet. **14–15:** A blessing pronounced by a priest. **14:** See Deut.

both you and your children.
15 You are blessed by the Lord,
  the maker of heaven and earth.
16 The heavens belong to the Lord,
  but the earth he has given to mankind.
17 It is not the dead who praise the Lord,
  not those who go down to the silent
    grave;
18 but we, the living, shall bless the Lord
  now and for evermore.

Praise the Lord.

116 1 I love the Lord, for he has
      heard me
and listened to my prayer;
2 he has given me a hearing
  and all my days I shall cry to him.
3 The cords of death bound me,
  Sheol held me in its grip.
  Anguish and torment held me fast;
4 then I invoked the Lord by name,
  'Lord, deliver me, I pray.'

5 Gracious is the Lord and righteous;
  our God is full of compassion.
6 The Lord preserves the
    simple-hearted;
  when I was brought low, he saved me.
7 My heart, be at peace once more,
  for the Lord has granted you full
    deliverance.
8 You have rescued me from death,
  my eyes from weeping,
  my feet from stumbling.
9 I shall walk in the presence of the Lord
  in the land of the living.

10 I was sure I should be swept away;
  my distress was bitter.
11 In my alarm I cried,
  'How faithless are all my
    fellow-creatures!'
12 How can I repay the Lord
  for all his benefits to me?
13 I shall lift up the cup of salvation
  and call on the Lord by name.
14 I shall pay my vows to the Lord
  in the presence of all his people.
15 A precious thing in the Lord's sight
  is the death of those who are loyal to
    him.
16 Indeed, Lord, I am your slave,
  I am your slave, your slave-girl's son;
  you have loosed my bonds.
17 To you I shall bring a thank-offering
  and call on the Lord by name.
18 I shall pay my vows to the Lord
  in the presence of all his people,
19 in the courts of the Lord's house,
  in the midst of you, Jerusalem.

Praise the Lord.

117 1 Praise the Lord, all nations,
      2 extol him, all you peoples;
for his love protecting us is strong,
the Lord's faithfulness is everlasting.

Praise the Lord.

115:18 **the living:** *so Gk; Heb. omits.*   116:3 **Sheol:** *or the underworld.*   116:10 **I was ... away:** *or I believed though I said.*

1.11 on *increase.* An abundance of children was seen as a sign of God's beneficent favor. **17:** In Sheol, the underworld of the *dead,* there is only silence; see Job 3.13, 18. **18:** See Ps. 113.2.

  Ps. 116: I love the Lord. A Thanksgiving Psalm, part of the Hallel; see Ps. 113 n. It presumes a recovery from serious illness (vv. 2–4) and the ensuing fulfillment of a vow to offer a sacrifice of thanks in the temple (vv. 17–20). **3:** *Sheol,* the place of the dead, is pictured as a trapper that has snared the poet in the *cords* of a noose. **4:** Calling a person, here the *Lord,* by name not only expresses a submission to God (v. 13) but also draws power from God. **5:** The key attributes of God in dealing with human beings: graciousness, righteousness, *full of compassion;* see 103.6–8 n. **13:** *Cup of salvation:* possibly a figurative expression or possibly an allusion to a sacrificial libation in fulfillment of a vow such as mentioned in Num. 15.1–10. **14:** The *vows* are fulfilled in the temple *in the presence of ... people.* **15:** In the Hebrew concept of Sheol, *death* severed all contact between God and the *loyal* ones whom God loves (117.2) and so their death is precious, i.e. costly, to God. Another possible interpretation is that they are like gold purified in the fire and hence costly; see Wisd. 3.1–8. **16:** *Your slave-girl's son:* a term of humility intensifying the force of *"your slave"* and meaning "slave born in your house." **17:** *Thank-offering:* see Lev. 7.12–15. **19:** *Lord's house:* the temple.

  Ps. 117: Praise the Lord. A Hymn, probably part of the temple liturgy. The shortest of the psalms, it is part of the Hallel (see Ps. 113 n.). **2:** *Praise the Lord* may belong with Ps. 118 as its opening words.

118

¹It is good to give thanks to the LORD,
for his love endures for ever.
²Let Israel say:
'His love endures for ever.'
³Let the house of Aaron say:
'His love endures for ever.'
⁴Let those who fear the LORD say:
'His love endures for ever.'

⁵When in distress I called to the LORD,
he answered me and gave me relief.
⁶With the LORD on my side, I am not afraid;
what can mortals do to me?
⁷With the LORD on my side, as my helper,
I shall see the downfall of my enemies.
⁸It is better to seek refuge in the LORD
than to trust in any mortal,
⁹better to seek refuge in the LORD
than to trust in princes.

¹⁰The nations all surrounded me,
but in the LORD's name I drove them off.
¹¹They surrounded me on every side,
but in the LORD's name I drove them off.
¹²They swarmed round me like bees;
they attacked me, as fire attacks brushwood,
but in the LORD's name I drove them off.
¹³They thrust hard against me so that I nearly fell,
but the LORD came to my help.
¹⁴The LORD is my refuge and defence,
and he has become my deliverer.

¹⁵Listen! Shouts of triumph
in the camp of the victors:
'With his right hand the LORD does mighty deeds;
¹⁶the right hand of the LORD raises up,
with his right hand the LORD does mighty deeds.'
¹⁷I shall not die; I shall live
to proclaim what the LORD has done.
¹⁸The LORD did indeed chasten me,
but he did not surrender me to death.
¹⁹Open to me the gates of victory;
I shall go in by them and praise the LORD.
²⁰This is the gate of the LORD;
the victors will enter through it.
²¹I shall praise you, for you have answered me
and have become my deliverer.
²²The stone which the builders rejected
has become the main corner-stone.
²³This is the LORD's doing;
it is wonderful in our eyes.
²⁴This is the day on which the LORD has acted,
a day for us to exult and rejoice.
²⁵LORD, deliver us, we pray;
LORD, grant us prosperity.
²⁶Blessed is he who enters in the name of the LORD;
we bless you from the house of the LORD.

118:13 **They:** cp. Gk; Heb. You.   118:15 **victors:** or righteous.   118:19 **victory:** or righteousness.   118:20 **victors:** or righteous.   118:24 **on . . . acted:** or the LORD has made.

Ps. 118: This is the LORD's doing. A Thanksgiving, originally possibly a king's thanksgiving hymn for victory in battle (vv. 10–14), sung in the temple. However, as the last of the "Egyptian Hallel" (see Ps. 113 n.), it was appropriate for use at the Passover. The psalm seems to be a dramatic ceremonial (see Neh. 12.27–43) with the following structure: a procession forms outside the temple and is invited to praise the LORD (vv. 1–4); the king or another individual in the name of the group describes dramatically how God came to the rescue when the nation confidently prayed for divine help (vv. 5–18); a dialogue between the leader of the procession outside the temple gates and the priests within (vv. 19–25); the blessing given by the priest to the procession gathered round the altar (vv. 26–27); resumption of the invitation (v. 1) to praise the LORD (vv. 28–29). **2–4:** Israel . . . house of Aaron . . . those who fear the LORD: see 115.9–11 n. **10–12:** In the LORD's name: by the power of the LORD. **20–21:** The condition for entering the temple is a righteous life which is attested by the fact that God has answered in time of need. **22:** In the context of the Exodus pilgrim-feasts—Passover, Weeks, and Booths—Israel was the stone rejected by the empire builders, Egypt. The verse is quoted frequently in the NT; see Matt. 21.42; Acts 4.11. **24:** Israelite festivals came to be viewed as a contemporary reenactment of a day on which God acted in past events: Passover as the Exodus; Weeks, the Sinai episode; Booths, the wilderness. Christian liturgy interprets "the day" to mean the Resurrection of Christ. **25:** Deliver us: Heb. Hosanna; see

27 The LORD is God; he has given us light.
Link the pilgrims with cords
   as far as the horns of the altar.
28 You are my God and I shall praise you;
my God, I shall exalt you.
29 It is good to give thanks to the LORD,
for his love endures for ever.

119 ¹ HAPPY are they whose way of
   life is blameless,
who conform to the law of the LORD.
² Happy are they who obey his
   instruction,
who set their heart on finding him;
³ who have done no wrong,
but have lived according to his will.
⁴ You, Lord, have laid down your
   precepts
that are to be kept faithfully.
⁵ If only I might hold a steady course,
keeping your statutes!
⁶ Then, if I fixed my eyes on all your
   commandments,
I should never be put to shame.
⁷ I shall praise you in sincerity of heart
as I learn your just decrees.
⁸ I shall observe your statutes;
do not leave me forsaken!

⁹ How may a young man lead a clean
   life?
By holding to your words.
10 With all my heart I seek you;
do not let me stray from your
   commandments.
11 I treasure your promise in my heart,
for fear that I might sin against you.
12 Blessed are you, LORD;
teach me your statutes.
13 I say them over, one by one,

all the decrees you have announced.
14 I have rejoiced in the path of your
   instruction
as one rejoices over wealth of every
   kind.
15 I shall meditate on your precepts
and keep your paths before my eyes.
16 In your statutes I find continual
   delight;
I shall not forget your word.

17 Grant this to me, your servant: let me
   live
so that I may keep your word.
18 Take the veil from my eyes, that I may
   see
the wonders to be found in your law.
19 Though I am but a passing stranger
   here on earth,
do not hide your commandments from
   me.
20 My heart pines continually
with longing for your decrees.
21 The proud have felt your censure;
cursed are those who turn from your
   commandments.
22 Set me free from scorn and insult,
for I have obeyed your instruction.
23 Rulers sit scheming together against
   me;
but I, your servant, shall study your
   statutes.
24 Your instruction is my continual
   delight;
I turn to it for counsel.

25 I lie prone in the dust;
revive me according to your word.

118:27 **cords:** *or* branches.

Matt. 21.9 and parallels. **27:** *Light:* possibly a reminiscence of a primitive celebration held at dawn. The four elevations at the corners *of the altar* were called *horns;* see Exod. 27.2; Lev. 4.7.

Ps. 119: Your law, O LORD, is my continual delight. A Wisdom meditation, didactic in nature, with many motifs of a Lament. Its unparalleled length arises from its being an acrostic (see Ps. 111 n.) with eight verses for each of the twenty-two letters of the Heb. alphabet. The word "law" and its synonyms—instruction, will, precept, statutes, commandments, decrees, word, promise, paths—occur in every verse. Frequent also is the plea that God teach the Law so that Israel may be faithful to God. Law and its synonyms are understood in the wide sense of divine teaching as found in the Pentateuch and in the prophets. There is very little logical development of thought but ideas are strung together loosely. The main thrust appears to be "How I love your precepts, O LORD." The elements of a Lament are: description of troubles and enemies, pleas for deliverance, vows both explicit and implicit (vv. 106, 175). Ability to withstand scorn, threats, and danger is tied to learning the way of God's statutes. The psalm is considered to be a late composition. **18:** Only an extraneous obstruction of vision, a *veil*, prevents a person from seeing the benefits of the *law.* **21:** The *proud* are the most averse to

26 I tell you of my plight and you answer
  me;
  teach me your statutes.
27 Show me the way set out in your
  precepts,
  and I shall meditate on your wonders.
28 Because of misery I cannot rest;
  renew my strength in accordance with
  your promise.
29 Keep falsehood far from me
  and grant me the grace of living by
  your law.
30 I have chosen the path of faithfulness;
  I have set your decrees before me.
31 I hold fast to your instruction;
  Lord, do not let me be put to shame.
32 I shall run the course made known in
  your commandments,
  for you set free my heart.

33 Teach me, Lord, the way of your
  statutes,
  and in keeping them I shall find my
  reward.
34 Give me the insight to obey your law
  and to keep it wholeheartedly.
35 Make me walk in the path of your
  commandments,
  for that is my desire.
36 Dispose my heart towards your
  instruction,
  not towards love of gain;
37 turn my eyes away from all that is
  futile;
  grant me life by your word.
38 Fulfil your promise for your servant,
  the promise made to those who fear
  you.
39 Turn away the taunts which I dread,
  for your decrees are good.
40 How I long for your precepts!
  By your righteousness grant me life.

41 Let your love descend on me, Lord,
  your deliverance as you have promised;
42 then I shall have an answer to the
  taunts aimed at me,
  because I trust in your word.
43 Do not rob me of my power to speak
  the truth,

for I put my hope in your decrees.
44 I shall heed your law continually,
  for ever and ever;
45 I walk in freedom wherever I will,
  because I have studied your precepts.
46 I shall speak of your instruction before
  kings
  and shall not be ashamed;
47 in your commandments I find
  continuing delight;
  I love them with all my heart.
48 I am devoted to your commandments;
  I love them, and meditate on your
  statutes.

49 Keep in mind the word spoken to me,
  your servant,
  on which you have taught me to fix my
  hope.
50 In my time of trouble my consolation is
  this:
  your promise has given me life.
51 Proud people treat me with insolent
  scorn,
  but I do not swerve from your
  commandments.
52 I have cherished your decrees from of
  old,
  and in them I find comfort, Lord.
53 Fury seizes me as I think of the wicked
  who forsake your law.
54 Your statutes are the theme of my song
  throughout my earthly life.
55 In the night I remember your name,
  Lord,
  and dwell upon your instruction.
56 This has been my lot,
  for I have kept your precepts.

57 You are my portion, Lord;
  I have promised to keep your words.
58 With all my heart I have tried to please
  you;
  fulfil your promise and be gracious to
  me.
59 I have considered my way of life

119:47 **with ... heart:** *prob. rdg, cp. Gk; Heb. omits.*
119:51 **commandments:** *prob. rdg; Heb. law.*
119:55 **instruction:** *prob. rdg; Heb. law.*

God's commandments. **55:** The darkness of *night* connotes the absence of God. **75:** If God's *decrees are just* their observance is beneficial and so God keeps *faith* in punishing transgressions. **83:** Leather flasks containing wine were hung from the ceiling, out of reach of children and rodents, where, exposed to heat and *smoke*, they eventually became brittle and useless. Though shriveled by age like an old wineskin, the psalmist can and turned back to your instruction;

⁶⁰ I have never delayed, but always made
   haste
to keep your commandments.

⁶¹ The wicked in crowds close round me,
but I do not forget your law.

⁶² At midnight I rise to give you thanks
for the justice of your decrees.

⁶³ I keep company with all who fear you,
with all who follow your precepts.

⁶⁴ Lord, the earth is filled with your
   unfailing love;
teach me your statutes.

⁶⁵ You have dealt kindly with your
   servant,
fulfilling your word, Lord.

⁶⁶ Give me insight, give me knowledge,
for I put my trust in your
   commandments.

⁶⁷ Before I was chastened I went astray,
but now I pay heed to your promise.

⁶⁸ You are good, and you do what is
   good;
teach me your statutes.

⁶⁹ I follow your precepts wholeheartedly,
though those who are proud blacken
   my name with lies;

⁷⁰ they are arrogant and unfeeling,
but I find my delight in your
   instruction.

⁷¹ How good for me to have been
   chastened,
so that I might be schooled in your
   statutes!

⁷² The law you have ordained means
   more to me
than a fortune in gold and silver.

⁷³ Your hands made me and formed me;
give me insight that I may learn your
   commandments.

⁷⁴ May all who fear you see me and be
   glad,
because I put my hope in your word.

⁷⁵ I know, Lord, that your decrees are
   just
and even in chastening you keep faith
   with me.

⁷⁶ Let your love comfort me,
as you have promised me, your servant.

⁷⁷ Extend your compassion to me, that I
   may live,
for your law is my delight.

⁷⁸ Put the proud to shame, for they
wrong me with lies;

but I shall meditate on your precepts.

⁷⁹ Let those who fear you turn to me,
that they may understand your
   instruction.

⁸⁰ Let me give my whole heart to your
   statutes,
so that I am not put to shame.

⁸¹ I long with all my heart for your
   deliverance;
I have put my hope in your word.

⁸² My sight grows dim with looking for
   your promise
and I cry, 'When will you comfort me?'

⁸³ Though I shrivel like a wineskin in the
   smoke,
I do not forget your statutes.

⁸⁴ How long must I, your servant, wait?
When will you execute judgement on
   my persecutors?

⁸⁵ The proud who flout your law
spread tales about me.

⁸⁶ All your commandments stand sure;
but the proud hound me with
   falsehood. Come to my help!

⁸⁷ They had almost swept me from the
   earth,
but I did not forsake your precepts.

⁸⁸ In your love grant me life,
that I may follow your instruction.

⁸⁹ Your word is everlasting, Lord;
it is firmly fixed in heaven.

⁹⁰ Your faithfulness endures for all
   generations,
and the earth which you have
   established stands firm.

⁹¹ Even to this day your decrees stand
   fast,
for all things serve you.

⁹² Had your law not been my delight,
I should have perished in my distress;

⁹³ never shall I forget your precepts,
for through them you have given me
   life.

⁹⁴ I am yours; save me,
for I have sought your precepts.

⁹⁵ The wicked lie in wait to destroy me;
but I shall ponder your instruction.

⁹⁶ I see that all things have an end,
but your commandment has no limit.

⁹⁷ How I love your law!
It is my study all day long.

119:70 **instruction:** *prob. rdg; Heb.* law.

98 Your commandment makes me wiser
  than my enemies,
  for it is my possession for ever.
99 I have more insight than all my
  teachers,
  for your instruction is my study;
100 I have more wisdom than those who
  are old,
  because I have kept your precepts.
101 I do not set foot on any evil path
  in my obedience to your word;
102 I do not swerve from your decrees,
  for you have been my teacher.
103 How sweet is your promise to my
  palate,
  sweeter on my tongue than honey!
104 From your precepts I learn wisdom;
  therefore I hate every path of
  falsehood.

105 Your word is a lamp to my feet,
  a light on my path;
106 I have bound myself by oath and
  solemn vow
  to keep your just decrees.
107 I am cruelly afflicted;
  LORD, revive me as you have promised.
108 Accept, LORD, the willing tribute of my
  lips,
  and teach me your decrees.
109 Every day I take my life in my hands,
  yet I never forget your law.
110 The wicked have set a trap for me,
  but I do not stray from your precepts.
111 Your instruction is my everlasting
  heritage;
  it is the joy of my heart.
112 I am resolved to fulfil your statutes;
  they are a reward that never fails.

113 I hate those who are not single-minded,
  but I love your law.
114 You are my hiding-place and my shield;
  in your word I put my hope.
115 Leave me alone, you evildoers,
  that I may keep the commandments of
  my God.
116 Support me as you have promised, that
  I may live;
  do not disappoint my hope.

117 Sustain me, that I may see deliverance;
  then I shall always be occupied with
  your statutes.
118 You reject all who stray from your
  statutes,
  for their whole talk is malice and lies.
119 In your sight the wicked are all scum of
  the earth;
  therefore I love your instruction.
120 The dread of you makes my flesh
  creep;
  I stand in awe of your decrees.

121 I have done what is just and right;
  you will not abandon me to my
  oppressors.
122 Stand surety for the welfare of your
  servant;
  do not let the proud oppress me.
123 My eyes grow weary looking for your
  deliverance,
  with waiting for the victory you have
  promised.
124 In your dealings with me, LORD, show
  your love
  and teach me your statutes.
125 I am your servant; give me insight
  to understand your instruction.
126 It is time for you to act, LORD,
  for your law has been broken.
127 Truly I love your commandments
  more than gold, even the finest gold.
128 It is by your precepts that I find the
  right way;
  I hate the paths of falsehood.

129 Your instruction is wonderful;
  therefore I gladly keep it.
130 Your word is revealed, and all is light;
  it gives understanding even to the
  untaught.
131 I pant, I thirst,
  longing for your commandments.
132 Turn to me and show me favour,
  just as you have decreed for those who
  love your name.

119:119 **In ... earth:** *so some MSS; others* You have
made an end of all the wicked on earth like scum.
119:128 **It ... precepts:** *prob. rdg, cp. Gk; Heb.* All
precepts of all.

still meditate on the law in good vigor. **99:** In the study of the Law, God is the inner teacher so that the psalmist
has more *insight* than academic *teachers*. **100:** Even though wisdom and old age were equated, the young who
kept the Law acquired *more wisdom* than the old who did not. **109:** The threat to *life* itself does not distract
the psalmist from attention to the Law. **113:** *Not single-minded:* those whose allegiance is divided, who have

133 Make my step firm according to your
 promise,
 and let no wrong have the mastery over
 me.
134 Deliver me from oppression by my
 fellows,
 that I may observe your precepts.
135 Let your face shine on your servant
 and teach me your statutes.
136 My eyes stream with tears
 because your law goes unheeded.

137 How just you are, Lord!
 How straight and true are your
 decrees!
138 How just is the instruction you give!
 It is firm and sure.
139 I am speechless with indignation
 at my enemies' neglect of your words.
140 Your promise has been well tested,
 and I love it, Lord.
141 I may be despised and of little account,
 but I do not forget your precepts.
142 Your justice is an everlasting justice,
 and your law is steadfast.
143 Though I am overtaken by trouble and
 anxiety,
 your commandments are my delight.
144 Your instruction is ever just;
 give me understanding that I may live.

145 With my whole heart I call; answer me,
 Lord.
 I shall keep your statutes.
146 I call to you; save me
 that I may heed your instruction.
147 Before dawn I rise to cry for help;
 I put my hope in your word.
148 Before the midnight watch my eyes are
 open
 for meditation on your promise.
149 In your love hear me,
 and give me life, Lord, by your decree.
150 My pursuers in their malice are close
 behind me,
 but they are far from your law.
151 Yet you are near, Lord,
 and all your commandments are
 steadfast.

152 I have long known from your
 instruction
 that you have given it everlasting
 foundations.
153 See in what trouble I am and set me
 free,
 for I do not forget your law.
154 Be my advocate and gain my acquittal;
 as you promised, give me life.
155 Such deliverance is beyond the reach of
 the wicked,
 because they do not ponder your
 statutes.
156 Great is your compassion, Lord;
 by your decree grant me life.
157 Though my persecutors and my foes
 are many,
 I have not swerved from your
 instruction.
158 I was cut to the quick when I saw
 traitors
 who had no regard for your word.
159 See how I love your precepts!
 In your love, Lord, grant me life.
160 Your word is founded in steadfastness,
 and all your just decrees are
 everlasting.

161 Rulers persecute me without cause,
 but it is your word that fills me with
 awe.
162 I am jubilant over your promise,
 like someone who finds much booty.
163 Falsehood I abhor and detest,
 but I love your law.
164 Seven times each day I praise you
 for the justice of your decrees.
165 Peace is the reward of those who love
 your law;
 no pitfalls beset their path.
166 I hope for your deliverance, Lord,
 and I fulfil your commandments;
167 gladly I heed your instruction
 and love it dearly.
168 I heed your precepts and your
 instruction,
 for all my life lies open before you.

169 Let my cry of joy reach you, Lord;

ambivalent feelings about the Law. **135:** *Let your face shine:* regard favorably. **140:** *Tested:* proved valid. **150:**
Though evildoers may apprehend the psalmist, they cannot overpower the Law, which is the psalmist's support.
164: *Seven times:* either a symbolic number meaning "always" (compare Matt. 18.21), or an allusion to a pious
regimen of prayer.

give me insight as you have promised.
170 Let my prayers for favour reach you;
be true to your promise and save me.
171 Let your praise pour from my lips,
for you teach me your statutes;
172 let the music of your promises be on
my tongue,
for your commandments are justice
itself.
173 May your hand be prompt to help me,
for I have chosen your precepts;
174 I long for your deliverance, LORD,
and your law is my delight.
175 Let me live to praise you;
let your decrees be my help.
176 I have strayed like a lost sheep;
come, search for your servant,
for I have not forgotten your
commandments.

120 *A song of the ascents*
1 I CALLED to the LORD in my
distress,
and he answered me.
2 'LORD,' I cried, 'save me from lying lips
and from the deceitful tongue.'
3 What has he in store for you, deceitful
tongue?
What more has he for you?
4 Nothing but a warrior's sharp arrows
and red-hot charcoal.

5 Wretched is my lot, exiled in Meshech,
dwelling by the tents of Kedar.
6 Too long have I lived
among those who hate peace.

7 I am for peace, but whenever I speak
of it,
they are for war.

121 *A song of the ascents*
1 IF I lift up my eyes to the hills,
where shall I find help?
2 My help comes only from the LORD,
maker of heaven and earth.
3 He will not let your foot stumble;
he who guards you will not sleep.
4 The guardian of Israel
never slumbers, never sleeps.
5 The LORD is your guardian,
your protector at your right hand;
6 the sun will not strike you by day
nor the moon by night.
7 The LORD will guard you against all
harm;
he will guard your life.
8 The LORD will guard you as you come
and go,
now and for evermore.

122 *A song of the ascents: for David*
1 I REJOICED when they said to
me,
'Let us go to the house of the LORD.'
2 Now we are standing
within your gates, Jerusalem:
3 Jerusalem, a city built
compactly and solidly.

120:4 **red-hot charcoal:** *lit.* live coals of desert broom.
122:3 **compactly and solidly:** *or* where people come
together in unity.

Ps. 120: God answered me. Either a Thanksgiving (v. 1) which contains a past lamentation (vv. 2–7) or a Lament with God's assurance of deliverance. The superscriptions (see Introduction) designate Pss. 120–134 as "Songs of Ascents." The phrase could mean the ascent of pilgrims to the city of Jerusalem, one of the highest points in Palestine, and hence a song for one of the great annual pilgrim-feasts designated in Exod. 23.14–17; Deut. 16.16. It could also mean the ascent of a procession within Jerusalem up the steps leading to the temple; hence the interpretation of the superscription as "Psalms of the Steps." The theme of exile (v. 5) among a hostile people (vv. 6–7) with the resultant longing for Jerusalem, the city of peace, possibly made this a Pilgrim Song. **3:** *What more:* a formula commonly used for a curse in Heb.; compare 1 Sam. 25.22. **4:** *Sharp arrows:* death in battle. **5:** *Meshech:* an ancient people to the north of Palestine (Gen. 10.2) from whom the final enemy of Israel would come; see Ezek. 38.2. *Kedar:* a land in the Syrian desert, perhaps a symbol of hardship; see S. of S. 1.5–6. **7:** See 55.21.

Ps. 121: The guardian of Israel. A Hymn, another Song of Ascents (see Ps. 120 n.), pointing to Mount Zion as the source of protection in the dangers of the pilgrimage to Jerusalem (vv. 2–6) as well as in life (vv. 7–8). **1:** Sanctuaries were built on *hills,* both to the Canaanite Baals (2 Kgs. 23.5) and to the God of Israel for whom the temple on Mount Zion was built. **4:** *Never sleeps:* the affirmation is in sharp contrast with the anxiety in 44.23. **5:** The defendant of an accused person stood at his or her *right hand* at a trial. **8:** *Come and go:* the performance of one's daily work; see Deut. 28.6.

4 There the tribes went up, the tribes of
the LORD,
to give thanks to the name of the LORD,
the duty laid on Israel.
5 For there the thrones of justice were
set,
the thrones of the house of David.

6 Pray for the peace of Jerusalem:
'May those who love you prosper;
7 peace be within your ramparts
and prosperity in your palaces.'
8 For the sake of these my brothers and
my friends,
I shall say, 'Peace be within you.'
9 For the sake of the house of the LORD
our God
I shall pray for your wellbeing.

123 *A song of the ascents*
1 I LIFT my eyes to you
whose throne is in heaven.
2 As the eyes of slaves follow their
master's hand
or the eyes of a slave-girl the hand of
her mistress,
so our eyes are turned to the LORD our
God,
awaiting his favour.

3 Show us your favour, LORD, show us
favour,
for we have suffered insult enough.
4 Too long have we had to suffer
the insults of the arrogant,
the contempt of the proud.

124 *A song of the ascents: for David*
1 IF the LORD had not been on
our side —
let Israel now say —

2 if the LORD had not been on our side
when our foes attacked,
3 then they would have swallowed us alive
in the heat of their anger against us.
4 Then the waters would have carried us
away
and the torrent swept over us;
5 then over us would have swept
the raging waters.

6 Blessed be the LORD, who did not leave
us
a prey for their teeth.
7 We have escaped like a bird
from the fowler's trap;
the trap is broken, and we have
escaped.
8 Our help is in the name of the LORD,
maker of heaven and earth.

125 *A song of the ascents*
1 THOSE who trust in the LORD
are like Mount Zion:
it cannot be shaken; it stands fast for
ever.
2 As the mountains surround Jerusalem,
so the LORD surrounds his people both
now and evermore.
3 Surely wicked rulers will not continue
to hold sway
in the land allotted to the righteous,
or the righteous may put
their hands to injustice.
4 Do good, LORD, to the good,
to those who are upright in heart.
5 But those who turn aside into crooked
ways,
may the LORD make them go the way
of evildoers!

Peace be on Israel!

Ps. 122: **Pray for the peace of Jerusalem.** A Hymn, sung by admiring pilgrims as they entered or departed
the walls of Jerusalem. **5:** *Thrones of justice:* where the king held court (1 Kgs. 7.7). **6–9:** Pilgrims *pray* for
Jerusalem as they leave. **6:** *Peace:* in Heb. *shalom,* has wide-ranging positive meaning, namely, well-being,
happiness, and prosperity.

Ps. 123: **Show us your favour, LORD.** A Lament of the community which returned humbled and lowly from
the Exile and was exposed to the contempt of its neighbors; see Neh. 2.19. **1:** See Ps. 121.1. **3–4:** A plea for
help.

Ps. 124: **Our help is in the name of the LORD.** A Thanksgiving. See Ps. 120 n. on Songs of Ascents. The theme
is the deliverance of the nation from its foes. **4–5:** The metaphor of *waters* is also found in 69.1–2, 15. **8:**
Compare 121.2.

Ps. 125: **Peace be on Israel.** A Lament; a Song of Ascents (see 120 n.). **1–3:** The security of those who trust
in God is as solid as Mount Zion, the rock on which the temple stood. **4–5:** A plea for help.

126

A song of the ascents

1 WHEN the LORD restored the
fortunes of Zion,
we were like people renewed in health.
2 Our mouths were full of laughter
and our tongues sang aloud for joy.
Then among the nations it was said,
'The LORD has done great things for
them.'
3 Great things indeed the LORD did for
us,
and we rejoiced.

4 Restore our fortunes, LORD,
as streams return in the Negeb.
5 Those who sow in tears
will reap with songs of joy.
6 He who goes out weeping,
carrying his bag of seed,
will come back with songs of joy,
carrying home his sheaves.

127

A song of the ascents: for Solomon

1 UNLESS the LORD builds the
house,
its builders labour in vain.
Unless the LORD keeps watch over the
city,
the watchman stands guard in vain.
2 In vain you rise early
and go late to rest,
toiling for the bread you eat;
he supplies the need of those he loves.

3 Sons are a gift from the LORD
and children a reward from him.
4 Like arrows in the hand of a warrior
are the sons of one's youth.
5 Happy is he

who has his quiver full of them;
someone like that will not have to back
down
when confronted by an enemy in court.

128

A song of the ascents

1 HAPPY are all who fear the
LORD,
who conform to his ways.
2 You will enjoy the fruit of your labours,
you will be happy and prosperous.

3 Within your house
your wife will be like a fruitful vine;
your sons round your table
will be like olive saplings.
4 Such is the blessing in store
for him who fears the LORD.

5 May the LORD bless you from Zion;
may you rejoice in the prosperity of
Jerusalem
all the days of your life.
6 And may you live to see your children's
children!

Peace be on Israel!

129

A song of the ascents

1 OFTEN since I was young have
I been attacked —
let Israel now say —
2 often since I was young have I been
attacked,
but never have my attackers prevailed.
3 They scored my back with scourges,
like ploughmen driving long furrows.

126:1 **like . . . health:** *or* like dreamers.
127:2 **those he loves:** *prob. rdg; Heb. adds an
unintelligible word.* 127:5 **in court:** *lit.* in the gate.

Ps. 126: **Restore our fortunes, LORD.** A Lament with a prayer for deliverance, possibly from the hardships
the community experienced in the first years after the return from Exile; see Neh. 5.1–5. **1–2:** To the returned
Exiles their new life of freedom at first seemed like a dream (see Tfn.) as they *sang*, in contrast to their stay
in Babylon; compare 137.2–4. **4:** In the *Negeb*, which is southern Israel or Palestine, water courses, dry during
most of the year, all at once fill up with streams of water from sudden rains in winter.

Ps. 127: **Without the LORD all is in vain.** A Wisdom Psalm. Ascription of this Song of Ascents (see Ps. 120 n.)
to Solomon may be because of his reputation for wisdom or because of his building exploits. **1–2:** God is the
true source of security and blessing. **3–5:** The blessing of having many children. **5:** In an Israelite *court,* which
was held in an open forum, the larger one's family, the greater influence one had.

Ps. 128: **May the LORD bless you from Zion.** A Wisdom Psalm; see Ps. 120 n. **1–4:** It is a frequent theme
of Wisdom teaching that the faithful are blessed with a devoted family. **5–6:** A prayer for Jerusalem and for
peace.

Ps. 129: **Let all who hate Zion be thrown back in confusion.** A Lament of the community in which an
individual speaks for the whole nation, apparently in a cultic setting. See Ps. 120 n. **1:** Israel was *young* in the

4 The LORD is victorious;
he has cut me free from the bonds of
the wicked.

5 Let all who hate Zion
be thrown back in confusion;
6 let them be like grass growing on the
roof,
which withers before it can shoot,
7 which will never fill a mower's hand
nor yield an armful for the harvester,
8 so that passers-by will never say to
them,
'The blessing of the LORD be on you!
We bless you in the name of the LORD.'

130 *A song of the ascents*
1 LORD, out of the depths I have
called to you;
2 hear my cry, Lord;
let your ears be attentive
to my supplication.
3 If you, LORD, should keep account of
sins,
who could hold his ground?
4 But with you is forgiveness,
so that you may be revered.

5 I wait for the LORD with longing;
I put my hope in his word.
6 My soul waits for the Lord
more eagerly than watchmen for the
morning.
Like those who watch for the morning,
7 let Israel look for the LORD.

For in the LORD is love unfailing,
and great is his power to deliver.
8 He alone will set Israel free
from all their sins.

131 *A song of the ascents: for David*
1 LORD, my heart is not proud,
nor are my eyes haughty;
I do not busy myself with great affairs
or things too marvellous for me.
2 But I am calm and quiet
like a weaned child clinging to its
mother.

3 Israel, hope in the LORD,
now and for evermore.

132 *A song of the ascents*
1 LORD, remember David
and all the adversity he endured,
2 how he swore an oath to the LORD
and made this vow to the Mighty One
of Jacob:
3 'I will not live in my house
nor will I go to my bed,
4 I will give myself no rest,
nor allow myself sleep,
5 until I find a sanctuary for the LORD,
a dwelling for the Mighty One of
Jacob.'

6 We heard of the Ark in Ephrathah;
we found it in the region of Jaar.

131:2 **to its mother:** *prob. rdg; Heb. adds* as a weaned
child clinging to me.

Exodus from Egypt and in the wandering in the wilderness. **3:** *Ploughmen driving long furrows:* apparently a
popular metaphor (also found in a Ugaritic text 62.4–5). **5–8:** A curse, prompted by the danger from foes. **6:**
In Palestine a house has a flat *roof* made of clay from which *grass* sprouts after a rain but quickly *withers* in
the sunshine that follows. See Ps. 37.2. **8:** See Ps. 118.26; Ruth 2.4.

Ps. 130: **LORD, hear my cry.** A Lament; see Ps. 120 n. This psalm is one of the seven "Penitential Psalms"
(others are: Pss. 6, 32, 38, 51, 102, 143), so called because they are used in the Christian liturgy on occasions
of mourning as an expression of repentance. **1:** *Depths:* affliction of the spirit because of sinfulness rather than
physical misery. **4:** God's forgiveness evokes reverence and worship. **6–7:** Those keeping a military or
shepherd's *watch* during the darkest hours before dawn *eagerly* await the security of the *morning*. **8:** *Set Israel
free:* compare Isa. 44.22.

Ps. 131: **I am calm and quiet.** A fragment of a Song of Ascents; see Ps. 120 n. The psalm may be by a woman
who compares her spirit to the quiet security of the child on her breast. **1b:** The allusion in these words of
humility is unclear. **2:** For the suggestion that God is like a *mother* see Isa. 66.7–13.

Ps. 132: **The LORD swore to David.** A Royal Psalm. It was probably used in a liturgical setting, possibly at
a coronation ceremony or at a processional ceremony, to commemorate the finding of the Ark (vv. 6–8; see
1 Sam. 6.13) and its transfer to Jerusalem (2 Sam. ch. 6). This latter use put it into the category of the Ascents;
see Ps. 120 n. **2:** *Mighty One:* a name for God. **5:** *Dwelling:* a shrine to house the Ark of the Covenant above
which God was considered to be present in a special way; see Exod. 25.22. **6:** *Ephrathah:* Bethlehem, David's

7 Let us enter his dwelling;
  let us bow down at his footstool.
8 Arise, LORD, and come to your
    resting-place,
  you and your powerful Ark.
9 Let your priests be clothed in
    righteousness
  and let your loyal servants shout for
    joy.
10 For your servant David's sake
  do not reject your anointed one.

11 The LORD swore this oath to David,
  an oath which he will not break:
  'A prince of your own line
  I will set on your throne.
12 If your sons keep my covenant
  and heed the teaching that I give them,
  their sons in turn for all time
  will occupy your throne.'
13 For the LORD has chosen Zion,
  desired her for his home:
14 'This is my resting-place for ever;
  here I shall make my home, for that is
    what I want.
15 I shall bless her with food in plenty
  and satisfy her needy with bread.
16 I shall clothe her priests with victory;
  her loyal servants will shout for joy.
17 There I shall make a king of David's
    line appear
  and prepare a lamp for my anointed
    one;
18 I shall cover his enemies with shame,

but on him there will be a shining
  crown.'

133 A song of the ascents: for David
  1 How GOOD and how pleasant
    it is
  to live together as brothers in unity!
2 It is like fragrant oil poured on the
    head
  and falling over the beard,
  Aaron's beard, when the oil runs down
  over the collar of his vestments.
3 It is as if the dew of Hermon were
    falling
  on the mountains of Zion.
  There the LORD bestows his blessing,
  life for evermore.

134 A song of the ascents
  1 COME, bless the LORD,
  all you his servants,
  who minister night after night
  in the house of the LORD.
2 Lift up your hands towards the
    sanctuary
  and bless the LORD.
3 May the LORD, maker of heaven and
    earth,
  bless you from Zion!

135 1 PRAISE the LORD.

  Praise the name of the LORD;

132:17 **make ... appear:** *lit.* make a horn shoot for
David.

---

birthplace. *Jaar:* Kiriath-jearim, a city in Judah to which the Philistines returned the Ark after capturing it in battle; see 1 Sam. 6.13–7.2. **7:** *Footstool:* the Ark; see v. 5. **8:** *Arise, LORD:* a ceremonial exclamation when moving the Ark; see 68.1 and compare Num. 10.35. **9:** This is possibly a rubric for the *priests* to put on sacred vestments, i.e. be *clothed in righteousness,* and for the assembly to *shout for joy,* i.e. start singing as the procession begins. **11–18:** Possibly an oracle by a temple prophet proclaiming God's promises to David and to Zion. **17:** God lights a *lamp* for David by establishing his successor (see 1 Kgs. 11.36).

  Ps. 133: How pleasant to live in unity. A Wisdom Psalm; see Introduction. The united community of Israel is seen to be as beneficent as the oil that conferred the blessings of the priesthood and the dew that brought refreshment in the heat. **2:** *Oil on the head* was part of the ceremony of priestly consecration which brought a person into a brotherly relationship of temple ministers; see Exod. 29.7. **3:** *Hermon* is the highest mountain in Syria, whose peak is almost always covered with snow and lost in mist. It was believed by the ancients to be the source of the refreshing *dew* that settled on the parched countryside to the south of Palestine.

  Ps. 134: The LORD bless you from Zion. A Benediction which closes the Songs of Ascents (Ps. 120 n.) with a blessing. It consists of a liturgical dialogue between pilgrims who leave and the priests who remain on duty in the temple at night. **1–2:** Encouragement given to the priests, the *servants of the LORD,* by the pilgrims. **3:** Blessing imparted by the priests in the name of the LORD, from whom all blessings in *heaven* and on *earth* come. *Maker of heaven and earth:* also used in 121.2 and 124.8.

  Ps. 135: Praise the LORD. A Hymn which begins and ends with a ritual call to worship. It is composed almost

give praise, you servants of the LORD,
2 who minister in the house of the LORD,
in the temple courts of our God.
3 Praise the LORD, for he is good;
sing psalms to his name, for that is
pleasing.
4 For the LORD has chosen Jacob to be
his own,
Israel as his treasured possession.

5 I know that the LORD is great,
that our God is above all gods.
6 Whatever the LORD wills,
that he does, in heaven and on earth,
in the sea and all the great deep.
7 He brings up the mist from the ends of
the earth,
makes clefts for the rain,
and brings the wind out of his
storehouses.

8 He struck down all the firstborn in
Egypt,
both of humans and of animals.
9 In Egypt he sent signs and portents
against Pharaoh and all his subjects.
10 He struck down mighty nations
and slew powerful kings:
11 Sihon king of the Amorites, King Og of
Bashan,
and all the kingdoms of Canaan.
12 He gave their land as a heritage
to his people Israel.
13 LORD, your name endures for ever;
your renown, LORD, will last to all
generations,
14 for the LORD will give his people
justice;
he has compassion on his servants.

15 The gods of the nations are idols of
silver and gold,
fashioned by human hands.
16 They have mouths that cannot speak

and eyes that cannot see;
17 they have ears that cannot hear,
and there is no breath in their mouths.
18 Their makers become like them,
and so do all who put their trust in
them.

19 House of Israel, bless the LORD;
house of Aaron, bless the LORD.
20 House of Levi, bless the LORD;
you that fear the LORD, bless the LORD.
21 Blessed from Zion be the LORD,
he who dwells in Jerusalem.

Praise the LORD.

136 1 It is good to give thanks to the
LORD,
for his love endures for ever.
2 Give thanks to the God of gods;
his love endures for ever.
3 Give thanks to the Lord of lords —
his love endures for ever;
4 who alone works great marvels —
his love endures for ever;
5 who made the heavens in wisdom —
his love endures for ever;
6 who spread out the earth on the
waters —
his love endures for ever.
7 He made the great luminaries —
his love endures for ever:
8 the sun to rule the day —
his love endures for ever;
9 the moon and the stars to rule the
night —
his love endures for ever.

10 Give thanks to him
who struck down the firstborn of the
Egyptians —

135:5 **God:** *so Scroll; Heb.* Lord.   135:7 **clefts:** *prob.*
rdg; Heb. lightnings.   135:9 **In Egypt:** *lit.* In your
midst, Egypt.

entirely of allusions to, or borrowing from, other psalms and passages of the Bible. **7:** In the absence of meteorological science, the formation of *mist* was a mystery. Also, rain was thought to fall from *clefts* opened by God in the vault containing the waters above the heaven; see Gen. 1.6–8. **8–12:** God's deeds in history. **10:** For the defeat of *kings* see Num. 21.21–35. **15–18:** Similar to 115.4–8. **19–21:** For the house of *Israel, Aaron,* etc., see 115.9–11 n.

Ps. 136: God's love endures forever. A Hymn. In the Jewish liturgy it is called "the Great Hallel" since it was recited at the Passover meal after the "Lesser Hallel," i.e. Pss. 113–118. In structure it is a litany; that is, the refrain, "his love endures for ever," in the second half of every verse, was sung by the congregation in response to the first half of the verse sung by a soloist. The basic structure is an introduction (vv. 1–3); God's marvelous work in creation (vv. 4–9), in the Exodus (vv. 10–15), in the wilderness (vv. 16–20), in the Conquest

his love endures for ever—
11 and brought Israel out from among
   them;
   his love endures for ever.
12 With strong hand and outstretched
   arm—
   his love endures for ever—
13 he divided the Red Sea in two—
   his love endures for ever—
14 and made Israel pass through it;
   his love endures for ever.
15 But Pharaoh and his host he swept into
   the Red Sea;
   his love endures for ever.
16 He led his people through the
   wilderness;
   his love endures for ever.
17 He struck down great kings;
   his love endures for ever.
18 He slew powerful kings;
   his love endures for ever:
19 Sihon king of the Amorites—
   his love endures for ever—
20 and Og the king of Bashan;
   his love endures for ever.
21 He gave their land to Israel—
   his love endures for ever—
22 a heritage to Israel his servant;
   his love endures for ever.
23 He remembered us when our fortunes
   were low—
   his love endures for ever—
24 and rescued us from our enemies;
   his love endures for ever.
25 He gives food to all mankind;
   his love endures for ever.
26 Give thanks to the God of heaven,
   for his love endures for ever.

137 ¹ By the rivers of Babylon we sat
          down and wept
   as we remembered Zion.
² On the willow trees there
   we hung up our lyres,

³ for there those who had carried us
   captive
   asked us to sing them a song,
   our captors called on us to be joyful:
   'Sing us one of the songs of Zion.'
⁴ How could we sing the LORD's song
   in a foreign land?

⁵ If I forget you, Jerusalem,
   may my right hand wither away;
⁶ let my tongue cling to the roof of my
   mouth
   if I do not remember you,
   if I do not set Jerusalem
   above my chief joy.

⁷ Remember, LORD, against the Edomites
   the day when Jerusalem fell,
   how they shouted, 'Down with it, down
   with it,
   down to its very foundations!'
⁸ Babylon, Babylon the destroyer,
   happy is he who repays you
   for what you did to us!
⁹ Happy is he who seizes your babes
   and dashes them against a rock.

138 *For David*
          ¹ I SHALL give praise to you,
             LORD, with my whole heart;
   in the presence of the gods I shall sing
   psalms to you.
² I shall bow down towards your holy
   temple;
   for your love and faithfulness I shall
   praise your name,
   for you have exalted your promise
   above the heavens.
³ When I called, you answered me
   and made me bold and strong.

136:13,15 **Red Sea:** or sea of Reeds.   137:2 **willow trees:** or poplars.

(vv. 21–22), in the time of the Judges (vv. 23–25); and a conclusion (v. 26). **17–20:** Num. 21.21–35; compare Ps. 135.11.

Ps. 137: We sat down and wept. A Lament sung during or after the Exile after the destruction of Jerusalem by the Babylonians in 587 B.C.E. **1:** *Rivers of Babylon:* the Tigris and Euphrates and the irrigation ditches which branched off from them. **3:** A group of psalms which extol Jerusalem, the "city of God" are called the *songs,* or *canticles, of Zion;* they are Pss. 46, 48, 76, 84, 87, and 122. **7:** *Edomites* (from a country to the southeast of Judah) allied themselves with the Babylonians in plundering Jerusalem after the *day* of its capture in June–July, 587 B.C.E.; see Ezek. 35.5; Obad. 10–14. **9:** In ancient warfare children were often cruelly killed.

Ps. 138: I shall give praise to you, LORD. A Thanksgiving Psalm, probably a royal one sung in the temple. **1:** *Gods* can mean the godlike beings or angels who make up the heavenly assembly. **2:** *Promise above the*

⁴Let all the kings of the earth praise
  you, LORD,
when they hear the words you have
  spoken;
⁵let them sing of the LORD's ways,
for great is the glory of the LORD.
⁶The LORD is exalted, yet he cares for
  the lowly
and from afar he takes note of the
  proud.

⁷Though I am compassed about by
  trouble,
you preserve my life,
putting forth your power against the
  rage of my enemies,
and with your right hand you save me.
⁸The LORD will accomplish his purpose
  for me.
Your love endures for ever, LORD;
do not abandon what you have made.

139

For the leader: for David: a psalm
¹LORD, you have examined me
  and you know me.
²You know me at rest and in action;
you discern my thoughts from afar.
³You trace my journeying and my
  resting-places,
and are familiar with all the paths I
  take.
⁴For there is not a word that I speak
but you, LORD, know all about it.
⁵You keep close guard behind and
  before me
and place your hand upon me.
⁶Knowledge so wonderful is beyond my
  grasp;
it is so lofty I cannot reach it.

⁷Where can I escape from your spirit,
where flee from your presence?
⁸If I climb up to heaven, you are there;
if I make my bed in Sheol, you are
  there.
⁹If I travel to the limits of the east,

or dwell at the bounds of the western
  sea,
¹⁰even there your hand will be guiding
  me,
your right hand holding me fast.
¹¹If I say, 'Surely darkness will steal over
  me,
and the day around me turn to night,'
¹²darkness is not too dark for you
and night is as light as day;
to you both dark and light are one.

¹³You it was who fashioned my inward
  parts;
you knitted me together in my mother's
  womb.
¹⁴I praise you, for you fill me with awe;
wonderful you are, and wonderful your
  works.
You know me through and through:
¹⁵my body was no mystery to you,
when I was formed in secret,
woven in the depths of the earth.
¹⁶Your eyes foresaw my deeds,
and they were all recorded in your
  book;
my life was fashioned
before it had come into being.
¹⁷How mysterious, God, are your
  thoughts to me,
how vast in number they are!
¹⁸Were I to try counting them,
they would be more than the grains of
  sand;
to finish the count, my years must
  equal yours.

¹⁹If only, God, you would slay the
  wicked!
If those murderers would but leave me
  in peace!
²⁰They rebel against you with evil intent

139:8 **Sheol:** *or* the underworld.   139:11 **and . . .
night:** *or, with Scroll,* night will close around me.
139:14 **you are:** *so Gk; Heb.* I am. **You . . . and
through:** *cp. Gk; Heb.* as I know full well.
139:20 **rebel . . . you:** *so one form of Gk; Heb.* speak of
you.

heavens: God offers everything to humankind. **6:** Not only does God stay *afar* from the *proud,* those who aspire
to be God's equals, but God also humbles them, in bringing them lower than they were.
Ps. 139: Examine me, God. A Lament (see Introduction). Life is a gift of God and open to God who knows
intimately the inner soul of the poet. The poet offers to be examined by the all-searching, all-knowing God.
2: *At rest . . . in action:* the totality of human actions. **8:** Although God's knowledge encompassed *Sheol* (Job
26.6), God was ordinarily considered absent from it (Job 3.13–19). The view expressed in this verse is unique.
15: *Depths of the earth:* the womb, the emphasis being on the mystery of the process that is at work. **16:** *Your*

and as your adversaries they rise in
    malice.
21 How I hate those that hate you, LORD!
    I loathe those who defy you;
22 I hate them with undying hatred;
    I reckon them my own enemies.

23 Examine me, God, and know my mind;
    test me, and understand my anxious
      thoughts.
24 Watch lest I follow any path that
    grieves you;
    lead me in the everlasting way.

140 *For the leader: a psalm: for David*
1 RESCUE me, LORD, from
      evildoers;
keep me safe from those who use
    violence,
2 whose hearts are bent on wicked
    schemes;
day after day they stir up bitter strife.
3 Their tongues are as deadly as serpents'
    fangs;
on their lips is spiders' poison.   [*Selah*

4 Guard me, LORD, from the clutches of
    the wicked;
keep me safe from those who use
    violence,
who plan to thrust me out of the way.
5 The arrogant set hidden traps for me;
    villains spread their nets
and lay snares for me along my path.
                        [*Selah*
6 I say to the LORD, 'You are my God;
    LORD, hear my plea for mercy.
7 LORD God, my strong deliverer,
    you shield my head on the day of
      battle.
8 LORD, frustrate the desires of the
    wicked;
do not let their plans succeed.   [*Selah*
9 'When those who beset me raise their
    heads,

may their conspiracies engulf them.
10 Let burning coals be rained on them;
    let them be plunged into the miry
      depths,
    never to rise again.
11 The slanderer will find no home in the
    land;
disaster will hound the violent to
    destruction.'

12 I know that the LORD will give to the
    needy their rights
and justice to the downtrodden.
13 The righteous will surely give thanks to
    your name;
the upright will continue in your
    presence.

141 *A psalm: for David*
1 LORD, I call to you, come to
      my aid quickly;
listen to me when I call.
2 May my prayer be like incense set
    before you,
the lifting up of my hands like the
    evening offering.

3 LORD, set a guard on my mouth;
    keep watch at the door of my lips.
4 Let not my thoughts incline to evil,
    to the pursuit of evil courses
with those who are evildoers;
let me not partake of their delights.

5 I would rather be beaten by the
    righteous
and reproved by those who are good.
My head will not be anointed with the
    oil of the wicked,
for while I live my prayer is against
    their wickedness.

139:20 **rise:** *so Scroll; Heb. obscure.*
140:3 **spiders':** *meaning of Heb. word uncertain.*
140:9 **When . . . heads:** *prob. rdg; Heb. obscure.*
141:5 **while I live:** *prob. rdg; Heb. still and.*

book: see 56.8 n. **21:** God's cause is the cause of God's faithful, and vice versa; compare Matt. 12.30.
    Ps. 140: Rescue me, LORD. A Lament (see Introduction), a lengthy appeal for deliverance from enemies. **1–2:**
A prayer for help. **3–7:** The entrapment by the wicked. **3:** *Tongues:* possibly an allusion to a curse; compare
109.28. **6:** The plea is based on the psalmist's confession: *you are my God.* **8–11:** A curse on the enemies.
12–13: The psalmist's trust.
    Ps. 141: Listen to my cry. A Lament (see Introduction), with the usual vow absent. **2:** The fragrant smoke
of *incense* rising from the altar was a symbol of *prayer* acceptable to God; see Rev. 5.8. *Lifting . . . hands* is
a gesture of supplication which the poet prays may be acceptable as an *evening offering* which God had
commanded; see Exod. 29.38–42. **3:** *Guard on my mouth:* against sinful words. **5:** Anointing oneself with oil

⁶When they are brought down through
   the power of their rulers
they will learn how acceptable are my
   words.
⁷As when one ploughs and breaks up
   the ground,
our bones are scattered at the mouth of
   Sheol.

⁸But my eyes are fixed on you, LORD
   God;
you are my refuge; do not leave me
   unprotected.
⁹Keep me from the trap set for me,
   from the snares of evildoers.
¹⁰Let the wicked fall into their own nets,
   whilst all alone I pass on my way.

142 A maskil: for David (when he was in
   the cave): a prayer
¹I CRY aloud to the LORD;
to the LORD I plead aloud for mercy.
²I pour out my complaint before him
and unfold my troubles in his presence.
³When my spirit is faint within me,
   you are there to watch over my steps.

In the path that I should take
   they have hidden a snare for me.
⁴I look to my right hand,
I find no friend by my side;
no way of escape is in sight,
   no one comes to rescue me.

⁵I cry to you, LORD,
and say, 'You are my refuge;
you are my portion
   in the land of the living.
⁶Give me a hearing when I cry,
   for I am brought very low.
Save me from those who harass me,
   for they are too strong for me.

⁷Set me free from prison
that I may praise your name.'
The righteous will place a crown on
   me,
when you give me my due reward.

143 A psalm: for David
¹LORD, hear my prayer;
listen to my plea;
in your faithfulness and righteousness
   answer me.
²Do not bring your servant to trial,
for no person living is innocent before
   you.
³An enemy has hunted me down,
has crushed me underfoot,
and left me to lie in darkness like those
   long dead.
⁴My spirit fails me
and my heart is numb with despair.
⁵I call to mind times long past;
I think over all you have done;
the wonders of your creation fill my
   mind.
⁶Athirst for you like thirsty land,
I lift my outspread hands to you. [Selah
⁷LORD, answer me soon;
my spirit faints.
Do not hide your face from me
or I shall be like those who go down to
   the abyss.
⁸In the morning let me know of your
   love,
for I put my trust in you.
Show me the way that I must take,
for my heart is set on you.
⁹Deliver me, LORD, from my enemies;
with you I seek refuge.

141:7 **Sheol:** or the underworld.   142:7 **place ...
on:** or crowd around.   143:9 **with ... refuge:** so one
MS; others to you have I hidden.

was a sign of prosperity in festivity; see 23.5; Ezek. 16.9. **7:** *Bones at the mouth of Sheol:* symbol of shameful
death.

   Ps. 142: I cry aloud to the LORD. A Lament (see Introduction). See Ps. 30.8 and 77.1. **4:** *Right hand:* see
109.6 n. **5:** *Land of the living:* this earth. **7:** The vow usual in a Lament. *Prison:* probably meant figuratively
for the feeling of being hemmed in by enemies. *Praise your name:* the vow as a motive for deliverance. *Reward:*
liberation and restoration to an honorable status surrounded by the *righteous.*

   Ps. 143: LORD, answer me soon. A Lament (see Introduction). This is the last of the so-called "Penitential
Psalms" (see Ps. 130 n.). The poet confesses that because of sins he or she does not deserve to be heard in
strict justice (vv. 1–2) but only in God's love (vv. 8, 10, 12). **1:** God shows *faithfulness and righteousness* in
listening to the pleas of the psalmist. **7:** *Hide your face:* see 10.11 n. *Abyss:* Sheol, the place of the dead. **8–12:**
An appeal to God's love for deliverance and for the destruction of the enemies. **8:** In the darkness and loneliness
of night God seemed absent, but *morning* was the true indication of God's *love.*

10 Teach me to do your will, for you are
    my God;
 by your gracious spirit guide me on
    level ground.
11 Revive me, LORD, for the honour of
    your name;
 be my deliverer; release me from
    distress.
12 In your love for me, destroy my
    enemies
 and wipe out all who oppress me,
 for I am your servant.

144 *For David*
 ¹ BLESSED be the LORD, my rock,
 who trains my hands for battle,
 my fingers for fighting;
 ² my unfailing help, my fortress,
 my strong tower and refuge,
 my shield in whom I trust,
 he who subdues nations under me.

³ LORD, what are human beings that you
    should care for them?
 What are frail mortals that you should
    take thought for them?
⁴ They are no more than a puff of wind,
 their days like a fleeting shadow.
⁵ LORD, part the heavens and come
    down;
 touch the mountains so that they pour
    forth smoke.
⁶ Discharge your lightning-flashes far
    and wide,
 and send your arrows humming.
⁷ Reach out your hands from on high;
 rescue me and snatch me from mighty
    waters,
 from the power of aliens
⁸ whose every word is worthless,
 whose every oath is false.

⁹ I shall sing a new song to you, my God,
 psalms to the music of a ten-stringed

harp.
10 God who gave victory to kings
 and deliverance to your servant David,
 rescue me from the cruel sword;
11 snatch me from the power of aliens
 whose every word is worthless,
 whose every oath is false.

12 Our sons in their youth will be like
    thriving plants,
 our daughters like sculptured corner
    pillars of a palace.
13 Our barns will be filled with every kind
    of provision;
 our sheep will bear lambs in thousands
    upon thousands;
14 the cattle in our fields will be fat and
    sleek.
 There will be no miscarriage or
    untimely birth,
 no cries of distress in our public places.
15 Happy the people who are so blessed!
 Happy the people whose God is the
    LORD!

145 *A psalm of praise: for David*
 ¹ I SHALL extol you, my God and
    King,
 and bless your name for ever and ever.
² Every day I shall bless you
 and praise your name for ever and
    ever.
³ Great is the LORD and most worthy of
    praise;
 his greatness is beyond all searching
    out.
⁴ One generation will commend your
    works to the next
 and set forth your mighty deeds.
⁵ People will speak of the glorious
    splendour of your majesty;

144:5 **and come down:** *or* so that they come down.
144:14 **no . . . birth:** *or* no invasion or exile.
145:5 **People . . . speak of:** *so Scroll.*

Ps. 144: Rescue me from the cruel sword. A Lament (see Introduction), probably by a king (vv. 10–11). The first part, vv. 1–11, is almost completely borrowed from, or inspired by, other psalms: vv. 1–2 = 18.2–3; v. 3 = 8.4–5; v. 4 = 39.5; v. 5 = 18.9; vv. 9–10 = 18.49–50. **9:** The vow usual in a Lament. **12–14:** The blessing of peace and prosperity promised to Israel for obeying the Law; see Deut. 28.1–12. **12:** *Like sculptured corner pillars:* statuesque.

Ps. 145: I shall extol you, my God and King. A Hymn, many of whose phrases are similar to other psalms and other parts of the Bible. It extols the goodness and greatness of God. The preceding six psalms (139–144) are Laments, but the ensuing and last six (145–150) are Hymns. This acrostic psalm (see Ps. 111 n.) lacks a verse for the Heb. letter *nun* in the MT, possibly as a result of a copyist's omission; its place would be between

I shall meditate on your wonderful
   deeds.
⁶People will declare your mighty and
   terrible acts,
and I shall tell of your greatness.
⁷They will recite the story of your
   abounding goodness
and sing with joy of your righteousness.

⁸The LORD is gracious and
   compassionate,
long-suffering and ever faithful.
⁹The LORD is good to all;
his compassion rests upon all his
   creatures.
¹⁰All your creatures praise you, LORD,
and your loyal servants bless you.
¹¹They talk of the glory of your kingdom
and tell of your might,
¹²to make known to mankind your
   mighty deeds,
the glorious majesty of your kingdom.
¹³Your kingdom is an everlasting
   kingdom,
and your dominion endures throughout
   all generations.

¹⁴In all his promises the LORD keeps
   faith,
he is unchanging in all his works;
the LORD supports all who stumble
and raises all who are bowed down.
¹⁵All raise their eyes to you in hope,
and you give them their food when it is
   due.
¹⁶You open your hand
and satisfy every living creature with
   your favour.
¹⁷The LORD is righteous in all his ways,
faithful in all he does;
¹⁸the LORD is near to all who call to him,
to all who call to him in sincerity.
¹⁹He fulfils the desire of those who fear
   him;
he hears their cry for help and saves
   them.

²⁰The LORD watches over all who love
   him,
but the wicked he will utterly destroy.
²¹My tongue will declare the praises of
   the LORD,
and all people will bless his holy name
for ever and ever.

146   ¹PRAISE the LORD.

My soul, praise the LORD.
²As long as I live I shall praise the
   LORD;
I shall sing psalms to my God all my
   life long.
³Put no trust in princes
or in any mortal, for they have no
   power to save.
⁴When they breathe their last breath,
they return to the dust,
and on that day their plans come to
   nothing.

⁵Happy is he whose helper is the God of
   Jacob,
whose hope is in the LORD his God,
⁶maker of heaven and earth,
the sea, and all that is in them;
who maintains faithfulness for ever
⁷and deals out justice to the oppressed.
The LORD feeds the hungry
and sets the prisoner free.
⁸The LORD restores sight to the blind
and raises those who are bowed down;
the LORD loves the righteous
⁹and protects the stranger in the land;
the LORD gives support to the fatherless
   and the widow,
but thwarts the course of the wicked.

¹⁰The LORD will reign for ever, Zion,
your God for all generations.
Praise the LORD.

145:14 **In all ... works:** *so Scroll.*   145:16 **and ...
favour:** *or* and satisfy the desire of every living
creature.

vv. 13 and 14. **8–9:** The unique attributes of God in dealing with Israel and all humanity; see 86.15. **14–20:**
God's responsive attention to the needs of the faithful. **21:** The praise of God, an echo of vv. 1–4.

   Ps. 146: My soul, praise the LORD. A Hymn. The last five of the psalms (146–150) begin and end with *Praise
the LORD,* Heb. *Hallelujah.* **1–2:** The praise of God. **3–4:** Compare 144.3–4. **4:** *Return to the dust:* see Gen.
3.19. **5–10:** The great deeds, past and present, of God the Creator. **6–9:** In extolling God's deeds on behalf
of the poor in the present there is a subtle allusion to God's acts on behalf of Israel, *the oppressed, the hungry,
the prisoner,* the *bowed down,* in the Exodus.

147 [1] PRAISE the LORD.

How good it is to sing psalms to our
God!
How pleasant and right to praise him!
[2] The LORD rebuilds Jerusalem;
he gathers in the scattered Israelites.
[3] It is he who heals the broken in spirit
and binds up their wounds,
[4] who numbers the stars one by one
and calls each by name.
[5] Mighty is our Lord and great his
power;
his wisdom is beyond all telling.
[6] The LORD gives support to the humble
and brings evildoers to the ground.

[7] Sing to the LORD a song of
thanksgiving,
sing psalms to the lyre in honour of
our God.
[8] He veils the sky in clouds
and provides rain for the earth;
he clothes the hills with grass.
[9] He gives food to the cattle
and to the ravens when they cry.
[10] The LORD does not delight in the
strength of a horse
and takes no pleasure in a runner's
fleetness;
[11] his pleasure is in those who fear him,
who wait for his steadfast love.

[12] Jerusalem, sing to the LORD;
Zion, praise your God,
[13] for he has strengthened your barred
gates;
he has blessed your inhabitants.
[14] He has brought peace to your realm
and given you the best of wheat in
plenty.
[15] He sends his command over the earth,
and his word runs swiftly.
[16] He showers down snow, white as wool,
and sprinkles hoar-frost like ashes;

[17] he scatters crystals of ice like crumbs;
he sends the cold, and the water stands
frozen;
[18] he utters his word, and the ice is
melted;
he makes the wind blow, and the water
flows again.
[19] To Jacob he reveals his word,
his statutes and decrees to Israel;
[20] he has not done this for other nations,
nor were his decrees made known to
them.

Praise the LORD.

148 [1] PRAISE the LORD.

Praise the LORD from the heavens;
praise him in the heights above.
[2] Praise him, all his angels;
praise him, all his hosts.
[3] Praise him, sun and moon;
praise him, all you shining stars.
[4] praise him, you highest heavens,
and you waters above the heavens.
[5] Let them praise the name of the LORD,
for by his command they were created;
[6] he established them for ever and ever
by an ordinance which will never pass
away.

[7] Praise the LORD from the earth,
you sea monsters and ocean depths;
[8] fire and hail, snow and ice,
gales of wind that obey his voice;
[9] all mountains and hills;
all fruit trees and cedars;
[10] wild animals and all cattle,
creeping creatures and winged birds.
[11] Let kings and all commoners,
princes and rulers over the whole earth,
[12] youths and girls,
old and young together,
[13] let them praise the name of the LORD,

148:7 **sea monsters:** *or* waterspouts.

Ps. 147: **How good it is to sing psalms to our God.** A Hymn, possibly two separate psalms joined together;
the Sept. and Vg. treat this psalm as two (vv. 1–11 and 12–20) with a Hallelujah (see Ps. 146 n.) in vv. 1 and
20. **1:** The praise of God. **2–11:** God's power in history and over nature; God's goodness to the faithful. **2:**
A clue to the postexilic date of the poem. **12–20:** God's special care of Jerusalem and Israel. **15:** God's word
here is presented as a messenger, an active power in the world.

Ps. 148: **Let all praise the name of the LORD.** A Hymn; see Ps. 146 n. **1–12:** All that God has created should
give praise. **2:** *Hosts:* the armies of angels; compare Matt. 26.53. **4:** *The highest heaven:* i.e. God's dwelling,
where God is enthroned above the vault and the heavenly reservoir of waters: see Gen. 1.6–8. **5:** Compare

for his name is high above all others,
and his majesty above earth and
heaven.
14 He has exalted his people in the pride
of power
and crowned with praise his loyal
servants,
Israel, a people close to him.

Praise the LORD.

149 1 PRAISE the LORD.

Sing to the LORD a new song,
his praise in the assembly of his loyal
servants!
2 Let Israel rejoice in their maker;
let the people of Zion exult in their
king.
3 Let them praise his name in the dance,
and sing to him psalms with
tambourine and lyre.
4 For the LORD accepts the service of his
people;
he crowns the lowly with victory.
5 Let his loyal servants exult in triumph;
let them shout for joy as they prostrate
themselves.
6 Let the high praises of God be on their
lips
and a two-edged sword in their hand

7 to wreak vengeance on the nations
and punishment on the heathen,
8 binding their kings with chains,
putting their nobles in irons,
9 carrying out the judgement decreed
against them —
this is glory for all his loyal servants.

Praise the LORD.

150 1 PRAISE the LORD.

Praise God in his holy place,
praise him in the mighty vault of
heaven;
2 praise him for his acts of power,
praise him for his immeasurable
greatness.
3 Praise him with fanfares on the
trumpet,
praise him on harp and lyre,
4 praise him with tambourines and
dancing,
praise him with flute and strings;
5 praise him with the clash of cymbals;
with triumphant cymbals praise him.

6 Let everything that has breath praise
the LORD!
Praise the LORD.

Gen. ch. 1 and Ps. 33.6. **13–14:** Israel has a very special place but should not be alone in praising the name of the LORD.

Ps. 149: Sing to the LORD a new song. A Hymn; see Ps. 146 n. It reflects a liturgical setting. **3:** *Dance* seems to have been part of religious ceremony; see 2 Sam. 6.14; Exod. 15.20. **4–9:** A military victory appears to be reflected.

Ps. 150: Let everything praise the LORD. A Hymn. This is the last of Hallelujah psalms (see Ps. 146 n.) and it also is a final doxology to Book 5 and to all the psalms. A festival seems to be the background (vv. 3–5). **1:** *Holy place:* the temple. **3–5:** The various musical instruments used in the temple liturgy are indicated. **6:** *Praise* from all living beings, the note on which the Psalter closes.

Proverbs

The Book of Proverbs is a distillate of centuries of Israelite instruction in the home, court, and school. Called by some a foreign body in the Bible, Proverbs ignores major religious themes (covenant, ancestors, Exodus, Sinai, David) and makes creative use of non-Israelite wisdom traditions, particularly Egyptian. In substance, it represents the results of a search for a divinely sustained cosmic order in the lessons derived from human experience. Prudence plus knowledge are thought to have been conferred by God, and these are regarded as an authoritative repository, entrusted to the care of parents, teachers, and royal counselors. All insight being deemed a gift of God, Proverbs was thought of as revealed wisdom and hence was incorporated into Scripture.

Four long collections and five short appendixes are represented. Several headings indicate royal patronage (1.1; 10.1; 25.1); these and others (22.17; 24.23; 30.1; 31.1) testify to many centuries in which material accumulated. Chapters 1–9, by far the most religious collection, are the latest; these chapters have occasional stylistic affinities with Deuteronomy and prophecy. The oldest collections, surely preexilic, are 10.1–22.16 and 25.1–29.27; these are basically "secular." The teachings generally reflect an agricultural economy and are "this worldly" and optimistic despite a rigid principle of retribution. There is a characteristic tendency toward sharp contrast, such as rich/poor, wise/fool, good/evil.

Advice to the reader

1 ¹ THE proverbs of Solomon son of
David, king of Israel,
² by which mankind will come to wisdom
and instruction,
will understand words that bring
understanding,
³ and will attain to a well-instructed
intelligence,
righteousness, justice, and probity.
⁴ The simple will be endowed with
shrewdness

and the young with knowledge and
discretion.
⁵ By listening to them the wise will
increase their learning,
those with understanding will acquire
skill
⁶ to understand proverbs and parables,
the sayings and riddles of the wise.

⁷ The fear of the LORD is the foundation
of knowledge;

1.7 **foundation:** or chief part, or beginning.

1.1–7.27: Advice to the reader. This section differs both stylistically and thematically from the subsequent ones. Only here are there discussions of single topics in long paragraphs and also linguistic affinities with Deut. and the Prophets. The personification of Wisdom and Folly as two women is a major theme of the chapters; the picture of Wisdom is a derivative of the portrait of Folly. It is not fully clear how one is to view the allusions to the "foreign woman," whether: (1) she may be a participant in a fertility cult, that is, a sacred prostitute; or (2) simply a loose woman, foreign because her bad behavior sets her apart. In either case, the chapters burn with the intense conviction that since all knowledge derives from God it instructs human beings in the path of life. The superscription (1.1) recalls a tradition, 1 Kgs. 4.29–34, that Solomon composed or compiled proverbs and songs.

1.2–6: Introduction to the several collections. The editor gives reasons for studying the proverbial traditions. **6:** The Heb. word for *proverb* (*mashal*) implies a "likeness" or, less likely, an authoritative word, while that for *riddle* (*ḥidah*) suggests an enigmatic saying.

1.7–9: Recommendation of wisdom. 7: This motto of the book occurs again at 9.10, and in other forms in Job 28.28 and Ecclus. 1.14. It is in creative tension with the anthropocentricity ("centering on humankind")

it is fools who scorn wisdom and
  instruction.

8 Attend, my son, to your father's
  instruction
  and do not reject your mother's
  teaching;
9 they become you like a garland on your
  head,
  a chain of honour for your neck.

10 My son, if sinners entice you, do not
  yield.
11 They may say: 'Join us and lie in wait
  for someone's blood;
  let us waylay some innocent person who
  has done us no harm.
12 We shall swallow them like Sheol
  though they are alive;
  though in health, they will be like those
  who go down to the abyss.
13 We shall take rich treasure of every sort
  and fill our houses with plunder.
14 Throw in your lot with us
  and share the common purse.'
15 My son, do not go along with them,
  stay clear of their ways;
16 they hasten hotfoot into crime,
  pressing on to shed blood.
17 (A net is spread in vain
  if any bird that flies can see it.)
18 It is for their own blood they lie in
  wait;
  they waylay no one but themselves.
19 Such is the fate of all who strive after
  ill-gotten gain:
  it robs of their lives all who possess it.

20 Wisdom cries aloud in the open air,
  and raises her voice in public places.

21 She calls at the top of the bustling
  streets;
  at the approaches to the city gates she
  says:
22 'How long will you simple fools be
  content with your simplicity?
23 If only you would respond to my
  reproof,
  I would fill you with my spirit
  and make my precepts known to you.
24 But because you refused to listen to my
  call,
  because no one heeded when I
  stretched out my hand,
25 because you rejected all my advice
  and would have none of my reproof,
26 I in turn shall laugh at your doom
  and deride you when terror comes,
27 when terror comes like a hurricane
  and your doom approaches like a
  whirlwind,
  when anguish and distress come upon
  you.

'The insolent delight in their insolence;
  the stupid hate knowledge.
28 When they call to me, I shall not
  answer;
  when they seek, they will not find me.
29 Because they detested knowledge
  and chose not to fear the LORD,
30 because they did not accept my counsel
  and spurned all my reproof,
31 now they will eat the fruits of their
  conduct
  and have a surfeit of their own devices;

1:12 **Sheol:** *or* the underworld.   1:19 **Such ... fate:**
prob. rdg; Heb. Such are the courses.
1:22 **simplicity:** *continuation of verse 22 transposed to*
follow verse 27.   1:27 **The insolent ... knowledge:**
transposed from end of verse 22.

of most Wisdom texts. *Fools:* a moral rather than an intellectual judgment. **8:** A metaphor for student, *my son*
derives from the family setting in which fathers and mothers instructed children in the way of the wise. The
term is used frequently in Egyptian Wisdom literature for "pupil." **9:** *Garland:* a motif common in Egyptian
Wisdom literature.

  1.10–19: Warning against the sinner's style of life. The attractiveness of evil is negated by its ultimate result;
compare Wisd. 2.1–22. **12:** *Sheol:* the shadowy realm of the dead. **17:** A popular proverb enforces the warning
against gullibly paying heed to the enticing criminal.

  1.20–33: Wisdom in the role of prophetess. In striking prophetic style personified Wisdom pleads for a
hearing and rebukes those who pay no heed. **20–21:** Unafraid of competition, Wisdom speaks publicly at the
gates, the center of economic and judicial activity. **23:** *Fill you . . . :* lit. "I will pour out my spirit upon you
. . . ," recalling prophetic language, e.g. Isa. 44.3; Joel 2.28–29. **24:** The *hand* of God may be *stretched out*
either to strengthen or save a people or else to punish them; the former is intended here. The outstretched hand
is a frequent Deuteronomic expression for God's saving deeds in defeating the enemies of Israel; the image

32 for simpletons who turn a deaf ear
    come to grief,
and the stupid are ruined by their own
    complacency.
33 But whoever listens to me will live
    without a care,
undisturbed by fear of misfortune.'

2 My son, if you take my words to heart
    and treasure my commandments deep
        within you,
2 giving your attention to wisdom
    and your mind to understanding,
3 if you cry out for discernment
    and invoke understanding,
4 if you seek for her as for silver
    and dig for her as for buried treasure,
5 then you will understand the fear of
        the Lord
    and attain to knowledge of God.
6 It is the Lord who bestows wisdom
    and teaches knowledge and
        understanding.
7 Out of his store he endows the upright
    with ability.
For those whose conduct is blameless he
    is a shield,
8 guarding the course of justice
    and keeping watch over the way of his
        loyal servants.

9 You will then understand what is right
        and just
    and keep only to the good man's path,
10 for wisdom will sink into your mind,
    and knowledge will be your heart's
        delight.
11 Discretion will keep watch over you,
    understanding will guard you,
12 to save you from the ways of evildoers,
    from all whose talk is subversive,
13 those who forsake the right road
    to walk in murky ways,
14 who take pleasure in doing evil
    and exult in wicked and subversive acts,
15 whose ways are crooked,

whose course is devious.

16 It will save you from the adulteress,
    from the loose woman with her smooth
        words,
17 who has forsaken the partner of her
        youth
    and forgotten the covenant of her God;
18 for her house is the way down to death,
    and her course leads to the land of the
        dead.
19 None who resort to her find their way
        back
    or regain the path to life.

20 See then that you follow the footsteps
        of the good
    and keep to the paths of the righteous;
21 for the upright will dwell secure in the
        land
    and the blameless remain there;
22 but the wicked will be cut off from the
        land,
    those who are perfidious uprooted
        from it.

3 My son, do not forget my teaching,
    but treasure my commandments in
        your heart;
2 for long life and years in plenty
    and abundant prosperity will they bring
        you.
3 Let your loyalty and good faith never
        fail;
    bind them about your neck,
    and inscribe them on the tablet of your
        memory.
4 So will you win favour and success
    in the sight of God and man.

5 Put all your trust in the Lord
    and do not rely on your own
        understanding.

2:9 **keep:** *prob. rdg; Heb.* probity.   2:16 **adulteress:**
lit. strange woman. **loose woman:** *lit.* alien woman.

is also found in prophetic texts, where the idea of punishment is prevalent (see Isa. 5.25; 9.17, 21; 10.4). **32:** *Turn a deaf ear:* turn away, i.e. waywardness. **33:** See 3.24–26.

2.1–22: The fruits of wisdom. By diligent attention to the precepts of the sages one becomes heir to (1) insight into religious knowledge; (2) divine protection, both from evil ways and from adulterers; and (3) the promise of the land, i.e. possessions. **3:** *Invoke understanding:* this passage comes near to personifying wisdom; see 1.1–7.27 n. **9:** The insight is moral, what is *right* and *just.* **16:** *Loose:* lit. alien; a moral rather than an ethnic term. **17:** As frequently elsewhere, *covenant* is the term for the relation between God and people.

3.1–12: Divine trustworthiness. The Lord's discipline, like that of one's natural parents, has the best interests

⁶At every step you take keep him in
  mind,
and he will direct your path.
⁷Do not be wise in your own estimation;
fear the LORD and turn from evil.
⁸Let that be medicine to keep you in
  health,
liniment for your limbs.
⁹Honour the LORD with your wealth
and with the firstfruits of all your
  produce;
¹⁰then your granaries will be filled with
  grain
and your vats will brim with new wine.
¹¹My son, do not spurn the LORD's
  correction
or recoil from his reproof;
¹²for those whom the LORD loves he
  reproves,
and he punishes the son who is dear to
  him.

¹³Happy is he who has found wisdom,
he who has acquired understanding,
¹⁴for wisdom is more profitable than
  silver,
and the gain she brings is better than
  gold!
¹⁵She is more precious than red coral,
and none of your jewels can compare
  with her.
¹⁶In her right hand is long life,
in her left are riches and honour.
¹⁷Her ways are pleasant ways
and her paths all lead to prosperity.
¹⁸She is a tree of life to those who grasp
  her,
and those who hold fast to her are safe.

¹⁹By wisdom the LORD laid the earth's
  foundations
and by understanding he set the
  heavens in place;

²⁰by his knowledge the springs of the
  deep burst forth
and the clouds dropped dew.

²¹My son, safeguard sound judgement
  and discretion;
do not let them out of your sight.
²²They will be a charm hung about your
  neck,
an ornament to grace your throat.
²³Then you will go on your way without
  a care,
and your foot will not stumble.
²⁴When you sit, you need have no fear;
when you lie down, your sleep will be
  pleasant.
²⁵Do not be afraid when fools are
  frightened
or when destruction overtakes the
  wicked,
²⁶for the LORD will be at your side,
and he will keep your feet from the
  trap.
²⁷Withhold from no one a favour due to
  him
when you have the power to grant it.
²⁸Do not say to your neighbour, 'Come
  back again;
you can have it tomorrow'—when you
  could give it now.
²⁹Devise no evil against the neighbour
living trustingly beside you.
³⁰Do not pick a quarrel with a man for
  no reason,
when he has done you no harm.
³¹Do not emulate a violent person
or choose to follow his example;
³²for one who is not straight is detestable
  to the LORD,
but those who are upright are in God's
  confidence.

3:10 **with grain:** *or* to overflowing.   3:12 **he
punishes:** *prob. rdg, cp. Gk; Heb.* like a father.
3:22 **charm:** *lit.* life.   3:24 **sit:** *so Gk; Heb.* lie down.

of human beings at heart. **9:** *Firstfruits:* See Exod. 22.29. This is the sole cultic injunction in Prov.

3.13–18: Praise of Wisdom. In the style almost of a hymn the author extols Wisdom as a precious treasure.
13: *Happy:* the word that usually introduces beatitudes, as in "wisdom psalms" (Pss. 1, 32, etc.). **16:** The image
is likely that of the Egyptian goddess Maat, who holds in her *right hand* the symbol of life and in her *left* the
scepter, symbolizing wealth and dignity.

3.19–20: Wisdom's role at creation. Wisdom was at God's side at the creation of the universe. This motif
is elaborated in 8.22–31. **20:** *Deep:* underground springs. In Israelite thought the sources of water were three:
rain, dew, and underground streams (see Gen. 7.11; 2 Sam. 1.21).

3.21–35: Admonition and warning. A series of exhortations to commendable behavior is followed by
specific prohibitions, particularly in regard to the treatment of neighbors. **32:** *Detestable:* the word in the cultic

33 The LORD's curse falls on the house of
   the wicked,
  but he blesses the home of the
   righteous.
34 Though God meets the scornful with
   scorn,
  to the humble he shows favour.
35 The wise win renown,
  but disgrace is the portion of fools.

4 Listen, my sons, to a father's
   instruction,
  consider attentively how to gain
   understanding;
2 it is sound learning I give you,
  so do not forsake my teaching.
3 When I was a boy, subject to my father,
  tender in years, my mother's only child,
4 he taught me and said to me:
  'Hold fast to my words with all your
   heart,
  keep my commandments, and you will
   have life.

5 'Get wisdom, get understanding;
  do not forget or turn a deaf ear to
   what I say.
6 Do not forsake her, and she will watch
   over you;
  love her, and she will safeguard you;
8 cherish her, and she will lift you high;
  if only you embrace her, she will bring
   you to honour.
9 She will set a becoming garland on
   your head;
  she will bestow on you a glorious
   crown.

10 'Listen, my son, take my words to heart,
  and the years of your life will be many.
11 I shall guide you in the paths of
   wisdom;
  I shall lead you in honest ways.
12 When you walk nothing will impede
   you,
  and when you run nothing will bring
   you down.

13 Cling to instruction and never let it go;
  guard it well, for it is your life.
14 Do not take to the course of the wicked
  or follow the way of evildoers;
15 do not set foot on it, but avoid it,
  turn from it, and go on your way.
16 For they cannot sleep unless they have
   done some wrong;
  unless they have been someone's
   downfall they lie sleepless.
17 The bread they eat is gained by crime,
  the wine they drink is got by violence.
18 While the course of the righteous is like
   morning light,
  growing ever brighter till it is broad
   day,
19 the way of the wicked is like deep
   darkness,
  and they do not know what has been
   their downfall.

20 'My son, attend to my words,
  pay heed to my sayings;
21 do not let them slip from your sight,
  keep them fixed in your mind;
22 for they are life to those who find
   them,
  and health to their whole being.
23 Guard your heart more than anything
   you treasure,
  for it is the source of all life.
24 Keep your mouth from crooked speech
  and banish deceitful talk from your
   lips.
25 Let your eyes look straight before you,
  fix your gaze on what lies ahead.
26 Mark out the path that your feet must
   take,
  and your ways will be secure.
27 Deviate to neither right nor left;
  keep clear of evil.

5 'My son, attend to my wisdom
  and listen with care to my counsel,

3:34 **humble:** *or* wretched.   4:6 **safeguard you:** *so
Gk; Heb. adds* ⁷The foundation of wisdom. Get wisdom,
get understanding though it cost all you have.

sense is usually rendered "abomination," and is frequent in Deut. Originally it had the limited sense of ritual
uncleanliness.

4.1–27: Threefold recommendation of Wisdom. The supreme acquisition, Wisdom is indeed a lover or bride
(vv. 1–9); a path of light enabling one to walk in the right way (vv. 10–19); and the pathway itself (vv. 20–27).
3: *When I . . . :* This formula, one of self-abnegation, is also found in Wisd. 7.1.

5.1–23: Warning against the loose woman. Belying a beautiful appearance, the adulteress leads a youth
to destruction. He must be able to recognize deceitfulness (vv. 1–6) in order to steer clear of embarrassment

2 so that you may preserve discretion
  and your lips safeguard knowledge.
3 For though the lips of an adulteress
  drip honey
  and her tongue is smoother than oil,
4 yet in the end she is as bitter as
  wormwood,
  as sharp as a two-edged sword.
5 Her feet tread the downward path
  towards death,
  the road she walks leads straight to
  Sheol.
6 She does not mark out the path to life;
  her course twists this way and that, but
  she is unconcerned.'

7 Now, my sons, listen to me
  and do not ignore what I say:
8 keep well away from her
  and do not go near the door of her
  house,
9 or you will surrender your vigour to
  others,
  the pride of your manhood to the
  heartless.
10 Strangers will batten on your wealth,
  and your hard-won gains pass to the
  family of another.
11 When you shrink to skin and bone
  you will end by groaning 12 and saying,
  'Oh, why did I hate correction
  and set my heart against reproof?
13 Why did I not listen to the voice of my
  teachers
  and pay heed to my instructors?
14 I was almost brought to ruin
  in the public assembly.'

15 Drink water from your own cistern,
  fresh water from your own spring.
16 Do not let your well overflow into the
  road,
  your runnels of water pour into the
  street.
17 Let them be for yourself alone,

not shared with strangers.
18 Let your fountain, the wife of your
  youth,
  be blessed; find your joy in her.
19 A lovely doe, a graceful hind, let her be
  your companion;
  her love will satisfy you at all times
  and wrap you round continually.
20 Why, my son, are you wrapped in the
  love of an adulteress?
  Why do you embrace a loose woman?
21 The Lord watches a man's ways,
  marking every course he takes.
22 He who is wicked is caught in his own
  iniquities,
  held fast in the toils of his own sin;
23 for want of discipline he will perish,
  wrapped in the shroud of his boundless
  folly.

6 My son, if you give yourself in pledge
  to another person
  and stand surety for a stranger,
2 if you are caught by your promise,
  trapped by some promise you have
  made,
3 this is what you must do, my son, to
  save yourself:
  since you have come into the power of
  another,
  bestir yourself, go and pester the man,
4 give yourself no rest,
  allow yourself no sleep.
5 Free yourself like a gazelle from a net,
  like a bird from the grasp of the
  fowler.

6 Go to the ant, you sluggard,
  observe her ways and gain wisdom.
7 She has no prince,
  no governor or ruler;

5:5 **Sheol:** *or* the underworld.   5:6 **but . . .**
unconcerned: *or* and she is restless.   5:19 **let . . .**
companion: *so Gk; Heb. omits.*   6:5 **net:** *so Gk; Heb.*
hand.

and loss (vv. 7–14), particularly since he should be faithful to a solicitous spouse (vv. 15–23). **6:** The metaphor
is that of restless turning *this way and that,* characteristic of the opportunist, who, irresponsible, *is unconcerned.*
15: *Cistern:* a metaphor for wife (see v. 18); a cistern was important for storing precious water. **21:** That God
watches all the ways of a person is a theme in the Egyptian work by Amen-em-ope and in Mesopotamian hymns
to the sun-god Shamash. That God sees everything is essential to the belief in a judgment after life, a theme
prominent in Egypt.

6.1–19: Various admonitions. Do everything possible to be free of standing surety for another's debt
(vv. 1–5); do not be a sluggard (vv. 6–11; compare 24.30–34); avoid scoundrels who by gestures belie their
words (vv. 12–15); shun detestable habits (vv. 16–19; these are described by metaphors of the body in

⁸but in summer she gathers in her store
of food
and lays in her supplies at harvest.
⁹How long, you sluggard, will you lie
abed?
When will you rouse yourself from
sleep?
¹⁰A little sleep, a little slumber,
a little folding of the hands in rest—
¹¹and poverty will come on you like a
footpad,
want will assail you like a hardened
ruffian.

¹²A scoundrel and knave is one
who goes around with crooked talk,
¹³a wink of the eye,
a nudge with the foot,
a gesture with the fingers.
¹⁴His mind is set on subversion;
all the time he plots mischief and sows
strife.
¹⁵That is why disaster comes upon him
suddenly;
in an instant he is broken beyond all
remedy.

¹⁶Six things the LORD hates,
seven are detestable to him:
¹⁷a proud eye, a false tongue,
hands that shed innocent blood,
¹⁸a mind given to forging wicked
schemes,
feet that run swiftly to do evil,
¹⁹a false witness telling a pack of lies,
and one who sows strife between
brothers.

²⁰My son, observe your father's
commands
and do not abandon the teaching of
your mother;
²¹wear them always next to your heart
and bind them close about your neck.

²²Wherever you turn, wisdom will guide
you;
when you lie down, she will watch over
you,
and when you wake, she will talk with
you.
²³For a commandment is a lamp, and
teaching a light,
reproof and correction point the way to
life,
²⁴to keep you from the wife of another
man,
from the seductive tongue of the loose
woman.
²⁵Do not be infatuated by her beauty
or let her glance captivate you;
²⁶for a prostitute can be had for the price
of a loaf,
but a married woman is after the prize
of a life.

²⁷Can a man kindle a fire in his bosom
without setting his clothes alight?
²⁸If a man walks on live coals,
will his feet not be scorched?
²⁹So is he who commits adultery with his
neighbour's wife;
no one can touch such a woman and go
free.
³⁰Is not a thief contemptible if he steals,
even to satisfy his appetite when he is
hungry?
³¹And, if he is caught, must he not pay
seven times over
and surrender all that his house
contains?
³²So one who commits adultery is a
senseless fool:
he dishonours the woman and ruins
himself;
³³he will get nothing but blows and
contumely

6:22 **wisdom:** *lit.* she.   6:24 **the wife . . . man:** *prob. rdg; Heb.* the evil woman.

---

vv. 16–18). **16:** *Six . . . seven:* a common literary device, perhaps growing out of the parallel structure of a Heb. verse (see 10.1–22.16 n.). The device usually means "the totality of," rather than the specific number mentioned, but see 30.15b–16, 18–19, 21–31. **19:** The climax of the section is in *false witness* and *one who sows strife. . . .*

6.20–35: Warning against adultery. What young persons learn in the family setting can shield them from adultery. Whoever succumbs to the allurements of a married person cannot expect forgiveness from the wronged spouse. **23:** The *commandment is a lamp,* that is, more than simply a mechanical law. The psalms similarly throb with joyous exultation over the gift of the divine commandments. See too Deut. 6.4–9. **27:** This appears to be an old proverb about *fire* and its ill effects, applied to the destructive work of passions left unrestrained. **31:** *Seven times over:* contrast Exod. 22.1–4.

and can never live down the disgrace;
³⁴ for a husband's anger is rooted in jealousy
and he will show no mercy when he takes revenge;
³⁵ compensation will not buy his forgiveness,
nor will a present, however large, purchase his connivance.

7 My son, keep my words;
store up my commands in your mind.
² Keep my commands if you would live,
and treasure my teaching as the apple of your eye.
³ Wear them like a ring on your finger;
inscribe them on the tablet of your memory.
⁴ Call wisdom your sister,
greet understanding as a familiar friend;
⁵ then they will save you from the adulteress,
from the loose woman with her seductive words.
⁶ I glanced out of the window of my house,
I looked down through the lattice,
⁷ and I saw among the simpletons,
among the young men there I noticed a lad devoid of all sense.
⁸ He was passing along the street at her corner,
stepping out in the direction of her house
⁹ at twilight, as the day faded,
at dusk as the night grew dark,
¹⁰ and there a woman came to meet him.
She was dressed like a prostitute, full of wiles,
¹¹ flighty and inconstant,
a woman never content to stay at home,
¹² lying in wait by every corner,
now in the street, now in the public squares.

¹³ She caught hold of him and kissed him;
brazenly she accosted him and said,
¹⁴ 'I had a sacrifice, an offering, to make
and I have paid my vows today;
¹⁵ so I came out to meet you,
to look for you, and now I have found you.
¹⁶ I have spread coverings on my couch,
coloured linen from Egypt.
¹⁷ I have perfumed my bed
with myrrh, aloes, and cassia.
¹⁸ Come! Let us drown ourselves in pleasure,
let us abandon ourselves to a night of love;
¹⁹ for my husband is not at home.
He has gone away on a long journey,
²⁰ taking a bag of silver with him;
he will not be home until full moon.'
²¹ Persuasively she cajoled him,
coaxing him with seductive words.
²² He followed her, the simple fool,
like an ox on its way to be slaughtered,
like an antelope bounding into the noose,
²³ like a bird hurrying into the trap;
he did not know he was risking his life
until the arrow pierced his vitals.
²⁴ But now, my sons, listen to me,
and attend to what I say.
²⁵ Do not let desire entice you into her ways,
do not stray down her paths;
²⁶ many has she wounded and laid low,
and her victims are without number.
²⁷ Her house is the entrance to Sheol,
leading down to the halls of death.

Wisdom and folly

8 HEAR how wisdom calls
and understanding lifts her voice.
² She takes her stand at the crossroads,
by the wayside, at the top of the hill;

7.27 **Sheol:** *or* the underworld.

7.1–27: Wisdom as a defense against loose people. The words of the sages will protect one from the seduction of one whose way of working is described by an observer, safely from a distance. **4:** *Sister:* probably bride, as in S. of S. 4.9–10, 12, and in Egyptian love literature. **14:** Having had an animal *sacrifice,* the jubilant one is now ready to enjoy the subsequent feast; see Lev. 7.15. Irony is intended in the contrast of ritual observance and personal dissoluteness. See also 15.8 and Isa. 1.11–17.

8.1–9.18: Wisdom and Folly personified as two women and contrasted. Wisdom seeks out individuals where they usually congregate, and hence is readily available to, and clearly understandable by, all who wish to respond (8.1–13). Wisdom enables monarchs to rule as befits true kings (vv. 14–16). Those who seek

³beside the gate, at the entrance to the city,
at the approach by the portals she cries aloud:
⁴'It is to you I call,
to all mankind I appeal:
⁵understand, you simpletons, what it is to be shrewd;
you stupid people, understand what it is to have sense.
⁶Listen! For I shall speak clearly,
you will have plain speech from me;
⁷for I speak nothing but truth,
and my lips detest wicked talk.
⁸All that I say is right,
not a word is twisted or crooked.
⁹All is straightforward to those with understanding,
all is plain to those who have knowledge.
¹⁰Choose my instruction rather than silver,
knowledge rather than pure gold;
¹¹for wisdom is better than red coral,
and no jewel can match her.

¹²'I am wisdom, I bestow shrewdness
and show the way to knowledge and discretion.
¹³To fear the LORD is to hate evil.
Pride, arrogance, evil ways,
subversive talk, all those I hate.
¹⁴From me come advice and ability;
understanding and power are mine.
¹⁵Through me kings hold sway
and governors enact just laws.
¹⁶Through me princes wield authority,
from me all rulers on earth derive their rank.
¹⁷Those who love me I love,
and those who search for me will find me.
¹⁸In my hands are riches and honour,
boundless wealth and prosperity.
¹⁹My harvest is better even than fine gold,
and my revenue better than choice silver.
²⁰I follow the course of justice
and keep to the path of equity.
²¹I endow with riches those who love me;
I shall fill their treasuries.

²²'The LORD created me the first of his works
long ago, before all else that he made.
²³I was formed in earliest times,
at the beginning, before earth itself.
²⁴I was born when there was yet no ocean,
when there were no springs brimming with water.
²⁵Before the mountains were settled in their place,
before the hills I was born,
²⁶when as yet he had made neither land nor streams
nor the mass of the earth's soil.
²⁷When he set the heavens in place I was there,
when he girdled the ocean with the horizon,
²⁸when he fixed the canopy of clouds overhead
and confined the springs of the deep,
²⁹when he prescribed limits for the sea
so that the waters do not transgress his command,
when he made earth's foundations firm.
³⁰Then I was at his side each day,
his darling and delight,
playing in his presence continually,

8:16 **rulers on earth:** *so some MSS; others* who rule in righteousness. 8:26 **streams:** *or* fields. **the mass:** *or* the first. 8:30 **darling:** *or* craftsman; *Heb. obscure.*

Wisdom find the object of their search and gain wealth and rewards beyond wealth (vv. 17–21). Created as the first of God's works, Wisdom delights in people even as God delights in Wisdom (vv. 22–36). Like a gracious host, Wisdom invites guests to house and table (9.1–6). The insolent reject Wisdom, whom the wise accept (vv. 7–12). By contrast, Stupidity (here understood as Folly in its most pejorative sense, vv. 13–18) invites fools to destruction. **13:** The verse has suffered in ancient copying. It was probably once a numerical saying, possibly reading: "Three things I hate, indeed four I loathe; pride, presumption, evil courses, and subversive talk." **22:** The emphasis on Wisdom's role *before all else* came into being is common in Egyptian and Babylonian texts; see also Col. 1.15–16 and Jn. 1.1–3. *Created:* acquired, possessed. **30:** *Darling:* the Heb. is uncertain; perhaps the meaning is master worker or confidant. If darling, the figure is of a child playing in the presence of a loving parent. The personification of Wisdom is of profound theological significance, for it corrects a faulty notion that God was thought of in Wisdom literature as somewhat remote from creation. A

31 playing over his whole world,
   while my delight was in mankind.

32 'Now, sons, listen to me;
   happy are those who keep to my ways.
33 Listen to instruction and grow wise;
   do not ignore it.
34 Happy the one who listens to me,
   watching daily at my threshold
   with his eyes on the doorway!
35 For whoever finds me finds life
   and wins favour with the LORD,
36 but whoever fails to find me deprives
   himself,
   and all who hate me are in love with
   death.'

9 Wisdom has built her house;
   she has hewn her seven pillars.
2 Now, having slaughtered a beast, spiced
   her wine,
   and spread her table,
3 she has sent her maidens to proclaim
   from the highest point of the town:
4 'Let the simple turn in here.'
   She says to him who lacks sense,
5 'Come, eat the food I have prepared
   and taste the wine that I have spiced.
6 Abandon the company of simpletons
   and you will live,
   you will advance in understanding.'

7 Correct an insolent person, and you
   earn abuse;
   reprove a bad one, and you will acquire
   his faults.
8 Do not reprove the insolent person or
   he will hate you;
   reprove a wise one, and he will be your
   friend.
9 Lecture a wise person, and he will grow
   wiser still;

teach a righteous one, and he will add
   to his learning.

10 The first step to wisdom is the fear of
   the LORD,
   and knowledge of the Most Holy One is
   understanding;
11 for through me your days will be
   increased
   and years be added to your life.
12 If you are wise, it will be to your
   advantage;
   if you are arrogant, you alone must
   bear the blame.

13 The Lady Stupidity is a flighty
   creature;
   a fool, she cares for nothing.
14 She sits at the door of her house,
   on a seat in the highest part of the
   town,
15 to invite the passers-by indoors
   as they hurry on their way:
16 'Turn in here, simpleton,' she says,
   and to him who lacks sense she says,
17 'Stolen water is sweet
   and bread eaten in secret tastes good.'
18 Little does he know that the dead are
   there,
   that her guests are in the depths of
   Sheol.

A collection of wise sayings

10 PROVERBS of Solomon:
   A wise son is his father's joy,
   but a foolish son is a sorrow to his
   mother.
2 No good comes of ill-gotten wealth;

9:18 **Sheol:** *or* the underworld.

development in the idea of personification can be traced from Job ch. 28, which asks about Wisdom's hiding place, through 8.22–31 (and 3.19–20), to Ecclus. 24.1–22 and Wisd. 7.22–8.21. In Ecclus. 24.23 Wisdom is identified with Torah; the Greeks typically understood Wisdom as an emanation of God (see Wisd.). **9.1:** From the mention of *seven pillars* it has been conjectured that the house is really the world and the pillars are those which support the sky. Yet the figure seems modeled after vv. 14–15. **10:** Contrast Wisdom as something to be learned with the inner knowledge of God as in Jer. 31.33–34. **17:** Stupidity quotes an old proverb, to which may be compared the Arabic saying that "everything forbidden is sweet."

10.1–22.16: A collection of wise sayings. The section consists of observations from experience in the form of miscellaneous one-line maxims. Each verse is in parallelism, i.e. it consists of two balanced parts, as is usual in Heb. verse. The observations have a secular tone, and their date is preexilic. These proverbs may have been used for instruction in the home and in school. The mention of Solomon does not imply his authorship, but

uprightness is a safeguard against
  death.
3 The LORD will not let the righteous go
  hungry,
but he thwarts the desires of the
  wicked.
4 Idle hands make for penury;
diligent hands make for riches.
5 A prudent son gathers crops in
  summer;
a son who sleeps at harvest is a source
  of disappointment.
6 Blessings are showered on the
  righteous;
the speech of the wicked conceals
  violence.
7 The righteous are remembered in
  blessings;
the name of the wicked falls into decay.
8 A person who is wise takes
  commandments to heart,
but the foolish talker comes to grief.
9 One whose life is pure lives in safety,
but one whose ways are crooked is
  brought low.
10 A wink of the eye causes trouble;
a frank rebuke promotes peace.
11 The words of the righteous are a
  fountain of life;
the speech of the wicked conceals
  violence.
12 Hate is always picking a quarrel,
but love overlooks every offence.
13 The possessor of understanding has
  wisdom on his lips;
a rod is in store for the back of the
  fool.
14 The wise store up knowledge;
when a fool speaks, ruin is imminent.
15 The wealth of the rich is a strong
  city,
but poverty spells disaster for the
  helpless.
16 The reward of the good leads to life;
the earnings of the wicked make for a
  bad end.
17 Heed admonition and you are on the
  road to life;
neglect reproof and you miss the way.
18 Lying lips conceal hatred;
anyone who defames another is foolish.

19 When there is too much talk, offence is
  never far away;
the prudent hold their tongues.
20 The tongue of the righteous is like
  pure silver;
the mind of the wicked is trash.
21 The teaching of the righteous guides
  many,
but fools perish through lack of sense.
22 The blessing of the LORD is what brings
  riches,
and he sends no sorrow with them.
23 Lewdness is entertainment for the
  stupid,
wisdom a delight to men of
  understanding.
24 What the wicked dread will overtake
  them;
what the righteous desire will be
  granted.
25 When the whirlwind has swept past, the
  wicked are gone,
but the righteous are firmly established
  for ever.
26 Like vinegar to the teeth or smoke to
  the eyes,
so is the lazy servant to his master.
27 The fear of the LORD brings length of
  days;
the years of the wicked are cut short.
28 The hope of the righteous blossoms;
the expectation of the wicked withers
  away.
29 The LORD is a refuge for the blameless,
but he brings destruction on evildoers.
30 The righteous man will never be
  shaken;
the wicked will not remain in the land.
31 Wisdom flows from the mouth of the
  righteous;
the subversive tongue will be torn out.
32 The righteous suit words to the
  occasion;
the wicked know only subversive talk.

11 False scales are an abomination to
the LORD,
but accurate weights win his favour.

10:10 **a frank ... peace:** *so Gk; Heb.* a foolish talker
comes to grief, *cp. verse 8.*

rather his royal sponsorship, or else possibly a literary type. **2:** Premature death was thought to be an indication
of divine disfavor. **3:** See also Ps. 37.25. **6:** The doctrine of reward and punishment is here almost mechanical,
in that calamity is understood as punishment for sin. **25:** *Whirlwind:* God uses natural phenomena to punish

2 When pride comes in, in comes contempt,
but wisdom goes hand in hand with modesty.

3 Integrity is a guide for the upright;
the perfidious are ruined by their own duplicity.

4 Wealth avails naught in the day of wrath,
but uprightness is a safeguard against death.

5 By uprightness the blameless keep their course,
but the wicked are brought down by their own wickedness.

6 Uprightness saves the righteous,
but the perfidious are trapped by their own lies.

7 When someone wicked dies, all his hopes perish,
and any expectation of affluence ends.

8 The righteous are rescued from disaster,
and the wicked plunge into it.

9 By their words the godless try to ruin others,
but when the righteous plead for them they are saved.

10 A city rejoices in the prosperity of the righteous,
and when the wicked perish there is jubilation.

11 By the blessing of the upright a city is raised to greatness,
but the words of the wicked tear it down.

12 One who belittles others is lacking in sense;
someone of understanding holds his peace.

13 A tale-bearer gives away secrets,
but a trustworthy person respects a confidence.

14 For want of skilful strategy an army is lost;
victory is the fruit of long planning.

15 Give a pledge for a stranger and you will suffer;
refuse to stand surety and stay safe.

16 A gracious woman gets honour;
a bold man gets only a fortune.

17 Kindness brings its own reward;
cruelty earns trouble for itself.

18 A wicked person earns a delusive profit,
but he who sows goodness reaps a sure reward.

19 Anyone set on righteousness finds life,
but the pursuit of evil leads to death.

20 The LORD detests the crooked heart,
but honesty wins his favour.

21 Depend upon it: an evildoer will not escape punishment,
but the righteous and all their offspring will go free.

22 Like a gold ring in a pig's snout
is a beautiful woman without good sense.

23 The righteous desire only what is good;
what the wicked hope for comes to nothing.

24 One may spend freely and yet grow richer;
another is tight-fisted, yet ends in poverty.

25 A generous person enjoys prosperity,
and one who refreshes others will be refreshed.

26 Whoever holds back his grain is cursed by the people,
but one who sells it earns their blessing.

27 Someone who seeks what is good wins much favour,
but one who pursues evil finds it recoils upon him.

28 Whoever relies on his wealth is riding for a fall,
but the righteous flourish like leaves sprouting.

29 One who brings trouble on his family inherits the wind,
and a fool becomes slave to one who is wise.

30 The fruit of the righteous is a tree of life,
but violence results in the taking of life.

11:6 **their own:** *so Gk; Heb. omits.*   **11:25 will be refreshed:** *prob. rdg, cp. Lat.; Heb. obscure.*
11:30 **violence:** *so Gk; Heb. a wise person.*

those with whom the deity is angry (see especially Ecclus. 39.28–31 and Wisd. 16–19). **11.9:** *Saved:* in the courts, when the righteous *plead* as advocates of the weak. **21:** The strong statement (compare 24.15–16) seems to counter doubt about retribution, as if one cannot always or truly depend on it; such questioning of the justice of God is a recurrent theme in Eccles. and the major theme of Job. **30:** *Tree of life* (see Gen. 3.22–24): a symbol for eternal life found also in Egypt and Babylonia. Here eternal life arises from righteous living. The motif of

31 If the righteous get their deserts on
  earth,
  how much more will the wicked and
  the sinner!

12 He who loves correction loves
     knowledge;
  he who hates reproof is stupid.
2 The good man wins the LORD's favour,
  the schemer his condemnation.
3 No one can be established by
  wickedness,
  but the roots of the righteous will not
  be disturbed.
4 A capable wife is her husband's crown;
  one who disgraces him is like a canker
  in his bones.
5 The purposes of the righteous are just;
  the schemes of the wicked are full of
  deceit.
6 The wicked by their words lay a
  murderous ambush,
  but the words of the upright save them.
7 Once the wicked are down, that is the
  end of them,
  but the line of the righteous continues.
8 Intelligence is commended,
  but a warped mind is despised.
9 It is better to be modest and earn one's
  living
  than to play the grandee on an empty
  stomach.
10 A right-minded person cares for his
  beast,
  but one who is wicked is cruel at heart.
11 Someone who cultivates his land has
  plenty to eat,
  but one who follows idle pursuits lacks
  sense.
12 The stronghold of the wicked crumbles
  like clay,
  but the righteous take lasting root.
13 The wicked are ensnared by their own
  offensive speech,
  but the righteous come safely through
  trouble.
14 People win success by their words;
  they get the reward their work merits.
15 A fool's conduct is right in his own
  eyes;
  to listen to advice shows wisdom.
16 A fool betrays his annoyance at once;
  a clever person who is slighted conceals

his feelings.
17 An honest witness comes out with the
  truth,
  but the false one with deceit.
18 Gossip is sharp as a sword,
  but the tongue of the wise brings
  healing.
19 Truthful speech stands firm for ever,
  but lies live only for a moment.
20 Those who plot evil delude themselves,
  but there is joy for those who seek the
  common good.
21 No mischief will befall the righteous,
  but the wicked get their fill of
  adversity.
22 The LORD detests a liar
  but delights in honesty.
23 A clever person conceals his knowledge,
  but a stupid one blurts out folly.
24 Diligence brings people to power,
  but laziness to forced labour.
25 An anxious heart is dispiriting;
  a kind word brings cheerfulness.
26 The righteous are freed from evil,
  but the wicked take a path that leads
  astray.
27 The lazy hunter puts up no game;
  those who are diligent reap a rich
  harvest.
28 The way of righteousness leads to life,
  but there is a well-worn path to death.

13 A wise son heeds a father's
     instruction;
  the arrogant will not listen to rebuke.
2 The good enjoy the fruit of
  righteousness,
  but violence is meat and drink for the
  perfidious.
3 One who minds his words preserves his
  life;
  one who talks too much faces ruin.
4 Those who are lazy and torn by
  appetite are unsatisfied,
  but the diligent grow prosperous.
5 The righteous hate falsehood;
  the actions of the wicked are base and
  disgraceful.

12:12 **The stronghold ... clay:** *prob. rdg; Heb.* The
wicked covet a stronghold of crumbling earth.
12:26 **are... evil:** *prob. rdg; Heb.* let him spy out his
friend.   12:27 **those ... harvest:** *prob. rdg; Heb.*
obscure.   13:1 **heeds:** *prob. rdg, cp. Syriac; Heb. omits.*

the beneficial effect of correction is frequent in Prov. and underwent further development in later literature.

6 Right conduct protects the honest,
but wickedness brings sinners down.
7 One pretends to be rich, although he
has nothing;
another has great wealth but affects
poverty.
8 One who is rich has to pay a ransom,
but one who is poor is immune from
threats.
9 The light of the righteous burns
brightly;
the lamp of the wicked will be
extinguished.
10 A brainless fool causes strife by his
presumption;
wisdom is found among friends in
council.
11 Wealth quickly won dwindles away,
but if amassed little by little it will grow.
12 Hope deferred makes the heart sick;
a wish come true is a tree of life.
13 To despise a word of advice is to ask
for trouble;
mind a command, and you will be
rewarded.
14 The teaching of the wise is a fountain
of life
offering escape from the snares of
death.
15 Good sense wins favour,
but perfidy leads to disaster.
16 Clever people do everything with
understanding,
but the stupid parade their folly.
17 An evil messenger causes trouble,
but a trusty envoy brings healing.
18 To refuse correction brings poverty and
humiliation;
one who takes reproof to heart comes
to honour.
19 Desire fulfilled is sweet to the taste;
stupid people detest mending their
ways.
20 Walk with the wise and learn wisdom;
mix with the stupid and come to harm.
21 Ill fortune pursues the sinner;
good fortune rewards the righteous.
22 A good man leaves an inheritance to
his descendants,
but the sinner's hoard passes to the
righteous.
23 The fallow land of the poor may yield
much grain,

but through injustice it may be stolen.
24 A father who spares the rod hates his
son,
but one who loves his son brings him
up strictly.
25 The righteous eat their fill,
but the bellies of the wicked are empty.

14 Wise women build up their homes,
but with their own hands the
foolish pull theirs down.
2 A person whose conduct is upright
fears the LORD;
the double-dealer scorns him.
3 The speech of a fool is a rod for his
own back;
the words of the wise are their
safeguard.
4 Where there are no oxen, the barn is
empty;
the strength of an ox ensures rich
crops.
5 A truthful witness does not deceive;
the perjurer produces a pack of lies.
6 The arrogant aspire in vain to wisdom,
while to those with understanding,
knowledge comes readily.
7 Avoid a stupid person;
you will not hear a word of sense from
him.
8 Someone who is clever will have the wit
to find the right way;
the folly of the stupid misleads them.
9 Fools are too arrogant to make amends;
the upright know what reconciliation
requires.
10 The heart knows its own bitterness,
and in its joy a stranger has no part.
11 The house of the wicked will be torn
down,
but the dwelling of the upright will
flourish.
12 A road may seem straightforward,
yet end as the way to death.
13 Even in laughter the heart can ache,
and mirth may end in sorrow.
14 Renegades reap the reward of their
conduct,

13:11 **quickly won:** *so Gk; Heb.* because of emptiness.
13:15 **leads to disaster:** *prob. rdg, cp. Gk; Heb.* is
enduring.   13:16 **do ... understanding:** *or* in their
understanding conceal everything.   14:3 **his ...**
back: *prob. rdg; Heb.* pride.

13.23: The land here is either that left uncultivated every seventh year (Lev. 25.1–7) or the marginal areas left

the good the reward of their
achievements.

15 A simpleton believes every word he
hears;
a clever person watches each step.
16 One who is wise is cautious and avoids
trouble,
but one who is stupid is reckless and
falls headlong.
17 Impatience runs into folly;
advancement comes by careful thought.
18 Simpletons wear the trappings of folly;
the clever are crowned with knowledge.
19 Evildoers cringe before the good,
the wicked at the door of the righteous.
20 The poor are not liked even by their
friends,
but the rich have friends in plenty.
21 Whoever despises the hungry does
wrong,
but happy are they who are generous
to the poor.
22 Do not those who intend evil go
astray,
while those with good intentions are
loyal and faithful?
23 The pains of toil bring gain;
mere talk yields nothing but need.
24 Their wealth is the crown of the wise,
folly the chief ornament of the stupid.
25 A truthful witness saves lives;
a slanderer utters nothing but lies.
26 One who is strong and trusts in the
fear of the LORD
will be a refuge for his children.
27 The fear of the LORD is a fountain of
life
offering escape from the snares of
death.
28 Many subjects make for a king's glory;
lack of them makes a prince of no
account.
29 To be patient shows great
understanding;
quick temper is the height of folly.
30 Peace of mind gives health of body,
but envy is a canker in the bones.
31 To oppress the poor is to insult the
Creator;

to be generous to the needy is to do
him honour.
32 Evildoers are brought down by their
wickedness;
the upright find refuge in their
honesty.
33 Wisdom is at home in a discerning
mind,
but in the heart of a fool it is
suppressed.
34 Righteousness raises a people to
greatness;
to pursue wrong degrades a nation.
35 A king shows favour to a prudent
servant;
his displeasure falls on those who fail
him.

15 A mild answer turns away anger,
but a sharp word makes tempers
rise.
2 The tongues of the wise spread
knowledge;
the stupid talk a lot of nonsense.
3 The eyes of the LORD are everywhere,
surveying everyone, good and evil.
4 A soothing word is a tree of life,
but a mischievous tongue breaks the
spirit.
5 A fool spurns his father's correction,
but whoever heeds a reproof shows
good sense.
6 In the houses of the righteous there is
ample wealth;
the gains of the wicked bring trouble.
7 The lips of the wise promote
knowledge;
the hearts of the stupid are dishonest.
8 The sacrifices of the wicked are
abominable to the LORD,
but the prayers of the upright win his
favour.
9 The conduct of the wicked is
abominable to the LORD,
but he loves the seeker after
righteousness.

14:17 advancement . . . thought: *prob. rdg; Heb.* a
person of careful thought is hated. 14:21 the
hungry: *so Gk; Heb.* his friend. 14:32 honesty: *so
Gk; Heb.* death.

for the poor (Lev. 19.9–10). **14.4:** *Empty:* of fodder. **31:** The attitude to the poor is ambivalent in Wisdom
literature, for it is usually assumed that one's external circumstances indicate interior life, and hence a rich
person was enjoying God's reward and a poor one divine punishment. On the other hand, the wise championed
the cause of the widow, the orphan, and the poor. **33:** The harsh judgment on the *fool* is moral, associating
folly with sin (13.10; 14.9; 15.5, 7). **15.3:** *Eyes . . . everywhere:* God's scrutiny of individuals (see also 15.11;

10 Punishment awaits the one who
   forsakes the right way;
   he who hates reproof will die.
11 Sheol and Abaddon lie open before the
   LORD;
   how much more does the human
   heart!
12 The arrogant do not take kindly to
   reproof;
   they will not consult the wise.
13 A glad heart makes a cheerful face;
   heartache crushes the spirit.
14 A discerning mind seeks knowledge,
   but the stupid feed on folly.
15 To the downtrodden every day is
   wretched,
   but to have a merry heart is a perpetual
   feast.
16 Better a pittance with the fear of the
   LORD
   than wealth with worry in its train.
17 Better a dish of vegetables if love goes
   with it
   than a fattened ox eaten amid hatred.
18 Bad temper provokes quarrels,
   but patience heals discord.
19 The path of the sluggard is a tangle of
   briars,
   but the road of the diligent is a
   highway.
20 A wise son brings joy to his father;
   a young fool despises his mother.
21 Folly may amuse the empty-headed;
   a person of understanding holds to a
   straight course.
22 Schemes lightly made come to nothing,
   but with detailed planning they
   succeed.
23 Someone may be pleased with his own
   retort;
   how much better is a word in season!
24 For the prudent the path of life leads
   upwards
   and keeps them clear of Sheol below.
25 The LORD will pull down the houses of
   the proud,

but maintain the widow's boundary
   stones.
26 Evil thoughts are an abomination to the
   LORD,
   but the words of the pure are pleasing.
27 He who is grasping brings trouble on
   his family,
   but he who spurns a bribe will enjoy
   long life.
28 The righteous think before they
   answer;
   but from the mouths of the wicked
   mischief pours out.
29 The LORD stands aloof from the
   wicked,
   but he listens to the prayer of the
   righteous.
30 A bright look brings joy to the heart,
   and good news warms the bones to the
   marrow.
31 Whoever listens to wholesome reproof
   will enjoy the society of the wise.
32 Whoever refuses correction is his own
   worst enemy,
   but one who listens to reproof learns
   sense.
33 Wisdom's discipline is the fear of the
   LORD,
   and humility comes before honour.

16 A mortal may order his thoughts,
   but the LORD inspires the words his
   tongue utters.
2 A mortal's whole conduct may seem
   right to him,
   but the LORD weighs up his motives.
3 Commit to the LORD all that you do,
   and your plans will be successful.
4 The LORD has made each thing for its
   own end;
   so he has made the wicked for a day of
   calamity.

15:11 **Sheol and Abaddon:** *or* Death and Destruction.
15:19 **diligent:** *so* Gk; *Heb.* upright.   15:24 **Sheol:**
or the underworld.   15:26 **the words ... pleasing:**
prob. rdg; Heb. pleasant words are pure.

20.27; 24.11–12) assures the working out of divine retribution (10.7). **8:** See also 21.3. **11:** *Abaddon:* lit.
destruction or perdition. That is, God who sees into the realm of the dead surely sees into the hearts of living
persons. **25:** *Maintain:* that is, the LORD preserves her property intact. **16.1:** Humankind proposes but God
disposes; compare the Egyptian Amen-em-ope 20.5–6, "If the human tongue [be] the rudder of the boat, the
All-Lord is its pilot." **2:** A similar saying occurs in 21.2; see also v. 25. Compare the statement in a Babylonian
work that what is good with humankind is evil with the gods, and what is evil to people is proper to a god.
4: The second half of the verse expresses the view that God is the source of evil as well as good. This view
is characteristic of Hebrew "monism," namely, that the ultimate source of evil as well as good is God (see Isa.

⁵One and all the proud are abominable
to the LORD;
depend upon it: they will not escape
punishment.
⁶Guilt is wiped out by loyalty and faith,
and the fear of the LORD makes mortals
turn from evil.
⁷When the LORD approves someone's
conduct,
he makes even his enemies live at peace
with him.
⁸Better a pittance honestly earned
than great gains ill gotten.
⁹Someone may plan his journey by his
own wit,
but it is the LORD who guides his steps.
¹⁰The king's mouth is an oracle;
he does not err when he passes
sentence.
¹¹Accuracy of scales and balances is the
LORD's concern;
all the weights in the bag are his
business.
¹²Wrongdoing is abhorrent to kings,
for a throne rests firmly on
righteousness.
¹³Honest speech is what pleases kings,
for they hold dear those who speak the
truth.
¹⁴A king's anger is a herald of death,
and the wise will appease it.
¹⁵In the light of the king's countenance is
life;
his favour is like a rain-cloud in the
spring.
¹⁶How much better than gold it is to get
wisdom,
and to gain discernment is more
desirable than silver.
¹⁷The highway of the upright avoids evil;
he who watches his step preserves his
life.
¹⁸Pride goes before disaster,
and arrogance before a fall.
¹⁹Better live humbly with those in
need
than divide the spoil with the proud.

²⁰He who is shrewd in business will
prosper,
but happy is he who puts his trust in
the LORD.
²¹The sensible person seeks advice from
the wise;
persuasive speech increases learning.
²²Good sense is a fountain of life to its
possessors,
but a fool is punished by his own folly.
²³The wise person's mind guides his
speech,
and what his lips impart increases
learning.
²⁴Kind words are like dripping honey:
sweetness to the palate and health for
the body.
²⁵A road may seem straightforward to
the one who is on it,
yet it may end as the way to death.
²⁶The labourer's appetite impels him to
work,
hunger spurs him on.
²⁷A scoundrel rakes up evil gossip;
it is like a scorching fire on his lips.
²⁸Disaffection sows strife,
and tale-bearing breaks up the closest
friendship.
²⁹Anyone given to violence will entice
others
and lead them into evil ways.
³⁰Anyone narrowing his eyes intends
dishonesty,
and one who pinches his lips is bent on
mischief.
³¹Grey hair is a crown of glory,
which is won by a virtuous life.
³²Better be slow to anger than a fighter,
better control one's temper than
capture a city.
³³The lots may be cast into the lap,
but the issue depends wholly on the
LORD.

17 Better a dry crust and amity with it
than a feast in a house full of
strife.

45.6–7). **9:** Human wisdom recognizes its limits (see 30.4). The limitation on the nature of human knowledge
can induce some despair in sages, for they can no longer perceive any purpose in life. This despair is increased
greatly in Eccles. **10:** The king functions as the ultimate source of appeal for redress (20.8; see 1 Kgs. 3.16–28).
12: The idea of righteousness as a royal pedestal is an Egyptian motif as well. **15:** *Rain-cloud:* the seasonal
rain was eagerly awaited to assure the grain crop; hence the comparison with the favorable countenance of
the king. **30:** *Narrowing:* restricting oneself to an evil purpose. *Pinches the lips:* acts secretly to achieve an
aim. **33:** The decision of God was learned by casting *lots* (called Urim and Thummim, Exod. 28.15 n.) which

2 Where the son is a wastrel, a prudent
  slave is master,
and shares the inheritance with the
  brothers.
3 The smelting pot for silver, the crucible
  for gold,
but the LORD it is who assays the heart.
4 A rogue gives a ready ear to
  mischievous talk,
and a liar listens to slander.
5 To sneer at the poor is to insult the
  Creator,
and whoever gloats over another's
  misfortune will answer for it.
6 Grandchildren are the crown of old
  age,
and parents are the pride of their
  children.
7 Fine talk is out of place in a boor,
how much more are false words from a
  noble character!
8 A bribe works like a charm for him
  who offers it;
wherever he turns he will prosper.
9 One who covers up another's offence
  seeks his goodwill,
but one who betrays a confidence
  disrupts a friendship.
10 A reproof makes more impression on a
  discerning person
than a hundred blows on one who is
  stupid.
11 An evil person is set only on rebellion,
so a messenger without mercy will be
  sent against him.
12 Better face a she-bear robbed of her
  cubs
than a fool in his folly.
13 If anyone repays evil for good,
evil will never depart from his house.
14 Stealing water starts a quarrel;
abandon a dispute before you come to
  blows.
15 To acquit the guilty and to condemn
  the innocent —
both are abominable to the LORD.
16 What use is money in the hands of a
  fool?
Can he buy wisdom if he has no
  sense?
17 A friend shows his friendship at all
  times,
and a brother is born to share troubles.

18 Whoever gives a guarantee is without
  sense;
as surety he surrenders himself to
  another.
19 One who likes giving offence likes
  strife.
One who builds a lofty entrance invites
  disaster.
20 A crooked heart will come to no good,
and a mischievous tongue will end in
  calamity.
21 Stupid offspring bring sorrow to
  parents,
and no father has joy of a boorish son.
22 A glad heart makes for good health,
but low spirits sap one's strength.
23 A wicked person produces a bribe from
  under his cloak
to pervert the course of justice.
24 Wisdom is never out of sight of those
  who are discerning,
but the stupid have their eyes on the
  ends of the earth.
25 A stupid son exasperates his father
and is a heartache to the mother who
  bore him.

26 To punish the innocent is not right,
and it is wrong to inflict blows on those
  of noble mind.
27 Experience uses few words;
discernment keeps a cool head.
28 Even a fool, if he keeps his mouth shut,
  will seem wise;
if he holds his tongue, he will seem
  intelligent.

18   A solitary person pursues his own
      desires;
he quarrels with every sound policy.
2 The foolish have no interest in seeking
  to understand,
but only in expressing their own
  opinions.
3 When wickedness comes in, in comes
  contempt;
with loss of honour comes reproach.
4 The words of the mouth are a gushing
  torrent,
but deep is the water in the well of
  wisdom.

18:4 **The words … wisdom:** *prob. rdg, inverting phrases.*

were in the care of priests. **17.8:** *Bribe:* the meaning here is a proper gift, not a dishonest one; the verse

5 It is wrong to show favour to the
   wicked,
to deprive the righteous of justice.
6 When the stupid man talks, contention
   follows;
his words provoke blows.
7 The tongue of a stupid person is his
   undoing;
his lips put his life in jeopardy.
8 A gossip's whispers are tasty morsels
   swallowed right down.

9 The lazy worker is own brother
to the man who enjoys destruction.
10 The name of the LORD is a tower of
   strength,
where the righteous may run for
   refuge.
11 The wealth of someone who is rich is
   his strong city;
he thinks it an unscalable wall.
12 Before disaster comes one may be
   proud;
before honour comes one must be
   humble.
13 To answer a question before you have
   heard it out
is both stupid and insulting.
14 A person's spirit sustains in sickness,
but who can endure if the spirit is
   crushed?
15 Knowledge comes to the discerning
   mind;
the wise ear listens to get knowledge.
16 A gift opens the door to the giver
and gains access to the great.
17 In a lawsuit the first speaker seems
   right,
until another comes forward to
   cross-examine him.
18 Cast lots, and settle a quarrel,
and so keep litigants apart.
19 A reluctant brother is more unyielding
   than a fortress,
and quarrels are as stubborn as the bars
   of a fortress.
20 Someone may live by the fruit of his
   tongue;
his lips may earn him a livelihood.
21 The tongue has power of life and
   death;
make friends with it and enjoy its
   fruits.

22 He who finds a wife finds a good thing;
he has won favour from the LORD.
23 The poor speak in a tone of entreaty;
the rich give a harsh answer.
24 Some companions are good only for
   idle talk,
but there is a friend who sticks closer
   than a brother.

19 Better to be poor and above
       reproach
than rich and double-tongued.

2 It is not good to have zeal without
   knowledge,
nor to be in too great a hurry and so
   miss the way.
3 When folly wrecks someone's life,
he rages in his heart against the LORD.
4 Wealth makes many new friends,
but someone without means loses any
   friend he has.
5 A false witness will not escape
   punishment;
the perjurer will not go free.
6 Many curry favour with the great;
a lavish giver has the world for his
   friend.
7 A pauper's brothers all dislike him;
how much more is he shunned by his
   friends!
The man who picks his words keeps to
   the point.
8 To learn sense is true self-love;
cherish discernment and make sure of
   success.
9 A false witness will not escape
   punishment;
the perjurer will perish.
10 A fool at the helm is out of place,
how much worse a slave in command of
   men of rank!
11 Forbearance shows intelligence;
to overlook an offence brings glory.
12 A king's rage is like a lion's roar,
but his favour is like dew on the grass.
13 A stupid son is a calamity to his father;
a nagging wife is like water endlessly
   dripping.
14 Home and wealth may come down
   from ancestors,
but a sensible wife is a gift from the
   LORD.

19:1 **rich:** *prob. rdg; so Syriac, cp.* 28:6; *Heb.* a fool.

commends generosity. **18.10–11:** The trust in God, here expressed in *name,* is more dependable than a trust

¹⁵Sloth leads to sleep
and negligence to starvation.
¹⁶Keeping the commandments keeps a
person safe,
but scorning the way of the LORD
brings death.
¹⁷He who is generous to the poor lends
to the LORD,
who will recompense him for his deed.
¹⁸Chastise your son while there is hope
for him;
only be careful not to flog him to
death.
¹⁹Anyone whose temper is violent must
bear the consequences;
try to save him, and you make matters
worse.
²⁰Listen to advice and accept instruction,
and in the end you will be wise.
²¹The human mind may be full of
schemes,
but it is the LORD's purpose that will
prevail.
²²Greed is a disgrace to a man;
better be poor than a liar.
²³The fear of the LORD is life;
he who is full of it will rest untouched
by evil.
²⁴The sluggard dips his hand into the
dish
but will not so much as lift it to his
mouth.
²⁵Strike an arrogant person,
and the simpleton learns prudence;
reprove someone who has
understanding,
and he understands what you mean.
²⁶He who expels his father evicts his
mother;
they have a son who brings shame and
disgrace on them.
²⁷A son who ceases to accept correction
is sure to turn his back on the teachings
of knowledge.
²⁸A lying witness makes a mockery of
justice,
and the talk of the wicked fosters
mischief.
²⁹There is a rod in pickle for the
arrogant,
and blows are ready for the fool's
back.

20 Wine is an insolent fellow, strong
drink a brawler,
and no one addicted to their company
grows wise.
²A king's threat is like a lion's roar;
one who ignores it puts his life in
jeopardy.
³To draw back from a dispute is
honourable,
but every fool comes to blows.
⁴The lazy man who does not plough in
autumn
looks for a crop at harvest and gets
nothing.
⁵Counsel in another's heart is like deep
water,
but a discerning person will draw it up.
⁶Many assert their loyalty,
but where will you find one to keep
faith?
⁷If someone leads a good and upright
life,
happy are his children after him!
⁸A king seated on his throne in
judgement
has an eye to sift out all that is evil.
⁹Who can say, 'I have a clear conscience;
I am purged from my sin'?
¹⁰A double standard in weights and
measures
is an abomination to the LORD.
¹¹By his actions a child reveals himself,
whether or not his conduct is innocent
and upright.
¹²An attentive ear, an observant eye,
the LORD made them both.
¹³Love sleep, and you will know poverty;
keep awake, and you will eat your fill.
¹⁴'A bad bargain!' says the buyer to the
seller,
but off he goes to brag about it.
¹⁵There is gold in plenty and a wealth of
red coral,
but informed speech is a rarity.
¹⁶Take the garment of anyone who
pledges his word for a stranger;
hold it as security for the unknown
person.
¹⁷Bread got by fraud may taste good,
but afterwards it turns to grit in the
mouth.

19:27 **A son:** *so Gk; Heb.* My son.

in wealth. See 2 Sam. 22.3; Ps. 18.2. **24:** See 17.17. **20.16:** *A garment:* demand a significant pledge if it is
made by one on behalf of a stranger. Ordinarily a garment taken in pledge had to be returned at sundown (Exod.

18 Counsel is the key to good planning;
　wars are won by statecraft.
19 A gossip will betray secrets,
　so have nothing to do with a
　　tale-bearer.
20 If anyone reviles his father and mother,
　his lamp will fail when darkness is
　　deepest.
21 If you begin by amassing possessions in
　　haste,
　they will bring you no blessing in the
　　end.
22 Do not think to repay evil for evil;
　wait for the LORD to deliver you.
23 A double standard in weights is an
　　abomination to the LORD,
　and false scales are unforgivable.
24 It is the LORD who directs a person's
　　steps;
　how can anyone understand the road
　　he travels?
25 It is dangerous to dedicate a gift rashly,
　to make a vow and then have second
　　thoughts.
26 A wise king sifts out the wicked
　and turns the wheel of fortune against
　　them.
27 The LORD shines into a person's soul,
　searching out his inmost being.
28 Loyalty and good faith preserve a king;
　his throne is upheld by justice.
29 The glory of young men is their
　　strength,
　the dignity of old men their grey hairs.
30 A good beating purges the mind of
　　evil,
　and blows chasten the inmost being.

21 The king's heart is in the LORD's
　　hand;
　like runnels of water, he turns it
　　wherever he will.
2 A person's whole conduct may be right
　in his own eyes,
　but the LORD weighs up his motives.
3 To do what is right and just
　is more acceptable to the LORD than
　　sacrifice.
4 Haughty looks and a proud heart—
　these sins brand the wicked.

5 Forethought and diligence lead to
　　profit
　as surely as rash haste leads to poverty.
6 He who makes a fortune by telling lies
　runs needlessly into the snares of death.
7 The wicked are caught up in their own
　　violence,
　because they refuse to do what is just.
8 The criminal's conduct is devious;
　straight dealing is a sign of integrity.
9 Better to live on a corner of the
　　housetop
　than share the house with a nagging
　　wife.
10 The wicked are set on evil;
　even friends do not arouse their pity.
11 Simpletons learn wisdom when the
　　insolent are punished;
　when the wise prosper they draw a
　　lesson from it.
12 The Just One deals effectively with the
　　wicked household,
　overturning the wicked to their ruin.
13 Whoever stops his ears at the cry of the
　　helpless
　will himself cry for help and not be
　　answered.
14 A gift given privily appeases anger;
　a present in secret allays great wrath.
15 When justice is done, honest folk
　　rejoice,
　but it causes dismay among evildoers.
16 If someone takes leave of common
　　sense
　he will come to rest in the company of
　　the dead.
17 Love pleasure and you will end in
　　want;
　one who loves wine and oil will never
　　grow rich.
18 The wicked serve as a ransom for the
　　righteous,
　so do the perfidious for the upright.
19 Better to live alone in the desert
　than with a nagging and ill-tempered
　　wife!

20:21 **by . . . haste:** *or, as otherwise read,* by wrongfully
withholding an inheritance.　　20:28 **justice:** *so Gk;
Heb.* loyalty.　　21:6 **snares:** *prob. rdg, cp. Gk; Heb.*
seekers.

22.26).　**25:** Gifts *dedicated* to sanctuaries were accompanied by solemn oaths, not to be taken lightly; see Ps.
15.4.　**27:** *Shines:* God plants moral discernment within everyone.　**21.3:** See Hos. 6.6; Mic. 6.6–8.　**9:** *Corner:*
may mean a room apart.　**18:** *Ransom:* the price society pays; righteous individuals are clearly discerned by
comparison with the unrighteous.

20 The wise man has a houseful of fine
and costly treasures;
the stupid man will fritter them away.
21 He who perseveres in right conduct
and loyalty
finds life, prosperity, and honour.
22 He who is wise can attack a city full of
armed men
and undermine its boasted strength.
23 Keep a guard over your lips and
tongue
and you keep yourself out of trouble.
24 The conceited man is haughty, his
name is insolence;
overweening conceit marks all he does.
25 The sluggard's cravings will be the
death of him,
because his hands refuse to work;
26 all day long his cravings go unsatisfied,
while the righteous give without stint.
27 Sacrifice from a wicked person is an
abomination to the LORD,
the more so when it is offered from
impure motives.
28 A lying witness will be cut short,
but a truthful witness will speak on.
29 A wicked person puts a bold face on it,
whereas one who is upright looks to his
ways.
30 Face to face with the LORD,
wisdom, understanding, counsel avail
nothing.
31 A horse may be made ready for the day
of battle,
but victory rests with the LORD.

22 A good name is more to be desired
than great riches;
esteem is better than silver or gold.
2 Rich and poor have this in common:
the LORD made them both.
3 A shrewd person sees trouble coming
and lies low;
the simpleton walks straight into it and
pays the penalty.
4 The fruit of humility is the fear of God
with riches and honour and life.
5 Snares and pitfalls lie in the path of the
crooked;

the cautious person will steer clear of
them.
6 Start a child on the right road,
and even in old age he will not leave it.
7 The rich lord it over the poor;
the borrower becomes the lender's
slave.
8 Whoever sows injustice will reap
trouble;
the rod of God's wrath will destroy
him.
9 One who is kindly will be blessed,
for he shares his food with the poor.
10 Banish the insolent, and strife goes too;
discord and disgrace are ended.
11 The LORD loves a person to be sincere;
by attractive speech a king's friendship
is won.
12 The LORD keeps watch over every claim
at law,
and upsets the perjurer's case.
13 The sluggard protests, 'There is a lion
outside;
I shall be killed if I go on the street.'
14 The mouth of an adulteress is like a
deep pit;
he whom the LORD has cursed will fall
into it.
15 Folly is deep-rooted in the hearts of
children;
a good beating will drive it out of them.
16 Oppression of the poor brings gain,
but giving to the rich leads only to
penury.

Thirty wise sayings

17 PAY heed and listen to the sayings of
the wise,
and apply your mind to the knowledge
I impart;
18 to keep them in your heart will give
pleasure,
and then you will always have them
ready on your lips.
19 I would have you trust in the LORD

22:8 **destroy him:** *prob. rdg; Heb.* come to an end.
22:11 **The LORD:** *so Gk; Heb.* omits.

22.17–24.22(34): Thirty wise sayings. This section is dependent on the Egyptian work by Amen-em-ope, from which ten sayings have been derived and adapted to the Israelite setting. **17–21:** A prologue. The MT's reading (v. 20), formerly rendered "excellent things," has been corrected to "thirty sayings"—a very minor change in the Heb.—on the basis of the Amen-em-ope, where, as here, there are found both prologue and conclusion (for the latter see 24.21–22). **17:** *To the sayings of the wise:* possibly a superscription belonging

and so I make these things known to
you now.
20 Here I have written out for you thirty
sayings,
full of knowledge and wise advice,
21 to impart to you a knowledge of the
truth,
that you may take back a true report to
him who sent you.

22 Never rob anyone who is helpless
because he is helpless,
nor ill-treat a poor wretch in court;
23 for the LORD will take up their cause
and rob of life those who rob them.

24 Never make friends with someone
prone to anger,
nor keep company with anyone
hot-tempered;
25 be careful not to learn his ways
and find yourself caught in a trap.
26 Never be one to give guarantees,
or to pledge yourself as surety for
another;
27 for if you cannot pay, beware:
your very bed will be taken from under
you.

28 Do not move the ancient boundary
stone
which your ancestors set up.

29 You see an artisan skilful at his craft:
he will serve kings, not common men.

23 When you sit down to dine with a
ruler,
give heed to what is before you.
2 Cut down your appetite
if you are a greedy person.
3 Do not hanker after his dainties,
for they are not what they seem.
4 Do not slave to get wealth;
be sensible, and desist.
5 Before you can look around it is gone!
It will surely grow wings

like an eagle, like a bird in the sky.

6 Do not go to dine with a miserly
person,
and do not hanker after his dainties;
7 for they will stick in your throat like a
hair.
He will bid you eat and drink,
but in his heart he does not mean it;
8 you will bring up the morsel you have
eaten,
and your compliments will have been
wasted.

9 Do not address yourself to a stupid
person,
for he will disdain your words of
wisdom.

10 Do not move an ancient boundary stone
or encroach on the land of the
fatherless:
11 they have a powerful Guardian
who will take up their cause against
you.

12 Apply your mind to instruction
and your ears to words of knowledge.
13 Do not withhold discipline from a boy;
take the stick to him, and save him
from death.
14 If you take the stick to him yourself,
you will be preserving him from Sheol.

15 My son, if you are wise at heart,
my heart in turn will be glad;
16 I shall rejoice with all my soul
when your lips utter what is right.

17 Do not try to emulate sinners;
emulate only those who fear the LORD
all their days;
18 do this, and you may look forward to
the future,
and your hopes will not be cut short.

22:21 **to impart ... truth:** *prob rdg; Heb adds* words of
truth.   23:7 **your throat:** *prob. rdg; Heb.* his throat.
23:14 **Sheol:** *or* the underworld.   23:18 **do this:**
prob. rdg, cp. Gk; Heb. omits.

elsewhere and misplaced here. **28:** The prohibition against removing a landmark is in Amen-em-ope, ch. 6;
compare Prov. 23.10; Deut. 19.14 and 27.17. **23.1:** *What:* i.e. who: in whose presence you are. **2:** *Cut down
your appetite:* lit. "put a knife to your throat." **5:** *Eagle:* Amen-em-ope here reads geese, but since Palestine
has no such fowl, the Heb. text substitutes eagle. **10:** *Ancient:* Amen-em-ope reads widow (in Heb. 'almana);
'*olam*, "ancient," is a scribe's error; "widow's boundary" is a more suitable parallel for *the land of the fatherless.*
11: The next-of-kin was responsible for the welfare of the defenseless victim of the powerful (see Lev. 25.25;

¹⁹Listen, my son, and become wise;
　set your mind on the right course.
²⁰Do not keep company with drunkards
　or those who are greedy for the
　fleshpots.
²¹The drunkard and the glutton will end
　in poverty;
　in a state of stupor they are reduced to
　rags.

²²Listen to your father, who gave you
　life,
　and do not despise your mother when
　she is old.
²³Buy truth, and do not sell it;
　buy wisdom, instruction, and
　understanding.
²⁴A good man's father will rejoice
　and he who has a wise son will delight
　in him.
²⁵Give your father and mother cause for
　delight;
　may she who bore you rejoice.

²⁶My son, pay attention to me
　and accept my guidance willingly.
²⁷A prostitute is a deep pit,
　a loose woman a narrow well;
²⁸the one lies in wait like a robber,
　the other is unfaithful with man after
　man.

²⁹Whose is the misery? Whose the
　remorse?
　Whose are the quarrels and the
　anxiety?
　Who gets the bruises without knowing
　why?
　Whose eyes are bloodshot?
³⁰Those who linger late over their wine,
　those always sampling some new spiced
　liquor.
³¹Do not gulp down the wine, the strong
　red wine,
　when the droplets form on the side of
　the cup.
³²It may flow smoothly
　but in the end it will bite like a snake
　and poison like a cobra.
³³Then your eyes will see strange
　sights,

your wits and your speech will be
　confused;
³⁴you become like a man tossing out at
　sea,
　like one who clings to the top of the
　rigging;
³⁵you say, 'If I am struck down, what do
　I care?
　If I am overcome, what of it?
　As soon as I wake up,
　I shall turn to the wine again.'

24 Do not emulate the wicked
　or desire their friendship;
²for violence is all they think of,
　and mischief is ever on their lips.

³Wisdom builds the house,
　good judgement makes it secure,
⁴knowledge fills the rooms
　with costly and pleasing furnishings.

⁵Wisdom prevails over strength,
　knowledge over brute force;
⁶for wars are won by skilful strategy,
　and victory is the fruit of detailed
　planning.

⁷Wisdom is too lofty for a fool to grasp;
　he remains tongue-tied in the public
　assembly.

⁸Whoever is bent on mischief
　gets a name for intrigue;
⁹the intrigues of the foolish misfire,
　and the insolent are odious to their
　fellows.

¹⁰If you have shown yourself weak at a
　time of crisis,
　how limited is your strength!
¹¹Rescue those being dragged away to
　death,
　and save those being hauled off to
　execution.
¹²If you say, 'But this person I do not
　know,'
　God, who fixes a standard for the
　heart, will take note;

23:34 **clings to:** *prob. rdg; Heb.* lies on.　　24:12 **I:** *so
Gk; Heb.* we.

Ruth 4.1–6); here the *guardian* is God but it may originally have been Pharaoh. **20:** *Fleshpots:* meat was eaten
by most people only on special occasions; hence the danger of greed when it was served. **27:** *Deep pit:* dug
as a trap for wild animals. **28:** See 7.12. **24.11–22:** Passive virtue is inadequate. See Ps. 82.4; Isa. 58.6, 7;

he who watches you will know;
he will repay everyone according to
what he does.

13 Eat honey, my son, for it is good,
and the honeycomb is sweet to your
palate.
14 Seek wisdom for yourself;
if you find it, you may look forward to
the future,
and your thread of life will not be cut
short.

15 Do not lie in wait like a felon at the
upright person's house,
or raid his homestead.
16 Though he may fall seven times, he is
soon up again,
but the rogue is brought headlong by
misfortune.

17 Do not rejoice at the fall of your
enemy;
do not gloat when he is brought down,
18 or the LORD will be displeased at the
sight,
and will cease to be angry with him.

19 Do not vie with evildoers
or emulate the wicked;
20 for those who are evil can expect no
future;
their lamp will be extinguished.

21 My son, fear the LORD and fear the
king.
Have nothing to do with persons of
high rank;
22 they will come to sudden disaster,
and who knows what their ruin will
entail?

23 More sayings of the wise:

Partiality in dispensing justice is
invidious.
24 A judge who pronounces the guilty
innocent

is cursed by nations, and peoples
denounce him;
25 but it will go well with those who
convict the guilty,
and they will be blessed with prosperity.
26 A straightforward answer
is as good as a kiss of friendship.

27 Put in order your work out of doors
and make everything ready on the
land;
after that build yourself a home.

28 Do not testify against your neighbour
without good reason
or misrepresent him in your evidence.
29 Do not say,
'I shall do to him as he has done to me;
I am paying off an old score.'

30 I passed by the field of an idle fellow,
by the vineyard of someone with no
sense.
31 I looked, and it was all overgrown with
thistles;
it was covered with weeds,
and its stone wall was broken down.
32 I saw and I took it to heart,
I considered and learnt the lesson:
33 a little sleep, a little slumber,
a little folding of the hands in rest—
34 and poverty will come on you like a
footpad,
want will assail you like a hardened
ruffian.

Other collections of wise sayings

25 MORE proverbs of Solomon, transcribed by the men of King Hezekiah
of Judah:

2 The glory of God is to keep things
hidden,
but the glory of kings is to fathom
them.

24:14 **thread of life:** or hope.   24:22 **they ... will
entail?:** or they will bring about disaster without
warning; who knows what their ruin may cause?

1 Jn. 3.16. **16:** Verse 22; Ps. 34.19. **17:** See Job 31.29; Obad. 12.
   24.23–34: Miscellaneous proverbs, plus a narrative about a sluggard. **30–31:** Compare Isa. 5.1–7. **34:**
Identical with 6.11.
   25.1–31.9: Other collections of wise sayings. Chapters 25–29 are a second collection of "Proverbs of
Solomon." The reign of Hezekiah was 715–687 B.C.E. The official phrase *men of King Hezekiah* suggests that

³ The heavens for height, the earth for depth:
  unfathomable likewise is the mind of a king.
⁴ Rid silver of its impurities,
  then it may go to the silversmith;
⁵ rid the king's presence of the wicked,
  and his throne will rest firmly on righteousness.
⁶ Do not push yourself forward at court
  or take your stand where the great assemble;
⁷ for it is better to be told, 'Come up here,'
  than to be moved down to make room for a nobleman.
  What you have witnessed ⁸ be in no hurry to tell everyone,
  or it will end in reproaches from your friend.
⁹ Argue your own case with your neighbour,
  but do not reveal another's secrets,
¹⁰ or he will reproach you when he hears of it
  and your indiscretion will then be beyond recall.

¹¹ Like apples of gold set in silver filigree
  is a word spoken in season.
¹² Like a golden ear-ring or a necklace of Nubian gold
  is a wise person's reproof in an attentive ear.
¹³ Like the coolness of snow in harvest time
  is a trusty messenger to those who send him;
  he brings new life to his masters.
¹⁴ Like clouds and wind that bring no rain
  is he who boasts of gifts he never gives.
¹⁵ A prince may be won over by patience,
  and a soft tongue may break down authority.
¹⁶ If you find honey, eat what you need and no more;
  a surfeit will make you sick.
¹⁷ Be sparing in visits to your neighbour's house;
  if he sees too much of you, he will come to dislike you.
¹⁸ Like a club, a sword, or a sharp arrow
  is a false witness who denounces his friend.
¹⁹ Like a decaying tooth or a sprained ankle
  is a perfidious person relied on in the day of trouble.
²⁰ Like one who dresses a wound with vinegar,
  so is the sweetest of singers to the heavy-hearted.
²¹ If your enemy is hungry, give him food;
  if he is thirsty, give him a drink of water;
²² for so you will heap live coals on his head,
  and the LORD will reward you.

²³ As the north wind holds back the rain,
  so an angry glance holds back slander.
²⁴ Better to live on a corner of the housetop
  than share the house with a nagging wife.
²⁵ Like cold water to the throat that is faint with thirst
  is good news from a distant land.
²⁶ Like a muddied spring or a polluted well
  is a righteous man who gives way to a wicked one.
²⁷ A surfeit of honey is bad for one,
  and the quest for glory is onerous.
²⁸ Like a city breached and defenceless
  is a man who cannot control his temper.

26 Like snow in summer or rain at harvest,
  honour is unseasonable when paid to a fool.

25:20 **one who dresses:** *prob. rdg; Heb. adds* a garment on a cold day.

this king took an active interest in the welfare of the Wisdom tradition, as had Solomon before him. **7:** Compare Lk. 14.7–11. **12:** *Nubian:* Ethiopian. **14:** In a climate characterized by seasonal rainfall the first *clouds* promising *rain* after the many dry months are greeted eagerly and become particularly disappointing when no rain falls. **15:** Compare Ecclus. 28.17. **22:** The image of *live coals* may have had a cultic origin in Egypt. The figure is used in Rom. 12.20. **26.1:** Rainfall in Palestine is limited to certain seasons, so that the weather is highly predictable.

2 Like a fluttering sparrow or a darting
    swallow,
  groundless abuse gets nowhere.
3 The whip for a horse, the bridle for a
    donkey,
  the rod for the back of a fool!
4 Do not answer a fool as his folly
    deserves,
  or you will grow like him yourself;
5 answer a fool as his folly deserves,
  or he will think himself wise.
6 Whoever sends a fool on an errand
  cuts his own leg off and displays the
    stump.
7 A proverb in the mouth of fools
  dangles helpless as the legs of the lame.
8 Like one who ties the stone into his
    sling
  is he who bestows honour on a fool.
9 Like a thorn-stick brandished by a
    drunkard
  is a proverb in the mouth of a fool.
10 Like an archer who shoots at any
    passer-by
  is one who hires a fool or a drunkard.
11 A fool who repeats his folly
  is like a dog returning to its vomit.
12 Do you see that man who thinks
    himself so wise?
  There is more hope for a fool than for
    him.
13 The sluggard protests, 'There is a lion
    in the road,
  a lion at large on the street.'
14 A door turns on its hinges,
  a sluggard on his bed.
15 A sluggard dips his hand into the dish
  but is too lazy to lift it to his mouth.
16 A sluggard is wiser in his own eyes
  than seven who answer sensibly.

17 Like someone who seizes a stray cur by
    the ears
  is he who meddles in a quarrel not his
    own.
18 Like a madman shooting at random
  his deadly darts and lethal arrows,
19 so is the man who deceives another
  and then says, 'It was only a joke.'

20 For lack of wood a fire dies down
  and for want of a tale-bearer a quarrel
    subsides.
21 Like coal for glowing embers and wood
    for the fire
  is a quarrelsome man for kindling

strife.
22 A gossip's whispers are tasty morsels
  swallowed right down.

23 Like glaze spread on earthenware
  is glib speech that covers a spiteful
    heart.
24 With his lips an enemy may speak you
    fair
  but in his heart he harbours deceit;
25 when his speech is fair, do not trust
    him,
  for seven abominations fill his mind;
26 he may cloak his enmity in
    dissimulation,
  but his wickedness will be exposed
    before the assembly.

27 Whoever digs a pit will fall into it;
  if he rolls a stone, it will roll back upon
    him.
28 A lying tongue is the enemy of the
    innocent,
  and smooth words bring about their
    downfall.

27 Do not praise yourself for
    tomorrow's success;
  you never know what a day may bring
    forth.
2 Let praise come from a stranger, not
    from yourself,
  from the lips of an outsider and not
    from your own.
3 Stone is a burden and sand a dead
    weight,
  but to be vexed by a fool is more
    burdensome than both.
4 Wrath is cruel and anger is a deluge;
  but who can stand up to jealousy?
5 Open reproof is better
  than love concealed.
6 The blows a friend gives are well
    meant,
  but the kisses of an enemy are
    perfidious.
7 Someone who is full may refuse honey
    from the comb,
  but to the hungry even bitter food
    tastes sweet.
8 Like a bird that strays from its nest

26:10 **passer-by:** *transposed from end of verse.*
26:17 **meddles:** *so* Lat.; Heb. is negligent *or* becomes
enraged.   26:28 **the innocent:** *prob. rdg;* Heb. its
crushed ones.   27:6 **perfidious:** *meaning of Heb.*
word uncertain.

is a man straying from his home.

9 Oil and incense bring joy to the heart,
but cares torment one's very soul.

10 Do not neglect your own friend or your father's.

Do not run to your brother's house
when you are in trouble.

Better a neighbour near at hand than a
brother far away!

11 Acquire wisdom, my son, and bring joy
to my heart;

I shall have an answer for my critics.

12 A shrewd person sees trouble coming
and lies low;

the simpleton walks right into it and
pays the penalty.

13 Take the garment of anyone who
pledges his word for a stranger;

hold it as security for the unknown
person.

14 If someone wakes another early with
effusive greetings,

he might as well curse him!

15 A constant dripping on a rainy day—
that is what a woman's nagging is like.

16 As well try to control the wind as to
control her!

As well try to pick up oil in one's
fingers!

17 As iron sharpens iron,
so one person sharpens the wits of
another.

18 He who guards the fig tree will eat its
fruit,

and he who watches his master's
interests will come to honour.

19 As someone sees his face reflected in
water,

so he sees his own mind reflected in
another's.

20 Sheol and Abaddon are insatiable;
so too the human eye is never satisfied.

21 The smelting pot is for silver, the
crucible for gold;

so the character is tested by praise.

22 You may pound a fool in a mortar with
a pestle,

but his folly will never be knocked out
of him.

23 Be careful to know the state of your
flock

and take good care of your herds;

24 for possessions do not last for ever,
nor will a crown endure to endless
generations.

25 The grass is cropped, new shoots are
seen,

and the green growth on the hills is
gathered in;

26 the lambs provide you with clothing,
and the he-goats with the price of a
field,

27 while the goats' milk is food enough for
your household

and sustenance for your servant-girls.

28 The wicked flee, even though no
one pursues,

but the righteous are as confident as
young lions.

2 It is the fault of a violent person that
quarrels start,

but they are settled by one who
possesses discernment.

3 A tyrant oppressing the poor
is like driving rain that ruins the crop.

4 Those who abandon God's law applaud
the wicked;

those who keep it contend with them.

5 Evildoers have no understanding of
justice,

but those who seek the LORD
understand it well.

6 Better to be poor and above reproach
than rich and crooked.

7 A discerning son observes God's law,
but one who keeps profligate company
brings disgrace on his father.

8 He who grows rich by lending at
discount or at interest

is saving for another who will be
generous to the poor.

9 If anyone turns a deaf ear to God's law,
even his prayer is an abomination.

10 He who tempts the upright into evil
ways

will himself land in the pit he has dug;

27:9 **but cares . . . soul:** *so Gk; Heb.*
obscure.　　27:19 **another's:** *or himself.*
27:20 **Sheol and Abaddon:** *or* Death and Destruction.
28:2 **a violent person:** *so Gk; Heb.* land. **start:** *prob. rdg, cp.*
Gk; Heb. her officers. **they are settled:** *so Gk; Heb.* a knowing
man thus prolongs.

26.4–5: The two proverbs supplement each other: they are not in contradiction. **27.13:** See 20.16 n. **15:** See
19.13. **28.6:** See 14.31 n.

but the honest will inherit a fortune.

11 The person who is rich may think
    himself wise,
but the discerning poor will see
    through him.

12 When the just triumph, morale is high,
but when the wicked come to the top,
    the people are downtrodden.

13 Conceal your offences, and you will not
    prosper;
confess and renounce them, and you
    will obtain mercy.

14 Happy are those who are scrupulous in
    conduct,
but if one hardens his heart he falls
    into misfortune!

15 Like a roaring lion or a prowling bear
is a wicked ruler governing a helpless
    people.

16 The leader who is stupid and grasping
    will perish;
he who detests ill-gotten gain will live
    long.

17 Anyone charged with bloodshed
will jump into a well to escape arrest.

18 Whoever leads an honest life will be
    safe,
but a rogue will fall into a pit.

19 Those who cultivate their land will have
    food in plenty,
but those who follow idle pursuits will
    have poverty in plenty.

20 Someone of steady character will enjoy
    many blessings,
but one in a hurry to get rich will not
    go unpunished.

21 It is invidious to show partiality;
wrong may be done for a crust of
    bread.

22 The miser is in a hurry to become
    rich,
never dreaming that want may overtake
    him.

23 Take someone to task and in the end
    win more thanks
than he who has a flattering tongue.

24 To rob your father or mother and say
    you do no wrong
is no better than murder.

25 A grasping person provokes quarrels,
but he who trusts in the LORD will
    prosper.

26 It is stupid to trust to one's own wits,
but he whose guide is wisdom will come

safely through.

27 He who gives to the poor will never
    want,
but he who turns a blind eye gets
    nothing but curses.

28 When the wicked come to the top,
    people go into hiding;
but, when they perish, the righteous
    come into power.

29 Someone still stubborn after much
    reproof
will suddenly be broken past mending.

2 When the righteous are in power the
    people rejoice,
but they groan when the wicked hold
    sway.

3 A lover of wisdom brings joy to his
    father,
but an associate of harlots squanders
    wealth.

4 By just government a king maintains a
    country,
but by extortion it can be brought to
    ruin.

5 To flatter a neighbour
is to spread a net for his feet.

6 An evildoer is ensnared by his sin,
but the doer of good will live and
    flourish.

7 The righteous are concerned for the
    claims of the helpless,
but the wicked cannot understand such
    concern.

8 Arrogance can inflame a city,
but wisdom averts the people's anger.

9 If a wise person goes to law with a fool,
he will meet with unceasing abuse and
    derision.

10 Bloodthirsty men hate those who are
    honest,
but the upright see to their interests.

11 The stupid give free rein to their
    anger;
the wise wait for it to cool.

12 If a ruler listens to what liars say,
all his ministers become wicked.

13 The poor and the oppressors have this
    in common:
it is the LORD who gives light to the
    eyes of both.

28:18 **into a pit:** *prob. rdg; Heb.* in one.
28:25 **grasping:** *or* self-important.   29:6 **will live:** *so
some MSS; others obscure.*

28.13: *Mercy:* from human beings. Divine mercy plays little role in Wisdom literature.

¹⁴If a king steadfastly deals out justice to
   the weak
his throne will be secure for ever.
¹⁵Rod and reprimand impart wisdom,
   but an uncontrolled youth brings shame
   on his mother.
¹⁶When the wicked are in power, sin is in
   power,
but the righteous will witness their
   downfall.
¹⁷Correct your son, and he will be a
   comfort to you
and bring you the delights you desire.
¹⁸With no one in authority, the people
   throw off all restraint,
but he who keeps God's law leads them
   on a straight path.
¹⁹Mere words will not keep a slave in
   order;
he may understand, but he will not
   respond.
²⁰Do you see someone over-eager to
   speak?
There is more hope for a fool than for
   him.
²¹Pamper a slave from childhood,
   and in the end he will prove
   ungrateful.
²²Someone prone to anger provokes
   quarrels
and a hothead is always committing
   some offence.
²³Pride will bring anyone low,
   but honour awaits the lowly.
²⁴He who goes shares with a thief is his
   own enemy:
he hears himself put on oath but
   divulges nothing.
²⁵Fear of men may prove a snare,
   but trust in the LORD is a tower of
   refuge.
²⁶Many seek audience of a ruler,
   but it is the LORD who decides each
   case.
²⁷The righteous cannot abide the unjust,
   nor can the wicked abide him whose
   conduct is upright.

30 Sayings of Agur son of Jakeh from
   Massa:

This is the great man's very word: I am
   weary, God,
I am weary and worn out;
²I am a dumb beast, scarcely a man,
   without a man's powers of
   understanding;
³I have not learnt wisdom,
   nor have I attained to knowledge of the
   Most Holy One.
⁴Who has ever gone up to heaven and
   come down again?
Who has cupped the wind in the hollow
   of his hands?
Who has bound up the waters in the
   fold of his garment?
Who has fixed all the boundaries of the
   earth?
What is his name or his son's name?
   Surely you know!

⁵God's every promise has stood the test:
   he is a shield to all who take refuge in
   him.
⁶Add nothing to his words,
   or he will convict you and expose you
   as a liar.
⁷Two things I ask of you—
   do not withhold them in my lifetime:
⁸put fraud and lying far from me;
   give me neither poverty nor wealth,
   but provide me with the food I need,
⁹for if I have too much I shall deny you
   and say, 'Who is the LORD?'
and if I am reduced to poverty I shall
   steal
and besmirch the name of my God.

¹⁰Never disparage a slave to his master,
   or he will speak ill of you and you will
   be held guilty.
¹¹There are certain people who defame
   their fathers
and speak ill of their own mothers.
¹²There are people who are pure in their
   own estimation,
yet are not cleansed of their filth.

29:18 **no one in authority:** *or* no prophecy.
30:1 **from Massa:** *prob. rdg (cp. 31:1); Heb.* the oracle.

30.1–14: An appendix. The skeptical words of Agur (vv. 1–4), a non-Israelite, are followed by pious advice
(vv. 5–6), a prayer (vv. 7–9), and a description of evil types (vv. 11–14). **1:** *Massa:* probably a place in Arabia
(Gen. 25.14). The word also means "oracle." *Weary . . . worn out:* Some interpreters read here the proper names
Ithiel and Ucal; the translation has altered the extremely difficult text. **3–4:** The style is ironical, scorning those
who know too much about God, but the mood is agonized sadness.

13 There are people—how haughty are
     their looks,
   how disdainful their glances!—
14 there are people whose teeth are
     swords,
   whose fangs are knives;
   they devour the wretched from the
     earth
   and the needy from among mankind.

15 The leech has two daughters;
   'Give,' says one, and 'Give,' says the
     other.

   Three things there are which will never
     be satisfied,
   four which never say, 'Enough!'
16 Sheol, a barren woman,
   a land thirsty for water,
   and fire that never says, 'Enough!'

17 The eye that mocks a father or scorns a
     mother's old age
   will be plucked out by the ravens of the
     valley
   or eaten by young vultures.

18 Three things there are which are too
     wonderful for me,
   four which are beyond my
     understanding:
19 the way of an eagle in the sky,
   the way of a serpent over rock,
   the way of a ship out at sea,
   and the way of a man with a girl.

20 The way of an unfaithful wife is this:
   she eats, then wipes her mouth
   and says, 'I have done nothing wrong.'

21 Under three things the earth shakes,
   four things it cannot bear:
22 a slave becoming king,
   a fool gorging himself,
23 a hateful woman getting wed,
   and a slave supplanting her mistress.

24 Four things there are which are
     smallest on earth

yet wise beyond the wisest:
25 ants, a folk with no strength,
   yet they prepare their store of food in
     the summer;
26 rock-badgers, a feeble folk,
   yet they make their home among the
     rocks;
27 locusts, which have no king,
   yet they all sally forth in formation;
28 the lizard, which can be grasped in the
     hand,
   yet it is found in the palaces of kings.

29 Three things there are which are stately
     in their stride,
   four which are stately as they move:
30 the lion, mighty among beasts,
   which will not turn tail for anyone;
31 the strutting cock, the he-goat,
   and a king going forth at the head of
     his army.

32 If you are churlish and arrogant
   and given to scheming, hold your
     tongue;
33 for as the pressing of milk produces
     curd,
   and the pressing of the nose produces
     blood,
   so the pressing of anger leads to strife.

31 Sayings of King Lemuel of Massa,
   which his mother taught him:

2 What shall I say to you, my son,
   child of my womb and answer to my
     prayers?
3 Do not give the vigour of your
     manhood to women,
   or consort with women who bring down
     kings.
4 Lemuel, it is not for kings, not for
   kings to drink wine,

30:16 **Sheol:** *or* The underworld.   30:17 **old age:**
prob. rdg; Heb. unintelligible.   30:22 **fool:** *or* boor.
30:27 **in formation:** *meaning of Heb. word uncertain.*
30:31 **strutting cock:** *or* charger; *meaning of Heb.
uncertain.* **going forth ... army:** *prob. rdg; Heb.
unintelligible.*   30:33 **anger:** *lit.* the nostrils.

30.15–33: Another appendix. Some of these numerical sayings may originally have been riddles (e.g.
vv. 15b–16). **18–19:** The point seems to be the absence of all trace of the movement made. **20:** *Eats:* commits
adultery. The words are to be taken as symbolic of sexual relations.
    31.1–9: The advice of the queen mother, here an appendix, is paralleled in Egyptian royal instructions. **1:**
Lemuel: he is unknown. **4–9:** Those whose situation is desperate resort to *strong* drink; the king must not

or for those who govern to crave strong liquor.
⁵ If they drink, they will forget rights and customs
and twist the law against all who are defenceless.
⁶ Give strong drink to the despairing and wine to the embittered of heart;
⁷ let them drink and forget their poverty and remember their trouble no more.
⁸ Speak up for those who cannot speak for themselves;
oppose any that go to law against them;
⁹ speak out and pronounce just sentence and give judgement for the wretched and the poor.

A good wife

¹⁰ WHO can find a good wife?
Her worth is far beyond red coral.
¹¹ Her husband's whole trust is in her, and children are not lacking.
¹² She works to bring him good, not evil, all the days of her life.
¹³ She chooses wool and flax and with a will she sets about her work.
¹⁴ Like a ship laden with merchandise she brings home food from far off.
¹⁵ She rises while it is still dark and apportions food for her household, with a due share for her servants.
¹⁶ After careful thought she buys a field and plants a vineyard out of her earnings.
¹⁷ She sets about her duties resolutely and tackles her work with vigour.
¹⁸ She sees that her business goes well,

and all night long her lamp does not go out.
¹⁹ She holds the distaff in her hand, and her fingers grasp the spindle.
²⁰ She is open-handed to the wretched and extends help to the poor.
²¹ When it snows she has no fear for her household,
for they are wrapped in double cloaks.
²² She makes her own bed coverings and clothing of fine linen and purple.
²³ Her husband is well known in the assembly,
where he takes his seat with the elders of the region.
²⁴ She weaves linen and sells it, and supplies merchants with sashes.
²⁵ She is clothed in strength and dignity and can afford to laugh at tomorrow.
²⁶ When she opens her mouth, it is to speak wisely;
her teaching is sound.
²⁷ She keeps her eye on the conduct of her household
and does not eat the bread of idleness.
²⁸ Her sons with one accord extol her virtues;
her husband too is loud in her praise:
²⁹ 'Many a woman shows how gifted she is;
but you excel them all.'
³⁰ Charm is deceptive and beauty fleeting; but the woman who fears the LORD is honoured.
³¹ Praise her for all she has accomplished; let her achievements bring her honour at the city gates.

31:17 **tackles her work:** *so Gk; Heb. omits.*

imbibe, for he is to vindicate the cause of the *poor* and so is not to impair his *judgement* by strong drink. **8–9:** A characteristic Hebrew concern for the lowly.

31.10–31: A capable wife. An acrostic poem on the ideal wife, possibly meant as instruction to girls (for other alphabetic poems see Lam. chs. 1–4; Pss. 9–10; 119, etc.). **10:** *Who . . . wife:* a rhetorical question, equivalent to the statement, "One who finds a capable wife . . ."

Ecclesiastes

This book stands alone in the Hebrew Bible, both in theology and style. It asserts that God and divine ways are inscrutable, and that this recognition is the only valid intellectual stance for humankind, who cannot comprehend why the same fate befalls the good and the bad, people and beasts. Since death ignores all distinctions, life in the long run is futile, profitless.

As in Egyptian royal instructions, the style depends on frequent references to personal experience and reflection. Despair over existence is expressed in repeated refrains and phrases, brief stories and maxims. In service of a basic pessimistic outlook, the author's favorite expressions are "futility," "under the sun," "labor and toil," "chasing the wind," "one's portion."

The book predates the entrance of vivid views of afterlife into Jewish thought. However, the Hebrew employed here is a late type (fourth or third century B.C.E.). The ascription of the book to Solomon is, therefore, unlikely; yet Solomon's name may have opened the way for its inclusion in the canon, while at the same time reinforcing the theme of life's absurdity.

The noun applied to the author, Hebrew *Qoheleth*, here rendered "Speaker," is taken by some to be a proper name. But the noun seems related to a root which means "to assemble," and the Greek name Ecclesiastes derives from the idea of someone addressing an assembly (see 1.1 n.). The place of composition was probably Palestine.

The book moves a step beyond Job in attacking overconfidence in excessive wisdom; yet it encourages people to enjoy life while they have the strength to do so. Glosses which relieve the gloom (and, indeed, the impiety) of the book seem to have been added in later times at 3.17; 7.18; 8.12–13; 11.9b; 12.9–14.

The futility of all endeavour

1 THE words of the Speaker, the son of David, king in Jerusalem.
² Futility, utter futility, says the Speaker, everything is futile. ³ What does anyone profit from all his labour and toil here under the sun? ⁴ Generations come and generations go, while the earth endures for ever.

⁵ The sun rises and the sun goes down; then it speeds to its place and rises there again. ⁶ The wind blows to the south, it veers to the north; round and round it goes and returns full circle. ⁷ All streams run to the sea, yet the sea never overflows; back to the place from which the streams ran they return to run again.

⁸ All things are wearisome. No one can describe them all, no eye can see them all, no ear can hear them all. ⁹ What has happened will happen again, and what has been done will be done again; there is nothing new under the sun. ¹⁰ Is there anything of which it can be said, 'Look, this is new'? No, it was already in existence, long before our time. ¹¹ Those who lived in the past are not remembered, and those who follow will not be remembered by those who follow them.

¹² I, the Speaker, ruled as king over Israel

1:1 **the Speaker:** *Heb.* Koheleth, *Gk* Ecclesiastes.
1:5 **then ... place:** *prob. rdg; Heb.* panting to its place.

1.1–6.12: The emptiness of all endeavor. Inasmuch as meaningless repetition characterizes life, there is no advantage to toil.

1.1–11: Title and prologue. 1: The unusual Heb. form for "*the Speaker*" indicates that an office, not a name is meant. **2:** The Heb. phrase *futility, utter futility* is a superlative, just as Song of Songs means "the best song." **3:** *Under the sun:* on earth. **4:** *Earth endures* while the "lord of the earth," humankind (see Gen. 1.28), passes on. **8:** *Things:* or words.

1.12–2.26: Neither wisdom nor pleasure is profitable. Since one fate comes to all, there is no gain in work, in Jerusalem; [13] and I applied my mind to study and explore by means of wisdom all that is done under heaven. It is a worthless task that God has given to mortals to keep them occupied. [14] I have seen everything that has been done here under the sun; it is all futility and a chasing of the wind. [15] What is crooked cannot become straight; what is not there cannot be counted. [16] I thought to myself, 'I have amassed great wisdom, surpassing all my predecessors on the throne at Jerusalem; I have become familiar with wisdom and knowledge.' [17] So I applied my mind to understanding wisdom and knowledge, madness and folly, and I came to see that this too is a chasing of the wind. [18] For in much wisdom is much vexation; the more knowledge, the more suffering.

2 I said to myself, 'Come, I will test myself with pleasure and get enjoyment'; but that too was futile. [2] Of laughter I said, 'It is madness!' And of pleasure, 'What is the good of that?' [3] I sought how to cheer my body with wine, and, though my mind was still guiding me with wisdom, how to pursue folly; I hoped to find out what was good for mortals to do under heaven during their brief span of life.

[4] I undertook great works; I built myself palaces and planted vineyards; [5] I made myself gardens and orchards, planted with every kind of fruit tree. [6] I constructed ponds from which to water a grove of growing trees; [7] I acquired male and female slaves, and I had my home-born slaves as well; I owned possessions, more flocks and herds than any of my predecessors in Jerusalem; [8] I also amassed silver and gold, the treasure of kings and provinces; I got for myself minstrels, male and female, and everything that affords delight. [9] I achieved greatness, surpassing all my predecessors in Jerusalem; and my wisdom stood me in good stead. [10] I did not refuse my eyes anything they coveted; I did not deny myself any pleasure. Indeed I found pleasure in all my labour, and for all my labour this was my reward. [11] I considered my handiwork, all my labour and toil: it was futility, all of it, and a chasing of the wind, of no profit under the sun.

[12] Then I considered wisdom and madness and folly. [13] I saw that wisdom is more profitable than folly, as light is more profitable than darkness: [14] the wise person has eyes in his head, but the fool walks in the dark. Yet I realized also that one and the same fate overtakes them both. [15] So I thought, 'I too shall suffer the fate of the fool. To what purpose have I been wise? Where is the profit? Even this', I said to myself, 'is futile. [16] The wise person is remembered no longer than the fool, because in the days to come both will have been forgotten. Alas, both wise and foolish are doomed to die!' [17] So I came to hate life, since everything that was done here under the sun was a trouble to me; for all is futility and a chasing of the wind. [18] I came to hate all my labour and toil here under the sun, since I should have to leave its fruits to my successor. What will the king's successor do? Will he do what has been done before? [19] Who knows whether he will be wise or foolish? Yet he will have in his control all the fruits of my labour and skill here under the sun. This too is futility.

[20] Then I turned and gave myself up to despair, as I reflected on all my labour and toil here under the sun. [21] For though someone toils with wisdom, knowledge, and skill he must leave it all to one who has spent no labour on it. This too is futility and a great wrong. [22] What reward does anyone have for all his labour, his planning, and his toil here under the sun? [23] His lifelong activity is pain and vexation to him; even in the night he has no peace of mind. This too is futility.

[24] To eat and drink and experience pleasure in return for his labours, this does not come from any good in a person: it comes from God. [25] For without God who can eat with enjoyment? [26] He gives wisdom and knowledge and joy to whosoever is pleasing

2:8 **everything ... delight:** *prob. rdg; Heb. adds two unintelligible words.* 2:12 **folly:** *the rest of verse 12 transposed to follow verse 18.* 2:18 **What will ... done before:** *see note on verse 12.*

knowledge, or sensuality. **13:** The occupation of the wise is dismissed as *a worthless task,* even if a gift of God. **14:** *Chasing:* or shepherding, with nothing to show for one's effort (Hos. 12.1). **16:** *Predecessors:* the fiction of Solomonic authorship is here abandoned; Solomon had only one predecessor in Jerusalem (cf. 2.7, 9). **2.10:** The author intends readers to assume that the king possessed the means and power of fulfilling his will, yet at the same time rendering a negative judgment on "Solomon and all his glory." **23:** *Peace of mind* is forbidden even the good person. **26:** Except for the refrain, this may be either a pious gloss or a quotation to be refuted.

to him, while to the one who fails to please him is given the task of gathering and amassing wealth only to hand it over to someone else who does please God. This too is futility and a chasing of the wind.

3 For everything its season, and for every activity under heaven its time:

2 a time to be born and a time to die;
a time to plant and a time to uproot;
3 a time to kill and a time to heal;
a time to break down and a time to build up;
4 a time to weep and a time to laugh;
a time for mourning and a time for dancing;
5 a time to scatter stones and a time to gather them;
a time to embrace and a time to abstain from embracing;
6 a time to seek and a time to lose;
a time to keep and a time to discard;
7 a time to tear and a time to mend;
a time for silence and a time for speech;
8 a time to love and a time to hate;
a time for war and a time for peace.

9 What profit has the worker from his labour? 10 I have seen the task that God has given to mortals to keep them occupied. 11 He has made everything to suit its time; moreover he has given mankind a sense of past and future, but no comprehension of God's work from beginning to end. 12 I know that there is nothing good for anyone except to be happy and live the best life he can while he is alive. 13 Indeed, that everyone should eat and drink and enjoy himself, in return for all his labours, is a gift of God. 14 I know that whatever God does lasts for ever; there is no adding to it, no taking away. And he has done it all in such a way that everyone must feel awe in his presence. 15 Whatever is has been already, and whatever is to come has been

already, with God summoning each event back in its turn.

16 Moreover I saw here under the sun that, where justice ought to be, there was wickedness; and where righteousness ought to be, there was wickedness. 17 I said to myself, 'God will judge the just and the wicked equally; for every activity and every purpose has its proper time.' 18 I said to myself, 'In dealing with human beings it is God's purpose to test them and to see what they truly are. 19 Human beings and beasts share one and the same fate: death comes to both alike. They all draw the same breath. Man has no advantage over beast, for everything is futility. 20 All go to the same place: all came from the dust, and to the dust all return. 21 Who knows whether the spirit of a human being goes upward or whether the spirit of a beast goes downward to the earth?' 22 So I saw that there is nothing better than that all should enjoy their work, since that is their lot. For who will put them in a position to see what will happen afterwards?

4 Again, I considered all the acts of oppression perpetrated under the sun; I saw the tears of the oppressed, and there was no one to comfort them. Power was on the side of their oppressors, and there was no one to afford comfort. 2 I accounted the dead happy because they were already dead, happier than the living who still have lives to live; 3 more fortunate than either I reckoned those yet unborn, who have not witnessed the wicked deeds done here under the sun. 4 I considered all toil and all achievement and saw that it springs from rivalry between one person and another. This too is futility and a chasing of the wind. 5 The fool folds his arms and wastes away. 6 Better one hand full, along with peace of mind, than two full, along with toil; that is a chasing of the wind.

7 Here again I saw futility under the sun:

3:17 **proper time:** *prob. rdg; Heb. adds* there.
3:18 **what . . . are:** *prob. rdg; Heb. adds* they to them.
4:3 **I reckoned:** *so Lat.; Heb. omits.*

3.1–15: On timeliness. Every deed, thought, or feeling has an appropriate moment, but individuals cannot discover it. **11:** *Sense of past and future:* one can know the facts of history and in a sense the events of the immediate future, yet can fail to grasp God's role in history.

3.16–4.3: Tears of the oppressed. Injustice abounds, and none comes to the defense of the weak, so that death is to be preferred to life. **16:** *Wickedness:* perhaps bribery at the court. **19:** Although people rule beasts, *death* strikes *both* of them indiscriminately. **21:** The sage is agnostic, recognizing that life after death is problematic. **4.1:** Compare Isa. 25.8 for the prophetic word of comfort to the tearful.

4.4–16: Advantages of community. Concerted effort is better than solitary endeavor. **5–6:** Two proverbs

[8]someone without a friend, without son or brother, toiling endlessly yet never satisfied with his wealth—'For whom', he asks, 'am I toiling and denying myself the good things of life?' This too is futile, a worthless task. [9]Two are better than one, for their partnership yields this advantage: [10]if one falls, the other can help his companion up again; but woe betide the solitary person who when down has no partner to help him up. [11]And if two lie side by side they keep each other warm; but how can one keep warm by himself? [12]If anyone is alone, an assailant may overpower him, but two can resist; and a cord of three strands is not quickly snapped.

[13]Better a poor and wise youth than an old and foolish king who will listen no longer to advice. [14]One who has been in prison may well rise to be king, though born a pauper in his future kingdom. [15]But I have studied all life here under the sun, and I saw his place taken by yet another young man, [16]and no limit set to the number of people he ruled. He in turn will give no joy to those who come after him. This too is futility and a chasing of the wind.

5 Go circumspectly when you visit the house of God. Better draw near in obedience than offer the sacrifice of fools, who sin without a thought. [2]Do not be impulsive in speech, nor be guilty of hasty utterance in God's presence. God is in heaven and you are on earth, so let your words be few. [3]Dreams come with much business; the voice of the fool comes with much chatter. [4]When you make a vow to God, do not be dilatory in paying it, for he has no use for fools. Whatever you vow, pay! [5]Better not vow at all than vow and fail to pay. [6]Do not let your tongue lead you into sin, and then say before the angel of God that it was unintentional, or God will be angry at your words, and all your achievements will be brought to nothing. [7]A profusion of dreams and a profusion of words are futile. Therefore fear God.

[8]If in some province you witness the oppression of the poor and the denial of right and justice, do not be surprised at what goes on, for every official has a higher one set over him, and the highest keeps watch over them all. [9]The best thing for a country is a king whose own lands are well tilled.

[10]No one who loves money can ever have enough, and no one who loves wealth enjoys any return from it. This too is futility. [11]When riches increase, so does the number of parasites living off them; and what advantage has the owner, except to feast his eyes on them? [12]Sweet is the sleep of a labourer whether he has little or much to eat, but the rich man who has too much cannot sleep.

[13]There is a singular evil here under the sun which I have seen: a man hoards wealth to his own hurt, [14]in that the wealth is lost through an unlucky venture, and the owner's son is left with nothing. [15]As he came from the womb of mother earth, so, naked as he came, must he return; all his toil produces nothing he can take away with him. [16]This too is a singular evil: exactly as he came, so shall he go, and what profit does he get when his labour is all for the wind? [17]What is more, all his days are overshadowed; gnawing anxiety and great vexation are his lot, sickness and resentment.

[18]This is what I have seen: that it is good and proper for a man to eat and drink and enjoy himself in return for his labours here under the sun, throughout the brief span of life which God has allotted him. [19]Moreover, it is a gift of God that everyone to whom he has granted wealth and riches and the power to enjoy them should accept his lot and rejoice in his labour. [20]He will not brood overmuch on the passing years, for God fills his time with joy of heart.

6 Here is an evil which I have seen under the sun, and it weighs heavily on the human race. [2]Consider someone to whom God grants wealth, riches, and substance,

---

4:10 **if one falls, the other:** *prob. rdg; Heb. obscure.* 5:1 *In Heb. 4:17.* 5:2 *In Heb. 5:1.* 5:9 **whose:** *prob. rdg; Heb. for.* 5:17 **gnawing anxiety:** *so Gk; Heb. he eats.* 5:20 **his:** *prob. rdg; Heb. omits.*

---

are employed in a didactic setting. **9–10:** In companionship there is *advantage,* some profit to one's action. **16:** Since memory is short, the one who *ruled* is soon forgotten.

5.1–7: Passive ethics. Act so as not to call God's attention to you. **6:** *Angel:* either death or the person responsible for collecting what was vowed. **7:** The motto of the wise was *fear* of God according to Prov. 1.7 and 9.10.

5.8–6.12: Oppression and anxiety. Society is so ordered that injustice will be observed by high officials; in money there is no profit, only sleeplessness. **15:** This verse may be a citation of Job 1.21. **19:** *Lot:* fate; lot and who lacks nothing that his heart is set on: if God has not given him the power to enjoy these things, but a stranger enjoys them instead, that is futility and a dire affliction. ³ Or someone may have a hundred children and live to a great age; but however many his days may be, if he does not gain satisfaction from the good things of life and in the end receives no burial, then I maintain that the stillborn child is in better case than he. ⁴ Its coming is a futile thing, it departs into darkness, and in darkness its name is hidden; ⁵ it has never seen the sun or known anything, yet its state is better than his. ⁶ What if the man should live a thousand years twice over, and have no enjoyment? Do not both go to the same place?

⁷ The end of all man's toil is but to fill his belly, yet his appetite is never satisfied. ⁸ What advantage then in facing life has the wise man over the fool, or what advantage has the pauper for all his experience? ⁹ It is better to be satisfied with what is before your eyes than to give rein to desire; this too is futility and a chasing of the wind.

¹⁰ Whatever exists has already been given a name; it is known what human beings are and they cannot contend with one who is stronger than they. ¹¹ The more words used the greater is the futility of it all; and where is the advantage to anyone? ¹² For who can know what is good for anyone in this life, this brief span of futile existence through which one passes like a shadow? What is to happen afterwards here under the sun, who can tell?

Wisdom and folly

7 A GOOD name smells sweeter than fragrant ointment, and the day of death is better than the day of birth. ² It is better to visit a house of mourning than a house of feasting; for to be mourned is the lot of everyone, and the living should take this to heart. ³ Grief is better than laughter: a sad face may go with a cheerful heart. ⁴ The thoughts of the wise are at home in the house of mourning, but a fool's thoughts in the

house of mirth. ⁵ It is better to listen to the rebukes of the wise than to the songs of fools. ⁶ For the laughter of fools is like the crackling of thorns under a pot. That too is futility. ⁷ Oppression drives the wise crazy, and a bribe corrupts the mind. ⁸ Better the end of anything than its beginning; better patience than pride! ⁹ Do not be quick to take offence, for it is fools who nurse resentment. ¹⁰ Do not ask why the old days were better than the present; for that is a foolish question. ¹¹ Wisdom is better than possessions and an advantage to all who see the sun. ¹² Better have wisdom behind you than money; wisdom profits by giving life to those who possess her.

¹³ Consider God's handiwork; who can straighten what he has made crooked? ¹⁴ When things go well, be glad; but when they go ill, consider this: God has set the one alongside the other in such a way that no one can find out what is to happen afterwards. ¹⁵ In my futile existence I have seen it all, from the righteous perishing in their righteousness to the wicked growing old in wickedness. ¹⁶ Do not be over-righteous and do not be over-wise. Why should you destroy yourself? ¹⁷ Do not be over-wicked and do not be a fool. Why die before your time? ¹⁸ It is good to hold on to the one thing and not lose hold of the other; for someone who fears God will succeed both ways. ¹⁹ Wisdom makes the possessor of wisdom stronger than ten rulers in a city. ²⁰ There is no one on earth so righteous that he always does right and never does wrong. ²¹ Moreover, do not pay attention to everything folk say, or you may hear your servant speak ill of you; ²² for you know very well how many times you yourself have spoken ill of others. ²³ All this I have put to the test of wisdom. I said, 'I am resolved to be wise,' but wisdom was beyond my reach — ²⁴ whatever has happened lies out of reach, deep down, deeper than anyone can fathom. ²⁵ I went on to reflect how I could know, enquire, and search for wisdom and for the reason in things, only to discover that it is folly to be wicked and madness to act like a fool. ²⁶ I find more bitter than death the

and fate are close in idea. **6.3:** *Great age* and many *children* were signs of God's favor and hence sources of happiness. A lack of proper *burial* was considered a curse. On the advantage of the *stillborn,* see Job 3.11.

7.1–12: Seven proverbs on relative value. The task of the wise was to evaluate various alternatives, in essence, to make distinctions as to better options. **12b:** This part of the verse may be a gloss, inasmuch as the author elsewhere (7.23–24) denies that wisdom can be known or that it profits anyone.

7.13–29: On premature death. One should not so behave as to bring about an early death, despite the fact woman whose heart is a net to catch and whose hands are fetters. He who is pleasing to God may escape her, but the sinner she will entrap. 27 'See,' says the Speaker, 'this is what I have found, reasoning things out one by one, 28 after searching long without success: I have found one man in a thousand worthy to be called upright, but I have not found one woman among them all. 29 This alone I have found: that God, when he made man, made him straightforward, but men invent endless subtleties of their own.'

8 Who here is wise enough? Who has insight into the meaning of anything? Wisdom lights up a person's face, and the boldness of his aspect is changed. 2 Do as the king commands you, and if you have to swear by God, 3 do not rush into it. Do not persist in something which displeases the king, and leave his presence, for he can do whatever he likes. 4 His word is sovereign, and who can call in question what he does? 5 Whoever obeys a command will come to no harm. One who is wise knows in his heart the right time and method for action.

6 Every enterprise has its time and method, although man is greatly troubled 7 by ignorance of the future; who can tell him what it will bring? 8 It is not in anyone's power to retain the breath of life, and no one has power over the day of death. In war no one can lay aside his arms, no wealth will save its possessor. 9 All this I have seen, having applied my mind to everything done under the sun, at a time when one person had power over another and could make him suffer.

10 It was then that I saw scoundrels approaching and even entering the holy place; and they went about the city priding themselves on having done right. This too is futility. 11 It is because sentence upon a wicked act is not promptly carried out that evildoers are emboldened to act. 12 A sinner may do wrong and live to old age, yet I know that it will be well with those who fear God: their fear of him ensures this. 13 But it will not be well with the evildoer, nor will his days lengthen like a shadow, because he does not fear God.

14 There is a futile thing found on earth: sometimes the just person gets what is due to the unjust, and the unjust what is due to the just. I maintain that this too is futility. 15 So I commend enjoyment, since there is nothing good for anyone to do here under the sun but to eat and drink and enjoy himself; this is all that will remain with him to reward his toil throughout the span of life which God grants him here under the sun.

16 I applied my mind to acquire wisdom and to observe the tasks undertaken on earth, when mortal eyes are never closed in sleep day or night; 17 and always I perceived that God has so ordered it that no human being should be able to discover what is happening here under the sun. However hard he may try, he will not find out; the wise may think they know, but they cannot find the truth of it.

9 To all this I applied my mind, and I understood — that the righteous and the wise and whatever they do are under God's control; but whether they will earn love or hatred they have no way of knowing. Everything that confronts them, everything is futile, 2 since one and the same fate comes to all, just and unjust alike, good and bad, ritually clean and unclean, to the one who offers sacrifice and to the one who does not. The good and the sinner fare alike, he who can take an oath and he who dares not. 3 This is what is wrong in all that is done here under the sun: that one and the same fate befalls everyone. The minds of mortals are full of evil; there is madness in their minds throughout their lives, and afterwards they go down to join the dead. 4 But for anyone who is counted among the living there is still hope: remember, a live dog is better than a dead lion. 5 True, the living know that they will die; but the dead know nothing. There is no more reward for

8:8 **retain ... life:** *or* restrain the wind.
8:10 **approaching ... entering:** *prob. rdg; Heb. obscure.* **priding themselves on:** *so many MSS; others* forgotten for.   8:12 **do wrong:** *prob. rdg; Heb. adds an unintelligible word.*   9:1 **and I understood:** *prob. rdg; Heb.* and to test. **futile:** *so Gk; Heb.* all.   9:2 **and bad:** *so Gk; Heb. omits.*

that relatively few persons can be trusted. **14:** The practice of divining the future is attacked. **26:** See Prov. 7.10–27. **28:** Ecclesiasticus 25.13–24 advances this misogynistic attitude considerably (see also Zech. 5.7–8). **29:** This verse affirms the goodness of humankind at creation.

8.1–9.6: The king and subjects. Respect for royal authority is prudent, even though injustice prevails. **12–13:** These verses seem to be a gloss affirming divine justice. **17:** God has sealed off from the wise the object of inquiry; hence the sage may be deceived because of the partial knowledge permitted the seeker.

them; all memory of them is forgotten. ⁶For them love, hate, rivalry, all are now over. Never again will they have any part in what is done here under the sun.

⁷Go, then, eat your food and enjoy it, and drink your wine with a cheerful heart; for God has already accepted what you have done. ⁸Always be dressed in white, and never fail to anoint your head. ⁹Enjoy life with a woman you love all the days of your allotted span here under the sun, futile as they are; for that is your lot while you live and labour here under the sun. ¹⁰Whatever task lies to your hand, do it with might; because in Sheol, for which you are bound, there is neither doing nor thinking, neither understanding nor wisdom.

¹¹One more thing I have observed here under the sun: swiftness does not win the race nor strength the battle. Food does not belong to the wise, nor wealth to the intelligent, nor success to the skilful; time and chance govern all. ¹²Moreover, no one knows when his hour will come; like fish caught in the destroying net, like a bird taken in a snare, so the people are trapped when misfortune comes suddenly on them.

¹³This too is an example of wisdom as I have observed it here under the sun, and I find it of great significance. ¹⁴There was once a small town with few inhabitants, which a great king came to attack; he surrounded it and constructed huge siege-works against it. ¹⁵There was in it a poor wise man, and he saved the town by his wisdom. But no one remembered that poor man. ¹⁶I thought, 'Surely wisdom is better than strength'; but a poor man's wisdom is despised, and his words go unheeded. ¹⁷A wise man speaking quietly is more to be heeded than a commander shouting orders among fools. ¹⁸Wisdom is better than weapons of war, but one mistake can undo many things done well.

10 Dead flies make the sweet ointment of the perfumer turn rancid and ferment; so a little folly can make wisdom lose its worth. ²The minds of the wise turn to the right, but the mind of a fool to the left. ³Even when he travels, the fool shows no sense and reveals to everyone how foolish he is.

⁴If the anger of the ruler flares up at you, do not leave your post; submission makes amends for grave offences. ⁵There is an evil that I have observed here under the sun, an error for which rulers are responsible: ⁶fools are given high office, while the rich occupy humble positions. ⁷I have seen slaves on horseback and men of high rank going on foot like slaves.

⁸He who digs a pit may fall into it, and he who breaks down a wall may be bitten by a snake. ⁹He who quarries stones may be hurt by them, and the woodcutter runs a risk of injury. ¹⁰If the axe is blunt for lack of sharpening, then one must use more force; the skilled worker has a better chance of success. ¹¹If a snake bites before it is charmed, the snake-charmer loses his fee.

¹²Wise words win favour, but a fool's tongue is his undoing. ¹³He begins by talking nonsense and ends in mischief run mad. ¹⁴A fool talks at great length; but no one knows what is coming, and what will come after that, who can tell? ¹⁵The fool wearies himself to death with his exertions; he does not even know the way to town!

¹⁶Woe betide the land when a slave becomes its king, and its princes begin feasting in the morning. ¹⁷Happy the land when its king is nobly born, and its princes feast at the right time of day, with self-control, and not as drunkards. ¹⁸If the owner is negligent the rafters collapse, and if his hands are idle the house leaks. ¹⁹The table has its pleasures, and wine makes for a cheerful life; but money meets all demands. ²⁰Do not speak ill of the king when you are at rest, or of a rich man even when you are in your bedroom, for

9:9 **futile . . . are:** *prob. rdg; Heb. adds* all your days, futile as they are. 9:10 **Sheol:** *or* the underworld. 10:15 **fool . . . death:** *prob. rdg; Heb. obscure.* 10:16 **slave:** *or* child.

9.7–12: The wise person's counsel. Enjoy your spouse, since time and chance befall everyone. **8:** The festive garment and the *anointed head* are signs of the good life. **10:** *Sheol:* the land of the dead, of shadowy existence, but not, in Hebrew thought, of punishment.

9.13–18: The waste of wisdom. The point of this passage is that a ready means of deliverance, the *wisdom* of the *poor* is not respected.

10.1–20: Maxims derived from experience. The whole of life is brought under Wisdom's control. **2:** *Right and left* are to be understood here in a moral sense. For a somewhat different use of *right* and *left,* see Matt. 25.33–46.

a bird may carry your voice, a winged creature may repeat what you say.

11 Send your grain across the seas, and in time you will get a return. ² Divide your merchandise among seven or perhaps eight ventures, since you do not know what disasters are in store for the world. ³ If the clouds are heavy with rain, they will shed it on the earth; whether a tree falls south or north, it must lie as it falls. ⁴ He who keeps watching the wind will never sow, and he who keeps his eye on the clouds will never reap. ⁵ As you do not know how a pregnant woman comes to have a body and a living spirit in her womb, so you do not know the work of God, the maker of all things. ⁶ In the morning sow your seed in good time, and do not let your hands slack off until evening, for you do not know whether this or that sowing will be successful, or whether both alike will do well.

⁷ The light of day is sweet, and pleasant to the eye is the sight of the sun. ⁸ However many years a person may live, he should rejoice in all of them. But let him remember the days of darkness, for they will be many. Everything that is to come will be futility.

Advice to a young man

⁹ DELIGHT in your youth, young man, make the most of your early days; let your heart and your eyes show you the way; but remember that for all these things God will call you to account. ¹⁰ Banish vexation from your mind, and shake off the troubles of the body, for youth and the prime of life are mere futility.

12 Remember your Creator in the days of your youth, before the bad times come and the years draw near when you will say, 'I have no pleasure in them,' ² before the sun and the light of day give place to darkness, before the moon and the stars grow dim, and the clouds return with the rain.

³ Remember him in the day when the guardians of the house become unsteady, and the strong men stoop, when the women grinding the meal cease work because they are few, and those who look through the windows can see no longer, ⁴ when the street doors are shut, when the sound of the mill fades, when the chirping of the sparrow grows faint and the songbirds fall silent; ⁵ when people are afraid of a steep place and the street is full of terrors, when the blossom whitens on the almond tree and the locust can only crawl and the caper-buds no longer give zest. For mortals depart to their everlasting home, and the mourners go about the street.

⁶ Remember your Creator before the silver cord is snapped and the golden bowl is broken, before the pitcher is shattered at the spring and the wheel broken at the well, ⁷ before the dust returns to the earth as it began and the spirit returns to God who gave it.

⁸ Utter futility, says the Speaker, everything is futile.

⁹ So the Speaker, in his wisdom, continued to instruct the people. He turned over many maxims in his mind and sought how best to set them out. ¹⁰ He chose his words to give pleasure, but what he wrote was straight truth. ¹¹ The sayings of the wise are sharp as goads, like nails driven home; they guide the assembled people, for they come from one shepherd. ¹² One further warning, my son:

12:4 **grows faint:** *prob. rdg; Heb. obscure.* **fall silent:** *prob. rdg; Heb. sink low.*   12:7 **spirit:** *or* breath.

11.1–10: Admonitions. Unable to foresee the result of a course of action, one must be willing to risk failure. Youth is to be especially prized. **8:** *Darkness:* Sheol; see 9.10 n.

12.1–8: A description of old age and death. By means of a rich store of metaphors, not all of them fully clear, the author characterizes the twilight years. **1:** The unusual Heb. word translated *Creator* can have a double meaning, one, "cistern," referring to one's wife (see Prov. 5.15 n.), the other "grave," thus hinting at the positive and negative themes of the book. **2:** *Clouds* may refer to poor eyesight. **3:** The *guardians . . .* are the arms; the *strong men* are the knees; the *women grinding* are the teeth; and the *windows* are the eyes. **4:** The *doors* are the ears, the *chirping . . .* is sleeplessness, the *songbirds* are the voice. **5:** *Almond . . . :* gray hair; *locust,* creaking of bones. Alternatively, the images may refer to a ruined house and to nature's indifference to human destiny. **6:** *Remember your Creator:* missing in Heb. *Cord* and *bowl:* life, and when broken, death. **7:** *To God who gave it:* 3.20–21. See also Gen. 3.19.

12.9–14: Postscript. One addition (vv. 9–12) praises the author for his integrity, and even suggests that the wisdom set forth is sufficient; hence *the writing of books* is discouraged. Earlier translations read, "of making there is no end to the writing of books, and much study is wearisome.

¹³ This is the end of the matter: you have heard it all. Fear God and obey his com-

mandments; this sums up the duty of mankind. ¹⁴ For God will bring everything we do to judgement, every secret, whether good or bad.

many books there is no end." **13–14:** A second addition reflects a usual piety, and is in tension with the rest of the book.

The Song of Songs

Unique in the Bible, this collection of songs sensitively touches several major chords in the love life of a young man and a maiden. It is an anthology which plays on a wide range of themes: love's awakening, the description of the beloved, the enticement, the surrender of the embrace, the pain of separation, the joy of coming together again, the wedding ceremony. The book was early regarded as fully allegorical, a view not surprising because of the presence of some obvious symbolism, as is noted.

In its own way, the book extols the virtues of deep rather than transient love. There is no discernible overall flow of action or plot, although the positioning of the various songs creates a definite dramatic effect.

The traditional ascription of authorship to King Solomon (1.1) may have come about because of the several appearances of his name in the text. Scholars have dated the songs as early as the tenth century B.C.E. and as late as the Greek period, the fourth century B.C.E., with a postexilic date at least for the final redaction the usual view. There are no historical allusions; the geographical ones are mainly from the Northern Kingdom (see 1.14 n.); the images are decidedly rural. The book is often referred to as Canticles.

1 SOLOMON'S song of songs:

Bride

2 May he smother me with kisses.

Your love is more fragrant than wine,
3 fragrant is the scent of your anointing oils,
and your name is like those oils poured out;
that is why maidens love you.
4 Take me with you, let us make haste;
bring me into your chamber, O king.

Companions

Let us rejoice and be glad for you;
let us praise your love more than wine,
your caresses more than rare wine.

Bride

5 Daughters of Jerusalem, I am dark and lovely,

like the tents of Kedar
or the tent curtains of Shalmah.
6 Do not look down on me; dark of hue I may be
because I was scorched by the sun,
when my mother's sons were displeased with me
and sent me to watch over the vineyards;
but my own vineyard I did not watch over!
7 Tell me, my true love,
where you mind your flocks,
where you rest them at noon,
that I may not be left picking lice
as I sit among your companions' herds.

1:2 *By its use of pronouns the Hebrew text implies different speakers, but does not indicate them specifically. They are suggested here by 'Bride' etc.* 1:3 **poured out:** *prob. rdg; Heb. word uncertain.* 1:4 **your chamber:** *so Syriac; Heb. his chamber.* **your caresses:** *so Syriac; Heb. they love you.*

1.1–11: Opening songs of man and woman, telling of their love. 1: *Song of songs:* Hebrew idiom for the best of songs. **2:** *Bride* (see Tfn.): the maiden appears more like a young lover than a bride, but the songs would be appropriate for a wedding, recalling early love and courtship. **4:** The girl is often portrayed as taking the initiative. *King:* bridegroom; see 3.11 n. **5:** *Daughters* (or "maidens") *of Jerusalem:* used in 2.7 and elsewhere. The bride is addressing the chorus-companions of v. 4 where the chorus is female, perhaps consisting of wedding guests (see 5.1 n.); in 8.8–9 the chorus is male. *Kedar:* in northern Arabia. *Shalmah:* a frequent correction of the text, which reads Solomon; possibly it was near Kedar. **6:** *Dark of hue:* She is more sunburned than city girls, but no less pretty. **7:** *That . . . lice:* the Heb. text here is obscure.

Bridegroom

8 If you do not know,
  O fairest of women,
  go, follow the tracks of the sheep
  and graze your young goats by the
    shepherds' huts.

9 I would compare you, my dearest,
  to a chariot-horse of Pharaoh.
10 Your cheeks are lovely between plaited
    tresses,
  your neck with its jewelled chains.

Companions

11 We shall make you braided plaits of
    gold
  set with beads of silver.

Bride

12 While the king reclines on his couch,
  my spikenard gives forth its scent.
13 My beloved is for me a sachet of myrrh
  lying between my breasts;
14 my beloved is for me a spray of henna
    blossom
  from the vineyards of En-gedi.

Bridegroom

15 How beautiful you are, my dearest,
  ah, how beautiful,
  your eyes are like doves!

Bride

16 How beautiful you are, my love,
  and how handsome!

Bridegroom

  Our couch is shaded with branches;
17 the beams of our house are of cedar,
  our rafters are all of pine.

Bride

2 I am a rose of Sharon,
  a lily growing in the valley.

Bridegroom

2 A lily among thorns
  is my dearest among the maidens.

Bride

3 Like an apple tree among the trees of
    the forest,
  so is my beloved among young men.
  To sit in his shadow is my delight,
  and his fruit is sweet to my taste.
4 He has taken me into the wine-garden
  and given me loving glances.
5 Sustain me with raisins, revive me with
    apples;
  for I am faint with love.
6 His left arm pillows my head, his right
    arm is round me.

Bridegroom

7 I charge you, maidens of Jerusalem,
  by the spirits and the goddesses of the
    field:
  Do not rouse or awaken love
  until it is ready.

Bride

8 Hark! My beloved! Here he comes,
  bounding over the mountains, leaping
    over the hills.
9 My beloved is like a gazelle
  or a young stag.
  There he stands outside our wall,
  peering in at the windows, gazing
    through the lattice.

10 My beloved spoke, saying to me:
  'Rise up, my darling;
  my fair one, come away.
11 For see, the winter is past!
  The rains are over and gone;
12 the flowers appear in the countryside;
  the season of birdsong is come,
  and the turtle-dove's cooing is heard in
    our land;
13 the green figs ripen on the fig trees
  and the vine blossoms give forth their
    fragrance.
  Rise up, my darling;
  my fair one, come away.'

Bridegroom

14 My dove, that hides in holes in the
    cliffs

2:1 rose: or asphodel. 2:7 by ... goddesses: or by
the gazelles and the hinds.

1.12–2.7: The lovers together. 14: En-gedi: on the western edge of the Dead Sea, the only southern Israelite
reference, except for Jerusalem, in the book. 2.1: Sharon: the coastal plain in north central Israel. 7: A refrain
(see 3.5; 8.4), perhaps marking the end of a section. Goddesses: see Tfn.

or in crannies on the terraced hillside,
let me see your face and hear your
  voice;
for your voice is sweet, your face is
  lovely.

Companions

15 Catch the jackals for us, the little
  jackals,
the despoilers of vineyards, for our
  vineyards are full of blossom.

Bride

16 My beloved is mine and I am his;
he grazes his flock among the lilies.
17 While the day is cool
and the shadows are dispersing,
turn, my beloved, and show yourself
a gazelle or a young stag
on the hills where aromatic spices
  grow.

3 Night after night on my bed
   I have sought my true love;
I have sought him, but I have not
  found him.
2 I said, 'I will rise and go the rounds of
  the city
through streets and squares,
seeking my true love.'
I sought him, but could not find him.
3 The watchmen came upon me,
as they made their rounds of the
  city.
'Have you seen my true love?' I asked
  them.
4 Scarcely had I left them behind
when I met my true love.
I held him and would not let him go
till I had brought him to my mother's
  house,
to the room of her who conceived me.

Bridegroom

5 I charge you, maidens of Jerusalem,
by the spirits and the goddesses of the
  field:
Do not rouse or awaken love
until it is ready.

Companions

6 Who is this coming up from the
  wilderness
like a column of smoke
from the burning of myrrh and
  frankincense,
of all the powdered spices that
  merchants bring?
7 Look! It is Solomon carried in his state
  litter,
escorted by sixty of Israel's picked
  warriors,
8 all of them skilled swordsmen,
all expert in handling arms,
each with his sword ready at his side
against the terrors of the night.

9 The palanquin which King Solomon
  had made for himself
was of wood from Lebanon.
10 Its uprights were made of silver,
its headrest of gold;
its seat was of purple stuff,
its lining of leather.

11 Come out, maidens of Jerusalem;
you maidens of Zion, welcome King
  Solomon,
wearing the crown which his mother
  placed on his head
on his wedding day, his day of joy.

2:15 **jackals:** *or* fruit-bats.   2:17 **on . . . grow:** *or* on
the rugged hills *or* on the hills of Bether.   3:5 **by
. . . goddesses:** *or* by the gazelles and the hinds.

2.8–17: The season for love. 11: It is spring, which is the time for love the world over. **15:** The import of
the verse is unclear; it is directed against someone or something interfering with the lovers. The image of the
vineyards is used for the maiden's physical charms; see 7.12, and, in 6.2, gardens.

3.1–5: Separation and reunion. Here the maiden finds her beloved; in a similar passage, 5.2–8, she does
not. **4:** *I held him:* see 1.4 n. *Mother's . . . room:* to bind symbolically her lovemaking to that of her parents;
see 8.2, 5. **5:** See 2.7 n.

3.6–11: Solomon's wedding procession. The legendary style of Solomon was perhaps the model for every
groom to aspire to, the way he would want a poet to picture his wedding. For another description of a royal
wedding, see Ps. 45. **6:** *Who is this:* the rhetorical question is used often as a stylistic device; see 6.10. **11:**
Perhaps the *crown* the groom wears as "king" on his wedding day still in modern times in the Near East accounts
for the allusions to the king and Solomon in the book; the maiden is nowhere referred to as queen.

Bridegroom

4 How beautiful you are, my dearest,
how beautiful!
Your eyes are doves behind your veil,
your hair like a flock of goats streaming
down Mount Gilead.
2 Your teeth are like a flock of ewes
newly shorn,
freshly come up from the dipping;
all of them have twins, and none has
lost a lamb.
3 Your lips are like a scarlet thread,
and your mouth is lovely;
your parted lips behind your veil
are like a pomegranate cut open.
4 Your neck is like David's tower,
which is built with encircling courses;
a thousand bucklers hang upon it,
and all are warriors' shields.
5 Your two breasts are like two fawns,
twin fawns of a gazelle
grazing among the lilies.
6 While the day is cool
and the shadows are dispersing,
I shall take myself to the mountains of
myrrh
and to the hill of frankincense.
7 You are beautiful, my dearest,
beautiful without a flaw.

8 Come with me from Lebanon, my
bride;
come with me from Lebanon.
Hurry down from the summit of
Amana,
from the top of Senir and Hermon,
from the lions' lairs, and the
leopard-haunted hills.

9 You have stolen my heart, my sister,
you have stolen it, my bride,
with just one of your eyes, one jewel of
your necklace.
10 How beautiful are your breasts, my
sister and bride!
Your love is more fragrant than wine,
your perfumes sweeter than any spices.

11 Your lips drop sweetness like the
honeycomb, my bride,
honey and milk are under your tongue,
and your dress has the scent of
Lebanon.
13 Your two cheeks are an orchard of
pomegranates,
an orchard full of choice fruits:
14 spikenard and saffron, aromatic cane
and cinnamon
with every frankincense tree,
myrrh and aloes
with all the most exquisite spices.
12 My sister, my bride, is a garden
close-locked,
a garden close-locked, a fountain
sealed.

Bride

15 The fountain in my garden is a spring
of running water
flowing down from Lebanon.
16 Awake, north wind, and come, south
wind!
Blow upon my garden to spread its
spices abroad,
that my beloved may come to his
garden
and enjoy the choice fruit.

Bridegroom

5 I have come to my garden, my sister
and bride;
I have gathered my myrrh and my
spices;
I have eaten my honeycomb and my
honey,
and drunk my wine and my milk.
Eat, friends, and drink deep,
till you are drunk with love.

Bride

2 I sleep, but my heart is awake.
Listen! My beloved is knocking:

4:13 *Verse 12 is transposed to follow verse 14.* **Your two
cheeks:** *prob. rdg; Heb.* Your shoots. **an orchard . . .
fruits:** *prob. rdg; Heb. adds* henna with spikenard.

4.1–12: The lover's description of the maiden. See also 6.4–10; 7.1–9 for similar endearments. **6:** *Mountains . . . hill:* breasts. **8:** Many commentators hold that this is an old poem from Lebanon, and hence the mention of Lebanese mountaintops. **9:** *My sister:* a term of endearment as in ancient Egypt, and used in 4.9–5.2; compare Prov. 7.4. *Bride:* See 1.2 n. **12:** *Garden close-locked:* her charms are closed to all but her beloved.
4.15–5.1: Sensitive metaphors. The maiden invites her young man to make love and he responds. **5.1:** *Friends:* the wedding guests; compare 8.13 n.
5.2–8: The maiden's dream song. A short dramatic dream sequence. It is kindred to 3.1–5, both passages

'Open to me, my sister, my dearest,
my dove, my perfect one;
for my head is drenched with dew,
my locks with the moisture of the
night.'

3 'I have put off my robe; must I put it
on again?
I have bathed my feet; must I dirty
them again?'

4 When my beloved slipped his hand
through the latch-hole,
my heart turned over.
5 When I arose to open for my beloved,
my hands dripped with myrrh;
the liquid myrrh from my fingers
ran over the handle of the latch.
6 I opened to my love,
but my love had turned away and was
gone;
my heart sank when he turned his
back.
I sought him, but could not find him,
I called, but there was no answer.
7 The watchmen came upon me,
as they made their rounds of the city.
They beat and wounded me,
and those on the walls stripped off my
cloak.
8 Maidens of Jerusalem, I charge you,
if you find my beloved, to tell him
that I am faint with love.

Companions

9 What is your beloved more than any
other,
O fairest of women?
What is your beloved more than any
other,
that you should give us this charge?

Bride

10 My beloved is fair and desirable,
a paragon among ten thousand.
11 His head is gold, finest gold.
His locks are like palm-fronds,
black as the raven.
12 His eyes are like doves beside pools of
water,

in their setting bathed as it were in
milk.
13 His cheeks are like beds of spices,
terraces full of perfumes;
his lips are lilies, they drop liquid
myrrh.
14 His arms are golden rods set with
topaz,
his belly a plaque of ivory adorned with
sapphires.
15 His legs are pillars of marble set on
bases of finest gold;
his aspect is like Lebanon, noble as
cedars.
16 His mouth is sweetness itself, wholly
desirable.
Such is my beloved, such is my darling,
O maidens of Jerusalem.

Companions

6 Where has your beloved gone,
O fairest of women?
Which way did your beloved turn,
that we may look for him with you?

Bride

2 My beloved has gone down to his
garden,
to the beds where balsam grows,
to delight in the gardens, and to pick
the lilies.
3 I am my beloved's, and my beloved is
mine;
he grazes his flock among the lilies.

Bridegroom

4 You are beautiful as Tirzah, my
dearest,
lovely as Jerusalem.
5 Turn your eyes away from me;
they dazzle me.
Your hair is like a flock of goats
streaming down Mount Gilead;
6 your teeth are like a flock of ewes
newly come up from the dipping,
all of them have twins, and none has
lost a lamb.
7 Your parted lips behind your veil

5:10 **desirable:** *or* ruddy.   5:16 **mouth:** *lit.* palate.
6:4 **lovely as Jerusalem:** *prob. rdg; Heb. adds* majestic
as the starry heavens *(see verse 10).*

dealing with the pain of separation and the search for the lover, here fruitless. **7:** Perhaps they mistook her for
a woman of the streets; contrast 3.3. **8:** See 2.7; 3.5; 2.5.
  5.9–7.9: Descriptions of the beloved. 10–16: The maiden describes the man, as he has described her in
4.1–7. **6.1:** The same theme as in 3.3 and 5.6. **4–10:** A description of the maiden; see 4.1–12 n. **4:** *Tirzah:*

are like a pomegranate cut open.
⁸ There may be three score princesses,
four score concubines, and young
    women past counting,
⁹ but there is one alone, my dove, my
    perfect one,
her mother's only child,
the favourite of the one who bore her.
Maidens see her and call her happy,
princesses and concubines sing her
    praises.
¹⁰ Who is this that looks out like the
    dawn,
beautiful as the moon, radiant as the
    sun,
majestic as the starry heavens?

¹¹ I went down to a garden of nut trees
to look at the green shoots of the
    palms,
to see if the vine had budded
or the pomegranates were in flower.
¹² I did not recognize myself:
she made me a prince
chosen from myriads of my people.

Companions

¹³ Come back, O Shulammite, come back;
come back, that we may gaze on you.

Bridegroom

How you love to gaze on the
    Shulammite,
as she moves between the lines of
    dancers!

7 How beautiful are your sandalled feet,
    O prince's daughter!
The curves of your thighs are like
    ornaments
devised by a skilled craftsman.
² Your navel is a rounded goblet
that will never lack spiced wine.
Your belly is a heap of wheat
encircled by lilies.
³ Your two breasts are like two fawns,

twin fawns of a gazelle.
⁴ Your neck is like a tower of ivory.
Your eyes are the pools in Heshbon,
beside the gate of the crowded city.
Your nose is like towering Lebanon
that looks towards Damascus.
⁵ You carry your head like Carmel;
your flowing locks are lustrous black,
tresses braided with ribbons.
⁶ How beautiful, how entrancing you are,
my loved one, daughter of delights!
⁷ You are stately as a palm tree,
and your breasts are like clusters of
    fruit.
⁸ I said, 'Let me climb up into the palm
to grasp its fronds.'
May I find your breasts like clusters of
    grapes on the vine,
your breath sweet-scented like apples,
⁹ Your mouth like fragrant wine
flowing smoothly to meet my caresses,
gliding over my lips and teeth.

Bride

¹⁰ I am my beloved's, his longing is all for
    me.
¹¹ Come, my beloved, let us go out into
    the fields
to lie among the henna bushes;
¹² let us go early to the vineyards
and see if the vine has budded or its
    blossom opened,
or if the pomegranates are in flower.
There I shall give you my love,
¹³ when the mandrakes yield their
    perfume,
and all choice fruits are ready at our
    door,
fruits new and old
which I have in store for you, my love.

8 If only you were to me like a brother
    nursed at my mother's breast!

6:12 **myriads:** *prob. rdg; Heb.* chariots.   6:13 *In Heb.*
7:1.   7:9 **mouth:** lit. palate. **over . . . teeth:** *so Gk;*
Heb. lips of sleepers.

the early residence of the northern kings (1 Kgs. 15.33). The maiden is compared to two capital cities. **8–9:**
She excels all the women of a king's harem. Perhaps 1 Kgs. 11.3, Solomon's harem, is here echoed. **10:** The
praise spoken by the harem women. **11–12:** Perhaps a fragment of a longer poem. Verse 12 is obscure.
6:13–7.9: Another praise of the beauty of the maiden. **13:** *Shulammite:* the name occurs only here in the book.
It seems related to the Heb. for Solomon. The meaning, often guessed at, is uncertain. The *dancers* are the
wedding dancers. **7.4:** *Heshbon:* a city in Moab east of the Jordan. **5:** *Carmel:* a famous mountain on the coast,
in the north.

7.10–8.4: Love's fulfillment. 10–13: The flowers are probably all symbols of awakening passion. **12:** See

Then if I came upon you outside, I
could kiss you,
and no one would despise me.
² I should lead you to the house of my
mother,
bring you to her who conceived me;
I should give you mulled wine to drink
and the fresh juice of my
pomegranates.
³ His left arm pillows my head, his right
arm is round me.

Bridegroom

⁴ I charge you, maidens of Jerusalem:
Do not rouse or awaken love
until it is ready.

Companions

⁵ Who is this coming up from the
wilderness
leaning on her beloved?

Bridegroom

Under the apple tree I roused you.
It was there your mother was in labour
with you,
there she who bore you was in labour.
⁶ Wear me as a seal over your heart,
as a seal upon your arm;
for love is strong as death,
passion cruel as the grave;
it blazes up like a blazing fire,
fiercer than any flame.
⁷ Many waters cannot quench love,
no flood can sweep it away;
if someone were to offer for love
all the wealth in his house,
it would be laughed to scorn.

Companions

⁸ We have a little sister
who as yet has no breasts.
What shall we do with our sister
when she is asked in marriage?
⁹ If she is a wall,
we shall build on it a silver parapet;
if she is a door,
we shall bar it with a plank of
cedarwood.

Bride

¹⁰ I am a wall, and my breasts are like
towers;
so in his eyes I am as one who brings
content.
¹¹ Solomon has a vineyard at Baal-hamon;
he has given his vineyard to others to
guard;
each is to bring for its fruit
a thousand pieces of silver.
¹² My vineyard is mine to give;
keep your thousand pieces, O Solomon;
those who guard the fruit shall have
two hundred.

Bridegroom

¹³ My bride, you sit in my garden,
and my friends are listening to your
voice.
Let me hear it too.

Bride

¹⁴ Come into the open, my beloved,
and show yourself like a gazelle or a
young stag
on the spice-bearing mountains.

8:2 **who conceived me:** *prob. rdg based on Gk; Heb.* who
taught me.   8:6 **the grave:** *Heb.* Sheol.

2.15 n. **13:** *Mandrakes:* an aphrodisiac; they were also an assurance of fertility (see Gen. 30.14–17). **8.2:** *House of my mother:* see 3.4 n. **4:** See 2.7 n.
   8.5a: A suggestion of a procession, perhaps the bridal march, using the same words as 3.6.
   8.5b–7: Authentic love. These verses could well be considered the theme of the whole book.
   8.8–12: The little sister. To her brothers who seek to protect her, the maiden responds with a statement of her chastity. **11:** *Solomon:* see 3.11 n. *Baal-hamon:* an unknown place. **12:** *Vineyard:* see 2.15 n. *Mine to give:* lit. my own before me. The verse perhaps means that the king sells the fruit of his vineyard for whatever he pleases, even great amounts, but her richer love is her own to give to whomever she pleases; see 8.7b. *Two hundred:* possibly the dowry.
   8.13–14: The lovers together. Perhaps a joyous wedding game is reflected. **13:** *My bride:* the words are not in the Heb. text, but have been added for clarity. *Friends:* see 5.1 n. The Heb. word here is a synonym of that in 5.1. **14:** See 2.9; 4.6 n.

THE BOOK OF THE PROPHET
Isaiah

There are three major collections of literature in the Book of Isaiah, reflecting different periods of Israel's political and religious history. Most of the material in chs. 1–39 is related to Isaiah of Jerusalem, an eloquent prophet whose career spanned four decades (ca. 742–701 B.C.E.) and the lives of four kings of Judah: Uzziah, (783–742 B.C.E.; see 1.1; 6.1), Jotham (742–735 B.C.E.; see 1.1), Ahaz (735–715 B.C.E.; see 1.1; 7.1–12), and Hezekiah (715–687 B.C.E.; see 1.1; 38.1–6). Throughout this period Judah was faced with one crisis after another, primarily because of the advance of the Assyrian Empire toward Egypt. Assyria swallowed up the Northern Kingdom of Israel (721 B.C.E.) and frequently threatened to conquer Judah (see chs. 7; 36–39). Isaiah interpreted these events in terms of the LORD's will, calling for trust in the LORD rather than political alliances (7.1–9; 30.1–5; 31.1–9).

The literature in chs. 1–39 consists primarily of prophetic speeches, reports of Isaiah's activities, and an historical appendix (chs. 36–39). Collections of Isaiah's speeches seem to have existed separately. When the words were recorded (perhaps by disciples; see 8.16) and gathered into one book the words of the collectors, editors, and of later writers were added. Many units in these chapters, therefore, are easily recognized as not being those of Isaiah, but written in different styles and reflecting later historical situations.

Chapters 40–55 are from an unknown prophet, now called Second Isaiah, active in Babylon toward the end of the Exile (587–539 B.C.E.), whose words were joined to those of Isaiah. This conclusion is based on the difference in historical situation, namely exiles receiving the promises of a return to their homeland, and not the inhabitants of Judah and Jerusalem threatened with imminent invasion. The glowing promises of this section have led to its often being called the "Book of the Consolation of Israel." One discerns in moving from the first (chs. 1–39) into this section, a change in religious ideas, especially now a clear affirmation, in theological language, that there is only one God for all peoples. Moreover, a different vocabulary is used, and the style has become more rhetorical and complex.

The final chapters of the book (56–66) reflect for the most part the life and thought of the postexilic community struggling against discouragement to reestablish its life in the promised land. The varying styles, religious ideas, and historical situations reflect diverse authors writing over a longer period of time. This section is often called "Trito-Isaiah" or "Third Isaiah."

Prophecies against Judah

1 THE vision which Isaiah son of Amoz had about Judah and Jerusalem during the reigns of Uzziah, Jotham, Ahaz, and Hezekiah, kings of Judah.

2 Let the heavens and the earth give ear,

for it is the LORD who speaks:
I reared children and brought
  them up,
but they have rebelled against me.
3 An ox knows its owner
and a donkey its master's stall;
but Israel lacks all knowledge,
my people has no discernment.

1.1: Superscription. The prophetic message frequently is designated as a *vision* (see 6.1–13; Ezek. 1.1–3; Amos 1.1) to indicate that it was a revelation from God. On the *kings of Judah,* see Introduction. *Uzziah:* compare 6.1.

1.2–31: A collection of speeches. Diverse speeches from different periods in Isaiah's life. They are a compendium of the prophet's thought. **2–3:** The prophetic message takes the form of a lawsuit in which God

4 You sinful nation, a people weighed
  down with iniquity,
a race of evildoers, children whose lives
  are depraved,
who have deserted the Lord,
spurned the Holy One of Israel,
and turned your backs on him!
5 Why do you invite more punishment,
  why persist in your defection?
Your head is all covered with sores,
  your whole body is bruised;
6 from head to foot there is not a sound
  spot in you —
nothing but weals and welts and raw
  wounds
which have not felt compress or
  bandage
or the soothing touch of oil.
7 Your country is desolate, your cities
  burnt down.
Before your eyes strangers devour your
  land;
it is as desolate as Sodom after its
  overthrow.
8 Only Zion is left,
like a watchman's shelter in a vineyard,
like a hut in a plot of cucumbers,
like a beleaguered city.
9 Had the Lord of Hosts not left us a
  few survivors,
we should have become like Sodom,
no better than Gomorrah.
10 Listen to the word of the Lord, you
  rulers of Sodom;
give ear to the teaching of our God,
  you people of Gomorrah:

11 Your countless sacrifices, what are they
  to me?
says the Lord.
I am sated with whole-offerings of rams
and the fat of well-fed cattle;
I have no desire for the blood of bulls,
of sheep, and of he-goats,
12 when you come into my presence.
Who has asked you for all this?
No more shall you tread my courts.
13 To bring me offerings is futile;
the reek of sacrifice is abhorrent to me.
New moons and sabbaths and sacred
  assemblies —
such idolatrous ceremonies I cannot
  endure.
14 I loathe your new moons and your
  festivals;
they have become a burden to me,
and I can tolerate them no longer.
15 When you hold out your hands in
  prayer,
I shall turn away my eyes.
Though you offer countless prayers,
I shall not listen;
there is blood on your hands.
16 Wash and be clean;
put away your evil deeds
far from my sight;
cease to do evil, 17 learn to do good.
Pursue justice, guide the oppressed;
uphold the rights of the fatherless,
and plead the widow's cause.

1:7 **Sodom:** *prob. rdg; Heb.* strangers.

is both plaintiff and judge with the *heavens and earth* as witnesses. The indictment is lack of *knowledge*. **4–9:** A woe (v. 4) indictment is elaborated into a warning to the people of Judah and Jerusalem. First comes the people's sinfulness, then the results of their rebellion, and finally, they are reminded that the Lord has stopped short of total destruction. **4:** The verse begins with the Heb. word *hoi* elsewhere translated "woe betide" (see 5.8–23 n.). **7–8:** This description of the destruction probably refers either to the invasion of Tiglath-pileser III in 734–732 B.C.E. (see 7.1–9 n.) or Sennacherib in 701 B.C.E. (see 36.1). **8:** In Palestine stones gathered in a vineyard are made into a small tower from which the *watchman* protects the fruit by warding off thieves and destructive animals. This *shelter* is useless when the vines are destroyed; just so is *Zion*, Jerusalem, in a land which will be devastated. The description here of Jerusalem's isolation is similar to Sennacherib's report of his siege of the city. **9:** Judah is compared to *Sodom* and *Gomorrah* both in their depravity (Gen. 18.20–33) and in their total destruction (Gen. 19.24–29). **10–17:** Instructions on the relationship between ritual and social justice (see Amos 5.21–27). **10:** *Teaching:* that is, "Torah," or "Law." **11–15:** The Lord rejects the rituals of the cult. **11:** The *fat* and the *blood* of animals were not to be eaten but used only for sacrifices, the former because it was considered a choice morsel, the latter because it was the vehicle of life; see Lev. 3.12–16. **12:** *My presence:* the temple. **13:** New *moons* occurred on the first day of each month; these days, like the *sabbaths*, were days of rest; see Num. 28.11–15. **15:** *Turn away my eyes:* refuse to look at. Hands held out *in prayer* do not draw God's benevolent gaze because there is *blood* on them. **16–17:** Instructions concerning the Lord's

18 Now come, let us argue this out,
   says the LORD.
   Though your sins are scarlet,
   they may yet be white as snow;
   though they are dyed crimson,
   they may become white as wool.
19 If you are willing to obey,
   you will eat the best that earth yields;
20 but if you refuse and rebel,
   the sword will devour you.
   The LORD himself has spoken.

21 How the faithful city has played the
      whore!
   Once the home of justice where
      righteousness dwelt,
   she is now inhabited by murderers.
22 Your silver has turned to dross
   and your fine liquor is diluted with
      water.
23 Your rulers are rebels, associates of
      thieves;
   every one of them loves a bribe
   and chases after gifts;
   they deny the fatherless their rights,
   and the widow's cause is never heard.

24 This therefore is the word of the Lord, the
   LORD of Hosts, the Mighty One of Israel:

   Alas for you! I shall secure a respite
      from my foes
   and wreak vengeance on my enemies.
25 Once again I shall act against you
   to refine away your dross as if with
      potash
   and purge all your impurities.

26 I shall make your judges what once
      they were
   and your counsellors like those of old.
   Then you will be called
   Home of Righteousness, the Faithful
      City.
27 Zion will be redeemed by justice
   and her returning people by
      righteousness.
28 Rebels and sinners alike will be broken
   and those who forsake the LORD will
      cease to be.

29 The sacred oaks in which you delighted
   will play you false,
   the garden-shrines of your fancy will
      fail you.
30 You will be like a terebinth with
      withered leaves,
   like a garden without water.
31 The strongest tree will flare up like
      tow,
   and what is made from it will go up in
      sparks;
   both will burn together
   with no one to quench the flames.

2 This is the message which Isaiah son of
   Amoz received in a vision about Judah
and Jerusalem.

2 In days to come
   the mountain of the LORD's house
   will be set over all other mountains,
   raised high above the hills.
   All the nations will stream towards it,

1:24 **Alas for you:** *prob. rdg; Heb.* Alas.   1:29 **play
you false:** *so some MSS; others* play them false.

expectations. **18–20:** If Israel repents it will be saved; if it continues to *rebel,* it will be punished. **21–28:** The corruption of Jerusalem (vv. 21–23) and judgment which will purge and purify the city (vv. 24–28). **21:** *The faithful city:* Jerusalem; see also v. 26. **25–27:** After a period of purification Judah will be restored. *Justice,* the quality by which a king rescues the oppressed, and *righteousness,* the state of right order and harmony in relationships, will be given by God. **27:** *Zion* was originally the mount where the temple was built; it became another name for Jerusalem. **29–31:** *The sacred oaks* (lit. "oaks"), the *garden-shrines* (lit. "gardens"), and the *terebinth* are the sacred places and symbols of fertility religion. This is one of the few passages in Isa. chs. 1–39 where judgment is announced on Israel because of pagan practices.

2.1: A second superscription. This verse probably served as the original title to a collection of Isaiah's speeches, perhaps Isa. chs. 2–5. Both the individual utterances of the prophets and the collections of their speeches are characterized as *the message* (lit. "the word"). *Vision:* see 1.1 n.

2.2–5: An announcement of eternal peace. The new age will begin when Mount Zion is elevated above *all other mountains,* i.e. recognized as the most holy place. The *nations* will come to be taught at the temple, turn their weapons into farming implements, and war will come to an end. The same vision of peace is found in Mic. 4.1–4; it is strikingly reversed in Joel 3.9–12. **2:** The *mountain* is Zion; the LORD's *house* is the temple

³and many peoples will go and say,
  'Let us go up to the mountain of the
    LORD,
  to the house of the God of Jacob,
  that he may teach us his ways
  and that we may walk in his paths.'
  For instruction comes from Zion,
  and the word of the LORD from
    Jerusalem.
⁴He will judge between the nations
  as arbiter among many peoples.
  They will beat their swords into
    mattocks
  and their spears into pruning-knives;
  nation will not lift sword against nation
  nor ever again be trained for war.
⁵Come, people of Jacob,
  let us walk in the light of the LORD.

⁶You have abandoned your people, the
    house of Jacob.
  Their towns are filled with traders from
    the east,
  and with soothsayers speaking like
    Philistines;
  the children of foreigners are
    everywhere.
⁷Their land is full of silver and gold,
  and there is no end to their treasures;
  their land is full of horses,
  and there is no end to their chariots.
⁸Their land is full of idols,
  and they bow down to their own
    handiwork,
  to objects their fingers have fashioned.
⁹Mankind will be brought low,
  everyone will be humbled.

¹⁰Get among the rocks and hide in the
    ground
  from the dread presence of the LORD
  and the splendour of his majesty.
¹¹Haughty looks will be cast down,
  loftiness brought low;
  the LORD alone will be exalted
  on that day.

¹²The LORD of Hosts has a day of doom
    in store
  for all that is proud and lofty,
  for all that is high and lifted up,
¹³for all the cedars of Lebanon, lofty and
    high,
  and all the oaks of Bashan,
¹⁴for all lofty mountains and all high
    hills,
¹⁵for every tall tower and every towering
    wall,
¹⁶for all ships of Tarshish and all stately
    vessels.
¹⁷Then will pride be brought low
  and loftiness humbled;
  the LORD alone will be exalted
  on that day.
¹⁸The idols will utterly pass away.
¹⁹Creep into caves in the rocks
  and openings in the ground
  from the dread presence of the LORD
  and the splendour of his majesty,
  when he arises to strike the world with
    terror.
²⁰On that day people will fling away
  the idols of silver and gold

2:9 **humbled:** *so Scroll; Heb. adds* and do not forgive them.   2:12 **high:** *cp. Gk; Heb.* low.

in Jerusalem. On the importance and holiness of Zion, see Pss. 48.1–2; 78.68–69; 87.1–7. **3:** As they approach Zion the *peoples* will be singing a pilgrim song (see Ps. 122). *Zion* is the source of both *instruction* (or "Torah," or "Law"), ordinarily understood as the responsibility of the priest, and the *word of the* LORD, the message of the prophet. **4:** Peace can result because there will be but one *judge* and *arbiter*, namely, Israel's God. See 11.3–4. **5:** The language of v. 3 is used in an admonition. On *light* as a symbol of the presence of the LORD, see 60.1–3.

2.6–22: The coming day of the LORD. On the day when the LORD comes to judge pride and idolatry, people will flee from God's wrath. The organization of the unit is difficult to discern, but there are refrains throughout (compare vv. 9, 11 with v. 17, and v. 10 with vv. 19, 21). Verse 22 is omitted from the Sept. **6–11:** An announcement of judgment because of foreign corruption, specifically, idolatry. **6–9:** The words are addressed to God. *Soothsayers:* divination was illegal (see Lev. 20.27; Deut. 18.10–11), yet was practiced (see 1 Sam. 28.3–20). **11:** As v. 12 indicates, *that day* is the day of the LORD, when, in popular expectation (Amos 5.18–20), the LORD would punish the enemies of Israel; the prophets of the eighth century declare, rather, that *on that day* the LORD would, instead, judge God's own people. (See also 13.6; 4.1; Amos 2.16; compare Jer. 17.16–18; Ezek. 30.3.) **12–19:** The day of the LORD is a *day of doom* for all that is *proud* in human culture. **13:** *Bashan* is a region in northeastern Transjordan, known for its *oaks.* **16:** On *ships of Tarshish* see Isa. 23.1, 14; 60.9;

which they have made and worship,
fling them to the dung-beetles and bats.
21 They themselves will creep into crevices
   in rocks
and crannies in cliffs
from the dread presence of the LORD
and the splendour of his majesty,
when he arises to strike the world with
   terror.
22 Do not rely on mere mortals. What are
   they worth?
No more than the breath in their
   nostrils.

3 The Lord, the LORD of Hosts,
  is about to strip Jerusalem and Judah
of every prop and stay,
2 warriors and soldiers,
judges, prophets, diviners, and elders,
3 captains of companies and men of good
   standing,
counsellors, skilled magicians, and
   expert enchanters.
4 I shall appoint youths to positions of
   authority,
and they will govern as the whim takes
   them.
5 The people will deal oppressively with
   one another,
everyone oppressing his neighbour;
the young will be arrogant towards
   their elders,
mere nobodies towards men of rank.
6 A man will take hold of his brother in
   his father's house,
saying, 'You have a cloak, you shall be
   our chief;
our stricken family shall be in your
   charge.'
7 But the brother will at once reply,

'I cannot heal society's wounds
when in my house there is neither
   bread nor cloak.
You shall not put me in authority over
   the people.'

8 Jerusalem is brought low,
Judah has come to grief,
for in word and deed they defied the
   LORD,
in open rebellion against his glory.
9 The look on their faces testifies against
   them;
like Sodom they proclaim their sins,
parading them openly.
Woe betide them! They have earned
   the disaster that strikes them.
10 Happy the righteous! All goes well with
   them;
they enjoy the fruit of their actions.
11 Woe betide the wicked! All goes ill with
   them;
they reap the reward they have earned.
12 Moneylenders strip my people bare,
and usurers lord it over them.
My people, those who guide you are
   leading you astray
and putting you on the path to ruin.
13 The LORD comes forward to argue his
   case,
standing up to judge his people.
14 The LORD opens the indictment
against the elders and officers of his
   people:
It is you that have ravaged the
   vineyard;

3:1 **prop and stay:** prob. rdg; Heb. adds all stay of bread
and all stay of water.   3:10 **Happy:** prob. rdg; Heb.
Say.   3:13 **his people:** so Gk; Heb. peoples.

Ezek. 27.25; Ps. 48.7. **22:** The breath in their nostrils; see Gen. 2.7; Ps. 104.29.

3.1–12: A threat of anarchy. The LORD will take away from Jerusalem and Judah all their leaders, and chaos
will result. **1:** Prop and stay refer to the leaders of the people. The phrase, "all stay of bread and all stay of
water" (Tfn.), interprets the prop and stay as referring to what supports life. **2:** The prophet lists all who might
give any direction, government officials, military leaders and charismatics. **4:** Compare Eccles. 10.16. Positions
of authority: that is, princes. **5:** Oppression and disorder result from the removal of leaders. **6–7:** The situation
finally will become so bad that the only requirement for election as chief will be the possession of a decent
outer cloak. The struggle for individual survival will be so intense that no one will take the responsibility of
providing for the welfare of the people. **8–12:** Chaos has resulted from rebellion against the LORD, especially
by Those who guide (the elders and officers, v. 14) who do not lead properly.

3.13–15: The LORD's indictment of the leaders. The LORD brings the people before the bar of justice as in
the Israelite court. **13:** Technical legal language is used to describe the LORD's appearance. People: The Revised
English Bible reads a singular with the Sept. **14:** Officers: princes. On the vineyard as a figure of speech

in your houses are the spoils taken
from the poor.
15 Is it nothing to you that you crush my
people
and grind the faces of the poor?
This is the word of the LORD of Hosts.

16 The LORD said:
Because the women of Zion give
themselves airs,
with heads held haughtily, with wanton
glances,
as they move with mincing gait
and jingling feet,
17 the Lord will smite with baldness the
women of Zion,
the LORD will make bare their
foreheads.

18 On that day the Lord will take away their
finery: anklets, discs, crescents, 19 pendants,
bracelets, coronets, 20 headbands, armlets,
necklaces, lockets, charms, 21 signet rings,
nose-rings, 22 fine dresses, mantles, cloaks,
flounced skirts, 23 scarves of gauze, kerchiefs
of linen, turbans, and flowing veils.

24 Instead of perfume there will be the
stench of decay;
there will be a rope instead of a girdle,
baldness instead of hair elegantly
coiled,
a loincloth of sacking instead of a fine
robe,

the mark of branding instead of beauty.
25 Zion, your men will fall by the sword,
your warriors in battle.
26 Zion's gates will mourn and lament,
and, stripped bare, she will sit on the
ground.

4 On that day seven women will take hold
of one man and say, 'We shall provide
our own food and clothing if only we may
bear your name. Take away our disgrace!'
2 On that day the plant that the LORD has
grown will become glorious in its beauty, and
the fruit of the land will be the pride and
splendour of the survivors of Israel.
3 Then those who are left in Zion, who remain in Jerusalem, every one whose survival
in Jerusalem was decreed will be called holy.
4 When the Lord washes away the filth of the
women of Zion and cleanses Jerusalem from
bloodstains by a spirit of judgement burning
like fire, 5 he will create a cloud of smoke by
day and a bright flame of fire by night over
the whole building on Mount Zion and over
all her assemblies; for his glory will be a canopy over all, 6 a cover giving shade by day
from the heat, a refuge and shelter from
storm and rain.

5 I shall sing for my beloved
my love song about his vineyard:
My beloved had a vineyard

3:15 word ... LORD: *prob. rdg, cp. Scroll; Heb.* word of
the Lord, the LORD.

representing Israel, see 5.1–7. **15:** The basic charge against the leaders is oppression of the people, especially
the poor.

3.16–24: Announcement of judgment against the women of Jerusalem. First, reasons for punishment are
given in terms of the posture of the *women of Zion;* next, a judgment is announced that fits the crime
(vv. 17–24). **17, 24:** The humiliations which the women will suffer are common to military defeat and exile.
18–23: The list of *finery* is a prose elaboration of vv. 17, 24.

3.25–4.1: Judgment against Jerusalem and her women. 25: The repeated pronoun *your* is feminine singular,
referring to Jerusalem; compare v. 26. **4.1:** With men killed in war (v. 25), women will be without husbands
and children, a reproach in the society of that day. To *take away* the *disgrace,* women will break all tradition
and beg men to marry them. On *disgrace,* see 54.4; Gen. 30.23; 2 Sam. 13.13.

4.2–6: A promise of Jerusalem's renewal. The hope for the future lies in *survivors* who have been purged
through punishment. **2:** The *plant* and the *fruit* are the *survivors* or the remnant. See 1.9 n. **3:** *Whose survival
was decreed:* Lit. "enrolled for life"; compare Exod. 32.32; Mal. 3.16; Dan. 12.1. **5–6:** The language of *cloud*
and *fire* recalls the tradition of Israel's journey through the wilderness from Egypt to the promised land (see
Exod. 13.21–22) and recalls the description of the *glory* of the LORD filling the wilderness Tabernacle (see Exod.
40.34–38; Ezek. 10.4).

5.1–7: The parable of the vineyard. Israel is indicted for its failure to respond to the LORD's nurture. First,
the prophet, acting as the friend of the bridegroom, sings a love song (vv. 1–2). Second, he assumes the role
of the vineyard's owner presenting a lawsuit (vv. 3–6). Third, he interprets the parable, applying it to Israel

high up on a fertile slope.
2 He trenched it, cleared it of stones,
and planted it with choice red vines;
in the middle he built a watch-tower
and also hewed out a wine vat.
He expected it to yield choice grapes,
but all it yielded was a crop of wild
grapes.

3 Now, you citizens of Jerusalem
and people of Judah,
judge between me and my vineyard.
4 What more could have been done for
my vineyard
than I did for it?
Why, when I expected it to yield choice
grapes,
did it yield wild grapes?

5 Now listen while I tell you
what I am about to do to my vineyard:
I shall take away its hedge
and let it go to waste,
I shall break down its wall
and let it be trampled underfoot;
6 I shall leave it derelict.
It will be neither pruned nor hoed,
but left overgrown with briars and
thorns.
I shall command the clouds
to withhold their rain from it.
7 The vineyard of the LORD of Hosts is
Israel,
Judah the plant he cherished.
He looked for justice but found
bloodshed,
for righteousness but heard cries of
distress.

8 Woe betide those who add house to
house
and join field to field,
until everyone else is displaced,

and you are left as sole inhabitants of
the countryside.
9 In my hearing the LORD of Hosts made
this solemn oath:
'Great houses will be brought to ruin,
fine mansions left uninhabited.
10 Five acres of vineyard will yield only a
gallon,
and ten bushels of seed return only a
peck.'

11 Woe betide those who rise early in the
morning
to go in pursuit of drink,
who sit late into the night
inflamed with wine,
12 at whose feasts there are harps and
lutes,
tabors and pipes and wine;
yet for the work of the LORD they have
never a thought,
no regard for what he has done.
13 Therefore my people shall go into
captivity
because they lack all knowledge of me.
The nobles are starving to death,
and the common folk die of thirst.
14 Therefore Sheol gapes with straining
throat
and opens her enormous jaws:
down go the nobility and people of
Jerusalem,
her noisy throng of revellers.
15 Mankind is brought low, everyone is
humbled,
and haughty looks are cast down.
16 But the LORD of Hosts is exalted by
judgement,
and by righteousness the Holy God
reveals his holiness.

5:9 made . . . oath: *prob. rdg; Heb. omits.*   5:10 Five
acres: *lit.* ten yokes. gallon: *lit.* bath. ten bushels: *lit.* a
homer. a peck: *lit.* an ephah.   5:14 Sheol: *or the*
underworld.

(v. 7). **1:** The *vineyard* is a common metaphor in love poetry (see S. of S. 1.6; 7.12; 8.12). **2:** The soil in Palestine
is shallow and full of *stones;* these the good farmer gathers and makes a *tower* from which he keeps *watch*
over the vineyard. *Wild:* i.e. sour. **3–6:** The vineyard's owner calls for the court to convene (v. 3), argues the
reasonableness of his complaint (vv. 4–5), and gives his judgment. **7:** The Heb. contains two plays on words,
mishpat . . . mispah ("justice" . . . "bloodshed") and *tzedakah . . . tze'akah* ("righteousness" . . . "cries of
distress"). *Justice* and *righteousness* often are used in parallel (see 1.21; Amos 5.24) to characterize the
standards of behavior which the LORD expects (see also 1.17, 26–27; 9.7; 16.5).
   5.8–23: A series of woe indictments. Each accusation begins with the cry *woe betide* (lit. "woe," vv. 8, 11,
18, 20, 21, 22). Isaiah 10.1–4 may also belong to this series. Each unit describes a group in terms of its immoral
actions. **8–10:** Against the rich who take the land of the poor. **11–17:** Against those whose pursuit of pleasure

17 Lambs will feed where fat bullocks once
     pastured,
   young goats will graze broad acres
     where cattle grew fat.

18 Woe betide those who drag wickedness
     and sin along,
   as with a sheep's tether or a heifer's
     rope,
19 who say, 'Let the LORD make haste:
   let him speed up his work that we may
     see it;
   let the purpose of the Holy One of
     Israel
   be soon fulfilled, that we may know it.'
20 Woe betide those who call evil good
     and good evil,
   who make darkness light and light
     darkness,
   who make bitter sweet and sweet bitter.
21 Woe betide those who are wise in their
     own sight
   and prudent in their own esteem.
22 Woe betide those heroic topers,
   those valiant mixers of drink,
23 who for a bribe acquit the guilty
   and deny justice to those in the right.

24 As tongues of fire lick up the stubble
   and chaff shrivels in the flames,
   so their root will moulder away
   and their opening buds vanish like fine
     dust;
   for they have spurned the instruction
     of the LORD of Hosts
   and rejected the word of the Holy One
     of Israel.
25 So the anger of the LORD is roused
   against his people,

and he has stretched out his hand to
     strike them down;
   the mountains trembled,
   and corpses lay like refuse in the
     streets.
   Yet for all this his anger has not
     abated,
   and his hand is still stretched out.

26 He will hoist a standard as a signal to a
     nation far away,
   he will whistle them up from the ends
     of the earth,
   and they will come with all speed.
27 None is weary, not one of them
     stumbles,
   no one slumbers or sleeps.
   None has his belt loose about his waist
   or a broken thong to his sandals.
28 Their arrows are sharpened and all
     their bows bent,
   their horses' hoofs are like flint,
   their chariot wheels like the whirlwind.
29 Their growling is like that of a lion,
   they growl like young lions;
   they roar as they seize their prey
   and carry it beyond reach of rescue.
30 Their roaring over it on that day
   will be like the roaring of the sea.
   Anyone who looks over the land sees
     darkness closing in,
   and the light overshadowed by the
     gathering clouds.

The calling of Isaiah

6 IN the year that King Uzziah died I saw
   the Lord seated on a throne, high and

5:17 **Lambs . . . grew fat:** *poss. rdg; Heb. unintelligible.*
5:30 **by . . . clouds:** *or* on the hilltops.

obscures their perception of the LORD's activity and the needs of the *people*. **14:** *Sheol:* netherworld. **18–19:**
Against those who dare the LORD to act. **20:** Against those who reverse morality. **21:** Against those who are
proud of their wisdom. **22–23:** Against drunkards who pervert justice.

5.26–30: An announcement of judgment. The LORD (*he*, v. 26) will call an enemy to punish the people.
26: The *nation far away* probably is Assyria. The invaders obey God as a dog obeys the *whistle* of its master.
27–28: The discipline and size of the army are fearful, and its sound becomes a roar as it comes nearer. **30:**
That day: see 2.11 n. The invaders will leave the land in the same chaos over which, before creation, *darkness*
and the *sea* spread; compare Gen. 1.1–2.

6.1–13: Isaiah's report of his call. The prophet reports his call as a vision of the LORD as king followed by
a dialogue in which he receives and reacts to the message. The main elements of the report are the vision
(vv. 1–4), the prophet's reaction emphasizing his unworthiness (v. 5), a purification ritual (vv. 6–7), the LORD's
call and Isaiah's acceptance (v. 8), and the prophet's commission (vv. 9–10). Finally there is the prophet's
intercession and the LORD's response that includes further details concerning the commission (vv. 11–13). Most
of these elements are found in the reports of other vocations, both of prophets (Jer. 1.4–10; Ezek. 1–3; 1 Kgs.

exalted, and the skirt of his robe filled the temple. ²Seraphim were in attendance on him. Each had six wings: with one pair of wings they covered their faces and with another their bodies, and with the third pair they flew. ³They were calling to one another,

'Holy, holy, holy is the LORD of Hosts:
the whole earth is full of his glory.'

⁴As each called, the threshold shook to its foundations at the sound, while the house began to fill with clouds of smoke. ⁵Then I said,

'Woe is me! I am doomed,
for my own eyes have seen the King,
the LORD of Hosts,
I, a man of unclean lips,
I, who dwell among a people of
unclean lips.'

⁶One of the seraphim flew to me, carrying in his hand a glowing coal which he had taken from the altar with a pair of tongs. ⁷He touched my mouth with it and said,

'This has touched your lips;
now your iniquity is removed
and your sin is wiped out.'

⁸I heard the Lord saying, 'Whom shall I send? Who will go for us?' ⁹I said: 'Here am I! Send me.' He replied: 'Go, tell this people:

However hard you listen, you will never
understand.

However hard you look, you will never
perceive.
¹⁰This people's wits are dulled;
they have stopped their ears and shut
their eyes,
so that they may not see with their eyes,
nor listen with their ears,
nor understand with their wits,
and then turn and be healed.'

¹¹I asked, 'Lord, how long?' And he answered,

'Until cities fall in ruins and are
deserted,
until houses are left without occupants,
and the land lies ruined and waste.'
¹²The LORD will drive the people far
away,
and the country will be one vast
desolation.
¹³Even though a tenth part of the people
were to remain,
they too would be destroyed
like an oak or terebinth
when it is felled,
and only a stump remains.
Its stump is a holy seed.

Isaiah and King Ahaz

7 WHEN Ahaz son of Jotham and grandson of Uzziah was ruler of Judah, King Rezin of Aram with Pekah son of Remaliah, king of Israel, marched on Jerusalem, but

6:10 This people's ... shut: *or* Dull this people's wits, stop their ears, and shut.

22.19–21), and of leaders such as Moses (Exod. 3.1–12) and Gideon (Judg. 6.11–17). The purpose of this report is to authenticate the prophet as the LORD's spokesman and to justify his uncompromising message of doom. **1:** *King Uzziah's death* was in 742 B.C.E. God's *throne* was considered to be above the Ark in the *temple;* see Exod. 25.16–22; Ezek. 10.1–5. **2:** The *seraphim* (lit. "fiery ones") perhaps are to be associated with the cherubim who appear as the LORD's attendants in Ezek. ch. 1 and elsewhere are associated with the Ark (Exod. 25.18–20). The seraphim *covered their faces* for fear of seeing God. **3:** The attendants were singing antiphonally a hymn to the holiness of the LORD. Isaiah frequently speaks of the LORD as "the Holy One of Israel" (1.4; 5.19, 24; 10.20). **4:** The *smoke* in the *house* (that is, the temple) should be associated with the "cloud" (Exod. 19.9) on Mount Sinai where the "glory of the LORD" was present; compare Ezek. 10.1–4. **5:** Before the Holy One all are unclean. Furthermore, according to OT tradition, no one could see God and live (Exod. 33.20). **6–7:** Other prophetic vocation reports also include rituals concerning the mouth; see Jer. 1.9–10; Ezek. 3.1–3. **8:** The questions are not addressed to the prophet; he overhears the LORD speaking to the heavenly council (see Ps. 82). **9–10:** The Heb. (see Tfn. at v. 10) reads literally as a commission to the prophet deliberately to prevent the people from hearing, seeing, understanding, and thus repenting. **11–13:** Isaiah's response is a prayer of intercession, but the LORD offers no hope until the land will have been destroyed.

7.1–9: Assurance given to Ahaz. Assyria invaded the lands to the west in 735 B.C.E. The kings of Israel, the was unable to reduce it. ²When it was reported to the house of David that the Aramaeans had made an alliance with the Ephraimites, king and people shook like forest trees shaking in the wind. ³The LORD said to Isaiah, 'Go out with your son Shear-jashub to meet Ahaz at the end of the conduit of the Upper Pool by the causeway leading to the Fuller's Field, ⁴and say to him: Remain calm and unafraid; do not let your nerve fail because of the blazing anger of Rezin with his Aramaeans and Remaliah's son, those two smouldering stumps of firewood. ⁵The Aramaeans with Ephraim and Remaliah's son have plotted against you: ⁶"Let us invade Judah and break her spirit," they said; "let us bring her over to our side, and set Tabeal's son on the throne." ⁷The Lord GOD has said:

This shall not happen now or ever,
⁸⁻⁹that the rule in Aram should belong to
   Damascus,
the rule in Damascus to Rezin,
or that the rule in Ephraim should
   belong to Samaria,
and the rule in Samaria to Remaliah's
   son.

(Within sixty-five years a shattered
   Ephraim shall cease to be a nation.)
Have firm faith, or you will fail to
   stand firm.'

¹⁰The LORD spoke further to Ahaz. ¹¹'Ask the LORD your God for a sign,' he said, 'whether from Sheol below or from heaven above.' ¹²But Ahaz replied: 'No, I will not put the LORD to the test by asking for a sign.' ¹³Then the prophet said: 'Listen, you house of David. Not content with wearing out the patience of men, must you also wear out the patience of my God? ¹⁴Because you do, the Lord of his own accord will give you a sign; it is this: A young woman is with child, and she will give birth to a son and call him Immanuel. ¹⁵By the time he has learnt to reject what is bad and choose what is good, he will be eating curds and honey; ¹⁶before that child has learnt to reject evil and choose good, the territories of those two kings before whom you now cringe in fear will lie desolate. ¹⁷The LORD will bring on you, on

7:3 **Shear-jashub:** *that is* A remnant will return.
7:14 **Immanuel:** *that is* God is with us.   7:17 **Judah:**
prob. rdg; Heb. adds the king of Assyria.

Northern Kingdom, and of Aram, i.e. Syria, had tried to organize a coalition of small nations to stop the invasion. When Ahaz, king of Judah, refused to join the coalition, the two kings laid siege to Jerusalem (about 734–732 B.C.E.). Ahaz decided to ask Assyria for help; thereupon Isaiah emerged to counsel Ahaz neither to fear the besiegers nor to seek the human help of Assyria, but rather to look to the LORD for aid. For the historical context, see 2 Kgs. 16.1–20. **1:** *Ahaz* reigned 735–715 B.C.E. *Aram:* Syria, with its capital at Damascus. **2:** *The house of David,* i.e. Judah, the Southern Kingdom, *shook* with fear because it was no military match for either of the attackers. **3:** *Shear-jashub* (see Tfn.) means either "a remnant will return" or "only a remnant will return"; see 10.21–22. **4:** *Smouldering stumps:* a scornful allusion to the destructive power of the two kings as being already extinguished. **6:** *Tabeal's son* — his own name is not given — probably was a rebel in Judah who agreed with the anti-Assyrian policies of the coalition. **8–9:** No nation, whatever its capitol and whoever its king, can prevail against Jerusalem, the city of God, whose ruler is the son of David. **9:** *Firm faith* (Heb. *ta'aminu*) and *stand firm* (*te'amenu*) are different forms of the same verb; this play on words is both reassurance and warning.

7.10–17: The sign of Immanuel. The historical context is the same as in 7.1–9. Here the prophet assures Ahaz that within a short time Aram and Israel will be destroyed. **10:** *The LORD spoke:* that is, through the prophet. **11–12:** A *sign* was a revelation of the divine will, and in the prophetic literature was most commonly concerned with the future. Prophets frequently performed sign acts or symbolic actions, such as giving their children dramatic names (7.3; 8.14; Hos. 1.2–9), to convey the word of the LORD to their people. *Put the LORD to the test:* i.e. expect God to perform an extraordinary feat on demand. **14:** *A young woman:* lit. "the young woman." The Heb. here, *'almah* (feminine of *'elem,* young man), refers to a girl of marriageable age, or one recently married (see Gen. 24.43; Exod. 2.8; Prov. 30.19; S. of S. 6.8). The NT references (Matt. 1.23; see also Lk. 1.27) to this verse are based on the early Gk. rendering of the passage. Many identifications have been proposed of the *young woman* and her *son:* the wife of Ahaz and her son the future king Hezekiah; the wife of Isaiah; collective Israel personified and sometimes called "virgin" (compare Jer. 14.17; Amos 5.2) or some unidentified Judean woman. **15–16:** *Curds and honey* probably refer to the infant's first solid food after mother's milk. Before the child ceases to be a toddler, the threat by the two kings will be ended.

your people, and on your father's house, a time the like of which has not been seen since Ephraim broke away from Judah.

18 'On that day the LORD will whistle up flies from the distant streams of Egypt and bees from the land of Assyria. 19 They will all come and settle in the steep wadis and in the clefts of the rock, swarming over the camel-thorn and stinkwort. 20 On that day the Lord will shave the head and body with a razor hired on the banks of the Euphrates, and it will remove the beard as well. 21 On that day a man will keep a young cow and two ewes, 22 and he will get so much milk that he eats curds; all who are left in the land will eat curds and honey. 23 On that day every place where there used to be a thousand vines worth a thousand pieces of silver will be given over to briars and thorns. 24 A man will go there only to hunt with bow and arrows, for briars and thorns will cover the whole land. 25 Daunted by the briars and thorns, no one will set foot on any of those hills once under the hoe. They will become a place where oxen are turned loose and sheep and goats can wander.'

8 The LORD said to me, 'Take a large writing tablet and write on it in common script "Maher-shalal-hash-baz".' 2 I had it witnessed for me by Uriah the priest and Zechariah son of Jeberechiah as reliable witnesses. 3 Then I lay with my wife, and she conceived and gave birth to a son. The LORD said to me, 'Call him Maher-shalal-hash-baz; 4 before the boy can say "Father" or "Mother", the wealth of Damascus and the spoils of Samaria will be carried off and presented to the king of Assyria.'

5 Once again the LORD spoke to me; he said:

6 Because this nation has rejected
  the waters of Shiloah, which flow softly
    and gently,
7 therefore the Lord will bring up against
  it
the mighty floodwaters of the
  Euphrates.
The river will rise in its channels
and overflow all its banks.
8 In a raging torrent mounting neck-high
it will sweep through Judah.
With his outspread wings
the whole expanse of the land will be
  filled,
for God is with us.
9 Take note, you nations; you will be
  shattered.
Listen, all you distant parts of the
  earth:
arm yourselves, and be shattered;
arm yourselves, and be shattered.
10 Devise your plans, but they will be
  foiled;

7:20 **Euphrates:** *prob. rdg; Heb. adds* with the king of Assyria.   8:1 **in ... script:** *lit.* with the pen of a human being. **Maher-shalal-hash-baz:** *that is* Speeding for spoil, hastening for plunder.   8:3 **my wife:** *lit.* the prophetess.   8:6 **gently:** *prob. rdg;* Heb. adds Rezin and the son of Remaliah.   8:7 **Euphrates:** *prob. rdg; Heb. adds* the king of Assyria and all his pomp.   8:8 **God is with us:** *Heb.* Immanuel. 8:9 **Take note:** *so Gk; Heb.* unintelligible.

7.18–25: The day of the LORD. Each announcement is introduced by *on that day* (vv. 18, 20, 21, 23). The first two speak of Assyria as the LORD's means of punishment; the remainder speak of the desolation that will result from Assyrian invasion. **20:** To *shave the head* was a sign of disgrace and/or mourning; see Neh. 13.25; Jer. 48.37. *Body:* lit. "feet," a euphemism for pubic hair.

8.1–4: The sign of Maher-shalal-hash-baz (speedy-spoiling-prompt-plundering). The prophet reports two "sign acts" (see 7.11–12), the writing of the name of a child before his conception, and the name of the child itself. The message of the name is that the threat to Judah (see 7.1–9 n.) will be ended by Assyria; the message of the inscription is that the promise can be trusted as a word of the LORD since it is known in advance. For other "sign acts" see also Hos. 1.2; Ezek. 4.1, 9; 5.1; 37.16; Jer. 13.4; etc. **2:** *Uriah:* see 2 Kgs. 16.10–16. **3:** The *prophetess* would have been Isaiah's wife, but elsewhere the term refers to a woman performing some official function; see 2 Kgs. 22.14; Exod. 15.20; Judg. 4.4; Neh. 6.14.

8.5–10: Judgments against the enemies of the LORD. 5–8: The prophet announces judgment upon Judah; Assyria will flood through the land. **6:** *This nation:* Judah. *Waters of Shiloah:* the stream fed by the spring Gihon which flowed alongside the hill Ophel and brought clean drinking water into a pool (7.3) in Jerusalem. **7–8:** Assyria will overrun the *land* like the *Euphrates* which, unlike Shiloah, overflows all its *channels*, including those made for irrigation. **9–10:** Contrary to appearances, the *plans* of God are being carried out and those of Assyria *foiled*.

propose what you will, but it will not be
   carried out;
for God is with us.

[11] This is what the LORD said to me when he
took me by the hand and charged me not to
follow the ways of this people: [12] 'You are not
to call alliance anything that this people calls
alliance; you must neither fear nor stand in
awe of what they fear. [13] It is the LORD of
Hosts whom you should hold sacred; he must
be the object of your fear and awe. [14] He will
become a snare, an obstacle, and a rock
against which the two houses of Israel will
strike and stumble, a trap and a snare to the
inhabitants of Jerusalem. [15] Over them many
will stumble and fall and suffer injury; they
will be snared and caught.'

[16] I shall tie up the message, I shall seal
   the instruction
so that it cannot be consulted by my
   disciples.
[17] I shall wait eagerly for the LORD,
who is hiding his face from the house
   of Jacob;
I shall watch longingly for him.
[18] Here I am with the children the LORD
   has given me
to be signs and portents in Israel,
sent by the LORD of Hosts who dwells
   on Mount Zion.
[19] People will say to you,
'Seek guidance from ghosts and
   familiar spirits
which squeak and gibber;
a nation may surely consult its gods,
consult its dead on behalf of the living
[20] for instruction or a message.'
They will surely say some such thing,
but what they say has no force.

[21] So despondency and fear will come
   over them,
and when they are afraid and fearful,
they will rebel against their king and
   their gods.
Whether they turn their gaze upwards
[22] or look down,
everywhere is distress and darkness
   inescapable,
constraint and gloom that cannot be
   avoided;

9 [1] for there is no escape for an
   oppressed people.

Formerly the lands of Zebulun and Naphtali
were lightly regarded, but afterwards honour was bestowed on Galilee of the Nations
on the road beyond Jordan to the sea.

[2] The people that walked in darkness
have seen a great light;
on those who lived in a land as dark as
   death
a light has dawned.
[3] You have increased their joy
and given them great gladness;
they rejoice in your presence
as those who rejoice at harvest,
as warriors exult when dividing spoil.

[4] For you have broken the yoke that
   burdened them,
the rod laid on their shoulders,
the driver's goad, as on the day of
   Midian's defeat.

8:10 **God is with us:** *Heb.* Immanuel.
8:11 **and . . . follow:** *or* and he turned me from
following.   8:14 **become a snare:** *prob. rdg; Heb.*
become a sanctuary.   8:21–22 *Meaning of Heb.*
uncertain.   9:1 *In Heb. 8:23.*   9:2 *In Heb. 9:1.*
9:3 **their joy and:** *prob. rdg; Heb.* the nation, not.

8.11–22: The role of the prophet among people who will not hear. 11–15: The prophet reports a private
message concerning his role; he is to *fear* (v. 13) only the LORD, who causes the people to *stumble* (v. 14;
compare 6.9–10 n.). **16–20:** Although it is not explicit in the translation, these words are addressed to the
prophet's disciples (see v. 19). **17:** Since the LORD *is hiding his face* there is no prophetic word to give. **18:**
The children are the ones mentioned in 7.3; 8.1–4; and possibly also 7.14. *Sign:* see 7.11–12 n. **19–20:** *Squeak*
and gibber: probably a mocking imitation of sounds made by necromancers to convey the alleged voice of
the dead. When people reject the words of a living prophet, they turn to *ghosts and familiar spirits* (see 1 Sam.
28.7). For the prohibition of consulting the dead, see Deut. 18.10–15.

   9.1–7: The great light, a new king. After an introductory note (v. 1), this poem captures the celebration and
hope following the birth of a new prince to continue the line of David. Three reasons for celebration are given:
(1) the *yoke* of the oppressor has been broken (v. 4), (2) the gear of battle has been destroyed (v. 5), and (3)
a new crown prince has been born (vv. 6–7). **1:** *Zebulun, Naphtali,* and *Galilee* probably refer to territories
taken by the Assyrians after 734 B.C.E. **4:** On *Midian's defeat,* see Judg. 7.15–25.

5 The boots of earth-shaking armies on
   the march,
the soldiers' cloaks rolled in blood,
all are destined to be burnt, food for
   the fire.

6 For a child has been born to us, a son
   is given to us;
he will bear the symbol of dominion on
   his shoulder,
and his title will be:
Wonderful Counsellor, Mighty Hero,
Eternal Father, Prince of Peace.
7 Wide will be the dominion
and boundless the peace
bestowed on David's throne and on his
   kingdom,
to establish and support it
with justice and righteousness
from now on, for evermore.
The zeal of the LORD of Hosts will do
   this.

Prophecies against Israel

8 THE Lord has sent forth his word
   against Jacob
and it will fall on Israel;
9 all the people will know,
Ephraim and the inhabitants of
   Samaria,
though in their pride and arrogance
   they say,
10 'The bricks have fallen down,
but we shall rebuild in dressed stone;
the sycomores are cut down,
but we shall grow cedars in their place.'
11 The LORD has raised their foes against
   them
and spurred on their enemies,
12 Aramaeans from the east, Philistines
   from the west,
and they have swallowed Israel in one
   mouthful.

For all this his anger has not abated;
his hand still threatens.
13 Yet the people did not come back to
   him who struck them,
nor seek guidance from the LORD of
   Hosts;
14 therefore on one day the LORD cut off
   from Israel
head and tail, palm-frond and reed.

(15 The aged and the honoured are the head;
the prophets who give false instruction are
the tail.)

16 Those who guide this people have led
   them astray,
and those who follow their guidance
   are engulfed.
17 That is why the Lord showed no mercy
   to their youths,
no compassion towards the fatherless
   and widows;
it is a nation of godless evildoers,
every one speaking impiety.
For all this his anger has not abated;
his hand still threatens.

18 Wicked men have been set ablaze like a
   fire
fed with briars and thorns,
kindled in the thickets of the forest;
they are wrapped in a pall of smoke.
19 The land is scorched by the fury of the
   LORD of Hosts,
and the people are like food for the
   fire.
20 On one side, a man is eating his fill
but yet remains hungry;
on another, a man is devouring

9:7 **Wide:** *so Gk; Heb. prefixes two unintelligible letters.*
9:11 **their foes:** *prob. rdg; Heb.* the foes of Rezin.
9:20 **and no one . . . brother:** *transposed from end of
verse 19.*

6: The verse begins with a birth announcement (Job 3.3; Jer. 20.15); it closes with a series of four crown names.
7: *Peace* means more than the absence of war; it means the presence of *justice and righteousness*.
   9.8–10.4: The LORD's outstretched hand. A series of four stanzas (9.8–12, 13–17, 18–21; 10.1–4; see also
5.24–25), each concluding with the same refrain, announces the LORD's unrelenting judgment upon his people.
For a similar series see Amos 4.6–12. Repeated disasters have not brought repentance; therefore the punishment continues. **8:** The *word* of the LORD spoken through a prophet is considered to be God's active power
which sets in motion the fulfilment of the prophecy (see Amos 1.2; Jer. 1.9–10). **9:** *Ephraim* was the Northern
Kingdom named after the leading tribe; *Samaria* was the capital city. **13–17:** Since Israel did not repent but
was misguided by its leaders, the LORD's anger continued. **14:** *Head and tail:* rulers and subjects, rich and poor.
15: A gloss interpreting the meaning of head and tail. **18–21:** The disaster is so severe that cannibalism results.

but is not satisfied;
each feeds on his own children's flesh,
and no one spares his own brother.

(Manasseh Ephraim, and Ephraim Manasseh
—together they are against Judah.)

21 For all this his anger has not abated;
his hand still threatens.

10 Woe betide those who enact unjust
laws
and draft oppressive edicts,
2 depriving the poor of justice,
robbing the weakest of my people of
their rights,
plundering the widow and despoiling
the fatherless!
3 What will you do when called to
account,
when devastation from afar confronts
you?
To whom will you flee for help,
and where will you leave your children
4 so that they do not cower among the
prisoners
or fall among the slain?
For all this his anger has not abated;
his hand still threatens.

5 The Assyrian! He is the rod I wield in
my anger,
the staff in the hand of my wrath.
6 I send him against a godless nation,
I bid him march against a people who
rouse my fury,
to pillage and plunder at will,
to trample them down like mud in the
street.
7 But this man's purpose is lawless,
and lawless are the plans in his mind;
for his thought is only to destroy
and to wipe out nation after nation.
8 'Are not my commanders all kings?' he
boasts.

9 'See how Calno has suffered the fate of
Carchemish.
Is not Hamath like Arpad, Samaria like
Damascus?
10 Before now I have overcome kingdoms
full of idols,
with more images than have Jerusalem
and Samaria,
11 and now, what I did to Samaria and
her worthless gods,
I shall do also to Jerusalem and her
idols.'

12 When the Lord has finished all that he
means to do against Mount Zion and Jerusalem, he will punish the king of Assyria for the
words which spring from his arrogance and
for his high and haughty mien, 13 because he
said:

By my own might I have done it,
and in my own far-seeing wisdom
I have swept aside the frontiers of
nations
and plundered their treasures;
like a bull I have trampled on their
inhabitants.
14 My hand has come on the wealth of
nations as on a nest,
and, as one gathers eggs that have been
abandoned,
so have I taken every land;
not a wing fluttered,
not a beak gaped, no cheep was heard.

15 Will the axe set itself up against the
hewer,
or the saw claim mastery over the
sawyer,
as if a stick were to brandish him who
raises it,
or a wooden staff to wield one who is
not wood?

10:5 the staff . . . wrath: prob. rdg; Heb. obscure.
10:12 he will punish: so Gk; Heb. I shall punish.

See Jer. 19.9. 10.1–4: This woe indictment (see 5.8–23) explains the punishment as arising from failure to give
the poor (v. 2) their legal rights.

10.5–19: Assyria, rod of God's anger. Assyria is the LORD's means of punishing the people, but that nation
also will be judged for its arrogance. 5: The Assyrian: lit. "woe Assyria." 6–7: God's purpose to punish Israel,
carried out by Assyria, is just, but Assyria's own purpose to plunder at will is lawless. 9: Calno, Carchemish,
Hamath, and Arpad are cities in northern Syria taken by Tiglath-pileser III in 734 B.C.E. 13–14: The king of
Assyria (v. 12) is quoted as boasting that everything he did was his own plan. 13: Frontiers: as the Assyrians
advanced they included conquered nations as provinces of their empire. 15: The question is rhetorical; Assyria

16 Therefore the Lord, the LORD of Hosts,
will inflict a wasting disease on the
king's frame,
on his sturdy frame from head to toe,
and in his body a fever like fire will
rage.
17 The Light of Israel will become a fire
and its Holy One a flame,
which in one day will burn up and
consume
his thorns and his briars;
18 his splendid forest and meadow will be
destroyed
as suddenly as someone falling in a fit;
19 what remain of the trees in his forest
will be so few
that a child might record them.

20 On that day the remnant of Israel, the survivors of Jacob, will lean no more on him who
scourged them; without wavering they will
lean on the LORD, the Holy One of Israel.

21 A remnant will return, a remnant of
Jacob,
to God their strength.
22 Israel, your people may be many as the
sands of the sea,
but only a remnant will return.
The instrument of final destruction
will overflow with justice,
23 for the Lord, the LORD of Hosts, will
bring final destruction
on the whole land.

24 Therefore these are the words of the Lord,
the LORD of Hosts: My people, you dwellers
in Zion, do not be afraid of the Assyrians,
though they beat you with their rod and lift
their staff against you as the Egyptians did;
25 for in a very short time my wrath will be
over and my anger will be finally spent.

26 Then the LORD of Hosts will brandish his
scourge at them as he did when he struck
Midian at the Rock of Oreb; he will lift his
staff against the Euphrates as he did against
Egypt.

27 On that day
the burden they laid on your shoulder
will be removed
and their yoke will be broken from off
your neck.

28 An invader from Rimmon has reached
Aiath,
has passed through Migron,
and left his baggage train at Michmash;
29 he has passed through Maabarah
and camped for the night at Geba.
Ramah is terrified, Gibeah of Saul is in
flight.
30 Bath-gallim, raise a shrill cry.
Hear it, Laish. Answer her, Anathoth.
31 Madmenah retreats;
the people of Gebim seek cover.
32 This day he will be at Nob;
he gives the signal to advance
against the mount of Zion,
the hill of Jerusalem.

33 The Lord, the LORD of Hosts,
will shatter the trees with a crash,
the tallest will be hewn down, the lofty
laid low,
34 the thickets of the forest will be felled
with the axe,
and Lebanon with its noble trees will
fall.

10:16 **from ... toe:** *transposed from verse 18; lit. from
neck to groin.* 10:25 **will be finally spent:** *prob.
rdg; Heb. obscure.* 10:27–28 **and their ... Rimmon:**
*prob. rdg; Heb. and their yoke from upon your neck,
and a yoke shall be broken because of oil.* (28)He.

is just a tool in the hand of the LORD. **16–19:** After the LORD, *the Light of Israel,* has used the Assyrians (v. 12),
they will be destroyed.

10.20–23: A remnant shall return. On the day of the LORD (*that day,* see 2.11 n.) those who are left in Israel
will trust the LORD and not Assyria. **21–22:** *A remnant will return:* The sentence is the name of Isaiah's son,
Shear-jashub (7.3). The idea of a remnant, a group which would survive the judgment, is very important in
Isaiah's thought (see 4.2–3; 11.11, 16; 28.5–6; 37.4, 31–32).

10.24–27: Deliverance from Assyria. The people of Jerusalem (*Zion,* v. 24) are not to fear the *Assyrians,*
for the LORD will treat them as he did the *Egyptians* (v. 24). **26:** *Midian:* see Judg. chs. 6–7; *Oreb:* Judg. 7.25.
Euphrates: The river is symbolic here of Assyria.

10.28–34: The advance of the Assyrians. The route of the invaders (vv. 28–32) is described as they approach
from the north toward Jerusalem. **30–34:** The destruction is the work of the LORD.

11 Then a branch will grow from the
stock of Jesse,
and a shoot will spring from his roots.
[2] On him the spirit of the LORD will
rest:
a spirit of wisdom and understanding,
a spirit of counsel and power,
a spirit of knowledge and fear of the
LORD;
[3] and in the fear of the LORD will be his
delight.
He will not judge by outward
appearances
or decide a case on hearsay;
[4] but with justice he will judge the poor
and defend the humble in the land
with equity;
like a rod his verdict will strike the
ruthless,
and with his word he will slay the
wicked.
[5] He will wear the belt of justice,
and truth will be his girdle.

[6] Then the wolf will live with the lamb,
and the leopard lie down with the kid;
the calf and the young lion will feed
together,
with a little child to tend them.
[7] The cow and the bear will be friends,
and their young will lie down together;
and the lion will eat straw like cattle.
[8] The infant will play over the cobra's
hole,
and the young child dance over the
viper's nest.
[9] There will be neither hurt nor harm in
all my holy mountain;

for the land will be filled with the
knowledge of the LORD,
as the waters cover the sea.

[10] On that day a scion from the root of
Jesse
will arise like a standard to rally the
peoples;
the nations will resort to him,
and his abode will be glorious.

[11] On that day the Lord will exert his power
a second time to recover the remnant of his
people from Assyria and Egypt, from Pathros and Cush, from Elam, Shinar, Hamath,
and the islands of the sea.

[12] He will hoist a standard for the nations
and gather those dispersed from Israel;
he will assemble Judah's scattered
people
from the four corners of the earth.
[13] Ephraim's jealousy will cease,
and enmity towards Judah will end.
Ephraim will not be jealous of Judah,
nor will Judah be hostile towards
Ephraim.
[14] They will swoop down on the Philistine
flank in the west
and together plunder the tribes of the
east:
Edom and Moab will be in their
clutches,
and Ammon will be subject to them.

11:4 **ruthless:** *prob. rdg; Heb.* land.   11:6 **will feed:**
so Scroll; Heb. and the buffalo.   11:8 **dance over:**
prob. rdg; Heb. obscure.

11.1–9: The appearance of the Davidic king. The prophet first announces the coming of a new king (v. 1),
describes him as the perfect king (vv. 2–5), and characterizes the results of his reign as perfect and complete
peace throughout all of nature (vv. 6–9). See 9.1–7. **1:** *Jesse* was the father of David (1 Sam. 16.1–20); the new
king continues the dynasty of David in fulfillment of the promise reported in 2 Sam. ch. 7. **2:** The same Heb.
word (*ruah,* a feminine noun) is translated by "spirit" and "breath." The *spirit,* or breath, of the LORD is found
throughout the Bible as an active and creative presence of God. It swept over the abyss at creation (Gen. 1.2);
it inspired God's servants (42.1; 61.1), judges (Judg. 3.10; 6.34), kings (1 Sam. 11.6), and prophets (2 Kgs. 2.9,
Mic. 3.8). **3–5:** The king was responsible for *justice,* especially the protection of the *poor* and the *humble.* See
Ps. 72. **6–9:** The rise of this messianic ruler has cosmic implications; all creatures, even natural enemies, will
be at peace with one another. **9:** See 65.25; Hab. 2.14.

11.10–16: The return of the exiles. The passage assumes the dispersion of the people of Israel among the
nations and looks toward the day of their return. **10:** *A scion from the root of Jesse:* lit. "the root of Jesse"; see
11.1 n. **11:** Most of the known countries of the civilized world (that is, the Near East) are listed. *Pathros* (see
Jer. 44.1, 15) was a section of upper Egypt; *Cush,* Ethiopia; *Shinar,* a name for Babylonia; *the islands of the
Sea* included the islands of the Mediterranean as well as the Aegean coast. **13–14:** The kingdom, reunited,

15 The LORD will divide the tongue of the
   Egyptian sea.
He will wave his hand over the
   Euphrates
to bring a mighty wind,
and will split it into seven wadis
so that it may be crossed dry-shod.
16 So there will be a causeway for the
   remnant of his people,
for the remnant rescued from Assyria,
as there was for the Israelites when
   they came up from Egypt.

12 On that day you will say:
   'I shall praise you, LORD.
Though you were angry with me,
your anger has abated,
and you have comforted me.
2 God is my deliverer.
I am confident and unafraid,
for the LORD is my refuge and defence
and has shown himself my deliverer.'

3 With joy you will all draw water
from the wells of deliverance.
4 On that day you will say:
'Give thanks to the LORD, invoke him
   by name,
make known among the peoples what
   he has done,
proclaim that his name is exalted.
5 Sing psalms to the LORD, for he has
   triumphed;
let this be known in all the world.

6 Cry out, shout aloud, you dwellers in
   Zion,
for the Holy One of Israel is among
   you in majesty.'

Prophecies against foreign nations

13 BABYLON: an oracle which Isaiah son
   of Amoz received in a vision.

2 On a wind-swept height hoist the
   standard,
sound the call to battle,
wave on the advance
towards the Nobles' Gate.
3 I have issued this order to my fighting
   men,
and summoned my warriors, all eager
   for my victory,
to give effect to my anger.
4 A tumult is heard on the mountains,
the sound of a vast multitude;
it is the clamour of kingdoms, of
   nations assembling.
The LORD of Hosts is mustering a host
   for war.
5 They come from a distant land, from
   beyond the horizon,
the LORD with the weapons of his
   wrath,
to lay the whole earth waste.
6 Wail, for the day of the LORD is at
   hand,

11:15 **mighty:** *so Gk; Heb.* glow.   12:2 **defence:** *prob. rdg; Heb.* defence of Yah.

will conquer its traditional enemies. **15–16:** The return of the *remnant* will be a new exodus, with natural phenomena more glorious than the first; see Exod. 14.21–22; Josh. 3.13–17. **15:** *The tongue of the Egyptian Sea:* the modern Gulf of Suez.

12.1–6: Two Thanksgiving hymns. Two brief hymns similar in form to psalms of Enthronement of the LORD (Pss. 47; 97) mark the end of the first major section of the Book of Isa. Each is introduced by ceremonial instructions to the congregation (vv. 1a and 4a) which link the songs to the previous section (11.11–16). **2b:** The language is common in hymns of Thanksgiving; see Exod. 15.2; Ps. 18.1–3. **3:** The verse can be read with 4a as liturgical instruction to temple priests. **4–6:** Typical invitations to give thanks and to sing; see Pss. 105.1; 148.13.

13.1–23.18: Prophecies against foreign nations. Most major sections are introduced with the word *oracle*, or "burden." See 13.1; 15.1; 17.1; 19.1; 21.1, 11, 13; 22.1; 23.1; 30.6.

13.1–22: Judgment on Babylon. Since Babylon did not develop into a ruling power until 612 B.C.E. when it destroyed Nineveh, the capital of Assyria, this oracle is probably later than Isaiah. The Medes, mentioned in v. 17, were united to the Persians under Cyrus in 550 B.C.E. Together they conquered Babylon in 539 B.C.E. Therefore, the prophecy belongs somewhere between the Exile in 587 B.C.E. and the conquest of Babylon by Cyrus. The oracle is in the poetic form of a dirge, i.e. a funeral lament, over Babylon. **3:** *My warriors:* the Medes (v. 17) and Persians who carry out God's purpose of overthrowing Babylon to bring back the captives from Exile. **5:** *Distant land:* Persia. **6:** *Day of the LORD:* see 2.11 n. Since Israel has been punished by God with the

devastation coming from the Almighty!
7 Because of it every hand will hang
    limp,
  every man's courage melt away;
8 they will writhe with terror;
  agonizing pangs will grip them,
  like a woman in labour.
  They will look aghast at each other,
  their faces livid with fear.

9 The day of the LORD is coming,
  that cruel day of wrath and fierce
    anger,
  to reduce the earth to desolation
  and destroy all the wicked there.
10 The stars of heaven in their
    constellations
  will give no light,
  the sun will be dark at its rising,
  and the moon will not shed its light.
11 I shall bring disaster on the world
  and due punishment on the wicked.
  I shall cut short insolent pride
  and bring down ruthless arrogance.
12 I shall make human beings scarcer than
    fine gold,
  more rare than gold of Ophir.
13 Then I shall make the heavens
    shudder,
  and the earth will be shaken to its
    foundations
  at the wrath of the LORD of Hosts,
  on the day of his blazing anger.
14 Like a gazelle pursued by a hunter
  or like a flock with no shepherd to
    round it up,
  every man will head back to his own
    people,
  each one will flee to his own land.
15 All who are found will fall by the
    sword,
  all who are taken will be thrust
    through;

16 their babes will be battered to death
    before their eyes,
  their houses looted and their wives
    raped.

17 I shall stir up the Medes against them;
  they cannot be bought off with silver,
  nor be tempted by gold;
18 they have no pity on little children
  and spare no mother's son.
19 Babylon, fairest of kingdoms,
  proud beauty of the Chaldaeans,
  will be like Sodom and Gomorrah
  when overthrown by God.
20 Never again will she be inhabited,
  no one will live in her throughout the
    ages;
  no Arab will pitch his tent there,
  no shepherds fold their flocks.
21 But marmots will have their lairs in
    her,
  and porcupines will overrun her
    houses;
  desert-owls will dwell there,
  and there he-goats will gambol;
22 jackals will occupy her mansions,
  and wolves her luxurious palaces.
  Her time draws very near;
  her days have not long to run.

14 The LORD will show compassion for Jacob and will once again make Israel his choice. He will resettle them on their native soil, where aliens will join them and attach themselves to Jacob's people. 2 Nations will escort Israel to her homeland, and she will take them over, both male and female, as slaves in the LORD's land; she will take her captors captive and lord it over her oppressors.
3 On the day when the LORD gives you re-

13:18 **they have:** Heb. prefixes bows will strike down young men to the ground.   13:22 **her mansions:** prob. rdg; Heb. her widows.

Exile, here the *day* is a judgment on its enemies. Before the Exile the day was a judgment exclusively on Israel; compare Amos 5.18. **9–16:** God's decisive judgments are accompanied by a disruption of order in *heaven*. The *day* brings darkness, destruction and death. **16:** Children were treated cruelly in ancient warfare; see Ps. 137.8–9. **17:** *Medes:* 13.1–22 n. above. **19:** *Chaldaeans:* the inhabitants of the southern part of Mesopotamia at the head of the Persian gulf, who extended their rule over all of Babylonia and Assyria under Nabopolassar, the father of Nebuchadnezzar. *Sodom and Gomorrah:* see Gen. 19.23–25. **20–22:** Babylon will not even be fit for pasture land; only wild beasts will live there.
  14.1–23: The return of the exiles and a satire on the fall of their oppressor. 1–2: The LORD will choose Israel (*Jacob*) once again, *resettle* the people on their land, and make the *captors* servants. Since this unit refers to the return from Exile and the conversion of pagan *nations,* it has affinities with the second part of Isaiah, namely, chs. 40–55, and perhaps its date of composition is the same (see Introduction). **3–23:** This dirge is

lief from your pain and trouble and from the cruel servitude imposed upon you, ⁴you will take up this taunt-song over the king of Babylon:

> See how still the oppressor has become,
> how still his raging arrogance!
> ⁵The LORD has broken the rod of the
>   wicked,
> the sceptre of rulers
> ⁶who in anger struck down peoples
> with unerring blows,
> who in fury trod nations underfoot
> with relentless persecution.

> ⁷The whole world rests undisturbed;
> it breaks into cries of joy.
> ⁸The very pines and the cedars of
>   Lebanon exult:
> 'Since you have been laid low,' they say,
> 'no woodman comes to cut us down.'

> ⁹Sheol below was all astir
> to greet you at your coming;
> she roused for you the ancient dead,
> all that were leaders on earth;
> she had all who had been kings of the
>   nations
> get up from their thrones.

> ¹⁰All greet you with these words:
> 'So you too are impotent as we are,
> and have become like one of us!'
> ¹¹Your pride has been brought down to
>   Sheol,
> to the throng of your victims;
> maggots are the mattress beneath you,
> and worms your coverlet.

> ¹²Bright morning star, how you have
>   fallen from heaven,
> thrown to earth, prostrate among the
>   nations!
> ¹³You thought to yourself:

> 'I shall scale the heavens
> to set my throne high above the mighty
>   stars;
> I shall take my seat on the mountain
>   where the gods assemble
> in the far recesses of the north.
> ¹⁴I shall ascend beyond the towering
>   clouds
> and make myself like the Most High!'

> ¹⁵Instead you are brought down to Sheol,
> into the depths of the abyss.
> ¹⁶Those who see you stare at you,
> reflecting as they gaze:
> 'Is this the man who shook the earth,
> who made kingdoms quake,
> ¹⁷who turned the world into a desert
> and laid its cities in ruins,
> who never set his prisoners free?'

> ¹⁸All the kings of every nation lie in
>   honour,
> each in his last resting-place.
> ¹⁹But you have been flung out without
>   burial
> like some loathsome carrion,
> a carcass trampled underfoot,
> a companion to the slain pierced by the
>   sword
> who have gone down to the stony abyss.
> ²⁰You will not be joined in burial with
>   those kings,
> for you have ruined your land,
> brought death to your people.
> That wicked dynasty will never again be
>   mentioned!
> ²¹Prepare the shambles for his children
> butchered for their fathers' sins;
> they will not rise and possess the earth
> or cover the world with their cities.

14:4 **his raging arrogance:** *so Scroll; Heb. obscure.*
14:9 **Sheol:** *or* The underworld.   14:11 **the throng of your victims:** *so Scroll; Heb.* the music of your lutes.
14:19 **carrion:** *prob. rdg, cp. Gk; Heb.* shoot.

referred to the king of Babylon in its prose introduction (vv. 3–4a) and conclusion (vv. 22–23), but the song itself (vv. 4b–21) could have been applied to any of Israel's oppressors. **4b–6:** The *oppressor* has fallen. **7–11:** Even the dead welcome his arrival and ridicule him (vv. 9–11). **9:** *Sheol:* the underworld where the "shades" of the dead dwelled. See Ezek. 32.17–32; Ps. 88. **12–15:** The tyrant placed himself *above the mighty stars* (v. 13) and now lies beneath the earth. **12:** *Bright morning star:* Heb. "Helal son of Shahar," possibly meaning "Day Star, son of Dawn," and reflecting the names of deities. **13:** *Mountain where the gods assemble:* lit. "Mountain of assembly"; in Canaanite mythology a place (usually Mount Zaphon, Pss. 48.2 (Tfn.); 89.12) where the gods met in council. **19–20:** To be left *without burial* as *carrion* was considered to be a *loathsome* curse which pursued and troubled a person even beyond death. Those *pierced by the sword* died an untimely death

22 I shall rise against them, declares the LORD of Hosts; I shall destroy what remains of Babylon, her name, her offspring, and her posterity, declares the LORD; 23 I shall make her a haunt of the bustard, a waste of marshland, and sweep her with the besom of destruction. This is the word of the LORD of Hosts.

24 The LORD of Hosts has sworn this oath:
'As I purposed, so most surely it will be;
as I planned, so it will take place:
25 I shall break the Assyrian in my own land
and trample him down on my mountains;
his yoke will be lifted from my people,
his burden taken from their shoulders.'
26 This is the plan prepared for the whole world,
this the hand stretched out over all the nations.
27 For the LORD of Hosts has prepared his plan:
who can frustrate it?
His is the hand that is stretched out,
and who can turn it back?

28 In the year King Ahaz died this oracle came from God:

29 Let none of you Philistines rejoice
because the rod that chastised you is broken;
for a viper will be born of a snake,
and its offspring will be a flying serpent.
30 The poor will graze their flocks in my meadows,

and the destitute will lie down in safety,
but your offspring I shall do to death by famine,
and your remnant I shall slay.
31 Wail in the gate, cry for help in the city,
let all Philistia be stricken with panic;
for a formidable foe is coming from the north,
with not one straggler in his ranks.
32 What answer is there for a nation's envoys?
It is that the LORD has established Zion,
and in her the afflicted among his people will find refuge.

15 Moab: an oracle.

On the night when Ar is laid waste,
Moab meets her doom;
on the night when Kir is laid waste,
Moab meets her doom.
2 The people of Dibon go up to the shrines to weep;
Moab is wailing over Nebo and over Medeba.
Every head is shaven, every beard cut off.
3 In their streets they wear sackcloth,
they cry out on the roofs;
in the public squares every one wails,
streaming with tears.
4 Heshbon and Elealeh cry out in distress,
their voices carry to Jahaz.

14:30 **remnant I:** *so Scroll; Heb.* remnant he.
15:2 **The people . . . go up:** *prob. rdg; Heb.* He has gone up to the house and Dibon.   15:3 **they cry out:** *prob. rdg, cp. Gk; Heb. omits.*

with their lives unfulfilled and so in some way were cursed by God. **21:** That *children* be cut off from life at an early age was considered to be a particularly heavy punishment for the *sins* of the fathers.

14.24–27: Judgment against Assyria. 24: *The LORD . . . planned* to act against Assyria; in doing so God will deliver the people. **27:** God's *hand is stretched* out in punishment of Assyria. Compare 5.25; 9.12, 17; 10.4.

14.28–32: Judgment against the Philistines. 28: *Ahaz died* about 715 B.C.E. **29:** Although the Philistines ceased to be a power in the time of David, they continued to exist as a thorn in Israel's side, rejoicing in their misfortunes and taking advantage of them; see Ezek. 25.15–17. The *rod that chastised* the Philistines probably was Sargon II, who died in 705 B.C.E. The *snake* is probably the Assyrian nation that will give birth to another tyrant ruler, or *viper*. **32:** *Zion* was deemed to be impregnable and inviolable.

15.1–16.14: Lament over Moab. Moab was the country immediately to the east of the Dead Sea. According to Gen. 19.36–38, the Moabites are descended from Lot and so related to the Israelites. The relations between the two peoples vacillated between close friendship and bitter hostility; see Ruth 1.1–2; 1 Sam. 22.3–4; 2 Sam. 8.2. This song at points carries a tone of authentic lament, but at others (16.6, 12) shows no regret over Moab's destruction. See Jer. ch. 48. **1–9:** All the cities of Moab mourn its death. **2–3:** *Weep, wailing, head . . . shaven,*

So Moab's stoutest warriors become
alarmed,
and their courage ebbs away.
5 My heart cries out for Moab,
whose fugitives have reached Zoar,
as far as Eglath-shelishiyah.
On the ascent to Luhith they go up
weeping;
on the road to Horonaim there are
cries of 'Disaster!'
6 The waters of Nimrim are desolate;
the grass is parched, the herbage dead,
not a green thing is left;
7 the people carry across the wadi
Arabim
their hard-earned wealth and hoarded
savings.
8 The cry of distress echoes round the
frontiers of Moab,
their wailing reaches Eglaim and
Beer-elim.
9 The waters of Dibon run with blood;
yet I have worse in store for Dibon:
a lion for the survivors of Moab,
and for the remnant of Admah.

16 The rulers of the land send a
present of lambs
from Sela by the wilderness
to the mount of Zion;
2 the women of Moab at the fords of the
Arnon
are like fluttering birds, like scattered
nestlings.
3 'Give us counsel, intervene for us;
let your shadow shield us at high noon
as if it were night.
Give the exiles shelter, do not betray
the fugitives;
4 let the exiles from Moab find a home
with you
and shelter them from the despoiler.'

When oppression has done its work
and the despoiling is over,
when the heel of the aggressor has
vanished from the land,
5 a trusted throne will be set up in
David's tent;
on it there will sit a true judge,

one who cares for justice and pursues
right.
6 We have heard how great is the
haughtiness of Moab,
we have heard of his pride, his
surpassing pride—
his boastful talk is groundless!
7 Therefore let Moab wail;
let all the Moabites wail indeed;
they will mourn for the prosperous
farmers of Kir-hareseth,
who face ruin;
8 the vineyards of Heshbon languish,
the vines of Sibmah,
whose red grapes used to overpower
the lords of the nations;
they reached as far as Jazer
and trailed out to the wilderness,
and their spreading branches crossed
the sea.
9 I shall weep for Sibmah's vines as I
weep for Jazer.
I shall drench you with tears, Heshbon
and Elealeh;
for the shouts of the enemy have fallen
on your summer fruits and harvest.
10 Joy and gladness will be banished from
the fields,
no more will they tread wine in the
winepresses;
I have silenced the shouting of the
harvesters.
11 Therefore my heart throbs
like a harp for Moab,
and my soul for Kir-hareseth.
12 Though the Moabites come to worship
and weary themselves at the shrines,
though they flock to their sanctuaries to
pray,
it will avail them nothing.

13 Those are the words which the LORD spoke
long ago about Moab; 14 and now he says: 'In
three years, as a hired labourer counts them
off exactly, the vast population in which
Moab glories will be brought into contempt;

15:5 **there are cries of:** *prob. rdg, cp. Lat.; Heb.
unintelligible.* 16:7 **they:** *prob. rdg; Heb.* you.

beard cut off, sackcloth: these were conventional signs of mourning. **9:** The Heb. words for *Dimon* and *blood*
are very similar; hence the play on words. **16.1–4a:** The *rulers* (v. 1) seek refuge in Jerusalem. **4:** *David's tent:*
the dynasty of David. **6–12:** Moab's *pride* (v. 6) is the reason for its trouble; not even *prayer* (v. 12) will help.
8: *Wilderness:* the Arabian desert to the east of Moab. *Sea:* the Dead Sea.

those who are left will be few and feeble and bereft of all honour.'

17 Damascus: an oracle.

Damascus will cease to be a city;
she will be reduced to a heap of ruins
2 for ever desolate.
Flocks will have her for their own
and lie there undisturbed.
3 No longer will Ephraim boast a
fortified city,
or Damascus a kingdom;
the remnant of Aram will share the fate
of Israel's glory.
This is the word of the LORD of Hosts.

4 On that day Jacob's glory will wane
and his prosperity waste away,
5 as when the reaper gathers the standing
grain,
harvesting the ears by armfuls,
or as when one gleans the ears in the
vale of Rephaim,
6 or as when an olive tree is beaten
and only gleanings are left on it,
two or three berries on the topmost
branch,
four or five on its fruitful boughs.
This is the word of the LORD the God
of Israel.

7 On that day all will look to their Maker,
turning their eyes to the Holy One of Israel;
8 they will not look to the altars, their own
handiwork, or to objects their fingers have
made, sacred poles and incense-altars.
9 On that day your strong cities will be deserted like the deserted cities of the Hivites

and the Amorites, which they abandoned at
Israel's approach, and they will become desolate.

10 You forgot the God who delivered you,
and did not keep in mind the rock,
your stronghold.
Plant then, if you will, your gardens in
honour of Adonis,
set out your cuttings for a foreign god;
11 though you protect them on the day
you plant them,
and though your seeds sprout next
morning,
yet the crop will disappear when
wasting disease comes
in a day of incurable pain.

12 Listen! It is the thunder of vast forces,
a thundering like the thunder of the
sea.
Listen! It is the roar of nations,
a roaring like the roar of mighty
waters.
13 At his rebuke, they flee far away,
driven before the wind like chaff on
the hills,
like thistledown before the storm.
14 At evening all is terror;
before morning it is gone.
Such is the fate of our plunderers,
the lot of those who despoil us.

18 There is a land of sailing ships
lying beyond the rivers of Cush;
2 it sends its envoys by the Nile

17:2 **for ever . . . own:** *so Gk; Heb.* The cities of Aroer
will be deserted for flocks.   17:9 **Hivites . . .
Amorites:** *prob. rdg, cp. Gk; Heb.* woodland and
hill-country.   17:12 **roaring . . . waters:** *so some MSS;
others add* peoples roar with the roar of great waters.

17.1–6: Judgment on the Syro-Ephraimitic coalition. In the context of the threat to Judah from Syria (*Aram*,
v. 3) and Israel (*Ephraim*, v. 3), the prophet announces judgment on these enemies. The date is 734–732 B.C.E.;
see 7.1–9 n. **1:** *Damascus:* capital of Syria. **3:** *Israel's glory* perhaps refers to its capital, Samaria. **5:** The *vale
of Rephaim* was northwest of Jerusalem; see Josh. 15.8; 18.16.

17.7–11: Concerning idolatry. 7–8: One day mortals will choose *their Maker* over what they have made.
8: *Sacred poles:* lit. "Asherim," cultic objects representing a Canaanite goddess. **9–11:** Idolatry results in
desolation. **10:** *Adonis* (lit. "pleasant plants") was a god of vegetation.

17.12–14: The thunder of the enemy. The approach of an unnamed army becomes a roar, but the LORD
blows the invader away. While the passage may refer to the unsuccessful Assyrian attack on Jerusalem (2 Kgs.
19.35–36) in 701 B.C.E., the language and concepts are common enough to lack a direct reference.

18.1–20.6: Relations with Egypt.

18.1–7: Response to the envoys from Ethiopia. This section ensues on an attempt by an Egyptian embassy
to establish a coalition against Assyria, about 714 B.C.E. Isaiah speaks against the attempt, holding that God,
not human treaties, controls history. **1:** *Beyond . . . Cush:* the Pharaohs of the Twenty-fifth Dynasty who, coming

in vessels of reed on the waters.
Go, swift messengers,
to a people tall and smooth-skinned,
to a people dreaded far and near,
a nation strong and aggressive,
whose land is scoured by rivers.
³All you inhabitants of the world, you
   dwellers on earth,
will see when the standard is hoisted on
   the mountains
and hear when the trumpet sounds.

⁴These were the words of the LORD to me:

From my dwelling-place I shall look on
   and do nothing
when the heat shimmers in the summer
   sun,
when the dew is heavy at harvest time.
⁵Before the vintage, when the budding
   is over
and the flower ripens into a berry,
the shoots will be cut down with
   pruning-knives,
the branches struck off and cleared
   away.
⁶All will be left to birds of prey on the
   hills
and to the wild beasts of the earth;
in summer those birds will make their
   home there,
in winter those wild beasts.

⁷At that time tribute will be brought to the
LORD of Hosts from a people tall and
smooth-skinned, dreaded near and far, a nation strong and aggressive, whose land is
scoured by rivers. They will bring it to the
place where the name of the LORD of Hosts
dwells, to Mount Zion.

19 Egypt: an oracle.

The LORD comes riding swiftly on a
   cloud,

and he descends on Egypt;
the idols of Egypt quail before him,
Egypt's courage melts within her.
²I shall incite Egyptian against Egyptian,
and they will fight one against another,
neighbour against neighbour,
city against city, kingdom against
   kingdom.
³Egypt's spirit will ebb away within her,
and I shall throw her counsels into
   confusion.
They will resort to idols and
   oracle-mongers,
to ghosts and spirits,
⁴but I shall hand Egypt over to a hard
   master,
and a fierce ruler will be king over
   them.
This is the word of the Lord, the LORD
   of Hosts.

⁵The waters of the Nile will disappear,
the river bed will be parched and dry,
⁶and its channels will give off a stench.
Egypt's canals will fail altogether;
reeds and rushes will wither away.
⁷The lotus beside the Nile
and everything sown along the river
   will dry up;
they will blow away and vanish.
⁸The fishermen will groan and lament;
all who cast their hooks into the Nile
and those who spread nets on the water
   will lose heart.
⁹The flax-dressers will be dejected,
the women carding and the men
   weaving grow pale.
¹⁰Egypt's spinners will be downcast,
and all her artisans sick at heart.

¹¹The princes of Zoan are no better than

18:4 **time:** *so Gk; Heb.* heat.   18:7 **from:** *so Scroll;*
Heb. omits.   19:7 **lotus . . . Nile:** *prob. rdg; Heb. adds*
the mouth of the Nile.   19:9 **grow pale:** *so Scroll;*
Heb. white linen.

from the area south of Egypt, are regarded as Ethiopians; *Cush* is the ordinary Heb. name for Ethiopia. **2:** *Vessels
of reed:* the Egyptians used boats made of papyrus, lined with pitch. **4–6:** As the seasons turn, the LORD will
act in the LORD's own time. **7:** Eventually even the Egyptians will bring *tribute* to the temple in Jerusalem.
   19.1–15: Judgment against Egypt. The LORD will bring internal chaos in Egypt, dry up the Nile, and cause
all who depended on it to suffer (vv. 1–10). The crucial decisions in history are made in the *counsels* of the
LORD to which the prophets are privy and the wise *counsellors* of kings are not (vv. 11–15). **1:** In Canaanite
mythology too the god Baal often is called "cloud rider"; see Pss. 104.3; 68.4 n. **2:** *Egyptian against Egyptian:*
The description of turbulence is so general that it cannot be identified with particular historical events. **4:** The
hard master may be an Egyptian tyrant or a foreign *king* who will conquer Egypt. **5–6:** Egypt depended upon

fools; Pharaoh's wisest counsellors give stupid advice.

How can you say to Pharaoh,
'I am descended from wise men;
I spring from ancient kings'?
12 Where are your wise men, Pharaoh,
to teach you and make known to you
what the LORD of Hosts has planned
for Egypt?
13 Zoan's princes are fooled,
the princes of Noph are dupes;
the chieftains of her clans have led
Egypt astray.
14 The LORD has infused into them
a spirit that distorts their judgement;
they make Egypt miss her way in all she
does,
as a vomiting drunkard will miss his
footing.
15 There will be nothing in Egypt that
anyone can do,
be they head or tail, palm-frond or
reed.

16 When that day comes the Egyptians will become weak as women; they will be terror-stricken when the LORD of Hosts raises his hand against them. 17 The land of Judah will throw the Egyptians into panic; the very mention of its name will cause dismay, because of the plans that the LORD of Hosts has laid against them.

18 When that day comes there will be five cities in Egypt speaking the language of Canaan and swearing allegiance to the LORD of Hosts, and one of them will be called the City of the Sun.

19 When that day comes there will be an altar dedicated to the LORD in the heart of Egypt, and a sacred pillar set up for the LORD at her frontier. 20 It will stand as a symbol and a reminder of the LORD of Hosts in Egypt; for they will appeal to him against their oppressors, and he will send a deliverer to champion their cause and come to their rescue. 21 The LORD will make himself known to the Egyptians. They will acknowledge the LORD when that day comes; they will worship him with sacrifices and grain-offerings, make vows to him, and fulfil them. 22 The LORD will strike down Egypt, and then bring healing; when they turn back to him he will respond to their prayers and heal them.

23 When that day comes there will be a highway between Egypt and Assyria. The Assyrians will link up with Egypt and the Egyptians with Assyria, and Egyptians will worship with Assyrians.

24 When that day comes Israel will rank as a third with Egypt and Assyria and be a blessing in the world. 25 This is the blessing the LORD of Hosts will give: 'Blessed be Egypt my people, Assyria my handiwork, and Israel my possession.'

20 IT was the year that King Sargon of Assyria sent his commander-in-chief to Ashdod, and he took it by storm. 2 Before that time the LORD had said to Isaiah son of Amoz, 'Strip the sackcloth from your waist and take off your sandals.' He had done so, and gone about naked and barefoot. 3 Now the LORD said, 'As my servant Isaiah has gone naked and barefoot for three years, a sign

19:14 **them:** *so Gk; Heb.* her.   19:18 **the City of the Sun:** *or* Heliopolis; *so some MSS; others* the City of Destruction.   19:23 **will worship with:** *or* will be subject to.   20:2 **to:** *so Gk; Heb.* through.

the regular floods of the Nile. The anticipated disaster is more serious than a drought. **11:** *Zoan:* the Greek Tanis, a city on the Nile delta; see Num. 13.22; Ezek. 30.14. The wise men of Egypt were renowned; see 1 Kgs. 4.30. **13:** *Noph:* Memphis, one of the ancient capitals of Egypt. **15:** Everyone in Egypt, from the highly placed (the *head,* the *palm-frond*) to the lowest (the *tail, reed* in the water) will be helpless.

19.16–25: Hope for the salvation of Egypt. Five paragraphs, each beginning with the same phrase (*When that day comes*), have been appended to the poem against Egypt. **16:** *That day:* day of the LORD; see 2.11 n. **18:** *City of the Sun:* the translation and identification are problematic. *Heliopolis* (Tfn.) was a later name for the city of On, center of sun worship and renowned as an educational center. **22:** The LORD will treat Egypt like Israel, i.e. will *strike* Israel with a *healing* punishment. **24–25:** *Israel, Egypt, and Assyria,* traditional enemies, will be reconciled on *that day,* and all will become the LORD's peoples.

20.1–6: A sign of Egypt's humiliation. When Egypt attempted to unite the small states of Palestine against Assyria (714–711 B.C.E.; see 18.1–7), Isaiah walked naked and barefoot, proclaiming himself as a sign of Egypt's failure. **1:** *Sargon:* Sargon II (722–705 B.C.E.). *Ashdod* was one of the Philistine cities taken by the Assyrians in 711 B.C.E. **3–6:** The prophet would have proclaimed these words as the interpretation of his and portent to Egypt and Cush, ⁴so will the king of Assyria lead away the captives of Egypt and the exiles of Cush naked and barefoot, young and old alike, with their buttocks shamefully exposed. ⁵All will be dismayed; their trust in Cush and their pride in Egypt will be disappointed. ⁶On that day those who dwell along this coast will say, "So much for all our hopes on which we relied, our hopes for help and deliverance from the king of Assyria! What escape is there for us?" '

21 'THE wilderness': an oracle.

A day of storms, sweeping through the Negeb,
coming from the wilderness, from a land of terror!
²A grim vision is shown to me:
the traitor betrayed, the spoiler despoiled.
Advance, Elam; up, Media, to the siege!
Throw off all weariness!
³At this vision my limbs writhe in anguish,
I am gripped by pangs like a woman in labour.
I am distraught past hearing, disquieted past seeing,
⁴my mind reels, sudden convulsions assail me.

The evening cool I longed for has become horrible to me:
⁵the banquet is set, the rugs are spread;
they are eating and drinking.
Rise, princes, burnish your shields.
⁶For these are the words of the Lord to me:
'Go, post a watchman to report what he sees.
⁷If it is a column of horsemen in pairs,
a column of donkeys, a column of camels,
he must be on the alert, fully on the alert.'

⁸Then the look-out cried:
'All day long I stand on the watch-tower, Lord,
and night after night I am at my post.
⁹There they come: a column of horsemen in pairs.'
A voice called back:
'Fallen, fallen is Babylon,
and all the images of her gods lie shattered on the ground.'
¹⁰My people, once trodden out on the threshing-floor,
what I have heard from the LORD of Hosts,
from the God of Israel, I have told you.

¹¹Dumah: an oracle.

One calls to me from Seir:
'Watchman, what is left of the night?
Watchman, what is left of it?'
¹²The watchman answered:
'Morning comes, and so does night.
Come back again and ask if you will.'

¹³'With the Arabs': an oracle.

You caravans of Dedan, that camp in the scrub with the Arabs,
¹⁴bring water to meet the thirsty.
You inhabitants of Tema, meet the fugitives with food,
¹⁵for they flee from the sword, the sharp edge of the sword,
from the bent bow, and from the press of battle.

¹⁶For these are the words of the Lord to me:
'Within a year, as a hired labourer counts off years exactly, all Kedar's glory will come to an end; ¹⁷few will be the archers left, the warriors of Kedar.'
The LORD the God of Israel has spoken.

20:6 **on which we relied:** so Scroll; Heb. to which we fled.   21:8 **the look-out:** so Scroll; Heb. a lion.

behavior. **3:** Sign: see 7.11–12 n. **4:** See 2 Sam. 10.1–5. **6:** The Palestinian coastal states which trusted Egypt have no escape.

21.1–10: A vision of the fall of Babylon. The poem was written by an anonymous prophet, active at the time of Babylon's fall in 539 B.C.E. In a vision he awaits a messenger with the news of the oppressor's demise. **2:** Elam and Media, powers east of Babylon, are encouraged to move against the spoiler. **10:** The news is for the people of Israel who have experienced the punishment of exile.

21.11–17: Speeches concerning Arabia. With the exception of Seir (Edom), the places mentioned are in Arabia.

22 'THE Valley of Vision': an oracle.

Tell me, what is amiss with you
that all of you have climbed up on the
　roofs?
2 You city full of tumult, you town in
　ferment
and filled with uproar,
your slain did not fall by the sword;
they did not die in battle.
3 All your commanders are in full flight,
fleeing in groups from the bow;
all your stoutest warriors dispersed in
　groups
have fled in all directions.
4 That is why I said: Turn your eyes
　away from me;
leave me to weep in misery.
Do not press consolation on me
for the ruin of my people.

5 For the Lord, the LORD of Hosts, has ordained a day of tumult, a day of trampling
and turmoil in the Valley of Vision, clamour
and cries among the mountains.

6 Elam took up the quiver,
horses were harnessed to the chariots of
　Aram,
Kir bared the shield.
7 Your fairest valleys were overrun by
　chariots
and the city gates were beset by
　horsemen;
8 the heart of Judah's defence was laid
　open.

On that day you checked the weapons stored
in the House of the Forest; 9 you filled all the
many pools in the City of David, collecting
water from the Lower Pool. 10 Then you surveyed the houses in Jerusalem, tearing some
down to repair and fortify the wall, 11 and
between the two walls you constructed a reservoir for the water of the Old Pool.

You did not look to the Maker of the
　city
or consider him who fashioned it long
　ago.
12 On that day the Lord, the LORD of
　Hosts,
called for weeping and beating the
　breast in mourning,
for shaving the head and putting on
　sackcloth.
13 Instead there was joy and
　merrymaking,
killing of cattle and slaughtering of
　sheep,
eating of meat and drinking of wine.
'Let us eat and drink,' you said, 'for
　tomorrow we die!'

14 Here are words revealed to me by the LORD
of Hosts:

Assuredly your wickedness will never be
　wiped out;
you will die for it.
This is the word of the Lord, the LORD
　of Hosts.

15 These were the words of the Lord, the
LORD of Hosts:

22:1 **Vision:** *or* Calamity. 　 22:3 **your stoutest**
warriors: *so Gk; Heb.* those found in you.
22:5 **Vision:** *or* Calamity. 　 22:6 **Aram:** *prob. rdg;*
Heb. man. 　 22:9 **you ... Pool:** *or* you took note of
the many breaches in the wall of the City of David,
and you collected water from the Lower Pool.

22.1–14: The LORD's day of judgment upon Jerusalem. The events here probably occurred in 701 B.C.E. when
Sennacherib of Assyria invaded Judah and besieged Jerusalem, but left without destroying the city (2 Kgs.
19.35–36). **1–4:** The *tumult* (v. 2) may have been the cries of alarm as the siege began, or the celebration when
the siege was lifted. **5–13:** The prophet sees the approach of the enemy as the coming *day* of the LORD's
judgment. **6:** *Elam, Aram* (the text is uncertain), and *Kir* (an unknown locality in Mesopotamia) may represent
troops in the Assyrian army. **8–13:** The people of Jerusalem trusted in their siege preparations instead of the
LORD; they ate and drank (v. 13) instead of praying and lamenting. **8:** The *House of the Forest* was an armory
built by Solomon (1 Kgs. 7.2; 10.17). **9–11:** According to 2 Kgs. 20.20 Hezekiah built a reservoir and water
conduit; such water systems were common in Palestinian cities, built in such a way as to provide water in case
of siege. **12–13:** The people fail to see the impending siege as a call to repentance. **14:** The LORD pronounces
a death sentence on the people.

22.15–25: Against an arrogant official. *Shebna*, the highest government official under the king (cf. Jer.

Go to the steward,
this Shebna, comptroller of the
household, and say:
16 What have you here, or whom have
you here,
that you have hewn out a tomb here
for yourself?
Why should he hew his tomb in an
eminent place,
and carve for himself a resting-place in
the rock?
17 The LORD is about to shake you out,
as a garment is shaken to rid it of lice;
18 he will roll you up tightly
and throw you like a ball
into a land of vast expanses.
There you will die,
and there your chariot of honour will
remain,
bringing disgrace on your master's
household.
19 I shall remove you from office
and pluck you from your post.

20 On that day I shall send for my servant
Eliakim son of Hilkiah; 21 I shall invest him
with your robe, equip him with your sash of
office, and invest him with your authority; he
will be a father to the inhabitants of Jerusalem and to the people of Judah. 22 I shall
place the key of David's palace on his shoulder; what he opens none will shut, and what
he shuts none will open. 23 He will be a seat
of honour for his father's family; I shall fasten him firmly in place like a peg. 24 On him
will hang the whole glory of the family, even
to the meanest members—all the paltriest of
vessels, whether bowl or pot. 25 On that day,
says the LORD of Hosts, the peg which was
firmly fastened in its place will be removed;
cut off, it will fall, and the load hanging on
it will be destroyed. The LORD has spoken.

23 TYRE: an oracle.

Wail, you ships of Tarshish, for the
harbour is destroyed;

the port of entry from Kittim is swept
away.
2 Lament, you people of the sea coast,
you merchants of Sidon,
3 whose envoys cross the great waters,
whose harvest is grain from Shihor,
whose revenue comes from trade
between nations.
4 In dismay Sidon, the sea-fortress, says:
'I no longer feel the anguish of labour
or bear children;
I have no young sons to rear, no
daughters to bring up.'
5 When the news reaches Egypt
her people will writhe in anguish at the
fate of Tyre.
6 Make your way to Tarshish;
wail, you dwellers by the sea.
7 Is this your bustling city of ancient
foundation,
the founder of colonies in distant parts?

8 Whose was this plan against Tyre,
a city with crowns in its gift,
whose merchants were princes,
whose traders the most honoured men
on earth?
9 The LORD of Hosts planned it to prick
every noble's pride
and humiliate all the most honoured
men on earth.
10 Take to the tillage of your fields, you
people of Tarshish;
for your market is lost.
11 The LORD has stretched out his hand
over the sea
and made kingdoms quake;
he has decreed the destruction of
Canaan's marts.
12 He has said, 'You will be busy no more,

22:17 **garment:** *prob. rdg; Heb.* man.   22:19 **and
pluck:** *so Syriac; Heb.* and he will drive.   23:3 **whose
envoys:** *prob. rdg, cp.* Scroll; *Heb.* they have filled you.
whose harvest: *prob. rdg; Heb.* the harvest of the Nile.
23:4 **the sea-fortress, says:** *prob. rdg; Heb.* for the sea
said, the sea-fortress saying.   23:10 **Take... fields:**
so Gk; Heb. Pass over your fields like the Nile. **market:**
prob. rdg; Heb. girdle.

20.1–6), has behaved arrogantly; he will not be buried in the magnificent grave he has prepared for himself,
but will be exiled after losing his office (vv. 15–19). He will be replaced by *Eliakim* (vv. 20–25; see 36.3, 11,
22; 37.2). **15:** The *comptroller of the household* (lit. "the one over the household") was the prime minister (see
Gen. 41.40). **21–24:** The symbols of authority and the duties of the prime minister are described. **25:** The verse
is enigmatic; it suggests that Eliakim himself eventually will be removed from office.

   23.1–18: Judgment against Tyre and Sidon. These were Phoenician seaports. **1–7:** The location of *Tarshish*
is uncertain; it was a distant Mediterranean port, perhaps on the southern coast of Spain and so a symbol for

you, the sorely oppressed city of Sidon.
Though you make your escape to
     Kittim,
even there you will find no respite.'

13 Look at this land, the destined home of
ships! The Chaldaeans (this was the people;
it was not Assyria) erected siege-towers, tore
down its palaces, and laid it in ruins.

14 Wail, you ships of Tarshish;
     for your haven is destroyed.

15 From that day Tyre will be forgotten for
seventy years, the span of one king's life. At
the end of the seventy years her plight will be
that of the harlot in the song:

16 Take your lyre, walk about the city,
     poor, forgotten harlot;
touch the strings sweetly, sing all your
     songs,
make men remember you once more.

17 At the end of seventy years the LORD will
turn again to Tyre; she will go back to her old
trade and hire herself out to every kingdom
on earth. 18 But the profits of her trading will
be dedicated to the LORD; they will not be
stored up or hoarded, but given to those who
worship the LORD, to purchase food in plenty
and fine apparel.

The Lord's judgement

24 BEWARE, the LORD is about to strip
     the earth,
split it and turn it upside down,
and scatter its inhabitants!

2 There will be the same fate for priest
     and people,
for master and slave, mistress and
     maid,
seller and buyer, borrower and lender,
     creditor and debtor.
3 The earth is empty and void
and stripped bare.
For this is the word that the LORD has
     spoken.
4 The earth dries up and withers,
the whole world wilts and withers,
the heights of the earth wilt.
5 The earth itself is desecrated by those
     who live on it,
for they have broken laws, disobeyed
     statutes,
and violated the everlasting covenant.
6 That is why a curse consumes the earth
and its inhabitants suffer punishment,
why the inhabitants of the earth
     dwindle
and only a few are left.

7 The new wine fails, the vines wilt,
and the revellers all groan in sorrow.
8 The merry beat of tambourines is
     silenced,
the shouts of revelry are hushed,
the joyful lyre is silent.
9 They drink wine but without songs;
liquor tastes bitter to the one who
     drinks it.
10 The city is shattered and in chaos,
every house barred, that none may
     enter.
11 In the streets there is a crying out for
     wine;
all joy has faded,

23:18 **worship**: *lit.* sit in the presence of.

the end of the earth. *Kittim*: probably Cyprus. **13**: This verse, the text of which is corrupt, relates the destruction
to the Babylonian period (see Ezek. chs. 27–28). **15**: *Seventy years* is symbolic of a long time.

24.1–27.13: The new age. The diverse materials collected in this section are strongly eschatological in
character, looking toward the final triumph of the LORD. There are announcements of the final judgment, prayers
of petition, and hymns. The literary style with the tendency toward apocalyptic (24.21–23) and the theological
perspective of final judgment (v. 21) indicate that this collection originated long after Isaiah of Jerusalem (see
Introduction).

24.1–23: The LORD's judgment on the earth. The first (vv. 1–6) and final (vv. 18b–23) sections of this chapter
constitute a single announcement of the LORD's intervention against all of creation. The remainder of the chapter
(vv. 7–18a) consists of additions to that poem. **1–6**: The LORD will judge the *earth itself* (v. 5) and destroy all
but a few of its inhabitants. **5**: *The everlasting covenant* may allude to the one with Noah (Gen. 9.1–17), but
in view of the reference to the *laws* and *statutes*, may well reflect the covenant on Sinai (Exod. chs. 19–24).
7–13: As nature suffers, *the city* (vv. 10, 12), probably Jerusalem, will become desolate; the same tragedy will

and merriment is banished from the
land.

12 Nothing but desolation is left in the
city;
its gates are smashed beyond repair.
13 So it will be throughout the world
among the nations,
as when an olive tree is beaten and
stripped
at the end of the vintage.

14 People raise their voices and cry aloud,
acclaiming in the west the majesty of
the LORD.
15 Therefore let the LORD be glorified in
the eastern regions,
and the name of the LORD the God of
Israel
in the coasts and islands of the sea.
16 From the ends of the earth we have
heard them sing,
ascribing beauty to the righteous
nation.

But I said: Depravity, depravity!
Woe betide me! Traitors deal
treacherously!
They are double-dyed traitors.
17 The hunter's scare, the pit, and the
trap
threaten all you inhabitants of the
earth.
18 Whoever runs from the rattle of the
scare
will fall into the pit,
and whoever climbs out of the pit
will be caught in the trap.
The windows of heaven above are
opened
and earth's foundations shake;
19 the earth is utterly shattered,
it is convulsed and reels wildly.
20 The earth lurches like a drunkard
and sways like a watchman's shelter;

the sins of its inhabitants weigh heavy
on it,
and it falls, to rise no more.

21 On that day the LORD will punish
in heaven the host of heaven,
and on earth the kings of the earth.
22 They are herded together,
and packed like prisoners in a
dungeon,
shut up in jail, punished over many
years.
23 The moon will grow pale
and the sun hide its face in shame;
for the LORD of Hosts has become king
on Mount Zion and in Jerusalem,
and is revealed in his glory to the
elders of his people.

25 LORD, you are my God;
I shall exalt you, I shall praise your
name,
for you have done wonderful things,
long-planned, certain and sure.
2 You have turned cities into heaps of
ruin,
fortified towns into rubble;
every mansion in the cities is swept
away,
never to be rebuilt.
3 For this many a cruel nation holds you
in honour,
the cities of ruthless peoples treat you
with awe.
4 Truly you have been a refuge to the
poor,
a refuge to the needy in their distress,
shelter from tempest, shade from heat.
For the blast of the ruthless is like an
icy storm
5 or a scorching drought;
you subdue the roar of the foe,

24:15 **the eastern regions:** *meaning of Heb. uncertain.*
25:5 **foe:** *prob. rdg; Heb. adds* heat in the shadow of a
cloud.

occur throughout the earth (v. 13). **14–18a:** Some are heard to praise the LORD and *righteousness* (v. 16), or
"the righteous one," but this is deceptive. **17–18a:** There is no escape from God's judgment; compare Amos
5.18–20. **18b–23:** The judgment has cosmic dimensions; afterward the LORD will become king in Jerusalem.
18b: *Windows of heaven:* see Gen. 7.11. **21:** *Host of heaven:* the stars, here conceived of as deities. See Jer.
19.13; Zeph. 1.5; Ps. 82.1, 6–7. **23:** On the enthronement of the LORD, see Pss. 47; 93; 96.
  25.1–5: A hymn of thanksgiving. Compare Ps. 145. Following the defeat of an oppressor, the community
gives thanks to the LORD who cares for the *poor* and *needy* (v. 4) by destroying the *ruthless* (v. 5). The hymn
begins by announcing the intention to *praise* (v. 1) God, and then consists of praise itself and reasons for praise.
5: The dominance of the *ruthless* is as fleeting as a *song.*

and the song of the ruthless dies away.

6 On this mountain the LORD of Hosts
will prepare
a banquet of rich fare for all the
peoples,
a banquet of wines well matured,
richest fare and well-matured wines
strained clear.
7 On this mountain the LORD will destroy
that veil shrouding all the peoples,
the pall thrown over all the nations.
8 He will destroy death for ever.
Then the Lord GOD will wipe away the
tears
from every face,
and throughout the world
remove the indignities from his people.
The LORD has spoken.

9 On that day the people will say:
'See, this is our God;
we have waited for him and he will
deliver us.
This is the LORD for whom we have
waited;
let us rejoice and exult in his
deliverance.'

10 For the hand of the LORD will rest on
this mountain,
but Moab will be trampled where he
stands,
as straw is trampled in the slush of a
midden.
11 In it Moab will spread out his hands
as a swimmer spreads his hands to
swim,
but his pride will be sunk

with every stroke of his hands.
12 The LORD will overthrow the
high-walled defences,
level them to the ground,
and bring them down to the dust.

26 On that day this song will be sung
in Judah:

We have a strong city
with walls and ramparts built for our
safety.
2 Open the gates! Let a righteous nation
enter,
a nation that keeps faith!
3 LORD, you keep those of firm purpose
untroubled because of their trust in you.
4 Trust in the LORD for ever,
for he is an eternal rock.
5 He has brought low
all who dwell high in a towering city;
he levels it to the ground
and lays it in the dust,
6 so that the oppressed and the poor
may tread it underfoot.

7 The path of the righteous is smooth,
and you, LORD, make level the way for
the upright.
8 We have had regard to the path
prescribed in your laws,
your name and your renown are our
heart's desire.
9 With all my heart I long for you in the
night,
at dawn I seek for you;
for, when your laws prevail on earth,

26:8 **We ... regard to:** *so Scroll; Heb.* We look to you.

25.6–12: Promise of the LORD's banquet. The unit is an announcement of salvation, with strong eschatological tones. It expects a ritual meal (v. 6), the end of suffering (vv. 7–8), and general rejoicing. The inclusion of *Moab* (vv. 10b–12) seems out of place and may be an addition. **6:** *This mountain:* Zion. Shared-offering sacrifices were those in which a part of the animal was burned on the altar to God, a part given to the priests, and a part eaten at the shrine by the offerer and his family as a sign of communion with the deity; see Num. ch. 7; 1 Sam. 9.13. Here this cultic feast is extended to symbolize the great, universal *banquet* given by God in which humanity and God will live in communion and harmony; compare, Isa. 55.1–3. **8:** This is one of the rare OT passages expressing the hope for the end of *death.*

26.1–6: A hymn of trust. See Ps. 24, especially vv. 7–10. The themes of 25.1–5 are resumed: *Judah* has confidence in the LORD because God has destroyed the enemy and cares for the *oppressed and the poor* (v. 6). **1–2:** An entrance or processional liturgy begins the psalm: see Ps. 118.19–20. **1:** The *strong city* is Jerusalem.

26.7–19: Prayers of petition and meditations. Reflections on the way of the *righteous* (v. 7; see Ps. 1), requests for divine help, and expressions of confidence in the LORD are concluded by an affirmation of hope for the resurrection of the dead (v. 19). **7–10:** The LORD cares for the *righteous* but destroys the *wicked* (v. 10).

the inhabitants of the world learn what
justice is.

10 The wicked are destroyed;
they have never learnt justice.
Corrupt in a land of honest ways,
they are blind to the majesty of the
LORD.

11 LORD, your hand is lifted high,
but they do not see your zeal for your
people
(let them see and be ashamed!);
let the fire reserved for your enemies
consume them.
12 LORD, you will bestow prosperity on us;
for in truth all our works are your
doing.
13 LORD our God,
other lords than you have been our
masters,
but you alone do we invoke by name.
14 Those who are dead will not live again,
those in their graves will not rise:
you punished and destroyed them,
and wiped out all memory of them.
15 LORD, you have enlarged the nation,
enlarged it and won honour for
yourself;
you have extended all the frontiers of
the country.

16 In distress, LORD, we sought you out,
chastened by the whisper of your
rebuke.
17 As a woman with child cries out in her
pains
when her time is near and she is in
labour,
so were we because of you, LORD.
18 We have been with child, we have been
in labour,

but have given birth to wind.
We have achieved no victories for the
land,
given birth to no one to inhabit the
world.
19 But your dead will live,
their bodies will rise again.
Those who sleep in the earth
will awake and shout for joy;
for your dew is a dew of sparkling
light,
and the earth will bring those long
dead to birth again.

20 Go, my people, enter your rooms,
and shut the doors after you;
withdraw for a little while,
until the LORD's wrath has passed.
21 The LORD is coming from his
dwelling-place
to punish the inhabitants of the earth
for their sins;
then the earth will reveal the blood
shed on it
and hide the slain no more.

27 On that day the LORD with his
cruel sword,
his mighty and powerful sword, will
punish
Leviathan that twisting sea serpent,
that writhing serpent Leviathan;
he will slay the monster of the deep.
2 On that day sing of the pleasant
vineyard.
3 I the LORD am its keeper,

26:11 **your people:** *prob. rdg, cp. Aram. (Targ.); Heb.
omits* your.   26:16 **we:** *prob. rdg; Heb.* they.
26:18 **in labour:** *prob. rdg, cp. Gk; Heb. adds* like. **given
birth to no ... world:** *or* the inhabitants of the world
have not fallen.   26:19 **their bodies:** *so Syriac; Heb.*
my body.   27:1 **twisting:** *or* primeval.

11–13: The poet prays for and expects the LORD to bless the people. **14–19:** The language concerning
resurrection is quite explicit, and may refer to the restoration of individuals; see Dan. 12.2. However, it may
be only figurative, referring to the restoration of the nation whose suffering has been described in the previous
verses; see Ezek. ch. 37.

26.20–27.1: The LORD's judgment on the dragon. The people are instructed to hide and watch the LORD
come in judgment (vv. 20–21), finally against the dragon of chaos (27.1). **27.1:** *Leviathan* and other sea
monsters, well-known in Canaanite and Mesopotamian mythology, occasionally appear in the OT, especially
in Pss., as symbols of the chaos and evil overcome by God; see 51.9–10; Amos 9.3; Ps. 74.13; Job 26.12–13.
The struggle against the monster or monsters is usually associated either with creation or with the end of the
world.

27.2–13: Words of salvation and judgment. The section is not a unified whole, but a collection of various
speeches announcing the LORD's intentions. **2–6:** The poem is a reinterpretation of the metaphors of the

I water it regularly,
for fear its leaves should wilt.
Night and day I tend it,
⁴but I get no wine.
I would as soon have briars and thorns.
Then as if in battle I would trample it
down,
⁵unless it grasps me as its refuge
and makes peace with me —
unless it makes its peace with me.

⁶In time to come Jacob's posterity will
take root
and Israel will bud and blossom,
and they will fill the whole earth with
fruit.

⁷Has the LORD struck them down
as he struck their enemies?
Have they been slaughtered
as their attackers were slaughtered?
⁸His quarrel with Jerusalem ends
by driving her into exile,
removing her by a cruel blast
like that of the east wind.
⁹This wipes out Jacob's iniquity,
and the removal of his sin has this
result:
he pounds to chalk all the altar stones,
and no sacred poles or incense-altars
are left standing.

¹⁰The fortified city is left solitary,
a homestead stripped bare, forsaken
like a wilderness;
the calf grazes and lies down there,
and eats up every twig.
¹¹The boughs grow dry and snap off
and women come and light their fires
with them.

They are a people without sense;
therefore their Maker will show them
no mercy,
he who formed them will show them no
favour.

¹²On that day the LORD will beat out the
grain,
from the streams of the Euphrates to
the wadi of Egypt;
but you Israelites will be gathered one
by one.

¹³On that day
a great trumpet will be sounded,
and those who are lost in Assyria
and those dispersed in Egypt will come
to worship the LORD on Jerusalem's
holy mountain.

Judah, Egypt, and Assyria

28 ALAS for the proud garlands of
Ephraim's drunkards,
fading flowers, lovely in their beauty,
on the heads of those who drip with
perfumes,
on those who are overcome with wine!
²The Lord has one at his bidding,
mighty and strong;
like a sweeping storm of hail, like a
destroying tempest,
like a torrent of water in overwhelming
flood
he will beat down on the land with
violence.

27:7 **their enemies:** *lit.* those who struck them down.
their attackers: *lit.* those who slew them.
28:1 **those ... perfumes:** *prob. rdg, cp. Scroll; Heb.* a
valley of fat things.

vineyard in 5.1–7; announcement of judgment has become promise of salvation. **7–11:** A very confusing
passage. The first part sees the judgment upon Israel as a purging punishment; the second part is an announcement of total judgment upon an unidentified *fortified city*. **12–13:** The *day* of the LORD will be a day of harvest
when the exiles will be brought home. **12:** *Wadi of Egypt:* a stream, dry except during the rainy season, flowing
from the Sinai peninsula into the Mediterranean fifty miles south of Gaza. It was considered to be the southern
boundary of Judah. **13:** The *great trumpet,* the horn which called people to worship, will summon the exiles
home to *Jerusalem.*

28.1–33.24: Indictments of Israel and Judah. The historical context of many of these speeches is the Assyrian
crisis of 705–701 B.C.E. when Hezekiah allied himself with Egypt against Assyria. The prophet criticized those
who favored the alliance and warned of disaster. Many of the speeches in this unit begin in Hebrew with a
cry "Woe"; see 28.1; 29.1; 29.15; 30.1; 31.1; 33.1.

28.1–6: Judgment against the Northern Kingdom. The speech probably dates before the fall of Samaria
(2 Kgs. 17.6) in 722–721 B.C.E. which signaled the end of the Northern Kingdom, *Ephraim.* **2:** The *one* must

³ The proud garlands of Ephraim's
   drunkards
will be trampled underfoot.
⁴ The fading flowers, lovely in their
   beauty,
on those who drip with perfumes,
will be like early figs ripe before
   summer.
Whoever sees them plucks them,
and their bloom is gone
while they lie in the hand.
⁵ On that day the LORD of Hosts shall be
   a lovely garland,
a fair diadem for the remnant of his
   people,
⁶ a spirit of justice for one who sits as a
   judge,
and of valour for those who repel
   enemy attacks at the gate.

⁷ These also lose their way through
   wine
and are set wandering by strong drink:
priest and prophet lose their way
   through strong drink
and are befuddled with wine;
they are set wandering by strong drink,
lose their way through tippling,
and stumble in judgement.
⁸ Every table is covered with vomit;
filth is everywhere.

⁹ Who is there that can be taught?
Who makes sense of what he hears?
They are babes newly weaned,
just taken from the breast.
¹⁰ A babble of meaningless noises,
mere sounds on every side!
¹¹ So through barbarous speech and a
   strange tongue
the Lord will address this people,
¹² a people to whom he once said,
'This is true rest; let the exhausted
   have rest.
This is repose,' but they would not
   listen.

¹³ Now to them the word of the LORD will
   be
a babble of meaningless noises,
mere sounds on every side.
And so, as they walk, they will fall
   backwards,
they will be injured, trapped, and
   caught.

¹⁴ Therefore listen to the word of the
   LORD,
you arrogant rulers of this people in
   Jerusalem.
¹⁵ You say, 'We have made a treaty with
   Death
and signed a pact with Sheol:
when the raging flood sweeps by,
it will not touch us;
for we have taken refuge in lies
and sheltered behind falsehood.'
¹⁶ Therefore these are the words of the
   Lord GOD:
I am laying a stone in Zion, a block of
   granite,
a precious corner-stone well founded;
he who has faith will not waver.
¹⁷ I shall use justice as a plumb-line
and righteousness as a plummet.
Then hail will sweep away your refuge
   of lies
and floodwaters carry away your
   shelter.
¹⁸ Your treaty with Death will be annulled
and your pact with Sheol will not stand;
the raging waters will sweep by,
and you will be like land overwhelmed
   by flood.
¹⁹ As often as it sweeps by, it will take you;
daily, morning and night, it will sweep
   by.
When you understand what you hear,

28:4 **those ... perfumes:** *prob. rdg, cp. Scroll; Heb.* a
valley of fat things. **plucks:** *prob. rdg; Heb.* sees.
28:6 **for those:** *prob. rdg; Heb.* omits for.   28:15 **Sheol:**
or the underworld.   28:16 **a block of granite:** *or* a
testing-stone.

be an Assyrian king. **5–6:** This promise of salvation for the *remnant* is a later addition.
   28.7–22: Judgment because of false prophets, priests, and leaders. The prophet ridicules drunken priests
and prophets, holding them responsible for his people's trouble (vv. 7–13), then he announces total destruction,
giving further reasons for it. **9–10:** The drunkards mimic the language of the prophet, as if his language were
the unintelligible babbling of infants, which the Heb. words imitate. **11–13:** The leaders, refusing to listen to
God through Isaiah, will be forced to listen to the LORD through the *barbarous speech and strange tongue* of
the Assyrians, their conquerors. **14:** The *word* is now addressed to *the rulers,* that is, the king and his advisers.
15: The *treaty* (or "covenant") which Isaiah ridicules may have been an agreement with Egypt for mutual aid

it will mean sheer terror.

20 As the saying goes: 'The bed is too
short for a person to stretch,
and the blanket too narrow for a cover.'

21 But the LORD will arise as he rose on
Mount Perazim
and storm with rage as he did in the
vale of Gibeon
to do what he must do, how strange a
deed;
to perform his task, an alien task!

22 But now have done with your
arrogance,
or your bonds will be tightened;
for I have heard destruction decreed
for the whole land by the Lord GOD of
Hosts.

23 Listen and hear what I say,
attend and hear my words.

24 Will the ploughman spend his whole
time ploughing,
breaking up his ground and harrowing
it?

25 Does he not, once he has levelled it,
broadcast the dill and scatter the
cummin?
Does he not put in the wheat and
barley in rows,
and vetches along the edge?

26 Does not his God instruct him and train
him aright?

27 Dill must not be threshed with a
threshing-sledge,
nor the cartwheel rolled over cummin;
but dill is beaten out with a rod,
and cummin with a flail.

28 Grain is crushed, but not too long or
too finely;

cartwheels rumble over it and thresh it,
but they do not grind it fine.

29 Even this knowledge comes from the
LORD of Hosts,
whose counsel is wonderful
and whose wisdom is great.

29 Woe betide Ariel! Ariel,
the city where David encamped.
When another year has passed,
with its full round of pilgrim-feasts,

2 then I shall reduce Ariel to sore straits.
There will be moaning and lamentation
when I make her my Ariel, my
fire-altar.

3 I shall encircle you with my army,
set a ring of outposts all round you,
and erect siege-works against you.

4 You will be brought low, you will speak
out of the ground,
and your words will issue from the
earth;
your voice will come ghostlike from the
ground,
and your words will squeak out of the
earth.

5 Yet the horde of your enemies will
crumble into dust,
the horde of ruthless foes will fly like
chaff.
Suddenly, all in an instant,

6 punishment will come from the LORD
of Hosts
with thunder and earthquake and a
great noise,
with storm and tempest and a flame of
devouring fire.

28:25 **wheat and barley:** *prob. rdg; Heb. adds an
unintelligible word.*

against Assyria. **16:** *Faith:* see 7.9 n. **17:** *Plumb-line:* see Amos 7.7–9. **20:** The proverb cited illustrates the
point: the treaty is not sufficient to save Israel. **21:** *Mount Perazim* was the site of one of David's victories over
the Philistines (2 Sam. 5.17–21). *Gibeon* was in Benjamin (Josh. 18.25); the allusion is uncertain, though Josh.
10.1–11 may be meant.

28.23–29: The parable of the farmer. No direct interpretation or application, such as in 5.1–7 and 2 Sam.
12.1–6, is given here; the point (v. 29) is that the farmer's wisdom symbolizes the divine *wisdom.* **27:** In the
Near East even today large grains like wheat, barley, etc. are threshed under a sledge pulled over the ears by
oxen or donkeys. *Dill* and *cummin* are too small and soft and would be lost or crushed in such a process.

29.1–8: Jerusalem under siege. 1–4: The occasion is probably Sennacherib's invasion of Judah in 701 B.C.E.
(2 Kgs. 18.13–35). **1:** *Ariel,* which probably means "lion of God," is a special name for Jerusalem, used only
by Isaiah. **5–8:** Promises of salvation from the enemy alternate with the promise of punishment, but the final
word is that Jerusalem will be delivered. According to his own reports, Sennacherib besieged Jerusalem but
left without destroying it. See 37.21–36.

7 The horde of all the nations warring
  against Ariel,
all who fight against her with their
  siege-works,
all who hem her in,
will fade as a dream, a vision of the
  night.
8 Like one who is hungry and dreams
  that he is eating,
but wakes to find himself empty,
or like one who is thirsty and dreams
  that he is drinking,
but wakes to find himself faint with
  thirst,
so will it be with the horde of nations
all warring against Mount Zion.

9 If you confuse yourselves,
you will stay confused;
if you blind yourselves,
you will stay blinded.
Be drunk but not with wine, reel but
  not with strong drink;
10 for the LORD has poured on you a
  spirit of deep stupor;
he has closed your eyes (that is, the
  prophets),
and muffled your heads (they are the
  seers).

11 The prophetic vision of it all has become
for you like the words in a sealed book. If you
hand such a book to one who can read and
say, 'Pray read this,' he will answer, 'I cannot;
it is sealed.' 12 Give it to one who cannot read
and say, 'Pray read this'; he will answer, 'I
cannot read.'

13 Then the Lord said:

Because this people worship me with
  empty words
and pay me lip-service
while their hearts are far from me,
and their religion is but a human
  precept, learnt by rote,
14 therefore I shall shock this people yet
  again,

adding shock to shock:
the wisdom of their wise men will
  vanish
and the discernment of the discerning
  will be lost.

15 Woe betide those who seek to hide
  their plans
too deep for the LORD to see!
When their deeds are done in the dark
they say, 'Who sees us? Who knows of
  us?'
16 How you turn things upside down,
as if the potter ranked no higher than
  the clay!
Will the thing made say of its maker,
  'He did not make me'?
Will the pot say of the potter, 'He has
  no skill'?

17 In but a very short time
Lebanon will return to garden land
and the garden land will be reckoned
  as common as scrub.
18 On that day the deaf will hear
when a book is read,
and the eyes of the blind will see
out of impenetrable darkness.
19 The lowly will once again rejoice in the
  LORD,
and the poor exult in the Holy One of
  Israel.
20-21 The ruthless will be no more,
the arrogant will cease to exist;
those who are quick to find mischief,
those who impute sins to others,
or lay traps for him who brings the
  wrongdoer into court,
or by falsehood deny justice to the
  innocent—
all these will be cut down.

22 Therefore these are the words of the LORD,
the deliverer of Abraham, about the house of
Jacob:

This is no time for Jacob to be shamed,

29:7 **siege-works:** *so Scroll; Heb.* strongholds.

29.9–24: Human ignorance and the LORD's plans. 9–10: The failure to see and hear comes from the LORD;
see 6.9–10 n. **11–12:** This seems to be a later prose addition to explain vv. 9–10. **13–14:** The punishment
for any religion without depth is a loss of *wisdom*. **13:** See Matt. 15.8–9; Mk. 7.6–7. *Religion:* lit. "their fear
of me." **15–16:** A woe indictment (see 5.8 n.) against those who think themselves more wise than God; see
30.1–2. **17–21:** The time will come when, hearing and sight restored, the *lowly* (v. 19) will have cause for
celebration, and the *ruthless* and *arrogant* (v. 20) will be destroyed.

no time for his face to grow pale;
23 for his descendants will hallow my
name
when they see what I have done in
their midst.
They will hold sacred the Holy One of
Jacob
and regard Israel's God with awe;
24 the confused will gain understanding,
and the obstinate accept instruction.

30 Woe betide the rebellious children!
says the LORD,
who make plans, but not of my
devising,
who weave schemes, but not inspired by
me,
so piling sin on sin.
2 Without consulting me they hurry
down to Egypt
to seek shelter under Pharaoh's
protection,
to take refuge under Egypt's shadow.
3 Pharaoh's protection will lead to
humiliation
and refuge under Egypt's shadow will
bring you disgrace.
4 Though his officers are at Zoan
and his envoys reach as far as Hanes,
5 that unprofitable nation will leave
everyone in sorry plight;
they will find neither help nor profit,
only humiliation and contempt.

6 'THE Beasts of the South': an oracle.

Through a land of hardship and
distress,
of lioness and roaring lion,
of sand-viper and venomous flying
serpent,
they convey their wealth on the backs
of donkeys
and their treasures on camels' humps
to an unprofitable people.

7 Worthless and futile is the help of
Egypt;
therefore have I given her this name:
Rahab Subdued.

8 Now in their sight write it on a tablet,
engrave it as an inscription
that it may be there in future days,
a testimony for all time to come.
9 They are a race of rebels, disloyal
children,
children who refuse to listen to the
LORD's instruction.
10 They say to the seers, 'You are not to
see,'
and to those who have visions,
'Do not produce true visions for us;
give us smooth words and illusory
visions.
11 Turn aside, leave the straight path,
and rid us of the Holy One of Israel.'

12 Therefore these are the words of the Holy
One of Israel:

You have rejected this warning
and put your trust in devious and
dishonest practices
on which you lean for support,
13 therefore you shall find this iniquity
like a crack running down
a high wall, which bulges out
and suddenly, all in an instant, comes
crashing down.
14 It crashes and breaks like an earthen
jar
shattered beyond repair,
so that among the fragments not a
shard is found
to take an ember from the hearth,
or to scoop water from a pool.

15 These are the words of the Lord GOD, the
Holy One of Israel:

29:23 **they see:** so Gk; Heb. he sees.   30:12 **devious:**
prob. rdg; Heb. oppressive.

30.1–18: The fruits of rebellion. These speeches are related to the period of Judah's alliance with Egypt
against Assyria, 705–701 B.C.E. **1–5:** Those who seek help from Egypt are indicted as *rebellious children*
(vv. 1–2) whose plans will fail. **4:** *Zoan* and *Hanes* were in the Nile delta. **6–7:** It is vain to seek the help of
Egypt (*Beasts of the South*). **7:** *Rahab Subdued* is a sarcastic title based on one of the names of the chaos dragon
slain by the deity. See 27.1 n. Rahab is often a synonym for Egypt. **8–18:** Several speeches concerning the
danger of rebellion against the LORD support the prophet's warnings against the Egyptian alliance. **8–11:** Isaiah
is commanded to write down his words so that when they come true it will be known that he was a prophet.
8: See 8.1–4, 16–18. **12–14:** Judgment is pronounced upon those who do not heed the prophetic *warning*

In calm detachment lies your safety,
your strength in quiet trust.
But you would have none of it; 16'No,'
you said,
'we shall take horse and flee.'
Therefore you will be put to flight!
'We shall ride apace,' you said.
Therefore swift will be the pace of your
pursuers!
17When a thousand flee at the challenge
of one,
you will flee at the challenge of five,
until you are left solitary as a mast on a
mountaintop,
a signal-post on a hill.
18Yet the LORD is waiting to show you his
favour,
and he yearns to have pity on you;
for the LORD is a God of justice.
Happy are all who wait for him!

19People of Zion, dwellers in Jerusalem, you
will weep no more. The LORD will show you
favour and answer you when he hears your
cry for help. 20The Lord may give you bread
of adversity and water of affliction, but he
who teaches you will no longer keep himself
out of sight, but with your own eyes you will
see him. 21If you stray from the path,
whether to right or to left, you will hear a
voice from behind you sounding in your ears
saying, 'This is the way; follow it.' 22You will
treat as things unclean your silver-plated images and your gold-covered idols; you will
loathe them like a foul discharge and call
them filth.

23The Lord will give rain for the seed you
sow in the ground, and as the produce of
your soil he will give you heavy crops. When
that day comes your cattle will graze in broad
pastures; 24the oxen and donkeys that
plough the land will be fed with well-sea-
soned fodder, winnowed with shovel and
fork. 25On every high mountain and lofty hill

streams of water will flow, on the day of massacre when fortresses fall. 26The moon will
shine as brightly as the sun, and the sun with
seven times its wonted brightness, like seven
days' light in one, on the day when the LORD
binds up the broken limbs of his people and
heals the wounds inflicted on them.

27See, the LORD himself comes from afar,
his anger blazing and his doom heavy.
His lips are charged with wrath
and his tongue is like a devouring fire.
28His breath is like a torrent in spate,
to load the nations with an evil yoke.
He sieves out the nations for
destruction;
he puts a bit in their mouths to lead the
peoples astray.

29But for you there will be songs,
as on a night of a sacred pilgrim-feast,
and gladness of heart as if one
marched to the sound of the pipe
on the way to the mountain of the
LORD, to the Rock of Israel.
30Then the LORD will make his voice
heard in majesty
and reveal his arm descending in fierce
anger
with devouring flames of fire,
amid cloudburst and tempests of rain
and hail.
31For at the voice of the LORD Assyria's
heart fails her,
as she feels the stroke of his rod;
32tambourines, lyres, and shaking
sistrums will keep time
with every stroke of his rod,
of the punishment which the LORD
inflicts on them.
33Topheth was made ready long ago
(it, too, was prepared for Molech);

30:27 **the LORD himself:** *lit.* the name of the LORD.
30:32 **punishment:** *so some MSS; others* foundation.

(v. 12). **15–18:** The people were admonished to be calm (v. 15), but they panicked and now find themselves
isolated (vv. 16–17); still it is not too late to be saved (v. 18). **15:** See 7.9. **16:** See Amos 2.14–16. **17:**
Signal-post: Jerusalem under siege.

30.19–26: Healing beyond punishment. Those who suffer *adversity* (v. 20) are encouraged to remain faithful
by the assurance that a punishment will purge them and by the promise of restored prosperity. The section
reflects the circumstances of the Exile and probably is a late expansion of v. 18.

30.27–33: Judgment against Assyria. The terrible approach of the LORD is announced (vv. 27–28), but there
will be rejoicing (v. 29), for the LORD comes to punish Assyria. **33:** The oracle is probably about 701 B.C.E.
Topheth was a place just outside of Jerusalem where human sacrifices had been offered to the god *Molech;*
see Lev. 18.21; 2 Kgs. 23.10.

its fire-pit, made deep and broad,
is a blazing mass of logs,
with the breath of the LORD like a
    stream of brimstone
setting it ablaze.

31 Woe betide those who go down to
    Egypt for help
and rely upon horses,
who put their trust in chariots because
    they are many,
and in horsemen because of their vast
    numbers,
but do not look to the Holy One of
    Israel
or seek guidance of the LORD!
2 Yet he too in his wisdom can bring
    trouble
and he does not take back his threats;
he will rise up against wrongdoers,
against all who go to the help of
    evildoers.
3 The Egyptians are mortals, not gods,
their horses are flesh, not spirit.
When the LORD stretches out his
    hand,
the helper will stumble
and the one who is helped will fall;
both will perish together.

4 This is what the LORD has said to me:

As a lion or a young lion growls over its
    prey
when the shepherds are called out in
    force,
and it is not scared at their shouting
or daunted by their clamour,
so the LORD of Hosts will come down to
    do battle
on the heights of Mount Zion.
5 Like a hovering bird the LORD of Hosts
will be a shield over Jerusalem;
he will shield and deliver her,
sparing and rescuing her.
6 Israel, you have been deeply disloyal,
    yet come back to him,

7 for on that day every one of you will
    spurn
the idols of silver and the idols of gold
which your own sinful hands have
    made.
8 Assyria will fall, but not by man's
    sword;
a sword that no mortal wields will
    devour him.
He will flee before the sword,
and his young warriors will be put to
    forced labour;
9 officers will be helpless from terror
and captains powerless to flee.
This is the word of the LORD
whose fire blazes in Zion,
whose furnace burns in Jerusalem.

32 A king will reign in righteousness
    and his ministers rule with justice,
2 each of them a refuge from the wind
and a shelter from the storm.
They will be like runnels of water in
    dry ground,
like the shade of a great rock in a
    thirsty land.
3 Then those who see will see clearly,
and those who hear will listen with
    care;
4 the impetuous mind will understand
    and know,
and the stammering tongue will speak
    fluently and plainly.
5 The scoundrel will no longer be
    thought noble,
nor the villain considered honourable;
6 for the scoundrel will speak like a
    scoundrel
hatching evil in his heart,
godless in all his conduct,
and a liar to the LORD;
he starves the hungry of their food
and deprives the thirsty of anything to
    drink.
7 The villain's tactics are villainous
and he devises infamous plans
to bring ruin on the poor with his lies

31.1–3: Against reliance on Egypt. The prophet again indicts those leaders who made a treaty with Egypt.
2–3: The LORD *in his wisdom* controls history; it is ridiculous to trust in these mere mortals.
    31.4–9: A promise to protect Jerusalem. As in the holy war, the LORD will *come down* on Zion and fight against *Assyria*. The speech should be associated with Sennacherib's invasion of 701 B.C.E. See 29.1–8; 37.21–38. **5:** Compare Deut. 32.11. **6–7:** The verses probably are a late addition.
    32.1–8: A messianic promise. When Israel's government is based on *justice*, eyes will be opened and all persons will be recognized for what they are. See Prov. 16.12–15. **1:** See 9.7; 11.3–5.

and deny justice to the needy.
8 But he who is of noble mind forms
     noble designs
and in those designs he stands firm.

9 You women who live at ease,
listen attentively to what I say;
you daughters without a care, mark my
     words.
10 You may be carefree now,
but you will be quaking at the turn of
     the year,
for the vintage will be a failure,
with no produce gathered in.
11 You women now at ease, be terrified;
tremble, you women without a care.
Strip yourselves bare,
and put on a loincloth of sacking.
12 Beat upon your breasts in mourning
for the pleasant fields and fruitful
     vines,
13 for my people's land with its yield of
     thorns and briars,
for every happy home in the bustling
     city.
14 Mansions are forsaken and the crowded
     streets deserted;
citadel and watch-tower are turned into
     open heath,
for ever the delight of wild asses and
     pasture for flocks,
15 until a spirit from on high is lavished
     upon us.

Then the wilderness will become
     garden land
and garden land will be reckoned as
     common as scrub.
16 Justice will make its home in the
     wilderness,
and righteousness dwell in the
     grassland;
17 righteousness will yield peace
and bring about quiet trust for ever.

18 Then my people will live in tranquil
     country,
dwelling undisturbed in peace and
     security;
19 it will be cool on the slopes of the forest
     then,
and cities will lie peaceful in the plain.
20 Happy will you be sowing everywhere
     beside water
and letting ox and donkey roam freely.

33 Woe betide you, destroyer, yourself
     undestroyed,
betrayer still unbetrayed!
After all your destroying, you will be
     destroyed;
after all your betrayals, you yourself
     will be betrayed.

2 LORD, show us your favour;
our hope is in you.
Uphold us every morning,
save us when troubles come.
3 At the crack of thunder peoples flee,
nations are scattered at your roar;
4 they are stripped of spoil as if stripped
     by young locusts,
like a swarm of locusts folk swarm over
     it.

5 The LORD is supreme, for he dwells on
     high;
he has filled Zion with justice and
     righteousness.
6 Her strength will be in your
     unchanging stability,
her deliverance in wisdom and
     knowledge;
her treasure is the fear of the LORD.
7 Listen, how the valiant cry out aloud
     for help,

33:1 **after all your betrayals:** *so Scroll; Heb.
unintelligible.*   33:2 **Uphold us:** *so some MSS; others
Uphold them.*   33:6 **her treasure:** *prob. rdg; Heb.* his
treasure.

32.9–14: A warning to complacent women. The women, now *carefree* (probably at the *vintage* festival,
v. 10), will, in a *year*, mourn the destruction of their fields and cities. See 3.16–24; Amos 4.1–3. **14:** *Citadel:*
the fortified hills in the old city of David.

32.15–20: A promise of peace with justice. The outpouring of the *spirit* reverses the desolation outlined
in the previous section. *Nature* will be fruitful and people will live in *righteousness* (v. 16) that leads to *peace*
(v. 17).

33.1–24: An exilic liturgy. It is impossible to identify the precise historical context of this psalm. The
apparently disjointed units in this collection of prayers probably reflect the use of the chapter in worship after
the time of Isaiah. The community in the midst of trouble looks to God for help. **1:** The *destroyer,* Babylon

and envoys sent to sue for peace weep
bitterly!
8 The highways are deserted, no one
travels the roads.
Covenants are broken, treaties are
flouted;
no one is held of any account.
9 The land is parched and wilting,
Lebanon is eroded and crumbling;
Sharon has become like a desert,
Bashan and Carmel are stripped bare.
10 Now I shall arise, says the LORD;
now I shall exalt myself, now lift myself
up.
11 You will conceive chaff, and bring forth
stubble;
a wind like fire will devour you.
12 Whole nations will be heaps of white
ash,
or like thorns cut down and set on fire.

13 You dwellers afar off, hear what I have
done;
acknowledge my might, you that are
near at hand.
14 Sinners in Zion quake with terror,
the godless are seized with trembling;
they ask,
'Can any of us live with a devouring
fire?
Can any of us live in perpetual flames?'
15 The person who behaves uprightly and
speaks the truth,
who scorns to enrich himself by
extortion,
who keeps his hands clean from
bribery,
who stops his ears against talk of
murder
and closes his eyes against looking at
evil—
16 he it is who will dwell on the heights,
his refuge a fastness in the cliffs,
his food assured and water never
failing him.

17 Your eyes will see a king in his

splendour
and look on a land stretching into the
distance.
18 You will call to mind what once you
feared:
'Where then is he that reckoned, where
is he that weighed,
where is he that counted the treasures?'
19 You will no longer see that barbarous
people,
that people whose language was so
obscure,
whose stuttering speech you could not
comprehend.

20 Look to Zion, city of our sacred feasts,
let your eyes rest on Jerusalem,
a secure abode, a tent that will never be
moved,
whose pegs will never be pulled up,
whose ropes will none of them be
snapped.
21 There we have the LORD in all his
majesty
in a place of rivers and broad streams;
but no galleys will be rowed there,
no stately ships sail by.
22 The LORD is our judge, the LORD our
lawgiver,
the LORD our king—he it is who will
save us.
23 (It may be said, 'Your rigging is slack;
it will not hold the mast firm in its
socket,
nor can it spread the sails.')
Then the blind will have a full share of
the spoil
and the lame will take part in the
pillage.
24 No one dwelling there will say, 'I am
sick';
the sins of the people who live there
will be pardoned.

33:8 **treaties:** *so Scroll; Heb.* cities. 33:23 **blind:**
prob. rdg, cp. Aram. (Targ.); Heb. obscure.

in 21.1–10, is not identified here. **5–6:** A hymn of praise. **7–9:** In the absence of the fear of the LORD human
order collapses and nature itself is *wilting.* **10–14:** Announcement of the LORD's intervention. When the LORD
appears nature is in turmoil and *sinners* (v. 14) are terrified. **15–16:** The description of those who will survive
the appearance of God resembles the liturgies for entrance into the temple. See Pss. 15; 24. **17–24:** Announcements of salvation. These lines probably stem from the postexilic period. **19:** *Stuttering speech:* a reversal of
the doom pronounced in 28.12–13. **21–24:** In the messianic age not an economy dependent on *stately ships*
but one dependent on the LORD's majesty will prevail in Zion: *no one* will be *sick* in body or oppressed by
want or sins; compare Ezek. 34.11–31; 47.1–12; Matt. 11.5.

Edom and Israel

34 APPROACH, you nations, and listen;
attend, you peoples;
let the earth listen and everything in it,
the world and all that it yields;
2 for the LORD's anger is against all the
nations
and his wrath against all their hordes;
he gives them over to slaughter and
destruction.
3 Their slain will be flung out,
stench will rise from their corpses,
and the mountains will run with their
blood.
4 All the host of heaven will crumble into
nothing,
the heavens will be rolled up like a
scroll,
and all their host fade away,
as the foliage withers from the vine
and the ripened fruit from the fig tree.

5 For my sword appears in heaven.
See how it descends in judgement on
Edom,
on a people whom I have doomed to
destruction.
6 The LORD has a sword sated with
blood,
gorged with fat, the fat of rams'
kidneys,
and with the blood of lambs and goats;
for the LORD has a sacrifice in Bozrah,
a great slaughter in Edom.
7 Wild oxen will go down also,
bull and bison together,
and their land will drink deep of blood
and their soil be enriched with fat.
8 For the LORD has a day of vengeance,
the champion of Zion has a time of
retribution.

9 Edom's torrents will be turned to pitch
and its soil to brimstone;
the land will become blazing pitch,

10 never to be quenched night or day;
smoke will rise from it for ever.
Age after age it will lie waste,
and no one will ever again pass
through it.
11 Horned owl and bustard will make it
their home;
it will be the haunt of screech-owl and
raven.
The LORD has stretched over it a
measuring line of chaos,
and its boundaries will be a jumble of
stones.
12 No king will be acclaimed there,
and all its princes will come to naught.
13 Its palaces will be overgrown with
thorns;
nettles and briars will cover its
strongholds.
It will be the lair of wolves, the haunt
of desert-owls.
14 Marmots will live alongside jackals,
and he-goats will congregate there.
There too the nightjar will return to
rest
and find herself a place for repose;
15 there the sand-partridge will make her
nest,
lay her eggs and hatch them,
and gather her brood under her wings;
there will the kites gather,
each with its mate.
16 Consult the book of the LORD and read
it:
not one of these will be missing,
not one will lack its mate,
for with his own mouth he has ordered
it
and by his spirit he has brought them
together.
17 He it is who has allotted each its place,
and his hand has measured out their
portions;
they will occupy it for all time,
and each succeeding generation will
dwell there.

34:5 **appears:** *so Scroll; Heb.* drinks.

34.1–35.10: Edom and Israel. Two poems, both of them exilic or postexilic, are juxtaposed to contrast the
expected devastation of *Edom* (34.1–17) with the glorious future in store for the exiles (35.1–10).
    34.1–17: The doom of Edom. Compare Ps. 137.7–9. **1–3:** The *nations* are called to observe the LORD's
wrath. **4:** The cosmos is in turmoil when the LORD appears. **5–8:** The LORD is coming to destroy *Edom,* as people
slaughter animals for sacrifice. **5:** *Sword:* see Ezek. ch. 21. **6:** *Bozrah* was a major city in northern Edom. **9–15:**
As the result of divine intervention, *Edom* will return to a state of chaos. **11:** *Chaos:* see Jer. 4.23–28. **16–17:**
The announcement is trustworthy, for it is written in the *book of the* LORD (probably prophetic books).

35

Let the wilderness and the parched
land be glad,
let the desert rejoice and burst into
flower.
2 Let it flower with fields of asphodel,
let it rejoice and shout for joy.
The glory of Lebanon is given to it,
the splendour too of Carmel and
Sharon;
these will see the glory of the LORD,
the splendour of our God.

3 Brace the arms that are limp,
steady the knees that give way;
4 say to the anxious, 'Be strong, fear not!
Your God comes to save you
with his vengeance and his retribution.'
5 Then the eyes of the blind will be
opened,
and the ears of the deaf unstopped.
6 Then the lame will leap like deer,
and the dumb shout aloud;
for water will spring up in the
wilderness
and torrents flow in the desert.
7 The mirage will become a pool,
the thirsty land bubbling springs;
instead of reeds and rushes, grass will
grow
in country where wolves have their lairs.

8 And a causeway will appear there;
it will be called the Way of Holiness.
No one unclean will pass along it;
it will become a pilgrim's way,
and no fool will trespass on it.
9 No lion will come there,
no savage beast go by;
not one will be found there.
But by that way those the LORD has
redeemed will return.
10 The LORD's people, set free, will come
back
and enter Zion with shouts of triumph,
crowned with everlasting joy.
Gladness and joy will come upon them,

while suffering and weariness flee away.

Jerusalem delivered

36

IN the fourteenth year of King Hezekiah's reign, King Sennacherib of Assyria attacked and captured all the fortified
towns of Judah. 2 From Lachish he sent his
chief officer with a strong force to King Hezekiah at Jerusalem. The officer halted by the
conduit of the Upper Pool on the causeway
leading to the Fuller's Field. 3 There Eliakim
son of Hilkiah, the comptroller of the household, came out to him, with Shebna the adjutant-general and Joah son of Asaph, the
secretary of state.

4 The chief officer said to them, 'Tell Hezekiah that this is the message of the Great
King, the king of Assyria: "What ground
have you for this confidence of yours? 5 Do
you think words can take the place of skill
and military strength? On whom then do you
rely for support in your rebellion against me?
6 On Egypt? Egypt is a splintered cane that
will run into a man's hand and pierce it if he
leans on it. That is what Pharaoh king of
Egypt proves to all who rely on him. 7 And if
you tell me that you are relying on the LORD
your God, is he not the god whose shrines
and altars Hezekiah has suppressed, telling
Judah and Jerusalem they must worship at
this altar?"

8 'Now, make a deal with my master the
king of Assyria: I shall give you two thousand
horses if you can find riders for them. 9 How
then can you reject the authority of even the
least of my master's servants and rely on
Egypt for chariots and horsemen? 10 Do you
think that I have come to attack this land and
destroy it without the consent of the LORD?
No; the LORD himself said to me, "Go up and
destroy this land." '

35:6 **flow:** *so Scroll; Heb. omits.*   35:8 **causeway:** *so
Scroll; Heb. adds and a road.* **a pilgrim's way:** *prob. rdg;
Heb. unintelligible.*   36:1–22; *Cp. 2 Kgs. 18:13–37;
2 Chr. 32:1–19.*   36:2 **his chief officer:** *or
Rab-shakeh.*   36:5 **Do you:** *so Scroll; Heb. Do I.*

35.1–10: God comes to save the exiles. This poem of the return from Exile resembles Second Isaiah; see
40.1–11; 42.17–18. **4:** *The anxious:* those discouraged by the long captivity. **8:** *Causeway:* highway.

36.1–39.8: Historical appendix. With some variants, this material, with the exception of 38.9–20, is found
in 2 Kgs. 18.13–20.19. The main theme is the relationship between Isaiah and King Hezekiah through several
crises.

36.1–22: First account of Sennacherib's attack. See 2 Kgs. 18.13–27. This account omits the report in 2 Kgs.
18.14–16 of Hezekiah's submission and tribute to the Assyrians. **1:** The *fourteenth year* of Hezekiah was
701 B.C.E. **2:** See 7.3. **3:** See 22.15–25. **6:** A reference to the alliance with Egypt; see 31.1–3. **11:** *Aramaic:*

[11] Eliakim, Shebna, and Joah said to the chief officer, 'Please speak to us in Aramaic, for we understand it; do not speak Hebrew to us within earshot of the people on the city wall.' [12] The chief officer answered, 'Is it to your master and to you that my master has sent me to say this? Is it not to the people sitting on the wall who, like you, will have to eat their own dung and drink their own urine?'

[13] Then he stood and shouted in Hebrew, 'Hear the message of the Great King, the king of Assyria! [14] These are the king's words: "Do not be taken in by Hezekiah. He is powerless to save you. [15] Do not let him persuade you to rely on the LORD, and tell you that the LORD will surely save you and that this city will never be surrendered to the king of Assyria." [16] Do not listen to Hezekiah, for this is what the king of Assyria says: "Make your peace with me, and surrender. Then every one of you will eat the fruit of his own vine and of his own fig tree, and drink the water of his own cistern, [17] until I come and take you to a land like your own, a land of grain and new wine, of bread and vineyards. [18] Beware that Hezekiah does not mislead you by telling you that the LORD will save you. Did any god of the nations save his land from the king of Assyria's power? [19] Where are the gods of Hamath and Arpad? Where are the gods of Sepharvaim? Where are the gods of Samaria? Did they save Samaria from me? [20] Among all the gods of these nations is there one who saved his land from me? So how is the LORD to save Jerusalem?" '

[21] The people remained silent and said not a word in reply, for the king had given orders that no one was to answer him. [22] Eliakim son of Hilkiah, comptroller of the household, Shebna the adjutant-general, and Joah son of Asaph, secretary, came to Hezekiah with their clothes torn and reported the words of the chief officer.

37 When King Hezekiah heard their report, he tore his clothes, put on sackcloth, and went into the house of the LORD.

[2] He sent Eliakim comptroller of the household, Shebna the adjutant-general, and the senior priests, all wearing sackcloth, to the prophet Isaiah son of Amoz, [3] to give him this message from the king: 'Today is a day of trouble for us, a day of reproof and contumely. We are like a woman who lacks the strength to bring to birth the child she is carrying. [4] It may be that the LORD your God will give heed to the words of the chief officer whom his master the king of Assyria sent to taunt the living God, and will confute the words which the LORD your God heard. Offer a prayer for those who still survive.'

[5] When King Hezekiah's officials came to Isaiah, [6] they were given this answer for their master: 'Here is the word of the LORD: Do not be alarmed at what you heard when the Assyrian king's minions blasphemed me. [7] I shall sap his morale till at a mere rumour he will withdraw to his own country; and there I shall make him fall by the sword.'

[8] Meanwhile the chief officer went back, and, having heard that the king of Assyria had moved camp from Lachish, he found him attacking Libnah. [9] But when the king learnt that King Tirhakah of Cush was on the way to engage him in battle, he sent messengers again to King Hezekiah of Judah [10] to say to him, 'How can you be deluded by your God on whom you rely when he promises that Jerusalem will not fall into the hands of the king of Assyria? [11] You yourself must have heard what the kings of Assyria have done to all countries: they utterly destroyed them. Can you then hope to escape? [12] Did their gods save the nations which my predecessors wiped out: Gozan, Harran, Rezeph, and the people of Eden living in Telassar? [13] Where are the kings of Hamath, of Arpad, and of Lahir, Sepharvaim, Hena, and Ivvah?'

[14] Hezekiah received the letter from the messengers and, having read it, he went up

36:19 **Where are the gods of Samaria?:** *prob. rdg, cp. Gk (Luc.) at 2 Kgs. 18:34; Heb. omits.*   37:1–38 *Cp. 2 Kgs. 19:1–37; 2 Chr. 32:20–22.*   37:9 **again:** *prob. rdg, cp. 2 Kgs. 19:9; Heb. and he heard.*

the international language of the Assyrian empire. **13:** *In Hebrew:* lit. "in Jewish" or "in the Judean language."

37.1–7: Hezekiah turns to Isaiah. See 2 Kgs. 19.1–7. The king and his officials, afraid and in mourning, consult Isaiah who announces the end of the siege and the death of Sennacherib. **1:** *Sackcloth:* symbol of mourning and repentance.

37.8–20: A second account of Sennacherib's attack. See 2 Kgs. 19.9–19. This narrative is another tradition of the events reported in 36.1–37.7. **9:** *Tirhakah* was a member of the royal house of Ethiopia, *Cush,* which gained control over Egypt to become the Twenty-fifth Dynasty. **14–20:** Instead of summoning Isaiah, Hezekiah to the temple and spread it out before the LORD [15] with this prayer: [16] 'LORD of Hosts, God of Israel, enthroned on the cherubim, you alone are God of all the kingdoms of the world; you made heaven and earth. [17] Incline your ear, LORD, and listen; open your eyes, LORD, and see; hear all the words that Sennacherib has sent to taunt the living God. [18] LORD, it is true that the kings of Assyria have laid waste every country, [19] and have consigned their gods to the flames. They destroyed them, because they were no gods but the work of men's hands, mere wood and stone. [20] Now, LORD our God, save us from his power, so that all the kingdoms of the earth may know that you alone, LORD, are God.'

[21] Isaiah son of Amoz sent Hezekiah the following message: 'This is the word of the LORD the God of Israel: I have heard your prayer to me concerning King Sennacherib of Assyria, [22] and this is the word which the LORD has spoken against him:

The virgin daughter of Zion disdains you,
she laughs you to scorn;
the daughter of Jerusalem tosses her head
as you retreat.
[23] Whom have you taunted and blasphemed?
Against whom did you raise an outcry,
casting haughty glances at the Holy One of Israel?
[24] You sent your servants to taunt the Lord;
you said: "With my countless chariots
I have ascended the mountain heights,
gone to the remote recesses of Lebanon.
I have felled its tallest cedars,
the finest of its pines;
I have reached the highest peak,
the most luxuriant forest.
[25] I have dug wells
and drunk the waters of a foreign land,

and with the sole of my foot I have dried up
all the streams of Egypt."

[26] 'Have you not heard?
Long ago I did it all.
In days gone by I planned it
and now I have brought it about,
till your fortified cities have crashed
into heaps of rubble.
[27] Their inhabitants, shorn of strength,
disheartened and put to shame,
were but as plants in the field,
frail as green herbs,
as grass on the rooftops blasted by the east wind.
[28] I know your rising up and your sitting down,
your going out and your coming in.
[29] The frenzy of your rage against me
and your arrogance have come to my ears.
I shall put a ring in your nose
and a bridle in your mouth,
and I shall take you back
by the way on which you came.

[30] 'This will be the sign for you: this year you will eat the leavings of the grain and in the second year what is self-sown; but in the third year you will sow and reap, plant vineyards and eat their fruit. [31] The survivors left in Judah will strike fresh root below ground and yield fruit above ground, [32] for a remnant will come out of Jerusalem and survivors from Mount Zion. The zeal of the LORD of Hosts will perform this.

[33] 'Therefore, this is the word of the LORD about the king of Assyria:

37:18 **every country:** *so Scroll; Heb. adds* and their country.   37:20 **are God:** *so Scroll; Heb. omits* God. 37:21 **I have heard:** *so Gk; Heb. omits.*   37:25 **of a foreign land:** *so Scroll; Heb. omits.*   37:27 **blasted ... east wind:** *so Scroll; Heb. obscure.*   37:28 **your rising up:** *so Scroll; Heb. omits.*   37:29 **The frenzy ... me:** *cp. Scroll; Heb. repeats* the frenzy of your rage against me.

goes to the temple to pray for help.

37.21–38: Isaiah's intervention. See 2 Kgs. 19.20–34. **21:** The king's prayer is answered. **22–29:** The prophet accuses Sennacherib of blasphemy, emphasizes the LORD's power, and promises that he will be led back to Assyria with a *ring* in his nose. **22:** *Virgin daughter of Zion:* prophetic term for Jerusalem. *Tosses her head:* gesture of contempt. **26:** Achievements claimed by Assyria were *planned* and *brought about* by God. **27:** Grass sprang up on the mud *roof-tops* of Palestinian houses but dried up quickly in the *east wind* from the desert. **30:** Either the sign is that after two years conditions of life will be normal; or it may be a proverb

He will not enter this city
or shoot an arrow there;
he will not advance against it with his
   shield
or cast up a siege-ramp against it.
34 By the way he came he will go back;
he will not enter this city.
This is the word of the LORD.
35 I shall shield this city to deliver it
for my own sake and for the sake of
   my servant David.'

36 The angel of the LORD went out and struck down a hundred and eighty-five thousand men in the Assyrian camp; when morning dawned, there they all lay dead. 37 King Sennacherib of Assyria broke camp and marched away; he went back to Nineveh and remained there. 38 One day, while he was worshipping in the temple of his god Nisroch, his sons Adrammelech and Sharezer assassinated him and made their escape to the land of Ararat. His son Esarhaddon succeeded him.

38 At this time Hezekiah became mortally ill, and the prophet Isaiah son of Amoz came to him with this message from the LORD: 'Give your last instructions to your household, for you are dying; you will not recover.' 2 Hezekiah turned his face to the wall and offered this prayer to the LORD: 3 'LORD, remember how I have lived before you, faithful and loyal in your service, always doing what was pleasing to you.' And he wept bitterly.

4 Then the word of the LORD came to Isaiah: 5 'Go and say to Hezekiah: "This is the word of the LORD the God of your father David: I have heard your prayer and seen your tears; I am going to add fifteen years to your life, 6 and I shall deliver you and this city from the king of Assyria. I shall protect this city." '

21 Isaiah told them to prepare a fig-plaster; when it was made and applied to the inflammation, Hezekiah recovered. 22 He asked Isaiah what proof there was that he would go up to the house of the LORD. 7 Isaiah replied, 'This will be your proof from the LORD that he will do what he has promised: 8 I shall bring back by ten steps the shadow cast by the setting sun on the stairway of Ahaz.' And the sun went back ten steps on the stairway down which it had gone.

9 A poem written by King Hezekiah of Judah on his recovery from his illness:

10 I said, In the prime of life I must pass
   away;
for the rest of my days I am consigned
   to the gates of Sheol.
11 I said, I shall no longer see the LORD
as I did in the land of the living;
I shall no longer see my fellow-men
as I did when I lived in the world.
12 My dwelling is taken from me,
pulled up like a shepherd's tent;
you have rolled up my life
like a weaver when he cuts the web
   from the thrum.
Day and night you torment me;
13 I am racked with pain till the morning.
All my bones are broken, as if by a
   lion;
day and night you torment me.
14 I twitter as if I were a swallow,
I moan like a dove.
My eyes are raised to heaven:
'Lord, pay heed; stand surety for me.'
15 How can I complain, what can I say to
   the LORD
when he himself has done this?
I shall wander to and fro all my life
   long

38:1–8,21,22 Cp. 2 Kgs. 20:1–11.   38:6 Verses 21,22 transposed to follow this verse; cp. 2 Kgs. 20:7,8. 38:7 **Isaiah replied:** prob. rdg, cp. 2 Kgs. 20:9; Heb. omits.   38:11 **as I did when . . . world:** so some MSS; others when I am with those who dwell in the underworld.   38:13 **I . . . pain:** so Scroll; Heb. I wait. 38:14 **a swallow:** so Gk; Heb. adds a wryneck. 38:15 **what . . . LORD:** prob. rdg, cp. Aram. (Targ.); Heb. what can he say to me.

that the change from adversity to prosperity is gradual. **32:** Remnant: see 10.21–22 n. **36:** An angel of the LORD appears in the Bible either as the presence of the LORD (Exod. 3.2–6) or as a messenger or agent of God's will in some event.

38.1–22: Hezekiah's illness. See 2 Kgs. 20.1–11. **3:** Hezekiah uses the language of the Lament; see Introduction to Pss. **4–6:** Isaiah gives an oracle of salvation promising healing for the king and deliverance for the city. **21–22:** The Revised English Bible has moved these verses from the end of the chapter to their more logical place in the narrative. **9–20:** The song ascribed here to Hezekiah is a typical individual Thanksgiving psalm, used in the temple service of thanksgiving for deliverance from suffering. See Pss. 32; 116.

in bitterness of soul.
16 Yet, Lord, because of you my soul will
live.
Give my spirit rest;
restore me and give me life.
17 Bitterness, not prosperity, had indeed
been my lot,
but your love saved me from the pit of
destruction;
for you have thrust all my sins behind
you.
18 Sheol cannot confess you,
Death cannot praise you,
nor can those who go down to the abyss
hope for your truth.
19 The living, only the living can confess
you
as I do this day, my God,
just as a father makes your faithfulness
known to his sons.
20 The LORD is at hand to save me;
so let the music of our praises resound
all our life long in the house of the
LORD.

39 At that time the king of Babylon, Merodach-baladan son of Baladan, sent
envoys with a gift to Hezekiah, for he heard
that he had been ill. 2 Hezekiah welcomed
them and showed them his treasury, the silver and gold, the spices and fragrant oil, his
entire armoury and everything to be found
in his storehouses; there was nothing in his
palace or in his whole realm that Hezekiah
did not show them.
3 The prophet Isaiah came to King Hezekiah and asked, 'What did these men say?
Where did they come from?' 'They came to
me from a distant country,' Hezekiah answered, 'from Babylon.' 4 'What did they see
in your palace?' Isaiah demanded. 'They saw
everything,' was the reply; 'there was nothing
in my storehouses that I did not show them.'
5 Isaiah said to Hezekiah, 'Hear the word of

the LORD of Hosts: 6 The time is coming, says
the LORD, when everything in your palace,
and all that your forefathers have amassed
till the present day, will be carried away to
Babylon; not a thing will be left. 7 And some
of your sons, your own offspring, will be
taken to serve as eunuchs in the palace of the
king of Babylon.' 8 Hezekiah answered, 'The
word of the LORD which you have spoken is
good,' for he was thinking to himself that
peace and security would last his lifetime.

Israel delivered and redeemed

40 COMFORT my people; bring comfort
to them,
says your God;
2 speak kindly to Jerusalem
and proclaim to her
that her term of bondage is served,
her penalty is paid;
for she has received at the LORD's hand
double measure for all her sins.

3 A voice cries:
'Clear a road through the wilderness
for the LORD,
prepare a highway across the desert for
our God.
4 Let every valley be raised,
every mountain and hill be brought
low,
uneven ground be made smooth,
and steep places become level.
5 Then will the glory of the LORD be
revealed
and all mankind together will see it.
The LORD himself has spoken.'

38:16 Yet ... rest: *prob. rdg; Heb. unintelligible.*
38:18 Sheol: *or* The underworld.   38:20 *Verses
21,22 transposed to follow verse 6.*   39:1–8 *Cp. 2 Kgs.
20:12–19.*   40:2 speak ... Jerusalem: *or* bid
Jerusalem be of good heart.

39.1–8: Hezekiah and ambassadors from Babylon. See 2 Kgs. 20.12–19. The Babylonian king sent *envoys*
to Hezekiah, ostensibly to inquire about his health, but probably to encourage rebellion against Assyria. The
date is probably 705–703 B.C.E. Isaiah criticizes the welcome given the Babylonians and announces judgment
against Hezekiah.

40.1–55.13: Words of hope. On Second Isaiah, see Introduction.

40.1–11: The prophet's commission. 1: This second part of Isaiah is known as "The Consolation of Israel"
because the prophet brings *comfort* to the captives in the Exile. **2:** *Term of bondage:* the Exile is over. **3:** The
voice that *cries,* here and in v. 6, is that of the LORD giving the prophet his mission (6.8; Jer. 1.7–10; Ezek.
2.1–3) to prepare the return from the captivity across the desert as in the Exodus. **4:** God will eliminate all
difficulties from the path of the returning captives. **5:** *The glory of the LORD,* i.e. the presence and power of God,

⁶A voice says, 'Proclaim!'
and I asked, 'What shall I proclaim?'
'All mortals are grass,
they last no longer than a wild flower
of the field.
⁷The grass withers, the flower fades,
when the blast of the LORD blows on
them.
Surely the people are grass!
⁸The grass may wither, the flower
fade,
but the word of our God will endure
for ever.'

⁹Climb to a mountaintop,
you that bring good news to Zion;
raise your voice and shout aloud,
you that carry good news to Jerusalem,
raise it fearlessly;
say to the cities of Judah, 'Your God is
here!'
¹⁰Here is the Lord GOD; he is coming in
might,
coming to rule with powerful arm.
His reward is with him,
his recompense before him.
¹¹Like a shepherd he will tend his flock
and with his arm keep them together;
he will carry the lambs in his bosom
and lead the ewes to water.

¹²WHO has measured the waters of the
sea in the hollow of his hand,
or with its span gauged the heavens?
Who has held all the soil of the earth in
a bushel,
or weighed the mountains on a balance,
the hills on a pair of scales?
¹³Who has directed the spirit of the
LORD?
What counsellor stood at his side to
instruct him?
¹⁴With whom did he confer to gain
discernment?
Who taught him this path of justice,
or taught him knowledge,
or showed him the way of wisdom?

¹⁵To him nations are but drops from a
bucket,
no more than moisture on the scales;
to him coasts and islands weigh as light
as specks of dust!
¹⁶Lebanon does not yield wood enough
for fuel,
beasts enough for a whole-offering.
¹⁷All the nations are as naught in his
sight;
he reckons them as less than nothing.

¹⁸What likeness, then, will you find for
God
or what form to resemble his?
¹⁹An image which a craftsman makes,
and a goldsmith overlays with gold
and fits with studs of silver?
²⁰Or should someone choose
mulberry-wood,
a wood that does not rot,
and seek out a skilful craftsman for the
task
of setting up an image and making it
secure?

[6]Each workman helps his comrade,
each encourages his fellow.
[7]The craftsman encourages the
goldsmith,
the gilder him who strikes the anvil;
he declares the soldering to be sound,
and fastens the image with nails
so that it will remain secure.

²¹Do you not know, have you not heard,
were you not told long ago,
have you not perceived ever since the
world was founded,
²²that God sits enthroned on the vaulted
roof of the world,
and its inhabitants appear as
grasshoppers?

40:9 you ... to Zion: or Zion, bringer of good news.
you that carry ... Jerusalem: or Jerusalem, bringer of
good news.   40:20 mulberry-wood: prob. rdg; Heb.
adds a contribution. Verses 6 and 7 of ch. 41 are
transposed to follow this verse.

will become manifest to all nations in the restoration of Israel. 6–8: Like First Isaiah (6.1–13), this prophet
overhears the discussion in the heavenly council. **40.12–31: The majestic Creator. 12–14:** Rhetorical questions stress the majesty (v. 12) and the wisdom
(vv. 13–14) of God. **15–17:** All nations are nothing before God. **15:** Coast and islands: lit. "islands." **16:**
Lebanon had the biggest forest of the largest trees known to the prophet's audience. The majesty and wisdom
of God are characterized by spatial metaphors. **18–20:** Probably an interpolation, with 41.6–7. No image
resembles or can be compared with God. **22:** The vaulted roof is the horizon or the dome over the earth.

He stretches out the skies like a
curtain,
spreads them out like a tent to live in;
23 he reduces the great to naught
and makes earthly rulers as nothing.
24 Scarcely are they planted, scarcely
sown,
scarcely have they taken root in the
ground,
before he blows on them and they
wither,
and a whirlwind carries them off like
chaff.
25 To whom, then, will you liken me,
whom set up as my equal?
asks the Holy One.
26 Lift up your eyes to the heavens;
consider who created these,
led out their host one by one,
and summoned each by name.
Through his great might, his strength
and power,
not one is missing.

27 Jacob, why do you complain,
and you, Israel, why do you say,
'My lot is hidden from the LORD,
my cause goes unheeded by my God'?
28 Do you not know, have you not heard?
The LORD, the eternal God,
creator of earth's farthest bounds,
does not weary or grow faint;
his understanding cannot be fathomed.
29 He gives vigour to the weary,
new strength to the exhausted.
30 Young men may grow weary and faint,
even the fittest may stumble and fall;
31 but those who look to the LORD will win
new strength,
they will soar as on eagles' wings;
they will run and not feel faint,
march on and not grow weary.

41 Listen in silence to me, all you
coasts and islands;
let the peoples come to meet me.
Let them draw near, then let them
speak up;
together we shall go to the place of
judgement.

2 Who has raised up from the east
one greeted by victory wherever he
goes,
making nations his subjects
and overthrowing their kings?
He scatters them with his sword like
dust
and with his bow like chaff driven
before the wind;
3 he puts them to flight and passes on
unscathed,
swifter than any traveller on foot.
4 Whose work is this, who has brought it
to pass?
Who has summoned the generations
from the beginning?
I, the LORD, was with the first of them,
and I am with those who come after.
5 Coasts and islands saw it and were
afraid,
the world trembled from end to end.

8 But you, Israel my servant,
Jacob whom I have chosen,
descendants of my friend Abraham,
9 I have taken you from the ends of the
earth,
and summoned you from its farthest
corners;
I have called you my servant,
have chosen you and not rejected you:

41:1 **come to meet me:** *prob. rdg, transposed, with slight
change, from end of verse 5; Heb. win new strength
(repeated from 40:31).*   41:5 *See note on verse 1.*
41:8 *Verses 6 and 7 transposed to follow 40:20.*

25–26: *Holy One* of Israel, the characteristic title given to God by Second Isaiah, has its foundation in the
inaugural vision of Isaiah of Jerusalem; see 6.3. It signifies that God is and acts beyond all earthly and/or profane
causality and motivation. Hence, the terms "creator" and *created* are used more frequently by Second Isaiah
than by any other OT writer; see 41.20, 42.5, etc. 27–31: Israel should not complain that God does not know
the people's circumstances (*lot*, v. 27), for God is able and willing to strengthen the *weary* (v. 31). 28: See Pss.
90.2; 147.5. 31: See Ps. 103.5.

41.1–29: The LORD in court. The framework of the chapter is a courtroom scene (*place of judgement*, v. 1)
in which it is the LORD who argues the case that God controls historical events. 1: *Coasts and islands:* all the
earth to the farthest reaches of the Mediterranean Sea, the then known world. 2: The one *from the east* of whom
these first four verses speak is Cyrus, whom the ancient world welcomed as a benevolent liberator from the
Babylonians. 4: God will be there when the last *generations* will cease to be. 8: In Second Isaiah, Israel is

10 have no fear, for I am with you;
  be not afraid, for I am your God.
  I shall strengthen you and give you
    help
  and uphold you with my victorious
    right hand.

11 Now all who defy you
  will be confounded and put to shame;
  all who set themselves against you
  will be as nothing and will vanish.
12 You will look for your assailants
  but you will not find them;
  those who take up arms against you
  will be reduced to nothing.
13 For I, the LORD your God,
  take you by the right hand
  and say to you, Have no fear;
  it is I who help you.
14 Have no fear, Jacob you worm and
    Israel you maggot.
  It is I who help you, declares the LORD;
  your redeemer is the Holy One of
    Israel.
15 See, I shall make of you a sharp
    threshing-sledge,
  new and studded with teeth;
  you will thresh mountains and crush
    them to dust
  and reduce the hills to chaff;
16 you will winnow them; the wind will
    carry them away
  and a gale will scatter them.
  Then you will rejoice in the LORD
  and glory in the Holy One of Israel.

17 The poor and the needy look for water
    and find none;
  their tongues are parched with thirst.
  But I the LORD shall provide for their
    wants;
  I, the God of Israel, shall not forsake
    them.
18 I shall open rivers on the arid heights,
  and wells in the valleys;
  I shall turn the desert into pools
  and dry land into springs of water;

19 I shall plant cedars in the wilderness,
  acacias, myrtles, and wild olives;
  I shall grow pines on the barren heath
  side by side with fir and box tree,
20 that everyone may see and know,
  may once for all observe and
    understand
  that the LORD himself has done this:
  it is the creation of the Holy One of
    Israel.

21 Come, open your plea, says the LORD,
  present your case, says Jacob's King;
22 let these idols come forward
  and foretell the future for us.
  Let them declare the meaning of these
    past events
  that we may reflect on it;
  let them predict the future to us
  that we may know what it holds.
23 Declare what is yet to happen;
  then we shall know you are gods.
  Do something, whether good or bad,
  anything that will strike us with dismay
    and fear.
24 You cannot! You are sprung from
    nothing,
  your works are non-existent.
  To choose you is outrageous!

25 I roused one from the north, and he
    has come;
  I called from the east one summoned
    in my name;
  he marches over rulers as if they were
    mud,
  like a potter treading clay.
26 Who has declared this from the
    beginning,
  that we might know it,
  or told us beforehand
  so that we might say, 'He was right'?
  Not one of you declared, not one
    foretold,
  no one heard a sound from you.
27 I am the first to appoint a messenger to
    Zion,

represented as a *servant chosen* anew by God, never to be *rejected*. **14:** The *redeemer* (Heb. *goel*) was the closest relative, whose duty it was to be the "avenger of blood" (Num. 35.19–29) in a murder, or to buy back a relative from slavery (Lev. 25.47–48), or to pay the relative's debt. The LORD acts as Israel's nearest kin who first ransomed them from Egypt by the mighty deeds of the Exodus and now will repeat the wonders. **18:** The return from captivity will be more wonderful than the Exodus because the LORD will not only furnish water in the wilderness (Num. 20.8–12) but will transform it into *pools*. **21:** *Plea . . . case:* language of a juridical process. The LORD challenges the idols to defend themselves in court. **25:** *One from the north . . . east:* Cyrus

a bringer of good news to Jerusalem.
28 When I look round there is no one,
and among those gods no one to give
counsel;
I ask a question and no one can
answer.
29 What empty things they all are!
Nothing they do amounts to anything,
their effigies are so much wind, mere
nothings.

42 Here is my servant, whom I
uphold,
my chosen one, in whom I take delight!
I have put my spirit on him;
he will establish justice among the
nations.
2 He will not shout or raise his voice,
or make himself heard in the street.
3 He will not break a crushed reed
or snuff out a smouldering wick;
unfailingly he will establish justice.
4 He will never falter or be crushed
until he sets justice on earth,
while coasts and islands await his
teaching.

5 These are the words of the LORD who
is God,
who created the heavens and stretched
them out,
who fashioned the earth
and everything that grows in it,
giving breath to its people
and life to those who walk on it:
6 I the LORD have called you with
righteous purpose
and taken you by the hand;
I have formed you, and destined you

to be a light for peoples,
a lamp for nations,
7 to open eyes that are blind,
to bring captives out of prison,
out of the dungeon where they lie in
darkness.
8 I am the LORD; the LORD is my name;
I shall not yield my glory to another
god,
nor my praise to any idol.
9 The earlier prophecies have come to
pass,
and now I declare new things;
before they unfold, I announce them to
you.

10 Sing a new song to the LORD,
sing his praise throughout the world,
you that sail the broad seas,
and you that inhabit the coasts and
islands.
11 Let the wilderness and its settlements
rejoice,
and the encampments where Kedar
lives.
Let the inhabitants of Sela shout for
joy,
let them cry out from the hilltops.
12 Let the coasts and islands ascribe glory
to the LORD;
let them sing his praise.
13 The LORD will go forth as a warrior,
a soldier roused to the fury of battle;
he will shout, he will raise the battle cry
and triumph over his foes.

14 Long have I restrained myself,
I kept silence and held myself in check;

42:6 **a light:** *or* a covenant.

---

from Persia. **28–29:** The trial demonstrates that the *gods* (v. 28) can neither speak nor act. **29:** A final sarcastic denial of the existence of other gods.

42.1–43.7: Israel, the servant of God. These poems (except possibly the hymn in 42.10–13) speak of the relationship between God and God's servant, and of the role of that servant.

42.1–4: First servant song. This and three other passages in Second Isaiah are generally acknowledged to have a unique orientation; the other three are 49.1–6; 50.4–11; 52.13–53.12. Here God speaks to introduce the *servant.* Some scholars argue that the servant is a particular individual, but both the language and context of this song urge that the servant is Israel. **1:** *Spirit:* see 11.2 n. **4:** *Teaching,* or "Law" (Heb. *Torah*), parallels *justice.* The servant will bring it to all peoples, the *coasts and islands.*

42.5–43.7: The Creator and God's servant Israel. 5–9: The creator God commissions the servant as a *light for peoples.* **6:** *With righteous purpose:* according to the divine plan. *Formed* is the same word used in Gen. 2.7 for the making of the first human being. **10–13:** *Kedar* and *Sela,* remote inhabited places in the desert of Arabia, the former to the north and the latter to the south, will praise the LORD along with the remote places to the west, the *coasts and islands.* **14–17:** God, like a *woman in labour* (v. 14), is straining to act to bring

now I groan like a woman in labour,
  panting and gasping.
15 I shall lay waste mountain and hill
  and shrivel up all their herbage.
  I shall change rivers into desert wastes
  and dry up every pool.
16 I shall lead the blind on their way
  and guide them along paths they do
    not know;
  I shall turn darkness into light before
    them
  and make straight their twisting roads.
  These things I shall do without fail.
17 Those who put their trust in an image,
  and say to idols, 'You are our gods,'
  will be repulsed in bitter shame.

18 You that are deaf, hear now;
  you that are blind, look and see.
19 Who is blind but my servant,
  who so deaf as the messenger I send?
  Who so blind as the one who has my
    trust,
  so deaf as the servant of the LORD?
20 You have seen much but perceived
    little,
  your ears are open but you hear
    nothing.
21 Though it pleased the LORD to further
    his justice
  by making his law great and glorious,
22 yet here is a people taken as spoil and
    plundered,
  all of them shut up in holes
  and hidden away in dungeons.
  They are carried off as spoil without
    hope of rescue,
  as plunder with no one to demand
    their return.
23 Who among you will pay heed to this?
  Who will give it close attention from
    now on?
24 Who handed over Jacob for plunder,
  who gave up Israel for spoil?
  Was it not the LORD, against whom they
    sinned?
  They would not follow his ways
  and refused obedience to his law;
25 so on Jacob he poured out his wrath,
  anger and the fury of battle.

It wrapped him in flames, yet he did
    not learn,
  burnt him, yet he did not lay it to
    heart.

43 But now, Jacob, this is the word of
    the LORD,
  the word of your Creator,
  of him who fashioned you, Israel:
  Have no fear, for I have redeemed
    you;
  I call you by name; you are mine.
2 When you pass through water I shall be
    with you;
  when you pass through rivers they will
    not overwhelm you;
  walk through fire, and you will not be
    scorched,
  through flames, and they will not burn
    you.
3 I am the LORD your God,
  the Holy One of Israel, your deliverer;
  I give Egypt as ransom for you,
  Nubia and Seba in exchange for you.
4 You are more precious to me than the
    Assyrians;
  you are honoured, and I love you.
  I would give the Edomites in exchange
    for you,
  and any other people for your life.

5 Have no fear, for I am with you;
  I shall bring your descendants from the
    east
  and gather you from the west.
6 To the north I shall say, 'Give them
    up,'
  and to the south, 'Do not obstruct
    them.
  Bring my sons and daughters from
    afar,
  bring them back from the ends of the
    earth:
7 everyone who bears my name,
  all whom I have created, whom I have
    formed,

42:15 **desert wastes:** *prob. rdg; Heb.* coasts and islands.
42:16 **on their way:** *prob. rdg; Heb. adds* which they do
not know.   42:19 **deaf as the servant:** *so some MSS;*
others blind as the servant.   42:24 **they sinned:** *so*
Gk; Heb. we sinned.

Israel out of captivity. **18–25:** God heals the deaf and blind Israelites, thereby reversing the action performed
by Isaiah at the LORD's command in 6.10. **22:** *People . . . taken as spoil:* Israel in the Exile. No human power,
but only God can *demand their return.* **43.1–7:** No price is too much for God to pay for Israel. **6–7:** Israel
brought back from Exile is a people newly *created* by God, God's own *sons* and *daughters.*

whom I have made for my glory.'

8 Bring forward this people,
a people who have eyes but are blind,
who have ears but are deaf.
9 All the nations are gathered together
and the peoples assembled.
Who among them can expound what
has gone before
or interpret this for us?
Let them produce their witnesses and
prove their case;
let people hearing them say, 'That is
the truth.'
10 The LORD declares, You are my
witnesses,
you are my servants chosen by me
to know me and put your trust in me
and understand that I am the Lord.
Before me no god existed,
nor will there be any after me.
11 I am the LORD,
and I alone am your deliverer.
12 I have made it known; I declared it,
I and no alien god among you,
and you are my witnesses, says the
LORD.
I am God; 13 from everlasting I am he.
None can deliver from my hand;
what I do, none can undo.

14 These are the words of the LORD your
Redeemer,
the Holy One of Israel:
For your sakes I shall send an army to
Babylon
and lay the Chaldaeans prostrate as
they flee;
their cry of triumph will turn to
lamentation.
15 Israel, I am the LORD, your Holy One,
your Creator and your King.

16 This is the word of the LORD,
who opened a way in the sea,
a path through mighty waters,
17 who drew on chariot and horse to their
destruction,
an army in all its strength;
they lay down, never to rise again;
they were extinguished, snuffed out
like a wick:
18 Stop dwelling on past events
and brooding over days gone by.
19 I am about to do something new;
this moment it will unfold.
Can you not perceive it?
Even through the wilderness I shall
make a way,
and paths in the barren desert.
20 The wild beasts will do me honour,
the wolf and the desert-owl,
for I shall provide water in the
wilderness
and rivers in the barren desert,
where my chosen people may drink,
21 this people I have formed for myself,
and they will proclaim my praises.

22 Yet, Jacob, you did not call upon me;
much less did you, Israel, weary
yourself in my service.
23 You did not bring me whole-offerings
from your flock
or honour me with your sacrifices;
I did not exact grain-offerings from
you
or weary you with demands for
frankincense.
24 You did not buy me aromatic cane with
your money
or sate me with the fat of your
sacrifices.
Rather you burdened me with your sins
and wearied me with your crimes.

25 I am the LORD;
for my own sake I wipe out your
transgressions

43:12 **I have ... known:** *prob. rdg; Heb. adds* and I will
deliver.   43:19 **paths:** *so Scroll; Heb.* rivers.

43.8–44.8: Israel can witness that the LORD is God. As in 41.1–29, the framework of these poems is the
legal process; the court will decide who is God and whether the LORD is a just God. **8–13:** In this court scene
God calls *blind* and *deaf* Israel as *witnesses* to prove that the LORD alone is God. **14:** *Redeemer:* see 41.14 n.
The LORD will *send* a power to *Babylon* to act for Israel's *sake. Holy One:* see 40.25–26 n. **19–21:** *Something
new* is another Exodus, not through the sea but through the desert. **22–28:** Israel's sins, which led to punishment, are now forgiven. **22–24:** Israel was not faithful in religious observances, including *whole-offerings* and
sacrifices (v. 23). **24:** *Aromatic cane:* a plant used in making incense and sacred anointing oil; see Exod.
30.23–25. **26:** *Cite ... argue:* Language of the legal process.

and remember your sins no more.

26 Cite me to appear, let us argue it out;
set forth your pleading and establish
  your innocence.

27 Your first forefather transgressed,
your spokesmen rebelled against me,

28 and your leaders desecrated my
  sanctuary;
that is why I put Jacob under solemn
  curse
and left Israel to be reviled.

44 Hear me now, Jacob my servant;
Israel, my chosen one, hear me.

2 Thus says the LORD your maker,
your helper, who fashioned you from
  birth:
Have no fear, Jacob my servant,
Jeshurun whom I have chosen,

3 for I shall pour down rain on thirsty
  land,
showers on dry ground.
I shall pour out my spirit on your
  offspring
and my blessing on your children.

4 They will grow up like a green
  tamarisk,
like willows by flowing streams.

5 This person will say, 'I am the LORD's';
that one will call himself a son of Jacob;
another will write the LORD's name on
  his hand
and the name of Israel will be added to
  his own.

6 Thus says the LORD, Israel's King,
the LORD of Hosts, his Redeemer:
I am the first and I am the last,
and there is no god but me.

7 Who is like me? Let him speak up;
let him declare his proof and set it out
  for me:
let him announce beforehand things to
  come,
let him foretell what is yet to be.

8 Take heart, have no fear.
Did I not tell you this long ago?
I foretold it, and you are my witnesses.
Is there any god apart from me,
any other deity? I know none!

9 Those who make idols are all less than
  nothing;
their cherished images profit nobody;
their worshippers are blind;
their ignorance shows up their
  foolishness.

10 Whoever makes a god or casts an
  image,
his labour is wasted.

11 All the votaries are put to shame;
the craftsmen are but mortals.
Let them all assemble and confront me;
they will be afraid and utterly shamed.

12 The blacksmith sharpens a graving tool
and hammers out his work hot from the coals
and shapes it with his strong arm. Should he
go hungry his strength fails; if he has no
water to drink he feels exhausted. 13 The
woodworker draws his line taut and marks
out a figure with a scriber; he planes the
wood and measures it with calipers, and he
carves it to the shape of a man, comely as the
human form, to be set up in a shrine.

14 A man plants a cedar and the rain makes
it grow, so that later on he will have a tree to
cut down; or he picks out in the forest an ilex
or an oak which he will raise into a stout tree
for himself. 15 It becomes fuel for his fire:
some of it he uses to warm himself, some he
kindles and bakes bread on it. Some he even
makes into a god, and prostrates himself; he
shapes it into an idol and bows down before

43:28 **your leaders . . . sanctuary:** *prob. rdg, cp. Gk;
Heb.* I have profaned holy princes.   44:4 **willows:** *or*
poplars.   44:7 **let him announce beforehand:** *prob.
rdg; Heb.* since my appointing an ancient people and.
44:8 **deity:** *lit.* rock.   44:12 **sharpens:** *so Gk; Heb.
omits.* **his work:** *prob. rdg; Heb.* he works.
44:13 **shrine:** *or* house.

27: *First forefather:* Jacob (Gen. 27.1–29; Hos. 12.2–4). *Your spokesmen:* rulers, priests, and prophets. **44.1–5:**
Israel is chosen as servant, and all will be proud to wear the name of the LORD and *Israel* (v. 5). **2:** *Jeshurun:*
a name for Israel; it appears also in Deut. 32.15; 33.5, 26. **3:** *Spirit:* see 11.1 n. **5:** The *name* of the owner was
tattooed *on the hand* of a Babylonian slave (see Rev. 13.16). **6–8:** The case is concluded. *There is no god* but
the LORD, and Israel can prove it. **6:** *Redeemer:* see 41.14 n.

44.9–20: Idols and idolators are ridiculous. This biting satire on idolatry appears to be an addition to the
preceding verses as a commentary on them. In the Hebrew, the entire unit is understood as prose. **10:** See 41.29;
45.20. **11:** See 1.29; 42.17. **12–20:** The procedures for making idols are reviewed to show that they are nothing
but human creations.

it. [16]One half of the wood he burns in the fire and on this he roasts meat, so that he may eat this and be satisfied; he also warms himself and he says, 'Good! I can feel the heat as I watch the flames.' [17]Then what is left of the wood he makes into a god, an image to which he bows down and prostrates himself; he prays to it and says, 'Save me; for you are my god.'

[18]Such people neither know nor understand, their eyes made too blind to see, their minds too narrow to discern. [19]Such a one will not use his reason; he has neither the wit nor the sense to say, 'Half of it I have burnt, and even used its embers to bake bread; I have roasted meat on them and eaten it; but the rest of it I turn into this abominable object; really I am worshipping a block of wood.' [20]He feeds on ashes indeed! His deluded mind has led him astray, and he cannot recover his senses so far as to say, 'This thing I am holding is a sham.'

[21]Jacob, remember all this;
    Israel, remember, for you are my
        servant:
    I have fashioned you, and you are in
        my service;
    Israel, never forget me.
[22]I have swept away your transgressions
        like mist,
    and your sins are dispersed like clouds;
    turn back to me, for I have redeemed
        you.
[23]Shout in triumph, you heavens, for it is
        the LORD's doing;
    cry out for joy, you lowest depths of
        the earth;
    break into songs of triumph, you
        mountains,
    you forest and all your trees;
    for the LORD has redeemed Jacob
    and through Israel he wins glory.

[24]Thus says the LORD, your Redeemer,
    who formed you from birth:

I am the LORD who made all things,
    by myself I stretched out the heavens,
    alone I fashioned the earth.
[25]I frustrate false prophets and their
        omens,
    and make fools of diviners;
    I reverse what wise men say
    and make nonsense of their wisdom.
[26]I confirm my servants' prophecies
    and bring about my messengers' plans.
    Of Jerusalem I say, 'She will be
        inhabited once more,'
    and of the towns of Judah, 'They will
        be rebuilt;
    I shall restore their ruins.'
[27]I say to the deep waters, 'Be dried up;
    I shall make your streams run dry.'
[28]I say to Cyrus, 'You will be my
        shepherd
    to fulfil all my purpose,
    so that Jerusalem may be rebuilt
    and the foundations of the temple be
        laid.'

45 Thus says the LORD to Cyrus his
        anointed,
    whom he has taken by the right hand,
    subduing nations before him
    and stripping kings of their strength;
    before whom doors will be opened
    and no gates barred:
[2]I myself shall go before you
    and level the swelling hills;
    I shall break down bronze gates
    and cut through iron bars.
[3]I shall give you treasures from dark
        vaults,
    and hoards from secret places,
    so that you may know that I am the
        LORD,
    Israel's God, who calls you by name.
[4]For the sake of Jacob my servant
    and Israel my chosen one
    I have called you by name

44:28 **be laid:** *prob. rdg, cp. Scroll; Heb.* you may be laid.

44.21–45.17: The election of Cyrus. The LORD announces that Israel will be ransomed through a foreign king. **24:** *Redeemer:* see 41.14 n. **28:** *Cyrus,* king of Persia (559–529 B.C.E.) and victor over Babylon (539 B.C.E.), issued the edict that *Jerusalem* and the *temple* be rebuilt; see Ezra 1.1–4. *Shepherd:* king; see Ezek. ch. 34. **45.1:** *Anointed* is the English equivalent of the Heb. *mashiah* (from which the word "Messiah" comes) and of the Gk. *christos* from which "Christ" is derived. Hebrew priests (Lev. 8.12–13) and kings (1 Sam. 16.12–13) were anointed with oil, signifying a commission given them by God. Cyrus is the only non-Israelite called "anointed" because he carried out God's purpose of liberating Israel. God leads Cyrus *by the hand* so that he may accomplish his task without fail. **4:** *A title:* "anointed."

and given you a title, though you have
not known me.

5 I am the LORD, and there is none
other;
apart from me there is no god.
Though you have not known me I shall
strengthen you,

6 so that from east to west
all may know there is none besides me:
I am the LORD, and there is none
other;

7 I make the light, I create the darkness;
author alike of wellbeing and woe,
I, the LORD, do all these things.

8 Rain righteousness, you heavens,
let the skies above pour it down,
let the earth open for it
that salvation may flourish
with righteousness growing beside it.
I, the LORD, have created this.

9 Will the pot contend with the potter,
or the earthenware with the hand that
shapes it?
Will the clay ask the potter what he is
making
or his handiwork say to him, 'You have
no skill'?

10 Will the child say to his father, 'What
are you begetting?'
or to his mother, 'What are you
bringing to birth?'

11 Thus says the LORD, Israel's Holy One,
his Maker:
Would you dare question me
concerning my children,
or instruct me in my handiwork?

12 I alone made the earth
and created mankind upon it.
With my own hands I stretched out the
heavens
and directed all their host.

13 With righteous purpose I have roused
this man,
and I shall smooth all his paths;
he it is who will rebuild my city
and set my exiles free—
not for a price nor for a bribe,
says the LORD of Hosts.

14 These are the words of the LORD:
Toilers of Egypt and Nubian merchants
and Sabaeans bearing tribute
will come into your power and be your
slaves,
will come and follow you in chains;
they will bow in submission before you,
and say,
'Surely God is with you, and there is no
other god.

15 How then can you be a God who hides
himself,
God of Israel, the Deliverer?'

16 All the makers of idols are confounded
and brought to shame,
they perish in confusion together.

17 But Israel has been delivered by the
LORD,
a deliverance for all time to come;
they will never be confounded, never
put to shame.

18 Thus says the LORD, the Creator of the
heavens,
he who is God,
who made the earth and fashioned it
and by himself fixed it firmly,
who created it not as a formless waste
but as a place to be lived in:
I am the LORD, and there is none other.

19 I did not speak in secret, in realms of
darkness;
I did not say to Jacob's people,
'Look for me in the formless waste.'
I the LORD speak what is right, I
declare what is just.

20 Gather together, come, draw near,
you survivors of the nations,
who in ignorance carry wooden idols in
procession,
praying to a god that cannot save.

21 Come forward and urge your case,
consult together:

45:9 **Will . . . contend:** *prob. rdg; Heb.* Ho! He has
contended. **his handiwork:** *prob. rdg; Heb.* your
handiwork.　　45:10 **Will . . . say:** *prob. rdg; Heb.* Ho!
You that say.　　45:11 **Would . . . question me:** *prob.
rdg; Heb.* obscure.　　45:14 **bearing tribute:** *or* men of
stature.　　45:21 **consult:** *so Lat.; Heb.* let them
consult.

13: *This man:* Cyrus.

45.18–25: Lawsuit against idolators. 18: The *formless waste* (better, "chaos") preceded, and is the alternative
to, creation. **20–21a:** Idolators are summoned as if to a court; see 41.21. **21b–25:** Note the clear statement
of monotheism.

who foretold this in days of old,
who stated it long ago?
Was it not I, the LORD?
There is no god but me,
none other than I, victorious and able
    to save.

22 From every corner of the earth
turn to me and be saved;
for I am God, there is none other.
23 By my life I have sworn,
I have given a promise of victory,
a promise that will not be broken;
to me every knee will bow,
by me every tongue will swear,
24 saying, 'In the LORD alone
are victory and might.
All who defy him
will stand ashamed in his presence,
25 but all Israel's descendants will be
    victorious
and will glory in the LORD.'

46 Bel has crouched down, Nebo
    stooped low:
their images, once carried in your
    processions,
have been loaded on to beasts and
    cattle,
a burden for the weary creatures;
2 though they stoop and crouch,
they are not able to bring the burden to
    safety,
but they themselves go into captivity.

3 Listen to me, house of Jacob
and all who remain of the house of
    Israel,
a load on me from your birth,
upheld by me from the womb:
4 Till you grow old I am the LORD,
and when white hairs come, I shall
    carry you still;
I have made you and I shall uphold
    you,

I shall carry you away to safety.
5 To whom will you liken me? Who is my
    equal?
With whom can you compare me?
    Where is my like?
6 Those who squander their bags of gold
and weigh out their silver with a
    balance
hire a goldsmith to fashion it into a
    god;
then they prostrate themselves before it
    in worship;
7 they hoist it shoulder-high and carry it
and set it down on its place;
there it must stand, it cannot stir from
    the spot.
Let a man cry to it as he will, it does
    not answer;
it cannot deliver him from his troubles.

8 Remember this and abandon hope;
consider it well, you rebels.
9 Remember all that happened long ago,
for I am God, and there is none other;
I am God, and there is no one like me.
10 From the beginning I reveal the end,
from ancient times what is yet to be;
I say, 'My purpose stands,
I shall accomplish all that I please.'
11 I summon a bird of prey from the
    east—
from a distant land a man to fulfil my
    design.
I have spoken and I shall bring it to
    pass,
I have planned it, and I shall carry it
    out.
12 Listen to me, you stubborn of heart,
for whom victory is far off:
13 I bring my victory near, mine is not far
    off,
and my deliverance will not be delayed;
In Zion I shall grant deliverance
for Israel my glory.

46:13 **for ... glory:** or and give my glory to Israel.

46.1–13: The LORD and the gods of Babylon. 1–7: The downfall of the Babylonian gods. **1:** *Bel* ("lord") is one of the titles of Marduk, the main Babylonian deity; *Nebo* (Babylonian Nabu), the god of wisdom, was considered Marduk's son. The liturgies of Babylonian cultic festivities, among them the New Year's celebration, included *processions* of *their images*. See also v. 7. **6–7:** See 44.9–20. **8–13:** The LORD has controlled the past and will control the future. **11:** The one *from the east* is Cyrus; see 41.2; in 44.28 he is "my shepherd"; in 45.1, "his anointed."

47.1–15: A funeral song for Babylon. The city of Babylon, personified as a dethroned queen reduced to slavery, is commanded to mourn, for nothing can stop the punishment the LORD plans for her. The poem is

47 Come down and sit in the dust,
  virgin daughter of Babylon.
Descend from your throne and sit on
    the ground,
daughter of the Chaldaeans;
never again will you be called
  tender and delicate.
2 Take the handmill, grind meal, remove
    your veil;
strip off your skirt, bare your thighs,
  wade through rivers,
3 so that your nakedness may be seen,
your shame exposed.
I shall take vengeance and show
  clemency to none,
4 says our Redeemer, the Holy One of
    Israel,
whose name is the LORD of Hosts.

5 Daughter of the Chaldaeans,
go into the darkness and sit in silence;
for never again will you be called
queen of many kingdoms.
6 I was angry with my people;
I dishonoured my own possession
and surrendered them into your power.
You showed them no mercy;
even on the aged you laid a very heavy
  yoke.
7 You said, 'I shall reign a queen for
    ever';
you gave no thought to your actions,
nor did you consider their outcome.

8 Now listen to this,
you lover of luxury, carefree on your
    throne,
saying to yourself,
'I am, and there is none other.
I shall never sit in widow's mourning,
never know the loss of children.'
9 Yet suddenly, in a single day,
both these things will come upon you;
they will both come upon you in full
  measure:
loss of children and widowhood,
despite your many sorceries, all your

countless spells.
10 Secure in your wicked ways
you thought, 'No one can see me.'
It was your wisdom and knowledge
that led you astray.
You said to yourself,
'I am, and there is none other.'
11 Therefore evil will overtake you,
and you will not know how to conjure it
  away;
disaster will befall you,
and you will not be able to avert it;
ruin all unforeseen
will suddenly come upon you.
12 Persist in your spells and your many
    sorceries,
in which you have trafficked all your
  life.
Maybe you can get help from them!
Maybe you will yet inspire terror!

13 In spite of your many wiles you are
    powerless.
Let your astrologers, your star-gazers
who foretell your future month by
    month,
persist, and save you!
14 But they are like stubble
and fire burns them up;
they cannot snatch themselves from the
    flame.
It is not a glowing coal to warm them,
not a fire for them to sit by!
15 So much for your magicians
with whom you have trafficked all your
    life:
they have wandered off, each his own
    way,
and there is not one to save you.

48 Hear this, you house of Jacob,
  who are called by the name of
    Israel,
and have sprung from the seed of
    Judah;

47:4 **says:** *so some Gk MSS; Heb. omits.*   47:9 **in full
measure:** *or* at random. **despite:** *or* because of.

a taunt song in *qinah* ("dirge") form. **1:** *Daughter of Babylon:* better, "daughter Babylon." **2:** To *grind meal*
was the work of slaves whose task required them to *strip off* outer clothes, especially in working around
irrigation *rivers,* i.e. canals. **4:** *Holy One:* see 40.25–26 n. *Redeemer:* see 41.14 n. **8:** Babylon describes herself
in the same terms as did the LORD; see 43.13. **9–12:** Magic, divination, and rituals for warding off evil were
important elements in Babylonian religion. These will not save Babylon. **10:** Her famous *wisdom* led Babylon
astray, for it led to arrogance. **13:** Astrology was a sophisticated art in Mesopotamia.
    48.1–22: Hear what the LORD will do. Just as the LORD controlled the past, so the God of Israel controls the

who swear by the name of the LORD
and invoke the God of Israel,
but not with honesty and sincerity,
[2] though you call yourselves citizens of
the Holy City
and lean for support on the God of
Israel,
whose name is the LORD of Hosts:
[3] Long ago I announced what would first
happen,
I revealed it with my own mouth;
suddenly I acted and it came about.
[4] Knowing your stubbornness,
your neck being as stiff as iron, your
brow like brass,
[5] I told you of these things long ago,
and declared them to you before they
happened,
so that you could not say, 'They were
my idol's doing;
my image, the god that I fashioned,
ordained them.'
[6] You have heard what I said; consider it
well,
and admit the truth of it.

From now on I show you new things,
hidden things you did not know before.
[7] They were not created long ago, but in
this very hour;
before today you had never heard of
them.
You cannot claim, 'I know them
already.'
[8] You neither heard nor knew;
your ears were closed long ago.

I knew that you were treacherous
and rebellious from your birth.
[9] For the sake of my own name I was
patient;
rather than destroy you I held myself
in check.
[10] I tested you, but not as silver is tested:
it was in the furnace of affliction I
purified you.
[11] For my honour's sake, for my own
honour I did it;
I will not let my name be profaned

or yield my glory to any other god.
[12] Listen to me, Jacob,
and Israel whom I have called:
I am the LORD; I am the first,
I am the last also.
[13] My hand founded the earth,
my right hand spread the expanse of
the heavens;
when I summoned them,
they came at once into being.
[14] Assemble, all of you, and listen;
which of you has declared what is
coming,
that he whom I love will carry out my
purpose against Babylon
and the Chaldaeans will be scattered?
[15] I myself have spoken, I have
summoned him,
I have brought him here, and his
mission will prosper.
[16] Draw near to me and hear this:
from the beginning I have never
spoken in secret,
and at its time of fulfilment I was
there.

[17] Thus says the LORD your Redeemer,
the Holy One of Israel:
I am the LORD your God:
I teach you for your own wellbeing
and lead you in the way you should go.
[18] If only you had listened to my
commands,
your prosperity would have rolled on
like a river,
your success like the waves of the sea;
[19] your children would have been like the
sand in number,
your descendants countless as its grains;
their name would never be erased or
blotted from my sight.

[20] Go out from Babylon, hasten away
from the Chaldaeans;

48:9 **patient:** *prob. rdg; Heb. adds* my praise.
48:11 **my name:** *so Gk; Heb. omits.*   48:14 **which of
you:** *so many MSS; others* which of them. **I:** *prob. rdg, cp.
Gk; Heb. adds* the LORD.   48:16 **I was there:** *prob.
rdg; Heb. adds* and now the Lord GOD has sent me, and
his spirit.

future. **3:** *With my own mouth:* that is, through the prophets. **4–5:** The purpose of prophecy was to show that
the LORD alone controls history. **6:** *New things:* the message of deliverance in Second Isaiah. **10:** See 1.25.
The furnace of affliction was the Babylonian Exile. **12–16:** The LORD promises to call Cyrus (*he whom I love,*
v. 14) to destroy Babylon. **12:** See 41.4. **17–21:** Israel's disobedience led to the exile, but now the LORD is
bringing *his servant Jacob* (v. 20) back home. **18:** *Your prosperity:* welfare, well-being. **20:** *Servant Jacob:* see

proclaim it with joyful song,
  sending out the news to the ends of the
    earth;
  tell them, 'The LORD has redeemed his
    servant Jacob.'
21 Though he led them through desert
    places,
  they suffered no thirst;
  he made water flow for them from the
    rock,
  for them he split the rock and streams
    gushed forth.

22 There is no peace for the wicked,
  says the LORD.

Israel a light to the nations

49 LISTEN to me, you coasts and
    islands,
  pay heed, you peoples far distant:
  the LORD called me before I was born,
  he named me from my mother's womb.
2 He made my tongue a sharp sword
  and hid me under the shelter of his
    hand;
  he made me into a polished arrow,
  in his quiver he concealed me.
3 He said to me, 'Israel, you are my
    servant
  through whom I shall win glory.'
4 Once I said, 'I have toiled in vain;
  I have spent my strength for nothing,
    and to no purpose.'
  Yet my cause is with the LORD
  and my reward with my God.
5 The LORD had formed me in the womb
    to be his servant,
  to bring Jacob back to him
  that Israel should be gathered to him,
  so that I might rise to honour in the
    LORD's sight
  and my God might be my strength.
6 And now the LORD has said to me:
  'It is too slight a task for you, as my
    servant,
  to restore the tribes of Jacob,

to bring back the survivors of Israel:
  I shall appoint you a light to the
    nations
  so that my salvation may reach earth's
    farthest bounds.'

7 These are the words of the Holy One,
    the LORD who redeems Israel,
  to one who is despised,
  and whom people abhor,
  the slave of tyrants:
  Kings will rise when they see you,
  princes will do homage,
  because of the LORD who is faithful,
  because of Israel's Holy One who has
    chosen you.

8 These are the words of the LORD:
  In the time of my favour I answered
    you;
  on the day of deliverance I came to
    your aid.
  I have formed you, and destined you
  to be a light for peoples,
  restoring the land
  and allotting once more its desolate
    holdings.
9 I said to the prisoners, 'Go free,'
  and to those in darkness, 'Come out
    into the open.'
  Along every path they will find pasture
  and grazing in all the arid places.
10 They will neither hunger nor thirst,
  nor will scorching heat or sun distress
    them;
  for one who loves them will guide them
  and lead them by springs of water.
11 I shall make every hill a path
  and raise up my highways.
12 They are coming: some from far away,
  some from the north and the west,
  and others from the land of Syene.
13 Shout for joy, you heavens; earth,
    rejoice;

49:5 **be gathered to him:** *or* not be swept away.
49:8 **light:** *or* covenant.

41.8 n. **22:** Probably a gloss.

49.1–6: Second servant song. See 42.1–4 n. The servant is the speaker; the servant's call and mission are
like those of a prophet. In vv. 1–4, the servant speaks as an individual, explicitly identified as Israel; however,
in vv. 5–6 the servant's mission is to *restore* Israel. **1, 5:** *Mother's womb:* see Jer. 1.5. *Named me:* see 43.1.
  49.7–26: The glorious return. 7: Royalty will *do homage* to the LORD's chosen. **8–13:** The people of Israel
will be restored to their land because the LORD *had pity on them* (v. 13). **9a:** *Prisoners . . . darkness:* the exiles
in Babylon. **9b–10:** The *arid places* between Babylon and Israel will provide water and food as Israel returns,

break into songs of triumph, you
    mountains,
for the LORD has comforted his people
and has had pity on them in their
    distress.

14 But Zion says,
'The LORD has forsaken me;
my Lord has forgotten me.'
15 Can a woman forget the infant at her
    breast,
or a mother the child of her womb?
But should even these forget,
I shall never forget you.
16 I have inscribed you on the palms of
    my hands;
your walls are always before my eyes.
17 Those who rebuild you make better
    speed
than those who pulled you down,
while those who laid you waste leave
    you and go.
18 Raise your eyes and look around:
they are all assembling, flocking back to
    you.
By my life I, the LORD, swear it:
you will wear them as your jewels,
and adorn yourself with them like a
    bride;
19 I did indeed make you waste and
    desolate,
I razed you to the ground,
but now the land is too small for its
    inhabitants,
while they who made you a ruin are far
    away.
20 Children born during your
    bereavement will say,
'Make room for us to live here,
the place is too cramped.'
21 Then you will say to yourself,
'Who bore these children for me,
bereaved and barren as I was?
Who reared them
when I was left alone, left by myself;
where did I get them?'

22 These are the words of the Lord GOD:

I shall beckon to the nations
and hoist my signal to the peoples,
and they will bring your sons in their
    arms
and your daughters will be carried on
    their shoulders;
23 kings will be your foster-fathers,
their princesses serve as your nurses.
They will bow to the earth before you
and lick the dust from your feet.
You will know that I am the LORD;
none who look to me will be
    disappointed.

24 Can spoil be snatched from the strong
    man,
or a captive liberated from the ruthless?
25 Yes, says the LORD,
the captive will be taken even from the
    strong,
and the spoil of the ruthless will be
    liberated;
I shall contend with all who contend
    against you
and deliver your children from them.
26 I shall make your oppressors eat their
    own flesh,
and they will be drunk with their own
    blood
as if with wine,
and all mankind will know
that I the LORD am your Deliverer,
your Redeemer, the Mighty One of
    Jacob.

50 These are the words of the Lord:
Is there anywhere a deed of
    divorce
by which I put your mother away?
Which creditor of mine was there
to whom I sold you?
No; for your own wickedness you were
    sold
and for your misconduct your mother
    was put away.

49:19 **I did . . . land:** *or* your wasted and desolate
land, your ruined countryside.   49:21 **as I was:** *so
Gk; Heb. adds* banished and exiled.   49:24 **ruthless:**
so Scroll; Heb. righteous.

as did the wilderness at the Exodus. **12:** *Syene:* a town at the southern end of Egypt; see Ezek. 29.10. **14–26:**
The LORD has not forgotten Jerusalem; Israel will return and *rebuild* it. **18:** *By my life:* an oath formula; see
Amos 4.2. **19–21:** The city cannot contain the enlarged population. **22:** The *signal,* formerly a sign of danger
(5.26; 13.2; 18.3; compare Jer. 6.1), is now a call for the return. **23:** See 49.7. **26:** *Redeemer:* see 41.14 n.
    50.1–3: Separation, not divorce. The Exile did not mark the end of the LORD's relationship with Israel, as
some say; God can do what God wills. **1:** *Put your mother away:* see Hos. 2.2–13; Jer. 3.1–10. *Deed of*

2 Why did I find no one when I came?
Why, when I called, did no one
answer?
Can my arm not reach out to deliver?
Do you think I lacked the power to
save?
Did I not by my rebuke dry up the sea
and turn rivers into desert,
the fish in them stinking for lack of
water
and dying of thirst?
3 Did I not clothe the heavens with
mourning,
and cover them with sackcloth?

4 The Lord GOD has given me
the tongue of one who has been
instructed
to console the weary
with a timely word;
he made my hearing sharp every
morning,
that I might listen like one under
instruction.
5 The Lord GOD opened my ears
and I did not disobey or turn back in
defiance.
6 I offered my back to the lash,
and let my beard be plucked from my
chin,
I did not hide my face from insult and
spitting.
7 But the Lord GOD is my helper;
therefore no insult can wound me;
I know that I shall not be put to shame,
therefore I have set my face like flint.
8 One who will clear my name is at my
side.
Who dare argue against me? Let us
confront one another.
Who will dispute my cause? Let him
come forward.

9 The Lord GOD is my helper;
who then can declare me guilty?
They will all wear out like a garment;
the moth will devour them.

10 Whoever among you fears the LORD,
let him obey his servant's commands.
The one who walks in dark places with
no light,
let him trust in the name of the LORD
and rely on his God.
11 But all who kindle a fire and set
firebrands alight,
walk by the light of your fire
and the firebrands you have set ablaze.
This is your fate at my hands:
you shall lie down in torment.

51 Listen to me,
all who follow after the right, who
seek the LORD:
consider the rock from which you were
hewn,
the quarry from which you were cut;
2 consider Abraham your father
and Sarah who gave you birth:
when I called him he was but one;
I blessed him and made him many.

3 The LORD has comforted Zion,
comforted all her ruined homes,
turning her wilderness into an Eden,
her arid plains into a garden of the
LORD.
Gladness and joy will be found in her,
thanksgiving and melody.

4 Pay heed to me, my people,
and listen to me, my nation,
for instruction will shine forth from me

50:4 **with . . . word:** *prob. rdg, cp. Gk; Heb. adds* he
aroused.   50:11 **set . . . alight:** *prob. rdg, cp. Gk; Heb.*
gird on firebrands.

---

divorce: see Deut. 24.1–4. The covenant is not broken since no *creditor* takes precedence over God. **2:** See
Exod. chs. 14–15.

50.4–9: Third servant song. See 42.1–4 n. The servant speaks concerning the servant's mission (v. 4) and
response to suffering (vv. 5–9). **4:** The prophet perhaps identifies himself with the servant, but it is still possible
to regard the servant as Israel, or at least faithful Israel. **5–7:** Confidence in the LORD enabled the servant to
endure abuse. **8:** The language comes from the court process.

50.10–11: Follow the servant. Israelites are admonished to be obedient like the servant, trusting in the LORD
and not in themselves.

51.1–16: Comfort to Zion. Several poems of different types present a common theme, Zion's salvation. **1–2:**
Abraham and *Sarah, the rock from which* Israel was *hewn,* were *made many* in accord with God's promise
(Gen. 12.1–3); the same promise and power are still active. **3:** The restoration of *Zion* will be like the creation

and my judgement will be a light to
    peoples.
5 In an instant I bring near my victory;
    my deliverance will appear
    and my arm will rule the peoples;
    coasts and islands will wait for me
    and look to me for protection.

6 Raise your eyes heavenwards;
    look on the earth beneath:
    though the heavens be dispersed as
        smoke
    and the earth wear out like a garment
    and its inhabitants die like flies,
    my deliverance will be everlasting
    and my saving power will remain
        unbroken.

7 Listen to me, my people who know
    what is right,
    you that lay my instruction to heart:
    do not fear the taunts of enemies,
    do not let their reviling dismay you;
8 for they will be like a garment
    devoured by grubs,
    like wool consumed by moths,
    but my saving power will last for ever
    and my deliverance to all generations.

9 Awake, awake! Arm of the LORD, put
    on strength;
    awake as you did in days of old, in ages
        long past.
    Was it not you who hacked Rahab in
        pieces
    and ran the dragon through?
10 Was it not you who dried up the sea,
    the waters of the great abyss,
    and made the ocean depths a path for
        the redeemed?
11 The LORD's people, set free, will come
        back
    and enter Zion with shouts of triumph,
    crowned with everlasting joy.
    Gladness and joy will come upon them,
    while suffering and weariness flee away.

12 I am he who comforts you;

why then fear man who must die,
    who must perish like grass?
13 Why have you forgotten the LORD your
        maker,
    who stretched out the heavens and
        founded the earth?
    Why are you in constant fear all the
        day long?
    Why dread the fury of the oppressors
    bent on your destruction?
    Where is the oppressors' fury?
14 He who cowers under it will soon be set
        free;
    he will not be consigned to a dungeon
    and die there lacking food.

15 I am the LORD your God, who stirred up
the sea so that its waves roared. The LORD of
Hosts is my name. 16 I have put my words in
your mouth and kept you covered under the
shelter of my hand. I who fixed the heavens
in place and established the earth say to Zion,
You are my people.

17 Arouse yourself; rise up, Jerusalem.
    From the LORD's hand you have drunk
    the cup of his wrath,
    drained to its dregs the bowl of
        drunkenness;
18 of all the sons you have borne
    there is not one to guide you,
    of all you have reared
    not one to take you by the hand.
19 This twofold disaster has overtaken
        you:
    havoc and ruin—who can condole with
        you?
    Famine and sword—who can comfort
        you?
20 Your children lie in a stupor at every
        street corner,
    like antelopes caught in a net.
    They are glutted with the wrath of the
        LORD,
    with the rebuke of your God.

51:5 **I bring near:** *prob. rdg; Heb. obscure.*
51:19 **who can comfort you:** *so Scroll; Heb.* who am I
to comfort you.

---

of *Eden* out of the primeval desert; see Gen. 2.5–9; Ezek. 36.35. **5:** Israel's restoration will inaugurate a new
era for all *peoples* who will look to the LORD for *protection.* **9:** *Rahab, the dragon:* see 30.7 n. **10:** The crossing
of the sea at the Exodus was also a new creation, like the slaying of the dragon of the great abyss at the original
creation. **16:** *You are my people:* see Hos. 1.8; 2.23.
    51.17–52.2: Awake, Jerusalem. The holy city earlier had been drunk with the LORD's wrath, but the drunken
binge is ended. Compare Jer. 13.13; 25.15–18; Ezek. 23.32–34; Lam. 4.21. **17–20:** The prophet calls for

21 Therefore listen to this in your
   affliction,
you that are drunk, but not with wine.
22 Thus says the LORD, your Lord and
   God,
who will plead his people's cause:
I take from your hand
the cup of drunkenness.
Never again will you drink from the
   bowl of my wrath;
23 I shall hand it to your tormentors,
those who said to you, 'Lie down for us
   to walk over you.'
You flattened your back like ground
   beneath their feet,
like a road for them to walk over.

52 Awake, awake, Zion, put on your
    strength;
Jerusalem, Holy City, put on your
   splendid garments!
For the uncircumcised and the unclean
will never again come into you.
2 Arise, captive Jerusalem, shake off the
   dust;
undo the ropes about your neck,
you captive daughter of Zion.

3 The LORD says, You were sold but no price
was paid, and without payment you will be
redeemed. 4 The Lord GOD says: At its beginning my people went down into Egypt to live
there, and in the end it was the Assyrians who
oppressed them. 5 But now what do I find
here? says the LORD. My people carried off
and no price paid, their rulers wailing, and
my name reviled increasingly all day long,
says the LORD. 6 But on that day my people

will know my name and know that it is I the
LORD who speak; here I am.

7 How beautiful on the mountains are
   the feet of the herald,
the bringer of good news,
announcing deliverance,
proclaiming to Zion, 'Your God has
   become king.'
8 Your watchmen raise their voices
and shout together in joy;
for with their own eyes they see
the LORD return to Zion.
9 Break forth together into shouts of
   joy,
you ruins of Jerusalem;
for the LORD has comforted his people,
he has redeemed Jerusalem.
10 The LORD has bared his holy arm
in the sight of all nations,
and the whole world from end to end
shall see the deliverance wrought by
   our God.

11 Go out, leave Babylon behind,
touch nothing unclean.
Leave Babylon behind, keep yourselves
   pure,
you that carry the vessels of the LORD.
12 But you will not come out in urgent
   haste
or leave like fugitives;
for the LORD will go before you,
your rearguard will be Israel's God.

13 My servant will achieve success,
he will be raised to honour, high and
   exalted.

Jerusalem to revive herself. **18:** *Take you by the hand:* give guidance and support. **21–23:** The LORD will take
the cup of *wrath* from Jerusalem and give it to her *tormentors.* **52.1–2:** The opening call to *awake* is reiterated,
now looking to the future instead of the past. **1:** *Uncircumcised:* foreigners. *Unclean:* Jews who do not observe
the ritual laws of cleanliness.

52.3–6: Israel sold and ransomed without money. A prose insertion. **4–5:** *Egypt* paid the price of Israel's
slavery by the plagues and death of its firstborn, but Babylon paid *no price* when it *carried* them *off* into Exile.
6: *That day:* the day of the LORD's deliverance; see 7.18–25 n. *Know my name:* see 43.1.

52.7–12: A pilgrim victory hymn. The song celebrates the joyful return of the LORD and the people to the
holy city. **7:** *Your God has become king:* see Pss. 47; 93; 96. **8–9:** *Watchmen* are the people left in the *ruins
of Jerusalem* at the time of its destruction by the Babylonians in 587 B.C.E. (2 Kgs. 25.8–12). They look for the
return of *the LORD* who was considered to have gone to Babylon with the captives; compare Ezek. 11.22–25;
43.1–7. **11:** See Ezra 1.7–11. **12:** The Israelites on their return from Babylon did not ask for an escort of soldiers
but trusted that the LORD would be their guard: see Ezra 8.21–23.

52.13–53.12: Fourth servant song. The suffering servant. See 42.1–4 n. Israel, the servant of God, has
suffered as a humiliated individual. However, the servant endured without complaint because it was vicarious

14-15 Time was when many were appalled at
you, my people;
so now many nations recoil at the sight
of him,
and kings curl their lips in disgust.
His form, disfigured, lost all human
likeness;
his appearance so changed he no
longer looked like a man.
They see what they had never been
told
and their minds are full of things
unheard before.

53 Who could have believed what we
have heard?
To whom has the power of the LORD
been revealed?

2 He grew up before the LORD like a
young plant
whose roots are in parched ground;
he had no beauty, no majesty to catch
our eyes,
no grace to attract us to him.
3 He was despised, shunned by all,
pain-racked and afflicted by
disease;
we despised him, we held him of no
account,
an object from which people turn away
their eyes.
4 Yet it was our afflictions he was
bearing,
our pain he endured,
while we thought of him as smitten by
God,
struck down by disease and misery.
5 But he was pierced for our
transgressions,
crushed for our iniquities;

the chastisement he bore restored us to
health
and by his wounds we are healed.
6 We had all strayed like sheep,
each of us going his own way,
but the LORD laid on him
the guilt of us all.

7 He was maltreated, yet he was
submissive
and did not open his mouth;
like a sheep led to the slaughter,
like a ewe that is dumb before the
shearers,
he did not open his mouth.
8 He was arrested and sentenced and
taken away,
and who gave a thought to his fate—
how he was cut off from the world of
the living,
stricken to death for my people's
transgression?
9 He was assigned a grave with the
wicked,
a burial-place among felons,
though he had done no violence,
had spoken no word of treachery.

10 Yet the LORD took thought for his
oppressed servant
and healed him who had given himself
as a sacrifice for sin.
He will enjoy long life and see his
children's children,
and in his hand the LORD's purpose will
prosper.

53:3 **we despised him:** *so Scroll; Heb.* one despised.
53:8 **arrested and sentenced and:** *or* without
protection and justice.   53:9 **a burial-place:** *so
Scroll; Heb.* in his deaths.   53:10 **healed ... himself:**
prob. rdg; Heb. obscure.

suffering (suffering for others). **13–15:** *Nations* and *kings* will be surprised to see the servant *exalted.* **53.1–3:**
The servant was unattractive and rejected. **2:** In traditional Hebrew thought, the good person prospers like a
tree by water but the wicked is like a *plant* growing in *parched ground;* see Ps. 1.3–6. **3:** *Turn away their eyes:*
lit. hide their faces, an expression used in relation to lepers, whose sickness, considered a sign of sin, made
them *despised.* **4–6:** The vicarious suffering expressed here is in contrast both to the traditional solidarity in
guilt of Exod. 20.5 and to individual responsibility proposed by the prophets at the time of the Exile; see Jer.
31.30; Ezek. ch. 18. **5:** *Health for us:* lit. "our peace," which means "general welfare." **7–9:** The servant was
condemned to death but did not complain. **8:** Although some legal process seems to be involved, the servant
does not receive a fair trial; see Jer. 39.5–6. **9:** The death probably refers to the destruction and Exile of Israel.
Compare Ezek. ch. 37. **10–12:** The theme of 52.13 is resumed. Israel, which has suffered for all humanity, will
now be granted its rightful place. **10:** *Long life* and *children's children* are the signs of a final vindication before
God; see Job 42.16–17.

11 By his humiliation my servant will
    justify many;
after his suffering he will see light and
    be satisfied;
it is their guilt he bears.

12 Therefore I shall allot him a portion
    with the great,
and he will share the spoil with the
    mighty,
because he exposed himself to death
and was reckoned among transgressors,
for he bore the sin of many
and interceded for transgressors.

54 Sing, barren woman who never
    bore a child;
break into a shout of joy, you that have
    never been in labour;
for the deserted wife will have more
    children
than she who lives with her husband,
says the LORD.
2 Enlarge the space for your dwelling,
extend the curtains of your tent to the
    full;
let out its ropes and drive the tent-pegs
    home;
3 for you will spread from your confines
    right and left,
your descendants will dispossess
    nations
and will people cities now desolate.

4 Fear not, you will not be put to shame;
do not be downcast, you will not suffer
    disgrace.
It is time to forget the shame of your
    younger days
and remember no more the reproach
    of your widowhood;
5 for your husband is your Maker;
his name is the LORD of Hosts.
He who is called God of all the earth,
the Holy One of Israel, is your
    redeemer.

6 The LORD has acknowledged you a wife
    again,
once deserted and heart-broken;
your God regards you as a wife still
    young,
though you were once cast off.
7 For a passing moment I forsook you,
but with tender affection I shall bring
    you home again.
8 In an upsurge of anger I hid my face
    from you for a moment;
but now have I pitied you with
    never-failing love,
says the LORD, your Redeemer.
9 For this to me is like the days of Noah;
as I swore that the waters of Noah's
    flood
should never again pour over the earth,
so now I swear to you
never again to be angry with you or
    rebuke you.
10 Though the mountains may move and
    the hills shake,
my love will be immovable and never
    fail,
and my covenant promising peace will
    not be shaken,
says the LORD in his pity for you.

11 Storm-battered city, distressed and
    desolate,
now I shall set your stones in the finest
    mortar
and lay your foundations with
    sapphires;
12 I shall make your battlements of red
    jasper
and your gates of garnet;
all your boundary stones will be
    precious jewels.
13 Your children will all be instructed by
    the LORD,
and they will enjoy great prosperity.

53:11 **humiliation:** or knowledge. **servant:** *prob. rdg;*
Heb. adds righteous. **light:** *so Scroll; Heb. omits.*
54:11 **sapphires:** *or* lapis lazuli.

54.1–17: Reassurance to Israel. A series of metaphors is used to repeat the promise that the nation will be
rebuilt and Israel's relationship to the LORD restored. **1–3:** Like a childless wife whose barrenness has ended,
Israel will need to *enlarge* her *tent* to make room for all her *descendants.* **1:** The *deserted wife* represents Israel
in Exile; the one *who lives with her husband* represents preexilic Israel. **4–10:** Like the *husband* (v. 5) of a
deserted wife, the LORD will acknowledge Israel as a *wife* (v. 6) and bring her home with *tender* affection (v. 7).
4: *Shame of your younger days:* see Ezek. ch. 16. **7:** *Tender affection:* lit. the affection of a mother for the child
of her womb. **8:** *I pitied you:* see Tfn. Hos. 1.6. **9:** See Gen. 9.8–17; compare Gen. 8.21–22. **10:** *Covenant
promising peace:* see Ezek. 34.25.

14 You will be restored triumphantly.
　You will be free from oppression
and have nothing to fear;
　you will be free from terror, for it will
　　not come near you.
15 Should anyone attack you, it will not be
　　my doing;
　for his attempt the aggressor will
　　perish.
16 It was I who created the smith
　to fan the coals in the fire
and forge weapons for every purpose;
　and I created the destroyer to deal out
　　havoc.
17 But the weapon that will prevail against
　　you has not been made,
and the accuser who rises in court
　against you will be refuted.
These benefits are enjoyed by the
　servants of the LORD;
their victory comes from me.
This is the word of the LORD.

55 Come for water, all who are
　　thirsty;
though you have no money, come, buy
　grain and eat;
come, buy wine and milk,
not for money, not for a price.
2 Why spend your money for what is not
　food,
　your earnings on what fails to satisfy?
Listen to me and you will fare well,
you will enjoy the fat of the land.
3 Come to me and listen to my words,
　hear me and you will have life:
I shall make an everlasting covenant
　with you
to love you faithfully as I loved David.
4 I appointed him a witness to peoples,
　a prince ruling over them;
5 and you in turn will summon nations
　you do not know,
and nations that do not know you will
　hasten to you,

because the LORD your God,
　Israel's Holy One, has made you
　glorious.

6 Seek the LORD while he is present,
　call to him while he is close at hand.
7 Let the wicked abandon their ways
　and the evil their thoughts:
let them return to the LORD, who will
　take pity on them,
and to our God, for he will freely
　forgive.
8 For my thoughts are not your thoughts,
　nor are your ways my ways.
This is the word of the LORD.
9 But as the heavens are high above the
　earth,
so are my ways high above your ways
and my thoughts above your thoughts.
10 As the rain and snow come down from
　the heavens
and do not return there without
　watering the earth,
making it produce grain
to give seed for sowing and bread to
　eat,
11 so is it with my word issuing from my
　mouth;
it will not return to me empty
without accomplishing my purpose
and succeeding in the task for which I
　sent it.

12 You will go out with joy
　and be led forth in peace.
Before you mountains and hills will
　break into cries of joy,
and all the trees in the countryside will
　clap their hands.
13 Pine trees will grow in place of
　camel-thorn,
myrtles instead of briars;
all this will be a memorial for the LORD,
a sign that for all time will not be cut
　off.

55.1–13: Admonitions and reassurance. The Book of Second Isaiah (chs. 40–55) concludes with invitations and instructions (vv. 1–9) and affirmations of the LORD's faithfulness, transcendence, and power (vv. 10–13). **1–2:** See 25.6–12 n. All are invited to the LORD's table. The language is both metaphorical and literal; those who *listen* (vv. 2–3) to the LORD will be fed. **3–5:** The *words* of the LORD give *life*. **3:** The *covenant* with David (2 Sam. ch. 7) is extended to the people as a whole. **4–5:** Israel has a mission to the nations. **6:** *Seek:* to request an oracle. See Amos 5.5–6, 14. *Call upon him:* to pray. **12–13:** Nature will celebrate as Israel comes out of Babylon.

56.1–66.24: A collection of postexilic poems. See Introduction. **56.1–8: The house of prayer for all nations.**

God's warnings to the restored community

56 THESE are the words of the LORD:
Maintain justice, and do what is
right;
for my deliverance is close at hand,
and my victory will soon be revealed.
² Happy is the person who follows these
precepts
and holds fast to them,
who keeps the sabbath unprofaned,
who keeps his hand from all
wrongdoing!
³ The foreigner who has given his
allegiance to the LORD must not say,
'The LORD will exclude me from his
people.'
The eunuch must not say,
'I am naught but a barren tree.'
⁴ These are the words of the LORD:
The eunuchs who keep my sabbaths,
who choose to do my will
and hold fast to my covenant,
⁵ will receive from me something better
than sons and daughters,
a memorial and a name in my own
house and within my walls;
I shall give them everlasting renown,
an imperishable name.
⁶ So too with the foreigners who give
their allegiance to me,
to minister to me and love my name
and become my servants,
all who keep the sabbath unprofaned
and hold fast to my covenant:
⁷ these I shall bring to my holy hill
and give them joy in my house of
prayer.
Their offerings and sacrifices
will be acceptable on my altar;
for my house will be called
a house of prayer for all nations.
⁸ This is the word of the Lord GOD,
who gathers those driven out of Israel:
I shall add to those who have already
been gathered.

⁹ All you beasts of the open country and
of the forest,
come and eat your fill.
¹⁰ For all Israel's watchmen are blind,
perceiving nothing;
they are all dumb dogs that cannot
bark,
dreaming, as they lie stretched on the
ground,
loving their sleep,
¹¹ greedy dogs that can never have
enough.
They are shepherds who understand
nothing,
all of them going their own way,
one and all intent on their own gain.
¹² 'Come,' says each of them, 'let me fetch
wine,
strong drink, and we shall swill it down;
tomorrow will be like today,
or better still!'

57 The righteous perish,
and no one is concerned;
all who are loyal to their faith are swept
away
and no one gives it a thought.
The righteous are swept away by the
onset of evil;
² those who have followed a straight
course
shall achieve peace at the last,
as they lie on their deathbeds.

³ Come near, you children of a
soothsayer.
You spawn of an adulterer and a
harlot,
⁴ who is the target of your jests?
Against whom do you open your
mouths
and stick out your tongues?
Children of sin, spawn of a lie,
⁵ you are burning with lust under the
sacred oaks,

57:3 **and a harlot:** *so Gk; Heb.* and she played the
harlot.

Converts to Judaism are welcomed and encouraged to obey the ritual laws. **4–5:** The law of Deut. 23.1–6
is superseded. **5:** Inscription and service among God's people will earn a *name* more lasting than begetting
sons and daughters. **7:** *Holy hill:* Mount Zion, on which the temple was built. The future community of God
will exclude no one because of arbitrary physical or ethnic conditions but will include all nations. **8:** See 11.12;
27.12; Ps. 147.2.

    56.9–57.13: Against corruption. 56.9–57.2: Israel's leaders are compared to dumb animals. **11:** *Shepherds:*
rulers; see Ezek. ch. 34. **57.3:** Idolatry was considered adultery against God. The Israelites practicing idolatry

under every spreading tree,
and sacrificing children in the wadis,
under the rocky clefts.

6 And you, woman,
your place is with the deceitful gods of
the wadi;
that is where you belong.
To them you have poured a libation
and presented an offering of grain.
In spite of this am I to relent?

7 On a high mountaintop
you have made your bed;
there too you have gone up to offer
sacrifice.

8 Beside door and doorpost you have put
up your sign.
Deserting me, you have stripped and
lain down
on the wide bed which you have made;
you drove bargains with men
for the pleasure of sleeping together
and making love.

9 You drenched your tresses with oil,
were lavish in your use of perfumes;
you sent out your procurers far and
wide
even down to the confines of Sheol.

10 Though worn out by your unending
excesses,
you never thought your plight
desperate.
You found renewed vigour
and so had no anxiety.

11 Whom do you fear so much, that you
should be false,
that you never remembered me or
spared me a thought?
Did I not keep silent and look away
while you showed no fear of me?

12-13 Now I shall expose your conduct
that you think so righteous.
Your idols will not help you when you
cry;
they will not save you.
The wind will carry them off, one and
all,

a puff of air will take them away;
but he who makes me his refuge will
possess the land
and inherit my holy hill.

14 Then the LORD will say:
Build up a highway, clear the road,
remove all that blocks my people's path.

15 These are the words of the high and
exalted One,
who is enthroned for ever, whose name
is holy:
I dwell in a high and holy place
and with him who is broken and
humble in spirit,
to revive the spirit of the humble,
to revive the courage of the broken.

16 I shall not be always accusing,
I shall not continually nurse my wrath,
else the spirit of the creatures whom I
made
would be faint because of me.

17 For a brief time I was angry at the guilt
of Israel.
I smote him in my anger and withdrew
my favour,
but he was wayward and went his own
way.

18 I have seen his conduct,
yet I shall heal him and give him relief;
I shall bring him comfort in full
measure,
and on the lips of those who mourn
him

19 I shall create words of praise.
Peace, peace, for all, both far and near;
I shall heal them, says the LORD.

20 But the wicked are like a storm-tossed
sea,
a sea that cannot be still,
whose waters cast up mud and dirt.

21 There is no peace for the wicked,
says my God.

57:17 For ... Israel: *prob. rdg, cp. Gk; Heb.* I was angry
at the guilt of his unjust gain.

are not children of the LORD but *spawn of an adulterer.* 5: *Sacred oaks:* trees used in pagan fertility cults.
Sacrificing children: see 30.33. 7–11: This alludes either literally to sexual immorality connected with the
fertility cult sacrifice or figuratively to the courting of foreign alliances and friendships with pagan nations, as
in Ezek. ch. 16. 7: See Ezek. 16.16; 23.41. 13: *Holy hill:* Zion, Jerusalem; see 56.7 n.; 65.11.
57.14–21: Consolation to the humble. God addresses the *broken and humble in spirit* (v. 15) to assure them
that they will be healed. 15: *Name is holy:* see 40.25–26 n. 16–19: The LORD summarizes the history of Israel's
guilt, punishment through the Exile, restoration, and peace. 20–21: The *wicked* are like a restless, troubled
sea.

58

Shout aloud without restraint;
  lift up your voice like a trumpet.
Declare to my people their
  transgression,
to the house of Jacob their sins,
2 although they ask guidance of me day
  after day
and say they delight in knowing my
  ways.
As if they were a nation which had
  acted rightly
and had not abandoned the just laws of
  their God,
they ask me for righteous laws
and delight in approaching God.

3 'Why should we fast, if you ignore it?
Why mortify ourselves, if you pay no
  heed?'
In fact you serve your own interests on
  your fast-day
and keep all your men hard at work.
4 Your fasting leads only to wrangling
  and strife
and to lashing out with vicious blows.
On such a day the fast you are keeping
is not one that will carry your voice to
  heaven.
5 Is this the kind of fast that I require,
a day of mortification such as this:
that a person should bow his head like
  a bulrush
and use sackcloth and ashes for a bed?
Is that what you call a fast,
a day acceptable to the LORD?
6 Rather, is not this the fast I require:
to loose the fetters of injustice,
to untie the knots of the yoke,
and set free those who are oppressed,
tearing off every yoke?
7 Is it not sharing your food with the
  hungry,
taking the homeless poor into your
  house,
clothing the naked when you meet
  them,
and never evading a duty to your
  kinsfolk?

8 Then your light will break forth like
  the dawn,
and new skin will speedily grow over
  your wound;
your righteousness will be your
  vanguard
and the glory of the LORD your
  rearguard.
9 Then, when you call, the LORD will
  answer;
when you cry to him, he will say, 'Here
  I am.'
If you cease to pervert justice,
to point the accusing finger and lay
  false charges,
10 if you give of your own food to the
  hungry
and satisfy the needs of the wretched,
then light will rise for you out of
  darkness
and dusk will be for you like noonday;
11 the LORD will be your guide continually
and will satisfy your needs in the bare
  desert;
he will give you strength of limb;
you will be like a well-watered garden,
like a spring whose waters never fail.
12 Buildings long in ruins will be restored
  by your own kindred
and you will build on ancient
  foundations;
you will be called the rebuilder of
  broken walls,
the restorer of houses in ruins.

13 If you refrain from sabbath journeys
and from doing business on my holy
  day,
if you call the sabbath a day of joy
and the LORD's holy day worthy of
  honour,
if you honour it by desisting from work
and not pursuing your own interests
or attending to your own affairs,
14 then you will find your joy in the
  LORD,
and I shall make you ride on the
  heights of the earth,

58.1–12: The true fasts, a prophetic Torah. The questions, admonitions, instructions, and contents of this postexilic oracle (v. 12) reflect the practice of the laity inquiring of priests or other cultic professionals concerning proper practices. See 1.10–20; Amos 5.21–24; Mic. 6.1–8. **5:** *Bow his head:* sign of sadness; *sackcloth and ashes:* sign of mortification and mourning. **6–10:** Proper fasting consists of acting against *injustice,* freeing the *oppressed,* providing clothes for the *naked,* and giving food to the *hungry.*

58.13–14: The rewards of observing the sabbath. See Exod. 20.8–11; Deut. 5.12–15.

and the holding of your father Jacob
   will be yours to enjoy.
The LORD himself has spoken.

59 The LORD's arm is not too short to
   save
nor his ear too dull to hear;
2 rather, it is your iniquities that raise a
   barrier
between you and your God;
it is your sins that veil his face,
so that he does not hear.
3 Your hands are stained with blood
and your fingers with crime;
your lips speak lies
and your tongues utter injustice.
4 No one sues with just cause,
no one makes an honest plea in court;
all rely on empty words, they tell lies,
they conceive mischief and bring forth
   wickedness.

5 They hatch snakes' eggs; they weave
   cobwebs.
Whoever eats those eggs will die,
for rottenness hatches from rotten eggs.
6 Their webs are useless for making
   cloth;
no one can use them for clothing.
Their works breed wickedness
and their hands are full of acts of
   violence.
7 They rush headlong into crime
in furious haste to shed innocent blood;
their schemes are harmful
and leave a trail of havoc and ruin.
8 They are strangers to the path of
   peace,
no justice guides their steps;
all the ways they choose are crooked;
no one who walks in them feels safe.

9 That is why justice is far removed from
   us,
and righteousness is out of our reach.
We look for light, but all is darkness;
for daybreak, but we must walk in deep
   gloom.

10 We grope like blind men along a wall,
feeling our way like those whose sight
   has gone;
we stumble at noonday as if it were
   nightfall,
like the dead in the desolate
   underworld.
11 All of us growl like bears,
we keep moaning like doves;
we wait for justice, but there is none,
for deliverance, but it is far from us.

12 Our transgressions against you are
   many,
and our sins bear witness against us;
our transgressions are on our minds,
and well we know our guilt:
13 we have rebelled and broken faith with
   the LORD,
we have relapsed and forsaken our
   God;
we have conceived lies in our hearts
and repeated them in slanderous and
   treacherous words.
14 Justice is rebuffed and flouted
while righteousness stands at a
   distance;
truth stumbles in court
and honesty is kept outside,
15 so truth is lost to sight,
and those who shun evil withdraw.

There was no justice,
and when the LORD saw it he was
   displeased.
16 He saw that there was no help
   forthcoming
and was outraged that no one
   intervened;
so his own might brought him the
   victory
and his righteousness supported him.
17 He put on righteousness as a
   breastplate
and salvation as a helmet on his head;
he put on the garments of vengeance
and wrapped zeal about him like a
   cloak.

59.1–21: A liturgy of repentance. The parts which comprise this unit may have once existed separately,
but together they are the words of a liturgical act of confession and forgiveness. **1–8:** *It is your iniquities:* the
prophet begins the service by indicting Israel for its sins. **5–6:** This is probably a proverb. *Snakes' eggs:*
malicious evil deeds; *weave cobwebs:* useless, unproductive schemes and plans. **9–15a:** The congregation
acknowledges its rebellion, which has left it in the dark. **15b–20:** The LORD punished Israel for its sins but now

18 According to their deeds he will repay:
for his adversaries, anger;
for his enemies, retribution!
19 So from the west the LORD's name will
be feared,
and his glory revered from the rising of
the sun.
His glory will come like a swift river
on which the wind of the LORD moves.
20 He will come as a redeemer to Zion
and to those in Jacob who repent of
their rebellion.
This is the word of the LORD.

21 This, says the LORD, is my covenant, which
I make with them: My spirit which rests on
you and my words which I have put into your
mouth will never fail you from generation to
generation of your descendants from now
on, for evermore. The LORD has said it.

Promise of the new Jerusalem

60 ARISE, shine, Jerusalem, for your
light has come;
and over you the glory of the LORD has
dawned.
2 Though darkness covers the earth
and dark night the nations,
on you the LORD shines
and over you his glory will appear;
3 nations will journey towards your light
and kings to your radiance.

4 Raise your eyes and look around:
they are all assembling, flocking back to
you;
your sons are coming from afar,
your daughters walking beside them.
5 You will see it, and be radiant with joy,
and your heart will thrill with gladness;
sea-borne riches will be lavished on you
and the wealth of nations will be yours.

6 Camels in droves will cover the land,
young camels from Midian and Ephah,
all coming from Sheba

laden with gold and frankincense,
heralds of the LORD's praise.
7 Kedar's flocks will all be gathered for
you,
rams of Nebaioth will serve your needs,
acceptable offerings on my altar;
I shall enhance the splendour of my
temple.

8 Who are these that sail along like
clouds,
that fly like doves to their dovecots?
9 They are vessels assembling from the
coasts and islands,
ships of Tarshish leading the convoy;
they bring your children from far away,
their silver and gold with them,
to the honour of the LORD your God,
the Holy One of Israel;
for he has made you glorious.

10 Foreigners will rebuild your walls
and their kings will be your servants;
though in my wrath I struck you down,
now in my favour I show you pity.
11 Your gates will stand open at all times;
day and night they will never be shut,
so that through them may be brought
the wealth of nations
and their kings under escort.

12 For the nation or kingdom which refuses to
serve you will perish; and there will be widespread devastation among such nations.

13 The glory of Lebanon will come to you,
pine, fir, and boxwood all together,
to adorn my holy sanctuary,
to honour the place where I stand.
14 The sons of your oppressors will come
forward to do homage,
all who reviled you will bow low at your
feet;

59:18 **retribution:** *so Gk; Heb. adds* he will repay: for
the coasts and islands, retribution.   59:19 **wind:** *or*
spirit.   60:1 **Jerusalem:** *so Gk; Heb. omits.*
60:6 **gold:** *or* golden spice.

redeems those who repent. **19:** *Spirit of the LORD:* see 11.2 n. **20:** *Redeemer:* see 41.14 n. **21:** This verse, which
is a later addition, affirms a *covenant* which shall not end.
60.1–22: The new Jerusalem. The LORD addresses the holy city, promising restoration and a glory greater
than in the past. The style and thought here resemble those of chs. 40–55. **1–3:** *Jerusalem* will *shine* with the
glory of the LORD. **6–7:** The riches of Arabia come by *camels* across the desert. **8–9:** The riches of the west,
coasts and islands, will come by ship. *Like clouds . . . doves:* white sails of *ships of Tarshish.* **10:** The great
reversal: *walls* destroyed by *foreigners* will be rebuilt by them; their *kings,* once tyrants, will now be *servants.*

they will address you as 'City of the
LORD,
Zion of the Holy One of Israel'.

¹⁵ No longer will you be deserted,
like a wife hated and neglected;
I shall make you an object of
everlasting acclaim,
and a source of never-ending joy.
¹⁶ You will suck the milk of nations
and be suckled at royal breasts.
Then you will know that I, the LORD,
am your Deliverer;
your Redeemer is the Mighty One of
Jacob.

¹⁷ For copper I shall bring you gold
and for iron I shall bring silver,
copper for timber and iron for stone;
I shall appoint peace to govern you
and make righteousness rule over you.
¹⁸ No longer will the sound of violence be
heard in your land,
nor havoc and ruin within your
borders;
but you will name your walls
Deliverance
and your gates Praise.

¹⁹ The sun will no longer be your light by
day,
nor the moon shine on you by night;
the LORD will be your everlasting light,
your God will be your splendour.
²⁰ Never again will your sun set
nor your moon withdraw her light;
but the LORD will be your everlasting
light
and your days of mourning will be
ended.

²¹ Your people, all of them righteous,
will possess the land for ever.
They are a shoot of my own planting,

a work of my own hands for my
adornment.
²² The few will become a thousand;
the handful, a great nation.
At its appointed time I the LORD shall
bring this swiftly to pass.

61 The spirit of the Lord GOD is upon
me
because the LORD has anointed me;
he has sent me to announce good news
to the humble,
to bind up the broken-hearted,
to proclaim liberty to captives,
release to those in prison;
² to proclaim a year of the LORD's favour
and a day of the vengeance of our
God;
to comfort all who mourn,
³ to give them garlands instead of ashes,
oil of gladness instead of mourners'
tears,
a garment of splendour for the heavy
heart.
They will be called trees of
righteousness,
planted by the LORD for his adornment.

⁴ Buildings long in ruins will be rebuilt
and sites long desolate restored;
they will repair the ruined cities
which for generations have lain
desolate.
⁵ Foreigners will serve as shepherds of
your flocks,
aliens will till your land and tend your
vines,
⁶ but you will be called priests of the
LORD
and be named ministers of our God.
You will enjoy the wealth of nations
and succeed to their riches.

61:2 **all who mourn:** *prob. rdg; Heb. adds* to appoint to
Zion's mourners.

13: *Glory of Lebanon:* the cedar trees used by Solomon to build the first temple; 1 Kgs. 5.6–10. **16:** *Redeemer:*
see 41.14 n. **18:** Ancient as well as modern *walls* and *gates* of Jerusalem had names. Here they are symbolic,
Deliverance being God's action protecting the city, and *Praise* being the people's action in entering God's
protection. The life of the city will be completely changed. **19–20:** The LORD will be a *light* of the city; compare
vv. 1–3. **21–22:** The *people* shall be reestablished in the *land*. **21:** Jerusalem is a new plant, a new creation,
at the LORD's *hands;* see 43.6–7 n.
61.1–11: Good news to the exiles. A prophetic voice proclaims consolation and salvation. **1:** *Spirit of the
LORD:* see 11.2 n. **3:** *Righteousness:* see 5.7 n. **4–9:** The prophet announces the restoration and return. **4:** See
Amos 9.14. **5–6:** Since *foreigners* will do the secular work, the Israelites will be their *priests,* i.e. intermediaries
between them and the LORD, offering sacrifices for them and giving them the Torah, or teaching; see Exod.

7 And so, because shame in double
  measure
and insults and abuse have been my
  people's lot,
they will receive in their own land a
  double measure of wealth,
and everlasting joy will be theirs.
8 For I the LORD love justice
and hate robbery and crime;
I shall grant them a sure reward
and make an everlasting covenant with
  them;
9 their posterity will be renowned among
  the nations
and their descendants among the
  peoples;
all who see them will acknowledge
that they are a race blessed by the
  LORD.
10 Let me rejoice in the LORD with all my
  heart,
let me exult in my God;
for he has robed me in deliverance
and arrayed me in victory,
like a bridegroom with his garland,
or a bride decked in her jewels.
11 As the earth puts forth her blossom
or plants in the garden burst into
  flower,
so will the Lord GOD make his victory
  and renown
blossom before all the nations.

62 For Zion's sake I shall not keep
    silent,
for Jerusalem's sake I shall not be
  quiet,
until her victory shines forth like the
  sunrise,
her deliverance like a blazing torch,
2 and the nations see your victory
and all their kings your glory.
Then you will be called by a new name
which the LORD himself will announce;
3 you will be a glorious crown in the
  LORD's hand,
a royal diadem held by your God.
4 No more will you be called Forsaken,

no more will your land be called
  Desolate,
but you will be named Hephzibah
and your land Beulah;
for the LORD will take delight in you
and to him your land will be linked in
  wedlock.
5 As a young man weds a maiden,
so will you be wedded to him who
  rebuilds you,
and as a bridegroom rejoices over the
  bride,
so will your God rejoice over you.

6 Jerusalem, on your walls I have posted
  watchmen,
who day and night without ceasing will
  cry:
'You that invoke the LORD's name,
take no rest, 7 and give no rest to him
until he makes Jerusalem
a theme of praise throughout the
  world.'

8 The LORD has sworn with raised right
  hand and mighty arm:
Never again will I give your grain to
  feed your foes,
never again let foreigners drink the
  vintage
for which you have toiled;
9 but those who harvest the grain will eat
  it
and give praise to the LORD,
and those who gather the grapes will
  drink the wine
within my sacred courts.

10 Pass through the gates, go out,
clear a road for my people;
build a highway, build it up,
remove the boulders;
hoist a signal for the peoples.
11 This is the LORD's proclamation
to earth's farthest bounds:

61:7 **shame:** *prob. rdg; Heb.* your shame. **and abuse:**
prob. rdg; Heb. they shout. **my people's:** *lit.* their.
62:4 **Hephzibah:** *that is* My delight is in her. **Beulah:**
that is Wedded.

19.5–6. **10–11:** The prophet (or perhaps Israel) responds to the promises with a hymn.
  62.1–12: New names for Jerusalem. See 60.1–22; 51.1–52.12. **2:** *New name:* signifies a new status and
relationship to God: see 43.1; Ezek. 48.35. **4:** Israel's *land* is an integral part of the promise and covenant with
God; Gen. 15.18–20; Deut. 6.10–24. **6–7:** Compare 21.12–13. The *watchmen* (prophets) must keep praying,
giving God *no rest* until the divine promises are fulfilled. **10–12:** Chapters 60.1–62.9 are summarized here.
The *Holy People* and the holy city will be reunited.

Tell the daughter of Zion,
'See, your deliverance comes.
His reward is with him,
his recompense before him.'
12 They will be called the Holy People,
the Redeemed of the LORD;
and you will be called Sought After,
City No Longer Forsaken.

The people's lament and God's response

63 'WHO is this coming from Edom,
from Bozrah with his garments
stained red,
one splendidly attired,
striding along with mighty power?'

It is I, proclaiming victory,
I, who am strong to save.

2 'Why are your clothes all red,
like the garments of one treading
grapes in the winepress?'

3 I have trodden the press alone,
for none of my people was with me.
I trod the nations in my anger,
I trampled them in my fury,
and their blood bespattered my
garments
and all my clothing was stained.
4 I resolved on a day of vengeance;
the year for redeeming my own had
come.
5 I looked for a helper but found none;
I was outraged that no one upheld me;
yet my own might brought me victory,
my fury alone upheld me.
6 I stamped on peoples in my anger,
I shattered them in my fury
and spilled their blood over the
ground.

7 I shall recount the LORD's unfailing
love,

the prowess of the LORD,
according to all he has done for us,
his great goodness to the house of
Israel,
what he has done for them in his
tenderness
and by his many acts of faithful love.
8 He said, 'Surely they are my people,
children who will not play me false';
and he became their deliverer
9 in all their troubles.
No envoy, no angel, but he himself
delivered them,
redeemed them in his love and pity;
he lifted them up and carried them
through all the days of old.
10 Yet they rebelled and grieved his holy
spirit;
so he turned hostile to them
and himself fought against them.

11 Then they recalled days long past
and him who drew out his people:
where is he who brought up from the
Nile
the shepherd of his flock?
Where is he who put within him
his holy spirit,
12 who sent his glorious power
to walk at Moses' right hand?
Where is he who divided the waters
before them,
to win for himself everlasting renown,
13 who brought them through the deep
sure-footed as horses in open country,
14 like cattle moving down into a valley
guided by the spirit of the LORD?
Thus you led your people
to win yourself a glorious name.

15 Look down from heaven and see

63:1 **striding:** *prob. rdg; Heb.* stooping.   63:3 **my
people:** *so Scroll; Heb.* peoples.   63:11 **him who
drew out:** *that is Moses whose name resembles the Heb.
verb meaning 'draw out'; cp. Exod. 2:10 and the note there.*
brought up: *so Scroll; Heb.* brought them up.
63:14 **guided:** *so Gk; Heb.* given rest.

63.1–6: The approach of the divine warrior. The prophet as watchman (62.6) asks a question (v. 1a) and the LORD, as a figure covered with the blood of the enemies, responds (1b–6). God alone has destroyed the nations in order to save the LORD's people; see ch. 34. **1:** *Bozrah:* see 34.6 n.

63.7–64.12: Praise and petition. This prayer begins with an emphasis upon praise for God's saving acts (63.7–14) and turns to pleas that God act again to restore Jerusalem and the temple (63.15–64.12). **7:** Hymns often begin with an expression of the intention to praise. See Ps. 89.1. **9–14:** The account of God's acts corresponds to Israel's history. **11:** *Spirit:* see 11.2 n.; Ps. 106.4. **12:** See Exod. chs. 14–15, especially 14.21 and 15.6. **13:** See also Ps. 106.9.

from the heights where you dwell holy
and glorious.
Where is your zeal, your valour,
your burning and tender love?
Do not stand aloof, [16]for you are our
Father.
Though Abraham were not to know us
nor Israel to acknowledge us,
you, LORD, are our Father;
our Redeemer from of old is your
name.
[17]Why, LORD, do you let us wander from
your ways
and harden our hearts until we cease to
fear you?
Turn again for the sake of your
servants,
the tribes that are your possession.
[18]Why have the wicked trespassed on
your sanctuary,
why have our enemies trampled on
your shrine?
[19]We have long been reckoned as beyond
your sway,
as if we had not been named your own.

64 Why did you not tear asunder the
heavens and come down,
that, when you appeared, the
mountains might shake,
[2]that fire might blaze as it blazes in
brushwood
when it makes water boil?
Then would your name be known to
your adversaries,
and nations would tremble before you.
[3]You surprised us with awesome things;
the mountains shook when you
appeared.
[4]Never has ear heard or eye seen
any other god who acts for those who
wait for him.
[5]You welcome him who rejoices to do
what is right,
who is mindful of your ways.
When you showed your anger, we
sinned
and, in spite of it, we have done evil
from of old.

[6]We all became like something unclean
and all our righteous deeds were like a
filthy rag;
we have all withered like leaves
and our iniquities carry us away like the
wind.
[7]There is no one who invokes you by
name
or rouses himself to hold fast to you;
for you have hidden your face from us
and left us in the grip of our iniquities.

[8]Yet, LORD, you are our Father;
we are the clay, you the potter,
and all of us are your handiwork.
[9]Do not let your anger pass all bounds,
LORD,
and do not remember iniquity for ever;
look on us all, look on your people.
[10]Your holy cities are a wilderness,
Zion a wilderness, Jerusalem desolate;
[11]our holy and glorious sanctuary,
in which our forefathers praised you,
has been burnt to the ground
and all that we cherished lies in ruins.
[12]Despite this, LORD, will you stand aloof,
will you keep silent and punish us
beyond measure?

Judgement and final salvation

65 I WAS ready to respond, but no one
asked,
ready to be found, but no one sought
me.
I said, 'Here am I! Here am I!'
to a nation that did not invoke me by
name.
[2]All day long I held out my hands
appealing to a rebellious people
who went their evil way,
in pursuit of their own devices;

63:15 **Do ... aloof:** *prob. rdg; Heb. obscure.*
63:18 **Why ... sanctuary:** *prob. rdg; Heb. For a little
while they possessed your holy people.*   64:1 *In Heb.
63:19b.*   64:2 *In Heb. 64:1.*   64:5 **in spite ... old:**
prob. rdg, cp. Gk; Heb. obscure.   64:7 **and left:** *so Gk;
Heb. unintelligible.*

15–19: The petitioner asks for reasons for God's absence. **16:** *Redeemer:* see 41.14 n. **17:** *Harden our hearts:*
since God controls all things, God must have caused Israel to go astray. Compare Exod. 14.4. **19:** *Named:* see
43.6–7 n. **64.1–4:** A prayer that God act as in the past. **5–7:** The community confesses its sins.
    65.1–25: The answer to the prayer. In the inherited organization of the book, this chapter appears as God's
response to the previous petition; sinners will be judged but the faithful redeemed. **1–7:** Non-Israelite or corrupt

³they were a people who provoked me
  perpetually to my face,
  offering sacrifice in the gardens,
  burning incense on brick altars.
⁴They crouch among graves,
  keeping vigil all night long,
  eating the flesh of pigs,
  their cauldrons full of a foul brew.
⁵'Keep clear!' they cry,
  'Do not touch me, for my holiness will
    infect you.'
  Such people are a smouldering fire,
  smoke in my nostrils all day long.
⁶Your record lies before me; I shall not
    keep silent;
  I shall fully repay ⁷your iniquities,
  both yours and your forefathers', says
    the LORD,
  for having sacrificed on the mountains
  and shamed me on the hills;
  I shall first measure out their reward
  and then repay them in full.

⁸These are the words of the LORD:
  As there is juice in a cluster of grapes
  and folk say, 'Do not destroy it; there is
    blessing in it,'
  so shall I act for the sake of my
    servants:
  I shall not destroy the whole nation.
⁹I shall give descendants to Jacob,
  and to Judah heirs who will possess my
    mountains;
  my chosen ones will take possession of
    the land,
  and those who serve me will live
    there.
¹⁰Flocks will range over Sharon,
  and the valley of Achor become a
    pasture for cattle;
  they will belong to my people who seek
    me.

¹¹But you that forsake the LORD
  and ignore my holy mountain,
  who spread a table for the god of Fate,
  and fill bowls of spiced wine in honour
    of Destiny,
¹²I shall destine you for the sword,

and you will all submit to slaughter,
  because, when I called, you did not
    respond,
  when I spoke, you would not listen.
  You did what was wrong in my sight,
  and chose what displeased me.
¹³Therefore these are the words of the
    Lord GOD:
  My servants will eat, while you go
    hungry;
  my servants will drink, while you go
    thirsty;
  my servants will rejoice, while you are
    put to shame;
¹⁴my servants in the gladness of their
    hearts
  will shout for joy,
  while you cry from an aching heart
  and wail from anguish of spirit.
¹⁵Your name will be used as a curse by
    my chosen ones:
  'May the Lord GOD give you over to
    death!'
  but his servants he will call by another
    name.
¹⁶Anyone in the land invoking a blessing
    on himself
  will do so by God whose name is Amen,
  and anyone in the land taking an oath
  will do so by God whose name is Amen,
  for past troubles are forgotten;
  they have vanished from my sight.

¹⁷See, I am creating new heavens and a
    new earth!
  The past will no more be remembered
  nor will it ever come to mind.
¹⁸Rejoice and be for ever filled with
    delight
  at what I create;
  for I am creating Jerusalem as a delight
  and her people as a joy;
¹⁹I shall take delight in Jerusalem
  and rejoice in my people;
  the sound of weeping, the cry of
    distress
  will be heard in her no more.

65:6–7 **I shall fully repay:** *prob. rdg, transposing* and
then repay *to follow* reward.

---

religious practices are condemned. **3:** *Sacrifice . . . incense:* that is, participation in fertility cults. **4:** *Crouch among graves:* probably a reference to consulting the spirits of the dead. *Keeping vigil:* awaiting a dream revelation; see Jer. 23.25–32. *Eating the flesh of pigs* was a violation of dietary law; see Deut. 14.8. **8–10:** Salvation is announced to those who *serve* and *seek* the LORD. **11–25:** God announces judgment against those who *forsake* God, but salvation to God's *servants*. **11:** *Fate, Destiny:* Aramaean gods.

20 No child there will ever again die in
    infancy,
no old man fail to live out his span of
    life.
He who dies at a hundred is just a
    youth,
and if he does not attain a hundred he
    is thought accursed!
21 My people will build houses and live in
    them,
plant vineyards and eat their fruit;
22 they will not build for others to live in
    or plant for others to eat.
They will be as long-lived as a tree,
and my chosen ones will enjoy the fruit
    of their labour.
23 They will not toil to no purpose
    or raise children for misfortune,
because they and their issue after them
    are a race blessed by the LORD.
24 Even before they call to me, I shall
    answer,
and while they are still speaking I shall
    respond.
25 The wolf and the lamb will feed
    together
and the lion will eat straw like the ox,
and as for the serpent, its food will be
    dust.
Neither hurt nor harm will be done in
    all my holy mountain,
says the LORD.

66 These are the words of the LORD:
The heavens are my throne and
    the earth is my footstool.
Where will you build a house for
    me,
where will my resting-place be?
2 These are all of my own making,
and all belong to me.
This is the word of the LORD.

The one for whom I have regard
is oppressed and afflicted,
one who reveres my word.

3 Sacrificing an ox is like killing a man,
slaughtering a sheep like breaking a

dog's neck,
making an offering of grain like
    offering pigs' blood,
burning frankincense as a token like
    worshipping an idol.
Because people have adopted these
    practices
and revelled in loathsome rites,
4 I in turn shall adopt a wilful course
and bring on them the very things they
    dread,
since, when I called, no one responded,
when I spoke, no one listened.
They did what was wrong in my sight
and chose what displeased me.

5 Hear the word of the LORD, you that
    revere his word:
Your fellow-countrymen, who are
    hostile to you
and spurn you because you bear my
    name, have said,
'Let the LORD show his glory,
that we may see you rejoice!'
But they themselves will be put to
    shame.
6 That roar from the city, that uproar in
    the temple,
is the sound of the LORD dealing
    retribution to his foes.

7 Without birth-pains Zion has given
    birth,
borne a son before the onset of labour.
8 Who has heard of anything like this?
Who has witnessed such a thing?
Can a country be born in a single day,
a nation be brought to birth in a trice?
Yet Zion, at the onset of her pangs,
    bore her children.
9 Shall I bring to the point of birth and
    not deliver?
says the LORD;
shall I who deliver close the womb?
says your God

10 Rejoice with Jerusalem and exult in
    her,

66:2 **belong to me:** so Gk; Heb. omits.

21: See Amos 9.14. See also Ezek. 28.26; Hos. 11.11. 25: Isaiah 11.9 is quoted at the end.
66.1–24: A collection of speeches. 1–2a: The LORD, who speaks, cannot be confined to one place. **2b–4:**
Those who sacrifice to idols will themselves be sacrificed. **5–9:** God's intervention has already begun and will
soon be evident. **5–6:** God's *foes* will be *put to shame*. **7–9:** Israel is being reborn. Unlike the *labour* of
childbirth, God will deliver the new Israel without prolonged *birth-pains* of further calamity and Israel will

all you that love her;
share her joy with all your heart,
all you that mourned over her.
11 Then you may suck comfort from her
  and be satisfied,
taking with enjoyment her plentiful
  milk.

12 These are the words of the LORD:
I shall make prosperity flow over her
  like a river,
and the wealth of nations like a stream
  in spate;
her babes will be carried in her arms
and dandled on her knees.
13 As a mother comforts her son
so shall I myself comfort you;
in Jerusalem you will find comfort.
14 At the sight your heart will be glad,
you will flourish like grass in spring;
the LORD will make his power known
  among his servants
and his indignation felt among his foes.

15 See, the LORD is coming in fire,
his chariots like a whirlwind,
bringing retribution with his furious
  anger
and with the flaming fire of his
  rebukes.
16 The LORD will judge with fire,
by his sword he will test all mankind,
and many will be slain by him.
17 Those who consecrate and purify
  themselves for garden-rites,
one after another in a magic ring,
those who eat swine flesh, rats, and vile
  vermin
will all meet their end,
says the LORD,
18 for I know their deeds and their
  thoughts.

I am coming to gather peoples of every
tongue; they will come to see my glory. 19 I
shall put a sign on them, and those survivors
I shall send to the nations, to Tarshish, Put,
and Lud, to Meshech, Rosh, Tubal, and Javan, distant shores which have never yet
heard of me or seen my glory; these will declare that glory among the nations. 20 From
every nation your countrymen will be
brought on horses, in chariots and wagons,
on mules and dromedaries, as an offering to
the LORD on my holy mountain Jerusalem,
says the LORD, just as the Israelites themselves bring grain-offerings in purified vessels to the LORD's house; 21 and some of them
I shall take for priests and for Levites, says
the LORD.

22 As the new heavens and the new earth
which I am making will endure before
  me,
says the LORD,
so will your posterity and your name
  endure.
23 Month after month at the new moon,
week after week on the sabbath,
all mankind will come to bow before
  me,
says the LORD.

24 As they go out they will see the corpses of
those who rebelled against me, where the
devouring worm never dies and the fire is
not quenched. All mankind will view them
with horror.

66:12 **her babes:** *prob. rdg; cp. Gk; Heb.* you will suck.
66:17 **one . . . ring:** *possible mng; Heb. obscure.*
66:18 **know:** *so Syriac; Heb. omits.* **I am coming:** *so Gk;*
Heb. It will come.   66:19 **Put:** *so Gk; Heb.*
unintelligible. **Meshech, Rosh;** *prob. rdg; Heb.* those who
draw the bow. **Javan:** *or* Greece.

continue to be fruitful in bearing children. **10–16:** God is coming to bring *prosperity* (v. 12) to God's people
and punishment to God's enemies. **15–16:** The LORD is a warrior who destroys by fire. **18–24:** God will *gather
peoples of every tongue* to Jerusalem. **18:** Not only Israel but all nations will see the *glory* of the LORD; see
v. 5. **19:** *Sign:* see 7.11–12 n. *Tarshish:* possibly Spain, at the extreme edge of the then known world; *Put* and
Lud: northern Africa; *Javan:* Ionia; *Meshech, Rosh, Tubal:* at the extremities of Asia Minor to the north of
Palestine. **21:** The priesthood will be reestablished. **22:** Creation will be reordered. **24:** The punishment of the
wicked shall not end. Outside the city there will be a horrible place of refuse, *corpses* and smoldering *fire*,
as it was in the Valley of Hinnom outside of the old Jerusalem.

THE BOOK OF THE PROPHET
Jeremiah

Jeremiah prophesied in Jerusalem mostly before the Babylonians destroyed the temple there in 587 B.C.E. but also for a short while after that event, and even, briefly, in Egypt among the fugitives from Judah. He foresaw this fall of the Southern Kingdom which occurred something over a century after the fall of the Northern Kingdom, Israel. He was no uninvolved spectator; loving his people, compelled by his God and undeterred either by ridicule or by persecution, he sought to salvage what he could from the national calamity. His major accomplishment as a prophet was his contribution to his people's maturation: Judah could survive, he knew, even without the Jerusalem sanctuary.

Chapters 1 to 20 contain two related types of matter: the tender prophet pleads with Israel for an appropriately loyal response, one that would enable a pardoning God to withhold a merited punishment; and he also reveals his dismay and sorrow at Israel's stubbornly heedless behavior and rebels against his need to pursue his seemingly futile mission to it. In chapters 21 to 45 a biographer, probably the prophet's disciple Baruch, records the dramatic course of Jeremiah's frustrating ministry. Both here and in the remaining section (chs. 46–52), messages of hope and consolation occasionally relieve the dreary forebodings.

Persons other than the prophet and his biographer may be responsible for certain passages, especially within the "prophecies against the nations" (chs. 46–51), but also elsewhere in the book. Some of the passages are written after the manner of Deuteronomy or in the style of the later chapters of Isaiah.

1 THE words of Jeremiah son of Hilkiah, one of the priests at Anathoth in Benjamin. ² The word of the LORD came to him in the thirteenth year of the reign of Josiah son of Amon, king of Judah. ³ It came also during the reign of Jehoiakim son of Josiah, king of Judah, until the end of the eleventh year of Zedekiah son of Josiah, king of Judah. In the fifth month the inhabitants of Jerusalem were carried off into exile.

Jeremiah's call and first visions

⁴ THIS word of the LORD came to me: ⁵ 'Before I formed you in the womb I chose you, and before you were born I consecrated you;

I appointed you a prophet to the nations.' ⁶ 'Ah! Lord GOD,' I answered, 'I am not skilled in speaking; I am too young.' ⁷ But the LORD said, 'Do not plead that you are too young; for you are to go to whatever people I send you, and say whatever I tell you to say. ⁸ Fear none of them, for I shall be with you to keep you safe.' This was the word of the LORD. ⁹ Then the LORD stretched out his hand, and touching my mouth said to me, 'See, I put my words into your mouth. ¹⁰ This day I give you authority over nations and kingdoms to uproot and to pull down, to destroy and to demolish, to build and to plant.'

¹¹ The word of the LORD came to me: 'What

1.1–3: A title page. 1: *Anathoth:* about three miles north of Jerusalem. *One of the priests:* a member of a priestly family though seemingly not of the Jerusalem priesthood; see 1 Kgs. 2.26–27. 2: *Thirteenth year of Josiah:* 627 B.C.E. 3: *Eleventh year of Zedekiah:* 587 B.C.E. *In the fifth month:* see 2 Kgs. 25.8, 11. But chs. 40–44 imply that Jeremiah's activity actually extended into later years.

1.4–19: The beginning of Jeremiah's career: 5: *I consecrated you:* set you apart. *To the nations:* chs. 46–51 are against the nations. 6: *I am too young* suggests inadequacy. 7: *Say whatever I tell you to say:* the thought is it that you see, Jeremiah?' 'A branch of an almond tree,' I answered. ¹²'You are right,' said the LORD to me, 'for I am on the watch to carry out my threat.'

¹³The word of the LORD came to me a second time: 'What is it that you see?' 'A cauldron on a fire,' I said; 'it is fanned by the wind and tilted away from the north.' ¹⁴The LORD said:

> From the north disaster will be let loose
> against all who live in the land.
> ¹⁵For now I am summoning all the
>   peoples
> of the kingdoms of the north,
> says the LORD;
> their kings will come
> and each will set his throne in place
> before the gates of Jerusalem;
> they will encircle her walls
> and besiege every town in Judah.
> ¹⁶I shall state my case against my people
> for all their wickedness in forsaking me,
> in burning sacrifices to other gods,
> and in worshipping the work of their
>   own hands.

> ¹⁷Brace yourself, Jeremiah;
> stand up and speak to them.
> Tell them everything I bid you;
> when you confront them
> do not let your spirit break,
> or I shall break you before their eyes.
> ¹⁸This day I make you a fortified city,
> an iron pillar, a bronze wall,
> to withstand the whole land,
> the kings and princes of Judah,
> its priests, and its people.
> ¹⁹Though they attack you, they will not
>   prevail,
> for I shall be with you to keep you safe.
> This is the word of the LORD.

God's appeal to Israel and Judah

2 THE word of the LORD came to me: ²Go, make this proclamation in the hearing of Jerusalem: These are the words of the LORD:

> I remember in your favour the loyalty
>   of your youth,
> your love during your bridal days,
> when you followed me through the
>   wilderness,
> through a land unsown.
> ³Israel was holy to the LORD,
> the firstfruits of his harvest;
> no one who devoured her went
>   unpunished,
> disaster overtook them.
> This is the word of the LORD.

⁴Listen to the word of the LORD, people of Jacob, all you families of Israel. ⁵These are the words of the LORD:

> What fault did your forefathers find in
>   me,
> that they went so far astray from me,
> pursuing worthless idols
> and becoming worthless like them;
> ⁶that they did not ask, 'Where is the
>   LORD,
> who brought us up from Egypt
> and led us through the wilderness,
> through a barren and broken country,
> a country parched and forbidding,
> where no one ever travelled,
> where no one made his home?'
> ⁷I brought you into a fertile land
> to enjoy its fruit and every good thing
>   in it;

1:11 **almond tree:** *Heb*. shaked.　　1:12 **on the watch:** *Heb*. shoked.

---

is dramatized in v. 9. **8:** *Fear none of them:* God fortifies the prophet in advance against the people's opposition, a thought which is developed in vv. 17–19. **10:** *To uproot . . . pull down . . . build . . . plant:* God's message has two aspects, the threat of disaster and consolation after calamity. **11–12:** What God threatens through the prophet will be brought to sure fulfillment. The early blooming *almond* (shaked) reminds Jeremiah that God is "watchful" (shoked) *to carry out the divine purpose.* **13–16:** Disaster looms from the north. **13:** In steam from a boiling *cauldron* the prophet sees an omen of national calamity. **15:** *Peoples of the kingdoms of the north:* the enemy, Babylon, is not directly identified until 20.4. While some, indeed, speculate that the distant Scythians are intended, more probably Jeremiah had in mind the Babylonians, the currently dominant Mesopotamian power. Similarly, in Amos 6.14, an unnamed nation can be identified as Assyria.

2.1–37: Israel's apostasy a fateful error. 2–3: *Through the wilderness . . . a land unsown:* before the entry into Canaan, Israel served God with undivided loyalty, and God protected Israel. **5–8:** In agricultural Canaan, the *fertile land,* Israel forgot God's solicitude, confused their God with the god Baal, and forfeited God's care.

but when you entered my land you
   defiled it
and made loathsome the home I gave
   you.
8 The priests no longer asked, 'Where is
   the LORD?'
Those who handled the law had no real
   knowledge of me,
the shepherds of the people rebelled
   against me;
the prophets prophesied in the name of
   Baal
and followed gods who were powerless
   to help.

9 Therefore I shall bring a charge against
   you once more,
says the LORD,
against you and against your
   descendants.
10 Cross to the coasts and islands of Kittim
   and see,
send to Kedar and observe closely,
see whether there has been anything
   like this:
11 has a nation ever exchanged its gods,
and these no gods at all?
Yet my people have exchanged their
   glory
for a god altogether powerless.
12 Be aghast at this, you heavens,
shudder in utter horror,
says the LORD.
13 My people have committed two sins:
they have rejected me,
a source of living water,
and they have hewn out for themselves
   cisterns,
cracked cisterns which hold no water.

14 Is Israel a slave? Was he born in
   slavery?
If not, why has he become spoil?
15 Lions roar loudly at him;
his land has been laid waste,

his towns razed to the ground and
   abandoned.
16 The people of Noph and Tahpanhes
will break your heads.
17 Is it not your rejection of the LORD
   your God
when he guided you on the way
that brings all this upon you?
18 And now, why should you make off to
   Egypt
to drink the waters of the Nile?
Or why make off to Assyria
to drink the waters of the Euphrates?
19 It is your own wickedness that will
   punish you,
your own apostasy that will condemn
   you.
See for yourselves how bitter a thing it
   is and how evil,
to reject the LORD your God,
to hold me in dread no longer.
This is the word of the Lord GOD of
   Hosts.

20 Many ages ago you shattered your yoke
   and snapped your traces,
crying, 'I will not serve you';
and you sprawled in promiscuous vice
on all the hilltops, under every
   spreading tree.
21 I planted you as a choice red vine,
a wholly pure strain,
yet now you are turned into a vine
that has reverted to its wild state!
22 Though you wash with soda and use
   soap lavishly,
the stain of your sin is still there for me
   to see.
This is the word of the Lord GOD.
23 How can you say, 'I am not defiled;
I have not followed the baalim'?
Look at your conduct in the valley;
recall what you have done:

2:15 **razed to the ground:** *so some MSS; others* burnt.
2:18 **Nile:** *Heb.* Shihor.

8: *Priests . . . shepherds* (rulers), and *prophets* all went astray. **9–13:** It was wholly unnatural behavior in that not even worshipers of idols, *no gods,* exchange those phantoms for others. **10:** *Kittim:* Cyprus. *Kedar:* in Arabia, east of Edom. **11:** *Their glory:* God. **13:** Water sources were either *living water,* a spring flowing from underground, or *cisterns,* dug out and plastered to collect and hold rainwater. **14–15:** The consequences of Israel's apostasy already in evidence. *Become spoil . . . razed . . . abandoned:* the allusions are either to the ruin wrought by Assyria about 721 B.C.E. in the Northern Kingdom, or else to the effects of some more recent invasion, possibly Necho's in 609 B.C.E.; see 22.10 n. **16:** *Noph and Tahpanhes:* Memphis and Daphne in Lower Egypt. **18:** *Drink the Nile . . . the Euphrates:* playing international politics is also disloyalty to God. **20:** *Promiscuous vice:* an example of, and a metaphor for, religious apostasy. **21:** Compare the vineyard parable

you have been like a she-camel,
twisting and turning as she runs,
24 rushing off into the wilderness,
snuffing the wind in her lust;
in her heat who can restrain her?
None need tire themselves out in
pursuit of her;
she is easily found at mating time.
25 Stop before your feet are bare
and your throat is parched.
But you said, 'No; I am desperate.
I love foreign gods and I must go after
them.'
26 As a thief is ashamed when he is found
out,
so the people of Israel feel ashamed,
they, their kings, their princes,
their priests, and their prophets,
27 who say to a block of wood, 'You are
our father'
and cry 'Mother' to a stone.
On me they have turned their backs
and averted their faces from me.
Yet in their time of trouble they say,
'Rise up and save us!'
28 Where are the gods you made for
yourselves?
In your time of trouble let them arise
and save you.
For you, Judah, have as many gods as
you have towns.

29 Why argue your case with me?
You are rebels, every one of you.
This is the word of the LORD.
30 In vain I punished your people—
the lesson was not learnt;
your sword devoured your prophets
like a ravening lion.
31 Have I shown myself to Israel
as some wilderness or waterless land?
Why do my people say, 'We have
broken away;
we shall come to you no more'?

32 Will a girl forget her finery
or a bride her wedding ribbons?

Yet times without number
my people have forgotten me.
33 You pick your way so well in search of
lovers;
even wanton women can learn from
you.
34 Yes, and there is blood on the corners
of your robe—
the life-blood of the innocent poor,
though you did not catch them
housebreaking.
For all these things I shall punish you.
35 You say, 'I am innocent;
surely his anger has passed away.'
But I shall challenge your claim
to have done no sin.
36 Why do you so lightly change your
course?
You will be let down by Egypt
as you were by Assyria;
37 you will go into exile from here
with your hands on your heads,
for the LORD rejects those on whom
you rely,
and from them you will gain nothing.

3 If a man divorces his wife and she leaves
him, and if she then becomes another's,
may he go back to her again? Is not that
woman defiled, a forbidden thing? You have
been unfaithful with many lovers, says the
LORD, and yet you would come back to me?

2 Look up to the bare heights and see:
where have you not been lain with?
Like an Arab lurking in the desert
you sat by the wayside to catch lovers;
you defiled the land
with your adultery and debauchery.
3 Therefore the showers were withheld

2:24 **rushing off into:** *prob. rdg; Heb.* a wild ass taught
in. 2:28 **towns:** *or* blood-spattered altars.
2:31 **Have . . . Israel:** *prob. rdg; Heb.* prefixes You, O
generation, see the word of the LORD. 2:33 **even
. . . from you:** *or* even at wantonness you have made
yourself expert. 2:34 **I shall punish you:** *poss. mng;
Heb. obscure.* 2:37 **those on whom:** *or* the things on
which. 3:1 **If a man:** *so Gk; Heb.* prefixes Saying.
woman: *so Gk; Heb.* land.

in Isa. 5.1–7. **23:** *Baalim:* the gods of the Canaanites. *The valley:* its name was Ben-hinnom; see 7.31. **27:**
Block of wood . . . a stone: idols. **30:** *In vain I punished your people:* brought defeat to your armies. *The lesson
that I was displeased was not learned;* see 3.3 n. *Your prophets,* e.g. Uriah (26.20–23). **34:** *The life-blood of
the innocent poor:* see 5.28. Social injustice too is infidelity. **36:** *Egypt . . . Assyria:* see vv. 16 and 18. **37:** *Your
hands on your heads:* disgraced; see 2 Sam. 13.19. *Those on whom you rely:* possibly Egypt; see 37.7.

3.1–10: A persistently inconstant people. Jeremiah condemns Judah, the wife faithless to God. **1:** A twice
divorced woman may not remarry her first husband; see Deut. 24.1–4. **3:** *Showers were withheld* but this

and the spring rain failed.
But yours was a prostitute's brazenness,
and you were resolved to show no
    shame.
⁴Not so long since you called me 'Father,
teacher of my youth',
⁵thinking, 'Will he keep up his anger for
    ever?
Will he rage to the end?'
This is how you spoke, but you have
    done evil
and gone unchallenged.

⁶In the reign of King Josiah the LORD said to
me: Do you see what apostate Israel has
done, how she went to every hilltop and under every spreading tree, and there committed adultery? ⁷Even after she had done all
this I thought she would come back to me,
but she did not. That faithless woman, her
sister Judah, saw it; ⁸she saw too that I had
put apostate Israel away and given her a certificate of divorce because she had committed
adultery. Yet that faithless woman, her sister
Judah, was not afraid; she too went and committed adultery. ⁹She defiled the land with
her casual prostitution and her adulterous
worship of stone and wood. ¹⁰In spite of all
this Judah, that faithless woman, has not
come back to me in sincerity, but only in
pretence. This is the word of the LORD.
¹¹The LORD said to me: Apostate Israel is less
to blame than that faithless woman Judah.
¹²Go and proclaim this message towards
the north:

Come back, apostate Israel,
says the LORD;
I shall no longer frown on you.
For my love is unfailing, says the LORD;
I shall not keep up my anger for ever.
¹³Only acknowledge your wrongdoing,
your rebellion against the LORD your
    God,
your promiscuous traffic with foreign
    gods
under every spreading tree,

and your disobedience to my
    commands.
This is the word of the LORD.

¹⁴Come back, apostate people, says the LORD,
for I am patient with you, and I shall take
you, one from each city and two from each
clan, and bring you to Zion. ¹⁵There I shall
give you shepherds after my own heart, and
they will lead you with knowledge and understanding. ¹⁶In those days, when you have
increased and become fruitful in the land,
says the LORD, no one will speak any more of
the Ark of the Covenant of the LORD; no one
will think of it or remember it or resort to it;
that will be done no more. ¹⁷At that time
Jerusalem will be called the Throne of the
LORD, and all nations will gather in Jerusalem to honour the LORD's name; never again
will they follow the promptings of their evil
and stubborn hearts. ¹⁸In those days Judah
will be united with Israel, and together they
will come from a northern land into the land
I gave their fathers as their holding.

¹⁹I said: How gladly would I treat you as
    a son,
giving you a pleasant land,
a holding fairer than that of any
    nation!
You would call me 'Father', I thought,
and never cease to follow me.
²⁰But like a woman who through illicit
    love has been unfaithful,
so you, Israel, were unfaithful to me.
This is the word of the LORD.

²¹Weeping is heard on the bare places,
Israel's people pleading for mercy,
because they have taken to crooked
    ways
and ignored the LORD their God.
²²Come back, you apostate people;
I shall heal your apostasy.

3:3 **brazenness:** *Heb.* brow.   3:8 **she saw:** *so one
MS; others* I saw.   3:18 **their fathers:** *so Gk; Heb.*
your fathers.

proved ineffective as discipline (see Amos 4.7–8). **6:** *The reign of King Josiah:* 640–609 B.C.E., in Jeremiah's
earlier period. **7–9:** *Judah saw that I had* delivered *Israel* over to the armies of Assyria (2 Kgs. 18.9–12) but
did not learn from that early example. **10:** *Has . . . come back . . . but only in pretence:* this may refer to the
reformation under Josiah in 621 B.C.E. (2 Kgs. 22.8–23.25); if so, the reformation is judged as halfhearted.
    3.11–4.2: An invitation to return, coupled with gleaming messianic promise. 11: *Apostate Israel is less to
blame:* the Northern Kingdom had no such earlier example to learn from (vv. 7–9 n.). **12:** *Towards the north:*
in the Assyrian captivity, Israel still survives as the ten tribes. (Later these were deemed "lost.") **22–25:** Jeremiah

Here we are coming to you,
for you are the LORD our God.

²³ There is no help in worship on the
hilltops,
no help from clamour on the heights;
truly in the LORD our God
lies Israel's salvation.

²⁴ From our early days
Baal has devoured
the fruits of our fathers' labours,
their flocks and herds, their sons and
daughters.

²⁵ Let us lie down in our shame, covered
by dishonour,
for we have sinned against the LORD
our God,
both we and our fathers,
from our early days even till now,
and we have not obeyed the LORD our
God.

4 Israel, if you will come back,
if you will come back to me, says the
LORD,
if you will banish your loathsome idols
from my sight,
and go astray no more,
² if you swear 'by the life of the LORD'
in truth, justice, and uprightness,
then the nations will pray to be blessed
like you
and in you they will boast.

³ These are the words of the LORD to the
people of Judah and Jerusalem:

Break up your ground that lies
unploughed,
do not sow among thorns;
⁴ circumcise yourselves to the service of
the LORD,
circumcise your hearts,
you people of Judah, you dwellers in
Jerusalem,
or the fire of my fury may blaze up
and burn unquenched,

because of your evil actions.

⁵ Declare this in Judah,
proclaim it in Jerusalem.
Blow the trumpet throughout the land.
Shout aloud the command: 'Assemble!
Let us move back to the fortified
towns.'
⁶ Raise the signal — to Zion!
Make for safety without delay,
for I am about to bring disaster out of
the north
and dire destruction.

⁷ A lion has risen from his lair,
the destroyer of nations;
he has broken camp and marched out
to devastate your land
and make your cities waste and empty.
⁸ Therefore put on sackcloth,
beat the breast and wail,
for the fierce anger of the LORD
is not averted from us.

⁹ On that day, says the LORD,
the courage of the king and his officers
will fail,
priests will be aghast and prophets
appalled.

¹⁰ I said: Ah, Lord GOD, you surely deceived
this people and Jerusalem in promising
peace while the sword is at our throats.

¹¹ At that time this people and Jerusalem
will be told:

A scorching wind from the desert
heights
sweeps down on my people;
it is no breeze for winnowing or for
cleansing.
¹² A wind too strong for these
will come at my bidding,
and now I shall state my case against
my people.

4:2 **like you and in you:** *prob. rdg; Heb.* like him and
in him.

---

imagines the response he desires. **22:** *Come back:* reconciliation was still possible.

4.3–4: The peril of stubborn disobedience. Ancient psychology located the emotions in the lower viscera,
and the mind in the heart; "uncircumcised heart" means a stubbornly closed mind. Jeremiah pleads for open
minds. The thought of v. 4 is repeated with a different symbol in v. 14.

4.5–31: More about the devastating foe from the north. See 1.13–16. Mostly the prophet speaks for God,
but in v. 13 (end), in vv. 19–21, and in v. 31 (end), he puts the words of anguished lamentation into the mouths
of his people, while in v. 10 and vv. 23–26 he breaks in with his own exclamations of dismay. **6:** God is the
self-declared moving force behind the invading armies. **9:** *Prophets:* these claim, like Jeremiah, to speak for

13 Like clouds the enemy advances,
like a whirlwind with his chariots;
his horses are swifter than eagles:
'Woe to us, for we are lost!'
14 Jerusalem, cleanse the wrongdoing
from your heart
and you may yet be saved.
How long will you harbour within you
your evil schemes?
15 News comes from Dan,
evil tidings from Mount Ephraim.
16 Tell this to the nations,
proclaim the doom of Jerusalem:
hordes of invaders are on the way from
a distant land,
giving voice against the cities of Judah.
17 As a field surrounded by guards
she is encircled by them,
because she has rebelled against me.
This is the word of the LORD.
18 Your own ways and deeds
have brought these things on you;
this is your punishment,
for your rebellion is seated deep within
you.

19 Oh, how I writhe in anguish,
how my heart throbs!
I cannot keep silence,
for I hear the sound of the trumpet,
the clamour of the battle cry.
20 Crash follows crash,
for the whole land goes down in ruin.
Suddenly my tents are thrown down,
the curtains in an instant.
21 How long must I see the standard
raised
and hear the trumpet-call?
22 My people are foolish, they know
nothing of me;
senseless children, lacking all
understanding,
clever only in wrongdoing,
but of doing right they know nothing.

23 I looked at the earth, and it was chaos,
at the heavens, and their light was
gone,

24 at the mountains, and they were reeling,
and all the hills rocked to and fro.
25 I looked: no one was there,
and all the birds of heaven had taken
wing.
26 I looked: the fertile land was
wilderness,
its towns all razed to the ground
before the LORD, before his fierce
anger.
27 These are the words of the LORD:
The whole land will be desolate,
and I shall make an end of it.
28 The earth will be in mourning for this
and the heavens above turn black;
for I have made known my purpose,
and I shall not relent or change it.

29 At the sound of the horsemen and
archers
every town is in flight;
people crawl into the thickets,
scramble up among the crags.
Every town is deserted,
no one lives there.

30 And you, what are you doing?
When you dress yourself in scarlet,
deck yourself out with gold ornaments,
and enlarge your eyes with antimony,
you are beautifying yourself to no
purpose.
Your lovers spurn you
and seek your life.
31 I hear a sound as of a woman in
labour,
the sharp cry of one bearing her first
child.
It is Zion, gasping for breath,
stretching out her hands.
'Ah me!' she cries. 'I am weary,
weary of slaughter.'

5 Go up and down the streets of
Jerusalem,

4:18 **your rebellion:** *prob. rdg; Heb. obscure.*   4:27 **I
shall:** *prob. rdg; Heb. adds* not.   4:30 **And you:** *so Gk;
Heb. adds* overwhelmed.

God, but, unlike Jeremiah, come promising peace (v. 10). **14:** *Heart:* see vv. 3–4 n. **15:** *Dan . . . Mount
Ephraim:* places north of Jerusalem, the first to fall to the invader. **22:** *My people:* after the imagined lamentation
Jeremiah speaks again as if for God; in vv. 23–26, the prophet puts his vision of the event in apocalyptic terms,
depicting a catastrophe whereby all becomes *chaos* as things were before creation. **27–28:** Here again appear
the words of the LORD, followed in v. 29 with another reference to the invader. **30:** *To no purpose:* flirtation
with prospective military allies (*your lovers*) will not avail.

see, take note;
search through her wide squares:
can you find anyone who acts justly,
anyone who seeks the truth,
that I may forgive that city?
² People may swear by the life of the
    LORD,
but in fact they perjure themselves.
³ LORD, are your eyes not set upon the
    truth?
You punished them,
but they took no heed;
you pierced them to the heart,
but they refused to learn.
They made their faces harder than
    flint;
they refused to repent.
⁴ I said, 'After all, these are the poor,
these are folk without understanding,
who do not know the way of the LORD,
the ordinances of their God.
⁵ I shall go to the great ones
and speak with them;
for they will know the way of the LORD,
the ordinances of their God.'
But they too have broken the yoke
and snapped their traces.
⁶ So a lion out of the scrub will strike
    them down,
a wolf from the plains will savage them;
a leopard will prowl about their towns
and maul any who venture out,
for their rebellious deeds are many,
their apostasies past counting.

⁷ How can I forgive you for all this?
Your children have forsaken me,
swearing by gods that are no gods.
I gave them all they needed,
yet they committed adultery
and frequented brothels;
⁸ each neighs after another man's wife,
like a well-fed and lusty stallion.
⁹ Shall I fail to punish them for this,
says the LORD,
shall I not exact vengeance on such a
    people?

¹⁰ Go along her rows of vines; destroy
    them,
make an end of them.
Lop off her green branches,
for they are not the LORD's.
¹¹ Faithless are Israel and Judah,
both faithless to me.
This is the word of the LORD.
¹² They have denied the LORD,
saying, 'He does not matter.
No harm will come to us;
we shall see neither sword nor famine.
¹³ The prophets will prove mere wind;
the word is not in them.'

¹⁴ Therefore, because they talk in this way,
these are the words of the LORD the God of
Hosts to me:

I shall make my words a fire in your
    mouth,
and it will burn up this people like
    brushwood.

¹⁵ Israel, I am bringing against you a
    distant nation,
an ancient people established long ago,
says the LORD,
a people whose language you do not
    know,
whose speech you will not understand;
¹⁶ they are all mighty warriors,
their jaws are a grave, wide open,
¹⁷ to devour your harvest and your food,
to devour your sons and your
    daughters,
to devour your flocks and your herds,
to devour your vines and your fig trees.
They will beat down with the sword
the walled cities in which you trust.

¹⁸ But in those days, the LORD declares, I shall

5:7 **frequented:** *so some MSS; others* gashed themselves
in.   5:10 **make:** *prob. rdg; Heb.* prefixes do not.
5:13 **in them:** *prob. rdg; Heb. adds* So may it be done to
them.   5:14 **they:** *prob. rdg; Heb.* you.   5:16 **their
jaws are:** *so Syriac; Heb.* their quiver is.

5.1–31: Deserved calamities. The people are at fault. **1:** The merit of even a few who act justly would enable
God to *forgive* Jerusalem; compare Gen. 18.28, 32. **3:** *Refused to learn:* disciplinary punishment had gone
unheeded (see 2.30 n.). **10:** *Go:* here and in v. 14 God seems to be making Jeremiah an executioner on God's
behalf. The *vines* are figurative; see 2.21 n. **11:** *Israel and Judah:* both kingdoms are mentioned, though Israel
has already long been in captivity. **12–13:** A challenge and a retort. *He does not matter* is to be understood
as denying the authenticity of the prophet's threatening *word.* Atheism in the Bible is largely a denial of divine
activity, not of God's existence. **14:** *To me:* to the prophet. *Fire in your mouth:* see v. 10 n. **15:** *Distant nation:*

not make an end of you. ¹⁹When it is asked, 'Why has the LORD our God done all this to us?' you are to answer, 'As you have forsaken the LORD and served alien gods in your own land, so you will serve foreigners in a land that is not your own.'

²⁰Announce this to the people of Jacob,
proclaim it in Judah:
²¹Listen, you foolish and senseless
people,
who have eyes and see nothing,
ears and hear nothing.
²²Have you no fear of me, says the LORD,
will you not tremble before me,
who set the sand as bounds for the sea,
a limit it never can pass?
Its waves may heave and toss, but they
are powerless;
roar as they may, they cannot pass.
²³But this people has a rebellious and
defiant heart;
they have rebelled and gone their own
way.
²⁴They did not say to themselves,
'Let us fear the LORD our God,
who gives the rains of autumn
and spring showers in their turn,
who brings us unfailingly
fixed harvest seasons.'
²⁵But your wrongdoing has upset
nature's order,
and your sins have kept away her
bounty.

²⁶For among my people there are
scoundrels
who, like fowlers, lay snares and set
deadly traps;
they prey on their fellows.
²⁷Their houses are full of fraud,
as a cage is full of birds.
They grow great and rich,
²⁸sleek and bloated;
they turn a blind eye to wickedness
and refuse to do justice;

the claims of the fatherless they do not
uphold,
nor do they defend the poor at law.
²⁹Shall I fail to punish them for this,
says the LORD;
shall I not exact vengeance
on such a people?

³⁰An appalling thing, an outrage,
has appeared in this land:
³¹prophets prophesy lies
and priests are in league with them,
and my people love to have it so!
How will you fare at the end of it all?

6 People of Benjamin, save yourselves,
flee from Jerusalem;
sound the trumpet in Tekoa,
light the beacon on Beth-hakkerem,
for calamity looms from the north
and great disaster.
²Zion, delightful and lovely,
her end is near —
³she against whom the shepherds will
come,
they and their flocks with them.
They will pitch their tents all around
her,
each grazing his own strip of pasture:
⁴'Prepare for battle against her;
come, let us attack her at noon.'
'Too late! The day declines
and the shadows lengthen.'
⁵'Come then, let us attack by night
and destroy her palaces.'

⁶These are the words of the LORD of
Hosts:
Cut down the trees of Jerusalem
and cast up siege-ramps against her,
a city ripe for punishment;
oppression is rampant within her.
⁷As a well keeps its water fresh,

5:19 **foreigners:** *or* foreign gods.   5:26 **who . . . snares:** *prob. rdg; Heb. unintelligible.*   5:31 **lies:** *or by a false god.*

---

see 1.15 n. **18:** *Shall not make an end:* Some regard this as a comforting addition. **21–23:** *See nothing . . . hear nothing . . . rebellious and defiant heart.* They are a people ignorant of the LORD of creation and willfully obtuse; see vv. 30–31 and 4.3–4 n. **27:** *Full of fraud:* full of possessions obtained by fraud. **29:** A refrain, see v. 9. **30–31:** These verses resume the thought of vv. 21–23. A similar theme is found in 6.13–15.

6.1–30: Calamity is near. 1: Jerusalem is no refuge for the tribe of Benjamin, and when Zion (Jerusalem) falls, *Tekoa* and *Beth-hakkerem* to the south will be exposed to attack. **3:** *Shepherds . . . their flocks:* used ironically for the hostile kings with their armies. **4–5:** These words are placed in the mouths of these "shepherds." **6–8:** *Oppression . . . wickedness . . . violence and outrage* will bring on the city's fate, unless

so she keeps fresh her wickedness.
Violence and outrage echo in her
   streets;
sickness and wounds ever confront me.
[8] Learn your lesson, Jerusalem,
   or I shall be estranged from you,
   and leave you devastated,
   a land without inhabitants.

[9] These are the words of the LORD of
   Hosts:
Glean like a vine the remnant of Israel;
   one last time, like a vintager,
   pass your hand over the branches.
[10] To whom shall I speak,
   to whom give warning? Who will hear
      me?
Their ears are blocked:
   they are incapable of listening;
   they treat the LORD's word as a
      reproach;
   it has no appeal for them.
[11] But I am full of the anger of the LORD,
   I cannot hold it back.
I must pour it out on the children in
   the street,
on the young men in their gatherings.
Man and wife alike will be caught in it,
   the ageing and the aged.
[12] Their houses will be turned over to
   others,
fields and women together,
because, says the LORD, I shall raise my
   hand
against the inhabitants of the land.
[13] For all, high and low,
   are out for ill-gotten gain;
prophets and priests are frauds,
   every one of them;
[14] they dress my people's wound,
   but on the surface only,
with their saying, 'All is well.'
All well? Nothing is well!
[15] They ought to be ashamed
because they practised abominations;
   yet they have no sense of shame,

they could never be put out of
   countenance.
Therefore they will fall with a great
   crash,
and be brought to the ground on the
   day of my reckoning.
The LORD has said it.

[16] These are the words of the LORD: Take
your stand and watch at the crossroads; enquire about the ancient paths; ask which is
the way that leads to what is good. Take that
way, and you will find rest for yourselves. But
they said, 'We refuse.' [17] I appointed watchmen to direct them. 'Listen for the trumpet-
call,' I used to say. But they said, 'We refuse.'
[18] Therefore hear, you nations, and all who
witness it take note of the plight of this people. [19] Let the earth listen: I am about to bring
ruin on them, the fruit of all their scheming; for they have given no heed to my words
and have spurned my instruction. [20] What
good is it to me if frankincense is brought
from Sheba and fragrant cane from a distant
land? Your whole-offerings are not acceptable to me, your sacrifices do not please me.
[21] Therefore these are the words of the LORD:

I shall set obstacles before this people
   which will bring them to the ground;
fathers and sons, friends and
   neighbours
will all perish together.

[22] These are the words of the LORD:

See, an army is coming from a
   northern land,
a great nation rouses itself from earth's
   farthest corners.
[23] Armed with bow and scimitar, they are
   cruel and pitiless;

6:9 **Glean:** *prob. rdg, cp. Gk; Heb.* Let them glean.
6:10 **blocked:** *lit.* uncircumcised.   6:15 **with a great
crash:** *or* among the fallen.   6:17 **them:** *so some
MSS; others* you.

she heeds the *lesson;* see 2.30 n. **10–12:** The prophet has no choice but to speak, while his people, unconcerned, cover their ears. **10:** *Their ears are blocked:* lit. "uncircumcised"; see 4.4. **11:** The prophet's *anger* is
a part of God's anger, and beyond the prophet's control; it spills over, causing havoc. **13–15:** *Prophets and
priests are frauds:* the thought of 5.31 is more fully developed here; see 5.30–31 n. **16–21:** The fate of an
unheeding people, for God asks obedience more than incense and offerings. Israel spurns God's *instruction*
(v. 19) and will perish. **16:** *Ancient paths:* Jeremiah does not claim to be proposing a new doctrine. *Find rest:*
he shares the common human yearning for security. **17:** *Watchmen:* prophets. **20:** *Sheba* was in Arabia. **22–26:**
Another dramatic projection of the northern foe (see 1.13–16; 4.5–31); vv. 24 and 25 are exclamations of the

bestriding their horses, they sound like
the thunder of the sea;
they are like men arrayed for battle
against you, Zion.
24 News of them has reached us
and our hands hang limp;
agony grips us, pangs as of a woman in
labour.
25 Do not go out into the country,
do not walk by the high road;
for the foe, sword in hand,
spreads terror all around.
26 Daughter of my people, wrap yourself
in sackcloth,
sprinkle ashes over yourself,
wail bitterly as one who mourns an only
son;
for in an instant the despoiler will be
upon us.

27 I have appointed you an assayer and
tester of my people;
you will know how to assay their
conduct:
28 arch-rebels all of them,
mischief-makers, corrupt to a man.
29 The bellows blow, the fire is ready;
lead, copper, and iron—in vain the
refiner refines;
the impurities are not removed.
30 Call them reject silver,
for the LORD has rejected them.

False religion and its punishment

7 THIS word came from the LORD to Jeremiah. 2 Stand at the gate of the LORD's
house and there make this proclamation:
Hear the word of the LORD, all you of Judah
who come in through these gates to worship
him. 3 These are the words of the LORD of
Hosts the God of Israel: Amend your ways

and your deeds, that I may let you live in this
place. 4 You keep saying, 'This place is the
temple of the LORD, the temple of the LORD,
the temple of the LORD!' This slogan of yours
is a lie; put no trust in it. 5 If you amend your
ways and your deeds, deal fairly with one
another, 6 cease to oppress the alien, the fatherless, and the widow, if you shed no innocent blood in this place and do not run after
other gods to your own ruin, 7 then I shall let
you live in this place, in the land which long
ago I gave to your forefathers for all time.

8 You gain nothing by putting your trust in
this lie. 9 You steal, you murder, you commit
adultery and perjury, you burn sacrifices to
Baal, and you run after other gods whom you
have not known; 10 will you then come and
stand before me in this house which bears my
name, and say, 'We are safe'? Safe, you think,
to indulge in all these abominations! 11 Do
you regard this house which bears my name
as a bandits' cave? I warn you, I myself have
seen all this, says the LORD.

12 Go to my shrine at Shiloh, which once I
made a dwelling for my name, and see what
I did to it because of the wickedness of my
people Israel. 13 Now you have done all these
things, says the LORD; though I spoke to you
again and again, you did not listen, and
though I called, you did not respond.
14 Therefore what I did to Shiloh I shall do to
this house which bears my name, the house
in which you put your trust, the place I gave
to you and your forefathers; 15 I shall fling
you away out of my presence, as I did with all
your kinsfolk, all Ephraim's offspring.

16 Offer up no prayer for this people, Jeremiah, raise no plea or prayer on their behalf,
and do not intercede with me, for I shall not
listen to you. 17 Do you not see what they are
doing in the towns of Judah and in the streets

6:29 **copper, and iron:** *transposed from after*
mischief-makers *in verse 28.*

---

dismayed Judeans. **27–30:** God speaks to Jeremiah. The prophet, like an *assayer*, tests his people, and finds
them to be utterly lacking in value.

7.1–10.25: False religion and its punishment.

7.1–8.3: The temple sermon (vv. 1–15), with supplements. To the Judeans assembled for worship at the
Jerusalem temple Jeremiah brings the alarming message that their confidence is misplaced, for God rejects their
worship and will reduce the temple and their land to ruins. The thought is expanded in vv. 21–28, 29–34,
and 8.1–3. **2:** *The LORD's house:* the Jerusalem temple. **3:** *Amend your ways . . . that I may:* God appeals for
repentance. **9–10:** The people break half of the Ten Commandments, and yet say, "We are safe," because they
are in the sanctuary. **12:** *Shiloh:* an earlier sanctuary. It was probably destroyed by the Philistines after the battle
of Eben-ezer (1 Sam. ch. 4). **15:** *Ephraim:* the Northern Kingdom, Israel (compare 2 Kgs. 18.9–12), of which
Ephraim was the leading tribe. **16:** *Offer up no prayer* (see 14.11) suggests that Jeremiah would have done so

of Jerusalem? [18]Children are gathering wood, fathers lighting the fire, women kneading dough to make crescent-cakes in honour of the queen of heaven; and drink-offerings are poured out to other gods—all to grieve me. [19]But is it I, says the LORD, whom they grieve? No; it is themselves, to their own confusion. [20]Therefore, says the Lord GOD, my anger and my fury will pour out on this place, on man and beast, on trees and crops, and it will burn unquenched.

[21]These are the words of the LORD of Hosts the God of Israel: Add your whole-offerings to your sacrifices and eat the flesh yourselves. [22]For when I brought your forefathers out of Egypt, I gave them no instructions or commands about whole-offering or sacrifice. [23]What I did command them was this: Obey me, and I shall be your God and you will be my people. You must conform to all my commands, if you are to prosper.

[24]But they did not listen; they paid no heed, and persisted in their own plans with evil and stubborn hearts; they turned their backs and not their faces to me, [25]from the day when your forefathers left Egypt until now. Again and again I sent to them all my servants the prophets; [26]but instead of listening and paying heed to me, they in their stubbornness proved even more wicked than their forefathers. [27]Tell them all this, but they will not listen to you; call them, but they will not respond. [28]Then say to them: This is the nation who did not obey the LORD their God or accept correction. Truth has perished; it is heard no more on their lips.

[29]Jerusalem, cut off your hair and throw
      it away;
  raise a lament on the bare heights.
  For the LORD has spurned and forsaken
  the generation that roused his wrath.

[30]The people of Judah have done what is wrong in my eyes, says the LORD. They set up their loathsome idols in the house which bears my name and so defiled it; [31]they have built shrines of Topheth in the valley of Ben-hinnom, at which to burn their sons and daughters. That was no command of mine; indeed it never entered my mind.

[32]Therefore the time is coming, says the LORD, when it will no longer be called Topheth or the valley of Ben-hinnom, but the valley of Slaughter; for the dead will be buried in Topheth until there is no room left. [33]So the corpses of this people will become food for the birds of the air and the wild beasts, with none to scare them away. [34]From the towns of Judah and the streets of Jerusalem I shall banish all sounds of joy and gladness, the voices of bridegroom and bride; for the whole land will become desert.

8 At that time, says the LORD, the bones of the kings of Judah, of the officers, priests, and prophets, and of all who have lived in Jerusalem, will be brought out from their graves. [2]They will be exposed to the sun, the moon, and all the host of heaven, which they loved and served and adored, from which they sought guidance and to which they bowed in worship. Those bones will not be gathered up and reburied; they will be dung spread over the ground. [3]All the survivors of this wicked race, wherever I have banished them, would rather die than live. This is the word of the LORD of Hosts.

[4]You are to say to them: These are the words of the LORD.

  Does someone fall and not get up,
    or default and not return?
  [5]Then why are this people so wayward,
    incurable in their waywardness?
  Why have they persisted in their
      treachery
  and refused to return?

7:25 **them:** *so one MS; others* you.   8:3 **them:** *so one MS; others add* those who are left.   8:5 **this people:** *so Gk; Heb. adds* Jerusalem.

if it were not prohibited, and that God would have found it hard to refuse him (see 15.1–2 n.). **17–18, 30–31:** These verses enlarge on the offensive acts listed briefly in v. 9, of running "after other gods." **18:** *Queen of heaven* was an astral deity variously identified as Ishtar, Venus, or some other love goddess of the ancient Near East. See also 44.17–19 and 32.29. **22:** *No commands about . . . sacrifice:* Jeremiah seems to reflect a tradition at direct variance with much of the Pentateuch. **23:** *I will be your God . . . you . . . my people;* the covenant arrangement is contingent, not on the temple cult, but on obedience to such ethical demands as those in vv. 5 and 6. **29:** *Cut off your hair:* a sign of mourning. **30–31:** *The house:* the temple. *Topheth in the Valley of Ben-hinnom* was outside the south wall of Jerusalem. **7.33–8.3:** For those long dead to lie unburied constituted a grave indignity to the person and a defilement of the land (see 22.19).

6 I have listened to them
and heard not one word of truth,
not one sinner crying remorsefully,
'What have I done?'
Each one breaks away in headlong
    career
as a war-horse plunges into battle.
7 The stork in the heavens
knows the time to migrate,
the dove and the swift and the wryneck
know the season of return;
but my people do not know
the ordinances of the LORD.
8 How can you say, 'We are wise,
we have the law of the LORD,'
when scribes with their lying pens
have falsified it?
9 The wise are put to shame;
they are dismayed and entrapped.
They have spurned the word of the
    LORD,
so what sort of wisdom is theirs?
10 Therefore I shall give their wives to
    other men
and their lands to new owners.
For all, high and low,
are out for ill-gotten gain;
prophets and priests are frauds,
every one of them;
11 they dress my people's wound,
but on the surface only,
with their saying, 'All is well.'
All well? Nothing is well!
12 They ought to be ashamed
because they have practised
    abominations,
yet they have no sense of shame,
they could never be put out of
    countenance.
Therefore they will fall with a great
    crash,
and be brought to the ground on the
    day of reckoning.
The LORD has said it.
13 I shall gather them all in, says the
    LORD;

there will be no grapes on the vine,
no figs on the fig tree;
even the foliage will be withered.
14 Why do we sit idle? Assemble!
Let us move to the fortified towns
and there meet our doom,
since the LORD our God has doomed
    us,
giving us a draught of bitter poison,
for we have sinned against him.
15 We hoped to prosper, but nothing went
    well;
we hoped for respite, but terror struck.
16 The snorting of their horses is heard
    from Dan;
at the neighing of their stallions the
    whole land trembles.
The enemy come; they devour the land
    and all its store,
city and citizens alike.
17 I am sending snakes against you,
vipers such as no one can charm,
and they will bite you.
This is the word of the LORD.
18 There is no cure for my grief;
I am sick at heart.
19 Hear my people's cry of distress
from a distant land:
'Is the LORD not in Zion?
Is her King no longer there?'
Why do they provoke me with their
    images
and with their futile foreign gods?
20 Harvest is past, summer is over,
and we are not saved.
21 I am wounded by my people's wound;
I go about in mourning, overcome with
    horror.
22 Is there no balm in Gilead,
no physician there?

8:12 **with a great crash:** *or* among the fallen.
8:13 **withered:** *so Gk; Heb. adds* so I have allowed men
to pass them by.   8:18 **There . . . grief:** *prob. rdg;
Heb. unintelligible.*

8.4–13: Unnatural conduct and its consequence. 8–9: They allow themselves to be misled by *scribes with
. . . lying pens:* a possible disparaging reference to Josiah's reform; see 3.10 n. **10–12:** These verses repeat
6.12–15 almost verbatim.

8.14–17: Consternation at the destroyer's approach. The people, or some among them, are speaking in
vv. 14–16; God speaks in v. 17. **16:** *Dan* was in the north, at the headwaters of the Jordan. **17:** *Vipers:* figurative
for irretrievable disaster.

8.18–9.1: An elegy. Jeremiah envisions his people in captivity and laments. God interrupts the captives'
dismayed exclamation with a challenge: *Why do they provoke me? 22: Is there no balm in Gilead?* This was

Why has no new skin grown over their wound?

9 Would that my head were a spring of water,
my eyes a fountain of tears,
that I might weep day and night
for the slain of my people.

2 Would that I had in the wilderness a wayside shelter,
that I might leave my people and go away!
They are all adulterers, a faithless mob.
3 The tongue is their weapon,
a bow ready bent.
Lying, not truth, holds sway in the land.
They proceed from one wrong to another
and care nothing for me.
This is the word of the LORD.

4 Be on your guard, each against his friend;
put no trust even in a brother.
Brother supplants brother as Jacob did,
and friend slanders friend.
5 They deceive their friends
and never speak the truth;
they have trained their tongues to lying;
deep in sin, they weary themselves going astray.
6 Wrong follows wrong, deceit follows deceit;
they refuse to acknowledge me.
This is the word of the LORD.
7 Therefore these are the words of the LORD of Hosts:
I shall refine and assay them.
How else should I deal with my people?
8 Their tongues are deadly arrows,
their mouths speak lies.
One person talks amicably to another,
while inwardly planning a trap.

9 Shall I fail to punish them for this,
says the LORD,
shall I not exact vengeance
on such a people?

10 Over the mountains I shall raise
weeping and wailing,
and over the open pastures I shall chant a dirge.
They are scorched and untrodden,
they hear no lowing of cattle;
birds of the air and beasts have fled
and are gone.
11 I shall make Jerusalem a heap of ruins,
a haunt of wolves,
and the towns of Judah waste, without inhabitants.

12 Who is wise enough to understand this, and who has the LORD's command to proclaim it? Why has the land become a dead land, scorched like the desert and untrodden? 13 The LORD said: It is because they rejected my law which I set before them; they neither obeyed me nor followed it. 14 They followed the promptings of their own stubborn hearts and followed the baalim as their forefathers had taught them. 15 Therefore these are the words of the LORD of Hosts the God of Israel: I shall give this people wormwood to eat and bitter poison to drink. 16 I shall disperse them among nations whom neither they nor their forefathers have known; I shall harry them with the sword until I have made an end of them.

17 These are the words of the LORD of Hosts:

Summon the wailing women to come,
send for the women skilled in keening
18 to come quickly and raise a lament for us,

9:1 *In Heb. 8:23.*   9:2 *In Heb. 9:1.*   9:3 **not truth, holds sway:** *so Gk; Heb.* not for truth, they hold sway.
9:17 **Summon:** *so Gk; Heb. prefixes* Consider and.

---

probably a proverbial expression. Gilead was perhaps a distribution point for the healing balm.

9.2–22: The fate in store for a chaotic society caring nothing for God. Cheating, treachery, slander, and deceit are deeply engrained (vv. 2–6 and 8); *therefore* God will *assay* and *punish* them (vv. 7, 9, 11). **2:** Repelled by his people's corruption, Jeremiah would *find a shelter in the wilderness.* **9:** See 5.29 n. **10:** Jeremiah bemoans the envisioned fate of his people as in 8.21 and 9.1. **13:** *My law:* perhaps an allusion to Deut., which formed the basis of Josiah's reform; see 3.10 n. If so, unlike 3.10 and 8.8, this passage (vv. 12–16) urges compliance with that law. It is often suggested that this and similar passages are a later editor's attempt to make of Jeremiah a supporter of the reform. **14:** *Baalim:* gods (5.19). **15:** *Wormwood:* a bitter drug. **17–21:** A continuation of the lament begun in v. 10. **17:** *Women skilled in keening:* professionally trained for ritual weeping and wailing.

that our eyes may stream with tears
and our eyelids be wet with weeping.
19 The sound of lamenting is heard from
Zion:
'How fearful is our ruin! How great
our shame!
We have left our land, our houses have
been overthrown.'
20 Listen, you women, to the words of the
LORD,
that your ears may catch what he says.
Teach your daughters the lament;
teach your neighbours this dirge:
21 'Death has climbed in through our
windows
and entered our palaces,
cutting off the children in the street
and the young men in the
thoroughfare.'
22 Corpses will fall and lie like dung in the
fields,
like swathes behind the reaper with no
one to gather them.

23 These are the words of the LORD:

Let not the wise boast of their wisdom,
nor the valiant of their valour;
let not the wealthy boast of their
wealth;
24 but if anyone must boast, let him boast
of this:
that he understands and acknowledges
me.
For I am the LORD, I show unfailing
love,
I do justice and right on the earth;
for in these I take pleasure.
This is the word of the LORD.

25 The time is coming, says the LORD, when I
shall punish all the circumcised, 26 Egypt and
Judah and Edom, Ammon and Moab, and all
who live in the fringes of the desert, for all
alike, the nations and Israel, are uncircumcised in heart.

10 Listen, Israel, to these words that the
LORD has spoken against you:

2 Do not fall into the ways of the nations,
do not be terrified by signs in the
heavens.
It is the nations who go in terror of
these.
3 For the carved images of the nations
are a sham;
they are nothing but timber cut from
the forest,
shaped by a craftsman with his chisel
4 and decorated with silver and gold.
They are made fast with hammer and
nails
to keep them from toppling over.
5 They are as dumb as a scarecrow in a
plot of cucumbers;
they have always to be carried,
for they cannot walk.
Do not be afraid of them: they can do
no harm,
nor have they any power to do good.

6 Where can one be found like you,
LORD?
You are great, and great is the might of
your name.
7 Who would not fear you, King of the
nations,
for fear is a fitting tribute for you?
Where among the wisest of the nations
and among all their royalty
can any be found like you?
8 One and all they are stupid and foolish,
learning their nonsense from a piece of
wood.
9 Beaten silver is brought from Tarshish
and gold from Ophir;
they are the work of craftsmen and
goldsmiths;

9:21 **Death:** or Plague. **in the thoroughfare:** so Gk;
Heb. adds (22)Speak, thus the saying of the LORD.
9:26 **who . . . desert:** or the dwellers in the desert who
clip the hair on their temples.   10:9 **Ophir:** so
Syriac; Heb. Uphaz.

19: How fearful . . . overthrown: words attributed to the stricken inhabitants of Zion.
    9.23–26: Closed minds. 23–24: To "know" God is to do as God does (22.16). **25–26:** The thought of 4.3–4,
there applied to Judah alone, is here generalized to include all the willfully obtuse. Egypt . . . Edom, Ammon,
Moab: except for the Philistines, all of Israel's neighbors practiced circumcision, but, like Judah, were also
uncircumcised in heart.
    10.1–16: The folly of idolatry and of other "ways of the nations." This passage is closely related in thought
to the satiric attack on the Babylonian gods and their deluded "witnesses" in Isa. chs. 40–48 (see especially
Isa. 44.9–20). **1–2:** Do not be terrified by signs in the heavens. "Omens" were connected with the prohibited

they are draped in violet and purple,
all made by skilled workers.
¹⁰But the LORD is God in truth,
a living God, an everlasting King.
The earth quakes under his fury;
no nation can endure his wrath.

¹¹You say this of them: The gods who did not
make heaven and earth will perish from the
earth and from under these heavens.

¹²God made the earth by his power,
fixed the world in place by his wisdom,
and by his knowledge unfurled the
skies.
¹³When he speaks in the thunder
the waters in the heavens are in tumult;
he brings up the mist from the ends of
the earth,
he opens rifts for the rain,
and brings the wind out of his
storehouses.
¹⁴Everyone is brutish and ignorant;
every goldsmith is discredited through
his idols;
for the figures he casts are a sham,
there is no breath in them.
¹⁵They are worthless, objects of mockery,
which perish when their day of
reckoning comes.
¹⁶Jacob's chosen God is not like these,
for he is the creator of the universe.
Israel is the people he claims as his
own;
the LORD of Hosts is his name.

¹⁷Gather up your goods and flee the
country,
for you are living under siege.
¹⁸These are the words of the LORD:
This time I shall throw out
the whole population of the land,
and I shall press them and squeeze
them dry.

¹⁹Oh, the pain of my wounds!
The injuries I suffer are cruel.
'I am laid low,' I said, 'and must endure
it.
²⁰My tent is wrecked, my tent-ropes all
severed,
my children have left me and are gone,
there is no one left to pitch my tent
again,
no one to put up its curtains.'
²¹The shepherds of the people are
brutish;
they never consult the LORD,
and so they do not act wisely,
and their entire flock is scattered.

²²Listen, a rumour comes flying,
a great uproar from the land of the
north,
an army to make Judah's cities desolate,
a haunt of wolves.
²³I am aware, LORD,
that no one's ways are of his own
choosing;
nor is it within his power
to determine his course in life.
²⁴Correct me, LORD, but with justice, not
in anger,
or you will bring me almost to nothing.
²⁵Pour out your fury on the nations
that have not acknowledged you,
on tribes that have not invoked you by
name;
for they have devoured Jacob
and made an end of him
and have left his home a waste.

11 THE word which came to Jeremiah
from the LORD: ²Listen to the terms
of this covenant and repeat them to the in-

10:11 *This verse is in Aramaic.*   10:13 **When ...
thunder:** *prob. rdg; Heb. obscure.* **rifts:** *prob. rdg; Heb.
lightnings.*   10:25 **for ... Jacob:** *so some MSS; others
add and they will devour him.*

worship of astral deities. **3–5:** See Isa. 40.18–20; 46.1–7. **9:** *Tarshish ... Ophir:* regions not clearly identifiable,
proverbially a source of precious metals. Tarshish is identified by some as in Spain; Ophir as in India, Arabia,
or Africa. **16:** The climactic point of the passage is made in this verse.

10.17–25: The threat of total captivity, the distress of the victims, and a plea for equity. 17–18: It is
uncertain which of two sieges is meant, the first (597) or the second (587). *This time* suggests the latter. **19–20:**
The heartfelt words *I am laid low, I said, and I must endure it,* seem to be spoken by Jeremiah himself. The
subsequent words of v. 20 are the imagined anguished cry of his collective people, personified as an individual.
Jeremiah had no *children*; see 16.2. The people speak again in v. 24. **21:** *Shepherds:* kings. **25:** *Jacob:* the
collective people. See Ps. 79.6–7 which may be the source of this verse.

11.1–15.9: Warnings and punishment.

habitants of Judah and the citizens of Jerusalem, ³telling them: These are the words of the LORD the God of Israel: A curse on everyone who does not observe the terms of this covenant ⁴which I enjoined on your forefathers when I brought them out of Egypt, from the smelting furnace. I said: If you obey me and do all that I command, you will become my people and I shall become your God. ⁵I shall thus make good the oath I swore to your forefathers, that I would give them a land flowing with milk and honey, the land you now possess.

I answered, 'Amen, LORD.'

⁶Then the LORD said: Proclaim these terms throughout the towns of Judah and in the streets of Jerusalem. Say: Listen to the terms of this covenant and carry them out. ⁷I gave solemn warning to your forefathers, from the time when I brought them out of Egypt till this day; I was at pains to warn them: Obey me, I said. ⁸But they did not obey; they paid no attention to me, and each followed the promptings of his own stubborn and wicked heart. So I brought on them all the penalties laid down in this covenant which I had enjoined upon them, but whose terms they did not observe.

⁹The LORD said to me: The inhabitants of Judah and the citizens of Jerusalem have entered into a conspiracy: ¹⁰they have gone back to the sins of their earliest forefathers and refused to listen to me. They have followed other gods and served them; Israel and Judah have broken the covenant which I made with their forefathers. ¹¹Therefore these are the words of the LORD: I am about to bring on them a disaster from which they cannot escape. They may cry to me for help, but I shall not listen. ¹²The inhabitants of the towns of Judah and of Jerusalem may go and cry for help to the gods to whom they have burnt sacrifices, but assuredly they will not save them in the hour of disaster. ¹³For you,

Judah, have as many gods as you have towns; you have set up as many altars to burn sacrifices to Baal as there are streets in Jerusalem. ¹⁴So, Jeremiah, offer up no prayer for this people; raise no plea or prayer on their behalf, for I shall not listen when they call to me in the hour of their disaster.

¹⁵What right has my beloved in my house
  with her shameless ways?
Can the flesh of fat offerings on the
  altar
ward off the disaster that threatens
  you?
Now you will feel sharp anguish.
¹⁶Once the LORD called you an olive tree,
  leafy and fair;
with a great roaring noise
he has set it on fire
and its branches are consumed.

¹⁷The LORD of Hosts who planted you has threatened you with disaster, because of the evil which Israel and Judah have done, provoking him to anger by burning sacrifices to Baal.

¹⁸It was the LORD who showed me, and so I knew; he opened my eyes to what they were doing. ¹⁹I had been like a pet lamb led trustingly to the slaughter; I did not realize they were hatching plots against me and saying, 'Let us destroy the tree while the sap is in it; let us cut him off from the land of the living, so that his name will be wholly forgotten.'

²⁰LORD of Hosts, most righteous judge,
  testing the heart and mind,
to you I have committed my cause;
let me see your vengeance on them.

²¹Therefore these are the words of the LORD

11:13 **altars**: *so Gk; Heb. adds* altars to the shameful thing.   11:15 **fat offerings**: *so Old Latin; Heb.* the many.   11:16 **fair**: *so Gk; Heb. adds* the fruit of.

11.1–17: The penalty of a breach of faith. Some scholars deny this section to Jeremiah because of its conventional style and substance. **3:** The terms of a covenant include the penalty (*curse*) which the party incurs who fails to meet the agreed-upon obligations. **5:** *Amen:* Heb. for "so be it." **8:** *All the penalties:* the "curse" in v. 3. **9:** *The inhabitants of Judah:* your own generation. **11–14:** *I shall not listen . . . offer up no prayer:* see 7.16 n. **15–16:** A metaphor of irrevocable doom. The offerings brought to the temple will not avail, for Judah, the choice *olive tree,* is to be utterly consumed.

11.18–12.6: A prayer of Jeremiah and what he learns. Jeremiah hears of plots against his life, seeks God's help, and is reassured. **18–19:** A narrative preamble. **20:** The prayer itself. **21–23:** The answer. **20:** *Heart:* lit. "kidneys," see 4.3–4 n. **21:** It is the people of his own village, *Anathoth* (1.1), who have threatened to kill him for his prophesying.

about the men of Anathoth who seek to take
your life, and say, 'Prophesy no more in the
name of the LORD or we shall kill you'—
²²these are his words: I am about to punish
them: their young men shall die by the
sword, their sons and daughters by famine.
²³Not one of them will survive; for in the year
of reckoning for them I shall bring disaster
on the people of Anathoth.

12 LORD, even if I dispute with you,
    you remain in the right;
yet I shall plead my case before you.
Why do the wicked prosper
and the treacherous all live at ease?
²You have planted them and their roots
    strike deep,
they grow and bear fruit.
You are ever on their lips,
yet far from their hearts.
³But you know me, LORD, you see me;
you test my devotion to you.
Drag them away like sheep to the
    shambles;
set them apart for the day of slaughter.

⁴How long must the country lie parched
and all its green grass wither?
No birds and beasts are left, because its
    people are so wicked,
because they say, 'God does not see
    what we are doing.'

⁵If you have raced with men running on
    foot
and they have worn you down,
how then can you hope to compete
    with horses?
If in easy country you fall headlong,
how will you fare in Jordan's dense
    thickets?
⁶Even your brothers and kinsmen deal
    treacherously with you,

they are in full cry after you;
do not trust them, for all the fair words
    they use.

⁷I have abandoned the house of Israel,
I have cast off my own people.
I have given my beloved
into the power of her foes.
⁸My own people have turned on me
like lions from the jungle;
they roar against me,
therefore I hate them.
⁹Is this land of mine a hyena's lair,
with birds of prey hovering all around
    it?
Come, all you wild beasts;
come, flock to the feast.

¹⁰Many shepherds have ravaged my
    vineyard
and trampled down my portion of land,
they have made my pleasant portion a
    desolate wilderness;
¹¹they have made it a desolation, to my
    sorrow.
The whole land is desolate, but no one
    pays heed.

¹²Plunderers have swarmed across the open
regions of the wilderness; a sword of the
LORD devours the land from end to end;
there is no peace for any living thing.

¹³Men sow wheat and reap thistles;
they sift but get no grain.
Their harvest is a disappointment to
    them
because of the fierce anger of the
    LORD.

¹⁴These are the words of the LORD about all

12:4 **what we are doing:** *so Gk; Heb.* our latter end.
12:9 **come:** *so some MSS; others* bring.   12:13 **Their:**
prob. rdg; Heb. Your.

12.1–6: Prayer and response. This passage, related in form and substance to 11.18–23, is in some disorder.
Verses 1–3 and the end of v. 4 are Jeremiah's prayer; v. 5 is what he takes to be the answer to his prayer. In
v. 4 *How long . . . wicked* concerns "the drought"; see 14.1–6. Verse 6 would follow best on 11.18. **1–2:**
Jeremiah is not here asking the broader question about the suffering of the righteous raised in Job; here the
wicked, the *treacherous* are specifically those who hatch plots against him; see v. 6 and 11.19. **4:** *God does
not see:* see 5.12–13 n. **5:** *If you:* you, Jeremiah. You have proved too soft for your task (see 20.14–18;
15.19–21 n.); but weightier challenges lie ahead.
    12.7–13: God explains the lamentable disaster. The conduct of the *people* left God no choice but to bring
on the enemy and lay waste the land. **9–10:** *Many shepherds:* foreign kings and their armies. *Pleasant portion:*
the land of Judah. God speaks in vv. 7–11; in vv. 12–13 the prophet interprets the events.
    12.14–17: An inclusive covenant. Were even Israel's *evil neighbours* to learn faithfully to worship God

those evil neighbours who encroach on the land which I allotted to my people Israel as their holding: I shall uproot them from their own soil. Also I shall uproot Judah from among them; 15but after I have uprooted them, I shall have pity on them again and bring each man back to his holding and land. 16If they will learn the ways of my people, swearing by my name, 'by the life of the LORD', as they taught my people to swear by the Baal, they will establish families among my people. 17But the nation that will not listen, I shall uproot and destroy. This is the word of the LORD.

13 These were the words of the LORD to me: Go and buy yourself a linen loincloth and wrap it round your body, but do not put it in water. 2So I bought one as instructed by the LORD and wrapped it round me. 3The LORD spoke to me a second time: 4Take the loincloth which you bought and are wearing and go now to Perath, where you are to hide it in a crevice in the rocks. 5I went and hid it at Perath, as the LORD had ordered me. 6A long time afterwards the LORD said to me: Set out now for Perath and fetch the loincloth which I told you to hide there. 7So I went to Perath and looked for the place where I had hidden it, but when I picked it up, I saw that it was ruined and no good for anything. 8The LORD spoke to me: 9Thus shall I ruin the enormous pride of Judah and Jerusalem. 10This wicked people who refuse to listen to my words, who follow the promptings of their stubborn hearts and go after other gods to serve and worship them, will become like this loincloth, no good for anything. 11Just as a loincloth is bound close to a man's body, so I bound all Israel and all Judah to myself, says the LORD, so that they should become my people to be a source of renown and praise and glory to me; but they did not listen.

12You are to say this to them: These are the words of the LORD the God of Israel: Wine jars should be filled with wine. They will answer, 'We are well aware that wine jars should be filled with wine.' 13Then say to them, These are the words of the LORD: I shall fill all the inhabitants of this land with wine until they are drunk—kings of David's line who sit on his throne, priests, prophets, and all who live in Jerusalem. 14I shall dash them one against the other, fathers and sons together, says the LORD; I shall show them no compassion or pity or tenderness, nor refrain from destroying them.

15Pay heed; be not too proud to listen,
  for it is the LORD who speaks.
16Ascribe glory to the LORD your God
  before the darkness falls,
  before your feet stumble
  against the hillside in the twilight,
  before he turns the light you look for
  to deep gloom and thick darkness.
17If in those depths you will not listen,
  then for very anguish I can only weep
    bitterly;
  my eyes must stream with tears,
  for the LORD's flock is carried off into
    captivity.
18Say to the king and the queen mother:
  Take a humble seat,
  for your proud crowns are fallen from
    your heads.
19The towns in the Negeb are besieged,
  and no one can relieve them;
  all Judah has been swept into exile,
  swept clean away.
20Look up and see
  those who are coming from the north.

13:17 **If . . . bitterly:** *or* If you will not listen to this, for very anguish I must weep in secret.   13:18 **from your heads:** *so Gk; Heb.* your pillows.

alone, they would form *families* (lit. "be built up") within God's people. Otherwise general havoc must ensue. The passage is related to the "Prophecies against the nations" in chs. 46–51, and may be an addition here.

13.1–14: The loincloth and the wine jars, two symbols. 1–11: As Jeremiah bound the *loincloth* about his waist, thus intimately God took Israel to God's own self in covenant. Israel spurned this love and would rot away like that garment. **4–7:** *Perath:* usually the river Euphrates, but here perhaps a nearer place with a like-sounding name. **11:** *To be a source of renown for me:* for the broad purpose of making God known among the nations; compare Isa. 55.5; Ezek. 36.23–24. **12–14:** A new meaning for an old saying: As *wine jars* are *filled with wine,* so too would the people of Jerusalem, who thereafter would be shattered.

13.15–27: A frantic plea to trust in God. 15–17: *Pay heed* before it is too late, or else I must weep *for very anguish.* The mood is elegiac as in 9.1 and elsewhere. **18–22:** One blow has already fallen, and another comes.

Where is the flock that was entrusted to
  you,
  the sheep that were your pride?
21 What will you say when your leaders
    are missing,
  though trained by you to be your head?
  Will not pangs seize you
  like the pangs of a woman in labour,
22 when you wonder,
  'Why has this happened to me'?
  For your many sins your skirts are
    stripped off you,
  your limbs uncovered.

23 Can a Nubian change his skin,
  or a leopard its spots?
  No more can you do good,
  you who are schooled in evil.
24 I shall scatter you like chaff
  before the desert wind.
25 This is your lot, your portion as a rebel,
  decreed by me, says the LORD,
  because you have quite forgotten me
  and trusted in false gods.
26 So I myself have torn off your skirts
  and laid bare your shame:
27 your adulteries, your lustful neighing,
  your wanton lewdness.
  On the hills and the open fields
  I have seen your foul deeds.
  Woe to you, Jerusalem, in your
    uncleanness!
  How long will you delay?

14 This came to Jeremiah as the word of
the LORD concerning the drought:

2 Judah droops, her towns languish,
  the inhabitants sit on the ground in
    mourning;
  and a crying goes up from Jerusalem.
3 Masters send their servants for water,
  but when they come to the pools they
    find none there,
  and go back with their vessels empty;
  disappointed and shamed, they uncover
    their heads.
4 Because the ground is cracked
  through lack of rain in the land,

  the farmers' hopes are wrecked;
  they uncover their heads in grief.
5 The hind calves in the open country,
  and because there is no grass
  she abandons her young.
6 Wild asses stand on the bare heights
  and snuff the wind as wolves do,
  and their eyes begin to fail for lack of
    herbage.

7 Though our sins testify against us,
  yet take action, LORD, for your own
    name's sake.
  Our disloyalties indeed are many;
  we have sinned against you.
8 Hope of Israel, their saviour in time of
    trouble,
  must you be like a stranger in the land,
  like a traveller breaking his journey to
    find a night's lodging?
9 Must you be like a man suddenly
    overcome,
  like a warrior powerless to save himself?
  You are in our midst, LORD, and we
    bear your name.
  Do not forsake us.

10 The LORD says of this people: They love to
stray from my ways; they wander where they
will. Therefore the LORD has no more pleasure in them; he remembers their guilt now,
and punishes their sins.

11 The LORD said to me: Do not pray for the
wellbeing of this people. 12 Though they fast,
I shall not listen to their cry; though they
sacrifice whole-offering and grain-offering,
I shall not accept them. I shall make an end
of them with sword, famine, and pestilence.
13 But I said: Ah, Lord GOD, the prophets
keep saying to them that they will see no
sword and suffer no famine; for you will give
them lasting prosperity in this place.
14 The LORD answered me: These are lies
the prophets are prophesying in my name. I
have not sent them; I have given them no

13:21 **leaders:** *transposed from next line.* 13:24 **you:**
prob. rdg; Heb. them. 13:25 **rebel:** *prob. rdg, cp. Gk;
Heb.* measures. 13:27 **How ... delay?:** *prob. rdg;
Heb. unintelligible.* 14:4 **Because ... cracked:** *prob.
rdg; Heb. obscure.*

18: *The king:* probably Jehoiachin. **19:** *Negeb:* southern Judah. **20:** *Entrusted to you:* to Jerusalem. **23:** The
power of habit. *Nubian:* a black-skinned people from the upper Nile region.

   14.1–15.9: Concerning the drought and other calamities. 7–9: Public confession and supplication. *For your
own name's sake:* that is, God should act because of who God is, to enhance divine glory in the world. **12:**
Their cry: the accompaniment of the ritual fasting, for relief from drought. **13:** *The prophets keep saying to*

charge; I have not spoken to them. The prophets are offering false visions, worthless augury, and their own day-dreams. ¹⁵ Therefore these are the words of the LORD about the prophets who, with no commission from me, prophesy in my name and say that neither sword nor famine will touch this land: By sword and by famine those prophets will meet their end. ¹⁶ The people to whom they prophesy will be flung out into the streets of Jerusalem, victims of famine and sword: they, their wives, their sons, and their daughters, and there will be no one to bury them. I shall pour down on them the disaster they deserve.

¹⁷ This is what you are to say to them:
Let my eyes stream with tears
ceaselessly night and day.
For the virgin daughter of my people,
struck by a cruel blow,
is grievously wounded.
¹⁸ If I go out into the open country,
I see those slain by the sword;
if I enter the city,
I see the victims of famine.
Prophet and priest alike
wander without rest in the land.

¹⁹ Have you spurned Judah utterly?
Do you loathe Zion?
Why have you wounded us past all
healing?
We hoped to prosper, but nothing went
well.
We hoped for respite, but terror
struck.
²⁰ We acknowledge our wickedness,
the guilt of our forefathers;
LORD, we have sinned against you.
²¹ Do not despise the place where your
name dwells
or bring contempt on your glorious
throne.
Remember your covenant with us and
do not make it void.

²² Can any of the false gods of the nations
give rain?
Or do the heavens of themselves send
showers?
Is it not in you, LORD our God,
that we put our hope?
You alone made all these things.

15 The LORD said to me: Even if Moses and Samuel stood before me, I would not be moved to pity this people. Banish them from my presence; let them be gone. ² Should they ask where to go, say to them: These are the words of the LORD:

Those who are for the plague shall go
to the plague,
and those for the sword to the sword;
those who are for famine to famine,
and those for captivity to captivity.

³ Four kinds of doom I ordain for them, says the LORD: the sword to kill, dogs to drag away, birds of prey and wild beasts to devour and destroy. ⁴ I shall make them abhorrent to all the kingdoms of the earth, because of the crimes committed in Jerusalem by Manasseh son of Hezekiah, king of Judah.

⁵ Who will take pity on you, Jerusalem,
who will offer you consolation?
Who will turn aside to ask about your
wellbeing?
⁶ You yourselves cast me off, says the
LORD,
you turned your backs on me,
so I stretched out my hand to bring
you to ruin;
I was weary of relenting.
⁷ I winnowed them and scattered them
in every town in the land;
I brought bereavement on them,
I destroyed my people;
they would not abandon their ways.

14:22 **made:** or did.

them; see 4.9 n. **17–18:** *This is what you are to say to them* is probably not in place, as a result of a copyist's blunder; the rest of vv. 17 and 18 is Jeremiah's private lament. **19–22:** Again a public prayer, as in vv. 7–9. **21:** *The place where your name dwells:* the usual Deuteronomic designation of the temple in Jerusalem. **22:** The reference to *rain* ties the prayer in with the context of drought (v. 1). **15.1–2:** Because of their reputed success in providing water and calling down a storm, Moses and Samuel (Exod. 17.1–7 and 1 Sam. 7.7–13) are cited as examples of persons who had influence with God. Now not even they, much less Jeremiah, could relieve the drought. **4:** The reference to King *Manasseh,* whose evil excesses his grandson Josiah sought to counter, may be a Deuteronomic addition (see 2 Kgs. 21.1–18). **5–9:** Probably written after 597 (possibly even

⁸I made widows among them more in
　　number
than the sands of the seas;
I brought upon the mother of young
　　warriors
a plunderer at noonday.
I made the terror of invasion fall upon
　　her
all in a moment.
⁹The mother of seven sons grew faint,
she sank into despair;
her light was quenched while it was yet
　　day;
she was left humbled and shamed.
The remnant I shall give to the sword,
to perish at the hand of their enemies.
This is the word of the LORD.

¹⁰ALAS, my mother, that ever you gave
　　birth to me,
a man doomed to strife
with the whole world against me!
I have borrowed from no one,
I have lent to no one,
yet everyone abuses me.

¹¹The LORD said:

Have I not utterly dismissed you?
Shall I not bring the enemy against you
in a time of trouble and distress?
¹²Can iron break steel from the north?
¹³I shall hand over your wealth as spoil,
and your treasure for no payment,
because of all your sin throughout your
　　borders.
¹⁴I shall make you serve your enemies
in a land you do not know;
for my anger is a blazing fire
and it will flare up against you.

¹⁵LORD, you know;
remember me, and vindicate me,
avenge me on my persecutors.

Be patient with me and do not put me
　　off,
see what reproaches I endure for your
　　sake.
¹⁶When I came on your words I
　　devoured them;
they were joy and happiness to me,
for you, LORD God of Hosts, have
　　named me yours.
¹⁷I have never kept company with
　　revellers,
never made merry with them;
because I felt your hand upon me I
　　have sat alone,
for you have filled me with indignation.
¹⁸Why then is my pain unending,
and my wound desperate, past all
　　healing?
You are to me like a brook that fails,
whose waters are not to be relied on.

¹⁹This was the LORD's answer:

If you turn back to me, I shall take you
　　back
and you will stand before me.
If you can separate the precious from
　　the base,
you will be my spokesman.
This people may turn again to you,
but you are not to turn to them.
²⁰To withstand them I shall make you
　　strong,
an unscaled wall of bronze.
Though they attack you, they will not
　　prevail,
for I am with you to save
and deliver you, says the LORD;
²¹I shall deliver you from the clutches of
　　the wicked,
I shall rescue you from the grasp of the
　　ruthless.

15:8 **brought:** *so Gk; Heb. adds* to them.　　15:12 **Can
... north:** *prob. rdg; Heb. adds* and bronze.

after 587) since the calamity has already occurred; compare 9.12. **9:** *Mother of seven:* the populous city
Jerusalem is here personified.
　　15.10–21: The prophet's lament and God's response. 10: Jeremiah gives vent to self-pity; see also 20.14–18.
11: The precise meaning of this is obscure. The verse may belong with the prayer continued in v. 15. **12–14:**
These verses seem to be a confused intrusion from 17.1–4. **15–18:** Jeremiah pleads before God like someone
on trial before a judge. **18:** *Why . . . ?* Jeremiah charges that God is not being fair, nor even trustworthy, like
Judean brooks which disappear in the dry season; see, too, Job 6.15–21. **19–21:** *The LORD's answer:* God has
not failed him; he has failed God. Jeremiah has been running away (see 12.5 n.) and must *turn back.* **19:**
Spokesman: prophet. **20:** *Wall of bronze:* as in 1.18–19.

Judgement on Judah

16 THE word of the LORD came to me: ²You are not to marry or to have sons and daughters in this place. ³For these are the words of the LORD about any sons and daughters born in this place, about the mothers who bear them and the fathers who beget them in this land: ⁴They shall die a horrible death; there must be no wailing for them and no burial; they will be dung spread over the ground. They will perish by sword or famine, and their corpses will be food for birds and beasts.

⁵For these are the words of the LORD: Do not enter a house where there is a funeral feast; do not go in to wail or to bring comfort, for, says the LORD, I have withdrawn my peace from this people, my love and compassion. ⁶High and low will die in this land, but there must be no burial, no wailing for them; no one is to gash himself or shave his head. ⁷No one is to offer the mourner a portion of bread to console him for the dead or give him a cup of consolation for the loss of his father or mother.

⁸Nor may you enter a house where there is feasting, to sit eating and drinking there. ⁹For these are the words of the LORD of Hosts, the God of Israel: In your own days and in the sight of you all, I shall silence in this place every sound of joy and gladness, the voices of bridegroom and bride.

¹⁰When you tell this people all these things they will ask you, 'Why has the LORD decreed that this great disaster is to come on us? What wrong have we done? What sin have we committed against the LORD our God?' ¹¹You are to answer: Because your forefathers forsook me, says the LORD, and followed other gods, serving and worshipping them. They forsook me and did not keep my law. ¹²And you yourselves have done worse than your forefathers; for each of you follows the promptings of his wicked and stubborn heart instead

of obeying me. ¹³So I shall fling you headlong out of this land into a country unknown to you and your forefathers; there serve other gods day and night, for I shall show you no favour.

¹⁴Therefore the time is coming, says the LORD, when people will no longer swear 'by the life of the LORD who brought the Israelites up from Egypt'; ¹⁵instead they will swear 'by the life of the LORD who brought the Israelites back from a northern land and from all the lands to which he had dispersed them'; and I shall bring them back to the soil which I gave to their forefathers.

¹⁶I shall send for many fishermen, says the LORD, and they will fish for them. After that I shall send for many hunters, and they will hunt them from every mountain and hill and from the crevices in the rocks. ¹⁷For my eyes are on all their ways; they are not hidden from my sight, nor is their wrongdoing concealed from me. ¹⁸I shall first make them pay double for the wrong they have done and the sin they have committed by defiling the land which belongs to me; they have filled my possession with their lifeless idols and abominations.

¹⁹LORD, my strength and my stronghold,
  my refuge in time of trouble,
to you the nations will come
  from the ends of the earth and say:
Our forefathers inherited only a
  sham,
an idol vain and worthless.
²⁰Can man make gods for himself?
  They would be no gods.
²¹Therefore I am teaching them,
  I shall teach them once for all
my power and my might,
  and they will learn that my name is the
  LORD.

16:7 **bread:** *so Gk; Heb.* to them. **give him:** *so Gk; Heb.* give them.

16.1–9: Jeremiah the solitary prophet. With no family of his own (vv. 1–4), alienated from his parental home (11.21; 12.6), renouncing human companionship (vv. 5 and 8), Jeremiah is the figure of loneliness. **5:** Like God, the prophet of God is to withdraw his *peace, love, and compassion.* **6:** *Gash himself, or shave his head:* rites of mourning. See 41.5; 47.5. **7:** Compare Ezek. 24.17; Hos. 9.4. **8:** See 15.17.

16.10–21: Mingled threat and promise. 10–13: The sense and language of threat are Deuteronomic; see 15.4 n. **13:** *Serve other gods:* contrast with this verse Jeremiah's message to the exiles in Babylonia in 29.12. **14–15:** Restoration promised; as in Isa. 52.10–12, the return from Babylonian captivity is equated with the ancient Exodus from Egypt. **18:** See 10.3–5, 8–9, 14–16. **19–21:** *The nations:* compare the broader purpose of calamity in 12.14–17 n. and 13.11 n.

17 The sin of Judah is recorded with an iron stylus,
engraved with a diamond point on the tablet of their hearts,
on the horns of their altars ²to witness against them.
Their altars and their sacred poles stand by every spreading tree,
on the heights ³and the hills in the mountain country.
I shall hand over your wealth as spoil,
and all your treasure for no payment,
because of sin throughout your borders.
⁴You will lose possession of the holding which I gave you.
I shall make you serve your enemies in a land you do not know;
for the fire of my anger is kindled by you
and it will burn for ever.

⁵These are the words of the LORD:

A curse on anyone who trusts in mortals
and leans for support on human kind,
while his heart is far from the LORD!
⁶He will be like a juniper in the steppeland;
when good comes he is unaware of it.
He will live among the rocks in the wilderness,
in a salt, uninhabited land.

⁷Blessed is anyone who trusts in the LORD,
and rests his confidence on him.
⁸He will be like a tree planted by the waterside,
that sends out its roots along a stream.
When the heat comes it has nothing to fear;
its foliage stays green.
Without care in a year of drought,
it does not fail to bear fruit.

⁹The heart is deceitful above any other thing,
desperately sick; who can fathom it?
¹⁰I, the LORD, search the mind and test the heart,
requiting each one for his conduct and as his deeds deserve.
¹¹Like a partridge
sitting on a clutch of eggs which it has not laid,
so is he who amasses wealth unjustly.
Before his days are half done it will leave him,
and he will be a fool at the last.

¹²A glorious throne, exalted from the beginning,
is the site of our sanctuary;
¹³LORD, on whom Israel's hope is fixed,
all who reject you will be put to shame;
those who forsake you will be inscribed in the dust,
for they have rejected the source of living water, the LORD.

¹⁴Heal me, LORD, and I shall be healed,
save me and I shall be saved;
for you are my praise.
¹⁵They say to me, 'Where is the word of the LORD?
Let it come, if it can!'
¹⁶It is not the prospect of disaster that makes me press after you,
and I did not desire this day of despair.
You know all that has passed my lips;
you are fully aware of it.
¹⁷Do not become a terror to me;
you are my refuge on an evil day.
¹⁸May my persecutors be foiled, not I;
may they, not I, be terrified.
Bring on them an evil day;
destroy them, destroy them utterly.

17:2 **to witness ... them:** *prob. rdg; Heb.* as their sons remember.   17:3 **for no payment:** *prob. rdg, cp. 15:13; Heb.* your shrines.   17:4 **You ... possession:** *prob. rdg; Heb.* obscure.   17:6 **a juniper:** *or* one who is a destitute person.   17:13 **who forsake you:** *so Lat.; Heb.* who forsake me.

17.1–18: Observations and prayers. 1–4: Judah, habituated in evil, is doomed. **1:** *Their hearts:* compare 4.3–4 n. and 31.33. *Horns:* the elevated corners of an altar. **5–8:** A clear affirmation of individual retribution; compare Ps. 1. **9–10:** Only God can clearly know the motives behind human conduct; human organs of thought and feeling are open to God. **10:** *As his deeds deserve* connects vv. 9–10 with vv. 5–8. **12–13:** A public confession. **12:** *The site:* the temple in Jerusalem; contrast 7.4 with its scorn of the temple. **13:** *Living water:* see, too, 2.13. **14–18:** A private prayer. **15:** "... *Let it come, if it can!*": see 5.12–13 n. **16:** *I did not desire this day of despair:* see 8.18–9.1 n.

19 These were the words of the LORD to me: Go and stand at the Benjamin Gate, through which the kings of Judah pass in and out, and stand also at all the gates of Jerusalem. 20 Say: Hear the words of the LORD, you kings of Judah, all you people of Judah, and all you citizens of Jerusalem who come in through these gates. 21 These are the words of the LORD: Do not put your lives at risk by carrying any load on the sabbath day or bringing it through the gates of Jerusalem. 22 You are not to bring any load out of your houses or do any work on the sabbath, but you are to keep the sabbath day holy as I commanded your forefathers. 23 They, however, did not obey or pay attention, but stubbornly refused to hear or receive instruction. 24 Now if you will obey me, says the LORD, and refrain from bringing any load through the gates of this city on the sabbath, and keep that day holy by doing no work on it, 25 then kings will come through the gates of this city, kings who will sit on David's throne. They will come riding in chariots or on horseback, escorted by their officers, by the people of Judah, and by the citizens of Jerusalem; and this city will be inhabited for ever. 26 People will come from the towns of Judah, the country round Jerusalem, the territory of Benjamin, the Shephelah, the hill-country, and the Negeb, bringing whole-offerings, sacrifices, grainofferings, and frankincense, bringing also thank-offerings to the house of the LORD. 27 But if you do not obey me by keeping the sabbath day holy and by carrying no load as you come through the gates of Jerusalem on the sabbath, then I shall set fire to the gates; it will consume the palaces of Jerusalem and will not be put out.

The potter and the clay

18 THESE are the words which came to Jeremiah from the LORD: 2 Go down now to the potter's house, and there I shall tell you what I have to say. 3 I went down to the potter's house, where I found him working at the wheel. 4 Now and then a vessel he was making from the clay would be spoilt in his hands, and he would remould it into another vessel to his liking.

5 Then the word of the LORD came to me: 6 Israel, can I not deal with you as this potter deals with his clay? says the LORD. House of Israel, you are clay in my hands like the clay in his. 7 At any moment I may threaten to uproot a nation or a kingdom, to pull it down and destroy it. 8 But if the nation which I have threatened turns back from its wicked ways, then I shall think again about the disaster I had in mind for it. 9 At another moment I may announce that I shall build or plant a nation or a kingdom. 10 But if it does evil in my sight by disobeying me, I shall think again about the good I had in mind for it.

11 Go now and tell the people of Judah and the citizens of Jerusalem that these are the words of the LORD: I am framing disaster for you and perfecting my designs against you. Turn back, every one of you, from his evil conduct; mend your ways and your actions. 12 But they will answer, 'Things are past hope. We must stick to our own plans, and each of us follow the promptings of his wicked and stubborn heart.'

13 Therefore these are the words of the LORD:

Enquire among the nations:
whoever heard the like of this?
The virgin Israel has done a thing most horrible.
14 Does the snow cease to fall from the rocky slopes of Lebanon?
Does the cool rain streaming in torrents ever fail?
15 No, but my people have forgotten me: they burn sacrifices to idols
which cause them to stumble as they tread the ancient ways,

17:19 **Benjamin:** *prob. rdg; Heb.* sons of the people.
17:25 **city, kings:** *prob. rdg; Heb. adds* and officers.
18:14 **fail:** *prob. rdg; Heb.* become uprooted.

17.19–27: The importance of sabbath rest. The passage seems not to come from Jeremiah, but comes from a time like that of Nehemiah when the sabbath received particular emphasis; see Neh. 13.15–22. **25:** *David's throne:* apparently it is conceived of as vacant at the time.

18.1–17: A lesson from the potter's shop. A last minute pardon is possible; before the fall of Jerusalem, an appropriate response could yet avert the doom, and hence the plea (v. 11): *turn back . . . from this evil conduct.* **12:** *Things are past hope:* because of the unnatural conduct of this unfaithful people it is now too late; see vv. 15–17.

and they take to byways and unmade
    roads;
16 their own land they lay waste,
    an object of lasting derision,
at which all passers-by shake their
    heads in horror.
17 As with a wind from the east
    I shall scatter them before their
      enemies.
In the hour of their downfall
    I shall turn my back and not my face
      towards them.

18 The cry was raised: 'Let us consider how to
deal with Jeremiah. There will still be priests
to guide us, still wise men to give counsel, still
prophets to proclaim the word. Let us invent
some charges against him; let us pay no heed
to anything he says.'

19 But pay heed, LORD,
    and hear what my opponents are saying
      against me.
20 Is good to be repaid with evil,
    that they have dug a pit for me?
Remember how I stood before you,
    interceding on their behalf
    to avert your wrath from them.
21 Therefore give their children over to
      famine,
leave them at the mercy of the sword.
Let their women be childless and
      widowed,
let their men be slain by pestilence,
    their young men cut down in battle.
22 Bring raiders on them without warning,
    and let screaming be heard from their
      houses.
They have dug a pit to catch me
    and have laid snares for my feet.
23 Well you know, LORD,
    all their murderous plots against me.
Do not blot out their wrongdoing
    or wipe away their sin from your sight;
when they are brought stumbling
      before you,
deal with them on the day of your
      anger.

19 These are the words of the LORD: Go
and buy from the potter an earthenware jar, and taking with you some of the
elders of the people and some priests, 2 go
out to the valley of Ben-hinnom, on which
the Gate of the Potsherds opens, and there
proclaim what I tell you. 3 Say: Hear the word
of the LORD, you princes of Judah and citizens of Jerusalem. These are the words of the
LORD of Hosts the God of Israel: I am about
to bring on this place such a disaster as will
ring in the ears of all who hear of it, 4 because
they have forsaken me, and made this a place
of alien worship. They have burnt sacrifices
to other gods whom neither they nor their
forefathers nor the kings of Judah ever
knew, and they have filled this place with the
blood of the innocent. 5 They have built
shrines to Baal, at which to burn their sons as
whole-offerings to Baal. That was no command of mine, a thing I never spoke of, nor
did it ever enter my mind.

6 Therefore the time is coming, says the
LORD, when it will no longer be called Topheth or the valley of Ben-hinnom, but the
valley of Slaughter. 7 In this place I shall
make void the plans of Judah and Jerusalem;
I shall make the people fall by the sword
before their enemies, at the hands of those
who seek to kill them; I shall give their
corpses to the birds and beasts to devour. 8 I
shall make this city a scene of desolation, an
object of astonishment, so that every passer-
by will be desolated and appalled at the sight
of all her wounds. 9 I shall make people eat
the flesh of their sons and their daughters;
they will devour one another's flesh in the
dire straits to which their enemies and those
who would kill them will reduce them in the
siege.

10 Then you are to smash the jar before the
eyes of the men who accompany you 11 and
say to them: These are the words of the LORD
of Hosts: Thus shall I smash this people and
this city as an earthen vessel is smashed beyond all repair, and the dead will be buried
in Topheth until there is no room left to bury
them. 12 That is how I shall deal with this

18.18–23: A private prayer.

19.1–20.6: A dramatic pronouncement and its consequences. 1: An earthenware jar: it is dramatically
reserved for the climax in v. 10. Elders ... and ... priests: they are both audience and witnesses. 2: Valley
of Ben-hinnom is chosen for its association with human sacrifice; see 7.30–31 n. Gate of the Potsherds: the
mention of pottery fragments anticipates the shattering of jars in vv. 10–11. 4–5: The innocent: their sons
(compare 2 Kgs. 21.1–7). 10–11: The shattering of the jar could have been interpreted as more than a dramatic

place and with those who live there, says the
LORD: I shall make this city like Topheth.
13 Because of their defilement, the houses of
Jerusalem and those of the kings of Judah
will be like the site of Topheth, every one of
the houses on whose roofs men have burnt
sacrifices to all the host of heaven and
poured drink-offerings to other gods.

14 When Jeremiah came in from Topheth,
where the LORD had sent him to prophesy, he
stood in the court of the LORD's house and
said to all the people: 15 These are the words
of the LORD of Hosts the God of Israel: I am
about to bring on this city and on all its dependent towns the whole disaster with which
I have threatened it, for its people have remained stubborn and refused to listen to me.

20 The priest Pashhur son of Immer,
the chief officer in the house of the
LORD, heard Jeremiah prophesying these
things, 2 and had him flogged and put him in
the stocks at the Upper Benjamin Gate, in the
house of the LORD. 3 When next morning
Pashhur released him from the stocks, Jeremiah said to him: The LORD has called you
not Pashhur but Magor-missabib. 4 For these
are the words of the LORD: I shall make you
a terror to yourself and to all your friends;
they will fall by the sword of the enemy before your very eyes. I shall hand over all
Judah to the king of Babylon, and he will
deport them to Babylon or put them to the
sword. 5 I shall give all this city's store of
wealth and riches and all the treasures of the
kings of Judah to their enemies; they will
seize them as spoil and carry them off to
Babylon. 6 You, Pashhur, and all your household will go into captivity. You will come to
Babylon; there you will die and there you will
be buried, you and all your friends to whom
you have been a false prophet.

Jeremiah's lament

7 YOU HAVE duped me, LORD,
and I have been your dupe;
you have outwitted me and prevailed.

All the day long I have been made a
    laughing-stock;
everyone ridicules me.
8 Whenever I speak I must needs cry
    out,
calling, 'Violence!' and 'Assault!'
I am reproached and derided all the
    time
for uttering the word of the LORD.
9 Whenever I said, 'I shall not call it to
    mind
or speak in his name again,'
then his word became imprisoned
    within me
like a fire burning in my heart.
I was weary with holding it under,
and could endure no more.
10 For I heard many whispering, 'Terror
    let loose!
Denounce him! Let us denounce him.'
All my friends were on the watch for a
    false step,
saying, 'Perhaps he may be tricked;
then we can catch him
and have our revenge on him.'
11 But the LORD is on my side,
a powerful champion;
therefore my persecutors will stumble
    and fall powerless.
Their abasement will be bitter when
    they fail,
and their dishonour will long be
    remembered.
12 But, LORD of Hosts, you test the
    righteous
and search the depths of the heart.
To you I have committed my cause;
let me see your vengeance on them.
13 Sing to the LORD, praise the LORD;
for he rescues the poor
from those who would do them wrong.

14 A curse on the day when I was born!
The day my mother bore me,
may it be for ever unblessed!

20:3 **Magor-missabib:** *that is* Terror let loose.
20:7 **have outwitted me:** *or* were too strong for me.
20:9 **call it:** *or* call him.

gesture, and may have reflected a view that regarded it as a hostile act. See v. 1 n.; Ps. 2.9. **14:** See 26.2.
20.3–6: When Jeremiah is *released* he puts an individual curse on his torturer, but without revoking his threat
to all Judah.
   20.7–13: A personal plaintive prayer. 7–9: Jeremiah insists that God has misused him. He would cease
speaking in God's name were the compulsion not beyond his power to resist. **10:** *Friends:* ironic. **11–12:** He
needs the LORD on his *side* and is torn between the wish to flee and the need to find refuge with his God.

¹⁵A curse on the man who brought word
　　to my father,
'A child is born to you, a son,'
　　and gladdened his heart!
¹⁶May that man fare like the cities
　　which the LORD overthrew without
　　　mercy.
　　May he hear cries of alarm in the
　　　morning
　　and uproar at noon,
¹⁷since death did not claim me before
　　birth,
　　and my mother did not become my
　　　grave,
　　her womb great with me for ever.
¹⁸Why did I come from the womb
　　to see only sorrow and toil,
　　to end my days in shame?

Warnings to kings and people

21 THE word which came from the
LORD to Jeremiah when King Zedekiah sent to him Pashhur son of Malchiah
and the priest Zephaniah son of Maaseiah
with this request: ²'King Nebuchadrezzar of
Babylon has declared war on us; enquire of
the LORD on our behalf. Perhaps the LORD
will perform a miracle as he has done in times
past, so that Nebuchadrezzar will raise the
siege.'

³But Jeremiah answered them: Tell Zedekiah ⁴that these are the words of the LORD
the God of Israel: I shall turn against you
your own weapons with which you are fighting the king of Babylon and the Chaldaeans
who are besieging you outside the wall; and
I shall bring them into the heart of this city.
⁵I myself shall fight against you in burning
rage and great fury, with an outstretched
hand and a strong arm. ⁶I shall strike down
those who live in this city, men and cattle
alike; they will die of a great pestilence. ⁷After that, says the LORD, I shall take King Zedekiah of Judah, his courtiers, and the people,
all in this city who survive pestilence, sword,
and famine, and hand them over to King
Nebuchadrezzar of Babylon, to their enemies and those who would kill them. He will
put them to the sword and show no pity or
mercy or compassion.

⁸You are to say further to this people:
These are the words of the LORD: I offer you
now a choice between the way of life and the
way of death. ⁹Whoever remains in this city
will die by sword, famine, or pestilence, but
whoever goes out and surrenders to the
Chaldaeans now laying siege to you will survive; he will escape with his life. ¹⁰I have set
my face against this city, determined to do
them harm, not good, says the LORD. It will
be handed over to the king of Babylon, and
he will burn it to the ground.

¹¹To the royal house of Judah:
　　Listen to the word of the LORD;
¹²house of David, these are the words of
　　the LORD:
　　Dispense justice betimes,
　　rescue the victim from his oppressor,
　　or the fire of my fury may blaze up
　　　and burn unquenchably
　　because of your evil actions.

¹³The LORD says: I am against you,
　　you inhabitants of the valley,
　　the rock in the plain,
　　who say, 'Who can come down upon
　　　us?
　　Who can penetrate our retreats?'
¹⁴I shall punish you as your deeds
　　deserve,
　　says the LORD,
　　I shall set fire to your heathland,
　　and it will devour everything round
　　　about.

22 These are the words of the LORD: Go
down to the palace of the king of
Judah with this message: ²King of Judah,

20.14–18: Inner fury. 14: See Job 3.3. He avoids a curse on his parents. **16:** *Cities:* Sodom and Gomorrah.
See Gen. 19.24–25.

　　21.1–23.8: The kings are denounced. 1–7: Jeremiah answers Zedekiah. **1:** *Pashhur:* not the same person
as in 20.1. **2:** *Nebuchadrezzar* is closer to the Akkadian original, *Nabû-kudurri-uṣur,* than the more familiar
spelling, Nebuchadnezzar (see Jer. 29.1; 2 Kgs. 24.1). *Declared war:* the final siege of Jerusalem was in
588–587. The king hopes for a *miracle* like the deliverance from Egypt. **5:** *Outstretched hand . . . strong arm:*
these words are here bitterly ironical; they commonly signify deliverance for Israel, as in Deut. 4.34. **7:** See
2 Kgs. 25.6–7, 18–21. **12:** *House of David:* all the Judean kings were of Davidic lineage. **13–14:** These verses
are apparently not in their original context. **13:** *Valley:* area around Jerusalem. **22.1–7:** These verses develop

occupant of David's throne, listen to the words of the LORD, you and your courtiers and your people who come in at these gates. ³ These are the words of the LORD: Deal justly and fairly, rescue the victim from his oppressor, do not ill-treat or use violence towards the alien, the fatherless, and the widow, and do not shed innocent blood in this place. ⁴ If you obey, then kings who succeed to David's throne will come riding through the gates of this palace in chariots and on horses, with their retinue of courtiers and subjects. ⁵ But if you do not obey my words, then by myself I solemnly swear, says the LORD, this palace will become a ruin. ⁶ For these are the words of the LORD about the royal house of Judah:

> Though you are dear to me as Gilead
> or as the crest of Lebanon,
> I swear that I shall turn you into a
>   wilderness,
> a land of towns no longer inhabited.
> ⁷ I shall consecrate an armed host to
>   fight against you,
> a destructive horde;
> they will cut down your choicest cedars,
> felling them for fuel.

⁸ People of many nations will pass by this city and say to one another, 'Why has the LORD done such a thing to this great city?' ⁹ The answer will be, 'Because they forsook their covenant with the LORD their God by worshipping other gods and serving them.'

> ¹⁰ Weep not for him who is dead nor
>   lament his loss.
> Weep rather for him who is going into
>   exile,
> for he will return no more,
> never again see the land of his birth.

¹¹ For these are the words of the LORD concerning Shallum son of Josiah, king of Judah, who succeeded his father on the throne and has gone from this place: He will never return; ¹² he will die in the place of his exile without ever seeing this land again.

> ¹³ Woe betide him who builds his palace
>   on unfairness
> and completes its roof-chambers with
>   injustice,
> compelling his countrymen to work
>   without payment,
> giving them no wage for their labour!
> ¹⁴ Woe to him who says,
> 'I shall build myself a spacious palace
> with airy roof-chambers and windows
>   set in it;
> it will be panelled with cedar
> and painted with vermilion.'
> ¹⁵ Though your cedar is so splendid,
> does that prove you a king?
> Think of your father: he ate and
>   drank,
> dealt justly and fairly; all went well with
>   him.
> ¹⁶ He upheld the cause of the lowly and
>   poor;
> then all was well.
> Did not this show he knew me? says the
>   LORD.
> ¹⁷ But your eyes and your heart are set on
>   naught but gain,
> set only on the innocent blood you can
>   shed,
> on the cruel acts of tyranny you
>   perpetrate.

¹⁸ Therefore these are the words of the LORD concerning Jehoiakim son of Josiah, king of Judah:

> For him no mourner will say, 'Alas,
>   brother, dear brother!'
> no one say, 'Alas, lord and master!'
> ¹⁹ He will be buried like a dead donkey,
>   dragged along and flung out
> beyond the gates of Jerusalem.

> ²⁰ Go up to Lebanon and cry aloud,
> make your voice heard in Bashan,

the thought of 21.11–12. **6:** *Gilead* and *Lebanon* are symbols for flourishing habitations; so, too, *cedars*, v. 7. **10–12:** Concerning Jehoahaz the son of Josiah. **10:** *For him who is dead:* this is King Josiah, whom Pharaoh Necho killed at Megiddo (2 Kgs. 23.28–30). *For him who is going into exile:* this is Jehoahaz who succeeded his father, Josiah, only to be deposed by Necho and brought to Egypt where he died (2 Kgs. 23.30–34). **11:** *Shallum* is the name used for Jehoahaz here and in 1 Chr. 3.15. **13–19:** Concerning Jehoiakim, son of Josiah, whom Necho made king after deposing Jehoahaz (see v. 18 and 2 Kgs. 23.34–36). **17–19:** Words addressed to Jehoiakim. **20–30:** The kings of Judah in exile. **20:** *Lebanon, Bashan, and Abarim* (the latter in Moab): these

cry aloud from Abarim,
  for all who love you are broken.
²¹ I spoke to you in your days of
    prosperous ease,
  but you said, 'I shall not listen.'
  Since your youth this is how you have
    behaved;
  you have never obeyed me.
²² A wind will carry away all your friends;
  those who love you will go into
    captivity.
  Then you will be abashed and put to
    shame
  for all your evil deeds.
²³ You dwellers in Lebanon, nestling
    among the cedars,
  how you will groan when pains come
    on you,
  like the pangs of a woman in labour!

²⁴ By my life, says the LORD, although you,
Coniah son of Jehoiakim, king of Judah, are
the signet ring on my right hand, I shall pull
you off ²⁵ and hand you over to those who
seek your life, to those you fear, to King Nebuchadrezzar of Babylon and to the Chaldaeans. ²⁶ I shall fling you headlong, you and the
mother who bore you, into another land, not
that of your birth, and there you will both
die. ²⁷ You will never come back to your own
land, the land for which you long.

²⁸ This man Coniah, then, is he a mere
puppet, despised and broken, a thing unwanted? Why else are he and his children
flung out headlong and hurled into a country they do not know?
²⁹ Land, land, land! Hear the words of the
LORD: ³⁰ These are the words of the LORD:
Write this man down as stripped of all honour, one who in his lifetime will not prosper,
nor leave descendants to sit in prosperity on
David's throne or rule again over Judah.

23 Woe betide the shepherds who let
the sheep of my flock scatter and be
lost! says the LORD. ² Therefore these are the
words of the LORD the God of Israel to the
shepherds who tend my people: You have
scattered and dispersed my flock. You have

not watched over them; but I am watching
you to punish you for your misdeeds, says the
LORD. ³ I myself shall gather the remnant of
my sheep from all the lands to which I have
dispersed them. I shall bring them back to
their homes, and they will be fruitful and
increase. ⁴ I shall appoint shepherds who will
tend them, so that never again will they know
fear or dismay or punishment. This is the
word of the LORD.

⁵ The days are coming, says the LORD,
  when I shall make a righteous Branch
    spring from David's line,
  a king who will rule wisely,
  maintaining justice and right in the
    land.
⁶ In his days Judah will be kept safe,
  and Israel will live undisturbed.
  This will be the name to be given to
    him:
  The LORD our Righteousness.

⁷ Therefore the time is coming, says the
LORD, when people will no longer swear 'by
the life of the LORD who brought the Israelites up from Egypt'; ⁸ instead they will swear
'by the life of the LORD who brought the
descendants of the Israelites back from a
northern land and from all the lands to
which he had dispersed them'; and they will
live on their own soil.

⁹ Of the prophets:

  Within my breast my heart gives way,
  there is no strength in my bones;
  because of the LORD, because of his
    holy words,
  I have become like a drunken man,
  like one overcome by wine.
¹⁰ For the land is full of adulterers,
  and because of them the earth lies
    parched,

22:22 **friends:** *or* leaders (*lit.* shepherds).
23:4 **punishment:** *or* be missing.   23:5 **righteous**
Branch: *or* legitimate Shoot.   23:8 **he:** *so Gk, cp.*
16:15; Heb. I.   23:10 **adulterers:** *or* idolaters.

areas were to the north and the east, the direction of exile or of flight. **21:** God speaks in this verse. **24–30:**
Concerning Jehoiachin (called *Coniah* here, but Jeconiah in 24.2 and 1 Chr. 3.16). **24:** *Signet ring:* a symbol
of authority (see Gen. 41.42; Hag. 2.23). **25–27:** See 2 Kgs. 24.8–17. **23.1–4:** The *shepherds* (kings) whom
God *will appoint;* see Ezek. 34.1–10. **5:** *Branch* is used also in Isa. 11.1 and Zech. 3.8 to designate the hoped
for ideal ruler from the tree of Jesse, father of David. **7–8:** A promise repeated from 16.14–15.
   23.9–40: Concerning prophets and prophecy. 10–12: Here God is speaking. See 2.8; 6.13. **13–15:** Prophets

the open pastures have dried up.
The lives they lead are wicked,
and the powers they possess are
misused.
11 For prophet and priest alike are
godless;
even in my house I have witnessed
their evil deeds.
This is the word of the LORD.
12 Therefore their path will turn slippery
beneath their feet;
they will be dispersed in the dark and
fall headlong,
for I shall bring disaster on them,
their day of reckoning.
This is the word of the LORD.
13 Among the prophets of Samaria
I found a lack of sense:
they prophesied in Baal's name
and led my people Israel astray.
14 Among the prophets of Jerusalem
I see a thing most horrible:
adulterers and hypocrites.
They encourage evildoers,
so that no one turns back from sin;
to me all her inhabitants
are like those of Sodom and Gomorrah.

15 These then are the words of the LORD of
Hosts about the prophets:

I shall give them wormwood to eat
and bitter poison to drink;
for from the prophets of Jerusalem
a godless spirit has spread to the whole
country.

16 These are the words of the LORD of Hosts:

Do not listen to what is prophesied to
you by the prophets,
who buoy you up with false hopes;
they give voice to their own fancies;
it is not the LORD's words they speak.
17 They say to those who spurn the word
of the LORD,
'Prosperity will be yours';
and to all who follow their stubborn
hearts they say,

'No harm will befall you.'
18 For which of them has stood in the
council of the LORD,
has been aware of his word and
listened to it?
Which of them has heeded his word
and obeyed?
19 See what a scorching wind has gone out
from the LORD,
a furious whirlwind
which whirls round the heads of the
wicked.
20 The LORD's anger is not to be turned
aside,
until he has fully accomplished his
purposes.
In days to come you will truly
understand.
21 I did not send these prophets,
yet they went in haste;
I did not speak to them,
yet they prophesied.
22 But if they had stood in my council,
they would have proclaimed my words
to my people
and turned them from their evil ways
and their evil doings.
23 Am I a God near at hand only, not a
God when far away?
24 Can anyone hide in some secret place
and I not see him?
Do I not fill heaven and earth?
This is the word of the LORD.

25 I have heard what the prophets say, the
prophets who speak lies in my name; they
cry, 'I have had a dream, I have had a
dream!' 26 How much longer will these
prophets be minded to prophesy lies and
give voice to their own inventions? 27 By these
dreams which they tell one another they
think they will make my people forget my
name, just as their fathers forgot my name
for the name of Baal. 28 If a prophet has a
dream, let him tell his dream; if he has my
word, let him speak my word faithfully.

23:23 **near at hand:** *so Gk; Heb. adds* says the LORD.
23:24 **see him:** *so Gk; Heb. adds* says the LORD.
23:27 **for the name of:** *or* by their worship of.

of Samaria is an allusion to times past, for, by Jeremiah's day, the *people Israel* had long been exiled, this after
the Assyrian conquest in 722. **19:** The *furious whirlwind* of the LORD's anger (v. 20) is not to be turned aside
by optimistic slogans. **22:** A prophet who has truly been admitted to intimacy with God (*stood in my council*)
brings word to *God's* people designed to *turn them from their evil ways.* **25–32:** Misdeeds of the self-appointed
prophets. **25:** They pass off mere *dreams* for true prophetic words. **26:** They *prophesy lies* and *give voice to*

Chaff and grain are quite distinct, says the LORD. ²⁹ Are not my words like fire, says the LORD; are they not like a hammer that shatters rock? ³⁰ Therefore I am against those prophets, the impostors who steal my words from the others, says the LORD. ³¹ I am against those prophets, says the LORD, who concoct words of their own and then say, 'This is his word.' ³² I am against those prophets, says the LORD, who deal in false dreams and relate them to mislead my people with wild and reckless falsehoods. It was not I who sent them or commissioned them, and they will do this people no good service. This is the word of the LORD.

³³ When you are asked by this people or by a prophet or a priest what is the burden of the LORD, you shall answer: You are the burden, and I shall throw you down, says the LORD. ³⁴ If anyone, prophet, priest, or layman, mentions 'the LORD's burden', I shall punish that person and his family. ³⁵ The form of words you shall use in speaking amongst yourselves is: 'What answer has the LORD given?' or, 'What has the LORD said?' ³⁶ You must never again mention 'the burden of the LORD'; for how can his word be a burden to anyone? But you pervert the words of the living God, the LORD of Hosts our God. ³⁷ This is the form you are to use in speaking to a prophet: 'What answer has the LORD given?' or, 'What has the LORD said?' ³⁸ But to any of you who do say 'the burden of the LORD', the LORD speaks thus: Because you say 'the burden of the LORD', though I sent to tell you not to say it, ³⁹ therefore I myself shall carry you like a burden and throw you away out of my sight, both you and the city which I gave to you and to your forefathers. ⁴⁰ I shall inflict on you endless reproach, endless shame which will never be forgotten.

24 ¹ THIS is what the LORD showed me: I saw two baskets of figs set out in front of the temple of the LORD. This was after King Nebuchadrezzar of Babylon had deported from Jerusalem Jeconiah son of Jehoiakim, king of Judah, with the officers of Judah, the craftsmen, and the smiths, and taken them to Babylon. ² In one basket the figs were very good, like those that are first ripe; in the other the figs were very bad, so bad that they were not fit to eat. ³ The LORD said to me, 'What are you looking at, Jeremiah?' 'Figs,' I answered, 'the good very good, and the bad so bad that they are not fit to eat.'

⁴ Then this word came to me from the LORD: ⁵ These are the words of the LORD the God of Israel: I count the exiles of Judah whom I sent away from this place to the land of the Chaldaeans as good as these good figs. ⁶ I shall look to their welfare, and restore them to this land; I shall build them up and not pull them down, plant them and not uproot them. ⁷ I shall give them the wit to know me, for I am the LORD; they will be my people and I shall be their God, for they will come back to me wholeheartedly.

⁸ But King Zedekiah of Judah, his officers, and the survivors of Jerusalem, both those who remain in this land and those who have settled in Egypt—all these I shall treat as bad figs, says the LORD, so bad that they are not fit to eat. ⁹ I shall make them abhorrent to all the kingdoms of the earth, a reproach, a byword, an object of taunting and cursing wherever I banish them. ¹⁰ I shall send sword,

23:36 **for . . . anyone:** *or* that is reserved for the man to whom he entrusts his message.   23:39 **carry . . . burden:** *or, with some MSS,* forget you.   24:1 **the smiths:** *or* the harem.   24:9 **abhorrent:** *so Gk; Heb. adds* a disaster.

their own fantasies, leading the people to apostasy. **28:** *Chaff . . . grain:* they are ignorant of the true intensity and power of God's words (see v. 9 and 20.9). **30:** *Steal my words:* they quote but distort the words of true prophets. **33–38:** In v. 33, there is a play on words, for *masa'* in Heb. is both something heavy to carry and also a prophetic message. In vv. 36, 38, the phrase *burden of the LORD* is regarded as offensive, an affront to the word of God, for God's word is not an unwelcome "burden." Hence, one should ask about God's *answer;* not God's *burden.*

24.1–10: Two baskets of figs suggests two groups within the people. One, the Judean exiles, will eventually be restored; the second, *survivors* still in *Jerusalem* (v. 8), will yet experience exile. For the literary form of a vision and its interpretation compare 1.11–12, 13–16. **1:** *In front of the temple:* like firstfruit offerings; see Deut. 26.1–4. *Jeconiah* (see 22.24–30 n.) was deported in 597 B.C.E (2 Kgs. 24.8–17). **6:** *Build them up . . . plant them:* after the threat comes the promise; see 1.10. **8:** This verse anticipates the events in ch. 43, with the wider dispersion of the conquered Judahites. See also 44.26–30. *Treat as bad figs:* See 29.17. **9:** *Abhorrent:* see 15.4; 29.18; 34.17. **10:** See 21.9; 27.8; Isa. 51.19.

famine, and pestilence against them until they have vanished from the land which I gave to them and to their forefathers.

25 This came to Jeremiah as the word concerning all the people of Judah in the fourth year of Jehoiakim son of Josiah, king of Judah, which was the first year of King Nebuchadrezzar of Babylon. ²This is what the prophet Jeremiah said to all Judah and all the inhabitants of Jerusalem: ³For twenty-three years, from the thirteenth year of Josiah son of Amon, king of Judah, up to the present day, I have been receiving the words of the LORD and speaking to you again and again, but you would not listen. ⁴Again and again the LORD has sent you all his servants the prophets, but you would not listen or show any inclination to listen. ⁵He promised that if each of you would turn from his wicked ways and evil conduct, then you would live for ever on the soil which the LORD gave to you and to your forefathers. ⁶You must not follow other gods, serving and worshipping them, nor must you provoke me to anger with the idols your hands have made; then I shall not harm you. ⁷But you would not listen to me, says the LORD; you provoked me to anger with the idols your hands had made and so brought harm upon yourselves.

⁸Therefore these are the words of the LORD of Hosts: Because you have not listened to my words, ⁹I shall summon all the tribes of the north, says the LORD, and I shall send for my servant King Nebuchadrezzar of Babylon. I shall bring them against this land and all its inhabitants and against all these nations round it; I shall exterminate them and make them an object of horror and astonishment, ruined for ever. ¹⁰I shall silence every sound of joy and gladness among them, the voices of bridegroom and bride, and the sound of the handmill; the light of every lamp will be quenched. ¹¹For seventy years this whole country will be a ruin, an object of horror, and these nations will be in subjection to the king of Babylon. ¹²When the seventy years are up, I shall punish the king of Babylon and his people, says the LORD, for all their misdeeds, and make the land of the Chaldaeans a waste for ever. ¹³I shall bring on that country all I have pronounced against it, all that is written in this scroll, all that Jeremiah has prophesied against all the nations. ¹⁴Mighty nations and great kings will reduce them to servitude, and thus I shall requite them for their actions and their deeds.

¹⁵These were the words of the LORD the God of Israel to me: Receive from my hand this cup of the wine of wrath, and make all the nations to whom I send you drink from it. ¹⁶When they have drunk they will vomit and become crazed; such is the sword which I am sending among them.

¹⁷I took the cup from the LORD's hand and made all the nations to whom he sent me drink it: ¹⁸Jerusalem and the towns of Judah, its kings and officers, turning them into a ruin, an object of horror, derision, and cursing, as they still are; ¹⁹Pharaoh king of Egypt, his courtiers, his officers, all his people, ²⁰and all his mixed crowd of followers, all the kings of the land of Uz, all the kings of the Philistines, of Ashkelon, Gaza, Ekron, and the remnant of Ashdod; ²¹also Edom, Moab, and the Ammonites, ²²all the kings of Tyre, of Sidon, and of the overseas coastlands; ²³also Dedan, Tema, Buz, and all who live in the fringes of the desert, ²⁴all the kings of Arabia living in the desert, ²⁵all the kings of Zimri, of Elam, and of the Medes, ²⁶all the kings of the north, neighbours or distant

25:23 **who live ... desert:** *or* who clip the hair on their temples.　　25:24 **kings of Arabia:** *so Gk; Heb.* adds and all the kings of the Arabs.

25.1–14: Ineffective warnings. Jeremiah, summarizing a twenty-three year effort, calls it a failure; he now foresees only disaster. **1:** *Fourth year:* 605 B.C.E., the year when Jeremiah dictated his prophecies to Baruch (36.1). The reference in v. 13 to "this scroll" suggests that possibly 25.1–14 is the conclusion of, or else the preface to, the second copy of the "scroll" mentioned in 36.27–32. **3:** *From the thirteenth year of Josiah:* see 1.2. **9:** *Babylon:* see 1.15 n. **11:** *Seventy:* actually Babylon fell in 539 B.C.E., fewer than *seventy years* from the destruction of Jerusalem in 587. Perhaps the seventy are reckoned (after the fact) to the rededication of the temple about 516 B.C.E. (see Ezra 6.15).

25.15–38: Worldwide devastation. All Judah's foes will sink in ruin along with it—a small measure of comfort. **15:** *Cup:* a frequent figure for experience; see Isa. 51.22–23; Mk. 14.36. *Wine of wrath:* a great disaster. **18:** *As they still are:* the words suggest a time of continuing decline. **20:** *Uz:* a place near Damascus.

from each other—all the kingdoms on the face of the earth. Last of all the king of Sheshak will have to drink.

²⁷ Say to them: These are the words of the LORD of Hosts the God of Israel: Drink this, get drunk, and be sick; fall down, never to rise again, because of the sword I am sending among you. ²⁸ If they refuse to accept the cup from you and to drink, say to them: These are the words of the LORD of Hosts: Most certainly you are to drink. ²⁹ I shall first punish the city which bears my name; do you think that you can be exempt? No, you will not be exempt, for I am summoning a sword against all the inhabitants of the earth. This is the word of the LORD of Hosts.

³⁰ Prophesy to them and tell them all I have said:

The LORD roars from on high,
he thunders from his holy
    dwelling-place.
He roars loudly against his land;
like those who tread the grapes he
    utters a shout
against all the inhabitants of the land.
³¹ The great noise reaches to the ends of
    the earth,
for the LORD brings a charge against
    the nations;
he arraigns all mankind
and has handed the wicked over to the
    sword.
This is the word of the LORD.

³² These are the words of the LORD of
    Hosts:
Ruin spreads from nation to nation,
a mighty tempest is blowing up
from the far corners of the earth.

³³ Those whom the LORD has slain on that day will lie scattered from one end of the earth to the other; they will not be mourned or taken up for burial; they will be dung spread over the ground.

³⁴ Wail, you shepherds, cry aloud,
    sprinkle yourselves with ashes, you
    masters of the flock.
It is your time to go to the slaughter,
    and you will fall like fine rams.
³⁵ The shepherds will have nowhere to
    flee,
    the flockmasters no way of escape.
³⁶ The shepherds cry out,
    the flockmasters wail,
    for the LORD is ravaging their pasture,
³⁷ and their peaceful homesteads lie in
    ruins
    beneath the LORD's fierce anger.
³⁸ They flee like a young lion abandoning
    his lair,
    for the land has become a waste
    under the sword of the oppressor
    and the fierce anger of the LORD.

26 AT the beginning of the reign of Jehoiakim son of Josiah, king of Judah, this word came from the LORD: ² These are the words of the LORD: Stand in the court of the LORD's house and speak to the inhabitants of all the towns of Judah who come to worship there. Tell them everything that I charge you to say to them; do not cut it short by one word. ³ Perhaps they may listen, and everyone may turn back from evil ways. If they do, I shall relent, and give up my plan to bring disaster on them for their evil deeds. ⁴ Say to them: These are the words of the LORD: If you do not obey me, if you do not live according to the law I have set before you, ⁵ and listen to the words of my servants the prophets, whom again and again I have been sending to you, though you have never listened to them, ⁶ then I shall do to this house as I did to Shiloh, and make this city an object of cursing to all nations on earth.

⁷ The priests, the prophets, and all the people heard Jeremiah say this in the LORD's

25:26 **Sheshak:** *a cipher for* Babylon.
25:34 **slaughter:** *so Gk; Heb. adds an unintelligible word.*
fine rams: *so Gk; Heb. a fine instrument.*
25:38 **sword:** *so some MSS; others heat.*

Ashkelon, Gaza, Ekron, Ashdod: Philistine cities. **23:** *Dedan, Tema, and Buz* were in central Arabia. **25:** *Zimri* is unknown. **29:** *City which bears my name:* Jerusalem. *All the inhabitants of the earth* is an apocalyptic phrase; see following note. **30–38:** This whole passage has the flavor of apocalypse, the prediction of a violent intervention of God into human history for judgment. **34:** *Shepherds:* rulers.

26.1–24: Jeremiah's arrest and release. Accused of a capital offense, Jeremiah is brought to trial, defends himself, finds support in a precedent, and is acquitted, though another prophet is executed for the same offense. **1:** *The beginning of the reign of Jehoiakim:* 609 B.C.E. **2–6:** An abstract of the temple sermon, more fully quoted house [8] and, when he came to the end of what the LORD had charged him to say to them, the priests and prophets and all the people seized him and threatened him with death. [9] 'Why', they demanded, 'do you prophesy in the LORD's name that this house will become like Shiloh and this city an uninhabited ruin?' The people all crowded round Jeremiah in the LORD's house. [10] When the chief officers of Judah heard what was happening, they went up from the royal palace to the LORD's house and took their places there at the entrance of the New Gate.

[11] The priests and the prophets said to the officers and all the people, 'This man deserves to be condemned to death, because he has prophesied against this city, as you yourselves have heard.' [12] Then Jeremiah said to all the officers and people, 'The LORD it was who sent me to prophesy against this house and this city all the things you have heard. [13] Now, if you mend your ways and your actions and obey the LORD your God, he may relent and revoke the disaster which he has pronounced against you. [14] But here I am in your hands; do with me whatever you think right and proper. [15] Only you may be certain that, if you put me to death, you and this city and those who live in it will be guilty of murdering an innocent man; for truly it was the LORD who sent me to you to say all this to you.'

[16] The officers and all the people then said to the priests and the prophets, 'This man ought not to be condemned to death, for he has spoken to us in the name of the LORD our God.' [17] Some of the elders of the land also stood up and said to the whole assembled people, [18] 'In the time of King Hezekiah of Judah, Micah of Moresheth was prophesying and said to all the people of Judah: "These are the words of the LORD of Hosts:

Zion will become a ploughed field,
Jerusalem a heap of ruins,
and the temple hill rough heath."

[19] 'Did King Hezekiah and all Judah put him to death? Did not the king show reverence for the LORD and seek to placate him, so that the LORD relented and revoked the disaster which he had pronounced on them? But we are on the point of inflicting great disaster on ourselves.'

[20] There was another man too who prophesied in the name of the LORD: Uriah son of Shemaiah, from Kiriath-jearim. He prophesied against this city and this land, just as Jeremiah had done. [21] King Jehoiakim with his bodyguard and all his officers heard what he said and sought to put him to death. On hearing of this, Uriah fled in fear to Egypt. [22] King Jehoiakim dispatched Elnathan son of Akbor with some others [23] to fetch Uriah from Egypt. When they brought him to the king, he had him put to the sword and his body flung into the burial-place of the common people. [24] But Ahikam son of Shaphan used his influence on Jeremiah's behalf to save him from death at the hands of the people.

Jeremiah opposes false prophets

27 At the beginning of the reign of Zedekiah son of Josiah, king of Judah, this word came to Jeremiah from the LORD: [2] These are the words of the LORD to me: Take the cords and crossbars of a yoke and put them on your neck. [3] Then send to the kings of Edom, Moab, Ammon, Tyre, and Sidon by their envoys who have come to King Zedekiah of Judah in Jerusalem, [4] and give them the following message for their masters: These are the words of the LORD of Hosts the God of Israel: Say to your masters: [5] It was I who by my great power and outstretched arm made the earth, along with mankind and the animals all over the earth, and I give it to whom I see fit. [6] Now I have handed over all these lands to my servant King Nebuchadnezzar of Babylon, and I

27:3 **Then send:** *so Gk (Luc.); Heb. adds* them.

in 7.1–15. **9:** Though Jeremiah said much more, what the people heard was: *This house shall become like Shiloh* (7.12 n.). The prophet had just laid the city under a curse; they must destroy him. **11:** *The officers and all the people* sit as a court in the temple gate. **12–15:** Jeremiah repeats the threat. **15:** *Truly it was the LORD who sent me* (see 1.4–10). His affirmation is here made explicit. **18–19:** *Hezekiah:* 715–687 B.C.E., about a century before this time. *Micah of Moresheth:* see Mic. 1.1. *Zion will become . . . rough heath:* the same phrase appears in Mic. 3.12. Hezekiah's *reverence for the LORD* is related not in the book of Mic. but in Isa. 37.14–21. **20:** *Uriah* is known only from this passage.

27.1–22: Jeremiah declares Nebuchadrezzar's success. 1: *Zedekiah* became king in 597 B.C.E. **3:** *Send:* send have given him even the creatures of the wild to serve him. 7 All nations will serve him, his son, and his grandson, until the destined hour of his own land comes; mighty nations and great kings will be subject to him. 8 If any nation or kingdom will not serve King Nebuchadnezzar of Babylon or submit to his yoke, I shall punish them with sword, famine, and pestilence, says the LORD, until I have ensured their destruction at his hand.

9 Therefore do not listen to your prophets, your diviners, your women dreamers, your soothsayers, and your sorcerers who keep on saying to you that you will not become subject to the king of Babylon. 10 Their prophecy to you is a lie; you will be carried away far from your native soil, and I shall banish you and you will perish. 11 But the nation which submits to the yoke of the king of Babylon and serves him I shall leave on their own soil, says the LORD; they will cultivate it and live there.

12 My message to King Zedekiah of Judah is no different: If you will submit to the yoke of the king of Babylon and serve him and his people, then you will save your lives. 13 Why should you and your people die by sword, famine, and pestilence, the fate with which the LORD has threatened any nation which does not serve the king of Babylon? 14 Do not listen to the prophets who say to you that you will not become subject to the king of Babylon. Their prophecy to you is a lie. 15 I have not sent them, says the LORD; they are prophesying falsely in my name; I shall banish you and you will perish, you and the prophets who prophesy to you.

16 I said to the priests and all this people: These are the words of the LORD: Do not listen to your prophets who tell you that very shortly the vessels of the LORD's house will be brought back from Babylon. Their prophecy to you is a lie. 17 Do not listen to them; serve the king of Babylon, and save your lives. Why should this city become a ruin? 18 If they are really prophets and have the word of the LORD, let them intercede with the LORD of

Hosts to grant that the things still left in the LORD's house, in the royal palace, and in Jerusalem, may not be carried off to Babylon. 19 For these are the words of the LORD of Hosts about the pillars, the Sea, the trolleys, and all the other furnishings still left in this city, 20 which King Nebuchadnezzar of Babylon did not take when he deported Jeconiah son of Jehoiakim, king of Judah, from Jerusalem to Babylon, together with all the nobles of Judah and Jerusalem. 21 These are the words of the LORD of Hosts the God of Israel about everything still left in the LORD's house, in the royal palace, and in Jerusalem: 22 They will be carried off to Babylon and remain there until I recall them, says the LORD; then I shall bring them back and restore them to this place.

28 That same year, at the beginning of the reign of King Zedekiah of Judah in the fifth month of the first year, Hananiah son of Azzur, the prophet from Gibeon, said to Jeremiah in the house of the LORD before the priests and all the people, 2 'These are the words of the LORD of Hosts the God of Israel: I shall break the yoke of the king of Babylon. 3 Within two years I shall restore to this place everything which King Nebuchadnezzar of Babylon took from the LORD's house and carried off to Babylon. 4 I shall also bring back to this place, says the LORD, Jeconiah son of Jehoiakim, king of Judah, and all the Judaean exiles who went to Babylon; for I shall break the yoke of the king of Babylon.'

5 The prophet Jeremiah gave this reply to Hananiah the prophet in the presence of the priests and all the people standing there in the LORD's house: 6 'May it be so! May the LORD indeed do this: may he fulfil all that you have prophesied, by bringing back the furnishings of the LORD's house together with all the exiles from Babylon to this place! 7 Only hear what I have to say to you and to all the people: 8 The prophets who preceded you and me from earliest times have foretold

28:1 **first:** *prob. rdg; Heb.* fourth.

---

word. *Their envoys* have come to draw Judah into an anti-Babylonian alliance. **7:** *The destined hour of his own land:* when Cyrus of Persia will break the power of Babylon (539 B.C.E.). **9:** *Prophets:* of these pagan nations. **12–15:** Jeremiah's word to *Zedekiah, king of Judah.* **16–22:** Jeremiah's word to the *priests* and *people.* **16:** *The vessels* were taken as loot in 597 (see vv. 19–20). *Very shortly:* within two years, according to 28.3. **17:** See 21.8–10.

28.1–17: Two types of prophets in conflict. Hananiah disputes Jeremiah's claims and hears God's adverse judgment. **1:** The same year as the events in ch. 27. **3:** Temple treasures. **6:** *May it be so!:* the Heb. word is *amen. May the LORD indeed do this:* although Jeremiah believes that it will not come about, he wishes that war, famine, and pestilence for many lands and for great kingdoms. ⁹If a prophet foretells prosperity, it will be known that the LORD has sent him only when his words come true.'

¹⁰Then the prophet Hananiah took the yoke from the neck of the prophet Jeremiah and broke it, ¹¹announcing to all the people, 'These are the words of the LORD: So shall I break the yoke of King Nebuchadnezzar of Babylon; I shall break it off the necks of all nations within two years.' Then the prophet Jeremiah went his way.

¹²After Hananiah had broken the yoke which had been on Jeremiah's neck, the word of the LORD came to Jeremiah: ¹³Go and say to Hananiah: These are the words of the LORD: You have broken bars of wood; in their place you will get bars of iron. ¹⁴For these are the words of the LORD of Hosts the God of Israel: I shall lay an iron yoke on the necks of all these nations, making them serve King Nebuchadnezzar of Babylon. They will be enslaved to him. I have given him even the creatures of the wild. ¹⁵Then Jeremiah said to Hananiah, 'Listen, Hananiah. The LORD never sent you, and you have led this nation to trust in false prophecies. ¹⁶Therefore these are the words of the LORD: I shall remove you from the face of the earth; within a year you will die, because you have preached rebellion against the LORD.' ¹⁷The prophet Hananiah died in the seventh month of that same year.

29 Jeremiah sent a letter from Jerusalem to the elders who were left among the exiles, to the priests, prophets, and all the people whom Nebuchadnezzar had deported from Jerusalem to Babylon, ²after King Jeconiah, with the queen mother and the eunuchs, the officers of Judah and Jerusalem, the craftsmen, and the smiths, had left Jerusalem. ³The prophet entrusted the letter to Elasah son of Shaphan and Gemariah son of Hilkiah, whom King Zedekiah of Judah had sent to Babylon to King Nebuchadnezzar. This is what he wrote:

⁴These are the words of the LORD of Hosts the God of Israel: To all the exiles whom I deported from Jerusalem to Babylon: ⁵Build houses and live in them; plant gardens and eat the produce; ⁶marry wives and rear families; choose wives for your sons and give your daughters to husbands, so that they may bear sons and daughters. Increase there and do not dwindle away. ⁷Seek the welfare of any city to which I have exiled you, and pray to the LORD for it; on its welfare your welfare will depend. ⁸For these are the words of the LORD of Hosts the God of Israel: Do not be deceived by the prophets and diviners among you, and pay no attention to the women whom you set to dream dreams. ⁹They prophesy falsely to you in my name; I did not send them. This is the word of the LORD.

¹⁰These are the words of the LORD: When a full seventy years have passed over Babylon, I shall take up your cause and make good my promise to bring you back to this place. ¹¹I alone know my purpose for you, says the LORD: wellbeing and not misfortune, and a long line of descendants after you. ¹²If you invoke me and come and pray to me, I shall listen to you: ¹³when you seek me, you will find me; if you search wholeheartedly, ¹⁴I shall let you find me, says the LORD. I shall restore your fortunes; I shall gather you from all the nations and all the places to which I have banished you, says the LORD, and restore you to the place from which I carried you into exile.

¹⁵You say that the LORD has raised up prophets for you in Babylon. ¹⁶These are the words of the LORD concerning the king who sits on the throne of David and all the people who live in this city, your fellow-countrymen who have not gone into exile with you. ¹⁷These are the words of the LORD of Hosts: I am bringing sword, famine, and pestilence on them, making them

---

29:2 **the smiths:** *or* the harem.

it would. **8–9:** Only when the words of a prophet foretelling prosperity *come true* will such a prophecy be recognized as authentic. **16:** *You will die . . . because you have preached rebellion against the LORD:* see Deut. 13.5.

29.1–32: Messages to the exiles. 1–23: The first letter. **2:** The time is after the first deportation in 597. **3:** The opportunity is the sending of envoys to Nebuchadnezzar. **10:** Babylon's *seventy years* are possibly reckoned (approximately) from the battle of Carchemish in 605 to the fall of Babylon in 539. **12:** *If you . . . pray to me I will listen to you:* even in Babylonia. **16–18:** *This city:* Jerusalem; still populous between the first and second like rotten figs, too bad to eat. ¹⁸I shall pursue them with sword, famine, and pestilence, and make them abhorrent to all the kingdoms of the earth, an object of execration and horror, of derision and reproach among all the nations to which I have banished them. ¹⁹Just as they did not listen to my words, says the LORD, when time and again I sent my servants the prophets, so you did not listen, says the LORD.

²⁰But now listen to the words of the LORD, all you exiles whom I have sent from Jerusalem to Babylon. ²¹These are the words of the LORD of Hosts the God of Israel about Ahab son of Kolaiah and Zedekiah son of Maaseiah, who prophesy lies to you in my name. I am handing them over to King Nebuchadrezzar of Babylon, and he will put them to death before your eyes. ²²Their names will be used by all the exiles of Judah in Babylon when they curse anyone; they will say: May the LORD treat you like Zedekiah and Ahab, whom the king of Babylon roasted to death in the fire! ²³For their conduct in Israel was an outrage: they committed adultery with their neighbours' wives, and prophesied in my name without my authority, and what they prophesied was false. I am he who knows and can testify. This is the word of the LORD.

²⁴To Shemaiah the Nehelamite. ²⁵These are the words of the LORD of Hosts the God of Israel: You have sent a letter on your own authority to Zephaniah son of Maaseiah the priest, in which you say: ²⁶'The LORD has appointed you to be priest in place of Jehoiada the priest, and it is your duty, as officer in charge of the LORD's house, to put every crazy person who poses as a prophet into the stocks and the pillory. ²⁷Why, then, have you not restrained Jeremiah of Anathoth, who acts the prophet among you? ²⁸On the strength of this he has sent us a message in Babylon to say, "Your exile will be long; build houses and live in them, plant gardens and eat their produce." '

²⁹When Zephaniah the priest read this letter to Jeremiah the prophet, ³⁰this word of the LORD came to Jeremiah: ³¹Send and tell all the exiles that these are the words of the LORD concerning Shemaiah the Nehelamite: Because Shemaiah has prophesied to you, though I did not send him, and has led you to trust in false prophecies, ³²these are now the words of the LORD: I shall punish Shemaiah and his posterity. He will leave no one to take his place in this nation and witness the wellbeing which I shall bestow on my people, says the LORD, because he has urged rebellion against me.

Promises of restoration for the people

30 THE word which came to Jeremiah from the LORD. ²These are the words of the LORD the God of Israel: Write on a scroll all that I have said to you. ³The time is coming when I shall restore the fortunes of my people, both Israel and Judah, says the LORD, and bring them back to take possession of the land which I gave to their ancestors.

⁴This is what the LORD has said to Israel and Judah. ⁵These are the words of the LORD:

We have heard a cry of terror, of fear
    without relief.
⁶Enquire and see: can a man bear a
    child?
Why then do I see every man
gripping his sides like a woman in
    labour?
Why has every face turned deadly pale?
⁷How awful is that day:

29:25 **authority:** *so Gk; Heb. adds* to all the people in Jerusalem. **the priest:** *so Gk; Heb. adds* and to all the priests.   29:26 **officer:** *so Gk; Heb.* officers.

deportations, it was yet to experience defeat and ruin; see 24.8–10. **21–23:** *Ahab . . . and Zedekiah:* two prophets in Babylonia not mentioned elsewhere. **22:** *May the Lord treat you like . . . :* this is a formula used in a curse, the counterpart of the formula for blessing in Gen. 48.20. **24–32:** The second letter. **28:** He (correctly) understood Jeremiah to be saying: *"Your exile will be long,"* that is, longer than Hananiah's predicted two years (28.3).

30.1–31.40: Hopes for the restoration of Jerusalem. It is sometimes argued that these chapters originally held out hope for the exiles of the Northern Kingdom alone. As we have them now, they clearly speak to the exiles of the Southern Kingdom, too. References to the restoration of Judah are necessarily later than the fall of Jerusalem. **4–7:** The concluding line, *Yet he will come through it safely,* contains the consolation that an

when has there been its like?
A time of anguish for Jacob,
yet he will come through it safely.

8 On that day, says the LORD of Hosts, I shall break their yoke off their necks and snap their cords; foreigners will no longer reduce them to servitude; 9 they will serve the LORD their God and David their king, whom I shall raise up for them.

10 But do not be afraid, Jacob my servant;
Israel, do not despair, says the LORD.
For I shall bring you back safe from afar,
and your posterity from the land where they are captives.
Jacob will be at rest once more,
secure and untroubled.
11 For I am with you to save you, says the LORD.
I shall make an end of all the nations among whom I have dispersed you,
but I shall not make an end of you.
I shall discipline you only as you deserve,
I shall not leave you wholly unpunished.

12 For these are the words of the LORD to Zion:

Your wound is past healing;
the blow you suffered was cruel.
13 There can be no remedy for your sore;
the new skin cannot grow.
14 All your friends have forgotten you;
they look for you no longer.
I have struck you down as an enemy strikes,
and have punished you cruelly,
because of your great wickedness, your flagrant sins.
15 Why complain of your injury,
that your sore cannot be healed?
Because of your great wickedness, your flagrant sins,
I have done this to you.

16 Yet all who devoured you will themselves be devoured;
all your oppressors will go into captivity;
those who plunder you will be plundered,
and those who despoil you I shall give up to be spoiled.
17 I shall cause the new skin to grow and heal your wounds, says the LORD,
although you are called outcast, Zion,
forsaken by all.

18 These are the words of the LORD:

I shall restore the fortunes of Jacob's clans
and show my love for his dwellings.
Every city will be rebuilt on its own mound,
every mansion will occupy its traditional site.
19 From them praise will be heard and sounds of merrymaking.
I shall increase them, they will not diminish;
I shall raise them to honour,
no longer to be despised.
20 Their children will be what once they were,
and their community will be established in my sight.
I shall punish all their oppressors.
21 A ruler will appear, one of themselves;
a governor will arise from their own number.
I shall myself bring him near and let him approach me,
for who dare risk his life by approaching me?
says the LORD.
22 So you will be my people,
and I shall be your God.
23 See what a scorching wind has gone out from the LORD,
a sweeping whirlwind

30:8 their necks . . . their cords: so Gk; Heb. your neck . . . your cords. 30:13 no: prob. rdg; Heb. adds one judging your case.

extreme crisis has been overcome. 8–11: The bright future. 9: *David their king:* the restoration of the monarchy to a descendant of David. 12–17: Again, Zion's disaster overcome. 18–24: The ruins will be restored and the kingdom reconstituted. 18: *Jacob's clans:* the ten northern tribes, not yet considered "lost" (3.12 n.). 21: *A ruler . . . from their own number;* the end of foreign domination. 22: *My people . . . your God:* this ancient formula reaffirms the covenant. 23–24: *The wicked* are those who hold God's people in captivity; see v. 16. The verses

which whirls round the heads of the
wicked.
24 The Lord's fierce anger is not to be
turned aside
until he has fully accomplished his
purposes.
In days to come you will understand.

31 At that time, says the Lord, I shall be
the God of all the families of Israel,
and they will be my people. 2 These are the
words of the Lord:

A people that escaped the sword
found favour in the wilderness.
The Lord went to give rest to Israel;
3 from afar he appeared to them:
I have dearly loved you from of old,
and still I maintain my unfailing care
for you.
4 Virgin Israel, I shall build you up
again,
and you will be rebuilt.
Again you will provide yourself with
tambourines,
and go forth with the merry throng of
dancers.
5 Again you will plant vineyards on the
hills of Samaria,
and those who plant them will enjoy
the fruit;
6 for a day will come when the watchmen
cry out on Ephraim's hills,
'Come, let us go up to Zion,
to the Lord our God.'

7 For these are the words of the Lord:

Break into shouts of joy for Jacob's
sake,
lead the nations, crying loud and clear,
sing out your praises and say:
'The Lord has saved his people;
he has preserved a remnant of Israel.'
8 See how I bring them from a northern
land;
I shall gather them from the far ends
of the earth,
among them the blind and lame,
the woman with child and the woman
in labour.

A vast company, 9 they come home,
weeping as they come,
but I shall comfort them and be their
escort.
I shall lead them by streams of water;
their path will be smooth, they will not
stumble.
For I have become a father to Israel,
and Ephraim is my eldest son.
10 Listen to the word of the Lord, you
nations,
announce it, make it known to
coastlands far away:
He who scattered Israel will gather
them again
and watch over them as a shepherd
watches his flock.
11 For the Lord has delivered Jacob
and redeemed him from a foe too
strong for him.
12 They will come with shouts of joy to
Zion's height,
radiant at the bounty of the Lord:
the grain, the new wine, and the oil,
the young of flock and herd.
They will be like a well-watered garden
and never languish again.
13 Girls will then dance for joy,
and men young and old will rejoice;
I shall turn their grief into gladness,
comfort them, and give them joy after
sorrow.
14 I shall satisfy the priests with the fat of
the land
and my people will have their fill of my
bounty.
This is the word of the Lord.

15 These are the words of the Lord:

Lamentation is heard in Ramah, and
bitter weeping:
Rachel weeping for her children
and refusing to be comforted, because
they are no more.

16 These are the words of the Lord to her:

31:3 **them:** *so Gk; Heb.* me.   31:7 **his:** *so Gk; Heb.*
your.   31:9 **I shall comfort them:** *so Gk; Heb.*
prayers for favour.

repeat 23.19–20. **31.1–22:** God's constant love for the Northern Kingdom. **4:** Dancing in *vineyards* was an
ancient ritual; see Judg. 21.19–21. **5:** *Samaria:* the capital of the Northern Kingdom. **6:** *Ephraim:* see 7.15 n.
Zion: The mention here suggests a future reunion of the two Hebrew kingdoms. **8:** *A northern land:* the distant
regions of Assyria; see 2 Kgs. 17.6. **15:** *Ramah:* a place in Benjamin. *Rachel* was the mother of Benjamin and

Cease your weeping,
shed no more tears;
for there will be a reward for your toil,
and they will return from the enemy's
land.
17 There will be hope for your posterity;
your children will return within their
own borders.

18 I listened intently;
Ephraim was rocking in his grief:
'I was like a calf unbroken to the yoke;
you disciplined me, and I accepted your
discipline.
Bring me back and let me return,
for you are the LORD my God.
19 Though I broke away I have repented:
now that I am submissive I beat my
breast;
in shame and remorse
I reproach myself for the sins of my
youth.'

20 Is Ephraim still so dear a son to me,
a child in whom I so delight
that, as often as I speak against him,
I must think of him again?
Therefore my heart yearns for him;
I am filled with tenderness towards
him.
This is the word of the LORD.

21 Build cairns to mark your way,
set up signposts;
make sure of the road,
the path which you will tread.
Come back, virgin Israel,
come back to your cities and towns.
22 How long will you waver, my wayward
child?
For the LORD has created a new thing
in the earth:
a woman will play a man's part.

23 These are the words of the LORD of Hosts
the God of Israel: Once more will these

words be heard in the land of Judah and in
her towns, when I restore their fortunes:

The LORD bless you,
abode of righteousness, holy mountain.
24 Ploughmen and shepherds with their
flocks
will live together in Judah and all her
towns.
25 For I have given deep draughts to the
thirsty,
and satisfied those who were faint with
hunger.

26 Thereupon I woke and looked about me,
and my sleep had been pleasant.
27 The days are coming, says the LORD,
when I shall sow Israel and Judah with the
seed of man and the seed of cattle. 28 As I
watched over them with intent to pull down
and to uproot, to demolish and destroy and
inflict disaster, so now I shall watch over
them to build and to plant. This is the word
of the LORD.
29 In those days it will no longer be said,

'Parents have eaten sour grapes
and the children's teeth are set on
edge';

30 for everyone will die for his own wrongdoing; he who eats the sour grapes will find his
own teeth set on edge.
31 The days are coming, says the LORD,
when I shall establish a new covenant with
the people of Israel and Judah. 32 It will not
be like the covenant I made with their forefathers when I took them by the hand to lead
them out of Egypt, a covenant they broke,
though I was patient with them, says the
LORD. 33 For this is the covenant I shall establish with the Israelites after those days, says
the LORD: I shall set my law within them,
writing it on their hearts; I shall be their God,
and they will be my people. 34 No longer need
they teach one another, neighbour or

31:32 **I was . . . them:** *or* I had authority over them.

Joseph, and the grandmother of Ephraim and Manasseh, tribes of the Northern Kingdom. **18–20:** Ephraim's
penitent words. **20:** See Hos. 11.8. **22:** *A woman will play a man's part:* The meaning is obscure. Perhaps it
is a reference to the mixed figure that the *virgin Israel* (v. 21) is God's *dear son* (v. 20), or that those regarded
as weak will be victorious. **23–25:** The restoration of Judah. **23:** *Abode of righteousness:* a probable designation
for Jerusalem, *the holy mountain;* see 33.16 for another use of righteousness. **26:** The prophet, or a reader,
reflects on the preceding lines. **27–40:** The fulfillment of gleaming promises. **28:** See 1.10. **31–34:** *A new
covenant:* unlike a usual covenant, it will not depend on external knowledge, nor be recorded on stone tablets,

brother, to know the LORD; all of them, high and low alike, will know me, says the LORD, for I shall forgive their wrongdoing, and their sin I shall call to mind no more.

35 These are the words of the LORD,
    who gave the sun for a light by day
    and the moon and stars in their courses
    for a light by night,
    who cleft the sea and its waves roared;
    the LORD of Hosts is his name.

36 Israel could no more cease to be a nation in my sight, says the LORD, than could this fixed order vanish before my eyes.

37 These are the words of the LORD: I could no more spurn the whole of Israel because of what they have done, than anyone could measure the heaven above or fathom the depths of the earth beneath. This is the word of the LORD.

38 The days are coming, says the LORD, when Jerusalem will be rebuilt in the LORD's honour from the Tower of Hananel to the Corner Gate. 39 The measuring line will then be laid straight out over the hill of Gareb and round Goath. 40 All the valley and every field as far as the wadi Kidron to the corner by the Horse Gate eastwards will be holy to the LORD. Never again will it be pulled down or demolished.

32 The word which came to Jeremiah from the LORD in the tenth year of King Zedekiah of Judah, which was the eighteenth year of Nebuchadrezzar. 2 At that time the forces of the Babylonian king were besieging Jerusalem, and the prophet Jeremiah was imprisoned in the court of the guardhouse attached to the royal palace. 3 King Zedekiah had imprisoned him after demanding what he meant by this prophecy: 'These are the words of the LORD: I shall give this city into the power of the king of Babylon, and he will capture it. 4 Nor will King Zede-

kiah of Judah escape from the Chaldaeans; he will be surrendered to the king of Babylon and will speak with him face to face and see him with his own eyes. 5 Zedekiah will be taken to Babylon and will remain there until the day I visit him, says the LORD. However much you fight against the Chaldaeans you will have no success.'

6 Jeremiah said: This word of the LORD came to me: 7 Hanamel son of your uncle Shallum is coming to you; he will say, 'Buy my field at Anathoth; as next-of-kin you have the right of redemption to buy it.' 8 Just as the LORD had foretold, my cousin Hanamel came to me in the court of the guardhouse and said, 'Buy my field at Anathoth in Benjamin. You have the right of redemption and possession as next-of-kin, so buy it for yourself.' I recognized that this instruction came from the LORD, 9 so I bought the field at Anathoth from my cousin Hanamel and weighed out the price for him, seventeen shekels of silver. 10 I signed and sealed the deed, had it witnessed, and then weighed the money on the scales. 11 I took my copies of the deed of purchase, both the sealed and the unsealed copies, 12 and handed them over to Baruch son of Neriah, son of Mahseiah, in the presence of Hanamel my cousin and the witnesses whose names were subscribed on the deed of purchase, and of the Judaeans sitting in the court of the guardhouse. 13 In their presence I gave my instructions to Baruch: 14 These are the words of the LORD of Hosts the God of Israel: Take these copies of the deed of purchase, both the sealed and the unsealed copies, and deposit them in an earthenware jar so that they may be preserved for a long time to come. 15 For these are the words of the LORD of Hosts the God

31:39 **Goath:** *or* Goah.   31:40 **the valley:** *prob. rdg;* Heb. *adds* the corpses and the buried bodies. 32:11 **the sealed:** *so Gk; Heb. adds* the command and the statutes.

but will be internal, written on the *hearts* of the people. **35–37:** That God could reject Israel is not conceivable. **38–40:** The places mentioned were in or near Jerusalem.

32.1–44: Jeremiah's confidence in a restored Judah. 1: *Tenth year:* 588, the year before Jerusalem fell; see 2 Kgs. 25.1–4. **2:** *Imprisoned* (see 38.2–6, 13). Yet Jeremiah had considerable freedom of movement. **7:** *Anathoth:* see 1.1. *Right of redemption:* land remained within the family; if anyone had to sell property the *next-of-kin* had the duty, as well as the right, to purchase it; see Lev. 25.25. **8:** When it happened *as the LORD had foretold* Jeremiah *knew that this instruction came from the LORD.* **11:** *The sealed and the unsealed:* clay tablets in Mesopotamia and papyrus rolls in Egypt were completed, with one copy open and one sealed for security. *Baruch:* see 36.4. **14:** *In an earthenware jar:* the Qumran (Dead Sea) Scrolls were similarly preserved. **15:** The meaning is that since not all of the people would be taken captive nor the kingdom be destroyed forever, of Israel: Houses, fields, and vineyards will again be bought and sold in this land.

¹⁶ After I handed over the deed of purchase to Baruch son of Neriah, I offered this prayer to the LORD: ¹⁷ Lord GOD, maker of the heavens and the earth by your great power and outstretched arm, nothing is impossible for you. ¹⁸ You keep faith with thousands but punish the children for the sins of their fathers. Great and mighty God whose name is the LORD of Hosts, ¹⁹ great in purpose and mighty in action, your eyes watch all the ways of mortals, rewarding each according to his conduct and as his deeds deserve. ²⁰ You worked signs and portents in Egypt and have continued them to this day, both in Israel and among all mankind, and have won for yourself renown that lives on to this day. ²¹ You brought your people Israel out of Egypt amid signs and portents, with a strong hand and an outstretched arm, and with great terror. ²² You gave them this land which you promised with an oath to their forefathers, a land flowing with milk and honey. ²³ They came and took possession of it, but they did not obey you or follow your law; they did not perform all you commanded them to do, and so you have brought on them this whole disaster: ²⁴ siege-ramps, and men advancing to take the city; and the city, victim of sword, famine, and pestilence, is given over to the attacking Chaldaeans. What you threatened has come true, as you see. ²⁵ And yet, Lord GOD, you have bidden me buy the field and have the deed witnessed, even though the city is to be given into the power of the Chaldaeans!

²⁶ These are the words of the LORD to Jeremiah: ²⁷ I am the LORD, the God of all mankind; is anything impossible for me? ²⁸ Therefore these are the words of the LORD: I am about to give this city into the hands of the Chaldaeans and of King Nebuchadrezzar of Babylon, and he will take it. ²⁹ The Chaldaeans assailing this city will enter and set it on fire; they will burn it down, together with the houses on whose roofs sacrifices have been burnt to Baal and drink-offerings poured out to other gods, by which I was provoked to anger.

³⁰ From their earliest days Israel and Judah have been doing what is wrong in my eyes, provoking me to anger by their idolatry, says the LORD. ³¹ For this city has so roused my anger and my fury, from the time it was built down to this day, that I mean to rid myself of it. ³² Israel and Judah, their kings, officers, priests, prophets, and the people of Judah and the citizens of Jerusalem, have provoked me to anger by their wrongdoing. ³³ They have turned their backs on me and averted their faces; though I taught them again and again, they would not hear or learn their lesson. ³⁴ They set up their loathsome idols in the house which bears my name and so defiled it. ³⁵ They built shrines to Baal in the valley of Ben-hinnom, at which to offer up their sons and daughters to Molech. That was no command of mine to them, nor did it ever enter my mind that they should do this abominable thing, so causing Judah to sin.

³⁶ Now, therefore, these are the words of the LORD the God of Israel to this city of which you say, 'It is being given over to the king of Babylon, by sword, famine, and pestilence':

³⁷ I shall gather them from all the lands to which I banished them in my furious anger and great wrath; I shall bring them back to this place and let them dwell there undisturbed. ³⁸ They will be my people and I shall be their God. ³⁹ I shall give them singleness of heart and one way of life so that they will fear me at all times, for their own good and the good of their children after them. ⁴⁰ I shall enter into an everlasting covenant with them, to follow them unfailingly with my bounty; I shall put fear of me into their hearts, and so they will not turn away from me. ⁴¹ It will be a joy to me to do them good, and faithfully with all my heart and soul I shall plant them in this land.

---

people would make use of the land they bought. **16–44:** The rest of the chapter enlarges on the theme already clearly stated and is thought to be a later supplement; the language is conventional. **16–25:** A prayer for enlightenment: God's actions are beyond challenge; *and yet* (v. 25) God has led the prophet to perform a wholly irrational act, so that one must wonder. **26–44:** God responds: After Judah has fared as it has indeed deserved, the relationship between God and the people will be restored. **35:** See 19.4–5. There "Baal," the Canaanite god, stands in place of the Moabite god *Molech* here. **39–40:** God will *give them singleness of heart,* so that they will *fear* (stand in awe of) God, by such divine initiative excluding all contingency from the arrangement. *An everlasting covenant* is, in fact, a divine commitment; see 31.31–34 n.

⁴²For these are the words of the LORD: As I brought upon this people all this great disaster, so shall I bring them all the prosperity which I now promise them. ⁴³Fields will again be bought and sold in this land of which you now say, 'It is a desolation abandoned by man and beast; it is given over to the Chaldaeans.' ⁴⁴Fields will be bought and sold, deeds signed, sealed, and witnessed, in Benjamin, in the neighbourhood of Jerusalem, in the towns of Judah, of the hill-country, of the Shephelah, and of the Negeb; for I shall restore their fortunes. This is the word of the LORD.

33 The word of the LORD came to Jeremiah a second time while he was still imprisoned in the court of the guardhouse: ²These are the words of the LORD who made the earth, who formed and established it; the LORD is his name: ³If you call to me I shall answer, and tell you great and mysterious things of which you are still unaware. ⁴These are the words of the LORD the God of Israel about the houses in this city and the royal palaces of Judah which are razed to the ground, about siege-ramp and sword, ⁵and the Chaldaean attackers who leave the houses full of corpses: I struck them down in anger and rage, and hid my face from this city because of all their wicked ways.

⁶Now I shall bring healing and care for her; I shall cure Judah and Israel, and let them see lasting peace and security. ⁷I shall restore their fortunes and rebuild them as once they were. ⁸I shall cleanse them of all the wickedness and sin that they have committed, and forgive all the evil deeds they have done in rebellion against me. ⁹This city will win me renown and praise and glory before all the nations of the world, as they hear of all the blessings I bestow on her; and they will be filled with awe and deeply moved because of all the blessings and the prosperity which I bring on her.

¹⁰These are the words of the LORD: You say of this place, 'It lies in ruins, without people or animals throughout the towns of Ju-

dah and the streets of Jerusalem. It is all a waste, inhabited by neither man nor beast.' ¹¹Yet in this place will be heard once more the sounds of joy and gladness, the voices of bridegroom and bride; here too will be heard voices shouting, 'Praise the LORD of Hosts, for the LORD is good; his love endures for ever,' as they offer praise and thanksgiving in the house of the LORD. For I shall restore the fortunes of the land as once they were. This is the word of the LORD.

¹²These are the words of the LORD of Hosts: In this place and in all its towns, now ruined and devoid of both people and animals, there will once more be sheepfolds where shepherds may keep their flocks. ¹³In the towns of the hill-country, of the Shephelah, of the Negeb, in Benjamin, in the neighbourhood of Jerusalem and the towns of Judah, flocks will once more pass under the shepherd's hand as he counts them. This is the word of the LORD.

¹⁴The days are coming, says the LORD, when I shall bestow on Israel and Judah all the blessings I have promised them. ¹⁵In those days, at that time, I shall make a righteous Branch spring from David's line; he will maintain law and justice in the land. ¹⁶In those days Judah will be kept safe and Jerusalem will live undisturbed. This will be the name given to him: The LORD our Righteousness.

¹⁷For these are the words of the LORD: David will never lack a successor on the throne of Israel, ¹⁸nor will there ever be lacking a levitical priest to present whole-offerings, to burn grain-offerings, and to make other offerings every day.

¹⁹This word came from the LORD to Jeremiah: ²⁰These are the words of the LORD: It would be as unthinkable to annul the covenant that I made for the day and the night, so that they should fall out of their proper order, ²¹as to annul my covenant with my servant David, so that he would have none of

33:2 **the earth:** *so Gk; Heb.* it.   33:9 **renown:** *prob. rdg; Heb. adds* of joy.

33.1–26: More comforting thoughts. These supplement chs. 30–32. With vv. 1–9 compare 32.36–44. **8:** *I shall cleanse them:* as in 31.34 God takes the initiative. **9:** *This city will win me renown:* see 13.11 n. **10:** The destruction is no longer a prospect, but now a reality; accordingly, the passage comes after 587. **11:** *'Praise the LORD of Hosts . . . ':* this phrase is a variant of Ps. 136.1. *Offer . . . thanksgiving:* the sacrifice of a thank-offering (Lev. 22.29) as acknowledgment of blessings received. **14–16:** See 23.5–6 and 31.23 n. **17–22:** The abiding stability of the Davidic and Levitical lines. **17:** That *David will never lack a successor* (see 2 Sam. 7.11–16) was an article of faith frequently invoked in postexilic times. **18:** *Nor will there ever be lacking a* his line to sit on his throne; likewise it would be unthinkable to annul my covenant with the levitical priests who minister to me. 22 Like the innumerable host of heaven or the countless sands of the sea, I shall increase the descendants of my servant David and the Levites who minister to me.

23 The word of the LORD came to Jeremiah: 24 Have you not observed how this people have said, 'It is the two families whom he chose that the LORD has rejected'? So others will despise my people and no longer regard them as a nation. 25 These are the words of the LORD: If there were no covenant for day and night, and if I had not established a fixed order in heaven and earth, 26 then I could spurn the descendants of Jacob and of my servant David, and not take any of David's line to be rulers over the descendants of Abraham, Isaac, and Jacob. But in my compassion I shall restore their fortunes.

Events under Jehoiakim and Zedekiah

34 THE word which came to Jeremiah from the LORD when King Nebuchadrezzar of Babylon and his whole army, along with all his vassal kingdoms and nations, were attacking Jerusalem and all her towns.

2 These are the words of the LORD the God of Israel: Go and say to King Zedekiah of Judah: These are the words of the LORD: I shall hand over this city to the king of Babylon and he will burn it to the ground. 3 You yourself will not escape; your capture is certain, and you will be delivered into his hands. You will see him with your own eyes, and he will speak to you face to face, and you will go to Babylon. 4 But listen to the LORD's word to you, King Zedekiah of Judah. This is his word: You will not die by the sword; 5 you will die a peaceful death, and they will kindle funeral fires in your honour like the fires kindled in former times for the kings your ancestors who preceded you. 'Alas, my lord!'

they will say as they beat their breasts in mourning for you. It is a promise I have made. This is the word of the LORD.

6 The prophet Jeremiah repeated all this to King Zedekiah of Judah in Jerusalem 7 while the army of the king of Babylon was attacking Jerusalem and the remaining towns in Judah, namely Lachish and Azekah, the only fortified towns left there.

8 The word that came to Jeremiah from the LORD after King Zedekiah had entered into an agreement with all the people in Jerusalem to proclaim freedom for their slaves: 9 everyone who had Hebrew slaves, male or female, was to set them free; no one was to keep a fellow-Jew in servitude. 10 All the officers and people, having entered this agreement to set free their slaves, both male and female, and not to keep them in servitude any longer, fulfilled its terms and let them go. 11 Afterwards, however, they changed their minds and forced back again into slavery the men and women whom they had freed.

12 Then this word came from the LORD to Jeremiah: 13 These are the words of the LORD the God of Israel: I made a covenant with your forefathers when I brought them out of Egypt, out of the land of slavery. These were its terms: 14 'Within seven years each of you must liberate any Hebrew who has sold himself to you as a slave and has served you for six years.' Your forefathers did not listen to me or obey me, 15 but recently you proclaimed freedom for the slaves and made an agreement in my presence, in the house that bears my name, and so did what is right in my eyes. 16 Now, however, you have renounced this agreement and profaned my name by taking back the slaves you had set free and forcing them all, both male and female, to become your slaves again.

17 Therefore these are the words of the LORD: After you had proclaimed freedom, a deliverance for your kinsmen and your neighbours, you did not obey me; so I shall proclaim a deliverance for you, says the

---

levitical priest: see 1 Sam. 2.35. 23–26: God will never spurn . . . the descendants of Abraham, Isaac, and Jacob or leave them without a legitimate ruler.

34.1–7: A warning to Zedekiah about his captivity. 1: The time is just before the final siege. 3: See the realities in 39.6–7. 5: You will not die by the sword: Jeremiah offers only this comfort to the king; compare his minimal promise (21.9) to those who would surrender to the Chaldeans. Funeral fires in your honour: contrast with 22.18–19. 7: Lachish and Azekah: southwest of Jerusalem.

34.8–22: The evils of slavery. 14: Within seven years: see Deut. 15.12. 16: The betrayal of the manumission

LORD, a deliverance to sword, pestilence, and famine, and I shall make you abhorrent to all the kingdoms of the earth. 18 You have violated my covenant and have not fulfilled the terms to which you yourselves had agreed before me; so I shall treat you like the calf which was cut in two for all to pass between the pieces, 19 the officers of Judah and Jerusalem, the eunuchs and priests, and all the people of the land. 20 I shall give them up to their enemies who seek their lives; their dead bodies will be food for birds of prey and wild beasts. 21 I shall deliver King Zedekiah of Judah and his officers to their enemies who seek their lives and to the army of the king of Babylon, which is now raising the siege. 22 I shall give the command, says the LORD, and bring them back to this city. They will attack it, capture it, and burn it to the ground. I shall make the towns and cities of Judah desolate and unpeopled.

35 This is the word which came to Jeremiah from the LORD in the days of Jehoiakim son of Josiah, king of Judah: 2 Go and speak to the Rechabites; bring them to one of the rooms in the house of the LORD and offer them wine to drink. 3 So I fetched Jaazaniah son of Jeremiah, son of Habazziniah, with his brothers and all his sons, the whole Rechabite family. 4 I brought them into the house of the LORD to the room of the sons of Hanan son of Igdaliah, the man of God; this adjoins the officers' room above that of Maaseiah son of Shallum, the keeper of the threshold. 5 I set bowls full of wine and drinking-cups before the Rechabites and invited them to drink; 6 but they said, 'We never drink wine, for our forefather Jonadab son of Rechab laid this charge on us: "You must never drink wine, neither you nor your children. 7 Do not build houses or sow seed or plant vineyards; you are to have none of

these things. Instead, you are to remain tent-dwellers all your days, so that you may live long on the soil where you are sojourners." 8 We have honoured all the commands of our forefather Jonadab son of Rechab and have drunk no wine all our lives, neither we, nor our wives, nor our sons, nor our daughters. 9 We have not built houses to live in, nor have we possessed vineyards or sown fields; 10 we have lived in tents, obeying and observing fully the charge which our forefather Jonadab laid on us. 11 But when King Nebuchadrezzar of Babylon invaded the land we said, "Let us go to Jerusalem to escape the advancing Chaldaean and Aramaean armies." And we have stayed in Jerusalem.'

12 Then the word of the LORD came to Jeremiah: 13 These are the words of the LORD of Hosts the God of Israel: Go and say to the Judaeans and the citizens of Jerusalem: Will you never accept correction and obey my words? says the LORD. 14 The command of Jonadab son of Rechab to his descendants not to drink wine has been honoured; to this day they do not drink wine, for they obey their ancestor's command. But though I have warned you time and again, you have not obeyed me. 15 Time and again I sent all my servants the prophets to say, 'Turn back every one of you from evil conduct, mend your ways, and cease to follow other gods and serve them; then you will remain in the land that I have given to you and to your forefathers.' Yet you did not obey or listen to me. 16 The descendants of Jonadab son of Rechab have honoured the command their forefather laid on them, but this people have not listened to me. 17 Therefore, these are the words of the LORD the God of Hosts, the God of Israel: Because they did not listen when I spoke to them or respond when I called them, I shall bring on Judah and on all the

agreement was a profanation of God's *name.* **17:** *Deliverance for you:* this is bitter irony. **18:** The dismembered covenant animal suggests the fate of one who breaches the covenant; see Gen. 15.10. **21:** The *raising of the siege* at the advance of an Egyptian army coming to Jerusalem's relief had produced the illusion of victory; thereupon the slaveholders, regretting their generous impulse, denounced the covenant (v. 8). **22:** The thought is more fully developed in 37.7–10. There, Pharaoh's diversionary campaign has failed and Jerusalem's end is in sight.

35.1–19: A lesson in loyalty. The members of the Rechabite order remain faithful to the rules laid down by their founder but Israel shows no such loyalty to God; compare Isa. 1.3. **6–7:** The group traced their beginnings to *Jonadab son of Rechab.* The Rechabites are otherwise known only from 2 Kgs. 10.15–28 and 1 Chr. 2.55. The abstentions mentioned are features of a nomadic society, *tent-dwellers;* see 2.2. Nazirites, too, abstained from products of the vine; see Num. 6.1–4 and Judg. 13.2–5. **16:** This verse contains the point citizens of Jerusalem the full disaster with which I threatened them.

18 To the Rechabites Jeremiah said: These are the words of the LORD of Hosts the God of Israel: Because you have kept the command of Jonadab your forefather, obeying all his instructions and carrying out all that he told you to do, 19 therefore these are the words of the LORD of Hosts the God of Israel: There will never be lacking in my service a man of the line of Jonadab son of Rechab.

36 IN the fourth year of Jehoiakim son of Josiah, king of Judah, this word came to Jeremiah from the LORD: 2 Take a scroll and write on it all the words I have spoken to you about Jerusalem, Judah, and all the nations, from the day that I first spoke to you during the reign of Josiah down to the present day. 3 Perhaps the house of Judah will be warned of all the disaster I am planning to inflict on them, and everyone will abandon his evil conduct; then I shall forgive their wrongdoing and their sin.

4 Jeremiah summoned Baruch son of Neriah, and Baruch wrote on the scroll at Jeremiah's dictation everything the LORD had said to him. 5 He gave Baruch this instruction: 'As I am debarred from going to the LORD's house, 6 you must go there and on a fast-day read aloud to the people the words of the LORD from the scroll you wrote at my dictation. You are to read them in the hearing of all those who come in from the towns of Judah. 7 Then perhaps they will petition the LORD, and everyone will abandon his evil conduct; for in great anger and wrath the LORD has threatened this people.' 8 Baruch son of Neriah did all that the prophet Jeremiah had told him, about reading from the scroll the words of the LORD in the LORD's house.

9 In the ninth month of the fifth year of the reign of Jehoiakim son of Josiah, king of Judah, all the people in Jerusalem and all who came there from the towns of Judah proclaimed a fast before the LORD. 10 Then in the LORD's house Baruch read aloud Jeremiah's words from the scroll to all the people; he read them from the room of Gemariah son of the adjutant-general Shaphan, which was in the upper court at the entrance to the New Gate of the LORD's house.

11 When Micaiah son of Gemariah, son of Shaphan, heard all the LORD's words from the scroll 12 he went down to the palace, to the chief adviser's room, where he found the officers all in session: Elishama the chief adviser, Delaiah son of Shemaiah, Elnathan son of Akbor, Gemariah son of Shaphan, Zedekiah son of Hananiah, and all the other officers. 13 Micaiah reported to them everything he had heard Baruch read from the scroll in the hearing of the people. 14 Then the officers sent Jehudi son of Nethaniah, son of Shelemiah, son of Cushi, to Baruch with this order: 'Come here and bring the scroll from which you read to the people.' When Baruch son of Neriah appeared before them with the scroll, 15 they said to him, 'Sit down and read it to us,' and he did so. 16 When they had listened to it, they turned to each other in alarm and said, 'We must certainly report this to the king.' 17 They asked Baruch to explain to them how he had come to write all this. 18 He answered, 'Jeremiah dictated every word of it to me, and I wrote it down with ink on the scroll.' 19 The officers said to him, 'You and Jeremiah must go into hiding so that no one may know where you are.' 20 When they had deposited the scroll in the room of Elishama the chief adviser, they went to the court and reported the whole affair to the king.

21 The king sent Jehudi for the scroll and, when he had fetched it from the room of Elishama the chief adviser, Jehudi read it out to the king and to all the officers in attendance on him. 22 Since it was the ninth month of the year, the king was sitting in his winter apartments with a fire burning in a brazier in front of him. 23 Every time Jehudi read three

36:2 **Jerusalem:** *so Gk; Heb.* Israel.   36:17 **all this:** *so Gk; Heb. adds* at his dictation.

of the chapter. **18–19:** On individual survival in the midst of general disaster, see also 39.16–18 and 45.5.

36.1–32: Jeremiah, amid difficulties, records his words. 1: *Fourth year:* 605 B.C.E. **2:** *The day that I first spoke to you:* see 1.2. **3:** The word *perhaps* suggests Jeremiah's motivation in that he goes on hoping that his repeated appeal may yet effect a change; see v. 7. **4–6:** Baruch's *instruction.* Jeremiah was probably hiding, fearing a fate like that of Uriah; see 26.20–23. The unspecified *fast-day* provides Baruch with a gathering of hearers. **9:** *Fifth year:* probably a mistake for the "fourth"; see 25.1 n. **12:** *The officers:* see 26.10. **16:** *Trembling:* see 26.9 n. The words were in themselves a threat to the people and the city. **19:** *Go into hiding:* the officers were or four columns of the scroll, the king cut them off with a penknife and threw them into the fire in the brazier. He went on doing so until the entire scroll had been destroyed on the fire. 24 Neither the king nor any of his courtiers showed any alarm or tore their clothes as they listened to these words; 25 and though Elnathan, Delaiah, and Gemariah begged the king not to burn the scroll, he refused to listen, 26 but ordered Jerahmeel, a royal prince, Seraiah son of Azriel, and Shelemiah son of Abdeel to arrest Baruch the scribe and the prophet Jeremiah. But the LORD had hidden them.

27 After the king had burnt the scroll with all that Baruch had written on it at Jeremiah's dictation, the word of the LORD came to Jeremiah: 28 Take another scroll and write on it everything that was on the first scroll which King Jehoiakim of Judah burnt. 29 You are to say to the king: These are the words of the LORD: You burnt that scroll and said, 'Why have you written here that the king of Babylon will come and destroy this land and exterminate both man and beast?' 30 Therefore these are the words of the LORD about King Jehoiakim of Judah: He will have no descendant to succeed him on the throne of David, and his dead body will be exposed to scorching heat by day and frost by night. 31 I shall punish him, his offspring, and his courtiers for their wickedness, and I shall bring down on them and on the citizens of Jerusalem and on the people of Judah all the disasters with which I threatened them, for they turned a deaf ear to me.

32 Then Jeremiah took another scroll and gave it to the scribe Baruch son of Neriah, who wrote on it at Jeremiah's dictation all the words of the book which Jehoiakim king of Judah had burnt in the fire; and much else was added to the same effect.

37 Zedekiah son of Josiah was set on the throne of Judah by King Nebuchadrezzar of Babylon, in place of Coniah son of Jehoiakim, 2 but neither he nor his courtiers nor the people of the land heeded the words which the LORD spoke through the prophet Jeremiah. 3 King Zedekiah, however, sent Jehucal son of Shelemiah and the priest Zephaniah son of Maaseiah to Jeremiah to say to him, 'Intercede on our behalf with the LORD our God.' 4 At the time Jeremiah was free to come and go among the people; he had not yet been committed to prison.

5 Meanwhile Pharaoh's army had marched out of Egypt, and when the Chaldaeans who were besieging Jerusalem were apprised of this they raised the siege. 6 Then the word of the LORD came to the prophet Jeremiah: 7 These are the words of the LORD the God of Israel: Take this message to the king of Judah who sent you to consult me: Pharaoh's army which marched out to your aid is on its way back to Egypt, its own land, 8 and the Chaldaeans will return to the attack. They will capture this city and burn it to the ground. 9 These are the words of the LORD: Do not delude yourselves by imagining that the Chaldaeans will go away and leave you alone. They will not; 10 supposing that you were to defeat the whole Chaldaean force now fighting against you, and only the wounded were left lying in their tents, even they would rise and burn down this city.

11 After the Chaldaean army raised the siege of Jerusalem in the face of the advance of Pharaoh's army, 12 Jeremiah was on the way out from Jerusalem to go into Benjamite territory to take possession of his holding among the people there. 13 Irijah son of Shelemiah, son of Hananiah, the officer of the guard, was at the Benjamin Gate when Jeremiah reached it, and he arrested the prophet, accusing him of defecting to the Chaldaeans. 14 'That is not true!' said Jeremiah. 'I am not going over to the Chaldaeans.' Irijah refused to listen but brought him under arrest before the officers. 15 The officers, furious with Jeremiah, had him flogged

not overtly hostile (see v. 25), but only frightened. **22:** *Ninth month:* Kislev, in midwinter. **23:** *Cut them . . . threw them into the fire:* he hoped to remove the curse by destroying the words. **24:** Once they had burned up the words they no longer *showed any alarm.* **32:** *Another scroll:* see 25.1 n. *Much else:* the written record continues beyond the fourth year (v. 1).

37.1–10: Jeremiah disappoints the king. 1: See 2 Kgs. 24.15–17. **3:** *Intercede on our behalf:* Zedekiah attributes to Jeremiah special intercessory qualities; see 7.16 n. and 15.1–2 n. **4:** *Not yet . . . committed to prison;* see v. 15. **5–8:** See 34.21–22.

37.11–16: Jeremiah is accused of desertion and imprisoned. 11: See v. 5. **12:** *His holding:* a part of the family inheritance from which, in 32.6–15, he buys a field. **13:** *The Benjamin Gate:* in the direction of and imprisoned in the house of Jonathan the scribe, which had been converted into a jail. ¹⁶Jeremiah was put into a vaulted pit beneath the house, and he remained there many days.

¹⁷King Zedekiah had Jeremiah brought to him and questioned him privately in the palace, asking if there was a word from the LORD. 'There is,' said Jeremiah; 'you will fall into the hands of the king of Babylon.' ¹⁸Jeremiah went on, 'What wrong have I done to you or your courtiers or this people, that you have thrown me into prison? ¹⁹Where are your prophets who prophesied that the king of Babylon would not attack you or this country? ²⁰I pray you now, my lord king, give me a hearing and let my petition be accepted: do not send me back to the house of Jonathan the scribe, or I shall die there.' ²¹Then King Zedekiah gave the order for Jeremiah to be committed to the court of the guardhouse, and as long as there was bread in the city he was granted a daily ration of one loaf from the Street of the Bakers. So Jeremiah remained in the court of the guardhouse.

38 Shephatiah son of Mattan, Gedaliah son of Pashhur, Jucal son of Shelemiah, and Pashhur son of Malchiah heard how Jeremiah was addressing all the people; he was saying: ²These are the words of the LORD: Whoever remains in this city will die by sword, famine, or pestilence, but whoever surrenders to the Chaldaeans will survive; he will escape with his life. ³These are the words of the LORD: This city will assuredly be delivered into the power of the king of Babylon's army, and be captured. ⁴The officers said to the king, 'This man ought to be put to death. By talking in this way he is demoralizing the soldiers left in the city and indeed the rest of the people. It is not the people's welfare he seeks but their ruin.' ⁵King Zedekiah said, 'He is in your hands; the king is powerless against you.' ⁶So they took Jeremiah and put him into the cistern in the court of the guard-

house, letting him down with ropes. There was no water in the cistern, only mud, and Jeremiah sank in the mud.

⁷⁻⁸Ebed-melech the Cushite, a eunuch, who was in the palace, heard that they had put Jeremiah into a cistern and he went to tell the king, who was seated at the Benjamin Gate. ⁹'Your majesty,' he said, 'these men have acted viciously in their treatment of the prophet Jeremiah. They have thrown him into a cistern, and he will die of hunger where he is, for there is no more bread in the city.' ¹⁰The king instructed Ebed-melech the Cushite to take three men with him and hoist Jeremiah out of the cistern before he perished. ¹¹Ebed-melech went to the palace with the men and took some tattered, cast-off clothes from a storeroom and lowered them with ropes to Jeremiah in the cistern. ¹²He called to Jeremiah, 'Put these old clothes under your armpits to pad the ropes.' Jeremiah did so, ¹³and they pulled him up out of the cistern with the ropes. Jeremiah remained in the court of the guardhouse.

¹⁴King Zedekiah sent for the prophet Jeremiah and had him brought to the third entrance of the LORD's house. 'I want to ask you something,' he said to him; 'hide nothing from me.' ¹⁵Jeremiah answered, 'If I speak out, you will certainly put me to death; if I offer advice, you will disregard it.' ¹⁶King Zedekiah secretly made this promise on oath to Jeremiah: 'By the life of the LORD who gave us our lives, I shall not put you to death, nor shall I hand you over to these men who are seeking your life.' ¹⁷Jeremiah said to Zedekiah, 'These are the words of the LORD the God of Hosts, the God of Israel: If you go out and surrender to the officers of the king of Babylon, you will live and this city will not be burnt down; you and your family will sur-

38:6 **into the cistern:** *prob. rdg; Heb.* adds Malchiah son of the king.   38:10 **three:** *so one MS; others* thirty.
38:11 **a storeroom:** *prob. rdg; Heb.* underneath the store.

Anathoth. **15:** *They had him flogged:* see 20.2. **16:** *A vaulted pit:* apparently a dungeonlike, unwholesome place.

37.17–21: Jeremiah speaks bluntly. 19: *Prophets:* like Hananiah (ch. 28).

38.1–13: Jeremiah is charged with sedition. 1: *Pashhur son of Malchiah:* he is mentioned in 21.1. **2–3:** Jeremiah's allegedly seditious speech may have been more extensive than the two verses quoted here. The same address probably appears in excerpts in 21.8–10, 32.3–5, and 34.2–5. **4:** *He is demoralizing the soldiers:* perhaps; but Jeremiah's goal is national survival. **5:** *Powerless:* the king vacillates, first assenting to the attempt on Jeremiah's life and then (v. 10) to his deliverance from mortal danger. **7:** *Cushite:* from Cush in Upper Egypt. **9:** *He will die of hunger:* beyond hunger, there was the likelihood of dying of suffocation in the mud.

vive. ¹⁸If, however, you do not surrender to the officers of the king of Babylon, this city will fall into the hands of the Chaldaeans, who will burn it down; you yourself will not escape them.' ¹⁹The king said to Jeremiah, 'I am afraid of the Judaeans who have gone over to the enemy. The Chaldaeans may give me up to them, and their treatment of me will be ruthless.' ²⁰Jeremiah answered, 'You will not be given up. If you obey the Lord in everything I tell you, all will be well with you and your life will be spared. ²¹But if you refuse to surrender, this is what the Lord has shown me: ²²all the women left in the king of Judah's palace will be led out to the officers of the king of Babylon. Those women will say to you:

"Your own friends have misled you
and proved too strong for you;
when your feet sank in the mud
they turned and left you."

²³All your women and children will be led out to the Chaldaeans and you yourself will not escape; you will be seized by the king of Babylon, and this city will be burnt down.'

²⁴Zedekiah said to Jeremiah, 'On pain of death let no one know about this conversation. ²⁵If the officers hear that I have been speaking with you and they come and say to you, "Tell us what you said to the king and what he said to you; hide nothing from us, and we shall not put you to death," ²⁶you must reply, "I was petitioning the king not to send me back to the house of Jonathan to die there." ' ²⁷The officers did all come and question Jeremiah, and he said to them just what the king had told him to say; so they left off questioning him and were none the wiser. ²⁸Jeremiah remained in the court of the guardhouse till the day Jerusalem fell.

39 In the tenth month of the ninth year of the reign of King Zedekiah of Judah, King Nebuchadrezzar of Babylon advanced with his whole army against Jerusalem, and they laid siege to it. ²In the fourth month of the eleventh year of Zede-

kiah, on the ninth day of the month, the city capitulated. ³All the officers of the king of Babylon came in and took their seats by the middle gate: Nergalsarezer of Simmagir, Nebusarsekim the chief eunuch, Nergalsarezer the commander of the frontier troops, and all the other officers of the king of Babylon. ⁴When King Zedekiah of Judah saw them, he and all his armed escort left the city by night and, fleeing by way of the king's garden through the gate called Between the Two Walls, they made their escape towards the Arabah. ⁵The Chaldaean soldiers set off in pursuit and overtook Zedekiah in the lowlands of Jericho. He was seized and brought before King Nebuchadrezzar of Babylon at Riblah in the territory of Hamath, where sentence was passed on him. ⁶The king of Babylon had Zedekiah's sons slain before his eyes at Riblah; he also had all the nobles of Judah put to death. ⁷Then Zedekiah's eyes were blinded, and he was bound in bronze fetters to be brought to Babylon. ⁸The Chaldaeans burnt the royal palace and the house of the Lord and the houses of the people, and demolished Jerusalem's walls. ⁹Nebuzaradan captain of the bodyguard deported to Babylon the rest of the people left in the city, those who had defected to him, and any remaining artisans. ¹⁰He left behind only the poorest class of people, those who owned nothing at all; to them he gave vineyards and fields.

¹¹King Nebuchadrezzar of Babylon sent orders about Jeremiah to Nebuzaradan captain of the guard. ¹²'Hold him,' he said, 'and take good care of him; let him come to no harm, but do for him whatever he asks.' ¹³So Nebuzaradan captain of the guard sent Nebushazban the chief eunuch, Nergalsarezer the commander of the frontier troops, and all the chief officers of the king of Babylon, ¹⁴and they fetched Jeremiah from the court of the guardhouse and handed him over to

38:28 **fell:** *so Gk; Heb. adds* when Jerusalem was captured.   39:3 **the chief eunuch:** *or* Rab-saris. **the commander ... troops:** *or* Rab-mag.   39:8 **of the Lord and the houses:** *prob. rdg; Heb. omits.* 39:9 **artisans:** *prob. rdg, cp.* 52:15; *Heb.* people who were left.   39:11 **to:** *so Lat.; Heb.* by.

38.14–28: Zedekiah again consults the prophet. 15: The substance is paraphrased in Lk. 22.67–68. **22–23:** The women of the court will taunt the king, but their fate will be no better. See 41.10. **28:** See 39.14.

39.1–14: Jeremiah is spared when Jerusalem falls. Verses 1–2 and 4–10 appear again in 52.4–16 and also in 2 Kgs. 25.1–12, where they stood originally. Only 11–14 here concern Jeremiah. **14:** *Gedaliah son of Ahikam:* the puppet governor appointed by Nebuchadrezzar; see 40.7. *His residence:* for the governor at

Gedaliah son of Ahikam, son of Shaphan, to take him out to his residence. So he stayed with his own people.

15 While Jeremiah was imprisoned the word of the LORD had come to him in the court of the guardhouse: 16 Go and say to Ebed-melech the Cushite: These are the words of the LORD of Hosts the God of Israel: I shall make good the words I have spoken against this city, foretelling ruin and not wellbeing, and when that day comes you will recall them. 17 But I shall preserve you on that day, says the LORD, and you will not be handed over to the men you fear. 18 I shall keep you safe, and you will not fall a victim to the sword; because you trusted in me you will escape with your life. This is the word of the LORD.

After the capture of Jerusalem

40 THE word which came from the LORD about Jeremiah: Nebuzaradan captain of the guard had taken him in chains to Ramah along with the other captives from Jerusalem and Judah who were being deported to Babylon. After he set Jeremiah free, 2 he said to him, 'The LORD your God threatened this place with disaster, 3 and has duly carried out his threat that this should happen to the people because they have sinned against the LORD and not obeyed him. 4 But as for you, Jeremiah, I am now removing the fetters from your wrists. If you so wish, come with me to Babylon, and I shall take good care of you; but if you prefer not to come, very well. The whole country lies before you; go wherever you think best.' 5 Before Jeremiah could answer, Nebuzaradan went on, 'Go back to Gedaliah son of Ahikam, son of Shaphan, whom the king of Babylon has appointed governor of the cities and towns of Judah, and stay with him among your people; or go anywhere else you choose.' Then the captain of the guard gave him provisions and a gift, and dismissed him. 6 Jeremiah went to Mizpah to Gedaliah son of

Ahikam and stayed with him among the people left in the land.

7 When all the captains of the armed bands in the countryside and their men heard that the king of Babylon had appointed Gedaliah son of Ahikam to be governor of the land, and had put him in charge of the poorer class of the population, the men, women, and children who had not been deported to Babylon, 8 they, together with their men, came to him at Mizpah; they were Ishmael son of Nethaniah, and Johanan and Jonathan sons of Kareah, Seraiah son of Tanhumeth, the sons of Ephai from Netophah, and Jezaniah of Beth-maacah. 9 Gedaliah son of Ahikam, son of Shaphan, gave them this assurance: 'Do not be afraid to serve the Chaldaeans. Settle down in the land, serve the king of Babylon, and all will be well with you. 10 I for my part am to stay in Mizpah and attend on the Chaldaeans whenever they come to us; you can harvest the wine, summer fruits, and oil, store them in jars, and settle in the towns you have taken over.'

11 Likewise when all the Judaeans who were in Moab, Ammon, Edom, and other countries, heard that the king of Babylon had left a remnant in Judah and had set over them Gedaliah son of Ahikam, son of Shaphan, 12 they came back to Judah from all the places where they had scattered and presented themselves before Gedaliah at Mizpah; and they gathered in a good harvest of wine and summer fruit.

13 Johanan son of Kareah and all the captains of the armed bands from the countryside came to Gedaliah at Mizpah 14 and said to him, 'Are you aware that Baalis king of the Ammonites has sent Ishmael son of Nethaniah to assassinate you?' But Gedaliah son of Ahikam would not believe them. 15 Then Johanan son of Kareah spoke privately to Gedaliah: 'Let me go, unknown to anyone else, and kill Ishmael son of Nethaniah. Why let him assassinate you, and so allow all the Juda-

40:5 **Jeremiah . . . went on:** *prob. rdg; Heb. unintelligible in context.*

Mizpah (40.6). The royal palace had been destroyed (v. 8).

39.15–18: Jeremiah praises Ebed-melech. See 38.7–13. **15:** *Had come:* before the fall of Jerusalem.
40.1–6: Jeremiah after the capture of Jerusalem. 1: *Ramah:* in Benjamin, a few miles north of Jerusalem.
2–3: Nebuzaradan's language here is much like that of Jeremiah in 44.2–6. **5:** *Ahikam, son of Shaphan:* he is mentioned in 26.24 and 2 Kgs. 22.12. **6:** *Mizpah:* see 39.14 n.
40.7–41.18: The assassination of Gedaliah. The date was probably 582 B.C.E. Some scholars call the event the "third revolt." The story is told more succinctly in 2 Kgs. 25.22–26. **9:** Compare this with Jeremiah's counsel

eans who have rallied round you to be scattered and the remnant of Judah to be lost?' [16] Gedaliah son of Ahikam answered him, 'Do no such thing. What you are saying about Ishmael is not true.'

41 In the seventh month Ishmael son of Nethaniah, son of Elishama, who was a member of the royal house, came with ten men to Gedaliah son of Ahikam at Mizpah. While they were eating together there, [2] Ishmael son of Nethaniah and his ten men rose and assassinated Gedaliah son of Ahikam, son of Shaphan, whom the king of Babylon had appointed governor of the land. [3] Ishmael also murdered all the Judaeans who were with Gedaliah in Mizpah as well as the Chaldaean soldiers stationed there.

[4] Next day, while the murder of Gedaliah was not yet common knowledge, [5] eighty men arrived from Shechem, Shiloh, and Samaria. They had shaved off their beards, torn their clothes, and gashed their bodies; they were carrying grain-offerings and frankincense to present to the house of the LORD. [6] Ishmael son of Nethaniah went out from Mizpah to meet them, weeping as he went, and when he met them he said, 'Come to Gedaliah son of Ahikam.' [7] But as soon as they were well inside the town, Ishmael son of Nethaniah and his men murdered them and threw their bodies into a cistern, [8] all except ten of them who said to Ishmael, 'Do not kill us, for we have a secret hoard in the country, wheat and barley, oil and honey.' So he held his hand and did not kill them with the others. [9] The cistern into which he threw all the bodies of those whom he had killed was the large one which King Asa had made when threatened by King Baasha of Israel, and this Ishmael son of Nethaniah filled with the slain. [10] He rounded up the rest of the people in Mizpah, that is the king's daughters and all who had remained in Mizpah when Nebuzaradan captain of the guard appointed Gedaliah son of Ahikam governor; and with these he set out to cross over to the Ammonites.

[11] When Johanan son of Kareah and the captains of the armed bands heard of all the crimes committed by Ishmael son of Nethaniah, [12] they mustered their men and set out to attack him. They came up with him by the great pool in Gibeon. [13] The people with Ishmael were glad when they saw Johanan son of Kareah and all the captains of the armed bands with him, [14] while those whom Ishmael had taken prisoner at Mizpah turned and joined Johanan son of Kareah. [15] But Ishmael son of Nethaniah escaped from Johanan with eight men to make his way to the Ammonites.

[16] Johanan son of Kareah and the captains of the armed bands took from Mizpah all the survivors whom he had rescued from Ishmael son of Nethaniah after the murder of Gedaliah son of Ahikam—men, both armed and unarmed, women, children, and eunuchs, whom he had brought back from Gibeon. [17] They started out and broke their journey at Kimham's holding near Bethlehem, on their way into Egypt [18] to escape the Chaldaeans. They were afraid of them because Ishmael son of Nethaniah had assassinated Gedaliah son of Ahikam, whom the king of Babylon had appointed governor of the country.

42 All the captains of the armed bands, including Johanan son of Kareah and Azariah son of Hoshaiah, together with the entire people, high and low, approached [2] the prophet Jeremiah and said, 'May our petition be acceptable to you: Intercede with the LORD your God on our behalf and on behalf of this remnant; as you see for yourself, only a few of us remain out of many.

41:1 **royal house:** *so Gk; Heb. adds* and the chief officers of the king.   41:9 **was . . . one:** *so Gk; Heb.* by the hand of Gedaliah.   42:1 **Azariah:** *so Gk, cp. 43:2; Heb.* Jezaniah.

in 27.12. **10:** *Attend on the Chaldaeans:* Gedaliah would represent them to the Chaldeans. **41.4:** *Shechem, Shiloh . . . Samaria:* These were once prominent northern cities, now again settled after war and destruction. **4–5:** Since Gedaliah's murder was *not yet common knowledge,* the mourning rites were perhaps in observance of a fast day of the seventh month. Seemingly, parts of *the house of the LORD* were still standing, or else they had been restored. **9:** *King Asa:* around 900 B.C.E.; see 1 Kgs. 15.16–22. **11–18:** The defeat of Ishmael. **12:** The *pool* in Gibeon is mentioned also in 2 Sam. 2.13. **17:** *Kimham's* father was named Barzillai; see 2 Sam. 19.31–40 and 1 Kgs. 2.7. *Bethlehem* was on the way to Egypt. **18:** *Escape:* the motive for the group's flight to Egypt was the fear of Babylonian reprisals for Ishmael's rebellious acts.

42.1–43.7: The fugitives consult Jeremiah, whether to proceed to Egypt for safety, or whether it would be safe to remain in Judea, but reject his answer. **2:** *Your:* Jeremiah's God, as though there was a special tie between

³ Pray that the LORD your God may tell us which way we are to take and what we ought to do.' ⁴ Jeremiah answered, 'I have heard your request. I shall pray to the LORD your God as you ask, and whatever answer the LORD gives I shall tell you, keeping nothing back.' ⁵ They said to Jeremiah, 'May the LORD be a true and faithful witness against us if we do not act exactly as the LORD your God sends you to tell us. ⁶ Whether it is favourable to us or not, we shall obey the LORD our God to whom we are sending you, in order that it may be well with us through our obedience to him.'

⁷ When after an interval of ten days the word of the LORD came to Jeremiah, ⁸ he summoned Johanan son of Kareah, all the captains of the armed bands who were with him, and all the people, both high and low, ⁹ and addressed them: These are the words of the LORD the God of Israel, to whom you sent me with your petition. ¹⁰ If you remain in this land, then I shall build you up and not pull you down, I shall plant you and not uproot you; I grieve for the disaster which I have inflicted on you. ¹¹ Do not be afraid of the king of Babylon whom you now fear. Do not be afraid of him, says the LORD, for I am with you, to save you and deliver you from his power. ¹² I shall show you compassion, so that he too has compassion on you, and will let you stay on your own soil. ¹³ But it may be that you will disobey the LORD your God and insist, 'We are not going to stay in this land. ¹⁴ No, we shall go to Egypt, where we shall see no sign of war, never hear the sound of the trumpet, and suffer no lack of food; it is there we shall live.' ¹⁵ In that case hear the word of the LORD, you remnant of Judah. These are the words of the LORD of Hosts the God of Israel: If you are determined to go to Egypt, if you do go and settle there, ¹⁶ then the sword you fear will overtake you there in Egypt, and the famine you dread will dog you, even in Egypt, and there you will die. ¹⁷ All who insist on going to settle in Egypt will die by sword, famine, or pestilence; not one will escape or survive the disaster I shall bring on them.

¹⁸ These are the words of the LORD of Hosts the God of Israel: As my anger and my wrath were poured out on the inhabitants of Jerusalem, so will my wrath be poured out on you when you go to Egypt; you will become an object of execration and horror, of cursing and reproach, and you will never see this place again. ¹⁹ To you, then, remnant of Judah, the LORD says: Do not go to Egypt. Make no mistake; I give you solemn warning this day. ²⁰ You deceived yourselves when you sent me to the LORD your God and said, 'Intercede for us with the LORD our God; tell us exactly what the LORD our God says and we shall do it.' ²¹ I have told it all to you today; but you have not obeyed the LORD your God in what he sent me to tell you. ²² So now be sure of this: you will die by sword, famine, and pestilence in the place where you want to go and live.

43 When Jeremiah had finished reporting to the people all that the LORD their God had sent him to say, ² Azariah son of Hoshaiah and Johanan son of Kareah and their party had the effrontery to say to Jeremiah, 'You are lying! The LORD our God has not sent you to forbid us to go and make our home in Egypt; ³ it is Baruch son of Neriah who is inciting you against us in order to put us in the power of the Chaldaeans, to be killed or deported to Babylon.'

⁴ Johanan son of Kareah and the captains of the armed bands and all the people refused to obey the LORD's command to stay in Judah. ⁵ Johanan and the captains collected the remnant of Judah, all who had returned from the countries among which they had been scattered to make their home in Judah —⁶ men, women, and children, including the king's daughters, everyone whom Nebuzaradan captain of the guard had left with Gedaliah son of Ahikam, son of Shaphan, as well as the prophet Jeremiah and Baruch son of Neriah; ⁷ and in defiance of the LORD's command they all went to Egypt and arrived at Tahpanhes.

⁸ The word of the LORD came to Jeremiah in Tahpanhes: ⁹ Take some large stones and set them in cement in the pavement at the

God and Jeremiah. 4: *To the LORD your God:* Jeremiah makes no distinction between their God and his. 10: *Remain in this land:* see 32.6–15. 14: *The trumpet:* the ram's horn warning of peril; see Ezek. 33.3. 19–20: See vv. 5–6. 43.3: The fugitives, strangely, hold Baruch responsible for Jeremiah's unwelcome answer. 6: *Jeremiah and Baruch:* they were taken to Egypt, apparently against their will. 7: *Tahpanhes:* Daphne, just west of the Sinai-Egypt border (2.16).

entrance to Pharaoh's palace in Tahpanhes. Let the Judaeans see you do it, 10 and say to them: These are the words of the Lord of Hosts the God of Israel: I shall send for my servant King Nebuchadrezzar of Babylon, and he will place his throne on these stones that I have set here, and spread his canopy over them. 11 He will come and vanquish Egypt:

> Those who are for the plague shall go
>   to the plague,
> those for captivity to captivity,
> and those for the sword to the sword.

12 He will set fire to the temples of the Egyptian gods, burning the buildings and carrying the gods into captivity. He will scour the land of Egypt as a shepherd scours his clothes to rid them of lice. He will come out of Egypt unscathed. 13 He will smash the sacred pillars of Beth-shemesh in Egypt and burn down the temples of the Egyptian gods.

44 The word that came to Jeremiah for all the Judaeans living in Egypt, at Migdol, Tahpanhes, Noph, and in the district of Pathros: 2 These are the words of the Lord of Hosts the God of Israel: You have seen all the disaster I brought on Jerusalem and on all the towns of Judah: today they lie in ruins and are left uninhabited, 3 all because of the wickedness of those who provoked me to anger by going after other gods, gods unknown to them, by burning sacrifices in their service. It was you and your forefathers who did this. 4 Constantly I sent all my servants the prophets to you with this warning: 'Do not do this abominable thing, which I detest.' 5 But your forefathers would not listen or pay any heed. They did not give up their wickedness or cease to burn sacrifices to other gods; 6 so my anger and wrath were poured out, and swept like fire through the towns of Judah and the streets of Jerusalem, until they became the desolate ruin they are today. 7 Now these are the words of the Lord the God of Hosts, the God of Israel: Why bring so great a disaster on yourselves? Why bring destruction on Judaeans, men and women,

children and babes, and leave yourselves without a survivor? 8 This is what comes of provoking me by your idol-worship in burning sacrifices to other gods in Egypt where you have made your home. You will destroy yourselves and become an object of cursing and reproach among all the nations on earth. 9 Have you forgotten the wickedness committed by your forefathers, by the kings of Judah and their wives, by yourselves and your wives in the land of Judah and in the streets of Jerusalem? 10 To this day no remorse has been shown, no reverence, no obedience to the law and the statutes which I set before you and your forefathers.

11 These, therefore, are the words of the Lord of Hosts the God of Israel: I have resolved to bring disaster on you and to exterminate all the people of Judah. 12 I shall deal with the remnant of Judah who decided to go to Egypt and make their home there; in Egypt they will all meet their end. Some will fall by the sword, others will meet their end by famine. High and low alike will die by sword or by famine and will be an object of execration and horror, of cursing and reproach. 13 I shall punish those who live in Egypt as I punished those in Jerusalem, by sword, famine, and pestilence. 14 Those who had remained in Judah came to make their home in Egypt, confident that they would return and live once more in Judah. But they will not return; not one of them will survive, not one escape.

15 Then all the men who knew that their wives were burning sacrifices to other gods, and the large crowd of women standing by, indeed all of the people who lived in Pathros in Egypt, answered Jeremiah: 16 'We are not going to listen to what you tell us in the name of the Lord. 17 We intend to fulfil all the vows by which we have bound ourselves: we shall burn sacrifices to the queen of heaven and pour drink-offerings to her as we used to do, we and our forefathers, our kings and leaders, in the towns of Judah and in the streets

43:10 **he will place:** *so Gk; Heb.* I shall place.
43:12 **He will set fire:** *so Gk; Heb.* I shall set fire.
44:14 **But . . . return:** *prob. rdg; Heb. adds* except fugitives.

43.8–44.30: Jeremiah in Egypt. 8–13: He forecasts Nebuchadrezzar's invasion of Egypt. **9:** *Stones:* to dramatize the message. **12:** *Will scour the land:* will leave no survivors. **13:** *Beth-shemesh:* lit. "house of the sun (God)." It was also called On (Gen. 41.45), and later, Heliopolis. It was near Tahpanhes. Nebuchadrezzar's forces did invade Egypt about 567 B.C.E. **44.1–30:** The faithlessness of the Judeans in Egypt. **1:** *Migdol:* near Tahpanhes; both were east of *Noph* (Memphis), while *Pathros* was in the south of Egypt. **17:** *Queen of heaven:*

of Jerusalem. Then we had food in plenty and were content; no disaster touched us. [18] But from the time we left off burning sacrifices to the queen of heaven and pouring drink-offerings to her, we have been in great want, and we have fallen victims to sword and famine.' [19] The women said, 'All the time we burnt sacrifices to the queen of heaven and poured drink-offerings to her, our husbands were fully aware that we were making crescent-cakes marked with her image and pouring drink-offerings to her.'

[20] When Jeremiah received this answer from all the people, men and women, he said, [21] 'The LORD did not forget those sacrifices which you and your forefathers, your kings and princes, and the people of the land burnt in the towns of Judah and in the streets of Jerusalem, and they mounted up in his mind [22] until he could no longer endure them, so wicked were your deeds, so abominable the things you did. Your land became a desolate waste, an object of horror and cursing, with no inhabitants, as it still is. [23] The disaster you now suffer has come on you because you burnt these sacrifices and sinned against the LORD, refusing to obey the LORD and conform to his law, statutes, and teachings.'

[24] Further, Jeremiah said to all the people, particularly the women: Listen to the word of the LORD, all you from Judah who live in Egypt. [25] These are the words of the LORD of Hosts the God of Israel: You women have made your actions match your words. You said, 'We shall carry out our vows to burn sacrifices to the queen of heaven and to pour drink-offerings to her.' Fulfil your vows by all means; carry them out! [26] But listen to the word of the LORD, all you from Judah who are settled in Egypt. I have sworn by my great name, says the LORD, that my name will never again be invoked by any of the Judaeans; in Egypt they will no longer swear 'by the life of the Lord GOD'. [27] I am on the watch to bring

you evil and not good, and all Judaeans who are in Egypt will meet their end by sword and famine until not one is left. [28] It is then that any survivors of Judah who made their home in Egypt will know whose word prevails, mine or theirs.

[29] This is the sign I give you, says the LORD, that I intend to punish you in this place, so that you may learn that my threat of disaster against you will prevail. [30] These are the words of the LORD: I shall hand over Pharaoh Hophra king of Egypt to his enemies and to those who seek his life, just as I handed over King Zedekiah of Judah to King Nebuchadrezzar of Babylon, his enemy who sought his life.

45 THE word which the prophet Jeremiah addressed to Baruch son of Neriah when Baruch wrote these words in a scroll at Jeremiah's dictation in the fourth year of Jehoiakim son of Josiah, king of Judah: [2] These are the words of the LORD the God of Israel concerning you, Baruch: [3] You said, 'Woe is me, for the LORD has added grief to my trials. I have worn myself out with my labours and have had no respite.' [4] This is what you shall say to Baruch: These are the words of the LORD: What I have built, I demolish; what I have planted, I uproot. So it will be with the whole earth. [5] You seek great things for yourself; leave off seeking them. I am about to bring disaster on all mankind, says the LORD, but wherever you go I shall let you escape with your life.

Prophecies against foreign nations

46 THIS came to the prophet Jeremiah as the word of the LORD about the nations.

44:19 **The women said:** *so Gk (Luc.); Heb. omits.*
44:25 **You women:** *so Gk; Heb. You and your wives.*
44:27 **until . . . left:** *prob. rdg; Heb. adds* [28] *Few will escape the sword in Egypt to return to Judah.*

see 7.18 n. **18:** *The time:* this is probably not an allusion to Josiah's reform (621 B.C.E.), but to some more recent period, such as the fall of Jerusalem in 587, or possibly even the earlier deportation in 597. **26–27:** *Meet their end:* contrast the doom on the exiles to Egypt with the hope extended to the exiles in Babylonia (24.6). **28:** *Prevails:* the *word* that is *theirs* is in vv. 16–17a. **29–30:** Jeremiah proposes a sign, that when Pharaoh *Hophra* will be taken by his enemies, God's punishment of these Judeans will be imminent. Hophra was deposed in 569, lost his life in 566. This prediction concludes the story of the Judeans in Egypt and the biography of Jeremiah.

45.1–5: The experience of Baruch. A warning against aggrandizement. See also ch. 36. **4:** God also knows failure and grief. **5:** Baruch needs to be satisfied simply to survive.

² Of Egypt: about the army of Pharaoh Necho king of Egypt at Carchemish on the river
Euphrates, which King Nebuchadrezzar of
Babylon defeated in the fourth year of Jehoiakim son of Josiah, king of Judah.

³ Hold shield and buckler ready
  and advance to battle;
⁴ harness the horses,
  let the riders mount;
  form up with your helmets on,
  your lances burnished;
  on with your coats of mail!
⁵ But now, what sight is this?
  They are broken and routed,
  their warriors defeated;
  they are in headlong flight
  without a backward look.
  Terror let loose!
  This is the word of the LORD.

⁶ Can the swiftest escape,
  the bravest save himself?
  In the north, by the river Euphrates,
  they stumble and fall.

⁷ Who is this rising like the Nile,
  like rivers turbulent in flood?
⁸ It is Egypt rising like the Nile,
  like rivers turbulent in flood.
  I shall arise and cover the earth, says
    Egypt;
  I shall destroy every city and its
    people.

⁹ Let the cavalry charge
  and the chariots drive furiously!
  Let the warriors attack,
  Cushites and men of Put bearing
    shields,
  Lydians with their bows ready strung!

¹⁰ That day belongs to the Lord, the GOD
    of Hosts,
  a day of vengeance, vengeance on his
    enemies;
  the sword will devour until sated,
  drunk with their blood.
  For the GOD of Hosts, the Lord, holds
    sacrifice
  in a northern land, by the river
    Euphrates.

¹¹ Virgin daughter of Egypt,
  go up into Gilead and fetch balm.
  You have tried many remedies, all in
    vain;
  no skin will grow over your wounds.
¹² The nations have heard your cry,
  and the earth echoes with your
    screams;
  warrior stumbles against warrior
  and both fall down together.

¹³ The word which the LORD spoke to the
prophet Jeremiah about the advance of King
Nebuchadrezzar of Babylon to harry the
land of Egypt:

¹⁴ Announce it in Egypt, proclaim it in
    Migdol,
  proclaim it in Noph and Tahpanhes.
  Say: Stand to! Be ready!
  For a sword devours all around you.
¹⁵ Why does Apis flee? Why does your
    bull-god not stand fast?
  Because the LORD has thrust him out.
¹⁶ The rabble of Egypt stumbles and falls,
    man against man;
  each says, 'Quick, back to our own
    people,

46:12 **your cry:** *so Gk; Heb.* your shame.
46:15 **Why does Apis . . . not:** *or* Why is your bull-god
laid low, why does he not.

46.1–51.64: Heathen nations will be destroyed. Compare 25.15–38. The Book of Jer. ends on a note of
comfort. Unlike the comfort in chs. 30–34 which stressed God's forgiving love and looked to the rehabilitation
of the exiled people, these chapters offer comfort through the elimination of actively or potentially hostile
nations. The prevailing tone is spiteful, yet sympathy is not lacking. **1:** The verse ascribes the ensuing chapters
to Jeremiah; compare 1.5, 10. Some scholars, however, question his authorship of the whole, others of the
individual parts. **2–26:** Two taunt songs (vv. 2–12 and 13–26) against Egypt. The proud might of Egypt (vv. 3–4
and 7–9) suffers inglorious defeat (vv. 5–6 and 11–12) at Carchemish. **2:** *Carchemish:* a place on the upper
Euphrates. There, in 605 B.C.E., *Nebuchadrezzar* of Babylonia defeated and wiped out *the army of Pharaoh
Necho* (II), an ally of the waning Assyrian power. **3:** Egypt is addressed. **9:** *Put:* in North Africa. **10:** *That day
belongs to the LORD:* in an old tradition the day was to be, as here, a time of God's triumph over enemies, the
foes of Israel. **11:** *Balm:* a healing medicine; see 8.22. **13:** The precise occasion of the passage is uncertain.
It may be that of 567 B.C.E.; see 43.13 n. **15:** *Apis:* a bull god, one of the chief deities of Egypt. With the scorn

to our native land, far from the
   oppressor's sword!'
17 Give Pharaoh of Egypt the title King
   Bombast,
   the man who missed his opportunity.

18 By my life, one will come,
   says the King whose name is the LORD
   of Hosts,
   one mighty as Tabor among the hills,
   as Carmel by the sea.
19 Get ready your baggage for exile,
   you native people of Egypt;
   Noph will become a waste,
   ruined and unpeopled.

20 Egypt was a lovely heifer,
   but a gadfly from the north attacked
   her.
21 The mercenaries in her land were like
   stall-fed calves;
   but they too turned tail and fled,
   not one of them standing his ground.
   The day of retribution has come upon
   them,
   their time of reckoning.

22 Egypt is hissing like a fleeing snake,
   for the enemy has come in force.
   They attack her with axes
   like fellers of trees.
23 They cut down her forest, says the
   LORD,
   for they cannot be numbered;
   more numerous than locusts,
   they are past counting.
24 The Egyptians are put to shame,
   enslaved to a northern race.

25 The LORD of Hosts the God of Israel
   has spoken:
   I am about to punish Amon god of
   Thebes,
   Egypt with her gods and her princes,
   Pharaoh and all who trust in him.
26 I shall deliver them to those bent on
   their destruction,

to King Nebuchadrezzar of Babylon
   and his troops;
   yet after this the land will be peopled as
   of old.
   This is the word of the LORD.

27 But, Jacob my servant, do not be
   afraid;
   Israel, do not be dismayed;
   from afar I shall bring you back safe,
   and your children from the land where
   they are captives.
   Jacob will be at rest once more,
   secure and untroubled.
28 Do not be afraid, Jacob my servant,
   says the LORD, for I am with you.
   I shall make an end of all the nations
   amongst whom I have dispersed you;
   but of you I shall not make an end.
   I shall discipline you only as you
   deserve,
   I shall not leave you wholly
   unpunished.

47 This came to the prophet Jeremiah
   as the word of the LORD concerning
the Philistines before Pharaoh's attack on
Gaza: 2 These are the words of the LORD:

   See how waters are rising from the
      north
   and swelling to a torrent in spate,
   flooding the land and all that is in it,
   towns and those who live in them.
   People cry out in alarm;
   wailing arises from all the inhabitants of
      the land.
3 At the noise of the pounding of his
      chargers' hoofs,
   the rattle of his chariots and their
      rumbling wheels,
   fathers have no thought for their
      children;
   their hands hang powerless,

46:22 **Egypt is hissing:** *cp. Gk; Heb. obscure.*
46:25 **Amon … Thebes:** *prob. rdg; Heb. adds and*
Pharaoh.

here, compare Isa. 46.1–2. **16:** The people speaking are foreign mercenaries. **18:** *Mighty:* these Palestinian
mountains, *Carmel* and *Tabor,* dominate their vicinities. **25:** *Amon:* a god worshiped at *Thebes* in southern
Egypt. **26:** The latter part of the verse is probably an addition, softening the judgment; see 48.47 and 49.6.
27–28: Reassurance to Israel; see 30.1–11.

   47.1–7: Concerning the Philistines. Pharaoh is mentioned only in v. 1. *From the north* (v. 2) suggests
Babylon, not Egypt, as the agent of God (v. 4) being sent to destroy Philistia. The chapter could refer to any
of the frequent occasions when Philistia was ground between the two major powers, e.g. during Necho's

⁴because the day has come
  for all Philistia to be despoiled,
and Tyre and Sidon destroyed to the
  last defender;
for the LORD is despoiling the
  Philistines,
that remnant of the isle of Caphtor.
⁵Gaza is shorn bare, Ashkelon ruined,
  the remnant of the Philistine power.
How long will you gash yourselves and
  cry:
⁶'Ah, sword in the hand of the LORD,
how long will it be before you rest?
Sheathe yourself, cease and be quiet.'
⁷How can it rest when the LORD has
  given it work to do
against Ashkelon and the sea coast?
There he has assigned the sword its
  task.

48 Of Moab. This is what the LORD of
  Hosts the God of Israel says:

Woe betide Nebo! It is laid waste;
Kiriathaim captured and put to shame,
Misgab reduced to shame and dismay;
²Moab's glory is no more.
In Heshbon they plot her downfall:
'Come, put an end to that nation.'
And you, the inhabitants of Madhmen,
  will also perish,
pursued by the sword.
³Cries of anguish arise from Horonaim:
'Havoc and utter destruction!'
⁴Moab is broken;
  their cries are heard as far as Zoar.
⁵On the ascent to Luhith
they go up weeping bitterly;
on the descent to Horonaim
an anguished cry of destruction is
  heard.
⁶Flee, escape with your lives
and become like one destitute in the
  wilderness.

⁷Because you trust in your defences and
  arsenals,
you too will be captured,
and Kemosh will go into exile,
his priests and those in attendance with
  him.
⁸A despoiler will come against every
  town;
no town will escape,
valley and tableland will be laid waste
  and plundered;
the LORD has spoken.
⁹Give a warning signal to Moab,
for she will be laid in ruins;
and her towns will become waste places
  with no inhabitant in them.
¹⁰A curse on all who are slack in doing
  the LORD's work!
A curse on all who withhold their
  swords from bloodshed!

¹¹From its earliest days Moab has been
  undisturbed
and never gone into exile.
It has been like wine settled on its lees,
not decanted from vessel to vessel;
its flavour remains unaltered
and its aroma stays unchanged.

¹²Therefore the days are coming, says the
LORD, when I shall send men to tilt the jars;
they will empty the vessels and smash the
jars. ¹³Moab will be let down by Kemosh as
Israel was let down by Bethel, a god in whom
they trusted.

¹⁴How can you say, 'We are warriors,
  men valiant in battle'?
¹⁵The spoiler of Moab and its towns has
  launched an attack,

47:7 **can it:** *so Gk; Heb.* can you.   48:6 **one
destitute:** *or* a juniper.   48:9 **Give ... signal:** *poss.
mng; Heb. obscure.* **laid in ruins:** *prob. rdg; Heb. obscure.*

---

campaign in 609 (see 2 Kgs. 23.29). **4:** *Tyre and Sidon,* Phoenician cities, seemingly allied with the Philistines
(27.3). *Caphtor:* Crete, or possibly Asia Minor; see Amos 9.7. *Gaza ... Ashkelon:* Philistine cities. **6:** Philistia
speaks here.

48.1–47: Of Moab. A collection of compositions concerning Moab, some threatening calamities, others
lamenting that people's distress. Neither the occasions nor the human agents of destruction are specified.
During the latter half of the seventh century and early in the sixth, Moab suffered from incursions of Arab tribes
from the east. When Jerusalem fell in 587, Moab afforded refuge to fugitives from Judah (see 40.11–12). **1–6:**
The chapter begins with what sounds like a dirge, sympathy for Moab in her plight; compare Isa. 15.1–8. **7:**
The tone becomes more hostile. *Kemosh:* the Moabite god; see vv. 13 and 46. *Will go into exile:* see also Isa.
46.2. **12:** *Smash the jars:* see 13.12–14; 19.11. **13:** *Bethel:* see Gen. 31.13. Here the word is a name for a

and the flower of its youth goes down
  to be slaughtered.

This is the word of the King whose name is
the LORD of Hosts.

16 Retribution on Moab is near at hand,
  disaster rushing swiftly on him.
17 Bewail him, all you his neighbours
  and all who knew his fame;
  and say, 'Alas! The commander's staff
  is broken,
  that splendid baton.'
18 Come down from your place of
  honour,
  sit on the parched ground, you natives
  of Dibon;
  for the spoiler of Moab has come
  against you
  and destroyed your citadels.
19 You that live in Aroer, stand by the
  road and watch,
  ask the man running away, the woman
  escaping,
  ask, 'What has happened?'

20 Moab is reduced to shame and dismay:
  wail and cry, proclaim by the Arnon
  that Moab is despoiled.

21 Judgement has come to the tableland, to
Holon and Jahaz, Mephaath 22 and Dibon,
Nebo and Beth-diblathaim 23 and Kiriathaim,
Beth-gamul, Beth-meon, 24 Kerioth and Boz-
rah, and to all the towns of Moab far and
near.

25 Moab's horn is hacked off
  and his strong arm is broken,
  says the LORD.

26 Make Moab drunk—he has defied the
  LORD.
  Let Moab overflow with his vomit
  and become in turn a butt for derision.
27 Was not Israel your butt?
  Yet was he ever in company with
  thieves,
  that each time you spoke of him
  you shook your head?

28 Leave your towns, you inhabitants of
  Moab,
  and find a home among the crags;
  become like a dove which nests
  in the rock-face at the mouth of a
  cavern.

29 We have heard of Moab's pride, and
  proud indeed he is,
  proud, presumptuous, overbearing,
  insolent.
30 I know his arrogance, says the LORD;
  his boasting is false, false are his deeds.
31 Therefore I shall wail over Moab,
  cry in anguish for the whole of Moab;
  I shall moan over the men of Kir-heres.
32 More than I wept for Jazer
  I shall weep for you, vine of Sibmah,
  whose branches spread out to the sea
  and reach as far as Jazer.
  The despoiler has fallen on your
  harvest and vintage;
33 gladness and joy are taken away
  from the garden land of Moab;
  I have dried up the flow of wine from
  the vats,
  and the shouts of those treading the
  grapes
  will echo no more.

34 Heshbon and Elealeh utter cries of anguish
which are heard in Jahaz; the sound carries
from Zoar to Horonaim and Eglath-shelishiyah; for the waters of Nimrim have become
a desolate waste. 35 In Moab I shall put an end
to their sacrificing at shrines and burning of
offerings to their gods, says the LORD.
36 Therefore I wail for Moab like a reed-pipe,
wail like a reed-pipe for the men of Kir-heres. Their accumulated wealth has vanished.
37 Every man's head is shorn in mourning,
every beard clipped, every hand gashed, and
every waist girded with sackcloth. 38 On all
Moab's roofs and in all her broad streets
nothing is heard but lamentation, for I have
broken Moab like an unwanted pot, says the

48:32 **as far as Jazer:** *prob. rdg, cp. Isa. 16:8; Heb.* the
sea of Jazer.   48:34 **and Elealeh:** *prob. rdg, cp. Isa.
15:4; Heb.* as far as Elealeh. **Horonaim and:** *so Gk;
Heb.* omits and.

deity rather than the place of a sanctuary. The betrayal alluded to is obscure. **17–24:** Further sympathy for
Moab. *Alas!:* the same Heb. word (*echah*) begins Lamentations. **25–39:** Again the hostile words are interspersed with sympathetic murmurs (see vv. 31–32, 34). **27:** *Shook your head:* this motion is a sign of scorn.
29–33, 36: These verses largely echo those of Isa. 16.6–11. **34:** Sites in Moab. **36:** *Kir-heres* (Kir-hareseth)

LORD. ³⁹Moab is dismayed and has turned away in shame. It has become a butt of derision and a cause of dismay to all round about.
⁴⁰For the LORD has spoken:

Like an eagle with outspread wings
he swoops down on Moab.
⁴¹Towns are captured, the strongholds taken;
on that day the spirit of Moab's warriors will fail
like the spirit of a woman in labour.
⁴²The Moabite nation will be destroyed,
for it vaunted itself against the LORD.
⁴³The hunter's scare, the pit, and the trap
threaten you dwellers in Moab,
says the LORD.
⁴⁴If anyone runs from the scare
he will fall into the pit;
if someone climbs out of the pit
he will be caught in the trap.
All this I shall bring on Moab
in the year of their reckoning.
This is the word of the LORD.
⁴⁵In the shadow of Heshbon
the fugitives stand helpless;
for fire has blazed out from Heshbon,
flames from within Sihon
devouring the braggarts of Moab,
both forehead and crown.
⁴⁶Woe betide you, Moab!
The people of Kemosh have vanished,
for your sons are taken into captivity,
your daughters led away captive.
⁴⁷Yet in days to come I shall restore
Moab's fortunes.
This is the word of the LORD.

Here ends the judgement on Moab.

49

Of the Ammonites. Thus says the LORD:

Has Israel no sons? Has he no heir?

Why then has Milcom inherited the land of Gad,
and why do Milcom's people live in its towns?
²Therefore a time is coming,
says the LORD,
when I shall make Rabbah of the Ammonites hear the battle cry,
when it will become a desolate mound
and its villages will be burnt to ashes;
then Israel will disinherit all who disinherited them,
says the LORD.

³Wail, Heshbon, for Ai is despoiled;
cry aloud, you villages round Rabbah!
Put on sackcloth and beat your breast,
and score your bodies with gashes,
for Milcom will go into exile,
and with him his priests and attendants.
⁴Why do you glory in your strength,
you wayward people who trust in your arsenals
and say, 'Who will dare attack me?'
⁵Beware, I am bringing terror on you
from every side,
says the Lord GOD of Hosts;
every one of you will be driven headlong
with no one to rally the fugitives.
⁶Yet after this I shall restore the fortunes of Ammon.
This is the word of the LORD.

⁷Of Edom. The LORD of Hosts has said:

Is wisdom no longer to be found in Teman?
Have her wise men lost all skill in counsel?

48:39 **dismayed:** *so Gk; Heb. adds* they howl.
49:3 **gashes:** *prob. rdg, cp. Aram. (Targ.); Heb.* fences.

---

ancient capital of Moab. **40–46:** Moab is to undergo irretrievable disaster. With vv. 43–44 compare Isa. 24.17–18. **45–46:** On Moab's sad plight, see also Num. 21.28–29. **45:** *Heshbon:* a border city. It is here in Moab, but in 49.3 it is in Ammon. *Sihon:* an Amorite king (Num. 21.21–31).

49.1–39: The seizure by the people of Ammon of Israelite territory will not go unpunished. The exact occasion is not known. **1:** *Gad:* on Ammon's northern border, east of the Jordan. *Milcom:* the Ammonite god. **2:** *Rabbah of the Ammonites:* the capital city, modern Amman. **3:** *Heshbon:* see 48.45 n. **6:** See, similarly, 48.47. **7–22:** *Of Edom:* except for her "arrogance" (v. 16) Edom's offense is not here specified. After the fall of Jerusalem and during the early Persian Period (sixth century), the Nabateans, nomadic peoples from Arabia, invaded and pushed the Edomites westward into southern Judah. **7:** "Men of the east," including *Edom,* were widely reputed for their *wisdom;* see 1 Kgs. 4.29–30. *Teman:* an Edomite city, at times used synonymously

Has their wisdom been dispersed
  abroad?
8 Turn and flee, people of Dedan,
take refuge in remote places;
for I shall bring retribution on Esau,
his day of reckoning.
9 If vintagers were to come to you
they would surely leave gleanings;
and if thieves were to raid your crops
  by night,
they would take only enough for their
  needs.
10 But I have ransacked Esau's treasure,
I have uncovered his hiding-places,
and he has nowhere to conceal himself.
His children, his kinsfolk, and his
  neighbours are despoiled;
there is no one to deliver him.
11 Am I to keep alive your fatherless
  children?
Are your widows to depend on me?

12 For these are the words of the Lord: Those
who were not doomed to drink the cup must
drink it none the less; are you alone to go
unpunished? You will not escape; you will
have to drink it. 13 For by my life, says the
Lord, Bozrah will become an object of horror and reproach, a desolation and a thing of
cursing; and all her towns will be desolate for
ever.

14 When a herald was sent among the
  nations crying,
'Gather and march against her,
prepare for battle,'
I heard this message from the Lord:
15 Look, I make you the least of all
  nations,
most despised of people.
16 Your overbearing arrogance and your
  insolent heart
have led you astray.
You, whose haunts are in the crannies
  of the rock,
you keep your hold on the hilltop.
Though you nest as high as an eagle,
even from there I shall bring you
  down.

This is the word of the Lord.
17 Edom will become an object of horror,
all who pass that way will be
  horror-struck,
astounded at the sight of all her
  wounds,
18 overthrown as she is like Sodom and
  Gomorrah and their neighbours,
says the Lord.
No one will live there,
no human being will make a home in
  her.

19 Like a lion coming up
from Jordan's dense thickets to the
  perennial pastures,
in a moment I shall chase the shepherd
  away
and round up the choicest of the rams.
For who is like me? Who can arraign
  me?
What shepherd can stand his ground
  before me?

20 Therefore listen to the Lord's purpose
against Edom and his plans against the people of Teman:

The young of the flock will be dragged
  off,
and their pasture will be aghast at their
  fate.
21 At the sound of their downfall the land
  quakes;
it cries out, and the sound is heard at
  the Red Sea.
22 Like an eagle with outspread wings
he will soar and swoop down against
  Bozrah,
and on that day the spirit of Edom's
  warriors
will be like the spirit of a woman in
  labour.

23 Of Damascus.

49:19 **the choicest of:** *prob. rdg; Heb.* who is chosen?
49:21 **Red Sea:** *or* sea of Reeds.

---

with Edom. **8:** *Esau:* the ancestor of Edom; see Gen. 25.29–30; 36.1. **9:** *Vintagers:* harvesters of grapes. **10:**
Ransacked: see Obad. 5–6. **12:** *Those who were not doomed:* i.e. not specifically "sentenced"; probably they
are included in the category of "all the inhabitants of the earth" in 25.29. **13:** *Bozrah:* a fortress city in the
northern part of Edom. **14–16:** See Obad. 1–4. **18:** *Sodom and Gomorrah and their neighbours:* see Deut.
29.23. **19:** *From Jordan's dense thickets:* God, like a lion, attacks Edom's *rams*, its leaders. **23–27:** *Damascus:*

Hamath and Arpad are covered with
confusion,
for they have heard news of disaster;
they are tossed up and down in anxiety
like the unresting sea.
24 Damascus has lost heart and turns to
flight;
trembling has seized her,
pangs like childbirth have gripped her.
25 How forlorn is the town of joyful song,
the place of gladness!
26 Therefore her young men will fall in
her streets
and all her warriors lie still in death
that day.
This is the word of the LORD of Hosts.
27 Then I shall kindle a fire within the
wall of Damascus
and it will devour Ben-hadad's palaces.

28 Of Kedar and the kingdoms of Hazor
which King Nebuchadrezzar of Babylon subdued. The LORD has said:

Come, attack Kedar,
despoil the eastern desert-dwellers.
29 Carry away their tents and their flocks,
the curtains of their tents and all their
goods,
and drive off their camels.
A cry will go up: 'Terror let loose!'
30 Flee and make your escape,
take refuge in remote places, you
people of Hazor,
says the LORD;
for King Nebuchadrezzar of Babylon
has laid his plans,
he has formed a design against you:
31 'Come, let us attack a nation at peace,
living in fancied security
with no barred gates,
dwelling in isolation.'

32 Their camels will be carried off as
booty,
their vast herds of cattle as plunder;
I shall scatter them to all the winds

to roam the fringes of the desert,
and from every side I shall bring
retribution on them,
says the LORD.
33 Hazor will become a haunt of wolves,
for ever desolate,
where no one will live,
no mortal make a home.
This is the word of the LORD.

34 This came to the prophet Jeremiah as the
word of the LORD concerning Elam, at the
beginning of the reign of King Zedekiah of
Judah: 35 Thus says the LORD of Hosts:

I shall break the bow of Elam,
the chief weapon of their might;
36 I shall bring four winds against Elam
from the four quarters of heaven;
I shall scatter them to all these winds,
and there will be no nation
to which the exiles from Elam do not
go.
37 I shall break Elam before their foes,
before those who are bent on their
destruction;
I shall vent my fierce anger upon them
in disaster;
I shall pursue them with the sword
until I make an end of them,
says the LORD.
38 Then I shall set my throne in Elam,
and destroy the king and his officers
there.
This is the word of the LORD.
39 Yet in days to come I shall restore the
fortunes of Elam.
This is the word of the LORD.

50 The word which the LORD spoke
about Babylon, the land of the Chaldaeans, through the prophet Jeremiah:

49:23 like: so some MSS, others in.
49:25 of gladness: so Syriac; Heb. of my gladness.
49:31 security: so Gk; Heb. adds says the LORD.
49:32 them ... desert: or to the wind those who clip
the hair on their temples.

the capital of Syria. 23: Except in v. 27, which is quoted from Amos 1.4, no reason for, or source of, the *disaster*
is given. *Hamath* and *Arpad* are neighboring cities. *Ben-hadad:* a royal Syrian name. 28–33: *Kedar:* an area
in the east of Palestine. 28: *Hazor:* a place unknown, but apparently in, or near, Kedar. 29: '*Terror let loose!*':
see 20.10; 46.5. 30: See 25.9. 31: See Ezek. 38.11; Deut. 33.28. 32: See Ezek. 12.14, 15. 33: *Wolves:* the
exact identification is uncertain here and in 10.22. 34–39: *Elam:* a country east of Babylonia, bordering on
Media and Persia, and a protectorate of Media, but having no known contact with Judah. 34: *Zedekiah:* he
began to reign around 597 B.C.E 38: *Throne:* see also 1.15. 39: A comforting addition.

2 Declare among the nations, make
      proclamation;
   keep nothing back, spread the news:
   Babylon is taken,
   Bel put to shame, Marduk dismayed;
   the idols of Babylon are put to shame,
   her false gods are dismayed.
3 A nation has come out of the north
      against her;
   it will make her land a desolate waste
   with no one living there;
   man and beast have fled and are gone.

4 In those days and at that time, says the
Lord, the people of Israel and the people of
Judah will come together, and in tears go in
search of the Lord their God; 5 they will ask
the way to Zion, turning their faces towards
her, and saying, 'Come, let us join ourselves
to the Lord in an everlasting covenant which
will never be forgotten.'

6 My people were lost sheep, whose shepherds let them stray and run wild on the
mountains; they wandered from mountain
to hill, forgetful of their fold. 7 All who came
on them devoured them; their enemies said,
'We incur no guilt, because they have sinned
against the Lord, the Lord who is the true
goal and the hope of their forefathers.'

8 Flee from Babylon, from the land of
      the Chaldaeans;
   go out like he-goats leading the flock.
9 I shall stir up a host of mighty nations
   and bring them against Babylon,
   marshalled against her from a northern
      land;
   and from the north she will be
      captured.
   Their arrows are like those of a skilled
      warrior
   who never returns empty-handed;
10 the Chaldaeans will be plundered,
   and all who plunder them will take
      their fill.

This is the word of the Lord.

11 You plundered my possession; but
      though you rejoice and exult,
   though you run free like a heifer
      during the threshing,
   though you neigh like a stallion,
12 your mother will be cruelly disgraced,
   she who bore you will be put to shame.
   Look at her, bringing up the rear of
      the nations,
   a wilderness, parched and barren,
13 uninhabited through the wrath of the
      Lord,
   an object of horror;
   all who pass by Babylon will be
      horror-struck
   and astounded at the sight of her many
      wounds.

14 Marshal your forces and encircle
      Babylon,
   you whose bows are ready strung;
   shoot at her, spare not your arrows,
   for she has sinned against the Lord.
15 On every side shout in triumph over
      her;
   she has surrendered,
   her bastions are thrown down, her walls
      demolished.
   This is the vengeance of the Lord;
   be avenged on her;
   as she has done, so do to her.
16 Destroy every sower in Babylon,
   every reaper with his sickle at harvest
      time.
   To escape the cruel sword
   everyone will turn back to his people,
   everyone flee to his own land.

17 Israel is a scattered flock
   harried and chased by lions:

50:2 **make proclamation:** *so Gk; Heb. adds* and raise a
standard, proclaim. 50:5 **let us join ourselves:** *so
Syriac; Heb.* they will join themselves.

50.1–51.64: Concerning Babylon. In 539 B.C.E. its capital fell before Cyrus the Persian. In part, chs. 50–51
anticipate those events, without, however, naming Persia, and in part they look back to them, but it is not always
clear whether the intention is future or past. **2:** *Babylon is taken.* But in vv. 3 and 9 the land is yet to be
conquered. *Bel,* "great god," is a title of *Marduk* (Merodach), god of the city of Babylon. **3:** *A nation out of
the north:* Media lay north of Babylon, Persia to the southeast: by 550 B.C.E., Cyrus of Persia had incorporated
the northern peoples into his expanding empire. **4–7:** The reunion of *Israel and . . . Judah:* these verses interrupt
the material concerning Babylon. **8:** *Flee from Babylon:* this is addressed to captive Judeans. **9–10:** God
assembles the nations of the north; see 51.27–28 n. The time is future. **11:** *My possession:* the land of Judah.
12: *Your mother:* Babylon, the capital city. **16:** *Everyone:* from a foreign land. **17–20:** Concern for Israel and

the Assyrian king was the first to
  devour him,
and now at the last his bones have been
  gnawed
by King Nebuchadrezzar of Babylon.

18 Therefore the LORD of Hosts the God of
Israel says this:

I shall punish the king of Babylon and
  his country
as once I punished the king of Assyria.
19 But I shall bring Israel back to his own
  pasture,
  to graze on Carmel and Bashan;
  on Ephraim's hills and in Gilead he will
    eat his fill.

20 In those days, says the LORD, when that
time comes, search will be made for the iniquity of Israel, but there will be none, and for
the sin of Judah, but it will not be found; for
those whom I leave as a remnant I shall pardon.

21 Attack the land of Merathaim;
  attack it and the inhabitants of Pekod;
  put them to the sword and utterly
    destroy them,
and do whatever I command you.
This is the word of the LORD.

22 The sound of war is heard in the land
  and great destruction!
23 See how the hammer of the whole
  world
  is hacked and broken,
how Babylon has become
  a thing of horror among the nations!
24 Babylon, you have set a snare for
  yourself
and have been trapped unawares.
There you are, you are caught,
  because you have challenged the LORD.
25 The LORD has opened his armoury
  and brought out the weapons of his
    wrath;
for this is work for the Lord the GOD
  of Hosts to do
in the land of the Chaldaeans.

26 Come against her from every quarter;
  throw open her granaries,
pile her like heaps of grain;
  destroy her completely,
  let no survivor be left.
27 Put all her warriors to the sword;
  let them be led to the slaughter.
Woe betide them, for their time has
    come,
  their day of reckoning!
28 I hear the fugitives escaping from the
    land of Babylon
to proclaim in Zion the vengeance of
    the LORD our God,
  the vengeance he takes for his temple.

29 Let your arrows whistle against
    Babylon,
all you whose bows are ready strung.
Besiege her on all sides;
  let no one escape.
Repay her in full for her misdeeds;
  as she has done, so do to her,
for she has insulted the LORD
  the Holy One of Israel.
30 Therefore her young men will fall in
    her streets,
and all her warriors lie still in death
    that day.
This is the word of the LORD.

31 I am against you, insolent city;
  for your time has come, your day of
    reckoning.
This is the word of the Lord GOD of
    Hosts.
32 The insolent one will stumble and fall
  and no one will lift her up;
I shall kindle fire in her towns
  and it will devour everything round
    about.

33 The LORD of Hosts has said this:

The peoples of Israel and Judah are
  both oppressed;
their captors all hold them fast
  and will not let go.
34 But they have a powerful advocate,

50:26 **from every quarter:** *prob. rdg; Heb.* at the end.

Judah; see vv. 4–7. God has already dealt with Assyria which had conquered Israel; now God will punish
Babylonia and will bring Israel back to its land, forgiven. **19:** *Carmel and Bashan . . . Ephraim and Gilead:* areas
west and east of the Jordan, formerly occupied by the Northern Kingdom. **21:** The attention reverts to Babylonia.
23: The conquests of Babylon, *the hammer of the whole world,* have been ended. **28:** *Vengeance . . . for his*

whose name is the LORD of Hosts;
he himself will take up their cause,
that he may give distress to the land
and turmoil to the inhabitants of
   Babylon.

35 A sword hangs over the Chaldaeans,
over the people of Babylon,
her officers and wise men,
says the LORD.
36 A sword hangs over the false prophets,
and they are made fools,
a sword over her warriors, and they
   despair,
37 a sword over her horses and her
   chariots
and over all the mixed rabble within
   her,
and they will become like women;
a sword over her treasures, and they
   will be plundered,
38 a sword over her waters, and they will
   dry up;
for it is a land of idols
that glories in its dreaded gods.

39 Therefore marmots and jackals will skulk
in it, desert-owls will haunt it; never more will
it be inhabited and age after age no one will
dwell in it. 40 It will be as when God overthrew
Sodom and Gomorrah along with their
neighbours, says the LORD; no one will live in
it, no human being will make a home there.

41 See, an army is coming from the north;
a great nation and mighty kings
rouse themselves from earth's farthest
   corners.
42 Armed with bow and scimitar,
they are cruel and pitiless;
bestriding their horses,
they sound like the thunder of the sea;
they are like men arrayed
for battle against you, Babylon.
43 News of them has reached the king of
   Babylon,
and his hands hang limp;
agony grips him,
pangs as of a woman in labour.
44 Like a lion coming up

from Jordan's dense thickets to the
   perennial pastures,
in a moment I shall chase the shepherd
   away
and round up the choicest of the rams.
For who is like me? Who can challenge
   me?
What shepherd can stand his ground
   before me?

45 Therefore listen to the LORD's purpose
against Babylon and his plans against the
land of the Chaldaeans:

The young of the flock will be dragged
   off,
and their pasture will be aghast at their
   fate.
46 At the sound of Babylon's capture the
   land quakes;
it cries out, and the sound is heard
   throughout the nations.

51 For thus says the LORD:

I shall raise a destructive wind
against Babylon and the inhabitants of
   Leb-kamai.
2 I shall send winnowers to Babylon
who will winnow her land empty;
for they will assail her from all sides
on the day of disaster.
3 How will the archer then string his bow
or put on his coat of mail?

Spare none of her young men, but
   utterly destroy her whole army
4 and let them fall dead in the land of
   the Chaldaeans,
slain in her streets.
5 Israel and Judah are not left widowed
by their God, by the LORD of Hosts;
but their land is full of guilt,
condemned by the Holy One of Israel.

6 Flee out of Babylon, each one for
   himself,
or you will perish for her sin;

50:44 **the choicest of:** *prob. rdg; Heb.* who is chosen?
51:1 **Leb-kamai:** *a cipher for* Chaldaea.

---

temple: see 51.11. **40, 44–46:** These verses quote 49.18–21, substituting Babylon here for Edom there. **41–43:**
These verses quote 6.22–24 almost exactly, here substituting Babylon for Zion. **44:** See vv. 40, 44–46 n. God
brings the Medes (51.11) to destroy Babylon and avenge the destruction of the temple; see Isa. 13.17–19. After
Media's defeat about 550 B.C.E., by Cyrus of Persia, the latter was a real threat to Babylon. **51:5:** *Not left*

for this is the LORD's day of vengeance,
and he is paying her full recompense.

7 Babylon has been a golden cup in the
LORD's hand
to make all the earth drunk;
the nations have drunk of her wine,
and that has made them mad.

8 Suddenly Babylon falls and is broken.
Wail for her!
Fetch balm for her wound;
perhaps she may be healed.

9 We tried to heal Babylon, but she is
past healing.
Leave her and let us be off, each to his
own country;
for her doom reaches to heaven
and mounts up to the skies.

10 The LORD has made our victory plain
to see;
come, let us proclaim in Zion
what the LORD our God has done.

11 Sharpen the arrows, fill the quivers.
The LORD has roused the spirit of the
king of the Medes;
for the LORD's purpose against Babylon
is to destroy it,
and his vengeance is vengeance for his
temple.

12 Raise the standard against Babylon's
walls,
mount a strong blockade,
post sentries, set an ambush;
for the LORD has both planned and
carried out
his threat against the inhabitants of
Babylon.

13 You opulent city, standing beside great
waters,
your end has come, your destiny is
certain.

14 The LORD of Hosts has sworn by
himself:
Surely I shall fill you with enemies
who will swarm like locusts,
and they will raise a shout of triumph
over you.

15 God made the earth by his power,
fixed the world in place by his
wisdom,

and by his knowledge unfurled the
skies.

16 When he speaks in the thunder
the waters in the heavens are in tumult;
he brings up the mist from the ends of
the earth,
he opens rifts for the rain,
and brings the wind out of his
storehouses.

17 Everyone is brutish and ignorant,
every goldsmith is discredited through
his idols;
for the figures he casts are a sham,
there is no breath in them.

18 They are worthless, mere objects of
mockery,
which perish when their day of
reckoning comes.

19 Jacob's chosen God is not like these,
for he is the creator of the universe.
Israel is the people he claims as his
own;
the LORD of Hosts is his name.

20 You are my battleaxe, my weapon of
war;
with you I shall break nations in
pieces,
and with you I shall destroy kingdoms.

21 With you I shall break horse and rider,
with you I shall break chariot and
charioteer,

22 with you I shall break man and wife,
with you I shall break old and young,
with you I shall break youth and
maiden,

23 with you I shall break shepherd and his
flock,
with you I shall break ploughman and
his team,
with you I shall break viceroys and
governors.

24 So shall I repay Babylon and the
people of Chaldaea
for all the wrong which they did in
Zion in your sight.
This is the word of the LORD.

51:11 **king:** *so Gk; Heb.* kings.   51:13 **destiny:** *lit.*
cutting off *(the thread of life).*   51:16 **When ...**
tumult: *prob. rdg; Heb. obscure.* **rifts:** *prob. rdg; Heb.*
lightnings.   51:19 **Israel:** *so many MSS; others omit.*

widowed by their God: the same metaphor is in Isa. 54.4–6. **6:** *Flee out of Babylon:* this is addressed to the
foreigners and the mercenaries; see 46.16 n. **7:** *Cup:* see 25.15–16. **10:** *Our victory:* the words are spoken
by the Judean exiles; see 50.28. **11:** See 50.28. **13:** *Great waters* refers to the Euphrates river. **15–19:** The same
as 10.12–16. **20–24:** Continues vv. 1–14. The Medes (or Persians) are God's *weapon* against Babylon. **25–33:**

25 I am against you, a destructive
    mountain
destroying the whole earth, says the
    LORD.
I shall stretch out my hand against you
and send you tumbling headlong from
    the rocks
and make you a burnt-out mountain.
26 No stone taken from you will be used
    as a corner-stone,
no stone for a foundation;
but you will be for ever desolate.
This is the word of the LORD.

27 Raise a standard on the earth,
blow a trumpet among the nations,
consecrate the nations for war against
    her,
summon the kingdoms of Ararat,
    Minni, and Ashkenaz,
appoint a commander against her,
bring up horses like a dark swarm of
    locusts.
28 For war against her consecrate the
    nations,
the king of the Medes, his viceroys and
    governors,
and all the lands under his sway.
29 The earth quakes and writhes;
for the LORD's designs against Babylon
    are fulfilled:
to make the land of Babylon an
    unpeopled waste.
30 Babylon's warriors have given up the
    fight;
they skulk in the forts,
their courage has failed,
they have become like women.
The buildings are set on fire,
the bars of the gates broken.
31 Runner speeds to meet runner,
messenger to meet messenger,
reporting to the king of Babylon
that every quarter of his city is taken,
32 the river-crossings are seized,
the guard-towers set on fire,
and the garrison stricken with panic.

33 For these are the words of the LORD of
Hosts the God of Israel:

Babylon is like a threshing-floor when it
    is trodden;
very soon harvest time will come for
    her.
34 'King Nebuchadrezzar of Babylon has
    devoured me
and sucked me dry;
he has set me aside like an empty jar.
Like a dragon he has gulped me down;
he filled his maw with my delicate flesh
and spewed me up.'
35 Every citizen of Zion will say,
'On Babylon be the violence done to
    me,
the vengeance taken on me!'
Jerusalem will say,
'My blood be on the Chaldaeans!'

36 Therefore the LORD says:

I shall plead your cause, I shall avenge
    you;
I shall dry up her river and make her
    waters fail.
37 Babylon will become a heap of ruins, a
    haunt of wolves,
an object of horror and astonishment,
    with no inhabitant.

38 Together they roar like young lions,
they growl like the whelps of a lioness.
39 I shall cause their drinking bouts to
    end in fever
and make them so drunk that they will
    writhe and toss,
then sink into unending sleep, never to
    wake again.
This is the word of the LORD.
40 I shall bring them down like lambs to
    the slaughter,
like rams and he-goats together.

51:27 **on the earth:** *or* in the land.   51:28 **king:** *so
Gk (cp. verse 11); Heb.* kings.

God summons a company of nations to avenge the *wrong* done *in Zion* (v. 24) and destroy Babylon. **25:**
Mountain: Babylon, so called because of a landmark, a terraced tower (ziggurat) of the Marduk temple there.
27–28: *Ararat, Minni, and Ashkenaz:* they were far to the north. Defeated by the Medes, they were later added
to the empire of Cyrus. The Heb. term for *commander* is a loan word from the Babylonian. **31:** Relay *runners*
report to the king Nabonidus, who was probably away at his oasis at Tema in Arabia when Babylon fell. **33:**
Trodden: grain was separated from straw by the treading of animals (Deut. 25.4). **34–35:** Jerusalem's plea.

41 Sheshak is captured,
the pride of the whole world taken.
How Babylon has become
a thing of horror among the nations!
42 The sea has surged over Babylon,
she is covered by its roaring waves.
43 Her towns have become waste places,
a land parched and barren,
a land where no one lives,
through which no human being travels.

44 I shall punish Bel in Babylon
and make him disgorge what he has
swallowed;
nations will never again come streaming
to him.
Babylon's wall has fallen.

45 My people, come out from her,
and let every one save himself
from the fierce anger of the LORD.
46 Then beware of losing heart;
fear no rumours spread abroad in the
land,
as rumour follows rumour,
a new one every year:
of violence on earth,
of ruler against ruler.

47 Therefore a time is coming
when I shall punish Babylon's idols;
her whole land will be put to shame,
and all her slain will lie fallen in her
midst.
48 The heavens and the earth
and all that is in them
will sing in triumph over Babylon;
for marauders from the north will
overrun her.
This is the word of the LORD.

49 Babylon in her turn must fall
because of Israel's slain,
as the slain of all the world
have fallen because of Babylon.

50 You that have escaped the sword,
go, do not linger.
Remember the LORD from afar
and let Jerusalem come to your
minds.

51 By the reproaches we have heard we
are put to shame
and our faces are covered with
confusion,
because foreigners have entered
the sacred courts of the LORD's house.

52 A time is coming therefore, says the
LORD,
when I shall punish her idols,
and throughout her land
the wounded will groan.
53 Were Babylon to reach the skies
and make strong her towers in the
heights,
I should still send marauders against
her.
This is the word of the LORD.
54 Cries of agony are heard from Babylon,
sounds of great destruction from
Chaldaea.
55 The advancing wave booms and roars
like mighty waters,
for the LORD is despoiling Babylon
and will silence the noise of the city.
56 Marauders march on Babylon herself,
her warriors are captured and their
bows broken;
for the LORD, a God of retribution, will
repay in full.
57 I shall make her princes and her wise
men drunk,
her viceroys and governors and
warriors,
and they will sink into unending sleep,
never to wake again.
This is the word of the King,
whose name is the LORD of Hosts.

58 The LORD of Hosts says:

The walls of broad Babylon will be
razed to the ground,
her lofty gates set on fire.
Worthless now is the thing for which
peoples toiled;
nations wore themselves out for a mere
nothing.

51:41 **Sheshak:** *a cipher for* Babylon.   51:49 **fall
because of:** *prob. rdg; Heb. omits* because of.

36–58: God responds. Babylon is doomed (if not already taken, vv. 41, 44). 41: *Sheshak:* Babylonia. 44: *Bel:*
also called Marduk, the god of Babylon; see Isa. 46.1–2. 45: *My people, come out:* from your captivity;
compare Isa. 48.20. 48: *From the north:* vv. 27–28 n. 51: *We:* the speaker and fellow exiles. 53: *Towers in
the heights:* see v. 25 n. and Gen. 11.4 n. 56: Israel's *God of retribution* will repay Babylon for its cruelty;

59 The instructions given by the prophet Jeremiah to the quartermaster Seraiah son of Neriah and grandson of Mahseiah, when he went to Babylon with King Zedekiah of Judah in the fourth year of his reign.

60 Jeremiah, having written on a scroll a full description of the disaster which would befall Babylon, 61 said to Seraiah, 'When you come to Babylon, see that you read all these words aloud; 62 then say, "LORD, you have declared your purpose to destroy this place and leave it with nothing living in it, man or beast; it will be desolate, for ever waste." 63 When you have finished reading the scroll, tie a stone to it and throw it into the middle of the Euphrates 64 with the words, "So will Babylon sink, never to rise again after the disaster which I am going to bring on her." '

Thus far are the collected sayings of Jeremiah.

The fall of Jerusalem

52 ZEDEKIAH was twenty-one years old when he came to the throne, and he reigned in Jerusalem for eleven years; his mother was Hamutal daughter of Jeremiah from Libnah. 2 Zedekiah did what was wrong in the eyes of the LORD, as Jehoiakim had done. 3 Jerusalem and Judah so angered the LORD that in the end he banished them from his sight.

Zedekiah rebelled against the king of Babylon. 4 In the ninth year of his reign, on the tenth day of the tenth month, King Nebuchadrezzar of Babylon advanced with his whole army against Jerusalem, invested it, and erected siege-towers against it on every side; 5 the siege lasted till the eleventh year of King Zedekiah. 6 In the fourth month of that year, on the ninth day of the month, while famine raged in the city and there was no food for the people, 7 the city capitulated. When King Zedekiah of Judah saw this, he and all his armed escort left the city by night and, fleeing through the gate called Between

the Two Walls near the king's garden, they made their way towards the Arabah, although the Chaldaeans were surrounding the city. 8 The Chaldaean soldiers set off in pursuit and overtook King Zedekiah in the lowlands of Jericho; his men had all abandoned him and scattered. 9 Zedekiah, when captured, was brought before the king of Babylon at Riblah in the territory of Hamath, where sentence was passed on him. 10 The king of Babylon had Zedekiah's sons slain before his eyes; he also put to death all the princes of Judah at Riblah. 11 Then Zedekiah's eyes were blinded, and the king of Babylon bound him with bronze fetters and brought him to Babylon, where he committed him to prison till the day of his death.

12 On the tenth day of the fifth month, in the nineteenth year of King Nebuchadrezzar of Babylon, Nebuzaradan, captain of the king of Babylon's bodyguard, came to Jerusalem, 13 and set fire to the house of the LORD and the royal palace, indeed all the houses in the city; every notable person's house was burnt down. 14 The whole Chaldaean force under the captain of the guard pulled down all the walls encircling Jerusalem. 15 Nebuzaradan, captain of the guard, deported the rest of the people left in the city, those who had defected to the king of Babylon, and the remaining artisans. 16 He left behind only the poorest class of people, to be vine-dressers and labourers.

17 The Chaldaeans broke up the bronze pillars in the house of the LORD, the trolleys, and the bronze Sea, and carried off all the metal to Babylon. 18 They removed also the pots, shovels, snuffers, tossing-bowls, saucers, and all the bronze vessels used in the service of the temple. 19 The captain of the guard took away the precious metal, whether gold or silver, of which the cups, firepans, tossing-bowls, pots, lampstands, saucers, and

52:7 **When ... he and:** *prob. rdg, cp. 39:4; Heb. omits.*
52:15 **Nebuzaradan:** *prob. rdg, cp. 39:9 and 2 Kgs. 25:11; Heb. prefixes* The poorest class of the people *(cp. verse 16).*

compare Isa. 47.6. **59–64:** A curse on Babylon. *59: Seraiah:* he appears to have been a brother to Jeremiah's disciple Baruch; see 32.12. *With king Zedekiah:* such a journey is unknown. The king may have gone in person to pay a vassal's homage to Nebuchadrezzar; see 29.3. *63: Throw it into the Euphrates:* set the process in motion. Compare the rinsing of the written curse in Num. 5.23. *64b: Thus far ... Jeremiah:* this half verse, apparently, once followed v. 58.

52.1–34: An appendix recapitulating Zedekiah's reign, Jerusalem's fall, deportations, Jehoichin's release. Only vv. 28–30 are new; the remainder of this chapter is taken almost verbatim from, one may see, 2 Kgs.

flagons were made. [20] The bronze of the two pillars, of the one Sea, and of the twelve oxen supporting it, which King Solomon had made for the house of the LORD, was beyond weighing. [21] One pillar was eighteen cubits high and twelve cubits in circumference; it was hollow, but the metal was four fingers thick. [22] It had a capital of bronze, five cubits high, and a decoration of network and pomegranates ran all round it, wholly of bronze. The other pillar, with its pomegranates, was exactly like it. [23] Ninety-six pomegranates were exposed to view and there were a hundred in all on the network all round.

[24] The captain of the guard took Seraiah the chief priest, Zephaniah the deputy chief priest, and the three on duty at the entrance; [25] he took also from the city a eunuch who was in charge of the fighting men, seven of those with right of access to the king who were still in the city, the adjutant-general whose duty was to muster the army for war, and sixty men of the people who were still there. [26] These Nebuzaradan, captain of the guard, brought to the king of Babylon at Riblah. [27] There, in the land of Hamath, the king had them flogged and put to death. So Judah went into exile from its own land.

[28] These were the people deported by Nebuchadrezzar in the seventh year of his reign: three thousand and twenty-three Judaeans. [29] In the eighteenth year, eight hundred and thirty-two people from Jerusalem; [30] in the twenty-third year, seven hundred and forty-five Judaeans were deported by Nebuzaradan the captain of the bodyguard: in all four thousand six hundred people.

[31] In the thirty-seventh year of the exile of King Jehoiachin of Judah, on the twenty-fifth day of the twelfth month, King Evil-merodach of Babylon in the year of his accession showed favour to King Jehoiachin of Judah. He released him from prison, [32] treated him kindly, and gave him a seat at table above the kings with him in Babylon. [33] Jehoiachin, discarding his prison clothes, lived as a pensioner of the king for the rest of his life. [34] For his maintenance a regular daily allowance was given him by the king of Babylon to the day of his death.

52:20 **supporting it:** *so Gk; Heb.* which were under the trolleys. 52:23 **exposed to view:** *mng of Heb. word uncertain.* 52:34 **to ... death:** *so Gk; Heb. adds* as long as he lived.

24.18–25.21, 27–30. Verses 4–16 occur also in Jer. 39.1–2, 4–10. **28–30:** The *seventh* and *eighteenth* years of Nebuchadrezzar mentioned here are at variance with the dating of the same events to his eighth and nineteenth years in 2 Kgs. 24.12; 25.8 (see also Jer. 52.12). However these discrepancies are resolved, the probable years are 597 and 587/6 B.C.E. The events of Nebuchadrezzar's *twenty-third* year (582) are otherwise unknown and unrecorded; perhaps there was some aftermath to the (undated) assassination of Gedaliah (40.7–41.18). No great numbers were deported, 4600 in all. **31–34:** The same as 2 Kgs. 25.27–30.

Lamentations

This collection of five carefully structured poems is unified by a common theme: lamentation over the fall of Jerusalem and its temple to the Babylonians in 587 B.C.E. Each poem except the last is an alphabetic acrostic.

With dirge-type rhythm, the mood is set by a number of unnamed voices. One voice comments on the condition of the city (1.1–11b), while another is that of the city herself, whose personification heightens the pathos (1.11c–22). A third voice is that of an individual who, though crushed, maintains an attitude of hope (ch. 3). At times the voice speaks in the plural, as in ch. 5. All these separate voices blend as one.

A very old tradition that Jeremiah was the author is based upon some similarities between his writings and Lamentations, but there are also profound differences; the poems have closer affinities to the national "laments," such as Pss. 44, 74, 80. The exact date after 587 and the place of composition are difficult to determine because the style and themes were used for many hundreds of years, even in Mesopotamian compositions antedating Hebrew literature.

Lamentations probably came to be used in the temple in liturgical mourning, a practice which continues in Jewish synagogue worship today.

Sorrows of captive Zion

1 How DESERTED lies the city,
once thronging with people!
Once great among nations,
now become a widow;
once queen among provinces,
now put to forced labour!

2 She weeps bitterly in the night;
tears run down her cheeks.
Among all who loved her
she has no one to bring her
comfort.
Her friends have all betrayed her;
they have become her enemies.

3 Judah has wasted away through
affliction
and endless servitude.
Living among the nations,
she has found no resting-place;
her persecutors all fell on her
in her sore distress.

4 The approaches to Zion mourn,
for no pilgrims attend her sacred feasts;
all her gates are desolate.
Her priests groan,
her maidens are made to suffer.
How bitter is her fate!

5 Her adversaries have become her
masters,
her enemies take their ease,
for the LORD has made her suffer
because of her countless sins.
Her young children are gone,
taken captive by an adversary.

6 All splendour has vanished
from the daughter of Zion.
Her princes have become like deer
that can find no pasture.
They run on, their strength spent,
pursued by the hunter.

7 In the days of Jerusalem's misery and
restlessness

1.1–22: The desolation of Zion (Jerusalem). This general lament introduces many of the themes of the book. **1:** *How:* lit. "alas, how . . ." From *greatness* to *widow*hood, from a *queen* to a slave are typical of the poet's stylistic contrasts. **3:** Even though *Judah* as a whole sometimes appears, the main focus is on Jerusalem and the temple. **5:** *Countless sins:* this theme of sin is to be contrasted with that of innocence, as in 3.52; or the sin of a specific group, as in 4.13; or the sins of the forebears, as in 5.7. **6:** *Daughter of Zion:* a term of

she called to mind
all the treasures which were hers
from days of old,
when her people fell into the power of
    adversaries
and she had no one to help her.
The adversaries looked on,
laughing at her downfall.

8 Jerusalem, greatly sinning,
was treated like a filthy rag.
All who had honoured her
held her cheap,
now they had seen her nakedness.
What could she do but groan
and turn away?

9 Uncleanness afflicted her body,
and she gave no thought to her fate.
Her fall was beyond belief
and there was no one to comfort her.
'Look, Lord, on my misery,
for the enemy has triumphed.'

10 The adversary stretched out his hand
to seize all her treasures.
Indeed she saw Gentiles
invade her sanctuary,
Gentiles forbidden by you to enter
the assembly, for it was yours.

11 All her people groaned,
they begged for bread;
they bartered their treasures for food
to regain their strength.
'Look, Lord, and see
how cheap I am accounted.

12 'Is it nothing to you, you passers-by?
If only you would look and see:
is there any agony like mine,
like these torments
which the Lord made me suffer
on the day of his fierce anger?

13 'From heaven he sent down fire,
which ran through my bones;
he spread out a net to catch my feet,
and turned me back;

he made me an example of desolation,
racked with sickness all day long.

14 'My sins were bound like a yoke
tied fast by his own hand;
set upon my neck,
it caused my strength to fail.
The Lord abandoned me to my sins,
and in their grip I could not stand.

15 'The Lord treated with scorn
all the mighty men within my walls;
he marshalled rank on rank against me
to crush my young warriors.
The Lord trod down, like grapes in the
    winepress,
the virgin daughter of Judah.

16 'This is why I weep over my plight,
why tears stream from my eyes:
because any who might comfort me and
    renew my strength
are far away from me;
my children have become desolate,
for the enemy is victorious.'

17 Zion lifted her hands in prayer,
but there was no one to comfort her;
the Lord ordered Jacob's enemies
to beset him on every side.
In their midst Jerusalem became
an unclean thing to be shunned.

18 'The Lord was in the right,
for I rebelled against his command.
Listen, all you nations,
and look on my agony:
my maidens and my young men
are gone into captivity.

19 'I called to my lovers,
but they let me down;
my priests and my elders
perished in the city
while seeking food
to keep themselves alive.

1:9 her fate: or her children after her.
1:14 bound: prob. mng; Heb. word unknown.
1:16 my plight: prob. rdg; Heb. my eye.

endearment for Zion, personifying the temple mount area. 7: The backward look seems to come after the passing of many years. 10: This verse is a stereotyped description of the enemy; see Ps. 74.4–8.
1.11c–22: The voice is now the city herself speaking. 12: You passers-by: perhaps the other nations; see v. 18. 15: Rank on rank against me: the role of the Lord as an enemy warrior, as in Isa. 10.5–11. 17: Here the observer in 1.1–11b again comments. 18: The city's confession of sin; see Deut. 28.15–68. Into captivity:

20 'LORD, see how sorely distressed I am.
My bowels writhe in anguish
and my heart within me turns over,
because I wantonly rebelled.
In the street the sword brings
    bereavement,
like the plague within the house.

21 'People have heard when I groan
with no one to comfort me.
My enemies, hearing of my plight,
all rejoiced at what you had done.
Hasten the day you have promised
when they will suffer as I do!

22 'Let all their evil deeds come before
 — you;
torment them in their turn,
as you have tormented me
on account of all my sins;
for I groan continually
and I am sick at heart.'

Zion's hope of relief after punishment

2 WHAT darkness the Lord in his anger
has brought on the daughter of Zion!
He hurled down from heaven to earth
the honour of Israel,
with scant regard for Zion his footstool
on the day of his anger.

2 The Lord overwhelmed without pity
all the dwellings of Jacob.
In his wrath he overthrew
the strongholds of the daughter of
    Judah;
he brought to the ground in dishonour
the kingdom and its rulers.

3 In his fierce anger he hacked off
the horn of Israel's pride;
he withdrew his protecting hand
at the approach of the enemy;
he blazed in Jacob like flaming fire

that rages far and wide.

4 In enmity he bent his bow;
like an adversary he took his stand,
and with his strong arm he slew
all those who had been his delight.
He poured out his fury like fire
on the tent of the daughter of Zion.

5 The Lord played an enemy's part
and overwhelmed Israel,
overthrowing all their mansions
and laying their strongholds in ruins.
To the daughter of Judah he brought
unending sorrow.

6 He stripped his tabernacle as if it were
    a garden,
and made the place of assembly a ruin.
In Zion the LORD blotted out all
    memory
of festal assembly and of sabbath;
king and priest alike he spurned
in the heat of his anger.

7 The Lord rejected his own altar
and abandoned his sanctuary.
The walls of Zion's mansions
he delivered into the power of the
    enemy;
in the LORD's house they raised shouts
as on a festal day.

8 The LORD was resolved to destroy
the wall of the daughter of Zion;
he took its measure with his line
and did not scruple to demolish it.
He made rampart and wall lament,
and both together lay dejected.

9 He has shattered the bars of her gates,
and the gates themselves have sunk into
    the ground.

2:6 **festal assembly:** *or* appointed seasons.

see 2 Kgs. 25.11. **21:** *Hasten the day:* though somewhat incongruous with v. 15, this is a call for God's wrath
on the enemy, as in 3.64–66; see also Ps. 83.9–18.

2.1–4.22: A compassionate God judges suffering Zion. Dire as the sufferings are, the LORD will have
compassion.

2.1–10: The fullness of calamity. 1: *What:* lit. "alas, how"; so too 1.1 and 4.1. The verse reminds God of
past favors, especially of partiality for the temple, which here, and in 1 Chr. 28.2, is likened to a *footstool,* a
figure of affectionate comfort. **3:** *Horn:* perhaps of the altar, as in Amos 3.14. **4–5:** See 1.15 n. **6:** *Blotted out
all memory:* see 1.7 n. **7:** *Shouts:* as in Ps. 74.4. **9bc:** Revelation and prophecy have ceased; compare Mic.
3.5–6.

Her king and rulers are exiled among
　　the Gentiles;
there is no direction from priests,
and her prophets have received
　no vision from the LORD.

10 The elders of Zion
sit on the ground in silence;
they have cast dust on their heads
and put on sackcloth.
The maidens of Jerusalem
bow their heads to the ground.

11 My eyes are blinded with tears,
my bowels writhe in anguish.
My bile is spilt on the earth
because of my people's wound,
as children and infants lie fainting
in the streets of the city.

12 They cry to their mothers,
'Where is there bread and wine?' —
as they faint like wounded things
in the streets of the city,
gasping out their lives
in their mothers' bosoms.

13 How can I cheer you? Whose plight is
　like yours,
daughter of Jerusalem?
To what can I compare you for your
　comfort,
virgin daughter of Zion?
For your wound gapes as wide as the
　ocean —
who can heal you?

14 The visions that your prophets saw for
　you
were a false and painted sham.
They did not bring home to you your
　guilt
so as to reverse your fortunes.
The visions they saw for you were
　delusions,
false and fraudulent.

15 All those who pass by
snap their fingers at you;
they hiss and wag their heads

at the daughter of Jerusalem, saying,
'Is this the city once called perfect in
　beauty,
the joy of the whole earth?'

16 All your enemies
jeer at you with open mouths;
they hiss and grind their teeth,
saying, 'Here we are,
this is the day we have waited for;
we have lived to see it.'

17 The LORD has done what he planned to
　do,
he has fulfilled his threat,
all that he decreed from days of old.
He has demolished without pity
and let the enemy rejoice over you,
filling your adversaries with pride.

18 Cry to the Lord from the heart
at the wall of the daughter of Zion;
let your tears run down like a torrent
day and night.
Give yourself not a moment's rest,
let your tears never cease.

19 Arise, cry aloud in the night;
at the beginning of every watch
pour out your heart like water
before the presence of the Lord.
Lift up your hands to him
for the lives of your children,
who are fainting with hunger
at every street corner.

20 'LORD, look and see:
who is it you have thus tormented?
Must women eat the fruit of their
　wombs,
the children they have held in their
　arms?
Should priest and prophet be slain
in the sanctuary of the Lord?

21 'There in the streets both young and
　old
lie prostrate on the ground.

2:18 **Cry . . . heart:** *prob. rdg; Heb.* Their heart cried to
the Lord.

2.11–16: An observer witnesses the distress. 12: The hunger: see 4.4–10. **13:** *Virgin:* the figure appears
also in Amos 5.2. **14:** *Your prophets:* here the false prophets, who prophesied peace; see Jer. 14.13–16. **15:**
All those who pass by: recalling the words of 1.12.

　2.17–19: Let the city weep. 17: *All that he decreed:* compare Jer. 23.20.

　2.20–22: The city's plea to God. 21: The day of the LORD (v. 22), anticipated by many prophets, is viewed

My maidens and my young men
have fallen by the sword;
you have slain them on the day of your
anger,
slaughtered them without pity.

22 'You summoned my enemies from
every side,
like men assembled for a festival;
on the day of the LORD's anger
no one escaped, not one survived.
All whom I have held in my arms and
reared
my enemies have destroyed.'

3 I am the man who has known
affliction
under the rod of the wrath of the
LORD.
2 It was I whom he led away
and left to walk
in darkness, where no light is.
3 Against me alone he has turned his
hand,
and so it is all day long.

4 He has wasted away my flesh and my
skin
and broken my bones;
5 he has built up as walls around me
bitterness and hardship;
6 he has cast me into a place of darkness
like those long dead.

7 He has hemmed me in so that I cannot
escape;
he has weighed me down with fetters.
8 Even when I cry out and plead for help
he rejects my prayer.
9 He has barred my road with blocks of
stone
and entangled my way.

10 He lies in wait for me like a bear
or a lion lurking in a covert.

11 He has forced me aside, thrown me
down,
and left me desolate.
12 He has bent his bow
and made me the target for his arrows;

13 he has pierced right to my kidneys
with shafts drawn from his quiver.
14 I have become a laughing-stock to all
nations,
the butt of their mocking songs all day.
15 He has given me my fill of bitter herbs
and made me drink deep of
wormwood.

16 He has broken my teeth on gravel;
racked with pain, I am fed on ashes.
17 Peace has gone from my life
and I have forgotten what prosperity is.
18 Then I cry out that my strength has
gone
and so has my hope in the LORD.

19 The memory of my distress and my
wanderings
is wormwood and gall.
20 I remember them indeed
and am filled with despondency.
21 I shall wait patiently
because I take this to heart:

22 The LORD's love is surely not
exhausted,
nor has his compassion failed;
23 they are new every morning,
so great is his constancy.
24 'The LORD', I say, 'is all that I have;
therefore I shall wait for him patiently.'

25 The LORD is good to those who look to
him,

3:19 **The memory . . . is:** or Remember my distress
and my wanderings, the.   3:20 **am filled with**
despondency: prob. original rdg, altered in Heb. to I sink
down.   3:22 **exhausted:** prob. rdg; Heb. unintelligible.

here as having occurred; see Joel 1.14–15 n.

   3.1–66: The lament of an individual in distress. See the similar themes in such psalms of lamentation as
Pss. 22; 69. The individual has traditionally been identified as Jeremiah; see Introduction.

   3.1–18: What life has become. 1: Wrath of the LORD: as in 2.4–5. **2–16:** Many metaphors describe the
techniques of the punishing God, literally inconsistent with one another, but thematically in accord. **14:**
Laughing-stock: see Jer. 20.7.

   3.19–33: A sensitive outpouring of trust in the LORD. The positive attitude here is unique in the book. **21:**
Wait patiently: the idea, a key one, recurs often in this section, but not elsewhere in the book; compare Pss.

to anyone who seeks him;
26 it is good to wait in patience
for deliverance by the LORD.
27 It is good for a man
to bear the yoke from youth.
28 Let him sit alone in silence
if it is heavy on him;
29 let him lie face downwards on the
ground,
and there may yet be hope;
30 let him offer his cheek to the smiter
and endure full measure of abuse.

31 For rejection by the Lord
does not last for ever.
32 He may punish, yet he will have
compassion
in the fullness of his unfailing love;
33 he does not willingly afflict
or punish any mortal.

34 To trample underfoot
prisoners anywhere on earth,
35 to deprive a man of his rights
in defiance of the Most High,
36 to pervert justice in the courts—
such things the Lord has never
approved.

37 Who can command and have it done
if the Lord has forbidden it?
38 Do not both bad and good proceed
from the mouth of the Most High?
39 Why should any man living complain,
any mortal who has sinned?

40 Let us examine our ways and test them
and turn back to the LORD;
41 let us lift up our hearts and our hands
to God in heaven, saying:
42 'We have sinned and rebelled,
and you have not forgiven.

43 'You have covered us in anger, pursued
us,
and slain without pity;
44 you have covered yourself with cloud
beyond reach of our prayers;
45 you have treated us as scum and refuse

among the nations.

46 'Our enemies all jeer at us
with open mouths.
47 Before us lie hunter's scare and pit,
devastation and ruin.'
48 My eyes run with streams of water
because of my people's wound.

49 My eyes stream with unceasing tears
and refuse all comfort,
50 while the LORD looks down
and sees from heaven.
51 My eyes ache
because of the fate of all the women of
my city.

52 Those who for no reason were my
enemies
drove me cruelly like a bird;
53 to silence me they thrust me alive into
the pit
and closed the opening with a boulder;
54 waters rose above my head,
and I said, 'My end has come.'

55 But I called, LORD, on your name
from the depths of the pit;
56 you heard my plea: 'Do not turn a deaf
ear
when I cry out for relief.'
57 You came near when I called to you;
you said, 'Have no fear.'

58 Lord, you pleaded my cause;
you came to my rescue.
59 You saw the injustice done to me,
LORD,
and gave judgement in my favour;
60 you saw all their vindictive behaviour,
all their plotting against me.

61 You heard their bitter scorn, LORD,
all their plotting,
62 the whispering and murmuring of my
adversaries
the livelong day.
63 See how, whether they sit or stand,
I am the object of their taunts.

69.3; 42.5. **29:** *Hope:* equivalent to waiting. **30:** Compare Isa. 50.6; Matt. 5.39.
　　3.34–47: The city or nation speaks as a prophet. 41: A de-emphasis on worship and a stress on morality,
as in Isa. 1.15–17.
　　　3.48–51: The afflicted individual again. 51: The only direct mention of the city in this chapter.
　　　3.52–66: The innocent one is hurt. 52: *No reason:* this motif is common in the psalms of lamentation, as

64 Pay them back for their deeds, LORD,
  pay them as they deserve.
65 Show them how hard your heart can be,
  how little concern you have for them.
66 Pursue them in anger and wipe them
    out
  from beneath your heavens, LORD.

4 How dulled is the gold,
  how tarnished the fine gold!
  The stones of the sanctuary lie strewn
  at every street corner.

2 See Zion's precious sons,
  once worth their weight in finest gold,
  now counted as clay jars,
  the work of any potter's hand.

3 Even whales uncover the teat
  and suckle their young;
  but the daughters of my people are
    heartless
  as the ostriches of the desert.

4 With thirst the sucking infant's tongue
  cleaves to the roof of its mouth;
  young children beg for bread,
  but no one offers them a crumb.

5 Those who once fed delicately
  are desolate in the streets;
  those brought up in purple garments
  now grovel on refuse heaps.

6 The penalty inflicted on my people is
    worse
  than the punishment of Sodom,
  which suffered overthrow in a moment,
  and no hands were wrung.

7 Her crowned princes were once purer
    than snow,
  whiter than milk;
  they were ruddier than branching
    coral;
  their limbs were lapis lazuli.

8 But their faces turned blacker than
    soot,

and no one knew them in the streets;
  the skin was shrivelled tight over their
    bones,
  dry as touchwood.

9 Those who died by the sword were
    more fortunate
  than those who died of hunger,
  who wasted away, deprived
  of the produce of the field.

10 With their own hands tender-hearted
    women
  boiled their own children;
  their children became their food
  on the day of my people's wounding.

11 The LORD glutted his rage
  and poured forth his fierce anger;
  he kindled a fire in Zion
  that burnt to the very foundations.

12 No one, neither the kings of the earth
  nor any other inhabitant of the world,
  believed that any adversary, any foe
  could penetrate within the gates of
    Jerusalem.

13 It happened for the sins of her
    prophets,
  for the crimes of her priests,
  who had shed within her walls
  the blood of the righteous.

14 They wandered blindly in the streets;
  they are so stained with blood
  that no one would touch
  even their garments.

15 'Go away! Unclean!' people cried to
    them.
  'Away! Do not come near!'
  They hastened away, wandering among
    the nations,

4:1 **The stones of the sanctuary:** or Bright gems.
4:3 **whales:** prob. rdg; Heb. wolves.   4:6 **penalty
inflicted on:** or iniquity of. **punishment:** or sin.
4:7 **than branching:** prob. rdg; Heb. branch than red.
4:15 **wandering . . . nations:** prob. rdg; Heb. adds they
said.

in Ps. 69.4. **64:** See 1.21 n.
  4.1–16: A return to the distressing conditions in Jerusalem, but here on a more personal level. **3–10:** A
vivid portrayal of the results of hunger. **3:** Heartless: see v. 10. As ostriches: see Job 39.13–18. **6:** Sodom: the
oft-used example of a wicked city; see Gen. 19.1–26. **10:** Their own children: see 2.20. **13:** See 1.5 n. Here
the blame is laid at the feet of the leaders: prophets (false, see 2.14 n.), priests, and elders (v. 16).

unable to find any resting-place.

16 The LORD himself scattered them,
    he thought of them no more;
    he showed no favour to priests,
    no pity for elders.

17 Still we strain our eyes,
    looking in vain for help.
    We have watched and watched
    for a nation that proved powerless to
        save.

18 When we go out, we take to byways
    to avoid the public streets;
    our days are all but finished,
    our end has come.

19 Our pursuers have shown themselves
        swifter
    than eagles in the heavens;
    they are hot on our trail over the hills,
    they waylay us in the wilderness.

20 The LORD's anointed, the breath of life
        to us,
    was caught in their traps;
    although we had thought to live among
        the nations,
    safe under his protection.

21 Rejoice and be glad, daughters of
        Edom,
    dwellers in the land of Uz.
    Yet the cup will pass to you in your
        turn,
    and when drunk you will expose your
        nakedness.

22 The punishment for your sin, daughter
        of Zion, is now complete,
    and never again will you be carried into
        exile.

But you, daughter of Edom, your sin
    will be punished,
and your guilt revealed.

A prayer for remembrance and restoration

5 REMEMBER, LORD, what has befallen
    us;
    look, and see how we are scorned.
2 The land we possessed is turned over
        to strangers,
    our homes to foreigners.
3 We are like orphans, without a father;
    our mothers are like widows.
4 We have to buy water to drink, water
        which is ours;
    our own wood can be had only for
        payment.
5 The yoke is on our necks, we are
        harassed;
    we are weary, but allowed no rest.
6 We came to terms, now with Egypt,
    now with Assyria, to provide us with
        food.
7 Our forefathers sinned; now they are
        no more,
    and we must bear the burden of their
        guilt.
8 Slaves have become our rulers,
    and there is no one to free us from
        their power.
9 We must bring in our food from the
        wilderness
    at the risk of our lives in the scorching
        heat.
10 Our skins are blackened as in a furnace
    by the ravages of starvation.

4:16 **scattered:** *or* destroyed.   4:18 **our . . . finished:**
prob. rdg; Heb. our end has drawn near, our days are
complete.   5:5 **The yoke:** *so Gk (Symm.); Heb. omits.*

4.17–20: A poet again cries out. The passage, deeply personal and sorrowful, is in the plural. **17:** *A nation
. . . powerless:* perhaps Egypt; see Jer. 37.5–7. **19–20:** Perhaps this is related to the incident told of the king,
that is, the LORD's anointed, in 2 Kgs. 25.4–7.

4.21–22: Criticism of Edom for its action at the time of the fall; see Obad. 10–15; Ps. 137.7. **22:** *Punishment
. . . complete:* this theme is also found in Isa. 40.2.

5.1–18: A prayer for remembrance and restoration. Many verses are paraphrases of passages in chs. 1; 2;
4. **6:** *Assyrians:* this is anachronistic; the Babylonians, conquerors of the Assyrians, had control at the time of
the fall of the city. The mention shows a powerful remembrance of the Assyrian conquest of the Northern
Kingdom (721 B.C.E.) and the siege of Jerusalem; see 2 Kgs. chs. 17–19. **7:** *Our forefathers sinned:* another
explanation of the fall of Jerusalem. On the sins of the parents being visited upon the children, see Jer. 31.29;

11 Women were raped in Zion,
    virgins ravished in the towns of Judah.
12 Princes were hung up by their hands;
    elders received no respect.
13 Young men toil, grinding at the mill;
    boys stagger under loads of wood.
14 Old men have left off their sessions at
    the city gate;
    young men no longer pluck the strings.
15 Joy has vanished from our hearts;
    our dancing is turned to mourning.
16 The garlands have fallen from our
    heads.
    Woe to us, sinners that we are!
17 This is why we are sick at heart;

all this is why our eyes grow dim:
18 Mount Zion is desolate
    and overrun with jackals.
19 LORD, your reign is for ever,
    your throne endures from age to
    age.
20 Why do you forget us so completely
    and forsake us these many days?
21 LORD, turn us back to you, and we shall
    come back;
    renew our days as in times long past.
22 But you have utterly rejected us;
    your anger against us has been great
    indeed.

see also 1.5 n. **14–18:** For a similar passage, see Isa. 24.7–13.

5.19–22: A final prayer for rescue. 21: *Turn us back:* unless the LORD restores the faithfulness of the city, it will have no success in turning back to God. **22:** The conclusion is indefinite, fittingly cautious after the mournful words of the rest of the book.

THE BOOK OF THE PROPHET
Ezekiel

Ezekiel, priest and prophet, began his ministry in the last years of the Kingdom of Judah and ended it during the Babylonian captivity following upon the destruction of Jerusalem in 587 B.C.E. His ministry bridges the greatest catastrophe and transformation the religion of Israel ever experienced: the transition from a religion identified with a land and a temple, with its sacrifices, to a religion identified with a community of people, thus leading ultimately to the full development of the synagogue where the study of the Law is paramount, the essential Judaism of today.

Beginning with the inaugural vision, dated 593 B.C.E. (1.2), and ending with the last securely dated oracle, 571 B.C.E. (29.17), Ezekiel contains the most complete chronology of any prophetic book. The dates do not follow in order, however, and only the oracle immediately following a given date can be attached to it with certainty. The dating of the oracles according to contemporary chronology in the annotations is an approximation, correlating the lunar calendar followed by the ancients with the modern solar calendar.

Ezekiel, the most unusual among a unique class of individuals, the prophets of Israel, dramatized his prophecies by bizarre actions that some interpreters see as simply literary devices to emphasize his message, but which others see as reflecting pathological states. Further, though he seems to be with the captives in Babylon (1.1–3; 3.11, etc.) he sometimes addresses his message to the Palestinian Jews (11.1–3), so that interpreters are divided between postulating a double ministry (first to the people in Palestine before the captivity and then to the captives in Babylonia after the destruction of Jerusalem) and holding a single ministry, but attributing the gift of clairvoyance to Ezekiel by which he was in contact with people and events in Palestine.

The key to Ezekiel's message is a very exalted idea of God; a God beyond human comprehension (1.4–28); a God whose hand guides the destinies of nations (chs. 25–32); a God who, for the sake of God's "holy name," forgives transgression and puts a new "spirit" within the people (36.22–26). Earlier prophets saw in human existence a cause and effect chain with this sequence: sin—punishment—repentance (condition)—redemption (at a price). Ezekiel sees the sequence as: sin—punishment—redemption (gratuitous)—repentance (free). Thus, with redemption once assured, a person is free to choose repentance without the coercion of punishment; Ezekiel's message, therefore, stresses also freedom of choice and human responsibility (ch. 18).

The MT account of Ezekiel is longer and more repetitious than that of the Sept., which is more concise and more strongly supported by the other versions, suggesting that the MT has undergone disturbance and dislocation in many passages. Moreover, chs. 40–48 are regarded by many scholars as an addition from a later hand and a later time (see 40.1–48.35 n.).

The calling of Ezekiel

1 On the fifth day of the fourth month in the thirtieth year, while I was among the exiles by the river Kebar, the heavens were opened and I saw visions from God. ² On the fifth day of the month in the fifth year of the exile of King Jehoiachin, ³ the word of the

1.1–3.21: Ezekiel empowered. He receives his commission to prophesy doom to the Israelites.
1.1–3: Superscription. 1–2: There is difficulty understanding the *thirtieth year*, especially in view of the *fifth year* (v. 2), since both dates seem to refer to the same event, i.e. the call of the prophet. The point of reference for both dates seems to be the capture of *Jehoiachin* by Nebuchadnezzar, king of Babylon, in 597 B.C.E. (2 Kgs.

LORD came to the priest Ezekiel son of Buzi, in Chaldaea by the river Kebar, and there the LORD's hand was upon him.

4 In my vision I saw a storm-wind coming from the north, a vast cloud with flashes of fire and brilliant light about it; and within was a radiance like brass, glowing in the heart of the flames. 5 In the fire was the likeness of four living creatures in human form. 6 Each had four faces and each four wings; 7 their legs were straight, and their hoofs were like the hoofs of a calf, glistening and gleaming like bronze. 8 Under the wings on each of the four sides were human hands; all four creatures had faces and wings, 9 and the wings of one touched those of another. They did not turn as they moved; each creature went straight forward. 10 This is what their faces were like: all four had a human face and a lion's face on the right, on the left the face of an ox and the face of an eagle. 11 Their wings were spread upwards; each living creature had one pair touching those of its neighbour, while one pair covered its body. 12 They moved forward in whatever direction the spirit went; they never swerved from their course. 13 The appearance of the creatures was as if fire from burning coals or torches were darting to and fro among them; the fire was radiant, and out of the fire came lightning.

15 As I looked at the living creatures, I saw wheels on the ground, one beside each of the four. 16 The wheels sparkled like topaz, and they were all alike: in form and working they were like a wheel inside a wheel, 17 and when they moved in any of the four directions they never swerved from their course. 18 I saw that they had rims, and the rims were covered with eyes all around. 19 When the living creatures moved, the wheels moved beside them; when the creatures rose from the ground, the wheels rose; 20 they moved in whichever direction the spirit went; and the wheels rose together with them, for the spirit of the creatures was in the wheels. 21 When one moved, the other moved; when one halted, the other halted; when the creatures rose from the ground, the wheels rose together with them, for the spirit of the creatures was in the wheels.

22 Above the heads of the living creatures was, as it were, a vault glittering like a sheet of ice, awe-inspiring, stretched over their

1:4 **brass:** *mng of Heb. word uncertain.*   1:11 **Their wings:** *so Gk; Heb. adds and their faces.* **those . . . neighbour:** *prob. rdg; Heb. unintelligible.* 1:13 **out . . . lightning:** *prob. rdg, cp. Gk; Heb. adds* 14 and the living creatures went out *(prob. rdg; Heb. obscure)* and in like rays of light.   1:15 **one . . . four:** *prob. rdg; Heb. obscure.*   1:16 **The wheels:** *so Gk; Heb. adds and their works.*   1:18 **I saw . . . had rims:** *prob. rdg; Heb. obscure.*

24.10–17). The first date then becomes 568 B.C.E. and the second 593 B.C.E. Scholars think that the thirtieth year refers either to a second call of the prophet, the one in Babylonia (see Introduction); or possibly, though less likely, to the date of the compilation of Ezekiel's many messages into a single book. Some conjecture that the call of another prophet whose work was in some way associated with that of Ezekiel was added. The *river Kebar* is probably an irrigation canal mentioned in Babylonian records. It flowed from the Euphrates through the old city of Nippur, where excavations have revealed ancient business contracts with Jewish names. See Ps. 137.1–6. There were two groups of *exiles*. The first, referred to here, was taken to Babylonia with King Jehoiachin. The second was deported by Nebuchadnezzar after his destruction of Jerusalem (12.11–12; 2 Kgs. 25.3–12); this date is set by some at 586, by others at 587 B.C.E. Jehoiachin was considered the rightful king, if a restoration were to take place; hence his captivity is the point of departure for all the dates in the book. **3:** *Ezekiel* means "God strengthens." *Hand of the LORD* is the symbol for Ezekiel's consciousness that his activity is divinely motivated. Compare 3.22; 37.1. *Chaldaea:* southern part of Babylonia.

1.4–28a: The throne-chariot vision. God's incomprehensible majesty, power, and mobility are conveyed in a visual metaphor that overwhelms the imagination. The frequent repetition of the words "like" and "appearance" indicates that this vision of God defies description. The vision is a fitting summary of God's activity in the book. **4:** *North:* mythological symbol for the dwelling of the gods; see Isa. 14.13. *Wind, cloud, fire* are all signs of God's presence as in Exod. 19.16; Ps. 18.10–14. **12:** *The Spirit* is God's purposeful power directing the activity of the universe and of humankind; see 1.20. **15–21:** *Wheels* are symbols of cosmic mobility, and the *eyes all around* signify an all-seeing intelligence guiding the movement of the most insensitive elements in the universe which respond to the same active spirit that moves the prophet, e.g. 3.14. **22:** The heads above them. 23 Under the vault their wings were spread straight out, touching one another, while one pair covered the body of each. 24 I heard, too, the noise of their wings; when they moved it was like the noise of a mighty torrent or a thunderclap, like the noise of a crowd or an armed camp; when they halted their wings dropped. 25 A voice was heard from above the vault over their heads, as they halted with drooping wings.

26 Above the vault over their heads there appeared, as it were, a sapphire in the shape of a throne, and exalted on the throne a form in human likeness. 27 From his waist upwards I saw what might have been brass glowing like fire in a furnace; and from his waist downwards I saw what looked like fire. Radiance encircled him. 28 Like a rainbow in the clouds after the rain was the sight of that encircling radiance; it was like the appearance of the glory of the LORD.

When I saw this I prostrated myself, and I 2 heard a voice: 1 'Stand up, O man,' he said, 'and let me talk with you.' 2 As he spoke, a spirit came into me and stood me on my feet, and I listened to him speaking. 3 He said to me, 'O man, I am sending you to the Israelites, rebels who have rebelled against me. They and their forefathers have been in revolt against me to this very day, 4 and this generation to which I am sending you is stubborn and obstinate. You are to say to them, "These are the words of the Lord GOD," 5 and they will know that they have a prophet among them, whether they listen or whether in their rebelliousness they refuse to listen.

6 'But you, O man, must not be afraid of them or of what they say, though they resist and reject you and you are sitting on scorpi-ons. There is nothing to fear in their rebellious words, nothing to make you afraid in their rebellious looks. 7 You must speak my words to them, whether they listen or whether in their rebelliousness they refuse to listen. 8 But you, O man, must heed what I say and not be rebellious like them. Open your mouth and eat what I am giving you.'

9 I saw a hand stretched out to me, holding a scroll. 10 He unrolled it before me, and it was written on both sides, back and front, with dirges and laments and words of woe.

3 1 Then he said to me, 'O man, eat what is in front of you; eat this scroll; then go and speak to the Israelites.' 2 I opened my mouth and he gave me the scroll to eat, 3 saying, 'O man, swallow this scroll I give you, and eat your fill.' I ate it, and it tasted as sweet as honey to me.

4 'O man,' he said to me, 'go to the Israelites and declare my message to them. 5 It is not to people whose speech is thick and difficult you are sent, but to Israelites. 6 I am not sending you to great nations whose speech is so thick and so difficult that you cannot make out what they say; had I sent you to them they would have listened to you. 7 But the Israelites will refuse to listen to you, for they refuse to listen to me; all of them are brazen-faced and stubborn-hearted. 8 But I shall make you a match for them. I shall make you as brazen and as stubborn as they are. 9 I shall make your brow like adamant, harder than flint. Do not fear them, do not be terrified by them, rebellious though they are.' 10 He went on: 'Listen carefully, O man, to all that I have

1:23 **while ... each:** *so some MSS; others repeat* one pair covered the body of each.   1:26 **sapphire:** *or* lapis lazuli.   2:1 **O man:** *lit.* son of man, *and so throughout the book when Ezekiel is addressed.*

ancients considered the sky a *vault* (Gen. 1.6), i.e. a solid roof over the world supporting the flood waters above which God was enthroned Lord over the universe and all in it. Compare Ps. 29.10. **28:** *Like ... the glory of the LORD* indicates that the description is a subjective vision rather than an objective presence of God such as that experienced at Sinai by all the people. See Exod. 19.17–20.

1.28b–3.21: Prophetic experience of the call and five commissions. There are possibly four calls: 1.28b–3.9; 3.10–11; 3.16–21; 3.22–27, which contain five commissions. **2.1:** *Man*, lit. "son of man," which means "a member of the human race." This expression is used over ninety times and contrasts human frailty with God's might and glory. Compare Job 14.1–5. **2–5:** *Spirit ... stood me*, i.e. bridged the distance between God and the prophet, and gave such power to his words and actions that the people *will know*, i.e. be unable to ignore, the reality of the divine message even though they *refuse to listen.* **2.8–3.3:** The *scroll* contains only *dirges* and *words of woe* because a prophet preaching well-being is suspect; see 13.10–16. Eating the scroll signifies assimilating God's message; the sweetness is the sense of fulfillment it brings; compare Pss. 19.9–10; 119.100–103. **3.4–9:** Ezekiel's boldness is attributed to God because it was acquired in carrying out his commission. **10–11:** Some interpreters conjecture that this repetition is a second call of Ezekiel; others, that to say to you, and take it to heart. ¹¹ Then go to your fellow-countrymen in exile and say to them, "These are the words of the Lord God," whether they listen or refuse to listen.'

¹² A spirit lifted me up, and I heard behind me a fierce rushing sound as the glory of the LORD rose from his place. ¹³ I heard the sound of the living creatures' wings brushing against one another, and the sound of the wheels beside them, a fierce rushing sound. ¹⁴ A spirit lifted me and carried me along, and I went full of exaltation, the power of the LORD strong upon me. ¹⁵ So I came to the exiles at Tel-abib who were settled by the river Kebar. For seven days I stayed there among them in a state of consternation.

¹⁶ At the end of seven days this word of the LORD came to me: ¹⁷ 'I have appointed you, O man, a watchman for the Israelites; you will pass to them the warnings you receive from me. ¹⁸ If I pronounce sentence of death on a wicked person and you have not warned him or spoken out to dissuade him from his wicked ways and so save his life, that person will die because of his sin, but I shall hold you answerable for his death. ¹⁹ But if you have warned him and he persists in his wicked ways, he will die because of his sin, but you will have discharged your duty. ²⁰ Again, if someone who is righteous goes astray and does wrong, and I cause his downfall, he will die because you have not warned him. He will die for his sin; the righteous deeds he has done will not be taken into account, and I shall hold you responsible for his death. ²¹ But if you have warned the righteous person not to sin and he does not sin, then he will have saved his life because he heeded the

warning, and you will have discharged your duty.'

The coming ruin of Jerusalem

²² THE LORD'S hand was upon me there, and he said to me, 'Rise, go out into the plain, and there I shall speak to you.' ²³ I arose, and when I went out into the plain, the glory of the LORD was there, like the glory which I had seen by the river Kebar, and I prostrated myself. ²⁴ Then a spirit came and set me on my feet. The LORD spoke to me: 'Go,' he said, 'and shut yourself up in your house. ²⁵ You will be tied and bound with ropes, O man, so that you cannot go out among the people. ²⁶ I shall make your tongue cleave to the roof of your mouth and you will be unable to speak and so rebuke them, that rebellious people. ²⁷ But when I have something to say to you, I shall give you back the power of speech. Then you will declare to them, "This is what the Lord God said." If anyone will listen, he may listen; and if anyone refuses to listen, he may refuse. Rebels indeed they are!

4 'O man, take a tile and lay it in front of you. Draw a city on it, the city of Jerusalem: ² portray it under siege, erect towers against it, raise a siege-ramp, put mantelets in position, and bring up battering-rams on every side. ³ Then take a griddle, and put it as if it were an iron wall between you and the city. Keep your eyes fixed on the city; it will be the besieged and you the besieger. This will be a sign to the Israelites.

3:12 **rose:** *prob. rdg; Heb. obscure.* 3:15 **by . . .
Kebar:** *so some MSS; others add* and where they were living.

it is the call of another prophet whose prophecy is added to that of Ezekiel's (see 1.1–2 n.); still others reason that it is editorial duplication. See Introduction. **14:** *Full of exaltation:* lit. "bitter in the fury of my spirit," the ecstasy of a religious experience. **15:** *Tel-abib:* a Jewish settlement in Babylonia. In 1.1, Ezekiel is already among the exiles when the vision takes place; here he is arriving after the vision. For possible explanation see vv. 10–12. **16:** How *the word of the LORD came* to Ezekiel is not clear; it need only imply his conviction that he spoke God's message to the people. **17–21:** The prophet as *watchman* has a long tradition in Israel; compare Isa. 21.6–12. Here it applies Ezekiel's principle of personal responsibility (see 18.1–32) to the prophetic office.

3.22–27: Ezekiel confined. To be *bound with ropes* (v. 25) may mean actual physical restraints; more probably it means discouragement, deterring the prophet from speaking and acting except when moved by special inspiration from God. Compare Ps. 22.16.

4.1–5.17: Actions symbolic of the judgment of Jerusalem. The prophecies given here as actions seem impossible to perform and so are probably dramatic allegories. Ezekiel, having received a command to speak in riddles and parables (17.2), acquired a reputation of dealing "only in figures of speech"; see 20.49. **1:** *Tile:* clay tablet. **3:** *Israelites,* lit. "house of Israel," embraces both the Northern Kingdom of Israel, as in v. 4, taken into captivity in 721 B.C.E. by the Assyrians, and the Southern Kingdom of Judah, as in v. 6; Ezekiel envisions

⁴'Next, lie on your left side, putting the weight of Israel's punishment on it; for as many days as you lie on that side you will be bearing their punishment. ⁵I ordain that you bear Israel's punishment for three hundred and ninety days, allowing one day for each year of their punishment. ⁶When you have completed these days, lie down again, this time on your right side, and bear Judah's punishment; I ordain for you forty days, one day for each year. ⁷Then fix your gaze towards the siege of Jerusalem and with bared arm prophesy against it. ⁸See how I tie you with ropes so that you cannot turn over from one side to the other until you complete your days of siege.

⁹'Take wheat, barley, beans, lentils, millet, and vetches, and mixing them all in one bowl make your bread from them. You are to eat it during the three hundred and ninety days you spend lying on your side. ¹⁰Twenty shekels' weight is your ration for a day, eaten at a set time each day. ¹¹You are to measure out your drinking water; you may drink a sixth of a hin at a set time each day. ¹²The bread you are to eat is to be baked like barley cakes, with human dung as fuel, and you must bake it where people can see you.' ¹³The LORD said, 'This is the unclean bread that the Israelites will eat among the peoples where I shall banish them.' ¹⁴I protested: 'Lord GOD, I have never been made unclean. Never in my whole life have I eaten what has died a natural death or been mauled by wild beasts; no tainted meat has ever passed my lips.' ¹⁵He answered, 'Very well; I shall allow you to use cow dung instead of human dung to bake your bread.'

¹⁶He then said, 'O man, I am cutting short their daily bread in Jerusalem; people will weigh out anxiously the bread they eat, and measure with dismay the water they drink. ¹⁷So their food and their water will run short until dismay spreads from one to another and they waste away because of their iniquity.

5 'O man, take a sharp sword, and use it like a razor to shave your head and your chin. Then take scales and divide the hair into three lots. ²When the siege comes to an end, burn one third of the hair in a fire in the centre of the city; cut up one third with the sword round about the city; scatter the last third to the wind, and I shall follow it with drawn sword. ³Take a few of these hairs and tie them up in a fold of your robe. ⁴Then take others, throw them into the fire and burn them.

'Say to all Israel: ⁵These are the words of the Lord GOD: This city of Jerusalem I have set among the nations, with lands all around her, ⁶but she has rebelled against my laws and my statutes more wickedly than those nations and lands; for her people have rejected my laws and refused to conform to my statutes.

⁷'The Lord GOD says: Since you have been more insubordinate than the nations around you and have not conformed to my statutes and have not kept my laws or even the laws of the nations around you, ⁸therefore, says the Lord GOD, I in turn shall be against you; in the sight of the nations I shall execute judgements in your midst, ⁹such judgements as I have never executed before, nor ever shall again, so abominable have all your offences been. ¹⁰Parents will eat their children and children their parents in your midst, Jerusalem; I shall execute judgements on you, and any who survive in you I shall scatter to the four winds. ¹¹As I live, says the Lord GOD, because you have defiled my holy place with all your vile and abominable rites, I in turn shall destroy you and show no pity; I shall spare no one. ¹²One third of your people will die by pestilence or perish by famine in your midst; one third will fall by the sword in the country round about; and one third I shall scatter to the four winds and follow with

5:4 **Say:** so Gk; Heb. obscure.   5:7 **or even:** some MSS but.

the ultimate restoration and reunion of the two; see 37.15–28. **4:** *Bearing their punishment:* representing the punishment of Israel in a symbolic manner. **5–6:** The number symbolism is uncertain, possibly referring to the duration of the exiles of the two kingdoms. **9:** Mixing different grains *all in one bowl* signifies the last of the food supply, the threat of famine. **12:** Contact with *human dung* made a person unclean (Deut. 23.13–14); here it indicates the ritual uncleanness of Babylon where pure cultic life was impossible. **5.1–17:** Shearing the prophet's hair and beard — symbols of dignity (2 Sam. 10.4–5) and of life (Num. 6.1–9) — is a sign of the degradation and massacre following the horrible siege. God's fury against Israel is a reflection of God's *jealousy*, i.e. God's desire that Israel worship no other deity; this theme is central in the book. For examples, read 6.13; 7.3, 8; 8.18; 20.8.

drawn sword. 13 When my anger is spent and my fury is abated I shall be appeased; when my fury against them is spent they will know that I, the LORD, have spoken in my jealousy. 14 I have reduced you to a ruin, an object of mockery to the nations around you, and all who pass by will see it. 15 You will be an object of mockery and abuse, an appalling lesson to the nations round about, when I pass sentence on you and execute judgement in anger and fury. I, the LORD, have spoken.

16 'When I loose the deadly arrows of famine against you, arrows of destruction, I shall shoot them to destroy you. I shall send one famine after another on you and cut off your daily bread; 17 I shall unleash famine and savage beasts on you, and they will leave you childless. Pestilence and bloodshed will sweep through you, and I shall bring the sword against you. I, the LORD, have spoken.'

God's judgement on the land

6 THIS word of the LORD came to me: 2 'O man, face towards the mountains of Israel and prophesy against them 3 and say: Mountains of Israel, listen to the word of the Lord GOD. He says this to the mountains and hills, the ravines and valleys: I am bringing a sword against you, and I shall destroy your shrines. 4 Your altars will be devastated, your incense-altars shattered, and I shall throw down your slain in front of your idols. 5 I shall lay the corpses of the Israelites before their idols and scatter your bones around your altars. 6 In all your settlements the blood-spattered altars will be laid waste and the shrines devastated. Your altars will be laid waste and devastated, your idols shattered and brought to an end, your incense-altars hewn down, and the gods you have made will be wiped out. 7 As the slain fall all about you, you will know that I am the LORD. 8 But among the nations there will be some of you that have survived the sword, and are scattered in for-

eign lands. 9 They will remember me in exile among the nations, when I destroy their wanton and wayward hearts and their eyes which rove wantonly after their idols. Then they will loathe themselves for the evil they have done with all their abominations. 10 Then they will know that I, the LORD, was uttering no vain threat when I said that I would inflict this evil on them.

11 'The Lord GOD says: Beat your hands together, stamp your feet, bemoan all your vile abominations, people of Israel, who will fall by sword, famine, and pestilence. 12 Those far away will die by pestilence; those nearer home will fall by the sword; any who survive or are spared will die by famine, and so at last my anger at them will be spent. 13 You will know that I am the LORD when their slain fall among the idols round their altars, on every high hill or mountaintop, under every spreading tree or leafy terebinth, wherever they have offered sweet-smelling sacrifices to appease all their idols. 14 I shall stretch out my hand over them and reduce the land in all their settlements to a desolate waste, more desolate than the desert of Riblah. Then they will know that I am the LORD.'

7 This word of the LORD came to me: 2 'O man, the Lord GOD says to the land of Israel: The end is coming on the four corners of the earth. 3 Now the end is upon you; I shall unleash my anger against you; I shall call you to account for your conduct and bring all your abominations on your own heads. 4 I shall neither show pity, nor spare you; I shall make you suffer for your conduct and the abominations that are in your midst. Then you will know that I am the LORD.

5 'The Lord GOD says: Disasters are com-

5:16 **against you:** *prob. rdg; Heb.* against them.
6:6 **blood-spattered altars:** *or* cities.   6:8 **But among:** *so Gk; Heb.* prefixes and I will leave.   6:9 **I destroy:** *so Lat.; Heb.* I am grieved with.
6:14 **Riblah:** *prob. rdg; Heb.* Diblah.

6.1–7.27: Oracles of judgment. Here punishment is announced in words rather than in symbolic actions. **3:** *Shrines:* lit. "high places," associated with mountaintops where worship was carried on. They were proscribed after Hezekiah centralized the cult in the Jerusalem temple (2 Kgs. 18.4), because the rituals tended toward the cults of the gods of the Canaanites. **5:** The touch of *corpses* which made a person unclean for worship will pollute the very altars. **8:** *Some that have survived:* the "remnant" (Isa. 4.3) will be the seed of the restoration. **11:** *Sword, famine, pestilence* are the traditional scourges by which God punishes the people; see Jer. 14.12; 27.8. **13:** *Leafy terebinth:* also associated with the worship of other gods. See 20.28; Hos. 4.13.

7.1–27: Judgment against the land. The day is near when all practitioners of evil in Israel will be destroyed and all human security will disintegrate: social life, vv. 10–11; economic life, vv. 12–19; religious life, ing, one after another. 6 The end is coming; it is roused against you. 7 Doom is coming upon you, dweller in the land; the time is coming, the day is near, a day of panic and not of rejoicing. 8 Very soon I shall vent my wrath on you and let my anger spend itself. I shall call you to account for your conduct and bring all your abominations on your own heads. 9 I shall neither show pity nor spare you; I shall make you suffer for your conduct and the abominations that are in your midst. Then you will know that it is I, the LORD, who struck you.

10 'The day is coming, doom is here; it has burst upon them. Injustice buds, insolence blossoms. 11 Violence leads to flagrant injustice. Is it not their fault, the fault of their turbulence and tumult? There is nothing but turmoil in them. 12 The time has come, the day has arrived; there is no joy for the buyer, no sorrow for the seller, for their turmoil has called forth my wrath. 13 The seller will not recover what he has sold in their lifetime, for because of all the turmoil the agreement will never be revoked, and because of their sin none will have a sure hold on life. 14 The trumpet has sounded and all are ready, but no one goes to war, for their turmoil has called forth my wrath.

15 'Outside is the sword, inside are pestilence and famine; those in the country will die by the sword, those in the city will be devoured by famine and pestilence. 16 If any escape like moaning doves and take to the mountains, there I shall slay them, each for his iniquity, 17 while every hand hangs limp and every knee turns to water. 18 They will go in sackcloth, shuddering from head to foot, with faces downcast and heads close shaved. 19 They will fling their silver into the street and treat their gold like so much filth; their silver and gold will not avail to save them on the day of the LORD's fury. Their hunger will not be satisfied, nor their bellies filled; for their iniquity will be the cause of their downfall. 20 Their beautiful jewellery, which was their pride and delight, they have made into vile, abominable images. Therefore I shall

treat their jewellery as so much filth, 21 I shall hand it over as plunder to foreigners and as booty to earth's most evil nations, who will defile it. 22 I shall turn my face from them, while brigands encroach on my treasured land to defile it 23 and create confusion, for the land is full of bloodshed and the city full of violence. 24 I shall let in the most ruthless of nations to take possession of the houses; I shall quell the pride of the strong, and their sanctuaries will be profaned. 25 Shuddering will come over my people, and they will look in vain for peace. 26 Tempest will follow upon tempest and rumour upon rumour. People will pester a prophet for a vision; there will be no more guidance from a priest, no counsel from elders. 27 The king will go mourning, the ruler will be clothed with terror, the hands of the people will shake with fright. I shall deal with them as they deserve, and call them to account for their conduct. Then they will know that I am the LORD.'

8 ON the fifth day of the sixth month in the sixth year, as I was sitting at home and the elders of Judah were sitting with me, suddenly I felt the power of the Lord GOD come upon me. 2 I saw what looked like a man; from the waist down he seemed to be all fire and from the waist up to shine and glitter like brass. 3 He stretched out what appeared to be a hand and took me by the forelock. In a vision from God a spirit lifted me up between earth and heaven, carried me to Jerusalem, and put me down at the entrance to the inner gate facing north, where stands the idolatrous image which arouses God's indignation. 4 The glory of the God of Israel was there, like the vision I had seen in the plain. 5 The LORD said to me, 'O man, look northwards.' I did so, and there to the north of the Altar Gate, at the entrance, was that idolatrous image. 6 'O man,' he said, 'do you see what they are doing? The monstrous abominations which the Israelites practise

7:7 **a day ... rejoicing:** *prob. rdg; Heb. obscure.*
7:23 **and create confusion:** *so Gk; Heb. obscure.*
bloodshed: *prob. rdg; Heb.* the judgement of bloodshed.

vv. 20–26; political life, v. 27. **12–14:** Neither the *buyer* getting a good bargain can rejoice nor the *seller* suffering a loss will grieve; total disaster will permanently nullify all loss or gain. **26–27:** In the catastrophe to follow, of all the community functions, only the work of the *prophet* will remain, it being a divine communication rather than a human effort.

8.1–11.25: God punishes Jerusalem for its abominations. 1–18: Rites such as these were considered by the prophet to be acts of sinful worship. **1:** *Sixth year:* September 17, 592 B.C.E. **3:** The *idolatrous image* may here are making me abandon my sanctuary, and you will see even greater abominations.'

⁷ Then he brought me to the entrance of the court, where I saw that there was a hole in the wall. ⁸ 'O man,' he said to me, 'dig through the wall.' I did so, and made an opening. ⁹ 'Go in,' he said, 'and see the vile abominations they practise here.' ¹⁰ I went in and saw figures of creeping things, beasts, and vermin, and all the idols of the Israelites, carved round the walls. ¹¹ Standing in front of them were seventy elders of Israel, with Jaazaniah son of Shaphan in the middle, and each held a censer from which rose the fragrant smoke of incense. ¹² He said to me, 'O man, do you see what the elders of Israel are doing in darkness, each at the shrine of his own carved image? They think that the LORD does not see them, that he has forsaken the land. ¹³ You will see even greater abominations practised by them,' he said.

¹⁴ Next he brought me to the gateway of the LORD's house which faces north; and there sat women wailing for Tammuz. ¹⁵ 'O man, do you see that?' he asked me. 'But you will see greater abominations than these.'

¹⁶ So he brought me to the inner court of the LORD's house, and there, by the entrance to the sanctuary of the LORD, between porch and altar, were some twenty-five men with their backs to the sanctuary and their faces to the east, prostrating themselves to the rising sun. ¹⁷ He said to me, 'O man, do you see that? Do you think it a trifling matter for Judah to practise these abominations here? They have filled the land with violence and have provoked me to anger again and again. Look at them at their worship, holding twigs to their noses. ¹⁸ I shall turn on them in my rage and show them no pity, nor spare them. Loudly though they cry to me, I shall not listen.'

9 A loud voice rang in my ears: 'Here they come, those appointed to punish the city, each carrying his weapon of destruction.' ² I saw six men approaching from the road that leads to the upper gate which faces north, each carrying a battle-club, and among them one was dressed in linen, with a writer's pen and ink at his waist; they advanced until they stood by the bronze altar. ³ The glory of the God of Israel had risen from above the cherubim where it rested, and had come to the terrace of the temple. He called to the man dressed in linen, with pen and ink at his waist. ⁴ 'Go through the city of Jerusalem,' said the LORD, 'and mark with a cross the foreheads of those who groan and lament over all the abominations practised there.' ⁵ To the others I heard him say, 'Follow him through the city and deal out death; show no pity; spare no one. ⁶ Kill and destroy men old and young, girls, little children, and women, but touch no one who bears the mark. Begin at my sanctuary.' So they began with the elders in front of the temple. ⁷ 'Defile the temple,' he said, 'and fill the courts with dead bodies; then go out and spread death in the city.'

⁸ While the killing went on, I was left alone, and I threw myself on the ground, crying out, 'Lord GOD, are you going to destroy all the Israelites who are left, in this outpouring of your anger on Jerusalem?' ⁹ He answered, 'The iniquity of Israel and Judah is very great indeed; the land is full of bloodshed, the city is filled with injustice. They are saying, "The LORD has forsaken the land and does not see." ¹⁰ But I shall show no pity, nor spare them; I shall make their conduct recoil on their own heads.' ¹¹ When the man dressed in linen, with pen and ink at his waist, returned he reported: 'I have carried out your orders.'

10 Then in my vision I saw, above the vault over the heads of the cherubim, as it were a sapphire in the shape of a throne.

9:3 **cherubim:** *so Gk; Heb.* cherub. 9:7 **go out:** *so Gk; Heb. adds* and they will go out.

have been that of the goddess Asherah, mentioned in 2 Kgs. 21.7. **7–11:** The imagery recalls the Egyptian Book of the Dead, with its descriptions of the cult of the god Osiris. **14–15:** The wailing for a god, here the Babylonian deity *Tammuz*, was a common element in rituals that recalled the dying and rising of a god. Such deities were generally associated with the dying and rejuvenation of vegetation. **17:** *Violence* is seen as the result of idolatry.

9.1–11: Purge of idolators in Jerusalem. 2: *Linen:* a ritually clean cloth worn by those in immediate service of God, priests in the temple (Lev. 16.3–4) and angels in heaven (Dan. 10.5; Rev. 15.6). **7:** *Dead bodies* made the temple unfit for any worship, legitimate or idolatrous.

10.1–22: God leaves the temple. In the Bible, abandonment by the LORD is the most terrible punishment known; see Deut. 31.16–17; Ps. 27.8–10. **1–4:** Unlike the individual and private vision of 1.28, *the glory of the LORD* here represents Israel's shared experience of the majesty of God. The symbolism of *cloud* conveys

[2] The LORD said to the man dressed in linen, 'Come in between the circling wheels under the cherubim, and take a handful of the burning embers lying among the cherubim; then throw it over the city.' As I watched he went in.

[3] The cherubim stood on the right side of the temple as the man entered, and a cloud filled the inner court. [4] The glory of the LORD rose high above the cherubim and moved to the terrace of the temple; and the temple was filled with the cloud, while the radiance of the glory of the LORD filled the court. [5] The sound of the wings of the cherubim could be heard as far as the outer court; it was as if God Almighty were speaking.

[6] When the man dressed in linen was told by the LORD to take fire from between the circling wheels and from among the cherubim, he went and stood by a wheel, [7] and one of the cherubim reached out to the fire that was in their midst and, taking some fire, handed it to the man dressed in linen, who received it and went away. [8] Under the wings of the cherubim there could be seen what looked like a human hand.

[9] I saw four wheels beside the cherubim, one wheel beside each cherub. In appearance they were like sparkling topaz, [10] and all four were alike, like a wheel inside a wheel. [11] When the cherubim moved in any of the four directions, they never swerved from their course; they went straight on in the direction in which their heads were turned, never swerving. [12] Their whole bodies, the backs, hands, and wings of all four of them, as well as the wheels, were covered all over with eyes, [13] and I could hear the whirring of the wheels. [14] Each had four faces: the first was a cherub's face, the second a human face, the third a lion's face, and the fourth an eagle's face.

[15] The cherubim raised themselves from the ground, those same living creatures I had seen by the river Kebar. [16] When they moved, the wheels moved beside them; when they lifted their wings and rose from the ground, the wheels did not move from their side. [17] When one halted, the other halted; when one rose, the other rose, for the spirit of the creatures was in the wheels.

[18] The glory of the LORD left the temple terrace and halted above the cherubim. [19] They spread their wings and raised themselves from the ground; I watched them go with the wheels beside them. They halted at the eastern gateway of the LORD's house, with the glory of the God of Israel over them. [20] These were the living creatures I had seen beneath the God of Israel at the river Kebar, and so I knew that they were cherubim. [21] Each had four faces and four wings, and what looked like human hands under their wings. [22] Their faces were like those I had seen in my vision by the river Kebar. They all moved straight forward.

11 A spirit lifted me up and brought me to the eastward-facing gate of the LORD's house. There by the gateway I saw twenty-five men, among them two of high office, Jaazaniah son of Azzur and Pelatiah son of Benaiah. [2] The LORD said to me, 'O man, these are the men who are planning mischief and offering bad advice in this city, [3] saying, "The time has not yet come to build; the city is a cooking pot and we are the meat in it." [4] Therefore', he said, 'prophesy against them, O man, prophesy.'

[5] The spirit of the LORD came upon me, and he told me to say, 'These are the words of the LORD: This is what you are saying to yourselves, you men of Israel; well do I know the thoughts that rise in your mind. [6] You have caused the death of many in this city, heaping the streets with the dead. [7] There-

10:1 **sapphire:** *or* lapis lazuli.
10:2 **under the cherubim:** *so Gk; Heb.* under the cherub.　10:4 **cherubim:** *Heb.* cherub.
10:12 **four of them:** *prob. rdg; Heb. adds* their wheels.
10:22 **by . . . Kebar:** *prob. rdg. Heb. adds* and them.

God's hiddenness (Exod. 16.10) and the brilliance of sapphire manifests the divine majesty (Exod. 24.9–10). Compare Isa. 6.1–5. **7:** Jerusalem, desecrated and put under the ban (Josh. 6.17 n.), must be completely destroyed by *fire* (5.2) coming from God's throne itself; a new city, holy to the LORD, may then rise in its place; see chs. 40–48. **19:** The LORD leaves by the *eastern gateway* in order to go eastward to the captives already in Babylon. The vision continues in 11.22–24.

11.1–25: False security of the inhabitants of Jerusalem. Jehoiachin and the most important people of Jerusalem were taken captive to Babylon in 597; those who remained congratulated themselves that they had God's favor and were therefore safe. Compare Jer. 24.1–10. **2–3:** The city's rulers, as secure and contented as *meat* in a bubbling *cooking pot,* express a confidence that the *time* will *come to build* in the city, thus giving fore, this is what the Lord GOD says: The bodies of your victims, they are the meat, and the city is the cooking pot. But I shall drive you out of the city. [8] You fear the sword, and it is a sword I shall bring on you, says the Lord GOD. [9] I shall drive you out of the city and hand you over to a foreign power; I shall bring you to justice. [10] You will fall by the sword when I bring you to judgement on the frontier of Israel; thus you will know that I am the LORD. [11] So the city will no longer be your cooking pot, nor you the meat in it; on the frontier of Israel I shall bring you to judgement. [12] Then you will know that I am the LORD. You have not conformed to my statutes, nor kept my laws, but have followed the laws of the nations round about you.'

[13] While I was prophesying, Pelatiah son of Benaiah fell dead; and I threw myself on the ground, crying aloud, 'Lord GOD, are you going to make an end of all the Israelites who are left?'

[14] This word of the LORD came to me: [15] 'O man, they are your brothers and your kinsmen, this whole people of Israel, to whom the inhabitants now in Jerusalem have said, "They are separated far from the LORD; the land has been made over to us to possess." [16] Say therefore: These are the words of the Lord GOD: When I sent them far away among the nations and dispersed them over the earth, for a little time I became their sanctuary in the countries to which they had gone. [17] Say therefore: These are the words of the Lord GOD: I shall gather you from among the nations and bring you together from the countries where you have been dispersed, and I shall give the land of Israel to you. [18] When they come there, they will abolish all the vile and abominable practices. [19] I shall give them singleness of heart and put a new spirit in them; I shall remove the heart of stone from their bodies and give them a heart of flesh, [20] so that they will conform to my statutes and keep my laws. They will be my people, and I shall be their God. [21] But those whose hearts are set on vile and abominable practices will be made to answer for all they have done. This is the word of the Lord GOD.'

[22] Then the cherubim lifted their wings, with the wheels beside them and the glory of the God of Israel above them. [23] The glory of the LORD rose up and left the city, and halted on the mountain to the east of it. [24] In a vision sent by the spirit of God, a spirit lifted me up and brought me back to the exiles in Chaldaea. After the vision left me, [25] I told the exiles all that the LORD had revealed to me.

The false prophets

12 THIS word of the LORD came to me: [2] 'O man, you are living among a rebellious people. They have eyes and see nothing; they have ears and hear nothing, because they are rebellious. [3] You must pack

11:16 **for ... time:** *or* in a limited way.   11:19 **in them:** *so Gk; Heb.* in you.   11:21 **those ... set on:** *prob. mng; Heb. obscure.*

the lie to Ezekiel's warning in 7.12–13. The key to this allegory is found in 24.3–7, 9–13. **7–9:** Those unjustly slain in Jerusalem by the rulers of the city are the *meat* in the *cooking pot,* i.e. their bodies will remain in Palestine, but the nobility will be taken beyond the *frontier of Israel* for examination: judgment. **13:** Pelatiah's death in the presence of the prophesying Ezekiel is considered proof by some interpreters of the prophet's double ministry, first before the destruction of Jerusalem in 587 B.C.E. and subsequently in Babylon. Those who admit only a Babylonian ministry explain the whole verse either as a vision the prophet had in Babylonia or as one he added when the oracles were gathered together in 563 B.C.E. See 1.1–2 n. **14–15:** The northern tribes having been in captivity since 721 B.C.E. (2 Kgs. 17.6) and a large portion of Judah since 597 B.C.E., *the inhabitants now in Jerusalem* consider the *whole people of Israel* as *separated far from the LORD,* i.e. away from God's presence in the temple. Hence, in their false security, they claim all the land as their exclusive property. **16–17:** Though distant from the temple, the captives indeed have the LORD (vv. 22–24) as *their sanctuary* until, as their next-of-kin, the LORD delivers them from captivity and gives them anew the *land.* **19–20:** Following a new Exodus (vv. 16–17), *God* will renew the covenant with Israel; by giving them a *new spirit* and a *heart of flesh, they will be* God's *people.* **23:** To fulfill the promises made in vv. 16–17, 19–20, the *glory of the LORD* leaves Jerusalem to be with the exiles in the *east.*

12.1–24.27: Jerusalem's fate predicted. This section contains further prophecies against all whose conduct makes Jerusalem's doom inevitable: the city's rulers and people, priests and prophets.

12.1–20: More symbols of exile. According to some interpreters, the prophet acts out his prediction of exile what you need, O man, for going into exile, and set off by day while they look on. When they see you leave for exile, it may be they will realize that they are rebellious. 4 Bring out your belongings, packed as if for exile; do it in the daytime in their presence, and then again at evening, still before them, leave home as if for exile; 5 break a hole through the wall, and carry your belongings out through it. 6 Shoulder your pack in their presence, and set off when dusk falls, with your face covered so that you cannot see the land, for I am making you a warning sign for the Israelites.'

7 I did exactly as I had been told. In the daytime I brought out my belongings, packed for exile; at evening with my own hands I broke through the wall, and when dusk fell I shouldered my pack and carried it out before their eyes.

8 Next morning this word of the LORD came to me: 9 'O man, the Israelites, that rebellious people, have asked you what you are doing. 10 Tell them that these are the words of the Lord GOD: This oracle concerns the ruler and all the people of Jerusalem. 11 Tell them that you are a sign to warn them; what you have done will be done to them; they will go as captives into exile. 12 In the dusk their ruler will shoulder his pack and go through a hole made to let him out, with his face covered so that he cannot see the land. 13 But I shall throw my net over him, and he will be caught in the meshes. I shall take him to Babylon, to the land of the Chaldaeans, where he will die without ever seeing it. 14 I shall scatter his bodyguard and drive all his squadrons to the four winds; I shall pursue them with drawn sword. 15 Then they will know that I am the LORD, when I disperse them among the nations and scatter them over the earth. 16 But I shall leave a few of them, survivors of the sword, famine, and pestilence, to describe all their abominations

to the peoples among whom they go. They will know that I am the LORD.'

17 THIS word of the LORD came to me: 18 'O man, as you eat your bread you are to tremble, and as you drink the water you are to shudder with fear. 19 Say to the people: This is what the Lord GOD says concerning the inhabitants of Jerusalem in the land of Israel: They will eat bread with fear and be filled with horror as they drink water; the land will be waste and empty because of the violence of all who live there. 20 Inhabited towns will be deserted, and the land will become a waste. Thus you will know that I am the LORD.'

21 This word of the LORD came to me: 22 'O man, what is this proverb current in the land of Israel: "Days pass and visions perish"? 23 Very well! Say to them: This is what the Lord GOD says: I have put an end to this proverb; it will never again be quoted in Israel. Rather say to them: The days are near when every vision will be fulfilled. 24 There will be no more false visions, no misleading divination among the Israelites, 25 for I, the LORD, shall say what I will, and it will be done. It will be put off no longer: you rebellious people, in your lifetime I shall do what I have said. This is the word of the Lord GOD.'

26 This word of the LORD came to me: 27 'O man, the Israelites say, "The visions which prophets now see are not to be fulfilled for many years: they are prophesying of a time far off." 28 Very well! Say to them: This is what the Lord GOD said: No word of mine will be delayed; whatever I say will be done. This is the word of the Lord GOD.'

13 This word of the LORD came to me: 2 'O man, prophesy against the prophets of Israel who are prophesying; say to those whose prophecies come from their own minds: Hear what the LORD says:

12:6 set off: so Gk; Heb. bring out.

---

before the inhabitants of Jerusalem in Palestine; according to others, he is in Babylon before the captives. **6:** The *face* was *covered* as a sign of grief, or to avoid recognition and thus escape ridicule. **12:** Ezekiel's dramatization (vv. 3–7) was already applied to Israel's departure into exile (vv. 10–11). Its reapplication here to the attempted escape of King Zedekiah (2 Kgs. 25.4–5) is probably a later addition, but possibly by the prophet himself. **13:** *There he will die:* the words seem to indicate that the writer is in Palestine, not Babylonia.

12.21–13.23: True and false prophecy. Without objective criteria to distinguish true from false prophecy, the common people are left confused. See 1 Kgs. 22.1–28; Jer. 28.1–15; Mic. 3.5. Two oracles (the first, vv. 21–25, and the second, vv. 26–28) reflect both ridicule suffered by the prophet and his own keen sensitivity and hurt. **22:** *Visions perish:* they are not fulfilled. **25:** Ezekiel feels that he speaks what the LORD wishes to *say*, i.e. that he is the mouth of God. **13.1–5:** Those *whose prophecies come from their own minds* are moved by

³These are the words of the Lord GOD: Woe betide the prophets bent on wickedness, who follow their own enthusiasms, for they have seen no vision! ⁴Your prophets, Israel, have been like jackals among ruins. ⁵They have not stepped into the breach to repair the broken wall for the Israelites, so that they might stand firm in battle on the day of the LORD. ⁶The vision is false, the divination a lie! They claim, "It is the word of the LORD," when it is not the LORD who has sent them, yet they expect him to confirm their prophecies! ⁷Is it not a false vision that you prophets have seen? Is not your divination a lie? You call it the word of the LORD, but it is not I who have spoken.

⁸'The Lord GOD says: Because what you say is false and your visions are a lie, therefore I have set myself against you, says the Lord GOD. ⁹I shall raise my hand against the prophets whose visions are false, whose divinations are a lie. They will have no place in the assembly of my people; their names will not be entered in the roll of Israel, nor will they set foot on her soil. Thus you will know that I am the Lord GOD.

¹⁰'This they deserve, for they have misled my people by saying that all is well when nothing is well. It is as if my people were building a wall and the prophets used whitewash for the daubing. ¹¹Tell these daubers that it will fall, for rain will pour down in torrents, and I shall send hailstones streaming down and unleash a storm-wind. ¹²When the wall collapses, it will be said, "Where is the plaster you used?" ¹³So this is what the Lord GOD says: In my rage I shall unleash a storm-wind; rain will come in torrents in my anger, hailstones in my fury, until all is destroyed. ¹⁴I shall overthrow the wall which you have daubed with whitewash and level it to the ground, laying bare its foundations. It will fall, and you will be destroyed with it: thus you will know that I am the LORD. ¹⁵I shall vent my rage on the wall and on those who daubed it with whitewash; and I shall say,

"Gone is the wall and gone those who daubed it, ¹⁶those prophets of Israel who prophesied to Jerusalem, who saw visions of well-being for her when there was no well-being." This is the word of the Lord GOD.

¹⁷'Now set your face, O man, against the women of your people whose prophecies come from their own minds; prophesy against them ¹⁸and say: This is the word of the Lord GOD: Woe betide you women who hunt men's lives by sewing magic bands on the wrists and putting veils over the heads of persons of every age! Are you to hunt the lives of my people and keep your own lives safe? ¹⁹You have dishonoured me in front of my people for some handfuls of barley and scraps of bread. By telling my people lies they wish to hear, you bring death to those who should not die, and keep alive those who should not live. ²⁰So this is what the Lord GOD says: I have set my face against your magic bands with which you hunt men's lives for the excitement of it. I shall tear them from your arms and set free those lives that you hunt just for excitement. ²¹I shall tear up your veils; I shall rescue my people from your clutches, and you will no longer have it in your power to hunt them. Thus you will know that I am the LORD. ²²With your lying you undermined the righteous, when I meant no hurt; you so strengthened the wicked that they would not abandon their evil ways and save themselves. ²³So never again will you see your false visions or practise divination. I shall rescue my people from your clutches; and thus you will know that I am the LORD.'

14 Some of the elders of Israel visited me, and while they were sitting in my presence ²this word of the LORD came to me, ³'O man, these people have set their hearts on their idols and keep their eyes fixed on the sinful things that cause their downfall. Am I to be consulted by such men? ⁴Speak to

13:18 **the wrists:** *so some MSS; others* my wrists.

their greed, and, far from exposing the community's weaknesses, conceal and exploit them; thus they live like *jackals* off the calamity of others. **6:** *Divination* was a common practice in antiquity. It was not unknown in Israel (Gen. 44.5; Exod. 28.15 n.) but was eventually forbidden (Lev. 19.26; Deut. 18.11). The divination of these prophets is a *lie* because it is not the LORD who has sent them. **10–11:** Plaster, not *whitewash,* gives mud-brick walls a hard, water-resistant coat that does not merely hide the faults of the wall. So, too, true prophets strengthen the community against a day of reckoning by not hiding its evil. **17–23:** Certain *women* seem to have practiced, for payment by *handfuls of barley and scraps of bread* (v. 19), idolatrous magic, divination, and sorcery of an unknown nature. See Mic. 3.5–11.

them, therefore, and tell them that this is what the Lord GOD says: If any Israelite, with his heart set on his idols and his eyes fixed on the sinful things that cause his downfall, comes to a prophet, I, the LORD, give him his answer, despite his gross idolatry. 5My answer will grip the hearts of the Israelites, who through their idols are all estranged from me.

6'So tell the Israelites that this is what the Lord GOD says: Repent, turn from your idols, turn your backs on all your abominations. 7If anyone, Israelite or resident alien, renounces me, setting his heart on idols and fixing his eyes on the sinful things that cause his downfall—if such a one comes to consult me through a prophet, I, the LORD, shall give him his answer directly. 8I shall set my face against him; I shall make him an example and a byword; I shall root him out from among my people. Thus you will know that I am the LORD.

9'If a prophet is deceived into making a prophecy, it is I, the LORD, who have deceived him; I shall stretch out my hand to destroy him and rid my people Israel of him. 10Both will be punished; the prophet and the person who consults him alike are guilty. 11Never again will the Israelites stray from their allegiance, never again defile themselves by their sins; they will be my people, and I shall be their God. This is the word of the Lord GOD.'

12THIS word of the LORD came to me: 13'O man, when a country sins by breaking faith with me, I stretch out my hand and cut short its daily bread. I send famine on it and destroy all the inhabitants along with their cattle. 14Even if these three men, Noah, Daniel, and Job, were there, they would by their righteousness save none but themselves. This is the word of the Lord GOD. 15If I were to turn wild beasts loose in a country to destroy the population, until it became a waste through which no one would pass for fear of the beasts, 16and if those three men were there, as I live, says the Lord GOD, they would not be able to save even their own sons and daughters; they would save themselves alone, and the country would become a waste. 17Or if I were to bring the sword upon that country, commanding it to pass through the land, so that I might destroy people and cattle, 18and if those three men were there, as I live, says the Lord GOD, they could save neither son nor daughter; they would save themselves alone. 19Or if I were to send pestilence on that land and pour out my fury on it in bloodshed, destroying people and cattle, 20and if Noah, Daniel, and Job were there, as I live, says the Lord GOD, they would save neither son nor daughter; they would by their righteousness save none but themselves.

21'The Lord GOD says: How much less hope is there for Jerusalem when I inflict on her these four terrible punishments of mine, sword, famine, wild beasts, and pestilence, to destroy both people and cattle! 22Yet some will be left in her, some survivors to be brought out, both men and women. Look at them as they come out to you, and see how they have behaved and what they have done. This will be consolation to you for the disaster I have brought on Jerusalem, for all I have inflicted on her. 23It will bring you consolation when you consider how they have behaved and what they have done; for you will know that it was not without good reason that I dealt thus with her. This is the word of the Lord GOD.'

14.1–23: Duplicity and personal responsibility. 7: Anyone who comes to consult a prophet while still practicing idolatry will receive an answer not from the prophet, but from the LORD—in punishment! **9:** A prophet who gives an answer to a known idolater is regarded as the idolater's accomplice. God, who as LORD of all allowed it, is considered to have *deceived* the prophet in order to *rid* the community of the prophet's influence. **14:** Three men were famous in the ancient world for their virtue and intercessory power: *Noah* (Gen. 6.9), *Job* (Job 42.7–10), and *Daniel,* a Canaanite hero, or possibly Daniel the biblical hero (Dan. 6.1–24). These three were not able to save their wicked contemporaries from God's anger in time of calamity. They would not be able to do so in the present situation. **21–23:** The *survivors* of the coming catastrophe will be evidence that God does not punish *without good reason.* That God is not capricious will be a source of hope to the exiles.

15.1–8: Parable of the wood of the vine. Israel is the vine cultivated by God, in contrast to the big trees, the nations. Unlike the big trees, a vine is valued only for its fruit and not for its wood, especially if it has been charred by flames, as Israel has been by sin and its punishment, the Exile. See Judg. 9.12–13; Jn. 15.1–11.

The people and their leaders condemned

15 THIS word of the LORD came to me:
²'O man, how is the vine better than any
    other tree,
  than a branch from a tree in the forest?
³Is wood got from it
  useful for making anything?
  Can one make it into a peg
  and hang something on it?
⁴If it is put on the fire for fuel,
  if its two ends are burnt by the fire
  and the middle is charred,
  is it fit for anything useful?
⁵Nothing useful could be made from it,
  even when whole;
  how much less is it useful for making
    anything
  when burnt and charred by fire!

⁶'The Lord GOD says: As the wood of the vine among all kinds of wood from the forest is useful only for burning, even so I treat the inhabitants of Jerusalem. ⁷I have set my face against them. They have escaped from the fire, but fire will burn them up. Thus you will know that I am the LORD when I set my face against them, ⁸and make the land a waste because they have broken faith. This is the word of the Lord GOD.'

16 This word of the LORD came to me:
²'O man, make Jerusalem see her abominable conduct. ³Tell her that these are the words of the Lord GOD to her: Canaan is the land of your ancestry and your birthplace; your father was an Amorite, your mother a Hittite. ⁴This is how you were treated when you were born: at birth your navel-string was not tied, you were not bathed in water and rubbed with oil; no salt was put on you, nor were you wrapped in swaddling clothes. ⁵No one cared enough for

you to do any of these things, or felt enough compassion; you were thrown out on the bare ground in your own filth on the day you were born. ⁶I came by and saw you kicking helplessly as you lay in your blood; I decreed that you should continue to live in your blood. ⁷I tended you like an evergreen plant growing in the fields; you throve and grew. You came to full womanhood; your breasts became firm and your hair grew, but you were still quite naked and exposed.

⁸'I came by again and saw that you were ripe for love. I spread the skirt of my robe over you and covered your naked body. I plighted my troth and entered into a covenant with you, says the Lord GOD, and you became mine. ⁹Then I bathed you with water to wash off the blood; I anointed you with oil. ¹⁰I gave you robes of brocade and sandals of dugong-hide; I fastened a linen girdle round you and dressed you in fine linen. ¹¹I adorned you with jewellery: bracelets on your wrists, a chain round your neck, ¹²a ring in your nose, pendants in your ears, and a splendid crown on your head. ¹³You were adorned with gold and silver, and clothed with linen, fine linen and brocade. Fine flour and honey and olive oil were your food; you became a great beauty and rose to be a queen. ¹⁴Your beauty was famed throughout the world; it was perfect because of the splendour I bestowed on you. This is the word of the Lord GOD.

¹⁵'Relying on your beauty and exploiting your fame, you played the harlot and offered yourself freely to every passer-by. ¹⁶You used some of your clothes to deck shrines in gay colours and there you committed fornication. ¹⁷You took the splendid gold and silver jewellery that I had given you, and made

16:4 **tied:** *prob. rdg, cp. one MS; others* cut.
16:15 **passer-by:** *Heb. has obscure addition.*
16:16 **fornication:** *Heb. has obscure addition.*

16.1–63: The marriage allegory of Jerusalem. The city's history is compared, in sexual imagery, to the biography of a woman in distinct stages of her life. **1–7:** Unlike other cities, Jerusalem had no epic legend of being founded by some god's commission. Rather, like an illegitimate foundling, Jerusalem was left as the result of the Amorite and Hittite movements in Palestine, known now as occurring in the second millennium B.C.E. The LORD *decreed* that Jerusalem *should continue to live,* by not destroying it during Joshua's conquest; see Josh. 15.63. **8–14:** The espoused maiden: Jerusalem, being *ripe for love* when taken by David (2 Sam. 5.6–8), became the "spouse" of the LORD when the Ark of the LORD, the symbol of the *covenant,* was moved into it (2 Sam. 6.12–19); Jerusalem *became a great beauty* when the temple and the palaces were built by Solomon (1 Kgs. 6.1–9.1). **15–19:** The flirtatious bride: because of commerce with other nations, Jerusalem committed the sin of being unfaithful to God and of adopting Canaanite religious practices (2 Kgs. 21.1–18).

for yourself male images with which you committed fornication. ¹⁸You covered them with your robes of brocade, and you offered up my oil and my incense to them. ¹⁹The food I had provided for you, the fine flour, the oil, and the honey, you set before them as an offering of soothing odour. This is the word of the Lord GOD.

²⁰⁻²¹'The sons and daughters whom you had borne to me you took and sacrificed to these images as their food. Was this slaughtering of my children, this handing them over and surrendering them to your images, any less a sin than your fornication? ²²With all your abominable fornication you never recalled those early days when you lay quite naked, kicking helplessly in your blood.

²³'Woe betide you! says the Lord GOD. After all the evil you had done ²⁴you set up a couch for yourself and erected a shrine in every open place. ²⁵You built your shrines at the top of every street and debased your beauty, offering your body to every passer-by in countless acts of harlotry. ²⁶You committed fornication with your lustful neighbours, the Egyptians, and provoked me to anger by your repeated harlotry.

²⁷'I stretched out my hand against you and reduced your territory. I gave you up to the will of your enemies, the Philistine women, who were disgusted by your lewd conduct. ²⁸Still unsatisfied, you committed fornication with the Assyrians, and still were not satisfied. ²⁹You committed many acts of fornication in Chaldaea, a land of traders, and even with this you were not satisfied.

³⁰'How you anger me! says the Lord GOD. You have done all this like the headstrong harlot you are. ³¹You have set up your couches at the top of every street and erected your shrines in every open place, but, unlike the common prostitute, you have scorned a fee. ³²You adulterous wife who receives strangers rather than her husband! ³³All prostitutes receive presents; but you give presents to all your lovers, bribing them to come from far and wide to commit fornication with you. ³⁴When you are so engaged you are the very opposite of those other women: no one runs after you, and you do not receive a fee; you give one!

³⁵'Listen, you harlot, to the word of the LORD. ³⁶The Lord GOD says: Because of your brazen excesses, exposing your naked body in fornication with your lovers, because of your abominable idols and the slaughter of the children you have offered to them, ³⁷I shall assemble all those lovers whom you charmed, all whom you loved and all whom you turned against. I shall gather them in from all around against you; I shall strip you before them, and they will see you altogether naked. ³⁸I shall bring you to trial for adultery and murder, and I shall give you over to blood spilt in fury and jealousy. ³⁹When I hand you over to them, they will demolish your couch and pull down your shrine; they will strip off your clothes, take away your splendid jewellery, and leave you stark naked. ⁴⁰They will bring up a mob to punish you; they will stone you and hack you to pieces with their swords. ⁴¹They will burn down your houses and execute judgement on you in the sight of many women. I shall put a stop to your harlotry, and never again will you pay a fee to your lovers. ⁴²Then I shall abate my fury, and my jealousy will turn away from you. I shall be calm and no longer be provoked to anger. ⁴³You never called to mind the days of your youth, but enraged me with all your doings; I in turn brought retribution on you for your conduct. This is the word of the Lord GOD.

'Did you not commit these obscenities, as well as all your other abominations? ⁴⁴Everyone who quotes proverbs will quote this one about you, "Like mother, like daughter." ⁴⁵You are a true daughter of a mother who rejected her husband and children. You are a true sister of your sisters who rejected their husbands and children. You are daughters of a Hittite mother and an Amorite father. ⁴⁶Your elder sister was Samaria, who lived with her daughters to the north of you; your younger sister was Sodom, who lived with her daughters to the south. ⁴⁷Did you not behave as they did and commit the same

16:19 **soothing odour:** *so Syriac; Heb. adds* and it was.

20–22: An unfeeling mother: even human sacrifices of children were offered; see 2 Kgs. 16.3; 17.17; Jer. 7.31. **23–34:** The adulterous wife: Jerusalem squandered the wealth of the LORD in order to attract trading and military partners (1 Kgs. 16.7–18). *Shrines* are the "high places," sanctuaries of Canaanite worship; see 6.3 n.; 2 Kgs. 21.3. **35–43:** The castoff and condemned woman: Jerusalem, having provoked God's anger, is punished by being attacked by its former allies, Egypt and Babylon. **45–52:** Jerusalem's sins exceed those of its sister abominations? Indeed you surpassed them in depraved conduct. ⁴⁸As I live, says the Lord GOD, your sister Sodom and her daughters never behaved as you and your daughters have done! ⁴⁹This was the iniquity of your sister Sodom: she and her daughters had the pride that goes with food in plenty, comfort, and ease, yet she never helped the poor in their need. ⁵⁰They grew haughty and committed what was abominable in my sight, and I swept them away, as you are aware. ⁵¹Nor did Samaria commit half the sins of which you have been guilty; you have committed more abominations than she. All the abominations you have committed have made your sister look innocent. ⁵²It is you that must bear the humiliation, for your sins have pleaded your sisters' cause; your conduct is so much more abominable than theirs that they appear innocent in comparison. Now you must bear your shame and humiliation and make your sisters look innocent.

⁵³'I shall restore the fortunes of Sodom and her daughters and of Samaria and her daughters (and I shall restore yours at the same time). ⁵⁴When you bring them comfort, you will bear your shame and be disgraced for all you have done. ⁵⁵After your sister Sodom and her daughters become what they were of old, and when your sister Samaria and her daughters become what they were of old, then you and your daughters will be restored likewise. ⁵⁶Did you not speak contemptuously of your sister Sodom in the days of your pride, ⁵⁷before your wickedness was exposed? Even so now you are despised by the daughters of Aram and all those nations around them, and the daughters of Philistia round about who also despise you. ⁵⁸You must bear the consequences of your lewd and abominable conduct. This is the word of the LORD.

⁵⁹'The Lord GOD says: I shall treat you as you have deserved, because you violated an oath and made light of a covenant. ⁶⁰But I shall call to mind the covenant I made with you when you were young, and I shall establish with you a covenant which will last for ever. ⁶¹You will remember your past conduct and feel ashamed when you receive your sisters, the elder and the younger. I shall give them to you as daughters, though they are not included in my covenant with you. ⁶²Thus I shall establish my covenant with you, and you will know that I am the LORD. ⁶³You will remember, and will be so ashamed and humiliated that you will never open your mouth again, once I have pardoned you for all you have done. This is the word of the Lord GOD.'

17 This word of the LORD came to me: ²'O man, pose this riddle, expound this parable to the Israelites. ³Tell them that these are the words of the Lord GOD:

A great eagle
  with broad wings and long pinions,
  in full plumage, richly patterned,
  came to Lebanon.
He took the very top of a cedar tree,
⁴plucked its highest twig;
  he carried it off to a land of traders,
  and planted it in a city of merchants.
⁵Then he took a native seed
  and put it in a prepared plot;
  he set it like a willow,
  a shoot beside abundant water.
⁶It sprouted and became a vine,
  sprawling low along the ground
  and bending its boughs towards him

16:47 **Indeed . . . conduct:** *prob. mng; Heb. obscure.*
16:57 **Aram:** *so some MSS; others* Edom.

cities Samaria and Sodom, and therefore, so will its *shame and humiliation.* **53–63:** Reconciliation, conversion, and new espousals await Jerusalem when once the city will recognize and return to its original condition. *Daughters of Aram:* perhaps the Assyrian cities of Asshur and Nineveh destroyed in 614 and 612 respectively. *Oath:* oath of loyalty to Nebuchadnezzar broken by Zedekiah; see 17.12–18.

17.1–24: Allegory of the cedar and the eagles portrays the drama of Zedekiah, the weak king of Judah, caught between the aggressiveness of the king of Babylon and the king of Egypt. **3–5:** Since allegory is an extended metaphor, a narrative with a continuous system of equivalents, the following identifications can possibly be made: *great eagle,* Nebuchadnezzar; *Lebanon,* city of Jerusalem; *top of a cedar tree,* dynasty of David; *highest twig,* King Jehoiachin; *land of traders,* Babylonia; *city of merchants,* Babylon; *native seed,* Zedekiah, Jehoiachin's uncle, placed upon the throne by Nebuchadnezzar in 597 B.C.E. (2 Kgs. 24.17). **6:** *Roots growing beneath him* is explained in v. 13, namely, when the king of Babylon put Zedekiah "on his oath." The kingdom was *sprawling low,* because most of its exalted citizens had been taken into captivity and

with its roots growing beneath him.
So it became a vine; it branched out
and sent forth shoots.

7 'But there was another great eagle
with broad wings and thick plumage;
and this vine gave its roots
a twist towards him;
from the bed where it was planted,
    seeking drink,
it pushed out its trailing boughs
    towards him,
8 though it had been set
in good ground beside abundant water
that it might branch out and be
    fruitful,
and become a noble vine.

9 'Tell them that the Lord GOD says:

Will such a vine flourish?
Will not its roots be torn up
and its fruit stripped off,
and all its freshly sprouted leaves
    wither,
until it is uprooted and carried away
with little effort and a small force?
10 If it is transplanted, will it flourish?
Will it not be utterly shrivelled,
as though by the touch of the east
    wind,
on the bed where it ought to sprout?'

11 This word of the LORD came to me: 12 'Say
to that rebellious people: Have you no idea
what all this means? The king of Babylon
came to Jerusalem, took its king and those in
high office, and brought them back with him
to Babylon. 13 He chose a prince of the royal
line and made a treaty with him, putting him
on his oath. He carried away the chief men
of the country, 14 so that it should become a
humble kingdom, submissive, ready to observe the treaty and keep it in force. 15 But
the prince rebelled against him and sent envoys to Egypt with a request for horses and
a large force of troops. Will such a man be
successful? Will he escape destruction if he
acts in this way? Can he violate a treaty and
escape unpunished? 16 As I live, says the Lord
GOD, I swear that he will die in Babylon, in
the land of the king who put him on the
throne, the king whose oath he disregarded,
whose treaty he violated. 17 No large army
will come from Pharaoh, no great force to be
a protection for him in battle, when siege-
ramps are thrown up and towers are built for
the destruction of many. 18 Because he violated a treaty and disregarded his oath, because he submitted, and yet did all these
things, he will not escape.

19 'The Lord GOD says: As I live, he has
made light of the oath sworn in my name and
has violated the covenant he made with me.
For this I shall bring retribution upon him.
20 Because he has broken faith with me I shall
throw my net over him, and he will be caught
in the meshes; I shall carry him to Babylon
and bring him to judgement there. 21 The
picked troops in all his squadrons will fall by
the sword; those who are left will be scattered
to all the winds. Thus you will know that it is
I, the LORD, who have spoken.

22 'The Lord GOD says:

I, too, shall take a slip
from the lofty crown of the cedar
and set it in the soil;
I shall pluck a tender shoot from the
    topmost branch
and plant it on a high and lofty
    mountain,
23 the highest mountain in Israel.
It will put out branches, bear its fruit,
and become a noble cedar.
Birds of every kind will roost under it,
perching in the shelter of its boughs.
24 All the trees of the countryside will
    know
that it is I, the LORD,
who bring low the tall tree
and raise the lowly tree high,
who shrivel up the green tree
and make the shrivelled tree put forth
    buds.
I, the LORD, have spoken; I shall do it.'

17:7 **another:** *so Gk; Heb.* one.

Zedekiah's power was very limited even over his officers (Jer. 38.5). **7:** *Another great eagle:* the Pharaoh
Psammetichus II of Egypt (594–588 B.C.E.). Zedekiah's request for military aid from Egypt (v. 15) is the *twist
towards him.* **19:** Ezekiel considers Zedekiah's breach of his loyalty oath to Nebuchadnezzar a rejection of
God's *covenant.* **22–24:** God's action in history—to *pluck* and to *plant*—is decisive, not the maneuverings
of kings.

18 This word of the Lord came to me: ²'What do you all mean by repeating this proverb in the land of Israel:

Parents eat sour grapes,
and their children's teeth are set on
edge?

³'As I live, says the Lord God, this proverb will never again be used by you in Israel. ⁴Every living soul belongs to me; parent and child alike are mine. It is the person who sins that will die.

⁵'Consider the man who is righteous and does what is just and right. ⁶He never feasts at mountain shrines, never looks up to idols worshipped in Israel, never dishonours another man's wife, never approaches a menstruous woman; ⁷he oppresses no one, he returns the debtor's pledge, he never commits robbery; he gives his food to the hungry and clothes to those who have none. ⁸He never lends either at discount or at interest, but shuns injustice and deals fairly between one person and another. ⁹He conforms to my statutes and loyally observes my laws. Such a one is righteous: he will live, says the Lord God.

¹⁰'He may have a son who is given to violence and bloodshed, one who turns his back on these commandments; ¹¹obeying none of them, he feasts at mountain shrines, dishonours another man's wife, ¹²oppresses the poor in their need; he commits robbery, he does not return the debtor's pledge, he looks up to idols, and joins in abominable rites; ¹³he lends both at discount and at interest. Such a one will not live; because he has committed all these abominations he must die. His blood be on his own head!

¹⁴'This person in turn may have a son who sees all his father's sins, but in spite of seeing them commits none of them. ¹⁵He never feasts at mountain shrines, never looks up to the idols worshipped in Israel, never dishonours another man's wife, ¹⁶oppresses no one, takes no pledge, does not rob; he gives his food to the hungry and clothes to those

who have none; ¹⁷he shuns injustice and never lends either at discount or at interest. He keeps my laws and conforms to my statutes. Such a one is not to die for his father's wrongdoing; he will live.

¹⁸'If his father has been guilty of oppression and robbery and lived an evil life in the community, and died because of his iniquity, ¹⁹you may ask, "Why is the son not punished for his father's iniquity?" Because he has always done what is just and right and has been careful to obey all my laws, he will live. ²⁰It is the person who sins that will die; a son will not bear responsibility for his father's guilt, nor a father for his son's. The righteous person will have his own righteousness placed to his account, and the wicked person his own wickedness.

²¹'If someone who is wicked renounces all his sinful ways and keeps all my laws, doing what is just and right, he will live; he will not die. ²²None of the offences he has committed will be remembered against him; because of his righteous conduct he will live. ²³Have I any desire for the death of a wicked person? says the Lord God. Is not my desire rather that he should mend his ways and live?

²⁴'If someone who is righteous turns from his righteous ways and commits every kind of abomination that the wicked practise, is he to do this and live? No, none of his former righteousness will be remembered in his favour; because he has been faithless and has sinned, he must die.

²⁵'You say that the Lord acts without principle? Listen, you Israelites! It is not I who act without principle; it is you. ²⁶If a righteous man turns from his righteousness, takes to evil ways, and dies, it is because of these evil ways that he dies. ²⁷Again, if a wicked man gives up his wicked ways and does what is just and right, he preserves his life; ²⁸he has seen his offences and turned his back on them all, and so he will not die; he will live. ²⁹"The

18:7 **the debtor's pledge:** *so Gk; Heb. unintelligible.*
18:10 **who turns ... commandments:** *prob. rdg; Heb. unintelligible.* 18:17 **injustice:** *so Gk; Heb.* the unfortunate. 18:18 **robbery:** *so Gk; Heb.* robbery of a brother.

18.1–32: The Lord's way is freedom. Maintaining right relations with God frees one from: (a) the past of one's parents, vv. 1–20; (b) the past of one's own life, vv. 21–32. Although individual responsibility is asserted by biblical authors before Ezekiel, as in Deut. 24.16; 2 Kgs. 14.6; Jer. 31.29–30, Ezekiel's challenging affirmation here stands in clear contrast to the strong formulations of the inherited doctrine found in Exod. 34.7; Lev. 26.39–40; Deut. 5.9. **2:** *This proverb,* restating, though somewhat cynically, the teaching of Exod. 20.5 and 34.7, seems to imply that the nation's recent calamities were an unjust application of the teaching by God.

Lord acts without principle," say the Israelites. No, it is you, Israel, that acts without principle, not I.
³⁰'Therefore I shall judge every one of you Israelites on his record, says the Lord GOD. Repent, renounce all your offences, or your iniquity will be your downfall. ³¹Throw off the load of your past misdeeds; get yourselves a new heart and a new spirit. Why should you Israelites die? ³²I have no desire for the death of anyone. This is the word of the Lord GOD.

19 'Raise a dirge over the rulers of Israel ²and say:

What a lioness was your mother
　among the lions!
She made her lair among the young
　lions
and reared her cubs.
³One of her cubs she singled out;
he grew into a young lion,
he learnt to tear his prey,
he devoured men.
⁴Then the nations raised a shout at
　him;
he was caught in their pit,
and they dragged him off
with hooks to Egypt.
⁵When she saw that her hope in him
was disappointed and dashed,
she took another of her cubs
and made a young lion of him.
⁶He prowled among the lions
and acted like a young lion.
He learnt to tear his prey,
he devoured men;
⁷he broke down their palaces,
laid their cities in ruins.
The land and all in it were aghast
at the sound of his roaring.
⁸From the regions all around
the nations raised a hue and cry;
they cast their net over him
and he was caught in their pit.
⁹With hooks they drew him into a cage

and brought him to the king of
　Babylon;
he was put in prison
that his roar might never again be
　heard
on the mountains of Israel.

¹⁰'Your mother was a vine
planted by the waterside.
It grew fruitful and luxuriant,
for there was water in plenty.
¹¹It had stout branches,
sceptres for those who bear rule.
It grew tall, finding its way through the
　foliage;
it was conspicuous for its height and
　many boughs.
¹²But it was torn up in anger
and thrown to the ground;
the east wind blighted it,
its fruit was blown off,
its strong branches were blighted,
and fire burnt it.
¹³Now it is transplanted in the wilderness,
in a dry and thirsty land;
¹⁴fire bursts forth from its own branches
and burns up its shoots.
It has no strong branch any more,
no sceptre for those who bear rule.'

This is a lament and it has passed into use as such.

20 ON the tenth day of the fifth month in the seventh year, some of the elders of Israel came to consult the LORD and were sitting with me. ²Then this word of the LORD came to me: ³'O man, say to the elders of Israel: The Lord GOD says: Do you come to consult me? As I live, I refuse to be consulted by you. This is the word of the Lord GOD.

18:32 **the Lord GOD:** *so Gk; Heb. adds* and bring back and live.　　19:5 **another:** *so Gk; Heb.* one.　　19:7 **he broke ... palaces:** *so Aram. (Targ.); Heb.* he knew his widows.　　19:10 **vine:** *prob. rdg; Heb. obscure.*　　19:14 **burns ... shoots:** *prob. rdg; Heb. adds* its fruit.

31–32: After repeated assurances that a "righteous one" will "surely live" (vv. 9, 17, 22), Ezekiel exhorts the reader to *get a new heart and a new spirit* and so turn and live; the prophet's message seems to have implications beyond the physical life of this world.

19.1–14: Laments on the royal house. The calamities of the Davidic dynasty are depicted allegorically in mournful poetic meter. **2:** *Lioness:* Judah (Gen. 49.9). **3:** *One of her cubs:* King Jehoahaz, taken captive by Pharaoh Necho in 609; see 2 Kgs. 23.30–34. **10:** *Vine:* Judah. **11:** *Stout branches:* may refer to the Davidic dynasty in general or to specific kings, probably Zedekiah or Jehoiachin.

20.1–44: Theology of Israel's history. The history of Israel, in the prophet's view, is the history of God's

⁴'Bring a charge against them, O man! Tell them of the abominations of their forefathers ⁵and say to them: The Lord God says: On the day I chose Israel, with uplifted hand I bound myself by oath to the descendants of Jacob and revealed myself to them in Egypt, declaring: I am the Lord your God. ⁶That day I swore with hand uplifted that I would bring them out of Egypt into the land I had sought out for them, a land flowing with milk and honey, the fairest of all lands. ⁷I told every one of them to cast away the loathsome things to which they looked up, and not to defile themselves with the idols of Egypt. I am the Lord your God, I said.

⁸'But in rebellion against me they refused to listen, and not one of them cast away the loathsome things to which he looked up or forsook the idols of Egypt. I resolved to pour out my wrath and exhaust my anger on them in Egypt. ⁹But then I acted for the honour of my name, that it might not be profaned in the sight of the nations among whom Israel was living: I revealed myself to them by bringing Israel out of Egypt.

¹⁰'I brought them out of Egypt and led them into the wilderness. ¹¹There I gave my statutes to them and taught them my laws; it is by keeping them that mortals have life. ¹²Further, I gave them my sabbaths to serve as a sign between us, so that they would know that I am the Lord who sanctified them. ¹³But the Israelites rebelled against me in the wilderness; they did not conform to my statutes, they rejected my laws, though it is by keeping them that mortals have life, and they totally desecrated my sabbaths. I resolved to pour out my wrath on them in the wilderness to destroy them. ¹⁴But then I acted for the honour of my name, that it might not be profaned in the sight of the nations who had seen me bring them out.

¹⁵'However, in the wilderness I swore to them with uplifted hand that I would not bring them into the land I had given them, that land flowing with milk and honey, the fairest of all lands. ¹⁶They loved to follow idols of their own, so they rejected my laws,

they would not conform to my statutes, and they desecrated my sabbaths. ¹⁷Yet I pitied them too much to destroy them and did not make an end of them in the wilderness. ¹⁸I warned their children in the wilderness not to conform to the rules and usages of their fathers, nor to defile themselves with their idols. ¹⁹I am the Lord your God, I said; you must conform to my statutes, you must observe my laws and act according to them. ²⁰You must keep my sabbaths holy, and they will become a sign between us; so you will know that I am the Lord your God.

²¹'But those children rebelled against me; they did not conform to my statutes or observe my laws, though obedience to them would have given life. Moreover they desecrated my sabbaths. Again I resolved to pour out my wrath and vent my anger on them in the wilderness. ²²But I stayed my hand. I acted for the honour of my name, so that it might not be profaned in the sight of the nations who had seen me bring them out of Egypt. ²³However, in the wilderness I swore to them with uplifted hand that I would disperse them among the nations and scatter them over the earth, ²⁴because they had disobeyed my laws, rejected my statutes, desecrated my sabbaths, and had regard only for the idols of their forefathers. ²⁵I even imposed on them statutes that were malign and laws which would not lead to life. ²⁶I let them defile themselves with gifts to idols; I made them surrender their eldest sons to them so that I might fill them with revulsion. Thus they would know that I am the Lord.

²⁷'Speak therefore, O man, to the Israelites; say to them: The Lord God says: Once again your forefathers reviled me and broke faith with me: ²⁸when I brought them into the land which I had sworn with uplifted hand to give them, they noted every hilltop and every leafy tree, and there they offered their sacrifices, there they presented the gifts which roused my anger, there they set out their offerings of soothing odour and poured out their drink-offerings. ²⁹I asked them: What is this bamah to which you go?

---

self-revelation, so that Israel might have life. **1:** August 14, 591 B.C.E. Compare 1.1; 8.1; 24.1. **9:** *Honour* of God's *name:* not vain concern for reputation, but acute awareness that Israel's welfare flows from, and is identified with, the name, i.e. the reality, of God. **20:** The observance of the *sabbaths* became at this time, and especially in captivity, a visible *sign* of fidelity to the covenant. **25–26:** The *surrender* of the *eldest sons* as *gifts to idols* is seen as one of the *laws* from God, inasmuch as God directs even the evil deeds of people to their own good. Sacrifices of human infants are condemned in v. 31 and in 16.20; also in Lev. 18.21; Jer. 7.31.

And 'bamah' has been the name for a shrine ever since.

30 'So tell the Israelites: The Lord GOD says: Are you defiling yourselves as your forefathers did, and lusting after their loathsome gods? 31 You are defiling yourselves to this very day with all your idols when you bring your gifts and pass your children through the fire. How then can I let you consult me, men of Israel? As I live, says the Lord GOD, I refuse to be consulted by you. 32 When you say to yourselves, "Let us become like the nations and tribes of other lands and worship wood and stone," you are thinking of something that can never be. 33 As I live, says the Lord GOD, I shall reign over you with a strong hand, with arm outstretched and wrath outpoured. 34 By my strong hand, an outstretched arm, and outpoured wrath I shall bring you out from the peoples and gather you from the lands where you have been dispersed. 35 I shall bring you into the Wilderness of the Peoples; there I shall confront you and bring you to judgement. 36 Even as I did in the wilderness of Egypt against your forefathers, so against you I shall state my case. This is the word of the Lord GOD.

37 'I shall make you pass under the rod, counting you as you enter. 38 I shall purge you of those who revolt and rebel against me. I shall take them out of the land where they now live, but they will not set foot on the soil of Israel. Thus you will know that I am the LORD.

39 'Now, you Israelites, the Lord GOD says: Go, each one of you, and serve your idols! But in days to come I shall punish you for your disobedience to me, and no more will you desecrate my holy name with your gifts and your idolatries. 40 But on my holy mountain, the lofty mountain of Israel, says the Lord GOD, there in the land all the Israelites will serve me. There I shall accept them; there I shall require your gifts and your choicest offerings, with all else that you consecrate to me. 41 I shall accept you when you make offerings with their soothing odour, after I have brought you out from the peoples and gathered you from the lands where you have been dispersed. I alone shall have your worship, and the nations will witness it. 42 'You will know that I am the LORD, when I bring you home to the soil of Israel, to the land which I swore with uplifted hand to give your forefathers. 43 There you will remember your past conduct and all the acts by which you defiled yourselves, and you will loathe yourselves for all the wickedness you have committed. 44 You will know that I am the LORD, when I deal with you Israelites, not as your wicked ways and your vicious deeds deserve, but as the honour of my name demands. This is the word of the Lord GOD.'

45 This word of the LORD came to me: 46 'O man, turn and face towards the south and utter your words towards it; prophesy to the scrubland of the Negeb. 47 Say to it: Listen to the word of the LORD. The Lord GOD says: I am about to kindle a fire in you, and it will consume all the wood, green and dry alike. Its fiery flame will not be put out, but from the Negeb northwards everyone will be scorched by it. 48 Everyone will see that it is I, the LORD, who have set it ablaze; it will not be put out.' 49 'Ah Lord GOD,' I cried; 'they are always saying of me, "He deals only in figures of speech." '

Threats against sinners

21 THIS word of the LORD came to me: 2 'O man, turn and face towards Jerusalem, and utter your words against her sanctuary; prophesy against the land of Israel. 3 Say to that land: The LORD says: I am against you; I shall draw my sword from the scabbard and make away with both righteous and wicked from among you. 4 It is because I intend to make away with righteous and wicked alike that my sword will be drawn from the scabbard against everyone, from the Negeb northwards. 5 All shall know that I, the LORD, have drawn my sword; it will

20:37 counting . . . enter: *prob. rdg; Heb. obscure.*
20:45 *In Heb. 21:1.*

34–36: The return from exile through the *Wilderness of the Peoples,* i.e. the desert of Syria, will be like the Sinai experience relived.

20.45–21.32: **Parable of the forest fire** is the oracle of doom in vv. 45–48. When the people object that Ezekiel *deals only in figures of speech* (v. 49), he gives an explanation (21.1–7). 46: According to some interpreters, Ezekiel, if in Babylon, could not *face south* and look toward Judah. See Introduction. *Negeb:* the southern part of Judah. 21.3: The consuming fire (20.47) is the *sword* which destroys Israel, both of which are never again be sheathed. ⁶Groan while they look on, O man, groan bitterly until you collapse. ⁷When they ask why you are groaning, say, "Because what I have heard is about to come. All hearts will melt, all hands will hang limp, all courage will fail, all knees will turn to water. See, it is coming; it is here!" This is the word of the Lord God.'

⁸The Lord said to me: ⁹'Prophesy, O man, and say: This is the word of the Lord:

A sword, a sword is sharpened and
  burnished,
¹⁰sharpened to kill and kill again,
  burnished to flash like lightning.
  (Look, the rod is brandished, my son,
  to defy all wooden idols!)
¹¹The sword is given to be burnished
  ready for the hand to grasp.
  The sword is sharpened,
  it is burnished,
  ready to be given into the slayer's hand.

¹²'Cry aloud and wail, O man; for it falls on my people, and on all Israel's rulers who are delivered over to the sword and are slain with my people. Therefore slap your thigh in remorse. ¹³(When the test comes, what if the rod does not in truth defy?) This is the word of the Lord God.

¹⁴'But you, O man, prophesy and strike
  your hands together;
  swing the sword twice, thrice:
  it is the sword of slaughter,
  the great sword of slaughter whirling
  about them.
¹⁵That their hearts may be fearful and
  many may stumble and fall,
  I have set the threat of the sword at all
  their gates,
  the threat of the sword flashing like
  lightning
  and drawn to kill.
¹⁶Be sharpened, turn right; be
  unsheathed, turn left,
  wherever your point is aimed.

¹⁷'I, too, shall strike my hands together and

abate my anger. I, the Lord, have spoken.'

¹⁸This word of the Lord came to me: ¹⁹'O man, trace out two roads by which the sword of the king of Babylon may come, both starting from the same land. Then make a signpost for the point where the highway forks. ²⁰Mark a road for the sword to come to the Ammonite city of Rabbah, and a road to Judah, with Jerusalem at its heart. ²¹At the parting of the ways where the road divides, the king of Babylon will halt to take the omens. He will cast lots with arrows, consult household gods, and inspect the livers of beasts. ²²The arrow marked "Jerusalem" will fall at his right hand: here, then, he will give the command for slaughter and sound the battle cry, set battering-rams against the gates, cast up siege-ramps, and build watchtowers. ²³The people will think that the auguries are groundless, the king of Babylon will remind me of their wrongdoing, and they will fall into his hand. ²⁴Therefore the Lord God says: Because you have kept me mindful of your wrongdoing by your open rebellion, and your sins have been revealed in everything you do, because you have kept yourselves in my mind, you will fall into the enemy's hand.

²⁵'And you, impious and wicked ruler of Israel, your fate has come upon you in the hour of final punishment. ²⁶The Lord God says: Off with the diadem! Away with the crown! All is overturned; raise the low and bring down the high. ²⁷Ruin! Ruin! I shall bring about such ruin as never was, until one comes who is the rightful ruler; and I shall install him.

²⁸O MAN, prophesy and say: The Lord God

21:10 **to flash:** *prob. rdg; Heb. unintelligible.* **the rod . . . idols:** *or* the rod is waved, my son, defying all wooden defences. 21:13 **When . . . defy:** *Heb. obscure.* 21:15 **the threat of the sword [flashing]:** *prob. rdg; Heb. obscure.* 21:16 **Be sharpened:** *so Aram. (Targ.); Heb.* Unify yourself. 21:20 **come to:** *so Gk; Heb.* come with. 21:22 **here, then:** *prob. rdg; Heb. adds* he must set battering-rams. 21:23 **groundless:** *so Gk; Heb. adds an unintelligible phrase.* 21:26 **diadem:** *lit.* turban.

attributed to God as the Lord of history. **8–17:** This song of *the sword* is a poetic description of the coming catastrophe. **20:** *Rabbah* is modern Amman, the capital of Jordan. **21:** Three forms of divination are used; the result of only one is given: arrows inscribed with alternatives, shaken in a quiver, and then drawn. **23–24:** The *auguries* do not bind the Lord but only keep God *mindful* of Israel's *rebellion*. **25:** *Wicked ruler:* Zedekiah. See 17.19–21; 2 Chr. 36.11–13; Jer. 52.2. **28–32:** The song of the *sword* depicts for Ammon the same fate says to the Ammonites and to their shameful god:

A sword, a sword drawn for slaughter,
burnished for destruction
to flash like lightning!
29 Your visions are false, your auguries a
lie,
which bid you bring it down
upon the necks of the impious and the
wicked;
their fate will come upon them
in the hour of final punishment.
30 Return the sword to the sheath.
I shall judge you in the place where
you were born,
the land of your origin.
31 I shall pour out my wrath on you;
I shall fan my blazing anger over you.
I shall hand you over to barbarous
men,
skilled in destruction.
32 You will become fuel for fire,
your blood will be shed within the land
and you will leave no memory behind.

'I, the LORD, have spoken.'

22 THIS word of the LORD came to me:
2 'O man, will you bring a charge
against her? Will you charge the murderous
city and bring home to her all her abominable deeds? 3 Say to her: The Lord GOD has
said: Woe betide the city that sheds blood
within her walls and brings her fate on herself, the city that makes idols for herself and
is defiled by them! 4 You are guilty because of
the blood you have shed, you are defiled because of the idols you have made. You have
shortened your days by this and hastened
your end. This is why I exposed you to the
contempt of the nations and the mockery of
every country. 5 Lands both far and near will
taunt you with your infamy and monstrous

disorder. 6 In you all the rulers of Israel have
used their power to shed blood; 7 in you fathers and mothers have been treated contemptuously, aliens have been oppressed, the
fatherless and the widow have been
wronged. 8 You have despised what I hold
sacred, and desecrated my sabbaths. 9 In you,
Jerusalem, perjurers have worked to procure
bloodshed; in you are men who have feasted
at mountain shrines and have committed
lewdness. 10 In you men have exposed their
fathers' nakedness; they have violated
women who were menstruating; 11 they have
committed an outrage with their neighbours'
wives and have lewdly defiled their own
daughters-in-law; they have ravished their
sisters, their own fathers' daughters. 12 In you
people have accepted bribes to shed blood.
You have exacted discount and interest, and
have oppressed your fellows for gain. You
have committed apostasy. This is the word of
the LORD GOD.

13 'See, I strike with my clenched fist at your
ill-gotten gains and at the bloodshed within
your walls. 14 Will your courage and strength
endure when I deal with you? I, the LORD,
have spoken and I shall act. 15 I shall disperse
you among the nations and scatter you over
the earth to rid you of your defilement. 16 I
shall sift you in the sight of the nations, and
you will know that I am the LORD.'

17 THIS word of the LORD came to me: 18 'O
man, to me all Israelites are but an alloy, their
silver debased with copper, tin, iron, and
lead. 19 Therefore, these are the words of the
Lord GOD: Because you are all alloyed, I shall
gather you into Jerusalem, 20 as silver, copper, iron, lead, and tin are gathered into a
crucible, where fire is blown to full heat to

21:28 **for destruction:** *prob. rdg; Heb. obscure.*
21:29 **it:** *prob. rdg; Heb.* you.   22:18 **their silver . . .
lead:** *prob. rdg; Heb.* copper, tin, iron, and lead inside a
crucible; they are an alloy, silver.

as for Judah in vv. 8–17.

22.1–31: The docket of crimes committed by the city and by various classes of citizens. Three indictments
are given, in legal form, each followed by an appropriate sentence: vv. 1–12, against the population of
Jerusalem in general, vv. 13–16 being the sentence; vv. 17–18, against all Israel, including those who took
refuge in the city, with the sentence in vv. 19–22; 23–30, against specific classes for their various abuses of
civic, religious and social authority or responsibility, with v. 31 as the sentence. **3:** *Sheds blood:* bloody
violence, or sins which demand the death penalty as in vv. 10–11. **10–11:** These acts, according to Lev.
18.6–30, are prohibited. **12:** Two forms of exacting *interest* were apparently in use: *discount* (lit. "bite"), taking
a cut at the time of loan; and *interest* (lit. "increase"), demanding at time of payment more than was lent. **19:**
Into Jerusalem: possibly an allusion to refugees fleeing before the advancing Babylonian army.

melt them. So shall I gather you in my anger and wrath, put you in it, and melt you; ²¹I shall gather you in Jerusalem and fan the fire of my anger until you are melted. ²²As silver is melted in a crucible so will you be melted, and you will know that I, the LORD, have poured out my anger on you.'

²³THIS word of the LORD came to me: ²⁴'O man, say to Jerusalem: You are like a land on which no rain has fallen, no shower has come in the time of my wrath. ²⁵The princes within her are like lions growling as they tear their prey. They devour the people, and seize their wealth and valuables; they make widows of many women within her. ²⁶Her priests give rulings which violate my law, and profane what is sacred to me. They do not distinguish between sacred and profane, and enforce no distinction between clean and unclean. They disregard my sabbaths, and I am dishonoured among them. ²⁷The city's leaders are like wolves tearing their prey, shedding blood and destroying people's lives to obtain ill-gotten gain. ²⁸Her prophets whitewash over the cracks, their vision is false and their divination a lie. They say, "This is the word of the Lord GOD," when the LORD has not spoken. ²⁹The common people resort to oppression and robbery; they ill-treat the unfortunate and the poor, they oppress the alien and deny him justice.

³⁰'I looked among them for a man who would build a barricade in the breach and withstand me, to avert the destruction of the land; but I found no such person. ³¹I poured out my wrath on them and utterly consumed them in my blazing anger. Thus I brought on them the punishment they had deserved. This is the word of the Lord GOD.'

23 This word of the LORD came to me: ²'O man, there were once two women, daughters of the same mother, ³who while they were still girls played the whore in Egypt. There they let their breasts be fondled and their virgin bosoms be pressed. ⁴The elder was named Oholah, her sister Oholibah. They became mine and gave birth to sons and daughters. Oholah is Samaria, Oholibah Jerusalem.

⁵'Though Oholah owed me obedience she played the whore and was infatuated with her Assyrian lovers, officers ⁶in blue, viceroys and governors, all of them handsome young men riding on horseback. ⁷She played the whore with all of them, the flower of Assyrian manhood; and because of her lust for all their idols she was defiled. ⁸She never gave up the ways she had learnt in Egypt, where men had lain with her while she was still young, had pressed her virgin bosom and overwhelmed her with their fornication. ⁹So I abandoned her to her lovers, the Assyrians, with whom she was infatuated. ¹⁰They ravished her, they took away her sons and daughters, and they put her to the sword. She became notorious among women, and judgement was executed on her.

¹¹'Oholibah, her sister, saw it, but she surpassed her sister in lust and outdid her in playing the whore. ¹²She too was infatuated with Assyrians, viceroys and governors, all handsome officers in full dress and riding on horseback. ¹³I saw that she too had let herself be defiled. Both had gone the same way, ¹⁴but she carried her fornication to greater lengths: she saw male figures carved on the

22:24 **on which . . . fallen:** *so Gk; Heb.* which has not been cleansed. 22:25 **The princes . . . are:** *so Gk; Heb.* The conspiracy of her prophets within her is.

23.1–49: Allegorical tale of two cities. Similar in literary form to ch. 16, but there the emphasis is on cultic infidelity, here on political instability. **1–3:** The *two women* are the two capital cities: Samaria standing for the Northern Kingdom Israel, and Jerusalem for the Southern Kingdom Judah. *Played the whore in Egypt* as *girls:* the ancestors of the two kingdoms descended into Egypt in search of food. The allegory suggests that their progeny, making use of Egypt's power and wealth (see Gen. chs. 40–50), fell into idolatry and were subsequently enslaved (Exod. 1.1–14). Such events set the pattern, allegorically, of the two women's adult life. **4:** *Oholah:* lit. "she who has a tent" (or: "her [own] tent"), that is, the Northern Kingdom; *Oholibah:* lit. "my tent [is] in her," is the Southern. "Tent" probably means the place of worship, Oholah having worship centers regarded as schismatic, e.g. Dan and Bethel (see 1 Kgs. 12.25–33), and Oholibah having the sanctuary in Jerusalem where the Ark was kept (2 Sam. 6.17). **5–10:** Because political alliances implied a lack of trust in God's power, the prophets considered reliance on them as playing the *whore.* God *abandoned* Samaria in 721 B.C.E., when it was destroyed by the Assyrians and its people were taken into captivity; see 2 Kgs. 17.5–6. **12:** Oholibah (Judah) was *infatuated* with *Assyrians,* when Ahaz, king of Judah (735–715 B.C.E.), courted their wall, sculptured forms of Chaldaeans picked out in vermilion, 15 with belts round their waists and flowing turbans on their heads. All had the appearance of high Babylonian officers, natives of Chaldaea. 16 When she set eyes on them she was infatuated, and sent messengers to Chaldaea for them. 17 The Babylonians came to her to share her bed, and defiled her with fornication; she was defiled by them until her love turned to revulsion. 18 When she made no secret that she was a whore and let herself be ravished, I recoiled with revulsion from her as I recoiled from her sister. 19 Remembering how in her youth she had played the whore in Egypt, she played the whore over and over again. 20 She was infatuated with their male prostitutes, whose members were like those of donkeys and whose seed came in floods like that of stallions. 21 So, Oholibah, you relived the lewdness of your girlhood in Egypt when you let your bosom be pressed and your breasts fondled.

22 'The Lord God has said: I shall rouse against you, Oholibah, those lovers of yours who have filled you with revulsion, and bring them against you from every side: 23 the Babylonians, all the Chaldaeans from Pekod, Shoa, and Koa, and with them all the Assyrians, handsome young men, viceroys and governors, commanders and officers, all on horseback. 24 They will advance against you with war-horses, with chariots and wagons, with a host drawn from the nations, armed with shield, buckler, and helmet; they will beset you on every side. I shall give them authority to judge, and they will use that authority to execute judgement on you. 25 I shall turn my jealous wrath against you, and they will bring their fury to bear on you. They will cut off your nose and ears, and those of you left will fall by the sword. They will take your sons and daughters, and those of you left will end in flames. 26 They will strip you of your clothes and take away your finery. 27 So I shall put a stop to your lewdness and the harlotry which you first learnt in Egypt. You will never cast longing eyes on such things again, never remember Egypt any more.

28 'The Lord God says: I am handing you over to those whom you hate, those who have filled you with revulsion; 29 and they will bring their fury to bear on you. They will take all you have earned and leave you stark naked; the body with which you have played the whore will be ravished. It is your lewdness and your fornication 30 that have brought this on you; it is because you adopted heathen ways, played the whore, and became defiled with idols. 31 As you have followed in your sister's footsteps, I shall put her cup into your hand.

32 'The Lord God says:

You will drink from your sister's cup,
a cup deep and wide,
charged to the very brim
with mockery and scorn.
33 It will be full of drunkenness and grief,
a cup of uttermost ruin,
the cup of your sister Samaria;
34 you will drink it to the dregs,
and then gnaw it into shreds
while you tear your breasts.

'This is my sentence, says the Lord God.

35 'The Lord God says: Because you have forsaken me and cast me behind your back, you will have to bear the guilt of your lewdness and fornication.'

36 The Lord said to me, 'O man, will you bring a charge against Oholah and Oholibah? Then tax them with their vile offences. 37 They have committed adultery, and there is blood on their hands. They have committed adultery with their idols and offered to them as food the children they had borne me. 38 Here is another thing they have done to me: they have polluted my sanctuary and desecrated my sabbaths. 39 They came into my sanctuary and desecrated it by slaughtering their sons as an offering to their idols; this they did in my house.

40 'Then also they would send for men from a far-off country, who would come at the messenger's bidding. For them you bathed your body, painted your eyes, decked yourself in your finery, 41 sat yourself on a splendid couch, and had a table placed before it on which you laid my incense and oil.

23:21 **fondled:** *prob. rdg; Heb. unintelligible.*
23:23 **officers:** *prob. rdg, cp. verses 5 and 12; Heb. obscure.*   23:25 **those . . . left:** *or* your successors.
23:38 **sanctuary:** *so Gk; Heb. adds* on that day.
23:39 **desecrated it:** *so Gk; Heb. adds* on that day.

favor (2 Kgs. 16.7–9). **32:** Samaria's fate (destruction of 721 B.C.E.) will be Jerusalem's *cup* in the destruction and captivity of 587 B.C.E. **40–44:** Unknown contemporary political events seem to be indicated. **42:** *Sabaeans:*

42 There was loud shouting from a carefree crowd. Besides ordinary folk, Sabaeans were there, brought in from the desert; they put bracelets on the harlots' arms and beautiful garlands on their heads. 43 I thought: Ah, that woman, grown old in adultery! Now they will commit fornication with her—her of all women! 44 They resorted to her as to a prostitute; they resorted to Oholah and Oholibah, those lewd women. 45 Upright men will condemn them for their adultery and bloodshed; they are adulterous, and have blood on their hands.

46 'The Lord GOD says: Bring up a mob to punish them; give them over to terror and pillage. 47 Let the mob stone them and hack them to pieces with their swords, kill their sons and daughters, and burn down their houses. 48 In this way I shall put an end to lewdness in the land, and all the women will take warning not to follow their lewd example. 49 When they punish you for your lewd conduct and you pay the penalty for your idolatries, you will know that I am the Lord GOD.'

The siege and capture of Jerusalem

24 THIS word of the LORD came to me on the tenth day of the tenth month in the ninth year: 2 'O man, write down as the name for this special day: This day the king of Babylon besieged Jerusalem. 3 Sing a song of derision to this body of rebels; say to them: These are the words of the Lord GOD:

Set a cauldron on the fire,
    set it on and pour in water.
4 Into it collect the pieces,
    every choice piece,
fill it with leg and shoulder, the best of
        the bones;
5 take the pick of the flock.
Pile the wood underneath;
    seethe the stew
and boil the bones in it.

6 'The Lord GOD says:

Woe betide the city running with blood,
    woe to the pot green with corrosion
    which will never come off!
Empty it, piece after piece,
    with no lot cast for any of them.
7 The city had blood in her midst
    and she poured it on the bare rock;
it was not shed on the ground
    for the dust to cover it.
8 I have spilt her blood on the bare rock
    so that it cannot be covered;
it will arouse anger
    and call out for vengeance.

9 'The Lord GOD says:

Woe betide the city running with blood!
    I myself shall make a great fire-pit.
10 Fill it with logs, kindle the fire;
    make an end of the meat,
    pour out all the broth and the bones
        with it.
11 Then set the pot empty on the coals
    so that its copper may be heated
        red-hot,
that the impurities in it may be melted
    and the corrosion burnt off.
12 Though you exhaust yourself with your
        efforts
    the corrosion is so deep it will not come
        off;
    only fire will rid it of corrosion.
13 When in your filthy lewdness I wished
        to cleanse you,
    you did not become clean,
    nor will you ever be clean again

23:43 her of all women: lit. and her.   23:44 They resorted to her: so one MS; others He resorted to her. 23:48 their: so Gk; Heb. your.   24:5 wood: prob. rdg, cp. verse 10; Heb. bones.   24:10 pour ... broth: prob. rdg; Heb. mix ointment. with it: prob. rdg; Heb. will be scorched.   24:12 Though... efforts: prob. rdg; Heb. obscure.

inhabitants of Sheba, a land of traders in the southwest corner of the Arabian peninsula, probably modern Yemen.

24.1–27: Jerusalem is besieged: Verses 1–14 are an elaboration and interpretation of 11.3–13. **1:** The date is probably January 15, 588 B.C.E.; compare 2 Kgs. 25.1. **3–5:** Into the *cauldron* (Jerusalem) is collected *every choice piece* (the nobility); the Babylonians apply the *fire* (siege), thus fulfilling in a tragic sense the optimistic allegory of 11.3. **6:** Their expected security destroyed, the nobles will be taken out *piece after piece* indiscriminately because the cauldron is full of *corrosion*. **7:** *Blood,* the source of life, and thus somehow divine, is to be covered by *dust* and forbidden to human contact. See Gen. 9.4–6; Lev. 17.13–14. Blood *poured on bare* until I have spent my anger against you.

¹⁴'I, the LORD, have spoken: The time is coming and I shall act. I shall not condone or pity or relent. You will be judged by your conduct and by what you have done. This is the word of the Lord GOD.'

¹⁵THIS word of the LORD came to me: ¹⁶'O man, I am taking from you at one stroke the dearest thing you have, but you are not to wail or weep or give way to tears. ¹⁷Suppress your grief, and observe no mourning for the dead. Wrap your turban on your head and put on your sandals. You are not to veil your beard in mourning or eat the bread of sorrow.'

¹⁸I spoke to the people in the morning. That evening my wife died, and next morning I did as I had been commanded. ¹⁹The people asked me what meaning my actions had for them. ²⁰I answered, 'This word of the LORD came to me: ²¹Tell the Israelites: The Lord GOD has said: I am about to desecrate my sanctuary, which has been your strong boast, the delight of your eyes, and your heart's desire, and the sons and daughters you have left behind will fall by the sword. ²²You are to do as I have done,' I said: 'you are not to cover your beard in mourning or eat the bread of sorrow. ²³Your turbans are to be on your heads and your sandals on your feet; you are not to wail or weep. Because of your wickedness you will pine away, groaning to each other. ²⁴Ezekiel will be a sign to warn you, says the LORD, and you are to do as he has done. When judgement befalls you, you will know that I am the Lord GOD.'

²⁵'Now, O man, I am taking from them at that time the stronghold whose beauty so gladdened them, the delight of their eyes, their heart's desire, and I am taking their sons and daughters. ²⁶When a fugitive then comes and brings the news to you, ²⁷you will recover the power of speech and, no longer dumb, you will speak with the fugitive. So you will be a warning to the people, and they will know that I am the LORD.'

Prophecies against foreign nations

25 THIS word of the LORD came to me: ²'O man, face towards the Ammonites and prophesy against them. ³Say this to them: Listen to the word of the Lord GOD. He says: Because you cried "Hurrah!" when my holy place was desecrated, when Israel's land was laid waste, and the people of Judah sent into exile, ⁴I am giving you into the possession of tribes from the east. They will pitch their tents and establish their camps among you; they will eat your crops and drink your milk. ⁵I shall turn Rabbah into a camel pasture and Ammon into a sheep-walk. Thus you will know that I am the LORD.

⁶'These are the words of the Lord GOD: Because you clapped your hands and stamped your feet and exulted over the land of Israel with spiteful contempt, ⁷I shall stretch out my hand over you and give you up to be plundered by the nations. I shall cut you off from other peoples, destroy you in every land, and bring you to ruin. Thus you will know that I am the LORD.

⁸'The Lord GOD says: Because Moab said, "Judah is like all other nations," ⁹I shall ex-

25:8 **Moab:** *so Gk; Heb. adds* and Seir.

rock shows flagrant disregard for life and its divine origin. **15–24:** Ezekiel, at the double tragedy of his wife's death and the impending destruction of the temple, is so numbed by grief that he cannot perform the ordinary rituals of mourning (v. 17) so important in the Near East. **26:** *When:* lit. "on the very day." The implication that fugitives could arrive so quickly again raises the question of where Ezekiel was preaching, in Babylon or in Palestine. See Introduction.

25.1–32.32: Judgment passed against enemy nations. The sin of the nations is twofold: the arrogance of powerful nations like Egypt, Tyre, and Babylon that exalt themselves at the expense of God; and the meanness of Israel's weak neighbors, Edom and Moab, that exalt themselves by preying on God's people. The first act in the restoration of Israel is the judgment passed upon the nations. See 36.7.

25.1–17: Oracles against Israel's neighbors. Apparently written after the destruction of Jerusalem, these oracles are cast in the form of a lawsuit against the nations, i.e. an indictment and a sentence: "because . . . therefore." **1–7:** *Ammonites:* people inhabiting the east side of the Jordan just north of the Dead Sea. Partners with Judah in the conspiracy against Nebuchadnezzar, they *exulted over* their prostrate ally. **4:** *Tribes from the east* are nomadic Arabs. **8–11:** *Moab:* directly south of Ammon and east of the Dead Sea. Most of its cities pose the flank of Moab and from one end to the other lay open its towns, the glory of the land: Beth-jeshimoth, Baal-meon, and Kiriathaim. ¹⁰ I shall give Moab and Ammon into the possession of tribes from the east, so that all memory of the Ammonites will be blotted out among the nations, ¹¹ and so that I may execute judgement upon Moab. Thus they will know that I am the LORD.

¹² 'The Lord GOD says: Because Edom exacted harsh revenge on Judah and by so doing incurred lasting guilt, ¹³ I shall stretch my hand out over Edom, says the Lord GOD, and destroy both people and animals in it, laying waste the land from Teman as far as Dedan; they will fall by the sword. ¹⁴ I shall wreak my vengeance on Edom through my people Israel. They will deal with Edom as my anger and fury demand, and it will feel my vengeance. This is the word of the Lord GOD.

¹⁵ 'The Lord GOD says: Because the Philistines have resorted to revenge, avenging themselves with spiteful contempt, and destroying to satisfy an age-long enmity, ¹⁶ I shall stretch out my hand over the Philistines, says the Lord GOD. I shall wipe out the Kerethites and destroy the other dwellers by the sea. ¹⁷ I shall take mighty vengeance upon them and punish them in my fury. When I exact my vengeance, they will know that I am the LORD.'

26 This word of the LORD came to me on the first day of the first month in the eleventh year: ² 'O man, since Tyre has said of Jerusalem,

"Aha! She who was the gateway of the nations is broken,
her gates lie open before me;
I prosper, she lies in ruin,"

³ the Lord GOD says:

I am against you, Tyre!
As the sea raises up its waves,
so shall I raise up many nations against you.
⁴ They will destroy the walls of Tyre
and overthrow her towers.
I shall scrape the soil off her
and leave her only bare rock;
⁵ she will be an island
where nets are spread to dry.
This is my word, says the Lord GOD.
She will become the prey of nations,
⁶ and her daughters on the mainland will be slain.
Then they will know that I am the LORD.

⁷ 'The Lord GOD says: From the north I am bringing against Tyre King Nebuchadrezzar of Babylon, king of kings. He will come with horses and chariots, cavalry, and a great force of infantry.

⁸ 'He will put to the sword
your daughters on the mainland.
He will set up siege-towers
and cast up siege-ramps against you,
and raise a screen of shields facing you.
⁹ He will launch his battering-rams on your walls
and break down your towers with his axes.
¹⁰ Dust will cover you
from his innumerable cavalry.
At the thunder of the horses
and of the chariot wheels
your walls will shake
when he enters your gates
as though entering a city that is breached.

26:1 **first month:** *so Gk; Heb. omits* first.

were situated on the *flank of Moab,* the steep but rounded eastern shore of that sea. **12–14:** Inhabiting the region south of the Dead Sea before the destruction of Jerusalem, *Edom* profited from Judah's tragedy by occupying the southern half of her territory. For traditional hostility between Judah and Edom see Gen. 27.41; 36.6–8. *Teman . . . Dedan:* Edomite cities to the southeast of the Dead Sea. **15–17:** The *Philistines* and a related group called *Kerethites* (both living on the Mediterranean coast, though by then greatly diminished) also plundered prostrate Judah.

26.1–21: Tyre will be swept from the sea. Tyre, an ancient Phoenician port (in modern Lebanon) was the heart of a commercial and cultural empire. Its traditional friendship with Israel (1 Kgs. ch. 5) wins it a fate less harsh. **1:** *Eleventh year:* approximately April 22, 587 B.C.E. **2:** Caravans to Tyre from Mesopotamia, Arabia, and Egypt had to pay duty to use Israelite territory as a *gateway.* **3:** Tyre, built on an island a half mile from shore, will be overrun by *nations,* just as it is washed by the *sea waves* in a storm. **8:** A *screen* of *shields:* probably

11 All your streets will be trampled
    by the hoofs of his horses.
He will put your people to the sword,
    and bring your strong pillars to the
        ground.
12 Your wealth will become spoil,
    your merchandise will be plundered.
Your walls will be levelled,
    and your fine houses pulled down;
the stones, timber, and rubble
    will be dumped in the sea.
13 I shall silence the chorus of your songs,
    and the sound of your harps will be
        heard no more.
14 I shall make you a bare rock,
    a place where nets are spread to dry.
You will never be rebuilt.

'I, the LORD, have spoken. This is the word
of the Lord GOD.

15 'THE Lord GOD says to Tyre: How the
coasts and islands will shake at the sound of
your downfall, while the wounded groan and
slaughter prevails in your midst! 16 Then the
sea-kings will descend from their thrones, lay
aside their cloaks, and strip off their bro-
caded robes. They will put on loincloths and
sit on the ground, shuddering incessantly,
aghast at your fate. 17 They will raise this
dirge over you:

    "How you are undone, swept from the
        seas,
you city of renown!
You whose strength lay in the sea,
you and your inhabitants,
who spread your terror throughout the
        world.
18 Now the coastlands shudder
    on the day of your downfall,
and the isles are appalled at your
        passing."

19 'For the Lord GOD says: When I make you
a desolate city, like cities where no one lives,
when I bring the primeval ocean up over you
and the great waters cover you, 20 I shall
thrust you down with those who go down to

the abyss, to the dead of all the ages; I shall
make you dwell in the underworld as in
places long desolate, with those that go down
to the abyss. So you will never again be inhabited or take your place in the land of the
living. 21 I shall bring destruction on you, and
you will be no more; people may look for you
but will never find you again. This is the
word of the Lord GOD.'

27 This word of the LORD came to me:
2 'O man, raise a dirge over Tyre
3 and say to her who is enthroned at the gateway to the sea, who carries the trade of the
nations to many coasts and islands: These are
the words of the Lord GOD:

Tyre, you declared,
    "I am perfect in beauty."
4 Your frontiers were on the high seas,
    your builders made your beauty
        perfect;
5 they used pine from Senir
    to fashion all your ribs;
they took a cedar from Lebanon
    to set up a mast for you.
6 They made your oars of oaks from
        Bashan;
for your deck they used cypress
    from the coasts of Kittim.
7 Your canvas was linen,
    patterned linen from Egypt
to serve you for sails;
    your awnings were violet and purple
    from the coasts of Elishah.
8 Men from Sidon and Arvad served as
        your oarsmen;
you had skilled men among you, Tyre,
    acting as your helmsmen.
9 You had skilled veterans from Gebal
    to caulk your seams.

'Every fully manned seagoing ship
    visited your harbour
    to traffic in your wares;
10 Persia, Lydia, and Put

26:14 **You will:** *so Gk; Heb.* She will.   26:17 **swept:**
so Gk; Heb. inhabited.   26:20 **or . . . place:** *so Gk;
Heb.* I shall give beauty.   27:6 **used:** *prob. rdg; Heb.*
adds ivory.

an offensive military technique. **14:** Tyre was not *rebuilt* after its destruction by Alexander in 332 B.C.E. **20:**
Abyss: Sheol, the place of the dead; see 31.15–18.

    27.1–28.19: Dirge over Tyre. The lament is in traditional dirge meter called the *qinah.* Tyre is like a stately
ship, carrying an expert crew, rich passengers and rare cargo, that founders. **5:** *Senir:* Mount Hermon near
Damascus. **6:** *Bashan:* plateau east of the Sea of Galilee mentioned for its oaks in Isa. 2.13. *Kittim:* Cyprus.
10–24: This section, in which the metaphor shifts from a ship to a fortified city and the language from poetry

supplied mercenaries for your army;
they arrayed shield and helmet in you,
and it was they who gave you your
    splendour.
¹¹ Men of Arvad and Cilicia manned your
    walls on every side,
men of Gammad were posted on your
    towers;
they arrayed their bucklers around
    your battlements,
making your beauty perfect.

¹² 'Tarshish was a source of your commerce,
from its abundant resources offering silver,
iron, tin, and lead as your staple wares. ¹³ Javan, Tubal, and Meshech dealt with you, offering slaves and bronze utensils as your
imports. ¹⁴ Men from Togarmah offered
horses, cavalry steeds, and mules as your
wares. ¹⁵ Rhodians dealt with you; many islands were a source of your commerce, paying their dues to you in ivory tusks and
ebony. ¹⁶ Edom was a source of your commerce, so many were your undertakings, and
offered purple garnets, brocade and fine
linen, black coral and red jasper, for your
wares. ¹⁷ Judah and Israel traded with you,
offering wheat from Minnith, and meal,
grape-syrup, oil, and balm as your imports.
¹⁸ Damascus was a source of your commerce,
so many were your undertakings, from its
abundant resources offering Helbon wine
and Suhar wool, ¹⁹ and casks of wine from
Izalla, in exchange for your wares; wrought
iron, cassia, and sweet cane were among your
imports. ²⁰ Dedan traded with you in coarse
woollens for saddle-cloths. ²¹ Arabia and all
the rulers of Kedar traded with you; they
were the source of your commerce in lambs,
rams, and goats. ²² Merchants from Sheba
and Raamah traded with you, offering all the
choicest spices, every kind of precious stone,
and gold as your wares. ²³ Harran, Kanneh,
and Eden, merchants from Asshur and all
Media, traded with you; ²⁴ they were your
dealers in choice stuffs: violet cloths and bro-
cades, in stores of coloured fabric rolled up
and tied with cords.

²⁵ 'Ships of Tarshish were the caravans
    for your imports;
you were deeply laden with full cargoes
    on the high seas.

²⁶ Your oarsmen brought you into many
    waters,
but an east wind wrecked you on the
    high seas.
²⁷ Your wealth, your wares, your imports,
your sailors and your helmsmen,
your caulkers, your merchants, and all
    your warriors,
all who were in the ship with you
were flung into the sea when it sank.
²⁸ Amid the cries of your helmsmen
the troubled waters tossed.
²⁹ When rowers disembark from their
    ships,
when sailors and the helmsmen, all
    together, go ashore,
³⁰ they mourn aloud over your fate
and cry out bitterly;
they throw dust on their heads
and sprinkle themselves with ashes.
³¹ At your plight they cut off their hair
and put on sackcloth;
they weep bitterly over you
with most bitter wailing.
³² In their lamentation they raise a dirge
and bewail you, saying:
"Who was like Tyre,
set in the midst of the sea?
³³ When your wares were unloaded off
    the seas
you met the needs of many nations;
with your vast resources and your
    imports
you enriched the kings of the earth.
³⁴ Now you are wrecked at sea,
sunk in deep water;
your wares and all your crew have gone
    down with you.
³⁵ All who dwell on the coasts and islands
are aghast at your fate;
horror is written on the faces of their
    kings
and their hair stands on end.
³⁶ Among the nations the merchants gasp
    at the sight of you;
destruction has come on you, and you
    shall be no more." '

27:13 **Javan:** *or* Greece.   27:15 **Rhodians:** *so Gk;*
Heb. Dedanites.   27:19 **casks . . . Izalla:** *prob. rdg;*
Heb. obscure.   27:23 **merchants from:** *so Gk; Heb.*
adds Sheba. **all Media:** *prob. rdg, cp. Aram. (Targ.); Heb.*
Kilmad.   27:32 **set:** *prob. rdg; Heb. obscure.*

to prose, is possibly an interpolation. **26:** The *east wind,* death-dealing on sea (Ps. 48.7) and land (Jer. 18.17)

28

This word of the LORD came to me: ²'O man, say to the ruler of Tyre: This is what the Lord GOD says:

In your arrogance you say,
"I am a god;
I sit enthroned like a god on the high
　seas."
Though you are a man and no god,
you give yourself godlike airs.
³What, are you wiser than Daniel?
Is no secret beyond your grasp?
⁴By your skill and shrewdness
you have amassed wealth,
gold and silver in your treasuries.
⁵By great skill in commerce
you have heaped up riches,
and with your riches your arrogance
　has grown.

⁶'The Lord GOD says:

Because you give yourself godlike airs,
⁷I am about to bring foreigners against
　you,
the most ruthless of nations;
they will draw their swords against your
　fine wisdom
and defile your splendour;
⁸they will thrust you down to
　destruction,
to a violent death on the high seas.
⁹When you face your attackers,
will you still say, "I am a god"?
You are a man and no god
in the hands of those who lay you low.
¹⁰You will die the death of the
　uncircumcised
at the hands of foreigners.

'I have spoken. This is the word of the Lord GOD.'

¹¹THIS word of the LORD came to me: ¹²'O man, raise this dirge over the king of Tyre,

and say to him: This is what the Lord GOD says:

You set the seal on perfection;
you were full of wisdom and flawless in
　beauty.
¹³In an Eden, a garden of God, you
　dwelt,
adorned with gems of every kind:
sardin and chrysolite and jade,
topaz, cornelian, and green jasper,
sapphire, purple garnet, and green
　feldspar.
Your jingling beads were of gold,
and the spangles you wore were made
　for you
on the day of your birth.
¹⁴I appointed a towering cherub as your
　guardian;
you were on God's holy mountain
and you walked proudly among stones
　of fire.
¹⁵You were blameless in your ways
from the day of your birth
until iniquity came to light in you.
¹⁶Your commerce grew so great
that lawlessness filled your heart
and led to wrongdoing.
I brought you down in disgrace
from the mountain of God,
and the guardian cherub banished you
from among the stones that flashed like
　fire.
¹⁷Your beauty made you arrogant;
you debased your wisdom to enhance
　your splendour.
I flung you to the ground,
I left you exposed to the gaze of kings.
¹⁸So great was the sin in your dishonest
　trading
that you desecrated your sanctuaries.
I kindled a fire within you,
and it devoured you.
I reduced you to ashes on the ground
for everyone to see.

alike, probably symbolizes Nebuchadnezzar, as in 17.10. **28.1–3:** Blinded by *arrogance,* the city scorned its national hero *Daniel,* who, a model of true wisdom (14.14 n.), had placed his sagacity at the service of the gods, of widows and orphans. **4–10:** Although it has *amassed wealth* for its own glorification and thinks its power and *wisdom* as unlimited as a god's, Tyre will suffer the fate of an ordinary mortal. **11–19:** Though Tyre had enjoyed familiarity with God, it scorned such honor in favor of its own *splendour,* achieved by *dishonest trading.* Some interpreters see in the passage allusions to unknown creation myths; others, an allegory on Tyre's ancient and long-standing alliance with Israel (1 Kgs. 5.1–18), ended when the high priest Jehoiada cast Queen Athaliah — daughter of the Tyrian princess Jezebel — out of the temple. See 2 Kgs. 11.13–16. Cut off from God's people, Tyre's doom was sealed.

¹⁹Among the nations all who knew you
were aghast:
destruction has come on you, and you
will be no more.'

²⁰This word of the LORD came to me: ²¹'O
man, face towards Sidon and prophesy
against her. ²²The Lord GOD says:

Sidon, I am against you
and I shall show my glory in your
midst.

'People will know that I am the LORD
when I execute judgement on her
and show my holiness in her.
²³I shall let loose pestilence on her
and bloodshed in her streets;
beset on all sides by the sword
the slain will fall within her walls.
Then people will know that I am the
LORD.

²⁴'No longer will the Israelites suffer from
the scorn of their neighbours, the pricking of
briars and scratching of thorns, and they will
know that I am the Lord GOD.
²⁵'The Lord GOD says: When I gather the
Israelites from the peoples among whom they
are dispersed, I shall show my holiness in
them for all the nations to see. They will live
on their own soil, which I gave to my servant
Jacob. ²⁶They will live there undisturbed,
build houses, and plant vineyards. When I
execute judgement on all their scornful neighbours, they will live undisturbed. Thus they
will know that I am the LORD their God.'

29 THIS word of the LORD came to me
on the twelfth day of the tenth month
in the tenth year: ²'O man, face towards

Pharaoh king of Egypt and prophesy against
him and the whole of Egypt. ³Say to them:
The Lord GOD says:

I am against you,
Pharaoh king of Egypt,
you great monster,
lurking in the streams of the Nile.
You have said, "My Nile is my own;
it was I who made it."
⁴But I shall put hooks in your jaws
and they will cling to your scales.
I shall haul you up out of its streams
with all its fish clinging to your scales.
⁵I shall fling you into the desert,
you and all the fish in your streams;
you will fall on the ground
with none to give you burial;
I shall give you as food
to beasts and birds.
⁶Then all who live in Egypt will know
that I am the LORD.
The support you gave the Israelites
was no better than a reed.
⁷When they grasped you, you splintered
in their hands
and tore their armpits;
when they leaned on you, you broke
and their limbs gave way.

⁸'The Lord GOD says: I am bringing a sword
on you to destroy both people and animals.
⁹Egypt will become a desolate waste land,
and they will know that I am the LORD. Because you said, "The Nile is mine; it was I
who made it," ¹⁰I am against you and your
Nile. I shall make Egypt desolate, wasted by
drought, from Migdol to Syene and as far as

29:3 **it was . . . it:** *so Syriac, cp. verse 9; Heb.* I even
made myself.   29:4 **they will cling:** *prob. rdg; Heb.*
make the fish of your streams cling.   29:6 **you:** *so
Gk; Heb.* they.   29:9 **you:** *so Gk; Heb.* he.

28.20–24: Sidon denounced. Sidon, a Phoenician city north of Tyre, merits punishment as an accomplice
in the fatal rebellion against Babylon; see Jer. 27.3.
28.25–26: Israel, restored, will experience God's holiness, and will witness it to the nations.
29.1–32.32: Egypt shall become a desolate waste. From Israel's beginning as a nation, Egypt either oppressed it like a slave master or abused it by fickle alliances; see 29.6–7. The reed conveys the latter idea for
it was abundant in the Nile and hence a symbol of Egypt. It promised support, but would break and pierce
the hand.
29.1–9: Oracle against Pharaoh, the monster and reed of the Nile. 1: January 7, 587 B.C.E. **3:** *Streams of
the Nile:* the Nile's several mouths in the delta. *Great monster:* the crocodile. **4:** *Clinging fish:* the dependent
nations. **6–7:** The *support no better than a reed* given to the *Israelites* may reflect Pharaoh Hophra's failure
to drive the Babylonians from Palestine, a little less than a year before this oracle. See Jer. 34.21–22; 37.1–10.
29.10–16: Israelites will never trust Egypt again. When finally converted, Israel will have a "new heart"

the frontier of Cush. ¹¹ Untrodden by people or animals, it will lie uninhabited for forty years. ¹² I shall make Egypt the most desolate of desolate lands, her cities the most derelict of derelict cities. For forty years they will lie derelict, and I shall scatter the Egyptians among the nations, dispersing them throughout the earth.

¹³ 'The Lord GOD says: At the end of forty years I shall gather the Egyptians from the peoples among whom they are scattered. ¹⁴ I shall restore the fortunes of Egypt and bring her people back to Pathros, the land of their origin, where they will be a petty kingdom. ¹⁵ It will become the most paltry of kingdoms and never again lord it over the nations, for I shall make the Egyptians too few to rule over them. ¹⁶ The Israelites, always mindful of their sin in turning to Egypt for help, will never trust Egypt again. They will know that I am the Lord GOD.'

¹⁷ This word of the LORD came to me on the first day of the first month in the twenty-seventh year: ¹⁸ 'O man, King Nebuchadrezzar of Babylon kept his army in the field against Tyre so long that everyone's head was rubbed bare and everyone's shoulder chafed. But no gain from Tyre accrued to him or to his army from their campaign. ¹⁹ This, therefore, is the word of the Lord GOD: I am now giving Egypt to King Nebuchadrezzar of Babylon. He will carry off its wealth, he will despoil and plunder it, and so his army will receive their wages. ²⁰ I have given him Egypt in payment for his service because they have spurned my authority. This is the word of the Lord GOD.

²¹ 'At that time I shall make Israel renew her strength, and give you back the power to speak among them, and they will know that I am the LORD.'

30 This word of the LORD came to me: ² 'O man, prophesy and say: The Lord GOD says:

Wail! Alas for the day!
³ A day is near,
a day of the LORD is near,
a day of cloud, a day of reckoning for
the nations!
⁴ A sword will come on Egypt,
and there will be anguish in Cush,
when the slain fall in Egypt,
when her wealth is seized,
her foundations are demolished.
⁵ Cush and Put and Lydia,
all the Arabs, Libyans, and peoples of
allied lands
will fall by the sword along with Egypt.

⁶ 'The LORD says:

Those who support Egypt will fall
and her boasted might will be brought
low;
from Migdol to Syene they will fall by
the sword.

This is the word of the Lord GOD.

⁷ 'They will be the most desolate of desolate lands, their cities the most derelict of derelict cities. ⁸ When I set Egypt on fire and all her helpers are shattered, they will know that I am the LORD. ⁹ When that day comes messengers will go out in ships from my presence to strike terror into Cush, still undisturbed, and anguish shall come on her in Egypt's hour. Now it is near.

¹⁰ 'The Lord GOD says:

I shall make an end of Egypt's hordes
at the hand of King Nebuchadrezzar of
Babylon.
¹¹ He and his people with him, the most
ruthless of nations,
will be brought to ravage the land.

30:5 **Libyans:** *so Gk; Heb.* Kub.   30:7 **their:** *prob. rdg, cp. Gk; Heb.* his.

and a "new spirit" from the LORD; it will then depend entirely on him. **10:** *Migdol:* at the northern boundary of Egypt. *Syene:* modern Aswan on the southern frontiers, near *Cush,* i.e. Ethiopia. **12:** *Forty years:* a round number.

29.17–21: Egypt as payment for Nebuchadrezzar. 17: The latest date for any oracle is April 26, 571 B.C.E. This date is also the latest secure one in the book. Since other oracles with earlier dates will follow, this one is placed here because its topic is the same as that of the preceding. **20:** In humbling Tyre, Nebuchadrezzar carries out God's purposes in history, and so deserves *payment.*

30.1–19: Day of the LORD for Egypt is near. 3: In the early prophetic writings, the *day* or the *day of the LORD* is the time of God's future decisive judgment which will bring doom either for Israel (Amos 5.18–20) or for the nations (Isa. 2.12). Later it represented the vindication of Israel against the nations (Joel 3.1–3).

They will draw their swords against
   Egypt
and fill the land with the slain.
[12] I shall turn the streams of the Nile into
   dry land
and sell Egypt into the power of evil
   men.

'By the hands of foreigners I shall lay waste
the land and everything in it. I, the LORD,
have spoken.
   [13] 'The Lord GOD says:

I shall make an end of the petty rulers
and wipe out the chieftains of Noph;
never again will a prince arise in Egypt.
I shall instil terror into that land:
[14] I shall lay Pathros waste and set fire to
   Zoan
and execute judgement on No.
[15] I shall vent my wrath on Sin,
   the bastion of Egypt,
and destroy the hordes of Noph.
[16] I shall set Egypt on fire,
and Syene will writhe in anguish;
the walls of No will be breached
and floodwaters will burst into it.
[17] The young men of On and Pi-beseth
   will fall by the sword
and the cities themselves will go into
   captivity.
[18] Daylight will fail in Tahpanhes
when I break the power of Egypt there;
there her boasted might will be brought
   to an end.
A cloud will cover her,
and her daughters will go into captivity.
[19] I shall execute judgement on Egypt,
and they will know that I am the LORD.'

[20] This word of the LORD came to me on the
seventh day of the first month in the eleventh
year: [21] 'O man, I have broken the arm of
Pharaoh king of Egypt, and it has not been
bound up with dressings or bandaged to
make it strong enough to wield a sword.
[22] The Lord GOD says: I am against Pharaoh
king of Egypt; I shall break both his arms, the
sound and the broken, and make the sword
fall from his hand. [23] I shall scatter the Egyp-

tians among the nations and disperse them
throughout the earth. [24] I shall strengthen
the arms of the king of Babylon and put my
sword in his hand; I shall break Pharaoh's
arms, and he will lie wounded and groaning
before him. [25] I shall give strength to the arms
of the king of Babylon, but Pharaoh's arms
will fall. All will know that I am the LORD,
when I put my sword into the hand of the
king of Babylon, and he stretches it out over
the land of Egypt. [26] I shall scatter the Egyptians among the nations and disperse them
throughout the earth, and they will know
that I am the LORD.'

31 On the first day of the third month in
the eleventh year this word of the
LORD came to me: [2] 'O man, say to Pharaoh
king of Egypt and to his hordes:

In your greatness, what are you like?
[3] Look at Assyria: it was a cedar in
   Lebanon,
towering high with its crown pushing
   through the foliage
and its fair branches overshadowing the
   forest.
[4] Springs nourished it, the underground
   waters made it lofty,
their streams washed the soil all round
   it
and sent channels of water to every tree
   in the country.
[5] So it grew taller than every other tree.
Its boughs were many, its branches
   far-spreading;
for water was abundant in the channels.
[6] In its boughs all the birds of the air
   had their nests,
under its branches all wild creatures
   bore their young,
and in its shade all great nations made
   their home.
[7] A splendid, great tree it was, with its
   far-spreading boughs,
for its roots were beside abundant
   waters.
[8] No cedar in God's garden eclipsed it,

30:15 **Noph:** *so Gk; Heb.* No.   30:16 **Syene:** *so Gk;*
Heb. Sin. **floodwaters . . . it:** *prob. rdg, cp. Gk; Heb.*
obscure.

30.20–26: The sword drops from Pharaoh's arm. 20: April 29, 587 B.C.E. **21:** Pharaoh's *sword arm* was
broken the year before when he was compelled to abandon his effort to lift the siege of Jerusalem. See 29.6–7 n.
22: *Both his arms* will be broken when Egypt will sink to complete military insignificance. This happened
following its conquest by Cambyses in 525 B.C.E.

no juniper could compare with its
  boughs,
and no plane tree had such
  branches;
not a tree in God's garden
  could rival its beauty.
  9 I, the LORD, made it beautiful
  with its mass of spreading boughs,
  the envy of every tree in Eden,
  the garden of God.

10 'The Lord GOD says: Because it grew so
high, raising its crown through the foliage,
and its pride mounted as it grew, 11 I handed
it over to a prince of the nations to deal with
it; I made an example of it as its wickedness
deserved. 12 Foreigners, the most ruthless of
nations, cut it down and left it lying. Its
sweeping boughs fell on the mountains and
in all the valleys, and its branches lay broken
beside every water-channel on earth. All the
peoples of the earth came out from under its
shade and left it. 13 On its fallen trunk the
birds all settled, the wild creatures all sought
shelter among its branches. 14 Never again
will the well-watered trees grow so high or
push their crowns up through the foliage.
Nor will the strongest of them, though well-
watered, attain their full height; for all have
been given over to death, to the world below,
to share the fate of mortals and go down to
the abyss.

15 'The Lord GOD says: When he went
down to Sheol, I dried up the deep, I
dammed its rivers, the great waters were held
back. I brought mourning on Lebanon for
him, and all the trees of the countryside
wilted. 16 I made nations shake at the sound
of his downfall, when I brought him down to
Sheol with those who go down to the abyss.
From this all the trees of Eden, the choicest
and best of Lebanon, all the well-watered
trees, drew comfort in the world below.

17 They too like him had gone down to Sheol,
to those slain by the sword, and those among
the nations who had lived in his shade.
  18 'Which among the trees of Eden was like
you in glory and greatness? Yet you will be
brought down with the trees of Eden to the
world below; you will lie with those who have
been slain by the sword, in the company of
the uncircumcised dead. So it will be with
Pharaoh and all his hordes. This is the word
of the Lord GOD.'

32 On the first day of the twelfth month
in the twelfth year this word of the
LORD came to me: 2 'O man, raise a dirge over
Pharaoh king of Egypt and say to him:

Young lion of the nations, your end has
  come.
You were like a monster in the waters
  of the Nile
scattering the water with its snout,
churning up the water with its feet
and muddying the streams.

3 'The Lord GOD says: When many nations
are assembled I shall spread my net over you,
and you will be hauled ashore in its meshes.
4 I shall fling you on land, dashing you on the
ground. I shall let all the birds of the air settle
upon you and all the wild beasts gorge themselves on you. 5 I shall leave your carcass on
the mountains, and fill the valleys with the
worms that feed on it. 6 I shall drench the
land with your blood as it pours out on the
mountains, and the ravines will be filled with
it. 7 When your light is quenched I shall veil
the sky and darken its stars; I shall veil the
sun with clouds, and the moon will give no
light. 8 I shall darken all the shining lights of
the sky above you and bring darkness over

31:10 **Because it grew:** *so Syriac; Heb.* Because you
grew.   31:15 **Sheol:** *or* the underworld.
32:2 **snout:** *prob. rdg; Heb.* streams.

31.1–18: Egypt, proud cedar of Lebanon, will be hewed down like Assyria. 8: Many commentators see in
God's garden a reference to a mythological earthly paradise; others, a symbol of God's care (Isa. 51.3) for the
nations in endowing them with material resources. **12:** Assyria's far-reaching administration broke down like
sweeping branches when the trunk is cut; so too will Egypt's. **15:** When Egypt *went down to Sheol* all the
dependent nations shook and *wilted*. **18:** *Slain by the sword:* those who suffered an untimely death.

32.1–32: A dirge over Egypt. This final prophecy against Egypt contains two oracles: vv. 1–16, a continuation of the monster allegory of ch. 29, and vv. 17–32, a dirge on the descent into Sheol of Pharaoh and his
hordes to join the company of the dishonored dead. **1:** March 3, 585 B.C.E. **2:** *Muddying the streams:* doing
violence to other nations by its violence. **3–4:** The monster Egypt will be *hauled* out of the Nile onto the *ground,*
to be seen and despoiled by the nations, called here *beasts* that *gorge* themselves on carrion. **5:** To leave the
flesh of the dead unburied was a great curse for the ancients. **7:** These phenomena suggest the judgment of

your land. This is the word of the Lord GOD.

9 'I shall cause disquiet to many peoples when I bring your broken army among the nations, into lands you have never known. 10 I shall appal many peoples with your fate; when I brandish my sword in the presence of their kings, their hair will stand on end. On the day of your downfall not a moment will pass without each trembling for his own fate. 11 For the Lord GOD has said: The king of Babylon's sword will come upon you. 12 I shall make your hordes of people fall by the sword of warriors who are of all men the most ruthless. They will shatter the pride of Egypt, and all her hordes will be wiped out. 13 I shall destroy all their cattle beside abundant waters. No foot or hoof will ever churn them up again. 14 Then I shall let their waters settle and their streams glide smooth as oil. This is the word of the Lord GOD. 15 When I have laid Egypt waste, and the whole land lies empty, when I strike down all who live there, they will know that I am the LORD.

16 'The women of the nations will raise this dirge, singing it as a dirge over Egypt and all her hordes. This is the word of the Lord GOD.'

17 On the fifteenth day of the first month in the twelfth year, this word of the LORD came to me:

18 'O man, raise a lament, you and the
    daughters of the nations,
  over Egypt's hordes and her nobility.
I shall consign them to the world
    below,
in company with those who go down to
    the abyss.
19 Are you better favoured than others?
Go down and lie with the
    uncircumcised dead.

20 'A sword is drawn. Those who marched with her, together with all her hordes, will descend into the company of those slain by the sword. 21 Warrior chieftains in Sheol speak to Pharaoh and his allies.

' "The uncircumcised dead, slain by the sword, have come down and lie there. 22 Assyria is there with all her company buried around her, all of them slain, victims of the sword. 23 Their graves are set in the farthest depths of the abyss, with her slain buried round about her, all victims of the sword, who once spread terror in the land of the living. 24 Elam is there with all her people buried around her, all of them slain, victims of the sword. They have gone down uncircumcised to the world below, who spread terror in the land of the living, but now bear disgrace with those who go down to the abyss. 25 A bed has been made for her in the midst of the slain. All her peoples are buried around her, all of them uncircumcised, victims of the sword. Those, who once spread terror in the land of the living, now bear disgrace with those who go down to the abyss, and are assigned a place in the midst of the slain. 26 Meshech and Tubal are there with all their hordes buried around them, all of them uncircumcised, slain by the sword, who once spread terror in the land of the living. 27 Do they not rest with warriors fallen uncircumcised, who have gone down to Sheol with their weapons, their swords laid under their heads and their shields over their bones, though the terror of the warriors once weighed heavily on the land of the living? 28 Pharaoh, you also will lie broken in the company of the uncircumcised dead, lying with those slain by the sword. 29 Edom is there, with her kings and all her princes, who, despite their might, have been laid with those slain by the sword. They will lie with the uncircumcised dead and with those who go down to the abyss. 30 All the princes of the north and the Sidonians are there, who, despite the terror inspired by their might, have gone down in shame with the slain. They lie uncircumcised with those slain by the sword, and they bear disgrace with those who go down to the abyss."

31 'Pharaoh will see them and be consoled for his lost hordes—Pharaoh who, with all his army, is slain by the sword, says the Lord GOD. 32 Though he spread terror throughout the land of the living, yet he with all his hordes is laid with those slain by the sword,

32:17 **first:** *so Gk; Heb. omits.*   32:18 **her nobility . . . them:** *prob. rdg; Heb. obscure.*   32:27 **and their shields:** *prob. rdg; Heb. unintelligible.*   32:32 **he spread:** *prob. rdg; Heb. I have spread.*

---

the day of the LORD; see Joel 2.1–2. **17:** Approximately April 27, 586 B.C.E. **21–32:** The *uncircumcised* were thought to be excluded from the community of Israel and its God, even after death. The Israelites are not included in this multitude. **26:** *Meshech and Tubal:* peoples from the area of Asia Minor.

in the company of the uncircumcised dead. This is the word of the Lord GOD.'

The watchman prepares for the restored kingdom

33 THIS word of the LORD came to me: 2'O man, say to your fellow-countrymen: When I bring a sword against a land, its people choose one of themselves to be their watchman, 3 and if he sees the enemy approach, he blows his trumpet to warn the people. 4 If anyone does not heed the warning and is overtaken by the sword, his fate be on his own head! 5 He ignored the alarm when he heard it. Had he taken heed, he would have escaped with his life. 6 But if the watchman does not blow his trumpet to give warning when he sees the approach of the enemy, and if anyone who is killed is caught with his sins on him, I shall hold the watchman answerable for his death.

7 'I have appointed you, O man, a watchman for the Israelites, and you must pass to them any warnings you receive from me. 8 If I pronounce sentence of death on a person because he is wicked and you do not speak out to dissuade him from his ways, that person will die because of his sin, but I shall hold you answerable for his death. 9 However, if you have warned him to give up his ways, and he persists in them, he will die because of his sin, but you will have saved yourself.

10 'O man, say to the Israelites: You complain, "We are burdened by our sins and offences; we are pining away because of them, and despair of life." 11 Tell them: As I live, says the Lord GOD, I have no desire for the death of the wicked. I would rather that the

wicked should mend their ways and live. Give them up, give up your evil ways. Israelites, why should you die?

12 'O man, say to your fellow-countrymen: When a righteous person transgresses, his righteousness will not save him. When a wicked person mends his ways, his former wickedness will not bring him down. When a righteous person sins, all his righteousness cannot save his life. 13 When I tell the righteous person that he will save his life, then if he presumes on his righteousness and does wrong, none of his righteous deeds will be remembered: but for the wrong he has done he will die. 14 When I pronounce sentence of death on the wicked, then if he mends his ways and does what is just and right — 15 if he restores the pledges he has taken, makes good what he has stolen, and, doing no more wrong, follows the rules that ensure life — he will live and not die. 16 None of the sins he has committed will be remembered against him; because he does what is just and right, he will live.

17 'Yet your fellow-countrymen say, "The Lord acts without principle," but in fact it is their ways which are unprincipled. 18 If a righteous man gives up his righteousness and does wrong, he will die because of it; 19 if a wicked man gives up his wickedness and does what is just and right, he will live. 20 Israel, how can you say that the Lord acts without principle, when I judge each one of you according to his deeds?'

21 In the twelfth year of our captivity, on the fifth day of the tenth month, a fugitive came from Jerusalem and reported that the city had fallen. 22 The evening before he arrived, the hand of the LORD had come upon me, but by the time the fugitive reached me

33.1–37.28: Israel to be restored; the kingdom established. The prophet assures Israel that the LORD will accomplish its redemption.

33.1–20: A prophet's responsibility. Ideas from preceding chapters are paralleled here: With 33.1–6, compare 3.4–11; with 33.7–9, compare 3.16–21; with 33.10–20, compare 18.1–32; with 33.23–29, compare 12.17–20. **1–6:** This particular definition of prophetic role is unique to Ezekiel. Nebuchadnezzar's advancing armies, described in v. 2 as the LORD bringing a sword against the land, probably suggested the oracle; life or death depended possibly on the warning of a watchman. On the watchman's importance in the hills of Palestine, see 2 Kgs. 9.17–28. **7–9:** Ezekiel is here presumably in Palestine, not in Babylonia. See Introduction.

33.21–22: Jerusalem's fall. The date varies; where the MT reads *twelfth* year or January 8, 585 B.C.E., the Syr. and Sept. read "eleventh" or January 19, 586 B.C.E. **22:** See 3.26–27 where Ezekiel seems not to be completely mute but only forbidden by the LORD to speak in certain circumstances. Compare 24.18–21, 26–27.

in the morning the LORD had given me back the power of speech. My speech was restored and I was no longer dumb.

²³ The word of the LORD came to me: ²⁴ 'O man, the inhabitants of these ruins on Israel's soil say, "When Abraham took possession of the land he was but one man; we are many, and surely the land has been granted to us." ²⁵ Tell them, therefore, that the Lord GOD says: You eat meat with the blood still in it, you worship idols, you shed blood; and yet you expect to possess the land! ²⁶ You resort to the sword, you commit abominations, you defile one another's wives, and yet you expect to keep possession of the land! ²⁷ Tell them that the Lord GOD says: As I live, those among the ruins will fall by the sword; those in the open country I shall give to wild beasts for food; those in dens and caves will die by pestilence. ²⁸ I shall make the land a desolate waste; her boasted might will be brought to an end, and the mountains of Israel will be an untrodden desert. ²⁹ When I make the land a desolate waste because of all the abominations they have committed, then they will know that I am the LORD.

³⁰ 'O man, your fellow-countrymen gather in groups and talk of you by the walls and in doorways, saying to one another, "Let us go and see what message there is from the LORD." ³¹ So my people will come in to you, as people are wont to do. They will sit down in front of you, and hear what you have to say, but they will not act on it. "Fine words!" they will say with insincerity, for their hearts are set on selfish gain. ³² To them you are no more than a singer of fine songs with a lovely voice and skill as a harpist. They will listen to what you say, but none of them will act on it. ³³ When it comes, as come it will, they will know that there has been a prophet in their midst.'

34 This word of the LORD came to me: ² 'Prophesy, O man, against the rulers of Israel. Prophesy and say to them: You

shepherds, these are the words of the Lord GOD: Woe betide Israel's shepherds who care only for themselves! Should not the shepherd care for the flock? ³ You consume the milk, wear the wool, and slaughter the fat beasts, but you do not feed the sheep. ⁴ You have not restored the weak, tended the sick, bandaged the injured, recovered the straggler, or searched for the lost; you have driven them with ruthless severity. ⁵ They are scattered abroad for want of a shepherd, and have become the prey of every wild beast. Scattered, ⁶ my sheep go straying over all the mountains and on every high hill; my flock is dispersed over the whole earth, with no one to enquire after them or search for them.

⁷ 'Therefore, you shepherds, hear the word of the LORD. ⁸ As surely as I live, says the Lord GOD, because for lack of a shepherd my sheep are ravaged by all the wild beasts and have become their prey, because my shepherds have not taken thought for the sheep, but have cared only for themselves and not for the sheep—⁹ therefore, you shepherds, hear the word of the LORD. ¹⁰ The Lord GOD says: I am against the shepherds and shall demand from them an account of my sheep. I shall dismiss those shepherds from tending my flock: no longer will they care only for themselves; I shall rescue my sheep from their mouths, and they will feed on them no more.

¹¹ 'For the Lord GOD says: Now I myself shall take thought for my sheep and search for them. ¹² As a shepherd goes in search of his sheep when his flock is scattered from him in every direction, so I shall go in search of my sheep and rescue them, no matter where they were scattered in a day of cloud and darkness. ¹³ I shall lead them out from the nations, gather them in from different lands, and bring them home to their own country. I shall shepherd them on the mountains of Israel and by her streams, wherever there is a settlement. ¹⁴ I shall feed them on

33.28: The desolation. Since the prediction of a *desolate waste* must be for the future, these words were spoken prior to the destruction of 587 B.C.E. The dates of v. 21 do not apply to this oracle.

33.30–33: The people listen, but do not heed. Such dubious pietism, blending *selfish gain* into a search for God's *message,* seems in vogue after the first capture of Jerusalem in 597 B.C.E.

34.1–31: The LORD as shepherd of the flock, Israel, is an image which Ezekiel inherited (Jer. 23.1–6) and passed on to those who followed him (Zech. 13.7), including Jesus (Matt. 18.12–14; Jn. 10.1–18). **6:** Worship at Canaanite *hill* shrines was encouraged or tolerated by most kings. See 2 Kgs. 12.3; 21.3; Jer. 50.6. **8:** *Wild beasts:* the hostile neighboring peoples. **10:** A play upon ideas; lit. "I will stop them from feeding the flock so that they may no longer feed themselves [upon it]." **11–14:** God will *tend* the flock: a continuation of divine good grazing-ground, and their pasture will be Israel's high mountains. There they will rest in good pasture, and find rich grazing on the mountains of Israel. 15 I myself shall tend my flock, and find them a place to rest, says the Lord God. 16 I shall search for the lost, recover the straggler, bandage the injured, strengthen the sick, leave the healthy and strong to play, and give my flock their proper food.

17 'The Lord God says to you, my flock: I shall judge between one sheep and another. As for you rams and he-goats, 18 are you not satisfied with grazing on the best pastures, that you must also trample down the rest with your feet? Or with drinking clear water, that you must also muddy the rest with your feet? 19 My flock has to graze on what you have trampled underfoot and drink what you have muddied. 20 Therefore, the Lord God says to them: Now I myself shall judge between the fat sheep and the lean. 21 You push aside the weak with flank and shoulder, you butt them with your horns until you have scattered them in every direction. 22 Therefore I shall save my flock, and they will be ravaged no more; I shall judge between one sheep and another.

23 'I shall set over them one shepherd to take care of them, my servant David; he will care for them and be their shepherd. 24 I, the Lord, shall be their God, and my servant David will be prince among them. I, the Lord, have spoken. 25 I shall make a covenant with them to ensure peace and prosperity; I shall rid the land of wild beasts, and people will live on the open pastures and sleep in the woods free from danger. 26 I shall settle them in the neighbourhood of my hill and bless them with rain in due season. 27 Trees in the countryside will bear their fruit, the ground will yield its produce, and my people will live in security on their own soil. When I break the bars of their yokes and rescue them from the power of those who have enslaved them they will know that I am the Lord. 28 They will never again be ravaged by the nations, nor will wild beasts devour them; they will live in security, free from terror. 29 I shall make their crops renowned, and they will never again be victims of famine in the land, nor bear any longer the taunts of the nations. 30 Then they will know that I, the Lord their God, am with them, and that they are my people Israel, says the Lord God. 31 You are my flock, the flock I feed, and I am your God. It is the word of the Lord God.'

35 This word of the Lord came to me: 2 'O man, face towards the hill-country of Seir and prophesy against it. 3 Say: These are the words of the Lord God:

Hill-country of Seir, I am against you:
I shall stretch out my hand to strike
    you
and reduce you to a desolate waste.
4 I shall lay your towns in ruins
and you will become a desolation.
Then you will know that I am the
    Lord;
5 for you have kept up an ancient feud
and handed over the Israelites to the
    sword
in the hour of their doom,
the hour of their final punishment.

6 'Therefore, as I live, says the Lord
    God,
I shall make blood your destiny, and it
    will pursue you;
you are most surely guilty of blood,
and it will pursue you.

35:6 **are ... guilty of:** *so Gk; Heb.* most surely hate.

saving action performed in the Exodus from Egypt. Compare Isa. 63.7–19. **17:** The Lord's judging *between one sheep and another* is a concrete application of the principle—not found explicit in other prophets—of individual responsibility (see 33.8–9). **18:** *Trample down . . . muddy:* images for abuse of power by exploiting the weak; see 32.2 for a similar indictment of Egypt. **20:** The *fat sheep* are the self-satisfied, hardhearted and insensitive people; see Deut. 32.15; Jer. 5.28. **23:** The *one shepherd* points to a renewed dynasty of David, uniting the two kingdoms separated after Solomon (see Hos. 1.11). **24:** Ezekiel envisions a restored Israel politically similar to the period after the Exodus. The ruler will be a *prince,* not an absolute king with power to dictate (2 Kgs. 16.10–18) in matters of worship and conduct as the kings had done. Compare 45.13–17 n.

35.1–15: The indictment of Edom. 1–5: A lawsuit is prepared for the recovery of the mountains of Israel (ch. 36). The defendant is *the hill-country of Seir,* which is Edom. The accusation is the oppression of Judah by occupying its lands extensively in its *hour of doom,* the destruction of 587 B.C.E. Compare Obad. 1–21. **6:** The verdict is: *guilty of blood;* and the sentence: *blood will pursue you,* with the Lord as avenger.

⁷I shall make the hill-country of Seir a
   desolate waste
and prevent anyone travelling to and
   fro in it;
⁸I shall cover your hills and valleys with
   the slain,
and those slain by the sword will fall
   into your streams.
⁹I shall make you desolate for ever,
and your cities will not be inhabited.
Then you will know that I am the
   LORD.

¹⁰'You say, "The two nations and the two
countries will be mine and I shall take possession of them, though the LORD has been
there." ¹¹Therefore, as I live, says the Lord
GOD, your anger and jealousy will be repaid,
for I shall do to you what you have done in
your hatred towards them. I shall be known
among you by the way I judge you; ¹²you will
know that I am the LORD. I have heard all
your blasphemous talk about the mountains
of Israel. You have said, "They are desolate
and have been given to us to devour." ¹³You
have boasted against me and spoken wildly.
I myself have heard you. ¹⁴The Lord GOD
says: I shall make you so desolate that the
whole world will gloat over you. ¹⁵I shall treat
you as you treated Israel my own possession
when you gloated over its desolation. Hill-
country of Seir, the whole of Edom, you will
be desolate. Then all will know that I am the
LORD.

36 'O man, prophesy to the mountains
      of Israel and say: Mountains of Is-
rael, hear the word of the LORD. ²The Lord
GOD says: The enemy has boasted over you,
"Aha! Now the ancient heights are ours."
³⁻⁴Therefore prophesy and say: These are
the words of the Lord GOD: You mountains
of Israel, all round you men gloated over you
and trampled you down when you were
seized and occupied by the rest of the nations; your name was bandied about in common gossip. Therefore, listen to the words of
the Lord GOD when he speaks to the mountains and hills, to the streams and valleys, to

ruined places and deserted cities, all plundered and despised by the rest of the surrounding nations. ⁵The Lord GOD says: In
the heat of my jealousy I have spoken out
against the rest of the nations, and against
Edom above all, for with hearts full of glee
and feelings of contempt they seized my land
as spoil. ⁶Therefore prophesy over the soil of
Israel; say to the mountains and hills, the
streams and valleys: The Lord GOD has said:
I have spoken my mind in jealous anger because you have had to endure the taunts of
the nations. ⁷Therefore, says the Lord GOD,
I swear with uplifted hand that the nations
round about you will in turn endure taunting. ⁸But you, mountains of Israel, will put
forth your branches and yield your fruit for
my people Israel, for their homecoming is
near. ⁹See now, I am for you, I shall turn to
you, and you will be tilled and sown. ¹⁰I shall
settle on you many people—the whole house
of Israel. The towns will again be inhabited
and the ruined places rebuilt. ¹¹I shall settle
in you many people and beasts; they will increase and be fruitful. I shall make you populous as in days of old, and more prosperous
than you were in your earliest times. Thus
you will know that I am the LORD. ¹²I shall
make my people Israel tread your paths
again. They will settle in you, and you will be
their possession. Never again will you leave
them childless.

¹³'The Lord GOD says: It is said that you
are a land that devours human beings and
leaves your nation childless. ¹⁴But never
again will you devour them or leave your
nation childless, says the Lord GOD. ¹⁵I shall
never let you hear again the taunts of the
surrounding nations, nor will you have to
suffer the scorn of foreigners. This is the
word of the Lord GOD.'

¹⁶This word of the LORD came to me: ¹⁷'O
man, when the Israelites were living on their
own soil they defiled it with their ways and
deeds; their ways were loathsome and un-

35:11 **among you:** so Gk; Heb. among them.
36:15 **foreigners:** so Gk; Heb. adds and you will no
more cause your tribes to fall.

35.10: *Will be mine:* second indictment. **11:** The verdict: guilty of *anger and jealousy;* the sentence: exact
retaliation; see Exod. 21.23–25.
   36.1–38: Mountains of Israel will be like a garden of Eden. 1–11: The mountains of Israel are personified
as successful plaintiffs. The verdict is the *heat* of the LORD's *jealousy against the rest of the nations* (v. 5); the
mountains in compensation are *to yield fruit* (v. 8) and have the LORD *settle many people* on them (v. 10), thus

clean in my sight. ¹⁸ I poured out my fury on them for the blood they had poured out on the land, and for the idols with which they had defiled it. ¹⁹ I scattered them among the nations, and they were dispersed in many lands. I passed a sentence on them which their ways and deeds deserved. ²⁰ But whenever they came among the nations, they caused my holy name to be profaned. It was said of them, "These are the LORD's people, and it is from his land they have gone into exile." ²¹ So I spared them for the sake of my holy name which the Israelites had profaned among the nations to whom they had gone.

²² 'Therefore tell the Israelites that the Lord GOD says: It is not for the sake of you Israelites that I am acting, but for the sake of my holy name, which you have profaned among the peoples where you have gone. ²³ I shall hallow my great name, which you have profaned among those nations. When they see that I reveal my holiness through you, they will know that I am the LORD, says the Lord GOD. ²⁴ I shall take you from among the nations, and gather you from every land, and bring you to your homeland. ²⁵ I shall sprinkle pure water over you, and you will be purified from everything that defiles you; I shall purify you from the taint of all your idols. ²⁶ I shall give you a new heart and put a new spirit within you; I shall remove the heart of stone from your body and give you a heart of flesh. ²⁷ I shall put my spirit within you and make you conform to my statutes; you will observe my laws faithfully. ²⁸ Then you will live in the land I gave to your forefathers; you will be my people, and I shall be your God.

²⁹ 'Having saved you from all that defiles you, I shall command the grain to be plentiful; I shall bring no more famine upon you. ³⁰ I shall make the trees bear abundant fruit and the ground yield heavy crops, so that you will never again have to bear among the nations the reproach of famine. ³¹ You will recall your wicked conduct and evil deeds, and you will loathe yourselves because of your wrongdoing and your abominations. ³² I assure you it is not for your sake that I am acting, says the Lord GOD, so feel the shame and disgrace of your ways, people of Israel.

³³ 'The Lord GOD says: When I have cleansed you of all your wrongdoing, I shall resettle the towns, and the ruined places will be rebuilt. ³⁴ The land now desolate will be tilled, instead of lying waste for every passerby to see. ³⁵ Everyone will say that this land which was waste has become like a garden of Eden, and the towns once ruined, wasted, and shattered will now be fortified and inhabited. ³⁶ The nations still left around you will know that it is I, the LORD, who have rebuilt the shattered towns and replanted the land laid waste; I, the LORD, have spoken and I shall do it.

³⁷ 'The Lord GOD says: Once again I shall let the Israelites pray to me for help. I shall make their people as numerous as a flock of sheep. ³⁸ As Jerusalem is filled with sheep offered as holy-gifts at times of festival, so will their ruined cities be filled with flocks of people. Then they will know that I am the LORD.'

37 The LORD's hand was upon me, and he carried me out by his spirit and set me down in a plain that was full of bones. ² He made me pass among them in every direction. Countless in number and very dry,

---

reversing the oracles of Israel's doom pronounced in chs. 6 and 7. **26–27:** The heart being for the ancients the seat of the conscious processes of knowing and willing, a *heart of stone* is imperceptive, chooses not to be aware of what the LORD has done and demanded, and does not know how to respond; by contrast a *heart of flesh* is a sensitive human heart fully aware of its relationship with God, and so capable of receiving a new measure of God's life-giving activity, a *new spirit.* **29–31:** In other prophets, the process of redemption involved the people's sin, their punishment, and, upon doing penance, their restoration. Ezekiel promises that God will redeem Israel out of sheer goodness, "for the sake of my holy name" (vv. 21–22), leading the people thereafter to repent.

37.1–14: The dry bones of Israel's hopes will live again. Central to the passage is a remarkable play on the Heb. word *ruah,* with its basic meaning, "breath," being applied in three contexts: (a) wind, the life-giving breath in nature; (b) the life-supporting breath of the nostrils in all creatures; (c) spirit, the life-creating power of God. Ezekiel does not refer directly to personal resurrection. The prophet's emphasis on individual responsibility and a person's continued life with God, which parallels national survival, at least raises the question. **2:** *Very dry:* lifeless a long time.

they covered the plain. [3] He said to me, 'O man, can these bones live?' I answered, 'Only you, Lord GOD, know that.' [4] He said, 'Prophesy over these bones; say: Dry bones, hear the word of the LORD. [5] The Lord GOD says to these bones: I am going to put breath into you, and you will live. [6] I shall fasten sinews on you, clothe you with flesh, cover you with skin, and give you breath, and you will live. Then you will know that I am the LORD.'

[7] I began to prophesy as I had been told, and as I prophesied there was a rattling sound and the bones all fitted themselves together. [8] As I watched, sinews appeared upon them, flesh clothed them, and they were covered with skin, but there was no breath in them. [9] Then he said to me, 'Prophesy to the wind, prophesy, O man, and say to it: These are the words of the Lord GOD: Let winds come from every quarter and breathe into these slain, that they may come to life.' [10] I prophesied as I had been told; breath entered them, and they came to life and rose to their feet, a mighty company.

[11] He said to me, 'O man, these bones are the whole people of Israel. They say, "Our bones are dry, our hope is gone, and we are cut off." [12] Prophesy, therefore, and say to them: The Lord GOD has said: My people, I shall open your graves and bring you up from them, and restore you to the land of Israel. [13] You, my people, will know that I am the LORD when I open your graves and bring you up from them. [14] Then I shall put my spirit into you and you will come to life, and I shall settle you on your own soil, and you will know that I the LORD have spoken and I shall act. This is the word of the LORD.'

[15] THIS word of the LORD came to me: [16] 'O man, take one leaf of a wooden tablet and write on it, "Judah and the Israelites associated with him". Then take another leaf and write on it, "Joseph, the leaf of Ephraim and all the Israelite tribes". [17] Now bring the two together to form one tablet; then they will be a folding tablet in your hand. [18] When your fellow-countrymen ask you to tell them what you mean by this, [19] say to them: The Lord GOD has said: I am taking the leaf of Joseph, which belongs to Ephraim and the other tribes of Israel, and joining to it the leaf of Judah. Thus I shall make them one tablet, and they will be one in my hand. [20] When the leaves on which you write are there in your hand for all to see, [21] say to them: The Lord GOD has said: I am going to take the Israelites from their places of exile among the nations; I shall assemble them from every quarter and restore them to their own soil. [22] I shall make them a single nation in the land, on the mountains of Israel, and one king will be over them all. No longer will they be two nations, no longer divided into two kingdoms. [23] They will never again be defiled with their idols, their loathsome ways, and all their acts of disloyalty. I shall save them from all their sinful backsliding and purify them. Thus they will be my people, and I shall be their God. [24] My servant David will be king over them; they will all have one shepherd. They will conform to my laws and my statutes and observe them faithfully. [25] They will live in the land which I gave to my servant Jacob, the land where your forefathers lived. They and their descendants will live there for ever, and my servant David is to be their prince for ever. [26] I shall make an everlasting covenant with them to ensure peace and prosperity. I shall greatly increase their numbers, and I shall put my sanctuary in their midst for all time. [27] They will live under the shelter of my dwelling; I shall be their God and they will be my people. [28] The nations will know that I the LORD am keeping Israel sacred to myself, because my sanctuary is in their midst for ever.'

38 THIS word of the LORD came to me: [2] 'O man, face towards Gog in the

37:5 **breath:** *or* wind *or* spirit.   37:14 **spirit:** *or* breath.   37:19 **joining:** *prob. rdg; Heb.* adds them. 37:23 **backsliding:** *so Gk (Symm.); Heb.* dwellings. 37:26 **an everlasting . . . prosperity:** *prob. rdg; Heb. adds* and I shall put them.

8–9: The perfect and more enduring new creation of human beings also occurs in two stages; compare Gen. 2.7. **11:** Israel's *bones are dry,* being completely *cut off* from the core of life, the covenant.

37.15–28: One nation (Israel), one king (David), and one God (the LORD). 16: *Joseph* is a synonym for the Northern Kingdom, Israel, sometimes called Ephraim after its leading tribe. **21–28:** God will unite the *two kingdoms* by a new *covenant,* and they will again be God's people. The description of the new land and new temple (chs. 40–48) should logically follow here.

38.1–39.29: Gog will be destroyed. God's triumph over the world includes primarily the triumph of Israel land of Magog, the prince of Rosh, Meshech, and Tubal, and prophesy against him. ³Say: These are the words of the Lord GOD: I am against you, Gog, prince of Rosh, Meshech, and Tubal. ⁴I shall put hooks in your jaws and turn you round. I shall lead you out, you and your whole army, horses and horsemen, all fully equipped, a great host with bucklers and shields, every man wielding a sword. ⁵With them will march the men of Persia, Cush, and Put, all with shields and helmets, ⁶Gomer and all its squadrons, Beth-togarmah with all its squadrons from the far recesses of the north—a great concourse of peoples with you. ⁷Be prepared; make ready, you and all the host which has rallied to you, and hold yourselves at my disposal. ⁸After a long time has passed you will be summoned; in years to come you will invade a land restored from ruin, whose people are gathered from many nations on the mountains of Israel that have been so long desolate. The Israelites, brought out from the nations, will all be living undisturbed; ⁹and you will come up, advancing like a hurricane; you will be like a cloud covering the land, you and all your squadrons, a great concourse of peoples.

¹⁰'The Lord GOD says: At that time a thought will enter your head and you will hatch an evil plan. ¹¹You will say, "I shall attack a land of open villages and fall upon a people living quiet and undisturbed, undefended by walls or barred gates." ¹²You will expect to come plundering, spoiling, and stripping bare the settlements which once lay in ruins, but are now inhabited by a people gathered out of the nations, a people acquiring livestock and goods, and making their home at the very centre of the world. ¹³Sheba and Dedan, the traders of Tarshish and her leading merchants, will say to you, "Is it for plunder that you have come? Have you mustered your host to get spoil, to carry off silver and gold, to take livestock and goods, to seize much booty?"

¹⁴'Therefore, O man, prophesy and say to Gog: The Lord GOD says: On that day when my people Israel are living undisturbed, will you not bestir yourself ¹⁵and come with many nations from your home in the far recesses of the north, all riding on horses, a large host, a mighty army? ¹⁶You will advance against my people Israel like a cloud that covers the earth. In the last days I shall bring you against my land, that the nations may know me, when they see me prove my holiness at Gog's expense.

¹⁷'The Lord GOD says: When I spoke in days of old through my servants the prophets, who prophesied in those days unceasingly, it was you whom I threatened to bring against Israel. ¹⁸On that day, when at length Gog invades Israel, says the Lord GOD, my wrath will boil over. ¹⁹In my jealousy and in the heat of my anger I swear that there will be a great earthquake throughout the land of Israel on that day, ²⁰and the fish in the sea and the birds in the air, the wild animals and all creatures that move on the ground, and every human being on the face of the earth will quake before me. Mountains will be overthrown, the terraced hills collapse, and every wall crash to the ground. ²¹I shall summon universal terror against Gog, says the Lord GOD, and his men will turn their swords against one another. ²²I shall bring him to judgement with pestilence and bloodshed; I shall pour torrential rain and hailstones as well as fire and brimstone on him and his squadrons and the whole concourse of peoples with him. ²³I shall show myself great and holy and make myself known to many nations. Then they will know that I am the LORD.

39 'O man, prophesy against Gog and say: The Lord GOD says: I am against you, Gog, prince of Rosh, Meshech, and Tubal. ²I shall turn you round and drive you on. I shall lead you from the far recesses of the north and bring you to the mountains of Is-

38:7 **my:** *so Gk; Heb.* their.   38:14 **bestir yourself:** *so Gk; Heb.* know.   38:21 **universal terror:** *so Gk; Heb.* for all my mountains a sword.

over all hostile evil forces. Resembling other biblical apocalypses (Isa. chs. 24–27; Dan. chs. 7–12; Zech. chs. 9–14), these verses are an early form of the genre.

38.1–39.7: Universal terror against Gog, who sets in motion against Israel all the forces of evil and hostility. **2:** *Gog* resembles all Israel's persecutors, a symbol of all wickedness menacing it, but neither he nor the land of *Magog* nor its place names can be identified with certainty. **4–13:** The *army of Gog* is composed of elements from the four corners of the author's world: Gomer, north; Ethiopia, south; Tarshish, west; Dedan, east; it is called out from the *far recesses of the north,* the mythological dwelling of good and evil. **12:** *Centre of the* rael. ³I shall strike the bow from your left hand and dash the arrows from your right hand. ⁴On the mountains of Israel you will fall, you and all your squadrons and allies. I shall give you as food to every kind of bird of prey and to the wild beasts. ⁵You will fall on the ground, for it is I who have spoken. This is the word of the Lord GOD. ⁶I shall send fire on Magog and on those who live undisturbed in the coasts and islands. Then they will know that I am the LORD. ⁷My holy name I shall make known in the midst of my people Israel and no longer let it be profaned; the nations will know that I, the LORD, am holy in Israel.

⁸'See, it is coming; it is here! says the Lord GOD; it is the day of which I have spoken. ⁹Those who live in Israel's towns will go out and gather weapons for fuel, bucklers and shields, bows and arrows, throwing-sticks and lances; for seven years they will kindle fires with them. ¹⁰They will take no wood from the fields, nor cut it from the forests, but will use the weapons to light their fires. Thus they will plunder those who plundered them and spoil their despoilers. This is the word of the Lord GOD.

¹¹'On that day, instead of a burial-ground in Israel, I shall assign to Gog the valley of Abarim east of the Dead Sea. There Gog with all his horde will be buried, and Abarim will be entirely blocked. It will be called the Valley of Gog's Horde. ¹²It will take the Israelites seven months to bury them and to purify the land, ¹³and all the people will share in the task. The day that I win myself honour will be a memorable day for them. This is the word of the Lord GOD. ¹⁴Men will be picked for the regular duty of going through the country to bury any left above ground, and so purify the land. They will begin their search at the end of the seven months: ¹⁵they will go up and down the country, and whenever one of them sees a human bone he is to put a marker beside it, until it has been buried in the Valley of Gog's Horde. ¹⁶So no

more will be heard of that great horde, and the land will be purified.

¹⁷'O man, the Lord GOD says: Cry to every bird that flies and to all the wild beasts: Assemble and come, gather from every side to my sacrifice, the great sacrifice I am preparing for you on the mountains of Israel. Eat flesh and drink blood, ¹⁸eat the flesh of warriors and drink the blood of the rulers of the earth; all these are your rams, sheep, hegoats, and bulls, and buffaloes of Bashan. ¹⁹You will sate yourselves with fat and drink yourselves drunk on blood at the sacrifice which I am preparing for you. ²⁰At my table you will eat your fill of horses and riders, of warriors and fighting men of every kind. This is the word of the Lord GOD.

²¹'I shall display my glory among the nations; all will see the judgement that I execute and the hand I lay upon them. ²²From that day forward the Israelites will know that I am the LORD their God, ²³and the nations will know that the Israelites went into exile for their iniquity in being unfaithful to me. I hid my face from them and handed them over to their enemies, and they fell, every one of them, by the sword. ²⁴I dealt out to them what their defilement and rebelliousness deserved, and I hid my face from them.

²⁵'The Lord GOD says: Now I shall restore the fortunes of Jacob and show my compassion for all Israel, and I shall be jealous for my holy name. ²⁶They will forget their shame and all their unfaithfulness to me, when they live once more in their homeland undisturbed and free from terror. ²⁷When I bring them back from the nations and gather them from the lands of their enemies, I shall make them exemplify my holiness for many nations to see. ²⁸They will know that I am the LORD their God, because, having sent them into exile among the nations, I bring them together again in their homeland and leave

39:11 **instead of:** *prob. rdg; Heb.* there.   39:16 **So ... horde:** *prob. rdg; Heb. obscure.*

---

world: Jerusalem; see 5.5. **39.7:** To *know* God or God's *name* is to experience God's reality and to acknowledge it by obedience.

   39.8–20: Evil turned to good in the complete slaughter of Gog. 8: The verse hearkens back to 38.17. **11:** '*Abarim:* play on words with '*oberim,* Heb. for "travelers," who will be *blocked* and so reminded of God's action. **15:** Unburied bodies make the land unclean. **17–20:** An evil army other than Gog's, which has been buried, is slaughtered and then offered as sacrifices for wild beasts, thus reversing the usual practice of animal sacrifices offered for human beings. The significance of this is not clear.

   39.21–29: End of the oracles. The only relation between this passage and Gog is the theme of Israel's exaltation after exile and the vindication of God's holiness in accomplishing it.

none of them behind. ²⁹No longer shall I hide my face from them, I who have poured out my spirit on Israel. This is the word of the Lord God.'

The new temple

40 AT the beginning of the year, on the tenth day of the month, in the twenty-fifth year of our exile, that is fourteen years after the city had fallen, on that very day the hand of the LORD came upon me and he brought me there. ²In a vision from God I was brought to the land of Israel and set on a very high mountain, on which were what seemed to be the buildings of a city to the south. ³He led me towards it, and I saw a man like a figure of bronze standing at the gate and holding a cord of linen thread and a measuring rod. ⁴'O man,' he said to me, 'look closely and listen carefully; note well all that I show you, for this is why you have been brought here. Tell the Israelites everything you see.'

⁵Right round the outside of the temple ran a wall. The length of the rod which the man was holding was six cubits, reckoning by the long cubit which was one cubit and a hand's breadth. He measured the thickness and the height of the wall; each was one rod.

⁶The man went to the gate which faced eastwards, and mounting its steps he measured the threshold of the gateway; its depth was one rod. ⁷Each cell was one rod long and one rod wide; and there was a space of five cubits between the cells. The threshold of the gateway at the end of the vestibule on the side facing the temple was one rod. ⁸He measured the vestibule of the gateway ⁹and it was eight cubits, with pilasters two cubits thick; the vestibule of the gateway lay at the end nearer the temple. ¹⁰Now the cells of the gateway, looking back eastwards, were three in number on each side, all of the same size, and their pilasters on either side were also identical in size. ¹¹He measured the entrance to the gateway; it was ten cubits wide, and the width of the gateway itself throughout its length was thirteen cubits. ¹²In front of the cells on each side lay a kerb, one cubit wide; each cell was six cubits by six. ¹³He measured the width of the gateway through the cell doors which faced one another, from the back of one cell to the back of the opposite cell; he made it twenty-five cubits, ¹⁴and the vestibule twenty cubits across; the gateway on every side projected into the court. ¹⁵From the front of the entrance gate to the outer face of the vestibule of the inner gate the distance was fifty cubits. ¹⁶Both cells and pilasters had embrasures all round inside the gateway, and the vestibule had windows all round within, and each pilaster was decorated with carved palm trees.

¹⁷The man brought me to the outer court, and I saw rooms and a pavement all round the court: there were thirty rooms along the pavement. ¹⁸The pavement ran up to the

---

Chs. 40—43 *In chapters 40—43 there are several Hebrew technical terms whose meaning is not certain and has to be determined, as well as may be, from the context.*
40:6 **one rod:** *so Gk; Heb. adds* and one threshold, one rod in width.   40:13 **back:** *so Gk; Heb.* roof.
40:14 **vestibule:** *prob. rdg; cp. Gk; Heb.* the pilasters. **twenty cubits:** *so Gk; Heb.* sixty cubits. **projected into:** *prob. rdg; Heb. adds* pilaster.

40.1–48.35: Revelation of "Utopia." It is described in a vision extending over eight chapters. Containing precise building plans, rubrics for ritual, and legal enactments—none of which was ever realized, and perhaps not meant to be—the passage aims to portray graphically the religious, social and political structures of a society termed "The LORD is there" (48.35). It is a religious Utopia, the ideal postexilic Jewish community in its relations with the LORD. Most interpreters agree that some of this material is not Ezekiel's but comes from the postexilic community that developed following his inspiration.

40.1–47: The new temple: its enclosure. 1: *Beginning of the year:* Heb., *r'os haššāna.* In modern Judaism this phrase would indicate the Feast of the New Year which is celebrated on the first day of the month of Tishri (September-October). In Ezekiel all dates are derived from an ancient religious calendar in which the year began in the spring, on the first day of the month of Nisan (March—April). Hence the *tenth day of the month* is probably April 28, 573 B.C.E. **5:** *The length of the rod* was about 10 feet 4 inches long. The long cubit, an ancient standard, was seven hands' breadth or 20.60 inches, and the newer cubit was six hands' breadth or 17.5 inches. In choosing the ancient measure, Ezekiel indicates a return to ancient standards (and/or possibly principles) in the new community. **6:** *Gate:* of the new temple. Built on a high mountain (17.23), the new temple rose above successive elevations of seven, eight and ten steps; see vv. 22, 26, 31, 34, 49. The temple stood on the last side of the gateways, as wide as they were long; this was the lower pavement. ¹⁹ He measured the width of the court from the front of the lower gateway to the outside of the inner gateway; it was a hundred cubits.

The man led me round to the north ²⁰ and I saw a gateway facing north belonging to the outer court, and he measured its length and its breadth. ²¹ Its cells, three on each side, together with its pilasters and its vestibule, were the same size as those of the first gateway, fifty cubits long by twenty-five wide. ²² So too its windows, and those of its vestibule, and its palm trees were the same size as those of the gateway which faced east; it was approached by seven steps with its vestibule facing them. ²³ A gate like that on the east side led to the inner court opposite the north gateway; he measured from gateway to gateway, and it was a hundred cubits.

²⁴ Then the man led me round to the south, where I saw a gateway facing south. He measured its cells, its pilasters, and its vestibule, and found it the same size as the others, ²⁵ fifty cubits long by twenty-five wide. Both gateway and vestibule had windows all round like the others. ²⁶ It was approached by seven steps with a vestibule facing them and palms carved on each pilaster. ²⁷ The inner court had a gateway facing south, and when he measured from gateway to gateway it was a hundred cubits.

²⁸ The man brought me into the inner court through the south gateway, measured it, and found it the same size as the others. ²⁹ So were its cells, pilasters, and vestibule, fifty cubits long by twenty-five wide. The court and its vestibule had windows all round. ³¹ Its vestibule faced the outer court; it had palm trees carved on its pilasters, and eight steps led up to it.

³² The man brought me to the inner court on the east side and measured the gateway, and he found it the same size as the others. ³³ So too were its cells, pilasters, and vestibule; it and its vestibule had windows all round, and it was fifty cubits long by twenty-five wide. ³⁴ Its vestibule gave on to the outer court and had a palm tree carved on each pilaster; eight steps led up to it.

³⁵ Then the man brought me to the north gateway and measured it and found it the same size as the others. ³⁶ So were its cells, pilasters, and vestibule, and it had windows all round; it was fifty cubits long by twenty-five wide. ³⁷ Its vestibule faced the outer court and had palm trees carved on the pilaster at each side; eight steps led up to it.

³⁸ Opening off the vestibule of the gateway was a room in which the whole-offerings were to be washed. ³⁹ On each side at the vestibule were two tables where the whole-offering, the purification-offering, and the reparation-offering were to be slaughtered. ⁴⁰ At the corner on the outside, on the way up to the entrance of the north gateway, stood two tables, and two more at the other corner of the vestibule of the gateway; ⁴¹ another four stood on each side at the corner of the gateway—eight tables in all, at which the slaughtering was to be done. ⁴² Four tables used for the whole-offering were of hewn stone, each one and a half cubits long by one and a half cubits wide and a cubit high; and on them they put the instruments used for the whole-offering and other sacrifices. ⁴³ The flesh of the offerings was on the tables, and rims a hand's breadth in width were fixed all round facing inwards.

⁴⁴ Then the man brought me right into the inner court, where there were two rooms, one at the corner of the north gateway, facing south, and one at the corner of the south gateway, facing north. ⁴⁵ This room facing south, the man told me, is for the priests in

40:19 **inner gateway:** *so Gk; Heb.* inner court.
40:19–20 **cubits . . . gateway:** *so Gk; Heb.* cubits, east and north, ²⁰ and the gate. 40:22 **and those of:** *prob. rdg; Heb. omits* those of. 40:23 **like . . . side:** *so Gk; Heb.* and to the east. 40:24 **its cells:** *so Gk; Heb. omits.* 40:29 **all round:** *so some MSS; others add* ³⁰ It had vestibules all round, and it was twenty-five cubits long by five wide. 40:37 **Its vestibule:** *so Gk; Heb.* Its pilasters. 40:38 **the vestibule of the gateway:** *prob. rdg; Heb.* pilasters, the gates. 40:44 **Then . . . rooms:** *so Gk; Heb.* And outside the inner gate singers' rooms in the inner court. **south gateway:** *so Gk; Heb.* east gateway.

elevation crowning the land as the LORD's throne; see 43.7. **25:** The *gateway* and *windows all round* enabled guards to keep out any one who might profane the temple. **39:** The emphasis on *purification-offering* and *reparation-offering,* expiatory sacrifices, stems from a keener sense of culpability and responsibility following the Exile. **45–46:** The *Levites* are divided into two ranks, those having *charge of the temple buildings,* performing work formerly done by foreign slaves, and a superior rank in *charge of altar* sacrifices; see 43.19; 44.10–15.

charge of the temple buildings. ⁴⁶The room facing north is for the priests in charge of the altar: that is, the descendants of Zadok, who alone of the Levites may come near to serve the LORD. ⁴⁷He measured the court; it was square, a hundred cubits each way, and the altar stood in front of the temple.

⁴⁸The man brought me into the vestibule of the temple, and measured a pilaster of the vestibule; it was five cubits on each side. The width of the gateway was fourteen cubits, and that of the corners of the gateway three cubits in each direction. ⁴⁹The vestibule was twenty cubits long by twelve wide; ten steps led up to it, and by the pilasters rose pillars, one on either side.

41 He brought me into the sanctuary and measured the pilasters; they were six cubits wide on each side. ²The entrance was ten cubits wide and its corners five cubits wide in each direction. He measured the length of the sanctuary; it was forty cubits, and its width twenty. ³He went into the inner sanctuary and measured the pilasters at the entrance: they were two cubits; the entrance itself was six cubits, and the corners of the entrance were seven cubits in each direction. ⁴Then he measured the room at the far end of the sanctuary; its length and its breadth were each twenty cubits. He said to me, 'This is the Holy of Holies.'

⁵The man measured the wall of the temple; it was six cubits high, and each arcade all round the temple was four cubits wide. ⁶The arcades were arranged in three tiers, each tier in thirty sections. In the wall all round the temple there were rebatements for the arcades, so that they could be supported without being fastened into the wall of the temple. ⁷The higher up the arcades were, the broader they were all round by the addition of the rebatements, one above the other all round the temple; the temple itself had a ramp running upwards on a base, and in this way there was access from the lowest to the highest tier by way of the middle tier.

⁸I saw the temple had a raised pavement all round it, and the foundations of the arcades were flush with it and measured a full rod, six cubits high. ⁹The outer wall of the

arcades was five cubits thick. There was an unoccupied area beside the terrace which was adjacent to the temple, ¹¹and the arcades opened on to this area, one opening facing north and one south; the unoccupied area was five cubits wide on all sides. ¹⁰There was a free space twenty cubits wide all round the temple. ¹²On the western side, at the far end of the free space, stood a building seventy cubits wide; its wall was five cubits thick all round, and its length ninety cubits.

¹³The man measured the temple; it was a hundred cubits long; the free space, the building, and its walls came to a hundred cubits in all. ¹⁴The east front of the temple along with the free space was a hundred cubits wide. ¹⁵He measured the length of the building at the far end of the free space to the west of the temple, and its corridors on each side: a hundred cubits.

The sanctuary, the inner shrine, and the outer vestibule were panelled; ¹⁶the embrasures around the three of them were framed with wood all round. From the ground up to the windows ¹⁷and above the door, in both the inner and outer chambers, round all the walls, inside and out, ¹⁸were carved figures, cherubim and palm trees, one palm tree between every pair of cherubim. Each cherub had two faces: ¹⁹one the face of a man, looking towards one palm tree, and the other the face of a lion, looking towards the palm tree on its other side. Such was the carving round the whole of the temple. ²⁰The cherubim and the palm trees were carved on the walls from the ground up to the top of the doorway. ²¹The doorposts of the sanctuary were square.

In front of the Holy Place was what seemed ²²an altar of wood, three cubits high and two

40:48 **fourteen . . . gateway:** *so Gk; Heb. omits.*
40:49 **twelve:** *so Gk; Heb.* eleven.   41:1 **side:** *so Gk; Heb. adds* the width of the tent.   41:3 **corners:** *so Gk; Heb.* width.   41:7 **by . . . rebatements:** *so Gk; Heb.* for the surrounding of the house.   41:9 **beside the terrace:** *prob. rdg; Heb.* between the arcades.
41:11 *Verses 10 and 11 transposed.*   41:10 **There . . . space:** *prob. rdg; Heb.* Between the rooms.
41:15–17 **the inner shrine . . . the door:** *prob. rdg, cp. Gk; Heb. unintelligible.*   41:18 **were . . . figures:** *prob. rdg; Heb.* measures ¹⁸and carving.   41:21 **The doorposts . . . square:** *prob. rdg; Heb. unintelligible.*

40.48–42.20: The new temple, like other ancient temples, had three well defined areas: the vestibule (vv. 48–49); the sanctuary (41.1–2); the Holy of Holies (41.4). **49:** Two *pillars* stood in front of Solomon's temple; see 1 Kgs. 7.21, 41. **41.12:** *On the western side . . . a building:* possibly a place for keeping animals destined for sacrifice. **22:** The *altar of wood* seems to be either the altar of incense or the *table* of the Presence cubits long; it was fitted with corner-posts, and its base and sides also were of wood. He told me that this was the table which stands before the LORD. 23 The sanctuary had a double door, as also had the Holy Place: 24 the double doors had hinged leaves, a pair for each door. 25 Carved on them were cherubim and palm trees like those on the walls. Outside there was a wooden cornice over the vestibule; 26 on both sides of the vestibule were embrasures, with palm trees carved at the corners.

42 Then the man took me to the outer court round by the north and brought me to the rooms facing the free space and facing the buildings to the north. 2 The length along the northern side was a hundred cubits, and the breadth fifty. 3 Facing the twenty cubits of free space which adjoined the inner court, and facing the pavement of the outer court, were corridors at three levels corresponding to each other. 4 In front of the rooms a passage, ten cubits wide and a hundred cubits long, ran towards the inner court; the entrances to the rooms faced north. 5 The upper rooms were narrower than the lower and middle rooms, because the corridors took building space from them. 6 For they were all at three levels and had no pillars such as the courts had, so that the lower and middle levels were recessed from the ground upwards. 7 An outside wall, fifty cubits long, ran parallel to the rooms and in front of them, on the side of the outer court, 8 and while the rooms adjacent to the outer court were fifty cubits long, those facing the sanctuary were a hundred cubits. 9 Below these rooms was an entry from the east on the way in from the outer court 10 where the wall of the court began.

On the south side, adjacent to the free space and the building, 11 were other rooms with a passage in front of them. These rooms corresponded, in length and breadth and in general character, to those facing north, 12 whose exits and entrances were the same as those of the rooms on the south. On the east-

ern approach, where the passages began, there was an entrance in the face of the inner wall.

13 The man said to me, 'The north and south rooms facing the free space are the consecrated rooms where the priests who approach the LORD are to eat the most sacred offerings. There they are to put these offerings as well as the grain-offering, the purification-offering, and the reparation-offering; for the place is holy. 14 When the priests have entered the Holy Place they must not go into the outer court again without leaving there the vestments they have worn while performing their duties. Those are holy vestments and they are to put on other garments before going to the place assigned to the people.'

15 When the man had finished measuring the inner temple, he brought me out through the gateway which faces east and measured the whole area. 16 He measured the east side with the measuring rod, and it was five hundred cubits. He turned 17 and measured the north side with his rod, and it was five hundred cubits. He turned to 18 the south side and measured it with his rod; it was five hundred cubits. 19 He turned to the west and measured it with his rod; it was five hundred cubits. 20 So he measured all four sides of the enclosing wall; in each direction it measured five hundred cubits. This marked off the sacred area from the secular.

43 The man led me to the gate which faced east, 2 and there, coming from the east, was the glory of the God of Israel. The sound of his coming was like that of a mighty torrent, and the earth was bright with his glory. 3 The form that I saw was the same as I had seen when he came to destroy the

41:22 **base:** *so Gk; Heb.* length.   41:26 **corners:** *prob. rdg; Heb. adds* and the arcades of the temple and the cornices.   42:2 **The length ... cubits:** *prob. rdg, cp. Gk; Heb. unintelligible.*   42:4 **and ... long:** *so Gk; Heb. unintelligible.*   42:10 **began:** *prob. rdg; Heb.* breadth. **south:** *so Gk; Heb.* east. 42:16,17,18,19,20 **cubits:** *prob. rdg; Heb.* rods. 42:17 **He turned to:** *so Gk; Heb.* round about. 42:18–19 *Some MSS place verse 18 after verse 19.*

bearing the twelve loaves of pure wheat flour, a witness to the covenant between the LORD and the twelve tribes; see Lev. 24.5–9. **42.1–14:** Accessory structures provide rooms for priests to eat their share of the sacrifices, for storing vestments and other supplies. The shape and disposition of the buildings are unclear. **15–20:** The temple area is holy, 500 cubits square, surrounded by a wall separating it from the profane, secular life.

43.1–12: The glory of the LORD returns to consecrate the new city. This occurrence is the high point of the vision. **1:** *Glory;* see 10.1–4 n. **2:** *The east:* the direction in which *the glory of the God of Israel* had departed city, the same I had seen by the river Kebar, and I prostrated myself.

4 As the glory of the LORD came to the temple by the east gate, 5 a spirit lifted me up and brought me into the inner court, and I saw the glory of the LORD fill the temple. 6 With the man standing beside me I heard someone speak to me from the temple 7 and say, 'O man, do you see the place of my throne, the place where I set my feet, and where I shall dwell among the Israelites for ever? Neither they nor their kings must ever defile my holy name again with their wanton idolatry, and with the monuments raised to dead kings. 8 They set their threshold by mine and their doorpost beside mine, with only a wall between me and them. They defiled my holy name with the abominations they committed; so I destroyed them in my anger. 9 But now they must put away their wanton idolatry and remove the monuments to their kings far from me, and I shall dwell among them for ever.

10 'Tell the Israelites, O man, about this temple, that they may be ashamed of their iniquities. 11 If they are ashamed of all they have done, you are to describe to them the temple and its fittings, its exits and entrances, all the details and particulars of its elevation and plan. Make a sketch for them to look at, so that they may keep them in mind and carry them out. 12 This is the plan of the temple to be built on the top of the mountain: all its precincts on every side shall be most holy.'

13 These were the dimensions of the altar in cubits (the cubit that is a cubit and a hand's breadth). This was the height of the altar: the base was a cubit high and projected a cubit; on its edge was a rim one span deep. 14 From the base to the cubit-wide ridge of the lower pedestal-block was two cubits, and from this smaller pedestal-block to the cubit-wide ridge of the larger pedestal-block was four cubits. 15 The altar-hearth was four cubits

high and was surmounted by four horns a cubit high. 16 The hearth was square, twelve cubits long and twelve cubits wide. 17 The upper pedestal-block was fourteen cubits long and fourteen cubits wide on its four sides, and the rim round it was half a cubit deep. The base of the altar projected a cubit, and there were steps facing east.

18 He said to me, 'O man, the Lord GOD says: Here are the regulations for the altar when it has been made, for sacrificing whole-offerings on it and for flinging the blood against it. 19 Only the levitical priests of the family of Zadok may come near to serve me, says the Lord GOD. You are to assign them a young bull for a purification-offering; 20 you must take some of the blood and apply it to the four horns of the altar, on the four corners of the upper pedestal, and all round the rim, and so purify and make expiation for the altar. 21 Then take the bull chosen as the purification-offering, and let the priests destroy it by fire in the proper place within the precincts, but outside the Holy Place.

22 'On the following day you are to present a he-goat without blemish as a purification-offering, and with it they are to purify the altar as they did with the bull. 23 When you have completed the purifying of the altar, you are to present a young bull without blemish and a ram without blemish. 24 Present them before the LORD, and have the priests throw salt on them and sacrifice them as a whole-offering to the LORD. 25 For seven days you are to offer a goat as a daily purification-offering, as well as a young bull, and a ram without blemish from the flock. 26 For seven days they are to make expiation for the altar, and, having pronounced it ritually clean,

43:7 **do you see:** *so Gk; Heb. omits.*
43:10 **iniquities:** *prob. rdg; Heb. adds* and they shall measure the proportions.   43:13 **the base ... high:** *prob. rdg; Heb. unintelligible.*   43:15 **a cubit high:** *Heb. omits.*

in 11.23. **3:** There is here no appearance of a form in human likeness or of living creatures as in 1.4–28. **7:** Now the LORD's *feet* will be *set* permanently in Jerusalem where earlier God had only sojourned in the temple. **8:** Unlike Solomon's temple, the new temple will not be a dependency of the king, surrounded by his buildings; see 1 Kgs. 7.1–12; 2 Kgs. 16.7–20.

43.13–27: Shape of the altar and its consecration. Since in cultic acts the altar represents God (Exod. 24.6–8), it will be a sign of God's permanent presence. **13–17:** Built in tiers on three platforms — 16, 14, and 12 cubits square — the altar resembles the Babylonian ziggurat, or sacred tower (Gen. 11.4 n.); it is 12 cubits or about 20½ ft. high. **15:** The significance of the *horns*, projections from the four corners of the altar, is not known. **18–26:** Zadokite *priests* were the descendants of Zadok, the priest who remained loyal to David (1 Kgs. 1.5–40). They will *consecrate* the *altar* — lit. "fill its hands" (with offerings), terminology used in consecrating they are to consecrate it. ²⁷ At the end of that time, on the eighth day and onwards, the priests will sacrifice on the altar your whole-offerings and your shared-offerings, and I shall accept you. This is the word of the Lord GOD.'

44 The man again brought me round to the outer gate of the sanctuary facing east. It was shut, and ² he said to me, 'This gate is to be kept closed and is not to be opened. No one may enter by it, for the LORD the God of Israel has entered by it. It must be kept shut. ³ Only the ruling prince himself may sit there to eat the sacrificial meal in the presence of the LORD. He is to come in and go out by the vestibule of the gate.'

⁴ The man brought me round by the north gate to the front of the temple, and I saw the glory of the LORD filling the LORD's house, and I prostrated myself. ⁵ He said to me, 'Note carefully, O man, look closely, and listen attentively to all I say to you, to all the rules and the regulations for the LORD's house. Take note of the entrance to the house and all the exits from the sanctuary. ⁶ Say to Israel: The Lord GOD says: Enough of all those abominations of yours, you Israelites! ⁷ You admit foreigners, uncircumcised in mind and body, into my sanctuary, so defiling my house, when you present to me the fat and blood which are my food. They have made my covenant void with your abominations. ⁸ Instead of keeping charge of my holy things yourselves, you have put these men in charge of my sanctuary.

⁹ The Lord GOD says: No foreigner, uncircumcised in mind and body, who may be living among the Israelites is to enter my sanctuary. ¹⁰ But the Levites, though they deserted me when the Israelites went astray after their idols and had to bear the punishment of their iniquity, ¹¹ may yet be servants in my sanctuary, having charge of the gates of the temple and serving in it. They are to slaughter the whole-offering and

the sacrifice for the people and be in attendance to serve them. ¹² Because they served the Israelites in the presence of their idols and caused the people to fall into sin, I have sworn with uplifted hand, says the Lord GOD, that they shall bear the punishment of their iniquity. ¹³ They shall not have access to me, to serve me as priests; nor shall they approach any of my holy or most holy things. They shall bear the shame of the abominable deeds they have committed. ¹⁴ I shall put them in charge of all the work which has to be done in the temple.

¹⁵ 'But the levitical priests of the family of Zadok who remained in charge of my sanctuary when the Israelites went astray from me, they shall approach and serve me. They shall stand before me, to present the fat and the blood, says the Lord GOD. ¹⁶ It is they who are to enter my sanctuary and approach my table to serve me and keep my charge.

¹⁷ 'When they come to the gates of the inner court they must put on linen garments; they must wear no wool when serving me at the gates of the inner court and inside it. ¹⁸ They are to wear linen turbans, and have linen drawers on their loins; they must not fasten their clothes with a belt, which might cause sweating. ¹⁹ Before going out to the people in the outer court, they are to remove the clothes they have worn while serving; leaving them in the sacred rooms, they are to put on other clothes, so that they do not by means of their clothing transmit holiness to the people.

²⁰ 'They must neither shave their heads nor let their hair grow long; they must keep their hair trimmed. ²¹ No priest may drink wine when he is to enter the inner court. ²² He may not marry a widow or a divorced woman, but

---

44:2 **he:** *prob. rdg; Heb.* the LORD.   44:5 **He:** *prob. rdg; Heb.* The LORD. **the entrance to:** *or* those who may enter. **the exits:** *or* those to be excluded.
44:7 **with:** *so Gk; Heb.* in addition to.

---

priests—setting it aside for sacred use. Compare Exod. 29.1–46. **27:** *Accept you:* be pleased with you. *Whole-offerings:* the sacrifice was completely burned. *Shared-offerings:* the offerer received a portion of it back and ate it as a sign of communion with God.

44.1–31: The personnel of the new temple receive guidelines for a worship free from profanation. **3:** For sacred meals following a sacrifice see Deut. 12.4–7. **7:** The Bible notes several instances of foreigners being taken into temple service; most to the point are Josh. 9.23–27; Ezra 2.43, 58; 8.20; Neh. 7.46, 60; 11.3, 21. Circumcision *of the body* is a sign of circumcision *of mind:* a willingness to love and serve the LORD by keeping the Law (see Deut. 10.12–20); foreigners, uncircumcised in both, would *void* the new covenant. **10–16:** Ezekiel seems to be a transition between Deut. (18.1–8) where all Levites are priests, and the later Priestly only a virgin of Israelite birth. He may, however, marry the widow of a priest.

23 'They are to teach my people to distinguish the sacred from the profane, and show them the difference between unclean and clean. 24 When disputes arise, let them take their place in court and decide each case according to my laws. At all my appointed seasons they must observe my rules and statutes, and they are to keep my sabbaths holy.

25 'They must not defile themselves by contact with any dead person, except father or mother, son or daughter, brother or unmarried sister. 26 After purification, they are to count off seven days and then they will be clean, 27 and when they re-enter the inner court to serve in the Holy Place, they are to present their purification-offering, says the Lord GOD.

28 'They are to own no holding in Israel; I am their holding. No possession is to be granted them in Israel; I am their possession. 29 The grain-offering, the purification-offering, and the reparation-offering are to be eaten by them. Everything in Israel devoted to God will be theirs. 30 The first of all the firstfruits and all your contributions of every kind are to belong wholly to the priests. You must give the first lump of your dough to the priests, so that a blessing may rest on your house.

31 'The priests must eat nothing, whether bird or beast, which has died a natural death or been killed by a wild animal.

45 'When you divide the land by lot among the tribes, you are to set apart for the LORD a sacred reserve, twenty-five thousand cubits in length and twenty thousand in width; the whole area is to be sacred. 2 Of this a square plot, five hundred cubits each way, must be devoted to the sanctuary, with fifty cubits of open land round it. 3 From the area set apart, measure off a space

twenty-five thousand cubits by ten thousand cubits, within which the sanctuary, the holiest place of all, will stand. 4 This part is sacred and is for the priests who serve in the sanctuary and who come near to serve the LORD. It will include room for their houses and a sacred plot for the sanctuary. 5 An area of twenty-five thousand by ten thousand cubits is to be for the Levites, the temple servants, and on it will stand the places in which they live. 6 You are to allot to the city an area of five thousand by twenty-five thousand cubits alongside the sacred reserve; this will belong to all Israel.

7 'On either side of the sacred reserve and of the city's share the ruler is to have land facing the sacred reserve and the city's share, running westwards and eastwards. It is to run alongside one of the tribal portions, and extend from the western to the eastern borders 8 of the land; it will be his share in Israel. The rulers of Israel will never oppress my people again, but they will assign the land to Israel, tribe by tribe.

9 'THE Lord GOD says: Enough, you rulers of Israel! Have done with lawlessness and robbery; do what is right and just. Give up evicting my people from their land, says the Lord GOD. 10 Your scales must be honest, as must your ephah and your bath. 11 There must be one standard for each, taking each as the tenth of a homer, and the homer must have its fixed standard. 12 Your shekel weight must contain twenty gerahs, and your mina be the sum of twenty and twenty-five and fifteen shekels.

13 'These are the contributions you are to set aside: out of every homer of wheat or of

44:26 **and then . . . clean:** *so Syriac; Heb.* omits.
44:28 **no holding:** *so Lat.; Heb.* omits no.
45:1 **twenty thousand:** *so Gk; Heb.* ten thousand.
45:5 **on it . . . live:** *so Gk; Heb.* twenty rooms.

source (Num. 3.5–10; 18.2) where they are assistants to the priests. **29:** *Devoted to God,* lit. "under the ban," Heb. ḥerem, is anything strictly reserved for sacred cultic use. **31:** See Lev. 22.8.

45.1–8: The new distribution of the land. Beginning here and ending in ch. 48, there is a graphic portrayal of the ideals of theocracy, a political system in which God is held to be the supreme ruler. **4:** Priests held such a position relative to the Tent of Meeting in the wilderness; see Num. 3.38. **7–8:** The rulers' property is so great because they must provide offerings for the cult; see v. 17. The ruler's role in the new nation is ambiguous, no mention being made of a king.

45.9–12: Weights and measures are standardized for use in the new temple.

45.13–46.24: Sacrifices, feasts, and ritual. The cult outlined in great detail. **13–17:** Out of taxes received, the ruler provides for certain sacrifices; in contrast to the meddling of past kings, this is the only privilege and barley, one sixth of an ephah. ¹⁴ For oil the rule is one tenth of a bath from every kor, at ten bath to the kor; ¹⁵ one sheep in every flock of two hundred is to be reserved by every Israelite clan. For a grain-offering, a whole-offering, and a shared-offering, to make expiation for them, says the Lord GOD, ¹⁶ all the people of the land must bring this contribution to the ruler in Israel. ¹⁷ He is to be responsible for the whole-offering, the grain-offering, and the drink-offering, at pilgrim-feasts, new moons, sabbaths, and every sacred season observed by Israel. He himself is to provide the purification-offering and the grain-offering, the whole-offering and the shared-offering, needed to make expiation for Israel.

¹⁸ 'The Lord GOD says: On the first day of the first month you are to take a young bull without blemish and purify the sanctuary. ¹⁹ The priest must take some of the blood from the purification-offering and put it on the doorposts of the temple, on the four corners of the altar pedestal, and on the gateposts of the inner court. ²⁰ You are to do the same on the seventh day of the month for the man who has sinned through inadvertence or ignorance. So you are to purify the temple.

²¹ 'On the fourteenth day of the first month you are to celebrate the pilgrim-feast of Passover, and for the seven days of the feast you must eat bread made without yeast. ²² On that day the ruler is to provide a bull as a purification-offering for himself and for all the people. ²³ During the seven days of the feast he is to offer daily as a whole-offering to the LORD seven bulls and seven rams, all without blemish, and one he-goat daily as a purification-offering. ²⁴ With every bull and ram he is to provide a grain-offering of one ephah, together with a hin of oil for each ephah.

²⁵ 'He is to do the same thing also for the pilgrim-feast which falls on the fifteenth day of the seventh month; this also will last seven days, and he must provide the same purification-offering and whole-offering and the same quantity of grain and oil.

46 'The Lord GOD says: The east gate of the inner court must remain closed during the six working days; it is to be opened only on the sabbath and at new moon. ² When the ruler comes through the porch of the gate from the outside, he is to take his stand by the gatepost, while the priests sacrifice his whole-offering and shared-offerings. At the threshold of the gate he is to bow down in worship and then go out, but the gate is not to be closed until evening. ³ On sabbaths and at new moons the people also must bow down before the LORD at the entrance to that gate.

⁴ 'On the sabbath the whole-offering which the prince brings to the LORD is to be six lambs without blemish and a ram without blemish. ⁵ The grain-offering is to be an ephah with the ram and whatever he can give with the lambs, together with a hin of oil to every ephah. ⁶ At the new moon it is to be a young bull without blemish, six lambs and a ram, all without blemish; ⁷ he is to provide as the grain-offering one ephah with the bull and one ephah with the ram, with the lambs whatever he can afford, adding a hin of oil for every ephah.

⁸ 'Whenever the ruler comes in, he is to enter through the porch of the gate and go out by the same way. ⁹ When the people come to worship before the LORD on festal days, anyone who enters by the north gate to worship must leave by the south gate, and anyone who enters by the south gate must leave by the north gate. He is not to turn back and go out through the gate by which he came in but to continue in the same direction. ¹⁰ The ruler will then be among them, going in when they go in and coming out when they come out.

¹¹ 'At pilgrim-feasts and on festal days the grain-offering is to be an ephah with a bull, an ephah with a ram, and as much as he can afford with a lamb, together with a hin of oil for every ephah.

45:14 **the rule is:** *prob. rdg; Heb. adds* the bath, the oil. **every kor:** *so Gk; Heb. adds* the homer is ten bath. **to the kor:** *so Lat.; Heb.* to the homer.   45:15 **clan:** *so Gk; Heb. unintelligible.*   45:16 **all ... bring:** *prob. rdg; Heb. unintelligible.*

duty allowed the new ruler; see 2 Kgs. 16.10–18. **18–20:** The rite here for purifying *the sanctuary* does not accord with Lev. 16.1–34. Comparable discrepancies in relation to the prescriptions of the Pentateuch concerning sacrifices created problems about the eligibility of the entire book for the canon, as is known from rabbinic literature. **21:** *Passover:* see Lev. 23.4–8; Deut. 16.1–8. **25:** Pilgrim-feast of Booths; see Exod. 23.16; Lev. 23.33–36; Deut. 16.13–15. **46.1–2:** The ruler may enter the *inner court* to watch the *priests* offer the

¹²'When the ruler provides a whole-offering or shared-offerings as a voluntary sacrifice to the LORD, the east gate is to be opened for him, and he will make his whole-offering and his shared-offerings as he does on the sabbath. When he goes out, the gate must be closed behind him.

¹³'You must provide a yearling lamb without blemish daily as a whole-offering to the LORD; you are to provide it every morning. ¹⁴With it every morning you must provide as a grain-offering one sixth of an ephah with a third of a hin of oil to moisten the flour. The LORD's grain-offering is an observance prescribed for all time. ¹⁵Every morning, as a regular whole-offering, a lamb is to be offered with the grain-offering and the oil.

¹⁶'The Lord GOD says: If the ruler makes a gift out of his property to any of his sons, it will belong to his sons, since it is part of the family property. ¹⁷But when he makes such a gift to one of his slaves, it will belong to the slave only until the year of manumission, when it will revert to the ruler; it is the property of his sons and will belong to them.

¹⁸'The ruler must not oppress the people by taking any part of their holdings of land; he is to endow his sons from his own property, so that my people may not be deprived of their holdings.'

¹⁹Then the man brought me through the entrance by the side of the gate to the rooms which face north, the rooms set apart for the priests, and, pointing to a place on their west side, ²⁰he said to me, 'This is the place where the priests boil the reparation-offering and the purification-offering and bake the grain-offering; they may not take it into the outer court, for fear of transmitting holiness to the people.'

²¹The man then brought me out into the outer court and led me across to the four corners of the court, at each of which there was a further court. ²²These four courts were vaulted and were the same size, forty cubits long by thirty cubits wide. ²³Round each of the four was a course of stonework, with fireplaces constructed close up against the stones. ²⁴'These are the kitchens', he said, 'where the attendants boil the people's sacrifices.'

47 The man brought me back to the entrance of the temple, and I saw a spring of water issuing towards the east from under the threshold of the temple; for the temple faced east. The water was running down along the south side, to the right of the altar. ²He took me out through the north gate and led me round by an outside path to the east gate of the court, and I saw water was trickling from the south side. ³With a line in his hand the man went out eastwards, and he measured off a thousand cubits and made me walk through the water; it came up to my ankles. ⁴Again he measured a thousand cubits and made me walk through the water; it came up to my knees. He measured another thousand and made me walk through the water; it was up to my waist. ⁵He measured another thousand, and it was a torrent I could not cross; the water had risen and was deep enough to swim in, a torrent impossible to cross. ⁶'Take note of this, O man,' he said, and led me back to the bank. ⁷When I got to the bank I saw a great number of trees on each side. ⁸He said to me, 'This water flows out to the region lying east, and down to the Arabah; it will run into the sea whose waters are noxious, and they will be made fresh.

47:2 the court: so Gk; Heb. unintelligible.

---

sacrifice which the ruler has provided. 13–15: This daily morning sacrifice was unfailingly offered in the temple until the last days of Jerusalem in 70 C.E., when, according to Josephus (B.J. VI, 2, 1), it was discontinued. 17: In the year of manumission — probably every fiftieth or jubilee year — all lands reverted to original ownership; see Lev. 25.8–55. 20: Transmitting holiness must be avoided both to insure the sacredness of the offering and to protect from danger those who are unprepared. See 44.19; 2 Sam. 6.6–7.

47.1–48.35: Life in the new land and the new city. Both land and city are to be so arranged that the vitality emanating from God in the temple may keep the tribes in unity.

47.1–12: Life-giving water flowing from the temple is a symbolism found in Ps. 36.8–9; Joel 3.18; Zech. 14.8; Rev. 22.1–2. 3–6: In powerful contrast to this visionary stream which increases as it flows from the temple into the desert is the spring Gihon, which still emerges from the hillside under the temple area and quickly dries out in the valley of the brook Kidron, which is ordinarily a wadi or a dry wash. 8–9: Arabah is the geological rift forming the Dead Sea and the valley south of it, a barren desert. Even the Dead Sea, in whose noxious waters (26 percent salt, besides a high mineral content) no life can survive, will be made fresh and

9 When any one of the living creatures that swarm upon the earth comes where the torrent flows, it will draw life from it. Fish will be plentiful, for wherever these waters come the sea will be made fresh, and where the torrent flows everything will live. 10 From Engedi as far as En-eglaim fishermen will stand on its shores and spread their nets. All kinds of fish will be there in shoals, like the fish of the Great Sea. 11 Its swamps and pools will not have their waters made fresh; they will be left to serve as salt-pans. 12 Beside the torrent on either bank fruitful trees of every kind will grow. Their leaves will not wither, nor will their fruit fail; they will bear fruit early every month, for the water for them flows from the sanctuary; their fruit is for food and their leaves for healing.

Division of the land among the tribes

13 'THE Lord GOD says: Here are the boundaries within which the twelve tribes of Israel will enter into possession of the land, Joseph receiving two portions. 14 The land which I swore with hand uplifted to give to your forefathers you are to divide with each other; it must be assigned to you by lot as your holding. 15 This is the frontier: on its northern side, from the Great Sea through Hethlon, Lebo-hamath, 16 Zedad, Berothah, and Sibraim, located between the frontiers of Damascus and Hamath, to Hazar-enan, near the frontier of Hauran. 17 The frontier will extend from the sea to Hazar-enan on the frontier of Damascus and northwards; this is its northern side. 18 The eastern side runs alongside the territories of Hauran, Damascus, and Gilead, and alongside the territory of Israel; Jordan forms the boundary to the eastern sea, to Tamar. This is the eastern boundary. 19 The southern side runs from Tamar to the waters of Meribah-by-Kadesh; the region assigned to you reaches the Great Sea. This is the southern side towards the

Negeb. 20 The western side is the Great Sea, which forms a boundary as far as a point opposite Lebo-hamath. This is the western side.

21 'You are to distribute this land among the tribes of Israel 22 and assign it by lot as a share for yourselves and for any aliens who are living in your midst and have children among you. They are to be treated like native-born Israelites and receive with you a share by lot among the tribes of Israel. 23 You are to give the alien his share in whatever tribe he is resident. This is the word of the Lord GOD.

48 'These are the names of the tribes: In the extreme north, in the direction of Hethlon, to Lebo-hamath and Hazar-enan, with Damascus on the northern frontier in the direction of Hamath, and so from the eastern boundary to the western, will be Dan: one portion.

2 'Bordering on Dan, from the eastern boundary to the western, will be Asher: one portion.

3 'Bordering on Asher, from the eastern boundary to the western, will be Naphtali: one portion.

4 'Bordering on Naphtali, from the eastern boundary to the western, will be Manasseh: one portion.

5 'Bordering on Manasseh, from the eastern boundary to the western, will be Ephraim: one portion.

6 'Bordering on Ephraim, from the eastern boundary to the western, will be Reuben: one portion.

7 'Bordering on Reuben, from the eastern boundary to the western, will be Judah: one portion.

47:9 **torrent:** *so Gk; Heb.* two torrents.
47:15–16 **Lebo-hamath, Zedad:** *prob. rdg, cp. Gk; Heb.* Lebo, Zedad, Hamath.   47:16 **Hazar-enan:** *prob. rdg, cp. 48:1; Heb.* Hazer-hattikon.   47:17 **northwards:** *so Gk; Heb.* adds northwards and the frontier of Hamath.
48:1 **from . . . western:** *so Gk; Heb.* the eastern corner is the sea.

will give life. The image symbol is the whole earth's receiving life and nourishment from the LORD's presence in the temple. **10:** *En-gedi, En-eglaim:* oases on the western shore of the Dead Sea at the mouth of the wadi Kidron, just south of Qumran. *Great Sea* is the Mediterranean.

47.13–48.35: Israel's boundaries and the tribal portions. Except along the River Jordan, these boundaries approximate the greatest extent of the kingdom under David, the ideal king. Since, in the past, the tribes east of the Jordan tended to isolate themselves, no territories are assigned there. See Josh. 22.10–29; Judg. 5.15–17. **21–23:** Other codes provide that *aliens* be treated like Israelites, but only here are they given a *share* among the tribes of Israel. **48.1–8:** Since they minister in the sanctuary, the portion of priests and Levites is adjacent to it. *Judah,* the leading southern tribe, is closest to the sanctuary. It is placed among the northern tribes with

8 'Bordering on Judah, from the eastern boundary to the western, will be the sacred reserve which you must set apart. Its breadth will be twenty-five thousand cubits and its length the same as that of the tribal portions, from the eastern boundary to the western, and the sanctuary is to be in the centre of it. 9 'The reserve which you must set apart for the LORD is to measure twenty-five thousand cubits by twenty thousand. 10 The reserve is to be apportioned thus: the priests will have an area measuring twenty-five thousand cubits on the north side, ten thousand on the west, ten thousand on the east, and twenty-five thousand in length on the south side; the sanctuary of the LORD is to be in the centre of it. 11 It is to be for the consecrated priests of the family of Zadok, who kept my charge and did not follow the Israelites when they went astray, as the Levites did. 12 The area set apart for the priests from the reserved territory will be most sacred, adjoining the territory of the Levites.

13 'The Levites are to have a portion running parallel to the border of the priests. It is to be twenty-five thousand cubits long by ten thousand wide; altogether, the length is to be twenty-five thousand cubits and the breadth ten thousand.

14 'They must neither sell nor exchange any part of it; it is the best of the land and must not be alienated, for it is holy to the LORD.

15 'The remaining strip, five thousand cubits in width by twenty-five thousand, is the city's secular land for dwellings and common land. The city will be in the middle, 16 and these are to be its dimensions: on the northern side four thousand five hundred cubits, on the southern side four thousand five hundred cubits, on the eastern side four thousand five hundred cubits, on the western side four thousand five hundred cubits. 17 The common land belonging to the city is to be two hundred and fifty cubits to the north, two hundred and fifty to the south, two hundred and fifty to the east, and two hundred and fifty to the west. 18 What is left parallel to the reserve, ten thousand cubits to the east and ten thousand to the west, will provide food for those who work in the city. 19 Those

who work in the city are to cultivate it; they may be drawn from any of the tribes of Israel. 20 You are to set apart as sacred the whole reserve, twenty-five thousand cubits square, as far as the holding of the city.

21 'What is left over on either side of the sacred reserve and the city holding is to be assigned to the ruler. Eastwards, what lies over against the reserved twenty-five thousand cubits, as far as the eastern side, and westwards, what lies over against the twenty-five thousand cubits to the western side, parallel to the tribal portions, is to be assigned to the ruler; the sacred reserve and the sanctuary itself will be in the centre. 22 The holding of the Levites and the holding of the city will be in the middle of that which is assigned to the ruler; it will be between the frontiers of Judah and Benjamin.

23 'The rest of the tribes: from the eastern boundary to the western will be Benjamin: one portion.

24 'Bordering on Benjamin, from the eastern boundary to the western, will be Simeon: one portion.

25 'Bordering on Simeon, from the eastern boundary to the western, will be Issachar: one portion.

26 'Bordering on Issachar, from the eastern boundary to the western, will be Zebulun: one portion.

27 'Bordering on Zebulun, from the eastern boundary to the western, will be Gad: one portion.

28 'Bordering on Gad, on the side of the Negeb, the frontier on the south stretches from Tamar to the waters of Meribah-by-Kadesh, to the wadi of Egypt as far as the Great Sea.

29 'That is the land which you are to allot as a holding to the tribes of Israel, and those will be their allotted portions. This is the word of the Lord GOD.

30-31 'These are to be the ways out of the city, the gates being named after the tribes of Israel. The northern side, four thousand five hundred cubits long, is to have three gates,

48:9 **twenty thousand:** *prob. rdg; Heb.* ten thousand.
48:18 **to the west:** *prob. rdg; Heb. adds* and it will be parallel to the sacred reserve.

whom it had formerly lived in hostile rivalry, to show the harmony in the new nation. **15:** Land used for daily existence, i.e. unconnected with the cult, is *secular,* and so separated from the sanctuary by the priests' land. **16–19:** Jerusalem, much larger in extent than at any time in history—5000 cubits square or 1.6 miles those of Reuben, Judah, and Levi; [32] the eastern side, four thousand five hundred cubits long, three gates, those of Joseph, Benjamin, and Dan; [33] the southern side, four thousand five hundred cubits long, three gates, those of Simeon, Issachar, and Zebulun; [34] the

western side, four thousand five hundred cubits long, three gates, those of Gad, Asher, and Naphtali. [35] The perimeter of the city will be eighteen thousand cubits, and for all time to come the city's name will be "The LORD is there".'

square — will be a "federal" district, with the names of all the twelve tribes on its gates (vv. 30–34). **35:** Unnamed till now, the city will be called "The LORD is there," in Heb. a contrast in assonance to its old Canaanite name *Yerushalaim*. For other names given Jerusalem by prophets as a sign of future transformation, see Isa. 1.26; 60.14; 62.2–4; Jer. 3.17; Zech. 8.3. The new city with its name expresses the paradoxical concept of God's absolute transcendence and intimate closeness.

THE BOOK OF
Daniel

The reports about Daniel in this book may contain elements about an older figure, or figures, with the same name: a king in an Ugaritic legend of the fourteenth century B.C.E.; the example, along with Noah and Job, of a righteous person in Ezek. 14.14; and a wise person who knows secrets in Ezek. 28.3; these three Daniels may reflect an ancient tradition about a single figure.

The book divides neatly into two parts. In chs. 1–6, Daniel is a young Jew at a foreign court, who, by his ability to interpret royal dreams, and through divine revelation, becomes a vizier to kings. In chs. 8–12, Daniel himself has the visions, and must turn to angels for interpretation. Chapter 7, belonging with chs. 1–6 in its idea of a succession of kingdoms, but also containing the first of the visions characteristic of the second section, unites the two parts. In language, too, ch. 7 provides a bridge between the two parts: Aramaic, rather than Hebrew, is found in 2.4–7.28; see 2.4 n. In chs. 1–6 Daniel has many of the characteristics of Joseph at the Pharaoh's court in Gen. ch. 41; in chs. 7–12 the author builds on elements from the Book of the Prophet Ezekiel to fashion the most fully developed example of apocalyptic literature in the Old Testament; see 8.17 n., 12.1 n., and the heavenly figures of ch. 7.

The stories and visions are set in the Babylonian and Persian periods (sixth–fourth centuries B.C.E.), but they reflect a later time, primarily that of the successors to Alexander the Great. Antiochus IV Epiphanes (175–163 B.C.E.) and his wars with the Egyptians (see 7.8 n.) are especially in view. In chs. 7–12, Antiochus, though anonymous as befits apocalyptic literature, emerges in more and more detail as the oppressor of the Jews. In the face of his intense persecution, the book gives great encouragement to the Jews by promising God's ultimate vindication of the righteous.

Additional stories in the Daniel tradition are found in the Sept. expansion of the book, and appear in the Apocrypha in The Prayer of Azariah and The Song of the Three; Daniel and Susanna; and Daniel, Bel, and the Snake.

Daniel and his companions

1 In the third year of the reign of King Jehoiakim of Judah, Nebuchadnezzar, the Babylonian king, came and laid siege to Jerusalem. ² The Lord handed King Jehoiakim over to him, together with all that was left of the vessels from the house of God; and he carried them off to the land of Shinar, to the temple of his god, where he placed the vessels in the temple treasury.

³ The king ordered Ashpenaz, his chief eunuch, to bring into the palace some of the Israelite exiles, members of their royal house and of the nobility. ⁴ They were to be young men free from physical defect, handsome in appearance, at home in all branches of knowledge, well-informed, intelligent, and so fitted for service in the royal court; and he was to instruct them in the writings and language of the Chaldaeans. ⁵ The king assigned them a daily allowance of fine food and wine from the royal table, and their training was to last for three years; at the end of that time

1.1–21: Daniel as a young man at a foreign court. See Introduction. The chronology is uncertain, and dates given are not necessarily precise. 1: *Third year of Jehoiakim:* 607 or 606 B.C.E. *Nebuchadnezzar* became king in 605; but see 2 Kgs. 24.1–6. The first deportation took place in 598; see 2 Kgs. 24.10–17. 2: *Shinar* was they would enter his service. [6] Among them were certain Jews: Daniel, Hananiah, Mishael, and Azariah. [7] To them the master of the eunuchs gave new names: Daniel he called Belteshazzar, Hananiah Shadrach, Mishael Meshach, and Azariah Abed-nego.

[8] Daniel determined not to become contaminated with the food and wine from the royal table, and begged the master of the eunuchs to excuse him from touching it. [9] God caused the master to look on Daniel with kindness and goodwill, [10] and to Daniel's request he replied, 'I am afraid of my lord the king: he has assigned you food and drink, and if he were to see you and your companions looking miserable compared with the other young men of your own age, my head would be forfeit.' [11] Then Daniel said to the attendant whom the master of the eunuchs had put in charge of Hananiah, Mishael, Azariah, and himself, [12] 'Submit us to this test for ten days: give us only vegetables to eat and water to drink; [13] then compare our appearance with that of the young men who have lived on the king's food, and be guided in your treatment of us by what you see for yourself.' [14] He agreed to the proposal and submitted them to this test. [15] At the end of the ten days they looked healthier and better nourished than any of the young men who had lived on the food from the king. [16] So the attendant took away the food assigned to them and the wine they were to drink, and gave them vegetables only.

[17] To all four of these young men God gave knowledge, understanding of books, and learning of every kind, and Daniel had a gift for interpreting visions and dreams of every kind. [18] At the time appointed by the king for introducing the young men to court, the master of the eunuchs brought them into the presence of Nebuchadnezzar. [19] The king talked with them all, but found none of them to compare with Daniel, Hananiah, Mishael, and Azariah; so they entered the royal service. [20] Whenever the king consulted them on any matter calling for insight and judgement, he found them ten times superior to all the magicians and exorcists in his whole kingdom.

[21] Daniel remained there until the accession of King Cyrus.

Daniel's wisdom

2 In the second year of his reign Nebuchadnezzar was troubled by dreams he had, so much so that he could not sleep. [2] He gave orders for the magicians, exorcists, sorcerers, and Chaldaeans to be summoned to expound to him what he had been dreaming. When they presented themselves before the king, [3] he said to them, 'I have had a dream, and my mind has been troubled to know what the dream was.' [4] The Chaldaeans, speaking in Aramaic, said, 'Long live the king! Relate the dream to us, your servants, and we shall give you the interpretation.' [5] The king answered, 'This is my firm decision: if you do not make both dream and interpretation known to me, you will be hacked limb from limb and your houses will be reduced to rubble. [6] But if you tell me the dream and its interpretation, you will be richly rewarded by me and loaded with honours. Tell me, then, the dream and its interpretation.' [7] They said again, 'Let the king relate the dream to his servants, and we shall

2:4 **Long live:** *from here to the end of ch. 7 the text is in Aramaic.*   2:5 **reduced to rubble:** *or forfeit.*

in southern Mesopotamia. **3:** *Ashpenaz* is otherwise unknown. **6:** *Hananiah, Mishael and Azariah* were common names; Azariah appears in Neh. 10.2, and Hananiah in Neh. 10.23. **7:** This was also the case with Joseph in Gen. 41.45. **8:** *Determined not to become contaminated:* compare 1 Macc. 1.62; see Ezek. 4.13; Hos. 9.3. **12:** The total abstinence from meat was a safeguard against eating forbidden meats such as pork. **17:** *Visions and dreams:* the practice of dream interpretation in Mesopotamia, and the special significance attributed to them, goes back to the third millennium. **20:** This verse anticipates the plots in chs. 2; 4; 5. *Magicians and exorcists:* the Heb. terms are borrowed from the ancient Akkadian, meaning, respectively, "interpreters of dreams" and "incantation officials." **21:** *First years of King Cyrus:* 539 B.C.E., sixty-eight years after the date (607 or 606) in v. 1.

2.1–49: The revelation of the future history of five world kingdoms. 1: *Second year:* 604 B.C.E. **2:** *Chaldaeans:* sages, rather than simply people from Chaldea. Chaldeans were found in great numbers in the Grecian lands, usually as astrologers and magicians. **4:** *In Aramaic:* either the author is deliberately following the format of the Book of Ezra, in which the center chapters are in Aram., or else the stories in this section were handed tell him the interpretation.' 8 The king rejoined, 'It is clear to me that you are trying to gain time, because you see that I have come to this firm decision: 9 if you do not make the dream known to me, there is but one verdict for you, and one only. What is more, you have conspired to tell me mischievous lies to my face in the hope that with time things may alter. Relate the dream to me, therefore, and then I shall know that you can give me its interpretation.' 10 The Chaldaeans answered, 'No one on earth can tell your majesty what you wish to know. No king, however great and powerful, has ever made such a demand of a magician, exorcist, or Chaldaean. 11 What your majesty asks is too hard; none but the gods can tell you, and they dwell remote from mortals.' 12 At this the king became furious, and in great rage he ordered all the wise men of Babylon to be put to death. 13 A decree was issued for the execution of the wise men, and search was made for Daniel and his companions.

14 As Arioch, captain of the royal bodyguard, set out to execute the wise men of Babylon, Daniel made a discreet and tactful approach to him. 15 He said, 'May I ask you, sir, as the king's representative, why his majesty has issued so peremptory a decree?' Arioch explained the matter, 16 and Daniel went to the king and begged to be allowed a certain time by which he would give the king the interpretation. 17 He then went home and made the matter known to Hananiah, Mishael, and Azariah, his companions, saying 18 they should implore the God of heaven to disclose this secret in his mercy, so that they should not be put to death along with the rest of the wise men of Babylon. 19 The secret was then revealed to Daniel in a vision by night, and he blessed the God of heaven 20 in these words:

'Blessed be God's name from age to
　　age,
for to him belong wisdom and power.
21 He changes seasons and times;
he deposes kings and sets up kings;
he gives wisdom to the wise
and knowledge to those who have
　　discernment;

22 he reveals deep mysteries;
he knows what lies in darkness;
with him light has its dwelling.
23 God of my fathers, to you I give thanks
　　and praise,
for you have given me wisdom and
　　power.
Now you have made known to me what
　　we asked;
you have given us the answer for the
　　king.'

24 Daniel therefore went to Arioch, whom the king had charged with the execution of the wise men of Babylon. He approached him and said, 'Do not put the wise men to death; bring me before the king and I shall tell him the interpretation of his dream.' 25 Greatly agitated, Arioch brought Daniel before the king. 'I have found among the Jewish exiles', he said, 'a man who will make known to your majesty the interpretation of your dream.' 26 The king asked Daniel (who was also called Belteshazzar), 'Are you able to make known to me what I saw in my dream and to interpret it?' 27 Daniel answered: 'No wise man, exorcist, magician, or diviner can tell your majesty the secret about which you ask. 28 But there is in heaven a God who reveals secrets, and he has made known to King Nebuchadnezzar what is to be at the end of this age. This is the dream and these are the visions that came into your head: 29 the thoughts that came to you, your majesty, as you lay on your bed, concerned the future, and he who reveals secrets has made known to you what is to be. 30 This secret has been revealed to me, not because I am wiser than anyone alive, but in order that your majesty may know the interpretation and understand the thoughts which have entered your mind.

31 'As you watched, there appeared to your majesty a great image. Huge and dazzling, it stood before you, fearsome to behold. 32 The head of the image was of fine gold, its chest and arms of silver, its belly and thighs of bronze, 33 its legs of iron, its feet part iron and part clay. 34 While you watched, you saw a stone hewn from a mountain by no human hand; it struck the image on its feet of iron

2:34 **from a mountain:** *so Gk; Aram. omits.*

down in Aram. **11:** *None but the gods:* this anticipates v. 47, in which the king recognizes Daniel's words as divinely given. **28:** *A God who reveals secrets:* see v. 22. **32:** The theme of a descending scale of metals representing ages of world history is also found in Greece, in Hesiod's *Works and Days*; in ancient Hindu and clay and shattered them. 35 Then the iron, the clay, the bronze, the silver, and the gold were all shattered into fragments, and as if they were chaff from a summer threshing-floor the wind swept them away until no trace of them remained. But the stone which struck the image grew and became a huge mountain and filled the whole earth.

36 'That was the dream; now we shall relate to your majesty its interpretation. 37 Your majesty, the king of kings, to whom the God of heaven has given the kingdom with its power, its might, and its honour, 38 in whose hands he has placed mankind wherever they live, the wild animals, and the birds of the air, granting you sovereignty over them all: you yourself are that head of gold. 39 After you there will arise another kingdom, inferior to yours, then a third kingdom, of bronze, which will have sovereignty over the whole world. 40 There will be a fourth kingdom, strong as iron; just as iron shatters and breaks all things, it will shatter and crush all the others. 41 As in your vision the feet and toes were part potter's clay and part iron, so it will be a divided kingdom, and just as you saw iron mixed with clay from the ground, so it will have in it something of the strength of iron. 42 The toes being part iron and part clay means that the kingdom will be partly strong and partly brittle. 43 As in your vision the iron was mixed with the clay, so there will be a mixing of families by intermarriage, but such alliances will not be stable: iron does not mix with clay. 44 In the times of those kings the God of heaven will establish a kingdom which will never be destroyed, nor will it ever pass to another people; it will shatter all these kingdoms and make an end of them, while it will itself endure for ever. 45 This is the meaning of your vision of the stone being hewn from a mountain by no human hand, and then shattering the iron, the bronze, the clay, the silver, and the gold. A mighty God has made known to your majesty what is to be

hereafter. The dream and its interpretation are true and trustworthy.

46 At this King Nebuchadnezzar prostrated himself and did homage to Daniel, and he gave orders that there should be presented to him a tribute of grain and soothing offerings. 47 'Truly,' he said, 'your God is indeed God of gods and Lord over kings, and a revealer of secrets, since you have been able to reveal this secret.' 48 The king then promoted Daniel to high position and bestowed on him many rich gifts. He gave him authority over the whole province of Babylon and put him in charge of all Babylon's wise men. 49 At Daniel's request the king appointed Shadrach, Meshach, and Abed-nego to administer the province of Babylon, while Daniel himself remained at court.

The fiery furnace

3 King Nebuchadnezzar made a gold image, ninety feet high and nine feet broad, and had it set up on the plain of Dura in the province of Babylon. 2 The king then summoned the satraps, prefects, governors, counsellors, treasurers, judges, magistrates, and all the provincial officials to assemble and attend the dedication of the image he had set up. 3 The satraps, prefects, governors, counsellors, treasurers, judges, magistrates, and all governors of provinces assembled for the dedication of the image King Nebuchadnezzar had set up, and they took their places in front of the image. 4 A herald proclaimed in a loud voice, 'Peoples and nations of every language, you are commanded, 5 when you hear the sound of horn, pipe, zither, triangle, dulcimer, a full consort of music, to prostrate yourselves and worship the gold image which King Nebuchadnezzar has set up. 6 Whosoever does not prostrate himself and worship will be thrown forthwith

3:1 **ninety . . . broad:** *lit.* sixty cubits high and six cubits broad.

mythology; and elsewhere. **37–40:** The four kingdoms are usually taken to be the Babylonian, the Median, the Persian, and the Macedonian Greek; compare 8.20–21. There is no confirming evidence for the opinion (9.1), found in Jer. 51.11, 28 as well, that the Medes existed as a world power quite separate from the Persians. **44:** The fifth kingdom will bring an end to world history as then known. **47:** Verse 22, alluded to here and in v. 28, is thereby a key theme of the story. **48:** Daniel's appointment is similar to that of Joseph in Gen. 41.41.

3.1–30: God delivers the three young men from the fiery furnace. The three are presented here as Daniel-like figures (see ch. 6), but do not appear again after this chapter. **1:** *An image:* the account does not give the exact nature of the statue but indicates that it is a major Babylonian god. *Dura:* a place name common into a blazing furnace.' 7 Accordingly, no sooner did the sound of horn, pipe, zither, triangle, dulcimer, a full consort of music, reach them than all the peoples and nations of every language prostrated themselves and worshipped the gold image set up by King Nebuchadnezzar.

8 Some Chaldaeans seized the opportunity to approach the king with a malicious accusation against the Jews. 9 They said, 'Long live the king! 10 Your majesty has issued a decree that everyone who hears the sound of horn, pipe, zither, triangle, dulcimer, a full consort of music, must fall down and worship the gold image; 11 and whoever does not do so will be thrown into a blazing furnace. 12 There are certain Jews whom you have put in charge of the administration of the province of Babylon. These men, Shadrach, Meshach, and Abed-nego, have disregarded your royal command; they do not serve your gods, nor do they worship the gold image you set up.' 13 In furious rage Nebuchadnezzar ordered Shadrach, Meshach, and Abed-nego to be fetched, and when they were brought into his presence, 14 he asked them, 'Is it true, Shadrach, Meshach, and Abed-nego, that you do not serve my gods or worship the gold image which I have set up? 15 Now if you are ready to prostrate yourselves as soon as you hear the sound of horn, pipe, zither, triangle, dulcimer, a full consort of music, and to worship the image that I have made, well and good. But if you do not worship it, you will be thrown forthwith into the blazing furnace; and what god is there that can deliver you from my power?' 16 Their reply to the king was: 'Your majesty, we have no need to answer you on this matter. 17 If there is a god who is able to save us from the blazing furnace, it is our God whom we serve; he will deliver us from your majesty's power. 18 But if not, be it known to your majesty that we shall neither serve your gods nor worship the gold image you have set up.'

19 At this Nebuchadnezzar was furious with them, and his face became distorted with anger. He ordered that the furnace should be heated to seven times its usual heat, 20 and commanded some of the strongest men in his army to bind Shadrach, Meshach, and Abed-nego and throw them into the blazing furnace. 21 Then, just as they were, in trousers, shirts, headdresses, and their other clothes, they were bound and thrown into the furnace. 22 Because the king's order was peremptory and the furnace exceedingly hot, those who were carrying the three men were killed by the flames; 23 and Shadrach, Meshach, and Abed-nego fell bound into the blazing furnace.

24 Then King Nebuchadnezzar, greatly agitated, sprang to his feet, saying to his courtiers, 'Was it not three men whom we threw bound into the fire?' They answered, 'Yes, certainly, your majesty.' 25 'Yet', he insisted, 'I can see four men walking about in the fire, free and unharmed; and the fourth looks like a god.' 26 Nebuchadnezzar approached the furnace door and called, 'Shadrach, Meshach, and Abed-nego, servants of the Most High God, come out!' When Shadrach, Meshach, and Abed-nego emerged from the fire, 27 the satraps, prefects, governors, and the king's courtiers gathered round them and saw how the fire had had no power to harm their bodies. The hair of their heads had not been singed, their trousers were untouched, and no smell of fire lingered about them.

28 Nebuchadnezzar declared: 'Blessed be the God of Shadrach, Meshach, and Abed-nego! He has sent his angel to save his servants who, trusting in him, disobeyed the royal command; they were willing to submit themselves to the fire rather than to serve or worship any god other than their own God. 29 I therefore issue this decree: anyone, whatever his people, nation, or language, if he speaks blasphemy against the God of Shadrach, Meshach, and Abed-nego, is to be hacked limb from limb and his house is to be

3:23 *The Prayer of Azariah and The Song of the Three* (*printed in the Revised English Bible Apocrypha*) *follow this verse in some translations of the Bible.*   3:28 **to the fire:** *so Gk; Aram. omits.*

in ancient Babylonia; the exact location cannot be determined. **17–18:** *But if not:* that is, even if God does not save us. The intention is not to imply that God cannot save, but that they can be saved only by the God they worship. **23:** At this point the Sept. introduces Shadrach, Meshach, and Abed-nego. Roman Catholic Bibles retain it here, but Protestant Bibles include it as a separate book of the Apocrypha, in this version called The Prayer of Azariah and The Song of the Three. **25:** *Like a god:* in v. 28, this fourth "person" is called an angel. **28–29:** The king's acknowledgment here is similar to the endings in 2.47; 4.37; 6.26–7.

reduced to rubble; for there is no other god who can save in such a manner.' ³⁰Then the king advanced the fortunes of Shadrach, Meshach, and Abed-nego in the province of Babylon.

Nebuchadnezzar's madness

4 KING Nebuchadnezzar to all peoples and nations of every language throughout the whole world: May your prosperity increase! ²It is my pleasure to recount the signs and wonders which the Most High God has worked for me:

³How great are his signs,
how mighty his wonders!
His kingdom is an everlasting kingdom,
his sovereignty endures through all
generations.

⁴I, Nebuchadnezzar, was living contentedly at home in the luxury of my palace, ⁵but as I lay on my bed, I had a dream which filled me with fear, and the fantasies and visions which came into my head caused me dismay. ⁶I issued an order summoning to my presence all the wise men of Babylon to make known to me the interpretation of the dream. ⁷When the magicians, exorcists, Chaldaeans, and diviners came in, I related my dream to them, but they were unable to interpret it for me. ⁸Finally there came before me Daniel, who is called Belteshazzar after the name of my god, a man in whom resides the spirit of the holy gods. To him also I related the dream: ⁹'Belteshazzar, chief of the magicians, you have in you, as I know, the spirit of the holy gods, and no secret baffles you; listen to what I saw in my dream, and tell me its interpretation.

¹⁰'This is the vision which came to me while I lay on my bed:

As I was looking,
there appeared a very lofty tree at the
centre of the earth;
¹¹the tree grew great and became strong;

its top reached to the sky,
and it was visible to earth's farthest
bounds.
¹²Its foliage was beautiful
and its fruit abundant,
and it yielded food for all.
Beneath it the wild beasts found
shelter,
the birds lodged in the branches,
and from it all living creatures fed.

¹³'This is what I saw in the vision which came to me while I lay on my bed:

There appeared a watcher,
a holy one coming down from heaven.
¹⁴In a mighty voice he cried,
"Hew down the tree, lop off the
branches,
strip away its foliage and scatter the
fruit;
let the wild beasts flee from beneath it
and the birds from its branches;
¹⁵but leave the stump with its roots in the
ground.

'"So, bound with iron and bronze
among the lush grass,
let him be drenched with the dew of
heaven
and share the lot of the beasts in their
pasture—
¹⁶his mind will cease to be human,
and he will be given the mind of a
beast.
Seven times will pass over him.
¹⁷The issue has been determined by the
watchers
and the sentence pronounced by the
holy ones.

'"Thereby the living will know that the Most High is sovereign in the kingdom of men: he gives the kingdom to whom he wills, and may appoint over it the lowliest of mankind."
¹⁸'This is the dream which I, King Nebu-

4:1 In Aram. 3:31.   4:4 In Aram. 4:1.   4:9 **listen to:** so Gk (Theod.); Aram. visions of.

4.1–37: Nebuchadnezzar loses and regains the throne. This chapter has the form of a letter; it turns from the first to the third person in vv. 19–33. **3:** The king's earlier reverence for Daniel's God (2.47 and 3.28–29) here emerges into full praise. **8:** Belteshazzar: the author either mistakenly or according to folk etymology considers Belteshazzar to contain the name of the Babylonian god Bel. Actually it is a shortened form of a simple name, "Balatshuuzur," meaning "guards his life." **13:** Watcher, holy one are synonyms for "angel." The first is not found in the Bible outside this chapter, but appears often in the Book of Enoch (in the Pseudepigrapha) as a term for archangel. The second is used in Dan. 8.13 for angel. **15:** The metaphor changes from a tree to chadnezzar, dreamt; now, Belteshazzar, tell me its interpretation, for, though not one of the wise men in all my kingdom is able to make its meaning known to me, you can do it, because in you is the spirit of the holy gods.'

19 Daniel, who was called Belteshazzar, was dumbfounded for a moment, dismayed by his thoughts; but the king said, 'Do not let the dream and its interpretation dismay you.' Belteshazzar answered, 'My lord, if only the dream applied to those who hate you and its interpretation to your enemies! 20 The tree which you saw grow great and become strong, reaching with its top to the sky and visible to earth's farthest bounds, 21 its foliage beautiful and its fruit abundant, a tree which yielded food for all, beneath which the wild beasts dwelt and in whose branches the birds lodged: 22 that tree, your majesty, is you. You have become great and strong; your power has grown and reaches the sky; your sovereignty extends to the ends of the earth. 23 Also, your majesty, you saw a watcher, a holy one, coming down from heaven and saying, "Hew down the tree and destroy it, but leave the stump with its roots in the ground. So, bound with iron and bronze among the lush grass, let him be drenched with the dew of heaven and share the lot of the beasts until seven times pass over him."

24 'This is the interpretation, your majesty: it is a decree of the Most High which affects my lord the king. 25 You will be banished from human society; you will be made to live with the wild beasts; like oxen you will feed on grass, and you will be drenched with the dew of heaven. Seven times will pass over you until you have acknowledged that the Most High is sovereign over the realm of humanity and gives it to whom he wills. 26 As the command was given to leave the stump of the tree with its roots, by this you may know that from the time you acknowledge the sovereignty of Heaven your rule will endure. 27 Your majesty, be advised by me: let charitable deeds replace your sins, generosity to the poor your wrongdoing. It may be that you will long enjoy contentment.'

28 All this befell King Nebuchadnezzar. 29 At the end of twelve months the king was walking on the roof of the royal palace at Babylon, 30 and he exclaimed, 'Is not this Babylon the great which I have built as a royal residence by my mighty power and for the honour of my own majesty?' 31 The words were still on his lips, when there came a voice from heaven: 'To you, King Nebuchadnezzar, the word is spoken: the kingdom has passed from you. 32 You are banished from human society; you are to live with the wild beasts and feed on grass like oxen. Seven times will pass over you until you have acknowledged that the Most High is sovereign over the realm of humanity and gives it to whom he will.' 33 At that very moment this judgement came upon Nebuchadnezzar: he was banished from human society to eat grass like oxen, and his body was drenched with the dew of heaven, until his hair became shaggy like an eagle and his nails grew like birds' claws.

34 At the end of the appointed time, I, Nebuchadnezzar, looked up towards heaven and I was restored to my right mind. I blessed the Most High, praising and glorifying the Ever-living One:

> His sovereignty is everlasting
> and his kingdom endures through all
>   generations.
> 35 All who dwell on earth count for
>   nothing;
> he does as he pleases with the host of
>   heaven
> and with those who dwell on earth.
> No one can oppose his power
> or question what he does.

36 At that very time I was restored to my right mind and, for the glory of my kingdom, my majesty and royal splendour returned to me. My courtiers and my nobles sought audience of me, and I was re-established in my kingdom and my power was greatly increased. 37 Now I, Nebuchadnezzar, praise and exalt and glorify the King of heaven; for all his acts are right and his ways are just, and

---

a beast to a human. **16:** *Times:* years, as in 7.25. **25:** *The Most High is sovereign:* see v. 30 n. **26:** *Heaven* as a euphemism for God, common in the Apocrypha, is not found elsewhere in the OT. **30–31:** The sin of pride is here given as the reason for his fall, as in Ezek. 31.10; see v. 27. **33:** A temporary lapse in the reign of Nebuchadnezzar is unknown, but does fit the last Babylonian king, Nabonidus, who (inexplicably) spent part of his reign at the north Arabian oasis of Taima. **34b–35:** These verses are an expansion of v. 3.

he can bring low those whose conduct is arrogant.

The writing on the wall

5 KING Belshazzar gave a grand banquet for a thousand of his nobles and he was drinking wine in their presence. ²Under the influence of the wine, Belshazzar gave orders for the vessels of gold and silver which his father Nebuchadnezzar had taken from the temple at Jerusalem to be fetched, so that he and his nobles, along with his concubines and courtesans, might drink from them. ³So those vessels belonging to the house of God, the temple at Jerusalem, were brought, and the king, the nobles, and the concubines and courtesans drank from them. ⁴They drank their wine and they praised their gods of gold, silver, bronze, iron, wood, and stone.

⁵Suddenly there appeared the fingers of a human hand writing on the plaster of the palace wall opposite the lamp, and the king saw the palm of the hand as it wrote. ⁶At this the king turned pale; dismay filled his mind, the strength went from his legs, and his knees knocked together. ⁷He called in a loud voice for the exorcists, Chaldaeans, and diviners to be brought in; then, addressing Babylon's wise men, he said, 'Whoever reads this writing and tells me its interpretation shall be robed in purple and have a gold chain hung round his neck, and he shall rank third in the kingdom.' ⁸All the king's wise men came, but they could neither read the writing nor make known to the king its interpretation. ⁹Then his deep dismay drove all colour from King Belshazzar's cheeks, and his nobles were in a state of confusion.

¹⁰Drawn by what the king and his nobles were saying, the queen entered the banqueting hall: 'Long live the king!' she said. 'Why this dismay, and why do you look so pale? ¹¹There is a man in your kingdom who has the spirit of the holy gods in him; he was known in your father's time to possess clear insight and godlike wisdom, so that King Nebuchadnezzar, your father, appointed him chief of the magicians, exorcists, Chaldaeans, and diviners. ¹²This Daniel, whom the king named Belteshazzar, is known to have exceptional ability, with knowledge and

insight, and the gift of interpreting dreams, explaining riddles, and unravelling problems; let him be summoned now and he will give the interpretation.'

¹³Daniel was then brought into the royal presence, and the king addressed him: 'So you are Daniel, one of the Jewish exiles whom my royal father brought from Judah. ¹⁴I am informed that the spirit of the gods resides in you and that you are known as a man of clear insight and exceptional wisdom. ¹⁵The wise men, the exorcists, have just been brought before me to read this writing and make known its interpretation to me, but they have been unable to give its meaning. ¹⁶I am told that you are able to furnish interpretations and unravel problems. Now, if you can read the writing and make known the interpretation, you shall be robed in purple and have a gold chain hung round your neck, and you shall rank third in the kingdom.' ¹⁷Daniel replied, 'Your majesty, I do not look for gifts from you; give your rewards to another. Nevertheless I shall read your majesty the writing and make known to you its interpretation.

¹⁸'My lord king, the Most High God gave a kingdom with power, glory, and majesty to your father Nebuchadnezzar; ¹⁹and, because of the power he bestowed on him, all peoples and nations of every language trembled with fear before him. He put to death whom he would and spared whom he would, he promoted them at will and at will abased them. ²⁰But, when he became haughty and stubborn and presumptuous, he was deposed from his royal throne and stripped of his glory. ²¹He was banished from human society, and his mind became like that of an animal; he had to live with the wild asses and to feed on grass like oxen, and his body was drenched with the dew of heaven, until he came to acknowledge that the Most High God is sovereign over the realm of humanity and appoints over it whom he will. ²²But although you knew all this, you, his son Belshazzar, did not humble your heart. ²³You have set yourself up against the Lord of heaven; his temple vessels have been fetched for you and your nobles, your concubines

5:10 **queen:** or queen mother.   5:12 **unravelling problems:** or unbinding spells.   5:16 **unravel problems:** or unbind spells.

5.1–31: **Corruption punished. 1:** *Belshazzar* was the son of Nabonidus, but is never referred to as king in Babylonian texts; he ruled as vice-regent while his father was away from the country; see 4.33 n. **7:** *Shall rank* and courtesans to drink from them. You have praised gods fashioned from silver, gold, bronze, iron, wood, and stone, which cannot see or hear or know, and you have not given glory to God, from whom comes your every breath, and in whose charge are all your ways. 24 That is why he sent the hand and why it wrote this inscription.

25 'The words inscribed were: "Mene mene tekel u-pharsin." 26 Their interpretation is this: mene, God has numbered the days of your kingdom and brought it to an end; 27 tekel, you have been weighed in the balance and found wanting; 28 u-pharsin, your kingdom has been divided and given to the Medes and Persians.' 29 Then at Belshazzar's command Daniel was robed in purple and a gold chain was hung round his neck, and proclamation was made that he should rank third in the kingdom.

30 That very night Belshazzar king of the Chaldaeans was slain, 31 and Darius the Mede took the kingdom, being then about sixty-two years old.

Daniel in the lion-pit

6 It pleased Darius to appoint a hundred and twenty satraps to be in charge throughout his kingdom, 2 and over them three chief ministers, to whom the satraps were to submit their reports so that the king's interests might not suffer; of these three ministers, Daniel was one. 3 Daniel outshone the other ministers and the satraps because of his exceptional ability, and it was the king's intention to appoint him over the whole kingdom. 4 Then the ministers and satraps began to look round for some pretext to attack Daniel's administration of the kingdom, but they failed to find any malpractice on his part, for he was faithful to his trust. Since they could discover neither negligence nor malpractice, 5 they said, 'We shall not find any ground for bringing a charge against this Daniel unless it is connected with his religion.' 6 These ministers and satraps, having watched for an opportunity to approach the king, said to him, 'Long live King Darius! 7 We, the ministers of the kingdom, prefects, satraps, courtiers, and governors, have taken counsel and all are agreed that the king should issue a decree and bring into force a binding edict to the effect that whoever presents a petition to any god or human being other than the king during the next thirty days is to be thrown into the lion-pit. 8 Now let your majesty issue the edict and have it put in writing so that it becomes unalterable, for the law of the Medes and Persians may never be revoked.' 9 Accordingly the edict was signed by King Darius.

10 When Daniel learnt that this decree had been issued, he went into his house. It had in the roof-chamber windows open towards Jerusalem; and there he knelt down three times a day and offered prayers and praises to his God as was his custom. 11 His enemies, on the watch for an opportunity to catch him, found Daniel at his prayers making supplication to his God. 12 They then went into the king's presence and reminded him of the edict. 'Your majesty,' they said, 'have you not issued an edict that any person who, within the next thirty days, presents a petition to any god or human being other than your majesty is to be thrown into the lion-pit?' The king answered, 'The matter has been determined in accordance with the law of the Medes and Persians, which may not be revoked.' 13 So they said to the king, 'Daniel, one of the Jewish exiles, has disregarded both your majesty

5:26 **mene**: *that is* numbered.   5:27 **tekel**: *that is* shekel *or* weight.   5:28 **u-pharsin**: *prob. rdg; Aram.* peres. *There is a play on three possible meanings:* half-mina *or* divisions *or* Persians.   5:31 *In Aram.* 6:1.

third: that is, after the king and crown prince; compare 2.48. **18–21:** A summary of ch. 4. **25:** *Mene mene tekel u-pharsin: tekel,* Heb. *shekel,* was a sixtieth of a *mene,* Heb. *mina. U* means "and"; *pharsin* means two *pheres,* with one *pheres* being a half-shekel. The weights, or coins, are here in descending value; this is in accord with the comparable descending values of the metals in 2.32. The weights are symbolic of the five kings after Nebuchadnezzar, including Belshazzar. **31:** See 2.37–40 n. No Darius is known as king of the Medes. The Persian king Darius ruled 522–486 B.C.E.

6.1–28: Daniel impresses Darius. The plot is a variant of that of ch. 3. **1:** *Darius:* see 5.31 n. *A hundred and twenty:* Persian sources refer to numbers of satrapies (province states) only up to twenty-nine; this text uses a typical biblical round number; compare Esther 8.9. **7:** A drastic form of punishment was to be thrown into *the lion-pit.* **8:** *The law of the Medes and Persians:* this phrase has passed into our everyday language to mean something unchangeable. **10:** *Open towards Jerusalem:* the sacred direction for Jewish prayer, as in 1 Kgs. 8.44.

and the edict, and is making petition to his God three times a day.' ¹⁴When the king heard this, he was greatly distressed; he tried to think of a way to save Daniel, and continued his efforts till sunset. ¹⁵The men watched for an opportunity to approach the king, and said to him, 'Your majesty must know that by the law of the Medes and Persians no edict or decree issued by the king may be altered.' ¹⁶Then the king gave the order for Daniel to be brought and thrown into the lion-pit; but he said to Daniel, 'Your God whom you serve at all times, may he save you.' ¹⁷A stone was brought and put over the mouth of the pit, and the king sealed it with his signet and with the signets of his nobles, so that no attempt could be made to rescue Daniel.

¹⁸The king went to his palace and spent the night fasting; no woman was brought to him, and sleep eluded him. ¹⁹He was greatly agitated and, at the first light of dawn, he rose and went to the lion-pit. ²⁰When he came near he called anxiously, 'Daniel, servant of the living God, has your God whom you serve continually been able to save you from the lions?' ²¹Daniel answered, 'Long live the king! ²²My God sent his angel to shut the lions' mouths and they have not injured me; he judged me innocent, and moreover I had done your majesty no injury.' ²³The king was overjoyed and gave orders that Daniel should be taken up out of the pit. When this was done no trace of injury was found on him, because he had put his faith in his God. ²⁴By order of the king those who out of malice had accused Daniel were brought and flung into the lion-pit along with their children and their wives, and before they reached the bottom the lions were upon them and devoured them, bones and all.

²⁵King Darius wrote to all peoples and nations of every language throughout the whole world: 'May your prosperity increase! ²⁶I have issued a decree that in all my royal domains everyone is to fear and reverence the God of Daniel,

for he is the living God, the everlasting,
  whose kingly power will never be
  destroyed;
  whose sovereignty will have no end—
²⁷a saviour, a deliverer, a worker of signs
  and wonders
in heaven and on earth,
  who has delivered Daniel from the
  power of the lions.'

²⁸Prosperity attended Daniel during the reigns of Darius and Cyrus the Persian.

Daniel's visions

7 In the first year that Belshazzar was king of Babylon, a dream and visions came to Daniel as he lay on his bed. Then he wrote down the dream, and here his account begins.

²In my vision during the night while I, Daniel, was gazing intently I saw the Great Sea churned up by the four winds of heaven, ³and four great beasts rising out of the sea, each one different from the others. ⁴The first was like a lion, but it had an eagle's wings. I watched until its wings were plucked off and it was lifted from the ground and made to stand on two feet as if it were a human being; it was also given the mind of a human being. ⁵Then I saw another, a second beast, like a bear. It had raised itself on one side, and it had three ribs in its mouth between its teeth. The command was given to it: 'Get up and gorge yourself with flesh.' ⁶After this as I gazed I saw another, a beast like a leopard with four wings like those of a bird on its back; this creature had four heads, and it was invested with sovereign power. ⁷Next in the night visions I saw a fourth beast, fearsome and grisly and exceedingly strong, with great iron teeth. It devoured and crunched, and it trampled underfoot what was left. It was different from all the beasts which went before it, and had ten horns. ⁸While I was considering the horns there appeared another horn, a little one,

---

14: Darius here knows Daniel immediately, which is in contrast to situations in earlier chapters. **26b–27:** This general hymn, similar to 4.34b–35, ends with a motif taken from the story; this is also the case in 2.23b. **28:** See 5.31 n.

7.1–12.13: Final manifestations. These form the second half of the book. Two separate themes—the four beasts and the heavenly visions—become united. **2:** *The Great Sea:* the ocean was viewed as the chaos dragon, slain by the deity; see e.g. Isa. 27.1 and Ps. 89.9–10 n. **4–7:** Compare the four creatures in Ezek. 1.5–10. According to v. 17, the beasts probably represent kingdoms; see 2.37–40. **8:** *A little horn:* the ten horns would

springing up among them, and three of the
first horns were uprooted to make room for
it. In this horn were eyes like human eyes,
and a mouth that uttered bombast. 9 As I was
looking,

thrones were set in place
and the Ancient in Years took his seat;
his robe was white as snow,
his hair like lamb's wool.
His throne was flames of fire
and its wheels were blazing fire;
10 a river of fire flowed from his
presence.
Thousands upon thousands served him
and myriads upon myriads were in
attendance.
The court sat, and the books were
opened.

11 Then because of the bombast the horn was
mouthing, I went on watching until the beast
was killed; its carcass was destroyed and consigned to the flames. 12 The rest of the beasts,
though deprived of their sovereignty, were
allowed to remain alive until an appointed
time and season. 13 I was still watching in visions of the night and I saw one like a human
being coming with the clouds of heaven; he
approached the Ancient in Years and was
presented to him. 14 Sovereignty and glory
and kingly power were given to him, so that
all peoples and nations of every language
should serve him; his sovereignty was to be
an everlasting sovereignty which was not to
pass away, and his kingly power was never to
be destroyed.

15 My spirit within me was troubled; and,
dismayed by the visions which came into my
head, I, Daniel, 16 approached one of those
who were standing there and enquired what
all this really signified; and he made known
to me its interpretation. 17 'These great
beasts, four in number,' he said, 'are four
kingdoms which will arise from the earth.
18 But the holy ones of the Most High will
receive the kingly power and retain possession of it always, for ever and ever.'

19 Then I wished to know what the fourth
beast really signified, the beast that was different from all the others, exceedingly fearsome with its iron teeth and bronze claws,
devouring and crunching, then trampling
underfoot what was left. 20 I wished also to
know about the ten horns on its head and
about the other horn which sprang up and at
whose coming three of them fell, the horn
which had eyes and a mouth uttering bombast and which in its appearance was more
imposing than the others. 21 As I still
watched, this horn was waging war on the
holy ones and proving too strong for them
22 until the Ancient in Years came. Then
judgement was pronounced in favour of the
holy ones of the Most High, and the time
came when the holy ones gained possession
of the kingly power.

23 The explanation he gave was this: 'The
fourth beast signifies a fourth kingdom
which will appear on earth. It will differ from
the other kingdoms; it will devour the whole
earth, treading it down and crushing it.
24 The ten horns signify ten kings who will
rise from this kingdom; after them will arise
another king, who will be different from his
predecessors; and he will bring low three
kings. 25 He will hurl defiance at the Most
High and wear down the holy ones of the
Most High. He will have it in mind to alter
the festival seasons and religious laws; and
the holy ones will be delivered into his power
for a time, and times, and half a time. 26 But

7:13 **human being:** *lit.* son of man.   7:25 **a time . . .
half a time:** *or* three and a half years.

represent a round number of successors of Alexander the Great in the Near East; see v. 24. The little horn would
be the contemporaneous persecutor of the Jews, Antiochus IV Epiphanes (see Introduction). See also 1 Macc.
1.41–50. **9–10:** A vision of heaven. **9:** *Ancient in Years:* God. On the scene depicted here, see 1 Kgs. 22.19
and Ezek. 1.26–28. **10:** *The court . . . the books:* the picture of a courtroom scene is found in other writings,
such as *Enoch* 47.3. **11–12:** A continuation of v. 8. **13–14:** A continuation of vv. 9–10. **13:** *Human being:*
lit. "son of humankind," traditionally translated "son of man." The term does not carry here all the levels of
meaning it later acquired, such as "messiah." **14:** The prerogatives are to be effective forever for the one like
a human being (v. 13), as anticipated in 2.44. **15:** A continuation of v. 12. **18:** *The holy ones:* the people
persecuted by Antiochus Epiphanes; see v. 27. In v. 14 such power was given to "the one like a human being."
21: *The Ancient in Years:* God would deliver the holy ones; compare the deliverance of the young men in
chs. 3 and 6. **25:** *A time and times and half a time:* three and a half years. *Time* means year; *times,* two years;
see 4.16.

when the court sits, he will be deprived of his sovereignty, so that it may be destroyed and abolished for ever. 27 The kingly power, sovereignty, and greatness of all the kingdoms under heaven will be given to the holy people of the Most High. Their kingly power will last for ever, and every realm will serve and obey them.'

28 Here the account ends. As for me, Daniel, my thoughts dismayed me greatly and I turned pale; but I kept these things to myself.

8 In the third year of the reign of King Belshazzar, a vision appeared to me, Daniel, following my earlier vision. 2 In this vision I was in Susa, the capital of the province of Elam, watching beside the Ulai canal. 3 I looked up and saw a ram with two horns standing by the canal. The two horns were long, with the longer of the two coming up after the other. 4 I watched the ram butting towards the west, the north, and the south. No beast could stand against it, and from its power there was no escape. It did as it pleased, and made a great display of strength.

5 While I pondered this, suddenly a he-goat came from the west skimming over the whole earth without touching the ground; it had a prominent horn between its eyes. 6 It approached the two-horned ram which I had seen standing by the canal, and charged it with impetuous force. 7 I saw it advance on the ram, working itself into a fury against it. Then it struck the ram and shattered both its horns; the ram was powerless to resist. The he-goat threw it to the ground and stamped on it, and there was no one to rescue the ram. 8 The he-goat in turn made a great display of its strength, but when it was at the height of its power its great horn broke, and in place of this there came up four prominent horns pointing towards the four quarters of heaven. 9 Out of one of them there emerged a little horn, which as it grew put forth its strength towards the south and the east and towards the fairest of all lands. 10 It aspired to be as great as the host of heaven, and it flung down to the earth some of the host, even some of the stars, and stamped on them. 11 It aspired to be as great as the Prince of the host, suppressed his regular offering, and even threw down his sanctuary. 12 The heavenly host was delivered up, and the little horn raised itself impiously against the regular offering and cast true religion to the ground; it succeeded in all that it did.

13 I heard a holy one speaking and another holy one answering. The one speaker said, 'How long will the period of this vision last? How long will the regular offering be suppressed and impiety cause desolation? How long will the Holy Place and the fairest of all lands be given over to be trodden down?' 14 The answer came, 'For two thousand three hundred evenings and mornings; then the Holy Place will be restored.'

15 All the while that I, Daniel, was seeing the vision, I was trying to understand it. Suddenly I saw standing before me one with the appearance of a man; 16 at the same time I heard a human voice calling to him across the bend of the Ulai, 'Gabriel, explain the vision to this man.' 17 He came to where I was standing; and at his approach I prostrated myself in terror. But he said to me, 'Understand, O man: the vision points to the time of the end.' 18 While he spoke to me, I lay face downwards in a trance, but at his touch I was made to stand up where I was. 19 'I shall make known to you', he said, 'what is to happen at the end of the period of wrath; for there is an end at the appointed time. 20 The two-horned ram

8:1 *Here the Hebrew text resumes (see note at 2:4)*.
8:12 **and the ... itself:** *prob. rdg; Heb. omits*.
8:13 **be suppressed:** *so Gk; Heb. omits*. **and impiety cause desolation:** *prob. rdg; Heb. obscure*. **fairest ... lands:** *prob. rdg, cp. verse 9; Heb. host*.

8.1–27: The ram, the goat and the little horn. This chapter (it reverts to Heb.) alludes to the same events as ch. 7, though on a lower level of literary quality. **1:** *My earlier vision:* that of ch. 7. **2:** *Susa:* a royal city in southern Persia, the area being named *Elam* after the ancient Elamites. *Ulai:* a river at or near Susa. **3:** *Ram* and the "goat" of v. 5 were probably signs of the zodiac. **5:** Alexander the Great's conquest of the East was remarkably swift, 334–323 B.C.E. **8:** *Four ... horns:* the successors to Alexander in Greece, Asia Minor, Syria and points east, and Egypt. **9:** Antiochus IV Epiphanes; see 7.8 n. **10–11:** See Isa. 14.12–16. **13:** *Regular offering suppressed:* as described in 1 Macc. 1.45. **14:** *Evenings and mornings:* this amounts to 1,150 days, a little less than the three and a half years of 7.25. **15:** *Appearance of a man:* not to be confused with the figure of 7.13. **16:** *Gabriel:* the name of an archangel; he appears often in the *Book of Enoch*. **17:** *The end* of time, when God would finally judge the world. A concern with what would happen at the end of time was a major

which you saw signifies the kings of Media
and Persia, 21 the he-goat is the king of
Greece, the great horn on its forehead being
its first king. 22 As for the horn which was
broken off and replaced by four other horns:
four kingdoms will rise out of that nation, but
they will lack its power.

23 'In the last days of those kingdoms,
   when their sin is at its height,
a king of grim aspect will appear, a
   master of stratagem.
24 His power will be great, and he will
   work havoc untold;
he will succeed in whatever he does.
He will work havoc on the mighty
   nations and the holy people.
25 By cunning and deceit
he will succeed in his designs;
he will devise great schemes
and wreak havoc on many when they
   least expect it.
He will challenge even the Prince of
   princes
and be broken, but by no human hand.
26 This revelation which has been given
of the evenings and the mornings is
   true;
but you must keep the vision secret,
for it points to days far ahead.'

27 As for me, Daniel, my strength failed and
I lay sick for some days. Then I rose and
attended to the king's business. But I was
perplexed by the revelation and no one could
explain it.

Interpreting Daniel's prophecy

9 In the first year of the reign of Darius
son of Ahasuerus (a Mede by birth, who
was appointed ruler over the kingdom of the
Chaldaeans) 2 I, Daniel, was reading the
scriptures and reflecting on the seventy years
which, according to the word of the LORD to
the prophet Jeremiah, were to pass while Jerusalem lay in ruins. 3 Then I turned to the
Lord God in earnest prayer and supplication
with fasting and with sackcloth and ashes. 4 I

prayed and made this confession to the LORD
my God:

'Lord, great and terrible God, keeping covenant and faith with those who love you and
observe your commandments, 5 we have
sinned, doing what was wrong and wicked;
we have rebelled and rejected your commandments and your decrees. 6 We have
turned a deaf ear to your servants the prophets, who spoke in your name to our kings and
princes, to our forefathers, and to all the
people of the land. 7 Lord, the right is on
your side; the shame, now as ever, belongs to
us, the people of Judah and the citizens of
Jerusalem, and to all the Israelites near and
far in every land to which you have banished
them for their disloyal behaviour towards
you. 8 LORD, the shame falls on us, on our
kings, our princes, and our forefathers. We
have sinned against you. 9 Compassion and
forgiveness belong to the Lord our God, because we have rebelled against him. 10 We
have not obeyed the LORD our God, in that
we have not conformed to the laws which he
laid down for our guidance through his servants the prophets. 11 All Israel has broken
your law and refused to obey your command,
so that the oath and curses recorded in the
law of Moses, the servant of God, have rained
down upon us; for we have sinned against
God. 12 He has made good the warning he
gave about us and our rulers, by bringing on
us and on Jerusalem a disaster greater than
has ever happened in all the world; 13 and this
whole disaster which has come upon us was
foretold in the law of Moses. Yet we have
done nothing to appease the LORD our God;
we have neither repented of our wrongful
deeds, nor remembered that you are true to
your word. 14 The LORD has kept strict watch
and has now brought the disaster upon us. In
all that he has done the LORD our God has
been just; yet we have not obeyed him.

15 'Now, Lord our God who brought your
people out of Egypt by a strong hand, winning for yourself a name that lives on to this
day, we have sinned, we have done wrong.

8:21 **Greece:** *Heb.* Javan.   8:24 **His power . . .**
great: *so Gk (Theod.); Heb. adds* and not with his power.

theme of apocalyptic literature. **23–25:** See 7.8 n. **23:** *Last days:* see v. 17. **25:** *By no human hand:* a theme
in 7.26.

  9.1–27: Daniel's prayer, and another vision of things to come. 1: Continuing the chronology of ch. 6. **2:**
The scriptures: this rare example of an interpretation of a scriptural text by another scriptural book apparently
alludes to Jer. 25.11–12; 29.10. **4–19:** This is a prayer of community confession of sins and a plea for

16 Lord, by all your saving deeds we beg that your wrath and anger may depart from Jerusalem, your own city, your holy hill; on account of our sins and our fathers' crimes, Jerusalem and your people have become a byword among all our neighbours. 17 Listen, our God, to your servant's prayer and supplication; for your own sake, Lord, look favourably on your sanctuary which lies desolate. 18 God, incline your ear to us and hear; open your eyes and look upon our desolation and upon the city that bears your name. It is not because of any righteous deeds of ours, but because of your great mercy that we lay our supplications before you. 19 Lord, hear; Lord, forgive; Lord, listen and act; God, for your own sake do not delay, because your city and your people bear your name.'

20 I was speaking and praying, confessing my own sin and the sin of my people Israel, and laying my supplication before the LORD my God on behalf of his holy hill; 21 indeed I was still praying, when the man Gabriel, whom I had already seen in the vision, flew close to me at the hour of the evening offering. 22 He explained to me: 'Daniel, I have now come to enlighten your understanding. 23 As you began your supplications a decree went forth, and I have come to make it known, for you are greatly beloved. Consider well the word, consider the vision: 24 seventy times seven years are marked out for your people and your holy city; then rebellion will be stopped, sin brought to an end, iniquity expiated, everlasting right ushered in, vision and prophecy ratified, and the Most Holy Place anointed.

25 'Know, then, and understand: from the time that the decree went forth that Jerusalem should be restored and rebuilt, seven of those seventy will pass till the appearance of one anointed, a prince; then for sixty-two it will remain restored, rebuilt with streets and conduits. At the critical time, 26 after the sixty-two have passed, the anointed prince

will be removed, and no one will take his part. The horde of an invading prince will work havoc on city and sanctuary. The end of it will be a cataclysm, inevitable war with all its horrors. 27 The prince will make a firm league with the many for one of the seventy; and, with that one half spent, he will put a stop to sacrifice and offering. And in the train of these abominations will come the perpetrator of desolation; then, in the end, what has been decreed concerning the desolation will be poured out.'

The angel's revelation

10 In the third year that Cyrus was king of Persia a revelation came to Daniel, who had been given the name Belteshazzar. The word was true, yet only after much struggle did understanding come to him in the course of the vision.

2 At that time I, Daniel, mourned for three whole weeks. 3 I refrained from all choice food; no meat or wine passed my lips, and I did not anoint myself until the three weeks had passed. 4 On the twenty-fourth day of the first month, I found myself on the bank of the great river, the Tigris, 5 and when I looked up I saw a man robed in linen with a belt of Ophir gold round his waist. 6 His body glowed like topaz, his face shone like lightning, his eyes flamed like torches, his arms and feet glittered like burnished bronze, and when he spoke his voice sounded like the voice of a multitude. 7 I, Daniel, alone saw the vision; those who were near me did not see it, but such great trepidation fell upon them that they crept away into hiding. 8 I was left by myself gazing at this great vision, and my strength drained away; and sapped of all

9:17 **for . . . Lord:** *so Gk (Theod.); Heb.* for the Lord's sake.   9:24 **seventy . . . years:** *Heb.* seventy weeks (*of years*).   9:27 **many:** *or* mighty.   10:5 **Ophir:** *so some MSS; others* Uphaz.

forgiveness, formed from a series of biblical phrases; compare Bar. 1.15–3.8. **21:** See 8.16 n. **24:** *Seventy times seven years:* equaling 490 years, the elapsed time since the destruction of Jerusalem (587 B.C.E.) mentioned in v. 2. The end will be like that in 7.26–27. **25:** *One anointed, a prince:* the first period of 49 years will be a time of waiting. The second period of 434 years will start with the appearance of one anointed as leader. **27:** The third period of 7 years will bring a religious persecution by a leader like the one described in 8.11–13. *That one half spent:* compare the three and a half years of 7.25. *The end:* see 8.17 n.

10.1–12.13: A detailed vision of the reigns of Alexander and his successors and of the end. 1: *Third year of Cyrus:* 536 B.C.E. **4:** Compare Ezek. 1.1. **5–6:** The passage uses some of the same terms as Ezek. 1.15–28. The *man* is probably the angel Gabriel. **7:** Compare Acts 9.7 for a vision seen by one person but not by his strength I became a sorry figure of a man. [9] I heard the sound of his words and, as I did so, I lay prone on the ground in a trance.

[10] Suddenly, at the touch of a hand, I was set, all trembling, on my hands and knees. [11] 'Daniel, man greatly beloved,' he said to me, 'attend to the words I am about to speak to you and stand upright where you are, for I am now sent to you.' When he spoke to me, I stood up trembling with apprehension. [12] He went on, 'Do not be afraid, Daniel, for from the very first day that you applied your mind to understanding, and to mortify yourself before your God, your prayers have been heard, and I have come in answer to them. [13] But the guardian angel of the kingdom of Persia resisted me for twenty-one days, and then, seeing that I had held out there, Michael, one of the chief princes, came to help me against the prince of the kingdom of Persia. [14] I have come to explain to you what will happen to your people at the end of this age; for this too is a vision for those days.'

[15] While he spoke in this fashion to me, I fixed my eyes on the ground and was unable to speak. [16] Suddenly one with a human appearance touched my lips; then I broke my silence and addressed him as he stood before me: 'Sir,' I said, 'at this vision anguish has gripped me, and I am sapped of all my strength. [17] How can I, my lord's servant, presume to talk with such as my lord, since my strength has now failed me and there is no more spirit left in me?'

[18] Again the figure touched me and put strength into me, [19] saying, 'Do not be afraid, man greatly beloved; all will be well with you. Take heart, and be strong.' As he spoke, my strength returned, and I said, 'Speak, sir, for you have given me strength.' [20] He said, 'Do you know why I have come to you? I am first going back to fight with the prince of Persia, and, as soon as I have left, the prince of Greece will appear: [21] I have no ally on my side for support and help, except Michael your prince. However I shall expound to you

11 what is written in the Book of Truth; [2] here and now I shall tell you what is true.

'Three more kings will appear in Persia, followed by a fourth who will far surpass all the others in wealth; and when by his wealth he has extended his power, he will mobilize the whole empire against the kingdom of Greece. [3] Then there will appear a warrior king, who will rule a vast kingdom and do whatever he pleases. [4] But once he is established, his kingdom will be broken up and divided to the four quarters of heaven. It will not pass to his descendants; nor will its power be comparable to his, for his kingdom will be uprooted and given to others besides his posterity.

[5] 'The king of the south will become strong; but one of his generals will surpass him in strength and win a greater dominion. [6] In the course of time the two will enter into an alliance, and to seal the agreement the daughter of the king of the south will be given in marriage to the king of the north, but she will not maintain her influence and their line will not last. She and those who escorted her, along with her child, and also her lord and master, will all be the victims of foul play. [7] Then another shoot from the same stock as hers will appear in his father's place. He will penetrate the defences of the king of the north, invade his fortress, and win a decisive victory. [8] He will carry away as booty to Egypt even the images of their gods cast in metal and their valuable vessels of silver and gold. Then for some years he will refrain from attacking the king of the north. [9] After that the king of the north will invade the southern kingdom and then retire to his own land.

[10] 'His sons will press on with the assembling of a large force of armed men. One of them will sweep on like an irresistible flood. In a second campaign he will press as far as

10:13 **prince:** *so Gk; Heb. omits.* Ch. 11: *Heb. adds* [1] and as for me, in the first year of Darius the Mede, I stood to support and help him.

---

companions. **13:** *Michael,* the guardian angel of Israel, came to the aid of Gabriel (vv. 5–6 n.) when the latter was battling the *guardian angel of the kingdom of Persia.* **20:** The battle of the angels reflects the battles of the people; *Greece* here is probably the kingdom of Antiochus IV Epiphanes, though it may be the empire of Alexander. **10.21–11.2:** *The Book of Truth* revealed. This was apparently an explanation of history and its fulfillment, and not the same as the book of 12.1. **11.2:** Since there were more than four kings in Persian history, it is not known which ones the author meant.

11.3–45: Alexander and his successors. 3–4: See Introduction and 8.8. **5–45:** The south is the Egyptian Ptolemaic kingdom and the north is the Syrian Seleucid kingdom. The struggles between the two countries are the enemy stronghold. ¹¹The king of the south, working himself up into a fury, will set out to do battle with the king of the north. He in turn will muster a large army, but it will be delivered into the hands of his enemy. ¹²At the capture of this force, the victor will be elated and will slaughter tens of thousands; yet he will not maintain his advantage. ¹³The king of the north will once more raise an army, one even greater than the last, and after a number of years he will advance with his huge force and a great baggage train.

¹⁴'During these times many will resist the king of the south, but some renegades among your own people will rashly attempt to give substance to a vision and will be brought to disaster. ¹⁵The king of the north will then come and cast up siege-ramps and capture a well-fortified city. The forces of the south will not stand up to him; even the flower of the army will not be able to hold their ground. ¹⁶The invader will do as he pleases and meet with no opposition. He will establish himself in the fairest of all lands, and it will come wholly into his power. ¹⁷He will resolve to advance with the full might of his kingdom; and, when he has agreed terms with the king of the south, he will give his young daughter in marriage to him, with a view to the destruction of the kingdom; but the treaty will not last nor will it be his purpose which is served. ¹⁸Then he will turn to the coasts and islands and take many prisoners, but a foreign commander will wear him down and put an end to his challenge; thus he will throw his challenge back at him. ¹⁹He will retreat to strongholds in his own country; there he will meet with disaster and be overthrown, and he will be seen no more.

²⁰'His successor will be one who will send out an officer with a royal escort to exact tribute; after but a brief time this king too will meet his end, yet neither openly nor in battle.

²¹'His place will be taken by a despicable creature, one who had not been given recognition as king; he will come when he is least

expected and seize the kingdom by smooth dissimulation. ²²As he advances, he will sweep away all forces of opposition, and even the Prince of the Covenant will be broken. ²³He will enter into alliances but dishonour them and, although only a few people are behind him, he will rise to power and establish himself ²⁴against all expectation. He will overrun the richest districts of the province, and succeed where all his ancestors failed, and distribute spoil, booty, and goods among his followers. He will frame stratagems against fortresses, but only for a time.

²⁵'He will rouse himself in all his strength and courage to lead a great army against the king of the south, who will fight back with a very large and powerful army; yet, hampered by treachery, the king of the south will not persist. ²⁶Those who eat at his board will be his undoing; his army will be swept away, and many will fall slain in battle. ²⁷The two kings, bent on mischief though seated at the same table, will lie to each other but with advantage to neither, for an end is yet to be at the appointed time. ²⁸Then the king of the north will return home with spoils in plenty, and with hostility in his heart against the Holy Covenant; he will work his will and return to his own country.

²⁹'At the appointed time he will once again invade the south, but he will have less success than he had before. ³⁰Ships of Kittim will sail against him, and he will suffer a rebuff. As he retreats he will vent his fury against the Holy Covenant, and on his return home will single out those who have forsaken it. ³¹Soldiers in his command will desecrate the sanctuary and citadel; they will abolish the regular offering, and will set up "the abominable thing that causes desolation". ³²By plausible promises he will win over those who are ready to violate the covenant, but the people who are faithful to their God will be resolute and take action. ³³Wise leaders of the nation will give

11:17 **when . . . south:** *prob. rdg; Heb. obscure.*
11:18 **will wear him down:** *prob. rdg; Heb. obscure.*

fairly accurately described. **21–45:** Antiochus IV Epiphanes, as in chs. 7–9, is the great oppressor. **22–23:** *Prince of the Covenant:* the Judean high priest Onias III deposed by Antiochus and supplanted by his brother Jason as part of the fraudulent *alliances*. **25–35:** The two campaigns of Antiochus against Egypt. **30:** *Ships of Kittim:* the Romans. They compelled Antiochus to withdraw from Egypt. On his return to Syria (168 B.C.E.), he desecrated the temple in Jerusalem (v. 31; see 9.27). **32:** *Fight back:* the Maccabean revolt; see 1 Macc. ch. 2.

guidance to the people at large, who for a while will fall victims to sword and fire, to captivity and pillage. [34] But these victims will have some help, though only a little, even if many who join them are insincere. [35] Some of these leaders will themselves fall victims for a time, so that they may be tested, refined, and made shining white; for an end is yet to be at the appointed time.

[36] 'The king will do as he pleases; he will exalt and magnify himself above every god, and against the God of gods he will utter monstrous blasphemies. Things will go well for him until the divine wrath is spent, for what is determined must be done. [37] Heedless of his ancestral gods and the god beloved of women, indeed heedless of all gods, for he will magnify himself above them all, [38] he will honour the god of fortresses, a god unknown to his ancestors, with gold and silver, gems and costly gifts. [39] He will garrison his strongest fortresses with aliens, the people of a foreign god. Those whom he favours he will load with honour, putting them into authority over the people and distributing land as a reward.

[40] 'At the time of the end, the king of the south will make a feint at the king of the north, but the king of the north will come storming against him with chariots and cavalry and a fleet of ships. He will pass through country after country, sweeping over them like a flood, [41] among them the fairest of all lands, and tens of thousands will fall victim; but these lands, Edom and Moab and the chief part of the Ammonites, will escape his clutches. [42] As he gets country after country into his grasp, not even Egypt will escape; [43] he will seize control of her hidden stores of gold and silver and of all her treasures; Libyans and Cushites will follow in subjection to him. [44] Then, alarmed by rumours from east and north, he will depart in a great rage to destroy and to exterminate many. [45] He will pitch his royal pavilion between the sea and the holy hill, the fairest of all hills; and he will meet his end with no one to help him.

The end of history

12 'AT that time there will appear
Michael the great captain,
who stands guarding your
　　fellow-countrymen;
and there will be a period of anguish
such as has never been known
ever since they became a nation till that
　　moment.
But at that time your people will be
　　delivered,
everyone whose name is entered in the
　　book:
[2] many of those who sleep in the dust of
　　the earth will awake,
some to everlasting life
and some to the reproach of eternal
　　abhorrence.
[3] The wise leaders will shine like the
　　bright vault of heaven,
and those who have guided the people
　　in the true path
will be like the stars for ever and ever.

[4] 'But you, Daniel, keep the words secret and seal the book until the time of the end. Many will rush to and fro, trying to gain such knowledge.'

[5] I, Daniel, looked and saw two others standing, one on this bank of the river and the other on the farther bank. [6] To the man robed in linen who was above the waters of the river I said, 'How long will it be until the end of these portents?' [7] The man robed in linen who was above the waters raised his right hand and his left heavenwards, and I heard him swear by him who lives for ever: 'It shall be for a time and times and half a time. When the power of the holy people is no longer being shattered, all these things will cease.'

[8] I heard, but I did not understand; so I said, 'Sir, what will be the outcome of these

---

11:35 **for an end ... time:** *prob. rdg; Heb. has different word order.* 12:6 **I:** *so Gk; Heb.* he.

35: *End:* see 8.17 n. **36–45:** Wars to occur as a result of the arrogance of Antiochus. **43:** *Cushites:* the peoples living south of Egypt in Nubia (roughly today's Sudan) and Ethiopia.
　　12.1–13: Concluding vision. 1: Apocalyptic literature seems to flow directly from historical events (here the wars brought on by Antiochus) to events of the end times. As in 9.26–27, the period before the very end would be the most distressful. *The book:* compare Ps. 69.28; see 10.21–11.2 n. **2:** This is a clear statement of resurrection, and unique in the OT. **4:** The book here seems to be that of 11.1, rather than 12.1. **6:** *Linen:* see

things?' ⁹He replied, 'Go your way, Daniel, for the words are to be kept secret and sealed till the time of the end. ¹⁰Many will purify themselves and be refined, making themselves shining white, but the wicked will continue in wickedness and none of them will understand; only the wise leaders will understand. ¹¹From the time when the regular offering is abolished and "the abomination of desolation" is set up, one thousand two hundred and ninety days will elapse. ¹²Happy are those who wait and live to see the completion of one thousand three hundred and thirty-five days! ¹³But you, Daniel, go your way till the end; you will rest, and then, at the end of the age, you will arise to your destiny.'

Ezek. 9.2. **7:** *Time, times, and a half:* three and a half years, as it is in 7.25. **11–12:** These figures, perhaps representing separate traditions, seem to be related to those of 7.25 and 8.14. **11:** See 9.27 n.

930

Hosea

In the Hebrew Bible, the Minor Prophets (so named because their books are shorter than Isaiah, Jeremiah, and Ezekiel) are called the Book of the Twelve and are treated as a literary unit. The ancients arranged the twelve writings in what they considered chronological order; Hosea is in the first position. While modern scholars see reasons to date some of these writings at times other than the ancient sequence suggests, they regard Hosea as indeed the earliest writing.

The first verse places Hosea in the latter part of the eighth century B.C.E., when the Assyrians were about to overrun the Northern Kingdom of Israel. That menace gives the book, addressed to the north, its tension. The prophet knows both the people's corruption and the LORD's love, and the book veers from judgment to love, from threats of destruction to promises of restoration.

A book such as Hosea can pose a problem for the reader in that it does not present a systematic argument. It consists of many poems and prose passages compiled into an anthology; hence there can be an impression of bewildering inconsistency. While it is uncertain that Hosea's message comes from his marriage, related in chs. 1–3, the experience narrated is searing and even bitter, though filled with his love. The portrait of the deity as partaking in human feelings and agonies makes Hosea one of the most moving of Old Testament books.

1 THE word of the LORD which came to Hosea son of Beeri during the reigns of Uzziah, Jotham, Ahaz, and Hezekiah, kings of Judah, and during the reign of Jeroboam son of Joash king of Israel.

Hosea's unfaithful wife

2 THIS is the beginning of the LORD's message given by Hosea. He said, 'Go and take an unchaste woman as your wife, and with this woman have children; for like an unchaste woman this land is guilty of unfaithfulness to the LORD.' 3 So he married Gomer daughter of Diblaim, and she conceived and bore him a son. 4 The LORD said to Hosea, 'Call him Jezreel, for in a little while I am going to punish the dynasty of Jehu for the blood shed in the valley of Jezreel, and bring the kingdom of Israel to an end. 5 On that day I shall break Israel's bow in the vale of Jezreel.'

6 Gomer conceived again and bore a daughter, and the LORD said to Hosea,

Call her Lo-ruhamah;
for I shall never again show love to Israel,
never again forgive them.

7 But Judah I shall love and save.
I shall save them not by bow or sword
or weapon of war,
not by horses and horsemen,
but I shall save them by the LORD their God.

8 After weaning Lo-ruhamah, Gomer conceived and bore a son; 9 and the LORD said,

Call him Lo-ammi;

1:6 **Lo-ruhamah:** *that is* Not loved. **never again forgive:** *or* I shall totally remove. 1:9 **Lo-ammi:** *that is* Not my people.

1.1: Introduction. *Hosea* means "rescue." The names of the kings place Hosea in the 740s B.C.E.

1.2–3.5: Hosea's unfaithful wife. The figure of the unhappy marriage sets forth God's dissatisfaction with Israel.

1.2–9: The three children. 4: *Jehu* became king in a bloody revolt at *Jezreel* in about 842 B.C.E. (see 2 Kgs. 9.1–10.31). Jezreel was the name both of a town and of the valley between Galilee and Samaria. **5:** *Break Israel's bow:* destroy its power. **7:** This apparently was added so as to apply to the Southern Kingdom Hosea's message addressed to the Northern.

for you are not my people,
and I shall not be your God.
10 The Israelites will be as countless as the
sands of the sea,
which can neither be measured nor
numbered;
it will no longer be said to them, 'You
are not my people';
they will be called Children of the
Living God.
11 The people of Judah and of Israel will
be reunited
and will choose for themselves one
leader;
they will spring up from the land,
for great will be the day of Jezreel.

2 You are to say to your brothers, 'You
are my people,'
and to your sisters, 'You are loved.'

2 Call your mother to account,
for she is no longer my wife
nor am I her husband.
Let her put an end to her infidelity
and banish the lovers from her bosom,
3 or else I shall strip her bare
and parade her naked as the day she
was born.
I shall make her bare as the wilderness,
parched as the desert,
and leave her to die of thirst.
4 I shall show no love towards her
children,
for they are the offspring of adultery.
5 Their mother has been promiscuous;
she who conceived them is shameless.
She says, 'I will go after my lovers,
who supply me with food and drink,
with my wool and flax, my oil and
perfumes.'
6 That is why I shall close her road with
thorn bushes
and obstruct her path with a wall,
so that she can no longer find a way
through.

7 Though she pursues her lovers
she will not overtake them,
though she looks for them
she will not find them.
At last she will say,
'I shall go back to my husband again,
for I was better off then than I am
now.'
8 She does not know that it was I who
gave her
the grain, the new wine, and fresh oil,
I who lavished on her silver and gold
which they used for the Baal.
9 That is why I am going to take back
my grain at the harvest and my new
wine at the vintage,
take away the wool and the flax
which I provided to cover her naked
body.
10 Now I shall reveal her shame to her
lovers,
and no one will rescue her from
me.
11 I shall put a stop to all her
merrymaking,
her pilgrimages, new moons, and
sabbaths,
all her festivals.
12 I shall ravage the vines and the fig
trees,
of which she says, 'These are the fees
which my lovers have paid me,'
and I shall leave them to grow wild
so that beasts may eat them.
13 I shall punish her for the holy days
when she burnt sacrifices to the baalim,
when she decked herself with her rings
and necklaces,
when, forgetful of me, she ran after
her lovers.
This is the word of the LORD.

1:9 *your God: lit.* to you.   1:10 *In Heb.* 2:1.
1:11 **Jezreel:** *that is* God sows.   2:6 **her road:** *so Gk;
Heb.* your road.

1.9: *You are not my people:* the LORD renounces the covenant (compare Exod. 6.7).

1.10–2.1: Restoration. 10: The substance of v. 9 is here reversed. See Gen. 22.17 and 32.12. **11:** *Reunited:*
the division into two kingdoms came after Solomon (see 1 Kgs. 12.1–20). *Jezreel* is here the son, standing for
God's restoration of Israel.

2.2–17: Israel, the promiscuous wife. 2: *Call to account:* the phrase comes from the law court. *She is no
longer my wife . . . :* The declaration implies a divorce proceeding. *Lovers* can often mean foreign nations
(compare Jer. 4.30; Ezek. ch. 16); here it may also mean alien gods. **8:** *Baal:* the Canaanite fertility god, whose
worship was viewed as disloyalty to the LORD. **11:** The list of rituals covers the various kinds of public worship. *Pilgrimages* are the pilgrim-feasts commanded in Exod. 23.14–17. **13:** *Baalim:* the plural of Baal.

14 But now I shall woo her,
　lead her into the wilderness,
　and speak words of encouragement to
　　her.
15 There I shall restore her vineyards to
　　her,
　turning the valley of Achor into a gate
　　of hope;
　there she will respond as in her
　　youth,
　as when she came up from Egypt.
16–17 On that day she will call me 'My
　　husband'
　and will no more call me 'My Baal';
　I shall banish from her lips the very
　　names of the baalim;
　never again will their names be
　　invoked.
　This is the word of the LORD.

18 Then I shall make a covenant on Israel's behalf with the wild beasts, the birds of the air, and the creatures that creep on the ground, and I shall break bow and sword and weapon of war and sweep them off the earth, so that my people may lie down without fear. 19 I shall betroth you to myself for ever, bestowing righteousness and justice, loyalty and love; 20 I shall betroth you to myself, making you faithful, and you will know the LORD. 21 At that time I shall answer, says the LORD; I shall answer the heavens and they will answer the earth, 22 and the earth will answer the grain, the new wine, and fresh oil, and they will answer Jezreel. 23 Israel will be my new sowing in the land, and I shall show love to Lo-ruhamah and say to Lo-ammi, 'You are my people,' and he will say, 'You are my God.'

3 The LORD said to me,

　Go again and bestow your love on a
　　woman
　loved by another man, an adulteress;
　love her as I, the LORD, love the
　　Israelites,
　although they resort to other gods
　and love the cakes of raisins offered to
　　idols.

2 So I bought her for fifteen pieces of silver, a homer of barley, and a measure of wine; 3 and I said to her,

　You will live in my house for a long
　　time
　and you will not lead an immoral life.
　You must have relations with no one
　　else,
　indeed not even with me.
4 So the Israelites will live for a long time
　without king or leader,
　without sacrifice or sacred pillar,
　without ephod or teraphim.
5 After that they will again seek
　the LORD their God and David their
　　king,
　and turn with reverence to the LORD
　and seek his bounty for the days to
　　come.

The Lord's case against Israel

4 ISRAEL, hear the word of the LORD;
　for the LORD has a charge to bring
　against the inhabitants of the land:

2:16–17 **she**: *so Gk; Heb.* you. **My Baal**: *also means* My husband.　**2:22 Jezreel**: *that is* God sows.　3:2 **wine**: *so Gk; Heb.* barley.

14–17: *Wilderness*: the place of the first encounter between God and Israel, and viewed by the prophet as a time of perfect faith and ideal relations. Compare Jer. 2.2–3. **15**: *Valley of Achor*: see Josh. 7.24–26. **16**: The word *Baal* means husband as well as being the name of the god; hence its use is forbidden here.

2.18–23: Restoring Israel's harmony with the earth. The LORD will resume the covenant relationship with Israel, as shown in the image of the new betrothal and by the new love for the children (compare 1.10–2.1). **23**: *My new sowing*: a play on the word Jezreel, which means "God sows"; see Tfn. at 1.11. Israel, not Jezreel, is God's sowing.

3.1–5: Redemption of the wife is achieved by *love* (v. 1) and a high cost (v. 2). *Fifteen pieces of silver* is about seven ounces, and a *homer* is nearly 11½ bushels; see p. xxviii. Love entails discipline: the woman (v. 3) and Israel (v. 4) must be kept from further sin before receiving the LORD's full *bounty*. **4**: Israel's distress arises from corruption caused by its kings and from observing Canaanite religious rituals. *Sacred pillar*: phallic representation of a male deity, here probably a symbol of the fertility god Baal.

4.1–9.17: God's case against Israel. The oracles in this section follow the literary form of a court trial in which God presses charges (4.1), passes a judicial sentence (5.1), and imposes a juridical penalty (5.9).

There is no good faith or loyalty,
no acknowledgement of God in the
    land.
2 People swear oaths and break them;
they kill and rob and commit adultery;
there is violence, one deed of blood
    after another.
3 Therefore the land will be desolate
and all who live in it will languish,
with the wild beasts and the birds of
    the air;
even the fish will vanish from the sea.
4 But it is not for mankind to bring
    charges,
not for them to prove a case;
it is my quarrel, and it is with you, the
    priest.
5 By day and by night you blunder on,
you and the prophet with you.
Your nation is brought to ruin;
6 want of knowledge has been the ruin of
    my people.
As you have rejected knowledge,
so will I reject you as a priest to me.
As you have forsaken the teaching of
    God,
so will I, your God, forsake your
    children.

7 The more priests there are,
the more they sin against me;
their dignity I shall turn into
    dishonour.
8 They feed on the sin of my people
and batten on their iniquity.
9 But people and priest will fare alike.
I shall punish them for their
    conduct
and repay them for their deeds.
10 They will eat but never be satisfied,
resort to prostitutes and never have
    children,
for they have abandoned the LORD
11 to give themselves to immorality.

Wine, old and new, steals my people's
    wits;
12 they ask advice from a piece of wood
and accept the guidance of the diviner's
    wand;
for a spirit of promiscuity has led them
    astray
and they are unfaithful to their God.
13 They sacrifice on mountaintops
and burn offerings on the hills,
under oak and poplar
and the terebinth's pleasant shade.
That is why your daughters turn to
    prostitution
and your sons' brides commit adultery.
14 I shall not punish your daughters for
    becoming prostitutes
or your sons' brides for their adultery,
because your men resort to whores
and sacrifice with temple-prostitutes.
A people so devoid of understanding
    comes to grief.
15 Israel, though you are adulterous,
let not Judah incur such guilt;
let her not come to Gilgal
or go up to Beth-aven
to swear by the life of the LORD.
16 Like a heifer, Israel has turned
    stubborn;
will the LORD now feed them
like lambs in a broad meadow?
17-18 Ephraim has associated with idols;
a drunken rabble,
they have devoted their lives to
    immorality,
preferring dishonour to glory.
19 The wind with its wings will carry them
    off,
and they will find their sacrifices a
    delusion.

4:4 **my quarrel:** *prob. rdg; Heb.* like my quarrel.
4:10 **have children:** *or* be wealthy.   4:17–18 **a**
drunken rabble: *prob. rdg; Heb.* unintelligible. **to glory:**
prob. rdg, cp. Gk; Heb. her shields.

4.1–4: General charge. The nation has broken the covenant. **1:** *Loyalty:* love between persons growing out
of fidelity to a covenant. *Acknowledgement of God:* the recognition of God in obedience and surrender,
resulting in a close personal relationship. **2:** The crimes are breaches of specific laws. **3:** The rupture of the
covenant meant the loss of natural vitality. Contrast 2.18–23, the vitality experienced in fidelity to the covenant.
4.5–5.7: Undermining religion. 5: The *prophet,* like the *priest* (v. 7), is here a religious functionary, and
unlike the charismatic Hosea. See Jer. 23.9–12. **6:** *Knowledge:* obedience to God's will; see 4.1 n. Hebrew
uses the same word for *knowledge* and *acknowledgement.* **11:** *Wine, old and new:* an allusion to a Canaanite
vintage festival. **13:** Fertility worship took place on *mountaintops* and under trees. **15:** *Gilgal:* an important
shrine town near Jericho. *Beth-aven:* lit. "house of iniquity," a sarcastic name for Bethel, "house of God,"
Israel's religious center; Gen. 28.16–19; 1 Kgs. 12.25–30. **17:** *Ephraim,* the main northern tribe, often means

5 Hear this, you priests, and listen,
　　Israel;
　let the royal house mark my words.
　Sentence is passed on you,
　for you have been a snare at Mizpah,
　a net spread out on Tabor,
2 and a deep pit at Shittim.
　I shall punish them all.
3 I have cared for Ephraim
　and not neglected Israel;
　but now Ephraim has become
　　promiscuous
　and Israel has brought defilement on
　　himself.
4 Their misdeeds have barred the way
　back to their God,
　for the spirit of immorality which is in
　　them
　prevents them from knowing the LORD.
5 Israel's arrogance cries out against
　　him;
　Ephraim's guilt is his downfall,
　and Judah in turn is brought down.
6 They go with sacrifices of sheep and
　　cattle
　to seek the LORD, but do not find him,
　for he has withdrawn from them.
7 They have deceived the LORD,
　for their children are bastards.
　Now an invader is set to devour their
　　fields.

8 Blow the trumpet in Gibeah,
　the horn in Ramah,
　raise the battle cry in Beth-aven:
　'We are with you, Benjamin!'
9 On the day of punishment
　Ephraim will be laid waste.
　This is the certain doom
　I have decreed for Israel's tribes.
10 Judah's rulers act like men
　who move their neighbour's boundary;
　on them I shall pour out
　my wrath like a flood.

11 Ephraim is an oppressor trampling on
　　justice,
　obstinately pursuing what is worthless.
12 But I am going to be a festering sore to
　　Ephraim,
　a canker to the house of Judah.

13 When Ephraim found that he was sick,
　and Judah found that he was covered
　　with sores,
　Ephraim turned to Assyria
　and sent envoys to the Great King.
　But he had no power to cure you
　or heal your sores.
14 I shall be fierce as a panther to
　　Ephraim,
　fierce as a lion to Judah;
　I shall maul the prey and go,
　carry it off beyond hope of rescue.
15 I shall return to my dwelling-place,
　until in remorse they seek me
　and search diligently for me in their
　　distress.

6 Come, let us return to the LORD.
　　He has torn us, but he will heal us,
　he has wounded us, but he will bind up
　　our wounds;
2 after two days he will revive us,
　on the third day he will raise us
　to live in his presence.
3 Let us strive to know the LORD,
　whose coming is as sure as the sunrise.
　He will come to us like the rain,
　like spring rains that water the earth.

4 How shall I deal with you, Ephraim?
　How shall I deal with you, Judah?
　Your loyalty to me is like the morning
　　mist,
　like dew that vanishes early.

5:2 **deep . . . Shittim:** *prob. rdg; Heb. obscure.*
5:5 **Ephraim's:** *prob. rdg; Heb. prefixes* Israel.

the whole Northern Kingdom. **5.1:** What events at *Mizpah* and *Tabor* are alluded to is not certain. **3–4:** *Cared for:* lit. "known"; expressive of God's active concern for Israel's well-being. See 4.1 n. **7:** *Bastards:* because they were born to parents who repudiated covenant with God, but also possibly because of actually being born from fertility cult unions.

　　5.8–6.6: Divine disappointment. The three parts of the poem are: punishment by political upheavals (5.8–15), Israel's apparent remorse (6.1–3), and the LORD's response (6.4–6). **8:** *Gibeah, Ramah,* and *Beth-aven* (see 4.15 n.) were cities in *Benjamin,* possibly annexed by the Northern Kingdom, and first targets of an invasion by the Southern Kingdom. **10:** *Judah's rulers* in calling the Assyrians against Israel were, in effect, taking land away from their *neighbors;* see 2 Kgs. 16.7–9. **13:** *Great King* was a title assumed by Assyrian kings.

　　6.1–6: Israel's apparent remorse. 1: *Torn:* the same Heb. word as *maul* (5.14). **2:** *Two days, third day:* that

5 That is why I have cut them to pieces
  by the prophets
and slaughtered them with my words:
my judgement goes forth like light.
6 For I require loyalty, not sacrifice,
  acknowledgement of God rather than
  whole-offerings.
7 At Admah they violated my covenant,
  there they played me false.
8 Gilead is a haunt of evildoers,
  marked by a trail of blood.
9 Like marauders lying in wait,
  priests are banded together
to do murder on the road to Shechem;
their behaviour is an outrage.
10 At Bethel I have seen a horrible
   thing:
there Ephraim became promiscuous
and Israel brought defilement on
  himself.
11 And for you, too, Judah, a harvest of
   reckoning will come.

When I am minded to restore the
  fortunes of my people,
7 1 when I am minded to heal Israel,
  the guilt of Ephraim stands revealed,
the wickedness of Samaria.
They have not kept faith;
they are thieves breaking into houses,
bandits raiding in the countryside,
2 unaware that I have their wickedness
  ever in mind.
Now their misdeeds encircle them;
they are ever before my eyes.
3 They divert the king with their
  wickedness
and princes with their treachery.
4 All of them are adulterers;
they are like an oven fire
which the baker does not have to stir
from the kneading of the dough until it
  has risen.

5 On their king's festal day the courtiers
  become inflamed with wine,
and he himself joins with arrogant
  men;
6 their hearts are heated like an oven by
  their intrigues.
During the night their passion
  slumbers,
but in the morning it flares up
like a blazing fire;
7 they are all as heated as an oven
and devour their rulers.
King after king falls from power,
but not one of them calls to me.

8 Ephraim is mixed up with aliens;
he is like a cake half done.
9 Foreigners feed on his strength,
but he is unaware;
grey hairs may come on him,
but he is unaware.
10 Israel's arrogance openly indicts them;
but they do not return to the LORD
   their God
nor, in spite of everything, do they seek
   him.
11 Ephraim is like a silly, senseless pigeon,
   now calling to Egypt,
   now turning to Assyria for help.
12 Wherever they turn, I shall cast my net
   over them
and bring them down like birds;
I shall take them captive when I hear
   them gathering.

13 Woe betide them, for they have strayed
   from me!
May disaster befall them for rebelling
   against me!

6:7 **At Admah:** *prob. rdg; Heb.* Like Adam.   6:10 **At**
Bethel: *prob. rdg; Heb.* In the house of Israel.
7:5 **their:** *so Aram. (Targ.); Heb.* our.   7:6 **are**
heated: *so Gk; Heb.* draw near.

is, soon; possibly, instead, the days of a pagan ritual observance. **6:** *Loyalty, acknowledgement of God:* see
4.1 n. The qualities that maintain the covenant are beyond mere ritual, and hence Israel's repentance is
unacceptable.

6.7–8.14: Israel's treachery. Influential persons, especially the king, have transgressed.

6.7–11: Murder and recklessness. 7: *Admah:* a city near the Dead Sea (see 11.8 n.). **8:** *Gilead:* east of the
Jordan. **9:** *Shechem* was the ancient central shrine, site of the kingdom's most solemn festivities. **11:** The
prophecy is applied here to the Southern Kingdom.

7.1–16: The evils of the kings. 1: *Samaria:* the capital. **4–6:** The people of Israel hide the evil intrigue in
their *hearts* like a *baker* who banks the *fire* in the *oven* after it has reached full intensity until the *dough* has
risen, i.e. is fully leavened and ready for baking. **7:** *Devour their rulers:* three of the six who ruled in the previous
twenty years were murdered. See 2 Kgs. 15.8–26. **11:** Hoshea, the last king of Israel, became a vassal of *Assyria*

I long to deliver them,
but they tell lies about me.
14 There is no sincerity in their cry to me;
for all their wailing on their beds
and gashing of themselves over grain
and new wine,
they are turning away from me.
15 Though I support and strengthen
them,
they plot evil against me.
16 Like a bow gone slack,
they relapse into useless worship;
their leaders will fall by the sword
because of their angry talk.
There will be derision at them in
Egypt.

8 Put the trumpets to your lips!
An eagle circles over the sanctuary of
the LORD;
they have violated my covenant
and rebelled against my instruction.
2 Israel cries to me for help:
'We acknowledge you as our God.'
3 But Israel rejects what is good,
and an enemy pursues him.
4 They make kings, but not on my
authority;
they set up rulers, but without my
knowledge;
from their silver and gold they have
made for themselves
idols for their own destruction.

5 Samaria, your calf-god is loathsome!
My anger burns against them!
How long must they remain guilty?
6 The calf was made in Israel;
a craftsman fashioned it and it is no
god;
it will be reduced to splinters.

7 Israel sows the wind and reaps the
whirlwind;
there are no heads on the standing
grain,
it yields no flour;

and, if it did yield any,
strangers would swallow it up.
8 Israel is swallowed up;
now among the nations
they are like a thing of no value.
9 Like a wild ass that goes its own way,
they have gone up to Assyria.
Ephraim has bargained for lovers;
10 because they have so bargained among
the nations
I will now round them up.
Soon they will have to abandon
the setting up of kings and rulers.
11 Ephraim has built altars everywhere
and they have become occasions for sin.
12 Though I give him many written laws,
they are treated as irrelevant;
13 though they sacrifice offerings of flesh
and eat them,
the LORD will not accept them.
Their guilt will be remembered
and their sins punished.
Let them go back to Egypt!

14 Israel has forgotten his Maker
and built palaces;
Judah has many walled cities,
but I shall burn his cities,
and fire will devour his citadels.

9 Do not rejoice, Israel, or exult like
other peoples;
for you have been unfaithful to your
God,
you have been attracted by a
prostitute's fee
on every threshing-floor heaped with
grain.
2 Threshing-floor and winepress will see
them no more,
there will be no new wine for them.
3 They will not dwell in the LORD's land:

7:14 **gashing of themselves:** *so many MSS; others*
rolling about.   7:16 **useless worship:** *prob. rdg, cp.*
Gk; Heb. obscure.   8:1 **An eagle:** *prob. rdg; Heb.* As an
eagle.   8:3 **Israel ... good:** *or* Israel is utterly
loathsome.   9:1 **or exult:** *so Gk; Heb.* to exultation.
9:2 **see:** *so Gk; Heb.* pasture.

but proved disloyal in seeking help from *Egypt;* see 2 Kgs. 17.1–6. **14:** *Howling* and *gashing* sarcastically
describe Canaanite rites (see 1 Kgs. 18.25–29).
8.1–14: False religion. Specific missteps are given. **4:** Though one strand of the OT tradition sees kingship
as the LORD's gift, another strand of it considers kingship as rebellion against the LORD. Hosea equates kingship
with idolatry. **5:** *Calf-god* alludes sarcastically to the statue of a bull (see 1 Kgs. 12.28–30).
9.1–13.16: Prosperity contrasted with exile. The poems use metaphors of agricultural plenty.
9.1–9: Untoward results of false worship. 1: *Rejoice* and *exult* are cultic acts. *Threshing-floor:* the place

Ephraim will go back to Egypt,
or eat unclean food in Assyria.
⁴They are not to pour out wine to the
LORD;
their sacrifices will not be pleasing to
him;
it would be like mourners' fare for
them,
and all who ate it would be polluted.
Their food must serve only to stay their
hunger;
it must not be offered in the house of
the LORD.
⁵What will you do on the festal day,
the day of the LORD's pilgrim-feast?
⁶For look, the people have fled from a
scene of devastation:
Egypt will receive them,
Memphis will be their grave.
Weeds will engulf their silver treasures,
and thorns their dwellings.

⁷The days of punishment have come,
the days of vengeance are here
and Israel knows it.
The prophet has become a fool,
the inspired seer a madman,
because of your great guilt and enmity.
⁸God appointed the prophet as a
watchman for Ephraim,
but he has become a fowler's trap on all
their ways.
There is enmity in the very temple of
God.
⁹They are deep in sin
as at the time of Gibeah.
Their guilt will be remembered
and their sins punished.

¹⁰I came upon Israel like grapes in the
wilderness;
as at the first ripe figs
I looked on their forefathers with joy,
but they resorted to Baal-peor
and consecrated themselves to a thing
of shame.

Ephraim became as loathsome as the
thing they loved.
¹¹Their honour will fly away like a bird:
no childbirth, no fruitful womb, no
conceiving!
¹²Even if they rear their children,
I will make them childless, without
posterity.
Woe betide them when I turn away
from them!

¹³As lions lead out their cubs, just to be
hunted,
so must Ephraim bring out his children
for slaughter.
¹⁴Give them whatever you, LORD, are
going to give.
Give them wombs that miscarry and dry
breasts.

¹⁵All their wickedness at Gilgal aroused
my hatred.
I shall drive them from my house
because of their evil deeds,
I shall love them no more, for all their
rulers are in revolt.
¹⁶Ephraim is struck down:
their root is withered, and they yield no
fruit;
if ever they give birth,
I shall slay the cherished offspring of
their womb.
¹⁷My God will reject them,
because they have not listened to him,
and they will become wanderers among
the nations.

God's judgement on Israel

10 ISRAEL is like a spreading vine with
ripening fruit:
the more his fruit, the more his altars;
the more beautiful his land, the more
beautiful his pillars.

9:13 **As lions ... hunted:** *prob. rdg; Heb. unintelligible.*

of Canaanite fertility worship at harvest time. **3:** *Unclean food:* In captivity it will be impossible to observe
ritual laws of cleanliness. **5:** *Pilgrim-feast:* see 2.11 n. **6:** *Memphis:* Egyptian city. **7–8:** A *prophet* attached to
a *temple* was a *trap* to the people in being concerned only with worship and in not warning people about their
guilt which would bring calamity, thereby making the prophet into a *fool*. See Ezek. 13.1–16. **9:** The allusion
to *Gibeah* may mean Saul, whose throne was also there (1 Sam. 10.26). See also Judg. ch. 19.

9.10–17: Israel's degeneration. 10: To find *grapes in the wilderness* was wondrous. *Baal-Peor:* see Num.
25.1–5; Ps. 106.28. **11:** Childlessness was a dishonor. **15:** *Gilgal:* see 4.15 n.; 12.11.

10.1–13.16: Israel's punishment and restoration. The LORD's efforts to redeem Israel have been frustrated.

2 They are false at heart;
now they must pay the penalty.
God himself will break down their
    altars
and demolish their sacred pillars.
3 Well may they say, 'We have no king,
because we do not fear the LORD;
and what could the king do for us?'
4 There is nothing but talk;
they swear false oaths and draw up
    treaties,
and litigation spreads like a poisonous
    weed
along the furrows of the fields.

5 The inhabitants of Samaria tremble
for the calf-god of Beth-aven;
the people mourn over it
and its priests lament,
distressed for the image of their god
which is carried away into exile.
6 It will be carried to Assyria
as tribute to the Great King;
disgrace will overtake Ephraim,
and Israel, lacking counsel, will be put
    to shame.
7 Samaria and her king are swept
    away
like flotsam on the water;
8 the shrines of Aven are destroyed,
the shrines where Israel sinned;
the altars are overgrown with thorns
    and thistles.
They will say to the mountains, 'Cover
    us,'
and to the hills, 'Fall upon us.'

9 Since the time of Gibeah Israel has
    sinned;
there they took their stand in rebellion.
Will not war overtake them in Gibeah?
10 I have come against the rebels to
    chastise them,
and the peoples will mass against them
to chastise them for their two shameful
    deeds.
11 Ephraim is like a heifer broken in,
which loves to thresh grain;
across that fair neck of hers I have laid
    a yoke.

I have harnessed Ephraim to the pole
    to plough,
that Jacob may harrow the land.
12 Sow justice, and reap loyalty.
Break up your fallow ground;
it is time to seek the LORD,
till he comes and rains justice on you.
13 You have ploughed wickedness
and reaped depravity;
you have eaten the fruit of treachery.

Because you have trusted in your
    chariots,
in the number of your warriors,
14 the tumult of war will arise against your
    people,
and all your fortresses will be
    overthrown
as Shalman overthrew Beth-arbel in the
    day of battle,
dashing mothers and babes to the
    ground.
15 So it is to be done to you, Bethel,
because of your great wickedness;
as swiftly as the passing of dawn,
the king of Israel will be swept away.

11 When Israel was a youth, I loved
    him;
out of Egypt I called my son;
2 but the more I called, the farther they
    went from me;
they must needs sacrifice to the baalim
and burn offerings to images.
3 It was I who taught Ephraim to walk,
I who took them in my arms;
but they did not know that 4 I secured
    them with reins
and led them with bonds of love,
that I lifted them like a little child to
    my cheek,
that I bent down to feed them.
5 Back they will go to Egypt,
the Assyrian will be their king;

10:2 **God himself:** *lit.* He.   10:5 **the image of their
god:** *lit.* their glory.   10:10 **I have come:** *prob. rdg,
cp. Gk; Heb.* By my desire.   10:11 **a yoke:** *prob. rdg;
Heb. omits.* **to plough:** *prob. rdg; Heb.* that Judah may
plough.   10:13 **chariots:** *so Gk; Heb.* way.   11:2 **I:**
so Gk; Heb. they. **me:** *so Gk; Heb.* them.   11:3 **I who
took:** *so Gk; Heb. unintelligible.* **my:** *so Gk; Heb.* his.

10.1–8: The fruits of idolatry. Cultic misdeeds produce political disasters. **2:** *Sacred pillars:* see 3.4 n. **5:**
Calf-god: see 8.5 n. **6:** *Great King:* see 5.13 n. **8:** *Aven:* see 4.15 n.
10.9–15: Punishment for rebellion. 9: *Gibeah:* see 9.9 n. **12:** *Fallow:* land uncultivated for a time, and by
implication, hardened and unproductive. **14:** The allusion to *Shalman's* destruction of *Beth-arbel* is obscure.
11.1–12.1: Parenting and ingratitude. 5: *Back . . . Egypt:* see 8.13; 9.3.

for they have refused to return to me.
⁶ The sword will be brandished in their
    cities
and it will make an end of their priests
and devour them because of their
    scheming.
⁷ My people are bent on rebellion,
but though they call in unison to Baal
he will not lift them up.

⁸ How can I hand you over, Ephraim,
how can I surrender you, Israel?
How can I make you like Admah
or treat you as Zeboyim?
A change of heart moves me,
tenderness kindles within me.
⁹ I am not going to let loose my fury,
I shall not turn and destroy Ephraim,
for I am God, not a mortal;
I am the Holy One in your midst.
I shall not come with threats.

¹⁰ They will follow the LORD
who roars like a lion, and when he
    roars,
his sons will speed out of the west.
¹¹ They will come speedily like birds out
    of Egypt,
like pigeons from Assyria,
and I shall settle them in their own
    homes.
This is the word of the LORD.
¹² The treachery of Ephraim encompasses
    me,
as does the deceit of the house of
    Israel;
and Judah is still restive under God,
still loyal to the idols he counts holy.

12 Ephraim feeds on wind,
        he pursues the east wind all day,
he piles up treachery and havoc;
he makes a treaty with Assyria
and carries tribute of oil to Egypt.

² The LORD has a charge to bring against
    Judah

and is resolved to punish Jacob for his
    conduct;
he will requite him for his misdeeds.
³ Even in the womb Jacob supplanted his
    brother,
and in manhood he strove with God.
⁴ He strove with the angel and prevailed;
he wept and entreated his favour.
God met him at Bethel
and spoke with him there.
⁵ The LORD the God of Hosts, the LORD
    is his name!

⁶ Turn back by God's help;
maintain loyalty and justice
and wait continually for your God.
⁷ False scales are in merchants' hands,
and they love to cheat.
⁸ Ephraim says,
'Surely I have become rich,
I have made my fortune,
but despite all my gains
the guilt of sin will not be found in me.'
⁹ Yet I have been the LORD your God
since your days in Egypt;
I shall make you live in tents yet again,
as in the days of the Tent of Meeting.

¹⁰ I spoke to the prophets;
it was I who gave vision after vision:
I declared my mind through them.
¹¹ In Gilead there was idolatry,
the people were worthless
and sacrificed to bull-gods in Gilgal;
their altars were like heaps of stones
beside a ploughed field.

¹² Jacob fled to the land of Aram;
Israel did service to win a wife,
to win her he tended sheep.

¹³ By a prophet the LORD brought Israel
    up from Egypt
and by a prophet Israel was tended.

11:7 **though ... Baal:** *prob. rdg; Heb. obscure.*
11:12 *In Heb. 12:1.*   12:4 **with him:** *so Gk; Heb.*
with us.

11.8: *Admah* and *Zeboyim:* destroyed with Sodom and Gomorrah (Deut. 29.23).

12.2–14: Jacob and Moses. 2–6: Just as *Jacob,* the tribal ancestor in whom Israel glories, sinned and *entreated* God's *favour,* so his descendants should *turn back* and *wait* on *God.* See especially Gen. 25.21–26; 32.22–32; 35.2–7; or 28.10–22. **7–9:** Israel's ill-gotten *gains* on its land do not have the power to prevent God from reducing the people to the poverty and loyalty of *tents* of the Exodus. **11:** In Palestine the soil is so shallow and stony that fields cleared for plowing are hedged with *heaps of stones. Idolatry* was practiced in

14 Ephraim gave bitter provocation;
he will be left to suffer for the blood he
   has shed;
his Lord will punish him for all his
   blasphemy.

13 Ephraim was a prince and a leader
   and he was exalted in Israel,
but, guilty of Baal-worship, he suffered
   death.
2 Yet now they sin more and more;
they cast for themselves images,
they use their silver to make idols,
all fashioned by craftsmen.
It is said of Ephraim:
'They offer human sacrifice and kiss
   calf-images.'
3 Therefore they will be like the morning
   mist,
like dew that vanishes early,
like chaff blown from the
   threshing-floor
or smoke from a chimney.

4 But since your days in Egypt
I have been the LORD your God;
you do not know any god but me,
any saviour other than me.
5 I cared for you in the wilderness,
in a land of burning heat.
6 They were fed and satisfied,
and, once satisfied, they grew proud,
and so they deserted me.
7 Now I shall be like a panther to them,
I shall prowl like a leopard by the
   wayside;
8 I shall come on them like a she-bear
   robbed of her cubs
and tear their ribs apart,
like a lioness I shall devour them on
   the spot,
like a wild beast I shall rip them up.

9 I have destroyed you, Israel;
who is there to help you?
10 Where now is your king that he may
   save you,

in all your cities where are your rulers?
'Give me a king and princes,' you said.
11 I gave you a king in my anger,
and in my wrath I took him away.

12 Ephraim's guilt is tied up in a scroll,
his sins are kept on record.
13 When the pangs of his birth came over
   his mother,
he showed himself a senseless child;
for at the proper time he could not
   present himself
at the mouth of the womb.
14 Shall I deliver him from the grave?
Shall I redeem him from death?
Where are your plagues, death?
Grave, where is your sting?
I shall put compassion out of my sight.
15 Though he flourishes among his
   brothers,
an east wind will come, a blast from the
   LORD
rising over the desert,
causing springs to fail and fountains to
   run dry.
The enemy will plunder his wealth,
all his costly treasures.
16 Samaria will become desolate
because she has rebelled against her
   God;
her babes will fall by the sword
and be dashed to the ground,
and pregnant women will be ripped up.

Repentance and restoration

14 RETURN, Israel, to the LORD your
   God;
for your iniquity has been your
   downfall.
2 Come back to the LORD
with your words of confession;

13:1 **Ephraim ... prince:** *meaning of Heb. uncertain.*
13:7 **I shall be:** *so Gk; Heb.* I was.   13:9 **who:** *so Gk;
Heb.* in me.   13:14 **the grave:** *Heb.* Sheol.
13:16 *In Heb.* 14:1.

the whole land. *Gilead* was east of the Jordan and *Gilgal,* west of it. **13:** *Prophet:* Moses.
13.1–16: The LORD's patience ends. 1: *Baal:* see 2.8 n. **9–11:** See 8.4 n. **12:** God's lawsuit against Israel ends
in a judicial conviction of *guilt,* sealed officially in a *scroll,* and entered on record, as was the judiciary custom.
See Isa. 8.16. **13:** The verse seems to be a proverb for congenital awkwardness and ineptitude ending in disaster.
14: *Where are your plagues:* quoted in 1 Cor. 15.55, though with the meaning altered from a rhetorical
question, implying a negative, into a strong affirmation. **15:** The *east wind* is dry and hot.
14.1–9: Repentance, forgiveness, and restoration. In a serenely confident poem, Hosea uses fertility images

say to him, 'You will surely take away
  iniquity.
Accept our wealth;
  we shall pay our vows with cattle from
  our pens.
³Assyria will not save us, nor shall we
  rely on horses;
what we have made with our own
  hands
we shall never again call gods;
for in you the fatherless find
  compassion.'

⁴I shall heal my people's apostasy;
I shall love them freely,
  for my anger is turned away from
  them.
⁵I shall be as dew to Israel
that they may flower like the lily,
  strike root like the poplar,
⁶and put out fresh shoots,

that they may be as fair as the olive
  and fragrant as Lebanon.
⁷Israel will again dwell in my shadow;
  they will grow vigorously like grain,
  they will flourish like a vine,
and be as famous as the wine of
  Lebanon.
⁸What further dealings has Ephraim
  with idols?
I declare it and affirm it:
I am the pine tree that shelters you;
  your prosperity comes from me.

⁹Let the wise consider these things and let
the prudent acknowledge them: the LORD's
ways are straight and the righteous walk in
them, while sinners stumble.

14:2 **surely:** *prob. rdg, cp. Gk; Heb.* all.   14:5 **poplar:**
prob. rdg; Heb. Lebanon.   14:7 **my:** *prob. rdg;*
Heb. its.   14:8 **What . . . Ephraim:** *prob. rdg, cp. Gk.*

as signs of God's favor and Israel's restoration and new life. **9:** A pious postscript from a later hand.

Joel

Few books can match Joel for drama. From the opening description of locust plagues, through pictures of ruin and restoration, visions and cosmic omens, and the war of the LORD against "a noisy throng in the valley of Decision," the poetry crackles with energy and stretches the mind with the visionary power of a remarkably gifted prophet.

We know nothing about this astonishing person, not even the date of his book. Some scholars place it as early as 600 B.C.E., others as late as 350. The references in 3.4–8 to foreign nations are too vague to allow precise dating, nor can the locust plague described in ch. 1 be identified by date. The picture of religious observances in chs. 1–2 leads most scholars to place Joel in the time of the second temple, perhaps 450–400 B.C.E.

Joel concentrates on God's ultimate victory, pursuing the eschatological implications of the locust plague and other contemporary events, and using a visionary, highly symbolic style. In Joel the prophetic manner carries on from the past, as in Ezekiel and Zechariah (chs. 1–6), toward such later apocalyptic books as Daniel and Revelation.

1

THE word of the LORD which came to Joel son of Pethuel.

The day of the Lord

2 HEAR this, you elders;
listen to me, all you inhabitants of the
  land!
Has the like of this happened in your
  days
or in the days of your forefathers?
3 Tell it to your children and let them
  tell it to theirs;
let one generation pass it on to another.
4 What the locust has left,
the swarmer devours;
what the swarmer has left,
the hopper devours;
and what the hopper has left,
the grub devours.

5 Wake up, you drunkards, and weep!
Mourn for the new wine,
all you wine-drinkers,
for it is denied to you.
6 A horde, vast and past counting,
has invaded my land;
they have teeth like a lion's
  teeth;
they have the fangs of a lioness.
7 They have laid waste my vines
and left my fig trees broken;
they have plucked them bare
and stripped them of their bark,
leaving the branches white.
8 Wail like a virgin in sackcloth,
wailing over the betrothed of her
  youth:
9 the grain-offering and drink-offering
  are cut off
from the house of the LORD.
Mourn, you priests, who minister to the
  LORD!
10 The fields are ruined, the ground
  mourns;
for the grain is ruined, the new wine
  has come to naught,
the oil has failed.

1.1: Title. The tone of the book may indicate that *Joel* was a temple prophet.
1.2–2.17: The day of the LORD (see 1.14–15 n.). A terrible locust plague seems the end of the world, and the people need to muster all their religious resources to meet it.
1.4–2.17: The locusts ruin the entire countryside, and all elements of the population are summoned to lament and repent. **4:** It is disputed whether the Heb. terms for *locust, swarmer, hopper,* and *grub* mean various kinds of locusts or successive stages of growth of one kind. **6–7:** The description of the locusts' ravages is poetically powerful. **9:** The gravity of the situation is indicated by the cessation of the regular sacrifices of the

943

11 Despair, you farmers, and lament, you
   vine-dressers,
   over the wheat and the barley;
   the harvest of the fields is lost.

12 The vines have come to naught,
   and the fig trees have failed;
   pomegranate, palm, and apple,
   every tree of the countryside is dried
      up,
   and all the people's joy
   has come to an end.

13 Put on sackcloth, you priests, and
      mourn;
   lament, you ministers of the altar;
   come, lie in sackcloth all night long,
   you ministers of my God;
   for grain-offerings and drink-offerings
   are withheld from the house of your
      God.

14 Appoint a solemn fast, proclaim a day
      of abstinence.
   You elders, gather all who live in the
      land
   to the house of the LORD your God,
   and cry out to him:

15 'The day is near,
   the day of the LORD: it comes
   as a mighty destruction from the
      Almighty.'

16 It is already before our eyes:
   food is cut off from the house of our
      God
   and there is neither joy nor gladness.

17 Under the clods the seeds have
      shrivelled,
   the water-channels are dry,
   the barns lie in ruins;
   for the harvests have come to naught.

18 How the cattle moan!
   The herds of oxen are distraught
   because they have no pasture;
   even the flocks of sheep waste away.

19 To you, LORD, I cry out;
   for fire has consumed the open
      pastures,
   flames have burnt up every tree in the
      countryside.

20 Even the beasts in the field look to you;
   for the streams are dried up,
   and fire has consumed the open
      pastures.

2 1–2 Blow the trumpet in Zion,
      sound the alarm on my holy
      mountain!
   Let all the inhabitants of the land
      tremble,
   for the day of the LORD is coming,
   a day of darkness and gloom is at hand,
   a day of cloud and dense fog.
   Like blackness spread over the
      mountains
   a vast and countless host appears;
   their like has never been known,
   nor will be in all the ages to come.

3 Their vanguard is a devouring fire,
   their rearguard a leaping flame;
   before them the land is a garden of
      Eden,
   but behind them it is a desolate waste;
   nothing survives their passing.

4 In appearance like horses,
   like cavalry they charge;

5 they bound over the peaks
   with a din like chariots,
   like crackling flames burning up
      stubble,
   like a vast host in battle array.

6 Nations tremble at their onset,
   every face is drained of colour.

7 Like warriors they charge,
   like soldiers they scale the walls;
   each keeps in line
   with no confusion in the ranks,

8 none jostling his neighbour;
   each keeps to his course.
   Weapons cannot halt their attack;

9 they burst into the city,
   race along the wall,
   climb into the houses,
   entering like thieves through the
      windows.

10 At their onset the earth shakes,
   the heavens shudder,
   sun and moon are darkened,

2:6 **drained of colour:** *meaning of Heb. uncertain.*

grain-offering and drink-offering. **12:** The fall harvest was possibly the occasion for a religious festival expressing the people's joy. **14–15:** The Pentateuch prescribes only one fast a year, the recurring Day of Atonement;
see Lev. 23.27. The day of the LORD was the future day of final judgment on the nations, and the purification
and restoration of Israel as described in ch. 3. Some see the plague of locusts as part of that future judgment,
which is conceived of as already beginning to arrive. **2.1:** The trumpet (Heb. shophar) was blown on the most

and the stars withhold their light.
11 The LORD thunders as he leads his
  host;
his is a mighty army,
countless are those who do his bidding.
Great is the day of the LORD and most
  terrible;
who can endure it?

12 Yet even now, says the LORD,
turn back to me wholeheartedly
with fasting, weeping, and mourning.
13 Rend your hearts and not your
  garments,
and turn back to the LORD your God,
for he is gracious and compassionate,
long-suffering and ever constant,
ready always to relent when he
  threatens disaster.
14 It may be he will turn back and relent
and leave a blessing behind him,
blessing enough for grain-offerings and
  drink-offerings
to be presented to the LORD your God.
15 Blow the trumpet in Zion,
appoint a solemn fast, proclaim a day
  of abstinence.
16 Gather the people together, appoint a
  solemn assembly;
summon the elders,
gather the children, even babes at the
  breast;
bid the bridegroom leave his
  wedding-chamber
and the bride her bower.
17 Let the priests, the ministers of the
  LORD,
stand weeping between the porch and
  the altar
and say, 'Spare your people, LORD;

do not expose your own people to
  insult,
to be made a byword by other nations.
Why should the peoples say,
"Where is their God?" '

Israel forgiven and restored

18 THEN the LORD showed his ardent love
  for his land,
and was moved with compassion for his
  people.
19 He answered their appeal and said:
I shall send you corn, new wine, and
  oil,
and you will have them in plenty.
I shall expose you no longer
to the reproach of other nations.
20 I shall remove the northern peril far
  from you
and banish it into a land arid and
  waste,
the vanguard into the eastern sea,
the rearguard into the western sea;
the stench and foul smell of it will go
  up.
He has done great things!
21 Earth, fear not, but rejoice and be glad;
for the LORD has done great things.
22 Fear not, you beasts in the field;
for the open pastures will be green,
the trees will bear fruit,
the fig and the vine yield their harvest.
23 People of Zion, rejoice,
be glad in the LORD your God,
who gives you food in due measure
by sending you rain,
the autumn and spring rains as of old.
24 The threshing-floors will be heaped
  with grain,

solemn occasions, especially at the new year. **10:** The plague of locusts in its density darkens the *sun* and *moon* which are the traditional conditions accompanying the day of the LORD in apocalyptic literature. See 2.30–31; Isa. 13.10. **12–14:** The LORD suggests the proper response, a genuine repentance (of the *heart*) and not merely an outward one (*garments*). *For he is gracious:* a frequent liturgical formula (compare Pss. 86.15; 103.8; 145.8). *Repent:* God frequently has a change of heart; see Gen. 6.6. *Blessing:* usually a tangible evidence of divine favor. **15–17:** The solemn ritual is proclaimed again. The *altar* stood in front of the temple. *Byword:* mockery (more generally, a sentential saying, like a proverb). If Israel is not spared, the Gentiles will infer that Israel's God is ineffectual.

2.18–3.21: Israel repents and is delivered. The poems in this section are arranged thematically rather than chronologically.

2.18–32: The day of the LORD has a positive side, for it is inaugurated by divine *love.* **20:** Danger in Palestine usually came from the north (compare Jer. 1.13–14; 4.6); the north is the mythological dwelling of evil (Isa. 14.13); the *northern peril* is a mythological monster, whose carcass stretches from east to west; see Ezek. 38.6.

the vats will overflow with new wine
and oil.
25 I shall recompense you for the years
that the swarmer has eaten,
hopper and grub and locust,
my great army which I sent against
you.
26 You will eat until you are satisfied,
and praise the name of the LORD your
God
who has done wonderful things for
you,
and my people will never again be put
to shame.
27 You will know that I am present in
Israel,
that I and no other am the LORD your
God;
and my people will never again be put
to shame.
28 After this I shall pour out my spirit on
all mankind;
your sons and daughters will prophesy,
your old men will dream dreams
and your young men see visions;
29 I shall pour out my spirit in those
days
even on slaves and slave-girls.
30 I shall set portents in the sky and on
earth,
blood and fire and columns of smoke.
31 The sun will be turned to darkness
and the moon to blood
before the coming of the great and
terrible day of the LORD.
32 Then everyone who invokes the LORD's
name will be saved:
on Mount Zion and in Jerusalem there
will be a remnant
as the LORD has promised,
survivors whom the LORD calls.

3 When that time comes, on that day
when I reverse the fortunes of Judah
and Jerusalem,
2 I shall gather all the nations together

and lead them down to the valley of
Jehoshaphat.
There I shall bring them to judgement
on behalf of Israel, my own people,
whom they have scattered among the
nations;
they have shared out my land
3 and divided my people by lot,
bartering a boy for a whore
and selling a girl for a drink of wine.

4 What are you to me, Tyre and Sidon and all
the districts of Philistia? Are you bent on taking vengeance on me? If you were to take
vengeance, I should make your deeds recoil
swiftly and speedily on your own heads. 5 You
have taken my silver and gold and carried off
my costly treasures to your temples; 6 you
have sold the people of Judah and Jerusalem
to the Greeks, and removed them far beyond
their own frontiers. 7 But I shall rouse them
to leave the places to which they have been
sold. I shall make your deeds recoil on your
own heads, 8 by selling your sons and your
daughters to the people of Judah, who will
then sell them to the Sabaeans, a distant nation. Those are the LORD's words.

9 Proclaim this amongst the nations:
Declare war, call your troops to arms!
Let all the fighting men advance to the
attack.
10 Beat your mattocks into swords
and your pruning-knives into spears.
Let even the weakling say, 'I am
strong.'
11 Muster, all you nations round about;
let them gather together there.
LORD, send down your champions!
12 Let the nations hear the call to arms
and march up to the valley of
Jehoshaphat.
There I shall sit in judgement

2:28 *In Heb. 3:1.*   3:1 *In Heb. 4:1.*
3:2 **Jehoshaphat:** *that is* The LORD has judged.

28: The LORD's *spirit,* the animating force behind the prophets, is to come on all Israel; compare Ezek.
36.26–27.

3.1–8: Punishment on Judah's oppressors. 1–2: An element in the day of the LORD is the reversal of the
condition of the *nations,* the oppressor, and *Israel,* the oppressed; the nations will be *gathered* for judgment,
just as they *scattered* Israel in carrying out God's judgment on them. **2:** *The Valley of Jehoshaphat* is probably
not any actual place but a hypothetical site for the final judgment; see Tfn. **4–8:** Merchants from *Tyre* and *Sidon*
and the region of *Philistia* came with the Seleucid armies to buy the Jews as slaves in order to sell them. See
1 Macc. 3.41; 2 Macc. 1.27; 8.11. But the talion (Exod. 21.23–24) will operate. *Sabaeans:* a people in Arabia.

3.9–21: The return of Paradise. 9–12: A battle is expected to precede the LORD's culminating victory. *Beat* on all the nations round about.

¹³Wield the knife, for the harvest is
　ripe;
come, tread the grapes,
for the winepress is full;
empty the vats, for they are full to the
　brim.

¹⁴A noisy throng in the valley of
　Decision!
The day of the LORD is at hand
in the valley of Decision:

¹⁵sun and moon are darkened
and the stars withhold their light.

¹⁶The LORD roars from Zion
and thunders from Jerusalem
so that heaven and earth shudder;
but the LORD is a refuge for his
　people,
a defence for Israel.

¹⁷Thus you will know that I am the LORD
　your God,
dwelling in Zion, my holy mountain;
Jerusalem will be holy,

and foreigners will never again set foot
in it.

¹⁸When that day comes,
the mountains will run with the new
　wine
and the hills flow with milk.
Every channel in Judah will be full of
　water;
a fountain will spring from the LORD's
　house
and water the wadi of Shittim.

¹⁹Egypt will become a desolation
and Edom a desolate waste,
because of the violence done to Judah
and the innocent blood shed in her
　land.

²⁰But Judah will be inhabited for ever,
Jerusalem for generation after
　generation.

²¹I shall avenge their blood,
the blood I have not yet avenged,
and the LORD will dwell in Zion.

---

your mattocks into swords, etc., exactly reverses the familiar saying in Isa. 2.4 and Mic. 4.3. **13:** The image
of the vintage for the final day is echoed in Isa. 63.1–3. **14:** *Decision:* against the nations and for Jerusalem.
17: The LORD's *dwelling* in *Jerusalem* gives the city its holy character. **18:** The picture of overflowing nature
is the antithesis of the ruin caused by the locusts (1.4–20; 2.3). *Shittim:* a valley some nineteen miles southwest
of Jerusalem. Compare a similar vision elaborated in Ezek. 47.1–12. **19:** *Egypt* and *Edom* will become sterile
in contrast to Israel's fertility. Edom and Egypt receive special condemnation, Edom because it despoiled Judah
after the latter was laid low by the Babylonians (587 B.C.E.) and Egypt because it deceived Judah with promised
help against the same Babylonians. See Jer. 49.7–22; Ezek. 25.12–14; Obad. 1–11.

Amos

Amos speaks against the Northern Kingdom of Israel with a severity not exceeded in the stern denunciations delivered by other prophets.

The narrative of his confrontation with Amaziah the priest of Bethel (7.10–17) in the time of Jeroboam II places him in the vicinity of 750 B.C.E. At that time Israel was in the midst of a prosperity which would end with its devastating conquest by the Assyrians about 722. But along with the high prosperity there had arisen a social and moral corruption which appeared especially abominable to Amos, a native of the poorer Southern Kingdom of Judah and a shepherd and grower of sycamore figs (7.14). Though in his view other nations were wicked (1.3–2.5), Israel was so deeply guilty of "monstrous sins" (5.12) that her doom, determined by the deity, was sealed and irrevocable.

Verses or passages here and there soften the otherwise unrelieved sternness of the words of Amos (for example, 5.14) by suggesting that a change of heart might still occur in time to save Israel from the divine judgment to come. Other passages (for example, 5.15) hold out at most a forlorn hope for Israel. More optimistically, the latter half of 9.8 and 9.13–15 assert that God's will to sustain Israel surpasses Israel's ability to go wrong. Such hopeful passages are often interpreted as additions to the book from a later hand. The "doxologies" in 4.13; 5.8–9; and 9.5–6 are sometimes also considered to be additions.

Although by his own statement (7.14) he was not the usual prophet, a striking series of visions (7.1–9; 8.1–3; 9.1–4) appear to reflect the personal experiences which culminated in his prophetic ministry, and determined the content of his message.

1 THE words of Amos, one of the sheep-farmers of Tekoa. He received these words in visions about Israel during the reigns of Uzziah king of Judah and Jeroboam son of Jehoash king of Israel, two years before the earthquake. ² He said,

The LORD roars from Zion
and thunders from Jerusalem;
the shepherds' pastures are dried up
and the choicest farmland is parched.

The sins of Israel and her neighbours

³ THESE are the words of the LORD:

For crime after crime of Damascus
I shall grant them no reprieve,

because they threshed Gilead
under threshing-sledges spiked with
basalt.
⁴ Therefore I shall send fire on Hazael's
house,
fire to consume Ben-hadad's palaces;
⁵ I shall crush the nobles of Damascus
and wipe out those who live in the vale
of Aven
and the sceptred ruler of Beth-eden;
the people of Aram will be carried to
exile in Kir.
It is the word of the LORD.

⁶ These are the words of the LORD:

1:2 **choicest farmland:** or summit of Carmel.
1:3 **basalt:** or iron. 1:5 **nobles:** or barred gates.

1.1: Title. *Sheep-farmers:* see 7.14 n. *Tekoa:* a small town southeast of Jerusalem. *Uzziah* reigned over Judah about 783–742 B.C.E. and *Jeroboam* (II) over Israel about 781–746 B.C.E. *Earthquake:* see Zech. 14.5.
1.2–2.16: Judgment upon Israel and surrounding nations. After an opening threat (v. 2; compare Joel 3.16), the oracles traverse the nations surrounding Israel. On a map, the reader will see how the LORD's judgment circles closer and closer until it strikes Israel (2.6). The episodes alluded to in these oracles are now unknown.
3–5: *Damascus:* a long-time enemy of Israel. *Gilead:* Israelite territory east of the Jordan. *Hazael* and *Ben-ha-*

For crime after crime of Gaza
I shall grant them no reprieve,
because they deported a whole
 community into exile
and delivered them to Edom.
7 Therefore I shall send fire on the walls
 of Gaza,
fire to consume its palaces.
8 I shall wipe out those who live in
 Ashdod
and the sceptred ruler of Ashkelon;
I shall turn my hand against Ekron,
and the Philistines who are left will
 perish.
It is the word of the Lord God.

9 These are the words of the Lord:

For crime after crime of Tyre
I shall grant them no reprieve,
because, ignoring the brotherly alliance,
they handed over a whole community
 to exile in Edom.
10 Therefore I shall send fire on the walls
 of Tyre,
fire to consume its palaces.

11 These are the words of the Lord:

For crime after crime of Edom
I shall grant them no reprieve,
because, sword in hand and stifling
 their natural affections,
they hunted down their kinsmen.
Their anger raged unceasingly,
their fury stormed unchecked.
12 Therefore I shall send fire on Teman,
fire to consume the palaces of Bozrah.

13 These are the words of the Lord:

For crime after crime of the
 Ammonites
I shall grant them no reprieve,
because in their greed for land
they ripped open the pregnant women
 in Gilead.
14 Therefore I shall set fire to the walls of
 Rabbah,

fire to consume its palaces
amid war cries on the day of battle,
with a whirlwind on the day of
 sweeping tempest;
15 then their king will go into exile,
he and his officers with him.
It is the word of the Lord.

2 These are the words of the Lord:

For crime after crime of Moab
I shall grant them no reprieve,
because they burnt to lime
the bones of the king of Edom.
2 Therefore I shall send fire on Moab,
fire to consume the palaces of Kerioth;
Moab will perish in uproar,
amid war cries and the sound of
 trumpets,
3 and I shall make away with its ruler
and with him slay all the officers.
It is the word of the Lord.

4 These are the words of the Lord:

For crime after crime of Judah
I shall grant them no reprieve,
because they have spurned the law of
 the Lord
and have not observed his decrees;
they have been led astray by the same
 false gods
their fathers followed.
5 Therefore I shall send fire on Judah,
fire to consume the palaces of
 Jerusalem.

6 These are the words of the Lord:

For crime after crime of Israel
I shall grant them no reprieve,
because they sell honest folk for silver
and the poor for a pair of sandals.
7 They grind the heads of the helpless
 into the dust
and push the humble out of their way.

1:13 **ripped . . . Gilead:** *or* invaded the plains of
Gilead. 2:1 **lime:** *or* ash. 2:7 **They grind:** *prob.
rdg; Heb. obscure.*

dad are royal names. *Aram:* Syria. *Kir:* see 9.7 n. **6–8:** *Gaza*, with *Ashdod, Ashkelon,* and *Ekron,* were Philistine
cities. *Edom:* see vv. 11–12. **9–10:** *Tyre:* a Phoenician seaport. **11–12:** Because *Edom* occupied Judah's
territory after the latter was conquered by the Babylonians in 587 B.C.E., the two became bitter enemies. Edom
lay south of Judah and southeast of the Dead Sea; its main cities were *Teman* and *Bozrah.* **13–15:** Living
adjacent to *Gilead,* east of the Jordan, the *Ammonites* had sporadic hostilities with the Hebrews. *Rabbah:* the
Ammonite capital. **2.1–3:** *Moab* was south of Ammon.

Father and son resort to the temple
girls,
so profaning my holy name.
8 Men lie down beside every altar
on garments held in pledge,
and in the house of their God they
drink wine
on the proceeds of fines.

9 It was I who destroyed the Amorite
before them;
he was as tall as the cedars,
as sturdy as the oak;
I destroyed his fruit above
and his root below.
10 It was I who brought you up out of
Egypt,
and for forty years led you in the
wilderness,
to take possession of the country of the
Amorite;
11 I raised up prophets from among your
sons,
Nazirites from among your young
men.
Israelites, is this not true?
says the LORD.
12 But you have made the Nazirites drink
wine,
and said to the prophets, 'You are not
to prophesy.'
13 Listen, I groan under the burden of
you,
as a wagon creaks under a full load.
14 Flight will be cut off for the swift,
the strong will not recover strength.
The warrior will not save himself,
15 the archer will not stand his
ground;
the swift of foot will not escape,
nor the horseman save himself.
16 On that day the bravest of warriors
will throw away his weapons and
flee.
It is the word of the LORD.

Israel's sins and threatened punishment

3 LISTEN, Israelites, to these words that
the LORD addresses to you, to the whole
nation which he brought up from Egypt:

2 You alone I have cared for
among all the nations of the world;
that is why I shall punish you
for all your wrongdoing.
3 Do two people travel together
unless they have so agreed?
4 Does a lion roar in the thicket
if he has no prey?
Does a young lion growl in his den
unless he has caught something?
5 Does a bird fall into a trap on the
ground
if no bait is set for it?
Does a trap spring from the ground
and take nothing?
6 If a trumpet sounds in the city,
are not the people alarmed?
If disaster strikes a city,
is it not the work of the LORD?

7 Indeed, the Lord GOD does nothing without
revealing his plan to his servants the prophets.

8 The lion has roared; who is not
frightened?
The Lord GOD has spoken; who will
not prophesy?
9 Upon the palaces of Ashdod
and upon the palaces of Egypt,
make this proclamation:
'Assemble on the hills of Samaria,
look at the tumult seething among her
people,
at the oppression in her midst;
10 what do they care for straight dealing
who hoard in their palaces
the gains of violence and plundering?'
This is the word of the LORD.

2:7 **the temple girls:** *lit.* the girl.   2:8 **God:** *or* gods.

2.8: *Garments held in pledge* (as collateral) were to be returned to the owner at night (Deut. 24.12–13). **9:** The *Amorites* (Gen. 15.16) were Canaanites. **11–12:** *Nazirites* vowed to abstain from wine (see Num. 6.2–4).

3.1–6.14: Israel is pronounced guilty. The three parts of the section begin with the word "Listen" (3.1; 4.1; 5.1).

3.1–15: Promised destruction. 2: *Cared:* see Hos. 5.3–4 n. **3–8:** A series of causes and effects in the form of questions. Verse 7 is in prose, and is regarded by some as a later addition since the passage is mostly in meter. **9–11:** The imperatives in v. 9 are plural, perhaps addressed to the prophets who are directed to *Ashdod*

¹¹Therefore these are the words of the Lord God:

> An enemy will encompass the land;
> your stronghold will be thrown down
> and your palaces sacked.

¹²These are the words of the Lord:

> As a shepherd rescues from the jaws of
> a lion
> a pair of shin-bones or the tip of an
> ear,
> so will the Israelites who live in Samaria
> be rescued,
> who repose on the finest beds and on
> divans from Damascus.

¹³Listen and testify against the
descendants of Jacob.
This is the word of the Lord God, the
God of Hosts.
¹⁴On the day when I deal with Israel for
their crimes,
I shall deal with the altars of Bethel:
the horns of the altar will be hacked off
and fall to the ground.
¹⁵I shall break down both winter houses
and summer residences;
the houses adorned with ivory will
perish,
and great houses will be no more.
This is the word of the Lord.

4 Listen to this word,
you Bashan cows on the hill of
Samaria,
who oppress the helpless and grind
down the poor,
who say to your lords, 'Bring us drink':
²the Lord God has sworn by his holiness
that your time is coming
when men will carry you away on
shields
and your children in fish-baskets.
³You will each be carried straight out
through the breaches in the wall
and thrown on a dunghill.

This is the word of the Lord.

⁴Come to Bethel—and infringe my law!
Come to Gilgal—and infringe it yet
more!
Bring your sacrifices for the morning,
your tithes within three days.
⁵Burn your thank-offering without
leaven;
announce publicly your
freewill-offerings;
for that is what you Israelites love to
do!
This is the word of the Lord God.

⁶It was I who brought starvation to all
your towns,
who spread famine through all your
settlements;
yet you did not come back to me.
This is the word of the Lord.

⁷It was I who withheld the heavy
showers from you
while there were still three months to
the harvest.
I would send rain on one town
and no rain on another;
rain would fall on one field,
another would be parched for lack of
it.
⁸From this town and that, people would
stagger to another
for water to drink, but would not find
enough;
yet you did not come back to me.
This is the word of the Lord.

⁹I struck you with black blight and red;
I dried up your gardens and vineyards;
the locust devoured your fig trees and
your olives;

3:11 **will encompass:** *prob. rdg; Heb.* and round.
3:12 **who repose … Damascus:** *prob. rdg; Heb.* obscure.
4:2 **on shields:** *or* with hooks. **in fish-baskets:** *or* with
fish-hooks.   4:3 **a dunghill:** *prob. rdg; Heb.* the
Harmon.   4:4 **within:** *or* on.   4:6 **starvation:** *lit.*
cleanness of teeth.   4:9 **I dried up:** *prob. rdg; Heb.*
to increase.

and *Egypt* as witnesses in a lawsuit against *Samaria*, Israel's capital. The latter was ringed by *hills*. **12:** This
bitterly ironic statement means that the *Israelites* who will be rescued from the impending catastrophe will be
merely a scrap, hardly worth the effort. **14:** *Altars* had projecting corners, called *horns*, possessing special
power. **15:** The *houses* symbolize the corruption of wealth. *Ivory:* luxurious decorations.
  4.1–13: "Prepare to meet your God." 1–3: The *Bashan cows* are the rich Samaritan women. Bashan was
famous for fine cattle (compare Ezek. 39.18; Ps. 22.12). **6a:** *Brought starvation:* lit. "kept teeth clean." **6b:** Hag.

yet you did not come back to me.
This is the word of the LORD.

10 I sent plague among you like the
    plagues of Egypt;
with the sword I slew
your young men and your troops of
    horses.
I made your camps stink in your
    nostrils;
yet you did not come back to me.
This is the word of the LORD.

11 I brought destruction among you
like the terrible destruction that befell
    Sodom and Gomorrah;
you were like a brand snatched from
    the burning;
yet you did not come back to me.
This is the word of the LORD.

12 Therefore, Israel, this is what I shall do
    to you;
and, because this is what I shall do,
Israel, prepare to meet your God.
13 It is he who fashions the mountains,
who creates the wind,
and declares his thoughts to mankind;
it is he who darkens the dawn with
    thick clouds
and marches over the heights of the
    earth—
his name is the LORD, the God of
    Hosts.

5 Listen, Israel, to these words, the dirge
  I raise over you:

2 She has fallen, to rise no more,
the virgin Israel,
prostrate on her own soil,
with no one to lift her up.

3 These are the words of the Lord GOD:

The city that marched out to war a
    thousand strong
will have but a hundred left,

and that which marched out a hundred
    strong
will have but ten left for Israel.

4 These are the words of the LORD to the
people of Israel:

If you would live, make your way to
    me, 5 not to Bethel;
do not go to Gilgal or pass on to
    Beersheba;
for Gilgal will surely go into exile
and Bethel come to nothing.
6 If you would live, make your way to the
    LORD,
or he will break out against Joseph's
    descendants like fire,
fire which will devour Bethel with no
    one to quench it.

8 He who made the Pleiades and Orion,
who turns deep darkness into dawn
and darkens day into night,
who summons the waters of the sea
and pours them over the earth—
the LORD is his name—
9 who makes destruction flash forth
    against the mighty
so that destruction comes upon the
    stronghold.

7 You that turn justice to poison
and thrust righteousness to the ground,
10 you that hate a man who brings the
    wrongdoer to court
and abominate him who speaks nothing
    less than truth:
11 for all this, because you levy taxes on
    the poor
and extort a tribute of grain from
    them,
though you have built houses of hewn
    stone,
you will not live in them;

4:10 **troops of:** *or* captured.   4:11 **the terrible:** *or*
God's.   5:8 *Verse 7 transposed to follow verse 9.*
5:9 **who makes . . . stronghold:** *or* who makes Taurus
rise after Capella, and Taurus set hard on the rising of
the Vintager.

2.17. **7:** Deut. 11.17. **10:** *Plagues:* compare Exod. 7.14–11.10; 12.29–32. **11:** Compare Gen. 19.24–28. **12:**
An oath, in which the threat (*this is what I will do*) is unspecified. **13:** The verse is hymnic in style.

    5.1–6.14: Death and exile. A miscellaneous group of poems unified by their pessimistic outlook. **1–2:** The
poetry of v. 2 has in Heb. the rhythm of the *dirge.*

    5.4–15: The possibility of life. The hope that the LORD holds out is hedged with qualifications. *Bethel* and
Gilgal were shrine towns in Benjamin; *Beersheba* a shrine town in Judah. As in vv. 21–27, Amos rejects Israel's

though you have planted pleasant
  vineyards,
you will not drink wine from them.
12 For I know how many are your crimes,
  how monstrous your sins:
you bully the innocent, extort ransoms,
and in court push the destitute out of
  the way.
13 In such a time, therefore, it is prudent
  to stay quiet,
for it is an evil time.

14 Seek good, and not evil,
  that you may live,
that the LORD, the God of Hosts, may
  be with you,
as you claim he is.
15 Hate evil, and love good;
  establish justice in the courts;
it may be that the LORD, the God of
  Hosts,
will show favour to the survivors of
  Joseph.

16 Therefore these are the words of the LORD,
the God of Hosts.

In all the public squares, there will be
  wailing,
the sound of grief in every street.
The farmer will be called to mourning,
and wailing proclaimed to those skilled
  in the dirge;
17 there will be wailing in every vineyard;
for I shall pass through your midst,
says the LORD.

18 Woe betide those who long for the day
  of the LORD!
What will the day of the LORD mean
  for you?
It will be darkness, not light;
19 it will be as when someone runs from a
  lion,
only to be confronted by a bear,

or as when he enters his house
and leans with his hand on the wall,
only to be bitten by a snake.
20 The day of the LORD is indeed
  darkness, not light,
a day of gloom without a ray of
  brightness.

21 I spurn with loathing your
  pilgrim-feasts;
I take no pleasure in your sacred
  ceremonies.
22 When you bring me your
  whole-offerings and your
  grain-offerings
I shall not accept them,
nor pay heed to your shared-offerings
  of stall-fed beasts.
23 Spare me the sound of your songs;
I shall not listen to the strumming of
  your lutes.
24 Instead let justice flow on like a river
and righteousness like a never-failing
  torrent.
25 Did you, people of Israel, bring me
  sacrifices and offerings
those forty years in the wilderness?
26 No! But now you will take up
  the shrine of your idol-king
and the pedestals of your images,
which you have made for yourselves,
27 and I shall drive you into exile beyond
  Damascus.

So says the LORD; the God of Hosts is his
name.

6 Woe betide those living at ease in
  Zion,
and those complacent on the hill of
  Samaria,

5:22 **stall-fed beasts:** or buffaloes.   5:26 **the shrine
... images:** prob. rdg; Heb. adds the star of your gods;
or Sakkuth your king and Kaiwan your star-god, the
images.

ritual worship. **14–15:** The word seek (make your way, vv. 4–6) reflects the ritual practice; the prophet insists
that such seeking be fully genuine and not merely formal. Amos goes beyond mere adherence to tradition,
demanding instead a new attitude: Hate evil, and love good.

    5.16–27: Rejection of the cult. 18: The day of the LORD: see Joel 1.14–15 n. **21–27:** The prophet rejects
the entire system of ritual, denying (vv. 25–26) that it was truly part of Israel's legacy from the formative
wilderness period. Justice and righteousness should replace the unacceptable ritualism.

    6.1–7: "Are they better?" Calneh, perhaps the same as Calno (Isa. 10.9) and Kanneh (Ezek. 27.23), was
a town in northern Syria. Hamath, an important Syrian center, was captured by the Assyrians in the 720s. Gath,
one of the five Philistine cities, was destroyed many times.

men of mark in the first of nations,
those to whom the people of Israel
have recourse!
2 Go over and look at Calneh,
travel on to great Hamath,
then go down to Gath of the
Philistines —
are they better than these kingdoms,
or is their territory greater than yours?
3 You thrust aside all thought of the evil
day
and hasten the reign of violence.
4 You loll on beds inlaid with ivory
and lounge on your couches;
you feast on lambs from the flock
and stall-fed calves;
5 you improvise on the lute
and like David invent musical
instruments,
6 you drink wine by the bowlful
and anoint yourselves with the richest
of oils;
but at the ruin of Joseph you feel no
grief.
7 Now, therefore, you will head the
column of exiles;
lounging and laughter will be at an
end.

8 The Lord GOD has sworn by himself:
I abhor the arrogance of Jacob,
I detest his palaces;
I shall abandon the city and its people
to their fate.

9 If ten are left in one house, they will die. 10 If
a relative and an embalmer take up a body to
carry it out of the house for burial, they will
call to someone in a corner of the house, 'Any
more there?' and he will answer, 'No'; then
he will add, 'Hush!' — for the name of the
LORD must not be mentioned.

11 When the LORD commands,
great houses will be reduced to rubble
and the small houses shattered.

12 Can horses gallop over rocks?
Can the sea be ploughed with oxen?
Yet you have turned into venom the
process of law,
justice itself you have turned into
poison.
13 Jubilant over a nothing, you boast,
'Have we not won power by our own
strength?'
14 Israel, I am raising a nation against
you,
and they will harry your land
from Lebo-hamath to the wadi of the
Arabah.
This is the word of the LORD the God
of Hosts.

Visions foretelling doom upon Israel

7 THIS was what the Lord GOD showed
me: it was a swarm of locusts hatching
when the later corn, which comes after the
king's early crop, was beginning to sprout.
2 As they devoured every trace of vegetation
in the land, I said, 'Lord GOD, forgive, I pray
you. How can Jacob survive? He is so small.'
3 The LORD relented. 'This will not happen,'
he said.

4 This was what the Lord GOD showed me:
the Lord GOD was summoning a flame of fire
to devour the great abyss, and to devour the
land. 5 I said, 'Lord GOD, cease, I pray you.
How can Jacob survive? He is so small.' 6 The
LORD relented. 'This also will not happen,' he
said.

7 This was what the Lord showed me: there
he was standing by a wall built with the aid of
a plumb-line, and he had a plumb-line in his
hand. 8 The LORD asked me, 'What do you
see, Amos?' 'A plumb-line', I answered. Then
the LORD said, 'I am setting a plumb-line in
the midst of my people Israel; never again
shall I pardon them. 9 The shrines of Isaac

6:8 by himself: so Gk; Heb. adds This is the word of
the LORD the God of Hosts.   6:13 nothing . . .
power: Heb. Lo-debar . . . Karnaim, making a word-play
on the two placenames.   7:4 a flame of fire: prob. rdg;
Heb. to contend with fire.

6.8–14: Punishment of Israel. The reduction of Israel to *rubble* (v. 11) is to be accompanied by the
demoralization of the people. **13:** *Nothing* and *power* represent city names; see Tfn. **14:** *Lebo-hamath* was in
the north, the *Arabah* in the south. The enemy overruns the land from one end to the other.

7.1–9.8: Visions foretelling doom upon Israel. A series of symbolic but accurate visions is interspersed with
a narrative and other oracles. **1–3:** A *locust* plague destroys the people's grain. *The king's early crop* has already
been harvested. **4–6:** *Abyss:* the waters beneath the earth; see Ps. 77.16–20. **7–9:** A *plumb-line* was used to
make sure a wall was vertical and hence stable.

will be desolated and the sanctuaries of Israel laid waste; and sword in hand I shall rise against the house of Jeroboam.'

10 AMAZIAH, the priest of Bethel, reported to King Jeroboam of Israel: 'Amos has conspired against you here in the heart of Israel; the country cannot tolerate all his words. 11 This is what he is saying: "Jeroboam will die by the sword, and the Israelites will assuredly be deported from their native land." ' 12 To Amos himself Amaziah said, 'Seer, go away! Off with you to Judah! Earn your living and do your prophesying there. 13 But never prophesy again at Bethel, for this is the king's sanctuary, a royal shrine.' 14 'I was no prophet,' Amos replied to Amaziah, 'nor was I a prophet's son; I was a herdsman and fig-grower. 15 But the LORD took me as I followed the flock and it was the LORD who said to me, "Go and prophesy to my people Israel." 16 So now listen to the word of the LORD. You tell me I am not to prophesy against Israel or speak out against the people of Isaac. 17 Now these are the words of the LORD: Your wife will become a prostitute in the city, and your sons and daughters will fall by the sword. Your land will be parcelled out with a measuring line, you yourself will die in a heathen country, and Israel will be deported from their native land.'

8 THIS was what the Lord GOD showed me: it was a basket of summer fruit. 2 'What is that you are looking at, Amos?' he said. I answered, 'A basket of ripe summer fruit.' Then the LORD said to me, 'The time is ripe for my people Israel. Never again shall I pardon them. 3 On that day, says the Lord GOD, the palace songs will give way to lamentation: "So many corpses, flung out everywhere! Silence!" '

4 Listen to this, you that grind the poor and suppress the humble in the land 5 while you say, 'When will the new moon be over so that

we may sell grain? When will the sabbath be past so that we may expose our wheat for sale, giving short measure in the bushel and taking overweight in the silver, tilting the scales fraudulently, 6 and selling the refuse of the wheat; that we may buy the weak for silver and the poor for a pair of sandals?' 7 The LORD has sworn by the arrogance of Jacob: I shall never forget any of those activities of theirs.

8 Will not the earth quake on account of
  this?
  Will not all who live on it mourn?
  The whole earth will surge and seethe
  like the Nile
  and subside like the river of Egypt.

9 On that day, says the Lord GOD,
  I shall make the sun go down at noon
  and darken the earth in broad daylight.
10 I shall turn your pilgrim-feasts into
  mourning
  and all your songs into lamentation.
  I shall make you all put sackcloth
  round your waists
  and have everyone's head shaved.
  I shall make it like mourning for an
  only son
  and the end of it like a bitter day.

11 The time is coming, says the Lord GOD,
  when I shall send famine on the land,
  not hunger for bread or thirst for
  water,
  but for hearing the word of the LORD.
12 People will stagger from sea to sea,
  they will range from north to east,
  in search of the word of the LORD,
  but they will not find it.

7:14 **I was no:** *or* I am no. **nor was I:** *or* nor am I. **son:** *or* disciple. **I was a:** *or* I am a. **fig-grower:** *lit.* pricker of sycomore-figs. 8:2 **ripe summer ... ripe for my people:** *a play on the Heb.* qais *('summer') and* qes *('end').* 8:5 **bushel:** *Heb.* ephah.

7.10–17: Amos' confrontation with Amaziah. *Bethel* was the main royal shrine in Israel. The narrative is about Amos, not by him; its origin is obscure. The charge against Amos was sedition. **14:** Amos' reply, *I was no prophet . . . nor was I a prophet's son,* asserts that he was not the usual "professional" prophet (see 1 Sam. 10.5), but rather someone specially called to prophesy. He terms himself a *herdsman and a fig-grower;* see 1.1, "sheep-farmer."

8.1–7: Summer fruit. This vision turns on a Heb. wordplay (see Tfn.). **4–7:** The mechanical observance of ritual, accompanied by derelictions from morality.

8.8–14: Cosmic catastrophe. 8: The allusion is to the annual flood of the *Nile.* **10:** *Pilgrim-feasts:* the festivals commanded in Exod. 23.14–17. *Sackcloth* and *shaved heads* were signs of *mourning.* **11:** *Hunger . . . for*

13 On that day fair maidens and young
    men
will faint from thirst;
14 all who take their oath by Ashimah,
    goddess of Samaria,
all who swear, 'As your god lives, Dan',
and, 'By the sacred way to Beersheba',
they all will fall to rise no more.

9 I saw the Lord standing by the altar, and
he said:

Strike the capitals so that the whole
    porch is shaken;
smash them down on the heads of the
    people,
and those who are left I shall put to the
    sword.
No fugitive will escape,
no survivor find safety.
2 Though they dig down to Sheol,
from there my hand will take them;
though they climb up to the heavens,
from there I shall bring them down.
3 If they hide on the summit of Carmel,
there I shall hunt them out and take
    them;
if they conceal themselves from my
    sight in the depths of the sea,
there at my command the sea serpent
    will bite them.
4 If they are herded off into captivity by
    their enemies,
there I shall command the sword to
    slay them;
I shall fix my eye on them
for evil, and not for good.

5 The LORD the God of Hosts —
at his touch the earth heaves,
and all who live on it mourn,
while the whole earth surges like the
    Nile
and subsides like the river of Egypt;

6 he builds his upper chambers in the
    heavens
and arches the vault of the sky over the
    earth;
he summons the waters of the sea
and pours them over the earth —
his name is the LORD.

7 Are not you Israelites like the Cushites
    to me?
says the LORD.
Did I not bring Israel up from Egypt,
and the Philistines from Caphtor, the
    Aramaeans from Kir?
8 Behold, I, the Lord GOD,
have my eyes on this sinful kingdom,
and I shall destroy it from the face of
    the earth.

A remnant spared and restored

YET I shall not totally destroy Jacob's
    posterity,
says the LORD.
9 No; I shall give the command,
and shake Israel among all the nations,
as a sieve is shaken to and fro
without one pebble falling to the
    ground.
10 They will die by the sword, all the
    sinners of my people,
who say, 'You will not let disaster
    approach
or overtake us.'
11 On that day I shall restore
David's fallen house;
I shall repair its gaping walls and
    restore its ruins;
I shall rebuild it as it was long ago,

8:14 **the sacred way to Beersheba:** *or, with Gk,* the life
of your god, Beersheba.   9:1 **those who are left:** *or*
their children.   9:2 **Sheol:** *or* the underworld.
9:5 **mourn:** *or* wither.   9:6 **upper chambers in:**
prob. rdg; Heb. stair up to.   9:11 **house:** *lit.* booth.

hearing the word: lack of a prophet who speaks for the LORD. **14:** *Ashimah:* a fertility goddess. Since *Dan* was
in the north and *Beersheba* in the south, when used together they were a frequent figure for all the land.
   9.1–8a: Destruction of the "chosen people." 2: *Sheol:* the place of the dead; compare Ps. 139.8. **3:** *Carmel:*
the famous mountain above modern Haifa. **7:** Since the LORD has dealt with other nations in the same way
as with Israel, Israel is not "chosen." *Cushites:* Ethiopians. *Caphtor:* Crete. *Aramaeans:* compare 1.3–5. *Kir* was
possibly in Mesopotamia; it appears both as the place of origin of the Aramaeans as here, and as the place
to which they were exiled (1.5; 2 Kgs. 16.9).
   9.8b–15: The future restoration of Israel. Many scholars believe that this glowing passage was added to
give a positive ending. **11:** *Fallen* suggests the period of the Babylonian conquest (587 B.C.E.) after which

¹²so that Israel may possess what is left of
    Edom
  and of all the nations who were once
    named as mine.

This is the word of the LORD, who will do this.

¹³A time is coming, says the LORD,
  when the ploughman will follow hard
    on the reaper,
  and he who treads the grapes after him
    who sows the seed.
  The mountains will run with fresh
    wine,

and every hill will flow with it.

¹⁴I shall restore the fortunes of my
    people Israel;
  they will rebuild their devastated cities
    and live in them,
  plant vineyards and drink the wine,
  cultivate gardens and eat the fruit.
¹⁵Once more I shall plant them on their
    own soil,
  and never again will they be
    uprooted
  from the soil I have given them.
  It is the word of the LORD your God.

David's dynasty came to an end. **12:** On the enmity of Judah and *Edom,* see 1.11–12 n. **13:** Fertility would be so great that the labors of the agricultural seasons would press on each other.

Obadiah

Nothing is known about this Obadiah. The similarities between vv. 1–9 and Jer. 49.7–22 suggest a common time of origin for both passages, and possibly a common prophetic circle.

The book consists of short poems of diverse origin, unified by the prediction that Israel's and Edom's national situations will be reversed. In the tradition (Gen. 25.24–26), Edom (Esau) was the twin brother of Israel (Jacob); according to Obadiah, Edom has not been his brother's keeper (v. 10), and now the LORD will punish Edom.

This latter theme suggests that the book originated shortly after the Babylonian sack of Jerusalem in 587 B.C.E., in which the Edomites apparently participated.

Edom's pride and downfall

THE vision of Obadiah: the words of the Lord GOD about Edom.

While envoys were being dispatched
among the nations, saying,
'Up! Let us attack Edom,'
I heard this message from the LORD:

2 I shall make you the least of all nations,
an object of utter contempt.
3 The pride in your heart has led you
astray,
you that haunt the crannies among the
rocks
and make your home on the heights,
saying to yourself, 'Who can bring me
to the ground?'
4 Though you soar as high as an eagle
and your nest is set among the stars,
even from there I shall bring you
down.
This is the word of the LORD.

5 If thieves or robbers were to come to
you by night,
though your loss might be heavy,
they would take only enough for their
needs;
if vintagers were to come to you,

would they not leave gleanings?
6 But see how Esau is ransacked,
their secret wealth hunted out!
7 All your former allies have pushed you
to the frontier,
your confederates have misled and
subjugated you,
those who eat at your table lay a snare
for your feet.
Where is his wisdom now?
8 This is the word of the LORD: On that
day
I shall destroy all the wise men of
Edom
and leave no wisdom on the mountains
of Esau.
9 Then your warriors, Teman, will be so
terror-stricken
that no survivors will be left on the
mountains of Esau.
10 For the violence done to your brother
Jacob
you will be covered with shame and cut
off for ever.
11 On the day when you stood aloof,
while strangers carried off his wealth,
while foreigners passed through his
gates
and shared out Jerusalem by lot,
you were at one with them.

1 **I heard:** *prob. rdg, so Gk; Heb.* we heard.

1: Title. Obadiah means "the LORD's servant."

1–4: Edom's pride and downfall. The poem describes the downfall by opposites: *contempt* and *pride, heights* and *the ground*. Edom's capital, Teman (v. 9), was in rocky hills.

5–7: Military conquest. 5: *Gleanings:* Harvesters were to leave fruit for the poor (Deut. 24.19–21). **6:** *Esau* was Edom's progenitor (Gen. 36.1) as *Jacob* (Obad. 10) was Israel's.

8–14: Edom's treachery. 8: Edom had a reputation for *wisdom*; the sages of 1 Kgs. 4.31 are regarded by

¹²Do not gloat over your brother when
  disaster strikes him,
or rejoice over Judah on the day of his
  ruin.
Do not boast when he suffers distress,
¹³or enter my people's gates on the day
  of their calamity.
Do not join in the gloating when
  calamity overtakes them,
or seize their treasure on the day of
  their calamity.
¹⁴Do not stand at the crossroads to cut
  down his fugitives,
or betray the survivors on the day of
  distress.
¹⁵The day of the Lord is at hand for all
  the nations.
You will be treated as you have treated
  others:
your deeds will recoil on your own
  head.

¹⁶The draught you, my people, have
  drunk on my holy mountain
all the nations will drink in turn;
they will drink and gulp it down
and be as though they had never been.

¹⁷But on Mount Zion there will be a
  remnant
which will be holy,
and Jacob will dispossess those that
  dispossessed them.
¹⁸Then the house of Jacob will be a fire,
the house of Joseph a flame,
and the house of Esau will be stubble;
they will set it alight and burn it up,
and the house of Esau will have no
  survivors.
Those are the Lord's words.

¹⁹My people will possess the Negeb, the
mountains of Esau, and the Shephelah of the
Philistines; they will possess the countryside
of Ephraim and Samaria, and Benjamin will
possess Gilead. ²⁰Exiles from Israel will possess Canaan as far as Zarephath, while exiles
from Jerusalem who are in Sepharad will
possess the towns of the Negeb. ²¹Those who
wield authority on Mount Zion will go up to
hold sway over the mountains of Esau, and
dominion will belong to the Lord.

20 **Exiles from:** *prob. rdg; Heb. adds* this army. **will
possess Canaan:** *prob. rdg; Heb.* which Canaan.

some as Edomites. **9:** *Teman:* the main Edomite city. **12–14:** On Edom's crimes at the time of the Babylonian
sack of Jerusalem, see Ezek. 35.1–36.7.

15–21: The punishment. 15: *The day of the Lord:* the time of the Lord's judgment on *all the nations.* **16:**
Draught: a symbol of divine wrath (see Jer. 25.15–28; Ps. 75.8). **19–21:** The areas mentioned are both in and
around Israel. The *Negeb* was the southern wilderness, *Shephelah* the Judean hills just east of the coastal plain.
Gilead was east of the Jordan. *Zarephath* was on the Phoenician coast. Sepharad, in Asia Minor, is a later Heb.
name for Spain.

Jonah

Unlike the other prophetic books, Jonah takes the form of a story. The reader should begin by enjoying it as a short story, without concern about its historical accuracy. Viewing the story as in a satiric vein may make it all the more enjoyable.

A prophet Jonah is mentioned in 2 Kgs. 14.25, yet with only the sketchiest information. We cannot be sure whether this story is or is not about that Jonah.

We cannot be certain of the date of composition of this book. The author's exaggerations (the size of Nineveh, 3.3; its response to Jonah's threat, 3.5–9) suggest that he wrote after Nineveh, destroyed in 612 B.C.E., was only a memory. This would mean a date at least later than 600 B.C.E. Since the book (like Ruth) opposes the exclusiveness found in Ezra and Nehemiah, it may have originated about 450–400 B.C.E.

The story has its own pungency. Traditionally, Jonah is viewed as a hero. Perhaps, however, as some modern scholars hold, the author had something other than a hero in mind, for his Jonah says the right things (1.9; 2.2–9; 4.2) but does not follow them. Jonah cannot conceive that God could care for anyone, human or animal, except an Israelite; he becomes quite upset when God forgives Nineveh. The book's message of God's universal concern is borne along by the irony of a petulant prophet who is disappointed by the success of his preaching.

Jonah's mission to Nineveh

1 THE word of the LORD came to Jonah son of Amittai: [2] 'Go to the great city of Nineveh; go and denounce it, for I am confronted by its wickedness.' [3] But to escape from the LORD Jonah set out for Tarshish. He went down to Joppa, where he found a ship bound for Tarshish. He paid the fare and went on board to travel with it to Tarshish out of the reach of the LORD.

[4] The LORD let loose a hurricane on the sea, which rose so high that the ship threatened to break up in the storm. [5] The sailors were terror-stricken; everyone cried out to his own god for help, and they threw things overboard to lighten the ship. Meanwhile Jonah, who had gone below deck, was lying there fast asleep. [6] When the captain came upon him he said, 'What, fast asleep? Get up and call to your god! Perhaps he will spare a thought for us, and we shall not perish.'

[7] The sailors said among themselves, 'Let us cast lots to find who is to blame for our misfortune.' They cast lots, and when Jonah was singled out [8] they wanted to be told how he was to blame. They questioned him: 'What is your business? Where do you come from? Which is your country? What is your nationality?' [9] 'I am a Hebrew,' he answered, 'and I worship the LORD the God of heaven, who made both sea and dry land.' [10] At this the sailors were even more afraid. 'What is this you have done?' they said, because they knew he was trying to escape from the LORD, for he had told them. [11] 'What must we do with you to make the sea calm for us?' they asked; for it was getting worse. [12] 'Pick me up and throw me overboard,' he replied; 'then the sea will go down. I know it is my fault that this great storm has struck you.' [13] Though the crew rowed hard to put back to land it was no use, for the sea was running higher and higher. [14] At last they called to the LORD, 'Do not let us perish, LORD, for this man's life; do not hold us responsible for the death of an innocent man, for all this, LORD, is what you yourself have brought about.' [15] Then they took Jonah and threw him overboard, and the raging of the sea subsided. [16] Seized

---

1.1–16: Jonah's flight by ship. 2: *Nineveh:* the capital of Assyria, far to the east. **3:** *Tarshish:* though often identified with Spain, it was probably a legendary place far to the west of Palestine. Jonah thus travels in the opposite direction from Nineveh. **9:** *Worship:* lit. "fear." Jonah seems not to see the disparity between his by a great fear of the LORD, the men offered a sacrifice and made vows to him. ¹⁷The LORD ordained that a great fish should swallow Jonah, and he remained in its belly for three days and three nights. 2 From the fish's belly Jonah offered this prayer to the LORD his God:

² 'In my distress I called to the LORD,
  and he answered me;
  from deep within Sheol I cried for
    help,
  and you heard my voice.
³ You cast me into the depths,
  into the heart of the ocean,
  and the flood closed around me;
  all your surging waves swept over me.
⁴ I thought I was banished from your
    sight
  and should never again look towards
    your holy temple.

⁵ 'The water about me rose to my neck,
  for the deep was closing over me;
  seaweed twined about my head
⁶ at the roots of the mountains;
  I was sinking into a world
  whose bars would hold me fast for
    ever.
  But you brought me up, LORD my God,
    alive from the pit.
⁷ As my senses failed I remembered the
    LORD,
  and my prayer reached you in your
    holy temple.

⁸ 'Those who cling to false gods
  may abandon their loyalty,

⁹ but I with hymns of praise
  shall offer sacrifice to you;
  what I have vowed I shall fulfil.
  Victory is the LORD's!'

¹⁰ The LORD commanded the fish, and it spewed Jonah out on the dry land. 3 A second time the word of the LORD came to Jonah: ²'Go to the great city of Nineveh; go and denounce it in the words I give you.' ³ Jonah obeyed and went at once to Nineveh. It was a vast city, three days' journey across, ⁴and Jonah began by going a day's journey into it. Then he proclaimed: 'In forty days Nineveh will be overthrown!' ⁵ The people of Nineveh took to heart this warning from God; they declared a public fast, and high and low alike put on sackcloth. ⁶ When the news reached the king of Nineveh he rose from his throne, laid aside his robes of state, covered himself with sackcloth, and sat in ashes. ⁷ He had this proclamation made in Nineveh: 'By decree of the king and his nobles, neither man nor beast is to touch any food; neither herd nor flock may eat or drink. ⁸ Every person and every animal is to be covered with sackcloth. Let all pray with fervour to God, and let them abandon their wicked ways and the injustice they practise. ⁹ It may be that God will relent and turn from his fierce anger: and so we shall not perish.' ¹⁰ When God saw what they did and how they gave up their wicked ways, he relented and did not inflict on them the punishment he had threatened. 4 This greatly displeased Jonah. In anger ²he prayed to the LORD: 'It is just as I feared, LORD, when I was still in my own

adherence to the LORD *who made both sea and dry land,* and his attempt to *escape* by sea (vv. 3, 10). **16:** The sailors' *fear* is religiously more productive than Jonah's (see v. 9 n.).

1.17–2.10: In the belly of the fish. Not a whale but simply a *great fish,* it, unlike the prophet, does whatever God commands. **2.1–9:** Jonah's prayer, in form very like some of the psalms, is felt by many scholars to have been added. The images of drowning, however, are appropriate to the story, and the author may have used an already familiar psalm. *Sheol* (v. 2) and *the pit* (v. 6) signify the place of the dead. In terms of the satire, v. 8 is deeply ironic, as is perhaps *victory* (v. 9).

3.1–10: The conversion of Nineveh. 1–2: This *second time,* Jonah is not told why he is to denounce Nineveh, as he was before (1.2). **4–5:** Nineveh was a large city by ancient standards, but not so *vast* as the storyteller measures. *Three days' journey* would be about fifty miles, a gross exaggeration of the size of Nineveh but consistent with the author's satire. When Jonah has gone only one-third of the way into the city, his work is finished! **10:** The sincerity of Nineveh's response (like that of the sailors', ch. 1) prompts God to *relent,* the word meaning to regret and to change a previous decision.

4.1–11: Jonah's conversation with God. 1: Jonah is angry over his success! **2:** Jonah quotes a conventional description of God's character, found in several other places (Exod. 34.6; Num. 14.18; Pss. 103.8; 145.8; Joel country, and it was to forestall this that I tried to escape to Tarshish. I knew that you are a gracious and compassionate God, long-suffering, ever constant, always ready to relent and not inflict punishment. ³ Now take away my life, LORD: I should be better dead than alive.' ⁴ 'Are you right to be angry?' said the LORD.

⁵ Jonah went out and sat down to the east of Nineveh, where he made himself a shelter and sat in its shade, waiting to see what would happen in the city. ⁶ The LORD God ordained that a climbing gourd should grow up above Jonah's head to throw its shade over him and relieve his discomfort, and he was very glad of it. ⁷ But at dawn the next day God ordained that a worm should attack the gourd, and it withered; ⁸ and when the sun came up God ordained that a scorching wind should blow from the east. The sun beat down on Jonah's head till he grew faint, and he prayed for death; 'I should be better dead than alive,' he said. ⁹ At this God asked, 'Are you right to be angry over the gourd?' 'Yes,' Jonah replied, 'mortally angry!' ¹⁰ But the LORD said, 'You are sorry about the gourd, though you did not have the trouble of growing it, a plant which came up one night and died the next. ¹¹ And should not I be sorry about the great city of Nineveh, with its hundred and twenty thousand people who cannot tell their right hand from their left, as well as cattle without number?'

4:6 **a climbing gourd:** *or* a castor-oil plant.

2.13), but he clearly wishes God were not so. **3:** Compare this death wish with those of Moses (Num. 11.15), of Elijah (1 Kgs. 19.4), and of Job (Job ch. 3). **6:** As the LORD had before ordained the fish (1.17), now a plant is *ordained* to shelter Jonah. *Gourd:* exactly what kind of plant is meant is unknown. **10:** The basic idea of being *sorry* is that the tears flow in compassionate grief. **11:** Since the *cattle* had previously repented (3.7–8), God is *sorry* for them too.

962

Micah

If the prophets have a single message, it may be summed up thus: God can be counted on to care. When the people have succumbed to corruption or to overweening pride, God's care shows itself in punishment; when they are in despair or have been overrun by an arrogant enemy, God's care shows itself in encouraging and restoring them. So especially with Micah.

The unity of the book lies in presenting a God who is concerned with human existence. That unity transcends a diversity of times and authors found in the book. Chapters 1–3 seem to come from the eighth century B.C.E., with portions from before 721, when the Assyrians demolished Israel and its capital, Samaria (see 1.5–6). Chapters 4–7 (except, perhaps, 5.5–6) seem to stem from the Babylonian Exile in the sixth century, or possibly even later.

The specific historical settings were helpful to the book's ancient readers, but not essential to them, for they were seeking its message of judgment and hope. These two elements appear alternately in the book. Judgment predominates in chs. 1–3, hope in chs. 4–5, judgment again in 6.1–7.6, and hope again in 7.7–20.

1 THE word of the LORD which came to Micah of Moresheth during the reigns of Jotham, Ahaz, and Hezekiah, kings of Judah; he received it in visions about Samaria and Jerusalem.

The rulers of Israel and Judah denounced

2 LISTEN, all you peoples;
let the earth and all who are in it give heed,
so that the Lord GOD, the Lord from his holy temple,
may bear witness among you.
3 Even now, the LORD is leaving his dwelling-place;
he comes down and walks on the heights of the earth.
4 At his touch mountains dissolve like wax before fire;
valleys are torn open
as when torrents pour down a hillside:

5 all this for Jacob's crime and Israel's sin.
What is the crime of Jacob? Is it not Samaria?
What is the sin of Judah? Is it not Jerusalem?
6 I shall reduce Samaria to a ruin in the open country,
a place for planting vines;
I shall hurl her stones into the valley and lay bare her foundations.
7 All her carved figures will be smashed,
all her images burnt with fire;
I shall reduce all her idols to rubble.
She amassed them out of earnings for prostitution,
and a prostitute's hire will they become once more.

8 That is why I lament and wail,

1:5 **sin of Judah:** *prob. rdg, so Gk; Heb.* shrines of Judah.

1.1: Title. *Micah* means "Who is like?" and is probably a contraction of Micaiah, "Who is like the LORD?" *Moresheth:* a town in Judah, about twenty-three miles southwest of Jerusalem. The names of the kings date the man Micah between about 740 and 700 B.C.E. *Samaria:* the capital of Israel, conquered by Assyria in 721 B.C.E.

1.2–3.12: The rulers of Israel and Judah denounced. Several of the poems accuse leaders, others deal with the people.

1.2–9: The crimes of Israel and Judah. The LORD *walks on the earth* to destroy *Samaria* and *Jerusalem.* **5:** The *crime* committed appears in v. 7. **6:** When a city was razed by an enemy, the site was leveled by pushing

963

despoiled and naked;
I howl like a wolf, mourn like a
desert-owl.
⁹Israel has suffered a deadly blow,
and now it has fallen on Judah;
it has reached the very gate of my
people,
even Jerusalem itself.
¹⁰Will you not tell it in Gath?
Will you not weep bitterly?
In Beth-aphrah sprinkle yourselves with
dust.
¹¹Take to the road, you that dwell in
Shaphir!
Have not the people of Zaanan gone
out
in shame from their city?
Beth-ezel is a place of lamentation;
she can lend you support no
longer.
¹²The people of Maroth are in the
depths of despair,
for disaster from the LORD has come
down
to the very gate of Jerusalem.
¹³You people of Lachish,
who first led the daughter of Zion into
sin,
harness the steeds to the chariots;
in you the crimes of Israel are to be
found.
¹⁴Therefore you must give parting gifts
to Moresheth-gath.
Beth-achzib has betrayed the kings of
Israel.
¹⁵And you too, people of Mareshah,
I shall send others to take your place;
and the glory of Israel will be hidden in
Adullam.

¹⁶Shave the hair from your head in
mourning
for the children who were your delight;
make yourself bald as a vulture,
for they have gone away from you into
exile.

2 Woe betide those who lie in bed
planning evil and wicked deeds,
and rise at daybreak to do them,
knowing that they have the power to do
evil!
²They covet fields and take them by
force;
if they want a house they seize it;
they lay hands on both householder
and house,
on a man and all he possesses.
³Therefore these are the words of the LORD:

I am planning disaster for this nation,
a yoke which you cannot remove from
your necks;
you will not walk haughtily,
for the hour of disaster will have come.

⁴On that day there will be heard this
verse about you,
this sorrowful lamentation:
'We are utterly despoiled,
for our people's land changes hands.
It is taken away from us;
our fields are parcelled out to
renegades.'
⁵Therefore there will be no one to allot
you

1:10 **Beth-aphrah:** *so Lat.; Heb.* Beth-le-aphrah.
1:11 **from their city:** *prob. rdg, cp. Gk; Heb.* nakedness.
1:14 **Beth-achzib has:** *prob. rdg; Heb.* The houses of
Achzib have.

the *stones* of its ruin into the valley surrounding it. **8:** The prophet probably acted out this verse; see Jer. 27.2;
28.10–11.
1.10–16: An invasion of Judah. The names of the towns seem to depict an invader's advance from the
southwest toward Jerusalem. **10:** *Gath:* a Philistine town. *Beth-aphrah:* northwest of Hebron; *dust* is a pun on
its name, "house of dust." **11:** *Shaphir:* probably near Beth-aphrah. *Zaanan:* perhaps near Lachish (v. 13); *gone
out* is a pun on the name. *Beth-ezel:* to the south of Beth-aphrah. **12:** *Maroth:* perhaps northeast of Beth-aphrah.
13: *Lachish:* an important fortress about thirty miles from Jerusalem; *to the chariots* may be a pun on the name.
The historical allusion is obscure. **14:** *Moresheth-gath:* the same as Moresheth, v. 1. *Beth-achzib:* east of
Moresheth; *betrayed* puns on the name. **15:** *Mareshah:* northeast of Lachish; *take your place* puns on the name.
Adullam: east of Achzib; its cave was once David's headquarters (2 Sam. 23.13). **16:** To *shave the hair* was
a sign of deep mourning.
2.1–5: Punishment for evil schemes. Those who *plan* wickedness (v. 1) will find that the LORD is *planning*
for them (v. 3). *Disaster:* the same Heb. word as *wicked,* v. 1. **5:** A Hebrew acquired valid possession of a *share*
of land by *lot:* see Num. 26.55; Josh. 14.2.

any share in the LORD's assembly.

6 'Do not hold forth,' they say, holding
  forth themselves.
But do not they hold forth about these
  things?
Do not they spin words?

7 House of Jacob, can one ask,
'Is the LORD's patience truly at an end?
Are these his deeds?
Does good not come of his words?
Is he not with those who are upright?'
8 But you are not my people;
you rise up as my enemy to my face,
to strip the cloaks from travellers who
  felt safe
or from men returning from the battle,
9 to drive the women of my people from
  their pleasant homes,
and rob their children of my glory for
  ever.
10 Up and be gone! This is no
  resting-place for you;
to defile yourselves you would commit
  any mischief however cruel.

11 If anyone had gone about uttering falsehood and lies, saying: 'I shall hold forth to
you about wine and strong drink,' his holding forth would be just what this people likes.

12 I shall assemble you, the whole house
  of Jacob;
I shall gather together those that are
  left in Israel.
I shall herd them like sheep into a fold,
like a flock in the pasture, moved away
  by men.
13 Their leader breaks out before them,
and they all break through the gate and
  go out
with their King going before them,
the LORD leading the way.

3 I said:

'Listen, you leaders of Jacob, rulers of
  Israel,

surely it is for you to know what is
  right,
2 and yet you hate good and love evil;
you flay the skin of my people
and tear the flesh from their bones.'
3 They devour the flesh of my people,
strip off their skin,
lay bare their bones;
they cut them up like flesh for the pot,
like meat for the cauldron.

4 Then they will call to the LORD, but he
  will not answer.
When that time comes he will hide his
  face from them,
so wicked are their deeds.

5 These are the words of the LORD about the
prophets who lead my people astray, who
promise prosperity in return for food, but
declare open war against those who give
them nothing to eat:

6 For you night will bring no vision,
  darkness no divination;
the sun will go down on the prophets,
daytime will be blackness over them.
7 Seers and diviners alike will be
  overcome with shame;
they will all put their hands over their
  mouths,
for there is no answer from God.
8 But I am full of strength, of justice and
  power,
to declare to Jacob his crime,
to Israel his sin.
9 Listen to this, leaders of Jacob,
you rulers of Israel,
who abhor what is right
and pervert what is straight,
10 building Zion with bloodshed,
Jerusalem with iniquity.
11 Her leaders sell verdicts for a bribe,
her priests give rulings for payment,

2:7 **his words:** so *Gk; Heb.* my words.　　2:8 **But you
are not:** *prob. rdg; Heb.* But yesterday. **my face:** *prob.
rdg; Heb.* omits my.　　3:3 **like flesh:** so *Gk; Heb.* as.
3:8 **full of strength:** *prob. rdg; Heb. adds* the spirit of
the LORD.

2.6–11: False prophecy. 6: *Hold forth:* a sarcastic word for prophecy. **7:** The false prophets cannot
understand how any *words* said in the name of the LORD would not be acceptable. Verses 8–10 show why.
2.12–3.4: Against the leaders. The metaphor of a flock begins (2.12) as if a promise of protection, but
becomes (3.1) a denunciation of the rulers. **4:** *Them:* the rulers.
3.5–12: Against the prophets. Because the professional prophets suit their oracles to their employers, they

her prophets practise divination for
    money,
yet claim the LORD's authority.
'Is not the LORD in our midst?' they say.
'No disaster can befall us.'
¹²Therefore, because of you
Zion will become a ploughed field,
Jerusalem a heap of ruins,
and the temple mount rough moorland.

God's people preserved

4 IN days to come
    the mountain of the LORD's house
will be established higher than all other
    mountains,
towering above other hills.
Peoples will stream towards it;
²many nations will go, saying,
'Let us go up to the mountain of the
    LORD,
to the house of Jacob's God,
that he may teach us his ways
and we may walk in his paths.'
For instruction issues from Zion,
the word of the LORD from Jerusalem.
³He will be judge between many peoples
and arbiter among great and distant
    nations.
They will hammer their swords into
    mattocks
and their spears into pruning-knives.
Nation will not take up sword against
    nation;
they will never again be trained for
    war.
⁴Each man will sit under his own vine
or his own fig tree, with none to cause
    alarm.
The LORD of Hosts himself has spoken.

⁵Other peoples may be loyal to their
    own deities,

but our loyalty will be for ever to the
    LORD our God.

⁶On that day, says the LORD,
I shall gather those who are lost;
I shall assemble the dispersed and those
    I have afflicted.
⁷I shall restore the lost as a remnant
and turn the outcasts into a mighty
    nation.
The LORD will be their king on Mount
    Zion
for ever from that time forward.
⁸And you, watch-tower of the flock, hill
    of Zion,
the promises made to you will be
    fulfilled,
and your former sovereignty will come
    again,
the dominion of Jerusalem.

⁹Why are you now crying out in
    distress?
Have you no king,
no counsellor left,
that you are seized with writhing like a
    woman in labour?
¹⁰Zion, writhe and shout like a woman in
    childbirth,
for now you must leave the city
and camp in the open country.
You must go to Babylon;
there you will be saved;
there the LORD will deliver you from
    your enemies.
¹¹But now many nations are massed
    against you;
they say, 'Let her suffer outrage;
let us gloat over Zion.'
¹²They do not know the LORD's thoughts
or understand his purpose;
for he has gathered them

will get *no answer from God* (v. 7). **12:** The verse is quoted in Jeremiah's trial (Jer. 26.18) as proof that prophets may say offensive things without being punished.

4.1–5.15: A contrite people is restored in the LORD's favor. Because these poems seem, in part, to presuppose the Babylonian Exile (beginning in 587 B.C.E.) they do not come from Micah's time, though 5.5–6 may. **1–3:** Identical with Isa. 2.2–4, the tone of the poem suggests a time after the sixth century B.C.E. **1:** *Mountain:* the hill on which the Jerusalem temple stands will be elevated to the highest position in the world. **4:** A figure of peace and security. **5:** In contradiction to v. 2, with its subordination of other peoples to the LORD, this verse is unusually tolerant of other deities.

4.6–13: Suffering and triumph. The poem moves back and forth between these two themes. **6–7:** The *remnant* are the survivors of the Babylonian conquest and Exile; see 5.3 and compare Ezek. 34.11–16. **9–11:** Suffering must be undergone in order that Judah *will be saved.* **12–13:** Judah will now triumph over these like sheaves to the threshing-floor.

13 Start your threshing, you people of
  Zion;
for I shall make your horns iron,
  your hoofs bronze,
and you will crush many peoples.
You are to devote their ill-gotten gain
  to the LORD,
their wealth to the LORD of all the
  earth.

5 Now withdraw behind your walls,
  you people of a walled city;
the siege is pressed home against you:
Israel's ruler is struck on the cheek with
  a rod.
2 But from you, Bethlehem in
  Ephrathah,
small as you are among Judah's clans,
from you will come a king for me over
  Israel,
one whose origins are far back in the
  past, in ancient times.
3 Therefore only until she who is
  pregnant has given birth
will he give up Israel;
and then those of the people that
  survive
will rejoin their brethren.
4 He will rise up to lead them
in the strength of the LORD,
in the majesty of the name of the LORD
  his God.
They will enjoy security, for then his
  greatness will reach
to the ends of the earth.
5 Then there will be peace.

Should the Assyrians invade our land,
should they overrun our strongholds,
we shall raise against them some seven
  or eight men
to be rulers and princes.
6 They will rule Assyria with the sword

and the land of Nimrod with drawn
  blades.
They will deliver us from the Assyrians,
should they invade our land,
should they encroach on our frontiers.
7 All that are left of Jacob,
dispersed among many peoples,
will be like dew from the LORD,
like copious rain on the grass,
which does not wait for mortal
  command
or linger for any mortal's bidding.
8 All that are left of Jacob among the
  nations,
dispersed among many peoples,
will be like a lion among the beasts of
  the forest,
like a young lion at large in a flock of
  sheep;
running through he will trample and
  tear,
with no rescuer in sight.
9 Your hand will be raised high over
  your foes,
and all your enemies will be destroyed!

10 On that day, says the LORD,
I shall slaughter your horses
and destroy your chariots.
11 I shall devastate the cities of your land
and raze your fortresses to the ground.
12 I shall destroy your sorcerers,
and there will be no more soothsayers
  among you.
13 I shall cut down your images and your
  sacred pillars;
you will no longer bow before things
  your hands have made.
14 I shall pull up your sacred poles

5:1 In Heb. 4:14. **Now ... city:** prob. rdg, cp. Gk; Heb.
Gash yourself, daughter of a band. **against you:** so Gk;
Heb. against us.   5:2 In Heb. 5:1.   5:5 **Then ...
peace:** or And he shall be a man of peace.

enemies. Horns and hoofs: The metaphor is of an animal tramping on grain to thresh it.
  5.1–6: A coming ruler. 1: Struck: some humiliation may have been part of the installation of a Hebrew king,
as it was in Babylon. **2:** Bethlehem in Ephrathah was David's city; his family was called Ephrathite (see 1 Sam.
17.12). The poem predicts the restoration (v. 4) of David's dynasty. The verse is paraphrased in Matt. 2.6. **3:**
Those ... that survive: the exiled Judeans. **5–6:** See Introduction. Judah will beat back an Assyrian threat.
Nimrod: equivalent to Assyria; see Gen. 10.8–12.
  5.7–15: Future security and fidelity. 10–15: Although the context appears to suggest that these verses are
addressed to Assyria, the prophets often denounced Israel for such illicit practices as those in vv. 12–14 (see
e.g. Isa. 2.6–8). If Israel, rather than Assyria, is addressed, these verses are a separate poem. **13:** Sacred pillars:
phallic symbols. **14:** Sacred poles: objects representing the Canaanite goddess Asherah. Their precise nature
is not known.

and demolish your blood-spattered
  altars.
15 In anger and fury I shall wreak
    vengeance
  on the nations who disobey me.

The Lord's case against his people

6 HEAR what the LORD is saying:

Stand up and state your case before the
  mountains;
let the hills hear your plea.
2 Hear the LORD's case, you mountains;
listen, you pillars that support the
  earth,
for the LORD has a case against his
  people,
and will argue it with Israel.

3 My people, what have I done to you?
How have I wearied you? Bring your
  charges!
4 I brought you up from Egypt,
I set you free from the land of slavery,
I sent Moses, Aaron, and Miriam to
  lead you.
5 My people, remember the plans
devised by King Balak of Moab,
and how Balaam son of Beor answered
  him;
consider the crossing from Shittim to
  Gilgal,
so that you may know the victories of
  the LORD.

6 What shall I bring when I come before
  the LORD,
when I bow before God on high?
Am I to come before him with
  whole-offerings,
with yearling calves?

7 Will the LORD be pleased with
    thousands of rams
  or ten thousand rivers of oil?
Shall I offer my eldest son for my
    wrongdoing,
  my child for the sin I have committed?

8 The LORD has told you mortals what is
    good,
  and what it is that the LORD requires of
    you:
only to act justly, to love loyalty,
to walk humbly with your God.

9 The LORD calls to the city
  (the fear of his name brings success):
  Listen, you tribe and assembled citizens,
10 can I forgive the false measure,
  the accursed short bushel?
11 Can I connive at misleading scales
  or a bag of fraudulent weights?
12 The rich men of the city are steeped in
    violence;
  her citizens are all liars,
  their tongues utter deceit.
13 But now I inflict severe punishment on
    you,
  bringing you to ruin for your sins:
14 you will eat, but not be satisfied;
  your food will lie heavy in your
    stomach;
  you will come to labour, but not bring
    forth;
  even if you bear a child
  I shall give it to the sword;
15 you will sow, but not reap;

6:2 **listen:** *prob. rdg; Heb. obscure.*   6:5 **consider the
crossing:** *prob. rdg; Heb. omits.*   6:9 **his name:** *so Gk;
Heb.* your name. **assembled citizens:** *prob. rdg; Heb.
unintelligible.*   6:10 **can I forgive:** *prob. rdg; Heb.
obscure.* **false measure:** *prob. rdg; Heb. adds* treasures of
wickedness. **bushel:** *Heb.* ephah.

6.1–16: God accuses a wayward people. The poem takes its form from a lawsuit.
  6.1–2: Preamble. The *mountains* and *hills* are called as witnesses to the trial. The Hebrews believed that
the earth rested upon *pillars* (compare Prov. 8.29).
  6.3–5: The LORD's past deeds. 4: *Aaron and Miriam:* brother and sister of *Moses* (see Exod. 4.14; 15.20).
5: *Balaam,* the Mesopotamian diviner, was called by *Balak* to curse the people of Israel but he blessed them
instead; see Num. chs. 22–24. *Shittim:* east of the Jordan, where Israel was encamped after the Balaam episode
(Num. 25.1). *Gilgal:* Israel's first stopping place after crossing the Jordan under Joshua (Josh. 4.19–5.9).
Victories: the word also means "righteousness." **7:** The overstatement suggests mild sarcasm or banter. *Eldest
son:* Israelites at one time offered human sacrifices to Molech (see 2 Kgs. 23.10; Jer. 32.35). **8:** Ritual is not
sufficient to fulfill God's demands. *Justly:* to obey the legal side of the covenant. The injunction is to *love,* rather

you will press the olives, but not use the
  oil;
you will tread the grapes, but not drink
  the wine.
16 You have kept the precepts of Omri
  and all the practices of Ahab;
you have adopted all their policies.
So I shall lay you utterly waste;
your citizens will be an object of horror,
and you will endure the insults aimed
  at my people.

Disappointment turned to hope

7 ALAS! I am now like the last
    gatherings of summer fruit,
the last gleanings of the vintage,
when there are no grapes left to eat,
none of those early figs I love so much.
2 The faithful have vanished from the
  land;
not one honest person is to be found.
All who remain lie in wait to do
  murder;
each one hunts his kinsman with a net.
3 They are bent on devising wrong—
the grasping officer, the venal judge,
and the powerful man who follows his
  own desires.
4 Their goodness is twisted like rank
  weeds
and their honesty like briars.
The day of their punishment has come;
now confusion seizes them.
5 Put no trust in a neighbour,
no confidence in a close friend.
Seal your lips even from your wife
  whom you love.
6 Son maligns father,
daughter rebels against mother,
daughter-in-law against mother-in-law,
and a person's enemies are found
  under his own roof.

7 But I shall watch for the LORD,
I shall wait for God my saviour;
my God will hear me.

8 My enemies, do not exult over me.
Though I have fallen, I shall rise again;
though I live in darkness, the LORD is
  my light.
9 Because I have sinned against the
  LORD,
I must bear his anger, until he
  champions my cause
and gives judgement for me,
until he brings me into the light,
and with gladness I see his justice.
10 When my enemies see it, they are
  confounded,
those who said to me, 'Where is the
  LORD your God?'
I shall gloat over them;
let them be trampled like mud in the
  streets.
11 That will be a day for rebuilding your
  walls,
a day when your boundaries will be
  extended,
12 a day when your people will return to
  you,
from Assyria to Egypt,
from Egypt to the Euphrates,
from every sea and every mountain.
13 The earth will be a waste because of its
  inhabitants;
this will be as their deeds deserve.

14 Shepherd your people with your crook,
the flock that is your own,
that lives apart on a moor with
  meadows all around;
let them graze in Bashan and Gilead, as
  in days gone by.
15 Show us miracles as in the days when
  you came out of Egypt.
16 Let nations see and be confounded by
  their impotence,
let them keep their mouths shut tight,

6:16 **You have kept:** *so Gk; Heb.* He has kept.
7:4 **Their . . . briars:** *prob. rdg; Heb. obscure.* **their
punishment:** *prob. rdg; Heb.* your watchmen, your
punishment.   7:12 **Assyria to:** *so one MS; others*
Assyria and the cities of.   7:15 **Show us:** *prob. rdg;
Heb.* I shall show him.

than merely to practice *loyalty.* **13–16:** The punishment precludes any prosperity. **16:** *Omri:* king of Israel
(1 Kgs. 16.16–28), about 876–869 B.C.E., father of *Ahab* (1 Kgs. 16.29–22.40). Exactly what is meant by the
precepts of Omri is not certain. Ahab fostered Baal worship in Israel; see 1 Kgs. 16.32–33.
     7.1–20: Penance and expectation of fulfillment. 1–6: Social chaos is vividly portrayed, from corrupt officials
(v. 3) to the failure of trust even within the family (vv. 5–6). **7–20:** Hope for the future comes from looking
to the LORD, who will restore Israel. **14–20:** The restoration of Israel. **14:** The figure of the LORD as a *shepherd*
(compare Ps. 23) protecting the flock was a familiar one. *Bashan* and *Gilead* were fertile grazing areas. **15:**

let their ears be stopped.

17 May they lick the dust like snakes,
  like creatures that crawl on the
    ground.
  Let them come trembling from their
    strongholds
  to the LORD our God;
  let them approach with awe and fear.

18 Who is a god like you? You take away
    guilt,
  you forgive the sins of the remnant of
    your people.

You do not let your anger rage for
    ever,
  for to be merciful is your true delight.
19 Once more you will show us
    compassion
  and wash away our guilt,
  casting all our sins into the depths of
    the sea.
20 You will show faithfulness to Jacob,
  unfailing mercy to Abraham,
  as you swore to our forefathers in days
    gone by.

7:19 **our sins:** *so Gk; Heb*. their sins.

Out of Egypt: the Exodus. **17:** *Lick the dust* is a figure for complete defeat; see Gen. 3.14. **18:** *Merciful* is the same Heb. word as "loyalty," 6.8 n. **20:** *Jacob* and *Abraham* are symbols for the descendants.

Nahum

Nahum stands at the end of an epoch. For 150 years, Assyria has oppressed the Near Eastern world, but now (612 B.C.E.) Nineveh, its capital, has fallen to the Babylonians (chs. 2–3). The victory over the Assyrians belongs to the LORD, who moves the earth and all its inhabitants (1.5). (Nahum does not seem to know that a terrible blow will fall on Judah from the Babylonians in 587 B.C.E.)

As a prophet, Nahum emphasizes two matters: Nineveh has received what it deserves at the LORD's hands, and, as a result, Judah can return to normal life. As a poet, Nahum is exceedingly gifted. Though neither especially profound nor original, he is capable of superb pictorial effects, as in 2.1–10, and of vivid metaphor, as in 2.11–13. The remains of an originally effective, though now disordered, acrostic poem (one in which each couplet begins with successive letters of the Hebrew alphabet) is to be found in 1.2–11.

1 AN oracle about Nineveh: the book of the vision of Nahum from Elkosh.

The vengeance of the Lord on his enemies

2 THE LORD is a jealous God, a God of vengeance;
the LORD takes vengeance and is quick to anger.
The LORD takes vengeance on his adversaries
and directs his wrath against his enemies.
3 The LORD is long-suffering and of great might,
but he will not let the guilty escape punishment.
His path is in the whirlwind and storm,
and the clouds are the fine dust beneath his feet.
4 He rebukes the sea and dries it up
and makes all the rivers fail.
Bashan and Carmel languish,
and on Lebanon the young shoots wither.

5 The mountains quake before him,
and the hills dissolve;
the earth is in tumult at his presence,
the world and all who live in it.
6 Who can stand before his wrath?
Who can resist the fury of his anger?
His rage is poured out like fire,
and the rocks are dislodged before him.
7 The LORD is a sure protection in time of trouble,
and cares for all who make him their refuge.
8 With a raging flood he makes an end of those who oppose him,
and pursues his enemies into darkness.

9 Why do you make plots against the LORD?
He will make an end of you,
and you will suffer affliction once and for all.
10 Like a thicket of tangled briars,
like dry stubble, they are utterly consumed.

1:8 those . . . him: *prob. rdg, cp. Gk; Heb.* her place.
1:10 tangled briars: *prob. rdg; Heb.* adds two *unintelligible words.* they . . . consumed: *prob. rdg; Heb.* for unto.

1.1: Title. *Nineveh:* see Introduction. *Nahum* means "comforted." The location of *Elkosh* is unknown.
1.2–11: Turbulence, oppression, and revenge are rampant. An acrostic; see Introduction. The imagery is cosmic in character (e.g. *whirlwind, storm, sea, earth, flood, darkness*); the victory over the unnamed but universal enemy is also in a cosmic setting. 4: *Bashan:* east of the Jordan. *Carmel:* a mountain range on the northern coast. *Lebanon:* mountains northwest of Canaan. All three places were notably fertile. 6: *Fire* and *rocks dislodged:* frequent images of the LORD's appearance (see e.g. Mic. 1.4). 9–11: *Wicked counsellor:* obscure; probably no specific individual is meant, unless it is Sennacherib, as some interpreters would have it.

11 From you, Nineveh, has come forth a
    wicked counsellor,
  one who plots evil against the LORD.

Israel and Judah rid of the invaders

12 THESE are the words of the LORD:

  Judah, though your punishment has
    been great,
  yet it will pass away and be gone.
  I have afflicted you, but I shall not
    afflict you again.
13 Now I shall break his yoke from your
    necks
  and snap the cords that bind you.

14 Nineveh, this is what the LORD has
    ordained for you:
  No more children will be born to you;
  I shall hew down image and idol
  in the temples of your gods;
  I shall prepare your grave,
  for you are of no account.

15 There on the mountains are the feet of
    the herald
  who proclaims good news!
  Keep your pilgrim-feasts, Judah,
  and fulfil your vows.
  The wicked will never again overrun
    you;
  they are totally destroyed.

2 2 The LORD will restore the pride of
    Jacob and Israel alike,
  for pillagers have despoiled them
  and ravaged their vines.

Nineveh's enemies triumphant

1 THE aggressor is coming against you.
  Man the ramparts, keep a watch on the
    road,
  brace yourselves, exert your strength!
3 The shields of their warriors are
    gleaming red,
  their fighting men are all in scarlet;

their chariots in battle line flash like
    fire.
  The squadrons of horse advance;
4 they charge madly on the city,
  they storm through the outskirts,
  like torches, like the zigzag of
    lightning.
5 The leaders display their prowess,
  rushing in headlong career;
  they dash to the city wall,
  and mantelets are set in position.
6 The floodgates of the rivers are
    opened,
  the palace topples down;
7 the train of captives goes into exile,
  their slave-girls are carried off,
  moaning like doves and beating their
    breasts.
8 Nineveh is like a pool of water ebbing
    away.
  The cry goes up, 'Stop! Stop!' but none
    turn back.

9 Spoil is taken, spoil of silver and gold;
  there is no end to its store,
  treasure costly beyond all desire.
10 Plundered, pillaged, despoiled!
  Courage failing and knees giving way,
  limbs in turmoil, and every face
    drained of colour!

11 Where now is the lion's den,
  the cave in which the lion cubs lived,
  to which lion, lioness, and cubs made
    their way
  with none to scare them?
12 The lion tore prey for its cubs,
  for its lionesses it broke its victim's
    neck;
  it filled its lairs with prey,
  its dens with flesh it had torn.

1:15 *In Heb. 2:1.*   2:1–2 *Verses 1 and 2 transposed.*
2:3 **flash:** *prob. rdg; Heb. obscure.* **squadrons of horse:**
so Gk; Heb. fir trees. **advance:** *prob. rdg; Heb.* are made
to quiver.   2:7 **the train . . . carried off:** *prob. rdg;*
Heb. obscure.   2:10 **drained of colour:** *meaning of*
Heb. uncertain.   2:11 **cave:** *prob. rdg; Heb.* pasture.

1.12–15; 2.2: No more shall Israel and Judah be overrun. 12: Judah was Assyria's vassal from about 734
until into Josiah's reign (640–609 B.C.E.). **15:** *There on the mountains:* compare Isa. 52.7. *Pilgrim-feasts:* the
three yearly festivals of Exod. 23.14–17; 34.23. **2.2:** Here, as elsewhere, the restoration of *Israel,* exiled after
being overrun in 721 B.C.E., is predicted.

2.1–3.19: The destruction of Nineveh. The poem is powerfully pictorial. We need not suppose that Nahum
was present; an active imagination is enough. **6:** *Floodgates:* the sluice-gates of the Tigris river, the opening
of which caused Nineveh to be flooded. **11–13:** The *lion* is often a metaphor of a ruthless nation; the use here

13 As you see, I am against you, says the
     LORD of Hosts;
   I shall smoke out your den,
   and the sword will devour your young
     lions.
   I shall cut off the prey you have taken
     on the earth,
   and the voices of your envoys will no
     more be heard.

3   Woe betide the blood-stained city,
      steeped in deceit,
   full of pillage, never empty of
     prey!
2 The crack of the whip, the rattle of
     wheels,
   the stamping of horses, swaying
     chariots, 3 rearing chargers,
   the gleam of swords, the flash of
     spears!
   Myriads of slain, heaps of corpses,
   bodies innumerable, and men
     stumbling over them—
4 all for the persistent harlotry of a
     harlot,
   the alluring mistress of sorcery,
   who by her harlotry and sorceries
   beguiled nations and peoples.
5 I am against you, says the LORD of
     Hosts,
   I shall tear off your skirts to your
     disgrace
   and expose your naked body to every
     nation,
   your shame to every kingdom.
6 I shall pelt you with loathsome
     filth;
   I shall hold you in contempt and make
     a spectacle of you.
7 Then all who see you will shrink from
     you and say,
   'Nineveh is laid waste!' Who will console
     her?
   Where shall I look for anyone to
     comfort you?

8 Will you fare better than No-amon,
   situated by the streams of the Nile
   and encompassed by water,
   whose rampart was the Nile, whose wall
     was water?
9 Cush and Egypt were a source of
   endless strength to her,

   Put and the Libyans were her
     allies.
10 Even she became an exile and went into
     captivity,
   even her infants were dashed to the
     ground at every street corner,
   her nobles were shared out by lot,
   all her great men were thrown into
     chains.
11 You also will drink the cup of wrath
     until you are overcome;
   you also will flee for refuge from the
     enemy.

12 All your fortifications are like the first
     ripe figs:
   shaken, they fall into the mouth of the
     eater.
13 Your troops behave like women.
   The gates of your country stand open
     to the enemy;
   fire has consumed the barred
     gates.

14 Draw yourselves water for the
     siege,
   strengthen your fortifications;
   go down into the clay, trample the
     mortar,
   repair the brickwork of the fort.
15 Even there the fire will consume
     you,
   and the sword will cut you off.

   Make yourselves as many as the
     locusts,
   make yourselves as many as the
     hoppers.
16 You have spies as numerous as the stars
     in the sky,
   like hoppers which raid and then fly
     away.
17 Your agents are like locusts,
   your commanders like the hoppers
   which lie dormant in the walls on a cold
     day;
   but when the sun rises, they make
     off,
   no one knows where.

2:13 **your den:** *prob. rdg; Heb.* her chariot.
3:6 **make ... you:** *or* treat you like dung.   3:9 **her**
allies: *so Gk; Heb.* your allies.   3:15 **cut you off:**
prob. rdg; Heb. adds and consume you like locusts.

is ironic. Assyrian kings hunting lions are portrayed on some relief sculptures. **3.8:** *No-amon:* Thebes in Egypt,
captured by the Assyrians in 662 B.C.E. **9:** *Cush:* Ethiopia. *Put:* west of Egypt, as was Libya. **10:** *Captivity:*

18 Your rulers slumber, king of Assyria,
  your leaders are asleep;
  your people are scattered over the
    mountains,
  with no one to round them up.
19 Your wounds cannot be relieved, your
    injury is mortal;

all who hear of your fate clap their
  hands in joy.
Who has not suffered your relentless
  cruelty?

3:18 **are asleep:** *prob. rdg; Heb.* dwell.

compare Isa. 20.4. *Shared out by lot:* see Joel 3.3; Obad. 11. **18–19:** Written in dirgelike rhythm, this poem is not dirgelike in its gloating joy.

974

Habakkuk

The end of Assyria as a world power (the Babylonians destroyed its capital, Nineveh, in 612 B.C.E.) seemed to many in Judah the beginning of a new age. But before long the conquering Babylonians (called Chaldeans in the Old Testament) made clear that they too were embarked on world domination. In 597 B.C.E. they conquered the Judeans. The allusion to the Chaldeans in 1.6 places 1.2–2.3 of this book within the period 612–597 B.C.E. We know nothing about Habakkuk other than his date.

The book's three sections are in different literary forms. The passage 1.2–2.3 is a dialogue, in which the prophet seriously questions God's justice, that is, how God can allow the wicked Chaldeans to triumph. Chapter 2.4–20 is a series of denunciations of human injustice, which begin with "Woe." Chapter 3 has the form of a psalm. The differing styles, plus the book's brevity, obstruct certainty that one hand produced the entire book. A basic unity is provided, however, by the themes of the justice of God and the need for human beings to have faithful confidence in God.

The dialogue section, though focused on theodicy, contains vivid descriptions of invading forces (1.5–11) and a splendid metaphor of a fisherman (1.14–16). The denunciations (2.4–20) excel in shrewd characterizations. The psalm (ch. 3) abounds in colorful cosmic symbols and images.

1 AN oracle which the prophet Habakkuk received in a vision.

Divine justice

2 How LONG, LORD, will you be deaf to
      my plea?
  'Violence!' I cry out to you,
    but you do not come to the rescue.
3 Why do you let me look on such
      wickedness,
    why let me see such wrongdoing?
  Havoc and violence confront me,
    strife breaks out, discord arises.
4 Therefore law becomes ineffective,
    and justice is defeated;
  the wicked hem in the righteous,
    so that justice is perverted.

5 Look around among the nations;
  see there a sight which will utterly
      astound you;
  you will not believe it when you are
      told

what is being done in your days:
6 I am raising up the Chaldaeans,
    that savage and impetuous nation,
  who march far and wide over the earth
    to seize and occupy what is not theirs.
7 Fear and terror go with them;
    they impose their own justice and
      judgements.
8 Their horses are swifter than leopards,
    keener than the wolves of the plain;
  their cavalry prance and gallop,
  swooping from afar like vultures to
      devour the prey.
9 Bent on violence, their whole army
      advances,
  a horde moving onward like an east
      wind;
  they round up captives countless as the
      sand.
10 They hold kings in derision,
    they make light of rulers;
    they laugh at every fortress

1:8 **plain:** *or* evening. **and gallop:** *so Scroll; Heb.* their cavalry.

1.1: Title. The meaning of the name is unknown; but some associate it with a word meaning "to embrace." The name appears also in the apocryphal book of Bel & Snake (vv. 33–39).

1.2–4: Internal discord. The prophet complains that God has allowed lawlessness to prevail in Judah.

1.5–11: God's solution. The *Chaldaeans:* the last dynasty of Babylon and often synonymous with it. They would punish Judah for its wickedness; yet they too were wicked. This "solution" by God is able to *astound* and to arouse the agonized questions in the next section.

and raise siege-works to capture them.
11 Then they sweep on like the wind and
are gone;
they ascribe their strength to their gods.

12 LORD, are you not from ancient times
my God and Holy One, who is
immortal?
LORD, you have appointed them to
execute judgement;
my Rock, you have commissioned them
to punish.
13 Your eyes are too pure to look on evil;
you cannot countenance wrongdoing.
Why then do you countenance the
treachery of the wicked?
Why keep silent when they devour
those who are more righteous?
14 You have made people like the fish of
the sea,
like creeping creatures with no ruler
over them.
15 The wicked haul them up with hooks
or catch them in their nets
or drag them in their trawls.
So they make merry and rejoice,
16 offering sacrifices to their nets
and burning offerings to their trawls,
for it is thanks to them that they live
sumptuously
and enjoy rich fare.
17 Are they to draw the sword every day
to slaughter the nations pitilessly?

2 I shall stand at my post,
I shall take up my position on the
watch-tower,
keeping a look-out to learn what he
says to me,
how he responds to my complaint.

2 The LORD gives me this answer:
Write down a vision, inscribe it clearly
on tablets,
so that it may be read at a glance.
3 There is still a vision for the appointed
time;
it will testify to the destined hour and
will not prove false.
Though it delays, wait for it,
for it will surely come before too long.
4 The reckless will lack an assured future,
while the righteous will live by being
faithful.
5 As for one who is conceited,
treacherous, and arrogant,
still less will he reach his goal;
his throat gapes as wide as Sheol
and he is insatiable as Death,
rounding up every nation,
gathering in all peoples to himself.
6 Surely with veiled taunts and insults
they will all turn on him and say,
'Woe betide the person who amasses
wealth that is not his
and enriches himself with goods taken
in pledge!'

7 Will not your debtors suddenly start
up?
Will not those be roused who will shake
you till you are empty?
Will you not fall a victim to them?
8 Because you yourself have plundered
many nations,

1:11 **ascribe:** *so Scroll; Heb.* are guilty.   1:12 **who is
immortal:** *prob. original rdg; altered in Heb. to* we shall
not die.   1:17 **the sword:** *so Scroll; Heb.* the net.
2:1 **he responds:** *prob. rdg; Heb.* I respond.   2:2 **so
that . . . glance:** *or* ready for a messenger to carry it
with speed.   2:5 **conceited:** *cp. Gk; Heb.* wine. **Sheol:**
or the underworld.   2:6 **his:** *prob. rdg; Heb. adds* till
when.

1.12–2.1: Is God just? The first question (v. 12) carries a subtle uncertainty. Is God in charge? Has God
indeed *appointed* the Chaldeans for *judgement, to punish?* How can God *countenance wrongdoing?* How can
the *wicked* be allowed to *devour those who are more righteous?* The images of fishing (vv. 14–16) imply the
insignificance of human beings before God and God's seeming unconcern at life's tragedies. **2.1:** The prophet
sees himself as the outpost of human consciousness to pick up God's faintest message to humanity and regards
himself as a responsible spokesman for humanity before God.

2.2–20: God's answer. 2: Habakkuk is to record the *vision,* so that others besides him can know it. *At a
glance:* older translations read: "that the one who runs may read." **4:** The vision contrasts what will happen
to the *reckless* (the Chaldeans) and to the *righteous.* The verse is quoted in Rom. 1.17 and Gal. 3.11, as well
as in rabbinic literature; here, *being faithful* implies fidelity or loyalty to the deity rather than a belief-centered
faith. **5:** A delineation of the *treacherous,* about whom a series of woes begins in v. 6b, is given. *Sheol:* the
place of the dead.

2.6–8: First woe. The exploiting creditor will be mercilessly exploited and despoiled. **8a:** See Isa. 33.1; Zech.

because of the bloodshed and violence
   you inflicted
on cities and all their inhabitants over
   the earth,
now the rest of the world will plunder
   you.

9 Woe betide the person who seeks unjust
   gain for his house,
building his nest on a height
to save himself from the onset of
   disaster!
10 Your schemes to overthrow many
   nations
will bring dishonour to your house
and put your own life in jeopardy.
11 The stones will cry out from the wall,
and from the timbers a beam will
   answer them.

12 Woe betide the person who has built a
   city with bloodshed
and founded a town on injustice,
13 so that nations toil for a pittance,
peoples weary themselves for a mere
   nothing!
Is not all this the doing of the Lord of
   Hosts?
14 The earth will be full of the knowledge
   of the Lord's glory
as the waters fill the sea.

15 Woe betide the person who makes his
   companions drink
the outpouring of God's wrath,
making them drunk to watch their
   naked orgies!
16 You will drink deep draughts,
not of glory but of shame,
drinking in your turn until you
   stagger.

The cup in the Lord's right hand is
   passed to you,
and your shame will exceed your glory.
17 The violence done to Lebanon will
   overwhelm you,
the havoc wrought on its beasts will
   shatter you,
because of the bloodshed and violence
   you inflicted
on cities and all their inhabitants over
   the earth.

18 What use is an idol after its maker has
   shaped it?
It is only an image, a source of lies!
What use is it when the maker trusts
   what he has made?
He is only making dumb idols!

19 Woe betide the person who says to a
   block of wood, 'Wake up,'
to a lifeless stone, 'Bestir yourself'!
Overlaid with gold and silver it may be,
but there is no breath in it.
20 The Lord is in his holy temple;
let all the earth be silent in his
   presence.

3 1 *A prayer of the prophet Habakkuk:*
according to shigionoth

2 Lord, I have heard of your fame;
Lord, I am in awe of what you have
   done.
Through all generations you have made
   yourself known,
and in your wrath you did not forget
   mercy.

2:16 **until you stagger:** *so Scroll; Heb. obscure.*
2:19 **Bestir yourself:** *prob. rdg; Heb. adds* he will teach.
3:2 **what you have done:** *prob. rdg; Heb. adds* in the
midst of the years quicken it.

2.8. **8b:** The phrase, *on cities and all their inhabitants,* recurs in v. 17.

  2.9–11: Second woe. The very attempts of the wicked to establish their honor and security become for them
shame and destruction.

  2.12–14: Third woe. Against those who turn the conquered into slave labor. Verse 14 is a liturgical formula
(see also v. 20).

  2.15–17: Fourth woe. Against the conqueror's extreme cruelty. The cup of *wrath* is usually a symbol of the
Lord's anger (Isa. 51.17–23; Jer. 25.15–29); here the conqueror is usurping the Lord's prerogative. *Lebanon:*
mountains northwest of Israel.

  2.18–20: Fifth woe. Against the folly of idolatry. **20:** A liturgical formula; see v. 14. *Be silent:* in awe; see
also Zeph. 1.7 and Zech. 2.13.

  3.1–19: Habakkuk's supplication. The text is poorly preserved (and hence the unusually large number of
corrections the translators have made). The poem seems to be an old cultic prayer, celebrating the Lord's march

³God comes from Teman,
the Holy One from Mount Paran;
[Selah
his radiance covers the sky,
and his splendour fills the earth.
⁴His brightness is like the dawn,
rays of light flash from his hand,
and thereby his might is veiled.
⁵Pestilence stalks before him,
and plague follows close behind.
⁶When he stands, the earth shakes;
at his glance the nations panic;
the everlasting mountains are riven,
the ancient hills sink down.
He journeys as he did of old.
⁷The tents of Cushan are wrecked,
the tent curtains of Midian flutter.

⁸LORD, are you angry with the streams?
Is your rage against the rivers,
your wrath against the sea,
that your steeds are mounted
and you ride your chariots to victory?
⁹You draw your bow from its case
and charge your quiver with arrows.
[Selah
You cleave the earth with streams;
¹⁰the mountains see you and writhe with
fear.
The torrent of water rushes by
and the deep thunders aloud.
¹¹At the gleam of your speeding arrows
and the glint of your flashing spear,
the sun forgets to turn in its course
and the moon stands still at its zenith.
¹²Furiously you traverse the earth;
in anger you trample down the nations.
¹³You go forth to save your people,
to save your anointed one.
You shatter the house of the wicked,

laying bare its foundations to the
bedrock. [Selah
¹⁴You pierce their chiefs with your
arrows;
their leaders are swept away by a
whirlwind,
as they open their jaws
to devour their wretched victims in
secret.
¹⁵When you tread the sea with your
steeds
the mighty waters foam.

¹⁶I hear, and my body quakes;
my lips quiver at the sound;
weakness overcomes my limbs,
and my feet totter in their tracks;
I long for the day of disaster
to dawn over our assailants.

¹⁷The fig tree has no buds,
the vines bear no harvest,
the olive crop fails,
the orchards yield no food,
the fold is bereft of its flock,
and there are no cattle in the stalls.
¹⁸Even so I shall exult in the LORD
and rejoice in the God who saves me.
¹⁹The LORD God is my strength;
he makes me as sure-footed as a hind
and sets my feet on the heights.

For the leader: with stringed instruments

3:7 **are wrecked:** *prob. rdg.* Heb. under wickedness I
have seen. 3:9 **and charge ... arrows:** *prob. rdg, cp.*
Gk (Luc.); Heb. obscure. 3:10 **aloud:** *prob. rdg;* Heb.
adds raised its hands on high. 3:13 **shatter:** *prob.*
rdg; Heb. adds a head from. **laying bare:** *so Lat.;* Heb.
bare places. **bedrock:** *prob. rdg;* Heb. neck.
3:14 **your arrows:** *prob. rdg;* Heb. his arrows.
3:16 **my feet:** *prob. rdg, cp. Gk;* Heb. which.

from the region of Sinai to save the people; see also Judg. 5.4; Deut. 33.2; and Ps. 68.7–8. **3:** *Teman:* equivalent
to Edom. *Paran:* see Num. 10.11–12. **7:** *Cushan ... Midian:* countries bordering on Edom. They lay along
the route of the LORD's march (see 3.1–19 n.). **8:** See Ps. 89.10 and Isa. 59.9–10. **9:** See Gen. 49.24. **13:** *Your*
anointed: it is uncertain whether this alludes to the king or the people. **15:** See Ps. 77.17–19; Isa. 43.16–17.
18–19: These verses may not be part of the original poem. They express confidence in God even in the face
of adversity, perhaps referring to 2.4.

Zephaniah

Two important events occurred during the reign of Josiah, when Zephaniah lived (1.1): Josiah's religious reform in 621 B.C.E. (see 2 Kgs. 22.1–23.30); and Assyria's complete disappearance as a power (see Introduction to Nahum). Zephaniah seems to know of neither of these events (unless 2.13–15 reflects the second); he can, therefore, be dated shortly before 621 B.C.E.

Corruption is the order of the day, and the LORD must root it out. The "day of the LORD" will bring an end to all this wickedness, both in Judah (1.4–18) and in other nations (2.1–15). Guilt falls on the ruling elements, who have deliberately pursued illicit religious practices (1.4–6; 3.4–5) and oppressed the common people (3.1–3). In destroying those responsible for Israel's misery, the LORD will entrust the land to the poor and humble, who better deserve it (3.11–20).

1 THIS is the word of the LORD which came to Zephaniah son of Cushi, son of Gedaliah, son of Amariah, son of Hezekiah, when Josiah son of Amon was king of Judah.

Doom on Judah and her neighbours

² I SHALL utterly destroy everything
  from the face of the earth,
  says the LORD.
³ I shall destroy human beings and
    animals,
  the birds of the air and the fish in the
    sea.
  I shall bring the wicked to their knees
  and wipe out all people from the earth.
  This is the word of the LORD.

⁴ I shall stretch my hand over Judah,
  over all who live in Jerusalem.
  I shall wipe out from that place the last
    remnant of Baal,
  every memory of the heathen priests,
⁵ those who bow down on the housetops
  to the host of heaven,
  those who swear by Milcom,

⁶ who have turned their backs on the
    LORD,
  who have neither sought the LORD nor
    consulted him.
⁷ Keep silent in the presence of the Lord
    GOD,
  for the day of the LORD is near.
  The LORD has prepared a sacrifice
  and set apart those he has invited.

⁸ On the day of the LORD's sacrifice
  I shall punish the royal house and its
    chief officers
  and all who appear in foreign apparel.
⁹ On that day I shall punish
  all who dance on the temple terrace,
  who fill their Lord's house
  with crimes of violence and fraud.
¹⁰ On that day, says the LORD,

1:3 **I shall bring ... knees:** *prob. rdg; Heb.* the ruins with the wicked.   1:4 **heathen priests:** *so Gk; Heb. adds* together with the *(legitimate)* priests.   1:5 **those ... heaven:** *prob. rdg, cp. Gk; Heb. adds* those who worship, who swear by the LORD.   1:9 **who dance ... terrace:** *or* who leap over the threshold. **Lord's:** *or* master's.

1.1: Title. *Zephaniah* means "the LORD protects." It is not sure that *Hezekiah* means the king of Judah of that name. *Josiah* reigned from about 640–609 B.C.E.

1.2–6: The great doom that is to come. A terrifyingly vivid portrayal of the end of Judah and of all living creatures. **2–3:** Contrast with the creation in Gen. ch. 1. **4–6:** *Judah* and *Jerusalem* will be destroyed because of their idolatrous worship. *Baal:* the Canaanite fertility god. *Host of heaven:* stars personified as gods. *Milcom:* an Ammonite god, possibly the same as Molech (or Moloch) to whom human sacrifice was made (see Lev. 20.2–5; Jer. 32.35).

1.7–18: The day of the LORD is the future day when the LORD will execute judgment over the earth; see Joel 1.14–15. Amos 5.18–20 implies that it was once thought to be a joyous day, but most of the prophets picture it as a time of terror. **7:** *Sacrifice:* the LORD *set apart those ... invited*, the Israelites, purifying them with

a sound of crying will be heard from
  the Fish Gate,
wailing from the Second Quarter of the
  city;
there will be a loud crash from the
  hills.
11 Those who live in the Lower Town will
  wail,
for all the merchants are destroyed,
and the dealers in silver are all wiped
  out.

12 At that time
I shall search Jerusalem by lantern-light
and punish all who are ruined by
  complacency
like wine left on its lees,
who say to themselves,
'The LORD will do nothing, neither
  good nor bad.'
13 Their wealth will be plundered,
  their houses laid in ruins;
they will build houses but not live in
  them,
they will plant vineyards but not drink
  the wine.

14 The great day of the LORD is near,
  near and coming fast;
no runner is so swift as that day,
  no warrior so fleet.
15 That day is a day of wrath,
  a day of anguish and torment,
a day of destruction and devastation,
a day of darkness and gloom,
a day of cloud and dense fog,
16 a day of trumpet-blasts and battle cries
against the fortified cities and lofty
  bastions.
17 I shall bring dire distress on the
  people;
they will walk like the blind
because of their sin against the LORD.
Their blood will be poured out like
  dust

and their bowels like dung;
18 neither their silver nor their gold
will avail to save them.
On the day of the LORD's wrath
by the fire of his jealousy
the whole land will be consumed;
for he will make a sudden and terrible
  end
of all who live in the land.

2 Humble yourself, unruly nation; be
  humble,
2 before you are driven away to
  disappear like chaff,
before the burning anger of the LORD
  comes upon you,
before the day of the LORD's anger
  comes upon you.
3 Seek the LORD,
all in the land who live humbly,
  obeying his laws;
seek righteousness, seek humility;
it may be that you will find
  shelter
on the day of the LORD's anger.

4 Gaza will be deserted,
Ashkelon left a waste;
the people of Ashdod will be driven out
  at noonday,
and Ekron will be uprooted.
5 Woe betide you Kerethites who live by
  the coast!
This word of the LORD is spoken
  against you:
Land of the Philistines, I shall crush
  you,
I shall lay you in ruins, bereft of
  inhabitants.

1:11 **Lower Town:** *lit.* Quarry.   1:14 **no runner ...
fleet:** *prob. rdg; Heb.* hark, the day of the LORD is
bitter; there the warrior cries aloud.   2:1 **Humble
... humble:** *prob. meaning; Heb. obscure.*   2:2 **you are
... disappear:** *prob. rdg; Heb. obscure.*   2:5 **I shall
crush you:** *prob. rdg; Heb.* Canaan.

punishment instead of ritual purifications; compare 1 Chr. 15.14; Job 1.5; Isa. 66.17. **10–11:** Various parts
of Jerusalem are named; the *Fish Gate* (Neh. 3.3) was the northern gate in the *Second Quarter,* but the location
of the *Lower Town* is uncertain. **15–18:** These verses are the basis of the medieval Latin hymn *Dies irae, dies
illa* ("a day of wrath will that day be"), which was for centuries (until Vatican Council II in the 1960s) part of
the Catholic Requiem Mass.

2.1–3.10: Oracles against nations and Jerusalem. 1–3: Zephaniah's predictions against the powerful (1.8,
11, 13; 3.3–4, 6) are balanced by comfort for the poor.

2.4–7: Against the Philistines. 4: Four Philistine cities are named. **5:** *Kereth* probably means Crete, from
which the Philistines came, settling on the *coastland.*

⁶Kereth will become pastures and
sheepfolds,
⁷and the coastland will belong to the
survivors of Judah.
They will pasture their flocks by the sea
and lie down at evening in the houses
at Ashkelon,
for the LORD their God will turn to
them
and restore their fortunes.

⁸I have heard the insults of Moab,
the taunts of the Ammonites,
how they reviled my people
and encroached on their frontiers.
⁹For this, by my life,
says the LORD of Hosts, the God of
Israel,
Moab shall become like Sodom,
Ammon like Gomorrah,
a mass of weeds, a heap of saltwort,
waste land for evermore.
Those of my people who survive will
plunder them,
the remnant of my nation will
dispossess them.

¹⁰This will be retribution for their pride, because they have insulted the people of the
LORD of Hosts and encroached upon their
land. ¹¹The LORD will bring terror on them;
he will reduce to beggary all the gods of the
earth. Then the nations in all the coasts and
islands will worship him, each in its own land.

¹²You Cushites also will be slain
by the sword of the LORD.

¹³He will stretch out his hand against the
north
and destroy Assyria,
making Nineveh a waste,
arid as the desert.
¹⁴Flocks will couch there,
and every kind of wild animal.
The horned owl and the bustard
will roost on her capitals;

the tawny owl will screech in the
window,
and the raven in the doorway.
¹⁵This is the city that exulted in her
security,
saying to herself, 'I and I alone am
supreme.'
And what is she now? A waste, a haunt
of wild animals,
at which every passer-by may jeer and
gesture!

3 Woe betide the tyrant city,
filthy and foul!
²She heeded no warning voice,
took no rebuke to heart;
she did not put her trust in the LORD,
nor did she draw near to her God.
³The leaders within her were roaring
lions,
her rulers wolves of the plain
that left nothing over till morning.
⁴Her prophets were reckless and
perfidious;
her priests profaned the sanctuary
and did violence to the law.
⁵But the LORD in her midst is just;
he does no wrong;
morning after morning he gives his
judgement,
every day without fail;
yet the wrongdoer knows no shame.

⁶I have wiped out this arrogant people;
their bastions are demolished.
I have destroyed their streets;
no one walks along them.
Their cities are laid waste,
abandoned and unpeopled.
⁷I said, 'Surely she will fear me;
she will take my instruction to heart,

2:6 **Kereth:** *so Gk; Heb.* adds the region of the sea.
2:7 **by the sea:** *prob. rdg; Heb.* upon them.   2:12 **the
sword of the LORD:** *prob. rdg; Heb.* my sword.
2:14 **tawny owl:** *prob. rdg; Heb.* voice. **in the doorway:**
prob. rdg; Heb. adds an unintelligible phrase.
3:3 **plain:** *or* evening.   3:6 **this . . . people:** *so Gk;
Heb.* nations.

2.8–12: Against Moab, Ammon, and the Cushites. See Amos 1.13–15 n., 2.1–3 n. **9:** *Like Sodom . . .
Gomorrah:* i.e. destroyed; see Gen. 19.24–28; Deut. 29.23; Isa. 1.9–10; Lam. 4.6; Amos 4.11. **10:** See v. 8;
Isa. 16.6; Jer. 48.29. **11:** See Isa. 45.23. **12:** *Cushites:* Ethiopians.

2.13–15: Against Assyria. See Introduction. The oracle begins in looking forward to Nineveh's destruction,
but ends as though this has already happened.

3.1–7: Against Jerusalem. In spite of warnings, the powerful (*rulers, priests, prophets*) have gone deeper into
wickedness, both civil and religious.

all the commands I laid on her
that her dwelling-place might escape
    destruction.'
But they hastened all the more
to perform their evil deeds.

8 Therefore wait for me, says the LORD,
wait for the day when I stand up to
    accuse you;
I have decided to gather nations
and assemble kingdoms,
in order to pour my wrath on them,
all my burning anger;
the whole earth will be consumed
by the fire of my jealousy.
9 Then I shall restore pure lips to all
    peoples,
that they may invoke the LORD by name
and serve him with one accord.
10 My worshippers, dispersed beyond the
    rivers of Cush,
will bring offerings to me.

A remnant preserved

11 ON that day, Jerusalem,
you will not be put to shame for any of
    the deeds
by which you have rebelled against me,
because I shall rid you then
of your proud and arrogant citizens,
and never again will you flaunt your
    pride
on my holy mountain.
12 I shall leave a remnant in you,
lowly and poor people.
The survivors in Israel will find refuge
in the LORD's name.
13 They will do no wrong, nor speak lies;
no words of deceit will pass their lips;
they will feed and lie down
with no one to terrify them.

14 Zion, cry out for joy;
raise the shout of triumph, Israel;

be glad, rejoice with all your heart,
daughter of Jerusalem!
15 The LORD has averted your
    punishment,
he has swept away your foes.
Israel, the LORD is among you as king;
never again need you fear disaster.

16 On that day this must be the message
    to Jerusalem:
Fear not, Zion, let not your hands hang
    limp.
17 The LORD your God is in your midst,
a warrior who will keep you safe.
He will rejoice over you and be glad;
he will show you his love once more;
he will exult over you with a shout of
    joy
18 as on a festal day.

I shall take away your cries of woe
and you will no longer endure
    reproach.
19 When that time comes;
I shall deal with all who oppress you;
I shall rescue the lost and gather the
    dispersed.
I shall win for my people praise and
    renown
throughout the whole world.
20 When that time comes I shall gather
    you
and bring you home.
I shall win you renown and praise
among all the peoples of the earth,
when I restore your fortunes before
    your eyes.
It is the LORD who speaks.

3:17 **he will show ... more:** *prob. rdg, cp. Gk; Heb.* he
will be silent in his love.   3:18 **as ... day:** *so Gk;*
Heb. obscure. **cries of woe:** *prob. rdg; Heb. obscure.*
endure reproach: *prob. rdg; Heb.* adds because of her.
3:19 **throughout ... world:** *prob. rdg; Heb.* adds their
shame.

3.8–10: The call to wait. The judgment on all the nations will end with their redemption (*pure lips*) and
worshiping the LORD. *My worshippers:* probably foreign nations, not scattered Judeans.

3.11–20: The humble shall inherit. 11–13: The fault of Jerusalem has lain in the *proud and arrogant*. With
their removal, the city will be left for the *poor*. **14–15:** *Raise the shout . . . rejoice:* a reflection of ceremonies
celebrating the LORD as *king*. **16–20:** The LORD's care will produce security for Judah. The future will be as
bright as the present is bleak.

Haggai

When the Exile in Babylon was lifted about 539 B.C.E., civil and religious life in Judah was at a low ebb. The temple (destroyed in 587) was in ruins, and the economy scarcely better. While the Persian rule proved more lenient than that of Babylonia, a simple return to the situation before the Exile was not possible.

By 520, the standard of living had improved, but there had been no progress in religious reestablishment. Along with Zechariah (see Introduction to Zechariah) Haggai addressed himself to this latter problem with such zeal that the rebuilding of the temple began within a month after his first oracle. Haggai saw a correlation between prosperity and piety, in that he tended to ascribe adverse conditions to the failure to build the temple and to predict favorable ones as a result of its construction. Moreover, he considered the restoration of David's dynasty necessary to Judah's full life, and hence the promise of kingship to Zerubbabel (2.20–23). The rebuilding of the temple was completed about 516 B.C.E., four years after Haggai began to prophesy.

Zerubbabel restorer of the temple

1 In the second year of King Darius, on the first day of the sixth month, the word of the LORD, spoken through the prophet Haggai, came to the governor of Judah Zerubbabel son of Shealtiel, and to the high priest Joshua son of Jehozadak. 2 'These are the words of the LORD of Hosts: This nation says that the time has not yet come for the house of the LORD to be rebuilt.' 3 Then this word came through Haggai the prophet: 4 'Is it a time for you yourselves to live in your well-roofed houses, while this house lies in ruins? 5 Now these are the words of the LORD of Hosts: Consider your way of life; 6 you have sown much but reaped little, you eat but never enough to satisfy, you drink but never enough to cheer you, you are clothed but never warm, and he who earns wages puts them into a purse with a hole in it.

7 'These are the words of the LORD of Hosts: Consider your way of life. 8 Go up into the hill-country, fetch timber, and build a house acceptable to me, where I can reveal my glory, says the LORD. 9 You look for much and get little and when you bring home the harvest I blast it away. And why? says the LORD of Hosts. Because my house lies in ruins, while each of you has a house he can hurry to. 10 It is your fault that the heavens withhold their moisture and the earth its produce. 11 So I have proclaimed a drought against land and mountain, against grain, new wine, and oil, and everything that the ground yields, against human beings and cattle and all the products of your labour.'

12 Zerubbabel son of Shealtiel, Joshua son of Jehozadak, the high priest, and all the rest of the people listened to the words of the LORD their God and to what the prophet Haggai said when the LORD their God sent him, and they were filled with fear because of the LORD. 13 So Haggai the LORD's messenger, as the LORD had commissioned him, said to the people: 'I am with you, says the LORD.' 14 Then the LORD stirred up the spirit of the governor of Judah Zerubbabel son of Shealtiel, of the high priest Joshua son of Jehozadak, and of the rest of the people, so that they went and set to work on the house of the LORD of Hosts their God 15 on the twenty-fourth day of the sixth month.

1:4 **well-roofed:** *or* well-panelled.

1.1–15: The first oracle, on the prompt rebuilding of the temple, was designed to shame the people into beginning the work despite obstacles. The date was late August, 520 B.C.E. *Darius* began his reign as Persian emperor in 522. The Persians allowed *Zerubbabel* and *Joshua* to share in the local rule, dividing the civil and priestly offices between them (see Ezra 5.1–2; Zech. chs. 3–4). **2:** According to Ezra chs. 3–4, though the returned exiles began to rebuild the temple on first coming to Jerusalem, they were compelled to stop. **9:** The nation's poor economic condition is attributed to the fact that the people have houses, but the LORD has not. **15:** The date is mid-September.

2 In the second year of King Darius, [1] on the twenty-first day of the seventh month, these words came from the LORD through the prophet Haggai: [2] 'Say to the governor of Judah Zerubbabel son of Shealtiel, to the high priest Joshua son of Jehozadak, and to the rest of the people: [3] Is there anyone still among you who saw this house in its former glory? How does it appear to you now? To you does it not seem as if it were not there? [4] But now, Zerubbabel, take heart, says the LORD; take heart, Joshua son of Jehozadak, high priest; take heart, all you people, says the LORD. Begin the work, for I am with you, says the LORD of Hosts, [5] and my spirit remains among you. Do not be afraid.

[6] 'For these are the words of the LORD of Hosts: In a little while from now I shall shake the heavens and the earth, the sea and the dry land. [7] I shall shake all the nations, and the treasure of all nations will come here; and I shall fill this house with splendour, says the LORD of Hosts. [8] Mine is the silver and mine the gold, says the LORD of Hosts, [9] and the splendour of this latter house will surpass the splendour of the former, says the LORD of Hosts. In this place I shall grant prosperity and peace. This is the word of the LORD of Hosts.'

[10] In the second year of Darius, on the twenty-fourth day of the ninth month, this word came from the LORD to the prophet Haggai: [11] 'These are the words of the LORD of Hosts: Ask the priests to give a ruling on this. [12] If someone who is carrying consecrated flesh in a fold of his robe lets the fold touch bread or broth or wine or oil or any food, will that also become consecrated?' The priests answered, 'No.' [13] Haggai went on, 'But if a person defiled by contact with a corpse touches any one of these things, will that become defiled?' 'It will,' answered the priests. [14] Haggai replied, 'In my view, so it is with this people and nation and all that they do, says the LORD; whatever offering they make here is defiled.

[15] 'Now look back over recent times down to this day: before one stone was laid on another in the LORD's temple, [16] how were you then? If someone came to a heap of grain expecting twenty measures, he found only ten; if he came to a wine vat to draw fifty measures, he found only twenty. [17] I blasted you and all your harvest with black blight and red and with hail, yet you had no mind to return to me, says the LORD. [18] Consider, from this day onwards, from this twenty-fourth day of the ninth month, the day when the foundations of the temple of the LORD are laid, consider: [19] will the seed still be diminished in the barn? Will the vine and the fig, the pomegranate and the olive still bear no fruit? Not so; from this day I shall bless you.'

[20] On that day, the twenty-fourth day of the month, the word of the LORD came to Haggai a second time: [21] 'Tell Zerubbabel, governor of Judah, I shall shake the heavens and the earth; [22] I shall overthrow the thrones of kings, break the power of heathen realms, overturn chariots and their riders; horses and riders will fall by the sword of their comrades. [23] On that day, says the LORD of Hosts, I shall take you, Zerubbabel son of Shealtiel, my servant, and shall wear you as a signet ring; for it is you whom I have chosen. This is the word of the LORD of Hosts.'

2:4 **the LORD of Hosts:** *so Gk; Heb. adds* [5] the thing I covenanted with you when you came out of Egypt.
2:6 **In . . . while:** *prob. rdg; Heb. obscure.* 2:16 **fifty measures:** *so Syriac; Heb. adds* winepress.
2:19 **diminished:** *prob. rdg; Heb. omits.*

2.1–9: The second oracle urges the builders on in the face of discouragement. The date is early October, 520. **3:** *Former glory:* since Solomon's temple was destroyed by the Babylonians in 587 B.C.E., some of the returnees might remember it. **6:** *Shake:* the verb often denotes an earthquake. Here it is used figuratively.

2.10–19: The third oracle comes on the day the foundations are laid (v. 18), in early December, 520. Its first part (vv. 10–14) has to do with ritual cleanliness. That which is *consecrated* (v. 12) does not affect what it touches, but that which is *defiled*, as a *corpse* is (v. 13), causes whatever it touches to become defiled. The second part (vv. 15–19) promises a change in economic fortune because of the work on the temple.

2.20–23: The fourth oracle, dated also in December, 520, is addressed to *Zerubbabel,* grandson of the exiled king Jehoiachin (the Jeconiah of 1 Chr. 3.17–19). By *shaking heaven and earth* God will crumple all human authority and effort, setting Judah in their place. **23:** *Signet ring:* a visible sign and seal which becomes the instrument of conveying authority and power. In Jer. 22.24, a king is called a signet ring. The symbol shows that Haggai considered Zerubbabel to be *chosen* by the LORD as the future king.

Zechariah

Zechariah is really two books, not one. In the first, chs. 1–8, the setting is Jerusalem, beginning life anew after the Exile in Babylon and in the process of reestablishing itself as a living and worshiping city. The second book, chs. 9–14, takes place much later; the book is in prose and poetry, some perhaps stemming from a time after the Maccabean War, which ended about 160 B.C.E.

Zechariah, in chs. 1–8, is as anxious as his contemporary, Haggai (see Introduction to Haggai), to revive the social and religious order of Jerusalem. He states his message partly in oracles (especially in chs. 7–8), but mostly in visions of the LORD's purification of Jerusalem (chs. 1–6). These highly symbolic visions foreshadow the style that apocalyptic books, such as Daniel and Revelation, would later develop.

Chapters 9–14, often called Deutero-Zechariah, are so diverse as to defy any unified description. Chapter 11.4–16 recalls the symbolic acts of earlier prophets (compare Jer. 13.1–11; Ezek. 4.1–5.4). The battle scene in 14.1–5 has an apocalyptic cast. Other oracles of threat and promise are quite similar to those of earlier prophets. But much of chs. 9–14 is extremely enigmatic.

Zechariah's commission

1 IN the eighth month of the second year of Darius, this word of the LORD came to the prophet Zechariah son of Berechiah, son of Iddo: ² The LORD was exceedingly angry with your forefathers. ³ Say therefore to the people: These are the words of the LORD of Hosts: If you return to me, I shall turn back to you, says the LORD of Hosts. ⁴ Do not be like your forefathers, who heard the prophets of old proclaim, 'These are the words of the LORD of Hosts: Turn back from your evil ways and your evil deeds.' They refused to listen and pay heed to me, says the LORD. ⁵ Your forefathers, where are they now? And the prophets, do they live for ever? ⁶ But did not the warnings and the decrees with which I charged my servants the prophets overtake your forefathers? They repented and said, 'The LORD of Hosts has fulfilled his intention, and has dealt with us as our lives and as our deeds deserved.'

Eight visions with their interpretations

⁷ ON the twenty-fourth day of the eleventh month, the month of Shebat, in the second year of Darius, the word of the LORD came to the prophet Zechariah son of Berechiah, son of Iddo.

⁸ In the night I had a vision in which I saw a man among the myrtles in a hollow; he was on a bay horse and behind him were other horses, bay, sorrel, and white. ⁹ 'What are these, sir?' I asked, and the angel who was talking with me answered, 'I shall show you what they are.' ¹⁰ Then the man standing among the myrtles said, 'They are those whom the LORD has sent to range throughout the world.'

¹¹ They reported to the angel of the LORD who was standing among the myrtles: 'We have ranged through the world, and the whole world is quiet and at peace.' ¹² The angel of the LORD then said, 'LORD of Hosts, how long will you withhold your compassion

1.1–6: Zechariah's commission. *Darius:* see Hag. 1.1–15 n. The date is October–November, 520 B.C.E. *Zechariah* means "the LORD remembers."

1.7–6.15: Eight visions with their interpretations. 7: The date is early February, 519 B.C.E.

1.8–17: Vision of the horsemen. The vision (vv. 8–12) is of riders on *horses* of four different colors, who *range throughout the world* as a patrol. To the *angel's* urging that it is time that the *wrath* be lifted from Jerusalem, the answer is a *comforting* oracle (vv. 14–17).

from Jerusalem and the towns of Judah, on which you have vented your wrath these seventy years?' 13 In answer the LORD spoke kind and comforting words to the angel who was talking with me. 14 This angel then said to me: Announce that these are the words of the LORD of Hosts: I am very jealous for Jerusalem and Zion, 15 but I am deeply angry with the nations that are enjoying their ease, because, although my anger was only mild, they aggravated the suffering. 16 Therefore these are the words of the LORD: I have returned to Jerusalem with compassion; my house is to be rebuilt there, says the LORD of Hosts, and the measuring line will be stretched over Jerusalem. 17 Proclaim once more: These are the words of the LORD of Hosts: My cities will again brim with prosperity; once again the LORD will comfort Zion, once again he will make Jerusalem the city of his choice.

18 I looked up and saw four horns. 19 I asked the angel who talked with me what they were, and he answered, 'These are the horns which scattered Judah, Israel, and Jerusalem.' 20 The LORD then showed me four smiths. 21 I asked what they were coming to do, and he said, 'Those horns scattered Judah so completely that no one could hold up his head; but these smiths have come to rout them, overthrowing the horns which the nations had raised against the land of Judah to scatter its people.'

2 I looked up and saw a man carrying a measuring line. 2 I asked him where he was going. 'To measure Jerusalem and discover its breadth and length,' he replied. 3 Then, as the angel who talked with me was going away, another angel came out to meet him 4 and said, 'Run to the young man there and tell him that Jerusalem will be without walls, so numerous will be the people and

cattle in it. 5 I myself shall be a wall of fire all round it, says the LORD, and a glorious presence within it.'

6 Away, away! Flee from the land of the north, says the LORD, for I have dispersed you to the four winds of heaven, says the LORD. 7 Away! Escape, you people of Zion who live in Babylon.

8 These are the words of the LORD of Hosts, spoken when he sent me on a glorious mission to the nations who have plundered you, for whoever touches you touches the apple of his eye: 9 I shall brandish my hand against them, and they will be plunder for those they enslaved. You will then know that the LORD of Hosts has sent me.

10 Shout aloud and rejoice, daughter of Zion! I am coming, I shall make my dwelling among you, says the LORD. 11 Many nations will give their allegiance to the LORD on that day and become his people, and he will dwell in your midst. Then you will know that the LORD of Hosts has sent me to you. 12 The LORD will claim Judah as his own portion in the holy land, and once again make Jerusalem the city of his choice.

13 Let all mortals be silent in the presence of the LORD! For he has bestirred himself and come out from his holy dwelling-place.

3 Then he showed me Joshua the high priest standing before the angel of the LORD, with Satan standing at his right hand to accuse him. 2 The angel said to Satan, 'The LORD silence you, Satan! May the LORD, who has chosen Jerusalem, silence you! Is not this man a brand snatched from the fire?' 3 Joshua was wearing filthy clothes as he stood before the angel, 4 who now said to

1:18 *In Heb.* 2:1.   2:8 **on a glorious mission:** *prob. rdg; Heb.* after glory.   3:2 **angel:** *prob. rdg, so Syriac; Heb.* LORD.

14: *Jealous:* exclusively concerned, or zealous. **15:** The LORD's *anger* against Jerusalem was *mild;* the *nations,* God's agents, went too far. **16:** *My house:* the temple. *Measuring line:* used in building, and hence a symbol of reconstruction.

1.18–21: Vision of the horns and smiths. *Horns* signify innate strength, especially as it is manifested in external activity, either good or evil. *Four* is obscure, but seems to mean Babylonia. The symbolism of the *smiths,* though their action is clear, is uncertain; they may suggest counterdestruction.

2.1–5: Vision of the man with the measuring line. The *measuring line* implies limits on the size of the city; the *angel,* however, says that Jerusalem will have no limits. It will be protected not by walls but by a *wall of fire,* the *glorious presence* of the LORD.

2.6–13: Oracle of promise to Jerusalem. 6–7: *Land of the north, Babylon:* see Joel 2.20 n. **10:** *Zion* was the hill on which the temple stood; *daughter* is a figure of speech for Jerusalem.

3.1–10; 4.4–5: Vision of Joshua's purification. In the trial, *Satan* (v. 1) is the Hebrew title of an angelic figure who, as in Job chs. 1–2, accuses wrongdoers before the heavenly court; see 1 Chr. 21.1 n. Joshua is purified those in attendance on him, 'Take off his filthy clothes.' Then to Joshua he said, 'See how I have taken away your guilt from you; and I shall clothe you in fine vestments. 5 Let a clean turban be put on his head,' he ordered. So while the angel of the Lord stood by, they put a clean turban on his head and clothed him in clean garments.

6 The angel gave Joshua this solemn charge: 7 'These are the words of the Lord of Hosts: If you conform to my ways and carry out your duties towards me, you are to administer my house and be in control of my courts, and I shall grant you the right to come and go amongst these in attendance here. 8 Listen, High Priest Joshua, you and your colleagues seated here before you, for they are an omen of good things to come: I shall now bring my servant, the Branch. 9–10 In a single day I shall wipe away the guilt of this land. On that day, says the Lord of Hosts, you are to invite each other to come and sit under your vines and fig trees.

'Here is the stone that I set before Joshua, a stone on which are seven eyes. I shall reveal its meaning to you, says the Lord of Hosts.'

4 4 I asked the angel of the Lord who talked with me, 'Sir, what are these?' 5 He answered, 'Do you not know what they are?' 'No, sir,' I answered. 'These seven', he said, 'are the eyes of the Lord which range over the whole earth.'

6 Then he said to me, 'This is the word of the Lord concerning Zerubbabel: Neither by force nor by strength, but by my spirit! says the Lord of Hosts. 7 How does a mountain, the greatest mountain, compare with Zerubbabel? It is no higher than a plain. He will bring out the stone called Foundation while the people shout, "All blessing be upon it!"'

8 There came this word from the Lord to me: 9 Zerubbabel with his own hands laid the foundation of this house; with his own hands he will finish it. So you will know that the Lord of Hosts has sent me to you. 10 Who has despised the day of small things? The people will rejoice when they see Zerubbabel holding the stone called Separation.

1 The angel who talked with me came back and roused me as someone is roused from sleep. 2 He asked me what I saw, and I answered, 'A lampstand entirely of gold, with a bowl on it. It holds seven lamps, and there are seven pipes for the lamps on top of it. 3 There are also two olive trees standing by it, one on the right and the other on the left. 11 What are these two olive trees on the right and on the left of the lampstand?' 12 I put a further question to him, 'What are the two sprays of olive beside the golden pipes which discharge the golden oil?' 13 He said, 'Do you not know what they mean?' 'No, sir,' I answered. 14 'These', he said, 'are the two consecrated with oil who attend the Lord of all the earth.'

5 I looked up again and saw a flying scroll. 2 He asked me what I saw, and I answered, 'I see a flying scroll, twenty cubits long and ten cubits wide.' 3 He told me: 'This is the curse which goes out over the whole land; for according to the writing on one side every thief will be swept away, and according to the writing on the other every perjurer will be swept away. 4 I have sent it out, says the Lord of Hosts, and it will enter the house of

4:4–11 *The verses traditionally numbered 4:1–3 are transposed to follow 4:10.*   4:5 **These seven ... earth:** *transposed from verse 10.*   4:2 **seven pipes:** *so Gk; Heb.* seven pipes each.   4:14 **two ... oil:** *lit.* two sons of oil.

of *guilt,* symbolized by his *filthy clothes.* **8–10:** *The Branch:* a title for the coming king, derived from Jer. 23.5; 33.15. See also 6.9–15 n. The accession of the king and the purification of the priesthood prepare Jerusalem for restoration. To *invite* neighbors to *sit under your vines and fig trees* (v. 10) is a sign of unusual prosperity (compare Mic. 4.4). *Seven eyes:* perhaps facets.

4.6–10: Oracle about Zerubbabel. *Zerubbabel* will build the temple by the aid of the *spirit* of the Lord. The two stones, *Foundation* and *Separation,* are taken to symbolize Judah's repossessing its land and being distinct from other peoples.

4.1–3, 11–14: Vision of the lampstand and olive trees. The *lampstand* has *seven* branches, a bowl-shaped *lamp* on each, a *bowl* as an oil reservoir over the whole, and *pipes* conducting oil from the bowl to each lamp. *Seven* symbolizes completeness. The *olive trees* probably stand for Joshua, the high priest, and Zerubbabel, the future king (see 4.6–10; 6.9–15 n.). By implication, the lampstand signifies the Lord's presence.

5.1–4: Vision of the flying scroll. The *scroll* contains a *curse* designed to remove all crime from the land. **2:** *Cubit:* about seventeen inches.

the thief and the house of the man who has committed perjury in my name; it will stay inside the house and demolish it, both timber and stone.'

⁵ The angel who talked with me came out and said, 'Look at this thing that is coming.' ⁶ I asked what it was, and he said, 'The thing that is coming is a barrel for measuring'; and he added, 'it is a symbol of the people's guilt throughout the land.' ⁷ Then its round, leaden cover was raised, and there was a woman sitting inside the barrel. ⁸ He said, 'This is Wickedness,' and he thrust her down into the barrel and pressed the leaden weight down on the opening.

⁹ I looked up again and saw two women coming forth with the wind in their wings (for they had wings like those of a stork), and they lifted up the barrel midway between earth and sky. ¹⁰ I asked the angel who talked with me where they were taking the barrel, ¹¹ and he answered, 'To build a house for it in the land of Shinar; once the house is ready, the barrel will be set there on the place prepared for it.'

6 I looked up again and saw four chariots coming out between two mountains, which were mountains of copper. ² The first chariot had bay horses, the second black, ³ the third white, and the fourth dappled. ⁴ I asked the angel who talked with me, 'Sir, what are these?' ⁵ He answered, 'These are the four winds of heaven; after attending the Lord of the whole earth, they are now going forth. ⁶ The chariot with the black horses is going to the land of the north, that with the white to the far west, that with the dappled to the south, ⁷ and that with the roan to the land of the east.' They were eager to set off and range over the whole earth. 'Go,' he said, 'range over the earth,' and they did so.

⁸ Then he called me to look and said, 'Those going to the land of the north have made my spirit rest on that land.'

⁹ THE word of the LORD came to me: ¹⁰ Receive the gifts from the exiles Heldai, Tobiah, and Jedaiah who have returned from Babylon, and go the same day to the house of Josiah son of Zephaniah. ¹¹ Take the silver and gold and make a crown; place it on the head of the high priest, Joshua son of Jehozadak, ¹² and say to him: These are the words of the LORD of Hosts: Here is a man whose name is Branch; he will branch out from where he is and rebuild the temple of the LORD. ¹³ It is he who will rebuild the temple, he who will assume royal dignity, who will sit on his throne as ruler. There will be a priest beside his throne, and there will be harmony between them. ¹⁴ The crown will serve as a memorial for Heldai, Tobiah, Jedaiah, and Josiah son of Zephaniah in the temple of the LORD.

¹⁵ Men from far away will come and work on the rebuilding of the temple of the LORD; so you will know that the LORD of Hosts has sent me to you. This will come about if you hearken with diligence to the LORD your God!

Joy and gladness in the coming age

7 THE word of the LORD came to Zechariah in the fourth year of King Darius, on the fourth day of Kislev, the ninth month. ² Bethel-sharezer sent Regem-melech to-

5:6 **a barrel for measuring:** *Heb.* an ephah. **guilt:** *so Gk; Heb.* eye.   6:3 **dappled:** *prob. rdg, cp. Gk; Heb. adds a word of uncertain meaning.*   6:6 **to the far west:** *prob. rdg; Heb.* behind them.   6:7 **and that ... east:** *prob. rdg, so Syriac; Heb. obscure.*   6:14 **Heldai:** *so Syriac; Heb.* Helem. **Josiah:** *so Syriac; Heb.* favour.

5.5–11: Vision of the barrel. *Wickedness* is symbolically removed from Judah. **6:** *Barrel:* container for an ephah, a dry measure equal to about 1⅓ bushels. **11:** *House:* a temple. *Shinar:* Babylon. Wickedness is returned to the place where the Jews suffered in Exile.

6.1–15: Vision of the chariots. As in the first vision (1.8–17), four differently colored *horses* go in the four directions. The symbolism of the colors is unknown. The crucial point of the patrol is the *north*, the direction of danger. Everything is ready for reestablishing the dynasty of David. **9–15:** Almost certainly, *Joshua* (v. 11) is an error, or deliberate substitution, for Zerubbabel. See 3.8–9; the *Branch* (royal power) is not Joshua; and in 4.6–10, Zerubbabel is to build the temple (compare v. 12). We do not know why the name Joshua was substituted. Some conjecture from 4.6 that Zerubbabel in some way offended.

7.1–8.23: Joy and gladness in the coming age. The oracles, taken together, give a wide-ranging answer to the question in 7.3, whether a fast in the *fifth month* (July–August) is still required. The date is mid-November, 518 B.C.E.

gether with his men to entreat the favour of the LORD. ³They were to say to the priests in the house of the LORD of Hosts and to the prophets, 'Am I to lament and fast in the fifth month as I have done these many years?' ⁴Then the word of the LORD of Hosts came to me: ⁵Say to all the people of the land and to the priests: When you fasted and lamented in the fifth and seventh months these past seventy years, was it indeed with me in mind that you fasted? ⁶And when you ate and drank, was it not to please yourselves? ⁷Was it not this that the LORD proclaimed through the prophets of old, while Jerusalem was populous and peaceful, as were the towns round about, and there were people settled in the Negeb and the Shephelah?

⁸The word of the LORD came to Zechariah: ⁹These are the words of the LORD of Hosts: Administer true justice, show kindness and compassion to each other, ¹⁰do not oppress the widow or the fatherless, the resident alien or the poor, and do not plot evil against one another. ¹¹But they refused to listen; they turned their backs defiantly on me, they stopped their ears so as not to hear. ¹²They were adamant in their refusal to accept the law and the teaching which the LORD of Hosts had sent by his spirit through the prophets of old; and in great anger the LORD of Hosts said: ¹³As they did not listen when I called, so I would not listen when they called. ¹⁴I drove them out among all the nations where they were strangers, leaving their land deserted behind them, so that no one came and went. Thus their pleasant land was turned into a desert.

8 The word of the LORD of Hosts came to me: ²These are the words of the LORD of Hosts: I have been very jealous for Zion, fiercely jealous for her. ³Now, says the LORD, I shall come back to Zion and dwell in Jerusalem. Jerusalem will be called the City of Faithfulness, and the mountain of the LORD of Hosts will be called the Holy Mountain. ⁴These are the words of the LORD of Hosts: Once again old men and women will sit in the streets of Jerusalem, each leaning on a stick

because of great age; ⁵and the streets of the city will be full of boys and girls at play. ⁶These are the words of the LORD of Hosts: Even if this may seem impossible to the remnant of this nation in those days, will it also seem impossible to me? This is the word of the LORD of Hosts. ⁷These are the words of the LORD of Hosts: I am about to rescue my people from the countries in the east and the west, ⁸and bring them back to live in Jerusalem. They will be my people, and I shall be their God, in faithfulness and justice.

⁹These are the words of the LORD of Hosts: Take heart, all who now hear the promise that the temple is to be rebuilt; you hear it from the prophets who were present when foundations for the house of the LORD of Hosts were laid. ¹⁰Before that time there was no hiring of people or animals; because of enemies, no one could go about his business in safety, for I had set everyone at odds with everyone else. ¹¹But I do not feel the same now towards the remnant of this people as I did in former days, says the LORD of Hosts. ¹²For they will sow in safety; the vine will yield its fruit and the soil its produce, and the heavens will give their moisture; with all these things I shall endow the remnant of this people. ¹³To the nations you, house of Judah and house of Israel, have become proverbial as a curse; now I shall save you, and you will become proverbial as a blessing. Courage! Do not lose heart.

¹⁴For these are the words of the LORD of Hosts: Whereas I resolved to bring disaster on you when your forefathers provoked my wrath, says the LORD of Hosts, and I did not relent, ¹⁵so I have resolved to do good again in these days to Jerusalem and to the house of Judah. Do not be afraid. ¹⁶This is what you must do: speak the truth to each other, administer true and sound justice in your courts. ¹⁷Do not plot evil against one another, and do not love perjury, for all these are things I hate. This is the word of the LORD.

¹⁸The word of the LORD of Hosts came to

7:13 **I called:** *prob. rdg; Heb.* he called.

7.4–14: **The first oracle** recapitulates the past. **5:** *Seventy years:* the length of the Exile (compare Jer. 25.11).

8.1–8: **The second oracle** describes a restored, *holy*, and happy Jerusalem. **2:** *Jealous:* see 1.14 n. **8:** *Justice:* lit. "righteousness."

8.9–13: **The third oracle** promises that the reconstruction of the temple will bring *blessing* to Judah, prosperous crops and security of life.

8.14–17: **The fourth oracle** sets out the quality of the social order.

me: 19 These are the words of the LORD of Hosts: The fasts of the fourth month, and of the fifth, seventh, and tenth months, are to become festivals of joy and gladness for the house of Judah. So love truth and peace.

20 These are the words of the LORD of Hosts: Nations and dwellers in many cities will come in the future; 21 people of one city will approach those of another and say, 'Let us go to entreat the favour of the LORD; let us resort to the LORD of Hosts; and I too shall go.' 22 Many peoples and mighty nations will resort to the LORD of Hosts in Jerusalem and entreat his favour. 23 These are the words of the LORD of Hosts: In those days, ten people from nations of every language will take hold of the robe of one Jew and say, 'Let us accompany you, for we have heard that God is with you.'

Judah's triumph over her enemies

9 AN oracle:

The word of the LORD is in the land of Hadrach;
it alights on Damascus,
for, no less than all the tribes of Israel,
the capital of Aram belongs to the LORD.
2 It alights also on Hamath which borders on Damascus,
and for all their wisdom it alights on Tyre and Sidon.
3 Tyre, who built herself a rampart,
has amassed silver like dust
and gold like the dirt on the streets.
4 But the Lord will take from her all she possesses;
he will break her power at sea,

and the city itself will be destroyed by fire.

5 Let Ashkelon see and be afraid;
Gaza will writhe in terror,
and Ekron's hope will come to naught.
Kings will vanish from Gaza,
and Ashkelon will be empty of people.
6 A mixed race will settle in Ashdod,
and I shall cut down the pride of the Philistines.

7 I shall stop them eating flesh with the blood still in it
and feeding on detestable things.
Those who survive will belong to our God;
they will be like a clan in Judah,
and Ekron will become like the Jebusites.
8 I shall post a garrison for my house
so that none may pass to and fro that way,
and no oppressor may ever again overrun them,
for now I am taking note of their suffering.

9 Daughter of Zion, rejoice with all your heart;
shout in triumph, daughter of Jerusalem!
See, your king is coming to you,
his cause won, his victory gained,
humble and mounted on a donkey,
on a colt, the foal of a donkey.

9:1 **capital:** *prob. rdg; Heb.* eye. **Aram:** *so one MS; others* Adam.   9:4 **power:** *or* wealth.   9:8 **of their suffering:** *prob. rdg; Heb.* with my eyes.

8.18–19: The fifth oracle alters *fasts* from times at which to "lament and abstain" (7.3) to *festivals of joy and gladness.*

8.20–23: The sixth oracle describes the growing adherence to the LORD of foreign nations. **23:** *Jew:* lit. a member of the tribe of Judah.

9.1–14.21: Deutero-Zechariah. See Introduction on this portion of the book.

9.1–8: The LORD's attack upon nations. 1: *Hadrach* and *Damascus* were in *Aram,* Syria. **2–4:** *Tyre* and *Sidon:* Phoenician ports on the Mediterranean. *Hamath:* a city inland from Sidon. **5–7:** *Ashkelon, Gaza, Ekron,* and *Ashdod* were *Philistine* cities, traditional enemies of Israel, which now become part of God's people. *Jebusites:* pre-Israelite inhabitants of Jerusalem who were assimilated into the Israelites after the capture of the city under David.

9.9–16: Judah goes to war. 9–10: *Daughter:* see 2.10 n. But here, it may be only a woman of Jerusalem. Some scholars think the *king* is Alexander the Great, sweeping through Palestine in 332 B.C.E. Others interpret the passage to mean a coming Jewish king (compare Matt. 21.4–5). *Ephraim:* the leading Israelite tribe of the

[10] He will banish the chariot from
    Ephraim,
  the war-horse from Jerusalem;
  the warrior's bow will be banished,
  and he will proclaim peace to the
    nations.
  His rule will extend from sea to sea,
  from the River to the ends of the earth.

[11] As for you, because of your blood
    covenant with me
  I shall release your people imprisoned
    in a waterless dungeon.
[12] Come back to the Citadel, you captives
    waiting in hope.
  Now is the day announced
  when I shall grant you twofold
    reparation.
[13] For my bow is strung, Judah;
  I have laid the arrow to it, Ephraim;
  I have roused your sons, Zion,
  and made you into a warrior's sword
  against the sons of Javan.

[14] The LORD will appear over them,
  and his arrow will flash forth like
    lightning;
  the Lord GOD will sound the trumpet
  and advance with the storm-winds of
    the south.
[15] The LORD of Hosts will protect them;
  they will prevail, trampling underfoot
    the sling-stones;
  they will be roaring drunk as if with
    wine,
  brimful as a bowl, drenched like the
    corners of the altar.
[16] On that day the LORD their God
  will save them, his own people, like a
    flock.
  For they are the precious stones in a
    crown
  which sparkle all about his land.
[17] What wealth is theirs, what beauty!
  Grain to strengthen young men,
  and new wine for maidens!

10 Ask the LORD for rain at the time
    of the spring rain,
  the LORD who makes the storm-clouds,
  and he will give the heavy rains
  and grass in the fields for everyone;
[2] for the household gods utter empty
    promises;
  diviners see false signs,
  they produce lies as dreams,
  and the comfort they offer is illusory.
  So the people are left to wander about
  like sheep in distress for lack of a
    shepherd.
[3] My anger burns against the shepherds,
  and I shall punish the leaders of the
    flock.

  The LORD of Hosts will care for his
    flock,
  the people of Judah,
  and transform them into his royal
    war-horses.
[4] From Judah will come corner-stone and
    tent-peg,
  the bow ready for battle, and all the
    commanders.
[5] Together they will be like warriors
  trampling the muddy tracks of the
    battlefield;
  they will fight because the LORD is with
    them,
  and they will put to rout even those on
    horseback.
[6] I shall give triumph to the house of
    Judah
  and victory to the house of Joseph;
  I shall restore them in my compassion
    for them,
  and they will be as though I had never
    cast them off;
  for I am the LORD their God and I
    shall answer them.
[7] So the Ephraimites will be like warriors,
  with hearts gladdened as if by wine;
  their children will see and be glad;

9:10 **He will banish:** *so Gk; Heb.* I shall banish.

Northern Kingdom, exiled in 722 B.C.E. *The River:* Euphrates. **15:** *Roaring drunk:* figure for the ecstatic exuberance of victors in battle; see 10.7; Ps. 78.65–66. The Israelites, covered with blood of the slain enemy, are compared to *corners of the altar* on which the blood of sacrifices was poured out daily, a symbol of overwhelming victory.

9.17–10.12: The restoration of Israel. 10.1: *Spring rain* strengthened crops against the heat. **2:** *Household gods:* idols, personal deities, who watched over families. Neither they nor *diviners,* but only the LORD gives real prosperity (v. 1). *Shepherd:* a leader. **3:** The *anger* may be against specific leaders of Judah. Compare Ezek. ch. 34. **6:** *House of Joseph:* often a term for northern Israel (see Amos 5.6, 15). The predicted restoration

their hearts will rejoice in the LORD.
8 I shall whistle to call them in,
for I have delivered them,
and they will be as many as they used
to be.
9 Though dispersed among the nations,
yet in far-off lands they will remember
me;
they will rear their children and return.
10 I shall bring them home from Egypt
and gather them from Assyria;
I shall lead them into Gilead and
Lebanon
until there is no more room for them.
11 They will pass through the sea of Egypt
and strike its waves;
all the depths of the Nile will become
dry.
The pride of Assyria will be brought
down,
and the sceptre of Egypt will be no
more.
12 But Israel's strength will be in the
LORD;
they will march proudly in his name.
This is the word of the LORD.

11 Lebanon, throw open your gates
so that fire may devour your
cedars.
2 Wail, every pine tree, for the cedars
have fallen,
the mighty trees are ravaged.
Wail, every oak of Bashan,
for the impenetrable forest is laid low.
3 Hark to the wailing of the shepherds!
Their rich pastures are ravaged.
Hark to the roar of the lions!
Jordan's dense thickets are ravaged.

4 These were the words of the LORD my God:
Be a shepherd to the flock destined for
slaughter. 5 Those who buy will slaughter

them and incur no guilt; those who sell will
then say, 'Praise the LORD, I have become
rich!' Even their shepherds feel no pity for
them. 6 For I shall no longer have pity on the
land's inhabitants, says the LORD. I am about
to put everyone into the power of his shepherd and his king, and when the land is
crushed I shall not rescue them from their
hands.

7 So I became a shepherd to the flock destined to be slaughtered by the dealers. I took
two staffs: one I called Favour and the other
Union, and so I looked after the flock. 8 In a
single month I got rid of the three shepherds; I had lost patience with the flock and
they had come to abhor me. 9 Then I said to
them, 'I shall not be a shepherd to you any
more. Any that are to die, let them die; any
that are missing, let them stay missing; and
the rest can devour one another.' 10 I took my
staff called Favour and snapped it in two,
annulling the covenant which the LORD had
made with all nations. 11 So it was annulled
that day, and the dealers who were watching
me knew that this was a word from the LORD.
12 I said to them, 'If it suits you, give me my
wages; otherwise keep them.' Then they
weighed out my wages, thirty silver pieces.
13 The LORD said to me, 'Throw it into the
treasury.' I took the thirty pieces of silver—
the princely sum at which I was paid off by
them!—and threw them into the house of
the LORD, into the treasury. 14 Then I broke
in two my second staff called Union, annulling the brotherhood between Judah and Israel.

15 The LORD said to me, 'Equip yourself
again as a shepherd, a worthless one; 16 for I
am about to install a shepherd in the land

10:11 **They:** so Gk; Heb. He. **sea of Egypt:** prob. rdg;
Heb. sea of distress.   11:6 **shepherd:** or neighbour.
11:10 **the LORD:** prob. rdg; Heb. I.   11:13 **into the
treasury:** so Syriac; Heb. to the potter.

includes the Northern Kingdom dispersed in 721 B.C.E., bringing the nation to its former unity. **10:** The place
of deportation in 721 was Assyria. After the Babylonian Exile, a colony of Jews lived in Egypt, at Elephantine.
Gilead and Lebanon are at the north and northeastern edges of Israel's former territory, where the roads from
Babylon and Assyria entered. **11:** Depths of the Nile: the wealth and fertility of Egypt.

    11.1–3: A short poem threatening destruction. 1: Cedars, useful lumber, were the hallmark of the prosperity
of Lebanon. **2:** Bashan: fertile area east of the Sea of Galilee. **3:** Compare Jer. 49.19.

    11.4–14: An allegorical narrative in which someone tending sheep gives up the job and breaks two
shepherd's staves. The action is symbolic of God, shepherd of the whole world, breaking first the covenant,
Favour (v. 10), with all nations (Gen. 9.1–17), and then the special covenant, Union (v. 14), with Israel (Exod.
24.8). **8:** The three shepherds here are specific leaders who cannot be identified. **12:** In Exod. 21.32, thirty
pieces of silver is the value of a slave. Thirty pieces of silver appears in Matt. 26.14–16 and parallels.

who will neither care about any that are gone missing, nor search for those that have strayed, nor heal the injured, nor nurse the sickly, but will eat the flesh of the fat beasts and throw away the broken bones.

17'Woe betide the worthless shepherd
   who abandons the sheep!
May a sword fall on his arm and on his
   right eye!
May his arm be all shrivelled,
   and his right eye be totally blind!'

Jerusalem a centre of worship for all

12 An oracle.
      This is the word of the LORD about Israel, the word of the LORD who spread out the heavens and founded the earth, and who formed the spirit in mortals. 2 I am about to make Jerusalem an intoxicating cup for all the nations pressing round her; and Judah will be caught up in the siege of Jerusalem. 3 On that day, when all the nations of the earth are gathered to attack her, I shall make Jerusalem a rock too heavy for any people to remove, and all who try to carry it will be torn by it. 4 On that day, says the LORD, I shall strike all their horses with panic and the riders with madness; I shall keep watch over Judah, while I strike with blindness all the horses of the other nations. 5 Then the families of Judah will say in their hearts, 'The inhabitants of Jerusalem find their strength in the LORD of Hosts, their God.'

6 On that day I shall make the families of Judah like a burning brazier in woodland, like a burning torch among the sheaves. They will consume all the surrounding nations, right and left, while the people of Jerusalem remain safe in their city. 7 The LORD will set free all the families of Judah first, so that the glory of David's line and of the citizens of Jerusalem may not surpass that of Judah.

8 On that day the LORD will shield the inhabitants of Jerusalem; on that day the weakest of them will be like David, and the line of David godlike, like the angel of the LORD going before them.

9 On that day I shall set about the destruction of every nation that attacks Jerusalem, 10 but I shall pour a spirit of pity and compassion on the house of David and the inhabitants of Jerusalem. Then they will look on me, on him whom they have pierced, and will lament over him as over an only child, and will grieve for him bitterly as for a firstborn son.

11 On that day the mourning in Jerusalem will be as great as the mourning over Hadadrimmon in the vale of Megiddo. 12 The land will mourn, each family by itself: the family of David by itself and its women by themselves; the family of Nathan by itself and its women by themselves; 13 the family of Levi by itself and its women by themselves; the family of Shimei by itself and its women by themselves; 14 all the remaining families by themselves and their women by themselves.

13 On that day a fountain will be opened for the line of David and for the inhabitants of Jerusalem, to remove their sin and impurity.

2 On that day, says the LORD of Hosts, I shall expunge the names of the idols from the land, and they shall be remembered no more; I shall also expel the prophets and the spirit of uncleanness from the land. 3 Thereafter, if anyone continues to prophesy, his parents, his own father and mother, will say to him, 'You are not to remain alive, for you have uttered lies in the LORD's name.' His own father and mother will run him through because he has prophesied. 4 On that day every prophet will be ashamed of his prophetic vision, and he will not wear a robe of coarse hair in order to deceive. 5 He will say, 'I am not a prophet, I am a worker on the land, for the land has been my possession from my

12:2 **and:** *so Lat.; Heb. adds* against.   12:5 **The inhabitants ... strength:** *prob. rdg; one Heb. MS* Inhabitants of Jerusalem, I am strong.   13:5 **for the land ... possession:** *prob. rdg; Heb.* for a man has made me his possession.

11.15–17: A *worthless shepherd* will ruin the flock.

12.1–14.21: Jerusalem repents and is delivered by the LORD. The oracles convey the themes of the LORD's triumph, not a chronology or systematic account. Some are extremely obscure. **3:** *Rock:* compare Dan. 2.33–35. **7:** Even the Davidic king's *glory* will not exceed that of the people. **10:** *Him whom they have pierced:* probably a contemporary allusion, now unrecoverable. Compare Jn. 19.37. **11:** *Hadad-rimmon:* a Canaanite fertility god, mourned in the seasonal death of vegetation. The *vale* was the most fertile plain near the city of *Megiddo* in northern Israel. **13.2–6:** The oracle marks the end of the professional *prophets*.

early days.' ⁶ If someone asks, 'What are these scars on your chest?' he will answer, 'I got them in the house of my friends.'

⁷ This is the word of the LORD of Hosts:
Sword, awake against my shepherd,
against him who works with me.
Strike the shepherd, and the sheep will
be scattered,
and I shall turn my hand against the
lambs.
⁸ This also is the word of the LORD:
It will happen throughout the land
that two thirds of the people will be
struck down and die,
while one third of them will be left
there.
⁹ Then I shall pass this third through the
fire;
I shall refine them as silver is refined
and assay them as gold is assayed.
They will invoke me by my name,
and I myself shall answer them;
I shall say, 'These are my people';
they will say, 'The LORD is my God.'

14 A day is coming for the LORD to act, and the plunder taken from you will be shared out while you stand by. ² I shall gather all the nations to make war on Jerusalem; the city will be taken, the houses ransacked, and the women raped. Half of the city will go into exile, but the rest of the population will not be taken away from the city. ³ Then the LORD will go out and fight against the nations, fighting as on a day of battle. ⁴ On that day his feet will stand on the mount of Olives, which lies to the east of Jerusalem, and the mount will be cleft in two by an immense valley running east and west; half the mount will move northwards and half southwards. ⁵ The valley between the hills will be blocked, for the new valley between them will reach as far as Asal. It will be blocked as it was by the earthquake in the time of King Uzziah of Judah. Then the LORD my God will appear attended by all the holy ones.
⁶ On that day there will be neither heat nor cold nor frost. ⁷ It will be one continuous day,

whose coming is known only to the LORD; there will be no distinction between day and night; even in the evening there will be light.

⁸ On that day, whether in summer or in winter, running water will issue from Jerusalem, half flowing to the eastern sea and half to the western sea. ⁹ The LORD will become king over all the earth; on that day he will be the only LORD and his name the only name. ¹⁰ The whole land will become like the Arabah from Geba to Rimmon south of Jerusalem. But Jerusalem will stand high in her place, and be full of people from the Benjamin Gate to the point where the former gate stood, to the Corner Gate, and from the Tower of Hananel to the king's winepresses. ¹¹ Jerusalem will be inhabited, and never again will a ban for her destruction be laid on her; all will live there in security.

¹² The LORD will strike with this plague all the nations who warred against Jerusalem: their flesh will rot while they are still standing on their feet, their eyes will rot in their sockets, and their tongues will rot in their mouths.

¹³ On that day a great panic sent by the LORD will fall on them, with everyone laying hands on his neighbour and attacking him. ¹⁴ Judah too will fight at Jerusalem, and the wealth of the surrounding nations will be gathered up — gold and silver and clothing in great quantities. ¹⁵ Plague will also be the fate of horse and mule, camel and donkey, the fate of every animal in those armies.

¹⁶ Any survivors among the nations which fought against Jerusalem are to go up year by year to worship the King, the LORD of Hosts, and to keep the pilgrim-feast of Tabernacles. ¹⁷ Should any of the families of the earth not go up to Jerusalem to worship the King, the LORD of Hosts, no rain will fall on them. ¹⁸ If any family of Egypt does not go up and enter the city, then the same disaster will overtake it as that which the LORD will inflict on any

14:5 **the hills:** *prob. rdg, so Syriac; Heb.* my hills. **It will . . . was by:** *or* You shall flee just as you fled before. 14:6 **cold:** *so Gk; Heb.* precious things.   14:18 **will overtake:** *so Gk; Heb. adds* not.

13.6: *Scars* from ecstatic activities (compare Hos. 7.14) will be given a false explanation. **7–9:** The *sheep* (Israel) will be scattered, but *one third* will survive as a purified remnant.

14.1–21: The LORD's battle against Jerusalem's enemies. 5: *Valley:* named the Kidron, between Jerusalem and the mount of Olives. *Earthquake:* compare Amos 1.1. *Holy ones:* probably angels. **8:** Compare Ezek. 47.1–12; Joel 3.18. **10:** The elevation of *Jerusalem* is similar to Isa. 2.2; Mic. 4.1. **16–19:** As in 8.20–23, nation which does not go up to keep the feast. ¹⁹This will be the punishment which befalls Egypt and any nation which does not go up to keep the feast of Tabernacles.

²⁰On that day 'Holy to the LORD' will be inscribed on the horses' bells, and the pots in the house of the LORD will be like the sacred bowls before the altar. ²¹Every pot in Jerusalem and Judah will be holy to the LORD of Hosts, and all who come to sacrifice will use them for boiling the flesh of the sacrifice. When that time comes, no longer will any trader be seen in the house of the LORD of Hosts.

foreigners worship the LORD at Jerusalem. *Tabernacles:* the autumn vintage feast, also called Booths. **20–21:** In the new age, everything, however common, is sanctified. *Holy to the LORD:* also inscribed on the rosette on the high priest's forehead (Exod. 28.36). **21:** *Trader:* lit. "Canaanite."

Malachi

After the return of the Judeans from the Exile in Babylon and the rebuilding of the temple was completed (see Introduction to Haggai), Judah, subject to the Persians, was without political defense, a royal dynasty, and other marks of a nation. Yet to live as the LORD's people, it was necessary to formulate laws to govern both civil and religious conduct, as permitted by the Persians. The book of Malachi reflects aspects of the problems and hardships that arose about 500–450 B.C.E.

Malachi (see 1.1 n.) delivers his message in a rather systematic regular form. First he gives a declaration from the LORD, then he proposes a question from his audience; he answers the question in the name of the LORD. The statement criticizes the behavior of people or priests, while the answer to a question contains both judgment and promise. In his view, Judah must live by the Law to maintain the people's purity and devotion to the LORD. The final day of the LORD will separate good from bad. Indeed, the issue of determining what are good and bad acts and who are good and bad persons, dominates the latest stage of Old Testament religion. At the same time that this stage fostered a confining legalism, it also fostered a religious devotion of great power and purity.

1 AN oracle. The word of the LORD to Israel through Malachi.

Religious decline and hope of recovery

2 I HAVE shown you love, says the LORD. But you ask, 'How have you shown love to us?' Is not Esau Jacob's brother? the LORD answers. Jacob I love, 3 but Esau I hate, and I have reduced his hill-country to a waste, and his ancestral land to desert pastures. 4 When Edom says, 'We are beaten down, but let us rebuild our ruined homes,' these are the words of the LORD of Hosts: If they rebuild, I shall pull down. They will be called a country of wickedness, a people with whom the LORD is angry for ever. 5 Your own eyes will see it, and you yourselves will say, 'The LORD's greatness reaches beyond the confines of Israel.'

6 A son honours his father and a slave his master. If I am a father, where is the honour due to me? If I am a master, where is the fear due to me? So says the LORD of Hosts to you, priests who despise my name. You ask, 'How have we despised your name?' 7 By offering defiled food on my altar. You ask, 'How have we defiled you?' By saying that the table of the LORD may be despised, 8 that if you offer a blind victim, there is nothing wrong, and if you offer a victim which is lame or sickly, there is nothing wrong. If you brought such a gift to your governor, would he receive you or show you favour? says the LORD of Hosts. 9 But now, if you placate God, he may show you mercy! If you do this, will he withhold his favour from you? So the LORD of Hosts has spoken. 10 Better far that one of you should close the great door altogether, to keep fire from being lit on my altar to no purpose! I have no pleasure in you, says the LORD of Hosts, nor will I accept any offering from you. 11 From farthest east to farthest west my name is great among the nations, and everywhere incense and pure offerings are presented to my name; for my name is great

1:1 **Malachi:** *or* my messenger. 1:3 **desert pastures:** *prob. rdg, cp. Gk; Heb. obscure.*

1.1: Title. *Malachi* means "my messenger" or "my angel," and is probably not a proper name (compare 3.1).

1.2–3.12: Religious decline and hope for recovery.

1.2–5: The LORD's hatred of Esau. The Edomites were descended from Esau, the Israelites from Jacob. They were brother nations, but their relations were dominated by hostility. See Gen. 25.19–23, Ezek. ch. 35, and Obad.

1.6–2.9: Against priests. Care for the details of sacrifice and ritual is a way to *honour* the LORD. **11:** In contrast to the impurity of worship in Judah, the LORD is worshiped in purity by all the Gentile nations. See, too, v. 14.

among the nations, says the LORD of Hosts. [12] But you profane me by thinking that the table of the LORD may be defiled, and you can offer on it food that you hold in no esteem. [13] You sniff scornfully at it, says the LORD of Hosts, and exclaim, 'How tiresome!' If you bring as your offering victims that are mutilated, lame, or sickly, am I to accept them from you? says the LORD. [14] A curse on the cheat who pays his vows by sacrificing a damaged victim to the Lord, though he has a sound ram in his flock! I am a great king, says the LORD of Hosts, and my name is held in awe among the nations.

2 And now, you priests, this decree is for you: [2] unless you listen to me and pay heed to the honouring of my name, says the LORD of Hosts, I shall lay a curse on you. I shall turn your blessings into a curse; yes, into a curse, because you pay no heed. [3] I shall cut off your arms, fling offal in your faces, the offal from your pilgrim-feasts, and I shall banish you from my presence. [4] Then you will know that I have issued this decree against you: my covenant with Levi falls, says the LORD of Hosts. [5] My covenant was with him: I bestowed life and welfare on him, and laid on him the duty of reverence; he revered me and lived in awe of my name. [6] The instruction he gave was true, and no word of injustice fell from his lips; he walked in harmony with me and in uprightness, and he turned many back from sin. [7] For men hang on the words of the priest and seek knowledge and instruction from him, because he is the messenger of the LORD of Hosts. [8] But you have turned aside from that course; you have caused many to stumble with your instruction; you have set at naught the covenant with the Levites, says the LORD of Hosts.

[9] So I in my turn shall make you despicable and degraded in the eyes of all the people, inasmuch as you disregard my ways and show partiality in your interpretation of the law.

[10] Have we not all one father? Did not one God create us? Why then are we faithless to one another by violating the covenant of our forefathers? [11] Judah is faithless, and abominable things are done in Israel and in Jerusalem; in marrying the daughter of a foreign god, Judah has violated the sacred place loved by the LORD. [12] May the LORD banish from the dwellings of Jacob any who do this, whether nomads or settlers, even though they bring offerings to the LORD of Hosts.

[13] Here is another thing you do: you weep and moan, drowning the LORD's altar with tears, but he still refuses to look at the offering or receive favourably a gift from you. [14] You ask why. It is because the LORD has borne witness against you on behalf of the wife of your youth. You have broken faith with her, though she is your partner, your wife by solemn covenant. [15] Did not the one God make her, both flesh and spirit? And what does the one God require but godly children? Keep watch on your spirit, and let none of you be unfaithful to the wife of your youth. [16] If a man divorces or puts away his wife, says the LORD God of Israel, he overwhelms her with cruelty, says the LORD of Hosts. Keep watch on your spirit, and do not be unfaithful.

[17] You have wearied the LORD with your talk. You ask, 'How have we wearied him?' By

1:12 **food:** *prob. rdg, cp. Aram.* (*Targ.*); *Heb. adds* its produce. 2:3 **cut off:** *so Gk; Heb.* rebuke. **and I ... presence:** *prob. rdg, cp. Gk; Heb.* and he will take you away to him.

12: *Profane:* to treat an object set aside for worship as if it were a matter of secular business, subject to scheming and bargaining. **2.1–2:** The business of *priests* is to convey God's *blessings* to people; dishonorable priests will have their blessings turned into *curses* that will fall upon themselves. **3:** Contact with *offal* made one unfit for worship; here the blemished sacrifices do the same (1.13). **4:** *Levi* was the priestly tribe, and the *covenant* acknowledged Levi's priestly functions.

2.10–16: Responsibility of Judah. Two aspects of covenants are discussed: the first (vv. 10–12) is Judah's *covenant* obligating fidelity to the LORD, and the second (vv. 13–16), divorce. **11:** *Daughters of a foreign god:* though this may mean foreign women, it more probably refers to the worship of alien deities. **13–16:** Divorce violates the covenant, for it entails inhuman *cruelty*. **14:** *Wife of your youth:* this probably means that men were faithlessly divorcing older women to take up with young ones; it may possibly be a protest against forced divorces of foreign wives, narrated in Ezra ch. 10, but this is unlikely.

2.17–3.5: The purifying of the priests. The prophet threatens that the priests, who ostensibly *seek* God's nearness, will be shocked and pained when the LORD actually comes near.

saying that all evildoers are good in the eyes of the LORD, that he is pleased with them, or by asking, 'Where is the God of justice?'

3 [1] I am about to send my messenger to clear a path before me. Suddenly the Lord whom you seek will come to his temple; the messenger of the covenant in whom you delight is here, here already, says the LORD of Hosts. [2] Who can endure the day of his coming? Who can stand firm when he appears? He is like a refiner's fire, like a fuller's soap; [3] he will take his seat, testing and purifying; he will purify the Levites and refine them like gold and silver, and so they will be fit to bring offerings to the LORD. [4] Thus the offerings of Judah and Jerusalem will be pleasing to the LORD as they were in former days, in years long past. [5] I shall appear before you in court, quick to testify against sorcerers, adulterers, and perjurers, against those who cheat the hired labourer of his wages, who wrong the widow and the fatherless, who thrust the alien aside and do not fear me, says the LORD of Hosts.

[6] I, the LORD, do not change, and you have not ceased to be children of Jacob. [7] Ever since the days of your forefathers you have been wayward and have not kept my laws. If you return to me, I shall turn back to you, says the LORD of Hosts. You ask, 'How can we return?' [8] Can a human being defraud God? Yet you defraud me. You ask, 'How have we defrauded you?' Why, over tithes and contributions. [9] There is a curse on you all, your entire nation, because you defraud me. [10] Bring the whole tithe into the treasury; let there be food in my house. Put me to the proof, says the LORD of Hosts, and see if I do not open windows in the sky and pour a blessing on you as long as there is need. [11] I shall forbid pests to destroy the produce of your soil, and your vines will not shed their fruit, says the LORD of Hosts. [12] All nations will count you happy, for yours will be a favoured land, says the LORD of Hosts.

The righteous triumphant

[13] YOU HAVE used hard words about me, says the LORD. Yet you ask, 'How have we spoken against you?' [14] You have said, 'To serve God is futile. What do we gain from the LORD of Hosts by observing his rules and behaving with humble submission? [15] We for our part count the arrogant happy; it is evildoers who prosper; they have put God to the proof and come to no harm.'

[16] Then those who feared the LORD talked together, and the LORD paid heed and listened. A record was written before him of those who feared him and had respect for his name. [17] They will be mine, says the LORD of Hosts, my own possession against the day that I appoint, and I shall spare them as a man spares the son who serves him. [18] Once more you will tell the good from the wicked, the servant of God from the person who does not serve him.

4 The day comes, burning like a furnace; all the arrogant and all evildoers will be stubble, and that day when it comes will set them ablaze, leaving them neither root nor branch, says the LORD of Hosts. [2] But for you who fear my name, the sun of righteousness will rise with healing in its wings, and you will break loose like calves released from the stall. [3] On the day I take action, you will tread down the wicked, for they will be as ashes under the soles of your feet, says the LORD of Hosts.

[4] Remember the law of Moses my servant, the rules and precepts which I told him to deliver to all Israel at Horeb.

3:1 **my messenger:** *Heb.* malachi.   3:3 **purifying:** *prob. rdg; Heb. adds* silver.   4:1 *In Heb.* 3:19.

3.6–12: Fraud. *Children of Jacob:* the people as a whole, not only the priests. *Tithe* is Heb. for a tenth. In Deut. 14.28, the tithe of produce every third year is given to the Levites to support them.

3.13–18: How and when the good will triumph over the bad. To the complaint that *evildoers prosper* (compare Job ch. 21), the answer is that the good are in the LORD's *possession;* when the LORD acts, the *good* will be separated from the *wicked.* **16:** *A record was written:* compare Exod. 32.32–34; Dan. 12.1.

4.1–6: The day of the LORD. The *day* is the time of distinction between *evildoers* and those who *fear* God's *name,* and its fire consumes rather than purifies; see Joel 1.14–15 n. The image of the *healing* winged *sun* (v. 2) may come, ultimately, from Egyptian symbolism. **4:** Obedience to the *law* is the criterion for surviving the day. *Horeb:* Mount Sinai. **5–6:** The expectation of the return of Elijah (2 Kgs. 2.11) before the end may have already been a popular tradition, as it became later, based on this passage (Matt. 11.13–14; Mk. 9.11–13; and in the

⁵ Look, I shall send you the prophet Elijah before the great and terrible day of the LORD comes. ⁶ He will reconcile parents to their children and children to their parents, lest I come and put the land under a ban to destroy it.

late Jewish expectations). He is probably not the same person as the messenger of 3.1. *Ban:* consignment to total destruction of anything or anyone connected with idolatry, including whole cities, as repugnant to God.

The Biblical Text with Annotations

THE APOCRYPHA

Introduction

The term 'Apocrypha', a Greek word meaning 'hidden (things)', was early used in different senses. It was applied to writings which were regarded as so important and precious that they must be hidden from the general public and preserved for initiates, the inner circle of believers. It also came to be applied to writings which were hidden not because they were too good, but because they were not good enough: because, that is, they were secondary, questionable, or heretical. A third usage may be traced to Jerome (ca. 342–420 C.E.). He was familiar with the scriptures in their Hebrew as well as their Greek form, and for him apocryphal books were those outside the Hebrew 'canon', the scriptures accepted as authoritative by the Jews.

It is the usage of Jerome that is adopted here. The Apocrypha in this translation consists of fifteen books or parts of books. They are works outside the canon adopted in Palestine; that is they form no part of the Hebrew scriptures, although the original language of some of them was Hebrew. They are all, except The Second Book of Esdras, in the Greek version of the Old Testament made for the Greek-speaking Jews in Egypt and known as the Septuagint. Gentile converts to Christianity overwhelmingly outnumbered those of Jewish origin, and so the Bible in Greek—the international language—with the extra books included in it, came to be adopted as the Bible of the early Church, and many early Christian writers quote them as scripture. With the exception of The First and Second Books of Esdras and The Prayer of Manasseh, the Roman Catholic Church recognizes these writings as part of the Old Testament, and designates them as deuterocanonical, that is added later to the canon. They are included in the Latin Vulgate Bible.

In Greek and Latin manuscripts of the Old Testament these books are dispersed throughout the Old Testament, generally in the places most in accord with their contents, and it was this arrangement which was traditionally followed by the Roman Catholic Church. The practice of collecting them into a separate unit dates back no farther than 1520 C.E., and explains why certain of the items are but fragments; they are passages not found in the Hebrew Bible, and so have been removed from the books in which they occur in the Greek version. To help the reader over this disunity and lack of context, the present revisers have adopted various devices used in The New English Bible: the name of Daniel appears in the titles of the stories of Susanna, and Bel and the Snake, as a reminder that these tales are to be read with The Book of Daniel; a note after the title of The Prayer of Azariah and The Song of the Three indicates that this item is to be found in the third chapter of the Greek form of Daniel; the six additions to the Book of Esther, which are disjointed as printed in older translations of the Apocrypha, are provided with a context by rendering the whole of the Greek version of Esther.

Due weight has been given to the variant readings given in critical editions of the Greek, the text of the ancient versions, and the suggestions of editors and commentators. The texts used for the revision were those edited by H. B. Swete in *The Old Testament in Greek according to the Septuagint,* and A. Rahlfs in his *Septuaginta.* In places these editions include two texts: the present revisers chose to use the Codex Sinaiticus text of Tobit together with the Old Latin version. They used Theodotion's version of the additions to The Book of Daniel, namely The Prayer of Azariah and The Song of the Three, Daniel and Susanna, and Daniel, Bel, and the Snake. The variant readings given in critical editions of the Greek were consulted throughout, and for Ecclesiasticus constant reference was made to the various forms of the Hebrew text. For The Second Book of Esdras, which apart from a few verses is not extant in Greek, the translation is based on the Latin text of R. L. Bensly's *The Fourth Book of Ezra.*

Alternative readings from Greek manuscripts and the evidence of early translations (*Vss.,* that is Versions) are given, as footnotes, only where they are significant either for text or for meaning. In a few places where the text seems to have suffered in the course of transmission and in its present form is obscure or even unintelligible, a slight change was made in the text and the rendering marked *prob. rdg.* Where an alternative interpretation was thought to deserve serious consideration it was recorded as a footnote with *or* as an indicator.

No attempt has been made to achieve consistency in the treatment of proper names. Familiar English forms have been used, especially when the reference is to well-known Old Testament characters or places.

In The First and Second Books of the Maccabees the dates given are reckoned according to the Greek or Seleucid era. As a help to the reader the nearest dates according to the Christian reckoning have been added at the foot of the page.

This revision of the Apocrypha shares with the rest of The Revised English Bible the aim of providing a rendering which is both faithful and idiomatic, conveying the meaning of the original in language which will be the closest natural equivalent. Every attempt has been made to avoid on the one hand free paraphrase, and on the other a formal fidelity that would result in a rendering which was all too obviously a translation. It is hoped that these documents, valuable in themselves and indispensable for the study of the New Testament, have been made more intelligible and more readily accessible.

The Place and Significance of the Apocrypha

The place of the Apocrypha in the biblical canon has been disputed since the first centuries of the Common Era, but the significance of the various writings for an understanding of Judaism in the Hellenistic and Roman periods and Early Christianity is no longer challenged.

Written between 250 B.C.E. and 100 C.E. by Jewish authors, the books classified in this volume as "Apocrypha" represent those works which are not included in the Hebrew canon, but which are found for the most part in the Greek translation of the Hebrew Bible, commonly referred to as the Septuagint. These include:

> The First Book of Esdras
> The Second Book of Esdras
> Tobit
> Judith
> The Rest of the Chapters of the Book of Esther
> The Wisdom of Solomon
> Ecclesiasticus or the Wisdom of Jesus Son of Sirach
> Baruch
> A Letter of Jeremiah
> The Prayer of Azariah and The Song of the Three
> Daniel and Susanna
> Daniel, Bel, and the Snake
> The Prayer of Manasseh
> The First Book of the Maccabees
> The Second Book of the Maccabees

Despite the rather simple definition given above, and the listing provided, it should be noted that there is no universal agreement as to the extent of the Old Testament canon, and therefore no agreement on the extent, or even the existence, of a separate category of books known as "Apocrypha." In Eastern Orthodox circles, for example, the canon encompasses all the books listed above, but also the Third and Fourth Books of the Maccabees and Psalm 151.

Although initially preserved within the Jewish community, the Septuagint emerged as the Scripture of the early church. As Judaism and Christianity defined themselves in the first several centuries C.E. (often with an eye toward each other), the Jewish community denied canonical status to the "extra" books. As a response to the Christian appropriation of the Septuagint, certain Jewish communities even commissioned alternate Greek translations which excluded the apocryphal books and gave a more literal rendering of the Hebrew text than the Septuagint. The early

Christians generally accepted the apocryphal books as part of their collection of authoritative writings. Augustine, for example, clearly held these books on a par with the rest of the "Old Testament." Almost exclusively from this point forward, it was the early church that preserved the material.

The issue of the canonical status of the books for Christians came to the fore when Jerome translated the Scriptures into Latin in the late fourth century. Having learned Hebrew, Jerome compared the Septuagint text with the Hebrew, noted the differences between the two collections, and recorded in his prefaces to the "extra" books that they were not considered canonical by the Jewish communities. Despite certain misgivings about the canonicity of books not found in the Hebrew Bible, Jerome included the apocryphal books in his translation (the Vulgate). It was this translation that became the standard for nearly all of western Christendom throughout the Middle Ages.

The next great challenge to the canonical status of the apocryphal books came during the Protestant Reformation of the sixteenth century. Protestant religious leaders, attempting both to ground their groups' religious identities in Scripture (and *only* Scripture) and to define themselves over against the Catholic church, rejected the apocryphal books. Their decision was based not only on the supposition that the shorter Hebrew canon was the older, and therefore more authoritative or "purer," form of the Old Testament, but also on the Catholic church's reliance on apocryphal books such as 2 Maccabees for their scriptural defense of the doctrines of purgatory and the saying of masses for the dead, both of which were major areas of dispute between the Protestants and Catholics. In response, the Catholic church at the Council of Trent in 1546 declared that all the books found in the Vulgate were canonical, and were to be received "with equal devotion and reverence." The exceptions to this affirmation were 1 and 2 Esdras and The Prayer of Manasseh, which were collected and, in editions published after the Council, printed together in an appendix which followed the New Testament. At a later time, the Catholic church did come to make a distinction between the "deuterocanonical" books (those accepted into the canon at a later date, but no less authoritative—the Apocrypha) and the "protocanonical" books (those found in the Hebrew canon), but the former books were interspersed with the latter, never grouped separately as they are in this edition.

Although Protestants do not accept the apocryphal books as canonical, several recent editions of the Christian Bible include, as this edition does, these "extra" books. Modern readers have come to understand that these works shed valuable light on the world out of which the latest books of the Old Testament and the entirety of the New Testament came. They reflect especially the thought worlds of the several types of Judaism that flourished at the turn of the eras. They also inform the reading of the rest of the biblical text; in fact, nearly all the literary forms found in the protocanonical books also appear in the deuterocanonicals.

History and historical fiction make up a substantial portion of the Apocrypha. While the history may be quite tendentious, or lapse occasionally into a propagandistic recounting of events, the First and Second Books of the Maccabees relay much valuable information about the Hasmonean revolts of the second century B.C.E. However, more prominent are those works of historical fiction such as Tobit, Judith, Daniel and Susanna, and Daniel, Bel, and the Snake. These works, which have their setting in the exilic period, purport to be descriptions of actual events, but are quite clearly fictional stories intended to encourage the reader to emulate the behavior of the characters in the story.

Examples of cultic poetry are The Prayer of Manasseh, allegedly the prayer of repentance offered by the wicked king (see 2 Chr. 33.11–13), and The Prayer of Azariah and The Song of the Three, additions to the Book of Daniel which claim to relate the words of Daniel's three friends as they stand in the furnace (see Dan. 3.23).

Two significant wisdom treatises, the Wisdom of Solomon and the Wisdom of Jesus Son of Sirach (Ecclesiasticus), are also part of the Apocrypha. Both clearly owe a great deal to the protocanonical wisdom texts, but they are just as clearly attempts to bring the Yahwistic wisdom reflected in the earlier texts into the cosmopolitan, overtly syncretistic Hellenistic age.

The Letter of Jeremiah demonstrates that the epistle was an acceptable form for the promulgation of a particular religious view in the last centuries B.C.E., long before Paul wrote his letters.

The Second Book of Esdras, especially chapters 3–14, is a Jewish apocalypse which addresses both the question of theodicy (primarily in the dialogues between Esdras and God) and the imminent end of the created order. Chapters 1–2 and 15–16 appear to have been added later, perhaps by Christians, but they also reflect the persistent hope for the renewal of creation found not only in the rest of the book, but also in nearly every apocalypse, including Daniel and Revelation.

Because a consensus has not been achieved concerning the canonical status of the Apocrypha, there is a sense in which its significance remains a disputed issue. But for all who are generally interested in the contexts of both the Old and New Testaments, these books are, along with the Dead Sea Scrolls and the other noncanonical Jewish literature, invaluable resources. The books of the Apocrypha have something in common with what came before them and with what followed them; they therefore act as a link between the Old and New Testaments and so help us to understand both.

THE FIRST BOOK OF

Esdras

First Esdras presents the material found in 2 Chr. chs. 35–36, the Book of Ezra (with one minor omission), and Nehemiah 7.38–8.12, dealing with Ezra. This material is at places presented in a sequence different from that found in the Masoretic Text. One section, 3.1–5.6, a story of a debate at the Persian court, is exceptional in completely lacking a parallel in Old Testament texts.

First Esdras is a Greek translation of a Hebrew-Aramaic original (no longer extant) that closely resembled the Masoretic Text. It differed, however, at several points (e.g. compare 1.11 n. and 2.13–15 n.), with some differences being enigmatic (e.g. 5.69 and 8.41). The exact relationship of the Hebrew-Aramaic original to the corresponding material in the Hebrew canon, and to a (hypothetical) common forerunner to these, cannot be determined. First Esdras is not related to the Septuagint translation of Ezra and Nehemiah. It is a curiosity that Josephus, for his history of the period, followed 1 Esdras.

A possible point of confusion lies in the name: 1 Esdras has also been called 2 Esdras (with 1 Esdras then being reserved for the Septuagint translation of Ezra-Nehemiah, originally a single book) and 3 Esdras (as in the Vulgate, where Ezra is 1 Esdras and Nehemiah is 2 Esdras). Others have called it the "Greek Ezra" (*Esdras* being a Greek rendering of the Hebrew *Ezra*).

Many scholars believe that 1 Esdras was written between 200 B.C.E. and 90 C.E., with sometime in the late second century B.C.E. a likely date.

The reader is invited to consult the annotations prepared for the parallel material in the Old Testament books, as indicated in the first paragraph above.

The reign of Josiah

1 JOSIAH celebrated the Passover to his Lord at Jerusalem, and the Passover victims were sacrificed on the fourteenth day of the first month. ² He installed the priests, duly robed in their vestments, in the temple of the Lord according to the order of daily service. ³ He commanded the Levites, who served the temple in Israel, to purify themselves for the Lord, before placing the sacred Ark in the Lord's house, which King Solomon son of David built. ⁴ Josiah said to them, 'You shall not carry it about on your shoulders any longer. Now you are to serve the Lord your God and minister to his people Israel: prepare yourselves, family by family and clan by clan, ⁵ in the manner prescribed by King David of Israel and provided for so magnificently by his son Solomon. Stand in the holy place according to your family groups, you Levites who are in divisions to act for your brother Israelites. ⁶ Sacrifice the Passover victims, and prepare the sacrifices for your kinsmen. Keep the Passover according to the command given by the Lord to Moses.'

⁷ For those who were present Josiah contributed thirty thousand lambs and kids and three thousand calves; they were given from the king's own resources to the people and to the priests and Levites in fulfilment of his promise. ⁸ The temple wardens, Chelkias, Zacharias, and Esyelus, gave the priests two

1.1–33: Josiah's Passover and his last days; parallel to 2 Chr. 35.1–27. Why 1 Esd. begins with this account is not known. Some speculate that the author wished to highlight the role of Josiah, and possibly to show a connection between his worthy acts and the return from the Exile in the days of Cyrus. The conclusion at 9.55 seems abrupt, as if more material was once included; possibly the beginning was also lost. 4: *It:* the Ark. *Family and clan:* see 1 Chr. chs. 24–26. 8: *Esyelus:* 2 Chr. 35.8 reads "Jehiel."

thousand six hundred sheep and three hundred calves for the Passover. [9] Jechonias, Samaeas, his brother Nathanael, Sabias, Ochielus, and Joram, high-ranking officers in the army, gave the Levites five thousand sheep and seven hundred calves for the Passover.

[10] This was the procedure: the priests and the Levites, bearing the unleavened bread, stood in all their splendour by clans [11] and by family groups before the people, to make offerings to the Lord as is laid down in the book of Moses. This took place in the morning. [12] The Passover victims were roasted over the fire in the prescribed way and the sacrifices boiled with fragrant herbs in the bronze vessels and cauldrons; [13] then portions were carried round to the whole assembly. After that the Levites made preparations for themselves and for their kinsmen, the priests of Aaron's line. [14] It was because the priests were engaged until nightfall in offering up the fat portions that the Levites made the preparations both for themselves and for their kinsmen, the priests of Aaron's line. [15] The temple singers, the sons of Asaph, were in their places according to the ordinances of David, and Asaph, Zacharias, and Eddinous of the royal court; [16] and the doorkeepers were at each gateway. There was no need for any of them to leave their posts, for their kinsmen, the Levites, made the preparations for them.

[17] Everything for the sacrifice to the Lord was completed that day: the celebration of the Passover [18] and the offering of the sacrifices on the Lord's altar, according to King Josiah's orders. [19] Israelites who were present at that time kept the Passover and the feast of Unleavened Bread for seven days. [20] No Passover like it had been celebrated in Israel since the time of the prophet Samuel; [21] none of the kings of Israel had kept such a Passover as was kept by Josiah, with the priests, Levites, and men of Judah, and all the Israelites who happened to be resident in Jerusalem. [22] It was in the eighteenth year of Josiah's reign that this Passover was celebrated.

[23] Josiah was deeply pious and his deeds

were upright in the sight of his Lord. [24] The events of his reign are to be found among earlier records, records of sin and rebellion against the Lord graver than anything perpetrated by any other nation or kingdom, and of offences against him which brought down his judgement on Israel.

[25] Some time after Josiah's act of worship had taken place, it happened that Pharaoh king of Egypt was advancing to open hostilities at Carchemish on the Euphrates. When Josiah marched out to confront him, [26] the Egyptian king sent him this message: 'What do you want with me, king of Judah? [27] It is not against you that the Lord God has sent me to fight; my campaign is on the Euphrates. On this occasion the Lord is with me. He is with me, speeding me on my way. Stand aside, and do not oppose the Lord.' [28] Josiah did not return to his chariot but set out to give battle, disregarding the words of the prophet Jeremiah, the spokesman of the Lord. [29] When he joined battle in the plain of Megiddo, Pharaoh's captains swept down on King Josiah. [30] 'I am badly wounded,' the king said to his servants; 'take me out of the battle.' They took him out of the line at once, [31] and when he had been put into his second chariot, he was brought back to Jerusalem. There he died and was buried in the ancestral tomb.

[32] Throughout Judah there was mourning for Josiah, and the prophet Jeremiah made lament for him. The lamentation for Josiah has been observed by the chief men and their wives from that day to this: an edict was issued to all the people of Israel that this should be done for all time. [33] These things are recorded in the annals of the kings of Judah; every deed of Josiah's which won him fame and showed his understanding of the law of the Lord, both what he did earlier and what is told of him here, is related in the book of the kings of Israel and Judah.

Exile and return

[34] His fellow-countrymen took Jeconiah son of Josiah and made him king in succession to his father. He was twenty-three years old,

---

11: *In the morning:* 2 Chr. 35.12 has "so with the bulls"; the Heb. words for "morning" and "bulls," having identical consonants, were easily confused. **22:** *The eighteenth year of Josiah's reign:* 621 B.C.E. **23–24:** Not paralleled in 2 Chr. **25:** *Pharaoh:* Necho (reigned 609–594 B.C.E.); 2 Chr. 35.20. In 609 the Egyptians moved north to attack *Carchemish,* to aid the Assyrians, who were making a last-ditch stand against the Medes and Babylonians.

35 and he reigned over Judah and Jerusalem for three months. Then the king of Egypt deposed him, 36 fined the nation a hundred talents of silver and one talent of gold, 37 and replaced him by his brother Joakim as king of Judah and Jerusalem. 38 Joakim imprisoned the leading men and had his brother Zarius arrested and brought back from Egypt.

39 Joakim was twenty-five years old when he became king of Judah and Jerusalem. He did what was wrong in the eyes of the Lord, 40 and King Nebuchadnezzar of Babylon marched against him, put him in bronze fetters, and took him away to Babylon. 41 Nebuchadnezzar also seized some of the sacred vessels of the Lord; he carried them off and placed them in his own temple at Babylon. 42 The stories about Joakim, his depraved and impious conduct, are recorded in the chronicles of the kings.

43 He was succeeded by his son Joakim, who was eighteen years old when he came to the throne. 44 He reigned in Jerusalem for three months and ten days, and he too did what was wrong in the eyes of the Lord. 45 A year later Nebuchadnezzar sent and had him brought to Babylon together with the sacred vessels of the Lord, 46 and he made Zedekiah king of Judah and Jerusalem.

Zedekiah was twenty-one years old, and he reigned for eleven years. 47 He did what was wrong in the eyes of the Lord and disregarded the advice of the prophet Jeremiah, the spokesman of the Lord. 48 King Nebuchadnezzar had made him swear by the Lord an oath of allegiance, but he renounced his oath and rebelled. He was stubborn and obstinate, and broke the commandments of the Lord God of Israel.

49 The leaders of both people and priests committed many impious and lawless acts. They outdid even the heathen in their abominable practices, and defiled the Lord's temple which had been consecrated in Jerusalem. 50 The God of their fathers sent his messenger to reclaim them, because he wished to spare them and his dwelling-place.

51 But they held his messengers in derision: they were scoffing at his prophets on the very day when the Lord spoke. 52 At last his anger was so roused against his people on account of their impieties that he ordered the Chaldaean kings to attack them. 53 The Lord handed them all over to their enemies, who put their young men to the sword around the holy temple, and spared neither young man nor maiden, neither the old nor the infant. 54 All the sacred vessels of the Lord, large and small, the furnishings of the Ark of the Lord, and the royal treasures were taken as spoil to Babylon. 55 The Lord's house was burnt down, the walls of Jerusalem razed to the ground, its towers set ablaze, 56 and all its splendours brought to ruin. Nebuchadnezzar transported to Babylon those who escaped the sword, 57 and they remained slaves to him and his sons until his empire fell to the Persians. This fulfilled the word of the Lord spoken by Jeremiah 58 that, until the land should have run the full term of its sabbaths, it should keep sabbath all the time of its desolation till the end of the seventy years.

2 In the first year of King Cyrus of Persia the Lord, to fulfil his word spoken through Jeremiah, 2 moved the heart of the king so that throughout his kingdom the following proclamation was made and at the same time issued in writing:

3 The decree of King Cyrus of Persia.

The Lord of Israel, the Most High Lord, has made me king of the world 4 and has charged me to build him a house at Jerusalem in Judaea. 5 Whoever among you, therefore, belongs to his people, may his Lord be with him! Let him go up to Jerusalem in Judaea and build the house of the Lord of Israel, the Lord who dwells in Jerusalem. 6 Throughout the country let assistance be given to each man by his neighbours with gold and silver 7 and other gifts, with horses and pack-animals, to-

1:54 **the furnishings of the Ark:** *in other MSS* the treasure chests.

1.34–58: The fall of Judah and Jerusalem; parallel to 2 Chr. 36.1–21. **38:** A confused version of 2 Chr. 36.4; see 2 Chr. 36.1–4, 9–11. The name *Zarius*, otherwise unknown, is likely an error for Jehoahaz, who was exiled to Egypt by Necho (2 Chr. 36.4). The "bringing back" of Zarius-Jehoahaz reflects further confusion. **43:** *He . . . Joakim:* for *Joakim*, read "Jehoiachin"; *eighteen* is correct, not eight (2 Chr. 36.9).

2.1–15: The ascendancy and decree of Cyrus; parallel to Ezra 1.1–11. **1:** *First year:* 539 B.C.E. **3:** *The Lord of Israel:* Ezra 1.2 has "The LORD the God of the heavens," a title perhaps more agreeable to the Persian rulers;

gether with anything else set aside as votive offerings for the temple of the Lord in Jerusalem.

8 Then the heads of the families of the tribes of Judah and Benjamin came forward, along with the priests, the Levites, and all who had been prompted by the Lord to go up and build his house in Jerusalem. 9 Their neighbours assisted with gifts of every kind, silver and gold, horses and pack-animals. Many were also moved to help with votive offerings in great quantity. 10 Moreover, the sacred vessels of the Lord which Nebuchadnezzar had removed from Jerusalem and placed in the temple of his idols were brought out by King Cyrus of Persia 11 and given into the charge of Mithradates his treasurer, 12 by whom they were handed over to Sanabassar, governor of Judaea. 13 Here is the list of them: a thousand gold cups, a thousand silver cups, twenty-nine silver censers, thirty gold bowls, two thousand four hundred and ten silver bowls, and a thousand other articles. 14 In all, five thousand four hundred and sixty-nine gold and silver vessels were sent back, 15 and they were brought by Sanabassar to Jerusalem from Babylon along with the exiles.

16 But when Artaxerxes was king of Persia, Belemus, Mithradates, Tabellius, Rathymus, Beeltethmus, Semellius the secretary, and their colleagues in office in Samaria and elsewhere, wrote the king the following letter denouncing the inhabitants of Judaea and Jerusalem:

17 To our Sovereign Lord Artaxerxes your servants Rathymus the Recorder, Semellius the Secretary, the other members of their council, and the magistrates in Coele-Syria and Phoenicia.

18 Be it known to your majesty that the Jews who left you to come up here have arrived in Jerusalem, and are rebuilding that rebellious and wicked city, repairing its streets and walls and laying the foundation of a temple. 19 Once this city is rebuilt and the walls are completed, they will never submit to paying tribute but will even rebel against your royal house. 20 Since work on the temple is in hand, we have thought it well not to overlook such an important matter 21 but to bring it to your majesty's attention, in order that, if it please your majesty, search may be made in the records left by your predecessors. 22 You will discover in the archives references to these matters; you will learn that this has been a rebellious city, a source of trouble to kings and cities. 23 From earliest times it has been a centre of armed resistance by the Jews, and for that reason it was laid in ruins. 24 Therefore we now submit to your majesty that, if this city be rebuilt and its walls rise again, you will be denied access to Coele-Syria and Phoenicia.

25 The king sent this reply:

To Rathymus the Recorder, Beeltethmus, Semellius the Secretary, and their colleagues in office in Samaria, Syria, and Phoenicia.

26 Having read the letter you sent me, I ordered search to be made, and that city, it was discovered, has a long history of opposition to the royal house, 27 and its inhabitants have been given to rebellion and

see 2 Chr. 36.23 and Ezra 5.11–12. **10:** *The temple of his idols* is pointedly monotheistic; compare Ezra 1.7, which has "in the temple of his gods." **12, 15:** *Sanabassar* is Sheshbazzar in Ezra 1.8. **13–15:** The inventory here is probably more accurate than the parallel in Ezra 1.9–11. The total here, 5,469, is correct, not the figure 5,400 in Ezra, though a miscellaneous category, "other vessels," is mentioned there.

2.16–30: Opposition to rebuilding the temple and the walls; parallel to Ezra 4.7, 11–24. The account is somewhat confusing. Verse 1 mentions Cyrus (died 529 B.C.E.) and v. 30, Darius I (521–486 B.C.E.); Cambyses (529–521 B.C.E.) is omitted. Artaxerxes (v. 16) reigned in 464–424 B.C.E. The section seems misplaced, perhaps belonging originally between the end of Ezra and the beginning of Nehemiah. **16:** *Beeltethmus:* the translator here mistook a title ("high commissioner," Ezra 4.9) for a personal name. **17:** These people ruled over the area which included Judea; the area, from Persian perspective, is called "Beyond-Euphrates" (Ezra 4.10). **18:** The *temple* is not mentioned in Ezra 4.14; 4.24, however, speaks of the cessation of building it. Many scholars believe that the mention of the temple here, in v. 30, and in Ezra 4.24 are late insertions, occasioned by the mention of sacred vessels (v. 10). The opposition at this time was to rebuilding the walls. **25:** *Beeltethmus:* see v. 16 n.

war. There have been powerful and ruthless kings ruling in Jerusalem who have exercised authority over Coele-Syria and Phoenicia and laid them under tribute. 28 I therefore command that the men of whom you write be prevented from rebuilding the city, and that measures be taken to enforce this order 29 and to check the spread of an evil likely to be troublesome to our royal house.

30 On receipt of the letter from King Artaxerxes, Rathymus, Semellius the secretary, and their colleagues hurried to Jerusalem with cavalry and a large body of other troops and stopped the builders. Work on the temple at Jerusalem remained at a standstill until the second year of the reign of King Darius of Persia.

A debate at the Persian court

3 KING Darius gave a great banquet for all his retainers, for all the members of his household, all the chief men of Media and Persia, 2 along with the whole body of satraps, commanders, and governors of his empire in the hundred and twenty-seven satrapies from India to Ethiopia. 3 After eating and drinking as much as they wanted, they withdrew. King Darius retired to his bedchamber, where he lay down and fell fast asleep.

4 Then the three young men of the king's personal bodyguard said among themselves: 5 'Let each of us name the thing he judges to be strongest, and to the one whose opinion appears wisest let King Darius give rich gifts and prizes: 6 he shall be robed in purple, drink from gold cups, and sleep on a golden bed; he shall have a chariot with gold-studded bridles, and a turban of fine linen, and a chain around his neck. 7 His wisdom shall give him the right to sit next to the king

and to bear the title Kinsman of Darius.' 8 Each then put his opinion in writing, affixed his seal, and placed it under the king's pillow. 9 'When the king wakes,' they said, 'the writing will be given him, and the king and the three chief men of Persia shall judge whose opinion is wisest; the award will be made to that man on the evidence of what he has written.'

10 One wrote, 'Wine is strongest.' 11 The second wrote, 'The king is strongest.' 12 The third wrote, 'Women are strongest, but truth conquers all.' 13 When the king awoke, he was handed what they had written. Having read it 14 he summoned all the chief men of Persia and Media, satraps, commanders, governors, and chief officers, 15 and took his seat in the council-chamber. What each of the three had written was then read out before them. 16 'Call the young men,' said the king, 'and let them explain their opinions.' They were summoned and, on coming in, 17 were asked to clarify what they had written.

The first, who spoke about the strength of wine, began: 18 'Sirs, how true it is that wine is strongest! It bemuses the wits of all who drink it: 19 king and orphan, slave and free, poor and rich, on them all it has the same effect. 20 It turns all thoughts to revelry and mirth; it brings forgetfulness of grief and debt. 21 It makes everyone feel rich; it cares nothing for king or satrap, but sets all men talking in millions. 22 When they are in their cups, they forget to be friendly to friends and relations, and before long are drawing their swords; 23 and when they awake after their wine, they cannot remember what they have done. 24 Sirs, is not wine the strongest, seeing that it makes men behave in this way?' With that he ended his speech.

4 Then the second, he who spoke of the strength of the king, began: 2 'Sirs, is not

3:3 **and fell fast asleep:** prob. rdg; Gk sleepless.

3.1–5.6: A debate at the Persian court. This interpolated story is unique to Esdras. It aggrandizes Zerubbabel. The author adapted a popular account of a debate, which originally contained only three statements (about wine, the king, and women). To that account was added the statement, "but truth conquers all" (v. 12), both in order to include a theme more akin to Jewish sensibilities, and also to introduce the return from the Babylonian Exile. The third speaker, Zerubbabel, proposes two separate statements, thus effacing the expected symmetry of three men and three statements.

3.1–17a: The setting of the debate. 1: Darius I, reigned 521–486 B.C.E. **2:** The hundred and twenty-seven satrapies: compare Esther 1.1; the number is greatly exaggerated; twenty would be accurate. **3:** Fell fast asleep: Josephus Ant. XI. 3.2 relates that the king suggested the debate after a sleepless night.

3.17b–24: Wine is strongest. 18: It bemuses the wits: compare Ecclus. 19.2.

4.1–12: The king is strongest. The passage is often misinterpreted as depicting the supposed arbitrary power man the strongest, man who subdues land and sea and everything in them? [3] But the strongest of men is the king; he is their lord and master, and they obey whatever command he gives them. [4] If he bids them make war on one another, they do so; if he dispatches them against his enemies, they march off and make their way over mountains and walls and towers. [5] They kill and are killed, but they never disobey the king's command. If they are victorious they bring everything, spoil and all else, to the king. [6] Again, take those who do not serve as soldiers or go to war, but work the land: they sow and reap, and lay the harvest before the king. They compel each other to pay him their tribute. [7] Though he is no more than one man, if he orders them to kill, they kill; if he orders them to release, they release. He orders them [8] to smite and they beat, to demolish and they demolish, to build and they build, [9] to cut down and they cut down, to plant and they plant. [10] People and troops all obey him. Further, while he himself is at table, whether he eats, drinks, or goes to sleep, [11] they stand in attendance round him and none can leave and see to his own affairs; in nothing whatever do they disobey. [12] Sirs, surely the king must be the strongest, when he commands such obedience!' With that he ended.

[13] The third, he who spoke about women and truth, was Zerubbabel; he began: [14] 'Sirs, it is true that the king is great, that men are many, and that wine is strong, but who rules over them? Who is the master? Women, surely! [15] The king and all his people, lords over land and sea, were born of women, [16] and from them they came. Women brought up the men who planted the vineyards which yield the wine. [17] They make the clothes men wear and they bring honour to men; without women men could not exist.

[18] 'If men have amassed gold and silver and all manner of beautiful things, and then see a woman with a lovely face and figure, [19] they leave it all to gape and stare at her with open mouth, and every one of them will prefer her above gold and silver or any thing of beauty. [20] A man will abandon his father who brought him up, abandon even his country, and become one with his wife. [21] To the end of his days he stays with her, forgetful of father, mother, and country. [22] Here is the proof that women are your masters: do you not toil and sweat and then bring all you earn and give it to your wives? [23] A man will take his sword and sally forth to plunder and steal, to sail on sea and river; [24] he confronts lions, he goes about in the dark; and when he has stolen and robbed and looted, he brings the spoil home to his beloved.

[25] 'A man loves his wife above father or mother. [26] For women's sakes many men have been driven out of their minds, many have become slaves, [27] many have perished or come to grief or taken to evil ways. [28] Now do you believe me? Certainly the king wields great authority; no country dare lift a finger against him. [29] Yet I watched him with Apame, his favourite concubine, daughter of the celebrated Bartacus. She was sitting on the king's right, [30] and she took the diadem off his head and put it on her own. She was slapping his face with her left hand, [31] and all the king did was gape at her open-mouthed. When she laughed at him he laughed; when she was cross with him he coaxed her to make it up with him. [32] Sirs, if women do as well as this, how can their strength be denied?' [33] The king and the chief men looked at one another.

Zerubbabel then went on to speak about truth: [34] 'Sirs, we have seen that women are strong. The earth is vast, the sky is lofty, yet the sun, swift in its course, moves through the circle of the sky and speeds home in a single day. [35] How great is the sun which can do this! But truth too is great; it is stronger than all else. [36] The whole earth calls on truth, and the sky praises her; all created things shake and tremble. With her there is no injustice. [37] There is injustice in wine, and in

of oriental rulers; rather, it is a general discourse on the power of those who govern, whoever or wherever they may be. Sources indicate that oriental rulers' powers were most usually circumscribed more effectively — though there were exceptions — than those of western rulers.

4.13–33: Women are strongest. 29: The identity of this *Apame* is uncertain. An Apame, daughter of Spitamenes, was given as wife to Seleucus Nicator, the Syrian ruler; and an Apame, daughter of Artabazus, was given to Ptolemy I Soter, the Egyptian king. *Bartacus* appears in various forms in manuscripts; the words *the celebrated* may be a corruption of an ancestral name, rather than the implication that Bartacus was well-known.

kings, and in women, injustice in all men and in all their works, whatever they may be. There is no truth in them, and in their injustice they shall perish. 38 But truth abides and remains strong for ever: she lives and is sovereign for ever and ever.

39 'There is no favouritism with her, no partiality; rather she exacts justice from everyone who is wicked or unjust. All approve what she does; 40 in her judgements there is no injustice. Hers are strength and royalty, the authority and majesty of all ages. Praise be to the God of truth!'

41 As Zerubbabel finished speaking, all the people shouted, 'Great is truth: truth is strongest!' 42 Then the king said to him, 'Ask what you will, even beyond what is laid down in the terms, and we shall grant it you. You have been proved to be the wisest, and you shall sit next to me and be called my Kinsman.' 43 Zerubbabel answered, 'Remember, O king, the vow you made on the day when you came to the throne: you promised to rebuild Jerusalem 44 and to send back all the vessels taken from there. Cyrus had set them aside, for when he vowed to destroy Babylon, at the same time he vowed to restore these vessels. 45 You also made a vow to rebuild the temple, burnt by the Edomites when Judaea had been ravaged by the Chaldaeans. 46 This is the favour I now beg of you, my lord king, this the magnanimous gesture I request: that you should perform the vow made by you to the King of heaven.'

47 King Darius stood up, embraced him, and wrote letters on his behalf, instructing all the treasurers, governors, commanders, and satraps to give safe conduct to him and to all those going up with him to rebuild Jerusalem. 48 He wrote also to all the governors in Coele-Syria and Phoenicia and to those in Lebanon ordering them to transport cedarwood from Lebanon to Jerusalem and help Zerubbabel build the city. 49 He gave all Jews going up from his kingdom to Judaea a written assurance of their liberties: no one in authority, whether satrap, governor, or treasurer, was to molest them in their homes. 50 All land which they might acquire was to be exempt from taxation, and the Edomites were to surrender the villages they had seized from the Jews. 51 Each year twenty talents were to be contributed to the building of the temple until it was completed, 52 and a further ten talents annually for the seventeen whole-offerings to be sacrificed every day on the altar in accordance with their law. 53–54 All who were going from Babylonia to build the city were to enjoy freedom, they and their descendants after them. The king gave orders in writing that all the priests going there should also receive maintenance and the vestments in which they would officiate; 55 that the Levites too should receive maintenance, until that day when the temple should be completed and Jerusalem rebuilt; 56 and that all who guarded the city should be given land and pay. 57 He sent back from Babylon the vessels which Cyrus had set aside. He reaffirmed all that Cyrus had commanded, and gave orders that everything should be restored to Jerusalem.

58 When the young man, Zerubbabel, went out, he turned to face the direction of Jerusalem, and looking heavenwards praised the King of heaven, saying:

59 'From you come victory and wisdom;
    yours is the glory, and I am your
    servant.
60 All praise to you, for you have given
    me wisdom;
  to you, Lord of our fathers, I ascribe
    praise.'

61 He took the letters and set out for Babylon. There his fellow-Jews, on receiving his report, 62 praised the God of their fathers who

4.34–42: Truth is strongest. 41: The Latin translation became an oft-quoted line: "Great is truth, and it prevails." **42:** *Sit next to me and be called my Kinsman:* see 3.7.

4.43–60: Permission granted to rebuild Jerusalem. 43–46: Darius' *vow.* This section contains historical improbabilities. It is unlikely that Darius would have made a vow (v. 43) such as here, particularly on his coronation day! Next, the vessels had already been sent back to Jerusalem in the days of Cyrus (2.1–15). Again, the idea that Cyrus *vowed to destroy Babylon* (v. 44) is contradicted by the fact that the city yielded to him without a struggle. Furthermore, not the *Edomites* (v. 45) but the Babylonians destroyed Jerusalem. Hence, this section is a literary construction to introduce the theme of the return to Zion. **58–60:** Like Daniel, Zerubbabel *turned to face the direction of Jerusalem* (compare Dan. 6.10). The prayer is kindred to that in Dan. 2.20–23.

4.61–5.6: The departure from Babylon. The Judeans leave Babylon; the Persian capital, where Zerubbabel had given them leave and liberty 63 to go up and rebuild Jerusalem and the temple which bore his name; and they feasted for seven days with music and rejoicing.

The returned Israelites

5 AFTER this the heads of families, tribe by tribe, were chosen to go up to Jerusalem with their wives, their sons and daughters, their male and female slaves, and their pack-animals. 2 Darius dispatched a thousand horsemen to escort them safely there, with a band of drums and flutes, 3 to which all their kinsmen danced. So he sent them off with their escort.

4 These are the names of the men who went up to Jerusalem, arranged according to their families and tribes and their allotted duties: 5 the priests, sons of Phineas son of Aaron, with Jeshua son of Josedek, son of Saraeas, and Joakim son of Zerubbabel, son of Sala-thiel, of the house of David of the line of Phares of the tribe of Judah; 6 it was Zerubba-bel who spoke wise words before King Darius of Persia. This was in the second year of his reign, in Nisan the first month.

7 These are the men from Judaea who re-turned from captivity and exile, those whom King Nebuchadnezzar of Babylon had taken to Babylon. 8 Each of them returned to his own town, whether to Jerusalem or else-where in Judaea. They were led by Zerubba-bel and Jeshua, Nehemiah, Zaraeas, Resaeas, Enenius, Mardochaeus, Beelsarus, Asphar-asus, Reelias, Roimus, and Baana.

9 The number of those of the nation who returned with their leaders was: the line of Phoros two thousand one hundred and sev-enty-two; the line of Saphat four hundred and seventy-two; 10 the line of Ares seven hundred and fifty-six; 11 the line of Phaath-moab, belonging to the line of Jeshua and Joab, two thousand eight hundred and twelve; 12 the line of Olamus one thousand two hundred and fifty-four; the line of Za-thui nine hundred and forty-five; the line of Chorbe seven hundred and five; the line of Banei six hundred and forty-eight; 13 the line of Bebae six hundred and twenty-three; the line of Argai one thousand three hundred and twenty-two; 14 the line of Adonikam six

hundred and sixty-seven; the line of Bagoi two thousand and sixty-six; the line of Adinus four hundred and fifty-four; 15 the line of Ater son of Hezekias ninety-two; the line of Keilan and Azetas sixty-seven; the line of Azurus four hundred and thirty-two; 16 the line of Annias one hundred and one; the line of Arom and the line of Bassa three hundred and twenty-three; the line of Arsi-phurith one hundred and twelve; 17 the line of Baeterus three thousand and five. The men of Bethlomon one hundred and twenty-three; 18 the men of Netophae fifty-five; the men of Anathoth one hundred and fifty-eight; the men of Bethasmoth forty-two; 19 the men of Cariathiarius twenty-five; the men of Caphira and Beroth seven hundred and forty-three; 20 the Chadiasans and Am-midaeans four hundred and twenty-two; the men of Kirama and Gabbes six hundred and twenty-one; 21 the men of Macalon one hun-dred and twenty-two; the men of Betolio fifty-two; the line of Niphis one hundred and fifty-six; 22 the line of Calamolalus and Onus seven hundred and twenty-five; the line of Jerechus three hundred and forty-five; 23 the line of Sanaas three thousand three hundred and thirty.

24 The priests: the line of Jeddu son of Jeshua, belonging to the line of Anasib, nine hundred and seventy-two; the line of Em-meruth one thousand and fifty-two; 25 the line of Phassurus one thousand two hundred and forty-seven; the line of Charme one thousand and seventeen.

26 The Levites: the line of Joshua, Cad-mielus, Bannus, and Sudius seventy-four. 27 The temple singers: the line of Asaph one hundred and forty-eight.

28 The door-keepers: the line of Salum, of Atar, of Tolman, of Dacubi, of Ateta, of Sabi, in all one hundred and thirty-nine.

29 The temple servitors: the line of Esau, of Asipha, of Taboth, of Keras, of Soua, of Pha-leas, of Labana, of Aggaba, 30 of Acud, of Uta, of Ketab, of Gaba, of Subai, of Anan, of Cathua, of Geddur, 31 of Jairus, of De-san, of Noeba, of Chaseba, of Gazera, of Ozius, of Phinoe, of Asara, of Basthae, of Asana, of Maani, of Naphisi, of Acum, of Achipha, of Asur, of Pharakim, of Baaloth, 32 of Meedda, of Coutha, of Charea, of Bar-

---

served in the court, was presumably at Susa. Perhaps Zerubbabel went from Susa to Babylon to find leaders and stimulate the return. **5.5:** The genealogy of Zerubbabel clashes with that in 1 Chr. 3.17–24.

5.7–46: Tally of returnees; parallel to Ezra 2.1–70 and Neh. 7.6–73, but with many differences. **24–25:**

chue, of Serar, of Thomi, of Nasith, of Atepha. 33 The descendants of Solomon's servants: the line of Asapphioth, of Pharida, of Je-eli, of Lozon, of Isdael, of Saphythi, 34 of Agia, of Phacareth, of Sabie, of Sarothie, of Masias, of Gas, of Addus, of Subas, of Apherra, of Barodis, of Saphat, of Allon. 35 The temple servitors and the descendants of Solomon's servants amounted to three hundred and seventy-two in all.

36 The following, who returned from Thermeleth and Thelsas with their leaders Chara, Athalar, and Alar, 37 were unable to prove by their families and descent that they were Israelites: the line of Dalan, the son of Tuban, and the line of Necodan amounting to six hundred and fifty-two.

38 From among the priests the claimants to the priesthood whose record could not be traced: the lines of Obdia, of Accos, and of Joddus who married Augia, one of the daughters of Pharzellaeus, and took his name. 39 When search was made for the record of their descent in the register it could not be traced, and so they were debarred from officiating. 40 Nehemiah the governor forbade them to partake of the sacred food until there should be a high priest wearing the breastpiece of Revelation and Truth.

41 They were in all: Israelites from twelve years old, not counting slaves male and female, forty-two thousand three hundred and sixty; 42 their slaves seven thousand three hundred and thirty-seven; musicians and singers two hundred and forty-five. 43 Their camels numbered four hundred and thirty-five, their horses seven thousand and thirty-six, their mules two hundred and forty-five, and their donkeys five thousand five hundred and twenty-five.

44 On their arrival at the temple of God in Jerusalem, certain of the heads of the families took a vow to put forth their best efforts to rebuild the house on its original site, 45 and to give to the sacred treasury one thousand minas of gold and five thousand minas of silver for the fabric and one hundred vestments for priests.

46 The priests, the Levites, and some of the people stayed in Jerusalem and its neighbourhood, while the temple musicians, the door-keepers, and all the rest of the Israelites lived in their villages.

47 WHEN it was the seventh month and the Israelites were settled in their homes, they came together with one accord in the broad square of the first gateway toward the east. 48 Jeshua son of Josedek and his fellow-priests, and Zerubbabel son of Salathiel and his colleagues set to work and made ready the altar of the God of Israel, 49 in order to offer on it whole-offerings as prescribed in the book of Moses, the man of God. 50 Other peoples of the land joined them, and they succeeded in setting up the altar on the original site; for in general the peoples in the land were hostile and too strong for them. Then they offered to the Lord sacrifices at the proper time and whole-offerings morning and evening. 51 They celebrated the feast of Tabernacles as decreed in the law, with the appropriate sacrifices each day, 52 and thereafter the regular offerings, and sacrifices on sabbaths, at new moons, and on all solemn feasts. 53 From the new moon of the seventh month, whoever had made a vow to God offered sacrifices to him, although the temple of God was not yet built. 54-55 Money was given to the stonemasons and carpenters; the Sidonians and Tyrians were supplied with food and drink, and with carts to bring cedar trees from the Lebanon, floating them down as rafts to the roadstead at Joppa. This was done on the written instructions of King Cyrus of Persia.

56 In the second month of the second year, Zerubbabel son of Salathiel came to the tem-

5:40 the governor: prob. mng (cp. Ezra 2:63); Gk and Attharias.

The priestly divisions here number four, but twenty-four in 1 Chr. 24.7–19. **40:** *Nehemiah the governor:* the name here (and in Neh. 8.9) is a late insertion, for it is missing from Ezra 2.1–70 and Neh. 7.6–73; see 9.49 n. *Revelation and Truth:* probably a rendering of Heb. "Urim" and "Thummim" (Exod. 28.30).

5.47–73: The setting up of the altar and the attempted construction of the temple; parallel to Ezra 3.1–4.5. In Ezra we read only of the foundation of the temple, whereas here there is apparently a more extensive effort, indeed, the construction of the entire edifice. **47:** *The seventh month:* Tishri (September–October). **51:** *The feast of Tabernacles as decreed in the law:* Lev. 23.33–43. *The appropriate sacrifices each day:* Num. 29.12–38. **52:** *The regular offerings . . . sabbaths . . . new moons . . . solemn feasts* follow the sequence of Num. 28.1–29.11. **56:** *The second month:* Iyyar (April–May).

ple of God in Jerusalem and began the work. There were with him Jeshua son of Josedek, their kinsmen, the levitical priests, and all who had returned to Jerusalem from captivity; 57 and they laid the foundation of the temple of God. This was at the new moon, in the second month of the second year after the return to Judaea and Jerusalem. 58 Levites who were aged twenty and upwards were appointed to supervise the works of the Lord. Jeshua, his sons and his kinsmen, his brother Cadoel, the sons of Jeshua Emadabun, and the sons of Joda son of Iliadun with their sons and kinsmen, all the Levites who were supervising co-operated in the work on the house of God.

While the builders built the Lord's temple, 59 the priests in their vestments with musical instruments and trumpets, and the Levites the sons of Asaph with their cymbals, took their places 60 singing to the Lord and praising him in the manner prescribed by King David of Israel. 61 They sang psalms in praise of the Lord, 'for his goodness and glory towards all Israel endures for ever'. 62 The people all sounded their trumpets and raised a great shout, and they sang to the Lord as the building rose.

63 But those of the priests, Levites, and heads of families who were old enough to have seen the former house came to the building of this house with cries of lamentation. 64 Though many were shouting and sounding the trumpets loudly for joy — 65 so loudly as to be heard from afar — the people could not hear the trumpets for the noise of lamentation.

66 The enemies of Judah and Benjamin heard the sound of the trumpets and came to see what it meant. 67 When they found the returned exiles rebuilding the temple for the Lord God of Israel, 68 they approached Zerubbabel and Jeshua and the heads of the families. 'We will build with you,' they said, 69 'for like you we obey your Lord and have sacrificed to him ever since the days of King Asbasareth of Assyria who brought us here.'

70 Zerubbabel, Jeshua, and the heads of the Israelite families replied: 'It is not for you to build the house for the Lord our God; 71 we alone shall build for the Lord of Israel, as King Cyrus of Persia commanded us.' 72 But the peoples of the land harassed and blockaded the men of Judaea, and interrupted the building. 73 By their plots, agitations, and riots they prevented its completion during the lifetime of King Cyrus. All building was held up for two years until Darius became king.

The temple rebuilt

6 IN the second year of the reign of Darius, the prophets Haggai and Zechariah son of Addo prophesied to the Jews in Judaea and Jerusalem, rebuking them in the name of the Lord God of Israel. 2 Then Zerubbabel son of Salathiel and Jeshua son of Josedek, with the prophets of the Lord at their side to help them, began at once to rebuild the Lord's house in Jerusalem. 3 Immediately Sisinnes, the governor-general of Syria and Phoenicia, together with Sathrabuzanes and their colleagues, came to them and asked, 4 'Who has given you authority to rebuild this house, to put on the roof and complete the whole work? Who are the builders engaged on this?' 5 But thanks to the Lord who protected the returned exiles, the elders of the Jews 6 were not prevented from building until such time as Darius should be informed and instructions issued.

7 Here is a copy of the letter sent to Darius by Sisinnes, the governor-general of Syria and Phoenicia, with Sathrabuzanes and their colleagues the authorities in Syria and Phoenicia:

To King Darius.
   Greeting.
8 Be these matters fully known to our lord the king: we went to the province of Judaea and to Jerusalem, its city, and there we found the elders of the Jews returned

5:72 harassed: *prob. rdg; Gk obscure.*

69: Compare 2 Kgs. 17.24–41. The name *Asbasareth* is hopelessly corrupt; the attempt at emendation (e.g. to Esarhaddon) is arbitrary. 73: *For two years until Darius became king:* as at 2.16, the eight-year reign of Cambyses is ignored. Some scholars believe that two separate returns, one under Cyrus led by Sheshbazzar, and a second under Zerubbabel, have become merged.

6.1–7.15: Building continued, correspondence with Darius, completion of the work, parallel to Ezra 5.1–6.22. 1: See Hag. 1.1–4; 2.1–4; Zech. 4.9; 6.15. Zechariah 1.1 reads "Zechariah son of Berechiah, son of Iddo." 2: *Jeshua* is the same as Joshua. 7: *Sisinnes* and *Sathrabuzanes* are Grecianized from Tattenai and from exile [9] building a great new house for their Lord with costly hewn stone and with beams set in the walls. [10] This work was carried on with all speed and the undertaking was making rapid headway under their direction; it was being executed in great splendour and with the utmost care. [11] We then enquired of these elders by whose authority they were building this house and laying such foundations. [12] We questioned them so that we could write and inform you who their leaders were, and we asked for a list of those in charge. [13] Their reply to us was: 'We are servants of the Lord who made heaven and earth. [14] This house was built and completed many years ago by a great and powerful king of Israel. [15] But when our fathers by their sin provoked the heavenly Lord of Israel to anger, he delivered them into the power of the Chaldaean monarch, King Nebuchadnezzar of Babylon. [16] The house was demolished and set on fire, and the people carried away captive to Babylon.

[17] 'But King Cyrus in the first year of his reign over Babylonia issued a decree that the house should be rebuilt. [18] He brought out again from the temple in Babylon the sacred vessels of gold and silver which Nebuchadnezzar had taken from the house at Jerusalem and set up in his own temple, and he handed them over to Zerubbabel and Sanabassar the governor, [19] with orders to take them all and restore them to the temple at Jerusalem, and to rebuild this temple of the Lord on its original site. [20] Then Sanabassar came and laid the foundations of the house of the Lord in Jerusalem; and from that time until now the rebuilding has continued and is still not completed.'

[21] Now, therefore, if it please your majesty, let search be made in the Babylonian royal archives, [22] and if it is found that the building of the Lord's house in Jerusalem was done with the approval of King Cyrus, and if our lord the king should so decide, let directions be issued to us on this matter.

[23] King Darius ordered search to be made in the archives deposited in Babylonia, and there was found in the citadel at Ecbatana in the province of Media a scroll containing the following memorandum:

[24] In the first year of his reign King Cyrus gave orders for the rebuilding of the Lord's house at Jerusalem, where they sacrifice with perpetual fire. [25] Its height was to be sixty cubits and its breadth sixty cubits, with three courses of hewn stone to one of new local timber, the cost to be defrayed from the royal treasury. [26] The sacred vessels, both gold and silver, which Nebuchadnezzar carried away from the house of the Lord at Jerusalem and brought to Babylon, were to be restored to the house in Jerusalem and placed where they had been in former times.

[27] Then Darius instructed Sisinnes, the governor-general of Syria and Phoenicia, with Sathrabuzanes, their colleagues, and the governors in office in Syria and Phoenicia, that they should see to it that the place was left unmolested and that the Lord's servant, Zerubbabel, governor of Judaea, and the elders of the Jews should be free to rebuild the house of the Lord on its original site. [28] 'I have also issued instructions', he went on, 'that it should be completely rebuilt, and that every effort be made to co-operate with the returned exiles in Judaea until the house of the Lord is finished. [29] From the tribute of Coele-Syria and Phoenicia a sufficient grant, payable to Zerubbabel the governor, is to be given to these men for sacrifices to the Lord, for bulls, rams, and lambs. [30] Similarly wheat, salt, wine, and olive oil as the priests in Jerusalem require to meet the needs of each day are to be provided regularly every year without question. [31] Let all this be expended in order that sacrifices and libations may be offered to the Most High God and intercession made for the king and his children.'

[32] Darius further decreed: 'If anyone contravenes or fails to observe anything written herein, let a beam be taken from his own house and let him be hanged on it, and his property shall be forfeit to the king. [33] May the Lord himself, therefore, whose name is invoked in this temple, utterly destroy any king or people who lifts a finger to delay the work or damage the Lord's house in Jerusa-

Shethar-bozenai (Ezra 5.3). The "letter" (vv. 8–22) is one of bureaucratic inquiry rather than hostility. **14:** *King:* Solomon. **18:** *Zerubbabel,* not mentioned in Ezra 5.14, is probably an addition. **19–20:** *Sanabassar:* see 2.12, 15 n. **23:** On *Ecbatana,* see Ezra 6.2 n. **32:** Contrast Ezra 6.11.

lem. ³⁴ I, Darius, the king, have directed that these decrees shall be strictly obeyed.'

7 Then, in compliance with the orders of King Darius, Sisinnes, governor-general of Coele-Syria and Phoenicia, with Sathrabuzanes and their colleagues, ² carefully supervised the sacred works, co-operating with the elders of the Jews and the temple officers. ³ Good progress was made with the sacred works, as the result of the prophecies of Haggai and Zechariah, ⁴ and they were finished as commanded by the Lord God of Israel and with the approval of Cyrus and Darius; ⁵ and the house was completed on the twenty-third of the month of Adar in the sixth year of King Darius.

⁶ The Israelites, priests, Levites, and the rest of the former exiles who had joined them carried out the directions in the book of Moses. ⁷ At the rededication of the temple of the Lord they offered one hundred bulls, two hundred rams, four hundred lambs, ⁸ and as a purification-offering for all Israel twelve he-goats corresponding to the number of the patriarchs of Israel. ⁹ The priests and the Levites robed in their vestments stood family by family to preside over the services of the Lord God of Israel according to the book of Moses, while the door-keepers were stationed at every gateway.

¹⁰ On the fourteenth day of the first month the Israelites who had returned from exile celebrated the Passover. The priests and the Levites were purified together; ¹¹ not all the returned exiles were purified with the priests, but the Levites were. ¹² They sacrificed the Passover victims for all the returned exiles, for their kinsmen the priests, and for themselves. ¹³ They were eaten by the Israelites who had returned from exile, and by all who had held aloof from the abominations of the peoples of the land and remained faithful to the Lord. ¹⁴ They celebrated the feast of Unleavened Bread for seven days, rejoicing before the Lord, ¹⁵ because he had changed the policy of the Assyrian king to-

wards them so that he supported them in their work for the Lord God of Israel.

Ezra in Jerusalem

8 It was after these events, when Artaxerxes was king of Persia, that Ezra came. He was the son of Saraeas son of Ezerias, son of Chelkias, son of Salemus, ² son of Zadok, son of Ahitub, son of Amarias, son of Ezias, son of Mareroth, son of Zaraeas, son of Savia, son of Bocca, son of Abishua, son of Phineas, son of Eleazar, son of Aaron the chief priest. ³ Ezra had come up from Babylon. He was a scribe expert in the law of Moses that had been given by the God of Israel. ⁴ The king held him in high regard and looked with favour on all the requests he made.

⁵ He was accompanied to Jerusalem by a number of Israelites, priests, Levites, temple singers, door-keepers, and temple servitors ⁶ in the fifth month of the seventh year of Artaxerxes' reign. They left Babylon at the new moon in the first month and reached Jerusalem at the new moon in the fifth month, for the Lord gave them a good journey. ⁷ Ezra's knowledge of the law of the Lord and the commandments was full and exact, so that he was able to instruct all Israel in all the ordinances and judgements.

⁸ The following is a copy of the mandate from King Artaxerxes to Ezra the priest, doctor of the law of the Lord:

⁹ King Artaxerxes to Ezra the priest, doctor of the law of the Lord.

Greeting.

¹⁰ I have graciously decided, and now command, that throughout our kingdom any of the Jewish nation and of the priests and Levites who so desire, may go with you

---

7:8 **purification-offering:** or sin-offering.   7:11 **not all . . . but:** *prob. rdg; Gk obscure; some witnesses omit* not. 8:2 **son of Mareroth . . . Savia:** *some MSS omit.*

7.2: *Carefully supervised . . . co-operating:* Ezra 6.13 depicts less enthusiasm, stating that the officials "carried out to the letter" their instructions. **5:** *The sixth year of Darius* was 516 B.C.E. **8:** Twelve *patriarchs:* Ezra 6.17 reads "tribes." **13:** Only those *who had returned from exile* celebrated, in contrast with Ezra 6.21, where "all who had held aloof from the peoples" are included. See also Neh. 9.2; 10.28. **15:** *Assyrian king* is not meant to be taken literally; it merely denotes an emperor from beyond the Euphrates.

8.1–9.55: The story of Ezra (Ezra 7.1–10.44; Neh. 7.73–8.12). Nehemiah is ignored. **1–67:** Ezra's return to Jerusalem, parallel to Ezra 7.1–8.36. **1:** *Artaxerxes* I reigned from 464–424 B.C.E. However, this is probably Artaxerxes II (404–359 B.C.E.). **6:** *The fifth month* was Ab (July–August), *the first month* was Nisan to Jerusalem. [11] I and my council of seven Friends have decreed that all who so choose may accompany you. [12] They are to consider the situation in Judaea and Jerusalem with regard to the law of the Lord. [13] They shall convey to Jerusalem for Israel's Lord the gifts which I and my Friends have vowed, together with all the gold and silver in Babylonia that may be found to belong to the Lord, [14] and the gifts provided by the nation for the temple of their Lord at Jerusalem. Let the gold and silver be expended on the purchase of bulls, rams, lambs, and the like, [15] so that sacrifices may be offered on the altar of their Lord in Jerusalem. [16] In whatever ways you and your colleagues may wish to use the gold and silver, let it be done in accordance with the will of your God. [17] You are to deliver the sacred vessels of the Lord which have been handed over for the service of the temple of your God in Jerusalem.

[18] Any other expenses you may incur for the needs of the temple of your God you shall defray from the royal treasury.

[19] I, Artaxerxes the king, hereby direct the treasurers of Syria and Phoenicia to supply exactly to Ezra the priest, doctor of the law of the Most High God, whatever he may request [20] up to one hundred talents of silver, and similarly up to one hundred sacks of wheat and one hundred casks of wine, and salt without limit. [21] Let all the requirements of God's law be diligently fulfilled in honour of the Most High God; otherwise wrath may befall the realm of the king and his sons. [22] You are also informed that no tribute or other impost is to be exacted from the priests, the Levites, the temple singers, the door-keepers, the temple servitors, or the lay officers of this temple; no one is authorized to impose any levy on them.

[23] Under the wise guidance of God you, Ezra, are to appoint judges and magistrates throughout Syria and Phoenicia to administer justice for all who acknowledge the law of your God; you must instruct those who do not know it. [24] Whoever transgresses the law of your God or the law of the king shall be duly punished, whether he be put to death or sentenced to a fine or imprisonment.

[25] Then Ezra the scribe said, 'Blessed is the Lord and he alone! He put this into the king's mind, to glorify his house in Jerusalem, [26] and has singled me out for honour in the eyes of the king and his counsellors, all his Friends and courtiers.

[27] 'Encouraged by the help of the Lord my God, I gathered men of Israel to go up with me. [28] These are the leaders according to families and divisions who went up with me from Babylon in the reign of King Artaxerxes: [29] from the line of Phineas, Gershom; from the line of Ithamar, Gamael; from the line of David, Attus son of Sechenias; [30] from the line of Phoros, Zacharias and with him a hundred and fifty men according to the register; [31] from the line of Phaath-moab, Eliaonias son of Zaraeas and with him two hundred men; [32] from the line of Zathoe, Sechenias son of Jezelus and with him three hundred men; from the line of Adin, Obeth son of Jonathan and with him two hundred and fifty men; [33] from the line of Elam, Jessias son of Gotholias and with him seventy men; [34] from the line of Saphatias, Zaraeas son of Michael and with him seventy men; [35] from the line of Joab, Abadias son of Jezelus and with him two hundred and twelve men; [36] from the line of Banias, Salimoth son of Josaphias and with him a hundred and sixty men; [37] from the line of Babi, Zacharias son of Bebae and with him twenty-eight men; [38] from the line of Astath, Joannes son of Hacatan and with him a hundred and ten men; [39] last came those from the line of Adonikam, by name Eliphalatus, Jeuel, and Samaeas, and with them seventy men; [40] from the line of Bago, Uthi son of Istalcurus and with him seventy men.

[41] 'I assembled them by the river Theras, and we encamped there for three days. I checked them, [42] and finding no one there who was a priest or a Levite, [43] I sent to Eleazar, Iduelus, Maasmas, [44] Elnathan, Samaeas, Joribus, Nathan, Ennatas, Zacharias, and Mosollamus, who were prominent and discerning men, [45] and instructed them to go to

(March–April). **41, 61**: *Theras*: Ezra 8.21, 31 reads "Ahava"; neither name can be identified, nor the location ascertained. **42**: *Levite*: Ezra 8.15, in contrast, speaks of their absence among the people and the priests. Perhaps the Ezra version makes better sense; we can assume that the priests were anxious to return to resume their cultic

Addaeus, the head of the treasury in the district. 46 I told them to speak with Addaeus and his colleagues and fellow-treasurers, asking that men should be sent to us to officiate in the house of our Lord. 47 Under the providence of our Lord they sent us discerning men from the line of Mooli son of Levi, son of Israel, Asebebias and his sons and brothers, eighteen men in all, 48 and Asebias and Annunus and his brother Hosaeas. Those of the line of Chanunaeus and their sons amounted to twenty men; 49 and those of the temple servitors whom David and the leading men appointed for the service of the Levites amounted to two hundred and twenty. A register of all those names was compiled.

50 'I made a vow there that the young men should fast before our Lord and ask from him a prosperous journey for ourselves, our children who accompanied us, and our pack-animals. 51 I was ashamed to apply to the king for an escort of infantry and cavalry to protect us against our enemies, 52 for we had told him that the might of our Lord would ensure a successful outcome for those who looked to him. 53 So once more we laid all these things before our Lord in prayer and found him gracious.

54 'Then I set apart twelve men from among the chiefs of the priestly families, Sarabias and Asamias and with them ten of their kinsmen. 55 I weighed out for them the silver and gold, and the sacred vessels for the house of our Lord which had been presented by the king, by his counsellors and courtiers, and by all Israel. 56 After weighing it, I handed over to them six hundred and fifty talents of silver, and silver vessels weighing a hundred talents, a hundred talents of gold, 57 and twenty gold dishes, and twelve vessels made of bronze so fine that it gleamed like gold. 58 I said, "Just as you are consecrated to the Lord, so too are the vessels; the silver and the gold are vowed to the Lord, the Lord of our fathers. 59 Guard them with all vigilance until you hand them over at Jerusalem, in the priests' rooms in the house of our Lord, to the chiefs of the priestly and levitical families and to the leaders of the clans of Israel." 60 The priests and the Levites who had custody of the silver, the gold, and the vessels which had been in Jerusalem brought them to the temple of the Lord.

61 'On the twelfth day of the first month we struck camp at the river Theras and, under the powerful protection afforded by our Lord, who saved us from every enemy attack on the way, we reached Jerusalem. 62 On our fourth day there, the silver and gold were weighed and handed over in the house of our Lord to the priest Marmathi son of Uri, 63 with whom was Eleazar son of Phineas; present with them were the Levites Josabdus son of Jeshua and Moeth son of Sabannus. Everything was counted and weighed, 64 and every weight recorded then and there.

65 'Those who had returned from captivity offered sacrifices to the Lord, the God of Israel: twelve bulls for all Israel, with ninety-six rams 66 and seventy-two lambs, and also twelve goats for a shared-offering, the whole as a sacrifice to the Lord. 67 They delivered the king's orders to the royal treasurers and the governors of Coele-Syria and Phoenicia, thereby adding lustre to the nation and the temple of the Lord.

68 'ONCE this business was concluded, the leaders came to me and said: 69 "The people of Israel, including even the rulers, priests, and Levites, have not kept themselves apart from the alien population of the land with all their unclean practices, that is to say the Canaanites, Hittites, Perizzites, Jebusites, Moabites, Egyptians, and Edomites. 70 Both they and their sons have intermarried with the women of these peoples, so that the holy race has become mixed with the alien population of the land. From the very beginning, the leaders and principal men have shared in this violation of the law."

71 'At this news I rent my clothes and sacred vestment, I tore my hair and beard and sat appalled and grieving. 72 All who were moved by the word of the Lord of Israel gathered round me, and I sat grief-stricken over this failure to observe the law; and I sat in grief until the evening sacrifice. 73 Then with my clothes and sacred vestment torn I rose from my fast and, kneeling down, held out my hands in supplication to the Lord. 74 "O Lord," I said, "I am covered with shame

duties in Jerusalem, whereas the subordinate Levites were less eager to leave their comforts in Babylonia. **51:** *I was ashamed*: contrast Neh. 2.7–9 for a different response in a similar situation.

8.68–9.36: The problem of mixed marriages; parallel to Ezra 9.1–10.44. **69:** *Unclean practices:* customs and confusion in your presence. 75 Our sins tower above us and our offences have reached high heaven 76 ever since the time of our forefathers; and today we are as deep in sin as ever. 77 Because of our sins and the sins of our forefathers, we, together with our brothers, our kings, and our priests, have been given into the power of the earthly rulers to be killed, taken captive, pillaged, and humiliated, down to this very day. 78 Yet even now, Lord, how great is your mercy! For we still have a root and a name in this your holy place. 79 Our light has been rekindled in the house of our Lord, and we have been given sustenance in the time of our enslavement. 80 Even when we were slaves we were not forsaken by our Lord, but he secured for us the favour of the kings of Persia: they have provided our sustenance 81 and added lustre to the temple of our Lord and restored the ruins of Zion, establishing us securely in Judaea and Jerusalem.

82 ' "Now, Lord, in the face of this, what are we to say? For we have broken your commandments given through your servants the prophets. You said: 83 'The land which you are going to occupy is a land defiled with the pollution of its heathen population; they have filled it with their impure ways. 84 Now therefore do not marry your daughters to their sons or take their daughters for your sons; 85 nor must you ever seek to be at peace with them. Only thus will you be strong and enjoy the good things of the land, and hand it on as an everlasting possession to your descendants.' 86 It is our evil deeds and great sins which have brought all our misfortunes on us. Although you, Lord, have lightened the burden of our sins 87 and given us firm roots in the land, yet we have fallen away again and broken your law by sharing in the impurity of the peoples of this land. 88 But you were not so angry with us as to destroy us, root, stock, and name. 89 O Lord of Israel, you are just; for we today are a root that is left. 90 In all our sin we are here before you; because of it we can no longer stand in your presence." '

91 While Ezra was praying and making confession, prostrate in tears before the temple, there gathered round him a vast throng from Jerusalem, men, women, and children, and there was widespread lamentation among the crowd. 92 One of the Israelites, Jechonias son of Jehiel, spoke up and said to Ezra: 'We have sinned against the Lord in taking foreign wives from the peoples of the land; yet there is still hope for Israel. 93 In this matter let us promise on oath to the Lord to get rid of our wives of foreign race together with their children, 94 in keeping with your judgement and the judgement of all who are obedient to the law of the Lord. 95 Get up and see to it; the matter is in your hands. Take strong action and we are with you!' 96 Ezra stood up and put the chiefs of the priestly and levitical families of all Israel on oath to act in this way.

9 Ezra then left the forecourt of the temple and went to the room of the priest Joanan grandson of Eliasib, 2 and there he stayed, eating no bread and drinking no water, for he was still mourning over the people's flagrant violations of the law. 3 A proclamation was issued throughout Judaea and Jerusalem that all the returned exiles were to assemble at Jerusalem. 4 If any failed to arrive within two or three days, as decided by the elders in office, they were to have their cattle confiscated for temple use and would themselves be excluded from the community of the exiles.

5 Three days later — it was the twentieth day of the ninth month — the men of Judah and Benjamin had assembled in Jerusalem, 6 where they all sat together in the broad space before the temple, shivering because winter had set in. 7 Ezra stood up and addressed them: 'In marrying foreign women you have broken the law and added to Israel's guilt. 8 Now acknowledge the majesty of the Lord God of our fathers: 9 do his will and cut yourselves off from the peoples of the land and from your foreign wives.'

10 The whole company assented loudly, 'We will do as you say! 11 But', they added, 'our numbers are great; it is the rainy season and we cannot stay out in the open. Besides, this is not the work of one or two days only, for the offence is rife amongst us. 12 Let the leaders of the community remain here, and let all members of our settlements who have foreign wives present themselves at a stated

viewed as idolatrous; see vv. 82–85 n. **82–85:** *You said:* the quotation is not found in Scripture, but Lev. 18.19–30, dealing with similar practices, contains like language. **9.1:** *Joanan* was actually the grandson of *Eliasib.* **5:** *The twentieth day of the ninth month:* Kislev (November–December). **6:** *Winter had set in:* Ezra time [13] accompanied by the elders and judges for each place, until the Lord's anger at what has been done is averted from us.' [14] Jonathan son of Azael and Hezekias son of Thocanus took charge on these terms, and Mosollamus, Levi, and Sabbataeus were their assessors.

[15] The returned exiles duly put all this into effect. [16] Ezra the priest selected, each by name, certain men, chiefs of their clans. They met in session to investigate the matter at the new moon in the tenth month, [17] and by the new moon of the first month the affair of the men who had taken foreign wives was brought to a conclusion.

[18] Among the priests, some of those who had come together were found to have married foreign women: [19] namely Mathelas, Eleazar, Joribus, and Joadanus of the line of Jeshua son of Josedek and his brothers. [20] They pledged themselves to dismiss their wives and to offer rams in expiation of their offence. [21] Of the line of Emmer: Ananias, Zabdaeus, Manes, Samaeus, Jereel, and Azarias; [22] of the line of Phaesus: Elionas, Massias, Ishmael, Nathanael, Okidelus, and Saloas. [23] Of the Levites: Jozabadus, Semis, Colius (this is Calitas), Phathaeus, Judah, and Jonas. [24] Of the temple singers: Eliasibus, Bacchurus. [25] Of the door-keepers: Sallumus and Tolbanes.

[26] Of the people of Israel there were, of the line of Phoros: Jermas, Jeddias, Melchias, Maelus, Eleazar, Asibias, and Bannaeas. [27] Of the line of Ela: Matthanias, Zacharias, Jezrielus, Oabdius, Jeremoth, and Aedias. [28] Of the line of Zamoth: Eliadas, Eliasimus, Othonias, Jarimoth, Sabathus, and Zardaeas. [29] Of the line of Bebae: Joannes, Ananias, Ozabadus, and Emathis. [30] Of the line of Mani: Olamus, Mamuchus, Jedaeus, Jasubus, Asaelus, and Jeremoth. [31] Of the line of Addi: Naathus, Moossias, Laccunus, Naidus, Matthanias, Sesthel, Balnuus, and Manasseas. [32] Of the line of Annas: Elionas, Asaeas, Melchias, Sabbaeas, and Simon Chosomaeus. [33] Of the line of Asom: Altannaeus, Matthias, Bannaeus, Eliphalat, Manasses, and Semi. [34] Of the line of Baani: Jeremias, Mom-

dis, Ismaerus, Juel, Mandae, Paedias, Anos, Carabasion, Enasibus, Mamnitanaemus, Eliasis, Bannus, Eliali, Somis, Selemias, and Nathanias. Of the line of Ezora: Sessis, Ezril, Azael, Samatus, Zambris, and Josephus. [35] Of the line of Nooma: Mazitias, Zabadaeas, Edaes, Juel, and Banaeas. [36] All these had married foreign women, whom they now dismissed together with their children.

[37] THE priests and Levites, with such Israelites as were in Jerusalem and its neighbourhood, settled down there. On the new moon of the seventh month, the other Israelites being now in their settlements, [38] the entire company assembled with one accord in the broad space in front of the east gateway of the temple precinct [39] and asked Ezra, priest and doctor of the law, to bring the law of Moses given by the Lord God of Israel. [40] At the new moon of the seventh month Ezra the high priest brought the law to the whole assembly, both men and women, and to all the priests, for them to hear it. [41] From daybreak until noon he read aloud from it in the square in front of the temple gateway, in the presence of both men and women, and all the company listened attentively to the law.

[42] Ezra, priest and doctor of the law, stood on the wooden platform which had been made for this purpose. [43] Beside him stood Mattathias, Sammus, Ananias, Azarias, Urias, Hezekias, and Baalsamus on his right, [44] and on his left Phaldaeus, Misael, Melchias, Lothasubus, Nabarias, and Zacharias. [45] Then in front of the whole assembly, for he was seated in a prominent place where everyone could see him, Ezra took up the book of the law, [46] and when he opened it they all stood. Ezra praised the Lord God, the Most High God of Hosts, the Almighty, [47] and all the people cried 'Amen, Amen.' They raised their hands and prostrated themselves in worship before the Lord. [48] Jeshua, Annus, Sarabias, Jadinus, Jacubus, Sabbataeas, Autaeas, Maeannas, Calitas, Azarias, Jozabdus, Ananias, and Phiathas, the Levites, taught the law of the Lord. They read the law of the Lord to the people, at the same time

---

10.9 mentions "heavy rain." **16:** *The tenth month* was Tebeth (December–January).

9.37–55: The reading of the law; parallel to Neh. 7.73–8.12. **37, 40:** *The new moon of the seventh month:* the first day of Tishri (September–October) was a day of "sacred assembly" (Lev. 23.24 and Num. 29.1), later called Rosh Hashanah, the New Year festival. **48:** *They read:* contrast v. 41, which states that Ezra *read it.* Apparently, the Levites relayed Ezra's words to those not within earshot, at the same time adding words of instilling into their minds the sense of what was read.

⁴⁹ The governor said to them all, to Ezra, high priest and doctor of the law, and to the Levites who taught the people: ⁵⁰ 'This day is holy to the Lord.' All were weeping as they listened to the law. ⁵¹ 'Go, therefore,' he continued, 'feast yourselves on rich food and sweet drinks, and send a share to those who have none, ⁵² for the day is holy to the Lord.

Let there be no sadness, for the Lord will give you glory.' ⁵³ The Levites enjoined the people: 'This day is holy; let there be no sadness.' ⁵⁴ So they all went away to eat and drink and make merry, and to distribute shares to those who had none. They held a great celebration, ⁵⁵ because the teaching given them had been instilled into their minds.

So they held their assembly.

9:49 **The governor:** *cp. 5:40; Gk* Attharates.

explanation and exhortation. **49:** The Heb. of Neh. 8.9 reads "Nehemiah the tirshata" (i.e. *governor*). Since the name Nehemiah is missing here, the name is probably a late insertion in Neh. 8.9 and in 1 Esd. 5.40. **51, 54:** The merriment and such phrases as *send a share to those who had none* are reminiscent of Esther 9.19 and 22, in connection with the Feast of Purim. **55:** The ending is so abrupt that it is believed that the continuation, probably paralleling Neh. 8.13–18 (or further), has been lost.

THE SECOND BOOK OF
Esdras

This book is known in the Vulgate as 4 Esdras. *Esdras* is the Greek form of the name *Ezra,* to whom the book is attributed. The Second Book of Esdras is distinctive in the Apocrypha as an apocalyptic book. "Apocalypse" means "unveiling"; and apocalyptic literature usually involves the disclosure of previously unknown truths about reality and the future in visions and highly symbolic language. In this literary genre, the author, under the pseudonym of a famous person of the past, describes events that are taking place in the author's own day. In this way consolation is offered to innocent sufferers by showing that what is happening is under God's Providence and that injustices will be reversed at the end of time, which is also described as revealed. For further information, see "Literary Forms of the Bible" (pp. *21–*22) and "The Apocalyptic Vision" (p. *181).

Second Esdras contains a core of seven visions (chs. 3–14). To these were added a prefix (chs. 1–2) and a suffix (chs. 15–16) which differ markedly in content. The core Jewish section was probably written in Judea in either Hebrew or Aramaic about 100 C.E.; the additions were written in Greek by Christian writers in the second and third centuries respectively.

A small fragment of the Greek has come down to us, but 2 Esdras survives only in ancient translations whose great number and variety reflect the popularity of the book in early centuries.

Echoing Old Testament Job and Habakkuk, the author of 2 Esdras dealt with the problem of human suffering. Though the work is particularly concerned with the fall of Jerusalem and the triumphs of the persecuting Roman Empire, the author also agonizes about the misery of human existence in general, finding some respite only in the conviction of restitution and reward in the world to come.

Roman Catholic tradition excludes 1 and 2 Esdras and the Prayer of Manasseh from its canon but accepts the rest of the Apocrypha.

Israel's rejection and glory to come

1 THE second book of the prophet Ezra son of Seraiah, son of Azariah, son of Hilkiah, son of Shallum, son of Zadok, son of Ahitub, ²son of Ahijah, son of Phinehas, son of Eli, son of Amariah, son of Aziah, son of Marimoth, son of Arna, son of Uzzi, son of Borith, son of Abishua, son of Phinehas, son of Eleazar, ³son of Aaron, of the tribe of Levi.

I, EZRA, was a captive in Media during the reign of King Artaxerxes of Persia ⁴when this word of the Lord came to me: ⁵Go to my people and proclaim their crimes; tell their children how they have sinned against me, and let them tell their children's children. ⁶My people have sinned even more than their fathers, for they have forgotten me and sacrificed to alien gods. ⁷Was it not I who brought them out of Egypt, out of the land where they were slaves? And yet they have aroused my anger and spurned my warnings.

⁸But it is for you, Ezra, to tear out your hair and to let every calamity loose on those

---

1.1–2.48: Israel's rejection and glory to come. Israel's past infidelity and its dire consequences are enumerated. God's fidelity is shown in a promised restoration.

1.1–3a: Ezra's lineage. The list varies slightly from Ezra 7.1–5 and 1 Esd. 8.1–2. **1:** *Ezra,* a priest and scribe in the OT (Ezra 7.11), is here termed a *prophet.*

1.3b–11: Ezra called to prophesy doom. 3: *Artaxerxes* II ruled from 404 to 359 B.C.E. **5:** *Proclaim their crimes:* make the people aware of their wickedness and condemn it; see Jer. 1.16. **8:** *Tear out your hair:* sign who have disobeyed my law. My people are beyond correction. 9 How much longer can I tolerate a people on whom I have lavished such great benefits? 10 Many are the kings I have overthrown for their sake; I struck down Pharaoh along with his court and his whole army. 11 Every nation that stood in their way I destroyed; in the east I routed the peoples of two provinces, Tyre and Sidon, and killed all Israel's enemies.

12 Say to them, 'These are the words of the Lord: 13 Was it not I who brought you through the sea, and made for you safe roads where no road had been? I gave you Moses as your leader, and Aaron as your priest; 14 I provided you with light from a pillar of fire; I performed great miracles among you. And yet you have forgotten me, says the Lord.

15–16 'These are the words of the Lord Almighty: The quails were a sign to you; I gave you a camp for your protection. Instead of celebrating the victory when I destroyed your enemies, all you did there was to grumble and complain, and from that day to this your complaints have never ceased. 17 Have you forgotten what benefits I conferred on you? When you were hungry and thirsty on your journey through the wilderness, you cried out: 18 "Why have you led us into this wilderness to kill us? Better for us to be slaves to the Egyptians than to perish here in this wilderness!" 19 Grieved at your complaints, I gave you manna for food; it was the bread of angels you were eating. 20 When you were thirsty, I split open the rock, and water flowed out in plenty. Against the summer heat I provided you with the shade of leafy trees. 21 I expelled those who opposed you, the Canaanites, Perizzites, and Philistines, and distributed their fertile lands among you. What more could I do for you? says the Lord.

22 'These are the words of the Lord Almighty: When you were in the wilderness, suffering thirst by the stream of bitter water

and cursing me, 23 I did not bring fire down on you for your blasphemy; instead I cast a log into the stream and made the water sweet. 24 Jacob, what am I to do with you? You have refused to obey me, Judah! I shall turn to other nations and give them my name, and they will keep my statutes. 25 Because you have forsaken me, I shall forsake you; when you implore me for mercy, I shall show you none; 26 when you pray to me, I shall not listen. You have stained your hands with blood; you hasten hotfoot to commit murder. 27 It is not that you have forsaken me: you have forsaken yourselves, says the Lord.

28 'These are the words of the Lord Almighty: Have I not pleaded with you as a father with his sons, as a mother with her daughters, or as a nursemaid with her children, 29 that you should be my people and I should be your God, that you should be my sons and I should be your father? 30 I gathered you as a hen gathers her brood under her wings. But now, what am I to do with you? I shall cast you out from my presence. 31 When you offer me sacrifice, I shall turn from you, for I have rejected your feasts, your new moons, and your circumcisions. 32 I sent my servants the prophets to you, but you took them and killed them and mutilated their bodies. For their murder I shall call you to account, says the Lord.

33 'These are the words of the Lord Almighty: Your house is forsaken. I shall toss you away like straw before the wind. 34 Your children will have no posterity, because like you they have ignored my commandments and done what I have condemned. 35 I shall hand over your homes to a people yet to come: a people who will trust me, though they have not known me; who will do my bidding, though I gave them no signs; 36 who never saw the prophets, and yet will keep in mind what the prophets taught of old. 37 I vow that this people yet to come shall have

of consternation and grief; see Ezra 9.3. **10:** *Pharaoh:* see Exod. 14.28. **11:** *Tyre* and *Sidon* were Phoenician cities, not provinces, to the west of Media and not *east;* Tyre was not destroyed until the time of Alexander (332 B.C.E.), which was after the reign of Artaxerxes.

1.12–21: God's past mercies recounted; these are events of the Exodus. **13:** See Exod. 14.29; 3.10; 28.1. **14:** See Exod. 13.21. **15:** See Exod. 16.13. **18:** See Num. 14.2–3. **19:** See Ps. 78.25. **20:** See Num. 20.11.

1.22–32: Israel to be rejected. 22–23: See Exod. 15.22–25. **24:** *I shall turn to other nations:* compare Matt. 21.43. Reflections of NT here show that the author of this preface was a Christian. **30–32:** Compare Matt. 23.34–37.

1.33–40: A new people replaces Israel. 35–37: *A people:* Gentile Christians; compare 1 Cor. 2.6–15.

my favour; their little ones will jump for joy, and though they themselves have not seen me with their eyes, they will perceive by the spirit and believe what I have said.'

38 Now, father Ezra, look with pride at the nation coming from the east. 39 The leaders I shall give them are Abraham, Isaac, and Jacob, Hosea and Amos, Micah and Joel, Obadiah and Jonah, 40 Nahum, Habakkuk, and Zephaniah, Haggai and Zechariah, and Malachi, who is also called the Lord's messenger.

2 These are the words of the Lord: I brought that people out of slavery and gave them commandments through my servants the prophets; but they shut their ears to the prophets, and allowed my precepts to become a dead letter. 2 The mother who bore them says: 'Go, my children; I am widowed and forsaken. 3 With joy I brought you up, but with mourning and sorrow I have lost you, because you have sinned against the Lord God and done what I have condemned. 4 But now, what can I do for you, widowed and forsaken as I am? Go, my children, ask the Lord for mercy.' 5 I call upon you, father Ezra, to add your testimony to hers that her children have refused to keep my covenant; 6 and let your words bring confusion on them. May their mother be despoiled, and may they themselves have no posterity. 7 Let them be dispersed among the nations and let their name vanish from the earth, because they have spurned my covenant.

8 Woe to you, Assyria, you harbourer of sinners! Remember, you evil nation, what I did to Sodom and Gomorrah: 9 their land lies buried under masses of pitch and heaps of ashes. So shall I deal with those who have disobeyed me, says the Lord Almighty.

10 These are the words of the Lord to Ezra: Tell my people that I shall give to them the kingdom of Jerusalem, which once I offered to Israel. 11 I shall also withdraw the splendour of my presence from Israel, and the home that was to be theirs for ever I shall give to my people. 12 The tree of life will spread its fragrance over them; they will neither toil nor grow weary. 13 Ask, and you will receive; pray that your short time of waiting may be cut shorter still. Even now the kingdom is ready for you; be vigilant! 14 I summon heaven and earth to witness: I have cancelled the evil and brought the good into being; for I am the Living One, says the Lord.

15 Mother, keep your children close to you. Rear them with gladness, as a dove rears her nestlings; teach them to walk without stumbling. You are my chosen one, says the Lord. 16 I shall raise up the dead from their resting-places and bring them out of their tombs, for I have acknowledged that they bear my name. 17 There is nothing to fear, mother of many children, for I have chosen you, says the Lord.

18 I shall send my servants Isaiah and Jeremiah to help you. As they prophesied, I have set you apart to be my people. I have made ready for you twelve trees laden with different kinds of fruit, 19 twelve fountains flowing with milk and honey, and seven great mountains covered with roses and lilies. There I shall fill your children with joy. 20 Champion the widow, defend the cause of the fatherless, give to the poor, protect the orphan, provide clothing for those who have none; 21 care for the weak and the helpless, and do not mock at the cripple; watch over the disabled, and bring the blind to the vision of my radiance. 22 Keep both old and young safe within your walls.

23 When you find the dead unburied, mark them with the sign and commit them to the tomb; and then, when I cause the dead to

---

38: *Father:* in rabbinic Judaism, Ezra is equated in eminence with both the ancestors and prophets.

2.1–9: God to destroy sinful Israel. 6: Jerusalem, Israel's *"mother city"* (see Ezek. ch. 16), was *despoiled* in 70 C.E. The writer views this as just retribution. **8:** *Assyria* probably stands for Rome. *Sodom:* see Gen. 19.24–25.

2.10–14: Israel's place given to others. 10: *My people:* the new people of 1.24, 35, 38. **12:** *Tree of life:* see Rev. 2.7 n.; 22.2, 14. **13:** *Ask:* compare Matt. 7.7. *Time of waiting:* Matt. 24.22. *Kingdom:* Matt. 25.34.

2.15–32: The new people exhorted. The church, addressed as *mother* (contrast 2.6), is admonished to good works (vv. 20–25) and patient endurance (vv. 26–32). **18:** *Send . . . Isaiah and Jeremiah:* compare 1.39–40. *As they prophesied:* see Isa. 65.1. *Twelve trees:* possibly an allusion to the twelve apostles. **19:** *Seven great mountains:* seven deacons of the early church; compare Acts 6.1–6. **23:** To bury the *dead* was an act of piety; *the sign* was possibly a Christian symbol which identified the dead person as belonging to God's protected rise, I shall give you the chief place. 24 Be calm, my people; your time of rest will come. 25 Be a good nursemaid to your children, and teach them to walk without stumbling. 26 Of servants whom I have given you, not one will be lost; I shall look for them from among your number. 27 Do not be anxious when the time of trouble and hardship comes; others will lament and be sad, but you will have happiness and plenty. 28 Though you become the envy of the nations, they will be powerless against you, says the Lord.

29 My power will protect you, and save your children from hell. 30 Be joyful, mother, you and your children, for I shall come to your rescue. 31 Remember your children who sleep in the grave; I shall bring them up from the depths of the earth, and show mercy to them; for I am merciful, says the Lord Almighty. 32 Keep your children close to you until I come; proclaim my mercy to them, for my grace which flows from gushing springs will never run dry.

33 I, EZRA, received on Mount Horeb a commission from the Lord to go to Israel; but when I came to them, they spurned me and rejected the Lord's command. 34 Therefore I say to you Gentiles, who hear and understand: 'Look forward to the coming of your shepherd; he who is to come at the end of the world is close at hand, and he will give you everlasting rest. 35 Be ready to receive the rewards of the kingdom, for light perpetual will shine on you throughout all time. 36 Flee from the shadow of this world, and receive the joy and splendour that await you. I bear witness openly to my Saviour. 37 It is he whom the Lord has appointed; receive him and be joyful, giving thanks to the One who has called you to the heavenly realms. 38 Arise, stand up and see the whole company of those who bear the Lord's mark and sit at his banquet. 39 They have moved out of the shadow of this world and have received shining robes from the Lord. 40 Take your full number, O Zion, and close the roll of those arrayed in white who have faithfully kept the law of the Lord. 41 The number of your children whom you so long desired is now complete. Pray that the Lord's kingdom may come, so that your people, whom he called when the world began, may be set apart as his own.'

42 I, Ezra, saw on Mount Zion a throng too vast to count, all singing hymns of praise to the Lord. 43 In the middle stood a young man. He was very tall, taller than any of the others, and was setting a crown on the head of each one of them; he towered above them all. Enthralled at the sight, 44 I asked the angel, 'My lord, who are these?' 45 He replied, 'They are those who have laid aside their mortal dress and put on the immortal, those who acknowledged the name of God. Now they are being given crowns and palms.' 46 I asked again, 'Who is the young man setting the crowns on their heads and giving them the palms?' 47 The angel replied, 'He is the Son of God, whom they acknowledged in this mortal life.' I began to praise those who had stood so valiantly for the Lord's name. 48 Then the angel said to me: 'Go and tell my people the many great and wonderful acts of the Lord God that you have seen.'

Ezra's first vision

3 IN the thirtieth year after the fall of Jerusalem, I, Salathiel (who am also Ezra), was in Babylon. Lying on my bed I was trou-

"people" (v. 38); see Rev. 14.1. **29:** *Hell:* lit. Gehenna, place of torment; compare Mk. 9.42–48.
　　2.33–48: Ezra turns to Gentiles, envisioning a faithful multitude. This is the most overtly Christian section of the book. **33:** Ezra receives his *commission* as the leader of the "new people of God" at *Mount Horeb* where Moses was called; see Exod. 3.1–12. **34:** The early Christians believed that *the end of the world* and the second coming of Jesus were *close at hand;* see 1 Thess. 4.15–18; 2 Thess. 2.1–2. **36:** The *shadow of this world* is the aspect of the world that passes away or changes; compare 1 Cor. 7.29–31; 1 Jn. 2.15–17. **38:** To *sit at his banquet* may be a symbol for accepting Christianity (Lk. 14.15–24; Rev. 19.9) or for the Eucharist (see 1 Cor. 10.21; 11.17–32). **40–41:** The *full number* of the righteous is regarded as determined by God. See 4.36–37 and compare Rev. 6.11. **42:** *On Mount Zion:* compare Heb. 12.22–23. *A throng . . . singing:* compare Rev. 7.9–12.
　　3.1–5.19: Vision I. 1–36: A difficult question is raised in these verses. Why does God allow Israel to suffer at the hands of a more wicked people? The writer prefaces the question by a survey of history stressing the origin of sin and the election of Israel. **1:** Mention of the *thirtieth year* after the destruction of Jerusalem by

bled and my mind filled with perplexity ²as I reflected on the desolation of Zion and the prosperity of those who lived in Babylon. ³I was deeply disturbed in spirit, and full of fear I addressed the Most High. ⁴'My Master and Lord,' I said, 'was it not you alone who in the beginning spoke the word that formed the world? At your command the dust ⁵brought forth Adam. His body was lifeless; yours were the hands that had moulded it, and you breathed the breath of life into it and he became a living person. ⁶You led him into paradise, which you yourself had planted before the earth came into being. ⁷You gave him your one commandment to obey; and when he disobeyed it, you made both him and his descendants subject to death.

'From him there sprang nations and tribes, peoples and families, too numerous to count. ⁸Each nation went its own way, sinning against you and treating you with scorn, and you did not stop them. ⁹Then, in course of time, you brought the flood upon the inhabitants of the earth and destroyed them. ¹⁰The same fate came upon all: death upon Adam, and the flood upon that generation. ¹¹But one man, Noah, you spared, together with his household and all the righteous descended from him.

¹²'The population of the earth expanded; families and peoples increased, nation upon nation. But once again they began to sin, more wickedly than those before them. ¹³When they sinned, you chose for yourself one of them; Abraham was his name. ¹⁴Him you loved, and to him alone, secretly at dead of night, you disclosed how the world would end. ¹⁵You made an everlasting covenant with him and promised never to abandon his descendants. ¹⁶You gave him Isaac, and to

Isaac you gave Jacob and Esau; of these you chose Jacob for yourself, and he grew to be a great nation; but Esau you rejected.

¹⁷'You rescued Jacob's descendants from Egypt and led them to Mount Sinai. ¹⁸There you made the heavens bow down, shook the earth, moved the world; you made the depths shudder and convulsed the whole creation. ¹⁹Your glory passed through the four gates of fire and earthquake, wind and frost, in order to give the commandments of the law to the Israelites, the race of Jacob. ²⁰But you did not take away their evil heart and thus enable your law to bear fruit in them; ²¹for the first man, Adam, burdened as he was with an evil heart, sinned and was overcome, and not only he but all who were descended from him. ²²So the weakness became inveterate, and although your law was in your people's hearts, a rooted wickedness was there too; thus the good came to nothing, and what was evil persisted.

²³'Years went by, and when the time came you raised up for yourself a servant, whose name was David. ²⁴You instructed him to build the city that bears your name and to offer to you there in sacrifice what was already your own. ²⁵This was done for many years, until the inhabitants of the city went astray, ²⁶behaving just like Adam and all his line; for they had the same evil heart. ²⁷And so you handed over your city into the power of your enemies.

²⁸'I had thought that perhaps those in Babylon lead better lives, and that is why Zion is in subjection. ²⁹But when I arrived here, I saw wickedness beyond reckoning, and with my own eyes I have seen evildoers in great numbers these thirty years. My heart sank ³⁰because I observed how you tolerate sin-

Nebuchadnezzar, i.e. 557/556 B.C.E. (see Jer. 52.4–11; compare Ezek. 1.1), may suggest that the book was written thirty years after the fall of Jerusalem to the Romans in 70 C.E. *Salathiel* is the Gk. form of Shealtiel, oldest son of King Jehoiachin and father of Zerubbabel (1 Chr. 3.17; Ezra 3.2). *Ezra* flourished a century after Shealtiel; the erroneous identification of the two may be an interpolation. **4–7:** Genesis chs. 1–3. According to rabbinic tradition, *paradise* was created before the *earth*. **7:** That Adam's sin made *him and his descendants subject to death* became heightened into the doctrine of "original sin." The view here is the earliest recording in Jewish literature; see vv. 20–22 for a fuller statement. **15:** The author stresses that God made *an everlasting covenant* with a representative of the fallen race, Abraham; see Gen. 15.18; 17.2–8. **19:** Speaking of God's appearance at Sinai (see Exod. 19.16–18; Ps. 68.7–8), the writer identifies *fire and earthquake, wind and frost* as *four gates* of heavenly regions, perhaps the gates of the four lowest of the "seven heavens" known in Jewish tradition. **20:** The *evil heart* is the rabbinical "evil yeṣer" or "evil inclination," considered, like its counterpart, the "good yeṣer," to be implanted in every person. That God had given Israel a law, but had not removed the evil nature inherited from Adam, the obstacle to its obedience, adds a new dimension to the writer's troubling ners and spare the godless, how you have destroyed your own people but preserved your enemies. You have given no indication [31] to anyone how your ways are to be understood. Is Babylon more virtuous than Zion? [32] Has any nation except Israel ever known you? What tribes have put their trust in your covenants as have the tribes of Jacob? [33] But they have seen no reward, no fruit for their labours. I have travelled far and wide among the nations and have seen how they prosper, heedless though they are of your commandments. [34] Now weigh our sins in the balance, therefore, against the sins of the rest of the world, and it will be clear which way the scale tips. [35] Has there ever been a time when the inhabitants of the earth did not sin against you? Has any nation ever kept your commandments like Israel? [36] You may indeed find a few individuals here and there who have done so, but nowhere a whole nation.'

4 Uriel, the angel who was sent to me, replied: [2] 'You are completely at a loss to understand this world; can you then expect to understand the way of the Most High?' [3] 'Yes, my lord,' I said.

'I have been sent', he continued, 'to propound to you three of the ways of this world, to give you three illustrations; [4] if you can explain to me any one of them, I shall show to you the way that you long to see and teach you why the heart is evil.'

[5] 'Speak on, my lord,' I said. 'Come then, weigh me a pound of fire,' he said, 'or measure me a bushel of wind, or call back for me a day that has passed.'

[6] 'How can you ask me to do that, something no man on earth can do?' I replied. [7] Then said he, 'Suppose I had asked you, "How many dwellings are there in the heart of the sea? Or how many streams to feed the depths? Or how many paths above the vault of heaven? Or where are the ways out of the grave, or the roads into paradise?" [8] You might have retorted, "I have not been down

into the deep, I have not yet descended into the grave, or ever ascended into heaven." [9] But, as it is, I have asked you only about fire, about wind, and about yesterday, things bound up with your experience and essential to your life; and yet you have failed to give me an answer. [10] If then', he went on, 'you cannot understand things you have grown up with, [11] how can you with your limited mind grasp the way of the Most High? A man corrupted by the corrupt world can never know the way of the incorruptible.'

[12] At those words I fell prostrate, exclaiming: 'Better never to have come into existence than be born into a world of evil and suffering we cannot explain!' [13] He replied, 'I went out into a wood, and the trees of the forest were devising a plot. [14] They said, "Come, let us make war on the sea, force it to retreat, and so win ground for more woods." [15] The waves of the sea had a similar plan: they said, "Come, let us attack and conquer the trees of the forest, and annex their territory." [16] The plan made by the trees came to nothing, for fire broke out and burnt them up. [17] So too the plot of the waves came to nothing, for the sand remained firm and blocked their way. [18] If you had to judge between the two, which would you pronounce right, and which wrong?'

[19] 'Both were wrong,' I answered; 'their plans were folly, for the land is assigned to the trees, and to the sea is allotted a place for its waves.'

[20] 'Yes,' he replied, 'you have judged rightly. Why then have you not done so with your own question? [21] Just as the land belongs to the trees and the sea to the waves, so dwellers on earth can understand earthly things and nothing beyond; only he who lives above the heavens can understand the things high above the heavens.'

[22] 'But, my lord, please tell me,' I asked, 'why have I been given the faculty of under-

4:21 he who lives: or those who live.

question. **28:** *Babylon* stands for Rome as in Rev. 14.8. **30:** Having laid the foundation, the writer now questions God in words reminiscent of Hab. 1.12–17.

4.1–5.19: The response: No one can comprehend God's ways. The human spirit is limited. The future age will show the answer. **1:** *Uriel* ("God is my light") is one of seven archangels who are God's "watchers" in *1 Enoch* 20.1. **4:** *If you can explain:* Echoing Job chs. 38–41, the passage goes on to stress Ezra's total inability to understand God's ways (v. 11). **7:** *The vault of heaven* (Gen. 1.6–7) was considered to support a reservoir of water; compare Ps. 29.10.

4.12–21: Parable of sea and forest depicts the folly of the quest. 21: Compare Isa. 55.8–9.

4.22–25: The seer objects, continues to question.

standing? 23 My question is not about the distant heavens, but about what happens every day before our eyes. Why has Israel been made a byword among the Gentiles? Why has the people you loved been put at the mercy of godless nations? Why has the law of our fathers been brought to nothing, and the written covenants made a dead letter? 24 We pass from the world like a flight of locusts, our life is but a vapour, and we are not worth the Lord's pity. 25 What then will he do for us who bear his name? Those are my questions.'

26 He answered: 'If you survive, you will see; if you live long enough, you will marvel. For this present age is passing away; 27 it is full of sorrow and weakness, too full to grasp what is promised in due time for the godly. 28 The evil about which you ask me has been sown, but the time for reaping is not yet. 29 Until the crop of evil has been reaped as well as sown, until the ground where it was sown has vanished, there will be no room for the field where the good is sown. 30 A grain of the evil seed was sown in the heart of Adam from the first; how much godlessness has it produced already! How much more will it produce before the harvest! 31 Reckon this up: if one grain of evil seed has produced so great a crop of godlessness, 32 how vast a harvest will there be when seeds beyond number have been sown!'

33 I asked, 'But when? How long have we to wait? Why are our lives short and miserable?' 34 He replied, 'Do not be in a greater hurry than the Most High himself. You are in a hurry for yourself alone; the Exalted One for many. 35 Are not these the very questions asked by the righteous in the storehouse of souls: "How long must we stay here? When will the harvest begin, the time when we get our reward?" 36 And the answer they got from the archangel Jeremiel was: "As soon as the tally of those like yourselves is complete. God has weighed the world in a balance, 37 he has measured and numbered the ages; he will move nothing, alter nothing, until the appointed measure is reached." '

38 'But, my master and lord,' I replied, 'we are all of us sinners through and through.

39 Can it be because of us, because of the sins of mankind, that the harvest and the reward of the just are delayed?' 40 'Go,' he said, 'ask a pregnant woman whether she can keep the child in her womb any longer once the nine months are up.' 41 'No, my lord, she cannot,' I said. He went on: 'The storehouses of souls in the world below are like the womb: 42 as a woman in labour is impatient to reach the end of the birth-pains, so they are impatient to give back all the souls entrusted to them since time began. 43 Then you will be shown all you wish to see.'

44 I said, 'If I have found favour with you and if it is possible for you to tell and for me to understand, 45 disclose to me one thing more: which is the longer — the future still to come, or the past that has gone by? 46 What is past I know, but not what is still to be.' 47 He said: 'Come, stand at my right hand, and I shall explain the vision you will see.'

48 I stood watching, and there passed before my eyes a blazing fire; when the flames had disappeared, there was still smoke left. 49 After that a dark rain-cloud passed before me; there was a heavy storm, and when it had gone over, there were still some raindrops left. 50 'Reflect on this,' said the angel. 'As the shower of rain filled a far greater space than the drops of water, and the fire more than the smoke, in the same way the past far exceeds the future in length; what remains is but raindrops and smoke.'

51 'Pray tell me,' I said, 'do you think that I shall live to see those days? Or in whose lifetime will they come?' 52 'If you ask me what signs will herald them,' he replied, 'I can tell you in part. But the length of your own life I am not commissioned to tell you; of that I know nothing.

5 'But to speak of the signs: a time is coming when the earth's inhabitants will be seized with great panic. The way of truth will be hidden from sight, and the land will be barren of faith. 2 Wickedness will increase beyond anything you yourself see or have ever heard of. 3 The country you now observe rul-

4:26 **if you live ... marvel:** *so one Vs.; Lat.* live, you will often marvel.

4.26–32: The future age to show the answer. 30: *Evil seed:* the evil yeṣer. See 3.20 n.

4.33–50: The seer asks when the new age will dawn. 35: Talmudic sources speak of a *storehouse of souls* of the righteous dead beneath the throne of God. **36:** *The archangel Jeremiel:* probably the archangel *Remiel* of 1 Enoch 20.1–8. **37:** *The appointed measure:* see 2.40–41 n. **44:** *Which is the longer:* the seer seeks to determine the end-time more closely.

ing the world will become a trackless desert, lying waste before men's eyes. ⁴After the third period (if the Most High grants you a long enough life) you will see universal disorder. The sun will suddenly begin to shine at night, and the moon by day. ⁵Trees will drip blood, stones will speak, nations will be in confusion, and the courses of the stars will be changed. ⁶A king unwelcome to the earth's inhabitants will bear rule. The birds will all fly away, ⁷the Dead Sea will cast up fish, and at night a voice will sound, unknown to the many but heard by all. ⁸Chasms will open in many places and spurt out incessant flames. Wild beasts will range far from their haunts, menstruous women will give birth to monsters, ⁹freshwater springs will run with brine, and everywhere friends will make war on one another. Then understanding will be hidden, and reason withdraw within her chamber. ¹⁰Many will seek her, but not find her; the earth will overflow with wickedness and vice. ¹¹One country will ask another, "Has justice, justice in action, ever passed your way?" and the answer will be "No!" ¹²In those days men will hope, but hope in vain; they will strive, but meet with no success.

¹³'Those are the signs I am allowed to tell you. But turn once more to prayer, continue to weep and fast for seven days; then again you will hear of greater signs than those.'

¹⁴I awoke with a start, trembling in every limb; my spirits faltered, and I was near to fainting. ¹⁵But the angel who had come and talked to me held me and put strength into me, and raised me to my feet.

¹⁶The next night Phaltiel, leader of the people, came to me and asked: 'Where have you been, and why that sad look? ¹⁷Have you forgotten that Israel in exile has been entrusted to your care? ¹⁸Rouse yourself; eat some food. Do not abandon us like a shepherd abandoning his flock to savage wolves.' ¹⁹I replied: 'Leave me, and do not come near me for the next seven days; after that you

may return.' On hearing this he went away.

Ezra's second vision

²⁰For seven days I fasted with tears and lamentations, as commanded by the angel Uriel. ²¹At the end of the seven days my mind was again deeply disturbed, ²²but I recovered the power of thought and began once more to address the Most High.

²³'My Master and Lord,' I said, 'out of all the forests on earth and all their trees, you have chosen one vine; ²⁴from all the lands in the whole world you have chosen one plot; and out of all the flowers in the world you have chosen one lily. ²⁵From all the depths of the sea you have filled one river for yourself, and of all the cities ever built you have set apart Zion as your own. ²⁶From all the birds that were created you have named for yourself one dove, and from all the animals that were fashioned you have taken one sheep. ²⁷Out of all the countless nations, you have adopted one for your own, and to this chosen people you have given a law approved above all others. ²⁸Why then, Lord, have you put this one people at the mercy of so many? Why have you humiliated this one stock more than all others, and dispersed your own people far and wide? ²⁹Those who reject your promises have trampled on the people who put their trust in your covenants. ³⁰If you are so deeply displeased with your people, yours should be the hand that punishes them.'

³¹When I had finished speaking, there was sent to me the angel who had visited me that earlier night. ³²'Listen to me,' he said, 'and I shall instruct you; attend carefully, and I shall tell you more.' ³³'Speak on, my lord,' I replied.

He began: 'You are in great sorrow of heart for Israel's sake. Do you love Israel more than Israel's Maker does?' ³⁴'No, my lord,' I answered, 'but sorrow has compelled

5:7 **Dead Sea:** or sea of Sodom.

4.51–5.12: Signs of end-time revealed. Compare Matt. 24.4–35; Mk. 13.3–31; Lk. 21.7–33. **5.3:** The country . . . ruling is Rome. **6:** Birds were thought capable of foreseeing disaster. **7:** Fish cannot live in the Dead Sea.

5.13–19: Vision ended, but further revelations promised. 13: Fasting accompanied by prayer and weeping seems to be set forth as a condition for receiving divine revelation. See 5.20; 6.35; 9.24; 12.51. **14:** I awoke: from the dream vision. **17–18:** The seer was regarded as the last prophet left in Babylon (12.42) to whom Israel was entrusted.

5.20–6.34: Vision II.

5.20–55: The seer's complaint and God's response. 20: Fasted: see 5.13 n. **23–30:** Drawing from OT me to speak; my heart is tortured every hour as I strive to understand the ways of the Most High and to fathom even part of his judgement.'

35 'You cannot,' he said to me. 'Why not, my lord?' I asked. 'Why then was I born? Why could not my mother's womb have been my grave? Then I should never have seen Jacob's trials and the utter exhaustion of Israel's people.'

36 He said, 'Count me the days that are not yet come, collect the scattered raindrops for me, make the withered flowers bloom again, 37 unlock for me the storehouses and let loose the winds shut up there, or give visible form to a voice — then I shall answer your question about the trials of Israel.'

38 'My master and lord,' I argued, 'how can there be anyone with such knowledge except the One whose dwelling is not among men? 39 I am only a fool; how can I answer your questions?'

40 'Just as you cannot do any of the things I have put to you,' he replied, 'so you will not be able to find out my judgement or the ultimate purpose of the love I have promised to my people.'

41 'But surely,' I objected, 'your promise, lord, is for those who are alive at the end. What is to be the fate of those who lived before us, or of ourselves, or of those who come after us?'

42 He said, 'I shall compare my judgement to a circle: the latest will not be too late, nor the earliest too early.'

43 To this I replied, 'Could you not have made all men, past, present, and future, at one and the same time? Then you could have held your assize with less delay.' 44 His answer to me was: 'Creation may not proceed faster than the Creator, nor could the world support at the same time all those created to live in it.'

45 'My lord,' I pointed out, 'you have just told me that you will at one and the same time restore to life every creature you ever made; how can that be? If all of them are to be alive at the same time and the world is to support them all then, it could support all of them together now.' 46 He replied, 'Think of a woman's womb: say to a woman, "If you give birth to ten children, why do you do so at intervals? Why not give birth to ten at one and the same time?"' 47 'No,' I said, 'that would be impossible; the births must take place at intervals.' 48 'True,' he answered; 'and I have made the earth's womb to bring forth at intervals those conceived in it. 49 An infant cannot give birth, nor can a woman who is too old; and I have made the same rule for the world I have created.'

50 I continued my questioning. 'Since you have now opened the way for me,' I said, 'may I ask: is our mother that you speak of still young, or is she already approaching old age?' 51 He replied, 'For an answer, ask any mother; 52 ask why the children she has borne later are not like those born earlier, but smaller. 53 She will tell you that those who were born in the vigour of her youth are very different from those born in her old age, when her womb is beginning to fail. 54 Think of it, then, like this: if you are smaller than those born before you, 55 and those who follow you are smaller still, the reason is that creation is growing old and losing the strength of its youth.'

56 I said, 'If I have found favour with you, my lord, show me through whom you will 6 judge your creation.' 1 He said to me, 'When the earth began, the gates of the world were not yet standing in place; no winds gathered and blew, 2 no thunder pealed, no lightning flashed; the foundations of paradise were not yet laid, 3 nor were its fair flowers there to see; the powers that move the stars were not established, nor the countless hosts of angels assembled, 4 nor the

5:41 **your promise:** so one Vs.; Lat. obscure.

imagery, the author stresses Israel's election as God's *chosen people,* v. 27. **35:** The seer is told that God's ways are beyond human comprehension. *Womb . . . grave:* compare Job 3.11; 10.18–19. **36–40:** Compare Job 38.24, 28, 34. If one cannot comprehend earthly things, how can one understand divine judgments? **40:** Instead of the angel (v. 31) God speaks to the troubled seer during the rest of Vision II. Such variation is found elsewhere (as in Gen. ch. 22) and is of limited significance, or none at all.

5.41–55: The seer asks about the end-time. 42: Just as no one is first or last or in the middle of those standing on a circle's circumference, so God's judgment embraces living and dead in a simultaneous action. **50–55:** *That creation is growing old,* hence, soon to end, is shown by the smaller stature of recent generations.

vast tracts of air lifted up on high; the divisions of the firmaments had not received their names. Zion had not yet been chosen as God's own footstool; 5 the present age had not been planned; the schemes of its sinners had not yet been outlawed, nor had God's seal yet been set on those who have laid up a treasure of faithfulness. 6 Then it was that I had my thought, and the whole world was created through me and through me alone; in the same way, through me and through me alone the end will be.'

7 'Tell me', I responded, 'about the interval that divides the ages. When will the first age end and the next begin?' 8 He said, 'The interval will be no bigger than that between Abraham and Abraham; for Jacob and Esau were his descendants, and Jacob's hand was grasping Esau's heel at the moment of their birth. 9 Esau's heel represents the end of the first age, and Jacob's hand the beginning of the next, 10 for the beginning of a man is his hand, and the end of a man is his heel; between the heel and the hand, Ezra, do not look for any interval.'

11 'My master and lord,' I said, 'if I have found favour with you, 12 make known to me the last of your signs, of which you showed me some part that former night.'

13 'Rise to your feet', he replied, 'and you will hear a voice, loud and resonant. 14–15 Do not be frightened if the place where you are standing shakes at the sound; it speaks of the end, and the earth's foundations will understand 16 that it is talking of them. They will tremble and shake, for they know that at the end they must be transformed.' 17 At this I stood up and listened. A voice began to speak, and the sound of it was like the sound of a mighty torrent. 18 The voice said: 'The time draws near when I shall come to judge earth's inhabitants, 19 the time when I shall enquire into the wickedness of wrongdoers, the time when Zion's humiliation will be over, 20 the time when a seal will be set on the age about to pass away. Then I shall perform

these signs: the books will be opened out against the vault of heaven, and all will see my judgement at the same moment. 21 Children only one year old will be able to talk, and pregnant women will give birth prematurely at three and four months to babes who will survive and dance about. 22 Fields that were sown will suddenly prove unsown, and barns that were full will suddenly be found empty. 23 A loud trumpet-blast will sound, striking sudden terror into all who hear it. 24 At that time friends will make war on friends as though on foes; the earth and its inhabitants will be terrified. Running streams will stand still, and for three hours cease to flow.

25 'Whoever is left after all I have foretold will be saved and see the salvation that I bring and the end of this world of mine. 26 They will see the men who were taken up into heaven without ever tasting death. Then will earth's inhabitants have a change of heart and come to a better mind. 27 Wickedness will be blotted out and deceit destroyed, 28 but faithfulness will flourish, corruption be overcome, and truth, so long unfruitful, will be revealed.'

29 While the voice was speaking, the ground where I stood gradually moved to and fro. 30 Then the angel said to me, 'These are the revelations I have brought you this night. 31 If once again you pray and fast for seven days, then I shall return to tell you even greater things. 32 For be sure your voice has been heard by the Most High; the Mighty God has seen your integrity and the chastity you have observed all your life. 33 That is why he has sent me to you with all these revelations, and with this message: Be confident, and have no fear! 34 Do not rush too hurriedly into unprofitable thoughts about the past; then you will not act hastily when the last age comes.'

6:31 greater things: Lat. adds by day.

5.56–6.34: Questions concerning the end-time. 6.6: See Gen. chs. 1 and 2; contrast Jn. 1.3. 7–10: As Jacob's hand grasped Esau's heel without interval (see Gen. 25.26), so the new age will follow this one immediately. 12: Compare 5.1–12. 17: The roar of the mighty torrent voices God's great power and majesty. See Ezek. 1.24; Rev. 1.15; 14.2; compare Ps. 29.3–4. 20: Books: heavenly records of human deeds; see Dan. 7.10; Rev. 20.12. 23: Trumpet-blast: see 1 Cor. 15.52; 1 Thess. 4.16 n. 26: Enoch (Gen. 5.24) and Elijah (2 Kgs. 2.11) did not experience death. Malachi 4.5–6 pictures a second Elijah who leads people to repent, i.e. to have a change of heart. 29: The quaking of the ground makes known God's presence in power; see Isa. 6.4; Jer. 10.10. 31: Fast: see 5.13 n.

Ezra's third vision

35 AFTER that I wept once more and I fasted for seven days as I did previously, thus completing the three weeks enjoined on me. 36 On the eighth night I was again troubled in mind, and began to address the Most High. 37 With spirit truly aflame and in agony of mind 38 I said: 'O Lord, at the beginning of creation you spoke the word. On the first day you said, "Let there be heaven and earth!" and your word accomplished its work. 39 At that time a wind was blowing, and there was encircling darkness with silence everywhere; there was as yet no sound of human voice. 40 Then you commanded a ray of light to be brought out of your treasure-chambers, to make your works visible from that time onwards.

41 'On the second day you created the angel of the firmament, and commanded him to make a barrier dividing the waters, so that one part of them should withdraw upwards and the other remain beneath.

42 'On the third day you ordered the waters to collect in a seventh part of the earth; the other six parts you made into dry land, and from it kept some to be sown and tilled for your service. 43 Your word went forth, and at once the work was done. 44 In an instant there appeared a vast profusion of fruits of every kind and taste that can be desired, with flowers of colours unsurpassed and scents mysterious in their fragrance. These were made on the third day.

45 'On the fourth day by your command were created the splendour of the sun, the light of the moon, and the stars in their appointed places; 46 and you ordered them to be at the service of mankind, whom you were about to create.

47 'On the fifth day you commanded the seventh part, where the water was collected, to bring forth living things, birds and fishes. At your command, 48 the dumb, lifeless water brought forth living creatures, and gave the nations cause to tell of your wonderful acts. 49 Then you set apart two creatures: to one you gave the name Behemoth and to the other Leviathan. 50 You put them in separate places, for the seventh part where the water was collected was not large enough to hold them both. 51 You assigned to Behemoth as his territory a part of the land which was made dry on the third day, a country of a thousand hills; 52 to Leviathan you gave the seventh part, the water. You have kept them to be food for whom you will and when you will.

53 'On the sixth day you ordered the earth to bring forth for you cattle, wild beasts, and creeping things. 54 To crown your work you created Adam, and gave him lordship over everything you had made. It is from Adam that we, your chosen people, are all descended.

55 'I have recited the whole story of the creation, O Lord, because you have said that it was for our sake you made this first world, 56 and that the rest of the nations descended from Adam are nothing, no better than spittle and, for all their numbers, no more than a drop from a bucket. 57 And yet, O Lord, those nations which count for nothing are today ruling over us and trampling us down. 58 We, your people, have been put into their power — your people, whom you have called your firstborn, your only son, your champion, and your best beloved. 59 Now if the world was made for us, why may we not take possession of our inheritance? How much longer must this go on?'

6:41 **angel:** *lit.* spirit. **firmament:** *or* vault of heaven.

6.35–9.25: Vision III. More questions about the end-time.

6.35–59: Was the world created for Israel? 35: *The three weeks:* apparently a week of fasting preceded each of the first three visions. **38–54:** Compare Gen. ch. 1. **41:** A Jewish belief that God governed the elements of the universe as well as people and nations through angels was widespread at this time; hence, Gen. 1.6 is here presumed to be addressed to an *angel of the firmament.* Compare Jude 6; Rev. 14.18; 16.5. **49:** *Behemoth . . . Leviathan:* compare Job 3.8; 40.15–41.34; Ps. 74.12–14. **55:** *For our sake you made this first world:* see 7.11. Not found in the canonical OT, this idea was deduced by the rabbis from such texts as Deut. 14.2. **58:** Israel is called the *firstborn* and *only son* because the Lord brought it into existence at the Exodus, which God did for no other nation; see Hos. 11.1; Jer. 31.9. **59:** Apocalyptic and apocryphal literature which describes the end-time is in part an answer to this question: *How much longer* before we *take possession of our inheritance?* See Ecclus. 36.1–17.

The angel instructs Ezra

7 WHEN I had finished speaking, there was sent to me the same angel as on the previous nights. 2 He addressed me, 'Rise to your feet, Ezra, and listen to the message I have brought you.' 3 'Speak on, my lord,' I replied.

He said: 'Imagine a sea set in a vast open space and spreading far and wide, 4 but the entrance to it narrow like the gorge of a river. 5 If anyone wishes to reach this sea, whether to set eyes on it or to gain control of it, how can he arrive at its broad, open waters without passing through the narrow gorge? 6 Or again, imagine a city built in a plain, a city full of every good thing, 7 but the entrance to it narrow and steep, with fire to the right and deep water to the left. 8 Between the fire and the water there is only one path, and that wide enough for but one person at a time. 9 If someone has been given this city as a legacy, how can he take possession of his inheritance except by passing through this dangerous approach?' 10 I agreed: 'That is the only way, my lord.'

The angel said: 'Such is the lot of Israel. 11 It was for Israel that I made the world, and when Adam transgressed my decrees the creation came under judgement. 12 The entrances to the present world were made narrow, painful, and arduous, few and evil, full of perils and grinding hardship. 13 But the entrances to the greater world are broad and safe, and lead to immortality. 14 Everyone must therefore enter this narrow and futile existence; otherwise they can never attain the blessings in store. 15 Then why are you so disquieted and perturbed, Ezra, at the thought that you are mortal and must die? 16 Why have you not turned your mind from the present to the future?'

17 'My master and lord,' I replied, 'in your law you have laid it down that the just shall inherit these blessings, but the ungodly shall perish. 18 The just, therefore, can endure this narrow life and look for the spacious life hereafter; but those who have lived a wicked life will have gone through the narrows without ever reaching the open spaces.'

19 He said: 'You are not a better judge than God, nor wiser than the Most High. 20 Better that many now living should perish, than that the law which God has set before them should be despised! 21 God has given clear instructions to all when they come into this world, telling them how to attain life and how to avoid punishment. 22 But the ungodly have refused to obey him; they have adopted their own futile devices 23 and made deceit and wickedness their goal; they have even denied the existence of the Most High and ignored his ways. 24 They have rejected his law and repudiated his promises; they have neither put faith in his decrees nor done what he commands. 25 Therefore, Ezra, it is emptiness for the empty, fullness for the full!

26 'Listen! The time will come when the signs I have foretold will be seen; the city which is now invisible will appear and the country now hidden be revealed. 27 Everyone who has been delivered from the calamities I have foretold will see for himself the wonderful things I shall do. 28 My son the Messiah will appear with his companions, bringing four hundred years of joy to all who survive. 29 At the end of that time my son the Messiah will die, and so will all mankind who draw breath. 30 Then the world will return to its original silence for seven days as at the beginning of creation; no one will be left alive. 31 After seven days the age which is not yet

7:26 **the city ... invisible:** *so some Vss.; Lat.* the city, the bride which is now seen.   7:28 **the Messiah:** *so some Vss.; Lat.* Jesus.

7.1–25: Because of sin the path to the next world is arduous. 1: *The same angel:* Uriel (4.1 n.). **11:** *When Adam transgressed:* judgment brought by Adam's sin explains why Israel does not enjoy the world made for it. See 6.55–59; compare 3.7 n.; 4.30.

7.17–25: The angel answers concerning punishment of wicked. 17: The seer thinks not only of Israel but of all human beings. The rabbis held that the Gentiles rejected God's *law* before it was offered to Israel. **18–25:** Even though the wicked have to go through the *narrows* like the just, they will *perish* because they *despised* the *law* and so *repudiated* God's *promises*.

7.26–(44): The angel speaks of the messianic kingdom and the end of the world. 26: *The signs:* see 5.1–12; 6.20–24. *The city ... the country:* the heavenly Jerusalem and paradise. See 8.52. **28:** In place of *four hundred years* some ancient versions have "thirty" or "one thousand," or omit the figure entirely. The idea of a temporary messianic reign is known from rabbinic sources. **31–32:** The age to come will awake when those who *sleep* awake will be aroused, and the age which is corruptible will cease to be. ³²The earth will give up those who sleep in it, and the dust those who rest there in silence; and the storehouses will give back the souls entrusted to them. ³³The Most High will be seen on the judgement-seat, and there will be an end of all pity and patience. ³⁴Judgement alone will remain, truth will stand firm, and faithfulness be strong. ³⁵The work of each man will come forward and its recompense be made known; good deeds will awake and wicked deeds will not be allowed to sleep. ⁽³⁶⁾The place of torment will appear, and over against it the place of rest; the furnace of hell will be displayed, and on the opposite side the paradise of joy.

⁽³⁷⁾'Then the Most High will say to the nations that have been raised from the dead: "Look and understand who it is you have denied and refused to serve, whose commandments you have despised. ⁽³⁸⁾Look on this side, and on that: here are joy and rest, there fire and torments." That is how he will speak to them on the day of judgement.

⁽³⁹⁾'That day will be without sun, moon, or stars; ⁽⁴⁰⁾without cloud, thunder, or lightning; wind, water, or air; darkness, evening, or morning; ⁽⁴¹⁾without summer, spring, or winter; without heat, frost, or cold; without hail, rain, or dew; ⁽⁴²⁾without noonday, night, or dawn; without brightness, light, or brilliance. There will be only the radiant glory of the Most High, by which all will see what lies before them. ⁽⁴³⁾That day will last for a week of years, as it were. ⁽⁴⁴⁾Such is the order that I have decreed for the judgement; but only to you have I given this revelation.'

⁽⁴⁵⁾I replied: 'My lord, I repeat what I said before: "How blest are the living who obey your decrees!" ⁽⁴⁶⁾But as for those for whom I have been praying, has there ever lived a man who has not sinned, who has never transgressed your covenant? ⁽⁴⁷⁾I see now that only to the few will the next world bring joy, while to the many it will bring torment. ⁽⁴⁸⁾For an evil heart has grown strong in us; it has estranged us from God's decrees, brought us into corruption and the paths of death, opened up to us the way to ruin, and carried us far away from life. This it has done, not merely to a few, but to almost all who have been created.'

⁽⁴⁹⁾The angel replied: 'Listen to me and I shall instruct and correct you yet further. ⁽⁵⁰⁾The Most High has made not one world but two, and for this reason: ⁽⁵¹⁾there are, as you say, not many who are just, but only a few, whereas the wicked are very numerous; well then, listen to the explanation. ⁽⁵²⁾Suppose you had a very few precious stones; would you add to their number by putting common lead and clay among them?' ⁽⁵³⁾'No, my lord,' I said, 'no one would do that.' ⁽⁵⁴⁾'Look at it also in this way,' he continued: 'enquire of the earth, ask her humbly, and she will give you the answer. ⁽⁵⁵⁾Say to her, "You produce gold, silver, and copper, iron, lead, and clay. ⁽⁵⁶⁾There is more silver than gold, more copper than silver, more iron than copper, more lead than iron, more clay than lead." ⁽⁵⁷⁾Then judge for yourself which things are valuable and desirable—those which are plentiful, or those which are rare.' ⁽⁵⁸⁾'My master and lord,' I said, 'what is plentiful is cheaper; the more rare is the more valuable.' ⁽⁵⁹⁾He replied, 'Consider then what follows from that: the owner of what is hard to get has more cause to be pleased than the owner of what is plentiful. ⁽⁶⁰⁾In the same

7:(36–105) *This passage, missing from the text of the Authorized (King James) Version, but found in ancient witnesses, has been restored.* 7:(48) **from ... decrees:** *lit.* from these.

---

in death will rise to new life. After the temporary messianic reign comes the resurrection (v. 32), and the judgment, hell and heaven (vv. 33–(44)). **32:** *The storehouses:* see 4.35 n. **34:** When the opportunity for obedience has passed, the final *judgement* is to be conducted with rigorous justice. **35:** Both *good* and *wicked deeds* will be brought to light and given the attention they deserve. **(36–105):** These verses are missing from the standard Vg., and thus from the King James Version, but are found in two Latin MSS. and in several secondary versions. The passage may have been omitted from the Vg. for doctrinal reasons because it excludes prayer on behalf of the dead; see 7.(105) n.

7.(37–44): Judgment Day described. Here judgment is not the end, but a prelude to subsequent blessings. See Matt. 25.46, which summarizes the discourse in Matt. ch. 24 on Judgment Day. **(42):** *The radiant glory* of God gives light at the judgment. Compare Isa. 60.19–20; Rev. 21.23.

7.(45–74): That few are to be saved is justified by angel but lamented by seer. (48): *Evil heart:* see 3.20 n.

way, when I fulfil my promise to the creation, I shall have joy in the few who are saved, because it is they who have made my glory prevail now, and through them my name has been made known. (61) I shall not grieve for the many who are lost, for even now they are no more than a vapour; they are like flame or smoke—they catch fire, blaze up, and then die out.'

(62) I said: 'Mother Earth, if the human mind, like the rest of creation, is but a product of the dust, why did you bring it forth? (63) It would have been better if the very dust had never come into being, for then the mind would never have been produced. (64) But, as it is, our mind grows up with us and we are tortured by it, for we realize we are doomed to die. (65) What sorrow for mankind; what happiness for the wild beasts! What sorrow for every mother's son; what joy for the cattle and flocks! (66) How much better their lot than ours! They have no judgement to expect, no knowledge of torment, no knowledge of salvation promised them after death. (67) What good to us is the promise of a future life if it is to be nothing but torture? (68) For everyone alive is burdened and defiled with wickedness, sinful through and through. (69) Would it not have been better for us if there had been no judgement awaiting us after death?'

(70) The angel replied: 'When the Most High was making the world and Adam and his descendants, he first of all planned the judgement and what goes with it. (71) Your own words, when you said that man's mind grows up with him, will give you the answer. (72) It was in spite of having a mind that the people of this world sinned, and that is why torment awaits them: they received the commandments, but did not keep them; they accepted the law, then violated it. (73) What defence will they be able to make at the judgement, what answer at the last day? (74) How patient the Most High has been with the inhabitants of this world, and for how long!—not for their own sake, but for the sake of the destined age to be.'

(75) 'If I have found favour with you, my lord,' I said, 'make this also plain to me: at death, when each one of us gives back his soul, shall we be kept in peace until the time when you begin to create your new world, or does our torment begin at once?' (76) 'That too I will explain to you,' he replied. 'Do not, however, include yourself among those who have despised my law, nor count yourself with those who are to be tormented. (77) You after all have a treasure of good works stored up with the Most High, though you will not be shown it until the last days. (78) But now to speak of death: when the Most High has pronounced final sentence for a person to die, the spirit leaves the body to return to the One who first gave it, that it may render adoration to the glory of the Most High. (79) As for those who have scornfully rejected the ways of the Most High, who have spurned his law, and who hate the godfearing, (80) their spirits enter no settled abode, but from then on must wander in torment, endless grief, and sorrow. And this for seven reasons. (81) First, they have held in contempt the law of the Most High. (82) Secondly, they have lost their chance of making a full repentance and so gaining life. (83) Thirdly, they can see the reward in store for those who have trusted the covenants of the Most High. (84) Fourthly, they begin to think of the torment that awaits them at the end. (85) Fifthly, they see that angels are guarding the abode of the other souls in undisturbed peace. (86) Sixthly, they see that they are soon to enter into torment. (87) The seventh cause for grief, the greatest cause of all, is this: at the sight of the Most High in his glory they break down in shame, waste away in remorse, and shrivel with fear, remembering how they sinned against him in their lifetime and how they are soon to be brought before him for judgement on the last day.

(88) 'As for those who have kept to the ways of the Most High, this is what is appointed for them when their time comes to leave their mortal bodies. (89) During their stay on earth they served the Most High in spite of great

---

(61): The *fire* in which the wicked *die out* is not one of annihilation (see v. (67)), but one in which their worth goes up in smoke. (64–68): The seer insists on the unity of the human race in doom; all share in the *wickedness* and *sorrow* of *every mother's son*; see also vv. (75–77). (70): According to rabbinic theology, paradise and hell which go with *judgement* were among seven things created before the world.

7.(75–101): State of the dead before judgment. (77): *Treasure of good works*: compare 8.33–36. (79–87): Wicked spirits *wander . . . in sorrow*, tormented by deep mental anguish. (85): *The other souls*: the righteous.

hardship and constant danger, and kept to the last letter the law given them by the Lawgiver. (90) Therefore the decision is this: (91) they shall rejoice greatly to see the glory of God, who will receive them as his own, and they shall enter into rest through seven appointed stages. (92) The first stage is their victory in the long struggle against their innate impulse to evil, so that it did not lead them astray from life into death. (93) The second is to see the souls of the wicked wandering endlessly and the punishment awaiting them. (94) The third is seeing the good report given of them by their Maker, that while they were alive they kept the law entrusted to them. (95) The fourth is to understand the rest which they are now to share in the storehouses, guarded by angels in undisturbed peace, and the glory awaiting them in the next age. (96) The fifth is the contrast between the corruptible world from which they have joyfully escaped and the future life that is to be their possession, between the cramped, arduous existence from which they have been set free and the spacious life which will soon be theirs to delight in for ever and ever. (97) The sixth will be the revelation that they are to shine like stars, never to fade or die, with faces radiant as the sun. (98) The seventh stage, the greatest of them all, will be the confident and joyful assurance which will be theirs, free from all fear and shame, as they press forward to see face to face the One whom they served in their lifetime, and from whom they are now to receive their reward in glory.

(99) 'What I have here set forth is the appointed destiny for the souls of the just; the torments I spoke of before are what the rebellious are to suffer!'

(100) I asked him: 'When souls are separated from their bodies, will they be given the opportunity to see what you have described to me?' (101) 'They will be allowed seven days,' he replied; 'for seven days they will be permitted to see the things I have told you, and after

that they will join the other souls in their abodes.'

(102) 'If I have found favour with you, my lord,' I said, 'tell me one thing more: on the day of judgement will the just be able to plead for the wicked, or by prayer win pardon for them from the Most High? (103) Can fathers do so for their sons, or sons for their parents? Can brothers pray for brothers, relatives and friends for their nearest and dearest?'

(104) 'Since you have found favour with me,' the angel replied, 'this too I will tell you. The day of judgement is decisive and sets its seal on the truth for all to see. In the present age a father cannot send his son in his place, nor a son his father, nor a master his slave, nor a man his best friend, to be ill for him, or sleep, or eat, or be cured for him. (105) In like manner no one shall ever ask pardon for another; every individual will be held responsible for his own wickedness or goodness when that day comes.'

36 (106) To this I replied: 'But how is it, then, that we read of intercessions in scripture? First, there is Abraham, who prayed for the people of Sodom; then Moses, who prayed for our ancestors when they sinned in the wilderness. 37 (107) Next, there is Joshua, who prayed for the Israelites in the time of Achan, 38 (108) as did Samuel in the time of Saul, David on account of the plague, and Solomon for those present at the dedication. 39 (109) Elijah prayed for rain for the people, and he prayed for one who had died, that he might be brought back to life. 40 (110) Hezekiah prayed for the nation in the time of Sennacherib; and there are many more besides. 41 (111) If, then, in an age when corruption had spread and wickedness increased, the just made entreaty for the wicked, why cannot it be the same on the day of judgement?'

42 (112) The answer he gave me was: 'The

7:(103) **friends:** *so some Vss.; Lat.* the faithful.
7:37 **Achan:** *Lat.* Achar.

7.(88–99): **The destiny of the just.** (92): *Innate impulse* refers to the evil *yeṣer:* see 3.20 n. (97): *Shine like stars, never to fade:* compare Dan. 12.3; Matt. 13.43. (101): *Abodes:* see 4.35 n.

7.(102–115): **No intercession can be made for the wicked at Judgment Day.** Compare Ezek. 18.4, 20. (105): See vv. (36–105) n. That the practice, later popular, of prayer for the dead is here excluded probably accounts for the omission of this section from some MSS. Its restoration has necessitated the double numbering of subsequent verses. (106): *Abraham:* see Gen. 18.23–32. *Moses:* see Exod. 32.11–14. (107): *Joshua:* see Josh. 7.6–9. (108): *Samuel:* see 1 Sam. 7.9; 12.19–25. *David:* see 2 Sam. 24.17. *Solomon:* see 1 Kgs. 8.22–30. (109): *Elijah:* see 1 Kgs. 18.41–45; 17.20–21. (110): *Hezekiah:* see 2 Kgs. 19.15–19. (112–115): Compare v. 35 n.

present world is not the end, and the glory of God does not stay in it continually. That is why the strong have prayed for the weak. 43 (113) But the day of judgement will be the end of the present world and the beginning of the eternal world to come, a world in which corruption will have disappeared, 44 (114) all excess will be abolished and unbelief eliminated, in which justice will be full-grown, and truth will have risen like the sun. 45 (115) On the day of judgement, therefore, there can be no mercy for those who have lost their case, no reversal for those who have won.'

46 (116) I replied, 'But this is my point, my first point and my last: how much better it would have been if the earth had never produced Adam at all, or, once it had done so, if he had been restrained from sinning! 47 (117) For what good does it do any of us to live in misery now and have nothing but punishment to expect after death? 48 (118) O Adam, what have you done? Though the sin was yours, the fall was not yours alone; it was ours also, the fall of all your descendants. 49 (119) What good is the promise of immortality to us, when we have committed mortal sins? 50 (120) What good is the hope of eternity, in the wretched and futile state to which we have come; 51 (121) or the prospect of dwelling in health and security, when we have lived such wicked lives? 52 (122) You say that the glory of the Most High will guard those who have led pure lives; but what help is that to us who have walked in the most wicked ways? 53 (123) What good is the revelation to us of paradise and its imperishable fruit, the source of perfect satisfaction and healing? For we shall never enter it, 54 (124) since we have made depravity our home. 55 (125) You say that those who have practised self-discipline will shine with faces brighter than the stars; but what good is that to us whose faces are darker than night? 56 (126) During a lifetime of iniquity we have never given a thought to the sufferings in store for us after death.'

57 (127) The angel replied, 'This is the thought for every man on earth to keep in mind during the battle of life: 58 (128) if he is defeated, he must accept the sufferings you have mentioned, but if he is victorious, the rewards I have been describing will be his. 59 (129) That was the way which Moses in his time urged the people to take, when he said, "Choose life and live!" 60 (130) But they believed neither him, nor the prophets after him, no, nor me when I spoke to them. 61 (131) There will be no sorrow over their damnation; but there will be joy for the salvation of those who have believed.'

62 (132) 'My lord,' I said, 'I know that the Most High is now called compassionate, because he has compassion on those yet unborn; 63 (133) and merciful, because he shows mercy to those who repent and live by his law; 64 (134) and patient, because he shows patience to those who have sinned, his own creatures as they are; 65 (135) and Benefactor, because he would rather give than demand; 66 (136) and rich in forgiveness, because again and again he forgives sinners, past, present, and to come. 67 (137) Without his continued forgiveness there could be no hope of life for the world and its inhabitants. 68 (138) He is called generous, because without his generosity in releasing sinners from their sins, not one ten-thousandth part of mankind could hope to be given life; 69 (139) and he is also called Judge, for unless he grants pardon to those who have been created by his word, and blots out their countless offences, 70 (140) only a very few of the entire human race would, I suppose, be spared.'

8 The angel said to me, 'The Most High has made this world for many, the next world for but a few. 2 Let me give you an illustration, Ezra: enquire of the earth, and it will tell you that it can produce an abundance of clay for making earthenware, but very little gold-dust. It is the same with the present world: 3 many have been created, but only a few will be saved.'

7.(116–131): **Lament on the sinful lot of humanity. (118):** *O Adam*: see 3.7 n. **(123):** The *imperishable fruit* comes from the restored tree of life. See Gen. 3.22–24; Ezek. 47.12; Rev. 22.2. **(125):** *Will shine*: see Dan. 12.3. **(126):** *A lifetime of iniquity*: see (64–68) n. **(129):** *Choose life*: see Deut. 30.19–20.

7.(132)–8.3: **The seer appeals to God's mercy. (132–140):** The divine attributes are apparently derived from Exod. 34.6–7 but here all involve the forgiveness of sin. **(139):** God is called *Judge* in the biblical sense of one who saves the oppressed, here from sin; compare Judg. 2.16–18. **8.1–3:** The seer is told strict justice will apply and *few will be saved.* Compare 7.(49–61) and Matt. 22.14.

Ezra's prayer and the answer

[4] I SAID: 'My soul, drink deep of understanding and eat your fill of wisdom! [5] Without your consent you came here, and against your will you depart; only a brief span of life is given you.

[6] 'O Lord above, if I may be allowed to approach you in prayer, implant a seed in our hearts and minds, and make it grow until it bears fruit, so that fallen man may obtain life. [7] For you alone are God, and by your hands we are all shaped in one mould, as your word declares. [8] The body moulded in the womb receives from you life and limbs; that which you create is kept safe amid fire and water, and for nine months the body moulded by you bears what you have created in it. [9] Both the womb which holds safely and that which is safely held will be kept safe only because you keep them so. And after the womb has delivered up what was created in it, [10] then, at your command, from the breasts the human body itself supplies milk, the fruit of the breasts. [11] For a certain time what has been made is nourished in that way; and afterwards in your mercy it is still cared for. [12] You bring it up to know your justice, train it in your law, and correct it by your wisdom. [13] It is your creature and you made it; you can put it to death or give it life, as you please. [14] But if you should lightly destroy what was fashioned by your command with so much labour, to what purpose was it created?

[15] 'And now let me say this: about mankind at large, you know best; but it is for your own people that I grieve, [16] for your inheritance that I mourn; my sorrow is for Israel, my distress for the descendants of Jacob. [17] For them and for myself, therefore, I shall address my prayer to you, since I perceive how low we have fallen, we who dwell in the land; [18] and I have heard how quickly your judgement will follow. [19] Hear, then, what I have to say, and consider the prayer which I make to you.'

This is the prayer offered by Ezra, before he was taken up to heaven: [20] 'O Lord, you inhabit eternity, to you the sky and the highest heavens belong; [21] your throne is beyond imagining, your glory past conceiving; you are attended by the host of angels, trembling [22] as they turn themselves into wind or fire at your bidding; your word is true, your declarations are constant, your commands mighty and terrible; [23] your glance dries up the depths, your anger melts the mountains, and your truth stands for ever: [24] hear, O Lord, the prayer of your servant, listen to my petition and attend to my words, for you it is who have fashioned me. [25] While I live, I must speak; while I have understanding, I must respond.

[26] 'Do not look upon the offences of your people, but rather look on those who have served you faithfully. [27] Pay heed not to the godless and their practices, but to those who have observed your covenant and suffered for it. [28] Do not think of those who all their lives have been untrue to you, but remember those who of their own will have acknowledged the fear due to you. [29] Do not destroy those who have lived like animals, but take account of those who have borne shining witness to your law. [30] Do not be angry with those considered worse than beasts, but show love to those who have put unfailing trust in your glory. [31] We and our fathers have lived evil lives, yet it is on account of us sinners that you are called merciful; [32] for if it is your desire to have mercy on us, sinners who have no just deeds to our credit, then indeed you will be called merciful. [33] The reward which will be given to the just, who have many good works stored up with you, will be no more than their own deeds have earned.

[34] 'What is man that you should be angry with him? Or the race of mortals that you should treat them so harshly? [35] The truth is, no one was ever born who did not sin, no one alive is innocent of offence. [36] Indeed, it is through your mercy shown towards those with no fund of good deeds to their name that your justice and kindness will be made known.'

[37] In reply to me the angel said: 'Some part

8.4–62: The seer prays for mercy upon the wicked but is denied. 4–19a: Why should nearly everyone, so carefully created and sustained by God, be doomed to perish? **6:** *Implant a seed:* give a sure inclination to righteousness which alone can offset the evil inclination; see 3.7 and 3.20 nn. **16:** *My sorrow is for Israel:* see the opening complaint, 3.4–36. **19b:** Because of its liturgical beauty, the following prayer appears separately in the special hymn section of many Latin MSS. under the title *Confessio Esdrae*. Hence, the superscription in the text: *this is the prayer*. **34:** Human beings are so insignificant that it is unworthy of God of what you have said is correct, and it will be as you say. ³⁸ You may be sure that I shall not give thought to sinners, to their creation, death, judgement, or damnation; ³⁹ but I shall have joy in the creation of the just, in their pilgrimage through this world, their salvation, and their final reward. ⁴⁰ So I have said, and so it is. ⁴¹ The farmer sows many seeds in the ground and plants many plants, but not all the seeds come up safely in due season, nor do all the plants strike root. It is the same in the world of men: not all who are sown will be saved.'

⁴² To that I replied: 'If I have found favour with you, let me speak. ⁴³ The farmer's seed may not come up, because you did not give it rain at the right time, or it may rot because of too much rain; ⁴⁴ but man, who was fashioned by your hands and called your image because he is made like you, and for whose sake you formed everything, will you really compare him with seed sown by a farmer? ⁴⁵ Do not be angry with us, Lord; but spare your people and show them pity, for it is your own creation you will be pitying.'

⁴⁶ He answered: 'The present is for those now alive, the future for those yet to come. ⁴⁷ It is not possible for you to love my creation with a love greater than mine — far from it! But never again rank yourself among the unjust, as so often you have done. ⁴⁸ Yet the Most High approves ⁴⁹ of the proper modesty you have shown; you have not sought great glory by including yourself among the godly. ⁵⁰ In the last days the inhabitants of the world will be punished for their arrogant lives by prolonged suffering. ⁵¹ But you should direct your thoughts to yourself and look to the glory awaiting those like you. ⁵² For all of you paradise lies open, the tree of life is planted, the age to come stands prepared, and rich abundance is in store; the city is already built, rest from toil is assured, goodness and wisdom are brought to perfection. ⁵³ From you the root of evil has been cut off; for you

disease is at an end and death abolished, hell is gone, and the corruption of the grave blotted out. ⁵⁴ All sorrows are at an end, and the treasure of immortality has been finally revealed.

⁵⁵ 'Ask no more questions, therefore, about the many who are lost; ⁵⁶ for when they were given freedom they used it to despise the Most High, to treat his law with contempt and abandon his ways. ⁵⁷ What is more, they trampled on the godly. ⁵⁸ "There is no God," they said to themselves, knowing full well that they must die. ⁵⁹ Yours, then, will be the joys I have predicted, theirs the thirst and torments already prepared. It is not that the Most High has wanted any man to be destroyed, ⁶⁰ but that those he created have themselves brought dishonour on their Creator's name, and shown ingratitude to the One who had put life within their reach. ⁶¹ That is why my judgement is now close at hand, ⁶² but I have not made this known to all — only to you and a few like you.'

⁶³ 'My lord,' I said, 'you have now revealed to me the many signs which you are to perform in the last days; but you have not shown me when that will be.'

9 The angel answered: 'Keep a careful check; when you see that some of the signs predicted have already passed, ² then you will understand that the time has come for the Most High to begin to judge the world he created. ³ When the world becomes the scene of earthquakes, insurrections, plots among the nations, unstable government, and panic among rulers, ⁴ then you will recognize these as the events foretold by the Most High since first the world began. ⁵ Just as everything that is done on earth has its beginning and end clearly marked, ⁶ so it is with the times which the Most High has determined: the beginning is marked by portents and miracles, the end by manifestations of power.

⁷ 'All who come safely through and escape

to be *angry with* them or to treat fragile *mortals harshly.* **37:** *It will be as you say:* the seer's prayer (v. 27) is accepted, but is turned to an opposite meaning: God will forget the doomed sinners and rejoice in the righteous. **41:** The *farmer* rejoices in the crop and disregards *the seeds* that fail. **46:** The seer's objection (vv. 43–44) seems dismissed as inapplicable to the future age. **47:** The angel asserts that God's *love* for the *creation* includes the doing of justice in vindication of those who have been trampled (v. 57). **52:** Now in existence, *paradise lies open* for contemplation. *Tree of life:* see 7.(123) n. **53:** *The root of evil:* see 3.20 n. **62:** *A few like you:* prophets like the seer, called apocalyptists because they have claimed to draw back the veil hiding the end-time.

8.63–9.13: Description of the end. 63: *The many signs:* see 5.1–13; 6.18–24. The present passage is a resumé. **9.1:** Keeping *a careful check* of the signs will enable the seer to judge the nearness of the end. **4:** The destruction, thanks to their good deeds or the faith they have shown, 8 will survive the dangers I have foretold and witness the salvation I shall bring to my land, the territory I have set apart from all eternity as my own. 9 Then those who have neglected my ways will be taken by surprise; their utter contempt for my ways will bring them lasting torment. 10 All who in their lifetime failed to acknowledge me in spite of the benefits I brought them, 11 all who disdained my law while freedom still was theirs, who scornfully dismissed the idea of penitence while the way was still open — 12 all these must learn the truth through torments after death. 13 Do not be curious any more, Ezra, to know how the godless will be tormented, but only how and when the just will be saved; the world is theirs and for their sake it exists.'

14 I answered, 15 'I repeat what I have said again and again: the lost outnumber the saved 16 as a wave exceeds a drop of water.'

17 The angel replied: 'The seed to be sown depends on the soil, the colour depends on the flower, the product on the craftsman, and the harvest on the farmer. There was a time 18 before the world had been created for men to live in, and I was planning it for the sake of those who now exist. No one then disputed my plan, 19 for no one existed. I supplied this world with unfailing food and a law not to be questioned; but those whom I created turned to corrupt ways of life. 20 I looked at my world and there it lay spoilt, at my earth and it was in danger from men's wicked plans. 21 I saw this and I was hard put to it to spare any at all; but I saved for myself one grape out of a cluster, one tree out of a large forest. 22 So then let it be: destruction for the many who were born in vain, and salvation for my grape and my tree, which have cost me such labour to bring to perfection.

23 'You, however, must wait seven days more, Ezra. Do not fast this time, 24 but go to a flowery field where no house stands, and eat only what grows there; taste no meat or wine, 25 and pray to the Most High the whole time. I shall then come and talk with you.'

Ezra's fourth vision

26 I WENT out, as the angel told me, to a field called Ardat. There I sat among the flowers; my food was what grew in the field, and I ate to my heart's content. 27 As I lay on the grass at the end of the seven days, I was troubled again in mind with all the same perplexities. 28 I broke my silence and addressed the Most High: 29 'Lord, you showed yourself to our fathers in the wilderness at the time of the exodus from Egypt, when they were travelling through a barren waste where no one ever trod, 30 and you said, "Hear me, Israel, listen to my words, you descendants of Jacob: 31 this is my law, which I am sowing among you to bear fruit and to bring you everlasting glory." 32 But our fathers, though they received the law, did not observe it; they disobeyed its commandments. Not that the fruit of the law perished — that was impossible, for it was yours; 33 rather, those who received it perished, because they failed to keep safe the seed that had been sown in them. 34 Now the usual way of things is that when seed is put into the earth, or a ship on the sea, or food or drink into a jar, then if the seed, or the ship, 35 or the contents of the jar should be destroyed, what held or contained them does not perish along with them. But with us sinners it is different: 36 destruction will come upon us, the recipients of the law, and upon our hearts, the vessel that held the law. 37 The law itself is not destroyed; it survives in all its glory.'

38 While turning over these things in my mind, I looked round and on my right I saw a woman in great distress, mourning and lamenting loudly; her dress was torn, and she had ashes on her head. 39 Breaking off my

writer expects to see and to *recognize* the end in the near future. **12:** *Learn the truth:* the real meaning of their ruinous but willful rebellion.

9.14–25: Summary. 14: *I repeat:* see 7.(140). **21:** Because of corruption (vv. 19–20), to spare even *one grape* in a vineyard is a marvelous act of grace. **23:** *Do not fast:* see 6.35 n.

9.26–10.59: Vision IV. Zion's present mourning and future glory. The transformation is sudden, complete, and terrifying.

9.26–37: The seer ponders the law's permanence and Israel's instability. 26: *Ardat:* an unidentifiable place, perhaps of mystic significance. **29:** See Exod. 19.9; 24.10; 24.15; Jer. 2.2. **33:** The whole generation that sinned at Sinai *perished* and did not enter the promised land; see Num. 32.13.

meditations, I turned to her ⁴⁰and asked: 'Why are you weeping? What is troubling you?' ⁴¹'Sir,' she replied, 'please leave me to my tears and my grief, for great is my bitterness of heart and great my affliction.' ⁴²'Tell me', I said, 'what has happened.' ⁴³'Sir, I was barren and childless throughout thirty years of marriage,' she replied; ⁴⁴'every hour of every day during those thirty years, night and day alike, I prayed to the Most High. ⁴⁵Then after thirty years God answered my prayer and had mercy on my affliction; he took note of my sorrow and granted me a son. What joy he brought to my husband and myself and to all our neighbours! What praise we gave to the Mighty God! ⁴⁶I took great pains over his upbringing, ⁴⁷and when he grew up I chose a wife for him and held a wedding feast.

10 'But when my son entered the bridal chamber, he fell down dead. ²We put out all the lights, and my neighbours all came to comfort me; I controlled my feelings till the evening of the following day. ³When everyone had stopped urging me to take comfort and control myself, I rose and stole away in the night, and came here, as you see, to this field. ⁴I have made up my mind never to return to the city; I shall stay here, neither eating nor drinking, but mourning and fasting all the time until I die.'

⁵At that I abandoned the reflections which occupied my mind and spoke sternly to the woman: ⁶'You are the most foolish of women,' I said; 'are you blind to the mourning and sufferings of our nation? ⁷It is for the anguish and affliction of Zion, the mother of us all, that you should mourn with such poignancy; ⁸you should share in our common mourning and anguish. But your anguish is for your one son. ⁹Ask the earth and she will tell you that she must mourn for the countless thousands who come to birth upon her. ¹⁰In the beginning all sprang from her, and there are more still to come; yet almost all her children go to perdition, and vast numbers of them are wiped out. ¹¹Who,

then, has the better right to be mourning—the earth, which has lost such vast numbers, or you, whose sorrow is for one only? ¹²You may say to me, "But my lamentation is different from that of the earth; I have lost the fruit of my womb, which I brought to birth in pain and travail, ¹³whereas it is only in the course of nature that the vast numbers now alive on earth should depart as they came." ¹⁴My answer is: at the cost of pain you have been a mother, but in the same way the earth has always been the mother of mankind, bearing fruit to earth's Creator.

¹⁵'Now, therefore, keep your sorrow to yourself, and bear your misfortunes bravely. ¹⁶If you will accept God's decree as just, then in due time you will receive your son again and win an honoured name among women. ¹⁷Go back, therefore, into the city to your husband.'

¹⁸'No,' she replied, 'I will not. I will never go back; I shall die here.'

¹⁹But I continued to argue with her. ²⁰'Do not do that,' I urged; 'let yourself be persuaded because of Zion's misfortunes, and take comfort from the sorrow of Jerusalem. ²¹You see how our sanctuary has been laid waste, our altar demolished, our temple destroyed. ²²Our harps are unstrung, our hymns silenced, our shouts of joy cut short; the light of the sacred lamp has been extinguished, and the Ark of our covenant has been plundered; the holy vessels are defiled, and the name which God has conferred on us is disgraced; our leading men have been treated with violence, our priests burnt alive, and the Levites taken into captivity; our virgins have been ravished and our wives violated, our godfearing men carried off, and our children left abandoned; our young men have been enslaved, and our strong warriors reduced to impotence. ²³Worst of all, Zion, once sealed with God's own seal, has forfeited its glory and been delivered into the hands of those who hate us. ²⁴Then throw off your own heavy grief, and lay aside all your sorrows; may the Mighty God restore you to

9.38–10.28: The woman in mourning. 38: *Ashes on her head,* like the torn *dress,* were a sign of grief. **10.2:** Weddings took place at night, hence, the *lights;* see Matt. 25.1–13. **7:** *Zion, the mother:* compare Bar. 4.8–20; Gal. 4.26. **16:** To *accept God's decree as just* is to submit humbly to God's will. The mother would receive her son back again after the resurrection in the new age; compare 2 Macc. 7.9, 23, 29. *An honoured name:* childbearing was regarded as a blessing, barrenness as a curse. **20–22:** These verses are a poignant enumeration of the misfortunes that attended the destruction of Jerusalem in 587 B.C.E.; see 2 Kgs. 25.8–12. *Hymns silenced:* compare Ps. 137.1–4. The *Ark* of the *covenant* was lost in the destruction. The holy vessels were defiled by his favour, may the Most High give you rest and peace after your troubles!'

25 Suddenly, as I was still speaking to the woman, I saw her face begin to shine brightly. Her countenance flashed like lightning, and I shrank from her in fear, and wondered what this meant. 26 All at once she uttered a great cry of terror that shook the earth. 27 I looked up and saw no longer a woman but a city, built on massive foundations. I was terrified and cried aloud, 28 'Where is the angel Uriel who came to me before? It is his doing that I have reached this state of panic, that my end is to be bodily corruption, and my prayers are met by reproach.'

29 I was still speaking when there appeared the angel who had come previously. When he saw me 30 lying unconscious, in a dead faint, he grasped me by my right hand, put strength into me, and raised me to my feet. 31 'What is the matter?' he asked. 'Why are you overcome? What has so disturbed you and troubled your mind?' 32 'You abandoned me,' I replied. 'I did as you told me: I came out to the fields; and what I have seen here and can still see is beyond my power to explain.'

33 'Stand up like a man,' he said, 'and I shall enlighten you.'

34 'Speak on, my lord,' I replied; 'only do not abandon me and leave me to die to no purpose. 35 I have seen and heard things beyond my knowledge and understanding— 36 unless this is all an illusion and a dream. 37 My lord, explain this state, I beg you.'

38 'Listen to me,' replied the angel, 'while I expound the things that terrify you; for the Most High has revealed many secrets to you. 39 He has seen your upright life, your unceasing grief for your people, and your deep mourning over Zion.

40 'Here, then, is the meaning of the vision. 41 A little while ago you saw a woman mourning and tried to console her; 42 now you no longer see that woman, but a complete city has appeared to you. 43 She told you about losing her son, and this is the explanation.

44 The woman you saw is Zion, which you now see as a city complete with its buildings. 45 She told you she was childless for thirty years; that was because three thousand years passed before any sacrifices were offered in Zion. 46 But then, after the three thousand years, Solomon built the city and offered the sacrifices; that was when the childless woman bore a son. 47 She took great trouble, she said, over his upbringing; that was the period when Jerusalem was inhabited. 48 She told you of the loss she suffered, how her son had died on the day he entered his bridal chamber; that was the destruction which has overtaken Jerusalem. 49 Such then was the vision you saw—the woman mourning for her son —and you tried to comfort her in her sufferings; this was the revelation you had to receive. 50 Seeing the sincerity of your grief and how you feel for her with all your heart, the Most High is now showing you her radiant glory and her surpassing beauty. 51 That was why I told you to stay in a field where no house has been built, 52 for I knew that the Most High intended to send you this revelation. 53 I told you to come to this field, where no foundation had been laid for any building, 54 because in the place where the city of the Most High was to be revealed no building made by man could stand.

55 'Have no fear, then, and set your mind at rest; go into the city, and see the great buildings in all their splendour, so far as your eyes have power to see them. 56 After that you will hear as much as your ears have power to hear. 57 You are more blessed than most, and few have such a name with the Most High as you have. 58 Stay here till tomorrow night, 59 when the Most High will show you in dreams and visions what he will do to earth's inhabitants in the last days.' So, as I had been told, I slept there that night and the next.

Ezra's fifth vision

11 On the second night I had a vision in my sleep: there, rising out of the sea, appeared an eagle with twelve wings and

---

being put to pagan worship (Ezra 1.7) or to profane use (see Dan. 5.2–3). **28:** *Uriel:* see 4.1 n.

10.29–59: The vision interpreted. 30: *In a dead faint:* compare Rev. 1.17. **33:** *Stand up:* see 5.15; 6.13, 17. **44:** *City:* the heavenly Jerusalem. **46–48:** *A son:* the earthly Jerusalem. His death symbolized Jerusalem's fall. **50:** Heavenly Zion continues, and its *radiant glory* will be seen; see Ezek. 40.2; 48.35; Heb. 11.10; Rev. 21.10.

11.1–12.51: Vision V. Rome to be destroyed. This strange vision with its bizarre and mysterious details is three heads. ²I saw it spread its wings over the whole earth; and all the winds of heaven blew upon it and clouds gathered about it. ³Out of its wings I saw opposing wings sprout, which proved to be only small and stunted. ⁴Its heads lay still; even the middle head, which was bigger than the others, lay still between them. ⁵As I watched, the eagle rose on its wings to establish itself as ruler over the earth and its inhabitants. ⁶I saw it bring into subjection everything under heaven; it encountered no protest at all from any creature on earth. ⁷I saw the eagle stand erect on its talons and address its wings: ⁸'Do not all wake together,' it said; 'sleep each of you in your place and wake up in your turn; ⁹the heads are to be kept till the last.' ¹⁰I saw that the sound was coming not from its heads but from the middle of its body. ¹¹I counted the opposing wings: there were eight of them.

¹²As I watched, one of the wings on its right side rose and became ruler over the whole earth. ¹³After a time its reign came to an end, and it disappeared, leaving no trace. Then the next arose and established its rule, holding sway for a long time. ¹⁴When its reign was coming to an end and it was about to disappear like the first, ¹⁵a voice could be heard addressing it: ¹⁶'You have held the world in your grasp; now listen to my message before your time comes to disappear. ¹⁷None of your successors will achieve a reign as long as yours, or even half as long.' ¹⁸Then the third wing arose, exercised power for a time like its predecessors, and like them disappeared. ¹⁹In the same way all the wings came to power one after the other, and in turn each disappeared.

²⁰As time went on, I saw the little wings on the right side also raise themselves up to seize power. Some achieved this, and at once passed from sight, ²¹while others arose but never attained to power. ²²At this point I noticed that two of the little wings were, like the twelve large ones, no longer to be seen; ²³nothing was left on the eagle's body except

the three motionless heads and six little wings. ²⁴As I watched, two of the six little wings separated from the rest and stationed themselves under the head on the right. The other four remained where they were, ²⁵and I saw them planning to rise up and seize power. ²⁶One rose, but disappeared immediately; ²⁷so too did the second, vanishing even more quickly than the first. ²⁸I saw the last two planning to make themselves the rulers; ²⁹but while they were still plotting, suddenly one of the heads woke from sleep, the one in the middle, the biggest of the three. ³⁰I saw how it joined with the other two heads, ³¹and along with them turned and devoured the two little wings which were planning to become rulers. ³²This head got the whole earth into its grasp, establishing an oppressive regime over all its inhabitants and a world-wide kingdom mightier than any of the wings had governed. ³³But after that I saw the middle head vanish as suddenly as the wings had done. ³⁴There were two heads left, and they also made themselves rulers over the earth and its inhabitants; ³⁵but, as I watched, the head on the right devoured the head on the left.

³⁶Then I heard a voice saying to me: 'Look carefully at what you see in front of you.' ³⁷I looked, and saw what seemed to be a lion roused out of the forest and roaring as it came. I heard it address the eagle in a human voice. ³⁸'Listen, you, to what I tell you!' it said. 'The Most High says: ³⁹Are you not the sole survivor of the four beasts to which I gave the rule over my world, intending through them to bring to an end the times I fixed? ⁴⁰⁻⁴¹You are the fourth beast to come, and you have conquered all who went before, dominating the whole world and holding it in the grip of fear and harsh oppression. You have lived long in the world, governing it with deceit and with no regard for truth. ⁴²You have trodden underfoot the gentle and injured the peaceful, hating the truthful

---

11:2 **clouds:** *so some Vss.; Lat. omits.*

more apocalyptic in tone than the previous ones.

11.1–12.3a: The mighty eagle and the strong lion. 1: *Rising out of the sea:* see Dan. 7.3; Rev. 13.1. As viewed from the east, Roman forces came from the Mediterranean. *An eagle:* the military emblem of Imperial Rome. **2:** *Spread its wings:* establish its dominion. **3:** *Opposing wings* probably symbolize rebellious army officers. Being *small and stunted,* unequal to the task, the rebellion hopelessly failed. **12:** The *wings* and heads (vv. 4, 29) seem to represent successive Roman rulers. **35:** *The head . . . devoured:* successful insurrection. **37:** *A lion:* the Messiah; see 12.31–32. **39:** *The four beasts* are those of Dan. 7.3 which the present passage recalls and loving liars; you have destroyed the homes of the prosperous, and razed to the ground the walls of those who had done you no harm. 43 Your insolence is known to the Most High, your pride to the Mighty One. 44 The Most High has surveyed the periods he has fixed: they are now at an end, and his ages have reached their completion. 45 Therefore, eagle, you must now disappear and be seen no more, you and your terrible great wings, your villainous small wings, your cruel heads, your grim talons, and your whole worthless carcass. 46 Then all the earth will be refreshed and relieved by being freed from your violence, and will look forward in hope to the judgement and mercy of its Creator.'

12 While the lion was still addressing the eagle, I looked 2 and saw the one remaining head disappear, and the two wings which had gone over to it arose and set themselves up as rulers. But their reign was short and troubled, 3 and when I looked they were already vanishing. Then the eagle's whole body burst into flames, filling the earth with terror.

So great was my agitation and alarm that I awoke. I said to myself: 4 'See the result of the attempt to discover the ways of the Most High! 5 I am weary of mind and utterly exhausted; the terrors I have experienced this night have bereft me of the last vestige of strength. 6 I shall now pray, therefore, to the Most High to be given strength to the end.' 7 I said: 'My Master and Lord, if I have found favour with you and am esteemed more just than most men, and if it is true that my prayers have reached your presence, 8 then give me strength. Reveal to me, my Lord, the precise interpretation of this terrifying vision, and set my soul fully at ease, 9 for you

have already judged me worthy to be shown the end of the present age.'

10 The angel answered: 'Here is the interpretation of your vision. 11 The eagle you saw rising out of the sea represents the fourth kingdom in the vision seen by your brother Daniel. 12 But he was not given the interpretation which I am now giving you or have already given you. 13 The days are coming when the earth will be under an empire more terrible than any before. 14 It will be ruled by twelve kings, one after another, 15 the second to come to the throne having the longest reign of all the twelve. 16 That is the meaning of the twelve wings you saw.

17 'As for the voice which you heard speaking from the middle of the eagle's body, and not from its heads, this is what it means: 18 after this second king's reign, great conflicts will arise, which will bring the empire into danger of collapse; yet it will not collapse then, but will be restored to its original power.

19 'As for the eight lesser wings which you saw growing from the eagle's wings, this is what they mean: 20 the empire will come under eight kings whose reigns will be brief and transient; 21 two of them will come and go just before the middle of the period, four will be kept back until shortly before its end, and two will be left until the end itself.

22 'As for the three heads which you saw sleeping, this is what they mean: 23 in the last years of the empire, the Most High will bring to the throne three kings, who will restore much of its strength, and rule over the earth 24 and its inhabitants more oppressively than any who preceded them. They are called the eagle's heads, 25 because they will bring to a

12:23 *who . . . rule: so some Vss.; Lat.* and he will restore . . . and they will rule.

(12.11). **43:** *Your insolence:* compare Dan. 5.20. **44:** The apocalyptic writers see the *periods* of human life before the *completion* of the end as *fixed* like the scenes of a pageant, brought on and removed from the stage of history by God, with no historical preparation, conditioning, or interconnection between them.

12.3b–39: The eagle vision interpreted. 11: *The fourth kingdom* of Dan. 7.7, 23 is here, as in rabbinic writings, understood to be the Roman Empire. **13:** The apocalyptic writers describe contemporary or past events as *days* that *are coming* to show that they had been foretold by the prophets and so were in God's plan. The objective was to provide consolation in the present trials and confidence in God's Providence for the future, as well as credibility in the descriptions of the end. Here the visions are set in the exilic period (1.3; 3.1) even though the seer is describing events that followed it and continued up to and beyond the time of the destruction of the second temple. **14:** *Twelve kings* are twelve emperors, beginning with Julius Caesar. **15:** *The second:* Augustus. **17:** See 11.10. **18:** The *great conflicts* seems to allude to the anarchy after Nero's death in 68 C.E. **19:** *Eight lesser wings:* see 11.3 n. **21:** *The period:* the duration of the empire. **22:** The three heads (see 11.1, head and consummate its long series of wicked deeds. 26 As for the greatest head, which you saw disappear, it signifies one of the kings; he will die in his bed, but in agony. 27 The two that survived will be destroyed by the sword; 28 one of them will fall victim to the sword of the other, who will himself fall by the sword in the last days.

29 'As for the two little wings that went over to the head on the right side, 30 this is what they mean: they are the ones whom the Most High has reserved until the last days, and their reign, as you saw, was short and troubled.

31 'As for the lion which you saw coming out of the forest, roused from sleep and roaring, and which you heard addressing the eagle, taxing it with its wicked deeds and words, 32 he is the Messiah whom the Most High has kept back until the end of the days; he will arise from the stock of David and will come and address those rulers, taxing them openly with their sins, their crimes, and their defiance. 33 First, he will bring them alive to judgement; then, after convicting them, he will destroy them. 34 But he will be merciful to the rest of my people, all who have survived in my land; he will set them free and give them joy, until the final day of judgement comes, about which I told you at the beginning.

35 'That is the vision you saw, and that its meaning. 36 It is the secret of the Most High, of which no one except yourself has proved worthy to be told. 37 You must therefore write in a book all you have seen, and deposit it in a hiding-place. 38 You must also disclose these secrets to those of your people whom you know to be wise enough to understand them and to keep them safe. 39 However, you must stay here for seven days more, to receive whatever revelation the Most High thinks fit to send you.' Then the angel left me.

40 When all the people heard that seven days had passed and I had not yet returned to the city, both high and low assembled and came to me and asked: 41 'What wrong or what injury have we done you, that you have abandoned us for good and settled in this place? 42 Out of all the prophets you are the only one left to us. You are like the last cluster in a vineyard, like a lamp in a dark place, or a safe harbour for a ship in a storm. 43 Have we not suffered enough already? 44 If you abandon us, we had far better have perished in the fire that destroyed Zion. 45 We are no better than those who died there.' And they wept aloud.

46 'Take courage, Israel,' I answered them; 'lay aside your grief, house of Jacob. 47 The Most High bears you in mind, the Mighty God has not forgotten you for ever. 48 I have not abandoned you, nor shall I leave you; I came here to pray for Zion in her desolation, and to beg for mercy for our sanctuary now fallen so low. 49 Go to your homes for the present, every one of you, and in a few days' time I shall come back to you.'

50 So the people returned to the city as I told them, 51 while I remained in the field. As commanded by the angel I stayed there for seven days, eating nothing but what grew in the field, and living on that for the whole of the time.

Ezra's sixth vision

13 THE seven days passed; and the following night I had a dream. 2 In my dream, a wind arose from the sea and set all its waves in turmoil. 3 As I watched, the wind brought a figure like that of a man out of the depths, and he flew with the clouds of heaven. Wherever he turned his face, everything he looked at trembled, 4 and wherever the sound of his voice reached, everyone who heard it melted as wax at the touch of fire.

12:32 of the days . . . address: so one Vs.; Lat. defective.
13:3 the wind . . . depths: so other Vss.; Lat. defective.

4, 29–35) may symbolize the Flavian emperors, Vespasian and his sons, Titus and Domitian. 31: The lion: see 11.37–12.3. 32: The verse implies the heavenly preexistence of the Messiah; compare Dan. 7.13–14. 34: The rest of my people are those who survive the messianic woes. See 7.26–28. 37–38: The book is to be put into a hiding place because of its esoteric contents which only the wise, i.e. the initiated, can understand and keep safe. Hence, the name Apocrypha, lit. "hidden," given to this class of books.

12.40–51: The seer comforts the people. 40: Seven days: see 9.23. 42: The apocalyptic writer puts Ezra into the category of the prophets; see 5.17–18 n. A lamp: see 2 Pet. 1.19. 50: Compare v. 39 and 9.24–26.

13.1–58: Vision VI. The Messiah's activity.

13.1–20: The man risen from the sea. 3: A figure like that of a man: the Messiah. See v. 32; compare Dan. 7.13. 4: Everyone . . . melted like wax suggests a divine manifestation. See Ps. 97.5; Mic. 1.4.

5 Next I saw a countless host of men gathering from the four winds of heaven to vanquish the man who had come up out of the sea. 6 I saw that the man hewed out for himself a great mountain, and flew on to it. 7 Though I tried to see from what region or place the mountain had been taken, I could not. 8 Then I saw that all who had gathered to fight against the man were greatly afraid, and yet they dared to fight. 9 When he saw the hordes advancing to the attack, he did not so much as lift a finger against them. He had no spear in his hand, no weapon at all; 10 only, as I watched, he poured out what appeared to be a stream of fire from his mouth, a breath of flame from his lips with a storm of sparks from his tongue. 11 These, the stream of fire, the breath of flame, and the great storm, combined into one mass which fell on the host prepared for battle, and burnt them all up. Of that enormous multitude suddenly nothing was to be discerned but dust and ashes and a reek of smoke. I was astounded at the sight.

12 After that, I saw the man come down from the mountain and summon to himself a different, a peaceful company. 13 He was joined by great numbers of men, some with joy on their faces, others with sorrow, some coming from captivity, and some bringing others to him as an offering. I woke up overcome by terror, and I prayed to the Most High: 14 'O Lord, from first to last you have revealed those wonders to me, and judged me worthy to have my prayers answered. 15 Now show me the meaning of this dream also. 16 How terrible it will be, to my thinking, for all who survive to those days, but how much worse for those who do not! 17 Those who do not survive will have the sorrow 18 of knowing what the last days have in store, yet without attaining it. 19 Those who do survive are to be pitied for the terrible dangers and many trials which those visions show they will have to face. 20 But perhaps after all it is better to endure the dangers and reach the goal than to vanish from the world like a cloud and never see what will happen at the last.'

21 'Yes,' he replied, 'I shall disclose the meaning of the vision, and tell you what you ask. 22 To your question about those who survive, the answer is this: 23 the very person from whom danger will then come will protect those exposed to the danger if they have good deeds and faith laid up to their credit with God Most Mighty. 24 You may rest assured that those who survive are more blessed than those who have died.

25 'This is what the vision means: the man you saw coming up from the heart of the sea 26 is he whom the Most High has held in readiness during many ages; through him he will deliver the world he has made, and he will determine the destiny of those who survive. 27 As for the breath of flame, the fire, and the storm you saw issuing from the mouth of the man, 28 so that without spear or any other weapon in his hand he crushed the onslaught of the hordes advancing to fight against him, the meaning is this: 29 the day is near when the Most High will start bringing deliverance to those on earth. 30 Its panic-stricken inhabitants 31 will plot hostilities against one another, city against city, region against region, nation against nation, kingdom against kingdom. 32 When that happens, and all the signs that I have shown you take place, then my son will be revealed, he whom you saw as a man coming up out of the sea. 33 At the sound of his voice all nations will leave their own territories and their separate wars, 34 and unite as you saw in your vision in one large host past counting, all intent on overpowering him. 35 When he takes his stand on the summit of Mount Zion, 36 then Zion, completed and fully built, will come and appear before all people, corresponding to the mountain which you saw hewn out, though not by human hands. 37 My son will convict of their godless deeds the nations that confront him; this will accord with the storm you saw.

13:26 **him:** *so one Vs.; Lat.* himself.

6: *Hewed out:* see Dan. 2.34, 45. **10:** *A breath of flame:* without weapon or allies the Messiah destroys his enemies supernaturally, i.e. by the words of judgment that come from his *mouth:* see Isa. 11.4; 2 Thess. 2.8. **13:** *As an offering:* see Isa. 66.20; compare Isa. 49.22. **18:** *What the last days have in store:* see 7.26–(44); 9.1–12. **19:** Compare Matt. 24.21–22. **20:** The just who *endure the dangers* of the *last days* seem to have an advantage over those who died before; compare 1 Thess. 4.15–18. See also v. 24.

13.21–58: The vision interpreted. 23: *The very person* is the Messiah, whose coming is presaged by the messianic woes. **26:** See 12.32 n. **27:** See vv. 9–11. **32:** *My son will be revealed:* see 7.28; compare Matt. 24.30. **35:** *Mount Zion* is thus the mountain hewed out (v. 6). **36:** *Zion:* the heavenly Jerusalem; see 7.26 and

38 He will reproach them to their face with their evil plotting and the torments they are soon to undergo; this is symbolized by the flame. And he will destroy them without effort by means of the law—and that is like the fire.

39 'You saw him assemble a company which was different and peaceful. 40 They are the ten tribes that were taken into exile in the days of King Hoshea, whom King Shalmaneser of Assyria made captive. Carrying them off beyond the river Euphrates, he deported them to a foreign country. 41 But then they resolved to leave behind the gentile population and go to a more distant region never yet inhabited, 42 and there at least to be obedient to their laws, which in their own country they had failed to keep. 43 As they passed through the narrow passages of the Euphrates, 44 the Most High performed miracles for them, halting the flow of the river until they had crossed over. 45 Their long journey through that region called Arzareth took a year and a half. 46 They have lived there ever since, until this final age. Now they are on their way back, 47 and once more the Most High is halting the river to let them cross.

'That is the meaning of the peaceful company you saw assembled. 48 With them too are the survivors of your own people, all who are found inside my sacred borders. 49 When the time comes, therefore, for him to destroy the assembled nations, he will protect those of your people who are left, 50 and then display to them countless portents.'

51 'My master and lord,' I said, 'explain to me why the man I saw came up out of the heart of the sea.' 52 He replied: 'It is beyond the power of anyone to explore the deep sea and discover what is in it; in the same way no one on earth can set eyes on my son and those who accompany him until the appointed day. 53 Such then is the meaning of your vision.

This revelation has been given to you, and to you alone, 54 because you have laid aside your own affairs, and devoted yourself entirely to mine and to the study of my law. 55 You have taken wisdom as your guide in life, and you have called understanding your mother. 56 That is why I have given this revelation to you: there is a reward for you with the Most High. In three more days' time I shall speak with you again, and tell you of momentous and wonderful things.'

57 So I went away to the field, glorifying and praising the Most High for the wonders he performed from time to time 58 and for his providential control of the passing ages and what happens in them. There I remained for three days.

Ezra's seventh vision

14 ON the third day I was sitting under an oak tree, when there came a voice from a bush in front of me: 'Ezra, Ezra!' it called. 2 'Here I am, Lord,' I answered, rising to my feet. 3 The voice went on: 'When my people was in slavery in Egypt, I revealed myself in the bush and spoke to Moses, 4 sending him to lead Israel out of Egypt. I brought him to Mount Sinai, where for many days I kept him with me. 5 I explained many wonderful things to him, showing him the secrets of the ages and the end of time, and I instructed him 6 what to make public and what to keep hidden. 7 To you also I now say: 8 Store up in your mind the signs I have shown you, the visions you have seen, and the interpretations you have heard. 9 You are about to be taken away from the world of men, and thereafter you will remain with my son and with those like you until the end of time. 10 The world has lost its youth, and time is growing old; 11 for the whole of time is in twelve divisions, of which nine divisions and

Rev. 21.2–4. **40:** *The ten tribes:* the Northern Kingdom, 2 Kgs. 17.3, 6. Perhaps an ideal group, including proselytes, is meant. **44:** *The Most High performed miracles* as in the original entrance into Canaan (Josh. 3.14–17). **45:** *Arzareth:* shortened transliteration of Heb. for "another land," taken from Deut. 29.28. **47:** See Isa. 11.15–16. **49:** *Those of your people who are left:* righteous Israel enlarged by the return of the ten tribes. **50:** *Countless portents* were to occur at the outset of the messianic age. See 5.1–13; 6.11–28. **52:** *Those who accompany:* probably angels, as in Matt. 24.31; 25.31; 2 Thess. 1.7. **57:** *The field:* Ardat (9.26).

14.1–48: Vision VII. The writing of the sacred books.

14.1–18: God admonishes Ezra to prepare to leave this life. 1: *A bush:* see Exod. 3.4. Ezra is set forth as a second Moses. **4:** *Many days:* forty days (Exod. 34.28). **6:** *What to keep hidden:* see v. 46 n. **8:** *Signs . . . visions . . . interpretations:* i.e. the contents of the preceding chapters. **9:** *To be taken away:* to be taken alive out of this world like Enoch and Elijah; see 6.26 n. **10:** Compare 5.50–55. **11–12:** *Nine divisions and half the tenth* half the tenth are already past; [12] so there remain only two and a half. [13] Now, therefore, set your house in order; admonish your nation, and give comfort to those of them who are lowly. Then take your leave of this corruptible life; [14] let go your earthly cares, and throw off your human burdens; shed your weak nature, [15] and put on one side the anxieties that vex you; then make haste to depart from this world of time. [16] However great the evils you have witnessed, there are worse to come. [17] As this ageing world grows ever more feeble, the more will evils increase for its inhabitants. [18] Truth will move farther away, and falsehood draw nearer. The eagle you saw in your vision is already on the wing.'

[19] 'Lord, if I may speak in your presence,' I replied, [20] 'I am to depart, by your command, after admonishing those of my people who are now alive; but who will give a warning to those born hereafter? The world is shrouded in darkness and its inhabitants are without light. [21] Because your law was destroyed in the fire, no one can know what you have done or intend to do. [22] If, then, I have found favour with you, send into me your holy spirit, and I shall put in writing the whole story of the world from the very beginning, everything that was contained in your law, so that all may have the possibility of finding the right path, and, if they so choose, of obtaining life in the last days.'

[23] 'Go,' he answered, 'call the people together, and tell them not to look for you for forty days. [24] Prepare a large number of writing tablets, and bring with you Seraiah and Dabri, Shelemiah, Ethan, and Asiel, five men all trained to write quickly. [25] On your return here, I shall light in your mind a lamp of understanding which will not go out until you have finished what you are to write. [26] When it is complete, some of it you must make public; the rest you must give to wise men to keep hidden. Tomorrow at this time you shall begin writing.'

[27] I went as I was ordered, called together all the people, and said: [28] 'Israel, listen to what I say. [29] At first our ancestors lived as aliens in Egypt; from there they were rescued [30] and given the law which imparts life. But they disobeyed it, and you have followed their example. [31] You were given a land of your own, the land of Zion; but, like your ancestors, you sinned and abandoned the ways laid down for you by the Most High. [32] Being a just judge, he took back in due time what he had given you. [33] Now you are here, and your fellow-countrymen are still farther away. [34] If, therefore, you direct your understanding and instruct your minds, you will be kept safe in life and meet with mercy after death. [35] For after death will come the judgement: we shall be restored to life, and then the names of the just will be known and the deeds of the godless exposed. [36] But no one must come near me now or look for me during the next forty days.'

[37] As instructed I took the five men with me, and we went out to the field and stayed there. [38] On the next day I heard a voice calling to me: 'Ezra, open your mouth and drink what I give you.' [39] I opened my mouth, and was handed a cup full of what seemed like water, except that its colour was the colour of fire. [40] I took it and drank, and, as soon as I had done so, understanding welled up in my mind, and wisdom increased within me. My memory remained fully active, [41] and I began to speak and went on without stopping. [42] The Most High gave understanding to the

had passed at the time the seer allegedly was writing, i.e. the reign of Artaxerxes II (404–359 B.C.E.; see 1.3 n.). What the measure of the divisions was is unknown but the two and a half divisions would have been greatly reduced at the time when the book appeared, approximately 100 C.E. See Introduction. **18:** *Eagle:* see ch. 11, especially 11.1 n.

14.19–26: The inspiration to restore Scriptures is granted. 20: *Without light:* without God's law (Ps. 19.8). **21:** *The fire:* Jerusalem's destruction; see 2 Kgs. 25.8–9. **23:** *Forty days:* see v. 1 n. and v. 4 n. **26:** *Some . . . make public:* publish the restored Heb. Scriptures (v. 45). *The rest . . . keep hidden:* see v. 46. As Moses, according to tradition, handed down an oral law to the sages, so Ezra is to preserve a number of secret (apocryphal) books for the future. See 12.37–38 n.

14.27–36: Ezra's last admonition to the people. 33: *Your fellow-countrymen:* perhaps the ten tribes. See 13.40 n., 41. **36:** See v. 23.

14.37–48: Ezra rewrites the holy books. 39: A *cup* of inspiration is given to Ezra enabling him to restore perfectly the Scriptures; compare Ezek. 3.1–3; Rev. 10.9–11. **42:** Until the Exile, the Heb. language was written five men, who took turns at writing down what was said, using characters which they had not known before. They continued at work throughout the forty days, writing all day, and taking food only at night. ⁴³ But as for me, I spoke all through the day, and even at night I did not break off. ⁴⁴ In the forty days, ninety-four books were written down. ⁴⁵ At the end of the time the Most High said to me: 'Make public the twenty-four books you wrote first; they are to be read by everyone, whether worthy to do so or not. ⁴⁶ But the last seventy books are to be kept back, and given to none but the wise among your people; ⁴⁷ they contain a stream of understanding, a fountain of wisdom, a flood of knowledge.' ⁴⁸ And this I did.

Prophecies and warnings

15 PROCLAIM to my people the words of prophecy which I give you to speak, says the Lord; ² have them written down, for they are trustworthy and true. ³ Do not be afraid of plots against you, and do not be troubled by the unbelief of your opponents; ⁴ for everyone who does not believe will die because of his unbelief.

⁵ Beware! says the Lord; I am letting loose over the earth terrible evils, sword and famine, death and destruction, ⁶ because evil men have spread their wickedness the whole world over, and it is filled to overflowing with their deeds of violence. ⁷ Therefore the Lord declares: ⁸ I shall no longer keep silent about their godless acts, nor shall I tolerate their wicked practices. See how the blood of innocent victims cries to me for vengeance, and

the souls of the just never cease to plead with me! ⁹ I shall most surely avenge them, says the Lord, and give ear to the plea of all the innocent blood that has been shed. ¹⁰ My people are being led like sheep to the slaughter. I shall allow them to remain in Egypt no longer, ¹¹ but shall rescue them with a strong hand and an outstretched arm; I shall strike the Egyptians with plagues, as I did once before, and bring ruin on their whole land. ¹² Shaken to its very foundations, how Egypt will mourn when scourged and chastised by plagues from the Lord! ¹³ How workers on the land will mourn when seed fails to grow and their trees are devastated by blight and hail and terrible storm! ¹⁴ Woe to the world and its inhabitants: ¹⁵ the sword that will destroy them is not far distant! With blade unsheathed, nation will rise against nation. ¹⁶ Stable government will be at an end; as one faction prevails over another, they will in their day of power care nothing for king or magnate. ¹⁷ Anyone wishing to visit a city will find himself unable to do so, ¹⁸ for rival ambitions will have reduced cities to chaos, demolishing houses and inspiring widespread fear. ¹⁹ Sword in hand, a man will attack his neighbour's house and plunder his possessions; when he is driven by famine and grinding misery, no pity will restrain him.

²⁰ See how I summon all the kings of the earth, God says, from the sunrise and the south wind, from the east and the south, to turn and repay what has been given to them. ²¹ I shall do to them as they are doing to my chosen ones even to the present day; I shall pay them back in their own coin.

15:4 **because . . . unbelief:** *or* in his unbelief.

in the Phoenician script. Between the sixth and fourth centuries B.C.E., the Aram. script was adopted and from it developed the square *characters* still used in writing Heb. To give the new script a sacred quality it is presented as revealed by God. **44–45:** The *ninety-four books* comprise the twenty-four books of the present Heb. canon, those written *first . . . to be read by everyone.* These twenty-four equal the thirty-nine of the Christian canon where the double books of Sam., Kgs., and Chr., as well as Ezra-Neh., are counted separately and the minor prophets are counted as twelve instead of as one book as in the Hebrew. **46:** *The last seventy books* include apocryphal and apocalyptic works such as the present one, to which the writer here ascribes great value as well as the authority of Moses (see v. 6) and Ezra. They are for the *wise,* i.e. the initiated.

15.1–16.78: Prophecies of doom. This section is considered a Christian appendix.

15.1–27: The coming vengeance. 3: *Do not be afraid:* compare Jer. 1.17; Ezek. 2.6. Other expressions in vv. 1–4 also imitate the "calls" of OT prophets. **8–9:** The Lord is considered the avenger of *blood* in the case of the *innocent;* compare Gen. 4.10–11; Rev. 6.9–10; 19.2. **10:** See Ps. 44.22. The chief wickedness to be avenged is the persecution of God's people. **11:** *I shall strike the Egyptians* may allude to the famine which almost decimated the population of Alexandria in Gallienus' reign (260–268 C.E.). *As I did once before* alludes to the ten plagues (Exod. 7.14–11.10; 12.28–36). **15:** *Nation . . . against nation:* compare Matt. 24.7; Mk. 13.8.

These are the words of the Lord God: [22] I shall show sinners no pity; the sword will not spare those murderers who stain the ground with innocent blood. [23] The Lord's anger has burst out in flame, scorching the earth to its foundations and consuming sinners like burning straw. [24] Woe to sinners who flout my commands! says the Lord; [25] I shall show them no mercy. Away from me, you rebels! Do not pollute my sanctuary with your presence. [26] The Lord well knows all who offend against him, and has consigned them to death and destruction. [27] Already calamities have spread over the world, and there is no escape for you; God will refuse to rescue you, because you have sinned against him.

[28] How terrible is the vision that comes from the east! [29] Hordes of dragons from Arabia will sally forth with countless chariots, and from the first day of their advance their hissing is borne across the land, so that all who hear them will tremble in fear. [30] The Carmanians, beside themselves with fury, will rush like wild boars out of a thicket, advancing in full force to do battle with them; they will devastate whole tracts of Assyria with their tusks. [31] But then the dragons will summon up their native fury and prove the stronger. Massing all their forces, they will fall on the Carmanians with overwhelming might [32] until, routed and their power silenced, the Carmanians turn to flight. [33] Their way will be blocked by a lurking enemy from Assyria, and when one of them is killed, terror and trembling will spread in their army and confusion among their kings.

[34] See the clouds stretching from east and north to south! Full of fury and tempest, their appearance is hideous. [35] They will clash together, letting loose a vast storm over the land; blood, shed by the sword, will reach as high as a horse's belly, [36] a man's thigh, or a camel's hock. [37] There will be terror and trembling throughout the world; those who see the fury rage will shudder, stricken with panic. [38] Then vast storm-clouds will approach from south and north, and others from the west. [39] But the winds from the east will be stronger still, and will hold in check the raging cloud and its leader; and the storm which was bent on destruction will be fiercely driven back to the south and west by the winds from the east. [40] Huge clouds, mighty and full of fury, will pile up and ravage the whole land and its inhabitants, and a terrible storm will sweep over all that is high and exalted, [41] with fire and hail and flying swords and a deluge of water which will flood all the plains and rivers. [42] They will flatten to the ground cities and walls, mountains and hills, trees in the woods and crops in the fields. [43] They will force their way to Babylon, and destroy her; [44] for they will encompass her when they get there, and let loose a storm in all its fury. The dust and smoke will reach the sky, and all the neighbouring cities will mourn over her. [45] Any who survive in her will be enslaved by her destroyers.

[46] And you, Asia, who have shared in the beauty and the glory of Babylon, [47] woe to you, miserable wretch! Like her you have dressed up your daughters as whores, to attract for your glorification the lovers who have always lusted for you. [48] You have imitated all the practices and schemes of that vile harlot. Therefore God says: [49] I shall unleash calamities on you—widowhood and poverty, famine, sword, and pestilence, to bring devastation to your homes with violence and death. [50] When the scorching heat bears down upon you, your strength and splendour will wither like a flower. [51] You will become a poor, weak woman, bruised, beaten, and wounded, unable any more to receive your wealthy lovers. [52] I should not be so fierce with you, says the Lord, [53] if you had not always killed my chosen ones, gloating over the blows you struck and hurling your drunken taunts at their corpses.

[54] Paint your face; beautify yourself! [55] The prostitute's hire shall be yours; you will get what you have earned. [56] What you do to my chosen people, God will do to you, says the Lord; he will consign you to a terrible fate.

15.28–63: Syria, Rome threatened. After a general announcement of doom, the text speaks of warfare against *Assyria,* i.e. the Roman province of Syria (v. 30). Again events of the third century C.E. seem reflected (see v. 11 n.), especially the attack of the Persian King Shapur I (241–273 C.E.) against Syria. **29:** *Dragons from Arabia* are apparently the armies of the Arabs of Palmyra. **30:** *The Carmanians* are the Sassanid Persians, Carmania (Kerman) being a Persian province. **43:** *Babylon:* Rome, as in Rev. 18.10. **46:** *Asia:* perhaps the Roman province of Asia, namely, the western end of Asia Minor, now Turkey. **48:** *That vile harlot:* see Rev. 14.8; 17.4–5. **49:** See Rev. 18.7–8.

57 Your children will perish from hunger, you will fall by the sword, your cities will be reduced to rubble, and all your people will fall on the field of battle. 58 Those who are on the mountains will be dying of hunger: their hunger and thirst will drive them to gnaw their own flesh and drink their own blood. 59 You will be foremost in misery; and there will be more still to come. 60 As the victors go past on their way home from the sack of Babylon, they will reduce your peaceful city to dust, destroy a great part of your territory, and bring much of your splendour to an end. 61 They will destroy you — you will be stubble to their fire. 62 They will completely devour you and your cities, your land and your mountains, and will burn down all your woodlands and your fruit trees. 63 They will carry off your sons as captives and plunder your possessions; not a trace will be left of your splendid beauty.

16 Woe to you, Babylon and Asia! Woe to you, Egypt and Syria! 2 Put on sackcloth and hair shirt and raise a cry of lamentation over your people, for destruction is close at hand. 3 The sword is let loose against you, and who will turn it aside? 4 Fire is let loose upon you, and who will extinguish it? 5 Calamities have been let loose against you, and who is to avert them? 6 Can anyone drive off a hungry lion in the forest, or put out a fire among stubble once it has begun to blaze? 7 Can anyone ward off an arrow shot by a strong archer? 8 When the Lord God sends calamities, who can avert them? 9 When his anger bursts into flame, who can extinguish it? 10 When the lightning flashes, who will not tremble? When it thunders, who will not quake with dread? 11 When the Lord threatens, is there anyone who will not be crushed to the ground at his approach? 12 The earth is shaken to its very foundations, and the sea is churned up from the depths; its waves and all the fish are in turmoil before the presence of the Lord and the majesty of his power. 13 Strong is his arm that bends the bow, and sharp the arrows he shoots; once they are on their way, nothing will stop them until they reach the ends of the earth. 14 Ca-

lamities are let loose, and will not turn back before they fetch up on earth. 15 The fire is alight and will not be put out until it has consumed earth's foundations. 16 An arrow shot by a powerful archer does not turn back; no more will the calamities let loose against the earth be recalled.

17 Alas, alas for me! Who will rescue me in those days? 18 At the onset of troubles, many will groan; at the onset of famine, many will die; at the onset of wars, empires will tremble; at the onset of bad times, all will be filled with terror. What will men do in the face of calamity? 19 Famine, plague, suffering, and hardship are scourges sent to teach them better ways; 20 but even so, they will not abandon their crimes or always keep the scourging in mind. 21 A time will come when food is so cheap that people will imagine peace and prosperity have arrived; but at that very moment the earth will become a hotbed of disasters — sword, famine, and anarchy. 22 Most of the inhabitants will die in the famine, while those who survive will be destroyed by the sword. 23 The dead will be thrown out like dung, and there will be no one to give them the last rites. The forsaken land will go to waste, and its cities to ruin; 24 no one will be left to cultivate the ground. 25 Trees will bear their fruits, but who will pick them? 26 Grapes will ripen, but who will tread them? There will be vast desolation everywhere. 27 A man will long to see a human face or hear a human voice, 28 for out of a whole city, only ten will survive, and in the countryside, only two will be left, hiding in the forest or in holes in the rocks. 29 As in an olive grove three or four olives might be left on each tree, 30 or as in a vineyard a few grapes might be overlooked by the sharp-eyed pickers, 31 so also in those days three or four will be overlooked by those who with sword in hand are searching the houses. 32 The forsaken land will go to waste and its fields be overrun with briars; thorns will grow over all the roads and paths, because there are no sheep to tread them. 33 Maidens will live in mourning with none to marry them; women will mourn because they have no husbands; their daughters will

16.1–34: Various powers denounced. Chapters 15 and 16 emulate the oracles against foreign nations by OT prophets such as Isaiah and Jeremiah. **1:** *Babylon:* Rome, as in 15.43. *Asia:* see 15.46 n. *Egypt:* see 15.11–19. **2:** *Sackcloth* was a sign of mourning and wearing a *hair shirt* next to the body a way of doing penance. **5:** A profusion of biblical phrases and stock apocalyptic ideas comprises the vague calamities here enumerated. **15:** See 2 Pet. 3.10. **19:** *Scourges sent to teach them:* compare Heb. 12.5–11.

mourn because they have no one to support them. [34] The young men who should have been bridegrooms will have been killed in the war, and the men who were married will have been wiped out by the famine.

[35] But you servants of the Lord, listen and learn. [36] This is the word of the Lord; take it to heart, and do not doubt what he says: [37] Calamities are close at hand, and will not be delayed. [38] When a woman is in the ninth month of her pregnancy and the moment of her child's birth is drawing near, there are two or three hours in which her womb suffers pangs of agony, and then the child comes from the womb without any further delay; [39] similarly, calamities will not defer their coming on the earth, and the world will groan under the pangs that beset it.

[40] My people, listen to my words; get ready for battle, and when the calamities surround you, behave as though you were strangers on earth. [41] The seller must expect to have to run for his life, the buyer to lose what he buys; [42] the merchant must expect to make no profit, the builder never to live in the house he builds. [43] The sower must not expect to reap, nor should he who prunes the vine expect to harvest the grapes. [44] Those who marry must not look for children; the unmarried must think of themselves as widowed. [45] For all who labour, labour in vain. [46] Their fruits will be gathered by foreigners, who will plunder their goods, pull down their houses, and take their sons captive, because only for captivity and famine will they bear children. [47] Any who make money do so only to have it plundered. The more care they lavish on their cities, houses, and property, and on their own persons, [48] the fiercer will be my indignation against their sins, says the Lord. [49] Like the indignation of a virtuous woman towards a prostitute, [50] so will be the indignation of justice towards wickedness decked out in finery; she will accuse her to her face, when the champion arrives to ex-

pose every sin on earth. [51] Therefore, do not imitate wickedness or her deeds; [52] in a very short time she will be swept away from the earth, and the reign of justice over us will begin.

[53] Let not the sinner deny that he has sinned; he will only bring burning coals on his own head if he says, 'I have committed no sin against the majesty of God.' [54] Everything that men do is known to the Lord; he knows their plans, their schemes, their inmost thoughts. [55] He said, 'Let the earth be made,' and it was made; 'Let the heavens be made,' and they were made. [56] The stars were fixed in their places by his word, and he knows the number of the stars. [57] He looks into the depths with their treasures; he has measured the sea and everything it contains. [58] By his word he confined the sea within the bounds of the waters and suspended the land above the water. [59] He spread out the sky like a vault, and fixed it firmly over the waters. [60] He provided springs in the desert, and pools on the mountaintops as the source of rivers flowing down to water the earth. [61] He created man, and put a heart in the middle of his body; he gave him breath, life, understanding, [62] and the very spirit of Almighty God who created all things and searches out secrets in secret places. [63] He knows well your plans and your inmost thoughts. Woe to sinners who try to conceal their sins! [64] The Lord will scrutinize all their deeds; he will call you all to account. [65] You will be covered with confusion, when your sins are brought into the open and your wicked deeds stand up to accuse you on that day. [66] What can you do? How will you hide your sins in the presence of God and his angels? [67] God is the judge; fear him! Abandon your sins, and have done with your wicked deeds for ever! Then God will set you free from all distress.

[68] Fierce flames are being kindled to consume you. A great horde will descend on you; they will seize some of you and compel

---

16.35–52: God's people warned of the coming disasters. 38: *A woman . . . in the ninth month of her pregnancy:* compare 4.40. *Pangs of agony:* calamities, as "birthpangs of the Messiah," presage the end of the present order; compare Jn. 16.21. **40–45:** In the *calamities* of the end, all stable economic and family life will cease so that *labour* to make it secure will be *in vain;* compare 1 Cor. 7.29–31. **51–52:** Do not *imitate wickedness:* compare 2 Pet. 3.11–13.

16.53–67: Sin cannot be hidden from God. 55–60: See Gen. 1.6–10.

16.68–78: God's persecuted people will be delivered. 68: *Fierce flames:* possibly the passage alludes to persecution of the Christians by the emperor Decius about 250 C.E.

you to eat food sacrificed to idols. 69 Those who give in to them will be derided, taunted, and humiliated. 70 In place after place and throughout the neighbouring cities there will be a violent attack on those who fear the Lord. 71 Their enemies will be like maniacs, plundering and destroying without mercy all who still fear the Lord, 72 destroying and plundering their possessions, and ejecting them from their homes. 73 Then it will be seen that my chosen ones have stood the test like gold in the assayer's fire.

74 Listen, you whom I have chosen, says the Lord: the days of harsh suffering are close at hand, but I shall rescue you from them. 75 Have done with fears and doubts! God is your guide. 76 As followers of my commandments and instructions, says the Lord God, you must not let your sins weigh you down or your wicked deeds gain the ascendancy. 77 Woe to those who are entangled in their sins and overrun with their wicked deeds! They are like a field where the path is entwined with bushes and brambles and there is no way through; 78 it is separated off in readiness for destruction by fire.

Tobit

This is the story of a pious Jew in exile who, after many misfortunes and trying events, finally sees the victory of God's Providence in a happy family reunion and a peaceful end.

Apart from the fascination of the tale itself, the book reflects aspects of Jewish piety during the Hellenistic period. The account is presented as history and as having taken place in Nineveh in the eighth century B.C.E. The many discrepancies with known facts of history suggest that the author uses Nineveh as a literary device, intending the blind Tobit to represent collective Israel who, in exile, is sorely tempted to lose faith in divine providence. The Israelites are admonished to remain faithful to the Torah so that they too may "see" at the end how God's designs are worked out in the ambiguities of history. The story belongs, therefore, to the category of Wisdom literature.

The author of Tobit is unknown. The story seems to be very old; differing versions have survived. This version was probably written in the early second century B.C.E. in Hebrew or Aramaic.

Tobit in exile

1 THIS is the story of Tobit son of Tobiel, son of Hananiel, son of Aduel, son of Gabael, son of Raphael, son of Raguel, of the family of Asiel, of the tribe of Naphtali. ² In the time of King Shalmaneser of Assyria he was taken captive from Thisbe which is south of Kedesh-naphtali in Upper Galilee above Hazor, beyond the road to the west, north of Peor.

³ I, TOBIT, have made truth and righteousness my lifelong guide. I did many acts of charity to my kinsmen, those of my nation who had gone with me into captivity at Nineveh in Assyria. ⁴ While I was quite young in my own country, Israel, the whole tribe of Naphtali my ancestor broke away from the dynasty of David and from Jerusalem, the city chosen out of all the tribes of Israel as the one place of sacrifice; it was there that God's dwelling-place, the temple, had been consecrated, built to last for all generations. ⁵ My kinsmen, the whole house of my ancestor Naphtali, sacrificed on the mountains of Galilee to the image of a bull-calf which King Jeroboam of Israel had set up in Dan.

⁶ At the festivals I, and I alone, made the frequent journey to Jerusalem prescribed as an eternal commandment for all Israel. I would hurry off to Jerusalem with the first-fruits of crops and herds, the tithes of the cattle, and the first shearings of the sheep; these I gave to the priests of Aaron's line for the altar, ⁷ while the tithe of wine, grain, olive oil, pomegranates, and other fruits I gave to the Levites ministering at Jerusalem. The second tithe for the six years I turned into money and brought it year by year to Jerusalem for distribution ⁸ among the orphans and widows and among the converts who had attached themselves to Israel. Every third year when I brought it and gave it to them, we held a feast in accordance with the command prescribed in the law of Moses and the instructions enjoined by Deborah the mother

1:2 **Shalmaneser:** *Gk* Enemessaros.

1.1–3.17: Tobit's tale of his misfortunes. His zealous efforts to live the Law earn him the persecution of the pagans and the jeers of the other Jews.

1.1–2: Introduction. 1: *Tobit:* perhaps an abbreviated form of the Heb. *Tobiah* (Gk. *Tobias,* v. 9), meaning "the LORD is good." **2:** The tribe of *Naphtali* was deported to *Assyria,* not by *Shalmaneser* but by his predecessor, Tiglath-pileser III (745–727 B.C.E.); see 2 Kgs. 15.29. *Thisbe* is located west-southwest of Lake Huleh in northern Palestine.

1.3–22: Tobit's virtuous life in exile. 3: *Nineveh:* capital of *Assyria.* **4:** The secession of the northern tribes from the *dynasty of David* (1 Kgs. ch. 12) took place about 922 B.C.E., 150 years before Tobit was born. **5:** *Mountains . . . bull-calf:* see 1 Kgs. 12.28–31. **6–8:** *Firstfruits . . . tithes:* an idealized picture of Jewish piety;

of Hananiel our grandfather; for on the death of my father I had been left an orphan.

⁹When I grew up, I took a wife from our kindred and had by her a son whom I called Tobias. ¹⁰After the deportation to Assyria in which I was taken captive and came to Nineveh, everyone of my family and nation ate gentile food; ¹¹but I myself scrupulously avoided doing so. ¹²And since I was wholeheartedly mindful of my God, ¹³the Most High endowed me with a presence which won me the favour of Shalmaneser, and I became his buyer of supplies. ¹⁴During his lifetime I used to travel to Media and buy for him there, and I deposited bags of money to the value of ten talents of silver with my kinsman Gabael son of Gabri in Media. ¹⁵When Shalmaneser died and was succeeded by his son Sennacherib, the roads to Media passed out of Assyrian control and I could no longer make the journey.

¹⁶In the days of Shalmaneser, I had done many acts of charity to my fellow-countrymen: I would share my food with the hungry ¹⁷and provide clothing for those who had none, and if I saw the dead body of anyone of my people thrown outside the wall of Nineveh, I gave it burial.

¹⁸I buried all those who fell victim to Sennacherib after his headlong retreat from Judaea, when the King of heaven brought judgement on him for his blasphemies. In his rage Sennacherib killed many of the Israelites, but I stole their bodies away and buried them, and when search was made for them by Sennacherib they were not to be found. ¹⁹One of the Ninevites disclosed to the king that it was I who had been giving burial to his victims and that I had gone into hiding. When I learnt that the king knew about me

and was seeking my life, I was alarmed and made my escape. ²⁰All that I possessed was seized and confiscated for the royal treasury; I was left with nothing but Anna my wife and my son Tobias.

²¹However, less than forty days afterwards the king was murdered by two of his sons, and when they sought refuge in the mountains of Ararat, his son Esarhaddon succeeded to the throne. He appointed Ahikar, my brother Anael's son, to oversee all the revenues of his kingdom, with control of the entire administration. ²²Then Ahikar interceded on my behalf and I came back to Nineveh; he had been chief cupbearer, keeper of the signet, comptroller, and treasurer when Sennacherib was king of Assyria, and Esarhaddon confirmed him in office. Ahikar was a relative of mine; he was my nephew.

Misfortune strikes Tobit and Sarah

2 DURING the reign of Esarhaddon, I returned to my house, and my wife Anna and my son Tobias were restored to me. At our festival of Pentecost, that is the feast of Weeks, a fine meal was prepared for me and I took my place. ²The table being laid and food in plenty put before me, I said to Tobias: 'My son, go out and, if you find among our people captive here in Nineveh some poor man who is wholeheartedly mindful of God, bring him back to share my meal. I shall wait for you, son, till you return.' ³Tobias went to look for a poor man of our people, but came straight back and cried, 'Father!' 'Yes, my son?' I replied. 'Father,' he answered, 'one of our nation has been murdered! His body is lying in the market-place; he has just been strangled.' ⁴I jumped up and

---

see Num. 18.12–13; Deut. 18.3–4. **10:** *Gentile food:* forbidden by the Law as unclean; see Deut. 14.3–21. **13:** *Shalmaneser* V: the successor of Tiglath-pileser III in 727 B.C.E. **14:** *Ten talents of silver:* 3000 shekels of silver. **15:** *Shalmaneser* V was followed by Sargon II (722–705 B.C.E.) and then only by *Sennacherib* (705–681 B.C.E.). Such historical inaccuracies suggest that the author intends, not history, but a story illustrative of Wisdom. **17:** A *dead body* left unburied was considered a curse, a punishment for an evil life, that somehow affected the peace of the deceased. See 2 Kgs. 9.10; Jer. 8.2; Ecclus. 44.14. **18:** God brought *judgement* on Sennacherib at the siege of Jerusalem. See 2 Kgs. 19.35–36; Isa. 37.36–37. **21:** *Two of his sons:* see 2 Kgs. 19.37. *Ahikar,* the hero of a popular ancient legend, was depicted as a wise and wealthy chancellor under several Assyrian kings. In the story he is said to have raised and educated a nephew, Nadab, who betrayed him. Eventually he was vindicated and the nephew was punished. Perhaps the author brings Ahikar into the story of Tobit because they were both tested by misfortune and finally restored to a happy state. See also 2.10; 11.18; and 14.10, where their tribulations are further recorded.

2.1–14: Tobit's misfortunes. 1: The Jewish feast of *Pentecost* (Gk. "fifty [days]") was observed seven weeks left my meal untasted. I took the body from the square and put it in one of the outbuildings until sunset when I could bury it; [5] then I went indoors, duly bathed myself, and ate my food in sorrow. [6] I recalled the words of the prophet Amos in the passage about Bethel:

> Your festivals shall be turned into
>   mourning,
> and all your songs into lamentation,

and I wept. [7] When the sun had gone down, I went and dug a grave and buried the body. [8] My neighbours jeered. 'Is he no longer afraid?' they said. 'He ran away last time, when they were hunting for him to put him to death for this very offence; and here he is again burying the dead!'

[9] That night, after bathing myself, I went into my courtyard and lay down to sleep by the courtyard wall, leaving my face uncovered because of the heat. [10] I did not know that there were sparrows in the wall above me, and their droppings fell, still warm, right into my eyes and produced white patches. I went to the doctors to be cured, but the more they treated me with their ointments, the more my eyes became blinded by the white patches, until I lost my sight. I was blind for four years; my kinsmen all grieved for me, and for two years Ahikar looked after me, until he moved to Elymais.

[11] At that time Anna my wife used to earn money by women's work, spinning and weaving, [12] and her employers would pay her when she took them what she had done. One day, the seventh of Dystrus, after she had cut off the piece she had woven and delivered it, they not only paid her wages in full, but also gave her a kid from their herd of goats to take home. [13] When my wife came into the house to me, the kid began to bleat, and I called out to her: 'Where does that kid come from? I hope it was not stolen? Return it to its owners; we have no right to eat anything stolen.' [14] But she assured me: 'It was given

me as a present, over and above my wages.' I did not believe her and insisted that she return it, and I blushed with shame for what she had done. Her rejoinder was: 'So much for all your acts of charity and all your good works! Everyone can now see what you are really like.'

3 In deep distress I groaned and wept aloud, and as I groaned I prayed: [2] 'O Lord, you are just and all your acts are just; in all your ways you are merciful and true; you are the Judge of the world. [3] Now bear me in mind, Lord, and look upon me. Do not punish me for the sins and errors which I and my fathers have committed. [4] We have sinned against you and disobeyed your commandments, and you have given us up to the despoiler, to captivity and death, until we have become a proverb and a byword; we are taunted by all the nations among whom you have scattered us. [5] I acknowledge the justice of your many judgements, the due penalty for our sins, for we have not carried out your commandments or lived in true obedience before you. [6] And now deal with me as you will. Command that my life be taken away from me so that I may be removed from the face of the earth and turned to dust. I would be better dead than alive, for I have had to listen to taunts I have not deserved and my grief is great. Lord, command that I be released from this misery; let me go to the eternal resting-place. Do not turn your face from me, Lord; I had rather die than live in such misery, listening to such taunts.'

[7] On the same day it happened that Sarah, the daughter of Raguel who lived at Ecbatana in Media, also had to listen to taunts, from one of her father's servant-girls. [8] Sarah had been given in marriage to seven husbands and, before the marriages could be duly consummated, each one of them had been killed by the evil demon Asmodaeus. The servant said to her: 'It is you who kill your husbands! You have already been given in marriage to seven, and you have not borne

---

2:6 **songs:** *so one Vs. (cp. Amos 8:10); Gk* ways.

---

after Passover (Lev. 23.15–21) at the time of the grain harvest. **5:** Tobit *bathed* himself because contact with a corpse made him ritually unclean and unfit for public worship (Num. 19.11–13). **10:** *Elymais* is Elam, a region north of the Tigris on the Persian Gulf. **12:** *Dystrus:* the fifth month of the Macedonian (and Hellenistic) calendar (about February). **14:** Tobit's wife expresses the view that Tobit suffered either because he was punished for secret sins or because virtue did not pay. See Job 2.9.

3.1–6: Tobit's prayer. 6: *Eternal resting-place:* Sheol. *Do not turn* your *face:* do not remove your favor.
3.7–10: Sarah's plight. 7: *Ecbatana:* the capital of *Media,* present-day Iran. **8:** *Asmodaeus* means "destroyer"

the name of any one of them. 9 Why punish us because they are dead? Go and join your husbands. I hope we never see son or daughter of yours!'

10 Deeply distressed at that, she went in tears to the roof-chamber of her father's house, meaning to hang herself. But she had second thoughts and said to herself: 'Perhaps they will taunt my father and say, "You had one dear daughter and she hanged herself because of her troubles," and so I shall bring my aged father in sorrow to his grave. No, I will not hang myself; it would be better to beg the Lord to let me die and not live on to hear such reproaches.' 11 Thereupon she spread out her hands towards the window in prayer saying: 'Praise be to you, merciful God, praise to your name for evermore; let all your creation praise you for ever! 12 And now I lift up my eyes and look to you. 13 Command that I be removed from the earth, never again to hear such taunts.

14 'You know, Lord, that I am a virgin, guiltless of intercourse with any man; 15 I have not dishonoured my name or my father's name in the land of my exile. I am my father's only child; he has no other to be his heir, nor has he any near kinsman or relative who might marry me and for whom I should stay alive. Already seven husbands of mine have died; what have I to live for any longer? But if it is not your will, Lord, to let me die, have regard to me in your mercy and spare me those taunts.'

16 At that very moment the prayers of both were heard in the glorious presence of God, 17 and Raphael was sent to cure the two of them: Tobit by removing the white patches from his eyes so that he might see God's light again, and Sarah daughter of Raguel by giving her in marriage to Tobias son of Tobit and by setting her free from the evil demon Asmodaeus, for it was the destiny of Tobias and of no other suitor to possess her. At the moment when Tobit went back into his house from the courtyard, Sarah came down from her father's roof-chamber.

Tobias's journey

4 THAT same day Tobit remembered the money he had deposited with Gabael at Rages in Media, 2 and he said to himself, 'I have asked for death; before I die I ought to send for my son Tobias and explain to him about this money.' 3 So he sent for Tobias and, when he came, said to him: 'When I die, give me decent burial. Honour your mother, and do not abandon her as long as she lives; do what will please her, and never grieve her heart in any way. 4 Remember, my son, all the hazards she faced for your sake while you were in her womb. When she dies, bury her beside me in the same grave.

5 'Keep the Lord in mind every day of your life, my son, and never deliberately do what is wrong or violate his commandments. As long as you live do what is right, and avoid evil ways; 6 for an honest life leads to success in any undertaking, and to all who do right the Lord will give good counsel.

7 'Distribute alms from what you possess and never with a grudging eye. Do not turn your face away from any poor man, and God will not turn away his face from you. 8 Let your almsgiving match your means. If you

and the name occurs only here in the Bible. **10:** Sarah's concern lest she bring her *aged father in sorrow to his grave* reflects a theme repeatedly expressed in the Joseph novelette about the aged Jacob, e.g. in Gen. 37.35; 42.38; 44.29. Premature death was deemed a curse.

3.11–15: Sarah's prayer. 15: This concern about a *near kinsman* reflects the clan law about marriage within the tribal group, a law with special significance in exile, where the maintenance of group identity was of great concern, lest the people disappear. Sarah here seems to be unaware of the existence of Tobias.

3.16–17: God hears the prayers of Tobit and Sarah. 16: A phrase like *at that very moment* suggests that the author is more interested in dramatic coincidence than historical probability. **17:** *Raphael* is a Heb. name meaning "God heals." An old tradition held that an angel was usually limited to a single errand. Here Raphael cures both at once.

4.1–9.6: Tobit sends for his son. Under the inspiration of the angel Raphael, Tobias himself is saved from danger and brings healing to others. His sage advice (4.3–20) reflects the morals of Judaism of the Hellenistic period.

4.1–5.3: Tobias is sent to retrieve Tobit's money. 1: *Rages* was a city in *Media* situated near modern Teheran. **3:** *Decent burial:* see 1.17 n. **5–19:** Wise counseling as in Prov. and Ecclus.

have little, do not be ashamed to give the little you can afford; ⁹you will be laying up sound insurance against the day of adversity. ¹⁰Almsgiving preserves the giver from death and keeps him from going down into darkness. ¹¹All who give alms are making an offering acceptable to the Most High.

¹²'Be on your guard, my son, against fornication; and above all choose your wife from the race of your ancestors. Do not take a foreign wife, one not of your father's tribe, for we are descendants of the prophets. My son, remember that back to the earliest days our ancestors, Noah, Abraham, Isaac, Jacob, all chose wives from their kindred. They were blessed in their children, and their descendants will possess the land. ¹³So you too, my son, must love your kindred; do not be too proud to take a wife from among the women of your own nation. Such pride breeds ruin and disorder, and the waster declines into poverty; waste is the mother of starvation.

¹⁴'Pay any man who works for you his wages that same day; let no one wait for his money. If you serve God, you will be repaid. Be circumspect, my son, in all that you do, and in all your behaviour be true to your upbringing. ¹⁵Do to no one what you yourself would hate. Do not drink to excess or let drunkenness become a habit. ¹⁶Share your food with the hungry, your clothes with those who have none. Whatever you have beyond your own needs, distribute in alms, and do not give with a grudging look. ¹⁷Pour out your wine and offer your bread on the tombs of the righteous; but give nothing to sinners. ¹⁸Seek advice from every sensible person; do not despise any advice that may be of use. ¹⁹Praise the Lord God at all times and ask him to guide your steps; then all you do and all you plan will be crowned with success. The heathen lack such guidance; it is the Lord himself who gives all good things and who humbles whomsoever he chooses to the lowly grave. Now remember those injunctions, my son; let them never be effaced from your mind.

²⁰'And now, my son, I should tell you that I have ten talents of silver on deposit with Gabael son of Gabri at Rages in Media. ²¹Do not be anxious because we have become poor; there is great wealth awaiting you, if only you fear God and avoid all wickedness and do what is good in the sight of the Lord your God.'

5 Tobias said: 'I will do all that you have told me, father. ²But how shall I be able to recover this money from Gabael, since he does not know me and I do not know him? What proof of identity shall I give him to make him trust me and give me the money? Besides, I do not know the roads which would get me to Media.' ³To this Tobit replied: 'He gave me his note of hand, and I divided it in two and we took one part each. I kept one half of it and put half with the money. It is all of twenty years since I deposited that money! Now, my son, find someone reliable to go with you, and we shall pay him his wages up to the time of your return; then go and recover the money from Gabael.'

⁴Tobias went out to look for someone who knew the way and would accompany him to Media, and found himself face to face with the angel Raphael. ⁵Not knowing he was an angel of God, he questioned him: 'Where do you come from, young man?' 'I am an Israelite,' he replied, 'one of your fellow-countrymen, and I have come here to find work.' Tobias asked, 'Do you know the road to Media?' ⁶'Yes,' he said, 'I have been there many times; I am familiar with all the routes, I know them well. I have frequently travelled into Media and used to stay with Gabael our fellow-countryman who lives there in Rages. It is two full days' journey to Rages from Ecbatana; for Rages is situated in the hills, and Ecbatana lies in the middle of the plain.' ⁷Tobias said: 'Wait for me, young man, while I go in and tell my father. I need you to go with me and I shall pay you for it.' ⁸'Very well, I shall wait,' he answered, 'only do not be long.'

Tobias went in and told his father. 'I have found a fellow-Israelite to accompany me,' he said. His father replied, 'Call him in; I

5:6 **in Rages:** *so one Vs. (cp. 4:1); Gk* in Ecbatana.

19: When Tobit urges his son to *remember those injunctions* he is voicing a constant theme of Jewish piety which viewed loyalty to God as an active remembrance of God's favors. **20:** *Ten talents:* see 1.14 n.

5.4–22: Azarias (Raphael) is hired as Tobias's guide. 6: The *journey to Rages from Ecbatana* cannot be made in *two full days* since it involves a distance of some 450 miles. Moreover, it is Ecbatana, not Rages, that is situated in mountainous terrain. Raphael's familiarity *with all the routes* seems to refer to the journey of his must find out the man's family and tribe and make sure, my son, that he will be a trustworthy companion for you.'

9 Tobias went out and called him: 'Young man, my father is asking for you.' When he entered, Tobit greeted him first. To Raphael's reply, 'May all be well with you!' Tobit retorted: 'How can anything be well with me any more? I am now blind; I cannot see the light of heaven, but lie in darkness like the dead who can no longer see the light. Though still alive, I am as good as dead. I hear voices, but I cannot see those speaking.' Raphael answered: 'Take heart; in God's design your cure is at hand. Take heart!' Tobit went on: 'My son Tobias wishes to travel to Media. Can you go with him as his guide? I shall pay you, my friend.' 'Yes,' he said, 'I can go with him. I know all the roads, for I have often been to Media. I have travelled over all the plains and mountains there and am familiar with the whole way.' 10 Tobit said to him, 'Tell me, my friend, what family and tribe do you belong to?' 11 He asked, 'Why do you need to know my tribe?' Tobit said, 'I wish to know whose son you are, my friend, and what your name is.' 12 'I am Azarias,' he replied, 'son of the older Ananias, one of your kinsmen.'

13 Tobit said to him: 'Welcome, may all be well with you! Do not be angry with me, my friend, for wanting to know all about you and your parentage. You are, as it turns out, a kinsman and a man of good and honourable family. I knew Ananias and Nathan, the two sons of the older Semelias. They used to go with me to Jerusalem and worship with me there; they were never led into error. Your kinsmen are worthy men; you come of a sound stock. You are indeed welcome.' 14 And he added: 'I shall pay you a drachma a day and allow you the same expenses as my son. 15 Accompany him, and I shall give you something over and above your wage.' 16 Raphael agreed: 'I shall go with him. Never fear; we shall travel there and back without mishap, for the road is not dangerous.' Tobit

said to him, 'God bless you, my friend!' He called his son and said: 'My son, get ready what you need for the journey and go with your kinsman. May God in heaven preserve you both on your journey there, and restore you to me safe and sound. May his angel safely escort you both, my son.' Before setting out Tobias kissed his father and mother, and Tobit wished him a safe journey.

17 Then his mother burst into tears. 'Why must you send my boy away?' she said to Tobit. 'Is he not the staff on which we lean? Do we not depend on him at every turn? 18 Why the haste to lay out money for money? For the sake of our boy write it off! 19 Let us be content to live the life appointed for us by the Lord.' 20 'Do not worry,' replied Tobit, 'our son will go safely and come back safely, and you will see him with your own eyes on the day of his return. Do not worry or be anxious about them, my dear. 21 A good angel will go with him; his journey will prosper and he will come back without mishap.' 22 At that she stopped weeping.

6 THE youth and the angel left the house together; the dog followed Tobias out and accompanied them. They travelled until night overtook them, and then camped by the river Tigris. 2 Tobias went down to bathe his feet in the river, and a huge fish leapt out of the water and tried to swallow his foot. He cried out, 3 and the angel said to him, 'Seize the fish and hold it fast.' So Tobias caught hold of it and dragged it up on the bank. 4 The angel said: 'Split open the fish and take out its gall, heart, and liver; keep them by you, but throw the guts away; the gall, heart, and liver can be used as remedies.' 5 Tobias split the fish open, and put its gall, heart, and liver on one side. He broiled and ate part of the fish; the rest he salted and kept.

They continued the journey together, and when they came near to Media 6 the youth asked the angel: 'Azarias, my friend, what remedy is there in the fish's heart and liver and in its gall?' 7 He replied: 'You can use the

---

life rather than to the geography of Persia. **9:** *I am now blind:* Tobit speaks for Israel, symbolically blind to the ways of God's Providence. The theme of the book is summed up in the appeal, *take heart,* directed to Israel. **12:** *Azarias* is the Gk. form of a Heb. name (*Azariah*) meaning "the LORD helps." **14:** A *drachma* was a normal day's wages.

6.1–17: Raphael guides Tobias to Ecbatana and they prepare to meet Sarah. 1: The *dog,* rarely noted in the Bible and even more rarely presented favorably, is introduced here to reinforce family atmosphere. See also 11.4 n. The *Tigris* river does not in fact cross the path of a journey from Nineveh to Ecbatana. **4:** Special heart and liver as a fumigation for any man or woman attacked by a demon or evil spirit; the attack will cease, and it will give no further trouble. 8 The gall is for anointing a person's eyes when white patches have spread over them; after one has blown on the patches, the eyes will recover.'

9 When he had entered Media and was already approaching Ecbatana, 10 Raphael said to the youth, 'Tobias, my friend.' 'Yes?' he replied. Raphael said: 'We must stay tonight with Raguel, who is a relative of yours. He has a daughter named Sarah, but no other children, neither sons nor daughters. 11 You as her next of kin have the right to marry her and inherit her father's property. 12 The girl is sensible, brave, and very beautiful indeed, and her father is an honourable man.' He went on: 'It is your right to marry her. Be guided by me, my friend; I shall speak to her father this very night and ask him to promise us the girl as your bride, and on our return from Rages we shall celebrate her marriage. I know that Raguel cannot withhold her from you or betroth her to another without incurring the death penalty according to the decree in the book of Moses; and he is aware that his daughter belongs by right to you rather than to any other man. Now be guided by me, my friend; we shall talk about the girl tonight and betroth her to you, and when we return from Rages we shall take her back with us to your home.'

13 At this Tobias protested: 'Azarias, my friend, I have heard she has already been given to seven husbands who died in the bridal chamber; the very night they went into the bridal chamber to her they died. 14 A demon kills them, I have been told. And now it is my turn to be afraid; he does her no harm, because he loves her, but he kills any man who tries to come near her. I am my father's only child, and I fear that, were I to die, grief for me would bring my father and mother to their grave; and they have no other son to bury them.'

15 Raphael said: 'But have you forgotten your father's instructions? He told you to take a wife from your father's kindred. Now be guided by me, my friend: marry Sarah, and do not worry about the demon. I am sure that this night she will be given to you as your wife. 16 When you enter the bridal chamber, take some of the fish's liver and its heart, and put them on the burning incense. The smell will spread, 17 and when it reaches the demon he will make off, never to be seen near her any more. When you are about to go to bed with her, both of you must first stand up and pray, beseeching the Lord of heaven to grant you mercy and protection. Have no fear; she was destined for you before the world was made. You will rescue her and she will go with you. I have no doubt you will have children by her and they will be very dear to you. Now do not worry!' When Tobias heard what Raphael said, and learnt that Sarah was his kinswoman and of his father's house, he was filled with love for her and set his heart on her.

Tobias weds Sarah

7 As THEY entered Ecbatana Tobias said, 'Azarias, my friend, take me straight to our kinsman Raguel.' So he took him to Raguel's house, where they found him sitting by the courtyard gate. They greeted him first, and he replied, 'Greetings to you, my friends. You are indeed welcome.' When he brought them into his house, 2 he said to Edna his wife, 'Is not this young man like my kinsman Tobit? 3 Edna questioned them, 'Friends, where do you come from?' 'We belong to the tribe of Naphtali, now in captivity at Nineveh,' they answered. 4 'Do you know our kinsman Tobit?' she asked, and they replied, 'Yes, we do.' 'Is he well?' she said. 5 'He is alive and well,' they answered, and Tobias added, 'He is my father.' 6 Raguel jumped up and, with tears in his eyes, he kissed him. 7 'God bless you, my boy,' he said, 'son of a good and upright father. But what a calamity that so

6:17 **be very dear to you:** *lit.* be like brothers to you.

---

medicinal qualities were often attributed to the internal organs of animals. **11:** Mosaic Law required a daughter who is heir to property to marry within her tribe (Num. 36.8), so as to prevent the gradual loss of a tribe's property and support. **12:** There is no mention of the *death penalty* in Num. 36.8. **14:** *To bury them:* the exiled Jew was continually preoccupied with the thought of burial because abandonment in death definitively confirmed God's abandonment of Israel in the Exile. **17:** *Stand up and pray:* the demon will be rendered powerless if passion is tempered by prayer.

7.1–15: Tobias and Sarah are married. Similar marriage arrangements are related in Gen. 24.15; 29.9–12;

just and charitable a man has lost his sight!' He embraced Tobias his kinsman and wept; [8] Edna his wife and their daughter Sarah also wept for Tobit.

Raguel slaughtered a ram from the flock and entertained them royally. They bathed and then, after washing their hands, took their places for the meal. Tobias said to Raphael, 'Azarias, my friend, ask Raguel to give me Sarah my kinswoman.' [9] Raguel overheard this and said to the young man: 'Eat and drink tonight, and enjoy yourself. [10] There is no one but yourself who should have my daughter Sarah; indeed I ought not to give her to anyone else, since you are my nearest kinsman. However, I must reveal the truth to you, my son: [11] I have given her in marriage to seven of our kinsmen, and they all died on their wedding night. My son, eat and drink now, and may the Lord deal kindly with you both.' Tobias answered, 'I shall not eat again or drink until you have disposed of this business of mine.' [12] Raguel said to him, 'I shall do so: I give her to you in accordance with the decree in the book of Moses, and Heaven itself has decreed that she shall be yours. Take your kinswoman; from now on you belong to her and she to you, from today she is yours for ever. May all go well with you both this night, my son; may the Lord of heaven grant you mercy and peace.'

[13] Raguel called for Sarah and, when she came, he took her by the hand and gave her to Tobias with these words: 'Receive my daughter as your wedded wife in accordance with the law, the decree written in the book of Moses; keep her and take her safely home to your father. And may the God of heaven grant you prosperity and peace.' [14] Then he sent for her mother and told her to fetch a roll of papyrus, and he wrote out and put his seal on a marriage contract giving Sarah to Tobias as his wife according to this decree. [15] After that they began to eat and drink.

[16] Raguel called his wife and said, 'My dear, get the other bedroom ready and take her in

there.' [17] Edna went and prepared the room as he had told her, and brought Sarah into it. She wept over her, and then drying her tears said: [18] 'Take heart, dear daughter; the Lord of heaven give you gladness instead of sorrow. Take heart, daughter!' Then she went out.

8 When they had finished eating and drinking and were ready for bed, the young man was escorted to the bedroom. [2] Tobias recalled what Raphael told him; he removed the fish's liver and heart from the bag in which he had them, and put them on the burning incense. [3] The smell from the fish kept the demon away, and he made off into Upper Egypt. Raphael followed him there and promptly bound him hand and foot.

[4] After they were left alone and the door was shut, Tobias got up from the bed, saying to Sarah, 'Rise, my love; let us pray and beseech our Lord to show us mercy and keep us in safety.' [5] She got up, and they began to pray that they might be kept safe. Tobias said: 'We praise you, God of our fathers, we praise your name for ever and ever. Let the heavens and all your creation praise you for ever. [6] You made Adam and also Eve his wife, who was to be his partner and support; and those two were the parents of the human race. This was your word: "It is not good for the man to be alone; let us provide a partner suited to him." [7] So now I take this my beloved to wife, not out of lust but in true marriage. Grant that she and I may find mercy and grow old together.' [8] They both said 'Amen, Amen,' [9] and they slept through the night.

Raguel rose and summoned his servants, and they went out and dug a grave, [10] for he thought, 'Tobias may be dead, and then we shall have to face scorn and taunts.' [11] When they had finished digging the grave, Raguel went into the house and called his wife: [12] 'Send one of the servant-girls', he said, 'to go in and see whether he is alive; for if he is

---

Exod. 2.16–21. **12:** *The decree . . .:* Num. 36.8. *Heaven itself has decreed:* the author strongly favors arranged marriages (see also 6.17), probably because in a foreign society romantic marriages were likely to involve non-Israelites or members of other tribes, thus weakening religious unity or tribal integrity.

7.16–8.21: The demon is cast out and the marriage is celebrated. 18: *Take heart, dear daughter* is an exhortation that is also directed toward exiled Israel. **8.3:** *Upper Egypt* is a wilderness, the traditional habitation of demons; see Lev. 16.8–10 for the ritual of driving the goat bearing sins into the wilderness. The demons are understood to be invaders of Israel from foreign parts. *Raphael* and the demon represent respectively the forces of order and chaos which are at war since the creation. **4:** *Let us pray:* see 6.17 n. **6:** *His partner:* see dead, let us bury him so that no one may know.' 13 They lit a lamp, opened the door, and sent a servant in; and she found them sound asleep together. 14 She came out and told them, 'He is alive and has come to no harm.'

15 Then Raguel praised the God of heaven: 'All praise to you, O God, all perfect praise! Let men praise you throughout the ages. 16 Praise to you for the joy you have given me: the thing I feared has not happened, but you have shown us your great mercy. 17 Praise to you for the mercy you have shown to these two, these only children. Lord, show them mercy, keep them safe, and grant them a long life of happiness and affection.' 18 And he ordered his servants to fill in the grave before dawn came.

19 Telling his wife to bake a great batch of bread, he went to the herd and brought two oxen and four rams and ordered his servants to get them ready; so they set about the preparations. 20 Then calling Tobias he said: 'You shall not stir from here for two weeks. Stay; eat and drink with us, and cheer my daughter's heart after all her suffering. 21 Here and now take half of all I possess, and may you have a safe journey back to your father; the other half will come to you both when I and my wife die. Be reassured, my son, I am your father and Edna is your mother; now and always we are as close to you as we are to your wife. You have nothing to fear, my son.'

9 Tobias sent for Raphael and said: 2 'Azarias, my friend, take four servants and two camels with you, and go to Rages. Make your way to Gabael's house, give him the note of hand and collect the money; then bring him with you to the wedding feast. 3–4 My father, as you know, will be counting the days, and if I am even one day late it will distress him. Yet you see what Raguel has sworn, and I cannot go against his oath.' 5 So Raphael went with the four servants and two camels to Rages in Media and stayed the night with Gabael. He delivered the note of

hand and informed him that Tobit's son Tobias had taken a wife and was inviting him to the wedding feast. At once Gabael counted out to him the bags with their seals intact, and they put them together. 6 They all made an early start and came to the wedding. Entering Raguel's house they found Tobias at the feast, and he jumped up and greeted Gabael. With tears in his eyes Gabael blessed him and said: 'Good and worthy son of a worthy father, that just and charitable man, may the Lord give Heaven's blessing to you, your wife, and your parents-in-law. Praise be to God, for I have seen my cousin Tobias, the very likeness of his father.'

Tobias's homecoming

10 Day by day Tobit was keeping count of the time Tobias would take for his journey there and for his journey back. When the time was up and his son had not made his appearance, 2 Tobit said: 'Perhaps he has been detained there? Or perhaps Gabael is dead and there is no one to give him the money?' 3 And he grew anxious. 4 Anna his wife said: 'My child has perished. He is no longer in the land of the living.' She began to weep, lamenting for her son: 5 'O my child, the light of my eyes, why did I let you go?' 6 Tobit said to her: 'Hush! Do not worry, my dear; he is all right. Something has happened there to distract them. The man who went with him is one of our kinsmen and can be trusted. My dear, do not grieve for him; he will soon be back.' 7 'Hush yourself!' she retorted. 'Do not try to deceive me. My child has perished.' Each day she would rush out to keep watch on the road her son had taken, and would listen to no one; and when she came indoors at sunset she was unable to sleep, but lamented and wept the whole night long.

After the two weeks of wedding celebrations which Raguel had sworn to hold for his daughter came to an end, Tobias ap-

Gen. 2.18; compare 1 Cor. 11.8–9. **21:** Tobias is asked to *take half* of Raguel's property now as a dowry; and the *other half* is to come to him as an inheritance.

9.1–6: Tobit's money is retrieved from Gabael. 5: The journey from Ecbatana to *Rages* would require about two weeks.

10.1–14.15: Tobias's homecoming. Sent to collect a debt of money for his father, the young Tobias brings him also a daughter (11.17) and healing for his eyes (11.14).

10.1–11.1: Tobias and Sarah leave Ecbatana. 4–5: When *Anna* calls Tobias the *light of my eyes* she is expressing the symbolic sight–blindness motif: Israel is blind to the meaning of history but light will come at proached him. 'Let me be on my way,' he said, 'for I am sure that my parents are thinking they will never see me again. I beg you, father, let me go home now to my father Tobit. I have already told you how I left him.' [8]Raguel replied: 'Stay, my son, stay with me, and I shall send messengers to your father to explain matters to him.' [9]But Tobias insisted: 'No, please let me go home to my father.' [10]Then without more ado Raguel handed over to Tobias Sarah his bride along with half of all that he possessed, male and female slaves, cattle and sheep, donkeys and camels, clothes, money, and household goods. [11]He bade them farewell. Embracing Tobias he said: 'Goodbye, my son, goodbye; a safe journey to you! May the Lord of heaven prosper you and Sarah your wife; and may I live to see your children.' [12]To his daughter Sarah he said: 'Honour your husband's father and mother; they are now your parents as much as if you were their own child. Go in peace, my daughter; as long as I live I hope to hear nothing but good news of you.' After bidding them both goodbye, he sent them on their way. Edna said to Tobias: 'My very dear cousin, may the Lord bring you safely home, you and my daughter Sarah, and may I live long enough to see your children. In the sight of the Lord I entrust my daughter to your keeping; do nothing to cause her distress throughout your life. Go in peace, my son. From now on I am your mother and Sarah is your beloved wife. May we all be blessed with prosperity to the end of our days!' She kissed them both goodbye and let them go.

11 Tobias parted from Raguel in good health and spirits, praising the Lord of heaven and earth, the King of all, for the success of his journey. He gave his blessing to Raguel and Edna his wife, saying, 'It is the Lord's command that I should honour you all your days.'

[2]When they reached Caserin close to Nineveh, Raphael said: 'You know how your father was when we left him. [3]Let us hurry on ahead of your wife and see that the house is ready before the others arrive'; [4]and as the two of them went on together he added, 'Bring the fish-gall in your hand.' The dog went with the angel and Tobias, following at their heels.

[5]Anna sat watching the road by which her son would return. [6]She caught sight of him coming and exclaimed to his father, 'Here he comes—your son and the man who went with him!' [7]Before Tobias reached his father's house Raphael said: 'I know for certain that his eyes will be opened. [8]Spread the fish-gall on them; this remedy will make the white patches shrink and peel off. Your father will get his sight back and see the light of day.' [9]Anna ran forward, flung her arms round her son, and said to him: 'Now that I have seen you again, my child, I am ready to die.' And she wept.

[10]As Tobit rose to his feet and came stumbling out through the courtyard gate, [11]Tobias went up to him with the fish-gall in his hand. He blew into his father's eyes and then, taking him by the arm and saying, 'Do not be alarmed, father,' [12]he applied the remedy carefully [13]and with both hands peeled off the patches from the corners of Tobit's eyes. Tobit threw his arms round him [14]and burst into tears. 'I can see you, my son, the light of my eyes!' he cried. 'Praise be to God, and praise to his great name and to all his holy angels. May his great name rest on us. Praised be all the angels for ever and ever. [15]He laid his scourge on me, and now, look, I see my son Tobias!'

Tobias went inside, rejoicing and praising God with all his might. He told his father about the success of his journey and the recovery of the money, and how he had married Raguel's daughter Sarah. 'She is on her way,' he said, 'quite close to the city gate.' [16]Tobit went out joyfully to meet his daughter-in-law at the gate, praising God as he went. At the sight of him passing through the city in full vigour and walking without anyone to guide his steps, the people of Nineveh were amazed; [17]and Tobit gave thanks to God before them all for his mercy in opening his eyes.

When he met Sarah, the wife of his son

---

the end. See 11.14. **9:** Tobias's plea to be allowed to *go home* is meant to be a model for all exiled Israelites who should yearn constantly for home.

11.2–18: Tobias arrives at home and cures Tobit's blindness. 2: *Caserin:* unknown. **4:** *Dog:* see 6.1 n. Only those who had seen Tobit's blindness go ahead and are present at the cure; this would include the dog! **14:** See 10.5 n. **15:** God's *scourge* on Israel was the Exile, but salvation is promised. **16:** Israel's vindication at the

Tobias, he blessed her and said to her: 'Come in, daughter, welcome! Praise be to God who has brought you to us. Blessings on your father and mother, and on my son Tobias, and blessings on you, my daughter. Come into your home, and may health, blessings, and joy be yours; come in, my daughter.' For all the Jews in Nineveh it was a day of joy, [18] and Ahikar and Nadab, Tobit's cousins, came to share his happiness. The joyful celebrations went on for a week, and many were the presents given to them.

12 After the wedding celebrations were over, Tobit sent for Tobias. 'My son,' he said, 'when you pay the man who went with you, see that you give him something extra, over and above his wages.' [2] Tobias asked: 'How much shall I pay him, father? It would not hurt to give him half the money he and I brought back. [3] He has kept me safe, cured my wife, helped me bring the money, and healed you. How much extra shall I pay him?' [4] Tobit replied, 'It would be right, my son, for him to be given half of all that he has brought with him.' [5] So Tobias called him and said, 'Half of all that you have brought with you is to be yours for your wages; take it, and may you fare well.'

[6] Then Raphael called them both aside and said to them: 'Praise God, and in the presence of all living creatures thank him for the good he has done you, so that they may sing hymns of praise to his name. Proclaim to all the world what God has done; pay him honour and give him willing thanks. [7] A king's secret ought to be kept, but the works of God should be publicly acknowledged. Acknowledge them, therefore, and pay him honour. Do good, and no evil will befall you. [8] Better prayer with sincerity, and almsgiving with righteousness, than wealth with wickedness. Better give alms than hoard up gold. [9] Almsgiving preserves from death and wipes out every sin. Givers of alms will enjoy long life; [10] but sinners and wrongdoers are their own enemies.

[11] 'I will tell you the whole truth, hiding nothing from you. I have already made it clear to you that while a king's secret ought to be kept, the works of God should be glorified in public. [12] Now Tobit, when you and Sarah prayed, it was I who brought your prayers to be remembered in the glorious presence of the Lord. [13] So too when you buried the dead: that day when without hesitation you got up from your meal to go and bury the dead man, I was sent to test you. [14] At the same time God sent me to cure both you and Sarah your daughter-in-law. [15] I am Raphael, one of the seven angels who stand in attendance on the Lord and enter his glorious presence.'

[16] Both of them were deeply shaken and prostrated themselves in fear. [17] But he said to them: 'Do not be afraid, peace be with you; praise God for ever. [18] It is no thanks to me that I have been with you; it was the will of God. To him all your life long sing hymns of praise. [19] Take note that I ate no food; what you saw was an apparition. [20] And now praise the Lord, give thanks to God here on earth; I am about to ascend to him who sent me. Write down everything that has happened to you.' [21] He then ascended and, when they rose to their feet, was no longer to be seen. [22] They sang hymns of praise to God, giving him thanks for the great deeds he had done when an angel of God appeared to them.

Tobit's thanksgiving and last words

13 In the fullness of his joy Tobit wrote this prayer:

Praise to the ever-living God and to his
    kingdom.
[2] He both punishes and shows mercy;
he brings men down to the grave
    below,
and he brings them up from the great
    destruction;
nothing can escape his power.

12:8 **sincerity:** or, in some texts, fasting.

---

end will astonish the nations, here represented by the people of Nineveh. **18:** *Ahikar* and *Nadab:* see 1.21 n.

12.1–22: Raphael is thanked and identifies himself. 2: *Half the money* apparently refers to half the sum retrieved from Gabael, i.e. five talents of silver. **6–10:** Raphael's exhortation is typical of Wisdom literature. **11–14:** *The whole truth* is that God's Providence works through human misfortune to *test* human beings, a theme that pervades Wisdom literature; see Wisd. 3.6; Prov. 17.3. **15:** *Seven angels:* nowhere do we find a complete list of these "chief" angels. Perhaps seven is a symbolic number, the full array of divine messengers.

13.1–18: Tobit praises God. 1–6: This is a prayer of thanksgiving in the hymnic style of many psalms. The

³Israelites, give him thanks in the sight
of the nations,
for, having scattered you among them,
⁴he has shown you his greatness there.
In the sight of every living creature
exalt him,
for he is our Lord and our God,
our Father and God for ever.

⁵Though for your wickedness he will
punish you,
yet he will show mercy to you all,
wherever you may be dispersed among
the nations.
⁶When you turn to him with all your
heart and soul
and act in loyal obedience to him,
then he will turn to you;
he will hide his face from you no
longer.
Consider now what he has done for
you,
and with full voice give him thanks;
praise the righteous Lord
and exalt the eternal King.

In the land of my exile I give thanks to
him
and declare his might and greatness to
a sinful nation.
Sinners, turn and do what is right in
his eyes;
who knows, he may yet welcome you
and show mercy.
⁷I shall exalt my God
and rejoice in the King of heaven.
⁸Let all men tell of his majesty
and in Jerusalem give him thanks.

⁹O Jerusalem, Holy City,
he will punish you for what your sons
have done,
but he will have mercy once more on
the righteous.
¹⁰Give thanks to the Lord for his
goodness
and praise to the eternal King.
Your sanctuary will be rebuilt for you
with rejoicing.
May he give happiness to all your
exiles
and cherish for all generations those in
distress.

¹¹Your radiance will shine to the ends of
the earth.
Many nations will come to you from
afar,
to your holy name from every corner
of the earth,
bearing gifts in their hands for the
King of heaven.
In you endless generations will utter
their joy;
the name of the chosen city will endure
for ever and ever.
¹²Accursed will be all who speak harshly
to you,
all who wreak destruction, pulling down
your walls,
overthrowing your towers, and burning
your houses;
but for ever blessed will be those who
rebuild you.
¹³Come then, be joyful for the righteous,
for they will all be gathered together
and will praise the eternal Lord.
¹⁴How happy will they be who love you
and happy those who rejoice in your
prosperity,
happy those who grieve for you in all
your afflictions!
They will rejoice over you
and behold all your joy for ever.

¹⁵My soul, praise the Lord, the great
King,
¹⁶for Jerusalem will be built again
to be his dwelling-place for all time.
How happy I shall be when the
remnant of my descendants
see your splendour and give thanks to
the King of heaven!
The gates of Jerusalem will be built of
sapphire and emerald,
and all the walls of costly stones.
The towers of Jerusalem will be built of
gold,
their battlements of the finest gold.
¹⁷The streets of Jerusalem will be paved
with garnets and jewels of Ophir.
¹⁸Jerusalem's gates will sing hymns of
joy
and all the houses in her will say,
'Alleluia! Praise to the God of Israel!'
In you, O Jerusalem, his holy name
will be praised for ever and ever.

topic is God's sovereignty which will ultimately be established in human history through the homecoming of
God's *scattered* people. **10**: The *sanctuary* is the temple in Jerusalem. **16–17**: See Rev. 21.18–21.

14 So ended Tobit's thanksgiving. He died peacefully at the age of a hundred and twelve, and was buried in Nineveh with all honour. [2] He was sixty-two years old when his eyes were damaged, and after he recovered his sight he lived in prosperity, doing acts of charity and never ceasing to praise God and to proclaim his majesty.

[3] When he was dying, he sent for his son Tobias and gave him these instructions: 'My son, you must take your children [4] and be off to Media with all haste, for I believe God's word spoken against Nineveh by Nahum. It will all come true; everything will happen to Asshur and Nineveh that was spoken by the prophets of Israel who were sent by God. Not a word of it will fall short; all will take place in due time. It will be safer in Media than in Assyria or Babylon. I know, I am convinced, that all God's words will be fulfilled. It will be so: not one of them will fail. Our countrymen who live in Israel will all be scattered and carried off into captivity out of that good land. The whole of Israel's territory with Samaria and Jerusalem will lie waste; and for a time the house of God will be in mourning, burnt to the ground.

[5] 'But God will have mercy on them again and bring them back to the land of Israel. They will rebuild the house of God, yet not as it was at first, not until the time of fulfilment comes. Then they will all return from their captivity and rebuild Jerusalem in splendour; then indeed God's house will be built in her as the prophets of Israel foretold. [6] All the nations in the whole world will be converted to the true worship of God; they will renounce the idols which led them astray into error, [7] and will praise the eternal God in righteousness. All the Israelites who survive at that time and are firm in their loyalty to God will be brought together; they will come to Jerusalem to take possession of the land of Abraham and will live there securely for ever. Those who love God in sincerity will rejoice; sinners and wrongdoers will disappear from the earth.

[8] 'My children, I give you this command: serve God in truth and do what is pleasing to him. [9] Teach your children to do what is right and give alms, to be mindful of God and praise his name sincerely at all times and with all their strength.

[10] 'Now, my son, you must leave Nineveh; do not stay here. Once you have laid your mother in the grave beside me, do not spend another night within the city boundaries, for I observe that the place is full of wickedness and shameless dishonesty. My son, think what Nadab did to Ahikar who brought him up: he forced him to hide in a living grave. Ahikar survived to see God requite the disgrace brought on him; he came out into the light of day, but Nadab passed into everlasting darkness for his attempt to kill Ahikar. Because he gave alms, Ahikar escaped from the deadly trap Nadab set for him, and it was Nadab who fell into the trap and was destroyed. [11] See what comes of almsgiving, my children; and see what comes of wickedness — death. But now my strength is failing.' They laid him on his bed and he died, and he was given honourable burial.

[12] When his mother died, Tobias buried her beside his father; then he and his wife and children went to Media, where they settled at Ecbatana with his father-in-law Raguel. [13] He honoured and cared for his wife's parents in their old age. He buried them at Ecbatana in Media, and he inherited the estate of Raguel as well as that of his father Tobit. [14] At the age of a hundred and seventeen he died, greatly respected. [15] Tobias lived long enough to hear of the destruction of Nineveh by King Ahasuerus of Media and to see the prisoners of war brought from there into Media. He praised God for all that he had done to the inhabitants of Nineveh and Asshur; before he died he rejoiced over the fate of Nineveh, and he praised the Lord God who lives for ever and ever. Amen.

14:10 **he gave alms:** *prob. rdg; Gk* I gave alms.

14.1–15: Tobit's final instructions to Tobias. 1: Tobit's peaceful death at an advanced age associates him with the patriarchs and matriarchs who, like him, kept the faith in a foreign environment. **4:** The book of *Nahum* describes the destruction of *Nineveh,* the capital of *Asshur,* Assyria. **5:** A second, and inferior, temple was built about 515 B.C.E.; see Hag. 1.1–15. **10:** *Ahikar . . . Nadab:* see 1.21 n. **15:** *Ahasuerus:* Xerxes I. *Nineveh* fell in 612 B.C.E. to an allied force of Medes under Cyaxares and of Babylonians, under Nabopolassar. The fall of Nineveh completes the vindication of Tobit's faith.

Judith

Judith is a good example of the Hebrew narrative art: vivid imagery; a paced combination of description and action; and resolute realism. The name Judith means "Jewess"; the heroine represents Israel's faith and spirit, strong and resourceful despite a weak and delicate appearance, which emerges triumphant from the drama of a confrontation between Israel, small and isolated, and all the great powers of the Near East.

There are historical contradictions in the story interpreted by some scholars as intended by the author to indicate unmistakably the fictional nature of the work, and thereby to point up the timeless quality of its contents.

Though set in earlier times, the narrative reflects conditions prevalent during the turmoil of the Hellenistic period described in 1 and 2 Maccabees: divine honors paid to kings (3.8); Jerusalem ruled by a high priest and a form of Sanhedrin (4.8; 15.8); and the like. This evidence of Hellenistic influence indicates a date of composition in the late second century B.C.E. The original language was probably Hebrew, even though most ancient surviving texts are Greek. The author and place of composition are unknown.

The intention of the author seems to be to reassert, at a moment of historical disarray, the Jewish conviction of God's commitment to the Jewish people's survival and victory in the odyssey of human existence. Judith exercises the same power that worked through Moses to free Israel from Egyptian bondage. Conversely, the author affirms that the proper response to God's action is an avoidance of political and religious involvement with pagan nations, and an uncompromising observance of the Torah in true Jewish fidelity and piety.

The Assyrian campaign

1 In the twelfth year of the reign of Nebuchadnezzar, who ruled the Assyrians from his great city of Nineveh, Arphaxad was ruling the Medes from Ecbatana. ²Arphaxad encircled Ecbatana with a wall built of hewn stones, each four and a half feet thick and nine feet long. He made the wall a hundred and five feet high and seventy-five feet thick, ³and at the city gates he set up towers a hundred and fifty feet high with foundations ninety feet thick; ⁴the gates themselves he made a hundred and five feet high, and he made them sixty feet wide to allow his army to march out in full force with the infantry in formation. ⁵It was in those days, then, that King Nebuchadnezzar waged war against King Arphaxad in the great plain on the borders of Ragau. ⁶All the inhabitants of the hill-country, all who lived along the Euphrates, the Tigris, and the Hydaspes, and, on the plain, King Arioch of Elam, these rallied to Nebuchadnezzar; and many tribes of the Chelodites joined forces with them.

1.1–7.32: The Assyrian invasion. The other nations capitulate and Jewish resistance is gradually broken.

1.1–6: Nebuchadnezzar wages war on Arphaxad. 1: *Nebuchadnezzar:* king of the Babylonians from 605–561 B.C.E. He directed the destruction of Jerusalem in 587 B.C.E.; see 2 Kgs. 25.1–9. His father had conquered the *Assyrians* and destroyed *Nineveh* in 612 B.C.E. The historically impossible combination here of Nebuchadnezzar and the Assyrians suggests that the author wished to combine Israel's traditional enemies to create a literary confrontation between faith and secular power. *Arphaxad* is unknown. **2–3:** *Ecbatana* was situated near present-day Hamadan in Iran. Its dimensions are exceedingly exaggerated, showing a high degree of fiction. **5:** *Ragau* is modern Rai, located near Teheran. **6:** The *Hydaspes* is a river near the eastern border of Persia. *Arioch* is unknown. The *Chelodites* are unknown.

⁷King Nebuchadnezzar of Assyria sent a summons to all the inhabitants of Persia, and to all who lived in the west: the inhabitants of Cilicia and Damascus, Lebanon and Antilebanon, all who lived along the coast, ⁸the peoples in Carmel and Gilead, Upper Galilee, and the great plain of Esdraelon, ⁹all who were in Samaria and its towns, and those to the west of the Jordan as far as Jerusalem, Betane, Chelus, Kadesh, and the wadi of Egypt, those who lived in Tahpanhes, Rameses, and the whole land of Goshen ¹⁰as far as Tanis and Memphis, and all the inhabitants of Egypt as far as the borders of Ethiopia. ¹¹But the king's summons was flouted by the entire region, and they did not join him for the campaign. They were not afraid of him; they regarded him as a mere man and, treating his envoys with contempt, they sent them back empty-handed.

¹²This roused Nebuchadnezzar to fury against the whole region; he swore by his throne and kingdom to exact vengeance from all the territories of Cilicia, Damascus, and Syria, and to put their inhabitants to the sword, along with the Moabites, the Ammonites, the people throughout Judaea, and everyone in Egypt, the whole region within the limits of the two seas.

¹³In the seventeenth year of his reign he marshalled his forces against King Arphaxad and defeated him in battle, with the complete rout of his army, all his cavalry and chariots. ¹⁴He occupied his towns, and advancing on Ecbatana he captured its towers, looted the bazaars, and reduced its splendour to abject ruin. ¹⁵He caught Arphaxad in the mountains of Ragau and ran him through with his spear, and so made an end of him. ¹⁶Then he and his combined forces, an immense host of warriors, went back with the spoil to Nine-

veh, where for four months he relaxed and feasted with his army.

2 In the eighteenth year, on the twenty-second day of the first month, there was a conference in King Nebuchadnezzar's palace about implementing his threat of vengeance on the whole region. ²Calling together all his officers and nobles, the king laid before them his secret plan for the region and declared his determination to put an end to the disaffection. ³It was resolved by them that everyone who had not obeyed the king's summons should die.

⁴When his plans were completed, King Nebuchadnezzar of Assyria summoned his commander-in-chief Holophernes, who was second only to himself, and said, ⁵'This is the decree of the Great King, lord of all the earth: Directly you leave my presence, you are to take under your command an army of seasoned troops, a hundred and twenty thousand infantry with a force of twelve thousand cavalry, ⁶and march against all the peoples of the west who have dared to disobey the order I issued. ⁷Bid them have earth and water ready in token of submission, for I am coming to vent my wrath on them. Every corner of their land will be overrun by my army, and I shall give them up to be plundered by my troops; ⁸their wounded will fill the ravines and wadis, and every river will be choked with their dead; ⁹and I shall send them into captivity to the ends of the earth. ¹⁰Go, and occupy all their territory for me. If they submit, hold them for me until the time comes to punish them. ¹¹But to those who resist show no mercy; throughout the whole region give them up to be slaughtered and plundered. ¹²By my life and royal power I have spoken and shall act accordingly. ¹³You are

1:15 **made an end of him:** *prob. rdg; Gk adds* up to that day.

1.7–12: **Persia and the western nations arouse Nebuchadnezzar's anger. 7—10:** The nations and towns listed represent the western portion of the Fertile Crescent—modern Syria, Lebanon, Palestine, and Egypt. *Betane* and *Chelus* are unknown. *Kadesh* may be in southern Palestine.

1.13–2.13: **Nebuchadnezzar defeats Arphaxad and declares war on the western nations. 14:** The Nebuchadnezzar of history did not capture *Ecbatana*. **2.1:** *The eighteenth year* of Nebuchadnezzar's reign is 587 B.C.E., the date when he ordered the destruction of Jerusalem. **4:** *Holophernes* is unknown as a famous Babylonian general; the name, indeed, is Persian and his presence adds the Persians to the artificial composite of Israel's enemies; see 1.1 n. **5:** Nebuchadnezzar's designation of himself as *lord . . .,* without reference to the rights of God, makes this a battle between the ungodly and the God-fearing. **7:** The offering of *earth and water* was a Persian expression for the provisioning of an invading and conquering army from the occupied country.

to obey these orders to the letter; see that you discharge them exactly as I your sovereign have commanded you, and do so without delay!'

14 Withdrawing from the royal presence, Holophernes summoned all the marshals, generals, and officers of the Assyrian army. 15 He mustered, as the king had commanded, a hundred and twenty thousand infantry and twelve thousand mounted archers, all picked men, 16 and marshalled them in the regular battle order of a great army. 17 He took an immense number of camels, donkeys, and mules for the baggage, innumerable sheep, oxen, and goats for provisions, 18 ample rations for every man, as well as a great quantity of gold and silver from the royal palace. 19 With his whole army he set off in advance of King Nebuchadnezzar to overrun the entire region to the west with his chariots, cavalry, and picked infantry. 20 Accompanying them went a motley host like a swarm of locusts, countless as the dust of the earth.

21 From Nineveh they marched for three days towards the plain of Bectileth, and encamped over against Bectileth near the mountain to the north of Upper Cilicia. 22 From there Holophernes pushed on into the hill-country with his whole army—infantry, cavalry, and chariots. 23 He devastated Put and Lud, and plundered all the people of Rassis, and the Ishmaelites on the edge of the desert south of the land of the Cheleans. 24 Then following the Euphrates he traversed Mesopotamia and destroyed every fortified town along the wadi Abron as far as the sea. 25 He occupied the territory of Cilicia, cutting down any who resisted. He marched south to the borders of Japheth which fronts Arabia. 26 He encircled the Midianites, set their encampments on fire, and plundered their sheepfolds. 27 He went down into the plain of Damascus at the time of the wheat harvest, and set fire to the crops; he slaughtered the flocks and herds, sacked the towns, laid waste the countryside, and put all the young men to the sword.

28 Fear and dread of him assailed the inhabitants of the coast at Sidon and Tyre, and the people of Sur and Okina, and of Jemnaan; terror seized the populations of Azotus and Ascalon.

3 1 They sent envoys to sue for peace. 2 'We, the servants of the Great King, Nebuchadnezzar, lie prostrate before you,' they said; 'do with us as you please. 3 Our homesteads, all our territory and wheatfields, our flocks and herds with every sheepfold in our encampments, all are yours to deal with as you will. 4 Our towns along with their inhabitants are yours to enslave; come and dispose of them as you think fit.'

5 When the envoys brought this message to Holophernes, 6 he went down with his army to the coast, where he established garrisons in all the fortified towns, and, at the same time, took from them picked men to serve as auxiliaries. 7 Both there and throughout the surrounding country he was welcomed with garlands and dancing and the sound of tambourines. 8 He demolished all their sanctuaries and cut down their sacred groves, for his commission was to destroy all the gods of the land, so that Nebuchadnezzar alone should be worshipped by every nation, and he alone be invoked as a god by men of every tongue and tribe.

9 Holophernes then advanced towards Esdraelon, near Dothan, which faces the Judaean ridge, 10 and encamped between Geba and Scythopolis, where he remained for a whole month to collect whatever supplies were needed for his army.

2:24 **following:** or crossing.　3:8 **sanctuaries:** so one Vs.; Gk borders.

2.14–3.10: Holophernes ravages the west as far as Palestine. 21: Three days to march from Nineveh to Bectileth (unknown city) in Upper Cilicia (southeastern Asia Minor) is impossible since the distance is about three hundred miles. **23:** Put and Lud are perhaps in Asia Minor. Rassis is unknown. Ishmaelites usually means Arabs. The Cheleans are unknown. **24–28:** The route of invasion is very erratic and most unlikely. Such an imposing list of victims is given for psychological and theological rather than historical purposes. **24:** The Abron is unknown. **25:** Japheth is unknown as a place name. **28:** Sur and Okina are perhaps Dor and Acco in western Galilee. Jemnaan may be Jamnia, this one on the Lake of Galilee; Azotus (Ashdod) and Ascalon (Ashkelon) are Philistine cities. **3.8:** The Babylonian rulers never claimed divine rights, but the Seleucid kings did (Dan. 3.1–7). The persecution of the Jews by the Seleucids seems to be alluded to here. See 1.1 n.; 2.4 n.; 2 Macc. 9.1–12. **9:** Esdraelon: the great plain that lies between Galilee and Samaria. **10:** Geba: a town in central Palestine. Scythopolis: Beth-shan, south of the Lake of Galilee.

Israelite resistance

4 A FULL report of the measures undertaken by Holophernes, King Nebuchadnezzar's commander-in-chief, how he had despoiled all the temples of the nations and razed them to the ground, reached the ears of the Israelites living in Judaea. ²His approach filled them with terror, and they trembled for the fate of Jerusalem and the sanctuary of the Lord their God. ³They had just returned from captivity, and only recently had all the people been reunited in Judaea, and the sacred vessels, the altar, and the temple been sanctified after their desecration. ⁴Accordingly they sent out a warning to the whole of Samaria, Cona, Beth-horon, Belmain and Jericho, Choba and Aesora, and the valley of Salem; ⁵the tops of all the high hills were occupied, the hill villages fortified, and stores of food from the newly harvested fields laid up in preparation for war. ⁶Joakim, high priest in Jerusalem at that time, wrote to the people of Bethulia and Bethomesthaim, which is opposite Esdraelon facing the plain near Dothan, ⁷directing them to hold the passes into the hill-country, because they gave access to Judaea; as the approaches were wide enough for only two men at most, it was easy to prevent the passage of an invader.

⁸The Israelites complied with the orders issued by Joakim the high priest and by the senate of all Israel in Jerusalem. ⁹They all cried to God with great fervour, fasting and humbling themselves; ¹⁰they put on sackcloth—they, their wives and children, their livestock, and every resident foreigner, hired labourer, and slave. ¹¹In Jerusalem the Israelites, men, women, and children, all prostrated themselves in front of the sanctuary, and, with ashes on their heads, spread out

their sackcloth before the Lord. They draped the altar in sackcloth, ¹²and with one voice they fervently implored the God of Israel not to allow their infants to be captured, their wives carried off, their ancestral cities destroyed, and the temple desecrated and dishonoured, so giving the heathen cause for gloating. ¹³The Lord heard their prayer and took pity on their distress.

For many days the entire population of Judaea and Jerusalem fasted before the temple of the Lord Almighty. ¹⁴Joakim the high priest and the priests who stood in the presence of the Lord, and all who served him, wore sackcloth when they offered the regular whole-offering and the votive and freewill-offerings of the people; ¹⁵they put ashes on their turbans, and they cried with all their might to the Lord to look favourably on the whole house of Israel.

5 When it was reported to Holophernes that the Israelites had prepared for war by closing the passes through the hill-country, fortifying all the heights, and putting obstructions in the plains, ²his anger knew no bounds. He summoned all the rulers of Moab and the Ammonite generals, and all the governors of the coastal region. ³'Tell me, you Canaanites,' he demanded, 'what people is this that lives in the hill-country? What are their cities? How large is their army, and wherein lies their power and strength? Who has set up as king at the head of their forces? ⁴Of all the people of the west, why do they alone disdain to come to meet me?'

⁵Achior, the commander of the Ammonites, replied: 'My lord, if you will allow your servant to speak, I shall give you the true facts about this people that lives close at hand in the hill-country; no lie will pass your servant's lips. ⁶They are descended from the

---

4.1–15: The Israelites prepare to defend their land and temple. 3: The Israelites could not have *just returned from captivity* because the return took place under the Persians, many years after Nebuchadnezzar; compare Ezra 1.1–11. The sanctification of the *altar* and *temple* may refer to the rededication of the temple under Judas Maccabeus in 164 B.C.E.; see 1 Macc. 4.52–55. Israel's history is here telescoped. **4:** *Cona, Belmain, Choba,* and *Aesora* are unknown; the *valley of Salem* is an archaic name for Jerusalem (Gen. 14.18). **6:** *Joakim* may refer to a high priest (named Joiakim) mentioned in Neh. 12.10–12, 26 but the circumstances there are quite different. *Bethulia,* mentioned frequently in Jdt., is not mentioned elsewhere in the Bible; this would be unthinkable if the story were historical. *Bethomesthaim* is unknown. **8:** There is no evidence of a *high priest* and a *senate* ruling in Jerusalem prior to Maccabean times (1 Macc. 12.6; 2 Macc. 11.27).

5.1–24: Achior, the Ammonite, briefs Holophernes on the history and religion of Israel. 3: Israel had generally controlled the *hill-country* where guerrilla tactics were effective; see Judg. 1.19. **5:** *Achior* plays the

Chaldaeans; [7] and at one time they settled in Mesopotamia, because they refused to worship the gods their fathers had worshipped in Chaldaea. [8] They abandoned the ways of their ancestors and worshipped the God of heaven, the God whom they acknowledge today. When they were driven from the presence of their fathers' gods, they fled to Mesopotamia and lived there for a long time. [9] Commanded by their God to leave their new home and move to Canaan, they settled there and acquired great wealth in gold and silver, and livestock in plenty.

[10] 'Because of a famine which spread throughout Canaan, they went down to Egypt, where they lived as long as they found food. While there, they multiplied so greatly that their numbers were past counting, [11] and the king of Egypt took precautionary action by setting them to labour at brickmaking and by reducing them to slavery. [12] They cried to their God, and he inflicted incurable plagues on the whole of Egypt. When the Egyptians expelled them, [13] their God dried up the Red Sea for them [14] and led them towards Sinai and Kadesh-barnea. They drove out all the inhabitants of the wilderness [15] and settled in the land of the Amorites, and by force of arms exterminated the whole population of Heshbon. Then they crossed the Jordan and took possession of the entire hill-country, [16] driving out the Canaanites, the Perizzites, the Jebusites, the Shechemites, and all the Girgashites; and there they lived for a long time.

[17] 'As long as they did not sin against their God, they prospered, for they had the support of a God who hates wickedness. [18] When, however, they strayed from the path he had marked out for them, they suffered heavy losses in many wars; they were carried captive to a foreign country, the sanctuary of their God was razed to the ground, and their towns were seized by enemies. [19] But now that they have turned again to their God, they have come back from the lands to which they had been dispersed; they have occupied Jerusalem, the site of their holy place, and have

settled in the hill-country, which lay uninhabited. [20] Now, my sovereign lord, if these people have fallen into the error of sinning against their God, and if we find that in so doing they have put themselves at a disadvantage, then we can go up and attack them. [21] But if these people have not violated their law, then let my lord leave them alone, for fear that the God they serve should defend and protect them, and we become the laughing-stock of the whole world.'

[22] When Achior finished speaking there were protests from all who stood round the tent. Holophernes' officers, together with the people from the coastal region and from Moab, demanded that Achior be hacked to pieces. [23] 'We are not going to be scared of the Israelites,' they said, 'a people incapable of putting a force of any strength in the field. [24] Let us march into the hill-country, Lord Holophernes; your great army will swallow them whole.'

6 When the uproar among the men surrounding the council had died down, Holophernes, the Assyrian commander-in-chief, addressed Achior in front of all the assembled foreigners: [2] 'And who are you, Achior, you and your Ephraimite mercenaries, to play the prophet in our presence as you have done today, telling us not to make war against this people, Israel, because their God will protect them? What god is there besides Nebuchadnezzar? [3] When he exerts his power he will wipe them off the face of the earth; their God will assuredly not come to their rescue. We who serve Nebuchadnezzar shall strike them down as if they were but one man. They will not be able to withstand the weight of our cavalry; [4] we shall overwhelm them. Their mountains will be drenched with their blood, and the plains filled with their dead. They cannot stand against us; they will perish without trace. So says King Nebuchadnezzar, lord of all the earth; he has spoken, and his words are no empty threat.

[5] 'As for you, Achior, you Ammonite mercenary, this is treasonable talk. You shall not

---

role of the "objective witness" who allows the author to recall the historical basis for Israel's uniqueness. **6:** *Chaldaeans:* a reference to Abraham's origin (Gen. 11.27–31). **7:** *Mesopotamia* here refers to the region around Harran where Abraham stopped on his way to the land of Israel (Gen. 11.31). The Bible makes no mention of any religious problems in this context, but later Jewish tradition does. **14:** *Kadesh-barnea:* Num. 20.1. **15:** *Heshbon:* Num. 21.25–26.

6.1–21: Holophernes condemns Achior. 2: It is important for the author that the issue be strictly religious, see my face again from this day until I have taken vengeance on that brood of fugitives from Egypt; [6] but when I come back my warriors will run you through with sword and spear and add you to their victims. [7] My men will now take you away to the hill-country and leave you in one of the towns in the passes; [8] you will be allowed to live until you share their fate. [9] If you are so confident that these places will not fall into our hands, you need not look downcast. I have spoken, and not a single word of mine will go unfulfilled.'

[10] Holophernes ordered the slaves standing by in the tent to seize Achior, escort him to Bethulia, and hand him over to the Israelites. [11] So laying hold of him they took him outside the camp into the plain, and from there up into the hill-country, until they arrived at the springs below Bethulia. [12] The moment the men of Bethulia sighted them, they picked up their weapons and sallied forth from the town to the top of the hill, and the slingers all pelted the enemy with stones to prevent them from coming up. [13] But they slipped through under cover of the hill, bound Achior and left him lying there at the foot, and then returned to their master.

[14] When the Israelites came down from the town and found Achior, they untied him and took him into Bethulia, where they brought him before the town magistrates [15] then in office, Ozias son of Mica, of the tribe of Simeon, and Chabris son of Gothoniel, and Charmis son of Melchiel. [16] The magistrates summoned the elders of the town, and all the young men and women also came running to the assembly. When Achior had been put in the centre of the crowd, Ozias questioned him as to what had happened. [17] He answered by telling them everything that had taken place in Holophernes' council, what he himself had said in the presence of the Assyrian commanders, and how Holophernes had boasted of what he would do to Israel. [18] At this the people prostrated themselves in worship and cried out to God: [19] 'O Lord, God of heaven, consider their arrogance; have pity on us and our nation in our humiliation;

show favour this day to your own people.' [20] Then they reassured Achior and commended him warmly. [21] Ozias brought him from the assembly to his own house, where he gave a feast for the elders; and all night long they invoked the help of the God of Israel.

7 THE next day Holophernes gave orders to his whole army together with all his allies to strike camp and march on Bethulia, to seize the passes up into the hill-country, and engage the Israelites in battle. [2] The entire force moved off, an army of a hundred and seventy thousand infantry and twelve thousand cavalry, not counting the baggage train of the infantry, an immense host. [3] They encamped in the valley near Bethulia, beside the spring; and their camp extended in breadth towards Dothan as far as Belbaim, and in length from Bethulia to Cyamon which faces Esdraelon. [4] The Israelites viewed the enemy's numbers with great alarm. 'These men will devour the whole country,' they said to one another; 'neither the high mountains nor the valleys, nor yet the hills, will ever be able to support the burden of them.' [5] Each man stood to arms; they lit beacons on their towers and remained on guard throughout the night.

[6] On the following day Holophernes led out all his cavalry in full view of the Israelites in Bethulia. [7] He reconnoitred the approaches to the town and in the course of his tour seized the springs which were its water supply; he stationed detachments of soldiers to picket them, before returning to his main force.

[8] The rulers of Esau's descendants and the Moabite leaders, along with the commanders of the coastal region, made a joint approach to him. [9] 'Be pleased to listen to our proposal,' they said, 'so that no disaster may befall the army of our lord. [10] These Israelites rely, not on their spears, but on the height of the mountains where they live, for it is no easy task to assault those mountain peaks. [11] Therefore, Lord Holophernes, avoid a

i.e. *what god is there?* **5:** *Egypt:* a derisive reference to the Exodus. **11:** *The springs below Bethulia:* this is of little help for identification, because most towns in Judah and Israel were built on a hill for defense and near a water supply. **19:** The enemy represents the *arrogance* of any human attempt to displace God in history.

7.1–18: Holophernes lays siege to Bethulia. 3: *Dothan:* a town in the plain of *Esdraelon;* see 3.9 n. *Belbaim . . . Cyamon:* unknown. **7:** Seizure of the *springs* was the first move in a siege, since the only other source of water was that collected in cisterns during the short rainy season; see v. 21. **8:** *Esau's descendants:* Edomites, pitched battle with them, and not one of your men will be lost. 12 Remain in the camp and keep all your soldiers in their quarters; but permit us, my lord, to take possession of the spring at the foot of the hill, 13 for that is where the whole population of Bethulia draws its water. When they are dying of thirst they will surrender the town. Meanwhile, we and our troops shall scale the neighbouring hills and make our camp there to see that not a man escapes from the place. 14 They and their wives and children will waste away with famine; even before the sword reaches them, the streets will be strewn with their corpses. 15 So you will make them pay dearly for rebelling against you and refusing to receive you peaceably.'

16 Their plan met with the approval of Holophernes and his entire staff, and he gave orders for it to be carried out. 17 A Moabite force, along with five thousand Assyrians, moved camp into the valley, where they seized the springs which were the Israelites' water supply. 18 Esau's descendants and the Ammonites went up into the hill-country and pitched camp opposite Dothan, and they sent a detachment south-east in the direction of Egrebel, which is near Chus by the wadi Mochmur. The rest of the Assyrian army, a vast host, made their camp on the plain; they filled the entire countryside, forming, with their tents and baggage train, an immense encampment.

19 The Israelites cried to the Lord their God. They were encircled by their enemies; there was no way of escape, and their courage failed. 20 For thirty-four days the whole Assyrian army, infantry, chariots, and cavalry, kept them blockaded. The people of Bethulia came to the end of their household supplies of water, 21 and the cisterns too were running dry; drinking water was so strictly rationed that there was never a day when their needs were satisfied. 22 Infants were listless, women and young men, faint with thirst,

collapsed in the streets and gateways from sheer exhaustion.

23 The people—young men, women, and children—all gathered round Ozias and the magistrates of the town, protesting loudly and saying in the presence of the elders: 24 'May God judge between us, for you have done us a great wrong in not suing for terms from the Assyrians. 25 Now we have no one to help us; God has sold us into their power, and they will find us struck down, all dead of thirst. 26 Surrender to them even now; let Holophernes' people and his army sack the whole town. 27 It is better for us to be carried off by them, for even as slaves we shall at least be alive, and we shall not have to watch our little ones dying before our eyes, the women and children at their last gasp. 28 We call heaven and earth to witness against you, we call our God, the Lord of our fathers, who is punishing us for our sins and the sins of our fathers. We pray that he may not let our forebodings come true this day.' 29 The whole assembly broke into a chorus of lamentation and cried loudly to the Lord God.

30 Ozias said to them, 'Courage, my friends! Let us hold out for five more days; by that time the Lord our God will again show us his mercy, for he will not abandon us for ever. 31 But if by the end of that time no help has reached us, I shall do what you ask.' 32 He dismissed the men, each to his post, and they went off to the walls and towers of the town; the women and children were sent to their homes. And throughout the town there was deep dejection.

Judith and Holophernes

8 NEWS of what was happening reached Judith, daughter of Merari who was the son of Ox, son of Joseph, son of Oziel, son of Helkias, son of Ananias, son of Gideon, son of Raphaim, son of Ahitob, son of Elias, son of Chelkias, son of Eliab, son of Nathanael,

7:17 **Moabite:** *so Old Lat.; Gk* Ammonite.

traditional enemies of Israel, are also added to the picture here; see 1.1 n. **18:** *Egrebel, Chus,* and *Mochmur* are located in the area southeast of Shechem.

7.19–32: The inhabitants of Bethulia contemplate surrender. 23–28: The complaints against *Ozias* are reminiscent of the bitter murmuring of the Israelites against Moses in the wilderness; see Num. 14.2–3.

8.1–13.20: Judith and Holophernes. Risking honor and life, she combines great faith, grim courage, and scrupulous observance of the Law in liberating Israel.

8.1–8: Judith is introduced. 1: *Judith* is the feminine form of Judah. Perhaps the name, which occurs passingly in Gen. 26.34, symbolizes the Jewish people. Judith's ancestors, aside from Israel (Jacob), cannot be son of Salamiel, son of Sarasadae, son of Israel. ² Her husband Manasses, who belonged to the same tribe and clan as she did, had died during the barley harvest. ³ While he was out in the fields supervising the binding of the sheaves, he suffered sunstroke; he took to his bed and died in Bethulia his native town and was buried beside his ancestors in the field between Dothan and Balamon. ⁴ For three years and four months Judith had lived in her house as a widow; ⁵ she had a shelter erected on the roof, and she put on sackcloth and always wore mourning. ⁶ After she became a widow she used to fast every day except sabbath eve, the sabbath itself, the eve of the new moon, the day of the new moon, and the Israelite feasts and days of public rejoicing. ⁷ She was beautiful and very attractive. Manasses had left her gold and silver, slaves and slave-girls, livestock and land, and she lived on her property. ⁸ No one had a word to say against her, for she was a deeply religious woman.

⁹ When Judith heard how the people, demoralized by the shortage of water, had made shameful demands on Ozias the magistrate, and how he had given them his oath to surrender the town to the Assyrians at the end of five days, ¹⁰ she sent her maid who had charge of everything she owned to ask Ozias, Chabris, and Charmis, the elders of the town, to come and see her.

¹¹ On their arrival she said: 'Listen to me, magistrates of Bethulia. It was wrong of you to speak as you did to the people today, binding yourselves and God in a solemn contract to surrender the town to our enemies unless the Lord sends relief within so many days. ¹² Who are you to put God to the test at a time like this, and to usurp his role in human affairs? ¹³ It is the Lord Almighty you are now putting to the proof! Will you never understand? ¹⁴ You are unable to plumb the depths of the human heart or grasp the way the mind works; how then can you fathom the Maker of mortal beings? How can you know

God's mind and understand his thought? No, my friends, do not provoke the anger of the Lord our God. ¹⁵ For even if he does not choose to help us within the five days, he has the power to shield us at any time he pleases, or equally he can let us be destroyed by our enemies. ¹⁶ It is not for you to impose conditions on the Lord our God, because God will neither yield to threats nor be bargained with like a mere mortal. ¹⁷ So while we wait for the deliverance which is his to give, let us appeal to him for help. If he sees fit, he will hear us.

¹⁸ 'At the present day there is not one of our tribes or clans, districts or towns, that worships man-made gods, or has done so within living memory. This did take place in days gone by, ¹⁹ and that was why our forefathers were abandoned to slaughter and pillage, and great was their downfall at the hand of the enemy. ²⁰ We, however, acknowledge no god but the Lord, and so have confidence that he will not spurn us or any of our nation. ²¹ If we should lose Bethulia, then all Judaea will be lost; the temple will be sacked, and God will hold us responsible for its desecration. ²² The slaughter and deportation of our fellow-countrymen and the devastation of our ancestral land will bring his judgement on our heads, wherever among the Gentiles we become slaves. Our masters will regard us with disgust and contempt. ²³ There will be no happy ending to our servitude, no return to favour; the Lord our God will use it to dishonour us.

²⁴ 'My friends, let us now set an example to our fellow-countrymen, for their lives depend on us, and with us rests the fate of the temple, its precincts, and the altar. ²⁵ Despite our peril let us give thanks to the Lord our God, for he is putting us to the test as he did our forefathers. ²⁶ Remember how he dealt with Abraham, and how he tested Isaac, and what happened to Jacob in Syrian Mesopotamia while he was working as a shepherd for his uncle Laban. ²⁷ The Lord is subjecting us to the same fiery ordeal by which he tested

identified. **3:** *Dothan:* 7.3 n. *Balamon:* unknown. **6:** The OT requires fasting only on the Day of Atonement. Rabbinic Judaism increased the number of fast days. Judith's fasting beyond the requirement implies an extraordinary piety.

8.9–36: Judith upbraids the magistrates and promises that God will deliver the city by her hand. 11–27: Judith's eloquent exhortation is an expression of what faith requires of Israel in the postexilic period of apparent abandonment by God. **12:** *Put God to the test:* to lay down *conditions* (v. 16) for God's action, e.g. to hold out for five days more (7.30). **18:** This favorable judgment was generally accurate in the period after the Exile. **25:** God puts Israel to the *test* by awaiting a response of fidelity. The argument is built on an antithesis: it is their loyalty, not taking vengeance on us: it is as a warning that he scourges his worshippers.'

28 Ozias replied, 'You have spoken from the wisdom of your heart, and what you say no one can deny. 29 This is not the first time you have given proof of your wisdom; throughout your life we have all recognized your good sense and sound judgement. 30 But the people were desperate with thirst, and drove us to make this promise and bind ourselves by an oath we may not break. 31 You are a devout woman; pray for us now and ask the Lord to send the rain to fill our cisterns, and then we shall be faint no more.'

32 'Listen to me,' said Judith. 'I am going to do something which will be remembered among our countrymen for all generations. 33 Be at the gate tonight; I shall go out with my maid and, before the day on which you have promised to surrender the town to our enemies, the Lord will deliver Israel by my hand. 34 But do not question me about my plan; I shall tell you nothing until I have accomplished what I mean to do.' 35 Ozias and the magistrates said to her, 'Go with our blessing, and may you have the guidance of the Lord God as you take vengeance on our enemies.' 36 They then left her roof-shelter and returned to their posts.

9 Judith prostrated herself; she put ashes on her head and uncovered the sackcloth she was wearing, and at the moment when the evening incense was being offered in the house of God at Jerusalem, she raised her voice and cried to the Lord: 2 'Lord, the God of my forefather Simeon, you put a sword in Simeon's hand for him to take vengeance on those foreigners who had stripped off a virgin's veil to defile her, uncovered her thighs to shame her, and violated her womb to dishonour her. Though you said, "Such a thing shall not be done," yet they did so. 3 That was why you gave up their rulers to be slain, and the bed they had disgraced with their treachery to be stained with blood; beneath your stroke both slaves and princes fell, even princes upon their thrones. 4 You gave their wives as booty, and their daughters as captives, and all the spoils to be apportioned among your beloved sons, who, aflame with zeal for your cause and aghast at the pollution of their blood, called on you for help. God, my God, hear also a widow's prayer. 5 All that happened then, and all that happened before and after, was your work. What is now and what is yet to be, you have planned; and what you have planned has come to pass. 6 The things you have foreordained present themselves and say, "We are here." All your ways are prepared beforehand: your judgement rests on foreknowledge.

7 'Here are the Assyrians massed in force, exultant in their horses and riders, boasting of the might of their infantry, confident in shield and javelin, bow and sling. They do not know that you are the Lord who stamps out wars; the Lord is your name. 8 Overthrow their strength by your power and crush their might in your anger, for their aim is to desecrate your temple, to defile the dwelling-place of your glorious name, and to lay low the horns of your altar with the sword. 9 See how arrogant they are! Bring down your wrath on their heads, and give to me, widow though I am, the strength to achieve my end. 10 Use the guile of my words to strike them down, the slave with the ruler, the ruler with the servant; shatter their pride by a woman's hand. 11 Your might lies not in numbers nor your sovereign power in strong men, but you are the God of the humble, the help of the poor, the support of the weak, the protector of the despairing, the deliverer of those who have lost all hope. 12 God of my forefather, God of Israel's heritage, Lord of heaven and earth, Creator of the waters, King of all your

not that human beings test God (v. 12) but, rather, God tests human beings. **27:** That suffering be viewed as a *warning* is a faith interpretation of history. **33:** The context and language are reminiscent of God's intervention to lead the people from Egypt by the *hand* of Moses (Exod. ch. 9). See also 13.14; 15.10.

9.1–14: Judith's prayer. 1: The time of the *evening* offering was considered a most propitious moment for prayer. See Exod. 30.8; 1 Kgs. 18.36. **2:** *Simeon* and Levi slaughtered the Shechemites for having violated their sister Dinah (Gen. ch. 34). But see also Gen. 49.5–7 where their violence is condemned. **4:** The *widow's prayer* is the object of special divine attention and care in the OT. See Deut. 10.18; Ecclus. 35.14–15. **7:** The *Assyrians*, *boasting* of their *might*, do not recognize that the *Lord* is the only true basis of power. See also 16.3. **10:** The pious Judith prays for the success of her deceit because trickery was considered a very honorable weapon in war; see Josh. 9.3–27.

creation, hear my prayer! [13] Grant that my deceiving words may wound and bruise those who harbour cruel designs against your covenant and against your temple, the summit of Zion, and the home and possession of your children. [14] May your whole nation, every tribe, be made aware that you are God, God of all power and might, and that you and you alone are Israel's shield.'

10 When Judith had ended this prayer to the God of Israel, [2] she rose from where she had been lying prostrate, called her maid, and went down into the house in which she spent her sabbaths and days of festival. [3] She removed the sackcloth she was wearing and laid aside her widow's dress. After bathing, she anointed herself with rich perfume. She arranged her hair elaborately, tied it with a ribbon, and arrayed herself in her gayest clothes, those she used to wear while her husband Manasses was still alive. [4] She put sandals on her feet and adorned herself with anklets, bracelets and rings, her ear-rings, and all her ornaments, and made herself very attractive, to catch the eye of any man who saw her. [5] She gave her maid a skin of wine and a flask of oil; she filled a bag with roasted grain, cakes of dried figs, and loaves of fine bread, packed up her utensils, and gave it all to her maid to carry.

[6] From the house they made their way to the town gate of Bethulia, where they found Ozias standing with Chabris and Charmis, the elders of the town. [7] When they beheld Judith transformed in appearance and quite differently dressed, they marvelled at her beauty and said to her, [8] 'The God of our fathers grant that you meet with favour and accomplish what you are undertaking, so that Israel may triumph and Jerusalem be exalted!' Judith bowed in worship to God [9] and then said, 'Give the order for the gate to be opened for me, and I shall go and carry out all we have spoken of.' They ordered the young men to do as she asked, [10] and when the gate was opened Judith went out, accompanied by her maid. The men of the town gazed after her until she had gone down the hillside and along the valley, where they lost sight of her.

[11] As the two women were making their way straight down the valley, they were confronted by an Assyrian outpost [12] who stopped Judith and questioned her: 'What is your nationality? Where have you come from, and where are you going?' 'I am a Hebrew,' she replied; 'but I am running away from my people, because they are about to fall into your hands and become your prey. [13] I am on my way to Holophernes, your commander-in-chief, with accurate information for him: I shall show him a route by which he can gain control of the entire hill-country without one of you suffering injury or worse.'

[14] The men listened to her story, looking at her face and marvelling at her beauty. [15] 'By coming down at once to see our master you have saved your life,' they said. 'You must go to his tent straight away; some of us will escort you and hand you over. [16] When you are in his presence, do not be afraid; just tell him what you have told us, and he will treat you well.' [17] They detailed a hundred of their number to accompany her and her maid, and the two women were conducted to Holophernes' tent.

[18] As THE news of her coming spread from tent to tent, men ran from all parts of the camp and gathered in a circle round her as she stood outside Holophernes' tent waiting for him to be told about her. [19] Admiration for her beauty led them to feel admiration for all Israelites; they said to each other, 'Who could despise a nation whose women are like these? We had better not leave a man of them alive, for if they get away they will be able to outwit the whole world.'

[20] Holophernes' bodyguard and all his attendants came out and escorted her into the tent, [21] where he was resting on his bed under a mosquito-net of purple interwoven with gold, emeralds, and precious stones. [22] When Judith was announced he came out to the front part of the tent, with silver lamps carried before him. [23] She entered his presence,

---

10.1–17: Judith goes to Holophernes. 1–2: *Went down into the house:* from the tent on the roof where she spent most of her time. See 8.5. **5:** Judith *packed up* her own food so that she would not be defiled by eating unclean food of the Gentiles; see 12.1–4. **12:** *Running away* from a city was not uncommon when a siege reached the decisive stage; see Jer. 38.19; 39.9; 2 Chr. 30.10.

10.18–11.23: Judith is welcomed by Holophernes and explains her errand. 19: *Outwit the whole world:*

and he and his attendants all marvelled at the beauty of her face. She prostrated herself and did obeisance to him, but his slaves raised her up.

11 'Do not be alarmed, madam,' said Holophernes; 'there is no cause for fear. I have never injured anyone who chose to serve Nebuchadnezzar, king of all the earth. ²I should never have raised my spear against your people in the hill-country had they not insulted me; they have brought it on themselves. ³Now tell me why you have run away from them and joined us. You have saved your life by coming. Be reassured! You are in no danger, this night or at any time; ⁴no one will harm you. On the contrary, you will enjoy the benefits that are accorded to the subjects of my master, King Nebuchadnezzar.'

⁵Judith replied, 'My lord, grant your slave a hearing and listen to what I have to say to you. The information I am giving you tonight is the truth. ⁶If you follow my advice, through you God will accomplish a great thing, and my lord will not fail to attain his ends: ⁷I swear this by the life of Nebuchadnezzar, king of all the earth, and by the living might of him who sent you to bring order to all creatures. Thanks to you and to your power, not only do men serve him, but wild animals, cattle, and birds will live at the disposal of Nebuchadnezzar and his whole house. ⁸We have heard how wise and clever you are; you are known throughout the world as a man of ability who has no peer in all the empire, a man of powerful intellect and amazing skill in the arts of war.

⁹'Now, we have heard about the speech that Achior made in your council; the men of Bethulia rescued him and he told them everything he had said in your presence. ¹⁰Do not disregard his words, my sovereign lord, but give them full weight. They are true: no punishment ever befalls our race nor does the sword subdue them, except when they sin against their God. ¹¹And yet, my lord, you are not to be thwarted and cheated of success; they are doomed to die, and sin has them in its power, for whenever they do wrong they arouse their God's anger. ¹²Since they have run out of food and their water supply is desperately low, they have decided to lay hands on their cattle, proposing to eat all the things that God by his laws has strictly prohibited; ¹³they have resolved to use up the firstfruits of the grain and the tithes of wine and oil, although these are dedicated and reserved for the priests who stand in attendance before our God in Jerusalem, and no layman may so much as touch them. ¹⁴They have sent to Jerusalem for permission from the senate, because even the people there have done this. ¹⁵As soon as ever the word comes and they act on it, that same day they will be given up to you to be destroyed.

¹⁶'When I learnt all this, my lord, I left them and made my escape; the things that God has sent me to do with you will be the wonder of the whole world, wherever men hear about them. ¹⁷For I, your servant, am a godfearing woman: day and night I worship the God of heaven. I shall stay with you now, my lord, and each night I shall go out into the valley and pray to God, and when they have committed their sins he will tell me. ¹⁸Immediately I bring you word, you may go out at the head of your army; you will meet with no resistance. ¹⁹I shall guide you across Judaea until you reach Jerusalem, and I shall set up your throne in the heart of the city. You will drive them like sheep that have lost their shepherd, and not a dog will so much as growl at you. I have been given foreknowledge of this; it has been revealed to me, and I have been sent to announce it to you.'

²⁰Judith's words delighted Holophernes and all those in attendance on him and, amazed at her wisdom, ²¹they declared, 'From one end of the earth to the other there

superb irony. The Assyrians note that the trap into which they are falling would make a very good trap! **11.3–4:** Holophernes guarantees freedom from *danger* to his prospective executioner! The Bible delights in showing how God uses evil people to bring about positive results. **6:** *Through you God will accomplish a great thing* has an altogether different meaning for Judith than for Holophernes. Judith's conversation is full of such delightful ambiguities. **13:** *Firstfruits . . . tithes* were reserved for priests by Mosaic Law. See Exod. 23.19; Lev. 23.15–21; 27.30. The requirements of the Law (see Deut. 26.1–15) seem to be extended here. Judith uses the same argument as Achior had done (5.17–21) but affirms Israel's guilt. It was commonly believed by the ancients that ritual transgression was followed by punishment. **17:** By going out *each night,* Judith is establishing a pattern of conduct that will permit her later escape (13.10).

is not a woman to compare with her for beauty of face or shrewdness of speech.' 22 Holophernes assured her, 'Your God has done well in sending you out from your people, to bring strength to us and destruction to those who have insulted my lord! 23 Your looks are striking and your words are wise. Do as you have promised, and your God shall be my god, and you shall live in King Nebuchadnezzar's palace and be renowned throughout the whole world.'

12 Holophernes then told them to bring her in where his silver was set out, and gave orders for a meal to be served to her from his own food and wine. 2 But Judith said, 'I must not eat of it for fear I should be breaking our law. What I have brought will be sufficient for my needs.' 3 'But', asked Holophernes, 'where can we get you a fresh supply of the same kind if you use up all you have with you? There is no one from your people here among us.' 4 Judith replied, 'As sure as you live, my lord, I shall not finish what I have with me before God accomplishes by my hand what he has purposed.'

5 Holophernes' attendants conducted her to a tent, and she slept until midnight. Shortly before the dawn watch she rose 6 and sent this request to Holophernes: 'May it please my lord to give orders for me to be allowed to go out and pray.' 7 Holophernes ordered his bodyguard not to prevent her. She stayed in the camp for three days, going out each night into the valley of Bethulia and bathing in the spring at the camp. 8 When she came up out of the water she would pray the Lord, the God of Israel, to prosper her undertaking to restore his people. 9 Then she returned to the camp purified, and remained in the tent until she took her evening meal.

10 On the fourth day Holophernes gave a banquet for his personal servants only; none of the army officers were invited. 11 He said to Bagoas, the eunuch in charge of all his personal affairs: 'Go to the Hebrew woman who is in your care, and persuade her to join us at our feast. 12 We shall lose face if we let such a woman go without enjoying her fa-

vours; if we do not win her, she will laugh us to scorn.' 13 Bagoas withdrew from Holophernes' presence and went in to Judith. 'Now, my fair one,' he said, 'do not be bashful; come along to my master and give yourself the honour of his company. Drink with us and enjoy yourself, and behave today like one of the Assyrian women in attendance at Nebuchadnezzar's palace.' 14 'Who am I to refuse my lord?' answered Judith. 'I am eager to do whatever pleases him, and it will be something to boast of till my dying day.' 15 She proceeded to dress herself up, putting on all her feminine finery. Her maid went ahead of her, and spread on the ground in front of Holophernes the fleeces which Bagoas had provided for her daily use, so that she might recline on them while eating.

16 As Judith came in and took her place, Holophernes was beside himself with desire for her. He trembled with passion and was filled with an ardent longing to possess her; indeed ever since he first set eyes on her he had been seeking an opportunity to seduce her. 17 He said to her, 'Drink, and join in our merriment.' 18 'Certainly I shall, my lord,' replied Judith, 'for today is the greatest day of my life.' 19 Then she took what her servant had prepared, and ate and drank in his presence. 20 Holophernes was entranced with her, and he drank a great deal of wine, more than he had ever drunk on any single day in his whole life.

13 When it grew late, Holophernes' servants made haste to withdraw, and Bagoas closed the tent from outside, shutting out the attendants from his master's presence, and they went off to their beds; the banquet had lasted so long that they were all exhausted. 2 Judith was now alone in the tent, with Holophernes lying sprawled on his bed, dead drunk. 3 Judith had told her maid to stand outside the sleeping apartment and wait for her to go out as she did on other days; she had said that she would be going out to pray, and had explained this to Bagoas also.

4 When all had left and not a soul re-

12.1–9: Judith prepares for the opportune moment. 2: Judith's scrupulous observance of the dietary laws reflects a norm of postexilic Jewish piety. **5–9:** That Holophernes is so easily manipulated is patently a literary device.

12.10–20: Holophernes invites Judith to a banquet. 11: *Bagoas* is a common Persian name (see 1.1 n.). A *eunuch* was usually in charge of the king's harem but in some cases he was also an important and influential court official (Gen. 37.36; Dan. 1.3).

mained, Judith stood beside Holophernes' bed and prayed silently: 'O Lord, God of all power, look favourably now on what I am doing to bring glory to Jerusalem, [5] for this is the moment to come to the aid of your heritage and to prosper my plan for crushing the enemies who have attacked us.' [6] She went to the bed-rail beside Holophernes' head, reached down his sword, [7] and drawing close to the bed she gripped him by the hair. 'Now give me strength, O Lord, God of Israel,' she said, [8] and struck at his neck twice with all her might and cut off his head. [9] She rolled the body off the bed and removed the mosquito-net from its posts; quickly she came out and gave Holophernes' head to her maid, [10] who put it in the food-bag. Then the two of them went out together as they always did when they went to pray. They passed through the camp, and went round the valley and up the hill to Bethulia till they approached its gates.

[11] From a distance Judith called to the guards: 'Open up! Open the gate! God, our God, is with us, still showing his strength in Israel and his might against our enemies. Today he has shown it!' [12] When the townspeople heard her voice, they hurried down to the gate and summoned the elders of the town. [13] Everyone, high and low, came running, hardly able to believe that Judith had returned. They opened the gate, and welcomed in the two women. Then, kindling a fire to give light, they gathered round them. [14] Judith raised her voice: 'Praise God! O praise him!' she cried. 'Give praise to God who has not withdrawn his mercy from the house of Israel, but has crushed our enemies by my hand this very night!' [15] She took the head from the bag and showed it to them. 'Look!' she said. 'The head of Holophernes, the Assyrian commander-in-chief! And here is the net under which he lay drunk! The Lord has struck him down by a woman's hand! [16] And I swear by the Lord who has brought me safely along the way I have travelled, that, though my face lured him to his destruction, he committed no sin with me, and my honour is unblemished.'

[17] The people were all astounded at what she had done; and bowing in worship to God, they spoke with one voice: 'Praise be to you, our God, who has this day humiliated the enemies of your people!' [18] Ozias addressed Judith: 'Daughter, the blessing of God Most High rests on you more than on any other woman on earth; praise be to the Lord God who created heaven and earth; under his guidance you struck off the head of the leader of our enemies. [19] As long as men commemorate the power of God, the sure hope which inspired you will never fade from their minds. [20] May God make your deed redound to your honour for ever, and may he shower blessings on you! You risked your life for our nation when it was faced with humiliation. Boldly you went to meet the disaster that threatened us, and firmly you held to God's straight road.' All the people responded, 'Amen, Amen.'

The triumph of Israel

14 JUDITH said to them: 'Listen to me, my friends; take this head and hang it out on the battlements. [2] Then at daybreak, as soon as the sun rises, let every able-bodied man among you arm himself; march out of the town with a leader before you, as if you were going down to the plain to attack the Assyrian outpost, but do not go down. [3] The men there will pick up their weapons and make for the camp to rouse their commanders, who will rush to Holophernes' tent. When he is not to be found, panic will seize them and they will flee from you; [4] pursue them, you and all who live within Israel's borders, and cut them down in their tracks. [5] But first of all, summon Achior the Ammonite to me, so that he may see for himself and identify the man who treated Israel with contempt and sent him to us as if to his death.'

13.1–20: Judith returns to Bethulia with the head of Holophernes. 6: *His sword:* a scimitar or dagger. **9:** Judith *removed the mosquito-net* as proof that she had been with Holophernes, since the men of Bethulia could scarcely have recognized him (v. 15). **14:** *By my hand:* 8.33 n. **15:** To be *struck . . . down by a woman's hand* was the ultimate disgrace for a warrior; see Judg. 9.54. **18–20:** Judith's victory is proof that power and violence can be conquered by faith and wisdom. The weak, oppressed, and demoralized postexilic Israel needs this reminder.

14.1–15.7: Judith directs the men of Bethulia in victory. 5: There is a double purpose in calling *Achior:* to *identify* the head of Holophernes and to *see* the defeat of the *man who treated Israel with contempt,* and

6 Achior was summoned from Ozias's house. He came, and when he saw Holophernes' head held by one of the men among the assembled people, he fell down in a faint. 7 After they revived him, he threw himself at Judith's feet and did obeisance to her. 'Your praises will be sung in every home in Judah and among all nations,' he declared; 'they will tremble when they hear your name. 8 And now tell me what you have done during these days.' So while the people listened, Judith told him everything from the day she left until that very moment. 9 As she ended her story, the people raised a shout of acclamation, making the town resound with their cheers. 10 Achior, realizing all that the God of Israel had done, believed wholeheartedly in him; he was circumcised, and admitted as a member of the community of Israel, as his descendants are to this day.

11 At dawn they hung Holophernes' head on the wall; then every man took up his weapons, and they marched out in companies towards the approaches to the town. 12 The moment the Assyrians set eyes on them, they passed word to their leaders, who went to the commanders, captains, and all the other officers. 13 They presented themselves at Holophernes' tent and said to his steward: 'Wake our master! These slaves have had the audacity to come down and offer battle. They are asking to be utterly wiped out.' 14 Bagoas went in and knocked at the screen of the inner tent, supposing that Holophernes was sleeping with Judith. 15 When there was no reply, he drew aside the screen, entered the sleeping apartment, and found the dead body sprawled over a footstool, with the head gone. 16 He gave a great cry, wailing and groaning aloud, and tearing his clothes. 17 He went into the tent which Judith had occupied, and not finding her there he burst out, shouting to the troops, 18 'The slaves have fooled us. One Hebrew woman has brought shame on King Nebuchadnezzar's house. Look! Holophernes is lying on the ground, headless!' 19 At his words the officers of the Assyrian army were appalled and tore their clothes, and the camp rang with their shouting and wild cries.

15 When news of those events spread to the men in the camp, they were thrown into confusion. 2 Terrified and panic-stricken and making no attempt to keep together, they streamed out as if by a common impulse, seeking to escape by any and every path across the plain and the hill-country, 3 while those who were encamped in the hills around Bethulia also took to flight. Thereupon all the fighting men of Israel poured out in pursuit. 4 Ozias sent messengers to Bethomesthaim, Choba, and Chola, and throughout the whole territory of Israel, to report what had happened and to encourage all to attack and destroy the enemy. 5 At this every man in Israel joined in the onslaught, cutting down the fugitives the whole way to Choba. So also the men from Jerusalem and the entire hill-country rallied in support, for word had reached them of what had happened to the enemy camp. The men of Gilead and Galilee outflanked the Assyrians and inflicted heavy losses on them, pressing on beyond Damascus and its surrounding district. 6 The rest of the inhabitants of Bethulia fell on the Assyrian camp and made themselves rich with the spoils. 7 When the Israelites returned from the slaughter, they helped themselves to what remained; there was a huge quantity, and the villages and hamlets in the hill-country and in the plain secured booty in plenty.

8 Joakim the high priest and the senate of Israel came from Jerusalem to see for themselves the great things the Lord had done for his people, and to greet Judith in person. 9 When they came into her presence, they all with one accord praised her: 'You are the glory of Jerusalem, the great pride of Israel, the great boast of our people! 10 With your own hand you have done all this, bestowing these benefits on Israel, and God has shown his approval. Blessings on you from the Lord Almighty, for all time to come!' And the people responded, 'Amen.'

11 The looting of the camp went on for thirty days. Judith was given Holophernes' tent, with all his silver, and his couches, bowls, and furniture. She loaded her mule, then got her wagons ready and piled the

thereby to have his witness to the vindication of Israel's God. 10: Achior's conversion to Judaism represents a more lenient view than that in Deut. 23.3. 13: *These slaves:* this is a contemptuous reference to Israel's condition in Egypt. 15.4: *Ozias:* a variant spelling of Uzziah. See 7.23. *Bethomesthaim, Choba,* and *Chola* have not been identified. See 4.4–6.

goods on them. [12] The Israelite women all came flocking to see her; they sang her praises, and some performed a dance in her honour. She took garlanded wands and distributed them among the women who accompanied her, [13] and she and those who were with her crowned themselves with olive leaves. Then, at the head of the people, she led the women in the dance; the men of Israel, in full armour, followed, all wearing garlands on their heads and singing hymns.

16 In the presence of all Israel, Judith began this hymn of praise and thanksgiving, which was echoed by the people:

[2] 'Strike up a song to my God with
　　tambourines;
sing to the Lord with cymbals;
raise a psalm of praise to him;
honour him and invoke his name.
[3] The Lord is a God who stamps out
　　wars;
he has brought me safe from my
　　pursuers;
he has stationed his camp among his
　　people.

[4] 'The Assyrian came from the
　　mountains of the north;
his armies came in such myriads
that his troops choked the valleys,
the cavalry covered the hills.
[5] He threatened to set my whole land on
　　fire,
to put my young men to the sword
and dash my infants to the ground,
to take my children as booty, my
　　maidens as spoil.

[6] 'The Lord Almighty has thwarted them
　　by a woman's hand.
[7] It was no young man that brought their
　　champion low;
no Titan struck him down,

no tall giant set upon him;
but Judith, Merari's daughter, disarmed
　　him by her beauty.
[8] To raise up the afflicted in Israel
she laid aside her widow's dress;
she anointed her face with perfume,
bound her hair with a ribbon,
and chose a linen gown to beguile him.
[9] Her sandal entranced his eye,
her beauty took his heart captive—
and the sword cut through his neck!

[10] 'The Persians shuddered at her daring,
the Medes were daunted by her
　　boldness.
[11] Then my lowly ones shouted in
　　triumph
and the enemy were dismayed;
my weak ones shouted
and the enemy cowered in fear;
they raised their voices and the enemy
　　took to flight.
[12] The sons of maidservants ran them
　　through,
wounding them like runaway slaves;
they were destroyed by the army of my
　　Lord.

[13] 'I will sing a new hymn to my God:
O Lord, you are great and glorious,
you are marvellous in your strength,
　　invincible.
[14] Let your whole creation serve you;
for you spoke, and all things came to
　　be;
you sent out your spirit, and it gave
　　them form;
none can oppose your word.
[15] Mountains will shake to their depths
　　like water,
rocks melt like wax at your presence;
but you still show compassion
to those who fear you.
[16] All sacrifices with their fragrance are
　　but a small thing,
all the fat for whole-offerings is of no
　　significance to you;

15.8–13: The heroism of Judith is extolled. 10: *Your own hand:* see 8.33 n. **12–13:** The festive expressions described here are in keeping with Greek, not Jewish, custom. **13:** *She led the women in the dance,* much as Miriam led the dance after Israel's victory over Egypt (Exod. 15.20). Many of the features of this triumph are borrowed from Israel's prototypal Exodus victory.

16.1–17: Judith's hymn of thanksgiving. 3: *Stamps out wars:* see 9.7 n. **4:** Assyria lies mostly east of the land of Israel but the route of invasion was from the *north.* **7:** *Titan:* Greek influence. **10:** *Persians . . . Medes:* see 1.1 n. **14:** Ps. 33.6.

but he who fears the Lord is great
    always.
17 Woe to the nations which attack my
    people!
The Lord Almighty will punish them
    on the day of judgement;
he will consign their bodies to fire and
    worms;
in pain they will weep for ever.'

18 They went to worship God at Jerusalem,
and as soon as the people were purified, they
presented their whole-offerings, freewill-offerings, and gifts. 19 Judith dedicated to God
all Holophernes' possessions which the people had given to her; the net, which she herself had taken from the sleeping apartment,
she gave to God as a votive offering. 20 For
three months the people continued their celebrations before the temple at Jerusalem;
and Judith remained with them.

21 At the end of that time they all returned
to their own homes. Judith went back to Bethulia, where she lived on her estate, and
throughout her lifetime was renowned in the
whole country. 22 Though she had many suit-
ors, she remained a widow all her days after
her husband Manasses died and was gathered to his fathers. 23 Her fame continued to
increase, and she lived on in her husband's
house until she was a hundred and five years
old. She gave her maid her liberty. She died
in Bethulia and was laid in the burial cave
beside her husband Manasses, 24 and Israel
observed mourning for seven days. Before
her death she divided her property among
all those who were most closely related to her
husband, and among her own nearest relations.

25 No one dared to threaten the Israelites
again in Judith's lifetime, or indeed for a
long time after her death.

17: The entire book is devoted to the theme of the inviolability of God's *people* in a world of hostility on the part of the godless nations. See 1.1 n.

   16.18–25: After a feast in Jerusalem, Judith returns to Bethulia. 19: *All Holophernes' possessions:* an example of detachment from worldly goods, perhaps to console the poverty-stricken postexilic Jews. **23–24:** A long life, praise from one's people, and generosity toward associates are all signs of a true Israelite.

THE REST OF THE CHAPTERS
OF THE BOOK OF
Esther
WHICH ARE FOUND NEITHER IN THE HEBREW
NOR IN THE SYRIAC

To the book of Esther, as found in the Hebrew, six sections were added either by the Greek translator, or by someone else only a short time later. These additions may be dated as coming from about 114 B.C.E.

When Jerome prepared his Latin Vulgate translation of the Old Testament from the Hebrew, he also translated these Greek additions to Esther, but grouped them together at the end of the Hebrew story. In the text here (see "Note"), the whole Greek version is reconstructed, with the additions inserted into their proper place in the story. (Compare the Book of Esther in the Old Testament.) It should be noted that the chapter and verse numbers here conform to Stephen Langton's arrangement of 1214 C.E., which followed Jerome's order of the text.

The account in the Greek version is substantially identical with the Hebrew. However, the Greek additions are significant because they supply an explicit religious element strangely lacking in the original, e.g. God is never mentioned in the Hebrew. The Greek version also inserts, through Mardochaeus' dream (10.4–9), an apocalyptic and cosmic element into the story; thereby the episode of a Jewish deliverance from a Persian pogrom becomes a sign of God's dramatic eleventh-hour victory over all secular powers at the end of history. Thus, the festival of Purim, to which the story of Esther purportedly gave rise, is made an occasion for expressing the Jewish hope of eventual deliverance from historical adversities.

NOTE. *The portions of the Book of Esther commonly included in the Apocrypha are extracts from the Greek version of the book, which differs substantially from the Hebrew text (translated in* The Revised English Bible: Old Testament). *In order that they may be read in their original sequence, the whole of the Greek version is here translated, those portions which are not normally printed in the Apocrypha being enclosed in square brackets, with the chapter and verse numbers in italic figures. The order followed is that of the Greek text, but the chapter and verse numbers are made to conform to those of the Authorized Version. Proper names are given in the form in which they occur in the Greek version.*

11 ² In the second year of the reign of Artaxerxes the Great King, on the first day of the month of Nisan, Mardochaeus son of Jairus, son of Semeius, son of Kisaeus, of the tribe of Benjamin, had a dream.

³ Mardochaeus, who was in the royal service at court, was a Jew living in the city of Susa and a man of high standing; ⁴ he was one of the exiles, a descendant of those whom King Nebuchadnezzar of Babylon had carried

11.2–12: Mardochaeus' dream. 2: *Artaxerxes* (Heb. Ahasuerus) is Xerxes I (485–464 B.C.E.). The *second year* of his reign is 484 B.C.E. The *first day of the month of Nisan* is about March 15. *Mardochaeus* (Heb. Mordecai) is obviously a Jew but his name is probably Babylonian. **3:** *Susa:* a city in Mesopotamia. **4:** This away from Jerusalem with King Jechonias of Judah. This was his dream: 5first came din and tumult, peals of thunder and an earthquake, turmoil on the earth. 6Then two great dragons appeared, each poised to grapple with the other. They gave a mighty roar, 7and every nation was roused by it to prepare for war and fight against the righteous nation. 8It was a day of darkness and gloom, distress and anguish, oppression and great turmoil on the earth. 9The whole righteous nation, dreading the evils in store, was troubled and prepared for death. 10They cried aloud to God, and in answer there came as though from a little spring a great river brimming with water. 11As the sun rose it grew light; the humble were exalted and they devoured those of high degree. 12After this dream, in which he saw what God had resolved to do, Mardochaeus woke; he pondered over the dream until nightfall, trying in every way to understand it.

12 Once, while Mardochaeus was taking his rest in the royal courtyard with Gabatha and Tharra, the two eunuchs in the king's service who were on guard in the courtyard, 2he overheard them deep in discussion. He listened carefully to discover what was on their minds, and found they were plotting violence against King Artaxerxes. He denounced them to the king, 3who had the two eunuchs interrogated; on their confessing, they were led away to execution. 4The king wrote an account of this affair to have it on record; Mardochaeus also wrote an account of it. 5The king gave him an appointment at court, and rewarded him for his services. 6But Haman son of Hamadathus, a Bugaean, who enjoyed the royal favour, looked for a chance to harm Mardochaeus and his people because of the king's two eunuchs.

A Jewess becomes queen in Persia

1 [THOSE events happened in the days of Artaxerxes, that Artaxerxes who ruled from India to Ethiopia, a hundred and twenty-seven provinces, 2at the time when he had taken his seat on the royal throne in the city of Susa. 3In the third year of his reign he gave a reception for the king's Friends and for others of various races, the Persian and Median nobles, and the leading provincial governors. 4Afterwards he put on display to them the wealth of his kingdom and the dazzling splendour of his riches for a hundred and eighty days. 5When these days of feasting were over, the king held a banquet for all the people of various races present in the city of Susa; it lasted six days and took place in the palace court, 6which was decorated with white curtains of linen and cotton stretched on cords of purple, and these were attached to blocks of gold and silver resting on stone and marble columns. There were gold and silver couches placed on a pavement of malachite, marble, and mother-of-pearl, and there were coverings of transparent weave elaborately embroidered with roses arranged in a circle. 7The cups were of gold and silver, and on display was a miniature cup made from a ruby worth thirty thousand talents. The wine, which was from the king's own cellar, was abundant and sweet. 8The drinking was according to no fixed rule, for the king had laid down that all the palace stewards should respect his wishes and those of the guests. 9Queen Astin gave a banquet for the women inside King Artaxerxes' palace.

deportation took place about 597 B.C.E., which would make Mardochaeus at least 113 years old at the time of his dream (v. 2)! Jechonias is Jehoiachin (2 Kgs. 24.12–13). **5–11:** The imagery of the dream is apocalyptic; the dragons (antagonists) are Mardochaeus and Haman, while the divinely decreed victory is effected through Esther (the little spring). See 10.6–9. **7:** Righteous nation: the Jews.

12.1–6: Mardochaeus discovers a plot against the king and is rewarded. 5: The Hebrew story (6.3) knows nothing of this reward. **6:** Haman has the villain's role. He is here identified as a Bugaean but in Esther 3.1 he is an Agagite. In 16.10 he is identified as a Macedonian although his father's name is Persian. It may be significant that Mardochaeus, like Saul, was a Benjaminite (11.2) while Haman was apparently an Amalekite (1 Sam. 15.8). Thus, there was a long previous historical basis for a blood feud between them.

1.1–9: Artaxerxes gives a lavish feast. 2: Susa was the winter residence of Persian kings; the official capital was Persepolis. **3:** King's Friends: see 1 Macc. 2.18 n. **7:** Thirty thousand talents: the sum is astronomical. The entire description seems to be greatly exaggerated. **9:** Queen Astin in the Hebrew account is called Vashti. She must have been a current favorite since Xerxes' official wife was Amestris.

[10]On the seventh day, when he was feeling merry, the king ordered Haman, Mazan, Tharra, Borazes, Zatholtha, Abataza, and Tharaba, the seven eunuchs who were in attendance on the king's person, [11]to bring the queen into his presence, so that he might place the royal diadem on her head and display her beauty to the officers and people of various races; for she was indeed a beautiful woman. [12]But Queen Astin refused to obey and accompany the eunuchs. This incensed the king and his anger flared up. [13]He said to his courtiers, 'You hear how Astin spoke. Give your ruling and judgement in the matter.' [14]Harkesaeus, Sarathaeus, and Malesear, the nobles of Persia and Media who were closest to the king and occupied the seats of honour by him, approached [15]and made known to him what, according to the law, should be done to Queen Astin for disobeying the royal command conveyed to her by the eunuchs.

[16]Muchaeus made this reply to the king and the nobles: 'Queen Astin has done wrong, not to the king alone, but also to all the nobles and officers of the king.' [17](For he had repeated to them what the queen had said and how she had defied the king.) [18]'Just as she defied King Artaxerxes, so now the nobles of Persia and Media will find that all the great ladies are emboldened to treat their husbands with disrespect, when they hear what she said to the king. [19]If it please your majesty, let a royal decree be issued once and for all, and let it be inscribed among the laws of the Medes and Persians, that Astin shall not come in again to the king; and let your majesty give her place as queen to another who is more worthy of it than she. [20]Let whatever law the king makes be proclaimed throughout the kingdom, and so all women, rich and poor alike, will give honour to their husbands.' [21]The advice pleased the king and the princes, and the king did as Muchaeus had proposed. [22]Dispatches were sent to all the provinces of the kingdom, to every province in its own language, in order that each man should be treated with deference in his own house.

2 Some time later, when the anger of King Artaxerxes had died down, he called Astin to mind, remembering what she had done and how he had given judgement against her. [2]So the king's attendants said: 'Let there be sought out for your majesty beautiful young virgins; [3]let your majesty appoint commissioners in every province of your kingdom to select these beautiful virgins and bring them to the women's quarters in the city of Susa. Have them placed under the care of the king's eunuch who has charge of the women, and let them be provided with cosmetics and everything else they need. [4]The girl who is most acceptable to the king shall become queen in place of Astin.' The advice pleased the king, and he acted on it.

[5]In the city of Susa there lived a Jew named Mardochaeus son of Jairus, son of Semeius, son of Kisaeus, of the tribe of Benjamin; [6]he had been taken into exile from Jerusalem when it was captured by King Nebuchadnezzar of Babylon. [7]He had a foster-child named Esther, the daughter of his father's brother Aminadab; and after the death of her parents he had brought her up, intending to make her his wife. She was a beautiful girl. [8]When the king's edict was proclaimed and many girls were brought to Susa to be committed to the care of Gai, who had charge of the women, Esther too was entrusted to him. [9]He found her pleasing and she received his special favour: he promptly supplied her with cosmetics and with her allowance of food, and also with seven maids assigned to her from the king's palace. She and her maids were accorded favourable treatment in the women's quarters.

[10]Esther had not disclosed her race or

1.10–22: Queen Astin disobeys Artaxerxes and is dethroned. 10: The Hebrew version attributes the king's *feeling merry* to drinking. *Eunuchs* were originally in charge of the king's harem but later they acquired positions of great influence (Jdt. 12.11 n.; Gen. 37.36; Dan. 1.3). **12:** Perhaps *Queen Astin refused* because the circumstances would have made her appearance degrading. **20:** Such naïvete may be due to the heavy drinking of these counselors!

2.1–14: Esther enters the competition to replace Queen Astin. 1–4: The scope of this contest serves to highlight the exceptional beauty of Esther. **3:** *Women's quarters:* the harem. **5:** Following the Hebrew version, the Greek text introduces *Mardochaeus* a second time; see 11.2–3. **7:** *Esther* is derived from the Babylonian goddess Ishtar, who was related to the god Marduk, from whom Mardochaeus' name was derived. **10:** Concealment of Esther's background is important for the development of the story line; see 7.4.

country, because Mardochaeus had forbidden her to do so. [11]Every day Mardochaeus would walk past the forecourt of the women's quarters to keep an eye on what was happening to Esther.

[12]The full period of preparation before a girl went to the king was twelve months: six months' treatment with oil of myrrh, and six months' with perfumes and cosmetics. At the end of this the girl went to the king. [13]She was handed to the person appointed and accompanied him from the women's quarters to the king's palace. [14]She entered the palace in the evening and returned in the morning to another part of the women's quarters, to be under the care of Gai, the king's eunuch in charge of the women. She did not go again to the king unless summoned by name.

[15]When the time came for Esther, the daughter of Aminadab, uncle of Mardochaeus, to go to the king, she neglected none of the instructions given her by the king's eunuch in charge of the women. Esther charmed all who saw her, [16]and when she went to King Artaxerxes in the twelfth month, that is, the month of Adar, in the seventh year of his reign, [17]the king fell in love with her. He treated her with greater favour than all the rest of the virgins, and put the queen's diadem on her head. [18] Then, to celebrate his marriage with Esther, the king gave a banquet lasting seven days for all the king's Friends and the officers. He also granted a remission of taxation to all the subjects of his kingdom.

Mardochaeus and Haman

[19]MARDOCHAEUS was in attendance in the court. [20]On his instructions Esther had not

disclosed her country; she was to fear God and keep the commandments, as she used to do when she was with him. So Esther made no change in her rule of life.

[21]Two of the king's eunuchs, officers of the bodyguard, were offended at the advancement of Mardochaeus and plotted to murder King Artaxerxes. [22]This became known to Mardochaeus, who told Esther, and she revealed the plot to the king. [23]The king interrogated the two eunuchs and had them hanged, and he ordered that the service Mardochaeus had rendered should be recorded to his honour in the royal archives.

3 It was after those events that King Artaxerxes promoted Haman, son of Hamadathus, a Bugaean, advancing him and giving him precedence above all the king's Friends. [2]Everyone at court did obeisance to Haman, for so the king had commanded it should be done; but Mardochaeus did not do obeisance. [3]The courtiers said, 'Mardochaeus, why do you flout his majesty's command?' [4]They challenged him day after day, and when he refused to listen they informed Haman that Mardochaeus was defying the king's order. Mardochaeus had told them he was a Jew. [5]Haman was furious when he learnt that Mardochaeus was not doing obeisance to him, and [6]he plotted to exterminate all the Jews throughout the kingdom.

[7]In the twelfth year of Artaxerxes' reign Haman made an order for lots to be cast, taking the days and months one by one, to decide on a day for the destruction of Mardochaeus's whole race. The lot fell on the thirteenth day of the month of Adar.

[3:7] **thirteenth:** *so some witnesses (cp.* [8:12]); *other witnesses read* fourteenth.

2.15–20: Esther wins the king's favor and is made queen. 16: *Adar:* February–March. *The seventh year:* four years after Queen Astin's dismissal; see 1.3. **18:** *King's Friends:* see 1 Macc. 2.18 n. **20:** *Esther made no change in her rule of life:* she maintained dietary laws and other such Jewish observances.

2.21–23: Mardochaeus saves the king's life. According to the Greek version (12.1–5), Mardochaeus was advanced only after he revealed the plot. The Heb. version (Esther 6.2–3), which is itself uncertain, makes a point of the fact that Mardochaeus was not rewarded for this service.

3.1–5.14: A plot against the Jews. Esther and Haman are pitted against each other as forces of good and evil.

3.1–6: Mardochaeus refuses homage to Haman. 2: The *obeisance* prescribed was certainly the normal deference required for the office of grand vizier or prime minister. But Mardochaeus, a Benjaminite, considers it irreligious to bow before an Agagite (see 12.6 n. above). Such defiance is presented as an ideal of Jewish attitudes toward Gentiles.

[8]Then Haman said to King Artaxerxes: 'Dispersed among the nations throughout your whole kingdom, there is one whose laws are different from those of every other nation. They flout your majesty's laws, and it is not in your majesty's interest to tolerate them. [9]If it please you, sire, let an order be issued for their destruction; and I shall make over to the royal treasury the sum of ten thousand talents of silver.' [10]The king drew off his signet ring and, handing it to Haman to seal the decree against the Jews, [11]he said, 'Keep the money, and deal with the people as you think fit.'

[12]On the thirteenth day of the first month the king's secretaries were summoned, and in accordance with Haman's instructions they wrote in the name of King Artaxerxes to his army commanders and governors of every province from India to Ethiopia; there were a hundred and twenty-seven provinces in all, and each was addressed in its own language. [13]Dispatches were sent by courier throughout the kingdom of Artaxerxes ordering the extermination of the Jewish race, on a given day of the twelfth month, Adar; and their goods were to be treated as spoil.]

13 THIS is a copy of the letter:

Artaxerxes the Great King to the Governors of the one hundred and twenty-seven provinces from India to Ethiopia and to their regional officials. [2]As ruler over many nations and master of the whole world, it is my will — not in the arrogance of power, but because my rule is equitable and mild — to ensure for my subjects a life permanently free from disturbance, to make my kingdom quiet and safe for travel to its farthest limits, and to re-

store the peace that all men desire. [3]I have enquired of my counsellors how this object might be achieved. Among us Haman is eminent for sound judgement, one whose worth is proved by his constant goodwill and steadfast loyalty, and who has gained the honour of the second place at our court. [4]He has represented to us that dispersed among all the races of the world is a disaffected people, opposed in its laws to every nation, and continually ignoring the royal ordinances, so that our perfected plans for the unified administration of the empire cannot be accomplished. [5]We understand that this nation stands quite alone in its continual hostility to the human race, that it evades the laws by its strange manner of life, and in disloyalty to our government commits the most grave offences, thus undermining the stability of our kingdom. [6]Accordingly we have given orders that all those who are designated to you in the indictments drawn up by Haman our vicegerent and second father shall, with their wives and children, be utterly destroyed by their enemies' swords without mercy or pity, on the thirteenth day of Adar, the twelfth month of the present year. [7]Therefore these persons, who have long been disaffected, shall in a single day meet a violent end, so that our government may henceforth be stable and untroubled.

3 [14][Copies of the dispatch were posted up in every province, and all the peoples were ordered to be ready for that day. [15]The matter was expedited also in Susa. The king and Haman caroused together, but in the city of Susa confusion reigned.

13:6 **thirteenth:** *prob. rdg; Gk* fourteenth; *see note on* [3:7].

3.7–13: Haman secures a royal edict to exterminate the Jews. 7: *Twelfth year:* about 474 B.C.E. In common practice important decisions were made by the impartial method of casting lots. The Babylonian word for "lot" is *pur* and this provides the name for the festival of Purim to which this story was later attached; see 9.25–26. *Thirteenth day:* about March 1; see 2.16 n. **8:** The standard complaint against the pious Jews was that they were *different;* see Wisd. 2.15; 1 Macc. ch. 2. **9:** *Ten thousand talents:* an astronomical sum; see 1.7 n. **12:** *First month:* Nisan (March–April). These *provinces* may have been subdivisions of the thirteen satrapies, or administrative districts, into which the Persian Empire was divided. **13:** *Adar:* see 2.16 n.

13.1–7; 3.14–15: Artaxerxes' edict to destroy the Jews. 4: *Disaffected people:* there is little doubt that the Jews, because of their adherence to distinctive customs ("strange manner of life"; v. 5), were viewed with a suspicion which lent credence to exaggerated and sometimes fantastic accusations. **6:** *Vicegerent:* an administrator in charge of royal affairs. *Adar:* see 2.16 n. **3.15:** *The king and Haman caroused together.* This was surely the height of Haman's triumph.

4 WHEN Mardochaeus learnt of all that had been done, he tore his clothes, put on sackcloth, and sprinkled himself with ashes. He rushed out through the city square, crying loudly: 'A nation that has committed no crime is being destroyed.' *2*He went right up to the palace gate, and there he halted, because no one wearing sackcloth and ashes was allowed to enter the courtyard. *3*In every province where the king's decree was posted up, there was a great cry of mourning and lamentation among the Jews, and they put on sackcloth and ashes. *4*When the queen's maids and eunuchs came in and told her, she was distraught at what she heard. She sent clothes for Mardochaeus and urged him to put off his sackcloth, but he refused. *5*Esther then summoned Hachrathaeus, the eunuch who waited upon her, and sent him to Mardochaeus to obtain accurate information for her. *7*Mardochaeus told him all that had happened, and how Haman had promised the king to pay ten thousand talents into the treasury to bring about the destruction of the Jews. *8*He also gave him a copy of the written decree for their destruction which had been posted up in Susa, that he might show it to Esther; and he told him to bid her go to the king to implore his favour and intercede for her people. 'Say to her,' he added, ' "Do not forget your humble origins and your upbringing in my house. Because Haman, who stands next to the king, has spoken against us and demanded our death, call on the Lord, and then speak to the king on our behalf and save our lives." ' *9*When Hachrathaeus came in and told Esther all Mardochaeus had said, *10*she bade him take back this message: *11*'Every nation in the kingdom knows that there is no hope for any person, man or woman, who enters the king's presence in the inner court without being summoned; only one to whom the king holds out the gold sceptre is spared. Further, I have not been summoned to go to the king these thirty days.'

*12*When Hachrathaeus delivered Esther's message, *13*Mardochaeus sent this reply: 'Do not imagine, Esther, that of all the Jews in the kingdom you alone will be safe. *14*If you remain silent at such a time as this, relief and deliverance for the Jews will come from another quarter, but you and your father's family will perish. And who knows whether it is not for a time like this that you have become queen?' *15*Esther gave the messenger this answer to take back to Mardochaeus: *16*'Go and assemble the Jews that are in Susa and hold a fast for me; for three days, night and day, take neither food nor drink, and I and my maids shall also fast. After that, in defiance of the law, I shall go to the king, even if it costs me my life.' *17*Mardochaeus then went away and did everything Esther had bidden him.]

13 *8*CALLING to mind all that the Lord had done, Mardochaeus uttered this prayer. *9*'O Lord, Lord and King, Ruler over all, for the whole creation is under your authority, and when it is your will to save Israel there is none who can oppose you: *10*you made heaven and earth and every wonderful thing under heaven; *11*you are Lord of all, and there is none who can resist you, the Lord. *12*You know all things; you know, Lord, that it was not from insolence or arrogance or vainglory that I refused to bow before this proud Haman, *13*for to save Israel I would gladly have kissed the soles of his feet! *14*But I acted in this way so as not to hold a man in greater honour than God; I shall not bow before any but you, my Lord, and it is not from arrogance that I refuse this homage. *15*Now, O Lord, God and King, God of Abraham, spare your people, for our enemies are bent on bringing us to ruin, and they have set their hearts upon the destruction of your chosen people, yours from the begin-

[4:5] **information for her:** *some witnesses add* *6*So he went out to Mardochaeus in the square opposite the city gate.

4.1–17: Esther is asked to plead for her kinsfolk. 1: *Tore his clothes:* sign of consternation; see 2 Kgs. 5.7; Matt. 26.65. *Sackcloth and . . . ashes:* sign of grief. **4:** Not knowing the reason for his grief, Esther *sent clothes for Mardochaeus.* **11:** Entrance without being summoned was considered a hostile action; also compare 2.14. **14:** The author is certain that Esther's good fortune is for providential reasons. Mardochaeus' exhortation is directed to all the more fortunate Jews in exile who might forget their responsibility for less fortunate compatriots.

13.8–18: Mardochaeus' prayer. The Hebrew account never mentions the name of God. The Greek additions furnish a religious dimension. **9:** The universal *authority* of God was a primary tenet of Israelite faith in the

ning. 16 Do not disregard your own possession which you ransomed and brought out of
Egypt for yourself. 17 Hear my prayer, and
have mercy on your heritage; turn our
mourning into feasting, that we may live to
sing of your name, O Lord. Do not put to
silence the lips that give you praise.' 18 The
Israelites cried aloud with all their might, for
death stared them in the face.

The triumph of the Jews

14 QUEEN Esther, in the grip of mortal
anxiety, sought refuge in the Lord.
2 She took off her royal robes and put on the
garb of distress and mourning. Instead of
rich perfumes she strewed ashes and dirt
over her head; she abased her body, and every part that she had delighted to adorn she
covered with her dishevelled hair. 3 Then she
prayed to the Lord God of Israel.

'O my Lord, you alone are our King; come
to my help who am alone and have no other
helper but you, 4 for I am taking my life in my
hands. 5 From my earliest days I have been
taught by my father's family and tribe that
you, Lord, chose Israel out of all the nations,
and from all who went before them you
chose our fathers as an everlasting possession, and you have performed for them
whatever you promised. 6 But now we have
sinned against you, and you have handed us
over to our enemies 7 because we paid honour to their gods. O Lord, you are just. 8 Yet
even now our enemies are not content that
we are in bitter servitude; they have taken a
vow 9 to annul the decree you have proclaimed and to destroy Israel, your possession, silencing those who praise you,
extinguishing the glory of your house and
the flame on your altar. 10 They would give
the heathen cause to sing the praises of their
worthless gods, and would have a mortal
king held in everlasting honour.

11 'Do not yield your sceptre, Lord, to gods
that have no real existence; let not our ene-

mies mock at our ruin, but turn their plot
against them, and make an example of the
man who planned it. 12 Be mindful of us,
Lord; reveal yourself in the time of our distress, and give me courage, O King of gods,
Sovereign over every power. 13 Put the right
words into my mouth when I enter this lion's
den, and divert his hatred to him who is our
enemy, so that there may be an end of him
and his associates.

14 'By your power save us, and help me who
am alone and have no one but you, Lord.
15 You know all things; you know that I hate
the splendour of the heathen; I abhor the
bed of the uncircumcised or of any Gentile.
16 You know in what straits I am: I loathe that
symbol of pride, the headdress that I wear
when I show myself in public, I loathe it as
one loathes a filthy rag and in private never
wear it. 17 I, your servant, have not eaten at
Haman's table, nor have I graced a banquet
of the king nor touched the wine of his drink-
offerings. 18 From the day of my preferment
until now I have known no joy except in you,
Lord God of Abraham. 19 O God, the all-
prevailing, give heed to the cry of those
driven to despair: deliver us from the power
of the wicked, and rescue me from what I
dread.'

15 ON the third day, after ending her
prayers, Esther put off the clothes
she had worn while she worshipped, and arrayed herself in her robes of state. 2 When
she was attired in all her splendour and had
invoked the all-seeing God, her preserver,
she took her two maids with her; 3 on one she
leaned for support, as befitted a fine lady,
4 while the other followed, bearing her train.
5 She was radiant and in the height of her
beauty; her face was as cheerful as it was
lovely, but her heart was constricted with
fear. 6 She passed through all the doors until
she stood in the royal presence. The king was

14:1 **in . . . anxiety:** or caught up in this deadly
struggle.

postexilic period when history seemed beyond divine plan and control. **12–14:** The story does not support
such pure motivation on the part of Mardochaeus (see 3.2 n.). **16:** The ultimate basis for Israel's confidence
is God's free choice of the nation, as expressed in the liberation from Egyptian bondage.

14.1–19: Esther's prayer. 5: Our fathers: the sons of Jacob who established the twelve tribes of Israel. **6–11:**
Even if Israel deserves to be punished (v. 6), God cannot permit the idolatrous enemies to claim victory (see
v. 11). **13:** Lion's den: the king's presence. **15–18:** Hate the splendour: an exaggeration to underline her
identification with the plight of Israel.

15.1–7: Esther dares to go to the king without being summoned. 3: Esther, knowing that her only chance seated on his throne in the full array of his majesty, all gold and precious stones, an awe-inspiring figure. [7]He looked up, his face aglow with regal dignity, and regarded her with towering anger. The queen sank down, changing colour and fainting, and she swooned on the shoulder of the maid who went before her.

[8]But the king's mood was changed by God to one of gentleness. In deep concern he started up from his throne and held her in his arms until she came to herself. He soothed her with reassuring words: [9]'Esther, what is it? Have no fear of me, your loving husband; [10]you shall not die, for our order is only for our subjects. You may approach.' [11]The king raised his gold sceptre and touched her neck; [12]then he kissed her and said, 'You may speak to me.' [13]She answered, 'My lord, I saw you like an angel of God; I was awestruck at your glorious appearance. [14]Your countenance is so full of grace, my lord, that I look in wonder.' [15]But while she was speaking she sank down fainting; [16]the king was distressed, and his attendants all tried to reassure her.

5 [3][THE king said, 'What is your wish, Esther? Whatever you request, up to half my kingdom, shall be given you.' [4]'This is a festive day for me,' she answered; 'if it please your majesty, will you come, and Haman with you, to a banquet I am preparing today?' [5]The king gave orders for Haman to be brought with all speed to meet Esther's wishes; and they both went to the banquet to which she had invited them. [6]Over the wine the king said to her, 'What is it, Queen Esther? Whatever you request shall be yours.' [7]She said, 'This is my petition and request: [8]if

I have found favour with your majesty, will your majesty and Haman come again tomorrow to the banquet that I shall prepare for you both? Tomorrow I shall do as I have done today.'

[9]Although Haman left the royal presence overjoyed and in the best of spirits, as soon as he saw Mardochaeus the Jew in the king's court he was furious. [10]When he arrived home, he sent for his friends and for Zosara, his wife, [11]and held forth to them about his wealth and the honours with which the king had invested him, and how he had advanced him to the chief position in the kingdom. [12]'The queen', Haman went on, 'had no one but myself come with the king to her banquet; and I am invited tomorrow. [13]Yet all this gives me no satisfaction so long as I see that Jew Mardochaeus at court.' [14]His wife Zosara and his friends said to him: 'Have a gallows set up, seventy-five feet high, and in the morning propose to the king that Mardochaeus be hanged on it. Then you can go with the king to the banquet and enjoy yourself.' This advice seemed good to Haman, and the gallows was made ready.

6 THAT night the Lord prevented the king from sleeping, so he ordered his secretary to bring the court chronicle and read it to him. [2]In it he found recorded an entry concerning Mardochaeus, how he had furnished information for the king about the two royal eunuchs on guard who had plotted to assassinate Artaxerxes. [3]When the king asked, 'What honour or favour did we confer on Mardochaeus?' his attendants said, 'You have not done anything for him.' [4]While the king was enquiring about Mardochaeus's ser-

[5:14] **seventy-five feet:** *lit.* fifty cubits.

before the powerful king was in a display of fear and weakness, *leaned for support.* **7:** *Towering anger:* this is explained in 4.11; it serves to heighten Esther's noble but risky intervention.

15.8–16: The king receives Esther graciously. 11: The *king* touching *her neck* with his *sceptre* was a sign of royal protection or forgiveness.

5.3–8: Esther's first banquet for the king and Haman. 4: A *banquet* is the special staging for Esther's request, serving the literary purpose of suspense. See v. 8.

5.9–14: Haman prepares a gallows for Mardochaeus. 9: *Haman* (like the Gentiles generally) was disturbed when he *saw* the "otherness" of *Mardochaeus* (the Jews). **14:** The completely unnecessary height of the *gallows* (*seventy-five feet*) is for literary effect and not meant to be taken literally.

6.1–11.1: The intended fate of the Jews falls on their persecutors.

6.1–14: Mardochaeus is exalted and Haman is humiliated. 3: *Not done anything for him:* but see 12.5. **4:** *Haman had just then entered:* a coincidence dear to folklore. **13:** *God . . . on his side:* recognition by Haman's friends that Providence has taken over.

vice to him, Haman appeared in the court-yard. 'Who is in the court?' said the king. As Haman had just then entered to propose to the king that Mardochaeus should be hanged on the gallows he had prepared, *5*the king's servants replied, 'Haman is standing there in the court.' 'Let him enter!' commanded the king. *6*Then he asked him, 'What shall I do for the man I wish to honour?' Haman thought, 'Whom other than myself would the king wish to honour?' *7*So he answered, 'For the man whom the king wishes to honour? *8*Let the king's attendants bring a robe of fine linen which the king himself has worn, and a horse on which the king rides. *9*Let both be handed over to one of the king's most noble Friends, and let him invest the man whom the king loves and mount him on the horse, and let him proclaim through the city square: "This shall be done for any man whom the king honours."' *10*The king said to Haman, 'Well spoken! Do this for Mardochaeus the Jew who serves in the courtyard. Let nothing be omitted of what you have proposed.' *11*Haman took the robe and the horse; he in-vested Mardochaeus, mounted him on horseback, and went through the city square proclaiming: 'See what is done for any man whom the king wishes to honour.'

*12*Mardochaeus then returned to the courtyard, while Haman hurried off home in grief with his head veiled. *13*When he told his wife Zosara and his friends what had hap-pened to him, the response he got was: 'If you have begun to be humiliated before Mar-dochaeus, and he is a Jew, your downfall is certain; you cannot get the better of him, because the living God is on his side.'

*14*While they were still talking, the eunuchs arrived and Haman was hurried off to the banquet Esther had prepared.

7 So the king and Haman went to the queen's banquet, *2*and on that sec-ond day, over the wine, the king said, 'What is it, Queen Esther? What is your petition? What is your request? You shall have it, up to half my kingdom.' *3*She answered: 'If I have found favour with your majesty, my petition and request is that my own life and the lives of my people be spared. *4*For we have been sold, I and my people, to be destroyed, plun-dered, and enslaved, we and our children, male and female—or so I have heard. Our adversary brings discredit on the king's court.' *5*The king demanded, 'Who is he that has dared to do such a thing?' *6*She answered, 'An enemy, this wicked Haman!' Haman stood dumbfounded before the king and queen. *7*The king rose from the banquet and went into the garden, while Haman began to plead with the queen, for he saw that things looked very black for him. *8*When the king returned from the garden, Haman in his en-treaties had flung himself across the queen's couch. The king exclaimed, 'What! You even assault the queen in my own palace?' At those words Haman turned away in despair. *9*Bugathan, one of the eunuchs, said to the king, 'There is actually a gallows seventy-five feet high, standing in Haman's grounds; he prepared it for Mardochaeus, the man who reported the plot against your majesty.' 'Let Haman be hanged on it!' said the king. *10*Ha-man was hanged on the gallows that had been prepared for Mardochaeus, and the king's anger subsided.

8 The same day King Artaxerxes gave Esther all that had belonged to Ha-man, the adversary of the Jews, and Mardo-chaeus was summoned to the king's presence, for Esther had revealed his rela-tionship to her. *2*The king took off his signet ring, which he had taken back from Haman, and gave it to Mardochaeus. Esther put Mar-dochaeus in charge of all Haman's property.

*3*Once again Esther addressed the king, falling at his feet and imploring him to thwart the wickedness of Haman and all he had devised against the Jews. *4*The king ex-tended his gold sceptre to her, and she rose and stood before the king. *5*'If it pleases you,' she said, 'and if I have found favour, let a writ be issued to recall the dispatches sent by Haman in pursuance of his plan to destroy the Jews in your kingdom. *6*For how can I bear to witness the ill-treatment of my peo-ple? How can I bear to survive the destruc-tion of my kindred?' *7*The king replied: 'What more do you want? To please you I have given you the whole of Haman's prop-

7.1–10: The second banquet results in Haman's death. 6: Haman is *dumbfounded,* not knowing that Esther is a Jewess.

8.1–12: Esther persuades the king to nullify his edict against the Jews. 2: With the *signet ring* Mardochaeus receives the office of prime minister vacated by Haman's death.

erty, and hanged him on the gallows because he threatened the lives of the Jews. *8* Now you may issue a writ in my name, in whatever terms you think fit, and seal it with my signet; no order written at the king's direction and sealed with his signet can be gainsaid.'

9 On the twenty-third day of the first month, Nisan, in the same year, the secretaries were summoned; and the Jews were informed in writing of the instructions given to the administrators and chief governors in the hundred and twenty-seven provinces from India to Ethiopia, to each province in its own language. *10* The writ was drawn up in the king's name and sealed with his signet, and dispatches were sent by courier. *11* By these dispatches permission was granted to the Jews in every city to observe their own laws and to defend themselves, and to deal as they wished with their opponents and enemies, *12* throughout the kingdom of Artaxerxes, in one day, the thirteenth of Adar, the twelfth month.]

16

The following is a copy of the letter:

From Artaxerxes the Great King to the Governors of the one hundred and twenty-seven provinces from India to Ethiopia, and to our loyal subjects.

Greeting.

2 Many who have been repeatedly honoured by the bountiful goodness of their benefactors have grown arrogant, *3* and not only attempt to injure our subjects but, unable to keep their insolence within bounds, even plot mischief against those same benefactors. *4* Not content with destroying gratitude among men, they are so carried away by the presumption of those who are strangers to good breeding that they even suppose they will escape the avenging justice of the all-seeing God. *5* Often, when the king's business has been entrusted to those he counts his friends, they have, by their plausibility, made those in supreme authority partners in the shedding of innocent blood and involved them in irreparable misfortunes, *6* for their malevolence with its misleading sophistries

has imposed upon the sincere goodwill of their rulers. *7* The evil brought about by those who wield power unworthily you can observe, not only in the accounts handed down to us from the past, but also in your familiar experience, *8* and the lesson can be applied to the future. Thus we shall ensure the peace and stability of the realm for the benefit of all; *9* we shall make no changes but shall always decide such matters as come to our notice with firmness and equity.

10 Now Haman son of Hamadathus, a Macedonian, an alien in fact with no Persian blood and not a trace of our kindly nature, was accepted by us *11* and enjoyed so fully the benevolence which we extend to every nation that he was given the title of Father and used to receive obeisance from everyone as second only to our royal throne. *12* But this man in his unbridled arrogance schemed to deprive us of our kingdom and our life; *13* by deceitfulness and tortuous cunning he sought to bring about the destruction of Mardochaeus, our constant benefactor who had saved our life, and of Esther, our blameless consort, together with their whole nation. *14* He thought, by these means, to catch us without support and transfer to the Macedonians the sovereignty now held by the Persians.

15 We find, however, that the Jews whom this double-dyed villain had consigned to extinction are no evildoers; on the contrary, they order their lives by the most just of laws *16* and are children of the living God, the Most High and Most Mighty, who for us as for our ancestors has maintained the kingdom in excellent order. *17* You will, therefore, disregard the letters sent by Haman son of Hamadathus, *18* because he, the contriver of all this, has been hanged at the gate of Susa, he and his whole household, for God who controls all things brought on him speedily the punishment he deserved.

19 Copies of this letter are to be posted up in all public places. The Jews are to live under their own laws, *20* and be given every assistance so that on the very same day, the

8.12: *The thirteenth of . . . Adar:* the date when the extermination of the Jews was to have taken place (3.7, 13).

16.1–24; 8.13–17: The king's letter brings joy to the Jews. 5–6: The king attributes his mistake to *misleading* advice from *friends.* **10:** *Macedonian:* see 12.6 n. Haman is called a Macedonian, a word synonymous with thirteenth day of Adar, the twelfth month, they may avenge themselves on their assailants in the time of oppression. ²¹God, who has all things in his power, has made that a day of joy, not of ruin, for his chosen people.

²²Therefore you also must keep it with all good cheer, as a notable day among your feasts of commemoration, ²³so that henceforth it may be a standing symbol of deliverance to us and our loyal Persians, but a reminder of destruction to those who plot against us. ²⁴Any city or country whatsoever which does not act upon these orders will incur our wrath and be destroyed with fire and sword. Not only will no man set foot in it, but it will also be shunned by beast and bird for all time.

8 ¹³[Let copies be posted up prominently throughout the kingdom, so that all the Jews may be prepared for that day, to fight against their enemies.

¹⁴MOUNTED couriers set out post-haste to do what the king commanded; and the decree was published also in Susa.

¹⁵When Mardochaeus went out in a royal robe, wearing a gold crown and a turban of fine linen dyed purple, the people in Susa rejoiced to see him. ¹⁶For the Jews all was light and gladness ¹⁷in every city and province, wherever the decree was posted up; there was joy and gladness for them, feasting and merrymaking. And many of the Gentiles were circumcised and professed Judaism, because of fear of the Jews.

9 ON the thirteenth day of Adar, the twelfth month, the decree drawn up by the king arrived. That same day the enemies of the Jews perished, ²for in their fear none offered resistance. ³The leading provincial governors, the princes, and the royal secretaries paid honour to the Jews out of fear of Mardochaeus, ⁴for they had received the king's decree that his name should be honoured throughout the kingdom. ⁶In the capital itself the Jews slaughtered five hundred men, ⁷including Pharsanestan, Del-

phon, Phasga, ⁸Pharadatha, Barsa, Sarbach, ⁹Marmasima, Ruphaeus, Arsaeus, and Zabuthaeus, ¹⁰the ten sons of Haman son of Hamadathus, the Bugaean and enemy of the Jews; and they took plunder.

¹¹When the number of those killed in Susa was reported to the king that day, ¹²he said to Esther, 'In the city of Susa the Jews have killed five hundred men; what do you suppose they have done in the surrounding country? Whatever further request you have, it shall be granted.' ¹³Esther replied, 'Let the Jews be permitted to do the same tomorrow, and hang up the bodies of Haman's ten sons.' ¹⁴He allowed this to be done, and he handed over the bodies of Haman's ten sons to the Jews of the city to be hung up. ¹⁵The Jews in Susa assembled on the fourteenth day of Adar also, and killed three hundred men, but they took no plunder.

¹⁶The rest of the Jews throughout the kingdom rallied in self-defence, and so had respite from their enemies, for they slaughtered fifteen thousand on the thirteenth of Adar, but they took no plunder. ¹⁷On the fourteenth of the month they rested, and made it a day of rest, with rejoicing and merrymaking. ¹⁸The Jews in the city of Susa had assembled also on the fourteenth day; they did not rest on that day, but they kept the fifteenth with rejoicing and merrymaking. ¹⁹That is why Jews who are dispersed over the remoter parts observe the fourteenth of Adar as a holiday with merrymaking, sending presents of food to one another; but those who live in the principal cities keep the fifteenth of Adar as a holiday, for merrymaking and sending presents of food to one another.

The festival of Purim founded

²⁰MARDOCHAEUS put these things on record in a book and sent it to the Jews in Artaxerxes' kingdom, both near and far, ²¹requiring them to establish these holidays, and to

[9:4] **the kingdom:** *some witnesses add from the Heb.* ⁵The Jews put their enemies to the sword. There was great slaughter and destruction, and they worked their will on those who hated them.

"enemy of the state." **12:** *Our kingdom:* an excessive charge not supported by the facts. **21:** The reversal of *ruin* into *joy* is an apocalyptic theme in late OT writings.

9.1–19: The Jews take vengeance on their enemies and establish a holiday. 1: *Thirteenth day:* see 8.12 n.
11–15: This is to explain why the urban Jews observed Purim for two days instead of the usual one; see v. 19.
9.20–10.3: Mardochaeus records the event; the Festival of Purim.

observe the fourteenth and fifteenth of Adar, [22]because these were the days on which the Jews had respite from their enemies; and they were to observe the whole month of Adar, in which came the change from sorrow to joy and from a time of mourning to holiday, as days for weddings and merrymaking, days for sending presents of food to friends and to the poor.

[23]The Jews welcomed the account which Mardochaeus wrote: [24]how Haman son of Hamadathus, the Macedonian, fought against them, how he made a decree and cast lots with intent to destroy them, [25]how he came before the king with a proposal to hang Mardochaeus, how all the evils which he had plotted against the Jews recoiled upon him, and how he and his sons were hanged. [26]This is why these days were named Purim, because in the Jews' language it means 'Lots'. Because of all that was written in this letter, because of all that they had experienced, and all that had happened and been done, [27]the Jews gladly undertook, on behalf of themselves, their descendants, and those who should join them, to observe these days without fail; [28]they were to be days of commemoration, duly celebrated generation after generation in every city, family, and province; further, these days of Purim were to be observed for all time, and the commemoration was never to cease throughout all ages.

[29]Queen Esther daughter of Aminadab, and Mardochaeus the Jew, recorded in writing all that they had done, and confirmed the letter about Purim; [30–31]they had made themselves responsible for this decision and staked their life upon the plan. [32]Esther established it for all time by her decree, and it was put on record.

10 The king made decrees for his kingdom over land and sea. [2]His strength and courage, his wealth and the splendour of his kingdom, are recorded in the book of the kings of the Persians and Medes. [3]Mardochaeus was viceroy for King Artaxerxes; he was a great man in the kingdom and honoured by the Jews. His way of life won him the affection of his whole nation.]

10 [4]MARDOCHAEUS said, 'This is God's doing, [5]for I have been reminded of the dream I had about these matters; every one of the visions I saw has been fulfilled. [6]There was the little spring which became a river, and there was light and sun and abundant water: the river is Esther, whom the king married and made queen; [7]the two dragons are Haman and myself; [8]the nations are those who combined to blot out all memory of the Jews; [9]my nation is Israel, which cried out to God and was delivered. The Lord has delivered his people, he has rescued us from all these evils. God performed great signs and portents, such as have never occurred among the nations. [10]He prepared two lots, one for the people of God and one for all the nations; [11]then came the hour and the time for these two lots to be cast, the judgement by God upon all the nations; [12]he remembered his people and gave the verdict for his heritage.

[13]'So they are to keep these days in the month of Adar, the fourteenth and fifteenth of that month, by assembling with joy and gladness before God from one generation of his people Israel to another for ever.'

11 [1]IN the fourth year of the reign of Ptolemy and Cleopatra, Dositheus, who declared he was a levitical priest, and Ptolemaeus his son, brought the foregoing letter about Purim; according to their declaration it was authentic and had been translated by Lysimachus son of Ptolemaeus, a resident in Jerusalem.

[9:27] **observe . . . days:** *prob. rdg; cp. Heb.*

22: This festival celebrates the Israelite conviction that the *sorrow* of oppression in all ages will be turned into *joy* through the fulfilment of God's promises. **26:** *Purim:* see 3.7 n. **32:** This insistence on authoritative establishment of the festival by Esther's *decree* suggests that its propriety was being questioned.

10.4–13: Mardochaeus interprets his dream. 6–7: see 11.5–11 n. **10–12:** Another interpretation of Purim is that human beings seem to control history, but God casts the decisive *lots*.

11.1: The translation of the Book of Esther. 1: *Fourth year:* probably 114 B.C.E. *Letter:* the Book of Esther as a whole.

The Wisdom of Solomon

The author of Wisdom purports to be King Solomon (9.8), but this ascription was regarded as a literary fiction by both Origen (182–251 C.E.) and Jerome (about 340–420). Rather, the author was an Alexandrian Jew, well read in Jewish tradition and in Greek thought, who wrote in Greek. The author used the Septuagint translation of the Bible, completed in the second century B.C.E., but was unacquainted with the ideas of Philo (20 B.C.E.–40 C.E.), possibly indicating that the book was written in the first century B.C.E.

Biblical Wisdom literature is the source of many ideas in the book, and biblical poetry, with its parallel clauses, the model of its style (at least in the first sections). The review of Israel's history is embellished by expansions, many of which are found in late Jewish literature.

Under the impact of the cosmopolitan culture and a variety of philosophies and mystery religions of the Hellenistic world, the faith of many was shaken. Moreover, as a result of persecution, the perennial problem of the wicked prospering and the good suffering rose to a crisis level.

The author, denouncing the Jewish skeptics of the day who have forsaken inherited beliefs and practices, seeks to safeguard the faith of the rest of the people. The author does so by proposing a religious philosophy of history (chs. 10–12; 16–19), by clearly affirming reward and punishment after death (chs. 1–5), and by identifying Wisdom with the traditional spirit of the Lord (1.4–7; 7.22–25). Aided by the Platonic distinction of body from soul and the Greek ideas of providence (6.7; 14.3), conscience (17.11), and the cardinal virtues (8.7), the author uses this synthesis to appeal also to the pagans to examine Judaism as a valid Wisdom and a way of life (1.1–2; 10.15–11.14).

Wisdom and human destiny

1 LOVE justice, you rulers of the earth; set your mind upon the Lord in the right way, and seek him in singleness of heart; ²for he is to be found by those who trust him without question, and he makes himself known to those who never doubt him. ³Dishonest thinking cuts people off from God, and if fools take liberties with his power he shows them up for what they are. ⁴Wisdom will not enter a shifty soul, nor make her home in a body that is mortgaged to sin. ⁵This holy spirit of discipline will shun falsehood; she cannot stay in the presence of unreason, and will withdraw at the approach of injustice.

⁶The spirit of wisdom is kindly towards mortals, but she will not hold a blasphemer blameless for his words, because God, who sees clearly into his heart and hears every word he speaks, is a witness of his inmost being. ⁷For the spirit of the Lord fills the whole earth, and that which holds all things

---

1.1–5.23: God rewards the righteous and punishes the ungodly.

1.1–11: Wisdom, the key to immortality, is incompatible with deceit. 1: *Rulers of the earth:* lit. rulers in general; compare 6.1. But the real addressees were Alexandrian Jews. **4:** Here and in subsequent passages (7.25–26), *Wisdom* attains the highest personification in the Bible. **5:** *Discipline* in Wisdom literature means religious instruction and correction. **6:** *Heart:* the center of intellect and will. *Inmost being:* lit. "kidneys," considered as the center of emotion and instinct. Together they signify each person's inner forces. **7:** The fact that God's spirit *fills the whole earth* guarantees the assertion in v. 6 that God knows and will punish all transgressions. Spirit is identified with Wisdom; compare Col. 1.17; Heb. 1.3.

together knows well everything that is said. [8] Hence no one can utter injustice and not be found out, nor will justice overlook him when she passes sentence. [9] The devices of a godless person will be brought to account, and a report of his words will come before the Lord as proof of his iniquity; [10] no muttered syllable escapes that vigilant ear. [11] Beware, then, of futile grumbling, and avoid all bitter talk; for even a secret whisper will not go unheeded, and a lying tongue brings destruction on its owner.

[12] Do not court death by a crooked life; do not draw disaster on yourselves by your own actions. [13] For God did not make death, and takes no pleasure in the destruction of any living thing; [14] he created all things that they might have being. The creative forces of the world make for life; there is no deadly poison in them. Death has no sovereignty on earth, [15] for justice is immortal; [16] but the godless by their deeds and words have asked death for his company. Thinking him their friend and pining for him, they have made a pact with him because they are fit members of his party.

2 They said to themselves in their deluded way: 'Our life is short and full of trouble, and when a person comes to the end there is no remedy; no one has been known to return from the grave. [2] By mere chance were we born, and afterwards we shall be as though we had never existed, for the breath in our nostrils is but a wisp of smoke; our reason is a mere spark kept alive by the beating of our hearts, [3] and when that goes out, our body will turn to ashes and the breath of our life disperse like empty air. [4] With the passing of time our names will be forgotten, and no one will remember anything we did. Our life will vanish like the last vestige of a cloud; and as a mist is chased away by the sun's rays and overborne by its heat, so too will life be dispersed. [5] A fleeting shadow—such is our life,

and there is no postponement of our end. Man's fate is sealed: no one returns.

[6] 'Come then, let us enjoy the good things while we can and, with all the eagerness of youth, make full use of the creation. [7] Let us have costly wines and perfumes to our heart's content, and let no flower of spring escape us. [8] Let us crown ourselves with rosebuds before they wither. [9] Let none of us fail to share in the good things that are ours; let us leave behind on every side traces of our revelry. This is the life for us, this our birthright.

[10] 'Down with the poor and honest man! Let us show no mercy to the widow, no reverence to the grey hairs of old age. [11] For us let might be right! Weakness is proved to be good for nothing. [12] Let us set a trap for the just man; he stands in our way, a check to us at every turn; he girds at us as breakers of the law, and calls us traitors to our upbringing. [13] He knows God, so he says; he styles himself "child of the Lord". [14] He is a living condemnation of all our way of thinking. [15] The very sight of him is an affliction to us, because his life is not like other people's, and the paths he follows are quite different. [16] He rejects us like base coin, and avoids us and our ways as if we were filth; he says that the just die happy, and boasts that God is his father. [17] Let us test the truth of his claim, let us see what will happen to him in the end; [18] for if the just man is God's son, God will stretch out a hand to him and save him from the clutches of his enemies. [19] Insult and torture are the means to put him to the test, to measure his forbearance and learn how long his patience lasts. [20] Let us condemn him to a shameful death, for, if what he says is true, he will have a protector.'

[21] So they argued, and how wrong they were! Blinded by their own malevolence, [22] they failed to understand God's hidden plan; they never expected that holiness of life would have its recompense, never thought

2:13 **child**: or servant.

1.12–16: God made all immortal. 13: See 2.23–24 and Ezek. 33.11. **16:** *The godless* are renegade Jews, the author's real opponents, for whom life is completely this-worldly, ended by *death*. See Isa. 28.15 for the image of a "pact" with death.

2.1–20: Philosophy of the deluded sinners and its consequences. 2–3: The explanations of life are derived from the science of the author's day. **4:** Since *no one will remember*, there is no difference whether one is good or evil. Compare Eccles. 2.24; 3.12; 9.7–9. **10–12:** The sinners' attitude toward the precepts of Judaism is slightly caricatured for the sake of emphasis. **15:** The charge that the *paths* of the Jews were *different* was common in antiquity; compare Esther 3.8. **18:** *God's son*: Ps. 22.8–9 is the common source of this verse and of Matt. 27.43.

that innocence would have its reward. 23 But God created man imperishable, and made him the image of his own eternal self; 24 it was the devil's spite that brought death into the world, and the experience of it is reserved for those who take his side.

3 But the souls of the just are in God's hand; no torment will touch them. 2 In the eyes of the foolish they seemed to be dead; their departure was reckoned as defeat, 3 and their going from us as disaster. But they are at peace, 4 for though in the sight of men they may suffer punishment, they have a sure hope of immortality; 5 and after a little chastisement they will receive great blessings, because God has tested them and found them worthy to be his. 6 He put them to the proof like gold in a crucible, and found them acceptable like an offering burnt whole on the altar. 7 In the hour of their judgement they will shine in glory, and will sweep over the world like sparks through stubble. 8 They will be judges and rulers over nations and peoples, and the Lord will be their King for ever. 9 Those who have put their trust in him will understand that he is true, and the faithful will attend upon him in love; they are his chosen, and grace and mercy will be theirs.

10 But the godless will meet with the punishment their evil thoughts deserve, because they took no heed of justice and rebelled against the Lord. 11 Wretched indeed is he who thinks nothing of wisdom and discipline; the hopes of such people are void, their labours unprofitable, their actions futile; 12 their wives are wanton, their children depraved, 13 their parenthood is under a curse. But blessed is the childless woman if she is innocent, if she has never slept with a man in sin; at the great assize of souls she will find a fruitfulness of her own. 14 Blessed also is the eunuch, if he has never done anything against the law and never harboured a wicked thought against the Lord; in return for his faith he will receive special favour, and a place in the Lord's temple to delight his heart the more. 15 Honest work bears glorious fruit, and wisdom grows from roots that are imperishable. 16 But the children of adultery are like fruit that never ripens; they have sprung from a union forbidden by the law and will come to nothing. 17 Even if they attain length of life, they will be held of no account, and at the end their old age will be without honour. 18 If they die young, they will have no hope, no consolation in the day of judgement; 19 the unjust generation has a harsh fate in store.

4 It is better to be childless, provided one is virtuous; for virtue held in remembrance is a kind of immortality, because it wins recognition from God, and also from mankind; 2 they follow the good person's example while it is with them, and when it is gone they mourn its loss. Through all time virtue makes its triumphal progress, crowned with victory in the contest for prizes that nothing can tarnish. 3 But the swarming progeny of the godless will come to no good; none of their bastard offshoots will strike deep root or take firm hold. 4 For a time their branches may flourish, but as they have no sure footing they will be shaken by the wind, and uprooted by the violence of the gales. 5 Their boughs will be snapped off half grown, and their fruit will be worthless, unripe, uneatable, and fit for nothing. 6 Children engendered in unlawful union are

2.21–24: **Causes of the sinners' misconceptions.** Wickedness leads to illogic. **23:** See Gen. 1.26. **24:** *Devil's spite* alludes either to the fall of Adam (Gen. ch. 3) or to Cain and Abel (Gen. ch. 4).

3.1–19: **Rewards of the righteous and punishment of the ungodly. 4:** The *immortality* reserved for the righteous is of the soul (see v. 1); it is a Greek concept and supplants the Jewish resurrection of the body (Dan. 12.2). **5–6:** The righteous were only *tested* with *chastisement,* not punished; compare Ps. 66.10; 2 Macc. 6.12–16. **7–8:** *The hour of their judgement* seems to allude to God's definitive intervention in favor of the just, i.e. Israel, at the end of time. *Shine in glory* and *sparks through stubble* are images of victory; see Obad. 18. **10:** The *punishment* will be appropriate to *their evil thoughts* and not arbitrary. **13:** Traditional Jewish belief in large families (see Gen. 30.23) is seemingly abandoned. Perhaps the author means that sinful unions are so bad that even childlessness is preferable; see 4.1. **14:** See Isa. 56.4–5. Whether the *Lord's temple* is in Jerusalem or heaven is unspecified. If the latter, it is one of the first indications in the Bible of heaven as the dwelling of the godly.

4.1–6: **The true hierarchy of virtues.** Compare Ecclus. 16.3. **2:** *Virtue* is *crowned with victory* like successful athletes at the Greek athletic games. **4–5:** Compare Pss. 1.3–5; 92.13–15; Ecclus. 23.25.

living evidence of their parents' sin when God brings them to account.

7 But the just person, even one who dies an untimely death, will be at rest. 8 It is not length of life and number of years which bring the honour due to age; 9 if people have understanding, they have grey hairs enough, and an unblemished life is the true ripeness of age. 10 There was once such a man who pleased God, and God accepted him and took him while still living from among sinners. 11 He was snatched away before his mind could be perverted by wickedness or his soul deceived by falsehood 12 (because evil is like witchcraft: it dims the radiance of good, and the waywardness of desire unsettles an innocent mind); 13 in a short time he came to the perfection of a full span of years. 14 His soul was pleasing to the Lord, who removed him early from a wicked world. 15 People see this but give it no thought; they do not lay to heart the truth, that those whom God has chosen enjoy his grace and mercy, and that he comes to the help of his holy people.

16 Even after his death the just person will shame the godless who are still alive; youth come quickly to perfection will shame the person who has grown old in sin. 17 The godless will see the end of the wise person, without understanding what the Lord had purposed for him and why he took him into safe keeping; 18 they will see it and make light of him, but it is they whom the Lord will laugh to scorn. In death their bodies will be dishonoured, and among the dead they will be an object of lasting contempt; 19 for he will fling them speechless to the ground, shake them from their foundations, and leave them barren as a desert; they will be in anguish, and all memory of them will perish. 20 So, on the day of reckoning for their sins, they will come cringing, convicted to their face by their own lawless actions.

5 Then the just man will take his stand, full of assurance, to confront those who oppressed him and made light of his sufferings; 2 at the sight of him there will be terror and confusion, and they will be astounded at his unforeseen deliverance. 3 Remorseful, groaning and gasping for breath, they will say among themselves: 'Was not this the man who was once our butt, a target for our contempt? 4 Fools that we were, we held his way of life to be madness and his end dishonourable. 5 To think he is now counted one of the sons of God and assigned a place of his own among God's people! 6 How far we strayed from the way of truth! The lamp of justice never gave us light, the sun never rose on us. 7 We roamed to our heart's content along the paths of wickedness and ruin, wandering through trackless deserts and ignoring the Lord's highway. 8 What good has pride been to us? What can we show for all our vaunted wealth? 9 All those things have passed like a shadow, like a messenger galloping by; 10 like a ship that cleaves the surging sea and, when she has passed, not a trace is to be found, no wake from her keel in the waves; 11 or as when a bird flies through the air, there is no sign of her passage, but with the stroke of her pinions she lashes the insubstantial breeze and parts it with the whirr and the rush of her beating wings, and so she passes through it, and thereafter it bears no mark of her assault; 12 or as when a shaft is shot at a target, the air is parted and instantly closes up again and no one can tell where the arrow passed. 13 So too with us, as soon as we were born we ceased to be; we had no token of virtue to show, and in our wickedness we frittered our lives away.' 14 The hope of the godless is like down flying on the wind, like spindrift swept before a storm, like smoke which the wind whirls away, transient like the memory of a guest who stayed but one day.

15 But the just live for ever; their reward is in the Lord's keeping, and the Most High has them in his care. 16 Therefore royal splendour will be theirs, and a fair diadem from the Lord himself; he will protect them with his right hand and shield them with his arm. 17 He will array himself from head to foot with the armour of his wrath, and make all creation his weapon against his enemies. 18 With the cuirass of justice on his breast, and

---

4.7–20: The fate of the righteous and the ungodly contrasted. 10–11: *Such a man:* Enoch *was snatched away* in this manner (Gen. 5.21–24).

5.1–14: Remorse of the ungodly. This confession of the ungodly is in deliberate contrast with what they used to say; see 2.1–20. **5:** *Sons of God* is a poetic variant for *God's* own *people.* **9:** *Passed like a shadow:* disappeared.

5.15–23: Fate of the righteous and of the ungodly. 16: Compare Isa. 62.3. **17–20:** Compare Ps. 7.11–14;

on his head the helmet of inflexible judgement, [19] he will take holiness for his invincible shield [20] and sharpen his relentless anger for a sword; and his whole world will join him in the fight against his frenzied foes. [21] The bolts of his lightning will fly straight upon the mark, they will leap upon the target as if his bow in the clouds were drawn in its full arc, [22] and the artillery of his resentment will let fly a fury of hail. The waters of the sea will rage over them, and the rivers wash them relentlessly away; [23] a great tempest will arise against them, and scatter them like chaff before a whirlwind. So lawlessness will make the whole world desolate, and evildoing will overturn the thrones of princes.

In praise of wisdom

6 HEAR then, you kings, take this to heart; lords of the wide world, learn this lesson; [2] give ear, you rulers of the multitude, who take pride in the myriads of your people. [3] Your authority was bestowed on you by the Lord, your power comes from the Most High. He will probe your actions and scrutinize your intentions. [4] Though you are servants appointed by the King, you have not been upright judges; you have not maintained the law or guided your steps by the will of God. [5] Swiftly and terribly he will descend on you, for judgement falls relentlessly on those in high places. [6] The lowest may find pity and forgiveness, but those in power will be called powerfully to account; [7] for he who is Master of all is obsequious to none, and shows no deference to greatness. Small and great alike are of his making, and all are under his providence equally; [8] but it is for those who wield authority that he reserves the sternest inquisition. [9] To you, then, who have absolute power I speak, in hope that you may learn wisdom and not go astray; [10] those who in holiness have kept a holy course will be accounted holy, and those who

have learnt that lesson will be able to make their defence. [11] Therefore be eager to hear me; long for my teaching, and you will learn.

[12] Wisdom shines brightly and never fades; she is readily discerned by those who love her, and by those who seek her she is found. [13] She is quick to make herself known to all who desire knowledge of her; [14] he who rises early in search of her will not grow weary in the quest, for he will find her seated at his door. [15] To meditate on her is prudence in its perfect shape, and to be vigilant in her cause is the short way to freedom from care; [16] she herself searches far and wide for those who are worthy of her, and on their daily path she appears to them with kindly intent, meeting them half-way in all their purposes.

[17] The true beginning of wisdom is the desire to learn, and a concern for learning means love towards her; [18] the love of her means the keeping of her laws; to keep her laws is a warrant of immortality; [19] and immortality brings a person near to God. [20] Thus desire for wisdom leads to a kingdom. [21] If, therefore, you value your thrones and your sceptres, you rulers of the nations, you must honour wisdom so that you may reign for ever.

[22] What wisdom is, and how she came into being, I shall tell you; I shall not conceal her mysteries from you. I shall trace out her course from her first beginnings, and bring the knowledge of her into the light of day; I shall not leave the truth untold. [23] Pale envy will not travel in my company, for the spiteful will have no share in wisdom. [24] Wise men in plenty are the world's salvation, and a prudent king is the sheet-anchor of his people. [25] Therefore learn what I have to teach you, and it will be for your good.

7 I too am a mortal like everyone else, descended from the first man, who was made of dust, [2] and in my mother's womb I was wrought into flesh during a ten-month space, compacted in blood from the seed of

---

Isa. 59.17. **21:** *Lightning* is a traditional representation of divine intervention; see Pss. 18.14; 114.6.

6.1–9.18: The nature of wisdom is explained.

6.1–11: Admonition to the rulers. 1: See 1.1 n. **4:** *Law:* compare 2.12. **6–8:** God *shows no deference to greatness; the sternest inquisition* is reserved for the mighty.

6.12–21: Wisdom desires to be found. Compare Prov. 1.20–33; ch. 8. **17–21:** A chain argument called "sorites" of which the Stoics were fond, concludes that wisdom is essential for rulers.

6.22–25: The true nature of wisdom. 23: Unlike the old philosophers or founders of mystery cults who hid their teachings out of *envy,* the author will reveal all.

7.1–6: Wisdom is not inherited. 1: Solomon, the wisest of all, was a *mortal* like the rest. **2:** *Ten* lunar *months* her husband and the pleasure that accompanies sleep. [3] When I was born, I breathed the common air and was laid on the earth that all mortals tread; and the first sound I uttered, as all do, was a cry; [4] they wrapped me up and nursed me and cared for me. [5] No king begins life in any other way; [6] for all come into life by a single path, and by a single path they go out again.

[7] Therefore I prayed, and prudence was given me; I called for help, and there came to me a spirit of wisdom. [8] I valued her above sceptre and throne, and reckoned riches as nothing beside her; [9] I counted no precious stone her equal, because compared with her all the gold in the world is but a handful of sand, and silver worth no more than clay. [10] I loved her more than health and beauty; I preferred her to the light of day, for her radiance is unsleeping. [11] So all good things together came to me with her, and in her hands was wealth past counting. [12] Everything was mine to enjoy, for all follow where wisdom leads; yet I was in ignorance that she is the source of them all. [13] What I learnt with pure intention I now share ungrudgingly, nor do I hoard for myself the wealth that comes from her. [14] She is an inexhaustible treasure for mortals, and those who profit by it become God's friends, commended to him by the gifts they derive from her instruction.

[15] God grant that I may speak according to his will, and that my own thoughts may be worthy of his gifts, for even wisdom is under God's direction and he corrects the wise; [16] we and our words, prudence and knowledge and craftsmanship, all are in his hand. [17] He it was who gave me true understanding of things as they are: a knowledge of the structure of the world and the operation of the elements; [18] the beginning and end of epochs and their middle course; the alternating solstices and changing seasons; [19] the cycles of the years and the constellations; [20] the nature of living creatures and behaviour of wild beasts; the violent force of winds and human thought; the varieties of plants and the virtues of roots. [21] I learnt it all, hidden or manifest, [22] for I was taught by wisdom, by her whose skill made all things.

In wisdom there is a spirit intelligent and holy, unique in its kind yet made up of many parts, subtle, free-moving, lucid, spotless, clear, neither harmed nor harming, loving what is good, eager, unhampered, beneficent, [23] kindly towards mortals, steadfast, unerring, untouched by care, all-powerful, all-surveying, and permeating every intelligent, pure, and most subtle spirit. [24] For wisdom moves more easily than motion itself; she is so pure she pervades and permeates all things. [25] Like a fine mist she rises from the power of God, a clear effluence from the glory of the Almighty; so nothing defiled can enter into her by stealth. [26] She is the radiance that streams from everlasting light, the flawless mirror of the active power of God, and the image of his goodness. [27] She is but one, yet can do all things; herself unchanging, she makes all things new; age after age she enters into holy souls, and makes them friends of God and prophets, [28] for nothing is acceptable to God but the person who makes his home with wisdom. [29] She is more beautiful than the sun, and surpasses every constella-

7:26 **the radiance ... from:** or the reflection of.

---

are nine calendar months. *Compacted in blood* alludes to the ancient view that the menstrual blood united with the sperm to form the fetus. **6:** *Single path* of entry and exit emphasizes the equality of all in the search for wisdom; see Eccles. 9.2.

7.7–14: The values of wisdom. 7: Solomon *prayed* for wisdom, a course open to all; see ch. 9. **11:** Solomon's *wealth* was as fabulous as his wisdom; see 1 Kgs. 3.13.

7.15–22a: The extent of wisdom. The presentation is in scientific and philosophical terms; compare 1 Kgs. 3.16–28; 5.7–12. **17:** *Things as they are:* the totality of human science and philosophy. *Structure of the world:* cosmology. *Elements:* the four elements of Greek science. **18–19:** *Beginning and end:* chronology. *Alternating . . . cycles:* astronomical knowledge. **20:** *Nature of living creatures:* zoology. *Human thought:* psychology. *Varieties of plants:* botany. *Virtues of roots:* medicine and magic (compare Josephus, *Ant.* VIII.4.6).

7.22b–8.1: Nature of wisdom. 22b–23: Wisdom has 3×7 ($= 21$, the most perfect number) qualities, many of them Greek philosophical terms, some being divine attributes: *all-powerful, all-surveying.* **24:** Wisdom *pervades and permeates all things* like the spirit or world-soul of the Stoics. **26:** The relationship between wisdom and God is described philosophically using the most immaterial images possible: *light, power, goodness.*

tion. Compared with the light of day, she is found to excel, 30 for day gives place to night,

8 but against wisdom no evil can prevail. ¹ She spans the world in power from end to end, and gently orders all things.

Solomon and wisdom

²WISDOM I loved; I sought her out when I was young and longed to win her for my bride; I was in love with her beauty. ³ She adds lustre to her noble birth, because it is given her to live with God; the Lord of all things has accepted her. ⁴ She is initiated into the knowledge that belongs to God, and she chooses what his works are to be. ⁵ If riches are a possession to be desired in life, what is richer than wisdom, the active cause of all things? ⁶ If prudence shows itself in action, who more than wisdom is the artificer of all that is? ⁷ If someone loves uprightness, the fruits of wisdom's labours are the virtues; temperance and prudence, justice and fortitude, these are her teaching, and life can offer nothing of more value than these. ⁸ If someone longs, perhaps, for great experience, she knows the past, she can infer what is yet to come; she understands the subtleties of argument and the solving of hard questions; she can read signs and portents and foretell what the different times and seasons will bring about.

⁹ So I determined to take her home to live with me, knowing that she would be my counsellor in prosperity and my comfort in anxiety and grief. ¹⁰ Through her, I thought, I shall win fame in the eyes of the people and honour among older men, young though I am. ¹¹ When I sit in judgement, I shall prove myself acute, and the great will admire me; ¹² when I say nothing, they will wait for me to speak; when I speak, they will attend and, though I talk at some length, they will lay a finger to their lips and listen. ¹³ Through her

I shall have immortality and leave an undying memory to those who come after me. ¹⁴ I shall govern peoples, and nations will become subject to me. ¹⁵ Tyrants, however dread, will be afraid when they hear of me; among my own people I shall show myself a good king, and on the battlefield a brave one. ¹⁶ When I come home, I shall find rest with her; for there is no bitterness in her company, no pain in life with her, only gladness and joy.

¹⁷ I turned this over in my mind, and I perceived that there is immortality in kinship with wisdom, ¹⁸ and in her friendship there is pure delight; that in doing her work is wealth inexhaustible, to be taught in her school gives understanding, and an honourable name is won by converse with her. So I went about in search of some way to win her for my own. ¹⁹ As a child I was born to excellence, and a noble soul fell to my lot; ²⁰ or rather, I myself was noble, and I entered into an undefiled body; ²¹ but I saw that there was no way to gain possession of her except by gift of God —and it was itself a mark of understanding to know from whom that gift must come. So I pleaded with the Lord, and from the depths of my heart I prayed to him in these words:

9 ¹ God of our forefathers, merciful Lord, who made all things by your word, ² and in your wisdom fashioned man to have sovereignty over your whole creation, ³ and to be steward of the world in holiness and righteousness, and to administer justice with an upright heart: ⁴ give me wisdom, who sits beside your throne, and do not refuse me a place among your servants. ⁵ I am your slave, your slave-girl's son, weak and with but a short time to live, too feeble to understand justice and law; ⁶ for let someone be never so perfect in the eyes of his fellows, if the wisdom that comes from you is wanting, he will be of no account. ⁷ You chose me to be king of your own people and judge of your sons

8.2–16: **Solomon desires to take Wisdom as his bride. 3–4:** *The Lord of all things* has *accepted* Wisdom as a collaborator; she lives with God and is God's agent in the creation of all things. **7:** The four virtues of Greek philosophy and the "cardinal virtues" of Christian morality—*temperance and prudence, justice and fortitude*—are founded on wisdom. **8:** In the academic sphere wisdom is central to *argument* (logic), *hard questions* (mathematics), *signs and portents* (religious insight), *times and seasons* (history). **11:** See 1 Kgs. 3.16–28. **12:** *Finger to their lips:* a sign of silence in admiration of the speaker; see Job 29.9.

8.17–21: **Solomon searches for wisdom. 19–20:** The preexistence of the soul is implied in *a noble soul fell to my lot;* compare 9.15. The best that can be said for a body is that it is *undefiled.* Both these doctrines are Platonic and foreign to the OT.

9.1–18: **Solomon's prayer.** Compare 1 Kgs. 3.6–9. **4:** Compare Prov. 8.30. **8:** The attribution of the book and daughters; [8] you told me to build a temple on your sacred mountain and an altar in the city which is your dwelling-place, a copy of the sacred tabernacle prepared by you from the beginning. [9] With you is wisdom, who is familiar with your works and was present when you created the universe, who is aware of what is acceptable to you and in keeping with your commandments. [10] Send her forth from your holy heaven, and from your glorious throne bid her come down, so that she may labour at my side and I may learn what is pleasing to you. [11] She knows and understands all things; she will guide me prudently in whatever I do, and guard me with her glory. [12] So my life's work will be acceptable, and I shall judge your people justly, and be worthy of my father's throne.

[13] How can any human being learn what is God's plan? Who can apprehend what is the will of the Lord? [14] The reasoning of mortals is uncertain, and our plans are fallible, [15] because a perishable body weighs down the soul, and its frame of clay burdens the mind already so full of care. [16] With difficulty we guess even at things on earth, and laboriously find out what lies within our reach; but who has ever traced out what is in heaven? [17] Who ever came to know your purposes, unless you had given him wisdom and sent your holy spirit from heaven on high? [18] Thus it was that those on earth were set on the right path, and mortals were taught what pleases you; thus were they kept safe by wisdom.

Wisdom in Israel's history

10 WISDOM it was who kept guard over the first father of the human race, created alone as he was; after he had sinned she saved him [2] and gave him the strength to rule over all things. [3] It was because a wicked man forsook her in his anger that he murdered his brother in a fit of rage, and so destroyed himself. [4] Through his fault the earth was overwhelmed by a flood, and again wisdom came to the rescue, teaching the one good man to pilot his plain wooden hulk. [5] When heathen nations leagued in wickedness were thrown into confusion, she it was who recognized one good man and kept him blameless in God's sight, giving him strength to resist his pity for his child. [6] She saved a good man when the godless were being destroyed, and he escaped the fire that rained down on the Five Cities, [7] cities whose wickedness is still attested by a smoking waste, by plants whose fruit can never ripen, and by a pillar of salt standing there as a memorial of a disbelieving soul. [8] They ignored wisdom and suffered for it, losing the power to recognize what is good and leaving for mankind a monument to their folly, such that their enormities can never be forgotten. [9] But wisdom brought her servants safely out of their troubles. [10] When a good man was a fugitive from his brother's anger, she it was who guided him on straight paths; she gave him a vision of God's kingdom and a knowledge of holy things; she prospered his labours and made his toil fruitful. [11] When others in their rapacity sought to exploit him, she stood by him and made him rich. [12] She kept him safe from his enemies, and preserved him from treacherous attacks; after his hard struggle she gave him victory, and taught him that godliness is the mightiest power of all. [13] It was she who refused to desert a good man when he was sold into slavery; she preserved him from sin and went down into the dungeon with him, [14] nor did she leave him when he was in chains until she had brought him

to Solomon is here clear in that the author claims to have built a *temple;* see 1 Kgs. 6.1. The *sacred mountain* is Mount Zion, identified in Jewish tradition with Mount Moriah, the site of the temple. The temple was an earthly *copy* of the divine *tabernacle,* an idea derived from Exod. 25.9, 40. **15:** *Perishable body . . . of clay* alludes to the Platonic doctrine that the material world is less than real and is a prison of the spirit. **17:** *Holy spirit* is identified with wisdom; compare 7.22.

10.1–21: From Adam to the Exodus. 1–2: Adam (Gen. 1.26–5.5). **3:** Cain and Abel (Gen. 4.1–16). **4:** Noah (Gen. 5.28–9.29). For the flood as Cain's *fault* see Josephus, *Ant.* I.2.2. **5a:** The Tower of Babel (Gen. 11.1–9). **5b:** Abraham (Gen. 11.26–25.10). **6–9:** Lot (Gen. ch. 19). The *Five Cities* are Sodom and Gomorrah and their confederates (Gen. 14.2; 19.20–33), located by Jewish tradition and some modern writers at the southern end of the Dead Sea. Natural phenomena embellished by legend account for *smoking waste* (heavy evaporation of Dead Sea); *fruit . . . never ripen* (apples of Sodom), and *pillar of salt* (salt deposit formation; Gen. 19.26). See Philo, *De Abrahamo,* 137–141; Josephus, *B.J.* IV.8.4. **10–12:** Jacob (Gen. 25.19–49.33, especially a kingdom's sceptre with authority over his persecutors; she gave the lie to his accusers, and bestowed on him undying fame.

15 It was wisdom who rescued a godfearing people, a blameless race, from a nation of oppressors; 16 she inspired a servant of the Lord, and with his signs and wonders he defied formidable kings. 17 She rewarded the labours of a godfearing people, she guided them on a miraculous journey, and became a covering for them by day and a blaze of stars by night. 18 She brought them over the Red Sea, leading them through its deep waters; 19 but their enemies she engulfed, and cast them up again out of the fathomless deep. 20 So the good despoiled the ungodly; they sang the glories of your holy name, O Lord, and with one accord praised your power, their champion; 21 for wisdom enabled the dumb to speak, and made the tongues of infants eloquent.

11 Wisdom, working through a holy prophet, gave them success in all they did. 2 They made their way across an unpeopled desert and pitched camp in untrodden wastes; 3 they stood firm against their enemies, and fought off hostile assaults. 4 When they were thirsty they cried to you, and water to slake their thirst was given them out of the hard stone of a rocky cliff. 5 The selfsame means by which their oppressors had been punished were used to help them in their hour of need: 6 those others found

their river no unfailing stream of water, but putrid and befouled with blood, 7 a punishment for their order that all the infants should be killed; to these, however, when they had lost hope, you gave abundant water. 8 So, from the thirst they then endured, they learnt how you had punished their enemies; 9 when they themselves were put to the test, though chastisement was tempered with mercy, they understood the tortures of the godless who were sentenced in anger. 10 Your own people you subjected to an ordeal, disciplining them like a father, but those others you put to the torture like a stern king passing sentence. 11 Whether at home or abroad, they were equally in distress, 12 for double misery had come upon them, and they groaned as they recalled the past. 13 When they heard that the means of their own punishment had been used to benefit your people, they saw your hand in it, Lord. 14 The man who long ago had been abandoned and exposed, whom they had rejected with contumely, became in the event the object of their wonder and admiration; their thirst was such as the godly never knew.

15 In return for the foolish imagination of those wicked people, which deluded them into worshipping reptiles incapable of reason, and mere vermin, you sent upon them in your vengeance mindless swarms 16 to teach them that the instruments of someone's sin are the instruments of his punishment.

chs. 28–31). **13–14:** Joseph (Gen. chs. 37–50). **15–21:** The Exodus (Exod. 1.1–15.21, especially chs. 12–15). **16:** *A servant:* Moses. *Formidable kings* are Pharaoh and others, as in Ps. 135.9–10. **17:** The cloud of Exod. 13.21 is thought of as a *covering;* see Num. 10.34 and Ps. 105.39. **20:** According to Josephus, *Ant.* II.16.6., the Egyptians were despoiled at the Red Sea. **21:** *Dumb* who *speak* and *eloquent infants* refer to the Jewish tradition that even infants and embryos joined in the song of Israel at the Red Sea; see Exod. 15.1–18.

11.1–14: The wandering in the wilderness (Exod. 15.22–17.16). **4:** Events of Exod. 17.1–7 are given according to an idealized version; compare Ps. 107.4–6. **5–7:** Before the Exodus, water was turned into *blood* for the Egyptians by the first plague (Exod. 7.19–25), a punishment, according to the author, for Pharaoh's decree that *all the infants* of the Israelites be *killed* by being drowned in the Nile. The Egyptians were thus punished by the sudden loss of drinking water but the Israelites were rewarded by finding it unexpectedly in the desert (Num. 20.11). Exodus states that the Pharaoh ordered only the male children to be drowned (Exod. 1.22) and the water was turned into blood not because of that decree, but because of Pharaoh's refusal to let Israel leave Egypt (Exod. 7.16–17). **13:** Exodus 32.12 also implies that the Egyptians could know what was occurring in the wilderness, and that the *means of their own punishment had been used to benefit your people.* **14:** Moses is the one *abandoned,* both in his exposure at birth (Exod. 2.1–10), and in his flight (Exod. 2.11–22).

11.15–20: The punishment of the Egyptians was appropriate. God could have chosen innumerable punishments. Instead, ironically, they were punished through the animals they worshiped. **15:** Exodus ch. 8 does not suggest that the Egyptians worshiped *reptiles* or *vermin.* Perhaps the author is exaggerating the practice of Egyptian temples. See Philo, *De Vita Contemplativa,* 8–9. *Mindless swarms* were the plagues of frogs, lice,

17 For your almighty hand, which created the world out of formless matter, was not without other resource: it could have let loose on those wicked people a horde of bears or ravening lions 18 or unknown ferocious monsters newly created, breathing out blasts of fire, or roaring and belching smoke, or flashing terrible sparks like lightning from their eyes, 19 beasts with power not only to exterminate them by the wounds they inflicted, but by their mere appearance to kill them with fright. 20 Even without these, a single breath would have sufficed to lay them low, with justice in pursuit and the breath of your power to blow them away; but you have set all things in order by measure and number and weight.

21 Great strength is yours to exert at any moment, and the power of your arm no one can resist, 22 for in your sight the whole world is like a grain that just tips the scale or like a drop of dew alighting on the ground at dawn. 23 But you are merciful to all because you can do all things; you overlook people's sins in order to bring them to repentance; 24 for all existing things are dear to you and you hate nothing that you have created— why else would you have made it? 25 How could anything have continued in existence, had it not been your will? How could it have endured unless called into being by you? 26 You spare all things because they are yours,

12 O Lord, who love all that lives; 1 for your imperishable breath is in every one of them.

2 For this reason you correct offenders little by little, disciplining them and reminding them of their sins, in order that they may abandon their evil ways and put their trust in you, Lord. 3 There were the ancient inhabitants of your holy land: 4 you hated them for their loathsome practices, their sorcery and unholy rites, 5 their pitiless killing of children, their cannibal feasts of human flesh and blood; 6 they were initiates of a secret ritual in which parents slaughtered their defenceless children. Therefore it was your will to destroy them at the hands of our forefathers, 7 so that the land which is of all lands most precious in your eyes might receive in God's children settlers worthy of it. 8 And yet you spared them because they too were human beings, and you sent hornets as the advance guard of your army to exterminate them by stages. 9 It was well within your power to have the godly overwhelm the godless in a pitched battle, or to wipe them out in an instant by fearsome beasts or with one relentless word. 10 But instead you carried out the sentence by stages to give them room for repentance, knowing well enough that they came of evil stock, that their wickedness was innate, and that their way of thinking would not change to the end of time, 11 for there was a curse on their race from the beginning.

Nor was it out of deference to anyone else that you gave them an amnesty for their misdeeds, 12 for no one can say 'What have you done?' Who can challenge your verdict? Who can bring a charge against you for destroying nations which were of your own making? Who can appear against you in court to plead the cause of the guilty? 13 For there is no other god but you; all the world is your concern, and there is none to whom you must prove the justice of your sentence. 14 There is no king or other ruler who can outface you on behalf of those whom you have punished. 15 But you are just and you order all things justly, counting it alien to your power to condemn anyone to undeserved punishment. 16 For your strength is the source of justice, and it is because you are Master of all that you are lenient to all. 17 You show your strength when people doubt whether your power is absolute; it is when they know it and yet are insolent that you punish them. 18 But you, with strength at your command, judge in mercy and rule us in great forbearance;

and locusts, Exod. chs. 8 and 10. **17:** *Formless matter* may imply the Platonic philosophical concept of preexistent matter out of which the world was made, but compare Gen. 1.2.

11.21–12.1: God is merciful to all creatures. See Ps. 145.9.

12.2–11: God was merciful even to the Canaanites. 3–8: The charge of *cannibal feasts* is unattested in the Bible, but it was part of the Greek philosophical attack on Greek mythology. On the gradual extermination of the *ancient inhabitants* of the holy land (Canaan) see Exod. 23.28–30; Deut. 7.20. **11:** Noah cursed *their race*, i.e. the Canaanites, Gen. 9.25.

12.12–21: God's leniency is not due to weakness or fear. God's mercy is an example and warning to the Jews. The author avoids mentioning the sins of the Israelites.

for the power is yours to exercise whenever you choose.

19 By acts like these you taught your people that he who is just must also be kind-hearted, and you have filled your children with hope by the offer of repentance for their sins. 20 If you used such care and such indulgence even in punishing your children's enemies who deserved to die, granting them time and opportunity to win free of their wickedness, 21 with what discrimination you passed judgement on your people, to whose forefathers you gave sworn covenants full of the promise of good!

22 So we are chastened by you, but you scourge our enemies ten thousand times more, so that we may lay your goodness to heart when we sit in judgement, and may hope for mercy when we ourselves are judged. 23 This is why the wicked who had lived their lives in heedless folly were tormented by you with their own abominations. 24 They had strayed far down the paths of error, taking for gods the most despised and hideous creatures; they were deluded like thoughtless infants. 25 And so, as though they were children who had not learnt reason, you imposed on them a sentence that made them ridiculous; 26 but those who are not disciplined by such derisive correction will experience the full weight of divine judgement. 27 They were indignant at their own sufferings, but, finding themselves chastised through the very creatures they had deemed to be gods, they recognized that the true God was he whom they had formerly refused to know. For this reason the full rigour of condemnation overtook them.

Indictment of idolatry

13 WHAT born fools were all who lived in ignorance of God! From the good things before their eyes they could not learn to know him who is, and failed to recognize the artificer though they observed his handiwork! 2 Fire, wind, swift air, the circle of the starry signs, rushing water, or the great lights in heaven that rule the world—these they accounted gods. 3 If it was through delight in the beauty of these things that people supposed them gods, they ought to have understood how much better is the Lord and Master of them all; for it was by the prime author of all beauty they were created. 4 If it was through astonishment at their power and influence, people should have learnt from these how much more powerful is he who made them. 5 For the greatness and beauty of created things give us a corresponding idea of their Creator. 6 Yet these people are not greatly to be blamed, for when they go astray they may be seeking God and really wishing to find him. 7 Passing their lives among his works and making a close study of them, they are persuaded by appearances because of the beauty of what they see. 8 Yet even so they do not deserve to be excused, 9 for with enough understanding to speculate about the universe, why did they not sooner discover its Lord and Master?

10 The really degraded ones are those whose hopes are set on lifeless things, who give the title of gods to the work of human hands, to gold and silver fashioned by art into images of living creatures, or to a useless stone carved by a craftsman long ago. 11 Suppose some skilled worker in wood fells with his saw a convenient tree and deftly strips off all the bark, then works it up elegantly into some household vessel suitable for everyday use; 12 and the bits left over from his work he uses to cook his food, and then eats his fill. 13 But among what is left over there is one useless piece, crooked and full of knots, and this he takes and carves to occupy his idle moments. He shapes it with leisurely skill into the image of a human being, 14 or else he gives it the form of some worthless creature, smearing it over with vermilion and raddling its surface with red paint, so that every flaw in it is daubed over. 15 Then he makes a suitable shrine for it and fixes it on the wall, securing it with nails. 16 It is he who has to

---

12.22–27: Severe punishment for the Egyptians. 23–24: Compare 11.15–16.

13.1–15.19: Heathen worship is foolishness.

13.1–9: The folly of deifying nature. 1: The argument for God's existence from design was popular among the Stoics. God is described in philosophical terms as one *who* really *is;* see Sept. Exod. 3.14. **2:** *Fire, wind,* etc. are aspects of nature worshiped by pagans and important to Greek philosophers; compare Deut. 4.19.

13.10–19: The worship of idols is inexcusable. See Isa. 44.9–20 and L. of Jer. This was a frequent theme in Jewish literature.

take the precautions on its behalf to save it from falling, for he well knows that it cannot fend for itself: it needs help, for it is only an image. 17 Yet he prays to it about his possessions and his wife and children, and feels no shame in addressing this inanimate object; 18 for health he appeals to a thing that is weak, for life he prays to a thing that is dead, for aid he asks help from something utterly incapable, for a prosperous journey from something that cannot put one foot before the other; 19 where earnings or business or success in handicraft are in question he asks effectual help from a thing whose hands are entirely ineffectual.

14 Again, the man who gets ready for a voyage and plans to set his course through the wild waves invokes a piece of wood more fragile than the ship which is to carry him. 2 Desire for gain invented the ship, and the shipwright with his skill built it; 3 but your providence, Father, is the pilot, for you have given it a pathway through the sea and a safe course among the waves, 4 showing that you can save from every danger, so that even the inexpert can put to sea. 5 It is your will that the things made by your wisdom should not lie unused; and therefore people entrust their lives even to the frailest spar, and passing through the billows on a mere raft come safe to land. 6 So in the beginning, when the proud race of giants was being brought to an end, the hope of mankind escaped on a raft and, piloted by your hand, bequeathed to the world a new breed of people. 7 While a blessing is on the wood through which right prevails, 8 the wooden idol made by human hands is accursed, and so is its maker — he because he made it, and the perishable thing because it was called a god. 9 Equally hateful to God are the godless and their ungodliness; 10 the doer and the deed will both be punished. 11 Therefore retribution will fall on the idols of the heathen, because although part of God's creation they have been made into an abomination, to make people stumble and to catch the feet of the foolish. 12 The devising of idols is the beginning of immorality; they are an invention which has blighted hu-

man life. 13 They did not exist from the beginning, nor will they be with us for ever; 14 superstition brought them into the world, and for good reason a speedy end is in store for them.

15 Some father, overwhelmed with untimely grief for the child suddenly taken from him, made an image of his child and honoured thenceforth as a god what was once a dead human being, handing on to his household the observance of rites and ceremonies. 16 Then this impious custom, established by the passage of time, was observed as law. Or again, graven images came to be worshipped at the command of despotic princes. 17 When people could not do honour to such a prince before his face because he lived too far away, they made a likeness of that distant face, and produced a visible image of the king they sought to honour, in order that by their zeal they might gratify the absent prince as though he were present. 18 Then the cult grows in fervour as those to whom the king is unknown are spurred on by ambitious craftsmen. 19 In his desire, it may be, to please the monarch, a craftsman skilfully distorts the likeness into an ideal form, 20 and the common people, beguiled by the beauty of the workmanship, take for an object of worship him whom lately they honoured as a man. 21 So this becomes a snare in the life of a people: enslaved by mischance or misgovernment, they confer on stocks and stones the name that none may share.

22 Then, not content with crass error in their knowledge of God, people live in the constant warfare of ignorance and call this monstrous evil peace. 23 They perform ritual killing of children and secret ceremonies and the frenzied orgies of unnatural cults; 24 the purity of life and marriage is abandoned; and a man treacherously murders a neighbour or by corrupting his wife breaks his heart. 25 All is chaos — bloody murder, theft and fraud, corruption, treachery, riot, perjury, 26 honest folk driven to distraction; ingratitude, depravity, sexual perversion,

14:2 **and the shipwright ... built it:** *other witnesses read* and wisdom was the shipwright who built it.

14.1–10: Folly of the idolatrous navigator. 1: The *piece of wood more fragile* is the protective idol of the ship. **6:** *Giants:* see Gen. 6.1–4. *Hope of mankind:* Noah and his family; see Gen. 5.28–9.29.

14.11–31: Origin and evil results of idolatry. 13: Unnatural idols *did not exist from the beginning* but were invented. **17:** The worship of the *prince,* or ruler cult, was popular in the Hellenistic world, particularly in Egypt. See Rom. 1.22–32 for similar licentious behavior in defiance of God and society.

breakdown of marriage, adultery, debauchery. 27 For the worship of idols, whose names it is wrong even to mention, is the beginning, the cause, and the end of every evil. 28 People either indulge themselves to the point of madness, or pass off lies as prophecies, or live dishonest lives, or break their oath without scruple. 29 They perjure themselves and expect no harm because the idols they trust in are lifeless. 30 But judgement will overtake them on two counts: both because in their devotion to idols they have thought wrongly about God, and also because in their contempt for religion they have deliberately perjured themselves. 31 It is not any power in what they swear by, but the nemesis of sin, that ever pursues the transgressions of the wicked.

15 But you, our God, are kind and true and patient, a merciful ruler of all that is. 2 Even if we sin, we are yours, since we acknowledge your power. But because we know that we are accounted yours we shall not sin. 3 To know you is the whole of righteousness, and to acknowledge your power is the root of immortality. 4 We have not been led astray by the perverted inventions of human skill or the barren labour of painters, by some gaudily coloured shape, 5 the sight of which arouses in fools a passionate desire for an image without life or breath. 6 They are in love with evil and do not deserve anything better to trust in, those who make such evil things, those who hanker after them, and those who worship them.

7 A potter laboriously kneading the soft clay shapes every vessel for our use. Out of the selfsame clay he fashions without distinction the pots that are to serve for clean uses and the opposite; and what the purpose of each one is to be, the moulder of the clay decides. 8 Then with ill-directed toil he makes a false god out of the same clay, this man who not long before was himself fashioned out of earth and soon returns to the place whence he was taken, when the living soul that was lent to him must be returned on demand.

9 His concern is not that he must one day fall sick or that his span of life is short; but he must vie with goldsmiths and silversmiths and emulate the workers in bronze, and he thinks it does him credit to contrive fakes. 10 His heart is ashes, his hope worth less than common earth, and his life cheaper than clay, 11 because he did not recognize by whom he himself was moulded, or who it was that inspired him with an active soul and breathed into him the breath of life. 12 No, he reckons this life of ours a game, and our existence a market where money can be made: 'By fair means or foul', he says, 'one must get a living.' 13 But this maker of fragile pots and idols from the same earthy stuff knows better than anyone that he is doing wrong.

14 The greatest fools of all, and worse than infantile, were the enemies and oppressors of your people, 15 for they supposed all their heathen idols to be gods, although they have eyes that cannot see, nostrils that cannot draw breath, ears that cannot hear, fingers that cannot feel, and feet that are useless for walking; 16 for it was a man who made them, one drawing borrowed breath who gave them their shape. But no human being has the power to shape a god in his own likeness: 17 he is only mortal, but what he makes with his impious hands is dead. So he is better than the objects of his worship, for at least he is alive—they never can be.

18 Moreover, these people worship animals, the most revolting animals. Compared with the rest of the brute creation, their divinities are the least intelligent. 19 Even as animals they are without a trace of beauty which might make them desirable. When God approved and blessed his work, they were left out.

Israel and the Egyptians

16 For that reason it was fitting that the oppressors were chastised by creatures like these: they were tormented by

15.1–6: Benefits of worshiping the true God. 1: See Exod. 34.6 and Sept. Deut. 32.4. **4:** Ancient statues were usually painted. **5:** Stories were told by Christian authors of the *passionate desire* aroused by a mere *image.*

15.7–19: The manufacture of idols. 7: Compare Isa. 45.9. **14–17:** *The greatest fools of all* in making *idols* were the Egyptians. **19:** Which *animals* worshiped by the Egyptians *were left out* of God's blessing is not clear, perhaps the unclean animals of 11.15 or the serpent cursed by God in Gen. 3.14–15.

16.1–19.22: A theology of history is developed.

16.1–23: The punishment of the Egyptians and wicked Israelites. The theme is similar to that of chs. 10–12.

swarms of vermin. [2] They were punished; but your own people you treated with kindness, sending quails for them to eat, a novel food to satisfy their hunger. [3] Your purpose was that whereas those others, hungry as they were, should turn in loathing even from essential food because the creatures sent against them were so repulsive, your people, after a short spell of scarcity, should partake of novel delicacies. [4] It was right that the scarcity falling on the oppressors should be inexorable, and that your people should learn by brief experience how their enemies were tortured.

[5] Even when fierce and venomous snakes attacked your people and the bites of writhing serpents were spreading death, your anger did not continue to the bitter end. [6] Their short-lived trouble was sent them as a lesson, and they were given a symbol of salvation to remind them of the requirements of your law. [7] Anyone turning towards it was saved, not by what he looked at but by you, the saviour of all. [8] In this way also you convinced our enemies that you are the deliverer from every evil. [9] Those others died from the bites of locusts and flies, and no remedy to save their lives was found, because they deserved to be punished by such creatures.

[10] But your people did not succumb to the fangs of snakes, however poisonous, because your mercy came to their aid and healed them. [11] It was to remind them of your decrees that they were bitten, and they were quickly healed for fear they might fall into deep forgetfulness and become unresponsive to your kindness. [12] It was neither herb nor poultice that cured them, but your all-healing word, O Lord. [13] You have the power of life and death, you bring a person down to the gates of death and you bring him up again. [14] In his wickedness a human being may kill, but he cannot bring back the breath of life that has gone or release a soul that death has arrested.

[15] But from your hand there is no escape; [16] for the godless who refused to acknowledge you were scourged by your mighty arm, they were pursued by unwonted storms of rain and hail falling in relentless torrents, and were utterly destroyed by fire. [17] Strangest of all, in water, that quenches everything, the fire burned more fiercely; creation itself fights to defend the righteous. [18] At one time the flame was moderated, so that it should not burn up the living creatures inflicted on the godless, who were to learn from this that it was by God's judgement they were pursued; [19] at another time it blazed even in water with more than the natural power of fire, to destroy the produce of a sinful land.

[20] In contrast to this your own people were given angels' food. You sent to them from heaven, without labour on their part, bread ready to eat, rich in every kind of delight and suited to every taste. [21] The sustenance you supplied showed the sweetness of your disposition towards your children, and the bread, serving the appetite of every person who ate it, was transformed into what each wished. [22] Though like snow and ice, yet it resisted fire and did not melt, to teach them that whereas their enemies' crops had been destroyed by fire blazing in the hail and flashing through the teeming rain, [23] that same fire had now forgotten its own power, in order that the godly might be fed.

[24] For creation, serving you its Maker, strains to punish the unrighteous and relaxes into benevolence towards those who put their trust in you. [25] It was so at that time too: it adapted itself endlessly in the service of your universal bounty, according to the desire of your suppliants. [26] So your people, whom you, Lord, have loved, were to learn that it is not by the growing of crops that mankind is nourished, but it is by your word that those who trust in you are sustained. [27] That substance, which fire did not destroy, simply melted away when warmed by the sun's first

---

2: *Quails:* Exod. 16.13; Num. 11.31; Ps. 78.27. **5–6:** Num. 21.4–9. **7:** This is based on Jewish exegesis of Num. 21.9. **9:** Exodus 10.17 may have suggested that the Egyptians *died from the bites of locusts and flies.* See Josephus, *Ant.* II.14.3. **16:** See Exod. 9.18–34. **17:** The strange quality of *fire* burning *in water* is derived from Jewish exegesis of Exod. 9.24. **18:** The author assumes that the frogs and lice of the earlier plagues survived to be spared by the hail. This is contrary to Exod. 8.13, 31. **20:** *Angels' food:* the manna of Exod. 16.4–21 ("bread from heaven") and Ps. 78.25 ("bread of angels"). It was described by Jewish tradition as *suited to every taste.* **22:** *Snow and ice:* "the manna," according to Sept. Num. 11.7–8.

16.24–29: Philosophical and moral lessons of the manna. 26: Compare Deut. 8.3. **27:** Manna could be baked, and was seemingly indestructible by *fire*, but it was *melted away when warmed by the sun's first rays;*

rays, 28 to teach us that we must rise before the sun to give you thanks and pray to you as daylight dawns. 29 The hope of the ungrateful will melt like wintry hoar-frost, and drain away like water that runs to waste.

17 Great are your judgements and hard to expound; and this was why uninstructed souls went astray. 2 The heathen imagined that they could lord it over your holy nation, but, prisoners of darkness and captives of unending night, they themselves lay immured each under his own roof, fugitives from eternal providence. 3 Thinking that their secret sins might escape detection beneath a dark pall of oblivion, they lay in disorder, dreadfully afraid, terrified by apparitions. 4 Not even the dark corner that hid them offered refuge from fear, but loud, unnerving noises resounded about them, and phantoms with faces grim and downcast passed before their eyes. 5 No fire, however intense, was strong enough to give them light, nor were the brilliant, flaming stars adequate to pierce that hideous darkness. 6 There shone on them only a terrifying blaze of no human making, and in their panic they thought the real world even worse than the sight their imagination conjured up. 7 The tricks of the sorcerer's art failed, and their boasted wisdom was exposed and put to shame; 8 for those who professed to drive out fear and trouble from sick souls were themselves sick with dread that made them ridiculous. 9 Even if there was nothing frightful to terrify them, yet having once been scared by the advance of the vermin and the hissing of the serpents, 10 they collapsed in terror, even refusing to look upon the air from which there could be no escape. 11 For wickedness proves a cowardly thing when condemned by an inner witness, and in the grip of conscience gives way to forebodings of disaster. 12 Fear is nothing but an abandonment of the aid that reason affords; 13 and hope, defeated by this inward weakness, capitulates in ignorance of the cause by which the torment comes.

14 So all that night, which really had no power over them because it came upon them from the powerless depths of hell, they slept the same haunted sleep, 15 now harried by portentous spectres, now paralysed by the treachery of their own souls; sudden and unforeseen, fear came upon them. 16 Thus someone would fall down wherever he was and be held captive, locked in a prison that had no bars. 17 Farmer or shepherd or a labourer toiling out in the wilderness, he was overtaken, and awaited the inescapable doom; the same chain of darkness bound all alike. 18 The whispering breeze, the sweet melody of birds in spreading branches, the steady noise of rushing water, 19 the headlong crash of rocks falling, the racing of creatures as they bound along unseen, the roar of savage wild beasts, or an echo reverberating from hollows in the hills — all these sounds paralysed them with fear. 20 The whole world was bathed in the bright light of day, and went about its tasks unimpeded; 21 those people alone were overspread with heavy night, fit image of the darkness that awaited them. But heavier than the darkness was the burden each was to himself.

18 For your holy ones, however, there shone a very great light. Their enemies, hearing their voices but not seeing them, counted them happy because they had not suffered as they themselves had; 2 they thanked them for their forbearance under provocation, and begged as a favour that they should part company. 3 In place of the darkness you provided a pillar of fire to be the guide of their uncharted journey, a sun that would not scorch them on that glorious expedition. 4 Their enemies did indeed deserve to lose the light of day and be imprisoned in darkness, for they had kept in durance your people, through whom the imperishable light of the law was to be given to the world.

5 They planned to kill the new-born infants among your holy people but, when one babe had been exposed and rescued, you deprived them of their children in requital, and drowned them all together in the swelling waves. 6 Of that night our forefathers were given warning in advance, so that, having

---

compare Exod. 16.21. **28:** Jewish morning prayers may be recited only after *daylight dawns*.

17.1–18.4: The plague of darkness (Exod. 10.21–23). **3:** *Secret sins,* attributed here to the ancient Egyptians, may allude to the mystery cults of the author's day; compare 14.23. **5:** The details are derived from the Jewish exegesis of Exod. 10.21. **7:** Compare Exod. 7.11, 22; 8.7, 18; 9.11. **18.3:** See Exod. 13.21; 14.24.

18.5–19: The Egyptians counsel death but are slain themselves. 5: *One babe:* Moses; see Exod. 1.15–2.10.

sure knowledge, they might be heartened by the promises which they trusted. ⁷Your people were looking for the deliverance of the godly and the destruction of their enemies; ⁸for you used the same means to punish our assailants and to make us glorious when we heard your call. ⁹The devout children of a virtuous race were offering sacrifices in secret, and covenanted with one accord to keep the law of God and to share alike in the same benefits and the same dangers; already they were singing their ancestral sacred songs of praise.

¹⁰In discordant contrast there came a clamour from their enemies, as piteous lamentation for their children spread abroad. ¹¹Master and slave were punished together with the same penalty; king and commoner suffered the selfsame fate. ¹²All alike had dead past counting, struck down by one common form of death; there were not even enough living to bury the dead; at one stroke the most precious of their offspring had perished. ¹³Relying on their magic arts, they had scouted all warnings; but when they saw the destruction of their firstborn, they acknowledged that your people have God as their Father.

¹⁴All things were lying in peace and silence, and night in her swift course was half spent, ¹⁵when your all-powerful word leapt from your royal throne in heaven into the midst of that doomed land like a relentless warrior, ¹⁶bearing the sharp sword of your inflexible decree; with his head touching the heavens and his feet on earth he stood and spread death everywhere. ¹⁷Then all at once nightmare phantoms appalled the godless, and fears unlooked-for beset them; ¹⁸flinging themselves half dead to the ground, one here, another there, they made clear why they were dying; ¹⁹for the dreams that tormented them had taught them before they died, so that they should not perish still ignorant of why they suffered.

²⁰The godly also had a taste of death when large numbers were struck down in the wilderness. But the divine wrath did not long continue, ²¹for a blameless man was quick to be their champion, bearing the weapons of his priestly ministry, prayer and the incense that propitiates; he withstood the divine anger and set a limit to the disaster, thus showing that he was indeed your servant. ²²He overcame the anger neither by bodily strength nor by force of arms; but by words he subdued the avenger, appealing to the sworn covenants made with our forefathers. ²³The dead were already fallen in heaps when he interposed himself and drove back the divine wrath, barring its line of attack on those still alive. ²⁴On his long-skirted robe the whole world was represented; the glories of the fathers were engraved on his four rows of precious stones; and your majesty was on the diadem upon his head. ²⁵To these the destroyer yielded, for they made him afraid. It was only a taste of the wrath, but it was enough.

19 But the godless were assailed by pitiless anger to the very end, for God knew their future also: ²how after allowing your people to go, and even urging their departure, they would have a change of heart and set out in pursuit. ³While they were still mourning, still lamenting at the graves of their dead, they rushed into another foolish decision, and pursued as runaways those whom they had entreated to leave. ⁴For a well-deserved fate was drawing them on to this conclusion and made them forget what had happened, so that they might suffer the torments still needed to complete their punishment, ⁵and so that your people might achieve an incredible journey but their enemies meet a strange death.

⁶The whole creation, with all its elements, was refashioned in subservience to your commands, in order that your servants might be preserved unscathed. ⁷They gazed at the

18:22 **anger:** *prob. rdg; Gk* crowd.

6: The night of the first Passover was so well known as to be called *that night;* see Exod. 12.42. **9:** *Ancestral sacred songs:* the first Passover is anachronistically pictured in the format of the author's own day at which Pss. 113–118 were sung. **12:** *Not even enough living:* exaggeration of Num. 33.3–4. **15:** *Word* of God is personified as the effective executor of God's will. Compare "God said" of Gen. 1.2–29. **17–19:** The content has no foundation in the Exodus story but is an embellishment of it. *Appalled the godless:* the firstborn who were to die. See Exod. 12.28–30.

18.20–25: The Israelite plague of death was stayed by Aaron (Num. 16.44–50).

19.1–21: God worked wonders at the time of the Exodus. The wicked Egyptians were grieved by them and cloud that overshadowed the camp, at dry land emerging where before was only water, at an open road leading out of the Red Sea, and a grassy plain in place of stormy waves, 8 across which the whole nation passed under the protection of your hand, after witnessing amazing portents. 9 They were like horses at pasture, like skipping lambs, as they praised you, O Lord, by whom they were rescued. 10 They still remembered their life in a foreign land: how instead of cattle the earth bred lice, and instead of fish the river disgorged swarms of frogs; 11 and how, at a later stage, they had seen a new sort of bird when, driven by appetite, they had begged for delicacies to eat, 12 and for their relief quails came up from the sea.

13 On the sinners, however, punishment came, heralded by violent thunderbolts. They suffered justly for their own wickedness, because their hatred of strangers was on a new level of bitterness. 14 While others there had been who refused to welcome strangers when they came to them, these made slaves of guests who were their benefactors. 15 There will indeed be a judgement for those whose reception of foreigners was hostile; 16 but these, after a festal welcome, oppressed with hard labour men who had earlier shared their rights. 17 They were struck with blindness also, like the men at the door of the one good man, when yawning darkness fell upon them and each went groping for his own doorway.

18 As the strings of a harp can make various tunes with different names though each string retains its own pitch, so the elements combined among themselves in different ways, as can be accurately inferred from the observation of what happened. 19 Land animals took to the water and creatures that swim migrated to dry land; 20 fire retained its normal power even in water, and water forgot its fire-quenching properties. 21 Flames on the other hand failed to consume the flesh of perishable creatures that walked in them, and the substance of heavenly food, like ice and prone to melt, no longer melted.

22 In everything, O Lord, you have made your people great and glorious, and in every time and place you have been their unfailing helper.

the Israelites liberated. **2:** See Exod. 12.31–33; 14.23–28. **10:** Read Exod. ch. 8. **12:** As usual, the murmurings of the Israelites prior to the *quails* are omitted. See 16.2 n. **13:** There are no *thunderbolts* in Exod. ch. 14, but see Ps. 77.16–19 and Josephus, *Ant.* II.16.3. **14:** *Others* are the Sodomites, Gen. ch. 19. **16:** The Israelites were given a *festal welcome* in Egypt at the time of Joseph (Gen. 47.1–12) and were *oppressed with hard labour* by a later Pharaoh (Exod. 1.8–11). **17:** Gen. 19.11; Exod. 10.21–23. **18–21:** God, dealing with the *elements* of nature as a musician with a *harp*, arranges and rearranges them to achieve the wonderful result.

19.22: The conclusion. God directs Israel's history.

Ecclesiasticus

OR THE WISDOM OF JESUS
SON OF SIRACH

Ecclesiasticus, literally meaning a "church book," is so called either because it was used extensively in church worship or because the early Christian church rather than the synagogue received it into the canon. It is the work of a Jewish Wisdom teacher of about 180 B.C.E. The book, also called the Wisdom of Sirach, or ben Sirach, or simply Sirach, after its author, Jesus the son of Sirach (see 50.27), stands in the Wisdom tradition of Proverbs, which, attempting to discover the patterns at work in the circumstances of human life, concludes that wisdom is God's gift. But unlike the sages of Proverbs, the author is also a close student of the Jewish Scriptures, especially the Torah (the Law). His work represents a fusion of wisdom and scribal piety.

Written in Hebrew, the original text was lost in the early centuries C.E. About two-thirds of the book in Hebrew was rediscovered in Cairo around 1896. Since then other partial Hebrew manuscripts have been found, among them short fragments in the Judean desert at Qumran and Masada; these discoveries seem to indicate that the Hebrew text of Cairo, though not identical with the original, does derive from the original text, not from a retranslation from the Greek, as was once supposed. The present English translation is made from the Greek version prepared by the author's grandson (see Preface and notes) but is influenced by the recent Hebrew finds. At many points the books had been expanded by later additions, and the omission of these additions from this translation explains why the verse numbers are not always in consecutive order.

Preface

A LEGACY of great value has come down to us through the law, the prophets, and the writers who followed in their steps, and Israel deserves recognition for its traditions of learning and wisdom. It is the duty of those who study the scriptures not only to become expert themselves, but also to use their scholarship for the benefit of the world outside through both the spoken and the written word. For that reason my grandfather Jesus, who had applied himself diligently to the study of the law, the prophets, and the other writings of our ancestors, and had gained a considerable proficiency in them, was moved to compile a book of his own on the themes of learning and wisdom, in order that, with this further help, scholars might make greater progress in their studies by living as the law directs.

You are asked, then, to read with sympathetic attention, and to make allowances wherever you think that, in spite of all the devoted work that has been put into the translation, some of the expressions I have used are inadequate. For what is said in Hebrew does not have the same force when

Preface. The preface was written by the grandson of the author of Ecclesiasticus, when he translated the book into Gk. for the use of Egyptian Jews who did not know Heb. It mentions the three divisions of the Heb. Scriptures: *the law, the prophets, and the other writings;* this is the earliest reference to the third division of the canon, though the limits of the *writings* were not to be defined for another two centuries; see Lk. 24.44. The translator, like the author, closely associates wisdom and study of Scripture. He asserts that a scholar should work not only for fellow specialists but for the *world outside;* the translator speaks of his grandfather but is also thinking of his own work. The *thirty-eighth year* of *King* Ptolemy *Euergetes* II Physcon of Egypt (one of the longest reigns in Egypt) was 132 B.C.E. This puts the original composition of Ecclus. about 180 B.C.E, shortly before the Maccabean uprising.

translated into another tongue. Not only the present work, but even the law itself, as well as the prophets and the other writings, are not a little different when spoken in the original.

When I came to Egypt and settled there in the thirty-eighth year of the reign of King Euergetes, I found much scope for giving instruction; and I thought it very necessary to spend some energy and labour on the translation of this book. Ever since then I have applied my skill night and day to complete it, and to publish it for the use of those who have made their home in a foreign land, and wish to study and so train themselves to live according to the law.

The ways of wisdom

1 ALL wisdom is from the Lord;
  she dwells with him for ever.
2 Who can count the sands of the sea,
  the raindrops, or the days of unending time?
3 Who can measure the height of the sky,
  the breadth of the earth, or the depth of the abyss?
4 Wisdom was first of all created things;
  intelligent purpose has existed from the beginning.
6 To whom has the root of wisdom been revealed?
  Who has understanding of her subtlety?
8 One alone is wise, the Lord most terrible,
  seated upon his throne.
9 It is he who created her, beheld and measured her,
  and infused her into all his works.
10 To everyone he has given her in some degree,
  but without stint to those who love him.

11 THE fear of the Lord brings honour and pride,
  cheerfulness and a garland of joy.
12 The fear of the Lord gladdens the heart;
  it brings cheerfulness and joy and long life.
13 Whoever fears the Lord, it will be well with him at the last,
  and on the day of his death blessings will be his.
14 The beginning of wisdom is the fear of the Lord;
  she is created with the faithful in their mother's womb,
15 she has built an everlasting home among mortals,
  and with their descendants she will keep faith.
16 The full measure of wisdom is the fear of the Lord;
  she gives to mortals deep draughts of her wine.
17 She fills her home with all that the heart can desire,
  and her storehouses with her produce.
18 Wisdom's garland is the fear of the Lord,
  flowering with peace and perfect health.
19 She showers down knowledge and discernment,
  and bestows high honour on those who hold fast to her.

1:3 **of the abyss:** *prob. rdg; Gk adds* or wisdom.
1:4 **from the beginning:** *some witnesses add* 5The fountain of wisdom is God's word on high, and her ways are eternal commandments. 1:6 **of her subtlety:** *some witnesses add* 7Who has discovered all that wisdom knows, or understood her wealth of experience?

1.1–10: The source of wisdom. The two major divisions of the book (chs. 1–23 and 24–51) are each introduced by a poem in praise of wisdom. See 24.1–22; Prov. 8.1–31; Job 28.1–28. **1:** *Wisdom* includes the knowledge of human beings (both practical and ethical), nature, and God. **2–3:** The immeasurability of nature suggests the infinite depth of wisdom. **4:** *Wisdom* existed before the creation and informs it (see v. 9); it was later identified with the divine creative word; Jn. 1.1–3. **6–10:** Against the tendency to make wisdom a human achievement, Ecclus. repeatedly (as here) affirms that it is God's gift. **10:** *Those who love him:* God's people Israel; see 24.7–8.

1.11–20: The definition of wisdom. Though much in Ecclus. is secular common sense, this poem equates the core of wisdom with the loyal and joyful reverence for the God of Israel. **11:** *The fear of the Lord:* reverent acceptance of God's lordship. **13:** Life's basic fairness to the wise person will be shown, if only *on the day of his death* (see 11.28). **15:** The *everlasting home* of wisdom is specifically Israel; see 24.7–8. **16–20:** The reward of wisdom is a full life in the present world; contrast such full life here with v. 13.

20 Wisdom is rooted in the fear of the
    Lord,
  and long life grows on her branches.

22 Unjust rage can never be excused;
  when anger tips the scale it is a person's
    downfall.
23 Until the right moment comes, he who
    is patient restrains himself,
  and afterwards cheerfulness breaks
    through again;
24 until the right moment he keeps his
    thoughts to himself,
  and later his good sense is on
    everyone's lips.
25 In wisdom's treasure house are wise
    proverbs,
  but godliness is detestable to a sinner.
26 If you long for wisdom, keep the
    commandments,
  and the Lord will give it you without
    stint.
27 The fear of the Lord is wisdom and
    instruction;
  fidelity and gentleness are his delight.
28 Do not disregard the fear of the Lord
  or approach him without sincerity.
29 Do not act a part before the eyes of the
    world;
  keep guard over your lips.
30 Never be arrogant, or you will fall
  and bring disgrace on yourself;
  the Lord will reveal your secrets
  and humble you before the assembly,
  because what prompted you was not the
    fear of the Lord:
  guile filled your heart.

2 My son, if you aspire to be a servant
   of the Lord,
prepare yourself for testing.

2 Set a straight course and keep to it,
  and do not be dismayed in the face of
    adversity.
3 Hold fast to him and never let go,
  if you would end your days in
    prosperity.
4 Bear every hardship that is sent you,
  and whenever humiliation comes, be
    patient;
5 for gold is assayed in the fire,
  and the chosen ones in the furnace of
    humiliation.
6 Trust him and he will help you;
  steer a straight course and fix your
    hope on him.

7 You that fear the Lord, wait for his
    mercy;
  do not stray, for fear you will fall.
8 You that fear the Lord, trust in him,
  and you will not be baulked of your
    reward.
9 You that fear the Lord, hope for
    prosperity
  and lasting joy and favour.
10 Consider the past generations and see:
  was anyone who trusted the Lord ever
    disappointed?
  Was anyone who stood firm in the fear
    of him ever abandoned?
  Did he ever ignore anyone who called
    to him?
11 For the Lord is compassionate and
    merciful;
  he forgives sins and saves in time of
    trouble.

12 Woe to faint hearts and nerveless hands

1:20 **on her branches:** *some witnesses add* 21 The fear of
the Lord drives away sins, and wherever it dwells it
averts his anger.   1:30 **because . . . the Lord:** *or*
because you had no concern for the fear of the Lord.

1.22–30: Signs of wisdom. 22–23: Self-control (*restrains himself*) is such a sign (see 6.2–4). **26–28:** Here,
as in the preceding poem (1.11–20), wisdom is identified with reverence. **29–30:** Public *disgrace* is a severe
punishment; one's reputation is a frequent theme.

    2.1–6: Testing and endurance. Testing of one's wholehearted devotion to God is here the central meaning
of suffering (as in 4.17; 33.1; Job chs. 1–2), in contrast to discipline for past transgressions (Prov. 3.11–12;
Job 5.17–19). **1:** *My son:* the usual address of teacher to student (Prov. 1.8). **3:** Though reward may be delayed,
the righteous will be vindicated before they *end* their *days*. **5:** Human beings and *gold* alike show their
wholeness through testing.

    2.7–11: God's promise confirmed by experience. Three lines beginning *You that fear the Lord* are balanced
by three with *Those who fear the Lord* (vv. 15–17); three *Woe*'s set in between complete the pattern
(vv. 12–14). **10:** The history of *the past generations* is part of the evidence of experience; see Job 8.8–10.

    2.12–14: Woe to the inconsistent. 12: The indecisiveness of a *double life* and of those who are *faint* and

and to the sinner who leads a double life!

13 Woe to the feeble-hearted! They have no faith,
and therefore will go unprotected.
14 Woe to you who have given up the struggle!
What will you do at the Lord's coming?

15 Those who fear the Lord never disobey his words,
and all who love him keep to his ways.
16 Those who fear the Lord try to do his will,
and all who love him steep themselves in the law.
17 Those who fear the Lord will always be ready;
they humble themselves before him and say,
18 'Let us fall into the Lord's hands, not into the hands of men,'
for his majesty is equalled by his mercy.

3 CHILDREN, listen to me, for I am your father;
do what I tell you, that you may be safe.
2 The Lord has given the father honour in his children's eyes
and confirmed a mother's rights in the eyes of her sons.
3 Respect for a father atones for sins;
4 to honour your mother is like laying up treasure.
5 He who respects his father will be made happy by children,
and when he prays, he will be heard.
6 He who honours his father will have a long life,
and he who obeys the Lord gives comfort to his mother;

7 he submits to his parents as though he were their servant.

8 Honour your father by deed and word,
so that you may receive his blessing;
9 for a father's blessing strengthens his children's houses,
but a mother's curse uproots their foundations.
10 Never seek honour at the cost of discredit to your father;
how can his discredit bring honour to you?
11 A man gets honour from his father's honour;
a mother's dishonour is disgrace to her children.
12 My son, look after your father in his old age,
and as long as he lives do nothing to grieve him.
13 Even if his mind fails, make allowances
and do not despise him because you are in your prime.
14 If you support your father it will never be forgotten
and will stand to your credit against your sins;
15 when you are in trouble, it will be remembered in your favour,
and your sins will melt away like frost in sunshine.
16 To leave your father in the lurch is like blasphemy;
to curse your mother is to provoke your Creator's wrath.

17 My son, in all you do be unassuming,
and those whom the Lord approves will love you.

---

feeble-hearted (v. 13) contrasts with the wholehearted decision of those who trust the Lord.
2.15–18: The character of the reverent. 15: From parallelism of the two poetic lines it is clear that *fear* and *love* of God are synonymous. **16:** The *law* of Israel is associated with wisdom throughout Ecclus., in contrast to Prov. **18:** See 2 Sam. 24.14; in contrast to Prov., Ecclus. refers frequently to God's *mercy*.
3.1–16: Respect for parents. The topic is drawn both from the sages (Prov. 10.1) and especially from the Law (Exod. 20.12; Deut. 5.16). **1:** *Safe*, lit. "saved," means doing well in this world. **2:** God's gift of position to parents joins divine authority to that of the teacher. The *mother's rights* are asserted with the father's. **3:** Atoning *for sin* here and in v. 30 means that a good deed cancels out a bad one; see vv. 14–15 and Dan. 4.27. **16:** Deserting one's parents is considered to be as serious as *blasphemy;* see Exod. 21.17. *Your Creator's wrath* is an expression of God's role in retribution. In closing, the poem returns to God's will, with which it began.
3.17–24: Need for humility. Students of the sages were often from wealthy and successful families; see v. 18.

18 The greater you are, the humbler must
    you be,
  and the Lord will show you favour;
20 for his power is great,
    yet he reveals his secrets to the humble.
21 Do not pry into things too hard for you
  or investigate what is beyond your
    reach.
22 Meditate on what the Lord has
    commanded;
  what he has kept hidden need not
    concern you.
23 Do not busy yourself with matters that
    are beyond you;
  even what has been shown you is above
    the grasp of mortals.
24 Many have been led astray by their
    theorizing,
  and evil imaginings have impaired their
    judgements.

26 Stubbornness will come to a bad end,
  and he who flirts with danger will lose
    his life.
27 Stubbornness brings a load of troubles;
    the sinner piles sin on sin.
28 When calamity befalls the arrogant,
    there is no cure;
  wickedness is too deeply rooted in
    them.

29 A sensible person will take a proverb to
    heart;
  an attentive audience is the desire of
    the wise.
30 As water quenches a blazing fire,
    so almsgiving atones for sin.
31 He who repays a favour is mindful of
    his future;
  when he is falling, he will have support
    at hand.

4 My son, do not cheat a poor person of
    his livelihood
  or keep him waiting with hungry eyes.
2 Do not tantalize one who is starving
  or drive him to desperation in his need.
3 If someone is desperate, do not add to
    his troubles
  or keep him waiting for the charity he
    asks.
4 Do not reject the appeal of someone in
    distress
  or turn your back on the poor;
5 when one begs for alms, do not look
    the other way,
  so giving him cause to curse you,
6 for if he curses you in his bitterness,
    his Creator will hear his prayer.
7 Make yourself popular in the assembly,
    and show deference to the great.
8 When anyone who is poor speaks to
    you, give him your attention
  and answer his greeting courteously.
9 Rescue the downtrodden from the
    oppressor
  and be firm when giving a verdict.
10 Be as a father to the fatherless
  and like a husband to their mother;
    then the Most High will call you his
    son,
  and greater than a mother's love will be
    his love for you.

11 WISDOM raises her sons to greatness
    and gives help to those who seek her.
12 To love her is to love life;
  those who rise early to greet her will be
    filled with joy.

3:18 **show you favour:** *some witnesses add* 19Many are
high and illustrious, but he reveals his secrets to the
humble.   3:24 **their judgements:** *some witnesses add*
25Without the apple of the eye, light is lacking; without
knowledge, wisdom is lacking.

21–24: The warning may be against Greek philosophy or against Jewish apocalyptic speculation. *What the Lord has commanded* — the Law — is sufficient study for one who is wise.

3.26–31: The stubborn and the sensible person. The destructive consequences of not following the warnings of vv. 17–24 are in contrast to the success of the teachable person. **28:** *Calamity* will not work a *cure*, i.e. repentance in the *arrogant*.

4.1–6: Responsibility to the poor. 1–2: Compare the proverb, "He who gives quickly gives twice." **6:** The curse was a prayer of special potency; see Num. 22.1–6.

4.7–10: On being a leader. Leadership requires concern for, and courtesy to, rich and poor alike. **10:** One becomes a *son* of God by acting as God does.

4.11–19: Wisdom gives life. The rewards of *greatness* (v. 11), *honour* (v. 13), and security (v. 15) are summed up as *life* (v. 12). **11:** *Sons:* those who put *wisdom* into practice, i.e. wisdom's disciples. **12:** The comparison of wisdom to an attractive woman was widespread (see Prov. chs. 8–9), and the more striking since the danger

13 He who holds fast to her will gain
   honour;
   the Lord's blessing rests on the house
   she enters.
14 To serve her is to serve the Holy One,
   and the Lord loves those who love her.
15 He who is obedient to her will give true
   judgement,
   and, because he listens to her, his home
   will be secure.
16 If he trusts her, he will possess her
   and bequeath her to his descendants.
17 At first she will lead him by tortuous
   ways,
   filling him with craven fears.
   Her discipline will be a torment to him,
   and her decrees a hard test,
   until he trusts her with all his heart;
18 then she will come straight back to him,
   bringing gladness and revealing to him
   her secrets.
19 But if he strays, she will abandon him
   and leave him to his fate.

20 BE on your guard at all times and
   beware of evil;
   do not be over-modest in your own
   cause,
21 for there is a modesty that leads to sin,
   as well as a modesty that brings honour
   and favour.
22 Do not be untrue to yourself in
   deference to another,
   or diffident to your own undoing.
23 Never remain silent when a word might
   put things right,
   and do not hide your wisdom,
24 for it is by the spoken word that
   wisdom is known,
   and learning finds expression in
   speech.
25 Do not argue against the truth,
   but have a proper sense of your own
   ignorance.

26 Never be ashamed to admit your
   mistakes,
   and do not try to swim against the
   current.
27 Do not let yourself be a doormat to a
   fool
   or curry favour with the powerful.
28 Fight to the death for truth,
   and the Lord God will fight on your
   side.

29 Do not be forward in your speech
   while slack and feeble in deeds.
30 Do not play the lion in your home
   or swagger among your servants.
31 Do not keep your hand wide open to
   receive,
   but closed when it is time to repay.

5 Do not rely on your money
   and say, 'This makes me
   self-sufficient.'
2 Do not yield to every impulse you can
   gratify
   or follow the desires of your heart.
3 Do not say, 'I have no master';
   the Lord, you may be sure, will call you
   to account.
4 Do not say, 'I sinned, yet nothing
   happened to me';
   it is only that the Lord is very patient.
5 Do not be so confident of pardon
   that you pile up sin on sin;
6 do not say, 'His compassion is so great
   he will pardon my sins, however many.'
   To him belong both mercy and anger,
   and sinners feel the weight of his
   retribution.
7 Turn back to the Lord without delay,
   and do not defer action from one day
   to the next;
   for the Lord's anger can suddenly pour
   out,

4:13 **she:** or he.

of a woman's lure was also a standard motif (9.2–9). **14:** Wisdom is not only common sense, it is also the worship of *the Holy One*. **17:** Nowhere else is the anguish of wisdom's *discipline* put so sharply; but see 6.18–21. **18:** Wisdom is not a public knowledge, but imparts its *secrets* to the few who earn it (39.7; Job 11.6).

4.20–31: False and inadequate humility. Just as true humility is praised (3.17–24), so both false humility, vv. 20–28, and its opposite, the fault of arrogance, vv. 29–31, are condemned. *Truth* (vv. 25, 28) is the balance. **26:** To try to justify one's *mistakes* is as useless as swimming against the *current*.

5.1–8: Reliance on God. Three sections (4.20–31; 5.1–7; 5.8–6.4) are held together by the frequent use of the negative command. In 5.1–6, six negatives show false bases of trust. **1:** *Do not rely:* this ties 5.1 to 5.8. **7:** Turning *back to the Lord* gives the true basis of trust. Though a delay of justice may be observed, nevertheless God will repay in this life.

and at the time of reckoning you will perish.

8 Do not rely on ill-gotten gains,
for they will not avail on the day of calamity.

Wisdom in human relations

9 Do NOT winnow in every wind
or walk along every path:
this is the mark of duplicity.

10 Stand firmly by what you know,
and be consistent in what you say.

11 Be quick to listen,
but over your answer take time.

12 Give an answer if you know what to say,
but if not, hold your tongue.

13 Through speaking come both honour and dishonour,
and the tongue can be its owner's downfall.

14 Do not get a name for tale-bearing
or lay traps with your tongue,
for, as there is shame in store for the thief,
so there is harsh censure for duplicity.

15 Avoid all faults, both great and small.

6 Do not change from a friend into an enemy,
for a bad name earns shame and disgrace:
this is the mark of duplicity.

2 Never let violent passions rouse you;
they will tear you apart like a bull,

3 they will devour your foliage, destroy your fruit,
and leave you a withered tree.

4 Evil passion ruins anyone who harbours it,
and gives his enemies cause to gloat over him.

5 Pleasant words win many friends,
and affable talk makes acquaintance easy.

6 Live at peace with everyone:

accept advice, however, from but one in a thousand.

7 When you make a friend, begin by testing him,
and be in no hurry to give him your trust.

8 Some friends are loyal when it suits them
but desert you in time of trouble.

9 Some friends turn into enemies
and shame you by making the quarrel public.

10 Another may sit at your table
but in time of trouble is nowhere to be found;

11 when you are prosperous, he is your second self
and talks familiarly with your servants,

12 but if you come down in the world, he turns against you
and you will not see his face again.

13 Hold your enemies at a distance,
and keep a wary eye on your friends.

14 A faithful friend is a secure shelter;
whoever finds one, finds a treasure.

15 A faithful friend is beyond price;
there is no measure of his worth.

16 A faithful friend is an elixir of life,
found only by those who fear the Lord.

17 Whoever fears the Lord directs his friendship aright,
for he treats a neighbour as himself.

18 My son, seek wisdom's instruction while you are young,
and you will still find her when your hair turns white.

19 Come to her like a farmer who ploughs and sows;
then wait for the good fruits she supplies.
If you cultivate her, you will labour for a little while,
but soon you will be enjoying the harvest.

6:2 **they ... bull:** *prob. mng; Gk obscure.*

5.9–6.4: Sincerity, integrity, and self-control. 9: To *winnow in every wind* means to be an opportunist. **6.2–3:** Control of *passions* rather than their free expression is real vitality. **4:** *Enemies* who *gloat:* a form of punishment.

6.5–17: Friendship. 5: *Pleasant words:* contrast with 5.10–14. **6–15:** *Friends,* false and true, are nearly universal themes of secular wisdom. **16–17:** This common-sense section ends on the religious note, fear of *the Lord.* On treating the *neighbour* as oneself, see 31.15.

20 How harsh she seems to the
 uninstructed!
The fool cannot abide her;
21 like a boulder she tests and strains his
 strength,
and he is not slow to let her drop.
22 Wisdom well deserves her name;
she is not accessible to many.

23 Listen, my son: accept my opinion
and do not reject my advice.
24 Put your feet in wisdom's fetters
and your neck into her collar.
25 Stoop to carry her on your shoulders
and do not chafe at her bonds.
26 Come to her wholeheartedly,
and with all your might keep to her
 ways.
27 Follow her track, and she will make
 herself known;
once you have grasped her, do not let
 her go.
28 In the end you will find the
 refreshment she offers;
she will transform herself for you into
 joy:
29 her fetters will become your strong
 defence
and her collar a splendid robe.
30 Her yoke is a golden ornament
and her bonds a violet cord;
31 you will put her on like a splendid robe
and wear her like a garland of joy.

32 If it is your wish, my son, you will be
 instructed;
if you give your mind to it, you will
 become clever;
33 if you are content to listen, you will
 learn;
if you are attentive, you will grow
 wise.
34 When you stand among the assembled
 elders,
see who is wise and stick close by him.
35 Listen gladly to every godly
 conversation;

let no wise maxim escape you.
36 If you discover anyone who is wise, rise
 early to visit him;
let your feet wear out his doorstep.
37 Ponder the decrees of the Lord
and study his commandments at all
 times.
He will instruct your mind,
and your desire for wisdom shall be
 met.

7 Do NO evil, and no evil will befall you;
2 keep clear of wrong, and it will avoid
 you.
3 Do not sow in the furrows of injustice,
for fear of reaping a sevenfold crop.

4 Do not ask the Lord for high office
or the king for preferment.
5 Do not pose as righteous before the
 Lord
or act the sage in the king's presence.
6 Do not aspire to be a judge;
you may lack the strength to root out
 injustice,
or you may be intimidated by rank
and so compromise your integrity.
7 Do not commit an offence against the
 community
and so incur a public disgrace.
8 Do not pile up sin on sin,
for just one is enough to make you
 guilty.
9 Do not say, 'All my gifts to God will be
 taken into account;
when I make an offering to the Most
 High he will accept it.'
10 Do not grow weary of praying
or neglect almsgiving.
11 Never laugh at anyone in his bitter
 humiliation,
for there is One who both humbles and
 exalts.
12 Do not plot to deceive your brother
or do the like to your friend.

6:30 **Her yoke:** so *Heb.; Gk* Upon her.

6.18–7.3: The struggle for, and choice of, wisdom. (Compare with 4.11–19.) **21:** *Boulder* that *tests . . . his strength:* perhaps a training exercise. **22:** An obscure Heb. pun may lie behind this verse. **23–31:** Slavery to wisdom (*fetters, collar,* v. 24) becomes a princely status (vv. 29–31). For *refreshment* (v. 28) and *yoke* (v. 30; compare 51.26), see Matt. 11.28–30. **32–33:** The fourfold *if* emphasizes freedom of choice. **34–37:** To *listen* to the wise (vv. 34–36) and to *study* the Law (v. 37) bring the same wisdom.

7.4–17: Warnings against pride. In this series of imperatives, the interplay of common sense and faith is noteworthy. **5:** Action *before the Lord* is paralleled to that *in the king's presence.*

13 Refuse ever to tell a lie;
   it is a habit from which no good comes.
14 Do not be loquacious among the
      assembled elders,
   and when you pray do not repeat
      yourself.
15 Do not resent manual labour;
   work on the land was ordained by the
      Most High.
16 Do not enlist in the ranks of sinners;
   remember that retribution will not
      tarry.
17 Humble yourself to the uttermost,
   for the doom of the ungodly is fire and
      worms.

18 Do not part with a friend for gain,
   or a true brother for all the gold of
      Ophir.
19 Do not miss the chance of a wise and
      good wife;
   her attractions are worth more than
      gold.
20 Do not ill-treat a servant who works
      honestly
   or a hireling whose heart is in his work.
21 Regard a good servant with deep
      affection
   and do not withhold his freedom from
      him.
22 Have you cattle? Take care of them,
   and if they bring you profit, do not
      part with them.
23 Have you sons? Discipline them
   and break them in from their earliest
      years.
24 Have you daughters? Keep a close
      watch over them,
   and do not look on them with
      indulgence.
25 Marry off your daughter, and you will
      have done well;

but give her to a sensible husband.
26 If you have a wife after your own
      heart, do not divorce her;
   but do not trust yourself to one you
      cannot love.
27 Honour your father with all your heart
   and do not forget your mother's
      birth-pangs.
28 Remember that your parents brought
      you into the world;
   how can you repay them for all that
      they have done?

29 Reverence the Lord wholeheartedly
   and show respect to his priests.
30 Love your Maker with all your might
   and do not leave his ministers without
      support.
31 Fear the Lord and honour the priest,
   and give them their due as you have
      been commanded:
   the firstfruits, the guilt-offering, and
      the shoulder of the victim,
   the sacred grain-offering, and the
      firstfruits of holy things.

32 Be open-handed also with the poor,
   that your blessedness may be complete.
33 Every living being appreciates
      generosity;
   do not withhold kindness even from the
      dead.
34 Do not turn your back on those who
      weep,
   but mourn with those who mourn.
35 Do not hesitate to visit the sick,
   for by such acts you will win affection.
36 In whatever you are doing, remember
      the end that awaits you;

7:18 **gain:** *prob. rdg; Gk* a trifle.
7:31 **guilt-offering:** *or* reparation-offering. **sacred
grain-offering:** *lit.* sacrifice of consecration.

14: See Matt. 6.7. **15:** *Work on the land* was widely praised as honorable (see Gen. 2.15), but in 38.25 it is seen as in conflict with study. **17:** *Fire and worms:* the underlying Gk. differs from the Heb., which speaks rather of death (worms) as the fate of all, and not as punishment for the impious.

7.18–28: How to act in life's closest relationships. 18: *Ophir:* a well-known source for gold, perhaps in southwest Arabia; see 1 Kgs. 9.28. **19:** *Do not miss the chance:* Heb. lit. "do not reject," alludes to divorce; see v. 26 and Deut. 24.1. **22:** The only nonpersonal relationship in the list. **24–25:** Marriage was arranged by the father; until then *daughters* were kept under close supervision. **27–28:** Here gratitude is the motive for honoring parents; contrast 3.1–16.

7.29–36: Religious duties. 29–31: In contrast to Prov., the priests and formal worship are important to the author; compare 50.1–21. **32–35:** Other religious duties are care for the *poor* and *sick. Kindness* to the *dead* means providing proper burial; see Tob. 1.17. **36:** The same closing advice as in v. 17.

then all your life you will never go
wrong.

8 Do not pit yourself against the great,
for fear of falling into their power.
[2] Do not quarrel with the rich,
for fear they will outbid you;
for gold has brought ruin on many
and has perverted the minds of kings.
[3] Do not argue with a garrulous person
and so add fuel to his fire.
[4] Never make fun of the ill-mannered,
or you may hear your ancestors
insulted.
[5] Do not taunt a repentant sinner;
remember that we are all guilty.
[6] Despise nobody in his old age;
some of us are growing old as well.
[7] Do not gloat over the death of anyone;
remember we all must die.

[8] Do not neglect the discourse of the
wise,
but apply yourself to their maxims;
from these you will gain instruction
and learn how to serve the great.
[9] Attend to the discourse of your elders,
for they themselves learned from their
fathers;
they can teach you to understand
and to have an answer ready when you
need one.

[10] Do not fan a sinner's embers into a
blaze,
for fear of being burnt in the flames.
[11] Do not let anyone's insolence bring you
to your feet;
he is but waiting to trap you with your
own words.
[12] Do not lend to someone more powerful
than yourself,
or, if you do, write off the loan as a
loss.

[13] Do not stand surety beyond your
means,
and, when you do stand surety, be
prepared to pay.
[14] Do not go to law with a judge;
in deference to his position he will be
given the verdict.
[15] Do not go on a journey with a reckless
man,
for you may find him a burden;
he will take the way he fancies,
and through his folly you also will come
to ruin.
[16] Do not fall out with a hot-tempered
man
or travel with him across the desert;
he thinks nothing of bloodshed,
and where no help is at hand he will set
upon you.
[17] Never discuss your plans with a fool,
for he cannot keep anything to himself.
[18] Do nothing private in the presence of a
stranger;
you do not know what use he will make
of it.
[19] Do not tell what is in your mind to all
comers
or accept favours from them.

9 Do not be jealous over your dear wife;
what you teach her may cause you
harm.
[2] Do not surrender yourself to a woman
for her to trample your strength
underfoot.
[3] Do not go near a loose woman
or you may fall into her snares.
[4] Do not keep company with a
dancing-girl
or you may be caught by her advances.
[5] Do not stare at a virgin
or you may be trapped into paying
damages for her.

8.1–19: Behavior toward various people. This section deals with a wider circle than 7.18–28. **1–7:** Wisdom
advises caution in difficult relationships; see also vv. 10–19. **3:** See Prov. 26.21. **8–9:** In contrast, toward the
wise and the *elders,* one can be open. **8:** Training for the service of *the great,* i.e. government service, was
an age-old function of wisdom teaching; here the maxim may be merely traditional, or it may apply to the
defense of Jewish interests before Hellenistic rulers. **9:** The chain of tradition was important to the ancients.
15: Caution in traveling comes from the author's own experience; see 39.4; 51.13. **19:** Here, as throughout
the chapter, except in vv. 8–9, the clue to wisdom is withholding oneself.
9.1–9: Behavior toward women. All that follows, aside from v. 1, urges holding oneself back from trouble.
1: *Do not be jealous,* i.e. have confidence, is the only positive advice. **2:** *Do not surrender yourself:* probably
alludes to one's wife; a warning against too much confidence. **5:** *Damages* would be paid to her father (Exod.

⁶ Never surrender yourself to prostitutes,
for fear of losing all you possess.
⁷ Do not gaze about you in the city
streets
or wander in its unfrequented areas.
⁸ Do not let your eye linger on a comely
figure
or stare at beauty not yours to possess.
Many have been seduced by the beauty
of a woman;
it kindles passion like fire.
⁹ Never sit down with another man's wife
or join her in a drinking party,
for fear of succumbing to her charms
and slipping into fatal disaster.

¹⁰ Do not desert an old friend;
a new one is not on a par with him.
A new friend is like new wine:
until it has matured, you do not enjoy
it.
¹¹ Do not envy a bad man his success;
you do not know what is in store for
him.
¹² Take no pleasure in the pleasures of
the ungodly;
remember that before they die
punishment will overtake them.
¹³ Keep clear of a man who has power to
kill,
and you will not be haunted by the fear
of death;
but if you should approach him, make
no false step
or you will risk losing your life.
Be aware that you are moving among
pitfalls,
or walking on the battlements of the
city.
¹⁴ Take the measure of your neighbours
as best you can,
and accept advice from those who are
wise.
¹⁵ Let your discussion be with intelligent
men

and all your talk about the law of the
Most High.
¹⁶ At table choose the company of good
men
whose pride is in the fear of the Lord.

¹⁷ A craftsman is recognized by the skill
of his hands
and a councillor by his words of
wisdom.
¹⁸ A garrulous person is the terror of his
town,
and one who is unguarded in his
speech is detested.

10 A wise ruler instructs his people
and gives them sound and orderly
government.
² Like ruler, like ministers;
like sovereign, like subjects;
³ a king lacking instruction is his people's
ruin,
but sound judgement in a prince
upholds a city.

The exercise of wisdom

⁴ THE government of the world is in the
hand of the Lord;
at the right time he will find the right
man to rule it.
⁵ In the Lord's hand is all human
success;
it is he who confers honour on the
legislator.

⁶ Do not be angry with your neighbour
for every offence,
and do not resort to acts of insolence.
⁷ Arrogance is hateful in the sight of
God and man,
and injustice is offensive to both.
⁸ Because of injustice, insolence, and
greed,
empire passes from nation to
nation.

22.16–17; Deut. 22.29). Financial and social risks rather than personal loyalty in marriage are stressed.
   9.10–16: Social behavior. 11: God's justice and the uncertainty of life are held together in this statement.
13: *Walking on the battlements:* exposing oneself to deadly weapons.
   9.17–10.3: The skill of rulers. The language shifts from command to description. **17:** A leader is like a
craftsman. **10.1–3:** The ideal *ruler* is one who provides *sound and orderly government. King* was a traditional
term in Wisdom, here equivalent to *ruler;* the Jews had no king at this time.
   10.4–11.28: Rulership and pride. A series of poems on pride repeatedly alludes to the ruler as a model of
the person tempted to pride. First Samuel 2.1–10 may have suggested many of the themes in this section. **4–5:**
Babylonian and Egyptian kings also claimed to be appointed by God. **6–11:** Against pride which destroys both

9 What has a mortal to be so proud of?
  He is only dust and ashes,
  subject even in life to bodily decay.
10 A long illness mocks the doctor's skill;
  today's king is tomorrow's corpse.
11 When anyone dies, he comes into an
    inheritance
  of maggots and vermin and worms.
12 The beginning of pride is to forsake
    the Lord,
  when the human heart revolts against
    its Maker;
13 as its beginning is sin,
  so persistence in it brings on a deluge
    of depravity.
  Therefore the Lord inflicts signal
    punishments on the proud
  and brings them to utter disaster.

14 The Lord overturns the thrones of
    princes
  and installs the meek in their place.
15 The Lord uproots nations
  and plants the humble in their place.
16 The Lord lays waste the territory of
    nations,
  destroying them to the very
    foundations of the earth;
17 some he shrivels away to nothing,
  so that all memory of them vanishes
    from the earth.
18 Pride was not the Creator's design for
    man
  nor violent anger for those born of
    woman.

19 What creature is worthy of honour?
    Man.
  What men? Those who fear the Lord.
  What creature is worthy of contempt?
    Man.
  What men? Those who break the
    commandments.
20 The members of the family honour
    their head;
  the Lord honours those who fear
    him.
22 The convert, the stranger, and the
    poor —
  their pride is in the fear of the Lord.

23 It is not right to despise a poor man
  whose judgement is sound,
  and it is wrong to honour a rich man
  who is a sinner.
24 The mighty, the judge, and the prince
  win high renown,
  but none is as great as he who fears the
    Lord.
25 When a wise servant is waited on by
    free men,
  the sensible person will not protest.

26 Do NOT be too clever to do a day's work
  or give yourself airs when you have
    nothing to live on.
27 It is better to work and have more than
    enough
  than to be full of conceit on an empty
    stomach.
28 My son, be modest, but keep your
    self-respect
  and value yourself at your true worth.
29 Who will speak up for anyone who is
    his own enemy,
  or respect someone who disparages
    himself?
30 The poor may be honoured for good
    sense,
  the rich for wealth.
31 If someone is honoured in poverty,
  how much more in wealth!
  If he is dishonoured in wealth, how
    much more in poverty!

11 Someone poor but wise can hold
    his head high
  and take his seat among the great.

2 Do not overrate one person for his
    good looks
  or be repelled by another's appearance.
3 The bee is small among winged
    creatures,
  yet her produce takes first place for
    sweetness.
4 Do not brag about your fine clothes

10:9 **even ... decay:** *prob. mng, based on Heb.; Gk
obscure.*   10:20 **fear him:** *some witnesses add* 21Fear
the Lord, and you will be accepted; be obstinate and
proud, and you will be rejected.   10:22 **convert:** *so
Heb.; Gk rich.*   10:23 **rich:** *so Syriac; Gk omits.*

mortal (v. 9) and *nation* (v. 8), the poet points to death which levels all, even the *king* (vv. 10–11). **14–18:**
Compare Isa. 40.15–17, 23–24. **19:** The same answer to opposite questions was a teaching device. **25:** There
is no literal implication here of freeing the slave; contrast 7.21. **30–31:** In themselves *poverty* and *wealth* are
neutral as true values but wealth does make a difference in the way a person is treated. **11.2–6:** The

or be elated when honours come your
way.
Remember, the Lord can perform
marvels
which are hidden from mortal eyes:
5 many a king has been reduced to sitting
on the ground,
while crowns have gone where least
expected;
6 many a ruler has been stripped of
every honour,
and the eminent have found themselves
at the mercy of others.

7 Do not find fault before examining the
evidence;
think first, and criticize afterwards.
8 Do not answer without first listening,
and do not interrupt while another is
speaking.
9 Never take sides in a quarrel not your
own
or become involved in the disputes of
the wicked.

10 My son, do not engage in too many
transactions;
attempting too much, you will come to
grief;
in pursuit you will not overtake;
in flight you will not escape.
11 One person slaves and toils and presses
on,
and yet falls farther behind.
12 Another is slow and in need of help,
poor in strength, rich only in poverty;
yet the Lord turns on him a kindly eye,
lifts him up out of his miserable plight,
13 and, to the amazement of many, raises
him to dignity.

14 Good fortune and bad, life and death,
poverty and wealth, all are from the
Lord.
17 His gifts to the devout endure;
his approval brings unending
prosperity.
18 Someone may grow rich by stinting and
sparing,

but what does he get for his pains?
19 When he says, 'I have earned my rest
and now I can live on my savings,'
he does not know how long it will be
before he must die and leave them to
others.

20 Stand by your contract and give your
mind to it;
grow old at your work.
21 Do not envy the wicked their
achievements;
trust the Lord and stick to your job,
for it is very easy for the Lord
to make the poor rich all in a moment.
22 Piety is rewarded by the Lord's blessing,
which blossoms in a single hour.
23 Do not say, 'What use am I?
What good can the future hold for
me?'
24 And do not say, 'I am self-sufficient;
nothing can ever go wrong for me.'
25 Hardship is forgotten in time of
prosperity,
and prosperity in time of hardship.
26 Even on the day a person dies it is easy
for the Lord
to give him what he deserves.
27 An hour's misery wipes out all memory
of delight,
and someone's end reveals how he has
lived.
28 Call no one happy before he dies,
for not until death is a person known
for what he is.

29 Do NOT invite all comers into your
home;
dishonesty wears many a guise.
30 A proud person's mind is like a decoy
partridge in its cage,
or like a spy watching for a false step;
31 he waits for a chance to twist good into
evil

11:14 **from the Lord:** *some witnesses add* 15From the
Lord come wisdom, understanding, and knowledge of
the law, love, and the doing of good works. 16Error
and darkness have been with sinners from their birth,
and evil grows old with them who delight in it.

unpredictability of life is a warning against pride. **7–9:** Discretion in judgment implies avoiding overinvolve-
ment. **10–13:** Overreaching oneself is self-destructive; compare vv. 2–6. **14–19:** God's gifts *endure* (v. 17);
one's own achievement may be snatched away (v. 19). **20–28:** This poem is a meditation on the popular
proverb, *Call no one happy before he dies* (v. 28). The skeptical proverb is given religious meaning.
    11.29–13.13: Caution against being taken advantage of. God is mentioned only in 12.2, 6 in this hard-

or to cast blame on praiseworthy
actions.
32 One spark kindles many coals,
and a plot laid by a bad man ends in
bloodshed.
33 Beware of a scoundrel and his evil
schemes,
or he may ruin your reputation forever.
34 Admit a stranger to your home and he
will stir up trouble
and estrange you from your own flesh
and blood.

12 If you do a good turn, make sure
to whom you are doing it;
then you will have credit for your
kindness.
2 A good turn done to a godfearing
person will be repaid,
if not by him, then by the Most High.
3 There is no prosperity for the
persistent wrongdoer
or for him who never gives alms.
4 Give to the godfearing, but never help
the sinner.
5 Keep your good works for the humble,
not the godless;
put away your bread, do not give him
any;
he will use your gift to get the better of
you,
and for every favour you have done
him
you will suffer a twofold injury;
6 for the Most High himself hates sinners
and sends the ungodly what they
deserve.
7 Give to anyone who is good, but never
help a sinner.

8 Prosperity does not reveal your
friends,
nor does adversity conceal your
enemies.
9 When all goes well with someone his
enemies are friendly;
when things go badly even a friend will
shun him.
10 Never trust an enemy;

he will turn vicious as surely as bronze
corrodes.
11 Even if he appears humble and
cringing,
keep your distance and be on your
guard.
Behave towards him like someone who
polishes a mirror
to ensure it does not tarnish.
12 Do not place him by your side,
or he will trip you up and supplant
you;
do not seat him at your right hand,
or he will thrust you out and take your
place;
and in the end you will admit the force
of my words
and recall my warning with regret.
13 Who sympathizes with a snake-charmer
when he is bitten,
or with those who deal with wild
animals?
14 So is it with the person who keeps bad
company
and is involved in another's wickedness.
15 He may stand by you for a while,
but if your fortunes decline, his
friendship will not last.

16 An enemy speaks honeyed words,
but in his heart he plans to topple you
into the ditch.
He may have tears in his eyes,
but given the chance he will not stop at
bloodshed.
17 If disaster overtakes you, you will find
him there ahead of you,
and while pretending to help, he will
catch you by the heel.
18 Then he will wag his head and rub his
hands
and with many a whispered slander
reveal his true colours.

13 Handle pitch and it will make you
dirty;
associate with the arrogant and you will
grow like them.
2 Do not lift a weight too heavy for you,

headed, practical section. **12.1–7:** Reciprocity in good deeds is urged. God's hatred of *sinners* is the motivation for the advice, *never help a sinner* (vv. 6–7); contrast Ezek. 18.23. **11:** The *mirror* was of metal and needed constant polishing; likewise, constant vigilance is the only protection from the corrosion (v. 10) of the enemy's wiles. **12:** The reference to *my warning* is a threat of "I told you so" from the teacher. **18:** *Wag his head:* a gesture of triumphant derision. **13.1:** The first line has become an English proverb. **2:** The *jug* of clay would

nor associate with someone greater and
richer than yourself.
How can a jug be friends with a kettle?
If they knock together, it will be
smashed.
3 A rich person does wrong, and then
adds insult to injury;
a poor person is wronged, and must
apologize into the bargain.
4 If you can serve his turn, a rich person
will exploit you,
but if you are in need, he will drop
you.
5 If you are in funds, he will be your
constant companion
and without a twinge of remorse drain
you dry.
6 He may need you, and then he will
deceive you
and be all smiles and encouragement,
paying you compliments and asking,
'What can I do for you?'
7 embarrassing you with his hospitality,
until he has drained you two or three
times over;
but he will end up by laughing at you.
Afterwards, when he sees you, he will
pass you by
and wag his head over you.

8 Take care not to be led astray
and humiliated when you are enjoying
yourself.
9 If a great man invites you, be slow to
accept,
and he will be the more pressing in his
invitation.
10 Do not push yourself forward, for fear
of a rebuff,
but do not keep aloof, or you may be
forgotten.
11 Do not presume to converse with him
as an equal,
and put no trust in his effusive
speeches;
the more he speaks, the more he is
testing you,
weighing you up even while he smiles.
12 The person who betrays a confidence is
without compunction

and will not spare you injury or
imprisonment.
13 Confide in no one and be on your
guard,
for you are walking with disaster.

15 Every living thing loves its like,
and every person his own sort.
16 All creatures flock together with their
kind,
and human beings stick close to their
fellows.
17 What has a wolf in common with a
lamb,
or a sinner with someone who fears
God?
18 What peace can there be between hyena
and dog,
what peace between rich and poor?
19 As lions prey on the wild asses of the
desert,
so the rich live off the poor.
20 As humility disgusts the proud,
so the rich are disgusted by the poor.

21 If a rich person staggers, he is steadied
by his friends;
a poor one falls, and his friends
promptly disown him.
22 When a rich person slips, many come
to his rescue;
if he says something outrageous, they
make excuses for him.
A poor one makes a slip, and at once
he is criticized;
even if he talks sense, he is not given a
hearing.
23 A rich person speaks, and all keep
silent;
then they praise his speech to the skies.
A poor one speaks, and they say, 'Who
is this?'
and if he stumbles, they push him
farther.

24 WEALTH untainted by sin is good;
poverty brought on by godless conduct
is evil.

13:13 **with disaster:** *some witnesses add* When you hear
this in your sleep, wake up! [14]Love the Lord all your
life, and appeal to him to keep you safe.

---

be broken by the metal *kettle*. **3–7:** The tactics of the *rich* require constant guard. **9:** The *great man* is the
political authority who is trying to extract information; see vv. 12–13.

13.15–23: The incompatibility of rich and poor. 21–23: Society readily supports the rich; compare v. 3
and contrast 10.23–24.

²⁵ It is the heart that changes the look on
the face
either for better or for worse.
²⁶ A cheerful face betokens someone in
good heart,
but the invention of proverbs involves
wearisome thought.

14 Happy is the one who has never let
slip a careless word,
who has never felt the sting of remorse!
² Happy is the one whose conscience
does not accuse him,
whose hopes have never been dashed!

³ Meanness and wealth do not go well
together:
what use is money to a miser?
⁴ He deprives himself only to hoard for
others;
on his possessions someone else will
lead a life of luxury.
⁵ How can anyone who is hard on
himself be kind to others?
His money brings him no enjoyment.
⁶ No one is worse than he who is
grudging to himself:
his niggardliness is its own retribution.
⁷ If ever he does good, he does it by
mistake,
and his villainy comes out at the finish.
⁸ He is hard who has a grudging eye,
who turns his back on need and looks
the other way.
⁹ The covetous eye is not satisfied with its
share;
greedy injustice shrivels the soul.
¹⁰ Someone with a miserly outlook
begrudges bread
and keeps a bare table.

¹¹ My son, treat yourself well if you can
afford it,
and present worthy sacrifices to the
Lord.

¹² Remember that death will not tarry;
the hour of your appointment with the
grave is undisclosed.
¹³ Before you die, treat your friend well;
reach out as far as you can to help him.
¹⁴ Do not miss a day's enjoyment
or forgo your share of innocent
pleasure.
¹⁵ Are you to leave to others all you have
laboured for
and let them draw lots for your
hard-earned wealth?
¹⁶ Give and take; pamper yourself;
expect no luxury in the grave.
¹⁷ The body wears out like a garment;
for the age-old sentence stands: you
shall die.
¹⁸ In the thick foliage of a spreading tree
some leaves fall and others grow in
their stead;
so too with the generations of flesh and
blood;
one dies and another comes to birth.
¹⁹ All human works decay and vanish,
and the worker follows them into
oblivion.

²⁰ HAPPY is he who gives his mind to
wisdom
and meditates on understanding;
²¹ happy is he who reflects on her ways
and ponders her secrets!
²² Stalk her like a hunter
and lie in wait by her paths.
²³ He who peeps in at her window
and listens at her door,
²⁴ who camps beside her house,
driving his tent-peg into her wall,
²⁵ who pitches his tent close by her,
having found a good place to live —
²⁶ that man will put his children under
her shade
and camp beneath her branches;
²⁷ sheltered by her from the heat,

13.24–14.2: True contentment. The harsh facts of the preceding section are balanced by the thought that
true happiness comes from within.

14.3–19: Wrong and right uses of money. 3–10: Money is useless to someone who is mean or to a *miser;*
it is a basic conviction of the author that if you cannot be good to yourself, you cannot be good to others; see
v. 5. **12:** The *grave:* lit. Hades, Heb. *Sheol,* the gloomy underworld. God knows the *hour* of death, but it is
hidden from human knowledge. **17:** The *age-old sentence:* see Gen. 2.17. **18:** Comparison of passing generations to falling *leaves* was widespread; compare Homer, *Iliad,* VI 145–50. **19:** Contrast Rev. 14.13.

14.20–15.10: The quest for wisdom. Compare with 4.11–19 and Prov. 8.32–9.6. **20:** *Happy* ("blessed" in
many earlier translations) introduces a set style of Wisdom speech which declares the way to the fullness of
life. **23:** *Peeps in:* is on familiar terms; contrast the etiquette of 21.23–24 ("a well-bred person stands outside").

he will dwell in her glory.

15 He who fears the Lord will act thus,
and if he masters the law, wisdom will be his.

2 She will come out to meet him like a mother;
she will receive him like a young bride.

3 For food she will give him the bread of understanding
and for drink the water of wisdom.

4 He will lean on her and will not fall,
he will rely on her and not be put to shame.

5 She will advance him above his neighbours
and find words for him when he speaks in the assembly.

6 He will be crowned with joy and exultation;
lasting renown will be his heritage from her.

7 Fools will never possess wisdom,
nor will sinners catch a glimpse of her.

8 She holds aloof from arrogance;
liars never call her to mind.

9 Praise is out of place on the lips of a sinner,
because it has not come from the Lord;

10 for praise is the outward expression of wisdom,
and the Lord himself prompts it.

11 Do not say, 'The Lord is to blame for my going astray';
it is for you to avoid what he hates.

12 Do not say, 'It was he who led me into error';
he has no use for a sinner.

13 The Lord hates every kind of vice;
you cannot love vice and still fear him.

14 When in the beginning God created the human race,

he left them free to take their own decisions:

15 if you choose, you can observe the commandments;
you can keep faith if you are so minded.

16 He has set before you fire and water:
reach out and make your choice.

17 Mortals are offered life or death:
whichever they prefer will be given them.

18 For great is the wisdom of the Lord;
he is mighty in power, all-seeing;

19 his eyes are on those who fear him;
no human action escapes his notice.

20 He has commanded no one to be impious;
to none has he given licence to sin.

16 Do NOT set your heart on a large family of ne'er-do-wells
or think yourself happy in sons who are godless.

2 However many your children, do not think yourself happy
unless the fear of the Lord is in them.

3 Do not count on their living to be old or rely on their number,
for one son can be better than a thousand.
Better indeed to die childless than to have ungodly children!

4 One person of good sense can establish a city,
but a tribe of lawless people can turn it into a desert.

5 Many such things have I seen with my own eyes,
and still weightier examples have come to my ears.

6 Where sinners assemble, fire breaks out;
retribution blazes up when a nation is disobedient.

24: The *tent peg*: a symbol of setting up a home. **15.1:** *Thus* ties 15.1–8 to 14.20–27. *Law* and *wisdom* coincide here as throughout the book. **6:** Compare this poetic glorification of the wise person with the pragmatic observation of wisdom's limits in 13.2–13. **9–10:** From wisdom springs *praise;* compare 1.11–20. *The sinner:* probably the Hellenized Jew careless about observation of the Law.

15.11–20: Freedom of choice. "Determinism" or "predestination" is strongly rejected, to make clear that God is not responsible for anyone's sin, which God *hates* (vv. 11, 13). **14–15:** The human race was created free and is still free; contrast Rom. 1.18–3.20; 7.1–25. **16–17:** Compare Deut. 30.19–20. **18–20:** Though God does not determine anyone's deeds, God's *eyes are on* the pious.

16.1–14: Retribution and reward. 1–3: A large family was held to be one of God's greatest gifts. **5:** *Seen*

7 There was no pardon for the giants of
old,
who rebelled in all their strength.
8 There was no reprieve for Lot's
adopted home,
abhorrent in its arrogance.
9 There was no mercy for the doomed
nation,
exterminated in its sin,
10 and no mercy for those six hundred
thousand warriors
assembled in stubborn defiance.
11 Even if there were but one stubborn
person,
it would be a miracle for him to escape
punishment,
for mercy and anger belong to the
Lord:
he shows his power now in forgiveness,
now in overflowing anger.
12 His mercy is great, but great also his
condemnation;
he judges each by what he has done.
13 He does not let the wrongdoer escape
with his plunder
or try the patience of the godly too
long.
14 He gives scope freely to his mercy,
and everyone is treated according to his
deeds.

17 Do not say, 'I am hidden from the
Lord;
who is there up above to give a thought
to me?
Among so many I shall not be noticed;
what am I in the immensity of
creation?'
18 Heaven itself, the highest heaven,
the abyss, and the earth are shaken at
his coming;
19 the mountains also and the foundations
of the world

quiver and tremble when he looks upon
them.
20 What mortal mind can grasp this
or comprehend his ways?
21 As a squall takes people unawares,
so his works for the most part are done
in secret.
22 'Who is to declare his acts of justice
or who will wait for them,
their fulfilment being so remote?'
23 These are the thoughts of a small
mind,
the absurdities of a senseless and
misguided person.

God in creation

24 My son, listen to me and acquire
knowledge;
pay heed to what I say.
25 I will offer you correct instruction
and teach you accurate knowledge.
26 When in the beginning the Lord
created his works
and, after making them, defined their
boundaries,
27 he disposed them in an eternal order
and fixed their domains for all time.
They do not grow hungry or weary,
or abandon their tasks;
28 one does not jostle another,
nor will they ever disobey his word.
29 Then the Lord looked at the earth
and filled it with his good things.
30 With every kind of living creature he
covered its surface,
and to the earth they must all return.

16:14 **his deeds:** *some witnesses add* 15The Lord made
Pharaoh too stubborn to acknowledge him, so that his
deeds might be published to the world. 16He displays
his mercy to the whole creation, and has assigned his
light and his darkness for human beings.

with my own eyes: the teacher's personal experience gives weight to tradition. **7:** The *giants:* see Gen. 6.4;
compare Bar. 3.26–28; Wisd. 14.6. **8:** *Lot's adopted home:* Sodom; see Gen. 19.23–25. **9:** *The doomed nation:*
the Canaanites; see Deut. 7.1–6 and Gen. 15.16. **10:** *Six hundred thousand:* rebellious Israelites; see 46.8;
Exod. 12.37; Num. 14.22–23. **11–14:** God's *mercy* and *anger* are in tension; the author is sure that mercy
will not provide an easy out for sinners.

16.17–23: God's universal knowledge. Only the *absurdities* of a *small mind* (v. 23) will lead to the wrong
view that anyone can escape God's notice because of the *immensity of God's creation* (v. 17).

16.24–30: God the Creator. This section, extending vv. 17–23, is drawn especially from Gen. ch. 1. **26–28:**
The orderly heavens are God's *works* (compare Isa. 40.26) which do not *grow hungry or weary.* **29–30:** In
contrast to the eternal heavens, the living beings on earth, even though *good,* are temporary.

17

The Lord created human beings
 from the earth
and to it he turns them back again.
2 He set a fixed span of life for mortals
and gave them authority over
 everything on earth.
3 He clothed them with power like his
 own
and made them in his own image.
4 He put the fear of them into all
 creatures
and granted them lordship over beasts
 and birds.
6 He fashioned tongues, eyes, and ears
 for them,
and gave them minds with which to
 think.
7 He filled them with understanding and
 knowledge
and showed them good and evil.
8 He kept watch over their hearts,
to display to them the majesty of his
 works.
10 They will praise his holy name,
proclaiming the grandeur of his works.
11 He gave them knowledge
and endowed them with the
 life-bringing law.
12 He established with them an everlasting
 covenant
and revealed to them his decrees.
13 Their eyes saw his glorious majesty,
and their ears heard the glory of his
 voice.
14 He said to them, 'Refrain from all
 wrongdoing,'
and he taught each his duty towards his
 neighbour.

15 Their conduct lies open before him at
 all times,

never hidden from his sight.
17 For every nation he appointed a ruler,
but Israel is the Lord's portion.
19 Whatever they do is as clear as the sun
 to him;
his eyes are always on their ways.
20 Their misdeeds are not hidden from
 the Lord;
he observes all their sins.
22 Charitable giving he treasures like a
 signet ring,
and kindness like the apple of his eye.
23 In the end he will arise and give the
 wicked their deserts,
bringing down retribution on their
 heads.
24 Yet he leaves a way open for the
 penitent to return to him
and endows the waverer with strength
 to endure.

25 Return to the Lord and have done with
 sin;
make your prayer in his presence and
 lessen your offence.
26 Come back to the Most High, renounce
 wrongdoing,
and hate intensely what he abhors.

17:4 **beasts and birds:** *some witnesses add* 5The Lord
gave them the use of the five faculties; as a sixth gift
he assigned to them mind, and as a seventh, reason,
the interpreter of those faculties.   17:8 **his works:**
some witnesses add 9To them it is given to boast for ever
of his marvels.   17:15–17 **his sight ... nation:** *some*
witnesses read his sight. 16Everyone from his youth
tended towards evil; they could not make themselves
hearts of flesh in place of their hearts of stone.
17When he dispersed the nations over all the earth, for
every nation.   17:17 **portion:** *some witnesses add* 18He
rears them with discipline as his firstborn, imparting to
them the light of love and never neglecting them.
17:20 **their sins:** *some witnesses add* 21The Lord who is
gracious and knows of what they are made has neither
rejected nor deserted them, but spared them.

17.1–14: God's creation of human beings. The recurring *He* (God) emphasizes that human beings are God's
creatures. **1:** The transitory nature of human beings links this poem to 16.24–30. **2–4:** Compare Gen. 1.26–28.
7: God showed all human beings *good and evil;* this knowledge links the universally human to the covenant
at Sinai (v. 12). **11:** The apex of creation is the *law,* which enables human beings to be fully human. **13:** *Glorious*
majesty: theophany on Sinai; see Exod. 19.16–19. **14:** *Duty towards* the *neighbour* is the core of the Law.

17.15–24: God's watchful care of God's people. This is the closing poem of the section beginning in 16.17,
the final answer to the absurdities of 16.17–23. **17:** A higher standard is set for *Israel,* which stands directly
under God, not under an earthly *ruler.* **23–24:** The familiar contrast between the righteous and the *wicked*
is modified by the introduction of the *penitent,* those who pass from the wicked group to the righteous. *Strength*
to endure: the phrase, from Isa. 40.31, ties the end of the section to its beginning, 16.17, which is drawn from
Isa. 40.27.

17.25–32: A call to repentance. This poem gives a practical application to what precedes. The sharp contrast

27 The living give him thanks,
but who will praise the Most High from
the grave?
28 When the dead cease to be, their
gratitude dies with them;
only when alive and well do they praise
the Lord.
29 How great is the Lord's mercy
and his forgiveness to those who turn
to him!
30 Not everything is within human reach,
for we are not immortal.
31 Is anything brighter than the sun? Yet
it suffers eclipse;
so flesh and blood have evil thoughts.
32 The Lord judges the armies of high
heaven,
and humankind, who are but dust and
ashes.

18 He who lives for ever is the
Creator of the whole universe;
2 the Lord alone will be proved supreme.
4 To whom is it given to unfold the story
of his works?
Who can fathom his mighty acts?
5 No one can measure his majestic power,
still less tell the full tale of his mercies.
6 They can neither be diminished nor
increased,
and the wonders of the Lord cannot be
fathomed.
7 When anyone finishes he is still only
beginning,
and when he stops he will still be at a
loss.

8 What is a human being, and what use is
he?
His good or evil deeds, what do they
signify?
9 His span of life is at the most a
hundred years;
10 compared with unending time, his few
years

are like one drop from the ocean or a
single grain of sand.
11 That is why the Lord is patient with
people;
that is why he lavishes his mercy upon
them.
12 He sees and knows the harsh fate in
store for them,
and therefore gives full play to his
forgiveness.
13 Their compassion is only for their own
kin,
but the Lord's compassion is for all
mankind.
He corrects, disciplines and teaches,
and brings them back as a shepherd
brings his flock.
14 He has compassion on those who accept
discipline
and are eager to obey his decrees.

Self-discipline

15 Do good, my son, but without scolding;
do not spoil your generosity with
hurtful words.
16 Does not the dew give respite from the
scorching heat?
So a word can do more than a gift.
17 Does not a kind word count for more
than a rich present?
With someone gracious you will find
both.
18 A graceless fool must always be
taunting,
and a grudging giver makes no eyes
sparkle.

19 Before you speak, learn;
before sickness comes, attend to your
health.

17:32 **The Lord ... ashes:** so *Syriac.* 18:2 **proved
supreme:** *some witnesses add* and there is none beside
him ³who can steer the world with a touch of his hand,
so that all things obey his will; as King of the universe,
he has power to fix the bounds between what is holy
and what is profane.

between human insignificance and God's greatness makes the point that pride is the basic sin. **27:** The *grave:*
see 14.12 n.

18.1–7: The limits of human knowledge. This poem expands the thought of 17.30–32.

18.8–14: God's compassion. 8: Contrast Ps. 8. **9:** The *hundred years* of a life span extend the seventy or
eighty of Ps. 90.10. **12:** The *harsh fate* is death. **13–14:** God is presented as a patient teacher; it is not accidental
that the author was a teacher himself.

18.15–18: The deed and the word. The theme of doing *good* is suggested by 18.13.

18.19–29: Looking ahead. Foresight is a central virtue of secular wisdom. **19:** The advice to *attend to your*

20 Before judgement, examine yourself,
   and you will find pardon in your hour
      of trial.
21 Before you fall ill, humble yourself;
   whenever you sin, show your penitence.
22 Let nothing hinder the prompt
      discharge of your vows;
   do not wait until death to be absolved.
23 Before you make a vow, give it due
      thought;
   do not be like those who try the Lord's
      patience.
24 Think of the wrath you must face in
      the hour of death,
   when the time of reckoning comes and
   he turns away his face.
25 Remember in time of plenty the time of
      famine,
   poverty and need in your days of
      wealth.
26 Between dawn and dusk times may
      alter;
   before the Lord all change comes
      quickly.
27 The wise are always on their guard;
   when sin is rife they will beware of
      negligence.
28 Everybody with sense makes
      acquaintance with wisdom,
   and to him who finds her she gives
      cause for thankfulness.
29 They who are trained in learning prove
      wise themselves
   and pour forth apt proverbs.

30 Do not let your passions be your guide;
   keep your lusts under control.
31 If you indulge yourself with all that
      passion fancies,
   it will give your enemies cause to gloat
      over you.
32 Do not revel in great luxury,
   or the expense of it may ruin you.
33 Squandering and drunkenness
   will leave you with nothing in your
      purse.

19 A drunken workman will never
         grow rich;

carelessness in small things leads by
   degrees to ruin.
2 Wine and women rob the wise of their
      wits,
   and a frequenter of prostitutes becomes
      more and more reckless;
3 decay and worms take possession of
      him;
   through his recklessness he is
      destroyed.

4 To trust anyone hastily shows a shallow
      mind,
   and to sin is to do oneself an injury.
5 To delight in wickedness is to court
      condemnation,
6 but evil loses its hold on him who hates
      gossip.
7 Never repeat what you hear,
   and you will never be the loser.
8 Tell no tales before friend or foe;
   unless silence makes you an accomplice,
      never betray a secret.
9 Suppose someone has heard you and
      learnt to distrust you,
   he will seize a chance to show his
      hatred.
10 Have you heard a rumour? Let it die
      with you.
   Never fear, it will not make you burst!
11 A fool with a rumour goes through
      agony
   like a woman in labour.
12 As painful as an arrow through the
      thigh
   is a rumour in the heart of a fool.
13 Put it to your friend; he may not have
      done it,
   or if he did, he will know not to do it
      again.
14 Put it to your neighbour; he may not
      have said it,
   or if he did, he will know not to say it
      again.
15 Put it to your friend; it will often turn
      out to be slander;
   so do not believe everything you
      hear.

health views illness in common-sense terms. **21:** Here illness is seen as punishment for sin. **24:** Since retribution, for Ecclus., is limited to this life, all will be repaid for their deeds before the *hour of death*. When God *turns away his face* from a person, it is always a sign of wrath; see Pss. 13.1; 44.24.
   18.30–19.17: Self-control. 30: The poem of 18.30–19.3 is a commentary on this popular proverb. **19.2:** *Wine and women* are frequently associated already in Egyptian wisdom. See Prov. 31.3–5. **4–17:** Self-control in speech is discussed in two sections: vv. 4–12 on not speaking and vv. 13–17 on proper speech, direct

16 Someone may let slip what he does not
    intend;
  is anyone's tongue free from guilt?
17 Put your case to your neighbour before
    you threaten him,
  and let the law of the Most High take
    its course.

20 All wisdom is the fear of the Lord
  and includes the fulfilling of the law.
22 To know about wickedness is not
    wisdom,
  nor is there good sense in the advice of
    sinners.
23 There is a cleverness that repels,
  and some fools are merely ignorant.
24 Better to lack brains and be godfearing
  than to have great intelligence and
    transgress the law.
25 A meticulous cleverness may lead to
    injustice,
  and crooked means may be used to
    uncover the right.
26 A scoundrel may bow his head and
    wear mourning,
  but at heart be an out-and-out fraud.
27 He hides his face and pretends to be
    deaf,
  but when no one is looking, he steals a
    march on you;
28 and if lack of strength prevents him
    from doing wrong,
  he will still harm you at the first
    opportunity.
29 You can tell a person by his appearance
  and recognize good sense at first
    sight.
30 His clothes, the way he laughs,
  his gait—these reveal his character.

20 A reproof may be untimely,
    and silence may show a man's good
    sense.
2 How much better to rebuke than to
  nurse one's anger!

Confession may save someone from
  losing face.
4 Like a eunuch longing to ravish a
    young girl
  is he who resorts to force to secure
    right.
5 One person is silent, and is reckoned to
    be wise;
  another chatters, and is detested for it.
6 There is the person who is silent, at a
    loss for an answer;
  another is silent, biding his time.
7 The wise are silent until the right
    moment,
  but a swaggering fool is always speaking
    out of turn.
8 The garrulous get themselves detested,
  and one who abuses his position
    arouses hatred.

9 SOME find profit in adversity,
  while good fortune may turn into loss.
10 Sometimes liberality does not benefit
    the giver;
  sometimes it brings a double return.
11 The quest for honour may lead some to
    loss of position,
  while others may rise from obscurity to
    eminence.
12 Someone may make a good bargain,
  yet pay for it seven times over.
13 A wise person endears himself when he
    speaks,
  but a fool makes himself agreeable to
    no purpose.

19:17 its course: some witnesses add without giving way
to anger. 18The fear of the Lord is the beginning of
acceptance by him, and wisdom wins love from him.
19The knowledge of the Lord's commandments is
discipline for life, and those who do what pleases him
pluck the fruit of the tree of immortality.
19:20 the law: some witnesses add and a knowledge of
his omnipotence. 21A servant who says to his master, 'I
will not do as you wish,' even if he does it later, angers
him who feeds him.   20:2 losing face: some witnesses
add 3How good it is to meet reproof with repentance,
and so escape deliberate sin!

confrontation of rumor. **17:** God's *law* is mentioned in closing, a typical pattern.

19.20–30: True wisdom and mere cleverness. This is the first of a series of observations; except for 21.1–11, after the initial reference (v. 20), God is not mentioned again until 23.1. Notice also the scarcity of imperatives. **22–28:** Clever knowledge (probably Hellenistic learning) that disregards God's *law* (v. 24) destroys human trust. Hiding the *face* (v. 27) was probably a begging technique. **29–30:** Wisdom includes the ability to judge character.

20.1–8: Qualities of silence and speaking. The poem searches for a middle way between the wrong silence of nursing *one's anger* (v. 2) and the wrong self-expression of resorting *to force to secure right* (v. 4).

20.9–17: Surprising outcomes. One who is wise expects the unexpected. **12:** *Seven times:* many times.

14 A gift from a fool will bring you no
profit;
   it looks bigger to him than to you.
15 He gives small gifts accompanied by
long lectures
   and opens his mouth as wide as the
   town crier.
   Today he gives a loan, and tomorrow
   demands it back.
   Such conduct is detestable!
16 The fool says, 'I have not one friend
   and I get no thanks for my kindnesses;
   those who eat my bread speak ill of
   me.'
17 How everyone will laugh at him—and
how often!

18 Better a slip on the floor than a slip of
the tongue;
   the downfall of the wicked comes just
   as suddenly.
19 An ill-mannered man is like an ill-timed
story,
   continually on the lips of the ill-bred.
20 A proverb will fall flat when uttered by
a fool;
   he is sure to bring it out at the wrong
   moment.

21 Poverty may keep someone from doing
wrong;
   when he goes to rest, conscience will
   not trouble him.
22 Diffidence may be someone's undoing,
   or a foolish appearance may bring him
   disaster.
23 Someone may be shamed into making
promises to a friend
   and needlessly turn him into an
   enemy.

24 A lie is an ugly blot on anyone's name
   and is continually on the lips of the
   ill-bred.
25 Better be a thief than a habitual liar,
   but both will come to a bad end.
26 A lying disposition brings disgrace,
   shame that can never be shaken off.

27 He that is wise in discourse advances
himself,
   and he that has sense is pleasing to the
   great.
28 He who cultivates his land heaps up a
harvest;
   he who pleases the great secures
   pardon for his offence.
29 Hospitality and gifts make the wise
blind;
   like a gag in the mouth they silence
   criticism.
30 Hidden wisdom and buried treasure—
   what is the use of either?
31 Better one who hides his folly
   than one who hides his wisdom!

21 My son, have you done wrong? Do
no more,
   and for your past wrongdoing ask
   pardon.
2 Avoid wrong as you would a viper,
   for it will bite you if you go near;
   its teeth are like a lion's teeth
   and can deprive men of their lives.
3 Every breach of the law is a two-edged
sword;
   the wound it inflicts is incurable.
4 Bullying and insolence are destroyers of
wealth;
   thus a proud man will be bereft of his
   home.
5 The Lord listens to the appeal of the
poor,
   and his verdict follows promptly.
6 To hate reproof is to go the way of
sinners,
   but whoever fears the Lord will repent
   wholeheartedly.
7 A great talker is known far and wide;
   a sensible person is aware of his own
   failings.
8 To build a house with borrowed money
   is like gathering the stones for one's
   own tomb.

20:31 **his wisdom:** *some witnesses add* 32Better to seek
the Lord with unremitting patience than to drive one's
way through life on one's own.

16–17: Fools are disappointed because they expect to be repaid for everything they do.
   20.18–31: Wise and foolish speech. 18: A popular proverb, known also from the Greek philosopher Zeno,
recorded in Diogenes Laertius, *Lives,* VII, 26. **21–23:** Improper shame (especially of a debtor who is not candid
to a creditor) will destroy a friendship. **30–31:** *Wisdom* must not be hidden; contrast the wise person's silence,
20.1–8.
   21.1–10: Warnings against sin. This section differs from the shrewd observations of 19.20–20.31 in its

9 An assembly of the wicked is like a
   bundle of tow;
   they end in flames.
10 The sinners' road is smoothly paved,
   but it leads straight down to the grave.

Folly and indiscretion

11 WHOEVER keeps the law keeps control
   of his thoughts;
   the fear of the Lord has its outcome in
   wisdom.
12 He who is not clever cannot be taught,
   but there is a cleverness which breeds
   bitterness.
13 The knowledge of the wise is like a
   river in full flood;
   advice from such is like a fountain of
   life.
14 A fool's mind is like a broken jug:
   it cannot retain anything it learns.
15 If an instructed man hears a wise
   saying,
   he applauds it and improves on it;
   if a dissolute man hears it, he is
   annoyed
   and flings it away out of his sight.
16 Listening to a fool is like travelling with
   a heavy pack,
   but delight is to be found in learned
   conversation.
17 The assembly welcomes a word from a
   wise man
   and ponders what he says.

18 To a fool, wisdom is like a derelict
   house;
   the knowledge of the stupid is a string
   of ill-digested sayings.
19 To the ignorant, instruction is like
   fetters,
   like a manacle on the right wrist.
21 To the wise, instruction is a gold
   ornament
   like a bracelet on the right arm.
20 A fool guffaws,

but a clever man smiles quietly, if
   at all.
22 A fool rushes into a house,
   while someone of experience hangs
   back politely.
23 A boor peers into a house from the
   doorstep,
   while a well-bred person stands outside.
24 It is bad manners to eavesdrop at
   doors;
   anyone with sense would think it an
   intolerable disgrace.
25 The glib only repeat what others have
   said,
   but the wise weigh every word.
26 Fools speak before they think,
   but the wise think before they speak.
27 When the ungodly curses his adversary,
   he is really cursing himself.
28 A tale-bearer blackens his own
   character
   and gets himself detested throughout
   the neighbourhood.

22 A sluggard is like a filthy stone:
   everyone jeers at his disgrace.
2 A sluggard is like a lump of dung:
   whoever picks it up shakes it off his
   hand.

3 There is shame in being father to an
   ill-mannered son,
   and the birth of a daughter means loss.
4 A sensible daughter wins a husband,
   but an immodest one is a grief to her
   father.
5 A brazen daughter brings shame on
   father and husband,
   and is despised by both.
6 Unseasonable talk is like music in time
   of mourning,
   but the lash of wisdom's discipline is
   always in season.

7 Teaching a fool is like mending pottery
   with paste,

frequent reference to the Lord. **8:** *A house:* a symbol of one's whole existence. **9:** See 16.6. **10:** The smooth
road leads quickly to one's destruction; see Prov. 14.12; Matt. 7.13.

21.11–28: The wise and the foolish. 12: See 19.20–30 on *cleverness.* **13:** The *river* and *fountain of life* are
contrasted to stagnant cistern water and even more to the *broken jug* (v. 14). **22–28:** Etiquette was a major
subject of ancient wisdom. **27:** *His adversary* is literally "Satan," but here the reference is to the human
adversary.

22.1–26: Bad experiences. 1–2: The *sluggard* or idler is frequently rebuked in Prov. (Prov. 10.4; 15.19;
24.30–34), but is a target of Ecclus. only here and in 33.24–28. **3–5:** The *daughter* meant *loss* because she

or like rousing a sleeper from heavy
slumber.
8 As well talk with someone dozing as
with a fool;
when you have finished, he will say,
'What was that?'
11 Weep for the dead: he has taken leave
of the light;
weep for the fool: he has taken leave of
his wits.
Weep less bitterly for the dead, for he
is at rest;
but the fool's life is worse than death.
12 Mourning for the dead lasts seven days;
for an impious fool it lasts all the days
of his life.

13 Do not prolong talk with a fool
or visit one who is stupid.
Beware of him, or you may be in
trouble
and find yourself bespattered when he
shakes himself.
Avoid him, if you are looking for
peace,
and you will not be worn out by his
folly.
14 What is heavier than lead?
What is its name but 'Fool'?
15 Sand, salt, and a lump of iron
are less of a burden than a stupid
person.

16 A tie-beam fixed firmly into a
building
is not shaken loose by an earthquake;
so a mind kept steadfast by sensible
advice
will not be daunted in a crisis.
17 A mind solidly backed by intelligent
thought
is like stucco decorating a well-prepared
wall.
18 As a fence set on a hilltop
will not stand against the wind,
so a mind made timid by foolish fancies
is not proof against any terror.

19 Prick the eye and tears will flow;

prick the heart and you will find it
sensitive.
20 Throw a stone at birds and you scare
them away;
taunt a friend and you destroy a
friendship.
21 If you have drawn your sword on a
friend,
do not despair; a way back is still open.
22 If you have quarrelled with a friend,
do not hold aloof, for there can still be
reconciliation.
But taunts, scorn, a secret betrayed, a
stab in the back —
these will make any friend keep his
distance.
23 Win your neighbour's confidence while
he is poor,
that you may share fully in his
prosperity;
stand by him in time of trouble,
that you may be his partner when he
comes into a fortune.
24 As furnace fumes and smoke precede
the flame,
so insults come before bloodshed.
25 I shall not be ashamed to protect a
friend,
nor shall I turn my back on him;
26 and if on his account harm should
befall me,
everyone who hears of it will beware of
him.

27 O FOR a sentry to guard my mouth
and a seal of discretion to close my lips,
to prevent them from being my
downfall,
to keep my tongue from causing my
ruin!

23 Lord, Father, and Ruler of my life,
do not abandon me to the tongue's
control
or allow it to bring about my downfall.

22:8 **'What was that?':** *some witnesses add* 9Children
nurtured in a good life do not show the low birth of
their parents; 10but those who run riot, haughty and
undisciplined, sully the good name of their family.
22:18 **a fence:** *or* pebbles.

could not carry on the family name. **7:** Ancient *paste* was not strong enough to mend *pottery*. **11–13:** These
imperatives are not the usual moral commands (as in 21.1) but shrewd observation of life. The *seven days* of
mourning (v. 12) were traditional (see Gen. 50.10); contrast 38.17. **19:** The *heart* is that of a friend who will
be hurt. **23:** The pairing of opposites (*prosperity, trouble*) was a favorite way of building proverbs.
   22.27–23.6: A prayer for self-control. 27: The *mouth* is viewed as a gate which needs a *sentry*. See Ps. 141.3

2 O for wisdom's rod to curb my
thoughts
and to discipline my mind,
that my shortcomings may not be
overlooked
or any sin of mine be condoned!
3 Then my errors would not multiply
or my sins increase in number,
humiliating me before my opponents
and giving my enemy cause to gloat.
4 Lord, Father, and God of my life,
do not let me wear a supercilious look.
5 Protect me from the onslaught of
desire;
6 let neither gluttony nor lust take hold
of me,
and do not give me over to
shamelessness.

7 Hear how to discipline the mouth, my
sons;
he that does so will never be caught
out.
8 It is by his own words that the sinner is
ensnared;
by his own scurrility and pride he is
tripped.
9 Do not accustom your mouth to oaths
or make a habit of using the Holy
One's name.
10 As a servant constantly questioned
under the lash
is never free from weals,
so also anyone who has oaths and the
sacred name forever on his lips
will never be clear of guilt.
11 One given to oaths is wicked to the
core;
the rod will never be far from his
house.
If he goes back on his word, he must
bear the blame;
if he wilfully neglects it, he sins twice
over;
if his oath was insincere, punishment
will overtake him

and his house will be filled with
trouble.
12 There is a kind of speech that is the
counterpart of death;
may it never be found among Jacob's
descendants!
The godly will keep clear of such
conduct
and will not wallow in sin.
13 Do not make a habit of coarse and
filthy talk,
or you will be bound to say something
sinful.
14 Remember your father and mother
when you take your seat among the
great;
otherwise you may forget yourself in
their presence
and through such habits make a fool of
yourself;
then you will wish you had never been
born,
and curse the day of your birth.
15 Someone addicted to scurrilous talk
will never learn better as long as he
lives.

16 Two KINDS of people add sin to sin,
and a third brings God's wrath on
himself.
Hot lust that blazes like a fire
can never be suppressed till life itself is
quenched.
A man whose whole body is given to
sensuality
never stops till the fire consumes him.
17 To the profligate every cake is as sweet
as the last,
and he will not leave off until he dies.
18 The man who strays from his own bed
says to himself, 'Who can see me?
All around is dark and the walls hide
me;
nobody can see me; why need I
worry?'

and compare Prov. 21.23. **23.1:** God is *Father* also in the closing prayer of 51.10. **4:** The *supercilious look*
may mean the eye of desire (the "bold looks" of 26.9 represents the same word).

23.7–15: Control of the tongue. 9–11: *Oaths* carried a special weight of punishment if not fulfilled. The
naming of the *Holy One* made an oath sacred, but such use of the holy name was to be avoided (see Exod.
20.7). **12–15:** Here the subject is restraint from vulgar talk.

23.16–27: Sins of lust.

23.16–21: The adulterous man. 16: A sequence of numbers (*two . . . a third*) was a favorite way of shaping
a proverb; compare 25.7; Prov. 30.15–31. The three *kinds of people* are put in a climactic order in vv. 16–18.

The Most High will take no note of my
sins.'
19 The eyes of human beings are all he
fears;
he forgets that the eyes of the Lord
are ten thousand times brighter than
the sun,
observing every step that mortals take
and penetrating to every secret place;
20 before all things were created, they
were known to him,
and so it is since their completion.
21 Such a man will pay the penalty in the
public street,
caught where he least expected it.

22 So too with the woman who is
unfaithful to her husband,
presenting him with an heir by another
man:
23 first, she disobeys the law of the Most
High;
secondly, she commits an offence
against her husband;
thirdly, she has prostituted herself
by bearing bastard children.
24 She shall be brought before the
assembly for judgement,
and the consequences will fall on her
children.
25 Her children will not take root,
nor will fruit grow on her branches.
26 A curse will rest on her memory,
and her shame will never be wiped out.
27 All who survive her will learn
that nothing is better than the fear of
the Lord,
nothing sweeter than obeying his
commandments.

In praise of wisdom

24 HEAR the praise of wisdom from
her own mouth,

as she speaks with pride among her
people,
2 before the assembly of the Most High
and in the presence of the heavenly
host:
3 'I am the word spoken by the Most
High;
it was I who covered the earth like a
mist.
4 My dwelling-place was in high heaven;
my throne was in a pillar of cloud.
5 Alone I made a circuit of the sky
and traversed the depths of the abyss.
6 The waves of the sea, the whole earth,
every people and nation were under my
sway.
7 Among them all I sought where I
might come to rest:
in whose territory was I to settle?
8 Then the Creator of all things laid a
command on me;
he who created me decreed where I
should dwell.
He said, "Make your home in Jacob;
enter on your heritage in Israel."
9 Before time began he created me,
and until the end of time I shall
endure.
10 In the sacred tent I ministered in his
presence,
and thus I came to be established in
Zion.
11 He settled me in the city he loved
and gave me authority in Jerusalem.
12 I took root among the people whom
the Lord had honoured
by choosing them to be his own
portion.

13 'There I grew like a cedar of Lebanon,
like a cypress on the slopes of Hermon,
14 like a date-palm at En-gedi,
like roses at Jericho.

23:27 **his commandments:** *some witnesses add* 28 To
follow God brings great honour; to win his approval
means length of days.

20: God's knowledge *before all things were created* is not in conflict with freedom of choice (15.11–20) in
the author's total view.

23.22–27: The adulterous woman. The penalty for adultery was death (Deut. 22.22). For the suspicion of
adultery on the part of a wife, and for the attendant consequences, see Num. 5.11–31.

24.1–22: Wisdom's praise. A hymn to wisdom introduces the second main part of the book; compare
1.1–10. **1:** The *people* are Israel. **2:** The *assembly* is the heavenly council; see Ps. 89.6–7. **3:** Wisdom speaks,
as in Prov. 8.22–36 on which much of this section is modeled. The *mist* represents the creative power of
wisdom, parallel to the spirit or wind of Gen. 1.2 (see Tfn. there); compare Gen. 2.6. **4:** *High heaven:* God's
throne above the reservoir of waters supported by the vault of the sky; see Gen. 1.6–8; Ps. 29.10. **7:** Wisdom

I grew like a fair olive tree in the vale,
or like a plane tree planted beside the
water.
15 Like cinnamon or camel-thorn I was
redolent of spices;
like choice myrrh I spread my
fragrance,
like galbanum, aromatic shell, and gum
resin,
like the smoke of frankincense in the
sacred tent.
16 Like a terebinth I spread out my
branches,
laden with honour and grace.
17 I put forth graceful shoots like the
vine,
and my blossoms were a harvest of
honour and wealth.

19 'Come to me, all you who desire me,
and eat your fill of my fruit.
20 To think of me is sweeter than honey,
to possess me sweeter than the
honeycomb.
21 Whoever feeds on me will hunger for
more;
whoever drinks from me will thirst for
more.
22 To obey me is to be safe from disgrace;
those who make me their business will
not go astray.'

23 All this is the book of the covenant of
God Most High,
the law laid on us by Moses,
a possession for the assemblies of Jacob.
25 It sends out wisdom in full flood like
the river Pishon
or like the Tigris at the time of
firstfruits;

26 it overflows like the Euphrates with
understanding
or like the Jordan at the harvest season.
27 It pours forth instruction like the Nile,
like the Gihon at the time of vintage.
28 No one has ever known wisdom fully
and from first to last no one has
fathomed her,
29 for her thoughts are vaster than the
ocean,
her purpose more profound than the
great abyss.

30 As for me, I was like a watercourse
leading from a river,
like a conduit into a pleasure garden.
31 I said, 'I will water my garden,
soaking its flower beds';
all at once my watercourse became a
river
and my river a sea.
32 I will again make learning shine like
the dawn,
that its light may be seen from afar.
33 I will again pour out my teaching like
prophecy
and bequeath it to future generations.
34 Truly, I have not toiled for myself
alone
but for all who seek wisdom.

25 THERE are three sights which warm
my heart

24:17 **honour and wealth:** *some witnesses add* 18 I give
birth to honourable love, to reverence, knowledge, and
holy hope; all these my eternal progeny I give to God's
elect (*prob. mng; Gk obscure*).   24:23 **assemblies of
Jacob:** *some witnesses add* 24 Never fail to be strong in the
Lord; hold fast to him, so that he may strengthen you.
The Lord Almighty is God alone, and beside him
there is no saviour.   24:25, 26, 27 **It:** *or* He.
24:27 **pours . . . Nile:** *so one Vs.; Gk* makes instruction
shine like light.

looked for a place to *come to rest,* but found it only in Israel (v. 8), which has God's law. **13–14:** The
massiveness and majesty of the *cedar* and *cypress,* the fruitfulness of the *date-palm,* the beauty of *roses,* and
the fairness of the *olive tree* are symbolic of wisdom. **15:** These were prized aromatic substances used in
worship. **19–22:** Wisdom's call is paralleled in 51.23–30, where a Wisdom teacher speaks; see also Prov.
9.1–6 and Matt. 11.28–30. **21:** Unlike food for the stomach which satiates, the use of wisdom creates hunger
for more and so brings continual enjoyment; contrast Jn. 6.35.

24.23–29: Wisdom and Law. This is the author's interpretation of Wisdom's speech above. **25–27:** The
productiveness of *wisdom* is compared to the *Jordan* and the four rivers of Gen. 2.10–14. The *Gihon* was
identified with the *Nile* (but see Tfn. at 24.27), which is at its height in the time of vintage.

24.30–34: The author's encounter with Wisdom. The life-giving symbolism of water is carried forward from
Wisdom (24.23–29) to the author.

25.1–2: A numerical saying. The main theme is marriage which is the final element in each series of three.

and are beautiful in the eyes of the
Lord and of men:
concord among brothers, amity among
neighbours,
and a man and wife who are
inseparable.
2 There are three kinds of men who
arouse my hatred
and disgust me by their manner of
life:
a poor man who boasts, a rich man who
lies,
and an old fool who commits adultery.

3 If you have not gathered wisdom in
your youth,
will you find it when you are old?
4 How well sound judgement befits grey
hairs,
as wise advice does those advanced in
years!
5 How well wisdom befits the aged,
and ripe counsel persons of eminence!
6 Long experience is the crown of the
aged,
and their pride is the fear of the Lord.

7 I can think of nine men I count happy,
and I can tell you of a tenth:
a man who delights in his children,
and one who lives to see the downfall
of his enemy.
8 Happy the husband of a sensible wife,
the farmer who does not plough with
ox and ass together,
he whose tongue never trips him,
and he who has never had to work for
his inferior!
9 Happy the man who has found a
friend,
and the speaker who has an attentive
audience!
10 How great is he who finds wisdom!
But no greater than he who fears the
Lord.
11 The fear of the Lord excels all other
gifts;

to whom can its possessor be
compared?

Domestic counsels

13 ANY wound but a wound in the heart,
any malice but a woman's!
14 Any disaster but one caused by hate,
any vengeance but the vengeance of an
enemy!
15 There is no venom deadlier than a
snake's
and no anger deadlier than a woman's.
16 I would sooner live with a lion or a
serpent
than share a house with a malicious
wife.
17 Her spite changes her expression,
making her look as surly as a bear.
18 Her husband goes to a neighbour for
his meals
and cannot repress a bitter sigh.

19 There is nothing so bad as a bad wife;
may the fate of the wicked overtake
her!
20 It is as easy for an old man to climb a
sand-dune
as for a quiet husband to live with a
garrulous wife.
21 Do not be enticed by a woman's beauty
or set your heart on possessing one
who has wealth.
22 If a man is supported by his wife
he must expect tantrums, effrontery,
and much humiliation.
23 Depression, downcast looks, and a
broken heart:
these are caused by a worthless wife.
Feeble of hand and weak at the knees

25:8 **the farmer ... together:** *so Heb.; Gk omits.*
25:9 **found a friend:** *so Vss.; Gk* found good sense.
25:11 **be compared:** *some witnesses add* 12 The fear of
the Lord is the source of love for him, and faith is the
source of adherence to him.   25:15 **venom:** *prob.
mng; Gk* head. **a woman's:** *so some Vss.; Gk* an enemy's.

25:3–6: Wisdom is the crown of old age. 6: *Experience* in a stable environment makes the advice of the
aged valuable.

25:7–11: A numerical saying. The speaker is the Wisdom teacher. **10:** *Wisdom* is here distinguished as a
lower stage than *fear of the Lord,* a distinction not usually made in this book. **11:** *Fear of the Lord* is the climactic
happiness.

25:13–26:18: The good and bad wife. Ecclesiasticus is not affirmative about women; his view is not merely

is the man whose wife fails to bring him
    happiness.
24 Sin began with a woman,
    and because of her we all die.
25 Do not leave a leaky cistern to drip
    or allow a worthless wife to say
        whatever she likes.
26 If she does not accept your control,
    bring the marriage to an end.

26 A good wife makes a happy
        husband;
    she doubles the length of his life.
2 A staunch wife is her husband's joy;
    he will live out his days in peace.
3 A good wife is a blessing;
    she is one of the Lord's gifts to those
        who fear him.
4 Rich or poor, they are in good heart,
    with always a smile on their faces.

5 Three things there are that alarm
        me,
    and a fourth I am afraid to face:
    scandalmongering in the city, a mob
        controlling the assembly,
    and false accusation — all harder to bear
        than death;
6 but a wife's jealousy of a rival brings
        heartache and grief,
    and everyone alike feels the lash of her
        tongue.
7 A bad wife is a yoke that chafes;
    controlling her is like handling a
        scorpion.
8 A drunken wife provokes much anger;
    she will not conceal her excesses.

9 A loose woman betrays herself by her
        bold looks;
    you can tell her by her glance.
10 Keep close watch over a headstrong
        daughter;
    if she finds you off your guard, she will
        take her chance.
11 Beware of her impudent looks
    and do not be surprised if she disobeys
        you.

12 As a parched traveller with gaping
        mouth
    drinks from any spring that offers,
    she will open her arms to every
        embrace
    and her quiver to every arrow.

13 A wife's charm is the delight of her
        husband,
    and her womanly skill puts flesh on his
        bones.
14 A silent wife is a gift from the Lord;
    her good breeding is more than money
        can buy.
15 A modest wife has infinite charm;
    no scales can weigh the worth of her
        self-control.
16 As beautiful as the sunrise in the Lord's
        heavens
    is a good wife in a well-ordered home.
17 As bright as the light on the sacred
        lampstand
    is a beautiful face with a stately figure.
18 Like a golden pillar on a silver base

26:3 **blessing:** *lit.* good portion.   26:18 **a firm foot:**
some witnesses add
19 My son, guard your health in the bloom of your
        youth,
    and do not waste your vigour on strange women.
20 Search the whole plain for a fertile plot;
    sow your own seed, trusting in your sound stock.
21 Then the children you leave behind
    will prosper, confident in their parentage.
22 A woman of the streets is no better than spittle;
    a married woman is a mortuary for her lovers.
23 A godless woman is a good match for a lawless
        husband,
    a godly one for a man who fears the Lord.
24 A brazen woman courts disgrace,
    but a virtuous daughter is modest even before
        her husband.
25 A headstrong woman is a shameless bitch,
    but a modest one fears the Lord.
26 A woman who honours her husband is accounted
        wise by all,
    but if she despises him, all know her as proud and
        godless.
    A good wife makes a happy husband;
    she doubles the length of his life.
27 A strident, garrulous wife is like a trumpet
        sounding the charge;
    in a home like hers a man lives in the confusions
        of war.

personal, but draws on an old Wisdom tradition. **24:** The *woman:* Eve (Gen. 3.1–24); apparently the earliest
interpretation of Gen. as teaching that *sin began with a woman.* **26:** Divorce was permitted in Deut. 24.1.
26.1–3: The long *life* of the husband is the direct result of his marriage to a good wife. **4:** Inner harmony is
important to marital relationships. **6:** The *rival* presupposes polygamy; see Lev. 18.18; Deut. 21.15–17; 1 Sam.
1.1–7. **9–12:** The disloyal wife is the theme of the poem, despite the word *daughter* (v. 10), which means wife.
13–18: Meditation on the good wife climaxes in appreciation of her physical beauty.

is a shapely leg with a firm foot.

28 Two THINGS grieve my heart,
and a third excites my anger:
a soldier in distress through
poverty,
the wise treated with contempt,
and someone deserting right conduct
for wrong—
for such a one the Lord will get ready
the sword.

29 How rare it is for a merchant to keep
clear of wrong
or a shopkeeper to be acquitted of
dishonesty!

27 Many have cheated for gain;
a money-grubber will always turn a
blind eye.
2 As a peg is fixed in the joint between
stones,
so dishonesty squeezes in between
selling and buying.
3 Unless a person holds resolutely to the
fear of the Lord,
his house will soon collapse in ruins.

4 Shake a sieve, and the rubbish
remains;
start an argument, and a man's faults
show up.
5 As the work of a potter is tested in the
kiln,
so a man is tried in debate.
6 As a tree's fruit reveals the skill of the
grower,
so the expression of a man's thoughts
reveals his character.
7 Do not praise a man till you hear him
in argument,
for that is the test.

8 If justice is what you seek, you will
succeed
and wear it like a splendid robe.
9 Birds of a feather roost together,
and honesty comes home to those who
practise it.
10 A lion lies in wait for its prey;
so does sin for those whose conduct is
evil.

11 The conversation of the godly is
constantly wise,
but a fool is as changeable as the
moon
12 Grudge every minute spent among
fools,
but linger among the thoughtful.
13 The conversation of fools provokes
disgust;
to them a life of licence is just a joke.
14 The chatter of the profane makes the
hair stand on end;
when such folk quarrel, others stop
their ears.
15 The quarrels of the proud lead to
bloodshed;
their abuse makes sorry hearing.

16 The betrayer of secrets forfeits all
trust;
he will never find an intimate friend.
17 Love your friend and keep faith with
him;
but if you betray his secrets, steer clear
of him,
18 for as one kills an enemy,
so you have killed your neighbour's
friendship.
19 As a bird that is allowed to fly out of
your hand,
your neighbour, once lost, will not be
caught again.
20 He has gone too far for you to pursue
him;
he has escaped like a gazelle from a
trap.
21 A wound may be bandaged, an insult
pardoned,
but the betrayer of secrets has
renounced all hope.

22 Someone who winks is plotting
mischief;
those who know him will keep their
distance.
23 He speaks sweetly enough to your face
and admires whatever you say,
but later he will change his tune
and use your own words to trip you.
24 There are many things I hate, but him
above all;

26.28–28.26: Types of sin. 26.29–27.3: Dishonesty destroys the merchant just as the *peg* (27.2) driven between the *stones* is the first step in tearing down the house. **27.16–21:** Betraying *secrets* has irreversible results; but contrast 22.21–22 which says that broken friendships can be restored. **22:** Winking was a frequent and the Lord will hate him too.

25 Throw a stone in the air and you throw
it on your own head;
and a treacherous blow means wounds
all round.
26 Dig a pit and you will fall into it;
set a trap and you will be caught by it.
27 The wrong anyone does recoils on him,
and he has no idea where it comes
from.
28 The arrogant deal in mockery and
taunts,
but like a lion retribution lies in wait
for them.
29 Those who rejoice at the downfall of
the good will be trapped,
and before they die they will be
consumed with pain.

30 Rage and anger, these also I abhor,
but a sinner has them ready at hand.

28 Whoever acts vengefully will face
the vengeance of the Lord,
who keeps strict account of sins.
2 Forgive your neighbour any wrong he
has done you;
then, when you pray, your sins will be
forgiven.
3 If anyone harbours anger against
another,
can he expect help from the Lord?
4 If he refuses mercy to his fellow,
can he ask forgiveness for his own sins?
5 If a mere mortal cherishes rage,
where is he to look for pardon?
6 Think of the end that awaits you, and
have done with hate;
think of mortality and death, and be
true to the commandments;
7 think of the commandments, and do
not be enraged at your neighbour;
think of the covenant of the Most High,
and overlook errors.

8 To avoid a quarrel is a setback for sin,
for quarrels are kindled by a hot
temper.

9 A sinner sets friends at odds
and spreads enmity where before there
was peace.
10 The more fuel, the fiercer the blaze;
the more stubborn the defence, the
fiercer the fight.
The greater a person, the greater his
anger;
the more his wealth, the higher his
temper will flare.
11 A hasty dispute kindles a fire;
a hasty quarrel leads to bloodshed.
12 Blow on a spark to make it glow,
or spit on it to put it out;
both results come from your
mouth.

13 Curses on tale-bearing and duplicity!
For they have been the ruin of many
who were living peaceably.
14 A third party's talk has wrecked the
lives of many
and driven them from country to
country;
it has destroyed strong cities
and overthrown the houses of the
great.
15 A third party's talk has brought divorce
on staunch wives
and deprived them of the fruits of their
industry;
16 whoever heeds it will never again find
rest
or live in peace of mind.
17 The lash of a whip raises weals,
but the lash of a tongue will break
bones.
18 Many have been killed by the edge of
the sword,
but not so many as by the tongue.
19 Happy are they who are sheltered from
its onslaught,
who have not been exposed to its fury,
who have not borne its yoke
or been chained with its fetters;
20 for its yoke is of iron,
its fetters are of bronze!
21 The death it inflicts is a horrible death;

symbol for deception; compare Prov. 6.12–13. **25:** The *stone* describes any deception which is self-destructive.
26: One digs a *pit* to trap another. **28.2–5:** Human forgiveness is prerequisite to receiving God's forgiveness;
compare Lev. 19.18; Matt. 5.7, 23–24; Mk. 11.25. **3:** *Help* means forgiveness. **13–26:** This poem on slander
is noteworthy for the tension between the shrewd observation that the righteous do suffer (the *staunch wives*,
v. 15) and the assertion of faith that the *godfearing* (v. 22) are protected from the power of slander.

better the grave than the tongue!
22 But it has no power over the godfearing;
they cannot be burnt in its flames.
23 Rather, those who desert the Lord fall victim to it;
among them it will blaze up and never be quenched.
It will launch itself against them like a lion
and tear them like a leopard.
24 As you enclose your garden with a thorn hedge,
and as you tie up securely your silver and gold,
25 so weigh your words and measure them,
and make for your mouth a door that locks.
26 Take care you are not tripped by your tongue
to fall before a waiting enemy.

29 He who is compassionate lends to his neighbour;
by giving a helping hand he fulfils the commandments.
2 Lend to your neighbour in his hour of need;
repay your neighbour punctually.
3 Be as good as your word and keep faith with him,
and your needs will always be met.
4 Many treat a loan as a windfall
and create trouble for those who helped them.
5 Until he gets a loan, a man kisses his neighbour's hand
and at the sight of his wealth drops his voice;
when repayment is due, he delays,
pays back only perfunctory promises,
and claims that times are hard.
6 If the creditor presses, he will get back scarcely half,
and will count himself lucky at that;
if he does not press, he has deprived himself of the money,
and made an enemy into the bargain.
The debtor will pay him back in curses and insults,

with dishonour in place of honour.
7 Because of such knavery many refuse to lend,
for fear of being parted from their money to no purpose.

8 Nevertheless be patient with the penniless,
and do not keep them waiting for your charity;
9 for the commandment's sake help the poor,
and in their need do not send them away empty-handed.
10 Be ready to lose money for a brother or a friend
rather than leave it to rust away under a stone.
11 Dispose of your treasure as commanded by the Most High;
that will benefit you more than gold.
12 Let almsgiving be the treasure in your strong-room,
and it will deliver you from every misfortune;
13 better than stout shield or strong spear,
it will arm you against the enemy.

14 A good person will stand surety for his neighbour;
only he who is lost to shame will let him down.
15 If someone stands surety for you, do not forget the favour;
he has staked his very self on your behalf.
16 A sinner ruins the property of his surety,
17 and one who is ungrateful leaves his rescuer in the lurch.
18 Standing surety has overturned the prosperity of many
and wrecked them like a storm at sea;
it has driven people of influence into exile
and set them wandering in foreign countries.
19 When a sinner involves himself in accepting surety,

29.1–28: Borrowing and lending. 1–7: Lending is encouraged in accord with the *commandments* (see Deut. 15.7–11), though the risks are clearly stated. **14–20:** Becoming *surety* for another is here favored within common-sense limits, in contrast to Prov., which warns against suretyship (Prov. 6.1–5; 11.15). In other words,

his pursuit of gain will land him in
lawsuits.

20 So help your neighbour to the best of
your ability,
but beware of becoming too deeply
involved.

21 The basis of life is water, bread, and
clothing,
and a home with decent privacy.

22 Better the life of the poor in his own
hut
than a sumptuous banquet in someone
else's house!

23 Rest content with whatever you have,
be it much or little,
and do not become known for living on
hospitality.

24 It is a miserable life going from house
to house,
keeping your mouth shut because you
are a visitor.

25 Without thanks you play the host and
hand round the drinks,
and into the bargain must listen to
things that rankle:

26 'Come here, you stranger, and lay the
table;
whatever you have there, hand it to
me.'

27 'Be off, stranger! Make way for a more
important guest;
my brother has come to stay, and I
need the guest room.'

28 Two things a sensitive person finds
hard to bear:
criticism at home and abuse from a
creditor!

30 A MAN who loves his son will not
spare the rod,
and then in his old age he may have joy
of him.

2 He who disciplines his son will find
profit in him
and take pride in him among his
acquaintances.

3 He who educates his son makes his
enemy envious
and will boast of him among friends.

4 When the father dies, it is as if he were
still alive,
for he has left behind a copy of
himself.

5 During his lifetime he saw and rejoiced,
and on his deathbed he had no regrets.

6 He has left an heir to take vengeance
on his enemies
and to repay friends for their kindness.

7 A man who coddles his son will
bandage every scratch
and be on tenterhooks at every cry.

8 An unbroken horse turns out stubborn,
and an unchecked son turns out
headstrong.

9 Pamper a boy and he will shock you;
join in his games and he will grieve
you.

10 Do not share his laughter, or you will
share his pain
and end by grinding your teeth.

11 While he is young do not give him
freedom
or overlook his errors.

12 While he is young break him in,
and beat him soundly while he is still a
child;
otherwise he may grow stubborn and
disobedient
and cause you distress.

13 Discipline your son and take pains with
him
or he may affront you by some
disgraceful act.

14 BETTER to be poor and healthy and fit

Ecclus. advocates surety, but not to the extent of deprivation. **21–28:** This praise of simplicity and warning against a life of imposition on the hospitality of others was directed to the teacher's upper-class clientele. **23:** The theme of being *content* is quite usual in both Jewish and Christian counsel (Phil. 4.11; 1 Tim. 6.8; Heb. 13.5).

30.1–13: Raising children. 1–6: Discipline and education (v. 3) will enable a child to carry on the family traditions, even to *taking vengeance on . . . enemies* (v. 6); the motive for discipline is the benefit to the parent. **7:** The author is making fun of the oversolicitous parent. **8–13:** Lack of discipline will produce a rebellious child.

30.14–20: Health better than wealth. 18: *Offerings of food placed on a tomb* were forbidden Jews; see Deut.

than to be rich and racked by disease.

15 Health and fitness are better than any
amount of gold,
and vigour of body than boundless
prosperity.

16 There is no wealth to compare with
bodily health,
no joy to surpass gladness of heart.

17 Better death than a life of misery,
eternal rest than a long illness.

18 Delicacies heaped before someone with
no appetite
are like offerings of food placed on a
tomb.

19 What use is a sacrifice to an idol
which can neither taste nor smell?
So it is with one afflicted by the Lord:

20 he gazes at the food before him and
groans
as a eunuch groans when he embraces
a virgin.

21 Do not abandon yourself to grief
or go out of your way to distress
yourself.

22 A merry heart keeps a person alive,
and joy lengthens his span of days.

23 Indulge yourself, take comfort,
and banish grief far from you;
for grief has been the death of many
and no advantage ever came of it.

24 Envy and anger shorten life,
and anxiety brings premature old age.

25 He who has a light heart has a good
appetite
and relishes the food he eats.

31 Wakeful nights make the rich
person lose weight,
when the cares of wealth drive sleep
away;

2 sleepless worry keeps him wide awake,
just as serious illness banishes sleep.

3 The rich man toils to amass a fortune,
and when he relaxes he enjoys every
luxury.

4 The poor man toils to make a slender
living,
and when he relaxes he finds himself in
want.

5 Passion for gold can never be right;
the pursuit of profit leads astray.

6 Because of gold many a one has met
his downfall
and found himself face to face with
ruin.

7 Gold is a pitfall to those who make it
their god,
and every fool is ensnared by it.

8 Happy are the rich who have remained
blameless
and have not let gold become their
guide!

9 Show us such a person, and we will
congratulate him;
he has performed a miracle among his
people.

10 Has anyone come through this test
unscathed?
Then he has good cause to be proud.
Has anyone had it in his power to sin
and refrained,
to do wrong and not done it?

11 Then he will be confirmed in his
prosperity,
and the assembly will hail him as a
benefactor.

12 WHEN seated at a grand table
do not smack your lips and exclaim,
'What a feast!'

13 Remember, it is a bad thing to have a
greedy eye.
There is no greater evil in creation
than the eye;

26.14, but compare Tob. 4.17. **19:** Compare Ps. 115.4–6. Sickness is heavy to bear because it is an affliction
from the *Lord.*

30.21–31.4: Enjoyment of the present. 21–25: In contrast to the frequent advice to restrain the emotions
in the face of insecurity (as in 11.29–13.13), here a relaxed self-expression in security is the ideal; compare
14.11–19. **31.1–4:** Indicatives (rather than the imperatives of 30.21–25) offer a sober comment on the difficulty
of enjoying the present.

31.5–11: Good and bad uses of money. The ambiguity of wealth is a problem in Ecclus. The temptations
are clearly stated. **10:** The rhetorical question seems to expect the answer "no." **11:** Yet financial security is
the proper reward for righteousness; compare v. 8.

31.12–21: Etiquette. Table manners was a subject of Wisdom teaching through the centuries. Moderation

for that reason it must shed tears at
every turn.
14 Do not reach for everything within
sight,
or jostle your fellow-guest at the
dish;
15 judge his feelings by your own,
and always behave with consideration.
16 Eat what is set before you, but not like
a beast;
do not munch your food and make
yourself objectionable.
17 Be the first to stop for good manners'
sake
and do not be a glutton, or you will
give offence.
18 If you are dining in a large company,
do not reach out your hand before
others.
19 A person of good upbringing is content
with little,
so when he goes to bed he is not short
of breath.
20 The moderate eater enjoys healthy
sleep:
he rises early, feeling refreshed;
but sleeplessness, nausea, and colic
are the lot of the glutton.
21 If you cannot avoid overeating at a
banquet,
leave the table and find relief by
vomiting.

22 Listen to me, my son; do not disregard
me,
and in the end my words will come
home to you.
In all you do avoid extremes,
and no illness will come your way.
23 Everyone has a good word for a liberal
host;
the evidence of his generosity is
convincing.
24 The whole town grumbles at a mean
host,

and there is sure evidence of his
meanness.
25 Do not use wine to prove your
manhood,
for wine has been the ruin of many.
26 As the furnace tests iron when it is
being tempered,
so wine tests character when boasters
are wrangling.
27 Wine puts life into anyone
who drinks it in moderation.
What is life to somebody deprived of
wine?
Was it not created to gladden the
heart?
28 Wine brings gaiety and high
spirits
if people know when to drink and
when to stop;
29 but wine in excess makes for bitter
feelings
and leads to offence and retaliation.
30 Drunkenness inflames a fool's anger to
his own hurt;
it saps his strength and exposes him to
injury.
31 At a banquet do not rebuke your
fellow-guest
or make him feel small while he is
enjoying himself.
That is no time to upbraid him
or pester him to pay his debts.

32 ARE you chosen to preside at a
feast? Do not put on airs;
mix with the others as one of them.
Look after them and only then sit down
yourself;
discharge your duties before you take
your place.
2 Let the enjoyment of others be your
pleasure,
and you will win a garland for good
manners.

---

is the key. **15:** This is a form of the "Golden Rule"; compare 6.17; Tob. 4.15; Matt. 7.12. **18:** The *before* is
temporal.
31.22–24: How to entertain. 23: The *liberal host* is the ideal.
31.25–31: Moderation in drinking. 26: *Wine,* which *tests character,* is not to be avoided but rightly used;
for Ecclesiasticus life was full of such tests. **27–28:** The good effects of *wine* point up the motif of enjoying
the moment; compare 30.21–25.
32.1–13: Behavior at banquets. 1–2: Presiding *at a feast* was a great honor.

3 When you are old, you are entitled to
   speak,
  but come to the point and do not
   interrupt the music.
4 Where entertainment is provided, do
   not keep up a stream of talk;
  it is the wrong moment to show off
   your wisdom.
5 Like a garnet set in a gold ring
  is a concert of music at a banquet.
6 Like an emerald in a setting of gold
  is tuneful music with good wine.

7 When you are young, speak if the need
   arises,
  but twice at the most, and only when
   asked.
8 Be brief, say much in few words,
  like someone who knows and can still
   hold his tongue.
9 In the company of the great do not
   make yourself their equal
  or go on chattering when another is
   speaking.
10 As lightning streaks ahead of thunder,
  so esteem goes before a modest person.
11 Leave in good time and do not be the
   last to go;
  go straight off home without lingering.
12 There you may amuse yourself to your
   heart's content
  without giving offence by arrogant talk.
13 And one thing more: give praise to
   your Maker,
  who has filled your cup with his
   benefits.

14 WHOEVER fears the Lord will accept his
   discipline;
  those diligent in their search for him
   win his approval.
15 Those who study the law will find
   satisfaction therein,
  but the law will prove a stumbling block
   to the insincere.

16 Those who fear the Lord discover his
   will
  and make his decrees shine out like a
   beacon.
17 A sinner does not accept criticism;
  he will find precedents to justify his
   choice.
18 A thoughtful person can always take a
   hint,
  but an arrogant upstart lacks all
   diffidence.
19 Never do anything without due
   thought,
  and once started do not change your
   mind.
20 Do not travel by a road full of
   obstacles
  and stumble along among its boulders.
21 Do not be careless on a clear road;
22 watch where you go.
23 Whatever you are doing, keep yourself
   safe,
  for this too is fulfilling the
   commandments.
24 To rely on the law is to heed its
   commandments;
  trust the Lord and suffer no loss.

33 No misfortune ever befalls him
   who fears the Lord:
  in trials he will be rescued time and
   again.
2 A wise person does not hate the law,
  but he who is insincere about it is like a
   skiff in a squall.
3 A sensible person puts his trust in the
   law,
  finding it reliable like the oracle of
   God.

4 If you want a hearing, prepare what
   you have to say;
  marshal your learning, then give your
   answer.

32.3: The right of the *old* to *speak* first was widely recognized. **4:** Incessant talkers disturb a concert and bore and annoy. **7:** The *young* are to speak *only when asked.* **13:** The poem closes on a religious note, as frequently, with *praise to your Maker.*
   32.14–33.6: Contrasts between the reverent person and the fool. 15: The receptiveness of the wise enables them to find *satisfaction* in *the law.* **17:** By contrast, the *sinner* is not receptive and cannot *accept criticism.* **18–24:** Foresight and self-reliance mark the wise. **33.1–2:** The staying power of the reverent derives from their trust in the Law. **3:** The *oracle of God:* the Urim and Thummim (see Exod. 28.15 n.), which were no longer in use. Ecclesiasticus holds that such oracles are no longer necessary since the *law* fully discloses God's will.

⁵The feelings of a fool turn like a
  cartwheel,
and his thoughts spin like an axle.
⁶A sarcastic friend is like a stallion
which neighs no matter who is on its
  back.
⁷Why is one day more important than
  another,
when every day in the year has its light
  from the sun?
⁸It was by the Lord's decision that they
  were distinguished;
he appointed the various seasons and
  festivals:
⁹some days he made high and holy,
and others he assigned to the common
  run of days.
¹⁰All mankind comes from the ground—
Adam himself was created out of
  earth—
¹¹yet in his great wisdom the Lord
  distinguished them
and made them go their various
  ways:
¹²some he blessed and lifted high,
some he hallowed and brought near to
  himself,
others he cursed and humbled
and removed from their place.
¹³As clay is in the potter's hands
to be moulded just as he chooses,
so are human beings in the hands of
  their Maker
to be dealt with as he decides.
¹⁴Good is the opposite of evil, and life of
  death;
so the sinner is the opposite of the
  godly.
¹⁵Look at all the works of the Most
  High—

they are in pairs, one the counterpart
  of the other.
¹⁶I, last of all, kept watch.
I was like a gleaner following the
  grape-pickers,
and by the Lord's blessing I arrived in
  time
to fill my winepress as full as any of
  them.
¹⁷Note that I did not toil for myself
  alone,
but for all who seek learning.
¹⁸Listen to me, you dignitaries among the
  people;
you leaders of the assembly, give me
  your attention.
¹⁹As long as you live, give no one power
  over yourself—
son or wife, brother or friend.
Do not give your possessions to
  another,
in case you change your mind and want
  them back.
²⁰As long as you have life and breath,
do not let anyone take your place.
²¹It is better for your children to ask help
  from you
than for you to be dependent on them.
²²In all that you do, keep the upper
  hand
and allow no stain on your reputation.
²³Let your life run its full course
and then, at the hour of death,
  distribute your property.

²⁴Fodder, the stick, and burdens for a
  donkey;
for a servant—bread, discipline, and
  work!

6: The *stallion* has no fixed loyalty to anyone.

33.7–15: God and the opposites. Classing things in pairs and opposites was a favorite way of finding order in the world. **8:** Pairs and distinctions exist *by the Lord's decision.* **13:** The varied vessels made of *clay* correspond to the various stations of human beings; compare Jer. 18.1–12; Rom. 9.19–23. **14–15:** The *sinner* is paired against the *godly* among the *works of the Most High;* yet sin remains a human responsibility; compare 15.11–20.

33.16–18: The author's task. In the light of vv. 11–13, the author now sets forth the mission given him by God. Ancient writers tended to glorify the old (compare chs. 44–50); here Ecclesiasticus boldly states that his teaching is as good as the old.

33.19–23: The father as property holder. 20: Do not *let anyone take your place* of authority. **21:** *Children* were dependent on their fathers until the latter's death.

33.24–31: Relations with slaves. 24–28: Bad and lazy slaves require stern treatment. The slave is made

25 Keep your slave at work, if you want
rest for yourself;
if you let him slack, he will be looking
for his liberty.
26 The ox is tamed by yoke and harness,
the bad servant by rack and torture.
27 Set him to work to keep him from
being idle,
for idleness is a great teacher of
mischief.
28 Give him work to do, for that is what
he is for,
and if he disobeys you, load him with
fetters.
29 Do not be too exacting towards
anyone
or do anything contrary to justice.
30 If you have only one servant, treat him
as you do yourself,
because you bought him at a high
price.
31 If you have only one servant, treat him
like a brother;
you will need him as much as you need
yourself.
If you ill-treat him and he takes to his
heels,
where will you go to look for him?

34 VAIN hopes delude the senseless,
and dreams give wings to a fool's
fancy.
2 Paying heed to dreams
is like clutching a shadow or chasing
the wind.
3 What you see in a dream is nothing but
a reflection,
the image of a face in a mirror.
4 Truth can no more come from illusion
than purity can come from impurity.
5 Divination, omens, and dreams are all
futile,

mere fantasies, like those of a woman
in labour.
6 Unless they are sent by intervention
from the Most High,
pay no attention to them.
7 Dreams have led many astray
and disappointed those who built their
hopes on them.
8 The law is perfect without such
illusions;
wisdom spoken by those faithful to the
law is complete.

9 He who is well travelled knows much,
and a person of experience
understands what he is talking about.
10 He who has little experience knows
little,
but travel increases a person's
resources.
11 In the course of my own journeyings I
have seen much
and understand more than I can put
into words.
12 I have often been in deadly danger
but escaped, thanks to the experience I
had gained.

True piety

13 THOSE who fear the Lord will live,
for their trust is in him who can keep
them safe.
14 Fear the Lord and have nothing else to
fear;
he whose trust is in him will never be
daunted.
15 How happy is he who fears the Lord!
He knows where to look for support.
16 The Lord keeps watch over those who
love him;

33:30 **at a high price:** *Gk* with blood.

---

parallel to the domestic animal. **29–31:** The stern verses (24–28) are balanced by advice about equable
relations with good servants.

    34.1–12: The unsubstantiality of dreams. 1: Empty *hopes delude* because they are an escape from reality.
5: The objection here stems from such practices by pagan peoples. **6:** Nonetheless, "true" dreams may be *sent*
by the *Most High.* **8:** Normally, however, the *wisdom* provided in the *law* is sufficient. **9:** Empirical experience,
rather than dreams, provides real knowledge. **11–12:** *Journeyings* or travels were a practical source of
experience (compare 51.13); the author's opposition to paganism does not prevent him from gaining knowledge of the world outside Judea.

    34.13–36.17: True piety is rightly expressed only in good conduct.

    34.13–17: A psalm of deliverance from fear. It is God who gives what the dream seekers (34.1–8) were
after.

he is their strong shield and firm support,

a shelter from scorching wind and noonday heat,

a safeguard against stumbling, a help against falling.

17 He raises the spirits and makes the eyes sparkle;

he gives healing and life and blessing.

18 A sacrifice from ill-gotten gains is tainted,

and the gifts of the wicked win no approval.

19 The Most High has no pleasure in the offerings of the godless,

nor do countless sacrifices win his forgiveness.

20 To offer a sacrifice from the possessions of the poor

is like killing a son before his father's eyes.

21 Bread is life to the destitute,

and to deprive them of it is murder.

22 To rob your neighbour of his livelihood is to kill him,

and he who defrauds a worker of his wages sheds blood.

23 WHEN one builds and another pulls down,

what have they gained except hard work?

24 When one prays and another curses, which is the Lord to listen to?

25 Bathe after touching a corpse and then touch it again,

and what have you gained by your washing?

26 So it is with the one who fasts for his sins

and goes and repeats his offence;

who will listen to his prayer?

What has he gained by his penance?

35 To keep the law is worth many offerings;

to heed the commandments is a shared-offering.

2 A kindness repaid is a grain-offering, and to give alms is a thank-offering.

3 The way to please the Lord is to keep clear of evil,

and to keep clear of wrongdoing is to make atonement.

4 Yet do not appear before the Lord empty-handed;

5 perform all the sacrifices, for they are commanded.

6 When the just person brings his offering of fat to the altar,

its fragrance rises to the presence of the Most High.

7 The sacrifice of the just is acceptable, and such a memorial will never be forgotten.

8 Be generous in your worship of the Lord

and do not stint the firstfruits of your labour.

9 Give all your gifts cheerfully,

and with gladness dedicate your tithe.

10 Give to the Most High as he has given to you,

as generously as your means allow,

11 for the Lord always repays

and you will be repaid seven times over.

12 Do not offer him a bribe, for he will not accept it,

and do not rely on an ill-gotten sacrifice.

The Lord is a judge

who is no respecter of persons.

13 He has no favourites at the expense of the poor,

and he listens to the prayer of the wronged.

34.18–26: Empty observances. 18: *A sacrifice:* this cannot substitute for moral obedience. **21–22:** Withholding *wages* was forbidden in Lev. 19.13. **24–26:** When the poor *curses* the rich, this will cancel out the latter's prayers; compare 35.17. Likewise, *penance,* in the form of ritual washing or fasting, is nullified by the repetition of the act which necessitated it. God, who *listens* to the *prayer* of the penitent, will not heed the prayer of the insincere.

35.1–11: Right sacrifice. 1: The moral commands come first in keeping *the law.* **4–5:** Nevertheless, the ceremonial acts are not to be neglected. **9–11:** The view here draws on the motivation of self-interest.

35.12–20: God's justice and mercy. 12: The *bribe* refers to the false sacrifices of 34.18–20. God *is no respecter of persons* toward the rich; compare Deut. 10.17–18. **13–17:** Delay of justice means that the *prayer*

14 He never ignores the appeal of the
   orphan
or of the widow as she pours out her
   complaint.
15 How the tears run down the widow's
   cheeks,
and her cries accuse him who caused
   them!
16 To be accepted a man must serve the
   Lord as he requires,
and then his prayer will reach the
   clouds.
17 The prayer of the humble pierces the
   clouds;
before it reaches its goal there is no
   comfort for him.
He does not desist until the Most High
   intervenes,
giving the just their rights and seeing
   justice done.
18 The Lord will not be slow,
neither will he be patient with the
   wicked,
until he breaks the bones of the
   merciless
and sends retribution on the heathen;
until he blots out the insolent, one and
   all,
and shatters the power of the unjust;
19 until he gives all people their deserts,
measuring their actions by their
   intentions;
until he gives his people their rights
and gladdens them with his mercy.
20 When affliction comes, mercy is as
   timely
as rain-clouds in a time of drought.

36 Look on us with pity, Lord God of
   all,
2 and strike fear into every nation.
3 Lift your hand against the heathen,
and let them behold your power.
4 As they have seen your holiness
   displayed among us,

so let us see your greatness displayed
   among them.
5 Let them learn, as we ourselves have
   learned,
that there is no god but you, O Lord.
6 Renew your signs, repeat your miracles,
win glory for your mighty hand and
   right arm.
7 Rouse your anger, pour out your
   wrath,
to destroy the adversary and wipe out
   the enemy.
8 Remember the day you have appointed
   and hasten it,
and give men cause to recount your
   wonders.
9 Let burning wrath devour the
   survivors,
and let the oppressors of your people
   meet their doom.
10 Crush the heads of hostile princes
who say, 'No one counts but us.'
11 Gather all the tribes of Jacob,
and grant them their inheritance, as
   you did long ago.
12 Have pity, Lord, on the people called
   by your name,
on Israel, whom you have named your
   firstborn.
13 Show mercy to the city of your
   sanctuary,
to the city of Jerusalem, your
   dwelling-place.
14 Fill Zion with the praise of your
   triumph
and the temple with your glory.
15 Acknowledge those you created at the
   beginning
and fulfil the prophecies spoken in
   your name.
16 Reward those who look to you in trust;
prove your prophets worthy of
   credence.
17 Listen, O Lord, to the prayer of your
   servants,

---

of *orphan* and *widow* may have to be very persistent; but God will see *justice done*. **18–20:** Perhaps by the metaphor of Israel as a widow (v. 14; Lam. 1.1), the justice of God toward Israel becomes the subject.
36.1–17: A prayer for Israel. In language of appeal to God this section takes up the theme of 35.18–20.
1: *God of all:* compare 50.22. **4:** God's *holiness* was shown in the punishment of Israel by exile. **6:** The *signs* and *miracles* are those of Exod. 7.14–11.10; 12.29–32; 14.1–15.21. **8:** The *day* of the Lord was both a popular and prophetic hope; see Amos 5.18–20. **9–11:** Some of the elements of the "day" were to *crush* the *oppressors* of Israel and to *gather* the dispersed *tribes of Jacob. Inheritance:* land of Israel. **12:** *Called by your name:* belonging to you. **17:** Along with the prophecies, the writer invokes the priestly blessing of *Aaron;* see Num. 6.23–26.

who claim Aaron's blessing on your
    people.
Let all who live on earth acknowledge
that you are the Lord, the eternal God.

Life in society

18 THE stomach will accept any food,
    but one food is better than another.
19 As the palate identifies game by its
    taste,
so the discerning mind detects lies.
20 A warped mind makes trouble,
    but he who has wide experience can get
    his own back.

21 A woman will take any man for
    husband,
but a man may prefer one girl to
    another.
22 A woman's beauty makes a man happy,
    and there is nothing he desires more.
23 If she has a kind and gentle tongue,
    then her husband has no peer among
    men.
24 He who acquires a wife has the
    beginnings of a fortune,
a helper to match his needs and a pillar
    to give him support.
25 Where there is no hedge, a vineyard is
    plundered;
where there is no wife, a man wanders
    about in misery.
26 Does anyone trust the swift-moving
    bandit
who swoops on town after town?
No more will they trust a homeless man
who lodges wherever night overtakes
    him.

37 Every friend says, 'I too am your
    friend';
but some are friends in name only.
2 What a mortal grief it is

when a dear friend turns into an
    enemy!
3 O propensity to evil, how did you creep
    in
to cover the earth with treachery?
4 A friend may be all smiles when you
    are joyful,
but turn against you when trouble
    comes.
5 Another shares your toil for the sake of
    a meal,
and yet may shield you against an
    enemy.
6 Do not forget a friend in the fight,
    and do not neglect him when
    prosperity comes your way.

7 Every counsellor says his advice is best,
    but he may have in view his own
    advantage.
8 Be on your guard against him who
    proffers advice;
find out first where his interest lies,
for his advice will be weighted in his
    own favour.
He may tip the scales against you;
9 he may say, 'Your road is clear,'
and then stand aside to see what befalls
    you.
10 Do not consult anyone who regards you
    with suspicion,
or reveal your intentions to those who
    envy you.
11 Never consult a woman about her rival
    or a coward about war,
a merchant about a bargain
or a buyer about a sale,
a grudging person about gratitude
or a hard-hearted person about a kind
    action,
an idler about work of any sort,
a seasonal worker about the end of the
    job,
or a lazy servant about an exacting
    task—

36.18–20: Discernment. Three proverbs introduce a collection of poems (36.18–39.11) about judgment and discrimination.

36.21–26: The married life. 21: The *woman* had no choice; marriage was arranged by the father. **24–26:** Despite negative remarks about women, Ecclesiasticus strongly disapproves of men who avoid marriage.

37.1–6: Choosing a friend. Compare 6.5–17. **1–4:** A true friend is hard to discern. **6:** The section ends with an imperative which sets the qualifications aside.

37.7–15: Choosing a counselor. As in 37.1–6, the main theme is watchfulness against the other's interest. **11:** Lists were a typical way of collecting wisdom; compare 25.7–10. *Rival:* see 26.6 n.

do not turn to them for any advice.
¹² Rely rather on a godfearing person
whom you know to be a keeper of the
commandments,
one who is with you heart and soul
and will show you sympathy if you have
a setback.
¹³ But trust your own judgement also,
for you have no more reliable
counsellor.
¹⁴ One's own mind has sometimes a way
of bringing word
better than seven watchmen posted on
a tower.
¹⁵ But above all pray to the Most High
to guide you on the path of truth.

¹⁶ Every undertaking begins in discussion,
and deliberation precedes every action.
¹⁷ The roots of choice are in the heart:
¹⁸ destiny takes four forms,
good and evil, life and death;
and always it is the tongue that decides
the issue.
¹⁹ Someone may be clever enough to
teach many
and yet be of no use to himself.
²⁰ A brilliant speaker may make enemies
and end by dying of hunger,
²¹ if the Lord has withheld grace and
charm
by depriving him of wisdom.
²² If someone is wise in the conduct of his
own life,
his good sense can be trusted when he
gives advice.
²³ If someone is wise and instructs his
people,
then his good sense can be trusted.
²⁴ A wise person will have praise heaped
on him,
and all who see him will count him
happy.

²⁵ Human life can be numbered in
days,
but the days of Israel are countless.
²⁶ A person who is wise will possess the
confidence of his people,
and his name will live for ever.

²⁷ My son, test yourself all your life long;
note what is bad for you, and do not
indulge in it;
²⁸ for not everything is good for everyone,
nor do we all enjoy the same things.
²⁹ Do not be greedy for every delicacy
or eat without restraint,
³⁰ for illness is a sure result of overeating,
and gluttony is next door to nausea.
³¹ Gluttony has been the death of many,
but he who is careful prolongs his life.

38 Value the services of a doctor
for he has his place assigned him
by the Lord.
² His skill comes from the Most High,
and he is rewarded by kings.
³ The doctor's knowledge gives him high
standing
and wins him the admiration of the
great.
⁴ The Lord has created remedies from
the earth,
and a sensible man will not disparage
them.
⁵ Was not water sweetened by a log,
and so the power of the Lord was
revealed?
⁶ The Lord has imparted knowledge to
mortals,
that by their use of his marvels he may
win praise;
⁷ by means of them the doctor relieves
pain
⁸ and from them the pharmacist
compounds his mixture.

13–14: Factors that warp others' insight do not apply in the same way to your own. **15:** The shrewd, practical section closes on a religious note; see also v. 12.

37.16–26: Productive and unproductive wisdom. 22: Success in managing one's own life is a mark of productive wisdom. **24:** Public reputation is another mark. **26:** Lasting fame is a third criterion.

37.27–31: Know your own limits. These verses make the generalized proverbs of 36.18–19 into literal rules for finding one's own dietary style.

38.1–15: The doctor. 3: Social *standing* is cited as proof of the validity of the doctor's work. **4:** Apparently some did *disparage* medicines (*remedies*), because they believed that faith alone should heal. Ecclesiasticus advocates both faith (compare vv. 9–11) and the doctor. **5:** For the *water sweetened by a log,* see Exod. 15.23–25.

There is no limit to the works of the
  Lord,
who spreads health over the whole
  world.

⁹ My son, in time of illness do not be
  remiss,
but pray to the Lord and he will heal
  you.
¹⁰ Keep clear of wrongdoing, amend your
  ways,
and cleanse your heart from all sin.
¹¹ Bring a fragrant offering and a
  memorial sacrifice of flour;
pour oil on the sacrifice; be as lavish as
  you can.
¹² And the doctor should be called;
keep him by you, for you need him
  also.
¹³ A time may come when your recovery
  is in his hands;
¹⁴ then he too will pray to the Lord
to grant success in relieving pain
and finding a cure to save the patient's
  life.
¹⁵ He who sins before his Maker
shows himself arrogant before the
  doctor.

¹⁶ My son, shed tears for one who has
  died;
raise a lament for your grievous loss.
Shroud the body with proper ceremony
and do not neglect his burial.
¹⁷ With bitter weeping and passionate
  wailing
make your mourning worthy of him.
Mourn for a few days and avoid
  criticism;
then take comfort in your grief,
¹⁸ for grief may lead to death,
and a grieving heart saps the strength.
¹⁹ With the burial, grief should pass;
a life of misery is an affliction to the
  heart.
²⁰ Do not abandon yourself to grief;
put it from you and think of your own
  end.

²¹ Never forget: there is no returning;
you cannot help the dead and can only
  harm yourself.
²² Remember that his fate will also be
  yours:
'Mine today, yours tomorrow.'
²³ When the dead is at rest, let his
  memory rest too;
be comforted for him as soon as his
  spirit departs.

²⁴ A SCHOLAR's wisdom comes of ample
  leisure;
to be wise he must be relieved of other
  tasks.
²⁵ How can one become wise who follows
  the plough,
whose pride is in wielding the goad,
who is absorbed in the task of driving
  oxen,
whose talk is all about cattle?
²⁶ He concentrates on ploughing his
  furrows,
and toils late to give the heifers their
  fodder.
²⁷ So it is with every craftsman and
  designer
working both day and night.
Such are those who make engravings
  on signets
and patiently vary the design;
they concentrate on making an exact
  likeness
and stay up to all hours to finish their
  task.
²⁸ So it is with the smith, sitting by his
  anvil,
intent on his ironwork.
The fiery vapours shrivel his flesh
as he wrestles in the heat of the
  furnace;
the hammer rings in his ears again and
  again,
and his eyes are on the pattern he is
  copying.
He concentrates on completing the task
and stays up late to give it a perfect
  finish.

38.16–23: Mourning for the dead. 16–17: *Proper ceremony* is important, partly because it makes possible
the psychological break with the dead which is so important; see vv. 20–23. *Mourning worthy of* the deceased
involves a sensitivity to public opinion on which the author constantly kept his eye. **18–23:** The finality of *your
own end* (v. 20) can help you to accept another's. **22:** The one who has died speaks a proverb.

38.24–39.11: Ordinary work and the work of the wise. 24: *Leisure* is to be used acquiring *wisdom*. **25–34:**
Farming (honored in 7.15, 22) and crafts allow no leisure for study. Yet later on Jewish scholars regularly

29 So it is with the potter, sitting at his work,
turning the wheel with his feet,
always engrossed in the task
of making up his tally of vessels;
30 he moulds the clay with his arm,
crouching forward to exert his strength.
He concentrates on finishing the glazing,
and stays up to clean out the furnace.

31 All those rely on their hands,
and each is skilful at his own craft.
32 Without them a city would have no inhabitants;
no settlers or travellers would come to it.
33 Yet they are not in demand at public discussions,
nor do they attain to high office in the assembly.
They do not sit on the judge's bench
or understand the decisions of the courts.
They cannot expound moral or legal principles
and are not ready with maxims.
34 But they maintain the fabric of this world,
and the practice of their craft is their prayer.

39 How different it is with one who devotes himself
to reflecting on the law of the Most High,
who explores all the wisdom of the past
and occupies himself with the study of prophecies!
2 He preserves the sayings of the famous
and penetrates the subtleties of parables.
3 He explores the hidden meaning of proverbs
and knows his way among enigmatic parables.
4 The great avail themselves of his services,

and he appears in the presence of rulers.
He travels in foreign countries,
learning at first hand human good and human evil.
5 He makes a point of rising early
to seek the Lord, his Maker;
he prays to the Most High,
asking pardon for his sins.
6 If it is the will of the mighty Lord,
he will be filled with a spirit of intelligence;
then he will pour forth wise sayings of his own
and give thanks to the Lord in prayer.
7 He is directed in his counsel and knowledge by the Lord,
whose secrets are his constant study.
8 In his teaching he will reveal his learning,
and his pride will be in the law of the Lord's covenant.
9 Many will praise his intelligence,
and it will never be forgotten.
The memory of him will not die,
and his name will live for ever and ever.
10 The nations will tell of his wisdom,
and the assembled people will sing his praise.
11 If he lives long, he will leave a name in a thousand;
when he goes to his long rest, his reputation is secure.

12 I HAVE still more thoughts to express;
I am as full as the moon at mid-month.
13 Listen to me, my devout sons, and blossom
like a rose planted by a stream.
14 Spread your fragrance like frankincense,
and bloom like a lily.
Scatter your fragrance; lift your voices in song,
praising the Lord for all he has done.
15 Ascribe majesty to his name
and give thanks to him with praise,
with harps and the singing of songs.

practiced a craft; compare Acts 18.3. **39.1:** The sage is a scholar of the Scriptures. In the threefold division of the Bible, the order is usually Law, Prophecy, and the Writings, the latter equivalent to Wisdom. Here the author, because of his own interest, puts *wisdom* before *prophecies*. **4:** The sage is also a shrewd, practical advisor in public affairs. *Travels:* see 34.11–12 n. **9–11:** Enduring *memory* is an important test to Ecclus.; compare 44.10–15.

Let these be your words of
thanksgiving:
16 'All that the Lord has done is excellent;
all that he commands will in due time
take place.'
17 Let no one ask, 'What is this?' or 'Why
is that?'
In due time all such questions will be
answered.

At his bidding the waters stood up like
a heap,
and his word created reservoirs for
them.
18 When he commands, his will is done,
and no one can thwart his saving
power.
19 The deeds of all mankind lie plain
before him,
and there is no hiding from his eyes.
20 From the beginning to the end of time
he keeps watch;
nothing is too marvellous or too
difficult for him.
21 Let no one ask, 'What is this?' or 'Why
is that?'
for everything has been created for its
own purpose.

22 His blessing is like a river in full flood
which soaks the parched ground.
23 As surely as he turned fresh water into
brine,
so shall the heathen incur his anger.
24 For the devout his ways are straight;
for the wicked they are full of pitfalls.
25 From the beginning good was created
for the good,
and evil for sinners.
26 The basic necessities of human life
are water, fire, iron, and salt,
flour, honey, and milk,
the juice of the grape, oil, and
clothing—
27 all these are good for the godfearing,
but turn to evil for sinners.

28 There are winds created to be agents of
retribution,
with great whips to give play to their
fury;
on the day of reckoning they exert
their force
and so allay the anger of their Maker.
29 Fire and hail, famine and pestilence,
all these were created for retribution;
30 beasts of prey, scorpions, and vipers,
and the avenging sword to destroy the
ungodly.
31 They delight in carrying out his
commandments,
always standing ready for his service on
the earth;
and when the time comes, they never
disobey his word.

32 I have been convinced of all this from
the beginning;
I have thought it over and left it in
writing:
33 all that the Lord has made is good,
and he supplies every need as it
arises.
34 Let no one say, 'This is less good than
that,'
for all things prove good at their
proper time.
35 Come now, sing with full heart and
voice,
and to the name of the Lord give
praise!

40 HARD work is the lot of every
mortal,
and a heavy yoke is laid on the children
of Adam
from the day when they come from
their mothers' womb
until the day of their return to the
earth, the mother of all;
2 troubled thoughts and fears are theirs,
and anxious expectation of the day of
their death.

39.12–35: God's works. 16–31: A psalm opposes skeptics with the argument that everything is good in its
time. The skeptics (vv. 17, 21, 34) represent the pessimistic facet in the Wisdom tradition (compare the
interpretation of "times" in Eccles. 3.1–11). **17:** The *water stood up* in being separated from the land, Gen.
1.9–10, or for the passage of the Red Sea (Exod. 14.21–23) or of the Jordan river (Josh. 3.16). **23:** The *fresh
water turned into brine* is a reference to the destruction of Sodom and Gomorrah, Gen. 19.25; compare Ps.
107.34. **26:** This list of ten necessities drawn from secular wisdom (compare 29.21) is used to show that God
made all things good, though they can be turned to evil by the sinner.

40.1–11: Suffering as the human lot. In striking contrast to the previous psalm, Ecclus. here recognizes the

3 Whether someone sits in royal
  splendour on a throne
or lies humbled in dust and ashes,
4 whether he wears the purple and a
  crown
or is clothed in sackcloth,
5 his life is nothing but anger and envy,
a troubled and anxious mind,
fear of death, and guilt, and
  contention.
Even at night when he goes to bed,
sleep brings fresh confusion to his
  mind.
6 There is little or no rest for him;
he is as confused in his sleep as in the
  daytime.
Disturbed by nightmares,
he fancies himself a fugitive from the
  line of battle;
7 and at the moment when he reaches
  safety, he wakes up,
amazed to find his fears groundless.

8 To all living creatures, human and
  animal—
and seven times over to sinners—
9 come death and bloodshed, quarrelling
  and the sword,
disaster, famine, havoc, and plague.
10 All these were created for the
  wicked,
on whose account the flood came.
11 All that is of earth returns to earth
  again,
and all that is of water finds its way
  back to the sea.

12 Bribery and injustice will vanish
  completely,
but good faith will stand for ever.
13 Wealth from wickedness will dry up like
  a wadi
and die away like a clap of thunder in a
  storm;
14 when the torrent rises, rocks are rolled
  away;
yet suddenly it ceases for ever.

15 The branches of an impious stock put
  out few shoots;
their tainted roots are planted on sheer
  rock.
16 The rush that grows on every river
  bank
dries up before any other grass.
17 But kindness is a paradise in its
  blessings,
and almsgiving lasts for ever.

18 To be employed and to be one's own
  master, both are sweet,
but to find a treasure is better still.
19 Offspring and the founding of a city
  perpetuate a name,
but better still is a perfect wife.
20 Wine and music gladden the heart,
but better still is the love of wisdom.
21 Flute and harp make pleasant melody,
but better still is a pleasant voice.
22 The eye likes to look on grace and
  beauty,
but better still on the green shoots in a
  cornfield.
23 A friend or companion is a welcome
  partner,
but better still to be man and wife.
24 Brothers and helpers are a stand-by in
  time of trouble,
but better still is almsgiving.
25 Gold and silver make a person stand
  firm,
but better still is good advice.
26 Wealth and strength uplift the heart,
but better still is the fear of the Lord.
To fear the Lord is to lack nothing,
never to be in need of support.
27 The fear of the Lord is a paradise in its
  blessings;
it affords better protection than high
  position.

28 My son, do not live the life of a beggar;
better die than beg!
29 When someone starts looking to
  another's table,

universality of suffering, even for the righteous. **5–7:** Ecclesiasticus avoids a religious interpretation of dreams
(compare 34.1–8); they are part of the human burden. **8–11:** At least the burden of suffering is greater for
sinners.

40.12–17: The victory of the good. To counteract the previous pessimistic observations, Ecclesiasticus here
affirms the transience of *bribery* and *injustice* and all evil, and the permanence of *good faith* and all good.

40.18–30: Good and bad things. 18–27: Eighteen good things are listed in a complex parallel pattern which
contrasts the good and the *better.* **26–27:** *The fear of the Lord* is the best. **28–30:** A beggar's life is the opposite

his existence is not worth calling life.
It is demoralizing to live on the food of
another,
and he who is wise and well disciplined
will guard against it.
30 He who has lost all shame speaks as if
begging were sweet,
but in his breast resentment burns.

41 How bitter the thought of you, O
Death,
to anyone at ease among his
possessions,
free from cares, prosperous in all
things,
and still vigorous enough to enjoy a
good meal!
2 How welcome your sentence, O Death,
to a destitute person whose strength is
failing,
who is worn down by age and endless
anxiety,
resentful and at the end of his
patience!
3 Do not fear death's sentence;
remember those before you and those
coming after.
4 This is the Lord's decree for all mortals;
why try to argue with the will of the
Most High?
Whether life lasts ten years, or a
hundred, or a thousand,
no questions will be asked about it in
the grave.

5 What a loathsome brood are the
children of sinners,
brought up in the haunts of the
godless!
6 Their inheritance disappears,
and their descendants live in lasting
disgrace.
7 A godless father is taunted by his
children
for the disgrace they endure on his
account.
8 Woe to you who are impious,
who have abandoned the law of God
Most High!

9 When you are born, you are born to a
curse,
and when you die, a curse is your lot.
10 All that is of earth returns to earth;
so too the godless go from curse to
destruction.
11 There is grief over the death of the
body,
but sinners have no good name to
survive them.
12 Take thought for your name: it will
outlive you
longer than thousands of great hoards
of gold.
13 The days of a good life are numbered,
but a good name lasts for all time.

14 BE true to your upbringing, my
children, and live in peace.
Hidden wisdom and buried treasure—
what is the use of either?
15 Better someone who hides his folly
than one who hides his wisdom!

16 Show deference, then, to my teaching:
shame is not appropriate on all
occasions,
nor are all things held in high repute
by everyone.
17 Be ashamed to be detected in
fornication by your parents,
or in lies by a ruler or prince;
18 in crime by a judge or magistrate,
or in a breach of God's law by the
assembly and people;
in dishonesty by a partner or friend,
19 or in theft by the neighbourhood.
Be ashamed of breach of oath or
contract.

Be ashamed of leaning your elbow on
the table,
of giving or receiving with ill grace,
20 of refusing to return a greeting,
or of ogling a prostitute.
21 Be ashamed of turning away a
relative,
of robbing someone of his rightful
share,

of a good thing. **30:** The inner conflict is the worst feature of begging.
  41.1–4: Acceptance of death. Regardless of one's wishes, one must accept the inevitable.
  41.5–13: Consequences that outlast death. 5–10: *Children* bear the consequences of their *godless father's*
life. **11–13:** A *good name* is the most lasting memorial; compare Prov. 22.1; Eccles. 7.1.
  41.14–42.8: Proper and improper shame. 17–23: Proper bases of shame are listed.

or of eyeing another man's wife.

22 Be ashamed of meddling with his
    slave-girl
  or of visiting her bed.
  Be ashamed of taunting your friends
  or following up your charity with a
    lecture.

23 Be ashamed of repeating what you have
    heard
  and of betraying a confidence.

24 Then you will show a proper sense of
    shame
  and be popular with everyone.

42 But at other times you must not be
    ashamed,
  or you will do wrong out of deference
    to others.

2 Do not be ashamed of the law and
    covenant of the Most High,
  or of acting justly even if you acquit the
    ungodly;

3 of settling an account with a partner or
    travelling companion,
  or of sharing an inheritance with the
    other heirs;

4 of using accurate weights and measures,
  or of acquiring possessions, many or
    few,

5 or of making a profit out of trade;
  of frequent disciplining of children,
  or of drawing blood from the back of a
    worthless servant.

6 If your wife is untrustworthy, bolt your
    door;
  where there are many hands, keep
    things under lock and key.

7 When you make a deposit, see it
    counted and weighed,
  and when you give or receive, have it
    all in writing.

8 Do not be ashamed to discipline the
    ignorant and foolish,
  or a greybeard on trial for fornication.
  You will be showing your sound
    upbringing

and win universal approval.

9 A daughter is a secret anxiety to her
    father,
  and worry about her keeps him awake
    at night:
  when she is young, for fear she may
    grow too old to marry,
  and when she is married, for fear her
    husband may divorce her;

10 when she is a virgin, for fear she may
    be seduced
  and become pregnant in her father's
    house;
  when she has a husband, for fear she
    may prove unfaithful,
  and after marriage, for fear she may be
    barren.

11 Keep close watch over a headstrong
    daughter,
  or she may give your enemies cause to
    gloat,
  making you the talk of the town, a
    byword among the people,
  shaming you in the eyes of the world.

12 Give her a bedroom without windows,
  a room that does not overlook the
    entrance.
  Do not let her display her beauty to any
    man,
  or sit gossiping in the women's
    quarters;

13 for out of clothes comes the moth,
  and out of woman comes woman's
    wickedness.

14 Better a man's wickedness than a
    woman's goodness;
  it is woman who brings shame and
    disgrace.

Wonders of creation

15 Now I SHALL call to mind the works of
    the Lord
  and describe what I have seen,

24: The conclusion is a secular rather than a religious one; but compare v. 18. **42.2–7:** Things not to be ashamed of are listed in contrast to 41.17–23. **8:** The conclusion parallels 41.24.

  42.9–14: Problems with women. 9–12: *Anxiety* for a *daughter* is sketched through the stages of her life. **13–14:** The generalizing conclusion is probably a popular proverb.

  42.15–43.33: The wonders of creation. This poem on the wonders of creation introduces 44.1–50.21, on the champions of Israel's past; Pss. 104 (creation) and 105–106 (Israel's past) exhibit a similar pattern. These concluding chapters make clear that the practical human wisdom of the earlier part of the book is to be seen in the framework of God's all-embracing, benign influence in all of nature, but especially in Israel's history

his works which by his word were
made.

16 As everything is illumined by the rays
of the sun,
so the works of the Lord are full of his
glory.

17 Even to the angels the Lord has not
given the power
to tell the full tale of the marvels
accomplished by the Lord Almighty,
so that the universe may stand firm in
his glory.

18 He fathoms both the abyss and the
human heart,
he is versed in their intricacies;
for the Most High possesses all
knowledge,
and the signs of the times are under his
eye.

19 He discloses both past and future,
and lays bare the traces of secret things.

20 No thought escapes his notice,
and not a single word is hidden from
him.

21 He has set in order the masterpieces of
his wisdom,
he who is One from eternity to
eternity;
nothing is added, nothing taken away,
and he needs none to give him counsel.

22 How pleasing is all that he has made,
even the smallest spark the eye can see!

23 His works endure, all of them active for
ever
and all responsive to their several
functions.

24 All things go in pairs, one the
counterpart of the other;
he has made nothing incomplete.

25 One thing supplements the virtues of
another.
Of his glory who can ever see too
much?

43 How splendid is the clear vault of
the sky,
how glorious the spectacle of the
heavens!

2 The sun comes into view proclaiming as
it rises
how marvellous it is, the handiwork of
the Most High.

3 At noon it parches the earth,
and no one can endure its blazing heat.

4 The stoker of a furnace works in the
heat,
but three times as hot is the
hill-scorching sun.
It breathes out fiery vapours;
the glare of its rays blinds the eyes.

5 Great is the Lord, its Creator,
whose word speeds it on its course.

6 He made the moon also to serve in its
turn,
a perpetual sign to mark the divisions
of time.

7 From the moon, feast days are
reckoned;
it is a light that wanes as it completes its
course.

8 The moon gives its name to the month;
it waxes marvellously as its phases
change,
a beacon to the armies of heaven,
shining in the vault of the sky.

9 The stars in their brilliance adorn the
heavens,
a glittering array in the heights of the
Lord.

10 At the Holy One's command each
stands in its place,
never defaulting at its post.

11 Look at the rainbow and praise its
Maker;
it shines with a surpassing beauty,

12 spanning the heavens with its gleaming
arc,
a bow bent by the hands of the Most
High.

13 His command speeds the snowstorm
and sends the swift lightning to execute
his sentence.

and in the lives of those who made it.

42.15–25: God's lordship in the creation. 15: The *works of the Lord* make up the whole visible universe.
18: The human *heart* (i.e. the mind) is considered to be as inscrutable as the *abyss*, the subterranean reservoir
of water. **24–25:** The appearance of *pairs* helps explain the apparent contradictions in life; compare 33.15.

43.1–26: Examples of God's work. Astonishment at the rapid yet controlled changes of the natural environment is the leading theme.

14 To that end the storehouses are
opened,
and the clouds fly out like birds.
15 By his mighty power the clouds are
massed
and the hailstones broken small.
16–17 The thunder of his voice makes the
earth writhe,
and on his appearing the hills are
shaken.
At his will the south wind blows,
the squall from the north and the
hurricane.
He scatters the snowflakes like birds
alighting;
they settle like a swarm of locusts.
18 The eye is dazzled by their beautiful
whiteness,
and the mind is entranced as they
fall.
19 He sprinkles hoar-frost on the earth
like salt,
and icicles congeal like pointed stakes.
20 A cold blast from the north
and ice freezes hard on the water,
settling on every pool
as though the water were putting on a
breastplate.
21 He consumes the hills, burns up the
wilderness,
and like fire shrivels the grass.
22 Cloudy weather quickly puts all to
rights,
and dew brings welcome relief after the
scorching heat.

23 In his design he curbed the deep
and planted islands there.
24 Those who sail the sea have tales of its
dangers
which astonish all of us who hear
them;
25 in it are strange and wonderful
creatures,
all kinds of living things and great sea
monsters.
26 By his own action his purpose succeeds,
and by his word all things are held
together.

27 However much we say, our words will
always fall short;
the end of the matter is: God is all.
28 Where can we find the skill to sing his
praises?
For he is greater than all his works.
29 The Lord is terrible and very great;
marvellous is his power.
30 Honour the Lord to the best of your
ability,
yet still is he high above all praise.
Summon all your strength to extol him,
and be untiring, for you will always fall
short.
31 Who has seen him, that he can describe
him?
Can anyone praise him as he truly is?
32 We have seen but a small part of his
works,
and there remain many mysteries
greater still.
33 The Lord has created all things,
and to the godly he has granted
wisdom.

Heroes of Israel's past

44 LET us now praise famous men,
the fathers of our people in their
generations;
2 to them the Lord assigned great glory,
his majestic greatness from of old.
3 Some held sway over kingdoms
and gained renown by their might.
Others were far-seeing counsellors
who spoke out with prophetic power.
4 Some guided the people by their
deliberations
and by their knowledge of the nation's
law,
giving instruction from their fund of
wisdom.
5 Some were composers of music;
some were writers of poetry.
6 Others were endowed with wealth and
strength,
living at ease in their homes.
7 All those won glory in their own
generation

43.27–33: God's power. This is the conclusion of 42.15–43.33. **27:** To say that *God is all* is a poetic exaggeration, for God is not the things God has created; compare Wisd. 1.7. **32:** What we have *seen* (nature) points beyond itself, to the *mysteries* of the invisible worlds and of God.

44.1–15: Introduction to the praises of heroes. 1–2: *Heroes* are remembered not for themselves, but because they reveal God's *majestic greatness*. **3–7:** The prominence of *far-seeing counsellors* here contrasts

and were the pride of their times.
8 Some there are who have left behind
    them a name
  to be commemorated in story.
9 Others are unremembered;
  they have perished as though they had
    never existed,
  as though they had never been born;
  so too it was with their children after
    them.
10 But not so our forefathers, men true to
    their faith,
  whose virtuous deeds have not been
    forgotten.
11 Their prosperity is handed on to their
    descendants,
  their inheritance to future
    generations.
12 Through them their children are within
    the covenants —
  the whole race of their descendants.
13 Their line will endure for all time;
  their glory will never die.
14 Their bodies are buried in peace
  and their name lives for ever.
15 Nations will tell of their wisdom,
  and the assembled people will sing their
    praise.

16 Enoch pleased the Lord and was taken
    up to heaven,
  an example of repentance to future
    ages.

17 Noah was found perfect and
    righteous,
  and thus he made amends in the time
    of God's wrath;
  that was why when the flood came
  a remnant survived on the earth.
18 An everlasting covenant was established
    with him,
  that never again should all life be swept
    away by a flood.

19 Abraham was the great father of a host
    of nations;
  no one has ever been found to equal
    him in fame.
20 He kept the law of the Most High;
  he entered into a covenant with him,
  setting the mark of it on his body.
  When put to the test he proved
    steadfast.
21 Therefore the Lord assured him on
    oath
  that through his descendants nations
    should find blessing,
  and that his family should be countless
    as the dust of the earth
  and be exalted as high as the stars;
  that their territories should extend
    from sea to sea,
  from the river to the ends of the earth.

22 To Isaac, for the sake of Abraham his
    father,
  he gave the same assurance
  of a blessing for all mankind and a
    covenant.
23 He made the blessing rest on the head
    of Jacob,
  who was confirmed in the blessings he
    had received
  and was given the land for his
    inheritance,
  divided into portions
  which were allotted to the twelve tribes.

45 From Jacob's stock the Lord raised
   up a man of faith
  who won favour in the eyes of all:
  Moses of blessed memory, beloved by
    God and his people.
2 The Lord made him equal in glory to
    the angels,
  giving him power to the terror of his
    enemies.
3 He sent sign after sign at his request,

---

with the actual functions of those who are named later. **9:** The *unremembered,* are powerful people who were disloyal to God, unless the author here acknowledges that there were pious people whose memory was forgotten among human beings.

44.16–18: Enoch and Noah. 16: *Enoch* also appears at 49.14 and may be a copyist's addition here. **17–18:** On the *covenant* with *Noah,* see Gen. 8.20–22; 9.8–17.

44.19–23: Abraham, Isaac, and Jacob. 20: Ecclesiasticus remembers *Abraham* because he *kept the law* (Gen. 26.5); contrast Rom. 4.1–25. The *mark* of the *covenant* was circumcision; see Gen. 17.10–14, 23–27.

45.1–5: Moses. 2: *Angels:* represents a weakened Gk. translation of Exod. 4.16; 7.1, where Moses is like a "god" to Aaron and Pharaoh; the same Heb. word *elohim* is translated by "god" and "angels." **3:** The *sign after sign* were the plagues of Egypt; see Exod. 7.14–11.10; 12.29–32. The revelation of *some part of* God's

so enhancing his reputation with the
  king.
He gave him a commission to his
  people
and revealed to him some part of his
  glory.
⁴ For his loyalty and humility he
  consecrated him,
choosing him above everyone else.
⁵ He let him hear his voice
and brought him into the dark cloud,
where face to face he gave him the
  commandments,
law which is the source of life and
  knowledge,
so that he might teach his covenant to
  Jacob,
his decrees to Israel.

⁶ He raised up Aaron of the tribe of
  Levi,
a holy man like his brother.
⁷ He made an everlasting covenant with
  him,
conferring on him the priesthood of
  the nation.
He honoured and adorned him,
clothing him in splendid vestments,
⁸ robing him in full and proud array.
He gave him the emblems of his
  station,
the linen trousers, the mantle, and the
  tunic.
⁹ Round his robe he put pomegranates
and a circle of many golden bells
to make music as he walked,
ringing aloud throughout the temple
as a reminder to his people.
¹⁰ He gave him the sacred vestment
  adorned with embroidery,
gold and violet and purple;
the oracle of judgement with the tokens
  of truth;
¹¹ the scarlet thread spun with a
  craftsman's art;
the precious stones, engraved like
  signets,
and mounted by the jeweller in a
  setting of gold,
with inscriptions to serve as reminders,

one for each of the tribes of Israel;
¹² the gold diadem upon his turban,
engraved like a signet with 'Holy to the
  Lord'.
A proud adornment! A miracle of art!
What rich decoration to delight the
  eyes!
¹³ Before him there had not been such
  things of beauty.
Only his family has ever worn them,
throughout the ages only his sons and
  his descendants.
¹⁴ Twice each day without fail
they present his sacrifice, a complete
  offering.

¹⁵ It was Moses who installed him
and anointed him with sacred oil,
to mark the everlasting covenant made
  with him
and with his descendants as long as the
  heavens endure,
that he should be the Lord's minister in
  the priestly office
and bless his people in his name.
¹⁶ The Lord chose him out of all mankind
to bring offerings to him,
incense and the fragrance of memorial
  sacrifice,
to make expiation for the people.
¹⁷ He entrusted to him his
  commandments,
with authority to pronounce legal
  decisions,
to teach Jacob his decrees
and enlighten Israel about his law.

¹⁸ Upstarts became envious of him
and conspired against him in the
  wilderness:
Dathan and Abiram with their
  supporters
and Korah's men inflamed with anger.
¹⁹ The Lord saw and was displeased;
in the heat of his wrath he destroyed
  them;

45:10 **the oracle . . . truth:** *or* the breastpiece of
judgement with the Urim and Thummim (*Exod.
28:30*).   **45:12 signet . . . Lord:** *cp.* Exod. 28:36; *lit.*
signet of holiness.

---

glory was that of Exod. 33.18–34.8. **4:** For Moses' *humility*, see Num. 12.3.

45.6–26: Aaron and Phinehas. As founder of the priestly line, Aaron receives far more attention than Moses;
compare the long treatment of Simon (50.1–21). **7–13:** For the *splendid vestments*, see Exod. 28.1–43; they
symbolize the glory of God's service. **15:** For Aaron's anointing with *sacred oil*, see Lev. 8.10–13. **18–22:** For

amid portents he consumed them with
blazing fire.

20 But he added to Aaron's glory
and gave him a heritage
by allotting to the priests the choicest
firstfruits,
thus ensuring that they above all should
have bread in plenty;

21 for they eat the sacrifices of the Lord,
which he gave to Aaron and his
descendants.

22 But Aaron was to have no holding in
the land of his people,
no portion among them was allotted to
him;
the Lord himself is his portion and
holding.

23 Phinehas son of Eleazar ranks third in
renown
for being zealous in reverence towards
the Lord,
and for standing firm with noble
courage
when the people defected;
by so doing he made expiation for
Israel.

24 Therefore a covenant was established
with him,
assuring him charge of the sanctuary
and the people,
conferring on him and on his
descendants
the high-priesthood for ever.

25 As by a covenant with David son of
Jesse of the tribe of Judah
the royal succession should always pass
from father to son,
so the priestly succession was to pass
from Aaron to his descendants.

26 Now praise the Lord who is
good
and gives you a crown of glory!
May he grant you a wise mind
to judge his people with justice,
so that their prosperity may never
vanish
and their glory may be passed on to
future generations!

46 Joshua son of Nun was a mighty
warrior
and the successor of Moses in the
prophetic office.
He well deserved his name
as a great saviour of the Lord's chosen
people.
He wrought vengeance on the enemies
who attacked them,
and so put Israel in possession of its
heritage.

2 How glorious he was when with
upraised hand
he brandished his sword against the
city!

3 He was fighting the Lord's battles
and none could oppose him.

4 Was it not through him that the sun
stood still
and made one day as long as two?

5 When the enemy was pressing him
hard on every side,
he called to the Most High, the Mighty
One;
his prayer was answered by the great
Lord,

6 who displayed his power in a storm of
hail.
Joshua overwhelmed the hostile nation
and crushed his assailants as they fled
down the pass,
that the nations should know the source
of his strength
and learn that he fought under the
eyes of the Lord,
for he followed where the Mighty One
led.

7 In the time of Moses he had proved his
faithfulness,
he and Caleb son of Jephunneh:
they stood their ground against the
assembled Israelites,
restrained the people from sin,
and silenced their wicked grumbling.

8 Out of six hundred thousand warriors
these two alone survived
to bring the people into their heritage,
into a land flowing with milk and
honey.

Dathan, Abiram, and *Korah,* see Num. 16.1–33. **23–26:** The defense of *Phinehas* (see Num. 25.1–13) may
reflect a challenge to the priestly line in the time of the author.

46.1–10: Joshua and Caleb. 1: For *Joshua's* succession to the *prophetic office,* see Deut. 34.9. **7:** The
faithfulness of Joshua and Caleb (see Num. 14.5–10) makes them exemplary.

9 The Lord gave Caleb strength,
which even in old age did not fail him,
and he was able to invade the
hill-country
and win possession of it for his
descendants.
10 Thus all Israel might see
how good it is to follow the Lord.

11 Then there are the judges, name after
famous name;
all of them rejected idolatry
and never turned away from the
Lord—
blessings be on their memory!
12 May their bones send forth new life
from the grave!
May the fame of the honoured dead be
matched by their sons!

13 Samuel was beloved by his Lord.
As prophet of the Lord he established
the monarchy
and anointed rulers over his people.
14 He dispensed justice according to the
law of the Lord,
and the Lord kept watch over the
people of Jacob.
15 By his fidelity he was proved a
trustworthy prophet;
his faithfulness to his vision was shown
by his words.
16 When enemies were pressing him hard
on every side,
he called to the mighty Lord,
offering a sucking-lamb in sacrifice.
17 Then the Lord thundered from
heaven,
making his voice heard in a mighty
sound,
18 and routed the leaders of the enemy,
all the lords of the Philistines.
19 Before the time came for his eternal
sleep,
Samuel called the Lord and his
anointed to witness:
'I have never taken anyone's property,

not so much as a pair of shoes';
and no man brought any charge against
him.
20 Even after he had gone to his rest he
prophesied
and made the king's fate known to him,
lifting up his voice in prophecy from
the ground
to wipe out the wickedness of the
people.

47 After him there arose Nathan
to prophesy in the reign of David.
2 As the choice fat is set aside from the
sacrifice,
so David was chosen out of all Israel.
3 He disported himself with lions as
though they were young goats,
with bears as though they were lambs.
4 While still a youth he killed a giant
and removed the shame of his people,
when he whirled his sling with its stone
and brought down the arrogant
Goliath;
5 for he called to the Lord Most High,
who gave strength to his right arm
to strike that mighty warrior down
6 and win victory for his people.
So they hailed him as conqueror of tens
of thousands,
and sang his praises for the blessings
bestowed by the Lord.
When he assumed the glorious crown,
7 he fought and subdued enemies on
every side;
he crushed the resistance of the
Philistines,
whose power remains broken to this
day.
8 In all he did he gave thanks,
ascribing glory to the Holy One, the
Most High;
with all his heart he sang hymns of
praise
to show his love for his Maker.

46:18 **the enemy:** *so Heb.; Gk* Tyre.

46.11–12: The judges.

46.13–20: Samuel. 15: Samuel's position as a *trustworthy prophet* (see 1 Sam. 3.19–21; 9.6) is based on his *fidelity* which all can emulate. **20:** Despite his opposition to divination (compare 34.5), Ecclus. includes the incident of the necromancer of En-dor among Samuel's achievements (see 1 Sam. 28.3–20).

47.1–11: Nathan and David. 1: Nathan (2 Sam. 7.1–17; 12.1–14) links the prophetic line of Samuel to Elijah. **8–11:** David's sponsorship of ceremonial worship (1 Chr. 23.1–6, 24–32) is mentioned in line with the author's interest in cult.

⁹He appointed musicians to stand before
the altar
and sing sweet music to the harp.
¹⁰He ordered the festivals with dignity
and fixed for all time the round of
sacred seasons,
when the Lord's holy name is praised
and the sanctuary resounds from dawn
to dusk.
¹¹The Lord pardoned his sins
and endowed him with great power for
ever:
by a covenant he gave him the kingship
and a glorious throne in Israel.

¹²He was succeeded by a wise son,
Solomon;
thanks to David his father, he lived in
spacious days.
¹³He reigned in an age of peace,
because on every side God gave him
tranquillity,
that he might build a house in God's
honour,
a sanctuary founded to last for ever.
¹⁴How wise you were, Solomon, in your
youth,
full of understanding like a brimming
river!
¹⁵Your mind embraced the whole world,
and you stored it with proverbs and
riddles.
¹⁶Your fame reached distant islands,
and you were beloved for your peaceful
reign.
¹⁷Your songs, your sayings, your
proverbs,
and the answers you gave were the
wonders of the world.
¹⁸In the name of the Lord God,
who is known as the God of Israel,
you amassed gold and silver
like so much tin and lead.
¹⁹But you took women to lie at your side
and let them usurp your authority.
²⁰You stained your reputation
and tainted your line.

You brought God's wrath on your
children
and there was outrage at your folly,
²¹because it divided the sovereignty
and in Ephraim a rebel dynasty came to
power.
²²But the Lord never ceases to be
merciful;
he does not destroy what he himself
has made;
he will never wipe out the offspring of
his chosen servant
or cut short the line of one who has
loved him.
So he granted a remnant to Jacob
and let a scion of David survive.

²³When Solomon rested with his
forefathers,
he left one of his sons to succeed him,
a man of weak mind, the fool of the
nation,
Rehoboam, whose policy drove the
people to revolt.
Jeroboam son of Nebat led Israel into
sin
and started Ephraim on its wicked
course.
²⁴Their sins increased beyond measure
until they were driven into exile from
their native land;
²⁵they explored every kind of wickedness
until punishment overtook them.

48 Then there arose Elijah, a prophet
like fire,
whose word blazed like a torch.
²He brought famine on the people,
and in his zeal reduced them in
number.
³By the word of the Lord he shut up the
sky,
and three times he called down fire
from heaven.
⁴How glorious you were, Elijah, in your
miracles!
Who else can boast such deeds?

47.12–22: Solomon. 14–17: Solomon was a model sage; see 1 Kgs. 3.6–12; 4.29–34. **19–20:** *Women* were Solomon's downfall; compare 9.2; 1 Kgs. 11.1–13. **21:** Solomon's greed and *folly* were the root of the *rebel* dynasty; 1 Kgs. 12.1–5.
47.23–25: Rehoboam and Jeroboam. See 1 Kgs. 12.1–20. **23:** Jeroboam *led Israel into sin* by initiating illicit worship; 1 Kgs. 12.28–31.
48.1–16: Elijah and Elisha. See 1 Kgs. 17.1–19.21; 21.1–29; 2 Kgs. 1.1–9.3.

⁵ By the word of the Most High
   you raised a corpse from death and the
      grave.
⁶ You sent kings and famous men
   from their sick-beds down to
      destruction.
⁷ You heard a rebuke at Sinai,
   a sentence of doom at Horeb.
⁸ You anointed kings for retribution,
   and a prophet to succeed you.
⁹ You were taken up to heaven in a fiery
      whirlwind,
   in a chariot drawn by horses of fire.
¹⁰ Scripture records that you are to come
      at the appointed time
   to allay the divine wrath before it
      erupts in fury,
   to reconcile father and son,
   and to restore the tribes of Jacob.

¹¹ Happy are those who see you,
   happy those who have fallen asleep in
      love!
   (For we also shall certainly live.)

¹² After Elijah had vanished in a
      whirlwind,
   Elisha was filled with his spirit.
   Throughout his life no ruler made him
      tremble,
   no one lorded it over him.
¹³ Nothing was too difficult for him,
   and even in the grave his body kept its
      prophetic power.
¹⁴ In life he worked miracles;
   in death also his deeds were marvellous.

¹⁵ Despite all this the people did not
      repent
   or renounce their sins,
   until they were carried off captive from
      their land
   and scattered over the whole world.
   Only a very small nation was left
   under a ruler from the house of
      David;
¹⁶ some of them did what was pleasing to
      the Lord,
   but others committed sin upon sin.

¹⁷ Hezekiah fortified his city
   and brought water within its walls;
   with tools of iron he cut through sheer
      rock
   and made cisterns for the water.
¹⁸ In his reign Sennacherib invaded the
      country,
   and from Lachish sent Rab-shakeh,
   who came with threats against Zion,
   boasting loudly in his arrogance.
¹⁹ At this the people were unnerved in
      heart and hand,
   and suffered the anguish of a woman
      in labour;
²⁰ they called to the merciful Lord,
   holding out their hands to him in
      supplication.
   From heaven the Holy One quickly
      answered their prayer:
   he sent Isaiah to the rescue,
²¹ he struck at the camp of the Assyrians
   and his angel destroyed them.
²² For Hezekiah did what was pleasing to
      the Lord
   and held firmly to the ways of David
      his ancestor
   as he was instructed to do by Isaiah,
   the great prophet whose vision could be
      trusted.
²³ In his time the sun went back,
   and he added many years to the king's
      life.
²⁴ With inspired power he saw the future
   and comforted the mourners in Zion.
²⁵ He revealed what was to be until the
      end of time,
   the secrets of things still to come.

49 The memory of Josiah is fragrant
      as incense
   blended by the perfumer's craft,
   sweet as honey to every palate
   or like music at a banquet.
² He followed a right course, reforming
      the nation
   and rooting out loathsome and lawless
      practices.
³ He was wholeheartedly loyal to the
      Lord

10: *Scripture records:* a reference to Mal. 4.5–6; compare 2 Esd. 6.26; Matt. 17.10–13. **11:** *Shall certainly live:* from the Gk., appears to speak of the resurrection; the Heb. is obscure here but probably did not affirm this belief, since elsewhere the author rejects this belief. **15:** *Scattered:* see 2 Kgs. 17.6.

48.17–25: Hezekiah and Isaiah. See 2 Kgs. chs. 18–20. **24:** See Isa. 40.1–2. **25:** The view that prophecy *revealed . . . secrets* for later times was widespread; compare Isa. 41.22–23; 44.7.

and in a lawless age made godliness
prevail.

4 Except David, Hezekiah, and Josiah,
all were guilty of wrongdoing,
for all abandoned the law of the Most
High.
So the royal line of Judah came to an
end;
5 they surrendered their power to others
and their glory to a foreign nation.
6 The chosen city, the city of the
sanctuary, was set on fire,
and its streets were left deserted, as
Jeremiah had foretold.
7 He was maltreated,
even though he was a prophet
consecrated from the womb
to uproot, to damage, and to demolish,
but also to build and to plant.

8 There was revealed to Ezekiel a vision
of the Glory
which was enthroned on the chariot of
the cherubim.
9 The Lord remembered his enemies and
sent a storm,
but to those who kept to the right path
he brought benefits.
10 May the bones of the twelve prophets
also
send forth new life from the grave!
For they put new heart into Jacob,
and by their confident hope delivered
the people.

11 How can we tell the greatness of
Zerubbabel,
who was like a signet ring on the Lord's
right hand?
12 Jeshua son of Jozadak was with him,

and in their day they rebuilt the house,
erecting a temple holy to the Lord,
destined for eternal glory.
13 Great also is the memory of Nehemiah,
who restored for us the fallen walls,
who reconstructed their barred gates,
and built again our ruined homes.

14 No one to equal Enoch has been
created on earth,
for from the earth he was taken up into
heaven.
15 No man has been born to be Joseph's
peer,
the ruler of his brothers and the
support of the people;
over his bones watch was kept.
16 Shem and Seth were honoured among
men,
but Adam holds pre-eminence over all
creation.

50 Greatest among his brothers and
the glory of his people
was the high priest Simon son of Onias
in whose lifetime the house was
repaired,
in whose days the temple was fortified.
2 He laid the foundation for the high
double wall,
the high retaining wall of the temple
precinct.
3 In his day a reservoir was dug,
a cistern broad as the sea.
4 He was concerned to ward off disaster
from his people
and made the city strong against siege.
5 How glorious he was as he processed
through the temple,
emerging from behind the veil of the
sanctuary!

49.1–7: Josiah and Jeremiah. 1–3: See 2 Kgs. 22.1–23.30. **7:** *Maltreated:* see Jer. 37.15–38. *Uproot . . .
plant:* see Jer. 1.10.

49.8–10: Ezekiel and the twelve prophets. 8: See Ezek. 1.1–28. **10:** The *twelve "minor" prophets* are
regarded as a single book. Some of the twelve lived after the return from captivity and encouraged the captives
to rebuild: see Zech. 1.16; Hag. 1.8; 2.3–9.

49.11–13: Zerubbabel, Joshua, and Nehemiah. Hag. 1.1; 2.2–4; Zech. chs. 3–4; Neh. 7.1. Note that Ezra
is not specifically named.

49.14–16: Ancient heroes. Rather oddly these early heroes are inserted at this point; see 44.16.

50.1–21: Simon the son of Onias. He was high priest about 225–200 B.C.E.; although there may have been
an earlier Simon, it is the consensus that this one, actually known to the author, is meant. **5–21:** These verses
describe the service on the Day of Atonement. On this day only, in connection with the blessing, the high priest
pronounced the sacred *name* of Yahweh (v. 20).

6 He was like the morning star appearing
   through a cloud
 or the full moon on festal days;
7 like the sun shining on the temple of
   the Most High
 or the light of the rainbow on the
   gleaming clouds;
8 like a rose in springtime
 or lilies by a fountain of water;
 like a green shoot upon Lebanon on a
   summer's day
9 or frankincense burning in the censer;
 like a cup all of beaten gold,
   decorated with every kind of precious
   stone;
10 like an olive tree laden with fruit
 or a cypress with its summit in the
   clouds.
11 When he assumed his resplendent
   vestments,
 robing himself in full and proud
   array,
 he went up to the holy altar,
   adding lustre to the court of the
   sanctuary.
12 While he received the sacrificial
   portions from the priests,
 as he stood by the altar hearth
 with his brother priests around him like
   a garland,
 he was like a young cedar of Lebanon
   in the midst of encircling palms.
13 All the priests of Aaron's line in their
   splendour
 stood before the whole assembly of
   Israel,
 holding the Lord's offering in their
   hands.
14 To complete the ceremonies at the
   altar
 and adorn the offering of the Most
   High, the Almighty,
15 he reached out his hand for the cup
 and made the libation from the blood
   of the grape,
 pouring its fragrance at the base of the
   altar
 to the Most High, the King of all.
16 Then the priests of Aaron's line
   shouted
 and blew their trumpets of beaten
   silver;

they sounded a mighty fanfare
 as a reminder before the Most High.
17 At once all the people prostrated
   themselves
 to worship their Lord, the Almighty,
   God Most High.
18 The choir broke into praise,
 in the full, sweet strains of resounding
   song,
19 while the people were making their
   petitions
 to the Lord Most High, the Merciful
   One,
 until the liturgy of the Lord was
   finished
 and the ritual complete.
20 Then Simon came down and raised his
   hands
 over the whole congregation of Israel
 to pronounce the Lord's blessing
 and to glory in his name;
21 and again they bowed in worship
 to receive the blessing from the Most
   High.

22 Now COME, let us praise the God of the
   universe,
 who everywhere works great wonders,
 who from our birth raises us up
 and deals with us in mercy.
23 May he grant us a joyful heart,
 and in our days send Israel lasting
   peace.
24 May he confirm his mercy towards us,
 and in his own good time grant us
   deliverance.

25 Two nations I detest,
 and a third is no nation at all:
26 the inhabitants of Mount Seir, the
   Philistines,
 and the senseless folk that live at
   Shechem.

27 I, Jesus son of Sirach Eleazar, of
   Jerusalem,
 whose mind became a fountain of
   wisdom,
 have provided in this book

50:26 **Mount Seir:** *cp. Heb.; Gk* the mountain of
Samaria.

50.22–24: **Conclusion to the praise of heroes. 23:** The language shows uneasiness about *lasting peace*.
50.25–26: **A fragment.** It is directed against the Idumeans, the Philistines, and the Samaritans.
50.27–29: **The author's conclusion.** Unlike other writers in the Apocrypha, he gives his own name.

instruction in good sense and understanding.

28 Happy the man who occupies himself with these things,
who lays them to heart and becomes wise!

29 If he follows them he will be equal to anything,
for the light of the Lord will shine on his path.

Epilogue

51 I SHALL give thanks to you, Lord and King;
I shall praise you, God my Saviour.
I give thanks to you

2 because you have been my protector and my helper,
rescuing me from destruction,
from the trap laid by a slanderous tongue
and from lips that invent lies.
In the face of my assailants you came to my help;

3 in the fullness of your mercy and honour you rescued me
from gnashing teeth waiting to devour me,
from hands that threatened my life,
from the many troubles I endured,

4 from the choking fire enveloping me,
from flames I had not kindled,

5 from the deep recesses of the grave,
from the foul tongue and the lying word—

6 a wicked slander spoken in the king's presence.
I came very near to death,
close to the brink of the grave.

7 On every side I was surrounded
and there was no one to help;
I looked for human aid and there was none.

8 Then I remembered your mercy, Lord,
what you did in days long past;
you deliver those who put their trust in you
and free them from the power of their enemies.

9 From the earth I sent up my prayer,
begging to be rescued from death.

10 I cried, 'Lord, you are my Father;
do not abandon me in time of trouble,
when I am helpless in the face of arrogance.

11 I shall praise you continually;
I shall sing hymns of thanksgiving.'
My petition was granted,

12 for you saved me from destruction,
bringing me out from my desperate plight.
Therefore I shall give you thanks and praise;
I shall bless the name of the Lord.

13 WHEN I was still young, before I set off on my travels,
in my prayers I asked openly for wisdom.

14 In the forecourt of the sanctuary I laid claim to her,
and I shall seek her to the end.

15 From the first blossom to the ripening of the grape
she has been the delight of my heart.
From my youth my steps have followed her without swerving.

16 I had hardly begun to listen when I was rewarded,
and I gained for myself much instruction.

17 I made progress in my studies;
all glory to God who gives me wisdom!

18 I determined to practise what I learnt;
I pursued goodness, and shall never regret it.

19 With all my might I strove for wisdom
and was scrupulous in whatever I did.
I spread out my hands to Heaven above,
deploring my shortcomings;

20 I set my heart on possessing wisdom,
and by keeping myself pure I found her.
With her I gained understanding from the first;
therefore I shall never be at a loss.

21 Because I passionately yearned to discover her,
a noble possession was mine:

22 as my reward the Lord gave me eloquence,
and with it I shall praise him.

51.1–30: Epilogue; two psalms. 1–12: This psalm is modeled after the psalms of deliverance; compare Ps.
18.1–19, 49. **13–30:** An acrostic (alphabetic) psalm. **13–22:** A young man searches for Wisdom, which is

23 YOU THAT are uninstructed,
   come to me and lodge in the house of
   instruction.
24 Why do you still lack these things
   and leave your great thirst
   unslaked?
25 I have made this proclamation:
   'Buy wisdom for yourselves without
   money.
26 Bend your neck to the yoke
   and be ready to accept instruction;
   you need not go far to find it.'
27 See for yourselves how little were my
   labours

compared with the great refreshment I
   have found.
28 Your instruction may cost you a large
   amount of silver,
   but it will bring you a large return in
   gold.
29 May you take delight in the Lord's
   mercy
   and never be ashamed of praising him.
30 Do your duty in good time,
   and he in his own time will give you
   your reward.

51:24 **Why ... things:** *prob. rdg; Gk obscure.*

personified as a beautiful woman; see 4.12 n. **23–30:** A Wisdom teacher invites pupils in language very similar
to the appeal of Wisdom; see 4.11–19; 24.19–22. **23:** The *house of instruction* was later the regular term for
rabbinical schools.

Baruch

This book carries the name of Baruch, Jeremiah's close friend and secretary (Jer. chs. 32 and 45). If that Baruch were indeed the author, the book would have come from the sixth century B.C.E., but a later date and different authorship seem involved. The book was probably written in Hebrew, but the original writing has not survived. It shows little or no unity respecting authorship, style, age, and even Greek translator or translators. The divergent viewpoints (compare 1.11 and 2.22 with 4.15, 25) and the book's dependence on later writings (i.e. 1.15–3.8 on Neh. ch. 9 and Dan. 9.4–19) suggest a date between 200 and 150 B.C.E., although a date as late as the first century B.C.E. is possible.

This anthology of prayers and hymns provides a rare glimpse of religion in the synagogues outside the land of Israel, reflecting devotion to the temple and the religious authority at Jerusalem, resistance to foreign idolatry, and continuous meditation on the Law and other sacred writings like Jeremiah, Isaiah (chs. 40–55, 60–62), Daniel, Proverbs, and Job.

After a narrative introduction (1.1–14), there follow a group confession of sins and lamentation in prose (1.15–3.8), then in poetic meter a hymnic praise of wisdom (3.9–4.4) and a medley of prophetic poems of hope or tender lament about Jerusalem (4.5–5.9).

A message to a conquered people

1 This is the book of Baruch son of Neriah, son of Mahseiah, son of Zedekiah, son of Hasadiah, son of Hilkiah, written by him in Babylon, ²on the seventh day of the month, in the fifth year after the capture and burning of Jerusalem by the Chaldaeans.

³Baruch read the book aloud to Jeconiah son of Joakim, king of Judah, and to the whole community assembled to hear it: ⁴the nobles, the princes of the royal blood, the elders, and all the people, high and low — in short, all who were living in Babylon by the river Soud. ⁵Then with tears and fasting they offered their prayers before the Lord. ⁶Each of them got together as much money as he could, ⁷and this was sent to Jerusalem, to the high priest Joakim son of Hilkiah, son of Shallum, and to the other priests and all the people who were with him there. ⁸At the same time, on the tenth day of the month of Sivan, Baruch took the vessels belonging to the house of the Lord which had been looted from the temple, and returned them to the land of Judah. These were the silver vessels which Zedekiah son of Josiah, king of Judah, had made, ⁹after King Nebuchadnezzar of Babylon deported Jeconiah from Jerusalem and carried him off to Babylon, along with the rulers, craftsmen, nobles, and the common people.

¹⁰They sent this message: The money we are sending you is to be used to buy whole-offerings, sin-offerings, and frankincense, and to provide grain-offerings; you are to offer them on the altar of the Lord our God, ¹¹with prayers for King Nebuchadnezzar of Bab-

1:9 **craftsmen:** *prob. rdg; Gk* prisoners.
1:10 **sin-offerings:** *or* purification-offerings.

1.1–14: Introduction. By means of a pseudohistorical setting this section unites the liturgical prayers and pilgrimages of the Jews in the Diaspora with those of their ancestors in the Babylonian Exile (587–539 B.C.E.). Historical difficulties are many, such as the *month* intended in v. 2. Too, *Joakim* the *high priest* (v. 7) is unknown to us except in the historical romance of Jdt. 4.6 (see n. there). The temple is presumed to be destroyed in v. 2 and to be already rebuilt by its devastator in v. 10. *Belshazzar* (v. 11) was actually the son of Nabonidus, not of *Nebuchadnezzar;* see Dan. 1.1 n., 5.1 n., 5.2, 13, 18, 22. (Nabonidus, the last king of Babylon, reigned from 555–539 B.C.E.) **2:** *Jerusalem* fell in July 587 B.C.E. and was burned to the ground by order of Nebuchadnezzar a month later (2 Kgs. 25.3, 8–9). **3:** *Jeconiah:* King Jehoiachin, considered the legitimate king by fellow exiles (see Ezek. 1.2). **4:** *The river Soud* was undoubtedly one of the many irrigation canals carrying water from the Euphrates. **5:** *Fasting* became more frequent in postexilic times (Dan. 9.3; Zech. 7.1–5). **8:** *Sivan:* third month ylon and for his son Belshazzar, that their life may last as long as the heavens are above the earth. [12] So the Lord will strengthen us and bring light to our eyes, and we shall live under the protection of King Nebuchadnezzar of Babylon and of Belshazzar his son; we shall give them service for many a day and find favour with them. [13] Pray also for us to the Lord our God, because we have sinned against him, and to this day the Lord's anger and wrath have not been averted from us.

[14] You shall read this book we are sending you, and on the feast day and throughout the festal season make confession in the house of the Lord [15] in these words: The right is on the side of the Lord our God; the shame, now as ever, belongs to us, the men of Judah and the citizens of Jerusalem, [16] to our kings and rulers, our priests and prophets, and to our forefathers. [17] We have sinned against the Lord [18] and disobeyed him; we paid no heed to the voice of the Lord our God and did not conform to the laws he laid down for us. [19] We have been disobedient to the Lord our God from the day he brought our forefathers out of Egypt until now; we have thoughtlessly disregarded his voice. [20] So we find ourselves in the grip of adversity, suffering under the curse which the Lord commanded his servant Moses to pronounce, when he led our forefathers out of Egypt to give us a land flowing with milk and honey, as it still is today. [21] Moreover, we refused to hear the Lord our God speaking in all the words of the prophets he sent us; [22] we went our own way, each to follow the promptings of his wicked heart, to serve other gods, and to do what was evil in the sight of the Lord our God.

2 The Lord has made good the warning he gave about us and about our judges in Israel, about our kings and rulers and the people of Israel and Judah. [2] Under the whole of heaven no such things have been done as were done in Jerusalem; they fulfilled what was foretold in the law of Moses: [3] that we should eat the flesh of our children, one his own son and another his own daughter. [4] The Lord made our nation subject to all the kingdoms round about; to all the peoples among whom he had scattered us our name was a byword, our land a wilderness. [5] Instead of rising high, our nation sank low, because in disregarding his voice we sinned against the Lord our God. [6] The right is on the side of the Lord our God; the shame, now as ever, belongs to us and to our forefathers. [7] All those disasters of which the Lord gave us warning have come upon us; [8] yet we did not entreat the Lord to turn each one of us from the thoughts of his wicked heart. [9] The Lord has kept strict watch and brought the disasters on us. In all that he has done to us he is just; [10] yet we did not heed his warning, nor did we conform to the laws he laid down for our guidance.

[11] Lord God of Israel, who brought your people out of Egypt by a strong hand, with signs and portents, with great power and arm uplifted, winning for yourself a name that lives on to this day, [12] now, Lord our God, we have broken all your commandments by our sin, our godlessness, and our injustice. [13] Turn your anger away from us, for we are left few in number among the heathen where you have scattered us. [14] Listen, Lord, to our prayer and supplication, deliver us for your own sake, and grant us favour with those who have taken us into exile, [15] so that the whole world may know you are the Lord our God, and yours is the name by which Israel and his posterity are called.

[16] Lord, look down from your holy dwelling-place and take thought for us; incline

(May–June). **11:** This request to pray for the foreigner *Nebuchadnezzar* reveals a broad-minded spirit of prayer reaching beyond national prejudice as well as a monotheistic faith in one God for all people; see Rom. 13.1–7. **14:** Those Jews so fortunate as to be living in Jerusalem are directed to *make* their humble *confession* of sin in the name of the exiles *on the feast day* of Tabernacles (Booths), the final harvest festival and victory celebration of the Lord's sovereignty (Lev. 23.33–43; Zech. 14.16–21).

   1.15–3.8: Penitential prayer of the exiles. From an original Heb. text, this prose lament recasts a popular prayer, preserved even more carefully in Dan. 9.4–19; see Ezra 9.6–15; Neh. ch. 9. Because of 2.17, this lament is to be dated around 180 B.C.E., the period of Ecclus., since both books are silent about the resurrection (Ecclus. 17.27–28; Ps. 6.5), which is explicitly stated in Dan. 12.1–3 and 2 Macc. ch. 7. The principal theme is that of God's justice and God's merciful fidelity in fulfilling the promises to Israel; see 1.15; 2.6. **20:** *Curse of Moses:* Deut. 28.15–37. **2.3:** *Eat the flesh of our children:* see 2 Kgs. 6.28; Lam. 2.20. **11:** Transition from your ear to us, Lord, and hear; [17] open your eyes, Lord, and see. The dead are in their graves, all breath gone from their bodies, and they cannot sing the Lord's praises or applaud his justice; [18] it is the living, mourning their fall from greatness, walking the earth bent and enfeebled, with eyes dimmed and with failing appetite—it is they, Lord, who will sing your praises and applaud your justice.

[19] Not for any righteous deeds of our forefathers and our kings do we lay before you our plea for pity, Lord our God. [20] You have vented on us that anger and wrath of which you warned us through your servants the prophets when you said: [21] 'These are the words of the Lord: Bow your shoulders and serve the king of Babylon, and you will remain in the land that I gave to your fathers; [22] but if you ignore the Lord's command to serve the king of Babylon, [23] then I shall banish from the cities of Judah and from the streets of Jerusalem the sound of joy and gladness, the voices of bridegroom and bride; the whole land will lie waste and abandoned.' [24] When we went against your command to serve the king of Babylon, you made good the warning given through your servants the prophets: the bones of our kings and of our fathers have been brought out from their resting-place, [25] thrown down, and exposed to the scorching heat by day and the frost by night. They died a painful death by famine, sword, and pestilence. [26] And because of the wickedness of Israel and Judah the house that bears your name has become what it is today.

[27] Yet, Lord our God, you have shown us all your wonted forbearance and all your great mercy. [28] This is as you promised through your servant Moses on the day you commanded him to write down your law in the presence of the Israelites, when you said: [29] 'If you will not heed what I say, this great

swarming multitude will be reduced to a mere handful among the heathen where I shall scatter them. [30] I know this stubborn people will not listen to me, but in the land of their exile they will come to their right mind [31] and know that I am the Lord their God. I shall give them a mind to understand and ears to hear. [32] They will praise me in the land of their exile and turn their thoughts to me; [33] recalling how their forefathers sinned against the Lord, they will repent of their stubbornness and their wicked practices. [34] Then I shall bring them again to the land that I swore to give to their forefathers, Abraham, Isaac, and Jacob, and they will rule over it. I shall increase their number: they will never dwindle away. [35] I shall enter into an everlasting covenant with them, that I become their God and they become my people. Never again shall I remove my people Israel from the land I have given them.'

3 Lord Almighty, God of Israel, to you the soul in anguish and the fainting spirit cry out. [2] Hear and have mercy, Lord, for we have sinned against you. [3] You are enthroned for ever; we are for ever passing away. [4] Now Lord Almighty, God of Israel, hear the prayer of the men of Israel and of the sons of those who sinned against you. They did not heed the voice of the Lord their God, and so we are in the grip of adversity. [5] Do not call to mind the misdeeds of our forefathers, but remember at this time your power and your name, [6] for you are the Lord our God, and we shall praise you, Lord. [7] It is for this that you have put into our hearts the fear of you: to make us call on your name. And we shall praise you in our exile, for we have renounced all the wrongdoing of our forefathers who sinned against you. [8] Today we are exiled in the lands where you have scattered us; you have made us a byword and a curse, to be punished for all the sins of our forefa-

3:4 **men:** *prob. rdg; Gk* dead.

the lament to Israel's petition. **17–18:** For the pious Jew the impossibility of praising God in Sheol is the greatest tragedy of death. Here it is given as a motive in asking God for deliverance. See Ps. 115.17–18. **21–24:** Jeremiah 7.34 and 27.12 are merged; to have rejected Jeremiah was to have disobeyed God. Jeremiah advised surrender to the Babylonians while the city was under siege, and was considered a traitor; see Jer. 26.16–19; 38.1–13. **35:** *Everlasting covenant:* see Jer. 31.31; Ezek. 37.26. This expression of hope reverts to a more primitive stage of "messianism," for it is silent about David and Jerusalem (2 Sam. 7.12–16; 1 Chr. chs. 28–29) and the glorious rule (Amos 9.11–15) over all nations (Isa. 2.1–4). **3.5–8:** Here reappears the old theology which held that social and religious solidarity implied collective guilt and demanded collective punishment (Josh. ch. 7) so that children were *punished for all the sins of* their ancestors. This view was condemned in its excessive form by Jeremiah (31.29) and Ezekiel (ch. 18). Compare Jn. 9.2.

thers, who rebelled against the Lord our God.

9 Israel, listen to the life-giving
  commandments;
  hear, and learn understanding.
10 Why is it, Israel, that you are in your
  enemies' country,
  grown old in a foreign land?
  Why have you shared defilement with
  the dead
11 and been numbered among those that
  lie in the grave?
12 Because you have forsaken the fountain
  of wisdom!
13 If only you had walked in God's ways,
  you would have lived in peace for ever.
14 Where is understanding, where is
  strength,
  where is intelligence? Learn that,
  and you will know where are length of
  days and life,
  where happiness and peace.

15 Who has discovered wisdom's
  dwelling-place,
  who has entered her treasure house?
16 Where are the rulers of the nations
  now?
  Where are those who had lordship over
  earth's wild beasts,
17 those who made their sport with the
  birds of the air?
  Where are the hoarders of silver and
  gold
  in which men put their trust,
  those whose greed knew no limit?
18 Where are the silversmiths with their
  patient skill
  and the secrets of their craft?
19 They have vanished, gone down to the
  grave,

and others have arisen to take their
  place.
20 The light of day dawned on a later
  generation;
  they dwelt in the land,
  but they did not learn the way of
  knowledge
21 or discover its paths; they did not lay
  hold of it;
  their children went far astray.
22 Wisdom was not heard of in Canaan
  or seen in Teman.
23 Hagar's descendants who sought for
  knowledge on earth,
  the merchants of Merran and Teman,
  the story-tellers, the seekers after
  understanding,
  not one of them discovered the way of
  wisdom
  or had any recollection of her paths.

24 Israel, how great is God's
  dwelling-place,
  how vast the extent of his domain!
25 Great and boundless it is, lofty and
  immeasurable.
26 There of old the giants were born,
  a famous race, mighty in stature, skilled
  in war.
27 But those were not chosen by God
  or shown the way of knowledge.
28 Their race perished for lack of insight;
  they perished in their folly.

29 Has anyone gone up to heaven and
  gained wisdom
  and brought her down from the
  clouds?
30 Has anyone crossed the sea and found
  her,
  or obtained her for fine gold?
31 No one can know the path

3.9–4.4: In praise of wisdom. This passage is in verse form like other Wisdom writings. Composed originally in Heb. during a peaceful period like that of Ecclus. (200–180 B.C.E.), it is related thematically to texts like Prov. ch. 1–9, Job 28.12–28, and Ecclus. ch. 24. Addressing Israel, the writer celebrates God's supreme gift of the Law as the source of all life (see Deut. 4.1–40; Ecclus. 24.19–34)—the extent of Baruch's "messianic" expectations. **10:** *Defilement with the dead:* contact with the Babylonians who do not know the Lord or the Law, the source of life; see Deut. 4.4; Ezek. 4.13; 7.21–22; Ps. 119.93. **22–23:** Israel's God-given *wisdom* excelled that of places famous for knowledge, like *Canaan,* from whom the invading Israelites learned city culture and its vices, or like *Teman* to the southeast (Job 4.1; Jer. 49.7), or the bedouin *descendants* of *Hagar* (Gen. ch. 16), or *Merran* (perhaps, Midian, renowned merchants, Gen. 37.28). **24:** *God's dwelling-place* is not the Jerusalem temple but the cosmos (Ezek. ch. 1; Isa. 40.21–28). **26:** *Giants* (Gen. 6.4) destroyed at the flood of Noah were popular figures in later Jewish literature.

or conceive the way that will lead to
her.

32 Only the omniscient God knows her;
the mind of God discovered her.
He who established the earth for all
time
filled it with four-footed animals.

33 He sent forth the light and it went on
its way;
he summoned it, and trembling it
obeyed.

34 The stars shone in their appointed
places and rejoiced;
he summoned them, and they
answered, 'We are ready,'
and joyfully they shone for their
Maker.

35 This is he who is our God;
there is none to compare with him.

36 Every way of knowledge he found out
and gave to Jacob his servant,
to Israel whom he loved.

37 After that, wisdom appeared on earth
and lived among men.

4 She is the book of God's
commandments,
the law that endures for ever.
All who hold fast to her will live,
but those who forsake her will die.

2 Return, you people of Jacob, and lay
hold of her;
set your course towards the radiance of
her light.

3 Do not yield up your glory to another
or your privileges to a foreign nation.

4 Happy are we, Israel,
for we know what is pleasing to God!

5 Take heart, my people, who keep
Israel's name alive.

6 You were sold to the heathen, but not
to be destroyed.
Because you excited God's wrath
you were handed over to the foe,

7 for you provoked your Maker
by sacrificing not to God but to
demons.

8 You forgot the eternal God who
nurtured you;

you caused sorrow to Jerusalem who
fostered you.

9 She saw how God's wrath had befallen
you
and said: Listen, you neighbours of
Zion;
God has brought on me great grief,

10 for I have witnessed the captivity of my
sons and daughters
inflicted on them by the Eternal.

11 With joy I brought them up,
but with tears and mourning I watched
them go.

12 Let no one exult over me, a widow,
forsaken by so many,
left desolate through the sins of my
children.
They turned away from the law of
God;

13 they would not learn his statutes,
nor would they follow his
commandments,
nor let God guide and train them in his
righteousness.

14 Come, you neighbours of Zion,
bear in mind the captivity of my sons
and daughters
inflicted on them by the Eternal;

15 for he let loose on them a nation from
afar,
a ruthless nation speaking a strange
tongue
and with no reverence for the old,
no pity for the young.

16 They carried off the widow's beloved
sons,
and left her in loneliness, bereft of her
daughters.

17 But I, how can I help you?

18 Only the One who brought the disasters
on you
can deliver you from the power of your
enemies.

19 Go your way, my children, go,
for I am left desolate.

20 I have stripped off the robes of
peaceful days
and put on the sackcloth of a suppliant;

4.5–5.9: Songs of encouragement and lament. These lyrics, composed originally in Gk. and showing the influence of Deut., Isa. chs. 40–66, and Jer., are unified by the recurring theme of God's eternity. **5:** *Keep Israel's name alive:* physically by new generations of children and spiritually by obedience to God. **8:** *Eternal God:* a recurring expression found only in the poetic section 3.8–5.9. In contrast, the word "Lord" is found only in the first section. **12:** The image of Jerusalem as a *widow*, as in Isa. ch. 54 or Lam. 1.1–2, symbolizes the

I shall call to the Eternal as long as I
live.

21 Take heart, my children! Cry out to
God,
and he will rescue you from tyranny
and from the power of your enemies.
22 I set my hope of your deliverance on
the Eternal;
the Holy One, your everlasting Saviour,
has filled me with joy
for the mercy soon to be granted you.
23 With mourning and tears I watched
you go,
but God will give you back to me
with gladness and joy for ever.
24 As the neighbours of Zion have now
seen your captivity,
so they will soon witness God's
deliverance of you,
which will come to you with the great
glory
and the radiance of the Eternal.
25 My children, endure in patience
the wrath God has brought on you;
your enemy has hunted you down,
but soon you will see him destroyed,
soon put your foot on his neck.
26 My pampered children have trodden
rough paths,
driven off like a flock seized by
raiders.

27 Take heart, my children! Cry out to
God,
for he who afflicted you will not forget
you.
28 Once you were resolved to go astray
from God;
now with tenfold zeal you must turn
back and seek him.
29 He who brought the disasters on you
will bring you everlasting joy when he
delivers you.

30 Take heart, Jerusalem! He who called
you by name will comfort you.

31 Wretched will they be who maltreated
you
and gloated over your fall;
32 wretched the cities where your children
were slaves;
wretched the city that received your
sons!
33 She that rejoiced over your downfall
and was jubilant at your ruin,
that same city will grieve at her own
desolation.
34 I shall strip her of the multitudes that
were her boast,
and turn her pride into grief.
35 Fire from the Eternal will be her doom
for many a day,
and for a long time to come she will be
the haunt of demons.

36 Jerusalem, look eastwards and see the
joy
that is coming to you from God.
37 They come, the sons from whom you
parted;
from east to west they come,
assembling at the word of the Holy
One
and rejoicing in the glory of God.

5 JERUSALEM, strip off your garment of
mourning and affliction,
and put on for ever the glorious
majesty, the gift of God.
2 Wrap about you his robe of
righteousness;
place on your head as a diadem the
splendour of the Eternal.
3 God will show your radiance to every
land under heaven;
4 from him you will receive for ever the
name
Righteous Peace, the Splendour of
Godliness.

5 Arise, Jerusalem, stand on the height;
look eastwards and see your children
assembled

seeming rejection by God. **24:** *Glory* and *radiance* indicate an extraordinary manifestation of God's wonder
from within Zion or Jerusalem (Isa. 60.2). **30:** *Called you by name* probably refers to God's own name (see
3.5), just as Jerusalem is to be clothed in God's robes (5.1–4), because God's redemptive action is to be revealed
within the city. **35:** Jerusalem's persecutors will be a desert, the traditional haunt of *demons* (Tob. 8.3; Lk.
11.24). **5.5–9:** These lines, reflecting Isa. 40.3–5 and 60.1–2, are quoted almost verbatim in the nonbiblical
Psalms of Solomon 11.2–7, dated around 50 B.C.E. Again the messianic prospects of Baruch are limited to the
ingathering of the exiles (see Jer. 31.7–14; Isa. 43.1–7).

from west to east at the word of the
Holy One,
rejoicing that God has remembered
them.
⁶They went away from you on foot,
led off by their enemies;
but God is bringing them home to
you,
borne aloft in glory, as on a royal
throne.
⁷All the high mountains and everlasting
hills

are to be made low as God
commanded,
and every ravine is to be filled and
levelled,
that Israel may walk securely in the
glory of God;
⁸and the woods and every fragrant tree
will give Israel shade at God's
command.
⁹He will lead Israel with joy
by the light of his glory,
in his mercy and his righteousness.

A LETTER OF
Jeremiah

This harangue against idolatry is repetitive, sarcastic, and impassioned. Possibly it originated as a synagogal sermon. Following a tradition known from 2 Macc. 2.1–4, the author attributed it to Jeremiah, who actually did write a letter to the exiles in Babylon (Jer. ch. 29). The writer drew upon Jer. 10.1–16 and other sources, mainly Isa. 44.9–20.

The period in which the book was written, according to v. 3, was seven generations after the beginning of the Babylonian Exile; that date could be about 317 B.C.E. Some scholars, however, tend to date the book in the Maccabean period, between 165 and 110 B.C.E.

If "Babylon" is taken as a cryptic name for the area outside Judea, the letter could have been intended for the Jews in the Greek dispersion.

The language of the original seems to have been Hebrew (v. 72 n.); since there are no extant Hebrew manuscripts, some scholars think it could have been Aramaic or Greek. A fragment in the Greek (vv. 43–44) turned up in one of the caves where the Dead Sea Scrolls were found; scholars date the manuscript to around 100 B.C.E.

The Latin Vulgate and the Authorized Version consider A Letter of Jeremiah to be ch. 6 of Baruch.

Two series of refrains divide the letter into paragraphs: vv. 16, 23, 29, 65, 69 and vv. 40, 44, 52, 56.

The folly of idolatry

6 A copy of a letter sent by Jeremiah to the captives who were to be taken to Babylon by the king of the Babylonians; it conveys a message entrusted to him by God.

2 It is because of the sins you have committed in the sight of God that you are being led away captive to Babylon by Nebuchadnezzar, king of the Babylonians. 3 Once you are in Babylon, your stay there will be long; it will last for many years, up to seven generations; afterwards I will lead you out from there in peace.

4 In Babylon you can now see gods carried on men's shoulders, gods made of silver, gold, and wood, which fill the nations with awe. 5 You must be careful, then, never to become like those foreigners. Do not be over-awed by the gods when you see them in the midst of a procession of worshippers, 6 but say in your hearts, 'To you alone, O Lord, is worship due.' 7 For my angel will be with you; your lives will be in his care.

8 The idols are plated with gold and silver. They have tongues fashioned by a craftsman: they are a sham and cannot speak. 9 The people take gold and make crowns for the heads of their gods, as one might for a girl fond of finery. 10 Sometimes the priests filch gold and silver from their gods and spend it on themselves; 11 they will even give some to the temple prostitutes. They dress up the idols in clothes like human beings, their gods of silver, gold, and wood; 12 but the gods, decked

6:1 etc. *The chapter and verse numbering is that of the Authorized (King James) Version, in which this forms chapter 6 of Baruch.*

6.1–73: The folly of idolatry. 1: Major Gk. MSS. do not include this opening inscription as v. 1 and therefore differ in the numbering of the verses, being one digit lower than the numbers that appear here. **3:** *Seven generations* may be symbolic of perfection or fullness, rounding out the Exile. But since this phrase differs from the phrase "seventy years" in Jer. 25.12, some scholars take it literally, and reckoning a generation as forty years (Num. 32.13), relate the 280 years to the fall of Jerusalem, either in 597 B.C.E. or in 587 B.C.E. (2 Kgs. 24.10–17; 25.1–12). Hence, L. of Jer. would then have been written in 317 or 307 B.C.E. See Introduction. **7:** *My angel:* an indirect reference to God's continuing protection (Exod. 23.20–23). **11:** Sacred *prostitutes* accommodated

1184

in purple though they are, cannot protect themselves against corrosion and moth. ¹³ The dust in the temple lies thick upon them, so that their faces have to be wiped clean. ¹⁴ Like the ruler of a land, the god holds a sceptre, yet he has no power to put to death anyone who offends him. ¹⁵ In his right hand he has a dagger and an axe, yet he is powerless to save himself from war and pillage. ¹⁶ Clearly they are not gods; therefore have no fear of them.

¹⁷ These gods, sitting in their temples, are of no more use than a broken pot. Their eyes get filled with dust from the feet of those who come in. ¹⁸ And just as the court of the guard-house is barricaded when a traitor awaits execution, so the priests secure their temples with doors and bolts and bars to guard against pillage by robbers. ¹⁹ The priests light lamps, more than they need for themselves —yet the idols can see none of them. ²⁰ They are like one of the beams of the temple, but, as men admit, their hearts are eaten out, for creatures crawl from the ground and devour both them and their vestments without their being aware of it. ²¹ Their faces are blackened by the smoke in the temple. ²² Bats and swallows and birds of all kinds perch on their bodies and heads, and cats do likewise. ²³ From all this you may be sure that they are not gods; therefore have no fear of them.

²⁴ Though embellished with gold plating, the idols will not shine unless someone rubs off the tarnish. Even when being cast they felt nothing. ²⁵ They were bought regardless of price, but there is no breath in them. ²⁶ As they lack feet they are carried on men's shoulders, which proclaims to all how worthless they are. ²⁷ Even those who serve them are put to shame because, if ever an idol topples to the ground, it does not get up by itself; nor, if anyone sets it up again, can it move by its own effort; and if it is tilted it cannot straighten itself. To set an offering before them is like setting it before the dead! ²⁸ The sacrifices made to gods are sold by the priests, who spend the proceeds on themselves. Their wives are no better; they take portions of the sacrifices and cure the meat,

and give no share to the needy or helpless. ²⁹ These offerings are handled by women who are menstruating or by mothers fresh from childbirth. Be assured by this that they are not gods; have no fear of them.

³⁰ For how can they be called gods, these gods of silver, gold, and wood, when it is women who serve them food? ³¹ In the temples are seated the priests, shaven and shorn, with their clothes rent and their heads uncovered. ³² They shout and howl before these gods of theirs, like mourners at a funeral feast. ³³ The priests clothe their wives and children with vestments they stripped from the gods. ³⁴ Should anyone do the gods either injury or service they are incapable of repaying it. They cannot set up or depose a king; ³⁵ so too they are quite unable to bestow wealth or money. Anyone making a vow to them and failing to honour it will never be called to account. ³⁶ They will never save anyone from death, never rescue the weak from the strong; ³⁷ never restore the sight of the blind, or rescue a person in distress. ³⁸ They neither pity the widow nor befriend the fatherless. ³⁹ They are like blocks from the quarry, these wooden things plated with gold and silver, and all who serve them will be discredited. ⁴⁰ How then can anyone suppose them to be gods or call them so?

Besides, even the Chaldaeans themselves bring these idols of theirs into disrepute; ⁴¹ for when they see a dumb man without the power of articulate speech, they bring him into the temple and ask Bel to give him speech, as if Bel could understand. ⁴² Because they themselves are void of understanding, they do not see the folly of it and abandon their idols. ⁴³ The women sit in the street with cords round them, burning bran for incense; and when one of them has been drawn aside by a passer-by and she has lain with him, she taunts her neighbour, who has not been thought as attractive as herself and whose cord has not been broken. ⁴⁴ Everything to do with these idols is a sham. How then can anyone suppose them to be gods or call them so?

⁴⁵ They are the products of the carpenter

male devotees for fertility rites in their temples. **28:** The *needy* were to be helped (Deut. 14.28–29). **29–32:** These actions at the pagan *temples* were forbidden to the Jews and indeed were repellent to them (Lev. 12.1–4; 15.19–20; 21.5, 11). **36–38:** These statue-gods do not possess the kindly power of the Lord (Ps. 146.7–9; Isa. 35.4–6). **40:** *Chaldaeans:* Babylonians. **41:** *Bel:* the same as Marduk, the main god of Babylon (see Bel & Snake). **43:** The Greek writer, Herodotus, verifies this practice, demanded of all Babylonian women, to ask and the goldsmith; they can be nothing but what the craftsmen intend them to be. 46 Even their makers' lives cannot be prolonged; how then can the things they make be gods? 47 It is a disgraceful sham they have bequeathed to posterity. 48 If war or disaster overtakes the idols, the priests discuss among themselves where they can hide with their gods. 49 How then can anyone fail to see that these are not gods, when they are powerless to save themselves from war or disaster? 50 Since they are nothing but wood plated all over with gold and silver, they will in such times be recognized for the shams they are. 51 To every nation and king it will be evident that these are not gods but the work of human hands, with no divine power in them whatsoever. 52 Will anyone still not admit that they are not gods?

53 They cannot set up a king over a country; they cannot provide rain; 54 they cannot decide a case or redress an injustice. They are as helpless as crows tossed about in mid-air. 55 When fire breaks out in a temple belonging to those wooden gods all gilded and silvered, their priests will run for safety, but the gods will go up in flames like timbers. 56 They cannot offer resistance to king or enemy. How then can anyone accept or believe that they are gods?

57 They cannot save themselves from thieves and robbers, these wooden gods, plated with gold and silver. 58 Any able-bodied person can strip them of their gold and silver and make off with the vestments in which they are arrayed; they can in no way help themselves. 59 Better a king who displays his courage than such a sham god, better a household pot that serves its owner's purpose, better even the door of a house that keeps the contents safe, or a wooden pillar in a palace!

60 Sun and moon and the stars that shine so brightly are sent to serve a purpose, and they obey. 61 So too, when the lightning flashes, it is seen far and wide. Likewise the wind blows in every land. 62 When God commands the clouds to travel over all the world, they accomplish their task; 63 and fire, when it is sent down from above to consume mountains and forests, carries out his bidding. But idols are not to be compared with any of these, either in appearance or in power. 64 It follows they are not to be considered gods or given that name, since they are incapable of pronouncing judgement or of conferring benefits on mankind. 65 Being assured, therefore, that they are not gods, have no fear of them.

66 They wield no power over kings, either to curse or to bless; 67 and they cannot provide the nations with signs in the heavens, either by shining like the sun or by giving light like the moon. 68 Wild beasts are better off; they at least can save themselves by taking cover. 69 From first to last there is no evidence that they are gods; so banish all fear of them.

70 These wooden gods of theirs, all plated with gold and silver, give no better protection than a scarecrow in a bed of cucumbers. 71 They are like a thorn bush in a garden, a perch for every bird, or like a corpse cast out in the dark. Such are their wooden gods, with their plating of gold and silver! 72 The purple and fine linen rotting on them proves that they are not gods; in the end they will themselves be eaten away, to the disgrace of the land.

73 Better, then, to be upright and have no idols, for such a one will be in no danger of disgrace.

6:54 **cannot . . . injustice:** *some witnesses read* cannot judge in their own cause, or redress an injustice done them.   6:72 **fine linen:** *prob. mng; Gk* marble.

the gods for fertility in their marriage. **67:** Idols cannot *provide . . . signs* (portents of their presence and activity) as God can do with natural phenomena; see Joel 2.30; Lk. 21.11, 25. **72:** The Gk. text (see Tfn.) apparently mistranslated a Heb. word meaning "linen."

The Prayer of Azariah
And the Song of the Three

AN ADDITION IN THE GREEK VERSION
OF DANIEL
BETWEEN 3.23 AND 3.24

The three most substantial of many additions to the Hebrew-Aramaic text of Daniel are: The Prayer of Azariah and The Song of the Three; Daniel and Susanna; and Daniel, Bel, and the Snake. Whether these materials were first written in Hebrew, Aramaic, or Greek is debated, but puns on two Greek words in Daniel and Susanna favor Greek as the original language of at least that addition. These additions were probably written during the second or first century B.C.E.

The work is made up of two probably independent parts: a prayer of Azariah (Abed-nego), vv. 1–22, and a hymn to God sung by the three companions of Daniel: Shadrach, Meshach, and Abed-nego, vv. 23–68. The addition echoes major biblical themes, reflecting especially the thought of Ps. 148 and the form of Ps. 136. The prayer and the song were used extensively in worship by churches in later centuries.

THEY walked in the heart of the fire, praising God and blessing the Lord.

The prayer

2 AZARIAH stood among the flames and began to pray aloud: 3 'Blessed are you and worthy of praise, Lord, the God of our fathers; your name is glorious for ever: 4 you are just in all you have done to us; all your works are true; your paths are straight, your judgements all true. 5 Just is the sentence in all that you have brought on us and on Jerusalem, the holy city of our ancestors; true and just the sentence you have passed upon our sins. 6 For we sinned and broke your law in rebellion against you; 7 in all we did we sinned. We did not heed your commandments, we did not keep them, we failed to do what you commanded for our good. 8 So in all the punishments you have sent on us, in all you have done to us, your judgements have been just,

9 in that you have handed us over to our enemies, detested rebels against your law, and to a wicked king, the vilest in all the world. 10 Now we are reduced to silence: shame and disgrace have befallen your servants and worshippers.

11 'For the sake of your honour do not abandon us for ever; do not annul your covenant. 12 Do not withdraw your mercy from us, for the sake of Abraham your friend, for the sake of Isaac your servant and Israel your holy one. 13 You promised them that their descendants should be as numerous as the stars in the sky, as the grains of sand on the seashore. 14 Yet, Lord, we have been made the smallest of all nations; for our sins we are today the most abject in the world. 15 Now we have no ruler, no prophet, no leader; there is no whole-offering, no sacrifice, no oblation, no incense, no place to make an offering before you and find mercy. 16 But because we come with contrite heart and humbled spirit,

1–27: **Azariah prays. 1:** *They:* Daniel's friends; see Dan. 3.23. **2:** *Azariah:* Abed-nego's Heb. name; see Dan. 1.7. **3–4:** Many OT passages declare that God was *just* in punishing Israel by the Babylonian Exile; see Neh. 9.33; Lam. 1.18. **9:** The *wicked king* in Dan. is Nebuchadnezzar (Dan. 3.19); in the writer's day, however, Antiochus IV Epiphanes was *the vilest* because he sacked Jerusalem and profaned the temple; see 1 Macc. 1.41–60. **11:** *For the sake of your honour:* compare Ezek. 36.22. **13:** *You promised:* see Gen. 15.5; 22.17. **14–15:** Judah, deprived of its *ruler,* was *the most abject* because God's covenant with the Davidic dynasty seemed to be broken. See 2 Sam. 7.13–16; Lam. 2.9; Hos. 3.4. **16–18:** *Be accepted:* a technical cult term applied to sacrifices pleasing to God. Qualities of the spirit are seen as the cultic equivalents of animal may we be accepted. ¹⁷As though we came with whole-offerings of rams and bullocks and with thousands of fat lambs, let our sacrifice be made before you this day, that we may obey you in everything, for no shame shall come to those who put their trust in you. ¹⁸Now we shall follow you with our whole heart, and in fear seek your presence. ¹⁹Do not put us to shame, but deal with us in your forbearance and in the greatness of your mercy. ²⁰Lord, Worker of wonders, deliver us, and let your name be glorified. May all who harm your servants be brought low; ²¹let them be put to shame, stripped of all power and sovereignty, and may their strength be crushed; ²²let them know that you alone are the Lord God, glorious over all the earth.'

²³THE king's servants who had thrown them into the furnace kept feeding it with naphtha, pitch, tow, and brushwood, ²⁴so that the flames, blazing above it to a height of seventy-five feet, ²⁵leapt out and burnt up those Chaldaeans who were caught near it. ²⁶But the angel of the Lord came down to join Azariah and his companions in the furnace; he scattered the flames ²⁷and made the heart of the furnace as if a moist wind were whistling through. The fire touched them not at all; it neither harmed nor distressed them.

The song

²⁸THEN with one voice the three who were in the furnace praised and glorified and blessed God:

²⁹Blessed are you, Lord, the God of our fathers;
worthy of praise, highly exalted for ever.
³⁰Blessed is your holy and glorious name;
highly to be praised, highly exalted for ever.

³¹Blessed are you, glorious in your holy temple;
most worthy to be glorified in hymns for ever.
³²Blessed are you, for, enthroned on the cherubim, you behold the depths;
worthy of praise, highly exalted for ever.
³³Blessed are you on your royal throne;
most worthy to be hymned, highly exalted for ever.
³⁴Blessed are you in the vault of heaven;
worthy to be glorified in hymns for ever.

³⁵Let his whole creation bless the Lord,
sing his praise and exalt him for ever.
³⁶Bless the Lord, you heavens;
sing his praise and exalt him for ever.
³⁷Bless the Lord, you that are his angels;
sing his praise and exalt him for ever.
³⁸Bless the Lord, all you waters above the heavens;
sing his praise and exalt him for ever.
³⁹Bless the Lord, all you his hosts;
sing his praise and exalt him for ever.
⁴⁰Bless the Lord, sun and moon;
sing his praise and exalt him for ever.
⁴¹Bless the Lord, you stars of heaven;
sing his praise and exalt him for ever.
⁴²Bless the Lord, all rain and dew;
sing his praise and exalt him for ever.
⁴³Bless the Lord, all winds that blow;
sing his praise and exalt him for ever.
⁴⁴Bless the Lord, fire and heat;
sing his praise and exalt him for ever.
⁴⁵Bless the Lord, searing blast and bitter cold;
sing his praise and exalt him for ever.
⁴⁶Bless the Lord, sleet and falling snow;
sing his praise and exalt him for ever.

17 that ... everything: *poss. mng; Gk obscure.*
24 seventy-five feet: *Gk forty-nine cubits.*   46 sleet: *prob. mng; Gk dew.*

sacrifices; compare 1 Sam. 15.22; Ps. 51.16–17; Hos. 6.6. **20–21:** God's *name* would *be glorified* by ending the power of Babylon and granting Israel deliverance from captivity as God had done at the time of the Exodus from Egypt. **23:** *Naphtha:* a natural petroleum substance. *Brushwood:* bundles of sticks. **25:** See Dan. 3.22. **26:** *The angel of the Lord* in the OT is often God in angelic form; see Gen. 16.7–14. **27:** In Israel, when a *moist wind* blows from the Mediterranean it brings refreshing coolness, in contrast to the hot wind which blows from the eastern desert.

28–68: A song of exaltation. The constant refrain recalls Ps. 136. **32:** *Cherubim:* winged heavenly creatures on which God rode; see 2 Sam. 22.11; Ps. 18.10. **35:** *Let ... creation bless:* after addressing the Lord (vv. 29–34; see Ps. 104), the song exhorts the whole creation, part by part (vv. 35–59), person by person (vv. 60–68), to *bless the Lord,* i.e. to *praise* God (compare Ps. 148). **38:** *Waters ... heavens:* see Gen. 1.7;

⁴⁷ Bless the Lord, you nights and days;
sing his praise and exalt him for ever.
⁴⁸ Bless the Lord, light and darkness;
sing his praise and exalt him for ever.
⁴⁹ Bless the Lord, frost and cold;
sing his praise and exalt him for ever.
⁵⁰ Bless the Lord, rime and snow;
sing his praise and exalt him for ever.
⁵¹ Bless the Lord, lightning and clouds;
sing his praise and exalt him for ever.

⁵² Let the earth bless the Lord,
sing his praise and exalt him for ever.
⁵³ Bless the Lord, you mountains and
hills;
sing his praise and exalt him for ever.
⁵⁴ Bless the Lord, all that grows in the
earth;
sing his praise and exalt him for ever.
⁵⁵ Bless the Lord, you flowing springs;
sing his praise and exalt him for ever.
⁵⁶ Bless the Lord, you seas and rivers;
sing his praise and exalt him for ever.
⁵⁷ Bless the Lord, you whales and
everything that moves in the waters;
sing his praise and exalt him for ever.
⁵⁸ Bless the Lord, all birds of the air;
sing his praise and exalt him for ever.
⁵⁹ Bless the Lord, you cattle and wild
beasts;
sing his praise and exalt him for
ever.

⁶⁰ Let all mankind bless the Lord,
sing his praise and exalt him for ever.
⁶¹ Israel, bless the Lord;
sing his praise and exalt him for ever.
⁶² Bless the Lord, you that are his priests;
sing his praise and exalt him for ever.
⁶³ Bless the Lord, you that are his
servants;
sing his praise and exalt him for ever.
⁶⁴ Bless the Lord, spirits and souls of the
righteous;
sing his praise and exalt him for ever.
⁶⁵ Bless the Lord, you that are devout and
humble in heart;
sing his praise and exalt him for ever.

⁶⁶ Hananiah, Azariah, and Mishael, bless
the Lord;
sing his praise and exalt him for ever.
He has rescued us from the grave,
he has saved us from the power of
death;
he has delivered us from the furnace of
burning flame,
from the very heart of the fire.
⁶⁷ Give thanks to the Lord, for he is
gracious,
for his mercy endures for ever.
⁶⁸ All who worship the Lord, bless the
God of gods,
sing his praise and give him thanks,
for his mercy endures for ever.

Ps. 148.4. **39:** *Hosts:* compare Ps. 148.2–3. **44–51:** See Ps. 148.8. **50:** *Rime:* a type of frost. **53:** See Ps. 148.9.
58–65: Compare Ps. 148.10–12.

Daniel and Susanna

The story of Susanna is a "detective story" from the second or first century B.C.E. It is about Daniel, and is an addition to that book.

A masterpiece of the storyteller's art, the tale combines effective characterization with suspenseful plot development to proclaim its moral that God does not desert the innocent who trust and pray.

Some interpreters see the story as a criticism of the judicial system, especially the need to examine witnesses more carefully (vv. 48–49) and to insure against perjury by inflicting adequate punishment (v. 62).

This addition to Daniel appears in different places in the versions. In the Septuagint and Vulgate a slightly variant form of the story follows the end as ch. 13. The story comes first in the Greek text of Theodotion and in other versions, perhaps because Daniel is described (v. 45) as a "young man." On original language, see Introduction to the Prayer of Azariah and The Song of the Three.

Innocence vindicated

IN Babylon there lived a man named Joakim, ²who had married Susanna daughter of Hilkiah, a very beautiful and devout woman. ³Her parents were godfearing people who had brought up their daughter according to the law of Moses. ⁴Joakim was very rich, and his house had adjoining it a fine garden; this was a regular meeting-place for the Jews, because he was the man of greatest distinction among them.

⁵Now that year the judges appointed were two of the community's elders; of such the Lord had said, 'Wickedness came forth from Babylon, from elders who were judges and were supposed to guide my people.' ⁶These men were constantly at Joakim's house, and everyone who had a case to be tried came to them there.

⁷At noon, when the people went away, Susanna would go and walk in her husband's garden. ⁸Every day the two elders used to see her entering the garden for her walk, and they were inflamed with lust. ⁹Their minds were perverted; their thoughts went astray and were no longer turned to God, and they did not keep in mind the demands of justice. ¹⁰Both were infatuated with her; but they did not disclose to each other what torments they suffered, ¹¹because they were ashamed to confess they wanted to seduce her. ¹²Day after day they watched eagerly for a sight of her.

¹³One day, having said, 'Let us go home; it is time to eat,' ¹⁴they left and went off in different directions; but turning back they found themselves face to face, and on questioning each other about this, they admitted their passion. Then they agreed on a time when they might find her alone.

¹⁵While they were watching for an opportune moment, Susanna went into the garden as usual, accompanied only by her two maids; it was very hot, and she felt a desire to bathe in the garden. ¹⁶No one else was there apart from the two elders, who had hidden and were spying on her. ¹⁷She said to the maids, 'Bring me olive oil and unguents, and shut the garden doors so that I may bathe.' ¹⁸They did as she said: they made fast the garden doors and went out by the side entrance for the things they had been told to bring; they did not see the elders, because they were in hiding.

¹⁹As soon as the maids had gone, the two elders got up and ran to Susanna. ²⁰'Look, the garden doors are shut,' they said, 'and no

1–64: God's direct intervention fills a youth with wisdom to confound the craftiness of old age, thus vindicating innocence.

1–14: Wicked elders lust after Susanna. 2: *Susanna* means "lily." **4:** Jewish names recorded on clay tablets in Babylonian archives show that some Jews became *rich* and rose to positions of *distinction* in their captivity in Babylon. **5:** *The Lord had said* may allude to Jer. 29.21–23.

one can see us! We are overcome with desire for you; consent, and yield to us. 21 If you refuse, we shall swear in evidence there was a young man with you and that was why you sent your maids away.' 22 Susanna groaned and said: 'It is a desperate plight I am in! If I do this, the penalty is death; if I do not, you will have me at your mercy. 23 My choice is made: I will not do it! Better to be at your mercy than to sin against the Lord!' 24 With that she called out at the top of her voice, but the two elders shouted her down, 25 and one of them ran and opened the garden door. 26 The household, hearing the uproar in the garden, rushed in through the side entrance to see what had happened to her. 27 When the elders had told their story, the servants were deeply shocked, for no such allegation had ever been made against Susanna.

28 Next day, when the people gathered at her husband Joakim's house, the two elders arrived, intent on their criminal design to have Susanna put to death. 29 In the presence of the people they said, 'Send for Susanna daughter of Hilkiah, Joakim's wife.' She was summoned, 30 and came with her parents and children and all her relatives. 31 Now Susanna was a woman of great beauty and delicate feeling. 32 She was closely veiled, but those scoundrels ordered her to be unveiled so that they might feast their eyes on her beauty. 33 Her family and all who saw her were in tears.

34 Then the two elders stood up before the people and put their hands on her head, 35 she meanwhile looking towards heaven through her tears, for her trust was in the Lord. 36 The elders said: 'As we were walking by ourselves in the garden, this woman came in with her two maids. She shut the garden doors and dismissed her maids, 37 and then a young man, who had been in hiding, came and lay with her. 38 We were in a corner of the garden, and when we saw this wickedness we ran towards them. 39 We saw them in the act, but we could not hold the man; he was too

strong for us, he opened the door and got clean away. 40 We seized the woman and asked who the young man was, but she would not tell us. That is our evidence.'

41 Because they were elders of the people and judges, the assembly believed them and condemned her to death. 42 Then raising her voice Susanna cried: 'Eternal God, you know all secrets and foresee all things, 43 you know that their evidence against me is false. And now I am to die, innocent though I am of the charges these wicked men have brought against me.'

44 The Lord heard her cry, 45 and as she was being led off to execution, God inspired a devout young man named Daniel to protest. 46 He shouted out, 'I will not have this woman's blood on my hands.' 47 At this the people all turned towards him and demanded, 'What do you mean?' 48 He stepped forward and said: 'Are you such fools, you Israelites, as to condemn a woman of Israel, without making careful enquiry and finding out the truth? 49 Reopen the trial; the evidence these men have given against her is false.'

50 Everyone hurried back, and the rest of the elders said to Daniel, 'Come, take your place among us and state your case, for God has given you the standing of an elder.' 51 He said, 'Separate these men and keep them at a distance from each other, and I shall examine them.' 52 When they had been separated, Daniel summoned one of them. 'You hardened reprobate,' he began, 'the sins of your past have now come home to you. 53 You have given unjust decisions, condemning the innocent and acquitting the guilty, although the Lord has said, "You must not cause the death of the innocent and guiltless." 54 Now, if you really saw this woman, then tell us, under what tree did you see them together?' He answered, 'Under a clove tree.' 55 Daniel retorted, 'Very good! This lie has cost you

54 **clove:** lit. mastic.   54–55 **clove . . . cleave:** *there is a play on words in the Greek.*

15–27: **Seduction attempted. 22:** For an unfaithful wife *the penalty* was *death* by stoning; see Lev. 20.10; Deut. 22.21–22. **23:** *Sin against the Lord:* see Gen. 39.9; Ps. 51.4. All sin is against God.

28–43: **Susanna condemned through perjury. 34:** To identify her as accused and themselves as witnesses of the crime and accusers, the elders *put their hands on her head;* see Lev. 24.14.

44–49: **Daniel intervenes. 46:** According to Jewish tradition a herald preceded one being led to execution and appealed for possible evidence of the convicted person's innocence. The entire community shared responsibility for *blood* shed in executions.

50–64: **Susanna is acquitted; her accusers, the two elders, are put to death. 50:** The invitation to Daniel your life, for already God's angel has received your sentence from God, and he will cleave you in two.' 56 He ordered him to stand aside, and told them to bring forward the other.

He said to him: 'Spawn of Canaan, no son of Judah, beauty has been your undoing and lust has perverted your heart! 57 So this is how the two of you have been treating the women of Israel, terrifying them into yielding to you! But here is a woman of Judah who would not submit to your villainy. 58 Now tell me, under what tree did you surprise them together?' 'Under a yew tree,' he replied. 59 Daniel said to him, 'Very good! This lie has cost you also your life, for the angel of God is waiting sword in hand to hew you down and destroy the pair of you.'

60 At that the whole assembly shouted aloud, praising God, the Saviour of those who trust in him. 61 They turned on the two elders, for out of their own mouths Daniel had convicted them of giving false evidence; 62 they dealt with them according to the law of Moses, putting them to death as they in their wickedness had intended to do to their neighbour. So an innocent life was saved that day. 63 Then Hilkiah and his wife gave praise for their daughter Susanna, as did also her husband Joakim and all her relatives, because she was found innocent of a shameful deed.

64 From that day forward Daniel was held in great esteem among the people.

58 **yew:** *lit.* oak.   58–59 **yew . . . hew:** *there is a play on words in the Greek.*

to take his place as an *elder* is undoubtedly said in sarcasm. **53:** See Exod. 23.7. **56:** *Spawn of Canaan* may be an allusion to the notorious sexual laxity of the Canaanites. **62:** Deuteronomy 19.16–21 requires that a false witness receive the treatment intended for the accused. During Alexander Jannaeus' reign (105–79 B.C.E.) the Sadducees sought to apply this law only in cases where the falsely accused was executed, but the Pharisees demanded stricter interpretation.

Daniel, Bel, and the Snake

The third major addition to the Book of Daniel consists of two related tales designed to ridicule heathen idolatry. In the first story (vv. 1–22), Daniel is again presented (see Daniel and Susanna) as a clever detective who exposes the deception practiced by the priests of Bel. Daniel thus exposes the Bel statue as lifeless, no god at all. In the second story (vv. 23–42), Daniel demonstrates that a serpent worshiped by the Babylonians, while a living being, is surely not divine.

The wisdom and courage of the faithful Daniel and the truth that God delivers the faithful are significant themes in both stories.

On date and original language, see Introduction to the Prayer of Azariah and The Song of the Three.

The destruction of Bel

WHEN King Astyages was gathered to his forefathers, he was succeeded on the throne by Cyrus the Persian. ² Daniel was a companion of the king and the most honoured of all the king's Friends.

³ The Babylonians had an idol called Bel, for which every day they provided twelve bushels of fine flour, forty sheep, and fifty gallons of wine. ⁴ The king went daily to bow down to it in worship; but Daniel bowed before his own God. When the king asked him, 'Why do you not bow down to Bel?' ⁵ he replied, 'Because I do not worship man-made idols; I worship the living God who created heaven and earth and is sovereign over all mankind.' ⁶ The king protested, 'How can you think Bel is not a living god? Do you not see how much he eats and drinks each day?' ⁷ Daniel laughed. 'Do not be deceived, your majesty,' he said; 'this Bel of yours is just clay inside and bronze outside, and has never eaten or drunk anything.'

⁸ Angered by this, the king summoned the priests of Bel and said to them, 'If you cannot tell me who it is that consumes these provisions, you shall die; ⁹ but if you can show it is Bel that eats them, then, for blasphemy against Bel, Daniel shall die.' Daniel said to the king, 'Let it be as you propose.' ¹⁰ (There were seventy priests of Bel, and in addition their wives and children.) When the king, along with Daniel, went into the temple of Bel, ¹¹ the priests said, 'We are now leaving; let your majesty set out the food yourself, with the wine you have mixed; then make fast the door and seal it with your signet. ¹² In the morning when you return, if you do not find that Bel has eaten it all, let us be put to death; but if Daniel's charges against us turn out to be false, then let him die.' ¹³ They treated the affair lightly, for beneath the table they had constructed a hidden entrance, by which they used to go in and eat up everything.

¹⁴ After the priests had gone, the king set out the food for Bel; and Daniel ordered his servants to bring ashes and sift them over the whole temple with only the king present. They then left the building, closed the door, sealed it with the royal signet, and went away. ¹⁵ During the night the priests, with their wives and children, came as usual and ate and drank everything.

¹⁶ Next morning the king was up early, and Daniel with him. ¹⁷ The king said, 'Are the seals intact, Daniel?' 'They are intact, your majesty,' he answered. ¹⁸ As soon as the door was opened, the king took one look at the

1–22: Daniel destroys an idol. 1: *King Astyages* was the last king of the Medes, defeated by *Cyrus the Persian* about 550 B.C.E. **2:** *King's Friends:* a technical term; see 1 Macc. 2.18 n. **3:** Cyrus became the king of the *Babylonians* by defeating Nabonidus, the last king of Babylon, in 539 B.C.E. *Bel:* the chief Babylonian god, also known as Marduk; see Jer. 51.44. **6:** Represented by a colossal image, Bel was believed a voracious eater.

table and cried aloud, 'Great are you, O Bel! In you there is no deception whatsoever.' [19] But Daniel laughed and held back the king from going in. 'Just look at the floor,' he said, 'and judge whose footprints these are.' [20] The king said, 'I see the footprints of men, women, and children.' In a rage [21] he had the priests arrested together with their wives and children, and they showed him the secret door through which it was their custom to go and eat what was on the table. [22] The king then put them to death, and he handed Bel over to Daniel, who destroyed both idol and temple.

The destruction of the snake

[23] THERE was a huge snake which the Babylonians worshipped. [24] The king said to Daniel, 'Bow down to him; you cannot say that this is not a living god.' [25] Daniel answered, 'I shall bow before the Lord my God, for he is a living God. [26] But give me authority, your majesty, and without using sword or staff I shall kill the snake.' 'I grant it,' replied the king. [27] Then Daniel took pitch and fat and hair, boiled them together, and made them into cakes, which he put into the mouth of the snake. The snake swallowed them and burst. Daniel said, 'See what things you people worship!'

[28] When they heard of this, the Babylonians in their indignation made common cause against the king. 'The king has turned Jew!' they cried. 'He has pulled down Bel, killed the snake, and put the priests to the sword.' [29] They went to the king. 'Hand Daniel over to us,' they demanded, 'or else we shall kill you and your family.' [30] The king, finding himself thus hard pressed, was compelled to hand him over.

[31] They threw Daniel into the lion-pit, and he was there for six days. [32] In the pit were seven lions, and every day two slaves and two sheep were fed to them; now, to make sure they would devour Daniel, they were given nothing.

[33] The prophet Habakkuk, who was in Judaea, had made a stew; he broke bread into the bowl, and he was on the way to his field, carrying it to the reapers, [34] when an angel of the Lord said to him, 'Habakkuk, carry that meal you have to Babylon for Daniel, who is in the lion-pit.' [35] 'My lord,' replied Habakkuk, 'I have never been to Babylon, and I do not know where the lion-pit is.' [36] The angel took the prophet by the head, and carrying him by his hair swept him to Babylon with the blast of his breath and set him down above the pit. [37] Habakkuk called out, 'Daniel, Daniel! Take the meal that God has sent you.' [38] Daniel said, 'You do indeed remember me, God; you never abandon those who love you.' [39] He got up and ate; and at once God's angel brought Habakkuk home again.

[40] On the seventh day the king went to mourn for Daniel, but when he arrived at the pit and looked in, there sat Daniel! [41] The king cried aloud, 'You are indeed great, Lord, the God of Daniel, and there is no god but you alone.' [42] He drew Daniel up, while those men who had plotted to destroy Daniel were flung into the pit, and then and there they were devoured before his eyes.

Historical sources confirm the huge food offerings (v. 3). **22:** *Put them to death:* see Dan. 2.12; 6.24. Ancient historians record that the Persian King Xerxes (485–464 B.C.E.) *destroyed both idol and temple* in 479 B.C.E.

23–42: The destruction of the snake. The serpent was often regarded in the ancient Near East as a religious symbol; see Num. 21.8; 2 Kgs. 18.4. There is no evidence that the Babylonians worshiped a live *snake*. Earlier English translations speak of "dragon," rather than snake.

28–42: Daniel rescued. 31: *The lion-pit:* see Dan. 6.16–24. **33:** *Habakkuk* lived a century earlier and hence could not have so served. **34:** *That meal:* see 1 Kgs. 17.4–6. **36:** For a precedent of a prophet carried *by his hair* see Ezek. 8.3. **38:** That God does not *abandon* those who remain faithful is the point of all three additions to the Hebrew Daniel; it was an assurance needed by the Jews during the Maccabean struggle against King Antiochus IV Epiphanes (175–164 B.C.E.).

The Prayer of Manasseh

This brief devotional piece conveys sincere repentance and deep religious feeling.

Manasseh, son of the good king Hezekiah, appears in 2 Kgs. 21.1–18 as a most wicked ruler who led Judah into gross idolatry, including human sacrifice, and perpetrated extensive violence. The Chronicler adds, however, that this evil king, after a very, very long reign, repented of his evil and called upon God for deliverance. Restored to his kingdom after being carried off to Babylon, he instituted partial reforms (2 Chr. 33.1–20).

Mention is made in 2 Chr. 33.19 of a prayer of Manasseh, but no prayer is given there. To fill this gap, some pious Jew composed a prayer such as Manasseh might have voiced.

The date and origin of the prayer are uncertain, but many place the composition in the second or first century B.C.E. and consider it originally written in Greek instead of Hebrew or Aramaic.

In Roman Catholic tradition, wherein the Apocrypha are regarded as canonical, this book is not so regarded.

Repentance

ALMIGHTY Lord,
God of our fathers,
of Abraham, Isaac, and Jacob, and of
  their righteous posterity,
2 who made heaven and earth in their
  manifold array,
3 who fettered the ocean by your word of
  command,
who closed the abyss
and sealed it with your fearful and
  glorious name—
4 before your power all things quake and
  tremble.
5 The majesty of your glory is more than
  can be borne;
none can endure the threat of your
  wrath against sinners.

6 Your promised mercy is beyond
  measure and none can fathom it;
7 for you are Lord Most High,
compassionate, patient, and of great
  mercy,
relenting when men suffer for their
  sins.
8 Therefore, Lord God of the righteous,
you appointed repentance not for
  Abraham, Isaac, and Jacob,
who were righteous and did not sin
  against you,
but for me, 9 whose sins outnumber the
  sands of the sea.
My transgressions abound, Lord, my
  transgressions abound,
and, because of the multitude of my
  wrongdoings,
I am not worthy to look up and gaze at
  the height of heaven.

7 **for their sins:** *some witnesses add*
For out of your great goodness, Lord,
you have promised repentance and remission
to those who have sinned against you,
and in your boundless mercy you have appointed
repentance for sinners as the way to salvation.

1–8: God is praised as mighty Creator (vv. 1–4) who offers forgiveness to the penitent (vv. 5–8). **1:** *Righteous posterity:* faithful Israelites, descendants of the patriarchs. **2–3:** *Word of command:* the creative "God said" of Gen. 1.6, 10. Compare Job 38.8–11. **5:** God's majesty was considered so awesome that no one could experience it and live. Compare Isa. 6.5; Ezek. 1.28–2.2. **6–8:** Since all *suffer for their sins* the possibility for *repentance* is a *mercy* from God; see also Tfn.

9–13a: Repentance. 9: *My wrongdoings:* Manasseh's sins; see 2 Kgs. 21.1–8. **10:** *Iron chain:* Manasseh's

10 Bowed down with many an iron chain,
   I grieve over my sins and find no relief,
   because I have provoked your anger
   and done what is wrong in your eyes,
   setting up idols and so multiplying
      offences.

11 Now my heart submits to you,
   imploring your great goodness.
12 I have sinned, Lord, I have sinned,
   and I acknowledge my transgressions.
13 I beg and beseech you,
   spare me, Lord, spare me;
   destroy me not with my transgressions
      on my head,

do not be angry with me for ever,
or store up punishment for me.
Do not condemn me to the depths of
   the earth,
for you, Lord, are the God of the
   penitent.
14 You will show your goodness towards
   me,
for, unworthy as I am, you will save me
   in your great mercy;
15 and I shall praise you continually all
   the days of my life.
The whole host of heaven sings your
   praise,
and yours is the glory for ever. Amen.

captivity in Babylon (2 Chr. 33.11).
   13b–15: Confidence in divine mercy followed by a doxology closes the prayer. **13b:** God stored up *punishment* by being *angry* and not giving a person repentance. **15:** To *praise* God *continually* with the lips as well as with a repentant and upright life was considered the object and fulfillment of human life and Israel's call; Ps. 51.13–17.

THE FIRST BOOK OF THE
Maccabees

The word Maccabee, possibly meaning "designated by God," was a popular epithet for Judas (1 Macc. 2.4), the third son of the priest Mattathias. The plural Maccabees came to allude to the Jewish guerrillas who, under Mattathias, revolted against the Seleucid kings of Syria then ruling the land of Israel. The revolt began in 167 B.C.E. This and three other books bear the name Maccabees; 1 and 2 Maccabees and the nonbiblical 4 Maccabees are about the revolt, but 3 Maccabees is not.

Written originally in Hebrew (only a Greek translation survived antiquity), 1 Maccabees summarizes the events (1.1–64) which spurred the revolt of Mattathias (2.1–70) and follows the course of the resistance as it was carried on by his sons, especially Judas (3.1–9.22), Jonathan (9.23–12.53), and Simon (13.1–16.24).

First Maccabees is a simple history written in the manner of the day by an unknown adherent of the Hasmonean kings descended from Simon. It is also meant to teach the author's contemporaries that by fidelity to the Law of God the Jewish people may expect continued divine support, for God is still active in Israel's history. The book was probably written about 100 B.C.E.

Background to the Maccabaean revolt

1 ALEXANDER of Macedon, the son of Philip, marched from the land of Kittim, defeated Darius, king of Persia and Media, and seized his throne, being already king of Greece. ²During the course of many campaigns, in which he captured strongholds and put kings to death, ³he traversed the earth to its remotest bounds and plundered countless nations. When at last the world lay quiet under his sway, his pride knew no limits; ⁴he built up an extremely powerful army and ruled over countries, nations, and princedoms, all of which rendered him tribute.

⁵The time came when Alexander fell ill, and, realizing that he was dying, ⁶he summoned his generals, nobles who had been brought up with him from childhood, and divided his empire among them while he was yet alive. ⁷At his death he had reigned for twelve years. ⁸His generals took over the government, each in his own province, ⁹and, when Alexander died, they all assumed royal crowns, and for many years the succession passed to their descendants. They brought untold miseries on the world.

¹⁰An offshoot of this stock was that impious man, Antiochus Epiphanes, son of King Antiochus. He had been a hostage in Rome before he succeeded to the throne in the year 137 of the Greek era.

¹¹At that time there emerged in Israel a group of renegade Jews, who inveigled many by saying, 'We should go and make an agree-

1:1 **being ... Greece:** *prob. mng; Gk obscure.*
1:10 **the year ... era:** *that is 175 B.C.E.*

1.1–64: Background to the Maccabean revolt. The author notes the spread of Greek power from Alexander the Great (356–323 B.C.E.) through his successors, down to Antiochus IV Epiphanes. This Seleucid king's harsh treatment of the Jews and brutal imposition of Hellenic culture upon them led Mattathias to revolt. **1:** *Kittim:* Macedonians. **3:** Alexander's army reached the *remotest bounds* of the author's Mediterranean world, the Beas river of the Punjab in northern India. In *his pride,* Alexander accepted divine honors. **7–9:** *Alexander died* at Babylon in June, 323 B.C.E., at the age of thirty-two. After *his death,* Alexander's *generals* fought over his empire. Three powers emerged, the Antigonids of Macedonia, the Ptolemies of Egypt, and the Seleucids of Syria. **10:** *Antiochus* IV, surnamed *Epiphanes,* i.e. "[God] manifest" but nicknamed "madman" (Gk. *epimanes*), was the son of Antiochus III, "the Great." On the father's defeat by the Romans at the battle of Magnesia (190 B.C.E.), the son was sent as a hostage to Rome to insure fidelity to the treaty of Apamea (188 B.C.E.). See 8.6–8. **11:**

ment with the Gentiles round about; nothing but disaster has been our lot since we cut ourselves off from them.' ¹²This proposal was widely approved, ¹³and some of the people in their enthusiasm went to the king and received authority to introduce pagan laws and customs. ¹⁴They built a gymnasium in the gentile style at Jerusalem; ¹⁵they removed their marks of circumcision and repudiated the holy covenant; they intermarried with Gentiles and sold themselves to evil.

¹⁶Once he was firmly established on his throne, Antiochus determined to become king of Egypt and so rule both kingdoms. ¹⁷He invaded Egypt with a powerful force of chariots, elephants, and cavalry, together with a great fleet. ¹⁸When battle was joined, King Ptolemy was routed with heavy loss and took flight. ¹⁹The fortified towns in Egypt were captured and the land pillaged.

²⁰On his return from the conquest of Egypt in the year 143 Antiochus marched up with a strong force against Israel and Jerusalem. ²¹In his arrogance he entered the temple and carried off the gold altar, the lampstand with all its fittings, ²²the table of the Bread of the Presence, the libation cups and bowls, the gold censers, the curtain, and the garlands. He stripped the gold plating from the front of the temple, ²³seized the silver and gold, the precious vessels, and whatever secret treasures he found, ²⁴and carried them all away when he left for his own country. He had caused much bloodshed, and he boasted arrogantly of what he had done.

²⁵Great was the mourning throughout Israel,
²⁶deep the groans of rulers and elders.
Girls and young men languished;
the beauty of our women was disfigured.
²⁷Every bridegroom took up the lament;
every bride sat mourning in her bridal chamber.
²⁸The land trembled for its inhabitants, and all the house of Jacob was wrapped in shame.

²⁹Two years later, the king sent a governor to put the towns of Judaea under tribute. When he arrived at Jerusalem with a powerful force ³⁰his language, though friendly, was full of guile, for once he had gained the city's confidence he launched a sudden and savage attack. Many of the Israelites were killed, ³¹and their city was sacked and set ablaze. On every side the houses and city walls were demolished; ³²the women and children were captured, and the livestock seized.

³³The City of David was turned into a citadel, enclosed by a high, stout wall with strong towers, ³⁴and garrisoned by impious foreigners and renegades. Having made themselves secure, ³⁵⁻³⁶they laid up a store of arms and provisions, and brought in the plunder they had collected from Jerusalem. They lurked there, a snare and threat to the temple and a perpetual menace to Israel.

³⁷They shed innocent blood all round the temple;
they defiled the holy place.
³⁸For fear of them the inhabitants of Jerusalem fled;
the city became the abode of aliens, and alien herself to her offspring:
her children forsook her.
³⁹Her temple lay desolate as a wilderness;
her festivals were turned to mourning,
her sabbaths to a reproach,
her honour to contempt.
⁴⁰Her present dishonour was equalled only by her past renown,
and her pride was turned to mourning.

⁴¹The king issued an edict throughout his

1:20 **143**: *that is* 169 B.C.E.

The *renegade Jews* were led by Jason (Joshua), the brother of the Jewish high priest Onias III; see 2 Macc. 4.7–20. **18**: *Ptolemy* VI Philometor (180–145 B.C.E.). **20–24**: *Antiochus* robbed the *temple* to replenish the royal treasury depleted by war. **29–32**: Antiochus invaded Egypt again in 168 B.C.E. Forced to retire by the Roman emissary Popilius Laenas, who threatened war with Rome, Antiochus vented his wrath on Judea, which he thought to be in revolt. See 2 Macc. 5.1–14. *Two years later* than Antiochus' first Egyptian campaign, i.e. in 167 B.C.E., Apollonius, chief of the Mysian mercenaries, was sent to put down the unruly city again; see 2 Macc. 5.23b–26. **33–34**: *Impious foreigners* (Seleucid troops) *and renegades* (Hellenizing Jews) now fortified the westernmost hill of Jerusalem. This citadel remained in their hands until 141 B.C.E., when Simon drove them out (1 Macc. 13.49–50). **37–40**: A lament similar to that of Ps. 79. **41–50**: Hoping to weld into a political empire: his subjects were all to become one people [42] and abandon their own customs. Everywhere the nations complied with the royal command, [43] and many in Israel willingly adopted the foreign cult, sacrificing to idols and profaning the sabbath. [44] The king sent agents to Jerusalem and the towns of Judaea with written orders that ways and customs foreign to the country should be introduced. [45] Whole-offerings, sacrifices, and drink-offerings were forbidden in the temple; sabbaths and feast days were to be profaned, [46] the temple and its ministers defiled. [47] Pagan altars, idols, and sacred precincts were to be established, swine and other unclean beasts to be offered in sacrifice. [48] The Jews were to leave their sons uncircumcised; they had to make themselves in every way abominable, unclean, and profane, [49] and so forget the law and change all their statutes. [50] The penalty for disobeying the royal command was death.

[51] Such were the terms of the edict issued by the king throughout his realm. He appointed superintendents over all the people, and instructed the towns of Judaea to offer sacrifice, town by town. [52] Those of the people who were ready to betray the law all thronged to their side in large numbers. Their wicked conduct throughout the land [53] drove Israel into hiding in every possible place of refuge.

[54] On the fifteenth day of the month of Kislev in the year 145, 'the abomination of desolation' was set up on the altar of the Lord. In the towns throughout Judaea pagan altars were built; [55] incense was offered at the doors of houses and in the streets. [56] Every scroll of the law that was found was torn up and consigned to the flames, [57] and anyone

discovered in possession of a Book of the Covenant or conforming to the law was by sentence of the king condemned to die. [58] Thus month after month these wicked men used their power against the Israelites whom they found in their towns. [59] On the twenty-fifth day of each month they offered sacrifice on the pagan altar which was on top of the altar of whole-offering. [60] In accordance with the royal decree, they put to death women who had had their children circumcised; [61] their babies, their families, and those who had performed the circumcisions were hanged by the neck.

[62] Yet many in Israel found strength to resist, taking a determined stand against the eating of any unclean food. [63] They welcomed death and died rather than defile themselves and profane the holy covenant. [64] Israel lay under a reign of terror.

2 IT was in those days that a certain Mattathias son of John, son of Symeon, came on the scene. He was a priest of the Joarib family from Jerusalem, now settled at Modin, [2] and he had five sons: John called Gaddis, [3] Simon called Thassis, [4] Judas called Maccabaeus, [5] Eleazar called Avaran, and Jonathan called Apphus.

[6] When Mattathias saw the sacrilegious acts committed in Judaea and, above all, in Jerusalem, [7] he said:

'Oh! Why was I born to see this,
the ruin of my people, the ruin of the
    Holy City,
to sit by while she was surrendered,
the holy place given up to foreigners?

1:54 **145:** *that is* 167 B.C.E.

---

unity the many ethnic and linguistic groupings over which he ruled, Antiochus IV decreed a common culture (Hellenism) and religion (the worship of Zeus Olympios) for all of his subjects. For Jews, conformity to the decree meant abandonment of the Mosaic Law and apostasy from the God of Israel. **54:** On December 7, 167 B.C.E., Antiochus built an altar to Zeus Olympios on the temple's altar of holocausts (see v. 59). This *abomination* replaced the Holy of Holies as the center of worship in the temple, and the worship of Zeus replaced that of Israel's God. **55:** Apparently, Jews adopted Grecian shrines for their streets and houses. **57:** *Book of the Covenant:* the Law of Moses. **59:** December 17, 167 B.C.E. **62–63:** See 2 Macc. 6.18–7.42 for examples.

2.1–70: Mattathias begins active resistance. What began under Mattathias' direction as armed resistance to the Hellenizing program eventually escalated into a war for autonomy led by his sons. **1:** *Joarib* headed one priestly division of twenty-four appointed for alternate duty in the temple. See 1 Chr. 24.1–19 (especially v. 7). *Modin* is modern el-Midyah, seven miles east of Lod. **2:** The surnames of Mattathias' sons have been explained as meaning "fortunate," "burning," "designated by Yahweh" (or "the hammerer," or "hammer-headed"),

8 Her temple is like a man robbed of
honour;
9 its glorious vessels are carried off as
spoil.
Her infants are slain in her streets,
her young men by the sword of the foe.
10 Is there any nation that has not
usurped her sovereignty,
any people that has not taken plunder
from her?
11 She has been stripped of all her
adornment;
she is no longer free, she is a slave.

12 'We see the temple, which is our splendour
and glory, laid waste and desecrated by the
Gentiles. 13 Why should we go on living?'
14 Mattathias and his sons tore their garments, put on sackcloth, and mourned loud
and long.

15 The king's officers who were enforcing
apostasy came to the town of Modin to see
that sacrifice was offered. 16 Many Israelites
went over to them, but Mattathias and all his
sons stood apart. 17 The officers addressed
Mattathias: 'You are a leader here, a man of
mark and influence in this town, with your
sons and brothers at your back. 18 Now you be
the first to come forward; carry out the king's
decree as all the nations have done, as well as
the leading men in Judaea and the people
left in Jerusalem. Then you and your sons
will be enrolled among the king's Friends;
you will all receive high honours, rich rewards of silver and gold, and many further
benefits.'

19 In a ringing voice Mattathias replied:
'Though every nation within the king's dominions obeys and forsakes its ancestral worship, though all have chosen to submit to his
commands, 20 yet I and my sons and my
brothers will follow the covenant made with
our forefathers. 21 Heaven forbid we should
ever abandon the law and its statutes! 22 We
will not obey the king's command, nor will we
deviate one step from our way of worship.'

23 As he finished speaking, a Jew came forward in full view of all to offer sacrifice on
the pagan altar at Modin, in obedience to the
royal decree. 24 The sight aroused the zeal of

Mattathias, and, shaking with passion and in
a fury of righteous anger, he rushed forward
and cut him down on the very altar. 25 At the
same time he killed the officer sent by the
king to enforce sacrifice, and demolished the
pagan altar. 26 So Mattathias showed his fervent zeal for the law, as Phinehas had done
when he killed Zimri son of Salu. 27 He
shouted for the whole town to hear, 'Follow
me, all who are zealous for the law and stand
by the covenant!' 28 Then he and his sons took
to the hills, leaving behind in the town all
they possessed.

29 At that time many who sought to maintain their religion and law went down to live
in the desert, 30 taking their children and
their wives and their livestock with them, for
their miseries were more than they could
bear. 31 Word soon reached the king's officers and the forces stationed in Jerusalem,
the city of David, that Israelites who had defied the king's order had gone down into
hiding-places in the desert. 32 A large body of
soldiers, setting off in pursuit, came upon
them, and drew up in battle order ready to
attack on the sabbath. 33 'There is still time,'
they shouted; 'come out, do as the king commands, and your lives will be spared.' 34 'We
will not come out,' was the reply; 'we will not
obey the king's command to profane the sabbath.' 35 Without more ado the attack was
launched, 36 but the Israelites did nothing in
reply; they neither hurled stones, nor barricaded their caves. 37 'Let us all meet death
with a clear conscience,' they said; 'we call
heaven and earth to witness it is contrary to
all justice that you are making away with us.'
38 So on the sabbath they were attacked and
massacred, men, women, and children, up to
a thousand in all, along with their livestock.

39 When Mattathias and his friends learnt
of it, their grief was very great, 40 and they
said to one another, 'If we all do as our brothers have done and refuse to fight the Gentiles
in defence of our lives as well as our laws and
customs, then they will soon wipe us off the
face of the earth.' 41 That day the decision was
taken that if anyone came to fight against

2:10 **usurped her sovereignty:** *or* occupied her
palaces.

"awake," and "favorite." **18:** Mattathias was offered the lowest of four honorary ranks of *the king's Friends*
(friends, honored friends, first, and preferred friends). See 10.65; 11.27; 2 Macc. 8.9. **24:** Mattathias obeyed
God's law. See Deut. 13.6–11. **26:** See Num. 25.6–15. **29–38:** Josephus (*Ant.* XII.6.2) records that Jews who
had met secretly in a cave to observe the sabbath were suffocated by setting fire to brush that had been piled

them on the sabbath, they would fight back, rather than all perish as their brothers in the caves had done.

42 They were joined at that time by a group of Hasidaeans, stalwarts of Israel, every one of them a volunteer in the cause of the law; 43 and all who were refugees from the troubles came to swell their numbers and add to their strength. 44 Now that they had an organized force, they turned the fierceness of their wrath on the guilty men and renegades; those who escaped their onslaught took refuge with the Gentiles.

45 Mattathias and his friends swept through the country, demolishing the pagan altars 46 and forcibly circumcising all the uncircumcised boys found within the frontiers of Israel. 47 They hunted down their arrogant enemies, and the cause prospered in their hands. 48 Thus they came to the defence of the law against the Gentiles and their kings and withheld power from the wicked.

49 As the time drew near for Mattathias to die, he said to his sons: 'Arrogance now stands secure and gives judgement against us; these are days of calamity and raging fury. 50 Now, my sons, be zealous for the law, and give your lives for the covenant made with your forefathers. 51 If you keep in mind the deeds they did in their generations, great glory and everlasting fame will be yours. 52 Did not Abraham prove faithful under trial, and so win credit as a righteous man? 53 Joseph, hard pressed though he was, kept God's commandment, and he became overlord of Egypt. 54 Phinehas, our forefather, never flagged in his zeal, and his was the covenant of an everlasting priesthood. 55 Joshua kept the law, and he became a judge in Israel. 56 Caleb bore witness before the congregation, and his reward was a share in

the land. 57 David was a man of loyalty, and he was granted the throne of an everlasting kingdom. 58 Elijah never flagged in his zeal for the law, and he was taken up to heaven. 59 Hananiah, Azariah, and Mishael had faith, and they were saved from the flames. 60 Daniel was a man of integrity, and he was rescued from the lions' jaws. 61 So bear in mind how in the history of the generations no one who trusts in Heaven ever lacks strength. 62 Do not fear a wicked man's threats; his success will turn to filth and worms. 63 Today he may be high in honour, but tomorrow not a trace of him will be found; he will have returned to the dust, and his schemes will have come to naught. 64 But you, my sons, draw your courage and strength from the law, for through it glory will be yours.

65 'Now here is Symeon your brother, whom I know to be wise in counsel; listen always to him, for he will be a father to you. 66 Judas Maccabaeus has been strong and brave from boyhood; he is to be your commander in the field, and wage war against the peoples. 67 Assemble to your side all who observe the law, and avenge your people's wrongs. 68 Repay the Gentiles in their own coin, and give heed to what the law decrees.'

69 Mattathias blessed them, and was gathered to his fathers. 70 He died in the year 146, and was buried by his sons in the family tomb at Modin; and there was great lamentation for him throughout Israel.

The war under Judas Maccabaeus

3 Judas Maccabaeus came forward to take his father's place. 2 He had the support of all his brothers and his father's followers,

2:70 146: *that is* 166 B.C.E.

at the mouth of the cave; see also 2 Macc. 6.11. **42:** The *Hasidaeans* ("Pious" or "Faithful") were the forerunners of both the Pharisees and the Essenes. **44:** Second Maccabees 8.1 estimates this *organized force* as numbering about 6,000. *Guilty men:* pagans. *Renegades:* apostate Jews. **48:** *They came to the defense of the law* by preventing the absorption of Judaism into a mixture of pagan and Jewish worship. **49–70:** Mattathias' deathbed scene recalls that of Jacob (Gen. ch. 49) and Moses (Deut. ch. 33). Mattathias urges imitation of those who remained faithful to God's word despite difficult circumstances: Abraham (Gen. ch. 22), Joseph (Gen. ch. 39), Phinehas (Num. ch. 25), Joshua (Josh. ch. 1), Caleb (Num. chs. 13–14), David (2 Sam. ch. 7), Elijah (1 Kgs. ch. 18; 2 Kgs. ch. 2), Hananiah, Azariah, Mishael (Dan. ch. 1), and Daniel (Dan. ch. 6). See similar praises in Ecclus. chs. 44–50. **62:** *Filth and worms* were the final lot of Antiochus (2 Macc. 9.5–10). **65:** Although *Symeon* was older, he became the leader of the people only after his brothers Judas and Jonathan had died. **70:** *Family tomb at Modin:* see 13.25–30.

3.1–9.73: The Jews regain religious freedom. Under Judas, the Jews defeat the forces of Antiochus and his and they carried on Israel's campaign with zest.

3 He enhanced his people's glory.
  Like a giant he put on his breastplate
  and girt himself with weapons of war.
  He waged many a campaign
  from a camp well guarded with the
    sword.
4 He was like a lion in his exploits,
  like a young lion roaring for prey.
5 He tracked down and pursued the
    renegades;
  he consumed with fire the troublers of
    his people.
6 The renegades cowered in fear of him,
  and all such wrongdoers were utterly
    confounded,
  while the cause of freedom prospered
    in his hands.
7 He roused many kings to anger,
  but to Jacob his deeds brought joy.
  He is remembered for ever in blessing.
8 He passed through the towns of
    Judaea,
  wiping out the apostates there;
  he turned wrath away from Israel.
9 His renown spread to the ends of the
    earth,
  and he rallied a people near to
    destruction.

10 Apollonius raised an army, consisting of Gentiles and a large contingent from Samaria, to wage war against Israel. 11 Informed of this, Judas marched out and in the encounter defeated and killed him. Many of the enemy fell; the survivors took flight. 12 From the arms which were captured, Judas obtained the sword of Apollonius, and for the rest of his life he used it in his campaigns.

13 When Seron, the commander of the army in Syria, heard that Judas had mustered a considerable force, all his loyal followers of military age, 14 he said, 'I shall make a name for myself and win renown throughout the empire by taking up arms against Judas and his followers, who set at naught the king's command.' 15 Seron was reinforced by a strong contingent of apostate Jews, who marched up with him to help wreak vengeance on Israel. 16 As he reached the pass of Beth-horon, Judas advanced to meet him with a handful of men, 17 who at the sight of the host coming against them said to Judas, 'How can so few of us fight against so many? Besides, we have had nothing to eat all day and are faint with hunger.'

18 Judas replied: 'Many can easily be overpowered by a few; Heaven can save just as well by few as by many. 19 Victory does not depend on numbers; strength is from Heaven alone. 20 Our enemies, inflated with insolence and lawlessness, are coming against us; they mean to kill us and our wives and children for the sake of the plunder they will get. 21 But we are fighting for our lives and for our laws and customs, 22 and Heaven will crush them before our eyes; you have no need to be afraid of them.'

23 As soon as he finished speaking, he launched a surprise attack, which overwhelmed Seron and his army. 24 They were pursued down the pass of Beth-horon as far as the plain; some eight hundred of them fell; the rest fled to Philistia.

25 Judas and his brothers came to be regarded with fear, and alarm spread among

son, purify the temple, punish persecutors and regain religious freedom. When persecution is renewed, Judas resumes the struggle. Jonathan continues the war with success.

3.1–9: A poetic preface praises Judas. 5: *Consumed with fire:* see 5.5, 35, 44. **7:** *Kings:* Antiochus IV Epiphanes (3.27), Antiochus V Eupator (6.28, but not mentioned by name; see 3.33 n.) and Demetrius I Soter (9.1). **8:** By purging the land, Judas mollified the divine *wrath.* See 2 Macc. 6.12–16. **9:** *Ends of the earth:* Rome; see 8.17–32.

3.10–24: Judas' early victories. 10: *Apollonius,* who had earlier sacked Jerusalem (1.29–35), now led a contingent including his Mysian mercenaries (2 Macc. 5.24) against Judea. **16:** Two towns, two miles apart, "Upper" and "Lower" *Beth-horon,* were connected by a pass which led from the coastal plains to the highlands north of Jerusalem. Judas ambushed Seron in the pass and defeated him with fewer men. **18–19:** First Maccabees never uses "God" or "Lord," but prefers *Heaven.* **24:** *Philistia:* the seacoast, once home of the Philistines.

3.25–37: Antiochus goes to Persia. As he prepares to leave, Antiochus makes provision for retaining control of Judea and Jerusalem. That the king gathered a powerful army in response to the exploits of Judas is an the Gentiles round about. 26 His fame reached the ears of the king, and the story of his battles was told in every nation. 27 Incensed by those reports, King Antiochus issued orders for the mobilization of all the forces of his empire, an immensely powerful army. 28 He opened his treasury and gave a year's pay to his troops, with a command to be prepared to serve as required. 29 But he found that his resources were running low; his income from tribute had dwindled as a result of the disaffection and violence he had brought on his empire by abolishing traditional laws and customs. 30 He was worried that, as had happened once or twice before, he might be short of money, both for his normal expenses and for the gifts he had been accustomed to distribute with an even more lavish hand than any of his predecessors on the throne.

31 Greatly disconcerted, he resolved to go to Persia and collect the tribute due from the provinces, and so raise a large sum of ready money. 32 He left Lysias, a distinguished member of the royal family, as viceroy of the territories between the Euphrates and the Egyptian frontier, 33 and he also appointed him guardian of his son Antiochus until his return. 34 He transferred to him half the armed forces, together with the elephants, and gave him detailed instructions about what he wanted done, especially in regard to the inhabitants of Judaea and Jerusalem. 35 Lysias was to dispatch a force against them so as to crush and destroy the power of Israel and those left in Jerusalem, and to blot out all memory of them from the place. 36 Foreigners were to be settled throughout the territory and the land was to be parcelled out

among them. 37 The remaining half of his forces the king retained and, setting out with them from Antioch, his capital, in the year 147, he crossed the Euphrates and marched through the upper provinces.

38 Lysias chose Ptolemaeus son of Dorymenes, with Nicanor and Gorgias, all three powerful members of the order of king's Friends, 39 and sent forty thousand infantry and seven thousand cavalry under their command to invade and devastate Judaea in accordance with the king's orders. 40 They set out with their entire force and occupied a position near Emmaus in the lowlands. 41 The traders of the region, impressed by what they heard of the army, came to the camp to buy the Israelites for slaves, bringing with them a very large quantity of silver and gold as well as a stock of fetters. The army was also reinforced by troops from Syria and Philistia.

42 When Judas and his brothers saw how much graver their plight had become with the enemy encamped inside their frontiers, and, further, when they learnt of the orders the king had given for the complete destruction of the nation, 43 they said among themselves, 'Let us restore the shattered fortunes of our people; let us fight for our nation and for the holy place.' 44 They gathered in full assembly both to prepare for battle and to pray and seek divine mercy and compassion.

45 Jerusalem lay deserted like a
    wilderness,
with none of her children going in or
    out.
The holy place was trodden underfoot;

3:37 147: *that is* 165 B.C.E.

exaggeration. A more likely reason was to quell a rebellion in the east, indicated by overdue tribute (v. 31), to secure the eastern frontier against the Parthians and to replenish his depleted treasury (vv. 29–30) by conquest. **29:** Antiochus' problems largely resulted from his imposition of Hellenic religion and customs on native populations. **31:** *Persia* in 1 and 2 Macc. is all the area east of the Tigris. **32:** *Lysias* belonged to the highest court order of the realm, "the king's relative." **33:** The *son* is *Antiochus* V Eupator (164–161 B.C.E.), who was then only seven. **37:** *Antioch* is modern Antakya in eastern Turkey. The *upper provinces* included the valleys of the Tigris and Euphrates.

3.38–4.27: Judas defeats the Seleucid generals. See 2 Macc. 8.8–29. **38:** *Ptolemaeus:* in 2 Macc. 8.8, he is governor of Coele-Syria and Phoenicia. His region included Judea. *Nicanor:* see 1 Macc. 7.26–50; 2 Macc. 8.9; 14.15. *Gorgias:* see 5.59; 2 Macc. 8.9; 10.14; 12.32–35. *King's Friends:* see 2.18 n. **40:** *Emmaus* is about twenty miles northwest of Jerusalem. **41:** Jews were to be sold as *slaves* to raise money for tribute (2 Macc. 8.10–11). The Greek translator probably misread Aram (= Syria) for Edom, the Heb. words being easily confused. The main body of troops was already from Syria. **43–46:** Because *the holy place,* the temple, was defiled by the pagans and apostates (v. 45), the Jews assembled for prayer at *Mizpah,* an ancient Israelite

aliens and heathen lodged in her
citadel.
Joy had been banished from Jacob,
and flute and harp were silent.

46 They assembled at Mizpah, which is opposite Jerusalem, for there in former times Israel had had a place of worship. 47 They
fasted that day, put on sackcloth, sprinkled
ashes on their heads, and tore their garments. 48 They unrolled the scroll of the law,
seeking there the guidance which Gentiles
seek from the images of their gods. 49 They
brought the priestly vestments, together with
the firstfruits and the tithes, and presented
Nazirites who had completed their vows,
50 and they cried aloud to Heaven: 'What
shall we do about these? Where shall we take
them? 51 Your holy place is trodden underfoot and profaned, and for your priests there
is only mourning and humiliation. 52 And
now, the Gentiles have gathered against us to
destroy us. You know the fate they plan for
us; 53 how can we withstand them unless you
come to our aid?' 54 The trumpets were
sounded, and a great shout was raised.

55 Judas then appointed leaders of the people, officers over thousands, hundreds, fif-
ties, and tens. 56 In accordance with the law,
he ordered back to their homes those who
were building their houses or were betrothed
or were planting vineyards or were faint-
hearted. 57 The army moved off and took up
position to the south of Emmaus. 58 There
Judas addressed them: 'Prepare for action
and show yourselves men. Be ready at dawn
to fight these Gentiles massed against us to
destroy us and our holy place. 59 Better we
should die fighting than look on while calamity overwhelms our people and the holy
place. 60 But it will be as Heaven wills.'

4 Gorgias, with a detachment of five thousand men and a thousand picked cavalry, set out by night 2 to launch a surprise
attack on the Jewish position; his guides were
men from the citadel. 3 But Judas had word

of it, and he and his soldiers moved out to
strike at the king's army in Emmaus 4 while
the troops under Gorgias's command were
still away from their base. 5 Gorgias reached
Judas's camp during the night, but, finding
no one there, began to search the hills for
them. 'These Jews', he said, 'are running
away from us.'

6 Daybreak saw Judas in the plain with
three thousand men, though they had not all
the armour or swords they needed. 7 They
found the gentile camp to be strongly fortified with breastworks, while mounted
guards, seasoned troops, patrolled round it.

8 Judas said to his men: 'Do not be afraid of
their numbers or panic at their onslaught.
9 Remember how our forefathers were saved
at the Red Sea, when pursued by Pharaoh
and his army. 10 Now let us call on Heaven to
favour our cause and, remembering the covenant made with our forefathers, to crush
this army which today opposes us. 11 Then all
the Gentiles will know there is One who liber-
ates and saves Israel.'

12 When the foreigners saw them advancing to the attack, 13 they moved out from their
camp to give battle. Sounding their trumpets,
Judas and his men 14 closed with them, and
the Gentiles broke and fled into the plain;
15 all who fell behind were put to the sword.
The pursuit was pressed as far as Gazara and
the lowlands of Idumaea, to Azotus and Jamnia; some three thousand of the enemy were
killed.

16 Judas and his force then broke off the
pursuit and withdrew. 17 He said to the people: 'Curb your desire for spoil; there is more
fighting ahead of us; 18 Gorgias and his force
are in the hills near by. Stand firm now
against our enemies and fight; after that,
plunder as much as you please.'

19 Before Judas had finished speaking, an
enemy patrol appeared, reconnoitring from
the hills. 20 They saw that their army had
been routed and their camp was being set on
fire, for the smoke that met their gaze

---

sanctuary eight miles north of Jerusalem. See Judg. 20.1; 1 Sam. 7.5; 10.17; Jer. 40.6. **48:** Unable to cast lots
(the Urim and Thummim of 1 Sam. 14.41) after the Exile (Ezra 2.63; Neh. 7.65), Israel sought guidance from
the Lord by reading *the scroll of the law.* **49–51:** The *Nazirites* could not complete *their vows* (see Num.
6.1–21), because the *holy place* (temple) was defiled. **55:** The *leaders* included Judas' brothers (2 Macc.
8.22–23). **56:** See Deut. 20.5–8. Second Maccabees 8.13 cites only cowardice. **4.2:** *Guides . . . from the
citadel:* renegade Jews probably; see 1.33–34 n. **6:** Second Maccabees 8.16 doubles Judas' army. **8–11:** See
2 Macc. 8.16–20, where the incidents cited in Judas' speech as motives for confidence are different. Ancient
authors reported what a speaker should have said rather than exact words. **15:** The defeated enemy fled to

showed what had happened. ²¹ They were panic-stricken as they took in the scene, and when, further, they saw the army of Judas in the plain, ready for action, ²² they fled one and all to Philistia.

²³ Judas turned back to plunder the camp, and large quantities of gold and silver, violet and purple stuffs, and great riches were seized. ²⁴ At their homecoming there were songs of thanksgiving and praise to Heaven, 'for it is right, because his mercy endures for ever'. ²⁵ That day saw a great deliverance for Israel.

²⁶ Those of the Gentiles who escaped with their lives went to Lysias and reported all that had happened. ²⁷ He was stunned at the news, bitterly disappointed that matters with Israel had not gone as he intended; they had turned out very differently from the king's instructions to him.

²⁸ The following year Lysias mustered sixty thousand picked infantry and five thousand cavalry to bring the war with the Jews to an end. ²⁹ Marching into Idumaea, they encamped at Bethsura, where Judas opposed them with ten thousand men. ³⁰ When he saw the strength of the enemy's army, he prayed: 'All praise to you, Saviour of Israel, who by the hand of your servant David broke the giant's onslaught and who delivered the Philistine army into the hands of Jonathan, Saul's son, and of his armour-bearer. ³¹ Now let this army be hemmed in by the power of your people Israel, and let the enemy's pride in their troops and mounted men be humbled; ³² fill them with cowardice, make their insolent strength melt away, let them reel under a crushing defeat; ³³ may they fall by the sword of those who love you. And let all who know your name praise you with songs of thanksgiving.'

³⁴ Battle was joined, and in the hand-to-hand fighting Lysias lost about five thousand men. ³⁵ When he saw his own army routed and Judas's army in fighting spirit, ready to live or to die nobly, he withdrew to Antioch, where he recruited a force of mercenaries, intending to return to Judaea with a much larger army.

³⁶ Judas and his brothers said: 'Now that our enemies have been crushed, let us go up to cleanse and rededicate the temple.' ³⁷ When the whole army had assembled, they went up to Mount Zion, ³⁸ where they found the temple laid waste, the altar desecrated, the gates burnt down, the courts overgrown like a thicket or wooded hillside, and the priests' rooms in ruin. ³⁹ They tore their garments, lamented loudly, put ashes on their heads, ⁴⁰ and threw themselves face downwards on the ground. They cried aloud to Heaven, and the ceremonial trumpets were sounded.

⁴¹ Then Judas detailed men to engage the citadel garrison while the temple was being cleansed. ⁴² He selected priests without blemish and faithful to the law, ⁴³ and they purified the temple, removing to an unclean place the stones which defiled it. ⁴⁴ They discussed what to do about the desecrated altar of whole-offerings, ⁴⁵ and rightly decided to demolish it, for fear it might become a lasting reproach to them because it had been defiled by the Gentiles. They therefore pulled down the altar, ⁴⁶ and stored away the stones in a

4:35 intending . . . army: *prob. mng; Gk obscure.*

the cities of the coastal lowlands: *Gazara* (Gezer), *Azotus* (Ashdod), and *Jamnia* (Jabneh). **23:** The *gold and silver* of the slave traders now fell to their intended victims (2 Macc. 8.25). **24:** See the refrain of Ps. 136. **26:** The survivors included Nicanor (2 Macc. 8.34–36).

4.28–35: Judas defeats Lysias at Bethsura. See 2 Macc. 11.1–12. **28–29:** *The following year,* 164 B.C.E., Lysias besieged *Bethsura* (Beth-zur), which was friendly toward Judas (2 Macc. 11.6–7). **30:** Judas encouraged his troops by recalling how, against all odds, David overcame Goliath (1 Sam. ch. 17) and Jonathan slew the Philistine outpost (1 Sam. ch. 14). **35:** Second Maccabees 11.13–15 notes that Lysias came to terms with the Jews some time after his devastating defeat in this battle.

4.36–61: The purification and dedication of the temple. Second Maccabees 10.1–8 reports that the death of Antiochus IV Epiphanes (6.1–16), and the accession of his son Antiochus V Eupator (6.17), preceded the temple's purification (4.36–51) and dedication (4.52–59) in December 164 B.C.E. (2 Macc. 9.1–29). **41:** *The citadel:* see 1.33–34 n. **42:** For earlier purifications of the temple see 2 Kgs. 23.4–25; 2 Chr. ch. 29. **43:** *The stones which defiled* the temple, those of the altar to Zeus Olympios (1.54, 59), were taken *to an unclean place,* i.e. a place for refuse (possibly the Kidron valley, see 2 Kgs. 23.4, 6, 12). **44:** The *altar of whole-offerings* had been *desecrated* by the altar to Zeus built upon it, but because it had been devoted to the worship of the Lord, suitable place on the temple hill, until there should arise a prophet to give a decision about them. 47 They took unhewn stones, as the law directs, and built a new altar on the model of the previous one. 48 They also repaired the temple and restored its interior, and they consecrated the temple courts. 49 New sacred vessels were made; the lampstand, the altar of incense, and the table were brought into the temple. 50 They burnt incense on the altar, and they lit the lamps on the lampstand to shine within the temple. 51 When they had set the Bread of the Presence on the table and spread out the curtains, their work was completed.

52 Early on the twenty-fifth day of the ninth month, the month of Kislev, in the year 148, 53 sacrifice was offered, as laid down by the law, on the newly constructed altar of whole-offerings. 54 On the anniversary of the day of its desecration by the Gentiles, on that very day it was dedicated with hymns of thanksgiving, to the music of harps and lutes and cymbals. 55 All the people prostrated themselves in worship and gave praise to Heaven for prospering their cause.

56 They celebrated the dedication of the altar for eight days; there was rejoicing as they brought whole-offerings and sacrificed shared-offerings and thank-offerings. 57 They decorated the front of the temple with gold garlands and ornamental shields. They renovated the gates and restored the priests' rooms, fitting them with doors. 58 At the lifting of the disgrace brought on them by the Gentiles there was very great rejoicing among the people.

59 Judas, his brothers, and the whole congregation of Israel decreed that, at the same season each year, the dedication of the altar should be observed with joy and gladness for eight days, beginning on the twenty-fifth of Kislev.

60 At that time they encircled Mount Zion with high walls and strong towers to prevent the Gentiles from coming in and overrunning it as they had done before. 61 Judas set a garrison there, and he also fortified Bethsura, so that the people should have a fortress facing Idumaea.

5 The Gentiles round about were greatly incensed when they heard of the building of the altar and rededication of the temple. 2 Determined to wipe out all of Jacob's race living among them, they set about the work of massacre and extermination.

3 Judas made war on the descendants of Esau in Idumaea and attacked Acrabattene, because they had encircled Israel. He inflicted a heavy and humiliating defeat on them and stripped their corpses of armour and weapons. 4 He remembered also the wrong done by the Baeanites, who with traps and road-blocks were continually ambushing the Israelites. 5 He shut them up in their forts and positioned his troops against them; then, calling down a solemn curse on them, he set ablaze the forts with all their occupants. 6 He crossed over to attack the Ammonites and was confronted by a strong force and a large crowd of people, all under the leadership of Timotheus. 7 In the course of many engagements, they broke before Judas's attack and were crushed. 8 After Judas had taken Jazer

4:52 148: *that is* 164 B.C.E.

the stones were sacred and could not be put to a secular use. **46:** Only a *prophet* could declare what should be done with *the stones,* but lack of a prophet is noted; see also 9.27; 14.41. **47:** The *law:* Exod. 20.25; Deut. 27.5–6. **53–54:** For the pertinent laws on *sacrifice,* see Exod. 29.38–41; Num. 7.10–88. **56–59:** The Jewish feast which commemorates the temple's *dedication* in December 164 B.C.E., takes its present name from the Heb. word *Hanukkah,* meaning "dedication." **60–61:** Judas took precautions against further efforts of Lysias (v. 35).

5.1–68: Judas rescues his persecuted coreligionists. The dedication of the temple and the Jewish exemption from the edict of Antiochus (2 Macc. 11.27–33) which followed Judas' victory over Lysias (1 Macc. 4.28–35) aroused the envy and hostility of neighboring peoples. Soon after Antiochus' death, a series of anti-Jewish incidents led Judas to undertake reprisals and to rescue and relocate those Jews in danger. **1:** *The Gentiles round about* are those of Idumea (vv. 3–5; 2 Macc. 10.14–23), Ammon (vv. 6–8; possibly 2 Macc. 8.30–33), Gilead (vv. 9–13, 24–54; 2 Macc. 12.10–31), Galilee (vv. 14–23), and the land of the Philistines (vv. 66–68; 2 Macc. 12.3–9). **2:** *Jacob's race* and similar archaic expressions in this chapter (e.g. *the descendants of Esau,* v. 3) are meant to evoke the memory of Israel's earlier conquest of the land, which the Jews still regarded as their own. **3:** The location of *Acrabattene* is unknown. **4:** *The Baeanites* are difficult to identify; perhaps they were nomads and its dependent villages, he returned to Judaea.

⁹The Gentiles in Gilead gathered against the Israelites within their territory, intent on destroying them; but the Israelites took refuge in the fortress of Dathema, ¹⁰from where they sent this letter to Judas and his brothers:

The Gentiles in this region have gathered to wipe us out. ¹¹With Timotheus in command of their army, they are preparing to come and seize the fortress where we have taken refuge. ¹²Therefore come now at once and rescue us from their clutches, for many of our number have already fallen. ¹³All our fellow-Jews in the region of Tubias have been massacred, their wives and children seized, and their property carried off, and about a thousand men have lost their lives.

¹⁴While the letter was being read, other messengers with their garments torn arrived from Galilee. ¹⁵'Ptolemais, Tyre and Sidon,' they reported, 'and all heathen Galilee have mobilized armies for our destruction.'

¹⁶When Judas and the people heard this, a full assembly was called to decide what should be done for their fellow-countrymen under persecution and enemy attack. ¹⁷Judas said to his brother Simon, 'You go to the rescue of your countrymen in Galilee with such troops as you need, while I and our brother Jonathan go to Gilead.' ¹⁸The remainder of the forces he left with Josephus son of Zacharias, and Azarias, a leading citizen, for the defence of Judaea. ¹⁹Their orders were: 'Take charge of the people, but on no account engage the Gentiles in battle while we are away.' ²⁰Simon was allotted three thousand men for the march on Galilee, and Judas eight thousand for the march on Gilead.

²¹Simon invaded Galilee and, after many battles, broke the resistance of the Gentiles. ²²Pursuing them as far as the gate of Ptole-

mais, he killed nearly three thousand of them, and stripped their corpses. ²³He brought back with him the Jews from Galilee and Arbatta, together with their wives and children and all they possessed, and amid great jubilation conducted them to Judaea.

²⁴Meanwhile Judas Maccabaeus and his brother Jonathan crossed the Jordan and made a three days' march through the desert. ²⁵They came upon some Nabataeans, who met them peaceably, and gave them a full account of what had happened to the Jews in Gilead: ²⁶many of them were held prisoner in the large fortified towns of Bozrah and Bezer, in Alema, Casphor, Maked, and Carnaim; ²⁷some were enclosed in the other towns of Gilead. 'Your enemies', they reported, 'are marshalling their forces to storm your strongholds tomorrow so as to capture them and destroy all the Jews in them in a single day.'

²⁸Judas and his army abruptly turned aside to Bozrah by way of the desert, and captured the town. He put the entire male population to the sword, plundered all their property, and set the place on fire. ²⁹Making a night march from Bozrah he came within reach of the fortress of Dathema. ³⁰When dawn broke, there in front of them were troops past counting; they were bringing up scaling-ladders and siege-engines to breach the fortress and begin the attack. ³¹When Judas saw that battle was joined, and heard a cry go up to heaven from the town, with the sound of trumpets and loud shouting, ³²he said to his men: 'Fight this day for our brothers!'

³³They advanced in three columns to take the enemy in the rear; they sounded the trumpets and cried aloud in prayer. ³⁴When the army of Timotheus realized it was Maccabaeus, they fled. In the heavy defeat inflicted on them, there fell that day nearly eight thousand of the enemy.

³⁵Judas then turned aside to Alema, which

5:35 **Alema:** *some witnesses read* Maapha.

and the mercenaries of 2 Macc. 10.14. **6:** *Ammonites:* people in the region near modern Amman, Jordan. **8:** Ancient *Jazer* was west and slightly north of Amman. **9:** *Gilead,* the area immediately east of the Jordan and to the north of the Jabbok river, extended north of the Yarmuk river in Hellenistic times. *Dathema:* location unknown. **11–13:** The letter exaggerates. Not all the Jews in *the region of Tubias,* i.e. Gilead, were massacred; see vv. 26–27. **14–15:** *Heathen Galilee:* the coastal region of Galilee, as the cities named indicate. **22:** *Ptolemais* is modern Acre, a coastal town north of Haifa. **23:** For their own protection against reprisals, the Jews from Galilee and Arbatta (i.e. Narbata, the coastal region just south of Galilee) resettled in Judea. **25:** The Nabataeans, an Arab people, grew rich as caravan traders. **26–36:** These towns were all located east of the he attacked and captured; he killed all the males, plundered the town, and set it on fire. 36 Moving from there, he occupied Casphor, Maked, Bezer, and the other towns of Gilead.

37 After these events Timotheus gathered another army and took up position opposite Raphon, on the far side of the wadi. 38 Judas sent spies to their camp, and they reported that all the Gentiles in the neighbourhood had rallied in very great strength to Timotheus, 39 who had also hired the help of Arab mercenaries. The enemy were encamped on the far side of the wadi, ready to give battle. So Judas marched to meet them.

40 As Judas and his army were approaching the wadi, Timotheus said to his officers: 'If he crosses over to our side first, we shall not be able to stand up to him; he will certainly get the better of us. 41 If, however, his courage fails him and he takes up a position on the other side of the river, then we will cross over and get the better of him.' 42 When Judas reached the wadi, he stationed the officers of the muster on its bank with instructions that the whole army should advance to the battle; no one was to be allowed to take up a fixed position. 43 Thus Judas forestalled the enemy by crossing to attack them at the head of all his people. The gentile army broke before him; one and all they threw away their weapons and sought refuge in the temple at Carnaim. 44 Judas captured the town and burnt the temple and everyone in it. With the overthrow of Carnaim, all resistance came to an end.

45 Judas assembled the Israelites who were in Gilead to escort them all back to Judaea. There was a great host of them, men high and low, women and children, together with their possessions. 46 They arrived at Ephron, a large and strongly fortified town on the road. It was impossible to bypass it on either side; the only route lay through the town. 47 The inhabitants, however, barricaded their gates with boulders and denied them passage. 48 Judas made peaceful overtures to them: 'We have to go through your territory to reach our own. No one will do you any harm: we will simply pass through on foot.' But they refused to open their gates to him.

49 Judas issued orders to those under his command: everyone was to halt where he was. 50 The fighting men took up battle positions and attacked the town all that day and all the night, until it fell into their hands. 51 They put every male to the sword, razed the town to the ground and plundered it, and then marched through it over the bodies of the slain. 52 They crossed the Jordan to the broad plain opposite Bethshan, 53 while Judas kept the stragglers together and encouraged the people all along the way till he arrived in Judaea. 54 With gladness and jubilation they went up to Mount Zion and offered whole-offerings, because they had returned in safety and without loss.

55 While Judas and Jonathan were in Gilead, and Simon their brother was besieging Ptolemais in Galilee, 56 their heroic military achievements were reported to the two commanders, Azarias and Josephus son of Zacharias, 57 and they said: 'We too must make a name for ourselves; let us undertake a campaign against the Gentiles in our neighbourhood.' 58 They gave orders to the forces in their command to advance on Jamnia. 59 When Gorgias and his men marched from the town to give battle, 60 Josephus and Azarias were put to rout and pursued to the frontier of Judaea, with the loss that day of some two thousand Israelites. 61 The people suffered this heavy defeat because those in command of them, thinking to play the hero themselves, had not obeyed Judas and his brothers. 62 Those men were not, however, of that family whose prerogative it was to bring deliverance to Israel.

63 The valiant Judas and his brothers won a great reputation throughout Israel and among all the Gentiles, wherever their fame spread, 64 and crowds flocked to acclaim them.

Sea of Galilee and just north of the Yarmuk river, but the precise location is not known in every instance. **37:** *Raphon* lay on a northern tributary of the Yarmuk. **39:** Perhaps these *mercenaries* were the Arabs of 2 Macc. 12.10–12. **42:** *The officers of the muster* were scribes, who could easily make notes of the laggards. **43:** The *temple* was that of Atargatis (the horned Astarte) *at Carnaim*, another city in the same region; see 2 Macc. 12.26. **46:** *Ephron* lay to the south of the Yarmuk, close to the Jordan. **52:** *Bethshan* is the Scythopolis of 2 Macc. 12.29–30, about four miles west of the Jordan and eighteen south of the Sea of Galilee. **54:** The victors arrived in time to celebrate the feast of Weeks (Pentecost); 2 Macc. 12.31. **55–64:** The punitive raids of 2 Macc. 12.3–9 preceded this incident. The defeat is here attributed to disobedience of orders, but 2 Macc. 12.40 notes a

⁶⁵ After this, Judas marched out with his brothers and made war on the descendants of Esau in the country to the south. He struck at Hebron and its villages, demolished its fortifications, and everywhere burnt down its forts. ⁶⁶ He then set out to invade Philistia and marched through Marisa. ⁶⁷ Several priests who, from a desire to distinguish themselves, had ill-advisedly gone into action, fell in the battle that day. ⁶⁸ Judas turned aside to Azotus in the territory of the Philistines; he pulled down their altars and burnt the images of their gods; he carried off spoil from the towns, and then went back to Judaea.

6 As King Antiochus made his way through the upper provinces he heard that in Persia there was a city, Elymais, famous for its wealth in silver and gold. ² Its temple was very rich, full of gold shields, coats of mail, and weapons left there by Philip's son Alexander, king of Macedon and the first to be king over the Greeks. ³ Antiochus came to the city, but in his attempt to take and plunder it he was unsuccessful because his plan had become known to the citizens. ⁴ They gave battle and drove him off; in bitter disappointment he withdrew towards Babylon.

⁵ In Persia a messenger brought him the news that the armies which had invaded Judaea had suffered defeat, ⁶ and that Lysias, who had marched up with an exceptionally strong force, had been flung back in open battle. Further, the strength of the Jews had increased through the capture of weapons, equipment, and spoil in plenty from the armies they destroyed; ⁷ they had pulled down the abomination built by him on the altar in Jerusalem and surrounded their temple with high walls as before; they had even fortified Bethsura, his city.

⁸ The king was dismayed and so sorely shaken by this report that he took to his bed, ill with grief at the miscarriage of his plans. ⁹ There he lay for many days, overcome again and again by bitter grief, and he realized that he was dying. ¹⁰ He summoned all his Friends and said: 'Sleep has deserted me; the weight of care has broken my heart. ¹¹ At first I asked myself: Why am I engulfed in this sea of troubles, I who was kind and well loved in the day of my power? ¹² But now I recall the wrong I did in Jerusalem: I carried off all the vessels of silver and gold that were there, and with no justification sent armies to wipe out the inhabitants of Judaea. ¹³ I know that is why these misfortunes have come upon me; and here I am, dying of bitter grief in a foreign land.'

¹⁴ He summoned Philip, one of his Friends, and appointed him regent over his whole empire, ¹⁵ giving him the crown, his royal robe, and the signet ring, with authority to bring up his son Antiochus and train him for the throne. ¹⁶ King Antiochus died in Persia in the year 149.

¹⁷ When Lysias learnt that the king was dead, he placed on the throne in succession to his father the young Antiochus, whom he had trained from boyhood, and he gave him the name Eupator.

¹⁸ MEANWHILE the garrison of the citadel was confining the Israelites to the neighbourhood of the temple, and, by harassing tactics, giving continual support to the Gentiles. ¹⁹ Judas determined to make an end of them; he gathered all the people together to lay

6:16 *149: that is* 163 B.C.E.

different reason for the casualties. **62:** The *family* is that of Mattathias and his sons. **65:** The *descendants of Esau:* Edomites. *Hebron* is twenty miles south of Jerusalem. **66:** *Marisa* lay west of Hebron. **67:** See vv. 55–64.

6.1–17: The death of Antiochus IV. See 2 Macc. 9.1–29. The author continues the story begun in 3.37. **1:** The *upper provinces* were in Mesopotamia and the Iranian plateau. *Elymais* is not a city but the country Elam, the area around Susa, particularly north and east of that city. **2:** Possibly the *temple* was that of Nanaea at Susa (see 2 Macc. 1.13). *Alexander:* the Great. **5–7:** Antiochus died after Lysias' defeat. The author merely summarizes 4.28–61 here. **10:** *Friends:* see 2.18 n. **12–13:** Obviously, these are the sentiments of the author and not those of Antiochus. **14–15:** Earlier, Antiochus had entrusted his son to Lysias (3.33), who faithfully declared the young Antiochus V Eupator king (v 17). Philip soon proved to be ambitious (vv. 55–56). **17:** *Eupator* means "of a good father."

6.18–63: Lysias' second Judean campaign. 18–27: To neutralize the citadel (1.33–34 n.), Judas besieged it. *King* Antiochus V Eupator (v. 22) was reminded of the garrison's loyalty to his *father,* Antiochus IV Epiphanes (v. 23), and of Judas' attacks on *all the neighbouring lands* (v. 25; 5.1–68). Actually, Lysias, the regent, was siege to the citadel [20] in the year 150, erecting emplacements and siege-engines against the enemy.

[21] But some of the beleaguered garrison escaped and were joined by a number of apostate Israelites. [22] They went to the king and complained: 'How long must we wait for you to support our cause and avenge our comrades? [23] We were happy to serve your father, to follow his instructions and obey his decrees. [24] And what was the result? Our own countrymen turned against us; indeed they put to death as many of us as they could lay hold of, and they robbed us of our property. [25] Nor are we the only ones to suffer at their hands; they have attacked all the neighbouring lands as well. [26] At this very moment the citadel in Jerusalem is closely invested, and they are intent on its capture. They have also fortified both the temple and Bethsura. [27] Unless your majesty quickly takes the initiative against them they will go to yet greater lengths. There will be no stopping them!'

[28] The king became furious as he listened. He assembled all his Friends, his generals, and cavalry commanders, [29] and he was joined by mercenary troops from other kingdoms and from overseas. [30] His forces numbered one hundred thousand infantry, twenty thousand cavalry, and thirty-two war elephants. [31] They advanced through Idumaea and laid siege to Bethsura, keeping up the attack for many days. They erected siege-engines, but the defenders, fighting back manfully, made a sortie and set them on fire.

[32] Judas now withdrew from the citadel and took up his position at Bethzacharia facing towards the royal encampment. [33] Early next morning the king broke camp and after a forced march along the Bethzacharia road he drew up his army in battle order and the trumpets were sounded. [34] The elephants were roused for combat with the blood of grapes and of mulberries. [35] The great beasts were distributed among the phalanxes; by each were stationed a thousand men, equipped with coats of chain-mail and

bronze helmets. Five hundred picked horsemen were also assigned to each animal; [36] they were stationed beforehand where the beast was, and wherever it went, they went also, never leaving its side. [37] Each animal had, by way of protection, a strong wooden turret fastened on its back with a special harness, and carried four fighting men as well as an Indian driver. [38] The rest of his cavalry Lysias stationed on either flank of the army, to harass the enemy while themselves protected by the phalanxes. [39] When the sun shone on the gold and bronze shields, the hills gleamed and flashed like blazing torches.

[40] Part of the king's army was deployed over the heights, and part over the low ground. They advanced steadily and in good order, [41] and trembling seized all who heard the din and clash of arms of this multitude on the march, for it was indeed a very great and powerful force.

[42] Judas drew near with his army and gave battle, and six hundred of the king's men were killed. [43] Eleazar Avaran saw that one of the elephants wore royal armour and stood out above all the rest, and, thinking that the king must be on it, [44] he gave his life to save his people and win for himself everlasting renown. [45] He ran boldly towards it, into the middle of the phalanx, dealing death right and left, so that the enemy fell back on either side before him. [46] He got in underneath the elephant, thrust at it from below, and killed it. It sank to the ground on top of him, crushing him to death. [47] When the Jews saw the strength and impetus of the royal forces, they gave ground before them.

[48] A part of the royal army marched up to Jerusalem to renew the engagement, and the king encamped against Judaea and Mount Zion. [49] He came to terms with the people of Bethsura, who abandoned the town, not having the food to withstand a siege, as it was a sabbatical year when the land was left fallow.

6:20 150: *that is* 162 B.C.E.   6:37 *four: prob. rdg; Gk* thirty-two.

in charge, since the king was then only ten years old (1.33 n.). 28–63: See 2 Macc. 13.1–26. 28: *Friends:* see 2.18 n. 29: These *mercenary troops* were Greek-speaking (2 Macc. 13.2). 30: The exaggerated numbers soften Judas' defeat. 31: Because of his elephants and cavalry, Lysias kept to the coastal plain until he reached Bethsura, which Judas had garrisoned (4.61); then Lysias swung in from the south through Idumea. 34: *Roused:* intoxicated. 43: *Eleazar* was Judas' brother (2.5). 47: On lower ground (v. 40), Judas' guerrillas were no match for the superior armament and professionalism of the king's soldiers. 49: On the *sabbatical year,* see Exod.

50 So Bethsura was occupied by the king, who detailed a garrison to hold it.

51 He then subjected the temple to a lengthy siege; he set up emplacements and siege-engines, with flamethrowers, catapults for discharging stones and barbed missiles, and slings. 52 The defenders for their part constructed engines to counter his engines, and put up a prolonged resistance. 53 But there was no food in the storerooms because it was the sabbatical year; those who from time to time had arrived in Judaea as refugees from the Gentiles had consumed all that remained of the provisions. 54 The shortage had been so severe that men had dispersed to their homes, leaving only a few in the temple.

55 Lysias heard that Philip, whom King Antiochus, before he died, had appointed to bring up his son Antiochus and train him for the throne, 56 had now returned from Persia and Media with the late king's expeditionary force and was seeking to take over the government. 57 Hastily he gave orders for departure, saying to the king and to the army officers and men: 'Every day we grow weaker, our provisions are running low, the place we are besieging is strong, and the affairs of the empire are pressing. 58 Let us now offer these men terms, and make peace with them and with their whole nation. 59 Let us guarantee them the right to follow their laws and customs as they used to do, for it was our abolition of these laws and customs that roused their resentment and led to all the troubles.'

60 The proposal having met with approval from both king and commanders, an offer of peace was sent and accepted. 61 The king and his commanders bound themselves by oath, and on the terms agreed the defenders emerged from their stronghold. 62 But when the king entered Mount Zion and saw how strongly the place was fortified, he went back on his oath, and ordered the demolition of the surrounding wall. 63 Then with all speed he departed for Antioch, where he found Philip in possession. In the ensuing battle Antiochus took the city by storm.

7 In the year 151, Demetrius son of Seleucus left Rome, and, landing with a handful of men at a town on the coast, there made himself king. 2 While he was on his way to the palace of his ancestors, the army placed Antiochus and Lysias under arrest, with a view to handing them over to him. 3 But when he was informed of their action, he said, 'Do not let me set eyes on them.' 4 The soldiers accordingly put them to death, and Demetrius ascended the throne of his kingdom.

5 All the apostates and renegades from Israel, led by Alcimus, who aspired to the high-priesthood, came to the king 6 with charges against their people. 'Judas and his brothers have wiped out everybody who supported you and have driven us from our country,' they said. 7 'Be pleased now to send a man you trust, to go and see what devastation they have brought on us and on the king's territory, and to punish them along with all who aid and abet them.' 8 The king chose one of the royal Friends, Bacchides, who was governor of the province of Beyond-Euphrates, a man of high standing in the empire and loyal to the king; 9 he and Alcimus the apostate, on whom the king had conferred the high-priesthood, were sent with orders to wreak vengeance on Israel. 10 They set out and

6:53 **in the storerooms:** *some witnesses read* in the temple. 7:1 **151:** *that is* 161 B.C.E.

23.10–11; Lev. 25.3–7. **55:** *King Antiochus:* IV Epiphanes. **60:** The *king,* i.e. Lysias (see vv. 18–27 n.), granted religious but not civil liberty. Second Maccabees 11.22–26, 27–33 describe the peace terms. **63:** Josephus says Antiochus captured and killed *Philip* (*Ant.* XII.9.7).

7.1–25: The expedition of Bacchides and Alcimus. 1: *Demetrius* I Soter (161–150 B.C.E.), whose hopes to succeed his uncle Epiphanes (175–164 B.C.E.) were frustrated earlier when the Romans instead recognized the young Eupator (164–161 B.C.E.), escaped from Rome, where he had been held hostage, and moved to claim the kingdom once ruled by his father *Seleucus* IV (187–175 B.C.E.). The coastal *town* was Tripolis (2 Macc. 14.1). **2:** As Demetrius marched on Antioch, the location of *the palace of his ancestors,* the citizens there and the army switched allegiance to him. **5–7:** The Jewish historian Josephus says (*Ant.* XII.9.7) that *Alcimus* (also called Jakeimos) succeeded Menelaus (2 Macc. 13.4–8) as high priest. Perhaps Judas was forced by his treaty with Lysias to accept the defiled Alcimus for a time (2 Macc. 14.3). The change of government may have seemed to Judas the opportunity for driving out Alcimus. **8:** *One of the royal Friends, Bacchides* (see 2.18 n.), governed the area between the *Euphrates* and Egypt (Lysias had the same territory; 3.32). The king planned to go east — as marched on Judaea with a large force. There Bacchides sent envoys with false offers of friendship, 11 but when Judas and his brothers saw how large an army had come they disregarded those offers.

12 A deputation of doctors of the law appeared before Alcimus and Bacchides, to ask for a just settlement. 13 The Hasidaeans were the first group in Israel to make overtures, 14 for they said, 'A priest of the family of Aaron is come with their forces, and he will not treat us unjustly.' 15 The language of Alcimus was conciliatory; he assured them on oath that no harm was intended to them or to their friends. 16 But once he had gained their confidence, he arrested sixty of them and put them to death all on one day. As scripture says:

17 The bodies of your saints were
    scattered;
all round Jerusalem their blood was
    shed,
and there was none to give them burial.

18 Fear and dread fell on the whole people. 'There is neither truth nor justice among them,' they said to one another; 'they have broken their agreement and the oath they swore.'

19 Bacchides then left Jerusalem and encamped in Bethzaith, where he issued orders for the arrest of many of those who had deserted to him, together with some of the people, and had them slaughtered and thrown into a great cistern. 20 He assigned the whole district to Alcimus and detailed troops to assist him, while he himself went back to the king.

21 Alcimus put up a strong fight for his high-priesthood, 22 and all the trouble-makers rallied to him. They gained control over Judaea and inflicted great damage on Israel. 23 When Judas saw the extent of the havoc which Alcimus and his followers had wrought among the Israelites, far worse than anything done by the Gentiles, 24 he went throughout the territory of Judaea and its environs, punishing deserters and debarring them from access to the country districts. 25 Judging that Judas and his supporters had grown too powerful for him to withstand, Alcimus returned to the king and accused them of atrocities.

26 Then the king dispatched Nicanor, one of his most distinguished commanders and a bitter enemy of Israel, with orders to wipe out that people. 27 Nicanor arrived at Jerusalem with a large force and sent envoys to Judas and his brothers with false offers of friendship: 28 'Let there be no quarrel between us,' he said; 'I propose to come with only a small escort to meet you as a friend.' 29 When he came, they greeted one another in friendly fashion, yet the enemy were preparing to kidnap Judas. 30 That Nicanor's visit involved duplicity became known to Judas, and taking alarm he refused to meet him again. 31 Realizing that his plot had been detected, Nicanor marched out to engage Judas near Capharsalama. 32 About five hundred of Nicanor's men were killed; the rest made good their escape to the City of David.

33 After those events, Nicanor went up to Mount Zion, where some of the priests and members of the senate came out from the holy place to extend a friendly welcome to him, and to show him the whole-offering which was being sacrificed for the king. 34 But he mocked and jeered at them and polluted them with his spittle, talking arrogantly 35 and vowing in anger: 'Unless Judas and his army are turned over to me at once, I shall burn down this house when I return victorious.' And he departed in a rage. 36 The priests went in again and stood in tears, facing the altar and the temple, and said, 37 'Lord, you chose this house to bear your

Epiphanes had (3.27–37) — to subdue the eastern provinces. **12–13:** Some of Judas' *Hasidaeans* (2.42; 2 Macc. 14.6) now left him, recognized Alcimus, and asked for *a just settlement*, i.e. terms for reconciliation. **16–17:** See Ps. 79.2–3. **19:** *Bethzaith* is about three and a half miles north of Bethsura. Bacchides thus fulfilled his commission (v. 9). **20–25:** Pushed from the cities by Alcimus' superior numbers, Judas denied him the countryside by guerrilla warfare.

7.26–50: Nicanor's defeat. See 2 Macc. 14.11–15.37. **26:** *Nicanor* had ample reason (3.38–4.25) to be Israel's *bitter enemy*. Formerly in charge of the king's elephants, he was now made governor of Judea (2 Macc. 14.12). **27–30:** Second Maccabees 14.18–30 records a brief period of peace and friendship between *Judas* and *Nicanor* which is omitted here. **31:** *Capharsalama* is about seven miles from Jerusalem. **32:** *City of David*: Jerusalem. **33:** The sacrifice offered for the king was proof of basic loyalty to the empire. **34–38:** Contrast name, to be a house of prayer and supplication for your people; [38] take vengeance on this man and his army, and let them perish by the sword. Let their blasphemy not be forgotten; grant them no reprieve.'

[39] Nicanor moved from Jerusalem and set up his camp at Beth-horon, where he was joined by an army from Syria. [40] Meanwhile Judas, encamping at Adasa with three thousand men, uttered this prayer: [41] 'When the followers of a certain king were guilty of blasphemy, your angel came forth and struck down one hundred and eighty-five thousand of them. [42] In the same way crush this army before us today. Let generations to come know that Nicanor has reviled your holy place; judge him as his wickedness deserves.'

[43] Battle was joined on the thirteenth of the month of Adar, and Nicanor's forces suffered a crushing defeat, he himself being the first to fall in the fighting. [44] Seeing Nicanor fall, his men threw away their arms and fled. [45] The Jews, with their trumpets sounding a signal behind the fleeing enemy, pursued them as far as Gazara, a day's journey from Adasa. [46] From every Judaean village round about, the inhabitants came out and, attacking the fugitives on the flanks, forced them back upon their pursuers, so that they all fell by the sword; not one of them survived. [47] The Jews gathered up the weapons of the slain and other spoils of war; they cut off Nicanor's head and that right hand he had stretched out so arrogantly, and brought them to be displayed at Jerusalem. [48] There was great public rejoicing, and that day was kept as a special day of jubilation. [49] It was ordained that the day, the thirteenth of Adar, should be celebrated annually. [50] Judaea then entered on a short period of peace.

8 Judas had had reports about the Romans: that they were renowned for their military power and for the favour they showed to those who became their allies, and that any who joined them could be sure of their friendship [2] and strong military support. He was told of the campaigns they had fought, and the valour they had shown in their conquest of the Gauls, whom they had laid under tribute. [3] He heard of their successes in Spain, where they had seized the silver and gold mines, [4] maintaining by perseverance and good judgement their hold on the entire country, distant though it was from their own land. There were kings from the ends of the earth who had marched against them, only to be beaten off, heavily defeated; others there were who paid them annual tribute.

[5] Philip, and Perseus king of Kittim, and all who had set themselves in opposition to the Romans had been crushed in battle and conquered. [6] Antiochus the Great, king of Asia, had advanced against them with one hundred and twenty elephants, with cavalry and chariots and an immense force, only to be totally defeated. [7] They had captured the king alive, and had required that he and his successors should pay a large annual tribute, give hostages, [8] and cede the territories of India, Media, and Lydia, together with some of their finest provinces; these they had taken from him and handed over to King Eumenes. [9] The Greeks planned to attack and destroy them, [10] but the Romans got to know of it and sent just one general against them. When battle was joined many of the

---

Nicanor's attitude with that expressed in Isa. 56.6–8. **41:** Judas refers to the angelic slaughter (plague may be meant) of Sennacherib's army besieging Jerusalem (2 Kgs. 19.35; 2 Macc. 15.22). **43:** *Adar:* March, 160 B.C.E. **49:** The feast of Nicanor was dropped from the Jewish calendar after the destruction of the temple in 70 C.E.

8.1–32: Judas' treaty with the Romans. Hoping to curb the Seleucids, Judas allied himself with the Romans, who seized the opportunity to befriend an enemy of Demetrius while extending their own influence. **2:** The Cisalpine *Gauls* were conquered very easily in the second century B.C.E. **5:** *Philip* V of Macedon (land of the *Kittim*) was defeated in 197 B.C.E.; *Perseus,* Philip's son, was defeated in 168 B.C.E. **6–8:** *Antiochus* (III) *the Great, king of Asia,* i.e. the lands at the eastern end of the Mediterranean, lost to Lucius Scipio at Magnesia (now western Turkey) in 190 B.C.E. The author uses an exaggerated report; Antiochus had only fifty-four *elephants* and was not captured. Under the treaty of Apamea (188 B.C.E.), Antiochus and his successors had to pay tribute (see 2 Macc. 8.10) and give hostages; see 1.10 n. **8:** Ionia (here by scribal error, *India*), Mysia (here, *Media*), and *Lydia,* territories in Asia Minor, were ceded to *Eumenes* II of Pergamum (in western Turkey), an ally of Rome at Magnesia. **9–10:** The Roman consul Lucius Mummius defeated the Achaean League of Greek city-states in 146 B.C.E. The author gets ahead of himself here; in 160 B.C.E., Judas would not have heard of

Greeks fell, and their women and children were made captive. The Romans plundered and annexed their territory, demolishing their strongholds and making the inhabitants slaves, as they remain to this day. [11] The other kingdoms and the islands, any who ever opposed them, they destroyed or reduced to slavery. [12] With their friends, however, and with all who relied on them for protection, they maintained firm friendship.

Thus they overcame rulers near and far, and all who heard of their reputation went in dread of them. [13] Those whom they wished to help and appoint as kings, became kings; those whom they wished to depose, they deposed. By such means they attained to great heights of power. [14] Yet for all this, not one of them ever gave himself the airs of a prince, assuming a crown or putting on the purple. [15] They had established a senate where each day three hundred and twenty senators met for deliberation, giving constant thought to the proper ordering of public affairs. [16] Every year they entrusted their government and the rule of all their dominions to one of their number, all obeying this one man without jealousy or envy.

[17] So Judas chose Eupolemus son of John, son of Accos, and Jason son of Eleazar, and sent them to Rome to make a treaty of friendship and alliance, [18] in order that the Romans might rid them of foreign oppression, for it was clear that the Greek empire was reducing Israel to abject slavery. [19] The envoys made the journey to Rome, a very long journey, and when they came into the senate house they spoke as follows: [20] 'Judas Maccabaeus, his brothers, and the Jewish people have sent us to conclude with you a treaty of alliance, so that we may be enrolled as your allies and friends.' [21] The Romans gave their approval to the proposal, [22] and the following is a copy of the reply which they inscribed on bronze tablets and sent to Jerusalem, so that the Jews might have a record there of the treaty:

[23] Success attend the Romans and the Jewish nation by sea and land for ever! May sword and foe be far from them! [24] But if an unprovoked attack is made on Rome or on any of her allies throughout her dominion, [25] then the Jewish nation shall afford them wholehearted support as occasion may require. [26] In accordance with Rome's decision Jews shall neither give nor supply provisions, arms, money, or ships to the enemies of Rome. They are to observe their commitments without compensation.

[27] In like manner, if an unprovoked attack is made on the Jewish nation, then the Romans shall afford them wholehearted support as occasion may require. [28] In accordance with Rome's decision there shall be given neither provisions, arms, money, nor ships to the enemies of the Jewish nation. These commitments are to be kept without breach of faith.

[29] Those are the terms of the treaty which the Romans have made with the Jewish people. [30] But if, hereafter, both parties agree to add or to rescind anything, what they decide shall be done; any such addition or rescindment shall be valid.

[31] To this the Romans added: 'As for the wrongs which King Demetrius is perpetrating against the Jews, we have written to him as follows: "Why have you so harshly oppressed our friends and allies the Jews? [32] If they bring any further complaint against you, we shall open hostilities against you by sea and by land in support of their cause." '

9 When Demetrius heard that Nicanor and his men had fallen in battle, he sent Bacchides and Alcimus a second time into Judaea, and with them the right wing of his army. [2] They marched along the Gilgal road, laid siege to Messaloth in Arbela, and captured it, inflicting heavy loss of life.

[3] In the first month of the year 152, they moved camp to Jerusalem, [4] and from there

9:3 152: *that is* 160 B.C.E.

---

this. **13:** Among the *kings* appointed by the Romans was Alexander Balas (10.1). **15–16:** It was three hundred (not *three hundred and twenty*) Roman senators, who did not meet *each day*, nor did they elect *one man,* but two consuls, who ruled jointly. While very pro-Roman in his report, the author has an imperfect knowledge of Rome's government. **17:** *John,* the father of *Eupolemus,* had earlier won concessions for the Jews from Antiochus III (2 Macc. 4.11). **22:** Josephus says that the *bronze tablets* were kept in Rome's capitol (*Ant.* XII.10.6); a copy was sent in a letter to Judas. **23–30:** The treaty follows the standard Roman form for a treaty between equals. **31:** This addition came separately; it is not part of the treaty.

9.1–22: The defeat and death of Judas. 1: As before (7.8–10), the king sent an army too large for Judas to they marched to Berea with twenty thousand infantry and two thousand cavalry. [5]Judas had established his camp at Alasa. He had with him three thousand picked troops, [6]but, when his men saw the size of the enemy forces, their courage failed and many deserted, until a mere eight hundred remained.

[7]Aware that his army had melted away and the campaign was going against him, Judas was greatly disheartened, for there was not time to reassemble his forces. Though himself despondent, [8]he said to those who were left, 'Let us take the offensive and see if we can defeat the enemy.' [9]His men tried to dissuade him: 'Impossible!' they said. 'No, we are too few. Let us save our lives now, and come back later to fight them when we have our comrades with us.' [10]But Judas replied: 'Heaven forbid that I should do such a thing as run away! If our time has come, let us die bravely for our fellow-countrymen, and leave no stain on our honour.'

[11]The Syrian army moved from its camp and took up its battle position against Judas's men. The cavalry was divided into two squadrons; the slingers and the archers went ahead of the main force, and the crack troops were in the front line. [12]Bacchides was on the right wing. The phalanx advanced with trumpets sounding and flanked by the two cavalry squadrons; [13]Judas's men also sounded their trumpets. The earth shook as the armies met, and the fighting went on from morning till night.

[14]When he saw that Bacchides and the main strength of his army were on the right flank, Judas with all his most valiant troops rallying to him [15]broke the Syrian right and pursued them as far as Mount Azotus. [16]The Syrians on the left, seeing their right wing broken, wheeled about and, following closely after Judas and his men, attacked them from the rear. [17]The fighting became very heavy, and many fell on both sides. [18]Judas was among the fallen; the rest of the Jews fled. [19]Jonathan and Simon carried Judas their brother away and laid him in the family tomb at Modin, [20]and there they wept over him. There was great grief throughout Israel, and the people mourned him for many days, saying,

[21]How is our champion fallen,
  the saviour of Israel!

[22]The rest of the history of Judas, his wars, exploits, and achievements—these were so numerous that they have not been recorded.

Jonathan: leader and high priest

[23]AFTER the death of Judas, the renegades in every part of Israel emerged from hiding, and all the evildoers reappeared, [24]and the country, afflicted at that time by a terrible famine, went over to their side. [25]Bacchides chose apostates to be in control of the land. [26]They searched out and hunted down the friends of Judas to bring them before Bacchides, who wreaked his vengeance on them and loaded them with indignities. [27]It was a time of harsh oppression for Israel, worse than any since the days when prophets ceased to appear among them. [28]So the friends of Judas all assembled and said to Jonathan, [29]'Since the death of your brother Judas there has not been a man like him to take the lead against our enemies, Bacchides and those of our own nation who are hostile to us. [30]Today, therefore, we have chosen

defeat in open battle. **2:** *Messaloth in Arbela:* about three miles west of Lake Gennesaret. **4–5:** *Berea* is located ten miles north of Jerusalem; *Alasa* is less than a mile away. **15:** *Mount Azotus* is a scribal error for Mount Hazor, some six miles from Berea; see 2 Sam. 13.23; Neh. 11.33. **19:** Later, Simon turned *the family tomb at Modin* into a monument; see 13.25–30. **22:** This verse echoes the stock phrase used of the kings (1 Kgs. 11.41).

9.23–73: Jonathan continues the struggle. Jonathan improves the Jewish position through political and military activity and fortifies Judea.

9.23–31: Jonathan replaces Judas. Passing over Simon, the elder brother, for reasons unknown to us, the Jews chose Jonathan to lead them. **24:** Since the king's men controlled food supplies, the *famine* brought about desertions to their side. **27:** Malachi is the last of the universally recognized *prophets* in the Bible (about 500–450 B.C.E.), but scholars discern the presence of later prophetic material in other books, as in Zech. chs. 9–14, which speak of the Greeks and describe conditions during the Greek period of the fourth and third centuries B.C.E. The author also notes the lack of a prophet in 4.46; 14.41.

you to succeed him as our ruler and our leader to fight our battles.' ³¹ From then Jonathan took over the leadership in the place of his brother Judas.

³² When this became known to Bacchides, he sought to kill Jonathan; ³³ but Jonathan, his brother Simon, and all who were with them got to know of it and took refuge in the wilderness of Tekoa, where they encamped by the pool of Asphar. ³⁴ Bacchides discovered this on the sabbath, and he crossed the Jordan with his whole army. ³⁵ Jonathan sent his brother John away in charge of the camp followers and appealed to his friends the Nabataeans to look after the baggage train, which was of some size. ³⁶ But the Jambrites, in a sortie from Medaba, kidnapped John and made off with the baggage. ³⁷ Some time afterwards, news was brought to Jonathan and his brother Simon that the Jambrites were celebrating an important wedding and bringing the bride, the daughter of one of the great nobles of Canaan, from Nadabath with a large retinue. ³⁸ The fate of their brother John still fresh in their minds, Jonathan and his men went up and hid themselves under cover of a hill. ³⁹ As they watched, there, coming to meet the bridal party in the middle of a bustling crowd and a train of baggage, was the bridegroom, escorted, to the sound of drums and musical instruments, by his friends and kinsmen all fully armed. ⁴⁰ Jonathan's men leapt from their ambush and cut them down; many fell, while the survivors made off into the hills, and the Jews took all their goods as spoil.

⁴¹ So the wedding was turned into mourning, and the sound of music to lamentation. ⁴² The blood of their brother fully avenged, Jonathan and Simon returned to the marshes by Jordan.

⁴³ Hearing of this, Bacchides came on the sabbath right to the banks of Jordan with a large force. ⁴⁴ Jonathan said to his men, 'Up, fight for our lives! Today we are in worse plight than ever: ⁴⁵ a battle in front, the waters of Jordan behind, to right and left marsh and thicket—there is no escape! ⁴⁶ Cry to Heaven to save you from the enemy.' ⁴⁷ Battle was joined, and Jonathan had raised his hand to strike down Bacchides, when the Syrian leader eluded him and got away. ⁴⁸ Then Jonathan and his men leapt into the Jordan and swam over to the other side; but the enemy did not pursue them across the river. ⁴⁹ That day the army of Bacchides lost about a thousand men.

⁵⁰ Bacchides returned to Jerusalem, and he fortified with high walls and barred gates a number of places in Judaea: Jericho's fortress, Emmaus and Beth-horon, Bethel, Timnath-pharathon, and Tephon, ⁵¹ in all of which he stationed garrisons to harass Israel. ⁵² He strengthened the towns of Bethsura and Gazara and the citadel, placing troops and stores of provisions in them. ⁵³ He took as hostages the sons of the leading men of the country and put them under guard in the citadel at Jerusalem.

⁵⁴ In the second month of the year 153, Alcimus gave orders for the wall of the inner
9:54 153: *that is* 159 B.C.E.

9.32–49: Jonathan escapes Bacchides. 33: The mountainous and deserted region about *Tekoa* enabled Jonathan to evade pursuit and to assemble his forces. **34:** This verse is a misplaced repetition of the substance of v. 43. **35:** *Nabataeans:* see 5.25 n. **36:** The *Jambrites,* probably an Arab tribe, were based at *Medaba,* a city some fifteen miles southeast of the Jordan's entrance into the Dead Sea. They not only *kidnapped John,* they killed him (vv. 38, 42). **37:** The Greek translator misread the original Heb. *kenaani,* "trader," as the ancient name for the Holy Land, Canaan. This was a great merchant's daughter. *Nadabath* (= Nabatha = Nebo) was a little town on Mount Nebo not far from Medaba. **42:** *Blood* vengeance was considered a duty by ancient Semitic peoples. In desert regions, it was a deterrent to the type of crime committed against John. **43:** *Bacchides* thought ambush *on the sabbath* would add to the surprise. **44–48:** When the trap was sprung, in one of the many loops of the Jordan where it enters the Dead Sea, Jonathan had to abandon his spoils and save his troops. Bacchides blocked his way; Jambrites probably pursued. Fighting his way through, Jonathan crossed to the west bank and the safety of his camp. Bacchides did not follow, perhaps pausing to pick up the spoils. **49:** A *thousand* casualties, the report of the partisan, seems exaggerated.

9.50–53: Bacchides fortifies Judea. Bacchides assured Seleucid control of Judea by fortifying strategic sites. *Timnath-pharathon, and Tephon* were in Samaria and governed the northern approaches to Judea. The *hostages* guaranteed the cooperation of their parents.

9.54–57: Alcimus dies. The author views the death of *Alcimus* as punishment for his ordering the destruction court of the temple to be demolished, thereby destroying the work of the prophets. ⁵⁵ But he had only begun the work of demolition, when he suffered a stroke which put a stop to his activities. Paralysed and with his speech impaired, he could not utter a word or give final instructions about his property, ⁵⁶ and subsequently he died in great agony. ⁵⁷ On learning that Alcimus was dead, Bacchides returned to the king, and for two years Judaea had peace.

⁵⁸ The renegades all took counsel together: 'Here are Jonathan and his people living in peace and security,' they said; 'if we bring back Bacchides now, he will lay hold of every one of them in a single night.' ⁵⁹ They went and conferred with Bacchides, ⁶⁰ who set off with a large force. At the same time he sent letters secretly to all his supporters in Judaea, with instructions to seize Jonathan and his men. But because the plan leaked out they were unable to do so, ⁶¹ and some fifty of the ringleaders of this villainy in Judaea were taken and put to death. ⁶² Jonathan and Simon withdrew with their men to Bethbasi in the desert, rebuilt its ruined fortifications, and strengthened it. ⁶³ Informed of this, Bacchides mustered his whole army, summoned his allies in Judaea, ⁶⁴ and marched against Bethbasi. He took up his position against it, erected siege-engines, and pressed the attack for many days. ⁶⁵ Jonathan left his brother Simon in the town and, slipping out into the country with a few men, ⁶⁶ attacked Odomera and his people and the Phasirites in their encampment. ⁶⁷ Gradually he gained the upper hand and began to advance towards Bethbasi with his forces.

Simon and his men made a sortie from the town, set fire to the siege-engines, ⁶⁸ and inflicted a shattering attack on Bacchides. They kept up such heavy pressure on him that his plans for an assault were frustrated. ⁶⁹ Incensed with the renegades at whose instance he had invaded the land, he had many of them put to death. He then decided to return to his own country.

⁷⁰ When Jonathan learnt of this, he sent envoys to Bacchides to secure peace terms and the return of prisoners. ⁷¹ Bacchides agreed and accepted Jonathan's proposals, swearing to him that as long as he lived he would harm him no more. ⁷² He handed over the prisoners he had taken earlier from Judaea, and then returned to his own country, never again to set foot on Jewish soil. ⁷³ So the war in Israel came to an end. Taking up residence in Michmash, Jonathan began to govern the people and root the apostates out of Israel.

10 In the year 160, Alexander Epiphanes son of Antiochus arrived by ship and took possession of Ptolemais, where he was welcomed and proclaimed king. ² On hearing of this King Demetrius raised a very large army and marched out to give battle. ³ At the same time he sent Jonathan a letter in friendly and flattering terms. ⁴ He said to himself, 'Let us forestall Alexander by making peace with the Jews before Jonathan comes to terms with him against us, ⁵ for Jonathan will not have forgotten all the harm we

10:1 **160:** *that is* 152 B.C.E.

of the *wall* separating the *inner court,* to which the Israelites had access, from the outer court, where Gentiles were permitted. **54:** The *prophets* whose work Alcimus destroyed were Haggai and Zechariah, who had brought about reconstruction of the temple (520–516 B.C.E.), after the Babylonian Exile. **57:** *Judaea had peace,* because Bacchides had effectively curbed Jewish resistance for a time.

9.58–73: Jonathan escapes and defeats Bacchides. 62: *Bethbasi* lay between Bethlehem and Tekoa, about three miles north and slightly east of the latter. **66:** *Odomera* and *the Phasirites* were presumably allies of Bacchides whom Jonathan surprised at night before they could join the siege at Bethbasi. **68–69:** Conditions elsewhere in the empire must have brought about the recall of Bacchides and forced him to make a treaty with the unruly Jonathan. See, similarly, 6.55–61. **70:** The *return of prisoners* did not include the hostages in the citadel (9.53; 10.6). **73:** From *Michmash,* eight miles northeast of Jerusalem, the emboldened Jonathan continued the purge of his enemies.

10.1–12.53: Jonathan is appointed high priest and wields both political and religious authority. Demetrius makes overtures.

10.1–21: Jonathan is courted by rival kings. 1: *Alexander* Balas (150–145 B.C.E.) also called *Epiphanes* (because he claimed Antiochus IV was his father) *took possession of Ptolemais* by treason, according to did him by our treatment of his brothers and of his nation.' ⁶So he granted him authority to raise and equip an army, conferred on him the title of ally, and gave orders for the hostages in the citadel to be handed over to him. ⁷Jonathan came to Jerusalem and read out the letter to all the people and also to the men of the garrison in the citadel, ⁸who were filled with apprehension on hearing that the king had given Jonathan authority to raise an army. ⁹They surrendered the hostages, who were then restored to their parents.

¹⁰Jonathan took up his quarters in Jerusalem and began to rebuild and renovate the city. ¹¹He instructed those engaged on the work to build the walls and surround Mount Zion with a fortification of squared stones, and this was done. ¹²The foreigners who occupied the strongholds built by Bacchides made good their escape, ¹³every man of them deserting his post and making off to his own country; ¹⁴only in Bethsura were there still left some of those who had abandoned the law and ordinances and found refuge there.

¹⁵When King Alexander heard of the promises made to Jonathan by Demetrius, and was given an account of the battles and heroic deeds of Jonathan and his brothers, and of the hardships they had endured, he exclaimed, ¹⁶'Where shall we ever find another man like this? Let us make him our Friend and ally at once.' ¹⁷He therefore wrote Jonathan the following letter:

¹⁸From King Alexander to his brother Jonathan.

Greeting.

¹⁹Reports have reached us of your valour and of how worthy you are to be our Friend. ²⁰Now this day we appoint you to be high priest of your nation with the title of king's Friend, to support our cause and to maintain friendship with us.

He also sent him a purple robe and a gold crown.

²¹Jonathan assumed the sacred vestments in the seventh month of the year 160 at the feast of Tabernacles; he gathered an army and got ready a large supply of weapons. ²²Demetrius was mortified at the news. ²³'How did we come to let Alexander forestall us in gaining the friendship and support of the Jews?' he demanded. ²⁴'I too shall write to them in cordial terms and offer honours and gifts to keep them on my side.' ²⁵So he sent the Jews the following message:

From King Demetrius to the Jewish nation. Greeting.

²⁶We have heard with much pleasure that you have honoured your agreements and remained in friendship with us and have not gone over to our enemies. ²⁷Continue now to keep faith with us, and we shall reward you well for what you do in our cause, ²⁸both by granting you numerous exemptions and by making you gifts.

²⁹I hereby release and exempt you and all Jews whatsoever from tribute, from the tax on salt, and from the crown-levy. ³⁰From today and hereafter I exempt you from the one-third of the grain harvest and the half of the fruit harvest due to me; from today and for all time, I shall no longer exact them from Judaea or from the three administrative districts, formerly part of Samaria and Galilee, which I now attach to Judaea. ³¹Jerusalem and its environs, with its tithes and tolls, shall be sacred and free of taxes. ³²I surrender also authority over the citadel in Jerusalem and grant the high priest the right to garrison it with men of his own choice. ³³All Jewish prisoners of war taken from Judaea into any part of my realm I now set at liberty without ransom. No one shall exact any

10:21 **160:** *that is* 152 B.C.E.

Josephus (*Ant.* XIII.2.1). **2:** Alexander lost this first battle. **6–14:** Jonathan took full advantage of Demetrius' situation and promises, even though he was going over to Alexander. **9:** *The hostages:* see 9.50–53 n. **10:** *Rebuild and renovate the city:* see 1.31; 4.60. **12:** *The foreigners* may have gone to help Demetrius. **14:** *Bethsura*, Gazara (11.41; 13.43) and the citadel at Jerusalem (*Ant.* XIII.21.1) received the renegade Jews. **20:** Jonathan already belonged to a priestly family (2.1). The *purple robe* and *gold crown* symbolized the high priesthood. The purple robe also identified Jonathan as a *king's Friend* (see 2.18 n.). **21:** For the *feast of Tabernacles*, see Lev. 23.33–36. By officiating, Jonathan implicitly declared himself for Alexander.

10.22–50: Demetrius appeals to the Jewish nation as a whole. 30: *The three . . . districts* (11.34) are Apherema (= Ephraim; Jn. 11.54), Lydda, and Ramathaim (= Arimathea, Mk. 15.43). **31:** Being *sacred*, Jerusalem could pay its taxes to God (via the temple) instead of to the king. **32:** Demetrius recognized the status levy whatsoever on the livestock of the Jews. 34 All their festivals, sabbaths, new moons, and appointed days, with three days preceding and following each festival, shall be days of exemption and release for all Jews in my kingdom; 35 no one shall have authority to impose on a Jew any exaction or burden whatsoever.

36 Jews shall be enlisted in the forces of the crown to the number of thirty thousand men; they shall receive the standard rate of army pay. 37 Some of them shall be stationed in the important royal strongholds, others placed in positions of trust in the kingdom. Their commanders and officers shall be of their own race, and they may follow their own customs, just as the king has ordered for Judaea.

38 The three districts annexed to Judaea from the territory of Samaria shall be so annexed as to be deemed under a single control and subject to no authority other than that of the high priest.

39 Ptolemais and the adjoining land I make over to the temple in Jerusalem, to meet the expenses proper to it. 40 I myself shall make an annual grant of fifteen thousand silver shekels, charged on my own royal accounts, to be drawn from such places as may prove convenient. 41 And the arrears of the subsidy, in so far as it has not been paid by the revenue officials, as it formerly was, shall henceforth be paid in for the needs of the temple. 42 Further, the five thousand silver shekels which used to be taken from the annual income of the temple are also remitted, because they belong to the ministering priests. 43 Whoever takes sanctuary in the temple at Jerusalem or in any part of its precincts, because of a debt to the crown or any other debt, shall be free from distraint on his person or on his property within my kingdom. 44 The cost of the rebuilding and renovation of the temple shall be borne by the royal revenue; 45 in addition, the repair of the walls of Jerusalem and its surrounding fortification, as well as of the fortresses in Judaea, shall become a charge on the royal revenue.

46 Jonathan and the people put no faith in those proposals when they heard them, and declined to accept them, for they recalled the great harm the king had done Israel and his harsh oppression of them. 47 They favoured Alexander, because he had been the first to make overtures of peace, and they remained his allies to the end.

48 King Alexander mustered large forces and took up position over against Demetrius. 49 When the two kings joined battle, Alexander's army was put to flight. Demetrius pursued with vigour, 50 pressing home the attack till sunset; but Demetrius fell that day.

51 Alexander sent envoys to Ptolemy, the king of Egypt, with this message: 52 'I have returned to my kingdom and now sit on the throne of my ancestors. I have assumed the government, defeated Demetrius, and made myself master of our country; 53 when I gave battle, he and his army were routed, and I occupy the throne of his kingdom. 54 Now let us form an alliance; make me your son-in-law by giving me your daughter in marriage, and both to you and to her I shall make gifts worthy of your royal state.'

55 King Ptolemy replied: 'It was a happy day when you returned to the land of your ancestors and ascended the throne of their realm. 56 I now accede to your request; but come to Ptolemais so that we may meet, and I shall become your father-in-law as you propose.'

57 In the year 162, Ptolemy set out from Egypt with his daughter Cleopatra, and arrived at Ptolemais, 58 where King Alexander met him. Ptolemy gave him his daughter in marriage, and the wedding was celebrated there in royal style with great pomp.

59 King Alexander wrote to Jonathan to come and meet him. 60 Jonathan went in state to Ptolemais, where he met the two kings; he presented them with silver and gold, and also made many gifts to their Friends; and so he won their favour.

61 There were some pestilent Jewish renegades who conspired to lodge complaints against Jonathan. The king, however, paid no heed to them, 62 but gave orders for Jona-

10:57 **162:** *that is* 150 B.C.E.

of *high priest* conferred on Jonathan by Alexander! **36:** Jewish soldiers would be paid *the standard rate,* but at the king's expense and not, as was customary, at Judea's. **39:** Demetrius gave away *Ptolemais,* which Alexander held (10.1).

10.51–66: Jonathan at Alexander's wedding. Alexander married Cleopatra Thea, daughter of Ptolemy VI than to be divested of the garment he wore and to be robed in purple, and this was done. 63 The king then seated him at his side, and bade his officers escort Jonathan into the centre of the city and proclaim that no one should bring any complaint against him or make trouble for him for any reason whatsoever. 64 When this proclamation was made and the men who had planned to lodge complaints saw Jonathan's splendour and the purple robe he wore, one and all decamped. 65 So, honoured by the king, enrolled in the first class of the order of king's Friends, and appointed a general and a provincial governor, 66 Jonathan returned to Jerusalem well pleased with his success.

67 In the year 165, Demetrius, the son of King Demetrius, arrived in the land of his fathers from Crete, 68 which greatly perturbed King Alexander when he heard of it, and made him return to Antioch. 69 Demetrius appointed as his commander Apollonius the governor of Coele-Syria, who raised a powerful force and encamped at Jamnia. From there he sent this message to Jonathan the high priest: 70 'You are alone in offering resistance to us, and your opposition is bringing me ridicule and disgrace. Why do you defy us up there in the hills? 71 Now if you have confidence in your forces, come down and meet us on the plain, and let us try conclusions with each other there, for I have the power of the cities behind me. 72 Make enquiries; find out who I am, and who are our allies. You will be told that you cannot stand your ground against us: your predecessors were routed twice in their own territory, 73 and now you will not be able to resist my cavalry and such a force as mine on the plain, where there is not so much as a stone or a pebble, or any place to which you can escape.'

74 Provoked by this message from Apollonius, Jonathan marched out from Jerusalem with ten thousand picked men and was joined by his brother Simon with reinforce-ments. 75 He laid siege to Joppa, where the citizens had closed the gates against him because Apollonius had a garrison there. 76 But when the fighting started, the citizens were frightened and opened the gates; so Jonathan became master of Joppa. 77 Hearing of this, Apollonius with three thousand cavalry and a large body of infantry marched to Azotus as if to pass through it, but at the same time, relying on his numerous cavalry, he advanced into the plain. 78 Jonathan pursued him as far as Azotus, where battle was joined. 79 Apollonius had left behind a thousand cavalry in concealment, 80 and Jonathan now discovered this ambush at his rear. Though surrounded by the enemy raining arrows on them from dawn till dusk, 81 his army stood firm as Jonathan had ordered, and the enemy's horses grew weary. 82 At that point, with the cavalry now exhausted, Simon led out his troops and engaged the enemy phalanx, which, routed by him, took to flight.

83 The horsemen scattered across the plain and the infantry fled to Azotus, where they sought refuge in the temple of Dagon their idol. 84 But Jonathan set fire to Azotus and its surrounding villages, and plundered them; the temple of Dagon, with those who had fled there, he burnt to the ground. 85 The numbers of those who fell by the sword, together with those who lost their lives in the fire, reached eight thousand. 86 Jonathan marched from Azotus, and encamped at Ascalon, where with great pomp the citizens came out to meet him. 87 He and his men returned to Jerusalem loaded with spoil.

88 When these events were reported to King Alexander, he conferred still greater honour on Jonathan, 89 sending him the gold clasp which it is the custom to present to the king's Kinsmen; he also granted him Accaron and all its environs as a personal gift.

11 The king of Egypt gathered a huge army, countless as the sand on the seashore, and with it a great fleet of ships; his

10:67 165: *that is* 147 B.C.E.

Philometor (180–145 B.C.E.). 65: *First . . . king's Friends:* see 2.18 n. *Governor:* presumably of Judea.

10.67–89: Jonathan defeats Apollonius. Demetrius II (145–139 and 129–125 B.C.E.), son of Demetrius I (161–150 B.C.E.), arrived in Cilicia to claim the Seleucid throne. **69:** This *Apollonius* had helped Demetrius I to escape from Rome. **71–73:** On the plains, the Jews often proved to be no match for the superior armaments— chariots, cavalry, elephants—of their enemies. **74–76:** Jonathan's capture of *Joppa* cut Apollonius' line of communications. **77–87:** Pretending to retreat even farther southward, Apollonius lured Jonathan into the plain. Trapped, Jonathan won anyway, with the help of Simon's fresh reserves. **89:** *The gold clasp* signifying Jonathan's new promotion fastened the recipient's purple cloak at the shoulder.

intention was to make himself master of Alexander's kingdom by a subterfuge and to add it to his own. ² He set out for Syria with protestations of peace, and the people of the towns proceeded to open their gates to him and went to meet him; this they had been ordered to do by King Alexander, because Ptolemy was his father-in-law.

³ As he continued his progress from town to town, Ptolemy left in each of them a detachment of troops as a garrison. ⁴ When he reached Azotus, he was shown the burnt-out temple of Dagon, the city itself and its ruined suburbs strewn with corpses, and, piled up along his way, the bodies of those burnt in the course of the fighting. ⁵ The people told the king that it was all Jonathan's doing, for they hoped he would find fault with him; but the king said nothing. ⁶ When Jonathan met him in state at Joppa, they exchanged greetings and passed the night there, and ⁷ Jonathan accompanied the king to the river Eleutherus before returning to Jerusalem. ⁸ King Ptolemy made himself master of the coastal towns as far as Seleucia-by-the-sea, all the time hatching designs hostile to Alexander.

⁹ He sent envoys to King Demetrius with this message: 'I propose that you and I should make a compact: I will give you my daughter, now Alexander's wife, and you shall reign over the kingdom of your father. ¹⁰ I regret having given my daughter to Alexander, for he has tried to kill me.' ¹¹ He maligned him in this way because he coveted his kingdom, ¹² and he took back his daughter and gave her to Demetrius. The estrangement between Ptolemy and Alexander turned to open enmity.

¹³ Ptolemy now entered Antioch, where he assumed the crown of Asia, in addition to the crown of Egypt which he already wore.

¹⁴ All this time King Alexander was in Cilicia, because the inhabitants of that region were in revolt, ¹⁵ but when he heard what had been taking place he marched against Ptolemy, who met him with a strong force. Alexander was defeated ¹⁶ and fled to Arabia for protection; King Ptolemy was triumphant. ¹⁷ Zabdiel, an Arab chieftain, cut off Alexander's head and sent it to Ptolemy. ¹⁸ On the third day after that, however, King Ptolemy died, and his garrisons in the fortresses were wiped out by the local inhabitants. ¹⁹ So in the year 167 Demetrius became king.

²⁰ At this time Jonathan mustered the Judaeans for an attack on the citadel in Jerusalem, and they constructed a large number of siege-engines for the purpose. ²¹ Some renegades, enemies of their own people, went to the king and reported that Jonathan was laying siege to the citadel, ²² news which excited the king's anger. At once he moved his quarters to Ptolemais, and, in a letter to Jonathan, ordered him to raise the siege and with all speed meet him for conference at Ptolemais.

²³ When Jonathan received this summons, he gave orders for the siege to be continued, and then, selecting elders of Israel and priests to accompany him, he set out on his dangerous mission. ²⁴ He took with him silver and gold, and robes, and many other gifts, with which he won the favour of Demetrius when they met at Ptolemais.

²⁵ Although certain renegade Jews tried to lodge complaints against Jonathan, ²⁶ the king treated him just as his predecessors had done and honoured him in the presence of all his Friends. ²⁷ He confirmed him in the high-priesthood and in all his former dignities, and bestowed on him the rank of head of the first class of king's Friends.

²⁸ Jonathan requested the king to exempt Judaea and the three Samaritan districts from tribute, promising in return three hundred talents. ²⁹ The king gave his consent, and on all these matters wrote as follows:

³⁰ From King Demetrius to his brother Jonathan, and to the Jewish nation.

Greeting.

³¹ This is what we have written in a letter

11:19 **167:** *that is* 145 B.C.E.   11:28 **three ... districts:** *prob. rdg; Gk* three districts and Samaria.

11.1–19: Alexander and Ptolemy fall out. 3: The garrisons indicate Ptolemy's treacherous intent. **6–7:** Apparently, Ptolemy deceived Jonathan. The *Eleutherus* river is the Nahr el-Kebir, nineteen miles north of Tripolis. **13:** Ptolemy did not want all of Asia (i.e. the Seleucid empire; see 8.6) but only Judea. He left the rest for Demetrius. **18:** Ptolemy died of wounds received in battle with Alexander at the Oenoparas river near Antioch. **19:** The sixteen-year-old *Demetrius* now began to call himself Nicator, "Conquerer," because of his success over Alexander.

11.20–53: Jonathan serves Demetrius. 20–27: Jonathan wins over the new king as he had Alexander to our Kinsman Lasthenes about you; we have had a copy made for your information:

32 'From King Demetrius to his respected cousin Lasthenes.

'Greeting.

33 'Since the Jewish people are well disposed towards us and observe their obligations to us, we are resolved to recognize their loyalty by becoming their benefactor. 34 We have, therefore, confirmed them in the possession of the lands of Judaea and the three districts Apherema, Lydda, and Ramathaim, which are now transferred from Samaria to Judaea, together with all the lands adjacent thereto, for the benefit of all who sacrifice at Jerusalem; this is a transfer of the annual payments which the king formerly received from these territories, from the produce of the soil and of the orchards. 35 Other of our revenues, the tithes and tolls now pertaining to us, the salt-pans, and the crown-levy, all these we shall cede to them.

36 'These concessions are from now irrevocable for all future time. 37 See to it then that you make a copy of them to be given to Jonathan for display in a prominent position on the holy mountain.'

38 When King Demetrius saw that the country was quiet under his rule and resistance at an end, he disbanded his forces, dismissing them all to their homes, with the exception of the foreign mercenaries he had recruited from the islands of the Gentiles. As a result the troops who had served under his predecessors all turned against him. 39 A certain Trypho, formerly of the party of Alexander, aware of the widespread disaffection towards Demetrius among the soldiers, went to Imalcue, the Arab chieftain, who had charge of the child Antiochus, Alexander's son, 40 and kept pressing him to hand the boy over to him to be made king in place of his father. He informed Imalcue of all the measures Demetrius was taking and of his unpopularity with his troops; and he remained there for some time.

41 Meanwhile Jonathan sent a request to King Demetrius that the garrisons which were constantly harassing Israel should be withdrawn from the citadel in Jerusalem and from the fortresses. 42 To this Demetrius replied: 'I will not only meet your request, but when opportunity arises I will do you and your people the highest honour. 43 Therefore be so good now as to send men to support me, for my own troops have all defected.'

44 Jonathan dispatched three thousand seasoned fighting men to Antioch, and the king was delighted at their coming. 45 The citizens, a hundred and twenty thousand strong, poured into the centre of the city bent on killing Demetrius, 46 and while they seized control of the streets and fighting broke out, the king took refuge in the palace. 47 He summoned the Jews to his aid, and at once they all rallied to him; they deployed throughout the city and slaughtered as many as a hundred thousand that day, 48 setting the city on fire and taking much booty. And thus the king's life was saved.

49 When the citizens saw that the Jews had the city completely at their mercy, their courage failed and they clamoured to the king 50 to accept their surrender and to stop the Jews making war on them and the city. 51 They threw down their weapons and made peace; and the Jews, now in high repute with the king and his subjects throughout the kingdom, returned to Jerusalem laden with booty. 52 But when King Demetrius was secure on his throne, with the country quiet under him, 53 he went back on all his prom-

---

(10.59–66). **30:** *Jonathan* was *brother* or relative to Demetrius as he had once been to Alexander (10.89). **31:** *Lasthenes* was leader of the Cretan mercenaries (10.67) and chief minister to the king. **32–37:** Many of the privileges promised by Demetrius I (10.25–45) were confirmed by his son, but nothing is said of the citadel. Demetrius also confirmed Jonathan in the dignities conferred by Alexander (10.20, 65). **38:** The *King* kept his Cretan *mercenaries* (see 10.67), but he dismissed his regular army without its normal peacetime pay. **39:** Diodotus *Trypho* changed sides frequently, having served Demetrius I, Alexander, Ptolemy, Demetrius II, and now Antiochus. **41:** Demetrius I had not kept his promise (10.32) to give *the citadel* to the high priest. The other *garrisons* are Bethsura (10.14) and Gazara (13.43). **43:** Trypho had sparked a revolt. **44–50:** Actually, the Cretan mercenaries put down the revolt, according to the ancient historians Diodorus and Josephus, but Jewish aid turned the tide in the king's favor. **53:** *Great harshness:* the demand for tribute (according to Josephus, *Ant.* XIII.5.3).

ises and became estranged from Jonathan; instead of repaying the benefits he had received, he treated him with great harshness. [54] After this Trypho returned, and with him Antiochus, a mere lad, who was now crowned king. [55] The soldiers, so contemptuously discharged by Demetrius, all rallied to Antiochus and fought against Demetrius until he was defeated and fled. [56] Trypho, who had captured the elephants, made himself master of Antioch.

[57] The young Antiochus in a letter to Jonathan confirmed him in the high-priesthood, with authority over the four districts, and appointed him one of the king's Friends. [58] He also sent him a service of gold plate, and conferred on him the right to drink from a gold cup, to be robed in purple, and to wear the gold clasp. [59] To Jonathan's brother Simon he assigned command of the area from the Ladder of Tyre to the Egyptian frontier.

[60] Jonathan made a tour through the country on the far side of the river, including the towns there, and the whole Syrian army gathered to his support. He went to Ascalon, where he was received with great honour by the citizens. [61] From there he went on to Gaza, but the inhabitants closed the gates against him; so he blockaded it, set fire to its suburbs, and plundered them. [62] The inhabitants of Gaza then sued for peace, and he granted them terms, taking the sons of their magistrates as hostages and sending them off to Jerusalem; he himself continued his progress through the country as far as Damascus.

[63] Jonathan heard that Demetrius's officers had arrived at Kedesh-in-Galilee with a large force to divert him from his objective. [64] He went to meet them, leaving his brother Simon in Judaea. [65] Simon took up position against Bethsura, which he succeeded in blockading after a prolonged attack. [66] Finally the inhabitants sued for terms, which Simon granted; he expelled them from the town, occupied it, and installed a garrison.

[67] Jonathan, who had encamped with his army by the lake of Gennesaret, marched out early in the morning into the plain of Hazor. [68] There in the plain were the gentile forces advancing to meet him; they had set an ambush for him in the hills, while they themselves made a frontal attack. [69] When the troops started up from the ambush and joined in the fighting, Jonathan's men took to their heels; [70] except for the two commanders, Mattathias son of Absalom and Judas son of Chalphi, not a man of them stood his ground. [71] Jonathan tore his clothes, threw dust on his head, and prayed. [72] Then he returned to the attack and utterly routed the enemy. [73] Seeing this, the fugitives of Jonathan's army rallied to him and joined in the pursuit as far as the enemy base at Kedesh; there they set up camp. [74] That day about three thousand of the Gentiles fell. Jonathan then returned to Jerusalem.

12 JONATHAN considered that the time was now opportune to select representatives and dispatch them on a mission to Rome to confirm and renew the treaty of friendship with that city. [2] He also sent letters to the same effect to Sparta and elsewhere. [3] The envoys, having reached Rome, entered the senate house, where they said: 'Jonathan the high priest and the Jewish people have sent us to renew their former pact of friendship and alliance.' [4] The Romans provided them with letters requiring the authorities in each place to accord them safe conduct to Judaea.

[5] This is a transcript of Jonathan's letter to the Spartans:

[6] From Jonathan the High Priest, the Senate of the Jews, the priests, and the rest of the Jewish people, to our brothers of Sparta.

Greeting.

[7] On a former occasion a letter from

11.54–74: Jonathan goes over to Antiochus. 54: *Antiochus* VI Epiphanes Dionysius was a *mere lad* dominated by his minister *Trypho*. **57:** *The four districts* probably included those of 10.30 n., 38; 11.34. **59:** *The Ladder of Tyre,* a series of mountainous ascents, lies north of Ptolemais. **61:** *Gaza* and other coastal cities were still in Demetrius' control. **63:** *Kedesh* was only twenty-two miles southeast of Tyre. **67:** *The plain of Hazor* is just west of the Jordan above the Sea of Galilee. **68:** Demetrius' generals Sarpedon and Palamedes set the ambush. **70:** Josephus says about fifty remained with *Mattathias* and *Judas* (*Ant.* XIII.5.7). **71:** *Tore his clothes . . . dust:* signs of distress.

12.1–23: The treaties with Sparta and Rome. 2: The defeat of the Achaean League by the Romans in 146 B.C.E. brought *Sparta* to new prominence in Greece. **6:** The *Senate* (Gk. *gerousia*) was the forerunner of

Arius your king to Onias the high priest acknowledged our kinship; a copy is given below. [8]Onias welcomed your envoy with full honours and accepted the letter in which the terms of alliance and friendship were set forth. [9]We do not regard ourselves as being in need of such alliances, since the sacred books we possess afford us encouragement. [10]Nevertheless, we now venture to make contact with you to renew our pact of brotherhood and friendship so that we may not become estranged, for many years have passed since your previous approach to us. [11]We never neglect any opportunity, on festal and other appropriate days, of making mention of you at our sacrifices and in our prayers, as it is right and proper to remember kinsmen; [12]and we rejoice at your fame.

[13]We ourselves have been under the constant pressure of hostile attacks on every side, as the surrounding kings have made war upon us. [14]During the course of these wars we had no wish to trouble you or our other allies and friends. [15]Having had the support of aid from Heaven, we have been saved from our enemies, and they have been humbled. [16]Accordingly, we have chosen Numenius son of Antiochus and Antipater son of Jason and have sent them to the Romans to renew our former friendship and alliance with them. [17]We have instructed them to bear our greetings to you also, and to deliver this letter regarding the renewal of our pact of brotherhood. [18]Now we ask you to favour us with a reply.

[19]This is the copy of the letter sent by the Spartans to Onias:

[20]From Arius, King of Sparta, to Onias the High Priest.

Greeting.

[21]A document has come to light which shows that Spartans and Jews are kinsmen, both being descended from Abraham. [22]Now that we have learnt of this, we beg you to write and tell us how your affairs prosper. [23]Our own response is this: 'What is yours, your livestock and every kind of property, is ours, and what is ours is yours.' We are instructing our envoys, therefore, to report to you in these terms.

[24]When Jonathan heard that Demetrius's generals had come with an even larger force to renew the attack, [25]he marched out from Jerusalem and met them in the region of Hamath, to give them no chance of setting foot on his territory. [26]Spies sent to the enemy camp reported on their return that dispositions were being made for a night assault. [27]At sunset Jonathan issued orders to his men that throughout the night they were to stay awake and stand to arms ready for battle; he also stationed outposts all round the camp. [28]The enemy were alarmed when they learnt that Jonathan and his men were prepared for their attack; their courage failed them and they withdrew, first lighting watch-fires in their camp. [29]Jonathan and his men saw the fires burning and did not realize what had happened until morning. [30]Though he took up the pursuit, he did not overtake them, for they had crossed the river Eleutherus. [31]Turning aside he attacked and plundered the Arabs called Zabadaeans. [32]He moved on to Damascus, marching through the whole country.

[33–34]Meanwhile Simon set out, and, after advancing as far as Ascalon and the neighbouring fortresses, he turned towards Joppa. He had heard that the inhabitants intended to hand over the fort to the supporters of Demetrius, but, before they could do so, he occupied it and placed a garrison there for its defence.

[35]On his return Jonathan convened the senate and with its agreement decided to build fortresses in Judaea, [36]to increase the height of the walls of Jerusalem, and to erect a high barrier which would cut off the citadel from the city and so isolate it that the garrison could neither buy nor sell. [37]The people assembled to rebuild the city, for the wall

---

the Sanhedrin. **7**: *Onias* I (about 300 B.C.E.) received the letter of *Arius* I (309–265 B.C.E.). **10**: A *pact of brotherhood* in the ancient world often resulted in the diplomatic fiction of a common ancestry (see v. 21). **16**: Possibly the *Jason* of 8.17.

12.24–38: Further military activity. 25: *The region of* the "entrance to *Hamath*" lay between the Lebanon and Anti-Lebanon ranges. **30**: *Eleutherus*: see 11.6–7 n. **36**: The defenses razed by Antiochus IV (1.31) and Antiochus V (6.62) were only partially rebuilt (10.10). *The citadel* was to be starved out. **37**: *Chaphenatha* is along the ravine to the east had partly collapsed; he also repaired the section called Chaphenatha. ³⁸Simon rebuilt Adida in the Shephelah, and strengthened it with barred gates.

³⁹Trypho now aspired to the sovereignty of Asia; he planned to assume the crown and launch an offensive against King Antiochus. ⁴⁰But fearing that Jonathan would resort to war to prevent this, he cast about for some means of capturing and killing him. He set off and reached Bethshan. ⁴¹Jonathan went out to confront him with forty thousand picked warriors, and he too reached Bethshan. ⁴²When Trypho saw the size of the force with Jonathan, he hesitated to take the offensive. ⁴³Instead he received Jonathan with full honours: he commended him to all his Friends, loaded him with gifts, and ordered his Friends and his troops to obey him as they would himself. ⁴⁴He said to him: 'Why have you put all these men to so much trouble? We are not at war! ⁴⁵Send them home now and choose a few to accompany you, and come with me to Ptolemais. I shall hand it over to you together with the other fortresses, a large number of troops, and all the officials, and then I shall take my leave. This is the sole purpose of my coming.' ⁴⁶Jonathan believed him and did as he said: he dismissed his forces, and they returned to Judaea. ⁴⁷He kept back three thousand men, of whom he left two thousand in Galilee, while a thousand accompanied him. ⁴⁸But as soon as Jonathan entered Ptolemais, the people closed the gates and seized him, and put to the sword everyone who had come with him.

⁴⁹Trypho sent a force of infantry and cavalry into Galilee to the great plain, to wipe out Jonathan's men, ⁵⁰who only now learnt that Jonathan had been seized and was lost, along with his escort; however, they put heart into one another and marched off in close formation, ready for battle. ⁵¹When their pursuers saw that they would fight for their lives they turned back. ⁵²Though all came safely home to Judaea, they were greatly afraid and mourned for Jonathan and those who were with him; the whole of Israel was plunged into grief. ⁵³The Gentiles round about were all bent on destroying them root and branch. 'The Jews have no leader or champion,' they said; 'so now is the time for us to attack, and we shall blot out all memory of them from among men.'

The leadership of Simon

13 WHEN a report reached Simon that Trypho had got together a large force for the invasion and destruction of Judaea, ²the people were reduced to a state of panic. Seeing this, Simon went up to Jerusalem, where he called an assembly ³and to afford them encouragement said: 'I do not need to remind you how much my brothers and I and my father's house have done for the laws and the holy place, what battles we have fought, what hardships we have endured. ⁴All my brothers have fallen in this cause, fighting for Israel; only I am left. ⁵Now Heaven forbid that I should grudge my life when danger threatens, for I am in no way a better man than my brothers. ⁶Rather, since the Gentiles in their hatred have all gathered to destroy us, I shall take up the cause of my nation and of the holy place, of your wives and children.' ⁷With these words he rekindled the spirit of the people, ⁸and they responded by calling out: 'You shall be our leader in place of Judas and your brother Jonathan. ⁹Fight our wars, and we shall do whatever you say.' ¹⁰Simon assembled all the fighting men and hurried on the completion of the walls until Jerusalem was fortified on every side. ¹¹Jonathan son of Absalom was sent with a considerable force to Joppa, where he drove out the inhabitants and remained in occupation of the town.

thought to have been in the new or "second quarter" of Jerusalem, northwest of the temple. **38:** *Adida,* northeast of Lydda, lay *in the Shephelah,* the foothills east of the coastal plain.

12.39–53: Jonathan is captured by Trypho. 41: Trypho's armed presence must have made *Jonathan* wary enough to bring troops. **43:** *Friends:* see 2.18 n. **49:** *The great plain:* Esdraelon. **52:** Their *grief* was premature; Jonathan died later (13.23).

13.1–16.24: The leadership of Simon. Simon's victories and relatively peaceful reign led the people to make his rule hereditary.

13.1–30: Simon becomes leader and frustrates Trypho. 3: *The holy place:* the temple. **4:** Eventually, all five *brothers* died violently (6.46; 9.18, 36–38; 13.23; 16.16). **11:** The *inhabitants* of *Joppa* were politically

¹²Trypho marched from Ptolemais at the head of a large force to invade Judaea, taking Jonathan with him under guard; ¹³Simon meanwhile established his camp at Adida on the edge of the plain. ¹⁴When Trypho learnt that Simon had come forward to take the place of his brother Jonathan and was about to offer battle, he sent envoys to him with this message: ¹⁵'We are detaining your brother Jonathan because of certain moneys owed by him to the royal treasury in connection with the offices he held. ¹⁶To ensure that once released he will not again revolt, send now one hundred talents of silver and two of his sons as hostages, and we shall let him go.' ¹⁷Although he was sure the proposal was a trick, Simon had the money and the children brought to him, fearing that otherwise he might arouse widespread animosity among the people, ¹⁸who would say, 'It was because you did not send the money and the children that Jonathan lost his life.' ¹⁹So he sent the children and the hundred talents; but Trypho broke his word and did not release Jonathan.

²⁰After this, Trypho set out to invade and ravage the country. He made a detour by way of Adora, and Simon with his army marched parallel with him everywhere he went. ²¹Meanwhile the garrison of the citadel kept sending emissaries to Trypho, urging him to come by the desert route and to send supplies. ²²Trypho prepared to dispatch the whole of his cavalry, but that night there was a severe storm, and they failed to get through because of the snow; so he withdrew into Gilead. ²³When he was near Bascama, he had Jonathan put to death and buried there. ²⁴Trypho then turned and went off to his own country.

²⁵Simon had the body of his brother brought for burial to Modin, the town of his forefathers. ²⁶There was great grief for Jonathan throughout Israel and the mourning lasted for many days. ²⁷Over the tomb of his father and brothers Simon raised a lofty monument, visible at a great distance and faced, back and front, with polished stone. ²⁸He erected seven pyramids, arranged in pairs, for his father and mother and four brothers. ²⁹He contrived an elaborate setting for the pyramids: he surrounded them with tall columns surmounted with trophies of armour as a perpetual memorial, and with carved ships alongside the trophies, plainly visible to those at sea. ³⁰This mausoleum which he made at Modin stands to the present day.

³¹Trypho now conspired against Antiochus the young king and put him to death. ³²He usurped the throne and assumed the crown of Asia, and he inflicted great damage on the country.

³³Simon rebuilt the fortresses of Judaea, furnishing them with high towers and with massive walls and barred gates; he also stocked the fortresses with provisions. ³⁴He selected delegates and sent them to King Demetrius to negotiate a remission of taxes for the country, on the ground that all Trypho's exactions had been exorbitant. ³⁵In reply to this request Demetrius sent a letter in the following terms:

³⁶From King Demetrius to Simon the High Priest and Friend of kings, and to the elders and nation of the Jews.

Greeting.

³⁷We have received the gold crown and the palm branch which you sent, and we are prepared to make a lasting peace with you and to instruct the revenue officers to grant you remissions of tax. ³⁸All our agreements with you stand confirmed, and the strongholds which you built shall remain yours. ³⁹For any errors of omission or commission we grant a free pardon, to take effect from the date of this letter. We remit the crown-levy which you owed us, and every other tax formerly exacted in Jerusalem is henceforth cancelled. ⁴⁰Any

unreliable (12.33–34); see, similarly, 11.66. **16:** The (ransom) money was in payment for the alleged debts, and the *hostages* were to assure Jonathan's compliance. **20:** *Adora* (Dura): five miles southwest of Hebron. **21:** The *garrison* needed *supplies* because of the siege (12.36). *The desert route* may have been via the Transjordan. **23:** *Bascama* was located northeast of the Sea of Galilee. "Gilead" in v. 22 is the Greek text's error for "Galilee."

13.31–42: Simon supports Demetrius II again. 31: Actually, *Trypho* arranged for *Antiochus* VI's doctors to kill him during an operation in 139 B.C.E., some four years after he had deposed him. **32:** *The crown of Asia* was that of the Seleucid empire (8.6). **36:** The letter repeats much of 11.33–37 (see 10.25–45). **37:** *The gold crown and the palm branch* signify homage and allegiance. **39:** These *errors* included support of Trypho.

of you who are suitable for enrolment in our retinue shall be so enrolled.

Let there be peace between us.

[41] In the year 170, Israel was released from the gentile yoke; [42] the people began to write on their contracts and agreements: 'In the first year of Simon, the great high priest, general, and leader of the Jews'.

[43] At that time Simon surrounded and closely invested Gazara with his troops. He constructed a siege-engine, and bringing it up to the town he made a breach in one of the towers and captured it. [44] The men on the siege-engine leapt from it into the town, and there was great commotion. [45] The defenders along with their wives and children climbed on to the city wall with their garments torn, clamouring loudly to Simon to grant them terms. [46] 'Do not treat us as our wickedness deserves,' they cried, 'but as your mercy prompts you.' [47] Simon agreed terms and called off the attack. But he expelled them from the town, and after purifying the houses in which there were idols, he made his entry with songs of thanksgiving and praise. [48] Everything which was polluted he threw out, and he settled there men who would keep the law. He strengthened the fortifications, and he built himself a residence in the town.

[49] The occupants of the citadel at Jerusalem were prevented from going in and out to buy and sell in the countryside; famine ensued, and many died of starvation. [50] The survivors cried out to Simon to accept their surrender; this he granted; then expelling them from the citadel he cleansed it from its defilement. [51] It was on the twenty-third day of the second month in the year 171 that the Jews entered the city amid a chorus of praise and the waving of palm branches, with lutes, cymbals, and zithers, with hymns and songs, to celebrate Israel's final riddance of a formidable enemy. [52] Simon decreed that this day should be observed as an annual festival. He strengthened the fortifications of the temple hill opposite the citadel, and he and his men made it their base. [53] In recognition of the fact that his son John had now reached manhood, he appointed him commander of all the forces, with Gazara as his headquarters.

14 In the year 172, King Demetrius mustered his army and moved into Media to obtain support for his war against Trypho. [2] When Arsakes king of Persia and Media heard that Demetrius had entered his territory, he dispatched one of his generals to take him alive. [3] The general marched out, defeated and captured Demetrius, and brought him to Arsakes, who kept him under guard.

[4] As long as Simon ruled, Judaea was undisturbed. He sought his nation's good, and they lived happily all through the glorious days of his reign. [5] Notable among his achievements was his capture of the port of Joppa to secure his communications overseas. [6] He extended his nation's borders and made himself master of the land. [7] Many prisoners of war were repatriated. He gained control over Gazara and Bethsura and over the citadel, from which he removed all pollution. None could withstand him.

[8] The people farmed the land in peace; it produced its crops, and the trees in the plains

13:41 **170:** *that is* 142 B.C.E.   13:43 **Gazara:** *prob. rdg:* Gk Gaza.   13:51 **171:** *that is* 141 B.C.E.   14:1 **172:** *that is* 140 B.C.E.

Remission of the *crown-levy* (tribute), in effect, meant liberation (see v. 41). **40:** Demetrius thought well of Jewish soldiers (11.41–51). **42:** This *first year* was that of Simon's high priesthood and not the beginning of a new era, as the author thought.

13.43–53: Simon takes Gazara and the citadel. While Demetrius and Trypho were occupied with each other, Simon decided to remove the last hostile strongholds in Judea: Gazara (vv. 43–48) and the citadel (vv. 49–53). **44:** The *siege-engine* was a tower as high as the city walls. **49:** The siege may have lasted three years; see 12.36; 13.21. **50:** The *defilement* was the presence of pagan shrines; see 1.54. **51:** This *enemy* had plagued Israel for over twenty-five years (1.33–36). **53:** *John Hyrcanus* (134–104 B.C.E.) succeeded Simon as high priest.

14.1–3: The Parthian capture of Demetrius. Demetrius II (reigned 145–139 B.C.E. and 129–125 B.C.E.) went east to dislodge the Parthian King Mithridates I (also known dynastically as Arsakes VI, 171–138 B.C.E.) from captured Seleucid territories, as well as to gain troops. Captured by treachery, Demetrius was a Parthian prisoner until released in 129 B.C.E. He was murdered in 125 B.C.E.

14.4–15: Simon's achievements. 6: Simon *extended* his *nation's borders* by the addition of Joppa, Gazara, their fruit. ⁹Old men sat in the streets, talking together of their blessings; and the young men arrayed themselves in splendid military style. ¹⁰Simon supplied the towns with food in plenty and equipped them with weapons for defence, so that his renown spread to the ends of the earth. ¹¹Peace was restored to the land, and throughout Israel there was great rejoicing. ¹²Everyone sat under his own vine and fig tree, and there was none to cause alarm. ¹³Those were days when no enemy was seen in the land and every hostile king was crushed. ¹⁴Simon gave his protection to the poor among the people; he fulfilled the demands of the law, and rid the country of renegades and evil men. ¹⁵He enhanced the splendour of the temple and furnished it with a wealth of sacred vessels.

¹⁶THE report of Jonathan's death reached Rome and even Sparta, and caused widespread grief. ¹⁷When they heard, however, that his brother Simon had succeeded him as high priest and was firmly in control of both country and towns, ¹⁸they sent him a renewal of the treaty of friendship and alliance they had established with his brothers Judas and Jonathan; this was inscribed on bronze tablets ¹⁹which were read before the assembly in Jerusalem. ²⁰The following is a copy of the letter which the Spartans sent:

From the magistrates and city of Sparta to the High Priest Simon, to the Senate, the priests, and the rest of the Jewish people, our brothers.

Greeting.

²¹The envoys sent to our people have informed us of your honour and fame, and their visit has given us much pleasure. ²²We have entered a record of the message they brought in the minutes of the public assembly; it reads: 'Numenius son of Antiochus and Antipater son of Jason came as envoys of the Jews to renew the treaty of friendship. ²³It was resolved by the public assembly to receive these men with honour and to place a copy of their address in the public archives, so that the people of Sparta might have it on permanent record. A copy of this document has been made for Simon the high priest.'

²⁴After this, Simon sent Numenius to Rome bearing a large gold shield, worth a thousand minas, to confirm the alliance with the Romans.

²⁵When the people heard an account of these events they asked themselves how they could show their gratitude to Simon and his sons, ²⁶for he, with his brothers and his father's family, had proved resolute in repulsing the enemies of Israel and ensuring the nation's freedom. ²⁷So the people had an inscription engraved on bronze tablets and placed on a monument on Mount Zion; this is a copy of the inscription:

On the eighteenth day of the month of Elul, in the year 172, the third year of Simon's high-priesthood, ²⁸at Asaramel, before a large assembly of priests, people, rulers of the nation, and elders of the land, the following resolution was passed: ²⁹'Whereas our land had been subject to frequent wars, Simon son of Mattathias, a priest of the Joarib family, and his brothers put their lives in jeopardy by their resistance to the enemies of the people, in order to safeguard the temple and the law, and they brought great glory to their nation. ³⁰Jonathan rallied the nation and became high priest, and then was gathered to his forefathers. ³¹When enemies resolved to invade and destroy the land and to make an assault on the temple, ³²Simon came forward and fought for his nation. He ex-

14:27 172: *that is* 140 B.C.E.

---

and Bethsura. Josephus adds Jamnia (*Ant.* XIII.6.7). **7:** Simon *repatriated* Galilean Jews (5.23). **8–15:** Simon's reign has the *blessings* promised for observance of the Law. See Lev. 26.3–4; Zech. 3.10; 8.4. **12:** That *everyone enjoy his own vine and fig tree* is an ancient expression for universal peace and contentment; see 1 Kgs. 4.25; Isa. 36.16; Mic. 4.4.

14.16–24: Renewal of alliances with Rome and Sparta. In antiquity, when leadership changed, treaties were renewable. **17–19:** The more important treaty with the Romans is placed first and summarized. **22:** These were also Jonathan's envoys (12.16). **24:** *After this* visit to Sparta, the envoys continued on to Rome.

14.25–49: The edict honoring Simon. The decree honors Simon in the way that Greek cities honored their benefactors. **27:** *Bronze tablets* preserved important documents (8.22 n.; 14.18). **28:** The Heb. phrase for *at Asaramel* means "as prince of the people of God." **32:** Simon's payment of soldiers with *his own money* pended large sums of his own money to arm the soldiers of his nation and to provide their pay. [33] He fortified the towns of Judaea, including Bethsura, a frontier town formerly used by the enemy as an arsenal, and he stationed in it a garrison of Jewish soldiers. [34] The coastal town of Joppa was also fortified, as was Gazara near Azotus, formerly occupied by the enemy. He settled Jews there, and provided these towns with everything requisite for their restoration.

[35] 'Simon's patriotism and his resolution to win renown for his nation were such that the people made him their leader and high priest, in recognition of his achievements, his just conduct, his loyalty towards the nation, and constant efforts to enhance its power. [36] In his time and under his leadership the Gentiles were successfully evicted from the land; so too were those who had occupied the City of David in Jerusalem and made for themselves a citadel from which they used to sally forth and bring defilement on the whole precinct of the temple and do violence to its purity. [37] He installed Jewish soldiers in it and fortified it for the greater security of the land and city; he also heightened the walls of Jerusalem. [38] In consideration of all this King Demetrius confirmed him in the office of high priest, [39] appointed him one of his Friends, and granted him the highest honours; [40] for he had heard that the Romans were addressing the Jews as friends, allies, and brothers and had received Simon's envoys with much honour.

[41] 'The Jews and their priests confirmed Simon as their leader and high priest in perpetuity until a true prophet should appear. [42] He was to be their general, and to have full charge of the temple and of the work of reconstruction; in addition the supervision of the country and of the arms and fortifications was to be entrusted to him. [43] He was to be obeyed by the whole people; all official documents throughout the land were to be drawn up in his name.

He was to be entitled to wear the purple robe and gold clasp.

[44] 'None of the people or the priests is to have authority to abrogate any of these decrees, to oppose commands issued by Simon, or to convene any assembly in the land without his permission; none of them is to be robed in purple or to wear the gold clasp. [45] Whoever contravenes these provisions or neglects any of them is to be liable to punishment.

[46] 'It was the unanimous decision of the people that Simon should officiate in the ways here laid down. [47] Simon accepted, and consented to be high priest, general, and ethnarch of the Jews and the priests, and to be the protector of them all.'

[48] This inscription, it was declared, should be engraved on bronze tablets and set up in a prominent position within the precincts of the temple, [49] and copies were to be placed in the treasury in the keeping of Simon and his sons.

15 Antiochus son of King Demetrius sent a letter from overseas to Simon, priest and ethnarch of the Jews, and to the whole nation. [2] It read:

From King Antiochus to Simon, High Priest and Ethnarch, and to the Jewish nation.

Greeting.

[3] Whereas certain rebels have seized control of my ancestral kingdom, now I have decided to assert my claim to it, so that I may restore it to its former state. For this I have recruited a large body of mercenaries and fitted out ships of war. [4] It is my intention to land in my country and to seek out and punish those who have ravaged my kingdom and laid waste many of its cities.

[5] Therefore I now confirm all the remissions which my royal predecessors granted you, whether of tribute or of other contributions. [6] I authorize you to mint your own coinage as currency for your country. [7] Je-

---

indicated his princely status, since it followed royal custom. **41:** The titles of *leader* and *high priest* were now made hereditary in Simon's family. For lack of prophecy see also 4.46; 9.27 n. **49:** As successors of Simon, *his sons* received copies of the decree.

15.1–14: Antiochus VII seeks Simon's support in his struggles with Trypho for the throne of Demetrius II. **1:** *Antiochus* VII Sidetes (138–129 B.C.E.) was the son of *Demetrius* I (161–150 B.C.E.) and brother of the captured Demetrius II (145–139, 129–125 B.C.E.). **6:** Although Antiochus added to previous fiscal concessions rusalem and the temple is to be free. All the arms you have prepared and the fortresses you have built and now occupy may remain in your hands. 8 All debts now owing to the royal treasury and all future liabilities thereto are cancelled from this time forward for ever. 9 When we have re-established our kingdom, we shall confer the highest honours on you and on your nation and temple, to make your country's fame apparent to the whole world.

10 In the year 174, Antiochus entered the land of his forefathers, and all the armed forces came over to him, leaving Trypho only a few supporters. 11 With Antiochus in pursuit of him, Trypho fled along the coastal road to Dor, 12 for he well knew how desperate was his position now that his troops had deserted. 13 Antiochus, with a hundred and twenty thousand trained soldiers and eight thousand horsemen under his command, laid siege to Dor. 14 He drew a cordon round the town, his ships joining in the blockade from the sea, and thus, both by land and sea, he exerted heavy pressure on it and prevented anyone from leaving or entering.

15 NUMENIUS and his party arrived from Rome with letters to the various kings and nations. That to Ptolemy read as follows:

16 From Lucius, Consul of the Romans, to King Ptolemy.
Greeting.
17 Envoys have come to us from our friends and allies the Jews. They were sent by Simon the high priest and the Jewish people, to renew their original treaty of friendship and alliance, 18 and they brought with them a gold shield valued at a thousand minas. 19 We have resolved, therefore, to write to kings and nations, that they do nothing to the detriment of the Jews; they must not make war on them

or on their cities or their country, nor are they to ally themselves with those who so make war. 20 We have decided to accept the shield from them. 21 If, therefore, any rebels have escaped from their country to you, they are to be handed over to Simon the high priest to be punished by him according to Jewish law.

22 The same message was sent to King Demetrius, to Attalus, Ariarathes, Arsakes, 23 Sampsakes, and the Spartans, and also to the following places: Delos, Myndos, Sicyon, Caria, Samos, Pamphylia, Lycia, Halicarnassus, Rhodes, Phaselis, Cos, Sideh, Aradus, Gortyna, Cnidus, Cyprus, and Cyrene. 24 A copy was written out for Simon the high priest.

25 KING Antiochus laid siege to Dor for the second time, and launched repeated attacks against it; he had siege-engines constructed and blockaded Trypho, preventing all movement in or out of the town.

26 Simon sent two thousand picked men to assist him, as well as silver and gold and much equipment. 27 But Antiochus refused the offer; instead, he repudiated all his previous agreements with Simon and broke off relations. 28 He sent Athenobius, one of the Friends, to convey this message: 'You are occupying Joppa and Gazara and the citadel in Jerusalem, cities that belong to my kingdom. 29 You have laid waste their territories and done great damage to the country, and you have made yourselves masters of many places in my kingdom. 30 Therefore I now demand the return of the cities you have seized and the surrender of the tribute exacted from places beyond the frontiers of Judaea over which you have assumed control. 31 Otherwise, you must pay five hundred talents of silver on their account, and another five hun-

15:10 **174:** *that is* 138 B.C.E.   15:25 **for the second time:** *some witnesses read* on the second day.

the right to coin money (see 10.26–35; 13.37–39), Simon seems never to have used it. The right was soon revoked (15.27). **10–14:** Antiochus married Cleopatra, the wife of his brother Demetrius. Trypho's troops deserted to her, and she transferred them to Antiochus' command. *Dor* lay fifteen miles south of Mount Carmel.

15.15–24: Return of the envoys. 16: *Lucius* Caecilius Metullus Calvus, who was *Consul* in 142 B.C.E., wrote (v. 16) to *Ptolemy* VIII (Euergetes II Physcon) of Egypt (145–116 B.C.E.). **22:** Copies of the *message* went to *Demetrius* II of Asia (145–139 and 129–125 B.C.E.), *Attalus* II of Pergamum (159–138 B.C.E.), *Ariarathes* V of Cappadocia (162–131 B.C.E.), *Arsakes* VI (Mithridates I, 171–138 B.C.E.) of Parthia, and to various free city-states.

15.25–36: Antiochus VII alienates Simon. 26–27: Josephus says the king accepted this aid (*Ant.* XIII.7.2).

dred as compensation for the destruction you have caused and for the loss of tribute from the cities. Failing this, we shall resort to war.'

³²Athenobius, the king's Friend, came to Jerusalem, and when he saw the magnificence of Simon's establishment, and the gold and silver vessels on his sideboard, and his display of wealth, he was amazed. He delivered the king's message, ³³to which Simon replied: 'We have neither occupied other people's land nor taken possession of other people's property; we have taken only our ancestral heritage, unjustly seized for a time by our enemies. ³⁴We have grasped the opportunity to reclaim our patrimony. ³⁵But with regard to Joppa and Gazara, which you demand, these towns were doing great damage among our people and in our land; for these we offer one hundred talents.'

Without a word, ³⁶Athenobius went off in anger to the king, who was furious when Athenobius told him what Simon had said, and described Simon's splendour and all else he had seen.

³⁷Meanwhile Trypho boarded a ship and made his escape to Orthosia. ³⁸The king appointed Kendebaeus as commander-in-chief of the coastal zone, and gave him infantry and cavalry, ³⁹with instructions to blockade Judaea, to rebuild Kedron and strengthen its gates, and to make war on our people; he himself would continue the pursuit of Trypho. ⁴⁰Kendebaeus arrived in Jamnia, and by invading Judaea began to harass our people, capturing and killing them. ⁴¹He rebuilt Kedron and stationed cavalry and foot-soldiers there to sally forth and patrol the roads of Judaea, as instructed by the king.

16 John went up from Gazara and reported to Simon, his father, the results of Kendebaeus's campaign. ²Simon summoned his two eldest sons Judas and John, and said to them: 'My brothers and I and my father's family have fought Israel's battles from our youth until this day, and many a time have we been successful in rescuing Israel. ³Now I am old, but mercifully

you are in the prime of life. Take my brother's place and mine, and go out and fight for our nation. And may help from Heaven be with you!'

⁴John levied twenty thousand warriors, foot-soldiers and cavalry, from the country and marched against Kendebaeus. After a night at Modin ⁵they advanced early next morning into the plain, where a large force of infantry and cavalry stood ready to meet them on the far side of a wadi. ⁶John and his troops were in position facing the enemy, when he realized that his men were afraid to cross the gully. So he himself led the way, and seeing this his men followed him across. ⁷John drew up his army with the cavalry in the centre of the infantry, for the opposing cavalry were very numerous. ⁸The trumpets sounded for the attack, and Kendebaeus and his army were routed; many fell, and the remainder took refuge in the fortress. ⁹John's brother Judas was wounded in the fighting, but John kept up the pursuit until Kendebaeus reached Kedron, which he had rebuilt. ¹⁰The fugitives fled to the forts in the open country round Azotus, whereupon John set fire to Azotus, and some two thousand of the enemy perished. He then returned to Judaea in safety.

¹¹Ptolemaeus son of Abubus had been appointed commander for the plain of Jericho. He had great wealth in silver and gold, ¹²for he was the high priest's son-in-law, ¹³but he became over-ambitious and, proposing to make himself master of the country, plotted to put Simon and his sons out of the way. ¹⁴When, in the course of a tour to inspect the towns in that region and to attend to their needs, Simon went down to Jericho with his sons Mattathias and Judas in the year 177, in the eleventh month, the month of Shebat, ¹⁵the son of Abubus, with treachery in his heart, received them at the small fort called Dok which he had built, and entertained them lavishly. But he had men in concealment there, ¹⁶and when Simon and his sons

16:14 **177:** *that is* 134 B.C.E.

30: The *places beyond the frontiers* probably include those of 11.34. **32:** *King's Friend:* see 2.18 n.

15.37–16.10: John Hyrcanus defeats Kendebaeus. 37: From *Orthosia,* north of Tripolis, Trypho went to Apamea where Antiochus captured and killed him. **38:** Simon held this post under Antiochus VI (11.59). **39:** *Kedron* lay three miles southeast of Jamnia. **16.3:** Simon was about sixty years *old.* **4:** This is the first mention of Maccabean *cavalry.* **6:** John's crossing recalls Judas' (5.40, 43).

16.11–24: John Hyrcanus succeeds his murdered father. 15: The hill fortress of *Dok* lay five miles northwest were drunk, Ptolemaeus and his accomplices started up and seized their weapons; bursting into the banqueting hall, they attacked Simon and killed him, along with his two sons and some of his servants. [17] It was an act of base treachery in which evil was returned for good.

[18] Ptolemaeus forwarded an account of his action to the king, with a request for troops to be sent to his assistance and for him to be given authority over the country and its towns. [19] He ordered some of his men to Gazara to make away with John, and he wrote to the senior officers of the army urging them to come over to him and be given silver and gold and gifts. [20] Other troops he detailed to seize control of Jerusalem and the temple hill. [21] But someone ran ahead and reported to John at Gazara that his father and brothers had been murdered, and that Ptolemaeus had sent men to kill him as well. [22] The news came as a great shock to John, and, learning of the plot against his life, he arrested and put to death the men who came to kill him.

[23] The rest of the story of John, his wars and the deeds of valour he performed, the walls he built, and his achievements, [24] are recorded in the annals of his high-priesthood from the time when he succeeded his father.

of Jericho. **16:** Josephus says the sons were killed later (*Ant.* XIII.8.1). **18:** *Ptolemaeus* appealed to Antiochus VII. **22:** Eventually, Ptolemaeus fled to Philadelphia (Amman). **23–24:** The wording recalls that used of the kings of Israel (1 Kgs. 14.19, 29). The *annals* have been lost.

THE SECOND BOOK OF THE

Maccabees

Second Maccabees is a shortened version of a five-volume historical work, now lost, by Jason of Cyrene (2 Macc. 2.19–32). To this shortened version, the "abbreviator" prefixed two letters (1.1–10a; 1.10b–2.18) which Judeans addressed to their Egyptian coreligionists, urging them to observe the feast celebrating the temple's rededication in 164 B.C.E. The abridgment of Jason's work exemplifies "pathetic history," a genre of writing which seeks not only to tell the story, but to arouse the reader's sympathetic emotions and give pleasure. With invented dialogue, exaggerated numbers, apparitions, and miracles, the "abbreviator" or Epitomist, as such a writer is technically called, traces the decline of the high priesthood (3.1–4.50), Antiochus Epiphanes' attempt to impose Hellenism upon the Jews (5.1–7.42), and Judas Maccabeus' successful resistance, culminating in his triumphal cleansing of the temple (8.1–10.8), and his subsequent struggles (10.9–15.39).

Second Maccabees was written in Greek in Egypt about 124 B.C.E. It covers the period approximately 180–160 B.C.E., and parallels the events narrated in 1 Macc. 1.10–7.50.

Preface

1 FROM the Jews in Jerusalem and in the country of Judaea to their Jewish kinsmen in Egypt.

Greeting and peace.

² May God prosper you, and may he keep in mind the covenant he made with Abraham, Isaac, and Jacob, his faithful servants. ³ May he give to you all hearts to worship him and to fulfil his purposes with high courage and willing spirit. ⁴ May he make your minds open to his law and ordinances. May he bring you peace, ⁵ and grant you an answer to your prayers; may he be reconciled to you and never forsake you in an evil hour. ⁶ Here and now we are praying for you.

⁷ In the reign of Demetrius, in the year 169, we wrote to you during the persecution and crisis that we Jews experienced after Jason and his followers defected from the holy land and the kingdom, ⁸ setting the temple porch on fire and spilling innocent blood. We prayed to the Lord and were answered; we brought a sacrifice and an offering of fine flour, we lit the lamps, and laid out the Bread of the Presence. ⁹ Now we instruct you to observe the celebration of a feast of Tabernacles in the month of Kislev.

¹⁰ Written in the year 188.

FROM the people of Jerusalem and Judaea, from the Senate, and from Judas: to Aris-

1:7 **169:** *that is* 143 B.C.E.   1:10 **188:** *that is* 124 B.C.E.

1.1–10a: The first letter. The Judeans urge those in Egypt to observe the feast (v. 9) which celebrates the rededication of the temple. This letter, written in 124 B.C.E. (= 188 in the Seleucid calendar) refers to an earlier letter of 143 B.C.E. (= 169 in the Seleucid calendar), which described the events from Jason's apostasy (4.7–5.10) to the temple's dedication (10.1–8; 1 Macc. 4.36–61) and probably informed the Egyptian Jews of Jonathan's death (1 Macc. 12.39–53; 13.23). **1–2:** The two-fold salutation includes the Hellenistic *greeting* and the Hebraic *peace*. **7–8a:** Jason slaughtered his own people (5.5–7) in the *holy land* (Zech. 2.12), thus also revolting against the Seleucid *kingdom*. **8b:** After purifying the temple, Judas and his followers *brought a sacrifice* there (10.3; 1 Macc. 4.50–51). **9:** A feast is now to take place in *Kislev* (December); it came to be called Hanukkah. The biblical *feast of Tabernacles,* which Hanukkah resembles at least in length (eight days), was in Tishri (September–October).

1.10b–2.18: The second letter. Written earlier, in 164 B.C.E., this letter urges Egyptian Jews to celebrate the dedication of the newly purified temple (10.1–8; 1 Macc. 4.36–59) even though not prescribed in the

1233

tobulus, tutor of King Ptolemy and a member of the family of anointed priests, and to the Jews in Egypt.

Greeting and health.

11 We have been rescued by God from great dangers, for which we give him profound thanks as our champion against the king; 12 God it was who drove out the enemy stationed in the Holy City.

13 When King Antiochus went into Persia with a force that seemed invincible, they were cut to pieces in the temple of the goddess Nanaea through a stratagem employed by her priests. 14 On the pretext of a ritual marriage with the goddess, Antiochus, escorted by his Friends, had come to the temple to secure the considerable treasure by way of dowry. 15 After this was laid out by the priests, he entered the temple precinct with a small bodyguard. As soon as he was inside, the priests shut the sanctuary; 16 then, opening a secret trapdoor in the panelled ceiling, they hurled stones at them, and the king fell as if struck by a thunderbolt. They hacked off limbs and heads and threw them to those outside. 17 Blessed in all things be our God, who handed over the godless to death!

18 We think it right and proper to inform you that we are about to celebrate the purification of the temple on the twenty-fifth of Kislev, so that you also may celebrate a feast of Tabernacles; this is in honour of the fire which appeared when Nehemiah offered sacrifices, after he had rebuilt the temple and the altar. 19 When our forefathers were being carried off to Persia, the devout priests of those days secretly took fire from the altar and concealed it inside a dry well. This proved a safe hiding-place and remained undiscovered. 20 After many years had passed, in God's good time Nehemiah was sent back by the king of Persia. He dispatched in search of the fire the descendants of the priests who had hidden it, and they reported to our people that they found, not fire, but a thick liquid. 21 Nehemiah told them to draw some out and bring it to him. When the materials of the sacrifice had been presented, he ordered the priests to sprinkle this liquid over the wood and the sacrifice. 22 This was done, and after some time the sun, till then hidden by clouds, began to shine and to everyone's astonishment there was a great blaze of fire on the altar. 23 While the sacrifice was burning, the priests offered prayer, they and all those present: Jonathan began and the rest responded, led by Nehemiah.

24 The prayer was in this style: 'Lord God, the Creator of all things, the terrible and mighty, the just and merciful, the only King, you alone are gracious; 25 you are the only Giver, the only just and omnipotent and eternal One, the Deliverer of Israel from every evil, who chose the patriarchs and set them apart. 26 Accept, we pray, this sacrifice on behalf of your whole people Israel; watch over them and sanctify them, for they are your own possession. 27 Bring together those of our people who are dispersed, set free those who are enslaved among the heathen, look favourably on those who are despised and detested; so let the heathen know that you are our God. 28 Punish with torments our arrogant and insolent oppressors, 29 and, as promised by Moses, plant your people in your holy land.' 30 The priests then chanted the hymns.

31 After the sacrifice had been consumed, Nehemiah ordered that what remained of the liquid be poured over some

Pentateuch, since Judas' victory was God's salvation for all Jews (2.17). **10:** *Aristobulus* was a Jewish "philosopher" of Alexandria, who "taught" Ptolemy VI Philometor (180–145 B.C.E.) by dedicating a book to him which "proved" that the Greeks derived their wisdom and philosophy from the Law and the Prophets. **11:** *The king* is Antiochus IV Epiphanes (175–164 B.C.E.). **13:** The Elamite goddess *Nanaea* (Anaitis) was identified with the Greek goddess Artemis in Hellenistic times. **16–17:** Actually, Antiochus was driven off, not killed (9.2). The letter writer's sources may have confused the king's representative with the *king* himself. **18:** Lighting candles, *fire,* is a special feature of the present feast of Hanukkah. The *temple* was *rebuilt* long before Nehemiah's time; see Ezra 3.1–2; 6.6–16. The fire at the time of Nehemiah's sacrifices is not found in the Book of Nehemiah but apparently comes from the apocryphal memoirs of Nehemiah (2.13), now lost. The purpose of the allusion is to emphasize the privileges of the temple and the continuity and orthodoxy of its worship. The many difficulties in the story that follows show its fictional character. **19:** The Exile (587 B.C.E.; see 2 Kgs. 25.11–12) was to Babylon, which later became part of the Persian Empire. **20:** *The king* who sent Nehemiah back to govern great stones. ³²At this a flame shot up, but it burnt itself out as soon as the fire on the altar outshone it.

³³These events became widely known. The king of Persia was told that, in the place where the exiled priests had hidden the fire, a liquid had appeared, which Nehemiah and his companions had used to burn up the materials of the sacrifice. ³⁴After he had verified this, the king had the site enclosed and declared it sacred. ³⁵The custodians he appointed received a share of the very substantial revenue the king derived from it. ³⁶Nehemiah and his companions called the liquid nephthar, which means 'purification'; but most people call it naphtha.

2 The records show that it was Jeremiah the prophet who ordered the exiles to hide the fire, in the way just described. ²After giving them the law, the prophet charged them not to neglect the ordinances of the Lord, or let their minds be led astray by the sight of gold and silver images in all their finery. ³In similar terms he appealed to them never to let the law be far from their hearts.

⁴It is recorded also that, in obedience to a divine command, the prophet gave orders for the Tent of Meeting and the Ark to accompany him, and he went off to the mountain from the top of which Moses had seen God's promised land. ⁵Arriving at the mountain, Jeremiah found a cave-dwelling into which he carried the Tent, the Ark, and the altar of incense; he then blocked up the entrance. ⁶Some of his companions went to mark out the way, but were unable to find it. ⁷Jeremiah learnt of this and took them to task. 'The place is to remain unknown', he said, 'until God finally gathers his people together and shows them his favour. ⁸The Lord will then bring these things to light once more, and his glory will appear together with the cloud, as it was revealed in the time of

Moses and also when Solomon prayed that the shrine might be worthily consecrated.'

⁹Further, it is related that Solomon, who had the gift of wisdom, offered a dedication sacrifice at the completion of the temple; ¹⁰and that, just as Moses had prayed to the Lord and fire had come down from heaven and burnt up the sacrificial offerings, so in answer to Solomon's prayer the fire came down and consumed the whole-offerings. ¹¹(Moses said, 'The sin-offering was burnt in the same way because it was not eaten.') ¹²The feast celebrated by Solomon went on for eight days.

¹³These same facts are set out in the official records and in the memoirs of Nehemiah. Just as Nehemiah collected the chronicles of the kings, the writings of prophets, the works of David, and royal letters about sacred offerings, to found his library, ¹⁴in the same way Judas has collected for us all the documents that had been dispersed as a result of the recent conflict. These are in our possession, ¹⁵and if ever you need any of them, send messengers for them.

¹⁶Since we are about to celebrate the purification of the temple, we are writing to impress upon you the duty of holding this festival. ¹⁷God has rescued his whole people and granted to all of us the holy land, the kingship, the priesthood, and the consecration, ¹⁸as he promised by the law. We have confidence that God will soon show us compassion and gather us from everywhere under heaven to the holy place, for he has delivered us from great evils and purified that place.

¹⁹JASON of Cyrene has set out in five books

1:31 **that what remained ... stones:** *so some witnesses; others read* that great stones should enclose what remained of the liquid. 1:32 **but ... outshone it:** *or* but hardly had the light been reflected from the altar, when it burnt itself out. 2:11 **sin-offering:** *or* purification-offering.

was Artaxerxes I Longimanus (464–424 B.C.E.). The *thick liquid* was naphtha, or petroleum (v. 36). **36:** The Persian word for the *liquid* is *neft. Nephthar* involves a play on this word and on the Heb. root *ṯhr,* "purify." **2.4–8:** This story is improbable, too; see Jer. 3.16. Moses' *mountain* was Nebo (Deut. 32.49). **9–10:** On the theme of *fire ... from heaven,* see Lev. 9.24; Judg. 6.21; 1 Kgs. 18.38; 2 Chr. 7.1. **11:** The meaning of this verse is not clear but see Lev. 10.16–20. **13:** The inclusion of the *royal letters* of Persian kings shows this collection was not limited to sacred books. For Nehemiah's *memoirs* see 1.18 n.

2.19–32: A summary of the five books. The abbreviator leaves responsibility for accuracy to Jason, while attempting to make one readable, memorable, pleasurable, and profitable book out of Jason's five. **19:** *Jason* the story of Judas Maccabaeus and his brothers, of the purification of the great temple, and of the dedication of the altar. 20 He has also given an account of the wars with Antiochus Epiphanes and with his son Eupator, 21 and he has described the apparitions from heaven which appeared to those who, in the cause of the Jewish religion, vied with one another in heroism. Few though they were, they ranged through the whole country, taking booty and routing the foreign hordes; 22 they recovered the world-renowned temple, liberated the city of Jerusalem, and reaffirmed the laws, which were in danger of being abolished. All this they achieved because the Lord showed them clemency and favour.

23 These five books of Jason I shall attempt to summarize in a single work; 24 for I was struck by the mass of statistics and the difficulty which the sheer bulk of the material occasions to those wishing to master the narratives of this history. 25 I have tried to provide entertainment for those who peruse for pleasure, an aid for students who must commit the facts to memory, and in general a service to readers. 26 The task which I have taken on myself in making this summary is no easy one; it means hard work and late nights, 27 just as the man who prepares a banquet and aims to satisfy his guests has no light task. Yet I shall gladly undergo this labour to earn general gratitude 28 and, while concentrating on the main points of my outline, I shall leave to the original author the minute discussion of every particular. 29 While the architect of a new house must concern himself with the whole of the structure, the man who paints in encaustic on the walls needs to discover only what is necessary for the ornamentation; I reckon it is much the same

with me. 30 It is the province of the original author of a history to take possession of the field, to spread himself in discussion, and to busy himself with matters of detail; 31 on the other hand, whoever makes an abridgement must be allowed to aim at conciseness of expression and to renounce an exhaustive treatment of the subject matter.

32 Here then, without further comment, I begin my narrative, for it would be absurd to give a lengthy introduction to the history and cut short the history itself.

Syrian oppression of the Jews

3 DURING the rule of the high priest Onias, the Holy City enjoyed unbroken peace and prosperity, and there was exemplary observance of the laws, because he was pious and hated wickedness. 2 The kings themselves held the sanctuary in honour and embellished the temple with the most magnificent gifts; 3 King Seleucus of Asia even met the whole cost of the sacrificial worship from his own revenues.

4 But a certain Simon, of the clan Bilgah, who had been appointed administrator of the temple, quarrelled with the high priest about the regulation of the city market. 5 Unable to get the better of Onias, he went to Apollonius son of Thrasaeus, then governor of Coele-Syria and Phoenicia, 6 and alleged that the treasury at Jerusalem was so packed with untold riches that the total of the accumulated balances was beyond all reckoning; it bore no relation to the account for the sacrifices, and he suggested that these balances might be brought under the control of the king. 7 In the course of a meeting with the king, Apollonius reported what he had been

3:4 **Bilgah:** *so some witnesses; others read* Benjamin.

is otherwise unknown. *Cyrene* (now in Libya) was culturally one with Egypt. **21:** This is the first appearance of the term Judaism (here translated as *Jewish religion;* see also 8.1; 14.38; Gal. 1.14) to describe a way of life; it is contrasted to Hellenism (4.13).

3.1–4.50: The decline of the priesthood. After the defeat of Magnesia (190 B.C.E.) and the consequent loss of most of Asia Minor, the Seleucid kings needed money badly to pay the indemnities forced on them by the treaty of Apamea (188 B.C.E.). Seleucus saw a chance to rob the rich treasury of Jerusalem's temple. The priesthood moves from Onias (3.1), to the usurper Jason (4.7), and then to Menelaus (4.23).

3.1–4.6: The story of Heliodorus and its aftermath. 1: *Onias* III, son of Simon II (Ecclus. 50.1–21), was a descendant, through Jedaiah (Ezra 2.36), of Joshua, the high priest of the postexilic community (Hag. 1.1). **3:** *Seleucus* IV Philopator (187–175 B.C.E.) was king of *Asia,* i.e. of lands bordering the eastern Mediterranean. **4:** *Bilgah* is one of the twenty-four divisions for priestly service listed in 1 Chr. 24.1–19. **5:** *Apollonius* was told about the riches, whereupon the king chose Heliodorus, his chief minister, to be sent with orders to effect the removal of these treasures.

8 Heliodorus set off at once, ostensibly to make a tour of inspection of the cities of Coele-Syria and Phoenicia, but in fact to carry out the king's design. 9 When he arrived at Jerusalem and had been cordially received by the high priest and the citizens, he disclosed the purpose of his visit: he told them about the allegations and asked if they were true. 10 The high priest explained that the deposits were held in trust for widows and orphans, 11 apart from what belonged to Hyrcanus son of Tobias, a man of very high standing. The matter was being misrepresented by the godless Simon; the total sum was four hundred talents of silver and two hundred of gold. 12 It was unthinkable, he said, that injury should be done to those who had relied on the sanctity of the place, on the dignity and inviolability of a temple held in reverence the whole world over. 13 But, in virtue of the king's orders, Heliodorus insisted that these deposits must without question be confiscated for the royal treasury.

14 On the day appointed, when he entered the temple to draw up an inventory, there was great distress throughout the city. 15 The priests, prostrating themselves in their vestments before the altar, prayed to Heaven, whose law had made deposits sacred, to keep them intact for their rightful owners. 16 The high priest's looks pierced every beholder to the heart, for his face and changing colour betrayed the anguish of his spirit. 17 Alarm and shuddering gripped him, and the pain he felt was clearly apparent to the onlookers. 18 The people flocked from their houses and rushed to join in universal supplication because of the dishonour which threatened the holy place. 19 Women in sackcloth, their breasts bare, thronged the streets; unmarried girls who were kept in seclusion ran to the gates or the walls, while others leaned out from windows; 20 with outstretched hands all made solemn entreaty to Heaven. 21 It was pitiful to see the crowd lying prostrate in utter disarray and the high priest in an agony of apprehension.

22 While the people were imploring the Lord Almighty to keep the deposits intact and safe for those who had lodged them, 23 Heliodorus proceeded to put into effect what had been decided. 24 But just as he was arriving with his escort at the treasury, the Ruler of spirits and of all power sent a mighty apparition, so that everyone who had dared to accompany Heliodorus collapsed in terror, stricken with panic before the might of God. 25 There appeared to them a horse, splendidly caparisoned, with a rider of terrifying aspect who was clad all in golden armour; it rushed fiercely at Heliodorus and, rearing up, attacked him with its hooves. 26 There also appeared to Heliodorus two young men of surpassing strength and glorious beauty, magnificently attired. Taking their stand on either side of him, they flogged him, raining on him blow after blow. 27 Suddenly, overwhelmed by a great darkness, he fell to the ground, and his men quickly took him up and placed him on a stretcher. 28 This man, who so recently had entered the treasury accompanied by his whole bodyguard and an attendant crowd, was now borne off utterly helpless, publicly compelled to acknowledge the sovereignty of God.

29 While Heliodorus lay speechless, deprived by this divine act of all hope of recovery, 30 the Jews were praising the Lord for the miracle he had performed in his holy place; the temple, which only a short time before was the scene of alarm and confusion, now overflowed with joy and gladness at the manifestation of the Lord Almighty.

31 Some of Heliodorus's companions lost no time in begging Onias to pray to the Most High that the life of their master, now lying at his very last gasp, might be spared. 32 Fearing that the king might suspect that Heliodorus had met with foul play at the hands of the Jews, the high priest offered a sacrifice for the man's recovery. 33 As the expiation was being made, the same young men, dressed as before, again appeared to Heliodorus, and

---

son of Menestheus (4.4, 21). *Coele-Syria:* southern Syria including Judea. **7:** *Heliodorus,* chancellor to Seleucus, later murdered the king in an unsuccessful bid to assume the regency. **11:** The temple's treasure was today's equivalent of several million dollars. **12:** Onias pleads a form of "sanctuary" or *inviolability* for the money (see, similarly, 1 Macc. 10.43). **22–36:** Miraculous apparitions are a feature of "pathetic" history. Some suggest Onias saved the treasure by conspiring with Heliodorus against Seleucus (see 4.2). **26:** *Two young men:* angels.

standing over him said: 'You should be very grateful to Onias the high priest; it is for his sake the Lord has spared your life. ³⁴ You have been scourged by God; now proclaim his mighty power to all men.' With these words they vanished.

³⁵ Heliodorus offered a sacrifice and made lavish freewill-offerings to the Lord who had spared his life; then, taking leave of Onias, he returned with his troops to the king. ³⁶ To everyone he bore witness of the miracles of the supreme God which he had seen with his own eyes.

³⁷ When the king asked him what sort of man would be suitable to send to Jerusalem another time, Heliodorus replied: ³⁸ 'If you have an enemy or someone plotting against your government, that is the place to send him; you will receive him back soundly flogged, if he survives at all, for beyond doubt there is a divine power surrounding the place. ³⁹ He whose habitation is in heaven watches over it himself and gives it his aid; those who approach the place with evil intent he strikes down and destroys.'

⁴⁰ So runs the story of Heliodorus and the preservation of the treasury.

4 BUT Simon, the man mentioned above, who in the matter of the money had laid information against his country, went on to slander Onias by alleging that he it was who had incited Heliodorus and so been the author of these troubles. ² He had the effrontery to accuse of conspiracy against the government one who was a benefactor of the city, a protector of his fellow-Jews, and a staunch upholder of the law. ³ The feud reached such a pitch that one of Simon's trusted adherents even resorted to murder. ⁴ Realizing how dangerous this rivalry had become and that Apollonius son of Menestheus, governor of Coele-Syria and Phoenicia, was encouraging Simon in his evil ways, ⁵ Onias had recourse to the king. He did not appear as an accuser of his fellow-citizens but rather as one concerned for the interests of all the Jews, both as a nation and as individuals. ⁶ He saw that unless the king intervened

there could be no peace in public affairs, nor would Simon be stopped in his mad course.

⁷ When, on the death of Seleucus, Antiochus known as Epiphanes succeeded to the throne, Jason, Onias's brother, procured for himself the office of high priest by underhand means. ⁸ In a petition to the king he promised him three hundred and sixty talents in silver coin immediately, and eighty talents from future revenue; ⁹ further, he undertook to pay an additional hundred and fifty talents if authority were given him to set up a gymnasium for the physical education of young men, and to enrol in Jerusalem a group to be known as 'Antiochenes'. ¹⁰ The king gave his assent; and Jason, as soon as he had secured the high-priesthood, made his fellow-Jews conform to the Greek way of life.

¹¹ He set aside the royal privileges accorded the Jews through the agency of John, the father of that Eupolemus who at a later date negotiated a treaty of friendship and alliance with the Romans. He abolished the institutions founded on the law and introduced practices which ran counter to it. ¹² He lost no time in establishing a gymnasium at the foot of the citadel itself, and he made the most outstanding of the young men adopt the hat worn by Greek athletes. ¹³ So with the introduction of foreign customs Hellenism reached a high point through the inordinate wickedness of Jason, an apostate and no true high priest. ¹⁴ As a result, the priests no longer showed any enthusiasm for their duties at the altar; they treated the temple with disdain, they neglected the sacrifices, and whenever the opening gong called them they hurried to join in the sports at the wrestling school in defiance of the law. ¹⁵ They placed no value on dignities prized by their forefathers, but cared above everything for Hellenic honours. ¹⁶ This brought misfortune upon them from every side, and the very people whose way of life they admired and tried so hard to emulate turned out to be vindictive enemies. ¹⁷ To act profanely

4:9 **enrol ... 'Antiochenes':** *or* enrol the inhabitants of Jerusalem as citizens of Antioch.

4.7–22: Jason as high priest introduces Hellenism. Antiochus IV Epiphanes (175–164 B.C.E.) sought to unify his disparate subjects by imposing Hellenistic culture and religion on them. **7:** *Seleucus* was assassinated by Heliodorus. **9:** The *gymnasium* gave youth an *education* in cultural, physical, and premilitary affairs. The *Antiochenes,* honorary citizens of Antioch, the Seleucid capital, were a corporation of Hellenized Jews who had certain political and commercial privileges. **11:** See 1 Macc. 8.17. **12:** The athlete's hat was the traditional against God's laws is no light matter, as will in due course become clear. [18] When the quinquennial games were being held at Tyre in the presence of the king, [19] the villainous Jason sent, as envoys to represent Jerusalem, Antiochenes bearing three hundred drachmas in silver for the sacrifice to Hercules. Even the bearers considered it improper that this money should be used for a sacrifice, and thought it should be spent differently. [20] Thanks to them, the money intended by its sender for the sacrifice to Hercules went in fact to fit out triremes.

[21] From Apollonius son of Menestheus, who was sent to Egypt for the coronation of King Philometor, Antiochus learnt that Philometor was now hostile to his interests. Anxious for his own security, he removed to Joppa, and then to Jerusalem, [22] where he was lavishly welcomed by Jason and the city, and received with torchlight processions and ovations. Afterwards he quartered his army in Phoenicia.

[23] Three years later, Jason sent Menelaus, brother of the Simon mentioned above, to convey money to the king and to carry out agreed decisions on some urgent business. [24] But Menelaus, once in the king's presence, flattered him with an air of authority, and diverted the high-priesthood to himself, outbidding Jason by three hundred talents in silver. [25] He arrived back with the royal mandate, but with nothing else to make him worthy of the high-priesthood; he had the passions of a cruel tyrant and the temper of a savage beast. [26] Jason, who had supplanted his own brother, was now supplanted in his turn and forced to seek refuge in Ammonite territory. [27] Menelaus continued to hold the high-priesthood but without ever paying any of the money he had promised the king, however often it was demanded by Sostratus, the commander of the citadel, [28] who was responsible for collecting the revenues. In consequence both were summoned to appear before the king. [29] Menelaus left as his deputy

in the high-priesthood his brother Lysimachus, while Sostratus left Crates, the commander of the Cypriot mercenaries, to act for him.

[30] While those events were taking place the inhabitants of Tarsus and Mallus rose in revolt, because their cities had been handed over as a gift to Antiochis, the king's concubine. [31] The king went off hurriedly to restore order, leaving Andronicus, one of his ministers, as regent. [32] Thinking to seize a favourable opportunity, Menelaus made a present to Andronicus of some of the gold plate which he had appropriated from the temple. Some he had already sold to Tyre and neighbouring cities. [33] When Onias learnt of it on good authority, he withdrew to sanctuary at Daphne near Antioch and denounced him. [34] For this, Menelaus approached Andronicus privately and urged him to have Onias put to death. The regent came to Onias and, though bent on treachery, greeted him and with assurances on oath persuaded him to leave the sanctuary in spite of his suspicions. Then at once, with no respect for justice, he made away with him.

[35] This wicked murder caused indignation and resentment not only among Jews but among many from other nations as well. [36] When the king returned from Cilicia, the Jews of Antioch sent him a petition about the indefensible killing of Onias, a crime detested equally by the Gentiles. [37] Antiochus, deeply grieved, was moved to pity and tears as he thought of the high character and disciplined conduct of the dead man. [38] His anger flared up and without more ado he stripped Andronicus of the purple and tore off his clothes; then leading him right round the city to that very place where he had committed the sacrilegious crime against Onias, he dispatched the murderer, who was thus repaid by the Lord with richly deserved punishment.

[39] Lysimachus, with the connivance of Menelaus, entered on a career of sacrilege

wide-brimmed hat of Hermes, god of gymnastic skill. **19:** The Tyrian god Melqart was, in Hellenistic fashion, assimilated to Heracles, the Roman *Hercules*. **20:** *Triremes* were warships with three banks of oars. **21–22:** Ptolemy VI *Philometor* (180–145 B.C.E.) planned to regain Judea for Egypt; Epiphanes prepared for the invasion by stationing troops in *Joppa* and other Phoenician ports.

4.23–50: Menelaus as high priest. Corruption marks the reign of Menelaus, who succeeded in driving out his rivals. **23:** *Three years later:* 171 B.C.E. *Simon:* see 3.4 n. **26:** *Jason* fled east of the Jordan. **30:** *Tarsus and Mallus,* which lay in Cilicia (on the southeast coast of Turkey), objected for reasons of revenue, not morality. **33:** *Onias* took refuge in the temple of Apollo(!) at *Daphne,* five miles southwest of Antioch.

and plunder in Jerusalem. When this became widely known and the people heard that much of the gold plate had been disposed of, they combined against Lysimachus. 40 As the crowds, now aroused and furious, were getting out of hand, Lysimachus armed some three thousand men and launched a vicious attack, led by a certain Auranus, a man advanced in years and no less in folly. 41 Recognizing that Lysimachus was behind the attack, some of the crowd seized stones, others blocks of wood, others again handfuls of burning embers that were lying about, and they hurled them indiscriminately at Lysimachus and his men. 42 The result was that many were wounded, some were killed, and the rout was complete; the temple robber himself they put to death near the treasury.

43 A charge was laid against Menelaus in connection with this incident 44 and, on the king's arrival at Tyre, three men sent by the Jewish senate stated their case before him. 45 Menelaus's cause being as good as lost, he promised Ptolemaeus son of Dorymenes a substantial sum of money if he would win over the king. 46 Ptolemaeus led the king aside into a colonnade, as though to take the air, and persuaded him to change his mind. 47 Menelaus, the author of all the mischief, was acquitted and the charges brought against him were dismissed, but the king condemned to death the unfortunate accusers, men who would have been let go as entirely innocent had they appeared even before Scythians. 48 At once those who had pleaded for their city, their people, and their sacred vessels, suffered this undeserved penalty. 49 It caused even some of the Tyrians to show their detestation of the crime by providing a splendid funeral for the victims. 50 Yet thanks to the cupidity of those in power, Menelaus, this arch-plotter against his fellow-citizens, continued in office and went from bad to worse.

5 About that time Antiochus undertook his second expedition against Egypt. 2 For nearly forty days apparitions were seen in the sky all over Jerusalem: galloping horsemen in golden armour, companies of spearmen standing to arms, 3 swordsmen at the ready, and squadrons of cavalry in battle order. Charges and countercharges were made in this direction and that; shields were brandished, spears massed, javelins hurled; breastplates and golden ornaments of every kind blazed with light. 4 That the phenomenon might portend good was the prayer of everyone.

5 On a false report of Antiochus's death, Jason at the head of no less than a thousand men launched a surprise attack on Jerusalem. The defenders on the wall were driven back and, with the city on the point of being taken, Menelaus sought refuge in the citadel. 6 Jason embarked upon an unsparing massacre of his fellow-citizens, for he did not grasp that success against one's own kin is the greatest of failures; he imagined that the trophies he raised marked the defeat of enemies, not of fellow-countrymen. 7 However, he failed to secure control of the government; all he achieved as the result of his scheming was dishonour, and once again he sought asylum in Ammonite territory. 8 His career came to a miserable end, for after being imprisoned by Aretas the ruler of the Arabs he fled from city to city, hunted by all, hated as a renegade against the laws, detested as the butcher of his country and his fellow-citizens, until he landed up in Egypt. 9 Then, having crossed by sea to Sparta, where he hoped to obtain shelter because of the Spartans' kinship with the Jews, he, who had driven so many into exile, himself died an exile. 10 He who had cast out so many to lie unburied was himself unmourned; he had no obsequies of any kind, no resting-place in the ancestral grave.

11 It was clear to the king, when news of those happenings reached him, that Judaea was in a state of insurrection, and he set out from Egypt in savage mood. He took Jerusalem by storm, 12 ordering his troops to cut down unsparingly everyone they met, and to slaughter those who took refuge in the

---

45: *Ptolemaeus*, the governor of the region, later opposed the Maccabean resistance (8.8; 1 Macc. 3.38).

47: The *Scythians*, who lived just north of the Black Sea, were notorious for their cruelty.

5.1–14: Jason's attack upon Jerusalem and its aftermath. 1: 168 B.C.E. 2–4: The Jewish historian Josephus describes similar celestial portents preceding the destruction of the temple in 70 C.E. (*B.J.* VI.5.3). 8: The charge brought before *Aretas* (Harith I, king of the Nabataeans), Jason's former protector, is not known. 9: For this fictional relationship, see 1 Macc. 12.1–23, especially v. 10 n. 11: Forced out of Egypt by the Romans, Antiochus was already in a *savage mood*.

houses. [13] Young and old were murdered, women and children massacred, girls and infants butchered. [14] At the end of three days the victims numbered eighty thousand: forty thousand killed in the fighting, and as many again sold into slavery.

[15] Not satisfied with this, and guided by Menelaus, who had turned traitor to both religion and country, the king had the audacity to enter the most holy temple on earth. [16] The villain laid his polluted hands on the sacred vessels, and profanely swept up the votive offerings which other kings had made to enhance the splendour and fame of the shrine.

[17] The pride of Antiochus passed all bounds. He did not understand that the sins of the people of Jerusalem had for a short time angered the Lord, and that this was the reason why the temple was left to its fate. [18] Had they not been guilty of many sinful acts, Antiochus would have fared no better than Heliodorus, who was sent by King Seleucus to inspect the treasury; like him, he would have been flogged and his presumption foiled at once. [19] But the Lord did not choose the nation for the sake of the sanctuary; he chose the sanctuary for the sake of the nation. [20] That was why the sanctuary itself had its part in the misfortunes that befell the nation, and afterwards shared its good fortune; it was abandoned when the Almighty was roused to anger, but restored again in all its splendour when the great Master was reconciled with his people.

[21] So Antiochus hastened back to Antioch, taking with him eighteen hundred talents from the temple. Carried away by arrogance he thought that he could make ships sail on dry land and men walk over the sea! [22] He left behind commissioners to oppress the people: in Jerusalem he left Philip, by race a Phryg-

ian, by disposition more barbarous than the man who appointed him, [23] and in Mount Gerizim, Andronicus; and in addition to these there was Menelaus, who was more brutally overbearing to the citizens than the others. Further, such was the king's hostility towards the Jewish population [24] that he sent Apollonius, commander of the Mysian mercenaries, with an army of twenty-two thousand men; his orders were to slaughter all the adult males and to sell the women and children into slavery. [25] When Apollonius arrived at Jerusalem, he pretended he had come in peace; waiting until the holy sabbath day and finding the Jews abstaining from work, he paraded his troops under arms. [26] All who came out to witness the spectacle he put to the sword; then, charging into the city with his soldiers, he cut down an even greater number of the people.

[27] BUT Judas, also called Maccabaeus, escaped with about nine others into the desert, where he and his companions lived in the mountains, fending for themselves like the wild animals, and all the while feeding on what vegetation they found there, so as to have no share in the pollution.

6 Not long afterwards King Antiochus sent an elderly Athenian to compel the Jews to give up their ancestral customs and to cease regulating their lives by the laws of God. [2] He was commissioned also to pollute the temple at Jerusalem and dedicate it to Olympian Zeus; the sanctuary on Mount Gerizim he was to dedicate to Zeus God of Hospitality, as requested by the local inhabitants.

[3] This evil onslaught bore hard on the people and tried them grievously, [4] for the Gentiles filled the temple with licentious revelry: they took their pleasure with prostitutes and had intercourse with women in the sacred

5.15–23a: Antiochus robs the temple. This misplaced incident belongs after Antiochus' first Egyptian campaign in 169 B.C.E. (1 Macc. 1.20–24). **16:** *Other kings* included Seleucus IV (3.3). **21:** The amount seems excessive. **22:** *Philip* appears again in 6.11; 8.8. He is not the Philip of 9.29; 1 Macc. 6.14, 55–63. **23a:** *Andronicus* is not the murderer of 4.31–38.

5.23b–27: Apollonius attacks Jerusalem; Judas flees. Epiphanes punished the revolt led by Jason and fortified Jerusalem. See 1 Macc. 1.29–36. Later, Judas defeated and killed Apollonius (1 Macc. 3.10–12). **27:** The story of Mattathias is omitted (1 Macc. ch. 2; especially v. 28).

6.1–17: The imposition of Hellenism. The author describes the religious persecution. See 1 Macc. 1.41–64. **2:** The Syrian deity, *ba'al šāmēm*, "Lord of Heaven," was identified with the supreme Greek divinity, *Zeus*. Erection of an altar to him on the temple's altar of holocausts constituted the "abomination" of 1 Macc. 1.54; Dan. 11.31. Josephus says the rival Samaritan temple *on Mount Gerizim* was dedicated to Zeus Hellenios (*Ant.*

precincts. Moreover, they introduced things which the law forbade, 5 and heaped the altar with offerings prohibited as impure. 6 No one was allowed to observe the sabbath or to keep the traditional festivals or even to admit to being a Jew at all. 7 Each month during the celebration of the king's birthday, the Jews were forcibly compelled to eat the entrails of sacrificial victims, and on the feast of Dionysus to wear ivy-wreaths and join the procession in his honour. 8 At the instigation of the inhabitants of Ptolemais a royal decree was published in the neighbouring Greek cities to the effect that they should adopt the same policy of compelling the Jews to eat the entrails, 9 and that they should put to death everyone who refused to conform to Greek ways.

The miserable fate of the Jews was there for all to see. 10 For instance, two women who had had their children circumcised were brought to trial; then, with their babies hanging at their breasts, they were paraded through the city and hurled headlong from the ramparts. 11 Other Jews, who had assembled secretly in nearby caves to observe the sabbath, were denounced to Philip and, since out of regard for the sanctity of the day they had scruples about defending themselves, they were burnt alive.

12 Now I beg my readers not to be disheartened by those tragic events, but to reflect that such penalties were inflicted for the discipline, not the destruction, of our race. 13 It is a sign of great benevolence that acts of impiety should not be overlooked for long but rather should meet their due recompense at once. 14 The Lord has not seen fit to deal with us as he does with other nations: with them he patiently holds his hand until they have reached the full extent of their sins, 15 but on us he inflicts retribution before our sins reach their limit. 16 So he never withdraws his mercy from us; although he may discipline his people by disaster, he does not desert them. 17 So much by way of reminder; I must now continue with my summary of events.

18 Eleazar, one of the leading teachers of the law, a man of great age and distinguished bearing, was being forced to open his mouth and eat pork; 19 but preferring death with honour to life with impiety, he spat it out and voluntarily submitted to the torture. 20 So should men act who have the courage to reject food which despite a natural desire to save their lives it is not lawful to eat. 21 Because of their long acquaintance with him, the officials in charge of this sacrilegious meal had a word with Eleazar in private; they urged him to bring meat which he was permitted to eat and had himself prepared; he need only pretend to comply with the king's order to eat the sacrificial meat. 22 In that way he would escape death by taking advantage of the clemency which their long-standing friendship merited. 23 But Eleazar made an honourable decision, one worthy of his years and the authority of old age, worthy of the grey hairs he had attained to and wore with such distinction, worthy of his faultless conduct from childhood, but above all worthy of the holy and God-given law; he replied at once: 'Send me to my grave! 24 If I went through with this pretence at my time of life, many of the young might believe that at the age of ninety Eleazar had turned apostate. 25 If I practised deceit for the sake of a brief moment of life, I should lead them astray and stain my old age with dishonour. 26 I might for the present avoid man's punishment, but alive or dead I should never escape the hand of the Almighty. 27 If I now die bravely, I shall show that I have deserved my long life 28 and leave to the young a noble example; I shall be teaching them how to die a good death, gladly and nobly, for our revered and holy laws.'

With these words he went straight to the torture, 29 while those who a short time before had shown him friendship now turned hostile because, to them, what he had said was madness. 30 When Eleazar was on the point of death from the blows he had received, he groaned aloud and said: 'To the Lord belongs all holy knowledge; he knows what terrible agony I endure in my body from this flogging, though I could have escaped death; yet he knows also that in my

6:8 At . . . Ptolemais: *some witnesses read* At the instigation of Ptolemaeus.

XIII.5.5). **5:** The *impure* offerings included swine; see v. 18; 7.1; Lev. 11.7; 1 Macc. 1.47. **7:** *Dionysus:* god of revelry, identified with Roman Bacchus; *ivy* was his symbol. **11:** See 1 Macc. 2.29–41.

6.18–7.42: Examples of martyrdom. Old men, women, and children willingly die for the *law.* The stories are typical "Acts of Martyrs," a literary form to encourage others under persecution. **26:** This verse hints at the

soul I suffer gladly, because I stand in awe of
him.'

³¹So he died; and by his death he left a
noble example and a memorial of virtue, not
only to the young but also to the great mass
of his countrymen.

7 Another incident concerned the arrest
of seven brothers along with their
mother. They were being tortured by the
king with whips and thongs to force them to
eat pork, contrary to the law. ²But one of
them, speaking for all, said: 'What do you
expect to learn by interrogating us? Rather
than break our ancestral laws we are prepared to die.' ³In fury the king ordered great
pans and cauldrons to be heated. ⁴This was
attended to without delay; meanwhile he
gave orders that the spokesman's tongue
should be cut out and that he should be
scalped and mutilated before the eyes of his
mother and six brothers. ⁵A wreck of a man,
but still breathing, he was taken at the king's
direction to the fire and roasted in one of the
pans. As the smoke from it streamed out, the
mother and her sons encouraged each other
to die nobly. ⁶'The Lord God is looking on,'
they said, 'and we may be sure he has compassion on us. Did not Moses say to Israel in
the song plainly denouncing apostasy, "He
will have compassion on his servants"?'

⁷After the first brother had died in this
way, the second was subjected to the same
indignities. The skin and hair of his head
were torn off, and he was asked: 'Will you
eat, or must we tear you limb from limb?'
⁸'Eat? Never!' he replied in his native language, and so he in turn underwent torture
like the first. ⁹With his final breath he said:
'Fiend though you are, you are setting us free
from this present life, and the King of the
universe will raise us up to a life everlastingly
made new, since it is for his laws that we are
dying.'

¹⁰After him the third was tortured. When
the question was put to him, he at once
showed his tongue, courageously held out his
hands, ¹¹and spoke nobly: 'The God of
heaven gave these to me, but his laws mean
far more to me than they do, and it is from
him that I trust to receive them again.' ¹²Both

the king himself and those with him were
astounded at the young man's spirit and his
utter disregard for suffering.

¹³When he too was dead, they tortured the
fourth in the same cruel manner. ¹⁴At the
point of death, he uttered these words: 'Better to be killed by men and to cherish God's
promise to raise us again! But for you there
will be no resurrection.'

¹⁵Next the fifth was dragged forward for
torture. ¹⁶Looking at the king, he said: 'Mortal as you are, you have authority among human beings and can do as you please. But do
not imagine that God has abandoned our
nation. ¹⁷Wait, and you will see how his
mighty power will torment you and your descendants!'

¹⁸After him the sixth was brought and he,
with his dying breath, said: 'Do not delude
yourself: it is through our own fault that we
suffer these things; we have sinned against
our God and brought these appalling events
on ourselves. ¹⁹But do not suppose you yourself will escape the consequences of trying to
contend with God.'

²⁰The mother was the most remarkable of
all, and she deserves to be remembered with
special honour. She watched her seven sons
perish within the space of a single day, yet she
bore it bravely, for she trusted in the Lord.
²¹She encouraged each in turn in her native
language; filled with noble resolution, her
woman's thoughts fired by a manly spirit, she
said to them: ²²'You appeared in my womb,
I know not how; it was not I who gave you life
and breath, not I who set in order the elements of your being. ²³The Creator of the
universe, who designed the beginning of
mankind and devised the origin of all, will in
his mercy give you back again breath and life,
since now you put his laws above every
thought of self.'

²⁴Antiochus felt that he was being treated
with contempt and suspected an insult in her
words. As the youngest brother was still left,
the king, not content with appealing to him,
even assured him on oath that once he abandoned his ancestral customs he would make
him rich and enviable by enrolling him as a
king's Friend and entrusting him with high

sinner's punishment after death, an advance on earlier ideas (see also Dan. 12.2). **7.1:** In this contrived story,
the chief persecutor, *king* Antiochus, appears himself. **6:** See Deut. 32.36. **8:** The martyrs refuse to speak Greek
(vv. 21, 27; 12.37; 15.29). **9–14:** The resurrection of the just appears throughout this story (see Dan. 12.1–3);
universal resurrection is not explicitly taught. **17:** The *descendants* are the king's successors. **24:** *Friend:* see

office. 25 Since the youth paid no regard whatsoever, the king summoned the mother and urged her to advise her boy to save his life. 26 After much urging from the king, she agreed to persuade her son. 27 She leant towards him and, flouting the cruel tyrant, said in their native language: 'Son, take pity on me, who carried you nine months in the womb, nursed you for three years, reared you and brought you up to your present age. 28 I implore you, my child, to look at the heavens and the earth; consider all that is in them, and realize that God did not create them from what already existed and that a human being comes into existence in the same way. 29 Do not be afraid of this butcher; accept death willingly and prove yourself worthy of your brothers, so that by God's mercy I may receive back both you and them together.'

30 She had barely finished when the young man spoke out: 'What are you all waiting for? I will not submit to the king's command; I obey the command of the law given through Moses to our forefathers. 31 And you, King Antiochus, who have devised all manner of atrocities for the Hebrews, you will not escape God's hand. 32 It is for our own sins that we are suffering, 33 and, though to correct and discipline us our living Lord is angry for a brief time, yet he will be reconciled with his servants. 34 But you, impious creature, most villainous of the human race, do not let vain hopes buoy you up or empty delusions carry you away when you lay hands on Heaven's servants. 35 You are not yet safe from the judgement of the omnipotent, all-seeing God. 36 My brothers, after a short period of pain, have under God's covenant drunk of the waters of everlasting life; but you by God's verdict will pay the just penalty of your brutal insolence. 37 I, like my brothers, surrender my body and my life for our ancestral laws. I appeal to God to show favour speedily to his people and by whips and scourges to bring you to admit that he alone is God. 38 May the Almighty's anger, which has justly

fallen on all our race, end with me and my brothers!'

39 Roused by this defiance, the king in his fury used him worse than the others, 40 and the young man, putting his whole trust in the Lord, died without having incurred defilement.

41 Last of all, after her sons, the mother died.

42 This then must conclude our account of the eating of the entrails and the monstrous tortures.

Judas Maccabaeus revolts

8 MEANWHILE Judas, who was called Maccabaeus, and his companions were making their way into the villages unobserved, summoning their kinsmen to their side and recruiting others who had remained faithful to the Jewish religion, until they had collected up to six thousand men. 2 They appealed to the Lord to look with compassion on his people whom all were trampling underfoot, to take pity on the temple now profaned by apostates, 3 and to have mercy on Jerusalem, which was being destroyed and would soon be levelled to the ground. They prayed him also to give ear to the blood that cried to him for vengeance, 4 to keep in mind the infamous massacre of innocent children and the blasphemous deeds against his name, and to show his hatred of wickedness.

5 Once his band of partisans was organized, the Gentiles found Maccabaeus invincible, now that the Lord's anger had changed to mercy. 6 Maccabaeus came on towns and villages without warning and burnt them down; he recaptured strategic positions, and inflicted many reverses on the enemy, 7 choosing the night-time as being especially favourable for these attacks. Everywhere there was talk of his heroism.

8 When Philip realized that the gains made by Judas, though small, were occurring with

7:36 **drunk:** *prob. rdg; Gk* fallen.

---

1 Macc. 2.18 n. **28:** This is the first biblical mention of creation from nothingness; see Gen. 1.1 n. **33:** See 5.17. **38:** See vicarious suffering also in Isa. 52.13–53.12.

   8.1–10.8: Judas Maccabaeus succeeds in purifying the temple. The Lord's anger (6.12–17) is appeased and turns to mercy (8.5), enabling Judas and his guerrillas to rededicate the temple.

   8.1–36: Judas' initial successes. See 1 Macc. 2.42–48. **2–3:** The guerrillas pray, then fight. Second Maccabees emphasizes the role of prayer in the victories. For similar descriptions of the evils faced, see 1 Macc. 1.24–28, 36–40; 2.7–12; 3.45, 50–53. **8–29, 34–36:** See 1 Macc. 3.38–4.27. **8:** *Philip:* see 5.22; 6.11. *Ptolemaeus:* see 4.45; 1 Macc. 3.38. In Hellenistic times, *Coele-Syria* designated first the Seleucid province increasing frequency, he wrote to Ptolemaeus, the governor of Coele-Syria and Phoenicia, asking for help in protecting the royal interests. [9] Ptolemaeus at once appointed Nicanor son of Patroclus, a member of the highest order of king's Friends, and sent him at the head of no fewer than twenty thousand troops of various nationalities to exterminate the whole population of Judaea; with him Ptolemaeus associated Gorgias, a general of wide military experience. [10] Nicanor purposed, by the sale of the Jews he would take prisoner, to pay off the two thousand talents due from the king as tribute to the Romans; [11] and he immediately made an offer of Jewish slaves to the coastal towns, undertaking to deliver them at the rate of ninety to the talent. But he had not reckoned with the punishment soon to overtake him from the Almighty.

[12] When word of Nicanor's advance reached Judas, and his men were informed that the enemy was at hand, [13] the fainthearted who doubted God's justice deserted and fled. [14] But the rest, disposing of their remaining possessions, joined in prayer to the Lord for deliverance from the godless Nicanor, who had put them up for sale even before any fighting took place; [15] and, if they could not ask this for their own merits, they did so on the ground of the covenants God had made with their forefathers, and because they bore his holy and majestic name.

[16] Maccabaeus assembled his followers, six thousand in number, and urged them not to give way to panic in the face of the enemy nor to be afraid of the great horde of Gentiles coming against them without just cause. They should fight nobly, [17] keeping before their eyes the outrages committed by the Gentiles against the holy temple, the callous indignities inflicted on Jerusalem, and, moreover, the suppression of the traditional Jewish institutions. [18] 'They rely on weapons and deeds of daring,' he said, 'but we put our trust in Almighty God, who is able with a nod to overthrow our present assailants and, if need be, the whole world.' [19] He went on to

recount to them the occasions when God had come to the help of their ancestors: how, in Sennacherib's time, one hundred and eighty-five thousand of the enemy were destroyed, [20] and how, on the occasion of the battle in Babylonia against the Galatians, all the Jews engaged in the combat had numbered no more than eight thousand, with four thousand Macedonians, yet, when the Macedonians were hard pressed, the eight thousand through Heaven's aid had destroyed one hundred and twenty thousand and taken much spoil.

[21] His words put heart into his men and made them ready to die for their laws and their country. He divided the army into four, [22] putting each of his brothers, Simon, Josephus, and Jonathan, in command of a division of fifteen hundred men. [23] Besides this, Judas appointed Eleazar to read aloud from the holy book; then, giving the signal for battle with the cry 'God is our help' and taking command of the leading detachment, he joined battle with Nicanor. [24] With the Almighty fighting on their side they slaughtered over nine thousand of the enemy, wounded and disabled the greater part of Nicanor's forces, and routed them completely. [25] They also seized the money of those who had come to buy them as slaves. After chasing the enemy a considerable way, they were forced to break off because of the lateness of the hour; [26] it was the day before the sabbath, and for that reason they did not continue the pursuit. [27] They collected the enemy's weapons and stripped the dead, then turned to keep the sabbath, offering thanks and praises loud and long to the Lord who had kept the first drops of his mercy to shed on them that day. [28] When the sabbath was over, they distributed some of the spoils among the victims of persecution and among the widows and orphans; the remainder they divided among themselves and their children. [29] This done, all together made suppli-

8:23 **Besides . . . book:** *prob. rdg; Gk obscure.*
8:27 **kept . . . day:** *so some witnesses; others read* brought them safely to that day and had appointed it as the beginning of mercy for them.

in the valley between the Lebanon and Anti-Lebanon mountains. **9:** Victory for *Nicanor* (vv. 14–15; 1 Macc. 3.38; 7.26–50), one of the *king's Friends* (see 1 Macc. 2.18 n.), would *exterminate the whole population of Judea* by destroying defenders of its distinctiveness and assimilating the survivors to Hellenism. **10:** The *tribute* may be arrears from the money owed by the treaty of Apamea (188 B.C.E.). **11:** Nicanor's offer was half the average price per slave in Greece. **13:** First Maccabees 3.56 gives the reasons of Deut. 20.5–8 for their departure. **14:** *Disposing of their . . . possessions* lest Nicanor confiscate them anyway. **19:** *Sennacherib's time:*

cation to the merciful Lord, praying him to be fully reconciled with his servants.

³⁰ The Jews now engaged the forces of Timotheus and Bacchides, killed over twenty thousand of them, and gained firm control of some of the high strongholds. They divided the immense booty, allocating to the victims of persecution, to the orphans and widows, as well as to the old, shares equal to their own. ³¹ All the enemy's weapons were carefully collected and stored at strategic points; the remainder of the spoils they brought into Jerusalem. ³² The officer commanding the bodyguard of Timotheus was put to death; he was an utterly godless man who had caused the Jews great suffering. ³³ During the victory celebrations in their ancestral capital, they burnt alive the men who had set fire to the sacred gates, including Callisthenes, who had taken refuge in some small house; so he received the due reward of his impiety.

³⁴ Thus Nicanor, that double-dyed villain who had brought along the thousand traders to buy the Jewish captives, ³⁵ was with the Lord's help humiliated by the very people whom he had dismissed as of no consequence. He threw off his magnificent garment, and all alone made his escape across country like a runaway slave; he was, indeed, exceedingly fortunate to reach Antioch after the destruction of his army. ³⁶ He who had undertaken to secure tribute for the Romans by taking prisoner the inhabitants of Jerusalem now proclaimed to the world that the Jews had a champion and were invulnerable, because they kept the laws this champion had given them.

9 It so happened that about this time Antiochus had returned in disorder from Persia. ² He had entered the city called Persepolis and attempted to plunder its temples and gain control of the place. But the populace rose and resorted to arms, with the result that Antiochus was defeated by the inhabitants and forced into a humiliating withdrawal. ³ When he was near Ecbatana, a report reached him of what had befallen Nicanor and the forces of Timotheus, ⁴ and this so roused his anger that he proposed to make the Jews suffer for the injury inflicted by those who had routed him; to this end he ordered his charioteer not to stop until he reached his destination.

But riding with him was the divine judgement! In his arrogance he said: 'Once I reach Jerusalem, I will make it one big Jewish graveyard.' ⁵ But the all-seeing Lord, the God of Israel, dealt him a fatal, invisible blow. No sooner had he uttered the words than he was seized with incurable pains in his bowels and acute internal suffering — ⁶ a punishment entirely fitting for one who had inflicted many unheard-of torments on the bowels of others. ⁷ Still he did not in the least abate his insolence; more arrogant than ever and breathing fiery threats against the Jews, he gave orders for more speed on his journey. But as the chariot hurtled along he fell from it, and so violent was his fall that he suffered agony in every limb. ⁸ He, who in his pretension to be superhuman had been thinking that he could command the waves of the sea and weigh high mountains on the scales, was brought to the ground and had to be carried on a stretcher. The power of God was thus made manifest to all. ⁹ Worms swarmed from the body of this godless man and, while he was still alive and in agony, his flesh rotted off, and the whole army was overwhelmed by the stench of decay. ¹⁰ It was so unbearably offensive that no one was able to convey the man who only a short time before had seemed to reach to the stars in the heavens.

¹¹ In this broken state, Antiochus began to moderate his monstrous arrogance; scourged by God and racked with incessant pain, he was coming to see things in their true light. ¹² He was unable to endure his own stench and cried, 'It is right for mortals to submit to God and not claim equality with him.' ¹³ Though the Lord would spare him no longer, the villain made him a solemn promise: he vowed ¹⁴ that the Holy City,

---

see 2 Kgs. 19.35. **20:** This incident is otherwise unknown. **30–33:** See 1 Macc. 5.6–13, 24–54. **30:** For *Timotheus* see 1 Macc. 5.6–8, 37–44; 2 Macc. 12.10–25, and for *Bacchides,* see 1 Macc. 7.8–20. **33:** *Callisthenes* is otherwise unknown. The fire may be that of 1 Macc. 1.31. **36:** *Champion:* God.

9.1–29: The death of the persecutor. The false god Epiphanes, "(Zeus) manifest," falls by the manifest power of the true God. See 1 Macc. 6.1–17. **8:** See v. 12; 5.21. **9–17:** Theology, rather than history, seems to be the object of the description of the king's last illness. The allusions are to Isa. 14.11; 66.24; Ecclus. 7.17; 19.3. For similar descriptions of the deaths of the impious, see Josephus on Herod the Great (*Ant.* XVII.6.5) and Acts which he had been hurrying to level to the ground and transform into a graveyard, he would publicly declare to be free; 15 to all the Jews, a people he had considered not worthy of burial but fit only to be thrown out with their children as carrion for birds and beasts, he would now give privileges equal to those enjoyed by the citizens of Athens; 16 the holy temple, which he had earlier plundered, he would adorn with the most magnificent gifts, and would replace all the sacred vessels on a much more lavish scale, and he would meet the cost of the sacrifices from his own revenues. 17 In addition, he would even turn Jew and visit every inhabited place to proclaim God's might.

18 When his pain in no way abated, because the just judgement of God had befallen him, he was in despair and wrote to the Jews the following letter, as a kind of olive branch:

19 From Antiochus, King and Chief Magistrate, to my worthy citizens, the Jews.

Warm greetings and good wishes for your health and prosperity.

20 May you and your children flourish and your affairs progress as you wish. As I have my hope in Heaven, 21 I keep an affectionate remembrance of your respect and goodwill.

On my way back from Persia, I suffered a troublesome illness, and so I have judged it necessary to provide for the general security of all. 22 Not that I despair of my condition—on the contrary I have good hopes of recovery—23 but I observed that my father, whenever he undertook a campaign east of the Euphrates, nominated a successor, 24 so that, if anything unforeseen should happen or if some untoward report should spread, his subjects would not be disturbed, since they would know to whom the government had been entrusted. 25 Further, I am well aware that the neighbouring princes, those on the frontiers of my kingdom, are waiting on events and watching for their opportunity. I have

therefore designated as king my son Antiochus, whom I frequently placed in your care and commended to most of you during my regular visits to the satrapies beyond the Euphrates. I have written to him and enclose a copy. 26 Wherefore most earnestly I urge each one of you to maintain your existing goodwill towards me and my son, remembering the services I have rendered to you, both as a community and as individuals. 27 I am confident my son will follow my policy of moderation and benevolence and will accommodate himself to your wishes.

28 So this murderer and blasphemer, suffering the greatest agony, such as he had made others suffer, met a pitiable end in the mountains of a foreign land. 29 His close friend Philip brought the body back, but being afraid of Antiochus's son he went over to Ptolemy Philometor in Egypt.

The temple rededicated

10 UNDER the Lord's guidance, Maccabaeus and his followers recovered the temple and city of Jerusalem, 2 and demolished the altars erected by the heathen in the public square, together with their sacred precincts. 3 When they had purified the sanctuary, they made another altar, and striking fire with flints they offered sacrifice for the first time in two whole years; they restored the incense, the lamps, and the Bread of the Presence. 4 This done, they prostrated themselves and prayed to the Lord that he would never again allow them to fall into such disasters but, were they ever to sin, would discipline them himself with clemency rather than hand them over to blasphemous and barbarous Gentiles. 5 The sanctuary was purified on the twenty-fifth of Kislev, the same day of the same month as that on which foreigners had profaned it. 6 The joyful celebration lasted for eight days, like the feast of Tabernacles, and they recalled how, only a

12.23 on Herod Agrippa. **18–27:** The letter is sent to Hellenized Jews or Antiochenes. Jews faithful to the Law would not remember Antiochus' *services* (v. 26) kindly. **23:** Antiochus III had appointed Seleucus IV to succeed him. **29:** *Philip:* see 1 Macc. 6.14–15.

10.1–8: Judas purifies the temple. See 1 Macc. 4.36–61. **2:** See 1 Macc. 1.47. **3:** The interval of *two whole years* is three in 1 Macc. 1.54; 4.52. For the *incense, lamps,* and *Bread,* see Exod. 30.7–8; 25.30. **5:** December 17, 164 B.C.E. **6:** Unable to celebrate the *feast of Tabernacles* properly while on the run (5.27; 6.6), Judas and his men now celebrate the temple's purification and rededication as a feast of Tabernacles in Kislev (1.9 n.).

short time before, they had kept that feast while living like wild animals in the mountains and caves. ⁷So carrying garlanded wands and flowering branches, as well as palm-fronds, they chanted hymns to the One who had so triumphantly achieved the purification of his own temple. ⁸A decree was passed by the public assembly that every year the entire Jewish nation should keep these days holy.

⁹We have already given an account of the end of Antiochus called Epiphanes. ¹⁰Now we shall describe what transpired under that godless man's son, Antiochus Eupator, in a brief summary of the evils brought about by his wars. ¹¹At his accession, Eupator appointed as vicegerent a man called Lysias who had succeeded Ptolemaeus Macron as governor-general of Coele-Syria and Phoenicia. ¹²Because of the injustice formerly done to the Jews, Ptolemaeus had taken the lead in treating them with justice and endeavoured to maintain amicable relations with them. ¹³For this he was denounced to Eupator by the king's Friends; on every side he heard himself called traitor, because he had previously abandoned Cyprus, which had been entrusted to him by Philometor, and had gone over to Antiochus Epiphanes. He still enjoyed power, but no longer respect, and he ended his life by taking poison.

¹⁴When Gorgias became governor of the region, he hired mercenaries and seized every opportunity of attacking the Jews. ¹⁵At the same time the Idumaeans, who controlled strategic strongholds, were also harassing them; they harboured fugitives from Jerusalem and made every effort to foment hostilities. ¹⁶But Maccabaeus and his men, after public prayers entreating God to fight on their side, launched an assault on the Idumaean strongholds. ¹⁷They pressed the attack vigorously and captured them, driving off those who manned the walls and cutting down everyone they encountered. No less than twenty thousand of the enemy were killed.

¹⁸But nine thousand or more took refuge in two exceedingly strong forts, which were fully equipped to withstand a siege. ¹⁹Maccabaeus left Simon and Josephus behind with Zacchaeus and his troops in sufficient strength to besiege them, while he himself set out for areas which were being hard pressed. ²⁰But Simon's men were avaricious, and when they were offered seventy thousand drachmas by some of those in the forts, they accepted the bribe and let them slip through their lines. ²¹On being informed of this, Maccabaeus denounced the men before the assembled leaders of the army for having sold their brothers for money by letting their enemies escape to fight again, ²²and he had them executed as traitors. He promptly reduced the two forts, ²³and his military operations were crowned with complete success. In the two strongholds he destroyed over twenty thousand of the enemy.

²⁴Timotheus, who had earlier suffered defeat at the hands of the Jews, now mustered a huge army of mercenaries and no small force of Asian cavalry, and marched on Judaea to take it by storm. ²⁵At his approach, Maccabaeus and his men made their prayer to God; they sprinkled dust on their heads and put sackcloth round their waists, ²⁶prostrated themselves on the altar-step and entreated God to show them favour—in the words of the law: 'to be an enemy of their enemies and an opponent of their opponents'.

7: *Palm-fronds:* symbols of independence found on Jewish coins of the period and later; see 1 Macc. 13.51. 8: This explains the letters of 1.1–10a; 1.10b–2.18.

10.9–13.26: The defeat of Lysias and others. Since Antiochus V Eupator was only about seven years old when his father died, the main actors are Lysias and various generals.

10.9–12.1: Battles with Seleucid generals. The events leading up to the treaty with Lysias are described. **11:** Although *Lysias* was regent and guardian of Antiochus V Eupator (164–161 B.C.E.), he had to struggle with Philip to maintain this post (1 Macc. 3.33; 6.14, 55–63). **12–13:** *Ptolemaeus* had governed *Cyprus* for the Egyptian king Ptolemy VI *Philometor* (180–145 B.C.E.), but deserted to *Epiphanes* when that Seleucid king's fleet approached Cyprus. **14–23:** See 1 Macc. 5.3–5. **14:** *Gorgias* was *governor* of Idumea (12.32). **17:** The *twenty thousand* here, "nine thousand" in v. 18, and "seventy thousand" in v. 20 all seem excessive. The author tends to inflate numbers. **22:** Once the evil is removed, God, who fights along with Judas (v. 16), *promptly* allows success. The author never loses sight of the source of victory. **24–38:** This incident, unparalleled in

27 After this prayer, they took up their weapons and, advancing a considerable distance from Jerusalem, halted near the enemy. 28 At first light the two armies came to grips. For the Jews success and victory were assured, not only because of their courage but still more because they had recourse to the Lord, whereas the other side had only their own fury to lead them into battle. 29 As the fighting grew fierce, there appeared to the enemy five magnificent figures in the sky, each riding a horse with a golden bridle. Placing themselves at the head of the Jews, 30 they formed a circle round Maccabaeus and kept him unharmed under the protection of their armour, while they launched arrows and thunderbolts at the enemy, who, confused and blinded, broke in complete disarray. 31 Twenty thousand five hundred of the infantry as well as six hundred cavalry were slain.

32 Timotheus himself fled to Gazara, a stoutly garrisoned stronghold under the command of Chaereas. 33 This outcome suited Maccabaeus and his men, and for four days they laid siege to the place. 34 The defenders, confident in the strength of their position, hurled horrible and wicked blasphemies at them 35 until, at dawn on the fifth day, twenty young men from the Maccabaean force, burning with rage at the blasphemy, bravely stormed the wall and in savage fury cut down all they encountered. 36 Under cover of this distraction others got up the same way and attacked the defenders, setting alight the towers and kindling fires on which they burnt the blasphemers alive. Others broke down the gates and let in the rest of the army, and thus the city was occupied. 37 Timotheus, who had hidden in a cistern, was killed along with his brother Chaereas and Apollophanes. 38 In celebration of their achievement, the Jews praised with hymns and thanksgivings the Lord who showers benefits on Israel and gives them the victory.

11 Very shortly afterwards, in anger at what had happened, the vicegerent Lysias, the king's guardian and Kinsman, 2 mustered about eighty thousand foot-soldiers, in addition to all his cavalry, and marched against the Jews. He planned to make Jerusalem a settlement for Gentiles, 3 with the temple subject to taxation like all gentile shrines and the high-priesthood up for auction each year. 4 Reckoning not at all with the might of God, he was carried away by the thought of his tens of thousands of infantry, his thousands of cavalry, his eighty elephants. 5 He invaded Judaea, and advancing on Bethsura, a fortified place about twenty miles distant from Jerusalem, he closely invested it.

6 When Maccabaeus and his men were informed that Lysias was besieging their strongholds, they and all the people, wailing and weeping, prayed the Lord to send a good angel to deliver Israel. 7 Maccabaeus himself was the first to take up arms, and he urged the others to share the danger with him and go to the rescue of their fellow-Jews. Readily they all set out together. 8 While they were still in the neighbourhood of Jerusalem, there appeared at their head a horseman arrayed in white and brandishing golden weapons. 9 With one voice they praised their merciful God and felt so strong in spirit that they could have attacked not only men but also the most savage animals, or even walls of iron. 10 Under the Lord's mercy and with their heavenly ally they came on in battle array. 11 Like lions they hurled themselves on the enemy, laid low eleven thousand foot-soldiers, as well as sixteen hundred cavalry, and put the remainder to flight. 12 Most of those who escaped had lost their weapons and were wounded, and Lysias himself saved his life, if not his honour, by ignominiously taking to his heels.

13 Yet Lysias was no fool, and as he took stock of the defeat he had suffered he realized that the Hebrews were invincible, because God in his power fought on their side. So he sent emissaries 14 to persuade the Jews to make a settlement on terms that were entirely acceptable, promising also to make the king well disposed towards them. 15 Out of regard for the general welfare, Maccabaeus agreed to all the proposals of Lysias, for the king had accepted whatever written terms Maccabaeus had forwarded to Lysias from the Jewish side.

1 Macc., belongs chronologically after 12.10–31; 1 Macc. 5.9–13, 24–54. **26:** See Exod. 23.22. **29–31:** Fighting for the Law, Judas gets help from heaven, i.e. he receives supernatural protection and truly miraculous military assistance. **11.1–15:** See 1 Macc. 4.28–35. This event preceded the death of Antiochus IV Epiphanes. **11:** First Maccabees 4.34 gives much lower numbers. **13:** The reason is the author's, not that of Lysias.

16 Lysias's letter to the Jews ran as follows:

From Lysias to the Jewish community.
Greeting.
17 Your representatives John and Absalom have laid before me the document a copy of which is attached, and have asked me to give my views on its contents. 18 Whatever required to be brought to the king's attention I have communicated to him, and what was within my own competence I have granted. 19 Provided, therefore, you maintain your goodwill towards the government, I for my part shall endeavour to promote your wellbeing for the future. 20 I have charged your representatives and mine to confer with you about the details. 21 Farewell.

The twenty-fourth day of Dioscorus in the year 148.

22 The king's letter was as follows:

From King Antiochus to his brother Lysias.
Greeting.
23 Now that our royal father has joined the company of the gods, we desire that our subjects shall be left undisturbed in the conduct of their own affairs. 24 It has been brought to our notice that the Jews are not prepared to accept our father's policy and adopt Greek ways; they prefer their own mode of life and request that they be allowed to observe their own laws. 25 It is our pleasure, therefore, that this nation like others shall continue undisturbed. We hereby decree that their temple be restored to them and that they be allowed to regulate their lives in accordance with their ancestral customs. 26 Have the goodness, therefore, to inform them of this and to ratify it, so that, apprised of our policy,

they may be reassured and manage their affairs to their own satisfaction.

27 The king's letter to the people ran thus:

From King Antiochus to the Senate of the Jews and to the Jewish people.
Greeting.
28 We trust that all is well with you; we ourselves prosper. 29 Menelaus has made plain to us that it is your wish to return to your homes. 30 We therefore declare an amnesty for all who return before the thirtieth day of Xanthicus. 31 The Jews may follow their own food-laws as heretofore, and none of them will be in any way victimized for any previous offence committed in ignorance. 32 I am sending Menelaus to reassure you. 33 Farewell.

The fifteenth day of Xanthicus in the year 148.

34 The Romans also sent the Jews a letter. It read as follows:

From Quintus Memmius, Titus Manilius, and Manius Sergius, envoys of the Romans, to the Jewish people.
Greeting.
35 We give our assent to all the concessions that Lysias, the king's Kinsman, has granted you. 36 Be pleased to examine carefully the questions which he reserved for reference to the king; and then send someone without delay, so that we may make suitable proposals on your behalf, for we are proceeding to Antioch. 37 Send messengers immediately, therefore, so that we also may know what is your opinion. 38 Farewell.

11:21 **148:** *that is* 164 B.C.E.   11:33 **148:** *that is* 164 B.C.E.   11:34 **Titus ... Sergius:** *so some MSS; others* Titus Manius.   11:38 **148:** *that is* 164 B.C.E.

16–38: The letters, except for vv. 22–26, belong to the peace negotiations. **17:** *John* may be Mattathias' son (1 Macc. 2.2). **18:** The king here is Epiphanes, not Eupator. **21:** This is March 164 B.C.E. **22–26:** This misplaced letter belongs to the peace negotiations following Lysias' second campaign against Judas (13.1–26; 1 Macc. 6.28–63). It confirms religious freedom for the Jews. Here the *king* is Antiochus V Eupator. The terms were forced on Lysias by political necessity (1 Macc. 6.55–63). **23:** The dynasty was considered to draw its origin from the gods; its rulers were given divine honors during their lifetime and so went to *join the company of the gods* after death. **27–33:** Antiochus retracts the hated edicts regarding food (6.7–8). *Xanthicus:* March–April. **34–38:** The *questions referred to the king* (see v. 18) are not known. *Quintus Memmius* is otherwise unknown. *Titus Manilius* and *Manius Sergius* are both well-known Roman diplomats active in the east at this time.

The fifteenth day of Xanthicus in the year 148.

12 After the conclusion of these agreements, Lysias left and went to the king. The Jews busied themselves on their farms, ²but they were prevented from leading stable and tranquil lives by some of the governors in the region, Timotheus and Apollonius son of Gennaeus, as well as Hieronymus and Demophon, and also by Nicanor, chief of the Cypriot mercenaries.

³A DASTARDLY atrocity was perpetrated by the inhabitants of Joppa: they invited the Jews living among them to embark with their wives and children in boats they had provided, giving no indication of any animosity towards them. ⁴As it was a public decision by the whole town and because they wished to live in peace and suspected nothing, the Jews accepted; but once out at sea the people of Joppa sank the boats, drowning no fewer than two hundred of the Jews. ⁵As soon as Judas learnt of this brutal treatment of his fellow-countrymen he issued orders to his troops, ⁶and, invoking God the just judge, he fell upon the murderers. Under cover of night he set the harbour of Joppa on fire, burnt the shipping, and put to the sword those who had taken refuge there. ⁷But finding that the town was closed against him he withdrew, with the intention nevertheless of returning to wipe out the entire community. ⁸When he learnt that the people of Jamnia planned to deal in the same way with the Jews living there, ⁹he made a night attack on the town and set both harbour and fleet alight, so that the glow of the flames was visible at Jerusalem, thirty miles away.

¹⁰When, in their advance against Timotheus, Judas and his men had marched more than a mile from Jamnia, they were set upon by not less than five thousand Arabs on foot, supported by five hundred horsemen. ¹¹Through God's help, the Jews were the victors in a hard-fought battle. The defeated nomads begged Judas to make an alliance with them, promising to supply cattle and to furnish the Jews with all other assistance. ¹²Accepting that they could indeed be useful in many ways, Judas agreed to make peace, and with assurances from him the Arabs went back to their tents.

¹³Judas also attacked Caspin, a walled and strongly fortified town inhabited by a mixed population of Gentiles. ¹⁴Confident in the strength of their walls and in their stock of provisions, the defenders treated Judas and his men with insolence, abusing them and uttering the most wicked blasphemies. ¹⁵But Judas's men invoked the great Ruler of the universe, who in the days of Joshua threw down the walls of Jericho without the aid of battering-ram or siege-engine; then in a fierce onslaught they rushed the wall ¹⁶and, by the will of God, captured the town. The carnage was indescribable; the nearby lake, a quarter of a mile wide, appeared to be overflowing with blood.

¹⁷From there they advanced about ninety-five miles until they reached Charax, which is inhabited by the Tubian Jews, as they are called. ¹⁸They did not catch Timotheus, for having had no success he had by that time withdrawn from the district, though in one place he left behind an exceedingly strong garrison. ¹⁹Dositheus and Sosipater, Maccabaeus's generals, set out for the stronghold and destroyed the garrison stationed there by Timotheus; it consisted of over ten thousand men. ²⁰Maccabaeus for his part grouped his forces in a number of detachments, appointed commanders for them, and hurried in pursuit of Timotheus, who had with him a hundred and twenty thousand infantry and two thousand five hundred cavalry. ²¹When Timotheus learnt of Judas's approach, he sent on the women and children with the rest of the baggage train to a town called Carnaim, this being an inaccessible place, hard to storm because all the ap-

---

12.2–45: Battles with neighboring peoples. See 1 Macc. 5.1–68. Harassment by neighboring peoples led to a series of Jewish punitive raids. **2:** For *Timotheus,* see 8.30–33; 10.24–38; 12.10–31; 1 Macc. 5.24–54. The other *governors* are otherwise unknown. **10:** This *mile* should not be measured from Joppa or Jamnia but from some unspecified point in Gilead. The verse abruptly introduces a sizeable fragment (vv. 10–31) from a narrative of Judas' battles with Timotheus (see v. 2) which seems to have become disarranged at some point in its transmission. **13:** *Caspin* is the Casphor of 1 Macc. 5.26, 36. **15:** *Walls of Jericho:* see Josh. 6.1–21. **17:** *Charax* is literally a fortified camp. These *Tubian Jews* lived in the region of Tubias, i.e. in Gilead (1 Macc. 5.13). **21–26:** For the battle near, and at, *Carnaim,* see 1 Macc. 5.37–44. *Atargatis* was the famed Syrian proaches to it were so narrow. ²²As soon as Judas's first detachment came into sight, panic seized the enemy, who were terrified at a hostile manifestation of the all-seeing One. In headlong flight they rushed in all directions, so that frequently they were injured by their own comrades and run through by the points of their swords. ²³Judas pressed the pursuit vigorously and cut down these wicked men, destroying up to thirty thousand of them. ²⁴Timotheus himself was taken prisoner by the troops of Dositheus and Sosipater, but with great cunning he begged them to let him go unmolested, pointing out that he held in his power the brothers of some of them and the parents of most of them, and it might well be that scant regard would be paid them. ²⁵On his repeated pledge to restore those hostages unharmed, they let him go in order to save their relatives.

²⁶Judas moved on Carnaim and the sanctuary of Atargatis, where he slaughtered twenty-five thousand people. ²⁷From this defeat and massacre of his enemies he marched on Ephron, a fortified town with a mixture of nationalities. Stalwart young men positioned themselves before the walls, where they put up a stout fight, while inside there was a great supply of engines of war and missiles. ²⁸But the Jews, invoking the Ruler whose might shatters the enemy's strength, made themselves masters of the town and laid low as many as twenty-five thousand of the defenders. ²⁹Leaving it behind, they pushed on to Scythopolis, some seventy-five miles from Jerusalem. ³⁰When the Jewish settlers there testified to the goodwill shown them by the people and the kindness with which they had been treated in times of misfortune, ³¹Judas and his men thanked them, charging them to be no less friendly to the Jews in the future. Then, as the feast of Weeks was near, they proceeded to Jerusalem.

³²Immediately after celebrating Pentecost, as the feast is called, they marched against Gorgias, the general in charge of Idumaea, ³³who came out with three thousand infantry and four hundred cavalry. ³⁴Battle was joined and a small number of Jews fell. ³⁵But one of the Tubian Jews, Dositheus by name, a cavalryman of great strength, caught hold of Gorgias by his cloak and was dragging the villain off by main force, with the object of taking him alive, when a Thracian horseman bore down on Dositheus and chopped off his arm, and Gorgias escaped to Marisa.

³⁶As the troop under Esdrias were exhausted by the prolonged fighting, Judas appealed to the Lord to show himself their ally and leader in battle; ³⁷then, raising the battle cry with hymns in his native language, he launched a surprise attack and put Gorgias's army to flight. ³⁸Regrouping his forces, Judas led them to the town of Adullam, and since the seventh day was at hand they purified themselves according to custom and kept the sabbath there. ³⁹Next day they went to collect the bodies of the fallen, as by now had become necessary, in order to take them for burial with their kinsfolk in their family graves. ⁴⁰On each one of the dead they found under the tunic amulets sacred to the idols of Jamnia, objects forbidden to Jews by the law. It was evident to all that here was the reason these men had fallen. ⁴¹So everyone praised the acts of the Lord, the just Judge and Revealer of secrets, ⁴²and turning to prayer they begged that every trace of this offence might be blotted out. The noble Judas exhorted the people to keep themselves free from wrongdoing, for they had seen with their own eyes what had happened because of the sin of those who had fallen. ⁴³He levied a contribution from each man, and sent to Jerusalem the total of two thousand silver drachmas to provide a sin-offering—a fit and proper act in which he took due account of the resurrection. ⁴⁴Had he not been ex-

12:27 **nationalities:** *some witnesses add* where Lysias had his headquarters. 12:43 **sin-offering:** *or* purification-offering.

goddess. **27–28:** Judas took *Ephron* because it refused him passage (1 Macc. 5.46–51). **29:** *Scythopolis* is the Bethshan of 1 Macc. 5.52. **31:** For the *feast of Weeks,* or Pentecost, see Exod. 34.22; Deut. 16.9–12. **32–45:** See 1 Macc. 5.55–62, according to which Judas went to the relief of the defeated Josephus and Azarias (*Esdrias,* v. 36). **40:** First Maccabees 5.61 gives a different reason for the defeat. Deuteronomy 7.25–26 forbade taking these idol *amulets.* **42–44:** Judas, by *prayer* and *sin-offering,* hoped to avoid guilt by association (Josh. ch. 7) for the living. The author sees this as Judas' prayer for the dead. Thus, those who had died piously in battling for God's Law (v. 45) needed to be cleansed of this sin before the resurrection of the just (vv. 43–44). Later, Christian theologians would see here the essence of their doctrine of Purgatory.

pecting the fallen to rise again, it would have been superfluous and senseless to pray for the dead; [45] but since he had in view the splendid reward reserved for those who die a godly death, his purpose was holy and devout. That was why he offered the atoning sacrifice, to free the dead from their sin.

13 In the year 149, information reached Judas and those with him that Antiochus Eupator was advancing on Judaea with a large army; [2] he was accompanied by Lysias, his guardian and vicegerent, bringing in addition a Greek force consisting of one hundred and ten thousand infantry, five thousand three hundred cavalry, twenty-two elephants, and three hundred chariots fitted with scythes.

[3] Menelaus, who had also joined them, kept egging Antiochus on. This he did most disingenuously, not for his country's good, but because he believed he would be established in office. [4] The King of kings, however, stirred up the anger of Antiochus against this wicked man, and when Lysias produced evidence that Menelaus was responsible for all the troubles, the king ordered him to be taken to Beroea and there executed in the manner customary at that place. [5] In Beroea there is a tower some seventy-five feet high, filled with ashes; it has a circular device sloping down sheer on all sides into the ashes. [6] This is where the citizens take anyone guilty of sacrilege or any other heinous crime, and thrust him to his doom; [7] and such was the fate of the renegade Menelaus, who, in accordance with his just deserts, was not even given burial in the earth. [8] Many a time he had desecrated the sacred ashes of the altar-fire, and by ashes he met his death.

[9] In savage arrogance the king came on, aiming to inflict sufferings on the Jews far worse than they had endured under his father. [10] When Judas learnt of this, he ordered the people to invoke the Lord day and night, and pray that now more than ever he would come to their aid, since law, country, and holy temple were all at risk; [11] and that he would not allow them, just when they had begun to revive, to fall into the hands of blaspheming Gentiles. [12] They all complied: for three days without respite they prayed to their merciful Lord, they wailed, they fasted, they prostrated themselves. Then, with many an exhortation, Judas called upon them to stand by him.

[13] After a council of war with the elders, he decided not to wait for the king's army to invade Judaea and take Jerusalem, but to march out and with God's help put matters to the test. [14] He committed the outcome to the Lord of the universe, and exhorted his troops to fight nobly to the death for law, temple, and city, for their country and their way of life. He pitched camp near Modin, [15] and giving his men the watchword 'Victory with God!' he launched a night attack towards the royal tent with a picked force of his bravest young warriors. As many as two thousand in the enemy camp were killed, and Judas's men stabbed to death the leading elephant and its driver. [16] In the end they reduced the whole camp to panic and confusion, and then made a successful withdrawal. [17] Through the help and protection which Judas had received from the Lord it was all over by daybreak.

[18] Now that he had had a taste of Jewish daring, the king resorted to stratagem in probing their positions. [19] He advanced on Bethsura, one of their strong forts, and was repulsed; he attacked again, and was defeated. [20] Judas meanwhile sent in supplies to the garrison. [21] A soldier in the Jewish ranks, Rhodocus by name, passed secret information to the enemy; but he was tracked down, caught, and put away. [22] A second time the king parleyed with the inhabitants of Beth-

13:1 **149:** *that is* 163 B.C.E.   13:5 **some . . . feet:** *Gk* fifty cubits.   13:15 **stabbed to death:** *prob. rdg, based on one version.*

13.1–26: Lysias' second campaign against Judas. See 1 Macc. 6.28–63. While 2 Macc. speaks of victories and notes the eventual success of Judas, 1 Macc. points out more realistically how close to disaster the Jews came. Only the threat of Philip's coup at Antioch (v. 23; 1 Macc. 6.55–63) brought Lysias to the terms of the letter in 2 Macc. 11.22–26. **2:** The figures here and in 1 Macc. 6.30 are inflated. **3:** *Antiochus* V Eupator was a minor; Lysias as regent made the decisions. **4:** *Beroea* is the name given to Aleppo by Seleucus I Nicator (305–281 B.C.E.). *Menelaus'* execution may have resulted from Lysias' frustration over Judas' subsequent victory, or it may have been due to Menelaus' failure to pay what he promised (4.27–28). **5–8:** The method of execution was Persian. **15:** See 8.23. Judas' brother Eleazar killed the *elephant* (1 Macc. 6.43–46). **18–23:** See 1 Macc. 6.31, 49–50, 55–63.

sura; after giving and receiving guarantees he took his departure; he attacked Judas and his men, but had the worst of it. ²³ He now received a report that Philip, who had been left in charge of affairs of state in Antioch, had made a mad bid for power. In consternation the king summoned the Jews, agreed to their terms, and took an oath to respect all their rights. After reaching this settlement he offered a sacrifice, paid honour to the sanctuary and its precincts, ²⁴ and received Maccabaeus in a friendly manner. He left Hegemonides as governor of the region from Ptolemais to Gerra, ²⁵ while he himself went to Ptolemais, where the inhabitants resented the treaty he had made, and in their anger wanted to repudiate the terms. ²⁶ Lysias mounted the rostrum and put forward the best defence he could. He won the people over, calmed them down, and, having thus gained their support, departed for Antioch.

Such was the course of the king's offensive and retreat.

14 AFTER three years had passed, information reached Judas and his followers that Demetrius son of Seleucus had sailed into the harbour at Tripolis with a powerful army and fleet, ² and, having disposed of Antiochus and his guardian Lysias, had taken control of the country.

³ A certain Alcimus, who had formerly been high priest, had willingly submitted to defilement at the time of the revolt. Realizing now that there was no guarantee whatsoever of his safety, nor any possibility of access to the holy altar, ⁴ he went to King Demetrius about the year 151 and presented him with a gold crown and a palm, together with some of the customary olive branches from the temple. On that occasion he kept silent. ⁵ But when Demetrius summoned him to his council and questioned him about the attitude and aims of the Jews, he seized the opportunity to forward his own misguided scheme, and replied: ⁶ 'Those Jews called Hasidaeans who

are led by Judas Maccabaeus are keeping the war alive and fomenting sedition; they refuse to let the kingdom have peace. ⁷ Thus, although I have been deprived of my hereditary dignity, by which I mean the high-priesthood, I have two motives in coming here today: ⁸ first, a genuine concern for the king's interests; and secondly, a regard for my fellow-citizens, since our whole race is suffering considerable hardship as a result of the senseless conduct of those people I have mentioned. ⁹ My advice to your majesty is to get to know the details of these matters and then, as befits your universal kindness and goodwill, make provision for our country and our beleaguered nation. ¹⁰ For as long as Judas remains alive there can be no peace for the state.'

¹¹ No sooner had he spoken in this vein than the other Friends, who were hostile to Judas, added fresh fuel to Demetrius's anger. ¹² There and then the king selected Nicanor, commander of the elephant corps, made him military governor of Judaea, and sent him ¹³ with a commission to make away with Judas and disperse his army, and to install Alcimus as high priest of the great temple. ¹⁴ The gentile population of Judaea, refugees from the attacks of Judas, now flocked to join Nicanor, supposing that defeat and misfortune for the Jews would spell prosperity for them.

¹⁵ When the Jews heard of Nicanor's offensive and the onset of the Gentiles, they sprinkled dust over themselves and prayed to him who has established his people for ever, who never fails to manifest himself and afford help when his chosen are in need. ¹⁶ At their leader's command, they moved forward immediately and made contact with the enemy at the village of Adasa. ¹⁷ Simon, the brother of Judas, had fought an engagement with Nicanor, but because the enemy came up unexpectedly he had suffered a slight reverse.

14:4 **151:** *that is* 161 B.C.E. 14:16 **Adasa:** *prob. rdg; cp. 1 Macc. 7:40.* 14:17 **came up:** *prob. rdg, based on one version.*

14.1–15.37: The victory of Maccabeus over Nicanor. Second Maccabees details the final major victory of Judas. See 1 Macc. ch. 7. **1–2:** *Demetrius* I Soter (161–150 B.C.E.) was the oldest surviving *son of Seleucus* IV (187–175 B.C.E.) and considered *Antiochus* IV Epiphanes (175–164 B.C.E.) and his son Antiochus V Eupator (164–161 B.C.E.) as usurpers. **3:** The author barely alludes to Bacchides' earlier expedition and its resultant establishment of *Alcimus* as *high priest* (1 Macc. 7.8–25). The *revolt* is probably the persecution of Epiphanes, which divided the Jews. **6:** The *Hasidaeans* (1 Macc. 2.42–43; 7.12–18) were forerunners of the parties of the Pharisees and the Essenes. **11:** *Friends:* See 1 Macc. 2.18 n. **12:** *Nicanor:* see 8.8–29; 1 Macc. 3.38–4.25; 7.26–50. **16–30:** The preliminary skirmishes (vv. 15–19) and the friendship of Nicanor for Judas are summa-

18 In spite of this, when Nicanor learnt how brave Judas and his troops were and how courageously they fought for their country, he shrank from deciding the issue by the sword; 19 so he sent Posidonius, Theodotus, and Mattathias to negotiate a settlement.

20 After a full consideration of the proposals Judas put them to his men, all of whom were in favour of accepting the terms. 21 On the day fixed for a private meeting of the leaders, a chariot advanced from each of the two lines, and seats were placed in position; 22 Judas posted armed men at strategic points ready to deal with any sudden treachery on the enemy's part. The discussion between the two leaders was harmonious. 23 Nicanor stayed some time in Jerusalem and behaved correctly. Dismissing the crowds that had flocked from round about, 24 he kept Judas close to himself at all times, for he had developed a real affection for him. 25 He urged him to marry and have children; so Judas married and settled down to the quiet life of an ordinary citizen.

26 Alcimus, observing their friendliness, got hold of a copy of the agreement they had concluded, and went to Demetrius and claimed that Nicanor was pursuing a policy detrimental to the interests of the state by appointing Judas, a man guilty of conspiracy, as king's Friend designate. 27 Incensed by these villainous slanders, the king wrote angrily to Nicanor expressing his dissatisfaction with the terms agreed upon; he ordered him to arrest Maccabaeus and send him to Antioch at once. 28 The instructions dismayed Nicanor, and he took it hard that he should have to go back on his agreement when the man had committed no offence; 29 but since there was no gainsaying the king, he watched for an opportunity of carrying out the order by some stratagem. 30 Maccabaeus, on his part, noticed that Nicanor had become less friendly towards him and no longer showed him the same civility. He realized that this coolness boded ill for him, and collecting a good number of his followers he went into hiding.

31 Recognizing that he had been outmanoeuvred by the resolute action of Judas, Nicanor appeared before the great and holy temple at the time when the priests were offering the regular sacrifices, and ordered them to surrender Judas. 32 Though the priests declared on oath that they did not know the whereabouts of the wanted man, 33 Nicanor stretched out his right hand towards the shrine and swore this oath: 'Unless you surrender Judas to me in chains, I shall level this sanctuary of God to the ground and destroy the altar; on this spot I shall build a temple to Dionysus for all the world to see'; 34 and with those words he left. Then the priests, their hands uplifted to Heaven, prayed to the constant champion of our nation: 35 'Lord, you have no need of anything in the world, yet it was your pleasure that among us there should be a shrine for your dwelling-place; 36 now, holy Lord from whom all holiness comes, keep this house, so recently purified, free from defilement for ever.'

37 A MAN called Razis, a member of the Jerusalem senate, was denounced to Nicanor. He was a patriot and very highly spoken of, one who for his loyalty was known as Father of the Jews. 38 In the early days of the revolt he had stood trial for practising the Jewish religion, and with no hesitation had risked life and limb for that cause. 39 Nicanor, wishing to demonstrate his hostility towards the Jews, sent more than five hundred soldiers to arrest Razis; 40 he reckoned that this would be a severe blow to the Jews. 41 The tower of his house was on the point of being captured by this mob of soldiers, the outer gate was being forced, and there were calls for fire to burn down the inner doors, when Razis, beset on every side, turned his sword on himself; 42 he preferred to die nobly rather than fall into the hands of evil men and be subjected to gross humiliation. 43 With everything happening so quickly, he misjudged the stroke and, now that troops were pouring through the doorways, he ran up without hesitation on to the wall and heroically threw himself down into the crowd. 44 They hurriedly gave way and he fell to the ground in the space they left. 45 He was still breathing and still ablaze with courage; streaming with blood and severely wounded as he was, he picked himself up and dashed through the crowd. Finally, standing on a sheer rock, 46 and now completely drained of blood, he tore out his entrails and with both hands flung them at

rized in 1 Macc. 7.27–30. **31–36:** See 1 Macc. 7.33–38. **38:** *Revolt:* see v. 3 n. **46:** Razis, too, believes in the

1255

the crowd. And thus, invoking him who disposes of life and breath to give them back to him again, he died.

15 NICANOR, advised that Judas and his men were in the neighbourhood of Samaria, planned to attack them on their day of rest, when it could be done without risk. ² Those Jews who were forced to accompany his army begged him not to carry out so savage and barbarous a massacre. 'Have regard for the day singled out and made holy by the all-seeing One,' they said. ³ The double-dyed villain retorted, 'Is there some ruler in the sky who has ordered the sabbath-day observance?' ⁴ The Jews declared, 'The living Lord himself is ruler in the sky, and he commanded the seventh day to be kept holy.' ⁵ 'And I am a ruler on earth,' countered Nicanor; 'I order you to take up arms and do your duty to the king.' However, he did not succeed in carrying out this outrage he had planned.

⁶ In his pretentious and extravagant conceit, Nicanor had resolved to erect a public trophy from the spoils taken from Judas's army. ⁷ But Maccabaeus's confidence never wavered, and he had not the least doubt that he would obtain help from the Lord. ⁸ He urged his men to have no fear of the gentile attack, but to bear in mind the aid they had received from Heaven in the past and look with confidence to the Almighty for the victory he would send them on this occasion also. ⁹ He drew encouragement for them from the law and the prophets and, by reminding them of the struggles they had already come through, filled them with a fresh ardour. ¹⁰ When he had roused their courage, he issued his orders, reminding them at the same time of the Gentiles' broken faith and perjury. ¹¹ He armed each one of them, not so much with shield and spear for protection, as with brave and reassuring words; and he cheered them all by recounting a dream he had had, a waking vision worthy of belief. ¹² What he had seen was this: there had appeared to him the former high priest Onias, a good and noble man of modest bearing and mild disposition, a ready and apt speaker, an exemplar from childhood of every virtue; with uplifted hands Onias was praying for the whole Jewish community. ¹³ Next there appeared in the same attitude a figure of great age and dignity, whose wonderful air of authority marked him as a man of the utmost distinction. ¹⁴ Onias then spoke: 'This is God's prophet Jeremiah,' he said, 'one who loves his fellow-Jews and constantly offers prayers for the people and for the Holy City.' ¹⁵ Extending his right hand Jeremiah presented a golden sword to Judas, saying as he did so, ¹⁶ 'Take this holy sword, a gift from God, and with it shatter the enemy.'

The Jews triumph

¹⁷ THE heroic words of Judas had the effect of evoking the bravery of everyone and of giving boys the courage of men. The Jews resolved not to undertake a long campaign, but nobly to go over to the offensive and decide the issue by fighting in close combat with all their courage. This they did because Jerusalem, their religion, and the temple were in peril. ¹⁸ Their fear was not chiefly for their wives and children, or for brothers and relatives, but first and foremost for the sacred shrine. ¹⁹ The distress of those shut up in Jerusalem was no less, for they were anxious about the outcome of a battle on open ground.

²⁰ All were awaiting the decisive struggle which lay ahead. The enemy had already concentrated his forces: his army drawn up in battle order, the elephants strategically positioned, and the cavalry ranged on the flanks. ²¹ Maccabaeus observed the deployment of the troops, the variety of their weapons, and the ferocity of the elephants, and raising his hands towards heaven he invoked the Lord, the worker of miracles; he knew that God grants victory to those who deserve it, not because of their military strength but as he himself decides. ²² This was his prayer: 'Lord, in the days of King Hezekiah of Judah you sent your angel and he destroyed as

resurrection of the just. **15.1–5:** Despite Nicanor's plan, Judas would fight on the sabbath if attacked (1 Macc. 2.41). **10:** The Gentiles had perjured themselves with the Hasidaeans (1 Macc. 7.12–18). Judas warned his followers what to expect if they surrendered. **12–16:** The vision of *Onias* III (3.1; 4.34) and *Jeremiah* represented the support of the Law (through the temple's priesthood) and the Prophets for Judas' cause. The author notes the intercessory prayer of the saints (vv. 12, 14). **22:** Judas refers to the angelic slaughter (probably by

1256

many as a hundred and eighty-five thousand men in Sennacherib's camp. ²³ Now, Ruler of heaven, send a good angel once again to go before us spreading fear and panic. ²⁴ May these blasphemers who are coming to attack your holy people be struck down by your strong arm!' Such was his prayer.

²⁵ Nicanor and his forces advanced to the sound of trumpets and war-songs, ²⁶ but Judas and his men engaged the enemy with invocations and prayers on their lips. ²⁷ Praying to God in their hearts and greatly cheered by his care, they killed no fewer than thirty-five thousand in hand-to-hand fighting.

²⁸ The action over, they were joyfully disbanding, when they discovered Nicanor lying dead in full armour, ²⁹ and with tumultuous shouts they praised the heavenly Ruler in their native language. ³⁰ Judas their leader, who had always fought body and soul on behalf of his fellow-countrymen, without ever losing his youthful patriotism, ordered that Nicanor's head and whole arm should be cut off and taken to Jerusalem. ³¹ On arrival there he called together the people, stationed the priests before the altar, sent for the men in the citadel, ³² and put on display the head of that villainous Nicanor and the hand which the bragging blasphemer had stretched out against the Almighty's holy temple. ³³ He cut out the godless Nicanor's tongue and swore he would feed it to the birds bit by bit; and he gave orders that the evidence of what Nicanor's folly had brought upon him should be hung up opposite the shrine. ³⁴ All made the sky ring with the praises of the Lord who had shown his power: 'Praise to him who has preserved his own sanctuary from defilement!' ³⁵ Judas hung Nicanor's head from the citadel, as a clear proof of the Lord's help for everyone to see. ³⁶ It was unanimously decreed that this day should never pass unnoticed, but that the thirteenth of the twelfth month, called Adar in Aramaic, should be duly celebrated; it is the eve of Mordecai's Day. ³⁷ Such, then, was the fate of Nicanor, and from that time Jerusalem has remained in the possession of the Hebrews.

AT this point I shall bring my work to an end. ³⁸ If it is found to be well written and aptly composed, that is what I myself aimed at; if superficial and mediocre, it was the best I could do. ³⁹ For, just as it is disagreeable to drink wine by itself or water by itself, whereas the mixing of the two produces a pleasant and delightful taste, so too variety of style in a literary work charms the ear of the reader. Let this, then, be my final word.

plague) of *Sennacherib's* army as it besieged Jerusalem (2 Kgs. 19.35; Isa. 37.36; 1 Macc. 7.41). **33:** Instead of having a public trophy or monument to Judas' defeat (v. 6), *Nicanor* became one to his own. **36:** The feast of Nicanor was struck from the Jewish calendar after the destruction of the temple in 70 C.E. For *Mordecai's Day,* see Esther 3.7; 9.20–23.

15.38–39: The Epitomist ends this version before the story of Judas' death (1 Macc. 9.1–22).

The Biblical Text with Annotations

THE NEW TESTAMENT

Introduction

The Revised English Bible, a revision of The New English Bible, carries forward the aim of its predecessor to provide English-speaking readers with a faithful rendering of the best available Greek text into modern English, incorporating the gains of modern biblical scholarship.

The earliest manuscripts of the books of the New Testament were written down within a generation of their first composition. But the transmission of the text has not been altogether straightforward, and there is no scholarly Greek text of the New Testament which commands universal acceptance at the present time. Those who prepared the first draft of The New English Bible New Testament usually started with the text originally published by Eberhard Nestle at the end of the nineteenth century. The translators considered variant readings on their merits and, having weighed the evidence, selected for translation in each passage the reading which, to the best of their judgement, seemed most likely to represent what the author wrote. In assessing the evidence, the translators took into account (a) manuscripts of the New Testament in Greek, (b) early translations into other languages, and (c) quotations from the New Testament by early Christian writers. These three sources of evidence were referred to as 'witnesses'. The complete text eventually followed was edited by R. V. G. Tasker and published as *The Greek New Testament* (Oxford and Cambridge University Presses, 1964). A notable contribution to New Testament biblical studies after the completion of The New English Bible was the publication of *Novum Testamentum Graece,* edited by Kurt Aland and others (Deutsche Bibelstiftung, Stuttgart, 26th ed. 1979), and this was a major point of reference for those engaged in the revision. The translators and revisers have taken into consideration not only the evidence presented in recent editions of the Greek text, but also the work of exegetical and literary scholarship, which is continuing all the time. The revisers have drawn attention in footnotes to variant readings which may result in significant alternative understanding or interpretation of the text, and in particular to those readings which were followed in The New English Bible, but which now seem to the revisers to be less probable than those used in this revision. They are well aware that their judgement is provisional, but they believe the text they have adopted to be an improvement on that underlying earlier translations.

In accordance with the original decision of the Joint Committee of the Churches, the translators and revisers attempted to use consistently the idiom of contemporary English, employing its natural vocabulary, constructions, and rhythms to convey the meaning of the Greek. The revision has been concerned to avoid archaisms, technical terms, and pretentious language as far as possible. The New English Bible and its revisers adopted the wholesome practice of the translators of the Authorized (King James) Version, who recognized no obligation to render the same Greek word everywhere by the same English word. This version claims to be a translation rather than a paraphrase, observing faithfulness to the meaning of the text without necessarily reproducing grammatical structure or translating word for word.

The revisers are conscious of the limitations and imperfections of their work. Anyone who has tried it will know that it is impossible to make a perfect translation. Only those who have long meditated on the Greek original are aware of the richness and subtlety of meaning that may lie even within what appears to be the most simple of sentences, or know the despair that can attend efforts to bring it out through the medium of a different language. All who have been involved in the work trust that under the providence of Almighty God this revision may build on the achievement of The New English Bible in opening yet further the truth of the scriptures.

The Gospels

Among the earliest Christians the word "gospel" was not used as the title of a book or as a designation for a class of literature. Instead, it was a term which meant "Good News" and referred to the message of salvation which those Christians proclaimed.

The gospel as proclamation was about Jesus Christ whose crucifixion and resurrection were at the center of the message, which also included stories about his deeds and reports of his teaching. As the Christian movement grew, a considerable body of tradition about Jesus developed and circulated in the first decades of the church's life. While that tradition was made up of individual units (e.g., single stories, independent sayings), there were soon collections and short accounts useful for instruction, liturgy, and other purposes in the church.

Between 70 and 100 C.E., several authors employed these elements to compose connected narrative accounts which came to be known as Gospels. The title "Gospel" probably derives from the opening words of one of these narrative documents, that attributed to Mark ("The beginning of the gospel . . ."); the title certainly reflects the fact that all of these books focus on Jesus Christ in whose life, death, and resurrection the church found the hope of salvation. Four of these narrative documents are found at the front of the New Testament where they were collectively identified as "The Gospel" and where in ancient manuscripts they were distinguished by the headings "According to Matthew," "According to Mark," "According to Luke," and "According to John."

Scholarly opinion varies about the type of literature to which these books belong. Some regard them as representative of a specific type of ancient biography, while—at an opposite pole—others regard the Gospel form as new and distinctively Christian. There were diverse types of biographies in the Graeco-Roman world for which praise of the subject was characteristic, and a citizen of that world who came upon our Gospels probably would have understood them in the context of ancient biographical literature. Other books with the word "gospel" in their titles circulated among early Christians, some similar in type to the canonical four, some quite different in form (see articles, "Literary Forms of the Bible," p. *12, "Early Christian Literature," p. *112).

That Matthew, Mark, Luke, and John bear a general resemblance to each other is clear. All are developed narratives which culminate in passion and resurrection accounts; they agree in beginning their story of Jesus' public career with the activity of John the Baptist. Between the Baptist's appearance and the passion, they relate encounters, mighty deeds, and teaching. Such similarities suggest that these books are connected. In fact, Matthew, Mark, and Luke are so closely related that they are usually regarded as being interdependent. However, in spite of the general resemblances mentioned above, there are also significant variances which separate John from the others. John's stories of wondrous deeds are largely different stories and appear to serve a different purpose; John presents Jesus' teaching in extended thematic discourses, in contrast to the collections of sayings and parables which characterize the other Gospels; in John, Jesus' ministry oscillates between Galilee and Jerusalem, while in the other Gospels the ministry is concentrated in Galilee until one fateful journey to Jerusalem at its close. Most scholars believe that, though certain common traditions lie behind the four Gospels, John is best understood as basically independent of the others.

For Matthew, Mark, and Luke, the similarities are pronounced. The narrative outlines hang on the same events reported in essentially the same order. So close are these three Gospels to each other that they are commonly called the "Synoptic Gospels," which means that they "see or view (their subject) together." A useful tool for understanding these Gospels is a Synopsis: a book in which Matthew, Mark, and Luke are each printed in its own order, but in a parallel column format which reveals the unified outline they possess. In fact, the agreement between the Synoptics is such as to be explicable only in terms of a *literary* relationship. When documents are said to have a literary relationship, that means that one has used the other as a source or that they have used a common source. The assertion of dependence between Gospels is not made lightly or arbitrarily, but only when very specific circumstances are present. Literary relationship is not demonstrated merely by the authors' knowledge of some of the same stories or by coincidence in general arrangement of materials. On the contrary, what is minimally required is the recording of a significant number of passages (1) *with the same basic content,* (2) *in substantially the same sequence,* and (3) *with a very high incidence of the same words.* By such demanding criteria, John simply does not relate to Matthew, Mark, and Luke in the way they relate to each other. The relationship between the Synoptic Gospels can best be understood on the basis of literary dependence.

The relationship between Matthew, Mark, and Luke is clearly literary, but it is also complicated. Not only are there compelling agreements which must be recognized, but occasional divergences in order appear, Matthew and Luke share considerable blocks of tradition not found in Mark, and each Gospel has distinctive materials. This complex set of data constitutes what is called the "synoptic problem," which is the need to explain both the similarities and differences between Matthew, Mark, and Luke. Any hypothesis advanced to deal with the problem must reckon with the fact that Mark is, in some sense, the "common denominator." Mark's position is such that the most natural way of describing synoptic relationships is to speak of the degree of agreement with Mark. For example, one theory is that Mark drew upon both Matthew and

Luke; another hypothesis is that both Matthew and Luke were dependent on Mark. Notice that in either case Mark is the "common denominator."

For most scholars, the solution which recommends itself most strongly is commonly known as the "two-source" or "two-document hypothesis." Mark, on this view, is the prior Gospel and was used by Matthew and Luke. Matthew and Luke are also believed to have drawn from a second source which contained teaching materials not found in Mark: a "Sayings Source" which is usually given the designation "Q" (for German *Quelle*, "source"). On any theory each evangelist (as the Gospel authors are called) is seen to have utilized unique traditions as well.

Though broad, general similarities characterize all four Gospels and the Synoptics have literary ties, the evangelists have unique points of view, so that each Gospel has its distinctive message. The Introductions to the Gospels (pp. 1267, 1304, 1327, 1365) provide suggestive indications of these special perspectives and purposes. In the interplay of likenesses and differences, we are able to sense the vibrant, changing, growing faith of the early Christian communities.

THE GOSPEL ACCORDING TO
Matthew

The Gospel of Matthew has long been regarded as the most Jewish of the Gospels: the author's preference for the term kingdom of Heaven (see 3.2 n.), description of Peter's commission in scribal categories (16.19 n.), and interest in the Law (5.17–19 nn.) are traits which point in this direction. Yet the Evangelist shows an anti-Pharisaic bias (e.g. ch. 23), probably intends 23.37–24.2 to imply the repudiation of Israel, and concludes the book with a scene which directs the disciples out into the Gentile mission (28.16–20). With good reason (see 16.18 n.; 18.1–19.1 nn.), this has also been called an "ecclesiastical" Gospel; on almost every page the author's concern for the life of the church may be detected.

The feature of the book which attracts immediate attention is the organization of the teaching tradition into five great discourses (chs. 5–7; 10; 13; 18; 24–25). A narrative section precedes each discourse. This scheme is prefaced by chs. 1–2, which introduce the Messiah-Son of David, and is climaxed by the concluding report of the crucifixion and resurrection in chs. 26–28.

The book was probably written about 90 C.E.

The ancestry of the Messiah

1 THE genealogy of Jesus Christ, son of David, son of Abraham.

2 Abraham was the father of Isaac, Isaac of Jacob, Jacob of Judah and his brothers, 3 Judah of Perez and Zarah (their mother was Tamar), Perez of Hezron, Hezron of Ram, 4 Ram of Amminadab, Amminadab of Nahshon, Nahshon of Salmon, 5 Salmon of Boaz (his mother was Rahab), Boaz of Obed (his mother was Ruth), Obed of Jesse; 6 and Jesse was the father of King David.

David was the father of Solomon (his mother had been the wife of Uriah), 7 Solomon of Rehoboam, Rehoboam of Abijah, Abijah of Asa, 8 Asa of Jehoshaphat, Jehoshaphat of Joram, Joram of Uzziah, 9 Uzziah of Jotham, Jotham of Ahaz, Ahaz of Hezekiah, 10 Hezekiah of Manasseh, Manasseh of Amon, Amon of Josiah; 11 and Josiah was the father of Jeconiah and his brothers at the time of the deportation to Babylon.

12 After the deportation Jeconiah was the father of Shealtiel, Shealtiel of Zerubbabel, 13 Zerubbabel of Abiud, Abiud of Eliakim, Eliakim of Azor, 14 Azor of Zadok, Zadok of Achim, Achim of Eliud, 15 Eliud of Eleazar, Eleazar of Matthan, Matthan of Jacob, 16 Jacob of Joseph, the husband of Mary, who gave birth to Jesus called Messiah.

17 There were thus fourteen generations in all from Abraham to David, fourteen from David until the deportation to Babylon, and fourteen from the deportation until the Messiah.

The birth and infancy of Jesus

18 THIS is how the birth of Jesus Christ came about. His mother Mary was betrothed to Joseph; before their marriage she found she

1.1–17: **Genealogy of the Messiah** (compare Lk. 3.23–38). **1:** Literally *Christ* (or *Messiah*, v. 17) means "anointed one" and was frequently used of the royal figure whose rule would bring about the final age of righteousness and justice. The genealogy presents Jesus as this ruler, descended from *King David* (vv. 1, 6) through the royal line (vv. 6–11). **2–11:** These names are drawn from Ruth 4.18–22; 1 Chr. 2.1–3.19. **17:** *Fourteen generations*: perhaps reflecting the numerical value of *David* in Heb.; *d* (4) + *v* (6) + *d* (4) = 14. *Messiah*: see v. 1 n.

1.18–25: **The birth of Jesus** (compare Lk. 1.26–38; 2.1–7). The theme of the miraculous birth pervades the was going to have a child through the Holy Spirit. 19 Being a man of principle, and at the same time wanting to save her from exposure, Joseph made up his mind to have the marriage contract quietly set aside. 20 He had resolved on this, when an angel of the Lord appeared to him in a dream and said, 'Joseph, son of David, do not be afraid to take Mary home with you to be your wife. It is through the Holy Spirit that she has conceived. 21 She will bear a son; and you shall give him the name Jesus, for he will save his people from their sins.' 22 All this happened in order to fulfil what the Lord declared through the prophet: 23 'A virgin will conceive and bear a son, and he shall be called Emmanuel,' a name which means 'God is with us'. 24 When he woke Joseph did as the angel of the Lord had directed him; he took Mary home to be his wife, 25 but had no intercourse with her until her son was born. And he named the child Jesus.

2 JESUS was born at Bethlehem in Judaea during the reign of Herod. After his birth astrologers from the east arrived in Jerusalem, 2 asking, 'Where is the new-born king of the Jews? We observed the rising of his star, and we have come to pay him homage.' 3 King Herod was greatly perturbed when he heard this, and so was the whole of Jerusalem. 4 He called together the chief priests and scribes of the Jews, and asked them where the Messiah was to be born. 5 'At Bethlehem in Judaea,' they replied, 'for this is what the prophet wrote: 6 "Bethlehem in the land of Judah, you are by no means least among the rulers of Judah; for out of you shall come a ruler to be the shepherd of my people Israel." '

7 Then Herod summoned the astrologers to meet him secretly, and ascertained from them the exact time when the star had appeared. 8 He sent them to Bethlehem, and said, 'Go and make a careful search for the child, and when you have found him, bring me word, so that I may go myself and pay him homage.'

9-10 After hearing what the king had to say they set out; there before them was the star they had seen rising, and it went ahead of them until it stopped above the place where the child lay. They were overjoyed at the sight of it 11 and, entering the house, they saw the child with Mary his mother and bowed low in homage to him; they opened their treasure chests and presented gifts to him: gold, frankincense, and myrrh. 12 Then they returned to their own country by another route, for they had been warned in a dream not to go back to Herod.

13 After they had gone, an angel of the Lord appeared to Joseph in a dream, and said, 'Get up, take the child and his mother and escape with them to Egypt, and stay there until I tell you; for Herod is going to search for the child to kill him.' 14 So Joseph got up, took mother and child by night, and sought refuge with them in Egypt, 15 where he stayed till Herod's death. This was to fulfil what the Lord had declared through the prophet: 'Out of Egypt I have called my son.'

16 When Herod realized that the astrologers had tricked him he flew into a rage, and gave orders for the massacre of all the boys aged two years or under, in Bethlehem and throughout the whole district, in accordance with the time he had ascertained from the astrologers. 17 So the words spoken through Jeremiah the prophet were fulfilled: 18 'A voice was heard in Rama, sobbing in bitter grief; it was Rachel weeping for her children, and refusing to be comforted, because they were no more.'

19 After Herod's death an angel of the Lord appeared in a dream to Joseph in Egypt 20 and said to him, 'Get up, take the child and his mother, and go to the land of Israel, for those who threatened the child's life are dead.' 21 So he got up, took mother and child with him, and came to the land of Israel.

1:21 **Jesus:** *that is* Saviour.

passage (vv. 18, 20, 23, 25). **20:** Both the *angel* ("messenger") and the *dream* are customary devices for reporting revelations (see 2.12–13, 22). **21, 23:** The chief significance of the account for Matthew lies in the pointedly explained names, *Jesus* and *Emmanuel*. **22–23:** See Isa. 7.14 n. Matthew frequently introduces OT quotations with a phrase like *to fulfil what the Lord declared through the prophet* (e.g. 2.15; 8.17; 27.9–10).

2.1–12: The infant Jesus in Bethlehem. 1: *Bethlehem,* the city of David, was the expected birthplace of the Messiah (vv. 4–6). *Reign of Herod:* 37 B.C.E.–4 B.C.E. **4:** *Scribes:* interpreters of Scripture, especially of the Law of Moses. **6:** Mic. 5.2. In the OT *shepherd* frequently means "ruler."

2.13–23: Escape and return. The story of the flight to Egypt is told only by Matt. **15:** Hos. 11.1. **16:** The

22 But when he heard that Archelaus had succeeded his father Herod as king of Judaea, he was afraid to go there. Directed by a dream, he withdrew to the region of Galilee, 23 where he settled in a town called Nazareth. This was to fulfil the words spoken through the prophets: 'He shall be called a Nazarene.'

John the Baptist and Jesus

3 IN the course of time John the Baptist appeared in the Judaean wilderness, proclaiming this message: 2 'Repent, for the kingdom of Heaven is upon you!' 3 It was of him that the prophet Isaiah spoke when he said,

A voice cries in the wilderness,
'Prepare the way for the Lord;
clear a straight path for him.'

4 John's clothing was a rough coat of camel's hair, with a leather belt round his waist, and his food was locusts and wild honey. 5 Everyone flocked to him from Jerusalem, Judaea, and the Jordan valley, 6 and they were baptized by him in the river Jordan, confessing their sins.

7 When he saw many of the Pharisees and Sadducees coming for baptism he said to them: 'Vipers' brood! Who warned you to escape from the wrath that is to come? 8 Prove your repentance by the fruit you bear; 9 and do not imagine you can say, "We have Abraham for our father." I tell you that God can make children for Abraham out of these stones. 10 The axe lies ready at the roots of the trees; every tree that fails to produce good fruit is cut down and thrown on the fire. 11 I baptize you with water, for repentance; but the one who comes after me is mightier than I am, whose sandals I am not worthy to remove. He will baptize you with the Holy Spirit and with fire. 12 His winnowing-shovel is ready in his hand and he will clear his threshing-floor; he will gather the wheat into his granary, but the chaff he will burn on a fire that can never be put out.'

13 Then Jesus arrived at the Jordan from Galilee, and came to John to be baptized by him. 14 John tried to dissuade him. 'Do you come to me?' he said. 'It is I who need to be baptized by you.' 15 Jesus replied, 'Let it be so for the present; it is right for us to do all that God requires.' Then John allowed him to come. 16 No sooner had Jesus been baptized and come up out of the water than the heavens were opened and he saw the Spirit of God descending like a dove to alight on him.

massacre is not reported elsewhere, but Herod's barbarity was notorious. **18:** Jer. 31.15. **22:** *Archelaus* ruled from 4 B.C.E. to 6 C.E. **23:** Probably Isa. 11.1 (which contains a Heb. word, *nezer*, translated "branch," similar to *Nazareth*) is the intended reference.

3.1–12: The work of the Baptist (Mk. 1.1–8; Lk. 3.1–18; Jn. 1.6, 15, 19–28). **1:** *Wilderness:* the arid Judean territory southeast of Jerusalem, including the lower *Jordan* valley (v. 6). **2:** *Repent:* to change one's mind (Gk.), to return, to turn around (Heb.). *Kingdom:* see Mk. 1.15 n. In Jewish piety, *Heaven* was an ordinary manner of referring to God. **3:** Isa. 40.3. **4:** Second Kings 1.8 attributes similar clothing to Elijah. **7:** *Baptism,* dipping in water, was an important ritual in the Dead Sea community and was also administered to Gentile converts to Judaism. The *Pharisees* were a predominantly lay Jewish movement marked by an elastic interpretation of the Law, though in terms of a special, inherited tradition; they accepted as authoritative not only the "books of Moses," but also other literature including the Prophets and other writings; they believed in such "new" doctrines as the resurrection; after the fall of Jerusalem (70 C.E.), they were the dominant force in Judaism. The *Sadducees,* who interpreted Scripture literally, were a priestly-oriented party who enjoyed considerable civil power in Roman times and were theologically conservative (e.g. they did not believe in the resurrection). There were other distinctive Jewish groups, including the Essenes (of whose literature and practices the Dead Sea Scrolls provide rich information); about these, the NT is silent. **9:** *Abraham for our father:* see Lk. 3.8 n. **11:** *Holy Spirit* and *fire:* see Lk. 3.16 n.

3.13–17: The baptism of Jesus (Mk. 1.9–11 n.; Lk. 3.21–22; Jn. 1.32–34). **14–15:** Jesus' baptism by John presented several problems to the early church. These verses show, first, that John was subordinate to Jesus (v. 14) and second, that Jesus' submission to baptism was not evidence of his sinfulness (vv. 6, 15). **16:** The origin of the *Spirit-dove* imagery is unknown; the Spirit's "hovering" over the deep in Gen. 1.2 is a frequently conjectured source. The descent of the *Spirit* appears to have marked Jesus' installation as Son in the primitive

[17] And there came a voice from heaven saying, 'This is my beloved Son, in whom I take delight.'

The temptation of Jesus

4 JESUS was then led by the Spirit into the wilderness, to be tempted by the devil. [2] For forty days and nights he fasted, and at the end of them he was famished. [3] The tempter approached him and said, 'If you are the Son of God, tell these stones to become bread.' [4] Jesus answered, 'Scripture says, "Man is not to live on bread alone, but on every word that comes from the mouth of God." '

[5] The devil then took him to the Holy City and set him on the parapet of the temple. [6] 'If you are the Son of God,' he said, 'throw yourself down; for scripture says, "He will put his angels in charge of you, and they will support you in their arms, for fear you should strike your foot against a stone." ' [7] Jesus answered him, 'Scripture also says, "You are not to put the Lord your God to the test." '

[8] The devil took him next to a very high mountain, and showed him all the kingdoms of the world in their glory. [9] 'All these', he said, 'I will give you, if you will only fall down and do me homage.' [10] But Jesus said, 'Out of my sight, Satan! Scripture says, "You shall do homage to the Lord your God and worship him alone." '

[11] Then the devil left him; and angels came and attended to his needs.

The first disciples

[12] WHEN he heard that John had been arrested, Jesus withdrew to Galilee; [13] and leaving Nazareth he went and settled at Capernaum on the sea of Galilee, in the district of Zebulun and Naphtali. [14] This was to fulfil the words of the prophet Isaiah about [15] 'the land of Zebulun, the land of Naphtali, the road to the sea, the land beyond Jordan, Galilee of the Gentiles':

[16] The people that lived in darkness
have seen a great light;
light has dawned on those
who lived in the land of death's dark
shadow.

[17] From that day Jesus began to proclaim the message: 'Repent, for the kingdom of Heaven is upon you.'

[18] JESUS was walking by the sea of Galilee when he saw two brothers, Simon called Peter and his brother Andrew, casting a net into the lake; for they were fishermen. [19] Jesus said to them, 'Come with me, and I will make you fishers of men.' [20] At once they left their nets and followed him.

[21] Going on farther, he saw another pair of brothers, James son of Zebedee and his brother John; they were in a boat with their father Zebedee, mending their nets. He called them, [22] and at once they left the boat and their father, and followed him.

[23] He travelled throughout Galilee, teaching in the synagogues, proclaiming the good news of the kingdom, and healing every kind of illness and infirmity among the people. [24] His fame spread throughout Syria; and they brought to him sufferers from various diseases, those racked with pain or possessed by demons, those who were epileptic or paralysed, and he healed them all. [25] Large crowds followed him, from Galilee and the Decapolis, from Jerusalem and Judaea, and from Transjordan.

3:17 **This ... Son:** *or* This is my only Son.
4:1 **tempted:** *or* tested.

tradition. **17:** On *Son, Beloved,* see Mk. 1.11 n.

4.1–11: The temptation (Mk. 1.12–13; Lk. 4.1–13). **1:** The *devil,* or *Satan,* (v. 10) is properly defined in v. 3 as the *tempter,* who is a personification of the evil force which opposes God. **2:** *Forty days and nights* is reminiscent of fasts of Moses (Exod. 34.28; Deut. 9.9, 18) and Elijah (1 Kgs. 19.8). **3, 6:** The issue at stake in the incident is: *if you are the Son of God,* what is the meaning of true sonship? **4:** Deut. 8.3. **5:** *Holy City:* Jerusalem. **6:** Ps. 91.11–12. **7:** Deut. 6.16. **8–9:** The world is conceived as under Satan's power until God's kingdom is realized (v. 17). **10:** Deut. 6.13.

4.12–25: The beginning of Jesus' ministry (Mk. 1.14–20; Lk. 4.14–15; 5.1–11; Jn. 1.35–51). **15–16:** Isa. 9.1–2. **17:** On *kingdom of Heaven,* see 3.2 n. and Mk. 1.15 n. **18–22:** See Mk. 1.16–20 n. **18:** *Simon called Peter:* compare 16.18; Jn. 1.42. **24:** *Demons:* spirits acting as agents of Satan to work evil. **25:** *Decapolis:* Gk. for "Ten Towns"; a confederation of ten independent cities, most of which were southeast of the Sea of Galilee.

The Sermon on the Mount

5 WHEN he saw the crowds he went up a mountain. There he sat down, and when his disciples had gathered round him ²he began to address them. And this is the teaching he gave:

³'Blessed are the poor in spirit;
  the kingdom of Heaven is theirs.
⁴Blessed are the sorrowful;
  they shall find consolation.
⁵Blessed are the gentle;
  they shall have the earth for their possession.
⁶Blessed are those who hunger and thirst to see right prevail;
  they shall be satisfied.
⁷Blessed are those who show mercy;
  mercy shall be shown to them.
⁸Blessed are those whose hearts are pure;
  they shall see God.
⁹Blessed are the peacemakers;
  they shall be called God's children.
¹⁰Blessed are those who are persecuted in the cause of right;
  the kingdom of Heaven is theirs.

¹¹'Blessed are you, when you suffer insults and persecution and calumnies of every kind for my sake. ¹²Exult and be glad, for you have a rich reward in heaven; in the same way they persecuted the prophets before you.

¹³'You are salt to the world. And if salt becomes tasteless, how is its saltness to be restored? It is good for nothing but to be thrown away and trodden underfoot.

¹⁴'You are light for all the world. A town that stands on a hill cannot be hidden. ¹⁵When a lamp is lit, it is not put under the meal-tub, but on the lampstand, where it gives light to everyone in the house. ¹⁶Like the lamp, you must shed light among your fellows, so that, when they see the good you do, they may give praise to your Father in heaven.

¹⁷'Do NOT suppose that I have come to abolish the law and the prophets; I did not come to abolish, but to complete. ¹⁸Truly I tell you: so long as heaven and earth endure, not a letter, not a dot, will disappear from the law until all that must happen has happened. ¹⁹Anyone therefore who sets aside even the least of the law's demands, and teaches others to do the same, will have the lowest place in the kingdom of Heaven, whereas anyone who keeps the law, and teaches others to do so, will rank high in the kingdom of Heaven. ²⁰I tell you, unless you show yourselves far

5:6 **to . . . prevail:** *or* to do what is right.   5:18 **until . . . happened:** *or* before all that it stands for is achieved.

5.1–7.29: The Sermon on the Mount is the first of five great discourses in Matt. (see Introduction). Matthew has organized traditions from various sources to develop the theme of the "higher righteousness" (v. 20 n.). **1:** *Mountain:* mountains are frequently associated with revelation (compare 17.1; 28.16); contrast Lk. 6.17. The Jewish teacher customarily *sat* when delivering instruction. *His disciples* seems to limit the audience (but see 7.28).

5.3–10: The Beatitudes (Lk. 6.20–23). **3:** *Blessed* introduces a form, popularly called a beatitude, which in the OT and Apoc. commends a type of behavior or attitude for which this-worldly happiness is the promised reward (Ps. 1.1–2; Prov. 8.32–34; Ecclus. 25.7–10). In vv. 3–10 (compare Rev. 1.3) the promise is eschatological; i.e. the rewards are related to God's coming realm of salvation (*kingdom*, v. 3) and the beatitudes become conditions for admission to that realm. *Poor in spirit* expresses the religious dimension of a form of Jewish piety for which "poverty" and "utter dependence on God" were synonymous. **6:** The text, *to see right prevail*, implies "to witness the final vindication of right"; Tfn. at v. 6, *to do what is right*, reflects the meaning the Gk. word *dikaiosyne* usually has for Matt.

5.11–16: The task of the disciples. 11–12: The disciples are to expect suffering, which is their lot as *prophets*; compare Lk. 6.22–23. **13–14:** Both *salt* and *light* are metaphors for the learning of the wise and should perhaps be regarded as "names" (see 16.18 n.); see Mk. 4.21; 9.50; Lk. 8.16; 11.33; 14.34–35. **13:** The word translated *becomes tasteless* can also mean "becomes foolish."

5.17–20: The permanence of the Law. 17: The *law* (the "Five Books of Moses") and the writings of the *prophets* are regarded as one body of Scripture (compare 11.13). The section strongly affirms the abiding validity of the Law. **18:** *Dot:* the allusion is to a mark which is a small part of a letter. **19:** A scribe who *sets* better than the scribes and Pharisees, you can never enter the kingdom of Heaven.

21 'You have heard that our forefathers were told, "Do not commit murder; anyone who commits murder must be brought to justice." 22 But what I tell you is this: Anyone who nurses anger against his brother must be brought to justice. Whoever calls his brother "good for nothing" deserves the sentence of the court; whoever calls him "fool" deserves hell-fire. 23 So if you are presenting your gift at the altar and suddenly remember that your brother has a grievance against you, 24 leave your gift where it is before the altar. First go and make your peace with your brother; then come back and offer your gift. 25 If someone sues you, come to terms with him promptly while you are both on your way to court; otherwise he may hand you over to the judge, and the judge to the officer, and you will be thrown into jail. 26 Truly I tell you: once you are there you will not be let out until you have paid the last penny.

27 'You have heard that they were told, "Do not commit adultery." 28 But what I tell you is this: If a man looks at a woman with a lustful eye, he has already committed adultery with her in his heart. 29 If your right eye causes your downfall, tear it out and fling it away; it is better for you to lose one part of your body than for the whole of it to be thrown into hell. 30 If your right hand causes your downfall, cut it off and fling it away; it is better for you to lose one part of your body than for the whole of it to go to hell.

31 'They were told, "A man who divorces his wife must give her a certificate of dismissal." 32 But what I tell you is this: If a man divorces his wife for any cause other than unchastity he involves her in adultery; and whoever marries her commits adultery.

33 'Again, you have heard that our forefathers were told, "Do not break your oath," and "Oaths sworn to the Lord must be kept." 34 But what I tell you is this: You are not to swear at all—not by heaven, for it is God's throne, 35 nor by the earth, for it is his footstool, nor by Jerusalem, for it is the city of the great King, 36 nor by your own head, because you cannot turn one hair of it white or black. 37 Plain "Yes" or "No" is all you need to say; anything beyond that comes from the evil one.

38 'You have heard that they were told, "An eye for an eye, a tooth for a tooth." 39 But what I tell you is this: Do not resist those who wrong you. If anyone slaps you on the right cheek, turn and offer him the other also. 40 If anyone wants to sue you and takes your shirt, let him have your cloak as well. 41 If someone in authority presses you into service for one mile, go with him two. 42 Give to anyone who asks; and do not turn your back on anyone who wants to borrow.

43 'You have heard that they were told, "Love your neighbour and hate your enemy." 44 But what I tell you is this: Love your enemies and pray for your persecutors; 45 only so can you be children of your heavenly Father, who causes the sun to rise on good and bad alike, and sends the rain on the

aside (interprets too freely) the demands may, in effect, nullify both letter and spirit of the Law. **20:** Show yourselves far better calls for a "higher righteousness" which the remainder of the Sermon describes. Scribes: interpreters of the Law; although there must have been Sadducean and other interpreters, Matt. probably refers here to legal specialists among the Pharisees (see 3.7 n.). Enter the kingdom: participate in the salvation accompanying God's rule (see Mk. 1.15 n.).

5.21–48: The meaning of the Law. A series of six statements characterized by the formula, You have heard . . . but what I tell you, gives the Law a more radical (usually, an inward) dimension. **21–26: On murder and anger. 21:** Exod. 20.13; Deut. 5.17, with some addition from the Jewish interpretative tradition. **23–24:** A restored relationship with God (through altar sacrifice in the Jerusalem temple) requires prior reconciliation with the brother (and, surely, sister); compare 6.14–15. **27–30: On adultery and lust. 27:** Exod. 20.14; Deut. 5.18. **29–30:** Compare 18.7–9 n.; Mk. 9.43–48. **31–32: On divorce.** Deuteronomy 24.1–4; first-century legal interpretation sometimes allowed men to divorce their wives for trivial reasons (see Mk. 10.12 n.). **32:** Other than unchastity (see also 19.9): omitted in Mk. 10.11; Lk. 16.18; 1 Cor. 7.10–11. Matthew's form agrees with a strict type of Pharisaic interpretation. **33–37: On oath taking. 33:** Lev. 19.12; Num. 30.2. **34–36:** Compare 23.16–22. **35:** The great King: God. **37:** This radical rule on oaths is carefully stated in Jas. 5.12. **38–42: On retaliation** (Lk. 6.29–30). **38:** Exod. 21.23–24, Lev. 24.19–20; Deut. 19.21. **43–48: On enemies** (Lk. 6.27–28, 32–36). **43:** Love your neighbour (Lev. 19.18) was central to Jewish, as well as Christian, ethical concern in innocent and the wicked. [46] If you love only those who love you, what reward can you expect? Even the tax-collectors do as much as that. [47] If you greet only your brothers, what is there extraordinary about that? Even the heathen do as much. [48] There must be no limit to your goodness, as your heavenly Father's goodness knows no bounds.

6 'BE careful not to parade your religion before others; if you do, no reward awaits you with your Father in heaven.

[2] 'So, when you give alms, do not announce it with a flourish of trumpets, as the hypocrites do in synagogues and in the streets to win the praise of others. Truly I tell you: they have their reward already. [3] But when you give alms, do not let your left hand know what your right is doing; [4] your good deed must be secret, and your Father who sees what is done in secret will reward you.

[5] 'Again, when you pray, do not be like the hypocrites; they love to say their prayers standing up in synagogues and at street corners for everyone to see them. Truly I tell you: they have their reward already. [6] But when you pray, go into a room by yourself, shut the door, and pray to your Father who is in secret; and your Father who sees what is done in secret will reward you.

[7] 'In your prayers do not go babbling on like the heathen, who imagine that the more they say the more likely they are to be heard. [8] Do not imitate them, for your Father knows what your needs are before you ask him.

[9] 'This is how you should pray:

Our Father in heaven,
 may your name be hallowed;
[10] your kingdom come,
 your will be done,
 on earth as in heaven.
[11] Give us today our daily bread.
[12] Forgive us the wrong we have done,
 as we have forgiven those who have
 wronged us.
[13] And do not put us to the test,
 but save us from the evil one.

[14] 'For if you forgive others the wrongs they have done, your heavenly Father will also forgive you; [15] but if you do not forgive others, then your Father will not forgive the wrongs that you have done.

[16] 'So too when you fast, do not look gloomy like the hypocrites: they make their faces unsightly so that everybody may see that they are fasting. Truly I tell you: they have their reward already. [17] But when you fast, anoint your head and wash your face, [18] so that no one sees that you are fasting, but only your Father who is in secret; and your Father who sees what is done in secret will give you your reward.

[19] 'Do NOT store up for yourselves treasure on earth, where moth and rust destroy, and thieves break in and steal; [20] but store up treasure in heaven, where neither moth nor rust will destroy, nor thieves break in and steal. [21] For where your treasure is, there will your heart be also.

[22] 'The lamp of the body is the eye. If your eyes are sound, you will have light for your whole body; [23] if your eyes are bad, your

6:11 **our ... bread:** or our bread for the morrow.
6:13 **from the evil one:** or from evil. *Some witnesses add* For yours is the kingdom and the power and the glory, for ever. Amen.

the first century. *Hate your enemy* is not found in the OT or Pharisaic, Rabbinic Judaism; some other source must be assumed. The positive teaching radicalizes the obligation to love, not only by including enemies (v. 44), but by appealing to God's impartial dealing with all persons (v. 45). **45:** *Children:* see Lk. 6.35 n. **46–47:** See 5.20. **48:** See Lev. 19.2. The verse summarizes vv. 21–48; only an unrestricted obedience, which measures itself by God's goodness, is true righteousness.

6.1–18: Sincere piety seeks to serve God unostentatiously, without the fanfare of the *hypocrites* (lit. "playactors," vv. 2, 5, 16). **2:** Giving *alms* was a special virtue in Judaism. *Synagogues:* see Lk. 4.16 n. **9–13:** The Lord's Prayer (compare the shorter form in Lk. 11.2–4) centers in the hope for the realization of God's rule and will (v. 10; see Mk. 1.15 n.). **9:** Romans 8.15 is an example of the importance early Christians attached to addressing God as *Father*. **11:** The Gk. word translated *daily* (Tfn. at 6.11: *for the morrow*) does not appear elsewhere and its meaning is uncertain; in context, the petition must be a statement of trust in the One whose rule is coming. **12, 14–15:** On forgiveness of others, see 18.21–35.

6.19–34: Trust in God and material possessions compared (Lk. 11.34–36; 12.22–31, 33–34). **22:** *Sound* and *bad* eyes probably contrast "generosity" and "stinginess." Generosity in acts of charity (v. 2 n.) is a way whole body will be in darkness. If then the only light you have is darkness, how great a darkness that will be.

24 'No one can serve two masters; for either he will hate the first and love the second, or he will be devoted to the first and despise the second. You cannot serve God and Money.

25 'This is why I tell you not to be anxious about food and drink to keep you alive and about clothes to cover your body. Surely life is more than food, the body more than clothes. 26 Look at the birds in the sky; they do not sow and reap and store in barns, yet your heavenly Father feeds them. Are you not worth more than the birds? 27 Can anxious thought add a single day to your life? 28 And why be anxious about clothes? Consider how the lilies grow in the fields; they do not work, they do not spin; 29 yet I tell you, even Solomon in all his splendour was not attired like one of them. 30 If that is how God clothes the grass in the fields, which is there today and tomorrow is thrown on the stove, will he not all the more clothe you? How little faith you have! 31 Do not ask anxiously, "What are we to eat? What are we to drink? What shall we wear?" 32 These are the things that occupy the minds of the heathen, but your heavenly Father knows that you need them all. 33 Set your mind on God's kingdom and his justice before everything else, and all the rest will come to you as well. 34 So do not be anxious about tomorrow; tomorrow will look after itself. Each day has troubles enough of its own.

7 'Do NOT judge, and you will not be judged. 2 For as you judge others, so you will yourselves be judged, and whatever measure you deal out to others will be dealt to you. 3 Why do you look at the speck of sawdust in your brother's eye, with never a thought for the plank in your own? 4 How can you say to your brother, "Let me take the speck out of your eye," when all the time there is a plank in your own? 5 You hypocrite!

First take the plank out of your own eye, and then you will see clearly to take the speck out of your brother's.

6 'Do not give dogs what is holy; do not throw your pearls to the pigs: they will only trample on them, and turn and tear you to pieces.

7 'Ask, and you will receive; seek, and you will find; knock, and the door will be opened to you. 8 For everyone who asks receives, those who seek find, and to those who knock, the door will be opened.

9 'Would any of you offer his son a stone when he asks for bread, 10 or a snake when he asks for a fish? 11 If you, bad as you are, know how to give good things to your children, how much more will your heavenly Father give good things to those who ask him!

12 'Always treat others as you would like them to treat you: that is the law and the prophets.

13 'Enter by the narrow gate. Wide is the gate and broad the road that leads to destruction, and many enter that way; 14 narrow is the gate and constricted the road that leads to life, and those who find them are few.

15 'Beware of false prophets, who come to you dressed up as sheep while underneath they are savage wolves. 16 You will recognize them by their fruit. Can grapes be picked from briars, or figs from thistles? 17 A good tree always yields sound fruit, and a poor tree bad fruit. 18 A good tree cannot bear bad fruit, or a poor tree sound fruit. 19 A tree that does not yield sound fruit is cut down and thrown on the fire. 20 That is why I say you will recognize them by their fruit.

21 'Not everyone who says to me, "Lord, Lord" will enter the kingdom of Heaven, but only those who do the will of my heavenly Father. 22 When the day comes, many will say to me, "Lord, Lord, did we not prophesy in your name, drive out demons in your name,

6:27 **add ... life:** *or* add one foot to your height.
6:28 **Consider ... spin:** *one witness reads* Consider the lilies: they neither card, nor spin, nor work.

---

of storing up *treasure in heaven* (v. 20). **24:** Lk. 16.13. **25–34:** God can be trusted from day to day (vv. 26, 30, 32); the person of faith (v. 30) is free to put God's rule first (v. 33).

7.1–14: General instructions. 1–5: Lk. 6.37–38, 41–42. **2:** Mk. 4.24. **7–11:** Lk. 11.9–13. **12:** The Golden Rule (Lk. 6.31) is a widespread principle in ancient ethical literature, including that of Judaism. A related summary of *the law and the prophets* is found in 22.34–40 (compare Mk. 12.28–34; Lk. 10.25–28 n.). **13–14:** Lk. 13.23–24.

7.15–23: Warnings against false leaders (Lk. 6.43–46). Since the *false prophets* appear as *sheep* (although they are *wolves* in disguise, v. 15) and confess Jesus as *Lord* (vv. 21–22), they represent a danger within the and in your name perform many miracles?" [23] Then I will tell them plainly, "I never knew you. Out of my sight; your deeds are evil!"

[24] 'So whoever hears these words of mine and acts on them is like a man who had the sense to build his house on rock. [25] The rain came down, the floods rose, the winds blew and beat upon that house; but it did not fall, because its foundations were on rock. [26] And whoever hears these words of mine and does not act on them is like a man who was foolish enough to build his house on sand. [27] The rain came down, the floods rose, the winds blew and battered against that house; and it fell with a great crash.'

[28] When Jesus had finished this discourse the people were amazed at his teaching; [29] unlike their scribes he taught with a note of authority.

Miracles and teaching

8 WHEN he came down from the mountain great crowds followed him. [2] And now a leper approached him, bowed before him, and said, 'Sir, if only you will, you can make me clean.' [3] Jesus stretched out his hand and touched him, saying, 'I will; be clean.' And his leprosy was cured immediately. [4] Then Jesus said to him, 'See that you tell nobody; but go and show yourself to the priest, and make the offering laid down by Moses to certify the cure.'

[5] As Jesus entered Capernaum a centurion came up to ask his help. [6] 'Sir,' he said, 'my servant is lying at home paralysed and racked with pain.' [7] Jesus said, 'I will come and cure him.' [8] But the centurion replied, 'Sir, I am not worthy to have you under my roof. You need only say the word and my servant will be cured. [9] I know, for I am myself under orders, with soldiers under me. I say to one, "Go," and he goes; to another, "Come here," and he comes; and to my servant, "Do this," and he does it.' [10] Jesus heard him with astonishment, and said to the people who were following him, 'Truly I tell you: nowhere in Israel have I found such faith. [11] Many, I tell you, will come from east and west to sit with Abraham, Isaac, and Jacob at the banquet in the kingdom of Heaven. [12] But those who were born to the kingdom will be thrown out into the dark, where there will be wailing and grinding of teeth.' [13] Then Jesus said to the centurion, 'Go home; as you have believed, so let it be.' At that very moment the boy recovered.

[14] Jesus then went to Peter's house and found Peter's mother-in-law in bed with fever. [15] So he took her by the hand; the fever left her, and she got up and attended to his needs.

[16] That evening they brought to him many who were possessed by demons; and he drove the spirits out with a word and healed all who were sick, [17] to fulfil the prophecy of Isaiah: 'He took our illnesses from us and carried away our diseases.'

[18] At the sight of the crowd surrounding him Jesus gave word to cross to the other side of the lake. [19] A scribe came up and said to him, 'Teacher, I will follow you wherever you go.' [20] Jesus replied, 'Foxes have their holes and birds their roosts; but the Son of Man has nowhere to lay his head.' [21] Another man,

church. **17–18:** 12.33–35. **19:** Compare 3.10; Lk. 3.9. **23:** Lk. 13.27; Ps. 6.8.

7.24–29: The wise and foolish builders (Lk. 6.47–49) concludes the Sermon, warning the faithful to hear and act on Jesus' words. Of the five discourses in Matt. (see Introduction), only that in ch. 10 fails to close with a parable. **28:** A phrase like *when Jesus had finished this discourse* marks the end of the four other collections in the book (11.1; 13.53; 19.1; 26.1).

8.1–9.38: Jesus' teaching and healing. While teaching is interspersed between narratives, this section is comprised primarily of a collection of ten miracles. **1–4: A leper healed** (Mk. 1.40–45; Lk. 5.12–16). **2:** A *leper* was the victim of a skin ailment (not Hansen's disease) which required isolation from society; the rules are given in Lev. ch. 13. *Make me clean:* the leper asks to be rendered ritually pure as well as healed. **5–13: The centurion's servant** (Lk. 7.1–10; compare Jn. 4.46–53). **5:** *Centurion:* a commander of a unit of about one hundred infantry in the Roman army. **6:** *Servant:* the Gk. may mean "servant" or "child." **11–12:** In Jewish thought, an eschatological *banquet* is a theme frequently connected with God's final rule; Lk. 13.28–30. **11:** Compare Ps. 107.2–3. **13:** A phrase like *as you have believed* is frequently associated with healing in the Gospels; usually, this faith seems to be simple confidence in Jesus' power to cure. **14–17: Peter's mother-in-law** (Mk. 1.29–34; Lk. 4.38–41). **17:** Isa. 53.4. **18:** Mk. 4.35. **19–22:** Lk. 9.57–60. **20:** *Son of Man:* see Mk.

one of his disciples, said to him, 'Lord, let me go and bury my father first.' 22 Jesus replied, 'Follow me, and leave the dead to bury their dead.'

23 Jesus then got into the boat, and his disciples followed. 24 All at once a great storm arose on the lake, till the waves were breaking right over the boat; but he went on sleeping. 25 So they came and woke him, saying: 'Save us, Lord; we are sinking!' 26 'Why are you such cowards?' he said. 'How little faith you have!' With that he got up and rebuked the wind and the sea, and there was a dead calm. 27 The men were astonished at what had happened, and exclaimed, 'What sort of man is this? Even the wind and the sea obey him.'

28 When he reached the country of the Gadarenes on the other side, two men came to meet him from among the tombs; they were possessed by demons, and so violent that no one dared pass that way. 29 'Son of God,' they shouted, 'what do you want with us? Have you come here to torment us before our time?' 30 In the distance a large herd of pigs was feeding; 31 and the demons begged him: 'If you drive us out, send us into that herd of pigs.' 32 'Go!' he said. Then they came out and went into the pigs, and the whole herd rushed over the edge into the lake, and perished in the water. 33 The men in charge of them took to their heels, and made for the town, where they told the whole story, and what had happened to the madmen. 34 Then the whole town came out to meet Jesus; and when they saw him they begged him to leave the district. 1 So he got into the boat and crossed over, and came to his own town.

9 2 Some men appeared, bringing to Jesus a paralysed man on a bed. When he saw their faith Jesus said to the man, 'Take heart, my son; your sins are forgiven.' 3 At this some of the scribes said to themselves, 'This man is blaspheming!' 4 Jesus realized what they were thinking, and said, 'Why do you harbour evil thoughts? 5 Is it easier to say, "Your sins are forgiven," or to say, "Stand up and walk"? 6 But to convince you that the Son of Man has authority on earth to forgive sins'—he turned to the paralysed man—'stand up, take your bed, and go home.' 7 And he got up and went off home. 8 The people were filled with awe at the sight, and praised God for granting such authority to men.

9 As HE went on from there Jesus saw a man named Matthew at his seat in the custom-house, and said to him, 'Follow me'; and Matthew rose and followed him.

10 When Jesus was having a meal in the house, many tax-collectors and sinners were seated with him and his disciples. 11 Noticing this, the Pharisees said to his disciples, 'Why is it that your teacher eats with tax-collectors and sinners?' 12 Hearing this he said, 'It is not the healthy who need a doctor, but the sick. 13 Go and learn what this text means, "I require mercy, not sacrifice." I did not come to call the virtuous, but sinners.'

14 Then John's disciples came to him with the question: 'Why is it that we and the Pharisees fast but your disciples do not?' 15 Jesus replied, 'Can you expect the bridegroom's friends to be sad while the bridegroom is with them? The time will come when the bridegroom will be taken away from them; then they will fast.

16 'No one puts a patch of unshrunk cloth on an old garment; for then the patch tears away from the garment, and leaves a bigger hole. 17 Nor do people put new wine into old wineskins; if they do, the skins burst, and then the wine runs out and the skins are ruined. No, they put new wine into fresh skins; then both are preserved.'

18 EVEN as he spoke, an official came up, who bowed before him and said, 'My daughter has just died; but come and lay your hand on her, and she will live.' 19 Jesus rose and went with him, and so did his disciples.

2.10 n. **23–27: Rebuke of a storm** (Mk. 4.35–41; Lk. 8.22–25). **28–34: The Gadarene demoniacs** (Mk. 5.1–20; Lk. 8.26–39). **28–29:** The *demons* (see Mk. 1.23 n.) recognize the *Son of God* (see 16.16 n.; Mk. 1.24 n.). **28:** *Gadarenes:* see Mk. 5.1 n. *Two men:* Mk. and Lk. report only one *possessed* person. **30:** *Pigs* are unclean animals in Mosaic law (Lev. 11.7; Deut. 14.8). **9.1–8: A paralytic;** see Mk. 2.1–12 nn.; Lk. 5.17–20. **9:** *Matthew:* called Levi in Mk. 2.14; Lk. 5.27. **10–13: Tax-collectors and sinners.** Mk. 2.15–17; Lk. 5.29–32. **10:** *Tax-collectors:* see Lk. 3.12 n. **13:** Hos. 6.6; quoted again in 12.7. **14–17: Fasting** (Mk. 2.18–22; Lk. 5.33–39). **14:** *John's disciples:* see Mk. 2.18 n. **16–17:** See Mk. 2.21–22 n. **18–26: Jairus' daughter and a woman with a chronic ailment** (Mk. 5.21–43; Lk. 8.40–56). See Mk. 5.21–43 n. **18:** *An official:* in Mk. 5.22, Lk. 8.41, a synagogue leader named Jairus. **22:** *Healed:* lit. "saved"; see Lk. 7.50 n. **23:** *Flute-players* provided

²⁰Just then a woman who had suffered from haemorrhages for twelve years came up from behind, and touched the edge of his cloak; ²¹for she said to herself, 'If I can only touch his cloak, I shall be healed.' ²²But Jesus turned and saw her, and said, 'Take heart, my daughter; your faith has healed you.' And from that moment she recovered.

²³When Jesus arrived at the official's house and saw the flute-players and the general commotion, ²⁴he said, 'Go away! The girl is not dead: she is asleep'; and they laughed at him. ²⁵After turning them all out, he went into the room and took the girl by the hand, and she got up. ²⁶The story became the talk of the whole district.

²⁷As he went on from there Jesus was followed by two blind men, shouting, 'Have pity on us, Son of David!' ²⁸When he had gone indoors they came to him, and Jesus asked, 'Do you believe that I have the power to do what you want?' 'We do,' they said. ²⁹Then he touched their eyes, and said, 'As you have believed, so let it be'; ³⁰and their sight was restored. Jesus said to them sternly, 'See that no one hears about this.' ³¹But as soon as they had gone out they talked about him all over the region.

³²They were on their way out when a man was brought to him, who was dumb and possessed by a demon; ³³the demon was driven out and the dumb man spoke. The crowd was astonished and said, 'Nothing like this has ever been seen in Israel.'

³⁵So Jesus went round all the towns and villages teaching in their synagogues, proclaiming the good news of the kingdom, and curing every kind of illness and infirmity. ³⁶The sight of the crowds moved him to pity: they were like sheep without a shepherd, harassed and helpless. ³⁷Then he said to his disciples, 'The crop is heavy, but the labour-ers too few; ³⁸you must ask the owner to send labourers to bring in the harvest.'

The Twelve are commissioned

10 THEN he called his twelve disciples to him and gave them authority to drive out unclean spirits and to cure every kind of illness and infirmity.

²These are the names of the twelve apostles: first Simon, also called Peter, and his brother Andrew; James son of Zebedee, and his brother John; ³Philip and Bartholomew, Thomas and Matthew the tax-collector, James son of Alphaeus, Thaddaeus, ⁴Simon the Zealot, and Judas Iscariot, the man who betrayed him.

⁵These twelve Jesus sent out with the following instructions: 'Do not take the road to gentile lands, and do not enter any Samaritan town; ⁶but go rather to the lost sheep of the house of Israel. ⁷And as you go proclaim the message: "The kingdom of Heaven is upon you." ⁸Heal the sick, raise the dead, cleanse lepers, drive out demons. You received without cost; give without charge.

⁹'Take no gold, silver, or copper in your belts, ¹⁰no pack for the road, no second coat, no sandals, no stick; the worker deserves his keep.

¹¹'Whatever town or village you enter, look for some suitable person in it, and stay with him until you leave. ¹²Wish the house peace as you enter it; ¹³if it is welcoming, let your peace descend on it, and if it is not, let your peace come back to you. ¹⁴If anyone will not receive you or listen to what you say, then as you leave that house or that town shake the dust of it off your feet. ¹⁵Truly I tell you: on

9:20 **edge:** *or* tassel.
9:33 **in Israel:** *some witnesses add* ³⁴But the Pharisees said, 'He drives out devils by the prince of devils.'
10:3 **Thaddaeus:** *some witnesses read* Lebbaeus.

accompaniment to the customary wailing of mourners. **27–31: Two blind men** (20.29–34; Mk. 10.46–52; Lk. 18.35–43). **32–33: A dumb man.** Tfn. at v. 34 may be borrowed from the story in 12.22–24.

9.35–38: A transition from the miracles of chs. 8–9 to the "missionary discourse" of ch. 10; compare 4.23–25. **36:** Mk. 6.34; Num. 27.17; 1 Kgs. 22.17.

10.1–11.1: The second (missionary) discourse. 1: Mk. 3.14–15; 6.7; Lk. 9.1. **2–4:** Mk. 3.16–19; Lk. 6.14–16. **2:** *Apostles:* commissioned representatives; this designation appears in Matt. only in this verse. **3:** *Thaddaeus:* as in Mk. 3.18, but see Tfn. at v. 3. Luke 6.16 and Acts 1.13 have "Judas the son of James." **4:** *Zealot:* see Mk. 3.18 n. **5–6:** Contrast the instruction in 28.19. **7–15:** Mk. 6.8–11; Lk. 9.2–5; 10.3–12. **7:** Compare the Baptist's (3.2) and Jesus' (4.17) messages. **8:** On the close relation of healing and God's rule, consider 12.28; Lk. 10.9; 11.20; the Gospels present the career of Jesus as the proclamation of God's rule joined the day of judgement it will be more bearable for the land of Sodom and Gomorrah than for that town.

16 'I send you out like sheep among wolves; be wary as serpents, innocent as doves.

17 'Be on your guard, for you will be handed over to the courts, they will flog you in their synagogues, 18 and you will be brought before governors and kings on my account, to testify before them and the Gentiles. 19 But when you are arrested, do not worry about what you are to say, for when the time comes, the words you need will be given you; 20 it will not be you speaking, but the Spirit of your Father speaking in you.

21 'Brother will hand over brother to death, and a father his child; children will turn against their parents and send them to their death. 22 Everyone will hate you for your allegiance to me, but whoever endures to the end will be saved. 23 When you are persecuted in one town, take refuge in another; truly I tell you: before you have gone through all the towns of Israel the Son of Man will have come.

24 'No pupil ranks above his teacher, no servant above his master. 25 The pupil should be content to share his teacher's lot, the servant to share his master's. If the master has been called Beelzebul, how much more his household!

26 'So do not be afraid of them. There is nothing covered up that will not be uncovered, nothing hidden that will not be made known. 27 What I say to you in the dark you must repeat in broad daylight; what you hear whispered you must shout from the housetops. 28 Do not fear those who kill the body, but cannot kill the soul. Fear him rather who is able to destroy both soul and body in hell.

29 'Are not two sparrows sold for a penny? Yet without your Father's knowledge not one of them can fall to the ground. 30 As for you, even the hairs of your head have all been counted. 31 So do not be afraid; you are worth more than any number of sparrows.

32 'Whoever will acknowledge me before others, I will acknowledge before my Father in heaven; 33 and whoever disowns me before others, I will disown before my Father in heaven.

34 'You must not think that I have come to bring peace to the earth; I have not come to bring peace, but a sword. 35 I have come to set a man against his father, a daughter against her mother, a daughter-in-law against her mother-in-law; 36 and a man will find his enemies under his own roof.

37 'No one is worthy of me who cares more for father or mother than for me; no one is worthy of me who cares more for son or daughter; 38 no one is worthy of me who does not take up his cross and follow me. 39 Whoever gains his life will lose it; whoever loses his life for my sake will gain it.

40 'To receive you is to receive me, and to receive me is to receive the One who sent me. 41 Whoever receives a prophet because he is a prophet will be given a prophet's reward, and whoever receives a good man because he is a good man will be given a good man's reward. 42 Truly I tell you: anyone who gives so much as a cup of cold water to one of these little ones because he is a disciple of mine, will certainly not go unrewarded.'

11 When Jesus had finished giving instructions to his twelve disciples, he went from there to teach and preach in the neighbouring towns.

Recognizing the Messiah

2 JOHN, who was in prison, heard what Christ was doing, and sent his own disciples 3 to put this question to him: 'Are you the one who is to come, or are we to expect someone else?' 4 Jesus answered, 'Go and report to John what you hear and see: 5 the blind recover

---

with healing activity. **15:** *Sodom and Gomorrah* (Gen. ch. 29) were the epitome of evil. **17–25:** 24.9–13; Mk. 13.9–13; Lk. 12.11–12; 21.12–17, 19. Persecution in both Jewish (v. 17) and Roman (v. 18) settings is assumed. **21:** See vv. 35–36. **24–25:** Lk. 6.40; Jn. 13.16. **25:** *Beelzebul:* Satan (see 9.34; 12.22; Mk. 3.22; Lk. 11.15). **26–33:** Lk. 12.2–9. **26–27:** Compare Mk. 4.22, 24–25 n.; Lk. 8.17; 12.2–3 n. **28:** See Lk. 12.5 n. **29–32: God's providence:** 6.26–33; Lk. 12.6–8. **34–36:** Lk. 12.51, 53; the proclamation of God's rule calls for a decision which draws lines of separation. **37–39:** Compare Lk. 14.26–27. **38–39:** *Cross* and *losing life* sayings are also connected in 16.24–25; Mk. 8.34–35; Lk. 9.23–24; *life* and *follow me* sayings, in Jn. 12.25–26. The associated ideas would be particularly meaningful in situations involving mission or persecution. **39:** Lk. 17.33. **40–42:** Jesus affirms his identification with his disciples. **11.1:** See 7.28 n.
 11.2–12.50: Claims and conflict.

their sight, the lame walk, lepers are made clean, the deaf hear, the dead are raised to life, the poor are brought good news — 6 and blessed are those who do not find me an obstacle to faith.'

7 When the messengers were on their way back, Jesus began to speak to the crowds about John: 'What was the spectacle that drew you to the wilderness? A reed swaying in the wind? 8 No? Then what did you go out to see? A man dressed in finery? Fine clothes are to be found in palaces. 9 But why did you go out? To see a prophet? Yes indeed, and far more than a prophet. 10 He is the man of whom scripture says,

> Here is my herald, whom I send ahead
> of you,
> and he will prepare your way before
> you.

11 'Truly I tell you: among all who have ever been born, no one has been greater than John the Baptist, and yet the least in the kingdom of Heaven is greater than he. 12 'Since the time of John the Baptist the kingdom of Heaven has been subjected to violence and violent men are taking it by force. 13 For until John, all the prophets and the law foretold things to come; 14 and John is the destined Elijah, if you will but accept it. 15 If you have ears, then hear.

16 'How can I describe this generation? They are like children sitting in the marketplace and calling to each other,

> 17 We piped for you and you would not
> dance.
> We lamented, and you would not
> mourn.

18 'For John came, neither eating nor drinking, and people say, "He is possessed"; 19 the Son of Man came, eating and drinking, and they say, "Look at him! A glutton and a drinker, a friend of tax-collectors and sin-ners!" Yet God's wisdom is proved right by its results.'

20 THEN he spoke of the towns in which most of his miracles had been performed, and denounced them for their impenitence. 21 'Alas for you, Chorazin!' he said. 'Alas for you, Bethsaida! If the miracles performed in you had taken place in Tyre and Sidon, they would have repented long ago in sackcloth and ashes. 22 But it will be more bearable, I tell you, for Tyre and Sidon on the day of judgement than for you. 23 As for you, Capernaum, will you be exalted to heaven? No, you will be brought down to Hades! For if the miracles performed in you had taken place in Sodom, Sodom would be standing to this day. 24 But it will be more bearable, I tell you, for the land of Sodom on the day of judgement than for you.'

25 At that time Jesus spoke these words: 'I thank you, Father, Lord of heaven and earth, for hiding these things from the learned and wise, and revealing them to the simple. 26 Yes, Father, such was your choice. 27 Everything is entrusted to me by my Father; and no one knows the Son but the Father, and no one knows the Father but the Son and those to whom the Son chooses to reveal him.

28 'Come to me, all who are weary and whose load is heavy; I will give you rest. 29 Take my yoke upon you, and learn from me, for I am gentle and humble-hearted; and you will find rest for your souls. 30 For my yoke is easy to wear, my load is light.'

Opposition to Jesus

12 ABOUT that time Jesus was going through the cornfields on the sabbath; and his disciples, feeling hungry, began to pluck some ears of corn and eat them.

11:12 **has been ... force:** or has been forcing its way forward, and men of force are seizing it.   11:26 **Yes ... such:** or Yes, I thank you, Father, that such.

11.2–19: Jesus and John the Baptist: see Lk. 7.18–35 nn. **2:** In prison: 14.3–4; Mk. 6.17–18. **5:** Isa. 29.18–19; 35.5–6; 61.1. **10:** Mal. 3.1. **12–15:** John's career marks the beginning of the fulfillment of God's promises; compare Lk. 16.16 n. **14:** John fulfills the prophecy on Elijah; Mal. 4.5; see Lk. 1.17. **19:** Its results: lit. "her deeds"; compare Lk. 7.35 n. **20–24: Judgment of Galilean cities** (Lk. 10.13–15). **21:** Tyre and Sidon: Gentile (Phoenician) cities condemned by the prophets (Jer. 47.4). Sackcloth and ashes: symbols of mourning. Sodom: see 10.15 n. **25–27: Thanksgiving for revelation.** See Lk. 10.21–22 n. **28–30:** An invitation modeled on those extended by the heavenly Wisdom (Lk. 7.35 n.); see Prov. 8.1–21 and Ecclus. 6.18–31. **12.1–14: Sabbath controversy** (Mk. 2.23–3.6 nn.; Lk. 6.1–11). **1:** Deut. 23.25.

2 When the Pharisees saw this, they said to him, 'Look, your disciples are doing what is forbidden on the sabbath.' 3 He answered, 'Have you not read what David did when he and his men were hungry? 4 He went into the house of God and ate the sacred bread, though neither he nor his men had a right to eat it, but only the priests. 5 Or have you not read in the law that on the sabbath the priests in the temple break the sabbath and they are not held to be guilty? 6 But I tell you, there is something greater than the temple here. 7 If you had known what this text means, "It is mercy I require, not sacrifice," you would not have condemned the innocent. 8 For the Son of Man is lord of the sabbath.'

9 He went on to another place, and entered their synagogue. 10 A man was there with a withered arm, and they asked Jesus, 'Is it permitted to heal on the sabbath?' (They wanted to bring a charge against him.) 11 But he said to them, 'Suppose you had one sheep, and it fell into a ditch on the sabbath; is there a single one of you who would not catch hold of it and lift it out? 12 Surely a man is worth far more than a sheep! It is therefore permitted to do good on the sabbath.' 13 Then he said to the man, 'Stretch out your arm.' He stretched it out, and it was made sound again like the other. 14 But the Pharisees, on leaving the synagogue, plotted to bring about Jesus's death.

15 Jesus was aware of it and withdrew, and many followed him. He healed all who were ill, 16 and gave strict instructions that they were not to make him known. 17 This was to fulfil Isaiah's prophecy:

18 Here is my servant, whom I have chosen,
    my beloved, in whom I take delight;
I will put my Spirit upon him,
    and he will proclaim justice among the nations.
19 He will not strive, he will not shout,
    nor will his voice be heard in the streets.
20 He will not snap off a broken reed,
    nor snuff out a smouldering wick,

until he leads justice on to victory.
21 In him the nations shall put their hope.

22 THEN they brought him a man who was possessed by a demon; he was blind and dumb, and Jesus cured him, restoring both speech and sight. 23 The bystanders were all amazed, and the word went round: 'Can this be the Son of David?' 24 But when the Pharisees heard it they said, 'It is only by Beelzebul prince of devils that this man drives the devils out.'

25 Knowing what was in their minds, he said to them, 'Every kingdom divided against itself is laid waste; and no town or household that is divided against itself can stand. 26 And if it is Satan who drives out Satan, he is divided against himself; how then can his kingdom stand? 27 If it is by Beelzebul that I drive out devils, by whom do your own people drive them out? If this is your argument, they themselves will refute you. 28 But if it is by the Spirit of God that I drive out the devils, then be sure the kingdom of God has already come upon you.

29 'Or again, how can anyone break into a strong man's house and make off with his goods, unless he has first tied up the strong man? Then he can ransack the house.

30 'He who is not with me is against me, and he who does not gather with me scatters.

31 'So I tell you this: every sin and every slander can be forgiven, except slander spoken against the Spirit; that will not be forgiven. 32 Anyone who speaks a word against the Son of Man will be forgiven; but if anyone speaks against the Holy Spirit, for him there will be no forgiveness, either in this age or in the age to come.

33 'Get a good tree and its fruit will be good; get a bad tree and its fruit will be bad. You can tell a tree by its fruit. 34 Vipers' brood! How can your words be good when you yourselves are evil? It is from the fullness of the heart that the mouth speaks. 35 Good people from their store of good produce good; and evil people from their store of evil produce evil.

36 'I tell you this: every thoughtless word

2: Exod. 20.10; Deut. 5.14. 3: 1 Sam. 21.1–7. 4: Lev. 24.7–9. 5: Num. 28.9–10. 7: Hos. 6.6; compare 9.13. 9–14: See Mk. 3.1–6 n. 11: Lk. 14.5. 15–21: Healing the sick. 18–21: Isa. 42.1–4. 22–29: Jesus and Satan (Mk. 3.22–27; Lk. 11.14–22). 23: Son of David: the Messiah (1.1 n.). 24–28: Beelzebul: Satan (v. 26). 27: Your own people ascribes the effective practice of exorcism to others. 30: Lk. 11.23; contrast Mk. 9.39–40 n. 31–32: See Mk. 3.29 n.; Lk. 12.10. Matthew may intend the saying to distinguish between slander of the earthly you speak you will have to account for on the day of judgement. [37] For out of your own mouth you will be acquitted; out of your own mouth you will be condemned.'

[38] At this some of the scribes and the Pharisees said, 'Teacher, we would like you to show us a sign.' [39] He answered: 'It is a wicked, godless generation that asks for a sign, and the only sign that will be given it is the sign of the prophet Jonah. [40] Just as Jonah was in the sea monster's belly for three days and three nights, so the Son of Man will be three days and three nights in the bowels of the earth. [41] The men of Nineveh will appear in court when this generation is on trial, and ensure its condemnation, for they repented at the preaching of Jonah; and what is here is greater than Jonah. [42] The queen of the south will appear in court when this generation is on trial, and ensure its condemnation; for she came from the ends of the earth to listen to the wisdom of Solomon, and what is here is greater than Solomon.

[43] 'When an unclean spirit comes out of someone it wanders over the desert sands seeking a resting-place, and finds none. [44] Then it says, "I will go back to the home I left." So it returns and finds the house unoccupied, swept clean, and tidy. [45] It goes off and collects seven other spirits more wicked than itself, and they all come in and settle there; and in the end that person's plight is worse than before. That is how it will be with this wicked generation.'

[46] He was still speaking to the crowd when his mother and brothers appeared; they stood outside, wanting to speak to him. [47] Someone said, 'Your mother and your brothers are standing outside; they want to speak to you.' [48] Jesus turned to the man who brought the message, and said, 'Who is my mother? Who are my brothers?' [49] and pointing to his disciples, he said, 'Here are my mother and my brothers. [50] Whoever does

the will of my heavenly Father is my brother and sister and mother.'

Parables

13 THAT same day Jesus went out and sat by the lakeside, [2] where so many people gathered round him that he had to get into a boat. He sat there, and all the people stood on the shore. [3] He told them many things in parables.

He said: 'A sower went out to sow. [4] And as he sowed, some of the seed fell along the footpath; and the birds came and ate it up. [5] Some fell on rocky ground, where it had little soil, and it sprouted quickly because it had no depth of earth; [6] but when the sun rose it was scorched, and as it had no root it withered away. [7] Some fell among thistles; and the thistles grew up and choked it. [8] And some of the seed fell on good soil, where it produced a crop, some a hundredfold, some sixtyfold, and some thirtyfold. [9] If you have ears, then hear.'

[10] The disciples came to him and asked, 'Why do you speak to them in parables?' [11] He replied, 'To you it has been granted to know the secrets of the kingdom of Heaven, but not to them. [12] For those who have will be given more, till they have enough and to spare; and those who have not will forfeit even what they have. [13] That is why I speak to them in parables; for they look without seeing, and listen without hearing or understanding. [14] The prophecy of Isaiah is being fulfilled in them: "You may listen and listen, but you will never understand; you may look and look, but you will never see. [15] For this people's mind has become dull; they have stopped their ears and shut their eyes. Otherwise, their eyes might see, their ears hear,

12:41 **will appear ... trial:** *or* will rise again with this generation at the judgement.   12:42 **The queen ... trial:** *or* The queen of the south will be raised to life with this generation at the judgement.

Jesus and *slander* of the risen Lord. **33–37:** 7.16–20; Lk. 6.43–45. **38–42:** The request for a *sign* (Lk. 11.29–32) is perhaps regarded as evil because its intent is to "test" (compare 4.7). **39–41:** Jonah 1.17; 3.5. The *sign of the prophet Jonah* for Matt. is interpreted by v. 40; compare Lk. 11.29 n. *Queen of the south:* 1 Kgs. 10.1–10. **43–45:** Lk. 11.24–26. **43:** Deserts were often associated with demons. **46–50:** Mk. 3.31–35; Lk. 8.19–21.

13.1–53a: The third discourse (see Introduction) is a collection of parables typically introduced by the phrase "the kingdom . . . is like." For *kingdom* see Mk. 1.15 n. (Mk. ch. 4; Lk. 8.4–18; 10.23–24; 13.18–21). **3:** On *parables,* see Mk. 4.2 n. **3–9: The sower** (Mk. 4.1–9; Lk. 8.4–8). **3–8:** See Mk. 4.3–8 n. **8:** See Mk. 4.8 n. **10–17: The use of parables** (Mk. 4.10–12; Lk. 8.9–10; 10.23–24). See Mk. 4.11 n., 13–20 n. **13:** In Matt. the use of parables is a consequence of the failure to "see" or "hear"; contrast Mk. 4.12 n. **14–16:** Isa. 6.9–10.

and their mind understand, and then they might turn to me, and I would heal them."

16 'But happy are your eyes because they see, and your ears because they hear! 17 Truly I tell you: many prophets and saints longed to see what you now see, yet never saw it; to hear what you hear, yet never heard it.

18 'Hear then the parable of the sower. 19 When anyone hears the word that tells of the Kingdom, but fails to understand it, the evil one comes and carries off what has been sown in his heart; that is the seed sown along the footpath. 20 The seed sown on rocky ground stands for the person who hears the word and accepts it at once with joy; 21 it strikes no root in him and he has no staying-power; when there is trouble or persecution on account of the word he quickly loses faith. 22 The seed sown among thistles represents the person who hears the word, but worldly cares and the false glamour of wealth choke it, and it proves barren. 23 But the seed sown on good soil is the person who hears the word and understands it; he does bear fruit and yields a hundredfold, or sixtyfold, or thirty-fold.'

24 Here is another parable he gave them: 'The kingdom of Heaven is like this. A man sowed his field with good seed; 25 but while everyone was asleep his enemy came, sowed darnel among the wheat, and made off. 26 When the corn sprouted and began to fill out, the darnel could be seen among it. 27 The farmer's men went to their master and said, "Sir, was it not good seed that you sowed in your field? So where has the darnel come from?" 28 "This is an enemy's doing," he re-plied. "Well then," they said, "shall we go and gather the darnel?" 29 "No," he answered; "in gathering it you might pull up the wheat at the same time. 30 Let them both grow to-gether till harvest; and at harvest time I will tell the reapers, 'Gather the darnel first, and tie it in bundles for burning; then collect the wheat into my barn.' " '

31 This is another parable he gave them: 'The kingdom of Heaven is like a mustard seed, which a man took and sowed in his field. 32 Mustard is smaller than any other seed, but when it has grown it is taller than other plants; it becomes a tree, big enough for the birds to come and roost among its branches.'

33 He told them also this parable: 'The kingdom of Heaven is like yeast, which a woman took and mixed with three measures of flour till it was all leavened.'

34 In all this teaching to the crowds Jesus spoke in parables; indeed he never spoke to them except in parables. 35 This was to fulfil the saying of the prophet:

I will open my mouth in parables;
I will utter things kept secret since the
    world was made.

36 Then he sent the people away, and went into the house, where his disciples came to him and said, 'Explain to us the parable of the darnel in the field.' 37 He replied, 'The sower of the good seed is the Son of Man. 38 The field is the world; the good seed stands for the children of the Kingdom, the darnel for the children of the evil one, 39 and the enemy who sowed the darnel is the devil. The harvest is the end of time, and the reapers are angels. 40 As the darnel is gathered up and burnt, so at the end of time 41 the Son of Man will send his angels, who will gather out of his kingdom every cause of sin, and all whose deeds are evil; 42 these will be thrown into the blazing furnace, where there will be wailing and grinding of teeth. 43 Then the righteous will shine like the sun in the kingdom of their Father. If you have ears, then hear.

44 'The kingdom of Heaven is like treasure which a man found buried in a field. He buried it again, and in joy went and sold everything he had, and bought the field.

13:35 **prophet:** *some witnesses add* Isaiah.

16–17: Lk. 10.23–24. **18–23:** An interpretation of the sower. See Mk. 4.13–20 n. **19:** The term *understand* here and in v. 23 is used to serve the view of Matt. that the disciples are persons of insight (contrast the tone of Mk. 4.13). **24–30: The weeds in the field. 25:** *Darnel:* a weed similar in appearance to wheat. **31–32: The mustard seed** (see Mk. 4.26–32 nn.; Lk. 13.18–19). **33: Yeast** (Lk. 13.20–21). Although a fermenting agent (*yeast*) is regularly a symbol for evil influence elsewhere (e.g. 16.6, 11; Gal. 5.8–9), here the metaphor suggests the idea of the irreversible power of the kingdom. *Three measures:* a very large amount is meant. **35:** While Ps. 78.2 is quoted, some MSS. attribute the words to Isa. (Tfn. v. 35). **36–43: An interpretation of the parable** of the weeds. **38:** The *evil one:* the devil. **43:** Dan. 12.3. **44–46: The treasure and the pearls** parables speak either (a) of the cost of participating in the realm of salvation or (b) of its value which makes even that cost

45 'Again, the kingdom of Heaven is like this. A merchant looking out for fine pearls 46 found one of very special value; so he went and sold everything he had and bought it.

47 'Again the kingdom of Heaven is like a net cast into the sea, where it caught fish of every kind. 48 When it was full, it was hauled ashore. Then the men sat down and collected the good fish into baskets and threw the worthless away. 49 That is how it will be at the end of time. The angels will go out, and they will separate the wicked from the good, 50 and throw them into the blazing furnace, where there will be wailing and grinding of teeth.

51 'Have you understood all this?' he asked; and they answered, 'Yes.' 52 So he said to them, 'When, therefore, a teacher of the law has become a learner in the kingdom of Heaven, he is like a householder who can produce from his store things new and old.'

53 WHEN Jesus had finished these parables he left that place, 54 and came to his home town, where he taught the people in their synagogue. In amazement they asked, 'Where does he get this wisdom from, and these miraculous powers? 55 Is he not the carpenter's son? Is not his mother called Mary, his brothers James, Joseph, Simon, and Judas? 56 And are not all his sisters here with us? Where does he get all this from?' 57 So they turned against him. Jesus said to them, 'A prophet never lacks honour, except in his home town and in his own family.' 58 And he did not do many miracles there, such was their want of faith.

Death of John the Baptist

14 It was at that time that reports about Jesus reached Herod the tetrarch. 2 'This is John the Baptist,' he said to his attendants; 'he has been raised from the dead, and that is why these miraculous powers are at work in him.'

3 Now Herod had arrested John, put him in chains, and thrown him into prison, on account of Herodias, his brother Philip's wife; 4 for John had told him: 'You have no right to her.' 5 Herod would have liked to put him to death, but he was afraid of the people, in whose eyes John was a prophet. 6 But at his birthday celebrations the daughter of Herodias danced before the guests, and Herod was so delighted 7 that he promised on oath to give her anything she asked for. 8 Prompted by her mother, she said, 'Give me here on a dish the head of John the Baptist.' 9 At this the king was distressed, but because of his oath and his guests, he ordered the request to be granted, 10 and had John beheaded in prison. 11 The head was brought on a dish and given to the girl; and she carried it to her mother. 12 Then John's disciples came and took away the body, and buried it; and they went and told Jesus.

More miracles and teaching

13 WHEN he heard what had happened Jesus withdrew privately by boat to a remote place; but large numbers of people heard of it, and came after him on foot from the towns. 14 When he came ashore and saw a large crowd, his heart went out to them, and he healed those who were sick. 15 As evening drew on, the disciples came up to him and said, 'This is a remote place and the day has gone; send the people off to the villages to buy themselves food.' 16 Jesus answered, 'There is no need for them to go; give them something to eat yourselves.' 17 'All we have here', they said, 'is five loaves and two fish.' 18 'Bring them to me,' he replied. 19 So he told the people to sit down on the grass; then, taking the five loaves and the two fish, he looked up to heaven, said the blessing, broke the loaves, and gave them to the disciples; and the disciples gave them to the people. 20 They all ate and were satisfied; and twelve baskets were filled with what was left over. 21 Some five thousand men shared in this meal, not counting women and children.

22 As soon as they had finished, he made the disciples embark and cross to the other

---

a joy. **47–50: The net.** The proclamation attracts both good and bad; their separation must wait for the final judgment. **51–52:** The disciple's resources now include both the *new* message of the kingdom and the *old* tradition based on the Law and the Prophets. See 7.24–29 n. **53a:** See 7.28 n.

13.53b–58: Jesus in Nazareth (Mk. 6.1–6; compare Lk. 4.16–30). **54:** *Home town:* Nazareth.

14.1–12: Herod and John (Mk. 6.14–29; Lk. 3.19–20; 9.7–9). **1:** *Herod:* Antipas (Lk. 3.1 n.).

14.13–21: Feeding of five thousand (Mk. 6.30–44; Lk. 9.10–17; Jn. 6.1–13). See Mk. 6.30–44 nn.

side ahead of him, while he dismissed the crowd; 23 then he went up the hill by himself to pray. It had grown late, and he was there alone. 24 The boat was already some distance from the shore, battling with a head wind and a rough sea. 25 Between three and six in the morning he came towards them, walking across the lake. 26 When the disciples saw him walking on the lake they were so shaken that they cried out in terror: 'It is a ghost!' 27 But at once Jesus spoke to them: 'Take heart! It is I; do not be afraid.'

28 Peter called to him: 'Lord, if it is you, tell me to come to you over the water.' 29 'Come,' said Jesus. Peter got down out of the boat, and walked over the water towards Jesus. 30 But when he saw the strength of the gale he was afraid; and beginning to sink, he cried, 'Save me, Lord!' 31 Jesus at once reached out and caught hold of him. 'Why did you hesitate?' he said. 'How little faith you have!' 32 Then they climbed into the boat; and the wind dropped. 33 And the men in the boat fell at his feet, exclaiming, 'You must be the Son of God.'

34 So they completed the crossing and landed at Gennesaret. 35 The people there recognized Jesus and sent word to all the country round. They brought to him all who were ill 36 and begged him to let them simply touch the edge of his cloak; and all who touched it were completely cured.

15 THEN Jesus was approached by a group of Pharisees and scribes from Jerusalem, with the question: 2 'Why do your disciples break the ancient tradition? They do not wash their hands before eating.' 3 He answered them: 'And what about you? Why do you break God's commandment in the interest of your tradition? 4 For God said, "Honour your father and mother," and "Whoever curses his father or mother shall be put to death." 5 But you say, "Whoever

says to his father or mother, 'Anything I have which might have been used for your benefit is set apart for God,' 6 must not honour his father or his mother." You have made God's law null and void out of regard for your tradition. 7 What hypocrites! How right Isaiah was when he prophesied about you: 8 "This people pays me lip-service, but their heart is far from me; 9 they worship me in vain, for they teach as doctrines the commandments of men." '

10 He called the crowd and said to them, 'Listen and understand! 11 No one is defiled by what goes into his mouth; only by what comes out of it.'

12 Then the disciples came to him and said, 'Do you know that the Pharisees have taken great offence at what you have been saying?' 13 He answered: 'Any plant that is not of my heavenly Father's planting will be rooted up. 14 Leave them alone; they are blind guides, and if one blind man guides another they will both fall into the ditch.'

15 Then Peter said, 'Tell us what that parable means.' 16 Jesus said, 'Are you still as dull as the rest? 17 Do you not see that whatever goes in by the mouth passes into the stomach and so is discharged into the drain? 18 But what comes out of the mouth has its origins in the heart; and that is what defiles a person. 19 Wicked thoughts, murder, adultery, fornication, theft, perjury, slander — these all proceed from the heart; 20 and these are the things that defile a person; but to eat without first washing his hands, that cannot defile him.'

21 JESUS then withdrew to the region of Tyre and Sidon. 22 And a Canaanite woman from those parts came to meet him crying, 'Son of David! Have pity on me; my daughter is tormented by a devil.' 23 But he said not a word

14:36 **edge:** *or* tassel. 15:14 **blind guides:** *some witnesses add* of blind men.

14.22–36: **Walking on the sea** (Mk. 6.45–56 and note; Jn. 6.16–21). The attempt of *Peter* to walk on the water (vv. 28–30), told only in Matt., illustrates both the power of faith and the way fear threatens faith. **33:** Unlike the report in Mk. 6.52 (see n.), the event awakens a confession of faith in its observers. For Matt., understanding is characteristic of the disciples (see 16.12 n.). A confession (16.16; Mk. 8.29) also follows the second account of a feeding and sea crossing in Matt. and Mk. (see Mk. 6.30–44 nn.); compare Jn. 6.16–21, 66–71.

15.1–20: **The ancient traditions** (Mk. 7.1–23). **2:** See Mk. 7.5 n. **4a:** Exod. 20.12; Deut. 5.16. **4b:** Exod. 21.17; Lev. 20.9. **8–9:** Isa. 29.13. **11:** *Defiled:* made ritually impure.

15.21–31: **Healings** (Mk. 7.24–31, 36–37). See Mk. 7.24–37 n. **22:** The story revolves around a non-Jewish (*Canaanite*) woman and the question of Jesus' mission (v. 24). Matthew thinks of a mission limited to Israel in reply. His disciples came and urged him: 'Send her away! See how she comes shouting after us.' 24 Jesus replied, 'I was sent to the lost sheep of the house of Israel, and to them alone.' 25 But the woman came and fell at his feet and cried, 'Help me, sir.' 26 Jesus replied, 'It is not right to take the children's bread and throw it to the dogs.' 27 'True, sir,' she answered, 'and yet the dogs eat the scraps that fall from their master's table.' 28 Hearing this Jesus replied, 'What faith you have! Let it be as you wish!' And from that moment her daughter was restored to health.

29 After leaving that region Jesus took the road by the sea of Galilee, where he climbed a hill and sat down. 30 Crowds flocked to him, bringing with them the lame, blind, dumb, and crippled, and many other sufferers; they put them down at his feet, and he healed them. 31 Great was the amazement of the people when they saw the dumb speaking, the crippled made strong, the lame walking, and the blind with their sight restored; and they gave praise to the God of Israel.

32 Jesus called his disciples and said to them, 'My heart goes out to these people; they have been with me now for three days and have nothing to eat. I do not want to send them away hungry; they might faint on the way.' 33 The disciples replied, 'Where in this remote place can we find bread enough to feed such a crowd?' 34 'How many loaves have you?' Jesus asked. 'Seven,' they replied, 'and a few small fish.' 35 So he ordered the people to sit down on the ground; 36 then he took the seven loaves and the fish, and after giving thanks to God he broke them and gave them to the disciples, and the disciples gave them to the people. 37 They all ate and were satisfied; and seven baskets were filled with what was left over. 38 Those who were fed numbered four thousand men, not counting women and children. 39 After dismissing the crowd, he got into a boat and went to the neighbourhood of Magadan.

16 The Pharisees and Sadducees came, and to test him they asked him to show them a sign from heaven. 2 He answered: 4 'It is a wicked, godless generation that asks for a sign; and the only sign that will be given it is the sign of Jonah.' With that he left them and went away.

5 In crossing to the other side the disciples had forgotten to take any bread. 6 So when Jesus said to them, 'Take care; be on your guard against the leaven of the Pharisees and Sadducees,' 7 they began to say to one another, 'We have brought no bread!' 8 Knowing what they were discussing, Jesus said, 'Why are you talking about having no bread? Where is your faith? 9 Do you still not understand? Have you forgotten the five loaves for the five thousand, and how many basketfuls you picked up? 10 Or the seven loaves for the four thousand, and how many basketfuls you picked up? 11 How can you fail to see that I was not talking about bread? Be on your guard, I said, against the leaven of the Pharisees and Sadducees.' 12 Then they understood: they were to be on their guard, not against baker's leaven, but against the teaching of the Pharisees and Sadducees.

Jesus the Son of God

13 WHEN he came to the territory of Caesarea Philippi, Jesus asked his disciples, 'Who do people say that the Son of Man is?' 14 They answered, 'Some say John the Baptist, others Elijah, others Jeremiah, or one of the prophets.' 15 'And you,' he asked, 'who do you say I am?' 16 Simon Peter answered: 'You are the Messiah, the Son of the living God.' 17 Then Jesus said: 'Simon son of Jonah, you are favoured indeed! You did not learn that from

16:2 **He answered:** *some witnesses here insert* 'In the evening you say, "It will be fine weather, for the sky is red"; 3 and in the morning you say, "It will be stormy today; the sky is red and lowering." You know how to interpret the appearance of the sky; can you not interpret the signs of the times?'

during Jesus' human career (see 10.5–6) but ultimately intended to reach out to all (see 28.19).

15.32–39: Feeding of four thousand (Mk. 8.1–10). See Mk. 6.30–44 nn. **36:** See Mk. 8.6.

16.1–12: Sea crossing and discussions (Mk. 8.11–21; Lk. 11.29; 12.1, 54–56). **1:** After a boat trip (15.39), the question of a *sign* is again raised. **2–3:** (Tfn. vv. 2–3). See Lk. 12.54–56 n. **4:** See 12.38–42 n., 39–41 n. **6:** *Leaven:* see Mk. 8.15 n. **12:** Understanding is characteristic of the disciples in this Gospel; contrast Mk. 8.17–18, 21 n.

16.13–23: Peter's confession and Jesus' prediction of his suffering (Mk. 8.27–33; Lk. 9.18–22). **13:** *Son of Man:* see Mk. 2.10 n. **14:** See Mk. 8.28 n. **16:** *Messiah:* see 1.1 n. *Son of (the living) God* is a title with a wide range of meanings — from "a person who lives according to God's will" (see Lk. 6.35 n.) to "a preexistent any human being; it was revealed to you by my heavenly Father. ¹⁸ And I say to you: you are Peter, the Rock; and on this rock I will build my church, and the powers of death shall never conquer it. ¹⁹ I will give you the keys of the kingdom of Heaven; what you forbid on earth shall be forbidden in heaven, and what you allow on earth shall be allowed in heaven.' ²⁰ He then gave his disciples strict orders not to tell anyone that he was the Messiah.

²¹ From that time Jesus began to make it clear to his disciples that he had to go to Jerusalem, and endure great suffering at the hands of the elders, chief priests, and scribes; to be put to death, and to be raised again on the third day. ²² At this Peter took hold of him and began to rebuke him: 'Heaven forbid!' he said. 'No, Lord, this shall never happen to you.' ²³ Then Jesus turned and said to Peter, 'Out of my sight, Satan; you are a stumbling block to me. You think as men think, not as God thinks.'

²⁴ Jesus then said to his disciples, 'Anyone who wishes to be a follower of mine must renounce self; he must take up his cross and follow me. ²⁵⁻²⁶ Whoever wants to save his life will lose it, but whoever loses his life for my sake will find it. What will anyone gain by winning the whole world at the cost of his life? Or what can he give to buy his life back? ²⁷ For the Son of Man is to come in the glory of his Father with his angels, and then he will give everyone his due reward. ²⁸ Truly I tell you: there are some of those standing here who will not taste death before they have seen the Son of Man coming in his kingdom.'

17 Six days later Jesus took Peter, James, and John the brother of James, and led them up a high mountain by themselves. ² And in their presence he was transfigured; his face shone like the sun, and his clothes became a brilliant white. ³ And they saw Moses and Elijah appear, talking with him. ⁴ Then Peter spoke: 'Lord,' he said, 'it is good that we are here. Would you like me to make three shelters here, one for you, one for Moses, and one for Elijah?' ⁵ While he was still speaking, a bright cloud suddenly cast its shadow over them, and a voice called from the cloud: 'This is my beloved Son, in whom I take delight; listen to him.' ⁶ At the sound of the voice the disciples fell on their faces in terror. ⁷ Then Jesus came up to them, touched them, and said, 'Stand up; do not be afraid.' ⁸ And when they raised their eyes there was no one but Jesus to be seen.

⁹ On their way down the mountain, Jesus commanded them not to tell anyone of the vision until the Son of Man had been raised from the dead. ¹⁰ The disciples put a question to him: 'Why then do the scribes say that Elijah must come first?' ¹¹ He replied, 'Elijah is to come and set everything right. ¹² But I tell you that Elijah has already come, and they failed to recognize him, and did to him as they wanted; in the same way the Son of Man is to suffer at their hands.' ¹³ Then the disciples understood that he meant John the Baptist.

¹⁴ When they returned to the crowd, a man

16:18 **powers of death:** *lit.* gates of Hades.
17:5 **This . . . Son:** *or* This is my only Son.

being of divine nature" (see Jn. 1.14). Although *Son of God* apparently was not a pre-Christian title for the *Messiah*, the OT contains evidence of a "divine kingship" motif which might contribute to the synonymous use of the two terms (see Mk. 1.1 n.). **18:** Simon is given a new name, *Rock,* and the name is explained (compare Gen. 32.28; also Matt. 5.13–14 n.). In both Gk. and Aram. the name (*Peter, "Rock"*) is a play on a common noun meaning "rock." In the Gospels the word *church* appears only here and in 18.17 (*congregation*). **19:** The *keys* may signify the office of doctor of the law (compare 23.13; Lk. 11.52); to *forbid* and to *allow* are functions of legal authorities (2.4 n.; 5.20 n.). **21:** *Jesus must suffer:* see Mk. 8.31 n.; compare 17.22–23; 20.18–19. **23:** *Satan:* tempter. *Stumbling block* may be "stumbling stone" in contrast to v. 18.

16.24–28: Following Jesus (Mk. 8.34–9.1; Lk. 9.23–27). See 10.38–39 n.; Mk. 8.34 n.

17.1–8: The transfiguration (Mk. 9.2–8; Lk. 9.28–36). The story is marked by a number of features characteristic of revelation scenes: the mountain (v. 1; see 5.1 n.), the cloud (v. 5; see, e.g. Exod. 24.15–18), the heavenly voice (v. 5). **2:** *Transfigured:* "changed in appearance," as the following words indicate (compare Lk. 9.29). *His face shone:* see Exod. 34.29–35. **3:** *Moses* and *Elijah:* see Mk. 8.28 n. **5:** *This is my Son:* see Mk. 1.11 n.

17.9–13: Elijah has come. 9–10: See Mk. 9.9–10 n. **13:** On the identification of John the Baptist as *Elijah,* see Mk. 6.15 n., 8.28 n.; Lk. 1.17 n.

came up to Jesus, fell on his knees before him, and said, [15]'Have pity, sir, on my son: he is epileptic and has bad fits; he keeps falling into the fire or into the water. [16]I brought him to your disciples, but they could not cure him.' [17]Jesus answered, 'What an unbelieving and perverse generation! How long shall I be with you? How long must I endure you? Bring him here to me.' [18]Then Jesus spoke sternly to him; the demon left the boy, and from that moment he was cured.

[19]Afterwards the disciples came to Jesus and asked him privately, 'Why could we not drive it out?' [20]He answered, 'Your faith is too small. Truly I tell you: if you have faith no bigger than a mustard seed, you will say to this mountain, "Move from here to there!" and it will move; nothing will be impossible for you.'

[22]THEY were going about together in Galilee when Jesus said to them, 'The Son of Man is to be handed over into the power of men, [23]and they will kill him; then on the third day he will be raised again.' And they were filled with grief.

[24]On their arrival at Capernaum the collectors of the temple tax came up to Peter and asked, 'Does your master not pay temple tax?' [25]'He does,' said Peter. When he went indoors Jesus forestalled him by asking, 'Tell me, Simon, from whom do earthly monarchs collect tribute money? From their own people, or from aliens?' [26]'From aliens,' said Peter. 'Yes,' said Jesus, 'and their own people are exempt. [27]But as we do not want to cause offence, go and cast a line in the lake; take the first fish you catch, open its mouth, and you will find a silver coin; take that and pay the tax for us both.'

Teaching about the kingdom

18 AT that time the disciples came to Jesus and asked, 'Who is the greatest in the kingdom of Heaven?' [2]He called a child, set him in front of them, [3]and said, 'Truly I tell you: unless you turn round and become like children, you will never enter the kingdom of Heaven. [4]Whoever humbles himself and becomes like this child will be the greatest in the kingdom of Heaven, [5]and whoever receives one such child in my name receives me. [6]But if anyone causes the downfall of one of these little ones who believe in me, it would be better for him to have a millstone hung round his neck and be drowned in the depths of the sea. [7]Alas for the world that any of them should be made to fall! Such things must happen, but alas for the one through whom they happen!

[8]'If your hand or your foot causes your downfall, cut it off and fling it away; it is better for you to enter into life maimed or lame, than to keep two hands or two feet and be thrown into the eternal fire. [9]And if your eye causes your downfall, tear it out and fling it away; it is better to enter into life with one eye than to keep both eyes and be thrown into the fires of hell.

[10]'See that you do not despise one of these little ones; I tell you, they have their angels in heaven, who look continually on the face of my heavenly Father.

[12]'What do you think? Suppose someone has a hundred sheep, and one of them strays, does he not leave the other ninety-nine on

17:20 **impossible for you:** *some witnesses add* [21]But there is no means of driving out this sort but prayer and fasting.   18:10 **Father:** *some witnesses add* [11]For the Son of Man came to save the lost.

17.14–20: An epileptic boy (Mk. 9.14–29; Lk. 9.37–43a). **20:** The importance of *faith* (see Mk. 9.23 n.), central to the narrative, is further heightened by the hyperbole of a minute faith which achieves the impossible (compare Lk. 17.6).

17.22–23: The second prediction (see 16.21) **of suffering** (Mk. 9.30–32; Lk. 9.43b–45) which in Mk. 9.32 meets with bewilderment, arouses *grief* in Matt. (v. 23).

17.24–27: The temple tax was required of every male Jew.

18.1–19.2: The fourth discourse (see Introduction) is sometimes described as a "book of church discipline." **1–14:** The pastoral responsibility of Christian leaders is the subject of this section, in which *children* (vv. 2–5) and *little ones* (vv. 6, 10, 14) are terms for simple Christian believers. **1–5:** Mk. 9.33–37; 10.15; Lk. 9.46–48; 18.17. The *greatest* is the one who can accept a position of humility. **6:** Mk. 9.42; Lk. 17.1–2. To cause the *downfall* of a *little one* (compare 5.19) is a heinous wrong. **7–9:** Mk. 9.43–48. The seriousness of causing sin is expressed in a series of effective hyperboles; such exaggerations as *millstones* around the neck (v. 6), amputated *hands* and *feet,* torn out *eyes* are meant seriously, but not literally. **10–14:** The parable of the lost sheep illustrates the unrelenting love the church leader is to show for the *little ones* in the flock (contrast Lk.

the hillside and go in search of the one that strayed? 13 Truly I tell you: if he should find it, he is more delighted over that sheep than over the ninety-nine that did not stray. 14 In the same way, it is not your heavenly Father's will that one of these little ones should be lost.

15 'If your brother does wrong, go and take the matter up with him, strictly between yourselves. If he listens to you, you have won your brother over. 16 But if he will not listen, take one or two others with you, so that every case may be settled on the evidence of two or three witnesses. 17 If he refuses to listen to them, report the matter to the congregation; and if he will not listen even to the congregation, then treat him as you would a pagan or a tax-collector.

18 'Truly I tell you: whatever you forbid on earth shall be forbidden in heaven, and whatever you allow on earth shall be allowed in heaven.

19 'And again I tell you: if two of you agree on earth about any request you have to make, that request will be granted by my heavenly Father. 20 For where two or three meet together in my name, I am there among them.'

21 Then Peter came to him and asked, 'Lord, how often am I to forgive my brother if he goes on wronging me? As many as seven times?' 22 Jesus replied, 'I do not say seven times but seventy times seven.

23 'The kingdom of Heaven, therefore, should be thought of in this way: There was once a king who decided to settle accounts with the men who served him. 24 At the outset there appeared before him a man who owed ten thousand talents. 25 Since he had no means of paying, his master ordered him to be sold, with his wife, his children, and everything he had, to meet the debt. 26 The man fell at his master's feet. "Be patient with me," he implored, "and I will pay you in full"; 27 and the master was so moved with pity that he let the man go and cancelled the debt. 28 But no sooner had the man gone out than

he met a fellow-servant who owed him a hundred denarii; he took hold of him, seizing him by the throat, and said, "Pay me what you owe." 29 The man fell at his fellow-servant's feet, and begged him, "Be patient with me, and I will pay you"; 30 but he refused, and had him thrown into jail until he should pay the debt. 31 The other servants were deeply distressed when they saw what had happened, and they went to their master and told him the whole story. 32 Then he sent for the man and said, "You scoundrel! I cancelled the whole of your debt when you appealed to me; 33 ought you not to have shown mercy to your fellow-servant just as I showed mercy to you?" 34 And so angry was the master that he condemned the man to be tortured until he should pay the debt in full. 35 That is how my heavenly Father will deal with you, unless you each forgive your brother from your hearts.'

On the road to Jerusalem

19 When Jesus had finished this discourse he left Galilee and came into the region of Judaea on the other side of the Jordan. 2 Great crowds followed him, and he healed them there.

3 Some Pharisees came and tested him by asking, 'Is it lawful for a man to divorce his wife for any cause he pleases?' 4 He responded by asking, 'Have you never read that in the beginning the Creator made them male and female?' 5 and he added, 'That is why a man leaves his father and mother, and is united to his wife, and the two become one flesh. 6 It follows that they are no longer two individuals: they are one flesh. Therefore what God has joined together, man must not separate.' 7 'Then why', they objected, 'did Moses lay it down that a man might divorce

18:15 **wrong:** *some witnesses add* to you.
18:22 **seventy times seven:** *or* seventy-seven times.
18:24 **talents:** *see p. xi* 18:28 **denarii:** *see p. xi.*

15.3–7 n.). **15–17:** This rule regulates relations between Christians; a similar rule was followed in the Dead Sea community. Compare Lk. 17.3–4 n. **17:** *Congregation:* or, "church"; see 16.18 n. **18:** See 16.19 n. **21–22:** Lk. 17.4. **23–35:** See 7.24–29 n. **23:** In light of the magnitude of the debt (v. 24) those *who served* the king would be officials of high rank. **24, 28:** The contrast between *ten thousand talents* (a huge sum) of v. 24 and the insignificant amount of v. 28 (*a hundred denarii*) makes the first debtor's action in vv. 28–30 intolerable. **35:** As in v. 15, the *brother* is for Matt. another Christian. **19.1:** This is the conclusion to ch. 18, the third discourse. See 7.28 n.

19.3–12: Marriage and divorce (see 5.31–32 n.; Mk. 10.2–12; Lk. 16.18; 1 Cor. 7.10–11). **3:** For *Pharisees* divorce was *lawful* but they disagreed about the grounds on which it may be allowed; see Mk. 10.3 n. **4–6:**

his wife by a certificate of dismissal?' ⁸He answered, 'It was because of your stubbornness that Moses gave you permission to divorce your wives; but it was not like that at the beginning. ⁹I tell you, if a man divorces his wife for any cause other than unchastity, and marries another, he commits adultery.'

¹⁰The disciples said to him, 'If that is how things stand for a man with a wife, it is better not to marry.' ¹¹To this he replied, 'That is a course not everyone can accept, but only those for whom God has appointed it. ¹²For while some are incapable of marriage because they were born so, or were made so by men, there are others who have renounced marriage for the sake of the kingdom of Heaven. Let those accept who can.'

¹³They brought children for him to lay his hands on them with prayer. The disciples rebuked them, ¹⁴but Jesus said, 'Let the children come to me; do not try to stop them; for the kingdom of Heaven belongs to such as these.' ¹⁵And he laid his hands on the children, and went on his way.

¹⁶A man came up and asked him, 'Teacher, what good must I do to gain eternal life?' ¹⁷'Good?' said Jesus. 'Why do you ask me about that? One alone is good. But if you wish to enter into life, keep the commandments.' ¹⁸'Which commandments?' he asked. Jesus answered, 'Do not murder; do not commit adultery; do not steal; do not give false evidence; ¹⁹honour your father and mother; and love your neighbour as yourself.' ²⁰The young man answered, 'I have kept all these. What do I still lack?' ²¹Jesus

said to him, 'If you wish to be perfect, go, sell your possessions, and give to the poor, and you will have treasure in heaven; then come and follow me.' ²²When the young man heard this, he went away with a heavy heart; for he was a man of great wealth.

²³Jesus said to his disciples, 'Truly I tell you: a rich man will find it hard to enter the kingdom of Heaven. ²⁴I repeat, it is easier for a camel to pass through the eye of a needle than for a rich man to enter the kingdom of God.' ²⁵The disciples were astonished when they heard this, and exclaimed, 'Then who can be saved?' ²⁶Jesus looked at them and said, 'For men this is impossible; but everything is possible for God.'

²⁷Then Peter said, 'What about us? We have left everything to follow you. How shall we fare?' ²⁸Jesus replied, 'Truly I tell you: in the world that is to be, when the Son of Man is seated on his glorious throne, you also will sit on twelve thrones, judging the twelve tribes of Israel. ²⁹And anyone who has left houses, or brothers or sisters, or father or mother, or children, or land for the sake of my name will be repaid many times over, and gain eternal life. ³⁰But many who are first will be last, and the last first.

20 'The kingdom of Heaven is like this. There was once a landowner who went out early one morning to hire labourers for his vineyard; ²and after agreeing to pay them the usual day's wage he sent them off

19:9 **adultery:** *some witnesses add* And the man who marries a woman so divorced commits adultery.
20:2 **the . . . wage:** *lit.* one denarius for the day.

See Mk. 10.6, 7–8 nn. **7–8:** See Mk. 10.4–5 n. **9:** See 5.32 n. **10–12:** *Marriage* and celibacy both fall within God's purpose; compare 1 Cor. 7.25–28.

19.13–15: Children and the kingdom (Mk. 10.13–16; Lk. 18.15–17). Compare 18.2–4.

19.16–30: Possessions and the kingdom (Mk. 10.17–31; Lk. 18.18–30). **16–17:** In Mk. 10.17–18 and Lk. 18.18–19 the opening exchange between Jesus and the man could be interpreted as implying that Jesus disclaimed being good; Matt., then, might be thought to correct this implication by reformulating these verses. Yet the point is the same in the three Gospels: for *life,* a person must look to the *One* (God) who *alone is good* and who gives the *commandments* with which the quest for life begins (Lev. 18.5). **18–19:** Exod. 20.12–16; Lev. 19.18; Deut. 5.16–20; compare 22.39; Rom. 13.8–9. **19:** Matthew has a special interest in the *love* commandment, which the parallel accounts omit in this narrative. **20, 22:** 'Only Matt. calls him a *young* man. **21:** The radical challenge (*go, sell, give*) makes the general counsel on almsgiving elsewhere (e.g. 6.22 n.) thoroughgoing. **24:** *Camel . . . eye of a needle* is a hyperbole which prepares for v. 26. **27, 29:** In contrast to those who hoard riches, the disciples *have left everything* and *will . . . gain eternal life.* **28:** Lk. 22.30. **30:** 20.16; Mk. 10.31; Lk. 13.30.

20.1–16: The laborers in the vineyard. The laborers are hired around 6 a.m. (v. 2), 9 a.m. (v. 3), noon (v. 5), 3 p.m. (v. 5), and 5 p.m. (v. 6). Only those hired in v. 2 are promised a specific amount (*the usual day's wage*). The surprise comes in vv. 9–10 when all receive the same sum, regardless of their working hours.

to work. ³Three hours later he went out again and saw some more men standing idle in the market-place. ⁴"Go and join the others in the vineyard," he said, "and I will pay you a fair wage"; so off they went. ⁵At midday he went out again, and at three in the afternoon, and made the same arrangement as before. ⁶An hour before sunset he went out and found another group standing there; so he said to them, "Why are you standing here all day doing nothing?" ⁷"Because no one has hired us," they replied; so he told them, "Go and join the others in the vineyard." ⁸When evening fell, the owner of the vineyard said to the overseer, "Call the labourers and give them their pay, beginning with those who came last and ending with the first." ⁹Those who had started work an hour before sunset came forward, and were paid the full day's wage. ¹⁰When it was the turn of the men who had come first, they expected something extra, but were paid the same as the others. ¹¹As they took it, they grumbled at their employer: ¹²"These latecomers did only one hour's work, yet you have treated them on a level with us, who have sweated the whole day long in the blazing sun!" ¹³The owner turned to one of them and said, "My friend, I am not being unfair to you. You agreed on the usual wage for the day, did you not? ¹⁴Take your pay and go home. I choose to give the last man the same as you. ¹⁵Surely I am free to do what I like with my own money? Why be jealous because I am generous?" ¹⁶So the last will be first, and the first last.'

¹⁷JESUS was journeying towards Jerusalem, and on the way he took the Twelve aside and said to them, ¹⁸'We are now going up to Jerusalem, and the Son of Man will be handed over to the chief priests and the scribes; they will condemn him to death ¹⁹and hand him over to the Gentiles, to be mocked and flogged and crucified; and on the third day he will be raised to life again.'

²⁰The mother of Zebedee's sons then approached him with her sons. She bowed before him and begged a favour. ²¹'What is it you want?' asked Jesus. She replied, 'Give orders that in your kingdom these two sons of mine may sit next to you, one at your right hand and the other at your left.' ²²Jesus turned to the brothers and said, 'You do not understand what you are asking. Can you drink the cup that I am to drink?' 'We can,' they replied. ²³'You shall indeed drink my cup,' he said; 'but to sit on my right or on my left is not for me to grant; that honour is for those to whom it has already been assigned by my Father.'

²⁴When the other ten heard this, they were indignant with the two brothers. ²⁵So Jesus called them to him and said, 'You know that, among the Gentiles, rulers lord it over their subjects, and the great make their authority felt. ²⁶It shall be not be so with you; among you, whoever wants to be great must be your servant, ²⁷and whoever wants to be first must be the slave of all—²⁸just as the Son of Man did not come to be served but to serve, and to give his life as a ransom for many.'

²⁹As they were leaving Jericho he was followed by a huge crowd. ³⁰At the roadside sat two blind men. When they heard that Jesus was passing by they shouted, 'Have pity on us, Son of David.' ³¹People told them to be quiet, but they shouted all the more, 'Sir, have pity on us; have pity on us, Son of David.' ³²Jesus stopped and called the men. 'What do you want me to do for you?' ³³he asked. 'Sir,' they answered, 'open our eyes.' ³⁴Jesus was deeply moved, and touched their eyes. At once they recovered their sight and followed him.

Jesus in the temple

21 THEY were approaching Jerusalem, and when they reached Bethphage at the mount of Olives Jesus sent off two disciples, ²and told them: 'Go into the village op-

20:9 **the . . . wage:** *lit.* one denarius each.
20:13 **You . . . day:** *lit.* You agreed on a denarius.

20.17–19: The third prediction of suffering (16.21; 17.22–23; Mk. 10.32–34 n.; Lk. 18.31–34).
  20.20–28: Position in the kingdom (Mk. 10.35–45; Lk. 22.24–27). **20:** The *mother* initiates the request in Matt., the *sons* in Mk. 10.35. **21:** *Right . . . left:* see Mk. 10.37 n. *Kingdom:* probably not, as some think, the church—but, as elsewhere, the realm over which God will ultimately and finally rule. **22:** *Cup:* see Mk. 10.38 n. **23:** Compare Mk. 10.40. **28:** *Ransom for many:* see Mk. 10.45 n.; see also 2 Macc. 7.37–38.
  20.29–34: Two blind men healed (Mk. 10.46–52; Lk. 18.35–43). **30:** *Two blind men:* contrast Mk. 10.46; Lk. 18.35. **30, 31:** *Son of David:* see 1.1 n. **34:** *Followed:* see Mk. 10.52 n.

posite, where you will at once find a donkey tethered with her foal beside her. Untie them, and bring them to me. ³If anyone says anything to you, answer, "The Master needs them"; and he will let you have them at once.' ⁴This was to fulfil the prophecy which says, ⁵'Tell the daughter of Zion, "Here is your king, who comes to you in gentleness, riding on a donkey, on the foal of a beast of burden."'

⁶The disciples went and did as Jesus had directed, ⁷and brought the donkey and her foal; they laid their cloaks on them and Jesus mounted. ⁸Crowds of people carpeted the road with their cloaks, and some cut branches from the trees to spread in his path. ⁹Then the crowds in front and behind raised the shout: 'Hosanna to the Son of David! Blessed is he who comes in the name of the Lord! Hosanna in the heavens!'

¹⁰When he entered Jerusalem the whole city went wild with excitement. 'Who is this?' people asked, ¹¹and the crowds replied, 'This is the prophet Jesus, from Nazareth in Galilee.'

¹²Jesus went into the temple and drove out all who were buying and selling in the temple precincts; he upset the tables of the moneychangers and the seats of the dealers in pigeons, ¹³and said to them, 'Scripture says, "My house shall be called a house of prayer"; but you are making it a bandits' cave.'

¹⁴In the temple the blind and the crippled came to him, and he healed them. ¹⁵When the chief priests and scribes saw the wonderful things he did, and heard the boys in the temple shouting, 'Hosanna to the Son of David!' they were indignant ¹⁶and asked him, 'Do you hear what they are saying?' Jesus answered, 'I do. Have you never read the text, "You have made children and babes at the breast sound your praise aloud"?' ¹⁷Then he left them and went out of the city to Bethany, where he spent the night.

¹⁸Next morning on his way to the city he felt hungry; ¹⁹and seeing a fig tree at the roadside he went up to it, but found nothing on it but leaves. He said to the tree, 'May you never bear fruit again!' and at once the tree withered away. ²⁰The disciples were amazed at the sight. 'How is it', they asked, 'that the tree has withered so suddenly?' ²¹Jesus answered them, 'Truly I tell you: if only you have faith and have no doubts, you will do what has been done to the fig tree. And more than that: you need only say to this mountain, "Be lifted from your place and hurled into the sea," and what you say will be done. ²²Whatever you pray for in faith you will receive.'

²³He entered the temple, and, as he was teaching, the chief priests and elders of the nation came up to him and asked: 'By what authority are you acting like this? Who gave you this authority?' ²⁴Jesus replied, 'I also have a question for you. If you answer it, I will tell you by what authority I act. ²⁵The baptism of John: was it from God, or from men?' This set them arguing among themselves: 'If we say, "From God," he will say,

21:3 **The Master ... once:** *or* "The Master needs them and will send them back without delay."

21.1–25.46: Jesus in Jerusalem (Mk. 11.1–13.37 n.; Lk. 19.28–21.38).

21.1–9: The entry into Jerusalem (Mk. 11.1–11; Lk. 19.28–38; Jn. 12.12–19). **1:** The *mount of Olives:* associated with the appearance of the Messiah. The Gospel writers understand the entry as a messianic claim, and the account has been influenced by the picture of the humble king in Zech. 9.9 (see v. 5 n.). **2:** Matthew speaks of two animals, presumably because of the interpretation of the prophecy recorded in v. 5. **5:** Isa. 62.11 and Zech. 9.9 are combined; Jn. 12.15 also quotes Zech. **9:** Ps. 118.25–26. *Hosanna,* lit. means "O, save!" In Jesus' day, it could be simply a shout of praise. *Son of David:* see 1.1 n.

21.10–17: Cleansing of the temple (Mk. 11.15–19; Lk. 19.45–48). **11:** *Prophet:* see 21.26, 46; Mk. 8.28 n. **12:** The *temple* area involved would be the so-called Court of the Gentiles, to which even non-Jews were admitted. *Money-changers* converted ordinary money into the Tyrian half-shekels required at the temple. *Pigeons:* for inexpensive animal sacrifices. See Mk. 11.15–16 n. **13:** See Isa. 56.7; Jer. 7.11. *Prayer* and *praise* (v. 16) are the true functions of the temple. Mark adds "for all nations" (see Mk. 11.17 n.). **16:** Ps. 8.2.

21.18–22: The cursing of the fig tree (Mk. 11.12–14, 20–25). **18–19:** The narrative is frequently taken as an "acted parable or allegory" of the rejection of Israel or as a development of the parable in Lk. 13.6–9. **20–22:** The story has attracted sayings about the power of *faith* and *prayer* which are also found elsewhere (17.20; Lk. 17.6).

21.23–27: Jesus' authority challenged (Mk. 11.27–33; Lk. 20.1–8). **25:** *From God:* lit. "from heaven" (a

"Then why did you not believe him?" 26 But if we say, "From men," we are afraid of the people's reaction, for they all take John for a prophet.' 27 So they answered, 'We do not know.' And Jesus said: 'Then I will not tell you either by what authority I act.

28 'But what do you think about this? There was a man who had two sons. He went to the first, and said, "My son, go and work today in the vineyard." 29 "I will, sir," the boy replied; but he did not go. 30 The father came to the second and said the same. "I will not," he replied; but afterwards he changed his mind and went. 31 Which of the two did what his father wanted?' 'The second,' they replied. Then Jesus said, 'Truly I tell you: tax-collectors and prostitutes are entering the kingdom of God ahead of you. 32 For when John came to show you the right way to live, you did not believe him, but the tax-collectors and prostitutes did; and even when you had seen that, you did not change your minds and believe him.

33 'Listen to another parable. There was a landowner who planted a vineyard: he put a wall round it, hewed out a winepress, and built a watch-tower; then he let it out to vine-growers and went abroad. 34 When the harvest season approached, he sent his servants to the tenants to collect the produce due to him. 35 But they seized his servants, thrashed one, killed another, and stoned a third. 36 Again, he sent other servants, this time a larger number; and they treated them in the same way. 37 Finally he sent his son. "They will respect my son," he said. 38 But when they saw the son the tenants said to one another, "This is the heir; come on, let us kill him, and get his inheritance." 39 So they seized him, flung him out of the vineyard, and killed him. 40 When the owner of the vineyard comes, how do you think he will deal with those tenants?' 41 'He will bring those bad men to a bad end,' they answered, 'and hand the vineyard over to other tenants, who will give him his share of the crop when the season comes.' 42 Jesus said to them, 'Have you never read in the scriptures: "The stone which the builders rejected has become the main corner-stone. This is the Lord's doing, and it is wonderful in our eyes"? 43 Therefore, I tell you, the kingdom of God will be taken away from you, and given to a nation that yields the proper fruit.'

45 When the chief priests and Pharisees heard his parables, they saw that he was referring to them. 46 They wanted to arrest him, but were afraid of the crowds, who looked on Jesus as a prophet.

22 JESUS spoke to them again in parables: 2 'The kingdom of Heaven is like this. There was a king who arranged a banquet for his son's wedding; 3 but when he sent his servants to summon the guests he had invited, they refused to come. 4 Then he sent other servants, telling them to say to the guests, "Look! I have prepared this banquet for you. My bullocks and fatted beasts have been slaughtered, and everything is ready. Come to the wedding." 5 But they took no notice; one went off to his farm, another to his business, 6 and the others seized the servants, attacked them brutally, and killed them. 7 The king was furious; he sent troops to put those murderers to death and set their town on fire. 8 Then he said to his servants, "The wedding banquet is ready; but the guests I invited did not deserve the honour.

21:43 **proper fruit:** *some witnesses add* 44 Any man who falls on this stone will be dashed to pieces; and if it falls on a man he will be crushed by it.

typical Jewish circumlocution to avoid the careless use of "God"; compare 3.2 n.). **26:** *Prophet:* see Mk. 8.28 n.

21.28–32: The parable of the two sons. 31: That religious outcasts (*tax-collectors* and *prostitutes*) should have priority over religious leaders is not a popular notion even in modern times. **32:** In this context, to *believe him* (*John* the Baptist) appears to assure entrance into the kingdom.

21.33–46: The evil tenants (Mk. 12.1–12; Lk. 20.9–19). **33:** If originally a *parable,* the story as now told has the marks of an allegory; see Mk. 4.2 n. The *vineyard* is a conventional symbol for Israel as the chosen people; compare Isa. 5.1–7. **34:** Early Christian readers would identify the *servants* as the prophets and the *tenants* as the Jewish leaders of the day. **37:** *Son:* Jesus. **42:** *The stone . . . is wonderful:* Ps. 118.22–23; see Mk. 12.10–11 n.; Acts 4.11; 1 Pet. 2.4, 7.

22.1–14: The wedding feast (Lk. 14.16–24). **2:** *Banquet:* see Lk. 14.15 n. **3:** *To summon the guests:* see Lk. 14.17 n. **5–6:** The feature of the *servants* being *attacked* is peculiar to Matt. (see Lk. 14.18–20); the rejection of John and Jesus probably suggested this embellishment. **7:** Here the tradition may reflect the destruction of

9 Go out therefore to the main thorough-fares, and invite everyone you can find to the wedding." 10 The servants went out into the streets, and collected everyone they could find, good and bad alike. So the hall was packed with guests.

11 'When the king came in to watch them feasting, he observed a man who was not dressed for a wedding. 12 "My friend," said the king, "how do you come to be here without wedding clothes?" But he had nothing to say. 13 The king then said to his attendants, "Bind him hand and foot; fling him out into the dark, the place of wailing and grinding of teeth." 14 For many are invited, but few are chosen.'

15 THEN the Pharisees went away and agreed on a plan to trap him in argument. 16 They sent some of their followers to him, together with members of Herod's party. 'Teacher,' they said, 'we know you are a sincere man; you teach in all sincerity the way of life that God requires, courting no man's favour, whoever he may be. 17 Give us your ruling on this: are we or are we not permitted to pay taxes to the Roman emperor?' 18 Jesus was aware of their malicious intention and said, 'You hypocrites! Why are you trying to catch me out? 19 Show me the coin used for the tax.' They handed him a silver piece. 20 Jesus asked, 'Whose head is this, and whose inscription?' 21 'Caesar's,' they replied. He said to them, 'Then pay to Caesar what belongs to Caesar, and to God what belongs to God.' 22 Taken aback by this reply, they went away and left him alone.

23 The same day Sadducees, who maintain that there is no resurrection, came to him and asked: 24 'Teacher, Moses said that if a man dies childless, his brother shall marry the widow and provide an heir for his

brother. 25 We know a case involving seven brothers. The first married and died, and as he was without issue his wife was left to his brother. 26 The same thing happened with the second, and the third, and so on with all seven. 27 Last of all the woman died. 28 At the resurrection, then, whose wife will she be, since they had all married her?' 29 Jesus answered: 'How far you are from the truth! You know neither the scriptures nor the power of God. 30 In the resurrection men and women do not marry; they are like angels in heaven.

31 'As for the resurrection of the dead, have you never read what God himself said to you: 32 "I am the God of Abraham, the God of Isaac, the God of Jacob"? God is not God of the dead but of the living.' 33 When the crowds heard this, they were amazed at his teaching.

34 Hearing that he had silenced the Sadducees, the Pharisees came together in a body, 35 and one of them tried to catch him out with this question: 36 'Teacher, which is the greatest commandment in the law?' 37 He answered, ' "Love the Lord your God with all your heart, with all your soul, and with all your mind." 38 That is the greatest, the first commandment. 39 The second is like it: "Love your neighbour as yourself." 40 Everything in the law and the prophets hangs on these two commandments.'

41 Turning to the assembled Pharisees Jesus asked them, 42 'What is your opinion about the Messiah? Whose son is he?' 'The son of David,' they replied. 43 'Then how is it', he asked, 'that David by inspiration calls him "Lord"? For he says, 44 "The Lord said to my Lord, 'Sit at my right hand until I put your

---

22:35 **one of them:** *some witnesses add* an expert in the law.

Jerusalem in 70 C.E. **11–14:** In light of v. 10, the expectation of "correct dress" may indicate that these verses are from a second "feast parable" which Matt. has appended to vv. 2–10.

22.15–22: Caesar's tax (Mk. 12.13–17; Lk. 20.20–26). **17:** Advice against paying such *taxes* would amount to treason; advice in favor of paying would be unpopular with Jewish nationalists.

22.23–33: A resurrection puzzle (Mk. 12.18–27; Lk. 20.27–40). **23:** On differences between *Sadducees* and *Pharisees* (v. 15), see 3.7 n. **24:** Deut. 25.5–10. **29:** *The scriptures:* apparently Exod. 3.6, which is quoted in v. 32 as proof of the resurrection.

22.34–40: The double commandment of love (Mk. 12.28–34; compare Lk. 10.25–28). **35:** Matthew attributes the motive of testing to the inquirers; compare Mk. 12.28; Lk. 10.27 n. **37:** Deut. 6.5. **39:** Lev. 19.18. **40:** Compare 7.12.

22.41–46: Messiah, son of David (Mk. 12.35–37; Lk. 20.41–44). **42:** *Messiah . . . the son of David:* see 1.1 n. **44:** Psalm 110.1 is interpreted to mean "God (*the Lord*) said to the Messiah (*my Lord*)"; compare Acts enemies under your feet.' " ⁴⁵If then David calls him "Lord", how can he be David's son?' ⁴⁶Nobody was able to give him an answer; and from that day no one dared to put any more questions to him.

23

JESUS then addressed the crowds and his disciples ²in these words: 'The scribes and the Pharisees occupy Moses' seat; ³so be careful to do whatever they tell you. But do not follow their practice; for they say one thing and do another. ⁴They make up heavy loads and pile them on the shoulders of others, but will not themselves lift a finger to ease the burden. ⁵Whatever they do is done for show. They go about wearing broad phylacteries and with large tassels on their robes; ⁶they love to have the place of honour at feasts and the chief seats in synagogues, ⁷to be greeted respectfully in the street, and to be addressed as "rabbi".

⁸'But you must not be called "rabbi", for you have one Rabbi, and you are all brothers. ⁹Do not call any man on earth "father", for you have one Father, and he is in heaven. ¹⁰Nor must you be called "teacher"; you have one Teacher, the Messiah. ¹¹The greatest among you must be your servant. ¹²Whoever exalts himself will be humbled; and whoever humbles himself will be exalted.

¹³'Alas for you, scribes and Pharisees, hypocrites! You shut the door of the kingdom of Heaven in people's faces; you do not enter yourselves, and when others try to enter, you stop them.

¹⁵'Alas for you, scribes and Pharisees, hypocrites! You travel over sea and land to win one convert; and when you have succeeded you make him twice as fit for hell as you are yourselves.

¹⁶'Alas for you, blind guides! You say, "If someone swears by the sanctuary, that is nothing; but if he swears by the gold in the sanctuary, he is bound by his oath." ¹⁷Blind fools! Which is the more important, the gold, or the sanctuary which sanctifies the gold? ¹⁸Or you say, "If someone swears by the altar, that is nothing; but if he swears by the offering that lies on the altar, he is bound by his oath." ¹⁹What blindness! Which is the more important, the offering, or the altar which sanctifies it? ²⁰To swear by the altar, then, is to swear both by the altar and by whatever lies on it; ²¹to swear by the sanctuary is to swear both by the sanctuary and by him who dwells there; ²²and to swear by Heaven is to swear both by the throne of God and by him who sits upon it.

²³'Alas for you, scribes and Pharisees, hypocrites! You pay tithes of mint and dill and cummin; but you have overlooked the weightier demands of the law—justice, mercy, and good faith. It is these you should have practised, without neglecting the others. ²⁴Blind guides! You strain off a midge, yet gulp down a camel!

²⁵'Alas for you, scribes and Pharisees, hypocrites! You clean the outside of a cup or a dish, and leave the inside full of greed and self-indulgence! ²⁶Blind Pharisee! Clean the inside of the cup first; then the outside will be clean also.

23:13 **you stop them:** *some witnesses add* ¹⁴Alas for you, scribes and Pharisees, hypocrites! You eat up the property of widows, while for appearance' sake you say long prayers. You will receive the severest sentence.

2.34–36. **45:** While the story may represent a stratum of tradition which rejected a son of David Christology, that cannot have been the intention of the evangelist, in light e.g. of chs. 1–2.

23.1–39: Alas for scribes and Pharisees (compare Lk. 11.42–54). **1:** It is difficult to decide whether ch. 23 is the climax of the reported controversy of the preceding chs. or the beginning of the final discourse in Matt. The fact that the Pharisees appear as Jesus' chief opponents in the synoptic Gospels—and especially in Matt.—probably reflects the situation after 70 C.E., when Pharisaism was the form of Judaism which the church normally confronted. In the very old traditions of the passion (beginning with ch. 26 and its parallels), not the Pharisees, but the politically important priestly and Sadducaic elements seem to be most prominent in the fateful final conflict. **2:** On *scribes* (vv. 13, 15, 23, 25, 27, 29; *teachers*, v. 34!), see 2.4 n.; 5.20 n. *Moses' seat:* at one time, a place provided in the synagogue for authoritative teaching. **5:** *Phylacteries* were small leather containers holding certain passages of Scripture; compare Exod. 13.9. **8–10:** *Rabbi, father, teacher:* titles for teachers of the Law. **13:** *Alas for:* see Lk. 6.24–26 n. *Shut the door:* compare 16.19 n.; Lk. 11.52. **16–22:** The purpose of oaths of the type described was to guard against the profaning of the holy sanctuary or altar (and, ultimately, the name of God) by broken oaths; compare 5.33–37. **23:** *Tithes* of such produce probably exceed the actual requirements of Deut. 14.22–23. *The weightier demands:* see Mic. 6.8. **24:** *Midge:* or, gnat. **27–32:**

27'Alas for you, scribes and Pharisees, hypocrites! You are like tombs covered with whitewash; they look fine on the outside, but inside they are full of dead men's bones and of corruption. 28 So it is with you: outwardly you look like honest men, but inside you are full of hypocrisy and lawlessness.

29'Alas for you, scribes and Pharisees, hypocrites! You build up the tombs of the prophets and embellish the monuments of the saints, 30 and you say, "If we had been living in the time of our forefathers, we should never have taken part with them in the murder of the prophets." 31 So you acknowledge that you are the sons of those who killed the prophets. 32 Go on then, finish off what your fathers began! 33 Snakes! Vipers' brood! How can you escape being condemned to hell?

34'I am sending you therefore prophets and wise men and teachers of the law; some of them you will kill and crucify, others you will flog in your synagogues and hound from city to city. 35 So on you will fall the guilt of all the innocent blood spilt on the ground, from the blood of innocent Abel to the blood of Zechariah son of Berachiah, whom you murdered between the sanctuary and the altar. 36 Truly I tell you: this generation will bear the guilt of it all.

37'O Jerusalem, Jerusalem, city that murders the prophets and stones the messengers sent to her! How often have I longed to gather your children, as a hen gathers her brood under her wings; but you would not let me. 38 Look! There is your temple, forsaken by God and laid waste. 39 I tell you, you will not see me until the time when you say, "Blessed is he who comes in the name of the Lord!"'

Warnings about the end

24 JESUS left the temple and was walking away when his disciples came and pointed to the temple buildings. 2 He answered, 'Yes, look at it all. Truly I tell you: not one stone will be left upon another; they will all be thrown down.'

3 As he sat on the mount of Olives the disciples came to speak to him privately. 'Tell us,' they said, 'when will this happen? And what will be the sign of your coming and the end of the age?'

4 Jesus replied: 'Take care that no one misleads you. 5 For many will come claiming my name and saying, "I am the Messiah," and many will be misled by them. 6 The time is coming when you will hear of wars and rumours of wars. See that you are not alarmed. Such things are bound to happen; but the end is still to come. 7 For nation will go to war against nation, kingdom against kingdom; there will be famines and earthquakes in many places. 8 All these things are the first birth-pangs of the new age.

9'You will then be handed over for punishment and execution; all nations will hate you for your allegiance to me. 10 At that time many will fall from their faith; they will betray one another and hate one another. 11 Many false prophets will arise, and will mislead many; 12 and as lawlessness spreads, the love of many will grow cold. 13 But whoever endures to the end will be saved. 14 And this gospel of the kingdom will be proclaimed throughout the earth as a testimony to all nations; and then the end will come.

23:32 **Go on ... began:** *or* You too must come up to your fathers' standards.   23:38 *Some witnesses omit* and laid waste.

Compare Lk. 11.44–48. **33:** 3.7; Lk. 3.7. **34–36:** See Lk. 11.49–51 n. **34:** *Teachers:* see 23.3 n. **35:** *Abel:* Gen. 4.8. *Son of Berachiah* (2 Chr. 24.20–22; Zech. 1.1) is not found in Lk. 11.51 (see n.); probably the identification is mistaken. **37–38:** See Lk. 13.34–35 n. **39:** For Matt., *until the time* looks forward to the end time; contrast Lk. 13.35 n. *Blessed ... Lord:* Ps. 118.26.

24.1–26.1a: The fifth (eschatological) discourse: See 23.1 n.; 7.28 n. Compare Mk. 13.1–37 n.

24.1–2: Temple's destruction predicted (Mk. 13.1–4; Lk. 21.5–7). Herod the Great instituted the building of a magnificent temple about 20 B.C.E.; although it was substantially complete, work on it still continued in Jesus' day (see Jn. 2.20). Several traditions suggest that Jesus foretold the temple's destruction (compare Jn. 2.19); another form of the prediction had it that Jesus himself would destroy the temple (compare 26.61; Mk. 14.58; 15.29; Acts 6.14). The destruction occurred in 70 C.E. as a consequence of the revolt against Rome.

24.3–41: Signs, false signs, and warnings (Mk. 13.3–37; Lk. 21.8–36). **3:** *Mount of Olives:* see 21.1 n. *Disciples:* in Mk. 13.3 (n.), only Peter, James, John, Andrew. **4–5:** Compare vv. 23–24; Acts 8.9–11. **8:** *Birth-pangs:* conventional imagery for suffering associated with the dawn of the *new age* (e.g. 1 Thess. 5.3). **13:** 10.22. **14:** See 28.18–20; Mk. 13.10.

15'So when you see "the abomination of desolation", of which the prophet Daniel spoke, standing in the holy place (let the reader understand), 16then those who are in Judaea must take to the hills. 17If anyone is on the roof, he must not go down to fetch his goods from the house; 18if anyone is in the field, he must not turn back for his coat. 19Alas for women with child in those days, and for those who have children at the breast! 20Pray that it may not be winter or a sabbath when you have to make your escape. 21It will be a time of great distress, such as there has never been before since the beginning of the world, and will never be again. 22If that time of troubles were not cut short, no living thing could survive; but for the sake of God's chosen it will be cut short.

23'If anyone says to you then, "Look, here is the Messiah," or "There he is," do not believe it. 24Impostors will come claiming to be messiahs or prophets, and they will produce great signs and wonders to mislead, if possible, even God's chosen. 25See, I have forewarned you. 26If therefore they tell you, "He is there in the wilderness," do not go out; or if they say, "He is there in the inner room," do not believe it. 27Like a lightning-flash, that lights the sky from east to west, will be the coming of the Son of Man.

28'Wherever the carcass is, there will the vultures gather.

29'As soon as that time of distress has passed,

the sun will be darkened,
the moon will not give her light,
the stars will fall from the sky,
the celestial powers will be shaken.

30'Then will appear in heaven the sign that heralds the Son of Man. All the peoples of the world will make lamentation, and they will see the Son of Man coming on the clouds of heaven with power and great glory. 31With a trumpet-blast he will send out his angels, and they will gather his chosen from the four winds, from the farthest bounds of heaven on every side.

32'Learn a lesson from the fig tree. When its tender shoots appear and are breaking into leaf, you know that summer is near. 33In the same way, when you see all these things, you may know that the end is near, at the very door. 34Truly I tell you: the present generation will live to see it all. 35Heaven and earth will pass away, but my words will never pass away.

36'Yet about that day and hour no one knows, not even the angels in heaven, not even the Son; no one but the Father alone.

37'As it was in the days of Noah, so will it be when the Son of Man comes. 38In the days before the flood they ate and drank and married, until the day that Noah went into the ark, 39and they knew nothing until the flood came and swept them all away. That is how it will be when the Son of Man comes. 40Then there will be two men in the field: one will be taken, the other left; 41two women grinding at the mill: one will be taken, the other left.

42'Keep awake, then, for you do not know on what day your Lord will come. 43Remember, if the householder had known at what time of night the burglar was coming, he would have stayed awake and not let his house be broken into. 44Hold yourselves ready, therefore, because the Son of Man will come at the time you least expect him.

45'Who is the faithful and wise servant, charged by his master to manage his household and supply them with food at the

24:33 *that . . . near:* or that he is near.

15: *"The abomination of desolation"* (see Dan. 9.27; 11.31; 12.11): a symbol of pagan profanation of the holy place. The comment *let the reader understand* calls attention to the cryptic character of this material. **18:** Lk. 17.31. **20:** Matthew alone shows concern about violating the rule limiting *sabbath* travel; compare Mk. 13.18. **21:** Dan. 12.1. **24:** Deut. 13.1–2. **26–28:** Lk. 17.23–24, 37. **29:** The portents described here have OT roots; e.g. Isa. 13.10. **30:** Dan. 7.13. **31:** Isa. 27.13; 1 Cor. 15.52; Deut. 30.4. **34:** Compare 10.23; 16.28. A late first-century Christian could have understood the saying literally only of the destruction of the temple, not of the end of the age; see v. 36. **35:** 5.18; Lk. 16.17. **37–41:** Lk. 17.26–27, 34–35; Gen. chs. 6–7.

24.42–26.1a: Parables of judgment.

24.43–44: The wakeful householder (Lk. 12.39–40). The "thief" motif was widespread; e.g. 1 Thess. 5.2; Rev. 3.3.

24.45–51: The trusty servant (Lk. 12.42–46).

proper time? 46 Happy that servant if his master comes home and finds him at work! 47 Truly I tell you: he will be put in charge of all his master's property. 48 But if he is a bad servant and says to himself, "The master is a long time coming," 49 and begins to bully the other servants and to eat and drink with his drunken friends, 50 then the master will arrive on a day when the servant does not expect him, at a time he has not been told. 51 He will cut him in pieces and assign him a place among the hypocrites, where there is wailing and grinding of teeth.

25 'When the day comes, the kingdom of Heaven will be like this. There were ten girls, who took their lamps and went out to meet the bridegroom. 2 Five of them were foolish, and five prudent; 3 when the foolish ones took their lamps, they took no oil with them, 4 but the others took flasks of oil with their lamps. 5 As the bridegroom was a long time in coming, they all dozed off to sleep. 6 But at midnight there came a shout: "Here is the bridegroom! Come out to meet him." 7 Then the girls all got up and trimmed their lamps. 8 The foolish said to the prudent, "Our lamps are going out; give us some of your oil." 9 "No," they answered; "there will never be enough for all of us. You had better go to the dealers and buy some for yourselves." 10 While they were away the bridegroom arrived; those who were ready went in with him to the wedding banquet; and the door was shut. 11 Later the others came back. "Sir, sir, open the door for us," they cried. 12 But he answered, "Truly I tell you: I do not know you." 13 Keep awake then, for you know neither the day nor the hour.

14 'It is like a man going abroad, who called his servants and entrusted his capital to them; 15 to one he gave five bags of gold, to another two, to another one, each according to his ability. Then he left the country. 16 The man who had the five bags went at once and employed them in business, and made a profit of five bags, 17 and the man who had the two bags made two. 18 But the man who had been given one bag of gold went off and dug a hole in the ground, and hid his master's money. 19 A long time afterwards their master returned, and proceeded to settle accounts with them. 20 The man who had been given the five bags of gold came and produced the five he had made: "Master," he said, "you left five bags with me; look, I have made five more." 21 "Well done, good and faithful servant!" said the master. "You have proved trustworthy in a small matter; I will now put you in charge of something big. Come and share your master's joy." 22 The man with the two bags then came and said, "Master, you left two bags with me; look, I have made two more." 23 "Well done, good and faithful servant!" said the master. "You have proved trustworthy in a small matter; I will now put you in charge of something big. Come and share your master's joy." 24 Then the man who had been given one bag came and said, "Master, I knew you to be a hard man: you reap where you have not sown, you gather where you have not scattered; 25 so I was afraid, and I went and hid your gold in the ground. Here it is—you have what belongs to you." 26 "You worthless, lazy servant!" said the master. "You knew, did you, that I reap where I have not sown, and gather where I have not scattered? 27 Then you ought to have put my money on deposit, and on my return I should have got it back with interest. 28 Take the bag of gold from him, and give it to the one with the ten bags. 29 For everyone who has will be given more, till he has enough and to spare; and everyone who has nothing will forfeit even what he has. 30 As for the useless servant, throw him out into the dark, where there will be wailing and grinding of teeth!"

31 'When the Son of Man comes in his glory

25.1–13: **The girls at the wedding celebration.** The parable uses the wedding customs of the time to urge preparedness for the kingdom. **1:** No doubt the early church thought of Jesus as the *bridegroom.* **13:** Matthew interprets the parable in this way to carry forward the theme of 24.42–44.

25.14–30: **The parable of the talents.** In contrast to the similar parable in Lk. 19.11–27 (see nn. there), immense sums are left in the hands of the servants. (In other, more literal, translations, "talents" appears rather than *bags of gold;* a talent was an ancient measure of money.)

25.31–46: **The sheep and the goats.** See 7.24–29 n. The parable begins with familiar images: *the Son of Man . . . in his glory* (v. 1; Dan. 7.13–15); the assembling of the *nations*—i.e. even Gentiles (v. 2; e.g. Isa.

and all the angels with him, he will sit on his glorious throne, ³²with all the nations gathered before him. He will separate people into two groups, as a shepherd separates the sheep from the goats; ³³he will place the sheep on his right hand and the goats on his left. ³⁴Then the king will say to those on his right, "You have my Father's blessing; come, take possession of the kingdom that has been ready for you since the world was made. ³⁵For when I was hungry, you gave me food; when thirsty, you gave me drink; when I was a stranger, you took me into your home; ³⁶when naked, you clothed me; when I was ill, you came to my help; when in prison, you visited me." ³⁷Then the righteous will reply, "Lord, when was it that we saw you hungry and fed you, or thirsty and gave you drink, ³⁸a stranger and took you home, or naked and clothed you? ³⁹When did we see you ill or in prison, and come to visit you?" ⁴⁰And the king will answer, "Truly I tell you: anything you did for one of my brothers here, however insignificant, you did for me." ⁴¹Then he will say to those on his left, "A curse is on you; go from my sight to the eternal fire that is ready for the devil and his angels. ⁴²For when I was hungry, you gave me nothing to eat; when thirsty, nothing to drink; ⁴³when I was a stranger, you did not welcome me; when I was naked, you did not clothe me; when I was ill and in prison, you did not come to my help." ⁴⁴And they in their turn will reply, "Lord, when was it that we saw you hungry or thirsty or a stranger or naked or ill or in prison, and did nothing for you?" ⁴⁵And he will answer, "Truly I tell you: anything you failed to do for one of these, however insignificant, you failed to do for me." ⁴⁶And they will go away to eternal punishment, but the righteous will enter eternal life.'

The trial and crucifixion of Jesus

26 WHEN Jesus had finished all these discourses he said to his disciples, ²'You know that in two days' time it will be Passover, when the Son of Man will be handed over to be crucified.'

³Meanwhile the chief priests and the elders of the people met in the house of the high priest, Caiaphas, ⁴and discussed a scheme to seize Jesus and put him to death. ⁵'It must not be during the festival,' they said, 'or there may be rioting among the people.'

⁶JESUS was at Bethany in the house of Simon the leper, ⁷when a woman approached him with a bottle of very costly perfume; and she began to pour it over his head as he sat at table. ⁸The disciples were indignant when they saw it. 'Why this waste?' they said. ⁹'It could have been sold for a large sum and the money given to the poor.' ¹⁰Jesus noticed, and said to them, 'Why make trouble for the woman? It is a fine thing she has done for me. ¹¹You have the poor among you always, but you will not always have me. ¹²When she poured this perfume on my body it was her way of preparing me for burial. ¹³Truly I tell you: wherever this gospel is proclaimed throughout the world, what she has done will be told as her memorial.'

¹⁴THEN one of the Twelve, the man called Judas Iscariot, went to the chief priests ¹⁵and said, 'What will you give me to betray him to you?' They weighed him out thirty silver pieces. ¹⁶From that moment he began to look for an opportunity to betray him.

¹⁷On the first day of Unleavened Bread the disciples came and asked Jesus, 'Where would you like us to prepare the Passover for you?' ¹⁸He told them to go to a certain man

2.2–4); the judging of the flocks (Ezek. 34.17). **40:** *Brothers* may be a technical term for "Christians"; see 18.35 n. **40, 45:** 10.42; Mk. 9.41. **26.1a:** See 7.28 n.

26.1b–27.66: The final conflict (Mk. 14.1–15.47; Lk. 22.1–23.56; Jn. chs. 12–19). See Lk. 22.1–23.56 n. **2:** See Mk. 14.1 n. **6–13:** Mk. 14.3–9 (similar stories in Lk. 7.36–50; Jn. 12.1–8). **7:** *Pour:* an act of social courtesy (compare Lk. 7.44–46 n.). **12:** The courtesy (v. 7) is given a significance that reaches beyond the woman's intention. **14–16:** Mk. 14.10–11; Lk. 22.3–6. **15:** *Thirty silver pieces:* compare Zech. 11.12–13.

26.17–19: Preparation for the Passover (Mk. 14.12–16; Lk. 22.7–13). In Roman fashion Matt. (and Mk.; Lk.) describes the preparation (Thursday during the day) and the meal (Thursday evening) as taking place within the one day. However, by Jewish reckoning (in which a new day began at sunset), the preparation (vv. 17–19) fell on Nisan 14; *evening* (v. 20) was viewed as a new day, Nisan 15 (*Passover,* v. 19). The crucifixion is thus also dated on Nisan 15 in the synoptic Gospels. John dates the final meal and the crucifixion on Nisan 14 (e.g.

in the city with this message: 'The Teacher says, "My appointed time is near; I shall keep the Passover with my disciples at your house." ' 19 The disciples did as Jesus directed them and prepared the Passover.

20 In the evening he sat down with the twelve disciples; 21 and during supper he said, 'Truly I tell you: one of you will betray me.' 22 Greatly distressed at this, they asked him one by one, 'Surely you do not mean me, Lord?' 23 He answered, 'One who has dipped his hand into the bowl with me will betray me. 24 The Son of Man is going the way appointed for him in the scriptures; but alas for that man by whom the Son of Man is betrayed! It would be better for that man if he had never been born.' 25 Then Judas spoke, the one who was to betray him: 'Rabbi, surely you do not mean me?' Jesus replied, 'You have said it.'

26 During supper Jesus took bread, and having said the blessing he broke it and gave it to the disciples with the words: 'Take this and eat; this is my body.' 27 Then he took a cup, and having offered thanks to God he gave it to them with the words: 'Drink from it, all of you. 28 For this is my blood, the blood of the covenant, shed for many for the forgiveness of sins. 29 I tell you, never again shall I drink from this fruit of the vine until that day when I drink it new with you in the kingdom of my Father.'

30 After singing the Passover hymn, they went out to the mount of Olives. 31 Then Jesus said to them, 'Tonight you will all lose faith because of me; for it is written: "I will strike the shepherd and the sheep of his flock will be scattered." 32 But after I am raised, I shall go ahead of you into Galilee.' 33 Peter replied, 'Everyone else may lose faith because of you, but I never will.' 34 Jesus said to him,

'Truly I tell you: tonight before the cock crows you will disown me three times.' 35 Peter said, 'Even if I have to die with you, I will never disown you.' And all the disciples said the same.

36 Jesus then came with his disciples to a place called Gethsemane, and he said to them, 'Sit here while I go over there to pray.' 37 He took with him Peter and the two sons of Zebedee. Distress and anguish overwhelmed him, 38 and he said to them, 'My heart is ready to break with grief. Stop here, and stay awake with me.' 39 Then he went on a little farther, threw himself down, and prayed, 'My Father, if it is possible, let this cup pass me by. Yet not my will but yours.'

40 He came back to the disciples and found them asleep; and he said to Peter, 'What! Could none of you stay awake with me for one hour? 41 Stay awake, and pray that you may be spared the test. The spirit is willing, but the flesh is weak.'

42 He went away a second time and prayed: 'My Father, if it is not possible for this cup to pass me by without my drinking it, your will be done.' 43 He came again and found them asleep, for their eyes were heavy. 44 So he left them and went away again and prayed a third time, using the same words as before. 45 Then he came to the disciples and said to them, 'Still asleep? Still resting? The hour has come! The Son of Man is betrayed into the hands of sinners. 46 Up, let us go! The traitor is upon us.'

47 He was still speaking when Judas, one of the Twelve, appeared, and with him a great crowd armed with swords and cudgels, sent by the chief priests and the elders of the nation. 48 The traitor had given them this sign:

Jn. 18.28). **18:** Jerusalem residents customarily provided visitors to the city with space for observing the Passover meal.

26.20–29: The Last Supper (Mk. 14.17–25; Lk. 22.14–38). **20:** *Sat down:* lit. "reclined," as was the custom at Passover meals. **21–25:** See also Jn. 13.21–30. **24:** The motif of Jesus' death as the fulfillment of the *scriptures* is prominent in the passion narrative of each Gospel. It is to be recognized particularly in the way several OT passages (e.g. Ps. 22) are introduced as part of the account (e.g. Matt. 27.46). **26–29:** See also 1 Cor. 11.23–26. **28:** The idea of sacrificial *blood* as the seal of a *covenant* relies on Exod. 24.8 (Zech. 9.11); see Lk. 22.17–19 n. *Many:* see Mk. 10.45 n.

26.30–46: Gethsemane (Mk. 14.26–42; Lk. 22.39–46). **30:** Jn. 18.1. *Passover hymn:* the concluding half of the "Hallel," Pss. 115–118. **31:** Zech. 13.7. **32:** 28.7–10, 16. **33–35:** Lk. 22.31–34; Jn. 13.36–38 place this prediction prior to the departure from the supper. **36–46:** See Lk. 22.40–46 n. **38–39:** Compare Jn. 12.27–28. **38:** Ps. 42.6. **39:** *Cup:* see Mk. 10.38 n.; Jn. 18.11. **42:** 6.10.

26.47–56: The arrest (Mk. 14.43–52; Lk. 22.47–53; Jn. 18.2–11). **48:** The *kiss* was a disciple's usual

'The one I kiss is your man; seize him.' 49 Going straight up to Jesus, he said, 'Hail, Rabbi!' and kissed him. 50 Jesus replied, 'Friend, do what you are here to do.' Then they came forward, seized Jesus, and held him fast.

51 At that moment one of those with Jesus reached for his sword and drew it, and struck the high priest's servant, cutting off his ear. 52 But Jesus said to him, 'Put up your sword. All who take the sword die by the sword. 53 Do you suppose that I cannot appeal for help to my Father, and at once be sent more than twelve legions of angels? 54 But how then would the scriptures be fulfilled, which say that this must happen?'

55 Then Jesus spoke to the crowd: 'Do you take me for a bandit, that you have come out with swords and cudgels to arrest me? Day after day I sat teaching in the temple, and you did not lay hands on me. 56 But this has all happened to fulfil what the prophets wrote.'

Then the disciples all deserted him and ran away.

57 JESUS was led away under arrest to the house of Caiaphas the high priest, where the scribes and elders were assembled. 58 Peter followed him at a distance till he came to the high priest's courtyard; he went in and sat down among the attendants, to see how it would all end.

59 The chief priests and the whole Council tried to find some allegation against Jesus that would warrant a death sentence; 60 but they failed to find one, though many came forward with false evidence. Finally two men 61 alleged that he had said, 'I can pull down the temple of God, and rebuild it in three days.' 62 At this the high priest rose and said to him, 'Have you no answer to the accusations that these witnesses bring against you?' 63 But Jesus remained silent. The high priest

then said, 'By the living God I charge you to tell us: are you the Messiah, the Son of God?' 64 Jesus replied, 'The words are yours. But I tell you this: from now on you will see the Son of Man seated at the right hand of the Almighty and coming on the clouds of heaven.' 65 At these words the high priest tore his robes and exclaimed, 'This is blasphemy! Do we need further witnesses? You have just heard the blasphemy. 66 What is your verdict?' 'He is guilty,' they answered; 'he should die.'

67 Then they spat in his face and struck him with their fists; some said, as they beat him, 68 'Now, Messiah, if you are a prophet, tell us who hit you.'

69 Meanwhile Peter was sitting outside in the courtyard when a servant-girl accosted him; 'You were with Jesus the Galilean,' she said. 70 Peter denied it in front of them all. 'I do not know what you are talking about,' he said. 71 He then went out to the gateway, where another girl, seeing him, said to the people there, 'He was with Jesus of Nazareth.' 72 Once again he denied it, saying with an oath, 'I do not know the man.' 73 Shortly afterwards the bystanders came up and said to Peter, 'You must be one of them; your accent gives you away!' 74 At this he started to curse and declared with an oath: 'I do not know the man.' At that moment a cock crowed; 75 and Peter remembered how Jesus had said, 'Before the cock crows you will disown me three times.' And he went outside, and wept bitterly.

27 WHEN morning came, the chief priests and the elders of the nation all met together to plan the death of Jesus. 2 They bound him and led him away, to hand him over to Pilate, the Roman governor.

3 When Judas the traitor saw that Jesus had

26:64 **The words are yours:** or It is as you say.

greeting of a teacher. **51:** John 18.10 identifies the one as Peter. **52:** Jer. 15.2; Rev. 13.10. **53:** Twelve legions: a legion was an infantry brigade numbering about five thousand soldiers.

26.57–75: Before the Jewish authorities (Mk. 14.53–72; Lk. 22.54–71; Jn. 18.12–27). The Gospel accounts of Jesus' appearance before Jewish officials are not entirely harmonious. Whatever proceedings took place before the native Council (v. 59 n.), the crucial outcome was the charge as transmitted for the Roman trial. **57:** Caiaphas: see Lk. 3.2 n. **59:** The Council (or Sanhedrin) of Jerusalem was Judea's highest native judicial tribunal. **60–61:** See 24.1–3 n. Two witnesses: see Num. 35.30; Deut. 19.15. **63:** Messiah, the Son of God: see 16.16 n. **64:** Dan. 7.13; Ps. 110.1. **65–66:** The claim to be the Messiah would not, in itself, be blasphemy; the penalty for blasphemy was death by stoning (Lev. 24.13–16). **75:** Compare v. 34.

27.1–31: Before Roman authority (Mk. 15.1–20; Lk. 23.1–25; Jn. 18.28–19.16). **2:** Pilate: see Lk. 3.1 n.

been condemned, he was seized with remorse, and returned the thirty silver pieces to the chief priests and elders. 4 'I have sinned,' he said; 'I have brought an innocent man to his death.' But they said, 'What is that to us? It is your concern.' 5 So he threw the money down in the temple and left; he went away and hanged himself.

6 The chief priests took up the money, but they said, 'This cannot be put into the temple fund; it is blood-money.' 7 So after conferring they used it to buy the Potter's Field, as a burial-place for foreigners. 8 This explains the name Blood Acre, by which that field has been known ever since; 9 and in this way fulfilment was given to the saying of the prophet Jeremiah: 'They took the thirty silver pieces, the price set on a man's head (for that was his price among the Israelites), 10 and gave the money for the potter's field, as the Lord directed me.'

11 Jesus was now brought before the governor; 'Are you the king of the Jews?' the governor asked him. 'The words are yours,' said Jesus; 12 and when the chief priests and elders brought charges against him he made no reply. 13 Then Pilate said to him, 'Do you not hear all this evidence they are bringing against you?' 14 but to the governor's great astonishment he refused to answer a single word.

15 At the festival season it was customary for the governor to release one prisoner chosen by the people. 16 There was then in custody a man of some notoriety, called Jesus Barabbas. 17 When the people assembled Pilate said to them, 'Which would you like me to release to you — Jesus Barabbas, or Jesus called Messiah?' 18 For he knew it was out of malice that Jesus had been handed over to him.

19 While Pilate was sitting in court a message came to him from his wife: 'Have nothing to do with that innocent man; I was much troubled on his account in my dreams last night.'

20 Meanwhile the chief priests and elders had persuaded the crowd to ask for the release of Barabbas and to have Jesus put to death. 21 So when the governor asked, 'Which of the two would you like me to release to you?' they said, 'Barabbas.' 22 'Then what am I to do with Jesus called Messiah?' asked Pilate; and with one voice they answered, 'Crucify him!' 23 'Why, what harm has he done?' asked Pilate; but they shouted all the louder, 'Crucify him!'

24 When Pilate saw that he was getting nowhere, and that there was danger of a riot, he took water and washed his hands in full view of the crowd. 'My hands are clean of this man's blood,' he declared. 'See to that yourselves.' 25 With one voice the people cried, 'His blood be on us and on our children.' 26 He then released Barabbas to them; but he had Jesus flogged, and then handed him over to be crucified.

27 THEN the soldiers of the governor took Jesus into his residence, the Praetorium, where they collected the whole company round him. 28 They stripped him and dressed him in a scarlet cloak; 29 and plaiting a crown of thorns they placed it on his head, and a stick in his right hand. Falling on their knees before him they jeered at him: 'Hail, king of the Jews!' 30 They spat on him, and used the stick to beat him about the head. 31 When they had finished mocking him, they stripped off the cloak and dressed him in his own clothes.

Then they led him away to be crucified. 32 On their way out they met a man from Cyrene, Simon by name, and pressed him into service to carry his cross.

33 Coming to a place called Golgotha (which means 'Place of a Skull'), 34 they offered him a drink of wine mixed with gall; but after tasting it he would not drink.

35 When they had crucified him they shared out his clothes by casting lots, 36 and then sat down there to keep watch. 37 Above his head was placed the inscription giving the charge against him: 'This is Jesus, the king of the Jews.' 38 Two bandits were crucified with

27:9 **They took:** *or* I took.   27:11 **The words are yours:** *or* It is as you say.   27:16,17 **Jesus Barabbas:** *many witnesses omit* Jesus *in both verses.*

3–10: Compare Acts 1.18–19. **9–10:** Jer. 32.6–13; Zech. 11.12–13. **11:** *King:* see Lk. 23.2 n. **15:** Such a *customary* release is reported only in the Gospels. **16:** *Barabbas:* probably, "son of the father." The man was a revolutionary (Mk. 15.7; Lk. 23.25). **24:** Deut. 21.6–9.

27.32–66: The crucifixion (Mk. 15.21–47; Lk. 23.26–54; Jn. 19.17–42). On crucifixion, see Mk. 15.20b–47 n. **32:** *Simon:* see Mk. 15.21 n.; contrast Jn. 19.17. **34:** Ps. 69.21; see Lk. 23.36 n. **35:** Ps. 22.18.

him, one on his right and the other on his left.

39 The passers-by wagged their heads and jeered at him, 40 crying, 'So you are the man who was to pull down the temple and rebuild it in three days! If you really are the Son of God, save yourself and come down from the cross.' 41 The chief priests with the scribes and elders joined in the mockery: 42 'He saved others,' they said, 'but he cannot save himself. King of Israel, indeed! Let him come down now from the cross, and then we shall believe him. 43 He trusted in God, did he? Let God rescue him, if he wants him — for he said he was God's Son.' 44 Even the bandits who were crucified with him taunted him in the same way.

45 From midday a darkness fell over the whole land, which lasted until three in the afternoon; 46 and about three Jesus cried aloud, 'Eli, Eli, lema sabachthani?' which means, 'My God, my God, why have you forsaken me?' 47 Hearing this, some of the bystanders said, 'He is calling Elijah.' 48 One of them ran at once and fetched a sponge, which he soaked in sour wine and held to his lips on the end of a stick. 49 But the others said, 'Let us see if Elijah will come to save him.'

50 Jesus again cried aloud and breathed his last. 51 At that moment the curtain of the temple was torn in two from top to bottom. The earth shook, rocks split, 52 and graves opened; many of God's saints were raised from sleep, 53 and coming out of their graves after his resurrection entered the Holy City, where many saw them. 54 And when the centurion and his men who were keeping watch over Jesus saw the earthquake and all that was happening, they were filled with awe and said, 'This must have been a son of God.'

55 A NUMBER of women were also present, watching from a distance; they had followed Jesus from Galilee and looked after him. 56 Among them were Mary of Magdala, Mary the mother of James and Joseph, and the mother of the sons of Zebedee.

57 When evening fell, a wealthy man from Arimathaea, Joseph by name, who had himself become a disciple of Jesus, 58 approached Pilate and asked for the body of Jesus; and Pilate gave orders that he should have it. 59 Joseph took the body, wrapped it in a clean linen sheet, 60 and laid it in his own unused tomb, which he had cut out of the rock. He then rolled a large stone against the entrance, and went away. 61 Mary of Magdala was there, and the other Mary, sitting opposite the grave.

62 Next day, the morning after the day of preparation, the chief priests and the Pharisees came in a body to Pilate. 63 'Your excellency,' they said, 'we recall how that impostor said while he was still alive, "I am to be raised again after three days." 64 We request you to give orders for the grave to be made secure until the third day. Otherwise his disciples may come and steal the body, and then tell the people that he has been raised from the dead; and the final deception will be worse than the first.' 65 'You may have a guard,' said Pilate; 'go and make the grave as secure as you can.' 66 So they went and made it secure by sealing the stone and setting a guard.

The resurrection

28 ABOUT daybreak on the first day of the week, when the sabbath was over, Mary of Magdala and the other Mary came to look at the grave. 2 Suddenly there was a violent earthquake; an angel of the Lord descended from heaven and came and rolled away the stone, and sat down on it. 3 His face shone like lightning; his garments were white as snow. 4 At the sight of him the guards

27:54 **a son of God:** or the Son of God.

38: Isa. 53.12. **39:** Ps. 22.7. **40:** 24.1–3 n. **43:** Ps. 22.8. **44:** Compare Lk. 23.39–43. **46:** This is the first verse of Ps. 22, the remembrance of which has influenced the crucifixion narrative at several points (e.g. vv. 35, 43). **47:** The anticipation of *Elijah's* return (see Mk. 6.15 n.) lies behind this apparent misunderstanding of the cry. **48:** Ps. 69.21. **51:** The rending of the *curtain* before the Holy of Holies may have signified to early Christians God's accessibility to all people at all times; see Exod. 26.31–33; Lev. 16.1–2. **54:** Whatever a Roman soldier might mean by *a son of God* (perhaps, "divine hero"; see Mk. 1.1 n.), the Gospel writer probably understood the words as a Christian confession (see Tfn. at this verse). **59:** Deut. 21.22–23. **60:** The *tomb* was a chamber cut into rock, with the entrance sealed by a wheel-like *stone*. **62–66:** Only Matt. has this tradition, which seems intended to counteract claims like that in 28.13.

28.1–15: The empty tomb (Mk. 16.1–8; Lk. 24.1–11; Jn. 20.1–18). **1:** See Mk. 16.1 n.; Lk. 23.55–56 n.

shook with fear and fell to the ground as though dead.

5 The angel spoke to the women: 'You', he said, 'have nothing to fear. I know you are looking for Jesus who was crucified. 6 He is not here; he has been raised, as he said he would be. Come and see the place where he was laid, 7 and then go quickly and tell his disciples: "He has been raised from the dead and is going ahead of you into Galilee; there you will see him." That is what I came to tell you.'

8 They hurried away from the tomb in awe and great joy, and ran to bring the news to the disciples. 9 Suddenly Jesus was there in their path, greeting them. They came up and clasped his feet, kneeling before him. 10 'Do not be afraid,' Jesus said to them. 'Go and take word to my brothers that they are to leave for Galilee. They will see me there.'

11 While the women were on their way, some of the guard went into the city and reported to the chief priests everything that had happened. 12 After meeting and conferring with the elders, the chief priests offered the soldiers a substantial bribe 13 and told them to say, 'His disciples came during the night and stole the body while we were asleep.' 14 They added, 'If this should reach the governor's ears, we will put matters right with him and see you do not suffer.' 15 So they took the money and did as they were told. Their story became widely known, and is current in Jewish circles to this day.

16 The eleven disciples made their way to Galilee, to the mountain where Jesus had told them to meet him. 17 When they saw him, they knelt in worship, though some were doubtful. 18 Jesus came near and said to them: 'Full authority in heaven and on earth has been committed to me. 19 Go therefore to all nations and make them my disciples; baptize them in the name of the Father and the Son and the Holy Spirit, 20 and teach them to observe all that I have commanded you. I will be with you always, to the end of time.'

2: *Stone:* 27.60 n. **4:** *Guards:* see 27.62–66. **7–10:** *Galilee:* 26.32. **8:** Contrast Mk. 16.8. **11–15:** 27.62–66; 28.4. **15:** *This day:* i.e. in Matt.'s time the charge of the stolen body was used to counter the proclamation of Jesus' resurrection.

28.16–20: Appearance and commissioning in Galilee. 16: *Mountain:* see 5.1 n. **19:** The command to go to *all nations* directs the church into the Gentile mission, beyond the limits of 10.5–6. **20:** *All that I have commanded:* compare chs. 5–7 (the Sermon on the Mount). *I will be with you:* compare 1.23; 18.20.

THE GOSPEL ACCORDING TO

Mark

Probably the oldest of the Gospels, Mark is a collection of traditions about Jesus brought together around 70 C.E. The import of the term "collection" should not mislead one to suppose that the material is presented haphazardly. On the contrary, the author depicts Jesus' early ministry as centered in Galilee, where he proclaims the imminence of the rule and salvation of God (the kingdom) and performs wonders; at its climax comes Peter's confession of faith and the first announcement of the passion (8.27–33). From that crucial point, the story moves relentlessly toward the cross and resurrection (chs. 14–16). Within this general framework, other "turning points" may also be found: e.g. 1.14; 3.6; 10.1.

Moreover, certain motifs can be identified as of special concern to the evangelist. Perhaps the most important of these, at least in the Galilean section, is the victory over demonic forces to be seen in Jesus' healing activity. While the power which achieves that victory is exercised publicly, another Markan idea has to do with maintaining secrecy with respect to Jesus' identity (e.g. 1.34 n.). And the reader discovers a remarkable obtuseness even among the disciples (e.g. 8.17; 9.32) as another theme.

The book's purpose is succinctly expressed: to proclaim the good news of Jesus Christ, the Son of God (1.1; 15.39).

John the Baptist and Jesus

1 THE beginning of the gospel of Jesus Christ the Son of God.

2 IN the prophet Isaiah it stands written:

I am sending my herald ahead of you;
he will prepare your way.
3 A voice cries in the wilderness,
'Prepare the way for the Lord;
clear a straight path for him.'

4 John the Baptist appeared in the wilderness proclaiming a baptism in token of repentance, for the forgiveness of sins; 5 and everyone flocked to him from the countryside of Judaea and the city of Jerusalem, and they were baptized by him in the river Jordan, confessing their sins. 6 John was dressed in a rough coat of camel's hair, with a leather belt round his waist, and he fed on locusts and wild honey. 7 He proclaimed: 'After me comes one mightier than I am, whose sandals I am not worthy to stoop down and unfasten. 8 I have baptized you with water; he will baptize you with the Holy Spirit.'

9 It was at this time that Jesus came from Nazareth in Galilee and was baptized in the

1:1 *Some witnesses omit* the Son of God.

1.1–8: The work of the Baptist (Matt. 3.1–12; Lk. 3.1–20; Jn. 1.6, 15, 19–28). **1:** By *gospel* (i.e. the good news) the author means not the book, but the proclamation of *Jesus Christ;* it begins with the ministry of John the Baptist (compare Acts 1.22). Behind the use of the *Son of God* title in the Markan community are influences as diverse as the Jewish expectation of a royal Messiah (see Matt. 1.1 n.) and Hellenistic ideas about wonderworking "divine heroes" and persons of divine nature. **2:** Mal. 3.1. **3:** Isa. 40.3. **4:** *Wilderness:* Matt. 3.1 n. *Baptism:* see Matt. 3.7 n. *Repentance:* see Matt. 3.2 n. **6:** Elijah is clothed similarly in 2 Kgs. 1.8. **7:** The Baptist's role in the Gospel is as the forerunner of Christ; hence, he is sometimes identified with Elijah (see 6.15 n.; 9.11–12; Matt. 11.14; 17.10–13). **8:** *Holy Spirit:* see Lk. 3.16 n.
1.9–11: The baptism of Jesus (Matt. 3.13–17; Lk. 3.21–22; Jn. 1.32–34). In early Christian tradition, the striking account of Jesus' baptism by John serves at least three significant purposes: it narrates his becoming the Son (see Matt. 3.16 n.); it explains the origin of the church's initiatory rite; and it provides a location in

Jordan by John. ¹⁰As he was coming up out of the water, he saw the heavens break open and the Spirit descend on him, like a dove. ¹¹And a voice came from heaven: 'You are my beloved Son; in you I take delight.'

¹²At once the Spirit drove him out into the wilderness, ¹³and there he remained for forty days tempted by Satan. He was among the wild beasts; and angels attended to his needs.

Proclaiming the kingdom

¹⁴AFTER John had been arrested, Jesus came into Galilee proclaiming the gospel of God: ¹⁵'The time has arrived; the kingdom of God is upon you. Repent, and believe the gospel.'

¹⁶Jesus was walking by the sea of Galilee when he saw Simon and his brother Andrew at work with casting-nets in the lake; for they were fishermen. ¹⁷Jesus said to them, 'Come, follow me, and I will make you fishers of men.' ¹⁸At once they left their nets and followed him.

¹⁹Going a little farther, he saw James son of Zebedee and his brother John in a boat mending their nets. ²⁰At once he called them; and they left their father Zebedee in the boat with the hired men and followed him.

²¹They came to Capernaum, and on the sabbath he went to the synagogue and began to teach. ²²The people were amazed at his teaching, for, unlike the scribes, he taught with a note of authority. ²³Now there was a man in their synagogue possessed by an unclean spirit. He shrieked at him: ²⁴'What do you want with us, Jesus of Nazareth? Have you come to destroy us? I know who you are—the Holy One of God.' ²⁵Jesus rebuked him: 'Be silent', he said, 'and come out of him.' ²⁶The unclean spirit threw the man into convulsions and with a loud cry left him. ²⁷They were all amazed and began to ask one another, 'What is this? A new kind of teaching! He speaks with authority. When he gives orders, even the unclean spirits obey.' ²⁸His fame soon spread far and wide throughout Galilee.

²⁹On leaving the synagogue, they went straight to the house of Simon and Andrew; and James and John went with them. ³⁰Simon's mother-in-law was in bed with a fever. As soon as they told him about her, ³¹Jesus went and took hold of her hand, and raised her to her feet. The fever left her, and she attended to their needs.

³²That evening after sunset they brought to him all who were ill or possessed by demons; ³³and the whole town was there, gathered at the door. ³⁴He healed many who suffered from various diseases, and drove out many demons. He would not let the demons speak, because they knew who he was.

³⁵Very early next morning he got up and went out. He went away to a remote spot and remained there in prayer. ³⁶But Simon and his companions went in search of him, ³⁷and when they found him, they said, 'Everybody is looking for you.' ³⁸He answered, 'Let us move on to the neighbouring towns, so that I can proclaim my message there as well, for

1:11 **You are ... Son:** or You are my only Son.
1:24 **Have you:** or You have.

Israel's history for the beginning of Jesus' activity. **10–11:** *Spirit, dove:* see Matt. 3.16 n. **11:** Ps. 2.7 (*Son*) and Isa. 42.1 (*Beloved,* meaning "chosen one") are combined.

1.12–13: The temptation (Matt. 4.1–11; Lk. 4.1–13). This brief account introduces a major concern of Mk.—the conflict of the *Spirit*-led Son with *Satan,* the evil one (3.22–30). **13:** *Forty days:* see Matt. 4.2 n. *Satan:* see Matt. 4.1 n. Whether Mk. meant the *beasts* to represent the dangers of the wilderness or the restoration of creation's harmony is not clear.

1.14–20: The beginning of Jesus' ministry (Matt. 4.12–22; Lk. 4.14–15; 5.1–11; Jn. 1.35–51). **15:** The *time* is the long-anticipated dawning of what is called the *kingdom of God*—which signifies God's final victory over evil, when the divine rule is fully established and the age of salvation is inaugurated. *Repent:* change your ways. **16–20:** The first disciples are called without any indication of prior acquaintance with Jesus. **16:** *Simon:* Peter (compare Matt. 4.18). **18:** *Followed:* became his disciples.

1.21–38: Jesus in Capernaum (Matt. 8.14–17; Lk. 4.31–43). **23:** *Unclean spirit:* a demon, believed to have power to cause illness; see v. 32. Such demons are allied with Satan (see 3.22–23) in opposition to God's will for humanity. **24:** The demon has knowledge not possessed by the people in the synagogue. **32:** *Sunset:* see Lk. 4.40 n. **34:** In Mk., Jesus repeatedly imposes silence about his identity, not only on demons (e.g. 3.12), but also on friends (e.g. 8.30).

that is what I came out to do.' ³⁹ So he went through the whole of Galilee, preaching in their synagogues and driving out demons.

⁴⁰ On one occasion he was approached by a leper, who knelt before him and begged for help. 'If only you will,' said the man, 'you can make me clean.' ⁴¹ Jesus was moved to anger; he stretched out his hand, touched him, and said, 'I will; be clean.' ⁴² The leprosy left him immediately, and he was clean. ⁴³ Then he dismissed him with this stern warning: ⁴⁴ 'See that you tell nobody, but go and show yourself to the priest, and make the offering laid down by Moses for your cleansing; that will certify the cure.' ⁴⁵ But the man went away and made the whole story public, spreading it far and wide, until Jesus could no longer show himself in any town. He stayed outside in remote places; yet people kept coming to him from all quarters.

2 After some days he returned to Capernaum, and news went round that he was at home; ² and such a crowd collected that there was no room for them even in the space outside the door. While he was proclaiming the message to them, ³ a man was brought who was paralysed. Four men were carrying him, ⁴ but because of the crowd they could not get him near. So they made an opening in the roof over the place where Jesus was, and when they had broken through they lowered the bed on which the paralysed man was lying. ⁵ When he saw their faith, Jesus said to the man, 'My son, your sins are forgiven.'

⁶ Now there were some scribes sitting there, thinking to themselves, ⁷ 'How can the fellow talk like that? It is blasphemy! Who but God can forgive sins?' ⁸ Jesus knew at once what they were thinking, and said to them,

'Why do you harbour such thoughts? ⁹ Is it easier to say to this paralysed man, "Your sins are forgiven," or to say, "Stand up, take your bed, and walk"? ¹⁰ But to convince you that the Son of Man has authority on earth to forgive sins'—he turned to the paralysed man—¹¹ 'I say to you, stand up, take your bed, and go home.' ¹² And he got up, and at once took his bed and went out in full view of them all, so that they were astounded and praised God. 'Never before', they said, 'have we seen anything like this.'

¹³ Once more he went out to the lakeside. All the crowd came to him there, and he taught them. ¹⁴ As he went along, he saw Levi son of Alphaeus at his seat in the custom-house, and said to him, 'Follow me'; and he rose and followed him.

¹⁵ When Jesus was having a meal in his house, many tax-collectors and sinners were seated with him and his disciples, for there were many of them among his followers. ¹⁶ Some scribes who were Pharisees, observing the company in which he was eating, said to his disciples, 'Why does he eat with tax-collectors and sinners?' ¹⁷ Hearing this, Jesus said to them, 'It is not the healthy who need a doctor, but the sick; I did not come to call the virtuous, but sinners.'

¹⁸ Once, when John's disciples and the Pharisees were keeping a fast, some people came and asked him, 'Why is it that John's disciples and the disciples of the Pharisees are fasting, but yours are not?' ¹⁹ Jesus replied, 'Can you expect the bridegroom's friends to fast while the bridegroom is with them? As long as he is with them, there can

---

1:41 **to anger:** *many witnesses read* with pity.

1.40–45: A leper healed (Matt. 8.1–4; Lk. 5.12–16). **40:** *Leper . . . make me clean:* see Matt. 8.2 n. **43–44a:** See v. 34 n. **44:** See Lev. 14.1–32. **45:** Matt. has no parallel to this verse, while Lk. recasts it, omitting the suggestion that *Jesus could no longer show himself in any town.*

2.1–3.6: Healing and conflict.

2.1–12: A paralytic (Matt. 9.1–8; Lk. 5.17–26). **4:** A *roof* of mud and branches is meant (contrast Lk. 5.19). **5:** The account assumes a connection between illness and sin; compare Jn. 9.2. *Faith:* see Matt. 8.13 n. **6:** *Scribes:* see Matt. 2.4 n. **10:** *Son of Man* in some NT contexts may be only the equivalent of a Semitic phrase meaning "human being." In most places, however, *Son of Man* is a title for an exalted figure who will serve as judge at the end of history (see Dan. 7.13–14). The expression is found almost exclusively in sayings attributed to Jesus. In some occurrences, the *Son of Man* is clearly identified with Jesus, even in his earthly humility and suffering.

2.13–17: Jesus, friend of outcasts (Matt. 9.9–13; Lk. 5.27–32). **15:** Eating with *tax-collectors* (see Lk. 3.12 n.) and other outcasts was a practice of Jesus' of which his opponents strongly disapproved.

2.18–22: Fasting (Matt. 9.14–17; Lk. 5.33–39). **18:** *John's disciples* developed into a continuing religious be no fasting. 20 But the time will come when the bridegroom will be taken away from them; that will be the time for them to fast.

21 'No one sews a patch of unshrunk cloth on to an old garment; if he does, the patch tears away from it, the new from the old, and leaves a bigger hole. 22 No one puts new wine into old wineskins; if he does, the wine will burst the skins, and then wine and skins are both lost. New wine goes into fresh skins.'

23 One sabbath he was going through the cornfields; and as they went along his disciples began to pluck ears of corn. 24 The Pharisees said to him, 'Why are they doing what is forbidden on the sabbath?' 25 He answered, 'Have you never read what David did when he and his men were hungry and had nothing to eat? 26 He went into the house of God, in the time of Abiathar the high priest, and ate the sacred bread, though no one but a priest is allowed to eat it, and even gave it to his men.'

27 He also said to them, 'The sabbath was made for man, not man for the sabbath: 28 so the Son of Man is lord even of the sabbath.'

3 On another occasion when he went to synagogue, there was a man in the congregation who had a withered arm; 2 and they were watching to see whether Jesus would heal him on the sabbath, so that they could bring a charge against him. 3 He said to the man with the withered arm, 'Come and stand out here.' 4 Then he turned to them: 'Is it permitted to do good or to do evil on the sabbath, to save life or to kill?' They had nothing to say; 5 and, looking round at them with anger and sorrow at their obstinate stupidity, he said to the man, 'Stretch out your arm.' He stretched it out and his arm was restored. 6 Then the Pharisees, on leaving the synagogue, at once began plotting with the men of Herod's party to bring about Jesus's death.

7 JESUS went away to the lakeside with his disciples. Great numbers from Galilee, Judaea 8 and Jerusalem, Idumaea and Transjordan, and the neighbourhood of Tyre and Sidon, heard what he was doing and came to him. 9 So he told his disciples to have a boat ready for him, to save him from being crushed by the crowd. 10 For he healed so many that the sick all came crowding round to touch him. 11 The unclean spirits too, when they saw him, would fall at his feet and cry aloud, 'You are the Son of God'; 12 but he insisted that they should not make him known.

13 Then he went up into the hill-country and summoned the men he wanted; and they came and joined him. 14 He appointed twelve to be his companions, and to be sent out to proclaim the gospel, 15 with authority to drive out demons. 16 The Twelve he appointed were: Simon, whom he named Peter; 17 the sons of Zebedee, James and his brother John, whom he named Boanerges, Sons of Thunder; 18 Andrew, Philip, Bartholomew, Matthew, Thomas, James son of Alphaeus, Thaddaeus, Simon the Zealot, 19 and Judas Iscariot, the man who betrayed him.

He entered a house, 20 and once more such a crowd collected round them that they had no chance even to eat. 21 When his family heard about it they set out to take charge of him. 'He is out of his mind,' they said.

22 The scribes, too, who had come down from Jerusalem, said, 'He is possessed by Beelzebul,' and, 'He drives out demons by the prince of demons.' 23 So he summoned them, and spoke to them in parables: 'How can

movement; see Acts 19.1–6. **21–22:** Such a radical distinction between the *new* and the *old* shows the seriousness of the reported conflict.

2.23–3.6: Sabbath controversy (Matt. 12.1–14; Lk. 6.1–11). Strict sabbath observance required refraining from all work and was of prime importance for first-century Jewish piety. **23:** Deut. 23.25. **24:** Exod. 20.10; Deut. 5.14. **26:** *Abiathar* is a slip of the memory; Abiathar's father, Ahimelech, was the priest in this instance (1 Sam. 21.1–6). On the rule involved, see Lev. 24.7–9. **27:** Deut. 5.12–14. **28:** *Son of Man:* see 2.10 n. **3.1–6:** While healing in general was prohibited on the sabbath, Pharisaic interpretation permitted treatment when a life was at stake.

3.7–12: Summary of activity and Jesus' rapport with the common people (Matt. 4.24–25; 12.15–16; Lk. 6.17–19).

3.13–19: The Twelve appointed (Matt. 10.1–4; Lk. 6.12–16). **18:** The *Zealot* movement was a group of violent revolutionaries.

3.20–30: Suspicion and accusation (Matt. 12.22–37; Lk. 11.14–23; 12.10). **22:** *Beelzebul:* Satan.

Satan drive out Satan? 24 If a kingdom is divided against itself, that kingdom cannot stand; 25 if a household is divided against itself, that house cannot stand; 26 and if Satan is divided and rebels against himself, he cannot stand, and that is the end of him.

27 'On the other hand, no one can break into a strong man's house and make off with his goods unless he has first tied up the strong man; then he can ransack the house. 28 'Truly I tell you: every sin and every slander can be forgiven; 29 but whoever slanders the Holy Spirit can never be forgiven; he is guilty of an eternal sin.' 30 He said this because they had declared that he was possessed by an unclean spirit.

31 Then his mother and his brothers arrived; they stayed outside and sent in a message asking him to come out to them. 32 A crowd was sitting round him when word was brought that his mother and brothers were outside asking for him. 33 'Who are my mother and my brothers?' he replied. 34 And looking round at those who were sitting in the circle about him he said, 'Here are my mother and my brothers. 35 Whoever does the will of God is my brother and sister and mother.'

Parables

4 ON another occasion he began to teach by the lakeside. The crowd that gathered round him was so large that he had to get into a boat on the lake and sit there, with the whole crowd on the beach right down to the water's edge. 2 And he taught them many things by parables.

As he taught he said:

3 'Listen! A sower went out to sow. 4 And it happened that as he sowed, some of the seed fell along the footpath; and the birds came and ate it up. 5 Some fell on rocky ground, where it had little soil, and it sprouted quickly because it had no depth of earth; 6 but when the sun rose it was scorched, and as it had no root it withered away. 7 Some fell among thistles; and the thistles grew up and choked the corn, and it produced no crop. 8 And some of the seed fell into good soil, where it came up and grew, and produced a crop; and the yield was thirtyfold, sixtyfold, even a hundredfold.' 9 He added, 'If you have ears to hear, then hear.'

10 When Jesus was alone with the Twelve and his other companions they questioned him about the parables. 11 He answered, 'To you the secret of the kingdom of God has been given; but to those who are outside, everything comes by way of parables, 12 so that (as scripture says) they may look and look, but see nothing; they may listen and listen, but understand nothing; otherwise they might turn to God and be forgiven.'

13 He went on: 'Do you not understand this parable? How then are you to understand any parable? 14 The sower sows the word. 15 With some the seed falls along the footpath; no sooner have they heard it than Satan comes and carries off the word which has been sown in them. 16 With others the seed falls on rocky ground; as soon as they hear the word, they accept it with joy, 17 but it strikes no root in them; they have no staying-power, and when there is trouble or persecution on account of the word, they quickly lose faith. 18 With others again the seed falls among thistles; they hear the word, 19 but worldly cares and the false glamour of wealth and evil desires of all kinds

---

29: A difficult saying (compare Matt. 12.31–32 n.; Lk. 12.10), which appears in several forms in early Christian literature, is interpreted by Mk. to prohibit *slander* against the power at work in Jesus (v. 30).

3.31–35: Jesus' true family (Matt. 12.46–50; Lk. 8.19–21). **31:** *Arrived:* see v. 21.

4.1–34: The use of parables (Matt. ch. 13; Lk. 8.4–18; 13.18–21). **2:** A *parable* is a realistic story or true-to-experience observation which points beyond the everyday situation it describes. The parable is to be contrasted with the allegory, which is a puzzle whose meaning is discovered by unlocking the symbolic significance of each detail in the story. The parable's message is found by letting the metaphor stimulate the imagination to see things (God's rule, human relations, life) in a new way. **3–8:** The procedure in farming was to sow the seed first and then to plow. Inevitably, some seed would fall on ground with an abundance of subsurface rock. **8:** The *yield* exceeds normal expectations. **11:** The *secret* probably is that God's rule is manifesting itself. Here, *parables* appears to mean "puzzles" and may mistranslate a Semitic word; if so, the translation had fateful consequences (vv. 13–20 n.). **12:** See Isa. 6.9–10; in Mk. (but see Matt. 13.13 n.), the parables are a cause of that hardening of human hearts which occurs within God's purpose (compare Jn. 12.40).

come in and choke the word, and it proves barren. [20] But there are some with whom the seed is sown on good soil; they accept the word when they hear it, and they bear fruit thirtyfold, sixtyfold, or a hundred-fold.'

[21] He said to them, 'Is a lamp brought in to be put under the measuring bowl or under the bed? No, it is put on the lampstand. [22] Nothing is hidden except to be disclosed, and nothing concealed except to be brought into the open. [23] If you have ears to hear, then hear.'

[24] He also said to them, 'Take note of what you hear; the measure you give is the measure you will receive, with something more besides. [25] For those who have will be given more, and those who have not will forfeit even what they have.'

[26] He said, 'The kingdom of God is like this. A man scatters seed on the ground; [27] he goes to bed at night and gets up in the morning, and meanwhile the seed sprouts and grows — how, he does not know. [28] The ground produces a crop by itself, first the blade, then the ear, then full grain in the ear; [29] but as soon as the crop is ripe, he starts reaping, because harvest time has come.'

[30] He said, 'How shall we picture the kingdom of God, or what parable shall we use to describe it? [31] It is like a mustard seed; when sown in the ground it is smaller than any other seed, [32] but once sown, it springs up and grows taller than any other plant, and forms branches so large that birds can roost in its shade.'

[33] With many such parables he used to give them his message, so far as they were able to receive it. [34] He never spoke to them except in parables; but privately to his disciples he explained everything.

Miracles

[35] THAT day, in the evening, he said to them, 'Let us cross over to the other side of the lake.' [36] So they left the crowd and took him with them in the boat in which he had been sitting; and some other boats went with him. [37] A fierce squall blew up and the waves broke over the boat until it was all but swamped. [38] Now he was in the stern asleep on a cushion; they roused him and said, 'Teacher, we are sinking! Do you not care?' [39] He awoke and rebuked the wind, and said to the sea, 'Silence! Be still!' The wind dropped and there was a dead calm. [40] He said to them, 'Why are you such cowards? Have you no faith even now?' [41] They were awestruck and said to one another, 'Who can this be? Even the wind and the sea obey him.'

5 So they came to the country of the Gerasenes on the other side of the lake. [2] As he stepped ashore, a man possessed by an unclean spirit came up to him from among the tombs [3] where he had made his home. Nobody could control him any longer; even chains were useless, [4] for he had often been fettered and chained up, but had snapped his chains and broken the fetters. No one was strong enough to master him. [5] Unceasingly, night and day, he would cry aloud among the tombs and on the hillsides and gash himself with stones. [6] When he saw Jesus in the distance, he ran up and flung himself down before him, [7] shouting at the top of his voice, 'What do you want with me, Jesus, son of the Most High God? In God's name do not torment me.' [8] For Jesus was already saying to him, 'Out, unclean spirit, come out of the man!' [9] Jesus asked him, 'What is your name?' 'My name is Legion,' he said, 'there are so many of us.' [10] And he implored Jesus not to send them out of the district. [11] There was a

13–20: In line with v. 11 (see n.), the parable is interpreted as an allegory. **21:** Matt. 5.15; Lk. 8.16. **22:** Matt. 10.26; Lk. 8.17; 12.2. **24–25:** Compare Matt. 7.2; 13.12; Lk. 6.38; 8.18; the use of these sayings at this place (vv. 10–12, 33–34) underlines the privileged knowledge of the chosen ones, the secret truth which they will one day make public (v. 22). **26–32:** Though all but invisible now, God's rule and salvation are sure to be fulfilled. **31:** The *mustard seed* (Matt. 13.31–32; Lk. 13.18–19) is proverbially, although not literally, the smallest seed. **32:** Compare Dan. 4.12. **34:** See vv. 24–25 n.

4.35–41: Rebuke of a storm (Matt. 8.23–27; Lk. 8.22–25).

5.1–20: The Gerasene demoniac (Matt. 8.28–34; Lk. 8.26–39). **1:** *Country of the Gerasenes* would mean Gerasa (Jerash), a city of the Decapolis (Matt. 4.25 n.). Matthew 8.28 has "Gadarenes"; manuscripts of all three synoptics show confusion about the location (see Tfn. at Lk. 8.26). A place on the southeast side of the Sea of Galilee is apparently meant. **2:** See 1.23. **6–7:** See Matt. 8.28–29 n. **9:** Power over a person was believed large herd of pigs nearby, feeding on the hillside, 12 and the spirits begged him, 'Send us among the pigs; let us go into them.' 13 He gave them leave; and the unclean spirits came out and went into the pigs; and the herd, of about two thousand, rushed over the edge into the lake and were drowned.

14 The men in charge of them took to their heels and carried the news to the town and countryside; and the people came out to see what had happened. 15 When they came to Jesus and saw the madman who had been possessed by the legion of demons, sitting there clothed and in his right mind, they were afraid. 16 When eyewitnesses told them what had happened to the madman and what had become of the pigs, 17 they begged Jesus to leave the district. 18 As he was getting into the boat, the man who had been possessed begged to go with him. 19 But Jesus would not let him. 'Go home to your own people,' he said, 'and tell them what the Lord in his mercy has done for you.' 20 The man went off and made known throughout the Decapolis what Jesus had done for him; and everyone was amazed.

21 As soon as Jesus had returned by boat to the other shore, a large crowd gathered round him. While he was by the lakeside, 22 there came a synagogue president named Jairus; and when he saw him, he threw himself down at his feet 23 and pleaded with him. 'My little daughter is at death's door,' he said. 'I beg you to come and lay your hands on her so that her life may be saved.' 24 So Jesus went with him, accompanied by a great crowd which pressed round him.

25 Among them was a woman who had suffered from haemorrhages for twelve years; 26 and in spite of long treatment by many doctors, on which she had spent all she had, she had become worse rather than better. 27 She had heard about Jesus, and came up behind him in the crowd and touched his cloak; 28 for she said, 'If I touch even his clothes, I shall be healed.' 29 And there and then the flow of blood dried up and she knew in herself that she was cured of her affliction. 30 Aware at once that power had gone out of him, Jesus turned round in the crowd and asked, 'Who touched my clothes?' 31 His disciples said to him, 'You see the crowd pressing round you and yet you ask, "Who touched me?" ' 32 But he kept looking around to see who had done it. 33 Then the woman, trembling with fear because she knew what had happened to her, came and fell at his feet and told him the whole truth. 34 He said to her, 'Daughter, your faith has healed you. Go in peace, free from your affliction.'

35 While he was still speaking, a message came from the president's house, 'Your daughter has died; why trouble the teacher any more?' 36 But Jesus, overhearing the message as it was delivered, said to the president of the synagogue, 'Do not be afraid; simply have faith.' 37 Then he allowed no one to accompany him except Peter and James and James's brother John. 38 They came to the president's house, where he found a great commotion, with loud crying and wailing. 39 So he went in and said to them, 'Why this crying and commotion? The child is not dead: she is asleep'; 40 and they laughed at him. After turning everyone out, he took the child's father and mother and his own companions into the room where the child was. 41 Taking hold of her hand, he said to her, 'Talitha cum,' which means, 'Get up, my child.' 42 Immediately the girl got up and walked about—she was twelve years old. They were overcome with amazement; 43 but he gave them strict instructions not to let anyone know about it, and told them to give her something to eat.

6 From there he went to his home town accompanied by his disciples. 2 When the sabbath came he began to teach in the synagogue; and the large congregation who heard him asked in amazement, 'Where does he get it from? What is this wisdom he has been given? How does he perform such mir-

---

to be gained by knowing his or her *name*. *Legion:* a Roman army unit of about five thousand soldiers. **11:** *Pigs:* see Matt. 8.30 n. **20:** *Decapolis:* see Matt. 4.25 n.

5.21–43: Jairus' daughter and a woman with a chronic ailment (Matt. 9.18–26; Lk. 8.40–56). Both narratives display the elements common to ancient miracle stories: description, cure, proof of cure (compare 5.1–16). **34:** On *healed,* see Lk. 7.50 n. **38:** The customary noisy mourning practices. **41:** *Talitha cum* is Aram.; the command is preserved in transliteration, perhaps in the belief that the strange-sounding phrase has special power.

6.1–6: Jesus in Nazareth (Matt. 13.53b–58; compare Lk. 4.16–30). **1:** *Home town:* Nazareth.

acles? ³Is he not the carpenter, the son of Mary, the brother of James and Joses and Judas and Simon? Are not his sisters here with us?' So they turned against him. ⁴Jesus said to them, 'A prophet never lacks honour except in his home town, among his relations and his own family.' ⁵And he was unable to do any miracle there, except that he put his hands on a few sick people and healed them; ⁶and he was astonished at their want of faith.

Death of John the Baptist

As HE went round the villages teaching, ⁷he summoned the Twelve and sent them out two by two with authority over unclean spirits. ⁸He instructed them to take nothing for the journey except a stick — no bread, no pack, no money in their belts. ⁹They might wear sandals, but not a second coat. ¹⁰'When you enter a house,' he told them, 'stay there until you leave that district. ¹¹At any place where they will not receive you or listen to you, shake the dust off your feet as you leave, as a solemn warning.' ¹²So they set out and proclaimed the need for repentance; ¹³they drove out many demons, and anointed many sick people with oil and cured them.

¹⁴Now King Herod heard of Jesus, for his fame had spread, and people were saying, 'John the Baptist has been raised from the dead, and that is why these miraculous powers are at work in him.' ¹⁵Others said, 'It is Elijah.' Others again, 'He is a prophet like one of the prophets of old.' ¹⁶But when Herod heard of it, he said, 'This is John, whom I beheaded, raised from the dead.'

¹⁷It was this Herod who had sent men to arrest John and put him in prison at the instance of his brother Philip's wife, Herodias, whom he had married. ¹⁸John had told him, 'You have no right to take your brother's wife.' ¹⁹Herodias nursed a grudge against John and would willingly have killed him, but she could not, ²⁰for Herod went in awe of him, knowing him to be a good and holy

man; so he gave him his protection. He liked to listen to him, although what he heard left him greatly disturbed.

²¹Herodias found her opportunity when Herod on his birthday gave a banquet to his chief officials and commanders and the leading men of Galilee. ²²Her daughter came in and danced, and so delighted Herod and his guests that the king said to the girl, 'Ask me for anything you like and I will give it to you.' ²³He even said on oath: 'Whatever you ask I will give you, up to half my kingdom.' ²⁴She went out and said to her mother, 'What shall I ask for?' She replied, 'The head of John the Baptist.' ²⁵The girl hurried straight back to the king with her request: 'I want you to give me, here and now, on a dish, the head of John the Baptist.' ²⁶The king was greatly distressed, yet because of his oath and his guests he could not bring himself to refuse her. ²⁷He sent a soldier of the guard with orders to bring John's head; and the soldier went to the prison and beheaded him; ²⁸then he brought the head on a dish, and gave it to the girl; and she gave it to her mother.

²⁹When John's disciples heard the news, they came and took his body away and laid it in a tomb.

Miracles of feeding and their significance

³⁰THE apostles rejoined Jesus and reported to him all that they had done and taught. ³¹He said to them, 'Come with me, by yourselves, to some remote place and rest a little.' With many coming and going they had no time even to eat. ³²So they set off by boat privately for a remote place. ³³But many saw them leave and recognized them, and people from all the towns hurried round on foot and arrived there first. ³⁴When he came ashore and saw a large crowd, his heart went out to

6:3 **the carpenter . . . Mary:** *some witnesses read* the son of the carpenter and Mary.　6:14 **and . . . saying:** *some witnesses read* and he said.

6.7–13: Mission of the Twelve (Matt. 9.35; 10.1, 9–11, 14; Lk. 9.1–6). **7:** See Matt. 10.8 n.

6.14–29: Herod and John (Matt. 14.1–12; Lk. 3.19–20; 9.7–9). **14:** The *Herod* meant is Antipas (see Lk. 3.1 n.); he was actually a client prince, not a *king*. **15:** *Elijah* was expected to return to introduce the age of salvation (Mal. 4.5–6; Ecclus. 48.10).

6.30–44: Feeding of five thousand (Matt. 14.13–21; Lk. 9.10–17; Jn. 6.1–13). Matthew 5.32–39 and Mk. 8.1–10 both have a second account of the feeding of a multitude (followed by a sea crossing); some believe the two accounts are variant forms of the same report. **30:** *Apostles:* see Matt. 10.2 n.

them, because they were like sheep without a shepherd; and he began to teach them many things. 35 It was already getting late, and his disciples came to him and said, 'This is a remote place and it is already very late; 36 send the people off to the farms and villages round about, to buy themselves something to eat.' 37 'Give them something to eat yourselves,' he answered. They replied, 'Are we to go and spend two hundred denarii to provide them with food?' 38 'How many loaves have you?' he asked. 'Go and see.' They found out and told him, 'Five, and two fish.' 39 He ordered them to make the people sit down in groups on the green grass, 40 and they sat down in rows, in companies of fifty and a hundred. 41 Then, taking the five loaves and the two fish, he looked up to heaven, said the blessing, broke the loaves, and gave them to the disciples to distribute. He also divided the two fish among them. 42 They all ate and were satisfied; 43 and twelve baskets were filled with what was left of the bread and the fish. 44 Those who ate the loaves numbered five thousand men.

45 As soon as they had finished, he made his disciples embark and cross to Bethsaida ahead of him, while he himself dismissed the crowd. 46 After taking leave of them, he went up the hill to pray. 47 It was now late and the boat was already well out on the water, while he was alone on the land. 48 Somewhere between three and six in the morning, seeing them labouring at the oars against a head wind, he came towards them, walking on the lake. He was going to pass by them; 49 but when they saw him walking on the lake, they thought it was a ghost and cried out; 50 for they all saw him and were terrified. But at once he spoke to them: 'Take heart! It is I; do not be afraid.' 51 Then he climbed into the boat with them, and the wind dropped. At this they were utterly astounded, 52 for they had not understood the incident of the loaves; their minds were closed.

53 So they completed the crossing and landed at Gennesaret, where they made fast.

54 When they came ashore, he was recognized at once; 55 and the people scoured the whole countryside and brought the sick on their beds to any place where he was reported to be. 56 Wherever he went, to village or town or farm, they laid the sick in the market-place and begged him to let them simply touch the edge of his cloak; and all who touched him were healed.

7 A GROUP of Pharisees, with some scribes who had come from Jerusalem, met him 2 and noticed that some of his disciples were eating their food with defiled hands — in other words, without washing them. 3 (For Pharisees and Jews in general never eat without washing their hands, in obedience to ancient tradition; 4 and on coming from the market-place they never eat without first washing. And there are many other points on which they maintain traditional rules, for example in the washing of cups and jugs and copper bowls.) 5 These Pharisees and scribes questioned Jesus: 'Why do your disciples not conform to the ancient tradition, but eat their food with defiled hands?' 6 He answered, 'How right Isaiah was when he prophesied about you hypocrites in these words: "This people pays me lip-service, but their heart is far from me: 7 they worship me in vain, for they teach as doctrines the commandments of men." 8 You neglect the commandment of God, in order to maintain the tradition of men.'

9 He said to them, 'How clever you are at setting aside the commandment of God in order to maintain your tradition! 10 Moses said, "Honour your father and your mother," and again, "Whoever curses his father or mother shall be put to death." 11 But you hold that if someone says to his father or mother, "Anything I have which might have been used for your benefit is Corban," ' (that

6:37 **denarii:** *see p. xxvii.*   6:56 **edge:** *or tassel.*
7:3 **washing their hands:** *some witnesses add* with the fist; *others add* frequently; *or* thoroughly.
7:9 **maintain:** *some witnesses read* establish.

37: *Two hundred denarii:* one denarius was about a day's wage. **41:** See 8.6 n.

6.45–56: Walking on the sea (Matt. 14.22–36; Jn. 6.15–21). **52:** The obtuseness of the disciples here contrasts sharply with the ending of the episode in Matt. 14.33 (see n.); in 8.14–21 the obtuseness theme is expanded.

7.1–23: The ancient traditions (Matt. 15.1–20). **3:** *Washing the hands* was an act of ritual purification. **5:** The *ancient tradition* (also, v. 13) was not only the OT but also the oral expansion of the Law accepted by the Pharisees (see Matt. 3.7 n.). **6–7:** Isa. 29.13. **10a:** Exod. 20.12; Deut. 5.16. **10b:** Exod. 21.17; Lev. 20.9. **11:**

is, set apart for God) [12] 'he is no longer allowed to do anything for his father or mother. [13] In this way by your tradition, handed down among you, you make God's word null and void. And you do many other things just like that.'

[14] On another occasion he called the people and said to them, 'Listen to me, all of you, and understand this: [15] nothing that goes into a person from outside can defile him; no, it is the things that come out of a person that defile him.'

[17] When he had left the people and gone indoors, his disciples questioned him about the parable. [18] He said to them, 'Are you as dull as the rest? Do you not see that nothing that goes into a person from outside can defile him, [19] because it does not go into the heart but into the stomach, and so goes out into the drain?' By saying this he declared all foods clean. [20] He went on, 'It is what comes out of a person that defiles him. [21] From inside, from the human heart, come evil thoughts, acts of fornication, theft, murder, [22] adultery, greed, and malice; fraud, indecency, envy, slander, arrogance, and folly; [23] all these evil things come from within, and they are what defile a person.'

[24] He moved on from there into the territory of Tyre. He found a house to stay in, and would have liked to remain unrecognized, but that was impossible. [25] Almost at once a woman whose small daughter was possessed by an unclean spirit heard of him and came and fell at his feet. [26] (The woman was a Gentile, a Phoenician of Syria by nationality.) She begged him to drive the demon out of her daughter. [27] He said to her, 'Let the children be satisfied first; it is not right to take the children's bread and throw it to the dogs.' [28] 'Sir,' she replied, 'even the dogs under the table eat the children's scraps.' [29] He said to her, 'For saying that, go, and you will find the demon has left your daughter.' [30] And when she returned home, she found the child lying in bed; the demon had left her.

[31] On his journey back from Tyrian territory he went by way of Sidon to the sea of Galilee, well within the territory of the Decapolis. [32] They brought to him a man who was deaf and had an impediment in his speech, and begged Jesus to lay his hand on him. [33] He took him aside, away from the crowd; then he put his fingers in the man's ears, and touched his tongue with spittle. [34] Looking up to heaven, he sighed, and said to him, 'Ephphatha,' which means 'Be opened.' [35] With that his hearing was restored, and at the same time the impediment was removed and he spoke clearly. [36] Jesus forbade them to tell anyone; but the more he forbade them, the more they spread it abroad. [37] Their astonishment knew no bounds: 'All that he does, he does well,' they said; 'he even makes the deaf hear and the dumb speak.'

8 THERE was another occasion about this time when a huge crowd had collected, and, as they had no food, Jesus called his disciples and said to them, [2] 'My heart goes out to these people; they have been with me now for three days and have nothing to eat. [3] If I send them home hungry, they will faint on the way, and some of them have a long way to go.' [4] His disciples answered, 'How can anyone provide these people with bread in this remote place?' [5] 'How many loaves have you?' he asked; and they answered, 'Seven.' [6] So he ordered the people to sit down on the ground; then he took the seven loaves, and after giving thanks to God he broke the bread and gave it to his disciples to distribute; and they distributed it to the people. [7] They had also a few small fish, which he blessed and ordered them to distribute. [8] They ate and were satisfied, and seven baskets were filled with what was left over. [9] The people numbered about four thousand. Then he dismissed them, [10] and at once got into the boat with his disciples and went to the district of Dalmanutha.

[11] Then the Pharisees came out and began

7:15 **that defile him:** *some witnesses here add* [16] If you have ears to hear, then hear.   8:10 **Dalmanutha:** *some witnesses read* Magedan; *others read* Magdala.

The technicalities of the *Corban* oath are unclear. **15:** *Defile:* render ritually impure.

7.24–37: Healings (Matt. 15.21–28). Jesus now appears in territory that is predominantly Gentile. **24–30:** See Matt. 15.22 n. **26:** *Phoenician:* or, as in Matt. 15.22, Canaanite. **31:** The itinerary described is strange. *Decapolis:* see Matt. 4.25 n. **34:** *Ephphatha* is transliterated Aram., compare 5.41 (see n.). **36:** See 1.34 n.

8.1–10: Feeding of four thousand (Matt. 15.32–39; compare 6.30–44). **6:** The words used are rather reminiscent of eucharistic language; see, e.g. Lk. 22.19, but also Acts 27.35.

to argue with him. To test him they asked him for a sign from heaven. ¹²He sighed deeply and said, 'Why does this generation ask for a sign? Truly I tell you: no sign shall be given to this generation.' ¹³With that he left them, re-embarked, and made for the other shore.

¹⁴Now they had forgotten to take bread with them, and had only one loaf in the boat. ¹⁵He began to warn them: 'Beware,' he said, 'be on your guard against the leaven of the Pharisees and the leaven of Herod.' ¹⁶So they began to talk among themselves about having no bread. ¹⁷Knowing this, he said to them, 'Why are you talking about having no bread? Have you no inkling yet? Do you still not understand? Are your minds closed? ¹⁸You have eyes: can you not see? You have ears: can you not hear? Have you forgotten? ¹⁹When I broke the five loaves among five thousand, how many basketfuls of pieces did you pick up?' 'Twelve,' they said. ²⁰'And how many when I broke the seven loaves among four thousand?' 'Seven,' they answered. ²¹He said to them, 'Do you still not understand?'

²²They arrived at Bethsaida. There the people brought a blind man to Jesus and begged him to touch him. ²³He took the blind man by the hand and led him out of the village. Then he spat on his eyes, laid his hands upon him, and asked whether he could see anything. ²⁴The man's sight began to come back, and he said, 'I see people — they look like trees, but they are walking about.' ²⁵Jesus laid his hands on his eyes

again; he looked hard, and now he was cured and could see everything clearly. ²⁶Then Jesus sent him home, saying, 'Do not even go into the village.'

The cross foreshadowed

²⁷JESUS and his disciples set out for the villages of Caesarea Philippi, and on the way he asked his disciples, 'Who do people say I am?' ²⁸They answered, 'Some say John the Baptist, others Elijah, others one of the prophets.' ²⁹'And you,' he asked, 'who do you say I am?' Peter replied: 'You are the Messiah.' ³⁰Then he gave them strict orders not to tell anyone about him; ³¹and he began to teach them that the Son of Man had to endure great suffering, and to be rejected by the elders, chief priests, and scribes; to be put to death, and to rise again three days afterwards. ³²He spoke about it plainly. At this Peter took hold of him and began to rebuke him. ³³But Jesus, turning and looking at his disciples, rebuked Peter. 'Out of my sight, Satan!' he said. 'You think as men think, not as God thinks.'

³⁴Then he called the people to him, as well as his disciples, and said to them, 'Anyone who wants to be a follower of mine must renounce self; he must take up his cross and follow me. ³⁵Whoever wants to save his life will lose it, but whoever loses his life for my sake and for the gospel's will save it. ³⁶What

8:26 **Do ... village:** *some witnesses read* Do not tell anyone in the village.

8.11–21: Sea crossing and discussions (Matt. 16.1–12; Lk. 11.29; 12.1). **12:** *No sign* is stronger than Matt. 12.38–42 (see nn.); 16.4; Lk. 11.29. **15:** *Leaven* is a conventional symbol for an evil influence; compare Matt. 13.33 n. **17–18, 21:** As in 6.52, the disciples are unable to understand. Verse 18 brings to mind the outsiders who could not grasp the parables in 4.11–12 (compare Jer. 5.21; Ezek. 12.2; Isa. 6.9–10; contrast Matt. 16.12).

8.22–26: Healing of a blind man. Mark probably intended this to be understood symbolically: the disciples' eyes (v. 18) are also gradually opened, as the following narrative shows (vv. 27–29).

8.27–33: Peter's confession and Jesus' prediction of his suffering (Matt. 16.13–23; Lk. 9.18–22). **27:** *Caesarea Philippi* locates the event on the edge of Gentile territory. **28:** The return of an ancient prophet (see 6.15 n.) or the coming of a prophet like Moses (Deut. 18.15) or the appearance of a true prophet (1 Macc. 4.46) in connection with the messianic age were popular expectations. **29:** *Messiah:* see Matt. 1.1 n. **31:** This is the first of three (see 9.31–32; 10.33–34) predictions of the suffering of the *Son of Man* (see 2.10 n.). These predictions probably reflect the way in which the cross and resurrection were preached by early missionaries, so that their present form may have been influenced by that preaching. From this point the story of Mk. moves forward with the cross clearly in view. **32:** Suffering and death were not a part of the popular program for the Messiah. **33:** *Satan:* see Matt. 4.1 n.

8.34–9.1: Following Jesus (Matt. 16.24–28; Lk. 9.23–27). See Matt. 10.38–39 n. **34:** The expression, to *take up a cross*, is more than a metaphor for burden-bearing or even "sacrificial living"; the possibility of actually dying must be among the terms of discipleship.

does anyone gain by winning the whole world at the cost of his life? [37] What can he give to buy his life back? [38] If anyone is ashamed of me and my words in this wicked and godless age, the Son of Man will be ashamed of him, when he comes in the glory of his Father with the holy angels.'

9 He said to them, 'Truly I tell you: there are some of those standing here who will not taste death before they have seen the kingdom of God come with power.'

[2] Six days later Jesus took Peter, James, and John with him and led them up a high mountain by themselves. And in their presence he was transfigured; [3] his clothes became dazzling white, with a whiteness no bleacher on earth could equal. [4] They saw Elijah appear and Moses with him, talking with Jesus. [5] Then Peter spoke: 'Rabbi,' he said, 'it is good that we are here! Shall we make three shelters, one for you, one for Moses, and one for Elijah?' [6] For he did not know what to say; they were so terrified. [7] Then a cloud appeared, casting its shadow over them, and out of the cloud came a voice: 'This is my beloved Son; listen to him.' [8] And suddenly, when they looked around, only Jesus was with them; there was no longer anyone else to be seen.

[9] On their way down the mountain, he instructed them not to tell anyone what they had seen until the Son of Man had risen from the dead. [10] They seized upon those words, and discussed among themselves what this 'rising from the dead' could mean. [11] And they put a question to him: 'Why do the scribes say that Elijah must come first?' [12] He replied, 'Elijah does come first to set everything right. How is it, then, that the scriptures say of the Son of Man that he is to endure great suffering and be treated with contempt? [13] However, I tell you, Elijah has already come and they have done to him what they wanted, as the scriptures say of him.'

[14] When they came back to the disciples they saw a large crowd surrounding them and scribes arguing with them. [15] As soon as they saw Jesus the whole crowd were overcome with awe and ran forward to welcome him. [16] He asked them, 'What is this argument about?' [17] A man in the crowd spoke up: 'Teacher, I brought my son for you to cure. He is possessed by a spirit that makes him dumb. [18] Whenever it attacks him, it flings him to the ground, and he foams at the mouth, grinds his teeth, and goes rigid. I asked your disciples to drive it out, but they could not.' [19] Jesus answered: 'What an unbelieving generation! How long shall I be with you? How long must I endure you? Bring him to me.' [20] So they brought the boy to him; and as soon as the spirit saw him it threw the boy into convulsions, and he fell on the ground and rolled about foaming at the mouth. [21] Jesus asked his father, 'How long has he been like this?' 'From childhood,' he replied; [22] 'it has often tried to destroy him by throwing him into the fire or into water. But if it is at all possible for you, take pity on us and help us.' [23] 'If it is possible!' said Jesus. 'Everything is possible to one who believes.' [24] At once the boy's father cried: 'I believe; help my unbelief.' [25] When Jesus saw that the crowd was closing in on them, he spoke sternly to the unclean spirit. 'Deaf and dumb spirit,' he said, 'I command you, come out of him and never go back!' [26] It shrieked aloud and threw the boy into repeated convulsions, and then came out, leaving him looking like a corpse; in fact, many said, 'He is dead.' [27] But Jesus took hold of his hand and raised him to his feet, and he stood up.

[28] Then Jesus went indoors, and his disciples asked him privately, 'Why could we not drive it out?' [29] He said, 'This kind cannot be driven out except by prayer.'

8:38 **me and my words:** *some witnesses read* me and mine. **Father ... angels:** *some witnesses read* Father and of the holy angels. 9:7 **This ... Son:** *or* This is my only Son. 9:29 **by prayer:** *some witnesses add* and fasting.

9.2–8: The transfiguration (Matt. 17.1–8; Lk. 9.28–36). See notes on Matt. 17.1–8.

9.9–13: Elijah has come (Matt. 17.9–13). **9–10:** Since death did not fit the conception held of the *Son of Man* (8.32), resurrection was also inconceivable. **11–13:** On *Elijah* and his identification with the Baptist, see 6.15 n.; 8.28 n.; Lk. 1.17 n.

9.14–29: An epileptic boy (Matt. 17.14–20; Lk. 9.37–43a). **23:** *One who believes:* faith, an important element in early Christian miracle stories, receives special stress in this account; the father's response (v. 24) is that of all who know their faith is incomplete. **29:** Only *prayer* succeeds in the difficult situation because only God's power is adequate.

Learning what discipleship means

30 THEY left that district and made their way through Galilee. Jesus did not want anyone to know, 31 because he was teaching his disciples, and telling them, 'The Son of Man is now to be handed over into the power of men, and they will kill him; and three days after being killed he will rise again.' 32 But they did not understand what he said, and were afraid to ask.

33 So they came to Capernaum; and when he had gone indoors, he asked them, 'What were you arguing about on the way?' 34 They were silent, because on the way they had been discussing which of them was the greatest. 35 So he sat down, called the Twelve, and said to them, 'If anyone wants to be first, he must make himself last of all and servant of all.' 36 Then he took a child, set him in front of them, and put his arm round him. 37 'Whoever receives a child like this in my name,' he said, 'receives me; and whoever receives me, receives not me but the One who sent me.'

38 John said to him, 'Teacher, we saw someone driving out demons in your name, and as he was not one of us, we tried to stop him.' 39 Jesus said, 'Do not stop him, for no one who performs a miracle in my name will be able the next moment to speak evil of me. 40 He who is not against us is on our side. 41 Truly I tell you: whoever gives you a cup of water to drink because you are followers of the Messiah will certainly not go unrewarded.

42 'If anyone causes the downfall of one of these little ones who believe, it would be better for him to be thrown into the sea with a millstone round his neck. 43 If your hand causes your downfall, cut it off; it is better for you to enter into life maimed than to keep both hands and go to hell, to the unquenchable fire. 45 If your foot causes your downfall, cut it off; it is better to enter into life crippled than to keep both your feet and be thrown into hell. 47 And if your eye causes your downfall, tear it out; it is better to enter into the kingdom of God with one eye than to keep both eyes and be thrown into hell, 48 where the devouring worm never dies and the fire is never quenched.

49 'Everyone will be salted with fire.

50 'Salt is good; but if the salt loses its saltness, how will you season it?

'You must have salt within yourselves, and be at peace with one another.'

10 ON leaving there he came into the regions of Judaea and Transjordan. Once again crowds gathered round him, and he taught them as was his practice. 2 He was asked: 'Is it lawful for a man to divorce his wife?' This question was put to test him. 3 He responded by asking, 'What did Moses command you?' 4 They answered, 'Moses permitted a man to divorce his wife by a certificate of dismissal.' 5 Jesus said to them, 'It was because of your stubbornness that he made this rule for you. 6 But in the beginning, at the creation, "God made them male and female." 7 "That is why a man leaves his father and

9:43 **unquenchable fire:** *some witnesses add* 44 where the devouring worm never dies and the fire is never quenched.   9:45 **into hell:** *some witnesses add* 46 where the devouring worm never dies and the fire is never quenched.   10:2 **He was asked:** *some witnesses read* Pharisees approached and asked him.

9.30–32: The second prediction (see 8.31 n.) **of suffering** (Matt. 17.22–23; Lk. 9.43b–45) is given; as often in Mk., the disciples still do not understand (see 8.17–18, 21 n.).

9.33–37: Greatness and servanthood (Matt. 18.1–5; Lk. 9.46–48). **35:** 10.43–44; Matt. 20.26–27; 23.11; Lk. 22.26. **37:** Matt. 10.40.

9.38–41: An exorcist who is not a disciple (Lk. 9.49–50). **39–40:** The saying assumes that the unnamed exorcist is friendly, as v. 41 perhaps shows. Matthew 12.30 and Lk. 11.23 preserve a similar saying which assumes the opposite, i.e. the one not clearly "with us" is "against us." **41:** See Matt. 10.42 for a somewhat different version of this verse.

9.42–50: On being an example (Matt. 18.6–9; Lk. 17.1–2). Mark uses the negative illustration of causing a *downfall* (v. 42) and the positive metaphor of *salt* which *seasons* (v. 50) to encourage exemplary living. **42–48:** See Matt. 18.7–9 n. **50:** Compare Matt. 5.13; Lk. 14.34–35.

10.1–12: Marriage and divorce (Matt. 19.1–12; compare Matt. 5.31–32 n.; Lk. 16.18; 1 Cor. 7.10–11). **1:** *Judaea and Transjordan* anticipates v. 32. **3:** The question is only a *test,* since the Law clearly allows divorce. **4–5:** The divorce provisions of Deut. 24.1–4 were provided to guide husbands whose *stubborness* resisted the intention of the Creator. **6:** Gen. 1.27. **7–8:** From Gen. 2.(21–)24 Jesus argues that in God's purpose mother, and is united to his wife, ⁸and the two become one flesh." It follows that they are no longer two individuals: they are one flesh. ⁹Therefore what God has joined together, man must not separate.'

¹⁰When they were indoors again, the disciples questioned him about this. ¹¹He said to them, 'Whoever divorces his wife and remarries commits adultery against her; ¹²so too, if she divorces her husband and remarries, she commits adultery.'

¹³They brought children for him to touch. The disciples rebuked them, ¹⁴but when Jesus saw it he was indignant, and said to them, 'Let the children come to me; do not try to stop them; for the kingdom of God belongs to such as these. ¹⁵Truly I tell you: whoever does not accept the kingdom of God like a child will never enter it.' ¹⁶And he put his arms round them, laid his hands on them, and blessed them.

¹⁷As he was starting out on a journey, a stranger ran up, and, kneeling before him, asked, 'Good Teacher, what must I do to win eternal life?' ¹⁸Jesus said to him, 'Why do you call me good? No one is good except God alone. ¹⁹You know the commandments: "Do not murder; do not commit adultery; do not steal; do not give false evidence; do not defraud; honour your father and mother." ' ²⁰'But Teacher,' he replied, 'I have kept all these since I was a boy.' ²¹As Jesus looked at him, his heart warmed to him. 'One thing you lack,' he said. 'Go, sell everything you have, and give to the poor, and you will have treasure in heaven; then come and follow me.' ²²At these words his face fell and he went away with a heavy heart; for he was a man of great wealth.

²³Jesus looked round at his disciples and said to them, 'How hard it will be for the wealthy to enter the kingdom of God!' ²⁴They were amazed that he should say this, but Jesus insisted, 'Children, how hard it is to enter the kingdom of God! ²⁵It is easier for a camel to pass through the eye of a needle than for a rich man to enter the kingdom of God.' ²⁶They were more astonished than ever, and said to one another, 'Then who can be saved?' ²⁷Jesus looked at them and said, 'For men it is impossible, but not for God; everything is possible for God.'

²⁸'What about us?' said Peter. 'We have left everything to follow you.' ²⁹Jesus said, 'Truly I tell you: there is no one who has given up home, brothers or sisters, mother, father or children, or land, for my sake and for the gospel, ³⁰who will not receive in this age a hundred times as much—houses, brothers and sisters, mothers and children, and land —and persecutions besides; and in the age to come eternal life. ³¹But many who are first will be last, and the last first.'

³²THEY were on the road going up to Jerusalem, and Jesus was leading the way; and the disciples were filled with awe, while those who followed behind were afraid. Once again he took the Twelve aside and began to tell them what was to happen to him. ³³'We are now going up to Jerusalem,' he said, 'and the Son of Man will be handed over to the chief priests and the scribes; they will condemn him to death and hand him over to the Gentiles. ³⁴He will be mocked and spat upon, and flogged and killed; and three days afterwards, he will rise again.'

³⁵James and John, the sons of Zebedee,

10:24 **how hard it is:** *some witnesses add* for those who trust in riches.

marriage establishes an indissoluble unity. **12:** This verse probably reflects a Gentile environment, since Jewish law provided only for divorce initiated by the husband.

10.13–16: Children and the kingdom (Matt. 19.13–15; Lk. 18.15–17). **15:** *Like a child:* with simple trust; see Matt. 18.3.

10.17–31: Possessions and the kingdom (Matt. 19.16–30; Lk. 18.18–30). **17–18:** *No one is good except God:* see Matt. 19.16–17 n. **19:** Exod. 20.12–16; Deut. 5.16–20. **21:** See Matt. 19.21 n. **25–27:** *Eye of a needle:* see Matt. 19.24 n. **28–30:** See Matt. 19.27, 29 n. **31:** Matt. 19.30; 20.16; Lk. 13.30.

10.32–34: The third prediction (see 8.31 n.) **of suffering** (Matt. 20.17–19; Lk. 18.31–34). The story must end in *Jerusalem* (v. 32) and the author has had the end in mind from the beginning. Yet, the geographical notice takes on increased importance through its connection with the third passion prediction (vv. 33–34) and by the subsequent attention to itinerary (v. 46; 11.1). The tension and drama mount as the account moves toward its climax.

10.35–45: Position in the kingdom (Matt. 20.20–28; Lk. 22.24–27). **35:** *James and John,* along with Peter, approached him and said, 'Teacher, we should like you to do us a favour.' 36'What is it you want me to do for you?' he asked. 37They answered, 'Allow us to sit with you in your glory, one at your right hand and the other at your left.' 38Jesus said to them, 'You do not understand what you are asking. Can you drink the cup that I drink, or be baptized with the baptism I am baptized with?' 39'We can,' they answered. Jesus said, 'The cup that I drink you shall drink, and the baptism I am baptized with shall be your baptism; 40but to sit on my right or on my left is not for me to grant; that honour is for those to whom it has already been assigned.'

41When the other ten heard this, they were indignant with James and John. 42Jesus called them to him and said, 'You know that among the Gentiles the recognized rulers lord it over their subjects, and the great make their authority felt. 43It shall not be so with you; among you, whoever wants to be great must be your servant, 44and whoever wants to be first must be the slave of all. 45For the Son of Man did not come to be served but to serve, and to give his life as a ransom for many.'

46They came to Jericho; and as he was leaving the town, with his disciples and a large crowd, Bartimaeus (that is, son of Timaeus), a blind beggar, was seated at the roadside. 47Hearing that it was Jesus of Nazareth, he began to shout, 'Son of David, Jesus, have pity on me!' 48Many of the people told him to hold his tongue; but he shouted all the more, 'Son of David, have pity on me.'

49Jesus stopped and said, 'Call him'; so they called the blind man: 'Take heart,' they said. 'Get up; he is calling you.' 50At that he threw off his cloak, jumped to his feet, and came to Jesus. 51Jesus said to him, 'What do you want me to do for you?' 'Rabbi,' the blind man answered, 'I want my sight back.' 52Jesus said to him, 'Go; your faith has healed you.' And at once he recovered his sight and followed him on the road.

The challenge to Jerusalem

11 THEY were now approaching Jerusalem, and when they reached Bethphage and Bethany, close by the mount of Olives, he sent off two of his disciples. 2'Go into the village opposite,' he told them, 'and just as you enter you will find tethered there a colt which no one has yet ridden. Untie it and bring it here. 3If anyone asks why you are doing this, say, "The Master needs it, and will send it back here without delay."' 4So they went off, and found the colt outside in the street, tethered beside a door. As they were untying it, 5some of the bystanders asked, 'What are you doing, untying that colt?' 6They answered as Jesus had told them, and were then allowed to take it. 7So they brought the colt to Jesus, and when they had spread their cloaks on it he mounted it. 8Many people carpeted the road with their cloaks, while others spread greenery which they had cut in the fields; 9and those in front

11:3 **The Master:** *or* Its owner.

---

are given unusual prominence in the Gospels (e.g. 1.16–20; 9.2). **37:** Seats on the *right* and *left* hands are reserved for persons of great authority. **38:** The *cup* immediately suggests 14.36; but as a metaphor for experiencing trouble, "drinking of a *cup*" was a familiar manner of speaking (e.g. Ps. 75.8; compare Jn. 18.11). Unless the phrase about *baptism* has been added as a way of referring specifically to Christian martyrdom, the saying alludes to the ancient picture of the sufferer as a victim of overwhelming "waves" of tribulation; compare Lk. 12.50. **40:** Compare Matt. 20.23. **45:** Lit. *ransom* is the sum paid to win freedom for slaves or captives; it is one of several metaphors employed to express the idea that Jesus' death effects salvation for humanity. The Heb. term for *many* is equivalent to "all" in some contexts.

10.46–52: Blind Bartimaeus healed (Matt. 20.29–34; Lk. 18.35–43). **46:** *Son of Timaeus* simply translates the Aram. name, *Bartimaeus*. **47:** *Son of David:* see Matt. 1.1 n. **52:** *Healed:* see Lk. 7.50 n. With Jerusalem and the cross so near, *followed him on the road* implies courageous discipleship.

11.1–13.37: Jesus in Jerusalem (Matt. 21.1–25.46; Lk. 19.28–21.38). From this point, the Gospel narrative becomes increasingly circumstantial with respect to sequence of events, locations (four place names in 11.1!), and time (especially in Mk. where the material is organized carefully, using the scheme of the "days of the last week"). Such attention to detail and the dramatic character of the reported events and controversies signal the approaching climax of the story.

11.1–11: The entry into Jerusalem (Matt. 21.1–9; Lk. 19.28–38; Jn. 12.12–19). **1:** See Matt. 21.1 n. **9–10:**

and those behind shouted, 'Hosanna! Blessed is he who comes in the name of the Lord! 10 Blessed is the kingdom of our father David which is coming! Hosanna in the heavens!'

11 He entered Jerusalem and went into the temple. He looked round at everything; then, as it was already late, he went out to Bethany with the Twelve.

12 On the following day, as they left Bethany, he felt hungry, 13 and, noticing in the distance a fig tree in leaf, he went to see if he could find anything on it. But when he reached it he found nothing but leaves; for it was not the season for figs. 14 He said to the tree, 'May no one ever again eat fruit from you!' And his disciples were listening.

15 So they came to Jerusalem, and he went into the temple and began to drive out those who bought and sold there. He upset the tables of the money-changers and the seats of the dealers in pigeons; 16 and he would not allow anyone to carry goods through the temple court. 17 Then he began to teach them, and said, 'Does not scripture say, "My house shall be called a house of prayer for all nations"? But you have made it a robbers' cave.' 18 The chief priests and the scribes heard of this and looked for a way to bring about his death; for they were afraid of him, because the whole crowd was spellbound by his teaching. 19 And when evening came they went out of the city.

20 Early next morning, as they passed by, they saw that the fig tree had withered from the roots up; 21 and Peter, recalling what had happened, said to him, 'Rabbi, look, the fig tree which you cursed has withered.' 22 Jesus answered them, 'Have faith in God. 23 Truly I tell you: if anyone says to this mountain, "Be lifted from your place and hurled into the sea," and has no inward doubts, but be-

lieves that what he says will happen, it will be done for him. 24 I tell you, then, whatever you ask for in prayer, believe that you have received it and it will be yours.

25 'And when you stand praying, if you have a grievance against anyone, forgive him, so that your Father in heaven may forgive you the wrongs you have done.'

27 THEY came once more to Jerusalem. And as he was walking in the temple court the chief priests, scribes, and elders came to him 28 and said, 'By what authority are you acting like this? Who gave you authority to act in this way?' 29 Jesus said to them, 'I also have a question for you, and if you give me an answer, I will tell you by what authority I act. 30 The baptism of John: was it from God, or from men? Answer me.' 31 This set them arguing among themselves: 'What shall we say? If we say, "From God," he will say, "Then why did you not believe him?" 32 Shall we say, "From men"?' — but they were afraid of the people, for all held that John was in fact a prophet. 33 So they answered, 'We do not know.' And Jesus said to them, 'Then I will not tell you either by what authority I act.'

12 He went on to speak to them in parables: 'A man planted a vineyard and put a wall round it, hewed out a winepress, and built a watch-tower; then he let it out to vine-growers and went abroad. 2 When the season came, he sent a servant to the tenants to collect from them his share of the produce. 3 But they seized him, thrashed him, and sent him away empty-handed. 4 Again, he sent them another servant, whom they beat about the head and treated outrageously, 5 and then another, whom they killed. He sent

11:25 **wrongs you have done:** *some witnesses add* 26 But if you do not forgive others, then the wrongs you have done will not be forgiven by your Father in heaven.

Ps. 118.25–26. *Hosanna:* see Matt. 21.9 n. **11:** Nearby *Bethany* seems to have served as Jesus' base for Jerusalem activities; only Mk. delays the cleansing of the temple to the next day (see Matt. 21.12; Lk. 19.45).

11.12–14: The cursing of the fig tree (Matt. 21.18–19). The story is in two parts, with the end in vv. 20–25. In Matt. the two parts are presented as a single unit following the cleansing of the temple. **14:** See Matt. 21.19 n.

11.15–19: Cleansing of the temple (Matt. 21.10–17; Lk. 19.45–48). **15–16:** Jesus' objections to the misuse of the temple agree with Jewish regulations of the time. On *temple, money-changers, pigeons,* see Matt. 21.12 n. **17:** *For all nations* probably indicates a concern for Gentile worship; see Matt. 21.12 n.; Isa. 56.7; Jer. 7.11; compare Matt. 21.13; Lk. 19.46.

11.20–25: The lesson of the fig tree. See Matt. 21.20–22 n.

11.27–33: Jesus' authority challenged (Matt. 21.23–27; Lk. 20.1–8). **30:** *From God:* see Matt. 21.25 n. **32:** *Prophet:* see 8.28 n.

12.1–12: The evil tenants (Matt. 21.33–46; Lk. 20.9–19). **1:** On *parables, vineyard,* see Matt. 21.33 n. **2:**

many others and they thrashed some and killed the rest. 6 He had now no one left to send except his beloved son, and in the end he sent him. "They will respect my son," he said; 7 but the tenants said to one another, "This is the heir; come on, let us kill him, and the inheritance will be ours." 8 So they seized him and killed him, and flung his body out of the vineyard. 9 What will the owner of the vineyard do? He will come and put the tenants to death and give the vineyard to others. 10 'Have you never read this text: "The stone which the builders rejected has become the main corner-stone. 11 This is the Lord's doing, and it is wonderful in our eyes"?'

12 They saw that the parable was aimed at them and wanted to arrest him; but they were afraid of the people, so they left him alone and went away.

13 A NUMBER of Pharisees and men of Herod's party were sent to trap him with a question. 14 They came and said, 'Teacher, we know you are a sincere man and court no one's favour, whoever he may be; you teach in all sincerity the way of life that God requires. Are we or are we not permitted to pay taxes to the Roman emperor? 15 Shall we pay or not?' He saw through their duplicity, and said, 'Why are you trying to catch me out? Fetch me a silver piece, and let me look at it.' 16 They brought one, and he asked them, 'Whose head is this, and whose inscription?' 'Caesar's,' they replied. 17 Then Jesus said, 'Pay Caesar what belongs to Caesar, and God what belongs to God.' His reply left them completely taken aback.

18 Next Sadducees, who maintain that there is no resurrection, came to him and asked: 19 'Teacher, Moses laid it down for us that if there are brothers, and one dies leaving a wife but no child, then the next should marry the widow and provide an heir for his brother. 20 Now there were seven brothers.

The first took a wife and died without issue. 21 Then the second married her, and he too died without issue; so did the third; 22 none of the seven left any issue. Finally the woman died. 23 At the resurrection, when they rise from the dead, whose wife will she be, since all seven had married her?' 24 Jesus said to them, 'How far you are from the truth! You know neither the scriptures nor the power of God. 25 When they rise from the dead, men and women do not marry; they are like angels in heaven.

26 'As for the resurrection of the dead, have you not read in the book of Moses, in the story of the burning bush, how God spoke to him and said, "I am the God of Abraham, the God of Isaac, the God of Jacob"? 27 He is not God of the dead but of the living. You are very far from the truth.'

28 Then one of the scribes, who had been listening to these discussions and had observed how well Jesus answered, came forward and asked him, 'Which is the first of all the commandments?' 29 He answered, 'The first is, "Hear, O Israel: the Lord our God is the one Lord, 30 and you must love the Lord your God with all your heart, with all your soul, with all your mind, and with all your strength." 31 The second is this: "You must love your neighbour as yourself." No other commandment is greater than these.' 32 The scribe said to him, 'Well said, Teacher. You are right in saying that God is one and beside him there is no other. 33 And to love him with all your heart, all your understanding, and all your strength, and to love your neighbour as yourself—that means far more than any whole-offerings and sacrifices.' 34 When Jesus saw how thoughtfully he answered, he said to him, 'You are not far from the kingdom of God.' After that nobody dared put any more questions to him.

35 As he taught in the temple, Jesus went on

12:6 *his beloved son:* or his only son.

On *servant, tenants,* see Matt. 21.34 n. **6:** *Son:* Jesus. **10–11:** Ps. 118.22–23. Early Christians applied this and other OT "stone sayings" to Jesus; compare 1 Pet. 2.6–8.

　　12.13–17: Caesar's tax (Matt. 22.15–22; Lk. 20.20–26). **14:** *Taxes:* see Matt. 22.17 n.

　　12.18–27: A resurrection puzzle (Matt. 22.23–33; Lk. 20.27–40). **18:** On differences between *Sadducees* and *Pharisees* (v. 13), see Matt. 3.7 n. **19:** Deut. 25.5–10. **24:** *Scriptures:* v. 26; see Matt. 22.30 n. **26:** Exod. 3.6.

　　12.28–34: The double commandment of love (Matt. 22.34–40; compare Lk. 10.25–28). **29–30:** Deut. 6.4–5; the verses comprise the "Jewish creed." **31:** Lev. 19.18. **32–34:** Compare Lk. 10.27 n.

　　12.35–37: Messiah, son of David (Matt. 22.41–46; Lk. 20.41–44). **35:** *Messiah . . . son of David:* see Matt. 1.1 n. **36:** Ps. 110.1; see Matt. 22.44 n. **37:** See Matt. 22.45 n.

to say, 'How can the scribes maintain that the Messiah is a son of David? 36 It was David himself who said, when inspired by the Holy Spirit, "The Lord said to my Lord, 'Sit at my right hand until I put your enemies under your feet.'" 37 David himself calls him "Lord"; how can he be David's son?'

There was a large crowd listening eagerly. 38 As he taught them, he said, 'Beware of the scribes, who love to walk up and down in long robes and be greeted respectfully in the street, 39 to have the chief seats in synagogues and places of honour at feasts. 40 Those who eat up the property of widows, while for appearance' sake they say long prayers, will receive a sentence all the more severe.'

41 As he was sitting opposite the temple treasury, he watched the people dropping their money into the chest. Many rich people were putting in large amounts. 42 Presently there came a poor widow who dropped in two tiny coins, together worth a penny. 43 He called his disciples to him and said, 'Truly I tell you: this poor widow has given more than all those giving to the treasury; 44 for the others who have given had more than enough, but she, with less than enough, has given all that she had to live on.'

Warnings about the end

13 As HE was leaving the temple, one of his disciples exclaimed, 'Look, Teacher, what huge stones! What fine buildings!' 2 Jesus said to him, 'You see these great buildings? Not one stone will be left upon another; they will all be thrown down.'

3 As he sat on the mount of Olives opposite the temple he was questioned privately by Peter, James, John, and Andrew. 4 'Tell us,' they said, 'when will this happen? What will be the sign that all these things are about to be fulfilled?'

5 Jesus began: 'Be on your guard; let no one mislead you. 6 Many will come claiming my name, and saying, "I am he"; and many will be misled by them. 7 When you hear of wars and rumours of wars, do not be alarmed. Such things are bound to happen; but the end is still to come. 8 For nation will go to war against nation, kingdom against kingdom; there will be earthquakes in many places; there will be famines. These are the first birth-pangs of the new age.

9 'As for you, be on your guard. You will be handed over to the courts; you will be beaten in synagogues; you will be summoned to appear before governors and kings on my account to testify in their presence. 10 Before the end the gospel must be proclaimed to all nations. 11 So when you are arrested and put on trial do not worry beforehand about what you will say, but when the time comes say whatever is given you to say, for it is not you who will be speaking, but the Holy Spirit. 12 Brother will hand over brother to death, and a father his child; children will turn against their parents and send them to their death. 13 Everyone will hate you for your allegiance to me, but whoever endures to the end will be saved.

14 'But when you see "the abomination of desolation" usurping a place which is not his (let the reader understand), then those who are in Judaea must take to the hills. 15 If anyone is on the roof, he must not go down into the house to fetch anything out; 16 if anyone is in the field, he must not turn back for his coat. 17 Alas for women with child in those days, and for those who have children at the breast! 18 Pray that it may not come in winter. 19 For those days will bring distress such as there has never been before since the beginning of the world which God created, and will never be again. 20 If the Lord had not cut short that time of troubles, no living thing

---

12.38–40: Warning against pride (see Matt. 23.6; Lk. 11.43; 20.45–47).

12.41–44: The widow's gift (Lk. 21.1–4). **41:** *Chest:* see Lk. 21.1 n. **42:** *Coins:* see Lk. 21.2 n.

13.1–37: The eschatological discourse. All three synoptic Gospels introduce at this point (Matt. 24.1; Lk. 21.5) a collection of sayings, some of which relate to the destruction of Jerusalem, some to the end of history. Standing immediately before the passion narrative (chs. 14–15), this chapter, built out of diverse traditions, serves as a solemn final message of judgment and warning.

13.1–2: Temple's destruction predicted (Matt. 24.1–3 n.; Lk. 21.5–7).

13.3–37: Signs, false signs, and warnings (Matt. 24.4–44; Lk. 21.8–36). **3:** *Mount of Olives:* Matt. 21.1 n. The limiting of the audience to *Peter, James, John,* and *Andrew* makes the discourse in Mk. secret teaching. **5–6:** See vv. 21–23. **8:** *Birth-pangs:* see Matt. 24.8 n. **9–13:** Matt. 10.17–21. **11:** Matt. 10.20; Lk. 12.11–12. **13:** Matt. 10.22. **14:** *"The abomination of desolation":* see Matt. 24.15 n. **16:** Lk. 17.31. **19:** Dan. 12.1.

could survive. However, for the sake of his own, whom he has chosen, he has cut short the time.

21 'If anyone says to you then, "Look, here is the Messiah," or, "Look, there he is," do not believe it. 22 Impostors will come claiming to be messiahs or prophets, and they will produce signs and wonders to mislead, if possible, God's chosen. 23 Be on your guard; I have forewarned you of it all.

24 'But in those days, after that distress,

> the sun will be darkened,
> the moon will not give her light;
> 25 the stars will come falling from the sky,
> the celestial powers will be shaken.

26 'Then they will see the Son of Man coming in the clouds with great power and glory, 27 and he will send out the angels and gather his chosen from the four winds, from the farthest bounds of earth to the farthest bounds of heaven.

28 'Learn a lesson from the fig tree. When its tender shoots appear and are breaking into leaf, you know that summer is near. 29 In the same way, when you see all this happening, you may know that the end is near, at the very door. 30 Truly I tell you: the present generation will live to see it all. 31 Heaven and earth will pass away, but my words will never pass away.

32 'Yet about that day or hour no one knows, not even the angels in heaven, not even the Son; no one but the Father.

33 'Be on your guard, keep watch. You do not know when the moment is coming. 34 It is like a man away from home: he has left his house and put his servants in charge, each with his own work to do, and he has ordered the door-keeper to stay awake. 35 Keep awake, then, for you do not know when the master of the house will come. Evening or midnight, cock-crow or early dawn — 36 if he comes suddenly, do not let him find you asleep. 37 And what I say to you, I say to everyone: Keep awake.'

The trial and crucifixion of Jesus

14 IT was two days before the festival of Passover and Unleavened Bread, and the chief priests and the scribes were trying to devise some scheme to seize him and put him to death. 2 'It must not be during the festival,' they said, 'or we should have rioting among the people.'

3 Jesus was at Bethany, in the house of Simon the leper. As he sat at table, a woman came in carrying a bottle of very costly perfume, pure oil of nard. She broke it open and poured the oil over his head. 4 Some of those present said indignantly to one another, 'Why this waste? 5 The perfume might have been sold for more than three hundred denarii and the money given to the poor'; and they began to scold her. 6 But Jesus said, 'Leave her alone. Why make trouble for her? It is a fine thing she has done for me. 7 You have the poor among you always, and you can help them whenever you like; but you will not always have me. 8 She has done what lay in her power; she has anointed my body in anticipation of my burial. 9 Truly I tell you: wherever the gospel is proclaimed throughout the world, what she has done will be told as her memorial.'

10 Then Judas Iscariot, one of the Twelve, went to the chief priests to betray him to them. 11 When they heard what he had come for, they were glad and promised him money; and he began to look for an opportunity to betray him.

12 Now ON the first day of Unleavened Bread, when the Passover lambs were being slaughtered, his disciples said to him, 'Where would you like us to go and prepare the Passover for you?' 13 So he sent off two of his disciples with these instructions: 'Go into the city, and a man will meet you carrying a jar of water. Follow him, 14 and when he enters a house

13:29 **the end is near:** *or* he is near. 13:33 **keep watch:** *some witnesses add* and pray. 14:5 **denarii:** *see p. xxvii.*

22: Deut. 13.1–2. 23: *Forewarned:* see vv. 5–6. 24–26: See Matt. 24.29 n. 26: Dan. 7.13. 27: Deut. 30.4; Isa. 60.4–5. 30: 9.1; see Matt. 24.34 n. Compare v. 32. 31: Compare Matt. 5.17; Lk. 16.17.

14.1–15.47: **The final conflict** (Matt. 26.1–27.66; Lk. 22.1–23.56; Jn. chs. 12–19). See Lk. 22.1–23.56 n. 1: *Passover* and *Unleavened Bread* were originally two festivals (see Lev. 23.5–6) which had coalesced as a celebration of the deliverance from Egypt (Exod. 12.1–20). 3–9: Matt. 26.6–13 (similar stories in Lk. 7.36–50; Jn. 12.1–8). 3: *Poured:* see Matt. 26.7 n. 8: See Matt. 26.12 n. 10–11: Matt. 26.14–16; Lk. 22.3–6.

give this message to the householder: "The Teacher says, 'Where is the room in which I am to eat the Passover with my disciples?'" [15] He will show you a large upstairs room, set out in readiness. Make the preparations for us there.' [16] Then the disciples went off, and when they came into the city they found everything just as he had told them. So they prepared the Passover.

[17] In the evening he came to the house with the Twelve. [18] As they sat at supper Jesus said, 'Truly I tell you: one of you will betray me—one who is eating with me.' [19] At this they were distressed; and one by one they said to him, 'Surely you do not mean me?' [20] 'It is one of the Twelve', he said, 'who is dipping into the bowl with me. [21] The Son of Man is going the way appointed for him in the scriptures; but alas for that man by whom the Son of Man is betrayed! It would be better for that man if he had never been born.'

[22] During supper he took bread, and having said the blessing he broke it and gave it to them, with the words: 'Take this; this is my body.' [23] Then he took a cup, and having offered thanks to God he gave it to them; and they all drank from it. [24] And he said to them, 'This is my blood, the blood of the covenant, shed for many. [25] Truly I tell you: never again shall I drink from the fruit of the vine until that day when I drink it new in the kingdom of God.'

[26] After singing the Passover hymn, they went out to the mount of Olives. [27] And Jesus said to them, 'You will all lose faith; for it is written: "I will strike the shepherd and the sheep will be scattered." [28] Nevertheless, after I am raised I shall go ahead of you into Galilee.' [29] Peter answered, 'Everyone else may lose faith, but I will not.' [30] Jesus said to him, 'Truly I tell you: today, this very night, before the cock crows twice, you yourself will disown me three times.' [31] But Peter insisted: 'Even if I have to die with you, I will never disown you.' And they all said the same.

[32] WHEN they reached a place called Gethsemane, he said to his disciples, 'Sit here while I pray.' [33] And he took Peter and James and John with him. Horror and anguish overwhelmed him, [34] and he said to them, 'My heart is ready to break with grief; stop here, and stay awake.' [35] Then he went on a little farther, threw himself on the ground, and prayed that if it were possible this hour might pass him by. [36] 'Abba, Father,' he said, 'all things are possible to you; take this cup from me. Yet not my will but yours.'

[37] He came back and found them asleep; and he said to Peter, 'Asleep, Simon? Could you not stay awake for one hour? [38] Stay awake, all of you; and pray that you may be spared the test. The spirit is willing, but the flesh is weak.' [39] Once more he went away and prayed. [40] On his return he found them asleep again, for their eyes were heavy; and they did not know how to answer him.

[41] He came a third time and said to them, 'Still asleep? Still resting? Enough! The hour has come. The Son of Man is betrayed into the hands of sinners. [42] Up, let us go! The traitor is upon us.'

[43] He was still speaking when Judas, one of the Twelve, appeared, and with him a crowd armed with swords and cudgels, sent by the chief priests, scribes, and elders. [44] Now the traitor had agreed with them on a signal: 'The one I kiss is your man; seize him and get him safely away.' [45] When he reached the spot, he went straight up to him and said, 'Rabbi', and kissed him. [46] Then they seized him and held him fast.

[47] One of the bystanders drew his sword, and struck the high priest's servant, cutting off his ear. [48] Then Jesus spoke: 'Do you take me for a robber, that you have come out with swords and cudgels to arrest me? [49] Day after day I have been among you teaching in the

14:39 **prayed:** *some witnesses add* using the same words. 14:41 **Enough:** *the meaning of the Greek cannot be confidently decided.*

14.12–16: Preparation for the Passover (Matt. 26.17–19; Lk. 22.7–13). **12:** See Matt. 26.17–19 n. **14–15:** See Matt. 26.18 n.

14.17–25: The Last Supper (Matt. 26.20–29; Lk. 22.14–23). **17–21:** See also Jn. 13.21–30. **18:** Ps. 41.9. *Sat:* see Matt. 26.20 n. **21:** *Scriptures:* see Matt. 26.24 n. **22–25:** See also 1 Cor. 11.23–26. **24:** *Blood of the covenant:* Matt. 26.28 n.; Lk. 22.17–19 n. *Many:* see Mk. 10.45 n.

14.26–42: Gethsemane (Matt. 26.30–46; Lk. 22.39–46). **26:** Jn. 18.1. *Hymn:* see Matt. 26.30 n. **27:** Zech. 13.7. **28:** See 16.7. **32–42:** See Lk. 22.40–46 n. **34–36:** Compare Jn. 12.27–28. **34:** Ps. 42.6. **36:** *Abba:* Aram. for "Father"; see Rom. 8.15; Gal. 4.6. *Cup:* see Mk. 10.38 n.; Jn. 18.11.

14.43–52: The arrest (Matt. 26.47–56; Lk. 22.47–53; Jn. 18.2–12). **44:** *Kiss:* see Matt. 26.48 n. **47:** *One:*

temple, and you did not lay hands on me. But let the scriptures be fulfilled.' 50 Then the disciples all deserted him and ran away.

51 Among those who had followed Jesus was a young man with nothing on but a linen cloth. They tried to seize him; 52 but he slipped out of the linen cloth and ran away naked.

53 THEN they led Jesus away to the high priest's house, where the chief priests, elders, and scribes were all assembling. 54 Peter followed him at a distance right into the high priest's courtyard; and there he remained, sitting among the attendants and warming himself at the fire.

55 The chief priests and the whole Council tried to find evidence against Jesus that would warrant a death sentence, but failed to find any. 56 Many gave false evidence against him, but their statements did not tally. 57 Some stood up and gave false evidence against him to this effect: 58 'We heard him say, "I will pull down this temple, made with human hands, and in three days I will build another, not made with hands." ' 59 But even on this point their evidence did not agree.

60 Then the high priest rose to his feet and questioned Jesus: 'Have you no answer to the accusations that these witnesses bring against you?' 61 But he remained silent and made no reply.

Again the high priest questioned him: 'Are you the Messiah, the Son of the Blessed One?' 62 'I am,' said Jesus; 'and you will see the Son of Man seated at the right hand of the Almighty and coming with the clouds of heaven.' 63 Then the high priest tore his robes and said, 'Do we need further witnesses? 64 You have heard the blasphemy. What is your decision?' Their judgement was unanimous: that he was guilty and should be put to death.

65 Some began to spit at him; they blindfolded him and struck him with their fists, crying out, 'Prophesy!' And the attendants slapped him in the face.

66 Meanwhile Peter was still below in the courtyard. One of the high priest's servant-girls came by 67 and saw him there warming himself. She looked closely at him and said, 'You were with this man from Nazareth, this Jesus.' 68 But he denied it: 'I know nothing,' he said; 'I have no idea what you are talking about,' and he went out into the forecourt. 69 The servant-girl saw him there and began to say again to the bystanders, 'He is one of them'; 70 and again he denied it.

Again, a little later, the bystanders said to Peter, 'You must be one of them; you are a Galilean.' 71 At this he started to curse, and declared with an oath, 'I do not know this man you are talking about.' 72 At that moment the cock crowed for the second time; and Peter remembered how Jesus had said to him, 'Before the cock crows twice, you will disown me three times.' And he burst into tears.

15 As soon as morning came, the whole Council, chief priests, elders, and scribes, made their plans. They bound Jesus and led him away to hand him over to Pilate. 2 'Are you the king of the Jews?' Pilate asked him. 'The words are yours,' he replied. 3 And the chief priests brought many charges against him. 4 Pilate questioned him again: 'Have you nothing to say in your defence? You see how many charges they are bringing against you.' 5 But, to Pilate's astonishment, Jesus made no further reply.

6 At the festival season the governor used to release one prisoner requested by the people. 7 As it happened, a man known as Barabbas was then in custody with the rebels who had committed murder in the rising. 8 When the crowd appeared and began asking for the usual favour, 9 Pilate replied, 'Would you like me to release the king of the Jews?' 10 For he knew it was out of malice that Jesus had been handed over to him. 11 But the chief priests incited the crowd to ask instead for the re-

14:65 **Prophesy:** *some witnesses add* Who hit you? *as in Matthew and Luke.*   14:68 **into the forecourt:** *some witnesses add* and a cock crowed.   15:2 **The words are yours:** *or* It is as you say.   15:8 **appeared:** *some witnesses read* shouted.

see Matt. 26.51 n. **51:** The *young man* appears only in Mk. and his identity is unknown.

14.53–72: Before the Jewish authorities (Matt. 26.57–75 n.; Lk. 22.54–71; Jn. 18.13–27). **55:** *Council:* See Matt. 26.59 n. **57–58:** 13.2; 15.29; see Matt. 24.1–3 n. **61:** *Messiah . . . Son:* see Matt. 16.16 n. **62:** Dan. 7.13; Ps. 110.1. **63–64:** *Blasphemy:* see Matt. 26.65–66 n. **72:** Compare v. 30.

15.1–20a: Before Roman authority (Matt. 27.1–31; Lk. 23.1–25; Jn. 18.28–19.16). **1:** *Pilate:* see Lk. 3.1 n. **2:** *King:* see Lk. 23.2 n. **6:** Matt. 27.15 n. **7:** *Barabbas:* Matt. 27.16 n.

lease of Barabbas. ¹²Pilate spoke to them again: 'Then what shall I do with the man you call king of the Jews?' ¹³They shouted back, 'Crucify him!' ¹⁴'Why, what wrong has he done?' Pilate asked; but they shouted all the louder, 'Crucify him!' ¹⁵So Pilate, in his desire to satisfy the mob, released Barabbas to them; and he had Jesus flogged, and then handed him over to be crucified.

¹⁶The soldiers took him inside the governor's residence, the Praetorium, and called the whole company together. ¹⁷They dressed him in purple and, plaiting a crown of thorns, placed it on his head. ¹⁸Then they began to salute him: 'Hail, king of the Jews!' ¹⁹They beat him about the head with a stick and spat at him, and then knelt and paid homage to him. ²⁰When they had finished their mockery, they stripped off the purple robe and dressed him in his own clothes.

THEN they led him out to crucify him. ²¹A man called Simon, from Cyrene, the father of Alexander and Rufus, was passing by on his way in from the country, and they pressed him into service to carry his cross.

²²They brought Jesus to the place called Golgotha, which means 'Place of a Skull', ²³and they offered him drugged wine, but he did not take it. ²⁴Then they fastened him to the cross. They shared out his clothes, casting lots to decide what each should have.

²⁵It was nine in the morning when they crucified him; ²⁶and the inscription giving the charge against him read, 'The King of the Jews'. ²⁷Two robbers were crucified with him, one on his right and the other on his left.

²⁹The passers-by wagged their heads and jeered at him: 'Bravo!' they cried, 'So you are the man who was to pull down the temple, and rebuild it in three days! ³⁰Save yourself and come down from the cross.' ³¹The chief priests and scribes joined in, jesting with one another: 'He saved others,' they said, 'but he cannot save himself. ³²Let the Messiah, the

king of Israel, come down now from the cross. If we see that, we shall believe.' Even those who were crucified with him taunted him.

³³At midday a darkness fell over the whole land, which lasted till three in the afternoon; ³⁴and at three Jesus cried aloud, 'Eloï, Eloï, lema sabachthani?' which means, 'My God, my God, why have you forsaken me?' ³⁵Hearing this, some of the bystanders said, 'Listen! He is calling Elijah.' ³⁶Someone ran and soaked a sponge in sour wine and held it to his lips on the end of a stick. 'Let us see', he said, 'if Elijah will come to take him down.' ³⁷Then Jesus gave a loud cry and died; ³⁸and the curtain of the temple was torn in two from top to bottom. ³⁹When the centurion who was standing opposite him saw how he died, he said, 'This man must have been a son of God.'

⁴⁰A NUMBER of women were also present, watching from a distance. Among them were Mary of Magdala, Mary the mother of James the younger and of Joses, and Salome, ⁴¹who had all followed him and looked after him when he was in Galilee, and there were many others who had come up to Jerusalem with him.

⁴²By this time evening had come; and as it was the day of preparation (that is, the day before the sabbath), ⁴³Joseph of Arimathaea, a respected member of the Council, a man who looked forward to the kingdom of God, bravely went in to Pilate and asked for the body of Jesus. ⁴⁴Pilate was surprised to hear that he had died so soon, and sent for the centurion to make sure that he was already dead. ⁴⁵And when he heard the centurion's report, he gave Joseph leave to take the body. ⁴⁶So Joseph bought a linen sheet, took him down from the cross, and wrapped him in

15:27 **on his left:** *some witnesses add* ²⁸So was fulfilled the text of scripture which says, 'He was reckoned among criminals.'   15:39 **a son of God:** *or* the Son of God.

15.20b–47: The crucifixion (Matt. 27.32–66; Lk. 23.26–54; Jn. 19.17–42). Crucifixion was a form of Roman punishment reserved for dangerous criminals; further, Judaism regarded anyone who was crucified as cursed (Deut. 21.23; see 15.27; Matt. 27.38; Lk. 23.32). **21:** *Simon* was probably a Jew from *Cyrene*. The mention of *Alexander* and *Rufus* suggests that they may have been known in the church of Mk. Contrast Jn. 19.17. **23:** Ps. 69.21; on *wine*, see Lk. 23.36 n. **24:** Ps. 22.18. **25:** *Nine in the morning:* contrast Jn. 19.14. **29:** See 14.57–58 n. **32b:** Contrast Lk. 23.39–43. **34:** See Matt. 27.46 n. **35:** *Elijah:* see Matt. 27.47 n. **36:** Ps. 69.21. **38:** *Curtain:* see Matt. 27.51 n. **39:** *Son of God:* see Matt. 27.54 n. **43:** *Council:* see Matt. 26.59 n. **46:** Deut. 21.22–23.

the sheet. Then he laid him in a tomb cut out of the rock, and rolled a stone against the entrance. 47 And Mary of Magdala and Mary the mother of Joses were watching and saw where he was laid.

The resurrection of Jesus

16 When the sabbath was over, Mary of Magdala, Mary the mother of James, and Salome bought aromatic oils, intending to go and anoint him; 2 and very early on the first day of the week, just after sunrise, they came to the tomb. 3 They were wondering among themselves who would roll away the stone for them from the entrance to the tomb, 4 when they looked up and saw that the stone, huge as it was, had been rolled back already. 5 They went into the tomb, where they saw a young man sitting on the right-hand side, wearing a white robe; and they were dumbfounded. 6 But he said to them, 'Do not be alarmed; you are looking for Jesus of Nazareth, who was crucified. He has been raised; he is not here. Look, there is the place where they laid him. 7 But go and say to his disciples and to Peter: "He is going ahead of you into Galilee: there you will see him, as he told you."' 8 Then they went out and ran away from the tomb, trembling with amazement. They said nothing to anyone, for they were afraid.

[And they delivered all these instructions briefly to Peter and his companions. Afterwards Jesus himself sent out by them, from east to west, the sacred and imperishable message of eternal salvation.]

[9 When he had risen from the dead, early on the first day of the week, he appeared first to Mary of Magdala, from whom he had driven out seven demons. 10 She went and carried the news to his mourning and sorrowful followers, 11 but when they were told that he was alive and that she had seen him they did not believe it.

12 Later he appeared in a different form to two of them while they were on their way into the country. 13 These also went and took the news to the others, but again no one believed them.

14 Still later he appeared to the eleven while they were at table, and reproached them for their incredulity and dullness, because they had not believed those who had seen him after he was raised from the dead. 15 Then he said to them: 'Go to every part of the world, and proclaim the gospel to the whole creation. 16 Those who believe it and receive baptism will be saved; those who do not believe will be condemned. 17 Faith will bring with it these miracles: believers will drive out demons in my name and speak in strange tongues; 18 if they handle snakes or drink any deadly poison, they will come to no harm; and the sick on whom they lay their hands will recover.'

19 So after talking with them the Lord Jesus was taken up into heaven and took his seat at the right hand of God; 20 but they went out to proclaim their message far and wide, and the Lord worked with them and confirmed their words by the miracles that followed.]

16:1 **When ... Salome:** *some witnesses omit, reading* And they went and bought ...   16:8 **afraid:** *at this point some of the most ancient witnesses bring the book to a close.* **And they delivered ... salvation:** *some witnesses add this passage, which in one of them is the conclusion of the book.* 16:9–20 *Some witnesses give these verses either instead of, or in addition to, the passage* And they delivered ... salvation *(here printed before verse 9), and so bring the book to a close. Others insert further additional matter.*

16.1–20: The empty tomb (Matt. 28.1–8; Lk. 24.1–9; Jn. 20.1–3). **1:** The *sabbath* ended at sunset on Saturday; compare Lk. 23.55–56 n. **3–4:** *Stone:* Matt. 27.60 n. **7:** See 14.28. Perhaps the verse originally prepared for an account (now lost) of a Galilean appearance; compare Matt. 28.16–20; Jn. ch. 21. **8:** Textual evidence seems to favor the view that the Gospel ended with the word *afraid* (see Tfnn. for vv. 8, 9–20). However, the phrase *for they were afraid* is more abrupt in Greek than in English, and many scholars believe that there must have been additional material. Verses 9–20 are found in numerous witnesses. **9–11:** Jn. 20.11–18; Matt. 28.9–10. **12–13:** Lk. 24.13–35. **14–16:** Matt. 28.16–20. **19:** Lk. 24.50–51. **20:** However the book may have originally ended (Tfn. at vv. 9–20), the church in which it was cherished was not left in fear (v. 8 n.), but *went out to proclaim their message far and wide.* If Mk. indeed ended at v. 8, the felt need which prompted additions was the absence of a resurrection appearance (found in Matt. 28.18, Lk. 24.15–27, and Jn. 20.14–17) which is foreshadowed in 14.28, but not thereafter directly narrated. The addition, or additions, provide both a resurrection appearance and also (v. 19) the ascension of the risen Christ to heaven (compare Acts 1.9–11).

THE GOSPEL ACCORDING TO

Luke

The Gospel of Luke was written about 90 C.E. by a Gentile Christian, one of the first church writers with a real awareness of himself as a literary figure (see 1.1–4 n.). Basic to the design of his work is the place that Luke assigns the career of Jesus in a more comprehensive view of the course of God's dealings with the human family. Jesus' ministry is the period in terms of which the previous and subsequent history of salvation is given meaning: it is the culmination of ancient Israel's promise and the ground of the church's hope and life.

After a lengthy introduction (1.1–4.13), Luke describes Jesus' career as a procession that begins in Galilee (4.14–9.50) and moves on the way to Jerusalem (9.51–19.27) where the nature of divine Sonship is fully revealed (19.28–24.53).

But the story of salvation does not end here. It is taken up again in a second volume (Acts of the Apostles) where, in the experience of the church, the way that once led to Jerusalem now extends to "the farthest corners of the earth" (Acts 1.8).

1 To THEOPHILUS : Many writers have undertaken to draw up an account of the events that have taken place among us, ²following the traditions handed down to us by the original eyewitnesses and servants of the gospel. ³So I in my turn, as one who has investigated the whole course of these events in detail, have decided to write an orderly narrative for you, your excellency, ⁴so as to give you authentic knowledge about the matters of which you have been informed.

The coming of Christ

⁵IN the reign of Herod king of Judaea there was a priest named Zechariah, of the division of the priesthood called after Abijah. His wife, whose name was Elizabeth, was also of priestly descent. ⁶Both of them were upright and devout, blamelessly observing all the commandments and ordinances of the Lord.

⁷But they had no children, for Elizabeth was barren, and both were well on in years.

⁸Once, when it was the turn of his division and he was there to take part in the temple service, ⁹he was chosen by lot, by priestly custom, to enter the sanctuary of the Lord and offer the incense; ¹⁰and at the hour of the offering the people were all assembled at prayer outside. ¹¹There appeared to him an angel of the Lord, standing on the right of the altar of incense. ¹²At this sight, Zechariah was startled and overcome by fear. ¹³But the angel said to him, 'Do not be afraid, Zechariah; your prayer has been heard: your wife Elizabeth will bear you a son, and you are to name him John. ¹⁴His birth will fill you with joy and delight, and will bring gladness to many; ¹⁵for he will be great in the eyes of the Lord. He is never to touch wine or strong drink. From his very birth he will be filled with the Holy Spirit; ¹⁶and he will bring back many Israelites to the Lord their God. ¹⁷He

1.1–4: **The preface** follows the form customary in the literature of the period (compare Acts 1.1–5). **1:** Both this Gospel and Acts are dedicated to an unknown *Theophilus* (lit. "lover of God"), perhaps a Roman official (v. 3, *your excellency*; see Acts 23.26). *Many* perhaps should be understood as "several" writers. **3:** *An orderly account* may imply some arrangement of materials other than a strictly chronological order.

1.5–80: **Preparation for Jesus' birth.**

1.5–25: **The birth of John the Baptist is promised. 5:** There were twenty-four *divisions of the priesthood,* to whom the privilege of temple service fell by rotation (v. 8). **7:** Compare Gen. 17.15–18.15. **9:** To *offer the* (morning or evening) *incense* was a highly cherished honor. **13:** *John:* see vv. 60, 63 n. **15:** There are OT will go before him as forerunner, possessed by the spirit and power of Elijah, to reconcile father and child, to convert the rebellious to the ways of the righteous, to prepare a people that shall be fit for the Lord.'

18 Zechariah said to the angel, 'How can I be sure of this? I am an old man and my wife is well on in years.'

19 The angel replied, 'I am Gabriel; I stand in attendance on God, and I have been sent to speak to you and bring you this good news. 20 But now, because you have not believed me, you will lose all power of speech and remain silent until the day when these things take place; at their proper time my words will be proved true.'

21 Meanwhile the people were waiting for Zechariah, surprised that he was staying so long inside the sanctuary. 22 When he did come out he could not speak to them, and they realized that he had had a vision. He stood there making signs to them, and remained dumb.

23 When his period of duty was completed Zechariah returned home. 24 His wife Elizabeth conceived, and for five months she lived in seclusion, thinking, 25 'This is the Lord's doing; now at last he has shown me favour and taken away from me the disgrace of childlessness.'

26 In the sixth month the angel Gabriel was sent by God to Nazareth, a town in Galilee, 27 with a message for a girl betrothed to a man named Joseph, a descendant of David; the girl's name was Mary. 28 The angel went in and said to her, 'Greetings, most favoured one! The Lord is with you.' 29 But she was deeply troubled by what he said and wondered what this greeting could mean. 30 Then the angel said to her, 'Do not be afraid, Mary, for God has been gracious to you; 31 you will conceive and give birth to a son, and you are

to give him the name Jesus. 32 He will be great, and will be called Son of the Most High. The Lord God will give him the throne of his ancestor David, 33 and he will be king over Israel for ever; his reign shall never end.' 34 'How can this be?' said Mary. 'I am still a virgin.' 35 The angel answered, 'The Holy Spirit will come upon you, and the power of the Most High will overshadow you; for that reason the holy child to be born will be called Son of God. 36 Moreover your kinswoman Elizabeth has herself conceived a son in her old age; and she who is reputed barren is now in her sixth month, 37 for God's promises can never fail.' 38 'I am the Lord's servant,' said Mary; 'may it be as you have said.' Then the angel left her.

39 Soon afterwards Mary set out and hurried away to a town in the uplands of Judah. 40 She went into Zechariah's house and greeted Elizabeth. 41 And when Elizabeth heard Mary's greeting, the baby stirred in her womb. Then Elizabeth was filled with the Holy Spirit 42 and exclaimed in a loud voice, 'God's blessing is on you above all women, and his blessing is on the fruit of your womb. 43 Who am I, that the mother of my Lord should visit me? 44 I tell you, when your greeting sounded in my ears, the baby in my womb leapt for joy. 45 Happy is she who has had faith that the Lord's promise to her would be fulfilled!'

46 And Mary said:

'My soul tells out the greatness of the
    Lord,

1:33 **Israel:** *lit.* the house of Jacob.   1:35 **the holy child . . . God:** *or* the child to be born will be called holy, Son of God.   1:37 **for God's . . . fail:** *some witnesses read* for with God nothing will prove impossible.   1:46 **Mary:** *a few witnesses read* Elizabeth.

provisions against *wine* and *strong drink* for priests (Lev. 10.8–11) and Nazirites (Num. 6.1–21). **17:** The words *spirit and power of Elijah* and allusions to Mal. 3.1; 4.5–6 suggest a near identification of the Baptist and Elijah (see Matt. 11.14; 17.10–13) not characteristic of Lk. outside this chapter. **19:** *Gabriel* (Dan. 8.16–17; 9.21–22) was regarded as the angel of highest rank, especially in the noncanonical book of *1 Enoch*. **25:** *Disgrace:* the shame associated with barrenness; see 1 Sam. 1.1–20; Ps. 113.9.

1.26–38: Jesus' birth promised (see Matt. 1.18–25). As in Matt., the story speaks of a miraculous birth (vv. 34–35), stresses Joseph's Davidic descent (vv. 27, 32), and emphasizes the child's names or titles (vv. 31, 32, 35). **32:** *Son of the Most High:* a title for the royal Messiah (see Matt. 1.1 n.) as is shown by the words, *throne of his ancestor David* (1 Chr. 17.7–14; Isa. 11.1–10). **35:** Not physical impregnation by a divine being, but a miraculous generation of life through the Spirit is meant.

1.39–56: Mary visits Elizabeth. 43: Luke, as here, frequently uses the title *Lord* for Jesus; but in vv. 45–46 it refers to God. **46–55:** The "Magnificat" reads like a very old hymn celebrating God's goodness to Israel

47 my spirit has rejoiced in God my
   Saviour;
48 for he has looked with favour on his
   servant,
   lowly as she is.
   From this day forward
   all generations will count me blessed,
49 for the Mighty God has done great
   things for me.
   His name is holy,
50 his mercy sure from generation to
   generation
   toward those who fear him.
51 He has shown the might of his arm,
   he has routed the proud and all their
   schemes;
52 he has brought down monarchs from
   their thrones,
   and raised on high the lowly.
53 He has filled the hungry with good
   things,
   and sent the rich away empty.
54-55 He has come to the help of Israel his
   servant,
   as he promised to our forefathers;
   he has not forgotten to show mercy
   to Abraham and his children's children
   for ever.'

56 Mary stayed with Elizabeth about three
months and then returned home.

57 WHEN the time came for Elizabeth's child to
be born, she gave birth to a son. 58 Her neighbours and relatives heard what great kindness the Lord had shown her, and they
shared her delight. 59 On the eighth day they
came to circumcise the child; and they were
going to name him Zechariah after his father, 60 but his mother spoke up: 'No!' she
said. 'He is to be called John.' 61 'But', they
said, 'there is nobody in your family who has
that name.' 62 They enquired of his father by
signs what he would like him to be called.
63 He asked for a writing tablet and to everybody's astonishment wrote, 'His name is
John.' 64 Immediately his lips and tongue
were freed and he began to speak, praising
God. 65 All the neighbours were overcome

with awe, and throughout the uplands of Judaea the whole story became common talk.
66 All who heard it were deeply impressed
and said, 'What will this child become?' For
indeed the hand of the Lord was upon him.

67 And Zechariah his father was filled with
the Holy Spirit and uttered this prophecy:

68 'Praise to the Lord, the God of Israel!
   For he has turned to his people and set
   them free.
69 He has raised for us a strong deliverer
   from the house of his servant David.
70 So he promised: age after age he
   proclaimed
   by the lips of his holy prophets,
71 that he would deliver us from our
   enemies,
   out of the hands of all who hate us;
72 that, calling to mind his solemn
   covenant,
   he would deal mercifully with our
   fathers.
73 'This was the oath he swore to our
   father Abraham,
74 to rescue us from enemy hands and set
   us free from fear,
   so that we might worship 75 in his
   presence
   in holiness and righteousness our whole
   life long.
76 'And you, my child, will be called
   Prophet of the Most High,
   for you will be the Lord's forerunner,
   to prepare his way
77 and lead his people to a knowledge of
   salvation
   through the forgiveness of their sins:
78 for in the tender compassion of our
   God
   the dawn from heaven will break upon
   us,
79 to shine on those who live in darkness,
   under the shadow of death,
   and to guide our feet into the way of
   peace.'

(vv. 54–55); compare 1 Sam. 2.1–10. **59:** Circumcision on the *eighth day* was prescribed in the Law (Lev. 12.3;
Lk. 2.21). **60, 63:** The emphasis shows that the meaning of the name *John* ("God is gracious") is important.
   1.67–79: The "Benedictus" celebrates the coming of the royal Messiah (v. 69), the fulfillment of the promise
to Abraham (vv. 73–75), and John's Elijah-like commission (vv. 76–77; Mal. 3.1; Isa. 40.3; see v. 17 n.).

[80] As the child grew up he became strong in spirit; he lived out in the wilderness until the day when he appeared publicly before Israel.

2 In those days a decree was issued by the emperor Augustus for a census to be taken throughout the Roman world. [2] This was the first registration of its kind; it took place when Quirinius was governor of Syria. [3] Everyone made his way to his own town to be registered. [4-5] Joseph went up to Judaea from the town of Nazareth in Galilee, to register in the city of David called Bethlehem, because he was of the house of David by descent; and with him went Mary, his betrothed, who was expecting her child. [6] While they were there the time came for her to have her baby, [7] and she gave birth to a son, her firstborn. She wrapped him in swaddling clothes, and laid him in a manger, because there was no room for them at the inn.

[8] Now in this same district there were shepherds out in the fields, keeping watch through the night over their flock. [9] Suddenly an angel of the Lord appeared to them, and the glory of the Lord shone round them. They were terrified, [10] but the angel said, 'Do not be afraid; I bring you good news, news of great joy for the whole nation. [11] Today there has been born to you in the city of David a deliverer—the Messiah, the Lord. [12] This will be the sign for you: you will find a baby wrapped in swaddling clothes, and lying in a manger.' [13] All at once there was with the angel a great company of the heavenly host, singing praise to God:

[14] 'Glory to God in highest heaven,
    and on earth peace to all in whom he
      delights.'

[15] After the angels had left them and returned to heaven the shepherds said to one another, 'Come, let us go straight to Bethlehem and see this thing that has happened, which the Lord has made known to us.'

[16] They hurried off and found Mary and Joseph, and the baby lying in the manger. [17] When they saw the child, they related what they had been told about him; [18] and all who heard were astonished at what the shepherds said. [19] But Mary treasured up all these things and pondered over them. [20] The shepherds returned glorifying and praising God for what they had heard and seen; it had all happened as they had been told.

[21] Eight days later the time came to circumcise him, and he was given the name Jesus, the name given by the angel before he was conceived.

[22] Then, after the purification had been completed in accordance with the law of Moses, they brought him up to Jerusalem to present him to the Lord [23] (as prescribed in the law of the Lord: 'Every firstborn male shall be deemed to belong to the Lord'), [24] and also to make the offering as stated in the law: 'a pair of turtle-doves or two young pigeons'.

[25] There was at that time in Jerusalem a man called Simeon. This man was upright and devout, one who watched and waited for the restoration of Israel, and the Holy Spirit was upon him. [26] It had been revealed to him by the Holy Spirit that he would not see death until he had seen the Lord's Messiah. [27] Guided by the Spirit he came into the temple; and when the parents brought in the child Jesus to do for him what the law required, [28] he took him in his arms, praised God, and said:

[29] 'Now, Lord, you are releasing your
    servant in peace,
    according to your promise.
[30] For I have seen with my own eyes
    the deliverance [31] you have made ready
    in full view of all nations:

2:2 **registration ... Quirinius:** *or* registration carried out while Quirinius.   2:7 **no ... inn:** *or* no other space in their lodging.   2:11 **the Messiah, the Lord:** *some witnesses read* the Lord's Messiah.

2.1–40: The birth of Jesus. 1: *Augustus* reigned from 30 B.C.E. to 14 C.E. **2:** The *registration* under *Quirinius* is dated in 6 or 7 C.E. by the first-century Jewish historian Josephus. **7:** The *firstborn* belong to God and must be redeemed (Exod. 13.1–2, 12–13); see vv. 22–24. *Swaddling clothes:* the cloth strips with which infants were wrapped. A *manger* (or small feed trough) would serve well as a crib. **11:** *Deliverer* (or, "Savior") may be a play on the name Jesus; compare Matt. 1.21. *Lord:* see 1.43 n. **13:** The *angel* who brings the message is joined by a *great company* (compare Dan. 7.10). **21:** *Eight days:* see 1.59 n. On *Jesus,* see v. 11 n. **22–24:** See v. 7 n.; Lev. 12.1–8. **25–26:** *The restoration of Israel* was expected of the Messiah (see Acts 1.6). **29:** *Releasing* suggests the freeing of a slave. **31–32:** The Messiah's function beyond Israel is stated in terms of Isa.

³²a light that will bring revelation to the
　Gentiles
　and glory to your people Israel.'

³³ The child's father and mother were full of
wonder at what was being said about him.
³⁴⁻³⁵ Simeon blessed them and said to Mary
his mother, 'This child is destined to be a sign
that will be rejected; and you too will be
pierced to the heart. Many in Israel will stand
or fall because of him; and so the secret
thoughts of many will be laid bare.'

³⁶ There was also a prophetess, Anna the
daughter of Phanuel, of the tribe of Asher.
She was a very old woman, who had lived
seven years with her husband after she was
first married, ³⁷ and then alone as a widow to
the age of eighty-four. She never left the
temple, but worshipped night and day with
fasting and prayer. ³⁸ Coming up at that very
moment, she gave thanks to God; and she
talked about the child to all who were looking
for the liberation of Jerusalem.

³⁹ When they had done everything prescribed in the law of the Lord, they returned
to Galilee to their own town of Nazareth.
⁴⁰ The child grew big and strong and full of
wisdom; and God's favour was upon him.

⁴¹ Now it was the practice of his parents to
go to Jerusalem every year for the Passover
festival; ⁴² and when he was twelve, they
made the pilgrimage as usual. ⁴³ When the
festive season was over and they set off for
home, the boy Jesus stayed behind in Jerusalem. His parents did not know of this; ⁴⁴ but
supposing that he was with the party they
travelled for a whole day, and only then did
they begin looking for him among their
friends and relations. ⁴⁵ When they could not
find him they returned to Jerusalem to look
for him; ⁴⁶ and after three days they found
him sitting in the temple surrounded by the
teachers, listening to them and putting questions; ⁴⁷ and all who heard him were amazed

at his intelligence and the answers he gave.
⁴⁸ His parents were astonished to see him
there, and his mother said to him, 'My son,
why have you treated us like this? Your father and I have been anxiously searching for
you.' ⁴⁹ 'Why did you search for me?' he said.
'Did you not know that I was bound to be in
my Father's house?' ⁵⁰ But they did not understand what he meant. ⁵¹ Then he went
back with them to Nazareth, and continued
to be under their authority; his mother treasured up all these things in her heart. ⁵² As
Jesus grew he advanced in wisdom and in
favour with God and men.

John the Baptist and Jesus

3 In the fifteenth year of the emperor Tiberius, when Pontius Pilate was governor of Judaea, when Herod was tetrarch of
Galilee, his brother Philip prince of Ituraea
and Trachonitis, and Lysanias prince of Abilene, ² during the high-priesthood of Annas
and Caiaphas, the word of God came to John
son of Zechariah in the wilderness. ³ And he
went all over the Jordan valley proclaiming a
baptism in token of repentance for the forgiveness of sins, ⁴ as it is written in the book
of the prophecies of Isaiah:

　A voice cries in the wilderness,
　'Prepare the way for the Lord;
　clear a straight path for him.
　⁵ Every ravine shall be filled in,
　and every mountain and hill levelled;
　winding paths shall be straightened,
　and rough ways made smooth;
　⁶ and all mankind shall see God's
　　deliverance.'

⁷ Crowds of people came out to be baptized

2:49 **in . . . house:** *or* about my Father's business.

52.10; 42.6; 49.6. **38:** *Liberation of Jerusalem:* see vv. 25–26 n.

2.41–52: Jesus in the temple as a boy. 41: Deuteronomy 16.16 required Jewish males to be in Jerusalem
every year for the Passover festival (see Mk. 14.1 n.), which celebrated Israel's escape from Egypt (Exod. ch. 12).
52: *Wisdom* (also v. 40) is a complex term which includes such meanings as "practical knowledge about life,"
"knowledge of the Law," and "revealed knowledge."

　3.1–20: The work of the Baptist (Matt. 3.1–12; Mk. 1.1–8; Jn. 1.6, 15, 19–28). **1:** *The fifteenth year of . . .*
Tiberius: 27 C.E. Roman governors ruled Judea after 6 C.E.; *Pilate's* tenure covered 26–36. *Herod* Antipas (a
son of Herod the Great), who ruled Galilee and Perea, is meant. **2:** *Annas* was an influential former high priest;
Caiaphas, his son-in-law, was high priest during Pilate's governorship. *Wilderness:* see Matt. 3.1 n. **3:** *Baptism:*
see Matt. 3.7 n. **4–6:** Isa. 40.3–5.

by him, and he said to them: 'Vipers' brood! Who warned you to escape from the wrath that is to come? ⁸Prove your repentance by the fruit you bear; and do not begin saying to yourselves, "We have Abraham for our father." I tell you that God can make children for Abraham out of these stones. ⁹Already the axe is laid to the roots of the trees; and every tree that fails to produce good fruit is cut down and thrown on the fire.'

¹⁰The people asked him, 'Then what are we to do?' ¹¹He replied, 'Whoever has two shirts must share with him who has none, and whoever has food must do the same.' ¹²Among those who came to be baptized were tax-collectors, and they said to him, 'Teacher, what are we to do?' ¹³He told them, 'Exact no more than the assessment.' ¹⁴Some soldiers also asked him, 'And what of us?' To them he said, 'No bullying; no blackmail; make do with your pay!'

¹⁵The people were all agog, wondering about John, whether perhaps he was the Messiah, ¹⁶but he spoke out and said to them all: 'I baptize you with water; but there is one coming who is mightier than I am. I am not worthy to unfasten the straps of his sandals. He will baptize you with the Holy Spirit and with fire. ¹⁷His winnowing-shovel is ready in his hand, to clear his threshing-floor and gather the wheat into his granary; but the chaff he will burn on a fire that can never be put out.'

¹⁸In this and many other ways he made his appeal to the people and announced the good news. ¹⁹But Herod the tetrarch, when he was rebuked by him over the affair of his brother's wife Herodias and all his other misdeeds, ²⁰crowned them all by shutting John up in prison.

The ancestry of the Messiah

²¹DURING a general baptism of the people, when Jesus too had been baptized and was praying, heaven opened ²²and the Holy Spirit descended on him in bodily form like a dove, and there came a voice from heaven, 'You are my beloved Son; in you I delight.'

²³When Jesus began his work he was about thirty years old, the son, as people thought, of Joseph son of Heli, ²⁴son of Matthat, son of Levi, son of Melchi, son of Jannai, son of Joseph, ²⁵son of Mattathias, son of Amos, son of Nahum, son of Esli, son of Naggai, ²⁶son of Maath, son of Mattathias, son of Semein, son of Josech, son of Joda, ²⁷son of Johanan, son of Rhesa, son of Zerubbabel, son of Shealtiel, son of Neri, ²⁸son of Melchi, son of Addi, son of Cosam, son of Elmadam, son of Er, ²⁹son of Joshua, son of Eliezer, son of Jorim, son of Matthat, son of Levi, ³⁰son of Symeon, son of Judah, son of Joseph, son of Jonam, son of Eliakim, ³¹son of Melea, son of Menna, son of Mattatha, son of Nathan, son of David, ³²son of Jesse, son of Obed, son of Boaz, son of Salma, son of Nahshon, ³³son of Amminadab, son of Arni, son of Hezron, son of Perez, son of Judah, ³⁴son of Jacob, son of Isaac, son of Abraham, son of Terah, son of Nahor, ³⁵son of Serug, son of Reu, son of Peleg, son of Eber, son of Shelah, ³⁶son of Cainan, son of Arphaxad, son of Shem, son of Noah, son of Lamech, ³⁷son of Methuselah, son of Enoch, son of Jared, son of Mahalaleel, son of Cainan, ³⁸son of Enosh, son of Seth, son of Adam, son of God.

3:22 **You are ... Son:** *or* You are my only Son. **You are ... delight:** *some witnesses read* You are my Son; this day I have begotten you.   3:33 **Amminadab:** *some witnesses add* son of Admin.

8: Descendants of *Abraham* share the promise made to him (Gen. 17.4–8; 22.18). **12:** *Tax-collectors* were private citizens who contracted with the Roman authorities to collect duties in a specific area; Jews who engaged in this "business" were regarded as traitors. **15–16:** See Mk. 1.7 n. **16:** *With the Holy Spirit and with fire* probably originally meant "with divine power and judgment"; for Lk., *fire* is symbolically identified with *Spirit* (see Acts 1.5; 2.1–5). **19:** See Mk. 6.17–20.

3.21–22: The baptism of Jesus (Matt. 3.13–17; Mk. 1.9–11 n.; Jn. 1.32–34). **21:** Jesus' *praying* is frequently mentioned by Lk. (e.g. 5.16; 9.18). **22:** *Spirit, dove:* see Matt. 3.16 n. *Beloved:* see Mk. 1.11 n.

3.23–38: Genealogy of Jesus (compare Matt. 1.1–17). Verse 20 formally closes the career of the Baptist; with v. 21 attention turns exclusively to Jesus whose genealogy is given. **23:** *Thirty years old* would mean shortly after 25 C.E., reckoning from Herod's death in 4 B.C.E. (Matt. 2.1–20). **31:** While descent from *David* is still important for the Messiah (Matt. 1.1 n.), vv. 23–31 do not trace Jesus' ancestry through David's royal progeny (as does Matt. 1.6–11). **38:** The genealogy extends beyond *Abraham* (i.e. beyond the Jewish limits of Matt. 1.1–17) to *Adam, son of God,* perhaps to affirm Jesus' kinship with all humanity.

The temptation of Jesus

4 ¹⁻² FULL of the Holy Spirit, Jesus returned from the Jordan, and for forty days he wandered in the wilderness, led by the Spirit and tempted by the devil.

During that time he ate nothing, and at the end of it he was famished. ³ The devil said to him, 'If you are the Son of God, tell this stone to become bread.' ⁴ Jesus answered, 'Scripture says, "Man is not to live on bread alone." '

⁵ Next the devil led him to a height and showed him in a flash all the kingdoms of the world. ⁶ 'All this dominion will I give to you,' he said, 'and the glory that goes with it; for it has been put in my hands and I can give it to anyone I choose. ⁷ You have only to do homage to me and it will all be yours.' ⁸ Jesus answered him, 'Scripture says, "You shall do homage to the Lord your God and worship him alone." '

⁹ The devil took him to Jerusalem and set him on the parapet of the temple. 'If you are the Son of God,' he said, 'throw yourself down from here; ¹⁰ for scripture says, "He will put his angels in charge of you," ¹¹ and again, "They will support you in their arms for fear you should strike your foot against a stone." ' ¹² Jesus answered him, 'It has been said, "You are not to put the Lord your God to the test." '

¹³ So, having come to the end of all these temptations, the devil departed, biding his time.

Jesus in Galilee

¹⁴ THEN Jesus, armed with the power of the Spirit, returned to Galilee; and reports about him spread through the whole countryside.

¹⁵ He taught in their synagogues and everyone sang his praises.

¹⁶ He came to Nazareth, where he had been brought up, and went to the synagogue on the sabbath day as he regularly did. He stood up to read the lesson ¹⁷ and was handed the scroll of the prophet Isaiah. He opened the scroll and found the passage which says,

¹⁸ 'The spirit of the Lord is upon me
  because he has anointed me;
  he has sent me to announce good news
    to the poor,
  to proclaim release for prisoners
  and recovery of sight for the blind;
  to let the broken victims go free,
¹⁹ to proclaim the year of the Lord's
    favour.'

²⁰ He rolled up the scroll, gave it back to the attendant, and sat down; and all eyes in the synagogue were fixed on him.

²¹ He began to address them: 'Today', he said, 'in your hearing this text has come true.' ²² There was general approval; they were astonished that words of such grace should fall from his lips. 'Is not this Joseph's son?' they asked. ²³ Then Jesus said, 'No doubt you will quote to me the proverb, "Physician, heal yourself!" and say, "We have heard of all your doings at Capernaum; do the same here in your own home town." ²⁴ Truly I tell you,' he went on: 'no prophet is recognized in his own country. ²⁵ There were indeed many widows in Israel in Elijah's time, when for three and a half years the skies never opened, and famine lay hard over the whole country; ²⁶ yet it was to none of these that Elijah was sent, but to a widow at Sarepta in the territory of Sidon. ²⁷ Again, in the time of the prophet Elisha there were many lepers in Israel, and not one of them was healed, but only Naa-

---

4.1–13: The temptation (Matt. 4.1–11; Mk. 1.12–13). Except for a different sequence of temptations, the account closely parallels Matt. 4.1–11 (see notes there). **13:** *Biding his time* implies the later renewal of the contest (see 22.3, 28, 31).

4.14–15: Jesus appears in Galilee (Matt. 4.12–17; Mk. 1.14–15). **14:** In Jesus' ministry, the *Spirit* is uniquely operative (3.22; 4.1, 18–21). The phrase *returned to Galilee*, i.e. home (see 2.39), prepares for the scene in vv. 16–30. **15:** *Taught in their synagogues:* see Matt. 9.35.

4.16–30: Jesus in Nazareth (compare Matt. 13.54–58; Mk. 6.1–6). **16:** Only Lk. places the *Nazareth* visit at the beginning of Jesus' ministry. The *synagogue* was a place for instruction in the Law and for nonsacrificial worship. *Sabbath* begins at sunset on Friday. **18–19:** Isa. 61.1–2; 58.6. **18:** *Spirit:* see 4.14 n. **20:** *Sat:* see Matt. 5.1 n. **25–27:** Two OT examples of God's goodness to non-Israelites are cited (1 Kgs. ch. 17; 2 Kgs. 5.1–19), thus emphasizing the universal reach of Jesus' mission.

man, the Syrian.' [28] These words roused the whole congregation to fury; [29] they leapt up, drove him out of the town, and took him to the brow of the hill on which it was built, meaning to hurl him over the edge. [30] But he walked straight through the whole crowd, and went away.

[31] Coming down to Capernaum, a town in Galilee, he taught the people on the sabbath, [32] and they were amazed at his teaching, for what he said had the note of authority. [33] Now there was a man in the synagogue possessed by a demon, an unclean spirit. He shrieked at the top of his voice, [34] 'What do you want with us, Jesus of Nazareth? Have you come to destroy us? I know who you are — the Holy One of God.' [35] Jesus rebuked him: 'Be silent', he said, 'and come out of him.' Then the demon, after throwing the man down in front of the people, left him without doing him any injury. [36] Amazement fell on them all and they said to one another: 'What is there in this man's words? He gives orders to the unclean spirits with authority and power, and they go.' [37] So the news spread, and he was the talk of the whole district.

[38] On leaving the synagogue he went to Simon's house. Simon's mother-in-law was in the grip of a high fever; and they asked him to help her. [39] He stood over her and rebuked the fever. It left her, and she got up at once and attended to their needs.

[40] At sunset all who had friends ill with diseases of one kind or another brought them to him; and he laid his hands on them one by one and healed them. [41] Demons also came out of many of them, shouting, 'You are the Son of God.' But he rebuked them and forbade them to speak, because they knew he was the Messiah.

[42] When day broke he went out and made his way to a remote spot. But the crowds went in search of him, and when they came to where he was they pressed him not to leave them. [43] But he said, 'I must give the good news of the kingdom of God to the other towns also, for that is what I was sent to do.' [44] So he proclaimed the gospel in the synagogues of Judaea.

5 One day as he stood by the lake of Gennesaret, with people crowding in on him to listen to the word of God, [2] he noticed two boats lying at the water's edge; the fishermen had come ashore and were washing their nets. [3] He got into one of the boats, which belonged to Simon, and asked him to put out a little way from the shore; then he went on teaching the crowds as he sat in the boat. [4] When he had finished speaking, he said to Simon, 'Put out into deep water and let down your nets for a catch.' [5] Simon answered, 'Master, we were hard at work all night and caught nothing; but if you say so, I will let down the nets.' [6] They did so and made such a huge catch of fish that their nets began to split. [7] So they signalled to their partners in the other boat to come and help them. They came, and loaded both boats to the point of sinking. [8] When Simon saw what had happened he fell at Jesus's knees and said, 'Go, Lord, leave me, sinner that I am!' [9] For he and all his companions were amazed at the catch they had made; [10] so too were his partners James and John, Zebedee's sons. 'Do not be afraid,' said Jesus to Simon; 'from now on you will be catching people.' [11] As soon as they had brought the boats to land, they left everything and followed him.

[12] He was once in a certain town where there was a man covered with leprosy; when he saw Jesus, he threw himself to the ground and begged his help. 'Sir,' he said, 'if only you will, you can make me clean.' [13] Jesus stretched out his hand and touched him, saying, 'I will; be clean.' The leprosy left him immediately. [14] Jesus then instructed him not to tell anybody. 'But go,' he said, 'show yourself to the priest, and make the offering laid down by Moses for your cleansing; that will certify the cure.' [15] But the talk about him spread ever wider, so that great crowds kept

4:34 **Have you:** or You have.

4.31–44: Jesus in Capernaum (Matt. 8.14–17; Mk. 1.21–38). **33:** *Demon:* see Mk. 1.23 n. **38:** *Simon:* Peter (see Matt. 4.18). **40:** *Sunset* on Saturday marks the end of sabbath; see v. 16 n. **44:** For Lk., *Judaea* sometimes means the entire "Holy Land" (including Galilee).

5.1–11: The first disciples called (compare Matt. 4.18–22; Mk. 1.16–20; Jn. 1.35–51; 21.1–8). **1:** *Lake of Gennesaret:* Sea of Galilee.

5.12–16: A leper healed (Matt. 8.1–4; Mk. 1.40–45). **12:** *Leprosy, clean:* see Matt. 8.2 n. **14:** See Lev. 14.1–32. **16:** *Prayer:* see 3.21 n.

gathering to hear him and to be cured of their ailments. ¹⁶ And from time to time he would withdraw to remote places for prayer.

¹⁷ One day as he was teaching, Pharisees and teachers of the law were sitting round him. People had come from every village in Galilee and from Judaea and Jerusalem, and the power of the Lord was with him to heal the sick. ¹⁸ Some men appeared carrying a paralysed man on a bed, and tried to bring him in and set him down in front of Jesus. ¹⁹ Finding no way to do so because of the crowd, they went up onto the roof and let him down through the tiling, bed and all, into the middle of the company in front of Jesus. ²⁰ When Jesus saw their faith, he said to the man, 'Your sins are forgiven you.'

²¹ The scribes and Pharisees began asking among themselves, 'Who is this fellow with his blasphemous talk? Who but God alone can forgive sins?' ²² But Jesus knew what they were thinking and answered them: 'Why do you harbour these thoughts? ²³ Is it easier to say, "Your sins are forgiven you," or to say, "Stand up and walk"? ²⁴ But to convince you that the Son of Man has the right on earth to forgive sins'—he turned to the paralysed man—'I say to you, stand up, take your bed, and go home.' ²⁵ At once the man rose to his feet before their eyes, took up the bed he had been lying on, and went home praising God. ²⁶ They were all lost in amazement and praised God; filled with awe they said, 'The things we have seen today are beyond belief!'

²⁷ Later, when he went out, he saw a tax-collector, Levi by name, at his seat in the custom-house, and said to him, 'Follow me.' ²⁸ Leaving everything, he got up and followed him.

²⁹ Afterwards Levi held a big reception in his house for Jesus; among the guests was a large party of tax-collectors and others. ³⁰ The Pharisees, some of whom were scribes, complained to his disciples: 'Why', they said,

'do you eat and drink with tax-collectors and sinners?' ³¹ Jesus answered them: 'It is not the healthy that need a doctor, but the sick; ³² I have not come to call the virtuous but sinners to repentance.'

³³ Then they said to him, 'John's disciples are much given to fasting and the practice of prayer, and so are the disciples of the Pharisees; but yours eat and drink.' ³⁴ Jesus replied, 'Can you make the bridegroom's friends fast while the bridegroom is with them? ³⁵ But the time will come when the bridegroom will be taken away from them; that will be the time for them to fast.'

³⁶ He told them this parable also: 'No one tears a piece from a new garment to patch an old one; if he does, he will have made a hole in the new garment, and the patch taken from the new will not match the old. ³⁷ No one puts new wine into old wineskins; if he does, the new wine will burst the skins, the wine will spill out, and the skins be ruined. ³⁸ New wine goes into fresh skins! ³⁹ And no one after drinking old wine wants new; for he says, "The old wine is good."'

6 One sabbath he was going through the cornfields, and his disciples were plucking the ears of corn, rubbing them in their hands, and eating them. ² Some Pharisees said, 'Why are you doing what is forbidden on the sabbath?' ³ Jesus answered, 'Have you not read what David did when he and his men were hungry? ⁴ He went into the house of God and took the sacred bread to eat and gave it to his men, though only the priests are allowed to eat it.' ⁵ He also said to them, 'The Son of Man is master of the sabbath.'

⁶ On another sabbath he had gone to synagogue and was teaching. There was a man in the congregation whose right arm was with-

5:17 Pharisees . . . Jerusalem: *some witnesses read* Pharisees and teachers of the law, who had come from every village in Galilee and from Judaea and Jerusalem, were sitting round him.

5.17–6.11: Healing and conflict.

5.17–26: A paralytic (Matt. 9.1–8; Mk. 2.1–12). **17:** *Power* may mean "Spirit"; see 4.14 n. **19:** *Tiling:* compare Mk. 2.4 n. **21:** *Scribes:* see Matt. 2.4 n. **24:** *Son of Man:* see Mk. 2.10 n.

5.27–32: Friend of outcasts (Matt. 9.9–13; Mk. 2.13–17). **27:** *A tax-collector* was despised; see 3.12 n. **29:** *Reception:* only Lk. clearly places the dinner in *Levi's* house (compare Matt. 9.10; Mk. 2.15).

5.33–39: Fasting and prayer (Matt. 9.14–17; Mk. 2.18–22). **33:** *John's disciples:* see Mk. 2.18 n. **36–38:** See Mk. 2.21–22 n. **39:** This may have been intended as sarcastic comment about the preference of Jesus' opponents for the old ways.

6.1–11: Sabbath controversy (Matt. 12.1–14; Mk. 2.23–3.6). See Mk. 2.23–3.6 n. **1:** Deut. 23.25. **2:** Exod. 20.10; Deut. 5.14. **3:** 1 Sam. 21.1–7. **4:** Lev. 24.7–9.

ered; 7 and the scribes and Pharisees were on the watch to see whether Jesus would heal him on the sabbath, so that they could find a charge to bring against him. 8 But he knew what was in their minds and said to the man with the withered arm, 'Stand up and come out here.' So he stood up and came out. 9 Then Jesus said to them, 'I put this question to you: is it permitted to do good or to do evil on the sabbath, to save life or to destroy it?' 10 He looked round at them all, and then he said to the man, 'Stretch out your arm.' He did so, and his arm was restored. 11 But they totally failed to understand, and began to discuss with one another what they could do to Jesus.

12 During this time he went out one day into the hill-country to pray, and spent the night in prayer to God. 13 When day broke he called his disciples to him, and from among them he chose twelve and named them apostles: 14 Simon, to whom he gave the name Peter, and Andrew his brother, James and John, Philip and Bartholomew, 15 Matthew and Thomas, James son of Alphaeus, and Simon who was called the Zealot, 16 Judas son of James, and Judas Iscariot who turned traitor.

17 He came down the hill with them and stopped on some level ground where a large crowd of his disciples had gathered, and with them great numbers of people from Jerusalem and all Judaea and from the coastal region of Tyre and Sidon, who had come to listen to him, and to be cured of their diseases. 18 Those who were troubled with unclean spirits were healed; 19 and everyone in the crowd was trying to touch him, because power went out from him and cured them all.

Jesus's sermon to the disciples

20 TURNING to his disciples he began to speak:

'Blessed are you who are in need;
the kingdom of God is yours.
21 Blessed are you who now go hungry;
you will be satisfied.
Blessed are you who weep now;
you will laugh.

22 'Blessed are you when people hate you and ostracize you, when they insult you and slander your very name, because of the Son of Man. 23 On that day exult and dance for joy, for you have a rich reward in heaven; that is how their fathers treated the prophets.

24 'But alas for you who are rich;
you have had your time of happiness.
25 Alas for you who are well fed now;
you will go hungry.
Alas for you who laugh now;
you will mourn and weep.
26 Alas for you when all speak well of
you;
that is how their fathers treated the
false prophets.

27 'But to you who are listening I say: Love your enemies; do good to those who hate you; 28 bless those who curse you; pray for those who treat you spitefully. 29 If anyone hits you on the cheek, offer the other also; if anyone takes your coat, let him have your shirt as well. 30 Give to everyone who asks you; if anyone takes what is yours, do not demand it back.

7–11: See Mk. 3.1–6 n.

6.12–16: The Twelve chosen (Matt. 10.1–4; Mk. 3.13–19). The choosing of the Twelve is a prelude to the sermon which follows; notice again the reference to *prayer* (3.21 n.). **13:** *Apostles:* see Matt. 10.2 n. **15:** *Zealot:* Mk. 3.18 n.

6.17–49: Sermon on the Plain. The Sermon in Lk. includes sayings also found in the Sermon on the Mount in Matt. chs. 5–7.

6.17–19: The setting. See Matt. 4.25; 12.15–21; Mk. 3.7–12. **17:** Contrast Matt. 5.1. Luke thinks of mountains for settings requiring privacy; public teaching tends to take place on *level ground*.

6.20–23: The Beatitudes (Matt. 5.3–12). On form, see Matt. 5.3 n. Unlike Matt., Lk. reports all these Beatitudes in the second person. Also, Lk. does not "spiritualize" the conditions described as *blessed;* see vv. 24–26 n.

6.24–26: The Woes (*Alas for you* . . .) represent a form which warns against qualities of life or types of behavior that have bad consequences; here, the warning has been heightened to eschatological threat. As vv. 20, 21, 24, 25 show, *in need* and *hungry* are understood literally by Lk.; contrast Matt. 5.3 n., 6 n.

31 'Treat others as you would like them to treat you. 32 If you love only those who love you, what credit is that to you? Even sinners love those who love them. 33 Again, if you do good only to those who do good to you, what credit is there in that? Even sinners do as much. 34 And if you lend only where you expect to be repaid, what credit is there in that? Even sinners lend to each other to be repaid in full. 35 But you must love your enemies and do good, and lend without expecting any return; and you will have a rich reward: you will be sons of the Most High, because he himself is kind to the ungrateful and the wicked. 36 Be compassionate, as your Father is compassionate.

37 'Do not judge, and you will not be judged; do not condemn, and you will not be condemned; pardon, and you will be pardoned; 38 give, and gifts will be given you. Good measure, pressed and shaken down and running over, will be poured into your lap; for whatever measure you deal out to others will be dealt to you in turn.'

39 He also spoke to them in a parable: 'Can one blind man guide another? Will not both fall into the ditch? 40 No pupil ranks above his teacher; fully trained he can but reach his teacher's level.

41 'Why do you look at the speck in your brother's eye, with never a thought for the plank in your own? 42 How can you say to your brother, "Brother, let me take the speck out of your eye," when you are blind to the plank in your own? You hypocrite! First take the plank out of your own eye, and then you will see clearly to take the speck out of your brother's.

43 'There is no such thing as a good tree producing bad fruit, nor yet a bad tree producing good fruit. 44 Each tree is known by its own fruit: you do not gather figs from brambles or pick grapes from thistles. 45 Good people produce good from the store of good within themselves; and evil people produce evil from the evil within them. For the words that the mouth utters come from the overflowing of the heart.

46 'Why do you call me "Lord, Lord" — and never do what I tell you? 47 Everyone who comes to me and hears my words and acts on them — I will show you what he is like. 48 He is like a man building a house, who dug deep and laid the foundations on rock. When the river was in flood, it burst upon that house, but could not shift it, because it had been soundly built. 49 But he who hears and does not act is like a man who built his house on the soil without foundations. As soon as the river burst upon it, the house collapsed, and fell with a great crash.'

Miracles and parables

7 WHEN he had finished addressing the people, he entered Capernaum. 2 A centurion there had a servant whom he valued highly, but the servant was ill and near to death. 3 Hearing about Jesus, he sent some Jewish elders to ask him to come and save his servant's life. 4 They approached Jesus and made an urgent appeal to him: 'He deserves this favour from you,' they said, 5 'for he is a friend of our nation and it is he who built us our synagogue.' 6 Jesus went with them; but when he was not far from the house, the centurion sent friends with this message: 'Do not trouble further, sir; I am not worthy to have you come under my roof, 7 and that is why I did not presume to approach you in person. But say the word and my servant will be cured. 8 I know, for I am myself under orders, with soldiers under me. I say to one, "Go," and he goes; to another, "Come here," and he comes; and to my servant, "Do this," and he does it.' 9 When Jesus heard this, he was astonished, and, turning to the crowd that was following him, he said, 'I tell you, not even in Israel have I found such faith.' 10 When the messengers returned to the house, they found the servant in good health.

11 Afterwards Jesus went to a town called

6.27–36: **Love of enemies** (Matt. 5.39–42, 44–48). **31:** The Golden Rule; see Matt. 7.12 n. **35:** Being children of God is shown by behavior which conforms to God's manner of dealing with persons.

6.37–46: **Judging others** (Matt. 7.1–5). **39:** Matt. 15.14. **40:** Matt. 10.24–25; Jn. 13.16. **43–46:** Proof of goodness (Matt. 7.16–21; 12.33–35).

6.47–49: **The wise and foolish builders** (Matt. 7.24–27).

7.1–10: **The centurion's servant** (Matt. 8.5–13). **2:** Centurion: see Matt. 8.5 n. In Lk., the sick person is clearly a servant; compare Matt. 8.6 n.

7.11–17: **The widow's son.** Compare 1 Kgs. 17.17–24; 2 Kgs. 4.32–37.

Nain, accompanied by his disciples and a large crowd. 12 As he approached the gate of the town he met a funeral. The dead man was the only son of his widowed mother; and many of the townspeople were there with her. 13 When the Lord saw her his heart went out to her, and he said, 'Do not weep.' 14 He stepped forward and laid his hand on the bier; and the bearers halted. Then he spoke: 'Young man, I tell you to get up.' 15 The dead man sat up and began to speak; and Jesus restored him to his mother. 16 Everyone was filled with awe and praised God. 'A great prophet has arisen among us,' they said; 'God has shown his care for his people.' 17 The story of what he had done spread through the whole of Judaea and all the region around.

18 When John was informed of all this by his disciples, 19 he summoned two of them and sent them to the Lord with this question: 'Are you the one who is to come, or are we to expect someone else?' 20 The men made their way to Jesus and said, 'John the Baptist has sent us to ask you, "Are you the one who is to come, or are we to expect someone else?"' 21 There and then he healed many sufferers from diseases, plagues, and evil spirits; and on many blind people he bestowed sight. 22 Then he gave them this answer: 'Go and tell John what you have seen and heard: the blind regain their sight, the lame walk, lepers are made clean, the deaf hear, the dead are raised to life, the poor are brought good news — 23 and happy is he who does not find me an obstacle to faith.'

24 After John's messengers had left, Jesus began to speak about him to the crowds: 'What did you go out into the wilderness to see? A reed swaying in the wind? 25 No? Then what did you go out to see? A man dressed in finery? Grand clothes and luxury are to be found in palaces. 26 But what did you go out to see? A prophet? Yes indeed, and far more than a prophet. 27 He is the man of whom scripture says,

Here is my herald, whom I send ahead of you,
and he will prepare your way before you.

28 'I tell you, among all who have been born, no one has been greater than John; yet the least in the kingdom of God is greater than he is.'

29 When they heard him, all the people, including the tax-collectors, acknowledged the goodness of God, for they had accepted John's baptism; 30 but the Pharisees and lawyers, who had refused his baptism, rejected God's purpose for themselves.

31 'How can I describe the people of this generation? What are they like? 32 They are like children sitting in the market-place and calling to each other,

We piped for you and you would not dance.
We lamented, and you would not mourn.

33 'For John the Baptist came, neither eating bread nor drinking wine, and you say, "He is possessed." 34 The Son of Man came, eating and drinking, and you say, "Look at him! A glutton and a drinker, a friend of tax-collectors and sinners!" 35 And yet God's wisdom is proved right by all who are her children.'

36 One of the Pharisees invited Jesus to a meal; he went to the Pharisee's house and took his place at table. 37 A woman who was living an immoral life in the town had learned that Jesus was a guest in the Pharisee's house and had brought oil of myrrh in a small flask. 38 She took her place behind him, by his feet, weeping. His feet were wet with her tears and she wiped them with her hair, kissing them and anointing them with the myrrh. 39 When his host the Pharisee saw this he said to himself, 'If this man were a real prophet, he would know who this woman is who is touching him, and what a bad character she is.' 40 Jesus took him up: 'Simon,' he said, 'I have something to say to you.' 'What

---

7.18–35: Jesus and John the Baptist (Matt. 11.2–19). The passage advances high claims for both Jesus and the Baptist. John's question (v. 19) elicits not only Jesus' testimony about his own works (vv. 22–23), but also his commendation of the Baptist (vv. 24–28). Verses 22–23 are based on Isa. 29.18–19; 35.5–6; 61.1. **27:** Mal. 3.1. **33:** *Possessed,* i.e. by a demon, out of his mind. **34:** *Tax-collectors:* see Lk. 3.12 n. **35:** *Wisdom* is the personified source of revelation as in Prov. 1.20–33; Ecclus. 24.1–23.

7.36–50: Dinner with a Pharisee (compare Matt. 26.6–13; Mk. 14.3–9; Jn. 12.1–8). **37:** Custom permitted is it, Teacher?' he asked. 41'Two men were in debt to a moneylender: one owed him five hundred silver pieces, the other fifty. 42As they did not have the means to pay he cancelled both debts. Now, which will love him more?' 43Simon replied, 'I should think the one that was let off more.' 'You are right,' said Jesus. 44Then turning to the woman, he said to Simon, 'You see this woman? I came to your house: you provided no water for my feet; but this woman has made my feet wet with her tears and wiped them with her hair. 45You gave me no kiss; but she has been kissing my feet ever since I came in. 46You did not anoint my head with oil; but she has anointed my feet with myrrh. 47So, I tell you, her great love proves that her many sins have been forgiven; where little has been forgiven, little love is shown.' 48Then he said to her, 'Your sins are forgiven.' 49The other guests began to ask themselves, 'Who is this, that he can forgive sins?' 50But he said to the woman, 'Your faith has saved you; go in peace.'

8 AFTER this he went journeying from town to town and village to village, proclaiming the good news of the kingdom of God. With him were the Twelve 2and a number of women who had been set free from evil spirits and infirmities: Mary, known as Mary of Magdala, from whom seven demons had come out, 3Joanna, the wife of Chuza a steward of Herod's, Susanna, and many others. These women provided for them out of their own resources.

4People were now gathering in large numbers, and as they made their way to him from one town after another, he said in a parable: 5'A sower went out to sow his seed. And as he sowed, some of the seed fell along the footpath, where it was trampled on, and the birds ate it up. 6Some fell on rock and, after coming up, it withered for lack of moisture. 7Some fell among thistles, and the thistles grew up with it and choked it. 8And some of the seed fell into good soil, and grew, and yielded a hundredfold.' As he said this he called out, 'If you have ears to hear, then hear.'

9His disciples asked him what this parable meant, 10and he replied, 'It has been granted to you to know the secrets of the kingdom of God; but the others have only parables, so that they may look but see nothing, hear but understand nothing.

11'This is what the parable means. The seed is the word of God. 12The seed along the footpath stands for those who hear it, and then the devil comes and carries off the word from their hearts for fear they should believe and be saved. 13The seed sown on rock stands for those who receive the word with joy when they hear it, but have no root; they are believers for a while, but in the time of testing they give up. 14That which fell among thistles represents those who hear, but their growth is choked by cares and wealth and the pleasures of life, and they bring nothing to maturity. 15But the seed in good soil represents those who bring a good and honest heart to the hearing of the word, hold it fast, and by their perseverance yield a harvest.

16'Nobody lights a lamp and then covers it with a basin or puts it under the bed. You put it on a lampstand so that those who come in may see the light. 17For there is nothing hidden that will not be disclosed, nothing concealed that will not be made known and brought into the open.

18'Take care, then, how you listen; for those who have will be given more, and those who have not will forfeit even what they think they have.'

19His mother and his brothers arrived but could not get to him for the crowd. 20He was told, 'Your mother and brothers are standing outside, and want to see you.' 21He replied,

7:47 her great . . . have been forgiven: or her sins, which are many, have been forgiven because she has loved much.

such intrusions on private parties. *Myrrh:* a fragrant substance. **40:** *Simon* was a name in common use. **44–46:** Special courtesies which the host might have provided are performed instead by the woman. **50:** In miracle stories the Gk. words here translated *saved you* mean "healed you" (e.g. 8.48).

8.1–3: Women disciples serve.

8.4–15: The parable of the sower and its meaning (Matt. 13.1–23; Mk. 4.1–20). **4:** On *parables,* see Mk. 4.2 n. **6:** See Mk. 4.3–8 n. **8:** See Mk. 4.8 n. **9–10:** *Look, hear:* see Mk. 4.12 n.; Matt. 13.13 n. **11–15:** See Mk. 4.13–20 n.

8.16–21: Miscellaneous sayings. 16–18: See Mk. 4.24–25 n. **16:** Matt. 5.15; Mk. 4.21. **17:** Matt. 10.26; Mk. 4.22. **18:** 19.26; Matt. 13.12; 25.29; Mk. 4.25. **19–21:** Matt. 12.46–50; Mk. 3.31–35.

'My mother and my brothers are those who hear the word of God and act upon it.'

²²One day he got into a boat with his disciples and said to them, 'Let us cross over to the other side of the lake.' So they put out; ²³and as they sailed along he fell asleep. Then a heavy squall struck the lake; they began to ship water and were in grave danger. ²⁴They came and roused him: 'Master, Master, we are sinking!' they cried. He awoke, and rebuked the wind and the turbulent waters. The storm subsided and there was calm. ²⁵'Where is your faith?' he asked. In fear and astonishment they said to one another, 'Who can this be? He gives his orders to the wind and the waves, and they obey him.'

²⁶So they landed in the country of the Gerasenes, which is opposite Galilee. ²⁷As he stepped ashore he was met by a man from the town who was possessed by demons. For a long time he had neither worn clothes nor lived in a house, but stayed among the tombs. ²⁸When he saw Jesus he cried out, and fell at his feet. 'What do you want with me, Jesus, Son of the Most High God?' he shouted. 'I implore you, do not torment me.' ²⁹For Jesus was already ordering the unclean spirit to come out of the man. Many a time it had seized him, and then, for safety's sake, they would secure him with chains and fetters; but each time he broke loose and was driven by the demon out into the wilds.

³⁰Jesus asked him, 'What is your name?' 'Legion,' he replied. This was because so many demons had taken possession of him. ³¹And they begged him not to banish them to the abyss.

³²There was a large herd of pigs nearby, feeding on the hillside; and the demons begged him to let them go into these pigs. He gave them leave; ³³the demons came out of the man and went into the pigs, and the herd rushed over the edge into the lake and were drowned.

³⁴When the men in charge of them saw what had happened, they took to their heels and carried the news to the town and countryside; ³⁵and the people came out to see what had happened. When they came to Jesus, and found the man from whom the demons had gone out sitting at his feet clothed and in his right mind, they were afraid. ³⁶Eyewitnesses told them how the madman had been cured. ³⁷Then the whole population of the Gerasene district was overcome by fear and asked Jesus to go away. So he got into the boat and went away. ³⁸The man from whom the demons had gone out begged to go with him; but Jesus sent him away: ³⁹'Go back home,' he said, 'and tell them what God has done for you.' The man went all over the town proclaiming what Jesus had done for him.

⁴⁰When Jesus returned, the people welcomed him, for they were all expecting him. ⁴¹Then a man appeared—Jairus was his name and he was president of the synagogue. Throwing himself down at Jesus's feet he begged him to come to his house, ⁴²because his only daughter, who was about twelve years old, was dying.

While Jesus was on his way he could hardly breathe for the crowds. ⁴³Among them was a woman who had suffered from haemorrhages for twelve years; and nobody had been able to cure her. ⁴⁴She came up from behind and touched the edge of his cloak, and at once her haemorrhage stopped. ⁴⁵Jesus said, 'Who was it who touched me?' All disclaimed it, and Peter said, 'Master, the crowds are hemming you in and pressing upon you!' ⁴⁶But Jesus said, 'Someone did touch me, for I felt that power had gone out from me.' ⁴⁷Then the woman, seeing that she was detected, came trembling and fell at his feet. Before all the people she explained why she had touched him and how she had been cured instantly. ⁴⁸He said to her, 'Daughter, your faith has healed you. Go in peace.'

⁴⁹While he was still speaking, a man came from the president's house with the message, 'Your daughter is dead; do not trouble the teacher any more.' ⁵⁰But Jesus heard, and

8:26 **Gerasenes:** *some witnesses read* Gergesenes; *others read* Gadarenes.   8:37 **Gerasenes:** *some witnesses read* Gergesene; *others read* Gadarene.   8:43 **years; and:** *some witnesses add* though she had spent all she had on doctors.   8:44 **edge:** *or* tassel.

8.22–25: Rebuke of a storm (Matt. 8.23–27; Mk. 4.35–41).

8.26–39: The Gerasene demoniac (Matt. 8.28–34; Mk. 5.1–20). **26:** *Gerasenes:* see Mk. 5.1 n. **28:** *Son:* see Matt. 8.28–29 n. **30:** On *name, Legion,* see Mk. 5.9 n. **32:** *Pigs:* see Matt. 8.30 n.

8.40–56: Jairus' daughter and a woman with a chronic ailment (Matt. 9.18–26; Mk. 5.21–43). See Mk. 5.21–43 n. **48:** *Healed:* see 7.50 n.

said, 'Do not be afraid; simply have faith and she will be well again.' [51]When he arrived at the house he allowed no one to go in with him except Peter, John, and James, and the child's father and mother. [52]Everyone was weeping and lamenting for her. He said, 'Stop your weeping; she is not dead: she is asleep'; [53]and they laughed at him, well knowing that she was dead. [54]But Jesus took hold of her hand and called to her: 'Get up, my child.' [55]Her spirit returned, she stood up immediately, and he told them to give her something to eat. [56]Her parents were astounded; but he forbade them to tell anyone what had happened.

Jesus and the Twelve

9 CALLING the Twelve together he gave them power and authority to overcome all demons and to cure diseases, [2]and sent them out to proclaim the kingdom of God and to heal the sick. [3]'Take nothing for the journey,' he told them, 'neither stick nor pack, neither bread nor money; nor are you to have a second coat. [4]When you enter a house, stay there until you leave that place. [5]As for those who will not receive you, when you leave their town shake the dust off your feet as a warning to them.' [6]So they set out and travelled from village to village, and everywhere they announced the good news and healed the sick.

[7]Now Herod the tetrarch heard of all that was happening, and did not know what to make of it; for some were saying that John had been raised from the dead, [8]others that Elijah had appeared, others again that one of the prophets of old had come back to life. [9]Herod said, 'As for John, I beheaded him; but who is this I hear so much about?' And he was anxious to see him.

[10]On their return the apostles gave Jesus an account of all they had done. Then he took them with him and withdrew privately to a town called Bethsaida, [11]but the crowds found out and followed. He welcomed them, and spoke to them about the kingdom of God, and cured those who were in need of healing. [12]When evening was drawing on, the Twelve came to him and said, 'Send the people off, so that they can go into the villages and farms round about to find food and lodging, for this is a remote place we are in.' [13]'Give them something to eat yourselves,' he replied. But they said, 'All we have is five loaves and two fish, nothing more — or do you intend us to go and buy food for all these people?' [14]For there were about five thousand men. Then he said to his disciples, 'Make them sit down in groups of about fifty.' [15]They did so and got them all seated. [16]Then, taking the five loaves and the two fish, he looked up to heaven, said the blessing over them, broke them, and gave them to the disciples to distribute to the people. [17]They all ate and were satisfied; and the scraps they left were picked up and filled twelve baskets.

[18]One day, when he had been praying by himself in the company of his disciples, he asked them, 'Who do the people say I am?' [19]They answered, 'Some say John the Baptist, others Elijah, others that one of the prophets of old has come back to life.' [20]'And you,' he said, 'who do you say I am?' Peter answered, 'God's Messiah.' [21]Then he gave them strict orders not to tell this to anyone. [22]And he said, 'The Son of Man has to endure great sufferings, and to be rejected by the elders, chief priests, and scribes, to be put to death, and to be raised again on the third day.'

[23]To everybody he said, 'Anyone who wants to be a follower of mine must renounce

---

9.1–6: Mission of the Twelve (see 10.1 n.; Matt. 9.35; 10.1, 9–11, 14; Mk. 6.7–13). **1–2:** *Cure, proclaim:* see Matt. 10.8 n.

9.7–9: Herod and Jesus (Matt. 14.1–2; Mk. 6.14–16). **7:** *Herod:* Antipas (see 3.1 n.). *John:* the Baptist. **8:** *Elijah:* see Mk. 6.15 n.

9.10–17: Feeding of five thousand (Matt. 14.13–21; Mk. 6.30–44; Jn. 6.1–13). See Mk. 6.30–44 n.; Lk. has only one account of such a feeding.

9.18–22: Peter's confession and Jesus' prediction of his suffering (Matt. 16.13–23; Mk. 8.27–33; Jn. 6.66–71). **18:** *Praying alone:* see 3.21 n. **19:** *John, Elijah:* see Mk. 8.28 n. **20:** *Messiah:* see Matt. 1.1 n. **22:** 9.44; 18.31–33; see Mk. 8.31 n.

9.23–27: Following Jesus (Matt. 16.24–28; Mk. 8.34–9.1). **23:** *Cross:* see Matt. 10.38–39 n. The addition of *day after day* in Lk. (compare Matt. 16.24; Mk. 8.34 n.) spiritualizes the meaning of *take up a cross.*

self; day after day he must take up his cross, and follow me. 24 Whoever wants to save his life will lose it, but whoever loses his life for my sake will save it. 25 What does anyone gain by winning the whole world at the cost of destroying himself? 26 If anyone is ashamed of me and my words, the Son of Man will be ashamed of him, when he comes in his glory and the glory of the Father and the holy angels. 27 In truth I tell you: there are some of those standing here who will not taste death before they have seen the kingdom of God.'

28 About a week after this he took Peter, John, and James and went up a mountain to pray. 29 And while he was praying the appearance of his face changed and his clothes became dazzling white. 30 Suddenly there were two men talking with him — Moses and Elijah — 31 who appeared in glory and spoke of his departure, the destiny he was to fulfil in Jerusalem. 32 Peter and his companions had been overcome by sleep; but when they awoke, they saw his glory and the two men who stood beside him. 33 As these two were moving away from Jesus, Peter said to him, 'Master, it is good that we are here. Shall we make three shelters, one for you, one for Moses, and one for Elijah?' but he spoke without knowing what he was saying. 34 As he spoke there came a cloud which cast its shadow over them; they were afraid as they entered the cloud, 35 and from it a voice spoke: 'This is my Son, my Chosen; listen to him.' 36 After the voice had spoken, Jesus was seen to be alone. The disciples kept silence and did not at that time say a word to anyone of what they had seen.

37 Next day when they came down from the mountain a large crowd came to meet him. 38 A man in the crowd called out: 'Teacher, I implore you to look at my son, my only child. 39 From time to time a spirit seizes him and with a sudden scream throws him into con-

vulsions so that he foams at the mouth; it keeps on tormenting him and can hardly be made to let him go. 40 I begged your disciples to drive it out, but they could not.' 41 Jesus answered, 'What an unbelieving and perverse generation! How long shall I be with you and endure you? Bring your son here.' 42 But before the boy could reach him the demon dashed him to the ground and threw him into convulsions. Jesus spoke sternly to the unclean spirit, cured the boy, and gave him back to his father. 43 And they were all struck with awe at the greatness of God.

Amid the general astonishment at all he was doing, Jesus said to his disciples, 44 'Listen to what I have to tell you. The Son of Man is to be given up into the power of men.' 45 But they did not understand what he said; its meaning had been hidden from them, so that they could not grasp it, and they were afraid to ask him about it.

46 An argument started among them as to which of them was the greatest. 47 Jesus, who knew what was going on in their minds, took a child, stood him by his side, 48 and said, 'Whoever receives this child in my name receives me; and whoever receives me receives the one who sent me. For the least among you all is the greatest.'

49 'Master,' said John, 'we saw someone driving out demons in your name, but as he is not one of us we tried to stop him.' 50 Jesus said to him, 'Do not stop him, for he who is not against you is on your side.'

The journey to Jerusalem

51 As THE time approached when he was to be taken up to heaven, he set his face resolutely towards Jerusalem, 52 and sent messengers ahead. They set out and went into a Samaritan village to make arrangements for him;

9:26 **me and my words:** *some witnesses read* me and mine. 9:31 **departure:** *lit.* exodus.

9.28–36: The transfiguration (Matt. 17.1–8; Mk. 9.2–8). See Matt. 17.1–8 nn. **28:** *To pray:* see 3.21 n. **31:** *Departure* may refer to death or to Jesus' death, resurrection, and ascension.

9.37–43a: An epileptic boy (Matt. 17.14–20; Mk. 9.14–29). Luke has greatly abbreviated the story.

9.43b–45: The second prediction (see 9.19) **of suffering** (Matt. 17.22–23; Mk. 9.30–32).

9.46–50: The true disciple (Matt. 18.1–5; Mk. 9.33–41). The true disciple is not embroiled in arguments about rank (v. 46) or privilege (vv. 49–50), but knows instead the joy of humble service (v. 48). **49–50:** See Mk. 9.39–40 n.; contrast 11.23.

9.51–19.27: The Lukan travel narrative. Perhaps taking a clue from brief but dramatic notices in Mk. 10.1, 32, Lk. has developed the journey to Jerusalem into a narrative which prepares, not only for the death and resurrection in the Holy City (see e.g. 13.33), but also for the subsequent journey of the church to the "farthest

53 but the villagers would not receive him because he was on his way to Jerusalem. 54 When the disciples James and John saw this they said, 'Lord, do you want us to call down fire from heaven to consume them?' 55 But he turned and rebuked them, 56 and they went on to another village.

57 As they were going along the road a man said to him, 'I will follow you wherever you go.' 58 Jesus answered, 'Foxes have their holes and birds their roosts; but the Son of Man has nowhere to lay his head.' 59 To another he said, 'Follow me,' but the man replied, 'Let me first go and bury my father.' 60 Jesus said, 'Leave the dead to bury their dead; you must go and announce the kingdom of God.' 61 Yet another said, 'I will follow you, sir; but let me first say goodbye to my people at home.' 62 To him Jesus said, 'No one who sets his hand to the plough and then looks back is fit for the kingdom of God.'

10 After this the Lord appointed a further seventy-two and sent them on ahead in pairs to every town and place he himself intended to visit. 2 He said to them: 'The crop is heavy, but the labourers are few. Ask the owner therefore to send labourers to bring in the harvest. 3 Be on your way; I am sending you like lambs among wolves. 4 Carry no purse or pack, and travel barefoot. Exchange no greetings on the road. 5 When you go into a house, let your first words be, "Peace to this house." 6 If there is a man of peace there, your peace will rest on him; if not, it will return to you. 7 Stay in that house, sharing their food and drink; for the worker deserves his pay. Do not move around from house to house. 8 When you enter a town and you are made welcome, eat the food provided for you; 9 heal the sick there, and say, "The kingdom of God has come upon you."

10 But when you enter a town and you are not made welcome, go out into its streets and say, 11 "The very dust of your town that clings to our feet we wipe off to your shame. Only take note of this: the kingdom of God has come." 12 I tell you, on the day of judgement the fate of Sodom will be more bearable than the fate of that town.

13 'Alas for you, Chorazin! Alas for you, Bethsaida! If the miracles performed in you had taken place in Tyre and Sidon, they would have repented long ago, sitting in sackcloth and ashes. 14 But it will be more bearable for Tyre and Sidon at the judgement than for you. 15 As for you, Capernaum, will you be exalted to heaven? No, you will be brought down to Hades!

16 'Whoever listens to you listens to me; whoever rejects you rejects me. And whoever rejects me rejects the One who sent me.'

17 The seventy-two came back jubilant. 'In your name, Lord,' they said, 'even the demons submit to us.' 18 He replied, 'I saw Satan fall, like lightning, from heaven. 19 And I have given you the power to tread underfoot snakes and scorpions and all the forces of the enemy. Nothing will ever harm you. 20 Nevertheless, do not rejoice that the spirits submit to you, but that your names are enrolled in heaven.'

21 At that moment Jesus exulted in the Holy Spirit and said, 'I thank you, Father, Lord of heaven and earth, for hiding these

9:54 **consume them:** *some witnesses add* as Elijah did. 9:55 **rebuked them:** *some witnesses add* 'You do not know', he said, 'to what spirit you belong; (56) for the Son of Man did not come to destroy men's lives but to save them.'   10:1 **seventy-two:** *some witnesses read* seventy.   10:9 **come upon you:** *or* come close to you.   10:11 **has come:** *or* has come close. 10:17 **seventy-two:** *some witnesses read* seventy. 10:21 **Holy Spirit:** *some witnesses omit* Holy.

corners of the earth" (Acts 1.8; see e.g. 9.51–10.24 with notes). For most of this section (see 18.15–17 n.) Lk. does not follow the order of Mk.

9.51–10.24: The mission of the seventy-two. 51: *Taken up:* see Acts 1.11. **52:** The enmity between Jews and *Samaritans* was ancient and deep, of the sort possible only where there are rival claims to being the true guardians of a common tradition (the Law of Moses). **57–62:** Three candidates who wish to *follow* in Jesus' way are introduced; in each case, the heavy demands of discipleship are presented (compare Matt. 8.19–22). **10.1:** Luke has two missions: of the Twelve (9.1–6; perhaps a symbolic mission to Israel) and of the *seventy-two* (perhaps, symbolically, to the Gentile nations). **2–12:** Compare Matt. 9.37–38; 10.7–16; Mk. 6.7–11. **9:** *Heal, kingdom:* see Matt. 10.8 n. **12:** *Sodom:* see Matt. 10.15 n. **13–15:** *Tyre, Sidon:* see Matt. 11.21 n. **16:** See Matt. 10.40–42 n.; Jn. 13.20. **18:** *I saw Satan fall* may report a vision of God's final victory or interpret the success of the disciples as a sign of that victory. **21–22:** Revelation to the humble (*simple*), rather than to the "*wise* of the world*" was a familiar theme, common in NT times, but with ancient roots; see e.g. Isa. 29.14; Prov.

things from the learned and wise, and revealing them to the simple. Yes, Father, such was your choice. ²² Everything is entrusted to me by my Father; no one knows who the Son is but the Father, or who the Father is but the Son, and those to whom the Son chooses to reveal him.'

²³ When he was alone with his disciples he turned to them and said, 'Happy the eyes that see what you are seeing! ²⁴ I tell you, many prophets and kings wished to see what you now see, yet never saw it; to hear what you hear, yet never heard it.'

²⁵ A LAWYER once came forward to test him by asking: 'Teacher, what must I do to inherit eternal life?' ²⁶ Jesus said, 'What is written in the law? What is your reading of it?' ²⁷ He replied, 'Love the Lord your God with all your heart, and with all your soul, with all your strength, and with all your mind; and your neighbour as yourself.' ²⁸ 'That is the right answer,' said Jesus; 'do that and you will have life.'

²⁹ Wanting to justify his question, he asked, 'But who is my neighbour?' ³⁰ Jesus replied, 'A man was on his way from Jerusalem down to Jericho when he was set upon by robbers, who stripped and beat him, and went off leaving him half dead. ³¹ It so happened that a priest was going down by the same road, and when he saw him, he went past on the other side. ³² So too a Levite came to the place, and when he saw him went past on the other side. ³³ But a Samaritan who was going that way came upon him, and when he saw him he was moved to pity. ³⁴ He went up and bandaged his wounds, bathing them with oil and wine. Then he lifted him on to his own

beast, brought him to an inn, and looked after him. ³⁵ Next day he produced two silver pieces and gave them to the innkeeper, and said, "Look after him; and if you spend more, I will repay you on my way back." ³⁶ Which of these three do you think was neighbour to the man who fell into the hands of the robbers?' ³⁷ He answered, 'The one who showed him kindness.' Jesus said to him, 'Go and do as he did.'

³⁸ While they were on their way Jesus came to a village where a woman named Martha made him welcome. ³⁹ She had a sister, Mary, who seated herself at the Lord's feet and stayed there listening to his words. ⁴⁰ Now Martha was distracted by her many tasks, so she came to him and said, 'Lord, do you not care that my sister has left me to get on with the work by myself? Tell her to come and give me a hand.' ⁴¹ But the Lord answered, 'Martha, Martha, you are fretting and fussing about so many things; ⁴² only one thing is necessary. Mary has chosen what is best; it shall not be taken away from her.'

11 At one place after Jesus had been praying, one of his disciples said, 'Lord, teach us to pray, as John taught his disciples.' ² He answered, 'When you pray, say,

Father, may your name be hallowed;
    your kingdom come.

10:21 **Yes . . . such:** *or* Yes, I thank you, Father, that such.
10:42 **only . . . necessary:** *some witnesses read* only few things are necessary, or rather, one alone.
11:2 **Father:** *some witnesses read* Our Father in heaven.
your kingdom come: *one witness reads* your kingdom come upon us; *some others have* your Holy Spirit come upon us and cleanse us; *some add* your will be done, on earth as in heaven.   11:3 **daily bread:** *or* bread for the morrow.

26.12; 1 Cor. 1.19–20. **23–24:** Matt. 13.16–17.

10.25–28: The double commandment of love (Matt. 22.34–40; Mk. 12.28–31). **27:** The commandments are taken from Deut. 6.5; Lev. 19.18. It is significant that, even while regarding the question as a *test* (v. 25), Luke can credit the lawyer with providing this summary of the Law; similar summaries can be found in Jewish sources of the period, as well as in Paul (Rom. 13.9–10; Gal. 5.14) and Jas. 2.8. **28b:** *Do . . . have life:* Lev. 18.5; the implication is that v. 27 comprehends the whole Law (compare Matt. 22.40; Rom. 10.5; 13.10).

10.29–37: The good Samaritan. The *priest* (v. 31) and the *Levite* (v. 32), as temple officials, represent highly visible members of the religious establishment. While their failure to act as neighbors would attract the attention of the hearers of the parable, the hearers would also know that contact with the body beside the road—if it was dead—would render them unfit for temple service. **33:** Among Jews nothing good would be expected of a *Samaritan* (see 9.52 n.), which makes his action all the more notable.

10.38–42: Mary and Martha. 38: The words *on their way* pick up the theme of the journey; see 9.51–19.27 n. *Martha* and *Mary* (vv. 38–39) are presumably the sisters mentioned in Jn. ch. 11.

11.1–13: On prayer. 1: The occasion for the Lord's Prayer is reported in this way only by Lk. **2–4:** See Matt.

³ Give us each day our daily bread.
⁴ And forgive us our sins,
for we too forgive all who have done us
wrong.
And do not put us to the test.'

⁵ Then he said to them, 'Suppose one of you
has a friend who comes to him in the middle
of the night and says, "My friend, lend me
three loaves, ⁶ for a friend of mine on a journey has turned up at my house, and I have
nothing to offer him"; ⁷ and he replies from
inside, "Do not bother me. The door is shut
for the night; my children and I have gone
to bed; and I cannot get up and give you what
you want." ⁸ I tell you that even if he will not
get up and provide for him out of friendship,
his very persistence will make the man get up
and give him all he needs. ⁹ So I say to you,
ask, and you will receive; seek, and you will
find; knock, and the door will be opened to
you. ¹⁰ For everyone who asks receives, those
who seek find, and to those who knock, the
door will be opened.

¹¹ 'Would any father among you offer his
son a snake when he asks for a fish, ¹² or a
scorpion when he asks for an egg? ¹³ If you,
bad as you are, know how to give good things
to your children, how much more will the
heavenly Father give the Holy Spirit to those
who ask him!'

Opposition and questioning

¹⁴ HE was driving out a demon which was
dumb; and when the demon had come out,
the dumb man began to speak. The people
were astonished, ¹⁵ but some of them said, 'It
is by Beelzebul prince of demons that he
drives the demons out.' ¹⁶ Others, by way of
a test, demanded of him a sign from heaven.
¹⁷ But he knew what was in their minds, and
said, 'Every kingdom divided against itself is
laid waste, and a divided household falls.
¹⁸ And if Satan is divided against himself,
how can his kingdom stand — since, as you

claim, I drive out the demons by Beelzebul?
¹⁹ If it is by Beelzebul that I drive out demons,
by whom do your own people drive them
out? If this is your argument, they themselves will refute you. ²⁰ But if it is by the
finger of God that I drive out the demons,
then be sure the kingdom of God has already
come upon you.

²¹ 'When a strong man fully armed is on
guard over his palace, his possessions are
safe. ²² But when someone stronger attacks
and overpowers him, he carries off the arms
and armour on which the man had relied and
distributes the spoil.

²³ 'He who is not with me is against me, and
he who does not gather with me scatters.

²⁴ 'When an unclean spirit comes out of
someone it wanders over the desert sands
seeking a resting-place; and if it finds none,
it says, "I will go back to the home I left." ²⁵ So
it returns and finds the house swept clean
and tidy. ²⁶ It goes off and collects seven
other spirits more wicked than itself, and
they all come in and settle there; and in the
end that person's plight is worse than before.'

²⁷ While he was speaking thus, a woman in
the crowd called out, 'Happy the womb that
carried you and the breasts that suckled you!'
²⁸ He rejoined, 'No, happy are those who
hear the word of God and keep it.'

²⁹ With the crowds swarming round him he
went on to say: 'This is a wicked generation.
It demands a sign, and the only sign that will
be given it is the sign of Jonah. ³⁰ For just as
Jonah was a sign to the Ninevites, so will the
Son of Man be to this generation. ³¹ The
queen of the south will appear in court when
the men of this generation are on trial, and
ensure their condemnation; for she came
from the ends of the earth to listen to the
wisdom of Solomon, and what is here is

11:4 **to the test:** *some witnesses add* but save us from the
evil one (*or* from evil).   11:11 **offer his son:** *some
witnesses add* a stone when he asks for bread, or.
11:31 **will appear ... trial:** *or* will be raised to life at
the judgement together with the men of this
generation.

6.9–13 n. **2:** *Father:* see Matt. 6.9 n. **3:** *Daily:* see Matt. 6.11 n. **9–13:** Matt. 7.7–11. **13:** Emphasis on the *Holy
Spirit* is a characteristic of Lk.; Matt. 7.11 has "give good things."
  11.14–36: Signs, Beelzebul, Jonah. 14–23: Matt. 12.22–30; Mk. 3.22–27. **15:** *Beelzebul:* Satan. **16:** The
demand for a *sign* (see Matt. 12.38–42 n.) could not be satisfied by exorcism, since there were other exorcists
(v. 19); the observers are challenged to see God's power (v. 20) bursting upon them in the activity of Jesus.
20: *Finger of God* is a lively metaphor which calls to mind Exod. 8.19 ("hand of God"); Matt. 12.28 reads instead
"Spirit of God." **23:** See Mk. 9.39–40 n. **24–26:** Matt. 12.43–45. **24:** *Desert:* see Matt. 12.43 n. **29–32:** Matt.
12.38–42. **29:** *Sign:* see Matt. 12.38–42 n. Luke has nothing like Matt. 12.40 and interprets the *sign of Jonah*

greater than Solomon. 32 The men of Nineveh will appear in court when this generation
is on trial, and ensure its condemnation; for
they repented at the preaching of Jonah; and
what is here is greater than Jonah.

33 'No one lights a lamp and puts it in a
cellar, but on the lampstand so that those
who come in may see the light. 34 The lamp
of your body is the eye. When your eyes are
sound, you have light for your whole body;
but when they are bad, your body is in darkness. 35 See to it then that the light you have
is not darkness. 36 If you have light for your
whole body with no trace of darkness, it will
all be full of light, as when the light of a lamp
shines on you.'

37 WHEN he had finished speaking, a Pharisee
invited him to a meal, and he came in and sat
down. 38 The Pharisee noticed with surprise
that he had not begun by washing before the
meal. 39 But the Lord said to him, 'You Pharisees clean the outside of cup and plate; but
inside you are full of greed and wickedness.
40 You fools! Did not he who made the outside make the inside too? 41 But let what is
inside be given in charity, and all is clean.

42 'Alas for you Pharisees! You pay tithes of
mint and rue and every garden herb, but
neglect justice and the love of God. It is these
you should have practised, without overlooking the others.

43 'Alas for you Pharisees! You love to have
the chief seats in synagogues, and to be
greeted respectfully in the street

44 'Alas, alas, you are like unmarked graves
which people walk over unawares.'

45 At this one of the lawyers said, 'Teacher,
when you say things like this you are insulting us too.' 46 Jesus rejoined: 'Alas for you
lawyers also! You load men with intolerable
burdens, and will not lift a finger to lighten
the load.

47 'Alas, you build monuments to the

prophets whom your fathers murdered,
48 and so testify that you approve of the deeds
your fathers did; they committed the murders and you provide the monuments.

49 'This is why the Wisdom of God said, "I
will send them prophets and messengers;
and some of these they will persecute and
kill"; 50 so that this generation will have to
answer for the blood of all the prophets shed
since the foundation of the world; 51 from the
blood of Abel to the blood of Zechariah who
met his death between the altar and the sanctuary. I tell you, this generation will have to
answer for it all.

52 'Alas for you lawyers! You have taken
away the key of knowledge. You did not go
in yourselves, and those who were trying to
go in, you prevented.'

53 After he had left the house, the scribes
and Pharisees began to assail him fiercely
and to ply him with a host of questions, 54 laying snares to catch him with his own words.

12

MEANWHILE, when a crowd of many
thousands had gathered, packed so
close that they were trampling on one another, he began to speak first to his disciples:
'Be on your guard against the leaven of the
Pharisees — I mean their hypocrisy. 2 There is
nothing covered up that will not be uncovered, nothing hidden that will not be made
known. 3 Therefore everything you have said
in the dark will be heard in broad daylight,
and what you have whispered behind closed
doors will be shouted from the housetops.

4 'To you who are my friends I say: do not
fear those who kill the body and after that
have nothing more they can do. 5 I will show
you whom to fear: fear him who, after he has

11:32 **The men . . . ensure:** *or* At the judgement the
men of Nineveh will rise again together with this
generation and will ensure.   11:33 **in a cellar:** *some
witnesses add* or under the measuring bowl.

as the prophet's preaching (v. 32). **33:** Matt. 5.15. **34–36:** *Eyes . . . sound . . . eyes . . . . bad:* see Matt. 6.22 n.
For Lk. the sayings speak of the *light* by which Jesus is seen; sound eyes are organs of spiritual perception.
11.37–54: Alas for Pharisees and lawyers (compare Matt. ch. 23). **38:** *Washing:* see Mk. 7.3 n. **42:** Mic.
6.8. **43:** 20.46; Mk. 12.38–39. **44:** *Graves* were believed to make a person ritually unclean (see Num. 19.16).
49–51: The introductory formula reads as if a document authored by the *Wisdom of God* is being quoted
(compare Mk. 7.10; 12.36). *Wisdom* (see Lk. 7.35 n.) was thought of as sending *prophets* in every generation
(vv. 49–50; e.g. Wisd. 7.27 and chs. 10–11). Matthew 23.34 attributes the saying to Jesus. **51:** *Abel to . . .
Zechariah:* from the first prophet to the last. **52:** *Key of knowledge:* see Matt. 16.19 n.; 23.13.
12.1–59: Encouragement and warning. 1–12: Matt. 10.26–33. **1:** *Leaven:* see Mk. 8.15 n. **2–3:** 8.17; see
Matt. 10.26–27; Mk. 4.22, 24–25 n. Here, the saying promises that *hypocrisy* (v. 1) will be exposed. **5:** *Him*

killed, has authority to cast into hell. Believe me, he is the one to fear.

6 'Are not five sparrows sold for twopence? Yet not one of them is overlooked by God. 7 More than that, even the hairs of your head have all been counted. Do not be afraid; you are worth more than any number of sparrows.

8 'I tell you this: whoever acknowledges me before others, the Son of Man will acknowledge before the angels of God; 9 but whoever disowns me before others will be disowned before the angels of God.

10 'Anyone who speaks a word against the Son of Man will be forgiven; but for him who slanders the Holy Spirit there will be no forgiveness.

11 'When you are brought before synagogues and state authorities, do not worry about how you will conduct your defence or what you will say. 12 When the time comes the Holy Spirit will instruct you what to say.'

13 Someone in the crowd said to him, 'Teacher, tell my brother to divide the family property with me.' 14 He said to the man, 'Who set me over you to judge or arbitrate?' 15 Then to the people he said, 'Beware! Be on your guard against greed of every kind, for even when someone has more than enough, his possessions do not give him life.' 16 And he told them this parable: 'There was a rich man whose land yielded a good harvest. 17 He debated with himself: "What am I to do? I have not the space to store my produce. 18 This is what I will do," said he: "I will pull down my barns and build them bigger. I will collect in them all my grain and other goods, 19 and I will say to myself, 'You have plenty of good things laid by, enough for many years to come: take life easy, eat, drink, and enjoy yourself.' " 20 But God said to him, "You fool, this very night you must surrender your life; and the money you have made, who will get it now?" 21 That is how it is with the man who piles up treasure for himself and remains a pauper in the sight of God.'

22 To his disciples he said, 'This is why I tell you not to worry about food to keep you alive or clothes to cover your body. 23 Life is more than food, the body more than clothes. 24 Think of the ravens: they neither sow nor reap; they have no storehouse or barn; yet God feeds them. You are worth far more than the birds! 25 Can anxious thought add a day to your life? 26 If, then, you cannot do even a very little thing, why worry about the rest?

27 'Think of the lilies: they neither spin nor weave; yet I tell you, even Solomon in all his splendour was not attired like one of them. 28 If that is how God clothes the grass, which is growing in the field today, and tomorrow is thrown on the stove, how much more will he clothe you! How little faith you have! 29 Do not set your minds on what you are to eat or drink; do not be anxious. 30 These are all things that occupy the minds of the Gentiles, but your Father knows that you need them. 31 No, set your minds on his kingdom, and the rest will come to you as well.

32 'Have no fear, little flock; for your Father has chosen to give you the kingdom. 33 Sell your possessions and give to charity. Provide for yourselves purses that do not wear out, and never-failing treasure in heaven, where no thief can get near it, no moth destroy it. 34 For where your treasure is, there will your heart be also.

35 'Be ready for action, with your robes hitched up and your lamps alight. 36 Be like people who wait for their master's return from a wedding party, ready to let him in the moment he arrives and knocks. 37 Happy are those servants whom the master finds awake when he comes. Truly I tell you: he will hitch up his robe, seat them at table, and come and wait on them. 38 If it is the middle of the night or before dawn when he comes and he still finds them awake, then are they happy indeed. 39 Remember, if the householder had known at what time the burglar was coming he would not have let his house be broken

12:25 **a day . . . life:** *or* a foot to your height.

who . . . *has authority:* probably Satan is intended; but see Heb. 10.30–31. **8:** The saying is ambiguous about the relation of Jesus (*me*) and the *Son of Man* (see Mk. 2.10 n.). **10:** See Matt. 12.31–32 n.; Mk. 3.29 n. **11–12:** 21.14–15; Matt. 10.19–20; Mk. 13.11. **13–14:** The title *Teacher* probably indicates identification of Jesus as a rabbi, who as an expert on the Law would be expected *to judge*. **20:** Jeremiah 17.11 has a similar saying about a man who gets his wealth unjustly. **22–31:** See Matt. 6.25–34 n. **32:** *Little flock:* the community of the Messiah. **33–34:** Matt. 6.19–21. **35:** *With robes hitched up* or gathered securely at the waist so as to *be ready for action.* **39–46:** Matt. 24.43–51.

into. ⁴⁰So hold yourselves in readiness, because the Son of Man will come at the time you least expect him.'

⁴¹Peter said, 'Lord, do you intend this parable specially for us or is it for everyone?' ⁴²The Lord said, 'Who is the trusty and sensible man whom his master will appoint as his steward, to manage his servants and issue their rations at the proper time? ⁴³Happy that servant if his master comes home and finds him at work! ⁴⁴I tell you this: he will be put in charge of all his master's property. ⁴⁵But if that servant says to himself, "The master is a long time coming," and begins to bully the menservants and maids, and to eat and drink and get drunk, ⁴⁶then the master will arrive on a day when the servant does not expect him, at a time he has not been told. He will cut him in pieces and assign him a place among the faithless.

⁴⁷'The servant who knew his master's wishes, yet made no attempt to carry them out, will be flogged severely. ⁴⁸But one who did not know them and earned a beating will be flogged less severely. Where someone has been given much, much will be expected of him; and the more he has had entrusted to him the more will be demanded of him.

⁴⁹'I have come to set fire to the earth, and how I wish it were already kindled! ⁵⁰I have a baptism to undergo, and what constraint I am under until it is over! ⁵¹Do you suppose I came to establish peace on the earth? No indeed, I have come to bring dissension. ⁵²From now on, a family of five will be divided, three against two and two against three; ⁵³father against son and son against father, mother against daughter and daughter against mother, mother-in-law against daughter-in-law and daughter-in-law against mother-in-law.'

⁵⁴He also said to the people, 'When you see clouds gathering in the west, you say at once, "It is going to rain," and rain it does. ⁵⁵And when the wind is from the south, you say, "It will be hot," and it is. ⁵⁶What hypocrites you are! You know how to interpret the appearance of earth and sky, but cannot interpret this fateful hour.

⁵⁷'Why can you not judge for yourselves what is right? ⁵⁸When you are going with your opponent to court, make an effort to reach a settlement with him while you are still on the way; otherwise he may drag you before the judge, and the judge hand you over to the officer, and the officer throw you into jail. ⁵⁹I tell you, you will not be let out until you have paid the very last penny.'

13 At that time some people came and told him about the Galileans whose blood Pilate had mixed with their sacrifices. ²He answered them: 'Do you suppose that, because these Galileans suffered this fate, they must have been greater sinners than anyone else in Galilee? ³No, I tell you; but unless you repent, you will all of you come to the same end. ⁴Or the eighteen people who were killed when the tower fell on them at Siloam—do you imagine they must have been more guilty than all the other people living in Jerusalem? ⁵No, I tell you; but unless you repent, you will all come to an end like theirs.'

⁶He told them this parable: 'A man had a fig tree growing in his vineyard; and he came looking for fruit on it, but found none. ⁷So he said to the vine-dresser, "For the last three years I have come looking for fruit on this fig tree without finding any. Cut it down. Why should it go on taking goodness from the soil?" ⁸But he replied, "Leave it, sir, for this one year, while I dig round it and manure it. ⁹And if it bears next season, well and good; if not, you shall have it down."'

¹⁰He was teaching in one of the synagogues on the sabbath, ¹¹and there was a woman there possessed by a spirit that had

---

48: The privilege of special knowledge (compare 8.18) carries the burden of special responsibility. **49–53:** Matt. 10.34–36. **49:** *Fire* is a symbol of judgment (compare 3.16 n.). **50:** *Baptism* is a metaphor for martyrdom (compare Mk. 10.38). **51:** *Peace,* though promised in 2.14, is not to be hoped for apart from decisions which produce *dissension.* **52–53:** See Mic. 7.6. **54–56:** The *clouds* blow in from the Mediterranean: the *hot,* scorching *wind* comes across the desert. People who know so much about the weather should be able to see the imminence of the kingdom in Jesus' ministry. **57–59:** Matt. 5.25–26.

13.1–9: The necessity of repentance. 1: *Pilate:* see 3.1 n. The allusion is to an uprising of *Galileans* in Jerusalem which is not reported in other sources. **2:** Those who *suffered this fate* might have been regarded as *greater sinners* since such a tragedy could be understood as God's judgment; see v. 4. **3, 5:** Jesus does not allow the view of v. 2 n. to become the basis for complacency; all are called to *repent.*

crippled her for eighteen years. She was bent double and quite unable to stand up straight. [12] When Jesus saw her he called her and said, 'You are rid of your trouble,' [13] and he laid his hands on her. Immediately she straightened up and began to praise God. [14] But the president of the synagogue, indignant with Jesus for healing on the sabbath, intervened and said to the congregation, 'There are six working days: come and be cured on one of them, and not on the sabbath.' [15] The Lord gave him this answer: 'What hypocrites you are!' he said. 'Is there a single one of you who does not loose his ox or his donkey from its stall and take it out to water on the sabbath? [16] And here is this woman, a daughter of Abraham, who has been bound by Satan for eighteen long years: was it not right for her to be loosed from her bonds on the sabbath?' [17] At these words all his opponents were covered with confusion, while the mass of the people were delighted at all the wonderful things he was doing.

[18] 'What is the kingdom of God like?' he continued. 'To what shall I compare it? [19] It is like a mustard seed which a man took and sowed in his garden; and it grew to be a tree and the birds came to roost among its branches.'

[20] Again he said, 'To what shall I compare the kingdom of God? [21] It is like yeast which a woman took and mixed with three measures of flour till it was all leavened.'

[22] He continued his journey through towns and villages, teaching as he made his way towards Jerusalem. [23] Someone asked him, 'Sir, are only a few to be saved?' His answer was: [24] 'Make every effort to enter through the narrow door; for I tell you that many will try to enter but will not succeed.

[25] 'When once the master of the house has got up and locked the door, you may stand outside and knock, and say, "Sir, let us in!"

but he will only answer, "I do not know where you come from." [26] Then you will protest, "We used to eat and drink with you, and you taught in our streets." [27] But he will repeat, "I tell you, I do not know where you come from. Out of my sight, all of you, you and your wicked ways!" [28] There will be wailing and grinding of teeth there, when you see Abraham, Isaac, Jacob, and all the prophets, in the kingdom of God, and you yourselves are driven away. [29] From east and west, from north and south, people will come and take their places at the banquet in the kingdom of God. [30] Yes, and some who are now last will be first, and some who are first will be last.'

[31] At that time a number of Pharisees came and warned him, 'Leave this place and be on your way; Herod wants to kill you.' [32] He replied, 'Go and tell that fox, "Listen: today and tomorrow I shall be driving out demons and working cures; on the third day I reach my goal." [33] However, I must go on my way today and tomorrow and the next day, because it is unthinkable for a prophet to meet his death anywhere but in Jerusalem.

[34] 'O Jerusalem, Jerusalem, city that murders the prophets and stones the messengers sent to her! How often have I longed to gather your children, as a hen gathers her brood under her wings; but you would not let me. [35] Look! There is your temple, forsaken by God. I tell you, you will not see me until the time comes when you say, "Blessings on him who comes in the name of the Lord!"'

14 ONE sabbath he went to have a meal in the house of one of the leading Pharisees; and they were watching him closely. [2] There, in front of him, was a man suffering from dropsy, [3] and Jesus asked the lawyers and the Pharisees: 'Is it permitted to heal people on the sabbath or not?' [4] They said nothing. So he took the man, cured him, and sent him away. [5] Then he turned to them

---

13.10–17: A sabbath story. 13: *Laid his hands on her:* compare 4.40; 5.13. **14–15:** Exod. 20.9; Deut. 5.13. See 14.5 n.; Jn. 5.10–12.

13.18–21: The kingdom of God. See notes on Mk. 4.26–32, 31, 32 and Matt. 13.33.

13.22–35: Continuing in the way. These verses are an interlude, during which the reader is reminded of the theme of the journey (vv. 22, 33); see 9.51–19.27 n. **23–24:** Matt. 7.13–14. **25–30:** Matt. 7.22–23; 8.11–12; 19.30; 25.10–12. **27:** Ps. 6.8. **29:** Ps. 107.3. On the banquet, see 14.15 n. **31:** *Herod:* Antipas (see 3.1 n.). **32–33:** *Today . . . tomorrow . . . the third day* is a conventional manner of speaking of a short period of time. **34–35:** This saying is a dirge which may be quoted as a lament of Wisdom (see 7.35 n.). **35:** For Lk., *until the time comes* appears to point to the entry into Jerusalem (see 19.38); compare Matt. 23.39 n. *Blessings . . . Lord:* Ps. 118.26.

and said, 'If one of you has a son or an ox that falls into a well, will he hesitate to pull him out on the sabbath day?' 6 To this they could find no reply.

7 When he noticed how the guests were trying to secure the places of honour, he spoke to them in a parable: 8 'When somebody asks you to a wedding feast, do not sit down in the place of honour. It may be that some person more distinguished than yourself has been invited; 9 and the host will come to say to you, "Give this man your seat." Then you will look foolish as you go to take the lowest place. 10 No, when you receive an invitation, go and sit down in the lowest place, so that when your host comes he will say, "Come up higher, my friend." Then all your fellow-guests will see the respect in which you are held. 11 For everyone who exalts himself will be humbled; and whoever humbles himself will be exalted.'

12 Then he said to his host, 'When you are having guests for lunch or supper, do not invite your friends, your brothers or other relations, or your rich neighbours; they will only ask you back again and so you will be repaid. 13 But when you give a party, ask the poor, the crippled, the lame, and the blind. 14 That is the way to find happiness, because they have no means of repaying you. You will be repaid on the day when the righteous rise from the dead.'

15 Hearing this one of the company said to him, 'Happy are those who will sit at the feast in the kingdom of God!' 16 Jesus answered, 'A man was giving a big dinner party and had sent out many invitations. 17 At dinner-time he sent his servant to tell his guests, "Come please, everything is now ready." 18 One after another they all sent excuses. The first said, "I have bought a piece of land, and I must go and inspect it; please accept my apologies." 19 The second said, "I have bought five yoke of oxen, and I am on my way to try them out; please accept my apologies." 20 The next said,

"I cannot come; I have just got married." 21 When the servant came back he reported this to his master. The master of the house was furious and said to him, "Go out quickly into the streets and alleys of the town, and bring in the poor, the crippled, the blind, and the lame." 22 When the servant informed him that his orders had been carried out and there was still room, 23 his master replied, "Go out on the highways and along the hedgerows and compel them to come in; I want my house full. 24 I tell you, not one of those who were invited shall taste my banquet." '

25 Once when great crowds were accompanying him, he turned to them and said: 26 'If anyone comes to me and does not hate his father and mother, wife and children, brothers and sisters, even his own life, he cannot be a disciple of mine. 27 No one who does not carry his cross and come with me can be a disciple of mine. 28 Would any of you think of building a tower without first sitting down and calculating the cost, to see whether he could afford to finish it? 29 Otherwise, if he has laid its foundation and then is unable to complete it, everyone who sees it will laugh at him. 30 "There goes the man", they will say, "who started to build and could not finish." 31 Or what king will march to battle against another king, without first sitting down to consider whether with ten thousand men he can face an enemy coming to meet him with twenty thousand? 32 If he cannot, then, long before the enemy approaches, he sends envoys and asks for terms. 33 So also, if you are not prepared to leave all your possessions behind, you cannot be my disciples.

34 'Salt is good; but if salt itself becomes tasteless, how will it be seasoned? 35 It is useless either on the land or on the dungheap; it can only be thrown away. If you have ears to hear, then hear.'

14:5 **son:** *some witnesses read* donkey.

14.1–14: **Jesus, a guest of a Pharisee.** See Mk. 3.1–6 n. **5:** The Dead Sea community prohibited such activity on the sabbath. **8–10:** Compare Prov. 25.6–7. **11:** See 18.14; Matt. 23.12.

14.15–24: **The Great Supper** (Matt. 22.1–10). **15:** The *feast* was a frequently used symbol of the joy of the *kingdom;* see 13.28–29. **17:** The *servant* bears a customary courtesy reminder to guests who have been invited previously. **18:** The excuses which follow are not frivolous, but the master's anger (v. 21) is understandable since the guests had had a prior notice. **21, 23:** Luke probably means for the two groups to represent (a) sinners among the Jews and (b) Gentiles.

14.25–35: **The cost of discipleship. 26:** *Hate* probably means "love less"; see Matt. 10.37. **27:** *Carry . . . cross:* see 9.23 n.; Mk. 8.34 n.; Matt. 10.38; 16.24. **34–35:** Compare Matt. 5.13; Mk. 9.50.

Finding the lost

15 ANOTHER time, the tax-collectors and sinners were all crowding in to listen to him; [2] and the Pharisees and scribes began murmuring their disapproval: 'This fellow', they said, 'welcomes sinners and eats with them.' [3] He answered them with this parable: [4] 'If one of you has a hundred sheep and loses one of them, does he not leave the ninety-nine in the wilderness and go after the one that is missing until he finds it? [5] And when he does, he lifts it joyfully on to his shoulders, [6] and goes home to call his friends and neighbours together. "Rejoice with me!" he cries. "I have found my lost sheep." [7] In the same way, I tell you, there will be greater joy in heaven over one sinner who repents than over ninety-nine righteous people who do not need to repent.

[8] 'Or again, if a woman has ten silver coins and loses one of them, does she not light the lamp, sweep out the house, and look in every corner till she finds it? [9] And when she does, she calls her friends and neighbours together, and says, "Rejoice with me! I have found the coin that I lost." [10] In the same way, I tell you, there is joy among the angels of God over one sinner who repents.'

[11] Again he said: 'There was once a man who had two sons; [12] and the younger said to his father, "Father, give me my share of the property." So he divided his estate between them. [13] A few days later the younger son turned the whole of his share into cash and left home for a distant country, where he squandered it in dissolute living. [14] He had spent it all, when a severe famine fell upon that country and he began to be in need. [15] So he went and attached himself to one of the local landowners, who sent him on to his farm to mind the pigs. [16] He would have been glad to fill his belly with the pods that the pigs were eating, but no one gave him anything. [17] Then he came to his senses: "How many of my father's hired servants have more food than they can eat," he said, "and here am I, starving to death! [18] I will go at once to my father, and say to him, 'Father, I have sinned against God and against you; [19] I am no longer fit to be called your son; treat me as one of your hired servants.' " [20] So he set out for his father's house. But while he was still a long way off his father saw him, and his heart went out to him; he ran to meet him, flung his arms round him, and kissed him. [21] The son said, "Father, I have sinned against God and against you; I am no longer fit to be called your son." [22] But the father said to his servants, "Quick! Fetch a robe, the best we have, and put it on him; put a ring on his finger and sandals on his feet. [23] Bring the fatted calf and kill it, and let us celebrate with a feast. [24] For this son of mine was dead and has come back to life; he was lost and is found." And the festivities began.

[25] 'Now the elder son had been out on the farm; and on his way back, as he approached the house, he heard music and dancing. [26] He called one of the servants and asked what it meant. [27] The servant told him, "Your brother has come home, and your father has killed the fatted calf because he has him back safe and sound." [28] But he was angry and refused to go in. His father came out and pleaded with him; [29] but he retorted, "You know how I have slaved for you all these years; I never once disobeyed your orders; yet you never gave me so much as a kid, to celebrate with my friends. [30] But now that this son of yours turns up, after running through your money with his women, you kill the fatted calf for him." [31] "My boy," said the father, "you are always with me, and everything I have is yours. [32] How could we fail to celebrate this happy day? Your brother here was dead and has come back to life; he was lost and has been found." '

Instructing the disciples

16 HE said to his disciples, 'There was a rich man who had a steward, and he received complaints that this man was squan-

---

15.1–32: Joy over repentant sinners. 1–2: *Tax-collectors:* see Mk. 2.15 n. **3–7:** Luke doubtless preserves the parable's original concern for outcasts; Matt. 18.10–14 (and n.) applies it differently. **12:** The *younger* son's *share* would be one-third; see Deut. 21.17. **13:** The rate of emigration of Jews from Palestine to the urban centers of the Gentile world was very high. **15–16:** Since *pigs* are unclean animals, everything about the job would have been repugnant. **20–23:** *Kiss, robe, ring,* and *fatted calf* show that the son is not only forgiven, but received with honor. **31:** The elder son is still accepted.

16.1–31: The uses of wealth. Except for vv. 16–18, the traditional units in ch. 16 seem to have been dering the property. [2] So he sent for him, and said, "What is this that I hear about you? Produce your accounts, for you cannot be steward any longer." [3] The steward said to himself, "What am I to do now that my master is going to dismiss me from my post? I am not strong enough to dig, and I am too proud to beg. [4] I know what I must do, to make sure that, when I am dismissed, there will be people who will take me into their homes." [5] He summoned his master's debtors one by one. To the first he said, "How much do you owe my master?" [6] He replied, "A hundred jars of olive oil." He said, "Here is your account. Sit down and make it fifty, and be quick about it." [7] Then he said to another, "And you, how much do you owe?" He said, "A hundred measures of wheat," and was told, "Here is your account; make it eighty." [8] And the master applauded the dishonest steward for acting so astutely. For in dealing with their own kind the children of this world are more astute than the children of light.

[9] 'So I say to you, use your worldly wealth to win friends for yourselves, so that when money is a thing of the past you may be received into an eternal home.

[10] 'Anyone who can be trusted in small matters can be trusted also in great; and anyone who is dishonest in small matters is dishonest also in great. [11] If, then, you have not proved trustworthy with the wealth of this world, who will trust you with the wealth that is real? [12] And if you have proved untrustworthy with what belongs to another, who will give you anything of your own?

[13] 'No slave can serve two masters; for either he will hate the first and love the second, or he will be devoted to the first and despise the second. You cannot serve God and Money.'

[14] The Pharisees, who loved money, heard all this and scoffed at him. [15] He said to them, 'You are the people who impress others with your righteousness; but God sees through you; for what is considered admirable in human eyes is detestable in the sight of God.

[16] 'The law and the prophets were until John: since then, the good news of the kingdom of God is proclaimed, and everyone forces a way in.

[17] 'It is easier for heaven and earth to come to an end than for one letter of the law to lose its force.

[18] 'A man who divorces his wife and marries another commits adultery; and anyone who marries a woman divorced from her husband commits adultery.

[19] 'There was once a rich man, who used to dress in purple and the finest linen, and feasted sumptuously every day. [20] At his gate lay a poor man named Lazarus, who was covered with sores. [21] He would have been glad to satisfy his hunger with the scraps from the rich man's table. Dogs used to come and lick his sores. [22] One day the poor man died and was carried away by the angels to be with Abraham. The rich man also died and was buried. [23] In Hades, where he was in torment, he looked up and there, far away, was Abraham with Lazarus close beside him. [24] "Abraham, my father," he called out, "take pity on me! Send Lazarus to dip the tip of his finger in water, to cool my tongue, for I am in agony in this fire." [25] But Abraham said, "My child, remember that the good things fell to you in your lifetime, and the bad to Lazarus. Now he has his consolation here and it is you who are in agony. [26] But that is not all: there is a great gulf fixed between us; no one can cross it from our side to reach you, and none may pass from your side to us." [27] "Then, father," he replied, "will you send him to my father's house, [28] where I have five brothers, to warn them, so that they may not come to this place of torment?" [29] But Abraham said, "They have Moses and the prophets; let them listen to them." [30] "No, father Abraham," he re-

assembled around the theme of wealth. **1–8:** This very difficult parable about a *dishonest steward* (v. 8) commends a scoundrel for having the good sense to act decisively in a time of crisis. **8:** *Master* (lit. "lord") may refer either to the rich man who discharged his steward or to Jesus. *Children of light* (compare Jn. 12.36; 1 Thess. 5.5; Eph. 5.8) are inheritors of the new age; the Dead Sea sect used "children of light" as a designation of itself as the community of the elect. **9:** The saying perhaps commends dispensing *wealth* in acts of charity. **13:** Matt. 6.24. **16:** *John* (the Baptist) marks the dividing line between the age of anticipation and the age of salvation. It is not clear on which side of the line John himself stands for Lk.; compare Matt. 11.12–15 n. **17:** *Letter*, lit. "stroke"; see Matt. 5.18 n. **18:** On *divorce*, see notes on Matt. 5.31–32. **19–31:** The "rich man-poor man" motif is found in similar stories from other sources. The primary theme is the reversal of fortunes in the world to come for the poor (righteous) and the rich (unrighteous). Their fates are seen as a motive for repentance.

plied, "but if someone from the dead visits them, they will repent." [31] Abraham answered, "If they do not listen to Moses and the prophets they will pay no heed even if someone should rise from the dead."'

17 He said to his disciples, 'There are bound to be causes of stumbling; but woe betide the person through whom they come. [2] It would be better for him to be thrown into the sea with a millstone round his neck than to cause the downfall of one of these little ones. [3] So be on your guard.

'If your brother does wrong, reprove him; and if he repents, forgive him. [4] Even if he wrongs you seven times in a day and comes back to you seven times saying, "I am sorry," you are to forgive him.'

[5] The apostles said to the Lord, 'Increase our faith'; [6] and the Lord replied, 'If you had faith no bigger than a mustard seed, you could say to this mulberry tree, "Be rooted up and planted in the sea"; and it would obey you.

[7] 'Suppose one of you has a servant ploughing or minding sheep. When he comes in from the fields, will the master say, "Come and sit down straight away"? [8] Will he not rather say, "Prepare my supper; hitch up your robe, and wait on me while I have my meal. You can have yours afterwards"? [9] Is he grateful to the servant for carrying out his orders? [10] So with you: when you have carried out all you have been ordered to do, you should say, "We are servants and deserve no credit; we have only done our duty."'

[11] In the course of his journey to Jerusalem he was travelling through the borderlands of Samaria and Galilee. [12] As he was entering a village he was met by ten men with leprosy. They stood some way off [13] and called out to him, 'Jesus, Master, take pity on us.' [14] When he saw them he said, 'Go and show yourselves to the priests'; and while they were on their way, they were made clean. [15] One of them, finding himself cured, turned back with shouts of praise to God. [16] He threw himself down at Jesus's feet and thanked him. And he was a Samaritan. [17] At this Jesus said: 'Were not all ten made clean? The other nine, where are they? [18] Was no one found returning to give praise to God except this foreigner?' [19] And he said to the man, 'Stand up and go on your way; your faith has cured you.'

[20] The Pharisees asked him, 'When will the kingdom of God come?' He answered, 'You cannot tell by observation when the kingdom of God comes. [21] You cannot say, "Look, here it is," or "There it is!" For the kingdom of God is among you!'

[22] He said to the disciples, 'The time will come when you will long to see one of the days of the Son of Man and will not see it. [23] They will say to you, "Look! There!" and "Look! Here!" Do not go running off in pursuit. [24] For like a lightning-flash, that lights up the earth from end to end, will the Son of Man be in his day. [25] But first he must endure much suffering and be rejected by this generation.

17:21 **For . . . among you!:** *or* For the kingdom of God is within you! *or* For the kingdom of God is within your grasp! *or* For suddenly the kingdom of God will be among you.

29, 31: The two ages of v. 16 are suggested by the appeal, on the one hand, to *Moses and the prophets,* and the hint, on the other hand, of one who will *rise from the dead.*

17.1–10: Faithful discipleship. 1–2: See Matt. 18.6 n., 7–9 n.; Mk. 9.42. **3–4:** Compare Matt. 18.15, 21–22. The responsibility for righting a wrong between members of the Christian community lies with the one who is wronged (v. 3) and has no limits (v. 4). Luke does not have the church discipline provisions of Matt. 18.16–17. **5–6:** Compare Matt. 17.20. The hyperbole of a *faith* which uproots trees corresponds to the hyperbolic challenges of vv. 2, 4.

17.11–19: Ten lepers on the way. 11: *Journey to Jerusalem:* see 13.22–35 n. *Through the border lands of Samaria and Galilee* is an attempt to translate a Gk. phrase which is grammatically and geographically difficult; Lk. is more interested in the journey than in its precise itinerary. **12:** *Leprosy:* see Matt. 8.2 n. **16:** That a *Samaritan* should be the one to show gratitude is a surprise; see 9.52 n.; 10.33 n.

17.20–37: The coming of the kingdom. 21: The verse is sufficiently ambiguous to invite alternative translations (see Tfn. for this verse). Compare Matt. 24.23. The *when* of the Pharisee's question (v. 20) provides the unifying thread for vv. 20–37, so that Lk. appears to understand v. 21 in a manner consistent with the futuristic thrust of the remaining verses. **23–24:** Compare Matt. 24.26–27; Mk. 13.21. **24:** The coming of the *Son of*

26 'As it was in the days of Noah, so will it be in the days of the Son of Man. 27 They ate and drank and married, until the day that Noah went into the ark and the flood came and made an end of them all. 28 So too in the days of Lot, they ate and drank, they bought and sold, they planted and built; 29 but on the day that Lot left Sodom, fire and sulphur rained from the sky and made an end of them all. 30 It will be like that on the day when the Son of Man is revealed.

31 'On that day if anyone is on the roof while his belongings are in the house, he must not go down to fetch them; and if anyone is in the field, he must not turn back. 32 Remember Lot's wife. 33 Whoever seeks to preserve his life will lose it; and whoever loses his life will gain it.

34 'I tell you, on that night there will be two people in one bed: one will be taken, the other left. 35 There will be two women together grinding corn: one will be taken, the other left.' 37 When they heard this they asked, 'Where, Lord?' He said, 'Where the carcass is, there will the vultures gather.'

18 He told them a parable to show that they should keep on praying and never lose heart: 2 'In a certain city there was a judge who had no fear of God or respect for man, 3 and in the same city there was a widow who kept coming before him to demand justice against her opponent. 4 For a time he refused; but in the end he said to himself, "Although I have no fear of God or respect for man, 5 yet this widow is so great a nuisance that I will give her justice before she wears me out with her persistence." ' 6 The Lord said, 'You hear what the unjust judge says. 7 Then will not God give justice to his chosen, to whom he listens patiently while

they cry out to him day and night? 8 I tell you, he will give them justice soon enough. But when the Son of Man comes, will he find faith on earth?'

9 Here is another parable that he told; it was aimed at those who were sure of their own goodness and looked down on everyone else. 10 'Two men went up to the temple to pray, one a Pharisee and the other a tax-collector. 11 The Pharisee stood up and prayed this prayer: "I thank you, God, that I am not like the rest of mankind — greedy, dishonest, adulterous — or, for that matter, like this tax-collector. 12 I fast twice a week; I pay tithes on all that I get." 13 But the other kept his distance and would not even raise his eyes to heaven, but beat upon his breast, saying, "God, have mercy on me, sinner that I am." 14 It was this man, I tell you, and not the other, who went home acquitted of his sins. For everyone who exalts himself will be humbled; and whoever humbles himself will be exalted.'

15 They brought babies for him to touch, and when the disciples saw them they rebuked them. 16 But Jesus called for the children and said, 'Let the children come to me; do not try to stop them; for the kingdom of God belongs to such as these. 17 Truly I tell you: whoever does not accept the kingdom of God like a child will never enter it.'

18 One of the rulers put this question to him: 'Good Teacher, what must I do to win eternal life?' 19 Jesus said to him, 'Why do you call me good? No one is good except God alone. 20 You know the commandments: "Do not commit adultery; do not murder; do not steal; do not give false evidence; honour your

17:35 **the other left:** *some witnesses add* 36 'There will be two men in the fields: one will be taken, the other left.'

Man (see Mk. 2.10 n.) will leave no room for guesses (v. 23), but will be self-illuminating. **27:** Matt. 24.37–39. Noah: Gen. chs. 6–7. **28–32:** *The days of Lot:* Gen. 19.1–29. **31:** Matt. 24.17–18; Mk. 13.15–16. **33:** The reference to *Lot's wife* (v. 32) gives the saying about saving and losing life an unusual setting; see Matt. 10.38–39 n. **34–35:** Matt. 24.40–41. **37:** Matt. 24.28.

   18.1–17: Preparation for the kingdom. 1: To *keep on praying* is a familiar theme (3.21 n.); *never to lose heart* may indicate that this parable is meant for a time of trouble (perhaps of persecution, vv. 6–7). **6–7:** The point is not that God must be worn down like the unjust judge, but rather that the prayers of the *chosen* will surely be heard by the Righteous Judge. Compare 11.11–13. **10:** *Pharisee:* Matt. 3.7 n. *Tax-collector:* Lk. 3.12 n. **11–12:** For the original hearers, the Pharisee would be a genuinely good man, fasting far beyond the Law's requirements, tithing above the literal commandment (Deut. 14.22–29). **14:** The *tax-collector,* who acknowledges sin and repents, is *acquitted;* see 15.7, 10. **15–17:** Matt. 19.13–15; 18.3; Mk. 10.13–16. For the first time since 9.51 Lk. again takes up the content and order of Mk.

   18.18–30: Possessions and the kingdom (Matt. 19.16–30; Mk. 10.17–31). **18–20a:** See Matt. 19.16–17 n.

father and mother." ' 21 The man answered, 'I have kept all these since I was a boy.' 22 On hearing this Jesus said, 'There is still one thing you lack: sell everything you have and give to the poor, and you will have treasure in heaven; then come and follow me.' 23 When he heard this his heart sank, for he was a very rich man. 24 When Jesus saw it he said, 'How hard it is for the wealthy to enter the kingdom of God! 25 It is easier for a camel to go through the eye of a needle than for a rich man to enter the kingdom of God.' 26 Those who heard asked, 'Then who can be saved?' 27 He answered, 'What is impossible for men is possible for God.'

28 Peter said, 'What about us? We left all we had to follow you.' 29 Jesus said to them, 'Truly I tell you: there is no one who has given up home, or wife, brothers, parents, or children, for the sake of the kingdom of God, 30 who will not be repaid many times over in this age, and in the age to come have eternal life.'

Jesus's challenge to Jerusalem

31 He took the Twelve aside and said, 'We are now going up to Jerusalem; and everything that was written by the prophets will find its fulfilment in the Son of Man. 32 He will be handed over to the Gentiles. He will be mocked, maltreated, and spat upon; 33 they will flog him and kill him; and on the third day he will rise again.' 34 But they did not understand this at all or grasp what he was talking about; its meaning was concealed from them.

35 As he approached Jericho a blind man sat at the roadside begging. 36 Hearing a crowd going past, he asked what was happen-

ing, 37 and was told that Jesus of Nazareth was passing by. 38 Then he called out, 'Jesus, Son of David, have pity on me.' 39 The people in front told him to hold his tongue; but he shouted all the more, 'Son of David, have pity on me.' 40 Jesus stopped and ordered the man to be brought to him. When he came up Jesus asked him, 41 'What do you want me to do for you?' 'Sir, I want my sight back,' he answered. 42 Jesus said to him, 'Have back your sight; your faith has healed you.' 43 He recovered his sight instantly and followed Jesus, praising God. And all the people gave praise to God for what they had seen.

19 Entering Jericho he made his way through the city. 2 There was a man there named Zacchaeus; he was superintendent of taxes and very rich. 3 He was eager to see what Jesus looked like; but, being a little man, he could not see him for the crowd. 4 So he ran on ahead and climbed a sycamore tree in order to see him, for he was to pass that way. 5 When Jesus came to the place, he looked up and said, 'Zacchaeus, be quick and come down, for I must stay at your house today.' 6 He climbed down as quickly as he could and welcomed him gladly. 7 At this there was a general murmur of disapproval. 'He has gone in to be the guest of a sinner,' they said. 8 But Zacchaeus stood there and said to the Lord, 'Here and now, sir, I give half my possessions to charity; and if I have defrauded anyone, I will repay him four times over.' 9 Jesus said to him, 'Today salvation has come to this house — for this man too is a son of Abraham. 10 The Son of Man has come to seek and to save what is lost.'

11 While they were listening to this, he went on to tell them a parable, because he was now close to Jerusalem and they thought the king-

---

18: Only Lk. makes the questioner a *ruler*. **20:** Exod. 20.12–16; Deut. 5.16–20. **22:** See Matt. 19.21 n. **25, 27:** On *camel, needle,* see Matt. 19.24 n. **28–30:** See Matt. 19.27, 29 n.

18.31–34: The third prediction of suffering. See 9.22, 44–45; Matt. 20.17–19; Mk. 10.32–34 n.

18.35–43: A blind man healed (Matt. 20.29–34; Mk. 10.46–52). **38:** *Son of David:* see Matt. 1.1 n. **42:** *Healed:* see 7.50 n. **43:** *Followed:* see Mk. 10.52 n.

19.1–10: Zacchaeus. 2: *Superintendent of taxes:* see 3.12 n. **7:** *Guest of a sinner:* see Mk. 2.15 n. On the restitution of illegal gain, see Lev. 6.1–7.

19.11–27: The parable of the pounds (compare Matt. 25.14–30). The use of the term "pounds" in English titles of this parable reflects the fact that the *sum of money* (v. 13) given the servants in Lk.'s version is modest; in contrast, Matt.'s parable of the "talents" speaks of enormous amounts (see Matt. 25.14–30 n.). **11:** *Close to Jerusalem* is the last of several notices which serve the "journey theme"; with v. 27 Lk.'s special section comes to a close (see 9.51–19.27 n.). Luke employs the parabolic tradition to prepare for (apparent) defeat rather than (immediate) victory in Jerusalem and to encourage patient and trustworthy service while waiting for the dom of God might dawn at any moment. ¹²He said, 'A man of noble birth went on a long journey abroad, to have himself appointed king and then return. ¹³But first he called ten of his servants and gave them each a sum of money, saying, "Trade with this while I am away." ¹⁴His fellow-citizens hated him and sent a delegation after him to say, "We do not want this man as our king." ¹⁵He returned however as king, and sent for the servants to whom he had given the money, to find out what profit each had made. ¹⁶The first came and said, "Your money, sir, has increased tenfold." ¹⁷"Well done," he replied; "you are a good servant. Because you have shown yourself trustworthy in a very small matter, you shall have charge of ten cities." ¹⁸The second came and said, "Your money, sir, has increased fivefold"; ¹⁹and he was told, "You shall be in charge of five cities." ²⁰The third came and said, "Here is your money, sir; I kept it wrapped up in a handkerchief. ²¹I was afraid of you, because you are a hard man: you draw out what you did not put in and reap what you did not sow." ²²"You scoundrel!" he replied. "I will condemn you out of your own mouth. You knew me to be a hard man, did you, drawing out what I never put in, and reaping what I did not sow? ²³Then why did you not put my money on deposit, and I could have claimed it with interest when I came back?" ²⁴Turning to his attendants he said, "Take the money from him and give it to the man with the most." ²⁵"But, sir," they replied, "he has ten times as much already." ²⁶"I tell you," he said, "everyone who has will be given more; but whoever has nothing will forfeit even what he has. ²⁷But as for those enemies of mine who did not want me for their king,

bring them here and slaughter them in my presence."'

²⁸WITH that Jesus set out on the ascent to Jerusalem. ²⁹As he approached Bethphage and Bethany at the hill called Olivet, he sent off two of the disciples, ³⁰telling them: 'Go into the village opposite; as you enter it you will find tethered there a colt which no one has yet ridden. Untie it and bring it here. ³¹If anyone asks why you are untying it, say, "The Master needs it." ' ³²The two went on their errand and found everything just as he had told them. ³³As they were untying the colt, its owners asked, 'Why are you untying that colt?' ³⁴They answered, 'The Master needs it.'

³⁵So they brought the colt to Jesus, and threw their cloaks on it for Jesus to mount. ³⁶As he went along people laid their cloaks on the road. ³⁷And when he reached the descent from the mount of Olives, the whole company of his disciples in their joy began to sing aloud the praises of God for all the great things they had seen:

³⁸'Blessed is he who comes as king in the
        name of the Lord!
    Peace in heaven, glory in highest
        heaven!'

³⁹Some Pharisees in the crowd said to him, 'Teacher, restrain your disciples.' ⁴⁰He answered, 'I tell you, if my disciples are silent the stones will shout aloud.'

⁴¹When he came in sight of the city, he wept over it ⁴²and said, 'If only you had known this day the way that leads to peace! But no; it is hidden from your sight. ⁴³For a time will come upon you, when your enemies

kingdom. **12 (also 15, 27):** The *noble* person on a *journey abroad,* to be *appointed king* may be an allusion to some historical incident involving Rome and a member of the Herodian dynasty. However, the rejected *king* (vv. 15, 27) of Lk. is intended allegorically as a reference to the Messiah. **13:** The *ten servants* introduced here dwindle to three in vv. 16, 18, 20; Matt. 25.14–15 also has only three.

19.28–21.38: Jesus in Jerusalem (Matt. 21.1–25.46; Mk. 11.1–13.37). See Mk. 11.1–13.37 n.

19.28–40: The entry into Jerusalem (Matt. 21.1–9; Mk. 11.1–11; Jn. 12.12–15). **28:** The *ascent to Jerusalem* marks the end of the "travel narrative" (see 9.51–19.27 n.) and the beginning of the final stage of Jesus' ministry. In Jerusalem, the Holy City, Jesus' Sonship is fully revealed and the stage is set for the new beginning which Acts reports (see Introduction). **29:** *Olivet:* see Matt. 21.1 n. **38:** Ps. 118.26; Lk. has Jesus acclaimed as *king* without mention of David (compare Matt. 21.9; Mk. 11.10), perhaps to emphasize that Jesus is more than a Davidic ruler (see 20.41–44). *Peace, glory* recall the angelic hymn in 2.14.

19.41–44: Prediction of Jerusalem's destruction. Luke writes after the fall of Jerusalem (70 C.E.), but the language of this oracle is natural to the threatened destruction (compare Ps. 137.9; Isa. 29.3–4; Jer. 6.6–8).

will set up siege-works against you; they will encircle you and hem you in at every point; [44]they will bring you to the ground, you and your children within your walls, and not leave you one stone standing on another, because you did not recognize the time of God's visitation.'

[45]Then he went into the temple and began driving out the traders, [46]with these words: 'Scripture says, "My house shall be a house of prayer"; but you have made it a bandits' cave.'

[47]Day by day he taught in the temple. The chief priests and scribes, with the support of the leading citizens, wanted to bring about his death, [48]but found they were helpless, because the people all hung on his words.

20 ONE day, as he was teaching the people in the temple and telling them the good news, the chief priests and scribes, accompanied by the elders, confronted him. [2]'Tell us', they said, 'by what authority you are acting like this; who gave you this authority?' [3]He answered them, 'I also have a question for you: tell me, [4]was the baptism of John from God or from man?' [5]This set them arguing among themselves: 'If we say, "From God," he will say, "Why did you not believe him?" [6]And if we say, "From man," the people will all stone us, for they are convinced that John was a prophet.' [7]So they answered that they could not tell. [8]And Jesus said to them, 'Then neither will I tell you by what authority I act.'

[9]He went on to tell the people this parable: 'A man planted a vineyard, let it out to vine-growers, and went abroad for a long time. [10]When the season came, he sent a servant to the tenants to collect from them his share of the produce; but the tenants thrashed him and sent him away empty-handed. [11]He tried again and sent a second servant; but they thrashed him too, treated him outrageously, and sent him away empty-handed. [12]He tried once more and sent a third; him too they wounded and flung out. [13]Then the owner of the vineyard said, "What am I to do? I will send my beloved son; perhaps they will respect him." [14]But when the tenants saw him they discussed what they should do. "This is the heir," they said; "let us kill him so that the inheritance may come to us." [15]So they flung him out of the vineyard and killed him. What, therefore, will the owner of the vineyard do to them? [16]He will come and put those tenants to death and give the vineyard to others.'

When they heard this, they said, 'God forbid!' [17]But he looked straight at them and said, 'Then what does this text of scripture mean: "The stone which the builders rejected has become the main corner-stone"? [18]Everyone who falls on that stone will be dashed to pieces; anyone on whom it falls will be crushed.'

[19]The scribes and chief priests wanted to seize him there and then, for they saw that this parable was aimed at them; but they were afraid of the people. [20]So they watched their opportunity and sent agents in the guise of honest men, to seize on some word of his that they could use as a pretext for handing him over to the authority and jurisdiction of the governor. [21]They put a question to him: 'Teacher,' they said, 'we know that what you speak and teach is sound; you pay deference to no one, but teach in all sincerity the way of life that God requires. [22]Are we or are we not permitted to pay taxes to the Roman emperor?' [23]He saw through their trick and said, [24]'Show me a silver piece. Whose head does it bear, and whose inscription?' 'Caesar's,' they replied. [25]'Very well then,' he said, 'pay to Caesar what belongs to Caesar, and to God what belongs to God.' [26]Thus their attempt to catch him out in public failed, and, taken aback by his reply, they fell silent.

[27]Then some Sadducees, who deny that

20:13 **my beloved son:** *or* my only son.

19.45–48: Cleansing of the temple (Matt. 21.10–17; Mk. 11.15–19; compare Jn. 2.12–22). See notes at parallel passages. **47–48:** Although relating the cleansing episode very briefly, Lk. depicts Jesus as "in control" of the temple.

20.1–8: Jesus' authority challenged (Matt. 21.23–27; Mk. 11.27–33). **4:** *From God:* see Matt. 21.25 n. **6:** *Prophet:* see Mk. 8.28 n.

20.9–18: The evil tenants (Matt. 21.33–43; Mk. 12.1–11). **9:** On *parable, vineyard,* see Matt. 21.33 n. **10:** On *servant, tenants,* see Matt. 21.34 n. **13:** *Son:* Jesus. **17:** Ps. 118.22; see Mk. 12.10–11 n. **18:** Isa. 8.14–15.

20.19–26: Caesar's tax (Matt. 22.15–22; Mk. 12.13–17). **22:** *Taxes:* see Matt. 22.17 n.

20.27–40: A resurrection puzzle (Matt. 22.23–33; Mk. 12.18–27). **27:** *Sadducees:* see Matt. 3.7 n.

there is a resurrection, came forward and asked: 28'Teacher, Moses laid it down for us that if there are brothers, and one dies leaving a wife but no child, then the next should marry the widow and provide an heir for his brother. 29 Now, there were seven brothers: the first took a wife and died childless; 30 then the second married her, 31 then the third. In this way the seven of them died leaving no children. 32 Last of all the woman also died. 33 At the resurrection, therefore, whose wife is she to be, since all seven had married her?' 34 Jesus said to them, 'The men and women of this world marry; 35 but those who have been judged worthy of a place in the other world, and of the resurrection from the dead, do not marry, 36 for they are no longer subject to death. They are like angels; they are children of God, because they share in the resurrection. 37 That the dead are raised to life again is shown by Moses himself in the story of the burning bush, when he calls the Lord "the God of Abraham, the God of Isaac, the God of Jacob". 38 God is not God of the dead but of the living; in his sight all are alive.'

39 At this some of the scribes said, 'Well spoken, Teacher.' 40 And nobody dared put any further question to him.

41 He said to them, 'How can they say that the Messiah is David's son? 42 For David himself says in the book of Psalms: "The Lord said to my Lord, 'Sit at my right hand 43 until I make your enemies your footstool.'" 44 Thus David calls him "Lord"; how then can he be David's son?'

45 In the hearing of all the people Jesus said to his disciples: 46 'Beware of the scribes, who like to walk up and down in long robes, and love to be greeted respectfully in the street, to have the chief seats in synagogues and places of honour at feasts. 47 These are the men who eat up the property of widows, while for appearance' sake they say long prayers; the sentence they receive will be all the more severe.'

Warnings about the end

21 As Jesus looked up and saw rich people dropping their gifts into the chest of the temple treasury, 2 he noticed a poor widow putting in two tiny coins. 3 'I tell you this,' he said: 'this poor widow has given more than any of them; 4 for those others who have given had more than enough, but she, with less than enough, has given all she had to live on.'

5 Some people were talking about the temple and the beauty of its fine stones and ornaments. He said, 6 'These things you are gazing at—the time will come when not one stone will be left upon another; they will all be thrown down.' 7 'Teacher,' they asked, 'when will that be? What will be the sign that these things are about to happen?'

8 He said, 'Take care that you are not misled. For many will come claiming my name and saying, "I am he," and, "The time has come." Do not follow them. 9 And when you hear of wars and insurrections, do not panic. These things are bound to happen first; but the end does not follow at once.' 10 Then he added, 'Nation will go to war against nation, kingdom against kingdom; 11 there will be severe earthquakes, famines and plagues in many places, and in the sky terrors and great portents.

12 'But before all this happens they will seize you and persecute you. You will be handed over to synagogues and put in prison; you will be haled before kings and governors for your allegiance to me. 13 This

---

28: Deut. 25.5–10. **35–36:** The mode of existence in the new age will be completely different than in this age. **36:** *Angels* are sometimes called *children of God* in the OT. **37:** Exod. 3.6.

20.41–44: Messiah, son of David (Matt. 22.41–46; Mk. 12.35–37). **41:** *Messiah . . . David's son:* see Matt. 1.1 n. **42–43:** Ps. 110.1; see Matt. 22.44 n. **44:** See Matt. 22.45 n.

20.45–47: Warning against pride. 46: 11.43; Matt. 23.6; Mk. 12.38–40.

21.1–4: The widow's gift (Mk. 12.41–44). **1:** Several *chests* were located in the section of the temple open to Jewish women. **2:** The value of the *coins* was too small to be meaningfully defined in terms of modern currency.

21.5–38: The eschatological discourse. See Mk. 13.1–37 n. **5–7:** The temple's destruction: see Matt. 24.1–3 n.; Mk. 13.1–4.

21.8–36: Signs, false signs, and warnings (Matt. 24.4–44; Mk. 13.5–7). **8:** 17.23; see Matt. 24.4–5 n.

will be your opportunity to testify. 14 So resolve not to prepare your defence beforehand, 15 because I myself will give you such words and wisdom as no opponent can resist or refute. 16 Even your parents and brothers, your relations and friends, will betray you. Some of you will be put to death; 17 and everyone will hate you for your allegiance to me. 18 But not a hair of your head will be lost. 19 By standing firm you will win yourselves life.

20 'But when you see Jerusalem encircled by armies, then you may be sure that her devastation is near. 21 Then those who are in Judaea must take to the hills; those who are in the city itself must leave it, and those who are out in the country must not return; 22 because this is the time of retribution, when all that stands written is to be fulfilled. 23 Alas for women with child in those days, and for those who have children at the breast! There will be great distress in the land and a terrible judgement on this people. 24 They will fall by the sword; they will be carried captive into all countries; and Jerusalem will be trampled underfoot by Gentiles until the day of the Gentiles has run its course.

25 'Portents will appear in sun and moon and stars. On earth nations will stand helpless, not knowing which way to turn from the roar and surge of the sea. 26 People will faint with terror at the thought of all that is coming upon the world; for the celestial powers will be shaken. 27 Then they will see the Son of Man coming in a cloud with power and great glory. 28 When all this begins to happen, stand upright and hold your heads high, because your liberation is near.'

29 He told them a parable: 'Look at the fig tree, or at any other tree. 30 As soon as it buds,

you can see for yourselves that summer is near. 31 In the same way, when you see all this happening, you may know that the kingdom of God is near.

32 'Truly I tell you: the present generation will live to see it all. 33 Heaven and earth will pass away, but my words will never pass away.

34 'Be on your guard; do not let your minds be dulled by dissipation and drunkenness and worldly cares so that the great day catches you suddenly 35 like a trap; for that day will come on everyone, the whole world over. 36 Be on the alert, praying at all times for strength to pass safely through all that is coming and to stand in the presence of the Son of Man.'

37 His days were given to teaching in the temple; every evening he would leave the city and spend the night on the hill called Olivet. 38 And in the early morning the people flocked to listen to him in the temple.

The last supper

22 The festival of Unleavened Bread, known as Passover, was approaching, 2 and the chief priests and the scribes were trying to devise some means of doing away with him; for they were afraid of the people.

3 Then Satan entered into Judas, who was called Iscariot, one of the Twelve; 4 and he went to the chief priests and temple guards to discuss ways of betraying Jesus to them. 5 They were glad and undertook to pay him a sum of money. 6 He agreed, and began to look for an opportunity to betray him to them without collecting a crowd.

7 Then came the day of Unleavened Bread,

21:38 **in the temple:** *some witnesses here insert the passage printed on p. 1393.*

12–17: Matt. 10.17–22. **14–15:** 12.11–12; Acts 6.10. **16:** 12.52–53. **17:** Matt. 10.22. **18:** 12.7; Matt. 10.30; Acts 27.34. **20:** Luke speaks, not of a cryptic "abomination of desolation" (Matt. 24.15 n.), but directly of the siege of Jerusalem in 70 C.E. **22:** Deut. 32.35. **24:** Isa. 63.18; Zech. 12.3 (Sept.). **25–26:** See Matt. 24.29 n. **27:** Dan. 7.13. **32:** 9.27; see Matt. 24.34 n. **33:** 16.17.

21.37–38: Summary. Luke apparently thinks of the final period in Jerusalem as longer than the "week" of Mk. (see Mk. 11.1–13.37 n.).

22.1–23.56: The final conflict (Matt. 26.1–27.66; Mk. 14.1–15.47; Jn. chs. 12–19). While individual episodes (e.g. 23.27–31) can be removed from the narrative leading up to the crucifixion, the outline of the passion story appears to have been fixed quite early and is carried by all four Gospels in much the same form. However, Lk. and Jn., when compared with Matt.-Mk., show sufficient dissimilarity in detail as to suggest the existence of more than one passion tradition. **1:** See Mk. 14.1 n. **3–6:** Matt. 26.14–16; Mk. 14.10–11. **3:** See 4.13 n.; *Satan* is not mentioned as the agent in Matt. or Mk.; compare Jn. 6.70–71; 13.2, 27.

22.7–13: Preparation for the Passover (Matt. 26.17–19; Mk. 14.12–16). **7–8:** See Matt. 26.17–19 n.

on which the Passover lambs had to be slaughtered, [8] and Jesus sent off Peter and John, saying, 'Go and prepare the Passover supper for us.' [9] 'Where would you like us to make the preparations?' they asked. [10] He replied, 'As soon as you set foot in the city a man will meet you carrying a jar of water. Follow him into the house that he enters [11] and give this message to the householder: "The Teacher says, 'Where is the room in which I am to eat the Passover with my disciples?' " [12] He will show you a large room upstairs all set out: make the preparations there.' [13] They went and found everything as he had said. So they prepared for Passover.

[14] When the hour came he took his place at table, and the apostles with him; [15] and he said to them, 'How I have longed to eat this Passover with you before my death! [16] For I tell you, never again shall I eat it until the time when it finds its fulfilment in the kingdom of God.'

[17] Then he took a cup, and after giving thanks he said, 'Take this and share it among yourselves; [18] for I tell you, from this moment I shall not drink the fruit of the vine until the time when the kingdom of God comes.' [19] Then he took bread, and after giving thanks he broke it, and gave it to them with the words: 'This is my body.

[21] 'Even now my betrayer is here, his hand with mine on the table. [22] For the Son of Man is going his appointed way; but alas for that man by whom he is betrayed!' [23] At that they began to ask among themselves which of them it could possibly be who was to do this.

[24] Then a dispute began as to which of them should be considered the greatest. [25] But he said, 'Among the Gentiles, kings lord it over their subjects; and those in authority are given the title Benefactor. [26] Not so with you: on the contrary, the greatest among you must bear himself like the youngest, the one who rules like one who serves. [27] For who is greater—the one who sits at table or the servant who waits on him? Surely

the one who sits at table. Yet I am among you like a servant.

[28] 'You have stood firmly by me in my times of trial; [29] and I now entrust to you the kingdom which my Father entrusted to me; [30] in my kingdom you shall eat and drink at my table and sit on thrones as judges of the twelve tribes of Israel.

[31] 'Simon, Simon, take heed: Satan has been given leave to sift all of you like wheat; [32] but I have prayed for you, Simon, that your faith may not fail; and when you are restored, give strength to your brothers.' [33] 'Lord,' he replied, 'I am ready to go with you to prison and to death.' [34] Jesus said, 'I tell you, Peter, the cock will not crow tonight until you have denied three times over that you know me.'

[35] He said to them, 'When I sent you out barefoot without purse or pack, were you ever short of anything?' 'No,' they answered. [36] 'It is different now,' he said; 'whoever has a purse had better take it with him, and his pack too; and if he has no sword, let him sell his cloak to buy one. [37] For scripture says, "And he was reckoned among transgressors," and this, I tell you, must be fulfilled in me; indeed, all that is written of me is reaching its fulfilment.' [38] 'Lord,' they said, 'we have two swords here.' 'Enough!' he replied.

[39] THEN he went out and made his way as usual to the mount of Olives, accompanied by the disciples. [40] When he reached the place he said to them, 'Pray that you may be spared the test.' [41] He himself withdrew from them about a stone's throw, knelt down, and began to pray: [42] 'Father, if it be your will, take this

22:16 **For ... shall I:** *some witnesses read* But I tell you, I shall not.   22:19 **my body:** *some witnesses add, in whole or in part, and with various arrangements, the following:* 'which is given for you; do this as a memorial of me.' [20] In the same way he took the cup after supper, and said, 'This cup, poured out for you, is the new covenant sealed by my blood.'   22:29–30 **and I now ... and sit:** *or* and as my Father gave me the right to reign, so I give you the right to eat and to drink at my table in my kingdom and to sit.

10–12: See Matt. 26.18 n.

22.14–38: The Last Supper (Matt. 26.20–29; Mk. 14.17–21). **15–20:** See also 1 Cor. 11.23–26. **17–19:** Luke apparently follows a special tradition which places the cup ahead of the loaf. If the variant in Tfn. for v. 19 represents the original text, the *new covenant* (v. 20) refers to Jer. 31.31; see Matt. 26.28 n. **21–23:** See also Jn. 13.21–30. **24–26:** Matt. 20.25–28; Mk. 10.42–45. **29:** Compare Acts 1.6–8. **30:** Matt. 19.28. **31–34:** Matt. 26.30–35 (see 33–35 n.); Mk. 14.26–31; Jn. 13.36–38. **31:** 4.13 n. **35:** 10.4. **37:** Isa. 53.12.

22.39–46: Gethsemane (Matt. 26.30–46; Mk. 14.26–42). **39:** Jn. 18.1. **40–46:** Several elements in this cup from me. Yet not my will but yours be done.'

[43] And now there appeared to him an angel from heaven bringing him strength, [44] and in anguish of spirit he prayed the more urgently; and his sweat was like drops of blood falling to the ground.

[45] When he rose from prayer and came to the disciples he found them asleep, worn out by grief. [46] 'Why are you sleeping?' he said. 'Rise and pray that you may be spared the test.'

The trial and crucifixion of Jesus

[47] WHILE he was still speaking a crowd appeared with the man called Judas, one of the Twelve, at their head. He came up to Jesus to kiss him; [48] but Jesus said, 'Judas, would you betray the Son of Man with a kiss?'

[49] When his followers saw what was coming, they said, 'Lord, shall we use our swords?' [50] And one of them struck at the high priest's servant, cutting off his right ear. [51] But Jesus answered, 'Stop! No more of that!' Then he touched the man's ear and healed him.

[52] Turning to the chief priests, the temple guards, and the elders, who had come to seize him, he said, 'Do you take me for a robber, that you have come out with swords and cudgels? [53] Day after day, I have been with you in the temple, and you did not raise a hand against me. But this is your hour — when darkness reigns.'

[54] Then they arrested him and led him away. They brought him to the high priest's house, and Peter followed at a distance. [55] They lit a fire in the middle of the courtyard and sat round it, and Peter sat among them. [56] A serving-maid who saw him sitting in the firelight stared at him and said, 'This man was with him too.' [57] But he denied it: 'I do not know him,' he said. [58] A little later a man noticed him and said, 'You also are one

of them.' But Peter said to him, 'No, I am not.' [59] About an hour passed and someone else spoke more strongly still: 'Of course he was with him. He must have been; he is a Galilean.' [60] But Peter said, 'I do not know what you are talking about.' At that moment, while he was still speaking, a cock crowed; [61] and the Lord turned and looked at Peter. Peter remembered the Lord's words, 'Tonight before the cock crows you will disown me three times.' [62] And he went outside, and wept bitterly.

[63] The men who were guarding Jesus mocked him. They beat him, [64] they blindfolded him, and kept asking him, 'If you are a prophet, tell us who hit you.' [65] And so they went on heaping insults upon him.

[66] As SOON as it was day, the elders of the people, chief priests, and scribes assembled, and he was brought before their Council. [67] 'Tell us,' they said, 'are you the Messiah?' 'If I tell you,' he replied, 'you will not believe me; [68] and if I ask questions, you will not answer. [69] But from now on, the Son of Man will be seated at the right hand of Almighty God.' [70] 'You are the Son of God, then?' they all said, and he replied, 'It is you who say I am.' [71] At that they said, 'What further evidence do we need? We have heard this ourselves from his own lips.'

23 With that the whole assembly rose and brought him before Pilate. [2] They opened the case against him by saying, 'We found this man subverting our nation, opposing the payment of taxes to Caesar, and claiming to be Messiah, a king.' [3] Pilate asked him, 'Are you the king of the Jews?' He replied, 'The words are yours.' [4] Pilate then said to the chief priests and the crowd, 'I find no case for this man to answer.' [5] But they

22:43–44 *Some witnesses omit* And now . . . ground.
22:51 **Stop! No more of that:** *or* Let them have their way.　　22:69 **of Almighty God:** *lit.* of the Power of God.
22:70 **It is . . . I am:** *or* You are right, for I am.
23:3 **The words are yours:** *or* It is as you say.

scene are reminiscent of the Lord's Prayer (e.g. vv. 40, 42, 46). **42:** *Cup:* see Mk. 10.38 n.

　　22.47–53: The arrest (Matt. 26.47–56; Mk. 14.43–52; Jn. 18.2–11). **47:** *Kiss:* see Matt. 26.48 n. **50:** *One:* see Matt. 26.51 n.

　　22.54–71: Before the Jewish authorities (Matt. 26.57–75; Mk. 14.53–72; Jn. 18.12–27). See Matt. 26.57–75 n. **61:** Compare v. 34. **63–65:** See Matt. 26.67–68; Mk. 14.65. **66:** *Council:* see Matt. 26.59 n. **67, 70:** *Messiah, Son:* see Matt. 1.1 n.; 16.16 n. **69:** Dan. 7.13; Ps. 110.1. *Son of Man:* see Mk. 2.10 n.

　　23.1–25: Before Roman authority (Matt. 27.1–31; Mk. 15.1–20; Jn. 18.28–19.16). **1:** *Pilate:* see 3.1 n. **2:** *Opposing payment* of Roman *taxes* and *claiming* to be *king* are obviously seditious; Lk. has made the charge quite clear (see v. 14). **4:** In Lk., Pilate pronounces Jesus innocent three times in the course of the hearing (vv. 4, insisted: 'His teaching is causing unrest among the people all over Judaea. It started from Galilee and now has spread here.'

6 When Pilate heard this, he asked if the man was a Galilean, 7 and on learning that he belonged to Herod's jurisdiction he remitted the case to him, for Herod was also in Jerusalem at that time. 8 When Herod saw Jesus he was greatly pleased; he had heard about him and had long been wanting to see him in the hope of witnessing some miracle performed by him. 9 He questioned him at some length without getting any reply; 10 but the chief priests and scribes appeared and pressed the case against him vigorously. 11 Then Herod and his troops treated him with contempt and ridicule, and sent him back to Pilate dressed in a gorgeous robe. 12 That same day Herod and Pilate became friends; till then there had been a feud between them.

13 Pilate now summoned the chief priests, councillors, and people, 14 and said to them, 'You brought this man before me on a charge of subversion. But, as you see, I have myself examined him in your presence and found nothing in him to support your charges. 15 No more did Herod, for he has referred him back to us. Clearly he has done nothing to deserve death. 16 I therefore propose to flog him and let him go.' 18 But there was a general outcry. 'Away with him! Set Barabbas free!' 19 (Now Barabbas had been put in prison for his part in a rising in the city and for murder.) 20 Pilate addressed them again, in his desire to release Jesus, 21 but they shouted back, 'Crucify him, crucify him!' 22 For the third time he spoke to them: 'Why, what wrong has he done? I have not found him guilty of any capital offence. I will therefore flog him and let him go.' 23 But they persisted with their demand, shouting that Jesus should be crucified. Their shouts prevailed, 24 and Pilate decided that they should have their way. 25 He released the man they asked for, the man who had been put in prison for insurrection and murder, and gave Jesus over to their will.

26 As THEY led him away to execution they

took hold of a man called Simon, from Cyrene, on his way in from the country; putting the cross on his back they made him carry it behind Jesus.

27 Great numbers of people followed, among them many women who mourned and lamented over him. 28 Jesus turned to them and said, 'Daughters of Jerusalem, do not weep for me; weep for yourselves and your children. 29 For the days are surely coming when people will say, "Happy are the barren, the wombs that never bore a child, the breasts that never fed one." 30 Then they will begin to say to the mountains, "Fall on us," and to the hills, "Cover us." 31 For if these things are done when the wood is green, what will happen when it is dry?'

32 There were two others with him, criminals who were being led out to execution; 33 and when they reached the place called The Skull, they crucified him there, and the criminals with him, one on his right and the other on his left. 34 Jesus said, 'Father, forgive them; they do not know what they are doing.'

They shared out his clothes by casting lots. 35 The people stood looking on, and their rulers jeered at him: 'He saved others: now let him save himself, if this is God's Messiah, his Chosen.' 36 The soldiers joined in the mockery and came forward offering him sour wine. 37 'If you are the king of the Jews,' they said, 'save yourself.' 38 There was an inscription above his head which ran: 'This is the king of the Jews.'

39 One of the criminals hanging there taunted him: 'Are not you the Messiah? Save yourself, and us.' 40 But the other rebuked him: 'Have you no fear of God? You are under the same sentence as he is. 41 In our case it is plain justice; we are paying the price for our misdeeds. But this man has done nothing wrong.' 42 And he said, 'Jesus, remember me when you come to your throne.' 43 Jesus answered, 'Truly I tell you: today you will be with me in Paradise.'

44 By now it was about midday and a dark-

23:18 **But there was:** *some witnesses read* 17 At festival time he was obliged to release one person for them; 18 and now there was.   23:34 *Some witnesses omit* Jesus said, 'Father . . . doing.'

14, 22); see Acts 3.13–14. **7:** *Herod:* Antipas (see 3.1 n.). The appearance before Antipas is found only in Lk.; see Acts 4.27–28. **8:** 9.9. **11:** Compare Matt. 27.27–31; Mk. 15.16–20; Jn. 19.2–3. **18:** *Barabbas:* Matt. 27.16 n.

23.26–56: The crucifixion (Matt. 27.32–66; Mk. 15.21–47; Jn. 19.17–42). On crucifixion, see Mk. 15.20b–47 n. **26:** *Simon:* see Mk. 15.21 n.; contrast Jn. 19.17. **29:** Compare 21.23. **30:** Hos. 10.8. **33:** Isa.

ness fell over the whole land, which lasted until three in the afternoon: ⁴⁵ the sun's light failed. And the curtain of the temple was torn in two. ⁴⁶ Then Jesus uttered a loud cry and said, 'Father, into your hands I commit my spirit'; and with these words he died. ⁴⁷ When the centurion saw what had happened, he gave praise to God. 'Beyond all doubt', he said, 'this man was innocent.'

⁴⁸ The crowd who had assembled for the spectacle, when they saw what had happened, went home beating their breasts.

⁴⁹ His friends had all been standing at a distance; the women who had accompanied him from Galilee stood with them and watched it all.

⁵⁰ Now there was a man called Joseph, a member of the Council, a good and upright man, ⁵¹ who had dissented from their policy and the action they had taken. He came from the Judaean town of Arimathaea, and he was one who looked forward to the kingdom of God. ⁵² This man now approached Pilate and asked for the body of Jesus. ⁵³ Taking it down from the cross, he wrapped it in a linen sheet, and laid it in a tomb cut out of the rock, in which no one had been laid before. ⁵⁴ It was the day of preparation, and the sabbath was about to begin.

⁵⁵ The women who had accompanied Jesus from Galilee followed; they took note of the tomb and saw his body laid in it. ⁵⁶ Then they went home and prepared spices and perfumes; and on the sabbath they rested in obedience to the commandment.

The resurrection

24 BUT very early on the first day of the week they came to the tomb bringing the spices they had prepared. ² They found that the stone had been rolled away from the tomb, ³ but when they went inside, they did not find the body of the Lord Jesus. ⁴ While they stood utterly at a loss, suddenly two men in dazzling garments were at their side.

⁵ They were terrified, and stood with eyes cast down, but the men said, 'Why search among the dead for one who is alive? ⁶ Remember how he told you, while he was still in Galilee, ⁷ that the Son of Man must be given into the power of sinful men and be crucified, and must rise again on the third day.' ⁸ Then they recalled his words ⁹ and, returning from the tomb, they reported everything to the eleven and all the others.

¹⁰ The women were Mary of Magdala, Joanna, and Mary the mother of James, and they, with the other women, told these things to the apostles. ¹¹ But the story appeared to them to be nonsense, and they would not believe them.

¹³ THAT same day two of them were on their way to a village called Emmaus, about seven miles from Jerusalem, ¹⁴ talking together about all that had happened. ¹⁵ As they talked and argued, Jesus himself came up and walked with them; ¹⁶ but something prevented them from recognizing him. ¹⁷ He asked them, 'What is it you are debating as you walk?' They stood still, their faces full of sadness, ¹⁸ and one, called Cleopas, answered, 'Are you the only person staying in Jerusalem not to have heard the news of what has happened there in the last few days?' ¹⁹ 'What news?' he said. 'About Jesus of Nazareth,' they replied, 'who, by deeds and words of power, proved himself a prophet in the sight of God and the whole people; ²⁰ and how our chief priests and rulers handed him over to be sentenced to death, and crucified him. ²¹ But we had been hoping that he was to be the liberator of Israel. What is more, this is the third day since it happened, ²² and now some women of our company have astounded us: they went early to the tomb, ²³ but failed to find his body, and returned with a story that they had seen a vision of

24:5 **who is alive:** *some witnesses add* He is not here: he has been raised.   24:11 **believe them:** *some witnesses add* ¹²Peter, however, got up and ran to the tomb, and, peering in, saw the wrappings and nothing more; and he went home amazed at what had happened.

53.12. **34:** *Forgive them:* compare Acts 7.60. **34:** Ps. 22.18. **36:** The *wine* probably offered as a sedative. **43:** *Paradise,* in Jewish thought, was the garden in which the righteous lived after death; compare Rev. 2.7. **45:** *Curtain:* see Matt. 27.51 n. **46:** Ps. 31.5. **49:** Ps. 38.11. **50:** *Council:* see Matt. 26.59 n. **53:** Deut. 21.22–23. **55–56:** The women delay the burial anointing because the sabbath has begun and work must be postponed (Deut. 5.12–14).

24.1–11: The empty tomb (Matt. 28.1–10; Mk. 16.1–8; Jn. 20.1–18). **2:** *Stone:* see Matt. 27.60 n. **6:** Contrast Matt. 28.7; Mk. 16.7; in Lk. the resurrection appearances are restricted to the vicinity of Jerusalem.

angels who told them he was alive. ²⁴ Then some of our people went to the tomb and found things just as the women had said; but him they did not see.'

²⁵ 'How dull you are!' he answered. 'How slow to believe all that the prophets said! ²⁶ Was not the Messiah bound to suffer in this way before entering upon his glory?' ²⁷ Then, starting from Moses and all the prophets, he explained to them in the whole of scripture the things that referred to himself.

²⁸ By this time they had reached the village to which they were going, and he made as if to continue his journey. ²⁹ But they pressed him: 'Stay with us, for evening approaches, and the day is almost over.' So he went in to stay with them. ³⁰ And when he had sat down with them at table, he took bread and said the blessing; he broke the bread, and offered it to them. ³¹ Then their eyes were opened, and they recognized him; but he vanished from their sight. ³² They said to one another, 'Were not our hearts on fire as he talked with us on the road and explained the scriptures to us?'

³³ Without a moment's delay they set out and returned to Jerusalem. There they found that the eleven and the rest of the company had assembled, ³⁴ and were saying, 'It is true: the Lord has risen; he has appeared to Simon.' ³⁵ Then they described what had happened on their journey and told how he had made himself known to them in the breaking of the bread.

³⁶ As they were talking about all this, there he was, standing among them. ³⁷ Startled and terrified, they thought they were seeing a ghost. ³⁸ But he said, 'Why are you so perturbed? Why do doubts arise in your minds?

³⁹ Look at my hands and feet. It is I myself. Touch me and see; no ghost has flesh and bones as you can see that I have.' ⁴¹ They were still incredulous, still astounded, for it seemed too good to be true. So he asked them, 'Have you anything here to eat?' ⁴² They offered him a piece of fish they had cooked, ⁴³ which he took and ate before their eyes.

⁴⁴ And he said to them, 'This is what I meant by saying, while I was still with you, that everything written about me in the law of Moses and in the prophets and psalms was bound to be fulfilled.' ⁴⁵ Then he opened their minds to understand the scriptures. ⁴⁶ 'So you see', he said, 'that scripture foretells the sufferings of the Messiah and his rising from the dead on the third day, ⁴⁷ and declares that in his name repentance bringing the forgiveness of sins is to be proclaimed to all nations beginning from Jerusalem. ⁴⁸ You are to be witnesses to it all. ⁴⁹ I am sending on you the gift promised by my Father; wait here in this city until you are armed with power from above.'

⁵⁰ Then he led them out as far as Bethany, and blessed them with uplifted hands; ⁵¹ and in the act of blessing he parted from them. ⁵² And they returned to Jerusalem full of joy, ⁵³ and spent all their time in the temple praising God.

24:36 **among them:** *some witnesses add* And he said to them, 'Peace be with you!'   24:39 **I have:** *some witnesses add* ⁴⁰After saying this he showed them his hands and feet.   24:51 **parted from them:** *some witnesses add* and was carried up into heaven.
24:52 **And they:** *some witnesses add* worshipped him and.

24.13–53: Appearances and commissioning. 27: *Moses and all the prophets:* v. 44; see Matt. 5.17 n. **30:** The scene obviously suggests a eucharistic setting. **34:** 1 Cor. 15.5. **36–43:** Jn. 20.19–29. **44:** Verse 27; Matt. 5.17 n. **46:** Hos. 6.2. **47–49:** Compare Matt. 28.18–20; Acts 1.4–8. **47:** *From Jerusalem:* v. 52 n. **49:** *Power from above:* compare Acts 1.8; 2.1–4. **50–51:** Acts 1.9–12. **52:** As the Gospel concludes, the disciples are in *Jerusalem* (compare Acts 1.12–14), but the reader is assured (v. 47) that what began in Galilee and culminated in the Holy City would now move out to "the farthest corners of the earth" (Acts 1.8).

THE GOSPEL ACCORDING TO

John

While the Gospel according to John stands in contrast to Matthew, Mark, and Luke in matters of theological perspective, arrangement of its contents, and its distinctive use of imagery and symbols, it nevertheless clearly belongs to the same form of literature as do the other three. Its author, whose identity is unknown, displays exact knowledge both of Palestinian topography and of the Judaism of the first Christian century. This Gospel seems to record a tradition independent of that reflected in Matthew, Mark, and Luke, a tradition which may well go back to John, the son of Zebedee (see 21.2 n.), to whom the book was ascribed in the late second century. In Christian tradition John has often been called "the spiritual" Gospel, because of its attention to the spiritual import of the incidents it reports.

The Gospel is frequently analyzed into "The Book of Signs" (1.19–12.50) and "The Book of Glory" (13.1–20.31), with 1.1–18 as a Prologue and ch. 21 as an Epilogue. A "sign" is an act of power by Jesus, which points to a truth inaccessible to sight and touch, but apprehensible by faith. Paradoxically, "glory," an Old Testament term signifying God's presence, is for the evangelist publicly manifest in the earthly career of Jesus—who, to eyes of faith, reveals himself as the Son of God in certain significant events and through his death and resurrection. The writer's aim is "that you may believe that Jesus is the Christ, the Son of God, and that through this faith you may have life by his name" (20.31).

The Gospel probably originated in Asia Minor, possibly at Ephesus, shortly before the end of the first century.

The coming of Christ

1 In the beginning the Word already was. The Word was in God's presence, and what God was, the Word was. ²He was with God at the beginning, ³and through him all things came to be; without him no created thing came into being. ⁴In him was life, and that life was the light of mankind. ⁵The light shines in the darkness, and the darkness has never mastered it.

⁶There appeared a man named John. He was sent from God, ⁷and came as a witness to testify to the light, so that through him all might become believers. ⁸He was not himself the light; he came to bear witness to the light. ⁹The true light which gives light to everyone was even then coming into the world.

¹⁰He was in the world; but the world, though it owed its being to him, did not recognize him. ¹¹He came to his own, and his own people would not accept him. ¹²But to all who did accept him, to those who put their trust in him, he gave the right to become children of God, ¹³born not of human stock,

1:3–4 **through him ... was life:** or without him no single thing was created. All that came to be was alive with his life.   1:9 **The true ... world:** or The true light was in being, which gives light to everyone entering the world.

1.1–18: The prologue. 1: The *Word* (Gk. *logos*) as the title of Jesus Christ (v. 17) appears only here in Jn.; compare 1 Jn. 1.1; Rev. 19.13. *Word* and related terms in earlier Jewish tradition (see Wisd. 9.1–4, 9, 17–18; Ecclus. 24.1–12) prepared the way for its use here to denote Jesus as revealer of the unseen God. **4:** *Life* in Jn. always means eternal (not merely natural) life (see 3.15). This *life* becomes *the light of* humanity in that it reveals God to them. **5:** The *darkness* symbolizes those death-dealing forces in history irreconcilably opposed to God. **6:** *John* (in Matt., Mk., Lk., "the Baptist") is in Jn. a *witness* (see 1.19–51 n.) to Jesus, but in every way less important than he (1.19–27; 3.25–30). **11:** *Own* (first occurrence): the Holy Land. *Own people:* the people of Israel. John may think of the earlier appearance of the Word in the Mosaic Law (see v. 17; compare Ecclus.

by the physical desire of a human father, but of God. 14 So the Word became flesh; he made his home among us, and we saw his glory, such glory as befits the Father's only Son, full of grace and truth.

15 John bore witness to him and proclaimed: 'This is the man of whom I said, "He comes after me, but ranks ahead of me"; before I was born, he already was.'

16 From his full store we have all received grace upon grace; 17 for the law was given through Moses, but grace and truth came through Jesus Christ. 18 No one has ever seen God; God's only Son, he who is nearest to the Father's heart, has made him known.

Testimony of the Baptist and the first disciples

19 THIS is the testimony John gave when the Jews of Jerusalem sent a deputation of priests and Levites to ask him who he was. 20 He readily acknowledged, 'I am not the Messiah.' 21 'What then? Are you Elijah?' 'I am not,' he replied. 'Are you the Prophet?' 'No,' he said. 22 'Then who are you?' they asked. 'We must give an answer to those who sent us. What account do you give of yourself?' 23 He answered in the words of the prophet Isaiah: 'I am a voice crying in the wilderness, "Make straight the way for the Lord."'

24 Some Pharisees who were in the deputation 25 asked him, 'If you are not the Messiah, nor Elijah, nor the Prophet, then why are you baptizing?' 26 'I baptize in water,' John replied, 'but among you, though you do not know him, stands the one 27 who is to come after me. I am not worthy to unfasten the strap of his sandal.' 28 This took place at Bethany beyond Jordan, where John was baptizing.

29 The next day he saw Jesus coming towards him. 'There is the Lamb of God,' he said, 'who takes away the sin of the world. 30 He it is of whom I said, "After me there comes a man who ranks ahead of me"; before I was born, he already was. 31 I did not know who he was; but the reason why I came, baptizing in water, was that he might be revealed to Israel.'

32 John testified again: 'I saw the Spirit come down from heaven like a dove and come to rest on him. 33 I did not know him; but he who sent me to baptize in water had told me, "The man on whom you see the Spirit come down and rest is the one who is to baptize in Holy Spirit." 34 I have seen it and have borne witness: this is God's Chosen One.'

35 The next day again, John was standing with two of his disciples 36 when Jesus passed by. John looked towards him and said, 'There is the Lamb of God!' 37 When the two disciples heard what he said, they followed Jesus. 38 He turned and saw them following; 'What are you looking for?' he asked. They

1:18 **God's only Son:** *some witnesses read* the only begotten God.   1:34 **this . . . One:** *some witnesses read* this is the Son of God.

24.1–3, 8, 23). **14:** *Flesh:* human. *Made his home* (lit. pitched his tent): perhaps an echo of the glory of God which filled the Tent of Meeting (Exod. 40.34–38). *Glory:* radiance; therefore, the presence of God. **16:** *Grace upon grace:* God's gift to humanity in Jesus Christ is added to that of the Mosaic Law. **18:** The generalization that *no one has ever seen God* is modified in 14.9; there, to have seen Jesus is equivalent to having seen God.
1.19–51: Testimonies to Jesus. The language of the courtroom, frequent in biblical literature (e.g. Isa. 43.10–13), is particularly important to the description of Jesus' public life in Jn. Thus *testimony* (v. 19 and elsewhere) has a quasi-juridical meaning and seems to point to the climax at 12.31–32 ("judgement for this world"). **19:** *The Jews* is the Evangelist's generalized name for the religious authorities who oppose Jesus (such as the chief priests, scribes, etc., of the Synoptics), not literally meant to include all Jews. The term probably also reflects tensions between the Johannine church and the synagogue late in the first century. **20–21:** *The Messiah:* see Matt. 1.1 n. *Elijah:* see Matt. 17.10–13; Mk. 6.15 n. *Prophet:* see 6.14 n.; Mk. 8.28 n. **23:** See Isa. 40.3. **24:** *Pharisees:* see Matt. 3.7 n. **27:** *To unfasten . . . his sandals:* the task of the slave who washed the master's feet. **28:** The exact location of this *Bethany* is unknown. **29:** *The Lamb of God* derives from Isa. 53.7–12, especially Isa. 53.7. See also 1 Cor. 5.7 where Jesus is identified with the paschal lamb of Exod. 12.3–10. Compare 19.14 n. **30:** Although Jesus appears in history after John, in reality *he already was,* i.e. already existed before John's time. In Jn., Jesus has always existed (1.1; 8.56–57). **32:** John does not narrate the baptism of Jesus as do Matt., Mk., Lk., but only the coming down of the Spirit which accompanied it; see

said, 'Rabbi,' (which means 'Teacher') 'where are you staying?' 39 'Come and see,' he replied. So they went and saw where he was staying, and spent the rest of the day with him. It was about four in the afternoon.

40 One of the two who followed Jesus after hearing what John said was Andrew, Simon Peter's brother. 41 The first thing he did was to find his brother Simon and say to him, 'We have found the Messiah' (which is the Hebrew for Christ). 42 He brought Simon to Jesus, who looked at him and said, 'You are Simon son of John; you shall be called Cephas' (that is, Peter, 'the Rock').

43-44 The next day Jesus decided to leave for Galilee. He met Philip, who, like Andrew and Peter, came from Bethsaida, and said to him, 'Follow me.' 45 Philip went to find Nathanael and told him, 'We have found the man of whom Moses wrote in the law, the man foretold by the prophets: it is Jesus son of Joseph, from Nazareth.' 46 'Nazareth!' Nathanael exclaimed. 'Can anything good come from Nazareth?' Philip said, 'Come and see.' 47 When Jesus saw Nathanael coming towards him, he said, 'Here is an Israelite worthy of the name; there is nothing false in him.' 48 Nathanael asked him, 'How is it you know me?' Jesus replied, 'I saw you under the fig tree before Philip spoke to you.' 49 'Rabbi,' said Nathanael, 'you are the Son of God; you are king of Israel.' 50 Jesus answered, 'Do you believe this because I told you I saw you under the fig tree? You will see greater things than that.' 51 Then he added, 'In very truth I tell you all: you will see heaven wide open and God's angels ascending and descending upon the Son of Man.'

Signs and discourses

2 TWO DAYS later there was a wedding at Cana-in-Galilee. The mother of Jesus was there, 2 and Jesus and his disciples were also among the guests. 3 The wine gave out, so Jesus's mother said to him, 'They have no wine left.' 4 He answered, 'That is no concern of mine. My hour has not yet come.' 5 His mother said to the servants, 'Do whatever he tells you.' 6 There were six stone water-jars standing near, of the kind used for Jewish rites of purification; each held from twenty to thirty gallons. 7 Jesus said to the servants, 'Fill the jars with water,' and they filled them to the brim. 8 'Now draw some off,' he ordered, 'and take it to the master of the feast'; and they did so. 9 The master tasted the water now turned into wine, not knowing its source, though the servants who had drawn the water knew. He hailed the bridegroom 10 and said, 'Everyone else serves the best wine first, and the poorer only when the guests have drunk freely; but you have kept the best wine till now.'

11 So Jesus performed at Cana-in-Galilee the first of the signs which revealed his glory and led his disciples to believe in him.

12 AFTER this he went down to Capernaum with his mother, his brothers, and his disciples, and they stayed there a few days. 13 As it was near the time of the Jewish Passover, Jesus went up to Jerusalem. 14 In the temple precincts he found the dealers in cattle, sheep, and pigeons, and the money-changers seated at their tables. 15 He made a whip of cords and drove them out of the temple,

Mk. 1.9–11 n. **34:** *Chosen One:* see Isa. 42.1. **35:** *Two . . . disciples:* see v. 40. **40:** *Andrew* appears more prominently in Jn. (6.8; 12.22) than in the Synoptics. **44:** *Bethsaida* lay north of the Lake of Galilee and east of the Jordan. **45:** Although *Nathanael* is sometimes identified with Bartholomew (Mk. 3.18), this identification is not justified by NT evidence. **49:** *King:* the Messiah (see Matt. 1.1 n.). **51:** Jacob's vision of *God's angels* mediating between heaven and earth (Gen. 28.12) provides this image about the *Son of Man* (see Mk. 2.10 n.).

2.1–12: First sign at Cana. 1: John envisages the events of 1.19–2.12 as encompassing a week. The author has previously (1.19–28, 29–34, 35–42, 42–51) indicated the first four days of Jesus' ministry; hence *two days later* (lit. "on the third day") here marks the conclusion of this week. *Cana* is nine miles north of Nazareth. *The mother of Jesus* appears again in 19.25–27. **4:** *Hour* in Jn. denotes the climactic moment of Jesus' passion and glorification (see also 12.27). **11:** *Signs:* see Introduction. *His glory:* see 12.23; 17.24. **12:** *Capernaum* (Mk. 1.21–28) is on the Lake of Galilee.

2.13–25: The cleansing of the temple. 13: John understands Jesus' ministry to have spanned three *Passovers* (see also 6.4; 11.55) of which this is the first. Contrast the Synoptics where only a single Passover is involved. On Passover, see Mk. 14.1 n. **14:** The *temple* here includes the entire area of which the sanctuary proper is the center; see v. 19 n. *Money-changers:* see Matt. 21.12 n. **15:** This action is symbolic; there are a good many sheep, cattle, and all. He upset the tables of the money-changers, scattering their coins. [16] Then he turned on the dealers in pigeons: 'Take them out of here,' he said; 'do not turn my Father's house into a market.' [17] His disciples recalled the words of scripture: 'Zeal for your house will consume me.' [18] The Jews challenged Jesus: 'What sign can you show to justify your action?' [19] 'Destroy this temple,' Jesus replied, 'and in three days I will raise it up again.' [20] The Jews said, 'It has taken forty-six years to build this temple. Are you going to raise it up again in three days?' [21] But the temple he was speaking of was his body. [22] After his resurrection his disciples recalled what he had said, and they believed the scripture and the words that Jesus had spoken.

[23] WHILE he was in Jerusalem for Passover many put their trust in him when they saw the signs that he performed. [24] But Jesus for his part would not trust himself to them. He knew them all, [25] and had no need of evidence from others about anyone, for he himself could tell what was in people.

3 ONE of the Pharisees, called Nicodemus, a member of the Jewish Council, [2] came to Jesus by night. 'Rabbi,' he said, 'we know that you are a teacher sent by God; no one could perform these signs of yours unless God were with him.' [3] Jesus answered, 'In very truth I tell you, no one can see the kingdom of God unless he has been born again.' [4] 'But how can someone be born when he is old?' asked Nicodemus. 'Can he enter his mother's womb a second time and be born?' [5] Jesus answered, 'In very truth I tell you, no one can enter the kingdom of God without being born from water and spirit. [6] Flesh can give birth only to flesh; it is spirit that gives birth to spirit. [7] You ought not to be astonished when I say, "You must all be born again." [8] The wind blows where it wills; you hear the sound of it, but you do not know where it comes from or where it is going. So it is with everyone who is born from the Spirit.'

[9] 'How is this possible?' asked Nicodemus. [10] 'You a teacher of Israel and ignorant of such things!' said Jesus. [11] 'In very truth I tell you, we speak of what we know, and testify to what we have seen, and yet you all reject our testimony. [12] If you do not believe me when I talk to you about earthly things, how are you to believe if I should talk about the things of heaven?

[13] 'No one has gone up into heaven except the one who came down from heaven, the Son of Man who is in heaven. [14] Just as Moses lifted up the serpent in the wilderness, so the Son of Man must be lifted up, [15] in order that everyone who has faith may in him have eternal life.

[16] 'God so loved the world that he gave his only Son, that everyone who has faith in him may not perish but have eternal life. [17] It was not to judge the world that God sent his Son

3:8 **wind** and **spirit** are translations of the same Greek word, which has both meanings. 3:13 Some witnesses omit who is in heaven.

"acted" prophecies in the OT (see e.g. Jer. 13.1–11). **16:** Market: see Zech. 14.21. **17:** In Jn. the term recalled (remembered) usually points to something associated with Jesus which was understood only in Christian reflection after his time (see v. 22; 12.16; 14.26). See Ps. 69.9. **19:** Temple here indicates the sanctuary itself; contrast v. 14. **20:** Forty-six years: see Matt. 24.1–3 n. The date would appear to be 27 C.E. **21:** His body: Jesus' risen body was to supersede the sanctuary; see Matt. 24.1–2 n. **23:** See 4.48 n.

3.1–21: Jesus with Nicodemus. 1: Pharisees: Matt. 3.7 n. Jewish Council: Judea's highest native court, called the Sanhedrin in other translations. Nicodemus reappears at 7.50; 19.39. **2:** Rabbi: see Matt. 23.8–10 n. **3:** The Gk. for again can also mean "from above." The expression kingdom of God, frequent in the Synoptics (see Mk. 1.15 n.), is found in Jn. only here and in v. 5. **5:** Water and spirit: baptism; see 1 Cor. 6.11. **6:** Flesh describes human life in its creaturely limitations, while spirit can reflect divine action on persons. The contrast between flesh and spirit, frequent in the Hellenistic world, is given a strongly religious turn here and in 6.63; 7.79. In 4.24, God is described as spirit. **8:** Wind, spirit: see Tfn. for this verse. **13:** Has gone up: writing after the resurrection, Jn. refers to the ascension as a past event. **14:** Lifted up is a term with a paradoxical double meaning which includes both Jesus' crucifixion and his glorification (see 8.28; 12.32, 34). On Moses and the serpent, see Num. 21.4–9; Wisd. 16.5–6. **16:** The giving of God's only Son in love may allude to Abraham's near sacrifice of Isaac (Gen. 22.1–12); see Rom. 8.32. In Jn. the world may denote humanity in a good sense (as here) but also in a pejorative sense as in 12.31. **17:** Although Jesus' purpose is to save rather than to condemn, into the world, but that through him the world might be saved.

18 'No one who puts his faith in him comes under judgement; but the unbeliever has already been judged because he has not put his trust in God's only Son. 19 This is the judgement: the light has come into the world, but people preferred darkness to light because their deeds were evil. 20 Wrongdoers hate the light and avoid it, for fear their misdeeds should be exposed. 21 Those who live by the truth come to the light so that it may be clearly seen that God is in all they do.'

22 AFTER this Jesus went with his disciples into Judaea; he remained there with them and baptized. 23 John too was baptizing at Aenon, near Salim, because water was plentiful in that region; and all the time people were coming for baptism. 24 This was before John's imprisonment.

25 John's disciples were engaged in a debate with some Jews about purification; 26 so they came to John and said, 'Rabbi, there was a man with you on the other side of the Jordan, to whom you bore your witness. Now he is baptizing, and everyone is flocking to him.' 27 John replied: 'One can have only what is given one from Heaven. 28 You yourselves can testify that I said, "I am not the Messiah; I have been sent as his forerunner." 29 It is the bridegroom who marries the bride. The bridegroom's friend, who stands by and listens to him, is overjoyed at hearing the bridegroom's voice. This is my joy and now it is complete. 30 He must grow greater; I must become less.'

31 He who comes from above is above all others; he who is from the earth belongs to the earth and uses earthly speech. He who comes from heaven 32 bears witness to what he has seen and heard, even though no one accepts his witness. 33 To accept his witness is to affirm that God speaks the truth; 34 for he whom God sent utters the words of God, so measureless is God's gift of the Spirit. 35 The Father loves the Son and has entrusted him with complete authority. 36 Whoever puts his faith in the Son has eternal life. Whoever disobeys the Son will not see that life; God's wrath rests upon him.

4 1–2 NEWS now reached the Pharisees that Jesus was winning and baptizing more disciples than John; although, in fact, it was his disciples who were baptizing, not Jesus himself. When Jesus heard this, 3 he left Judaea and set out once more for Galilee. 4 He had to pass through Samaria, 5 and on his way came to a Samaritan town called Sychar, near the plot of ground which Jacob gave to his son Joseph; 6 Jacob's well was there. It was about noon, and Jesus, tired after his journey, was sitting by the well.

8 His disciples had gone into the town to buy food. 7 Meanwhile a Samaritan woman came to draw water, and Jesus said to her, 'Give me a drink.' 9 The woman said, 'What! You, a Jew, ask for a drink from a Samaritan woman?' (Jews do not share drinking vessels with Samaritans.) 10 Jesus replied, 'If only you knew what God gives, and who it is that is asking you for a drink, you would have asked him and he would have given you living water.' 11 'Sir,' the woman said, 'you have no bucket and the well is deep, so where can you get "living water"? 12 Are you greater than Jacob our ancestor who gave us the well and drank from it himself, he and his sons and his cattle too?' 13 Jesus answered, 'Everyone who drinks this water will be thirsty again; 14 but whoever drinks the water I shall give will never again be thirsty. The water that I shall give will be a spring of water within him, welling up and bringing eternal

3:25 some Jews: *some witnesses read* a Jew.
3:31 from heaven: *some witnesses add* is above all and.
4:9 Jews ... Samaritans: *some witnesses omit these words.*

Jn. is aware of Jesus' role as *judge* (5.22; 9.39).

3.22–36: Jesus and John. 22: The statement that Jesus *baptized* is qualified in 4.2. **23:** *Aenon* (Aram. for "springs"): like *Salim,* probably a Samaritan village. **24:** Mark 1.14, however, states that Jesus began his ministry after John's arrest. **29:** *The bridegroom* imagery recalls the OT theme of God's marriage with Israel (Hos. chs. 1–2). For Jesus' self-designation as the bridegroom see Mk. 2.19–20; compare Matt. 25.1–13. The imagery appears also in Rev. 19.7; 21.2.

4.1–42: Jesus and the Samaritans. 5: *Sychar* is probably Shechem, connected with *Jacob* in Gen. 33.18–19. **7, 9:** After the fall of the kingdom of Israel (721 B.C.E.) the population was mixed, though largely Gentile. The descendants are the *Samaritans.* Rebuffed by the Jews returning from the Babylonian Exile (Neh. 3.20), the Samaritans built their own temple on Mount Gerizim (v. 20). **10:** *Living water,* from a spring (contrasted in Jer.

life.' 15 'Sir,' said the woman, 'give me this water, and then I shall not be thirsty, nor have to come all this way to draw water.'

16 'Go and call your husband,' said Jesus, 'and come back here.' 17 She answered, 'I have no husband.' Jesus said, 'You are right in saying that you have no husband, 18 for though you have had five husbands, the man you are living with now is not your husband. You have spoken the truth!' 19 'Sir,' replied the woman, 'I can see you are a prophet. 20 Our fathers worshipped on this mountain, but you Jews say that the place where God must be worshipped is in Jerusalem.' 21 'Believe me,' said Jesus, 'the time is coming when you will worship the Father neither on this mountain nor in Jerusalem. 22 You Samaritans worship you know not what; we worship what we know. It is from the Jews that salvation comes. 23 But the time is coming, indeed it is already here, when true worshippers will worship the Father in spirit and in truth. These are the worshippers the Father wants. 24 God is spirit, and those who worship him must worship in spirit and in truth.' 25 The woman answered, 'I know that Messiah' (that is, Christ) 'is coming. When he comes he will make everything clear to us.' 26 Jesus said to her, 'I am he, I who am speaking to you.'

27 At that moment his disciples returned, and were astonished to find him talking with a woman; but none of them said, 'What do you want?' or, 'Why are you talking with her?' 28 The woman left her water-jar and went off to the town, where she said to the people, 29 'Come and see a man who has told me everything I ever did. Could this be the Messiah?' 30 They left the town and made their way towards him.

31 MEANWHILE the disciples were urging him, 'Rabbi, have something to eat.' 32 But he said, 'I have food to eat of which you know nothing.' 33 At this the disciples said to one another, 'Can someone have brought him

food?' 34 But Jesus said, 'For me it is meat and drink to do the will of him who sent me until I have finished his work.

35 'Do you not say, "Four months more and then comes harvest"? But look, I tell you, look around at the fields: they are already white, ripe for harvesting. 36 The reaper is drawing his pay and harvesting a crop for eternal life, so that sower and reaper may rejoice together. 37 That is how the saying comes true: "One sows, another reaps." 38 I sent you to reap a crop for which you have not laboured. Others laboured and you have come in for the harvest of their labour.'

39 Many Samaritans of that town came to believe in him because of the woman's testimony: 'He told me everything I ever did.' 40 So when these Samaritans came to him they pressed him to stay with them; and he stayed there two days. 41 Many more became believers because of what they heard from his own lips. 42 They told the woman, 'It is no longer because of what you said that we believe, for we have heard him ourselves; and we are convinced that he is the Saviour of the world.'

Jesus the giver of life

43 WHEN the two days were over Jesus left for Galilee; 44 for he himself had declared that a prophet is without honour in his own country. 45 On his arrival the Galileans made him welcome, because they had seen all he did at the festival in Jerusalem; they had been at the festival themselves.

46 Once again he visited Cana-in-Galilee, where he had turned the water into wine. An officer in the royal service was there, whose son was lying ill at Capernaum. 47 When he heard that Jesus had come from Judaea into Galilee, he went to him and begged him to go down and cure his son, who was at the point of death. 48 Jesus said to him, 'Will none of you ever believe without seeing signs and portents?' 49 The officer pleaded with him,

2.13 with cistern water), here symbolizes the Holy Spirit. **16:** *Husband:* a play on words is involved, since the same Gk. word means both "husband" and "man." **23:** God is to be worshiped in *spirit* and *truth,* rather than by visits to cultic holy places. **24:** That *God is spirit* does not mean for Jn. that God is remote from history; rather, it affirms God's involvement in history. **35:** Compare Matt. 9.37–38.

4.43–54: Second sign at Cana. See 2.1–11. **44:** See Mk. 6.4. **45:** *In Jerusalem:* see 2.23. **46:** This *officer* was probably in the employ of Herod Antipas (see Lk. 3.1 n.). **48:** John exhibits an ambivalence with respect to *signs,* which provide the substance of 1.19–12.50 (the Book of Signs; see Introduction). Here, Jn. attempts to establish limits to their significance; *signs and portents* cannot produce real faith, for Jesus is no mere wonder-worker.

'Sir, come down before my boy dies.' ⁵⁰'Return home,' said Jesus; 'your son will live.' The man believed what Jesus said and started for home. ⁵¹ While he was on his way down his servants met him with the news that his child was going to live. ⁵² So he asked them at what time he had begun to recover, and they told him, 'It was at one o'clock yesterday afternoon that the fever left him.' ⁵³ The father realized that this was the time at which Jesus had said to him, 'Your son will live,' and he and all his household became believers.

⁵⁴ This was the second sign which Jesus performed after coming from Judaea into Galilee.

5 SOME time later, Jesus went up to Jerusalem for one of the Jewish festivals. ² Now at the Sheep Gate in Jerusalem there is a pool whose Hebrew name is Bethesda. It has five colonnades ³ and in them lay a great number of sick people, blind, lame, and paralysed. ⁵ Among them was a man who had been crippled for thirty-eight years. ⁶ Jesus saw him lying there, and knowing that he had been ill a long time he asked him, 'Do you want to get well?' ⁷ 'Sir,' he replied, 'I have no one to put me in the pool when the water is disturbed; while I am getting there, someone else steps into the pool before me.' ⁸ Jesus answered, 'Stand up, take your bed and walk.' ⁹ The man recovered instantly; he took up his bed, and began to walk.

That day was a sabbath. ¹⁰ So the Jews said to the man who had been cured, 'It is the sabbath. It is against the law for you to carry your bed.' ¹¹ He answered, 'The man who cured me, he told me, "Take up your bed and walk."' ¹² They asked him, 'Who is this man who told you to take it up and walk?' ¹³ But the man who had been cured did not know who it was; for the place was crowded and Jesus had slipped away. ¹⁴ A little later Jesus found him in the temple and said to him,

'Now that you are well, give up your sinful ways, or something worse may happen to you.' ¹⁵ The man went off and told the Jews that it was Jesus who had cured him.

¹⁶ It was for doing such things on the sabbath that the Jews began to take action against Jesus. ¹⁷ He defended himself by saying, 'My Father continues to work, and I must work too.' ¹⁸ This made the Jews all the more determined to kill him, because not only was he breaking the sabbath but, by calling God his own Father, he was claiming equality with God.

¹⁹ To this charge Jesus replied, 'In very truth I tell you, the Son can do nothing by himself; he does only what he sees the Father doing: whatever the Father does, the Son does. ²⁰ For the Father loves the Son and shows him all that he himself is doing, and will show him even greater deeds, to fill you with wonder. ²¹ As the Father raises the dead and gives them life, so the Son gives life as he chooses. ²² Again, the Father does not judge anyone, but has given full jurisdiction to the Son; ²³ it is his will that all should pay the same honour to the Son as to the Father. To deny honour to the Son is to deny it to the Father who sent him.

²⁴ 'In very truth I tell you, whoever heeds what I say and puts his trust in him who sent me has eternal life; he does not come to judgement, but has already passed from death to life. ²⁵ In very truth I tell you, the time is coming, indeed it is already here, when the dead shall hear the voice of the Son of God, and those who hear shall come to life. ²⁶ For as the Father has life in himself, so by his gift the Son also has life in himself. ²⁷ 'As Son of Man he has also been given authority to pass judgement. ²⁸ Do not be sur-

5:3 **paralysed:** *some witnesses add* waiting for the disturbance of the water; *some also add* ⁴for from time to time an angel came down into the pool and stirred up the water. The first to plunge in after this disturbance recovered from whatever disease had afflicted him.

5.1–15: Cure of a cripple on the sabbath. 1: *One of the Jewish festivals:* possibly Pentecost. **2:** In addition to the four *colonnades* which surrounded the pool, a fifth divided it in half. **14:** Since Jesus' admonition, *give up your sinful ways,* comes after the healing, it is not intended to connect the man's disability with sin (see 9.3). Rather, it teaches that the purpose of the healing is to lead to a new life.

5.16–30: Jesus' divine Sonship. For Jn., Jesus is the Son of God in that he exercises uniquely divine prerogatives which show he is one with the Father (10.30; 17.11, 22). **17:** God *continues to work* even on the sabbath in sustaining the world. **19–30:** That the *Son . . . does only what he sees the Father doing* (v. 19) is explained in the following verses. First (vv. 21, 24–26), as the *Son,* he *gives life* (v. 21). Second (vv. 22, 27–30), as *Son of Man* (see Mk. 2.10 n.), he is the judge of human beings at the final resurrection (vv. 28–29).

prised at this, because the time is coming when all who are in the grave shall hear his voice ²⁹ and come out: those who have done right will rise to life; those who have done wrong will rise to judgement. ³⁰ I cannot act by myself; I judge as I am bidden, and my sentence is just, because I seek to do not my own will, but the will of him who sent me.

³¹'If I testify on my own behalf, that testimony is not valid. ³² There is another who bears witness for me, and I know that his testimony about me is valid. ³³ You sent messengers to John, and he has testified to the truth. ³⁴ Not that I rely on human testimony, but I remind you of it for your own salvation. ³⁵ John was a brightly burning lamp, and for a time you were ready to exult in his light. ³⁶ But I rely on a testimony higher than John's: the work my Father has given me to do and to finish, the very work I have in hand, testifies that the Father has sent me. ³⁷ And the Father who has sent me has borne witness on my behalf. His voice you have never heard, his form you have never seen; ³⁸ his word has found no home in you, because you do not believe the one whom he sent. ³⁹ You study the scriptures diligently, supposing that in having them you have eternal life; their testimony points to me, ⁴⁰ yet you refuse to come to me to receive that life.

⁴¹'I do not look to men for honour. ⁴² But I know that with you it is different, for you have no love of God in you. ⁴³ I have come accredited by my Father, and you have no welcome for me; but let someone self-accredited come, and you will give him a welcome. ⁴⁴ How can you believe when you accept honour from one another, and care nothing for the honour that comes from him who alone is God? ⁴⁵ Do not imagine that I shall be your accuser at the Father's tribunal. Your accuser is Moses, the very Moses on whom you have set your hope. ⁴⁶ If you believed him you would believe me, for it was of me that he wrote. ⁴⁷ But if you do not believe what he wrote, how are you to believe what I say?'

Bread from heaven

6 Some time later Jesus withdrew to the farther shore of the sea of Galilee (or Tiberias), ² and a large crowd of people followed him because they had seen the signs he performed in healing the sick. ³ Jesus went up the hillside and sat down with his disciples. ⁴ It was near the time of Passover, the great Jewish festival. ⁵ Looking up and seeing a large crowd coming towards him, Jesus said to Philip, 'Where are we to buy bread to feed these people?' ⁶ He said this to test him; Jesus himself knew what he meant to do. ⁷ Philip replied, 'We would need two hundred denarii to buy enough bread for each of them to have a little.' ⁸ One of his disciples, Andrew, the brother of Simon Peter, said to him, ⁹ 'There is a boy here who has five barley loaves and two fish; but what is that among so many?' ¹⁰ Jesus said, 'Make the people sit down.' There was plenty of grass there, so the men sat down, about five thousand of them. ¹¹ Then Jesus took the loaves, gave thanks, and distributed them to the people as they sat there. He did the same with the fish, and they had as much as they wanted. ¹² When everyone had had enough, he said to his disciples, 'Gather up the pieces left over, so that nothing is wasted.' ¹³ They gathered them up, and filled twelve baskets with the pieces of the five barley loaves that were left uneaten.

¹⁴ When the people saw the sign Jesus had performed, the word went round, 'Surely this must be the Prophet who was to come into the world.' ¹⁵ Jesus, realizing that they meant to come and seize him to proclaim him king, withdrew again to the hills by himself.

¹⁶ At nightfall his disciples went down to

6:7 **denarii:** *see p. xxvii.*

5.31–47: Further testimonies to Jesus. See 1.19–51 and n. The preceding material seems to be regarded as Jesus' testimony to himself; now other witnesses are evoked. **32:** *Another:* God; see 8.18. **33–35:** *John:* see 1.35–39. **36–37:** Jesus' *work:* for example, 2.1–11. **39–40:** The *scriptures:* see, for example, 6.45. The passage may reflect debate with opponents over the proper interpretation of OT passages. **45:** The appeal to *Moses* refers specifically to Deut. 18.15, or possibly to the Pentateuch as a whole.

6.1–15: The sign of the bread. 3: *Hillside:* a frequent motif; see Matt. 5.1 n. John may wish to contrast Jesus, who takes his disciples onto the mountain with him, with Moses, who ascended alone according to Exod. 19.10–24. **7:** The sum of money was the equivalent of two hundred days' wages. **14:** The *Prophet* here, as in 1.21, 25, is the one like Moses (see Deut. 18.15). **15:** The avoidance of being proclaimed *king* probably is intended to clarify for the reader that Jesus was not a political figure; see 18.33–37.

the sea, [17] and set off by boat to cross to Capernaum. Though darkness had fallen, Jesus had not yet joined them; [18] a strong wind was blowing and the sea grew rough. [19] When they had rowed about three or four miles they saw Jesus walking on the sea and approaching the boat. They were terrified, [20] but he called out, 'It is I; do not be afraid.' [21] With that they were ready to take him on board, and immediately the boat reached the land they were making for.

[22] NEXT morning the crowd was still on the opposite shore. They had seen only one boat there, and Jesus, they knew, had not embarked with his disciples, who had set off by themselves. [23] Boats from Tiberias, however, had come ashore near the place where the people had eaten the bread over which the Lord gave thanks. [24] When the crowd saw that Jesus had gone as well as his disciples, they went on board these boats and made for Capernaum in search of him. [25] They found him on the other side. 'Rabbi,' they asked, 'when did you come here?' [26] Jesus replied, 'In very truth I tell you, it is not because you saw signs that you came looking for me, but because you ate the bread and your hunger was satisfied. [27] You should work, not for this perishable food, but for the food that lasts, the food of eternal life.

'This food the Son of Man will give you, for on him God the Father has set the seal of his authority.' [28] 'Then what must we do', they asked him, 'if our work is to be the work of God?' [29] Jesus replied, 'This is the work that God requires: to believe in the one whom he has sent.'

[30] They asked, 'What sign can you give us, so that we may see it and believe you? What is the work you are doing? [31] Our ancestors had manna to eat in the desert; as scripture says, "He gave them bread from heaven to eat." ' [32] Jesus answered, 'In very truth I tell you, it was not Moses who gave you the bread from heaven; it is my Father who gives you the true bread from heaven. [33] The bread

that God gives comes down from heaven and brings life to the world.' [34] 'Sir,' they said to him, 'give us this bread now and always.' [35] Jesus said to them, 'I am the bread of life. Whoever comes to me will never be hungry, and whoever believes in me will never be thirsty. [36] But you, as I said, have seen and yet you do not believe. [37] All that the Father gives me will come to me, and anyone who comes to me I will never turn away. [38] I have come down from heaven, to do not my own will, but the will of him who sent me. [39] It is his will that I should not lose even one of those he has given me, but should raise them all up on the last day. [40] For it is my Father's will that everyone who sees the Son and has faith in him should have eternal life; and I will raise them up on the last day.'

[41] At this the Jews began to grumble because he said, 'I am the bread which came down from heaven.' [42] They said, 'Surely this is Jesus, Joseph's son! We know his father and mother. How can he say, "I have come down from heaven"?' [43] 'Stop complaining among yourselves,' Jesus told them. [44] 'No one can come to me unless he is drawn by the Father who sent me; and I will raise him up on the last day. [45] It is written in the prophets: "They will all be taught by God." Everyone who has listened to the Father and learned from him comes to me.

[46] 'I do not mean that anyone has seen the Father; he who has come from God has seen the Father, and he alone. [47] In very truth I tell you, whoever believes has eternal life. [48] I am the bread of life. [49] Your ancestors ate manna in the wilderness, yet they are dead. [50] I am speaking of the bread that comes down from heaven; whoever eats it will never die. [51] I am the living bread that has come down from heaven; if anyone eats this bread, he will live for ever. The bread which I shall give is my own flesh, given for the life of the world.' [52] This led to a fierce dispute among the

6:23 *Some witnesses omit* over which the Lord gave thanks.   6:36 **you ... have seen:** *some witnesses add* me.

6.16–21: Jesus walks on the sea of Galilee. 18: The incident of the storm is described tersely compared with Mk. 6.47–51. 20: The scene focuses on Jesus' words, *"It is I* (lit. 'I am'); *do not be afraid"* (see 8.24 n.).
6.22–71: The bread of life. 26–28: The crowd fails to see beyond the material "sign" of the miraculous feeding to the *food of eternal life* which *the Son of Man will give.* 31: On *manna,* see Exod. 16.14. The quotation is from Ps. 78.24. 32–33: Jesus, sent by God (3.31), is *the real bread from heaven. 32: Moses:* compare v. 14 n. 35: *Never be thirsty:* see 4.14–15. 37b: See 17.2, 7, 24. 45: See Isa. 54.13; Jer. 31.33–34 for the experiential, inner knowledge of God. 51–54: Notice the allusion to Jesus' words over the bread and wine at the Last Supper

Jews. 'How can this man give us his flesh to eat?' they protested. [53] Jesus answered them, 'In very truth I tell you, unless you eat the flesh of the Son of Man and drink his blood you can have no life in you. [54] Whoever eats my flesh and drinks my blood has eternal life, and I will raise him up on the last day. [55] My flesh is real food; my blood is real drink. [56] Whoever eats my flesh and drinks my blood dwells in me and I in him. [57] As the living Father sent me, and I live because of the Father, so whoever eats me will live because of me. [58] This is the bread which came down from heaven; it is not like the bread which our fathers ate; they are dead, but whoever eats this bread will live for ever.'

[59] Jesus said these things in the synagogue as he taught in Capernaum. [60] On hearing them, many of his disciples exclaimed, 'This is more than we can stand! How can anyone listen to such talk?' [61] Jesus was aware that his disciples were grumbling about it and asked them, 'Does this shock you? [62] Then what if you see the Son of Man ascending to where he was before? [63] It is the spirit that gives life; the flesh can achieve nothing; the words I have spoken to you are both spirit and life. [64] Yet there are some of you who have no faith.' For Jesus knew from the outset who were without faith and who was to betray him. [65] So he said, 'This is why I told you that no one can come to me unless it has been granted to him by the Father.'

[66] From that moment many of his disciples drew back and no longer went about with him. [67] So Jesus asked the Twelve, 'Do you also want to leave?' [68] Simon Peter answered him, 'Lord, to whom shall we go? Your words are words of eternal life. [69] We believe and know that you are God's Holy One.' [70] Jesus answered, 'Have I not chosen the twelve of you? Yet one of you is a devil.' [71] He meant Judas son of Simon Iscariot. It was he who would betray him, and he was one of the Twelve.

The great controversy

7 AFTER that Jesus travelled around within Galilee; he decided to avoid Judaea because the Jews were looking for a chance to kill him. [2] But when the Jewish feast of Tabernacles was close at hand, [3] his brothers said to him, 'You should leave here and go into Judaea, so that your disciples may see the great things you are doing. [4] No one can hope for recognition if he works in obscurity. If you can really do such things as these, show yourself to the world.' [5] For even his brothers had no faith in him. [6] Jesus answered: 'The right time for me has not yet come, but any time is right for you. [7] The world cannot hate you; but it hates me for exposing the wickedness of its ways. [8] Go up to the festival yourselves. I am not going to this festival, because the right time for me has not yet come.' [9] So saying he stayed behind in Galilee.

[10] Later, when his brothers had gone to the festival, he went up too, not openly, but in secret. [11] At the festival the Jews were looking for him and asking where he was, [12] and there was much murmuring about him in the crowds. 'He is a good man,' said some. 'No,' said others, 'he is leading the people astray.' [13] No one talked freely about him, however, for fear of the Jews.

[14] WHEN the festival was already half over, Jesus went up to the temple and began to teach. [15] The Jews were astonished: 'How is it', they said, 'that this untrained man has such learning?' [16] Jesus replied, 'My teaching is not my own but his who sent me. [17] Whoever chooses to do the will of God will know whether my teaching comes from him or is

7:8 **not going:** *some witnesses read* not yet going.

(see 1 Cor. 11.24). **63:** Until Jesus' glorification (v. 62; 7.39), his words are not known as *spirit and life* (see 2.22; 12.16). **68–69:** Peter's profession of faith; see Matt. 16.13–16 where no mention is made of disciples who have withdrawn from Jesus. **70–71:** In Matt. 16.23, Jesus addresses Peter as "Satan"; here, Judas is identified as *a devil.*

7.1–36: The feast of Tabernacles. 2: *Tabernacles* (or Booths) was a thanksgiving festival, associated with Israel's wandering in the wilderness, held for seven days in September–October (Lev. 23.39–43; Deut. 16.13–15). In Jn. chs. 7–8, it provides the background in terms of which Jesus' self-revelation is interpreted (see v. 37 n.; 8.12 n.). **6:** *The right time:* the moment determined by God's will. John consistently conceives of a preordained schedule of events in the career of Jesus. **8:** *I am not going* (up) involves a play on words in that it can also refer to Jesus' ascension (20.17). **15:** Jesus apparently lacks formal schooling in Scripture and, merely my own. ¹⁸Anyone whose teaching is merely his own seeks his own glory; but if anyone seeks the glory of him who sent him, he is sincere and there is nothing false in him.

¹⁹'Did not Moses give you the law? Yet not one of you keeps it. Why are you trying to kill me?' ²⁰The crowd answered, 'You are possessed! Who wants to kill you?' ²¹Jesus replied, 'I did one good deed, and you are all taken aback. ²²But consider: Moses gave you the law of circumcision (not that it originated with Moses, but with the patriarchs) and you circumcise even on the sabbath. ²³Well then, if someone can be circumcised on the sabbath to avoid breaking the law of Moses, why are you indignant with me for making someone's whole body well on the sabbath? ²⁴Stop judging by appearances; be just in your judgements.'

²⁵This prompted some of the people of Jerusalem to say, 'Is not this the man they want to put to death? ²⁶Yet here he is, speaking in public, and they say not one word to him. Can it be that our rulers have decided that this is the Messiah? ²⁷Yet we know where this man comes from; when the Messiah appears no one is to know where he comes from.' ²⁸Jesus responded to this as he taught in the temple: 'Certainly you know me,' he declared, 'and you know where I come from. Yet I have not come of my own accord; I was sent by one who is true, and him you do not know. ²⁹I know him because I come from him, and he it is who sent me.' ³⁰At this they tried to seize him, but no one could lay hands on him because his appointed hour had not yet come. ³¹Among the people many believed in him. 'When the Messiah comes,' they said, 'is it likely that he will perform more signs than this man?'

³²The Pharisees overheard these mutterings about him among the people, so the chief priests and the Pharisees sent temple police to arrest him. ³³Then Jesus said, 'For a little longer I shall be with you; then I am going away to him who sent me. ³⁴You will look for me, but you will not find me; and where I am, you cannot come.' ³⁵So the Jews said to one another, 'Where does he intend to go, that we should not be able to find him? Will he go to the Dispersion among the Gentiles, and teach Gentiles? ³⁶What does he mean by saying, "You will look for me, but you will not find me; and where I am, you cannot come"?'

³⁷ON the last and greatest day of the festival Jesus stood and declared, 'If anyone is thirsty, let him come to me and drink. ³⁸Whoever believes in me, as scripture says, "Streams of living water shall flow from within him." ' ³⁹He was speaking of the Spirit which believers in him would later receive; for the Spirit had not yet been given, because Jesus had not yet been glorified.

⁴⁰On hearing his words some of the crowd said, 'This must certainly be the Prophet.' ⁴¹Others said, 'This is the Messiah.' But others argued, 'Surely the Messiah is not to come from Galilee? ⁴²Does not scripture say that the Messiah is to be of the family of David, from David's village of Bethlehem?' ⁴³Thus he was the cause of a division among the people. ⁴⁴Some were for arresting him, but no one laid hands on him.

⁴⁵The temple police went back to the chief priests and Pharisees, who asked them, 'Why have you not brought him?' ⁴⁶'No one ever spoke as this man speaks,' they replied.

7:28 **Certainly . . . come from:** *or* Do you know me? And do you know where I come from?   7:37–38 **If anyone . . . within him:** *or* If anyone is thirsty, let him come to me; whoever believes in me, let him drink. As scripture says, "Streams of living water shall flow from within him."

therefore, is regarded as *untrained*. **19:** The polemic against the *law* is heightened as the Gospel proceeds; see 8.17 n.; 10.34. **21:** See 5.1–9. **26:** *Our rulers:* that is, leaders. **27:** The hidden character of the Messiah was a motif, too, in the *Enoch* literature (ancient Jewish writings that were ascribed to Enoch and that claimed to reveal the course of future history); it is possibly alluded to in Mk. 8.28; Matt. 24.23–27, as well. **33–36:** The theme of *going away,* with the significant overtone of Jesus' ascension, recurs in 8.21; 13.33.

7.37–52: Jesus, the source of living water. 37–38: At Tabernacles (see 7.2 n.), water was carried in a gold pitcher from the spring of Siloam and was poured out as a petition for rain. Translation alternatives for this passage are shown in the text and Tfn. In contrast to the text, the Tfn. presents Jesus (not the believer) as the source of *living water,* a symbol of the Spirit. *Scripture:* see Isa. 12.3; Pss. 78.15–16; 105.41. **39:** See Jn. 14.15–16. The giving of the *Spirit* is the result of Jesus' death and glorification. **42:** 2 Sam. 7.12–14; Mic. 5.2. That Jesus was descended from King David was a significant motif in early Christology (see Matt. 1.1 n.; Rom.

47 The Pharisees retorted, 'Have you too been misled? 48 Has a single one of our rulers believed in him, or any of the Pharisees? 49 As for this rabble, which cares nothing for the law, a curse is on them.' 50 Then one of their number, Nicodemus (the man who once visited Jesus), intervened. 51 'Does our law', he asked them, 'permit us to pass judgement on someone without first giving him a hearing and learning the facts?' 52 'Are you a Galilean too?' they retorted. 'Study the scriptures and you will find that the Prophet does not come from Galilee.'

8 12 ONCE again Jesus addressed the people: 'I am the light of the world. No follower of mine shall walk in darkness; he shall have the light of life.' 13 The Pharisees said to him, 'You are witness in your own cause; your testimony is not valid.' 14 Jesus replied, 'My testimony is valid, even though I do testify on my own behalf; because I know where I come from, and where I am going. But you know neither where I come from nor where I am going. 15 You judge by worldly standards; I pass judgement on no one. 16 If I do judge, my judgement is valid because it is not I alone who judge, but I and he who sent me. 17 In your own law it is written that the testimony of two witnesses is valid. 18 I am a witness in my own cause, and my other witness is the Father who sent me.' 19 'Where is your father?' they asked him. Jesus replied, 'You do not know me or my Father; if you knew me you would know my Father too.'

20 Jesus was teaching near the treasury in the temple when he said this; but no one arrested him, because his hour had not yet come.

21 Again he said to them, 'I am going away.

You will look for me, but you will die in your sin; where I am going, you cannot come.' 22 At this the Jews said, 'Perhaps he will kill himself: is that what he means when he says, "Where I am going, you cannot come"?' 23 Jesus continued, 'You belong to this world below, I to the world above. Your home is in this world, mine is not. 24 That is why I told you that you would die in your sins; and you will die in your sins unless you believe that I am what I am.' 25 'And who are you?' they asked him. Jesus answered, 'What I have told you all along. 26 I have much to say about you — and in judgement. But he who sent me speaks the truth, and what I heard from him I report to the world.'

27 They did not understand that he was speaking to them about the Father. 28 So Jesus said to them, 'When you have lifted up the Son of Man you will know that I am what I am. I do nothing on my own authority, but in all I say, I have been taught by my Father. 29 He who sent me is present with me, and has not left me on my own; for I always do what is pleasing to him.' 30 As he said this, many put their faith in him.

31 Turning to the Jews who had believed him, Jesus said, 'If you stand by my teaching, you are truly my disciples; 32 you will know the truth, and the truth will set you free.' 33 'We are Abraham's descendants,' they replied; 'we have never been in slavery to anyone. What do you mean by saying, "You will become free"?' 34 'In very truth I tell you,' said Jesus, 'that everyone who commits sin is a slave. 35 The slave has no permanent standing in the household, but the son belongs to

7:52 **the Prophet does not:** *most witnesses read* the prophets do not. **Galilee:** *some witnesses here insert the passage 7:53—8:11, which is printed on p. 1393.*
8:25 **What . . . along:** *or* Why should I speak to you at all?

1.3; 2 Tim. 2.8). **52:** On 7.53—8.11, see Tfn. for this verse.

8.12–30: Jesus, the light of the world. 12: At Tabernacles (see 7.2 n.) the temple court was brightly illuminated; Jesus is described as the *light* (see 1.4 n., 9; 3.19; 9.5; 12.46) who brings *life* to humanity (1.4). **14:** See 5.31. **17:** By referring to the *law* as *your own*, Jn. has Jesus dissociate himself from the Mosaic institutions (see 7.19) or from Judaism (see 1.19 n.). **19:** See 14.7; 16.3. **20:** *In the treasury:* see Lk. 21.1 n. **21:** See 7.33–36 and n. *Your sin:* the refusal to believe in Jesus as the Son of God (see also v. 24). **24:** *I am what I am* (lit. "I am"): perhaps this is an echo of Exod. 3.14 used to indicate Jesus' divine nature (see vv. 28, 58; 13.19). **25:** The meaning of Jesus' reply is not sufficiently clear for any translation to be regarded as secure (see Tfn. for this verse). **28:** *Lifted up* is another term with extended meaning. Jesus is lifted up on the cross, but this is also his exaltation or glorification (12.32).

8.31–59: Further controversies. 32: *Set you free:* from sin. The saving *truth* is not abstract but rather that found in the gospel and apprehended by faith. **35:** This seems to be a parenthetical remark by Jn., not a word it for ever. ³⁶ If then the Son sets you free, you will indeed be free.

³⁷ 'I know that you are descended from Abraham, yet you are bent on killing me because my teaching makes no headway with you. ³⁸ I tell what I have seen in my Father's presence; you do what you have learned from your father.' ³⁹ They retorted, 'Abraham is our father.' 'If you were Abraham's children', Jesus replied, 'you would do as Abraham did. ⁴⁰ As it is, you are bent on killing me, because I have told you the truth, which I heard from God. That is not how Abraham acted. ⁴¹ You are doing your own father's work.'

They said, 'We are not illegitimate; God is our father, and God alone.' ⁴² Jesus said to them, 'If God were your father, you would love me, for God is the source of my being, and from him I come. I have not come of my own accord; he sent me. ⁴³ Why do you not understand what I am saying? It is because my teaching is beyond your grasp. ⁴⁴ Your father is the devil and you choose to carry out your father's desires. He was a murderer from the beginning, and is not rooted in the truth; there is no truth in him. When he tells a lie he is speaking his own language, for he is a liar and the father of lies. ⁴⁵ But because I speak the truth, you do not believe me. ⁴⁶ Which of you can convict me of sin? If what I say is true, why do you not believe me? ⁴⁷ He who has God for his father listens to the words of God. You are not God's children, and that is why you do not listen.'

⁴⁸ The Jews answered, 'Are we not right in saying that you are a Samaritan, and that you are possessed?' ⁴⁹ 'I am not possessed,' said Jesus; 'I am honouring my Father, but you dishonour me. ⁵⁰ I do not care about my own glory; there is one who does care, and he is judge. ⁵¹ In very truth I tell you, if anyone obeys my teaching he will never see death.'

⁵² The Jews said, 'Now we are certain that you are possessed. Abraham is dead and so are the prophets; yet you say, "If anyone obeys my teaching he will never taste death."

⁵³ Are you greater than our father Abraham? He is dead and the prophets too are dead. Who do you claim to be?'

⁵⁴ Jesus replied, 'If I glorify myself, that glory of mine is worthless. It is the Father who glorifies me, he of whom you say, "He is our God," ⁵⁵ though you do not know him. But I know him; if I were to say that I did not know him I should be a liar like you. I do know him and I obey his word. ⁵⁶ Your father Abraham was overjoyed to see my day; he saw it and was glad.' ⁵⁷ The Jews protested, 'You are not yet fifty years old. How can you have seen Abraham?' ⁵⁸ Jesus said, 'In very truth I tell you, before Abraham was born, I am.' ⁵⁹ They took up stones to throw at him, but he was not to be seen; and he left the temple.

Seeing and believing

9 As HE went on his way Jesus saw a man who had been blind from birth. ² His disciples asked him, 'Rabbi, why was this man born blind? Who sinned, this man or his parents?' ³ 'It is not that he or his parents sinned,' Jesus answered; 'he was born blind so that God's power might be displayed in curing him. ⁴ While daylight lasts we must carry on the work of him who sent me; night is coming, when no one can work. ⁵ While I am in the world I am the light of the world.'

⁶ With these words he spat on the ground and made a paste with the spittle; he spread it on the man's eyes, ⁷ and said to him, 'Go and wash in the pool of Siloam.' (The name means 'Sent'.) The man went off and washed, and came back able to see.

⁸ His neighbours and those who were accustomed to see him begging said, 'Is not this the man who used to sit and beg?' ⁹ Some said, 'Yes, it is.' Others said, 'No, but it is someone like him.' He himself said, 'I am the man.' ¹⁰ They asked him, 'How were your eyes opened?' ¹¹ He replied, 'The man called Jesus made a paste and smeared my eyes with

9:4 **we:** *some witnesses read* I.

of Jesus; compare Heb. 3.3–6. **48:** *Samaritan:* a term of abuse; see 4.7, 9 n. **56:** *He saw it:* similarly 12.41 with respect to Isaiah. The Christ, who was preexistent, already existed in Abraham's time and Isaiah's. Later Jewish tradition (based on Gen. 15.13–17) portrays Abraham as having had the entire future history of his descendants revealed to him. **58:** *I am:* see 8.24 n. The preexistent Christ preceded Abraham.

9.1–41: Cure of a blind man on the sabbath. This "sign" reveals Jesus as the light of humanity, who not only restores physical sight, but confers spiritual sight through faith and baptism. **2–3:** Compare Lk. 13.1–5. **6:** A ritual "anointing." **7:** *Siloam:* Heb. *shiloah*, lit. "sent," but denoting "conduit." John wishes to associate it, and told me to go to Siloam and wash. So I went and washed, and found I could see.' ¹²'Where is he?' they asked. 'I do not know,' he said.

¹³The man who had been blind was brought before the Pharisees. ¹⁴As it was a sabbath day when Jesus made the paste and opened his eyes, ¹⁵the Pharisees too asked him how he had gained his sight. The man told them, 'He spread a paste on my eyes; then I washed, and now I can see.' ¹⁶Some of the Pharisees said, 'This man cannot be from God; he does not keep the sabbath.' Others said, 'How could such signs come from a sinful man?' So they took different sides. ¹⁷Then they continued to question him: 'What have you to say about him? It was your eyes he opened.' He answered, 'He is a prophet.'

¹⁸The Jews would not believe that the man had been blind and had gained his sight, until they had summoned his parents ¹⁹and questioned them: 'Is this your son? Do you say that he was born blind? How is it that he can see now?' ²⁰The parents replied, 'We know that he is our son, and that he was born blind. ²¹But how it is that he can now see, or who opened his eyes, we do not know. Ask him; he is of age; let him speak for himself.' ²²His parents gave this answer because they were afraid of the Jews; for the Jewish authorities had already agreed that anyone who acknowledged Jesus as Messiah should be banned from the synagogue. ²³That is why the parents said, 'He is of age; ask him.'

²⁴So for the second time they summoned the man who had been blind, and said, 'Speak the truth before God. We know that this man is a sinner.' ²⁵'Whether or not he is a sinner, I do not know,' the man replied. 'All I know is this: I was blind and now I can see.' ²⁶'What did he do to you?' they asked. 'How did he open your eyes?' ²⁷'I have told you already,' he retorted, 'but you took no notice. Why do you want to hear it again? Do you also want to become his disciples?' ²⁸Then they became abusive. 'You are that man's disciple,' they said, 'but we are disciples of Mo-

ses. ²⁹We know that God spoke to Moses, but as for this man, we do not know where he comes from.'

³⁰The man replied, 'How extraordinary! Here is a man who has opened my eyes, yet you do not know where he comes from! ³¹We know that God does not listen to sinners; he listens to anyone who is devout and obeys his will. ³²To open the eyes of a man born blind —that is unheard of since time began. ³³If this man was not from God he could do nothing.' ³⁴'Who are you to lecture us?' they retorted. 'You were born and bred in sin.' Then they turned him out.

³⁵Hearing that they had turned him out, Jesus found him and asked, 'Have you faith in the Son of Man?' ³⁶The man answered, 'Tell me who he is, sir, that I may put my faith in him.' ³⁷'You have seen him,' said Jesus; 'indeed, it is he who is speaking to you.' ³⁸'Lord, I believe,' he said, and fell on his knees before him.

³⁹Jesus said, 'It is for judgement that I have come into this world—to give sight to the sightless and to make blind those who see.' ⁴⁰Some Pharisees who were present asked, 'Do you mean that we are blind?' ⁴¹'If you were blind,' said Jesus, 'you would not be guilty, but because you claim to see, your guilt remains.'

Victory over death

10 'In very truth I tell you, the man who does not enter the sheepfold by the door, but climbs in some other way, is nothing but a thief and a robber. ²He who enters by the door is the shepherd in charge of the sheep. ³The door-keeper admits him, and the sheep hear his voice; he calls his own sheep by name, and leads them out. ⁴When he has brought them all out, he goes ahead of them and the sheep follow, because they know his voice. ⁵They will not follow a stranger; they will run away from him, because they do not recognize the voice of strangers.'

9:35 **Son of Man:** *some witnesses read* Son of God.

Jesus and the pool, both *sent* by God; Jn. sees baptismal symbolism in the incident. **22:** *Banned from the synagogue:* the practice of expelling Jewish Christians apparently arose near the end of the first century. See also v. 34. **29:** The issue of *where he* (Jesus) *comes from* is raised in different, "earthly" ways by Jesus' opponents (see also 7.27, 41–42); Jn. intends the question to elicit the response: "From God" (v. 33; 8.42). **35–38:** The dialogue is often viewed as reflecting the late first-century baptismal interrogation of the neophyte.

10.1–21: Jesus, the good shepherd. 2: God is spoken of often as the shepherd; see Isa. 40.11; Jer. 23.3;

[6] This was a parable that Jesus told them, but they did not understand what he meant by it.

[7] So Jesus spoke again: 'In very truth I tell you, I am the door of the sheepfold. [8] The sheep paid no heed to any who came before me, for they were all thieves and robbers. [9] I am the door; anyone who comes into the fold through me will be safe. He will go in and out and find pasture.

[10] 'A thief comes only to steal, kill, and destroy; I have come that they may have life, and may have it in all its fullness. [11] I am the good shepherd; the good shepherd lays down his life for the sheep. [12] The hired man, when he sees the wolf coming, abandons the sheep and runs away, because he is not the shepherd and the sheep are not his. Then the wolf harries the flock and scatters the sheep. [13] The man runs away because he is a hired man and cares nothing for the sheep.

[14] 'I am the good shepherd; I know my own and my own know me, [15] as the Father knows me and I know the Father; and I lay down my life for the sheep. [16] But there are other sheep of mine, not belonging to this fold; I must lead them as well, and they too will listen to my voice. There will then be one flock, one shepherd. [17] The Father loves me because I lay down my life, to receive it back again. [18] No one takes it away from me; I am laying it down of my own free will. I have the right to lay it down, and I have the right to receive it back again; this charge I have received from my Father.'

[19] These words once again caused a division among the Jews. [20] Many of them said, 'He is possessed, he is out of his mind. Why listen to him?' [21] Others said, 'No one possessed by a demon could speak like this. Could a demon open the eyes of the blind?'

[22] It was winter, and the festival of the Dedication was being held in Jerusalem. [23] As Jesus was walking in the temple precincts, in Solomon's Portico, [24] the Jews gathered round him and asked: 'How long are you going to keep us in suspense? Tell us plainly: are you the Messiah?' [25] 'I have told you,' said Jesus, 'and you do not believe. My deeds done in my Father's name are my credentials, [26] but because you are not sheep of my flock you do not believe. [27] My own sheep listen to my voice; I know them and they follow me. [28] I give them eternal life and they will never perish; no one will snatch them from my care. [29] My Father who has given them to me is greater than all, and no one can snatch them out of the Father's care. [30] The Father and I are one.'

[31] Once again the Jews picked up stones to stone him. [32] At this Jesus said to them, 'By the Father's power I have done many good deeds before your eyes; for which of these are you stoning me?' [33] 'We are not stoning you for any good deed,' the Jews replied, 'but for blasphemy: you, a man, are claiming to be God.' [34] Jesus answered, 'Is it not written in your law, "I said: You are gods"? [35] It is those to whom God's word came who are called gods—and scripture cannot be set aside. [36] Then why do you charge me with blasphemy for saying, "I am God's son," I whom the Father consecrated and sent into the world?

[37] 'If my deeds are not the deeds of my Father, do not believe me. [38] But if they are, then even if you do not believe me, believe the deeds, so that you may recognize and know that the Father is in me, and I in the Father.'

[39] This provoked them to make another attempt to seize him, but he escaped from their clutches.

[40] Jesus withdrew again across the Jordan, to

10:29 **My Father . . . snatch them:** *some witnesses read* That which my Father has given me is greater than all, and no one can snatch it.   10:33 **claiming . . . God:** *or* claiming to be a god.

Ps. 23.1. **11:** The ancient ideal of a *good shepherd* (as in Ezek. 34.23) is regarded as fulfilled in Jesus. **16:** *Other sheep:* Gentiles. **17–18:** A series of key expressions — *lay down, receive it back,* and *right* — reflect a major motif that the anticipated crucifixion and vindication of Jesus are not imposed by human decision, but result from Jesus' *free* decision in obedience to God's will. **21:** An allusion to the incident in ch. 9.

    10.22–39: Further controversy. 22: *Dedication,* Hanukkah, a Jewish feast held in December, commemorated the reconsecration of the temple (164 B.C.E.) after its profanation by Antiochus Epiphanes (167 B.C.E.). **24–38:** This exchange can call to mind the trial scene before the Sanhedrin (see Lk. 22.66–71). Here, too, the issue is raised whether Jesus claims to be Messiah (vv. 24–31) or the Son of God (vv. 33–38). **34:** *You are gods:* an allusion to Ps. 82.6.

the place where John had been baptizing earlier, and stayed there [41] while crowds came to him. 'John gave us no miraculous sign,' they said, 'but all that he told us about this man was true.' [42] And many came to believe in him there.

11 There was a man named Lazarus who had fallen ill. His home was at Bethany, the village of Mary and her sister Martha. [2] This Mary, whose brother Lazarus had fallen ill, was the woman who anointed the Lord with ointment and wiped his feet with her hair. [3] The sisters sent a message to him: 'Sir, you should know that your friend lies ill.' [4] When Jesus heard this he said, 'This illness is not to end in death; through it God's glory is to be revealed and the Son of God glorified.' [5] Therefore, though he loved Martha and her sister and Lazarus, [6] he stayed where he was for two days after hearing of Lazarus's illness.

[7] He then said to his disciples, 'Let us go back to Judaea.' [8] 'Rabbi,' his disciples said, 'it is not long since the Jews there were wanting to stone you. Are you going there again?' [9] Jesus replied, 'Are there not twelve hours of daylight? Anyone can walk in the daytime without stumbling, because he has this world's light to see by. [10] But if he walks after nightfall he stumbles, because the light fails him.'

[11] After saying this he added, 'Our friend Lazarus has fallen asleep, but I shall go and wake him.' [12] The disciples said, 'Master, if he is sleeping he will recover.' [13] Jesus had been speaking of Lazarus's death, but they thought that he meant natural sleep. [14] Then Jesus told them plainly: 'Lazarus is dead. [15] I am glad for your sake that I was not there; for it will lead you to believe. But let us go to him.' [16] Thomas, called 'the Twin', said to his fellow-disciples, 'Let us also go and die with him.'

[17] ON his arrival Jesus found that Lazarus had already been four days in the tomb. [18] Bethany was just under two miles from Jerusalem, [19] and many of the Jews had come from the city to visit Martha and Mary and condole with them about their brother. [20] As soon as Martha heard that Jesus was on his way, she went to meet him, and left Mary sitting at home.

[21] Martha said to Jesus, 'Lord, if you had been here my brother would not have died. [22] Even now I know that God will grant you whatever you ask of him.' [23] Jesus said, 'Your brother will rise again.' [24] 'I know that he will rise again', said Martha, 'at the resurrection on the last day.' [25] Jesus said, 'I am the resurrection and the life. Whoever has faith in me shall live, even though he dies; [26] and no one who lives and has faith in me shall ever die. Do you believe this?' [27] 'I do, Lord,' she answered; 'I believe that you are the Messiah, the Son of God who was to come into the world.'

[28] So saying she went to call her sister Mary and, taking her aside, she said, 'The Master is here and is asking for you.' [29] As soon as Mary heard this she rose and went to him. [30] Jesus had not yet entered the village, but was still at the place where Martha had met him. [31] When the Jews who were in the house condoling with Mary saw her hurry out, they went after her, assuming that she was going to the tomb to weep there.

[32] Mary came to the place where Jesus was, and as soon as she saw him she fell at his feet and said, 'Lord, if you had been here my brother would not have died.' [33] When Jesus saw her weeping and the Jews who had come with her weeping, he was moved with indignation and deeply distressed. [34] 'Where have you laid him?' he asked. They replied, 'Come and see.' [35] Jesus wept. [36] The Jews said, 'How dearly he must have loved him!' [37] But some of them said, 'Could not this man, who opened the blind man's eyes, have done something to keep Lazarus from dying?'

[38] Jesus, again deeply moved, went to the

11:25 *Some witnesses omit* and the life

10.40–11.54: The supreme sign: Lazarus' resurrection. 40: See 1.28. **11.1:** This *Bethany* (contrast 1.28) was a town near Jerusalem (see v. 18). *Mary and her sister Martha* appear in Lk. 10.38–42. **2:** On Mary's anointing of Jesus, see 12.1–8 and nn. *Lord:* a title rare in Jn. before the postresurrection narratives (see 6.23, and probably 4.1); it is frequent in Lk.–Acts, and in Paul's letters. **4:** *Son of God:* see 5.16–30 n. **9:** *This world's light:* the sun, but with the overtone that even daylight is a sign through which Jesus reveals himself as the true light. **17:** It was popularly held that corruption of the body began the third day after death; hence, the point of *four days* is to assert that Lazarus was truly dead and his resurrection real. **25:** *I am the resurrection and I am the life:* This, like other sayings in Jn. (e.g. 3.13; 5.25; 17.10 n.; perhaps 4.38), is best understood if the speaker tomb. It was a cave, with a stone placed against it. 39 Jesus said, 'Take away the stone.' Martha, the dead man's sister, said to him, 'Sir, by now there will be a stench; he has been there four days.' 40 Jesus said, 'Did I not tell you that if you have faith you will see the glory of God?' 41 Then they removed the stone.

Jesus looked upwards and said, 'Father, I thank you for hearing me. 42 I know that you always hear me, but I have spoken for the sake of the people standing round, that they may believe it was you who sent me.'

43 Then he raised his voice in a great cry: 'Lazarus, come out.' 44 The dead man came out, his hands and feet bound with linen bandages, his face wrapped in a cloth. Jesus said, 'Loose him; let him go.'

45 Many of the Jews who had come to visit Mary, and had seen what Jesus did, put their faith in him. 46 But some of them went off to the Pharisees and reported what he had done.

47 Thereupon the chief priests and the Pharisees convened a meeting of the Council. 'This man is performing many signs,' they said, 'and what action are we taking? 48 If we let him go on like this the whole populace will believe in him, and then the Romans will come and sweep away our temple and our nation.' 49 But one of them, Caiaphas, who was high priest that year, said, 'You have no grasp of the situation at all; 50 you do not realize that it is more to your interest that one man should die for the people, than that the whole nation should be destroyed.' 51 He did not say this of his own accord, but as the high priest that year he was prophesying that Jesus would die for the nation, 52 and not for the nation alone but to gather together the scattered children of God. 53 So from that day on they plotted his death.

54 Accordingly Jesus no longer went about openly among the Jews, but withdrew to a town called Ephraim, in the country bordering on the desert, and stayed there with his disciples.

The Passover in Jerusalem

55 The Jewish Passover was now at hand, and many people went up from the country to Jerusalem to purify themselves before the festival. 56 They looked out for Jesus, and as they stood in the temple they asked one another, 'What do you think? Perhaps he is not coming to the festival.' 57 Now the chief priests and the Pharisees had given orders that anyone who knew where he was must report it, so that they might arrest him.

12 Six days before the Passover festival Jesus came to Bethany, the home of Lazarus whom he had raised from the dead. 2 They gave a supper in his honour, at which Martha served, and Lazarus was among the guests with Jesus. 3 Then Mary brought a pound of very costly perfume, pure oil of nard, and anointed Jesus's feet and wiped them with her hair, till the house was filled with the fragrance. 4 At this, Judas Iscariot, one of his disciples—the one who was to betray him—protested, 5 'Could not this perfume have been sold for three hundred denarii and the money given to the poor?' 6 He said this, not out of any concern for the poor, but because he was a thief; he had charge of the common purse and used to pilfer the money kept in it. 7 'Leave her alone,' said Jesus. 'Let her keep it for the day of my burial. 8 The poor you have always among you, but you will not always have me.'

9 Learning he was there the Jews came in large numbers, not only because of Jesus but

12:5 denarii: see p. xxvii.   12:8 Some witnesses omit The poor . . . have me.

---

is viewed as the risen Christ. **40:** This remark reflects Jesus' previous statements to the disciples (v. 4) and Martha (vv. 25–26). *Glory of God:* see Introduction. **45–48:** John views the raising of Lazarus as the chief basis of the hostility which caused Jesus' death (but, on the other hand, see 10.17–18 n.). **47:** John alone ascribes to the *Pharisees* a role in the ordeal of Jesus (see 18.3), probably reflecting the tension between Christianity and Pharisaic Judaism when this Gospel was written about 90 C.E. **49:** *Caiaphas* was high priest from 18 to 36 C.E. **52:** *The scattered children of God* probably denotes the Gentiles. **54:** *Ephraim:* not the well-known region, but a town which cannot now be located.

11.55–12.50: Conclusion of Jesus' public ministry. 55: This is the third *Passover* in Jesus' public life (see 2.13 n.; 6.4). **12.1:** See Mk. 14.3–9 for a different account of Jesus' anointing. **3:** That Mary *anointed Jesus' feet* (rather than head) is strange; compare Lk. 7.37–38, perhaps a related tradition. **9–11:** The raising of Lazarus also to see Lazarus whom he had raised from the dead. [10] The chief priests then resolved to do away with Lazarus as well, [11] since on his account many Jews were going over to Jesus and putting their faith in him.

[12] THE next day the great crowd of pilgrims who had come for the festival, hearing that Jesus was on the way to Jerusalem, [13] went out to meet him with palm branches in their hands, shouting, 'Hosanna! Blessed is he who comes in the name of the Lord! Blessed is the king of Israel!' [14] Jesus found a donkey and mounted it, in accordance with the words of scripture: [15] 'Fear no more, daughter of Zion; see, your king is coming, mounted on a donkey's colt.' [16] At the time his disciples did not understand this, but after Jesus had been glorified they remembered that this had been written about him, and that it had happened to him.

[17] The people who were present when he called Lazarus out of the tomb and raised him from the dead kept telling what they had seen and heard. [18] That is why the crowd went to meet him: they had heard of this sign that he had performed. [19] The Pharisees said to one another, 'You can see we are getting nowhere; all the world has gone after him!'

[20] AMONG those who went up to worship at the festival were some Gentiles. [21] They approached Philip, who was from Bethsaida in Galilee, and said to him, 'Sir, we should like to see Jesus.' [22] Philip went and told Andrew, and the two of them went to tell Jesus. [23] Jesus replied: 'The hour has come for the Son of Man to be glorified. [24] In very truth I tell you, unless a grain of wheat falls into the ground and dies, it remains that and nothing more; but if it dies, it bears a rich harvest. [25] Whoever loves himself is lost, but he who hates himself in this world will be kept safe for eternal life. [26] If anyone is to serve me, he must follow me; where I am, there will my servant be. Whoever serves me will be honoured by the Father.

[27] 'Now my soul is in turmoil, and what am I to say? "Father, save me from this hour"? No, it was for this that I came to this hour. [28] Father, glorify your name.' A voice came from heaven: 'I have glorified it, and I will glorify it again.' [29] The crowd standing by said it was thunder they heard, while others said, 'An angel has spoken to him.' [30] Jesus replied, 'This voice spoke for your sake, not mine. [31] Now is the hour of judgement for this world; now shall the prince of this world be driven out. [32] And when I am lifted up from the earth I shall draw everyone to myself.' [33] This he said to indicate the kind of death he was to die.

[34] The people answered, 'Our law teaches us that the Messiah remains for ever. What do you mean by saying that the Son of Man must be lifted up? What Son of Man is this?' [35] Jesus answered them: 'The light is among you still, but not for long. Go on your way while you have the light, so that darkness may not overtake you. He who journeys in the dark does not know where he is going. [36] Trust to the light while you have it, so that you may become children of light.' After these words Jesus went away from them into hiding.'

[37] IN spite of the many signs which Jesus had performed in their presence they would not believe in him, [38] for the prophet Isaiah's words had to be fulfilled: 'Lord, who has believed what we reported, and to whom has the power of the Lord been revealed?' [39] And there is another saying of Isaiah which explains why they could not believe: [40] 'He has blinded their eyes and dulled their minds, lest they should see with their eyes, and perceive with their minds, and turn to me to heal them.' [41] Isaiah said this because he saw his glory and spoke about him.

[42] For all that, even among those in author-

is linked by these verses to the messianic entry in vv. 12–19; in Jewish tradition, the advent of the Messiah was related to the resurrection of the dead. **12–19:** Jesus' entry into the city is interpreted as messianic by citing Zech. 9.9. **13:** *Hosanna:* see Matt. 21.9 n. **16:** *Remembered:* see 2.17 n. **20:** *Some Gentiles* (lit. Greeks): possibly Gentiles who acknowledged the God of Israel; see Acts 10.2 n. **23:** *Hour:* see 2.4 n. **27:** *My soul is in turmoil* introduces a scene reminiscent of the Synoptic narrative of Jesus' suffering in Gethsemane (see Mk. 14.32–42). **31–32:** *Judgement for this world:* see 1.19–51 n. **35–36:** The theme of judgment and salvation is restated in terms of *light* and *darkness* (see 1.5; 3.19–21). **37–43:** John concludes the Book of Signs (see Introduction) by noting that Jesus' own people did not respond to him. **38–41:** Jesus' lack of success with fellow Jews is explained by two citations from the prophet Isaiah (53.1; 6.10). Moreover, Jn. interprets Isa. 6.1–13 ity many believed in him, but would not acknowledge him on account of the Pharisees, for fear of being banned from the synagogue. [43] For they valued human reputation rather than the honour which comes from God.

[44] JESUS proclaimed: 'To believe in me, is not to believe in me but in him who sent me; [45] to see me, is to see him who sent me. [46] I have come into the world as light, so that no one who has faith in me should remain in darkness. [47] But if anyone hears my words and disregards them, I am not his judge; I have not come to judge the world, but to save the world. [48] There is a judge for anyone who rejects me and does not accept my words; the word I have spoken will be his judge on the last day. [49] I do not speak on my own authority, but the Father who sent me has himself commanded me what to say and how to speak. [50] I know that his commands are eternal life. What the Father has said to me, therefore — that is what I speak.'

Farewell discourses

13 IT was before the Passover festival, and Jesus knew that his hour had come and that he must leave this world and go to the Father. He had always loved his own who were in the world, and he loved them to the end.

[2] The devil had already put it into the mind of Judas son of Simon Iscariot to betray him. During supper, [3] Jesus, well aware that the Father had entrusted everything to him, and that he had come from God and was going back to God, [4] rose from the supper table, took off his outer garment and, taking a towel, tied it round him. [5] Then he poured water into a basin, and began to wash his disciples' feet and to wipe them with the towel.

[6] When he came to Simon Peter, Peter said to him, 'You, Lord, washing my feet?' [7] Jesus replied, 'You do not understand now what I am doing, but one day you will.' [8] Peter said, 'I will never let you wash my feet.' 'If I do not wash you,' Jesus replied, 'you have no part with me.' [9] 'Then, Lord,' said Simon Peter, 'not my feet only; wash my hands and head as well!'

[10] Jesus said to him, 'Anyone who has bathed needs no further washing; he is clean all over; and you are clean, though not every one of you.' [11] He added the words 'not every one of you' because he knew who was going to betray him.

[12] After washing their feet he put on his garment and sat down again. 'Do you understand what I have done for you?' he asked. [13] 'You call me Teacher and Lord, and rightly so, for that is what I am. [14] Then if I, your Lord and Teacher, have washed your feet, you also ought to wash one another's feet. [15] I have set you an example: you are to do as I have done for you. [16] In very truth I tell you, a servant is not greater than his master, nor a messenger than the one who sent him. [17] If you know this, happy are you if you act upon it.

[18] 'I am not speaking about all of you; I know whom I have chosen. But there is a text of scripture to be fulfilled: "He who eats bread with me has turned against me." [19] I tell you this now, before the event, so that when it happens you may believe that I am what I am. [20] In very truth I tell you, whoever receives any messenger of mine receives me; and receiving me, he receives the One who sent me.'

[21] After saying this, Jesus exclaimed in deep distress, 'In very truth I tell you, one of you is going to betray me.' [22] The disciples looked at one another in bewilderment: which of them could he mean? [23] One of them, the disciple he loved, was reclining close beside Jesus. [24] Simon Peter signalled to him to find out which one he meant. [25] That

13:10 **needs ... washing:** *some witnesses read* needs only to wash his feet.

as a preview of Christ's glorification. **44–50:** The message of the Book of Signs (see Introduction) is recapitulated in these verses.

13.1–30: The Last Supper. 1: *His hour had come:* an important theme of the Johannine passion narrative is that Jesus *knew* in advance all that was to happen to him (see 16.28; 18.4; 19.28). **3–5:** Jesus washes his disciples' feet to symbolize the humiliation of his death, which is the sole source of forgiveness of sins and of fellowship with him (v. 8). **7:** The contrast between the disciples' limited understanding before Jesus' death and their future understanding, to take place *one day,* is frequent; see 2.22; 12.16; 16.12. **11:** *Betray him:* 6.64. **18:** See Ps. 41.9. **19:** *I am:* see 8.24 n. **23:** *The disciple he loved:* see 18.15 n. **27:** The words *Satan entered* disciple leaned back close to Jesus and asked, 'Lord, who is it?' 26 Jesus replied, 'It is the one to whom I give this piece of bread when I have dipped it in the dish.' Then he took it, dipped it in the dish, and gave it to Judas son of Simon Iscariot. 27 As soon as Judas had received it Satan entered him. Jesus said to him, 'Do quickly what you have to do.' 28 No one at the table understood what he meant by this. 29 Some supposed that, as Judas was in charge of the common purse, Jesus was telling him to buy what was needed for the festival, or to make some gift to the poor. 30 As soon as Judas had received the bread he went out. It was night.

31 WHEN he had gone out, Jesus said, 'Now the Son of Man is glorified, and in him God is glorified. 32 If God is glorified in him, God will also glorify him in himself; and he will glorify him now. 33 My children, I am to be with you for a little longer; then you will look for me, and, as I told the Jews, I tell you now: where I am going you cannot come. 34 I give you a new commandment: love one another; as I have loved you, so you are to love one another. 35 If there is this love among you, then everyone will know that you are my disciples.'

36 Simon Peter said to him, 'Lord, where are you going?' Jesus replied, 'I am going where you cannot follow me now, but one day you will.' 37 Peter said, 'Lord, why cannot I follow you now? I will lay down my life for you.' 38 Jesus answered, 'Will you really lay down your life for me? In very truth I tell you, before the cock crows you will have denied me three times.

14 'Set your troubled hearts at rest. Trust in God always; trust also in me. 2 There are many dwelling-places in my Father's house; if it were not so I should have told you; for I am going to prepare a place for you. 3 And if I go and prepare a place for you, I shall come again and take you to myself, so that where I am you may be also; 4 and you know the way I am taking.' 5 Thomas said, 'Lord, we do not know where you are going, so how can we know the way?' 6 Jesus replied, 'I am the way, the truth, and the life; no one comes to the Father except by me. 7 'If you knew me you would know my Father too. From now on you do know him; you have seen him.' 8 Philip said to him, 'Lord, show us the Father; we ask no more.' 9 Jesus answered, 'Have I been all this time with you, Philip, and still you do not know me? Anyone who has seen me has seen the Father. Then how can you say, "Show us the Father"? 10 Do you not believe that I am in the Father, and the Father in me? I am not myself the source of the words I speak to you: it is the Father who dwells in me doing his own work. 11 Believe me when I say that I am in the Father and the Father in me; or else accept the evidence of the deeds themselves. 12 In very truth I tell you, whoever has faith in me will do what I am doing; indeed he will do greater things still because I am going to the Father. 13 Anything you ask in my name I will do, so that the Father may be glorified in the Son. 14 If you ask anything in my name I will do it.

15 'If you love me you will obey my commands; 16 and I will ask the Father, and he will give you another to be your advocate, who will be with you for ever — 17 the Spirit of truth. The world cannot accept him, because the world neither sees nor knows him; but you know him, because he dwells with you and will be in you. 18 I will not leave you bereft; I am coming back to you. 19 In a little while the world will see me no longer, but you will see me; because I live, you too will live. 20 When that day comes you will know that I am in my Father, and you in me and I in you. 21 Anyone who has received my commands and obeys them — he it is who loves me; and he who loves me will be loved by my Father; and I will love him and disclose myself to him.'

22 Judas said — the other Judas, not Iscariot

13:32 *Some witnesses omit* If God . . . in him.
14:3 **also:** *some witnesses add* you know where I am going.   14:7 **If you . . . too:** *some witnesses read* If you know me you will know my Father too.   14:14 **If you ask:** *some witnesses add* me.   14:17 **will be:** *some witnesses read* is.

him prepare the reader to see that Jesus' confrontation in 18.2–6 is really with Satan. See also Lk. 22.3.   **13.31–14.31: Jesus' farewell discourse.** This final message is partly repeated later in chs. 15–16. **33:** See 7.34; 8.21. **34:** Jesus' death for his friends (15.13) makes the observance of the *new commandment* of love for each other possible. **14.1:** The words *set your troubled hearts at rest* (repeated at v. 27) state the theme of the discourse; i.e. Jesus' departure is to make possible the mutual indwelling of Father, Son, and disciples (see vv. 2, 20, 23). **13–14:** The phrases *in my name* and *I will do* indicate the belief that Jesus and the Father are

—'Lord, how has it come about that you mean to disclose yourself to us and not to the world?' 23 Jesus replied, 'Anyone who loves me will heed what I say; then my Father will love him, and we will come to him and make our dwelling with him; 24 but whoever does not love me does not heed what I say. And the word you hear is not my own: it is the word of the Father who sent me. 25 I have told you these things while I am still with you; 26 but the advocate, the Holy Spirit whom the Father will send in my name, will teach you everything and remind you of all that I have told you.

27 'Peace is my parting gift to you, my own peace, such as the world cannot give. Set your troubled hearts at rest, and banish your fears. 28 You heard me say, "I am going away, and I am coming back to you." If you loved me you would be glad that I am going to the Father; for the Father is greater than I am. 29 I have told you now, before it happens, so that when it does happen you may have faith. 30 'I shall not talk much longer with you, for the prince of this world approaches. He has no rights over me; 31 but the world must be shown that I love the Father and am doing what he commands; come, let us go!

15 'I AM the true vine, and my Father is the gardener. 2 Any branch of mine that is barren he cuts away; and any fruiting branch he prunes clean, to make it more fruitful still. 3 You are already clean because of the word I have spoken to you. 4 Dwell in me, as I in you. No branch can bear fruit by itself, but only if it remains united with the vine; no more can you bear fruit, unless you remain united with me.

5 'I am the vine; you are the branches. Anyone who dwells in me, as I dwell in him, bears much fruit; apart from me you can do noth-

ing. 6 Anyone who does not dwell in me is thrown away like a withered branch. The withered branches are gathered up, thrown on the fire, and burnt.

7 'If you dwell in me, and my words dwell in you, ask whatever you want, and you shall have it. 8 This is how my Father is glorified: you are to bear fruit in plenty and so be my disciples. 9 As the Father has loved me, so I have loved you. Dwell in my love. 10 If you heed my commands, you will dwell in my love, as I have heeded my Father's commands and dwell in his love.

11 'I have spoken thus to you, so that my joy may be in you, and your joy complete. 12 This is my commandment: love one another, as I have loved you. 13 There is no greater love than this, that someone should lay down his life for his friends. 14 You are my friends, if you do what I command you. 15 No longer do I call you servants, for a servant does not know what his master is about. I have called you friends, because I have disclosed to you everything that I heard from my Father. 16 You did not choose me: I chose you. I appointed you to go on and bear fruit, fruit that will last; so that the Father may give you whatever you ask in my name. 17 This is my commandment to you: love one another.

18 'If the world hates you, it hated me first, as you know well. 19 If you belonged to the world, the world would love its own; but you do not belong to the world, now that I have chosen you out of the world, and for that reason the world hates you. 20 Remember what I said: "A servant is not greater than his master." If they persecuted me, they will also persecute you; if they have followed my teaching, they will follow yours. 21 All this will they do to you on my account, because they do not know the One who sent me.

15:18 it hated . . . well: or bear in mind that it hated me first.

so related (vv. 9–10) that petitionary prayer may be directed to the Son. See 15.16 n.; 16.23–26 n. **26:** The advocate is identified as the Holy Spirit sent in Jesus' name by God (compare vv. 16–17). Compare 1 Jn. 2.1 n. **28:** The Father is greater than I: see v. 10; 5.19–30 n.

15.1–17: The abiding of Christians in Jesus and in one another. 1: Jesus, the true vine, fulfills the prophetic images of Israel as vineyard (Isa. 5.1–7) and vine (Jer. 2.21; Ezek. 19.10–14). **4:** The invitation to dwell in me implies obedience to Jesus' commands (v. 10), especially that of love for each other (v. 17). **14:** The title friend denotes great intimacy; it was bestowed on Abraham (Isa. 41.8; Jas. 2.23). **16:** In this passage (see 16.23–26 n.), the efficacy of prayer in my name is presented as a product of the close union with Jesus (see v. 4 n.) to which the disciples have been called.

15.18–27: The Christian is separated from the world. 18: The world: a term often ambivalent, here indicates Jesus' enemies, as in 12.31; 14.17; 16.33; 17.9; see 3.16 n. **20:** The servant, master saying occurs several times

22 'If I had not come and spoken to them, they would not be guilty of sin; but now they have no excuse for their sin: 23 whoever hates me, hates my Father also. 24 If I had not done such deeds among them as no one else has ever done, they would not be guilty of sin; but now they have seen and hated both me and my Father. 25 This text in their law had to come true: "They hated me without reason."

26 'When the advocate has come, whom I shall send you from the Father — the Spirit of truth that issues from the Father — he will bear witness to me. 27 And you also are my witnesses, because you have been with me from the first.

16 'I have told you all this to guard you against the breakdown of your faith. 2 They will ban you from the synagogue; indeed, the time is coming when anyone who kills you will suppose that he is serving God. 3 They will do these things because they did not know either the Father or me. 4 I have told you all this so that when the time comes for it to happen you may remember my warning. I did not tell you this at first, because then I was with you; 5 but now I am going away to him who sent me. None of you asks me, "Where are you going?" 6 Yet you are plunged into grief at what I have told you. 7 Nevertheless I assure you that it is in your interest that I am leaving you. If I do not go, the advocate will not come, whereas if I go, I will send him to you. 8 When he comes, he will prove the world wrong about sin, justice, and judgement: 9 about sin, because they refuse to believe in me; 10 about justice, because I go to the Father when I pass from your sight; 11 about judgement, because the prince of this world stands condemned.

12 'There is much more that I could say to you, but the burden would be too great for you now. 13 However, when the Spirit of truth comes, he will guide you into all the truth; for he will not speak on his own au-

thority, but will speak only what he hears; and he will make known to you what is to come. 14 He will glorify me, for he will take what is mine and make it known to you. 15 All that the Father has is mine, and that is why I said, "He will take what is mine and make it known to you."

16 'A LITTLE while, and you see me no more; again a little while, and you will see me.' 17 Some of his disciples said to one another, 'What does he mean by this: "A little while, and you will not see me, and again a little while, and you will see me," and by this: "Because I am going to the Father"?' 18 So they asked, 'What is this "little while" that he is talking about? We do not know what he means.'

19 Jesus knew that they were wanting to question him, and said, 'Are you discussing that saying of mine: "A little while, and you will not see me, and again a little while, and you will see me"? 20 In very truth I tell you, you will weep and mourn, but the world will be glad. But though you will be plunged in grief, your grief will be turned to joy. 21 A woman in labour is in pain because her time has come; but when her baby is born she forgets the anguish in her joy that a child has been born into the world. 22 So it is with you: for the moment you are sad; but I shall see you again, and then you will be joyful, and no one shall rob you of your joy. 23 When that day comes you will ask me nothing more. In very truth I tell you, if you ask the Father for anything in my name, he will give it you. 24 So far you have asked nothing in my name. Ask and you will receive, that your joy may be complete.

25 'Till now I have been using figures of speech; a time is coming when I shall no longer use figures, but tell you of the Father

16:23 **if you ask ... you:** *some witnesses read* if you ask the Father for anything, he will give it you in my name.

with varying interpretations; see 13.16 (compare 12.26); Matt. 10.24; Lk. 6.40. **25:** See Pss. 35.19; 69.4.

16.1–15: Jesus' departure; the sending of the advocate. 4: *Remember:* 2.17 n. **7–11:** As the one who represents the risen Christ, the *advocate* is here assigned a three-fold task: to pass judgment on the sin of the world, to testify to Jesus' presence with God, and to attest to God's condemnation of the powers of evil. See also v. 13; 14.26.

16.16–33: Jesus' return to the disciples. 16: *You will see me* is a promise which includes Christ's postresurrection appearances, his presence through the Spirit, and his second (final) coming. **23–26:** John now completes the teaching on prayer *in my name* (see 14.13–14 n.; 15.16 n.): it is a form of prayer which arises from Jesus' glorification and the gift of the Spirit (vv. 13–14); it is heard because of the intimacy between God and in plain words. 26 When that day comes you will make your request in my name, and I do not say that I shall pray to the Father for you, 27 for the Father loves you himself, because you have loved me and believed that I came from God. 28 I came from the Father and have come into the world; and now I am leaving the world again and going to the Father.' 29 His disciples said, 'Now you are speaking plainly, not in figures of speech! 30 We are certain now that you know everything, and do not need to be asked; because of this we believe that you have come from God.'

31 Jesus answered, 'Do you now believe? 32 I warn you, the hour is coming, has indeed already come, when you are to be scattered, each to his own home, leaving me alone. Yet I am not alone, for the Father is with me. 33 I have told you all this so that in me you may find peace. In the world you will have suffering. But take heart! I have conquered the world.'

17 THEN Jesus looked up to heaven and said:

'Father, the hour has come. Glorify your Son, that the Son may glorify you. 2 For you have made him sovereign over all mankind, to give eternal life to all whom you have given him. 3 This is eternal life: to know you the only true God, and Jesus Christ whom you have sent.

4 'I have glorified you on earth by finishing the work which you gave me to do; 5 and now, Father, glorify me in your own presence with the glory which I had with you before the world began.

6 'I have made your name known to the men whom you gave me out of the world. They were yours and you gave them to me, and they have obeyed your command. 7 Now they know that all you gave me has come from you; 8 for I have taught them what I

learned from you, and they have received it: they know with certainty that I came from you, and they have believed that you sent me.

9 'I pray for them; I am not praying for the world but for those whom you have given me, because they belong to you. 10 All that is mine is yours, and what is yours is mine; and through them is my glory revealed.

11 'I am no longer in the world; they are still in the world, but I am coming to you. Holy Father, protect them by the power of your name, the name you have given me, that they may be one, as we are one. 12 While I was with them, I protected them by the power of your name which you gave me, and kept them safe. Not one of them is lost except the man doomed to be lost, for scripture has to be fulfilled.

13 'Now I am coming to you; but while I am still in the world I speak these words, so that they may have my joy within them in full measure. 14 I have delivered your word to them, and the world hates them because they are strangers in the world, as I am. 15 I do not pray you to take them out of the world, but to keep them from the evil one. 16 They are strangers in the world, as I am. 17 Consecrate them by the truth; your word is truth. 18 As you sent me into the world, I have sent them into the world, 19 and for their sake I consecrate myself, that they too may be consecrated by the truth.

20 'It is not for these alone that I pray, but for those also who through their words put their faith in me. 21 May they all be one; as you, Father, are in me, and I in you, so also may they be in us, that the world may believe that you sent me. 22 The glory which you gave me I have given to them, that they may be

17:11 **protect ... given me:** *some witnesses read* protect by the power of your name those whom you have given me.   17:12 **protected ... gave me:** *some witnesses read* protected by the power of your name those whom you have given me.

the believer. **32:** Mark 14.27 and Matt. 26.31 connect this prophecy with the Gethsemane scene; see Zech. 13.7.

17.1–8: Jesus prays for the revelation of God's glory. 1: Jesus' intercession has a high-priestly character reminiscent of Rom. 8.34 and the Letter to Hebrews. He does not pray for himself, except perhaps in v. 5, but for the completion of his mission, to reveal the unseen God, who can be seen in the Son.

17.9–19: Jesus' intercession for the disciples. 10: *Through them is my glory revealed* refers to the disciples' postresurrection faith, which grasps Jesus' identity as the Son of God. **12:** *The man doomed to be lost* is Judas (see 6.70–71). **19:** *I consecrate myself* expresses Jesus' self-offering to God through his death.

17.20–26: Jesus' intercession for future Christians. 20: *Through their words:* i.e. the gospel handed down by the first disciples, which provides the occasion for the gift of faith to future Christians (see Rom. 10.10–17).

one, as we are one; 23 I in them and you in me, may they be perfectly one. Then the world will know that you sent me, and that you loved them as you loved me.

24 'Father, they are your gift to me; and my desire is that they may be with me where I am, so that they may look upon my glory, which you have given me because you loved me before the world began. 25 Righteous Father, although the world does not know you, I know you, and they know that you sent me. 26 I made your name known to them, and will make it known, so that the love you had for me may be in them, and I in them.'

The trial and crucifixion of Jesus

18 AFTER this prayer, Jesus went out with his disciples across the Kedron ravine. There was a garden there, and he and his disciples went into it. 2 The place was known to Judas, his betrayer, because Jesus had often met there with his disciples. 3 So Judas made his way there with a detachment of soldiers, and with temple police provided by the chief priests and the Pharisees; they were equipped with lanterns, torches, and weapons. 4 Jesus, knowing everything that was to happen to him, stepped forward and asked them, 'Who is it you want?' 5 'Jesus of Nazareth,' they answered. Jesus said, 'I am he.' And Judas the traitor was standing there with them. 6 When Jesus said, 'I am he,' they drew back and fell to the ground. 7 Again he asked, 'Who is it you want?' 'Jesus of Nazareth,' they repeated. 8 'I have told you that I am he,' Jesus answered. 'If I am the man you want, let these others go.' 9 (This was to make good his words, 'I have not lost one of those you gave me.') 10 Thereupon Simon Peter drew the sword he was wearing and struck at the high priest's servant, cutting off his right

ear. The servant's name was Malchus. 11 Jesus said to Peter, 'Put away your sword. This is the cup the Father has given me; shall I not drink it?'

12 THE troops with their commander, and the Jewish police, now arrested Jesus and secured him. 13 They took him first to Annas, father-in-law of Caiaphas, the high priest for that year — 14 the same Caiaphas who had advised the Jews that it would be to their interest if one man died for the people. 15 Jesus was followed by Simon Peter and another disciple. This disciple, who was known to the high priest, went with Jesus into the high priest's courtyard, 16 but Peter stayed outside at the door. So the other disciple, the high priest's acquaintance, went back and spoke to the girl on duty at the door, and brought Peter in. 17 The girl said to Peter, 'Are you another of this man's disciples?' 'I am not,' he said. 18 As it was cold, the servants and the police had made a charcoal fire, and were standing round it warming themselves. Peter too was standing with them, sharing the warmth.

19 The high priest questioned Jesus about his disciples and about his teaching. 20 Jesus replied, 'I have spoken openly for all the world to hear; I have always taught in synagogues or in the temple, where all Jews congregate; I have said nothing in secret. 21 Why are you questioning me? Question those who heard me; they know what I said.' 22 When he said this, one of the police standing near him struck him on the face. 'Is that the way to answer the high priest?' he demanded. 23 Jesus replied, 'If I was wrong to speak what I did, produce evidence to prove it; if I was right, why strike me?'

24 So Annas sent him bound to Caiaphas the high priest.

23: *The world will know:* the complete unity of the believers will challenge the world to recognize Jesus' mission from God.

18.1–11: The garden. 1: *The Kedron ravine* lay between Mount Moriah to the west, and the mount of Olives to the east. John lacks the place name Gethsemane (Mk. 14.32) and Jesus' prayer and struggle (Mk. 14.33–42); but see 12.27 n. **3:** See 11.47 n. **4:** *Knowing everything:* compare 10.17–18 n. **9:** *His words:* see 6.39; 17.12. **11:** The words seem to echo Jesus' prayer in Mk. 14.36; Matt. 26.39, 42; Lk. 22.42.

18.12–27: Interrogation by Annas. 12: The Gk. term for *troops* (lit. "cohort") may imply Roman intervention. **13:** *Annas* had been high priest from 6–15 C.E. **14:** *The same Caiaphas:* see 11.49 (and n.)–51. **15:** *Another* is plausibly the same *disciple* as in 20.2–10, the friend of Peter (13.23–25; 21.7, 20–24), possibly John, the son of Zebedee. **20:** The tradition consistently records the claim that Jesus taught openly in the temple; see Matt. 26.55; Mk. 14.49; Lk. 22.53. **24:** John apparently omits an official Jewish trial, substituting for it an

25 Meanwhile, as Simon Peter stood warming himself, he was asked, 'Are you another of his disciples?' But he denied it: 'I am not,' he said. 26 One of the high priest's servants, a relation of the man whose ear Peter had cut off, insisted, 'Did I not see you with him in the garden?' 27 Once again Peter denied it; and at that moment a cock crowed.

28 FROM Caiaphas Jesus was led into the governor's headquarters. It was now early morning, and the Jews themselves stayed outside the headquarters to avoid defilement, so that they could eat the Passover meal. 29 So Pilate came out to them and asked, 'What charge do you bring against this man?' 30 'If he were not a criminal', they replied, 'we would not have brought him before you.' 31 Pilate said, 'Take him yourselves and try him by your own law.' The Jews answered, 'We are not allowed to put anyone to death.' 32 Thus they ensured the fulfilment of the words by which Jesus had indicated the kind of death he was to die.

33 Pilate then went back into his headquarters and summoned Jesus. 'So you are the king of the Jews?' he said. 34 Jesus replied, 'Is that your own question, or have others suggested it to you?' 35 'Am I a Jew?' said Pilate. 'Your own nation and their chief priests have brought you before me. What have you done?' 36 Jesus replied, 'My kingdom does not belong to this world. If it did, my followers would be fighting to save me from the clutches of the Jews. My kingdom belongs elsewhere.' 37 'You are a king, then?' said Pilate. Jesus answered, ' "King" is your word. My task is to bear witness to the truth. For this I was born; for this I came into the world, and all who are not deaf to truth listen to my voice.' 38 Pilate said, 'What is truth?' With those words he went out again to the Jews and said, 'For my part I find no case against

him. 39 But you have a custom that I release one prisoner for you at Passover. Would you like me to release the king of the Jews?' 40 At this they shouted back: 'Not him; we want Barabbas!' Barabbas was a bandit.

19 Pilate now took Jesus and had him flogged; 2 and the soldiers plaited a crown of thorns and placed it on his head, and robed him in a purple cloak. 3 Then one after another they came up to him, crying, 'Hail, king of the Jews!' and struck him on the face.

4 Once more Pilate came out and said to the Jews, 'Here he is; I am bringing him out to let you know that I find no case against him'; 5 and Jesus came out, wearing the crown of thorns and the purple cloak. 'Here is the man,' said Pilate. 6 At the sight of him the chief priests and the temple police shouted, 'Crucify! Crucify!' 'Take him yourselves and crucify him,' said Pilate; 'for my part I find no case against him.' 7 The Jews answered, 'We have a law; and according to that law he ought to die, because he has claimed to be God's Son.'

8 When Pilate heard that, he was more afraid than ever, 9 and going back into his headquarters he asked Jesus, 'Where have you come from?' But Jesus gave him no answer. 10 'Do you refuse to speak to me?' said Pilate. 'Surely you know that I have authority to release you, and authority to crucify you?' 11 'You would have no authority at all over me', Jesus replied, 'if it had not been granted you from above; and therefore the deeper guilt lies with the one who handed me over to you.'

12 From that moment Pilate tried hard to release him; but the Jews kept shouting, 'If you let this man go, you are no friend to Caesar; anyone who claims to be a king is opposing Caesar.' 13 When Pilate heard what

informal hearing; but see 10.24–38 n.

18.28–19.16: Jesus and Pilate. 28: The site of the trial was either the Fortress Antonia, which was connected with the temple area, or the palace which had been built by Herod and was sometimes used as the *Governor's headquarters.* In Jn. the *Passover* meal was celebrated in the evening following Jesus' crucifixion, in apparent contradiction to the other Gospels (see Matt. 26.17 n.). **31:** *We are not allowed:* under Roman rule, the Council lacked the authority to execute criminals, though some commentators have raised questions about the full accuracy of the statement. **32:** See 3.14; 8.28; 12.32. **33:** The implication of *king of the Jews* is ambiguous. Either it might be a purely religious title ("king of Israel," see 1.49) or, on the contrary, it could carry the political connotation of opposition to Rome. **40:** *Bandit:* probably, a revolutionary. **19.1–5:** John highlights Jesus' royalty by locating his mockery as king in the center of his trial by Romans. **11:** John views Pilate as the appointed instrument of the divine will in these predetermined events. *Who handed me over:* either the high priest (18.28, they were saying, he brought Jesus out and took his seat on the tribunal at the place known as The Pavement (in Hebrew, 'Gabbatha'). ¹⁴ It was the day of preparation for the Passover, about noon. Pilate said to the Jews, 'Here is your king.' ¹⁵ They shouted, 'Away with him! Away with him! Crucify him!' 'Am I to crucify your king?' said Pilate. 'We have no king but Caesar,' replied the chief priests. ¹⁶ Then at last, to satisfy them, he handed Jesus over to be crucified.

Jesus was taken away, ¹⁷ and went out, carrying the cross himself, to the place called The Skull (in Hebrew, 'Golgotha'); ¹⁸ there they crucified him, and with him two others, one on either side, with Jesus in between.

¹⁹ Pilate had an inscription written and fastened to the cross; it read, 'Jesus of Nazareth, King of the Jews'. ²⁰ This inscription, in Hebrew, Latin, and Greek, was read by many Jews, since the place where Jesus was crucified was not far from the city. ²¹ So the Jewish chief priests said to Pilate, 'You should not write "King of the Jews", but rather "He claimed to be king of the Jews".' ²² Pilate replied, 'What I have written, I have written.'

²³ When the soldiers had crucified Jesus they took his clothes and, leaving aside the tunic, divided them into four parts, one for each soldier. The tunic was seamless, woven in one piece throughout; ²⁴ so they said to one another, 'We must not tear this; let us toss for it.' Thus the text of scripture came true: 'They shared my garments among them, and cast lots for my clothing.'

That is what the soldiers did. ²⁵ Meanwhile near the cross on which Jesus hung, his mother was standing with her sister, Mary wife of Clopas, and Mary of Magdala. ²⁶ Seeing his mother, with the disciple whom he loved standing beside her, Jesus said to her,

'Mother, there is your son'; ²⁷ and to the disciple, 'There is your mother'; and from that moment the disciple took her into his home.

²⁸ After this, Jesus, aware that all had now come to its appointed end, said in fulfilment of scripture, 'I am thirsty.' ²⁹ A jar stood there full of sour wine; so they soaked a sponge with the wine, fixed it on hyssop, and held it up to his lips. ³⁰ Having received the wine, he said, 'It is accomplished!' Then he bowed his head and gave up his spirit.

³¹ Because it was the eve of the sabbath, the Jews were anxious that the bodies should not remain on the crosses, since that sabbath was a day of great solemnity; so they requested Pilate to have the legs broken and the bodies taken down. ³² The soldiers accordingly came to the men crucified with Jesus and broke the legs of each in turn, ³³ but when they came to Jesus and found he was already dead, they did not break his legs. ³⁴ But one of the soldiers thrust a lance into his side, and at once there was a flow of blood and water. ³⁵ This is vouched for by an eyewitness, whose evidence is to be trusted. He knows that he speaks the truth, so that you too may believe; ³⁶ for this happened in fulfilment of the text of scripture: 'No bone of his shall be broken.' ³⁷ And another text says, 'They shall look on him whom they pierced.'

³⁸ After that, Joseph of Arimathaea, a disciple of Jesus, but a secret disciple for fear of the Jews, asked Pilate for permission to remove the body of Jesus. He consented; so Joseph came and removed the body. ³⁹ He was joined by Nicodemus (the man who had visited Jesus by night), who brought with him a mixture of myrrh and aloes, more than half

19:14 **It was ... Passover:** *or* It was Friday in Passover.   19:29 **hyssop:** *one witness reads* a javelin.

35) or, perhaps, Judas (13.2). **13:** *Took his seat:* the Gk. is ambiguous; it could mean that Pilate seated Jesus *on the tribunal.* **14:** *About noon:* the time when the paschal lamb was slaughtered by the priests; Jesus is the "paschal lamb"; see also 1.29 n.

19.17–37: Events on Calvary. 17: Unlike the Synoptics, Jn. does not mention Simon of Cyrene (Mk. 15.21 n.). His account also omits the mockery at the cross, the darkness, the tearing of the temple curtain, and the centurion's remark (see Mk. 15.29–39). **19:** John ascribes to the Romans a bitter irony in this scornful *inscription* about Jesus' kingship; see Matt. 27.37; Mk. 15.26; Lk. 23.38. **23:** *His clothes:* see Ps. 22.18. **25–27:** John alone mentions the presence of Jesus' *mother* and her relationship to the beloved disciple. **34:** In the *blood and water* Jn. perceives a deep theological significance (see 7.38–39; 1 Jn. 5.6, 8); the author intends this as a symbol of the gift of the Spirit or, possibly, of baptism. **35:** This *eyewitness* is the beloved disciple of v. 26. **36:** Compare Exod. 12.46. **37:** See Zech. 12.10.

19.38–42: Jesus' burial. 39: *Nicodemus:* see 3.1. John omits the presence of the women (compare Matt.

a hundredweight. [40]They took the body of Jesus and following Jewish burial customs they wrapped it, with the spices, in strips of linen cloth. [41]Near the place where he had been crucified there was a garden, and in the garden a new tomb, not yet used for burial; [42]and there, since it was the eve of the Jewish sabbath and the tomb was near at hand, they laid Jesus.

The resurrection

20 EARLY on the first day of the week, while it was still dark, Mary of Magdala came to the tomb. She saw that the stone had been moved away from the entrance, [2]and ran to Simon Peter and the other disciple, the one whom Jesus loved. 'They have taken the Lord out of the tomb,' she said, 'and we do not know where they have laid him.' [3]So Peter and the other disciple set out and made their way to the tomb. [4]They ran together, but the other disciple ran faster than Peter and reached the tomb first. [5]He peered in and saw the linen wrappings lying there, but he did not enter. [6]Then Simon Peter caught up with him and went into the tomb. He saw the linen wrappings lying there, [7]and the napkin which had been round his head, not with the wrappings but rolled up in a place by itself. [8]Then the disciple who had reached the tomb first also went in, and he saw and believed; [9]until then they had not understood the scriptures, which showed that he must rise from the dead.

[10]So the disciples went home again; [11]but Mary stood outside the tomb weeping. And as she wept, she peered into the tomb, [12]and saw two angels in white sitting there, one at the head, and one at the feet, where the body of Jesus had lain. [13]They asked her, 'Why are you weeping?' She answered, 'They have taken my Lord away, and I do not know where they have laid him.' [14]With these words she turned round and saw Jesus standing there, but she did not recognize him. [15]Jesus asked her, 'Why are you weeping? Who are you looking for?' Thinking it was the gardener, she said, 'If it is you, sir, who removed him, tell me where you have laid him, and I will take him away.' [16]Jesus said, 'Mary!' She turned and said to him, 'Rabbuni!' (which is Hebrew for 'Teacher'). [17]'Do not cling to me,' said Jesus, 'for I have not yet ascended to the Father. But go to my brothers, and tell them that I am ascending to my Father and your Father, to my God and your God.' [18]Mary of Magdala went to tell the disciples. 'I have seen the Lord!' she said, and gave them his message.

[19]Late that same day, the first day of the week, when the disciples were together behind locked doors for fear of the Jews, Jesus came and stood among them. 'Peace be with you!' he said; [20]then he showed them his hands and his side. On seeing the Lord the disciples were overjoyed. [21]Jesus said again, 'Peace be with you! As the Father sent me, so I send you.' [22]Then he breathed on them, saying, 'Receive the Holy Spirit! [23]If you forgive anyone's sins, they are forgiven; if you pronounce them unforgiven, unforgiven they remain.'

[24]One of the Twelve, Thomas the Twin, was not with the rest when Jesus came. [25]So the others kept telling him, 'We have seen the Lord.' But he said, 'Unless I see the mark of the nails on his hands, unless I put my finger into the place where the nails were, and my

27.61; Mk. 15.47; Lk. 23.55–56). **40:** In accordance with *Jewish burial customs* the corpse was not eviscerated, as in Egyptian mummification; thus, Jesus' body would remain intact.

20.1–23: The first Easter. 1: *The first day* (Sunday) became the Christian day of worship (1 Cor. 16.2) rather than Saturday. **2:** *The other disciple:* see 18.15 n. *Lord:* see 11.2 n. **6–8:** Peter's reaction shows that inspection of the empty tomb did not in itself cause faith in Jesus' resurrection; however, the *disciple* (v. 2) whom Jn. favors above Peter *saw and believed.* **9:** That without Christian faith the disciples *had not understood the scriptures* is crucial, since it shows that the OT in itself had not led them to anticipate Jesus' resurrection. **14:** Mary *did not recognize him* because she did not yet have faith in the risen Jesus. **17:** Jesus' prohibition, *do not cling to me,* shows that Mary's gesture of adoration is premature, because his glorification is incomplete. **22:** *Breathed on them* recalls God's creative action in Gen. 2.7. **23:** The risen Lord bestows the power to forgive sins on the church.

20.24–29: Thomas. This account of Thomas' doubt and ensuing faith invites belief which is not dependent on physical evidence.

hand into his side, I will never believe it.'
²⁶A week later his disciples were once again in the room, and Thomas was with them. Although the doors were locked, Jesus came and stood among them, saying, 'Peace be with you!' ²⁷Then he said to Thomas, 'Reach your finger here; look at my hands. Reach your hand here and put it into my side. Be unbelieving no longer, but believe.' ²⁸Thomas said, 'My Lord and my God!' ²⁹Jesus said to him, 'Because you have seen me you have found faith. Happy are they who find faith without seeing me.'

³⁰There were indeed many other signs that Jesus performed in the presence of his disciples, which are not recorded in this book. ³¹Those written here have been recorded in order that you may believe that Jesus is the Christ, the Son of God, and that through this faith you may have life by his name.

21 SOME time later, Jesus showed himself to his disciples once again, by the sea of Tiberias. This is how it happened. ²Simon Peter was with Thomas the Twin, Nathanael from Cana-in-Galilee, the sons of Zebedee, and two other disciples. ³'I am going out fishing,' said Simon Peter. 'We will go with you,' said the others. So they set off and got into the boat; but that night they caught nothing.

⁴Morning came, and Jesus was standing on the beach, but the disciples did not know that it was Jesus. ⁵He called out to them, 'Friends, have you caught anything?' 'No,' they answered. ⁶He said, 'Throw out the net to starboard, and you will make a catch.' They did so, and found they could not haul the net on board, there were so many fish in it. ⁷Then the disciple whom Jesus loved said to Peter, 'It is the Lord!' As soon as Simon Peter heard him say, 'It is the Lord,' he fastened his coat about him (for he had stripped) and plunged into the sea. ⁸The rest of them came on in the boat, towing the net full of fish. They were only about a hundred yards from land.

⁹When they came ashore, they saw a charcoal fire there with fish laid on it, and some bread. ¹⁰Jesus said, 'Bring some of the fish you have caught.' ¹¹Simon Peter went on board and hauled the net to land; it was full of big fish, a hundred and fifty-three in all; and yet, many as they were, the net was not torn. ¹²Jesus said, 'Come and have breakfast.' None of the disciples dared to ask 'Who are you?' They knew it was the Lord. ¹³Jesus came, took the bread and gave it to them, and the fish in the same way. ¹⁴This makes the third time that Jesus appeared to his disciples after his resurrection from the dead.

¹⁵After breakfast Jesus said to Simon Peter, 'Simon son of John, do you love me more than these others?' 'Yes, Lord,' he answered, 'you know that I love you.' 'Then feed my lambs,' he said. ¹⁶A second time he asked, 'Simon son of John, do you love me?' 'Yes, Lord, you know I love you.' 'Then tend my sheep.' ¹⁷A third time he said, 'Simon son of John, do you love me?' Peter was hurt that he asked him a third time, 'Do you love me?' 'Lord,' he said, 'you know everything; you know I love you.' Jesus said, 'Then feed my sheep.

¹⁸'In very truth I tell you: when you were young you fastened your belt about you and walked where you chose; but when you are old you will stretch out your arms, and a stranger will bind you fast, and carry you where you have no wish to go.' ¹⁹He said this to indicate the manner of death by which Peter was to glorify God. Then he added, 'Follow me.'

²⁰Peter looked round, and saw the disciple whom Jesus loved following—the one who at supper had leaned back close to him to ask the question, 'Lord, who is it that will betray you?' ²¹When he saw him, Peter asked, 'Lord, what about him?' ²²Jesus said, 'If it should be my will that he stay until I come, what is it to you? Follow me.'

20:31 **believe**: *witnesses read different tenses, some implying* continue to believe, *others* come to believe.

20.30–31: The first conclusion of the Gospel. See 21.1–25 n. **30:** Although Jn. is aware of *many other signs*, he has recounted only seven. **31:** The purpose of the Gospel is expressly stated here.

21.1–25: The epilogue. This chapter is sometimes regarded as a later appendix. **2:** *The sons of Zebedee*, prominent in Matt., Mk., Lk., are now mentioned for the first time in Jn.; some scholars think this points to John, the son of Zebedee, as the source of this Gospel's tradition. **7:** Note this Gospel's apparent preference for the beloved *disciple* over *Peter*. **12:** Hesitation or doubt appears in all accounts of the disciples' postresurrection experiences (see Matt. 28.17; Lk. 24.37–38; Jn. 20.25). **15–17:** Peter is given a unique task among the

²³That saying of Jesus became current among his followers, and was taken to mean that that disciple would not die. But in fact Jesus did not say he would not die; he only said, 'If it should be my will that he stay until I come, what is it to you?'

²⁴It is this same disciple who vouches for what has been written here. He it is who wrote it, and we know that his testimony is true.

²⁵There is much else that Jesus did. If it were all to be recorded in detail, I suppose the world could not hold the books that would be written.

21:24 **is true:** *some witnesses here insert the passage printed below.*

An incident in the temple*

8 ⁵³AND they all went home, ¹while Jesus went to the mount of Olives. ²At daybreak he appeared again in the temple, and all the people gathered round him. He had taken his seat and was engaged in teaching them ³when the scribes and the Pharisees brought in a woman caught committing adultery. Making her stand in the middle ⁴they said to him, 'Teacher, this woman was caught in the very act of adultery. ⁵In the law Moses has laid down that such women are to be stoned. What do you say about it?' ⁶They put the question as a test, hoping to frame a charge against him. Jesus bent down and wrote with his finger on the ground. ⁷When they continued to press their question he sat up straight and said, 'Let whichever of you is free from sin throw the first stone at her.' ⁸Then once again he bent down and wrote on the ground. ⁹When they heard what he said, one by one they went away, the eldest first; and Jesus was left alone, with the woman still standing there. ¹⁰Jesus again sat up and said to the woman, 'Where are they? Has no one condemned you?' ¹¹She answered, 'No one, sir.' 'Neither do I condemn you,' Jesus said. 'Go; do not sin again.'

* *This passage, which in most editions of the New Testament is printed in the text of John, 7:53—8:11, has no fixed place in our witnesses. Some of them do not contain it at all. Some place it after Luke 21:38, others after John 7:36, or 7:52, or 21:24.* 8:9 **they went away:** *some witnesses add* convicted by their conscience.

disciples (see Matt. 16.18; Lk. 22.31–32). **20:** See 13.23–25. **22:** *Until I come* probably has more than one meaning: see 16.16 n. **24:** *This same disciple* refers to the one on whose authority the Gospel of John rests.

7.53–8.11: The woman accused of adultery. 1: The terms *mount of Olives, daybreak* (v. 2), *the scribes and the Pharisees* (v. 3) are expressions more typical of the Synoptics, than of Jn. **5:** See Lev. 20.10; Deut. 22.20–21. **6:** The *question* was a *test* in that it posed a dilemma for Jesus: whether to show mercy or to advocate the death penalty. What, if anything, Jesus *wrote on the ground* is unimportant in the story. **11:** *Do not sin again:* see 5.14.

Acts of the Apostles

With this book the author of the third Gospel continues the story of the birth of the Christian church. Acts shows a wide acquaintance with the Hellenistic world, its customs and political organizations; and its good, if not artistic, Greek betrays the hand of a cosmopolitan author, whom tradition has identified as Luke, a physician (Col. 4.14; 2 Tim. 4.11). Written to show how God continues to fulfill the divine plan for the salvation of humankind, a plan which our author understands to have begun with Israel, Acts follows the church from its origin at Pentecost (ch. 2) through the geographical progression which Jesus himself had announced (1.8). Led by God's Spirit, the church moved from a small Jewish group centered in Jerusalem to a worldwide movement embracing Rome, the capital of the world (ch. 28). This shift from Jewish to Gentile mission was a primary interest of the author, who details how admission of the first Gentiles (ch. 10) led to a council (ch. 15) whose decision opened Christian fellowship to all people. Following ancient custom, Luke has composed summaries (e.g. 2.42–43; 5.12–16; 9.31–32) and speeches (e.g. 2.14–36; 3.12–26; 5.35–39; 7.2–53; 10.34–43; 15.13–21; 17.22–31; 28.25–28) as a method of informing the reader about the meaning of the events that are narrated. Our author may have had some sources available (e.g. the "we" sections: 16.10–18; 20.5–15; 21.1–18; 27.1–28.16; collections of local traditions from Palestine and Antioch), but they have been worked so skillfully into the narrative that their reconstruction is very difficult. That these sources were incomplete, however, is indicated by the inexact chronological references throughout the narrative, and by the fact that information contained in Paul's letters seems not to have been available to the author. Despite the fact, Acts stands as a mighty witness to the conviction that there is a divine working within human history to accomplish God's saving purpose for humankind.

1 In the first part of my work, Theophilus, I gave an account of all that Jesus did and taught from the beginning ² until the day when he was taken up to heaven, after giving instructions through the Holy Spirit to the apostles whom he had chosen. ³ To these men he showed himself after his death and gave ample proof that he was alive: he was seen by them over a period of forty days and spoke to them about the kingdom of God. ⁴ While he was in their company he directed them not to leave Jerusalem. 'You must wait', he said, 'for the gift promised by the Father, of which I told you; ⁵ John, as you know, baptized with water, but within the next few days you will be baptized with the Holy Spirit.'

⁶ When they were all together, they asked him, 'Lord, is this the time at which you are to restore sovereignty to Israel?' ⁷ He answered, 'It is not for you to know about dates or times which the Father has set within his own control. ⁸ But you will receive power when the Holy Spirit comes upon you; and you will bear witness for me in Jerusalem, and throughout all Judaea and Samaria, and even in the farthest corners of the earth.'

⁹ After he had said this, he was lifted up before their very eyes, and a cloud took him from their sight. ¹⁰ They were gazing intently into the sky as he went, and all at once there stood beside them two men robed in white, ¹¹ who said, 'Men of Galilee, why stand there looking up into the sky? This Jesus who has been taken from you up to heaven will come

1.1–5: Preface. 1: *Theophilus* (lit. "lover of God" or "loved by God") was probably a patron who would sponsor the distribution of this book. 2: These instructions are summarized in Lk. 24.44–49. 3: *Forty days* is a general number; see Lk. 4.1–2. 4: On the *gift promised* (concerning baptism), see Lk. 3.16; Isa. 44.2–5; Ezek. 39.28–29; Joel 2.28–29. 5: In Lk. 3.16 this saying is attributed to John the Baptist.

1.6–14: Jesus' ascension. 6: *All together* may imply table-fellowship; compare 10.41. On the problem of when and how God's *sovereignty* is realized, see Lk. 7.20–23; 19.11; 21.5–36. 7: *Dates or times:* see 1 Thess.

in the same way as you have seen him go.'

The church in Jerusalem

¹²THEY then returned to Jerusalem from the hill called Olivet, which is near the city, no farther than a sabbath day's journey. ¹³On their arrival they went to the upstairs room where they were lodging: Peter and John and James and Andrew, Philip and Thomas, Bartholomew and Matthew, James son of Alphaeus, Simon the Zealot, and Judas son of James. ¹⁴All these with one accord were constantly at prayer, together with a group of women, and Mary the mother of Jesus, and his brothers.

¹⁵It was during this time that Peter stood up before the assembled brotherhood, about one hundred and twenty in all, and said: ¹⁶'My friends, the prophecy in scripture, which the Holy Spirit uttered concerning Judas through the mouth of David, was bound to come true; Judas acted as guide to those who arrested Jesus—¹⁷he was one of our number and had his place in this ministry.' ¹⁸(After buying a plot of land with the price of his villainy, this man fell headlong and burst open so that all his entrails spilled out; ¹⁹everyone in Jerusalem came to hear of this, and in their own language they named the plot Akeldama, which means 'Blood Acre'.) ²⁰'The words I have in mind', Peter continued, 'are in the book of Psalms: "Let his homestead fall desolate; let there be none to inhabit it." And again, "Let his charge be given to another." ²¹Therefore one of those who bore us company all the while the Lord Jesus was going about among us, ²²from his baptism by John until the day when he was taken up from us—one of those must now join us as a witness to his resurrection.'

²³Two names were put forward: Joseph, who was known as Barsabbas and bore the added name of Justus, and Matthias. ²⁴Then they prayed and said, 'You know the hearts of everyone, Lord; declare which of these two you have chosen ²⁵to receive this office of ministry and apostleship which Judas abandoned to go where he belonged.' ²⁶They drew lots, and the lot fell to Matthias; so he was elected to be an apostle with the other eleven.

2 THE day of Pentecost had come, and they were all together in one place. ²Suddenly there came from the sky what sounded like a strong, driving wind, a noise which filled the whole house where they were sitting. ³And there appeared to them flames like tongues of fire distributed among them and coming to rest on each one. ⁴They were all filled with the Holy Spirit and began to talk in other tongues, as the Spirit gave them power of utterance.

⁵Now there were staying in Jerusalem devout Jews drawn from every nation under heaven. ⁶At this sound a crowd of them gathered, and were bewildered because each one heard his own language spoken; ⁷they were amazed and in astonishment exclaimed, 'Surely these people who are speaking are all Galileans! ⁸How is it that each of us can hear them in his own native language? ⁹Parthians, Medes, Elamites; inhabitants of Mesopotamia, of Judaea and Cappadocia, of Pontus and Asia, ¹⁰of Phrygia and Pamphylia, of Egypt and the districts of Libya around Cyrene; visitors from Rome, both Jews and proselytes; ¹¹Cretans and Arabs—all of us hear them telling in our own tongues the great things God has done.' ¹²They were all amazed and perplexed, saying to one an-

---

5.1. **8:** Compare 28.14 n. **12:** *Sabbath day's journey:* the travel permitted Jews, about a thousand paces. **13:** *Upstairs* (upper) *room* was a normal meeting place (see 20.8), not necessarily to be identified with the locus of the Last Supper. **14:** *Jesus' brothers* are named in Mk. 6.3. Hitherto they had not been his followers; compare Mk. 3.21. *Group of women:* compare Lk. 8.1–3; 23.49.

1.15–26: Replacement of Judas. 16: *Bound to come true:* see 2.23 n. **17:** *One of our number:* see Lk. 6.12–16. **18:** The meaning of *fell headlong* is uncertain; Papias (an early second-century Christian) took it to mean "became swollen." According to Matt. 27.5 Judas hanged himself. **20:** See Pss. 69.25; 109.8. **23:** *Added name:* many Jews bore two names, one Jewish (*Joseph*), the other Latin or Greek (*Justus*).

2.1–47: Pentecost. 1: *Pentecost,* fifty days following Passover, was a harvest festival which at this time celebrated the covenant (Lev. 23.15–21). **2–3:** *Wind* and *fire* are meant to be understood symbolically, not literally. **4:** It is not clear whether *other tongues* means languages (vv. 6, 8, 11) or ecstatic speaking (v. 13). **9–11:** Examples are given illustrating the universality expressed in v. 5. **14–36: Peter's sermon. 14:** *Addressed* other, 'What can this mean?' ¹³Others said contemptuously, 'They have been drinking!'

¹⁴But Peter stood up with the eleven, and in a loud voice addressed the crowd: 'Fellow-Jews, and all who live in Jerusalem, listen and take note of what I say. ¹⁵These people are not drunk, as you suppose; it is only nine in the morning! ¹⁶No, this is what the prophet Joel spoke of: ¹⁷"In the last days, says God, I will pour out my Spirit on all mankind; and your sons and daughters shall prophesy; your young men shall see visions, and your old men shall dream dreams. ¹⁸Yes, on my servants and my handmaids I will pour out my Spirit in those days, and they shall prophesy. ¹⁹I will show portents in the sky above, and signs on the earth below—blood and fire and a pall of smoke. ²⁰The sun shall be turned to darkness, and the moon to blood, before that great, resplendent day, the day of the Lord, shall come. ²¹Everyone who calls on the name of the Lord on that day shall be saved."

²²'Men of Israel, hear me: I am speaking of Jesus of Nazareth, singled out by God and made known to you through miracles, portents, and signs, which God worked among you through him, as you well know. ²³By the deliberate will and plan of God he was given into your power, and you killed him, using heathen men to crucify him. ²⁴But God raised him to life again, setting him free from the pangs of death, because it could not be that death should keep him in its grip. ²⁵'For David says of him:

I foresaw that the Lord would be with
    me for ever,
with him at my right hand I cannot be
    shaken;
²⁶therefore my heart is glad
    and my tongue rejoices;
moreover, my flesh shall dwell in hope,
²⁷for you will not abandon me to death,
    nor let your faithful servant suffer
    corruption.

²⁸You have shown me the paths of life;
    your presence will fill me with joy.

²⁹'My friends, nobody can deny that the patriarch David died and was buried; we have his tomb here to this very day. ³⁰It is clear therefore that he spoke as a prophet who knew that God had sworn to him that one of his own direct descendants should sit on his throne; ³¹and when he said he was not abandoned to death, and his flesh never saw corruption, he spoke with foreknowledge of the resurrection of the Messiah. ³²Now Jesus has been raised by God, and of this we are all witnesses. ³³Exalted at God's right hand he received from the Father the promised Holy Spirit, and all that you now see and hear flows from him. ³⁴For it was not David who went up to heaven; his own words are: "The Lord said to my Lord, 'Sit at my right hand ³⁵until I make your enemies your footstool.'" ³⁶Let all Israel then accept as certain that God has made this same Jesus, whom you crucified, both Lord and Messiah.'

³⁷When they heard this they were cut to the heart, and said to Peter and the other apostles, 'Friends, what are we to do?' ³⁸'Repent', said Peter, 'and be baptized, every one of you, in the name of Jesus the Messiah; then your sins will be forgiven and you will receive the gift of the Holy Spirit. ³⁹The promise is to you and to your children and to all who are far away, to everyone whom the Lord our God may call.'

⁴⁰He pressed his case with many other arguments and pleaded with them: 'Save yourselves from this crooked age.' ⁴¹Those who accepted what he said were baptized, and some three thousand were added to the number of believers that day. ⁴²They met constantly to hear the apostles teach and to share the common life, to break bread, and to pray.

⁴³A sense of awe was felt by everyone, and many portents and signs were brought about

2:33 **at:** or by.

---

is the same word as "utterance" (v. 4); the Spirit also empowers Peter's words. **17–21:** Joel 2.28–32a. **22:** Proof of Jesus' divine mission by *miracles* is a regular part of Lukan theology; compare 10.38; Lk. 4.16–27. **23:** *Plan of God* is a regular motif of Lukan theology; compare Lk. 22.22. **25–28:** Ps. 16.8–11a. **30:** The language reflects Ps. 132.11. **32:** *Witnesses:* to qualify as an apostle one had to have seen the risen Jesus; see 1 Cor. 9.1; 15.3–8. **36:** This verse says nothing about the time at which *Jesus* became *Messiah;* for Luke, Jesus was Messiah already during his lifetime, see 10.38; Lk. 4.18. **37–41: Response to the sermon. 38:** Baptism and reception of the *Holy Spirit* are usually simultaneous; when they are not, it is due to special reasons; see 8.16–17; 10.47; 19.1–6. **42–47: Summary of early Christian life. 42:** *Break bread* refers to common meals which included through the apostles. 44 All the believers agreed to hold everything in common: 45 they began to sell their property and possessions and distribute to everyone according to his need. 46 One and all they kept up their daily attendance at the temple, and, breaking bread in their homes, they shared their meals with unaffected joy, 47 as they praised God and enjoyed the favour of the whole people. And day by day the Lord added new converts to their number.

3 ONE day at three in the afternoon, the hour of prayer, Peter and John were on their way up to the temple. 2 Now a man who had been a cripple from birth used to be carried there and laid every day by the temple gate called Beautiful to beg from people as they went in. 3 When he saw Peter and John on their way into the temple, he asked for alms. 4 They both fixed their eyes on him, and Peter said, 'Look at us.' 5 Expecting a gift from them, the man was all attention. 6 Peter said, 'I have no silver or gold; but what I have I give you: in the name of Jesus Christ of Nazareth, get up and walk.' 7 Then, grasping him by the right hand he helped him up; and at once his feet and ankles grew strong; 8 he sprang to his feet, and started to walk. He entered the temple with them, leaping and praising God as he went. 9 Everyone saw him walking and praising God, 10 and when they recognized him as the man who used to sit begging at Beautiful Gate they were filled with wonder and amazement at what had happened to him.

11 While he still clung to Peter and John all the people came running in astonishment towards them in Solomon's Portico, as it is called. 12 Peter saw them coming and met them with these words: 'Men of Israel, why be surprised at this? Why stare at us as if we had made this man walk by some power or godliness of our own? 13-14 The God of Abraham, Isaac, and Jacob, the God of our fathers, has given the highest honour to his servant Jesus, whom you handed over for trial and disowned in Pilate's court — disowned the holy and righteous one when Pilate had decided to release him. You asked for the reprieve of a murderer, 15 and killed the Prince of life. But God raised him from the dead; of that we are witnesses. 16 The name of Jesus, by awakening faith, has given strength to this man whom you see and know, and this faith has made him completely well as you can all see.

17 'Now, my friends, I know quite well that you acted in ignorance, as did your rulers; 18 but this is how God fulfilled what he had foretold through all the prophets: that his Messiah would suffer. 19 Repent, therefore, and turn to God, so that your sins may be wiped out. Then the Lord may grant you a time of recovery 20 and send the Messiah appointed for you, that is, Jesus. 21 He must be received into heaven until the time comes for the universal restoration of which God has spoken through his holy prophets from the beginning. 22 Moses said, "The Lord God will raise up for you a prophet like me from among yourselves. Listen to everything he says to you, 23 for anyone who refuses to listen to that prophet must be cut off from the people." 24 From Samuel onwards, every prophet who spoke predicted this present time.

25 'You are the heirs of the prophets, and of

3:22 **a prophet like me:** *or* a prophet as he raised up me.

the Eucharist. **44—45:** It was a usual practice in religious communities, including Qumran, to hold everything in common. Such common ownership (Gk., *koina*) was an expression of community (Gk., *koinonia*).

3.1—4.31: Apostolic activity and Jewish persecution.

3.1—10: Peter heals a cripple. 1: Herod's *temple,* an entire complex of courtyards and buildings, was still under construction. **2:** The exact location of the *gate called Beautiful* is unknown. **6:** Typically for Acts, *the name of Jesus Christ* implies acting in his full power and authority; see 4.10, 18, 30. **8:** Jesus' word in Matt. 10.8 begins to receive its fulfillment.

3.11—26: Peter's second sermon. 11: *Solomon's Portico* was a colonnade on the east side of the great court of the temple, the "Court of the Gentiles." **13:** *Servant* as a title for Jesus is taken from Isa. 52.13—53.11, and is used only three other times in the NT, all in Acts (v. 26; 4.27, 30). *The God of Abraham:* see Exod. 3.6, 15. The reference shows that the church is the continuation of Israel. **14:** On *Pilate's decision,* see Lk. 23.4a, 13—25. **15:** *Witnesses* to resurrection; see 2.32 n. **17:** *You acted in ignorance:* compare Lk. 23.34. **18:** See 2.23 n. **20:** *Send the Messiah:* Peter implies Jesus will return when the Jews turn to Jesus; compare Rom. 11.25—31. **22:**

that covenant which God made with your fathers when he said to Abraham, "And in your offspring all the families on earth shall find blessing." 26 When God raised up his servant, he sent him to you first, to bring you blessing by turning every one of you from your wicked ways.'

4 They were still addressing the people when the chief priests, together with the controller of the temple and the Sadducees, broke in on them, 2 annoyed because they were proclaiming the resurrection from the dead by teaching the people about Jesus. 3 They were arrested and, as it was already evening, put in prison for the night. 4 But many of those who had heard the message became believers, bringing the number of men to about five thousand.

5 Next day the Jewish rulers, elders, and scribes met in Jerusalem. 6 There were present Annas the high priest, Caiaphas, John, Alexander, and all who were of the high-priestly family. 7 They brought the apostles before the court and began to interrogate them. 'By what power', they asked, 'or by what name have such men as you done this?' 8 Then Peter, filled with the Holy Spirit, answered, 'Rulers of the people and elders, 9 if it is about help given to a sick man that we are being questioned today, and the means by which he was cured, 10 this is our answer to all of you and to all the people of Israel: it was by the name of Jesus Christ of Nazareth, whom you crucified, and whom God raised from the dead; through him this man stands here before you fit and well. 11 This Jesus is the stone, rejected by you the builders, which has become the corner-stone. 12 There is no salvation through anyone else; in all the world no other name has been granted to mankind by which we can be saved.'

13 Observing that Peter and John were un-educated laymen, they were astonished at their boldness and took note that they had been companions of Jesus; 14 but with the man who had been cured standing in full view beside them, they had nothing to say in reply. 15 So they ordered them to leave the court, and then conferred among themselves. 16 'What are we to do with these men?' they said. 'It is common knowledge in Jerusalem that a notable miracle has come about through them; and we cannot deny it. 17 But to stop this from spreading farther among the people, we had better caution them never again to speak to anyone in this name.' 18 They then called them in and ordered them to refrain from all public speaking and teaching in the name of Jesus.

19 But Peter and John replied: 'Is it right in the eyes of God for us to obey you rather than him? Judge for yourselves. 20 We cannot possibly give up speaking about what we have seen and heard.'

21 With a repeated caution the court discharged them. They could not see how they were to punish them, because the people were all giving glory to God for what had happened. 22 The man upon whom this miracle of healing had been performed was over forty years old.

23 As soon as they were discharged the apostles went back to their friends and told them everything that the chief priests and elders had said. 24 When they heard it, they raised their voices with one accord and called upon God.

'Sovereign Lord, Maker of heaven and earth and sea and of everything in them, 25 you said by the Holy Spirit, through the mouth of David your servant,

Why did the Gentiles rage
and the peoples hatch their futile plots?
26 The kings of the earth took their stand

4:1 **the chief priests:** *some witnesses omit* chief.
4:6 **John:** *some witnesses read* Jonathan.

Compare Deut. 18.15–19; Lev. 23.29. **25:** Compare Gen. 22.18. *Offspring* here refers to Jesus, as in Gal. 3.16. **26:** That the Jews were the first to whom God *sent* the Son is a common theme in Acts; see Mk. 7.27; Rom. 1.16; 2.9.

4.1–31: Peter and John arrested, then freed. 1: *The controller of the temple* headed the Levitical guard which kept order in the temple precincts. *Sadducees:* See Matt. 3.7 n. **2:** See 23.6–8; Lk. 20.27. **5–22:** Hearing before Jewish authorities. **5:** Members of these groups constituted the Sanhedrin, the ruling council of the Jews. **6:** The office of *high priest* was no longer of lifetime tenure; because of its political prestige, it was granted and removed by Rome. The author may mean *Annas* (Lk. 3.2 n.) or Ananias (23.2 n.). Neither was in office at this time, although the former still had great influence. **7:** See 12.11–12. **11:** Ps. 118.22; compare 1 Pet. 2.7–8. **23–31: Return of Peter and John. 24:** *Sovereign Lord* (Gk., *despota*), used also in Lk. 2.29, is a Hellenistic and the rulers made common cause against the Lord and against his Messiah.

27 'They did indeed make common cause in this very city against your holy servant Jesus whom you anointed as Messiah. Herod and Pontius Pilate conspired with the Gentiles and with the peoples of Israel 28 to do all the things which, under your hand and by your decree, were foreordained. 29 And now, O Lord, mark their threats, and enable those who serve you to speak your word with all boldness. 30 Stretch out your hand to heal and cause signs and portents to be done through the name of your holy servant Jesus.'

31 When they had ended their prayer, the building where they were assembled rocked, and all were filled with the Holy Spirit and spoke God's word with boldness.

32 THE whole company of believers was united in heart and soul. Not one of them claimed any of his possessions as his own; everything was held in common. 33 With great power the apostles bore witness to the resurrection of the Lord Jesus, and all were held in high esteem. 34 There was never a needy person among them, because those who had property in land or houses would sell it, bring the proceeds of the sale, 35 and lay them at the feet of the apostles, to be distributed to any who were in need. 36 For instance Joseph, surnamed by the apostles Barnabas (which means 'Son of Encouragement'), a Levite and by birth a Cypriot, 37 sold an estate which he owned; he brought the money and laid it at the apostles' feet.

5 But a man called Ananias sold a property, 2 and with the connivance of his wife Sapphira kept back some of the proceeds, and brought part only to lay at the apostles' feet. 3 Peter said, 'Ananias, how was it that Satan so possessed your mind that you lied to the Holy Spirit by keeping back part of the price of the land? 4 While it remained unsold, did it not remain yours? Even after it was turned into money, was it not still at your own disposal? What made you think of doing this? You have lied not to men but to God.' 5 When Ananias heard these words he dropped dead; and all who heard were awestruck. 6 The younger men rose and covered his body, then carried him out and buried him.

7 About three hours passed, and his wife came in, unaware of what had happened. 8 Peter asked her, 'Tell me, were you paid such and such a price for the land?' 'Yes,' she replied, 'that was the price.' 9 Peter said, 'Why did the two of you conspire to put the Spirit of the Lord to the test? Those who buried your husband are there at the door, and they will carry you away.' 10 At once she dropped dead at his feet. When the young men came in, they found her dead; and they carried her out and buried her beside her husband.

11 Great awe fell on the whole church and on all who heard of this. 12 Many signs and wonders were done among the people by the apostles. All the believers used to meet by common consent in Solomon's Portico; 13 no one from outside their number ventured to join them, yet people in general spoke highly of them. 14 An ever-increasing number of men and women who believed in the Lord were added to their ranks. 15 As a result the sick were carried out into the streets and laid there on beds and stretchers, so that at least Peter's shadow might fall on one or another as he passed by; 16 and the people from the towns round Jerusalem flocked in, bringing those who were ill or harassed by unclean spirits, and all were cured.

4:33 **all . . . esteem:** or grace was strongly at work in them all.

prayer formula. **25–26:** Compare Ps. 2.1–2. **27:** *Herod* Antipas: see Mk. 6.14 n. *Herod and Pontius Pilate:* see Lk. 23.6–12. **30:** *Cause signs and portents:* the further narrative of Acts shows the author felt this prayer was granted. **31:** See 2.1–4.

4.32–5.12: Communal life. 32–37: All property was held in common. **32:** See 2.44–45 n. **34:** As 5.4 makes clear, such disposal of personal property was not mandatory, but was done at the prompting of the Spirit. **36:** *Joseph . . . Barnabas:* see 11.22–26; 13.2–3.

5.1–12: Ananias and Sapphira. This story is intended to show the powerful and immediate presence of the Spirit with the early church, represented in the person of the apostles: compare vv. 15–16. **4:** See 4.34. The sin is that they *lied,* rather than any refusal to turn property over to the apostles. **12:** Along with vv. 15–16, this shows that the prayer in 4.30 was answered. **13:** *Solomon's Portico:* see 3.11 n.

5.13–42: Further Jewish persecution. 17: Despite such opposition by Jewish authorities, especially the

17 Then the high priest and his colleagues, the Sadducean party, were goaded by jealousy 18 to arrest the apostles and put them in official custody. 19 But during the night, an angel of the Lord opened the prison doors, led them out, and said, 20 'Go, stand in the temple and tell the people all about this new life.' 21 Accordingly they entered the temple at daybreak and went on with their teaching.

When the high priest arrived with his colleagues they summoned the Sanhedrin, the full Council of the Israelite nation, and sent to the jail for the prisoners. 22 The officers who went to the prison failed to find them there, so they returned and reported, 23 'We found the jail securely locked at every point, with the warders at their posts by the doors, but on opening them we found no one inside.' 24 When they heard this, the controller of the temple and the chief priests were at a loss to know what could have become of them, 25 until someone came and reported: 'The men you put in prison are standing in the temple teaching the people.' 26 Then the controller went off with the officers and fetched them, but without use of force, for fear of being stoned by the people.

27 When they had been brought in and made to stand before the Council, the high priest began his examination. 28 'We gave you explicit orders', he said, 'to stop teaching in that name; and what has happened? You have filled Jerusalem with your teaching, and you are trying to hold us responsible for that man's death.' 29 Peter replied for the apostles: 'We must obey God rather than men. 30 The God of our fathers raised up Jesus; after you had put him to death by hanging him on a gibbet, 31 God exalted him at his right hand as leader and saviour, to grant Israel repentance and forgiveness of sins. 32 And we are witnesses to all this, as is the Holy Spirit who

is given by God to those obedient to him.'
33 This touched them on the raw, and they wanted to put them to death. 34 But a member of the Council rose to his feet, a Pharisee called Gamaliel, a teacher of the law held in high regard by all the people. He had the men put outside for a while, 35 and then said, 'Men of Israel, be very careful in deciding what to do with these men. 36 Some time ago Theudas came forward, making claims for himself, and a number of our people, about four hundred, joined him. But he was killed and his whole movement was destroyed and came to nothing. 37 After him came Judas the Galilean at the time of the census; he induced some people to revolt under his leadership, but he too perished and his whole movement was broken up. 38 Now, my advice to you is this: keep clear of these men; let them alone. For if what is being planned and done is human in origin, it will collapse; 39 but if it is from God, you will never be able to stamp it out, and you risk finding yourselves at war with God.'

40 Convinced by this, they sent for the apostles and had them flogged; then they ordered them to give up speaking in the name of Jesus, and discharged them. 41 The apostles went out from the Council rejoicing that they had been found worthy to suffer humiliation for the sake of the name. 42 And every day they went steadily on with their teaching in the temple and in private houses, telling the good news of Jesus the Messiah.

The church moves outwards

6 DURING this period, when disciples were growing in number, a grievance arose on the part of those who spoke Greek,

5:31 **at his right hand:** or with his right hand.
6:1 **those who spoke Greek:** lit. the Hellenists.

---

priestly party, the masses of Jews remained sympathetic; see vv. 14, 26. **19:** *Angel:* compare 12.6–10. **27–32: Peter before the Council. 29:** What *Peter* says is a summary of the whole apostolic tradition. **30:** *Hanging . . . on a gibbet* (regarded as equivalent to crucifixion): compare Deut. 21.22–23; Gal. 3.13. **33–39: Gamaliel's advice. 33:** There is some question as to whether the Romans permitted the Jews to exercise such punishment at that time; see Jn. 18.31. **34:** As a *Pharisee* (see Matt. 23.7 n.), *Gamaliel* (see 22.3 n.) belonged to a movement which opposed both the theology and politics of the Sadducees. **36–37:** *Theudas's* rebellion occurred some years after Gamaliel is reported to have made this speech, and long after *Judas* led his uprising about 6 C.E. **40:** *Flogged:* see Deut. 25.1–3. Rabbinic law sets thirty-nine lashes as the maximum (see 2 Cor. 11.24), although sentences of fewer were usual. **41:** Compare Lk. 6.22; 9.23; 1 Pet. 4.14–18.

6.1–7.60: The Hellenists and Stephen.

6.1–7: Choosing the Seven. 1: Luke uses the word *disciples* as equivalent to Christians. *Widows:* see 1 Tim.

against those who spoke the language of the Jews; they complained that their widows were being overlooked in the daily distribution. [2] The Twelve called the whole company of disciples together and said, 'It would not be fitting for us to neglect the word of God in order to assist in the distribution. [3] Therefore, friends, pick seven men of good repute from your number, men full of the Spirit and of wisdom, and we will appoint them for this duty; [4] then we can devote ourselves to prayer and to the ministry of the word.' [5] This proposal proved acceptable to the whole company. They elected Stephen, a man full of faith and of the Holy Spirit, along with Philip, Prochorus, Nicanor, Timon, Parmenas, and Nicolas of Antioch, who had been a convert to Judaism, [6] and presented them to the apostles, who prayed and laid their hands on them.

[7] The word of God spread more and more widely; the number of disciples in Jerusalem was increasing rapidly, and very many of the priests adhered to the faith.

[8] Stephen, full of grace and power, began to do great wonders and signs among the people. [9] Some members of the synagogue called the Synagogue of Freedmen, comprising Cyrenians and Alexandrians and people from Cilicia and Asia, came forward and argued with Stephen, [10] but could not hold their own against the inspired wisdom with which he spoke. [11] They then put up men to allege that they had heard him make blasphemous statements against Moses and against God. [12] They stirred up the people and the elders and scribes, set upon him and seized him, and brought him before the Council. [13] They produced false witnesses who said, 'This fellow is for ever saying things against this holy place and against the law. [14] For we have heard him say this Jesus of Nazareth will destroy this place and alter the customs handed down to us by Moses.' [15] All who were sitting in the Council fixed

their eyes on him, and his face seemed to them like the face of an angel.

7 Then the high priest asked him, 'Is this true?' [2] He replied, 'My brothers, fathers of this nation, listen to me. The God of glory appeared to Abraham our ancestor while he was in Mesopotamia, before he had settled in Harran, [3] and said: "Leave your country and your kinsfolk, and come away to a land that I will show you." [4] Thereupon he left the land of the Chaldaeans and settled in Harran. From there, after his father's death, God led him to migrate to this land where you now live. [5] He gave him no foothold in it, nothing to call his own, but promised to give it as a possession for ever to him and to his descendants after him, though he was then childless. [6] This is what God said: "Abraham's descendants shall live as aliens in a foreign land, held in slavery and oppression for four hundred years. [7] And I will pass judgement", he said, "on the nation whose slaves they are; and after that they shall escape and worship me in this place." [8] God gave Abraham the covenant of circumcision, and so, when his son Isaac was born, he circumcised him on the eighth day; and Isaac was the father of Jacob, and Jacob of the twelve patriarchs.

[9] 'The patriarchs out of jealousy sold Joseph into slavery in Egypt, but God was with him [10] and rescued him from all his troubles. He gave him wisdom which so commended him to Pharaoh king of Egypt that he appointed him governor of Egypt and of the whole royal household.

[11] 'When famine struck all Egypt and Canaan, causing great distress, and our ancestors could find nothing to eat, [12] Jacob heard that there was food in Egypt and sent our fathers there. This was their first visit. [13] On the second visit Joseph made himself known to his brothers, and his ancestry was disclosed

6:1 **those who spoke the language of the Jews:** *lit.* the Hebrews.

5.3 n., 9 n. **3:** *Your number* is addressed to the Hellenists (see Tfn. to 6.1), not all believers. **6:** It is evident from the following verses that they were ordained as evangelists, rather than as table overseers; compare 21.8. Paul and Barnabas were set apart for mission in the same way (13.3). This passage has nothing to do with the later "diaconate" as a church order.

6.8–15: Stephen is brought before the Council. 8: By performing *wonders and signs, Stephen* functioned as an evangelist, rather than as a table waiter; see v. 2; see also 2.43; 14.3. **11:** Jesus also was charged with blasphemy; see Mk. 14.64. **12:** The people here oppose Stephen; compare 5.26. **14:** *Destroy this place:* see Matt. 24.1–2 n. A similar charge of trying to *alter the customs* was leveled against Paul (21.21).

7.1–53: Stephen's speech. 3: Gen. 12.1. **5:** See Gen. 12.7; 17.8; for other discussions of Abraham, see Rom.

to Pharaoh. ¹⁴Joseph sent for his father Jacob and the whole family, seventy-five persons in all; ¹⁵and Jacob went down into Egypt. There he and our fathers ended their days. ¹⁶Their remains were later removed to Shechem and buried in the tomb for which Abraham paid a sum of money to the sons of Hamor at Shechem.

¹⁷'Now as the time approached for God to fulfil the promise he had made to Abraham, our people in Egypt grew and increased in numbers. ¹⁸At length another king, who knew nothing of Joseph, ascended the throne of Egypt. ¹⁹He employed cunning to harm our race, and forced our ancestors to expose their children so that they should not survive. ²⁰It was at this time that Moses was born. He was a fine child, and pleasing to God. For three months he was nursed in his father's house; ²¹then when he was exposed, Pharaoh's daughter adopted him and brought him up as her own son. ²²So Moses was trained in all the wisdom of the Egyptians, a powerful speaker and a man of action.

²³'He was approaching the age of forty, when it occurred to him to visit his fellow-countrymen the Israelites. ²⁴Seeing one of them being ill-treated, he went to his aid, and avenged the victim by striking down the Egyptian. ²⁵He thought his countrymen would understand that God was offering them deliverance through him, but they did not understand. ²⁶The next day he came upon two of them fighting, and tried to persuade them to make up their quarrel. "Men, you are brothers!" he said. "Why are you ill-treating one another?" ²⁷But the man who was at fault pushed him away. "Who made you ruler and judge over us?" he said. ²⁸"Are you going to kill me as you killed the Egyptian yesterday?" ²⁹At this Moses fled the country and settled in Midianite territory. There two sons were born to him.

³⁰'After forty years had passed, an angel appeared to him in the flame of a burning bush in the desert near Mount Sinai. ³¹Moses was amazed at the sight, and as he approached to look more closely, the voice of the Lord came to him: ³²"I am the God of your fathers, the God of Abraham, Isaac, and Jacob." Moses was terrified and did not dare to look. ³³Then the Lord said to him, "Take off your sandals; the place where you are standing is holy ground. ³⁴I have indeed seen how my people are oppressed in Egypt and have heard their groans; and I have come down to rescue them. Come now, I will send you to Egypt."

³⁵'This Moses, whom they had rejected with the words, "Who made you ruler and judge?"—this very man was commissioned as ruler and liberator by God himself, speaking through the angel who appeared to him in the bush. ³⁶It was Moses who led them out, doing signs and wonders in Egypt, at the Red Sea, and for forty years in the desert. ³⁷It was he who said to the Israelites, "God will raise up for you from among yourselves a prophet like me." ³⁸It was he again who, in the assembly in the desert, kept company with the angel, who spoke to him on Mount Sinai, and with our forefathers, and received the living utterances of God to pass on to us.

³⁹'Our forefathers would not accept his leadership but thrust him aside. They wished themselves back in Egypt, ⁴⁰and said to Aaron, "Make us gods to go before us. As for this fellow Moses, who brought us out of Egypt, we do not know what has become of him." ⁴¹That was when they made the bull-calf and offered sacrifice to the idol, and held festivities in honour of what their hands had made. ⁴²So God turned away from them and gave them over to the worship of the host of heaven, as it stands written in the book of the prophets: "Did you bring me victims and offerings those forty years in the desert, you people of Israel? ⁴³No, you carried aloft the shrine of Moloch and the star of the god Rephan, the images which you had made for your adoration. I will banish you beyond Babylon."

7:37 **like me:** *or* as he raised up me.

ch. 4; Gal. ch. 3. **6:** *Four hundred years:* Gen. 15.13; but according to Exod. 12.40, it was 430 years. **14:** *Seventy-five persons* are reported in Gen. 46.27 Sept. **16:** This is at variance with the OT, according to which *Abraham* bought the cave of Machpelah (Gen. 23) at Hebron. The purchase from *Hamor* was made by Jacob (Gen. 33.19) and provided Joseph's burial place at *Shechem* (Josh. 24.32). **22:** *Powerful speaker:* the opposite is reported in Exod. 4.10. In accordance with Hellenistic-Jewish practice, Moses is described in terms of the Hellenistic "divine hero"; see 14.11 n.; 28.6 n. **23:** Later Jewish tradition divided Moses' life into three periods of forty years each. **32:** Exod. 3.6. **33:** Exod. 3.5. **34:** Exod. 3.7. **37:** Deut. 18.15. **40:** Exod. 32.1–6. **42–43:**

44'Our forefathers had the Tent of the Testimony in the desert, as God commanded when he told Moses to make it after the pattern which he had seen. 45 In the next generation, our fathers under Joshua brought it with them when they dispossessed the nations whom God drove out before them, and so it was until the time of David. 46 David found favour with God and begged leave to provide a dwelling-place for the God of Jacob; 47 but it was Solomon who built him a house. 48 However, the Most High does not live in houses made by men; as the prophet says: 49 "Heaven is my throne and earth my footstool. What kind of house will you build for me, says the Lord; where shall my resting-place be? 50 Are not all these things of my own making?"

51'How stubborn you are, heathen still at heart and deaf to the truth! You always resist the Holy Spirit. You are just like your fathers! 52 Was there ever a prophet your fathers did not persecute? They killed those who foretold the coming of the righteous one, and now you have betrayed him and murdered him. 53 You received the law given by God's angels and yet you have not kept it.'

54 This touched them on the raw, and they ground their teeth with fury. 55 But Stephen, filled with the Holy Spirit, and gazing intently up to heaven, saw the glory of God, and Jesus standing at God's right hand. 56 'Look!' he said. 'I see the heavens opened and the Son of Man standing at the right hand of God.' 57 At this they gave a great shout, and stopped their ears; they made a concerted rush at him, 58 threw him out of the city, and set about stoning him. The witnesses laid their coats at the feet of a young man named Saul. 59 As they stoned him Ste-

phen called out, 'Lord Jesus, receive my spirit.' 60 He fell on his knees and cried aloud, 'Lord, do not hold this sin against them,' and 8 with that he died. 1 Saul was among those who approved of his execution.

The church in Judaea and Samaria

THAT day was the beginning of a time of violent persecution for the church in Jerusalem; and all except the apostles were scattered over the country districts of Judaea and Samaria. 2 Stephen was given burial by devout men, who made a great lamentation for him. 3 Saul, meanwhile, was harrying the church; he entered house after house, seizing men and women and sending them to prison.

4 As for those who had been scattered, they went through the country preaching the word. 5 Philip came down to a city in Samaria and began proclaiming the Messiah there. 6 As the crowds heard Philip and saw the signs he performed, everyone paid close attention to what he had to say. 7 In many cases of possession the unclean spirits came out with a loud cry, and many paralysed and crippled folk were cured; 8 and there was great rejoicing in that city.

9 A man named Simon had been in the city for some time and had captivated the Samaritans with his magical arts, making large claims for himself. 10 Everybody, high and low, listened intently to him. 'This man', they said, 'is that power of God which is called "The Great Power".' 11 They listened because they had for so long been captivated by his magic. 12 But when they came to believe

7:46 **for ... Jacob:** *some witnesses read* for the house of Jacob.

See Amos 5.25–27. **48:** For Stephen, building the temple dishonored God. **49:** Isa. 66.1–2; compare 1 Kgs. 8.29. **51:** For a similar attack, see Jesus' words in Matt. 23.13–36. **53:** *The law given by God's angels:* contrast Gal. 3.19, where the intention seems to be to reduce the Law's importance.

7.54–60: The stoning of Stephen. 56: *Son of Man:* see Lk. 12.8 n.; 22.69; Mk. 2.10 n. **58:** *Stoning* was the punishment for blasphemy; see Lev. 24.10–16. *Saul* (Paul) appears here for the first time in the Acts account. **59:** *Receive my spirit:* compare Lk. 23.46. **60:** *Do not hold this sin:* compare Lk. 23.34. The account here seems intended to stress the similarity of Stephen's death to that of Jesus'.

8.1–40: The mission spreads beyond Jerusalem. 1: The *violent persecution* was apparently directed only against the Hellenistic Jews who shared Stephen's views. **3:** See 9.1, 21; 22.4; 26.10–11; 1 Cor. 15.9; Gal. 1.13, 23; Phil. 3.6. **5:** *Samaria* is the area of the former Northern Kingdom of Israel, settled by non-Jews when it fell to Assyria (see 2 Kgs. 17.24–41). **6:** Like Stephen, *Philip*, one of the Seven, performed *signs* and preached, thus doing the apostolic work; compare 4.30; 6.8 n. **8:** *Great rejoicing:* the Samaritans had a lively expectation of the coming of a redeemer; compare Jn. 4.25. **9–24:** *Simon* the magician. **9:** His *magical arts* put *Simon* in competition with the wonder-working disciples of Jesus; compare Mk. 13.22. Such competition was common,

Philip, with his good news about the kingdom of God and the name of Jesus Christ, men and women alike were baptized. [13] Even Simon himself believed, and after his baptism was constantly in Philip's company. He was captivated when he saw the powerful signs and miracles that were taking place.

[14] When the apostles in Jerusalem heard that Samaria had accepted the word of God, they sent off Peter and John, [15] who went down there and prayed for the converts, asking that they might receive the Holy Spirit. [16] Until then the Spirit had not come upon any of them; they had been baptized into the name of the Lord Jesus, that and nothing more. [17] So Peter and John laid their hands on them, and they received the Holy Spirit.

[18] When Simon observed that the Spirit was bestowed through the laying on of the apostles' hands, he offered them money [19] and said, 'Give me too the same power, so that anyone I lay my hands on will receive the Holy Spirit.' [20] Peter replied, 'You thought God's gift was for sale? Your money can go with you to damnation! [21] You have neither part nor share in this, for you are corrupt in the eyes of God. [22] Repent of this wickedness of yours and pray the Lord to forgive you for harbouring such a thought. [23] I see that bitter gall and the chains of sin will be your fate.' [24] Simon said to them, 'Pray to the Lord for me, and ask that none of the things you have spoken of may befall me.'

[25] After giving their testimony and speaking the word of the Lord, they took the road back to Jerusalem, bringing the good news to many Samaritan villages on the way.

[26] Then the angel of the Lord said to Philip, 'Start out and go south to the road that leads down from Jerusalem to Gaza.' (This is the desert road.) [27] He set out and was on his way when he caught sight of an Ethiopian. This man was a eunuch, a high official of the Kandake, or queen, of Ethiopia, in charge of all her treasure; he had been to Jerusalem on a pilgrimage [28] and was now returning home, sitting in his carriage and reading aloud from the prophet Isaiah. [29] The Spirit said to Philip, 'Go and meet the carriage.' [30] When Philip ran up he heard him reading from the prophet Isaiah and asked, 'Do you understand what you are reading?' [31] He said, 'How can I without someone to guide me?' and invited Philip to get in and sit beside him.

[32] The passage he was reading was this: 'He was led like a sheep to the slaughter; like a lamb that is dumb before the shearer, he does not open his mouth. [33] He has been humiliated and has no redress. Who will be able to speak of his posterity? For he is cut off from the world of the living.'

[34] 'Please tell me', said the eunuch to Philip, 'who it is that the prophet is speaking about here: himself or someone else?' [35] Then Philip began and, starting from this passage, he told him the good news of Jesus. [36] As they were going along the road, they came to some water. 'Look,' said the eunuch, 'here is water: what is to prevent my being baptized?' [38] and he ordered the carriage to stop. Then they both went down into the water, Philip and the eunuch, and he baptized him. [39] When they came up from the water the Spirit snatched Philip away; the eunuch did not see him again, but went on his way rejoicing. [40] Philip appeared at Azotus, and toured the country, preaching in all the towns till he reached Caesarea.

9 SAUL, still breathing murderous threats against the Lord's disciples, went to the high priest [2] and applied for letters to the synagogues at Damascus authorizing him to arrest any followers of the new way whom he found, men or women, and bring them to Jerusalem. [3] While he was still on the road and nearing Damascus, suddenly a light

8:36 **baptized:** *some witnesses add* [37]Philip said, 'If you wholeheartedly believe, it is permitted.' He replied, 'I believe that Jesus Christ is the Son of God.'

and recognized as valid, in the Hellenistic world. **14–15:** Acts pictures Jerusalem as the continuing center of the church, overseeing all its operations. **16:** *Spirit had not* yet *come:* see 2.38 n. **17:** *Received the Holy Spirit:* compare 10.44–46 n. **26–40:** *Philip and the Ethiopian eunuch.* **27:** In ancient times, *Ethiopia*, peopled by the Nubians, centered in what is now the Sudan; compare Ps. 68.31. *Eunuch:* compare Isa. 56.3–5. **28:** *Reading aloud* was the common practice, even when reading alone. **32:** Isa. 53.7–8. Isaiah ch. 53 was a key passage in the earliest Christian proclamation (compare Matt. 8.17; Jn. 12.38; 1 Pet. 2.22–25). **38:** *They both went down into the water:* baptism of adults was by immersion, as Rom. 6.3–4 ("By baptism we were buried with him . . .") indicates.

9.1–30: Saul converted. For other accounts of this conversion, see chs. 22; 26. **3:** There is no hint in Acts from the sky flashed all around him. ⁴He fell to the ground and heard a voice saying, 'Saul, Saul, why are you persecuting me?' ⁵'Tell me, Lord,' he said, 'who you are.' The voice answered, 'I am Jesus, whom you are persecuting. ⁶But now get up and go into the city, and you will be told what you have to do.' ⁷Meanwhile the men who were travelling with him stood speechless; they heard the voice but could see no one. ⁸Saul got up from the ground, but when he opened his eyes he could not see; they led him by the hand and brought him into Damascus. ⁹He was blind for three days, and took no food or drink.

¹⁰There was in Damascus a disciple named Ananias. He had a vision in which he heard the Lord say: 'Ananias!' 'Here I am, Lord,' he answered. ¹¹The Lord said to him, 'Go to Straight Street, to the house of Judas, and ask for a man from Tarsus named Saul. You will find him at prayer; ¹²he has had a vision of a man named Ananias coming in and laying hands on him to restore his sight.' ¹³Ananias answered, 'Lord, I have often heard about this man and all the harm he has done your people in Jerusalem. ¹⁴Now he is here with authority from the chief priests to arrest all who invoke your name.' ¹⁵But the Lord replied, 'You must go, for this man is my chosen instrument to bring my name before the nations and their kings, and before the people of Israel. ¹⁶I myself will show him all that he must go through for my name's sake.'

¹⁷So Ananias went and, on entering the house, laid his hands on him and said, 'Saul, my brother, the Lord Jesus, who appeared to you on your way here, has sent me to you so that you may recover your sight and be filled with the Holy Spirit.' ¹⁸Immediately it was as if scales had fallen from his eyes, and he regained his sight. He got up and was baptized, ¹⁹and when he had eaten his strength returned.

He stayed some time with the disciples in Damascus. ²⁰Without delay he proclaimed Jesus publicly in the synagogues, declaring him to be the Son of God. ²¹All who heard were astounded. 'Is not this the man', they said, 'who was in Jerusalem hunting down those who invoke this name? Did he not come here for the sole purpose of arresting them and taking them before the chief priests?' ²²But Saul went from strength to strength, and confounded the Jews of Damascus with his cogent proofs that Jesus was the Messiah.

²³When some time had passed, the Jews hatched a plot against his life; ²⁴but their plans became known to Saul. They kept watch on the city gates day and night so that they might murder him; ²⁵but one night some disciples took him and, lowering him in a basket, let him down over the wall.

²⁶On reaching Jerusalem he tried to join the disciples, but they were all afraid of him, because they did not believe that he really was a disciple. ²⁷Barnabas, however, took him and introduced him to the apostles; he described to them how on his journey Saul had seen the Lord and heard his voice, and how at Damascus he had spoken out boldly in the name of Jesus. ²⁸Saul now stayed with them, moving about freely in Jerusalem. ²⁹He spoke out boldly and openly in the name of the Lord, talking and debating with the Greek-speaking Jews. But they planned to murder him, ³⁰and when the brethren discovered this they escorted him down to Caesarea and sent him away to Tarsus.

³¹MEANWHILE the church, throughout Judaea, Galilee, and Samaria, was left in peace to build up its strength, and to live in the fear of the Lord. Encouraged by the Holy Spirit, it grew in numbers.

³²In the course of a tour Peter was making throughout the region he went down to visit God's people at Lydda. ³³There he found a

9:29 **Greek-speaking Jews:** *lit.* Hellenists.

that Paul at this time suffered inner turmoil; Phil. 3.6 indicates he felt no guilt while pursuing the law. **4:** *Persecuting me:* Jesus identifies himself with the church Paul is tormenting; compare Lk. 10.16. **7:** The details of who *heard* and who saw are reversed in 22.9. **12:** Mutually confirming visions or dreams also appear in Hellenistic religious literature. **15:** *The people of Israel:* Acts reports that Paul regularly preached to the Jews (13.15; 14.1; 17.1–2); his own letters give a different impression (Gal. 1.16; 2.8). **17:** Compare 22.12–16. **20:** At this point, the account in Acts begins to diverge significantly from Paul's account of these events in Gal. 1.13–2.10. **23–25: Plot against Saul. 23:** With a *plot against his life,* the prediction in v. 16 begins its fulfillment. **25:** Compare 2 Cor. 11.32–33. **26–30: Saul in Jerusalem. 27:** Paul gives a different account of these events in Gal. 1.16–20.

9.31–43: Peter performs two miracles. Mighty deeds were understood to accredit authoritative persons; see man named Aeneas who had been bedridden with paralysis for eight years. ³⁴ Peter said to him, 'Aeneas, Jesus Christ cures you; get up and make your bed!' and immediately he stood up. ³⁵ All who lived in Lydda and Sharon saw him; and they turned to the Lord.

³⁶ In Joppa there was a disciple named Tabitha (in Greek, Dorcas, meaning 'Gazelle'), who filled her days with acts of kindness and charity. ³⁷ At that time she fell ill and died; and they washed her body and laid it in a room upstairs. ³⁸ As Lydda was near Joppa, the disciples, who had heard that Peter was there, sent two men to him with the urgent request, 'Please come over to us without delay.' ³⁹ At once Peter went off with them. When he arrived he was taken up to the room, and all the widows came and stood round him in tears, showing him the shirts and coats that Dorcas used to make while she was with them. ⁴⁰ Peter sent them all outside, and knelt down and prayed; then, turning towards the body, he said, 'Tabitha, get up.' She opened her eyes, saw Peter, and sat up. ⁴¹ He gave her his hand and helped her to her feet. Then he called together the members of the church and the widows and showed her to them alive. ⁴² News of it spread all over Joppa, and many came to believe in the Lord. ⁴³ Peter stayed on in Joppa for some time at the house of a tanner named Simon.

10 At Caesarea there was a man named Cornelius, a centurion in the Italian Cohort, as it was called. ² He was a devout man, and he and his whole family joined in the worship of God; he gave generously to help the Jewish people, and was regular in his prayers to God. ³ One day about three in the afternoon he had a vision in which he clearly saw an angel of God come into his room and say, 'Cornelius!' ⁴ Cornelius stared at him in terror. 'What is it, my lord?' he asked. The angel said, 'Your prayers and acts of charity have gone up to heaven to speak

for you before God. ⁵ Now send to Joppa for a man named Simon, also called Peter: ⁶ he is lodging with another Simon, a tanner, whose house is by the sea.' ⁷ When the angel who spoke to him had gone, he summoned two of his servants and a military orderly who was a religious man, ⁸ told them the whole story, and ordered them to Joppa.

⁹ Next day about noon, while they were still on their way and approaching the city, Peter went up on the roof to pray. ¹⁰ He grew hungry and wanted something to eat, but while they were getting it ready, he fell into a trance. ¹¹ He saw heaven opened, and something coming down that looked like a great sheet of sailcloth; it was slung by the four corners and was being lowered to the earth, ¹² and in it he saw creatures of every kind, four-footed beasts, reptiles, and birds. ¹³ There came a voice which said to him, 'Get up, Peter, kill and eat.' ¹⁴ But Peter answered, 'No, Lord! I have never eaten anything profane or unclean.' ¹⁵ The voice came again, a second time: 'It is not for you to call profane what God counts clean.' ¹⁶ This happened three times, and then the thing was taken up into heaven.

¹⁷ While Peter was still puzzling over the meaning of the vision he had seen, the messengers from Cornelius had been asking the way to Simon's house, and now arrived at the entrance. ¹⁸ They called out and asked if Simon Peter was lodging there. ¹⁹ Peter was thinking over the vision, when the Spirit said to him, 'Some men are here looking for you; ²⁰ get up and go downstairs. You may go with them without any misgiving, for it was I who sent them.' ²¹ Peter came down to the men and said, 'You are looking for me? Here I am. What brings you here?' ²² 'We are from the centurion Cornelius,' they replied, 'a good and religious man, acknowledged as such by the whole Jewish nation. He was directed by a holy angel to send for you to his house and hear what you have to say.' ²³ So

14.11 n. **35:** In Acts, miracles validly lead to faith; but compare Jn. 20.29; Mk. 8.12; Matt. 16.4. **36:** For similarities between this account and a miracle of Jesus, see Mk. 5.37–42. **39:** On *widows,* compare 1 Tim. 5.3 n., 9 n.

10.1–48: Peter and Cornelius. 1: *Caesarea,* the Roman capital of the provinces of Judea and Samaria, was the official residence of the procurators who ruled them. A *centurion* commanded one hundred soldiers. A *cohort* was a military unit, part of a legion. **2:** *Worship of God,* lit. he was a God-fearer: a term applied to Gentiles who observed Jewish rites without becoming converts; compare 13.50; 16.14. **14:** *Profane or unclean:* see Lev. ch. 11. **15:** The voice annuls Jewish food laws, and thus the distinction between Jew and Gentile; see also v. 28; Mk. 7.1–23. **17:** *Cornelius:* see vv. 3–5. **19–22:** This is another case of mutually confirming visions;

Peter asked them in and gave them a night's lodging.

Next day he set out with them, accompanied by some members of the congregation at Joppa, 24 and on the following day arrived at Caesarea. Cornelius was expecting them and had called together his relatives and close friends. 25 When Peter arrived, Cornelius came to meet him, and bowed to the ground in deep reverence. 26 But Peter raised him to his feet and said, 'Stand up; I am only a man like you.' 27 Still talking with him he went in and found a large gathering. 28 He said to them, 'I need not tell you that a Jew is forbidden by his religion to visit or associate with anyone of another race. Yet God has shown me clearly that I must not call anyone profane or unclean; 29 that is why I came here without demur when you sent for me. May I ask what was your reason for doing so?'

30 Cornelius said, 'Three days ago, just about this time, I was in the house here saying the afternoon prayers, when suddenly a man in shining robes stood before me. 31 He said: "Cornelius, your prayer has been heard and your acts of charity have spoken for you before God. 32 Send to Simon Peter at Joppa, and ask him to come; he is lodging in the house of Simon the tanner, by the sea." 33 I sent to you there and then, and you have been good enough to come. So now we are all met here before God, to listen to everything that the Lord has instructed you to say.'

34 Peter began: 'I now understand how true it is that God has no favourites, 35 but that in every nation those who are god-fearing and do what is right are acceptable to him. 36 He sent his word to the Israelites and gave the good news of peace through Jesus Christ, who is Lord of all. 37 I need not tell you what has happened lately all over the land of the Jews, starting from Galilee after the baptism proclaimed by John. 38 You know how God anointed Jesus of Nazareth with the Holy Spirit and with power. Because God was with him he went about doing good and healing

all who were oppressed by the devil. 39 And we can bear witness to all that he did in the Jewish countryside and in Jerusalem. They put him to death, hanging him on a gibbet; 40 but God raised him to life on the third day, and allowed him to be clearly seen, 41 not by the whole people, but by witnesses whom God had chosen in advance — by us, who ate and drank with him after he rose from the dead. 42 He commanded us to proclaim him to the people, and affirm that he is the one designated by God as judge of the living and the dead. 43 It is to him that all the prophets testify, declaring that everyone who trusts in him receives forgiveness of sins through his name.'

44 Peter was still speaking when the Holy Spirit came upon all who were listening to the message. 45 The believers who had come with Peter, men of Jewish birth, were amazed that the gift of the Holy Spirit should have been poured out even on Gentiles, 46 for they could hear them speaking in tongues of ecstasy and acclaiming the greatness of God. Then Peter spoke: 47 'Is anyone prepared to withhold the water of baptism from these persons, who have received the Holy Spirit just as we did?' 48 Then he ordered them to be baptized in the name of Jesus Christ. After that they asked him to stay on with them for a time.

11 News came to the apostles and the members of the church in Judaea that Gentiles too had accepted the word of God; 2 and when Peter came up to Jerusalem those who were of Jewish birth took issue with him. 3 'You have been visiting men who are uncircumcised,' they said, 'and sitting at table with them!' 4 Peter began by laying before them the facts as they had happened.

5 'I was at prayer in the city of Joppa,' he said, 'and while in a trance I had a vision: I saw something coming down that looked like a great sheet of sailcloth, slung by the four corners and lowered from heaven till it reached me. 6 I looked intently to make out

see 9.12 n. **23:** *Some members:* in 11.12 there are six who function as witnesses at this turning point in the life of the church. **30:** *Three days ago:* the Gk. is obscure for this. **34–35:** These verses justify the Gentile mission which now begins. **36–38:** *Lord of all,* as well as *doing good* and *healing,* were claims commonly made for deities and rulers in the Hellenistic world. **41:** *Who ate and drank:* compare 1.6; Lk. 24.30, 42. **42:** *As judge:* compare 17.31. **43:** *All the prophets:* see 3.24. *Everyone:* compare 13.39. **44–46:** The coming of the *Holy Spirit* is here identified with *speaking in tongues of ecstasy:* see 8.15–17 where the same may be implied. **48:** *Baptized:* see 2.38 n.

11.1–18: Peter in Jerusalem. 2: Of *Jewish birth* (or, of the circumcision party): compare Gal. 2.12. **12:** These what was in it and I saw four-footed beasts, wild animals, reptiles, and birds. [7]Then I heard a voice saying to me, "Get up, Peter, kill and eat." [8]But I said, "No, Lord! Nothing profane or unclean has ever entered my mouth." [9]A voice from heaven came a second time: "It is not for you to call profane what God counts clean." [10]This happened three times, and then they were all drawn up again into heaven. [11]At that very moment three men who had been sent to me from Caesarea arrived at the house where I was staying; [12]and the Spirit told me to go with them. My six companions here came with me and we went into the man's house. [13]He told us how he had seen an angel standing in his house who said, "Send to Joppa for Simon Peter. [14]He will speak words that will bring salvation to you and all your household." [15]Hardly had I begun speaking, when the Holy Spirit came upon them, just as upon us at the beginning, [16]and I recalled what the Lord had said: "John baptized with water, but you will be baptized with the Holy Spirit." [17]God gave them no less a gift than he gave us when we came to believe in the Lord Jesus Christ. How could I stand in God's way?'

[18]When they heard this their doubts were silenced, and they gave praise to God. 'This means', they said, 'that God has granted life-giving repentance to the Gentiles also.'

[19]MEANWHILE those who had been scattered after the persecution that arose over Stephen made their way to Phoenicia, Cyprus, and Antioch, bringing the message to Jews only and to no others. [20]But there were some natives of Cyprus and Cyrene among them, and these, when they arrived at Antioch, began to speak to Gentiles as well, telling them the good news of the Lord Jesus. [21]The power of the Lord was with them, and a great many became believers and turned to the Lord.

[22]The news reached the ears of the church in Jerusalem; and they sent Barnabas to Antioch. [23]When he arrived and saw the divine grace at work, he rejoiced and encouraged them all to hold fast to the Lord with resolute hearts, [24]for he was a good man, full of the Holy Spirit and of faith. And large numbers were won over to the Lord.

[25]He then went off to Tarsus to look for Saul; [26]and when he had found him, he brought him to Antioch. For a whole year the two of them lived in fellowship with the church there, and gave instruction to large numbers. It was in Antioch that the disciples first got the name of Christians.

[27]During this period some prophets came down from Jerusalem to Antioch, [28]and one of them, Agabus by name, was inspired to stand up and predict a severe and world-wide famine, which in fact occurred in the reign of Claudius. [29]So the disciples agreed to make a contribution, each according to his means, for the relief of their fellow-Christians in Judaea. [30]This they did, and sent it off to the elders, entrusting it to Barnabas and Saul.

12 It was about this time that King Herod launched an attack on certain members of the church. [2]He beheaded James, the brother of John, [3]and, when he saw that the Jews approved, proceeded to

11:11 **I was:** *some witnesses read* we were.
11:12 **with them:** *some witnesses add* making no distinctions; *others add* without any misgiving, *as in* 10:20.

companions are apparently to help Peter in his presentation. **15:** *At the beginning:* i.e. Pentecost; compare 2.1–4 (and nn.); 10.44–46 (and n.). **16:** See 1.5 n. **18:** *Repentance* is also used as a synonym for faith in 5.31.

11.19–30: Expanding missionary activity among Gentiles. 19: *Antioch,* the third largest city in the Roman Empire, was the official residence of the Roman administrator of the province of Syria. Here, it now becomes the center of the Gentile mission. **20:** For the first time, *Gentiles* are evangelized as a general practice. Verses 19–20 reflect Acts' missionary scheme: first to *Jews,* then to *Gentiles.* **22:** *They sent Barnabas,* apparently because the Gentile mission was still regarded with suspicion; compare 15.1; Gal. 2.11–14. **26:** *The name of Christians,* coined by outsiders, was not necessarily derisive in intent, as some interpreters assert. **27:** *Prophets:* compare 13.1; 15.32; 21.9. **28:** *Agabus:* see 21.10–12. *Claudius* was emperor of Rome in 41–54 C.E. Although there was a famine in Palestine about 46–48, there is no other record of a *world-wide famine.* **29:** There is some confusion as to when the *contribution* was sent. According to this account, it was sent prior to the apostolic council (ch. 15). According to Gal. 2.10, it occurred after the council, as is implied in Acts 24.17; compare Rom. 15.25–29. The reference to Claudius (v. 28) makes either time possible.

12.1–25: Herod's persecution. 1: *Herod* Agrippa I ruled as *king* of Judea 41–44 C.E., by the appointment arrest Peter also. This happened during the festival of Unleavened Bread. 4 Having secured him, he put him in prison under a military guard, four squads of four men each, meaning to produce him in public after Passover. 5 So, while Peter was held in prison, the church kept praying fervently to God for him.

6 On the very night before Herod had planned to produce him, Peter was asleep between two soldiers, secured by two chains, while outside the doors sentries kept guard over the prison. 7 All at once an angel of the Lord stood there, and the cell was ablaze with light. He tapped Peter on the shoulder to wake him. 'Quick! Get up!' he said, and the chains fell away from Peter's wrists. 8 The angel said, 'Do up your belt and put on your sandals.' He did so. 'Now wrap your cloak round you and follow me.' 9 Peter followed him out, with no idea that the angel's intervention was real: he thought it was just a vision. 10 They passed the first guard-post, then the second, and reached the iron gate leading out into the city. This opened for them of its own accord; they came out and had walked the length of one street when suddenly the angel left him.

11 Then Peter came to himself. 'Now I know it is true,' he said: 'the Lord has sent his angel and rescued me from Herod's clutches and from all that the Jewish people were expecting.' 12 Once he had realized this, he made for the house of Mary, the mother of John Mark, where a large company was at prayer. 13 He knocked at the outer door and a maidservant called Rhoda came to answer it. 14 She recognized Peter's voice and was so overjoyed that instead of opening the door she ran in and announced that Peter was standing outside. 15 'You are crazy,' they told her; but she insisted that it was so. Then they said, 'It must be his angel.'

16 Peter went on knocking, and when they opened the door and saw him, they were astounded. 17 He motioned to them with his hand to keep quiet, and described to them how the Lord had brought him out of prison. 'Tell James and the members of the church,' he said. Then he left the house and went off elsewhere.

18 When morning came, there was consternation among the soldiers: what could have become of Peter? 19 Herod made careful search, but failed to find him, so he interrogated the guards and ordered their execution.

Afterwards Herod left Judaea to reside for a while at Caesarea. 20 He had for some time been very angry with the people of Tyre and Sidon, who now by common agreement presented themselves at his court. There they won over Blastus the royal chamberlain, and sued for peace, because their country drew its supplies from the king's territory. 21 On an appointed day Herod, attired in his royal robes and seated on the rostrum, addressed the populace; 22 they responded, 'It is a god speaking, not a man!' 23 Instantly an angel of the Lord struck him down, because he had usurped the honour due to God; he was eaten up with worms and so died.

24 Meanwhile the word of God continued to grow and spread; 25 and Barnabas and Saul, their task fulfilled, returned from Jerusalem, taking John Mark with them.

Paul's work among the Gentiles

13 THERE were in the church at Antioch certain prophets and teachers: Barnabas, Simeon called Niger, Lucius of Cyrene, Manaen, a close friend of Prince Herod, and Saul. 2 While they were offering

12:25 **from Jerusalem:** *some witnesses read* to Jerusalem.

of the Emperor Claudius. **2:** *James, John:* see Mk. 1.19. On the fate of *John,* the NT is silent. **10:** The wondrous opening of locked doors is a widespread theme in Hellenistic stories. **12:** *John Mark:* 12.25; 13.5, 13; Col. 4.10; Philem. 24; 2 Tim. 4.11. **15:** In popular thought, each person had a (guardian) *angel* who was identical in appearance to the person. **17:** From this point on, *James,* Jesus' brother, emerges as the leader of the church in Jerusalem (compare Gal. 1.19; 2.12), and there is no further mention of the Twelve. Peter reappears only at 15.7. **20:** Since the time of Solomon, Phoenicia *drew its supplies* from Judea; see 1 Kgs. 5.9–11; Ezek. 27.17. **23:** Josephus (a first-century Jewish historian) confirms Herod's sudden death (*Ant.* XIX, 8.2) and the detail that he was acclaimed as divine. After the death of Herod Agrippa I, Judea reverted to an imperial province, ruled by governors; see 23.24.

13.1–14.28: Paul's missionary travels (first journey). 1–3: Barnabas and Saul set apart. 1: *Niger* means black. *Prince Herod* is Herod Antipas, the Tetrarch, not the Herod of 12.1. **2:** Acts' conviction that the *Holy* worship to the Lord and fasting, the Holy Spirit said, 'Set Barnabas and Saul apart for me, to do the work to which I have called them.' ³Then, after further fasting and prayer, they laid their hands on them and sent them on their way.

⁴These two, sent out on their mission by the Holy Spirit, came down to Seleucia, and from there sailed to Cyprus. ⁵Arriving at Salamis, they declared the word of God in the Jewish synagogues; they had John with them as their assistant. ⁶They went through the whole island as far as Paphos, and there they came upon a sorcerer, a Jew who posed as a prophet, Barjesus by name. ⁷He was in the retinue of the governor, Sergius Paulus, a learned man, who had sent for Barnabas and Saul and wanted to hear the word of God. ⁸This Elymas the sorcerer (so his name may be translated) opposed them, trying to turn the governor away from the faith. ⁹But Saul, also known as Paul, filled with the Holy Spirit, fixed his eyes on him ¹⁰and said, 'You are a swindler, an out-and-out fraud! You son of the devil and enemy of all goodness, will you never stop perverting the straight ways of the Lord? ¹¹Look now, the hand of the Lord strikes: you shall be blind, and for a time you shall not see the light of the sun.' At once mist and darkness came over his eyes, and he groped about for someone to lead him by the hand. ¹²When the governor saw what had happened he became a believer, deeply impressed by what he learnt about the Lord.

¹³Sailing from Paphos, Paul and his companions went to Perga in Pamphylia; John, however, left them and returned to Jerusalem. ¹⁴From Perga they continued their journey as far as Pisidian Antioch. On the sabbath they went to synagogue and took their seats; ¹⁵and after the readings from the law and the prophets, the officials of the synagogue sent this message to them: 'Friends, if you have

anything to say to the people by way of exhortation, let us hear it.' ¹⁶Paul stood up, raised his hand for silence, and began.

'Listen, men of Israel and you others who worship God! ¹⁷The God of this people, Israel, chose our forefathers. When they were still living as aliens in Egypt, he made them into a great people and, with arm outstretched, brought them out of that country. ¹⁸For some forty years he bore with their conduct in the desert. ¹⁹Then in the Canaanite country, after overthrowing seven nations, whose lands he gave them to be their heritage ²⁰for some four hundred and fifty years, he appointed judges for them until the time of the prophet Samuel.

²¹'It was then that they asked for a king, and God gave them Saul son of Kish, a man of the tribe of Benjamin. He reigned for forty years ²²before God removed him and appointed David as their king, with this commendation: "I have found David the son of Jesse to be a man after my own heart; he will carry out all my purposes." ²³This is the man from whose descendants God, as he promised, has brought Israel a saviour, Jesus. ²⁴John had made ready for his coming by proclaiming a baptism in token of repentance to the whole people of Israel; ²⁵and, nearing the end of his earthly course, John said, "I am not the one you think I am. No, after me comes one whose sandals I am not worthy to unfasten."

²⁶'My brothers, who come of Abraham's stock, and others among you who worship God, we are the people to whom this message of salvation has been sent. ²⁷The people of Jerusalem and their rulers did not recognize Jesus, or understand the words of the prophets which are read sabbath by sabbath; indeed, they fulfilled them by condemning him. ²⁸Though they failed to find grounds

13:18 **he ... conduct:** *some witnesses read* he sustained them.

Spirit guided the church is again evident here. **3:** The laying on of *hands* commissioned persons for special tasks; compare 6.6. **4–12: Elymas confounded. 4:** Travelers at that time *sailed* on any available boat; passenger ships plying regular routes were unknown. **6:** *Paphos* was the capital of Cyprus. **8:** The meaning of *Elymas* is unknown. **9:** *Paul,* a Latin name, would be appropriate for a Roman citizen (22.25–29); but see 1.23 n. **11:** Acts' opposition to magic is clear here; compare also 8.9–11; 19.13–20. **13–15: To Pisidian Antioch. 13:** There was some altercation accompanying *John*'s leaving, as 15.38 makes clear. **14:** *Pisidian Antioch,* a remotely situated Roman colony (see 16.12 n.), was in the southern part of the province of Galatia, as were the other cities visited on this "journey." **16–41: Paul's sermon. 17:** As did Peter (13.25) and Stephen (7.2–50), Paul recounts the origins of the Jewish people as the necessary presupposition of understanding the Christian faith. **18b–19a:** Compare Deut. 7.1. **22:** Compare 1 Sam. 13.14; Ps. 89.21. **25:** Compare Mk. 1.7; Lk. 3.16.

for the sentence of death, they asked Pilate to have him executed. ²⁹When they had carried out all that the scriptures said about him, they took him down from the gibbet and laid him in a tomb. ³⁰But God raised him from the dead; ³¹and over a period of many days he appeared to those who had come up with him from Galilee to Jerusalem, and they are now his witnesses before our people.

³²'We are here to give you the good news that God, who made the promise to the fathers, ³³has fulfilled it for the children by raising Jesus from the dead, as indeed it stands written in the second Psalm: "You are my son; this day I have begotten you." ³⁴Again, that he raised him from the dead, never to be subjected to corruption, he declares in these words: "I will give you the blessings promised to David, holy and sure." ³⁵This is borne out by another passage: "You will not let your faithful servant suffer corruption." ³⁶As for David, when he had served the purpose of God in his own generation, he died and was gathered to his fathers, and suffered corruption; ³⁷but the one whom God raised up did not suffer corruption. ³⁸You must understand, my brothers, it is through him that forgiveness of sins is now being proclaimed to you. ³⁹It is through him that everyone who has faith is acquitted of everything for which there was no acquittal under the law of Moses. ⁴⁰Beware, then, lest you bring down upon yourselves the doom proclaimed by the prophets: ⁴¹"See this, you scoffers, marvel, and begone; for I am doing a deed in your days, a deed which you will never believe when you are told of it."'

⁴²As they were leaving the synagogue they were asked to come again and speak on these subjects next sabbath; ⁴³and after the congregation had dispersed, many Jews and gentile worshippers went with Paul and Barnabas, who spoke to them and urged them to hold fast to the grace of God.

⁴⁴On the following sabbath almost the whole city gathered to hear the word of God. ⁴⁵When the Jews saw the crowds, they were filled with jealous resentment, and contradicted what Paul had said with violent abuse. ⁴⁶But Paul and Barnabas were outspoken in their reply. 'It was necessary', they said, 'that the word of God should be declared to you first. But since you reject it and judge yourselves unworthy of eternal life, we now turn to the Gentiles. ⁴⁷For these are our instructions from the Lord: "I have appointed you to be a light for the Gentiles, and a means of salvation to earth's farthest bounds."' ⁴⁸When the Gentiles heard this, they were overjoyed and thankfully acclaimed the word of the Lord, and those who were marked out for eternal life became believers. ⁴⁹Thus the word of the Lord spread throughout the region. ⁵⁰But the Jews stirred up feeling among those worshippers who were women of standing, and among the leading men of the city; a campaign of persecution was started against Paul and Barnabas, and they were expelled from the district. ⁵¹They shook the dust off their feet in protest against them and went to Iconium. ⁵²And the disciples were filled with joy and with the Holy Spirit.

14 At Iconium they went together into the Jewish synagogue and spoke to such purpose that Jews and Greeks in large numbers became believers. ²But the unconverted Jews stirred up the Gentiles and poisoned their minds against the Christians. ³So Paul and Barnabas stayed on for some time, and spoke boldly and openly in reliance on the Lord, who confirmed the message of his grace by enabling them to work signs and miracles. ⁴The populace was divided, some siding with the Jews, others with the apostles. ⁵A move was made by Gentiles and Jews together, with the connivance of the city authorities, to maltreat them and stone them, ⁶and when they became aware of this, they made their escape to the Lycaonian cities of Lystra and Derbe and the surrounding coun-

13:33 **for the children:** *some witnesses read* for our children; *others read* for us their children.

33: Ps. 2.7. 35–37: Compare 2.25–31. 35: Ps. 16.10. 41: Hab. 1.5. Paul's more sophisticated Christology, and his eschatological concerns, characteristic of his letters, are absent from this sermon. **42–52: Paul and Barnabas turn to Gentiles. 46:** This point is repeated in 18.6 and 28.28; compare also 19.8–9. **50:** The risen Jesus had foretold such persecution of Paul; see 9.16. **51:** They thus follow a command of Jesus: Lk. 9.5; compare 10.10–11. **14.1–7: On to Iconium. 1:** *Iconium*, like Antioch a Roman colony, was a commercial center for its area (see 13.14 n.). **4:** Paul and Barnabas are called *apostles* only here and in v. 14; the term is normally reserved in Acts for the leaders in Jerusalem (compare 15.2), although Paul himself claimed to be try. 7 There they continued to spread the good news.

8 At Lystra a cripple, lame from birth, who had never walked in his life, 9 sat listening to Paul as he spoke. Paul fixed his eyes on him and, seeing that he had the faith to be cured, 10 said in a loud voice, 'Stand up straight on your feet'; and he sprang up and began to walk. 11 When the crowds saw what Paul had done, they shouted, in their native Lycaonian, 'The gods have come down to us in human form!' 12 They called Barnabas Zeus, and Paul they called Hermes, because he was the spokesman. 13 The priest of Zeus, whose temple was just outside the city, brought oxen and garlands to the gates, and he and the people were about to offer sacrifice.

14 But when the apostles Barnabas and Paul heard of it, they tore their clothes and rushed into the crowd shouting, 15 'Men, why are you doing this? We are human beings, just like you. The good news we bring tells you to turn from these follies to the living God, who made heaven and earth and sea and everything in them. 16 In past ages he has allowed all nations to go their own way; 17 and yet he has not left you without some clue to his nature, in the benefits he bestows: he sends you rain from heaven and the crops in their seasons, and gives you food in plenty and keeps you in good heart.' 18 Even with these words they barely managed to prevent the crowd from offering sacrifice to them.

19 Then Jews from Antioch and Iconium came on the scene and won over the crowds. They stoned Paul, and dragged him out of the city, thinking him dead. 20 The disciples formed a ring round him, and he got to his feet and went into the city. Next day he left with Barnabas for Derbe.

21 After bringing the good news to that town and gaining many converts, they returned to Lystra, then to Iconium, and then to Antioch, 22 strengthening the disciples and encouraging them to be true to the faith.

They warned them that to enter the kingdom of God we must undergo many hardships. 23 They also appointed for them elders in each congregation, and with prayer and fasting committed them to the Lord in whom they had put their trust.

24 They passed through Pisidia and came into Pamphylia. 25 When they had delivered the message at Perga, they went down to Attalia, 26 and from there sailed to Antioch, where they had originally been commended to the grace of God for the task which they had now completed. 27 On arrival there, they called the congregation together and reported all that God had accomplished through them, and how he had thrown open the gates of faith to the Gentiles. 28 And they stayed for some time with the disciples there.

15 SOME people who had come down from Judaea began to teach the brotherhood that those who were not circumcised in accordance with Mosaic practice could not be saved. 2 That brought them into fierce dissension and controversy with Paul and Barnabas, and it was arranged that these two and some others from Antioch should go up to Jerusalem to see the apostles and elders about this question.

3 They were sent on their way by the church, and travelled through Phoenicia and Samaria, telling the full story of the conversion of the Gentiles, and causing great rejoicing among all the Christians.

4 When they reached Jerusalem they were welcomed by the church and the apostles and elders, and they reported all that God had accomplished through them. 5 But some of the Pharisaic party who had become believers came forward and declared, 'Those Gentiles must be circumcised and told to keep the law of Moses.'

6 The apostles and elders met to look into this matter, 7 and, after a long debate, Peter rose to address them. 'My friends,' he said, 'in

an apostle: see 1 Cor. 9.1; Gal. 1.1. **8–20: Paul and Barnabas at Lystra. 8:** *Lystra* was also a Roman colony. **11:** The idea of "divine heroes" was common in the Hellenistic world; great deeds were attributed to divine power in such persons; compare 28.6 n. **12:** *Zeus:* the Greek high god. *Hermes,* the god who, in Greek mythology, brought messages from the gods. **15:** Ps. 146.6; compare Acts 4.24. Peter also rejected any attribute of divinity (10.26). **19:** See 2 Cor. 11.25. **21–28: Return to Antioch. 23:** *Prayer and fasting:* compare 13.3. **28:** Such inexact time references are typical of Acts, and make the construction of historical chronology impossible.

15.1–35: The apostolic council. 2: This is the *controversy* with which Paul's letter to the Galatians deals, although in that letter, it occurs much later in Paul's career (see Gal. 2.1). **7:** According to Gal. 2.7–8, Peter the early days, as you yourselves know, God made his choice among you: from my lips the Gentiles were to hear and believe the message of the gospel. [8] And God, who can read human hearts, showed his approval by giving the Holy Spirit to them as he did to us. [9] He made no difference between them and us; for he purified their hearts by faith. [10] Then why do you now try God's patience by laying on the shoulders of these converts a yoke which neither we nor our forefathers were able to bear? [11] For our belief is that we are saved in the same way as they are: by the grace of the Lord Jesus.'

[12] At that the whole company fell silent and listened to Barnabas and Paul as they described all the signs and portents that God had worked among the Gentiles through them.

[13] When they had finished speaking, James summed up: 'My friends,' he said, 'listen to me. [14] Simon has described how it first happened that God, in his providence, chose from among the Gentiles a people to bear his name. [15] This agrees with the words of the prophets: as scripture has it,

[16] Thereafter I will return and rebuild the
   fallen house of David;
   I will rebuild its ruins and set it up
   again,
[17] that the rest of mankind may seek the
   Lord,
   all the Gentiles whom I have claimed
   for my own.
   Thus says the Lord, who is doing this
[18] as he made known long ago.

[19] 'In my judgement, therefore, we should impose no irksome restrictions on those of the Gentiles who are turning to God; [20] instead we should instruct them by letter to abstain from things polluted by contact with idols, from fornication, from anything that has been strangled, and from blood. [21] Moses, after all, has never lacked spokesmen in

every town for generations past; he is read in the synagogues sabbath by sabbath.'

[22] Then, with the agreement of the whole church, the apostles and elders resolved to choose representatives and send them to Antioch with Paul and Barnabas. They chose two leading men in the community, Judas Barsabbas and Silas, [23] and gave them this letter to deliver:

From the apostles and elders to our brothers of gentile origin in Antioch, Syria, and Cilicia. Greetings!

[24] We have heard that some of our number, without any instructions from us, have disturbed you with their talk and unsettled your minds. [25] In consequence, we have resolved unanimously to send to you our chosen representatives with our well-beloved Barnabas and Paul, [26] who have given up their lives to the cause of our Lord Jesus Christ; [27] so we are sending Judas and Silas, who will, by word of mouth, confirm what is written in this letter. [28] It is the decision of the Holy Spirit, and our decision, to lay no further burden upon you beyond these essentials: [29] you are to abstain from meat that has been offered to idols, from blood, from anything that has been strangled, and from fornication. If you keep yourselves free from these things you will be doing well. Farewell.

[30] So they took their leave and travelled down to Antioch, where they called the congregation together and delivered the letter. [31] When it was read, all rejoiced at the encouragement it brought, [32] and Judas and Si-

15:14 **Simon:** Gk Simeon.   15:20 **from fornication . . . blood:** some witnesses omit from fornication; others omit from anything that has been strangled; some add (after blood) and to refrain from doing to others what they would not like done to themselves.
15:29 **from anything . . . fornication:** some witnesses omit from anything that has been strangled; some omit and from fornication; and some witnesses add and refrain from doing to others what you would not like done to yourselves.

was sent to the Jews. **8:** Compare 10.44–45; 11.15. The conversion of Cornelius is the classic example in Acts. **10:** That the law was not universally regarded as a burdensome yoke is clear from Ps. 19.7–11. **13:** James is at this time clearly the head of the mother church in Jerusalem; see 12.17 n. **14:** Simon: although the Gk. here transliterates the Semitic name Simeon and 13.1 associates a person of that name with Antioch, Luke clearly refers at this point to Peter. **20:** Paul does not mention any such compromise (see Gal. 2.6, 9–10); he seems to contradict it in 1 Cor. 8.8; 10.27. **24–29: The apostolic letter. 24:** Without any instructions: a different impression is given in Gal. 2.12 ("from James"). **29:** Observance of these rules would make possible table-fellowship with law-observing Jewish Christians; see Lev. chs. 17–18.

las, who were themselves prophets, said much to encourage and strengthen the members. 33 After spending some time there, they took their leave with the good wishes of the brethren, to return to those who had sent them. 35 But Paul and Barnabas stayed on at Antioch, where, along with many others, they taught and preached the word of the Lord.

36 AFTER a while Paul said to Barnabas, 'Let us go back and see how our brothers are getting on in the various towns where we proclaimed the word of the Lord.' 37 Barnabas wanted to take John Mark with them; 38 but Paul insisted that the man who had deserted them in Pamphylia and had not gone on to share in their work was not the man to take with them now. 39 The dispute was so sharp that they parted company. Barnabas took Mark with him and sailed for Cyprus. 40 Paul chose Silas and started on his journey, commended by the brothers to the grace of the Lord. 41 He travelled through Syria and Cilicia bringing new strength to the churches.

16 He went on to Derbe and then to Lystra, where he found a disciple named Timothy, the son of a Jewish Christian mother and a gentile father, 2 well spoken of by the Christians at Lystra and Iconium. 3 Paul wanted to take him with him when he left, so he had him circumcised out of consideration for the Jews who lived in those parts, for they all knew that his father was a Gentile. 4 As they made their way from town to town they handed on the decisions taken by the apostles and elders in Jerusalem and enjoined their observance. 5 So, day by day, the churches grew stronger in faith and increased in numbers.

6 They travelled through the Phrygian and Galatian region, prevented by the Holy Spirit from delivering the message in the province of Asia. 7 When they approached the Mysian

border they tried to enter Bithynia, but, as the Spirit of Jesus would not allow them, 8 they passed through Mysia and reached the coast at Troas. 9 During the night a vision came to Paul: a Macedonian stood there appealing to him, 'Cross over to Macedonia and help us.' 10 As soon as he had seen this vision, we set about getting a passage to Macedonia, convinced that God had called us to take the good news there.

11 We sailed from Troas and made a straight run to Samothrace, the next day to Neapolis, 12 and from there to Philippi, a leading city in that district of Macedonia and a Roman colony. Here we stayed for some days, 13 and on the sabbath we went outside the city gate by the riverside, where we thought there would be a place of prayer; we sat down and talked to the women who had gathered there. 14 One of those listening was called Lydia, a dealer in purple fabric, who came from the city of Thyatira; she was a worshipper of God, and the Lord opened her heart to respond to what Paul said. 15 She was baptized, and her household with her, and then she urged us, 'Now that you have accepted me as a believer in the Lord, come and stay at my house.' And she insisted on our going.

16 Once, on our way to the place of prayer, we met a slave-girl who was possessed by a spirit of divination and brought large profits to her owners by telling fortunes. 17 She followed Paul and the rest of us, shouting, 'These men are servants of the Most High God, and are declaring to you a way of salvation.' 18 She did this day after day, until, in exasperation, Paul rounded on the spirit. 'I command you in the name of Jesus Christ to

15:33 **sent them:** *some witnesses add* 34But Silas decided to remain there.   16:6 **through . . . region:** *or* through Phrygia and the Galatian region.
16:13 **where . . . prayer:** *some witnesses read* where there was a recognized place of prayer.

15.36–18.22: Paul's further missionary travels (second journey). 36–41: Paul and Barnabas separate. 36: See 14.28 n. **38:** See 13.13. **39:** In Gal. 2.13, Paul's dispute with *Barnabas* turned on the more basic issue of table-fellowship between Jewish and Gentile Christians. **16.1–5: Timothy chosen. 1:** *Timothy* was a trusted associate (2 Cor. 1.19; Rom. 16.21), whom Paul often sent on important errands; see 1 Cor. 4.17; 16.10. **3:** Paul did not think circumcision necessary for Christians; see Gal. 2.3; 5.11; 6.15. **6–10: Paul's vision. 7:** *Bithynia* was the northernmost province in Asia Minor. **9:** Paul continues his westward movement; this seems to have been his overall strategy (see Rom. 15.19 n.). *Macedonia* was a Roman province in northern Greece. **11–15: Lydia converted. 11:** *Samothrace* is an island about halfway between *Troas* and *Neapolis*. **12:** As a *Roman colony*, *Philippi* was a military outpost and had a civil government modeled after Rome. **14:** *Worshipper of God:* see 10.2 n. **16–40: Trouble in Philippi. 18:** In using the *name of Jesus Christ*, Paul literally fulfills the come out of her,' he said, and it came out instantly.

¹⁹ When the girl's owners saw that their hope of profit had gone, they seized Paul and Silas and dragged them to the city authorities in the main square; ²⁰ bringing them before the magistrates, they alleged, 'These men are causing a disturbance in our city; they are Jews, ²¹ and they are advocating practices which it is illegal for us Romans to adopt and follow.' ²² The mob joined in the attack; and the magistrates had the prisoners stripped and gave orders for them to be flogged. ²³ After a severe beating they were flung into prison and the jailer was ordered to keep them under close guard. ²⁴ In view of these orders, he put them into the inner prison and secured their feet in the stocks.

²⁵ About midnight Paul and Silas, at their prayers, were singing praises to God, and the other prisoners were listening, ²⁶ when suddenly there was such a violent earthquake that the foundations of the jail were shaken; the doors burst open and all the prisoners found their fetters unfastened. ²⁷ The jailer woke up to see the prison doors wide open and, assuming that the prisoners had escaped, drew his sword intending to kill himself. ²⁸ But Paul shouted, 'Do yourself no harm; we are all here.' ²⁹ The jailer called for lights, rushed in, and threw himself down before Paul and Silas, trembling with fear. ³⁰ He then escorted them out and said, 'Sirs, what must I do to be saved?' ³¹ They answered, 'Put your trust in the Lord Jesus, and you will be saved, you and your household,' ³² and they imparted the word of the Lord to him and to everyone in his house. ³³ At that late hour of the night the jailer took them and washed their wounds, and there and then he and his whole family were baptized. ³⁴ He brought them up into his house, set out a meal, and rejoiced with his whole household in his new-found faith in God.

³⁵ When daylight came, the magistrates sent their officers with the order, 'Release those men.' ³⁶ The jailer reported these instructions to Paul: 'The magistrates have sent an order for your release. Now you are free

to go in peace.' ³⁷ But Paul said to the officers: 'We are Roman citizens! They gave us a public flogging and threw us into prison without trial. Are they now going to smuggle us out by stealth? No indeed! Let them come in person and escort us out.' ³⁸ The officers reported his words to the magistrates. Alarmed to hear that they were Roman citizens, ³⁹ they came and apologized to them, and then escorted them out and requested them to go away from the city. ⁴⁰ On leaving the prison, they went to Lydia's house, where they met their fellow-Christians and spoke words of encouragement to them, and then they took their departure.

17 THEY now travelled by way of Amphipolis and Apollonia and came to Thessalonica, where there was a Jewish synagogue. ² Following his usual practice Paul went to their meetings; and for the next three sabbaths he argued with them, quoting texts of scripture ³ which he expounded and applied to show that the Messiah had to suffer and rise from the dead. 'And this Jesus', he said, 'whom I am proclaiming to you is the Messiah.' ⁴ Some of them were convinced and joined Paul and Silas, as did a great number of godfearing Gentiles and a good many influential women.

⁵ The Jews in their jealousy recruited some ruffians from the dregs of society to gather a mob. They put the city in an uproar, and made for Jason's house with the intention of bringing Paul and Silas before the town assembly. ⁶ Failing to find them, they dragged Jason himself and some members of the congregation before the magistrates, shouting, 'The men who have made trouble the whole world over have now come here, ⁷ and Jason has harboured them. All of them flout the emperor's laws, and assert there is a rival king, Jesus.' ⁸ These words alarmed the mob and the magistrates also, ⁹ who took security from Jason and the others before letting them go.

¹⁰ As soon as darkness fell, the members of the congregation sent Paul and Silas off to Beroea; and, on arrival, they made their way

prayer of 4.30. **19:** Paul may refer to this episode in 1 Thess. 2.2. **22:** Paul suffered three such floggings at the hands of the Romans, who used rods (see 2 Cor. 11.25). **26:** *A violent earthquake . . . the doors burst open:* see 12.10 n. **37:** Paul's letters do not mention his *Roman* citizenship. **38–39:** Flogging Roman citizens was forbidden; hence, *the magistrates* were *alarmed* and *came and apologized to them.* See 22.24 n. **17.1–9: Paul in Thessalonica:** this city, the capital of the province of Macedonia, became an important Christian center to the synagogue. 11 The Jews here were more fair-minded than those at Thessalonica: they received the message with great eagerness, studying the scriptures every day to see whether it was true. 12 Many of them therefore became believers, and so did a fair number of Gentiles, women of standing as well as men. 13 But when the Thessalonian Jews learnt that the word of God had now been proclaimed by Paul in Beroea, they followed him there to stir up trouble and rouse the rabble. 14 At once the members of the congregation sent Paul down to the coast, while Silas and Timothy both stayed behind. 15 Paul's escort brought him as far as Athens, and came away with instructions for Silas and Timothy to rejoin him with all speed.

16 While Paul was waiting for them at Athens, he was outraged to see the city so full of idols. 17 He argued in the synagogue with the Jews and gentile worshippers, and also in the city square every day with casual passers-by. 18 Moreover, some of the Epicurean and Stoic philosophers joined issue with him. Some said, 'What can this charlatan be trying to say?' and others, 'He would appear to be a propagandist for foreign deities'—this because he was preaching about Jesus and the Resurrection. 19 They brought him to the Council of the Areopagus and asked, 'May we know what this new doctrine is that you propound? 20 You are introducing ideas that sound strange to us, and we should like to know what they mean.' 21 Now, all the Athenians and the resident foreigners had time for nothing except talking or hearing about the latest novelty.

22 Paul stood up before the Council of the Areopagus and began: 'Men of Athens, I see that in everything that concerns religion you are uncommonly scrupulous. 23 As I was going round looking at the objects of your worship, I noticed among other things an altar bearing the inscription "To an Unknown God". What you worship but do not know—this is what I now proclaim.

24 'The God who created the world and everything in it, and who is Lord of heaven and earth, does not live in shrines made by human hands. 25 It is not because he lacks anything that he accepts service at our hands, for he is himself the universal giver of life and breath—indeed of everything. 26 He created from one stock every nation of men to inhabit the whole earth's surface. He determined their eras in history and the limits of their territory. 27 They were to seek God in the hope that, groping after him, they might find him; though indeed he is not far from each one of us, 28 for in him we live and move, in him we exist; as some of your own poets have said, "We are also his offspring." 29 Being God's offspring, then, we ought not to suppose that the deity is like an image in gold or silver or stone, shaped by human craftsmanship and design. 30 God has overlooked the age of ignorance; but now he commands men and women everywhere to repent, 31 because he has fixed the day on which he will have the world judged, and justly judged, by a man whom he has designated; of this he has given assurance to all by raising him from the dead.'

32 When they heard about the raising of the dead, some scoffed; others said, 'We will hear you on this subject some other time.' 33 So Paul left the assembly. 34 Some men joined him and became believers, including Dionysius, a member of the Council of the Areopagus; and also a woman named Damaris, with others besides.

17:19 **to ... Areopagus:** *or* to Mars' Hill.
17:22 **before ... Areopagus:** *or* in the middle of Mars' Hill.   17:26 **determined ... history:** *or* fixed the ordered seasons.

(1 Thess. 1.8). **10–14: Trouble in Beroea. 13:** Similar events are reported in 13.50; 14.19. **15–34: Paul in Athens. 16:** *Athens,* although less important commercially and politically at this time than Corinth, remained the intellectual center of the western world, and an important city for ancient tourists. **17:** *The city square* lay north of the Acropolis. **18:** Many ancient deities had descriptive names, e.g. Fate, Victory, Wisdom; some of Paul's listeners apparently assumed that *Resurrection* also referred to a specific goddess. **19:** The *Areopagus,* or Mars Hill, lies south of the market and west of the Acropolis. There is no hint of any formal legal trial, although *the Council of Areopagus* was the highest court in Athens. **22–34:** Paul's witness in *Athens.* **23:** No *altar* with this specific wording has been found. **24:** Compare 7.48; this was a regular point made by Jewish preachers as well as Stoic philosophers. **25:** That the gods need nothing was a commonplace belief among Greek philosophers and religious thinkers. **28:** The quotation is from Aratus' (a fourth-century B.C.E. poet) *Phaenomena* 5. **31:** That Jesus would come at the end as judge was a common early Christian theme; see 10.42;

18 After this he left Athens and went to Corinth. [2] There he met a Jew named Aquila, a native of Pontus, and his wife Priscilla; they had recently arrived from Italy because Claudius had issued an edict that all Jews should leave Rome. Paul approached them [3] and, because he was of the same trade, he made his home with them; they were tentmakers and Paul worked with them. [4] He also held discussions in the synagogue sabbath by sabbath, trying to convince both Jews and Gentiles.

[5] Then Silas and Timothy came down from Macedonia, and Paul devoted himself entirely to preaching, maintaining before the Jews that the Messiah is Jesus. [6] When, however, they opposed him and resorted to abuse, he shook out the folds of his cloak and declared, 'Your blood be on your own heads! My conscience is clear! From now on I shall go to the Gentiles.' [7] With that he left, and went to the house of a worshipper of God named Titius Justus, who lived next door to the synagogue. [8] Crispus, the president of the synagogue, became a believer in the Lord, as did all his household; and a number of Corinthians who heard him believed and were baptized. [9] One night in a vision the Lord said to Paul, 'Have no fear: go on with your preaching and do not be silenced. [10] I am with you, and no attack shall harm you, for I have many in this city who are my people.' [11] So he settled there for eighteen months, teaching the word of God among them.

[12] But when Gallio was proconsul of Achaia, the Jews made a concerted attack on Paul and brought him before the court. [13] 'This man', they said, 'is inducing people to worship God in ways that are against the law.' [14] Paul was just about to speak when Gallio declared, 'If it had been a question of crime or grave misdemeanour, I should, of course, have given you Jews a patient hearing, [15] but if it is some bickering about words and names and your Jewish law, you may settle it yourselves. I do not intend to be a judge of these matters.' [16] And he dismissed them from the court. [17] Then they all attacked Sosthenes, the president of the synagogue, and beat him up in full view of the tribunal. But all this left Gallio quite unconcerned.

[18] Paul stayed on at Corinth for some time, and then took leave of the congregation. Accompanied by Priscilla and Aquila, he sailed for Syria, having had his hair cut off at Cenchreae in fulfilment of a vow. [19] They put in at Ephesus, where he parted from his companions; he himself went into the synagogue and held a discussion with the Jews. [20] He was asked to stay longer, but he declined [21] and set sail from Ephesus, promising, as he took leave of them, 'I shall come back to you if it is God's will.' [22] On landing at Caesarea, he went up and greeted the church; and then went down to Antioch. [23] After some time there he set out again on a journey through the Galatian country and then through Phrygia, bringing new strength to all the disciples.

[24] THERE arrived at Ephesus a Jew named Apollos, an Alexandrian by birth, an eloquent man, powerful in his use of the scriptures. [25] He had been instructed in the way of the Lord and was full of spiritual fervour; and in his discourses he taught accurately the facts about Jesus, though the only baptism he knew was John's. [26] He now began to speak boldly in the synagogue, where Priscilla and Aquila heard him; they took him in hand and expounded the way to him in greater detail.

18:24 **an eloquent man:** *or* a learned man.
18:26 **the way:** *some witnesses read* the way of God.

Matt. 13.41; 16.27; 2 Cor. 5.10. **18.1–17: Paul in Corinth. 1:** *Corinth,* the capital of the province of Achaia and a major port for east-west trade, had a wide reputation for low morals. **2:** On *Aquila* and *Priscilla* (or Prisca), see Rom. 16.3; 1 Cor. 16.19. *Claudius'. . . edict* is reported to have been issued about 49 C.E. **3:** Paul regularly earned his own living; see 20.33–34; 1 Cor. 4.12; 1 Thess. 2.9; compare 2 Cor. 11.7–10. **6:** See 13.46; 28.28. **9:** Such a *vision* was not uncommon for Paul; see 2 Cor. 12.1–5. For another such *vision,* see 22.17–21. **12:** *Gallio,* the older brother of the philosopher Seneca, *was proconsul* (governor) *of Achaia* about 51–53 C.E. **18–22: Return to Antioch. 18:** *Cenchreae* was the port on the east side of the Isthmus of Corinth. **19:** *Ephesus* was the chief city of the province of Asia. **22:** The Greek for *went up* (taken with the landing at Caesarea) implies Paul visited *the church* in Jerusalem, rather than going directly to Antioch, although there is no hint as to why such a visit should be made.

18.23–21.17: Paul's final missionary travels (third journey). 24–28: Apollos the Alexandrian. 24: *Apollos:* see 1 Cor. 1.12; 3.4–6, 22; 4.6; 16.12. **25:** Apparently disciples of John the Baptist continued an active mission

27 Finding that he wanted to go across to Achaia, the congregation gave him their support, and wrote to the disciples there to make him welcome. From the time of his arrival, he was very helpful to those who had by God's grace become believers, 28 for he strenuously confuted the Jews, demonstrating publicly from the scriptures that the Messiah is Jesus.

19 While Apollos was at Corinth, Paul travelled through the inland regions till he came to Ephesus, where he found a number of disciples. 2 When he asked them, 'Did you receive the Holy Spirit when you became believers?' they replied, 'No, we were not even told that there is a Holy Spirit.' 3 He asked, 'Then what baptism were you given?' 'John's baptism,' they answered. 4 Paul said, 'The baptism that John gave was a baptism in token of repentance, and he told the people to put their trust in one who was to come after him, that is, in Jesus.' 5 On hearing this they were baptized into the name of the Lord Jesus; 6 and when Paul had laid his hands on them, the Holy Spirit came upon them and they spoke in tongues of ecstasy and prophesied. 7 There were about a dozen men in all.

8 During the next three months he attended the synagogue and with persuasive argument spoke boldly about the kingdom of God. 9 When some proved obdurate and would not believe, speaking evil of the new way before the congregation, he withdrew from them, taking the disciples with him, and continued to hold discussions daily in the lecture hall of Tyrannus. 10 This went on for two years, with the result that the whole population of the province of Asia, both Jews and Gentiles, heard the word of the Lord. 11 God worked extraordinary miracles through Paul: 12 when handkerchiefs and scarves which had been in contact with his skin were carried to the sick, they were cured of their diseases, and the evil spirits came out of them.

13 Some itinerant Jewish exorcists tried their hand at using the name of the Lord Jesus on those possessed by evil spirits; they would say, 'I adjure you by Jesus whom Paul proclaims.' 14 There were seven sons of Sceva, a Jewish chief priest, who were doing this, 15 when the evil spirit responded, 'Jesus I recognize, Paul I know, but who are you?' 16 The man with the evil spirit flew at them, overpowered them all, and handled them with such violence that they ran out of the house battered and naked. 17 Everybody in Ephesus, Jew and Gentile alike, got to know of it, and all were awestruck, while the name of the Lord Jesus gained in honour. 18 Moreover many of those who had become believers came and openly confessed that they had been using magical spells. 19 A good many of those who formerly practised magic collected their books and burnt them publicly, and when the total value was reckoned up it came to fifty thousand pieces of silver. 20 In such ways the word of the Lord showed its power, spreading more and more widely and effectively.

21 When matters had reached this stage, Paul made up his mind to visit Macedonia and Achaia and then go on to Jerusalem. 'After I have been there,' he said, 'I must see Rome also.' 22 He sent two of his assistants, Timothy and Erastus, to Macedonia, while he himself stayed some time longer in the province of Asia.

23 It was about this time that the Christian movement gave rise to a serious disturbance. 24 There was a man named Demetrius, a silversmith who made silver shrines of Artemis, and provided considerable employment for the craftsmen. 25 He called a meeting of them and of the workers in allied trades, and addressed them: 'As you men know, our prosperity depends on this industry. 26 But this fellow Paul, as you can see and hear for yourselves, has perverted crowds of people with

(compare 19.3); this is all we hear of it directly in the NT. **27:** Writing letters of introduction was one way of guarding against false or unauthorized missionaries; Paul refers to this practice in 2 Cor. 3.1. **19.1–41: Paul's mission in Ephesus. 2:** This is a key question, since the presence of the *Holy Spirit* is the sign of true Christian faith; compare 11.15–18. **3:** See 18.25 n. **4:** Compare 13.24; Mk. 1.4, 7; Lk. 3.3–16. **6:** The presence of *tongues* and prophecy is a sign of the presence of the *Spirit*; compare 2.4–11; 10.46. **8:** *Kingdom of God:* see 20.25; 28.23, 31; the phrase also occurs in Paul's letters (e.g. 1 Cor. 4.20; 6.9–10; Gal. 5.21); it was central in Jesus' preaching (see Mk. 1.15 n.). **9:** Compare 13.46; 18.6. **14:** There is no other record of a *Sceva* having been chief priest. **19:** *Books* of *magic* from Ephesus enjoyed a worldwide reputation, and were eagerly sought and highly prized. **20:** Luke refers on other occasions as well to the Christian faith overcoming the practice of magic: 8.9–13; 13.8–11. **24:** *Artemis* was a fertility goddess whose temple was one of the seven wonders his propaganda, not only at Ephesus but also in practically the whole of the province of Asia; he tells them that gods made by human hands are not gods at all. 27 There is danger for us here; it is not only that our line of business will be discredited, but also that the sanctuary of the great goddess Artemis will cease to command respect; and then it will not be long before she who is worshipped by all Asia and the civilized world is brought down from her divine pre-eminence.'

28 On hearing this, they were enraged, and began to shout, 'Great is Artemis of the Ephesians!' 29 The whole city was in an uproar; they made a concerted rush into the theatre, hustling along with them Paul's travelling companions, the Macedonians Gaius and Aristarchus. 30 Paul wanted to appear before the assembly but the other Christians would not let him. 31 Even some of the dignitaries of the province, who were friendly towards him, sent a message urging him not to venture into the theatre. 32 Meanwhile some were shouting one thing, some another, for the assembly was in an uproar and most of them did not know what they had all come for. 33 Some of the crowd explained the trouble to Alexander, whom the Jews had pushed to the front, and he, motioning for silence, attempted to make a defence before the assembly. 34 But when they recognized that he was a Jew, one shout arose from them all: 'Great is Artemis of the Ephesians!' and they kept it up for about two hours.

35 The town clerk, however, quietened the crowd. 'Citizens of Ephesus,' he said, 'all the world knows that our city of Ephesus is temple warden of the great Artemis and of that image of her which fell from heaven. 36 Since these facts are beyond dispute, your proper course is to keep calm and do nothing rash. 37 These men whom you have brought here as offenders have committed no sacrilege and uttered no blasphemy against our goddess. 38 If, therefore, Demetrius and his craftsmen have a case against anyone, there

are assizes and there are proconsuls; let the parties bring their charges and counter-charges. 39 But if it is a larger question you are raising, it will be dealt with in the statutory assembly. 40 We certainly run the risk of being charged with riot for this day's work. There is no justification for it, and it would be impossible for us to give any explanation of this turmoil.' 41 With that he dismissed the assembly.

20 WHEN the disturbance was over, Paul sent for the disciples and, after encouraging them, said goodbye and set out on his journey to Macedonia. 2 He travelled through that region, constantly giving encouragement to the Christians, and finally reached Greece. 3 When he had spent three months there and was on the point of embarking for Syria, a plot was laid against him by the Jews, so he decided to return by way of Macedonia. 4 He was accompanied by Sopater son of Pyrrhus from Beroea, Aristarchus and Secundus from Thessalonica, Gaius of Derbe, and Timothy, and from Asia Tychicus and Trophimus. 5 These went ahead and waited for us at Troas; 6 we ourselves sailed from Philippi after the Passover season, and five days later rejoined them at Troas, where we spent a week.

7 On the Saturday night, when we gathered for the breaking of bread, Paul, who was to leave next day, addressed the congregation and went on speaking until midnight. 8 Now there were many lamps in the upstairs room where we were assembled, 9 and a young man named Eutychus, who was sitting on the window-ledge, grew more and more drowsy as Paul went on talking, until, completely overcome by sleep, he fell from the third storey to the ground, and was picked up dead. 10 Paul went down, threw himself upon him, and clasped him in his arms. 'Do not distress yourselves,' he said to them; 'he is alive.' 11 He

20:6 **after ... season:** *lit.* after the days of Unleavened Bread.

of the ancient world and a major tourist attraction. **26:** Demetrius seems to identify the images of Artemis with the goddess herself; compare 17.24–25. **29:** The *theatre,* recovered through excavation, had places for about 29,000 people. **34:** This is an indication of the anti-Semitism prevalent in many parts of the ancient world; compare 16.20–21. **20.1–6: Return to Greece. 2–4:** This journey, with its change of plans, appears to be reflected in 1 Cor. 16.5–9; 2 Cor. 1.15–2.13; 7.5–7. **4:** The many traveling companions imply Paul is bringing the collection to Jerusalem; compare 24.17. **7–12: Eutychus survives. 7:** *Saturday night* may also be translated "Sunday," when Christian gatherings were usually held; see 1 Cor. 16.2. The *breaking of bread* was a regular Christian act (see 2.42), and probably included the Eucharist. **10:** The Greek implies Paul restored him to life;

then went upstairs, broke bread and ate, and after much conversation, which lasted until dawn, he departed. 12 And they took the boy home, greatly relieved that he was alive.

13 We went on ahead to the ship and embarked for Assos, where we were to take Paul aboard; this was the arrangement he had made, since he was going to travel by road. 14 When he met us at Assos, we took him aboard and proceeded to Mitylene. 15 We sailed from there and next day arrived off Chios. On the second day we made Samos, and the following day we reached Miletus. 16 Paul had decided to bypass Ephesus and so avoid having to spend time in the province of Asia; he was eager to be in Jerusalem on the day of Pentecost, if that were possible. 17 He did, however, send from Miletus to Ephesus and summon the elders of the church. 18 When they joined him, he spoke to them as follows.

'You know how, from the day that I first set foot in the province of Asia, I spent my whole time with you, 19 serving the Lord in all humility amid the sorrows and trials that came upon me through the intrigues of the Jews. 20 You know that I kept back nothing that was for your good: I delivered the message to you, and taught you, in public and in your homes; 21 with Jews and Gentiles alike I insisted on repentance before God and faith in our Lord Jesus. 22 Now, as you see, I am constrained by the Spirit to go to Jerusalem. I do not know what will befall me there, 23 except that in city after city the Holy Spirit assures me that imprisonment and hardships await me. 24 For myself, I set no store by life; all I want is to finish the race, and complete the task which the Lord Jesus assigned to me, that of bearing my testimony to the gospel of God's grace.

25 'One thing more: I have gone about among you proclaiming the kingdom, but now I know that none of you will ever see my face again. 26 That being so, I here and now declare that no one's fate can be laid at my door; I have kept back nothing; 27 I have disclosed to you the whole purpose of God. 28 Keep guard over yourselves and over all the flock of which the Holy Spirit has given you charge, as shepherds of the church of the Lord, which he won for himself by his own blood. 29 I know that when I am gone, savage wolves will come in among you and will not spare the flock. 30 Even from your own number men will arise who will distort the truth in order to get the disciples to break away and follow them. 31 So be on the alert; remember how with tears I never ceased to warn each one of you night and day for three years.

32 'And now I commend you to God and to the word of his grace, which has power to build you up and give you your heritage among all those whom God has made his own. 33 I have not wanted anyone's money or clothes for myself; 34 you all know that these hands of mine earned enough for the needs of myself and my companions. 35 All along I showed you that it is our duty to help the weak in this way, by hard work, and that we should keep in mind the words of the Lord Jesus, who himself said, "Happiness lies more in giving than in receiving." '

36 As he finished speaking, he knelt down with them all and prayed. 37 There were loud cries of sorrow from them all, as they folded Paul in their arms and kissed him; 38 what distressed them most was his saying that they would never see his face again. Then they escorted him to the ship.

21 We tore ourselves away from them and, putting to sea, made a straight run and came to Cos; next day to Rhodes, and thence to Patara. 2 There we found a ship bound for Phoenicia, so we went aboard and sailed in her. 3 We came in sight of Cyprus and, leaving it to port, we continued our voyage to Syria and put in at Tyre, where the ship was to unload her cargo. 4 We sought out the disciples and stayed there a week. Warned by the Spirit, they urged Paul to abandon his visit to Jerusalem. 5 But when

20:28 of the Lord ... blood: *some witnesses read* of God, which he won for himself by the blood of his Own.

compare 1 Kgs. 17.21–22. **13–16: On to Miletus. 14–15:** *Mitylene, Chios* and *Samos* are located on offshore islands. **17–38: Paul's farewell to the Ephesian elders. 19:** Paul's Corinthian correspondence refers to his *sorrows* (2 Cor. 1.5–10) and *trials* (1 Cor. 15.32) in Ephesus. **20:** See 2 Cor. 4.2. **23:** See 9.16; for one form of such a warning, see 21.10–11. **25:** *Proclaiming the kingdom:* see 19.8 n. The latter part of this verse anticipates Paul's imprisonment and death. **27:** On everything happening according to the *purpose of God,* compare 2.23 (and n.); 4.28; 13.48. **29:** Similar trouble at Ephesus is described in Rev. 2.1–7. *Wolves:* see Matt. 7.15 (and 15–23 n.). **35:** This saying of Jesus does not appear in any of the Gospels. **21.1–17: To** our time ashore was ended, we left and continued our journey; and they and their wives and children all escorted us out of the city. We knelt down on the beach and prayed, [6]and then bade each other goodbye; we went on board, and they returned home.

[7]We made the passage from Tyre and reached Ptolemais, where we greeted the brotherhood and spent a day with them. [8]Next day we left and came to Caesarea, where we went to the home of Philip the evangelist, who was one of the Seven, and stayed with him. [9]He had four unmarried daughters, who possessed the gift of prophecy. [10]When we had been there several days, a prophet named Agabus arrived from Judaea. [11]He came to us, took Paul's belt, bound his own feet and hands with it, and said, 'These are the words of the Holy Spirit: Thus will the Jews in Jerusalem bind the man to whom this belt belongs, and hand him over to the Gentiles.' [12]When we heard this, we and the local people begged and implored Paul to abandon his visit to Jerusalem. [13]Then Paul gave his answer: 'Why all these tears? Why are you trying to weaken my resolution? I am ready, not merely to be bound, but even to die at Jerusalem for the name of the Lord Jesus.' [14]So, as he would not be dissuaded, we gave up and said, 'The Lord's will be done.'

[15]At the end of our stay we packed our baggage and took the road up to Jerusalem. [16]Some of the disciples from Caesarea came along with us, to direct us to a Cypriot named Mnason, a Christian from the early days, with whom we were to spend the night. [17]On our arrival at Jerusalem, the congregation welcomed us gladly.

[18]Next day Paul paid a visit to James; we accompanied him, and all the elders were present. [19]After greeting them, he described in detail all that God had done among the Gentiles by means of his ministry. [20]When they heard this, they gave praise to God. Then they said to Paul: 'You observe,

brother, how many thousands of converts we have among the Jews, all of them staunch upholders of the law. [21]Now they have been given certain information about you: it is said that you teach all the Jews in the gentile world to turn their backs on Moses, and tell them not to circumcise their children or follow our way of life. [22]What is to be done, then? They are sure to hear that you have arrived. [23]Our proposal is this: we have four men here who are under a vow; [24]take them with you and go through the ritual of purification together, and pay their expenses, so that they may have their heads shaved; then everyone will know that there is nothing in the reports they have heard about you, but that you are yourself a practising Jew and observe the law. [25]As for the gentile converts, we sent them our decision that they should abstain from meat that has been offered to idols, from blood, from anything that has been strangled, and from fornication.' [26]So Paul took the men, and next day, after going through the ritual of purification with them, he went into the temple to give notice of the date when the period of purification would end and the offering be made for each of them.

Paul's work in Jerusalem

[27]BUT just before the seven days were up, the Jews from the province of Asia saw him in the temple. They stirred up all the crowd and seized him, [28]shouting, 'Help us, men of Israel! This is the fellow who attacks our people, our law, and this sanctuary, and spreads his teaching the whole world over. What is more, he has brought Gentiles into the temple and profaned this holy place.' [29]They had previously seen Trophimus the Ephesian with him in the city, and assumed that Paul had brought him into the temple.

[30]The whole city was in a turmoil, and people came running from all directions. They

21:25 **from anything ... strangled:** *some witnesses omit.*

Jerusalem via Caesarea. 8: Compare 8.40. *Evangelist:* compare Eph. 4.11; 2 Tim. 4.5 n. *The Seven:* see 6.5. **10:** *Agabus* acts out his message as did the OT prophets; see Jer. chs. 27–28; Ezek. ch. 4; Isa. ch. 20.

21.18–22.29: Paul arrested in Jerusalem. 18–26: Paul undergoes ritual purification. 20–25: These verses are written as though the events surrounding the apostolic council had not happened, and as if Paul had not known of the letter sent to the Gentile churches; see ch. 15. **21:** As far as Paul's conduct in Acts is concerned, these charges are false, as v. 26 and 16.3 affirm. **23:** *A vow:* perhaps the Nazirite; see 18.18; Num. 6.1–21. **26:** Compare Num. 6.13–21. **27–40: Paul arrested in the temple. 28:** Compare the charges against Stephen: 6.13–14. *Into the temple:* into the Court of the Israelites. Gentiles were permitted only in the outer court. **30:**

seized Paul and dragged him out of the temple, and at once the doors were shut. ³¹They were bent on killing him, but word came to the officer commanding the cohort that all Jerusalem was in an uproar. ³²He immediately took a force of soldiers with their centurions and came down at the double to deal with the riot. When the crowd saw the commandant and his troops, they stopped beating Paul. ³³As soon as the commandant could reach Paul, he arrested him and ordered him to be shackled with two chains; he enquired who he was and what he had been doing. ³⁴Some in the crowd shouted one thing, some another, and as the commandant could not get at the truth because of the hubbub, he ordered him to be taken to the barracks. ³⁵When Paul reached the steps, he found himself carried up by the soldiers because of the violence of the mob; ³⁶for the whole crowd was at their heels yelling, 'Kill him!'

³⁷Just before he was taken into the barracks Paul said to the commandant, 'May I have a word with you?' The commandant said, 'So you speak Greek? ³⁸Then you are not the Egyptian who started a revolt some time ago and led a force of four thousand terrorists out into the desert?' ³⁹Paul replied, 'I am a Jew from Tarsus in Cilicia, a citizen of no mean city. May I have your permission to speak to the people?' ⁴⁰When this was given, Paul stood on the steps and raised his hand to call for the attention of the people. As soon as quiet was restored, he addressed them in the Jewish language:

22 'Brothers and fathers, give me a hearing while I put my case to you.' ²When they heard him speaking to them in their own language, they listened more quietly. ³'I am a true-born Jew,' he began, 'a native of Tarsus in Cilicia. I was brought up in this city, and as a pupil of Gamaliel I was thoroughly trained in every point of our ancestral law. I have always been ardent in

God's service, as you all are today. ⁴And so I persecuted this movement to the death, arresting its followers, men and women alike, and committing them to prison, ⁵as the high priest and the whole Council of Elders can testify. It was they who gave me letters to our fellow-Jews at Damascus, and I was on my way to make arrests there also and bring the prisoners to Jerusalem for punishment. ⁶What happened to me on my journey was this: when I was nearing Damascus, about midday, a great light suddenly flashed from the sky all around me. ⁷I fell to the ground, and heard a voice saying: "Saul, Saul, why do you persecute me?" ⁸I answered, "Tell me, Lord, who you are." "I am Jesus of Nazareth, whom you are persecuting," he said. ⁹My companions saw the light, but did not hear the voice that spoke to me. ¹⁰"What shall I do, Lord?" I asked, and he replied, "Get up, and go on to Damascus; there you will be told all that you are appointed to do." ¹¹As I had been blinded by the brilliance of that light, my companions led me by the hand, and so I came to Damascus.

¹²'There a man called Ananias, a devout observer of the law and well spoken of by all the Jews who lived there, ¹³came and stood beside me, and said, "Saul, my brother, receive your sight again!" Instantly I recovered my sight and saw him. ¹⁴He went on: "The God of our fathers appointed you to know his will and to see the Righteous One and to hear him speak, ¹⁵because you are to be his witness to tell the world what you have seen and heard. ¹⁶Do not delay. Be baptized at once and wash away your sins, calling on his name."

¹⁷'After my return to Jerusalem, as I was praying in the temple I fell into a trance ¹⁸and saw him there, speaking to me. "Make haste", he said, "and leave Jerusalem quickly, for they will not accept your testimony about me." ¹⁹"But surely, Lord," I answered, "they

The doors separated the Court of the Israelites from the Court of the Gentiles, into which Paul was now dragged. **32:** The Roman *soldiers* charged with keeping order in the temple were stationed in the Tower of Antonia, a fortress adjoining the temple at the northwest corner. **35:** The *steps* led up into the Tower of Antonia; there were two flights. **38:** The Jewish historian Josephus puts the original army of this *Egyptian* at thirty thousand, but his attempt to conquer Jerusalem was defeated by the procurator Felix (23.34), and only a portion of the revolutionaries escaped. **22.1–21: Paul's speech in Jerusalem. 3:** *Gamaliel* (see 5.34) enjoyed some fame as a rabbi, but is not mentioned in any of Paul's letters nor by the contemporary Jewish writers, Philo and Josephus. **5:** The *Council of Elders* is the Sanhedrin; see Matt. 26.59 n. **6–11:** Compare 9.3–9; 26.13–16. **7:** *Persecute me:* see 9.4 n. **12:** *Ananias:* compare 9.10–16, although his attitude to the *law* is not mentioned there. **14:** *Appointed you:* Paul expressly denied he received his commission from a human source (Gal. 1.1). **18:** *Leave* know that I imprisoned those who believe in you and flogged them in every synagogue; [20] when the blood of Stephen your witness was shed I stood by, approving, and I looked after the clothes of those who killed him." [21] He said to me, "Go, for I mean to send you far away to the Gentiles." '

[22] Up to this point the crowd had given him a hearing; but now they began to shout, 'Down with the scoundrel! He is not fit to be alive!' [23] And as they were yelling and waving their cloaks and flinging dust in the air, [24] the commandant ordered him to be brought into the barracks, and gave instructions that he should be examined under the lash, to find out what reason there was for such an outcry against him. [25] But when they tied him up for the flogging, Paul said to the centurion who was standing there, 'Does the law allow you to flog a Roman citizen, and an unconvicted one at that?' [26] When the centurion heard this, he went and reported to the commandant: 'What are you about? This man is a Roman citizen.' [27] The commandant came to Paul and asked, 'Tell me, are you a Roman citizen?' 'Yes,' said he. [28] The commandant rejoined, 'Citizenship cost me a large sum of money.' Paul said, 'It was mine by birth.' [29] Then those who were about to examine him promptly withdrew; and the commandant himself was alarmed when he realized that Paul was a Roman citizen and that he had put him in irons.

Paul's trials

[30] THE following day, wishing to be quite sure what charge the Jews were bringing against Paul, he released him and ordered the chief priests and the entire Council to assemble. He then brought Paul down to stand before them.

23 With his eyes steadily fixed on the Council, Paul said, 'My brothers, all my life to this day I have lived with a perfectly clear conscience before God.' [2] At this the high priest Ananias ordered his attendants to strike him on the mouth. [3] Paul retorted, 'God will strike you, you whitewashed wall! You sit there to judge me in accordance with the law; then, in defiance of the law, you order me to be struck!' [4] The attendants said, 'Would you insult God's high priest?' [5] 'Brothers,' said Paul, 'I had no idea he was high priest; scripture, I know, says: "You shall not abuse the ruler of your people." '

[6] Well aware that one section of them were Sadducees and the other Pharisees, Paul called out in the Council, 'My brothers, I am a Pharisee, a Pharisee born and bred; and the issue in this trial is our hope of the resurrection of the dead.' [7] At these words the Pharisees and Sadducees fell out among themselves, and the assembly was divided. [8] (The Sadducees deny that there is any resurrection or angel or spirit, but the Pharisees believe in all three.) [9] A great uproar ensued; and some of the scribes belonging to the Pharisaic party openly took sides and declared, 'We find no fault with this man; perhaps an angel or spirit has spoken to him.' [10] In the mounting dissension, the commandant was afraid that Paul would be torn to pieces, so he ordered the troops to go down, pull him out of the crowd, and bring him into the barracks.

[11] The following night the Lord appeared to him and said, 'Keep up your courage! You

Jerusalem quickly, implying Paul did not preach in Jerusalem, agrees with Gal. 1.16–20; but see 9.28–29. **19–20:** In a situation like this, the testimony of a Jewish convert to the Christian faith could be expected to carry considerable weight. **21:** The immediate occasion of Paul's arrest was temple profanation (21.28); here the point at issue seems to be Paul's association with *Gentiles* and the resulting dissolution of the law. Later the charge will concern resurrection (23.6). **22–29: Reaction to Paul's speech. 24–25:** It was Roman practice to obtain testimony from slaves and noncitizens by torture (*flogging*), on the assumption that lying in such circumstances was not likely. **27:** The penalty for falsely claiming citizenship was death.

22.30–24.27: Paul and Felix. 23.1–10: Paul before the Council. 1: The *clear conscience* mentioned here apparently is meant to include the events recited in 22.19–20; Paul refers to his persecution of Christians in his letters, but does not relate it to a *clear conscience.* **2:** The *high priest Ananias* entered that office about 48 C.E., was deposed during the rule of Felix, and was murdered in 66 C.E.; see 4.6 n. **5:** Exod. 22.28. This continues Acts' picture of Paul as a true follower of the law; compare 16.3; 22.26; 24.14; Lk. 24.44. For Luke, the Christian faith is the true fulfillment of Judaism. **6:** See 22.21 n. **8:** On *Sadducees* and *resurrection,* see 4.2; Matt. 3.7 n.; Lk. 20.27–38. **11:** Key events in Paul's life were revealed to him by the *Lord,* or by the Holy Spirit;

have affirmed the truth about me in Jerusalem, and you must do the same in Rome.'

12 When day broke, the Jews banded together and took an oath not to eat or drink until they had killed Paul. 13 There were more than forty in the conspiracy; 14 they went to the chief priests and elders and said, 'We have bound ourselves by a solemn oath not to taste food until we have killed Paul. 15 It is now up to you and the rest of the Council to apply to the commandant to have him brought down to you on the pretext of a closer investigation of his case; we have arranged to make away with him before he reaches you.'

16 The son of Paul's sister, however, learnt of the plot and, going to the barracks, obtained entry, and reported it to Paul, 17 who called one of the centurions and said, 'Take this young man to the commandant; he has something to report.' 18 The centurion brought him to the commandant and explained, 'The prisoner Paul sent for me and asked me to bring this young man to you; he has something to tell you.' 19 The commandant took him by the arm, drew him aside, and asked him, 'What is it you have to report?' 20 He replied, 'The Jews have agreed on a plan: they will request you to bring Paul down to the Council tomorrow on the pretext of obtaining more precise information about him. 21 Do not listen to them; for a party more than forty strong are lying in wait for him, and they have sworn not to eat or drink until they have done away with him. They are now ready, waiting only for your consent.' 22 The commandant dismissed the young man, with orders not to let anyone know that he had given him this information.

23 He then summoned two of his centurions and gave them these orders: 'Have two hundred infantry ready to proceed to Caesarea, together with seventy cavalrymen and two hundred light-armed troops; parade them three hours after sunset, 24 and provide mounts for Paul so that he may be conducted under safe escort to Felix the governor.' 25 And he wrote a letter to this effect:

26 From Claudius Lysias to His Excellency the Governor Felix. Greeting.

27 This man was seized by the Jews and was on the point of being murdered when I intervened with the troops, and, on discovering that he was a Roman citizen, I removed him to safety. 28 As I wished to ascertain the ground of their charge against him, I brought him down to their Council. 29 I found that their case had to do with controversial matters of their law, but there was no charge against him which merited death or imprisonment. 30 Information, however, has now been brought to my notice of an attempt to be made on the man's life, so I am sending him to you without delay, and have instructed his accusers to state their case against him before you.

31 Acting on their orders, the infantry took custody of Paul and brought him by night to Antipatris. 32 Next day they returned to their barracks, leaving the cavalry to escort him the rest of the way. 33 When the cavalry reached Caesarea, they delivered the letter to the governor, and handed Paul over to him. 34 He read the letter, and asked him what province he was from; and learning that he was from Cilicia 35 he said, 'I will hear your case when your accusers arrive.' He ordered him to be held in custody at his headquarters in Herod's palace.

24 FIVE days later the high priest Ananias came down, accompanied by some of the elders and an advocate named Tertullus, to lay before the governor their charge against Paul. 2-3 When the prisoner was called, Tertullus opened the case.

'Your excellency,' he said to Felix, 'we owe it to you that we enjoy unbroken peace, and it is due to your provident care that, in all kinds of ways and in all sorts of places, improvements are being made for the good of this nation. We appreciate this, and are most grateful to you. 4 And now, not to take up too much of your time, I crave your indulgence

---

see 18.9–10; 20.23; 22.17–21. **12–22: A plot against Paul. 12–13:** Such a *conspiracy* is repeated in 25.3 (compare 9.23); it was possible under Jewish law to be released from such an *oath*. **16:** That Paul's nephew was able to obtain *entry* was not unusual; see Matt. 11.2; 25.36. **23–35: Paul is taken to Felix. 23:** *Caesarea:* see 10.1 n. **24:** Antonius *Felix,* probably a freed slave of the mother of Emperor Claudius, was procurator about 52–55 C.E.; his reputation as procurator was not a good one. **35:** The exact location of *Herod's palace* is unknown. **24.1–9: Jewish charges against Paul. 1:** Compare 23.30, *Ananias:* see 23.2 n. **2:** Historically, for a brief statement of our case. 5 We have found this man to be a pest, a fomenter of discord among the Jews all over the world, a ringleader of the sect of the Nazarenes. 6 He made an attempt to profane the temple and we arrested him. 8 If you examine him yourself you can ascertain the truth of all the charges we bring against him.' 9 The Jews supported the charge, alleging that the facts were as he stated.

10 The governor then motioned to Paul to speak, and he replied as follows: 'Knowing as I do that for many years you have administered justice to this nation, I make my defence with confidence. 11 As you can ascertain for yourself, it is not more than twelve days since I went up to Jerusalem on a pilgrimage. 12 They did not find me in the temple arguing with anyone or collecting a crowd, or in the synagogues or anywhere else in the city; 13 and they cannot make good the charges they now bring against me. 14 But this much I will admit: I am a follower of the new way (the "sect" they speak of), and it is in that manner that I worship the God of our fathers; for I believe all that is written in the law and the prophets, 15 and in reliance on God I hold the hope, which my accusers too accept, that there is to be a resurrection of good and wicked alike. 16 Accordingly I, no less than they, train myself to keep at all times a clear conscience before God and man.

17 'After an absence of several years I came to bring charitable gifts to my nation and to offer sacrifices. 18 I was ritually purified and engaged in this service when they found me in the temple; I had no crowd with me, and there was no disturbance. But some Jews from the province of Asia were there, 19 and if they had any charge against me, it is they who ought to have been in court to state it.

20 Failing that, it is for these persons here present to say what crime they discovered when I was brought before the Council, 21 apart from this one declaration which I made as I stood there: "The issue in my trial before you today is the resurrection of the dead." '

22 Then Felix, who was well informed about the new way, adjourned the hearing. 'I will decide your case when Lysias the commanding officer comes down,' he said. 23 He gave orders to the centurion to keep Paul under open arrest and not to prevent any of his friends from making themselves useful to him.

24 Some days later Felix came with his wife Drusilla, who was a Jewess, and sent for Paul. He let him talk to him about faith in Christ Jesus, 25 but when the discourse turned to questions of morals, self-control, and the coming judgement, Felix became alarmed and exclaimed, 'Enough for now! When I find it convenient I will send for you again.' 26 He also had hopes of a bribe from Paul, so he sent for him frequently and talked with him. 27 When two years had passed, Felix was succeeded by Porcius Festus. Wishing to curry favour with the Jews, Felix left Paul in custody.

25 THREE days after taking up his appointment, Festus went up from Caesarea to Jerusalem, 2 where the chief priests and the Jewish leaders laid before him their charge against Paul. 3 They urged Festus to support them in their case and have Paul sent to Jerusalem, for they were plotting

24:6 **arrested him:** *some witnesses add* It was our intention to try him under our law; 7 but Lysias the commandant intervened and forcibly removed him out of our hands, (8)ordering his accusers to come before you.

Palestine at this time was wracked with murder and revolt. Such praise is, however, rhetorical convention. **4:** This is a further example of Hellenistic rhetorical convention. **6:** The *attempt to profane the temple* was a baseless charge; see 21.26, 29. **10–21: Paul's defense. 10:** *For many years:* Felix was procurator for about three years in this province, but, again, this is rhetorical convention. **15:** Only the Pharisees among his *accusers* accepted the *resurrection:* see 23.8. **17:** Compare Rom. 15.25–27. While this may be historically true, the bringing of charitable gifts was not given as the reason for this trip to Jerusalem in 19.21; see 11.29 n. **21:** See 22.21 n. **22–27: Discussion between Paul and Felix. 24:** *Drusilla,* the daughter of Herod Agrippa (see 12.1 (and n.)–23), was one of three noble ladies Felix married, this one having deserted her husband, King Azizus of Emesa, for him. **26:** This accords with the way Felix is described by ancient historians. This also informs us why Paul, though innocent, was not released. There was no legal way he could compel a decision to be rendered.

25.1–26.32: Paul and Festus. 1–5: Festus goes to Jerusalem. 1: Little is known of Porcius *Festus:* he probably to kill him on the way. ⁴ Festus, however, replied, 'Paul is in safe custody at Caesarea, and I shall be leaving Jerusalem shortly myself; ⁵ so let your leading men come down with me, and if the man is at fault in any way, let them prosecute him.'

⁶ After spending eight or ten days at most in Jerusalem, he went down to Caesarea, and next day he took his seat in court and ordered Paul to be brought before him. ⁷ When he appeared, the Jews who had come down from Jerusalem stood round bringing many grave charges, which they were unable to prove. ⁸ Paul protested: 'I have committed no offence against the Jewish law, or against the temple, or against the emperor.' ⁹ Festus, anxious to ingratiate himself with the Jews, turned to Paul and asked, 'Are you willing to go up to Jerusalem and stand trial on these charges before me there?' ¹⁰ But Paul said, 'I am now standing before the emperor's tribunal; that is where I ought to be tried. I have committed no offence against the Jews, as you very well know. ¹¹ If I am guilty of any capital crime, I do not ask to escape the death penalty; if, however, there is no substance in the charges which these men bring against me, it is not open to anyone to hand me over to them. I appeal to Caesar!' ¹² Then Festus, after conferring with his advisers, replied, 'You have appealed to Caesar: to Caesar you shall go!'

¹³ Some days later King Agrippa and Bernice arrived at Caesarea on a courtesy visit to Festus. ¹⁴ They spent some time there, and during their stay Festus raised Paul's case with the king. 'There is a man here', he said, 'left in custody by Felix; ¹⁵ and when I was in Jerusalem the chief priests and elders of the Jews brought a charge against him, demanding his condemnation. ¹⁶ I replied that it was not Roman practice to hand a man over before he had been confronted with his accusers and given an opportunity of answering

the charge. ¹⁷ So when they had come here with me I lost no time, but took my seat in court the very next day and ordered the man to be brought before me. ¹⁸ When his accusers rose to speak, they brought none of the charges I was expecting; ¹⁹ they merely had certain points of disagreement with him about their religion, and about someone called Jesus, a dead man whom Paul alleged to be alive. ²⁰ Finding myself out of my depth in such discussions, I asked if he was willing to go to Jerusalem and stand trial there on these issues. ²¹ But Paul appealed to be remanded in custody for his imperial majesty's decision, and I ordered him to be detained until I could send him to the emperor.' ²² Agrippa said to Festus, 'I should rather like to hear the man myself.' 'You shall hear him tomorrow,' he answered.

²³ Next day Agrippa and Bernice came in full state and entered the audience-chamber accompanied by high-ranking officers and prominent citizens; and on the orders of Festus, Paul was brought in. ²⁴ Then Festus said, 'King Agrippa, and all you who are in attendance, you see this man: the whole body of the Jews approached me both in Jerusalem and here, loudly insisting that he had no right to remain alive. ²⁵ It was clear to me, however, that he had committed no capital crime, and when he himself appealed to his imperial majesty, I decided to send him. ²⁶ As I have nothing definite about him to put in writing for our sovereign, I have brought him before you all and particularly before you, King Agrippa, so that as a result of this preliminary enquiry I may have something to report. ²⁷ There is no sense, it seems to me, in sending on a prisoner without indicating the charges against him.'

26 Agrippa said to Paul: 'You have our permission to give an account of yourself.' Then Paul stretched out his hand and began his defence.

---

assumed office about 55 C.E. **3:** *Plotting to kill him:* see 23.12–15. **6–12: Paul appeals to Caesar. 6:** This is Paul's second hearing in *Caesarea;* see 24.1–21. **9:** *Paul* was a similar pawn to Felix (24.24–26); this verse again explains why Paul, though innocent, was not released. **11:** In this way, the words of the Lord to Paul (23.11) began their fulfillment. Little is known, apart from this verse, about the circumstances surrounding an *appeal to Caesar* in the time of the Roman Empire. **13–22: Agrippa and Festus. 13:** *King* Marcus Julius *Agrippa* II, king of some territories in northern Palestine, was the son of Herod Agrippa I (12.1–5, 20–23), and a brother of Drusilla (24.24). *Bernice,* a widow at this time, was another of Agrippa's sisters; their constant companionship was an ancient scandal. **16:** Festus himself did not hold to this *practice* in Paul's case, nor did Felix; see 24.18–19. **23–27: Preliminary inquiry instituted. 25:** The commandant in Jerusalem had come to the same decision (23.29); the Pharisees, too, had declared him innocent (23.9). **26.1–32: Paul makes his**

2 'I consider myself fortunate, King Agrippa, that it is before you I am to make my defence today on all the charges brought against me by the Jews, 3 particularly as you are expert in all our Jewish customs and controversies. I beg you therefore to give me a patient hearing.

4 'My life from my youth up, a life spent from the first among my nation and in Jerusalem, is familiar to all Jews. 5 Indeed they have known me long enough to testify, if they would, that I belonged to the strictest group in our religion: I was a Pharisee. 6 It is the hope based on the promise God made to our forefathers that has led to my being on trial today. 7 Our twelve tribes worship with intense devotion night and day in the hope of seeing the fulfilment of that promise; and for this very hope I am accused, your majesty, and accused by Jews. 8 Why should Jews find it incredible that God should raise the dead?

9 'I myself once thought it my duty to work actively against the name of Jesus of Nazareth; 10 and I did so in Jerusalem. By authority obtained from the chief priests, I sent many of God's people to prison, and when they were condemned to death, my vote was cast against them. 11 In all the synagogues I tried by repeated punishment to make them commit blasphemy; indeed my fury rose to such a pitch that I extended my persecution to foreign cities.

12 'On one such occasion I was travelling to Damascus with authority and commission from the chief priests; 13 and as I was on my way, your majesty, at midday I saw a light from the sky, more brilliant than the sun, shining all around me and my companions. 14 We all fell to the ground, and I heard a voice saying to me in the Jewish language, "Saul, Saul, why do you persecute me? It hurts to kick like this against the goad." 15 I said, "Tell me, Lord, who you are," and the Lord replied, "I am Jesus, whom you are persecuting. 16 But now, get to your feet. I

have appeared to you for a purpose: to appoint you my servant and witness, to tell what you have seen and what you shall yet see of me. 17 I will rescue you from your own people and from the Gentiles to whom I am sending you. 18 You are to open their eyes and to turn them from darkness to light, from the dominion of Satan to God, so that they may obtain forgiveness of sins and a place among those whom God has made his own through faith in me."

19 'So, King Agrippa, I did not disobey the heavenly vision. 20 I preached first to the inhabitants of Damascus, and then to Jerusalem and all the country of Judaea, and to the Gentiles, calling on them to repent and turn to God, and to prove their repentance by their deeds. 21 That is why the Jews seized me in the temple and tried to do away with me. 22 But I have had God's help to this very day, and here I stand bearing witness to the great and to the lowly. I assert nothing beyond what was foretold by the prophets and by Moses: 23 that the Messiah would suffer and that, as the first to rise from the dead, he would announce the dawn both to the Jewish people and to the Gentiles.'

24 While Paul was thus making his defence, Festus shouted at the top of his voice, 'Paul, you are raving; too much study is driving you mad.' 25 'I am not mad, your excellency,' said Paul; 'what I am asserting is sober truth. 26 The king is well versed in these matters, and I can speak freely to him. I do not believe that he can be unaware of any of these facts, for this has been no hole-and-corner business. 27 King Agrippa, do you believe the prophets? I know you do.' 28 Agrippa said to Paul, 'With a little more of your persuasion you will make a Christian of me.' 29 'Little or much,' said Paul, 'I wish to God that not only you, but all those who are listening to me today, might become what I am — apart from these chains!'

30 With that the king rose, and with him the governor, Bernice, and the rest of the com-

---

defense. This speech sums up Paul's career as portrayed in Acts. 1: When Paul spoke to King *Agrippa*, the prophecy of Jesus about Paul's career (9.15) was fulfilled; compare Lk. 21.12. 2–3: Such an introduction was a Hellenistic rhetorical convention; see 24.2–3, 10. 4: See 22.3. 5: See 23.6; Phil. 3.5. 7: *Twelve tribes worship . . . in the hope:* see 24.14–15. 8: See 22.21 n. 9–11: See 8.3 n. 12–15: See 9.3–6; 22.4–10. 14: *To kick . . . against the goad* comes from a Greek proverb. 16–18: According to 22.14–15, Paul received his commission from Ananias (see 9.6); the present account conforms more closely to Paul's own account (Gal. 1.1, 15–17). 21: *Do away with me:* see 21.30–32. 22: The *prophets* and *Moses:* see 23.5 n. 23: See Mk. 8.31 n. for parallels; Lk. 24.44–47. *First to rise:* see 1 Cor. 15.20–23. 28: *Christian:* see 11.26 n. 30–32: **Paul's innocence recog-**

pany, [31] and after they had withdrawn they talked it over. 'This man', they agreed, 'is doing nothing that deserves death or imprisonment.' [32] Agrippa said to Festus, 'The fellow could have been discharged, if he had not appealed to the emperor.'

Paul's journey to Rome

27 WHEN it was decided that we should sail for Italy, Paul and some other prisoners were handed over to a centurion named Julius, of the Augustan Cohort. [2] We embarked in a ship of Adramyttium, bound for ports in the province of Asia, and put out to sea. Aristarchus, a Macedonian from Thessalonica, came with us. [3] Next day we landed at Sidon, and Julius very considerately allowed Paul to go to his friends to be cared for. [4] Leaving Sidon we sailed under the lee of Cyprus because of the head winds, [5] then across the open sea off the coast of Cilicia and Pamphylia, and so reached Myra in Lycia.

[6] There the centurion found an Alexandrian vessel bound for Italy and put us on board. [7] For a good many days we made little headway, and we were hard put to it to reach Cnidus. Then, as the wind continued against us, off Salmone we began to sail under the lee of Crete, [8] and, hugging the coast, struggled on to a place called Fair Havens, not far from the town of Lasea.

[9] By now much time had been lost, and with the Fast already over, it was dangerous to go on with the voyage. So Paul gave them this warning: [10] 'I can see, gentlemen, that this voyage will be disastrous; it will mean heavy loss, not only of ship and cargo but also of life.' [11] But the centurion paid more attention to the captain and to the owner of the ship than to what Paul said; [12] and as the harbour was unsuitable for wintering, the majority were in favour of putting to sea, hoping, if they could get so far, to winter at

Phoenix, a Cretan harbour facing south-west and north-west. [13] When a southerly breeze sprang up, they thought that their purpose was as good as achieved, and, weighing anchor, they sailed along the coast of Crete hugging the land. [14] But before very long a violent wind, the Northeaster as they call it, swept down from the landward side. [15] It caught the ship and, as it was impossible to keep head to wind, we had to give way and run before it. [16] As we passed under the lee of a small island called Cauda, we managed with a struggle to get the ship's boat under control. [17] When they had hoisted it on board, they made use of tackle to brace the ship. Then, afraid of running on to the sandbanks of Syrtis, they put out a sea-anchor and let her drift. [18] Next day, as we were making very heavy weather, they began to lighten the ship; [19] and on the third day they jettisoned the ship's gear with their own hands. [20] For days on end there was no sign of either sun or stars, the storm was raging unabated, and our last hopes of coming through alive began to fade.

[21] When they had gone for a long time without food, Paul stood up among them and said, 'You should have taken my advice, gentlemen, not to put out from Crete: then you would have avoided this damage and loss. [22] But now I urge you not to lose heart; not a single life will be lost, only the ship. [23] Last night there stood by me an angel of the God whose I am and whom I worship. [24] "Do not be afraid, Paul," he said; "it is ordained that you shall appear before Caesar; and, be assured, God has granted you the lives of all who are sailing with you." [25] So take heart, men! I trust God: it will turn out as I have been told; [26] we are to be cast ashore on an island.'

[27] The fourteenth night came and we were still drifting in the Adriatic Sea. At midnight the sailors felt that land was getting nearer,

27:17 **put . . . sea-anchor:** *or* lowered the mainsail.

---

nized. 31: This is the third time Paul's innocence has been implied (see 23.9; 25.25; also 23.29; compare Lk. 23.4 n.). **32:** Not enough is known of Roman law to determine whether a prisoner who had *appealed to the emperor* could be released by some other judicial officer. This verse implies such a prisoner could not.

27.1–28.31: Paul taken to Rome. 5–6: *Myra in Lycia* was an important way station for grain ships that regularly brought wheat from Egypt to Rome. *Alexandria* was the chief city of Egypt. **8:** The exact locations of *Fair Havens* and *Lasea* are unknown. **9:** *The Fast* probably refers to the Jewish Day of Atonement, which comes in early fall, a risky time for sailing. By November, all sailing ceased due to winter storms. **15:** Ancient ships had severely limited capabilities of beating into the wind. **17:** The meaning of *tackle* is unsure. How such a *ship* was braced is also unclear. **23–24:** See 23.11 n. **24:** Divine rescue from danger at sea was attributed

^{28}so they took a sounding and found twenty fathoms. Sounding again after a short interval they found fifteen fathoms; ^{29}then, fearing that we might be cast ashore on a rugged coast, they let go four anchors from the stern and prayed for daylight to come. ^{30}The sailors tried to abandon ship; they had already lowered the ship's boat, pretending they were going to lay out anchors from the bows, ^{31}when Paul said to the centurion and the soldiers, 'Unless these men stay on board you cannot reach safety.' ^{32}At that the soldiers cut the ropes of the boat and let it drop away.

^{33}Shortly before daybreak Paul urged them all to take some food. 'For the last fourteen days', he said, 'you have lived in suspense and gone hungry; you have eaten nothing. ^{34}So have something to eat, I beg you; your lives depend on it. Remember, not a hair of your heads will be lost.' ^{35}With these words, he took bread, gave thanks to God in front of them all, broke it, and began eating. ^{36}Then they plucked up courage, and began to take food themselves. ^{37}All told there were on board two hundred and seventy-six of us. ^{38}After they had eaten as much as they wanted, they lightened the ship by dumping the grain into the sea.

^{39}When day broke, they did not recognize the land, but they sighted a bay with a sandy beach, on which they decided, if possible, to run ashore. ^{40}So they slipped the anchors and let them go; at the same time they loosened the lashings of the steering-paddles, set the foresail to the wind, and let her drive to the beach. ^{41}But they found themselves caught between cross-currents and ran the ship aground, so that the bow stuck fast and remained immovable, while the stern was being pounded to pieces by the breakers. ^{42}The soldiers thought they had better kill the prisoners for fear that any should swim away and escape; ^{43}but the centurion was determined to bring Paul safely through, and prevented them from carrying out their plan. He gave orders that those who could swim should jump overboard first and get to land; ^{44}the rest were to follow, some on planks, some on parts of the ship. And thus it was that all came safely to land.

28 Once we had made our way to safety, we identified the island as Malta. ^{2}The natives treated us with uncommon kindness: because it had started to rain and was cold they lit a bonfire and made us all welcome. ^{3}Paul had got together an armful of sticks and put them on the fire, when a viper, driven out by the heat, fastened on his hand. ^{4}The natives, seeing the snake hanging on to his hand, said to one another, 'The man must be a murderer; he may have escaped from the sea, but divine justice would not let him live.' ^{5}Paul, however, shook off the snake into the fire and was none the worse. ^{6}They still expected him to swell up or suddenly drop down dead, but after waiting a long time without seeing anything out of the way happen to him, they changed their minds and said, 'He is a god.'

^{7}In that neighbourhood there were lands belonging to the chief magistrate of the island, whose name was Publius. He took us in and entertained us hospitably for three days. ^{8}It so happened that this man's father was in bed suffering from recurrent bouts of fever and dysentery. Paul visited him and, after prayer, laid his hands on him and healed him; ^{9}whereupon the other sick people on the island came and were cured. ^{10}They honoured us with many marks of respect, and when we were leaving they put on board the supplies we needed.

^{11}Three months had passed when we put to sea in a ship which had wintered in the island; she was the *Castor and Pollux* of Alexandria. ^{12}We landed at Syracuse and spent three days there; ^{13}then we sailed up the coast and arrived at Rhegium. Next day a south wind sprang up and we reached Puteoli in two days. ^{14}There we found fellow-

to many Hellenistic deities. **37:** The number is well within the capacity of such a ship. **39–44:** Paul reports suffering three earlier shipwrecks and drifting once twenty-four hours at sea (2 Cor. 11.25), but Acts gives no report of these incidents.

28.1–10: Paul at Malta. 1: Sometime after leaving Cauda, the wind must have shifted to the east; a continuing northeast wind would have landed them on the coast of Africa (27.17), not *Malta*. **6:** Much of what Paul did and said in 27.9–28.10 would make him appear to be a Hellenistic divine hero, or even a god.

28.11–15: On to Rome. 11: *Three months:* probably between November and February. Sailing resumed in late February or early March. **13:** Grain ships from Egypt unloaded at *Puteoli,* the major Roman harbor for foreign trade. **14:** When Paul reached *Rome,* the prophecy of 23.11 was fulfilled, as well as the program

Christians and were invited to stay a week with them. And so to Rome. [15] The Christians there had had news of us and came out to meet us as far as Appii Forum and the Three Taverns, and when Paul saw them, he gave thanks to God and took courage.

[16] WHEN we entered Rome Paul was allowed to lodge privately, with a soldier in charge of him. [17] Three days later he called together the local Jewish leaders, and when they were assembled, he said to them: 'My brothers, I never did anything against our people or against the customs of our forefathers; yet I was arrested in Jerusalem and handed over to the Romans. [18] They examined me and would have liked to release me because there was no capital charge against me; [19] but the Jews objected, and I had no option but to appeal to Caesar; not that I had any accusation to bring against my own people. [20] This is why I have asked to see and talk to you; it is for loyalty to the hope of Israel that I am in these chains.' [21] They replied, 'We have had no communication about you from Judaea, nor has any countryman of ours arrived with any report or gossip to your discredit. [22] We should like to hear from you what your views are; all we know about this sect is that no one has a good word to say for it.'

[23] So they fixed a day, and came in large numbers to his lodging. From dawn to dusk he put his case to them; he spoke urgently of the kingdom of God and sought to convince them about Jesus by appealing to the law of Moses and the prophets. [24] Some were won over by his arguments; others remained unconvinced. [25] Without reaching any agreement among themselves they began to disperse, but not before Paul had spoken this final word: 'How well the Holy Spirit spoke to your fathers through the prophet Isaiah [26] when he said, "Go to this people and say: You may listen and listen, but you will never understand; you may look and look, but you will never see. [27] For this people's mind has become dull; they have stopped their ears and closed their eyes. Otherwise, their eyes might see, their ears hear, and their mind understand, and then they might turn again, and I would heal them." [28] Therefore take note that this salvation of God has been sent to the Gentiles; the Gentiles will listen.'

[30] He stayed there two full years at his own expense, with a welcome for all who came to him; [31] he proclaimed the kingdom of God and taught the facts about the Lord Jesus Christ quite openly and without hindrance.

28:28 **listen:** *some witnesses add* [29] After he had spoken, the Jews went away, arguing vigorously among themselves.

outlined in 1.8; see also Rom. 15.22–24, 28. **15:** Though Paul had never been to Rome, he and the *Christians there* knew about each other; see Rom. 1.8; 15.14–16. The NT tells us nothing about the origin of the Christian congregation in Rome.

28.16–31: Paul in Rome. 17: This was the original accusation by the Jews from Asia; see 21.28. **18:** *No capital charge;* see 23.29; 25.25; 26.31. **23:** *Kingdom of God:* see 19.8 n. **26:** Isa. 6.9–10 Sept.; compare Mk. 4.12 and parallels. This is similar to Stephen's condemnation of the Jews (7.51–53). **28:** As the whole narrative has shown, this is a major theme of Acts; see 13.46 n. **31:** The story which began with Jesus in Galilee (the Gospel of Luke) has now moved through Jerusalem to Rome, and, in the author's view, will continue to the ends of the earth (1.8). Although we would like to know the outcome of Paul's imprisonment, that information is not essential for the author's purpose. The author has had in mind a story that remains incomplete until the fulfillment of God's plan in the remote future. Meanwhile, disciples will be proclaiming *the kingdom of God and* teaching *the facts about the Lord Jesus Christ.*

THE LETTER OF PAUL TO THE
Romans

The longest of Paul's letters (and first in the New Testament sequence) contains the fullest and most balanced statement of his theology. For a year or two Paul had been collecting relief money for the Christian poor in Jerusalem (15.16; 1 Cor. 16.1; 2 Cor. 8.4; 9.1). Now, perhaps because of Judaizers (see Introduction to Galatians), he has decided that he can no longer work in his old territory (from Syria to Illyricum; 15.19, 23). He proposes to visit Rome, after he has delivered this collection (15.25), in order to open a new mission farther west ("Spain"; 15.24, 28). To introduce himself to the Romans, a church he has never visited, he fills this impressive letter with insights derived from past crises in his eventful ministry. Perhaps he also intends to scotch any rumors that labeled him as antinomian (3.8, 31; 7.12; chs. 13–14) or anti-Jewish (3.1–3; chs. 9–11).

As to the date: the collection project implies the chronological sequence—1 Corinthians, 2 Corinthians, chs. 1–9, Romans—over a period of perhaps two years. The Judaizing crisis suggests that Galatians immediately preceded Romans. Opinions about the year vary from 48 C.E. to 58 C.E.

The gospel of Christ

1 From Paul, servant of Christ Jesus, called by God to be an apostle and set apart for the service of his gospel.

² This gospel God announced beforehand in sacred scriptures through his prophets. ³⁻⁴ It is about his Son: on the human level he was a descendant of David, but on the level of the spirit—the Holy Spirit—he was proclaimed Son of God by an act of power that raised him from the dead: it is about Jesus Christ our Lord. ⁵ Through him I received the privilege of an apostolic commission to bring people of all nations to faith and obedience in his name, ⁶ including you who have heard the call and belong to Jesus Christ.

⁷ I send greetings to all of you in Rome, who are loved by God and called to be his people. Grace and peace to you from God our Father and the Lord Jesus Christ.

⁸ Let me begin by thanking my God, through Jesus Christ, for you all, because the story of your faith is being told all over the world. ⁹ God is my witness, to whom I offer the service of my spirit by preaching the gospel of his Son: God knows that I make mention of you in my prayers continually, ¹⁰ and am always asking that by his will I may, somehow or other, at long last succeed in coming to visit you. ¹¹ For I long to see you; I want to bring you some spiritual gift to make you strong; ¹² or rather, I want us to be encouraged by one another's faith when I am with you, I by yours and you by mine.

¹³ Brothers and sisters, I should like you to know that I have often planned to come, though so far without success, in the hope of achieving something among you, as I have in the rest of the gentile world. ¹⁴ I have an obligation to Greek and non-Greek, to learned and simple; ¹⁵ hence my eagerness to declare the gospel to you in Rome as well. ¹⁶ For I am not ashamed of the gospel. It is the saving

1:3–4 **Son of God . . . dead:** or Son of God with full power at his resurrection from the dead.

1.1–7: Salutation. Greek letters began with the names of the sender and the recipient. **1:** *Apostle:* see 1 Cor. 9.1 n. **5:** Paul here affirms his apostleship to the *nations,* i.e. Gentiles. **7:** The word *grace* (i.e God's favor) replaces the usual and similar-sounding Greek salutation; *peace* is the Jewish salutation (e.g. Matt. 10.13).

1.8–15: Opening thanksgiving. Next in an ancient Greek letter there was usually a prayer for the recipient's health. Similarly, Paul begins all his letters, except the angry Gal. (and 2 Cor. chs. 10–13 if that is indeed a separate letter; see annotation at 2 Cor. 10.1–13.14), by *thanking . . . God* for the addressees, mentioning in the process the major themes of the letter.

1.16–17: The thesis of the letter is that the *righteousness of God* gives unmerited acceptance to (i.e. justifies)

power of God for everyone who has faith — the Jew first, but the Greek also — [17] because in it the righteousness of God is seen at work, beginning in faith and ending in faith; as scripture says, 'Whoever is justified through faith shall gain life.'

God's judgement on sin

[18] DIVINE retribution is to be seen at work, falling from heaven on all the impiety and wickedness of men and women who in their wickedness suppress the truth. [19] For all that can be known of God lies plain before their eyes; indeed God himself has disclosed it to them. [20] Ever since the world began his invisible attributes, that is to say his everlasting power and deity, have been visible to the eye of reason, in the things he has made. Their conduct, therefore, is indefensible; [21] knowing God, they have refused to honour him as God, or to render him thanks. Hence all their thinking has ended in futility, and their misguided minds are plunged in darkness. [22] They boast of their wisdom, but they have made fools of themselves, [23] exchanging the glory of the immortal God for an image shaped like mortal man, even for images like birds, beasts, and reptiles. Like Jeremiah

[24] For this reason God has given them up to their own vile desires, and the consequent degradation of their bodies. [25] They have exchanged the truth of God for a lie, and have offered reverence and worship to created things instead of to the Creator. Blessed is he for ever, Amen. [26] As a result God has given them up to shameful passions. Among them women have exchanged natural intercourse for unnatural, [27] and men too, giving up natural relations with women, burn with lust for one another; males behave indecently with males, and are paid in their own persons the fitting wage of such perversion.

[28] Thus, because they have not seen fit to acknowledge God, he has given them up to their own depraved way of thinking, and this leads them to break all rules of conduct. [29] They are filled with every kind of wickedness, villainy, greed, and malice; they are one mass of envy, murder, rivalry, treachery, and malevolence; gossips [30] and scandalmongers; and blasphemers, insolent, arrogant, and boastful; they invent new kinds of vice, they show no respect to parents, [31] they are without sense or fidelity, without natural affection or pity. [32] They know well enough the just decree of God, that those who behave like this deserve to die; yet they not only do these things themselves but approve such conduct in others.

2 You have no defence, then, whoever you may be, when you sit in judgement — for in judging others you condemn yourself, since you, the judge, are equally guilty. [2] We all know that God's judgement on those who commit such crimes is just; [3] and do you imagine — you that pass judgement on the guilty while committing the same crimes yourself — do you imagine that you, any more than they, will escape the judgement of God? [4] Or do you despise his wealth of kindness and tolerance and patience, failing to see that God's kindness is meant to lead you to repentance? [5] In the obstinate impenitence of your heart you are laying up for yourself a store of retribution against the day of retribution, when God's just judgement will be revealed, [6] and he will pay everyone for what he has done. [7] To those who pursue glory, honour, and immortality by steady persistence in well-doing, he will give eternal life; [8] but the retribution of his wrath awaits those who are governed by selfish ambition, who refuse obedience to truth and take evil for their guide. [9] There will be affliction and distress for every human being who is a wrongdoer, for the Jew first and for the Greek also; [10] but for everyone who does right there will be glory, honour, and peace, for the Jew first

1:17 **Whoever . . . life:** *or* The righteous shall live by faith.

the believer on the basis of the person's *faith* (i.e. trust). **16:** *Jew first:* see 2.9–10 n. **17:** *The righteousness of God . . . ending in faith:* the book's theme; see 3.22. *Scripture:* Hab. 2.4 (Gal. 3.11).

1.18–32: The depravity of the Gentiles. "The heavens tell out the glory of God" (Ps. 19.1), but human beings have *refused to honour* God (v. 21). **19:** *All that may be known,* i.e. except God's special revelation to Jews and Christians. **23:** For the Jewish scorn of idols see Isa. 44.13–20; Wisd. chs. 13–15. **24–28:** Therefore *God has given them up* (vv. 24, 26, 28) to increasing wickedness that leads to death. **29–31:** See Gal. 5.19–21.

2.1–16: The Jews will be judged also, although they presume to *sit in* moral *judgement* over the Gentiles. **5:** God's wrath, already evident (1.18), will culminate in *the day of retribution* (see 1 Cor. 1.8 n.). **9–10:**

and also for the Greek. [11] God has no favourites.

[12] Those who have sinned outside the pale of the law of Moses will perish outside the law, and all who have sinned under that law will be judged by it. [13] None will be justified before God by hearing the law, but by doing it. [14] When Gentiles who do not possess the law carry out its precepts by the light of nature, then, although they have no law, they are their own law; [15] they show that what the law requires is inscribed on their hearts, and to this their conscience gives supporting witness, since their own thoughts argue the case, sometimes against them, sometimes even for them. [16] So it will be on the day when, according to my gospel, God will judge the secrets of human hearts through Christ Jesus.

The Jews and their law

[17] BUT as for you who bear the name of Jew and rely on the law: you take pride in your God; [18] you know his will; taught by the law, you know what really matters; [19] you are confident that you are a guide to the blind, a light to those in darkness, [20] an instructor of the foolish, and a teacher of the immature, because you possess in the law the embodiment of knowledge and truth. [21] You teach others, then; do you not teach yourself? You proclaim, 'Do not steal'; but are you yourself a thief? [22] You say, 'Do not commit adultery'; but are you an adulterer? You abominate false gods; but do you rob shrines? [23] While you take pride in the law, you dishonour God by breaking it. [24] As scripture says, 'Because of you the name of God is profaned among the Gentiles.'

[25] Circumcision has value, provided you keep the law; but if you break the law, then your circumcision is as if it had never been. [26] Equally, if an uncircumcised man keeps the precepts of the law, will he not count as circumcised? [27] He may be physically uncircumcised, but by fulfilling the law he will pass judgement on you who break it, for all your written code and your circumcision. [28] It is not externals that make a Jew, nor an external mark in the flesh that makes circumcision. [29] The real Jew is one who is inwardly a Jew, and his circumcision is of the heart, spiritual not literal; he receives his commendation not from men but from God.

3 Then what advantage has the Jew? What is the value of circumcision? [2] Great, in every way. In the first place, the Jews were entrusted with the oracles of God. [3] What if some of them were unfaithful? Will their faithlessness cancel the faithfulness of God? [4] Certainly not! God must be true though all men be proved liars; for we read in scripture, 'When you speak you will be vindicated; when you are accused, you will win the case.'

[5] Another question: if our injustice serves to confirm God's justice, what are we to say? Is it unjust of God (I speak of him in human terms) to bring retribution upon us? [6] Certainly not! If God were unjust, how could he judge the world?

[7] Again, if the truth of God is displayed to his greater glory through my falsehood, why should I any longer be condemned as a sinner? [8] Why not indeed 'do evil that good may come', as some slanderously report me as saying? To condemn such men as these is surely just.

[9] Well then, are we Jews any better off? No, not at all! For we have already drawn up the indictment that all, Jews and Greeks alike, are under the power of sin. [10] Scripture says:

There is no one righteous; no, not one;
[11] no one who understands, no one who
　　seeks God.
[12] All have swerved aside, all alike have
　　become debased;

3:9 **No, not at all:** *or* Not altogether.

Because of the advantage of having special knowledge of God (3.2; 9.4–5), *the Jew is first*. **11–16:** But Jews and Gentiles equally are *judged* by their actions (v. 12; see Matt. 7.20–21; Gal. 3.21; Jas. 1.22–25), the Jews under the *law of Moses* (v. 12) as found in Scripture, the Gentiles by the same standard as *inscribed on their hearts* (v. 15; see v. 29; 2 Cor. 3.2–3 n.). **16:** *Day:* see v. 5 n.

2.17–29: The immorality of the adherents of the law. 21–22: Exod. 20.3–6, 14–15. **24:** Isa. 52.5; Ezek. 36.20. **25:** *Circumcision* is the symbol of God's covenant with Judaism (Gen. 17.11). **26:** See 1 Cor. 7.19; Gal. 5.6. **29:** *Circumcision . . . of the heart:* see Deut. 10.16; Jer. 4.4.

3.1–8: Jews have the advantage of God's *oracles* (v. 2), i.e. the Scriptures, and the unalterable promises they contain. **4:** Ps. 51.4. **8:** *Slanderously:* see 6.1 n.

3.9–20: But all are equally guilty, for the law itself condemns its followers (5.13; 7.7–11; Gal. 3.10). **10–18:**

there is no one to show kindness: no,
not one.

13 Their throats are open tombs,
they use their tongues for treachery,
adders' venom is on their lips,
14 and their mouths are full of bitter
curses.

15 Their feet hasten to shed blood,
16 ruin and misery mark their tracks,
17 they are strangers to the path of peace,
18 and reverence for God does not enter
their thoughts.

19 Now all the words of the law are addressed, as we know, to those who are under the law, so that no one may have anything to say in self-defence, and the whole world may be exposed to God's judgement. 20 For no human being can be justified in the sight of God by keeping the law: law brings only the consciousness of sin.

21 But now, quite independently of law, though with the law and the prophets bearing witness to it, the righteousness of God has been made known; 22 it is effective through faith in Christ for all who have such faith — all, without distinction. 23 For all alike have sinned, and are deprived of the divine glory; 24 and all are justified by God's free grace alone, through his act of liberation in the person of Christ Jesus. 25 For God designed him to be the means of expiating sin by his death, effective through faith. God meant by this to demonstrate his justice, because in his forbearance he had overlooked the sins of the past — 26 to demonstrate his justice now in the present, showing that he is himself just and also justifies anyone who puts his faith in Jesus.

27 What room then is left for human pride? It is excluded. And on what principle? The keeping of the law would not exclude it, but faith does. 28 For our argument is that people are justified by faith quite apart from any question of keeping the law.

29 Do you suppose God is the God of the Jews alone? Is he not the God of Gentiles also? Certainly, of Gentiles also. 30 For if the Lord is indeed one, he will justify the circumcised by their faith and the uncircumcised through their faith. 31 Does this mean that we are using faith to undermine the law? By no means: we are upholding the law.

Abraham's faith

4 WHAT, then, are we to say about Abraham, our ancestor by natural descent? 2 If Abraham was justified by anything he did, then he has grounds for pride. But not in the eyes of God! 3 For what does scripture say? 'Abraham put his faith in God, and that faith was counted to him as righteousness.'

4 Now if someone does a piece of work, his wages are not 'counted' to be a gift; they are paid as his due. 5 But if someone without any work to his credit simply puts his faith in him who acquits the wrongdoer, then his faith is indeed 'counted as righteousness'. 6 In the same sense David speaks of the happiness of the man whom God 'counts' as righteous, apart from any good works: 7 'Happy are they', he says, 'whose lawless deeds are forgiven, whose sins are blotted out; 8 happy is the man whose sin the Lord does not count against him.'

9 Is this happiness confined to the circumcised, or is it for the uncircumcised also? We have just been saying: 'Abraham's faith was

3:25 **designed him to be:** *or* set him forth as.

Pss. 14.1–3; 5.9; 140.3; 10.7; Isa. 59.7–8; Ps. 36.1. **19:** *Words of the law:* here Scripture as a whole (contrast v. 21). **20:** Ps. 143.2 (Gal. 2.16); *sin:* see 7.7–13 n.

3.21–31: God's gracious acceptance (i.e. justifying, vv. 24, 26, 28, 30; see Gal. 2.16 n.) of the believer is now revealed. **21–22:** *Law and the prophets:* Scripture, which later included a third part, Writings. God's justifying depends on the believer's trust (i.e. *faith*) in Christ. *All:* both Jews and Gentiles (see vv. 29–30). **24:** *Act of liberation* (from sin) applies the metaphor of freeing from slavery to God's deed in Christ. **25–26:** The past *sins* of the believer are not ignored, since God is *just*. Instead, now using the language of sacrifice, Christ's death is God's way of cleansing the believer's sins (4.25; 5.9). **27–28:** *The keeping of the law* could be an achievement leading to *pride*. However, salvation is a gift resting on *faith:* thus pride is *excluded*. **31:** God's basic intention in the *law* is accomplished by *faith*.

4.1–12: Abraham was justified by his faith and not by *anything he did* (v. 2). **3:** Paul finds his understanding of *faith* confirmed by Gen. 15.6 (Sept.; Gal. 3.6). **6:** *David:* the traditional author of the Psalter. **7–8:** Ps. 32.1–2.

counted as righteousness.' ¹⁰ In what circumstances was it so counted? Was he circumcised at the time, or not? He was not yet circumcised, but uncircumcised; ¹¹ he received circumcision later as the sign and hallmark of that righteousness which faith had given him while he was still uncircumcised. It follows that he is the father of all who have faith when uncircumcised, and so have righteousness 'counted' to them; ¹² and at the same time he is the father of the circumcised, provided they are not merely circumcised, but also follow that path of faith which our father Abraham trod while he was still uncircumcised.

¹³ It was not through law that Abraham and his descendants were given the promise that the world should be their inheritance, but through righteousness that came from faith. ¹⁴ If the heirs are those who hold by the law, then faith becomes pointless and the promise goes for nothing; ¹⁵ law can bring only retribution, and where there is no law there can be no breach of law. ¹⁶ The promise was made on the ground of faith in order that it might be a matter of sheer grace, and that it might be valid for all Abraham's descendants, not only for those who hold by the law, but also for those who have Abraham's faith. For he is the father of us all, ¹⁷ as scripture says: 'I have appointed you to be father of many nations.' In the presence of God, the God who makes the dead live and calls into being things that are not, Abraham had faith. ¹⁸ When hope seemed hopeless, his faith was such that he became 'father of many nations', in fulfilment of the promise, 'So shall your descendants be.' ¹⁹ His faith did not weaken when he considered his own body, which was as good as dead (for he was about a hundred years old), and the deadness of Sarah's womb; ²⁰ no distrust made him doubt God's

promise, but, strong in faith, he gave glory to God, ²¹ convinced that what he had promised he was able to do. ²² And that is why Abraham's faith was 'counted to him as righteousness'.

²³ The words 'counted to him' were meant to apply not only to Abraham ²⁴ but to us; our faith too is to be 'counted', the faith in the God who raised Jesus our Lord from the dead; ²⁵ for he was given up to death for our misdeeds, and raised to life for our justification.

Life in Christ

5 THEREFORE, now that we have been justified through faith, we are at peace with God through our Lord Jesus Christ, ² who has given us access to that grace in which we now live; and we exult in the hope of the divine glory that is to be ours. ³ More than this: we even exult in our present sufferings, because we know that suffering is a source of endurance, ⁴ endurance of approval, and approval of hope. ⁵ Such hope is no fantasy; through the Holy Spirit he has given us, God's love has flooded our hearts.

⁶ It was while we were still helpless that, at the appointed time, Christ died for the wicked. ⁷ Even for a just man one of us would hardly die, though perhaps for a good man one might actually brave death; ⁸ but Christ died for us while we were yet sinners, and that is God's proof of his love towards us. ⁹ And so, since we have now been justified by Christ's sacrificial death, we shall all the more certainly be saved through him from final retribution. ¹⁰ For if, when we were God's enemies, we were reconciled to him through

5:1 **we are at peace:** *some witnesses read* let us continue at peace.   5:2 **we exult:** *or* let us exult.   5:3 **we even exult:** *or* let us even exult.

10–11: He was not circumcised until Gen. 17.11, 24.

4.13–25: Faith and not law was the basis of God's *promise* to *Abraham* and to his *descendants* (compare Gal. 3.16–18). **15:** *Retribution, breach of law:* see 3.10–20; 5.13–20; 7.7–11. **17:** Gen. 17.5. *Nations:* see 1.5 n. **18:** Gen. 15.5. **19:** Gen. 17.17; 18.11. **22–23:** See v. 3. **24:** *To us:* see 15.4 n.; Gal. 3.29. **25:** See 3.25–26 n.; 5.9.

5.1–11: Peace and reconciliation. *God* accepts us on the basis of our *faith* (v. 1). God's *love* (v. 5) expressed in *Christ's* death (vv. 6–10) and communicated by the *Spirit* (v. 5), gives assurance to our *hope* (vv. 2, 4, 5) of salvation (on the triads God, Christ, Spirit and faith, hope, love, see 1 Cor. 12.4–6 n. and 13.13 n.). **3:** *Sufferings:* see 2 Cor. 4.8–11; 11.23–30; 12.10. **5:** *Spirit:* see ch. 8; 2 Cor. 5.5 n. **8–10:** As *sinners* we were God's *enemies* (v. 10), but by God's unique *love* (see Jn. 15.13) we are now *reconciled,* and we shall surely be acquitted in the Last Judgment. **9:** See 3.25–26 n.

the death of his Son, how much more, now that we have been reconciled, shall we be saved by his life! [11] But that is not all: we also exult in God through our Lord Jesus, through whom we have now been granted reconciliation.

[12] What does this imply? It was through one man that sin entered the world, and through sin death, and thus death pervaded the whole human race, inasmuch as all have sinned. [13] For sin was already in the world before there was law; and although in the absence of law no reckoning is kept of sin, [14] death held sway from Adam to Moses, even over those who had not sinned as Adam did, by disobeying a direct command—and Adam foreshadows the man who was to come. [15] But God's act of grace is out of all proportion to Adam's wrongdoing. For if the wrongdoing of that one man brought death upon so many, its effect is vastly exceeded by the grace of God and the gift that came to so many by the grace of the one man, Jesus Christ. [16] And again, the gift of God is not to be compared in its effect with that one man's sin; for the judicial action, following on the one offence, resulted in a verdict of condemnation, but the act of grace, following on so many misdeeds, resulted in a verdict of acquittal. [17] If, by the wrongdoing of one man, death established its reign through that one man, much more shall those who in far greater measure receive grace and the gift of righteousness live and reign through the one man, Jesus Christ.

[18] It follows, then, that as the result of one misdeed was condemnation for all people, so the result of one righteous act is acquittal and life for all. [19] For as through the disobedience of one man many were made sinners, so through the obedience of one man many will be made righteous.

[20] Law intruded into this process to multiply law-breaking. But where sin was multiplied, grace immeasurably exceeded it, [21] in order that, as sin established its reign by way of death, so God's grace might establish its reign in righteousness, and result in eternal life through Jesus Christ our Lord.

Baptism into Christ

6 WHAT are we to say, then? Shall we persist in sin, so that there may be all the more grace? [2] Certainly not! We died to sin: how can we live in it any longer? [3] Have you forgotten that when we were baptized into union with Christ Jesus we were baptized into his death? [4] By that baptism into his death we were buried with him, in order that, as Christ was raised from the dead by the glorious power of the Father, so also we might set out on a new life.

[5] For if we have become identified with him in his death, we shall also be identified with him in his resurrection. [6] We know that our old humanity has been crucified with Christ, for the destruction of the sinful self, so that we may no longer be slaves to sin, [7] because death cancels the claims of sin. [8] But if we thus died with Christ, we believe that we shall also live with him, [9] knowing as we do that Christ, once raised from the dead, is never to die again: he is no longer under the dominion of death. [10] When he died, he died to sin, once for all, and now that he lives, he lives to God. [11] In the same way you must regard yourselves as dead to sin and alive to God, in union with Christ Jesus.

[12] Therefore sin must no longer reign in your mortal body, exacting obedience to the body's desires. [13] You must no longer put any part of it at sin's disposal, as an implement for doing wrong. Put yourselves instead at the disposal of God; think of yourselves as raised

---

5.12–21: Adam and Christ, *disobedience* (Gen. 2.17; 3.6) and *obedience* (v. 19), *sin* and *righteousness, condemnation* (Gen. 3.19) and *acquittal, death* for *all people* and *life* for *all*—these are Paul's contrasts (compare 1 Cor. 15.21–23, 45–49). **13:** See v. 20. **14:** *Adam, the man who was to come:* see 1 Cor. 15.45–49 n. **20:** The *law* of Moses *intruded* (Gal. 3.17–20) and, by specifying sin (v. 13; 3.20), made it more flagrant (see 7.7–13 n.).

6.1–14: Dying and rising with Christ. 1: *Sin* to obtain *more grace* (also v. 15; 3.8)? The idea is ludicrous and probably represents one of several ways Paul's gospel was twisted by his opponents (see Introduction). **3–4:** *Baptism* means dying to sin and rising to life *into union with Christ.* **6:** *Crucified:* see Gal. 5.24; 6.14. **12–14:** The basis of Paul's ethic is expressed here. That God has freed us from sin's power (v. 7) is the meaning of Christ's death; therefore we must live as if we are indeed free. *Obedience* to sin is unthinkable. See 8.5–13; Gal. 5.16–25.

from death to life, and yield your bodies to God as implements for doing right. 14 Sin shall no longer be your master, for you are no longer under law, but under grace.

15 What then? Are we to sin, because we are not under law but under grace? Of course not! 16 You know well enough that if you bind yourselves to obey a master, you are slaves of the master you obey; and this is true whether the master is sin and the outcome death, or obedience and the outcome righteousness. 17 Once you were slaves of sin, but now, thank God, you have yielded wholehearted obedience to that pattern of teaching to which you were made subject; 18 emancipated from sin, you have become slaves of righteousness 19 (to use language that suits your human weakness). As you once yielded your bodies to the service of impurity and lawlessness, making for moral anarchy, so now you must yield them to the service of righteousness, making for a holy life.

20 When you were slaves of sin, you were free from the control of righteousness. 21 And what gain did that bring you? Things that now make you ashamed, for their end is death. 22 But now, freed from the commands of sin and bound to the service of God, you have gains that lead to holiness, and the end is eternal life. 23 For sin pays a wage, and the wage is death, but God gives freely, and his gift is eternal life in union with Christ Jesus our Lord.

The role of the law

7 You must be aware, my friends — I am sure you have some knowledge of law — that a person is subject to the law only so long

as he is alive. 2 For example, a married woman is by law bound to her husband while he lives; but if the husband dies, she is released from the marriage bond. 3 If, therefore, in her husband's lifetime she gives herself to another man, she will be held to be an adulteress; but if the husband dies, she is free of the law and she does not commit adultery by giving herself to another man. 4 So too, my friends, through the body of Christ you died to the law and were set free to give yourselves to another, to him who rose from the dead so that we may bear fruit for God. 5 While we lived on the level of mere human nature, the sinful passions evoked by the law were active in our bodies, and bore fruit for death. 6 But now, having died to that which held us bound, we are released from the law, to serve God in a new way, the way of the spirit in contrast to the old way of a written code.

7 What follows? Is the law identical with sin? Of course not! Yet had it not been for the law I should never have become acquainted with sin. For example, I should never have known what it was to covet, if the law had not said, 'You shall not covet.' 8 Through that commandment sin found its opportunity, and produced in me all kinds of wrong desires. In the absence of law, sin is devoid of life. 9 There was a time when, in the absence of law, I was fully alive; but when the commandment came, sin sprang to life and I died. 10 The commandment which should have led to life proved in my experience to lead to death, 11 because in the commandment sin found its opportunity to seduce me,

6:17 **to which . . . subject:** *or* which was handed on to you.

6.15–23: No slave can serve two masters, and by God's mercy the *slaves of sin* (v. 17) have become the *slaves of righteousness* (v. 18). Once again, obedience to sin is out of the question. **15:** See v. 1 n. **22:** *Holiness:* a consecrated life (as in v. 19).

7.1–6: The marriage law as an analogy. How is it that the Christian is not "under law, but under . . . grace" (6.14–15)? **4–6:** In the same way we have *died to the law* and thus are free of the *law. Fruit* is a conventional metaphor for "the product of a manner of life."

7.7–13: The law and sin contrasted. Paul often speaks (especially in Gal.; see Gal. 3.19–20 n.) as if he thought of *the law* as *identical with sin* (v. 7; compare "died to sin" in Rom. 6.10 with "died to the law" in v. 4). Here, however, he makes his most positive assessment of the law: it is *holy and just and good* (v. 12), since it reflects God's intentions. But in practice the law is powerless against *sin* and even encourages it (v. 8; compare 5.13, 20; Gal. 3.21–22). **7–8:** "*You shall not covet*" (Exod. 20.17; Deut. 5.21) is the only commandment in the Decalogue which restricts a person's thoughts; here *sin* finds *its opportunity.* **9–11:** Paul speaks of leaving childhood and assuming responsibility under the law in terms reminiscent of the Eden story (Gen. 3.1–19; 2 Cor. 11.3). **11:** *Seduce:* trick (Gen. 3.13).

and through the commandment killed me. [12] So then, the law in itself is holy and the commandment is holy and just and good.

[13] Are we therefore to say that this good thing caused my death? Of course not! It was sin that killed me, and thereby sin exposed its true character: it used a good thing to bring about my death, and so, through the commandment, sin became more sinful than ever. [14] We know that the law is spiritual; but I am not: I am unspiritual, sold as a slave to sin. [15] I do not even acknowledge my own actions as mine, for what I do is not what I want to do, but what I detest. [16] But if what I do is against my will, then clearly I agree with the law and hold it to be admirable. [17] This means that it is no longer I who perform the action, but sin that dwells in me. [18] For I know that nothing good dwells in me — my unspiritual self, I mean — for though the will to do good is there, the ability to effect it is not. [19] The good which I want to do, I fail to do; but what I do is the wrong which is against my will; [20] and if what I do is against my will, clearly it is no longer I who am the agent, but sin that has its dwelling in me.

[21] I discover this principle, then: that when I want to do right, only wrong is within my reach. [22] In my inmost self I delight in the law of God, [23] but I perceive in my outward actions a different law, fighting against the law that my mind approves, and making me a prisoner under the law of sin which controls my conduct. [24] Wretched creature that I am, who is there to rescue me from this state of death? [25] Who but God? Thanks be to him through Jesus Christ our Lord! To sum up then: left to myself I serve God's law with my mind, but with my unspiritual nature I serve the law of sin.

Life through the Spirit

8 IT follows that there is now no condemnation for those who are united with Christ Jesus. [2] In Christ Jesus the life-giving law of the Spirit has set you free from the law of sin and death. [3] What the law could not do, because human weakness robbed it of all potency, God has done: by sending his own Son in the likeness of our sinful nature and to deal with sin, he has passed judgement against sin within that very nature, [4] so that the commandment of the law may find fulfilment in us, whose conduct is no longer controlled by the old nature, but by the Spirit.

[5-6] Those who live on the level of the old nature have their outlook formed by it, and that spells death; but those who live on the level of the spirit have the spiritual outlook, and that is life and peace. [7] For the outlook of the unspiritual nature is enmity with God; it is not subject to the law of God and indeed it cannot be; [8] those who live under its control cannot please God.

[9] But you do not live like that. You live by the spirit, since God's Spirit dwells in you; and anyone who does not possess the Spirit

8:3 **and to deal with sin:** *or* and as a sacrifice for sin.

7.14–25: The divided self. In his *inmost self* (v. 22) Paul knows that the law is *spiritual* (v. 14), *admirable* (v. 16), and a *delight* (v. 22). But sin enslaves his body so that it acts *against* his *will* (vv. 15–17, 20). **14:** *Unspiritual:* lit. "fleshly." Here and in ch. 8 Paul contrasts "flesh" and "spirit"; compare 8.4, 5–8, 9–10 nn.; Gal. 5.16–17; 2 Cor. 4.7–5.5; 1 Cor. 15.39–53. **17, 20:** Paul thinks of *sin* as a power and occasionally personifies it: *no longer I* but *sin* acts. But as chs. 1–3 show, one is still responsible for one's actions. **23, 25:** *A different law, the law of sin:* a foreign principle, sin's command. **24–25:** Paul expresses both ultimate despair at being in a *state of death* and simultaneously his profoundest *thanks* for God's *rescue* (see 8.1–4).

8.1–4: God's act of rescue has turned the tables. Divided by sin we could only expect *condemnation* and *death*. But Christ, by sharing our *sinful nature* and dealing *with sin* (see Tfn. at v. 3 and 3.25–26 n.), has diverted the expected condemnation to *sin* itself and given us new life instead. **1:** Paul's language is fluid. The believer is *united with Christ* (lit. "in Christ") since the *Spirit* "dwells within" the believer (v. 9). Paul also speaks of Christ "dwelling within" the believer (v. 10 and Gal. 2.20; Eph. 3.17). **3:** *Sending his own son:* see v. 32 and 5.8. The phrase, *in the likeness of our sinful nature* (compare Phil. 2.7), does not mean that Paul doubted Jesus' full humanity. On the contrary, his argument requires it. **4:** Now *controlled . . . by the Spirit,* our *conduct* can fulfill the Law's basic requirement: love (see 13.8–10; Gal. 5.14, 22). *Old nature:* lit. "flesh" (see 7.14 n.).

8.5–11: The old life and the new. 5–8: Those whose lives are directed by their *old nature* (see Gal. 5.19–21) live in *enmity* with God (see 5.10) and can only expect *death*. **9–10:** But for those who live *by the spirit* (see 7.14 n.), *the Spirit is* their *life. Christ is in you, the Spirit dwells in you:* see v. 1 n. *The body is dead,* i.e. mortal, of Christ does not belong to Christ. ¹⁰ But if Christ is in you, then although the body is dead because of sin, yet the Spirit is your life because you have been justified. ¹¹ Moreover, if the Spirit of him who raised Jesus from the dead dwells in you, then the God who raised Christ Jesus from the dead will also give new life to your mortal bodies through his indwelling Spirit.

¹² It follows, my friends, that our old nature has no claim on us; we are not obliged to live in that way. ¹³ If you do so, you must die. But if by the Spirit you put to death the base pursuits of the body, then you will live.

¹⁴ For all who are led by the Spirit of God are sons of God. ¹⁵ The Spirit you have received is not a spirit of slavery, leading you back into a life of fear, but a Spirit of adoption, enabling us to cry 'Abba! Father!' ¹⁶ The Spirit of God affirms to our spirit that we are God's children; ¹⁷ and if children, then heirs, heirs of God and fellow-heirs with Christ; but we must share his sufferings if we are also to share his glory.

¹⁸ For I reckon that the sufferings we now endure bear no comparison with the glory, as yet unrevealed, which is in store for us. ¹⁹ The created universe is waiting with eager expectation for God's sons to be revealed. ²⁰ It was made subject to frustration, not of its own choice but by the will of him who subjected it, yet with the hope ²¹ that the universe itself is to be freed from the shackles of mortality and is to enter upon the glorious liberty of the children of God. ²² Up to the present, as

we know, the whole created universe in all its parts groans as if in the pangs of childbirth. ²³ What is more, we also, to whom the Spirit is given as the firstfruits of the harvest to come, are groaning inwardly while we look forward eagerly to our adoption, our liberation from mortality. ²⁴ It was with this hope that we were saved. Now to see something is no longer to hope: why hope for what is already seen? ²⁵ But if we hope for something we do not yet see, then we look forward to it eagerly and with patience.

²⁶ In the same way the Spirit comes to the aid of our weakness. We do not even know how we ought to pray, but through our inarticulate groans the Spirit himself is pleading for us, ²⁷ and God who searches our inmost being knows what the Spirit means, because he pleads for God's people as God himself wills; ²⁸ and in everything, as we know, he co-operates for good with those who love God and are called according to his purpose. ²⁹ For those whom God knew before ever they were, he also ordained to share the likeness of his Son, so that he might be the eldest among a large family of brothers; ³⁰ and those whom he foreordained, he also called, and those whom he called he also justified, and those whom he justified he also glorified.

³¹ With all this in mind, what are we to say? If God is on our side, who is against us? ³² He

8:24 **why hope for:** *some witnesses read* why endure.
8:28 **and in everything . . . God:** *or* and, as we know, all things work together for good for those who love God; *some witnesses read* and we know God himself co-operates for good with those who love God.

because of *sin* (see 5.12). **11:** The *indwelling Spirit* is our promise (see 2 Cor. 1.22; 5.5) of a resurrection like Christ's.

8.12–17: God's adopted children. Compare Gal. 4.5–7. **12–13:** See 6.12–14 n. **14–16:** Paul's previous use of slavery motifs (3.24; 6.15–23; 7.14) makes his new language dramatic. Sin made us slaves; the Spirit *makes us* God's *children*. Thus we can call God "*Father*" (notably in the Lord's Prayer) with the Aram. word that Jesus used, "*Abba.*" **16:** See vv. 26–27. **17:** Christ is *heir* to all God's promises (Gal. 3.16), and we also, as we are found in him (Gal. 3.29) and share his suffering (Phil. 3.10–11). In v. 29 Paul even calls us Christ's *brothers.*

8.18–25: The liberation of the whole creation. Just as we share in Christ's sufferings (v. 17), so all of nature suffers with us (v. 22). And the whole *universe,* ourselves included, now waits eagerly to be *freed* from *mortality* and to *enter* upon the *glorious liberty* (v. 21) which is our heritage (v. 17). **20:** God *subjected it:* see Gen. 3.17. **23:** *Firstfruits:* see 1 Cor. 15.20 n. and 2 Cor. 5.5. *Groaning:* see 2 Cor. 5.2. **24–25:** See 2 Cor. 5.6–7.

8.26–30: God's loving care supports us in *our weakness* (i.e. suffering) by the Spirit's intercession (vv. 26–28) and by the revelation of God's plans for us (vv. 29–30). **26:** *We do not . . . know how . . . to pray* until the Spirit teaches us to say "Father" (v. 15; compare Lk. 11.1–2) and gives us ecstatic speech (see 1 Cor. chs. 12–14). **28–29:** The final goal of God's purpose for us is *likeness* to *his Son* (see 2 Cor. 3.18; Eph. 4.13). **30:** For Paul's own experience see Gal. 1.15–16.

8.31–39: Our ultimate trust in God's love. The notions of someone *against us* (v. 31) and someone who did not spare his own Son, but gave him up for us all; how can he fail to lavish every other gift upon us? ³³Who will bring a charge against those whom God has chosen? Not God, who acquits! ³⁴Who will pronounce judgement? Not Christ, who died, or rather rose again; not Christ, who is at God's right hand and pleads our cause! ³⁵Then what can separate us from the love of Christ? Can affliction or hardship? Can persecution, hunger, nakedness, danger, or sword? ³⁶'We are being done to death for your sake all day long,' as scripture says; 'we have been treated like sheep for slaughter'—³⁷and yet, throughout it all, overwhelming victory is ours through him who loved us. ³⁸For I am convinced that there is nothing in death or life, in the realm of spirits or superhuman powers, in the world as it is or the world as it shall be, in the forces of the universe, ³⁹in heights or depths—nothing in all creation that can separate us from the love of God in Christ Jesus our Lord.

Israel and the Gentiles in God's plan

9 I AM speaking the truth as a Christian; my conscience, enlightened by the Holy Spirit, assures me that I do not lie when I tell you ²that there is great grief and unceasing sorrow in my heart. ³I would even pray to be an outcast myself, cut off from Christ, if it would help my brothers, my kinsfolk by natural descent. ⁴They are descendants of Israel, chosen to be God's sons; theirs is the glory of the divine presence, theirs the covenants, the law, the temple worship, and the promises. ⁵The patriarchs are theirs, and from them by natural descent came the Messiah. May God, supreme above all, be blessed for ever! Amen.

⁶It cannot be that God's word has proved false. Not all the offspring of Israel are truly Israel, ⁷nor does being Abraham's descendants make them all his true children; but, in the words of scripture, 'It is through the line of Isaac's descendants that your name will be traced.' ⁸That is to say, it is not the children of Abraham by natural descent who are children of God; it is the children born through God's promise who are reckoned as Abraham's descendants. ⁹For the promise runs: 'In due season I will come, and Sarah shall have a son.'

¹⁰And that is not all: Rebecca's children had one and the same father, our ancestor Isaac; ¹¹yet, even before they were born, when they as yet had done nothing, whether good or ill, in order that the purpose of God, which is a matter of his choice, might stand firm, based not on human deeds but on the call of God, ¹²she was told, 'The elder shall be servant to the younger.' ¹³That accords with the text of scripture, 'Jacob I loved and Esau I hated.'

¹⁴What shall we say to that? Is God to be charged with injustice? Certainly not! ¹⁵He says to Moses, 'I will show mercy to whom I will show mercy, and have pity on whom I will have pity.' ¹⁶Thus it does not depend on human will or effort, but on God's mercy. ¹⁷For in scripture Pharaoh is told, 'I have raised you up for this very purpose, to exhibit my power in my dealings with you, and to spread my fame over all the earth.' ¹⁸Thus he not only shows mercy as he chooses, but also makes stubborn as he chooses.

¹⁹You will say, 'Then why does God find fault, if no one can resist his will?' ²⁰Who do you think you are to answer God back? Can

9:5 **Messiah:** *Gk* Christ. **Messiah . . . for ever:** *or* Messiah, who is God, supreme above all and blessed for ever; *or* Messiah, who is supreme above all. Blessed be God for ever!   9:7 **all . . . children:** *or* all children of God.

will bring a charge (v. 33) suggest the heavenly court at the Last Judgment. **31:** Ps. 118.6. **35:** Paul's *hardships* (2 Cor. 11.23–28) were, of course, not unique to him. **36:** Ps. 44.22. **38–39:** *Death* is but one of the forces which attempt to separate us from God (see 1 Cor. 2.6–8 n.).

9.1–5: Paul's anguish at Israel's unbelief. 3: *Outcast:* see 1 Cor. 16.22 n.; Exod. 32.32. **4:** *Descendants of Israel:* of Jacob, renamed Israel (Gen. 32.28). The name emphasizes God's special choice. *Sons:* see e.g. Exod. 4.22; Jer. 31.9. *Glory:* see Exod. 16.10; 24.16; 40.34. *Covenants:* see e.g. Gen. 6.18; 9.9; 17.7; Exod. 19.5; 34.10. *Law:* notably Exod. 20.1–17; Deut. 5.1–21. *Promises:* see 4.13–21.

9.6–29: God never intended that the promises should descend to more than a *remnant* (v. 27) of *Abraham's descendants,* for of Abraham's sons only Isaac was chosen (compare Gal. 4.21–5.1) and of Isaac's sons, only *Jacob.* **7:** Gen. 21.12. **9:** Gen. 18.10. **12:** Gen. 25.23. **13:** Mal. 1.2–3. **14–23:** Not injustice but mercy lies behind God's choices, for human beings have no claims against God's supreme sovereignty. **15:** Exod. 33.19.

the pot say to the potter, 'Why did you make me like this?'? ²¹Surely the potter can do what he likes with the clay. Is he not free to make two vessels out of the same lump, one to be treasured, the other for common use?

²²But if it is indeed God's purpose to display his retribution and to make his power known, can it be that he has with great patience tolerated vessels that were objects of retribution due for destruction, ²³precisely in order to make known the full wealth of his glory on vessels that were objects of mercy, prepared from the first for glory?

²⁴We are those objects of mercy, whom he has called from among Jews and Gentiles alike, ²⁵as he says in Hosea: 'Those who were not my people I will call my people, and the unloved I will call beloved. ²⁶In the very place where they were told, "You are no people of mine," they shall be called sons of the living God.' ²⁷But about Israel Isaiah makes this proclamation: 'Though the Israelites be countless as the sands of the sea, only a remnant shall be saved, ²⁸for the Lord's sentence on the land will be summary and final'; ²⁹as also he said previously, 'If the Lord of Hosts had not left us descendants, we should have become like Sodom, and no better than Gomorrah.'

³⁰Then what are we to say? That Gentiles, who made no effort after righteousness, nevertheless achieved it, a righteousness based on faith; ³¹whereas Israel made great efforts after a law of righteousness, but never attained to it. ³²Why was this? Because their efforts were not based on faith but, mistakenly, on deeds. They tripped over the 'stone' ³³mentioned in scripture: 'Here I lay in Zion a stone to trip over, a rock to stumble against; but he who has faith in it will not be put to shame.'

10 Friends, my heart's desire and my prayer to God is for their salvation.

²To their zeal for God I can testify; but it is an ill-informed zeal. ³For they ignore God's way of righteousness, and try to set up their own, and therefore they have not submitted themselves to God's righteousness; ⁴for Christ is the end of the law and brings righteousness for everyone who has faith.

⁵Of righteousness attained through the law Moses writes, 'Anyone who keeps it shall have life by it.' ⁶But the righteousness that comes by faith says, 'Do not say to yourself, "Who can go up to heaven?"' (that is, to bring Christ down) ⁷or, "Who can go down to the abyss?"' (to bring Christ up from the dead). ⁸And what does it say next? 'The word is near you: it is on your lips and in your heart'; and that means the word of faith which we proclaim. ⁹If the confession 'Jesus is Lord' is on your lips, and the faith that God raised him from the dead is in your heart, you will find salvation. ¹⁰For faith in the heart leads to righteousness, and confession on the lips leads to salvation.

¹¹Scripture says, 'No one who has faith in him will be put to shame': ¹²there is no distinction between Jew and Greek, because the same Lord is Lord of all, and has riches enough for all who call on him. ¹³For 'Everyone who calls on the name of the Lord will be saved.' ¹⁴But how could they call on him without having faith in him? And how could they have faith without having heard of him? And how could they hear without someone to spread the news? ¹⁵And how could anyone spread the news without being sent? As scripture says, 'How welcome are the feet of the messengers of good news!' ¹⁶It is true that not all have responded to the good news; as Isaiah says, 'Lord, who believed when they heard us?' ¹⁷So then faith does come from hearing, and hearing through the word of Christ.

¹⁸I ask, then: Can it be that they never

17: Exod. 9.16. **20:** Isa. 29.16; 45.9. **21:** Jer. 18.6. **24–26:** Now, as the church's mission shows, Gentiles are also *called*. Paul finds the promise in Hos. 1.10; 2.23. **27–28:** Isa. 10.22–23. *Remnant, descendants* (v. 29) prepare for 11.1–12. **29:** Isa. 1.9. *Sodom* and *Gomorrah:* Gen. 19.24–25.

9.30–10.10: God's righteousness comes by faith. 30: See 3.22; 10.20; Gal. 2.16; Phil. 3.9. **33:** Paul equates Christ with "the *stone* which the builders rejected" (Ps. 118.22), which he relates to Isa. 8.14–15; 28.16. Compare 1 Pet. 2.4 (and n.)–8. **10.4:** See 3.21–26; Gal. 3.19, 24. **5:** Although *anyone who keeps* the law will indeed be saved (Lev. 18.5; Gal. 3.12), the task is beyond our strength (3.9–20; 7.7–25). **6–10:** Deut. 9.4 and 30.12–14 are interpreted to mean that the *faith* which *leads to righteousness* and the *confession* of Christ that *leads to salvation* (v. 10) are now available. **9:** Compare Phil. 2.11.

10.11–21: Israel has been deaf to the *good news* of Christ. **11:** See 9.33; Isa. 28.16. **12:** See 3.29; Gal. 3.28. **13:** Joel 2.32 (*Lord* is taken to mean Christ). **15:** Isa. 52.7. **16:** Isa. 53.1. **17:** *Word of Christ:* the preaching about heard? Of course they did: 'Their voice has sounded all over the world, and their words to the ends of the earth.' [19] I ask again: Can it be that Israel never understood? Listen first to Moses: 'I will use a nation that is no nation to stir you to envy, and a foolish nation to rouse your anger.' [20] Isaiah is still more daring: 'I was found', he says, 'by those who were not looking for me; I revealed myself to those who never asked about me'; [21] while of Israel he says, 'All day long I have stretched out my hands to a disobedient and defiant people.'

11 I ASK, then: Has God rejected his people? Of course not! I am an Israelite myself, of the stock of Abraham, of the tribe of Benjamin. [2] God has not rejected the people he acknowledged of old as his own. Surely you know what scripture says in the story of Elijah—how he pleads with God against Israel: [3] 'Lord, they have killed your prophets, they have torn down your altars, and I alone am left, and they are seeking my life.' [4] But what was the divine word to him? 'I have left myself seven thousand men who have not knelt to Baal.' [5] In just the same way at the present time a 'remnant' has come into being, chosen by the grace of God. [6] But if it is by grace, then it does not rest on deeds, or grace would cease to be grace.

[7] What follows? What Israel sought, Israel has not attained, but the chosen few have attained it. The rest were hardened, [8] as it stands written: 'God has dulled their senses; he has given them blind eyes and deaf ears, and so it is to this day.' [9] Similarly David says:

May their table be a snare and a trap, their downfall and their retribution!

[10] May their eyes become darkened and blind!
Bow down their backs unceasingly!

[11] I ask, then: When they stumbled, was their fall final? Far from it! Through a false step on their part salvation has come to the Gentiles, and this in turn will stir them to envy. [12] If their false step means the enrichment of the world, if their falling short means the enrichment of the Gentiles, how much more will their coming to full strength mean!

[13] It is to you Gentiles that I am speaking. As an apostle to the Gentiles, I make much of that ministry, [14] yet always in the hope of stirring those of my own race to envy, and so saving some of them. [15] For if their rejection has meant the reconciliation of the world, what will their acceptance mean? Nothing less than life from the dead! [16] If the first loaf is holy, so is the whole batch. If the root is holy, so are the branches. [17] But if some of the branches have been lopped off, and you, a wild olive, have been grafted in among them, and have come to share the same root and sap as the olive, [18] do not make yourself superior to the branches. If you do, remember that you do not sustain the root: the root sustains you.

[19] You will say, 'Branches were lopped off so that I might be grafted in.' [20] Very well: they were lopped off for lack of faith, and by faith you hold your place. Put away your pride, and be on your guard; [21] for if God did not spare the natural branches, no more will he spare you. [22] Observe the kindness and the severity of God—severity to those who fell away, divine kindness to you provided that you remain within its scope; otherwise you too will be cut off, [23] whereas they, if they do

---

Christ. **18:** Ps. 19.4. **19–21:** The message is so simple that (*foolish*) Gentiles understand it; Israel, however, has failed to respond because they are a *disobedient* and *defiant* people (v. 21). **19:** Deut. 32.21. *Envy:* see 11.11, 14. **20–21:** Isa. 65.1–2.

   11.1–12: Israel's rejection is not complete as long as a *"remnant"* (v. 5) exists, i.e. the church. **1:** *Israelite myself:* see 9.4 n.; 2 Cor. 11.22; Phil. 3.5. **2–4:** *Elijah* mistakenly believed that Israel's rebellion was complete (1 Kgs. 19.10, 14, 18). **2:** Ps. 94.14. **6:** See 4.4–5; Gal. 3.18. **7–12:** At present God *has dulled* Israel's *senses* (vv. 7–10, 25), but only to allow time to call the *Gentiles*, who will in turn *stir* Israel *to envy* (v. 11; 10.19). **8:** Isa. 29.10; Deut. 29.4 (compare Mk. 4.10–12). **9–10:** Ps. 69.22–23. *David:* see 4.6 n.

   11.13–24: Israel is God's olive tree (Jer. 11.16; Hos. 14.6). **13:** See 1.5; 15.16; Gal. 1.16; 2.9. **14:** See 1 Cor. 9.22. **15:** Without Israel God has achieved the *reconciliation of the world* (5.10–11), but when Israel receives God's *acceptance*, what a glorious consummation! **16:** *First loaf* (Num. 15.20–21) and *root* probably mean the ancestors (patriarchs) (v. 28; 9.5). **17:** *The branches . . . lopped off* are the Jews, who lack faith (v. 20); the Gentiles are shoots from a *wild olive . . . grafted in* "against all nature" (v. 24). **21–22:** Compare 1 Cor. 10.12.

not continue faithless, will be grafted in, since it is in God's power to graft them in again. 24 For if you were cut from your native wild olive and against nature grafted into the cultivated olive, how much more readily will they, the natural olive branches, be grafted into their native stock!

25 There is a divine secret here, my friends, which I want to share with you, to keep you from thinking yourselves wise: this partial hardening has come on Israel only until the Gentiles have been admitted in full strength; 26 once that has happened, the whole of Israel will be saved, in accordance with scripture:

From Zion shall come the Deliverer;
  he shall remove wickedness from Jacob.
27 And this is the covenant I will grant
  them,
  when I take away their sins.

28 Judged by their response to the gospel, they are God's enemies for your sake; but judged by his choice, they are dear to him for the sake of the patriarchs; 29 for the gracious gifts of God and his calling are irrevocable. 30 Just as formerly you were disobedient to God, but now have received mercy because of their disobedience, 31 so now, because of the mercy shown to you, they have proved disobedient, but only in order that they too may receive mercy. 32 For in shutting all mankind in the prison of their disobedience, God's purpose was to show mercy to all mankind.

33 How deep are the wealth
  and the wisdom and the knowledge of
    God!
  How inscrutable his judgements,
  how unsearchable his ways!
34 'Who knows the mind of the Lord?
  Who has been his counsellor?'
35 'Who has made a gift to him first,

and earned a gift in return?'
36 From him and through him and for
  him all things exist —
  to him be glory for ever! Amen.

Christian service and the community

12 THEREFORE, my friends, I implore you by God's mercy to offer your very selves to him: a living sacrifice, dedicated and fit for his acceptance, the worship offered by mind and heart. 2 Conform no longer to the pattern of this present world, but be transformed by the renewal of your minds. Then you will be able to discern the will of God, and to know what is good, acceptable, and perfect.

3 By authority of the grace God has given me I say to everyone among you: do not think too highly of yourself, but form a sober estimate based on the measure of faith that God has dealt to each of you. 4 For just as in a single human body there are many limbs and organs, all with different functions, 5 so we who are united with Christ, though many, form one body, and belong to one another as its limbs and organs.

6 Let us use the different gifts allotted to each of us by God's grace: the gift of inspired utterance, for example, let us use in proportion to our faith; 7 the gift of administration to administer, the gift of teaching to teach, 8 the gift of counselling to counsel. If you give to charity, give without grudging; if you are a leader, lead with enthusiasm; if you help others in distress, do it cheerfully.

9 Love in all sincerity, loathing evil and holding fast to the good. 10 Let love of the Christian community show itself in mutual affection. Esteem others more highly than yourself.

11 With unflagging zeal, aglow with the Spirit, serve the Lord. 12 Let hope keep you joyful; in trouble stand firm; persist in

---

24: The restoration of Israel will be swifter than the mission to the Gentiles.

11.25–36: The salvation of all humankind, both Gentiles and Jews, will be accomplished by God's *mercy* (v. 32). **25–27:** *Hardening:* see vv. 8, 10. *Gentiles . . . in full strength* and *the whole of Israel:* corporately but not necessarily every individual. *Scripture:* Isa. 59.20–21; 27.9. **34:** Isa. 40.13 (1 Cor. 2.16). **35:** Job 41.11. **36:** See 1 Cor. 8.6; Col. 1.16.

12.1–8: The dedicated life. 1: See 6.13, 16, 19. *A living sacrifice:* in contrast to the offering of a dead animal. **2:** See 8.5–13. **3:** *Grace . . . given me:* Paul's apostleship (see 1.5). *Measure of faith:* the amount and nature of the spiritual gifts (v. 6) received by faith. **4–8:** The passage is a reworking of 1 Cor. 12.4–31. **6:** *In proportion to our faith:* see v. 3 n.

12.9–21: The greatness of love (see 1 Cor. ch. 13).

prayer; [13]contribute to the needs of God's people, and practise hospitality. [14]Call down blessings on your persecutors—blessings, not curses. [15]Rejoice with those who rejoice, weep with those who weep. [16]Live in agreement with one another. Do not be proud, but be ready to mix with humble people. Do not keep thinking how wise you are.

[17]Never pay back evil for evil. Let your aims be such as all count honourable. [18]If possible, so far as it lies with you, live at peace with all. [19]My dear friends, do not seek revenge, but leave a place for divine retribution; for there is a text which reads, 'Vengeance is mine, says the Lord, I will repay.' [20]But there is another text: 'If your enemy is hungry, feed him; if he is thirsty, give him a drink; by doing this you will heap live coals on his head.' [21]Do not let evil conquer you, but use good to conquer evil.

13 Every person must submit to the authorities in power, for all authority comes from God, and the existing authorities are instituted by him. [2]It follows that anyone who rebels against authority is resisting a divine institution, and those who resist have themselves to thank for the punishment they will receive. [3]Governments hold no terrors for the law-abiding but only for the criminal. You wish to have no fear of the authorities? Then continue to do right and you will have their approval, [4]for they are God's agents working for your good. But if you are doing wrong, then you will have cause to fear them; it is not for nothing that they hold the power of the sword, for they are God's agents of punishment bringing retribution on the offender. [5]That is why you are obliged to sub-

mit. It is an obligation imposed not merely by fear of retribution but by conscience. [6]That is also why you pay taxes. The authorities are in God's service and it is to this they devote their energies.

[7]Discharge your obligations to everyone; pay tax and levy, reverence and respect, to those to whom they are due. [8]Leave no debt outstanding, but remember the debt of love you owe one another. He who loves his neighbour has met every requirement of the law. [9]The commandments, 'You shall not commit adultery, you shall not commit murder, you shall not steal, you shall not covet,' and any other commandment there may be, are all summed up in the one rule, 'Love your neighbour as yourself.' [10]Love cannot wrong a neighbour; therefore love is the fulfilment of the law.

[11]Always remember that this is the hour of crisis: it is high time for you to wake out of sleep, for deliverance is nearer to us now than it was when first we believed. [12]It is far on in the night; day is near. Let us therefore throw off the deeds of darkness and put on the armour of light. [13]Let us behave with decency as befits the day: no drunken orgies, no debauchery or vice, no quarrels or jealousies! [14]Let Christ Jesus himself be the armour that you wear; give your unspiritual nature no opportunity to satisfy its desires.

14 ACCEPT anyone who is weak in faith without debate about his misgivings. [2]For instance, one person may have faith

13:10 **the fulfilment of the law:** *or* the whole content of the law.

13: *Hospitality:* see 16.2 n. **14:** See Matt. 5.44. **16:** Prov. 3.7. **17a:** Prov. 20.22; 1 Thess. 5.15. **17b:** Prov. 3.4 (Sept.); 2 Cor. 8.21. **19:** *Do not seek revenge:* Lev. 19.18; Matt. 5.39. *Leave a place for:* leave it to. *A text:* Deut. 32.35. **20:** Prov. 25.21–22 (Matt. 5.44). *Live coals:* deep shame and remorse.

13.1–7: The Christian's duty to the state is to be an obedient subject (compare Wisd. 6.1–5; 1 Pet. 2.13–17; 3.13). Paul had experienced both the benefits of the Roman government and its *punishment* (v. 2; see 2 Cor. 11.25 n.), but since he believed that the government's *authority comes from God,* he counseled obedience. **6–7:** See Mk. 12.17.

13.8–10: Love sums up the law. 9: *The commandments:* Exod. 20.13–15, 17; Deut. 5.17–19, 21 (see Rom. 7.7). *One rule:* Lev. 19.18 (compare Mk. 12.31; Matt. 19.18; Gal. 5.14).

13.11–14: The end of the age approaches. 11: We must *wake* and put the obligation of love into action. The passage is a reworking of 1 Thess. 5.1–8. **12:** *Armour:* see 1 Thess. 5.8; Eph. 6.14–17. **14:** See 6.12–14 n.; Gal. 3.27 n.

14.1–23: Love respects the scruples of others. Those who remain in bondage to laws about *meat* (vv. 6, 21), *wine* (v. 21), and sabbath observance (vv. 5–6) are *weak in faith* (v. 1). Paul regards these scruples as unnecessary (v. 14), but counsels tolerance based on *love* (v. 15). Paul here adapts 1 Cor. 8.7–13 and strong enough to eat all kinds of food, while another who is weaker eats only vegetables. 3 Those who eat meat must not look down on those who do not, and those who do not eat meat must not pass judgement on those who do; for God has accepted them. 4 Who are you to pass judgement on someone else's servant? Whether he stands or falls is his own Master's business; and stand he will, because his Master has power to enable him to stand.

5 Again, some make a distinction between this day and that; others regard all days alike. Everyone must act on his own convictions. 6 Those who honour the day honour the Lord, and those who eat meat also honour the Lord, since when they eat they give thanks to God; and those who abstain have the Lord in mind when abstaining, since they too give thanks to God.

7 For none of us lives, and equally none of us dies, for himself alone. 8 If we live, we live for the Lord; and if we die, we die for the Lord. So whether we live or die, we belong to the Lord. 9 This is why Christ died and lived again, to establish his lordship over both dead and living. 10 You, then, why do you pass judgement on your fellow-Christian? And you, why do you look down on your fellow-Christian? We shall all stand before God's tribunal; 11 for we read in scripture, 'As I live, says the Lord, to me every knee shall bow and every tongue acknowledge God.' 12 So, you see, each of us will be answerable to God.

13 Let us therefore cease judging one another, but rather make up our minds to place no obstacle or stumbling block in a fellow-Christian's way. 14 All that I know of the Lord Jesus convinces me that nothing is impure in itself; only, if anyone considers something impure, then for him it is impure. 15 If your fellow-Christian is outraged by what you eat, then you are no longer guided by love. Do not by your eating be the ruin of one for whom Christ died! 16 You must not let what you think good be brought into disrepute; 17 for the kingdom of God is not eating and drinking, but justice, peace, and joy, inspired

by the Holy Spirit. 18 Everyone who shows himself a servant of Christ in this way is acceptable to God and approved by men.

19 Let us, then, pursue the things that make for peace and build up the common life. 20 Do not destroy the work of God for the sake of food. Everything is pure in itself, but it is wrong to eat if by eating you cause another to stumble. 21 It is right to abstain from eating meat or drinking wine or from anything else which causes a fellow-Christian to stumble. 22 If you have some firm conviction, keep it between yourself and God. Anyone who can make his decision without misgivings is fortunate. 23 But anyone who has misgivings and yet eats is guilty, because his action does not arise from conviction, and anything which does not arise from conviction is sin.

15 1 Those of us who are strong must accept as our own burden the tender scruples of the weak, and not just please ourselves. 2 Each of us must consider his neighbour and think what is for his good and will build up the common life. 3 Christ too did not please himself; to him apply the words of scripture, 'The reproaches of those who reproached you fell on me.' 4 The scriptures written long ago were all written for our instruction, in order that through the encouragement they give us we may maintain our hope with perseverance. 5 And may God, the source of all perseverance and all encouragement, grant that you may agree with one another after the manner of Christ Jesus, 6 and so with one mind and one voice may praise the God and Father of our Lord Jesus Christ.

7 In a word, accept one another as Christ accepted us, to the glory of God. 8 Remember that Christ became a servant of the Jewish people to maintain the faithfulness of God by making good his promises to the patriarchs, 9 and by giving the Gentiles cause to glorify God for his mercy. As scripture says, 'Therefore I will praise you among the Gentiles and sing hymns to your name'; 10 and again, 'Gen-

14:23 *See note on 16:27.*

10.27–11.1 for the benefit of the Romans. **5:** Compare Gal. 4.10. **7:** See Gal. 2.20; 2 Cor. 5.15. **8:** *Live . . . die:* see Phil. 1.20–21. **10:** *Tribunal:* final judgment (see 2.5, 16; 2 Cor. 5.10). **11:** Isa. 45.23 (Phil. 2.10–11). **14:** See Mk. 7.18–19.

15.1–13: To put others first is to imitate Christ. 3: See Phil. 2.5–8; 2 Cor. 8.9. *Scripture:* Ps. 69.9. **4:** See 4.23–24; 1 Cor. 9.10; 10.11. **8:** Christ was born a Jew, obedient to the law (Gal. 4.4–5), so as to *maintain* God's *faithfulness* to the *promises to the patriarchs* (see 4.13–21; 9.4–13). **9–12:** As a result the *Gentiles* share tiles, join in celebration with his people'; [11] and yet again, 'All Gentiles, praise the Lord; let all peoples praise him.' [12] Once again, Isaiah says, 'The Scion of Jesse shall come, a ruler who rises to govern the Gentiles; on him shall they set their hope.' [13] And may God, who is the ground of hope, fill you with all joy and peace as you lead the life of faith until, by the power of the Holy Spirit, you overflow with hope.

[14] My friends, I have no doubt in my own mind that you yourselves are full of goodness and equipped with knowledge of every kind, well able to give advice to one another; [15] nevertheless I have written to refresh your memory, and written somewhat boldly at times, in virtue of the gift I have from God. [16] His grace has made me a minister of Christ Jesus to the Gentiles; and in the service of the gospel of God it is my priestly task to offer the Gentiles to him as an acceptable sacrifice, consecrated by the Holy Spirit.

[17] In Christ Jesus I have indeed grounds for pride in the service of God. [18] I will venture to speak only of what Christ has done through me to bring the Gentiles into his allegiance, by word and deed, [19] by the power of signs and portents, and by the power of the Holy Spirit. I have completed the preaching of the gospel of Christ from Jerusalem as far round as Illyricum. [20] But I have always made a point of taking the gospel to places where the name of Christ has not been heard, not wanting to build on another man's foundation; [21] as scripture says,

Those who had no news of him shall see,
and those who never heard of him shall understand.

[22] That is why I have been prevented all this time from coming to you. [23] But now I have no further scope in these parts, and I have been longing for many years to visit you [24] on my way to Spain; for I hope to see you in passing, and to be sent on my way there with your support after having enjoyed your company for a while. [25] But at the moment I am on my way to Jerusalem, on an errand to God's people there. [26] For Macedonia and Achaia have resolved to raise a fund for the benefit of the poor among God's people at Jerusalem. [27] They have resolved to do so, and indeed they are under an obligation to them. For if the Jewish Christians shared their spiritual treasures with the Gentiles, the Gentiles have a clear duty to contribute to their material needs. [28] So when I have finished this business and seen the proceeds safely delivered to them, I shall set out for Spain and visit you on the way; [29] I am sure that when I come it will be with a full measure of the blessing of Christ.

[30] I implore you by our Lord Jesus Christ and by the love that the Spirit inspires, be my allies in the fight; pray to God for me [31] that I may be saved from unbelievers in Judaea and that my errand to Jerusalem may find acceptance with God's people, [32] in order that by his will I may come to you in a happy frame of mind and enjoy a time of rest with you. [33] The God of peace be with you all. Amen.

Greetings

16 I COMMEND to you Phoebe, a fellow-Christian who is a minister in the church at Cenchreae. [2] Give her, in the fellowship of the Lord, a welcome worthy of

15:33 *See note on 16:27.*   16:1 **minister:** *or* deacon.

in God's promises: Ps. 18.49; Deut. 32.43; Ps. 117.1; Isa. 11.10. **12:** *Scion of Jesse:* Messiah; see Matt. 1.1 n.

15.14–21: A polite postscript lest the Romans consider him presumptuous (see Introduction; 1.12). **14:** *One another:* perhaps an indication that they have no apostolic leader. **19:** *Signs and portents:* see 2 Cor. 12.12; Gal. 3.5. *Jerusalem . . . Illyricum:* Paul has been moving round the Mediterranean Sea systematically. He hopes that this program will carry him to Rome and Spain (v. 24). **20:** Paul makes it a principle not to work where other missionaries have preceded him (see 1 Cor. 3.10–15; 2 Cor. 10.15–16). **21:** Isa. 52.15.

15.22–33: Paul plans to visit Rome on his way to Spain. **22–23:** See 1.10–13. *No further scope:* see Introduction and v. 19 n. **25:** Paul's *errand* is the collection (see Introduction). **26:** Galatia is not mentioned. Paul's angry letter to them may have resulted in their abandoning the project (contrast 2 Cor. 8.1–9.15 n.; 8.10–11 n.). **30–32:** Presumably Paul's fears were justified and this visit to *Jerusalem* resulted in his arrest (Acts 21.17–24.27).

16.1–23: The closing greetings are unusually numerous. Paul lists people known by the Romans who could

God's people, and support her in any business in which she may need your help, for she has herself been a good friend to many, including myself.

³Give my greetings to Prisca and Aquila, my fellow-workers in Christ Jesus. ⁴They risked their necks to save my life, and not I alone but all the gentile churches are grateful to them. ⁵Greet also the church that meets at their house.

Give my greetings to my dear friend Epaenetus, the first convert to Christ in Asia, ⁶and to Mary, who worked so hard for you. ⁷Greet Andronicus and Junia, my fellow-countrymen and comrades in captivity, who are eminent among the apostles and were Christians before I was.

⁸Greetings to Ampliatus, my dear friend in the fellowship of the Lord, ⁹to Urban my comrade in Christ, and to my dear Stachys. ¹⁰My greetings to Apelles, well proved in Christ's service, to the household of Aristobulus, ¹¹to my countryman Herodion, and to those of the household of Narcissus who are in the Lord's fellowship. ¹²Greet Tryphaena and Tryphosa, who work hard in the Lord's service, and dear Persis who has worked hard in his service for so long. ¹³Give my greetings to Rufus, an outstanding follower of the Lord, and to his mother, whom I call mother too. ¹⁴Greet Asyncritus, Phlegon, Hermes, Patrobas, Hermas, and any other Christians who are with them. ¹⁵Greet Philologus and Julia, Nereus and his sister, and Olympas, and all God's people who are with them.

¹⁶Greet one another with the kiss of peace. All Christ's churches send you their greetings.

¹⁷I implore you, my friends, keep an eye on those who stir up quarrels and lead others astray, contrary to the teaching you received. Avoid them; ¹⁸such people are servants not of Christ our Lord but of their own appetites, and they seduce the minds of simple people with smooth and specious words. ¹⁹The fame of your obedience has spread everywhere, and this makes me happy about you. I want you to be expert in goodness, but innocent of evil, ²⁰and the God of peace will soon crush Satan beneath your feet. The grace of our Lord Jesus be with you!

²¹Greetings to you from my colleague Timothy, and from Lucius, Jason, and Sosipater my fellow-countrymen. ²²(I Tertius, who took this letter down, add my Christian greetings.) ²³Greetings also from Gaius, my host and host of the whole congregation, and from Erastus, treasurer of this city, and our brother Quartus.

²⁵To him who has power to make you stand firm, according to my gospel and the proclamation of Jesus Christ, according to the revelation of that divine secret kept in silence for long ages ²⁶but now disclosed, and by the eternal God's command made known to all nations through prophetic scriptures, to bring them to faith and obedience — ²⁷to the only wise God through Jesus Christ be glory for endless ages! Amen.

16:7 **Junia:** *or* Junias.   16:15 **Julia:** *or* Julias.
16:20 **The grace . . . with you:** *These words are omitted at this point in some witnesses; in some, these or similar words are given as verse 24, and in some others after verse 27.*
16:23 *After this verse some witnesses add* ²⁴The grace of our Lord Jesus Christ be with you all! Amen.
16:27 *After this verse some witnesses add* The grace of our Lord Jesus Christ be with you! *Some witnesses place verses 25–27 at the end of chapter 14, one other places them at the end of chapter 15, and others omit them altogether.*

vouch for him. Nothing is known about most of these persons. **2:** *Welcome:* Christian travelers depended on the hospitality of other Christians (see 12.13). **3–5:** *Prisca* and *Aquila* were in Ephesus (1 Cor. 16.19); now they are back (Acts 18.2) at Rome. *House:* see v. 23 n. **7:** *Apostles:* see 1 Cor. 9.1 n. **16:** The Christian *kiss* of ceremonial greeting (1 Cor. 16.20; 2 Cor. 13.12; 1 Thess. 5.26; 1 Pet. 5.14) became a part of the church's liturgy (see 1 Cor. 16.22 n.). **17–18:** See Gal. 1.6–9; 6.12–13; 2 Cor. 11.12–15; Phil. 3.2–3, 18–19. **19:** *Expert, innocent:* see 1 Cor. 14.20; Matt. 10.16; Jer. 4.22. **20:** *Satan,* the serpent, will be crushed (Gen. 3.15); see 1 Cor. 15.25. *Grace . . . :* see 2 Cor. 13.14 n. **21:** *Timothy:* see 1 Cor. 16.10 n. **22:** Paul dictated (compare 1 Cor. 1.16 n.) this letter to the scribe *Tertius.* **23:** *Gaius:* the Christian of 1 Cor. 1.14? *Host:* early Christians worshiped in houses (v. 5), not yet in churches.

    16.25–27: The benediction echoes some of the major themes of the letter (compare 1.2–6). **25:** *Gospel:* see 2.16; Gal. 1.6–9. *Secret:* see 1 Cor. 2.6–7; Col. 1.26–27. **26:** *All nations:* see 1.5 n.

THE FIRST LETTER OF PAUL TO THE

Corinthians

This letter gives a uniquely comprehensive picture of an early Christian congregation and of its founder (3.6, 10), Paul. It contains the earliest written tradition of Jesus' resurrection (15.3–8) and of the Lord's Supper (11.23–26), as well as the moving "hymn" on Christian love (ch. 13). This is apparently the second letter Paul wrote to the Corinthians. The previous letter, mentioned in 5.9, is lost (unless 2 Cor. 6.14–7.1 is a surviving fragment), but the Corinthians' reply to that letter provides the subject matter for chs. 7–16 of the present letter: marriage (7.1–24), celibacy (7.25–40), food offered to idols (8.1–11.1), worship (11.2–34), spiritual gifts (especially glossolalia, the gift of tongues; chs. 12–14), bodily resurrection (ch. 15), the "collection" of money for the Jerusalem Christians (16.1–11), and Apollos (16.12). But first Paul reasserts his authority at Corinth by dealing with three disciplinary lapses which have occurred there: congregational factions (chs. 1–4), a case of immorality (ch. 5), and lawsuits among Christians (ch. 6).

The letter was written from Ephesus (16.8). Paul's directions about the "collection" date the letter a year or so before 2 Cor. chs. 1–9 (see 2 Cor. 8.10; 9.2 and Introduction to Rom.).

1 FROM Paul, apostle of Christ Jesus by God's call and by his will, together with our colleague Sosthenes, ²to God's church at Corinth, dedicated to him in Christ Jesus, called to be his people, along with all who invoke the name of our Lord Jesus Christ wherever they may be—their Lord as well as ours.

³Grace and peace to you from God our Father and the Lord Jesus Christ.

⁴I am always thanking God for you. I thank him for his grace given to you in Christ Jesus; ⁵I thank him for all the enrichment that has come to you in Christ. You possess full knowledge and you can give full expression to it, ⁶because what we testified about Christ has been confirmed in your experience. ⁷There is indeed no single gift you lack, while you wait expectantly for our Lord Jesus Christ to reveal himself. ⁸He will keep you firm to the end, without reproach on the day of our Lord Jesus. ⁹It is God himself who called you to share in the life of his Son Jesus Christ our Lord; and God keeps faith.

True and false wisdom

¹⁰I APPEAL to you, my friends, in the name of our Lord Jesus Christ: agree among yourselves, and avoid divisions; let there be complete unity of mind and thought. ¹¹My friends, it has been brought to my notice by Chloe's people that there are quarrels among you. ¹²What I mean is this: each of you is saying, 'I am for Paul,' or 'I am for Apollos'; 'I am for Cephas,' or 'I am for Christ.' ¹³Surely Christ has not been divided! Was it Paul who was crucified for you? Was it in Paul's name that you were baptized? ¹⁴Thank God, I never baptized any of you,

1.1–3: Salutation: see Rom. 1.1–7 nn. **1:** *Sosthenes* is unknown (but see Acts 18.17).

1.4–9: Opening thanksgiving: see Rom. 1.8–15 n. **8:** The *day* refers to Christ's impending (7.29, 31) return to end the present age (2 Thess. 1.7–2.12) and to establish the kingdom (15.23–26, 50) in a time of severe testing (3.13–15; 4.5; 5.5).

1.10–4.21: Paul's apostolic authority. In the face of divided loyalties Paul asserts his authority as founder (3.5–15), teacher (2.6–7; 3.1–2), and father (4.14–15) of the congregation.

1.10–17: Factiousness in Corinth. 11: *Chloe's people* are slaves or employees of this unknown lady. **12:** *Apollos:* the principal missionary at Corinth after Paul (3.4–6; 4.6; 16.12; see Acts 18.24–19.1). *Cephas:* the Aram. equivalent of "Peter" (meaning "rock"; see Matt. 16.18). **14–17:** Baptism was not unimportant to Paul except Crispus and Gaius; 15 no one can say you were baptized in my name. 16 I did of course baptize the household of Stephanas; I cannot think of anyone else. 17 Christ did not send me to baptize, but to proclaim the gospel; and to do it without recourse to the skills of rhetoric, lest the cross of Christ be robbed of its effect.

18 The message of the cross is sheer folly to those on the way to destruction, but to us, who are on the way to salvation, it is the power of God. 19 Scripture says, 'I will destroy the wisdom of the wise, and bring to nothing the cleverness of the clever.' 20 Where is your wise man now, your man of learning, your subtle debater of this present age? God has made the wisdom of this world look foolish! 21 As God in his wisdom ordained, the world failed to find him by its wisdom, and he chose by the folly of the gospel to save those who have faith. 22 Jews demand signs, Greeks look for wisdom, 23 but we proclaim Christ nailed to the cross; and though this is an offence to Jews and folly to Gentiles, 24 yet to those who are called, Jews and Greeks alike, he is the power of God and the wisdom of God.

25 The folly of God is wiser than human wisdom, and the weakness of God stronger than human strength. 26 My friends, think what sort of people you are, whom God has called. Few of you are wise by any human standard, few powerful or of noble birth. 27 Yet, to shame the wise, God has chosen what the world counts folly, and to shame what is strong, God has chosen what the world counts weakness. 28 He has chosen things without rank or standing in the world, mere nothings, to overthrow the existing order. 29 So no place is left for any human pride in the presence of God. 30 By God's act you are in Christ Jesus; God has made him our wisdom, and in him we have our righteousness, our holiness, our liberation. 31 There-

fore, in the words of scripture, 'If anyone must boast, let him boast of the Lord.'

2 So it was, my friends, that I came to you, without any pretensions to eloquence or wisdom in declaring the truth about God. 2 I resolved that while I was with you I would not claim to know anything but Jesus Christ — Christ nailed to the cross. 3 I came before you in weakness, in fear, in great trepidation. 4 The word I spoke, the gospel I proclaimed, did not sway you with clever arguments; it carried conviction by spiritual power, 5 so that your faith might be built not on human wisdom but on the power of God.

6 Among the mature I do speak words of wisdom, though not a wisdom belonging to this present age or to its governing powers, already in decline; 7 I speak God's hidden wisdom, his secret purpose framed from the very beginning to bring us to our destined glory. 8 None of the powers that rule the world has known that wisdom; if they had, they would not have crucified the Lord of glory. 9 Scripture speaks of 'things beyond our seeing, things beyond our hearing, things beyond our imagining, all prepared by God for those who love him'; 10 and these are what God has revealed to us through the Spirit. For the Spirit explores everything, even the depths of God's own nature. 11 Who knows what a human being is but the human spirit within him? In the same way, only the Spirit of God knows what God is. 12 And we have received this Spirit from God, not the spirit of the world, so that we may know all that God has lavished on us; 13 and, because we are interpreting spiritual truths to those who have the Spirit, we speak of these gifts of God in words taught us not by our human wisdom but by the Spirit. 14 An unspiritual person refuses what belongs to the Spirit of God; it is folly to him; he cannot grasp it,

2:1 **declaring . . . God:** *some witnesses read* declaring God's secret purpose.

(see 6.11; Rom. 6.3–4), but the actual rite he usually left to his assistants. **14:** *Crispus:* see Acts 18.8. *Gaius:* see Rom. 16.23 n. **16:** Paul dictated his letters (see 16.21–24 n. and Rom. 16.22 n.). Here he corrects himself. *Stephanas:* see 16.15–17 n.

1.18–2.5: The paradox of the cross: God saves through weakness and in spite of folly, revealing in *Christ nailed to the cross* (v. 23) God's true *power* and *wisdom* (v. 24). **19:** Isa. 29.14. **22:** *Signs* (or miracles): see Mk. 8.11–12. *Wisdom:* see 2.4–8. **31:** Jer. 9.24 (2 Cor. 10.17). **2.3–4:** See 2 Cor. 10.10.

2.6–16: The true wisdom of God is given by the Spirit. **6–8:** *This present age* (in contrast to the coming age or kingdom): see 1.8 n. The *governing powers* (or "elemental spirits" or "authorities") are demonic astral or planetary beings that *rule the world* (Gal. 4.3, 9; Rom. 8.38–39; Col. 1.16). By crucifying Christ they have brought their own coming destruction upon themselves (15.24; Col. 2.14–15). **9:** Perhaps Isa. 64.4. **13:** See because it needs to be judged in the light of the Spirit. 15 But a spiritual person can judge the worth of everything, yet is not himself subject to judgement by others. 16 Scripture indeed asks, 'Who can know the mind of the Lord or be his counsellor?' Yet we possess the mind of Christ.

Servants of Christ

3 BUT I could not talk to you, my friends, as people who have the Spirit; I had to deal with you on the natural plane, as infants in Christ. 2 I fed you on milk, instead of solid food, for which you were not yet ready. Indeed, you are still not ready for it; 3 you are still on the merely natural plane. Can you not see that as long as there is jealousy and strife among you, you are unspiritual, living on the purely human level? 4 When one declares, 'I am for Paul,' and another, 'I am for Apollos,' are you not all too human?

5 After all, what is Apollos? What is Paul? Simply God's agents in bringing you to faith. Each of us performed the task which the Lord assigned to him: 6 I planted the seed, and Apollos watered it; but God made it grow. 7 It is not the gardeners with their planting and watering who count, but God who makes it grow. 8 Whether they plant or water, they work as a team, though each will get his own pay for his own labour. 9 We are fellow-workers in God's service; and you are God's garden.

Or again, you are God's building. 10 God gave me the privilege of laying the foundation like a skilled master builder; others put up the building. Let each take care how he builds. 11 There can be no other foundation than the one already laid: I mean Jesus Christ himself. 12 If anyone builds on that foundation with gold, silver, and precious stones, or with wood, hay, and straw, 13 the work that each does will at last be brought to light; the day of judgement will expose it. For that day dawns in fire, and the fire will test the worth of each person's work. 14 If anyone's building survives, he will be rewarded;

15 if it burns down, he will have to bear the loss; yet he will escape with his life, though only by passing through the fire. 16 Surely you know that you are God's temple, where the Spirit of God dwells. 17 Anyone who destroys God's temple will himself be destroyed by God, because the temple of God is holy; and you are that temple.

18 Make no mistake about this: if there is anyone among you who fancies himself wise — wise, I mean, by the standards of this age — he must become a fool if he is to be truly wise. 19 For the wisdom of this world is folly in God's sight. Scripture says, 'He traps the wise in their own cunning,' 20 and again, 'The Lord knows that the arguments of the wise are futile.' 21 So never make any human being a cause for boasting. For everything belongs to you — 22 Paul, Apollos, and Cephas, the world, life, and death, the present and the future, all are yours — 23 and you belong to Christ, and Christ to God.

4 We are to be regarded as Christ's subordinates and as stewards of the secrets of God. 2 Now stewards are required to show themselves trustworthy. 3 To me it matters not at all if I am called to account by you or by any human court. Nor do I pass judgement on myself, 4 for I have nothing on my conscience; but that does not prove me innocent. My judge is the Lord. 5 So pass no premature judgement; wait until the Lord comes. He will bring to light what darkness hides and disclose our inward motives; then will be the time for each to receive commendation from God.

6 My friends, I have applied all this to Apollos and myself for your benefit, so that you may take our case as an example, and learn the true meaning of 'nothing beyond what stands written', and may not be inflated with pride as you take sides in support of one against another. 7 My friend, who makes you so important? What do you possess that was not given you? And if you received it as a gift, why take the credit to yourself?

8 No doubt you already have all you could

3:9 We . . . service: or We are God's fellow-workers.

chs. 12–14. 15: See 4.3–5. 16: Isa. 40.13.

3.1–23: Teachers and pupils. 1–2: Infants: see 13.11; 14.20. 3–4: See 1.12. 8: Pay: see vv. 14–15 n. 10: See Rom. 15.20 n. 13: The day: see 1.8 n. 14–15: Good work will be rewarded, but even a bad worker will escape, i.e. be saved. 16: Surely you know: Paul had instructed them (possibly in his previous letter; see Introduction and 2 Cor. 6.16). 19: Job 5.13. 20: Ps. 94.11. 22: See 1.12.

4.1–13: The humility of the apostles. 5: See 1.8 n.; 5.12–13 n.; Matt. 13.24–30, 36–43. 6: Builders (see desire; you have come into your fortune already! Without us you have come into your kingdom. How I wish you had indeed come into your kingdom; then you might share it with us! [9] For it seems to me God has made us apostles the last act in the show, like men condemned to death in the arena, a spectacle to the whole universe — to angels as well as men. [10] We are fools for Christ's sake, while you are sensible Christians! We are weak; you are powerful! You are honoured; we are in disgrace! [11] To this day we go hungry and thirsty and in rags; we are beaten up; we wander from place to place; [12] we wear ourselves out earning a living with our own hands. People curse us, and we bless; they persecute us, and we submit; [13] they slander us, and we try to be conciliatory. To this day we are treated as the scum of the earth, as the dregs of humanity.

[14] I am not writing this to shame you, but to bring you to reason; for you are my dear children. [15] You may have thousands of tutors in Christ, but you have only one father; for in Christ Jesus you are my offspring, and mine alone, through the preaching of the gospel. [16] I appeal to you therefore to follow my example. [17] That is why I have sent Timothy, who is a dear son to me and a trustworthy Christian, to remind you of my way of life in Christ, something I teach everywhere in all the churches. [18] There are certain persons who are filled with self-importance because they think I am not coming to Corinth. [19] I shall come very soon, if it is the Lord's will;

and then I shall take the measure of these self-important people, not by what they say, but by what they can do, [20] for the kingdom of God is not a matter of words, but of power. [21] Choose, then: am I to come to you with a rod in my hand, or with love and a gentle spirit?

Sexual immorality

5 I ACTUALLY hear reports of sexual immorality among you, immorality such as even pagans do not tolerate: the union of a man with his stepmother. [2] And you are proud of yourselves! You ought to have gone into mourning; anyone who behaves like that should be turned out of your community. [3] For my part, though I am absent in body, I am present in spirit, and have already reached my judgement on the man who did this thing, as if I were indeed present: [4] when you are all assembled in the name of our Lord Jesus, and I am with you in spirit, through the power of our Lord Jesus you are [5] to consign this man to Satan for the destruction of his body, so that his spirit may be saved on the day of the Lord.

[6] Your self-satisfaction ill becomes you. Have you never heard the saying, 'A little leaven leavens all the dough'? [7] Get rid of the old leaven and then you will be a new batch of unleavened dough. Indeed you already are, because Christ our Passover lamb has been sacrificed. [8] So we who observe the festival must not use the old leaven, the leaven of

5.10–11) besides Paul and *Apollos* should fear judgment. **8–13:** With biting irony Paul contrasts his humiliating hardships with their complacency. **9:** *Arena:* compare 15.32. *Angels:* see 6.2–3 n. **12:** *Earning a living with our own hands* (see Acts 18.3) is an especially bitter complaint (see 2 Cor. 11.7–10 n.).

4.14–21: Paul's fatherly authority extends itself to the Corinthians by means of *Timothy's* mission and Paul's impending visit. **15:** *Tutors* were normally slaves who supervised a child's conduct outside of school; their temporary (Gal. 3.24) authority derived from the charge's *father*. **17:** *Timothy:* see 16.10 n. **18–19:** Sternly Paul speaks of his visit as *very soon;* his actual plans are more elaborate (16.5–9). **20:** *Power,* i.e. of the Spirit (2.4).

5.1–13: A case of sexual immorality. 1: Paul has received *reports* (possibly from Chloe's people; see 1.11) about a Christian who is living with his stepmother, who may have been widowed. Neither Roman nor Jewish law (Lev. 18.8; 20.11) permitted such a *union*. **2:** The Corinthians' pride (also v. 6) is worse than the sin itself. Perhaps the experiments in sexual asceticism discussed in ch. 7 (see 7.36–38 n.) have created the problem here. **3–5:** Paul orders a formal assembly to expel the offender (see 2 Cor. 2.5–11 n.). Excluded from the table-fellowship he becomes Satan's prey. His death (11.30 n.) will end his sin, but, like all Christians, he has been marked for salvation *on the day* (1.8 n.). **6:** *Leaven,* i.e. yeast, was both useful (Matt. 13.33) and, like mold, corrupting. **7–8:** Writing perhaps near Passover (16.8 n.), Paul compares the expulsion of the immoral person to the Jewish custom of discarding all household leaven before baking the *unleavened* (Passover) *bread* (Deut. 16.1, 3–4). This leads him to speak of Christ as the lamb sacrificed at Passover (v. 7; Deut. 16.2; Exod. 12.21;

depravity and wickedness, but only the un-leavened bread which is sincerity and truth.

⁹ In my letter I wrote that you must have nothing to do with those who are sexually immoral. ¹⁰ I was not, of course, referring to people in general who are immoral or extor-tioners or swindlers or idolaters; to avoid them you would have to withdraw from soci-ety altogether. ¹¹ I meant that you must have nothing to do with any so-called Christian who leads an immoral life, or is extortionate, idolatrous, a slanderer, a drunkard, or a swindler; with anyone like that you should not even eat. ¹²⁻¹³ What business of mine is it to judge outsiders? God is their judge. But within the fellowship, you are the judges: 'Root out the wrongdoer from your commu-nity.'

Lawsuits among Christians

6 IF one of your number has a dispute with another, does he have the face to go to law before a pagan court instead of before God's people? ² It is God's people who are to judge the world; surely you know that. And if the world is subject to your judgement, are you not competent to deal with these trifling cases? ³ Are you not aware that we are to judge angels, not to mention day to day af-fairs? ⁴ If therefore you have such everyday disputes, how can you entrust jurisdiction to outsiders with no standing in the church? ⁵ I write this to shame you. Can it be that there is not among you a single person wise enough to give a decision in a fellow-Christian's cause? ⁶ Must Christian go to law with Chris-tian—and before unbelievers at that? ⁷ In-deed, you suffer defeat by going to law with one another at all. Why not rather submit to

wrong? Why not let yourself be defrauded? ⁸ But instead, it is you who are wronging and defrauding, and fellow-Christians at that! ⁹ Surely you know that wrongdoers will never possess the kingdom of God. Make no mis-take: no fornicator or idolater, no adulterer or sexual pervert, ¹⁰ no thief, extortioner, drunkard, slanderer, or swindler will possess the kingdom of God. ¹¹ Such were some of you; but you have been washed clean, you have been dedicated to God, you have been justified through the name of the Lord Jesus and through the Spirit of our God.

¹² 'I am free to do anything,' you say. Yes, but not everything does good. No doubt I am free to do anything, but I for one will not let anything make free with me. ¹³ 'Food is for the belly and the belly for food,' you say. True; and one day God will put an end to both. But the body is not for fornication; it is for the Lord—and the Lord for the body. ¹⁴ God not only raised our Lord from the dead; he will also raise us by his power. ¹⁵ Do you not know that your bodies are limbs and organs of Christ? Shall I then take parts of Christ's body and make them over to a prosti-tute? Never! ¹⁶ You surely know that anyone who joins himself to a prostitute becomes physically one with her, for scripture says, 'The two shall become one flesh'; ¹⁷ but any-one who joins himself to the Lord is one with him spiritually. ¹⁸ Have nothing to do with fornication. Every other sin that one may commit is outside the body; but the fornica-tor sins against his own body. ¹⁹ Do you not know that your body is a temple of the in-dwelling Holy Spirit, and the Spirit is God's gift to you? You do not belong to yourselves; ²⁰ you were bought at a price. Then honour God in your body.

Jn. 1.29). **9:** *Letter:* see Introduction. **12–13:** Church discipline applies only to church members. Judgment in these matters is an exception to Paul's rule that Christians should not judge others until they judge the world in the new age (4.5; 6.2). *Root out:* v. 2; Deut. 22.21, 24.

6.1–11: Lawsuits among Christians. It is shameful that quarrelling believers should seek justice from a *pagan court.* **2–3:** In the age to come Christians will *judge the world* and *judge angels.* For Paul, *angels,* i.e. "messengers," are fearsome embodiments of supernatural power. They may be good (2 Cor. 11.14) or from Satan (2 Cor. 12.7). **9–11:** *The wrongdoers* of the world (this list of vices is stereotyped; see Gal. 5.19–24) will have no part in *the kingdom* (1.8 n.), but believers have been washed (in baptism) and made holy.

6.12–20: Conclusion (to chs. 1–6) **and preface** (to chs. 7–15). **12:** *"I am free . . ."* is a slogan of the Corinthians (10.23). **13:** *"Food is for the belly . . ."* is another of their slogans (see chs. 8–10). *Body* not *for fornication:* ch. 7. **14:** See ch. 15. **15:** *Limbs and organs of Christ:* see 12.12–13 n. **16:** Gen. 2.24 (1 Cor. ch. 7; Mk. 10.6–8; Eph. 5.31). **19:** The *gift* of the *Spirit:* see chs. 12–14. **20:** *Bought at a price:* like slaves set free (see 7.23; Rom. 3.24 n.).

Sex, marriage, and divorce

7 Now FOR the matters you wrote about. You say, 'It is a good thing for a man not to have intercourse with a woman.' ²Rather, in the face of so much immorality, let each man have his own wife and each woman her own husband. ³The husband must give the wife what is due to her, and equally the wife must give the husband his due. ⁴The wife cannot claim her body as her own; it is her husband's. Equally, the husband cannot claim his body as his own; it is his wife's. ⁵Do not deny yourselves to one another, except when you agree to devote yourselves to prayer for a time, and to come together again afterwards; otherwise, through lack of self-control, you may be tempted by Satan. ⁶I say this by way of concession, not command. ⁷I should like everyone to be as I myself am; but each person has the gift God has granted him, one this gift and another that.

⁸To the unmarried and to widows I say this: it is a good thing if like me they stay as they are; ⁹but if they do not have self-control, they should marry. It is better to be married than burn with desire.

¹⁰To the married I give this ruling, which is not mine but the Lord's: a wife must not separate herself from her husband — ¹¹if she does, she must either remain unmarried or be reconciled to her husband — and the husband must not divorce his wife.

¹²To the rest I say this, as my own word, not as the Lord's: if a Christian has a wife who is not a believer, and she is willing to live with him, he must not divorce her; ¹³and if a woman has a husband who is not a believer, and he is willing to live with her, she must not divorce him. ¹⁴For the husband now belongs to God through his Christian wife, and the wife through her Christian husband. Otherwise your children would not belong to God, whereas in fact they do. ¹⁵If however the unbelieving partner wishes for a separation,

it should be granted; in such cases the Christian husband or wife is not bound by the marriage. God's call is a call to live in peace. ¹⁶But remember: a wife may save her husband; and a husband may save his wife.

¹⁷However that may be, each one should accept the lot which the Lord has assigned him and continue as he was when God called him. That is the rule I give in all the churches. ¹⁸Was a man called with the marks of circumcision on him? Let him not remove them. Was he uncircumcised when he was called? Let him not be circumcised. ¹⁹Circumcision or uncircumcision is neither here nor there; what matters is to keep God's commands. ²⁰Everyone should remain in the condition in which he was called. ²¹Were you a slave when you were called? Do not let that trouble you; though if a chance of freedom should come, by all means take it. ²²Anyone who received his call to be a Christian while a slave is the Lord's freedman, and, equally, every free man who has received the call is a slave in the service of Christ. ²³You were bought at a price; do not become slaves of men. ²⁴So, my friends, everyone is to remain before God in the condition in which he received his call.

²⁵About the unmarried, I have no instructions from the Lord, but I give my opinion as one who by the Lord's mercy is fit to be trusted. ²⁶I think the best way for a man to live in a time of stress like the present is this — to remain as he is. ²⁷Are you bound in marriage? Do not seek a dissolution. Has your marriage been dissolved? Do not seek a wife. ²⁸But if you do marry, you are not doing anything wrong, nor does a girl if she marries; it is only that those who marry will have hardships to endure, and my aim is to spare you.

7:21 **though if ... take it:** *or* but even if a chance of freedom should come, choose rather to make good use of your servitude.

7.1–16: "Should we not avoid sex and marriage?" Some such question probably stood in the Corinthians' letter to Paul (see Introduction). **1:** *It is a good thing . . .:* probably a Corinthian slogan. **2–5:** Paul urges full conjugal rights, permitting only temporary asceticism. **6–9:** Paul is unmarried and because of the nearness of the day (1.8 n.; 7.29, 31), considers this preferable. But it is a *gift,* not a rule. The distractions of married life (7.32–34) are infinitely preferable to moral lapses. **10:** *The Lord's:* Jesus' (see Mk. 10.2–12); contrast vv. 12, 25. **12–16:** The *divorce* even of unbelieving partners is not encouraged.

7.17–24: Stay as you are. The end of this age is near (vv. 29, 31). Therefore believers should not try to change their outward condition. **19:** See Rom. 2.25–29.

7.25–38: "Should our celibate couples abandon their vows?" (See 7.1–16 n.). **25:** *Unmarried:* lit. "virgins"

²⁹ What I mean, my friends, is this: the time we live in will not last long. While it lasts, married men should be as if they had no wives; ³⁰ mourners should be as if they had nothing to grieve them, the joyful as if they did not rejoice; those who buy should be as if they possessed nothing, ³¹ and those who use the world's wealth as if they did not have full use of it. For the world as we know it is passing away.

³² I want you to be free from anxious care. An unmarried man is concerned with the Lord's business; his aim is to please the Lord. ³³ But a married man is concerned with worldly affairs; his aim is to please his wife, ³⁴ and he is pulled in two directions. The unmarried woman or girl is concerned with the Lord's business; her aim is to be dedicated to him in body as in spirit. But the married woman is concerned with worldly affairs; her aim is to please her husband.

³⁵ In saying this I am thinking simply of your own good. I have no wish to keep you on a tight rein; I only want you to be beyond criticism and be free from distraction in your devotion to the Lord. ³⁶ But if a man feels that he is not behaving properly towards the girl to whom he is betrothed, if his passions are strong and something must be done, let him carry out his intention by getting married; there is nothing wrong in it. ³⁷ But if a man is steadfast in his purpose and under no obligation, if he is free to act at his own discretion, and has decided in his own mind to respect her virginity, he will do well. ³⁸ Thus he who marries his betrothed does well, and he who does not marry does better.

³⁹ A wife is bound to her husband as long as he lives. But if the husband dies, she is free to marry whom she will, provided the marriage is within the Lord's fellowship. ⁴⁰ But she is better off as she is; that is my opinion, and I believe that I too have the Spirit of God.

Food offered to idols

8 Now ABOUT meat consecrated to heathen deities.

Of course 'We all have knowledge,' as you say. 'Knowledge' inflates a man, whereas love builds him up. ² If anyone fancies that he has some kind of knowledge, he does not yet know in the true sense of knowing. ³ But if anyone loves God, he is known by God.

⁴ Well then, about eating this consecrated meat: of course, as you say, 'A false god has no real existence, and there is no god but one.' ⁵ Even though there be so-called gods, whether in heaven or on earth — and indeed there are many such gods and many such lords — ⁶ yet for us there is one God, the Father, from whom are all things, and we exist for him; there is one Lord, Jesus Christ, through whom are all things, and we exist through him.

⁷ But not everyone possesses this knowledge. There are some who have been so accustomed to idolatry that they still think of this meat as consecrated to the idol, and their conscience, being weak, is defiled by eating it.

7:33–34 **his wife ... girl is concerned:** *some witnesses read* his wife. ³⁴ There is this difference between the wife and the virgin; the unmarried woman is concerned.   7:36–38 **But if ... better:** *or* But if a man feels open to criticism about his daughter, because she has reached puberty and the normal course ought to be followed, he may do as he wishes: let the marriage take place; there is nothing wrong in it. ³⁷ But if a man is steadfast in his purpose and under no obligation, if he is free to act at his own discretion, and has decided in his own mind to keep the girl unmarried, he will do well. ³⁸ Thus he who gives his daughter in marriage does well, and he who does not does better. *Or* But if a man has a partner in celibacy and feels that he is not behaving properly towards her, if, that is, his instincts are too strong for him, and something must be done, let him do what he wishes: let them marry; there is nothing wrong in it. ³⁷ But if a man is steadfast in his purpose and under no obligation, if he is free to act at his own discretion, and has decided in his own mind to keep his partner in her virginity, he will do well. ³⁸ Thus he who marries his partner does well, and he who does not marry her does better.

(referring to both sexes); see vv. 36–38 n. **26–34:** Paul reiterates the argument of vv. 17–24. **36–38:** Apparently some Corinthians had chosen to undertake mutual vows of celibacy as engaged couples or like the marital ascetics of v. 5.

7.39–40: An afterthought to vv. 1–16.

8.1–11.1: "Surely there is no harm in eating meat consecrated to a heathen deity?" (See 7.1–16 n.). The extent of consecration varied from full temple sacrifice to the merest slaughterhouse gesture.

8.1–13: Love is superior to knowledge (also ch. 13). **1–4:** The Corinthians' slogans (see also 10.23) defend their freedom. **6:** Mal. 2.10; Eph. 4.6; Col. 1.16; Jn. 1.3. **7–13:** Out of loving concern for the *weak* mature

8 Certainly food will not bring us into God's presence: if we do not eat, we are none the worse, and if we do eat, we are none the better. 9 But be careful that this liberty of yours does not become a pitfall for the weak. 10 If one of them sees you sitting down to a meal in a heathen temple—you with your 'knowledge'—will not his conscience be emboldened to eat meat consecrated to the heathen deity? 11 This 'knowledge' of yours destroys the weak, the fellow-Christian for whom Christ died. 12 In sinning against your brothers and sisters in this way and wounding their conscience, weak as it is, you sin against Christ. 13 Therefore, if food be the downfall of a fellow-Christian, I will never eat meat again, for I will not be the cause of a fellow-Christian's downfall.

9 AM I not free? Am I not an apostle? Have I not seen Jesus our Lord? Are not you my own handiwork in the Lord? 2 If others do not accept me as an apostle, you at least are bound to do so, for in the Lord you are the very seal of my apostleship.

3 To those who would call me to account, this is my defence: 4 Have I no right to eat and drink? 5 Have I not the right to take a Christian wife about with me, like the rest of the apostles and the Lord's brothers and Cephas? 6 Are only Barnabas and I bound to work for our living? 7 Did you ever hear of a man serving in the army at his own expense? Or planting a vineyard without eating the fruit? Or tending a flock without using the milk? 8 My case does not rest on these human analogies, for the law says the same; 9 in the law of Moses we read, 'You shall not muzzle an ox while it is treading out the grain.' Do you suppose God's concern is with oxen? 10 Must not the saying refer to us? Of course it does: the ploughman should plough and the thresher thresh in hope of sharing the produce. 11 If we have sown a spiritual crop

for you, is it too much to expect from you a material harvest? 12 If you allow others those rights, have not we a stronger claim?

But I have never availed myself of any such right. On the contrary, I put up with all that comes my way rather than offer any hindrance to the gospel of Christ. 13 You must know that those who are engaged in temple service eat the temple offerings, and those who officiate at the altar claim their share of the sacrifice. 14 In the same way the Lord gave instructions that those who preach the gospel should get their living by the gospel. 15 But I have never taken advantage of any such right, nor do I intend to claim it in this letter. I had rather die! No one shall make my boast an empty boast. 16 Even if I preach the gospel, I can claim no credit for it; I cannot help myself; it would be agony for me not to preach. 17 If I did it of my own choice, I should be earning my pay; but since I have no choice, I am simply discharging a trust. 18 Then what is my pay? It is the satisfaction of preaching the gospel without expense to anyone; in other words, of waiving the rights my preaching gives me.

19 I am free and own no master; but I have made myself everyone's servant, to win over as many as possible. 20 To Jews I behaved like a Jew, to win Jews; that is, to win those under the law I behaved as if under the law, though not myself subject to the law. 21 To win those outside that law, I behaved as if outside the law, though not myself outside God's law, but subject to the law of Christ. 22 To the weak I became weak, to win the weak. To them all I have become everything in turn, so that in one way or another I may save some. 23 All this I do for the sake of the gospel, to have a share in its blessings.

24 At the games, as you know, all the runners take part, though only one wins the prize. 25 You also must run to win. Every ath-

8:12 *some witnesses omit* weak as it is.

Christians should limit their own *liberty*. **10:** People often entertained their friends with a *meal* at some *temple*, using meat previously sacrificed. The affair was largely social; thus Christians might attend (see 10.27).

9.1–27: Paul's own self-restraint extends to other matters as well. **1:** An *apostle* has both *seen* the resurrected *Jesus* (15.5–9) and received from him a missionary task (see Gal. 1.16).

9.3–12a: Paul's right to financial support. 5: *The Lord's brothers:* see Mk. 6.3; Gal. 1.19. **6:** *Barnabas:* see Acts 4.36; Gal. 2.1. *Work:* tent-making (Acts 18.3). **9:** Deut. 25.4. **10:** The promises of Scripture apply to the new Israel (see 10.11; Rom. 15.4).

9.12b–18: The Gospel free of charge. 13: See Deut. 18.1–4; this was also true in pagan cults. **14:** Matt. 10.10. **15–18:** *Boast, satisfaction:* see 2 Thess. 3.7–9; 2 Cor. 11.7–10 n.

9.19–27: The highest goal requires self-sacrifice. 19–23: In his behavior Paul has a higher purpose than lete goes into strict training. They do it to win a fading garland; we, to win a garland that never fades. ²⁶For my part, I am no aimless runner; I am not a boxer who beats the air. ²⁷I do not spare my body, but bring it under strict control, for fear that after preaching to others I should find myself disqualified.

10 Let me remind you, my friends, that our ancestors were all under the cloud, and all of them passed through the Red Sea; ²so they all received baptism into the fellowship of Moses in cloud and sea. ³They all ate the same supernatural food, ⁴and all drank the same supernatural drink; for they drank from the supernatural rock that accompanied their travels—and that rock was Christ. ⁵Yet most of them were not accepted by God, for the wilderness was strewn with their corpses.

⁶These events happened as warnings to us not to set our desires on evil things as they did. ⁷Do not be idolaters, like some of them; as scripture says, 'The people sat down to feast and rose up to revel.' ⁸Let us not commit fornication; some of them did, and twenty-three thousand died in one day. ⁹Let us not put the Lord to the test as some of them did; they were destroyed by the snakes. ¹⁰Do not grumble as some of them did; they were destroyed by the Destroyer.

¹¹All these things that happened to them were symbolic, and were recorded as a warning for us, upon whom the end of the ages has come. ¹²If you think you are standing firm, take care, or you may fall. ¹³So far you have faced no trial beyond human endurance; God keeps faith and will not let you be tested beyond your powers, but when the test comes he will at the same time provide a way out and so enable you to endure.

¹⁴So THEN, my dear friends, have nothing to do with idolatry. ¹⁵I appeal to you as sensible people; form your own judgement on what I say. ¹⁶When we bless the cup of blessing, is it not a means of sharing in the blood of Christ? When we break the bread, is it not a means of sharing in the body of Christ? ¹⁷Because there is one loaf, we, though many, are one body; for it is one loaf of which we all partake.

¹⁸Consider Jewish practice: are not those who eat the sacrificial meal partners in the altar? ¹⁹What do I imply by this? That meat consecrated to an idol is anything more than meat, or that an idol is anything more than an idol? ²⁰No, I mean that pagan sacrifices are offered (in the words of scripture) 'to demons and to that which is not God'; and I will not have you become partners with demons. ²¹You cannot drink the cup of the Lord and the cup of demons. You cannot partake of the Lord's table and the table of demons. ²²Are we to provoke the Lord? Are we stronger than he is?

²³'We are free to do anything,' you say. Yes, but not everything is good for us. We are free to do anything, but not everything builds up the community. ²⁴You should each look after the interests of others, not your own.

²⁵You may eat anything sold in the meat market without raising questions of conscience; ²⁶'for the earth is the Lord's and all that is in it'.

²⁷If an unbeliever invites you to a meal and you accept, eat whatever is put before you, without raising questions of conscience. ²⁸But if somebody says to you, 'This food has

10:9 **the Lord:** *some witnesses read* Christ.
10:17 **Because ... body:** *or* For we, many as we are, are one loaf, one body.

consistency: to *win* persons for Christ. **27:** The *body* is not an enemy; Paul is speaking figuratively of his disciplined life. *Disqualified:* see 10.5–13.

10.1–13: It is possible to provoke God and perish; baptism and the Lord's Supper do not prevent sin or excuse from judgment. **1–2:** *Cloud:* see Exod. 13.21. *Sea:* see Exod. 14.22. **3:** *Food:* manna (Exod. 16.4–35). **4:** *Drink:* water from the *rock* (Exod. 17.6; Num. 20.11). Legend had it that the *rock* followed the Israelites in their *travels.* Paul identifies the source of this life-giving water with *Christ* (compare Jn. 4.14). **5:** Num. 14.29–30. **7:** Exod. 32.4, 6. **8–10:** Num. 25.1–18; 21.5–6; 16.41, 49. **11:** *End:* compare 1.8 n.

10.14–22: Danger from demons. *Idols* indeed are nothing (8.4), but *demons* use them as camouflage (Deut. 32.17). Thus eating food consecrated to heathen gods is defiance of God (Deut. 32.21). **16–17:** See 11.23–26; Mk. 14.22–25. **20:** Deut. 32.17. **21:** See 2 Cor. 6.15–16.

10.23–11.1: Paul closes the section on idol meat (8.1–11.1) with directions which allow freedom, if it is restrained by love. **23:** Another Corinthian slogan (compare 8.1–4 n.). **26:** Pss. 24.1; 50.12. **27:** See 8.10 n. **10.28–11.1:** See 8.7–13.

been offered in sacrifice,' then, out of consideration for him and for conscience' sake, do not eat it — [29] not your conscience, I mean, but his.

'What?' you say. 'Is my freedom to be called in question by another's conscience? [30] If I partake with thankfulness, why am I blamed for eating food over which I have said grace?' [31] You may eat or drink, or do anything else, provided it is all done to the glory of God; [32] give no offence to Jews, or Greeks, or to the church of God. [33] For my part I always try to be considerate to everyone, not seeking my own good but the good of the many, so that they may be saved.

11 [1] Follow my example as I follow Christ's.

Public worship

[2] I COMMEND you for always keeping me in mind, and maintaining the tradition I handed on to you. [3] But I wish you to understand that, while every man has Christ for his head, a woman's head is man, as Christ's head is God. [4] A man who keeps his head covered when he prays or prophesies brings shame on his head; [5] but a woman brings shame on her head if she prays or prophesies bareheaded; it is as bad as if her head were shaved. [6] If a woman does not cover her head she might as well have her hair cut off; but if it is a disgrace for her to be cropped and shaved, then she should cover her head. [7] A man must not cover his head, because man is the image of God, and the mirror of his glory, whereas a woman reflects the glory of man. [8] For man did not originally spring from woman, but woman was made out of man; [9] and man was not created for woman's sake, but woman for the sake of man; [10] and therefore a woman must have the sign of her authority on her head, out of regard for the angels. [11] Yet in the Lord's fellowship woman is as essential to man as man to woman. [12] If

woman was made out of man, it is through woman that man now comes to be; and God is the source of all.

[13] Judge for yourselves: is it fitting for a woman to pray to God bareheaded? [14] Does not nature herself teach you that while long hair disgraces a man, [15] it is a woman's glory? For her hair was given as a covering.

[16] And if anyone still insists on arguing, there is no such custom among us, or in any of the congregations of God's people.

[17] In giving you these instructions I come to something I cannot commend: your meetings tend to do more harm than good. [18] To begin with, I am told that when you meet as a congregation you fall into sharply divided groups. I believe there is some truth in it, [19] for divisions are bound to arise among you if only to show which of your members are genuine. [20] The result is that when you meet as a congregation, it is not the Lord's Supper you eat; when it comes to eating, [21] each of you takes his own supper, one goes hungry and another has too much to drink. [22] Have you no homes of your own to eat and drink in? Or are you so contemptuous of the church of God that you shame its poorer members? What am I to say? Can I commend you? On this point, certainly not!

[23] For the tradition which I handed on to you came to me from the Lord himself: that on the night of his arrest the Lord Jesus took bread, [24] and after giving thanks to God broke it and said: 'This is my body, which is for you; do this in memory of me.' [25] In the same way, he took the cup after supper, and said: 'This cup is the new covenant sealed by my blood. Whenever you drink it, do this in memory of me.' [26] For every time you eat this bread and drink the cup, you proclaim the death of the Lord, until he comes.

[27] It follows that anyone who eats the bread or drinks the cup of the Lord unworthily will

11:3 **is man:** *or* is her husband.　　11:7 **a woman . . . man:** *or* a woman reflects her husband's glory.

11.2–16: "Is it necessary for women to worship with their heads covered?" (See 7.1–16 n.). Christian women enjoyed considerable freedom, including the right to preach (prophesy, v. 5), but worship without *covering the head* may have reminded Paul of pagan cults. **7:** *Image:* Gen. 1.26. **8–12:** See Gen. 2.18, 21–24. **10:** A woman must wear a veil as a *sign of her authority* or power. These *angels* (see 6.2–3 n.) are perhaps the lustful spirits of a legend based on Gen. 6.1–4. **16:** See 14.36–38 n.

11.17–34: The Lord's Supper properly observed. Paul has more news (v. 18) of their dissensions (compare 1.11–12). The Lord's Supper was then a full meal; the Corinthians' greed shattered the "one body" (10.16–17) with dire consequences (v. 30). **17:** Contrast v. 2. **23–25:** This is the earliest written account of the Lord's Supper (compare Mk. 14.22–25; Lk. 22.14–20). **23:** *Handed on:* see 15.3 n. **25:** *Covenant, blood:* Exod. 24.8.

be guilty of offending against the body and blood of the Lord. [28] Everyone must test himself before eating from the bread and drinking from the cup. [29] For he who eats and drinks eats and drinks judgement on himself if he does not discern the body. [30] That is why many of you are feeble and sick, and a number have died. [31] But if we examined ourselves, we should not fall under judgement. [32] When, however, we do fall under the Lord's judgement, he is disciplining us to save us from being condemned with the rest of the world.

[33] Therefore, my friends, when you meet for this meal, wait for one another. [34] If you are hungry, eat at home, so that in meeting together you may not fall under judgement. The other matters I will settle when I come.

Spiritual gifts

12 About gifts of the Spirit, my friends, I want there to be no misunderstanding.

[2] You know how, in the days when you were still pagan, you used to be carried away by some impulse or other to those dumb heathen gods. [3] For this reason I must impress upon you that no one who says 'A curse on Jesus!' can be speaking under the influence of the Spirit of God; and no one can say 'Jesus is Lord!' except under the influence of the Holy Spirit.

[4] There are varieties of gifts, but the same Spirit. [5] There are varieties of service, but the same Lord. [6] There are varieties of activity, but in all of them and in everyone the same God is active. [7] In each of us the Spirit is seen to be at work for some useful purpose. [8] One, through the Spirit, has the gift of wise speech, while another, by the power of the same Spirit, can put the deepest knowledge

into words. [9] Another, by the same Spirit, is granted faith; another, by the one Spirit, gifts of healing, [10] and another miraculous powers; another has the gift of prophecy, and another the ability to distinguish true spirits from false; yet another has the gift of tongues of various kinds, and another the ability to interpret them. [11] But all these gifts are the activity of one and the same Spirit, distributing them to each individual at will.

[12] Christ is like a single body with its many limbs and organs, which, many as they are, together make up one body; [13] for in the one Spirit we were all brought into one body by baptism, whether Jews or Greeks, slaves or free; we were all given that one Spirit to drink.

[14] A body is not a single organ, but many. [15] Suppose the foot were to say, 'Because I am not a hand, I do not belong to the body,' it belongs to the body none the less. [16] Suppose the ear were to say, 'Because I am not an eye, I do not belong to the body,' it still belongs to the body. [17] If the body were all eye, how could it hear? If the body were all ear, how could it smell? [18] But, in fact, God appointed each limb and organ to its own place in the body as he chose. [19] If the whole were a single organ, there would not be a body at all; [20] in fact, however, there are many different organs, but one body. [21] The eye cannot say to the hand, 'I do not need you,' or the head to the feet, 'I do not need you.' [22] Quite the contrary: those parts of the body which seem to be more frail than others are indispensable, [23] and those parts of the body which we regard as less honourable are treated with special honour. The parts we are modest about are treated with special respect, [24] whereas our respectable parts have no such need. But God has combined the various parts of the body, giving special honour to

30: They had expected to live until Christ's return (v. 26; 15.51); Paul explains why some had died (see 5.3–5 n.).

12.1–14.40: "Ecstatic utterance in worship is the gift of the Spirit, is it not?" (See 7.1–16 n.) Paul's long response occupies chs. 12–14.

12.1–31: Other and better gifts. Ecstatic speaking in *tongues* (v. 10) is indeed a *gift,* but it is not the only gift. Of all the Spirit's *gifts* it ranks last (vv. 10, 28, 30). **2–3:** Not all ecstatic speech is from the Spirit; some is pagan. **4–6:** *Spirit . . . Lord . . . God:* the triad foreshadows the later doctrine of the Trinity. **7:** *Useful:* the test is utility (compare Matt. 7.16–20). **9:** *Faith* here (and in 13.2) is a special gift, rather than the characteristic of every believer (as in 1.21; 2.5; 3.5). **10:** *Prophecy:* preaching (14.1–5). *Distinguish . . . spirits:* see vv. 2–3. **12–13:** Christians are "in Christ" (Rom. 8.1 n.), not separately but "corporately." Paul speaks of the church as the *body* of Christ (v. 27) and of Christians as its differing but mutually dependent "members." **14–26:** Paul argues that a church whose members exhibit but one spiritual gift is like a body composed solely of an *eye*

1458

the humbler parts, 25 so that there might be no division in the body, but that all its parts might feel the same concern for one another. 26 If one part suffers, all suffer together; if one flourishes, all rejoice together.

27 Now you are Christ's body, and each of you a limb or organ of it. 28 Within our community God has appointed in the first place apostles, in the second place prophets, thirdly teachers; then miracle-workers, then those who have gifts of healing, or ability to help others or power to guide them, or the gift of tongues of various kinds. 29 Are all apostles? All prophets? All teachers? Do all work miracles? 30 Do all have gifts of healing? Do all speak in tongues of ecstasy? Can all interpret them? 31 The higher gifts are those you should prize.

But I can show you an even better way.

13 I may speak in tongues of men or of angels, but if I have no love, I am a sounding gong or a clanging cymbal. 2 I may have the gift of prophecy and the knowledge of every hidden truth; I may have faith enough to move mountains; but if I have no love, I am nothing. 3 I may give all I possess to the needy, I may give my body to be burnt, but if I have no love, I gain nothing by it.

4 Love is patient and kind. Love envies no one, is never boastful, never conceited, 5 never rude; love is never selfish, never quick to take offence. Love keeps no score of wrongs, 6 takes no pleasure in the sins of others, but delights in the truth. 7 There is nothing love cannot face; there is no limit to its faith, its hope, its endurance.

8 Love will never come to an end. Prophecies will cease; tongues of ecstasy will fall silent; knowledge will vanish. 9 For our knowledge and our prophecy alike are partial, 10 and the partial vanishes when wholeness comes. 11 When I was a child I spoke like a child, thought like a child, reasoned like a child; but when I grew up I finished with childish things. 12 At present we see only puzzling reflections in a mirror, but one day we shall see face to face. My knowledge now is partial; then it will be whole, like God's knowledge of me. 13 There are three things that last for ever: faith, hope, and love; and the greatest of the three is love.

14 Make love your aim; then be eager for the gifts of the Spirit, above all for prophecy. 2 If anyone speaks in tongues he is talking with God, not with men and women; no one understands him, for he speaks divine mysteries in the Spirit. 3 On the other hand, if anyone prophesies, he is talking to men and women, and his words have power to build; they stimulate and they encourage. 4 Speaking in tongues may build up the speaker himself, but it is prophecy that builds up a Christian community. 5 I am happy for you all to speak in tongues, but happier still for you to prophesy. The prophet is worth more than one who speaks in tongues — unless indeed he can explain its meaning, and so help to build up the community. 6 Suppose, my friends, that when I come to you I speak in tongues: what good shall I do you unless what I say contains something by way of revelation, or enlightenment, or prophecy, or instruction?

7 Even with inanimate things that produce sounds — a flute, say, or a lyre — unless their notes are distinct, how can you tell what tune is being played? 8 Or again, if the trumpet-call is not clear, who will prepare for battle? 9 In the same way, if what you say in tongues yields no precise meaning, how can anyone tell what is being said? You will be talking to empty air. 10 There are any number of different languages in the world; nowhere is without language. 11 If I do not know the speaker's language, his words will be gibberish to me, and mine to him. 12 You are, I know, eager for gifts of the Spirit; then aspire above all to excel in those which build up the church.

13 Anyone who speaks in tongues should

13:3 *give my ... burnt: some witnesses read* seek glory by self-sacrifice.

or an *ear.* **27:** See Rom. 12.4–5; Eph. 1.22–23; Col. 1.18–24. **28–30:** Roughly parallel to vv. 8–10.

13.1–13: Love, the best gift of all. This famous chapter is closely linked to chs. 12 and 14. **1:** *Tongues ... of angels:* ecstatic speech. *Angels:* see 6.2–3 n. *Gong ... cymbal:* mere noisemakers used in pagan cults. **2:** *Prophecy:* see 12.10 n. *Faith:* see 12.9 n.; Mk. 11.22–23. **3:** *Burnt:* perhaps as a martyr (Dan. 3.19–23; 2 Macc. 7.2–6). **4–6, 11:** Paul betrays his opinion of the Corinthians' pride in their special gifts. **12:** *Mirror:* ancient metal mirrors gave distorted *reflections.* **13:** *Faith, hope,* and *love:* a favorite triad for Paul (1 Thess. 1.3; 5.8; Rom. 5.1–5; Col. 1.4–5).

14.1–40: Rational preaching is of far more value than ecstatic utterance. 1: *Love:* for love's sake they ought pray for the ability to interpret. ¹⁴If I use such language in prayer, my spirit prays, but my mind is barren. ¹⁵What then? I will pray with my spirit, but also with my mind; I will sing hymns with my spirit, but with my mind as well. ¹⁶Suppose you are praising God with the spirit alone: how will an ordinary person who is present be able to say 'Amen' to your thanksgiving, when he does not know what you are saying? ¹⁷Your prayer of thanksgiving may be splendid, but it is no help to the other person. ¹⁸Thank God, I am more gifted in tongues than any of you, ¹⁹but in the congregation I would rather speak five intelligible words, for the benefit of others as well as myself, than thousands of words in the language of ecstasy.

²⁰Do not be children in your thinking, my friends; be infants in evil, but in your thinking be grown-up. ²¹We read in the law: 'I will speak to this people through strange tongues, and by the lips of foreigners; and even so they will not heed me, says the Lord.' ²²Clearly then these 'strange tongues' are not intended as a sign for believers, but for unbelievers, whereas prophecy is designed not for unbelievers but for believers. ²³So if the whole congregation is assembled and all are using the 'strange tongues' of ecstasy, and some uninstructed persons or unbelievers should enter, will they not think you are mad? ²⁴But if all are uttering prophecies, the visitor, when he enters, hears from everyone something that searches his conscience and brings conviction, ²⁵and the secrets of his heart are laid bare. So he will fall down and worship God, declaring, 'God is certainly among you!'

²⁶To sum up, my friends: when you meet for worship, each of you contributing a hymn, some instruction, a revelation, an ecstatic utterance, or its interpretation, see that all of these aim to build up the church. ²⁷If anyone speaks in tongues, only two should

speak, or at most three, one at a time, and someone must interpret. ²⁸If there is no interpreter, they should keep silent and speak to themselves and to God. ²⁹Of the prophets, two or three may speak, while the rest exercise their judgement upon what is said. ³⁰If someone else present receives a revelation, let the first speaker stop. ³¹You can all prophesy, one at a time, so that all may receive instruction and encouragement. ³²It is for prophets to control prophetic inspiration, ³³for God is not a God of disorder but of peace.

As in all congregations of God's people, ³⁴women should keep silent at the meeting. They have no permission to talk, but should keep their place as the law directs. ³⁵If there is something they want to know, they can ask their husbands at home. It is a shocking thing for a woman to talk at the meeting.

³⁶Did the word of God originate with you? Or are you the only people to whom it came? ³⁷If anyone claims to be inspired or a prophet, let him recognize that what I write has the Lord's authority. ³⁸If he does not acknowledge this, his own claim cannot be acknowledged.

³⁹In short, my friends, be eager to prophesy; do not forbid speaking in tongues; ⁴⁰but let all be done decently and in order.

The resurrection of the dead

15 AND now, my friends, I must remind you of the gospel that I preached to you; the gospel which you received, on which you have taken your stand, ²and which is now bringing you salvation. Remember the terms in which I preached the gospel to you —for I assume that you hold it fast and that your conversion was not in vain.

³First and foremost, I handed on to you

14:38 **If . . . acknowledged:** *some witnesses read* If he refuses to recognize this, let him refuse!

to make themselves understood when they *pray* (vv. 13–17). **16:** Christians adopted *"Amen"* (lit. "so be it"), the Jewish response to prayer (e.g. Neh. 8.6; Ps. 106.48). **18:** Probably the Corinthians had learned ecstatic utterance from Paul (see also 2 Cor. 12.1–4 n.). **20:** See 2.6; 3.1–2; 13.11. **21:** Isaiah 28.11–12 is cited as *law,* rather than prophet; see Rom. 3.19 n. **23–25:** This form of worship was not closed to *visitors,* as the Lord's Supper (11.23–32) presumably was. **34–35:** In view of 11.5 many consider these verses not by Paul, but a later insertion (compare 1 Tim. 2.11–12). **36–38:** For another abrupt closing of a difficult discussion see 11.16.

15.1–58: "Are Christians resurrected in bodily form?" (See 7.1–16 n.). **1–11:** An early Christian creed (vv. 3–5) serves to *remind* them that Christ's resurrection is basic to the *gospel* message. **3:** *Handed on, received:* Paul uses a traditional Jewish formula (also at 11.23) to emphasize that he is transmitting traditions which antedate his own ministry. *Scriptures* (here and in v. 4) probably means the OT in general. Later tradition the tradition I had received: that Christ died for our sins, in accordance with the scriptures; [4] that he was buried; that he was raised to life on the third day, in accordance with the scriptures; [5] and that he appeared to Cephas, and afterwards to the Twelve. [6] Then he appeared to over five hundred of our brothers at once, most of whom are still alive, though some have died. [7] Then he appeared to James, and afterwards to all the apostles.

[8] Last of all he appeared to me too; it was like a sudden, abnormal birth. [9] For I am the least of the apostles, indeed not fit to be called an apostle, because I had persecuted the church of God. [10] However, by God's grace I am what I am, and his grace to me has not proved vain; in my labours I have outdone them all—not I, indeed, but the grace of God working with me. [11] But no matter whether it was I or they! This is what we all proclaim, and this is what you believed.

[12] Now if this is what we proclaim, that Christ was raised from the dead, how can some of you say there is no resurrection of the dead? [13] If there is no resurrection, then Christ was not raised; [14] and if Christ was not raised, then our gospel is null and void, and so too is your faith; [15] and we turn out to have given false evidence about God, because we bore witness that he raised Christ to life, whereas, if the dead are not raised, he did not raise him. [16] For if the dead are not raised, it follows that Christ was not raised; [17] and if Christ was not raised, your faith has nothing to it and you are still in your old state of sin. [18] It follows also that those who have died within Christ's fellowship are utterly lost. [19] If it is for this life only that Christ has given us hope, we of all people are most to be pitied.

[20] But the truth is, Christ was raised to life —the firstfruits of the harvest of the dead. [21] For since it was a man who brought death into the world, a man also brought resurrection of the dead. [22] As in Adam all die, so in Christ all will be brought to life; [23] but each in proper order: Christ the firstfruits, and afterwards, at his coming, those who belong to Christ. [24] Then comes the end, when he delivers up the kingdom to God the Father, after deposing every sovereignty, authority, and power. [25] For he is destined to reign until God has put all enemies under his feet; [26] and the last enemy to be deposed is death. [27] Scripture says, 'He has put all things in subjection under his feet.' But in saying 'all things', it clearly means to exclude God who made all things subject to him; [28] and when all things are subject to him, then the Son himself will also be made subject to God who made all things subject to him, and thus God will be all in all.

[29] Again, there are those who receive baptism on behalf of the dead. What do you suppose they are doing? If the dead are not raised to life at all, what do they mean by being baptized on their behalf?

[30] And why do we ourselves face danger hour by hour? [31] Every day I die: I swear it by my pride in you, my friends—for in Christ Jesus our Lord I am proud of you. [32] With no more than human hopes, what would have been the point of my fighting those wild beasts at Ephesus? If the dead are never raised to life, 'Let us eat and drink, for tomorrow we die.'

[33] Make no mistake: 'Bad company ruins good character.' [34] Wake up, be sober, and

---

cited Isa. 52.13–53.12 for Jesus' death and Ps. 16.10 (Acts 2.31) for his resurrection. **7:** *James:* Jesus' brother (Gal. 1.19; Mk. 6.3). **8:** *Appeared to me:* see 9.1; Gal. 1.16; Acts 9.3–6. *Abnormal birth* is obscure; Paul may have been ridiculed for his appearance (2 Cor. 10.10; Gal. 4.13–14). **9:** *Persecuted:* see Gal. 1, 13–14. **10:** *Grace:* God's graciousness. **11:** Paul asserts the unity of the proclamation, despite differences among proclaimers.

15.12–34: Believing the Gospel means believing in resurrection. Paul is discussing only those few (11.30) who have died since becoming Christians (vv. 18, 23, 51–53 n.; 1 Thess. 4.13–18). **20:** As the *firstfruits* ritually symbolized the whole *harvest* (Lev. 23.10), so Christ's resurrection pledges the resurrection of Christians. **21–22:** See vv. 45–49 n.; Gen. 2.17. **23:** *Coming:* see 1.8 n.; 1 Thess. 2.19 n. **24–28:** Paul summarizes briefly the events of Christ's rule. **24–25:** *Sovereignty . . . enemies:* see 2.6–8 n. **26:** Perhaps at this point those from past ages held prisoner by *death* are released for judgment (see 6.2–3 n.). **27:** Ps. 8.6. **29:** Apparently Christians underwent *baptism* vicariously for previously deceased loved ones to insure their resurrection. **31:** *Die:* risk death. **32:** Paul does not explain what or who the *beasts* were (compare 4.9). *Let us eat:* Isa. 22.13. **33:** Doubters are *bad company,* quoting the Greek poet Menander.

stop sinning: some of you have no knowledge of God—to your shame I say it.

35 But, you may ask, how are the dead raised? In what kind of body? 36 What stupid questions! The seed you sow does not come to life unless it has first died; 37 and what you sow is not the body that shall be, but a bare grain, of wheat perhaps, or something else; 38 and God gives it the body of his choice, each seed its own particular body. 39 All flesh is not the same: there is human flesh, flesh of beasts, of birds, and of fishes—all different. 40 There are heavenly bodies and earthly bodies; and the splendour of the heavenly bodies is one thing, the splendour of the earthly another. 41 The sun has a splendour of its own, the moon another splendour, and the stars yet another; and one star differs from another in brightness. 42 So it is with the resurrection of the dead: what is sown as a perishable thing is raised imperishable. 43 Sown in humiliation, it is raised in glory; sown in weakness, it is raised in power; 44 sown a physical body, it is raised a spiritual body.

If there is such a thing as a physical body, there is also a spiritual body. 45 It is in this sense that scripture says, 'The first man, Adam, became a living creature,' whereas the last Adam has become a life-giving spirit. 46 Observe, the spiritual does not come first; the physical body comes first, and then the spiritual. 47 The first man is from earth, made of dust: the second man is from heaven. 48 The man made of dust is the pattern of all who are made of dust, and the heavenly man is the pattern of all the heavenly. 49 As we have worn the likeness of the man made of dust, so we shall wear the likeness of the heavenly man.

50 What I mean, my friends, is this: flesh and blood can never possess the kingdom of God, the perishable cannot possess the imperishable. 51 Listen! I will unfold a mystery: we shall not all die, but we shall all be changed 52 in a flash, in the twinkling of an eye, at the last trumpet-call. For the trumpet will sound, and the dead will rise imperishable, and we shall be changed. 53 This perishable body must be clothed with the imperishable, and what is mortal with immortality. 54 And when this perishable body has been clothed with the imperishable and our mortality has been clothed with immortality, then the saying of scripture will come true: 'Death is swallowed up; victory is won!' 55 'O Death, where is your victory? O Death, where is your sting?' 56 The sting of death is sin, and sin gains its power from the law. 57 But thanks be to God! He gives us victory through our Lord Jesus Christ.

58 Therefore, my dear friends, stand firm and immovable, and work for the Lord always, work without limit, since you know that in the Lord your labour cannot be lost.

Plans and greetings

16 Now ABOUT the collection in aid of God's people: you should follow the instructions I gave to our churches in Galatia. 2 Every Sunday each of you is to put aside and keep by him whatever he can afford, so that there need be no collecting when I come. 3 When I arrive, I will give letters of introduction to persons approved by you, and send them to carry your gift to Jerusalem. 4 If it seems right for me to go as well, they can travel with me.

5 I shall come to Corinth after passing through Macedonia—for I am travelling by

15:54 *Some witnesses omit* this perishable body has been clothed with the imperishable and.

15.35–58: "How are the dead raised?" The immortality of the soul freed of its bodily prison was an idea natural to Greeks. The Corinthians seem to have balked at the idea of bodily resurrection. Paul agrees that the *flesh* has no part in the ultimate realm of salvation (v. 50), arguing that there are many kinds of bodies and that Christians will receive bodies made not of flesh, but of spirit. **45–49:** Speculation based on Gen. chs. 1–2 featured an ideal Man (Heb. *Adam*, meaning "human being") who would initiate the Age to Come. Thus Paul contrasts Christ as the *last Adam* (v. 45) or *second man* (v. 47) with the sinful and mortal *first man* (see vv. 21–22; Rom. 5.12–19; compare Phil. 2.6–11). *Dust:* Gen. 2.7. **51–53:** Most Christians (Paul included) will survive until Christ's return (see 1.8 n.), but *all,* whether living or dead, must receive spirit bodies. **52:** See 1 Thess. 4.15–17. **54–55:** Isa. 25.8; Hos. 13.14. **56:** *Law:* see Rom. 5.13; 7.7–8; Gal. 3.21–22.

16.1–11: "How is the offering for Jerusalem to be collected?" (See 7.1–16 n.). **1:** *Collection:* see Introduction to Rom. *Galatia:* see Rom. 15.26 n. and Introduction to Gal. **2:** *No collecting:* each Christian will have way of Macedonia—⁶and I may stay some time with you, perhaps even for the whole winter; and then you can help me on my way wherever I go next. ⁷I do not want this to be a flying visit; I hope to spend some time with you, if the Lord permits. ⁸But I shall remain at Ephesus until Pentecost, ⁹for a great opportunity has opened for effective work, and there is much opposition.

¹⁰If Timothy comes, see that you put him at his ease; for it is the Lord's work that he is engaged on, as I am myself; ¹¹so no one must slight him. Speed him on his way with your blessing; for he is to join me, and I am waiting for him with our friends. ¹²As for our friend Apollos, I urged him strongly to go to Corinth with the others, but he was quite determined not to go at present; he will go when the time is right.

¹³Be on the alert; stand firm in the faith; be valiant, be strong. ¹⁴Let everything you do be done in love.

¹⁵One thing more, my friends. You know that the Stephanas family were the first con-

verts in Achaia, and have devoted themselves to the service of God's people. ¹⁶I urge you to accept the leadership of people like them, of anyone who labours hard at our common task. ¹⁷It is a great pleasure to me that Stephanas, Fortunatus, and Achaicus have arrived, because they have done what you had no chance to do; ¹⁸they have raised my spirits— and no doubt yours too. Such people deserve recognition.

¹⁹Greetings from the churches of Asia. Many greetings in the Lord from Aquila and Prisca and the church that meets in their house. ²⁰Greetings from the whole brotherhood. Greet one another with the kiss of peace.

²¹This greeting is in my own hand—Paul. ²²If anyone does not love the Lord, let him be outcast.

Marana tha—Come, Lord!

²³The grace of the Lord Jesus be with you. ²⁴My love to you all in Christ Jesus.

16:12 **but . . . not to go:** *or* but it was clearly not the will of God that he should go.

a sum ready. **3–4:** Compare with the delegates in Acts 20.4. **5:** *Macedonia:* see 2 Cor. 1.8–2.13 n. **8:** *Pentecost:* the "fiftieth" day after Passover; it fell in May–June. **10:** *Timothy:* a trusted assistant of Paul's (4.17; 2 Thess. 1.1; 1 Thess. 1.1; 3.2, 6; Phil. 1.1; 2.19; 2 Cor. 1.1, 19; Rom. 16.21; Col. 1.1; Philem. 1). **11:** *Our friends* (the others, v. 12): Timothy is one of a group of traveling church workers.

16.12: "When can Apollos return to us?" This is the final item from the Corinthians' letter (see Introduction). *Apollos:* see 1.12 n.

16.13–24: Final directions. 15–17: *Stephanas* (1.16), with *Fortunatus* and *Achaicus* (otherwise unknown), probably brought the Corinthians' letter to Paul (see Introduction). **19:** *Aquila, Prisca:* see Rom. 16.3–5 n. **20:** *Kiss:* see v. 22 n.; Rom. 16.16 n. **21–24:** Having finished dictating (see 1.16 n.), Paul "signs" the letter with a short paragraph (see 2 Thess. 3.17; Gal. 6.11; Col. 4.18). **22:** *Outcast:* lit. anathema, i.e. cursed. *Marana tha* is Aram. for *Come, O Lord.* The kiss of peace (v. 20), the anathema, and this invocation (compare Rev. 22.20) perhaps echo an early Lord's Supper liturgy.

THE SECOND LETTER OF PAUL TO THE
Corinthians

In the interval between 1 and 2 Corinthians Paul experienced two crises: (a) A visit to Corinth to deal with a sudden disciplinary problem was a painful failure (2.1). Retreating to Ephesus he wrote the Corinthians a severe letter (2.3–4; 7.8), now lost (see 10.1–13.14 n.), and sent it by Titus, one of his assistants. (b) Then Paul apparently underwent a crisis that caused him to despair of his life (1.8–10). When he was again able to travel, he went to Troas (2.12) and then to Macedonia (2.13; 7.5–6) before meeting Titus again. Titus had good news: the Corinthians had had a change of heart (7.7–12). Gratefully Paul wrote 2 Cor. chs. 1–9, urging forgiveness for the one who had caused the first crisis (2.5–11) and painting a joyful picture of the Christian life enjoyed despite sufferings like his second crisis (2.14–7.4). His remarks on the "collection" (chs. 8–9) dates chs. 1–9 between 1 Corinthians and Romans.

Chapters 10–13, which contain valuable autobiographical material, are so angry and "boastful" that many believe Paul wrote them on quite another occasion. In any case, these chapters respond to news of Jewish-Christian interlopers in Corinth, a topic not mentioned in chs. 1–9.

1 FROM Paul, apostle of Christ Jesus by God's will, and our colleague Timothy, to God's church at Corinth, together with all God's people throughout the whole of Achaia.

2 Grace and peace to you from God our Father and the Lord Jesus Christ.

3 Praise be to the God and Father of our Lord Jesus Christ, the all-merciful Father, the God whose consolation never fails us! 4 He consoles us in all our troubles, so that we in turn may be able to console others in any trouble of theirs and to share with them the consolation we ourselves receive from God. 5 As Christ's suffering exceeds all measure and extends to us, so too it is through Christ that our consolation has no limit. 6 If distress is our lot, it is the price we pay for your consolation and your salvation; if our lot is consolation, it is to help us to bring you consolation, and strength to face with fortitude the same sufferings we now endure. 7 And our hope for you is firmly grounded; for we know that if you share in the suffering, you share also in the consolation.

8 In saying this, my friends, we should like you to know how serious was the trouble that came upon us in the province of Asia. The burden of it was far too heavy for us to bear, so heavy that we even despaired of life. 9 Indeed, we felt in our hearts that we had received a death sentence. This was meant to teach us to place reliance not on ourselves, but on God who raises the dead. 10 From such mortal peril God delivered us; and he will deliver us again, he on whom our hope is fixed. Yes, he will continue to deliver us, 11 while you co-operate by praying for us. Then, with so many people praying for our deliverance, there will be many to give thanks on our behalf for God's gracious favour towards us.

Paul's concern for the church at Corinth

12 THERE is one thing we are proud of: our conscience shows us that in our dealings with others, and above all in our dealings with

---

1.1–7: **Salutation and thanksgiving:** see Rom. 1.1–7 nn. and 1.8–15 n. Paul *praises* God for his escape from danger and for Titus' good news (see Introduction). **1:** *Timothy:* see 1 Cor. 16.10 n.

1.8–2.13: **Explanation for a change in travel plans.** Apparently in his "severe" letter (see Introduction) Paul had threatened an immediate return visit. He later decided to wait for Titus' firsthand report, which he finally you, our conduct has been governed by a devout and godly sincerity, by the grace of God and not by worldly wisdom. 13–14 There is nothing in our letters to you but what you can read and understand. You do understand us in some measure, but I hope you will come to understand fully that you have as much reason to be proud of us, as we of you, on the day of our Lord Jesus.

15 It was because I felt so confident about all this that I had intended to come first of all to you and give you the benefit of a double visit: 16 I meant to visit you on my way to Macedonia and, after leaving Macedonia, to return to you, and you could then have sent me on my way to Judaea. 17 That was my intention; did I lightly change my mind? Or do I, when framing my plans, frame them as a worldly man might, first saying 'Yes, yes' and then 'No, no'? 18 God is to be trusted, and therefore what we tell you is not a mixture of Yes and No. 19 The Son of God, Christ Jesus, proclaimed among you by us (by Silvanus and Timothy, I mean, as well as myself), was not a mixture of Yes and No. With him it is always Yes; 20 for all the promises of God have their Yes in him. That is why, when we give glory to God, it is through Christ Jesus that we say 'Amen'. 21 And if you and we belong to Christ, guaranteed as his and anointed, it is all God's doing; 22 it is God also who has set his seal upon us and, as a pledge of what is to come, has given the Spirit to dwell in our hearts.

23 I appeal to God as my witness and stake my life upon it: it was out of consideration for you that I did not after all come to Corinth. 24 It is not that we have control of your faith; rather we are working with you for your happiness. For it is by that faith that you stand.

2 1 So I made up my mind that my next visit to you must not be another painful one. 2 If I cause pain to you, who is left to cheer me up, except you whom I have offended? 3 This is precisely the point I made in my letter: I did not want, I said, to come and be made miserable by the very people

who ought to have made me happy; and I had sufficient confidence in you all to know that for me to be happy is for all of you to be happy. 4 That letter I sent you came out of great distress and anxiety; how many tears I shed as I wrote it! Not because I wanted to cause you pain; rather I wanted you to know the love, the more than ordinary love, that I have for you.

5 Any injury that has been done has not been done to me; to some extent (I do not want to make too much of it) it has been done to you all. 6 The penalty on which the general meeting has agreed has met the offence well enough. 7 Something very different is called for now: you must forgive the offender and put heart into him; the man's distress must not be made so severe as to overwhelm him. 8 I urge you therefore to reassure him of your love for him. 9 I wrote, I may say, to see how you stood the test, whether you fully accepted my authority. 10 But anyone who has your forgiveness has mine too; and when I speak of forgiving (so far as there is anything for me to forgive), I mean that as the representative of Christ I have forgiven him for your sake. 11 For Satan must not be allowed to get the better of us; we know his wiles all too well.

12 When I came to Troas, where I was to preach the gospel of Christ, and where an opening awaited me for serving the Lord, 13 I still found no relief of mind, for my colleague Titus was not there to meet me; so I took leave of the people and went off to Macedonia. 14 But thanks be to God, who continually leads us as captives in Christ's triumphal procession, and uses us to spread abroad the fragrance of the knowledge of himself! 15 We are indeed the incense offered by Christ to God, both among those who are on the way to salvation, and among those who are on the way to destruction: 16 to the latter it is a

---

1:12 **devout:** *some witnesses read* frank.   1:17 **That was ... mind?:** *or* In forming this intention, did I act irresponsibly?   2:10 **as the representative:** *or* in the presence.

---

obtained in Macedonia (2.13; 7.6). **8–10:** *Trouble:* see Introduction. *Us, we, ourselves:* see 10.11 n. **13:** See 10.10; 2 Pet. 3.16. **14:** *Day:* see 1 Cor. 1.8 n. **17–20:** *Amen* (see 1 Cor. 14.16 n.) can mean yes. **19:** *Silvanus:* an assistant of Paul's (see 1 Thess. 1.1; 2 Thess. 1.1; as "Silas," Acts 15.22–18.5). **21–22:** *Christ . . . God . . . Spirit:* see 1 Cor. 12.4–6 n. **22:** *Pledge:* see 5.5 n. **2.1–4:** *Visit, letter:* see Introduction. **5–11:** The offending Corinthian has been disciplined (for a possible comparison see 1 Cor. 5.1–5) and he is now in need of *forgiveness.* **12–13:** The narrative of Paul's movements resumes in 7.5.

2.14–7.4: The apostle's ministry of suffering occupies the main section of the letter. **14:** See 1 Cor. 4.9. **15:**

deadly fume that kills, to the former a vital fragrance that brings life. Who is equal to such a calling? 17 We are not adulterating the word of God for profit as so many do; when we declare the word we do it in sincerity, as from God and in God's sight, as members of Christ.

Paul's commission as an apostle

3 ARE we beginning all over again to produce our credentials? Do we, like some people, need letters of introduction to you, or from you? 2 No, you are all the letter we need, a letter written on our heart; anyone can see it for what it is and read it for himself. 3 And as for you, it is plain that you are a letter that has come from Christ, given to us to deliver; a letter written not with ink but with the Spirit of the living God, written not on stone tablets but on the pages of the human heart.

4 It is in full reliance upon God, through Christ, that we make such claims. 5 There is no question of our having sufficient power in ourselves: we cannot claim anything as our own. The power we have comes from God; 6 it is he who has empowered us as ministers of a new covenant, not written but spiritual; for the written law condemns to death, but the Spirit gives life.

7 The ministry that brought death, and that was engraved in written form on stone, was inaugurated with such glory that the Israelites could not keep their eyes on Moses, even though the glory on his face was soon to fade. 8 How much greater, then, must be the glory of the ministry of the Spirit! 9 If glory accompanied the ministry that brought condemnation, how much richer in glory must be the ministry that brings acquittal! 10 Indeed, the glory that once was is now no glory at all; it

is outshone by a still greater glory. 11 For if what was to fade away had its glory, how much greater is the glory of what endures! 12 With such a hope as this we speak out boldly; 13 it is not for us to do as Moses did: he put a veil over his face to keep the Israelites from gazing at the end of what was fading away. 14 In any case their minds had become closed, for that same veil is there to this very day when the lesson is read from the old covenant; and it is never lifted, because only in Christ is it taken away. 15 Indeed to this very day, every time the law of Moses is read, a veil lies over the mind of the hearer. 16 But (as scripture says) 'Whenever he turns to the Lord the veil is removed.' 17 Now the Lord of whom this passage speaks is the Spirit; and where the Spirit of the Lord is, there is liberty. 18 And because for us there is no veil over the face, we all see as in a mirror the glory of the Lord, and we are being transformed into his likeness with ever-increasing glory, through the power of the Lord who is the Spirit.

4 SINCE God in his mercy has given us this ministry, we never lose heart. 2 We have renounced the deeds that people hide for very shame; we do not practise cunning or distort the word of God. It is by declaring the truth openly that we recommend ourselves to the conscience of our fellow-men in the sight of God. 3 If our gospel is veiled at all, it is veiled only for those on the way to destruction; 4 their unbelieving minds are so blinded by the god of this passing age that the gospel of the glory of Christ, who is the image of God, cannot dawn upon them and bring them light. 5 It is not ourselves that we proclaim; we proclaim Christ Jesus as Lord, and ourselves as your servants for Jesus's sake.

3:18 see ... mirror: or reflect like a mirror.

For Paul as a sacrifice compare Phil. 2.17. **17:** *Adulterating ... for profit:* lit. "huckstering," thus corrupting in order to "peddle."

3.1–18: The power of the new covenant; the impotence of the old. **1:** *All over again* implies some previous self-defense and criticism of it. Paul has his rivals in mind (see 10.1–13.14 n.), who carry *letters* of accreditation. **2–3:** The idea of the Corinthians as Paul's living credentials suggests Jer. 31.33, the law written on *hearts* rather than on *stone tablets* (Exod. 34.1, 4). **6:** The *written law* both *condemns to death* (Rom. 3.9–20) and is powerless to *give life* (Gal. 3.21–22). **7–18:** See Exod. 34.29–35. Moses' veil symbolically prevents Judaism from seeing that the law's original *glory* has come to an *end.* **16:** Exod. 34.34. **18:** *Are transformed:* are now at the present time being transfigured. *With ever-increasing glory:* by increasing degrees.

4.1–15: The apostle's faithfulness shown by his sufferings. **3:** *Veiled:* Paul's critics may have called him obscure. *Destruction:* see 2.15–16. **4:** *The god of this passing age,* i.e. Satan (see 1 Cor. 1.8 n.). *Image of God*

⁶For the God who said, 'Out of darkness light shall shine,' has caused his light to shine in our hearts, the light which is knowledge of the glory of God in the face of Jesus Christ.

⁷But we have only earthenware jars to hold this treasure, and this proves that such transcendent power does not come from us; it is God's alone. ⁸We are hard pressed, but never cornered; bewildered, but never at our wits' end; ⁹hunted, but never abandoned to our fate; struck down, but never killed. ¹⁰Wherever we go we carry with us in our body the death that Jesus died, so that in this body also the life that Jesus lives may be revealed. ¹¹For Jesus's sake we are all our life being handed over to death, so that the life of Jesus may be revealed in this mortal body of ours. ¹²Thus death is at work in us, but life in you.

¹³But scripture says, 'I believed, and therefore I spoke out,' and we too, in the same spirit of faith, believe and therefore speak out; ¹⁴for we know that he who raised the Lord Jesus to life will with Jesus raise us too, and bring us to his presence, and you with us. ¹⁵Indeed, all this is for your sake, so that, as the abounding grace of God is shared by more and more, the greater may be the chorus of thanksgiving that rises to the glory of God.

¹⁶No wonder we do not lose heart! Though our outward humanity is in decay, yet day by day we are inwardly renewed. ¹⁷Our troubles are slight and short-lived, and their outcome is an eternal glory which far outweighs them, ¹⁸provided our eyes are fixed, not on the things that are seen, but on the things that are unseen; for what is seen is transient, what is unseen is eternal. 5 ¹We know that if the earthly frame that houses us today is demolished, we possess a building which God has provided—a house not made by human hands, eternal and in heaven. ²In this present body we groan, yearning to be covered by our heavenly habitation put on over this one, ³in the hope that, being thus clothed, we shall not find ourselves naked. ⁴We groan indeed, we who are enclosed within this earthly frame; we are oppressed because we do not want to have the old body stripped off. What we want is to be covered by the new body put on over it, so that our mortality may be absorbed into life immortal. ⁵It is for this destiny that God himself has been shaping us; and as a pledge of it he has given us the Spirit.

⁶Therefore we never cease to be confident. We know that so long as we are at home in the body we are exiles from the Lord; ⁷faith is our guide, not sight. ⁸We are confident, I say, and would rather be exiled from the body and make our home with the Lord. ⁹That is why it is our ambition, wherever we are, at home or in exile, to be acceptable to him. ¹⁰For we must all have our lives laid open before the tribunal of Christ, where each must receive what is due to him for his conduct in the body, good or bad.

The message of reconciliation

¹¹WITH this fear of the Lord before our eyes we address our appeal to men and women. To God our lives lie open, and I hope that in your heart of hearts they lie open to you also. ¹²This is not another attempt to recommend ourselves to you: we are rather giving you a chance to show yourselves proud of us; then you will have something to say to those whose pride is all in outward show and not in in-

recalls Adam (see Gen. 1.27; 1 Cor. 15.45–49 n.; Phil. 2.6). **6:** Gen. 1.3. Paul associates *light* and *glory* with possession of the Spirit (5.5). **8–11:** Daily hardships (see Mk. 8.34) produce likeness to Christ (see Phil. 3.10–11); Paul's *mortal body* is becoming like his Lord's (see 3.18). **12:** Paul accepts more than his proper share of suffering so as to provide them with *life* (see 1.6). **13:** Ps. 116.10.

4.16–5.10: Our changing bodies. 16: *Day by day* our suffering is eroding our *outward humanity* (i.e. our flesh bodies), but simultaneously we are *inwardly renewed* by spirit. (By contrast, in 1 Cor. 15.42–57 this change of bodies is considered to occur instantly at Christ's return.) **18:** *Things . . . seen:* the external body; *things . . . unseen:* the interior possession of the Spirit. **5.1–4:** Figuratively, the body is our home, or alternatively, our clothing. **1:** Our spirit body is *eternal* and destined for life *in heaven*. **2–4:** Paul is *yearning* for the change to be completed and suffering ended (see Rom. 8.23). Unbelievers, since they do not receive spirit bodies, are *naked* at death. **5:** The *pledge* is the down payment which puts a contract in force and implies further payments (in this case, of *the Spirit;* so also 1.22). **6–8:** Phil. 1.21–24.

5.11–6.10: The reconciling ministry of Christ and his apostles. **12:** *Another attempt:* see 3.1 n. **13:** *If . . .*

ward worth. ¹³ If these are mad words, take them as addressed to God; if sound sense, as addressed to you. ¹⁴ For the love of Christ controls us once we have reached the conclusion that one man died for all and therefore all mankind has died. ¹⁵ He died for all so that those who live should cease to live for themselves, and should live for him who for their sake died and was raised to life. ¹⁶ With us therefore worldly standards have ceased to count in our estimate of anyone; even if once they counted in our understanding of Christ, they do so now no longer. ¹⁷ For anyone united to Christ, there is a new creation: the old order has gone; a new order has already begun.

¹⁸ All this has been the work of God. He has reconciled us to himself through Christ, and has enlisted us in this ministry of reconciliation: ¹⁹ God was in Christ reconciling the world to himself, no longer holding people's misdeeds against them, and has entrusted us with the message of reconciliation. ²⁰ We are therefore Christ's ambassadors. It is as if God were appealing to you through us: we implore you in Christ's name, be reconciled to God! ²¹ Christ was innocent of sin, and yet for our sake God made him one with human sinfulness, so that in him we might be made

6 one with the righteousness of God. ¹ Sharing in God's work, we make this appeal: you have received the grace of God; do not let it come to nothing. ² He has said:

> In the hour of my favour I answered you;
> on the day of deliverance I came to your aid.

This is the hour of favour, this the day of deliverance.

³ Lest our ministry be brought into discredit, we avoid giving any offence in anything. ⁴ As God's ministers, we try to recommend ourselves in all circumstances by our steadfast endurance: in affliction, hardship, and distress; ⁵ when flogged, imprisoned, mobbed; overworked, sleepless, starving. ⁶ We recommend ourselves by innocent behaviour and grasp of truth, by patience and kindliness, by gifts of the Holy Spirit, by unaffected love, ⁷ by declaring the truth, by the power of God. We wield the weapons of righteousness in right hand and left. ⁸ Honour and dishonour, praise and blame, are alike our lot: we are the impostors who speak the truth, ⁹ the unknown men whom all men know; dying we still live on; disciplined by suffering, we are not done to death; ¹⁰ in our sorrows we have always cause for joy; poor ourselves, we bring wealth to many; penniless, we own the world.

¹¹ We have spoken very frankly to you, friends in Corinth; we have opened our heart to you. ¹² There is no constraint on our part; any constraint there may be is in you. ¹³ In fair exchange then (if I may speak to you like a father) open your hearts to us.

Church life and discipline

¹⁴ DO NOT team up with unbelievers. What partnership can righteousness have with wickedness? Can light associate with darkness? ¹⁵ Can Christ agree with Belial, or a

5:13 **If these . . . to you:** *or* If we speak in ecstasy, it is to God's glory; if we speak sober sense, it is to your advantage.   5:17 **For anyone . . . begun:** *or* When anyone is united to Christ he is a new creature: his old life is over; a new life has already begun.
5:19 **God . . . himself:** *or* God was reconciling the world to himself by Christ.

mad words (lit. "If we are beside ourselves"): in ecstasy (see 12.1–4 n.). **14:** *Love of Christ:* Christ's love for us. *One man:* Christ, the second Adam (see 1 Cor. 15.45–49 n.), represents *all* humanity. In principle the old humanity has ended. **15:** See Mk. 8.35. **16:** *Once,* before his conversion, Paul thought of Jesus as a crucified criminal. **17:** For Christians the new life *has already begun* (see 4.16 n.). **18–20:** By extension the apostle shares Christ's *reconciling* ministry. **19–21:** *In Christ* (v. 19): through Christ as his agent. Christ accepted the *sinfulness* of human beings that those *in Christ* might *no longer* have their *misdeeds* held *against* them (v. 19; Rom. 3.21–26). **6.2:** Isa. 49.8. *This . . . hour:* see 5.17 n. **3:** *Discredit:* see 3.1 n. **4–5:** See 11.23–29. *In all circumstances:* see 1 Cor. 9.19–23. **6:** Paul here emphasizes his *patience and kindliness* by alluding to the abundance of personal sufferings he has undergone, all specified in v. 5. **7:** *Weapons:* see Eph. 6.14–17; 1 Thess. 5.8. **8–10:** The apostle's ministry (like Jesus') is full of paradoxes (see 4.8–12; 1 Cor. 4.9–13).

    6.11–13: Paul appeals with open heart to the Corinthians for complete reconciliation free of *constraint*. (For their past disagreements see Introduction.) Paul here reaches the climax of 2.14–7.4.

    6.14–7.1: Avoid unbelievers. The section is very probably misplaced (see 7.2–4 n. and Introduction to believer join with an unbeliever? [16]Can there be a compact between the temple of God and idols? And the temple of the living God is what we are. God's own words are: 'I will live and move about among them; I will be their God, and they shall be my people.' [17]And therefore, 'Come away and leave them, separate yourselves, says the Lord; touch nothing unclean. Then I will accept you, [18]says the Lord Almighty; I will be a father to you, and

7 you shall be my sons and daughters.' [1]Such are the promises that have been made to us, dear friends. Let us therefore cleanse ourselves from all that can defile flesh or spirit and, in the fear of God, let us complete our consecration.

[2]MAKE a place for us in your hearts! We have wronged no one, ruined no one, exploited no one. [3]My words are no reflection on you. I have told you before that, come death, come life, your place in our hearts is secure. [4]I am speaking to you with great frankness, but my pride in you is just as great. In all our many troubles my cup is full of consolation and overflows with joy.

[5]Even when we reached Macedonia we still found no relief; instead trouble met us at every turn, fights without and fears within. [6]But God, who brings comfort to the downcast, has comforted us by the arrival of Titus, [7]and not merely by his arrival, but by his being so greatly encouraged about you. He has told us how you long for me, how sorry you are, and how eager to take my side; and that has made me happier still.

[8]Even if I did hurt you by the letter I sent, I do not now regret it. I did regret it; but now that I see the letter gave you pain, though only for a time, [9]I am happy — not because of the pain but because the pain led to a change of heart. You bore the pain as God would have you bear it, and so you came to no harm from what we did. [10]Pain borne in God's way

brings no regrets but a change of heart leading to salvation; pain borne in the world's way brings death. [11]You bore your pain in God's way, and just look at the results: it made you take the matter seriously and vindicate yourselves; it made you indignant and apprehensive; it aroused your longing for me, your devotion, and your eagerness to see justice done! At every point you have cleared yourselves of blame. [12]And so, although I did send you that letter, it was not the offender or his victim that most concerned me. My aim in writing was to help to make plain to you, in the sight of God, how truly you are devoted to us. [13]That is why we have been so encouraged.

But besides being encouraged ourselves, we have also been delighted beyond everything by seeing how happy Titus is: you have all helped to set his mind completely at rest. [14]Anything I may have said to him to show my pride in you has been justified. Every word we addressed to you bore the mark of truth, and the same holds of the proud boast we made in the presence of Titus; that also has proved true. [15]His heart warms all the more to you as he recalls how ready you all were to do what he asked, meeting him as you did in fear and trembling. [16]How happy I am now to have complete confidence in you!

The collection for the church in Jerusalem

8 WE must tell you, friends, about the grace that God has given to the churches in Macedonia. [2]The troubles they have been through have tried them hard, yet in all this they have been so exuberantly happy that from the depths of their poverty they have shown themselves lavishly open-handed. [3]Going to the limit of their resources, as I can testify, and even beyond that limit, [4]they

1 Cor.). **15:** *Belial:* Satan. **16−18:** Paul links together a chain of texts: Lev. 26.12; Ezek. 37.27; Isa. 52.11; 2 Sam. 7.14. **7.1:** *Complete our consecration,* i.e. our dedication to holiness.

7.2−4: Paul continues his plea. These verses would follow on 6.13, if 6.14−7.1 are misplaced (see Introduction to 1 Cor.).

7.5−16: Paul's narrative resumes from 2.13. (For the sequence of events see Introduction.) **8:** Although Paul was sorry that he had sent the "severe" letter, the effect in the end was healthful. **12:** *The offender:* see 2.5−11 n. *His victim:* probably Paul. **14:** What Paul wrote to the Corinthians was angry; what he *said* to Titus expressed pride. **15−16:** Paul prepares for 8.6−8, 16−17.

8.1−9.15: The offering for the poor of the Jerusalem church (see Introduction to Rom.). Reconciliation assumed, Paul now turns to the collection. **1−5:** Paul describes the generosity of the Macedonians (see Phil.

begged us most insistently, and on their own initiative, to be allowed to share in this generous service to their fellow-Christians. ⁵And their giving surpassed our expectations; for first of all they gave themselves to the Lord and, under God, to us. ⁶The upshot is that we have asked Titus, since he has already made a beginning, to bring your share in this further work of generosity also to completion. ⁷You are so rich in everything—in faith, speech, knowledge, and diligence of every kind, as well as in the love you have for us—that you should surely show yourselves equally lavish in this generous service! ⁸This is not meant as an order; by telling you how keen others are I am putting your love to the test. ⁹You know the generosity of our Lord Jesus Christ: he was rich, yet for your sake he became poor, so that through his poverty you might become rich.

¹⁰Here is my advice, and I have your interests at heart. You made a good beginning last year both in what you did and in your willingness to do it. ¹¹Now go on and finish it. Be as eager to complete the scheme as you were to adopt it, and give according to your means. ¹²If we give eagerly according to our means, that is acceptable to God; he does not ask for what we do not have. ¹³There is no question of relieving others at the cost of hardship to yourselves; ¹⁴it is a question of equality. At the moment your surplus meets their need, but one day your need may be met from their surplus. The aim is equality; ¹⁵as scripture has it, 'Those who gathered more did not have too much, and those who gathered less did not have too little.'

¹⁶I thank God that he has made Titus as keen on your behalf as we are! ¹⁷So keen is he that he not only welcomed our request; it is by his own choice he is now leaving to come to you. ¹⁸With him we are sending one of our company whose reputation for his services to the gospel among all the churches is high. ¹⁹Moreover they have duly appointed him to travel with us and help in this beneficent work, by which we do honour to the Lord himself and show our own eagerness to serve. ²⁰We want to guard against any criticism of our handling of these large sums; ²¹for our aims are entirely honourable, not only in the Lord's eyes, but also in the eyes of men and women.

²²We are sending with them another of our company whose enthusiasm we have had repeated opportunities of testing, and who is now all the more keen because of the great confidence he has in you. ²³If there is any question about Titus, he is my partner and my fellow-worker in dealings with you; as for the others, they are delegates of the churches and bring honour to Christ. ²⁴So give them, and through them the churches, clear evidence of your love and justify our pride in you.

9 About this aid for God's people, it is superfluous for me to write to you. ²I know how eager you are to help and I speak of it with pride to the Macedonians, telling them that Achaia had everything ready last year; and most of them have been fired by your zeal. ³My purpose in sending these friends is to ensure that what we have said about you in this matter should not prove to be an empty boast. I want you to be prepared, as I told them you were; ⁴for if I bring men from Macedonia with me and they find you are not prepared, what a disgrace it will be to us, let alone to you, after all the confidence we have shown! ⁵I have accordingly thought it necessary to ask these friends to go on ahead to Corinth, to see that your promised bounty is in order before I come; it will then be awaiting me as genuine bounty, and not as an extortion.

⁶Remember: sow sparingly, and you will reap sparingly; sow bountifully, and you will reap bountifully. ⁷Each person should give as he has decided for himself; there should be no reluctance, no sense of compulsion;

8:7 **the love . . . us:** *some witnesses read* the love we have for you, *or* the love which we have kindled in your hearts.

4.15–18) to spur the Corinthians on (contrast 9.2). **6:** See vv. 16–17 n. **7:** See 1 Cor. 12.8–10. **9:** *Became poor:* see Phil. 2.5–11. **10–11:** *Finish, complete* suggests that the dispute between Paul and the Corinthians interrupted the collection project. **14:** *Surplus:* contrast v. 2. **15:** Exod. 16.18. **16–17:** Titus will precede Paul (see 9.4–5 n.). **18–24:** *One of our company:* lit. "the brother." This unidentified missionary has been *appointed* (probably by Jerusalem) to help with the collection (*this beneficent work*). He and *another* colleague of v. 22 are called "apostles" (*delegates*) in v. 23. **20:** On the Corinthians' suspicions about Paul and money see 12.16–18; 11.7–10 n. **21:** Prov. 3.4 (Sept.). **9.2:** See 8.1–5 n. **4–5:** Paul will come with representatives *from*

God loves a cheerful giver. [8] And it is in God's power to provide you with all good gifts in abundance, so that, with every need always met to the full, you may have something to spare for every good cause; [9] as scripture says: 'He lavishes his gifts on the needy; his benevolence lasts for ever.' [10] Now he who provides seed for sowing and bread for food will provide the seed for you to sow; he will multiply it and swell the harvest of your benevolence, [11] and you will always be rich enough to be generous. Through our action such generosity will issue in thanksgiving to God, [12] for as a piece of willing service this is not only a contribution towards the needs of God's people; more than that, it overflows in a flood of thanksgiving to God. [13] For with the proof which this aid affords, those who receive it will give honour to God when they see how humbly you obey him and how faithfully you confess the gospel of Christ; and they will thank him for your liberal contribution to their need and to the general good. [14] And as they join in prayer on your behalf, their hearts will go out to you because of the richness of the grace which God has given you. [15] Thanks be to God for his gift which is beyond all praise!

The challenge to Paul's authority

10 I, Paul, appeal to you by the gentleness and magnanimity of Christ — I who am so timid (you say) when face to face with you, so courageous when I am away from you. [2] Spare me when I come, I beg you, the need for that courage and self-assurance, which I reckon I could confidently display against those who assume my behaviour to be dictated by human weakness. [3] Weak and hu-

man we may be, but that does not dictate the way we fight our battles. [4] The weapons we wield are not merely human; they are strong enough with God's help to demolish strongholds. [5] We demolish sophistries and all that rears its proud head against the knowledge of God; we compel every human thought to surrender in obedience to Christ; [6] and we are prepared to punish any disobedience once your own obedience is complete.

[7] Look facts in the face. Is someone convinced that he belongs to Christ? Let him think again and reflect that we belong to Christ as much as he does. [8] Indeed, if I am boasting too much about our authority — an authority given by the Lord to build your faith, not pull it down — I shall make good my boast. [9] So you must not think of me as one who tries to scare you by the letters he writes. [10] 'His letters', so it is said, 'are weighty and powerful; but when he is present he is unimpressive, and as a speaker he is beneath contempt.' [11] People who talk in that way should reckon with this: my actions when I come will show the same man as my letters showed while I was absent.

[12] We should not dare to class ourselves or compare ourselves with any of those who commend themselves. What fools they are to measure themselves on their own, to find in themselves their standard of comparison! [13] As for us, our boasting will not go beyond the proper limits; and our sphere is determined by the limit God laid down for us, which permitted us to come as far as Corinth. [14] We are not overstretching our commission, as we would be if we had never come to you; but we were the first to reach as far as Corinth in the work of the gospel of Christ. [15] And we do not boast of work done where

---

Macedonia. From *Corinth* they will sail to Jerusalem (1 Cor. 16.3–4). **7:** Prov. 22.8 (Sept.). **9:** Ps. 112.9. **15:** *Gift . . . beyond all praise:* God's son (see Rom. 8.32).

10.1–13.14: Paul's boast against false apostles. Because of the tone of chs. 10–13, some have taken them to be part of the "severe" letter which preceded 2 Cor. chs. 1–9 (see Introduction). However, the problem of traveling Jewish "apostles" in chs. 10–13 is more probably subsequent to chs. 1–9. On the lack of an opening thanksgiving see Rom. 1.8–15 n. Note the accusations against Paul: unethical (v. 2), weak (v. 3), boastful (v. 8), brave from a distance but ineffectual in person (vv. 1, 10–11), an amateur "apostle" (11.7–11), a man without pedigree (11.22–23), a nobody (12.11).

10.1–18: Paul's bold counterattack. 1: On Christ's humility see Phil. 2.5–8, especially v. 8. **2:** *Behavior . . . dictated by human weakness:* unethical action. **3–4:** Paul adopts phrases by which his opponents have disparaged him: *weak, merely human. Weapons:* see 6.7; Eph. 6.14–17; 1 Thess. 5.8. **8:** Words meaning *boasting* appear nineteen times in 10.8–12.9. **9–10:** See 2.3–4; 11.6 n. **11:** *I, my:* lit. "we," "our." Here, as often, the plural stands primarily for Paul. **15–16:** *Our . . . sphere:* see Rom. 15.20 n. *Lands that lie beyond* others have laboured, work beyond our proper sphere. Our hope is rather that, as your faith grows, we may attain a position among you greater than ever before, but still within the limits of our sphere. 16 Then we can carry the gospel to lands that lie beyond you, never priding ourselves on work already done in anyone else's sphere. 17 If anyone would boast, let him boast of the Lord. 18 For it is not the one who recommends himself, but the one whom the Lord recommends, who is to be accepted.

Paul speaks as a fool

11 I SHOULD like you to bear with me in a little foolishness; please bear with me. 2 I am jealous for you, with the jealousy of God; for I betrothed you to Christ, thinking to present you as a chaste virgin to her true and only husband. 3 Now I am afraid that, as the serpent in his cunning seduced Eve, your thoughts may be corrupted and you may lose your single-hearted devotion to Christ. 4 For if some newcomer proclaims another Jesus, not the Jesus whom we proclaimed, or if you receive a spirit different from the Spirit already given to you, or a gospel different from the gospel you have already accepted, you put up with that well enough. 5 I am not aware of being in any way inferior to those super-apostles. 6 I may be no speaker, but knowledge I do have; at all times we have made known to you the full truth.

7 Or was this my offence, that I made no charge for preaching the gospel of God, humbling myself in order to exalt you? 8 I robbed other churches—by accepting support from them to serve you. 9 If I ran short while I was with you, I did not become a charge on anyone; my needs were fully met by friends from Macedonia; I made it a rule,

as I always shall, never to be a burden to you. 10 As surely as the truth of Christ is in me, nothing shall bar me from boasting about this throughout Achaia. 11 Why? Because I do not love you? God knows I do.

12 And I shall go on doing as I am doing now, to cut the ground from under those who would seize any chance to put their vaunted apostleship on the same level as ours. 13 Such people are sham apostles, confidence tricksters masquerading as apostles of Christ. 14 And no wonder! Satan himself masquerades as an angel of light, 15 so it is easy enough for his agents to masquerade as agents of good. But their fate will match their deeds.

16 I repeat: let no one take me for a fool; but if you must, then give me the privilege of a fool, and let me have my little boast like others. 17 In boasting so confidently I am not speaking like a Christian, but like a fool. 18 So many people brag of their earthly distinctions that I shall do so too. 19 How gladly you put up with fools, being yourselves so wise! 20 If someone tyrannizes over you, exploits you, gets you in his clutches, puts on airs, and hits you in the face, you put up with it. 21 And you call me a weakling! I admit the reproach.

But if there is to be bravado (and I am still speaking as a fool), I can indulge in it too. 22 Are they Hebrews? So am I. Israelites? So am I. Abraham's descendants? So am I. 23 Are they servants of Christ? I am mad to speak like this, but I can outdo them: more often overworked, more often imprisoned, scourged more severely, many a time face to face with death. 24 Five times the Jews have given me the thirty-nine strokes; 25 three times I have been beaten with rods; once I was stoned; three times I have been shipwrecked, and for twenty-four hours I was

11:3 lose ... devotion: *some witnesses read* lose your purity and single-hearted devotion.

you, i.e. to the west, perhaps Spain (Rom. 15.23–28). **17:** Jer. 9.24 (1 Cor. 1.31).

11.1–15: Satan's apostles. 1: *Foolishness:* see v. 16. **2:** See Hos. 2.19–20; Eph. 5.26–27. **3:** Paul compares his opponents to the serpent of Gen. 3.4; see vv. 13–15 n. **5:** The *super-apostles* are paid (vv. 7–10) preachers (v. 6), Jewish-Christians (vv. 22–23) probably from Jerusalem. **6:** See 10.10; 1 Cor. 2.3. **7–10:** Apparently Paul's practice was to accept money for himself but never to ask for it (see 1 Cor. 9.12b–18). The Corinthians, unlike the *Macedonians* (Phil. 4.14–18), had not offered to support him. Ironically, he is now criticized for not receiving support as a "true" apostle should. **13–15:** See also Gal. 5.12, a passage only slightly more intemperate.

11.16–33: Paul's credentials are his hardships. 21–23: *Hebrews:* Aram. speaking. *Israelites:* Jews by birth (see Rom. 9.4 n.). Compare Phil. 3.4–6. So well did Paul adapt himself to his environment (1 Cor. 9.19–23) that at times he had to assert his Jewish pedigree. **24:** *Thirty-nine strokes:* see Acts 5.40 n. **25:** *Rods:* a Roman adrift on the open sea. ²⁶ I have been constantly on the road; I have met dangers from rivers, dangers from robbers, dangers from my fellow-countrymen, dangers from foreigners, dangers in the town, dangers in the wilderness, dangers at sea, dangers from false Christians. ²⁷ I have toiled and drudged and often gone without sleep; I have been hungry and thirsty and have often gone without food; I have suffered from cold and exposure.

²⁸ Apart from these external things, there is the responsibility that weighs on me every day, my anxious concern for all the churches. ²⁹ Is anyone weak? I share his weakness. If anyone brings about the downfall of another, does my heart not burn with anger? ³⁰ If boasting there must be, I will boast of the things that show up my weakness. ³¹ He who is blessed for ever, the God and Father of the Lord Jesus, knows that what I say is true. ³² When I was in Damascus, the commissioner of King Aretas kept the city under observation to have me arrested; ³³ and I was let down in a basket, through a window in the wall, and so escaped his clutches.

12 It may do no good, but I must go on with my boasting; I come now to visions and revelations granted by the Lord. ² I know a Christian man who fourteen years ago (whether in the body or out of the body, I do not know — God knows) was caught up as far as the third heaven. ³ And I know that this same man (whether in the body or apart from the body, I do not know — God knows) ⁴ was caught up into paradise, and heard words so secret that human lips may not repeat them. ⁵ About such a man I am ready to boast; but I will not boast on my own account, except of my weaknesses. ⁶ If I chose to boast, it would not be the boast of a fool, for I

should be speaking the truth. But I refrain, because I do not want anyone to form an estimate of me which goes beyond the evidence of his own eyes and ears. ⁷ To keep me from being unduly elated by the magnificence of such revelations, I was given a thorn in my flesh, a messenger of Satan sent to buffet me; this was to save me from being unduly elated. ⁸ Three times I begged the Lord to rid me of it, ⁹ but his answer was: 'My grace is all you need; power is most fully seen in weakness.' I am therefore happy to boast of my weaknesses, because then the power of Christ will rest upon me. ¹⁰ So I am content with a life of weakness, insult, hardship, persecution, and distress, all for Christ's sake; for when I am weak, then I am strong.

Paul's final appeal

¹¹ I am being very foolish, but it was you who drove me to it; my credentials should have come from you. In nothing did I prove inferior to those super-apostles, even if I am a nobody. ¹² The signs of an apostle were there in the work I did among you, marked by unfailing endurance, by signs, portents, and miracles. ¹³ Is there any way in which you were treated worse than the other churches — except this, that I was never a charge on you? Forgive me for being so unfair!

¹⁴ I am now getting ready to pay you a third visit; and I am not going to be a charge on you. It is you I want, not your money; parents should make provision for their children, not children for their parents. ¹⁵ I would gladly spend everything for you — yes, and spend myself to the limit. If I love you overmuch, am I to be loved the less? ¹⁶ All very well, you

12:6–7 **ears ... given:** *some witnesses read* ears, ⁷and because of the magnificence of the revelations themselves. Therefore to keep me from being unduly elated I was given.

punishment (see Acts 16.22). *Stoned:* see Acts 14.19. **32–33:** See Acts 9.23–25. Aretas IV was king of Nabataea.

    12.1–10: Paul's visions and "thorn in the flesh." **1–4:** Paul was given to *visions and revelations* (see v. 7; 5.13); he could also speak in tongues (see 1 Cor. 14.18). **2:** *Christian man:* Paul (v. 7). *The third heaven* may mean the highest; or else the third of seven, as the Jews viewed heaven. **4:** *Paradise:* the heavenly Eden. **7:** *Thorn in my flesh:* some suggest a recurrent illness (compare Gal. 4.13–14); others, a human adversary (*messenger of Satan*). **9:** Just as the *power of Christ* was expressed in weakness, Paul understands that his own *weakness* is transformed into strength by means of *grace.* (Compare Phil. 2.5–11; 3.7–11.) **10:** See 11.23–30; 4.7–12; 1 Cor. 4.11–13; Rom. 8.35.

    12.11–21: Paul's fatherly concern for his congregation. **11:** *Super-apostles:* see 11.5 n. **12:** *Signs, portents, and miracles:* see Rom. 15.19; Gal. 3.5. **13–15:** See 11.7–10 n. **14:** *Third visit:* see 13.1–2 n. *Parents, children:*

say; I did not myself prove a burden to you, but I did use a confidence trick to take you in. 17 Was it one of the men I sent to you that I used to exploit you? 18 I begged Titus to visit you, and I sent our friend with him. Did Titus exploit you? Have we not both been guided by the same Spirit, and followed the same course?

19 Perhaps you have been thinking all this time that it is to you we are addressing our defence. No; we are speaking in God's sight, and as Christians. Our whole aim, dear friends, is to build you up. 20 I fear that when I come I may find you different from what I wish, and you may find me to be what you do not wish. I fear I may find quarrelling and jealousy, angry tempers and personal rivalries, backbiting and gossip, arrogance and general disorder. 21 I am afraid that when I come my God may humiliate me again in your presence, that I may have cause to grieve over many who were sinning before and have not repented of their unclean lives, their fornication and sensuality.

13 This will be my third visit to you. As scripture says, 'Every charge must be established on the evidence of two or three witnesses': 2 to those who sinned before, and to everyone else, I repeat the warning I gave last time; on my second visit I gave it in person, and now I give it while absent. It is that when I come this time, I will show no leniency. 3 Then you will have the proof you seek

of the Christ who speaks through me, the Christ who, far from being weak with you, makes his power felt among you. 4 True, he died on the cross in weakness, but he lives by the power of God; so you will find that we who share his weakness shall live with him by the power of God.

5 Examine yourselves: are you living the life of faith? Put yourselves to the test. Surely you recognize that Jesus Christ is among you? If not, you have failed the test. 6 I hope you will come to see that we have not failed. 7 Our prayer to God is that you may do no wrong, not that we should win approval; we want you to do what is right, even if we should seem failures. 8 We have no power to act against the truth, but only for it. 9 We are happy to be weak at any time if only you are strong. Our prayer, then, is for your amendment. 10 In writing this letter before I come, my aim is to spare myself, when I do come, any sharp exercise of authority—authority which the Lord gave me for building up and not for pulling down.

11 And now, my friends, farewell. Mend your ways; take our appeal to heart; agree with one another; live in peace; and the God of love and peace will be with you. 12 Greet one another with the kiss of peace. 13 All God's people send you greetings.

14 The grace of the Lord Jesus Christ, and the love of God, and the fellowship of the Holy Spirit, be with you all.

compare 1 Cor. 4.14–15. **18:** *Begged Titus:* see 8.6, 16–17 n. *Our friend:* see 8.18–24 n. **20–21:** All the old difficulties spring to Paul's mind (see 1 Cor. 1.11; 5.1; 6.12–20), but the lists are partly stereotyped (see 1 Cor. 6.9–11 n.; Rom. 1.29–31; Gal. 5.19–21). *Humiliate:* perhaps an echo of 2.1.

13.1–14: Final warnings, greetings and blessing. 1–2: Paul's approaching visit (see 9.4–5 n.) will be his *third.* The first was the founding visit (see 10.14); his *second visit* was "painful" (see Introduction). The *three witnesses* (Deut. 19.15) may be the three visits: the Corinthians have one chance left. **12:** *Kiss:* see Rom. 16.16 n. **14:** This is the fullest form of Paul's usual benediction (see 1 Cor. 12.4–6 n.).

THE LETTER OF PAUL TO THE
Galatians

Freedom is the message of this extremely important letter. The immediate issue is whether Christians should observe Jewish law. Paul's churches in Galatia (perhaps at Iconium, Lystra, and Derbe; Acts ch. 14) had been visited by Christian Jews who preached at least a partial observance of Mosaic law. Paul cites circumcision (5.2; 6.12) and the ritual calendar (4.10). Apparently they presented both themselves and Paul as subject to the authority of the Jerusalem Church. Paul asserts his divine commission and complete freedom from Jerusalem, giving us valuable autobiographical information (1.10–2.14). He attacks "legalism" as a denial in principle of the divine acceptance ("justification") which can depend only on utter trust ("faith") in Christ (2.15–3.29). The Mosaic law is for "slaves," whereas Christians are God's adopted children (ch. 4); their acting in love supersedes the law (5.13–6.10). Sarcastically, Paul accuses the Judaizers of seeking to give Christianity the appearance of a Jewish sect only to avoid persecution (6.12).

The date of the letter is a problem. Many of the same issues (and phrases) appear in Romans, suggesting that the interval between the two was not great. Because these issues are more urgent here in Galatians, this letter is the earlier.

1 FROM Paul, an apostle commissioned not by any human authority or human act, but by Jesus Christ and God the Father who raised him from the dead. ²I and all the friends now with me send greetings to the churches of Galatia.

³Grace to you and peace from God the Father and our Lord Jesus Christ, ⁴who gave himself for our sins, to rescue us out of the present wicked age as our God and Father willed; ⁵to him be glory for ever and ever! Amen.

One gospel for all

⁶I AM astonished to find you turning away so quickly from him who called you by grace, and following a different gospel. ⁷Not that it is in fact another gospel; only there are some who unsettle your minds by trying to distort the gospel of Christ. ⁸But should anyone, even I myself or an angel from heaven,

preach a gospel other than the gospel I preached to you, let him be banned! ⁹I warned you in the past and now I warn you again: if anyone preaches a gospel other than the gospel you received, let him be banned!

¹⁰Now do I sound as if I were asking for human approval and not for God's alone? Am I currying favour with men? If I were still seeking human favour, I should be no servant of Christ.

¹¹I must make it clear to you, my friends, that the gospel you heard me preach is not of human origin. ¹²I did not take it over from anyone; no one taught it me; I received it through a revelation of Jesus Christ.

¹³You have heard what my manner of life was when I was still a practising Jew: how savagely I persecuted the church of God and

1:3 **God . . . Christ:** *some witnesses read* God our Father and the Lord Jesus Christ. 1:6 **from him . . . grace:** *some witnesses read* from Christ who called you by grace, *or* from him who called you by the grace of Christ.

1.1–5: Salutation. See Rom. 1.1–7 nn. **1:** From the first line Paul emphasizes again and again that he is an *apostle* independent of human authority. **3–5:** See Rom. 1.7 n. and 1.8–15 n. **4:** See 2.20; 1 Cor. 15.3. *Age:* see 1 Cor. 2.6–8 n.

1.6–10: The Galatian apostasy from God. **8–9:** *Angel:* see 2 Cor. 11.14. *Banned:* lit. "anathema"; compare 1 Cor. 16.22 n.; 5.2–5. **10:** 1 Thess. 2.4; 1 Cor. 9.19–23.

1.11–17: Paul's gospel is from God not human beings. **12:** Compare 1 Cor. 15.8 and 2 Cor. 12.1–4 n. with tried to destroy it; [14] and how in the practice of our national religion I outstripped most of my Jewish contemporaries by my boundless devotion to the traditions of my ancestors. [15] But then in his good pleasure God, who from my birth had set me apart, and who had called me through his grace, chose [16] to reveal his Son in and through me, in order that I might proclaim him among the Gentiles. Immediately, without consulting a single person, [17] without going up to Jerusalem to see those who were apostles before me, I went off to Arabia, and afterwards returned to Damascus.

[18] Three years later I did go up to Jerusalem to get to know Cephas, and I stayed two weeks with him. [19] I saw none of the other apostles, except James, the Lord's brother. [20] What I write is plain truth; God knows I am not lying!

[21] Then I left for the regions of Syria and Cilicia. [22] I was still unknown by sight to the Christian congregations in Judaea; [23] they had simply heard it said, 'Our former persecutor is preaching the good news of the faith which once he tried to destroy,' [24] and they praised God for what had happened to me.

2 Fourteen years later, I went up again to Jerusalem with Barnabas, and we took Titus with us. [2] I went in response to a revelation from God; I explained, at a private interview with those of repute, the gospel which I preach to the Gentiles, to make sure that the race I had run and was running should not be in vain. [3] Not even my companion Titus, Greek though he is, was compelled to be circumcised. [4] That course was urged only as a concession to certain sham Christians, intruders who had sneaked in to spy on the liberty we enjoy in the fellowship of Christ Jesus. These men wanted to bring us into bondage, [5] but not for one moment did I yield to their dictation; I was determined that the full truth of the gospel should be maintained for you.

[6] As for those reputed to be something (not that their importance matters to me: God does not recognize these personal distinctions) — these men of repute, I say, imparted nothing further to me. [7] On the contrary, they saw that I had been entrusted to take the gospel to the Gentiles as surely as Peter had been entrusted to take it to the Jews; [8] for the same God who was at work in Peter's mission to the Jews was also at work in mine to the Gentiles.

[9] Recognizing, then, the privilege bestowed on me, those who are reputed to be pillars of the community, James, Cephas, and John, accepted Barnabas and myself as partners and shook hands on it: the agreement was that we should go to the Gentiles, while they went to the Jews. [10] All they asked was that we should keep in mind the poor, the very thing I have always made it my business to do.

[11] But when Cephas came to Antioch, I opposed him to his face, because he was clearly in the wrong. [12] For until some messengers came from James, he was taking his meals with gentile Christians; but after they came he drew back and began to hold aloof, because he was afraid of the Jews. [13] The other Jewish Christians showed the same lack of principle; even Barnabas was carried away and played false like the rest. [14] But when I saw that their conduct did not square with the truth of the gospel, I said to Cephas in front of the whole congregation, 'If you, a Jew born and bred, live like a Gentile, and

2:4–5 **bondage ... for you:** *or, following some witnesses,* bondage; [5] I yielded to their demand for the moment, to ensure that gospel truth should not be prevented from reaching you.   2:12 **the Jews:** *or* the advocates of circumcision.

1 Cor. 15.3 n. **13–14:** See Phil. 3.4–6 and compare Acts 8.3; 22.3–5; 26.4–11. **15–16:** *From my birth:* see Jer. 1.5. *In me and through me:* Gk. lit. "in me" (see v. 12 n.). **17:** Paul denies that he is a *Jerusalem* apostle.

1.18–24: Paul's first visit to Jerusalem. 18: *Cephas:* see 1 Cor. 1.12 n. **19:** *James:* see Mk. 6.3; Acts 15.13.

2.1–10: Paul's second visit to Jerusalem confirms his apostolic freedom (compare Acts 15.2–29). **1:** *Barnabas:* see Acts 4.36. *Titus:* see Introduction to 2 Cor. **2:** *Those of repute:* see v. 9. **3–9:** Conservative Jewish-Christians demanded that *Titus* be *circumcised,* but the Jerusalem apostles did not make circumcision a requirement for *Gentiles.* **9:** *John:* see Mk. 1.19. **10:** This request probably inaugurated the "collection" for the *poor* (see Introduction to Rom.).

2.11–21: Paul argues with Peter over table-fellowship between Jewish and Gentile Christians, asserting that God's acceptance comes through trust (*faith*) and not by legal observances. **12:** *James:* see 1.19 n. *Jews:* perhaps Jewish Christians who advocated circumcision; see vv. 3–5. **13:** *Other Jewish Christians:* those at Antioch.

not like a Jew, how can you insist that Gentiles must live like Jews?'

15 We ourselves are Jews by birth, not gentile sinners; 16 yet we know that no one is ever justified by doing what the law requires, but only through faith in Christ Jesus. So we too have put our faith in Jesus Christ, in order that we might be justified through this faith, and not through actions dictated by law; for no human being can be justified by keeping the law.

17 If then, in seeking to be justified in Christ, we ourselves no less than the Gentiles turn out to be sinners, does that mean that Christ is a promoter of sin? Of course not! 18 On the contrary, it is only if I start building up again all I have pulled down that I prove to be one who breaks the law. 19 For through the law I died to law—to live for God. 20 I have been crucified with Christ: the life I now live is not my life, but the life which Christ lives in me; and my present mortal life is lived by faith in the Son of God, who loved me and gave himself up for me. 21 I will not nullify the grace of God; if righteousness comes by law, then Christ died for nothing.

The freedom of faith

3 You STUPID Galatians! You must have been bewitched—you before whose eyes Jesus Christ was openly displayed on the cross! 2 Answer me one question: did you receive the Spirit by keeping the law or by believing the gospel message? 3 Can you really be so stupid? You started with the spiritual; do you now look to the material to make you perfect? 4 Is all you have experienced to come to nothing—surely not! 5 When God gives you the Spirit and works miracles among you, is it because you keep the law, or is it because you have faith in the gospel message?

6 Look at Abraham: he put his faith in God, and that faith was counted to him as righteousness. 7 You may take it, then, that it is those who have faith who are Abraham's sons. 8 And scripture, foreseeing that God would justify the Gentiles through faith, declared the gospel to Abraham beforehand: 'In you all nations shall find blessing.' 9 Thus it is those with faith who share the blessing with faithful Abraham.

10 On the other hand, those who rely on obedience to the law are under a curse; for scripture says, 'Cursed is everyone who does not persevere in doing everything that is written in the book of the law.' 11 It is evident that no one is ever justified before God by means of the law, because we read, 'He shall gain life who is justified through faith.' 12 Now the law does not operate on the basis of faith, for we read, 'He who does this shall gain life by what he does.' 13 Christ bought us freedom from the curse of the law by coming under the curse for our sake; for scripture says, 'Cursed is everyone who is hanged on a gibbet.' 14 The purpose of this was that the blessing of Abraham should in Jesus Christ be extended to the Gentiles, so that we might receive the promised Spirit through faith.

15 My friends, let me give you an illustration. When a man's will and testament has been duly executed, no one else can set it aside or add a codicil. 16 Now, the promises were pronounced to Abraham and to his 'issue'. It does not say 'issues' in the plural, but 'your issue' in the singular; and by 'issue' is meant Christ. 17 My point is this: a testament, or covenant, had already been validated by God; a law made four hundred and thirty years later cannot invalidate it and so render

15–21: This section summarizes Paul's basic argument (compare Rom. 3.9–26). 16: See 3.6–14. Justified: accepted by God as righteous (see Rom. 1.16–17 n.; 3.20). No human being . . . justified: Ps. 143.2. 17–18: Paul and Cephas indeed break the law (e.g. by eating with Gentiles); the real transgressor, however, is the adherent of the law (see 3.10). 20: Compare 6.14, 17.

3.1–18: Abraham's faith foreshadows the Christian's trust in Christ (Rom. ch. 4.). 1: Openly displayed, i.e. in Paul's preaching (see 1 Cor. 1.18–24). 2: Receive the Spirit: see 2 Cor. 5.5 n. 3: The material: keeping the law. 5: Miracles: see 1 Cor. 12.10; 2 Cor. 12.12. 6: Gen. 15.6. 8: Gen. 12.3; 18.18. 10: See Rom. 3.9–20. Scripture: Deut. 27.26. 11: Hab. 2.4 (Rom. 1.17). 12: Lev. 18.5 (Rom. 10.5). 13: Deut. 21.23 (compare 2 Cor. 5.21). 16: Issue: see e.g. Gen. 17.1–8. 17: Testament and covenant translate a single Gk. word, which in the Sept. (e.g. Gen. 9.9; 17.7) frequently refers to God's irrevocable promises (vv. 16–18, 21) offered with certain conditions (v. 22), and in common Greek to a will by which heirs (v. 29) receive their inheritance (v. 18). Exodus 12.40 (Sept.) gives four hundred and thirty years as the interval between Abraham and Moses.

its promises ineffective. ¹⁸ If the inheritance is by legal right, then it is not by promise; but it was by promise that God bestowed it as a free gift on Abraham.

¹⁹ Then what of the law? It was added to make wrongdoing a legal offence; it was an interim measure pending the arrival of the 'issue' to whom the promise was made. It was promulgated through angels, and there was an intermediary; ²⁰ but an intermediary is not needed for one party acting alone, and God is one.

²¹ Does the law, then, contradict the promises? Of course not! If a law had been given which had power to bestow life, then righteousness would indeed have come from keeping the law. ²² But scripture has declared the whole world to be prisoners in subjection to sin, so that faith in Jesus Christ should be the ground on which the promised blessing is given to those who believe.

²³ Before this faith came, we were close prisoners in the custody of law, pending the revelation of faith. ²⁴ The law was thus put in charge of us until Christ should come, when we should be justified through faith; ²⁵ and now that faith has come, its charge is at an end.

²⁶ It is through faith that you are all sons of God in union with Christ Jesus. ²⁷ Baptized into union with him, you have all put on Christ like a garment. ²⁸ There is no such thing as Jew and Greek, slave and freeman, male and female; for you are all one person in Christ Jesus. ²⁹ So if you belong to Christ, you are the 'issue' of Abraham and heirs by virtue of the promise.

Life under the law

4 THIS is what I mean: so long as the heir is a minor, he is no better off than a slave, even though the whole estate is his; ² he is subject to guardians and trustees until the date set by his father. ³ So it was with us: during our minority we were slaves, subject to the elemental spirits of the universe, ⁴ but when the appointed time came, God sent his Son, born of a woman, born under the law, ⁵ to buy freedom for those who were under the law, in order that we might attain the status of sons.

⁶ To prove that you are sons, God has sent into our hearts the Spirit of his Son, crying 'Abba, Father!' ⁷ You are therefore no longer a slave but a son, and if a son, an heir by God's own act.

⁸ Formerly, when you did not know God, you were slaves to gods who are not gods at all. ⁹ But now that you do acknowledge God — or rather, now that he has acknowledged you — how can you turn back to those feeble and bankrupt elemental spirits? Why do you propose to enter their service all over again? ¹⁰ You keep special days and months and seasons and years. ¹¹ I am afraid that all my hard work on you may have been wasted.

¹² PUT yourselves in my place, my friends, I beg you, as I put myself in yours. You never did me any wrong: ¹³ it was bodily illness, as you will remember, that originally led to my bringing you the gospel, ¹⁴ and you resisted any temptation to show scorn or disgust at my physical condition; on the contrary you welcomed me as if I were an angel of God, as you might have welcomed Christ Jesus himself. ¹⁵ What has become of the happiness you felt then? I believe you would have torn out your eyes and given them to me, had that been possible! ¹⁶ Have I now made myself your enemy by being frank with you?

¹⁷ Others are lavishing attention on you, but without sincerity: what they really want is

3:19 **added ... offence:** or added to restrain offences. 4:3 **to ... universe:** or to elementary notions belonging to this world.   4:9 **bankrupt ... spirits:** or threadbare elementary notions.

3.19–4.7: The law as temporary guardian of God's children. **19–20:** See Rom. 3.20; 5.13; 7.7–8. Here, by contrast with Rom. 7.12, 22, Paul suggests that God is not directly responsible for the *law*. Instead, the *law* came from the *angels* (Deut. 33.2 Sept.; see 1 Cor. 6.2–3 n.) with Moses as their *intermediary*. **22:** *Scripture:* see v. 10 n. **24–25:** *Put in charge of us:* lit. "was our tutor"; see 1 Cor. 4.15 n. **27:** *Put on Christ:* see Rom. 13.14; Col. 3.10–12. **28:** See 1 Cor. 7.18–22; Col. 3.11. **29:** *Christ* stands corporately for the new Israel, the church (see 6.16 n.). *Promise:* see vv. 17–18. **4.1–2:** See 3.24–25 n. **3:** *Elemental spirits:* see 1 Cor. 2.6–8 n. **6–7:** See Rom. 8.14–17.

4.8–20: A reminder of the Galatians' conversion. **8–10:** At the instigation of the Judaizers (see Introduction) they *keep* the Jewish ritual calendar, which Paul connects with astrology and the worship of demonic *spirits* (v. 3). **13:** Paul appears to attribute his original visit in Galatia to physical weakness rather than to design. *Illness:*

to isolate you so that you may lavish attention on them. [18] To be the object of sincere attentions is always good, and not just when I am with you. [19] You are my own children, and I am in labour with you all over again until you come to have the form of Christ. [20] How I wish I could be with you now, for then I could modify my tone; as it is, I am at my wits' end about you.

Freedom through Christ

[21] TELL me now, you that are so anxious to be under law, will you not listen to what the law says? [22] It is written there that Abraham had two sons, the one by a slave, the other by a free-born woman. [23] The slave's son was born in the ordinary course of nature, but the free woman's through God's promise. [24] This is an allegory: the two women stand for two covenants. The one covenant comes from Mount Sinai; that is Hagar, and her children are born into slavery. [25] Sinai is a mountain in Arabia and represents the Jerusalem of to-day, for she and her children are in slavery. [26] But the heavenly Jerusalem is the free woman; she is our mother. [27] For scripture says, 'Rejoice, O barren woman who never bore a child; break into a shout of joy, you who have never been in labour; for the deserted wife will have more children than she who lives with her husband.'

[28] Now you, my friends, like Isaac, are children of God's promise, [29] but just as in those days the natural-born son persecuted the spiritual son, so it is today. [30] Yet what does scripture say? 'Drive out the slave and her son, for the son of the slave shall not share the inheritance with the son of the free woman.' [31] You see, then, my friends, we are no slave's children; our mother is the free

woman. [1] It is for freedom that Christ set us free. Stand firm, therefore, and refuse to submit again to the yoke of slavery.

[2] Mark my words: I, Paul, say to you that if you get yourself circumcised Christ will benefit you no more. [3] I impress on you once again that every man who accepts circumcision is under obligation to keep the entire law. [4] When you seek to be justified by way of law, you are cut off from Christ: you have put yourselves outside God's grace. [5] For it is by the Spirit and through faith that we hope to attain that righteousness which we eagerly await. [6] If we are in union with Christ Jesus, circumcision makes no difference at all, nor does the lack of it; the only thing that counts is faith expressing itself through love.

[7] You were running well; who was it hindered you from following the truth? [8] Whatever persuasion was used, it did not come from God who called you. [9] 'A little leaven', remember, 'leavens all the dough.' [10] The Lord gives me confidence that you will not adopt the wrong view; but whoever it is who is unsettling your minds must bear God's judgement. [11] As for me, my friends, if I am still advocating circumcision, then why am I still being persecuted? To do that would be to strip the cross of all offence. [12] Those agitators had better go the whole way and make eunuchs of themselves!

Guidance by the Spirit

[13] YOU, MY friends, were called to be free; only beware of turning your freedom into licence for your unspiritual nature. Instead, serve one another in love; [14] for the whole law is summed up in a single commandment: 'Love your neighbour as yourself.' [15] But if you go on fighting one another, tooth and

see 2 Cor. 12.7 n. **15:** Possibly Paul had eye trouble (see 6.11, "these big letters"). **19:** *Labour:* a metaphor depicting Paul as an expectant "mother" awaiting the rebirth of the Galatians.

4.21–5.1: The allegory of Sarah and Hagar (compare Rom. 9.6–13). **22:** *Slave:* Hagar, mother of Ishmael (Gen. 16.15). *Free-born:* Sarah, mother of Isaac (Gen. 21.2–3). **23:** *Promise:* see Gen. 17.15–21. **25–28:** Paradoxically the Jews (who count Isaac as their ancestor) are called *children* of *Hagar;* the church is the promised heir *like Isaac.* **27:** Isa. 54.1. **29:** *Persecuted:* see Gen. 16.12; 21.9–10. *Today:* see 5.11; 1 Thess. 2.14–16. **30:** Gen. 21.10.

5.2–12: The Judaizers' message is slavery. 3: The Judaizers apparently preached *circumcision* but not the *entire law* (see 6.12–13). **9:** *Leaven:* see 1 Cor. 5.6 n. **11:** Paul's own troubles (see 4.29; 6.14, 17 n.) refute the Judaizers' allegation that *circumcision* was actually part of his gospel also (see 6.12 n.). *Cross:* see 1 Cor. 1.18–2.5.

5.13–25: The ethics of freedom is not *licence* but *love.* **13:** Mk. 10.43. **14:** Lev. 19.18 (see Rom. 13.8–10;

nail, all you can expect is mutual destruction.

16 What I mean is this: be guided by the Spirit and you will not gratify the desires of your unspiritual nature. 17 That nature sets its desires against the Spirit, while the Spirit fights against it. They are in conflict with one another so that you cannot do what you want. 18 But if you are led by the Spirit, you are not subject to law.

19 Anyone can see the behaviour that belongs to the unspiritual nature: fornication, indecency, and debauchery; 20 idolatry and sorcery; quarrels, a contentious temper, envy, fits of rage, selfish ambitions, dissensions, party intrigues, 21 and jealousies; drinking bouts, orgies, and the like. I warn you, as I warned you before, that no one who behaves like that will ever inherit the kingdom of God.

22 But the harvest of the Spirit is love, joy, peace, patience, kindness, goodness, fidelity, 23 gentleness, and self-control. Against such things there is no law. 24 Those who belong to Christ Jesus have crucified the old nature with its passions and desires. 25 If the Spirit is the source of our life, let the Spirit also direct its course.

26 We must not be conceited, inciting one another to rivalry, jealous of one another.

6 1 If anyone is caught doing something wrong, you, my friends, who live by the Spirit must gently set him right. Look to yourself, each one of you: you also may be tempted. 2 Carry one another's burdens, and in this way you will fulfil the law of Christ.

3 If anyone imagines himself to be somebody when he is nothing, he is deluding himself. 4 Each of you should examine his own conduct, and then he can measure his achievement by comparing himself with him-self and not with anyone else; 5 for everyone has his own burden to bear.

6 When anyone is under instruction in the faith, he should give his teacher a share of whatever good things he has.

7 Make no mistake about this: God is not to be fooled; everyone reaps what he sows. 8 If he sows in the field of his unspiritual nature, he will reap from it a harvest of corruption; but if he sows in the field of the Spirit, he will reap from it a harvest of eternal life. 9 Let us never tire of doing good, for if we do not slacken our efforts we shall in due time reap our harvest. 10 Therefore, as opportunity offers, let us work for the good of all, especially members of the household of the faith.

11 LOOK how big the letters are, now that I am writing to you in my own hand. 12 It is those who want to be outwardly in good standing who are trying to force circumcision on you; their sole object is to escape persecution for the cross of Christ. 13 Even those who do accept circumcision are not thoroughgoing observers of the law; they want you to be circumcised just in order to boast of your submission to that outward rite. 14 God forbid that I should boast of anything but the cross of our Lord Jesus Christ, through which the world is crucified to me and I to the world! 15 Circumcision is nothing; uncircumcision is nothing; the only thing that counts is new creation! 16 All who take this principle for their guide, peace and mercy be upon them, the Israel of God!

17 In future let no one make trouble for me, for I bear the marks of Jesus branded on my body.

18 The grace of our Lord Jesus Christ be with you, my friends. Amen.

6:14 **which:** or whom.   6:16 **the … God:** or and upon the whole Israel of God.

Mk. 12.31). **16–17:** *Unspiritual nature:* lit. "flesh" (compare 1 Cor. 15.35–53; Rom. 7.14–25; 7.14 n.). **19–24:** The lists are stereotyped (see Col. 3.1–15; compare Col. 3.18–4.1 n.). **24:** *Crucified:* see Rom. 6.6.

5.26–6.10: Appeal for love and generosity. 6.2: *The law of Christ* is love (see 5.14 n.). **6:** A *teacher* should be paid (see 1 Cor. 9.4–14). **7–10:** *Sow* and *reap* echo 2 Cor. 9.6–10 on the collection project (see Rom. 15.25–26 nn.).

6.11–18: Conclusion. 11: See 1 Cor. 16.21–24 n. **12:** *Circumcision* would prevent *persecution* by bringing Christians under the legal protection enjoyed by Judaism (see 5.11 n.). **13:** See 5.3 n. **14:** *Cross:* see 3.1; 5.24; Phil. 3.10. **16:** *Israel of God:* the church (see 4.25–28 n.). **17:** *Marks:* scars received in Jesus' service (see 2 Cor. 4.10–11; 11.23–28). **18:** See 2 Cor. 13.14 n.

THE LETTER OF PAUL TO THE
Ephesians

The main theme of the letter to the Ephesians is the church, the body of Christ, in which Jew and Gentile have been united and made "a single new humanity" (2.15). The letter presents itself as written by Paul during a time of imprisonment (3.1), and its close relationship to Colossians has led many to suppose a common situation for both: Paul's captivity in Rome (61–63 C.E.).

The best and earliest manuscripts lack the words "at Ephesus" in 1.1. Therefore, some scholars have offered the suggestion that it was originally intended for many churches, not just the one at Ephesus.

Moreover, there is some basis on which doubts have arisen that the letter was written by Paul himself. Thus, though there are points of contact in thought and wording with every Pauline letter (except perhaps 2 Thessalonians) and especially with Colossians, yet in many instances these points of contact also reflect differences. For example, Eph. 2.8–10 is closely related to the thought of Romans, but does not mention justification, which is central to that epistle. Again, the "revealed secret" is conceived differently in Colossians and in Ephesians; in Colossians, it is the union of Christ and his people (Col. 1.27); in the latter, it is the union of Jew and Gentile in the one church (Eph. 3.6). Accordingly, many (perhaps most) modern scholars regard Ephesians as the work of a member of the Pauline "school" and date it around 100 C.E.

1 ¹ From Paul, by the will of God apostle of Christ Jesus, to God's people at Ephesus, to the faithful, incorporate in Christ Jesus. ² Grace to you and peace from God our Father and the Lord Jesus Christ.

The glory of Christ in the church

³ Blessed be the God and Father of our Lord Jesus Christ, who has conferred on us in Christ every spiritual blessing in the heavenly realms. ⁴ Before the foundation of the world he chose us in Christ to be his people, to be without blemish in his sight, to be full of love; ⁵ and he predestined us to be adopted as his children through Jesus Christ. This was his will and pleasure ⁶ in order that the glory of his gracious gift, so graciously conferred on us in his Beloved, might redound to his praise. ⁷ In Christ our release is secured and our sins forgiven through the shedding of his blood. In the richness of his grace ⁸ God has lavished on us all wisdom and insight. ⁹ He has made known to us his secret purpose, in accordance with the plan which he determined beforehand in Christ, ¹⁰ to be put into effect when the time was ripe: namely, that the universe, everything in heaven and on earth, might be brought into a unity in Christ.

¹¹ In Christ indeed we have been given our

1:1 **at Ephesus:** *some witnesses omit.*   1:4–5 **sight . . . he:** *or* sight. In his love ⁵he.

1.3–14: Praise of God. The greeting (vv. 1–2) is followed not by the usual thanksgiving, but by a long prayer of praise for what God has done in Christ. Praise of God is frequent in the OT and in Jewish prayer; compare 2 Cor. 1.3–4. **3:** In the NT, the phrase *in the heavenly realms* (or a variation of it) occurs only in this letter (1.20; 2.6; 3.10; 6.12). Apocalyptic literature speaks of a series of heavens (frequently seven) extending above and beyond the earth, with the throne of God in the highest heaven. At times, the *heavenly realms* were thought of as accessible to human beings only in the future age to come, but at other times as immediately available to the dead. Here the faithful, through union with Christ (2.6), share his exaltation *in the heavenly realms* (see v. 14 n.). **4:** The choosing of a "people of God" (the church) is traced back beyond creation. *Without blemish:* see Col. 1.22 n. **10:** Although the main theme of the letter is the church, here the universe is viewed as intended for the *unity* destined to be achieved *in Christ*. **11–13:** In the preceding verses "we" includes all Christians.

1481

share in the heritage, as was decreed in his design whose purpose is everywhere at work; for it was his will [12] that we, who were the first to set our hope on Christ, should cause his glory to be praised. [13] And in Christ you also —once you had heard the message of the truth, the good news of your salvation, and had believed it—in him you were stamped with the seal of the promised Holy Spirit; [14] and that Spirit is a pledge of the inheritance which will be ours when God has redeemed what is his own, to his glory and praise.

[15] Because of all this, now that I have heard of your faith in the Lord Jesus and the love you bear towards all God's people, [16] I never cease to give thanks for you when I mention you in my prayers. [17] I pray that the God of our Lord Jesus Christ, the all-glorious Father, may confer on you the spiritual gifts of wisdom and vision, with the knowledge of him that they bring. [18] I pray that your inward eyes may be enlightened, so that you may know what is the hope to which he calls you, how rich and glorious is the share he offers you among his people in their inheritance, [19] and how vast are the resources of his power open to us who have faith. His mighty strength was seen at work [20] when he raised Christ from the dead, and enthroned him at his right hand in the heavenly realms, [21] far above all government and authority, all power and dominion, and any title of sovereignty that commands allegiance, not only in this age but also in the age to come. [22] He put all things in subjection beneath his feet, and gave him as head over all things to the church [23] which is his body, the fullness

of him who is filling the universe in all its parts.

God's grace to Gentiles

2 YOU ONCE were dead because of your sins and wickedness; [2] you followed the ways of this present world order, obeying the commander of the spiritual powers of the air, the spirit now at work among God's rebel subjects. [3] We too were once of their number: we were ruled by our physical desires, and did what instinct and evil imagination suggested. In our natural condition we lay under the condemnation of God like the rest of mankind. [4] But God is rich in mercy, and because of his great love for us, [5] he brought us to life with Christ when we were dead because of our sins; it is by grace you are saved. [6] And he raised us up in union with Christ Jesus and enthroned us with him in the heavenly realms, [7] so that he might display in the ages to come how immense are the resources of his grace, and how great his kindness to us in Christ Jesus. [8] For it is by grace you are saved through faith; it is not your own doing. It is God's gift, [9] not a reward for work done. There is nothing for anyone to boast of; [10] we are God's handiwork, created in Christ Jesus for the life of good deeds which God designed for us.

[11] Remember then your former condition, Gentiles as you are by birth, 'the uncircumcised' as you are called by those who call

1:12 **who ... Christ:** *or* who already looked forward in hope to Christ.   1:23 **body ... parts:** *or* body, filled as he is with the full being of God, who is imparting to all things that same fullness.

This passage, however, suggests a contrast between *we* (v. 11) and *you* (v. 13), with *we* here meaning Jewish Christians (*first . . . Christ*) and *you* (*in Christ . . . also*), later Gentile converts. *Seal . . . Holy Spirit* means baptism. **14:** *The pledge:* see 2 Cor. 5.5 n. The present possession of the Spirit is the guarantee of the coming full possession of their *inheritance*. Then the redemption of God's people will be complete.

1.15–23: Thanksgiving and prayer. 20: *Enthroned him at his right hand:* see Ps. 110.1; the NT frequently applies this OT verse to the ascended Christ (e.g. Acts 2.33–34). **21:** *Government . . . authority . . . title:* see 1 Cor. 2.6–8 n.; Col. 1.16. **22–23:** *Head, body:* see Col. 1.18 n. The *subjection* of all to Christ is expressed by a paraphrase of Ps. 8.6, one of the favorite proof texts of the early church; compare 1 Cor. 15.27. On Christ as the *fullness* of God, see Col. 1.19 n. Here the church is conceived of as the fullness of Christ.

2.1–10: The passage from "death" to "life." 2: Compare 1 Cor. 2.12; 2 Cor. 4.4; Gal. 1.4. The *commander* is Satan. An extrabiblical book (see *2 Enoch* 29.5) regarded the *air* as Satan's dwelling place. **8–10:** The emphasis on *grace* is in conformity with Paul's teaching. But the view here (and in v. 5) that salvation is already accomplished diverges from normal Pauline thought in which salvation belongs to the future (Rom. 5.10) or is at most only in process (see 1 Cor. 1.18). Such differences may support the opinion that Ephesians is a late product of a Pauline "school" (see Introduction).

themselves 'the circumcised' because of a physical rite. [12] You were at that time separate from Christ, excluded from the community of Israel, strangers to God's covenants and the promise that goes with them. Yours was a world without hope and without God. [13] Once you were far off, but now in union with Christ Jesus you have been brought near through the shedding of Christ's blood. [14] For he is himself our peace. Gentiles and Jews, he has made the two one, and in his own body of flesh and blood has broken down the barrier of enmity which separated them; [15] for he annulled the law with its rules and regulations, so as to create out of the two a single new humanity in himself, thereby making peace. [16] This was his purpose, to reconcile the two in a single body to God through the cross, by which he killed the enmity. [17] So he came and proclaimed the good news: peace to you who were far off, and peace to those who were near; [18] for through him we both alike have access to the Father in the one Spirit.

[19] Thus you are no longer aliens in a foreign land, but fellow-citizens with God's people, members of God's household. [20] You are built on the foundation of the apostles and prophets, with Christ Jesus himself as the corner-stone. [21] In him the whole building is bonded together and grows into a holy temple in the Lord. [22] In him you also are being built with all the others into a spiritual dwelling for God.

Paul's prayer

3 WITH this in mind I pray for you, I, Paul, who for the sake of you Gentiles am now the prisoner of Christ Jesus — [2] for

surely you have heard how God's gift of grace to me was designed for your benefit. [3] It was by a revelation that his secret purpose was made known to me. I have already written you a brief account of this, [4] and by reading it you can see that I understand the secret purpose of Christ. [5] In former generations that secret was not disclosed to mankind; but now by inspiration it has been revealed to his holy apostles and prophets, [6] that through the gospel the Gentiles are joint heirs with the Jews, part of the same body, sharers together in the promise made in Christ Jesus. [7] Such is the gospel of which I was made a minister by God's unmerited gift, so powerfully at work in me. [8] To me, who am less than the least of all God's people, he has granted the privilege of proclaiming to the Gentiles the good news of the unfathomable riches of Christ, [9] and of bringing to light how this hidden purpose was to be put into effect. It lay concealed for long ages with God the Creator of the universe, [10] in order that now, through the church, the wisdom of God in its infinite variety might be made known to the rulers and authorities in the heavenly realms. [11] This accords with his age-long purpose, which he accomplished in Christ Jesus our Lord, [12] in whom we have freedom of access to God, with the confidence born of trust in him. [13] I beg you, then, not to lose heart over my sufferings for you; indeed, they are your glory.

[14] With this in mind, then, I kneel in prayer to the Father, [15] from whom every family in heaven and on earth takes its name, [16] that out of the treasures of his glory he may grant you inward strength and power through his

2:16 **cross . . . enmity:** *or* cross. Thus in his own person he put to death the enmity.

2.11–22: The unity of all humankind in Christ. 14–15: The Mosaic law had been a *barrier* between Jew and Gentile. *A single new humanity:* lit. one new human being (Gk. *anthropos*). **17:** See Isa. 57.19. **20:** The symbolism changes abruptly from that of a body (v. 16; 1.22–23) to that of a building (vv. 20–22). *Cornerstone:* see Isa. 28.16; Ps. 118.22; compare Matt. 21.42 and parallels.

3.1–13: Paul's apostolate. 1: *Prisoner:* see Introduction. **3:** *Revelation:* see Gal. 1.15–16. The *brief account* probably refers not to an earlier letter, but to 2.11–22. **5–6:** *Revealed . . . apostles:* some take this passage as an indication that Paul did not write the letter (see Introduction), because in Gal. 2.8–9 he distinguishes between his commission to preach to the Gentiles and that of the Jerusalem apostles to preach to the Jews (compare Rom. 11.13). *Prophets:* see 1 Cor. 12.28; Rom. 12.6. The secret, *now . . . revealed,* is that the Gentiles are one with the Jews in the *body* of Christ, the church. **10:** The secret is not only to be made known on earth but also among the angelic powers (see Col. 1.16 n.); this is to be done by *the church,* which has a heavenward dimension. See 6.12.

3.14–21: Prayer and doxology. 14–15: A play on the Gk. words for *father* (*pater*) and *family* (*patria*) stresses

Spirit, ¹⁷that through faith Christ may dwell in your hearts in love. With deep roots and firm foundations ¹⁸may you, in company with all God's people, be strong to grasp what is the breadth and length and height and depth ¹⁹of Christ's love, and to know it, though it is beyond knowledge. So may you be filled with the very fullness of God.

²⁰Now to him who is able through the power which is at work among us to do immeasurably more than all we can ask or conceive, ²¹to him be glory in the church and in Christ Jesus from generation to generation for evermore! Amen.

Christian conduct

4 I IMPLORE you then—I, a prisoner for the Lord's sake: as God has called you, live up to your calling. ²Be humble always and gentle, and patient too, putting up with one another's failings in the spirit of love. ³Spare no effort to make fast with bonds of peace the unity which the Spirit gives. ⁴There is one body and one Spirit, just as there is one hope held out in God's call to you; ⁵one Lord, one faith, one baptism; ⁶one God and Father of all, who is over all and through all and in all.

⁷But each of us has been given a special gift, a particular share in the bounty of Christ. ⁸That is why scripture says:

He ascended into the heights;
he took captives into captivity;
he gave gifts to men.

⁹Now, the word 'ascended' implies that he also descended to the lowest level, down to the very earth. ¹⁰He who descended is none other than he who ascended far above all heavens, so that he might fill the universe. ¹¹And it is he who has given some to be apostles, some prophets, some evangelists, some pastors and teachers, ¹²to equip God's people for work in his service, for the building up of the body of Christ, ¹³until we all attain to the unity inherent in our faith and in our knowledge of the Son of God—to mature manhood, measured by nothing less than the full stature of Christ. ¹⁴We are no longer to be children, tossed about by the waves and whirled around by every fresh gust of teaching, dupes of cunning rogues and their deceitful schemes. ¹⁵Rather we are to maintain the truth in a spirit of love; so shall we fully grow up into Christ. He is the head, ¹⁶and on him the whole body depends. Bonded and held together by every constituent joint, the whole frame grows through the proper functioning of each part, and builds itself up in love.

¹⁷Here then is my word to you, and I urge it on you in the Lord's name: give up living as pagans do with their futile notions. ¹⁸Their minds are closed, they are alienated from the life that is in God, because ignorance prevails among them and their hearts have grown hard as stone. ¹⁹Dead to all feeling, they have abandoned themselves to vice, and there is no indecency that they do not practise. ²⁰But that is not how you learned Christ. ²¹For were you not told about him, were you not as Christians taught the truth as it is in Jesus? ²²Renouncing your former way of life, you must lay aside the old human nature which, deluded by its desires, is in process of decay: ²³you must be renewed in mind and spirit, ²⁴and put on the new nature created in God's likeness, which shows itself in the upright and devout life called for by the truth.

²⁵Then have done with falsehood and speak the truth to each other, for we belong to one another as parts of one body.

²⁶If you are angry, do not be led into sin;

4:9 **descended . . . earth:** *or* descended to the regions beneath the earth.

the relationship of God to all creation. The families *in heaven* are the angels. **21:** This juxtaposition of *the church* and *Christ Jesus* is unique in the NT; yet, it flows naturally from the image of the *church* as the body of *Christ*.

4.1–16: Christian unity. 1: *Prisoner:* see Introduction. **7:** The rich variety of individual gifts contributes to the unity of the church. **8–9:** *Captives into captivity:* the author means the angelic powers; see Col. 2.15. In the manner of rabbinic exegesis, the wording of Ps. 68.18 is altered to accommodate it to its new interpretation; the "ascent" is applied to Christ and is understood as implying a prior "descent" in the incarnation. Less probably, even the translation of the Tfn. for this verse might be adopted, in which case a "descent into hell" would be involved; compare 1 Pet. 3.19–20 n. **11–13:** *He . . . has given* the ministries of the church. *Evangelists:* missionary preachers.

4.17–5.20: Exhortation to the Christian life. 21: *The truth* may refer to the inherited teachings of the do not let sunset find you nursing your anger; 27 and give no foothold to the devil.

28 The thief must give up stealing, and work hard with his hands to earn an honest living, so that he may have something to share with the needy.

29 Let no offensive talk pass your lips, only what is good and helpful to the occasion, so that it brings a blessing to those who hear it. 30 Do not grieve the Holy Spirit of God, for that Spirit is the seal with which you were marked for the day of final liberation. 31 Have done with all spite and bad temper, with rage, insults, and slander, with evil of any kind. 32 Be generous to one another, tender-hearted, forgiving one another as God in Christ forgave you.

5 In a word, as God's dear children, you must be like him. 2 Live in love as Christ loved you and gave himself up on your behalf, an offering and sacrifice whose fragrance is pleasing to God.

3 Fornication and indecency of any kind, or ruthless greed, must not be so much as mentioned among you, as befits the people of God. 4 No coarse, stupid, or flippant talk: these things are out of place; you should rather be thanking God. 5 For be very sure of this: no one given to fornication or vice, or the greed which makes an idol of gain, has any share in the kingdom of Christ and of God. 6 Let no one deceive you with shallow arguments; it is for these things that divine retribution falls on God's rebel subjects. 7 Have nothing to do with them. 8 Though you once were darkness, now as Christians you are light. Prove yourselves at home in the light, 9 for where light is, there is a harvest of goodness, righteousness, and truth. 10 Learn to judge for yourselves what is pleasing to the Lord; 11 take no part in the barren deeds of darkness, but show them up for what they are. 12 It would be shameful even to mention what is done in secret. 13 But everything is shown up by being exposed to the light, and whatever is exposed to the light itself becomes light. 14 That is why it is said:

Awake, sleeper,
rise from the dead,
and Christ will shine upon you.

15 Take great care, then, how you behave: act sensibly, not like simpletons. 16 Use the present opportunity to the full, for these are evil days. 17 Do not be foolish, but understand what the will of the Lord is. 18 Do not give way to drunkenness and the ruin that goes with it, but let the Holy Spirit fill you: 19 speak to one another in psalms, hymns, and songs; sing and make music from your heart to the Lord; 20 and in the name of our Lord Jesus Christ give thanks every day for everything to our God and Father.

Christian relationships

21 BE subject to one another out of reverence for Christ.

22 Wives, be subject to your husbands as though to the Lord; 23 for the man is the head of the woman, just as Christ is the head of the church. Christ is, indeed, the saviour of that body; 24 but just as the church is subject to Christ, so must women be subject to their husbands in everything.

25 Husbands, love your wives, as Christ loved the church and gave himself up for it, 26 to consecrate and cleanse it by water and word, 27 so that he might present the church to himself all glorious, with no stain or wrinkle or anything of the sort, but holy and without blemish. 28 In the same way men ought to love their wives, as they love their own bodies. In loving his wife a man loves himself. 29 For no one ever hated his own body; on the contrary, he keeps it nourished and warm, and that is how Christ treats the church, 30 because it is his body, of which we are living parts. 31 'This is why' (in the words of scripture) 'a man shall leave his father and mother and be united to his wife, and the two shall become one flesh.' 32 There is hidden here a great truth, which I take to refer to Christ

5:19 **hymns, and:** *some witnesses add* spiritual.

historical *Jesus.* **5.1–2:** To *be like* God: lit. "be imitators" of God. *Fragrance . . . pleasing to God:* see Lev. 2.9. **8:** *Darkness . . . light:* see 1 Thess. 5.4–7 n. **14:** These lines (compare Isa. 60.1) may have been drawn from an early Christian baptismal hymn; see v. 19.

    5.21–6.9: Christian domestic life. The Christianizing of the lists of household virtues (see Col. 3.18–4.1 n.) is especially clear here in the treatment of marriage. **26:** Baptism is seen as the nuptial bath preparing the bride for her husband. The *word* may refer to the liturgical formula, including the invocation of the name of Jesus, pronounced over the candidate; see 1 Cor. 6.11. **31:** See Gen. 2.24. **32–33:** The *great truth . . .*

and to the church. 33 But it applies also to each one of you: the husband must love his wife as his very self, and the wife must show reverence for her husband.

6 Children, obey your parents; for it is only right that you should. 2 'Honour your father and your mother' is the first commandment to carry a promise with it: 3 'that it may be well with you and that you may live long on the earth.'

4 Fathers, do not goad your children to resentment, but bring them up in the discipline and instruction of the Lord.

5 Slaves, give single-minded obedience to your earthly masters with fear and trembling, as if to Christ. 6 Do it not merely to catch their eye or curry favour with them, but as slaves of Christ do the will of God wholeheartedly. 7 Give cheerful service, as slaves of the Lord rather than of men. 8 You know that whatever good anyone may do, slave or free, will be repaid by the Lord.

9 Masters, treat your slaves in the same spirit: give up using threats, and remember that you both have the same Master in heaven; there is no favouritism with him.

The Christian's armoury

10 FINALLY, find your strength in the Lord, in his mighty power. 11 Put on the full armour provided by God, so that you may be able to stand firm against the stratagems of the devil. 12 For our struggle is not against human foes, but against cosmic powers, against the authorities and potentates of this dark age, against the superhuman forces of evil in the heavenly realms. 13 Therefore, take up the armour of God; then you will be able to withstand them on the evil day and, after doing your utmost, to stand your ground. 14 Stand fast, I say. Fasten on the belt of truth; for a breastplate put on integrity; 15 let the shoes on your feet be the gospel of peace, to give you firm footing; 16 and, with all these, take up the great shield of faith, with which you will be able to quench all the burning arrows of the evil one. 17 Accept salvation as your helmet, and the sword which the Spirit gives you, the word of God. 18 Constantly ask God's help in prayer, and pray always in the power of the Spirit. To this end keep watch and persevere, always interceding for all God's people. 19 Pray also for me, that I may be granted the right words when I speak, and may boldly and freely make known the hidden purpose of the gospel, 20 for which I am an ambassador — in chains. Pray that I may speak of it boldly, as is my duty.

21 YOU WILL want to know how I am and what I am doing; Tychicus will give you all the news. He is our dear brother and trustworthy helper in the Lord's work. 22 I am sending him to you on purpose to let you have news of us and to put fresh heart into you.

23 Peace to the community and love with faith, from God the Father and the Lord Jesus Christ. 24 God's grace be with all who love our Lord Jesus Christ with undying love.

6:24 **Christ . . . love:** *or* Christ, grace and immortality.

hidden is that Gen. 2.24 can be taken to allude collectively to the union of Christ and the church in one body; but the verse *applies also to each one,* that is, it also speaks directly of the united relation of *husband* and *wife.*

6.10–20: The Christian battle. 11, 13–17: *Armour:* see 1 Thess. 5.8 n. **12:** *Cosmic powers:* see 1 Cor. 2.6–8 n.; Col. 1.6 n. **20:** *In chains:* a prisoner; see Introduction.

6.21–24: Final greetings and blessing. 21: *Tychicus:* a companion of Paul; see Col. 4.7–8.

THE LETTER OF PAUL TO THE
Philippians

The church of Philippi was the first Paul founded on the continent of Europe (Acts 16.11–40; 1 Thess. 2.2). His cordial relations with it can be seen from the unusual warmth of this letter and from the fact that it was the only one of his churches from which he accepted support (Phil. 4.15–16).

The letter was written from prison (1.7, 13, 17) and together with Colossians, Ephesians, and Philemon makes up the group known as the Captivity Letters. Two major imprisonments of Paul are recorded in Acts, one at Caesarea (23.33–26.32), the other at Rome (28.16–31), and Rome has traditionally been identified as the place from which Philippians was written.

However, the differences in thought between Colossians (also usually assigned to the Roman imprisonment) and Philippians make it difficult to ascribe both of these letters to the same period. Moreover, Philippians speaks of four journeys made by friends between the place of Paul's imprisonment and Philippi and of a fifth which is about to take place (2.25–26)—an unlikely number considering the great distance between Rome and Philippi. On the other hand, if one of Paul's many imprisonments (2 Cor. 11.23) occurred during his three-year stay at Ephesus (Acts 20.31), so many trips are easier to understand; Ephesus and Philippi were only about ten days apart. Inscriptions discovered at Ephesus show that members of the Praetorian Guard and of the imperial establishment were stationed in the Roman province of Asia; consequently, the references in 1.13 and 4.22 are as consistent with an origin in Ephesus as in Rome.

If composition at Ephesus is accepted, Philippians belongs to the period of Paul's "third missionary journey," and may be dated around 56 C.E.

It is not certain that the present document was always a unit; it may have been assembled from as many as three originally distinct letters: a note of thanks for the gift sent through Epaphroditus (4.10–20); a letter motivated by Paul's concern for the church in the face of potentially disruptive persons whose position is not clearly defined (1.1–3.1a; 4.2–9, 21–23); and a letter warning against false teachers about whose doctrines the apostle has become better informed (3.1b–4.1).

1 FROM Paul and Timothy, servants of Christ Jesus, to all God's people at Philippi, who are incorporate in Christ Jesus, with the bishops and deacons.

2 Grace to you and peace from God our Father and the Lord Jesus Christ.

3 I thank my God every time I think of you; 4 whenever I pray for you all, my prayers are always joyful, 5 because of the part you have taken in the work of the gospel from the first day until now. 6 Of this I am confident, that he who started the good work in you will bring it to completion by the day of Christ Jesus. 7 It is only natural that I should feel like this about you all, because I have great affection for you, knowing that, both while I am

1:1 **bishops and deacons:** *or* overseers and assistants.

1.1–2: Greeting. 1: *Bishops and deacons* are mentioned only here in the certainly authentic letters of Paul. (The Pastoral Epistles are sometimes regarded as not by Paul; see Introduction to 1 Tim.) Later ecclesiastical developments should not be read into the terms here. Bishops (lit. "overseers") are those who exercise supervision; deacons are probably their assistants.

1.3–11: Thanksgiving and prayer. 5: *The part you have taken:* their support of Paul; see 2.25; 4.15–16. **6:** *The day of Christ Jesus:* the Parousia; see 1 Thess. 2.19 n. **7:** *Prison:* see Introduction.

kept in prison and when I am called on to defend the truth of the gospel, you all share in this privilege of mine. [8] God knows how I long for you all with the deep yearning of Christ Jesus himself. [9] And this is my prayer, that your love may grow ever richer in knowledge and insight of every kind, [10] enabling you to learn by experience what things really matter. Then on the day of Christ you will be flawless and without blame, [11] yielding the full harvest of righteousness that comes through Jesus Christ, to the glory and praise of God.

Paul in prison

[12] My friends, I want you to understand that the progress of the gospel has actually been helped by what has happened to me. [13] It has become common knowledge throughout the imperial guard, and indeed among the public at large, that my imprisonment is in Christ's cause; [14] and my being in prison has given most of our fellow-Christians confidence to speak the word of God fearlessly and with extraordinary courage.

[15] Some, it is true, proclaim Christ in a jealous and quarrelsome spirit, but some do it in goodwill. [16] These are moved by love, knowing that it is to defend the gospel that I am where I am; [17] the others are moved by selfish ambition and present Christ from mixed motives, meaning to cause me distress as I lie in prison. [18] What does it matter? One way or another, whether sincerely or not, Christ is proclaimed; and for that I rejoice.

Yes, and I shall go on rejoicing; [19] for I know well that the issue will be my deliverance, because you are praying for me and the Spirit of Jesus Christ is given me for support. [20] It is my confident hope that nothing will daunt me or prevent me from speaking boldly; and that now as always Christ will display his greatness in me, whether the verdict be life or death. [21] For to me life is Christ, and death is gain. [22] If I am to go on living in the body there is fruitful work for me to do. Which then am I to choose? I cannot tell. [23] I am pulled two ways: my own desire is to depart and be with Christ — that is better by far; [24] but for your sake the greater need is for me to remain in the body. [25] This convinces me: I am sure I shall remain, and stand by you all to ensure your progress and joy in the faith, [26] so that on my account you may have even more cause for pride in Christ Jesus — through seeing me restored to you.

Unity and witness

[27] WHATEVER happens, let your conduct be worthy of the gospel of Christ, so that whether or not I come and see you for myself I may hear that you are standing firm, united in spirit and in mind, side by side in the struggle to advance the gospel faith, [28] meeting your opponents without so much as a tremor. This is a sure sign to them that destruction is in store for them and salvation for you, a sign from God himself; [29] for you have been granted the privilege not only of believing in Christ but also of suffering for him. [30] Your conflict is the same as mine; once you saw me in it, and now you hear I am in it still.

2 If then our common life in Christ yields anything to stir the heart, any consola-

1:13 **the imperial guard:** or the Residency.

11: The *harvest* does not consist in *righteousness* but is produced by it, and Jesus is its source.

1.12–30: Paul's situation and prospects. 13: The Gk. word translated *the imperial guard* has several possible meanings: the *guard* itself, the guard's headquarters in Rome, or the Residency of the provincial governor (see Tfn. for this verse). **15–18:** In contrast to the situation in Corinth, where doctrinal differences occasioned factionalism, here the *ambition* of those who *proclaim Christ in a jealous ... spirit* seems to be personal. **19:** Whether *deliverance* here means ultimate salvation or only release from prison is uncertain; as vv. 20, 25–26 show, Paul views both freedom and execution as possible outcomes of his situation. **21:** See Gal. 2.20. *Death is gain* for it will make Paul's union with Christ even closer (v. 23). Here Paul views the state of the Christian between death and the Parousia as superior to life in the world. This view does not contradict, but rather complements the futuristic resurrection hope expressed in 3.21. **28:** *Opponents:* in 3.1–11 they are "Judaizers," that is, Christians who advocated the observance of Jewish law by Christians; here they are outsiders, pagans who denied the religious hopes and contentions of Christians, or scorned Christians for their way of life.

2.1–11: Call to unity and humility. Except for what appears to be a minor disagreement mentioned in 4.2, the church of Philippi seems to have been an unusually harmonious congregation. The tone here suggests not tion of love, any participation in the Spirit, any warmth of affection or compassion, ²fill up my cup of happiness by thinking and feeling alike, with the same love for one another and a common attitude of mind. ³Leave no room for selfish ambition and vanity, but humbly reckon others better than yourselves. ⁴Look to each other's interests and not merely to your own.

⁵Take to heart among yourselves what you find in Christ Jesus: ⁶'He was in the form of God; yet he laid no claim to equality with God, ⁷but made himself nothing, assuming the form of a slave. Bearing the human likeness, ⁸sharing the human lot, he humbled himself, and was obedient, even to the point of death, death on a cross! ⁹Therefore God raised him to the heights and bestowed on him the name above all names, ¹⁰that at the name of Jesus every knee should bow—in heaven, on earth, and in the depths—¹¹and every tongue acclaim, "Jesus Christ is Lord," to the glory of God the Father.'

¹²So you too, my friends, must be obedient, as always; even more, now that I am absent, than when I was with you. You must work out your own salvation in fear and trembling; ¹³for it is God who works in you, inspiring both the will and the deed, for his own chosen purpose.

¹⁴Do everything without grumbling or argument. ¹⁵Show yourselves innocent and above reproach, faultless children of God in a crooked and depraved generation, in which you shine like stars in a dark world ¹⁶and proffer the word of life. Then you will be my pride on the day of Christ, proof that I did not run my race in vain or labour in vain. ¹⁷But if my life-blood is to be poured out to complete the sacrifice and offering up of your faith, I rejoice and share my joy with you all. ¹⁸You too must rejoice and share your joy with me.

Paul's plans

¹⁹I HOPE, in the Lord Jesus, to send Timothy to you soon; it will cheer me up to have news of you. ²⁰I have no one else here like him, who has a genuine concern for your affairs; ²¹they are all bent on their own interests, not on those of Christ Jesus. ²²But Timothy's record is known to you: you know that he has been at my side in the service of the gospel like a son working under his father. ²³So he is the one I mean to send as soon as I see how things go with me; ²⁴and I am confident, in the Lord, that I shall be coming myself before long.

²⁵I have decided I must also send our brother Epaphroditus, my fellow-worker and comrade, whom you commissioned to attend to my needs. ²⁶He has been missing you all, and was upset because you heard he

2:20 **no one ... who has:** *or* no one else here who sees things as I do, and has.

the presence of factions, but the apostle's encouragement of a healthy community spirit. **6–11:** In the view of most scholars, Paul has here incorporated into his letter an ancient Christian hymn. The hymn exalts the saving work of Christ. But because it speaks of a Christ who *made himself nothing* (v. 7) and *humbled himself* (v. 8), Paul quotes it to set forth Christ as the primary example of the humility which he here urges upon the Philippians. The hymn consists of two strophes, vv. 6–8 and 9–11; the words *death on a cross* (v. 8) were probably added by Paul. The first strophe presents a downward movement, from heavenly preexistence to human life; the second describes the exaltation of the obedient Jesus. **7:** *Made himself nothing* (lit. emptied himself): instead of clinging to a divine state of existence he assumed that of a *slave* in the incarnation. **7–8:** The phrases *bearing the human likeness* and *sharing the human lot* are probably intended to suggest that, while truly human, he was something more, i.e. the preexistent being who "was in the form of God" (v. 6). **9:** *Raised him to the heights:* a contrast to the "he humbled himself" of v. 8. *The name above all names:* the title "Lord." **10:** *Heaven, earth, the depths* probably reflect a view of a three-tiered universe ruled by angelic spirits who join in confessing Jesus' lordship.

2.12–18: The work of salvation. 12–13: *Fear and trembling:* a reverential attitude, since the work of salvation with which they must cooperate is actually the work of God. **17:** Paul again speaks of the possibility of his execution. In relation to the Philippians' *faith*, which is spoken of as a sacrificial gift (see Rom. 12.1), his own blood, shed in execution, would be like the drink-offering poured out *to complete the sacrifice*, as in Exod. 29.40; Num. 28.7. Through it all Paul hopes he will live to see the day of Christ, i.e. the Second Coming (v. 16).

2.19–3.1a: Timothy and Epaphroditus. 19: *Timothy:* see 1 Cor. 16.10 n.

was ill. 27 Indeed he was dangerously ill, but God was merciful to him; and not only to him but to me, to spare me one sorrow on top of another. 28 For this reason I am all the more eager to send him and give you the happiness of seeing him again; that will relieve my anxiety as well. 29 Welcome him then in the fellowship of the Lord with wholehearted delight. You should honour people like him; 30 in Christ's cause he came near to death, risking his life to render me the service you could not

3 give. 1 And now, my friends, I wish you joy in the Lord.

The Christian's goal

TO REPEAT what I have written to you before is no trouble to me, and it is a safeguard for you. 2 Be on your guard against those dogs, those who do nothing but harm and who insist on mutilation — 'circumcision' I will not call it; 3 we are the circumcision, we who worship by the Spirit of God, whose pride is in Christ Jesus, and who put no confidence in the physical. 4 It is not that I am myself without grounds for such confidence. If anyone makes claims of that kind, I can make a stronger case for myself: 5 circumcised on my eighth day, Israelite by race, of the tribe of Benjamin, a Hebrew born and bred; in my practice of the law a Pharisee, 6 in zeal for religion a persecutor of the church, by the law's standard of righteousness without fault.

7 But all such assets I have written off because of Christ. 8 More than that, I count everything sheer loss, far outweighed by the gain of knowing Christ Jesus my Lord, for whose sake I did in fact forfeit everything. I count it so much rubbish, for the sake of gaining Christ 9 and finding myself in union with him, with no righteousness of my own based on the law, nothing but the righteousness which comes from faith in Christ, given by God in response to faith. 10 My one desire is to know Christ and the power of his resurrection, and to share his sufferings in growing conformity with his death, 11 in hope of somehow attaining the resurrection from the dead.

12 It is not that I have already achieved this. I have not yet reached perfection, but I press on, hoping to take hold of that for which Christ once took hold of me. 13 My friends, I do not claim to have hold of it yet. What I do say is this: forgetting what is behind and straining towards what lies ahead, 14 I press towards the finishing line, to win the heavenly prize to which God has called me in Christ Jesus.

15 We who are mature should keep to this way of thinking. If on any point you think differently, this also God will make plain to

3:3 **who worship ... God:** *some witnesses read* who worship God in the spirit; *one reads* whose worship is spiritual.

29: See 1 Cor. 16.18. **30:** Epaphroditus' *risking his life* may refer to the illness which he contracted while on his mission to Paul (vv. 26–27). **3.1a:** This sentence reads like a concluding statement and, taken with the quite different tone of the ensuing section, suggests that one letter breaks off here and the following is a fragment of another letter.

3.1b–4.1: Warning against false teachers. See note on 3.1a. Here Paul's tone is sharp, as he speaks of opponents who threaten the faith of the Philippians. **2:** *Dogs* was a Jewish term of contempt for pagans, applied here to those who disturb the peace of the church. These may be Jewish Christian missionaries, as their insistence on *circumcision* suggests. Paul contends that physical circumcision is only *mutilation*. **3:** See Jer. 4.4; Rom. 2.28–29. **4:** Paul could cite *grounds ... for confidence* similar to his opponents', but he regards it all as worthless. **5:** *Pharisee:* see Matt. 3.7 n. **6:** *Persecutor:* see Acts 8.3; 9.1; Gal. 1.13; 2.23. **9:** If in terms of *righteousness ... based on the law* he could claim to have been *without fault* (v. 6), Paul's conversion did not arise merely from despair at fulfilling the law as is sometimes supposed. But he now believes that *righteousness,* far from being earned, can only be the gift which God gives to all who believe in Christ. **10:** *To know Christ* is to have not merely intellectual knowledge but to experience his *power* and to be united with him by sharing his *sufferings.* **12–13:** Paul's statement that he has not *already achieved this* or *yet reached perfection* may indicate that the false teachers he is opposing have claimed such achievement for themselves. If so, their errors may have included not only Judaizing practices but Gnostic views such as that expressed in 2 Tim. 2.18. "Judaizing" alludes to a tendency on the part of Christians to imitate a legalistic Judaism. Gnostics believed themselves to be in possession of a supernatural revelation by which they escaped the bondage of evil, material existence. **15–16:** Probably these verses are ironic, directed against those who thought they had you. 16 Only let our conduct be consistent with what we have already attained.

17 Join together, my friends, in following my example. You have us for a model; imitate those whose way of life conforms to it. 18 As I have often told you, and now tell you with tears, there are many whose way of life makes them enemies of the cross of Christ. 19 They are heading for destruction, they make appetite their god, they take pride in what should bring shame; their minds are set on earthly things. 20 We, by contrast, are citizens of heaven, and from heaven we expect our deliverer to come, the Lord Jesus Christ. 21 He will transfigure our humble bodies, and give them a form like that of his own glorious body, by that power which enables him to make all things subject to himself. 1 This, my dear friends, whom I love and long for, my joy and crown, this is what it means to stand firm in the Lord.

2 Euodia and Syntyche, I appeal to you both: agree together in the Lord. 3 Yes, and you too, my loyal comrade, I ask you to help these women, who shared my struggles in the cause of the gospel, with Clement and my other fellow-workers, who are enrolled in the book of life.

4 I wish you joy in the Lord always. Again I say: all joy be yours.

5 Be known to everyone for your consideration of others.

The Lord is near; 6 do not be anxious, but in everything make your requests known to God in prayer and petition with thanksgiving. 7 Then the peace of God, which is beyond all understanding, will guard your hearts and your thoughts in Christ Jesus.

8 And now, my friends, all that is true, all that is noble, all that is just and pure, all that is lovable and attractive, whatever is excellent and admirable — fill your thoughts with these things.

9 Put into practice the lessons I taught you, the tradition I have passed on, all that you heard me say or saw me do; and the God of peace will be with you.

Thanks and greetings

10 It is a great joy to me in the Lord that after so long your care for me has now revived. I know you always cared; it was opportunity you lacked. 11 Not that I am speaking of want, for I have learned to be self-sufficient whatever my circumstances. 12 I know what it is to have nothing, and I know what it is to have plenty. I have been thoroughly initiated into fullness and hunger, plenty and poverty. 13 I am able to face anything through him who gives me strength. 14 All the same, it was kind of you to share the burden of my troubles.

15 You Philippians are aware that, when I set out from Macedonia in the early days of my mission, yours was the only church to share with me in the giving and receiving; 16 more than once you contributed to my needs, even at Thessalonica. 17 Do not think I set my heart on the gift; all I care for is the interest mounting up in your account. 18 I have been paid in full; I have all I need and more, now that I have received from Epaphroditus what you sent. It is a fragrant offering, an acceptable sacrifice, pleasing to God. 19 And my God will supply all your needs out

---

already achieved perfection. **17:** *My example:* see 1 Cor. 11.1. **18–19:** *Enemies of the cross:* Paul's invective is too general (*appetite . . . shame*) for one to deduce what practices are being attacked.

4.2–9: Final exhortations. 3: *Comrade:* this translates the Gk. word *syzygos,* which can serve as, and may here be, a proper name. The OT concept of a *book of life* from which names were struck out at the time of death (see Exod. 32.32; Ps. 69.28) is transformed; the book becomes a list of those who are destined to everlasting life (see Rev. 3.5; 13.8). **5:** *The Lord is near:* an allusion to the Parousia; see 1 Thess. 2.19 n.

4.10–20: Thanks for the Philippians' gift; see Introduction. **10–14:** The main reason for Paul's *joy* about the gift is its evidence of the Philippians' devotion to him. Without being ungracious, he states that he is indifferent to material wants. **11–13:** *To be self-sufficient:* this ideal of Greek philosophy is realized by Paul, not by his own efforts, but *through* God *who gives* him *strength* (v. 13). **15:** Through commercial terms, Paul tells the Philippians that their support of him is payment for the spiritual goods they received through his ministry. *Yours . . . only:* from the Philippians alone did he accept financial aid. **18:** *Paid in full:* Paul's words imply a receipt for payment. Possibly, he intends a delicate indication that he does not expect to receive anything more from them. The gift, now described in terms of OT sacrifice, is a *fragrant offering* (see Lev. 1.9), *an acceptable sacrifice* (see Lev. 1.3).

of the magnificence of his riches in Christ Jesus. 20 To our God and Father be glory for ever and ever! Amen.

21 Give my greetings, in the fellowship of Christ Jesus, to each one of God's people. My colleagues send their greetings to you, 22 and so do all God's people here, particularly those in the emperor's service.

23 The grace of our Lord Jesus Christ be with your spirit.

4.21–23: Final greetings. 22: *The emperor's service:* lit. Caesar's household; see Introduction.

THE LETTER OF PAUL TO THE
Colossians

Colossae was a city of the Roman province of Asia, east of Ephesus and near Laodicea and Hierapolis. It had been evangelized by Epaphras (see 1.7). The unity, stability, and survival of the church were threatened by doctrinal diversity, especially by a faction which had blended together with the Christian gospel some pagan and marginal Jewish elements. This amalgam detracted from the uniqueness and supremacy of Christ through the worship of heavenly beings. The principal aim of Colossians is to assert the preeminence of Christ.

Paul's authorship of Colossians is sometimes questioned because of the differences in style, vocabulary, and doctrine between it and his undisputed letters. Those who uphold its authenticity explain these differences as due to the new situation to which he addresses himself and to the maturing of his thought. If authentic, Colossians probably dates from the Roman imprisonment of Paul (61–63 C.E.). The certainly genuine Letter to Philemon has several points of contact with Colossians (see Introduction to Philemon).

1 From Paul, by the will of God apostle of Christ Jesus, and our colleague Timothy, [2] to God's people at Colossae, our fellow-believers in Christ.

Grace to you and peace from God our Father.

[3] In all our prayers to God, the Father of our Lord Jesus Christ, we thank him for you, [4] because we have heard of your faith in Christ Jesus and the love you bear towards all God's people; [5] both spring from that hope stored up for you in heaven of which you learned when the message of the true gospel first [6] came to you. That same gospel is bearing fruit and making new growth the whole world over, as it does among you and has done since the day when you heard of God's grace and learned what it truly is. [7] It was Epaphras, our dear fellow-servant and a trusted worker for Christ on our behalf, who taught you this, [8] and it is he who has brought

us news of the love the Spirit has awakened in you.

The supremacy of Christ

[9] This is why, ever since we first heard about you, we have not ceased to pray for you. We ask God that you may receive from him full insight into his will, all wisdom and spiritual understanding, [10] so that your manner of life may be worthy of the Lord and entirely pleasing to him. We pray that you may bear fruit in active goodness of every kind, and grow in knowledge of God. [11] In his glorious might may he give you ample strength to meet with fortitude and patience whatever comes; [12] and to give joyful thanks to the Father who has made you fit to share the heri-

1:7 **our behalf:** *some witnesses read* your behalf.
1:11–12 **patience . . . thanks:** *or* patience, and joy whatever comes; [12] and to give thanks.

1.3–14: Thanksgiving and prayer. 9–10: True *wisdom* and *understanding* produce a *worthy manner of life.* Probably there is an implied contrast with the false wisdom which involved the worship of spiritual powers (see 1.16 n.). **12–14:** In the OT *the heritage of God's people* was the land. Here the *heritage* is *in the realm of light,* i.e. a share in Christ's *kingdom.* As Israel was delivered in the Exodus from Egypt, so too the Christians have been rescued. The words *release* (lit. redemption), *heritage,* and *rescued* draw upon the Exodus tradition to interpret Christian experience as release from the *domain of darkness,* i.e. of evil and evil powers.

1.15–20: A hymn to Christ. Most scholars agree that these verses are taken over and modified by Paul from an earlier hymn. Hence, many currents of thought, even pagan, are suggested as lying behind the hymn. The dominant source of its themes, however, is probably the OT and noncanonical Jewish Wisdom literature.

tage of God's people in the realm of light.

¹³ He rescued us from the domain of darkness and brought us into the kingdom of his dear Son, ¹⁴ through whom our release is secured and our sins are forgiven. ¹⁵ He is the image of the invisible God; his is the primacy over all creation. ¹⁶ In him everything in heaven and on earth was created, not only things visible but also the invisible orders of thrones, sovereignties, authorities, and powers: the whole universe has been created through him and for him. ¹⁷ He exists before all things, and all things are held together in him. ¹⁸ He is the head of the body, the church. He is its origin, the first to return from the dead, to become in all things supreme. ¹⁹ For in him God in all his fullness chose to dwell, ²⁰ and through him to reconcile all things to himself, making peace through the shedding of his blood on the cross—all things, whether on earth or in heaven.

²¹⁻²² Formerly you yourselves were alienated from God, his enemies in heart and mind, as your evil deeds showed. But now by Christ's death in his body of flesh and blood God has reconciled you to himself, so that he may bring you into his own presence, holy and without blame or blemish. ²³ Yet you must persevere in faith, firm on your foun-

dations and never to be dislodged from the hope offered in the gospel you accepted. This is the gospel which has been proclaimed in the whole creation under heaven, the gospel of which I, Paul, became a minister.

²⁴ It is now my joy to suffer for you; for the sake of Christ's body, the church, I am completing what still remains for Christ to suffer in my own person. ²⁵ I became a servant of the church by virtue of the task assigned to me by God for your benefit: to put God's word into full effect, ²⁶ that secret purpose hidden for long ages and through many generations, but now disclosed to God's people. ²⁷ To them he chose to make known what a wealth of glory is offered to the Gentiles in this secret purpose: Christ in you, the hope of glory.

²⁸ He it is whom we proclaim. We teach everyone and instruct everyone in all the ways of wisdom, so as to present each one of you as a mature member of Christ's body. ²⁹ To this end I am toiling strenuously with all the energy and power of Christ at work in me. ¹ I want you to know how strenuous are my exertions for you and the Laodiceans, and for all who have never set eyes on me. ² My aim is to keep them in good heart

1:16 **for him:** *or* with him as its goal.   1:20 **to himself:** *or* to their goal in him.

Israel's developed portrait of divine Wisdom (see Prov. 8.22–31; Ecclus. 24.1–22) is the forerunner of the portrayal of Christ as creator and redeemer. **15:** *The image of the invisible God:* see Wisd. 7.26. *His is the primacy over all creation:* see Prov. 8.22. **16:** Since all else was *created through him* (see Wisd. 7.22) *and for him,* he is superior to all, as the source and end of their being. *Invisible orders:* in the religious currents of the time, it was believed that many divine beings (*thrones, sovereignties, authorities, and powers*) existed; in some thought, these were represented as angelic beings (compare 1 Cor. 2.6–8 n.). The passage subordinates such spiritual beings to Christ, for they too are created things (v. 15). **18:** In the earlier Pauline letters Christ and Christians form one body (see 1 Cor. 12.12); in Col. and Eph. a distinction is made between the *body* (the church) and its *head* (Christ). Also distinctive is the fact that here *church* means the entire Christian community, not simply a local church as in the earlier Pauline usage. *The first to return from the dead:* lit. the firstborn from the dead. **19:** The entire *fullness* of God dwells in Christ. This has been interpreted by some scholars as a rebuttal of the notion that God's attributes were distributed among many angelic beings who mediate between God and humanity. Others doubt that that concept was current so early as to have called forth a rebuttal from Paul. **20:** The whole created order (*all things*) is understood as having been estranged from God, and rebellious; this estrangement has been overcome by the reconciliation effected by the death of Christ (*the shedding of his blood on the cross*).

1.21–23: The reconciled community. The universal reconciliation (1.20) is here applied to the local church. **22:** *Without . . . blemish:* the phrase draws on OT sacrificial requirements (Exod. 12.5; Lev. 9.3; and often).

1.24–2.5: The apostle's suffering and dedication. 24: The expression *what still remains for Christ to suffer* does not imply a lack in sufferings of the historical Jesus; rather, these afflictions are to be borne by the apostle and are "Christ's" because they will be endured *for the sake of Christ's body,* i.e. the church. The passage also reflects the apocalyptic notion that God's victory over evil would be preceded by a period of trial and suffering;

and united in love, so that they may come to the full wealth of conviction which understanding brings, and grasp God's secret, which is Christ himself, [3]in whom lie hidden all the treasures of wisdom and knowledge. [4]I tell you this to make sure no one talks you into error by specious arguments. [5]I may be absent in body, but in spirit I am with you, and rejoice to see your unbroken ranks and the solid front which your faith in Christ presents.

True and false teaching

[6]THEREFORE, since you have accepted Christ Jesus as Lord, live in union with him. [7]Be rooted in him, be built in him, grow strong in the faith as you were taught; let your hearts overflow with thankfulness. [8]Be on your guard; let no one capture your minds with hollow and delusive speculations, based on traditions of human teaching and centred on the elemental spirits of the universe and not on Christ.

[9]For it is in Christ that the Godhead in all its fullness dwells embodied, [10]it is in him you have been brought to fulfilment. Every power and authority in the universe is subject to him as head. [11]In him also you were circumcised, not in a physical sense, but by the stripping away of the old nature, which is Christ's way of circumcision. [12]For you were buried with him in baptism, and in that baptism you were also raised to life with him through your faith in the active power of God, who raised him from the dead. [13]And although you were dead because of your sins and your uncircumcision, he has brought you to life with Christ. For he has forgiven us all our sins; [14]he has cancelled the bond which was outstanding against us with its legal demands; he has set it aside, nailing it to the cross. [15]There he disarmed the cosmic powers and authorities and made a public spectacle of them, leading them as captives in his triumphal procession.

[16]ALLOW no one, therefore, to take you to task about what you eat or drink, or over the observance of festival, new moon, or sabbath. [17]These are no more than a shadow of what was to come; the reality is Christ's. [18]You are not to be disqualified by the decision of people who go in for self-mortification and angel-worship and access to some visionary world. Such people, bursting with the futile conceit of worldly minds, [19]lose their hold upon the head; yet it is from the head that the whole body, with all its joints and ligaments, has its needs supplied, and thus knit together grows according to God's design. [20]Did you not die with Christ and pass beyond reach of the elemental spirits of the universe? Then why behave as though you were still living the life of the world? Why let people dictate to you: [21]'Do not handle this, do not taste that, do not touch the other'— [22]referring to things that must all perish as they are used? That is to follow human rules and regulations. [23]Such conduct may have an air of wisdom, with its forced piety, its self-mortification, and its severity to the body; but it is of no use at all in combating sensuality.

3 Were you not raised to life with Christ? Then aspire to the realm above, where Christ is, seated at God's right hand, [2]and fix your thoughts on that higher realm, not on

2:8 **and centred ... universe:** or and elementary ideas belonging to this world.   2:15 **he disarmed ... of them:** or he stripped himself of his physical body, and thereby made a public spectacle of the cosmic powers and authorities.   2:20 **elemental ... universe:** or elementary ideas belonging to this world.

see Rev. 6.11; 1 Thess. 3.3 n. **2.1:** *Laodiceans:* neighbors of the Colossians. **3:** The notion that these *treasures lie hidden* in Christ is possibly derived from Prov. 2.3–5, which likens wisdom to buried treasure; see also Isa. 45.3.

2.6–23: Warning against false teaching. 8: *The elemental spirits of the universe:* see v. 20; 1 Cor. 2.6–8 n.; Gal. 4.3, 9. **11–12:** Beyond the partial stripping off of flesh in *circumcision, baptism* causes one to be totally divested of *the old nature* (lit. the body of flesh). **15:** Since the angelic powers were thought to be the guardians of the law (compare Gal. 3.19), its nullification means the end of their dominion. *Captives* were paraded in a public victory celebration; compare Eph. 4.8. **16–18:** The false teaching specified in these verses includes both Jewish and pagan religious practices. *Access to some visionary world* probably refers to the experience claimed in some pagan mystery cults.

3.1–17: The demands of life in Christ. 3: *Died:* abandoned your former life; compare Rom. 6.1–11. **4:** Although Paul emphasizes the present sharing in Christ's risen life, he nevertheless continues to look forward this earthly life. ³ You died; and now your life lies hidden with Christ in God. ⁴ When Christ, who is our life, is revealed, then you too will be revealed with him in glory.

Christian conduct

⁵ So PUT to death those parts of you which belong to the earth—fornication, indecency, lust, evil desires, and the ruthless greed which is nothing less than idolatry; ⁶ on these divine retribution falls. ⁷ This is the way you yourselves once lived; ⁸ but now have done with rage, bad temper, malice, slander, filthy talk—banish them all from your lips! ⁹ Do not lie to one another, now that you have discarded the old human nature and the conduct that goes with it, ¹⁰ and have put on the new nature which is constantly being renewed in the image of its Creator and brought to know God. ¹¹ There is no question here of Greek and Jew, circumcised and uncircumcised, barbarian, Scythian, slave and freeman; but Christ is all, and is in all.

¹² Put on, then, garments that suit God's chosen and beloved people: compassion, kindness, humility, gentleness, patience. ¹³ Be tolerant with one another and forgiving, if any of you has cause for complaint: you must forgive as the Lord forgave you. ¹⁴ Finally, to bind everything together and complete the whole, there must be love. ¹⁵ Let Christ's peace be arbiter in your decisions, the peace to which you were called as members of a single body. Always be thankful. ¹⁶ Let the gospel of Christ dwell among you in all its richness; teach and instruct one another with all the wisdom it gives you. With psalms and hymns and spiritual songs, sing from the heart in gratitude to God. ¹⁷ Let every word and action, everything you do, be in the name of the Lord Jesus, and give thanks through him to God the Father.

¹⁸ WIVES, be subject to your husbands; that is your Christian duty. ¹⁹ Husbands, love your wives and do not be harsh with them. ²⁰ Children, obey your parents in everything, for that is pleasing to God and is the Christian way. ²¹ Fathers, do not exasperate your children, in case they lose heart. ²² Slaves, give entire obedience to your earthly masters, not merely to catch their eye or curry favour with them, but with single-mindedness, out of reverence for the Lord. ²³ Whatever you are doing, put your whole heart into it, as if you were doing it for the Lord and not for men, ²⁴ knowing that there is a master who will give you an inheritance as a reward for your service. Christ is the master you must serve. ²⁵ Wrongdoers will pay for the wrong they do; there will be no favouritism. 4 ¹ Masters, be just and fair to your slaves, knowing that you too have a master in heaven.

² Persevere in prayer, with minds alert and with thankful hearts; ³ and include us in your prayers, asking God to provide an opening for the gospel, that we may proclaim the secret of Christ, for which indeed I am in prison. ⁴ Pray that I may make the secret plain, as it is my duty to do.

⁵ Be wise in your dealings with outsiders, but use your opportunities to the full. ⁶ Let your words always be gracious, never insipid; learn how best to respond to each person you meet.

News and greetings

⁷ YOU WILL hear all my news from Tychicus, our dear brother and trustworthy helper and fellow-servant in the Lord's work. ⁸ I am sending him to you for this purpose, to let you know how we are and to put fresh heart into you. ⁹ With him comes Onesimus, our trustworthy and dear brother, who is one of yourselves. They will tell you all that has happened here.

¹⁰ Aristarchus, Christ's captive like myself, sends his greetings; so does Mark, the cousin of Barnabas (you have had instructions about

to the Parousia (see 1 Thess. 2.19 n.). **5:** Paradoxically, those who are in Christ have died (v. 3) but they must *put to death* (give up completely) what is earthly in them. **10:** *In the image:* see Gen. 1.26–27. **11:** *Barbarian:* non-Greek and hence—like a *Scythian*—uncivilized.

3.18–4.1: Christian domestic ethics. These counsels are paralleled by the lists of household virtues found in both pagan and Jewish literature. Paul gives them a Christian tone by his additions, such as *out of reverence for the Lord* (v. 22).

4.2–18: Final admonition, greetings, and blessing. Among those greeted, note especially *Tychicus* (v. 7), *Onesimus* (v. 9), and *Archippus* (v. 17); see Philem. 1 and Introduction to Philem.

him; if he comes, make him welcome), [11] and Jesus Justus. Of the Jewish Christians, these are the only ones working with me for the kingdom of God, and they have been a great comfort to me. [12] Greetings from Epaphras, servant of Christ, who is one of yourselves. He prays hard for you all the time, that you may stand fast, as mature Christians, fully determined to do the will of God. [13] I can vouch for him, that he works tirelessly for you and the people at Laodicea and Hierapolis. [14] Greetings to you from our dear friend Luke, the doctor, and from Demas. [15] Give our greetings to the Christians at Laodicea,

and to Nympha and the congregation that meets at her house. [16] Once this letter has been read among you, see that it is read also to the church at Laodicea, and that you in turn read my letter to Laodicea. [17] Give Archippus this message: 'See that you carry out fully the duty entrusted to you in the Lord's service.'

[18] I add this greeting in my own hand— Paul. Remember I am in prison. Grace be with you.

4:15 **Nympha ... her house:** *some witnesses read* Nymphas ... his house.

THE FIRST LETTER OF PAUL TO THE
Thessalonians

According to Acts 17.1–18.5, Paul came to Thessalonica (modern Salonica) with Silas and Timothy during his second missionary journey, after leaving Philippi. His stay of three weeks was spent in preaching the messiahship of Jesus in the local synagogue. Some Jews and many "God-fearing" Gentiles were converted. Jews precipitated a riot, and charged the missionaries with acting against the laws of the emperor. Consequently, the Christians sent Paul and Silas by night to the neighboring town of Beroea. Success in preaching there prompted the Jews of Thessalonica to come and create a disturbance similar to that made in their own city, and for safety's sake Paul was constrained to leave alone for Athens. He next went to Corinth where he was joined by Silas and Timothy.

This picture does not correspond with the one found in the letter itself. The letter presupposes a much longer stay at Thessalonica (2.7–9; see Phil. 4.16) and a church predominantly composed of converts from paganism (1.9); the letter does not speak of any persecution suffered by Paul in the city; it states that it was from Athens that Paul sent Timothy back to Thessalonica (3.1). The letter was probably written from Corinth just after Timothy's completion of his mission (3.6). While at Corinth (Acts 18.12) Paul was brought before the tribunal of the Roman Gallio, whose term as proconsul was around 51–52 c.e.; if that information is reliable 1 Thessalonians, written around 51 c.e., is the first of the Pauline epistles.

The letter deals primarily with questions concerning the Parousia (the future coming of Christ): its time (e.g. 5.1–2), the suffering of Christians in relation to it (e.g. 3.3), and the destiny of those who die in advance of its arrival (e.g. 4.13–14).

1 FROM Paul, Silvanus, and Timothy to the church of the Thessalonians who belong to God the Father and the Lord Jesus Christ. Grace to you and peace.

2 We always thank God for you all, and mention you in our prayers. 3 We continually call to mind, before our God and Father, how your faith has shown itself in action, your love in labour, and your hope of our Lord Jesus Christ in perseverance. 4 My dear friends, beloved by God, we are certain that he has chosen you, 5 because when we brought you the gospel we did not bring it in mere words but in the power of the Holy Spirit and with strong conviction. You know what we were like for your sake when we were with you.

6 You, in turn, followed the example set by us and by the Lord; the welcome you gave the message meant grave suffering for you, yet you rejoiced in the Holy Spirit; 7 and so you have become a model for all believers in Macedonia and in Achaia. 8 From you the word of the Lord rang out; and not in Macedonia and Achaia alone, but everywhere your faith in God has become common knowledge. No

1.1: Greeting. *Silvanus* is the Latinized form of the name "Silas" used in Acts, for example, Acts 15.39. *Timothy:* see 1 Cor. 16.10 n., Acts 16.1–3. Of all his coworkers Timothy is the one most frequently mentioned by Paul. The letter is written in the name of all three, yet *Paul* is clearly the principal writer; see 3.5; 5.27. *Grace . . . peace:* see Rom. 1.7 n.

1.2–10: Thanksgiving for a fruitful ministry. 5: *The power of the Holy Spirit* may refer not only to the force inherent in the apostolic preaching, but also to certain miracles accompanying it; see Rom. 15.19. **6:** Paul comforts the Thessalonians in their *grave suffering* by the *example set* by Paul and Jesus. **7:** *Macedonia:* the Roman province in northern Greece of which Thessalonica was the capital. *Achaia:* the province in southern words of ours are needed; [9]everyone is spreading the story of our visit to you: how you turned from idols to be servants of the true and living God, [10]and to wait expectantly for his Son from heaven, whom he raised from the dead, Jesus our deliverer from the retribution to come.

Paul and the church at Thessalonica

2 YOU KNOW for yourselves, my friends, that our visit to you was not fruitless. [2]Far from it! After all the injury and outrage which as you know we had suffered at Philippi, by the help of our God we declared the gospel of God to you frankly and fearlessly in face of great opposition. [3]The appeal we make does not spring from delusion or sordid motive or from any attempt to deceive; [4]but God has approved us as fit to be entrusted with the gospel. So when we preach, we do not curry favour with men; we seek only the favour of God, who is continually testing our hearts. [5]We have never resorted to flattery, as you have cause to know; nor, as God is our witness, have our words ever been a cloak for greed. [6]We have never sought honour from men, not from you or from anyone else, [7]although as Christ's own envoys we might have made our weight felt; but we were as gentle with you as a nurse caring for her children. [8]Our affection was so deep that we were determined to share with you not only the gospel of God but our very selves; that is how dear you had become to us! [9]You remember, my friends, our toil and drudgery; night and day we worked for a living, rather than be a burden to any of you while we proclaimed to you the good news of God.

[10]We call you to witness, yes and God himself, how devout and just and blameless was our conduct towards you who are believers. [11]As you well know, we dealt with each one of you as a father deals with his children; [12]we appealed to you, we encouraged you, we urged you, to live lives worthy of the God who calls you into his kingdom and glory.

[13]We have reason to thank God continually because, when we handed on God's message, you accepted it, not as the word of men, but as what it truly is, the very word of God at work in you who are believers. [14]You, my friends, have followed the example of the Christians in the churches of God in Judaea: you have been treated by your own countrymen as they were treated by the Jews, [15]who killed the Lord Jesus and the prophets and drove us out, and are so heedless of God's will and such enemies of their fellow-men [16]that they hinder us from telling the Gentiles how they may be saved. All this time they have been making up the full measure of their guilt. But now retribution has overtaken them for good and all!

[17]My friends, when for a short spell you were lost to us — out of sight but not out of mind —

Greece from which Paul writes. **10:** The expectation of the early return of the resurrected Jesus is a dominant motif in the letter. Confidently *to wait* for Jesus' appearance from heaven is made possible by faith in his resurrection.

2.1–12: Defense of the missionaries' conduct. 2: *We had suffered at Philippi:* see Acts 16.19–24. **3–6:** Paul and his companions were not like the itinerant pagan preachers; the latter were frequently mercenary charlatans who traded on flattery and deceit. **9:** Unlike the charlatans (vv. 3–6 n.), it was Paul's practice not to accept support from the churches which he founded (see 1 Cor. 9.3–18). Philippi was the exception (see Phil. 4.15–16); Paul accepted their freely offered gifts, abstaining from any demand of support.

2.13–16: Consequences of accepting the gospel. The persecution of the Thessalonian church is compared to that of the churches of Judea by the Jews. **14–16:** Some scholars regard these verses as an addition from a much later time, containing a reference to the Roman destruction of the temple in 70 C.E. **16:** *Full measure of their guilt:* the concept is that divine punishment is deferred until the sins which call it forth have reached their climax. Swift chastisement was a sign of mercy; see 2 Macc. 6.14–15. The *retribution* which *has overtaken* the Jews is probably their obduracy in unbelief. For a similar view of moral evil as the punishment for previous sin, see Rom. 1.18, 24, 26, 28.

2.17–3.13: Paul's concern for the church. 17–18: Paul's mention of his repeated desire to return to Thessalonica is probably a response to a charge that he had not done so because he feared being caught in the persecution there (2.13–16). *Satan:* see Matt. 4.1 n. The precise circumstances (illness, opposition?) in we were exceedingly anxious to see you again. ¹⁸So we made up our minds to visit you—I, Paul, more than once—but Satan thwarted us. ¹⁹For what hope or joy or triumphal crown is there for us when we stand before our Lord Jesus at his coming? What indeed but you? ²⁰You are our glory and our joy.

3 So when we could bear it no longer, we decided to stay on alone at Athens, ²and sent Timothy, our colleague and a fellow-worker with God in the service of the gospel of Christ, to encourage you to stand firm for the faith ³and under all these hardships remain unshaken. You know that this is our appointed lot, ⁴for when we were with you we warned you that we were bound to suffer hardship; and so it has turned out, as you have found. ⁵This was why I could bear it no longer and sent to find out about your faith; I was afraid that the tempter might have tempted you and our labour might be wasted.

⁶But now Timothy has just returned from his visit to you, bringing good news of your faith and love. He tells us that you always think kindly of us, and are as anxious to see us as we are to see you. ⁷So amid all our difficulties and hardships we are reassured, my friends, by the news of your faith. ⁸It is the breath of life to us to know that you stand firm in the Lord. ⁹What thanks can we give to God in return for you? What thanks for all the joy you have brought us, making us rejoice before our God ¹⁰while we pray most earnestly night and day to be allowed to see you again and to make good whatever is lacking in your faith?

¹¹May our God and Father himself, and our Lord Jesus, open the way for us to come to you; ¹²and may the Lord make your love increase and overflow to one another and to everyone, as our love does to you. ¹³May he make your hearts firm, so that you may stand before our God and Father holy and faultless when our Lord Jesus comes with all those who are his own.

Christian conduct

4 AND now, friends, we have one thing to ask of you, as fellow-Christians. We passed on to you the tradition of the way we must live if we are to please God; you are indeed already following it, but we beg you to do so yet more thoroughly. ²You know the rules we gave you in the name of the Lord Jesus. ³This is the will of God, that you should be holy: you must abstain from fornication; ⁴each one of you must learn to gain mastery over his body, to hallow and honour it, ⁵not giving way to lust like the pagans who know nothing of God; ⁶no one must do his fellow-Christian wrong in this matter, or infringe his rights. As we impressed on you before, the Lord punishes all such offences. ⁷For God called us to holiness, not to impurity. ⁸Anyone therefore who flouts these rules is flouting not man but the God who bestows on you his Holy Spirit.

⁹About love of the brotherhood you need no words of mine, for you are yourselves taught by God to love one another, ¹⁰and you are in fact practising this rule of love towards all your fellow-Christians throughout Macedonia. Yet we appeal to you, friends, to do better still. ¹¹Let it be your ambition to live quietly and attend to your own business; and to work with your hands, as we told you, ¹²so that you may command the respect of those outside your own number, and at the same time never be in want.

Christ's return

¹³WE wish you not to remain in ignorance, friends, about those who sleep in death; you

which Paul sees Satan's activity are not known. **19:** *His coming:* Gk. *parousia,* ordinarily used of the "coming" of a king on a visit. This is the earliest instance in the NT of the use of "Parousia" for the coming of the resurrected Jesus in glory. Although it is frequent in later NT literature, Paul's use of it in the sense here intended is confined to 1 and 2 Thess. and 1 Cor. 15.23. **3.3:** The *hardships* are not only necessary to Christian life, but are the inevitable accompaniments of the near approach of the end of time and, thus, constitute *our appointed lot.* A similar view of pre-Messianic tribulations is found in the Judaism of the time. **5:** *Tempter:* Satan; compare 2.18. **13:** *All those who are his own:* lit. all his holy ones, probably meaning the "angels"; see also Zech. 14.5.

4.1–12: An exhortation to Christian living. 4: *Body:* the Gk. word can also mean "wife." **9:** *Taught by God:*

should not grieve like the rest of mankind, who have no hope. ¹⁴We believe that Jesus died and rose again; so too will God bring those who died as Christians to be with Jesus.

¹⁵This we tell you as a word from the Lord: those of us who are still alive when the Lord comes will have no advantage over those who have died; ¹⁶when the command is given, when the archangel's voice is heard, when God's trumpet sounds, then the Lord himself will descend from heaven; first the Christian dead will rise, ¹⁷then we who are still alive shall join them, caught up in clouds to meet the Lord in the air. Thus we shall always be with the Lord. ¹⁸Console one another, then, with these words.

5 About dates and times, my friends, there is no need to write to you, ²for you yourselves know perfectly well that the day of the Lord comes like a thief in the night. ³While they are saying, 'All is peaceful, all secure,' destruction is upon them, sudden as the pangs that come on a woman in childbirth; and there will be no escape. ⁴But you, friends, are not in the dark; the day will not come upon you like a thief. ⁵You are all children of light, children of day. We do not belong to night and darkness, ⁶and we must not sleep like the rest, but keep awake and sober. ⁷Sleepers sleep at night, and drunkards get drunk at night, ⁸but we, who belong to the daylight, must keep sober, armed with

the breastplate of faith and love, and the hope of salvation for a helmet. ⁹God has not destined us for retribution, but for the full attainment of salvation through our Lord Jesus Christ. ¹⁰He died for us so that awake or asleep we might live in company with him. ¹¹Therefore encourage one another, build one another up—as indeed you do.

Final instructions and greetings

¹²WE beg you, friends, to acknowledge those who are working so hard among you, and are your leaders and counsellors in the Lord's fellowship. ¹³Hold them in the highest esteem and affection for the work they do.

Live at peace among yourselves. ¹⁴We urge you, friends, to rebuke the idle, encourage the faint-hearted, support the weak, and be patient with everyone.

¹⁵See to it that no one pays back wrong for wrong, but always aim at what is best for each other and for all.

¹⁶Always be joyful; ¹⁷pray continually; ¹⁸give thanks whatever happens; for this is what God wills for you in Christ Jesus.

¹⁹Do not stifle inspiration ²⁰or despise prophetic utterances, ²¹but test them all; keep hold of what is good ²²and avoid all forms of evil.

²³May God himself, the God of peace,

---

see Jer. 31.33–34. **11–12:** These injunctions were probably motivated by irresponsibility similar to that described in 2 Thess. 3.6–11.

4.13–18: The destiny of the Christian dead. 13–14: Possibly Timothy had brought a report about a concern over the fate of those who had died before the Parousia (see 2.19 n.); this passage answers that concern. **15:** *A word from the Lord* probably means that Paul believes he speaks here with the authority of the Lord; compare 1 Cor. 14.37. **16:** An archangel is a chief angel. *God's trumpet sounds:* see Exod. 19.16, 19. That a trumpet call would usher in the final salvation is derived from Isa. 27.13; see also Matt. 24.31; 1 Cor. 15.52. At the Parousia of the monarch (see 2.19 n.), the townspeople went out of the city to receive their ruler. Since the Lord *will descend from heaven,* the Christians will meet him *in the air.*

5.1–11: Uncertainty about the time of the Parousia: 1–2: The precise time of the final saving intervention of God was a characteristic concern of apocalyptic thought; see Dan. 9.24–27. Paul considers such preoccupation useless. In the OT, *the day of the Lord* is God's future judgment day (see Amos 5.18; Joel 2.14–15 n.). Here, since the judgment comes with the Parousia, the Lord is Jesus. *Like a thief in the night:* the point of the comparison is its unexpectedness; compare Matt. 24.43–44; Lk. 12.39–40. **3:** *Pangs . . . a woman in childbirth:* compare Isa. 13.8; Jer. 6.24. **4–7:** A similar contrast between people of *light* and those of *darkness,* appears in the Dead Sea Scrolls. **8:** Aspects of God's judgment are described as pieces of divine armor (Isa. 59.17; Wisd. 5.17–20). Here and in Eph. 6.13–17 the Christians' preparedness for salvation is similarly described. **10:** *Awake or asleep:* alive or dead.

5.12–28: Final admonitions and blessing. 12: *Leaders and counsellors:* see Rom. 12.6–8. **23:** *Spirit, soul,* and *body:* the complete human being, not three separate aspects of a person.

make you holy through and through, and keep you sound in spirit, soul, and body, free of any fault when our Lord Jesus Christ comes. 24 He who calls you keeps faith; he will do it.

25 Friends, pray for us also.

26 Greet all our fellow-Christians with the kiss of peace.

27 I adjure you by the Lord to have this letter read to them all.

28 The grace of our Lord Jesus Christ be with you!

1502

THE SECOND LETTER OF PAUL TO THE
Thessalonians

Paul's authorship of 2 Thessalonians has been disputed on several grounds. First, the literary similarities with 1 Thessalonians have suggested to some that an anonymous author, writing in Paul's name, copied from the authentic letter. If, however, one supposes that Paul wrote the second letter very shortly after the first, that hypothesis loses much of its force.

A second and more substantial argument is that in 1 Thessalonians Paul, while emphasizing that the Parousia (see 1 Thess. 2.19 n.) will come unexpectedly, speaks as if it were near; 2 Thessalonians, on the other hand, indicates that there will be a considerable delay between this letter and the Parousia, and the author gives detailed signs which must occur first. However, these signs are not incompatible with the view that the Parousia will take place within the lifetime of those to whom the apostle writes, or that it will occur unexpectedly even though preceded by such signs.

Third, the strongest argument for inauthenticity is that this letter speaks against the teaching that "the day of the Lord is already here" (2.2). It is difficult to suppose that this latter view, which treats the Parousia as a present spiritual experience, would flourish in Thessalonica at the same time as the opposite, the fervent expectation of the Lord's coming as a future event, found in 1 Thessalonians. Nevertheless, it is possible that Paul responded to a new problem which arose after the writing of the earlier letter.

1 From Paul, Silvanus, and Timothy to the church of the Thessalonians who belong to God our Father and the Lord Jesus Christ.

2 Grace to you and peace from God the Father and the Lord Jesus Christ.

3 Friends, we are always bound to thank God for you, and it is right that we should, because your faith keeps on increasing and the love you all have for each other grows ever greater. 4 Indeed we boast about you among the churches of God, because your faith remains so steadfast under all the persecutions and troubles you endure. 5 This points to the justice of God's judgement; you will be proved worthy of the kingdom of God, for which indeed you are suffering. 6 It is just that God should balance the account by sending affliction to those who afflict you, 7 and relief to you who are afflicted, and to us

as well, when the Lord Jesus is revealed from heaven with his mighty angels 8 in blazing fire. Then he will mete out punishment to those who refuse to acknowledge God and who will not obey the gospel of our Lord Jesus. 9 They will suffer the penalty of eternal destruction, cut off from the presence of the Lord and the splendour of his might, 10 when on the great day he comes to reveal his glory among his own and his majesty among all believers; and therefore among you, since you believed the testimony we brought you.

11 With this in mind we pray for you always, that our God may count you worthy of your calling, and that his power may bring to fulfilment every good purpose and every act inspired by faith, 12 so that the name of our Lord Jesus may be glorified in you, and you in him, according to the grace of our God and the Lord Jesus Christ.

1.3–12: Thanksgiving and encouragement. 4: *Persecutions:* see 1 Thess. 2.13–16. **7–8:** The imagery of *blazing fire* in connection with Jesus being *revealed from heaven* is related to OT statements about God coming in judgment; see Ps. 97.3; Isa. 66.15. The association of the *angels* with the fire may be derived from a Jewish tradition arising from Deut. 33.2–3 (Sept.). See also the extra-biblical *2 Enoch* 29.3.

Christ's return

2 Now ABOUT the coming of our Lord Jesus Christ, when he is to gather us to himself: I beg you, my friends, ²do not suddenly lose your heads, do not be alarmed by any prophetic utterance, any pronouncement, or any letter purporting to come from us, alleging that the day of the Lord is already here. ³Let no one deceive you in any way. That day cannot come before the final rebellion against God, when wickedness will be revealed in human form, the man doomed to destruction. ⁴He is the adversary who raises himself up against every so-called god or object of worship, and even enthrones himself in God's temple claiming to be God. ⁵Do you not remember that I told you this while I was still with you? ⁶You know, too, about the restraining power which ensures that he will be revealed only at his appointed time; ⁷for already the secret forces of wickedness are at work, secret only for the present until the restraining hand is removed from the scene. ⁸Then he will be revealed, the wicked one whom the Lord Jesus will destroy with the breath of his mouth and annihilate by the radiance of his presence. ⁹The coming of the wicked one is the work of Satan; it will be attended by all the powerful signs and miracles that falsehood can devise, ¹⁰all the deception that sinfulness can impose on those doomed to destruction, because they did not open their minds to love of the truth and so find salvation. ¹¹That is why God puts them under a compelling delusion, which makes them believe what is false, ¹²so that all who have not believed the truth but made sinfulness their choice may be brought to judgement.

¹³WE are always bound to thank God for you, my friends beloved by the Lord. From the beginning of time God chose you to find salvation in the Spirit who consecrates you and in the truth you believe. ¹⁴It was for this that he called you through the gospel we brought, so that you might come to possess the splendour of our Lord Jesus Christ.

¹⁵Stand firm then, my friends, and hold fast to the traditions which you have learned from us by word or by letter. ¹⁶And may our Lord Jesus Christ himself and God our Father, who has shown us such love, and in his grace has given us such unfailing encouragement and so sure a hope, ¹⁷still encourage and strengthen you in every good deed and word.

Christian conduct

3 AND now, friends, pray for us, that the word of the Lord may have everywhere the swift and glorious success it has had among you, ²and that we may be rescued from wrong-headed and wicked people; for not all have faith. ³But the Lord keeps faith, and he will strengthen you and guard you

2:13 **From ... chose you:** *some witnesses read* God chose you as his firstfruits.

2.1–12: The delay of the Parousia. The portrayal of the events to precede the Parousia has points of contact with Mk. ch. 13 and parallels, and with some OT descriptions of the evils which will come before the arrival of God's kingdom. **2:** *Prophetic utterance* (lit. a spirit): the word of one who claims to be speaking under the influence of the Spirit; see 1 Thess. 5.19–21. *Purporting to come from us:* possibly a forged *letter. The day . . . is already here:* see Introduction and 2 Tim. 2.18 n. **3:** *The final rebellion against God* (lit. the apostasy): a falling away from the faith; see Matt. 24.10. Similarly, during the persecution by Antiochus IV Epiphanes (175–164 B.C.E.) many Jews abandoned the God of Israel; see 1 Macc. 2.15. The figure of Antiochus has influenced Paul's description of *the man doomed to destruction;* this "man" is an evil imitation of Jesus, and his coming is described in terms similar to that of Jesus; see v. 9 and 1.7. **4:** See the descriptions of Antiochus in Dan. 11.36–37 and of the prince of Tyre in Ezek. 28.2. The search for "the" historical person or institution fitting Paul's prediction has been fruitless. **6–7:** Some force, specified only as *the restraining hand* or *the restraining power* is holding back the revelation of the wicked person. **8:** *With the breath of his mouth* is a figure for the destroying word of judgment; see Isa. 11.4. **9–10:** The author's dismay at the *wicked one's* likeness to Jesus continues. On *signs and miracles* at the *coming,* see Mk. 13.22. **11–12:** The *delusion* under which the sinners fall is seen as God's punishment for their refusal to accept the truth.

2.13–3.5: Exhortation to steadfastness. 15: Although the Thessalonian letters were written early in Christian experience (see Introduction to 1 Thess.), the church already had a body of material which could be referred to as *traditions.*

from the evil one; [4] and in the Lord we have confidence about you, that you are doing and will continue to do what we tell you. [5] May the Lord direct your hearts towards God's love and the steadfastness of Christ.

[6] These are our instructions to you, friends, in the name of our Lord Jesus Christ: hold aloof from every Christian who falls into idle habits, and disregards the tradition you received from us. [7] You yourselves know how you ought to follow our example: you never saw us idling; [8] we did not accept free hospitality from anyone; night and day in toil and drudgery we worked for a living, rather than be a burden to any of you—[9] not because we do not have the right to maintenance, but to set an example for you to follow. [10] Already during our stay with you we laid down this rule: anyone who will not work shall not eat. [11] We mention this because we hear that some of you are idling their time away, minding everybody's business but their own. [12] We instruct and urge such people in the name of the Lord Jesus Christ to settle down to work and earn a living.

[13] My friends, you must never tire of doing right. [14] If anyone disobeys the instructions given in my letter, single him out, and have nothing to do with him until he is ashamed of himself. [15] I do not mean treat him as an enemy, but admonish him as one of the family.

[16] May the Lord of peace himself give you peace at all times and in all ways. The Lord be with you all.

[17] This greeting is in my own handwriting; all genuine letters of mine bear the same signature—Paul.

[18] The grace of our Lord Jesus Christ be with you all.

3.6–18: Treatment of the idlers. 6: Some in the community are refusing to work and becoming public charges, regarding themselves as released from ordinary obligations since this age is to endure only briefly. **17:** *My own handwriting:* see 1 Cor. 16.21–24 n.

THE FIRST LETTER OF PAUL TO
Timothy

The letters to Timothy and Titus, commonly called the "Pastoral Epistles" because they contain much material related to the pastoral oversight of churches, form a distinct grouping within the collection of Pauline correspondence. Closely similar to one another in content, diction, and theology, they differ enough from the other Pauline letters to raise a question about their true authorship. Lacking many of the typical Pauline theological motifs, such as justification by faith and redemption through the death of Christ on the cross, they use other terms in a way foreign to Paul. Faith, for example, does not define a relationship to Christ, but signifies a body of doctrine which must be kept free of perversion. Problems of church order also emerge, and are discussed in a detail absent from Paul's other letters. The travels presumed in the Pastoral Epistles cannot be fitted into the framework of Paul's journeys as detailed in Acts, but that is also true of some genuine letters (e.g. Rom. 15.19), and is not a telling argument for non-Pauline authorship. Most persuasive against Paul's authorship, however, are the language and style of these three letters. Bearing clear marks of typical Hellenistic diction, they do not contain stylistic traits displayed by the epistles to the Romans, Galatians, or Corinthians (traits such as the frequent use of rhetorical questions and complex sentence structure). Similar differences are to be noted in the vocabulary of Paul and the Pastorals. Containing a plea to believers to live quiet lives of moral and doctrinal purity, the Pastorals are probably best understood as compositions of a group who looked to Paul for leadership in religious matters, and who, after his death, sought to meet new problems in a way Paul, as they thought, would have met them.

Timothy, to whom the first of the Pastorals is addressed, was the child of a Jewish mother and a Gentile father (Acts 16.1), and a trusted friend of Paul; see 1 Cor. 16.10 n. He shared in the task of Christian proclamation (2 Cor. 1.19) and, on at least one occasion, was sent by Paul to clear up some problems within a Christian congregation (1 Cor. 4.17). This letter also contains the earliest evidence we have of the emergence of formal leadership within the church, concentrated in the offices of bishop and elder.

1 FROM Paul, apostle of Christ Jesus by command of God our Saviour and Christ Jesus our hope, 2 to Timothy his true-born son in the faith.

Grace, mercy, and peace to you from God the Father and Christ Jesus our Lord.

Paul's charge to Timothy

3 WHEN I was starting for Macedonia, I urged you to stay on at Ephesus. You were to instruct certain people to give up teaching erroneous doctrines 4 and devoting themselves to interminable myths and genealogies, which give rise to mere speculation, and do not further God's plan for us, which works through faith.

5 This instruction has love as its goal, the

1:4 **do not . . . faith:** *or* do not promote the faithful discharge of God's stewardship.

1.1–2: Salutation. 1: On *Timothy,* see the Introduction. *God our Saviour* is typical of the Pastorals (e.g. 1 Tim. 2.3; Ti. 1.3; 3.4), and reflects OT usage more than Paul's, for whom Christ is savior (Phil. 3.20).
1.3–20: The struggle for faith. 3: *Starting for Macedonia:* such a journey cannot be fitted into what we know of Paul's journeys from Acts. On *Ephesus,* see Acts 18.19 n.; 19.23–41. **4:** The presence of teachers of *erroneous doctrines* (v. 3) is a major concern of the author. The nature of the false teaching cannot be simply stated, but included: *myths and genealogies* (as here), asceticism (e.g. 4.2–3), and a dangerous mysticism

love which springs from a pure heart, a good conscience, and a genuine faith. [6] Through lack of these some people have gone astray into a wilderness of words. [7] They set out to be teachers of the law, although they do not understand either the words they use or the subjects about which they are so dogmatic.

[8] We all know that the law is an admirable thing, provided we treat it as law, [9] recognizing that it is designed not for good citizens, but for the lawless and unruly, the impious and sinful, the irreligious and worldly, for parricides and matricides, murderers [10] and fornicators, perverts, kidnappers, liars, perjurers—in fact all whose behaviour flouts the sound teaching [11] which conforms with the gospel entrusted to me, the gospel which tells of the glory of the ever-blessed God.

[12] I give thanks to Christ Jesus our Lord, who has made me equal to the task; I thank him for judging me worthy of trust and appointing me to his service—[13] although in the past I had met him with abuse and persecution and outrage. But because I acted in the ignorance of unbelief I was dealt with mercifully; [14] the grace of our Lord was lavished upon me, along with the faith and love which are ours in Christ Jesus.

[15] Here is a saying you may trust, one that merits full acceptance: 'Christ Jesus came into the world to save sinners'; and among them I stand first. [16] But I was mercifully dealt with for this very purpose, that Jesus Christ might find in me the first occasion for displaying his inexhaustible patience, and that I might be typical of all who were in future to have faith in him and gain eternal life. [17] To the King eternal, immortal, invisible, the only God, be honour and glory for ever and ever! Amen.

[18] In laying this charge upon you, Timothy my son, I am guided by those prophetic utterances which first directed me to you. Encouraged by them, fight the good fight [19] with faith and a clear conscience. It was through spurning conscience that certain persons made shipwreck of their faith, [20] among them Hymenaeus and Alexander, whom I consigned to Satan, in the hope that through this discipline they might learn not to be blasphemous.

Christian conduct

2 FIRST of all, then, I urge that petitions, prayers, intercessions, and thanksgivings be offered for everyone, [2] for sovereigns and for all in high office so that we may lead a tranquil and quiet life, free to practise our religion with dignity. [3] Such prayer is right, and approved by God our Saviour, [4] whose will it is that all should find salvation and come to know the truth. [5] For there is one God, and there is one mediator between God and man, Christ Jesus, himself man, [6] who sacrificed himself to win freedom for all mankind, revealing God's purpose at God's good time; [7] of this I was appointed herald and apostle (this is no lie, it is the truth), to instruct the Gentiles in the true faith.

[8] It is my desire, therefore, that everywhere prayers be said by the men of the congregation, who shall lift up their hands with a pure intention, without anger or argument. [9] Women must dress in becoming manner, modestly and soberly, not with elaborate

---

(2 Tim. 2.18). *Myths:* see 2 Tim. 4.4; Ti. 1.14. *Genealogies* may refer to Gnostic or Jewish speculations; the meaning is not sure. *God's plan:* see Eph. 1.10; 3.9. **5:** *Good conscience,* along with clear conscience, is a characteristic virtue in the Pastorals. **10:** Such lists of vices were common in the Hellenistic world; for other NT examples see 6.4–5; 2 Tim. 3.2–5; Ti. 3.3; Rom. 1.29–31; Gal. 5.19–21. *Sound teaching,* a characteristic phrase in the Pastorals, occurs nowhere else in the NT, but frequently in other contemporary authors. **13:** *I had met him:* Christ and his church are identified in similar language in Acts 9.4–5. *Persecution:* see Acts 26.11; 1 Cor. 15.9; Gal. 1.13. **15:** *A saying you may trust* is a formula that probably introduces traditional material. *I stand first:* see 1 Cor. 15.9. **17:** *Eternal,* lit. "of the ages": this language is typical of Hellenistic descriptions of god(s), as well as Jewish ascriptions of praise. **20:** *I consigned to Satan:* the meaning is unclear; see 1 Cor. 5.5; compare Job 2.6–8.

  2.1–15: Advice on prayer. 1: This is not an exhaustive list of kinds of prayer; see Phil. 4.6. **4:** *Come to know the truth:* see 2 Tim. 3.7 n. *All* (persons) points to the universality of the Christian community grounded in God's saving will; see vv. 1, 6; 4.10. **5:** *One God:* see Deut. 6.4–9, a passage repeated daily by pious Jews. *One mediator* intends to validate Jesus among the many mediators proclaimed in the Hellenistic world. **8:** *Everywhere* may refer to regular liturgical services. **9:** This verse (and v. 8) probably refers to dress and conduct in hair-styles, not adorned with gold or pearls or expensive clothes, [10]but with good deeds, as befits women who claim to be religious. [11]Their role is to learn, listening quietly and with due submission. [12]I do not permit women to teach or dictate to the men; they should keep quiet. [13]For Adam was created first, and Eve afterwards; [14]moreover it was not Adam who was deceived; it was the woman who, yielding to deception, fell into sin. [15]But salvation for the woman will be in the bearing of children, provided she continues in faith, love, and holiness, with modesty.

3 Here is a saying you may trust: 'To aspire to leadership is an honourable ambition.' [2]A bishop, therefore, must be above reproach, husband of one wife, sober, temperate, courteous, hospitable, and a good teacher; [3]he must not be given to drink or brawling, but be of a forbearing disposition, avoiding quarrels, and not avaricious. [4]He must be one who manages his own household well and controls his children without losing his dignity, [5]for if a man does not know how to manage his own family, how can he take charge of a congregation of God's people? [6]He should not be a recent convert; conceit might bring on him the devil's punishment. [7]He must moreover have a good reputation with the outside world, so that he may not be exposed to scandal and be caught in the devil's snare.

[8]Deacons, likewise, must be dignified, not indulging in double talk, given neither to excessive drinking nor to money-grubbing. [9]They must be men who combine a clear conscience with a firm hold on the mystery of the faith. [10]And they too must first undergo scrutiny, and only if they are of unimpeach-

able character may they serve as deacons. [11]Women in this office must likewise be dignified, not scandalmongers, but sober, and trustworthy in every way. [12]A deacon must be the husband of one wife, and good at managing his children and his own household. [13]For deacons with a good record of service are entitled to high standing and the right to be heard on matters of the Christian faith.

[14]I am hoping to come to you before long, but I write this [15]in case I am delayed, to let you know what is proper conduct in God's household, that is, the church of the living God, the pillar and bulwark of the truth. [16]And great beyond all question is the mystery of our religion:

He was manifested in flesh,
vindicated in spirit,
seen by angels;
he was proclaimed among the nations,
believed in throughout the world,
raised to heavenly glory.

False teaching

4 THE Spirit explicitly warns us that in time to come some will forsake the faith and surrender their minds to subversive spirits and demon-inspired doctrines, [2]through the plausible falsehoods of those whose consciences have been permanently branded.

3:1 **Here ... trust:** *some witnesses read* There is a popular saying. 3:11 **Women ... office:** *or* Their wives. 4:1 **in time to come:** *or* in the last times. 4:2 **branded:** *or* seared.

worship; compare 1 Pet. 3.3–5. **11–15:** These verses, dealing with liturgical services, reflect the position of women in some areas of the Hellenistic religious world; they are hardly to be taken as legislative. **13:** See 1 Cor. 11.3–16. **14:** See Gen. 3.6; also 2 Cor. 11.3. That for Paul himself *Adam* also sinned is clear from Rom. 5.12–14. **15:** The meaning of the first half of this verse is unclear.

3.1–16: Leadership in the church. 2: *Bishop* is not used in a technical sense; see Ti. 1.5–9, where bishop and elder are identified. The virtues are common ideals in the Hellenistic world. **8:** We cannot tell from the NT what different duties were given to bishops, elders, and *deacons*. Paul could describe his apostleship as a diaconate ("ministry" in 2 Cor. 4.1) and thus deacons may have had responsibility for preaching; see also v. 9; 4.6; Acts 6.4 ("ministry"); also Acts 6.2 ("to assist in the distribution"), 6 n. **9:** *Mystery* refers to the content of the Christian faith as revealing God's plan for humanity; see v. 16, where the content is Christ, as in Col. 1.27. **16:** This verse is probably an early Christian hymn, or confession of faith. The rhythm of the Greek points to three couplets, rather than two stanzas.

4.1–16: True service to Christ. 1: See 2 Tim. 3.1–9; 4.3–4; the point is made throughout the NT. **2:** In the

3 They will forbid marriage, and insist on abstinence from foods which God created to be enjoyed with thanksgiving by believers who have come to knowledge of the truth. 4 Everything that God has created is good, and nothing is to be rejected provided it is accepted with thanksgiving, 5 for it is then made holy by God's word and by prayer.

6 By offering such advice as this to the brotherhood you will prove to be a good servant of Christ Jesus, nurtured in the precepts of our faith and of the sound instruction which you have followed. 7 Have nothing to do with superstitious myths, mere old wives' tales. Keep yourself in training for the practice of religion; 8 for while the training of the body brings limited benefit, the benefits of religion are without limit, since it holds out promise not only for this life but also for the life to come. 9 Here is a saying you may trust, one that merits full acceptance. 10 'This is why we labour and struggle, because we have set our hope on the living God, who is the Saviour of all' — the Saviour, above all, of believers.

11 Insist on these things in your teaching. 12 Let no one underrate you because you are young, but be to believers an example in speech and behaviour, in love, fidelity, and purity. 13 Until I arrive devote yourself to the public reading of the scriptures, to exhortation, and to teaching. 14 Do not neglect the spiritual endowment given you when, under the guidance of prophecy, the elders laid their hands on you.

15 Make these matters your business, make them your absorbing interest, so that your progress may be plain to all. 16 Persevere in them, keeping close watch on yourself and on your teaching; by doing so you will save both yourself and your hearers.

Church discipline

5 NEVER be harsh with an older man; appeal to him as if he were your father. Treat the younger men as brothers, 2 the older women as mothers, and the younger as your sisters, in all purity.

3 Enrol as widows only those who are widows in the fullest sense. 4 If a widow has children or grandchildren, they should learn as their first duty to show loyalty to the family and so repay what they owe to their parents and grandparents; for that has God's approval. 5 But a widow in the full sense, one who is alone in the world, puts all her trust in God, and regularly, night and day, attends the meetings for prayer and worship. 6 A widow given to self-indulgence, however, is as good as dead. 7 Add these instructions to the rest, so that the widows may be above reproach. 8 And if anyone does not make provision for his relations, and especially for members of his own household, he has denied the faith and is worse than an unbeliever.

9 A widow under sixty years of age should not be put on the roll. An enrolled widow must have been the wife of one husband, 10 and must have gained a reputation for good deeds, by taking care of children, by showing hospitality, by washing the feet of God's people, by supporting those in distress

4:8–10 **for while ... Saviour of all':** *or* for 'While the training of the body brings limited benefit, the benefits of religion are without limit, since it holds out promise not only for this life but also for the life to come.' 9 That is a saying you may trust, one that merits full acceptance. 10 This is why we labour and struggle, because we have set our hope on the living God, who is the Saviour of all. 4:14 **prophecy ... on you:** *or* prophecy, you were ordained as an elder.

Hellenistic world, slaves were sometimes *branded* to indicate ownership. **3:** *Which God created to be enjoyed:* see Acts 10.15. Some contemporary sects thought that anything material was evil; only the spiritual was good. Jewish ritual purity may also be involved; compare Ti. 1.14. **4:** *Everything that God has created is good:* see Rom. 14.14; 1 Cor. 10.25–26. **6:** *Sound instruction:* see 1.10 n. **7:** *Superstitious myths:* see 1.4. **9:** *Here is a saying you may trust* may refer to v. 8. **10:** *Saviour of all:* see 2.4 n. **12:** *You are young* could, in that time, be applied to anyone under forty. **14:** *The elders* laying *their hands on* someone conferred a task; see e.g. Acts 6.6; 13.3.

5.1–16: General admonitions. 1–2: On personal relations. This kind of advice was popular in the Hellenistic world. **3–16:** On *widows*. **3:** There were no governmental provisions for the care of the destitute in the Hellenistic world, though care of widows was an obligation for Jews (Exod. 22.22; Deut. 24.17–22). The church early assumed this responsibility (Acts 6.1). **9:** This is our earliest evidence of an ecclesiastical order of *widows,*

—in short, by doing good at every opportunity.

¹¹ Do not admit younger widows to the roll; for if they let their passions distract them from Christ's service they will want to marry again, ¹² and so be guilty of breaking their earlier vow to him. ¹³ Besides, in going round from house to house they would learn to be idle, indeed worse than idle, gossips and busybodies, speaking of things better left unspoken. ¹⁴ For that reason it is my wish that young widows should marry again, have children, and manage a household; then they will give the enemy no occasion for scandal. ¹⁵ For there have in fact been some who have taken the wrong turning and gone over to Satan.

¹⁶ If a Christian woman has widows in her family, she must support them; the congregation must be relieved of the burden, so that it may be free to support those who are widows in the full sense.

¹⁷ Elders who give good service as leaders should be reckoned worthy of a double stipend, in particular those who work hard at preaching and teaching. ¹⁸ For scripture says, 'You shall not muzzle an ox while it is treading out the grain'; besides, 'The worker earns his pay.'

¹⁹ Do not entertain a charge against an elder unless it is supported by two or three witnesses. ²⁰ Those who do commit sins you must rebuke in public, to put fear into the others. ²¹ Before God and Christ Jesus and the angels who are his chosen, I solemnly charge you: maintain these rules, never prejudging the issue, but acting with strict impartiality. ²² Do not be over-hasty in the laying on of hands, or you may find yourself implicated in other people's misdeeds; keep yourself above reproach.

²³ Stop drinking only water; in view of your frequent ailments take a little wine to help your digestion.

²⁴ There are people whose offences are so obvious that they precede them into court, and others whose offences have not yet caught up with them. ²⁵ So too with good deeds; they may be obvious, but, even if they are not, they cannot be concealed for ever.

6 All who wear the yoke of slavery must consider their masters worthy of all respect, so that the name of God and the Christian teaching are not brought into disrepute. ² Slaves of Christian masters must not take liberties with them just because they are their brothers. Quite the contrary: they must do their work all the better because those who receive the benefit of their service are one with them in faith and love.

Final instructions

THIS is what you are to teach and preach. ³ Anyone who teaches otherwise, and does not devote himself to sound precepts—that is, those of our Lord Jesus Christ—and to good religious teaching, ⁴ is a pompous ignoramus with a morbid enthusiasm for mere speculations and quibbles. These give rise to jealousy, quarrelling, slander, base suspicions, ⁵ and endless wrangles—all typical of those whose minds are corrupted and who have lost their grip of the truth. They think religion should yield dividends; ⁶ and of course religion does yield high dividends, but only to those who are content with what they have. ⁷ We brought nothing into this world, and we can take nothing out; ⁸ if we have food and clothing let us rest content. ⁹ Those who want to be rich fall into temptations and snares and into many foolish and harmful desires which plunge people into ruin and destruction. ¹⁰ The love of money is the root of all evil, and in pursuit of it some have wandered from the faith and spiked themselves on many a painful thorn.

¹¹ But you, man of God, must shun all that, and pursue justice, piety, integrity, love, fortitude, and gentleness. ¹² Run the great race

---

an order well known by the third century; see Acts 9.39. **12:** *Breaking their earlier vow* may imply a promise by a widow not to remarry. **13:** *Going round from house to house* was apparently one of a widow's duties, perhaps as a Christian visitor.

5.17–6.21: Advice on proper conduct. 17: *Elders* shared *teaching* duties with bishops; see 3.2 (and n.); Ti. 1.5, 7 nn. **18:** Deut. 25.4; see 1 Cor. 9.9; Lk. 10.7. **19:** *Two or three witnesses:* see Deut. 19.15; Matt. 18.16; 2 Cor. 13.1. **23:** Timothy may have drunk *only water* as an ascetic practice; the validity of such a practice is here denied; compare 4.3. **6.1:** For mention of *slavery* in the NT, see Ti. 2.9–10; 1 Cor. 7.21–22; Eph. 6.5–8; Col. 3.22–25; Philem. 15–16; 1 Pet. 2.18–25. **3:** See 1.10 n. **5:** The following teachings reflect Hellenistic moral maxims and teachings. **7:** See Job 1.21; Eccles. 5.15. **8:** To *rest content* with little was a popular Stoic of faith and take hold of eternal life, for to this you were called, when you confessed your faith nobly before many witnesses. ¹³ Now in the presence of God, who gives life to all things, and of Jesus Christ, who himself made that noble confession in his testimony before Pontius Pilate, I charge you ¹⁴ to obey your orders without fault or failure until the appearance of our Lord Jesus Christ ¹⁵ which God will bring about in his own good time. He is the blessed and only Sovereign, King of kings and Lord of lords; ¹⁶ he alone possesses immortality, dwelling in unapproachable light; him no one has ever seen or can ever see; to him be honour and dominion for ever! Amen.

¹⁷ Instruct those who are rich in this world's goods not to be proud, and to fix their hopes not on so uncertain a thing as money, but on God, who richly provides all things for us to enjoy. ¹⁸ They are to do good and to be rich in well-doing, to be ready to give generously and to share with others, ¹⁹ and so acquire a treasure which will form a good foundation for the future. Then they will grasp the life that is life indeed.

²⁰ Timothy, keep safe what has been entrusted to you. Turn a deaf ear to empty and irreligious chatter, and the contradictions of 'knowledge' so-called, ²¹ for by laying claim to it some have strayed far from the faith.
Grace be with you all!

ideal. **10:** This proverb about *love of money* was widely known and popular in the Hellenistic world; but it is not to be construed that money in itself is *evil*; see vv. 17–19 n. **13:** See Jn. 18.36–37. **15–16:** This may be a fragment of an early Christian hymn. *King of kings and Lord of lords*: see Deut. 10.17. **17–19:** As in v. 10, it is not wealth, but attachment to it, that is condemned. Compare Matt. 6.19–21 (and 22 n.). **20:** *What has been entrusted to you* refers to sound Christian doctrine in its totality. *Contradictions* (lit. antitheses) were a favorite construction of Hellenistic philosophers, occasionally used to test another's skill in thinking.

THE SECOND LETTER OF PAUL TO
Timothy

Of the three Pastorals, this one is the closest to Pauline style and thought, and has the best claim to authenticity. It is sometimes suggested that the letter has incorporated fragments of genuine Pauline correspondence. However, attempts to isolate such fragments have not proved generally convincing. For more detailed information on this letter, see the Introduction to 1 Timothy.

1 FROM Paul, apostle of Christ Jesus by the will of God, whose promise of life is fulfilled in Christ Jesus, 2 to Timothy his dear son.

Grace, mercy, and peace to you from God the Father and Christ Jesus our Lord.

3 I give thanks to the God of my forefathers, whom I worship with a clear conscience, when I mention you in my prayers as I do constantly night and day; 4 when I remember the tears you shed, I long to see you again and so make my happiness complete. 5 I am reminded of the sincerity of your faith, a faith which was alive in Lois your grandmother and Eunice your mother before you, and which, I am confident, now lives in you.

The gospel of Jesus Christ

6 THAT is why I remind you to stir into flame the gift from God which is yours through the laying on of my hands. 7 For the spirit that God gave us is no cowardly spirit, but one to inspire power, love, and self-discipline. 8 So never be ashamed of your testimony to our Lord, nor of me imprisoned for his sake, but through the power that comes from God accept your share of suffering for the sake of the gospel. 9 It is he who has brought us salvation and called us to a dedicated life, not for any merit of ours but for his own purpose

and of his own grace, granted to us in Christ Jesus from all eternity, 10 and now at length disclosed by the appearance on earth of our Saviour Jesus Christ. He has broken the power of death and brought life and immortality to light through the gospel.

11 Of this gospel I have been appointed herald, apostle, and teacher. 12 That is the reason for my present plight; but I am not ashamed of it, because I know whom I have trusted, and am confident of his power to keep safe what he has put into my charge until the great day. 13 Hold to the outline of sound teaching which you heard from me, living by the faith and love which are ours in Christ Jesus. 14 Keep safe the treasure put into our charge, with the help of the Holy Spirit dwelling within us.

15 As you are aware, everyone in the province of Asia deserted me, including Phygelus and Hermogenes. 16 But may the Lord's mercy rest on the house of Onesiphorus! He has often relieved me in my troubles; he was not ashamed to visit a prisoner, 17 but when he came to Rome took pains to search me out until he found me. 18 The Lord grant that he find mercy from the Lord on the great day! You know as well as anyone the many services he rendered at Ephesus.

1:12 **what . . . charge:** or what I have put into his charge.   1:13 **Hold . . . teaching:** or Take as your model the sound teaching.

1.1−2: **Salutation.** On Timothy, see Introduction to 1 Tim. Compare 1 Tim. 1.1 n.

1.3−18: **Timothy's gifts and responsibilities. 3−5:** It was Hellenistic custom to include an opening prayer in a private letter, a custom followed in all Pauline and sub-Pauline letters except Gal., 1 Tim., and Ti. **5:** On Timothy's *mother,* see Acts 16.1. **6:** See 1 Tim. 4.14 (n.). **10:** *Saviour,* a title widely applied to deities and rulers in the Hellenistic world, is used both for Christ (Ti. 2.13; 3.6) and for God (see 1 Tim. 1.1 n.) in the Pastorals. **12:** *What he has put into my charge:* see 1 Tim. 6.20 n. **13:** *Sound* (or wholesome) *teaching:* see 1 Tim. 1.10 n. **15:** *Asia* was the Roman *province* of which Ephesus was the chief city. **18:** *The Lord* (i.e. Jesus) *grant . . .*; *from the Lord* (i.e. God); see Matt. 25.34−36.

Charge to Timothy

2 TAKE strength, my son, from the grace of God which is ours in Christ Jesus. ²You heard my teaching in the presence of many witnesses; hand on that teaching to reliable men who in turn will be qualified to teach others.

³Take your share of hardship, like a good soldier of Christ Jesus. ⁴A soldier on active service must not let himself be involved in the affairs of everyday life if he is to give satisfaction to his commanding officer. ⁵Again, no athlete wins a prize unless he abides by the rules. ⁶The farmer who does the work has first claim on the crop. ⁷Reflect on what I am saying, and the Lord will help you to full understanding.

⁸Remember the theme of my gospel: Jesus Christ, risen from the dead, born of David's line. ⁹For preaching this I am exposed to hardship, even to the point of being fettered like a criminal; but the word of God is not fettered. ¹⁰All this I endure for the sake of God's chosen ones, in the hope that they too may attain the glorious and eternal salvation which is in Christ Jesus.

¹¹Here is a saying you may trust:

If we died with him, we shall live with
    him;
¹²if we endure, we shall reign with him;
    if we disown him, he will disown us;
¹³if we are faithless, he remains faithful,
    for he cannot disown himself.

¹⁴Keep on reminding people of this, and charge them solemnly before God to stop disputing about mere words; it does no good, and only ruins those who listen. ¹⁵Try hard to show yourself worthy of God's approval, as a worker with no cause for shame; keep strictly to the true gospel, ¹⁶avoiding empty and irreligious chatter; those who indulge in it will stray farther and farther into godless

ways, ¹⁷and the infection of their teaching will spread like gangrene. Such are Hymenaeus and Philetus; ¹⁸in saying that our resurrection has already taken place they are wide of the truth and undermine people's faith. ¹⁹But God has laid a foundation-stone, and it stands firm, bearing this inscription: 'The Lord knows his own' and 'Everyone who takes the Lord's name upon his lips must forsake wickedness.' ²⁰Now in any great house there are not only utensils of gold and silver, but also others of wood or earthenware; the former are valued, the latter held cheap. ²¹Anyone who cleanses himself from all this wickedness will be a vessel valued and dedicated, a thing useful to the master of the house, and fit for any honourable purpose.

²²Turn from the wayward passions of youth, and pursue justice, integrity, love, and peace together with all who worship the Lord in singleness of mind; ²³have nothing to do with foolish and wild speculations. You know they breed quarrels, ²⁴and a servant of the Lord must not be quarrelsome; he must be kindly towards all. He should be a good teacher, tolerant, ²⁵and gentle when he must discipline those who oppose him. God may then grant them a change of heart and lead them to recognize the truth; ²⁶thus they may come to their senses and escape from the devil's snare in which they have been trapped and held at his will.

3 Remember, the final age of this world is to be a time of turmoil! ²People will love nothing but self and money; they will be boastful, arrogant, and abusive; disobedient to parents, devoid of gratitude, piety, ³and natural affection; they will be implacable in their hatreds, scandalmongers, uncontrolled and violent, hostile to all goodness, ⁴perfidious, foolhardy, swollen with self-importance. They will love their pleasures more than their God. ⁵While preserving the outward

2:26 **trapped ... will:** *or* trapped, and be made subject to God's will.

2.1–26: The way to wholehearted Christian service. 2: Apostolic tradition was transmitted in the manner described in this verse; see 1.14. **11–13:** These verses appear to be a fragment of an early Christian hymn. **11:** *A saying you may trust:* see 1 Tim. 1.15 n. *If we died with him:* see Rom. 6.8. **12:** *If we disown him:* see Matt. 10.33. **13:** *He remains faithful:* see Rom. 3.3–4. **18:** Some apparently thought that the *resurrection has already taken place* in some spiritual or mystical experience, perhaps at baptism; contrast 1 Cor. 15.50–55. **19:** The first quotation reflects Num. 16.5 Sept.; the second a variety of OT verses, e.g. Isa. 26.13; Ps. 6.8–9. **22:** *Passions of youth:* see 1 Tim. 4.12 n. **23:** See 1 Tim. 1.4; Ti. 3.9. **25:** The *truth:* see 3.7 n.

3.1–17: Admonitions to stand fast amid error and persecution. 1: Christians believed *the final age* had already begun; compare Acts 2.16–21. **2–4:** See 1 Tim. 1.10 n.

form of religion, they are a standing denial of its power. Keep clear of them. 6 They are the sort that insinuate themselves into private houses and there get silly women into their clutches, women burdened with sins and carried away by all kinds of desires, 7 always wanting to be taught but incapable of attaining to a knowledge of the truth. 8 As Jannes and Jambres opposed Moses, so these men oppose the truth; their warped minds disqualify them from grasping the faith. 9 Their successes will be short-lived; like those opponents of Moses, they will come to be recognized by everyone for the fools they are.

10 But you, my son, have observed closely my teaching and manner of life, my resolution, my faithfulness, patience, and spirit of love, and my fortitude 11 under persecution and suffering—all I went through at Antioch, at Iconium, at Lystra, and the persecutions I endured; and from all of them the Lord rescued me. 12 Persecution will indeed come to everyone who wants to live a godly life as a follower of Christ Jesus, 13 whereas evildoers and charlatans will progress from bad to worse, deceiving and deceived. 14 But for your part, stand by the truths you have learned and are assured of. Remember from whom you learned them; 15 remember that from early childhood you have been familiar with the sacred writings which have power to make you wise and lead you to salvation through faith in Christ Jesus. 16 All inspired scripture has its use for teaching the truth and refuting error, or for reformation of manners and discipline in right living, 17 so that the man of God may be capable and equipped for good work of every kind.

4 Before God, and before Christ Jesus who is to judge the living and the dead, I charge you solemnly by his coming appearance and his reign, 2 proclaim the message,

press it home in season and out of season, use argument, reproof, and appeal, with all the patience that teaching requires. 3 For the time will come when people will not stand sound teaching, but each will follow his own whim and gather a crowd of teachers to tickle his fancy. 4 They will stop their ears to the truth and turn to fables. 5 But you must keep your head whatever happens; put up with hardship, work to spread the gospel, discharge all the duties of your calling.

6 As for me, my life is already being poured out on the altar, and the hour for my departure is upon me. 7 I have run the great race, I have finished the course, I have kept the faith. 8 And now there awaits me the garland of righteousness which the Lord, the righteous Judge, will award to me on the great day, and not to me alone, but to all who have set their hearts on his coming appearance.

Final instructions

9 Do your best to join me soon. 10 Demas, his heart set on this present world, has deserted me and gone to Thessalonica; Crescens is away in Galatia, Titus in Dalmatia; apart from Luke 11 I have no one with me. Get hold of Mark and bring him with you; he is a great help to me. 12 Tychicus I have sent to Ephesus. 13 When you come, bring the cloak I left with Carpus at Troas, and the books, particularly my notebooks.

14 Alexander the coppersmith did me a great deal of harm. The Lord will deal with him as he deserves, 15 but you had better be on your guard against him, for he is bitterly opposed to everything we teach. 16 At the first hearing of my case no one came into court to support me; they all left me in the lurch; I

4:10 **Galatia:** *or* Gaul.

3.7: The *truth* here means the Christian gospel, as in 2.25; 1 Tim. 2.4; Ti. 1.1. **8:** *Jannes and Jambres* are the names ancient Jewish tradition gave to the Egyptian magicians of Pharaoh's court who opposed Moses; see Exod. 7.11; 9.11. **10:** On Paul as a model for faith, see also Acts 20.18–21. **11:** *All I went through:* see 2 Cor. 11.23–27. *At Antioch:* see Acts 13.50–51. *At Iconium:* see Acts 14.2–7. *At Lystra:* see Acts 14.19–20. **13:** The Gk. word translated *charlatans* can also mean magicians; see v. 8 n. **15:** *Sacred writings:* see v. 16 n. **16:** *Scripture* refers to the OT; the NT had not yet been assembled.

4.1–5: Charge to Timothy. 1: *Jesus who is to judge:* see Acts 10.42. **3:** *Sound teaching:* see 1 Tim. 1.10 n. **4:** *Fables* (or "myths"); see 1 Tim. 1.4; 4.7; Ti. 1.14. **5:** *Work to spread the Gospel* (or, Do the work of an evangelist); see Acts 21.8; Eph. 4.11, where such an office is mentioned.

4.6–22: Concluding personal remarks. 7: Compare Phil. 2.16–17. **8:** *The garland* was the prize given the winner of a race or other Greek athletic contest. **10:** On *Titus,* see the Introduction to Ti. **13:** On *Troas,* see

pray that it may not be counted against them.
[17] But the Lord stood by me and lent me
strength, so that I might be his instrument in
making the full proclamation of the gospel
for the whole pagan world to hear; and thus
I was rescued from the lion's jaws. [18] The
Lord will rescue me from every attempt to do
me harm, and bring me safely into his heavenly kingdom. Glory to him for ever and
ever! Amen.

[19] Greetings to Prisca and Aquila, and the
household of Onesiphorus.

[20] Erastus stayed behind at Corinth, and
Trophimus I left ill at Miletus. [21] Do try to get
here before winter.

Greetings from Eubulus, Pudens, Linus,
and Claudia, and from all the brotherhood
here.

[22] The Lord be with your spirit. Grace be
with you all!

Acts 16.8; 20.6; 2 Cor. 2.12. **14:** *Deal with him* (i.e. pay him): see Ps. 28.4; Rom. 2.6. **17:** *Rescued from the lion's jaws* may be used figuratively here, as it is in Ps. 22.21. **19:** *Prisca and Aquila:* see Acts 18.2 n. **21:** During the *winter,* travel by sea was hazardous; see Acts 27.9 (and n.)–44; 28.11 n.

THE LETTER OF PAUL TO
Titus

Titus, like Timothy, was a trusted friend and companion of Paul. Born of Gentile parents (Gal. 2.3), he accompanied Paul to the Apostolic Council in Jerusalem (Gal. 2.1; see also Acts 15), and played a significant role in collecting money from the Corinthians (2 Cor. 8.6, 16–23) for the poor in Jerusalem (see Gal. 2.10). This document is the earliest evidence we have for the presence of the Christian faith on the island of Crete. For more information on this letter, see the Introduction to 1 Timothy.

1 FROM Paul, servant of God and apostle of Jesus Christ, marked as such by the faith of God's chosen people and the knowledge of the truth enshrined in our religion [2] with its hope of eternal life, which God, who does not lie, promised long ages ago, [3] and now in his own good time has openly declared in the proclamation entrusted to me by command of God our Saviour.

[4] To Titus, my true-born son in the faith which we share. Grace and peace to you from God the Father and Jesus Christ our Saviour.

Christian discipline

[5] MY intention in leaving you behind in Crete was that you should deal with any outstanding matters, and in particular should appoint elders in each town in accordance with the principles I have laid down: [6] Are they men of unimpeachable character? Is each the husband of one wife? Are their children believers, not open to any charge of dissipation or indiscipline? [7] For as God's steward a bishop must be a man of unimpeachable character. He must not be overbearing or short-tempered or given to drink; no brawler, no money-grubber, [8] but hospitable, right-minded, temperate, just, devout, and self-controlled. [9] He must keep firm hold of the true doctrine, so that he may be well able both to appeal to his hearers with sound teaching and to refute those who raise objections.

[10] There are many, especially among Jewish converts, who are undisciplined, who talk wildly and lead others astray. [11] Such men must be muzzled, because they are ruining whole families by teaching what they should not, and all for sordid gain. [12] It was a Cretan prophet, one of their own countrymen, who said, 'Cretans were ever liars, vicious brutes, lazy gluttons' — [13] and how truly he spoke! All the more reason why you should rebuke them sharply, so that they may be restored to a sound faith, [14] instead of paying heed to Jewish myths and to human commandments, the work of those who turn their backs on the truth.

1:1 **apostle . . . knowledge:** *or* apostle of Jesus Christ, to bring God's chosen people to faith and to knowledge.

1.1–4: Salutation. 1: *Knowledge of the truth:* see 2 Tim. 3.7 n. **3:** *His own good time* (or, at the appropriate time): the early Christians saw in the history of Israel and the coming of Jesus the unfolding of God's plan for the salvation of humanity. In accordance with this plan, Jesus was sent at the time God found appropriate; see Rom. 5.6; Gal. 4.4; Eph. 1.10. **4:** On *Titus,* see Introduction to 1 Tim.

1.5–16: The need for Christian discipline. 5: *Elders:* in 1 Tim. 3.1–7, a similar list describes the qualifications of a bishop; see 1 Tim. 3.2 n. **7:** *Bishop* seems identical here to "elder" in v. 5. **9:** *Sound teaching:* see 1 Tim. 1.10 n. **10–11:** The problems here are similar to those discussed in 1 Tim. 1.3–4; 6.4–5; 2 Tim. 2.14, 16; 3.6–7. **12:** *Cretan prophet:* probably Epimenides (sixth century B.C.E.). **14:** *Jewish myths and human commandments:* see 1 Tim. 4.3 n. **15:** *To the pure:* probably meant here in the sense that a person's inner quality determines whether what that person perceives and expresses will be good or evil; see Matt. 7.16–18. Compare Rom. 14.14, where it refers to dietary practices.

15 To the pure all things are pure; but nothing is pure to tainted disbelievers, tainted both in reason and in conscience. 16 They profess to know God but by their actions deny him; they are detestable and disobedient, disqualified for any good work.

2 For your part, what you say must be in keeping with sound doctrine. 2 The older men should be sober, dignified, and temperate, sound in faith, love, and fortitude. 3 The older women, similarly, should be reverent in their demeanour, not scandalmongers or slaves to excessive drinking; they must set a high standard, 4 and so teach the younger women to be loving wives and mothers, 5 to be temperate, chaste, busy at home, and kind, respecting the authority of their husbands. Then the gospel will not be brought into disrepute.

6 Urge the younger men, similarly, to be temperate 7 in all things, and set them an example of good conduct yourself. In your teaching you must show integrity and seriousness, 8 and offer sound instruction to which none can take exception. Any opponent will be at a loss when he finds nothing to say to our discredit.

9 Slaves are to respect their masters' authority in everything and to give them satisfaction; they are not to answer back, 10 nor to pilfer, but are to show themselves absolutely trustworthy. In all this they will add lustre to the doctrine of God our Saviour.

11 For the grace of God has dawned upon the world with healing for all mankind; 12 and by it we are disciplined to renounce godless ways and worldly desires, and to live a life of temperance, honesty, and godliness in the present age, 13 looking forward to the happy fulfilment of our hope when the splendour of our great God and Saviour Christ Jesus will appear. 14 He it is who sacrificed himself for us, to set us free from all wickedness and to make us his own people, pure and eager to do good.

15 These are your themes; urge them and argue them with an authority which no one can disregard.

3 Remind everyone to be submissive to the government and the authorities, and to obey them; to be ready for any honourable work; 2 to slander no one, to avoid quarrels, and always to show forbearance and a gentle disposition to all.

3 There was a time when we too were lost in folly and disobedience and were slaves to passions and pleasures of every kind. Our days were passed in malice and envy; hateful ourselves, we loathed one another. 4 'But when the kindness and generosity of God our Saviour dawned upon the world, 5 then, not for any good deeds of our own, but because he was merciful, he saved us through the water of rebirth and the renewing power of the Holy Spirit, 6 which he lavished upon us through Jesus Christ our Saviour, 7 so that, justified by his grace, we might in hope become heirs to eternal life.' 8 That is a saying you may trust.

Final instructions

SUCH are the points I want you to insist on, so that those who have come to believe in God may be sure to devote themselves to good works. These precepts are good in themselves and also useful to society. 9 But avoid foolish speculations, genealogies, quarrels, and controversies over the law; they are unprofitable and futile.

2:13 **of our great . . . Saviour:** or of the great God and our Saviour.   3:5 **water . . . power of:** or water of rebirth and of renewal by.   3:8 **devote . . . good in themselves:** or engage in honest employment. This is good in itself.

2.1–3.2: All Christians must lead disciplined lives. 1: *Sound doctrine:* see 1 Tim. 1.10 n. **5:** *Respecting the authority of their husbands:* see 1 Tim. 2.11–14. **9:** *Slaves:* see 1 Tim. 6.1 n. **10:** *God our Saviour:* see 1 Tim. 1.1 n. **11–12:** *For all:* see 1 Tim. 2.4 n. These ideals also characterized the doctrine of much Hellenistic philosophy, although it did not speak of doing them by God's grace. **13:** *God* and *Saviour* were titles regularly applied in the Hellenistic world to gods and emperors. **14:** *His own people, pure:* see Exod. 19.5; Deut. 7.6; 14.2. **3.1:** See Rom. 13.1–7; 1 Tim. 2.2. Cretans had a reputation as a turbulent people.

3.3–8a: God is generous in mercy. 4: *God our Saviour:* see 1 Tim. 1.1 n. Hellenistic rulers frequently claimed *generosity* as a characteristic of their acts. **5:** *Water of rebirth* means baptism; see Eph. 5.26; 1 Pet. 1.3. **8:** *Saying . . . trust:* see 1 Tim. 1.15 n. The phrase refers here to vv. 4–7.

3.8b–15: Concluding exhortations. 8b–11: These verses serve as a summary of the author's counsel; we do not possess sufficient information to specify exactly what is meant by the references to *foolish speculations,*

10 If someone is contentious, he should be allowed a second warning; after that, have nothing more to do with him, 11 recognizing that anyone like that has a distorted mind and stands self-condemned in his sin.

12 Once I have sent Artemas or Tychicus to you, join me at Nicopolis as soon as you can, for that is where I have decided to spend the winter. 13 Do your utmost to help Zenas the lawyer and Apollos on their travels, and see that they are not short of anything. 14 And our own people must be taught to devote themselves to good works to meet urgent needs; they must not be unproductive.

15 All who are with me send you greetings. My greetings to our friends in the faith. Grace be with you all!

3:14 **devote . . . needs:** *or* engage in honest employment to produce the necessities of life.

genealogies, quarrels, and controversies over the law (see 1 Tim. 1.4 n.). **10:** See Matt. 18.15–17; 2 Thess. 3.14–15. The word translated *contentious* later means "heretical"; it appears only here in the NT; it is probably not meant in the formal sense it later acquired, but simply designates one whose views the author finds unacceptable. **12:** It is uncertain to which of several cities named *Nicopolis* this refers. **13:** *Apollos:* see Acts 18.24–19.1; he is also mentioned frequently in 1 Cor. chs. 1–4.

THE LETTER OF PAUL TO
Philemon

This most personal of all the Pauline letters—his plea for a runaway slave—was written during an imprisonment of the apostle, probably his house arrest at Rome (61–63 C.E.). Philemon was a leading member of his community, at whose house the Christians met for worship. That he was a resident of Colossae is indicated by Col. 4.7–9. It tells that Paul's companion Tychicus would carry his letter to the Colossians, and "with him comes Onesimus," the slave mentioned in Philem. 11–16.

Onesimus has run away; the penalty for this on recapture was severe. Paul is sending him back and appeals to Philemon to receive Onesimus without punishment. He does not speak against the institution of slavery, but reminds Philemon that since Onesimus has become a Christian their relations have changed—they are now brothers in Christ.

FROM Paul, a prisoner of Christ Jesus, and our colleague Timothy, to Philemon our dear friend and fellow-worker, 2 together with Apphia our sister, and Archippus our comrade-in-arms, and the church that meets at your house.

3 Grace to you and peace from God our Father and the Lord Jesus Christ.

4 I thank my God always when I mention you in my prayers, 5 for I hear of your love and faith towards the Lord Jesus and for all God's people. 6 My prayer is that the faith you hold in common with us may deepen your understanding of all the blessings which belong to us as we are brought closer to Christ. 7 Your love has brought me much joy and encouragement; through you God's people have been much refreshed.

A runaway slave

8 ACCORDINGLY, although in Christ I might feel free to dictate where your duty lies, 9 yet, because of that same love, I would rather appeal to you. Ambassador as I am of Christ Jesus, and now his prisoner, 10 I, Paul, appeal to you about my child, whose father I have become in this prison. I mean Onesimus, 11 once so useless to you, but now useful indeed, both to you and to me. 12 In sending him back to you I am sending my heart. 13 I should have liked to keep him with me, to look after me on your behalf, here in prison for the gospel, 14 but I did not want to do anything without your consent, so that your kindness might be a matter not of compulsion, but of your own free will. 15 Perhaps this is why you lost him for a time to receive him back for good — 16 no longer as a slave, but as more than a slave: as a dear brother, very dear to me, and still dearer to you, both as a man and as a Christian.

17 If, then, you think of me as your partner in the faith, welcome him as you would welcome me. 18 If he did you any wrong and owes you anything, put it down to my account. 19 Here is my signature: Paul. I will

1–3: **Salutation.** The form is usual in ancient letters. **2:** *Church . . . at your house:* as yet no church edifices existed.

4–7: **Prayer of thanksgiving.** Such prayers are usual in Paul's letters; see Rom. 1.8–15, where he begins with "thanking my God."

8–21: **The plea for Onesimus. 10:** *Child . . . father:* see 1 Cor. 4.15. **11:** *Useless . . . useful indeed:* the name Onesimus means "the useful one"; the verse puns on the name. **13–14:** Perhaps Paul is here hinting that Philemon should send the slave back to continue his service to the apostle. **15–16:** Paul acknowledges Philemon's right to have Onesimus *back for good,* although the apostle's own hope is expressed in v. 14. In any case, Philemon will henceforth know Onesimus as a *brother,* rather than merely a *slave.* **19:** The repay you—not to mention that you owe me your very self. ²⁰Yes, brother, I am asking this favour of you as a fellow-Christian; set my mind at rest.

²¹I write to you confident that you will meet my wishes; I know that you will in fact do more than I ask. ²²And one last thing: have a room ready for me, for I hope

through the prayers of you all to be restored to you.

²³Epaphras, a captive of Christ Jesus like myself, sends you greetings. ²⁴So do my fellow-workers Mark, Aristarchus, Demas, and Luke.

²⁵The grace of the Lord Jesus Christ be with your spirit!

signature is this verse and perhaps the following ones: see 1 Cor. 16.21–24 n. *Owe me:* an allusion to Paul's conversion of Philemon. **23–24:** These companions of Paul are mentioned also in Col. 4.10, 11, 14.

A LETTER TO

Hebrews

While the final paragraphs (see 13.18–25 n.) imply that Hebrews is a letter, in style and content it is a sermonic tract, an "exhortation" (13.22). The readers have endured great suffering because of their faith (10.32–34) and are now admonished to continue firm in their hope of salvation (e.g. 7.19), although apathy or even apostasy may seem the easier way. For backsliders into sin there is no second chance for salvation (6.4–8; 10.26–31).

The basis and content of hope is God's gift of the Son (ch. 1), and the first chs. (1.1–10.18) expound the significance of Christ's faithfulness (e.g. 2.18; 5.8–10) and death. The thesis is that Christ is the great high priest (8.1–2), the mediator of a new covenant (e.g. 8.6–13) who offers the one truly effective sacrifice (e.g. 9.11–14, 25–28). The last chs. (10.19–13.17) urge Christians to follow in "the new and living way" provided by Christ (10.20), as God's pilgrim people, "seekers after the city which is to come" (13.14).

There have been many attempts to name the person who wrote this tract (some early Christians even assigned it to Paul), but the author remains anonymous. In spite of the traditional title the addressees were probably Gentile Christians. Earliest evidence of its use comes from Rome at the end of the first century, one possible clue as to its date and origin.

Jesus, divine and human

1 WHEN in times past God spoke to our forefathers, he spoke in many and varied ways through the prophets. ² But in this the final age he has spoken to us in his Son, whom he has appointed heir of all things; and through him he created the universe. ³ He is the radiance of God's glory, the stamp of God's very being, and he sustains the universe by his word of power. When he had brought about purification from sins, he took his seat at the right hand of God's Majesty on high, ⁴ raised as far above the angels as the title he has inherited is superior to theirs.

⁵ To which of the angels did God ever say, 'You are my son; today I have become your father,' or again, 'I shall be his father, and he will be my son'? ⁶ Again, when he presents the firstborn to the world, he says, 'Let all God's angels pay him homage.' ⁷ Of the angels he says:

> He makes his angels winds,
> and his ministers flames of fire;

⁸ but of the Son:

> Your throne, O God, is for ever and
> ever,
> and the sceptre of his kingdom is the
> sceptre of justice.
> ⁹ You have loved right and hated wrong;
> therefore, O God, your God has set you
> above your fellows
> by anointing you with oil, the token of
> joy.

1:6 **Again ... presents:** or And when he again presents.   1:9 **therefore ... your God:** or therefore God who is your God.

1.1–3.6a: The supremacy of Christ and the significance of his suffering.

1.1–14: Christ's supremacy over the angels. 2–3a: See Jn. 1.1–3; Wisd. 7.25. **3:** The idea of Christ's exaltation to a position of supreme authority (*right hand*) in the heavenly "court" is derived from Ps. 110.1 which is quoted in v. 13; 5.6; 7.21 where it is applied to Christ. **4:** Jesus' *title* is "Son"; see vv. 2–3, 5. **5:** Ps. 2.7 (see Matt. 3.17); 2 Sam. 7.14. **6:** Deut. 32.43 Sept. (see Ps. 97.7). **7:** Ps. 104.4. **8–9:** Ps. 45.6–7.

10 And again:

> By you, Lord, were earth's foundations
>   laid of old,
> and the heavens are the work of your
>   hands.
> 11 They will perish, but you remain;
>   like clothes they will all wear out.
> 12 You will fold them up like a cloak,
>   they will be changed like any garment.
> But you are the same, and your years
>   will have no end.

13 To which of the angels has he ever said, 'Sit at my right hand until I make your enemies your footstool'? 14 Are they not all ministering spirits sent out in God's service, for the sake of those destined to receive salvation?

2 That is why we are bound to pay all the more heed to what we have been told, for fear of drifting from our course. 2 For if God's word spoken through angels had such force that any violation of it, or any disobedience, met with its proper penalty, 3 what escape can there be for us if we ignore so great a deliverance? This deliverance was first announced through the Lord, and those who heard him confirmed it to us, 4 God himself adding his testimony by signs and wonders, by miracles of many kinds, and by gifts of the Holy Spirit distributed at his own will.

5 For it is not to angels that he has subjected the world to come, which is our theme. 6 There is somewhere this solemn assurance:

> What is man, that you should
>   remember him,
> a man, that you should care for him?
> 7 You made him for a short while
>   subordinate to the angels;
> with glory and honour you crowned
>   him;
> 8 you put everything in subjection
>   beneath his feet.

For in subjecting everything to him, God left

nothing that is not made subject. But in fact we do not yet see everything in subjection to man. 9 What we do see is Jesus, who for a short while was made subordinate to the angels, crowned now with glory and honour because he suffered death, so that, by God's gracious will, he should experience death for all mankind.

10 In bringing many sons to glory it was fitting that God, for whom and through whom all things exist, should make the pioneer of their salvation perfect through sufferings; 11 for he who consecrates and those who are consecrated are all of one stock. That is why he does not shrink from calling men his brothers, 12 when he says, 'I will make your fame known to my brothers; in the midst of the assembly I will praise you'; 13 and again, 'I will keep my trust fixed on him'; and again, 'Here am I, and the children whom God has given me.' 14 Since the children share in flesh and blood, he too shared in them, so that by dying he might break the power of him who had death at his command, that is, the devil, 15 and might liberate those who all their life had been in servitude through fear of death. 16 Clearly they are not angels whom he helps, but the descendants of Abraham. 17 Therefore he had to be made like his brothers in every way, so that he might be merciful and faithful as their high priest before God, to make expiation for the sins of the people. 18 Because he himself has passed through the test of suffering, he is able to help those who are in the midst of their test.

Jesus, the faithful high priest

3 THEREFORE, brothers in the family of God, partners in a heavenly calling, think of Jesus, the apostle and high priest of the faith we profess: 2 he was faithful to God who appointed him, as Moses also was faithful in God's household; 3 but Jesus has been

2:9 **so that ... will:** *some witnesses read* so that, apart from God.

1.10–12: Ps. 102.25–27. **13:** Ps. 110.1.

2.1–18: **The significance of Christ's suffering. 2:** See e.g. Acts 7.53. **3–4:** There is a triple witness to salvation: Christ, the apostles, and God, whose power is manifest in many wondrous deeds and in diverse spiritual gifts. **6–8:** Ps. 8.4–6 Sept. **10:** See 5.8–10. **11:** Christ, the priest *who consecrates,* and *those who are consecrated* are all children of God. **12:** Ps. 22.22. **13:** Isa. 8.17–18. **17:** See 4.14–5.10. **18:** Christ's sacrifice is effective for salvation because he, through the trials of temptation and persecution, is able to identify fully with human suffering. See 4.15.

3.1–6a: **Christ's supremacy over Moses. 1:** Christ is God's *apostle* to humanity, and as *high priest* he is the counted worthy of greater honour than Moses, as the founder of a house enjoys more honour than his household. 4 Every house has its founder; and the founder of all is God. 5 Moses indeed was faithful as a servant in God's whole household; his task was to bear witness to the words that God would speak; 6 but Christ is faithful as a son, set over the household. And we are that household, if only we are fearless and keep our hope high.

7 'TODAY', therefore, as the Holy Spirit says —

Today if you hear his voice,
8 do not grow stubborn as in the
    rebellion,
at the time of testing in the desert,
9 where your forefathers tried me and
    tested me,
though for forty years they saw the
    things I did.
10 Therefore I was incensed with that
    generation
and said, Their hearts are for ever
    astray;
they would not discern my ways;
11 so I vowed in my anger,
    they shall never enter my rest.

12 See to it, my friends, that no one among you has the wicked and faithless heart of a deserter from the living God. 13 Rather, day by day, as long as that word 'today' sounds in your ears, encourage one another, so that no one of you is made stubborn by the wiles of sin. 14 For we have become partners with Christ, if only we keep our initial confidence firm to the end. 15 When scripture says, 'Today if you hear his voice, do not grow stubborn as in the rebellion,' 16 who was it that heard and yet rebelled? All those, surely,

whom Moses had led out of Egypt. 17 And with whom was God indignant for forty years? With those, surely, who had sinned, whose bodies lay where they fell in the desert. 18 And to whom did he vow that they should not enter his rest, if not to those who had refused to believe? 19 We see, then, it was unbelief that prevented their entering.

4 What we must fear, therefore, is that, while the promise of entering his rest remains open, any one of you should be found to have missed his opportunity. 2 For indeed we have had the good news preached to us, just as they had. But the message they heard did them no good, for it was not combined with faith in those who heard it. 3 Because we have faith, it is we who enter that rest of which he has said: 'As I vowed in my anger, they shall never enter my rest.' Yet God's work had been finished ever since the world was created. 4 Scripture somewhere says of the seventh day: 'God rested from all his work on the seventh day' — 5 and in the passage above we read: 'They shall never enter my rest.' 6 This implies that some are to enter it, and since those who first heard the good news failed to enter through unbelief, 7 once more God sets a day. 'Today', he says, speaking so many years later in the words already quoted from the Psalms: 'Today if you hear his voice, do not grow stubborn.' 8 If Joshua had given them rest, God would not have spoken afterwards of another day. 9 Therefore, a sabbath rest still awaits the people of God; 10 anyone who enters God's rest, rests from his own work, as God did from his. 11 Let us, then, make every effort to enter that rest, so that no one may fall by following the old example of unbelief.

12 The word of God is alive and active. It cuts more keenly than any two-edged sword,

mediator between God and human beings. **2–6:** The author supports Christ's supremacy by arguing that, while Moses was a servant in *God's . . . household* (Num. 12.7), Jesus is the master's *son.*

3.6b–4.13: The danger of unbelief. Characteristically, this author turns from theological exposition (1.1–3.6a) to ethical exhortation, beginning with a lengthy exposition of Scripture (3.7–11) which is applied to the readers' present needs. **6b:** God's people must keep their *hope high* lest they fall into unbelief (see vv. 14, 18–19; 4.11). **7–11:** Ps. 95.7–11. **12–13:** Israel's misadventures in the wilderness should serve as warning to Christians who may be faced with the temptation to apathy or apostasy. **14:** Christians are *partners with Christ* if they remain loyal children in God's household; see v. 1; 2.11–17. **15:** See vv. 7–8. **17:** Num. 14.29. **18:** The *rest* which awaited those who were obedient (v. 11; Num. 14.22–23) was the promised land of Canaan. **4.1–2:** God's *rest* (3.18) is interpreted as the final promised salvation which Christians, like Israel, can attain only by faithfulness. **3:** Ps. 95.11. **4:** Gen. 2.2. **5:** See v. 3. **6:** Israel disobeyed, but the promise was renewed. **7:** Ps. 95.7–8 (see 3.7–11). **8:** Joshua's settlement of Canaan (Deut. 31.7; Josh. ch. 22) did not fulfil the promise, for it had to be issued again "through . . . David" (v. 7); see Ps. 95.7–8. **12–13:** The *word of God* piercing so deeply that it divides soul and spirit, joints and marrow; it discriminates among the purposes and thoughts of the heart. [13] Nothing in creation can hide from him; everything lies bare and exposed to the eyes of him to whom we must render account.

[14] Since therefore we have a great high priest who has passed through the heavens, Jesus the Son of God, let us hold fast to the faith we profess. [15] Ours is not a high priest unable to sympathize with our weaknesses, but one who has been tested in every way as we are, only without sinning. [16] Let us therefore boldly approach the throne of grace, in order that we may receive mercy and find grace to give us timely help.

5 For every high priest is taken from among men and appointed their representative before God, to offer gifts and sacrifices for sins. [2] He is able to bear patiently with the ignorant and erring, since he too is beset by weakness; [3] and because of this he is bound to make sin-offerings for himself as well as for the people. [4] Moreover nobody assumes the office on his own authority: he is called by God, just as Aaron was. [5] So it is with Christ: he did not confer on himself the glory of becoming high priest; it was granted by God, who said to him, 'You are my son; today I have become your father'; [6] as also in another place he says, 'You are a priest for ever, in the order of Melchizedek.' [7] In the course of his earthly life he offered up prayers and petitions, with loud cries and tears, to God who was able to deliver him from death. Because of his devotion his

prayer was heard: [8] son though he was, he learned obedience through his sufferings, [9] and, once perfected, he became the source of eternal salvation for all who obey him, [10] and by God he was designated high priest in the order of Melchizedek.

Jesus and Melchizedek

[11] About Melchizedek we have much to say, much that is difficult to explain to you, now that you have proved so slow to learn. [12] By this time you ought to be teachers, but instead you need someone to teach you the ABC of God's oracles over again. It comes to this: you need milk instead of solid food. [13] Anyone who lives on milk is still an infant, with no experience of what is right. [14] Solid food is for adults, whose perceptions have been trained by long use to discriminate between good and evil.

6 [1-2] Let us stop discussing the rudiments of Christianity. We ought not to be laying the foundation all over again: repentance from the deadness of our former ways and faith in God, by means of instruction about cleansing rites and the laying on of hands, the resurrection of the dead and eternal judgement. Instead, let us advance towards maturity; [3] and so we shall, if God permits. [4] For when people have once been enlightened, when they have tasted the heavenly gift and have shared in the Holy Spirit, [5] when they have experienced the goodness of God's word and the spiritual power of the age to come, [6] and then after all this have fallen away, it is impossible to bring them afresh to

probes and judges all *creation*.

4.14–5.10: Christ, the great high priest. This is the author's most important way of interpreting the meaning of Christ's redemptive work. The development of the idea is interrupted temporarily by exhortations (5.11–6.12; see 3.6b–4.13 n.), but then resumed at 6.13. **14–16:** God's *mercy* and *grace* are sure because Christ himself withstood the trials of *our weaknesses . . . without sinning,* and thereby serves as the effective mediator between human beings and God. See 2.17–18. **5.1–4:** See Exod. 28.1; Lev. 9.7; 16.6. **5:** See 1.5 n. **6:** Ps. 110.4. See 7.1–10 n. **7–8:** See the stories of Jesus' passion, e.g. Matt. 26.36–46. **9–10:** See 9.24–28.

5.11–6.12: Warning against backsliding. 11–14: The explanation of Melchizedek's priesthood is deferred (see ch. 7). First, the readers need to be nurtured by the *milk* of some basic instruction about discerning *good* and *evil*. **6.1–3:** Certain *rudiments of Christianity,* like *faith, repentance, resurrection* and *judgement,* ought to be self-evident. (It is not clear what *cleansing rites and the laying on of hands* refer to.) Once the basic Christian doctrines have been understood, it is essential that one *advance towards maturity,* i.e. give oneself over to that perfect consecration to God's service which Christ's sacrifice has made possible (10.12–14). **4–8:** For sins committed after baptism no amount of repentance will suffice; backsliders have no second chance (see 10.26–31; 2 Pet. 2.20–22). They remain under a curse like Adam (vv. 7–8; see Gen. 1.11–12; 3.17–18).

repentance; for they are crucifying to their own hurt the Son of God and holding him up to mockery. [7] When the soil drinks in the rain that falls often upon it, and yields a crop for the use of those who cultivate it, it receives its blessing from God; [8] but if it bears thorns and thistles, it is worthless and a curse hangs over it; it ends by being burnt.

[9] Yet although we speak as we do, we are convinced that you, dear friends, are in a better state, which makes for your salvation. [10] For God is not so unjust as to forget what you have done for love of his name in rendering service to his people, as you still do. [11] But we should dearly like each one of you to show the same keenness to the end, until your hope is fully realized. [12] We want you not to be lax, but to imitate those who, through faith and patience, receive the promised inheritance.

[13] When God made his promise to Abraham, because he had no one greater to swear by he swore by himself: [14] 'I vow that I will bless you abundantly and multiply your descendants.' [15] Thus it was that Abraham, after patient waiting, obtained the promise. [16] People swear by what is greater than themselves, and making a statement on oath sets a limit to what can be called in question; [17] and so, since God desired to show even more clearly to the heirs of his promise how immutable was his purpose, he guaranteed it by an oath. [18] Here, then, are two irrevocable acts in which God could not possibly play us false. They give powerful encouragement to us, who have laid claim to his protection by grasping the hope set before us. [19] We have that hope as an anchor for our lives, safe and secure. It enters the sanctuary behind the curtain, [20] where Jesus has entered on our behalf as forerunner, having become high priest for ever in the order of Melchizedek.

7 THIS Melchizedek, king of Salem, priest of God Most High, met Abraham returning from the defeat of the kings and blessed him; [2] and Abraham gave him a tithe of everything as his share. His name, in the first place, means 'king of righteousness'; next he is king of Salem, that is, 'king of peace'. [3] He has no father, no mother, no ancestors; his life has no beginning and no end. Bearing the likeness of the Son of God, he remains a priest for all time.

[4] Consider now how great he must be for the patriarch Abraham to give him his tithe from the finest of the spoil. [5] The descendants of Levi who succeed to the priestly office are required by the law to tithe the people, that is, their fellow-countrymen, although they too are descendants of Abraham. [6] But Melchizedek, though he does not share their ancestry, tithed Abraham himself and gave his blessing to the man who had been given the promises; [7] and, beyond all dispute, it is always the lesser who is blessed by the greater. [8] Moreover, in the one instance tithes are received by men who must die; but in the other, by one whom scripture affirms to be alive. [9] It might even be said that Levi, the receiver of tithes, was himself tithed through Abraham; [10] for he was still in his ancestor's loins when Melchizedek met him. [11] Now if perfection had been attainable

6:6 **crucifying:** *or* crucifying again.   6:18 **They give ... grasping:** *or* They give to us, who have laid claim to his protection, a powerful encouragement to grasp.

9–12: Here the writer addresses those who, however, still show *faith, hope* and *love* and for whom *salvation* is still in prospect if they remain true to their baptismal vows.

6.13–10.18: The new covenant. The writer now returns (see 4.14–5.10) to the theological discussion. The author's aim in what follows is to demonstrate that Christ mediates, and by his death effectively seals, a new covenant for forgiveness of sins (10.16–18). This point is made by contrasting the redemptive character of Jesus' life, death, and exaltation with the inferior rites of the Jewish sacrificial system.

6.13–8.13: Christ is a new high priest. 13–18: *Two irrevocable acts* show God's faithfulness to Abraham, God's promise and God's oath; see Gen. 22.16–17. **19–20:** *The curtain* of the temple in Jerusalem guarded its inmost sanctuary, which was entered only once a year and only by the high priest; see 9.1–5. This priestly function of opening an approach to God for the people is now served by Jesus; see 4.14–5.10. **7.1–10:** *Melchizedek* (see Gen. 14.17–20) is called *a priest for all time* (v. 3) because Scripture happens to say nothing about either his birth or his death. He is thus the prototype of Christ, the eternal high priest (see vv. 23–25). **8:** The Levitical priests are mortal, Melchizedek is not. **11–14:** The inferiority of the old priesthood required the institution of a new order of priests which, in turn, involved *a change of law*. Under the old law priests through the levitical priesthood (on the basis of which the people were given the law), there would have been no need for another kind of priest to arise, described as being in the order of Melchizedek, instead of in the order of Aaron. ¹²But a change of priesthood must mean a change of law; ¹³for he who is spoken of here belongs to a different tribe, no member of which has ever served at the altar. ¹⁴It is beyond all doubt that our Lord is sprung from Judah, a tribe to which Moses made no reference in speaking of priests.

¹⁵What makes this still clearer is that a new priest has arisen, one like Melchizedek; ¹⁶he owes his priesthood not to a system of rules relating to descent but to the power of a life that cannot be destroyed. ¹⁷For here is the testimony: 'You are a priest for ever, in the order of Melchizedek.' ¹⁸The earlier rules are repealed as ineffective and useless, ¹⁹since the law brought nothing to perfection; and a better hope is introduced, through which we draw near to God.

²⁰⁻²²Notice also that no oath was sworn when the other men were made priests; but for this priest an oath was sworn in the words addressed to him: 'The Lord has sworn and will not go back on his word, "You are a priest for ever." ' In the same way, God's oath shows how superior is the covenant which Jesus guarantees. ²³There have been many levitical priests, because death prevents them from continuing in office; ²⁴but Jesus holds a perpetual priesthood, because he remains for ever. ²⁵That is why he is able to save completely those who approach God through him, since he is always alive to plead on their behalf.

²⁶Such a high priest is indeed suited to our need: he is holy, innocent, undefiled, set apart from sinners, and raised high above the heavens. ²⁷He has no need to offer sacrifices daily, as the high priests do, first for their own sins and then for those of the people; he did this once for all when he offered up himself. ²⁸The high priests appointed by the law are men in all their weakness; but the priest appointed by the words of the oath which supersedes the law is the Son, who has been made perfect for ever.

8 My main point is: this is the kind of high priest we have, and he has taken his seat at the right hand of the throne of Majesty in heaven, ²a minister in the real sanctuary, the tent set up by the Lord, not by man. ³Every high priest is appointed to offer gifts and sacrifices; hence, of necessity, this one too had something to offer. ⁴If he were on earth, he would not be a priest at all, since there are already priests to offer the gifts prescribed by the law, ⁵although the sanctuary in which they minister is only a shadowy symbol of the heavenly one. This is why Moses, when he was about to put up the tent, was instructed by God: 'See to it that you make everything according to the pattern shown you on the mountain.' ⁶But in fact the ministry which Jesus has been given is superior to theirs, for he is the mediator of a better covenant, established on better promises.

⁷Had that first covenant been faultless, there would have been no occasion to look for a second to replace it. ⁸But God finds fault with his people when he says, 'The time is coming, says the Lord, when I shall conclude a new covenant with the house of Israel and the house of Judah. ⁹It will not be like the covenant I made with their forefathers when I took them by the hand to lead them out of Egypt; because they did not abide by the terms of that covenant, and so I aban-

7:25 **completely:** *or* for all time.

were chosen only from the tribe of Levi (see Num. 18.21–24), but Jesus was from the tribe of Judah. **15–19:** Christ's priesthood depends on no legal statute of the Pentateuch, but rather on the uniqueness of his own person as God's eternal Son (see 1.1–4; 13.8). Therefore he secures for the people *a better hope* (v. 19). **17:** Ps. 110.4. **20–25:** The author resumes the argument that Jesus' priestly office was conferred by a divine oath (Ps. 110.4; see 6.13–18). Because death does not terminate his service he is *able to save completely* (v. 25). **26–28:** The preceding argument is summarized: Christ's priestly mediation is alone redemptive because he is God's *Son,* himself without sin, *appointed* to his office *by . . . the oath,* not *the law,* and because he offers the *once for all* sacrifice of his own life and subsequently is *raised high above the heavens* to be with God. See 9.11–12.

8.1–13: Christ exercises his priesthood in the Lord's sanctuary, not in a human sanctuary. This intensifies the author's view that there is a new covenant by which the old cultus has been rendered obsolete, a theme developed in several ways in the tract. **8–12:** Jer. 31.31–34.

doned them, says the Lord. [10] For this is the covenant I shall make with Israel after those days, says the Lord: I shall set my laws in their understanding and write them on their hearts; I shall be their God, and they will be my people. [11] They will not teach one another, each saying to his fellow-citizen and his brother, "Know the Lord!" For all of them will know me, high and low alike; [12] I shall pardon their wicked deeds, and their sins I shall remember no more.' [13] By speaking of a new covenant, he has pronounced the first one obsolete; and anything that is becoming obsolete and growing old will shortly disappear.

9 THE first covenant had its ordinances governing divine service and its sanctuary, but it was an earthly sanctuary. [2] An outer tent, called the Holy Place, was set up to contain the lampstand, the table, and the Bread of the Presence. [3] Beyond the second curtain was the tent called the Most Holy Place. [4] Here were a gold incense-altar and the Ark of the Covenant plated all over with gold, in which were kept a gold jar containing the manna, and Aaron's staff which once budded, and the tablets of the covenant; [5] and above the Ark were the cherubim of God's glory, overshadowing the place of expiation. These we need not discuss in detail now.

[6] Under this arrangement, the priests are continually entering the first tent in the performance of their duties; [7] but the second tent is entered by the high priest alone, and that only once a year. He takes with him the blood which he offers for himself and for the people's inadvertent sins. [8] By this the Holy Spirit indicates that so long as the outer tent still stands, the way into the sanctuary has not been opened up. [9] All this is symbolic, pointing to the present time. It means that the prescribed offerings and sacrifices cannot give the worshipper a clear conscience and so

bring him to perfection; [10] they are concerned only with food and drink and various rites of cleansing—external ordinances in force until the coming of the new order.

[11] But now Christ has come, high priest of good things already in being. The tent of his priesthood is a greater and more perfect one, not made by human hands, that is, not belonging to this created world; [12] the blood of his sacrifice is his own blood, not the blood of goats and calves; and thus he has entered the sanctuary once for all and secured an eternal liberation. [13] If sprinkling the blood of goats and bulls and the ashes of a heifer consecrates those who have been defiled and restores their ritual purity, [14] how much greater is the power of the blood of Christ; through the eternal Spirit he offered himself without blemish to God. His blood will cleanse our conscience from the deadness of our former ways to serve the living God.

[15] That is why the new covenant or testament of which he is mediator took effect once a death had occurred, to bring liberation from sins committed under the former covenant; its purpose is to enable those whom God has called to receive the eternal inheritance he has promised them. [16] Now where there is a testament it is necessary for the death of the testator to be established; [17] for a testament takes effect only when a death has occurred: it has no force while the testator is still alive. [18] Even the former covenant itself was not inaugurated without blood, [19] for when Moses had told the assembled people all the commandments as set forth in the law, he took the blood of calves, with water, scarlet wool, and marjoram, and sprinkled the law book itself and all the people, [20] saying, 'This is the blood of the covenant which God commanded you to keep.' [21] In the same way he sprinkled the blood over the tent and all the vessels of divine

9:11 **things . . . being:** *some witnesses read* things to be.

9.1–10.18: A new and better sacrifice is offered by Christ. 1–10: These verses provide an idealized picture of the earthly place of sacrifice. **1–5:** See Exod. chs. 25–26. **6–9:** Under the old system only the *high priest* is permitted into the inmost *sanctuary* (beyond the second curtain). There the priest must first atone for the priest's own personal and familial sins (v. 7; Lev. ch. 16). **10–12:** The new covenant brings a *new order* (v. 10), for with *Christ* as *high priest* (v. 11) the annual rites are replaced by one perfect sacrifice effective for *eternal liberation* (v. 12). **13–14:** This priest's sacrificial offering is *without blemish* (see 4.15; 5.9) and it therefore achieves an inward cleansing for God's people. **15–22:** God's *new covenant* with the people is compared to a human *testament* which is operative *only when* the testator's *death has occurred*. Similarly, the *new covenant* is inaugurated by Christ's death. **18–22:** Exod. 24.3–8.

service. ²²Indeed, under the law, it might almost be said that everything is cleansed by blood, and without the shedding of blood there is no forgiveness.

Jesus, the final sacrifice

²³If, then, the symbols of heavenly things required those sacrifices to cleanse them, the heavenly things themselves required still better sacrifices; ²⁴for Christ has not entered a sanctuary made by human hands which is only a pointer to the reality; he has entered heaven itself, to appear now before God on our behalf. ²⁵It was not his purpose to offer himself again and again, as the high priest enters the sanctuary year after year with blood not his own; ²⁶for then he would have had to suffer repeatedly since the world was created. But as it is, he has appeared once for all at the climax of history to abolish sin by the sacrifice of himself. ²⁷Just as it is our human lot to die once, with judgement to follow, ²⁸so Christ was offered once to bear the sins of mankind, and will appear a second time, not to deal with sin, but to bring salvation to those who eagerly await him.

10 THE law contains but a shadow of the good things to come, not the true picture. With the same sacrifices offered year after year for all time, it can never bring the worshippers to perfection. ²If it could, these sacrifices would surely have ceased to be offered, because the worshippers, cleansed once for all, would no longer have any sense of sin. ³Instead, by these sacrifices sins are brought to mind year after year, ⁴because they can never be removed by the blood of bulls and goats.

⁵That is why, at Christ's coming into the world, he says:

Sacrifice and offering you did not
  desire,

but you have prepared a body for me.
⁶Whole-offerings and sin-offerings you
  did not delight in.
⁷Then I said, 'Here I am: as it is written
  of me in the scroll,
I have come, O God, to do your will.'

⁸First he says, 'Sacrifices and offerings, whole-offerings and sin-offerings, you did not desire or delight in,' although the law prescribes them. ⁹Then he adds, 'Here I am: I have come to do your will.' He thus abolishes the former to establish the latter. ¹⁰And it is by the will of God that we have been consecrated, through the offering of the body of Jesus Christ once for all.

¹¹Daily every priest stands performing his service and time after time offering the same sacrifices, which can never remove sins. ¹²Christ, having offered for all time a single sacrifice for sins, took his seat at God's right hand, ¹³where he now waits until his enemies are made his footstool. ¹⁴So by one offering he has perfected for ever those who are consecrated by it. ¹⁵To this the Holy Spirit also adds his witness. First he says, ¹⁶'This is the covenant which I will make with them after those days, says the Lord: I will set my laws in their hearts and write them on their understanding'; ¹⁷then he adds, 'and their sins and wicked deeds I will remember no more.' ¹⁸And where these have been forgiven, there are no further offerings for sin.

¹⁹So NOW, my friends, the blood of Jesus makes us free to enter the sanctuary with confidence ²⁰by the new and living way which he has opened for us through the curtain, the way of his flesh. ²¹We have a great priest set over the household of God; ²²so let

9:28 **to bear the sins:** or to remove the sins.
10:1 **sacrifices ... perfection:** or sacrifices offered year after year it can never bring the worshippers to perfection for all time.   10:12 **for all time ... seat:** or a single sacrifice for sins, took his seat for all time.
10:20 **curtain ... flesh:** or curtain of his flesh.

23–28: The main points of the discussion are again summarized (see vv. 26–28), and attention is directed to the salvation which awaits believers (v. 28). **10.1–18:** The *law* does not lead to salvation. It betrays its own inferiority in dealing with sin by providing for repeated sacrifices. In contrast, Christ's sacrifice is *once for all* (v. 10), therefore, self-validating. **5–7:** Ps. 40.6–8 Sept., cited as Jesus' own words. **8–10:** In Christ's sacrifice the old system is annulled and God's people are now *consecrated* for true obedience. **12–13:** Ps. 110.1. **16–17:** Jer. 31.33–34. **18:** See vv. 11–12.

10.19–13.17: Exhortations to live as God's pilgrim people. The theological discussion now gives way entirely to practical appeals. The hope enshrined in the new covenant and sealed by Christ's sacrifice should sustain and shape the life of God's people in this world. **19–39:** The author renews the plea that Christians us make our approach in sincerity of heart and the full assurance of faith, inwardly cleansed from a guilty conscience, and outwardly washed with pure water. 23 Let us be firm and unswerving in the confession of our hope, for the giver of the promise is to be trusted. 24 We ought to see how each of us may best arouse others to love and active goodness. 25 We should not stay away from our meetings, as some do, but rather encourage one another, all the more because we see the day of the Lord drawing near.

26 For if we deliberately persist in sin after receiving the knowledge of the truth, there can be no further sacrifice for sins; there remains 27 only a terrifying expectation of judgement, of a fierce fire which will consume God's enemies. 28 Anyone who flouts the law of Moses is put to death without mercy on the evidence of two or three witnesses. 29 Think how much more severe a penalty will be deserved by anyone who has trampled underfoot the Son of God, profaned the blood of the covenant by which he was consecrated, and insulted God's gracious Spirit! 30 For we know who it is that said, 'Justice is mine: I will repay'; and again, 'The Lord will judge his people.' 31 It is a terrifying thing to fall into the hands of the living God.

32 Remember those early days when, newly enlightened, you met the test of great suffering and held firm. 33 Some of you were publicly exposed to abuse and tormented, while others stood loyally by those who were so treated. 34 For indeed you shared the sufferings of those who were in prison, and you cheerfully accepted the seizure of your possessions, knowing that you had a better, more lasting possession. 35 Do not, therefore, throw away your confidence, for it carries a great reward. 36 You need endurance in order to do God's will and win what he has promised. 37 For, in the words of scripture,

> very soon he who is to come will come;
> he will not delay;
> 38 and by faith my righteous servant shall
> find life;

> but if anyone shrinks back,
> I take no pleasure in him.

39 But we are not among those who shrink back and are lost; we have the faith to preserve our life.

Faith in times past

11 FAITH gives substance to our hopes and convinces us of realities we do not see.
2 It was for their faith that the people of old won God's approval.
3 By faith we understand that the universe was formed by God's command, so that the visible came forth from the invisible.
4 By faith Abel offered a greater sacrifice than Cain's; because of his faith God approved his offerings and attested his goodness; and through his faith, though he is dead, he continues to speak.
5 By faith Enoch was taken up to another life without passing through death; he was not to be found, because God had taken him, and it is the testimony of scripture that before he was taken he had pleased God. 6 But without faith it is impossible to please him, for whoever comes to God must believe that he exists and rewards those who seek him.
7 By faith Noah took good heed of the divine warning about the unseen future, and built an ark to save his household. Through his faith he put the whole world in the wrong, and made good his own claim to the righteousness which comes of faith.
8 By faith Abraham obeyed the call to leave his home for a land which he was to receive as a possession; he went away without knowing where he was to go. 9 By faith he settled as an alien in the land which had been promised him, living in tents with Isaac and Jacob, who were heirs with him to the same promise. 10 For he was looking forward to a city with firm foundations, whose architect and builder is God.

11:1 **substance:** *or* assurance.

---

remain *firm* and *unswerving* (v. 23) in the face of their difficulties. The exalted Christ is their *new and living way* to God (compare Jn. 14.6). **26–31:** See 6.4–8 n. **28:** See e.g. Deut. 17.6. **30:** Deut. 32.35–36; Ps. 135.14. **31:** See 12.29. **32–39:** Earlier post-conversion zeal should not be abandoned. **37–38:** Hab. 2.3–4.

11.1–40: Examples of faith from Scripture are rehearsed to support the preceding exhortations. **1:** *Faith,* in this writer's view, means primarily holding fast to hope. See e.g. vv. 22–23; 6.11–12, 19; 7.18–19. **3:** Gen. ch. 1. **4:** Gen. 4.3–10. **5:** Gen. 5.21–24. **7:** Gen. 6.13–22. **8–9:** Gen. 12.1–8. **10:** The *city* is the new, spiritual

¹¹ By faith even Sarah herself was enabled to conceive, though she was past the age, because she judged that God who had promised would keep faith. ¹² Therefore from one man, a man as good as dead, there sprang descendants as numerous as the stars in the heavens or the countless grains of sand on the seashore.

¹³ All these died in faith. Although they had not received the things promised, yet they had seen them far ahead and welcomed them, and acknowledged themselves to be strangers and aliens without fixed abode on earth. ¹⁴ Those who speak in that way show plainly that they are looking for a country of their own. ¹⁵ If their thoughts had been with the country they had left, they could have found opportunity to return. ¹⁶ Instead, we find them longing for a better country, a heavenly one. That is why God is not ashamed to be called their God; for he has a city ready for them.

¹⁷ By faith Abraham, when put to the test, offered up Isaac: he had received the promises, and yet he was ready to offer his only son, ¹⁸ of whom he had been told, 'Through the line of Isaac your descendants shall be traced.' ¹⁹ For he reckoned that God had power even to raise from the dead — and it was from the dead, in a sense, that he received him back.

²⁰ By faith Isaac blessed Jacob and Esau and spoke of things to come. ²¹ By faith Jacob, as he was dying, blessed each of Joseph's sons, and bowed in worship over the top of his staff.

²² By faith Joseph, at the end of his life, spoke of the departure of Israel from Egypt, and gave instructions about his burial.

²³ By faith, when Moses was born, his parents hid him for three months, because they saw what a fine child he was; they were not intimidated by the king's edict. ²⁴ By faith Moses, when he grew up, refused to be called a son of Pharaoh's daughter, ²⁵ preferring to share hardship with God's people rather than enjoy the transient pleasures of sin. ²⁶ He considered the stigma that rests on God's Anointed greater wealth than the treasures of Egypt, for his eyes were fixed on the coming reward. ²⁷ By faith he left Egypt, with no fear of the king's anger; for he was resolute, as one who saw the invisible God.

²⁸ By faith he celebrated the Passover and the sprinkling of blood, so that the destroying angel might not touch the firstborn of Israel. ²⁹ By faith they crossed the Red Sea as though it were dry land, whereas the Egyptians, when they attempted the crossing, were engulfed.

³⁰ By faith the walls of Jericho were made to fall after they had been encircled on seven successive days. ³¹ By faith the prostitute Rahab escaped the fate of the unbelievers, because she had given the spies a kindly welcome.

³² Need I say more? Time is too short for me to tell the stories of Gideon, Barak, Samson, and Jephthah, of David and Samuel and the prophets. ³³ Through faith they overthrew kingdoms, established justice, saw God's promises fulfilled. They shut the mouths of lions, ³⁴ quenched the fury of fire, escaped death by the sword. Their weakness was turned to strength, they grew powerful in war, they put foreign armies to rout. ³⁵ Women received back their dead raised to life. Others were tortured to death, refusing release, to win resurrection to a better life. ³⁶ Others, again, had to face jeers and flogging, even fetters and prison bars. ³⁷ They were stoned to death, they were sawn in two, they were put to the sword, they went about clothed in skins of sheep or goats, deprived, oppressed, ill-treated. ³⁸ The world was not worthy of them. They were refugees in deserts and on the mountains, hiding in

11:11 **though she was:** *some witnesses add* barren and.
11:37 **stoned to death:** *some witnesses add* they were tested.

Jerusalem; see e.g. Rev. ch. 21. **11:** Gen. 18.9–15; 21.2. **12:** Gen 15.5; 22.17–18. **13–16:** Faith is hopeful pilgrimage toward the city of God, i.e. into God's presence; see 13.14. **17:** Gen. ch. 22. **18:** Gen. 21.12. **19:** Isaac was offered but did not die (Gen. 22.13). **20:** Gen. 27.27–29, 39–40. **21:** Gen. ch. 48; 47.31 Sept. **22:** Gen. 50.24–25. **23:** Exod. 2.2; 1.22. **24–26:** Moses' suffering is regarded as obedience to the example of Jesus, *God's Anointed,* who also shared the lot of *God's people* (see Rom. 15.3; Exod. 2.10–15). **27:** Exod. 12.40–51. **28:** Exod. 12.21–30. **29:** Exod. 14.5–31. **30:** Josh. ch. 6. **31:** The basis is Josh. 2.1–21; 6.22–25. **32:** *Gideon:* Judg. chs. 6–8. *Barak:* Judg. chs. 4–5. *Samson:* Judg. chs. 13–16. *Jephthah:* Judg. chs. 11–12. *David:* 1 Sam. chs. 16–30; 2 Sam. chs. 1–24; 1 Kgs. 1.1–2.12. *Samuel:* 1 Sam. chs. 1–12; 15.1–16.13. **33–34:** *Lions . . . fire:* see Dan. chs. 6; 3. **35:** 1 Kgs. 17.17–24; 2 Kgs. 4.25–37; 2 Macc. 6.18–7.42. **36:** Jer. 20.2; 37.15; 38.6–13.

caves and holes in the ground. [39] All these won God's approval because of their faith; and yet they did not receive what was promised, [40] because, with us in mind, God had made a better plan, that only with us should they reach perfection.

Faith today

12 WITH this great cloud of witnesses around us, therefore, we too must throw off every encumbrance and the sin that all too readily restricts us, and run with resolution the race which lies ahead of us, [2] our eyes fixed on Jesus, the pioneer and perfecter of faith. For the sake of the joy that lay ahead of him, he endured the cross, ignoring its disgrace, and has taken his seat at the right hand of the throne of God. [3] Think of him who submitted to such opposition from sinners: that will help you not to lose heart and grow faint. [4] In the struggle against sin, you have not yet resisted to the point of shedding your blood. [5] You have forgotten the exhortation which addresses you as sons:

My son, do not think lightly of the
    Lord's discipline,
or be discouraged when he corrects
    you;
[6] for whom the Lord loves he disciplines;
he chastises every son whom he
    acknowledges.

[7] You must endure it as discipline: God is treating you as sons. Can anyone be a son and not be disciplined by his father? [8] If you escape the discipline in which all sons share, you must be illegitimate and not true sons. [9] Again, we paid due respect to our human fathers who disciplined us; should we not submit even more readily to our spiritual Father, and so attain life? [10] They disciplined us

for a short time as they thought best; but he does so for our true welfare, so that we may share his holiness. [11] Discipline, to be sure, is never pleasant; at the time it seems painful, but afterwards those who have been trained by it reap the harvest of a peaceful and upright life. [12] So brace your drooping arms and shaking knees, [13] and keep to a straight path; then the weakened limb will not be put out of joint, but will regain its former powers.

The fruit of righteousness

[14] AIM at peace with everyone and a holy life, for without that no one will see the Lord. [15] Take heed that there is no one among you who forfeits the grace of God, no bitter, noxious weed growing up to contaminate the rest, [16] no immoral person, no one worldly-minded like Esau. He sold his birthright for a single meal, [17] and you know that afterwards, although he wanted to claim the blessing, he was rejected; though he begged for it to the point of tears, he found no way open for a change of mind.

[18] IT is not to the tangible, blazing fire of Sinai that you have come, with its darkness, gloom, and whirlwind, [19] its trumpet-blast and oracular voice, which the people heard and begged to hear no more; [20] for they could not bear the command, 'If even an animal touches the mountain, it must be stoned to death.' [21] So appalling was the sight that Moses said, 'I shudder with fear.'

[22] No, you have come to Mount Zion, the city of the living God, the heavenly Jerusalem, to myriads of angels, [23] to the full concourse and assembly of the firstborn who are enrolled in heaven, and to God the judge of

12:1 **restricts:** *some witnesses read* distracts.   12:2 **For the sake . . . him:** *or* In place of the joy that was open to him.

37: 2 Chr. 24.20–21; 1 Kgs. 19.10; Jer. 26.23; 2 Macc. 5.27. **38:** 2 Macc. 6.11; 10.6. **40:** The *better plan* was for a new covenant mediated by Christ (9.15–28).

   12.1–17: The discipline of faith. 1: The readers, like the *witnesses* just recalled (ch. 11), should *run . . . the race* for salvation with disciplined *resolution;* see 10.39. **2:** Jesus' *joy* was to be seated at God's *right hand.* See 1.3 n. **5–6:** Prov. 3.11–12. **11–13:** After dealing with *discipline* in a familial context (vv. 7–10), the author returns to the analogy of the athletic contest (see vv. 1–2). **12:** Isa. 35.3. **15:** Deut. 29.18 Sept. **16–17:** Gen. 25.29–34; 27.30–40.

   12.18–29: The true worship of God is enabled by the new covenant, not by the old. **18–21:** The old covenant produces fear; see Exod. 19.12–22; 20.18–20. **22–29:** Glorious as the new covenant is (vv. 22–24, 28), there is all the more reason for the disobedient to fear. **22:** See 11.10 n.

all, and to the spirits of good men made perfect, 24 and to Jesus the mediator of a new covenant, whose sprinkled blood has better things to say than the blood of Abel. 25 See that you do not refuse to hear the voice that speaks. Those who refused to hear the oracle speaking on earth found no escape; still less shall we escape if we reject him who speaks from heaven. 26 Then indeed his voice shook the earth, but now he has promised, 'Once again I will shake not only the earth, but the heavens also.' 27 The words 'once again' point to the removal of all created things, of all that is shaken, so that what cannot be shaken may remain. 28 The kingdom we are given is unshakeable; let us therefore give thanks to God for it, and so worship God as he would be worshipped, with reverence and awe; 29 for our God is a devouring fire.

13 NEVER cease to love your fellow-Christians. 2 Do not neglect to show hospitality; by doing this, some have entertained angels unawares. 3 Remember those in prison, as if you were there with them, and those who are being maltreated, for you are vulnerable too.

4 Marriage must be honoured by all, and the marriage bond be kept inviolate; for God's judgement will fall on fornicators and adulterers.

5 Do not live for money; be content with what you have, for God has said, 'I will never leave you or desert you.' 6 So we can take courage and say, 'The Lord is my helper, I will not fear; what can man do to me?'

7 Remember your leaders, who spoke God's message to you. Keep before you the outcome of their life and follow the example of their faith.

8 Jesus Christ is the same yesterday, today, and for ever. 9 So do not be swept off your course by all sorts of outlandish teachings; it is good that we should gain inner strength from the grace of God, and not from rules about food, which have never benefited those who observed them.

10 Our altar is one from which the priests of the sacred tent have no right to eat. 11 As you know, the animals whose blood is brought by the high priest into the sanctuary as a sin-offering have their bodies burnt outside the camp. 12 Therefore, to consecrate the people by his own blood, Jesus also suffered outside the gate. 13 Let us then go to him outside the camp, bearing the stigma that he bore. 14 For here we have no lasting city, but we are seekers after the city which is to come. 15 Through Jesus let us continually offer up to God a sacrifice of praise, that is, the tribute of lips which acknowledge his name.

16 Never neglect to show kindness and to share what you have with others; for such are the sacrifices which God approves.

17 Obey your leaders and submit to their authority; for they are tireless in their care for you, as those who must render an account. See that their work brings them happiness, not pain and grief, for that would be no advantage to you.

18 Pray for us. We are sure that our conscience is clear, and our desire is always to do what is right. 19 I specially ask for your prayers, so that I may be restored to you the sooner.

20 May the God of peace, who brought back from the dead our Lord Jesus, the great Shepherd of the sheep, through the blood of an eternal covenant, 21 make you perfect in all goodness so that you may do his will; and may he create in us what is pleasing to him, through Jesus Christ, to whom be glory for ever and ever! Amen.

22 I beg you, friends, bear with my appeal;

24: Christ's blood means forgiveness, not revenge; see Gen. 4.10. 26: Hag. 2.6. 29: Deut. 4.24.

13.1–17: Concluding admonitions. 1: See 10.24. 2: Itinerant Christian teachers should be accommodated; see 3 Jn. 5–8. The mention of *angels* recalls Gen. chs. 18–19. 3: See Matt. 25.31–46. The Christians' pilgrimage toward heaven (see e.g. v. 14) does not exempt them from being actively concerned about the welfare of those in distress, for during the time of their pilgrimage they still *are vulnerable*. 5: Josh. 1.5. 6: Ps. 118.6. 7: The *leaders* mentioned here are probably not the heroes and heroines of faith cataloged in ch. 11, but Christian preachers and teachers, perhaps including both the original apostles (2.3) and those who now exercise leadership in the church (v. 17). 8: See 1.12. 9: See Col. 2.16–23. 11: *Sin-offering . . . outside:* see Lev. 16.27, where it is called a *purification-offering*. 12–14: Christians are a pilgrim people consecrated by Christ, *seekers after* the new Jerusalem (see 11.10). 15–16: The true *sacrifice of praise* (see Lev. 7.12) is offered by Christians and is manifest in their conduct. See Jas. 1.27.

13.18–25: Epistolary conclusion. Some or all of these last paragraphs may have been added by a later editor, for this is after all a short letter. 23 I have news for you: our friend Timothy has been released; and if he comes in time he will be with me when I see you.

24 Greet all your leaders and all God's people. Greetings to you from our Italian friends.

25 God's grace be with you all!

for the writing overall has more characteristics of a homily than of a letter. **23:** *Timothy:* see Acts 16.1 n.

HEBREWS 13:25

A LETTER OF
James

This writer is concerned to rescue sinners from their "erring ways" (5.20) by providing a manual for Christian conduct. Many topics are handled in fairly miscellaneous fashion, although four points receive more sustained attention: the evil of showing partiality (2.1–12), the need for works along with faith (2.14–26), the danger of loose talk (3.1–12), and the sins of the rich (4.13–5.6). This manual has been sent out to the church as a whole, and its purpose is completely practical. Doctrinal matters are not taken up, and the content of the moral advice does not reveal much about the author's own theological point of view. Most of the teaching is common to other Hellenistic Wisdom literature of the day.

If the writing is indeed from James, the Lord's brother (see 1.1 n.), a date no later than about 60 C.E. is required. However, because the ritual and cultic concerns attributed to James elsewhere (see Gal. 2.12) are absent and because the overall cast is so Hellenistic, many scholars question the traditional view of authorship. Some have held that the tract is of Jewish origin, subsequently lightly Christianized. More often, it is ascribed to a Christian writer of the late first or early second century. There is no consensus as to the place of writing.

1 FROM James, a servant of God and the Lord Jesus Christ. Greetings to the twelve tribes dispersed throughout the world.

Faith under trial

2 MY friends, whenever you have to face all sorts of trials, count yourselves supremely happy 3 in the knowledge that such testing of your faith makes for strength to endure. 4 Let endurance perfect its work in you that you may become perfected, sound throughout, lacking in nothing. 5 If any of you lacks wisdom, he should ask God and it will be given him, for God is a generous giver who neither grudges nor reproaches anyone. 6 But he who asks must ask in faith, with never a doubt in his mind; for the doubter is like a wave of the sea tossed hither and thither by the wind. 7 A man like that should not think he will receive anything from the Lord. 8 He is always in two minds and unstable in all he does.

9 The church member in humble circumstances does well to take pride in being exalted; 10 the wealthy member must find his pride in being brought low, for the rich man will disappear like a wild flower; 11 once the sun is up with its scorching heat, it parches the plant, its flower withers, and what was lovely to look at is lost for ever. So shall the rich man fade away as he goes about his business.

12 Happy is the man who stands up to trial! Having passed that test he will receive in reward the life which God has promised to those who love him. 13 No one when tempted should say, 'I am being tempted by God'; for God cannot be tempted by evil and does not himself tempt anyone. 14 Temptation comes when anyone is lured and dragged away by his own desires; 15 then desire conceives and

1.1: Salutation. *James:* probably the brother of Jesus (Matt. 13.55; see Jude 1), although this is not specified. The church is in the world like the *twelve tribes* of Israel.

1.2–27: Miscellaneous topics: *endurance* (vv. 2–4), *wisdom* (vv. 5–8), wealth (vv. 9–11), *trial* (v. 12), *temptation* (vv. 13–15), God's beneficence (vv. 16–18), *human anger* (vv. 19–21), true *religion* (vv. 22–27). **2–4:** *Endurance:* see 5.7–11; Prov. 3.11–12. **5–8:** *Wisdom* is understood by James as moral purity; see 3.13–17. *Faith* is belief in God; see 2.19. **9–11:** The theme of the *wealthy* and the *humble* is important in this tract; see 2.1–7; 4.13–5.6. **10–11:** Isa. 40.6–7. **12:** Outward trials: see Dan. 12.12 Sept.; Rev. 2.10; 1 Pet.

gives birth to sin, and sin when it is full-grown breeds death.

¹⁶ Make no mistake, my dear friends. ¹⁷ Every good and generous action and every perfect gift come from above, from the Father who created the lights of heaven. With him there is no variation, no play of passing shadows. ¹⁸ Of his own choice, he brought us to birth by the word of truth to be a kind of firstfruits of his creation.

¹⁹ Of that you may be certain, my dear friends. But everyone should be quick to listen, slow to speak, and slow to be angry. ²⁰ For human anger does not promote God's justice. ²¹ Then discard everything sordid, and every wicked excess, and meekly accept the message planted in your hearts, with its power to save you.

²² Only be sure you act on the message, and do not merely listen and so deceive yourselves. ²³ Anyone who listens to the message but does not act on it is like somebody looking in a mirror at the face nature gave him; ²⁴ he glances at himself and goes his way, and promptly forgets what he looked like. ²⁵ But he who looks into the perfect law, the law that makes us free, and does not turn away, remembers what he hears; he acts on it, and by so acting he will find happiness.

²⁶ If anyone thinks he is religious but does not bridle his tongue, he is deceiving himself; that man's religion is futile. ²⁷ A pure and faultless religion in the sight of God the Father is this: to look after orphans and widows in trouble and to keep oneself untarnished by the world.

Love your neighbour as yourself

2 My friends, you believe in our Lord Jesus Christ who reigns in glory and you must always be impartial. ² For instance, two visitors may enter your meeting, one a well-dressed man with gold rings, and the other a poor man in grimy clothes. ³ Suppose you pay special attention to the well-dressed man and say to him, 'Please take this seat,' while to the poor man you say, 'You stand over there, or sit here on the floor by my footstool,' ⁴ do you not see that you are discriminating among your members and judging by wrong standards? ⁵ Listen, my dear friends: has not God chosen those who are poor in the eyes of the world to be rich in faith and to possess the kingdom he has promised to those who love him? ⁶ And yet you have humiliated the poor man. Moreover, are not the rich your oppressors? Is it not they who drag you into court ⁷ and pour contempt on the honoured name by which God has claimed you?

⁸ If, however, you are observing the sovereign law laid down in scripture, 'Love your neighbour as yourself,' that is excellent. ⁹ But if you show partiality, you are committing a sin and you stand convicted by the law as offenders. ¹⁰ For if a man breaks just one commandment and keeps all the others, he is guilty of breaking all of them. ¹¹ For he who said, 'You shall not commit adultery,' said also, 'You shall not commit murder.' If you commit murder you are a breaker of the law, even if you do not commit adultery as well. ¹² Always speak and act as men who are to be judged under a law which makes them free. ¹³ In that judgement there will be no mercy for the man who has shown none. Mercy triumphs over judgement.

¹⁴ WHAT good is it, my friends, for someone to say he has faith when his actions do nothing to show it? Can that faith save him? ¹⁵ Suppose a fellow-Christian, whether man or woman, is in rags with not enough food for the day, ¹⁶ and one of you says, 'Goodbye, keep warm, and have a good meal,' but does

1:17 **no variation . . . shadows:** *some witnesses read* no variation, or shadow caused by change.   1:21 **Then discard . . . and meekly accept:** *or* Then meekly discard . . . and accept.   2:3 **Please . . . seat:** *or* Do take this comfortable seat.

5.4. **18:** As *firstfruits* Christians are heralds of a new age; see Rom. 8.23; 11.16. **19–21:** On *anger*, see 3.1–12. **21:** The *message* is the gospel. **22–25:** On moral action, see 2.14–26. **25:** The gospel is *the perfect law . . . that makes us free,* and demands studied attention and obedience. **26:** On false speech, see 3.1–12. **27:** True *religion* is defined here, not as doctrine or knowledge or ritual, but as moral action. *World:* see 2.5; 3.6; 4.4.

2.1–13: On partiality and privilege. No favors should be accorded the rich. **5:** See 1 Cor. 1.26–31. **6–7:** Christians are reminded of the social and economic exploitation for which rich nonbelievers are responsible; see 5.4–6. *The honoured name* is "Christ." **8:** The *sovereign law:* either *scripture* as a whole or the love commandment in particular (Lev. 19.18). **11:** Exod. 20.13–14. **12:** *Free:* see 1.25 n. **13:** See e.g. Matt. 5.7.

2.14–26: On faith and works. 14–17: If *faith* only means belief in God (see v. 19) it is as meaningless as nothing to supply their bodily needs, what good is that? [17] So with faith; if it does not lead to action, it is by itself a lifeless thing.

[18] But someone may say: 'One chooses faith, another action.' To which I reply: 'Show me this faith you speak of with no actions to prove it, while I by my actions will prove to you my faith.' [19] You have faith and believe that there is one God. Excellent! Even demons have faith like that, and it makes them tremble. [20] Do you have to be told, you fool, that faith divorced from action is futile? [21] Was it not by his action, in offering his son Isaac upon the altar, that our father Abraham was justified? [22] Surely you can see faith was at work in his actions, and by these actions his faith was perfected? [23] Here was fulfilment of the words of scripture: 'Abraham put his faith in God, and that faith was counted to him as righteousness,' and he was called 'God's friend'. [24] You see then it is by action and not by faith alone that a man is justified. [25] The same is true also of the prostitute Rahab. Was she not justified by her action in welcoming the messengers into her house and sending them away by a different route? [26] As the body is dead when there is no breath left in it, so faith divorced from action is dead.

Christian speaking

3 My friends, not many of you should become teachers, for you may be certain that we who teach will ourselves face severer judgement. [2] All of us go wrong again and again; a man who never says anything wrong is perfect and is capable of controlling every part of his body. [3] When we put a bit into a horse's mouth to make it obey our will, we can direct the whole animal. [4] Or think of a ship: large though it may be and driven by gales, it can be steered by a very small rudder on whatever course the helmsman chooses. [5] So with the tongue; it is small, but its pretensions are great.

What a vast amount of timber can be set ablaze by the tiniest spark! [6] And the tongue is a fire, representing in our body the whole wicked world. It pollutes our whole being, it sets the whole course of our existence alight, and its flames are fed by hell. [7] Beasts and birds of every kind, creatures that crawl on the ground or swim in the sea, can be subdued and have been subdued by man; [8] but no one can subdue the tongue. It is an evil thing, restless and charged with deadly venom. [9] We use it to praise our Lord and Father; then we use it to invoke curses on our fellow-men, though they are made in God's likeness. [10] Out of the same mouth come praise and curses. This should not be so, my friends. [11] Does a fountain flow with both fresh and brackish water from the same outlet? [12] My friends, can a fig tree produce olives, or a grape vine produce figs? No more can salt water produce fresh.

The sin of envy

[13] WHICH of you is wise or learned? Let him give practical proof of it by his right conduct, with the modesty that comes of wisdom. [14] But if you are harbouring bitter jealousy and the spirit of rivalry in your hearts, stop making false claims in defiance of the truth. [15] This is not the wisdom that comes from above; it is earth-bound, sensual, demonic. [16] For with jealousy and rivalry come disorder and the practice of every kind of evil. [17] But the wisdom from above is in the first

---

if one were to wish the needy well without lending a hand. **18:** *Someone:* a hypothetical inquirer who misunderstands the point that the same person must give evidence of both faith and action (v. 17). **21:** See Gen. 22.9–19; Heb. 11.17–19. **23:** Jewish teaching (see 1 Macc. 2.52) associated Gen. ch. 22 with the commendation of Abraham's *righteousness* in Gen. 15.6. Whereas Paul interpreted *counted* (Gen. 15.6) to mean God's free gift of acquittal (Rom. 4.3–5), here it is interpreted as God's acceptance of Abraham's works. *Friend:* a common description of Abraham; see 2 Chr. 20.7; Isa. 41.8. **25:** *Rahab:* see Josh. ch. 2; 6.17; Heb. 11.31.

3.1–12: On the evils of the tongue. 6: See 1.27. *Course of our existence:* a phrase borrowed from the Hellenistic mystery religions, used here to describe the orderly design of human life. **7:** See Gen. 9.2–3. Elsewhere it is presumed one's tongue can be controlled (vv. 2–4; 1.26). **9:** *In God's likeness:* see Gen. 1.26–27.

3.13–5.20: Miscellaneous topics.

3.13–18: On true wisdom. The essence of wisdom is moral uprightness. **17:** See Paul's description of love,

place pure; and then peace-loving, considerate, and open-minded; it is straightforward
and sincere, rich in compassion and in deeds
of kindness that are its fruit. ¹⁸ Peace is the
seed-bed of righteousness, and the peacemakers will reap its harvest.

4 What causes fighting and quarrels
among you? Is not their origin the appetites that war in your bodies? ² You want what
you cannot have, so you murder; you are
envious, and cannot attain your ambition, so
you quarrel and fight. You do not get what
you want, because you do not pray for it. ³ Or,
if you do, your requests are not granted, because you pray from wrong motives, in order
to squander what you get on your pleasures.
⁴ Unfaithful creatures! Surely you know that
love of the world means enmity to God?
Whoever chooses to be the world's friend
makes himself God's enemy. ⁵ Or do you suppose that scripture has no point when it says
that the spirit which God implanted in us is
filled with envious longings? ⁶ But the grace
he gives is stronger; thus scripture says, 'God
opposes the arrogant and gives grace to the
humble.' ⁷ Submit then to God. Stand up to
the devil, and he will turn and run. ⁸ Come
close to God, and he will draw close to you.
Sinners, make your hands clean; you whose
motives are mixed, see that your hearts are
pure. ⁹ Be sorrowful, mourn, and weep.
Turn your laughter into mourning and your
gaiety into gloom. ¹⁰ Humble yourselves before the Lord, and he will exalt you.

¹¹ Friends, you must never speak ill of one
another. He who speaks ill of a brother or
passes judgement on him speaks ill of the law
and judges the law. But if you judge the law,
you are not keeping it but sitting in judgement upon it. ¹² There is only one lawgiver
and judge: he who is able to save life or destroy it. So who are you to judge your neighbour?

The danger of wealth

¹³ Now a word with all who say, 'Today or the
next day we will go off to such and such a
town and spend a year there trading and
making money.' ¹⁴ Yet you have no idea what
tomorrow will bring. What is your life after
all? You are no more than a mist, seen for a
little while and then disappearing. ¹⁵ What
you ought to say is: 'If it be the Lord's will,
we shall live to do so and so.' ¹⁶ But instead,
you boast and brag, and all such boasting is
wrong. ¹⁷ What it comes to is that anyone who
knows the right thing to do and does not do
it is a sinner.

5 Next a word to you who are rich. Weep
and wail over the miserable fate overtak-
ing you: ² your riches have rotted away; your
fine clothes are moth-eaten; ³ your silver and
gold have corroded, and their corrosion will
be evidence against you and consume your
flesh like fire. You have piled up wealth in an
age that is near its close. ⁴ The wages you
never paid to the men who mowed your
fields are crying aloud against you, and the
outcry of the reapers has reached the ears of
the Lord of Hosts. ⁵ You have lived on the
land in wanton luxury, gorging yourselves —
and that on the day appointed for your
slaughter. ⁶ You have condemned and murdered the innocent one, who offers no resistance.

Patience and prayer

⁷ You must be patient, my friends, until the
Lord comes. Consider: the farmer looking
for the precious crop from his land can only
wait in patience until the early and late rains
have fallen. ⁸ You too must be patient and
stout-hearted, for the coming of the Lord is
near. ⁹ My friends, do not blame your troubles on one another, or you will fall under
judgement; and there at the door stands the

---

1 Cor. ch. 13. **18:** See Prov. 11.30; 13.2; Phil. 1.11.

4.1–5: On friendship with the world. 3: See Matt. 17.20. **4:** See 1.27; 2.23. **5:** It is unclear what *scripture*
reference is meant.

4.6–10: On drawing near to God. 6: Prov. 3.34; see 1 Pet. 5.5. **7–8:** See 1 Pet. 5.8–9; Heb. 10.22. **9–10:**
The penitent sinner receives God's forgiveness.

4.11–12: On judging a neighbor. The *law* demands love, not judgment (Lev. 19.18; see 2.9–13).

4.13–5.6: On the sins of the rich. 13–17: Traveling merchants are criticized for their worldliness. **5.1–6:**
Wealthy landholders are criticized for their greed and indifference to social justice. Compare Ecclus. 29.10–13.
6: See Wisd. 2.10–20.

5.7–11: On patience. 7: *The Lord:* perhaps a reference to God (v. 4; 3.9), but probably a reference to Christ's
return. **9:** See 4.11–12.

Judge. ¹⁰As a pattern of patience under ill-treatment, take the prophets who spoke in the name of the Lord. ¹¹We count those happy who stood firm. You have heard how Job stood firm, and you have seen how the Lord treated him in the end, for the Lord is merciful and compassionate.

¹²ABOVE all things, my friends, do not use oaths, whether 'by heaven' or 'by earth' or by anything else. When you say 'Yes' or 'No', let it be plain Yes or No, for fear you draw down judgement on yourselves.

¹³Is anyone among you in trouble? Let him pray. Is anyone in good heart? Let him sing praises. ¹⁴Is one of you ill? Let him send for the elders of the church to pray over him and anoint him with oil in the name of the Lord;

¹⁵the prayer offered in faith will heal the sick man, the Lord will restore him to health, and if he has committed sins they will be forgiven. ¹⁶Therefore confess your sins to one another, and pray for one another, that you may be healed. A good man's prayer is very powerful and effective. ¹⁷Elijah was a man just like us; yet when he prayed fervently that there should be no rain, the land had no rain for three and a half years; ¹⁸when he prayed again, the rain poured down and the land bore crops once more.

¹⁹My friends, if one of you strays from the truth and another succeeds in bringing him back, ²⁰you may be sure of this: the one who brings a sinner back from his erring ways will be rescuing a soul from death and cancelling a multitude of sins.

10: See Heb. 11.32–38. **11:** See Job ch. 1; 42.10–16.

5.12: On oaths. See Matt. 5.34–37.

5.13–18: On prayer. 14: See Mk. 6.13. **15:** See 1 Cor. 13.2. **17–18:** First Kings chs. 17–18 says nothing about Elijah's prayers; the reference is to noncanonical Jewish traditions.

5.19–20: On restoring sinners. 19: The *truth:* the gospel; see 1.18. **20:** See 1 Pet. 4.8 n.

THE FIRST LETTER OF
Peter

This letter is directed to congregations of predominantly Gentile Christians scattered throughout several Roman provinces in Asia Minor. It is an appeal to Christians to "stand fast" in the gospel (5.12) and to rejoice in whatever sufferings they are called upon to endure for their faith (4.12–16).

Following the salutation (1.1–2) a prefatory section focuses on the reality and responsibilities of the new life in Christ (1.3–2.10). Subsequently, a number of specific exhortations are issued which deal with the conduct of Christians in their daily affairs (2.11–4.6) and with their relationships to others in the church itself (4.7–11). Finally, the writer summarizes the meaning of suffering as a Christian (4.12–19) and concludes with some specific matters (5.1–14).

If Peter himself wrote this letter, or caused it to be written by Silvanus (5.12), it perhaps reflects Nero's persecution of Christians about 64 C.E. Some scholars, however, believe the good Greek style and the theological point of view preclude Petrine authorship or sponsorship. In this case the author would be an anonymous Christian concerned for the church's tribulations during the reign either of Domitian (81–96 C.E.) or of Trajan (98–117 C.E.), and would perhaps be using some traditional liturgical and catechetical materials (1.3–4.11).

1 FROM Peter, apostle of Jesus Christ, to the scattered people of God now living as aliens in Pontus, Galatia, Cappadocia, Asia, and Bithynia, ²chosen in the foreknowledge of God the Father, by the consecrating work of the Holy Spirit, for obedience to Jesus Christ and sprinkling with his blood.

Grace and peace to you in fullest measure.

Peter gives thanks

³PRAISED be the God and Father of our Lord Jesus Christ! In his great mercy by the resurrection of Jesus Christ from the dead, he gave us new birth into a living hope, ⁴the hope of an inheritance, reserved in heaven for you, which nothing can destroy or spoil or wither. ⁵Because you put your faith in God, you are under the protection of his power until the salvation now in readiness is revealed at the end of time.

⁶This is cause for great joy, even though for a little while you may have had to suffer trials of many kinds. ⁷Even gold passes through the assayer's fire, and much more precious than perishable gold is faith which stands the test. These trials come so that your faith may prove itself worthy of all praise, glory, and honour when Jesus Christ is revealed.

⁸You have not seen him, yet you love him; and trusting in him now without seeing him, you are filled with a glorious joy too great for words, ⁹while you are reaping the harvest of your faith, that is, salvation for your souls.

The calling of a Christian

¹⁰THIS salvation was the subject of intense

1.1–2: Salutation. Christians are temporary residents of this world, for they belong to God; see 2.9–10. *Sprinkling with his blood* refers to baptism into Christ's death; see Heb. 9.13–14.

1.3–9: The new birth. 4: Our *inheritance* is God's continuing love, accepted through baptism. **5:** *Salvation* is sure, but comes fully only in the future. **6:** The *trials* faced by Christians could include even persecution; see Introduction.

1.10–12: The testimony of the prophets. Salvation has always been God's purpose; even the prophets preached the gospel; see 1.23–25.

search by the prophets who prophesied about the grace of God awaiting you. 11 They tried to find out the time and the circumstances to which the spirit of Christ in them pointed, when it foretold the sufferings in Christ's cause and the glories to follow. 12 It was disclosed to them that these matters were not for their benefit but for yours. Now they have been openly announced to you through preachers who brought you the gospel in the power of the Holy Spirit sent from heaven. These are things that angels long to glimpse.

13 Your minds must therefore be stripped for action and fully alert. Fix your hopes on the grace which is to be yours when Jesus Christ is revealed. 14 Be obedient to God your Father, and do not let your characters be shaped any longer by the desires you cherished in your days of ignorance. 15 He who called you is holy; like him, be holy in all your conduct. 16 Does not scripture say, 'You shall be holy, for I am holy'?

17 If you say 'Father' to him who judges everyone impartially on the basis of what they have done, you must live in awe of him during your time on earth. 18 You know well that it was nothing of passing value, like silver or gold, that bought your freedom from the futility of your traditional ways. 19 You were set free by Christ's precious blood, blood like that of a lamb without mark or blemish. 20 He was predestined before the foundation of the world, but in this last period of time he has been revealed for your sake. 21 Through him you have come to trust in God who raised him from the dead and gave him glory, and so your faith and hope are fixed on God. 22 Now that you have purified your souls by obedience to the truth until you feel sincere affection towards your fellow-Christians, love one another wholeheartedly with all your strength. 23 You have been born again, not of mortal but of immortal parentage, through the living and enduring word of God. 24 As scripture says:

All mortals are like grass;
    all their glory like the flower of the
        field;
    the grass withers, the flower falls;
25 but the word of the Lord endures for
        evermore.

And this 'word' is the gospel which was preached to you.

2 Then away with all wickedness and deceit, hypocrisy and jealousy and malicious talk of any kind! 2 Like the newborn infants you are, you should be craving for pure spiritual milk so that you may thrive on it and be saved; for 3 surely you have tasted that the Lord is good.

4 So come to him, to the living stone which was rejected by men but chosen by God and of great worth to him. 5 You also, as living stones, must be built up into a spiritual temple, and form a holy priesthood to offer spiritual sacrifices acceptable to God through Jesus Christ. 6 For you will find in scripture:

I am laying in Zion a chosen
    corner-stone of great worth.
Whoever has faith in it will not be put
    to shame.

7 So for you who have faith it has great worth; but for those who have no faith 'the stone which the builders rejected has become the corner-stone', 8 and also 'a stone to trip over, a rock to stumble against'. They trip because they refuse to believe the word; this is the fate appointed for them.

9 But you are a chosen race, a royal priesthood, a dedicated nation, a people claimed by God for his own, to proclaim the glorious deeds of him who has called you out of darkness into his marvellous light. 10 Once you were not a people at all; but now you are God's people. Once you were outside his mercy; but now you are outside no longer.

1:11 **the time:** *or* the person.

1.13–2.10: The responsibilities of obedient children. 13–16: Hope should conform one's life to the holiness of God; see Lev. 11.44–45; Eph. 2.1–3. **17:** *Father:* the Lord's Prayer. **20:** See 1.10–12 n. **21:** See 1.2–3. **22:** *Now . . . purified:* in baptism; see vv. 1–2 n., 4 n. **25:** The *gospel* is that God remains active for salvation (Isa. 40.6–9); see 1.10–12. **2.2:** *Pure . . . milk:* the Lord's goodness (2.3); see Ps. 34.8. **4:** *The living stone:* the risen Christ; see Ps. 118.22; Isa. 8.14; 28.16, passages frequently applied to Christ in the early church. **5:** Since Christ is a new *temple,* replacing the one in Jerusalem (see Jn. 2.19–22), Christians are its *living stones,* and are a new *priesthood,* replacing the Jerusalem priests. *Spiritual sacrifices:* Christian obedience (see Rom. 12.1). **6:** Isa. 28.16. **7:** Ps. 118.22. **8:** Unbelievers will be judged; see Isa. 8.14–15. **9–10:** See the images in Isa. 43.20–21; Exod. 19.6; Hos. chs. 1–2. God's people are not passive.

The Christian household

¹¹ DEAR friends, I appeal to you, as aliens in a foreign land, to avoid bodily desires which make war on the soul. ¹² Let your conduct among unbelievers be so good that, although they now malign you as wrongdoers, reflection on your good deeds will lead them to give glory to God on the day when he comes in judgement.

¹³ Submit yourselves for the sake of the Lord to every human authority, whether to the emperor as supreme, ¹⁴ or to governors as his deputies for the punishment of those who do wrong and the commendation of those who do right. ¹⁵ For it is God's will that by doing right you should silence ignorance and stupidity.

¹⁶ Live as those who are free; not however as though your freedom provided a cloak for wrongdoing, but as slaves in God's service. ¹⁷ Give due honour to everyone: love your fellow-Christians, reverence God, honour the emperor.

¹⁸ Servants, submit to your masters with all due respect, not only to those who are kind and forbearing, but even to those who are unjust. ¹⁹ It is a sign of grace if, because God is in his thoughts, someone endures the pain of undeserved suffering. ²⁰ What credit is there in enduring the beating you deserve when you have done wrong? On the other hand, when you have behaved well and endured suffering for it, that is a sign of grace in the sight of God. ²¹ It is your vocation because Christ himself suffered on your behalf, and left you an example in order that you should follow in his steps. ²² 'He committed no sin, he was guilty of no falsehood.' ²³ When he was abused he did not retaliate, when he suffered he uttered no threats, but delivered himself up to him who judges justly. ²⁴ He carried our sins in his own person on the gibbet, so that we might cease to live for sin and begin to live for righteousness. By his wounds you have been healed. ²⁵ You were straying like sheep, but now you

have turned towards the Shepherd and Guardian of your souls.

3 In the same way you women must submit to your husbands, so that if there are any of them who disbelieve the gospel they may be won over without a word being said, ² by observing your chaste and respectful behaviour. ³ Your beauty should lie, not in outward adornment—braiding the hair, wearing gold ornaments, or dressing up in fine clothes—⁴ but in the inmost self, with its imperishable quality of a gentle, quiet spirit, which is of high value in the sight of God. ⁵ This is how in past days the women of God's people, whose hope was in him, used to make themselves attractive, submitting to their husbands. ⁶ Such was Sarah, who obeyed Abraham and called him master. By doing good and showing no fear, you have become her daughters.

⁷ In the same way, you husbands must show understanding in your married life: treat your wives with respect, not only because they are physically weaker, but also because God's gift of life is something you share together. Then your prayers will not be impeded.

⁸ Finally, be united, all of you, in thought and feeling; be full of brotherly affection, kindly and humble. ⁹ Do not repay wrong with wrong, or abuse with abuse; on the contrary, respond with blessing, for a blessing is what God intends you to receive. As scripture says:

¹⁰ If anyone wants to love life
  and see good days
  he must restrain his tongue from evil
  and his lips from deceit;
¹¹ he must turn from wrong and do good,
  seek peace and pursue it.
¹² The Lord has eyes for the righteous,
  and ears open to their prayers;

2:19,20 **a sign of grace:** *or* creditable.
2:21 **suffered:** *some witnesses read* died.   2:24 **on the gibbet:** *or* to the gibbet.

2.11–4.6: **Christian conduct in the world. 11–12:** *As aliens:* see 1.1–2 n.; Rom. 12.2. **13–15:** *Human authority:* the political order, which deserves support when it functions for the public good. See also Rom. 13.1–7. **16–17:** See Rom. 6.15–23. **18–25:** The death of Christ, identified here with that of the "suffering servant" of Isa. 53.5–12, is first advanced as an *example* (v. 21) of trust (see Eph. 6.5–8; Col. 3.22–25). **24–25:** Christ's death is also redemptive (see 3.18; Rom. 5.6–11; Col. 2.14). **3.1–7:** See Eph. 5.21–33; Col. 3.18–19. **6:** Gen. 18.12. **8–12:** *Affection* for each other is the sign of the new birth; see 1.22. **9:** Lk. 6.27–28; Rom. 12.17. **10:** Ps. 34.12–16.

but the face of the Lord is set against wrongdoers.

13 Who is going to do you harm if you are devoted to what is good? 14 Yet if you should suffer for doing right you may count yourselves happy. Have no fear of other people: do not be perturbed, 15 but hold Christ in your hearts in reverence as Lord. Always be ready to make your defence when anyone challenges you to justify the hope which is in you. But do so with courtesy and respect, 16 keeping your conscience clear, so that when you are abused, those who malign your Christian conduct may be put to shame. 17 It is better to suffer for doing right, if such should be the will of God, than for doing wrong.

18 Christ too suffered for our sins once and for all, the just for the unjust, that he might bring us to God; put to death in the body, he was brought to life in the spirit. 19 In the spirit also he went and made his proclamation to the imprisoned spirits, 20 those who had refused to obey in the past, while God waited patiently in the days when Noah was building the ark; in it a few people, eight in all, were brought to safety through the water. 21 This water symbolized baptism, through which you are now brought to safety. Baptism is not the washing away of bodily impurities but the appeal made to God from a good conscience; and it brings salvation through the resurrection of Jesus Christ, 22 who is now at the right hand of God, having entered heaven and received the submission of angels, authorities, and powers.

The final testing

4 SINCE Christ endured bodily suffering, you also must arm yourselves with the same disposition. When anyone has endured bodily suffering he has finished with sin, 2 so that for the rest of his days on earth he may live, not to satisfy human appetites, but to do what God wills. 3 You have spent time enough in the past doing what pagans like to do. You lived then in licence and debauchery, drunkenness, orgies and carousal, and the forbidden worship of idols. 4 Now, when you no longer plunge with the pagans into all this reckless dissipation, they cannot understand it and start abusing you; 5 but they will have to give account of themselves to him who is ready to pass judgement on the living and the dead. 6 That was why the gospel was preached even to the dead: in order that, although in the body they were condemned to die as everyone dies, yet in the spirit they might live as God lives.

7 The end of all things is upon us; therefore to help you to pray you must lead self-controlled and sober lives. 8 Above all, maintain the fervour of your love for one another, because love cancels a host of sins. 9 Be hospitable to one another without grumbling. 10 As good stewards of the varied gifts given you by God, let each use the gift he has received in service to others. 11 Are you a speaker? Speak as one who utters God's oracles. Do you give service? Give it in the strength which God supplies. In all things let God be glorified through Jesus Christ; to him belong glory and power for ever and ever. Amen.

12 DEAR friends, do not be taken aback by the fiery ordeal which has come to test you, as though it were something extraordinary. 13 On the contrary, in so far as it gives you a share in Christ's sufferings, you should re-

---

3:14 **Have ... people:** or Do not fear what other people fear. 3:18 **suffered:** some witnesses read died. **for our sins:** some witnesses read for sins. 3:21 **from a good conscience:** or for a good conscience. 4:6 **although ... lives:** or although in the body they suffered judgement by human standards, in the spirit they might be given life in accordance with God's purpose.

3.13–17: See 2.11–12. **18:** See 2.24–25 n. **19–20:** Imprisoned spirits: either Noah's disobedient contemporaries (Gen. chs. 6–9), or specifically the disobedient Nephilim (see Gen. 6.1–4 n.); perhaps both. The idea is that the gospel is withheld from no one; but the exact meaning remains problematic. **21–22:** As water was decisive in Noah's career, so it is in saving the Christian, the latter through baptism. **4.3:** The past: before conversion to Christ. **5:** For Christ as judge, see Acts 10.42; 2 Tim. 4.1. **6:** See 3.19–20 n.

4.7–11: Christian conduct in the church. 7: The end: the day of judgment and salvation; see 1.5, 7, 13. **8:** Where love is active sin subsides. See Prov. 10.12; Ecclus. 3.30; Jas. 5.19–20. **9:** Be hospitable: to Christian travellers; see Heb. 13.2 n.

4.12–19: The meaning of suffering as a Christian. 12: Ordeal: persecution; fiery implies "bitter." **13–19:**

joice; and then when his glory is revealed, your joy will be unbounded. ¹⁴ If you are reviled for being Christians, count yourselves happy, because the Spirit of God in all his glory rests upon you. ¹⁵ If you do suffer, it must not be for murder, theft, or any other crime, nor should it be for meddling in other people's business. ¹⁶ But if anyone suffers as a Christian, he should feel it no disgrace, but confess that name to the honour of God.

¹⁷ The time has come for the judgement to begin; it is beginning with God's own household. And if it is starting with us, how will it end for those who refuse to obey the gospel of God? ¹⁸ Scripture says: 'It is hard enough for the righteous to be saved; what then will become of the impious and sinful?' ¹⁹ So let those who suffer according to God's will entrust their souls to him while continuing to do good; their Maker will not fail them.

The Christian community

5 Now I APPEAL to the elders of your community, as a fellow-elder and a witness to Christ's sufferings, and as one who has shared in the glory to be revealed: ² look after the flock of God whose shepherds you are; do it, not under compulsion, but willingly, as God would have it; not for gain but out of sheer devotion; ³ not lording it over your charges, but setting an example to the flock.

⁴ So when the chief shepherd appears, you will receive glory, a crown that never fades.

⁵ In the same way the younger men should submit to the older. You should all clothe yourselves with humility towards one another, because 'God sets his face against the arrogant but shows favour to the humble.' ⁶ Humble yourselves, then, under God's mighty hand, and in due time he will lift you up. ⁷ He cares for you, so cast all your anxiety on him.

⁸ Be on the alert! Wake up! Your enemy the devil, like a roaring lion, prowls around looking for someone to devour. ⁹ Stand up to him, firm in your faith, and remember that your fellow-Christians in this world are going through the same kinds of suffering. ¹⁰ After your brief suffering, the God of all grace, who called you to his eternal glory in Christ, will himself restore, establish, and strengthen you on a firm foundation. ¹¹ All power belongs to him for ever and ever! Amen.

Final greetings

¹² I WRITE you this brief letter through Silvanus, whom I know to be a trustworthy colleague, to encourage you and to testify that this is the true grace of God; in this stand fast.

¹³ Greetings from your sister church in Babylon, and from my son Mark. ¹⁴ Greet one another with a loving kiss.

Peace to you all who belong to Christ!

Joyful acceptance of undeserved suffering demonstrates trust in God's ultimate faithfulness; see 2.18–25 n. **14:** Isa. 11.2. **16:** *Christian:* see Acts 11.26 n. **18:** Prov. 11.31.

5.1–14: Concluding matters. 1–7: Harmony should prevail as the church awaits in hope the coming of Christ, *the chief shepherd* (see also 2.25). **5:** Prov. 3.34. **7:** Ps. 55.22. **8–11:** The church under persecution must stand united against unbelief (*the devil;* see Job. 1.7). **12:** *Silvanus,* the stenographer, is probably "Silas" (Acts 15.22). **13:** *From your sister church in Babylon:* the church in Rome; see Rev. 17.1–5, 15. In early Christian tradition *Mark* was regarded as Peter's spiritual heir; see Acts 12.12. **14:** *Loving kiss:* a liturgical gesture, the "holy kiss" (e.g. Rom. 16.16).

THE SECOND LETTER OF

Peter

In form, this writing is Peter's "last will and testament," a passionate attempt to support orthodox Christian doctrines, especially beliefs in the glorious return of Christ. The purpose, style, and point of view sharply distinguish this testament from 1 Peter, and most scholars have concluded that it was written in Peter's name by a later church figure interested in representing its teaching as well-established apostolic tradition. The salutation (1.1–2) is followed by a preface which stresses the writer's authority (1.3–15). In 1.16–3.10 there are various arguments assembled to show that the hope of the Lord's coming is sure, and the readers are admonished in conclusion to be ready for that day (3.11–18).

Virtually all the arguments in 2 Peter duplicate those in Jude 3–18. The majority of interpreters believe that the author of 2 Peter has drawn on Jude in formulating this appeal. That 2 Peter used Jude (not Jude, 2 Peter) is suggested by the absence from 2 Peter of a passage in Jude 9 which alludes to a legend about Moses' body; that 2 Peter omitted this seems to scholars more likely than that Jude added it. Dependence on Jude and the association of Paul's letters with Scripture (3.16) suggest a date for 2 Peter well into the second century, perhaps about 150 C.E.

1 FROM Simeon Peter, servant and apostle of Jesus Christ, to those who share equally with us in the privileges of faith through the righteousness of our God and Saviour Jesus Christ.

2 Grace and peace be yours in fullest measure, through knowledge of God and of Jesus our Lord.

Living in the last days

3 GOD's divine power has bestowed on us everything that makes for life and true religion, through our knowledge of him who called us by his own glory and goodness. 4 In this way he has given us his promises, great beyond all price, so that through them you may escape the corruption with which lust has infected the world, and may come to share in the very being of God.

5 With all this in view, you should make every effort to add virtue to your faith, knowledge to virtue, 6 self-control to knowledge, fortitude to self-control, piety to forti-

tude, 7 brotherly affection to piety, and love to brotherly affection.

8 If you possess and develop these gifts, you will grow actively and effectively in knowledge of our Lord Jesus Christ. 9 Whoever lacks them is wilfully blind; he has forgotten that his past sins were washed away. 10 All the more then, my friends, do your utmost to establish that God has called and chosen you. If you do this, you will never stumble, 11 and there will be rich provision for your entry into the eternal kingdom of our Lord and Saviour Jesus Christ.

12 I shall keep reminding you of all this, although you know it and are well grounded in the truth you possess; 13 yet I think it right to keep on reminding you as long as I still lodge in this body. 14 I know I must soon leave it, as our Lord Jesus Christ told me. 15 But I will do my utmost to ensure that after I am gone you will always be able to call these things to mind.

16 It was not on tales, however cleverly concocted, that we relied when we told you about

---

1.1–2: Salutation.

1.3–15: The writer's purpose and authority. 9: *Sins* are *washed away* at baptism. **12:** *The truth:* Christian doctrine; see Jude 5. **13–14:** Perhaps a reference to the prediction of Jn. 21.18–19. **15:** The view that Mark's Gospel is derived from Peter may be reflected here.

1544

the power of our Lord Jesus Christ and his coming; rather with our own eyes we had witnessed his majesty. [17] He was invested with honour and glory by God the Father, and there came to him from the sublime Presence a voice which said: 'This is my Son, my Beloved, on whom my favour rests.' [18] We ourselves heard this voice when it came from heaven, for we were with him on the sacred mountain.

[19] All this confirms for us the message of the prophets, to which you will do well to attend; it will go on shining like a lamp in a murky place, until day breaks and the morning star rises to illuminate your minds.

[20] BUT first note this: no prophetic writing is a matter for private interpretation. [21] It was not on any human initiative that prophecy came; rather, it was under the compulsion of the Holy Spirit that people spoke as messengers of God.

God's judgement on false teaching

2 IN the past there were also false prophets among the people, just as you also will have false teachers among you. They will introduce their destructive views, disowning the very Master who redeemed them, and bringing swift destruction on their own heads. [2] They will gain many adherents to their dissolute practices, through whom the way of truth will be brought into disrepute. [3] In their greed for money they will trade on your credulity with sheer fabrications.

But judgement has long been in preparation for them; destruction waits for them with unsleeping eyes. [4] God did not spare the angels who sinned, but consigned them to the dark pits of hell, where they are held for judgement. [5] Nor did he spare the world in ancient times (except for Noah, who proclaimed righteousness, and was preserved with seven others), but brought the flood upon that world with its godless people. [6] God reduced the cities of Sodom and Gomorrah to ashes, condemning them to total ruin as an object-lesson for the ungodly in future days. [7] But he rescued Lot, a good man distressed by the dissolute habits of the lawless society in which he lived; [8] day after day every sight and sound of their evil ways tortured that good man's heart. [9] The Lord knows how to rescue the godly from their trials, and to keep the wicked under punishment until the day of judgement.

[10] Above all he will punish those who follow their abominable lusts and flout authority. Reckless and headstrong, they are not afraid to insult celestial beings, [11] whereas angels, for all their superior strength and power, employ no insults in seeking judgement against them before the Lord.

[12] These men are like brute beasts, mere creatures of instinct, born to be caught and killed. They pour abuse upon things they do not understand; they will perish like the beasts, [13] suffering hurt for the hurt they have inflicted. To carouse in broad daylight is their idea of pleasure; while they sit with you at table they are an ugly blot on your company, because they revel in their deceits. [14] They have eyes for nothing but loose women, eyes never resting from sin. They lure the unstable to their ruin; experts in mercenary greed, God's curse is on them! [15] They have abandoned the straight road and gone astray. They have followed in the steps of Balaam son of Bosor, who eagerly accepted payment for doing wrong, [16] but had his offence brought home to him when a dumb beast spoke with a human voice and checked the prophet's madness.

[17] These men are springs that give no water, mists driven by a storm; the place reserved for them is blackest darkness. [18] They utter empty bombast; they use sensual lusts and debauchery as a bait to catch people who have only just begun to escape from their pagan associates. [19] They promise them freedom, but are themselves slaves of corruption; for people are the slaves of whatever has

1:17 **This ... Beloved:** *or* This is my only Son.
2:4 **consigned ... hell:** *some witnesses read* consigned them to darkness and chains in hell.   2:15 **Bosor:** *some witnesses read* Beor.

1.16–3.10: The hope of the Lord's coming is no myth. 16–18: Peter was one of those present at the transfiguration, Matt. 17.1–8. **19:** Christ will dawn as the *morning star* on the *day* of his return. **20–21:** See 3.16 n.

2.1–22: False teachers will be punished. See Jude 4, 5–16 nn. **7–8:** See Gen. 19.4–29. **11:** In Jude 9 the angel Michael is named, but here the reference is more general (see Introduction). **18–22:** New converts are especially vulnerable to false teaching. Backsliders are worse off than are the unconverted. See also Heb. 6.4–6;

mastered them. [20] If they escaped the world's defilements through coming to know our Lord and Saviour Jesus Christ and entangled themselves in them again, and were mastered by them, their last state would be worse than the first. [21] Better for them never to have known the right way, than, having known it, to turn back and abandon the sacred commandment entrusted to them! [22] In their case the proverb has proved true: 'The dog returns to its vomit,' and 'The washed sow wallows in the mud again.'

The coming end

3 THIS, dear friends, is now my second letter to you. In both I have been recalling to you what you already know, to rouse you to honest thought. [2] Remember the predictions made by God's own prophets, and the commandment given by the Lord and Saviour through your apostles.

[3] First of all, note this: in the last days there will come scoffers who live self-indulgent lives; they will mock you and say: [4] 'What has happened to his promised coming? Our fathers have been laid to rest, but still everything goes on exactly as it always has done since the world began.'

[5] In maintaining this they forget that there were heavens and earth long ago, created by God's word out of water and with water; [6] and that the first world was destroyed by water, the water of the flood. [7] By God's word the present heavens and earth are being reserved for burning; they are being kept until the day of judgement when the godless will be destroyed.

[8] Here is something, dear friends, which you must not forget: in the Lord's sight one day is like a thousand years and a thousand years like one day. [9] It is not that the Lord is slow in keeping his promise, as some suppose, but that he is patient with you. It is not his will that any should be lost, but that all should come to repentance.

[10] But the day of the Lord will come like a thief. On that day the heavens will disappear with a great rushing sound, the elements will be dissolved in flames, and the earth with all that is in it will be brought to judgement. [11] Since the whole universe is to dissolve in this way, think what sort of people you ought to be, what devout and dedicated lives you should live! [12] Look forward to the coming of the day of God, and work to hasten it on; that day will set the heavens ablaze until they fall apart, and will melt the elements in flames. [13] Relying on his promise we look forward to new heavens and a new earth, in which justice will be established.

[14] In expectation of all this, my friends, do your utmost to be found at peace with him, unblemished and above reproach. [15] Bear in mind that our Lord's patience is an opportunity for salvation, as Paul, our dear friend and brother, said when he wrote to you with the wisdom God gave him. [16] He does the same in all his other letters, wherever he speaks about this, though they contain some obscure passages, which the ignorant and unstable misinterpret to their own ruin, as they do the other scriptures.

[17] So, dear friends, you have been forewarned. Take care not to let these unprincipled people seduce you with their errors; do not lose your own safe foothold. [18] But grow in grace and in the knowledge of our Lord and Saviour Jesus Christ. To him be glory both now and for all eternity!

3:10 **will be brought to judgement:** *lit.* will be found.

10.26–31. **22:** *Dog returns to its vomit:* see Prov. 26.11.

3.1–10: Predicted events have occurred. See Acts 20.29–30. **1:** *Second letter:* the first is presumed to be 1 Pet. **3–4:** See 2.1–3. **5–7:** See Gen. 1.1–10; chs. 7–8. **8:** Ps. 90.4. **10:** Compare e.g. Matt. 24.43–44; Zeph. 1.18; 3.8.

3.11–18: Exhortations to prepare for the end. 12: See Isa. 34.4. **13:** See e.g. Isa. 65.17; Rev. 21.1ff. **14:** See Jude 24. **15:** See v. 9. Perhaps Paul's letters to the Thessalonians are in mind, or passages like 1 Cor. 1.7–9. **16:** Heretics are false interpreters of the *scriptures* (see 1.19–21), within which Paul's letters are included (see Introduction).

THE FIRST LETTER OF
John

Unlike 2 and 3 John, this book is not a letter but a tract, occasioned by the denial of the reality of the incarnation (2.22; 4.2–3, 15) by some heretical Christians (2.19). These claim to be superior in knowing God (2.3–4), in love for God (4.20), and in communion with God (1.6).

The treatise may well be from the same hand that wrote 2 and 3 John. Its style and themes also recall those of the Fourth Gospel: centrality of the incarnation, the mission of the only Son, the Word (1.1). Still, no mention is made of the Holy Spirit as personal (Jesus is the "one who . . . will plead our cause" in 2.1), or of "glory," or of "judging," all important in the Gospel. This may indicate that the tract had an earlier origin than the Gospel, or that it was written by a different author from the same school of thought. Tradition has associated the tract with Asia Minor and the name of John.

The main body of the book is enclosed between a prologue (1.1–4) and an epilogue (5.13–21). Three aspects of God are developed in concentric circles: God is "Light" (1.5–2.27), "Righteous" (2.28–4.6), "Love" (4.7–5.12).

1 IT was there from the beginning; we have heard it; we have seen it with our own eyes; we looked upon it, and felt it with our own hands: our theme is the Word which gives life. ² This life was made visible; we have seen it and bear our testimony; we declare to you the eternal life which was with the Father and was made visible to us. ³ It is this which we have seen and heard that we declare to you also, in order that you may share with us in a common life, that life which we share with the Father and his Son Jesus Christ. ⁴ We are writing this in order that our joy may be complete.

Fellowship, obedience, and forgiveness

⁵ HERE is the message we have heard from him and pass on to you: God is light, and in him there is no darkness at all. ⁶ If we claim to be sharing in his life while we go on living in darkness, our words and our lives are a lie. ⁷ But if we live in the light as he himself is in the light, then we share a common life, and the blood of Jesus his Son cleanses us from all sin.

⁸ If we claim to be sinless, we are self-deceived and the truth is not in us. ⁹ If we confess our sins, he is just and may be trusted to forgive our sins and cleanse us from every kind of wrongdoing. ¹⁰ If we say we have committed no sin, we make him out to be a liar and his word has no place in us.

2 My children, I am writing this to you so that you should not commit sin. But if anybody does, we have in Jesus Christ one who is acceptable to God and will plead our

1.1–4: The prologue. 1: The impersonal *it* refers to *the Word which gives life,* which may denote the gospel, since *Word* is not as clearly a title for Jesus Christ as in Jn. (see Jn. 1.1, 14 nn.). However, *from the beginning* (the creation) suggests the preexistence of Christ (see 2.13–14). As in Jn. 1.14, the pronoun *we* indicates the apostolic witnesses, who attest their personal experience of Jesus' earthy life. The *theme* is that announced in Jn. 1.1–18. 2: *This life,* described as *eternal, which was with* God (see Jn. 1.1–2), has become *visible* through the incarnation (see Jn. 1.14). 3: The key Gk. term behind the phrase *share . . . in a common life* is found only here and in vv. 6–7 in Johannine literature, but is characteristic of Paul (e.g. 1 Cor. 1.9). However, the idea of *life which we share with* God and Christ is very Johannine (see Jn. 5.26; 14.6). 4: The *joy* communicated by Christ is mentioned in Jn. 15.11; 16.22; 17.13.

1.5–2.27: God is Light. 5: *Light* and *darkness,* a frequent antithesis in Jn., signify truth and error and reflect a moral dualism (see Jn. 1.5; 3.19). 7: The *common life* is not created by human goodwill, but by Christ's redemptive act (see Rev. 1.5). 9: James 5.16 also urges the confession of *sins.* 2.1: *One who . . . will plead* cause with the Father. ²He is himself a sacrifice to atone for our sins, and not ours only but the sins of the whole world.

³It is by keeping God's commands that we can be sure we know him. ⁴Whoever says, 'I know him,' but does not obey his commands, is a liar and the truth is not in him; ⁵but whoever is obedient to his word, in him the love of God is truly made perfect. This is how we can be sure that we are in him: ⁶whoever claims to be dwelling in him must live as Christ himself lived.

⁷Dear friends, it is no new command that I am sending you, but an old command which you have had from the beginning; the old command is the instruction which you have already received. ⁸Yet because the darkness is passing away and the true light already shining, it is a new command that I write and it is true in Christ's life and in yours.

⁹Whoever says, 'I am in the light,' but hates his fellow-Christian, is still in darkness. ¹⁰He who loves his fellow-Christian dwells in light: there is no cause of stumbling in him. ¹¹But anyone who hates his fellow is in darkness; he walks in the dark and has no idea where he is going, because the darkness has made him blind.

¹²I write to you, children, because your
   sins have been forgiven for his sake.
¹³I write to you, fathers, because you
   know him who is and has been from
   the beginning.
I write to you, young men, because you
   have conquered the evil one.

I have written to you, children, because
   you know the Father.
¹⁴I have written to you, fathers, because
   you know him who is and has been
   from the beginning.

I have written to you, young men,
   because you are strong; God's word
   remains in you, and you have
   conquered the evil one.

¹⁵Do not set your hearts on the world or what is in it. Anyone who loves the world does not love the Father. ¹⁶Everything in the world, all that panders to the appetites or entices the eyes, all the arrogance based on wealth, these spring not from the Father but from the world. ¹⁷That world with all its allurements is passing away, but those who do God's will remain for ever.

The danger of false teaching

¹⁸CHILDREN, this is the last hour! You were told that an antichrist was to come. Well, many antichrists have already appeared, proof to us that this is indeed the last hour. ¹⁹They left our ranks, but never really belonged to us; if they had, they would have stayed with us. They left so that it might be clear that none of them belong to us.

²⁰What is more, you have been anointed by the Holy One, and so you all have knowledge. ²¹It is not because you are ignorant of the truth that I have written to you, but because you do know it, and know that lies never come from the truth.

²²Anyone who denies that Jesus is the Christ is nothing but a liar. He is the antichrist, for he denies both the Father and the Son: ²³to deny the Son is to be without the Father; to acknowledge the Son is to have the Father too. ²⁴You must therefore keep hold of what you heard at the beginning; if what you heard then still dwells in you, you will

2:9 **fellow-Christian:** *lit.* brother.   2:19 **none of them:** *or* not all of them.   2:20 **you all have knowledge:** *some witnesses read* you have all knowledge.

our cause (i.e. an advocate): the Gospel of John (e.g. 14.16–17) calls the Holy Spirit the "advocate." **2:** Only here and at 4.10 in Johannine literature is Jesus called *a sacrifice to atone for our sins.* The meaning is that by Jesus' death (see 1.7) God has revealed gracious, loving forgiveness of humanity. The atoning power of Christ's death is limitless. **5:** John 14.15 and 15.10 assert that Christian love implies obedience. **7–8:** The *old* yet *new command:* see Jn. 13.34. **16:** *The world* here is opposed to God (see Jn. 3.16 n.) and is exemplified by three common evil tendencies in human beings: lust, avarice, arrogant self-sufficiency. **18:** *Antichrist,* found only in 1 and 2 Jn., is a personification of "enmity to Christ." **20–21:** The presence of the Spirit in the Christian brings *knowledge* of divine *truth* (see Jn. 14.26; 16.13–15). **22–23:** The denial of the incarnation is the basic yourselves dwell both in the Son and in the Father. [25] And this is the promise that he himself gave us, the promise of eternal life.

[26] So much for those who would mislead you. [27] But as for you, the anointing which you received from him remains with you; you need no other teacher, but you learn all you need to know from his anointing, which is true and no lie. Dwell in him as he taught you to do.

[28] Even now, children, dwell in him, so that when he appears we may be confident and unashamed before him at his coming. [29] You know that God is righteous; then recognize that everyone who does what is right is his child.

How Christians live together

3 CONSIDER how great is the love which the Father has bestowed on us in calling us his children! For that is what we are. The reason why the world does not recognize us is that it has not known him. [2] Dear friends, we are now God's children; what we shall be has not yet been disclosed, but we know that when Christ appears we shall be like him, because we shall see him as he is. [3] As he is pure, everyone who has grasped this hope makes himself pure.

[4] To commit sin is to break God's law: for sin is lawlessness. [5] You know that Christ appeared in order to take away sins, and in him there is no sin. [6] No one who dwells in him sins any more; the sinner has neither seen him nor known him.

[7] Children, do not be misled: anyone who does what is right is righteous, just as Christ is righteous; [8] anyone who sins is a child of the devil, for the devil has been a sinner from the first; and the Son of God appeared for the very purpose of undoing the devil's work. [9] No child of God commits sin, because the divine seed remains in him; indeed because he is God's child he cannot sin. [10] This is what

shows who are God's children and who are the devil's: anyone who fails to do what is right or love his fellow-Christians is not a child of God.

[11] The message you have heard from the beginning is that we should love one another. [12] Do not be like Cain, who was a child of the evil one and murdered his brother. And why did he murder him? Because his own actions were wrong, and his brother's were right.

[13] Friends, do not be surprised if the world hates you. [14] We know we have crossed over from death to life, because we love our fellow-Christians. Anyone who does not love is still in the realm of death, [15] for everyone who hates a fellow-Christian is a murderer, and murderers, as you know, do not have eternal life dwelling within them. [16] This is how we know what love is: Christ gave his life for us. And we in our turn must give our lives for our fellow-Christians. [17] But if someone who possesses the good things of this world sees a fellow-Christian in need and withholds compassion from him, how can it be said that the love of God dwells in him?

[18] Children, love must not be a matter of theory or talk; it must be true love which shows itself in action. [19] This is how we shall know that we belong to the realm of truth, and reassure ourselves in his sight [20] where conscience condemns us; for God is greater than our conscience and knows all.

[21] My dear friends, if our conscience does not condemn us, then we can approach God with confidence, [22] and obtain from him whatever we ask, because we are keeping his commands and doing what he approves. [23] His command is that we should give our allegiance to his Son Jesus Christ and love

3:2 **we are ... like him:** or we are God's children, though he has not yet appeared; what we shall be we know, for when he does appear we shall be like him. **when Christ appears:** or when it is disclosed.
3:19–20 **reassure ... than our conscience:** or convince ourselves in his sight that even if our conscience condemns us, God is greater than our conscience.

heresy attacked by the author. **27:** Jeremiah 31.33–34 promises a new covenant when human beings will be divinely taught and *need no other teacher.*

2.28–4.6: God is the Holy One. 28: This is the only place in the Johannine writings which speaks unambiguously of Christ's (future) coming; but see Jn. 16.16 n. **3.1–3:** *The love that the Father has bestowed* by Jesus' redemptive mission has made the Christian one of God's children; yet being such children remains a mystery and a *hope* until Christ appears. **9:** *The divine seed* is probably the Spirit of v. 24 and 4.13. The Christian *cannot sin* in the fundamental sense because of continuing union with God (v. 6); that, in fact, the Christian commits sin is affirmed in 1.8–10. **12:** *Cain:* Gen. 4.3–8. **19–20:** A life spent in loving service for others proves our union with God, whose love and mercy keeps us from despair, even if our *conscience* one another, as Christ commanded us. ²⁴Those who keep his commands dwell in him and he dwells in them. And our certainty that he dwells in us comes from the Spirit he has given us.

Spirits of truth and error

4 My dear friends, do not trust every spirit, but test the spirits, to see whether they are from God; for there are many false prophets about in the world. ²The way to recognize the Spirit of God is this: every spirit which acknowledges that Jesus Christ has come in the flesh is from God, ³and no spirit is from God which does not acknowledge Jesus. This is the spirit of antichrist; you have been warned that it was to come, and now here it is, in the world already!

⁴Children, you belong to God's family, and you have the mastery over these false prophets, because God who inspires you is greater than the one who inspires the world. ⁵They belong to that world, and so does their teaching; that is why the world listens to them. ⁶But we belong to God and whoever knows God listens to us, while whoever does not belong to God refuses to listen to us. That is how we can distinguish the spirit of truth from the spirit of error.

Love one another

⁷My dear friends, let us love one another, because the source of love is God. Everyone who loves is a child of God and knows God, ⁸but the unloving know nothing of God, for God is love. ⁹This is how he showed his love among us: he sent his only Son into the world that we might have life through him. ¹⁰This is what love really is: not that we have loved God, but that he loved us and sent his Son as a sacrifice to atone for our sins. ¹¹If God thus loved us, my dear friends, we also must love one another. ¹²God has never been seen by anyone, but if we love one another, he him-

self dwells in us; his love is brought to perfection within us.

¹³This is how we know that we dwell in him and he dwells in us: he has imparted his Spirit to us. ¹⁴Moreover, we have seen for ourselves, and we are witnesses, that the Father has sent the Son to be the Saviour of the world. ¹⁵If anyone acknowledges that Jesus is God's Son, God dwells in him and he in God. ¹⁶Thus we have come to know and believe in the love which God has for us.

God is love; he who dwells in love is dwelling in God, and God in him. ¹⁷This is how love has reached its perfection among us, so that we may have confidence on the day of judgement; and this we can have, because in this world we are as he is. ¹⁸In love there is no room for fear; indeed perfect love banishes fear. For fear has to do with punishment, and anyone who is afraid has not attained to love in its perfection. ¹⁹We love because he loved us first. ²⁰But if someone says, 'I love God,' while at the same time hating his fellow-Christian, he is a liar. If he does not love a fellow-Christian whom he has seen, he is incapable of loving God whom he has not seen. ²¹We have this command from Christ: whoever loves God must love his fellow-Christian too.

Obedience to the truth

5 EVERYONE who believes that Jesus is the Christ is a child of God. To love the parent means to love his child. ²It follows that when we love God and obey his commands we love his children too. ³For to love God is to keep his commands; and these are not burdensome, ⁴because every child of God overcomes the world. Now, the victory by which the world is overcome is our faith, ⁵for who is victor over the world but he who believes that Jesus is the Son of God?

⁶This is he whose coming was with water and blood: Jesus Christ. He came, not by the water alone, but both by the water and by the

---

condemns us. **4.1–6:** The author's admonition to *test the spirits* is an example of the church's distinction between types of "spiritual phenomena" (see 1 Cor. 12.3; 1 Thess. 5.19–22).

    4.7–5.21: God is Love. While 1 Jn. in many respects displays a less sophisticated theology than the Fourth Gospel, this cannot be said of its understanding of Christian love. **8–10:** The statement that *God is love* is not a definition of God, but a description of God's redemptive action in Christ. **11–12:** The way to "see" the invisible God (compare Jn. 1.14, 18) in this life is to *love one another.* **14–16:** The authenticity of our love is derived from our grasp of the reality of the incarnation and our redemption by Christian faith. The theme of the mutual indwelling of God and the believer is characteristically Johannine (see 3.24; Jn. 15.5). **5.1:** Faith blood; and to this the Spirit bears witness, because the Spirit is truth. 7–8 In fact there are three witnesses, the Spirit, the water, and the blood, and these three are in agreement. 9 We accept human testimony, but surely the testimony of God is stronger, and the testimony of God is the witness he has borne to his Son. 10 He who believes in the Son of God has the testimony in his own heart, but he who does not believe God makes him out to be a liar by refusing to accept God's witness to his Son. 11 This is the witness: God has given us eternal life, and this life is found in his Son. 12 He who possesses the Son possesses life; he who does not possess the Son of God does not possess life.

Final instructions and encouragement

13 YOU HAVE given your allegiance to the Son of God; this letter is to assure you that you have eternal life.

14 We can approach God with this confi-dence: if we make requests which accord with his will, he listens to us; 15 and if we know that our requests are heard, we also know that all we ask of him is ours.

16 If anyone sees a fellow-Christian com-mitting a sin which is not a deadly sin, he should intercede for him, and God will grant him life — that is, to those who are not guilty of deadly sin. There is such a thing as deadly sin, and I do not suggest that he should pray about that. 17 Although all wrongdoing is sin, not all sin is deadly sin.

18 We know that no child of God commits sin; he is kept safe by the Son of God, and the evil one cannot touch him.

19 We know that we are of God's family, but that the whole world lies in the power of the evil one.

20 We know that the Son of God has come and given us understanding to know the true God; indeed we are in him who is true, since we are in his Son Jesus Christ. He is the true God and eternal life. 21 Children, be on your guard against idols.

in the incarnate Son as *the Christ* enables us to recognize others as God's children and leads to true Christian love. **4:** The acknowledgment by *our faith* of Jesus' true character (v. 5) is the means *by which the world* (which opposes God) *is overcome.* **6:** Jesus was proclaimed the Son of God after his baptism with water (Matt. 3.17); but Jn. 19.34–35 attests that *by water and blood* Jesus was revealed as the Savior. **7–8:** An ancient trinitarian formula (which identifies "Father, Word, and Spirit" as "heavenly witnesses") was a gloss inserted into this passage in some Latin versions. **13:** This statement of purpose recalls Jn. 20.31. **14–15:** Christian *confidence* in being heard is an important element of petitionary prayer. **16:** The *deadly sin,* not specified by the author, is of such a nature as to defy forgiveness, possibly that cited in 2.18–29.

THE SECOND LETTER OF

John

This is a real letter, written to a specific Christian community by "the Elder." Someone of authority in one local church, the author feels a certain responsibility for the faith of another community. It is all but impossible to discover the date, place of origin, or destination of this note. Its purpose is to alert the church addressed to the dangers of the heretical denial of the incarnation. To counter these dangers, it urges fidelity to the traditional commandment of mutual love, which involves obedience to apostolic authority. Stylistic similarities suggest that this writer also composed 3 John and also may be the author of 1 John.

Truth and love

THE Elder to the Lady chosen by God and to her children whom I love in the truth, and not I alone but all who know the truth. ² We love you for the sake of the truth that dwells among us and will be with us for ever.

³ Grace, mercy, and peace will be with us from God the Father and from Jesus Christ the Son of the Father, in truth and love.

⁴ I was very glad to find that some of your children are living by the truth, in accordance with the command we have received from the Father. ⁵ And now, Lady, I have a request to make of you. Do not think I am sending a new command; I am recalling the one we have had from the beginning: I ask that we love one another. ⁶ What love means is to live according to the commands of God. This is the command that was given you from the beginning, to be your rule of life.

⁷ Many deceivers have gone out into the world, people who do not acknowledge Jesus Christ as coming in the flesh. Any such person is the deceiver and antichrist. ⁸ See to it that you do not lose what we have worked for, but receive your reward in full.

⁹ Anyone who does not stand by the teaching about Christ, but goes beyond it, does not possess God; he who stands by it possesses both the Father and the Son. ¹⁰ If anyone comes to you who does not bring this teaching, do not admit him to your house or give him any greeting; ¹¹ for he who greets him becomes an accomplice in his evil deeds.

¹² I have much to write to you, but I do not care to put it down on paper. Rather, I hope to visit you and talk with you face to face, so that our joy may be complete. ¹³ The children of your Sister, chosen by God, send you greetings.

1–3: Address and wish. 1: *Elder:* a term used elsewhere to designate the leader(s) of a local church (see Acts 14.23; 20.17; 1 Tim. 5.17; Ti. 1.5). The community addressed is called *the Lady,* which in Gk. is the feminine equivalent of "Lord." The title may be related to the familiar imagery of the church as the "bride of Christ" (see 2 Cor. 11.2; Eph. 5.26–27; Rev. 19.7). The phrase *chosen by God* (used here of the church) indicates Jesus in Jn. 1.34. **2:** The *truth* is the divine presence; its possession is assured by fidelity to the *teaching about Christ* (v. 9).

4–12: The body of the letter. 4: Since only *some* are *living by the truth,* the heresy has made serious inroads into the community. **5:** The writer's remedy is faithfulness to the *command* of mutual love (see 1 Jn. 2.7–10; Jn. 13.34). **6:** This association of *love* with *the commands of God* is characteristic of Johannine thought (see Jn. 14.23). **7:** See 1 Jn. 2.22. *Antichrist:* see 1 Jn. 2.18 n. **9:** The heretic *goes beyond it* by minimizing the reality of the incarnation.

13: Final greeting. *The children of your Sister:* the members of the Elder's church.

THE THIRD LETTER OF
John

This genuine letter is addressed to an individual member of a Christian church whose leader, Diotrephes, has refused to receive the emissaries of the Elder led by Demetrius. Gaius, the addressee, a man of probity, is asked to provide hospitality for Demetrius and his companions. The author is the same Elder who wrote 2 John, as the vocabulary and style indicate; also, the two letters are of equal length.

Trouble in the church

THE Elder to dear Gaius, whom I love in the truth.

² Dear friend, above all I pray that things go well with you, and that you may enjoy good health: I know it is well with your soul. ³ I was very glad when some fellow-Christians arrived and told me of your faithfulness to the truth; indeed you live by the truth. ⁴ Nothing gives me greater joy than to hear that my children are living by the truth.

⁵ Dear friend, you show a fine loyalty in what you do for our fellow-Christians, though they are strangers to you. ⁶ They have testified to your kindness before the congregation here. Please help them on their journey in a manner worthy of the God we serve. ⁷ It was for love of Christ's name that they went out; and they would accept nothing from unbelievers. ⁸ Therefore we ought to support such people, and so play our part in spreading the truth.

⁹ I wrote to the congregation, but Diotrephes, who enjoys taking the lead, will have nothing to do with us. ¹⁰ So when I come, I will draw attention to the things he is doing: he lays nonsensical and spiteful charges against us; not content with that, he refuses to receive fellow-Christians himself, and interferes with those who would receive them, and tries to expel them from the congregation.

¹¹ Dear friend, follow good examples, not bad ones. The well-doer is a child of God; the evildoer has never seen God.

¹² Demetrius is well spoken of by everyone, and even by the truth itself. I add my testimony, and you know that my testimony is true.

¹³ I had much to write to you, but I do not care to set it down with pen and ink. ¹⁴ I hope to see you very soon, when we will talk face to face. Peace be with you. Your friends here send you greetings. Greet each of our friends by name.

1–2: Address and prayer. 1: *Gaius,* an exemplary Christian, has already aided itinerant preachers (v. 6). To *love in the truth* is to love as a Christian.

3–14: The body of the letter. 4: In 2 Jn. 4 the phrase *living by the truth* means obedience to God. **5:** The writer recommends Demetrius (v. 12) and his associates to Gaius' care as *our fellow-Christians.* **9:** *Diotrephes* is not heretical but he is a foe of the Elder, overambitious, unjust, and uncharitable. **11:** The Christian *well-doer* is called *a child of God* in 1 Jn. 3.9. **13–14:** See 2 Jn. 12–13. The note ends with a wish of *peace,* the sum total of all Christ's blessings.

A LETTER OF

Jude

Most New Testament letters are addressed to one or more specific congregations. This author, however, writes to all Christians. Following the salutation (vv. 1–2) the author gives reasons for writing: to urge Christians everywhere to defend the faith against false teaching (v. 3) and to oppose "the enemies of religion" (v. 4). In vv. 5–16 the effectiveness of God's judgment of evil is stressed, while in vv. 17–23 the readers are urged to take action to prevent themselves and others from falling into error. An impressive doxology (vv. 24–25) gives assurance of God's aid in holding fast to the faith.

Although concerned to safeguard right doctrine, the author offers no systematic refutation of false teaching, but rather condemns the immorality of those who espouse it. A similar tactic and some of the same points are present in 2 Peter (see Introduction there). The author calls himself "Jude" the "brother of James," and probably means for the readers to infer that he is therefore one of the brothers of Jesus himself (see Matt. 13.55; Mk. 6.3). Most scholars, however, believe that the style, content, and probable date of this tract (late first or early second century) require the conclusion that Jude's name has been used by a later writer to lend authority to this urgent appeal.

The danger of false belief

FROM Jude, servant of Jesus Christ and brother of James, to those whom God has called, who live in the love of God the Father and are kept safe for the coming of Jesus Christ.

² Mercy, peace, and love be yours in fullest measure.

³ My friends, I was fully intending to write to you about the salvation we share, when I found it necessary to take up my pen and urge you to join in the struggle for that faith which God entrusted to his people once for all. ⁴ Certain individuals have wormed their way in, the very people whom scripture long ago marked down for the sentence they are now incurring. They are enemies of religion; they pervert the free favour of our God into licentiousness, disowning Jesus Christ, our only Master and Lord.

⁵ You already know all this, but let me re-mind you how the Lord, having once for all delivered his people out of Egypt, later destroyed those who did not believe. ⁶ Remember too those angels who were not content to maintain the dominion assigned to them, but abandoned their proper dwelling-place; God is holding them, bound in darkness with everlasting chains, for judgement on the great day. ⁷ Remember Sodom and Gomorrah and the neighbouring towns; like the angels, they committed fornication and indulged in unnatural lusts; and in eternal fire they paid the penalty, a warning for all.

⁸ In the same way these deluded dreamers continue to defile their bodies, flout authority, and insult celestial beings. ⁹ Not even the archangel Michael, when he was disputing with the devil for possession of Moses' body,

1 **kept ... coming:** or in the safe keeping.
4 **disowning ... Lord:** or disowning our one and only Master, and Jesus Christ our Lord.   5 **the Lord:** some witnesses read Jesus; others read God.

1–2: Salutation. See Introduction.

3–4: Preface. 3: The *faith* is the Christian doctrinal tradition entrusted to God's people (perhaps a specific reference to the apostles). **4:** A warning against *certain* false teachers who, in particular, deny that Jesus is *Master and Lord:* see 2 Jn. 7. *Scripture:* see vv. 14–15 n., 17–18 n.

5–16: The judgment of God. 5: See Num. 14.11–35. **6:** See Gen. 6.1–4; Deut. 32.8; *1 Enoch* (an ancient noncanonical book) chs. 6–10; 18.14–16; 21.2. **7:** See Gen. 19.23–25; Deut. 29.23; Wisd. 10.6. **8:** Angelic powers, in this writer's view, deserve respect; contrast Eph. 1.21–22; Col. 2.15–19. **9:** The literary source of presumed to condemn him in insulting words, but said, 'May the Lord rebuke you!' [10] But these people pour abuse on whatever they do not understand; the things that, like brute beasts, they do understand by their senses prove their undoing. [11] Alas for them! They have followed the way of Cain; for profit they have plunged into Balaam's error; they have rebelled like Korah, and they share his fate.

[12] These people are a danger at your love-feasts with their shameless carousals. They are shepherds who take care only of themselves. They are clouds carried along by a wind without giving rain, trees fruitless in autumn, dead twice over and pulled up by the roots. [13] They are wild sea waves, foaming with disgraceful deeds; they are stars that have wandered from their courses, and the place reserved for them is an eternity of blackest darkness.

[14] It was against them that Enoch, the seventh in descent from Adam, prophesied when he said: 'I saw the Lord come with his myriads of angels, [15] to bring all mankind to judgement and to convict all the godless of every godless deed they had committed, and of every defiant word they had spoken against him, godless sinners that they are.'

[16] They are a set of grumblers and malcontents. They follow their lusts. Bombast comes rolling from their lips, and they court favour to gain their ends. [17] But you, my friends, should remember the predictions made by the apostles of our Lord Jesus Christ. [18] They said to you: 'In the final age there will be those who mock at religion and follow their own ungodly lusts.'

[19] These people create divisions; they are worldly and unspiritual. [20] But you, my friends, must make your most sacred faith the foundation of your lives. Continue to pray in the power of the Holy Spirit. [21] Keep yourselves in the love of God, and look forward to the day when our Lord Jesus Christ in his mercy will give eternal life.

[22] There are some doubting souls who need your pity. [23] Others you should save by snatching them from the flames. For others your pity must be mixed with fear; hate the very clothing that is contaminated with sensuality.

[24] Now to the One who can keep you from falling and set you in the presence of his glory, jubilant and above reproach, [25] to the only God our Saviour, be glory and majesty, power and authority, through Jesus Christ our Lord, before all time, now, and for evermore. Amen.

9 **to condemn . . . words:** or to charge him with blasphemy.
19 **These . . . unspiritual:** or These people draw a line between spiritual and unspiritual persons, although they themselves are unspiritual, not spiritual.
23 **Others you . . . fear:** some witnesses read There are some whom you should snatch from the flames. Show pity to doubting souls with fear.

the legend referred to is now lost, but perhaps stood in the incompletely preserved writing, "Assumption of Moses." **11:** *Cain* symbolizes lust and self-indulgence (e.g. Wisd. 10.3). *Balaam's error* was covetousness (Num. chs. 22–24); *Korah* led a rebellion against Moses and Aaron (Num. ch. 16). **12–13:** *Love-feasts* were church meals probably separate from the "Lord's Supper." *Dead twice over:* see Rev. 20.14; 21.8. For other images used here, see Prov. 25.14; Isa. 14.12–15; 57.20; the nonbiblical book *1 Enoch* 18.12–16; 21.3ff. **14–15:** See the nonbiblical book *1 Enoch* 1.1–9; 5.4; 27.2; 60.8; 93.2.

17–23: The need for right doctrine. 17–18: See e.g. Paul in Acts 20.29–30. **20:** *Sacred faith:* see v. 3 n. **21–22:** *The day* of Christ's return will bring both mercy and judgment. **23:** Fleshly lusts should be despised; see Zech. 3.2–7.

24–25: Doxology. See Rom. 16.25–27.

The Revelation

OF JOHN

The Revelation of John encourages Christians to keep faith in the face of trial and persecution. The author is a Christian prophet, John, who is persecuted himself and writes from exile on the island of Patmos in the Aegean Sea to churches in what is now western Turkey. He often employs the visionary and symbolic language characteristic of apocalyptic ("unveiling," revelatory) literature to give his readers confidence that God, not Satan or the Roman emperor, is the Lord of history. Though there are symbolic images that seem to refer to Nero (54–68 C.E.) and parts may have been written before the fall of Jerusalem in 70 C.E., the book in its present form probably was written during the reign of Domitian (81–96 C.E.), a period when emperor worship was geographically extensive and coercive.

Among New Testament writings, Revelation is unique as a thoroughly apocalyptic document; it has forerunners in parts of such Old Testament books as Daniel, Isaiah, and Zechariah. Its very structure and language seem strongly influenced by Ezekiel. Like other apocalyptic writings composed in times of crisis and danger and portraying a struggle between God and God's adversaries, Revelation veils its message to hide it from pagan foes. Yet, the purpose of the symbols is to unveil or reveal to believers the ultimate divine victory and to encourage their loyalty to God. Steeped in Old Testament references, many of the seemingly cryptic statements are clarified when the reader consults these Scriptures.

The structure of Revelation is dominated by series of sevens, the biblical number of fullness or completeness. In powerful imagery and sometimes moving liturgical language, history is portrayed as unfolding toward that ultimate fullness of God's triumph in a new heaven and new earth. God and the Lamb (Jesus Christ) are "the first and the last." To them belong "praise and honor, glory and might forever." Such a message, though rooted in the first century, has been spiritually uplifting to poets, musicians, artists, and ordinary Christians through the ages.

1 THIS is the revelation of Jesus Christ, which God gave him so that he might show his servants what must soon take place. He made it known by sending his angel to his servant John, ² who in telling all that he saw has borne witness to the word of God and to the testimony of Jesus Christ.

³ Happy is the one who reads aloud the words of this prophecy, and happy those who listen if they take to heart what is here written; for the time of fulfilment is near.

Christ's messages to seven churches

⁴ JOHN, to the seven churches in the province of Asia.

Grace be to you and peace, from him who is, who was, and who is to come, from the

1.1–3: The foreword. The opening declares the ultimate source of the revelation, its purpose (to *show . . . what must soon take place*), and the manner of its mediation to John (see 22.6, 16). 1: *Servants* (lit. slaves) is a recurrent way of speaking of God's agents (compare Amos 3.7). The delivery of the revelation by an *angel* reflects the motif in postexilic prophecy that God's distant majesty required mediating messengers (see Zech. 1.19). 2: Here *the word of God* means God's message; in 19.13 (see Jn. 1.1) Jesus is the Word of God. 3: *Happy* (or, blessed) introduces one of seven blessings in Rev.; here (as in 22.7) it blesses those who read and hear the revelation in public worship.

1.4–8: Greeting, confession, and doxology. 4: The traditional greeting of *grace* and *peace* (see Rom. 1.7 n.) is expanded into a confession of God's past, present, and future reign, as well as of the lordship of Jesus Christ; they, not Satan or Caesar, are the true rulers of history. The *seven spirits* (see 3.1; 4.5; 5.6) point to the fullness seven spirits before his throne; [5] and from Jesus Christ, the faithful witness, the first-born from the dead and ruler of the kings of the earth.

To him who loves us and has set us free from our sins with his blood, [6] who has made of us a royal house to serve as the priests of his God and Father—to him be glory and dominion for ever! Amen.

[7] Look, he is coming with the clouds; everyone shall see him, including those who pierced him; and all the peoples of the world shall lament in remorse. So it shall be. Amen.

[8] 'I am the Alpha and the Omega,' says the Lord God, who is, who was, and who is to come, the sovereign Lord of all.

[9] I, John, your brother, who share with you in the suffering, the sovereignty, and the endurance which are ours in Jesus, was on the island called Patmos because I had preached God's word and borne my testimony to Jesus. [10] On the Lord's day the Spirit came upon me; and I heard behind me a loud voice, like the sound of a trumpet, [11] which said, 'Write down in a book what you see and send it to the seven churches: to Ephesus, Smyrna, Pergamum, Thyatira, Sardis, Philadelphia, and Laodicea.' [12] I turned to see whose voice it was that spoke to me; and when I turned I saw seven lampstands of gold. [13] Among the lamps was a figure like a man, in a robe that came to his feet, with a golden girdle round his breast. [14] His hair was as white as snow-white wool, and his eyes flamed like fire; [15] his feet were like burnished bronze refined in a furnace, and his voice was like the sound of a mighty torrent. [16] In his right hand he held seven stars, and from his mouth came a sharp, two-edged sword; his face shone like the sun in full strength.

[17] When I saw him, I fell at his feet as though I were dead. But he laid his right hand on me and said, 'Do not be afraid. I am the first and the last, [18] and I am the living One; I was dead and now I am alive for evermore, and I hold the keys of death and Hades. [19] Write down therefore what you have seen, what is now, and what is to take place hereafter.

[20] 'This is the secret meaning of the seven stars you saw in my right hand, and of the seven gold lamps: the seven stars are the angels of the seven churches, and the seven lamps are the seven churches themselves.

2 'To THE angel of the church at Ephesus write:

'"These are the words of the One who holds the seven stars in his right hand, who

---

of God's reigning power (*throne.*) **5:** *Faithful witness* (or, *martyr*) implies Jesus' faithfulness unto death. *Firstborn from the dead:* see Rom. 8.29; Col. 1.15, 18; compare Ps. 89.27. *Ruler of the kings:* see 11.15–18; 19.16. **6:** *Royal house* and *priests* apply OT political and cultic designations of Israel to Christians; see Exod. 19.6; Isa. 61.6; compare Rev. 5.10; 1 Pet. 2.9. **7:** *Coming with the clouds:* see Dan. 7.13; Matt. 24.30. *Pierced, lament:* Zech. 12.10; compare Jn. 19.37. *So it shall be* translates the Heb. *Amen.* **8:** *Alpha* and *Omega* (applied again to God in 21.6 and to Jesus in 22.13) are the first and last letters of the Gk. alphabet; compare "first" and "last" in 1.17; Isa. 44.6; 48.12.

1.9–20: John's vision and commission. 10: *The Lord's day:* Sunday. *The Spirit came upon me* reflects ecstatic experience; see Ezek. 3.12. *Trumpet:* compare Exod. 19.16, 19; as related to the end-time see Matt. 24.37; 1 Cor. 15.52; 1 Thess. 4.16. **11:** *Write down:* compare Isa. 30.8. **12:** *Seven . . . lampstands* (see Exod. 25.37; Zech. 4.2) are identified in v. 20 as the seven churches. These churches, named in v. 11, stood on a great road that circumscribed the west-central region of the province of Asia. **13–15:** *Like a man* (lit. "Son of Man"; see 14.14): a figure in Dan. 7.13; here and especially in the Gospels it is applied to Jesus; the description of him (see Dan. 7.9–10, 12–13; 10.5–6; Ezek. 1.24–8; 43.2) expresses priesthood, kingship, eternity, omniscience, strength. **16:** *Right hand* is a symbol of power; Christ, not Caesar, holds the *seven stars* (identified in v. 20 as the angels, perhaps guardian angels, of the churches); the stars are perhaps contrasted with the seven stars which appear on Roman coins as a symbol of imperial power. *Sword* suggests the power of his word; see Isa. 11.4; 49.2; Eph. 6.17; Heb. 4.12. *Shining face:* compare Dan. 10.6; Matt. 13.43; 17.2. **17:** *Fell at his feet:* compare Dan. 10.9; Ezek. 1.28; Matt. 17.6; Lk. 5.8. **17–18:** The affirmation that Christ is *first* and *last* (see v. 8 n.) here includes his victory over death.

2.1–3.22: The seven letters. Each contains initial descriptions of Christ, followed by encouragement, admonition, and promise.

2.1–7: Ephesus: Roman Asia's chief city. **1:** *Angel:* see 1.20. *One:* the risen Christ; see 1.17–18. *Stars:* see walks among the seven gold lamps: ²I know what you are doing, how you toil and endure. I know you cannot abide wicked people; you have put to the test those who claim to be apostles but are not, and you have found them to be false. ³Endurance you have; you have borne up in my cause and have never become weary. ⁴However, I have this against you: the love you felt at first you have now lost. ⁵Think from what a height you have fallen; repent, and do as once you did. If you do not, I will come to you and remove your lamp from its place. ⁶Yet you have this much in your favour: you detest as I do the practices of the Nicolaitans. ⁷You have ears, so hear what the Spirit says to the churches! To those who are victorious I will give the right to eat from the tree of life that stands in the garden of God."

⁸'To the angel of the church at Smyrna write:

' "These are the words of the First and the Last, who was dead and came to life again: ⁹I know how hard pressed and poor you are, but in reality you are rich. I know how you are slandered by those who claim to be Jews but are not; they are really a synagogue of Satan. ¹⁰Do not be afraid of the sufferings to come. The devil will throw some of you into prison, to be put to the test, and for ten days you will be hard pressed. Be faithful till death, and I will give you the crown of life. ¹¹You have ears, so hear what the Spirit says to the churches! Those who are victorious cannot be harmed by the second death."

¹²'To the angel of the church at Pergamum write:

' "These are the words of the One who has the sharp, two-edged sword: ¹³I know where you live; it is where Satan is enthroned. Yet you are holding fast to my cause, and did not deny your faith in me even at the time when Antipas, my faithful witness, was put to death in your city, where Satan has his home. ¹⁴But I have a few matters to bring against you. You have in Pergamum some that hold to the teaching of Balaam, who taught Balak to put temptation in the way of the Israelites; he encouraged them to eat food sacrificed to idols and to commit fornication. ¹⁵In the same way you also have some who hold to the teaching of the Nicolaitans. ¹⁶So repent! If you do not, I will come to you quickly and make war on them with the sword that comes out of my mouth. ¹⁷You have ears, so hear what the Spirit says to the churches! To anyone who is victorious I will give some of the hidden manna; I will also give him a white stone, and on it will be written a new name, known only to him who receives it."

¹⁸'To the angel of the church at Thyatira write:

' "These are the words of the Son of God, whose eyes flame like fire, and whose feet are like burnished bronze: ¹⁹I know what you are doing, your love and faithfulness, your service and your endurance; indeed of late you have done even better than you did at first. ²⁰But I have this against you: you tolerate that Jezebel, the woman who claims to be a

1.16 n., 1.20. *Lamps* (lampstands): see 1.12 n., 1.20. **2:** *Apostles:* missionaries; on *false* apostles, compare 2 Cor. 11.12–15. **4:** *Love . . . at first:* initial, waning enthusiasm; see Jer. 2.2; Hos. 2.14–16. **6:** The *Nicolaitans* apparently taught that Christians were free to eat meat offered to idols and to practice immorality; see vv. 14–15. **7:** *The tree of life* (Gen. 2.9; 3.22) suggests paradise restored; see 22.14.

2.8–11: Smyrna. Modern Izmir. **8:** *The First . . . Last:* see 1.8, 17–18 nn. **9:** *Poor, but in reality you are rich:* see the opposite in 3.17. *Synagogue of Satan* refers to false Jews who spurred the authorities to persecute those who refused to worship at Smyrna's emperor cult shrine. **10:** *Ten days:* a short period; see Dan. 1.12. *Crown of life:* an athletic symbol of ultimate victory; see 3.11; Jas. 1.12 (translated "gift of life"). **11:** *Second death:* final condemnation; see 20.14; 21.8.

2.12–17: Pergamum. That it was the first center of emperor worship in Asia Minor may explain *where Satan is enthroned* (v. 13). **12:** The *two-edged sword:* see 1.16 n. **14–15:** *Balaam* (see Num. chs. 22–24; 31.16), here related to the *Nicolaitans* (vv. 6 n., 15), was regarded in NT times as the forerunner of all corrupt teachers. **17:** *Manna:* bread from heaven (see Exod. ch. 16). Jews believed that the gift of manna would be repeated in the messianic age; see *2 Baruch* 29.8 (noncanonical); compare Jn. 6.47–51. *White* (like "light" and "brightness") is a frequent symbol for good in Rev.; see 1.14; 3.5; 7.9; 19.14; 20.11. The *white stone* may be related to the lot-casting Urim and Thummim; see Exod. 28.15 n. Is it here for those who "cast their lot" with God? *A new name:* compare Isa. 62.2; see 3.12 n.

2.18–29: Thyatira. A city renowned for its trade guilds and idolatrous feasts (see Acts 16.14). **18:** *Fire . . .*

prophetess, whose teaching lures my servants into fornication and into eating food sacrificed to idols. ²¹ I have given her time to repent, but she refuses to repent of her fornication. ²² So I will throw her on a bed of pain, and I will plunge her lovers into terrible suffering, unless they renounce what she is doing; ²³ and her children I will kill with pestilence. This will teach all the churches that I am the searcher of men's hearts and minds, and that I will give to each of you what his deeds deserve. ²⁴ And now I speak to the rest of you in Thyatira, all who do not accept this teaching and have had no experience of what they call the deep secrets of Satan. On you I impose no further burden; ²⁵ only hold fast to what you have, until I come. ²⁶ To him who is victorious, to him who perseveres in doing my will to the end, I will give authority over the nations — ²⁷ that same authority which I received from my Father — and he will rule them with a rod of iron, smashing them to pieces like earthenware; ²⁸ and I will give him the star of dawn. ²⁹ You have ears, so hear what the Spirit says to the churches!"

3 'To the angel of the church at Sardis write:
' "These are the words of the One who has the seven spirits of God and the seven stars; I know what you are doing; people say you are alive, but in fact you are dead. ² Wake up, and put some strength into what you still have, because otherwise it must die! For I have not found any work of yours brought to completion in the sight of my God. ³ Remember therefore the teaching you received; observe it, and repent. If you do not wake up, I will come upon you like a thief, and you will not know the moment of my coming. ⁴ Yet

you have a few people in Sardis who have not polluted their clothing, and they will walk with me in white, for so they deserve. ⁵ Anyone who is victorious will be robed in white like them, and I shall never strike his name off the roll of the living; in the presence of my Father and his angels I shall acknowledge him as mine. ⁶ You have ears, so hear what the Spirit says to the churches!"

⁷ 'To the angel of the church at Philadelphia write:
' "These are the words of the Holy One, the True One, who has David's key, so that when he opens the door, no one can shut it, and when he shuts it, no one can open it: ⁸ I know what you are doing. I have set before you an open door which no one can shut. I know your strength is small, yet you have observed my command and have not disowned my name. ⁹ As for those of Satan's synagogue, who falsely claim to be Jews, I will make them come and fall at your feet; and they will know that you are my beloved people. ¹⁰ Because you have kept my command to stand firm, I will also keep you from the ordeal that is to fall upon the whole world to test its inhabitants. ¹¹ I am coming soon; hold fast to what you have, and let no one rob you of your crown. ¹² Those who are victorious I shall make pillars in the temple of my God; they will remain there for ever. I shall write on them the name of my God, and the name of the city of my God, that new Jerusalem which is coming down out of heaven from my God, and my own new name. ¹³ You have ears, so hear what the Spirit says to the churches!"

¹⁴ 'To the angel of the church at Laodicea write:

bronze: see Dan. 10.6. **20:** *Jezebel:* name of Ahab's wicked, idolatrous queen (1 Kgs. 16.31; 18.1–5; 19.1–3; 21.5–24). **23:** *Her children:* those who follow her teaching. *Searcher . . . deeds:* compare Jer. 17.10. **24:** *Deep secrets of Satan:* heretical teachings (see v. 20). **27:** See Ps. 2.9. **28:** *Star of dawn:* Christ himself (see 22.16).

3.1–6: Sardis. A city known as carefree, wealthy, immoral. **1:** *Alive . . . dead:* nominal, not true, Christians. **3:** *Like a thief:* 1 Thess. 5.1–2 n.; Matt. 24.42–44. **4:** *Polluted their clothing* is an image of unfaithfulness; the faithful are *in white* (see 2.17 n.). **5:** *The roll of the living:* a register of the faithful (see 13.8; 17.8; 20.12, 15; compare Exod. 32.32; Ps. 69.28; Dan. 12.1; Mal. 3.16; Lk. 10.20); see Phil. 4.3 n. ("book of life"). *Shall acknowledge:* compare Matt. 10.32.

3.7–13: Philadelphia. A small city (compare v. 8). **7:** *David's key:* symbol of authority; see Isa. 22.22. **9:** *Satan's synagogue:* see 2.9 n. *Fall at your feet:* compare Isa. 49.23; 60.14. **10:** *Ordeal:* see 7.14; Dan. 12.1; Mk. 13.19–20. It refers to the three and a half years of the beast's rule; see 13.5–10. **12:** *New Jerusalem:* see 21.2. *New name:* see 2.17; 19.12; 22.4 n.; compare Ezek. 48.35.

3.14–22: Laodicea. A proud and wealthy city near Colossae (Col. 4.13–16). **14:** Here, as in 2 Cor. 1.20, Jesus is the *Amen,* God's "Yes" to humanity's hope (see Isa. 65.16; compare 1.7 n.). *The source:* compare Jn.

' "These are the words of the Amen, the faithful and true witness, the source of God's creation: 15 I know what you are doing; you are neither cold nor hot. How I wish you were either cold or hot! 16 Because you are neither one nor the other, but just lukewarm, I will spit you out of my mouth. 17 You say, 'How rich I am! What a fortune I have made! I have everything I want.' In fact, though you do not realize it, you are a pitiful wretch, poor, blind, and naked. 18 I advise you to buy from me gold refined in the fire to make you truly rich, and white robes to put on to hide the shame of your nakedness, and ointment for your eyes so that you may see. 19 All whom I love I reprove and discipline. Be whole-hearted therefore in your repentance. 20 Here I stand knocking at the door; if any-one hears my voice and opens the door, I will come in and he and I will eat together. 21 To anyone who is victorious I will grant a place beside me on my throne, as I myself was victorious and sat down with my Father on his throne. 22 You have ears, so hear what the Spirit says to the churches!" '

Visions of heaven

4 AFTER this I had a vision: a door stood open in heaven, and the voice that I had first heard speaking to me like a trumpet said, 'Come up here, and I will show you what must take place hereafter.' 2 At once the Spirit came upon me. There in heaven stood a throne. On it sat One 3 whose appearance was like jasper or cornelian, and round it was a rainbow, bright as an emerald. 4 In a circle about this throne were twenty-four other thrones, and on them were seated twenty-four elders, robed in white and wearing gold crowns. 5 From the throne came flashes of lightning and peals of thunder. Burning be-fore the throne were seven flaming torches, the seven spirits of God, 6 and in front of it stretched what looked like a sea of glass or a sheet of ice.

In the centre, round the throne itself, were four living creatures, covered with eyes in front and behind. 7 The first creature was like a lion, the second like an ox, the third had a human face, and the fourth was like an eagle in flight. 8 Each of the four living crea-tures had six wings, and eyes all round and in-side them. Day and night unceasingly they sing:

'Holy, holy, holy is God the sovereign Lord of all, who was, and is, and is to come!'

9 Whenever the living creatures give glory and honour and thanks to the One who sits on the throne, who lives for ever and ever, 10 the twenty-four elders prostrate them-selves before the One who sits on the throne and they worship him who lives for ever and ever. As they lay their crowns before the throne they cry:

11 'You are worthy, O Lord our God, to receive glory and honour and power, be-cause you created all things; by your will they were created and have their being!'

5 I saw in the right hand of the One who sat on the throne a scroll with writing on both sides, and sealed with seven seals. 2 And

1.3; Col. 1.15–18; Heb. 1.2. **17:** *Rich . . . poor:* contrast with 2.9; compare Hos. 12.8. **18:** Famous for its wealth, wool, and medical school, Laodicea is now to receive true *gold . . . white robes . . . ointment* from Christ. **19:** *Reprove:* see Prov. 3.11–12; Heb. 12.5–6. **20:** To *eat together* can refer both to the Lord's Supper (see Matt. 26.26–29) and to the future messianic banquet. **21:** The faithful will share Christ's *throne* and power; compare 2.26–27; Lk. 22.30.

4.1–5.14: A vision of the heavenly worship (see Isa. 6.1–3).

4.1–11: The praise of God the Creator. 1: *Voice:* compare 1.10. *Trumpet:* see 1.11 n. *Come up here:* the writer is transplanted to heaven, a conventional motif in ancient apocalyptic literature. **2:** *Throne:* a symbol of sovereignty occurring more than forty times in Rev.; compare Ezek. 1.26–28; Jer. 17.12. **4:** *Twenty-four elders* may refer to the twelve tribes and twelve apostles, symbolizing the unity of old and new covenant peoples: see 21.13–14. **5:** *Lightning . . . thunder:* compare Exod. 19.16. *Seven spirits:* see 1.5 n. **6:** *Sea of glass:* probably conceived as before the "throne" in the heavenly temple; see 1 Kgs. 7.23–26. *Four living creatures* (see Ezek. 1.5) symbolize the created world. *Covered with eyes* (see Ezek. 1.18) symbolizes all-seeing watchful-ness. **7:** *Lion . . . ox . . . human face . . . eagle* (see Ezek. 1.10): in later Christian tradition, related respectively to Mk., Lk., Matt., and Jn. **8:** *Holy, holy, holy:* see Isa. 6.3. **10:** *The One:* see vv. 2, 9. *Throne:* see v. 2 n.

I saw a mighty angel proclaiming in a loud voice, 'Who is worthy to break the seals and open the scroll?' ³But there was no one in heaven or on earth or under the earth able to open the scroll to look inside it. ⁴And because no one was found worthy to open the scroll and look inside, I wept bitterly. ⁵One of the elders said to me: 'Do not weep; the Lion from the tribe of Judah, the shoot growing from David's stock, has won the right to open the scroll and its seven seals.'

⁶Then I saw a Lamb with the marks of sacrifice on him, standing with the four living creatures between the throne and the elders. He had seven horns and seven eyes, the eyes which are the seven spirits of God sent to every part of the world. ⁷The Lamb came and received the scroll from the right hand of the One who sat on the throne. ⁸As he did so, the four living creatures and the twenty-four elders prostrated themselves before the Lamb. Each of the elders had a harp; they held golden bowls full of incense, the prayers of God's people, ⁹and they were singing a new song:

'You are worthy to receive the scroll and break its seals, for you were slain and by your blood you bought for God people of every tribe and language, nation and race. ¹⁰You have made them a royal house of priests for our God, and they shall reign on earth.'

¹¹As I looked I heard, all round the throne and the living creatures and the elders, the voices of many angels, thousands on thousands, myriads on myriads. ¹²They proclaimed with loud voices:

'Worthy is the Lamb who was slain, to receive power and wealth, wisdom and might, honour and glory and praise!'

¹³Then I heard all created things, in heaven, on earth, under the earth, and in the sea, crying:

'Praise and honour, glory and might, to him who sits on the throne and to the Lamb for ever!'

¹⁴The four living creatures said, 'Amen,' and the elders prostrated themselves in worship.

The seven seals

6 I WATCHED as the Lamb broke the first of the seven seals, and I heard one of the four living creatures say in a voice like thunder, 'Come!' ²There before my eyes was a white horse, and its rider held a bow. He was given a crown, and he rode forth, conquering and to conquer.

³The Lamb broke the second seal, and I heard the second creature say, 'Come!' ⁴Out came another horse, which was red. Its rider was given power to take away peace from the earth that men might slaughter one another; and he was given a great sword.

⁵He broke the third seal, and I heard the third creature say, 'Come!' There, as I looked, was a black horse, and its rider was holding in his hand a pair of scales. ⁶I heard what sounded like a voice from among the four living creatures; it said, 'A day's wage for a quart of flour, a day's wage for three quarts of barley-meal! But do not damage the olive and the vine!'

⁷He broke the fourth seal, and I heard the fourth creature say, 'Come!' ⁸There, as I

5:6 *standing . . . elders:* or standing in the middle of the throne, inside the circle of living creatures and the circle of elders.

5.1–14: The praise of the Lamb the Redeemer. 1: *A scroll . . . sealed:* see Isa. 29.11; Ezek. 2.9–10. The *seven seals* are to be opened to reveal the secrets of the future. **5:** *Lion from the tribe of Judah* (see Gen. 49.9), *the shoot* (descendant) *from David's stock* (see Isa. 11.1) are messianic titles. **6:** *Lamb with the marks of sacrifice* refers to Jesus' death, though now he is at the *throne;* see 3.21. The title *Lamb* appears nearly thirty times in Rev.; compare Isa. 53.7; Jn. 1.29, 36 (though a different Gk. word is used). *Seven horns* and *seven eyes* portray authority and omniscience; see Zech. 4.10; Dan. 7.7–8, 20. **8:** *Incense . . . and prayers:* see Ps. 141.2. **9:** *By your blood you bought:* redemption was won at the cost of Christ's life; see 1.5; 12.11; 1 Cor. 6.19–20. **10:** *A royal house of priests:* see 1.6 n. **12:** *Worthy is the Lamb:* the Redeemer is offered the same kind of worship as the Creator. The Lamb, not the beast (emperor), shares the divine sovereignty.

6.1–17: The opening of the first six seals. As the first four seals are opened, horses with riders (compare Zech. 1.7–17; 6.1–8) appear, portraying coming disasters; all six correspond to the scheme of Mk. 13.7–8, 24–25 (compare Lev. 26.21–39). **2:** *A white horse, and its rider* (in 19.11 the rider is Jesus) symbolize victory. **4:** *Another horse, which was red,* promotes war. **5–6:** *A black horse* brings a famine of grain. **7–8:** *Another* looked, was another horse, sickly pale; its rider's name was Death, and Hades followed close behind. To them was given power over a quarter of the earth, power to kill by sword and famine, by pestilence and wild beasts.

⁹ He broke the fifth seal, and I saw beneath the altar the souls of those who had been slaughtered for God's word and for the testimony they bore. ¹⁰ They gave a great cry: 'How long, sovereign Lord, holy and true, must it be before you will vindicate us and avenge our death on the inhabitants of the earth?' ¹¹ They were each given a white robe, and told to rest a little longer, until the number should be complete of all their brothers in Christ's service who were to be put to death, as they themselves had been.

¹² I watched as the Lamb broke the sixth seal. There was a violent earthquake; the sun turned black as a funeral pall and the moon all red as blood; ¹³ the stars in the sky fell to the earth, like figs blown off a tree in a gale; ¹⁴ the sky vanished like a scroll being rolled up, and every mountain and island was dislodged from its place. ¹⁵ The kings of the earth, the nobles and the commanders, the rich and the powerful, and all men, slave or free, hid themselves in caves and under mountain crags; ¹⁶ and they called out to the mountains and the crags, 'Fall on us, hide us from the One who sits on the throne and from the wrath of the Lamb, ¹⁷ for the great day of their wrath has come, and who can stand?'

7 After that I saw four angels stationed at the four corners of the earth, holding back its four winds so that no wind should blow on land or sea or on any tree. ² I saw another angel rising from the east, bearing the seal of the living God. To the four angels who had been given the power to ravage land and sea, he cried out: ³ 'Do no damage to land

or sea or to the trees until we have set the seal of our God upon the foreheads of his servants.' ⁴ I heard how many had been marked with the seal — a hundred and forty-four thousand from all the tribes of Israel: ⁵ twelve thousand from the tribe of Judah, twelve thousand from the tribe of Reuben, twelve thousand from the tribe of Gad, ⁶ twelve thousand from the tribe of Asher, twelve thousand from the tribe of Naphtali, twelve thousand from the tribe of Manasseh, ⁷ twelve thousand from the tribe of Simeon, twelve thousand from the tribe of Levi, twelve thousand from the tribe of Issachar, ⁸ twelve thousand from the tribe of Zebulun, twelve thousand from the tribe of Joseph, and twelve thousand from the tribe of Benjamin.

⁹ After that I looked and saw a vast throng, which no one could count, from all races and tribes, nations and languages, standing before the throne and the Lamb. They were robed in white and had palm branches in their hands, ¹⁰ and they shouted aloud:

'Victory to our God who sits on the throne,
    and to the Lamb!'

¹¹ All the angels who stood round the throne and round the elders and the four living creatures prostrated themselves before the throne and worshipped God, ¹² crying:

'Amen! Praise and glory and wisdom,
    thanksgiving and honour, power and
    might, be to our God for ever! Amen.'

¹³ One of the elders turned to me and asked, 'Who are these all robed in white, and where

6:9 **beneath:** *or* at the foot of.

---

horse, sickly pale bears *Death, and Hades* (in 1.18 *Hades* is translated as "Death's domain"; compare Ezek. 5.12). **9–11:** Breaking the fifth seal discloses the souls of the martyred dead crying out for vengeance; see Ps. 79.5–10; contrast Lk. 23.34; Acts 7.60. *Beneath the altar* may reflect a Jewish saying: "The souls of the righteous are kept safely under the throne of glory." *Until the number should be complete:* compare 2 Esd. 4.35–37. **12–17:** Breaking the sixth seal brings cosmic catastrophe. **12:** See Joel 2.31; Acts 2.20. **14:** Isa. 34.4. **15:** Isa. 2.10. **16:** Hos. 10.8. **17:** Joel 2.11; Mal. 3.2.

    7.1–17: The marking of God's servants falls between the sixth and seventh seals, securing the faithful from destruction. **1:** *Its four winds:* see Zech. 6.5. **3:** *Set the seal . . . upon the foreheads:* see Ezek. 9.4. **4:** *A hundred and forty-four thousand* is a "perfect" number (12 × 12 × 1000); it may symbolize Israel's future full participation in Christ (compare Rom. 9.25–27) or the return of the ten "lost" tribes; see 2 Esd. 13.40–48. **9:** With *a vast throng . . . from all . . . nations* the seer points beyond Israel (vv. 4–8) to the Gentile world (see do they come from?' ¹⁴ I answered, 'My lord, it is you who know.' He said to me, 'They are those who have passed through the great ordeal; they have washed their robes and made them white in the blood of the Lamb. ¹⁵ That is why they stand before the throne of God and worship him day and night in his temple; and he who sits on the throne will protect them with his presence. ¹⁶ Never again shall they feel hunger or thirst; never again shall the sun beat on them or any scorching heat, ¹⁷ because the Lamb who is at the centre of the throne will be their shepherd and will guide them to springs of the water of life; and God will wipe every tear from their eyes.'

8 Now when the Lamb broke the seventh seal, there was silence in heaven for about half an hour.

The seven trumpets

² I saw the seven angels who stand in the presence of God: they were given seven trumpets.

³ Another angel came and stood at the altar, holding a golden censer. He was given much incense to offer with the prayers of all God's people on the golden altar in front of the throne, ⁴ and the smoke of the incense from the angel's hand went up before God with his people's prayers. ⁵ The angel took the censer, filled it with fire from the altar, and threw it down on the earth; and there came peals of thunder, lightning-flashes, and an earthquake.

⁶ The seven angels who held the seven trumpets prepared to blow them.

⁷ The first angel blew his trumpet. There came hail and fire mingled with blood, and

this was hurled upon the earth; a third of the earth was burnt, a third of the trees, and all the green grass.

⁸ The second angel blew his trumpet. What looked like a great mountain flaming with fire was hurled into the sea; a third of the sea was turned to blood, ⁹ a third of the living creatures in it died, and a third of the ships on it were destroyed.

¹⁰ The third angel blew his trumpet. A great star shot from the sky, flaming like a torch, and fell on a third of the rivers and springs; ¹¹ the name of the star was Wormwood. A third of the water turned to wormwood, and great numbers of people died from drinking the water because it had been made bitter.

¹² The fourth angel blew his trumpet. A third part of the sun was struck, a third of the moon, and a third of the stars, so that a third part of them turned dark and a third of the light failed to appear by day or by night.

¹³ As I looked, I heard an eagle calling with a loud cry as it flew in mid-heaven: 'Woe, woe, woe to the inhabitants of the earth at the sound of the other trumpets which the next three angels must now blow!'

9 The fifth angel blew his trumpet. I saw a star that had fallen from heaven to earth, and the star was given the key to the shaft of the abyss. ² He opened it, and smoke came up from it like smoke from a great furnace and darkened the sun and the air. ³ Out of the smoke came locusts over the earth, and they were given the powers of scorpions. ⁴ They were told not to do damage to the grass or to any plant or tree, but only to those people who had not received God's seal on their foreheads. ⁵ They were given permission to torment them for five months

Dan. 7.14). **12:** Note the seven-fold ascription; compare 5.12. **14:** *The great ordeal:* see 3.10 n. *The blood of the Lamb:* see 5.9 n.; 1 Jn. 1.7. **15:** Compare 21.3. **16:** 21.4; Ps. 121.6; Isa. 25.8; 49.10. **17:** *Shepherd:* see Ps. 23.1–2; Ezek. 34.23. *Springs of the water of life:* see 21.6; 22.1, 17; compare Jn. 4.10; 7.37–38.

8.1–5: The opening of the seventh seal introduces the *seven trumpets* (v. 2). **1:** *Silence in heaven:* the calm before the storm. **2:** *Seven angels:* probably the seven archangels; compare Tob. 12.15. **3:** *Incense:* see Ps. 141.2. *Golden altar:* see Exod. 30.1–3. **5:** *Took the censer . . . and threw it:* compare Ezek. 10.2.

8.6–9.21: The first six trumpets proclaim catastrophes in nature as judgment on the wicked. **6–13:** Compare the plagues in Egypt, as in Exod. 7.17–21; 9.23, 25; 10.21–23. **6–7:** In connection with several trumpet blasts, a *third* of creation is affected. **8–9:** The volcanic island of Thera, visible from Patmos, may have suggested a *mountain flaming with fire . . . hurled into the sea.* **10:** *Great star:* shooting star or meteor. **11:** *Wormwood:* a bitter drug; see Jer. 9.15; 23.15. **13:** The three *woes* correspond to the last three trumpet blasts. **9.1:** Since stars were identified as angels (1.20), *a star that had fallen* may refer to Satan as a fallen angel: see v. 11; Isa. 14.12–16; Lk. 10.18. **2–3:** *Locusts:* compare Exod. 10.12–15; Joel 1.4; 2.10. **4:** *Seal on their foreheads:* see with torment like a scorpion's sting; but they were not to kill them. 6During that time people will seek death, but will not find it; they will long to die, but death will elude them.

7In appearance the locusts were like horses equipped for battle. On their heads were what looked like gold crowns; their faces were like human faces 8and their hair like women's hair; they had teeth like lions' teeth 9and chests like iron breastplates; the sound of their wings was like the noise of many horses and chariots charging into battle; 10they had tails like scorpions, with stings in them, and in their tails lay their power to injure people for five months. 11They had for their king the angel of the abyss, whose name in Hebrew is Abaddon, and in Greek Apollyon, the Destroyer.

12The first woe has now passed; but there are still two more to come.

13The sixth angel blew his trumpet. I heard a voice coming from the horns of the golden altar that stood in the presence of God. 14To the sixth angel, who held the trumpet, the voice said: 'Release the four angels held bound at the Great River, the Euphrates!' 15So the four angels were let loose, to kill a third of mankind; they had been held in readiness for this very year, month, day, and hour. 16And their squadrons of cavalry numbered twice ten thousand times ten thousand; this was the number I heard.

17This was how I saw the horses and their riders in my vision: they wore breastplates, fiery red, turquoise, and sulphur-yellow; the horses had heads like lions' heads, and from their mouths issued fire, smoke, and sulphur. 18By these three plagues, the fire, the smoke, and the sulphur that came from their mouths, a third of mankind was killed. 19The power of the horses lay in their mouths and in their tails; for their tails had heads like serpents, and with them they inflicted injuries.

20The rest of mankind who survived these plagues still did not renounce the gods their hands had made, or cease their worship of demons and of idols fashioned from gold, silver, bronze, stone, and wood, which cannot see or hear or walk; 21nor did they repent of their murders, their sorcery, their fornication, or their robberies.

10 I saw another mighty angel coming down from heaven. He was wrapped in cloud, with a rainbow over his head; his face shone like the sun and his legs were like pillars of fire. 2In his hand he held a little scroll which had been opened. He planted his right foot on the sea and his left on the land, 3and gave a great shout like the roar of a lion; when he shouted, the seven thunders spoke. 4I was about to write down what the seven thunders had said, but I heard a voice from heaven saying, 'Put under seal what the seven thunders have said; do not write it down.' 5Then the angel whom I saw standing on the sea and the land raised his right hand towards heaven 6and swore by him who lives for ever, who created heaven and earth and the sea and everything in them: 'There shall be no more delay; 7when the time comes for the seventh angel to sound his trumpet, the hidden purpose of God will have been fulfilled, as he promised to his servants the prophets.'

8The voice which I had heard from heaven began speaking to me again; it said, 'Go and take the scroll which is open in the hand of the angel who stands on the sea and the land.' 9I went to the angel and asked him to give me the little scroll. He answered, 'Take it, and eat it. It will turn your stomach sour, but in your mouth it will taste as sweet as honey.' 10I took the scroll from the angel's hand and ate it, and in my mouth it did taste as sweet as honey, but when I swallowed it my stomach turned sour.

11Then I was told, 'Once again you must utter prophecies over many nations, races, languages, and kings.'

7.3 n. **7:** *Like horses:* see Joel 2.4. **8:** *Teeth like lions':* Joel 1.6. **9:** *Chariots:* Joel 2.5. **11:** *Abaddon* (or, Destruction) in the OT is equivalent to Sheol or Hades; see Job 26.6; 28.22; Prov. 15.11. **13:** *Golden altar:* see Exod. 30.1–3. **14:** *The four angels* (not those in 7.2) are here at the *Euphrates,* whence Rome feared a Parthian invasion; compare "the kings from the east" in 16.12. **20:** Compare the view of idolatry here with Ps. 115.4–7; 135.15–17; Dan. 5.23. As frequently in the Bible, idolatry leads (v. 21) to further sin.

10.1–11.14: The little scroll and the two witnesses. This section falls between the sixth and seventh trumpets. **4:** *Put under seal . . . do not write:* see Dan. 12.4, 9. **5–6:** *The angel . . . swore:* Dan. 12.7. **8–10:** On the eating of the scroll compare Ezek. 2.8–3.3. **11:** The writer's sweet-sour (vv. 8–10; sweet for the faithful,

11 I was given a long cane to use as a measuring rod, and was told: 'Go and measure the temple of God and the altar, and count the worshippers. ²But leave the outer court of the temple out of your measurements; it has been given over to the Gentiles, and for forty-two months they will trample the Holy City underfoot. ³I will give my two witnesses authority to prophesy, dressed in sackcloth, for those twelve hundred and sixty days.' ⁴They are the two olive trees and the two lamps that stand in the presence of the Lord of the earth. ⁵If anyone tries to injure them, fire issues from their mouths and consumes their enemies; so shall anyone die who tries to do them injury. ⁶These two have the power to shut up the sky, so that no rain falls during the time of their prophesying; and they have power to turn water into blood and to afflict the earth with every kind of plague whenever they like. ⁷But when they have completed their testimony, the beast that comes up from the abyss will wage war on them and will overcome and kill them. ⁸Their bodies will lie in the street of the great city, whose name in prophetic language is Sodom, or Egypt, where also their Lord was crucified. ⁹For three and a half days people from every nation and tribe, language, and race, gaze on their corpses and refuse them burial. ¹⁰The earth's inhabitants gloat over them; they celebrate and exchange presents, for these two prophets were a torment to them. ¹¹But at the end of the three and a half days the breath of life from God came into their bodies, and they rose to their feet, to the terror of those who saw them. ¹²A loud voice from heaven was heard saying to them, 'Come up here!' and they ascended to heaven in a cloud, in full view of their enemies. ¹³At that moment there was a violent earthquake, and a tenth of the city collapsed. Seven thousand people were killed in the earthquake; the rest, filled with fear, did homage to the God of heaven.

¹⁴The second woe has now passed; but the third is soon to come.

¹⁵Then the seventh angel blew his trumpet. Voices in heaven were heard crying aloud:

'Sovereignty over the world has passed to our Lord and his Christ, and he shall reign for ever!'

¹⁶The twenty-four elders, who sit on their thrones before God, prostrated themselves before him in adoration, ¹⁷saying:

'O Lord God, sovereign over all, you are and you were; we give you thanks because you have assumed full power and entered upon your reign. ¹⁸The nations rose in wrath, but your day of wrath has come. Now is the time for the dead to be judged; now is the time for rewards to be given to your servants the prophets, to your own people, and to all who honour your name, both small and great; now is the time to destroy those who destroy the earth.'

¹⁹God's sanctuary in heaven was opened, and within his sanctuary was seen the ark of his covenant. There came flashes of lightning

---

sour for the faithless) *prophecies* (see Jer. 1.10) unfold in chs. 12–22. **11.1–14:** The scene seems to reflect material from the time of the Jewish War (66–70 C.E.) prior to the destruction of the Jerusalem temple in 70 C.E. **1:** *Measure the temple:* see Ezek. 40.3–42.20; Zech. 2.1–5. **2:** *Forty-two months* is equivalent to 1,260 days, or three and a half years, or "a time and times and half a time"; see Dan. 7.25 n.; 9.27 n.; 12.7. Daniel divides seven years in half, with three and a half years of acute persecution prior to 168 B.C.E. (when Antiochus IV set up an image of Zeus in the temple), and three and a half years of deliverance after. These events came to be regarded as foreshadowing the time of the Antichrist. **3–6:** *Two witnesses:* probably Elijah (see 1 Kgs. 17.1; Mal. 4.5–6) and Moses (see Exod. 7.17–21; Deut. 18.15–18); compare Mk. 9.11–13. It was a Jewish expectation that Elijah and Moses would return before the end of the age. In v. 4 Elijah and Moses are the *olive trees* and *lamps* (though in Zech. ch. 4 these symbols represent Zerubbabel and Joshua). **7:** *The beast . . . from the abyss:* see 17.7–8 n. **8:** *The great city . . . Sodom, or Egypt,* is here Jerusalem; see Isa. 1.9–10; Ezek. 23.27. **11:** *The breath of life . . . came into their bodies:* see Ezek. 37.5, 10. **12:** See 2 Kgs. 2.11. **14:** *Second woe:* see 8.13 for the prediction of three woes, associated with the last trumpet blasts.

11.15–19: The seventh trumpet brings the heavenly proclamation of God's sovereignty, indirectly introducing the final woe of chs. 12–19. **15:** *Our Lord and his Christ:* note v. 18, and compare Ps. 2.1–2. **19:** *Ark of God's covenant:* see 1 Kgs. 8.1–6.

and peals of thunder, an earthquake, and a violent hailstorm.

Seven visions

12 AFTER that there appeared a great sign in heaven: a woman robed with the sun, beneath her feet the moon, and on her head a crown of twelve stars. ²She was about to bear a child, and in the anguish of her labour she cried out to be delivered. ³Then a second sign appeared in heaven: a great, fiery red dragon with seven heads and ten horns. On his heads were seven diadems, ⁴and with his tail he swept down a third of the stars in the sky and hurled them to the earth. The dragon stood in front of the woman who was about to give birth, so that when her child was born he might devour it. ⁵But when she gave birth to a male child, who is destined to rule all nations with a rod of iron, the child was snatched up to God and to his throne. ⁶The woman herself fled into the wilderness, where she was to be looked after for twelve hundred and sixty days in a place prepared for her by God.

⁷Then war broke out in heaven; Michael and his angels fought against the dragon. The dragon with his angels fought back, ⁸but he was too weak, and they lost their place in heaven. ⁹The great dragon was thrown down, that ancient serpent who led the whole world astray, whose name is the Devil, or Satan; he was thrown down to the earth, and his angels with him.

¹⁰I heard a loud voice in heaven proclaim: 'This is the time of victory for our God, the time of his power and sovereignty, when his Christ comes to his rightful rule! For the accuser of our brothers, he who day and night accused them before our God, is overthrown. ¹¹By the sacrifice of the Lamb and by the witness they bore, they have conquered him; faced with death they did not cling to life. ¹²Therefore rejoice, you heavens and you that dwell in them! But woe to you, earth and sea, for the Devil has come down to you in great fury, knowing that his time is short!'

¹³When the dragon saw that he had been thrown down to the earth, he went in pursuit of the woman who had given birth to the male child. ¹⁴But she was given the wings of a mighty eagle, so that she could fly to her place in the wilderness where she was to be looked after for three and a half years, out of reach of the serpent. ¹⁵From his mouth the serpent spewed a flood of water after the woman to sweep her away with its spate. ¹⁶But the earth came to her rescue: it opened its mouth and drank up the river which the dragon spewed from his mouth. ¹⁷Furious with the woman, the dragon went off to wage war on the rest of her offspring, those who keep God's commandments and maintain

13 their witness to Jesus. ¹He took his stand on the seashore.

Then I saw a beast rising out of the sea. It had ten horns and seven heads; on the horns

12:11 **the witness they bore:** *or* the word of God to which they bore witness.

12.1–17: The woman, child, and dragon. The struggle between Satan and God's people is described in imagery possibly drawn from a widespread ancient myth. **1:** Here, the *woman* represents Israel from whom Jesus sprang (v. 5). *Twelve stars:* the twelve tribes. **2:** *The anguish of her labour:* see Isa. 66.7; Mic. 4.9–10. **3:** *A great, fiery red dragon:* Satan (see v. 9; compare descriptions of the beast in 13.1). *Ten horns:* see Dan. 7.7. **5:** *A male child:* Jesus, *destined to rule all nations* (see 2.27; 19.15; Ps. 2.9); reference is made only to his birth and ascension! **6:** The *woman,* now probably seen as Jewish Christians, is to be safe during the three and a half years of Satan's persecution (see v. 14; 11.2 n.; compare Mk. 13.14–20). **7–17:** Though still active for a short time (vv. 12, 14), the dragon is portrayed as defeated (see Lk. 10.18; Jn. 12.31). **7:** The archangel *Michael* is Israel's champion (see Dan. 10.13, 21; 12.1). **9:** *That ancient serpent:* an allusion to Gen. 3.1, 14–15. **10:** *The accuser:* Satan; see Job 1.6–12; Zech. 3.1. **11:** *Sacrifice of the lamb:* lit. blood; see 5.9 n. **12:** *Rejoice, you heavens:* compare Isa. 44.23; 49.13. **14:** *Wings of a mighty eagle:* see Exod. 19.4. **17:** *The rest of her offspring* (probably Gentile Christians): Jewish Christians are "sealed" but others must bear "the great ordeal" (compare ch. 7).

13.1–18: The two beasts. Chapters 4–5 portrayed God and the Lamb; chs. 12–13 portray their evil counterparts, the dragon and the beast (Satan and Rome). **1:** The *beast* is Rome. The empire is identified with the emperor Nero whose return was popularly expected; his persecution of Christians made him a dreaded figure (see ch. 17; compare Dan. 7.1–6). *Ten horns:* (Parthian) kings who conspire with Nero; compare 17.12; Dan. 7.7. *Seven heads:* seven hills of Rome or seven kings (see 17.9–10). *A blasphemous name:* the divine title were ten diadems, and on each head was a blasphemous name. ² The beast I saw resembled a leopard, but its feet were like a bear's and its mouth like a lion's. The dragon conferred it on his own power, his throne, and great authority. ³ One of the heads seemed to have been given a death blow, yet its mortal wound was healed. The whole world went after the beast in wondering admiration, ⁴ and worshipped the dragon because he had conferred his authority on the beast; they worshipped the beast also. 'Who is like the beast?' they said. 'Who can fight against it?'

⁵ The beast was allowed to mouth bombast and blasphemy, and was granted permission to continue for forty-two months. ⁶ It uttered blasphemies against God, reviling his name and his dwelling-place, that is, those who dwell in heaven. ⁷ It was also allowed to wage war on God's people and to defeat them, and it was granted authority over every tribe, nation, language, and race. ⁸ All the inhabitants of the earth will worship it, all whose names have not been written in the book of life of the Lamb, slain since the foundation of the world.

⁹ You have ears, so hear! ¹⁰ Whoever is to be made prisoner, to prison he shall go; whoever is to be slain by the sword, by the sword he must be slain. This calls for the endurance and faithfulness of God's people.

¹¹ Then I saw another beast; it came up out of the earth, and had two horns like a lamb's, but spoke like a dragon. ¹² It wielded all the authority of the first beast in its presence, and made the earth and its inhabitants worship this first beast, whose mortal wound had been healed. ¹³ It worked great miracles, even making fire come down from heaven to earth, where people could see it. ¹⁴ By the miracles it was allowed to perform in the presence of the beast it deluded the inhabitants of the earth, and persuaded them to erect an image in honour of the beast which had been wounded by the sword and yet lived. ¹⁵ It was allowed to give breath to the image of the beast, so that it could even speak and cause all who would not worship the image to be put to death. ¹⁶ It caused everyone, small and great, rich and poor, free man and slave, to have a mark put on his right hand or his forehead, ¹⁷ and no one was allowed to buy or sell unless he bore this beast's mark, either name or number. ¹⁸ (This calls for skill; let anyone who has intelligence work out the number of the beast, for the number represents a man's name, and the numerical value of its letters is six hundred and sixty-six.)

14 I LOOKED, and there on Mount Zion stood the Lamb, and with him were a hundred and forty-four thousand who had his name and the name of his Father written on their foreheads. ² I heard a sound from heaven like a mighty torrent or a great peal of thunder; what I heard was like harpists playing on their harps. ³ They were singing a new song before the throne and the four living creatures and the elders, and no one could learn it except the hundred and forty-four thousand ransomed from the earth. ⁴ These are men who have kept themselves chaste and have not defiled themselves with women; these follow the Lamb wherever he

13:8 **written ... world:** *or* written, since the foundation of the world, in the book of life of the slain Lamb.   13:10 **whoever ... slain by the sword:** *or* whoever takes the sword to slay.   13:18 **the numerical ... letters:** *lit.* his number.

claimed by the emperor. **2:** On the animals, see Dan. 7.4–6. *The dragon ... conferred ... power:* i.e. Satan works through the beast. **3:** *Death blow ... wound was healed* (see vv. 12, 14) points to Nero's rumored survival of suicide and return (see 17.8; compare with Jesus in 1.18; 5.6). **5:** *Bombast:* boastful words (see Dan. 7.8). *Forty-two months:* see 11.2 n. **7:** Compare 5.9; Dan. 7.21. **8:** *Book of life:* see 3.5 n. ("roll of the living"). **9–10:** This may indicate that Christians are not to strike a blow in their own defense; compare Matt. 26.52; Jer. 15.2. **11–18:** The second *beast* (called "the false prophet" in 19.20) may refer to the priesthood that supported emperor worship (see v. 12); compare Dan. 3.1–7; 2 Thess. 2.9–10. **16:** *A mark put on:* compare the marking of the faithful (see 7.3; 14.1). **18:** In Heb., the letters of the name "Nero Caesar" have numerical values which total *six hundred and sixty-six*.

14.1–20: Three visions of reassurance, admonition, and the harvest. 1–5: The *ransomed* (v. 3). **1:** *Mount Zion:* the heavenly Jerusalem; see Heb. 12.22. *A hundred and forty-four thousand:* here, not Israel (as in 7.4–8), but those *ransomed from the earth* (v. 3). **3:** *A new song:* see 5.8–10. **4:** *Chaste:* lit. virgins. It may mean celibacy, either literally or symbolically (see 2.20–22; compare 2 Cor. 11.2; Matt. 19.12); it could refer to abstinence from such pollutions as are prohibited in Deut. 27.20–30. *Firstfruits:* see Exod. 23.19; Jas. 1.18.

goes. They have been ransomed as the first-fruits of mankind for God and the Lamb. [5] No lie was found on their lips; they are without fault.

[6] Then I saw an angel flying in mid-heaven, with an eternal gospel to proclaim to those on earth, to every race, tribe, language, and nation. [7] He spoke in a loud voice: 'Fear God and pay him homage, for the hour of his judgement has come! Worship him who made heaven and earth, the sea and the springs of water!'

[8] A second angel followed, saying, 'Fallen, fallen is Babylon the great, who has made all nations drink the wine of God's anger roused by her fornication!'

[9] A third angel followed, saying in a loud voice, 'Whoever worships the beast and its image and receives its mark on his forehead or hand, [10] he too shall drink the wine of God's anger, poured undiluted into the cup of his wrath. He shall be tormented in sulphurous flames in the sight of the holy angels and the Lamb. [11] The smoke of their torment will rise for ever; there will be no respite day or night for those who worship the beast and its image, or for anyone who receives the mark of its name.' [12] This calls for the endurance of God's people, all those who keep his commands and remain loyal to Jesus.

[13] I heard a voice from heaven say, 'Write this: "Happy are the dead who henceforth die in the faith of the Lord!" "Yes," says the Spirit, "let them rest from their labours, for the record of their deeds goes with them."'

[14] As I looked there appeared a white cloud, on which was seated a figure like a man; he had a gold crown on his head and a sharp sickle in his hand. [15] Another angel came out of the temple and called in a loud voice to him who sat on the cloud: 'Put in your sickle and reap, for harvest time has come and earth's crop is fully ripe.' [16] So the one who sat on the cloud swept over the earth with his sickle and the harvest was reaped.

[17] Another angel came out of the heavenly sanctuary, and he also had a sharp sickle. [18] Then from the altar came yet another, the angel who has authority over fire, and he called aloud to the one with the sharp sickle: 'Put in your sharp sickle, and gather in earth's grape harvest, for its clusters are ripe.' [19] So the angel swept over the earth with his sickle and gathered in its grapes, and threw them into the great winepress of God's wrath. [20] The winepress was trodden outside the city, and for a distance of two hundred miles blood flowed from the press to the height of horses' bridles.

The seven bowls

15 THEN I saw in heaven another great and astonishing sign: seven angels with seven plagues, the last plagues of all, for with them the wrath of God was completed. [2] I saw what looked like a sea of glass shot through with fire. Standing beside it and holding the harps which God had given them were those who had been victorious against the beast, its image, and the number of its name. [3] They were singing the song of Moses, the servant of God, and the song of the Lamb:

'Great and marvellous are your deeds,
O Lord God, sovereign over all;
just and true are your ways,
O King of the ages.
[4] Who shall not fear you, Lord,
and do homage to your name?
For you alone are holy.
All nations shall come and worship
before you,
for your just decrees stand revealed.'

[5] After this, as I looked, the sanctuary of the

14:13 **the dead ... the Spirit**: *some witnesses read* the dead who die trusting in the Lord! Henceforth", says the Spirit.

They are here the first part of the ransomed, with the whole to come later. **6–13**: Judgment and warning. **8**: *Babylon the great* (see Isa. 21.9): here, Rome is meant (see ch. 18). **10**: *Wine of God's anger*: see Jer. 25.15–16. *Sulphurous flames*: see 19.20; 20.10. **11**: *Smoke of their torment*: compare Isa. 34.10. **14–20**: *The harvest* (v. 15): a familiar symbol of judgment (see Joel 3.13; Matt. 13.30). **14**: *A figure like a man* (lit. "Son of Man"): see 1.13–15 n. **17–20**: *Grape harvest* (v. 18): see 19.15; Isa. 63.1–6.

15.1–8: Introduction to the seven plagues of the seven bowls. 2: *A sea of glass*: see 4.6 n. *Those who* (like Jesus) *had been victorious*: the martyred faithful (compare Jn. 16.31–33). **3**: *Song of Moses . . . song of the Lamb* combines the first deliverer, Moses (see Exod. 15.1–18; Ps. 145.17), with the second, Jesus (the new exodus, a central NT theme): Moses' victory over Pharaoh foreshadows victory over the beast; compare Ps. 145.17.

heavenly Tent of Testimony was opened, [6]and from it came the seven angels with the seven plagues. They were robed in fine linen, pure and shining, and had golden girdles round their breasts. [7]One of the four living creatures gave to the seven angels seven golden bowls full of the wrath of God who lives for ever. [8]The sanctuary was filled with smoke from the glory of God and from his power, so that no one could enter it until the seven plagues of the seven angels were completed.

16 I heard a loud voice from the sanctuary say to the seven angels, 'Go and pour out the seven bowls of God's wrath on the earth.'

[2]The first angel went and poured out his bowl on the earth; and foul malignant sores appeared on the men that wore the mark of the beast and worshipped its image.

[3]The second angel poured out his bowl on the sea; and the sea turned to blood like the blood from a dead body, and every living thing in it died.

[4]The third angel poured out his bowl on the rivers and springs, and they turned to blood.

[5]And I heard the angel of the waters say, 'You are just in these your judgements, you who are, and were, O Holy One; [6]for they shed the blood of your people and your prophets, and blood you have given them to drink. They have what they deserve!' [7]I heard a voice from the altar cry, 'Yes, Lord God, sovereign over all, true and just are your judgements!'

[8]The fourth angel poured out his bowl on the sun; and it was allowed to burn people with its flames. [9]They were severely burned, and cursed the name of God who had the power to inflict such plagues, but they did not repent and do him homage.

[10]The fifth angel poured out his bowl on the throne of the beast; and its kingdom was plunged into darkness. Men gnawed their tongues in agony, [11]and cursed the God of heaven for their pain and sores, but they would not repent of what they had done.

[12]The sixth angel poured out his bowl on the Great River, the Euphrates; and its water was dried up to prepare a way for the kings from the east.

[13]I saw three foul spirits like frogs coming from the mouths of the dragon, the beast, and the false prophet. [14]These are demonic spirits with power to work miracles, sent out to muster all the kings of the world for the battle on the great day of God the sovereign Lord. [15]('See, I am coming like a thief! Happy the man who stays awake, and keeps his clothes at hand so that he will not have to go naked and ashamed for all to see!') [16]These spirits assembled the kings at the place called in Hebrew Armageddon.

[17]The seventh angel poured out his bowl on the air; and out of the sanctuary came a loud voice from the throne, which said, 'It is over!' [18]There followed flashes of lightning and peals of thunder, and a violent earthquake, so violent that nothing like it had ever happened in human history.

The destruction of Babylon

[19]THE great city was split in three, and the cities of the nations collapsed in ruin. God did not forget Babylon the great, but made her drink the cup which was filled with the

---

4: Compare Ps. 86.9–10; Jer. 10.7. **5:** *Tent of Testimony:* forerunner of the temple (see Exod. 40.34). **8:** *Filled with smoke:* see Isa. 6.4.

16.1–21: The seven bowls of God's wrath (similar to the ten plagues of Exod. chs. 7–11). **1:** *A loud voice from the sanctuary . . . pour:* compare Isa. 66.6; Ps. 69.24. **2:** *Sores:* see Exod. 9.10–11; Deut. 28.27. **3–4:** *Sea . . . springs . . . turned to blood:* see Exod. 7.17–21. **5:** *You are just:* see Ps. 119.137. **7:** *A voice from the altar:* see 6.9–10. **8–12:** While the plagues here are not fully parallel to those in Exod., on the fifth (v. 10, *darkness*), compare Exod. 10.21–23. **10:** *The throne of the beast:* Rome. **12:** *Dried up:* compare Exod. 14.21; Isa. 11.15–16. Perhaps the drying up of the *Euphrates* alludes to opening the way for the expected return of Nero with the *kings from the east*. See 13.1, 3 nn.; 17.15–18. **13:** *Dragon . . . beast . . . false prophet:* a trinity of evil over against God, the Lamb and the Spirit (the inspirer of true prophets). **14:** *All the kings of the world* (not the kings from the east; compare 17.15–18; 19.19–21): see Ps. 2; Joel 3.2; Zech. 14.1–3. **15:** *Like a thief:* 1 Thess. 5.1–2 n. **16:** *Armageddon* ("Hill of Megiddo," a strategic military post in antiquity; see Judg. 5.19; 2 Kgs. 23.29–30; 2 Chr. 35.22); in apocalyptic literature, the scene of the final battle between good and evil (compare 19.17–21). **17–21:** The seventh bowl pours out judgments similar to the seven trumpets (chs. 8–11).

fierce wine of his wrath. [20]Every island vanished, and not a mountain was to be seen. [21]Huge hailstones, weighing as much as a hundredweight, crashed down from the sky on the people; and they cursed God because the plague of hail was so severe.

17 ONE of the seven angels who held the seven bowls came and spoke to me; 'Come,' he said, 'I will show you the verdict on the great whore, she who is enthroned over many waters. [2]The kings of the earth have committed fornication with her, and people the world over have made themselves drunk on the wine of her fornication.' [3]He carried me in spirit into the wilderness, and I saw a woman mounted on a scarlet beast which was covered with blasphemous names and had seven heads and ten horns. [4]The woman was clothed in purple and scarlet, and decked out with gold and precious stones and pearls. In her hand she held a gold cup full of obscenities and the foulness of her fornication. [5]Written on her forehead was a name with a secret meaning: 'Babylon the great, the mother of whores and of every obscenity on earth.' [6]I saw that the woman was drunk with the blood of God's people, and with the blood of those who had borne their testimony to Jesus.

At the sight of her I was greatly astonished. [7]But the angel said to me, 'Why are you astonished? I will tell you the secret of the woman and of the beast she rides, with the seven heads and the ten horns. [8]The beast you saw was once alive, and is alive no longer, but has yet to ascend out of the abyss before going to be destroyed. All the inhabitants of the earth whose names have not been written in the book of life since the foundation of the world will be astonished to see the beast, which once was alive, and is alive no longer, and has still to appear.

[9]'This calls for a mind with insight. The seven heads are seven hills on which the woman sits enthroned. [10]They also represent seven kings: five have already fallen, one is now reigning, and the other has yet to come. When he does come, he is to last for only a little while. [11]As for the beast that once was alive and is alive no longer, he is an eighth — and yet he is one of the seven, and he is going to destruction. [12]The ten horns you saw are ten kings who have not yet begun to reign, but who for a brief hour will share royal authority with the beast. [13]They have a single purpose and will confer their power and authority on the beast. [14]They will wage war on the Lamb, but the Lamb will conquer them, for he is Lord of lords and King of kings, and those who are with him are called and chosen and faithful.'

[15]He continued: 'The waters you saw, where the great whore sat enthroned, represent nations, populations, races, and languages. [16]As for the ten horns you saw, and the beast, they will come to hate the whore. They will strip her naked and leave her destitute; they will devour her flesh and burn her up. [17]For God has put it into their minds to carry out his purpose, by making common cause and conferring their sovereignty on the beast until God's words are fulfilled. [18]The woman you saw is the great city that holds sway over the kings of the earth.'

18 After this I saw another angel coming down from heaven; he possessed

17:10 **kings:** or emperors.

19: *Babylon:* Rome. *Fierce wine:* 14.10 n. **21:** *Hail:* Exod. 9.23.

    17.1–18: The future fall of Babylon/Rome. 1: The description of a great, sinful city as a *whore* goes back to the prophets (compare Isa. 23.16; Ezek. 16.15; Nah. 3.4); here, the city is Rome, destroyed by the beast (Nero) in v. 16; contrast the bride (New Jerusalem) in 19.7; 21.2, 9. *Enthroned over many waters* echoes Jer. 51.13. **2:** *Fornication:* here, emperor worship, not just idolatry in general. **3:** *A woman . . . on a scarlet beast:* the city, Rome, and its imperial power. *Blasphemous names:* see 13.1 n. *Seven heads . . . ten horns:* defined in vv. 9–12. **4:** *A gold cup:* see Jer. 51.7. **6:** *Drunk with the blood* may once have referred to the Jewish War (see 11.1–14 n.); here it is applied to later persecution. **7–18:** The *beast* destroys the *whore*. **7–8:** This perhaps identifies Domitian as the "returned Nero"; see 13.1, 3 nn. **9:** Rome was built on *seven hills*. **10:** *Seven kings:* This is difficult to decipher; probably Domitian (81–96 C.E.) is seen as the *one . . . now reigning*. **11:** *An eighth — and yet he is one of the seven:* Nero. **12:** The *ten kings* are Nero's companions from the east; see 16.12 n. **14:** *Will wage war on the Lamb:* i.e. in the future (see 19.19–21), but before that they will destroy Rome (vv. 16–18). *Lord of lords:* Deut. 10.17; Dan. 2.47. **16:** *Burn her up:* see 18.16; Nero was suspected of starting the destructive fire in Rome in 64 C.E.

great authority and the earth shone with his splendour. ² In a mighty voice he proclaimed, 'Fallen, fallen is Babylon the great! She has become a dwelling for demons, a haunt for every unclean spirit, for every unclean and loathsome bird. ³ All the nations have drunk the wine of God's anger roused by her fornication; the kings of the earth have committed fornication with her, and merchants the world over have grown rich on her wealth and luxury.'

⁴ I heard another voice from heaven saying: 'Come out from her, my people, lest you have any part in her sins and you share in her plagues, ⁵ for her sins are piled high as heaven, and God has not forgotten her crimes. ⁶ Pay her back in her own coin, repay her twice over for her deeds! Give her a potion twice as strong as the one she mixed! ⁷ Measure out torment and grief to match her pomp and luxury! "I am a queen on my throne!" she says to herself. "No widow's weeds for me, no mourning!" ⁸ That is why plagues shall strike her in a single day, pestilence, bereavement, and famine, and she shall perish in flames; for mighty is the Lord God who has pronounced her doom!'

⁹ The kings of the earth who committed fornication with her and wallowed in her luxury will weep and wail over her, as they see the smoke of her burning. ¹⁰ In terror at her torment they will keep their distance and say, 'Alas, alas for you great city, mighty city of Babylon! In a moment your doom has come upon you!'

¹¹ The merchants of the world will weep and mourn for her, because no one buys their cargoes any more, ¹² cargoes of gold and silver, precious stones and pearls, purple and scarlet cloth, silks and fine linens; all sorts of fragrant wood, and all kinds of objects made of ivory or of costly woods, bronze, iron, or marble; ¹³ cinnamon and spice, incense, perfumes, and frankincense; wine, oil, flour and wheat, cattle and sheep, horses, chariots, slaves, and human lives. ¹⁴ 'The harvest you longed for', they will say, 'is gone from you; all the glitter and glamour are lost, never to be found again!' ¹⁵ The traders in all these goods, who grew rich on her, will keep their distance in terror at her torment; weeping and mourning ¹⁶ they will say: 'Alas, alas for the great city that was clothed in fine linen and purple and scarlet, decked out with gold and precious stones and pearls! ¹⁷ So much wealth laid waste in a moment!'

All the sea-captains and voyagers, the sailors and those who made a living on the sea, stayed at a distance; ¹⁸ as they saw the smoke of her burning, they cried out, 'Was there ever a city like the great city?' ¹⁹ They threw dust on their heads and, weeping and mourning, they cried aloud: 'Alas, alas for the great city, where all who had ships at sea grew rich from her prosperity! In a single hour she has been laid waste!'

²⁰ But let heaven exult over her; exult, God's people, apostles and prophets, for he has imposed on her the sentence she passed on you!

²¹ Then a mighty angel picked up a stone like a great millstone and hurled it into the sea, saying, 'Thus shall Babylon, the great city, be sent hurtling down, never to be seen again! ²² The sound of harpists and minstrels, flute-players and trumpeters, shall no more be heard in you; no more shall craftsmen of any trade be found in you, or the sound of the mill be heard in you; ²³ no more shall the light of the lamp appear in you, no more the voices of the bridegroom and bride be heard in you! Your traders were once the merchant princes of the world, and with your sorcery you deceived all the nations.' ²⁴ The blood of the prophets and of God's people was found in her, the blood of all who had been slain on earth.

19 After this I heard what sounded like a vast throng in heaven shouting:

18.1–24: **The fall of and lament over Babylon** (compare the dirge over Tyre in Ezek. chs. 26–27). Elements of several OT prophecies against Babylon are woven into a condemnation of Rome. **2:** *Fallen, fallen:* see Isa. 13.19–22; 21.9. **4:** *Come out from her:* compare Jer. 50.8; 51.45. **7–8:** Compare the boast with Isa. 47.7–9. **9–10:** See Ezek. 26.16–18. **11:** Ezek. 27.31. **12–16:** Ezek. 27.15–16. Rome's power as a world trade center is vividly depicted in the list of rich goods. **17–20:** Contrast vv. 17–19 with v. 20. **18:** *Was there ever a city:* see Ezek. 27.32. **19:** *Dust on their heads:* see Ezek. 27.30. **21:** *A great millstone:* compare Jer. 51.63–64. **22–24:** See Jer. 25.10.

19.1–5: **Rejoicing over Rome's destruction. 1:** *Hallelujah:* "Praise God" (Heb.), found only in this ch. in the NT.

'Hallelujah! Victory and glory and power belong to our God, ²for true and just are his judgements! He has condemned the great whore who corrupted the earth with her fornication; he has taken vengeance on her for the blood of his servants.'

³Once more they shouted:

'Hallelujah! The smoke from her burning will rise for ever!'

⁴The twenty-four elders and the four living creatures bowed down and worshipped God who sits on the throne; they cried: 'Amen! Hallelujah!'

⁵THERE came a voice from the throne saying: 'Praise our God, all you his servants, you that fear him, both small and great!' ⁶And I heard what sounded like a vast throng, like the sound of a mighty torrent or of great peals of thunder, and they cried:

'Hallelujah! The Lord our God, sovereign over all, has entered on his reign! ⁷Let us rejoice and shout for joy and pay homage to him, for the wedding day of the Lamb has come! His bride has made herself ready, ⁸and she has been given fine linen, shining and clean, to wear.'

(The fine linen signifies the righteous deeds of God's people.)

⁹THE angel said to me, 'Write this: "Happy are those who are invited to the wedding banquet of the Lamb!"' He added, 'These are the very words of God.' ¹⁰I prostrated myself to worship him, but he said, 'You must not do that! I am a fellow-servant with you and your brothers who bear their witness to Jesus. It is God you must worship. For those who bear witness to Jesus have the spirit of prophecy.'

More visions

¹¹I SAW heaven wide open, and a white horse appeared; its rider's name was Faithful and True, for he is just in judgement and just in war. ¹²His eyes flamed like fire, and on his head were many diadems. Written on him was a name known to none but himself; ¹³he was robed in a garment dyed in blood, and he was called the Word of God. ¹⁴The armies of heaven followed him, riding on white horses and clothed in fine linen, white and clean. ¹⁵Out of his mouth came a sharp sword to smite the nations; for it is he who will rule them with a rod of iron, and tread the winepress of the fierce wrath of God the sovereign Lord. ¹⁶On his robe and on his thigh was written the title: 'King of kings and Lord of lords'.

¹⁷I saw an angel standing in the sun. He cried aloud to all the birds flying in midheaven: 'Come, gather together for God's great banquet, ¹⁸to eat the flesh of kings, commanders, and warriors, the flesh of horses and their riders, the flesh of all, the free and the slave, the small and the great!' ¹⁹I saw the beast and the kings of the earth with their armies mustered to do battle against the rider and his army. ²⁰The beast was taken prisoner, along with the false prophet who had worked miracles in its presence and deluded those who had received the mark of the beast and worshipped its image. The two of them were thrown alive into the lake of fire with its sulphurous flames. ²¹The rest were killed by the sword which came out of the rider's mouth, and the birds all gorged themselves on their flesh.

20 I saw an angel coming down from heaven with the key to the abyss and a great chain in his hand. ²He seized the dragon, that ancient serpent who is the Devil, or Satan, and chained him up for a thousand years; ³he threw him into the abyss, shutting and sealing it over him, so that he might not

---

19.6–10: The marriage of the Lamb. 7–8: The OT sometimes sees Israel as God's *bride* (e.g. Jer. 2.2); here the *bride* of the Lamb is the church (compare 2 Cor. 11.2; Eph. 5.25–33). **10:** *God you must worship:* there is to be no worship of angelic beings; see 22.8–9; Col. 2.18.

19.11–21: Christ's victory over the beast. 11: *A white horse:* see 6.2. **12:** *Eyes . . . like fire:* see 2.18. **13:** *A garment dyed in blood:* see Isa. 63.1–6. *The Word of God:* see 1.2 n. **15:** *A sharp sword:* see 1.16 n.; 2.12. *A rod of iron:* Ps. 2.9. *Winepress:* see 14.10 n., 17–20. **16:** *Lord of lords:* Deut. 10.17; Dan. 2.47. **17–21:** Compare Ezek. 39.17–20. **19:** The final battle anticipated in 16.14–16. **20:** *The lake of fire:* see 14.10; 20.10.

20.1–15: The events of the last judgment. 2–4: With *Satan* bound (v. 2), the martyred dead (others later; see v. 5) are to rise and reign with Christ (following a Jewish messianic expectation). **2:** *Thousand years:* the seduce the nations again till the thousand years were ended. After that he must be let loose for a little while.

⁴I saw thrones, and on them sat those to whom judgement was committed. I saw the souls of those who, for the sake of God's word and their witness to Jesus, had been beheaded, those who had not worshipped the beast and its image or received its mark on forehead or hand. They came to life again and reigned with Christ for a thousand years, ⁵though the rest of the dead did not come to life until the thousand years were ended. This is the first resurrection. ⁶Blessed and holy are those who share in this first resurrection! Over them the second death has no power; but they shall be priests of God and of Christ, and shall reign with him for the thousand years.

⁷When the thousand years are ended, Satan will be let loose from his prison, ⁸and he will come out to seduce the nations in the four quarters of the earth. He will muster them for war, the hosts of Gog and Magog, countless as the sands of the sea. ⁹They marched over the breadth of the land and laid siege to the camp of God's people and the city that he loves. But fire came down on them from heaven and consumed them. ¹⁰Their seducer, the Devil, was flung into the lake of fire and sulphur, where the beast and the false prophet had been flung to be tormented day and night for ever.

¹¹I saw a great, white throne, and the One who sits upon it. From his presence earth and heaven fled away, and there was no room for them any more. ¹²I saw the dead, great and small, standing before the throne; and books were opened. Then another book, the book of life, was opened. The dead were judged by what they had done, as recorded in these books. ¹³The sea gave up the dead that were in it, and Death and Hades gave up the dead in their keeping. Everyone was judged on the record of his deeds. ¹⁴Then Death and Hades were flung into the lake of fire. This lake of fire is the second death; ¹⁵into it were flung any whose names were not to be found in the book of life.

21 I SAW a new heaven and a new earth, for the first heaven and the first earth had vanished, and there was no longer any sea. ²I saw the Holy City, new Jerusalem, coming down out of heaven from God, made ready like a bride adorned for her husband. ³I heard a loud voice proclaiming from the throne: 'Now God has his dwelling with mankind! He will dwell among them and they shall be his people, and God himself will be with them. ⁴He will wipe every tear from their eyes. There shall be an end to death, and to mourning and crying and pain, for the old order has passed away!'

⁵The One who sat on the throne said, 'I am making all things new!' ('Write this down,' he said, 'for these words are trustworthy and true.') ⁶Then he said to me, 'It is done! I am the Alpha and the Omega, the beginning and the end. To the thirsty I will give water from the spring of life as a gift. ⁷This is the victors' heritage; and I will be their God and they will be my children. ⁸But as for the cowardly, the faithless, and the obscene, the murderers,

millennium (from Latin *mille,* thousand, and *annus,* year). **4:** *Thrones . . . judgement:* see Dan. 7.9, 22, 27; Matt. 19.28; Lk. 22.30. **6:** *The second death:* defined in v. 14; see 2.11. **7:** The short release of Satan (see v. 3) may follow the Babylonian legend of Tiamat, the sea monster of chaos who is to be released at the end of history to be defeated again by Marduk, the god of light. **8:** *The hosts of Gog and Magog* (see Ezek. chs. 38–39) are identified with *the nations* who gather for the final battle against God's people; this also provides an opportunity to depict a final siege of *the city,* i.e. Jerusalem (v. 9); see Zech. ch. 14. **9:** *Fire came down:* compare 2 Kgs. 1.10–12. **10:** The *Devil, beast,* and *false prophet* are defeated forever. **11–15:** Here is the last judgment by the *books* (see 3.5 n.; compare Dan. 7.9–10; Matt. 16.27; 25.31–46; Rom. 2.6) in connection with the "second resurrection" (see v. 5); and *Death* and *Hades* (Death's domain; see 1.18) are vanquished (see 21.4).

21.1–21: The new heaven and earth and the new Jerusalem. 1: The future holds promise of a transformation so complete that there will be *a new heaven and . . . earth;* see Isa. 65.17; 66.22; Rom. 8.19–21. *No longer any sea:* perhaps, as in Babylonian legend, the sea is regarded as hostile. **2:** The *new Jerusalem* is not in heaven but comes down from it (see v. 10; 3.12). *Bride:* see 19.7–8 n. **3:** *God . . . dwelling* with humanity: compare Ezek. 37.27. **4:** *Wipe every tear:* see 7.17; Isa. 25.8; 35.10. **5:** Only here and in 1.8 does God (*the One*) speak. *All things new:* Isa. 43.19. **6:** *Alpha* and *Omega:* see 1.8 n. *To the thirsty . . . water:* see 7.17 n.; 22.1; Isa. 55.1. **7:** *Their God . . . my children:* Pss. 2.7; 89.27–28.

fornicators, sorcerers, idolaters, and liars of every kind, the lake that burns with sulphurous flames will be their portion, and that is the second death.'

The new Jerusalem

9 ONE of the seven angels who held the seven bowls full of the seven last plagues came and spoke to me. 'Come,' he said, 'and I will show you the bride, the wife of the Lamb.' 10 So in the spirit he carried me away to a great and lofty mountain, and showed me Jerusalem, the Holy City, coming down out of heaven from God. 11 It shone with the glory of God; it had the radiance of some priceless jewel, like a jasper, clear as crystal. 12 It had a great and lofty wall with twelve gates, at which were stationed twelve angels; on the gates were inscribed the names of the twelve tribes of Israel. 13 There were three gates to the east, three to the north, three to the south, and three to the west. 14 The city wall had twelve foundation-stones, and on them were the names of the twelve apostles of the Lamb.

15 The angel who spoke with me carried a gold measuring rod to measure the city, its gates, and its wall. 16 The city had four sides, and it was as wide as it was long. Measured by his rod, it was twelve thousand furlongs, its length and breadth and height being equal. 17 Its wall was one hundred and forty-four cubits high, by human measurements, which the angel used. 18 The wall was built of jasper, while the city itself was of pure gold, bright as clear glass. 19 The foundations of the city wall were adorned with precious stones of every kind, the first of the foundation-stones being jasper, the second lapis lazuli, the third

chalcedony, the fourth emerald, 20 the fifth sardonyx, the sixth cornelian, the seventh chrysolite, the eighth beryl, the ninth topaz, the tenth chrysoprase, the eleventh turquoise, and the twelfth amethyst. 21 The twelve gates were twelve pearls, each gate fashioned from a single pearl. The great street of the city was of pure gold, like translucent glass.

22 I saw no temple in the city, for its temple was the sovereign Lord God and the Lamb. 23 The city did not need the sun or the moon to shine on it, for the glory of God gave it light, and its lamp was the Lamb. 24 By its light shall the nations walk, and to it the kings of the earth shall bring their splendour. 25 The gates of the city shall never be shut by day, nor will there be any night there. 26 The splendour and wealth of the nations shall be brought into it, 27 but nothing unclean shall enter, nor anyone whose ways are foul or false; only those shall enter whose names are inscribed in the Lamb's book of life.

22 Then the angel showed me the river of the water of life, sparkling like crystal, flowing from the throne of God and of the Lamb 2 down the middle of the city's street. On either side of the river stood a tree of life, which yields twelve crops of fruit, one for each month of the year. The leaves of the trees are for the healing of the nations. 3 Every accursed thing shall disappear. The throne of God and of the Lamb will be there, and his servants shall worship him; 4 they shall see him face to face and bear his name on their foreheads. 5 There shall be no more night, nor will they need the light of lamp or sun, for the Lord God will give them light; and they shall reign for ever.

10: *Showed me . . . the Holy City:* compare Ezek. 40.2. **12–14:** The juxtaposition of *twelve tribes* (v. 12) and *twelve apostles* (v. 14) points to old and new covenant peoples; see 4.4 n. **15:** *A gold measuring rod:* see Ezek. 40.5. **16:** The dimensions correspond to the temple's Holy of Holies, but there is no longer to be a temple (see 21.22) and all (as priests; see 1.6 n.; Isa. 61.6), not only the high priest, have access to God. **18–20:** Exod. 28.15–21; Isa. 54.11–12.

   21.22–22.5: A city of light and life. 23: *Did not need the sun:* see Isa. 60.19. **24:** Isa. 60.3, 5. **25:** Isa. 60.11. **26:** Isa. 60.3–9. **27:** *Nothing unclean:* see Isa. 52.1. **22.1:** *The river of the water of life:* compare Ezek. 47.1–12, where it flows from the temple; here it flows from the *throne* (see Zech. 14.7–8). **2:** *A tree of life:* see 2.7 n.; Ezek. 47.7. *Healing of the nations:* compare Ezek. 47.12, Sept.; also Isa. 49.6. **3:** *Every accursed thing shall disappear:* in Gen. 3.17–18 it is humanity that is accursed; now humankind is redeemed in a new paradise with access to the tree of life. **4:** *See . . . face to face:* Ps. 17.15; 1 Cor. 13.12. *Name on their foreheads:* see 3.12 n.; in Exod. 28.36–38 the high priest has "Holy to the Lord" on his forehead, but now all are priests and bear God's name.

Conclusion

6 HE said to me, 'These words are trustworthy and true. The Lord God who inspires the prophets has sent his angel to show his servants what must soon take place. 7 And remember, I am coming soon!'

Happy is the man who takes to heart the words of prophecy contained in this book! 8 It was I, John, who heard and saw these things. When I had heard and seen them, I prostrated myself to worship the angel who had shown them to me. 9 But he said, 'You must not do that! I am a fellow-servant with you and your brothers the prophets and with those who take to heart the words of this book. It is God you must worship.' 10 He told me, 'Do not seal up the words of the prophecy that are in this book, for the time of fulfilment is near. 11 Meanwhile, let the evildoers persist in doing evil and the filthy-minded continue in their filth, but let the good persevere in their goodness and the holy continue in holiness.'

12 'I am coming soon, and bringing with me my recompense to repay everyone according to what he has done! 13 I am the Alpha and the Omega, the first and the last, the beginning and the end.'

14 Happy are those who wash their robes clean! They shall be free to eat from the tree of life and may enter the city by the gates. 15 Outside are the perverts, the sorcerers and fornicators, the murderers and idolaters, and all who love and practise deceit.

16 'I, Jesus, have sent my angel to you with this testimony for the churches. I am the offspring of David, the shoot growing from his stock, the bright star of dawn.'

17 'Come!' say the Spirit and the bride.

'Come!' let each hearer reply.

Let the thirsty come; let whoever wishes accept the water of life as a gift.

18 I, John, give this warning to everyone who is listening to the words of prophecy in this book: if anyone adds to them, God will add to him the plagues described in this book; 19 if anyone takes away from the words in this book of prophecy, God will take away from him his share in the tree of life and in the Holy City, which are described in this book.

20 He who gives this testimony says: 'Yes, I am coming soon!'

Amen. Come, Lord Jesus!

21 The grace of the Lord Jesus be with all.

22:15 **perverts:** *lit.* dogs.

22.6–21: Final admonitions and promises. 6: *Sent his angel:* see 1.1; 22.16. **7:** *I am coming soon:* see 16.15. **8:** *I, John:* see Introduction; 1.1, 4, 9. **9:** *You must not:* see 19.10 n. **10:** *Do not seal up . . . the time . . . is near:* the command to conceal in Dan. 8.26; 12.4, 9 is reversed because of the anticipation of the imminent end. **11:** There is no time for change; compare Dan. 12.10. **12:** *Repay everyone:* see 20.11–15 n.; compare Isa. 40.10; Jer. 17.10. **14:** *Who wash their robes:* see 7.14. **15:** *Outside:* compare Matt. 8.12. *Perverts:* lit. "dogs"; compare Phil. 3.2. *Sorcerers:* lit. poisoners; see 21.8. **16:** *I, Jesus:* see 1.1–2. *Offspring of David . . . shoot:* see 5.5 n. *Star of dawn:* see 2.28; compare Num. 24.17. **17:** *The bride:* see 19.7–8 n. **18–19:** *If anyone adds . . . if anyone takes away:* compare Deut. 4.2; 12.32. **20:** *Come, Lord Jesus:* compare 1 Cor. 16.22 n.

Select Index to People, Places, and Themes in the Bible

This index is designed to enable the reader to locate *persons, places,* and *ideas* in the Bible. Biblical books (such as Job, Micah, Isaiah) do not appear, but references are listed to passages of primary significance concerning the men: Job in Ezekiel and James; Micah in Jeremiah; and Isaiah in Kings, Chronicles, and in some of the books of the Apocrypha and the New Testament. Passing mention of principal characters such as even Abraham in Gen. 50.24, for example, is not included. Therefore, since the index is necessarily selective, it is suggested that a complete concordance to the Bible be consulted.

Sabbath: Gen. 2.2–3; Exod. 16.22–30; 20.8–11;
23.12; 31.12–17; 34.21; Lev. 19.3, 30; 23.3;
26.2; Num. 15.32–36; 28.9–10; Deut. 5.12–15;
Neh. 10.31; 13.15–22; Isa. 1.13; 56.2–4; 58.13;
Jer. 17.19–27; Ezek. 20.12–24; 22.8, 26; 46.1–
4; 1 Macc. 2.32–38; Matt. 12.1–14; Mk. 2.23–
3.6; Lk. 6.1–11; Acts 13.27, 42, 44
Sabbatical and Jubilee Years: Exod. 23.10–11; Lev.
25.1–7, 10–54; 26.34–35, 43; 27.17–24; Deut.
ch. 15; 31.10–11; 1 Macc. 6.49, 53–54
Sackcloth: Gen. 37.34; Neh. 9.1; Esther 4.1–4; Job
16.15; Pss. 30.11; 35.13; Isa. 15.3; 58.5; Jer.
49.3; Dan. 9.3; Jonah 3.5; Matt. 11.21
Sacrifice, Human: Gen. 22.2; Exod. 13.13; Lev.
18.21; 20.2–5; Deut. 12.31; 1 Kgs. 16.34;
2 Kgs. 3.27; 16.3; 23.10; Ps. 106.37–38; Jer.
7.31; 19.5; 32.35; Ezek. 16.20–21; Wisd.
12.3–6
Sacrifice/Offering: Gen. 31.54; Exod. 3.18; 5.17;
20.24–25; 23.18; 29.10–28; 34.15; Lev. chs.
1–7; 8.11–12, 22–35; 9.5–7; Num. chs. 28–29;
Deut. 12.13–28; 1 Sam. 2.29; 15.22; Ezra 4.2;
Neh. 4.2; Pss. 4.5; 40.6; 51.16–17; 54.6;
107.22; 116.17; 118.27; Prov. 15.8; 21.3;
Eccles. 5.1; 9.2; Isa. 1.11; Jer. 6.20; Ezek.
39.17; Dan. 8.11; Hos. 6.6; 8.13; Amos 5.25;
Hab. 1.16; Zeph. 1.7; Ecclus. 34.18–35.11;
Matt. 9.13; 12.7; Mk. 9.49; 12.33; Acts 7.42;
14.13; Rom. 12.1; 1 Cor. 5.7; 8.4; 10.20; Eph.
5.2; Phil. 2.17; 4.18; Heb. 9.26; 10.26; 13.15;
1 Pet. 2.5; Rev. 2.14, 20
Sadducees: Matt. 3.7; 22.23–33; Acts. 4.1–2; 23.6–8
Salamis: Acts 13.5
Salathiel: See Shealtiel
Salem: Gen. 14.18; Heb. 7.1–4; see also Jerusalem
Salome (daughter of Herodias): Matt. 14.3–11; Mk.
6.21–28
Salome (wife of Zebedee): Matt. 27.56; Mk. 16.1
Salt, Covenant of: Lev. 2.13; Num. 18.19; 2 Chr.
13.5
Salvation/Save: Exod. 14.30; Pss. 34.6; 68.19–20;
95.1; Isa. 45.17–25; Jer. 3.22–23; Matt. 1.21;
19.25–26; Lk. 1.68–79; 7.50; 19.9–10; Jn.
3.17; Acts 4.12; Rom. 1.16; 5.9–10; 10.9–10;
1 Cor. 1.18, 21; Eph. 2.5, 8; 1 Thess. 5.8–9;
1 Tim. 1.15; 2.15; 2 Tim. 2.10
Samaria/Samaritans: 1 Kgs. 16.23–28; 2 Kgs. 17.1–
6, 24–41; Ps. 78.67–72; Isa. 7.9; 8.4; Jer.
23.13–14; Hos. 7.1; 8.5–6; Amos 3.9; 4.1; 6.1;
8.14; Mic. 1.1–7; Matt. 10.5; Lk. 9.51–56;
10.33; 17.11–19; Jn. 4.1–42; 8.48; Acts 1.8;
8.1–8; 9.31
Samos: Acts 20.15
Samson: Judg. 13.24; 14.1–16.30; Heb. 11.32
Samuel: 1 Sam. ch. 1; 2.18–26; 3.1–4.1; 7.3–12.25;
13.8–15; 15.1–16.13; 19.18–24; 25.1; 28.3–20;
Ps. 99.6; Jer. 15.1; 2 Esd. 7.38(108); Ecclus.
46.13–20; Acts 3.24; 13.20; Heb. 11.32
Sanballat: Neh. 2.10; 4.1–2, 7–8; 6.1–14; 13.28
Sanhedrin: See Jewish Council
Sapphira: Acts 5.1–12
Sarah/Sarai: Gen. 11.29–12.20; ch. 16; 17.15–

18.15; 20.2–21.12; ch. 23; 24.34–36; 25.7–10;
49.31; Isa. 51.2; Rom. 4.19; 9.9; 1 Pet. 3.6
Sardis: Rev. 1.11; 3.1, 4
Sargon II: Isa. 20.1
Satan: 1 Chr. 21.1; Job 1.6; 2.1–7; Zech. 3.1–2;
Matt. 4.3–11; 12.26; 16.23; Mk. 4.15; Lk.
10.18; 13.16; 22.3, 31; Jn. 13.27; Acts 5.3;
26.18; Rom. 16.20; 1 Cor. 5.5; 7.5; 2 Cor.
2.11; 11.14; 12.7; 2 Thess. 2.9; 1 Tim. 1.20;
Rev. 2.13, 24; ch. 20
Saul: 1 Sam. chs. 9–11; chs. 13–22; ch. 26; 28.3–
25; ch. 31; 2 Sam. 1.5–10; 2 Esd. 7.38(108);
Ecclus. 46.19–20; Acts 13.21
Saul of Tarsus: See Paul
Save/Saviour: See Salvation
Sayings: See Proverbs
Sceptre: Gen. 49.10; Esther 4.11; Ps. 45.6; Matt.
27.29
Sceva: Acts 19.14
Scorpion: Deut. 8.15; Lk. 10.19; 11.12; Rev. 9.5
Scourge: See Flog
Scribes (doctors of the Law): 1 Chr. 27.32; Ezra
4.8; Neh. 8.4; Jer. 36.32; Ecclus. 38.24–39.11;
Matt. 8.19; 13.52; Mk. 12.38; Acts 4.5; 6.12;
23.9
Scroll of the covenant: 2 Kgs. 23.2
Secundus: Acts 20.4
Second Coming: See Parousia
Seed: Gen. 1.11; 47.19; Deut. 28.38; Ps. 126.6;
Eccles. 11.6; Isa. 30.23; 55.10; Matt. 13.3–23;
13.24–39; 17.20; Mk. 4.26–32; 1 Cor. 15.20–
23, 35–38
Seir: Gen. 36.8–9; Deut. 2.1–12; Josh. 24.4; Ezek.
ch. 35; Ecclus. 50.26; see also Edom
Sennacherib: 2 Kgs. 18.13; 2 Chr. 32.1; Isa. 36.1;
37.37; 2 Esd. 7.40(110); Tob. 1.15, 18
Seraphim: Isa. 6.2–6
Sergius Paulus: Acts 13.6–12
Sermon on the Mount: Matt. 5.3–7.27
Serpent: Gen. 3.1–15; Exod. 4.3; 7.9–15; Num.
21.6–9; 2 Kgs. 18.4; Deut. 14.29; 30.6; Wisd.
16.5–6; Bel & Snake; Mk. 16.18; Lk. 10.19;
Jn. 3.14; 2 Cor. 11.3; Rev. 12.9
Servant Songs: Isa. 42.1–4; 49.1–6; 50.4–11;
52.13–53.12
Seth: Gen. 4.25–5.8
Seven Evangelists: Acts 6.1–6
Seven Churches: Rev. 1.4, 11, 20; chs. 2–3
Shadrach, Meshach and Abed-nego: Dan. 1.6–7;
2.49; 3.12–30; S. of Three 66; 1 Macc. 2.59
Shallum (king of Israel): 2 Kgs. 15.8–15
Shalmaneser V: 2 Kgs. 17.3; 18.9; Tob. 1.2, 15
Shamgar: Judg. 3.31; 5.6
Shaphan: 2 Kgs. 22.3–14; Jer. 26.24; 39.14
Sharon: 1 Chr. 27.29; S. of S. 2.1; Isa. 35.2
Shealtiel: 1 Chr. 3.18; Ezra 3.2, 8; 5.2; Neh. 12.1;
Hag. 1.1, 12, 14; 2.2; 2 Esd. 3.1; Matt. 1.12;
Lk. 3.27
Shear-jashub: Isa. 7.3
Sheba: See Sabaeans/Seba/Sheba
Sheba (son of Bichri): 2 Sam. 20.1–22

THE NEW OXFORD

BIBLE MAPS

Prepared by Oxford Cartographers
and based on the Oxford Bible Atlas.

MAP 1

The Land of Canaan Abraham to Moses

GAD, etc.   Tribes of Israel

EDOM, etc   Kingdoms encountered by the Israelites in the 13th century, B.C.

2   Cities mentioned in Numbers and Deuteronomy, but not in Genesis.

20 Miles

20 Kilometres

0   10   20

THE GREAT SEA

(The Western Sea)

A R A M
(S Y R I A)

• Damascus

Mt. Hermon (Sirion, Senir)

Mt. Lebanon

ARGOB

B A S H A N

• Karnaim
• Ashtaroth
• Golan
• Edrei
• Ramoth-gilead

GESHUR

MAACAH

• Ijon
• Laish (Dan)
• Abel
• Beth-anath?
• Kedesh
• Kanah
• Merom
Hazor•
• Aduru

N

• Sidon

Tyre • Uzu

• Achzib
• Acco

R. Jordan

Sea of Chinnereth

Chinnereth•
• Madon

HAVVOTH-JAIR

• Yanoam
Beth-yerah (Philoteria)
• Japhia
• Anaharath?
• Shunem

G I L E A D

• Ham
• Pella (Pella)

• Beth-shean
• Rehob

M A N A S S E H

Jordan

G r a d

• Janoah

A S H E R

• Shimron
• Hannathon
• Achshaph?

Mt. Carmel

• Jokneam
• Dor

• Megiddo
• Taanach
• Beth-haggan (En-gannim)
• Ibleam
• Dothan

Aruna•
• Migdal
Gath of• Arubboth
Sharon • Yehem
• Socoh

• Tirzah
• Mt. Ebal

hill country of E P H R A I M

Sharon

of Sharon

33° 30'
36° 30'
36°
35° 30'
35°
34° 30'
33° 30'
33°
32° 30'

V W X Y Z

2 3 4

MAP 1

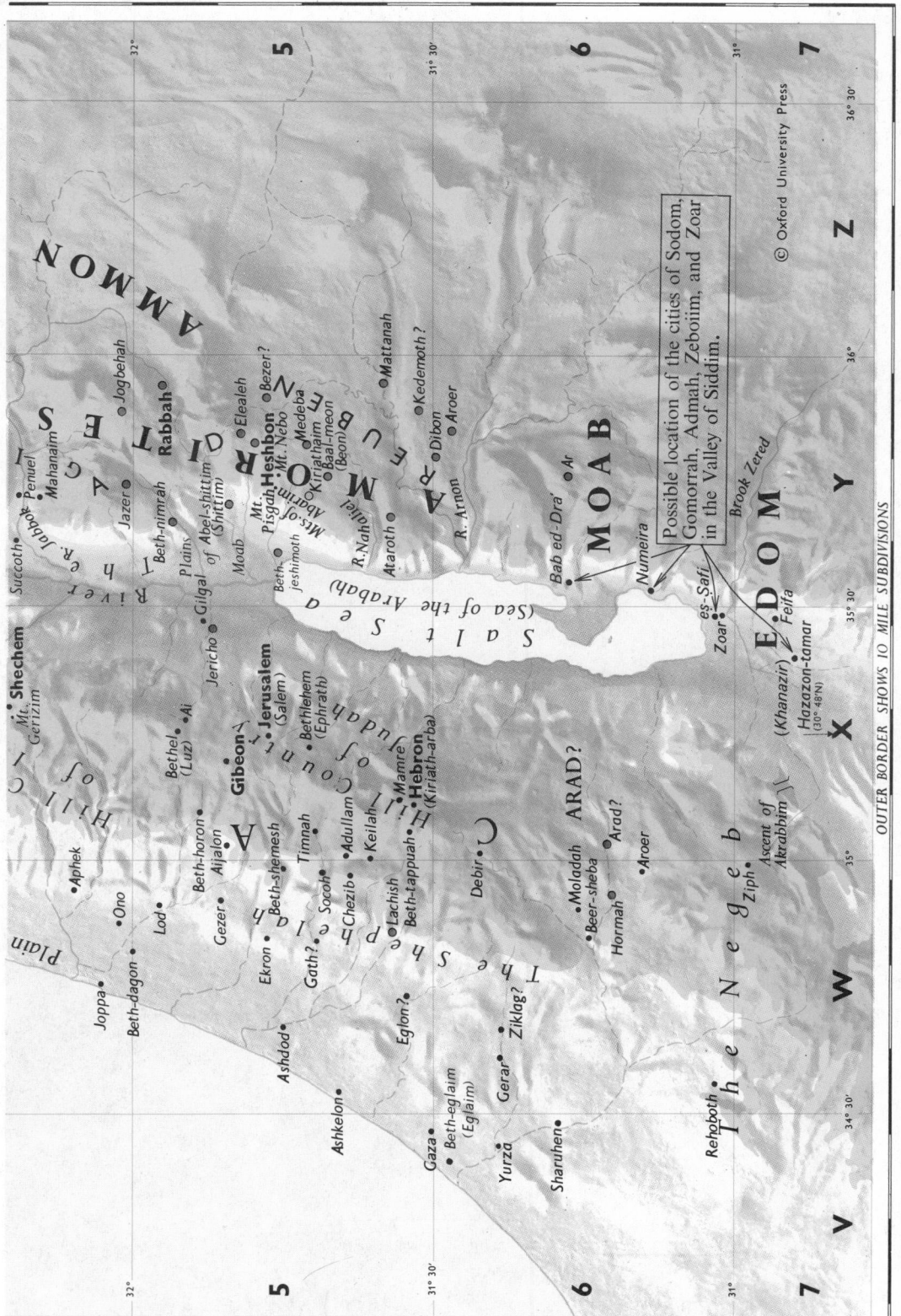

Possible location of the cities of Sodom, Gomorrah, Admah, Zeboiim, and Zoar in the Valley of Siddim.

OUTER BORDER SHOWS 10 MILE SUBDIVISIONS

MAP 2

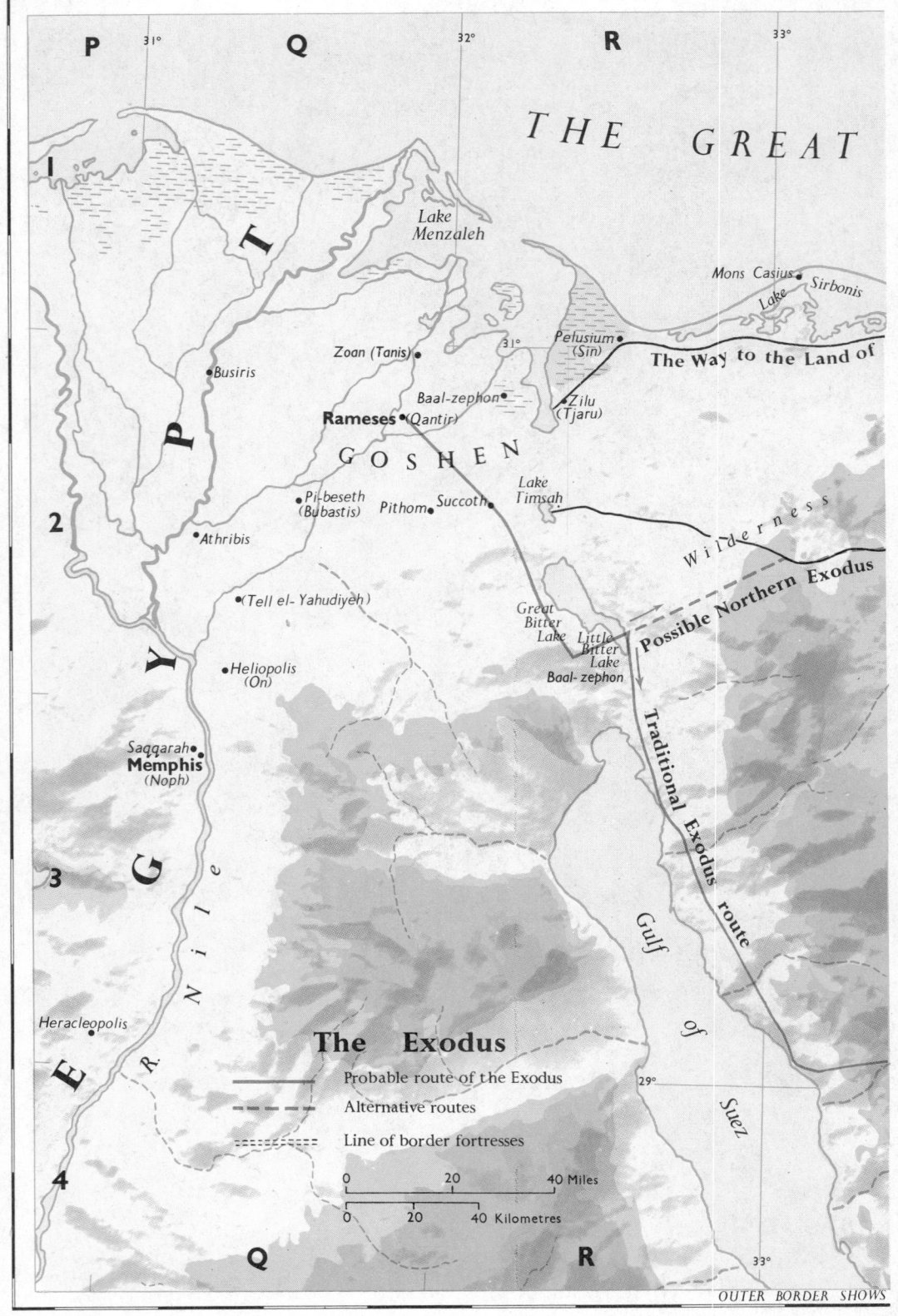

P   31°   Q   32°   R   33°

THE GREAT

I
P
T

Lake
Menzaleh

Mons Casius · Lake Sirbonis

Busiris

Zoan (Tanis) ·

Pelusium
(Sin) ·

31°

Zilu
(Tjaru)

Baal-zephon ·

The Way to the Land of

Rameses · (Qantir)

G O S H E N

Y
P
2

Pi-beseth
(Bubastis) ·   Pithom · Succoth ·

Athribis ·

Lake
Timsah

Wilderness

·(Tell el- Yahudiyeh)

Possible Northern Exodus

Heliopolis
(On) ·

Great
Bitter
Lake   Little
Bitter
Lake
Baal- zephon ·

Traditional Exodus route

Saqqarah ·
Memphis
(Noph)

G
E
3

Gulf

of

Heracleopolis ·

R. Nile

The   Exodus

Probable route of the Exodus

Alternative routes

Line of border fortresses

Suez   29°

4
Q   R   33°

0   20   40 Miles
0   20   40 Kilometres

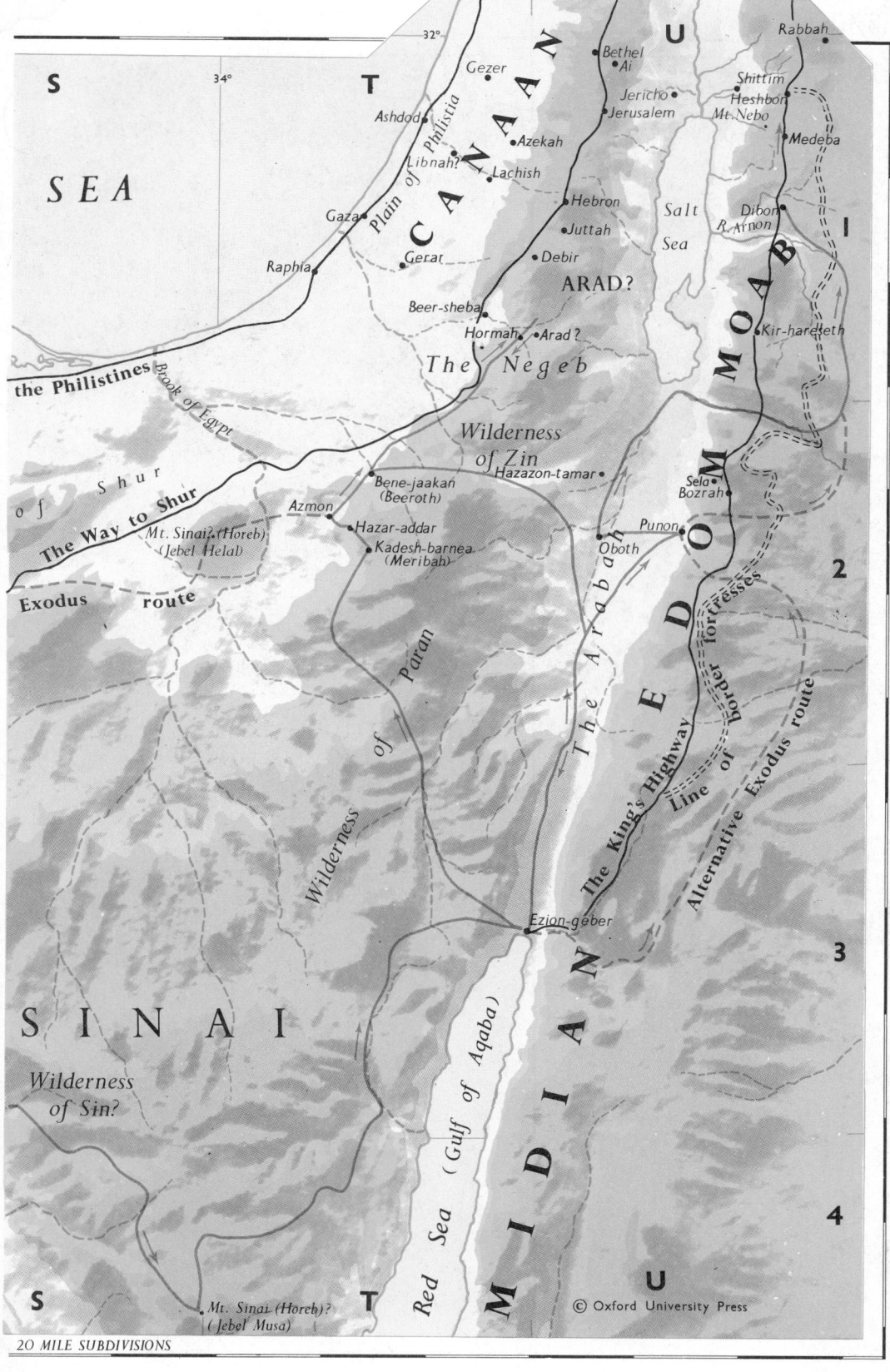

S

SEA

the Philistines

S I N A I

Wilderness
of Sin?

20 MILE SUBDIVISIONS

34°

32°

T

CANAAN

Plain of Philistia

U

Gezer

Bethel
Ai

Jericho
Jerusalem

Shittim
Heshbon
Mt. Nebo

Rabbah

Ashdod

Azekah

Libnah?
Lachish

Gaza

Hebron

Juttah

Salt
Sea

Medeba

Dibon
R. Arnon

I

Raphia

Gerar

Debir

ARAD?

Beer-sheba

Hormah   Arad ?

Kir-hareseth

The   Negeb

Wilderness
of Zin

Brook of Egypt

Shur

Bene-jaakan
(Beeroth)

Hazazon-tamar

Sela
Bozrah

of

The Way to Shur

Azmon

Hazar-addar

Kadesh-barnea
(Meribah)

Punon

Oboth

Exodus   route

Mt. Sinai? (Horeb)
(Jebel Helal)

Wilderness

of

Paran

Wilderness

The Arabah

E D O M

M O A B

2

Line of border fortresses

The King's Highway

Alternative Exodus route

Ezion-geber

3

Red Sea (Gulf of Aqaba)

M I D I A N

4

Wilderness
of Sin?

Mt. Sinai (Horeb)?
(Jebel Musa)

Red

T

U

© Oxford University Press

MAP 3

Israel in Canaan

Joshua to Samuel and Saul

ASHER, etc. Tribes of Israel
● Cities of Refuge
■ Philistine cities

20 Miles

20 Kilometres

V   W   X   Y   Z

Sidon

Tyre

Ahlab

Mt. Lebanon

Valley of Lebanon

Baal-gad?

Mt. Hermon

Damascus

Misrephoth-maim

Achzib

Acco

Abdon

Rehob

Beth-anath?

Yiron

Merom

Waters of Merom

Kedesh

Dan (Laish)

Beth-rehob

R. Jordan

NAPHTALI

Hazor

Sea of Chinnereth

Chinnereth

BASHAN

Ashtaroth

Golan

Edrei

Tob

Ramoth-gilead

HAVVOTH-JAIR

MANASSEH

GILEAD

Jabesh-gilead?

Abel-meholah

Tabbath?

Zaphon?

Jordan Arabah

Kamon?

Beth-shean

Beer

La kkum

Hammath

Rimmon

Madon

Mt. Tabor

Shimron

Hannathon

Achshaphot?

ZEBULUN

Cabul

Aphik

Hill of Moreh

En-dor

Shunem

Jezreel

V. of Jezreel

ISSACHAR

Y of Israel

Country

Mt. Gilboa

Bezek

Thebez

Tirzah

Mt. Ebal

En-gannim (Beth-haggan)

Ibleam

Taanach

Megiddo

Dor

Jokneam

Harosheth-ha-goiim

Naphath-Dor

Nahalol

Mt. Carmel

R. Kishon

MANASSEH

Socoh

Hepher?

THE   GREAT   SEA

MAP 3

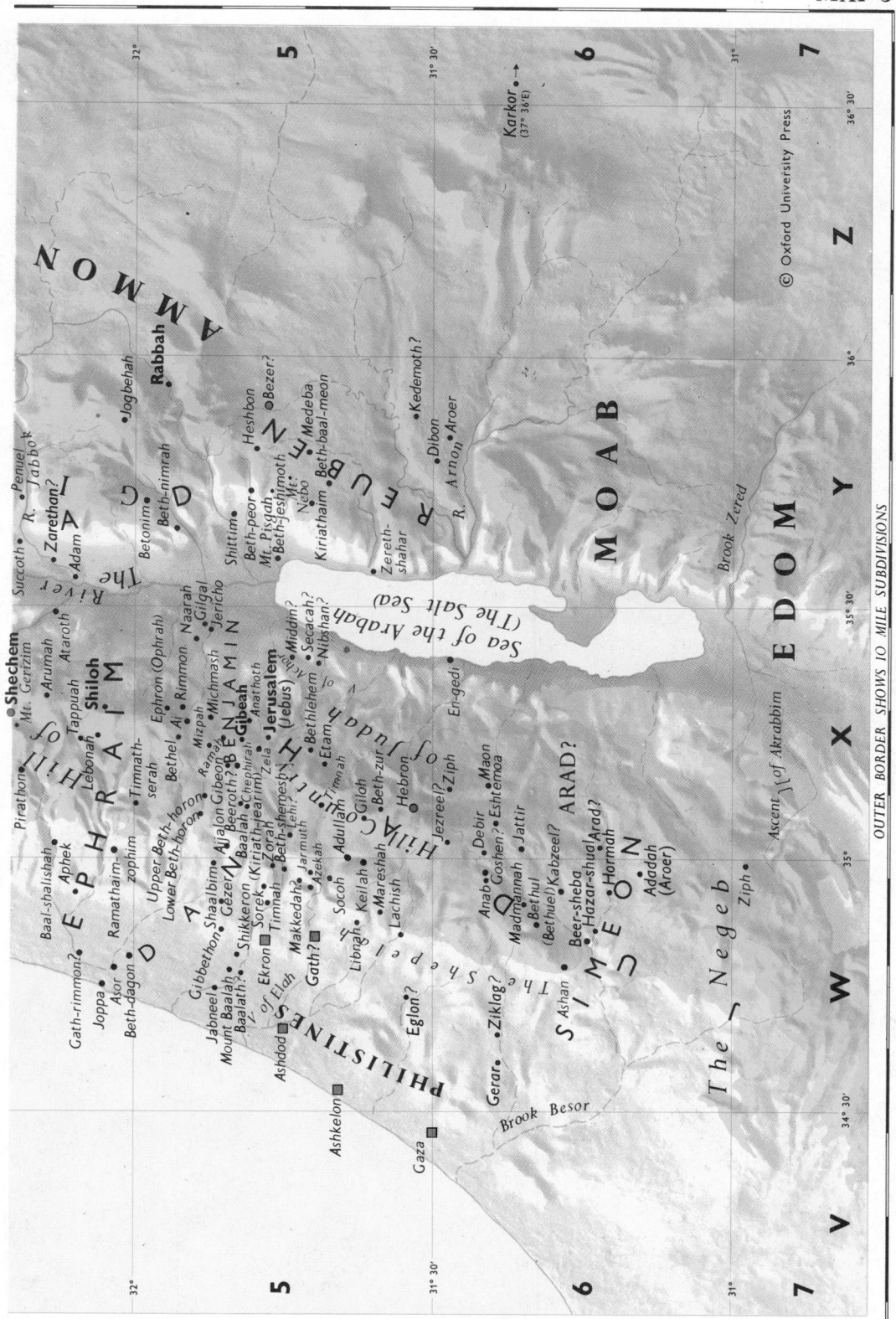

AMMON

Rabbah

Jogbehah

Succoth• R. Penuel
Jabbok
Zarethan? GILEAD
Adam

The River Jordan

Shechem
Mt. Gerizim •Arumah
Piraton• Tappuah Shiloh
Lebonah• Timnath-
serah
EPHRAIM
Baal-shalishah
Aphek
Asor
Beth-dagon
Ramathaim
zophim
Upper Beth-horon
Lower Beth-horon
Gibbethon Shaalbim
Jabneel Gezer
Mount Baalah
Baalath?
Shikkeron (Kiriath-jearim)
Ekron Timnah
Sorek Zorah
Makkedah?
Azekah
Libnah?
Gath? Socoh Keilah
Eglon? Mareshah
Lachish

Betonim
Beth-nimrah

Shittim
Beth-peor•
Mt. Pisgah
Beth-jeshimoth
Kiriathaim Mt.
Nebo
Zereth-
shahar

Heshbon
Bezer?
REUBEN
Medeba
Beth-baal-meon

•Kedemoth?

Dibon Aroer
Arnon•
R. Arnon

Karkor→
(37° 36'E)

MOAB

EDOM

Brook Zered

Ephron (Ophrah)
Bethel• Al• Rimmon Naarah
Mizpah Gilgal
Ramah Jericho
Gibeon BENJAMIN
Beeroth? Michmash
Baalah (Kiriath-jearim) Anathoth
Chephirah Gibeah
Jerusalem
Zela (Jebus)
Beth-shemesh Etam?
Jarmuth Bethlehem
Adullam Beth-zur?
Giloh Tekoa
Timnah Hebron
Jezreel?
Ziph

Midin?
Secacah?
Nibshan?

Sea of the Arabah
(The Salt Sea)

En-gedi

Maon
Debir •Eshtemoa
Goshen? Jattir
Anab• Madmannah
Bethul ARAD?
(Bethel) Kabzeel?
Beer-sheba Arad?
Hazar-shual Hormah
Adadah
(Aroer)
Ziph•

SIMEON

The Negeb

Ashdod
PHILISTINES
Ashkelon

Gaza

Gerar•
Ziklag?
Ashan

Brook Besor

Ascent of Akrabbim

OUTER BORDER SHOWS 10 MILE SUBDIVISIONS

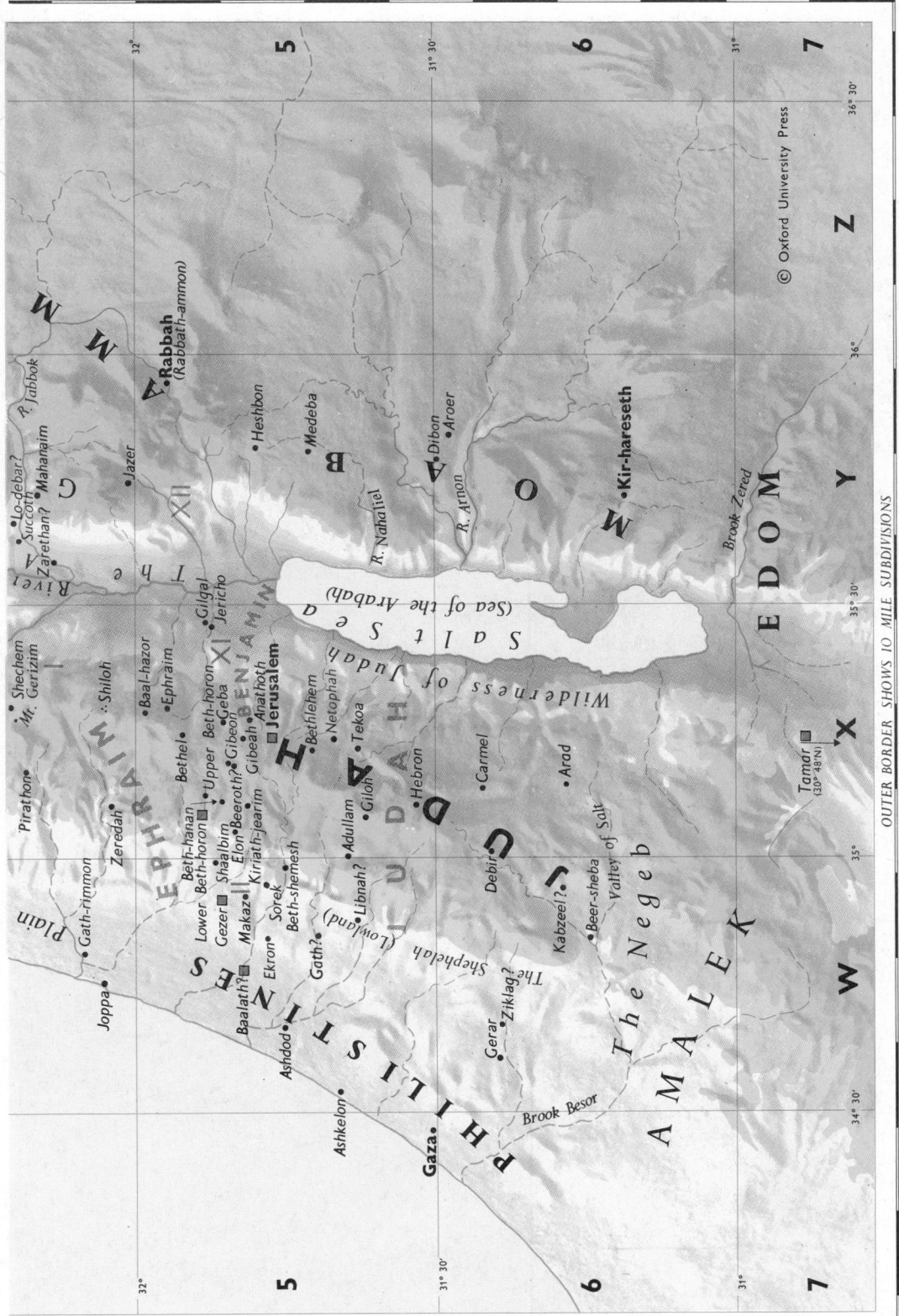

MAP 4

OUTER BORDER SHOWS 10 MILE SUBDIVISIONS

© Oxford University Press

Rabbah
(Rabbath-ammon)

A M M O N

R. Jabbok

Lo-debar?
Succoth
Zarethan?
Mahanaim
Jazer
Heshbon
Medeba
Dibon
Aroer

Kir-hareseth

E D O M

Brook Zered

R. Nahaliel
R. Arnon

M O A B

Salt Sea
(Sea of the Arabah)

Wilderness of Judah

R i v e r   J o r d a n

T h e   G

XII

Shechem
Mt. Gerizim
Shiloh
Baal-hazor
Ephraim
Bethel
Upper Beth-horon
Gibeon Geba
Gilgal
Jericho
BENJAMIN
XI
Anathoth
Jerusalem
Gibeah
Bethlehem
Netophah
Tekoa

E P H R A I M

Pirathon
Zeredah
Gath-rimmon
Joppa

Plain

Lower Beth-horon
Beth-hanan
Gezer
Makaz
Shaalbim
Elon
Beeroth?
Kiriath-jearim
Adullam
Giloh?
Hebron
Carmel
Arad

J U D A H

Ekron
Gath?
Sorek
Beth-shemesh
Libnah?
Debir
Kabzeel?

The Shephelah (Lowland)

Beer-sheba
Valley of Salt

The Negeb

Baalath?
Ashdod

P H I L I S T I N E S

Ashkelon
Gaza
Gerar
Ziklag?
Brook Besor

A M A L E K

Tamar
(30° 48'N)

X

W

Y

Z

32°
31° 30'
31°
36° 30'
36°
35° 30'
35°
34° 30'

5
6
7

MAP 5

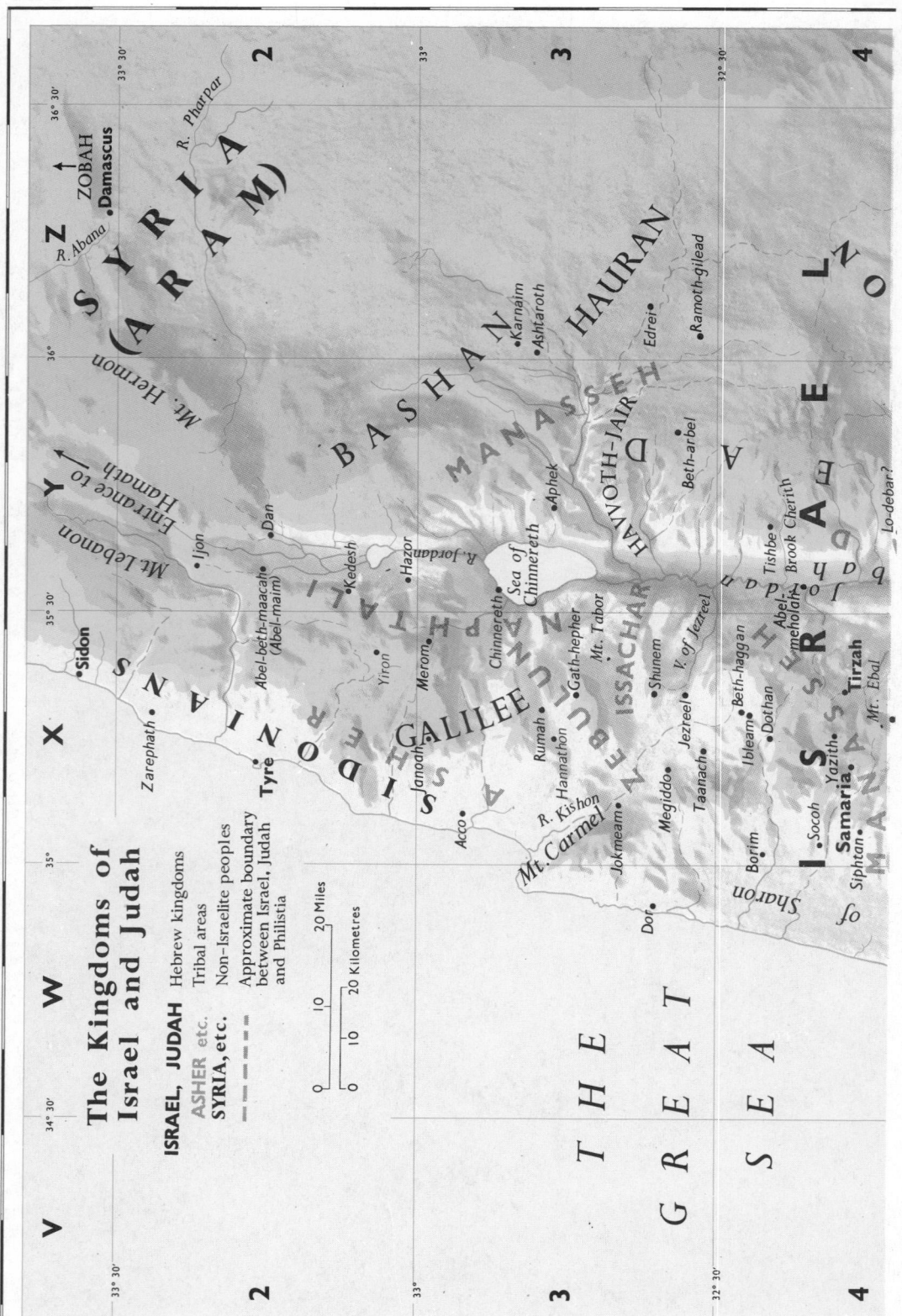

The Kingdoms of Israel and Judah

ISRAEL, JUDAH Hebrew kingdoms
ASHER etc. Tribal areas
SYRIA, etc. Non-Israelite peoples
– – – Approximate boundary between Israel, Judah and Philistia

20 Miles
20 Kilometres

SYRIA (ARAM)

ZOBAH
•Damascus
R. Pharpar
R. Abana
Mt. Hermon
Entrance to Hamath
Mt Lebanon

SIDONIANS
•Sidon
Zarephath•
Tyre•

BASHAN
HAURAN
Karnaim•
•Ashtaroth
Edrei•
•Ramoth-gilead

MANASSEH
HAVVOTH-JAIR
•Beth-arbel

NAPHTALI
Ijon•
•Dan
Kedesh•
•Hazor
R. Jordan
Sea of Chinnereth
Aphek•

ASHER
Abel-beth-maacah•
(Abel-maim)

GALILEE
Yiron•
Merom•
Chinnereth•
Janoah•

ZEBULUN
Rumah•
R. Hannathon
Gath-hepher•
Mt. Tabor

ISSACHAR
Shunem•
V. of Jezreel
Jezreel•

Acco•
R. Kishon
Mt. Carmel
Jokmeam•
Megiddo•
Taanach•
Ibleam•
Dothan•
Beth-haggan•

Tishbe•
Abel-
meholah•
Brook Cherith
•Lo-debar?

ISRAEL
Samaria.
•Borim
•Socoh
Yazith•
Siphtan•
Tirzah
Mt. Ebal

MANASSEH
of Sharon

Dor•

THE GREAT SEA

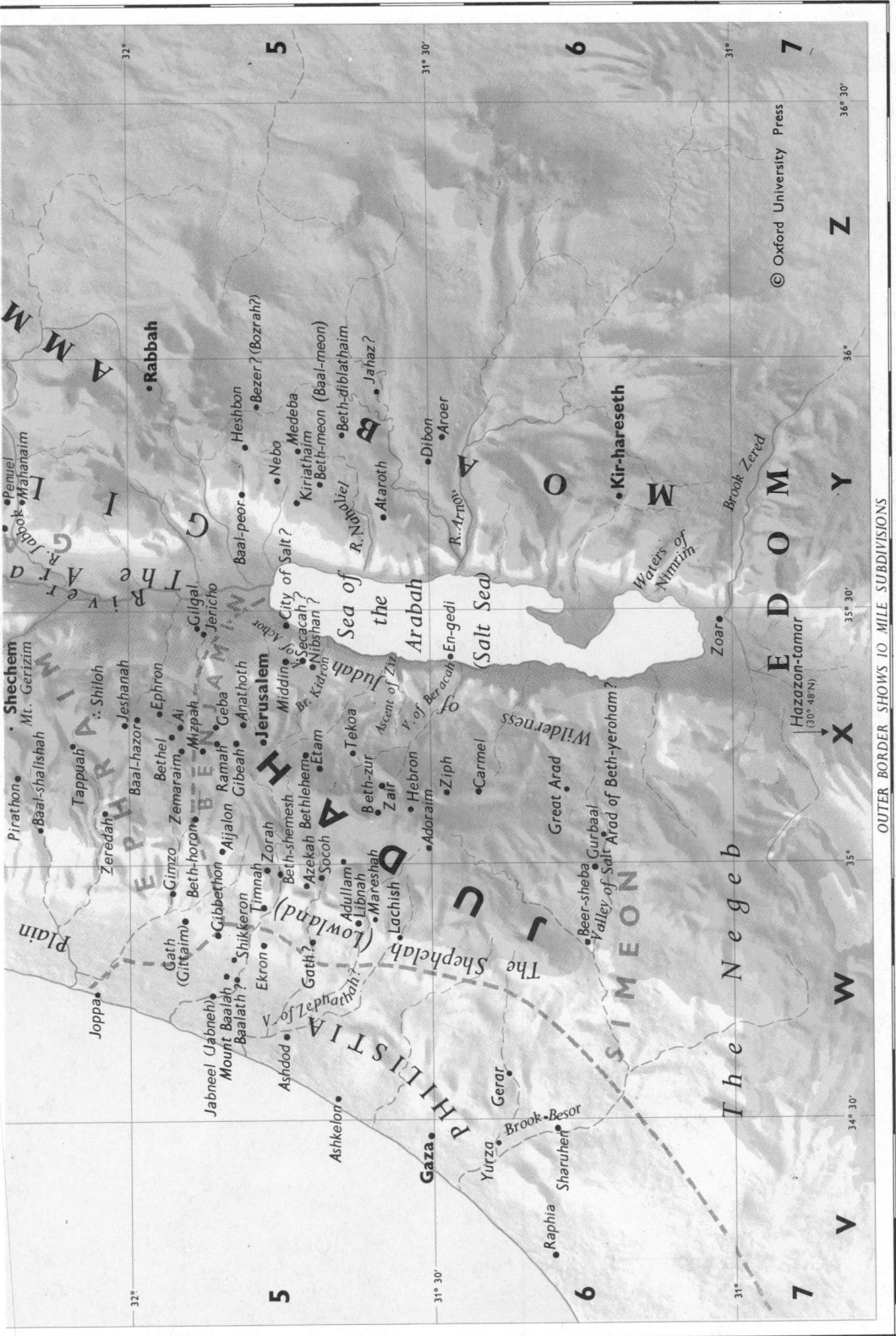

MAP 5

© Oxford University Press

OUTER BORDER SHOWS 10 MILE SUBDIVISIONS

AMM
Rabbah

GILEAD
The River Jabbok
R. Jabbok
Penuel • Mahanaim
The River
Heshbon
Nebo •
Medeba
Kiriathaim
Beth-meon (Baal-meon)
Beth-diblathaim
Bezer? (Bozrah?)
Jahaz?
Baal-peor •
Beth-peor?

EPHRAIM
Mt. Gerizim
Shechem •
Piathon •
Baal-shalishah •
Tappuah?
Zeredah •
Shiloh
Jeshanah
Ephron
Baal-hazor
Bethel •
Ai •
Gimzo •
Zemaraim
Beth-horon
Mizpah
Aijalon • Geba
Gibeah
Ramah
Anathoth

Penuel

Gilgal
Jericho
Adam
City of Salt?
Achor
Middin? •
Secacah?
Beth-hoglah
Nibshan?
Br. Kidron

JERUSALEM
Jerusalem
BENJAMIN
JUDAH
Ephron
Geba •

Etam
Tekoa
Ascent of Ziz
V. of Berachah
Beth-zur
Hebron
Zior •
Ziph •
Carmel •
Adoraim
En-gedi

JUDAH

Wilderness of Zin
Sea of the Arabah (Salt Sea)
Waters of Nimrim
R. Nimrim

MOAB
Ataroth •
Dibon •
Aroer •
Kir-hareseth
Brook Zered
R. Arnon

EDOM
Zoar •
Hazozon-tamar
(30° 48'N)

V
PHILISTIA
Joppa •
Jabneel (Jabneh) •
Mount Baalah •
Baalath?
Ashdod •
Ekron •
Gath (Gittaim) •
Shikkeron •
Gibbethon •
Gath? •
Timnah •
Zorah •
Beth-shemesh •
Azekah • Bethlehem
Socoh
Libnah
Adullam
Mareshah
Lachish
Shikkeron
V. of Zephathath?

ASHKELON
Ashkelon •
Gaza •

The Shephelah (Lowland)
SIMEON
Beer-sheba •
Gerbaal •
Valley of Salt
Great Arad
Arad of Beth-yeroham?

The Negeb

X
Y
Z

W

Gerar •
Yurza •
Sharuhen •
Brook Besor
Raphia •

5
6
7

MAP 6

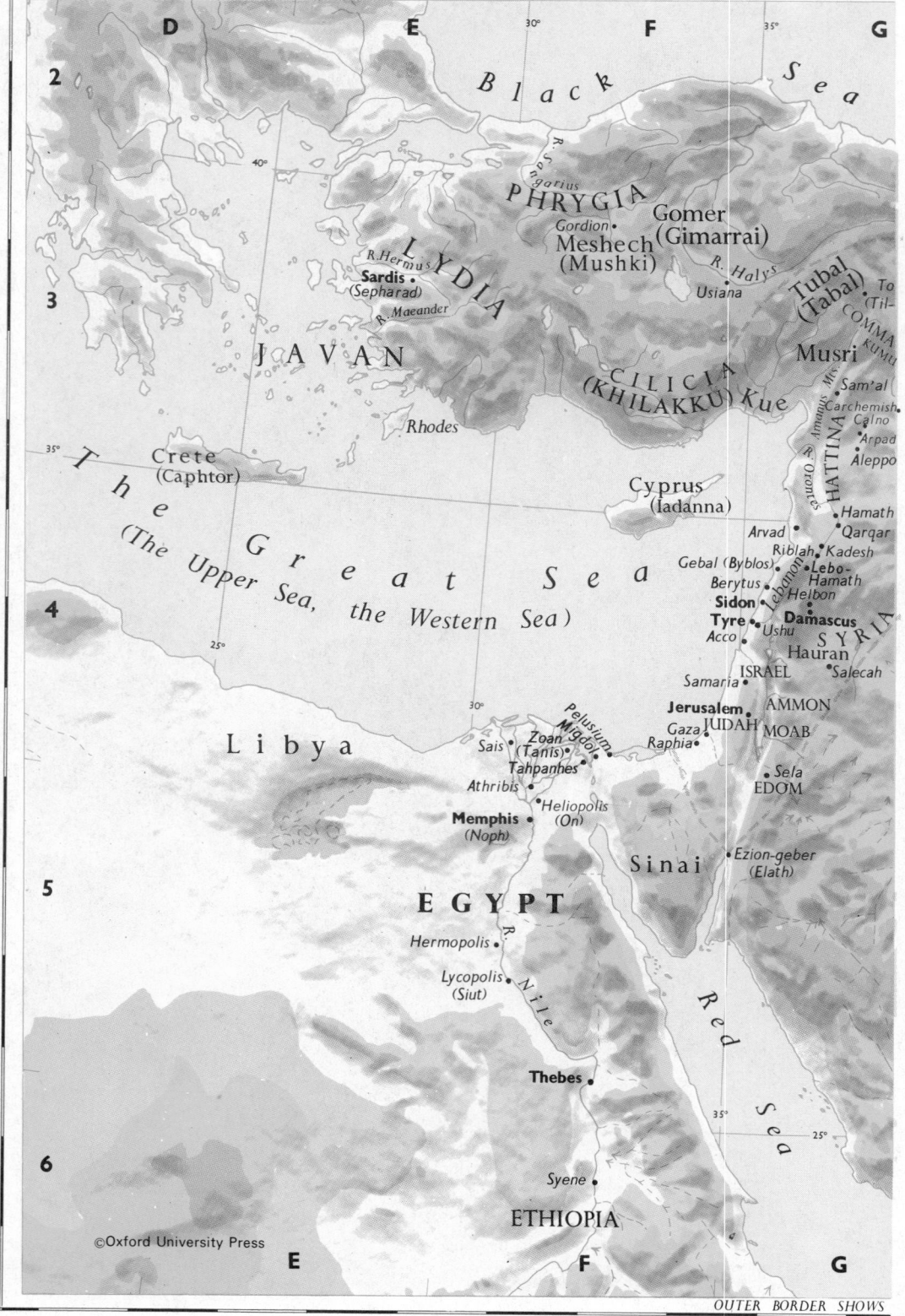

D   E   30°   F   35°   G

2   *B l a c k*   *S e a*

40°

PHRYGIA

Gomer
(Gimarrai)

Gordion •   Meshech   *R. Sangarius*
(Mushki)   *R. Halys*

Sardis •   LYDIA   *Usiana* •   Tubal
(Sepharad)   (Tabal)   To
(Til-
COMMA
KUMU

3   *R. Hermus*   Musri   *Amanus Mts.*

R. Maeander   Sam'al •

JAVAN   CILICIA   Carchemish •
(KHILAKKU) Kue   Calno •
Arpad •

35°   *Rhodes*   Aleppo •   *R. Orontes*

T h e   Crete   Cyprus   Hamath •
(Caphtor)   (Iadanna)   Qarqar •

G r e a t   Arvad •   Riblah • Kadesh •
Gebal (Byblos) •   Lebo-
S e a   Berytus •   Hamath
Helbon •   *Lebanon*   HATTINA

4   *(The Upper Sea,   the Western Sea)*   **Sidon** •
25°   **Tyre** •   **Damascus**
Acco •   *Ushu*   SYRIA
Hauran
Samaria •   ISRAEL   Salecah •

L i b y a   Jerusalem   AMMON
30°   Gaza • JUDAH MOAB
Pelusium   Raphia •
Sais •   Zoan   Migdol
(Tanis)   • Sela
Tahpanhes •   EDOM
Athribis •
Heliopolis
Memphis •   (On)   *S i n a i*   Ezion-geber •
(Noph)   (Elath)

5   *R e d*
E G Y P T

Hermopolis •

Lycopolis •   *R. Nile*
(Siut)   *S e a*

35°   25°

6

©Oxford University Press

E   F   G

MAP 6

2

3

H   J   K

Caspian Sea

40°

50°

40°

garmah garimmu)

•*Milid (Melitene)*

GENE KHUR.

R. Balikh

ARARAT (URARTU)

L. Van   *Turushpa (Tuspar)*

N a i r i

L. Urmia

Minni (Mannai)

•*Haran* *Gozan*

Beth-eden (Bit-adini)

Dur-sharrukin

A S S Y R I A

Nineveh

Calah   *Upper Zab*

Arbela

•*Tiphsah*

Asshur•   *Lower Zab*

•*Arrapkha*

MADAI (MEDES)

•*Ecbatana*

•*Rezeph*

R. Habor

R. Euphrates

R. Tigris

R. Adhaim

R. Diyala

•*Tadmor (Tadmar)*

E L A M

K e d a r (Qidri)

Sippar•
Cuthah•
Babylon•
Borsippa•

Pekod (Puqudu)

•*Susa (Shushan)*

•*Nippur*

A R A B I A

BABYLONIA

Erech (Uruk) •*Larsa*

Ur•

•*Dumah*

The Lower (Eastern) Sea

4

5

•*Tema*

The Near East

in the time of the

Assyrian Empire

•*Dedan*

– – – Approximate extent of Assyrian domination
in the latter part of the 8th. century.

(Later, under Esarhaddon (681-669), Assyria conquered Egypt.)

50°

25°

0   100   200 Miles

0   100   200 Kilometres

SHEBA (SABA)   OPHIR

6

H   J

© Oxford University Press

100 MILE SUBDIVISIONS

MAP 7

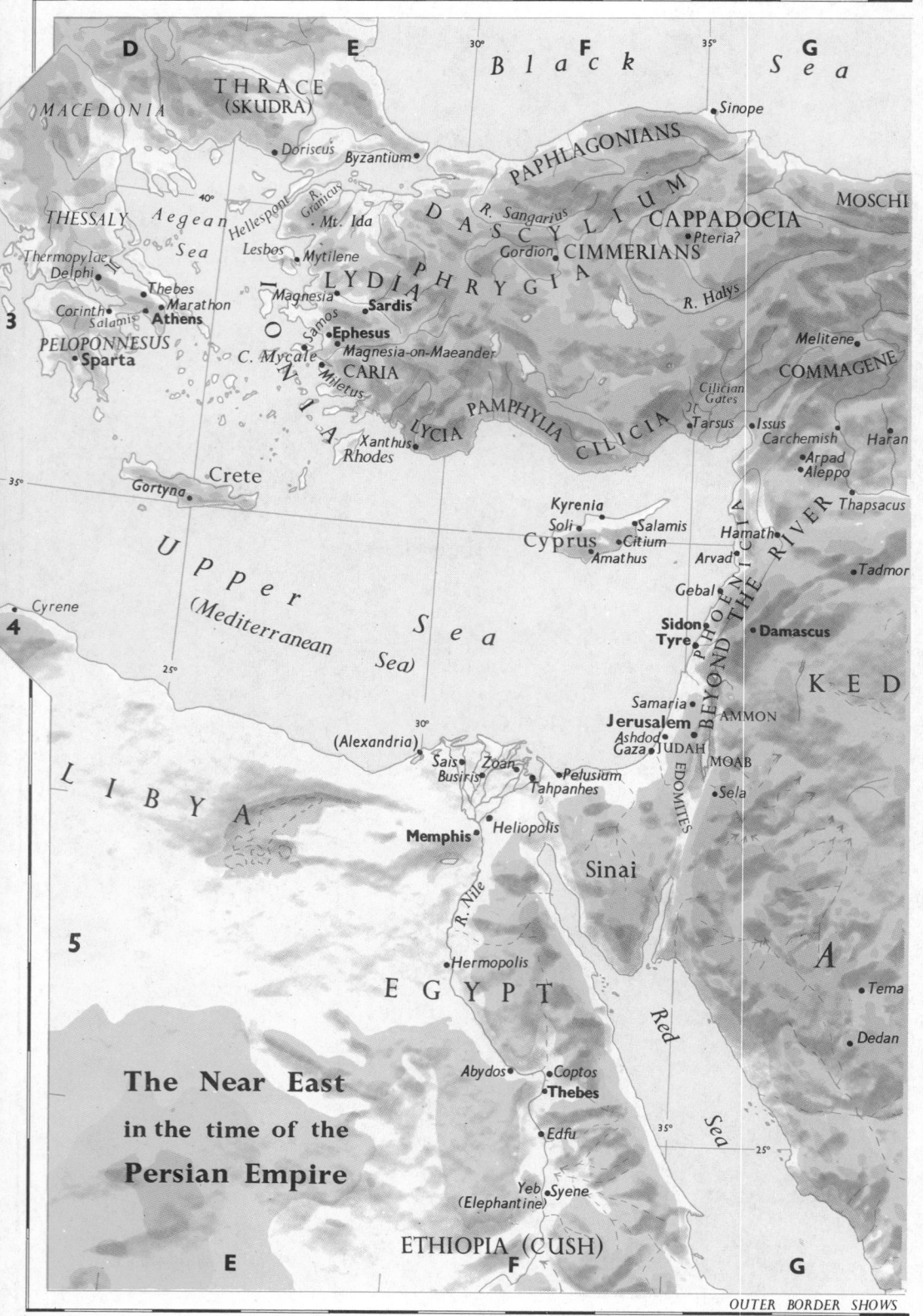

D E 30° F ck G

B l a Sea

Sinope

T H R A C E
(SKUDRA)

MACEDONIA

Doriscus
Byzantium

PAPHLAGONIANS

R. Sangarius

D A S C Y L I U M   CAPPADOCIA   MOSCHI

40° *Aegean* *Hellespont* *R. Granicus* *Mt. Ida*

THESSALY *Sea* *Lesbos* *Mytilene* Gordion CIMMERIANS *Pteria?*

Thermopylae L Y D I A   P H R Y G I A   *Melitene*
Delphi *Magnesia* **Sardis** *R. Halys*

3 *Thebes* *Marathon* **Athens** *Samos* **Ephesus** COMMAGENE
Corinth *Salamis* *C. Mycale* *Magnesia-on-Maeander* *Tarsus* *Issus*
PELOPONNESUS **Sparta** *Miletus* CARIA PAMPHYLIA CILICIA *Carchemish* *Haran*
I O N I A   *Cilician* *Arpad*
L Y C I A   *Gates* *Aleppo*

Xanthus *Thapsacus*
Rhodes

35° *Gortyna* Crete *Kyrenia* *Tadmor*
Soli *Salamis* *Hamath*
U p p e r   Cyprus *Citium* *Arvad*
Amathus *Gebal*
(Mediterranean S e a   **Sidon** **Damascus**
Cyrene **Tyre**
4 25° Sea) K E D

Samaria AMMON
(Alexandria) 30° **Jerusalem**
L I B Y A   *Sais* *Zoan* *Ashdod* JUDAH MOAB
Busiris *Pelusium* *Gaza*
Tahpanhes EDOMITES *Sela*

Memphis *Heliopolis*

Sinai A

5 *Tema*

Hermopolis

E G Y P T   *Dedan*

R. Nile Red

Abydos *Coptos*
The Near East **Thebes** 35° 25°

in the time of the *Edfu* Sea

Persian Empire *Yeb* *Syene*
(Elephantine)

E ETHIOPIA (CUSH) F G

MAP 7

H Caucasus Mountains **J** **K**

COLCHI

Trapezus
(MESHECH)

Hyrcanian

Sea

40°

(Caspian Sea)

R. Cyrus

R. Araxes

L. Van

ARMENIA
(URARTU)

L. Urmia

Astrabad   Zadrakarta
(Gorgan)   (Turang Tepe)

(Damghan)

ASSYRIA

MEDIA

HYRCANIA

PARTHIA

Nineveh   Arbela

R. Tigris

Asshur   Arrapkha

Rages
(Rhagae)

Ecbatana
(Achmetha)

SAGARTIA

Behistun
(Bisutun)

R. Euphrates

BABYLONIA

Eshnunna
Der

Sippar

Babylon
Borsippa   Nippur

ELAM
(SUSIANA)

Gabae
(Isfahan)

Susa
(Shushan)

Erech (Uruk)
Larsa
Ur

Parsagarda
(Pasargadae)

Anshan (Tall-i Malyan)

Persepolis

Dumah

PERSIS
(PERSIA)

AR

RABIA

Lower
Sea (Persian Gulf)

50°

55°

25°

0   100   200 Miles

0   100   200 Kilometres

© Oxford University Press

H   **J**   **K**

100 MILE SUBDIVISIONS

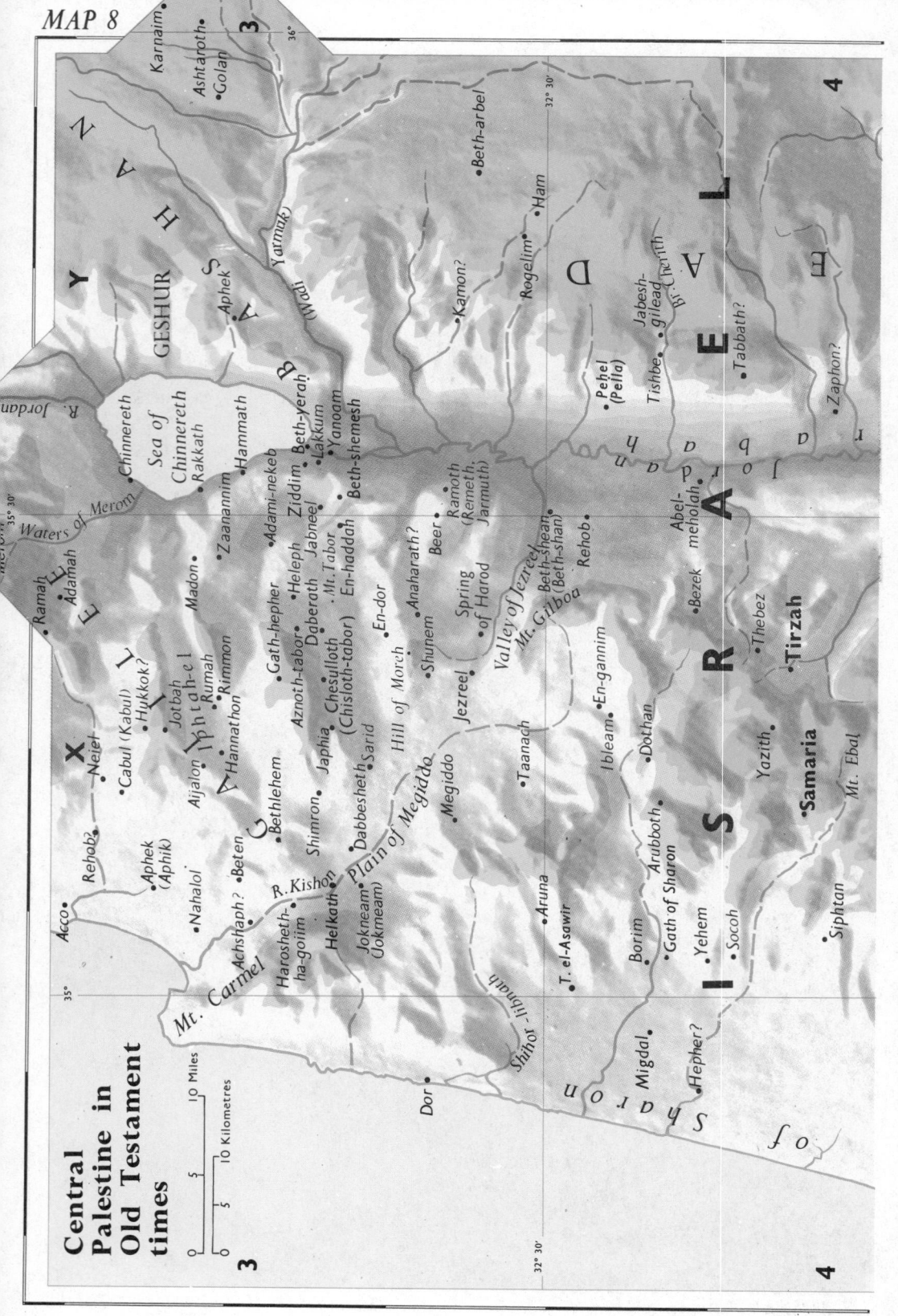

MAP 8

Central Palestine in Old Testament times

3

0   5   10 Miles

0   5   10 Kilometres

Acco•

Nahalol•

Aphek (Aphik)•

Rehob?•

Neiel•

Cabul (Kabul)•

Hukkok?•

Jotbah•

Aijalon•

Beten•

Achshaph?•

R. Kishon

Helkath•

Harosheth-ha-goiim•

Mt. Carmel

Bethlehem•

Shimron•

Hannathon•

Iphtah-el•

Rimmon•

Madon•

Ramah•

Adamah•

Waters of Merom

R. Jordan

Chinnereth•

Sea of Chinnereth

Rakkath•

Hammath•

Zaanannim•

Adami-nekeb•

Gath-hepher•

Heleph•

Ziddim•

Beth-yerah•

Lakkum•

Yanoam•

Beth-shemesh•

Aphek•

GESHUR

Yarmuk

(Wadi)

Golan•

Ashtaroth•

Karnaim•

Beth-arbel•

Ham•

Kamon?•

Rogelim•

Jabesh-gilead•

Tishbe•

Pehel (Pella)•

Tabbath?•

Zaphon?•

Abel-meholah•

Bezek•

Thebez•

Tirzah

Samaria

Mt. Ebal

Yazith•

Siphtan•

Hepher?•

Migdal•

Dor•

of Sharon

Shihor

Jibni

T. el-Asawir•

Aruna•

Borim•

Gath of Sharon•

Yehem•

Socoh•

Arubboth•

En-gannim•

Dothan•

Ibleam•

Taanach•

Megiddo•

Jezreel•

Plain of Megiddo

Dabbesheth•

Sarid•

Japhia•

Chesulloth (Chisloth-tabor)•

Daberath•

Aznoth-tabor•

Mt. Tabor

En-haddah•

Jabneel•

Hill of Moreh

Shunem•

En-dor•

Anaharath?•

Beer•

Spring of Harod

Valley of Jezreel

Mt. Gilboa

Beth-shean (Beth-shan)•

Rehob•

Ramoth (Remeth, Jarmuth)•

Jordan

Jordan

ISRAEL

GILEAD

32° 30'

35°

35° 30'

32° 30'

36°

4

MAP 8

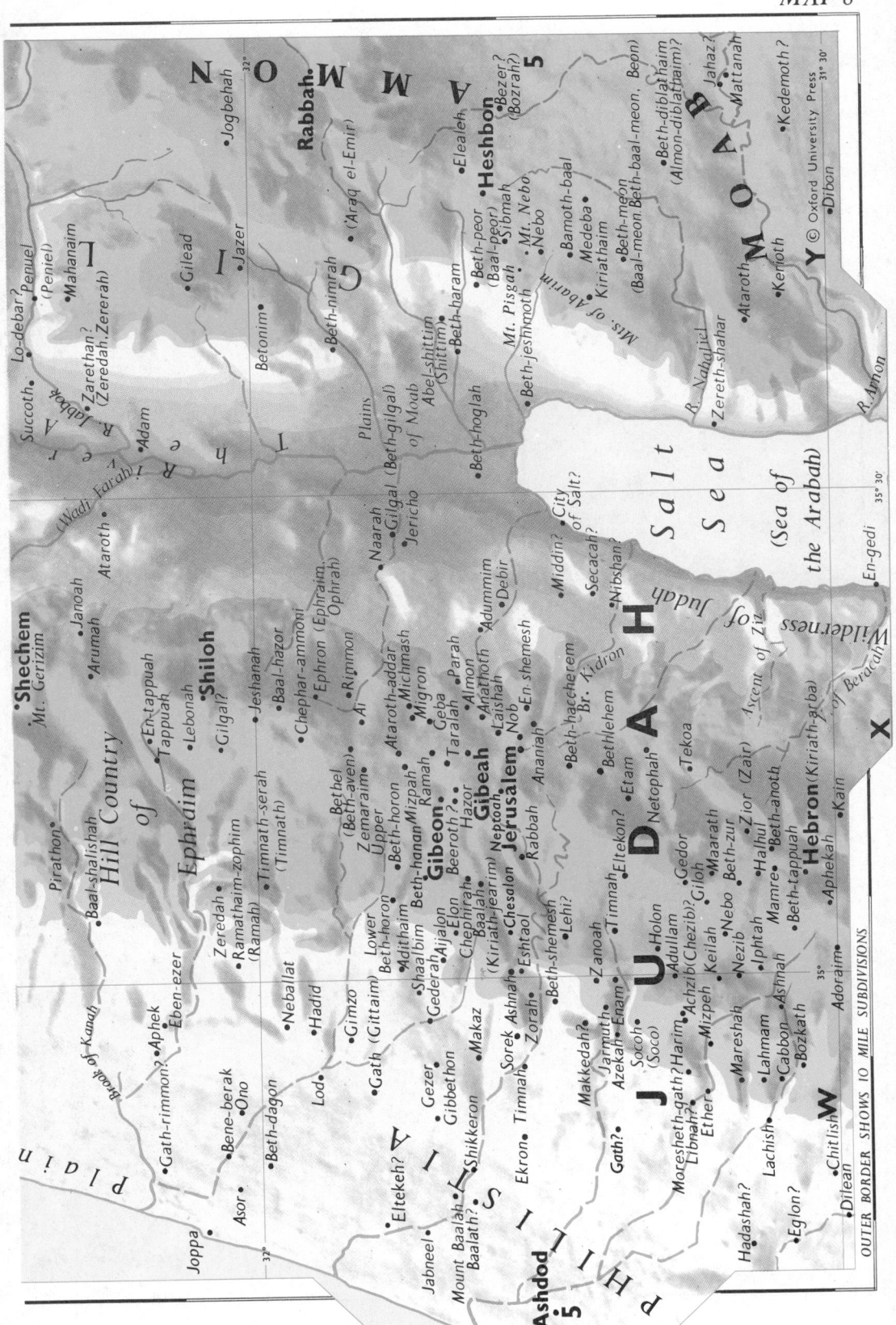

OUTER BORDER SHOWS 10 MILE SUBDIVISIONS

N
M O A B
Rabbah
Jogbehah
'Araq el-Emir
Beth-diblathaim
(Almon-diblathaim?)
Bezer? (Bozrah?)
Jahaz?
Heshbon
Mattanah
Kedemoth?
Elealeh
Beth-meon (Baal-meon. Beon)
Beth-nimrah
Gilead
Jazer
Beth-meon. Beth-baal-meon)
Bamoth-baal
Baal-peor (Baal-peor?)
Mt. Nebo
Nebo
Medeba
Sibmah
Kiriathaim
Atoroth
Kerioth
Lo-debar? Penuel (Peniel)
Mahanaim
Zarethan? (Zeredah.Zererah)
Adam
Atoroth
Betonim
Beth-nimrah
Abel-shittim (Shittim)
Beth-peor
Beth-haram
Mt. Pisgah
Beth-jeshimoth
Dibon
R. Nahaliel
Zereth-shahar
R. Arnon
Succoth
R. Jabbok
(Wadi Farah)
Plains of Moab
Beth-hoglah
Naarah
Gilgal Beth-gilgal
Gilgal
Jericho
City of Salt?
Secacah?
Nibshan?
Middin?
En-gedi
Salt Sea (Sea of the Arabah)
Shechem
Mt. Gerizim
Janoah
Arumah
En-tappuah
Tappuah
Lebonah
Shiloh
Gilgal?
Jeshanah
Baal-hazor
Chephar-ammoni
Ephron (Ephraim. Ophrah)
Rimmon
Ai
Bethel (Beth-aven)
Zemaraim
Ataroth-addar
Michmash
Migron
Geba
Anathoth
Almon
Laishah
Nob
En-shemesh
Debir
Adummim
Br. Kidron
Wilderness of Judah
Hill Country of Ephraim
Pirathon
Baal-shalishah
Zeredah
Ramathaim-zophim (Ramah)
Timnath-serah (Timnath)
Beth-horon Upper
Beth-horon Lower
Mizpah
Ramah
Gibeon
Beeroth?
Hazor
Gibeah
Jerusalem
Ananiah
Rabbah
Beth-haccherem
Neptoah
Bethlehem
Netophah
Etam
Tekoa
Adoni
Eben-ezer
Aphek
Brook of Kanah
Gath-rimmon?
Bene-berak
Ono
Beth-dagon
Lod
Neballat
Hadid
Gimzo
Gath (Gittim)
Aditham
Shaalbim
Gederah
Aijalon
Elon
Chephirah
Baalah (Kiriath-jearim)
Chesalon
Eshtaol
Zorah
Beth-shemesh
Lehi?
Zanoah
Enam
Timnah
Eltekon?
Gedor
Giloh
Maarath
Beth-zur
Nebo
Beth-anoth
Halhul
Mamre
Beth-tappuah
Hebron (Kiriath-arba)
Kain
Aphekah
Zior (Zair)
Ascent of Ziz
Ziph
Joppa
Asor
Jabneel
Mount Baalah? Baalath?
Eltekeh?
Gezer
Gibbethon
Shikkeron
Makaz
Sorek Ashnah
Ekron
Timnah
Gath?
Azekah Jarmuth
Socoh (Soco)
Adullam
Achzib Chezib?
Harim?
Mizpeh Keilah
Nezib
Iphtah
Mareshah
Lahmam
Cabbon Ashnah
Bozkath
Hadashah?
Lachish
Chitlish?
Dilean
Eglon?
Makkedah?
Moresheth-gath? Libnah?
Ether
Adoraim
Ashdod
Plain
Ephraim
Judah
Dan
Simeon
Philistia
Plain

31° 30'
32°
31° 30'
35° 30'
35°
X
Y
W
5
5

MAP 9

Jerusalem in Old Testament times

Medieval and Turkish
Jerusalem

Approximate lines of City Walls:
— of original Zion (2 Sam 5:7)
— extended under the Kings
— extended after the Exile
(by Maccabees, 2nd Cent.B.C.?)
...... Eastern wall of Nehemiah's city
Modern roads

Original Rock Contours are shown

0   300 Metres
0   300 Yards

Tower of Hananel
→Baris

TEMPLE □ALTAR

? PALACE

Solomon's Wall

Post-exilic
Jewish tombs
Monument of
Benei Hezir

Tombs

Central (Cheesemakers) Valley

Solomon's Wall

UPPER
CITY

?MISHNA
(SECOND QUARTER)

CITY OF DAVID (LOWER CITY)

Manasseh's Wall

Gate

Water
shaft

Gihon Spring

Wall of Hezekiah (Manasseh) ?

OPHEL

Upper
Pool

Wall of Zion

Conduit

Old Conduit

Mount of Olives

Pre-exilic Judean tombs

Hezekiah's

SILOAM

Gate

Lower Pool

Old Pool

The lines of the
southern walls of the city
after the Exile are uncertain

Hinnom Valley (?Topheth)

En-rogel
Spring

© Oxford University Press

OUTER BORDER SHOWS

MAP 9

Jerusalem in New Testament times

Medieval and Turkish Jerusalem

Approximate lines of City Walls:
under Herod the Great
added by Agrippa I
Wall of Aelia
Modern roads

Original Rock Contours are shown

0 — 300 Metres
0 — 300 Yards

Tomb of Helena Princess of Adiabene

OUTWORK OF UNCERTAIN ORIGIN

ROYAL CAVERNS

BEZETHA

Damascus Gate

? Fullers Tower

Pool of Bethzatha (Bethesda)

Pool

ANTONIA TOWER

Arch

Pool

Emmaus →

? Psephinus

TEMPLE

Portico

G Shishan Gate

Gethsemane

Jewish Tombs
Golgotha ?

Warren's Gate G

C. of I.
C. of Priests
C. of W.

? Beautiful Gate

Solomon's Portico

Court of Gentiles

Gate (by Wilson's Arch)

Western Wall

B

Tombs
Monument of Benei Hezir

Pool

Pinnacle of Temple

? Hippicus

Phasael ? Mariamme

Gennath Gate

Royal Portico

G

Ophlas

ROYAL PALACE
? Gabbatha
PRAE-TORIUM

Gate (by Robinson's Arch)

Plaza

Triple (Huldah) Gate

Mount of Olives

TURKISH WALL

Aqueduct

Tyropoeon Valley

Herodian Street

G

Gihon Spring

Kidron Valley

Bethany →

Pool

Pool of Siloam

Conduit

Bethlehem

Essene Gate G

? Solomon's Pool

Tekoa Gate G

Hinnom Valley

B = Bridge
C. of I. = Court of Israel
C. of Priests = Court of Priests
C. of W. = Court of Women
G = Gate
Gᶜ = Gate of Coponius = Barclay's Gate
G* = Double (Huldah) Gate

© Oxford University Press

200 YARD SUBDIVISIONS

MAP 10

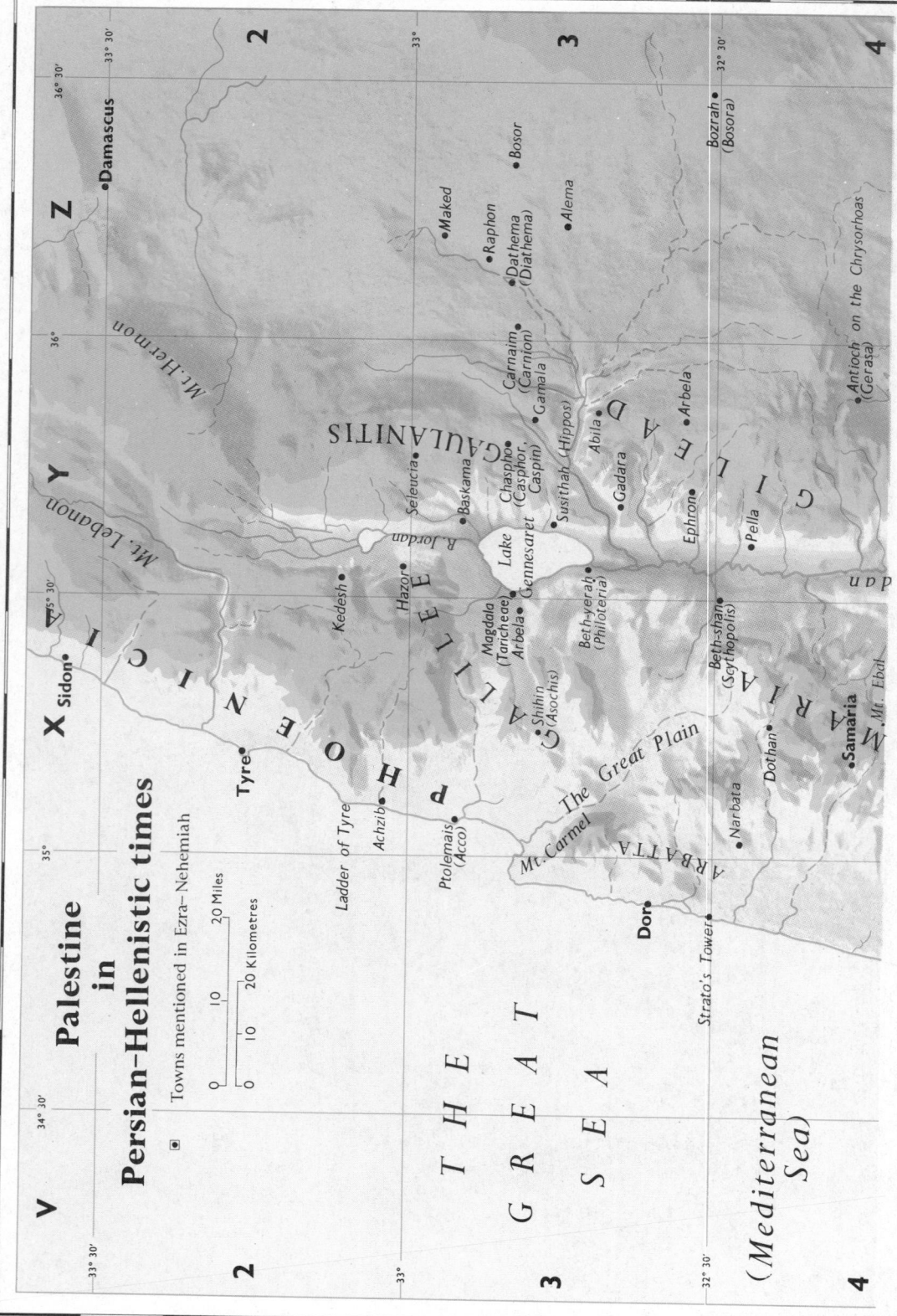

Palestine in Persian-Hellenistic times

▣ Towns mentioned in Ezra–Nehemiah

20 Miles
20 Kilometres

Damascus

Mt. Hermon

Mt. Lebanon

Sidon

PHOENICIA

Tyre

Ladder of Tyre

Achzib

Ptolemais (Acco)

Kedesh

Hazor

Seleucia

GAULANITIS

Baskama

Maked

Raphon

Dathema (Diathema)

Bosor

Alema

Carnaim (Carnion)

Gamala

Susithah (Hippos)

Abila

Gadara

Ephron

Pella

Arbela

GILEAD

Antioch on the Chrysorhoas (Gerasa)

R. Jordan

Lake Gennesaret

Chaspho (Casphor, Caspin)

Magdala (Tarichee) Arbela

Beth-yerah (Philoteria)

Beth-shan (Scythopolis)

GALILEE

Shihin (Asochis)

SAMARIA

Samaria

Mt. Ebal

Dothan

Narbata

ARBATTA

Mt. Carmel

The Great Plain

Dor

Strato's Tower

THE GREAT SEA

(Mediterranean Sea)

0   10   20
0   10   20

MAP 10

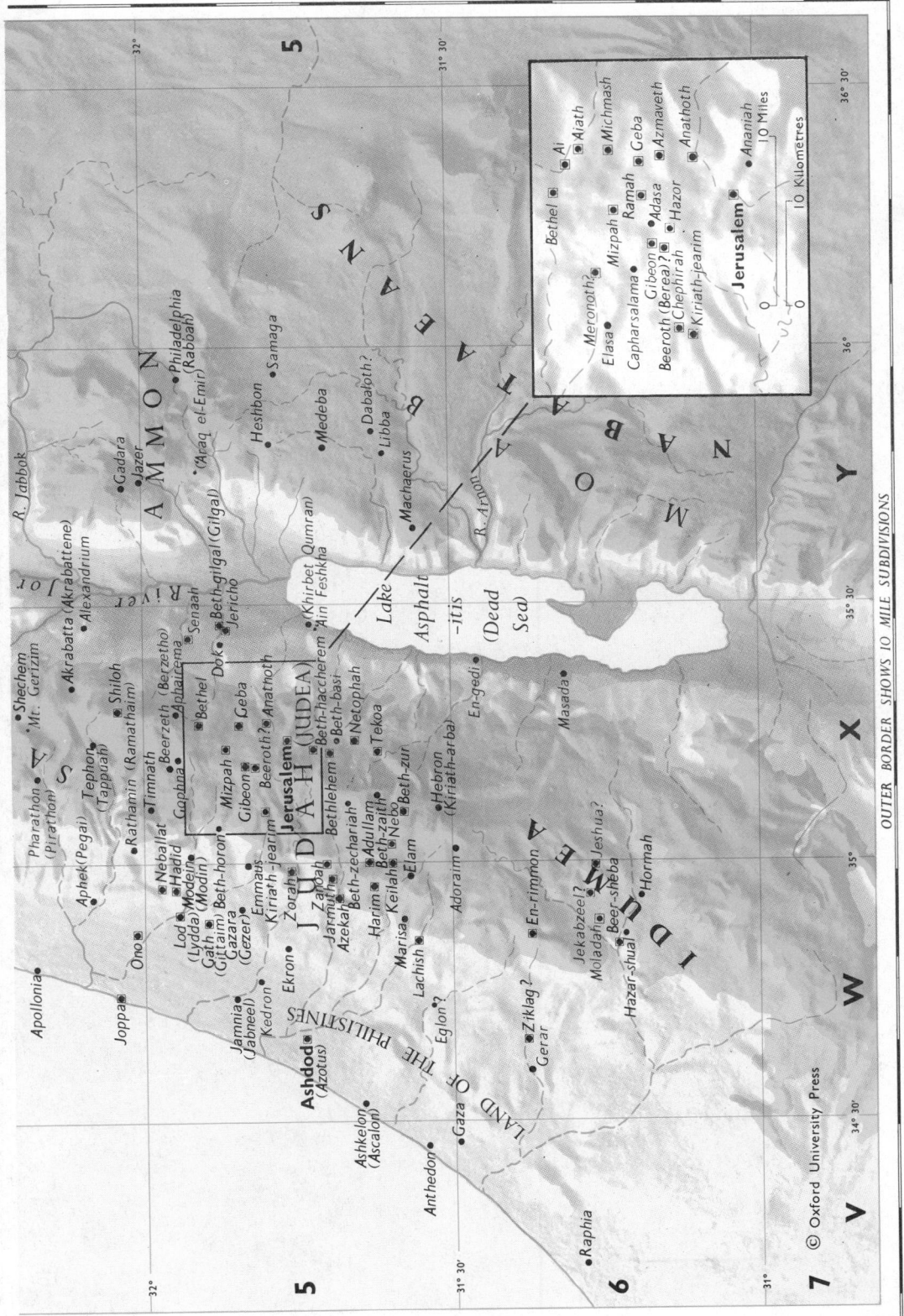

Inset map:

Bethel • Ai • Aiath
• Michmash
Meronoth? • Ramah • Geba
Elasa • • Mizpah • Azmaveth • Anathoth
Capharsalama • Gibeon • Adasa
Beeroth (Berea?) • • • Hazor • Ananiah
Chephirah • • Anathoth
Kiriath-jearim • Anathoth

Jerusalem

0 10 Miles
0 10 Kilomètres

AMMON

R. Jabbok
Gadara
Jazer
Akrabatta (Akrabattene)
Alexandrium
Philadelphia (Rabbah)
'Araq el-Emir
Heshbon • Samaga
Medeba
Dabaloth?
Libba
Machaerus

SAMARIA

Shechem
• Mt. Gerizim
Pharathon (Pirathon)
Tephon (Tappuah)
Aphek (Pegai)
Rathamin (Ramathaim)
Shiloh
Timnath
Beerzeth (Berzetho)
Beth-gilgal (Gilgal)
Senaah
Jericho
Dok
Bethel • Aphaerema
Geba
Gophna
Beeroth? • Anathoth

JUDAH (JUDEA)

Mizpah
Gibeon
Jerusalem
Beth-haccherem
Beth-basi
Anathoth
Netophah
Tekoa
Beth-zur

Ono
Neballat
Lod (Lydda)
Hadid • Modein
Gath • Beth-horon
Gazara (Gezer)
Emmaus
Kiriath-jearim
Zorah • Bethlehem
Zanoah
Jarmuth
Beth-zechariah
Adullam
Harim
Beth-zaith
Azekah
Keilah
Nebo
Elam
Marisa
Lachish

Hebron (Kiriath-arba)
Adoraim

NABATAEANS

MOAB
R. Arnon

(Khirbet Qumran)
'Ain Feshkha
Lake Asphaltitis
(Dead Sea)

En-gedi
Masada

IDUMAEA

En-rimmon
Jeshua?
Hormah
Jekabzeel? • Moladah?
Beer-sheba
Hazar-shual

Apollonia

Joppa

Jamnia (Jabneel)
Kedron
Ekron

LAND OF THE PHILISTINES

Ashdod (Azotus)

Ashkelon (Ascalon)
Anthedon

Gaza
Eglon?
Ziklag?
Gerar

Raphia

Jordan River

© Oxford University Press

OUTER BORDER SHOWS 10 MILE SUBDIVISIONS

V   W   X   Y

5   6   7

MAP 11

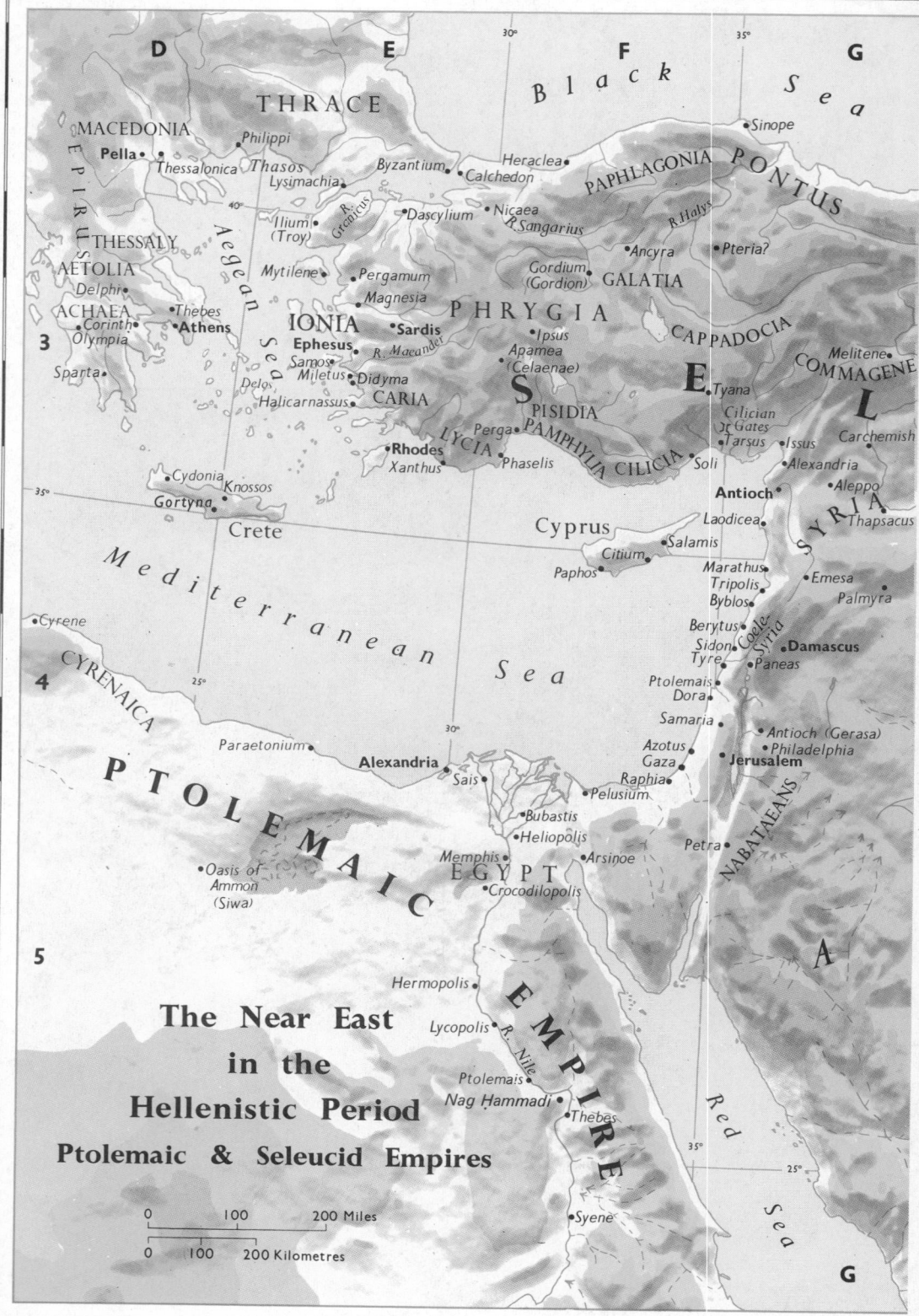

The Near East
in the
Hellenistic Period
Ptolemaic & Seleucid Empires

D · E · 30° · F · 35° · G

Black Sea

MACEDONIA
Pella·
Thessalonica
THRACE
Philippi
Thasos
Byzantium·
Heraclea
Calchedon
Sinope·
PAPHLAGONIA
PONTUS
EPIRUS
Lysimachia
Ilium (Troy)
R. Granicus
Dascylium
Nicaea
R. Sangarius
Ancyra·
R. Halys
Pteria?·
THESSALY
AETOLIA
Delphi
Mytilene
Pergamum
Magnesia
Gordium (Gordion)
GALATIA
CAPPADOCIA
COMMAGENE
Melitene·
ACHAEA
Corinth
Thebes·
Athens
Olympia
IONIA
Ephesus
Sardis·
PHRYGIA
Ipsus·
Apamea (Celaenae)
S
E
L
Sparta·
Samos
Miletus
Didyma
CARIA
Tyana·
Cilician Gates
Tarsus·
Issus·
Carchemish
Delos·
Halicarnassus
R. Maeander
PISIDIA
LYCIA
PAMPHYLIA
CILICIA
Perga
Phaselis
Soli·
Alexandria·
Aleppo·
SYRIA
Thapsacus
Rhodes
Xanthus
Antioch
Laodicea·
Cydonia·
Knossos
Gortyna
Crete
Cyprus
Citium·
Salamis·
Paphos·
Marathus·
Tripolis·
Byblos·
Emesa·
Palmyra·
Mediterranean Sea
Berytus·
Sidon·
Tyre·
Coele Syria
Damascus
Paneas·
Cyrene·
CYRENAICA
Ptolemais·
Dora·
Samaria·
Antioch (Gerasa)·
Philadelphia·
Jerusalem
Paraetonium·
Alexandria
Sais·
Azotus·
Gaza·
Raphia·
Pelusium·
PTOLEMAIC
Bubastis·
Heliopolis·
Arsinoe·
Petra·
NABATAEANS
A
Memphis·
Oasis of Ammon (Siwa)·
EGYPT
Crocodilopolis·
Hermopolis·
Lycopolis·
EMPIRE
R. Nile
Red Sea
Ptolemais·
Nag Hammadi·
Thebes·
Syene·
G

0 · 100 · 200 Miles
0 · 100 · 200 Kilometres

MAP 11

40°

H

J

50°

K

L

Trapezus

R. Cyrus

R. Araxes

H y r c a n i a n   S e a

40°

ARMENIA

L. Van

L. Urmia

H Y R C A N I A

Astrabad *Zadrakarta*
(Gorgan) *(Turang Tepe)*

Nisibis

E

Gaugamela

Arbela

M

E

Hecatompylus (?)

Rages
(Rhagae)

D

I

A

P A R T H I A

U

R. Euphrates

C

Ecbatana

Dura-Europus

R. Tigris

I

Gabae

D

E

Ctesiphon

Seleucia

Babylon

E

B A B Y L O N I A

Nippur

M

SUSIANA

Susa

P

Uruk

I

Parsagarda

Persepolis

R

R

A

B

I

A

P E R S I S

E

P e r s i a n

50°

G u l f

55°

25°

H

J

K

© Oxford University Press.

MAP 12

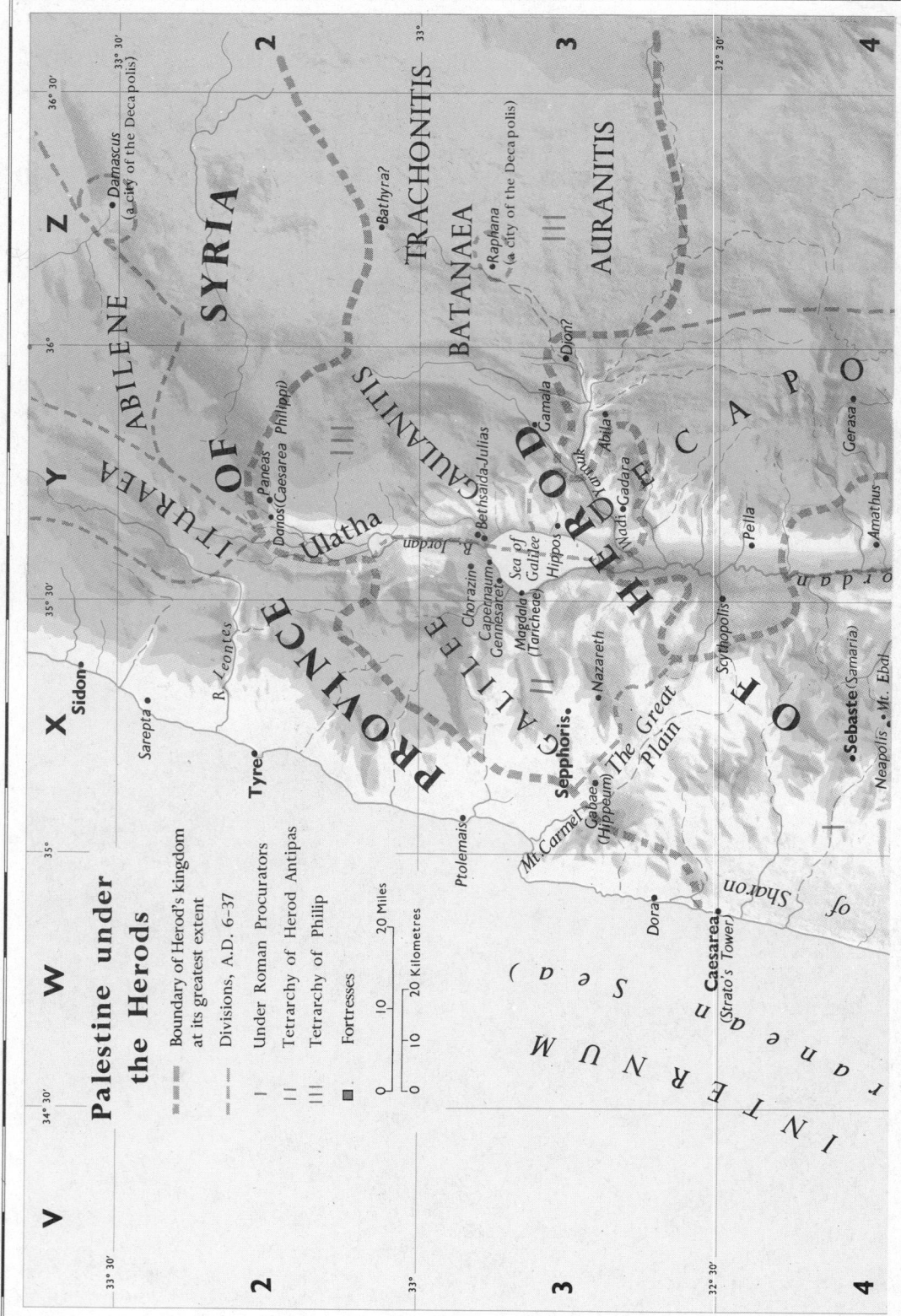

Palestine under the Herods

Boundary of Herod's kingdom at its greatest extent

Divisions, A.D. 6–37

I   Under Roman Procurators

II   Tetrarchy of Herod Antipas

III   Tetrarchy of Philip

■   Fortresses

0   10   20 Miles
0   10   20 Kilometres

Map labels

SYRIA

PROVINCE OF SYRIA

ABILENE

ITURAEA

TRACHONITIS

BATANAEA

AURANITIS

GAULANITIS

DECAPOLIS

HEROD

GALILEE

Damascus (a city of the Decapolis)

Bathyra?

Raphana (a city of the Decapolis)

Dion?

Gamala

Abila

Dan (Caesarea Philippi)

Paneas

Ulatha

Bethsaida-Julias

Jordan

Sea of Galilee

Hippos

Wadi Yarmuk

Gadara

Gerasa

Amathus

Pella

Chorazin

Capernaum

Gennesaret

Magdala (Tarichea)

Nazareth

The Great Plain

Sepphoris

Gabae (Hippeum)

Mt. Carmel

Scythopolis

Sebaste (Samaria)

Mt. Ebal

Neapolis

Jordan

Sidon

Sarepta

R. Leontes

Tyre

Ptolemais

Dora

Caesarea (Strato's Tower)

of Sharon

INTERNUM MARE (Mediterranean Sea)

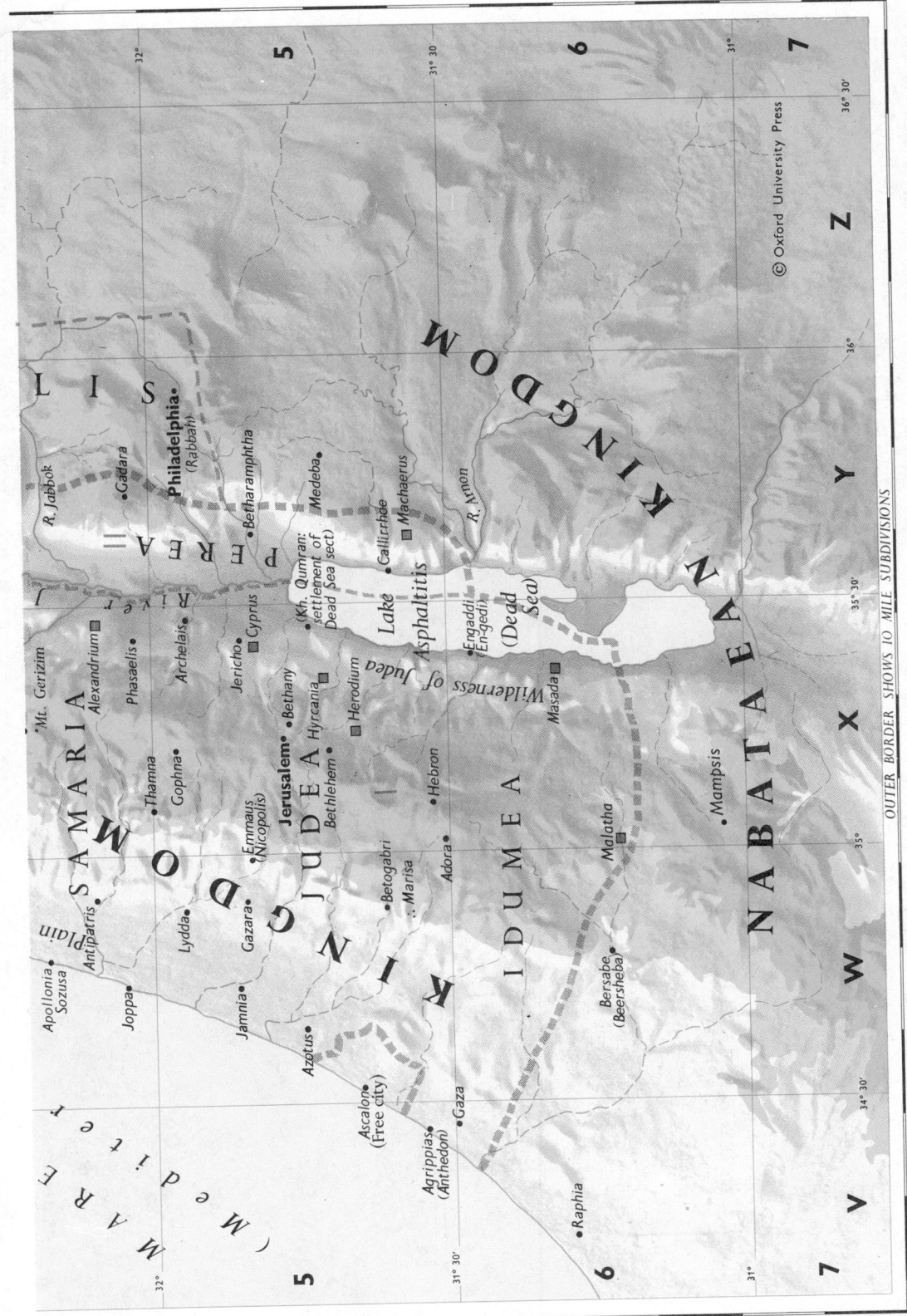

MAP 12

OUTER BORDER SHOWS 10 MILE SUBDIVISIONS

© Oxford University Press

NABATAEAN KINGDOM

KINGDOM

IDUMEA

SAMARIA

JUDEA

PEREA

DECAPOLIS

Wilderness of Judea

Lake Asphaltitis (Dead Sea)

MARE (Mediter)

Jordan River

R. Jabbok

R. Arnon

Mt. Gerizim

Apollonia Sozusa
Antiparis
Joppa
Jamnia
Azotus
Ascalone (Free city)
Agrippias (Anthedon)
Gaza
Raphia
Bersabe (Beersheba)
Malatha
Mampsis
Masada
Adora
Hebron
Betogabri
Marisa
Gazara
Lydda
Thamna
Gophna
Emmaus (Nicopolis)
Bethlehem
Jerusalem
Bethany
Hyrcania
Herodium
Jericho
Archelais
Cyprus
Phasaelis
Alexandrium
(Kh. Qumran: settlement of Dead Sea sect)
Engaddi En-gedi
Callirrhoe
Machaerus
Medeba
Betharamphtha
Gadara
Philadelphia (Rabbah)

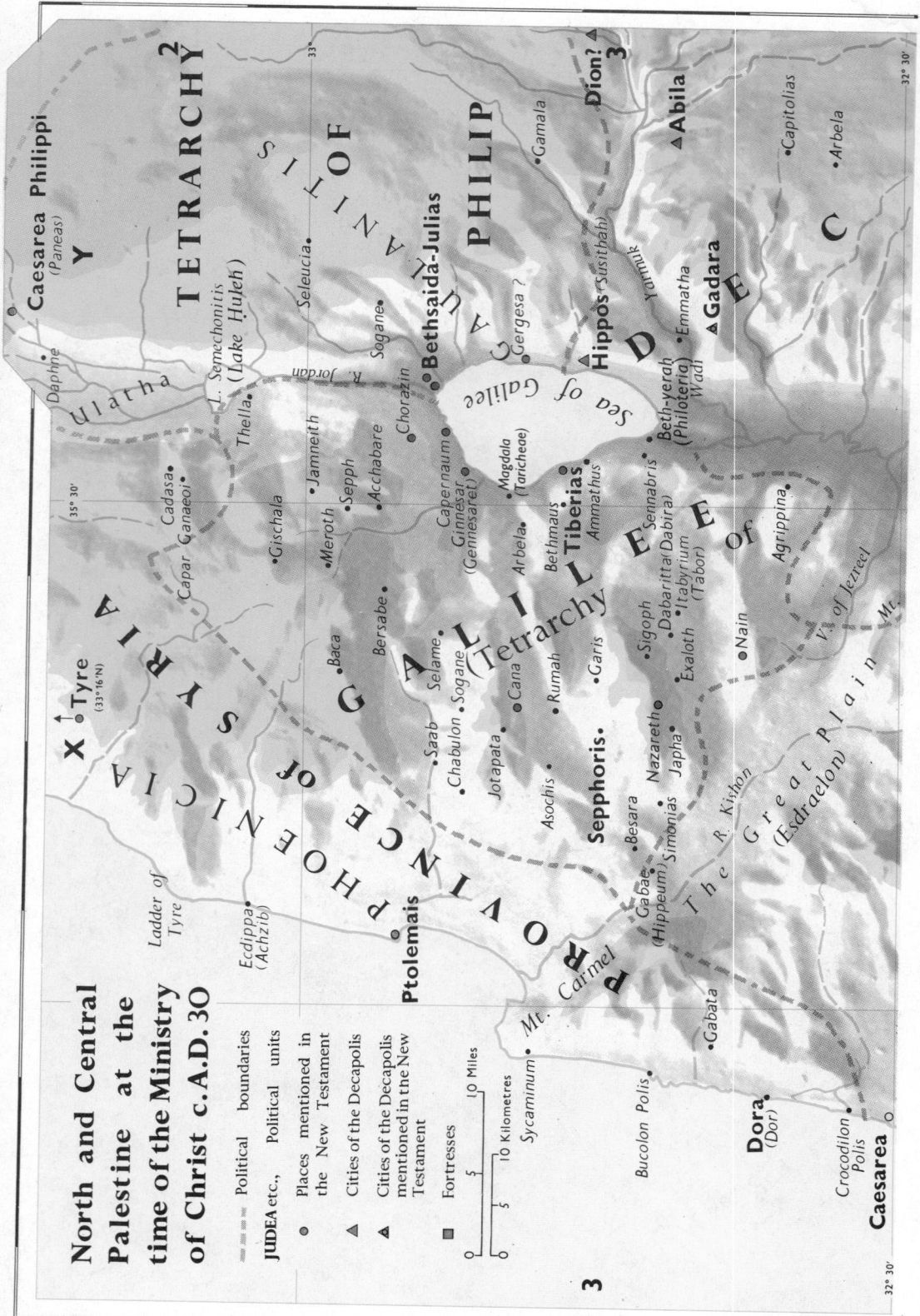

MAP 13

North and Central Palestine at the time of the Ministry of Christ c.A.D. 30

JUDEA etc., Political units

- Political boundaries
- Places mentioned in the New Testament
- Cities of the Decapolis
- Cities of the Decapolis mentioned in the New Testament
- Fortresses

0 5 10 Miles
0 5 10 Kilometres

PHOENICIA

PROVINCE of SYRIA

Tyre (33°16'N)

Ladder of Tyre

Ecdippa (Achzib)

Ptolemais

Sycaminum

Bucolon Polis

Dora (Dor)

Crocodilon Polis

Caesarea

Mt. Carmel

The Great Plain (Esdraelon)

Gabata

Gabae (Hippeum)

Simonias

Besara

Asochis

Sepphoris.

Japha

Nazareth

Exaloth

Jotapata

Cana

Rumah

Garis

Sigoph

Dabaritta(Dabira)

Itabyrium (Tabor)

Nain

V. of Jezreel

Mt.

R. Kishon

Chabulon Sogane

Selame

Saab

Baca

Bersabe

Meroth

Sepph

Acchabare

Jamneith

Gischala

Cadasa

Capar Ganeoi

Thella

L. Semechonitis (Lake Huleh)

Ulatha

Daphne

Caesarea Philippi (Paneas)

TETRARCHY 2

OF GAULANITIS

Seleucia

Sogane

Chorazin

Bethsaida-Julias

R. Jordan

PHILIP

Gergesa?

Gamala

Dion? 3

Abila

Capitolias

Arbela

GALILEE of

GAULANITIS

Sea of Galilee

Capernaum

Ginnesar (Gennesaret)

Magdala (Tarichede)

Bethmaus

Arbela

Tiberias

Ammathus

Sennabris

Amnathus

Agrippina

Hippos (Susithah)

Yarmuk

Beth-yerah (Philoteria) Wadi

Emmatha

Gadara

D E C A

GALILEE of

(Tetrarchy)

3

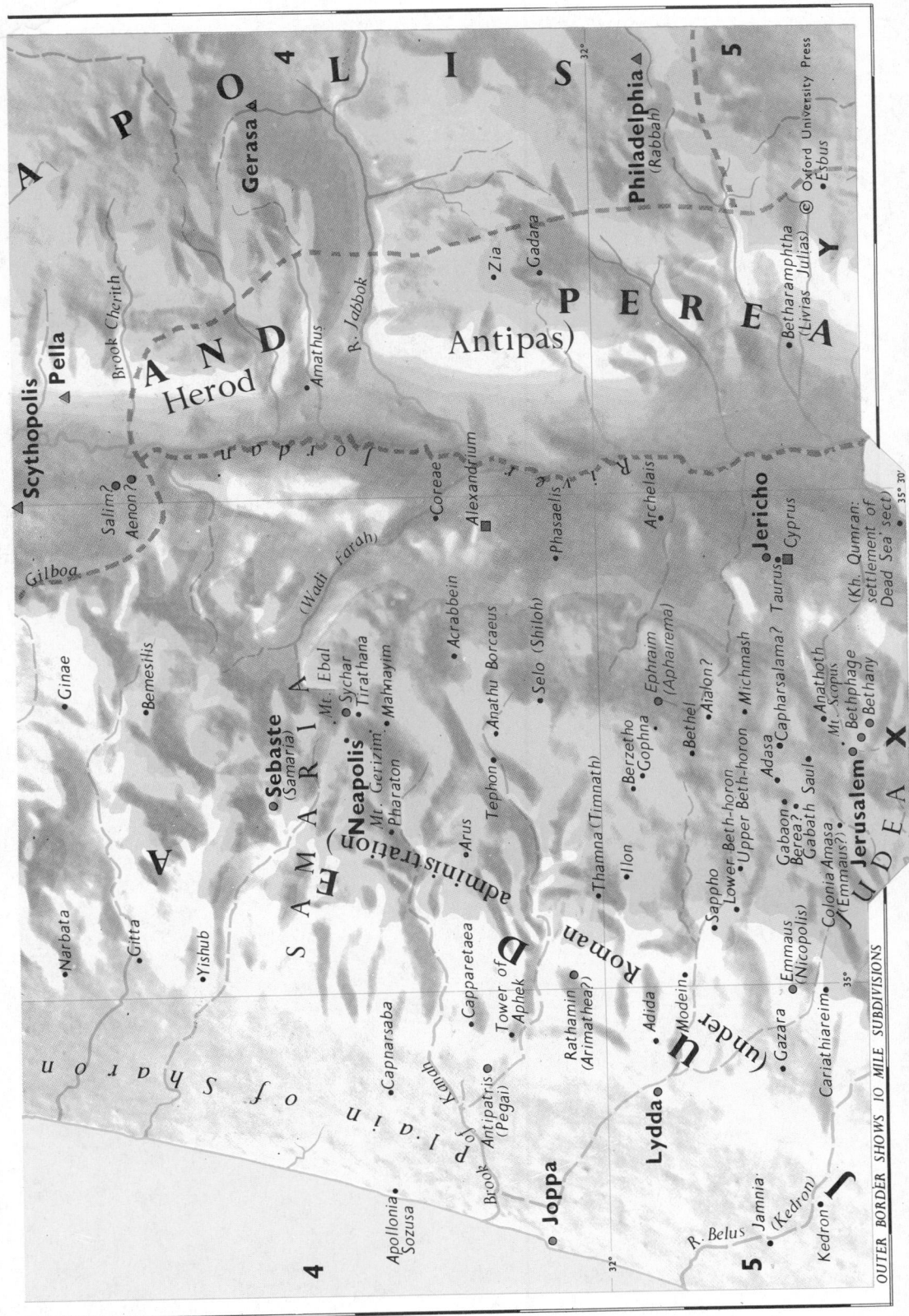

MAP 13

APOLIS

AND

Herod

PERE

Antipas)

Gerasa▲

4

Philadelphia▲
(Rabbah)

5

© Oxford University Press

Esbus▲

·Zia

·Gadara

·Betharamphtha
(Livias Julias)

Brook Cherith

▲Pella

▲Scythopolis

·Amathus

R. Jabbok

R. Jabbok

Jordan River

·Coreae

Alexandrium▪

·Phasaelis

Archelais·

Jericho▪
Cyprus▪

Gilboa

Salim?
Aenon?●

(Wadi Farah)

·Acrabbein

·Anathu Borcaeus

·Selo (Shiloh)

Taurus▪

(Kh. Qumran:
settlement of
Dead Sea sect)

35° 30'

·Ginae

·Bemesilis

Mt. Ebal
·Sychar
Tirathana
·Malhnayim

·Ephraim
(Apharema)

·Michmash

·Anathoth
Mt. Scopus

Bethphage
·Bethany

Sebaste●
(Samaria)

Neapolis●
Mt. Gerizim·
Pharaton·

·Tephon
·Arus

·Berzetho
·Gophna

·Bethel

·Aialon?

·Adasa
·Capharsalama?

·Lower Beth-horon
·Upper Beth-horon

Saul·

·Jerusalem
(UDEA X

SAMARIA

E

(Administration)

·Thamna (Timnath)

·Ilon

·Sappho

Gabaon·
Berea?·
Gabath
·Colonia Amasa
(Emmaus)

·Narbata

·Gitta

·Yishub

·Capnarsaba

·Capparetaea

Tower of
·Aphek

·Rathamin
(Arimathea?)

·Adida

·Modein

·Emmaus
(Nicopolis)

35°

·Cariathiareim

Roman
administration
(under

D
U

Plain of Sharon

·Apollonia
Sozusa

Brook of Kanah

·Antipatris
(Pegai)

·Gazara

Joppa●

Lydda●

·Jamnia

R. Belus

Kedron· ·(Kedron)

4

32°

32°

5

MAP 14

R. Po
B
45°
Pola
Ravenna
Ariminum
C
PANNONIA
Siscia
DACIA
D
Sirmium
Singidunum
Viminacium
E
Istros

2
Perusia
ITALY
Ancona
ILLYRICUM
(DALMATIA)
R. Danube
Oescus
MOESIA
Novae
Tomi

ROME
Ostia
Antium
Tarracina
Three Taverns
Forum of Appius
(Appii Forum)
Salonae
Naissus
Sardica
Philippopolis
THRACE
Odessus
Mesembria

Capua
Puteoli
Neapolis
Pompeii
Paestum
Beneventum
Canusium
Brundisium
Scodra
Scupi
Dyrrhachium
Apollonia
MACEDONIA
Beroea
Thessalonica
Philippi
Neapolis
Samothrace
Egnatian Way
Byzantium
Nicomedia
Nicaea
Prusa
Bosphorus

Capreae
(Capri)
Tarentum
Sybaris
Croton
Corcyra
THESSALY
Larissa
40
Troas
(Alexandria)
Lesbos
Assos
Mitylene
Adramyttium
Cyzicus
ASIA

R
O
M
A
N
Panormus
Messana
SICILY
Rhegium
Catana
Syracuse
Nicopolis
Actium
ACHAIA
Corinth
Cenchreae
Athens
Olympia
Sparta
(Lacedaemon)
Chios
Samos
Pergamum
Smyrna
Ephesus
Sardis
Philadelphia
Laodicea
Miletus
Colossae
Thyatira

Malta
(Melita)
Paul's Journey to Rome
Mediterranean
35°
Cos
Cnidus
Rhodes
Rhodes
Patara
Myra
LYCIA

(Mare Internum, Mare Nostrum)
CRETE
Phoenix
Cauda
Fair Havens
Lasea
Salmone
Sea

Lepcis Magna
15°
Greater
Syrtis
Cyrene
CYRENAICA
LIBYA
20°
25°
Alexandria
Canopus
Sais
Naucratis
30°
EGYPT

4
AFRICA

Oxyrhynchus

Paul's 1st Journey

Beroea
Philippi
Neapolis
Thessalonica
Troas
Athens
Cenchreae
Corinth
Ephesus
Antioch
Iconium
Lystra
Derbe
Antioch
Caesarea

Paul's 2nd Journey

Philippi
Troas
Assos
Mitylene
Chios
Ephesus
Samos
Miletus
Cos
Rhodes
Patara
Corinth
Antioch
Ptolemais
Tyre
Caesarea
Jerusalem

Paul's 3rd Journey

Antioch
Iconium
Lystra
Derbe
Attalia
Perga
Paphos
Salamis

OUTER BORDER SHOWS

MAP14

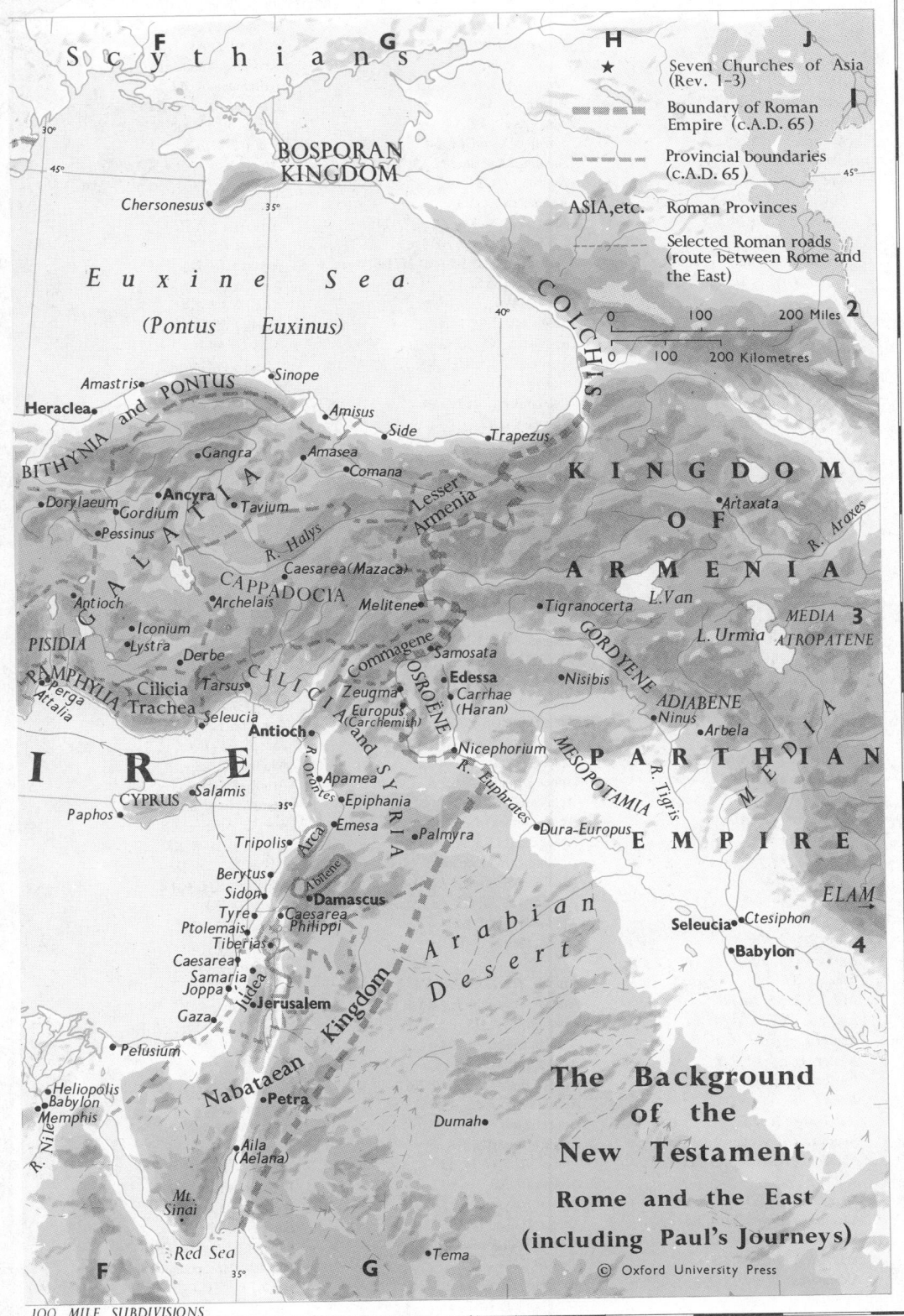

S c y t h i a n G s

H J I

★ Seven Churches of Asia (Rev. 1–3)

BOSPORAN KINGDOM

Boundary of Roman Empire (c.A.D. 65)

Provincial boundaries (c.A.D. 65)

ASIA,etc. Roman Provinces

Chersonesus 35°

30° 45°

Selected Roman roads (route between Rome and the East)

45°

E u x i n e S e a

(Pontus Euxinus)

40° COLCHIS

0 100 200 Miles 2

0 100 200 Kilometres

Amastris PONTUS Sinope

Heraclea BITHYNIA and

Amisus

Side

Trapezus

Gangra Amasea

Dorylaeum Ancyra Tavium Comana

K I N G D O M

Gordium GALATIA Pessinus

Lesser Armenia

Artaxata R. Araxes

O F

R. Halys

Antioch Caesarea (Mazaca) CAPPADOCIA

Archelais Melitene

Tigranocerta L.Van

A R M E N I A

3

L. Urmia MEDIA ATROPATENE

PISIDIA Iconium Lystra

Commagene Samosata

GORDYENE

Derbe CILICIA Tarsus OSROÊNE Edessa

Nisibis

ADIABENE Ninus

PAMPHYLIA Cilicia Trachea

Zeugma Carrhae (Haran) Europus (Carchemish)

MESOPOTAMIA

Arbela

Perga Attalia Seleucia

Nicephorium

R. Tigris

P A R T H I A N

I R E Antioch

R. Orontes Apamea

R. Euphrates

Dura-Europus

M E D I A

E M P I R E

CYPRUS Salamis 35° Epiphania

Emesa Palmyra

Paphos Tripolis

ELAM

Arca

Berytus Abilene

Sidon Damascus

Tyre Caesarea Philippi Ptolemais

Seleucia Ctesiphon

Babylon

4

Tiberias

Caesarea Samaria Joppa Judea Jerusalem

A r a b i a n

D e s e r t

Gaza

Pelusium

Nabataean Kingdom Petra

Dumah

Heliopolis Babylon Memphis

R. Nile

The Background

of the

New Testament

Aila (Aelana)

Mt. Sinai

Rome and the East

(including Paul's Journeys)

Red Sea 35°

Tema

© Oxford University Press

F G

INDEX TO MAPS